THE SPORT AMERICANA®

Hockey Card

PRICE GUIDE

By

DR. JAMES BECKETT

NUMBER 4

EDGEWATER BOOK COMPANY • CLEVELAND

SPORT AMERICANA is a registered trademark

EDGEWATER BOOK COMPANY
P.O. BOX 40238
CLEVELAND, OHIO 44140

BECKETT is a registered trademark of

BECKETT PUBLICATIONS
DALLAS, TEXAS

Manufactured in Canada

First Printing

ISBN 0-937424-77-3

OTABIND The pages in this book open easily and lie flat, a result of the Otabind bookbinding process. Otabind combines advanced adhesive technology and a free-floating cover to achieve books that last longer and are bound to stay open.

Bound to stay open

The Sport Americana Hockey Card Price Guide
Table of Contents

About the Author 10
How To Use This Book 10
Hockey Cards Year in Review 12
Introduction 18
How to Collect 19
  Obtaining Cards 20
  Preserving Your Cards 20
  Collecting vs. Investing 21
Terminology 22
  Glossary/Legend 23
Understanding Card Values 32
  Determining Value 32
  Regional Variation 33
  Set Prices 33
  Scarce Series 34
Grading Your Cards 34
  Centering 35
  Corner Wear 35
  Creases 35
  Alterations 38
  Categorization of Defects 38
Condition Guide 39
  Grades 39
Centering 36
Corner Wear 37
Selling Your Cards 41
Interesting Notes 42
Advertising 43
Additional Reading 43
Prices in this Guide 46
History of Hockey Cards 46
Finding Out More 48
Acknowledgments 811

Pro

Action/Panini Freaks
  1992-93 Promos 52
  1992-93 52
  1992-93 Stickers 53
Action Packed
  1989-90 Prototypes 53
  1993 HOF Induction 53
  1993 Prototypes 54
Alberta Int'l. Team Canada
  1991-92 54
  1992-93 54
  1993-94 55
All World M. Lemieux Promos 55
Amer. Licorice Sour Punch Caps 56
Arena Draft Picks 56
BayBank Bobby Orr 57
Bazooka 57
Blackhawks
  1960-61 57
  1986-87 Coke 58
  1987-88 Coke 58
  1988-89 Coke 58
  1989-90 Coke 59
  1990-91 Coke 59
  1991-92 Coke 60
  1993-94 Coke 60
Bleachers 23K Manon Rheaume 60
Blues
  1971-72 Postcards 61
  1987-88 Kodak 61
  1988-89 Kodak 62
  1989-90 Kodak 62

  1990-91 Kodak 62
  1991-92 Postcards 63
Bowman
  1990-91 63
  1990-91 Hat Tricks 65
  1991-92 65
  1992-93 68
Bruins
  1970-71 Team Issue 74
  1971-72 Team Issue 74
  1983-84 Team Issue 74
  1988-89 Sports Action 75
  1989-90 Sports Action 75
  1989-90 Sports Action Update 75
  1990-91 Sports Action 76
  1991-92 Sports Action 76
  1991-92 Sports Action Legends 76
C55 Sweet Caporal 77
C55 77
C56 78
C57 79
C144 Champ's Cigarettes 79
Canadian National Juniors 80
Canadiens
  1967-68 IGA 80
  1968-69 IGA 80
  1968-69 Postcards BW 81
  1969-71 Postcards Color 81
  1970-72 Pins 81
  1971-72 Postcards 82
  1972-73 Postcards 82
  1973-74 Postcards 82
  1974-75 Postcards 83
  1975-76 Postcards 83
  1976-77 Postcards 83
  1977-78 Postcards 84
  1978-79 Postcards 84
  1979-80 Postcards 84
  1980-81 Postcards 85
  1981-82 Postcards 85
  1982-83 Postcards 85
  1982-83 Steinberg 86
  1983-84 Postcards 86
  1984-85 Postcards 86
  1985-86 Placemats 87
  1985-86 Postcards 87
  1985-86 Provigo 88
  1986-87 Postcards 88
  1987-88 Postcards 89
  1987-88 Vachon Stickers 89
  1988-89 Postcards 90
  1989-90 Kraft 91
  1989-90 Provigo Figurines 91
  1991-92 Postcards 91
  1992-93 Postcards 92
  1993-94 Molson 92
  1993-94 Postcards 92
Canucks
  1970-71 Royal Bank 93
  1971-72 Royal Bank 93
  1972-73 Nalley's 93
  1972-73 Royal Bank 94
  1973-74 Royal Bank 94
  1974-75 Royal Bank 94
  1975-76 Royal Bank 95
  1976-77 Royal Bank 95
  1977-78 Royal Bank 95
  1978-79 Royal Bank 96

  1979-80 Royal Bank 96
  1980-81 Silverwood Dairy 97
  1980-81 Team Issue 97
  1981-82 Silverwood Dairy 97
  1981-82 Team Issue 98
  1983-84 98
  1984-85 98
  1985-86 98
  1986-87 99
  1987-88 Shell Oil 99
  1988-89 Mohawk 100
  1989-90 Mohawk 100
  1990-91 Mohawk 100
  1990-91 Molson 101
  1991-92 Autograph Cards 101
  1991-92 Molson 101
  1991-92 Team Issue 8x10 102
  1992-93 Road Trip Art 102
Capitals
  1984-85 Pizza Hut 103
  1985-86 Pizza Hut 103
  1986-87 Kodak 103
  1986-87 Police 103
  1987-88 Kodak 104
  1988-89 Smokey 104
  1989-90 Kodak 104
  1990-91 Kodak 105
  1990-91 Smokey 105
  1991-92 Junior 5x7 105
  1991-92 Kodak 106
  1992-93 Kodak 106
Champion Postcards 106
Chex Photos 107
Clark Candy Mario Lemieux 107
Classic
  1991 Draft Promos 107
  1991 Draft 108
  1992 Draft Promos 108
  1992 Draft 109
  1992 Draft Gold Promo 110
  1992 Draft Gold 110
  1992 Draft LPs 110
  1992-93 Manon Rheaume C3 Presidential ... 110
  1992-93 Manon Rheaume Promo 111
  1993 Pro Prospects Previews 111
  1993 Pro Prospects Prototypes 111
  1993 Pro Prospects 111
  1993 Pro Prospects BCs 113
  1993 Pro Prospects LPs 114
  1993 Draft Promos 114
  1993 Draft Manon Rheaume Promo 114
  1993 Draft 115
  1993 Draft Class of '94 116
  1993 Draft Crash Numbered 116
  1993 Draft Team Canada 116
  1993 Draft Top Ten 117
  1994 Draft Day 117
  1994 Draft Previews 117
  1994 Pro Prospects Promo 117
  1994 Pro Prospects Prototype 118
  1994 Pro Prospects 118
  1994 Pro Prospects International Heroes 120
Coca-Cola
  1964-65 Caps 120
  1965-66 121
  1965-66 Booklets 122
  1977-78 122
  1994 Mac's Milk Gretzky POGs 122

Colgate
1970-71 Stamps 123
1971-72 Heads 124
Crescent Ice Cream
1923-24 Selkirks 124
1924-25 Selkirks 124
1924-25 Tigers 125
Dad's Cookies 125
Devils
1984-85 Postcards 126
1985-86 Postcards 126
1986-87 Police 127
1988-89 Carretta 127
1989-90 128
1990-91 128
1991-92 Teams Carvel 128
Disney Mighty Ducks 128
Donruss
1993-94 129
1993-94 Elite 134
1993-94 Ice Kings 135
1993-94 Rated Rookies 135
1993-94 Special Print 136
1993-94 Team Canada 136
1993-94 Team USA 137
Ducks Milk Caps 137
Durivage
1992-93 Panini 137
1993-94 Score 138
EA Sports 139
El Producto Discs 141
Enor Mark Messier 141
Esso
1970-71 Power Players 141
1983-84 143
1988-89 All-Stars 144
Exhibits Canadian 144
Flames
1982-83 Dollars 145
1985-86 Red Rooster Police 145
1986-87 Red Rooster Police 146
1987-88 Red Rooster Police 146
1990-91 IGA/McGavin's 146
1991-92 IGA 147
1992-93 IGA 147
Fleury Hockey Tips 148
Flyers
1972 Mighty Milk 148
1983-84 J.C. Penney 148
1986-87 Postcards 149
1990-91 Postcards 149
1991-92 J.C. Penney 150
1992-93 J.C. Penney 150
Frito Lay
1971-72 150
1988-89 Stickers 151
Future Trends
1991-92 Canada '72 Promos 151
1991-92 Canada '72 151
1992 Promo Sheet 152
1992 '76 Canada Cup 153
Gillette 154
Hall of Fame
1983 Postcards 155
1985-87 Cards 157
1992-93 Legends 158
Heroes Stand-Ups 159
High-5 Previews 159
High Liner
1992-93 Stanley Cup 160
1993-94 Greatest Goalies 160
Hockey Wit 161

Holland Creameries 162
Hull Collection UMD 162
Humpty Dumpty
1992-93 I 163
1992-93 II 163
Islanders Islander News
1984 164
1985 164
1985 Trottier 165
Jets
1984-85 Police 166
1985-86 Police 166
1985-86 Silverwood Dairy 166
1988-89 Police 167
1989-90 Safeway 167
1990-91 IGA 168
1991-92 IGA 168
Jofa/Koho 168
Kahn's Stingers
1975-76 169
1976-77 169
Kellogg's
1972 Iron-On Transfers 169
1984-85 Accordion Discs 169
1992 Trophies 170
Kenner Starting Lineup 171
Kings
1980-81 Card Night 171
1984-85 Smokey 171
1987-88 Team Issue 4x6 172
1988-89 Smokey 172
1989-90 Smokey 172
1989-90 Smokey Gretzky 8x10 173
1990-91 Smokey 173
Kraft
1986-87 Drawings 173
1989-90 174
1989-90 All-Stars Stickers 175
1990-91 175
1991-92 176
1992-93 178
1993-94 179
1993-94 Recipes 180
La Patrie 180
Leaf
1993-94 Mario Lemieux Large Promo ... 181
1993-94 181
1993-94 Freshman Phenoms 186
1993-94 Mario Lemieux 186
1993-94 Gold All-Stars 187
1993-94 Painted Warriors 187
1993-94 Gold Rookies 187
1993-94 Hat Trick Artists 188
1993-94 Studio Signature 188
Letraset Action Replays 189
Lightning
1992-93 Sheraton 190
1993-94 Kash n'Karry 190
1993-94 Season in Review 190
Lipton Soup 191
Mac's Milk 191
Maple Leafs
1963-64 White Border 192
1965-66 White Border 192
1968-69 White Border 192
1969-70 White Border Glossy 192
1969-70 White Border Matte 193
1970-71 Postcards 193
1971-72 Postcards 193
1972-73 Postcards 193
1973-74 Postcards 194
1974-75 Postcards 194

1975-76 Postcards 195
1976-77 Postcards 195
1977-78 Postcards 195
1978-79 Postcards 196
1979-80 Postcards 196
1980-81 Postcards 196
1981-82 Postcards 197
1982-83 Postcards 197
1983-84 Postcards 198
1984-85 Postcards 198
1985-86 Postcards 199
1987-88 Postcards 199
1987-88 PLAY 199
1988-89 PLAY 200
Mariners San Diego WHA 200
McDonald's Stickers 201
Nationals Ottawa WHA 201
Neilson's Gretzky 201
NHL Action Stamps 202
Nordiques
1973-74 Team Issue 204
1983-84 Postcards 204
1985-86 Provigo 205
1986-87 Yum-Yum 205
1987-88 205
1987-88 Yum-Yum 206
1988-89 General Foods 206
1989-90 General Foods 206
1989-90 Police 207
1990-91 Team Issue 207
North Stars
1972-73 Glossy Photos 208
1978-79 Cloverleaf Dairy 208
1984-85 Postcards 208
1984-85 7-Eleven 209
1985-86 Postcards 209
1985-86 7-Eleven 209
1986-87 7-Eleven 210
1987-88 Postcards 210
Oilers
1979-80 Postcards 211
1981-82 Red Rooster 211
1981-82 West Edmonton Mall 211
1982-83 Red Rooster 212
1983-84 Dollars 212
1983-84 McDonald's 212
1984-85 213
1984-85 Red Rooster 213
1985-86 Red Rooster 213
1986-87 Red Rooster 214
1986-87 Team Issue 214
1987-88 Team Issue 215
1988-89 Tenth Ann. 215
1990-91 IGA 216
1991-92 IGA 217
1992-93 217
1992-93 IGA 218
O'Keefe Maple Leafs 218
O-Pee-Chee
1933-34 V304A 219
1933-34 V304B 219
1935-36 V304C 219
1936-37 V304D 220
1937-38 V304E 220
1939-40 V301-1 221
1940-41 V301-2 222
1968-69 222
1968-69 Puck Stickers 224
1969-70 224
1969-70 Stamps 226
1969-70 Four-in-One 226
1969-70 Team Booklets 227

1970-71 227
1970-71 Deckle................................229
1971-72 229
1971-72 Topps Booklets..................231
1971-72 Posters................................231
1972-73 232
1972-73 Player Crests......................234
1972-73 Team Canada......................235
1972-73 Team Logos 235
1973-74 235
1973-74 Rings..................................237
1973-74 Team Logos 238
1973-74 WHA Posters 238
1974-75 NHL......................................238
1974-75 WHA....................................242
1975-76 NHL......................................242
1975-76 WHA....................................246
1976-77 NHL......................................246
1976-77 WHA....................................250
1977-78 NHL......................................251
1977-78 WHA....................................253
1978-79 254
1979-80 257
1980-81 259
1980-81 Super 262
1981-82 263
1982-83 265
1983-84 268
1984-85 271
1985-86 273
1985-86 Topps Box Bottoms............275
1986-87 276
1986-87 Topps Box Bottoms............278
1987-88 278
1987-88 Topps Box Bottoms............279
1987-88 Minis 280
1988-89 280
1988-89 Box Bottoms......................282
1988-89 Minis 282
1988-89 Sticker Back Cards 283
1989-90 283
1989-90 Topps Box Bottoms............286
1989-90 Sticker Back Cards 286
1990-91 287
1990-91 Box Bottoms......................290
1990-91 Red Army............................290
1990-91 Premier 291
1991-92 Topps 292
1991-92 Inserts................................298
1991-92 Premier 299
1992-93 301
1992-93 Trophy Winners..................306
1992-93 25th Anniv. Inserts............306
1992-93 Premier 307
1992-93 Premier Star Performers 308
1992-93 Premier Top Rookies 309
1993 Canadiens Panel......................309
1993 Canadiens Hockey Fest 309
1993-94 Premier Black Gold 310
1993-94 Premier Team Canada........311

Parkhurst
1951-52 311
1952-53 312
1953-54 313
1954-55 314
1955-56 315
1957-58 316
1958-59 316
1959-60 317
1960-61 317
1961-62 318
1962-63 318

1963-64 319
1991-92 320
1991-92 PHC......................................323
1992-93 Previews..............................323
1992-93 324
1992-93 Cherry Picks 328
1992-93 Cherry Picks Sheet 328
1992-93 Emerald Ice........................329
1992-93 Parkie Reprints..................329
1992-93 Parkie Sheets......................329
1992-93 Arena Tour Sheets..............330
1993-94 330
1993-94 Emerald Ice........................334
1993-94 Calder Candidates..............334
1993-94 East/West Stars 335
1993-94 Cherry's Playoff Heroes 335
1993-94 First Overall........................336
1993-94 Parkie Reprints..................336
1993-94 Parkie Reprints Case Inserts 337
1993-94 USA/Canada Gold................337
1994 Missing Link............................338
1994 Missing Link Autograph..........339
1994 Missing Link Future Stars 340
1994 Missing Link Pop-Ups..............340
1994-95 340

Penguins
1971-72 Postcards............................343
1974-75 Postcards............................343
1977-78 Puck Bucks 343
1983-84 Heinz Photos......................344
1984-85 Heinz Photos......................344
1986-87 Kodak 344
1987-88 Kodak 345
1989-90 Foodland............................345
1990-91 Foodland............................345
1991-92 Coke/Elby's........................346
1991-92 Foodland............................346
1992-93 Coke/Clark..........................347
1992-93 Foodland............................347
1993-94 Foodland............................347

Pepsi-Cola Caps 348

Pinnacle
1991-92 349
1991-92 B..353
1992-93 354
1992-93 Team Pinnacle....................359
1992-93 Team 2000..........................359
1992-93 Promo Sheet........................360
1992-93 Eric Lindros........................360
1993 Power * 361
1993-94 Daigle Entry Draft..............361
1993-94 I Samples............................361
1993-94 II Hobby Samples................361
1993-94 362
1993-94 All-Stars..............................367
1993-94 Captains..............................368
1993-94 Expansion............................369
1993-94 Masks..................................369
1993-94 Nifty Fifty............................370
1993-94 Super Rookies......................370
1993-94 Team Pinnacle....................370
1993-94 Team 2001..........................371

Popsicle
1975-76 371
1976-77 372

Post
1968-69 Marbles..............................372
1970-71 Shooters..............................373
1981-82 Standups..............................373
1982-83 Cereal 373

PowerPlay
1993-94 376

1993-94 Gamebreakers....................379
1993-94 Global Greats......................379
1993-94 Netminders..........................380
1993-94 Point Leaders......................380
1993-94 Rising Stars 380
1993-94 Rookie Standouts................381
1993-94 Second Year Stars 381
1993-94 Slapshot Artists 382

Pro Set
1990-91 382
1990-91 Player of the Month 389
1991-92 NHL Awards Special 389
1991-92 NHL Sponsor Awards..........389
1991-92 HOF Induction 390
1991-92 Preview................................390
1991-92 391
1991-92 CC..395
1991-92 St. Louis Midwest 396
1991-92 Player of the Month 396
1991-92 Platinum..............................396
1991-92 Platinum PC........................399
1991-92 Platinum HOF 75th 399
1991-92 Puck Candy Promos............400
1991-92 Puck Candy 400
1991-92 Gazette 400
1991-92 Opening Night 401
1991-92 Rink Rat 401
1992-93 401
1992-93 Award Winners....................403
1992-93 Gold Team Leaders 404
1992-93 Rookie Goal Leaders 404

Pro-Sport All-Stars 405

Puffy Stickers................................405

Quaker Oats
1938-39 Photos................................406
1973-74 WHA....................................406

Rangers Marine Midland Bank 407

Red Wings
1970-71 Marathon............................407
1991-92 Little Caesars......................408

Roadrunners Phoenix WHA
1975-76 408
1976-77 408

Rockies
1976-77 Puck Bucks 409
1981-82 Postcards............................409

Royal Desserts Hockey 410

Russian National Team
1983 410
1987 410
1989 411

Russians Stars in NHL 411

Russian Stars Red Ace
1991-92 411
1992 412
1992-93 412

Sabres
1973-74 Bells....................................413
1979-80 Bells....................................413
1980-81 Milk Panels..........................413
1981-82 Milk Panels..........................413
1982-83 Milk Panels..........................414
1984-85 Blue Shield..........................414
1985-86 Blue Shield..........................414
1986-87 Blue Shield..........................415
1987-88 Blue Shield..........................415
1987-88 Wonder Bread/Hostess 415
1988-89 Blue Shield..........................416
1988-89 Wonder Bread/Hostess 416
1989-90 Blue Shield..........................417
1989-90 Campbell's..........................417
1990-91 Blue Shield..........................418

1990-91 Campbell's.............................418
1991-92 Blue Shield...........................419
1991-92 Pepsi/Campbell's..................419
1992-93 Blue Shield...........................419
1992-93 Jubilee Foods........................420
1993-94 Noco.....................................420
Sargent Promotions Stamps
1970-71..421
1971-72..422
1972-73..423
Score
1990-91 Promos..................................425
1990-91..425
1990-91 Traded..................................429
1990-91 Hottest/Rising Stars...............429
1990-91 Young Superstars....................430
1991 National/FanFest.........................431
1991-92 American...............................431
1991-92 Canadian...............................436
1991-92 Bobby Orr..............................444
1991-92 Rookie/Traded.......................444
1991-92 Eric Lindros............................445
1991-92 Hot Cards..............................446
1991-92 Young Superstars....................446
1991-92 Kellogg's...............................447
1992-93..447
1992-93 Canadian Promo Sheets..........454
1992-93 Canadian Olympians...............454
1992-93 Sharpshooters.........................454
1992-93 USA Greats.............................455
1992-93 Young Superstars....................455
1993-94 Samples.................................456
1993-94..456
1993-94 Black's...................................464
1993-94 Gold Rush..............................464
1993-94 Dream Team...........................465
1993-94 Dynamic Duos Canadian.........465
1993-94 Dynamic Duos U.S..................465
1993-94 Franchise...............................466
1993-94 International Stars...................466
1994-95 Hobby Samples.......................467
1994-95..467
1994-95 Gold Line...............................470
1994-95 Check It.................................471
1994-95 Dream Team...........................471
1994-95 Franchise...............................472
1994-95 Team Canada.........................472
Seasons Patches
1992-93..473
1993-94..474
Senators Kraft Sheets..................474
7-Eleven
1984-85 Discs......................................475
1985-86 Credit Cards...........................475
Sharks Los Angeles WHA.............476
Sharks San Jose Sports Action....476
Shirriff
1960-61 Coins.....................................476
1961-62 Salada Coins..........................477
1962-63 Metal Coins............................478
1968-69 Coins.....................................479
Sport-Flash..................................480
Stadium Club
1991-92..480
1992-93..485
1993-94..491
1993-94 First Day Issue.......................496
1993-94 All-Stars................................497
1993-94 Finest....................................498
1993-94 Master Photos.........................498
1993-94 Team USA...............................499
Star Pics Prospects......................499

Sweet Caporal...............................500
TCMA..500
Team Canada L'Equipe WHA.........501
Titrex Guy Lafleur
1993 Insert...501
1994..501
Topps
1954-55..502
1957-58..502
1958-59..503
1959-60..504
1960-61..504
1960-61 Stamps..................................505
1961-62..505
1962-63..506
1962-63 Hockey Bucks.........................507
1963-64..507
1964-65..508
1965-66..509
1966-67..510
1966-67 USA Test................................511
1967-68..511
1968-69..512
1969-70..513
1970-71..514
1970-71 OPC Sticker Stamps................515
1971-72..515
1972-73..517
1973-74..519
1974-75..519
1975-76..522
1976-77..525
1976-77 Glossy Inserts.........................527
1977-78..527
1977-78 O-Pee-Chee Glossy..................529
1978-79..529
1979-80..531
1979-80 Team Inserts...........................533
1980-81..534
1980-81 Posters...................................536
1981-82..536
1984-85..538
1985-86..539
1985-86 Sticker Inserts.........................540
1986-87..540
1986-87 Sticker Inserts.........................542
1987-88..542
1987-88 Sticker Inserts.........................543
1988-89..544
1988-89 Sticker Inserts.........................545
1989-90..546
1989-90 Sticker Inserts.........................547
1990-91..547
1990-91 Team Scoring Leaders.............550
1991-92 Bowman Preview Sheet...........550
1991-92 Team Scoring Leaders.............551
1992-93..551
1992-93 Gold......................................557
TCMA..557
1993-94 Premier Promo Sheet..............558
1993-94 OPC Premier...........................558
1993-94 OPC Premier Gold...................564
1993-94 Premier Black Gold.................565
1993-94 Premier Finest.........................565
1993-94 Premier Team USA...................566
Toronto Stars
1963-64..566
1964-65..566
Toronto Sun..................................567
Tri-Globe
1991 Fedorov......................................569
1991-92 Kamensky...............................569
1991-92 Bure......................................570

1991-92 Semenov...............................570
1991-92 Irbe.......................................570
1992 From Russia With Puck................571
Triumph Postcards........................571
Ultimate
1991 Draft Promos...............................572
1991 Draft...572
1991-92 Original Six.............................573
1991-92 Original Six Box Bottoms.........574
Ultra
1992-93..574
1992-93 All-Stars................................577
1992-93 Award Winners.......................577
1992-93 Imports..................................578
1992-93 Jeremy Roenick......................578
1992-93 Rookies..................................579
1993-94..579
1993-94 All-Rookies.............................583
1993-94 All-Stars................................584
1993-94 Award Winners.......................584
1993-94 Adam Oates............................584
1993-94 Premier Pivots........................585
1993-94 Prospects...............................585
1993-94 Red Light Specials...................585
1993-94 Scoring Kings.........................586
1993-94 Speed Merchants....................586
1993-94 Wave of the Future.................586
Upper Deck
1990-91 Promos..................................587
1990-91..587
1990-91 Holograms..............................591
1990-91 Sheets....................................591
1991-92..592
1991-92 Award Winner Holograms.......597
1991-92 Box Bottoms...........................598
1991-92 Euro-Stars..............................598
1991-92 Brett Hull Heroes....................598
1991-92 Sheets....................................599
1991-92 Kings Season Ticket................600
1991-92 McDonald's............................600
1991-92 World Junior Tournament........601
1992-93..602
1992-93 All-Rookie Team.....................609
1992-93 All-World Team......................609
1992-93 Ameri/Can Holograms............609
1992-93 Calder Candidates..................610
1992-93 Euro-Rookie Team..................610
1992-93 Euro-Rookies..........................611
1992-93 Euro-Stars..............................611
1992-93 Wayne Gretzky Heroes...........611
1992-93 Gordie Howe Heroes..............612
1992-93 Gordie Howe Selects...............612
1992-93 World Junior Grads.................613
1992-93 Sheets....................................613
1992-93 Flyers Sheets...........................614
1992-93 McDonald's............................615
1992-93 Best of the Blues.....................616
1993 Locker All-Stars...........................616
1993-94..617
1993-94 Award Winners.......................623
1993-94 Wayne Gretzky Box Bottom.....624
1993-94 Future Heroes.........................624
1993-94 Gretzky's Great Ones..............624
1993-94 Hat Tricks...............................625
1993-94 McDonald's............................625
1993-94 Next In Line............................626
1993-94 NHLPA/Roots..........................626
1993-94 NHL's Best..............................626
1993-94 SP..627
1993-94 Program of Excellence............628
1993-94 Silver Skates Hobby................629
1993-94 Silver Skates Retail.................629

1994 NHLPA/Be A Player 629
Vachon 630
V128-1 Paulins Candy 631
V128-2 Paulins Candy 632
V129...632
V130 Maple Crispette 633
V145-1 633
V145-2 634
V252 Canadian Gum 635
V288 Hamilton Gum 635
V356 Worldwide Gum 635
V357 Ice Kings 636
V357-2 Ice Kings Premiums 637
Whalers
1984-85 Junior Wendy's.........................637
1985-86 Junior Wendy's.........................637
1988-89 Junior Ground Round 638
1989-90 Junior Milk 638
1990-91 Jr. 7-Eleven 639
1991-92 Jr. 7-Eleven 639
1992-93 Dairymart.................................640
1993-94 Coke 640
Wonder Bread Premium Photos 640
York
1960-61 Premium Photos 640
1961-62 Yellow Backs.............................641
1962-63 Iron-On Transfers......................641
1963-64 White Backs..............................642
1967-68 Action Octagons 642
Zellers Masters of Hockey 643

Stickers

O-Pee-Chee
1981-82 643
1982-83 645
1983-84 647
1984-85 649
1985-86 651
1986-87 653
1987-88 655
1988-89 657
1989-90 659
Panini
1979 660
1987-88 663
1988-89 666
1989-90 669
1990-91 671
1991-92 673
1992-93 676
1993-94 678

Minors/Juniors (Leagues)

Air Canada
1991-92 SJHL 680
1991-92 SJHL All-Stars 683
British Columbia JHL
1991-92 684
1992-93 686
Juniors Blue Tint...................................687
Laval Dairy
1951-52 QSHL 689
1951-52 Subset 690
1951-52 Lac St. Jean 690
MPS Photographics SJHL...................691
ProCards
1988-89 AHL 692
1988-89 IHL 694
1989-90 AHL 695
1989-90 IHL 697

1990-91 AHL/IHL......................................699
1991-92 AHL/CHL/IHL..............................702
Quebec Int. Pee Wees
1992-93 706
1992-93 Gold 717
St. Lawrence Sales 718
7th Inn. Sketch
1989-90 OHL 718
1990 Memorial Cup 720
1990-91 OHL 721
1990-91 WHL 723
1990-91 QMJHL 726
1991 CHL Award Winners........................727
1991 Memorial Cup 728
1991-92 OHL 729
1991-92 WHL 731
1991-92 QMJHL 734
Union Oil WHL 736

Minors/Juniors (Teams)

Amos Les Forestiers AAA
1993-94 736
Arizona Icecats
1990-91 736
1991-92 737
1992-93 737
Belleville Bulls
1983-84 738
1984-85 738
Brandon Wheat Kings
1982-83 738
1983-84 739
1984-85 739
1985-86 740
1988-89 740
1989-90 740
1992-93 741
Brockville Braves
1987-88 741
1988-89 742
Cincinnati Cyclones
1991-92 742
Clarkson Knights
1992-93 742
Cleveland
1960-61 Barons 743
1992-93 Lumberjacks 743
1993-94 Lumberjacks 744
1993-94 Lumberjacks Postcards 744
Dallas Freeze
1992-93 744
Detroit Jr. Red Wings
1993-94 745
Drummondville Voltigeurs
1993-94 745
Ferris State Bulldogs
1991-92 745
Flint Spirits
1988-89 746
Fort Worth Fire
1992-93 746
Fredericton
1981-82 Express 746
1982-83 Express 747
1983-84 Express 747
1984-85 Express 748
1985-86 Express 748
1986-87 Express 748
1992-93 Canadiens 749
Greensboro
1991-92 Monarchs...................................749

1992-93 Monarchs...................................750
Guelph Storm
1993-94 750
Halifax Citadels
1990-91 750
Hamilton
1975-76 Fincups 751
1992-93 Canucks 751
Indianapolis
1981-82 Checkers 752
1982-83 Checkers 752
1992-93 Ice...752
Kamloops Blazers
1986-87 753
1987-88 753
1988-89 754
Kansas City Blades
1990-91 754
Kelowna Wings
1984-85 754
Kingston
1981-82 Canadians 755
1982-83 Canadians 755
1983-84 Canadians 756
1984-85 Canadians 756
1985-86 Canadians 757
1986-87 Canadians 757
1987-88 Canadians 758
1993-94 Frontenacs 758
Kitchener Rangers
1982-83 758
1983-84 759
1984-85 759
1985-86 760
1986-87 760
1987-88 760
1988-89 761
1990-91 761
1993-94 762
Knoxville Cherokees
1993-94 762
Lake Superior State Lakers
1991-92 763
Lethbridge Hurricanes
1989-90 763
London Knights
1985-86 763
1986-87 764
Maine Black Bears
1992-93 764
1993-94 765
Medicine Hat Tigers
1982-83 765
1983-84 765
1985-86 766
Michigan State
1993-94 766
Michigan Tech Huskies
1990-91 767
1991-92 767
Milwaukee Admirals
1981-82 768
Minnesota Golden Gophers
1991-92 768
1992-93 768
1993-94 769
Minnesota-Duluth
1985-86 769
1993-94 770
1993-94 Commemorative 770
Moncton
1983-84 Alpines 770

1984-85 Golden Flames 771
1985-86 Golden Flames 771
1986-87 Golden Flames 772
1987-88 Hawks 772
1990-91 Hawks 772
1991-92 Hawks 773
Nashville Knights
1989-90 773
Newmarket Saints
1990-91 774
Niagara Falls Thunder
1988-89 774
1989-90 774
1993-94 775
North Bay Centennials
1982-83 775
1983-84 775
1993-94 776
Nova Scotia Voyageurs
1977-78 776
1983-84 776
Nova Scotia Oilers
1984-85 777
1985-86 777
Oklahoma City Blazers
1992-93 777
Oshawa Generals
1980-81 778
1981-82 778
1982-83 779
1983-84 779
1991-92 779
1991-92 Sheet 780
1992-93 Sheet 780
1993-94 780
Ottawa 67's
1982-83 781
1984-85 781
1992 25th Anniversary 782
Peoria Riverman
1992-93 Coke/Kroger 782
1993-94 783
Peterborough Petes
1991-92 783
1993-94 783
Phoenix Roadrunners
1992-93 784
1993-94 784
Portland Winter Hawks
1987-88 785
Quebec Citadelle
1950 785
Quebec Aces QHSL
1963-64 785
Quebec Remparts
1980-81 786
Raleigh Icecaps
1992-93 786
Rayside-Balfour Jr. Canadiens
1989-90 787
1990-91 787
1991-92 787
Regina Pats
1981-82 788
1982-83 788
1983-84 788
1987-88 789
1988-89 789
1989-90 790
Rhode Island Reds
1935-36 790

Richmond Renegades
1990-91 790
1991-92 790
1992-93 791
1993-94 791
Rochester Amerks
1963-64 792
Rochester Americans
1991-92 Dunkin' Donuts 792
1991-92 Kodak 792
1992-93 Dunkin' Donuts 793
1992-93 Kodak 793
St. John's Maple Leafs
1992-93 794
Salt Lake City Golden Eagles
1988-89 794
San Diego Gulls
1992-93 794
Saskatoon Blades
1981-82 795
1983-84 795
Sault Ste. Marie Greyhounds
1981-82 795
1982-83 796
1983-84 796
1984-85 797
1987-88 797
1993-94 798
1969-70 798
Seattle Thunderbirds
1993-94 798
Sioux City Musketeers
1974-75 799
Spokane Chiefs
1989-90 799
Springfield Indians
1983-84 800
1984-85 800
Sudbury Wolves
1984-85 800
1985-86 801
1987-88 801
1988-89 802
1989-90 802
1990-91 802
1991-92 803
1992-93 803
1993-94 804
Tacoma Rockets
1992-93 804
1993-94 804
Toledo Storm
1993-94 805
Tulsa Oilers
1992-93 805
Victoria Cougars
1981-82 806
1982-83 806
1983-84 806
1984-85 807
1989-90 807
Waterloo Black Hawks
1993-94 808
Western Michigan
1992-93 808
1993-94 808
Wheeling Thunderbirds
1992-93 809
Windsor Spitfires
1989-90 809
1992-93 810
1993-94 810

Index to Advertisers

Baseball Card Baron 823
Beverly Hills Baseball Card Shop 823
Bleachers Sports Cards 821
Books N Stuff 823
Breakaway Cards 820
Brom Enterprise 823
Byron's Hockeyland 3
Can-Am Card Co. 817
Cartomania 823
Champions Cartes 823
Check Swing Sportscards 823
Collectors Books & Cards 819
Edwards Baseball Cards Plus 823
Golden Age Collectables 821
Great Canadian Card Co. 823
Hockey Immortals 822
John Furniss 818
Ken Collins 819
Larry Suverison 823
Let's Collect 824
Lincoln Heights Coin & Stamp 822
Michael Chark 820
Mr. Hockey USA 819
Oldies & Goodies 817
One If By Cards, Two If By Comics 823
Porky's Sports Emporium 823
Portland Sports Card Co. 823
Pro's Choice 823
Sports Collectors Heaven 824
Sports Fever 823
The Bullpen 823
Two Capitals Card Co. 823

About the Author

Jim Beckett, the leading authority on sports card values in the United States, maintains a wide range of activities in the world of sports. He possesses one of the finest collections of sports cards and autographs in the world, has made numerous appearances on radio and television, and has been frequently cited in many national publications. He was awarded the first "Special Achievement Award" for Contributions to the Hobby by the National Sports Collectors Convention in 1980, the "Jock-Jaspersen Award" for Hobby Dedication in 1983, and the "Buck Barker, Spirit of the Hobby" Award in 1991.

Dr. Beckett is the author of *The Sport Americana Baseball Card Price Guide, The Official Price Guide to Baseball Cards, The Sport Americana Price Guide to Baseball Collectibles, The Sport Americana Baseball Memorabilia and Autograph Price Guide, The Sport Americana Football Card Price Guide, The Official Price Guide to Football Cards, The Sport Americana Hockey Card Price Guide, The Official Price Guide to Hockey Cards, The Sport Americana Basketball Card Price Guide and Alphabetical Checklist, The Official Price Guide to Basketball Cards,* and *The Sport Americana Baseball Card Alphabetical Checklist.* In addition, he is the founder, publisher, and editor of *Beckett Baseball Card Monthly, Beckett Basketball Monthly, Beckett Football Card Monthly, Beckett Hockey Monthly, Beckett Focus on Future Stars, Beckett Tribute* and *Beckett Racing Monthly* magazines dedicated to advancing the card collecting hobby.

Jim Beckett received his Ph.D. in Statistics from Southern Methodist University in 1975. Prior to starting Beckett Publications in 1984, Dr. Beckett served as an Associate Professor of Statistics at Bowling Green State University and as a Vice President of a consulting firm in Dallas, Texas. He currently resides in Dallas with his wife, Patti, and their daughters, Christina, Rebecca, and Melissa.

How to Use this Book

Isn't it great? Every year this book gets bigger and bigger, packed with all the new sets coming out. But even more exciting is that every year there are more attractive choices and, sub-

A propos de l'auteur

Jim Beckett, l'autorité incontestée aux Etats-Unis concernant l'évaluation des cartes sportives, maintient une variété étendue d'activités dans le monde sportif.

Il possède l'une des plus fameuses collections de cartes et d'autographes du monde; il est passé de nombreuses fois à la radio et à la télévision et a été fréquemment cité dans des publications à l'échelon national. Il reçut la première récompense "Special Achievement Award" pour sa contribution à ce passe-temps au cours de l'assemblée nationale de 1980 des collectionneurs de cartes sportives; en 1983 il reçut la récompense "Jock-Jaspersen Award" pour sa consécration à ce passe-temps, et en 1991 le "Buck Barker, Spirit of the Hobby".

Le Dr. Beckett est l'auteur du Guide des prix des cartes de base-ball américain (*The Sport Americana Baseball Card Price Guide*), du Guide officiel des prix des cartes de base-ball (*The Official Price Guide to Baseball Cards*), du Guide des prix des objets de collection relatifs au base-ball en Amérique (*The Sport Americana Price Guide to Baseball Collectibles*), du Mémoire du base-ball américain et de la valeur des autographes (*The Sport Americana Baseball Memorabilia and Autograph Price Guide*), du Guide des prix des cartes de football américain, (*The Sport Americana Football Card Price Guide*), du Recueil officiel des prix des cartes de football (*The Official Price Guide to Football Cards*), du Guide des prix des cartes de hockey américain (*The Sport Americana Hockey Card Price Guide*), du Recueil officiel des prix des cartes de hockey (*The Official Price Guide to Hockey Cards*), du Guide des prix et du relevé alphabétique des cartes de basket-ball (*Sport Americana Basketball Card Price Guide and Alphabetical Checklist*), du Guide officiel des prix des cartes de basket-ball (*The Official Price Guide to Basketball Cards*), et du Relevé alphabétique du base-ball américain (*The Sport Americana Alphabetical Baseball Card Checklist*). En outre, il est le fondateur, éditeur et auteur du mensuel sur les cartes de base-ball "*Beckett Baseball Card Monthly*", du mensuel sur le basket-ball "*Beckett Basketball Monthly*", du mensuel sur les cartes de football "*Beckett Football Card Monthly*", du mensuel sur le hockey "*Beckett Hockey Monthly*" et de la revue consacrée aux futures vedettes sportives "*Focus on Future Stars*", des magazines "*Beckett Tribute*" et du mensuel sur les courses "Beckett Racing Monthly",

sequently, more interest in the cards we love so much. This edition has been enhanced and expanded from the previous edition. The cards you collect — who they depict, what they look like, where they are from, and (most importantly to many of you) what their current values are — are enumerated within. Many of the features contained in the other Beckett Price Guides have been incorporated into this volume since condition grading, terminology, and many other aspects of collecting are common to the card hobby in general. We hope you find the book both interesting and useful in your collecting pursuits.

The Beckett Guide has been successful where other attempts have failed because it is complete, current and valid. This price guide contains not just one, but three prices by condition for all the hockey cards listed. These account for most of the hockey cards in existence. The prices were added to the card lists just prior to printing and reflect not the author's opinions or desires but the going retail prices for each card, based on the marketplace (sports memorabilia conventions and shows, sports card shops, hobby papers, current mail-order catalogs, local club meetings, auction results, and other firsthand reportings of actually realized prices).

What is the BEST Price Guide available on the market today? Of course card sellers will prefer the Price Guide with the highest prices, while card buyers will naturally prefer the one with the lowest prices. Accuracy, however, is the true test. Use the Price Guide used by more collectors and dealers than all the others combined. Look for the Beckett name. I won't put my name on anything I won't stake my reputation on. Not the lowest and not the highest — but the most accurate, with integrity.

To facilitate your use of this book, read the complete introductory section on the following pages before going to the pricing pages. Every collectible field has its own terminology; we've tried to capture most of these terms and definitions in our glossary. Please read carefully the section on grading and the condition of your cards, as you will not be able to determine which price column is appropriate for a given card without first knowing its condition.

magazines dédiés à l'évolution de la collection des cartes.

Jim Beckett obtint un doctorat en statistiques en 1975 à l'université "Southern Methodist University". Avant de lancer Beckett Publications en 1984, le Dr. Beckett était professeur associé au département des Statistiques de l'université "Bowling Green State University" et vice-président d'une société de conseil à Dallas, Texas. Actuellement, il habite à Dallas avec son épouse Patti et ses filles Christina, Rebecca et Melissa.

Comment utiliser ce livre

 N'est-ce-pas super ? Chaque année, ce livre devient de plus en plus volumineux, grâce aux nouveaux jeux publiés de façon continue. Mais ce qui est encore plus intéressant est le fait que chaque année, il existe des sélections plus attirantes qui, par conséquent, suscitent plus d'intérêt. Cette édition est encore meilleure et plus complète que la précédente. Les cartes que vous collectionnez — les joueurs qu'elles montrent, l'apparence des cartes, leur origine, et (le plus important pour la plupart d'entre vous) leur valeur actuelle — tout cela est énuméré dans cette édition. Maintes caractéristiques contenues dans les autres guides Beckett ont été incorporées dans ce volume, puisque le classement en fonction de l'état, la terminologie, et de nombreuses autres caractéristiques d'une collection sont communes à ce passe-temps. Nous espérons que vous trouverez ce livre à la fois intéressant et utile dans la poursuite de vos collections.

Le Guide Beckett a réussi là où d'autres essais ont échoué parce qu'il est complet, d'actualité, et valable. Ce guide des prix ne contient pas seulement un, mais trois prix en fonction de leur condition, pour toutes les cartes de hockey inventoriées. Ces règles s'appliquent à pratiquement chaque carte de hockey existante. Les prix ont été ajoutés aux listes des cartes immédiatement avant de passer à l'imprimerie, et reflètent, non pas les opinions ou les désirs de l'auteur, mais les prix de vente courants au détail pour chaque carte, en fonction de marché (salons et événements sportifs, magasins spécialisés, journaux spécialisés, catalogues de vente par correspondance, réunions de clubs régionaux, résultats de ventes aux enchères, et autres renseignements de première main de prix réellement pratiqués).

Hockey Cards Year in Review

A collecting season usually stands out in our minds because of a singular, special event. A player ascends from star to superstar, and his cards follow. A set or trend redefines our hobby. A team dominates all comers.

The 1993-94 hockey season went above and beyond. All of the above events combined to raise the year into the realm of the significant. Not many seasons can be looked back upon and termed turning points in both collecting and the sport as a whole. But 1993-94 earned the credentials to qualify as a pivotal campaign in both fields.

Expansion into Anaheim and Miami, the Stars' team skate from Minnesota to Dallas and conference realignment brought in new fans and let old fans see the game in a new light. Wayne Gretzky netted another piece of immortality by breaking Gordie Howe's NHL career goal-scoring record. The New York Rangers rose to the top of the hockey world by claiming the Stanley Cup and erasing a 54-year-old curse. Then their coach, Mike Keenan, made off-season news by leaving the Rangers and signing with the St. Louis Blues.

The card market also underwent some major changes for the 1993-94 season. Pro Set's bid for a new licensing agreement was passed over by the NHL and the NHL Players' Association. Pro Set's spot was then filled by long-time baseball card producer Leaf Inc. Ironically, Leaf almost acquired Pro Set's popular Parkhurst brand name, which was picked up by Upper Deck after lengthy negotiations.

The biggest change in the market occurred when the NHL/NHLPA limited each manufacturer to just two brands. The two organizations created the rule to keep order in the ever-growing card industry.

The "two brand" rule hit Topps the hardest. Counting releases under its sister banner O-Pee-Chee, Topps produced five sets (Bowman, OPC, OPC Premier, Stadium Club and Topps) in 1992-93. The ruling forced the veteran cardmaker to pull the popular Bowman and merge Topps, OPC and OPC Premier into Topps/OPC Premier.

Manufacturers responded to the two-brand limitation like Pavel Bure attacks a double-team. They forged equal parts of power and finesse into

Quel est le MEILLEUR guide des prix actuellement disponible sur le marché? Evidemment les marchands de cartes choisiront le guide avec les prix les plus élevés — tandis que les acheteurs préféreront celui avec les prix les plus bas. L'exactitude cependant, est le véritable critère. Utilisez le guide des prix choisi par la plupart des collectionneurs et des revendeurs plutôt que tous les autres guides réunis. Recherchez le nom Beckett. Je refuse d'associer mon nom à quoi que ce soit qui puisse tâcher ma réputation. Non pas le prix le plus bas ou le plus élevé — mais le plus équitable, avec intégrité.

Pour vous faciliter l'usage du livre, lisez complètement l'introduction qui suit avant d'aller aux pages contenant les prix. Chaque secteur de pièces de collection possède sa propre terminologie; nous avons essayé d'incorporer la plupart de ces termes et définitions dans notre glossaire. Veuillez lire avec attention la partie relative au classement et à l'état de vos cartes, faute de quoi il ne vous sera pas possible de déterminer quelle colonne de prix correspond à quelle carte sans d'abord connaître l'état de celle-ci.

Compte-rendu des cartes de hockey pour l'année 1993-94

Pour nous, les collectionneurs de cartes de hockey, une saison est en général remarquable à cause d'un seul événement spécial. De champion, un joueur passe à l'état de superchampion, et ses cartes suivent. Un jeu ou une tendance redéfinissent notre passe-temps. Une équipe domine toutes les autres.

La saison de hockey 1993-94 a surpassé toutes les autres. Une combinaison des événements cités ci-dessus a rendu l'année inoubliable. Il existe peu de saisons qui peuvent être considérées comme un tournant aussi bien pour le passe-temps que pour le sport en général. L'année 1993-94 a pourtant gagné ses galons comme saison d'importance primordiale en ces deux aspects-là.

L'expansion vers Anaheim et Miami, l'équipe Stars patinant de Minnesota à Dallas et le regroupement de la conférence ont causé un flux de nouveaux supporters et permis aux supporters existants de voir le jeu sous un nouvel aspect.

the most diverse array of products ever. Eleven regular issue sets rolled off the presses, and then came the kicker — 74 insert sets that dazzled even the most show-savvy hobbyist.

New material (1992-present) drew most of the activity last season, and the wealth of sets and inserts quickly escalated into a weekly, and sometimes daily, battle for market share. A set could fly off of dealers' shelves one month and then battle for attention the next. Random inserts served as market indicators. Wax prices rose or fell depending on the fortunes of their inserts.

Meeting Expectations

Leaf series I and Donruss series I were among the most awaited sets the hockey card market has ever seen. Leaf lived up to its billing, but began to slow down around mid-season, a trend created somewhat by its own success. Leaf (and Upper Deck II as well) offered such hot inserts that dealers were prompted to break down boxes en masse to meet the demand. Eventually, supply began to catch up with demand, affecting the movement of regular sets and inserts.

Donruss series I stayed on a roll the entire season. Collectors perceived scarcity with a press run of 10,000 cases and flocked to inserts such as Elites and Special Prints.

The performance of Donruss series II illustrated why only the strong prospered in 1993-94. A press run of 4,000 cases and the success of series I sent expectations through the roof. Maybe no set could have lived up to such hype. But the player selection never gave series II a chance to match series I, and it proved to be an issue deserving more modest expectations.

With the two-brand restriction in place, manufacturers were challenged to introduce new lines while staying within the guidelines. After experiencing success with these brands in other sports, Topps and Upper Deck used Finest and SP, respectively, as inserts in second series packs.

One-per-pack parallel sets grew in number while they diminished in popularity. Parkhurst, Topps, OPC and Score (second series only) included some kind of special foil version of all regular issue cards in packs, but dealers reported heated interest only in the key superstars.

The annual World Junior Championships subset, once the sole province of Upper Deck, was opened up to all manufacturers. Donruss, Pinnacle

Wayne Gretzky devint un peu plus « immortel » en brisant le record de buts marqués par Gordie Howe durant sa carrière NHL. Les New York Rangers atteignirent le sommet du monde du hockey en capturant la Coupe Stanley et éradicant une malédiction de 54 ans. Enfin, leur entraîneur, Mike Keenan, choqua tout le monde en brisant son contrat et en signant avec les St. Louis Blues.

Le marché des cartes de hockey subit également quelques changements importants durant la saison 1993-94. La NHL et l'Association des joueurs NHL (NHLPA) refusèrent l'offre de Pro Set pour un nouvel accord de licence. La place de Pro Set fut alors prise par Leaf Inc., un producteur de cartes de base-ball de longue date. Ironiquement, Leaf réussit presque à acquérir la marque connue Parkhurst de Pro Set, qui fut capturée par Upper Deck après d'ardues négociations.

Le marché fut chambardé de la façon la plus remarquable lorsque les NHL et NHLPA limitèrent la production de chaque fabricant à deux marques. Les deux organisations émirent cette règle pour maintenir un peu d'ordre dans l'industrie croissante des cartes.

La règle des « deux marques » nuisit le plus à Topps. En comptant les jeux émis sous sa marque parallèle, O-Pee-Chee, Topps produisit 5 jeux en 1992-93 (Bowman, OPC, OPC Premier, Stadium Club et Topps). La règle força ce fabricant de cartes expérimenté à éliminer la marque populaire Bowman et fusionner Topps, OPC et OPC Premier en Topps / OPC Premier.

La loi du plus fort

Les fabricants réagirent à la limitation aux deux marques comme Pavel Bure attaque une double équipe. Ils combinèrent puissance et finesse pour lancer les gammes de produits les plus diversifiés jamais produites. Onze jeux d'émission régulière sortirent de presse, suivis du bouquet : 74 jeux d'insertion qui épatèrent les collectionneurs même les plus blasés.

Durant la dernière saison, les nouveautés (de 1992 au présent) connurent le plus de succès, et le flot de jeux et d'insertions provoquèrent rapidement, chaque semaine et parfois chaque jour, des échauffourées pour capter une partie du marché. Parfois un jeu disparaissait en vitesse des rayons des marchands en un mois particulier, pour ne pas se vendre du tout le mois d'après. Des insertions au hasard servaient d'indicateurs du marché. Les prix

and Parkhurst stepped in, closing the door on Upper Deck's three-year exclusive rights to present the sole RCs of several key young players.

Upper Deck and Parkhurst Products Inc., teamed up to produce the season's most unique card set in The Missing Link. The 180-card issue is an interpretation of what the never-produced 1956-57 Parkhurst set might have looked like. Collectors took notice of the excellent player selection and random inserts, not to mention the number of cases produced, 3,912.

Out With the Old

Collectors became more selective with vintage material (pre-1978) partly because of the drawing power of brand-new cards. Many dealers and collectors simply chose to put their money into cheaper, faster moving new issues rather than commit to older material. Count an old hand with a new face among the fast-moving crowd: the Parkhurst Missing Link set attracted collectors looking for vintage stars at less-than-vintage prices.

As they tend to do, some stars bucked the trend away from the blue-chip arena. Players such as Jean Beliveau, Henri Richard and Tim Horton generated new collector interest. Hall of Famers Maurice Richard, Terry Sawchuk, Bobby Hull, Glenn Hall, Johnny Bower and Dickie Moore also commanded attention. And as a whole, off-grade material continued to sell well.

Even the 1980s, home to hot cards of many of today's top players, were affected by the rush for new cards. Many hobbyists apparently had acquired their 1980s superstars when they were more affordable. Exceptions, again, were big names like Wayne Gretzky, Doug Gilmour and Patrick Roy.

Cherry Picking

Randomness played a reduced role in the well-devised plan that propelled the year's top inserts. Success hinged primarily on the channel of distribution.

To boost sales, cardmakers package different inserts for Canada and the United States. Because the Canadian market is smaller, and because Canadian foil is sometimes difficult to find in the United States, the inserts produced for Canada are perceived to be in shorter supply than their U.S. counterparts. Demand, therefore, is higher in the larger and more influential U.S. market, causing prices to rise substantially.

de la cire augmentaient ou diminuaient suivant la bonne fortune de leurs insertions.

Aucun jeu n'a jamais été attendu avec autant d'impatience que les Leaf de première série et Donruss de première série. Leaf remplit toutes ses promesses, mais les ventes commencèrent à ralentir vers la mi-saison, les jeux tombant victime de leur propre succès. Leaf (ainsi qu'Upper Deck II) offrit des insertions que étaient tellement en demande que les détaillants n'hésitaient pas à ouvrir et séparer des tas de boîtes pour satisfaire à la demande. Enfin, l'offre dépassa la demande et les jeux réguliers aussi bien que les insertions ne se vendirent plus.

La vente des Donruss de première série se maintint durant toute la saison. Avec une sortie de presse de seulement 10.000 caisses, les collectionneurs remarquèrent la pénurie et se ruèrent sur des insertions telles qu'Elites et Special Prints.

La performance de Donruss Série II illustra pourquoi seulement les forts purent survivre en 1993-94. Une sortie de presse de 4.000 caisses et la réussite de la première série dépassèrent toutes espérances. Il est possible qu'aucun jeu n'aurait pu se montrer à la hauteur d'un tel battage publicitaire. Mais à cause d'une sélection de joueurs décevante, la deuxième série n'eut jamais une chance et déçut même la plus modeste des espérances.

Une fois la restriction des deux marques bien établie, les fabricants devaient répondre au défi de lancer deux lignes tout en respectant les directives. Topps et Upper Deck utilisèrent respectivement Finest et SP comme insertions dans les paquets de deuxième série, ayant eu du succès avec ces marques dans d'autres sports.

Les jeux « un par paquet » crûrent en nombre, tout en diminuant en popularité. Parkhurst, Topps, OPC et Score (deuxième série seulement) inclurent une version spéciale aluminium de tous les paquets de cartes d'émission régulière, mais les détaillants indiquèrent que celles-ci se vendaient mal, sauf en ce qui concerne les plus grands champions.

Le jeu auxiliaire annuel World Junior Championships, jadis le domaine exclusif d'Upper Deck, fut ouvert à tous les fabricants. Donruss, Pinnacle et Parkhurst ne se firent pas prier, coupant court à trois années de droit exclusif d'Upper Deck de présenter l'unique carte Rookie de plusieurs jeunes joueurs importants.

Upper Deck et Parkhurst Products Inc. s'allièrent pour produire le jeu de cartes le plus orig-

The year's most popular insert set was Cherry's Playoff Heroes, found only in Parkhurst series II Canadian packs. Speculation of less than 1,000 cases produced proved to be a little low, but the supply was indeed short enough that, in combination with a strong player selection, the set was attractive to collectors. Other Canadian-only inserts did similarly well: Parkhurst First Overall, Score Canadian Dynamic Duos, OPC Premier Black Gold and Team Canada, and Upper Deck Program of Excellence.

Retail-only distribution also proved alluring to collectors in some cases. In particular, Ultra retail pack inserts fared well, powered in part by the success of Ultra retail inserts in other sports. Series I All-Rookies performed steady, yet strong, but superstars Pavel Bure and Sergei Fedorov picked up the pace for series II Speed Merchants.

Sweet Redemption

The season also saw the introduction of randomly inserted redemption cards, a popular feature of many sets in other sports. In a pure finesse move, Score marketed the first NHL card of No. 1 pick Alexandre Daigle by randomly inserting a series I card that could be exchanged for one of Daigle in a Senators' jersey. The card was numbered 496 to be the last card of the first series, but it isn't considered part of the complete set since it could not be pulled from packs.

Upper Deck ran several similar programs. Two separate 10-card Silver Skates inserts sets came in series II packs, one set for hobby packs and one for retail packs. To appease hobbyists, UD randomly inserted cards redeemable for complete sets of the retail insert with either silver or gold foil stamping. The gold foil versions were available only through the redemption card.

Similarly, Parkhurst inserted 20 Calder Candidates cards in series II packs. The redemption offer provided the complete set, and it was the only way to pocket the gold foil Candidates.

Topps followed suit with a number of redemption programs for Finest, Stadium Club Master Photos and Black Gold cards.

The unique distribution method had a singular effect on the performance of complete sets. As the season progressed, some collectors began to drift toward regular issues, especially when the redeemed sets hit the market. For example, the Topps Black Gold issues were outperformed by

inal de la saison, The Missing Link. Ce jeu de 180 cartes est une interprétation de ce qu'aurait pu être le jeu Parkhurst 1956-57, qui ne fut jamais produit. Les collectionneurs remarquèrent les excellentes sélections de joueurs et insertions, sans mentionner la quantité de caisses produites, au nombre de 3.912.

Fi du passé

Les cartes d'époque (avant 1978) s'écoulèrent mal, dû en partie à l'attraction des cartes nouvelles. Beaucoup de détaillants et de collectionneurs élurent de simplement investir en de nouvelles émissions meilleur marché, s'écoulant plus vite, plutôt qu'en de jeux plus anciens, se vendant moins vite. Un vieux de la vieille profita d'une remise à neuf, rejoignant les cartes qui s'écoulent vite : le jeu The Missing Link de Parkhurst attira les collectionneurs recherchant des champions d'époque à un prix modique.

Comme il arrive assez souvent, certains champions ne suivirent pas les tendances. Les collectionneurs renouvelèrent leur intérêt en des joueurs comme Jean Beliveau, Henri Richard et Tim Horton. Les joueurs du Hall de la Gloire Maurice Richard, Terry Sawchuck, Bobby Hull, Glenn Hall, Johnny Bower et Dickie Moore eurent aussi leur part de succès. Et généralement, les cartes hors catégorie continuèrent à bien se vendre.

Même les années 80, contenant les cartes prisées des meilleurs joueurs d'aujourd'hui, connurent une baisse d'intérêt. Beaucoup de collectionneurs avaient apparemment acquis leurs champions des années 80 alors qu'ils étaient à un prix plus abordable. Ici aussi, Wayne Gretzky, Doug Gilmour et Patrick Roy furent des exceptions.

Sélections Cherry

Le hasard ne joua pas un très grand rôle dans le plan bien conçu qui encourageait les ventes des meilleurs jeux d'insertion de l'année. La réussite dépendit surtout des voies de distribution.

Pour encourager les ventes, les fabricants de cartes produisent des insertions différentes pour le Canada et les États-Unis. Parce que le marché canadien est moins étendu et que l'aluminium canadien est parfois difficile à trouver aux États-Unis, les insertions produites pour le Canada laissent l'impression de ne pas être aussi nombreuses que leurs équivalents américains. De ce fait, la demande est donc plus élevée dans le marché américain, plus

their OPC counterparts, which offered no redemption program and held their value throughout the season.

Cards weren't the only collectibles being shuttled between collectors and cardmakers. For the first time since the 1920s, a manufacturer offered equipment in exchange for cards. Pinnacle randomly inserted series II cards good for skates, sticks and jerseys, some of which were signed by spokesman Eric Lindros.

Drawing Cards

Even as our hobby grows more complicated, on-ice performance still drives a player's cards. New hobby stars emerged last season, and a few perennial favorites kept rolling on.

Last season likely will be remembered as the year of the goalie. **Dominik Hasek**, **Mike Richter**, **Martin Brodeur**, **John Vanbiesbrouck** and **Arturs Irbe** all boosted their cards with career years. Because of the wealth of choices, collectors could pull most of their cards from common boxes throughout the season. Hasek and Brodeur rose to the top of their class, winning the Vezina and Calder trophies, respectively.

Ottawa's **Alexandre Daigle**, the No. 1 overall pick in 1993, opened the season as the class of the rookie crop. Yet Daigle quickly took a back seat to fab freshmen such as **Mikael Renberg**, **Alexei Yashin** and **Jason Arnott**.

Renberg, the Flyers' strapping winger, led all rookies with 38 goals and 82 points. Daigle's claim to fame occurred when he appeared in a nurse's uniform in a Score series I advertisement. The advertisement focused on the Daigle redemption card in series I, a strong mover until several other companies released him in their regular issue sets.

The New York Rangers as a whole sparked interest as they rolled to their first Cup in 54 years. To go along with Richter, **Mark Messier**, **Adam Graves**, **Brian Leetch**, **Sergei Zubov** and **Alexei Kovalev** all had collectors scrambling in hopes that the Cup would affect their card values.

Sergei Fedorov stepped up as the Red Wings' leader after **Steve Yzerman** was lost to injuries, and announced with two-way authority that he's one of the game's premier players. Fedorov claimed the Hart trophy as the league's MVP, as well as the Selke for Best Defensive Forward. Collectors responded by scrambling after his 1993-94 inserts and best Rookie Card (1990-91 OPC Premier #30).

grand et ayant plus d'influence, causant une hausse substantielle des prix.

Le jeu d'insertion Playoff Heroes de Cherry, uniquement trouvé dans les paquets canadiens Parkhurst de deuxième série, connut le plus de succès. La spéculation que seulement 1.000 caisses avaient été produites n'était pas tout à fait correcte, mais la provision était assez limitée et la sélection des joueurs tellement bonne que les collectionneurs trouvèrent le jeu irrésistible. D'autres jeux d'insertion, publiés uniquement pour le marché canadien, connurent autant de succès : First Overall de Parkhurst, Canadian Dynamic Duos de Score, Black Gold et Team Canada d'OPC Premier, et Program of Excellence d'Upper Deck.

Les collectionneurs se sentirent également attirés par les paquets destinés uniquement à la vente au détail. En particulier, les paquets d'insertion détail d'Ultra eurent beaucoup de succès, dû en partie au succès des paquets d'insertion détail Ultra dans d'autres sports. Les All-Rookies de première série ne se vendirent pas aussi bien à cause d'une sélection médiocre de joueurs, mais les superchampions Pavel Bure et Sergei Fedorov encouragèrent la vente des Speed Merchants de deuxième série.

Cartes d'échange

Durant la saison, des cartes d'échange insérées au hasard furent lancées sur le marché, un détail connaissant beaucoup de succès dans d'autres sports. Dans un geste rempli de finesse, Score lança la première carte NHL d'Alexandre Daigle, sélection n° 1, en insérant au hasard une carte de première série pouvant être échangée contre une carte de Daigle en tricot des Senators. La carte portait le numéro 496 pour être la dernière carte de la première série, mais n'est pas considérée comme faisant partie du jeu complet, puisqu'elle ne pouvait pas être retirée des paquets.

Upper Deck lança plusieurs programmes similaires. Deux jeux d'insertion séparés de 10 cartes Silver Skates étaient disponibles dans des paquets de deuxième série, un jeu pour les paquets passe-temps et un pour les paquets distribués au détail. Pour apaiser les collectionneurs, Upper Deck inséra au hasard des cartes échangeables contre des jeux complets d'insertion, vendus au détail, avec de l'aluminium estampé argenté ou doré. Les versions dorées ne pouvaient être obtenues qu'avec la carte d'échange.

De même, Parkhurst inséra 20 cartes Calder

Wayne Gretzky rode his timeless grace to another scoring title and claimed the all-time NHL record for goals scored. Many collectors turned their attention to his odd-ball items and his recent inserts. Past and present greatness make Gretzky and **Patrick Roy** the most popular players across the breadth of the hobby.

Pavel Bure continued to thrill collectors as he streaked to the goal scoring title by lighting the lamp 60 times. While the Russian Rocket's RC (1990-91 Upper Deck #526) didn't soar into the stratosphere, his inserts and some regular issue cards were a must for most collectors.

Mike Modano almost single-handedly turned many Texans into hockey fans. The superstar-in-waiting arrived with his long-anticipated 50-goal season, and turned up the heat on his 1990-91 OPC Premier RC #74.

The Rookie Cards of Toronto's **Doug Gilmour** (1984-85 OPC #185), **Wendel Clark** (1986-87 Topps/OPC #149) and **Dave Andreychuk** (1984-85 T/O #17) inched upward throughout the season. Gilmour's RC moved into a tie with Yzerman's as the top cards in the set. Clark and Quebec's **Mats Sundin** traded teams in the off-season, a deal that promises to affect their hobby standing.

Cam Neely may have edged Bure for the goal race had he stayed healthy all season. The Boston right winger scored 50 goals in 49 games, but went down in March with another knee injury. Collectors rekindled their interest in most of Neely's older cards, especially his condition sensitive 1985-86 OPC #228.

Speaking of being banged up, many of the league's drawing cards sat out a good part of the season due to injuries. Sidelined superstars included **Mario Lemieux**, **Pat LaFontaine**, **Eric Lindros** and **Teemu Selanne**. While they watched, new hobby favorites emerged and other, more fortunate stars supplied collectors with even more highlights.

Mike Hersh is a longtime collector living in Cherry Hill, N.J.

Candidates dans des paquets de deuxième série. L'offre d'échange concernait le jeu entier et était la seule manière d'obtenir les Calder Candidates en version aluminium doré.

Topps fit de même avec un nombre de programmes d'échange contre des cartes Finest, Stadium Club Master Photos et Black Gold.

Cette voie de distribution unique eut un effet bizarre sur la performance de jeux complets. Au fur et à mesure que la saison progressait, la valeur de certains de ces jeux spéciaux eut tendance à baisser, surtout lorsque les jeux échangés apparurent sur le marché. Par exemple, les émissions Black Gold de Topps furent généralement ignorées, alors que leurs équivalents OPC, n'offrant aucun programme d'échange, maintinrent leur valeur durant toute la saison.

Les collectionneurs et fabricants n'échangeaient pas seulement des cartes. Pour la première fois depuis les années 20, un fabricant offrit de l'équipement en échange contre des cartes. Pinnacle inséra au hasard des cartes de deuxième série pouvant être échangées contre des patins, des crosses et des tricots, parfois même signés par le porte-parole Eric Lindros.

Cartes favorites

Même si notre passe-temps devient plus compliqué, ce qui vend une carte est encore toujours la performance sur glace du joueur. La saison dernière a vu naître de nouveaux champions, alors que quelques favoris de toujours se maintiennent.

La saison passée sera probablement notée dans les annales comme l'année du Gardien de but. **Dominik Hasek**, **Mike Richter**, **Martin Brodeur**, **John Vanbiesbrouck** et **Arturs Irbe** renforcèrent tous la vente de leurs cartes par des années de professionnalisme. Hasek et Brodeur se hissèrent au sommet de leur catégorie, gagnant respectivement les trophées Vezina et Calder.

Alexandre Daigle d'Ottawa, la sélection n° 1 de 1993, inaugura la saison comme un des meilleurs dans la masse des débutants. Daigle dut cependant rapidement céder le terrain à des joueurs débutants tels que **Mikael Renberg**, **Alexei Yashin** et **Jason Arnott**.

Introduction

Welcome to the exciting world of sports card collecting, America's fastest growing avocation. You have made a good choice in buying this book, since it will open up to you the entire panorama of this field in the simplest, most concise way.

It is estimated that a third of a million different sports cards have been issued during the past century. And the number of total cards put out by all manufacturers last year has been estimated at several billion, with an initial wholesale price of more than $1 billion. Sales of older cards by dealers may account for a like amount. With all that cardboard available in the marketplace, it should be no surprise that several million sports fans like you collect sports cards today.

The growth of *Beckett Baseball Card Monthly*, *Beckett Basketball Monthly*, *Beckett Football Card Monthly*, *Beckett Hockey Monthly* and *Beckett Focus on Future Stars* is another indication of this rising crescendo of popularity for sports cards. Founded in 1984 by Dr. James Beckett, the author of this Price Guide, *Beckett Baseball Card Monthly* has grown to the pinnacle of the sports card hobby, with more than half a million readers anxiously awaiting each enjoyable issue.

So collecting sports cards — while still pursued as a hobby with youthful exuberance by kids in the neighborhood — also has taken on the trappings of an industry, with thousands of full- and part-time card dealers, as well as vendors of supplies, clubs and conventions. In fact, each year since 1980, thousands of hobbyists have assembled for a National Sports Collectors Convention, at which hundreds of dealers have displayed their wares, seminars have been conducted, autographs have been penned by sports notables, and millions of cards have changed hands. These colossal affairs have been staged in Los Angeles, Detroit, St. Louis, Chicago, New York, Anaheim, Arlington (Texas), San Francisco, Atlantic City, Houston and Atlanta. So sports card collecting really is national in scope!

This increasing interest has been reflected in card values. As more collectors compete for available supplies, card prices (especially for premium-grade cards) rise. A national publication indicated a "very strong advance" in sports card prices during the past decade, and a quick perusal of the prices in

Introduction

Bienvenue au monde passionnant des collectionneurs de cartes sportives, le passe-temps connaissant le taux de croissance le plus élevé aux États-Unis. Vous avez bien choisi en achetant ce livre, car il vous présentera, de la manière la plus simple et la plus succinte, le panorama complet de cette activité.

Il est estimé qu'environ trois cent mille différentes cartes sportives ont été émises au cours du siècle dernier. Et le nombre total des cartes publiées par tous les fabricants l'année dernière a été estimé à quelques milliards, avec un prix brut initial de plus d'un milliard de dollars. Les ventes de cartes plus anciennes par les revendeurs doivent vraisemblablement se chiffrer à un montant pareil. Avec toutes les différentes cartes sur le marché, il ne serait pas étonnant que plusieurs millions d'admirateurs sportifs tels que vous collectionnent des cartes sportives aujourd'hui,.

La croissance des revues mensuelles Beckett sur les cartes de base-ball (*Beckett Baseball Card Monthly*), le basket-ball (*Beckett Basketball Card Monthly*), les cartes de football (*Beckett Football Card Monthly*), le hockey (*Beckett Hockey Monthly)* et la concentration sur les vedettes futures (*Beckett Focus on Future Stars*), est une autre indication de la popularité croissante des cartes sportives. Fondé en 1984 par le Dr. James Beckett, l'auteur de ce Guide des prix, *Beckett Baseball Card Monthly* a atteint le sommet du passe-temps concernant la collection de cartes sportives, avec plus d'un demi-million de lecteurs attendant impatiemment chaque numéro agréable et instructif.

Ainsi, la collection de cartes sportives — bien que toujours perçu avec exubérance comme un passe-temps par les gamins du voisinage — s'est également développée en une industrie avec des milliers de revendeurs à plein temps et à temps partiel, des vendeurs d'accessoires de tous genres, des clubs et des salons. En fait, chaque année depuis 1980, des milliers d'amateurs se réunissent durant le Congrès national des collectionneurs sportifs, au cours duquel des centaines de revendeurs exposent leurs articles, des groupes de travail s'organisent, des autographes sont accordés par des vedettes du monde du sport, et des millions de cartes changent de mains. Ces événements à grande échelle ont lieu à Los Angeles, Détroit, Saint Louis, Chicago, New

this book compared to the figures in earlier editions of this Price Guide will quickly confirm this. Which brings us back around to the book you have in your hands. It is the best annual guide available to this exciting world of sports cards. Read it and use it. May your enjoyment and your card collection increase in the coming months and years.

How to Collect

Each collection is personal and reflects the individuality of its owner. There are no set rules on how to collect cards. Since card collecting is a hobby or leisure pastime, what you collect, how much you collect, and how much time and money you spend collecting are entirely up to you. The funds you have available for collecting and your own personal taste should determine how you collect. Information and ideas presented here are intended to help you get the most enjoyment from this hobby.

It is impossible to collect every card ever produced. Therefore, beginners as well as intermediate and advanced collectors usually specialize in some way. One of the most popular aspects of this hobby is that individual collectors can define and tailor their collecting methods to match their own tastes. To give you some ideas of the various approaches to collecting, we will list some of the more popular areas of specialization.

Many collectors select complete sets from particular years. For example, they may concentrate on assembling complete sets from all the years since their birth or since they became avid sports fans. They may try to collect a card for every player during that specified period of time.

Many others wish to acquire only certain players. Usually such players are the superstars of the sport, but occasionally collectors will specialize in all the cards of players who attended a particular college or came from a certain town. Some collectors are only interested in the first cards or Rookie Cards of certain players.

Another fun way to collect cards is by team. Most fans have a favorite team, and it is natural for that loyalty to be translated into a desire for cards of the players on that favorite team. For most of the recent years, team sets (all the cards from a given team for that year) are readily available at a reasonable price.

York, Anaheim, Arlington (Texas), San Francisco, Atlantic City, Houston et Atlanta. La collection de cartes sportives s'est donc vraiment développée sur un plan national.

Cet intérêt croissant s'est reporté sur la valeur des cartes. Alors que plus de collectionneurs rivalisent pour les éléments disponibles, les prix des cartes ont augmenté (en particulier pour les cartes en parfait état). Le prix des cartes de hockey a considérablement augmenté durant la dernière décennie, et un examen rapide des prix dans ce livre comparé aux indications des éditions antérieures de ce guide des prix le confirmera. Ceci nous ramène donc au livre que vous avez entre les mains. Il s'agit du meilleur guide annuel mis à la disposition du monde passionnant des cartes de hockey. Lisez-le et apprenez à vous en servir. Puissent votre satisfaction et votre collection de cartes s'accroître durant les mois et années à venir.

Comment collectionner

Chaque collection est personnelle et reflète l'individualité du propriétaire. Il n'existe pas de règles établies pour la collection de cartes. Puisque c'est un passe-temps, ce que vous collectionnez et comment, combien de temps et d'argent vous y consacrez, sont à votre entière discrétion. Les fonds que vous réservez à votre collection et votre appréciation personnelle devraient déterminer votre façon de procéder. Les informations et idées présentées ici ont l'intention de vous aider à profiter au maximum de ce passe-temps.

Il est impossible de collectionner toutes les cartes produites à ce jour. Par conséquent, les débutants tout aussi bien que les collectionneurs moyens ou avancés se spécialisent habituellement d'une certaine façon. L'une des raisons que ce passe-temps est populaire est que les collectionneurs individuels peuvent définir et façonner leurs méthodes de collection afin de satisfaire leurs goûts propres. Afin de vous donner quelques idées relatives aux diverses approches d'une collection, nous allons établir une liste de quelques-uns des secteurs de spécialisation les plus populaires.

Beaucoup de collectionneurs choisissent des séries complètes d'années particulières. Par exemple, ils peuvent se concentrer sur la collection de séries complètes de toutes les années depuis leur naissance ou depuis qu'ils ont commencé à

Obtaining Cards

Several avenues are open to card collectors. Cards can still be purchased in the traditional way: by the pack at the local discount, grocery and convenience stores. But there are also thousands of card shops across the country that specialize in selling cards individually or by the pack, box, or set. Another alternative is the thousands of card shows held each month around the country, which feature anywhere from five to 800 tables of sports cards and memorabilia for sale. For many years, it has been possible to purchase complete sets of sports cards through mail-order advertisers found in traditional sports media publications, such as *The Sporting News, Hockey Digest, Street & Smith* yearbooks, and others. These sets also are advertised in card collecting periodicals. Many collectors will begin by subscribing to at least one of the hobby periodicals. In fact, subscription offers can be found in the advertising section of this book.

Most serious card collectors obtain old (and new) cards from one or more of several main sources: (1) trading or buying from other collectors or dealers; (2) responding to sale or auction ads in the hobby publications; (3) buying at a local hobby store; and/or (4) attending sports collectibles shows or conventions. We advise that you try all four methods since each has its own distinct advantages: (1) trading is a great way to make new friends; (2) hobby periodicals help you keep up with what's going on in the hobby (including when and where the conventions are happening); (3) stores provide the opportunity to enjoy personalized service and consider a great diversity of material in a relaxed sports-oriented atmosphere; and (4) shows allow you to choose from multiple dealers and thousands of cards under one roof in a competitive situation.

Preserving Your Cards

Cards are fragile. They must be handled properly in order to retain their value. Careless handling can easily result in creased or bent cards. It is, however, not recommended that tweezers or tongs be used to pick up your cards, since such utensils might mar or indent card surfaces and thus reduce those cards' conditions and values. In general, your cards should be handled directly as little as possible. This is sometimes easier to say than to do.

Although there are still many who use custom boxes, storage trays, or even shoe boxes, plastic sheets are the preferred method of many collectors

s'intéresser activement au sport. Ils peuvent essayer de collectionner une carte pour chaque joueur durant cette période spécifique.

Beaucoup d'autres souhaitent acquérir seulement certains joueurs. Habituellement ces joueurs sont les super-vedettes du sport, mais occasionnellement des collectionneurs se spécialiseront dans toutes les cartes des joueurs qui ont étudié dans une université particulière ou qui sont originaires d'une certaine ville. Quelques collectionneurs s'intéressent seulement aux premières cartes, dites "Rookie Cards", de certains joueurs.

Une autre façon amusante de collectionner les cartes est de le faire par équipe. La plupart des admirateurs ont une équipe favorite et il est normal que cette admiration se reporte sur le désir de posséder les cartes de cette équipe favorite. Des jeux de cartes par équipe (toutes les cartes d'une certaine équipe pour une certaine année) peuvent être acquis à un prix raisonnable pour la plupart des années récentes.

L'obtention des cartes

Les collectionneurs peuvent obtenir leurs cartes de différentes façons. Les cartes peuvent encore être achetées de façon traditionnelle : par paquet dans les magasins de demi-gros, les épiceries et les magasins de voisinage. Mais il existe également des milliers de magasins de cartes dans le pays qui se spécialisent dans la vente de cartes individuelles ou par paquet, boîte ou jeu. Une autre alternative est offerte par les milliers de salons de cartes ouverts chaque mois partout dans le pays, comportant entre 5 à 800 tables de cartes sportives et de souvenirs à acheter. Depuis beaucoup d'années, il est également possible d'acheter des jeux de cartes à la suite d'annonces de vente par correspondance publiées dans les revues sportives telles que *The Sporting News, Hockey Digest, Street & Smith Yearbooks*, et bien d'autres. Ces jeux sont également mis en publicité dans des périodiques de collections de cartes. Beaucoup de collectionneurs commenceront par s'abonner à au moins un de ces périodiques spécialisés dans ce passe-temps et qui offrent de bons renseignements à jour. En fait, dans la section publicitaire de ce livre, vous trouverez des offres d'abonnements.

La plupart des collectionneurs de cartes sérieux obtiennent les cartes anciennes (et nouvelles) d'une ou de plusieurs sources principales: (1) échange avec ou achat d'autres collectionneurs

for storing cards. A collection stored in plastic pages in a three-ring album allows you to view your collection at any time without the need to touch the card itself.

Cards also can be kept in single holders (of various types and thickness) designed for the enjoyment of each card individually. For a large collection, some collectors may use a combination of the above methods. When purchasing plastic sheets for your cards, be sure that you find the pocket size that fits the cards snugly. Don't put your 1951 Bowmans in a sheet designed to fit 1981 Topps. Most hobby and collectibles shops and virtually all collectors' conventions will have these plastic pages available in quantity for the various sizes offered, or you can purchase them directly from the advertisers in this book. Also, remember that pocket size isn't the only factor to consider when looking for plastic sheets. Other factors such as safety, economy, appearance, availability, or personal preference also may indicate which types of sheets a collector may want to buy.

Damp, sunny and/or hot conditions — no, this is not a weather forecast — are three elements to avoid in extremes if you are interested in preserving your collection. Too much (or too little) humidity can cause gradual deterioration of a card. Direct, bright sun (or fluorescent light) over time will bleach out the color of a card. Extreme heat accelerates the decomposition of the card. On the other hand, many cards have lasted more than 50 years without much scientific intervention. So be cautious, even if the above factors typically present a problem only when present in the extreme. It never hurts to be prudent.

Collecting vs. Investing

Collecting individual players and collecting complete sets are both popular vehicles for investment and speculation. Most investors and speculators stock up on complete sets or on quantities of players they think have good investment potential. There is obviously no guarantee in this book, or anywhere else for that matter, that cards will outperform the stock market or other investment alternatives in the future. After all, sports cards do not pay quarterly dividends and cards cannot be sold at their "current values" as easily as stocks and bonds. Nevertheless, investors have noticed a favorable long-term trend in the past performance of sports collectibles, and certain cards and sets have outper-

ou revendeurs; (2) réponse à des annonces de ventes ou de ventes aux enchères dans des revues sur les passe-temps; (3) achat dans un magasin spécialisé du quartier, et/ou (4) visite aux expositions ou salons de pièces de collection sportives. Nous vous conseillons d'essayer ces quatre méthodes car chacune d'elles possède ses propres avantages: (1) l'échange est une façon agréable de se faire de nouveaux amis; (2) les périodiques spécialisés vous aident à vous tenir au courant de l'actualité concernant votre passe-temps (y compris où et quand ont lieu les salons); (3) les magasins spécialisés offrent un service personnalisé et une grande diversité de matériel dans une atmosphère détendue et sportive; et (4) les salons vous permettent de choisir parmi une multitude de vendeurs et des milliers de cartes, réunis sous le même toit dans une situation compétitive.

Conserver vos cartes

Les cartes sont fragiles. Elles doivent être manipulées proprement de façon à conserver leur valeur. Une manipulation sans précaution peut facilement aboutir à des cartes fripées ou pliées. Il n'est toutefois pas recommandé d'utiliser des petites pinces ou des pincettes pour prendre les cartes, car de tels ustensiles pourraient endommager ou marquer la surface des cartes et, par conséquent, amoindrir la qualité de ces cartes et diminuer leur valeur. En général, vos cartes devraient être aussi peu que possible manipulées directement. C'est parfois plus vite dit que fait.

Bien que beaucoup de collectionneurs utilisent encore des boîtes spéciales, des tiroirs de rangement et même des boîtes à chaussure, la méthode préférée de beaucoup d'autres est de ranger les cartes entre des feuilles de plastique. Une collection rangée entre des feuilles de plastique dans un album vous permet d'admirer votre collection à tout moment sans devoir toucher les cartes.

Les cartes peuvent aussi être rangées dans des porte-cartes individuels (plusieurs types et épaisseurs existent) permettant de regarder chaque carte séparément. Des collectionneurs possédant une collection importante utilisent parfois une combinaison de ces méthodes. En achetant ces porte-cartes de plastique, faites attention de prendre une taille adaptée aux cartes. Ne classez pas vos cartes de hockey Bowman 1951 dans un feuillet conçu pour recevoir les cartes hockey Topps 1981. La plupart des magasins de passe-temps et de collections et

formed just about any other investments in some years.

Some of the obvious questions are: Which cards? When to buy? When to sell? The best investment you can make is in your own education. The more you know about your collection and the hobby, the more informed the decisions you will be able to make. We're not selling investment tips. We're selling information about the current value of hockey cards. It's up to you to use that information to your best advantage.

Terminology

 Each hobby has its own language to describe its area of interest. The terminology traditionally used for trading cards is derived from the American Card Catalog, published in 1960 by Nostalgia Press. That catalog, written by Jefferson Burdick (who is called the "Father of Card Collecting" for his pioneering work), uses letter and number designations for each separate set of cards. The letter used in the ACC designation refers to the generic type of card. While both sport and non-sport issues are classified in the ACC, we shall confine ourselves to the sport issues. The following list defines the letters and their meanings as used by the American Card Catalog.

(none) or N - 19th Century U.S. Tobacco
B - Blankets
C - Canadian Tobacco
D - Bakery Inserts Including Bread
E - Early Candy and Gum
F - Food Inserts
H - Advertising
M - Periodicals
PC - Postcards
R - Candy and Gum since 1930
V - Canadian Candy

Following the letter prefix and an optional hyphen are one-, two-, or three-digit numbers, 1-999. These typically represent the company or entity issuing the cards. In several cases, the ACC number is extended by an additional hyphen and another one- or two-digit numerical suffix. For example, the 1933-34 Canadian Gum hockey card issue carries an ACC designation of V252. The "V" indicates a Canadian candy. The "252" is the ACC

virtuellement tous les salons de collectionneurs auront une multitude de feuillets de plastique disponibles pour les diverses tailles offertes, ou vous pouvez les commander directement des sociétés faisant de la publicité dans ce livre. Souvenez-vous aussi que le fait que les feuillets sont de dimension poche n'est pas l'unique facteur à considérer. D'autres facteurs, tels la sécurité, le prix, l'apparence, la disponibilité ou une préférence personnelle peuvent aussi jouer un rôle dans la décision de l'acheteur.

L'humidité, le soleil, la chaleur — non, il ne s'agit pas de prévisions météorologiques — sont trois éléments à éviter au plus haut point si vous avez l'intention de protéger votre collection. Trop d'humidité (ou pas assez) peut causer une dégradation graduelle d'une carte. L'ensoleillement direct, (ou une lumière fluorescente) peut décolorer une carte. Une chaleur extrême accélère la décomposition de la carte. D'un autre côté, de nombreuses cartes ont passé le cap des 50 ans sans beaucoup d'intervention scientifique. Donc, faites attention, même si les facteurs présentés ci-dessus ne sont typiquement que des extrêmes, il ne nuit jamais d'être prudent.

Collectionner par opposition à investir

Faire collection de joueurs individuels et collectionner des jeux complets sont tous deux des moyens populaires d'investissement et de spéculation. La plupart des investisseurs et des spéculateurs conservent les cartes en jeux complets ou les cartes des joueurs qu'ils estiment avoir un bon potentiel d'investissement. Il n'y a évidemment aucune garantie ni dans ce livre, ni ailleurs, que les cartes l'emporteront un jour sur la bourse ou sur d'autres solutions d'investissement. Après tout, les cartes de hockey ne paient pas de dividendes trimestriels et ne peuvent être vendues aussi facilement "au prix courant" que des actions et obligations. Quoiqu'il en soit, les investisseurs ont remarqué une tendance à long terme favorable de beaucoup de pièces de collection sportives, et il existe des cartes et des jeux qui, durant certaines années, ont pratiquement battu tout autre investissement.

Quelques questions viennent à l'esprit : quelles cartes acheter ? Quand ? A quel point les revendre ? Le meilleur investissement que vous puissiez faire est d'étendre vos connaissances. Plus

designation for Canadian Gum.

Like other traditional methods of identification, this system provides order to the process of cataloging cards; however, most serious collectors learn the ACC designation of the popular sets by repetition and familiarity, rather than by attempting to "figure out" what they might or should be.

From 1951 forward, collectors and dealers commonly refer to all sets by their year, maker, type of issue and any other distinguishing characteristic. For example, such a characteristic could be an unusual issue or one of several regular issues put out by a specific maker in a single year. Regional issues are usually referred to by year, maker, and sometimes, by title or theme of the set.

Glossary/Legend

Our glossary defines terms frequently used in the card collecting hobby. Many of these terms also are common to other types of sports memorabilia collecting. Some terms may have several meanings, depending on use and context.

ACO - Assistant Coach.

ACO/GM - Assistant Coach/General Manager.

ACTION SCENES CARD - a special type of card showing an action photo of a player or players with a description.

ADAMS - Trophy awarded to NHL's coach of the year.

AGM - Assistant General Manager.

AHL - American Hockey League.

ALL-STAR CARD - A card portraying an All-Star player of the previous year that says "All Star" on its face. Sometimes denoted as AS in the price listings.

ALPH - Alphabetical.

AP - Action Picture.

ART - All-Rookie Team or Art card.

AS - All-Star.

AS1 - First Team All-Star.

AS2 - Second Team All-Star.

ATG - All-Time Great card.

AW - Award Winner.

BL - Bloodlines.

BRICK - A group of cards, usually 50 or more, having common characteristics, that is intended to be bought, sold, or traded as a unit. Dealers usually place a star or superstar card on top as a selling tool.

BYNG - Lady Byng trophy, award for NHL's most gentlemanly player.

vous en savez sur votre collection et passe-temps, plus vos décisions seront valables. Nous ne sommes pas ici pour vous vendre des conseils en matière d'investissement. Nous vendons des informations au sujet de la valeur actuelle des cartes de hockey. C'est à vous d'utiliser ces informations au mieux de vos intérêts.

Terminologie

Chaque passe-temps possède son propre langage pour décrire sa zone d'intérêt. La terminologie traditionnellement utilisée pour le commerce des cartes provient du Catalogue de la carte américaine, "American Card Catalog" (ACC), publié en 1960 par Nostalgia Press. Ce catalogue, écrit par Jefferson Burdick (appelé le "Père de la collection des cartes" pour son travail innovateur), se sert d'appellations par lettre et chiffre pour chaque jeu de cartes. La lettre utilisée dans l'ACC s'applique au type générique de carte. Alors que les émissions de cartes sportives et non-sportives sont toutes deux identifiées dans l'ACC, nous nous concentrerons sur les cartes sportives. La liste suivante identifie les lettres et leur signification dans l'utilisation qui en est faite par le "American Card Catalog":

(none) ou N - tabac U.S. du 19ème siècle

B - "Blankets" (couvertures)

C - "Canadian Tobacco" (tabac canadien)

D - "Bakery Inserts Including Bread" (en complément avec les articles de boulangerie, y compris avec le pain)

E - "Early Candy and Gum" (anciens bonbons et chewing-gum)

F - "Food Inserts" (en complément avec de la nourriture)

H - "Advertising" (publicité)

M - "Periodicals" (périodiques)

PC - "Postcards" (cartes postales)

R - "Candy and Gum since 1930" (bonbons et chewing-gum depuis 1930)

V - "Canadian Candy" (bonbon canadien)

A la suite de la lettre préfixe et d'un trait d'union optionnel il y a des nombres de un, deux, ou trois chiffres, 1-999. Ceux-ci représentent typiquement la compagnie ou l'entité émettant les cartes. Dans plusieurs cas, le nombre ACC est suivi

CALDER - Trophy awarded to NHL's Rookie of the Year.

CAMPBELL - Campbell Trophy winner.

CAN - Canada or Team Canada.

CAPT - Captain.

CC - Canada Cup or Collectible Card.

CHC - Chairman Hockey Committee.

CHECKLIST - A list of the cards contained in a particular set. The list is always in numerical order if the cards are numbered. Some unnumbered sets are artificially numbered in alphabetical order, or by team and alphabetically within the team for convenience.

CL - Checklist card. A card that lists in order the cards and players in the set or series. Older checklist cards in Mint condition that have not been checked off are very desirable.

CHL - Central Hockey League or Canadian Hockey League (also known as the Junior Leagues).

CLANCY - Trophy awarded for humanitarian contributions.

CO - Coach(es) card.

CO/MG - Coach/Manager.

COIN - A small disc of metal or plastic portraying a player in its center.

COLLECTOR - A person who engages in the hobby of collecting cards primarily for his own enjoyment, with any profit motive being secondary.

COLLECTOR ISSUE - A set produced for the sake of the card itself with no product or service sponsor. It derives its name from the fact that most of these sets are produced for sale directly to the hobby market.

COMBINATION CARD - A single card depicting two or more players (but not a team card).

COMMON CARD - The typical card of any set; it has no premium value accruing from subject matter, numerical scarcity, popular demand, or anomaly.

CONVENTION ISSUE - A set produced in conjunction with a sports collectibles convention to commemorate or promote the show.

COR - Corrected card.

COUNTERFEIT - An unauthorized reproduction of a card. Sometimes only very close inspection reveals the difference between a real and a fake card.

COUPON - See Tab.

CPL - Career point leader.

CREASE - A wrinkle on the card, usually caused by bending the card. Creases are a common

d'un trait d'union complémentaire et d'un autre suffixe composé d'un ou deux chiffres. Par exemple, la carte de hockey émise par la gomme canadienne "Canadian Gum" en 1933-34 porte la référence ACC: V252. Le "V" indique qu'il s'agit d'un bonbon canadien. Le nombre "252" est la désignation ACC pour "Canadian Gum".

De même que les autres méthodes traditionnelles d'identification, le système procure une façon de cataloguer les cartes; toutefois, la plupart des collectionneurs sérieux apprennent la désignation ACC des séries populaires plutôt par répétition et familiarité que par une tentative de se représenter ce que cela pourrait ou devrait être.

Depuis 1951, les collectionneurs et les revendeurs réfèrent ordinairement aux jeux de cartes d'après leur année, le fabricant, le type d'émission et toute autre caractéristique. Par exemple, une telle caractéristique pourrait être une émission inhabituelle, ou l'une de plusieurs émissions régulières lancée par un fabriquant précis au cours d'une seule année. Des émissions régionales ont souvent comme référence leur année, leur émetteur, et quelquefois le titre ou le sujet du jeu.

Glossaire/Légende

Notre glossaire définit des termes fréquemment utilisés dans la collection de cartes. Beaucoup de ces termes sont aussi communs à d'autres genres de collection dans le monde du sport. Quelques termes peuvent avoir différentes significations, en fonction de leur usage ou du contexte.

ACO - entraîneur adjoint.

ACO/GM - entraîneur adjoint / directeur général.

ACTION SCENES CARD - carte de scènes d'action: un type spécial de carte montrant une photo d'un ou de plusieurs joueurs en action, accompagnée d'une explication.

ADAMS - trophée accordé à l'entraîneur NHL de l'année (NHL: "National Hockey League: Ligue nationale du hockey).

AGM - directeur général adjoint.

AHL - "American Hockey League" : Ligue américaine du hockey.

ALL-STAR CARD - carte représentant un joueur "All-Star" de l'année précédente : vedette toutes catégories, précisant "All-Star" côté face. Parfois il est seulement précisé AS sur les listes de prix.

ALPH - alphabétique.

defect from careless handling.

CRUNCH - Crunch Crew.

CZE - Czechoslovokia.

DEALER - A person who engages in buying, selling and trading sports collectibles or supplies. A dealer also may be a collector, but as a dealer, he anticipates a profit.

DECKLE EDGE - Jagged edge found on a special OPC 1970-71 set.

DIE-CUT - A card with part of its stock partially cut, allowing one or more parts to be folded or removed. After removal or appropriate folding, the remaining part of the card frequently can be made to stand up.

DIR - Director of Player Personnel.

DISC - A circular-shaped card.

DISPLAY CARD - A sheet, usually containing three to nine cards, that is printed and used by the manufacturer to advertise and/or display the packages containing his products and cards. The backs of display cards are blank or contain advertisements.

DISPLAY SHEET - A clear, plastic page that is punched for insertion into a binder (with standard three-ring spacing) containing pockets for displaying cards. Many different styles of sheets exist with pockets of varying sizes to hold the many differing card formats. The vast majority of current cards measure 2-1/2 by 3-1/2 inches and fit in nine-pocket sheets.

DOUBLE - Two-trophy card.

DP - Double Print (a card that was printed in double the quantity compared to the other cards in the same series).

DT - Dream Team.

E - East.

EJ - Euro Junior.

ERR - Error card. A card with erroneous information, spelling, or depiction on either side of the card. Most errors are never corrected by the producing card company.

EXHIBIT - The generic name given to thick stock, postcard-size cards with single color obverse pictures. The name is derived from the Exhibit Supply Co. of Chicago, the principal manufacturer of this type of card. These are also known as Arcade cards since they were found in many arcades.

FP - Franchise Player.

FULL SHEET - A complete sheet of cards that has not been cut up into individual cards by the

AP - "Action Picture" : photo d'action.

ART - équipe "All-Rookie team" ou carte ART.

AS - "All-Star".

AS1 - première équipe "All-Star".

AS2 - deuxième équipe "All-Star".

ATG - carte "All-Time Great".

AW - "Award Winner" : gagnant d'une récompense.

BL - lignées.

BRICK - paquet de cartes contenant normalement au moins 50 cartes avec des caractéristiques communes, destinées à être achetées, vendues ou échangées en temps qu'unité. En général, les revendeurs placent une carte vedette ou super-vedette en première pour causer la vente.

BYNG - trophée Lady Byng, récompense remise au joueur NHL le plus honorable.

CALDER - trophée remis au débutant NHL de l'année.

CAMPBELL - gagnant du trophée Campbell.

CAN - le Canada ou équipe Canadienne.

CAPT - Capitaine

CC - "Canada Cup" ou "Collectible Card" : carte spéciale de collection.

CHC - "Chairman Hockey Committee".

CHECKLIST - liste des cartes contenues dans une série précise. La liste est toujours en ordre numérique si les cartes sont numérotées. Quelques séries non numérotées sont classées artificiellement par ordre alphabétique ou par équipe, et ordre alphabétique à l'intérieur de chaque équipe pour des raisons pratiques.

CL - "Checklist Card" carte qui inventorie dans l'ordre les cartes et les joueurs d'un jeu ou d'une série. Les cartes anciennes et en parfaite condition qui n'ont pas été inventoriées sont particulièrement désirables.

CHL - "Central Hockey League" ou "Canadian Hockey League" : Ligue centrale du hockey ou Ligue canadienne du hockey (aussi nommée "Junior League" : ligue junior).

CLANCY - trophée NHL attribué pour contributions humanitaires.

CO - "Coach" : carte de l'entraîneur.

CO/MG - Entraîneur / Directeur.

COIN - petit disque de métal ou de plastique représentant un joueur en son centre.

COLLECTOR - collectionneur: une personne dont le passe-temps de collectionner les cartes n'est tout d'abord que pour sa propre satisfaction, la recherche du gain ne venant qu'en second plan.

manufacturer. Also called an uncut sheet.

G - Gold.

GAME CARD - Scarce special insert cards issued in 1962-63 Parkhurst.

GG - Good Guy.

GM - General Manager.

GOALIE CARD - Cards of goalies, even average ones, command slight premiums.

GW - Game Winner.

HALL OF FAMER - (HOFer) A card that portrays a player who has been inducted into the Hall of Fame.

HART - Hart Trophy, awarded to the NHL's Most Valuable Player.

HERO - Upper Deck Heroes of Hockey.

HIGH NUMBER - The cards in the last series of numbers in a year in which such higher-numbered cards were printed or distributed in significantly lesser quantities than the lower-numbered cards. The high-number designation refers to a scarcity of the high-numbered cards. Not all years have high numbers in terms of this definition.

HL - Highlight card.

HOB - Hobey Baker Award, given annually to the collegiate Player of the Year.

HOF - Acronym for Hall of Fame.

HOLOGRAM - Inserts produced by Pro Set, Upper Deck and Score.

HOR - Horizontal pose on card as opposed to the standard vertical orientation found on most cards.

HT - Hat Trick.

IA - In Action card. A special type of card depicting a player in an action photo. Denoted in the Price Guide as "IA

ID - Idols.

IHL - International Hockey League.

INSERT - A special card or other collectible (often a poster or sticker) contained and sold in the same package along with cards of a major set. Sometimes called a BONUS or CHASE CARD.

IRS - International Rising Star.

ISSUE - Synonymous with set, but usually used in conjunction with a manufacturer, e.g., a Topps issue.

JENN - Jennings Trophy awarded to team with most outstanding goaltending.

LAYERING - The separation or peeling of one or more layers of the card stock, usually at the corner of the card.

COLLECTOR ISSUE - jeu émis pour la carte en soi, sans support d'aucun produit ou service. L'origine de l'appellation vient du fait que la plupart de ces jeux sont produits pour être commercialisés directement.

COMBINATION CARD - carte décrivant à elle seule deux ou plusieurs joueurs (mais n'étant pas une carte d'équipe).

COMMON CARD - carte-type de n'importe quelle série; elle ne possède pas de valeur spéciale en fonction de la matière du sujet, d'une rareté numérique, d'une demande populaire ou d'une anomalie.

CONVENTION ISSUE - série produite en rapport avec un salon de pièces de collection sportives, pour commémorer ou promouvoir le salon.

COR - carte corrigée.

COUNTERFEIT - reproduction non autorisée d'une carte. Quelquefois seulement une vérification très attentive révèle la différence entre une carte authentique et une imitation.

COUPON - voir TAB.

CPL - "Career Point Leader" : meneur en nombre de points.

CREASE - faux pli sur la carte, habituellement la conséquence d'une courbure de la carte. Ces faux plis sont un défaut provenant d'une manipulation sans ménagement.

CRUNCH - Equipe "Crunch".

CZE - la Tchécoslovaquie.

DEALER - personne qui s'occupe d'acheter, vendre et échanger des accessoires et objets de collection se rapportant aux sport. Ce revendeur peut aussi être un collectionneur, mais en tant que revendeur il envisage de gagner de l'argent.

DECKLE EDGE - bordure dentelée trouvée sur une série particulière O-Pee-Chee de 1970-71.

DIE-CUT - carte partiellement coupée, permettant ainsi d'en plier ou supprimer une ou plusieurs parties. La partie restante de la carte peut souvent être placée de manière à rester debout.

DIR - directeur de personnel des joueurs.

DISC - carte en forme de cercle.

DISPLAY CARD - feuille contenant habituellement de trois à neuf cartes, imprimée et utilisée par le fabricant pour faire de la publicité et/ou faire voir les emballages contenant ses produits et cartes. Le dos de ces feuilles est vierge ou contient des publicités.

DISPLAY SHEET - feuille de plastique transparent, poinçonnée afin de s'insérer dans un

LBM - Little Big Men.

LEGITIMATE ISSUE - A set produced to promote or boost sales of a product or service, e.g., bubblegum, cereal, cigarettes, etc. Most collector issues are not legitimate issues in this sense.

LID - A circular-shaped card (possibly with tab) that forms the top of the container for the product being promoted.

LL - League Leader card.

MAJOR SET - A set produced by a national manufacturer of cards containing a large number of cards. Usually 132 or more different cards comprise a major set.

MAST - Masterson Trophy, awarded for perseverance, sportsmanship and dedication.

MC - Members Choice.

MD - Managing Director.

MEM - Memorial card.

MEMORIAL CUP - Award given to the overall champions of the Junior Leagues.

MG - Manager card.

MINI - A small card or stamp (for example, the 1988-89 O-Pee-Chee mini-set).

MVP - Abbreviation for Most Valuable Player.

NHL - National Hockey League.

NNO - No number on card.

NOBIO - No Biography.

NOR - Norris Trophy, awarded to NHL's outstanding defenseman.

NOTCHING - The grooving of a card, usually caused by fingernails, rubber bands, or bumping card edges against other objects, which reduces the condition and value of the card.

NYI - New York Islanders.

NYR - New York Rangers.

OBVERSE - The front, face, or pictured side of the card.

OHL - Ontario Hockey League.

OLY - Olympic card.

OPC - O-Pee-Chee.

ORIG6 - Original Six.

OTG - Old Time Great.

P1 - First Printing.

P2 - Second Printing.

P3 - Third Printing.

PANEL - An extended card that is composed of two or more individual cards. Often the panel forms the back part of the container for the product being promoted.

PATRICK - Patrick Trophy, awarded for outstanding service to U.S. hockey.

classeur (convenant au classeur normal à trois anneaux) avec des poches pour classer les cartes. De nombreux styles différents de ces feuilles existent avec des poches de tailles variées afin de convenir à des formats différents de cartes. La plupart des cartes récentes mesurent 2 1/2" x 3 1/2" et sont adaptées aux feuillets à deux poches.

DOUBLE - carte à deux trophées.

DP - "Double Print": une carte imprimée au double de la quantité des autres cartes des mêmes séries.

DT - "Dream Team".

E - Est.

EJ - "Euro Junior".

ERR - carte erronée. Une carte avec des informations, une orthographe, ou une représentation inexactes d'un côté ou de l'autre. La majorité des erreurs ne sont jamais corrigées par la société émettant les cartes.

EXHIBIT - nom générique donné à des cartes d'un matériel épais, de la taille d'une carte postale, avec des images monochromes sur une face. Le nom vient de la société "Exhibit Supply Co." de Chicago, le fabricant principal de cette sorte de cartes. Elles sont également connues sous le nom "Arcade" parce qu'elles étaient trouvées sous beaucoup d'arcades marchandes.

FP - "Franchise Player" : joueur franchise.

FULL SHEET - feuille complète de cartes qui n'a pas été coupée par le fabricant pour séparer les cartes. On l'appelle aussi une feuille entière ou brute.

G - or.

GAME CARD - cartes rares émises comme complément spécial par Parkhurst en 1962-63.

GG - "Good Guy".

GM - directeur général.

GOALIE CARD - les cartes des gardiens de buts, même moyens, valent légèrement plus.

GW - "Game Winner" : gagnant du match.

HALL OF FAMER - (HOFer) une carte représentant un joueur qui est entré au "Hall of Fame" (Galerie de la renommée).

HART - le trophée Hart, accordé au joueur le plus précieux de la Ligue nationale du hockey.

HERO - "Upper Deck Heroes of Hockey".

HIGH NUMBER - cartes de la dernière série de chiffres d'une année durant laquelle de telles cartes à numérotage élevé furent imprimées ou distribuées en bien plus grande quantité que les cartes à numérotage bas. La désignation « High Number »

PB - Parkie's Best.

PC - Prefix for Pro Set Platinum inserts.

PEARSON - Lester B. Pearson Award, given to NHL's Outstanding Player as voted on by the Players Association.

PERIPHERAL SET - A loosely defined term that applies to any non-regular issue set. This term is most often used to describe food issue, giveaway, regional or sendaway sets that contain a fairly small number of cards and are not accepted by the hobby as major sets.

PHC - Parkhurst Collectible.

PLASTIC SHEET - A clear, plastic page that is punched for insertion into a binder (with standard three-ring spacing) containing pockets for displaying cards. Many different styles of sheets exist with pockets of varying sizes to hold the many differing card formats.

POY - Player of the Year.

PP - Platinum Performer.

PR - President or public relations.

PREMIUM - A card, sometimes on photographic stock, that is purchased or obtained in conjunction with (or redeemed for) another card or product. This term applies mainly to older products, as newer cards distributed in this manner generally are lumped together as peripheral sets.

PREMIUM CARDS - A class of products introduced recently that are intended to have higher quality card stock and photography than regular cards, but more limited production and higher cost. Defining what is and isn't a premium card is somewhat subjective.

PRO - Profiles.

PROMOTIONAL SET - A set, usually containing a small number of cards, issued by a national card producer and distributed in limited quantities or to a select group of people such as major show attendees or dealers with wholesale accounts. Presumably, the purpose of a promo set is to stir up demand for an upcoming set. Also called a preview, prototype or test set.

PS - Play Smart.

PSPOY - Pro Set Player of the Year.

PT - Point.

PUZ - Puzzle.

QMJHL - Quebec Major Junior Hockey League.

RARE - A card or series of cards of very limited availability. Unfortunately, "rare" is a subjective

dénote une rareté de cartes à numérotage élevé. Cette catégorie n'existe pas pour toutes les années.

HL - carte "Highlight".

HOB - récompense "Hobey Baker", accordée au Joueur collégial de l'année.

HOF - "Hall of Fame".

HOLOGRAM - cartes de complément produites par Pro Set, Upper Deck et Score.

HOR - carte horizontale, par opposition à l'orientation traditionnelle verticale de la majeure partie des cartes.

HT - "Hat Trick".

IA - "In Action Card" : type spécial de carte montrant un joueur en action. Ce type de carte est identifié dans le Guide des prix comme "IA".

ID - idoles.

IHL - "International Hockey League" : Ligue internationale du hockey.

INSERT - carte spéciale ou autre pièce de collection (par exemple, une affiche ou un autocollant) contenue dans le même paquet de cartes d'une série importante. Parfois appelée "Bonus Card" ou "Chase Card".

IRS - Vedette internationale ascendante.

ISSUE - synonyme de "set" : jeu, mais habituellement utilisé en rapport avec un fabricant, comme "Topps issue" (jeu émis par Topps).

JENN - "Jennings Trophy" : trophée accordé à l'équipe ayant marqué le plus de buts.

LAYERING - séparation ou décollement d'une ou de plusieurs couches du matériau de fabrication des cartes, normalement au coin de la carte.

LBM - "Little Big Men".

LEGITIMATE ISSUE - jeu produit pour promouvoir ou lancer les ventes d'un produit ou d'un service, comme le chewing-gum, les céréales, les cigarettes etc... Beaucoup de jeux de collection ne tombent pas dans cette catégorie.

LID - carte circulaire (parfois équipée d'une patte), constituant le dessus du récipient contenant le produit en promotion.

LL - "League Leader card" : carte de chef de ligue.

MAJOR SET - un jeu produit par un fabricant national de cartes, contenant un grand nombre de cartes. Habituellement, au moins 132 différentes cartes composent un "Major Set".

MAST - "Masterson Trophy" : trophée accordé pour persévérance, sportivité et dévouement.

MC - les choix des membres.

MD - directeur d'administration.

term sometimes used indiscriminately. Rare cards are harder to obtain than scarce cards.

RB - Record Breaker card.

REGIONAL - A card issued and distributed only in a limited geographical area of the country. The producer is not a major, national producer of trading cards.

RET - Retired card.

REVERSE - The back or narrative side of the card.

REV NEG - Reversed or flopped photo side of the card. This is a major type of error card, but only some are corrected.

RK - Rookie subset card.

RLL - Rookie League Leader.

ROOKIE CARD - A player's first appearance on a regular-issue card from one of the major card companies. Each company has only one regular-issue set, and that is the traditional set that is widely available. Until the recent growth of the hockey card market, which saw several manufacturers begin producing NHL cards, each player had only one Rookie Card (RC). A Rookie Card cannot be a Record Breaker, All-Star, Action Scenes, trophy winner or other special card.

ROSS - Art Ross trophy, awarded to NHL's points scoring leader.

ROY - Acronym for Rookie of the Year.

RR - Rated Rookie or Rookie Report.

RS - Russian Star.

SA - Super Action (1981-82 O-Pee-Chee and Topps).

SCARCE - A card or series of cards of limited availability. This subjective term is sometimes used indiscriminately to promote or hype value. Scarce cards are not as difficult to obtain as rare cards.

SELKE - Frank J. Selke Trophy, awarded to NHL's best defensive forward.

SEMIHIGH - A card from the next to last series of a sequentially issued set. It has more value than an average card and generally less value than a high number. A card is not called semihigh unless the next to last series in which it exists has an additional premium attached to it.

SERIES - The entire set of cards issued by a particular producer in a particular year, e.g., the 1971-72 Topps series. Also, within a particular set, series can refer to a group of (consecutively numbered) cards printed at the same time, e.g., the last series of the 1972-73 O-

MEM - carte commémorative.

MEMORIAL CUP - récompense remise à l'ensemble des champions des ligues cadettes.

MG - "Manager Card" : carte de directeur.

MINI - petite carte ou timbre (par exemple, le mini-jeu O-Pee-Chee 1988-89).

MVP - abréviation pour "Most Valuable Player" : le joueur le plus précieux.

NHL - "National Hockey League" : Ligue nationale du hockey.

NNO - carte non numérotée.

NOBIO - pas de biographie.

NOR - "Norris Trophy" : trophée accordé au meilleur joueur de défense NHL.

NOTCHING - rainures sur une carte, généralement provoquées par les ongles, des élastiques, ou des coups occasionnés aux tranches des cartes par d'autres objets, et qui diminuent l'état et la valeur de la carte.

NOTR - "No Trade Reference".

NYI - l'équipe "New York Islanders".

NYR - l'équipe "New York Rangers".

OBVERSE - avant, côté face, ou côté imagé de la carte.

OHL - "Ontario Hockey League" : Ligue de hockey de l'Ontario.

OLY - carte olympique.

OPC - O-Pee-Chee.

ORIG6 - six originaux (les).

OTG - "Old Time Great": meilleur joueur du temps passé.

P1 - première édition.

P2 - seconde édition.

P3 - troisième édition.

PANEL - carte agrandie, composée de deux ou de plusieurs cartes individuelles. Souvent ce panneau constitue le dos d'une boîte d'un produit en promotion.

PATRICK - trophée Patrick, récompense remise pour un service extraordinaire rendu au hockey américain.

PC - préfixe pour les cartes insérées Pro Set Platinum.

PEARSON - le trophée Lester B. Pearson, accordé au meilleur joueur de la NHL suite au vote de la Players Association.

PERIPHERAL SET - terme général qui s'applique à n'importe quel jeu non-réglementaire. La plupart du temps, ce terme décrit des jeux inclus avec de la nourriture, donnés gratuitement, régionaux ou à recevoir par courrier. Ces jeux ne

Pee-Chee issue (#'s 290 through 341) encompasses the WHA subset.

SET - One each of the entire run of cards of the same type produced by a particular manufacturer during a single season. In other words, if you have a complete set of 1985-86 Topps cards, then you have every card from #1 up to and including #165; i.e., all the different cards that were produced.

SHOW - A large gathering of dealers and collectors at a single location for the purpose of buying, selling, and trading sports cards and memorabilia. Shows are open to the public and sometimes also feature autograph guests, door prizes, films, contests, etc. The more formal term is "convention."

SL - Sidelines.

SMART - Play Smart.

SMYTHE - Conn Smythe Trophy, awarded to most outstanding player in the NHL playoffs.

SP - Single or Short Print (a card which was printed in lesser quantity compared to the other cards in the same series; see also DP and TP).

SPECIAL CARD - A card that portrays something other than a single player or team; for example, a card that portrays the previous year's statistical leaders or the results from the previous year's postseason action.

SPH - Sensational Sophomore.

SR - Super Rookie. Also, Scouting Report.

SS - Soviet Star.

STAMP - Adhesive-backed papers depicting a player. The stamp may be individual or in a sheet of many stamps. Moisture must be applied to the adhesive in order for the stamp to be attached to another surface.

STANLEY CUP - Trophy awarded to NHL championship team.

STAR CARD - A card that portrays a player of some repute, usually determined by his ability, but sometimes referring to sheer popularity.

STICKER - A card with a removable layer that can be affixed to (stuck onto) another surface.

STOCK - The cardboard or paper on which the card is printed.

SUPER ACTION - Card type similar to In Action. Abbreviated in the Price Guide as SA.

SUPERSTAR CARD - A card that portrays a superstar, e.g., a Hall of Fame member or a player whose current performance eventually will warrant Hall of Fame consideration.

contiennent que peu de cartes et ne sont pas reconnus par les collectionneurs comme étant des "major sets".

PHC - "Parkhurst Collectible".

PLASTIC SHEET - feuille de plastique transparent, poinçonnée afin de s'insérer dans un classeur (convenant au classeur normal à trois anneaux) avec des poches pour disposer les cartes. De nombreux styles différents de ces feuilles existent avec des poches de tailles variées afin de convenir à des formats différents de cartes.

POY - joueur de l'année.

PP - joueur exceptionnel.

PR - président ou relations publiques.

PREMIUM - une carte, parfois sur papier photo, qui est achetée ou obtenue en relation avec/ou contre la remise d'une autre carte ou d'un autre produit. Ce terme s'applique surtout aux produits plus anciens, car les cartes plus neuves distribuées de cette manière sont généralement groupées comme des "peripheral sets".

PREMIUM CARDS - ligne de produits introduite récemment, dont le papier et la photographie sont supposés être de meilleure qualité mais la production est limitée et plus onéreuse. Le terme "premium card" est quelque peu subjectif.

PRO - profiles.

PROMOTIONAL SET - jeu contenant habituellement un petit nombre de cartes, émis par un fabricant national de cartes et distribué en quantités limitées ou à des groupes particuliers, comme par exemple aux personnes qui assistent aux salons importants ou aux revendeurs.

L'émission d'un jeu promotionnel est censé créer de l'intérêt pour un jeu sous production. Également appelé un jeu de première, prototype ou test.

PS - "Play Smart".

PSPOY - "Pro Set Player of the Year" : Pro Set Joueur de l'Année.

PT - point.

PUZ - énigme.

QMJHL - "Quebec Major Junior Hockey League".

RARE - une carte ou des séries de cartes d'une disponibilité très limitée. Malheureusement, le mot "rare" est un terme parfois utilisé à tort et àtravers. Les cartes rares sont plus difficiles à trouver que les cartes à édition limitée.

RB - "Record Breaker card": carte d'un joueur battant des records.

SWE - Sweden.

TAB - A card portion set off from the rest of the card, usually with perforations, that may be removed without damaging the central character or event depicted by the card.

TC - Team Checklist.

TEAM CARD - A card that depicts an entire team.

TECH - Technician card.

TEST SET - A set, usually containing a small number of cards, issued by a national card producer and distributed in a limited section or sections of the country. Presumably, the purpose of a test set is to measure market appeal for a particular type of card.

THER - Athletic therapists.

THN - The Hockey News.

TL - Team Leader card.

TP - Triple Print (a card that was printed in triple the quantity compared to the other cards in the same series).

TR - Trade or Traded or Trainer.

TRIMMED - A card cut down from its original size. Trimmed cards are undesirable to most collectors, and are, therefore, much less valuable than otherwise identical untrimmed cards.

TRIPLE - Three-trophy card.

TW - Trophy Winners.

UER - Uncorrected error.

VARIATION - One of two or more cards from the same series with the same card number (or player with identical pose if the series is unnumbered) differing from one another in some aspect, from the printing, stock or other feature of the card. This is most often caused when the manufacturer of the cards notices an error in a particular card, corrects the error and then resumes the print run. In this case there will be two versions or variations of the same card. Sometimes one of the variations is relatively scarce. Variations also can result from accidental or deliberate design changes, information updates, photo substitutions, etc.

VERT - Vertical pose on card.

VEZINA - Trophy awarded to NHL's outstanding goaltender.

VP - Vice president.

W - West.

WALES - Prince of Wales Trophy Winner.

WB - World Junior Best.

WHA - World Hockey Association.

WHL - Western Hockey League.

REGIONAL - une carte émise et distribuée seulement dans un secteur géographique limité du pays. Le producteur n'est pas un producteur national important de cartes trouvées dans le commerce.

RET - carte retirée de la circulation.

REVERSE - dos ou le côté descriptif de la carte.

REV NEG - la photo est reversée sur la carte. Cette erreur est fréquente, mais peu de cartes sont corrigées.

RK - carte d'un jeu secondaire des débutants.

RLL - "Rookie League Leader": meneur débutant.

ROOKIE CARD - la première apparition d'un joueur dans une série normale d'une des principales compagnies produisant des cartes. Chaque compagnie ne publie qu'une série normale, et c'est cette série qui, par tradition, est largement disponible. Jusqu'au récent développement important du marché des cartes de hockey, durant lequel plusieurs fabricants commencèrent la production de cartes NHL, chaque joueur n'avait seulement qu'une carte de débutant ou "Rookie Card" (RC). Une carte de débutant ne peut pas être une carte de joueur battant des records (Record Breaker), de vedette toutes catégories (All-Star), de scènes d'actions (Action scenes), d'un gagnant de trophée ou une autre carte "spéciale".

ROSS - trophée Art Ross, accordé au joueur NHL ayant marqué le plus de buts.

ROY - initiales pour "Rookie of the Year", ou débutant de l'année.

RR - joueurs débutants classés ou "Rookie Report".

RS - vedette Russe.

SA - "Super Action" (O-Pee-Chee et Topps de 1981-82).

SCARCE - une carte ou une série de cartes d'une disponibilité limitée. Ce terme est quelquefois utilisé à tort et à travers pour pousser ou exagérer la valeur. Les cartes à tirage limité ne sont pas aussi difficiles à trouver que les cartes dites "rares".

SELKE - trophée Frank J. Selke, accordé au meilleur défense-avant NHL.

SEMIHIGH - carte de l'avant-dernière série d'un jeu de cartes émis en séquence. Celle-ci a davantage de valeur que la carte moyenne et, en général, moins de valeur qu'une carte à numérotage élevé. Une carte n'est pas appelée "Semihigh" à moins que l'avant-dernière série dans laquelle elle se trouve ne se vende plus chère.

WJC - World Junior Championship.
YG - Young Guns.
4X - Quadruple exposure card.
50/50 - 50 goals in 50 games.
***** - Multi-sport set.

Understanding Card Values

Determining Value

Why are some cards more valuable than others? Obviously, the economic laws of supply and demand are applicable to sports card collecting, just as they are to any other field where a commodity is bought, sold or traded in a free, unregulated market.

Supply (the number of cards available on the market) is less than the total number of cards originally produced, since attrition diminishes that original quantity. Each year a percentage of cards is typically thrown away, destroyed or otherwise lost to collectors. This percentage is much, much smaller today than it was in the past because more and more people have become increasingly aware of the value of sports cards.

For those who collect only Mint condition cards, the supply of older cards can be quite small indeed. Until recently, collectors were not so conscious of the need to preserve the condition of their cards. For this reason, it is difficult to know exactly how many 1957-58 Topps hockey cards are currently available, Mint condition or otherwise. It is generally accepted that there are fewer 1957-58 Topps available than 1967-68, 1977-78, or 1987-88 Topps hockey cards. If demand was equal for each of these sets, the law of supply and demand would increase the price for the least available sets. Demand, however, is never equal for all sets, so price correlations can be complicated.

The demand for a card is influenced by many factors. These include: (1) the age of the card; (2) the number of cards printed; (3) the player(s) portrayed on the card; (4) the attractiveness and popularity of the set; and (5) the physical condition of the card.

In general, (1) the older the card, (2) the fewer the number of the cards printed, (3) the more famous, popular and talented the player, (4) the more attractive and popular the set, and (5) the better the condition of the card, the higher the value

SERIES - la production totale de cartes émises par un producteur particulier au cours d'une année déterminée, par exemple les séries Topps 1971-72. Egalement, à l'intérieur d'un paquet particulier, les séries peuvent s'appliquer à un groupe de cartes (dont les nombres se suivent) imprimées en même temps. Par exemple, les dernières séries O-Pee-Chee 1972-73 (numéros 290 à 341) renferment la sous-collection de l'Association mondiale du hockey.

SET - chaque tirage complet de cartes de la même espèce produites par un certain fabricant au cours d'une seule année. Autrement dit, si vous possédez un "set" ou jeu complet de cartes de hockey Topps pour 1985-86, vous avez toutes les cartes du numéro 1 au numéro 165 inclus; c'est à dire : toutes les différentes cartes émises.

SHOW - une réunion importante de revendeurs et de collectionneurs dans le but d'acheter, de vendre et parfois d'échanger des cartes et objets de collection. Ces assemblées sont ouvertes au public et ont quelquefois au programme des invités accordant des autographes, des remises de prix, des films, des concours, etc. Le terme plus formel est "salon".

SL - activités hors jeu.

SMART - "Play Smart": expression qui s'adresse aux jeunes pour les exhorter à mener une vie morale: non à la drogue, non au crime, etc.

SMYTHE - le trophée Conn Smythe, accordé au meilleur joueur des finales NHL.

SP - impression unique ou limitée (une carte qui a été imprimée en quantité moindre par comparaison aux autres cartes des mêmes séries; voir aussi DP et TP).

SPECIAL CARD - une carte qui représente autre chose qu'un seul joueur ou une équipe; par exemple, une carte qui représente les meilleurs joueurs d'après les statistiques de l'année précédente, ou les résultats de l'arrière saison précédente.

SPH - sophomore sensationnel.

SR - "Super Rookie": super débutant ou pronostic sur les capacités des joueurs.

SS - "Soviet Star": vedette soviétique.

STAMP - timbre de papier enduit de colle, représentant un joueur. Peut être émis individuellement ou en feuille. Il faut humidifier la partie enduite de colle pour appliquer le timbre.

STANLEY CUP - trophée accordé à l'équipe NHL championne.

STAR CARD - carte qui représente un joueur

of the card will be. There are exceptions to all but one of these factors: the condition of the card. Given two cards similar in all respects except condition, the one in the best condition will always be valued higher.

While those guidelines help to establish the value of a card, the countless exceptions and peculiarities make any simple, direct mathematical formula to determine card values impossible.

Regional Variation

Since the market varies from region to region, card prices of local players may be higher. This is known as a regional premium. How significant the premium is — and if there is any premium at all — depends on the local popularity of the team and the player.

The largest regional premiums usually do not apply to superstars, who often are so well known nationwide that the prices of their key cards are too high for local dealers to realize a premium.

Lesser stars often command the strongest premiums. Their popularity is concentrated in their home region, creating local demand that greatly exceeds overall demand.

Regional premiums can apply to popular retired players and sometimes can be found in the areas where the players grew up or starred in college.

A regional discount is the converse of a regional premium. Regional discounts occur when a player has been so popular in his region for so long that local collectors and dealers have accumulated quantities of his key cards. The abundant supply may make the cards available in that area at the lowest prices anywhere.

Set Prices

A somewhat paradoxical situation exists in the price of a complete set vs. the combined cost of the individual cards in the set. In nearly every case, the sum of the prices for the individual cards is higher than the cost for the complete set. This is prevalent especially in the cards of the last few years. The reasons for this apparent anomaly stem from the habits of collectors and from the carrying costs to dealers. Today, each card in a set normally is produced in the same quantity as all others in its set.

Many collectors pick up only stars, superstars and particular teams. As a result, the dealer is left with a shortage of certain player cards and an abun-

d'une certaine réputation, ordinairement en fonction de son talent, mais aussi parfois purement à cause de sa popularité.

STICKER - carte avec une pellicule amovible, pouvant être appliquée sur une autre surface (autocollant).

STOCK - carton ou papier employé pour l'impression de la carte.

SUPER ACTION - carte similaire à celle représentant une action (IN ACTION). Abréviation dans le Guide des prix: SA.

SUPERSTAR CARD - carte représentant une super-vedette, par exemple, un membre du Hall of Fame, ou un joueur dont les performances devraient le faire entrer au Hall of Fame.

SWE - la Suède

TAB - portion de la carte séparée du reste de la carte, d'habitude avec des perforations, et qui peut être enlevée sans abîmer le caractère principal ou l'événement décrit sur la carte.

TC - "Team Checklist" : carte de contrôle d'équipe.

TEAM CARD - carte montrant une équipe au complet.

TECH - "Technician Card" : carte de technique.

TEST SET - jeu contenant habituellement un petit nombre de cartes, émis par un fabricant national de cartes dans une région limitée du pays. Probablement, le but de cette expérience est d'évaluer le marché pour un modèle particulier de carte.

THER - spécialiste en thérapie athlétique.

THN - "The Hockey News".

TL - "Team Leader card" : carte de chef d'équipe.

TP - "Triple Print": carte imprimée au triple de la quantité des autres cartes des mêmes séries.

TR - échange ou échangé ou entraîneur.

TRIMMED - une carte diminuée de taille par rapport à sa taille d'origine. Ces cartes sont sans intérêt pour la plupart des collectionneurs, et par conséquent ont moins de valeur que les mêmes cartes de taille normale.

TRIPLE - carte à trois trophées.

TW - "Trophy Winners" : gagnants d'un trophée.

UER - erreur non corrigée.

VARIATION - une, deux ou plusieurs cartes d'une même série portant le même numéro (ou un joueur dans la même pose si la série n'est pas numérotée) quelque peu différentes les unes des autres, soit par l'impression, soit par les matériaux

dance of others. He therefore incurs an expense in simply "carrying" these less desirable cards in stock. On the other hand, if he sells a complete set, he gets rid of large numbers of cards at one time. For this reason, he generally is willing to receive less money for a complete set. By doing this, he recovers all of his costs and also makes a profit.

The disparity between the price of the complete set and the sum of the individual cards also has been influenced by the fact that some of the major manufacturers now are pre-collating card sets. Since "pulling" individual cards from the sets of all three manufacturers involves a specific type of labor (and cost), the singles or star card market is not affected significantly by pre-collation.

Set prices also do not include rare card varieties, unless specifically stated. Of course, the prices for sets do include one example of each type for the given set, but this is the least expensive variety.

Scarce Series

Scarce series occur because certain O-Pee-Chee and Topps sets were made available to the public each year in more than one series of finite numbers of cards, as opposed to all cards of the set being available for purchase at one time. At some point during the season, interest in the current year's cards usually waned. Consequently, the manufacturers produced smaller numbers of these later-series cards. Specific series information, if any, is included above the price list for each set.

We are always looking for information or photographs of printing sheets of cards for research. Each year, we try to update the hobby's knowledge of distribution anomalies. Please let us know at the address in this book if you have firsthand knowledge that would be helpful in this pursuit.

Grading Your Cards

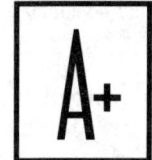

Each hobby has its own grading terminology — stamps, coins, comic books, record collecting, etc. Collectors of sports cards are no exception. The one invariable criterion for determining the value of a card is its condition: The better the condition of the card, the more valuable it is. Condition grading, however, is subjective. Individual card dealers and collectors differ in the strictness of their grading, but the stated condition

employés, soit par une autre caractéristique. Ceci arrive en général quand le fabricant relève et corrige une erreur sur une (ou plusieurs) cartes, puis continue à les imprimer. En ce cas, il y aura deux versions de la même carte. Parfois, l'une des versions a un tirage relativement limité. Les variations peuvent aussi résulter d'un changement accidentel ou volontaire du dessin, d'une mise à jour d'informations, d'une substitution des photos, etc.

VERT - pose verticale sur la carte.

VEZINA - trophée accordé au meilleur gardien de but NHL.

VP - vice-président.

W - ouest.

WALES - gagnant du trophée "Prince of Wales".

WB - "World Junior Best".

WHA - "World Hockey Association" : Association mondiale du hockey.

WHL - "Western Hockey League" : Ligue de hockey de l'ouest.

WJC - "World Junior Campionship".

YG - "Young Guns".

4X - "quadruple exposure card": une carte à quatre poses.

50/50 - 50 buts durant 50 jeux.

* - jeu couvrant multiples sports

Connaissance de la valeur des cartes

L'évaluation

Pourquoi certaines cartes ont-elles plus de valeur que d'autres? Visiblement, la loi économique de l'offre et de la demande s'applique à la collection des cartes comme à n'importe quel autre domaine où une marchandise est achetée, vendue ou échangée dans un marché libre et non réglé.

Le volume disponible (le nombre de cartes sur le marché) est inférieur au nombre total de cartes originellement produites du fait d'un phénomène d'attrition. Chaque année un pourcentage de cartes est typiquement jeté, détruit, ou de toute façon perdu pour les collectionneurs. Ce pourcentage est beaucoup moins important aujourd'hui qu'il ne l'était dans le passé parce que de plus en plus de gens ont pris davantage conscience de la valeur de leurs cartes sportives.

Pour ceux qui ne collectionnent que les cartes

of a card should be determined without regard to whether it is being bought or sold.

No allowance is made for age. A 1953-54 card is judged by the same standards as a 1993-94 card.

Centering

Current centering terminology uses numbers representing the percentage of border on either side of the main design. Obviously, centering is diminished in importance for borderless cards such as Stadium Club.

Slightly Off-Center (60/40): A slightly off-center card is one that upon close inspection is found to have one border bigger than the opposite border. This degree once was offensive only to purists, but now some hobbyists try to avoid cards that are anything other than perfectly centered.

Off-Center (70/30): An off-center card has one border that is noticeably more than twice as wide as the opposite border.

Badly Off-Center (80/20 or worse):: A badly off-center card has virtually no border on one side of the card.

Miscut: A miscut card actually shows part of the adjacent card in its larger border and consequently a corresponding amount of its card is cut off.

Corner Wear

Corner wear is the most scrutinized grading criteria in the hobby. These are the major categories of corner wear:

Corner with a slight touch of wear: The corner still is sharp, but there is a slight touch of wear showing. On a dark-bordered card, this shows as a dot of white.

Fuzzy corner: The corner still comes to a point, but the point has just begun to fray. A slightly "dinged" corner is considered the same as a fuzzy corner.

Slightly rounded corner: The fraying of the corner has increased to where there is only a hint of a point. Mild layering may be evident. A "dinged" corner is considered the same as a slightly rounded corner.

Rounded corner: The point is completely gone. Some layering is noticeable.

Badly rounded corner: The corner is completely round and rough. Severe layering is evident.

Creases

A third common defect is the crease. The

en état absolument parfait, le volume de cartes plus anciennes peut évidemment devenir assez réduit. Jusqu'à une période récente, les collectionneurs n'avaient pas autant conscience de la nécessité de préserver l'état de leurs cartes. Pour cette raison, il est difficile de savoir exactement combien de cartes de hockey Topps 1957-58 sont actuellement disponibles — qu'elles soient en parfait état ou non. Il est généralement accepté qu'il y a moins de cartes de hockey Topps disponibles pour 1957-58 que pour 1967-68, 1977-78 ou 1987-88. S'il y avait la même demande pour chacun de ces jeux, la loi de l'offre et de la demande augmenterait le prix des jeux les moins disponibles. Toutefois, la demande n'est jamais égale pour tous les jeux, donc la corrélation du prix est compliquée.

La désirabilité d'une carte est influencée par de nombreux facteurs. Cela comprend: (1) l'âge de la carte; (2) le nombre de cartes imprimées; (3) le ou les joueurs représentés sur la carte; (4) l'attraction ou la popularité exercées par ce jeu de cartes, et (5) la condition physique de la carte.

Généralement, (1) plus la carte est ancienne, (2) moins il en a été imprimé, (3) plus le joueur est connu et a du talent, (4) plus le jeu est attrayant et populaire, et (5) plus l'état de la carte est bon, plus le prix de la carte sera élevé. Il existe des exceptions pour tous ces facteurs sauf un; l'état dans lequel se trouve la carte. Prenez deux cartes similaires en tout sauf leur état, celle en meilleur état vaudra toujours davantage.

Alors que ces directives aident à définir la valeur d'une carte, d'innombrables exceptions et particularités font qu'il est impossible d'établir une formule mathématique simple pour établir la valeur des cartes.

Variations régionales

Le marché variant de région en région, le prix des cartes des joueurs régionaux peut être plus élevé. Ce phénomène est connu sous le nom de «prime régionale». Le montant de la prime — le cas échéant — dépend de la popularité locale de l'équipe et du joueur.

Les primes régionales les plus importantes ne s'appliquent, en général, pas aux toutes grandes vedettes, qui sont souvent tellement connues dans le pays que les prix de leurs cartes principales est extrêmement élevé, ne permettant pas aux commerçants régionaux de réclamer une prime.

Les étoiles moins connues peuvent souvent

Centering

Well-centered

Slightly Off-centered

Off-centered

Badly Off-centered

Miscut

Corner Wear

The partial cards shown at right have been photographed at 300%. This was done in order to
magnify each card's corner wear to such a degree
that differences could be shown on a printed
page.

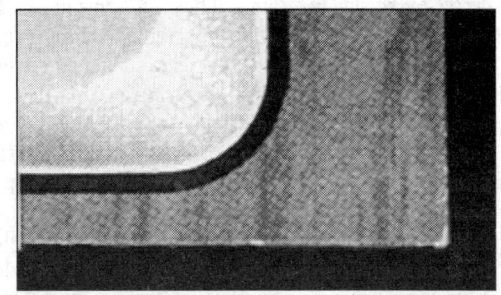

*This 1966-67 Topps Paul Henderson card has a
slight touch of wear. The corner is still sharp, but the
woodgrain borders shows extremely slight fraying.*

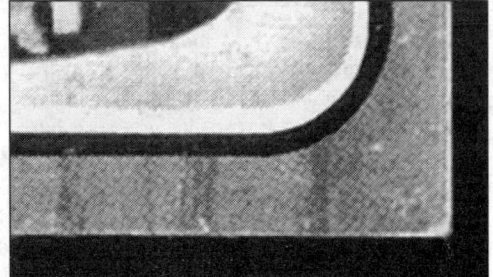

*This 1966-67 Topps Gordie Howe
All-Star card has a fuzzy corner. Although it still
comes to a point, the corner has begun to fray.
A slightly dinged corner is considered the same
as a fuzzy corner.*

*This 1966-67 Topps Gordie Howe
All-Star card has a slightly rounded corner,
evident by the lack of a point and flaking on both
edges. A "dinged" corner is considered the same
as a slightly rounded corner.*

*This 1966-67 Topps Gordie Howe
All-Star card displays a badly rounded corner.
Notice the heavy wear and excessive fraying.*

*This 1966-67 Topps Montreal
Canadians Team card displays creasing.
Notice the slight hairline creases, as well as
the thick crease in the corner.*

degree of creasing in a card is difficult to show in a drawing or picture. On giving the specific condition of an expensive card for sale, the seller should note any creases additionally. Creases can be categorized as to severity according to the following scale.

Light Crease: A light crease is a crease that is barely noticeable upon close inspection. In fact, when cards are in plastic sheets or holders, a light crease may not be seen (until the card is taken out of the holder). A light crease on the front is much more serious than a light crease on the card back only.

Medium Crease: A medium crease is noticeable when held and studied at arm's length by the naked eye, but does not overly detract from the appearance of the card. It is an obvious crease, but not one that breaks the picture surface of the card.

Heavy Crease: A heavy crease is one that has torn or broken through the card's picture surface, e.g., puts a tear in the photo surface.

Alterations

Deceptive Trimming: This occurs when someone alters the card in order (1) to shave off edge wear, (2) to improve the sharpness of the corners, or (3) to improve centering — obviously their objective is to falsely increase the perceived value of the card to an unsuspecting buyer. The shrinkage usually is evident only if the trimmed card is compared to an adjacent full-sized card or if the trimmed card is itself measured.

Obvious Trimming: Obvious trimming is noticeable and unfortunate. It is usually performed by non-collectors who give no thought to the present or future value of their cards.

Deceptively Retouched Borders: This occurs when the borders (especially on those cards with dark borders) are touched up on the edges and corners with magic marker or crayons of appropriate color in order to make the card appear to be Mint.

Categorization of Defects— Miscellaneous Flaws

The following are common minor flaws that, depending on severity, lower a card's condition by one to four grades and often render it no better than Excellent-Mint: bubbles (lumps in surface), gum and wax stains, diamond cutting (slanted borders), notching, off-centered backs, paper wrinkles, scratched-off cartoons or puzzles, rubber band

obtenir les meilleures primes. Elles sont surtout bien connues dans leur région, créant une demande locale bien plus élevée que la demande générale.

Des primes régionales peuvent être demandées pour un joueur populaire en retraite, et sont parfois exigées dans la région où le joueur a passé sa jeunesse ou a joué durant ses études.

Un décompte régional est l'opposé d'une prime régionale. Des décomptes régionaux sont donnés lorsqu'un joueur a été connu dans sa région durant si longtemps que les collectionneurs et distributeurs locaux ont accumulé une quantité importante de ses cartes principales. Une abondance de cartes permet de vendre celles-ci dans la région au prix le plus bas.

Le prix des jeux de cartes

Une situation en quelque sorte paradoxale survient dans le prix d'un jeu complet en fonction de la valeur combinée des cartes individuelles de ce jeu. Dans presque chaque cas, le total des prix des cartes individuelles est plus élevé que le prix du jeu complet. Ceci est particulièrement évident en ce qui concerne les cartes émises depuis peu d'années. Les raisons de cette apparente anomalie proviennent des habitudes des collectionneurs et du coût des inventaires des revendeurs. Aujourd'hui, chaque carte d'un jeu est en principe produite dans la même quantité que toutes les autres cartes de ce jeu.

Beaucoup de collectionneurs n'achètent que des vedettes, des super-vedettes, et certaines équipes. Il en résulte que le revendeur se retrouve avec un manque ou un surplus de cartes de certains joueurs. Il subit donc des frais, simplement pour "stocker" ces cartes moins recherchées. D'un autre côté, s'il vend un jeu complet, il se défait d'un grand nombre de cartes à la fois. Pour cette raison, il accepte en général de se faire payer moins cher pour un jeu complet. En agissant ainsi, il couvre toutes ses dépenses et en même temps fait un bénéfice.

La différence entre le prix d'un jeu complet et le total des prix individuels des cartes a également été influencée par le fait que certains des principaux fabricants collationnent maintenant d'avance les jeux de cartes. Etant donné que de "soustraire" des cartes individuelles des jeux des trois fabricants implique un effort spécifique (et des frais), le marché des cartes individuelles ("singles") de vedettes n'est pas affecté de façon significative par cette pré-collation.

marks, scratches, surface impressions and warping.

The following are common serious flaws that, depending on severity, lower a card's condition at least four grades and often render it no better than Good: chemical or sun fading, erasure marks, mildew, miscutting (severe off-centering), holes, bleached or retouched borders, tape marks, tears, trimming, water or coffee stains and writing.

Condition Guide

Grades

Mint (Mt) - A card with no flaws or wear. The card has four perfect corners, 60/40 or better centering from top to bottom and from left to right, original gloss, smooth edges and original color borders. A Mint card does not have print spots, color or focus imperfections.

Near Mint-Mint (NrMt-Mt) - A card with one minor flaw. Any one of the following would lower a Mint card to Near Mint-Mint: one corner with a slight touch of wear, barely noticeable print spots, color or focus imperfections. The card must have 60/40 or better centering in both directions, original gloss, smooth edges and original color borders.

Near Mint (NrMt) - A card with one minor flaw. Any one of the following would lower a Mint card to Near Mint: one fuzzy corner, or two to four corners with slight touches of wear, 70/30 to 60/40 centering, slightly rough edges, minor print spots, color or focus imperfections. The card must have original gloss and original color borders.

Excellent-Mint (ExMt) - A card with two or three fuzzy, but not rounded, corners and centering no worse than 80/20. The card may have no more than two of the following: slightly rough edges, very slightly discolored borders, minor print spots, color or focus imperfections. The card must have original gloss.

Excellent (Ex) - A card with four fuzzy but definitely not rounded corners and centering no worse than 80/20. The card may have a small amount of original gloss lost, rough edges, slightly discolored borders and minor print spots, color or focus imperfections.

Very Good (Vg) - A card that has been handled but not abused: slightly rounded corners with slight layering, slight notching on edges, a significant amount of gloss lost from the surface but no

En plus, les prix des jeux ne comprennent pas de variétés de cartes rares, à moins que ce ne soit spécifiquement précisé. Evidemment, les prix des jeux incluent un exemplaire de chaque espèce pour le jeu en question, mais il s'agit de la variété la moins chère.

Séries à faible tirage

Il existe des séries à faible tirage du fait que O-Pee-Chee et Topps ont, chaque année, rendu certains jeux disponibles au public dans plus d'une série de nombres définis de cartes, par opposition à toutes les cartes d'un jeu pouvant être achetées d'un coup. A un certain point au cours de la saison, l'intérêt pour les cartes de l'année s'est affaibli. En conséquence, les fabricants ont produit un plus petit nombre de ces cartes plus récentes. Des renseignements sur des séries particulières, le cas échéant, sont indiqués au-dessus des listes de prix pour chaque jeu.

Dans le cadre de nos études des cartes, nous sommes constamment à la recherche de renseignements ou de photos de feuilles d'impression de cartes. Chaque année, nous nous efforçons de mettre à jour les connaissances concernant les anomalies de distribution. Merci d'adresser tous renseignements qui pourraient aider nos efforts à l'adresse indiquée dans ce Guide.

La notation de vos cartes

Chaque passe-temps possède sa propre terminologie de notation —timbres, pièces de monnaie, bandes dessinées, disques, etc. Les collectionneurs de cartes sportives n'échappent pas à cette règle. Un critère invariable pour évaluer une carte est son état: plus la carte est en bon état, plus sa valeur est élevée. Toutefois, la notation de l'état d'une carte est subjective. Les revendeurs de cartes individuelles et les collectionneurs diffèrent quant à l'infaillibilité de leur système de notation, mais l'état de la carte devrait être établi sans considérer s'il s'agit d'un achat ou d'une vente.

Aucune exception n'est faite pour l'âge de la carte. Une carte de 1953-54 est jugée selon les mêmes critères qu'une carte de 1993-94.

scuffing and moderate discoloration of borders. The card may have a few light creases.

Good (G), **Fair** (F), **Poor** (P) - A well-worn, mishandled or abused card: badly rounded and layered corners, scuffing, most or all original gloss missing, seriously discolored borders, moderate or heavy creases, and one or more serious flaws. The grade of Good, Fair or Poor depends on the severity of wear and flaws. Good, Fair and Poor cards generally are used only as fillers.

The most widely used grades are defined above. Obviously, many cards will not perfectly fit one of the definitions.

Therefore, categories between the major grades known as in-between grades are used, such as Good to Very Good (G-Vg), Very Good to Excellent (VgEx), and Excellent-Mint to Near Mint (ExMt-NrMt). Such grades indicate a card with all qualities of the lower category but with at least a few qualities of the higher category.

The Sport Americana Hockey Card Price Guide lists each card and set in three grades, with the middle grade valued at about 40%-45% of the top grade, and the bottom grade valued at about 10%-15% of the top grade.

The value of cards that fall between the listed columns can also be calculated using a percentage of the top grade. For example, a card that falls between the top and middle grades (Ex, ExMt or NrMt in most cases) generally will be valued at anywhere from 50% to 90% of the top grade.

Similarly, a card that falls between the middle and bottom grades (G-Vg, Vg or VgEx in most cases) generally will be valued at anywhere from 20% to 40% of the top grade.

There are also cases where cards are in better condition than the top grade or worse than the bottom grade. Cards that grade worse than the lowest grade generally are valued at 5%-10% of the top grade.

When a card exceeds the top grade by one — such as NrMt-Mt when the top grade is NrMt, or Mint when the top grade is NrMt-Mt — a premium of up to 50% is possible, with 10%-20% the usual norm.

When a card exceeds the top grade by two — such as Mint when the top grade is NrMt, or NrMt-Mt when the top grade is ExMt — a premium of 25%-50% is the usual norm. But certain condition sensitive cards or sets, particularly those from the pre-war era, can bring premiums of up to 100% or

Le centrage

La terminologie actuelle de centrage utilise des chiffres représentant le pourcentage de marge de chaque côté du dessin principal. Il est évident que l'importance du centrage est moindre lorsqu'il s'agit de cartes sans marges, telle la Stadium Club.

Légèrement décentrée (60/40) : une carte légèrement décentrée est une carte qui, lors d'une inspection sérieuse, révèle une marge plus importante d'un côté que du côté opposé. Ce phénomène n'offusquait jadis que les perfectionnistes, mais aujourd'hui certains collectionneurs évitent les cartes qui ne sont pas parfaitement centrées.

Décentrée (70/30) : une carte décentrée possède une marge qui est visiblement plus de deux fois plus large que la marge opposée.

Très décentrée (80/20 ou pire) : une carte très décentrée n'a pratiquement aucune marge d'un côté.

Mal coupée : une carte mal coupée montre une partie de la carte adjacente du côté de sa marge la plus large et, par conséquent, il lui manque la même portion sur le côté opposé.

Usure des coins

L'usure des coins est un des critères les plus fréquemment appliqués lors de l'évaluation des cartes. Les catégories principales d'usure de coin sont :

Coin légèrement usé: l'angle est encore aigu, mais un certain degré d'usure est visible. Sur une carte à bords noirs, ceci se manifeste comme un point blanc.

Coin duveteux: un coin duveteux possède encore un angle correct, mais la pointe commence à s'effilocher. Un coin légèrement entaillé tombe dans la même catégorie qu'un duveteux.

Coin légèrement arrondi: l'effilochage du coin s'est augmentée au point qu'il n'existe plus qu'un indice d'angle pointu. Les couches de la carte peuvent être légèrement visibles. Un coin entaillé tombe dans la même catégorie qu'un coin légèrement arrondi.

Coin arrondi: la pointe n'existe plus. Les couches sont visibles jusqu'à un certain point.

Coin très arrondi: le coin est totalement arrondi et rugueux. Les couches sont très visibles.

Plis

Le troisième défaut commun est le pli. L'ampleur du pli d'une carte est difficile à montrer

even more.

Unopened packs, boxes and factory-collated sets are considered Mint in their unknown (and presumed perfect) state. Once opened, however, each card can be graded (and valued) in its own right by taking into account any defects that may be present in spite of the fact that the card has never been handled.

Selling Your Cards

Just about every collector sells cards or will sell cards eventually. Someday, you may be interested in selling your duplicates or maybe even your whole collection. You may sell to other collectors, friends or dealers. You may even sell cards you purchased from a certain dealer back to that same dealer. In any event, it helps to know some of the mechanics of the typical transaction between buyer and seller.

Dealers will buy cards in order to resell them to other collectors who are interested in the cards. Dealers will always pay a higher percentage for items that (in their opinion) can be resold quickly, and a much lower percentage for those items that are perceived as having low demand and hence are slow moving. In either case, dealers must buy at a price that allows for the expense of doing business and a margin for profit.

If you have cards for sale, the best advice we can give is that you get several offers for your cards — either from card shops or at a card show — and take the best offer, all things considered. Note, the "best" offer may not be the one for the highest amount. And remember, if a dealer really wants your cards, he won't let you get away without making his best competitive offer. Another alternative is to place your cards in an auction as one or several lots.

Many people think nothing of going into a department store and paying $15 for an item of clothing for which the store paid $5. But if you were selling your $15 card to a dealer and he offered you $5 for it, you might think his mark-up unreasonable. To complete the analogy: most department stores (and card dealers) that consistently pay $10 for $15 items eventually go out of business. An exception is when the dealer has lined up a willing buyer for the item(s) you are attempting to sell, or if the cards are so Hot that it's likely he'll have to hold

sur un dessin ou une photo. En décrivant l'état spécifique d'une coûteuse carte à vendre, le vendeur devrait en outre préciser s'il y a des plis. L'importance des plis peut être classée selon l'échelle suivante.

Léger pli: un léger pli est un pli qui est à peine détectable au cours d'une inspection soigneuse. En fait, quand les cartes sont dans des feuillets ou présentoirs en plastique, un léger pli peut bien ne pas être visible (jusqu'à ce que la carte soit retirée du feuillet ou porte-cartes). Un léger pli côté face est beaucoup plus sérieux qu'un léger pli au dos de la carte seulement.

Pli moyen: un pli moyen est détectable quand la carte est tenue et examinée à longueur de bras à l'oeil nu, mais ne détruit pas exagérément l'apparence de la carte. C'est un pli sans aucun doute, mais qui n'affecte pas la surface de l'image représentée par la carte.

Pli prononcé: un pli prononcé a déchiré ou brisé la surface de l'image, par exemple une cassure sur la surface d'une photo.

Altérations

Rognure trompeuse: il y a rognure trompeuse quand une personne retouche la carte dans le but (1) de faire disparaître l'usure des bords, (2) d'améliorer l'angle des coins, ou (3) d'améliorer le centrage. Assurément, le but est de faussement augmenter la valeur de la carte aux yeux de l'acheteur sans soupçons. La diminution de la taille de la carte ne devient généralement évidente que lorsque la carte rognée est comparée à une carte de taille complète, ou en mesurant la carte rognée.

Rognure évidente: ce type de rognure est détectable — et malheureux. Elle est généralement effectuée par des non-collectionneurs qui n'accordent aucune attention à la valeur actuelle ou future de leurs cartes.

Marges trompeusement retouchées: ceci arrive quand les marges (particulièrement pour les cartes avec des marges sombres) sont retouchées sur leurs bords et les coins avec un marqueur ou un pastel de même couleur afin de faire croire à une carte en parfait état.

Classification des défauts - Diverses imperfections

Les défauts mineurs suivants sont fréquents et, selon la sévérité du problème, peuvent faire baisser la notation d'une carte de un à quatre

the cards for only a short period of time.

In those cases, an offer of up to 75 percent of book value still will allow the dealer to make a reasonable profit considering the short time he will need to hold the merchandise. In general, however, most cards and collections will bring offers in the range of 25 to 50 percent of retail price. Also consider that most material from the last five to 10 years is plentiful. If that's what you're selling, don't be surprised if your best offer is well below that range.

Interesting Notes

The first card numerically of an issue is the single card most likely to obtain excessive wear. Consequently, you typically will find the price on the #1 card (in NrMt or Mint condition) somewhat higher than might otherwise be the case. Similarly, but to a lesser extent (because normally the less important, reverse side of the card is the one exposed), the last card numerically in an issue also is prone to abnormal wear. This extra wear and tear occurs because the first and last cards are exposed to the elements (human element included) more than any other cards. They generally are end cards in any brick formations, rubber bandings, stackings on wet surfaces, and like activities.

Sports cards have no intrinsic value. The value of a card, like the value of other collectibles, can be determined only by you and your enjoyment in viewing and possessing these cardboard treasures.

Remember, the buyer ultimately determines the price of each card. You are the determining price factor because you have the ability to say "No" to the price of any card by not exchanging your hardearned money for a given card. When the cost of a trading card exceeds the enjoyment you will receive from it, your answer should be "No." We assess and report the prices. You set them!

We are always interested in receiving the price input of collectors and dealers from around the country. We happily credit major contributors. We welcome your opinions, since your contributions assist us in ensuring a better guide each year. If you would like to join our survey list for the next editions of this book and others authored by Dr. Beckett, please send your name and address to Dr. James Beckett, 15850 Dallas Parkway, Dallas, TX 75248.

niveaux, lui donnant une notation ne dépassant souvent pas Excellent-Mint (excellente-parfaite) : bulles sur la surface, taches de chewing-gum et de cire, découpage diamant (bords en biais), entailles, dos décentré, papier fripé, dessins ou puzzles effacés sur le dos, impression d'un élastique, éraflures, marques en surface et distorsion.

Les défauts majeurs suivants sont fréquents et, selon la sévérité du problème, peuvent faire baisser la notation d'une carte d'au moins quatre niveaux, lui donnant souvent une notation ne dépassant pas Good (bon état) : décoloration dû au soleil ou à un produit chimique, marque d'effacement, moisissure, découpage incorrect (décentrage sérieux), trous, bords blanchis ou retouchés, marque de bande adhésive, déchirure, découpage des bords, taches d'eau ou de café et traces d'écriture.

Guide de l'état d'une carte

Notations

Mint (Mt) - Parfait. Une carte sans aucun défaut ni usure. Quatre coins parfaits, centrage de 60/40 ou mieux de haut en bas et de droite à gauche, brillant d'origine, marges lisses et couleur original du bord. Une carte parfaite n'a ni taches d'impression ni imperfections de couleur ou de mise au point.

Near Mint-Mint (NrMt-Mt) - Presque parfait-Parfait. Carte démontrant un défaut mineur. Un des défauts suivants fera baisser la notation d'une carte en parfait état à Presque parfait-Parfait : coin démontrant une légère trace d'usure, des taches d'impression et des imperfections de couleur ou de mise au point. Le centrage doit être au moins 60/40 dans les deux directions, brillant d'origine, marges lisses et couleur originale du bord.

Near Mint (NrMt) - Presque parfait. Carte démontrant un défaut mineur. Un des défaut suivants fera baisser la notation d'une carte en parfait état à Presque Parfait : un coin duveteux ou deux à quatre coins avec de légères traces d'usure, centrage de 70/30 à 60/40, marges légèrement rugueuses, légères taches d'impression et imperfections de couleur ou de mise au point. La carte doit avoir le brillant d'origine et la couleur originale du bord.

Advertising

Within this Price Guide, you will find advertisements for sports memorabilia material, mail-order and retail sports collectibles establishments. All advertisements were accepted in good faith based on the reputation of the advertiser; however, neither the author, the publisher, the distributors nor the other advertisers in this Price Guide accept any responsibility for any particular advertiser not complying with the terms of his or her ad.

Readers also should be aware that prices in advertisements are subject to change over the annual period before a new edition of this volume is issued each spring. When replying to an advertisement late in the hockey year, the reader should take this into account, and contact the dealer by phone or in writing for up-to-date price information. Should you come into contact with any of the advertisers in this guide as a result of their advertisement herein, please mention this source as your contact.

Additional Reading

With the increase in popularity of the hobby in recent years, there has been a corresponding increase in available literature. Below is a list of the books and periodicals that receive our highest recommendation and that we hope will further advance your knowledge and enjoyment of our great hobby.

The Sport Americana Baseball Card Price Guide by Dr. James Beckett (Sixteenth Edition, $16.95, released 1994, published by Edgewater Book Company) — the most comprehensive Price Guide and checklist ever issued on baseball cards.

The Official Price Guide to Baseball Cards by Dr. James Beckett (Fourteenth Edition, $6.99, released 1994, published by The House of Collectibles) — an abridgment of *The Sport Americana Price Guide* in a convenient and economical pocket-size format providing Dr. Beckett's pricing of the major baseball sets since 1948.

The Sport Americana Price Guide to Baseball Collectibles by Dr. James Beckett (Second Edition,

Excellent-Mint (ExMt) - Excellent-Parfait. Carte avec deux à trois coins duveteux mais pas arrondis, centrage maximum 80/20. La carte ne peut avoir plus de deux des défauts suivants : marges légèrement rugueuses, bords très légèrement décolorés, taches d'impression et imperfections de couleur ou de mise au point mineures. La carte doit avoir le brillant d'origine.

Excellent (Ex) - carte avec quatre coins duveteux mais pas arrondis, et centrage de maximum 80/20. La carte peut avoir perdu un peu de son brillant original, des marges rugueuses, des bords légèrement décolorés et des taches d'impression et imperfections de couleur et de mise au point mineures.

Very Good (Vg) - Très bon état. Carte ayant été manipulée mais pas maltraitée : coins légèrement arrondis avec couches un peu visibles, bords légèrement entaillés, perte significative de brillant en surface sans éraflures, et décoloration modérée du bord. La carte peut avoir quelques plis légers.

Good (G) - **Bon état, Fair (F)** - **Passable, Poor (P)** Mauvais état. Carte usée, maltraitée ou malmenée : coins arrondis et effilochés, éraflures, disparition de presque tout ou de tout le brillant, bords sérieusement décolorés, plis moyens à grands, et un ou plus d'un défaut sérieux. Les notations Good, Fair et Poor dépendent de la sévérité de l'usure et des défauts. Ces cartes-là ne sont, en général, employées que pour combler un vide.

Les notations employées le plus souvent ont été expliquées ci-dessus. Il est évident que beaucoup de cartes ne correspondent pas exactement àune de ces définitions.

Pour cette raison, des catégories entre ces principales notations, appelées des notations intermédiaires, sont souvent utilisées, telles que "de bon àtrès bon" (G-Vg), "de très bon à excellent" (Vg-Ex), "d'excellent-parfait àpresque parfait" (ExMt-NrMt). De telles notations indiquent une carte avec toutes les qualité s de la catégorie la plus basse, mais avec au moins quelques qualités de la catégorie plus élevée.

Le Guide des prix des cartes Sport Americana Hockey classe chaque carte et jeu dans trois catégories, avec la valeur de la catégorie moyenne estimée à 40-45 % de la catégorie supérieure, et la valeur de la catégorie inférieure estimée à 10-15 % de la catégorie supérieure.

La valeur des cartes classées entre les colonnes affichées peut aussi être calculée en utilisant un

$12.95, released 1988, published by Edgewater Book Company) — the complete guide and checklist with up-to-date values for box cards, coins, labels, Canadian cards, stamps, stickers, pins, etc.

The Sport Americana Football Card Price Guide by Dr. James Beckett (Eleventh Edition, $16.95, released 1994, published by Edgewater Book Company) — the most comprehensive Price Guide and checklist ever issued on football cards. No serious football card hobbyist should be without it.

The Official Price Guide to Football Cards by Dr. James Beckett (Fourteenth Edition, $6.99, released 1994, published by The House of Collectibles) — an abridgment of *The Sport Americana Price Guide* listed above in a convenient and economical pocket-size format providing Dr. Beckett's pricing of the major football sets since 1948.

The Official Price Guide to Hockey Cards by Dr. James Beckett (Fourth Edition, $6.99, released 1994, published by The House of Collectibles) — an abridgment of *The Sport Americana Price Guide* in a convenient and economical pocket-size format providing Dr. Beckett's pricing of the major hockey sets since 1951.

The Sport Americana Basketball Card Price Guide and Alphabetical Checklist by Dr. James Beckett (Third Edition, $14.95, released 1993, published by Edgewater Book Company) — the most comprehensive combination Price Guide and alphabetical checklist ever issued on basketball cards.

The Official Price Guide to Basketball Cards by Dr. James Beckett (Fourth Edition, $6.99, released 1994, published by The House of Collectibles) — an abridgment of *The Sport Americana Price Guide* in a convenient and economical pocket-size format providing Dr. Beckett's pricing of the major basketball sets since 1948.

The Sport Americana Baseball Card Alphabetical Checklist by Dr. James Beckett (Sixth Edition, $15.95, released 1994, published by Edgewater Book Company) — an alphabetical listing, by the last name of the player portrayed on the card, of virtually all baseball cards (major league and minor league) produced up through the 1994 major sets.

The Sport Americana Price Guide to the Non-Sports Cards 1930-1960 by Christopher Benjamin (Second Edition, $14.95, released 1993, published by Edgewater Book Company) — the definitive guide to virtually all popular non-sports American tobacco and bubblegum cards issued between

pourcentage de la catégorie supérieure. Par exemple, la valeur d'une carte classée entre les catégories supérieure et moyenne (dans la plupart des cas Ex, ExMt ou NrMt) sera estimée à entre 50 % et 90 % de la catégorie supérieure.

De même, la valeur d'une carte classée entre les catégories moyenne et inférieure (dans la plupart des cas G-Vg, Vg ou VgEx) sera généralement estimée à entre 20 % et 40 % de la catégorie supérieure.

Il existe aussi des cas ou une carte est en meilleur état que la catégorie supérieure ou en pire état que la catégorie inférieure. La valeur des cartes classées plus bas que la catégorie inférieure est en général estimée à entre 5 % et 10 % de la catégorie supérieure.

Lorsqu'une carte excède la catégorie supérieure d'un niveau, tel que NrMt-Mt lorsque la catégorie supérieure est NrMt, ou Mint lorsque la catégorie supérieure est NrMt-Mt, une prime pouvant atteindre 50 % est possible, de 10 à 20 % étant la norme habituelle.

Lorsqu'une carte excède la catégorie supérieure de deux niveaux, tel que Mint lorsque la catégorie supérieure est NrMt, ou NrMt-Mt lorsque la catégorie supérieure est ExMt, une prime d'entre 25 à 50 % est la norme habituelle. Mais certains jeux ou cartes dont l'état est important, surtout ceux de la période d'avant-guerre, peuvent obtenir des primes d'au moins 100 % ou même plus.

Les paquets, boîtes, et jeux non ouverts et collationnés par le fabricant sont considérés parfaits dans leur état non connu (et supposé parfait). Cependant, une fois le paquet ouvert, chaque carte peut être individuellement notée (et évaluée) en tenant compte de tous les défauts qui peuvent être détectés en dépit du fait que la carte n'ait jamais été manipulée.

La vente de vos cartes

Pratiquement tous les collectionneurs vendent ou vendront éventuellement des cartes. Un jour, vous pouvez avoir envie de vendre vos doubles ou peut-être même votre entière collection. Vous pouvez vendre à d'autres collectionneurs, à des amis ou des revendeurs. Vous pouvez même revendre des cartes achetées d'un certain revendeur à ce même revendeur. Dans tous les cas, il est utile de connaître certains des mécanismes d'une transac-

1930 and 1960. In addition to cards, illustrations and prices for wrappers also are included.

The Sport Americana Price Guide to the Non-Sports Cards by Christopher Benjamin (Fourth Edition, $14.95, released 1992, published by Edgewater Book Company) — the definitive guide to all popular non-sports American cards. In addition to cards, illustrations and prices for wrappers also are included. This volume covers non-sports cards from 1961 to 1992.

The Sport Americana Baseball Address List by Jack Smalling (Eighth Edition, $13.95, released 1994, published by Edgewater Book Company) — the definitive guide for autograph hunters, giving addresses and deceased information for virtually all Major League Baseball players past and present.

The Sport Americana Team Baseball Card Checklist by Jeff Fritsch (Sixth Edition, $12.95, released 1992, published by Edgewater Book Company) — includes all Topps, Bowman, Donruss, Fleer, Score, Play Ball, Goudey, and Upper Deck cards, with the players portrayed on the cards listed with the teams for whom they played. The book is invaluable to the collector who specializes in an individual team because it is the most complete baseball card team checklist available.

The Sport Americana Team Football and Basketball Card Checklist by Jeff Fritsch and Jane Fritsch-Gavin (Second Edition, $12.95, released 1993, published by Edgewater Book Company) — the book is invaluable to the collector who specializes in an individual team because it is the most complete football and basketball card team checklist available.

Beckett Baseball Card Monthly, published and edited by Dr. James Beckett — contains the most extensive and accepted monthly Price Guide, collectible glossy superstar covers, colorful feature articles, "who's Hot and who's Not" section, Convention Calendar, tips for beginners, "Readers Write" letters to and responses from the editor, information on errors and varieties, autograph collecting tips and profiles of the sport's Hottest stars. Published every month, *BBCM* is the hobby's largest paid circulation periodical. *Beckett Football Card Monthly*, *Beckett Basketball Monthly*, *Beckett Hockey Monthly*, *Beckett Focus on Future Stars*, *Beckett Tribute* and *Beckett Racing Monthly* were built on the success of *BBCM*.

tion typique entre acheteur et vendeur.

Les revendeurs achèteront des cartes dans le but de les revendre à d'autres collectionneurs de cartes. Les revendeurs paieront toujours un pourcentage plus élevé pour des objets qui (à leur avis) peuvent se revendre rapidement, et un pourcentage nettement plus faible pour des objets réputés comme étant peu recherchés et donc ne se revendant que lentement. Dans l'un et l'autre cas, les revendeurs doivent acheter à un prix qui couvre leurs dépenses et leur permettent de faire un bénéfice.

Si vous avez des cartes à vendre, le meilleur conseil que nous puissions vous donner est de prendre plusieurs offres pour vos cartes dans des magasins de cartes ou des salons, et de n'accepter que la meilleure, toutes choses considérées. Notez que la "meilleure" offre n'est pas forcément celle du montant le plus élevé. Et souvenez-vous, si un revendeur désire absolument vos cartes, il ne vous lâchera pas avant de vous avoir fait son offre la plus concurrentielle. Une autre formule est de placer vos cartes dans une vente aux enchères en un lot ou en plusieurs lots.

Beaucoup de gens ne trouvent rien à redire au fait de se rendre dans un grand magasin et de payer $15.00 pour un article vestimentaire pour lequel le magasin a payé $5.00. Par contre, si vous vouliez vendre votre carte de $15.00 à un revendeur qui vous en offrirait $5.00, vous pourriez penser que sa marge n'est pas raisonnable. Afin de compléter l'analogie: la plupart des grandes surfaces (et les revendeurs de cartes) qui paient $10.00 pour des objets valant $15.00 font éventuellement faillite. Il peut y avoir une exception quand le revendeur connaît un acheteur pour la marchandise que vous essayez de lui vendre, ou si les cartes sont tellement précieuses qu'il ne les gardera probablement que pendant très peu de temps.

En ce cas, une offre de jusqu'à 75 % de l'évaluation indiquée dans le livre lui permettra encore de faire un bénéfice raisonnable, considérant qu'il ne conservera la marchandise que pendant très peu de temps.

Cependant, la plupart des cartes et des collections apporteront en général des offres de l'ordre de 25 % à 50 % du prix de détail. N'oubliez pas non plus que la marchandise des cinq à dix dernières années existe en grande quantité. Si c'est ce que vous vendez, ne soyez pas surpris si votre meilleure offre tombe bien en-dessous de ce niveau.

Prices in this Guide

Prices found in this guide reflect current retail rates just prior to the printing of this book. They do not reflect the FOR SALE prices of the author, the publisher, the distributors, the advertisers, or any card dealers associated with this guide. No one is obligated in any way to buy, sell or trade his or her cards based on these prices. The price listings were compiled by the author from actual buy/sell transactions at sports conventions, sports card shops, buy/sell advertisements in the hobby papers, for sale prices from dealer catalogs and price lists, and discussions with leading hobbyists in the United States and Canada. All prices are in U.S. dollars.

History of Hockey Cards

Hockey cards have been produced for much longer periods than football or basketball cards — a fact no doubt influenced by hockey's predominance in Canada as its national pastime. Cigarette companies issued hockey cards from 1910 to 1913. While three distinct cigarette card sets have been identified, the manufacturers of these sets have not been determined. During the 1920s, four candy hockey sets and one cigarette hockey set were issued; none were in color. It was not until the 1930s that the Canadian gum companies started issuing card premiums with their chewing gum. World Wide Gum Co. and the familiar O-Pee-Chee were among these early Canadian hockey issuers. Bee Hive photos made their first appearance during the 1930s also. This Canadian chewing-gum card awakening parallels Goudey and National Chicle emerging as gum card issuers in the United States.

The recent history of hockey cards begins with the post-World War II Parkhurst issues of the 1950s and early 1960s. Parkhurst issued hockey card sets from 1951 through 1964, except for the 1956-57 season. Topps started issuing hockey cards in 1954. Then after a two-year hiatus, it issued cards regularly from the 1957-58 season to the present with the exception of a break for the

Notes d'intérêt

La première carte d'une édition est la seule à endurer une usure anormale. En conséquence, vous devriez trouver le prix sur la carte n° 1 (NrMt ou en condition parfaite) plus élevé qu'il ne devrait l'être autrement. De la même façon, mais à un niveau moindre (parce que l'envers de la carte, le côté normalement le moins important, est celui qui est exposé) la dernière carte d'une édition, dans l'ordre numérique, est aussi sujette à une usure anormale. Cette usure et ces éraflures supplémentaires se produisent parce que les premières et dernières cartes sont plus exposées aux éléments (élément humain compris) que les autres cartes. Il y a généralement des cartes de protection dessus et dessous chaque paquet, supportant les élastiques, le rangement sur des surfaces humides, et autres situations du même genre.

Les cartes sportives n'ont pas de valeur intrinsèque. La valeur d'une carte, comme la valeur de tout objet de collection, ne peut être déterminée que par vous-même et le plaisir que vous avez à regarder et posséder ces trésors de carton.

Souvenez-vous, l'acheteur est celui qui détermine le prix de chaque carte en dernier ressort. Vous êtes le facteur déterminant parce que vous avez la possibilité de dire "non" pour le prix de n'importe quelle carte en refusant d'échanger votre argent durement gagné pour une certaine carte. Lorsque le prix d'une carte trouvée dans le commerce dépasse le plaisir que vous en recevrez, votre réponse devrait être "non". Nous évaluons et indiquons des prix. Vous les déterminez !

Nous sommes toujours intéressés à entendre l'opinion des prix des collectionneurs ou revendeurs du pays. Nous reconnaissons volontiers nos collaborateurs importants. Votre avis est le bienvenu, d'autant plus que vos contributions nous aident à publier, chaque année, une édition encore améliorée de notre Guide. Si vous désirez faire partie de notre liste de sondage pour les futures éditions de ce livre ainsi que d'autres écrits par le Dr. Beckett, veuillez envoyer vos nom et adresse à: Dr. James Beckett, 15850 Dallas Parkway, Dallas, Texas 75248.

1982-83 and 1983-84 seasons. During the 1950s, Topps typically issued cards of players from American teams while Parkhurst issued cards with players from the two Canadian teams existing at the time, Montreal and Toronto. From the 1960-61 season until its demise after the 1963-64 season, Parkhurst issued cards of the two Canadian teams plus Detroit, while Topps issued cards of the remaining three American teams. Beginning with the 1964-65 season, Topps issued players from all teams in the NHL.

Topps attempted to produce a 66-card set aimed strictly at the American market, with no French on the cards, in 1966-67. This test issue, now quite scarce, is very similar to the regular 1966-67 Topps set and includes a Bobby Orr card.

O-Pee-Chee re-entered the hockey card market in 1968, and has issued sets from the 1968-69 season to the present. O-Pee-Chee sets are larger in size compared to Topps sets, perhaps a reflection of the relative popularity of hockey in Canada as compared to the United States. O-Pee-Chee also issued separate card sets containing World Hockey Association players for a four-year period between the 1974-75 and 1977-78 seasons. During recent years, beginning with the 1974-75 season, the Topps cards have been nearly identical to the O-Pee-Chee cards (the OPCs have white backs, the Topps gray).

In 1990-91, the NHL card market saw five new major sets: Bowman, O-Pee-Chee Premier, Pro Set, Score and Upper Deck. Most represented significant improvements over the quality of previous sets, and all enjoyed moderate to superb levels of success. Needless to say, this reflects the growing interest in hockey cards. Score and Upper Deck issued Canadian and French sets, respectively, which drew attention from collectors due to their perceived relative scarcity. Score's debut sets were partially fueled by the inclusion of ultratalented prospect Eric Lindros. Upper Deck matched Score by including a Canadian National Junior Championship subset (featuring Lindros, Pat Falloon and Scott Niedermayer, who were the top three picks, respectively, in the 1991 NHL draft) in its high number set.

The 1991-92 hockey card season saw the decline in interest in Canadian and French versions. Overall, the hockey card market enjoyed further growth, at least in the area of supply. All seven major 1990-91 sets returned, and four new "pre-

Publicité

Vous trouverez de la publicité dans ce Guide des prix pour le matériel en relation avec les sports, la vente par correspondance et les établissements de vente au détail d'objets de collection en rapport avec les sports. Toutes les publicités ont été acceptées de bonne foi, basées sur la réputation de leur initiateur; toutefois, ni l'auteur, ni l'éditeur, ni les distributeurs ou autres personnes faisant de la publicité dans le Guide des prix n'acceptent quelque responsabilité que ce soit à l'égard d'un personne faisant de la publicité et qui ne se conformerait pas aux termes de ladite publicité.

Les lecteurs devraient être également conscients que les prix contenus dans les publicités peuvent changer durant l'année précédant la sortie de chaque édition au printemps. Répondant à une publicité tard dans la saison de hockey, le lecteur devrait tenir compte de cela et prendre contact avec le revendeur par téléphone ou par courrier pour obtenir des renseignements courants sur les prix. Si vous contactez des personnes faisant de la publicité dans ce guide, voudriez-vous s'il vous plaît leur faire savoir que ce guide est à l'origine de votre prise de contact.

Lectures supplémentaires

Avec l'accroissement de popularité de ce passe-temps au cours des années récentes, il s'est avéré un accroissement identique de littérature disponible sur le sujet. A suivre, il y a une liste de livres et de périodiques que nous recommandons chaudement et qui, espérons-le, augmenteront votre savoir et votre plaisir pour ce qui est de ce magnifique passe-temps.

The Sport Americana Baseball Card Price Guide par le Dr. James Beckett (seizième édition, $16.95, publiée en 1994, éditée par Edgewater Book Company) — le Guide des prix/inventaire le plus complet jamais publié sur les cartes de base-ball.

The Official Price Guide to Baseball Cards par le Dr. James Beckett (quatorzième édition, $6.99 publiée en 1994, éditée par The House of Collectibles) — un abrégé du *Sport Americana Baseball Card Price Guide* dans un format de poche pratique et économique, indiquant les prix, par le Dr. Beckett,

mium" sets made their debuts: Pro Set Platinum, Parkhurst (also produced by Pro Set), Score Pinnacle and Topps Stadium Club. Overall, the values of the new sets generally remained stable or decreased because of overproduction. It will be interesting to see how the card companies respond to what appears to be a saturated new card market.

The 1992-93 hockey card season will be remembered for two things: the pervasiveness of insert card sets and the come-from-behind success of Bowman. The five returning licensees joined with newcomer Fleer to produce 12 regular sets and a staggering 31 insert sets. In reaction to the overproduction of recent years, Topps drastically curtailed its shipments of Bowman hockey. This reduction of supply, along with a number of short-printed insert cards, made the set wildly popular with collectors, and may signal the start of a new direction in card manufacturing.

The 1993-94 card season was drastically affected by a joint decision from the NHL and the NHLPA to limit licensees to two brands each. The new regulations were particularly tough on Topps, which released five sets in 1992-93 (including two through sublicensee, OPC). The company responded by dropping both base products and the Bowman line, leaving only Stadium Club, Topps and OPC Premier.

After experiencing financial troubles, Pro Set was denied a new license. The rights to the Parkhurst brand, which had served as Pro Set's pre-mium product, were sold to Upper Deck. The company continued the revival of that grand old name as a super-premium line in late 1993. Upper Deck also broke with tradition by issuing its base brand set in two distinct series. And in the place of Pro Set, the NHL and NHLPA awarded the fifth license to Leaf Brands, which released a two series, super-premium product, as well as a premium series under the Donruss imprint.

Finding Out More

The above has been a thumbnail sketch of card collecting from its inception to the present. It is dif-ficult to tell the whole story in just a few pages — there are several other good sources of information. Serious collectors should subscribe to at least one of the excellent hobby periodicals. We also suggest that collectors visit their local card shop(s) and also attend a sports collectibles show in their area. Card

des principaux jeux de base-ball depuis 1948.

The Sport Americana Price Guide to Baseball Collectibles par le Dr. James Beckett (deuxième édi-tion, $12.95, publiée en 1988, éditée par Edgewater Book Company) — un guide et inven-taire complets indiquant la valeur courante des boîtes de cartes, pièces, étiquettes, cartes canadi-ennes, timbres, autocollants, pinn's, etc.

The Sport Americana Football Card Price Guide par le Dr. James Beckett (onzième édition, $16.95, publiée en 1994, éditée par Edgewater Book Company) — le guide des prix/inventaire le plus compréhensif jamais publié sur les cartes de foot-ball. Il n'y a pas un sérieux amateur de cartes de football qui puisse s'en passer.

The Official Price Guide to Football Cards par le Dr. James Beckett (quatorzième édition, $6.99, publiée en 1994, éditée par The House of Collectibles) — un abrégé du *Sport Americana Football Card Price Guide* précédemment décrit, édité dans un format de poche pratique et économique indiquant les prix, par le Dr. Beckett, des principaux jeux de football depuis 1948.

The Official Price Guide to Hockey Cards par le Dr. James Beckett (quatrième édition, $6.99, pub-liée en 1994, éditée par House of Collectibles) — un abrégé du *Sport Americana Price Guide* dans un format de poche pratique et économique et indi-quant les prix, par le Dr. Beckett, des principaux jeux de hockey depuis 1951.

The Sport Americana Basketball Card Price Guide and Alphabetical Checklist par le Dr. James Beckett (troisième édition, $14.95, publiée en 1993, éditée par Edgewater Book Company) — le guide des prix/inventaire alphabétique le plus com-plet jamais publié sur les cartes de basket-ball.

The Official Price Guide to Basketball Cards par le Dr. James Beckett (quatrième édition, $6.99, publiée en 1994, éditée par The House of Collectibles) — un abrégé du *Sport Americana Price Guide* précédemment décrit, dans un format de poche pratique et économique, indiquant les prix, par le Dr. Beckett, des principaux jeux de basket-ball depuis 1948.

The Sport Americana Baseball Card Alphabetical Checklist par le Dr. James Beckett (sixième édition, $15.95, publiée en 1994, éditée par Edgewater Book Company) — un inventaire alphabétique, d'après le nom de famille du joueur montré sur la carte, de pratiquement toutes les cartes de base-ball (équipes majeures et minimes) produites jusqu'aux jeux importants de 1994.

The Sport Americana Price Guide to the Non-Sports Cards 1930-1960 par Christopher Benjamin et Dennis W. Eckes ($14.95, publié en 1993, édité par Edgewater Book Company) — le guide détermi-

collecting is still a young and informal hobby. You can learn more about it in either place. After all, smart dealers realize that spending a few minutes teaching beginners about the hobby often pays off for them in the long run.

Acknowledgments

A great deal of diligence, hard work, and dedicated effort went into this year's volume. The high standards to which we hold ourselves, however, could not have been met without the expert input and generous amount of time contributed by many people. Our sincere thanks are extended to each and every one of you.

A complete list of these invaluable contributors appears after the Price Guide section.

nant de virtuellement toutes les cartes populaires non-sportives de tabac américain et chewing-gum émises entre 1930 et 1960. En plus de ces cartes, des illustrations et des prix d'emballages sont aussi inclus.

The Sport Americana Price Guide to the Non-Sports Cards par Christopher Benjamin (quatrième édition, deuxième partie, $14.95, publiée en 1992, publiée par Edgewater Book Company) —le guide déterminant de toutes les cartes non-sportives américaines. En plus des cartes, des illustrations et des prix d'emballages sont inclus. Ce tome couvre les cartes non-sportives de 1961 à 1992.

The Sport Americana Baseball Address List par Jack Smalling (huitième édition, $13.95, publiée en 1994, éditée par Edgewater Book Company) — le guide déterminant des chasseurs d'autographes, donnant les adresses et informations défuntes de virtuellement tous les joueurs, passés et présents, de ligues majeures de base-ball.

The Sport Americana Team Baseball Card Checklist par Jeff Fritsch (sixième édition, $12.95, publiée en 1992, éditée par Edgewater Book Company) — comprend toutes les cartes Topps, Bowman, Donruss, Fleer, Score, Play Ball, Goudey, et Upper Deck avec le portrait des joueurs sur les cartes inventoriées et les équipes pour lesquelles ils ont joué. Le livre est inestimable pour le collectionneur qui se spécialise dans une équipe unique parce qu'il contient l'inventaire disponible le plus complet des cartes de base-ball.

The Sport Americana Team Football and Basketball Card Checklist par Jeff Fritsch et Jane Fritsch-Gavin (seconde édition, $12.95, publiée en 1993, éditée par Edgewater Book Company) — le livre est inestimable pour le collectionneur qui se spécialise dans une équipe unique parce qu'il contient l'inventaire disponible le plus complet des cartes de football et de basket-ball.

Beckett Baseball Card Monthly, édité et rédigé par le Dr. James Beckett — il s'agit du guide des prix mensuel le plus étendu et accepté, avec, en couverture, images brillantes et à collectionner des super-vedettes, articles d'un caractère coloré, "qui est en vue et qui ne l'est pas", calendrier des conventions, conseils pour débutants, "les lecteurs écrivent": lettres à l'éditeur et ses réponses, information sur les erreurs et variations, conseils pour collectionner les autographes, profils des vedettes de sports les plus en vue. Publié chaque mois, *BBCM* est le périodique payant de passe-temps au plus haut tirage. *Beckett Football Card Monthly, Beckett Basketball Monthly, Beckett Hockey Monthly, Beckett Focus on Future Stars, Beckett Tribute et Beckett Racing Monthly.* sont basés sur le succès de *BBCM*.

Prix indiqués dans le guide

Les prix trouvés dans ce guide sont le reflet actuel des prix de détail précédant immédiatement la mise de ce livre à l'imprimerie. Ils ne sont pas le reflet du prix "A VENDRE" par l'auteur, l'éditeur, les distributeurs, les personnes faisant de la publicité, ou tous revendeurs de cartes en rapport avec ce guide. Absolument personne n'est obligé, en aucune manière, d'acheter, vendre ou échanger sa ou ses cartes en se basant sur ces prix. Les listes de prix ont été établies par l'auteur à partir de transactions réelles ventes/achats aux congrès sportifs, magasins de cartes sportives, ventes/achats mis en publicité dans les journaux de passe-temps, prix de ventes indiqués dans des catalogues de revendeurs et listes de prix, et des discussions avec ceux qui sont en tête de file de ce passe-temps aux Etats-Unis et au Canada. Tous les prix sont indiqués en dollars U.S.

L'histoire des cartes de hockey

Les cartes de hockey sont en production depuis beaucoup plus longtemps que les cartes de football ou de basket-ball — un fait qui a sans aucun doute été influencé par la prédominance du hockey au Canada en temps que passe-temps national. Les marques de cigarettes ont émis des cartes de hockey de 1910 à 1913. Alors que trois jeux de cartes distincts de marques de cigarettes ont pu être identifiés, les fabricants de ces jeux n'ont pas pu être définis. Au cours des années 20, quatre jeux de hockey ont été produits par des marques de bonbons, et un jeu par une marque de cigarettes; pas un seul en couleur. Ce n'est pas avant les années 30 que les marques canadiennes de gommes ont commencé à émettre des cartes distribuées en prime avec leur chewing-gum. "World Wide Gum Company" et la familière société "O-Pee-Chee" font partie de ces premiers émetteurs canadiens. Les photos "Bee Hive" ont fait leur première apparition pendant les années 30 également. Les cartes de chewing-gum sont apparues au Canada en même temps que les sociétés Goudey et National Chicle, émettrices de cartes de chewing-gum, se sont formées aux Etats-Unis.

L'histoire récente des cartes de hockey commence avec les émissions de Parkhurst après la deuxième guerre mondiale au cours des années 50 et au début des années 60. Parkhurst a émis des jeux de cartes de hockey de 1951 à 1964, sauf pour la saison 1956-57. Topps a commencé à faire des cartes de hockey en 1954. Puis, après deux années de relâche, Topps a émis régulièrement des cartes depuis la saison 1957-58 jusqu'à maintenant, à l'exception d'un arrêt durant les saisons 1982-83 et 1983-84. Au cours des années 50, Topps a surtout produit des cartes de joueurs des équipes américaines alors que Parkhurst a émis des cartes de joueurs des deux équipes canadiennes existantes à l'époque, Montréal et Toronto. De la saison 1960-61 jusqu'à sa fin après la saison 1963-64, Parkhurst a produit des cartes des deux équipes canadiennes et de l'équipe de Détroit, tandis que Topps produisait les cartes des trois équipes américaines subsistantes. A partir de la saison 1964-65, Topps a fait des cartes des joueurs de toutes les équipes de la NHL.

En 1966-67, Topps a essayé de faire un jeu des cartes-66 consacré exclusivement au marché américain, sans un mot en français sur les cartes. Cette édition d'essai, pas spécialement à tirage limité, est très ressemblante au jeu normal Topps 1966-67 et comprend une carte de Bobby Orr.

O-Pee-Chee revient au marché de la carte de hockey en 1968, et a émis des jeux de la saison 1968-69 jusqu'à maintenant. Les jeux de O-Pee-Chee sont d'une taille plus importante que ceux de Topps, sans doute une conséquence de la popularité relative du hockey au Canada par rapport aux Etats-Unis. O-Pee-Chee a également produit des jeux de cartes distincts concernant les joueurs de l'association mondiale de hockey durant une période de quatre années entre 1974-75 et 1977-78. Au cours des années récentes, à partir de la saison 1974-75, les cartes Topps ont été pratiquement identiques aux cartes O-Pee-Chee (les cartes OPC ont un dos blanc, et les cartes Topps un dos gris).

En 1990-91, le marché des cartes NHL a vu l'arrivée de cinq nouveaux jeux principaux: "Bowman", "O-Pee-Chee Premier", "Pro Set", "Score" et "Upper Deck". La plupart présentent des améliorations substantielles par rapport à la qualité des jeux précédents, et tous ont goûté un succès allant du modéré à l'extrême. Sans aucun doute, ceci reflète un intérêt croissant dans les cartes de hockey. Score et Upper Deck ont sorti des jeux canadiens et français, respectivement, qui ont attiré l'attention des collectionneurs à cause d'un tirage relativement limité. Les premiers jeux de Score se sont, en partie, vendus grâce à l'inclusion de l'étoile montante, Eric Lindros. Upper Deck a maintenu le niveau avec Score en incluant un sous-jeu, dans les chiffres élevés ("high number") pour le championnat canadien "Canadian National Junior Championship" (représentant Lindros, Pat Falloon et Scott Neidermayer, les trois meilleurs choix, respectivement, du repêchage NHL 1991).

La saison de cartes de hockey 1991-92 a subi un déclin d'intérêt dans les versions canadiennes et françaises. En général, le marché des cartes de hockey a grandi, tout au moins en ce qui concerne la quantité de cartes. Les sept jeux 1990-91 les plus importants ont à nouveau été publiés, et quatre nouveaux jeux "premium" ont été lancés : Pro Set Platinum, Parkhurst (aussi produit par Pro Set), Score Pinnacle et Topps Stadium Club. Généralement, les valeurs des nouveaux jeux sont restées stables ou ont diminué à cause de la surproduction. Il sera intéressant de voir comment les producteurs de cartes réagiront à ce qui paraît être un marché inondé de nouvelles cartes.

La saison des cartes de Hockey 1992-93 restera en mémoire pour deux raisons: l'envahissement des jeux de cartes encart et le succès obtenu à la dernière minute par Bowman. Les cinq concessionnaires de licence réapparaissant se sont joints au nouvel arrivant Fleer pour produire douze jeux réguliers et un étonnant jeu encart de trente et une cartes. Réagissant sur la surproduction des années récentes, Topps a sévèrement diminué les envois de hockey Bowman. Cette réduction de stock, associée à une impression insuffisante de cartes encart, ont rendu le jeu très populaire aux yeux des collectionneurs et peut signaler le début d'une nouvelle direction dans le production de cartes. La saison des cartes 1993-94 a été énormément touchée par la décision commune de la part de la NHL et de la NHLPA, limitant les concessionnaires de licence à deux catégories chacun. Les nouveaux règlements ont surtout affecté Topps, qui a sorti cinq jeux en 92-93 (y compris deux jeux à travers le sous-concessionnaire OPC). La société a réagi en abandonnant les produits de base et la série Bowman, gardant seulement les séries Stadium Club, Topps et OPC Premier. Après avoir souffert des problèmes financiers, Pro Set s'est vu refusée une nouvelle licence. Les droits à la marque Parkhurst, qui représentait le produit à prime de Pro Set, furent vendus à Upper Deck. Vers la fin de 1993, cette société continuait encore le renouveau de cet ancien nom illustre comme ligne de produits à super-prime. Upper Deck rompit aussi avec la tradition en offrant son jeu de marque de base en deux séries distinctes. Enfin, les NHL et NHLPA décernèrent la cinquième licence, non à Pro Set, mais à Leaf Brands, qui lança un produit à super-prime en deux séries, ainsi qu'une série prime Donruss

Pour plus d'informations

Le texte précédent ne représente qu'une description sommaire de l'art de collectionner les cartes, de sa naissance jusqu'à nos jours. Ces quelques pages ne permettent pas de documenter l'histoire entière — il existe plusieurs autres sources fiables d'information. Nous recommandons au collectionneur appliqué de s'abonner à une ou plusieurs bonnes publications spécialisées en ce passe-temps, et de régulièrement fréquenter les boutiques de cartes et les salons de pièces de collection sportives régionaux. La collection de cartes est un passe-temps non-structuré, se développant plus chaque jour. Vous pouvez apprendre à mieux le connaître en visitant fréquemment les deux lieux mentionnés ci-avant. Après tout, un fournisseur de cartes avisé réalise que les quelques minutes passées à enseigner un débutant s'avèrent souvent profitables dans le futur.

Remerciements

Le volume de cette année a requis beaucoup de zèle, d'application et d'effort. Nos standards supérieurs n'auraient, cependant, pas pu être atteints sans la collaboration experte et le temps généreusement contribué par de nombreuses personnes. Nos sincères remerciements s'adressent à chacun de vous. Une liste complète de nos précieux collaborateurs apparaît après la section "Guide des prix".

1992-93 Action/Panini Freaks Promos

Produced by Action Cards in conjunction with Panini, these promo cards were issued to preview the set. The regular issue cards were sold in seven-card foil packs that included one sticker. The cards measure the standard size (2 1/2" by 3 1/2"). The fronts feature colorful cartoon pictures of futuristic hockey players with white borders. The player's name appears in a bottom stripe. The fictional team logo is in the lower right corner. The horizontal backs have a multi-colored block design and display biography, player information, and statistics. The Atomic Hockey League logo is printed on the right edge while the word "promo" appears in a colored circle at the upper right corner. These cards are unnumbered and checklisted below alphabetically by the fictional player's last name.

	MINT	EXC	G-VG
COMPLETE SET (2)	2.00	.80	.20
COMMON PLAYER (1-2)	1.00	.40	.10
☐ 1 Everett(Smokey) Garrett Los Angeles Pollution	1.00	.40	.10
☐ 2 Steve Koop Vancouver Kamikaze	1.00	.40	.10

1992-93 Action/Panini Freaks

Produced by Action Cards in conjunction with Panini, this 100-card standard-size (2 1/2" by 3 1/2") set was sold in packs featuring seven cards plus one sticker. The cards have real bubble gum scent. The fronts present colorful caricatures of imaginary hockey players by using cartoons to portray exaggerated hockey scenes. Team logos are placed in a small yellow box in the lower right corner. A long

the right side is a hockey stick caricature. On a white block set on a colored panel, the horizontal backs carry biography, player profile, and AHL (Atomic Hockey League) statistics. The card number and AHL logo are superimposed on a yellow stripe that runs down the right side. The cards are checklisted below alphabetically according to teams as follows: Boston Stranglers (2-10), Chicago Gangsters (11-19), Detroit Unemployed (20-28), Los Angeles Pollution (29-37), Montreal Flying Hasbeens (38-46), New York Scums (47-55), Ottawa Mountees (56-64), Quebec Frogs (65-73), Toronto Gold Plated (74-82), and Vancouver Kamikazes (83-91). The set closes with a topical subset (92-100).

	MINT	EXC	G-VG
COMPLETE SET (100)	10.00	4.00	1.00
COMMON PLAYER (1-100)	.15	.06	.01
☐ 1 A game in the AHL Checklist A	.25	.10	.02
☐ 2 Glenn Harvey	.15	.06	.01
☐ 3 Chuck(Aaaaarrrggghhh) Manson	.15	.06	.01
☐ 4 Drakk Kula	.15	.06	.01
☐ 5 Tex Leetch	.15	.06	.01
☐ 6 The Stuntson Brothers	.15	.06	.01
☐ 7 Jack the Strapper	.15	.06	.01
☐ 8 Evil Zattan	.15	.06	.01
☐ 9 Ted Knives	.15	.06	.01
☐ 10 Levy Waite	.15	.06	.01
☐ 11 Wolfee Bag	.15	.06	.01
☐ 12 Real Capote	.15	.06	.01
☐ 13 Shirley(High Scream) Vanilli	.15	.06	.01
☐ 14 Charlie Horse	.15	.06	.01
☐ 15 XXXX	.15	.06	.01
☐ 16 Doug Hunter	.15	.06	.01
☐ 17 Andy Glover	.15	.06	.01
☐ 18 Samantha Puck	.15	.06	.01
☐ 19 Pete Soup	.15	.06	.01
☐ 20 HV-151001	.15	.06	.01
☐ 21 Hercule(Pumping Iron) Samson	.15	.06	.01
☐ 22 Victor Laforce	.15	.06	.01
☐ 23 Brad Luck	.15	.06	.01
☐ 24 Pierrot Rinfrette	.15	.06	.01
☐ 25 Bernie Turcotte (40 Percent)	.15	.06	.01
☐ 26 Redd Neck	.15	.06	.01
☐ 27 Johnny Bolling	.15	.06	.01
☐ 28 Ted Gumbee	.15	.06	.01
☐ 29 Neil Moony	.15	.06	.01
☐ 30 Typhonse Allaire	.15	.06	.01
☐ 31 Wayne Grizzly	1.00	.40	.10
☐ 32 Nico(IQ) Brainstein	.15	.06	.01
☐ 33 Everett(Smokey) Garrett	.15	.06	.01
☐ 34 Frank Geiger	.15	.06	.01
☐ 35 Ernest Murphy	.15	.06	.01
☐ 36 Theo Beausoleil	.15	.06	.01
☐ 37 Power-22	.15	.06	.01
☐ 38 Jack Dummy	.15	.06	.01
☐ 39 Chris (Preacher) Window	.15	.06	.01
☐ 40 Mach Five	.15	.06	.01
☐ 41 Great Sesame	.15	.06	.01
☐ 42 Phil Boulet	.15	.06	.01
☐ 43 Darn Yarn	.15	.06	.01
☐ 44 Jim Fish	.15	.06	.01
☐ 45 Walter Walker	.15	.06	.01
☐ 46 Yvan Trilock	.15	.06	.01
☐ 47 M.D. Grichman	.15	.06	.01
☐ 48 Greg Proctor	.15	.06	.01
☐ 49 Max(Arson) Burn	.15	.06	.01
☐ 50 Bud(Raw) Butcher	.15	.06	.01
☐ 51 Dry Klean	.15	.06	.01
☐ 52 Herbert Picks	.15	.06	.01
☐ 53 Rod Heint	.15	.06	.01
☐ 54 Jack Hill	.15	.06	.01
☐ 55 Dave Save	.15	.06	.01
☐ 56 Boulhouboulhou Boulhou	.15	.06	.01
☐ 57 Pete Puzzle	.15	.06	.01
☐ 58 Michael Dundee	.15	.06	.01
☐ 59 Robert Rubber	.15	.06	.01
☐ 60 Kurt Spider	.15	.06	.01
☐ 61 Joe Cooker	.15	.06	.01
☐ 62 Mgwo Khull	.15	.06	.01
☐ 63 Satan Claus	.15	.06	.01
☐ 64 Benny Hull	.15	.06	.01

☐ 65	Jacques Baloune	.15	.06	.01
☐ 66	Gino Azzaro	.15	.06	.01
☐ 67	Don Nutts	.15	.06	.01
☐ 68	Rikki Lindrock	.15	.06	.01
☐ 69	Jim Trek	.15	.06	.01
☐ 70	Mark Max	.15	.06	.01
☐ 71	Charly Moffet	.15	.06	.01
☐ 72	Ben Crepeault	.15	.06	.01
☐ 73	Billy Bilodeau Jr.	.15	.06	.01
☐ 74	Raven Spitberg	.15	.06	.01
☐ 75	Goofy Mandell	.15	.06	.01
☐ 76	Rick Shark	.15	.06	.01
☐ 77	Buddy Selleck	.15	.06	.01
☐ 78	Oscar F. Fecks	.15	.06	.01
☐ 79	Jack Flash	.15	.06	.01
☐ 80	Alphonse Cadorette	.15	.06	.01
☐ 81	Jeff McFly	.15	.06	.01
☐ 82	Cammy Lyon	.15	.06	.01
☐ 83	Magayashi Shiyagama	.15	.06	.01
☐ 84	Martin Chauze	.15	.06	.01
☐ 85	Colonel Snaps	.15	.06	.01
☐ 86	Tommy Mito	.15	.06	.01
☐ 87	Will Van Hish	.15	.06	.01
☐ 88	Redd(Alert) Cannon	.15	.06	.01
☐ 89	Hiro Gotakaka	.15	.06	.01
☐ 90	Mami Blohead	.15	.06	.01
☐ 91	Steve Koop	.15	.06	.01
☐ 92	Mister Ron Royce	.15	.06	.01
☐ 93	NY-Studebaker Cup	.15	.06	.01
☐ 94	Rich Cash	.15	.06	.01
☐ 95	Terence Hell	.15	.06	.01
☐ 96	Kelly Nails	.15	.06	.01
☐ 97	Kandy Striker	.15	.06	.01
☐ 98	Ray Padds	.15	.06	.01
☐ 99	Rudolph Richter	.15	.06	.01
☐ 100	Atomic Hockey League Checklist B	.15	.06	.01

1992-93 Action/Panini Freaks Stickers

This standard-size (2 1/2" by 3 1/2") ten-sticker subset was included in the seven-card Hockey Freaks foil packs. One sticker was inserted in each pack. The borderless fronts have the team logos set in a peel-off silver foil sticker. There are promotional blurbs on the plain, white backs. The stickers are numbered on the back with an "SP" prefix.

		MINT	EXC	G-VG
COMPLETE SET (10)		3.00	1.20	.30
COMMON PLAYER (1-10)		.50	.20	.05
☐ 1	Detroit Unemployed	.50	.20	.05
☐ 2	Boston Stranglers	.50	.20	.05
☐ 3	Chicago Gangsters	.50	.20	.05
☐ 4	Quebec Frogs	.50	.20	.05
☐ 5	Vancouver Kamikazes	.50	.20	.05
☐ 6	Toronto Gold Plated	.50	.20	.05
☐ 7	Montreal Flying Hasbeens	.50	.20	.05
☐ 8	Ottawa Mountees	.50	.20	.05
☐ 9	Los Angeles Pollution	.50	.20	.05
☐ 10	New York Scums Logo Checklist	.50	.20	.05

1989-90 Action Packed Prototypes

This three-card set was produced by Action Packed to show the NHL and NHLPA a sample in order to obtain a license for hockey cards. The cards are unnumbered and listed below in alphabetcial order. Reportedly only 1000 cards of Gretzky and Lemieux were produced and only 300 of Yzerman. These cards are standard size (2 1/2" by 3 1/2") with the rounded corners.

		MINT	EXC	G-VG
COMPLETE SET (3)		450.00	180.00	45.00
COMMON PLAYER (1-3)		125.00	50.00	12.50
☐ 1	Wayne Gretzky	150.00	60.00	15.00
☐ 2	Mario Lemieux	125.00	50.00	12.50
☐ 3	Steve Yzerman	250.00	100.00	25.00

1993 Action Packed HOF Induction

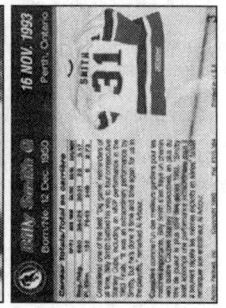

This special limited edition set was produced by Action Packed to commemorate the 1993 Hockey Hall Of Fame induction on November 16, 1993, and honors the ten inductees. It was given to attendees at the induction and was on sale at the Hockey Hall of Fame. The fronts feature embossed color and black-and-white borderless photos, a silver embossed Stanley Cup, and the words "Action Packed." The horizontal backs carry the inductee's name, a short biography, the date "November 16, 1993," and a brief career summary in French and English. The cards measure the standard size (2 1/2" by 3 1/2") and are numbered on the back. This set was released in a special black cardboard display featuring all ten cards (in two rows of five) and which could be placed in a black cardboard sleeve with the Hall of Fame logo and the words "1993 Hockey Hall of Fame Induction, November 16, 1993" printed in silver letters on the front. The back of the sleeve gives the set serial number out of a total of 5,000 sets produced.

	MINT	EXC	G-VG
COMPLETE SET (10)........................	50.00	20.00	5.00
COMMON PLAYER (1-10)................	4.00	1.60	.40
☐ 1 Edgar Laprade.......................	6.00	2.40	.60
☐ 2 Guy Lapointe.........................	8.00	3.25	.80
☐ 3 Billy Smith............................	10.00	4.00	1.00
☐ 4 Steve Shutt	8.00	3.25	.80
☐ 5 John D'Amico	4.00	1.60	.40
☐ 6 Al Shaver.............................	4.00	1.60	.40
☐ 7 Seymour Knox III	4.00	1.60	.40
☐ 8 Frank Griffiths	4.00	1.60	.40
☐ 9 Fred Page............................	4.00	1.60	.40
☐ 10 Al Strachan	4.00	1.60	.40

1993 Action Packed Prototypes

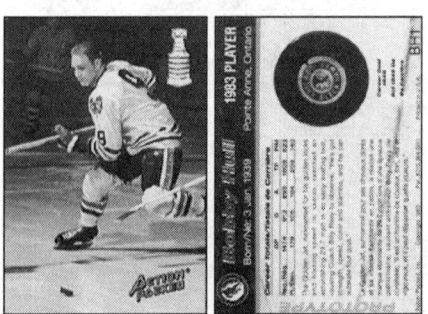

Both prototype cards measure the standard size (2 1/2" by 3 1/2") and feature Bobby Hull. The first card has a borderless embossed color photo, while the second card has the same design but is all in gold. Both cards feature a silver Stanley Cup in the upper right corner. The horizontal backs carry biographical (in English and French) and statistical information, the Blackhawks logo on a puck, and the word "Prototype" printed vertically on the left. The cards are numbered on the back with a "BH" prefix.

	MINT	EXC	G-VG
COMPLETE SET (2)..........................	10.00	4.00	1.00
COMMON CARD (1-2)	5.00	2.00	.50
☐ 1 Bobby Hull	5.00	2.00	.50
(Color)			
☐ 2 Bobby Hull	6.00	2.40	.60
(Gold)			

1991-92 Alberta International Team Canada

This 24-card set features the Canadian National Team and a bonus card of Vladislav Tretiak, the honorary captain of the Soviet Olympic team during the Pre-Olympic Hockey Tour. The cards are slightly smaller than standard size, measuring approximately 2 7/16" by 3 1/2". The front design has color head shots against a blue background, with no borders on the sides of the picture. A black stripe with the words "Collector's Edition" in orange and a white stripe border the picture above, and white and gray stripes border the picture below. Red and white diagonals overlay the gray stripe, and the player's name appears in an orange box that casts a black shadow. The backs have a similar design, with biography and statistics replacing the player photo. The cards are numbered on both sides in the lower right corner.

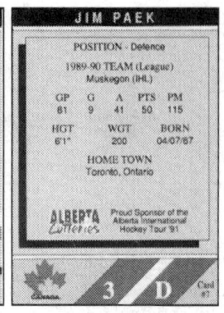

	MINT	EXC	G-VG
COMPLETE SET (24)........................	15.00	6.00	1.50
COMMON PLAYER (1-23)................	.60	.24	.06
☐ 1 Craig Billington	1.00	.40	.10
☐ 2 Doug Dadswell......................	.60	.24	.06
☐ 3 Greg Andrusak	.60	.24	.06
☐ 4 Karl Dykhuis.........................	.75	.30	.07
☐ 5 Gord Hynes	.75	.30	.07
☐ 6 Ken MacArthur	.60	.24	.06
☐ 7 Jim Paek	.75	.30	.07
☐ 8 Brad Schlegel	.60	.24	.06
☐ 9 Dave Archibald	.60	.24	.06
☐ 10 Stu Barnes	.75	.30	.07
☐ 11 Brad Bennett	.60	.24	.06
☐ 12 Todd Brost	.60	.24	.06
☐ 13 Jose Charbonneau	.60	.24	.06
☐ 14 Jason Lafreniere	.75	.30	.07
☐ 15 Chris Lindberg	.75	.30	.07
☐ 16 Ken Priestlay	.60	.24	.06
☐ 17 Stephane Roy	.75	.30	.07
☐ 18 Randy Smith	.60	.24	.06
☐ 19 Todd Strueby	.60	.24	.06
☐ 20 Vladislav Tretiak...................	2.50	1.00	.25
☐ 21 Dave King CO	.75	.30	.07
☐ 22 Wayne Fleming	.60	.24	.06
☐ 23 Checklist Card	.75	.30	.07
☐ NNO Title Card	.75	.30	.07

1992-93 Alberta International Team Canada

This 22-card set features the Canadian National Team as well as bonus cards of Mike Myers, honorary captain of the team, and of Vladislav Tretiak, honorary captain of Russia's National Team. The cards are slightly smaller than standard size, measuring 2 1/2" by 3 7/16". The fronts feature posed action shots that are full-bleed on the left and bottom. The pictures are bordered by a red stripe on top carrying the player's name, and by a blue stripe on the right carrying the year and "Canada's National Team." At the intersection of the two stripes in the upper right corner is a yellow block displaying the player's uniform number. The backs carry biographical information (on a yellow panel), player profile, and season-by-season statistics. The cards are unnumbered and checklisted below in alphabetical order.

	MINT	EXC	G-VG
COMPLETE SET (22)	12.00	5.00	1.20
COMMON PLAYER (1-22)	.50	.20	.05
□ 1 Dominic Amodeo	.50	.20	.05
□ 2 Mark Astley	.50	.20	.05
□ 3 Adrian Aucoin	.75	.30	.07
□ 4 Mark Bassen	.50	.20	.05
□ 5 Eric Bellerose	.75	.30	.07
□ 6 Mike Brewer	.50	.20	.05
□ 7 Dany Dube CO	.50	.20	.05
□ 8 Mike Fountain	.75	.30	.07
□ 9 Todd Hlushko	.75	.30	.07
□ 10 Hank Lammens	.75	.30	.07
□ 11 Derek Laxdal	.75	.30	.07
□ 12 Derek Mayer	.50	.20	.05
□ 13 Keith Morris	.50	.20	.05
□ 14 Mike Myers	3.00	1.20	.30
(SNL comedian and star of Wayne's World)			
□ 15 Jackson Penney	.50	.20	.05
□ 16 Garth Premak	.50	.20	.05
□ 17 Tom Renney CO	.50	.20	.05
□ 18 Allain Roy	.75	.30	.07
□ 19 Stephane Roy	.75	.30	.07
□ 20 Trevor Sim	.50	.20	.05
□ 21 Vladislav Tretiak	1.50	.60	.15
□ 22 Title Card	.75	.30	.07

1993-94 Alberta International Team Canada

This 23-card set measures the standard-size (2 1/2" by 3 1/2") and features players on the 1994 Canadian National Hockey Team. The white-bordered fronts feature posed black-and-white photos of the players on ice. The photo is set on a gold-colored background that bleeds through to highlight the suited-up player. The player's name and uniform number appear within the black stripe at the top; the logo for the team rests at the lower right. The white horizontal backs carry the player's name and uniform number at the top, followed below by biography, statistics, and career highlights. The logo for the sponsor, Alberta Lotteries, appears with the team logo in the gold-colored stripe on the right. The cards are unnumbered and checklisted below in alphabetical order.

	MINT	EXC	G-VG
COMPLETE SET (23)	12.00	5.00	1.20
COMMON PLAYER (1-23)	.40	.16	.04
□ 1 Adrian Aucoin	.60	.24	.06
□ 2 Todd Brost	.40	.16	.04
□ 3 Dany Dube	.40	.16	.04
□ 4 David Harlock	.40	.16	.04
□ 5 Corey Hirsch	1.00	.40	.10

□ 6 Todd Hlushko	.60	.24	.06
□ 7 Fabian Joseph	.40	.16	.04
□ 8 Paul Kariya	4.00	1.60	.40
□ 9 Chris Kontos	.60	.24	.06
□ 10 Manny Legace	.75	.30	.07
□ 11 Brett Lindros	5.00	2.00	.50
□ 12 Ken Lovsin	.40	.16	.04
□ 13 Jason Marshall	.60	.24	.06
□ 14 Derek Mayer	.40	.16	.04
□ 15 Dwayne Norris	.60	.24	.06
□ 16 Tom Renney CO	.40	.16	.04
□ 17 Russ Romaniuk	.40	.16	.04
□ 18 Brian Savage	.60	.24	.06
□ 19 Trevor Sim	.40	.16	.04
□ 20 Chris Therien	.40	.16	.04
□ 21 Todd Warriner	1.00	.40	.10
□ 22 Craig Woodcroft	.40	.16	.04
□ 23 Title Card	.60	.24	.06

1992-93 All World Mario Lemieux Promos

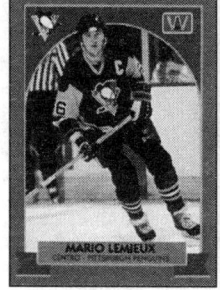 

This set consists of six standard-size (2 1/2" by 3 1/2") cards. All cards feature the same color action photo of Mario Lemieux, skating with stick in both hands. On the first three cards, the top of the photo is oval-shaped and framed by yellow stripes. The space above the oval as well as the stripe at the bottom carrying player information are purple. The outer border is green. Inside green borders, the horizontal back has a color close-up photo, biography and statistics. On the second three cards listed below, the player photo is tilted slightly to the right and framed by a thin green border. Yellow stripes above and below the picture carry information, and the outer border is black-and-white speckled. The back has a similar design and displays a close-up color head shot and biographical and statistical information on a pastel green panel. All cards are numbered as number 1. The cards were issued three different ways, in Spanish, French, and English. The design and concept of these cards is very similar to the 1992 All World Troy Aikman promos.

	MINT	EXC	G-VG
COMPLETE SET (6)	20.00	8.00	2.00
COMMON PLAYER (1A-1F)	5.00	2.00	.50
□ 1A Mario Lemieux (Green border; English)	5.00	2.00	.50
□ 1B Mario Lemieux (Green border; French)	5.00	2.00	.50
□ 1C Mario Lemieux (Green border; Spanish)	5.00	2.00	.50
□ 1D Mario Lemieux (Speckled border; English)	5.00	2.00	.50
□ 1E Mario Lemieux (Speckled border;	5.00	2.00	.50

French)

		MINT	EXC	G-VG
☐ 1F	Mario Lemieux .... (Speckled border; Spanish)	5.00	2.00	.50

1993 American Licorice Sour Punch Caps

Printed in Canada and sponsored by the American Licorice Co., these individually wrapped cards were inserted in specially-marked packages of 4 1/2 oz. Sour Punch Candy Straws. Each package contained one card, measuring the standard size (2 1/2" by 3 1/2") with two punch-out caps, each measuring 1 1/2" in diameter. One cap carries the Sour Punch logo and where appropriate, a flavor, while the other cap features a color player portrait with a black border. The cards are numbered on the front, and the backs are blank. There is a special promotion cap featuring Bobby Hull with no number, but the letter "P." This promo cap was used by the American Licorice sales brokerage as a sales sample.

		MINT	EXC	G-VG
COMPLETE SET (8)..........................		5.00	2.00	.50
COMMON PLAYER (1-8)...................		.25	.10	.02
☐ 1	Theoren Fleury .... Sour Apple Cap	.50	.20	.05
☐ 2	Guy Lafleur .... Blue Raspberry Cap	1.25	.50	.12
☐ 3	Chris Chelios........................... Strawberry Cap	.75	.30	.07
☐ 4	Stan Mikita............................. Sour Apple Cap	1.25	.50	.12
☐ 5	Rocket Richard .... Strawberry Cap	1.50	.60	.15
☐ 6	Steve Thomas .... Blue Raspberry Cap	.50	.20	.05
☐ 7	Checklist 1 .... Sour Punch Cap Logo	.25	.10	.02
☐ 8	Checklist 2 .... Sour Punch Cap Logo	.25	.10	.02
☐ P	Bobby Hull .... Sour Punch Cap Logo	1.00	.40	.10

1991 Arena Draft Picks

The 1991 Arena Draft Picks boxed set consists of 33 standard-size (2 1/2" by 3 1/2") cards. The set was produced in English as well as French versions, with both versions currently carrying the same values. One thousand cards signed by each player were randomly inserted throughout the sets with approximately ten sets or two per case. These autographed cards are valued at 25 to 50 times the values listed below. Moreover, a Pat Falloon hologram was produced in conjunction with this set,

although its release came much later. The Falloon hologram is not included in the complete set price below. The production run was reported to be 198,000 English and 99,000 French sets, and each set was issued with a numbered certificate of authenticity. The full-bleed fronts have a white background and show the hockey player in an action pose wearing a tuxedo. The player's name and position appear at the card top, while the round drafted and a silver stripe appear at the bottom of the front. The back has a second pose with the player again clad in a tuxedo, as well as brief biography, player profile, and statistics. The first 31 player cards feature 1st round (1-17), 2nd round (18-30), and 3rd round (31) draft picks. A combo card (32) and an unnumbered checklist card (33) complete the set. The checklist card carries a quote by Teddy Roosevelt. The player cards are numbered on the back.

		MINT	EXC	G-VG
COMPLETE SET (33)........................		3.00	1.20	.30
COMMON PLAYER (1-32)................		.04	.02	.00
☐ 1	Pat Falloon .... San Jose Sharks	.40	.16	.04
☐ 2	Scott Niedermayer .... New Jersey Devils	.40	.16	.04
☐ 3	Scott Lachance .... New York Islanders	.15	.06	.01
☐ 4	Peter Forsberg UER .... Philadelphia Flyers	.75	.30	.07
☐ 5	Alek Stojanov .... Vancouver Canucks	.07	.03	.01
☐ 6	Richard Matvichuk................. Minnesota North Stars	.10	.04	.01
☐ 7	Patrick Poulin......................... Hartford Whalers	.15	.06	.01
☐ 8	Martin Lapointe...................... Detroit Red Wings	.15	.06	.01
☐ 9	Tyler Wright .... Edmonton Oilers	.10	.04	.01
☐ 10	Philippe Boucher.................... Buffalo Sabres	.10	.04	.01
☐ 11	Pat Peake .... Washington Capitals	.25	.10	.02
☐ 12	Markus Naslund UER .... Pittsburgh Penguins	.15	.06	.01
☐ 13	Brent Bilodeau .... Montreal Canadiens	.10	.04	.01
☐ 14	Glen Murray .... Boston Bruins	.20	.08	.02
☐ 15	Niklas Sundblad .... Calgary Flames	.07	.03	.01
☐ 16	Trevor Halverson.................... Washington Capitals	.07	.03	.01
☐ 17	Dean McAmmond .... Chicago Blackhawks	.10	.04	.01
☐ 18	Rene Corbet .... Quebec Nordiques	.10	.04	.01
☐ 19	Eric Lavigne .... Washington Capitals	.07	.03	.01
☐ 20	Steve Staios .... St. Louis Blues	.10	.04	.01
☐ 21	Jim Campbell .... Montreal Canadiens	.10	.04	.01
☐ 22	Jassen Cullimore................... Vancouver Canucks	.07	.03	.01
☐ 23	Jamie Pushor.......................... Detroit Red Wings	.07	.03	.01

		NRMT	VG-E	GOOD
☐ 24	Donevan Hextall	.07	.03	.01
	New Jersey Devils			
☐ 25	Andrew Verner	.10	.04	.01
	Edmonton Oilers			
☐ 26	Jason Dawe	.10	.04	.01
	Buffalo Sabres			
☐ 27	Jeff Nelson	.10	.04	.01
	Washington Capitals			
☐ 28	Darcy Werenka	.07	.03	.01
	New York Rangers			
☐ 29	Francois Groleau	.04	.02	.00
	Calgary Flames			
☐ 30	Guy Leveque	.10	.04	.01
	Los Angeles Kings			
☐ 31	Yanic Perreault	.12	.05	.01
	Toronto Maple Leafs			
☐ 32	Pat Falloon and	.25	.10	.02
	Scott Lachance			
☐ HOL06	Pat Falloon	2.00	.80	.20
	Hologram			
☐ NNO	Checklist Card	.04	.02	.00

1991-92 BayBank Bobby Orr

 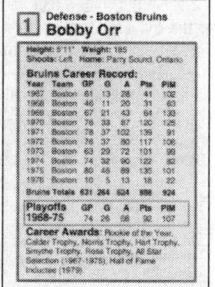

These promotional cards were sponsored by BayBank and measure 2 1/2" by 3 1/2". A player card and a sponsor advertisement were packaged inside a hockey puck-shaped holder (bearing the Bruin logo) and passed out to ticket holders on BayBank Night at the Bruins game. The fronts of both cards have a color action player photo framed by a blue and green inner border design. The white outer border on card 1 is slightly thicker than on card 2, and the positions of the player's name and the sponsor name are reversed when one compares the two cards. Against a pale green background, the back presents biography, statistics (career and playoffs), and career awards. The card number appears in a green box in the upper left corner.

		MINT	EXC	G-VG
COMPLETE SET (2)		12.00	5.00	1.20
COMMON CARD (1-2)		6.00	2.40	.60
☐ 1	Bobby Orr	6.00	2.40	.60
	(Skating with Flyer in pursuit)			
☐ 2	Bobby Orr	6.00	2.40	.60
	(Skating alone with puck)			

1971-72 Bazooka

The 1971-72 Bazooka set contains 36 cards. The cards, nearly identical in design to the 1971-72 Topps and 1971-72 O-Pee-Chee hockey cards, were distributed in 12 three-card panels as the bottoms of Bazooka bubble gum boxes. The cards are numbered at the bottom of each obverse. The cards are blank backed. The panels of three are in numerical

order, e.g., cards 1-3 are a panel, cards 4-6 form a panel, etc. The prices below refer to cut-apart individual cards; values for panels are 50 percent more than the values below.

		NRMT	VG-E	GOOD
COMPLETE SET (36)		2500.00	1000.00	250.00
COMMON PLAYER (1-36)		20.00	8.00	2.00
☐ 1	Phil Esposito	200.00	80.00	20.00
☐ 2	Frank Mahovlich	125.00	50.00	12.50
☐ 3	Ed Van Impe	20.00	8.00	2.00
☐ 4	Bobby Hull	200.00	80.00	20.00
☐ 5	Henri Richard	75.00	30.00	7.50
☐ 6	Gilbert Perreault	125.00	50.00	12.50
☐ 7	Alex Delvecchio	75.00	30.00	7.50
☐ 8	Denis DeJordy	25.00	10.00	2.50
☐ 9	Ted Harris	20.00	8.00	2.00
☐ 10	Gilles Villemure	25.00	10.00	2.50
☐ 11	Dave Keon	75.00	30.00	7.50
☐ 12	Derek Sanderson	50.00	20.00	5.00
☐ 13	Orland Kurtenbach	25.00	10.00	2.50
☐ 14	Bob Nevin	20.00	8.00	2.00
☐ 15	Yvan Cournoyer	75.00	30.00	7.50
☐ 16	Andre Boudrias	20.00	8.00	2.00
☐ 17	Frank St.Marseille	20.00	8.00	2.00
☐ 18	Norm Ullman	75.00	30.00	7.50
☐ 19	Garry Unger	25.00	10.00	2.50
☐ 20	Pierre Bouchard	20.00	8.00	2.00
☐ 21	Roy Edwards	20.00	8.00	2.00
☐ 22	Ralph Backstrom	20.00	8.00	2.00
☐ 23	Guy Trottier	20.00	8.00	2.00
☐ 24	Serge Bernier	20.00	8.00	2.00
☐ 25	Bert Marshall	20.00	8.00	2.00
☐ 26	Wayne Hillman	20.00	8.00	2.00
☐ 27	Tim Ecclestone	20.00	8.00	2.00
☐ 28	Walt McKechnie	20.00	8.00	2.00
☐ 29	Tony Esposito	150.00	60.00	15.00
☐ 30	Rod Gilbert	75.00	30.00	7.50
☐ 31	Walt Tkaczuk	25.00	10.00	2.50
☐ 32	Roger Crozier	25.00	10.00	2.50
☐ 33	Ken Schinkel	20.00	8.00	2.00
☐ 34	Ron Ellis	20.00	8.00	2.00
☐ 35	Stan Mikita	150.00	60.00	15.00
☐ 36	Bobby Orr	750.00	300.00	75.00

1970-71 Blackhawks

BRYAN CAMPBELL

This 14-card set measures approximately 4" by 6". The fronts feature borderless posed color player photos except at the bottom, where a white bar carries the player's name. The backs are blank. The cards are unnumbered and checklisted below in alphabetical order.

		NRMT	VG-E	GOOD
COMPLETE SET (14)		50.00	20.00	5.00
COMMON PLAYER (1-14)		3.00	1.20	.30
☐ 1	Lou Angotti	3.00	1.20	.30
☐ 2	Bryan Campbell	3.00	1.20	.30
☐ 3	Bobby Hull	10.00	4.00	1.00
	Bill Wirtz			
	Stan Mikita			
☐ 4	Dennis Hull	5.00	2.00	.50
☐ 5	Tommy Ivan	3.00	1.20	.30

Billy Reay

			MINT	EXC	G-VG
☐	6	Doug Jarrett	3.00	1.20	.30
☐	7	Keith Magnuson	3.00	1.20	.30
☐	8	Hubert Martin	3.00	1.20	.30
☐	9	Stan Mikita	10.00	4.00	1.00
☐	10	Eric Nesterenko	5.00	2.00	.50
☐	11	Jim Pappin	3.00	1.20	.30
☐	12	Allan Pinder	3.00	1.20	.30
☐	13	Paul Shmyr	3.00	1.20	.30
☐	14	William White	3.00	1.20	.30

1986-87 Blackhawks Coke

This 24-card set of Chicago Blackhawks was sponsored by Coca-Cola, whose company logo appears at the bottom corner on the card front. The cards measure approximately 3 1/2" by 6 1/2" and feature borderless color posed photos of the players. The player's name and brief biographical information is given beneath the picture between the Coke logos. The backs are blank. The cards are unnumbered and we have checklisted them below in alphabetical order.

			MINT	EXC	G-VG
	COMPLETE SET (24)		18.00	7.25	1.80
	COMMON PLAYER (1-24)		.60	.24	.06
☐	1	Murray Bannerman	.75	.30	.07
☐	2	Marc Bergevin	.60	.24	.06
☐	3	Keith Brown	.75	.30	.07
☐	4	Dave Donnelly	.60	.24	.06
☐	5	Curt Fraser	.60	.24	.06
☐	6	Steve Larmer	3.00	1.20	.30
☐	7	Steve Ludzik	.60	.24	.06
☐	8	Dave Manson	1.25	.50	.12
☐	9	Bob Murray	.60	.24	.06
☐	10	Troy Murray	1.00	.40	.10
☐	11	Gary Nylund	.60	.24	.06
☐	12	Jack O'Callahan	.60	.24	.06
☐	13	Ed Olczyk	1.00	.40	.10
☐	14	Rick Paterson	.60	.24	.06
☐	15	Wayne Presley	.75	.30	.07
☐	16	Rich Preston	.60	.24	.06
☐	17	Bob Sauve	.75	.30	.07
☐	18	Denis Savard	3.00	1.20	.30
☐	19	Al Secord	.75	.30	.07
☐	20	Mike Stapleton	.60	.24	.06
☐	21	Darryl Sutter	1.00	.40	.10
☐	22	Bill Watson	.60	.24	.06
☐	23	Behn Wilson	.60	.24	.06
☐	24	Doug Wilson	1.50	.60	.15

1987-88 Blackhawks Coke

This 30-card set of Chicago Blackhawks was sponsored by Coca-Cola, whose company logo appears at the bottom

corner on the card front. The cards measure approximately 3 1/2" by 6 1/2" and feature borderless color posed photos of the players. The player's name and brief biographical information is given beneath the picture between the Coke logos. The backs are blank. The cards are unnumbered and we have checklisted them below in alphabetical order.

			MINT	EXC	G-VG
	COMPLETE SET (30)		18.00	7.25	1.80
	COMMON PLAYER (1-30)		.60	.24	.06
☐	1	Murray Bannerman	.75	.30	.07
☐	2	Marc Bergevin	.60	.24	.06
☐	3	Keith Brown	.75	.30	.07
☐	4	Glen Cochrane	.60	.24	.06
☐	5	Curt Fraser	.60	.24	.06
☐	6	Steve Larmer	2.50	1.00	.25
☐	7	Mark LaVarre	.60	.24	.06
☐	8	Steve Ludzik	.60	.24	.06
☐	9	Dave Manson	1.00	.40	.10
☐	10	Bob Mason	.75	.30	.07
☐	11	Bob McGill	.60	.24	.06
☐	12	Bob Murdoch CO	.60	.24	.06
☐	13	Bob Murray	.60	.24	.06
☐	14	Troy Murray	1.00	.40	.10
☐	15	Brian Noonan	1.00	.40	.10
☐	16	Gary Nylund	.60	.24	.06
☐	17	Darren Pang	1.00	.40	.10
☐	18	Wayne Presley	.75	.30	.07
☐	19	Everett Sanipass	.60	.24	.06
☐	20	Denis Savard	2.50	1.00	.25
☐	21	Mike Stapleton	.60	.24	.06
☐	22	Darryl Sutter CO	1.00	.40	.10
☐	23	Duane Sutter	.75	.30	.07
☐	24	Steve Thomas	1.00	.40	.10
☐	25	Wayne Thomas CO	.60	.24	.06
☐	26	Rick Vaive	.75	.30	.07
☐	27	Dan Vincelette	.75	.30	.07
☐	28	Bill Watson	.60	.24	.06
☐	29	Behn Wilson	.60	.24	.06
☐	30	Doug Wilson	1.50	.60	.15

1988-89 Blackhawks Coke

This 25-card set of Chicago Blackhawks was sponsored by Coca-Cola, whose company logo appears at the bottom corner on the card front. The cards measure approximately 3 1/2" by 6 1/2" and feature borderless color posed photos of the players. The player's name and brief biographical information is given beneath the picture between the Coke logos. The backs are blank. The cards are unnumbered and we have checklisted them below in alphabetical order. The set features an early card of Ed Belfour pre-dating his Rookie Cards by two years.

	MINT	EXC	G-VG
COMPLETE SET (25)	18.00	7.25	1.80
COMMON PLAYER (1-25)	.50	.20	.05

ED BELFOUR

		MINT	EXC	G-VG
☐	1 Ed Belfour	7.50	3.00	.75
☐	2 Keith Brown	.75	.30	.07
☐	3 Bruce Cassidy	.50	.20	.05
☐	4 Mike Eagles	.50	.20	.05
☐	5 Dirk Graham	1.00	.40	.10
☐	6 Mike Hudson	1.00	.40	.10
☐	7 Mike Keenan CO	1.50	.60	.15
☐	8 Steve Larmer	1.50	.60	.15
☐	9 Dave Manson	1.00	.40	.10
☐	10 Jacques Martin CO	.50	.20	.05
☐	11 Bob McGill	.50	.20	.05
☐	12 E.J. McGuire CO	.50	.20	.05
☐	13 Troy Murray	.75	.30	.07
☐	14 Brian Noonan	.75	.30	.07
☐	15 Darren Pang	.75	.30	.07
☐	16 Wayne Presley	.50	.20	.05
☐	17 Everett Sanipass	.50	.20	.05
☐	18 Denis Savard	2.00	.80	.20
☐	19 Duane Sutter	.75	.30	.07
☐	20 Steve Thomas	.75	.30	.07
☐	21 Rick Vaive	.75	.30	.07
☐	22 Dan Vincelette	.50	.20	.05
☐	23 Jimmy Waite	1.25	.50	.12
☐	24 Doug Wilson	1.50	.60	.15
☐	25 Trent Yawney	.75	.30	.07

1989-90 Blackhawks Coke

JEREMY ROENICK

This 27-card set was sponsored by Coke. The cards were issued in a photo album consisting of five unperforated sheets measuring approximately 12" by 12". The first four sheets have six players each, while the last sheet features the three coaches. If the cards were cut, they would measure approximately 4" by 6". The fronts have posed color player photos, shot from the waist up against a blue

background. Biographical information appears below the picture between two Coke logos. The backs are blank. The cards are unnumbered and checklisted below according to the order they appear in the photo album. The set features an early card of Jeremy Roenick pre-dating his Rookie Cards by one year.

		MINT	EXC	G-VG
COMPLETE SET (27)		18.00	7.25	1.80
COMMON PLAYER (1-27)		.50	.20	.05
☐	1 Denis Savard	2.00	.80	.20
☐	2 Troy Murray	.75	.30	.07
☐	3 Steve Larmer	1.50	.60	.15
☐	4 Doug Wilson	1.50	.60	.15
☐	5 Bob Murray	.50	.20	.05
☐	6 Jeremy Roenick	7.50	3.00	.75
☐	7 Duane Sutter	.75	.30	.07
☐	8 Greg Gilbert	.50	.20	.05
☐	9 Trent Yawney	.50	.20	.05
☐	10 Bob McGill	.50	.20	.05
☐	11 Jacques Cloutier	.75	.30	.07
☐	12 Bob Bassen	.50	.20	.05
☐	13 Steve Thomas	.75	.30	.07
☐	14 Adam Creighton	.75	.30	.07
☐	15 Wayne Van Dorp	.50	.20	.05
☐	16 Dirk Graham	.75	.30	.07
☐	17 Mike Hudson	.75	.30	.07
☐	18 Al Secord	.75	.30	.07
☐	19 Alain Chevrier	.50	.20	.05
☐	20 Wayne Presley	.50	.20	.05
☐	21 Steve Konroyd	.50	.20	.05
☐	22 Everett Sanipass	.50	.20	.05
☐	23 Keith Brown	.75	.30	.07
☐	24 Dave Manson	.75	.30	.07
☐	25 Mike Keenan CO	1.25	.50	.12
☐	26 E.J. McGuire CO	.50	.20	.05
☐	27 Jacques Martin CO	.50	.20	.05

1990-91 Blackhawks Coke

This 28-card set was sponsored by Coke, and the cards were issued in a photo album consisting of five unperforated sheets measuring approximately 11 3/4" by 12 1/4". The first four sheets have six players each, while the last sheet features the four coaches. If the cards were cut, they would measure approximately 3 1/2" by 6". The fronts have posed color player photos, shot from the waist up against a blue background. Biographical information appears below the picture between two Coke logos. The backs are blank. The cards are unnumbered and checklisted below according to the order they appear in the photo album.

		MINT	EXC	G-VG
COMPLETE SET (28)		15.00	6.00	1.50
COMMON PLAYER (1-28)		.50	.20	.05
☐	1 Dirk Graham	.75	.30	.07
☐	2 Troy Murray	.75	.30	.07
☐	3 Steve Larmer	1.25	.50	.12
☐	4 Doug Wilson	1.25	.50	.12
☐	5 Chris Chelios	2.50	1.00	.25
☐	6 Jeremy Roenick	4.00	1.60	40
☐	7 Steve Thomas	.75	.30	.07
☐	8 Greg Gilbert	.50	.20	.05
☐	9 Trent Yawney	.50	.20	.05
☐	10 Bob McGill	.50	.20	.05
☐	11 Jacques Cloutier	.60	.24	.06
☐	12 Jocelyn Lemieux	.50	.20	.05
☐	13 Michel Goulet	1.00	.40	.10
☐	14 Adam Creighton	.75	.30	.07
☐	15 Mike McNeill	.50	.20	.05
☐	16 Ed Belfour	3.00	1.20	.30
☐	17 Mike Hudson	.75	.30	.07
☐	18 Greg Millen	.75	.30	.07
☐	19 Stu Grimson	.75	.30	.07
☐	20 Wayne Presley	.50	.20	.05
☐	21 Steve Konroyd	.50	.20	.05
☐	22 Mike Peluso	.50	.20	.05
☐	23 Keith Brown	.60	.24	.06
☐	24 Dave Manson	.75	.30	.07
☐	25 Mike Keenan CO	1.00	.40	.10

		MINT	EXC	G-VG
☐ 26	Darryl Sutter CO	.75	.30	.07
☐ 27	E.J. McGuire CO	.50	.20	.05
☐ 28	Vladislav Tretiak CO	2.00	.80	.20

1991-92 Blackhawks Coke

The 1991-92 Chicago Blackhawks Photo Album was sponsored by Coke. The album measures approximately 11 5/8" by 12 1/4". The first four glossy pages feature six 3 1/2" by 6" posed color player photos, while the inside of the back cover displays four coaches' photos. The photos are attractive full body shots in Chicago Original Six uniforms. Player information appears below the picture between two Coke logos. The backs are blank. The cards are unnumbered and checklisted below in alphabetical order.

		MINT	EXC	G-VG
	COMPLETE SET (28)	15.00	6.00	1.50
	COMMON PLAYER (1-28)	.50	.20	.05
☐ 1	Ed Belfour	2.00	.80	.20
☐ 2	Keith Brown	.60	.24	.06
☐ 3	Rod Buskas	.50	.20	.05
☐ 4	Chris Chelios	1.50	.60	.15
☐ 5	Karl Dykhuis	.75	.30	.07
☐ 6	Greg Gilbert	.50	.20	.05
☐ 7	Michel Goulet	1.00	.40	.10
☐ 8	Dirk Graham	.75	.30	.07
☐ 9	Stu Grimson	.60	.24	.06
☐ 10	Mike Hudson	.60	.24	.06
☐ 11	Mike Keenan GM/CO	1.00	.40	.10
☐ 12	Steve Konroyd	.50	.20	.05
☐ 13	Frantisek Kucera	.50	.20	.05
☐ 14	Steve Larmer	1.00	.40	.10
☐ 15	Brad Lauer	.50	.20	.05
☐ 16	Jocelyn Lemieux	.50	.20	.05
☐ 17	Bryan Marchment	.50	.20	.05
☐ 18	Dave McDowall CO	.50	.20	.05
☐ 19	Brian Noonan	.60	.24	.06
☐ 20	Mike Peluso	.50	.20	.05
☐ 21	Rich Preston CO	.50	.20	.05
☐ 22	Jeremy Roenick	2.50	1.00	.25
☐ 23	Steve Smith	.75	.30	.07
☐ 24	Mike Stapleton	.50	.20	.05
☐ 25	Brent Sutter	.75	.30	.07
☐ 26	Darryl Sutter CO	.75	.30	.07
☐ 27	John Tonelli	.60	.24	.06
☐ 28	Jimmy Waite	.60	.24	.06

1993-94 Blackhawks Coke

Sponsored by Coca-Cola, the 1993-94 Chicago Blackhawks Photo Album measures approximately 11 1/2" by 12 1/4". Each of the four glossy pages features two rows with three player cards per row; the final six player cards are printed

on the inside of the back cover. The cards are unperforated, but if they were cut, they would measure approximately 3 1/2" by 6". The photos are full-body color shots of the players in action. In the wider bottom border appears player identification between two Coke logos. The backs are blank. The cards are unnumbered and checklisted below according to the order they appear in the photo album.

		MINT	EXC	G-VG
	COMPLETE SET (30)	12.00	5.00	1.20
	COMMON PLAYER (1-30)	.35	.14	.03
☐ 1	Joe Murphy	.60	.24	.06
☐ 2	Chris Chelios	1.00	.40	.10
☐ 3	Rich Sutter	.35	.14	.03
☐ 4	Frantisek Kucera	.35	.14	.03
☐ 5	Jeff Shantz	.50	.20	.05
☐ 6	Brian Noonan	.35	.14	.03
☐ 7	Michel Goulet	.75	.30	.07
☐ 8	Jeremy Roenick	2.00	.80	.20
☐ 9	Dave Christian	.50	.20	.05
☐ 10	Patrick Poulin	.50	.20	.05
☐ 11	Brent Sutter	.50	.20	.05
☐ 12	Cam Russell	.35	.14	.03
☐ 13	Stephane Matteau	.50	.20	.05
☐ 14	Ed Belfour	1.50	.60	.15
☐ 15	Neil Wilkinson	.35	.14	.03
☐ 16	Eric Weinrich	.35	.14	.03
☐ 17	Christian Ruuttu	.35	.14	.03
☐ 18	Kevin Todd	.35	.14	.03
☐ 19	Jeff Hackett	.50	.20	.05
☐ 20	Steve Smith	.50	.20	.05
☐ 21	Jocelyn Lemieux	.35	.14	.03
☐ 22	Keith Carney	.35	.14	.03
☐ 23	Troy Murray	.50	.20	.05
☐ 24	Darin Kimble	.35	.14	.03
☐ 25	Dirk Graham	.50	.20	.05
☐ 26	Bob Pulford GM	.50	.20	.05
☐ 27	Darryl Sutter CO	.50	.20	.05
☐ 28	Paul Baxter ACO	.35	.14	.03
☐ 29	Rich Preston ACO	.35	.14	.03
☐ 30	Phil Myre ACO	.35	.14	.03

1993 Bleachers 23K Manon Rheaume

This four-card set measures the standard size (2 1/2" by 3 1/2") and features posed and action, color player photos with 23 Karat gold borders. The production run was reported to be 10,000 numbered sets and 1,500 uncut numbered strips. The player's name and the card title appear in a gold oval below the picture. Another gold oval above the picture is printed with "23KT" and is outlined in black. Six black stars accent the top of the card. The backs carry a serial number ("X of 10,000"), biographical information, player profile, career highlights, and a gold foil facsimile autograph within multi-colored blocks. The title

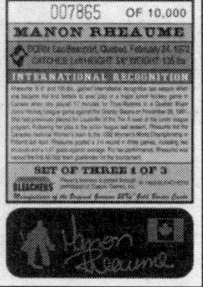

		MINT	EXC	G-VG
☐ 11	Mike Murphy	1.25	.50	.12
☐ 12	Gerry Odrowski	1.25	.50	.12
☐ 13	Danny O'Shea	1.25	.50	.12
☐ 14	Mike Parizeau	1.25	.50	.12
☐ 15	Noel Picard	1.25	.50	.12
☐ 16	Barclay Plager	3.00	1.20	.30
☐ 17	Bill Plager	2.00	.80	.20
☐ 18	Bob Plager	3.00	1.20	.30
☐ 19	Phil Roberto	1.25	.50	.12
☐ 20	Gary Sabourin	1.25	.50	.12
☐ 21	Frank St. Marseille	1.25	.50	.12
☐ 22	Floyd Thomson	1.25	.50	.12
☐ 23	Garry Unger	3.00	1.20	.30
☐ 24	Ernie Wakely	1.25	.50	.12
☐ 25	Tom Woodcock TR	1.25	.50	.12

card features a full-bleed, color action photo. The words "The Original 23 Karat Genuine Gold Border Cards" are printed on the photo near the bottom. The back is bright blue with a yellow hockey player silhouette. It carries promotional information. The cards are numbered on the back.

	MINT	EXC	G-VG
COMPLETE SET (4)	30.00	12.00	3.00
COMMON PLAYER (1-3)	10.00	4.00	1.00
☐ 1 Manon Rheaume	10.00	4.00	1.00
Trois-Rivieres			
☐ 2 Manon Rheaume	10.00	4.00	1.00
Atlanta Knights			
☐ 3 Manon Rheaume	10.00	4.00	1.00
Tampa Bay			
☐ NNO Manon Rheaume	10.00	4.00	1.00
Title Card			

1971-72 Blues Postcards

This 25-card set measures approximately 3 1/2" by 5 1/2" and features full-bleed color action player photos. A facsimile autograph appears near the bottom. The backs are white and carry limited biographical information and the St. Louis Blues logo. The cards are unnumbered and checklisted below in alphabetical order.

	NRMT	VG-E	GOOD
COMPLETE SET (25)	35.00	14.00	3.50
COMMON PLAYER (1-25)	1.25	.50	.12
☐ 1 Al Arbour CO	5.00	2.00	.50
☐ 2 John Arbour	1.25	.50	.12
☐ 3 Carl Brewer	3.00	1.20	.30
☐ 4 Jacques Caron	1.25	.50	.12
☐ 5 Terry Crisp	3.00	1.20	.30
☐ 6 Andre Dupont	2.00	.80	.20
☐ 7 Jack Egers	1.25	.50	.12
☐ 8 Larry Hornung	1.25	.50	.12
☐ 9 Brian Lavender	1.25	.50	.12
☐ 10 Gordon Marchant ATR	1.25	.50	.12
Alex McPherson ATR			

1987-88 Blues Kodak

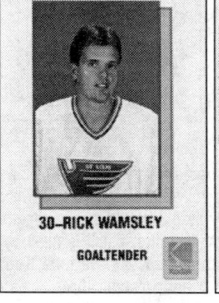
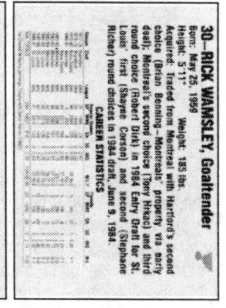

The 1987-88 St. Louis Blues Team Photo Album was sponsored by Kodak in conjunction with KMOX Radio. The set consists of three large sheets, each measuring approximately 11" by 8 1/4" and joined together to form one continuous sheet. The first panel is filled by a team photo. While the second panel presents three rows of five cards each, the third panel presents two rows of five cards, with one player card and four Kodak coupons completing the third row of the panel. After perforation, the cards measure approximately 2 3/16" by 3". They feature color posed photos bordered in blue, shadowed by an orange border on the right and bottom of the picture. Player information and a Kodak logo fill the space below the picture. The back has biographical and statistical information in a horizontal format. We have checklisted the names below in alphabetical order, with the uniform number to the right of the name. The set features an early card of Cliff Ronning pre-dating his Rookie Cards by two years.

	MINT	EXC	G-VG
COMPLETE SET (26)	25.00	10.00	2.50
COMMON PLAYER (1-26)	.75	.30	.07
☐ 1 Brian Benning 2	1.25	.50	.12
☐ 2 Tim Bothwell 6	.75	.30	.07
☐ 3 Charlie Bourgeois 4	.75	.30	.07
☐ 4 Paul Cavallini 14	1.50	.60	.15
☐ 5 Gino Cavallini 17	1.50	.60	.15
☐ 6 Michael Dark 26	.75	.30	.07
☐ 7 Doug Evans 32	.75	.30	.07
☐ 8 Todd Ewen 21	1.25	.50	.12
☐ 9 Bernie Federko 24	2.50	1.00	.25
☐ 10 Ron Flockhart 12	.75	.30	.07
☐ 11 Doug Gilmour 9	6.00	2.40	.60
☐ 12 Gaston Gingras 23	.75	.30	.07
☐ 13 Tony Hrkac 18	1.25	.50	.12
☐ 14 Mark Hunter 20	1.25	.50	.12
☐ 15 Jocelyn Lemieux 16	.75	.30	.07
☐ 16 Tony McKegney 10	.75	.30	.07
☐ 17 Rick Meagher 22	1.25	.50	.12
☐ 18 Greg Millen 29	1.25	.50	.12
☐ 19 Robert Nordmark 27	.75	.30	.07
☐ 20 Greg Paslawski 28	.75	.30	.07
☐ 21 Herb Raglan 25	.75	.30	.07

☐ 22	Rob Ramage 5	1.25	.50	.12
☐ 23	Cliff Ronning 7	3.00	1.20	.30
☐ 24	Brian Sutter 11	1.50	.60	.15
☐ 25	Perry Turnbull 19	.75	.30	.07
☐ 26	Rick Wamsley 30	1.25	.50	.12

1988-89 Blues Kodak

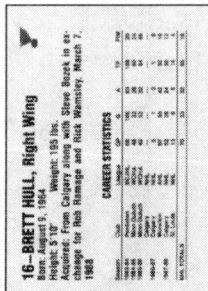

The 1988-89 St. Louis Blues Team Photo Album was sponsored by Kodak. It consists of three large sheets, each measuring approximately 11" by 8 1/4" and joined together to form one continuous sheet. The first panel is filled by a picture of hockey gear intermingled with various Kodak products. While the second panel presents three rows of five cards each, the third panel presents two rows of five cards, with five Kodak coupons completing the left over portion of the panel. After perforation, the cards measure approximately 2 3/16" by 3". They feature color posed photos bordered in yellow, shadowed by a blue border on the right and bottom of the picture. Player information and a Kodak logo fill the space below the picture. The back has biographical and statistical information in a horizontal format. The cards are listed below by sweater number, which is prominently displayed on the card front.

		MINT	EXC	G-VG
COMPLETE SET (25)		25.00	10.00	2.50
COMMON PLAYER		.75	.30	.07
☐ 2	Brian Benning	1.00	.40	.10
☐ 4	Gordie Roberts	.75	.30	.07
☐ 5	Dave Richter	.75	.30	.07
☐ 6	Tim Bothwell	.75	.30	.07
☐ 7	Cliff Ronning	1.50	.60	.15
☐ 9	Peter Zezel	1.00	.40	.10
☐ 10	Tony McKegney	.75	.30	.07
☐ 14	Paul Cavallini	1.00	.40	.10
☐ 15	Craig Coxe	.75	.30	.07
☐ 16	Brett Hull	10.00	4.00	1.00
☐ 17	Gino Cavallini	1.00	.40	.10
☐ 18	Tony Hrkac	1.00	.40	.10
☐ 20	Tom Tilley	.75	.30	.07
☐ 21	Todd Ewen	.75	.30	.07
☐ 22	Rick Meagher	1.00	.40	.10
☐ 23	Gaston Gingras	.75	.30	.07
☐ 24	Bernie Federko	1.50	.60	.15
☐ 25	Herb Raglan	.75	.30	.07
☐ 26	Mike Lalor	.75	.30	.07
☐ 27	Sergio Momesso	1.25	.50	.12
☐ 28	Greg Paslawski	.75	.30	.07
☐ 29	Greg Millen	1.00	.40	.10
☐ 30	Vincent Riendeau	1.25	.50	.12
☐ 32	Doug Evans	.75	.30	.07
☐ 35	Steve Tuttle	.75	.30	.07

1989-90 Blues Kodak

This 25-card set of St. Louis Blues measures approximately 2 3/8" by 3 1/2" and has a portrait shot of the player

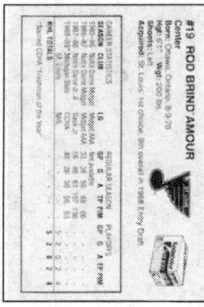

ROD BRIND'AMOUR • Center

surrounded by yellow borders. Players pictured in their white home sweaters are shown against a blue background whereas players in their away blue sweaters are shown against a dark yellow background. Only Tony Twist and Kelly Chase are shown with the yellow background. The players name and position appears underneath the photo. The backs of the cards have biographical and statistical information about the players portrayed. The set is arranged by sweater numbers in the checklist below. Among the stars featured in this set are Brett Hull and Adam Oates. The set features early cards of Rod Brind'Amour and Curtis Joseph pre-dating their Rookie Cards by one year. The set was supposedly passed out to the first 15,000 ticket-holders at the Blues vs. Buffalo Sabres game on February 27th.

		MINT	EXC	G-VG
COMPLETE SET (25)		25.00	10.00	2.50
COMMON PLAYER		.50	.20	.05
☐ 1	Pat Jablonski	1.00	.40	.10
☐ 4	Gordie Roberts	.50	.20	.05
☐ 6	Tony Twist	.75	.30	.07
☐ 9	Peter Zezel	.90	.36	.09
☐ 10	Dave Lowry	.50	.20	.05
☐ 12	Adam Oates	5.00	2.00	.50
☐ 14	Paul Cavallini	.75	.30	.07
☐ 15	Paul MacLean	.75	.30	.07
☐ 16	Brett Hull	6.00	2.40	.60
☐ 17	Gino Cavallini	.75	.30	.07
☐ 19	Rod Brind'Amour	5.00	2.00	.50
☐ 20	Tom Tilley	.50	.20	.05
☐ 21	Jeff Brown	1.50	.60	.15
☐ 22	Rick Meagher	.75	.30	.07
☐ 23	Adrien Plavsic	.50	.20	.05
☐ 25	Herb Raglan	.50	.20	.05
☐ 26	Mike Lalor	.50	.20	.05
☐ 27	Sergio Momesso	.90	.36	.09
☐ 30	Vincent Riendeau	1.00	.40	.10
☐ 31	Curtis Joseph	5.00	2.00	.50
☐ 35	Steve Tuttle	.50	.20	.05
☐ 38	Dominic Lavoie	.50	.20	.05
☐ 39	Kelly Chase	.75	.30	.07
☐ 40	Dave Thomlinson	.50	.20	.05
☐ NNO	Brian Sutter CO	.90	.36	.09

1990-91 Blues Kodak

This 25-card set was sponsored by Kodak in conjunction with KMOX Radio. The cards measure the standard size (2 1/2" by 3 1/2"). On an orangish-yellow card face, the fronts feature color head and shoulders shots against a blue background. Thin white and red borders enclose the pictures, and the player's name and position appear at the card bottom between two team logos. The horizontally oriented backs carry biography, career statistics, team logo, and sponsor logo. The cards are unnumbered and checklisted below in alphabetical order.

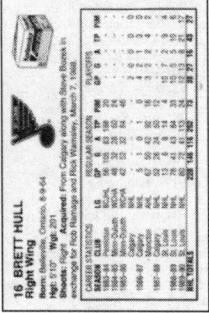

	MINT	EXC	G-VG
COMPLETE SET (25)	20.00	8.00	2.00
COMMON PLAYER (1-25)	.50	.20	.05

			MINT	EXC	G-VG
☐	1	Bob Bassen	.50	.20	.05
☐	2	Rod Brind'Amour	2.50	1.00	.25
☐	3	Jeff Brown	1.25	.50	.12
☐	4	David Bruce	.50	.20	.05
☐	5	Gino Cavallini	.75	.30	.07
☐	6	Paul Cavallini	.75	.30	.07
☐	7	Geoff Courtnall	1.25	.50	.12
☐	8	Robert Dirk	.50	.20	.05
☐	9	Glen Featherstone	.90	.36	.09
☐	10	Brett Hull	4.50	1.80	.45
☐	11	Curtis Joseph	3.00	1.20	.30
☐	12	Dave Lowry	.50	.20	.05
☐	13	Paul MacLean	.50	.20	.05
☐	14	Mario Marois	.50	.20	.05
☐	15	Rick Meagher	.75	.30	.07
☐	16	Sergio Momesso	.75	.30	.07
☐	17	Adam Oates	3.00	1.20	.30
☐	18	Vincent Riendeau	.90	.36	.09
☐	19	Cliff Ronning	1.00	.40	.10
☐	20	Harold Snepsts	.90	.36	.09
☐	21	Scott Stevens	1.50	.60	.15
☐	22	Brian Sutter CO	.75	.30	.07
☐	23	Rich Sutter	.50	.20	.05
☐	24	Steve Tuttle	.50	.20	.05
☐	25	Ron Wilson	.50	.20	.05

1991-92 Blues Postcards

This 22-card set measures approximately 3 1/2" by 5 1/2". The horizontal and vertical fronts feature glossy, full-bleed color action player photos. The white backs carry the player's name, position and statistics in the upper left corner. The postcards are unnumbered and checklisted below in alphabetical order.

	MINT	EXC	G-VG
COMPLETE SET (22)	15.00	6.00	1.50
COMMON PLAYER (1-22)	.60	.24	.06

☐	1	Murray Baron	.60	.24	.06
☐	2	Bob Bassen	.60	.24	.06
☐	3	Jeff Brown	1.25	.50	.12
☐	4	Garth Butcher	1.00	.40	.10
☐	5	Gino Cavallini	.60	.24	.06
☐	6	Paul Cavallini	.60	.24	.06
☐	7	Kelly Chase	.60	.24	.06
☐	8	Dave Christian	1.00	.40	.10
☐	9	Nelson Emerson	1.25	.50	.12
☐	10	Brett Hull	4.00	1.60	.40
☐	11	Pat Jablonski	1.00	.40	.10
☐	12	Curtis Joseph	2.00	.80	.20
☐	13	Darin Kimble	.60	.24	.06
☐	14	Dave Lowry	.60	.24	.06
☐	15	Michel Mongeau	.60	.24	.06
☐	16	Adam Oates	2.00	.80	.20
☐	17	Rob Robinson	.60	.24	.06
☐	18	Brendan Shanahan	3.00	1.20	.30
☐	19	Rich Sutter	1.00	.40	.10
☐	20	Ron Sutter	1.00	.40	.10
☐	21	Ron Wilson	.60	.24	.06
☐	22	Rick Zombo	.60	.24	.06

1990-91 Bowman

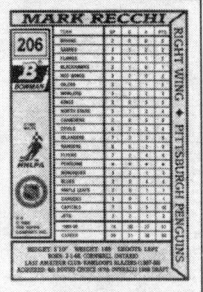

The 1990-91 Bowman set contains 264 cards measuring the standard size (2 1/2" by 3 1/2"). The fronts feature color photos with variegated borders in green, yellow, and red. The team name and player's name appear in black lettering below the picture. The backs are tinted blue with black lettering on gray card stock, and provide biographical information and career statistics. The cards are numbered on the back and are arranged alphabetically according to team name as follows: Chicago Blackhawks (1-13). St. Louis Blues (14-26), Boston Bruins (27-40), Montreal Canadiens (41-53), Vancouver Canucks (54-65), Washington Capitals (66-78), New Jersey Devils (79-90), Calgary Flames (91-103), Philadelphia Flyers (104-114), New York Islanders (115-127), Winnipeg Jets (128-139), Los Angeles Kings (140-152), Toronto Maple Leafs (153-164), Quebec Nordiques (165-175), Minnesota North Stars (176-188), Edmonton Oilers (189-201), Pittsburgh Penguins (202-213), New York Rangers (214-226), Detroit Red Wings (227-238), Buffalo Sabres (239-250), and Hartford Whalers (251-62). Topps also produced a high-gloss Tiffany version of this Bowman set that was only available to hobby dealers in complete set cases; supposedly just 3000 Tiffany sets were produced. The Tiffany versions are valued at five times the prices listed below. The key Rookie Cards in this set are Ed Belfour, Alexander Mogilny, Mark Recchi, Jeremy Roenick, and Kevin Stevens.

	MINT	EXC	G-VG
COMPLETE SET (264)	15.00	6.75	1.90
COMPLETE FACT.SET (264)	15.00	6.75	1.90
COMMON PLAYER (1-264)	.05	.02	.01

☐	1	Jeremy Roenick	1.50	.65	.19
☐	2	Doug Wilson	.08	.04	.01

☐ 3	Greg Millen	.05	.02	.01
☐ 4	Steve Thomas	.08	.04	.01
☐ 5	Steve Larmer	.08	.04	.01
☐ 6	Denis Savard	.08	.04	.01
☐ 7	Ed Belfour	1.50	.65	.19
☐ 8	Dirk Graham	.08	.04	.01
☐ 9	Adam Creighton	.05	.02	.01
☐ 10	Keith Brown	.05	.02	.01
☐ 11	Jacques Cloutier	.05	.02	.01
☐ 12	Al Secord UER (Photo actually Duane Sutter)	.05	.02	.01
☐ 13	Troy Murray	.05	.02	.01
☐ 14	Kelly Chase	.05	.02	.01
☐ 15	Dave Lowry	.05	.02	.01
☐ 16	Adam Oates	.15	.07	.02
☐ 17	Sergio Momesso	.15	.07	.02
☐ 18	Paul MacLean	.05	.02	.01
☐ 19	Peter Zezel	.05	.02	.01
☐ 20	Vincent Riendeau	.15	.07	.02
☐ 21	Dave Thomlinson	.05	.02	.01
☐ 22	Paul Cavallini	.05	.02	.01
☐ 23	Rod Brind'Amour	.60	.25	.08
☐ 24	Brett Hull	.75	.35	.09
☐ 25	Jeff Brown	.08	.04	.01
☐ 26	Dominic Lavoie	.05	.02	.01
☐ 27	Andy Brickley	.05	.02	.01
☐ 28	Bob Sweeney	.05	.02	.01
☐ 29	Cam Neely	.25	.11	.03
☐ 30	Bob Carpenter	.05	.02	.01
☐ 31	Ray Bourque	.20	.09	.03
☐ 32	Rejean Lemelin	.08	.04	.01
☐ 33	Craig Janney	.20	.09	.03
☐ 34	Bob Beers	.10	.05	.01
☐ 35	Andy Moog	.10	.05	.01
☐ 36	Dave Poulin	.08	.04	.01
☐ 37	Brian Propp	.08	.04	.01
☐ 38	John Byce	.05	.02	.01
☐ 39	John Carter	.05	.02	.01
☐ 40	Dave Christian	.05	.02	.01
☐ 41	Shayne Corson	.08	.04	.01
☐ 42	Chris Chelios	.08	.04	.01
☐ 43	Mike McPhee	.05	.02	.01
☐ 44	Guy Carbonneau	.08	.04	.01
☐ 45	Stephane Richer	.08	.04	.01
☐ 46	Petr Svoboda UER (Photo actually Chris Chelios)	.05	.02	.01
☐ 47	Russ Courtnall	.08	.04	.01
☐ 48	Sylvain Lefebvre	.05	.02	.01
☐ 49	Brian Skrudland	.05	.02	.01
☐ 50	Patrick Roy	1.00	.45	.13
☐ 51	Bobby Smith	.08	.04	.01
☐ 52	Mathieu Schneider	.25	.11	.03
☐ 53	Stephan Lebeau	.35	.16	.04
☐ 54	Petri Skriko	.05	.02	.01
☐ 55	Jim Sandlak	.05	.02	.01
☐ 56	Doug Lidster	.05	.02	.01
☐ 57	Kirk McLean	.25	.11	.03
☐ 58	Brian Bradley	.08	.04	.01
☐ 59	Greg Adams Vancouver Canucks	.05	.02	.01
☐ 60	Paul Reinhart	.05	.02	.01
☐ 61	Trevor Linden	.25	.11	.03
☐ 62	Adrien Plavsic	.05	.02	.01
☐ 63	Igor Larionov	.35	.16	.04
☐ 64	Steve Bozek	.05	.02	.01
☐ 65	Dan Quinn	.05	.02	.01
☐ 66	Mike Liut	.08	.04	.01
☐ 67	Nick Kypreos	.05	.02	.01
☐ 68	Michal Pivonka	.25	.11	.03
☐ 69	Dino Ciccarelli	.08	.04	.01
☐ 70	Kevin Hatcher	.08	.04	.01
☐ 71	Dale Hunter	.08	.04	.01
☐ 72	Don Beaupre	.08	.04	.01
☐ 73	Geoff Courtnall	.08	.04	.01
☐ 74	Rob Murray	.05	.02	.01
☐ 75	Calle Johansson	.05	.02	.01
☐ 76	Kelly Miller	.05	.02	.01
☐ 77	Mike Ridley	.08	.04	.01
☐ 78	Alan May	.05	.02	.01
☐ 79	Bob Brooke	.05	.02	.01
☐ 80	Viacheslav Fetisov	.15	.07	.02
☐ 81	Sylvain Turgeon	.05	.02	.01
☐ 82	Kirk Muller	.08	.04	.01
☐ 83	John MacLean	.08	.04	.01
☐ 84	Jon Morris	.05	.02	.01
☐ 85	Brendan Shanahan	.30	.14	.04
☐ 86	Peter Stastny	.08	.04	.01
☐ 87	Bruce Driver	.05	.02	.01
☐ 88	Neil Brady	.05	.02	.01
☐ 89	Patrik Sundstrom	.05	.02	.01
☐ 90	Eric Weinrich	.15	.07	.02
☐ 91	Joe Nieuwendyk	.15	.07	.02
☐ 92	Sergei Makarov	.40	.18	.05
☐ 93	Al MacInnis	.10	.05	.01
☐ 94	Mike Vernon	.08	.04	.01
☐ 95	Gary Roberts	.20	.09	.03
☒ 96	Doug Gilmour	.35	.16	.04
☐ 97	Joe Mullen	.10	.05	.01
☐ 98	Rick Wamsley	.05	.02	.01
☐ 99	Joel Otto	.05	.02	.01
☐ 100	Paul Ranheim	.10	.05	.01
☐ 101	Gary Suter	.08	.04	.01
☐ 102	Theoren Fleury	.25	.11	.03
☐ 103	Sergei Priakin	.05	.02	.01
☐ 104	Tony Horacek	.05	.02	.01
☐ 105	Ron Hextall	.08	.04	.01
☐ 106	Gord Murphy	.05	.02	.01
☐ 107	Pelle Eklund	.05	.02	.01
☐ 108	Rick Tocchet	.08	.04	.01
☐ 109	Murray Craven	.05	.02	.01
☐ 110	Doug Sulliman	.05	.02	.01
☐ 111	Kjell Samuelsson	.05	.02	.01
☐ 112	Ilkka Sinisalo	.05	.02	.01
☐ 113	Keith Acton	.05	.02	.01
☐ 114	Mike Bullard	.05	.02	.01
☐ 115	Doug Crossman	.05	.02	.01
☐ 116	Tom Fitzgerald	.05	.02	.01
☐ 117	Don Maloney	.05	.02	.01
☐ 118	Alan Kerr	.05	.02	.01
☐ 119	Mark Fitzpatrick	.15	.07	.02
☐ 120	Hubie McDonough	.05	.02	.01
☐ 121	Randy Wood	.05	.02	.01
☐ 122	Jeff Norton	.05	.02	.01
☐ 123	Pat LaFontaine	.30	.14	.04
☐ 124	Pat Flatley	.05	.02	.01
☐ 125	Joe Reekie	.05	.02	.01
☐ 126	Brent Sutter	.08	.04	.01
☐ 127	David Volek	.05	.02	.01
☐ 128	Shawn Cronin	.10	.05	.01
☐ 129	Dale Hawerchuk	.08	.04	.01
☐ 130	Brent Ashton	.05	.02	.01
☐ 131	Bob Essensa	.20	.09	.03
☐ 132	Dave Ellett	.05	.02	.01
☐ 133	Thomas Steen	.08	.04	.01
☐ 134	Doug Smail	.05	.02	.01
☐ 135	Fredrik Olausson	.08	.04	.01
☐ 136	Dave McIlwain UER (Card says shoots right, should say left)	.05	.02	.01
☐ 137	Pat Elynuik	.05	.02	.01
☐ 138	Teppo Numminen	.15	.07	.02
☐ 139	Paul Fenton	.05	.02	.01
☐ 140	Tony Granato	.08	.04	.01
☐ 141	Tomas Sandstrom	.08	.04	.01
☐ 142	Rob Blake	.50	.23	.06
☐ 143	Wayne Gretzky	1.25	.55	.16
☐ 144	Kelly Hrudey	.08	.04	.01
☐ 145	Mike Krushelnyski	.05	.02	.01
☐ 146	Steve Duchesne	.08	.04	.01
☐ 147	Steve Kasper	.05	.02	.01
☐ 148	John Tonelli	.08	.04	.01
☐ 149	Dave Taylor	.08	.04	.01
☐ 150	Larry Robinson	.08	.04	.01
☐ 151	Todd Elik	.20	.09	.03
☐ 152	Luc Robitaille	.30	.14	.04
☐ 153	Al Iafrate	.08	.04	.01
☐ 154	Allan Bester	.05	.02	.01
☐ 155	Gary Leeman	.05	.02	.01
☐ 156	Mark Osborne	.05	.02	.01
☐ 157	Tom Fergus	.05	.02	.01
☐ 158	Brad Marsh	.08	.04	.01
☐ 159	Wendel Clark	.15	.07	.02
☐ 160	Daniel Marois	.05	.02	.01
☐ 161	Ed Olczyk	.05	.02	.01
☐ 162	Rob Ramage	.05	.02	.01
☐ 163	Vincent Damphousse	.08	.04	.01
☐ 164	Lou Franceschetti	.05	.02	.01
☐ 165	Paul Gillis	.05	.02	.01
☐ 166	Craig Wolanin	.05	.02	.01
☐ 167	Marc Fortier	.05	.02	.01
☐ 168	Tony McKegney	.05	.02	.01
☐ 169	Joe Sakic	.50	.23	.06
☐ 170	Michel Petit	.05	.02	.01
☐ 171	Scott Gordon	.05	.02	.01
☐ 172	Tony Hrkac	.05	.02	.01
☐ 173	Bryan Fogarty	.05	.02	.01
☐ 174	Mike Hough	.05	.02	.01
☐ 175	Claude Loiselle	.05	.02	.01
☐ 176	Ulf Dahlen	.08	.04	.01
☐ 177	Larry Murphy	.08	.04	.01
☐ 178	Neal Broten	.08	.04	.01
☐ 179	Don Barber	.05	.02	.01
☐ 180	Shawn Chambers	.05	.02	.01
☐ 181	Clark Donatelli UER	.05	.02	.01

(Born 11/22/67,
should be 11/22/65;
'77-78 U.S. Olympic team)

☐ 182	Brian Bellows	.08	.04	.01
☐ 183	Jon Casey	.08	.04	.01
☐ 184	Neil Wilkinson	.15	.07	.02
☐ 185	Aaron Broten	.05	.02	.01
☐ 186	Dave Gagner	.08	.04	.01
☐ 187	Basil McRae	.08	.04	.01
☐ 188	Mike Modano	1.00	.45	.13
☐ 189	Grant Fuhr	.10	.05	.01
☐ 190	Martin Gelinas	.15	.07	.02
☐ 191	Jari Kurri	.10	.05	.01
☐ 192	Geoff Smith	.05	.02	.01
☐ 193	Craig MacTavish	.08	.04	.01
☐ 194	Esa Tikkanen	.08	.04	.01
☐ 195	Glenn Anderson	.10	.05	.01
☐ 196	Joe Murphy	.30	.14	.04
☐ 197	Petr Klima	.08	.04	.01
☐ 198	Kevin Lowe	.08	.04	.01
☐ 199	Mark Messier	.35	.16	.04
☐ 200	Steve Smith	.08	.04	.01
☐ 201	Craig Simpson	.08	.04	.01
☐ 202	Rob Brown	.05	.02	.01
☐ 203	Wendell Young	.05	.02	.01
☐ 204	Mario Lemieux	1.00	.45	.13
☐ 205	Phil Bourque	.05	.02	.01
☐ 206	Mark Recchi	1.00	.45	.13
☐ 207	Zarley Zalapski	.08	.04	.01
☐ 208	Kevin Stevens	1.00	.45	.13
☐ 209	Tom Barrasso	.10	.05	.01
☐ 210	John Cullen	.08	.04	.01
☐ 211	Paul Coffey	.15	.07	.02
☐ 212	Bob Errey	.05	.02	.01
☐ 213	Tony Tanti	.05	.02	.01
☐ 214	Carey Wilson	.05	.02	.01
☐ 215A	Brian Leetch ERR	1.00	.45	.13
	(Name spelled eetch)			
☐ 215B	Brian Leetch COR	.50	.23	.06
☐ 216	Darren Turcotte	.25	.11	.03
☐ 217	Brian Mullen	.08	.04	.01
☐ 218	Mike Richter	1.00	.45	.13
☐ 219	Troy Mallette	.05	.02	.01
☐ 220	Mike Gartner	.10	.05	.01
☐ 221	Bernie Nicholls	.10	.05	.01
☐ 222	John Vanbiesbrouck	.15	.07	.02
☐ 223	John Ogrodnick	.05	.02	.01
☐ 224	Paul Broten	.05	.02	.01
☐ 225	James Patrick	.05	.02	.01
☐ 226	Mark Janssens	.05	.02	.01
☐ 227	Randy McKay	.05	.02	.01
☐ 228	Marc Habscheid	.05	.02	.01
☐ 229	Jimmy Carson	.08	.04	.01
☐ 230	Yves Racine	.15	.07	.02
☐ 231	Dave Barr	.05	.02	.01
☐ 232	Shawn Burr	.05	.02	.01
☐ 233	Steve Yzerman	.35	.16	.04
☐ 234	Steve Chiasson	.08	.04	.01
☐ 235	Daniel Shank	.05	.02	.01
☐ 236	John Chabot	.05	.02	.01
☐ 237	Gerard Gallant	.05	.02	.01
☐ 238	Bernie Federko	.08	.04	.01
☐ 239	Phil Housley	.08	.04	.01
☐ 240	Alexander Mogilny	1.00	.45	.13
☐ 241	Pierre Turgeon	.30	.14	.04
☐ 242	Daren Puppa	.08	.04	.01
☐ 243	Scott Arniel	.05	.02	.01
☐ 244	Christian Ruuttu	.05	.02	.01
☐ 245	Doug Bodger	.05	.02	.01
☐ 246	Dave Andreychuk	.20	.09	.03
☐ 247	Mike Foligno	.08	.04	.01
☐ 248	Dean Kennedy	.05	.02	.01
☐ 249	Dave Snuggerud	.05	.02	.01
☐ 250	Rick Vaive	.05	.02	.01
☐ 251	Todd Krygier	.05	.02	.01
☐ 252	Adam Burt	.05	.02	.01
☐ 253	Scott Young	.05	.02	.01
☐ 254	Ron Francis	.10	.05	.01
☐ 255	Peter Sidorkiewicz	.05	.02	.01
☐ 256	Dave Babych	.05	.02	.01
☐ 257	Pat Verbeek	.08	.04	.01
☐ 258	Ray Ferraro	.08	.04	.01
☐ 259	Chris Govedaris	.05	.02	.01
☐ 260	Brad Shaw	.05	.02	.01
☐ 261	Kevin Dineen	.08	.04	.01
☐ 262	Dean Evason	.05	.02	.01
☐ 263	Checklist 1-132	.05	.02	.01
☐ 264	Checklist 133-264	.05	.02	.01

1990-91 Bowman Hat Tricks

This 22-card standard size (2 1/2" by 3 1/2") set was issued
as an insert in the 1990-91 Bowman hockey wax packs. This
set honored the 14 players (1-14) who scored three or more
goals (a hat trick) in a game at least twice during the 1989-
90 regular season and the eight players (15-22) who
performed the feat during the 1990 NHL playoffs. The fronts
of the cards have a glossy sheen to them while the backs
talk about the hat tricks of the players. There are two Mike
Gartner cards as he had hat tricks for two different teams.

		MINT	EXC	G-VG
COMPLETE SET (22)		5.00	2.00	.50
COMMON PLAYER (1-22)		.15	.06	.01
☐ 1	Brett Hull	1.00	.40	.10
☐ 2	Mario Lemieux	1.50	.60	.15
☐ 3	Rob Brown	.15	.06	.01
☐ 4	Mark Messier	.50	.20	.05
☐ 5	Steve Yzerman	.60	.24	.06
☐ 6	Vincent Damphousse	.25	.10	.02
☐ 7	Kevin Dineen	.15	.06	.01
☐ 8	Mike Gartner UER	.35	.14	.03
	(Pictured with Minnesota, identified as Maple Leaf)			
☐ 9	Pat LaFontaine	.50	.20	.05
☐ 10	Gary Leeman	.15	.06	.01
☐ 11	Stephane Richer	.15	.06	.01
☐ 12	Luc Robitaille	.50	.20	.05
☐ 13	Steve Thomas	.15	.06	.01
☐ 14	Rick Tocchet	.25	.10	.02
☐ 15	Dino Ciccarelli	.25	.10	.02
☐ 16	John Druce	.15	.06	.01
☐ 17	Mike Gartner	.35	.14	.03
☐ 18	Tony Granato	.25	.10	.02
☐ 19	Jari Kurri	.25	.10	.02
☐ 20	Bernie Nicholls	.15	.06	.01
☐ 21	Tomas Sandstrom	.25	.10	.02
☐ 22	Dave Taylor	.15	.06	.01

1991-92 Bowman

The 1991-92 Bowman hockey set contains 429 cards
measuring the standard size (2 1/2" by 3 1/2"). On a white
card face, the fronts display color action player photos
enclosed by blue and tan border stripes. The player's name
appears in a purple stripe below the picture. The backs are
colorful (displaying blue, green, and red fading to yellow
sections) and present biography and statistics (career and
for the 1990-91 season). The season statistics are broken
down to show the player's performance against each NHL
team. The cards are numbered on the back and checklisted
below according to teams as follows: Hartford Whalers (1-
20), Buffalo Sabres (21-40), Detroit Red Wings (41-57),
New York Rangers (58-71, 73-77), San Jose Sharks (72,
122), Pittsburgh Penguins (78-95), Edmonton Oilers (96-

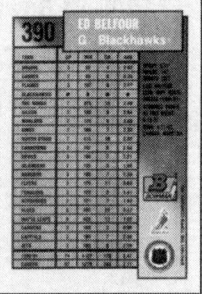

116), Minnesota North Stars (117-121, 123-132), Quebec Nordiques (133-152), Toronto Maple Leafs (153-172), Los Angeles Kings (173-192), Winnipeg Jets (193-211), New York Islanders (212-229), Philadelphia Flyers (230-248), Calgary Flames (249-270), New Jersey Devils (271-289), Washington Capitals (290-308), Vancouver Canucks (309-327), Montreal Canadiens (328-346), Boston Bruins (347-366), St. Louis Blues (367-385), and Chicago Blackhawks (386-404). Subsets feature first round playoff action (405-412), semi-finals (413-415), conference finals (416-418), and Stanley Cup finals (419-424). Notable Rookie Cards in the set are John LeClair and Corey Millen.

	MINT	EXC	G-VG
COMPLETE SET (429)	12.00	5.50	1.50
COMPLETE FACT.SET (429)	15.00	6.75	1.90
COMMON PLAYER (1-429)	.05	.02	.01

☐ 1 John Cullen	.05	.02	.01
☐ 2 Todd Krygier	.05	.02	.01
☐ 3 Kay Whitmore	.05	.02	.01
☐ 4 Terry Yake	.08	.04	.01
☐ 5 Randy Ladouceur	.05	.02	.01
☐ 6 Kevin Dineen	.08	.04	.01
☐ 7 Jim McKenzie	.05	.02	.01
☐ 8 Brad Shaw	.05	.02	.01
☐ 9 Mark Hunter	.05	.02	.01
☐ 10 Dean Evason	.05	.02	.01
☐ 11 Mikael Andersson	.05	.02	.01
☐ 12 Pat Verbeek	.08	.04	.01
☐ 13 Peter Sidorkiewicz	.05	.02	.01
☐ 14 Mike Tomlak	.05	.02	.01
☐ 15 Zarley Zalapski	.05	.02	.01
☐ 16 Rob Brown	.05	.02	.01
☐ 17 Sylvain Cote	.05	.02	.01
☐ 18 Bobby Holik	.08	.04	.01
☐ 19 Daryl Reaugh	.05	.02	.01
☐ 20 Paul Cyr	.05	.02	.01
☐ 21 Doug Bodger	.05	.02	.01
☐ 22 Dave Andreychuk	.15	.07	.02
☐ 23 Clint Malarchuk	.08	.04	.01
☐ 24 Darrin Shannon	.05	.02	.01
☐ 25 Christian Ruuttu	.05	.02	.01
☐ 26 Uwe Krupp	.05	.02	.01
☐ 27 Pierre Turgeon	.20	.09	.03
☐ 28 Kevin Haller	.10	.05	.01
☐ 29 Dave Snuggerud	.05	.02	.01
☐ 30 Alexander Mogilny	.40	.18	.05
☐ 31 Dale Hawerchuk	.08	.04	.01
☐ 32 Mike Ramsey	.05	.02	.01
☐ 33 Darcy Wakaluk	.30	.14	.04
☐ 34 Tony Tanti	.05	.02	.01
☐ 35 Jay Wells	.05	.02	.01
☐ 36 Mikko Makela	.05	.02	.01
☐ 37 Daren Puppa	.08	.04	.01
☐ 38 Benoit Hogue	.05	.02	.01
☐ 39 Rick Vaive	.05	.02	.01
☐ 40 Grant Ledyard	.05	.02	.01
☐ 41 Steve Yzerman HT	.15	.07	.02
☐ 42 Steve Yzerman	.25	.11	.03
☐ 43 Shawn Burr	.05	.02	.01
☐ 44 Yves Racine	.05	.02	.01
☐ 45 Johan Garpenlov	.05	.02	.01
☐ 46 Keith Primeau	.15	.07	.02
☐ 47 Tim Cheveldae	.08	.04	.01
☐ 48 Brad McCrimmon	.05	.02	.01
☐ 49 Dave Barr	.05	.02	.01
☐ 50 Sergei Fedorov	.75	.35	.09
☐ 51 Brent Fedyk	.08	.04	.01
☐ 52 Jimmy Carson	.08	.04	.01
☐ 53 Paul Ysebaert	.05	.02	.01
☐ 54 Rick Zombo	.05	.02	.01
☐ 55 Bob Probert	.08	.04	.01
☐ 56 Gerard Gallant	.05	.02	.01
☐ 57 Kevin Miller	.08	.04	.01
☐ 58 Randy Moller	.05	.02	.01
☐ 59 Kris King	.05	.02	.01
☐ 60 Corey Millen	.20	.09	.03
☐ 61 Brian Mullen	.08	.04	.01
☐ 62 Darren Turcotte	.05	.02	.01
☐ 63 Ray Sheppard	.08	.04	.01
☐ 64 David Shaw	.05	.02	.01
☐ 65 Troy Mallette	.05	.02	.01
☐ 66 James Patrick	.05	.02	.01
☐ 67 Mark Janssens	.05	.02	.01
☐ 68 John Vanbiesbrouck	.10	.05	.01
☐ 69 Joey Kocur	.05	.02	.01
☐ 70 Mike Richter	.25	.11	.03
☐ 71 John Ogrodnick	.05	.02	.01
☐ 72 Kelly Kisio	.05	.02	.01
☐ 73 Normand Rochefort	.05	.02	.01
☐ 74 Mike Gartner	.10	.05	.01
☐ 75 Brian Leetch	.35	.16	.04
☐ 76 Bernie Nicholls	.08	.04	.01
☐ 77 Jan Erixon	.05	.02	.01
☐ 78 Larry Murphy	.08	.04	.01
☐ 79 Joe Mullen	.10	.05	.01
☐ 80 Tom Barrasso	.08	.04	.01
☐ 81 Paul Coffey	.15	.07	.02
☐ 82 Jiri Hrdina	.05	.02	.01
☐ 83 Mark Recchi	.30	.14	.04
☐ 84 Randy Gilhen	.05	.02	.01
☐ 85 Bob Errey	.05	.02	.01
☐ 86 Scott Young	.05	.02	.01
☐ 87 Mario Lemieux	.75	.35	.09
☐ 88 Ulf Samuelsson	.08	.04	.01
☐ 89 Frank Pietrangelo	.05	.02	.01
☐ 90 Ron Francis	.08	.04	.01
☐ 91 Paul Stanton	.05	.02	.01
☐ 92 Kevin Stevens	.30	.14	.04
☐ 93 Bryan Trottier	.08	.04	.01
☐ 94 Phil Bourque	.05	.02	.01
☐ 95 Jaromir Jagr	.50	.23	.06
☐ 96 Petr Klima HT	.10	.05	.01
☐ 97 Adam Graves	.25	.11	.03
☐ 98 Esa Tikkanen	.08	.04	.01
☐ 99 Norm Maciver	.15	.07	.02
☐ 100 Craig MacTavish	.05	.02	.01
☐ 101 Bill Ranford	.08	.04	.01
☐ 102 Martin Gelinas	.05	.02	.01
☐ 103 Charlie Huddy	.05	.02	.01
☐ 104 Petr Klima	.05	.02	.01
☐ 105 Ken Linseman	.05	.02	.01
☐ 106 Steve Smith	.08	.04	.01
☐ 107 Craig Simpson	.08	.04	.01
☐ 108 Chris Joseph	.05	.02	.01
☐ 109 Joe Murphy	.08	.04	.01
☐ 110 Jeff Beukeboom	.05	.02	.01
☐ 111 Grant Fuhr	.08	.04	.01
☐ 112 Geoff Smith	.05	.02	.01
☐ 113 Anatoli Semenov	.05	.02	.01
☐ 114 Mark Messier	.25	.11	.03
☐ 115 Kevin Lowe	.08	.04	.01
☐ 116 Glenn Anderson	.08	.04	.01
☐ 117 Bobby Smith	.08	.04	.01
☐ 118 Doug Smail	.05	.02	.01
☐ 119 Jon Casey	.08	.04	.01
☐ 120 Gaetan Duchesne	.05	.02	.01
☐ 121 Neal Broten	.05	.02	.01
☐ 122 Brian Hayward	.05	.02	.01
☐ 123 Brian Propp	.08	.04	.01
☐ 124 Mark Tinordi	.08	.04	.01
☐ 125 Mike Modano	.30	.14	.04
☐ 126 Marc Bureau	.05	.02	.01
☐ 127 Ulf Dahlen	.08	.04	.01
☐ 128 Chris Dahlquist	.05	.02	.01
☐ 129 Brian Bellows	.08	.04	.01
☐ 130 Mike Craig	.05	.02	.01
☐ 131 Dave Gagner	.08	.04	.01
☐ 132 Brian Glynn	.05	.02	.01
☐ 133 Joe Sakic	.25	.11	.03
☐ 134 Owen Nolan	.15	.07	.02
☐ 135 Everett Sanipass	.05	.02	.01
☐ 136 Jamie Baker	.10	.05	.01
☐ 137 Mats Sundin	.25	.11	.03
☐ 138 Craig Wolanin	.05	.02	.01
☐ 139 Kip Miller	.05	.02	.01
☐ 140 Steven Finn	.05	.02	.01
☐ 141 Tony Hrkac	.05	.02	.01
☐ 142 Curtis Leschyshyn	.05	.02	.01
☐ 143 Mike McNeil	.05	.02	.01
☐ 144 Mike Hough	.05	.02	.01

☐	145	Alexei Gusarov	.10	.05	.01
☐	146	Jacques Cloutier	.05	.02	.01
☐	147	Shawn Anderson	.05	.02	.01
☐	148	Stephane Morin	.05	.02	.01
☐	149	Bryan Fogarty	.05	.02	.01
☐	150	Scott Pearson	.05	.02	.01
☐	151	Ron Tugnutt	.05	.02	.01
☐	152	Randy Velischek	.05	.02	.01
☐	153	David Reid	.05	.02	.01
☐	154	Rob Ramage	.05	.02	.01
☐	155	Dave Hannan	.05	.02	.01
☐	156	Wendel Clark	.20	.09	.03
☐	157	Peter Ing	.05	.02	.01
☐	158	Michel Petit	.05	.02	.01
☐	159	Brian Bradley	.08	.04	.01
☐	160	Rob Cimetta	.05	.02	.01
☐	161	Gary Leeman	.05	.02	.01
☐	162	Aaron Broten	.05	.02	.01
☐	163	Dave Ellett	.05	.02	.01
☐	164	Peter Zezel	.05	.02	.01
☐	165	Daniel Marois	.05	.02	.01
☐	166	Mike Krushelnyski	.05	.02	.01
☐	167	Luke Richardson	.05	.02	.01
☐	168	Scott Thornton	.05	.02	.01
☐	169	Mike Foligno	.05	.02	.01
☐	170	Vincent Damphousse	.08	.04	.01
☐	171	Todd Gill	.05	.02	.01
☐	172	Kevin Maguire	.05	.02	.01
☐	173	Wayne Gretzky HT	.50	.23	.06
☐	174	Tomas Sandstrom HT	.15	.07	.02
☐	175	John Tonelli	.08	.04	.01
☐	176	Wayne Gretzky	1.00	.45	.13
☐	177	Larry Robinson	.08	.04	.01
☐	178	Jay Miller	.05	.02	.01
☐	179	Tomas Sandstrom	.08	.04	.01
☐	180	John McIntyre	.05	.02	.01
☐	181	Brad Jones	.05	.02	.01
☐	182	Rob Blake	.15	.07	.02
☐	183	Kelly Hrudey	.08	.04	.01
☐	184	Marty McSorley	.08	.04	.01
☐	185	Todd Elik	.05	.02	.01
☐	186	Dave Taylor	.08	.04	.01
☐	187	Steve Kasper	.05	.02	.01
☐	188	Luc Robitaille	.15	.07	.02
☐	189	Bob Kudelski	.08	.04	.01
☐	190	Daniel Berthiaume	.05	.02	.01
☐	191	Steve Duchesne	.08	.04	.01
☐	192	Tony Granato	.08	.04	.01
☐	193	Bob Essensa	.08	.04	.01
☐	194	Phil Sykes	.05	.02	.01
☐	195	Paul MacDermid	.05	.02	.01
☐	196	Dave McLlwain	.05	.02	.01
☐	197	Phil Housley	.08	.04	.01
☐	198	Pat Elynuik	.05	.02	.01
☐	199	Randy Carlyle	.05	.02	.01
☐	200	Thomas Steen	.05	.02	.01
☐	201	Teppo Numminen	.05	.02	.01
☐	202	Danton Cole	.05	.02	.01
☐	203	Doug Evans	.05	.02	.01
☐	204	Ed Olczyk	.05	.02	.01
☐	205	Moe Mantha	.05	.02	.01
☐	206	Scott Arniel	.05	.02	.01
☐	207	Rick Tabaracci	.05	.02	.01
☐	208	Bryan Marchment	.10	.05	.01
☐	209	Mark Osborne	.05	.02	.01
☐	210	Fredrik Olausson	.08	.04	.01
☐	211	Brent Ashton	.05	.02	.01
☐	212	Ray Ferraro	.08	.04	.01
☐	213	Mark Fitzpatrick	.08	.04	.01
☐	214	Hubie McDonough	.05	.02	.01
☐	215	Joe Reekie	.05	.02	.01
☐	216	Bill Berg	.05	.02	.01
☐	217	Wayne McBean	.05	.02	.01
☐	218	Pat Flatley	.05	.02	.01
☐	219	Jeff Hackett	.05	.02	.01
☐	220	Derek King	.08	.04	.01
☐	221	Craig Ludwig	.05	.02	.01
☐	222	Pat LaFontaine	.20	.09	.03
☐	223	David Volek	.05	.02	.01
☐	224	Glenn Healy	.08	.04	.01
☐	225	Jeff Norton	.05	.02	.01
☐	226	Brent Sutter	.08	.04	.01
☐	227	Randy Wood	.05	.02	.01
☐	228	Gary Nylund	.05	.02	.01
☐	229	Dave Chyzowski	.05	.02	.01
☐	230	Rick Tocchet	.08	.04	.01
☐	231	Ken Wregget	.05	.02	.01
☐	232	Terry Carkner	.05	.02	.01
☐	233	Martin Hostak	.05	.02	.01
☐	234	Ron Hextall	.08	.04	.01
☐	235	Gord Murphy	.05	.02	.01
☐	236	Scott Mellanby	.05	.02	.01
☐	237	Pete Peeters	.08	.04	.01
☐	238	Ron Sutter	.05	.02	.01
☐	239	Murray Craven	.05	.02	.01
☐	240	Kjell Samuelsson	.05	.02	.01
☐	241	Pelle Eklund	.05	.02	.01
☐	242	Mark Pederson	.05	.02	.01
☐	243	Murray Baron	.05	.02	.01
☐	244	Keith Acton	.05	.02	.01
☐	245	Derrick Smith	.05	.02	.01
☐	246	Mike Ricci	.15	.07	.02
☐	247	Dale Kushner	.05	.02	.01
☐	248	Normand Lacombe	.05	.02	.01
☐	249	Theoren Fleury HT	.15	.07	.02
☐	250	Sergei Makarov HT	.15	.07	.02
☐	251	Paul Ranheim	.05	.02	.01
☐	252	Joe Nieuwendyk	.10	.05	.01
☐	253	Mike Vernon	.08	.04	.01
☐	254	Gary Suter	.08	.04	.01
☐	255	Doug Gilmour	.25	.11	.03
☐	256	Paul Fenton	.05	.02	.01
☐	257	Roger Johansson	.05	.02	.01
☐	258	Stephane Matteau	.05	.02	.01
☐	259	Frantisek Musil	.05	.02	.01
☐	260	Joel Otto	.05	.02	.01
☐	261	Tim Sweeney	.05	.02	.01
☐	262	Al MacInnis	.10	.05	.01
☐	263	Gary Roberts	.08	.04	.01
☐	264	Sergei Makarov	.08	.04	.01
☐	265	Carey Wilson	.05	.02	.01
☐	266	Ric Nattress	.05	.02	.01
☐	267	Robert Reichel	.15	.07	.02
☐	268	Rick Wamsley	.05	.02	.01
☐	269	Brian MacLellan	.05	.02	.01
☐	270	Theoren Fleury	.15	.07	.02
☐	271	Claude Lemieux	.08	.04	.01
☐	272	John MacLean	.08	.04	.01
☐	273	Viacheslav Fetisov	.08	.04	.01
☐	274	Kirk Muller	.08	.04	.01
☐	275	Sean Burke	.08	.04	.01
☐	276	Alexei Kasatonov	.05	.02	.01
☐	277	Claude Lemieux	.08	.04	.01
☐	278	Eric Weinrich	.05	.02	.01
☐	279	Patrik Sundstrom	.05	.02	.01
☐	280	Zdeno Ciger	.05	.02	.01
☐	281	Bruce Driver	.05	.02	.01
☐	282	Laurie Boschman	.05	.02	.01
☐	283	Chris Terreri	.08	.04	.01
☐	284	Ken Daneyko	.05	.02	.01
☐	285	Doug Brown	.05	.02	.01
☐	286	Jon Morris	.05	.02	.01
☐	287	Peter Stastny	.08	.04	.01
☐	288	Brendan Shanahan	.25	.11	.03
☐	289	John MacLean	.08	.04	.01
☐	290	Mike Liut	.08	.04	.01
☐	291	Michal Pivonka	.08	.04	.01
☐	292	Kelly Miller	.05	.02	.01
☐	293	John Druce	.05	.02	.01
☐	294	Calle Johansson	.05	.02	.01
☐	295	Alan May	.05	.02	.01
☐	296	Kevin Hatcher	.08	.04	.01
☐	297	Tim Bergland	.05	.02	.01
☐	298	Mikhail Tatarinov	.05	.02	.01
☐	299	Peter Bondra	.08	.04	.01
☐	300	Al Iafrate	.08	.04	.01
☐	301	Nick Kypreos	.05	.02	.01
☐	302	Dino Ciccarelli	.08	.04	.01
☐	303	Dale Hunter	.08	.04	.01
☐	304	Don Beaupre	.08	.04	.01
☐	305	Jim Hrivnak	.05	.02	.01
☐	306	Stephen Leach	.05	.02	.01
☐	307	Dimitri Khristich	.08	.04	.01
☐	308	Mike Ridley	.08	.04	.01
☐	309	Sergio Momesso	.05	.02	.01
☐	310	Kirk McLean	.20	.09	.03
☐	311	Greg Adams	.05	.02	.01
☐	312	Adrien Plavsic	.05	.02	.01
☐	313	Cliff Ronning	.08	.04	.01
☐	314	Garry Valk	.05	.02	.01
☐	315	Troy Gamble	.05	.02	.01
☐	316	Gino Odjick	.08	.04	.01
☐	317	Doug Lidster	.05	.02	.01
☐	318	Geoff Courtnall	.08	.04	.01
☐	319	Tom Kurvers	.05	.02	.01
☐	320	Robert Kron	.05	.02	.01
☐	321	Jyrki Lumme	.05	.02	.01
☐	322	Jay Mazur	.05	.02	.01
☐	323	Dave Capuano	.05	.02	.01
☐	324	Petr Nedved	.25	.11	.03
☐	325	Steve Bozek	.05	.02	.01
☐	326	Igor Larionov	.08	.04	.01
☐	327	Trevor Linden	.25	.11	.03
☐	328	Shayne Corson	.08	.04	.01
☐	329	Eric Desjardins	.08	.04	.01
☐	330	Stephane Richer	.08	.04	.01

☐ 331	Brian Skrudland	.05	.02	.01
☐ 332	Sylvain Lefebvre	.05	.02	.01
☐ 333	Stephan Lebeau	.15	.07	.02
☐ 334	Mike Keane	.05	.02	.01
☐ 335	Patrick Roy UER	.50	.23	.06
	(Photo actually			
	Jean Claude Bergeron)			
☐ 336	Brent Gilchrist	.05	.02	.01
☐ 337	Andre Racicot	.10	.05	.01
☐ 338	Guy Carbonneau	.08	.04	.01
☐ 339	Mike McPhee	.05	.02	.01
☐ 340	Andrew Cassels	.08	.04	.01
☐ 341	Petr Svoboda	.05	.02	.01
☐ 342	Denis Savard	.08	.04	.01
☐ 343	Mathieu Schneider	.08	.04	.01
☐ 344	John LeClair	.20	.09	.03
☐ 345	Tom Chorske	.05	.02	.01
☐ 346	Russ Courtnall	.08	.04	.01
☐ 347	Ken Hodge Jr. HT	.10	.05	.01
☐ 348	Cam Neely HT	.13	.06	.02
☐ 349	Randy Burridge	.05	.02	.01
☐ 350	Glen Wesley	.05	.02	.01
☐ 351	Chris Nilan	.08	.04	.01
☐ 352	Jeff Lazaro	.05	.02	.01
☐ 353	Wes Walz	.05	.02	.01
☐ 354	Rejean Lemelin	.08	.04	.01
☐ 355	Craig Janney	.15	.07	.02
☐ 356	Ray Bourque	.15	.07	.02
☐ 357	Bob Sweeney	.05	.02	.01
☐ 358	Dave Christian	.05	.02	.01
☐ 359	Dave Poulin	.08	.04	.01
☐ 360	Garry Galley	.08	.04	.01
☐ 361	Andy Moog	.10	.05	.01
☐ 362	Ken Hodge Jr.	.05	.02	.01
☐ 363	Jim Wiemer	.05	.02	.01
☐ 364	Petri Skriko	.05	.02	.01
☐ 365	Don Sweeney	.05	.02	.01
☐ 366	Cam Neely	.15	.07	.02
☐ 367	Brett Hull HT	.20	.09	.03
☐ 368	Gino Cavallini	.05	.02	.01
☐ 369	Scott Stevens	.10	.05	.01
☐ 370	Rich Sutter	.05	.02	.01
☐ 371	Glen Featherstone	.05	.02	.01
☐ 372	Vincent Riendeau	.05	.02	.01
☐ 373	Dave Lowry	.05	.02	.01
☐ 374	Rod Brind'Amour	.15	.07	.02
☐ 375	Brett Hull	.50	.23	.06
☐ 376	Dan Quinn	.05	.02	.01
☐ 377	Tom Tilley	.05	.02	.01
☐ 378	Paul Cavallini	.05	.02	.01
☐ 379	Bob Bassen	.05	.02	.01
☐ 380	Mario Marois	.05	.02	.01
☐ 381	Darin Kimble	.05	.02	.01
☐ 382	Ron Wilson	.05	.02	.01
☐ 383	Garth Butcher	.05	.02	.01
☐ 384	Adam Oates	.20	.09	.03
☐ 385	Jeff Brown	.08	.04	.01
☐ 386	Jeremy Roenick HT	.20	.09	.03
☐ 387	Tony McKegney	.05	.02	.01
☐ 388	Troy Murray	.05	.02	.01
☐ 389	Dave Manson	.08	.04	.01
☐ 390	Ed Belfour	.40	.18	.05
☐ 391	Steve Thomas	.08	.04	.01
☐ 392	Michel Goulet	.08	.04	.01
☐ 393	Trent Yawney	.05	.02	.01
☐ 394	Adam Creighton	.05	.02	.01
☐ 395	Steve Larmer	.08	.04	.01
☐ 396	Jimmy Waite	.08	.04	.01
☐ 397	Dirk Graham	.05	.02	.01
☐ 398	Chris Chelios	.08	.04	.01
☐ 399	Mike Hudson	.05	.02	.01
☐ 400	Doug Wilson	.08	.04	.01
☐ 401	Greg Gilbert	.05	.02	.01
☐ 402	Wayne Presley	.05	.02	.01
☐ 403	Jeremy Roenick	.50	.23	.06
☐ 404	Frantisek Kucera	.05	.02	.01
☐ 405	Blackhawks/North Stars	.07	.03	.01
	Playoff Action			
☐ 406	Blues/Red Wings	.10	.05	.01
	Playoff Action (Adam Oates)			
☐ 407	Flames/Oilers	.07	.03	.01
	Playoff Action			
☐ 408	Penguins/Devils	.07	.03	.01
	Playoff Action			
☐ 409	Rangers/Capitals	.07	.03	.01
	Playoff Action			
☐ 410	Bruins/Whalers	.07	.03	.01
	Playoff Action			
☐ 411	Canadiens/Sabres	.07	.03	.01
	Playoff Action			
☐ 412	Kings/Canucks	.07	.03	.01
	Playoff Action			
☐ 413	Penguins/Capitals	.07	.03	.01

	Playoff Action			
☐ 414	Bruins/Canadiens	.07	.03	.01
	Playoff Action			
☐ 415	North Stars/Blues	.07	.03	.01
	Playoff Action			
☐ 416	Kings/Oilers	.07	.03	.01
	Playoff Action			
☐ 417	North Stars/Oilers	.07	.03	.01
	Playoff Action			
☐ 418	Bruins/Penguins	.10	.05	.01
	Playoff Action (Kevin Stevens)			
☐ 419	Game 1 Cup Finals	.07	.03	.01
☐ 420	Game 2 Cup Finals	.07	.03	.01
☐ 421	Game 3 Cup Finals	.07	.03	.01
☐ 422	Game 4 Cup Finals	.10	.05	.01
	(Kevin Stevens)			
☐ 423	Game 5 Cup Finals	.07	.03	.01
☐ 424	Game 6 Cup Finals	.07	.03	.01
☐ 425	Mario Lemieux MVP	.40	.18	.05
	(Smythe)			
☐ 426	Checklist 1-108	.05	.02	.01
☐ 427	Checklist 109-216	.05	.02	.01
☐ 428	Checklist 217-324	.05	.02	.01
☐ 429	Checklist 325-429	.05	.02	.01

1992-93 Bowman

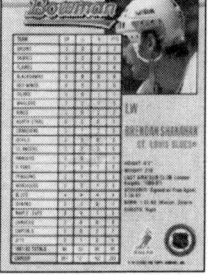

The 1992-93 Bowman hockey set contains 441 cards and measures the standard size (2 1/2" by 3 1/2"). Reportedly only 2,000 16-box wax cases were produced. One of 45 gold-foil engraved cards was inserted in each 15-card jumbo pack. These gold-foil cards feature 44 All-Stars (Campbell Conference on cards 199-220 and Wales Conference on cards 222-243) and a special card commemorating Mario Lemieux as the winner of the Conn Smythe trophy (440). The 18 gold-foil All-Stars which were single printed are listed in the checklist below as SP. The basic card fronts feature color action player photos with white borders. A magenta bar at the top left corner carries the Bowman "B". A gradated turquoise bar at the bottom right displays the player's name. The backs have a burlap-textured background and carry a close-up photo, a yellow and white statistics box presenting the player's performance vs. other teams, and biography. The cards are numbered on the back. The only noteworthy Rookie Card in the set is Guy Hebert. There are a number of non-glossy Eric Lindros (No. 442) cards on the market. These are unauthorized releases.

	MINT	EXC	G-VG
COMPLETE SET (442)	350.00	160.00	45.00
COMMON PLAYER (1-442)	.25	.11	.03
COMMON FOIL (199-220)	1.50	.65	.19
COMMON FOIL (222-243)	1.50	.65	.19
☐ 1 Wayne Gretzky	8.00	3.60	1.00
Los Angeles Kings			
☐ 2 Mike Krushelnyski	.25	.11	.03
Toronto Maple Leafs			
☐ 3 Ray Bourque	.60	.25	.08
Boston Bruins			
☐ 4 Keith Brown	.25	.11	.03

Chicago Blackhawks			
☐ 5 Bob Sweeney UER	.25	.11	.03
(Photo on back actually Don Sweeney)			
Boston Bruins			
☐ 6 Dave Christian	.25	.11	.03
St. Louis Blues			
☐ 7 Frantisek Kucera	.25	.11	.03
Boston Bruins			
☐ 8 John LeClair	.25	.11	.03
Montreal Canadiens			
☐ 9 Jamie Macoun	.25	.11	.03
Toronto Maple Leafs			
☐ 10 Bob Carpenter	.25	.11	.03
Boston Bruins			
☐ 11 Garry Galley	.25	.11	.03
Philadelphia Flyers			
☐ 12 Bob Kudelski	.30	.14	.04
Los Angeles Kings			
☐ 13 Doug Bodger	.25	.11	.03
Buffalo Sabres			
☐ 14 Craig Janney	.50	.23	.06
St. Louis Blues			
☐ 15 Glen Wesley	.25	.11	.03
Boston Bruins			
☐ 16 Daren Puppa	.30	.14	.04
Buffalo Sabres			
☐ 17 Andy Brickley	.25	.11	.03
Boston Bruins			
☐ 18 Steve Konroyd	.25	.11	.03
Hartford Whalers			
☐ 19 Dave Poulin	.30	.14	.04
Boston Bruins			
☐ 20 Phil Housley	.30	.14	.04
Winnipeg Jets			
☐ 21 Kevin Todd	.25	.11	.03
New Jersey Devils			
☐ 22 Tomas Sandstrom	.30	.14	.04
Los Angeles Kings			
☐ 23 Pierre Turgeon	1.50	.65	.19
New York Islanders			
☐ 24 Steve Smith	.30	.14	.04
Chicago Blackhawks			
☐ 25 Ray Sheppard	.40	.18	.05
Detroit Red Wings			
☐ 26 Stu Barnes	.25	.11	.03
Winnipeg Jets			
☐ 27 Grant Ledyard	.25	.11	.03
Buffalo Sabres			
☐ 28 Benoit Hogue UER	.25	.11	.03
New York Islanders			
(Photo of Dennis Vaske on back)			
☐ 29 Randy Burridge	.25	.11	.03
Washington Capitals			
☐ 30 Clint Malarchuk	.30	.14	.04
St. Louis Blues			
☐ 31 Steve Duchesne	.30	.14	.04
Philadelphia Flyers			
☐ 32 Guy Hebert	1.50	.65	.19
Buffalo Sabres			
☐ 33 Steve Kasper	.25	.11	.03
Los Angeles Kings			
☐ 34 Alexander Mogilny	3.00	1.35	.40
New York Rangers			
☐ 35 Marty McSorley	.30	.14	.04
Los Angeles Kings			
☐ 36 Doug Weight	.50	.23	.06
Montreal Canadiens			
☐ 37 Dave Taylor	.30	.14	.04
Los Angeles Kings			
☐ 38 Guy Carbonneau	.30	.14	.04
Montreal Canadiens			
☐ 39 Brian Benning	.25	.11	.03
Quebec Nordiques			
☐ 40 Nelson Emerson	.40	.18	.05
Los Angeles Kings			
☐ 41 Craig Wolanin	.25	.11	.03
Quebec Nordiques			
☐ 42 Kelly Hrudey	.30	.14	.04
Los Angeles Kings			
☐ 43 Chris Chelios	.50	.23	.06
Chicago Blackhawks			
☐ 44 Dave Andreychuk	.60	.25	.08
Buffalo Sabres			
☐ 45 Russ Courtnall	.30	.14	.04
Montreal Canadiens			
☐ 46 Stephane Richer	.30	.14	.04
New Jersey Devils			
☐ 47 Petr Svoboda	.25	.11	.03
Buffalo Sabres			
☐ 48 Barry Pederson	.25	.11	.03
Boston Bruins			
☐ 49 Claude Lemieux	.30	.14	.04
New Jersey Devils			
☐ 50 Tony Granato	.30	.14	.04
Los Angeles Kings			
☐ 51 Al MacInnis	.35	.16	.04
Calgary Flames			
☐ 52 Luciano Borsato	.25	.11	.03
Winnipeg Jets			
☐ 53 Sergei Makarov	.40	.18	.05
Calgary Flames			
☐ 54 Bobby Smith	.30	.14	.04
Minnesota North Stars			
☐ 55 Gary Suter	.30	.14	.04
Calgary Flames			
☐ 56 Tom Draper	.25	.11	.03
Buffalo Sabres			
☐ 57 Corry Millen	.25	.11	.03
Los Angeles Kings			
☐ 58 Joe Mullen	.35	.16	.04
Pittsburgh Penguins			
☐ 59 Joe Nieuwendyk	.50	.23	.06
Calgary Flames			
☐ 60 Brian Hayward	.25	.11	.03
San Jose Sharks			
☐ 61 Steve Larmer	.35	.16	.04
Chicago Blackhawks			
☐ 62 Cam Neely	.60	.25	.08
Boston Bruins			
☐ 63 Ric Nattress	.25	.11	.03
Toronto Maple Leafs			
☐ 64 Denis Savard	.30	.14	.04
Montreal Canadiens			
☐ 65 Gerald Diduck	.25	.11	.03
Vancouver Canucks			
☐ 66 Pat Jablonski	.25	.11	.03
St. Louis Blues			
☐ 67 Brad McCrimmon	.25	.11	.03
Detroit Red Wings			
☐ 68 Dirk Graham	.25	.11	.03
Chicago Blackhawks			
☐ 69 Joel Otto	.25	.11	.03
Calgary Flames			
☐ 70 Luc Robitaille	.75	.35	.09
Los Angeles Kings			
☐ 71 Dana Murzyn	.25	.11	.03
Vancouver Canucks			
☐ 72 Jocelyn Lemieux	.25	.11	.03
Chicago Blackhawks			
☐ 73 Mike Hudson	.25	.11	.03
Chicago Blackhawks			
☐ 74 Patrick Roy UER	4.00	1.80	.50
(Games played vs. Edmonton was 2, not 32)			
Montreal Canadiens			
☐ 75 Doug Wilson	.30	.14	.04
San Jose Sharks			
☐ 76 Wayne Presley	.25	.11	.03
Buffalo Sabres			
☐ 77 Felix Potvin UER	10.00	4.50	1.25
('91-92 season record was 0-2-1, not 0-3-1)			
Toronto Maple Leafs			
☐ 78 Jeremy Roenick	4.00	1.80	.50
Chicago Blackhawks			
☐ 79 Andy Moog	.35	.16	.04
Boston Bruins			
☐ 80 Joe Kocur	.25	.11	.03
New York Rangers			
☐ 81 Neal Broten	.30	.14	.04
Minnesota North Stars			
☐ 82 Shayne Corson	.30	.14	.04
Montreal Canadiens			
☐ 83 Doug Gilmour	2.50	1.15	.30
Toronto Maple Leafs			
☐ 84 Rob Zettler	.25	.11	.03
San Jose Sharks			
☐ 85 Bob Probert	.25	.11	.03
Detroit Red Wings			
☐ 86 Mike Vernon	.30	.14	.04
Calgary Flames			
☐ 87 Rick Zombo	.25	.11	.03
St. Louis Blues			
☐ 88 Adam Creighton	.25	.11	.03
New York Islanders			
☐ 89 Mike McPhee	.25	.11	.03
Montreal Canadiens			
☐ 90 Ed Belfour	1.00	.45	.13
Chicago Blackhawks			
☐ 91 Steve Chiasson	.25	.11	.03
Detroit Red Wings			
☐ 92 Dominic Roussel	.40	.18	.05
Philadelphia Flyers			
☐ 93 Troy Murray	.25	.11	.03
Winnipeg Jets			
☐ 94 Jari Kurri	.35	.16	.04

Los Angeles Kings			
☐ 95 Geoff Smith	.25	.11	.03
Edmonton Oilers			
☐ 96 Paul Ranheim	.25	.11	.03
Calgary Flames			
☐ 97 Rick Wamsley	.25	.11	.03
Toronto Maple Leafs			
☐ 98 Brian Noonan	.25	.11	.03
Chicago Blackhawks			
☐ 99 Kevin Lowe	.30	.14	.04
Edmonton Oilers			
☐ 100 Josef Beranek	.50	.23	.06
Edmonton Oilers			
☐ 101 Michel Petit	.25	.11	.03
Calgary Flames			
☐ 102 Craig Billington	.25	.11	.03
New Jersey Devils			
☐ 103 Steve Yzerman	2.50	1.15	.30
Detroit Red Wings			
☐ 104 Glenn Anderson	.30	.14	.04
Toronto Maple Leafs			
☐ 105 Perry Berezan	.25	.11	.03
San Jose Sharks			
☐ 106 Bill Ranford	.30	.14	.04
Edmonton Oilers			
☐ 107 Randy Ladouceur	.25	.11	.03
Hartford Whalers			
☐ 108 Jimmy Carson	.30	.14	.04
Detroit Red Wings			
☐ 109 Gary Roberts	.40	.18	.05
Calgary Flames			
☐ 110 Checklist 1-110	.25	.11	.03
☐ 111 Brad Shaw	.25	.11	.03
Hartford Whalers			
☐ 112 Pat Verbeek	.30	.14	.04
Hartford Whalers			
☐ 113 Mark Messier	1.00	.45	.13
New York Rangers			
☐ 114 Grant Fuhr	.30	.14	.04
Toronto Maple Leafs			
☐ 115 Sylvain Cote	.25	.11	.03
Washington Capitals			
☐ 116 Mike Sullivan	.25	.11	.03
San Jose Sharks			
☐ 117 Steve Thomas	.30	.14	.04
New York Rangers			
☐ 118 Craig MacTavish	.25	.11	.03
Edmonton Oilers			
☐ 119 Dave Babych	.25	.11	.03
Vancouver Canucks			
☐ 120 Jim Waite	.30	.14	.04
Chicago Blackhawks			
☐ 121 Kevin Dineen	.30	.14	.04
Philadelphia Flyers			
☐ 122 Shawn Burr	.25	.11	.03
Detroit Red Wings			
☐ 123 Ron Francis	.30	.14	.04
Pittsburgh Penguins			
☐ 124 Garth Butcher	.25	.11	.03
St. Louis Blues			
☐ 125 Jarmo Myllys	.25	.11	.03
San Jose Sharks			
☐ 126 Doug Brown	.25	.11	.03
New Jersey Devils			
☐ 127 James Patrick	.25	.11	.03
New York Rangers			
☐ 128 Ray Ferraro	.25	.11	.03
New York Islanders			
☐ 129 Terry Carkner	.25	.11	.03
Philadelphia Flyers			
☐ 130 John MacLean	.30	.14	.04
New Jersey Devils			
☐ 131 Randy Velischek	.25	.11	.03
Quebec Nordiques			
☐ 132 John Vanbiesbrouck	.75	.35	.09
New York Rangers			
☐ 133 Dean Evason	.25	.11	.03
San Jose Sharks			
☐ 134 Patrick Flatley	.25	.11	.03
New York Rangers			
☐ 135 Petr Klima	.25	.11	.03
Edmonton Oilers			
☐ 136 Geoff Sanderson	2.50	1.15	.30
Hartford Whalers			
☐ 137 Joe Reekie	.25	.11	.03
New York Rangers			
☐ 138 Kirk Muller	.30	.14	.04
Montreal Canadiens			
☐ 139 Brian Mullen	.30	.14	.04
San Jose Sharks			
☐ 140 Daniel Berthiaume	.25	.11	.03
Boston Bruins			
☐ 141 David Shaw	.25	.11	.03
Minnesota North Stars			

☐ 142 Pat LaFontaine	1.50	.65	.19
Buffalo Sabres			
☐ 143 Ulf Dahlen	.25	.11	.03
Minnesota North Stars			
☐ 144 Esa Tikkanen	.30	.14	.04
Edmonton Oilers			
☐ 145 Viacheslav Fetisov	.30	.14	.04
New Jersey Devils			
☐ 146 Mike Gartner	.50	.23	.06
New York Rangers			
☐ 147 Brent Sutter	.30	.14	.04
Chicago Blackhawks			
☐ 148 Darcy Wakaluk	.30	.14	.04
Minnesota North Stars			
☐ 149 Brian Leetch	1.50	.65	.19
New York Rangers			
☐ 150 Craig Simpson	.30	.14	.04
Edmonton Oilers			
☐ 151 Mike Modano	1.50	.65	.19
Minnesota North Stars			
☐ 152 Bryan Trottier	.35	.16	.04
Pittsburgh Penguins			
☐ 153 Larry Murphy	.30	.14	.04
Pittsburgh Penguins			
☐ 154 Pavel Bure	10.00	4.50	1.25
Vancouver Canucks			
☐ 155 Kay Whitmore	.25	.11	.03
Hartford Whalers			
☐ 156 Darren Turcotte	.25	.11	.03
New York Rangers			
☐ 157 Frantisek Musil	.25	.11	.03
Calgary Flames			
☐ 158 Mikael Andersson	.25	.11	.03
Tampa Bay Lightning			
☐ 159 Rick Tocchet	.30	.14	.04
Pittsburgh Penguins			
☐ 160 Scott Stevens	.35	.16	.04
New Jersey Devils			
☐ 161 Bernie Nicholls	.30	.14	.04
Edmonton Oilers			
☐ 162 Peter Sidorkiewicz	.25	.11	.03
Tampa Bay Lightning			
☐ 163 Scott Mellanby	.25	.11	.03
Edmonton Oilers			
☐ 164 Alexander Semak	.25	.11	.03
New Jersey Devils			
☐ 165 Kjell Samuelsson	.25	.11	.03
Pittsburgh Penguins			
☐ 166 Kelly Kisio	.25	.11	.03
San Jose Sharks			
☐ 167 Sylvain Turgeon	.25	.11	.03
Montreal Canadiens			
☐ 168 Rob Brown	.25	.11	.03
Chicago Blackhawks			
☐ 169 Gerard Gallant	.25	.11	.03
Detroit Red Wings			
☐ 170 Jyrki Lumme	.25	.11	.03
Vancouver Canucks			
☐ 171 Dave Gagner	.30	.14	.04
Minnesota North Stars			
☐ 172 Tony Tanti	.25	.11	.03
Buffalo Sabres			
☐ 173 Zarley Zalapski	.25	.11	.03
Hartford Whalers			
☐ 174 Joe Murphy	.30	.14	.04
Edmonton Oilers			
☐ 175 Ron Sutter	.25	.11	.03
St. Louis Blues			
☐ 176 Dino Ciccarelli	.30	.14	.04
Washington Capitals			
☐ 177 Jim Johnson	.25	.11	.03
Minnesota North Stars			
☐ 178 Mike Hough	.25	.11	.03
Quebec Nordiques			
☐ 179 Pelle Eklund	.25	.11	.03
Philadelphia Flyers			
☐ 180 John Druce	.25	.11	.03
Washington Capitals			
☐ 181 Paul Coffey	.50	.23	.06
Los Angeles Kings			
☐ 182 Ken Wregget	.25	.11	.03
Pittsburgh Penguins			
☐ 183 Brendan Shanahan	1.50	.65	.19
St. Louis Blues			
☐ 184 Keith Acton	.25	.11	.03
Philadelphia Flyers			
☐ 185 Steven Finn	.25	.11	.03
Quebec Nordiques			
☐ 186 Brett Hull	5.00	2.30	.60
St. Louis Blues			
☐ 187 Rollie Melanson	.25	.11	.03
Montreal Canadiens			
☐ 188 Derek King	.30	.14	.04

	New York Rangers			
☐ 189	Mario Lemieux	6.00	2.70	.75
	Pittsburgh Penguins			
☐ 190	Mathieu Schneider	.30	.14	.04
	Montreal Canadiens			
☐ 191	Claude Vilgrain	.25	.11	.03
	New Jersey Devils			
☐ 192	Gary Leeman	.25	.11	.03
	Calgary Flames			
☐ 193	Paul Cavallini......................	.25	.11	.03
	St. Louis Blues			
☐ 194	John Cullen	.25	.11	.03
	Hartford Whalers			
☐ 195	Ron Hextall	.30	.14	.04
	Philadelphia Flyers			
	(Traded to Quebec)			
☐ 196	David Volek	.25	.11	.03
	New York Rangers			
☐ 197	Gordie Roberts....................	.25	.11	.03
	Pittsburgh Penguins			
☐ 198	Dale Craigwell	.25	.11	.03
	San Jose Sharks			
☐ 199	Ed Belfour	4.00	1.80	.50
	AS FOIL			
	Chicago Blackhawks			
☐ 200	Brian Bellows	25.00	11.50	3.10
	AS FOIL SP			
	Minnesota North Stars			
☐ 201	Chris Chelios......................	2.00	.90	.25
	AS FOIL			
	Chicago Blackhawks			
☐ 202	Tim Cheveldae....................	20.00	9.00	2.50
	AS FOIL SP			
	Detroit Red Wings			
☐ 203A	Vincent Damphousse........	3.00	1.35	.40
	AS FOIL ERR			
	(Team name missing			
	on card back)			
	Edmonton Oilers			
☐ 203B	Vincent Damphousse........	3.00	1.35	.40
	AS FOIL COR			
	Edmonton Oilers			
☐ 204	Dave Ellett..........................	1.50	.65	.19
	AS FOIL			
	Toronto Maple Leafs			
☐ 205	Sergei Fedorov....................	55.00	25.00	7.00
	AS FOIL SP			
	Detroit Red Wings			
☐ 206	Theoren Fleury	1.50	.65	.19
	AS FOIL			
	Calgary Flames			
☐ 207	Wayne Gretzky	15.00	6.75	1.90
	AS FOIL			
	Los Angeles Kings			
☐ 208	Phil Housley........................	1.50	.65	.19
	AS FOIL			
	Winnipeg Jets			
☐ 209	Brett Hull............................	8.00	3.60	1.00
	AS FOIL			
	St. Louis Blues			
☐ 210	Trevor Linden......................	16.00	7.25	2.00
	AS FOIL SP			
	Vancouver Canucks			
☐ 211	Al MacInnis	9.00	4.00	1.15
	AS FOIL SP			
	Calgary Flames			
☐ 212	Kirk McLean	32.00	14.50	4.00
	AS FOIL SP			
	Vancouver Canucks			
☐ 213	Adam Oates	3.00	1.35	.40
	AS FOIL			
	St. Louis Blues			
☐ 214	Gary Roberts......................	15.00	6.75	1.90
	AS FOIL SP			
	Calgary Flames			
☐ 215	Larry Robinson	1.50	.65	.19
	AS FOIL			
	Los Angeles Kings			
☐ 216	Luc Robitaille.....................	4.00	1.80	.50
	AS FOIL			
	Los Angeles Kings			
☐ 217	Jeremy Roenick	50.00	23.00	6.25
	AS FOIL SP			
	Chicago Blackhawks			
☐ 218	Mark Tinordi	1.50	.65	.19
	AS FOIL			
	Minnesota North Stars			
☐ 219	Doug Wilson	1.50	.65	.19
	AS FOIL			
	San Jose Sharks			
☐ 220	Steve Yzerman	6.00	2.70	.75
	AS FOIL			
	Detroit Red Wings			
☐ 221	Checklist 111-220	.25	.11	.03

☐ 222	Don Beaupre	15.00	6.75	1.90
	AS FOIL SP			
	Washington Capitals			
☐ 223	Ray Bourque	3.00	1.35	.40
	AS FOIL			
	Boston Bruins			
☐ 224	Rod Brind'Amour UER	20.00	9.00	2.50
	AS FOIL SP			
	(Apostrophe in last			
	name is missing)			
	Philadelphia Flyers			
☐ 225	Randy Burridge	9.00	4.00	1.15
	AS FOIL SP			
	Washington Capitals			
☐ 226	Paul Coffey.........................	20.00	9.00	2.50
	AS FOIL SP			
	Los Angeles Kings			
☐ 227	John Cullen	9.00	4.00	1.15
	AS FOIL SP			
	Hartford Whalers			
☐ 228	Eric Desjardins	15.00	6.75	1.90
	AS FOIL SP			
	Montreal Canadiens			
☐ 229	Ray Ferraro	9.00	4.00	1.15
	AS FOIL SP			
	New York Rangers			
☐ 230	Kevin Hatcher.....................	1.50	.65	.19
	AS FOIL			
	Washington Capitals			
☐ 231	Jaromir Jagr	9.00	4.00	1.15
	AS FOIL			
	Pittsburgh Penguins			
☐ 232	Brian Leetch	20.00	9.00	2.50
	AS FOIL SP			
	New York Rangers			
☐ 233	Mario Lemieux	14.00	6.25	1.75
	AS FOIL			
	Pittsburgh Penguins			
☐ 234	Mark Messier	5.00	2.30	.60
	AS FOIL			
	New York Rangers			
☐ 235	Alexander Mogilny	7.00	3.10	.85
	AS FOIL			
	Buffalo Sabres			
☐ 236	Kirk Muller	2.50	1.15	.30
	AS FOIL			
	Montreal Canadiens			
☐ 237	Owen Nolan........................	1.50	.65	.19
	AS FOIL			
	Quebec Nordiques			
☐ 238	Mike Richter.......................	6.00	2.70	.75
	AS FOIL			
	New York Rangers			
☐ 239	Patrick Roy	10.00	4.50	1.25
	AS FOIL			
	Montreal Canadiens			
☐ 240	Joe Sakic............................	18.00	8.00	2.30
	AS FOIL SP			
	Quebec Nordiques			
☐ 241	Kevin Stevens	3.00	1.35	.40
	AS FOIL			
	Pittsburgh Penguins			
☐ 242	Scott Stevens.....................	1.50	.65	.19
	AS FOIL			
	New Jersey Devils			
☐ 243	Brian Trottier......................	9.00	4.00	1.15
	AS FOIL SP			
	New York Rangers			
☐ 244	Joe Sakic............................	.75	.35	.09
	Quebec Nordiques			
☐ 245	Daniel Marois	.25	.11	.03
	New York Islanders			
☐ 246	Randy Wood	.25	.11	.03
	Pittsburgh Penguins			
☐ 247	Jeff Brown...........................	.30	.14	.04
	St. Louis Blues			
☐ 248	Peter Bondra.......................	.30	.14	.04
	Washington Capitals			
☐ 249	Peter Stastny......................	.30	.14	.04
	New Jersey Devils			
☐ 250	Tom Barrasso	.35	.16	.04
	Pittsburgh Penguins			
☐ 251	Al Iafrate	.30	.14	.04
	Washington Capitals			
☐ 252	James Black........................	.25	.11	.03
	Hartford Whalers			
☐ 253	Jan Erixon	.25	.11	.03
	New York Rangers			
☐ 254	Brian Lawton.......................	.25	.11	.03
	San Jose Sharks			
☐ 255	Luke Richardson	.25	.11	.03
	Edmonton Oilers			
☐ 256	Rich Sutter	.25	.11	.03

St. Louis Blues
☐ 257 Jeff Chychrun UER.............. .25	.11	.03

(Misspelled Chychurn
on card front)
Los Angeles Kings
☐ 258 Adam Oates........................ .75 .35 .09
Boston Bruins
☐ 259 Tom Kurvers...................... .25 .11 .03
New York Islanders
☐ 260 Brian Bellows .... .30 .14 .04
Minnesota North Stars
☐ 261 Trevor Linden .... .75 .35 .09
Vancouver Canucks
☐ 262 Vincent Riendeau .... .25 .11 .03
St. Louis Blues
☐ 263 Peter Zezel .... .25 .11 .03
Toronto Maple Leafs
☐ 264 Rich Pilon .... .25 .11 .03
New York Islanders
☐ 265 Paul Broten .... .25 .11 .03
New York Rangers
☐ 266 Gaetan Duchesne .... .25 .11 .03
Minnesota North Stars
☐ 267 Doug Lidster .... .25 .11 .03
Vancouver Canucks
☐ 268 Rod Brind'Amour .... 1.00 .45 .13
Philadelphia Flyers
☐ 269 Jon Casey .... .30 .14 .04
Minnesota North Stars
☐ 270 Pat Elynuik .... .25 .11 .03
Winnipeg Jets
☐ 271 Kevin Hatcher................... .30 .14 .04
Washington Capitals
☐ 272 Brian Propp....................... .30 .14 .04
Minnesota North Stars
☐ 273 Tom Fergus .... .25 .11 .03
Vancouver Canucks
☐ 274 Steve Weeks .... .25 .11 .03
New York Islanders
☐ 275 Calle Johansson................. .25 .11 .03
Washington Capitals
☐ 276 Russ Romaniuk................... .25 .11 .03
Winnipeg Jets
☐ 277 Greg Paslawski .... .25 .11 .03
Quebec Nordiques
☐ 278 Ed Olczyk .... .25 .11 .03
Winnipeg Jets
☐ 279 Rod Langway .... .25 .11 .03
Washington Capitals
☐ 280 Murray Craven .... .25 .11 .03
Hartford Whalers
☐ 281 Guy Larose....................... .25 .11 .03
Toronto Maple Leafs
☐ 282 Paul MacDermid .... .25 .11 .03
Washington Capitals
☐ 283 Brian Bradley..................... .30 .14 .04
Tampa Bay Lightning
☐ 284 Paul Stanton .... .25 .11 .03
Pittsburgh Penguins
☐ 285 Kirk McLean...................... .75 .35 .09
Vancouver Canucks
☐ 286 Andrei Lomakin.................. .25 .11 .03
Philadelphia Flyers
☐ 287 Randy Carlyle.................... .25 .11 .03
Winnipeg Jets
☐ 288 Donald Audette .... .25 .11 .03
Buffalo Sabres
☐ 289 Dan Quinn .... .25 .11 .03
Philadelphia Flyers
☐ 290 Mike Keane .... .25 .11 .03
Montreal Canadiens
☐ 291 Dave Ellett....................... .25 .11 .03
Toronto Maple Leafs
☐ 292 Joe Juneau UER................. 3.50 1.55 .45
(Card back says shoots
right, should be left)
Boston Bruins
☐ 293 Phil Bourque .... .25 .11 .03
Pittsburgh Penguins
☐ 294 Michal Pivonka.................... .30 .14 .04
Washington Capitals
☐ 295 Fredrik Olausson.................. .30 .14 .04
Winnipeg Jets
☐ 296 Randy McKay .... .25 .11 .03
New Jersey Devils
☐ 297 Don Beaupre .... .30 .14 .04
Washington Capitals
☐ 298 Steve Leach........................ .25 .11 .03
Boston Bruins
☐ 299 Teppo Numminen .... .25 .11 .03
Winnipeg Jets
☐ 300 Viacheslav Kozlov .... 3.50 1.55 .45
Detroit Red Wings
☐ 301 Kevin Haller .... .25 .11 .03

Montreal Canadiens
☐ 302 Jaromir Jagr .... 3.50 1.55 .45
Pittsburgh Penguins
☐ 303 Dale Hunter........................ .30 .14 .04
Washington Capitals
☐ 304 Bob Errey .... .25 .11 .03
Pittsburgh Penguins
☐ 305 Nicklas Lidstrom.................. .40 .18 .05
Detroit Red Wings
☐ 306 Bob Essensa .... .30 .14 .04
Winnipeg Jets
☐ 307 Sylvain Lefebvre................. .25 .11 .03
Montreal Canadiens
☐ 308 Dale Hawerchuk .... .30 .14 .04
Buffalo Sabres
☐ 309 Dave Snuggerud .... .25 .11 .03
San Jose Sharks
☐ 310 Michel Goulet..................... .30 .14 .04
Chicago Blackhawks
☐ 311 Eric Desjardins................... .25 .11 .03
Montreal Canadiens
☐ 312 Thomas Steen .... .30 .14 .04
Winnipeg Jets
☐ 313 Scott Niedermayer .... 1.00 .45 .13
New Jersey Devils
☐ 314 Mark Recchi...................... 1.50 .65 .19
Philadelphia Flyers
☐ 315 Gord Murphy...................... .25 .11 .03
Boston Bruins
☐ 316 Sergio Momesso .... .25 .11 .03
Vancouver Canucks
☐ 317 Todd Elik.......................... .25 .11 .03
Minnesota North Stars
☐ 318 Louie DeBrusk..................... .25 .11 .03
Edmonton Oilers
☐ 319 Mike Lalor......................... .25 .11 .03
Winnipeg Jets
☐ 320 Jamie Leach....................... .25 .11 .03
Pittsburgh Penguins
☐ 321 Darryl Sydor....................... .30 .14 .04
Los Angeles Kings
☐ 322 Brent Gilchrist.................... .25 .11 .03
Montreal Canadiens
☐ 323 Alexei Kasatonov................. .25 .11 .03
New Jersey Devils
☐ 324 Rick Tabaracci..................... .25 .11 .03
Winnipeg Jets
☐ 325 Wendel Clark..................... .60 .25 .08
Toronto Maple Leafs
☐ 326 Vladimir Konstantinov.......... .25 .11 .03
Detroit Red Wings
☐ 327 Randy Gilhen...................... .25 .11 .03
New York Rangers
☐ 328 Owen Nolan....................... .40 .18 .05
Quebec Nordiques
☐ 329 Vincent Damphousse .... .50 .23 .06
Edmonton Oilers
☐ 330 Checklist 221-331 .... .25 .11 .03
☐ 331 Yves Racine .... .25 .11 .03
Detroit Red Wings
☐ 332 Jacques Cloutier .... .25 .11 .03
Quebec Nordiques
☐ 333 Greg Adams....................... .30 .14 .04
Vancouver Canucks
☐ 334 Mike Craig .... .25 .11 .03
Minnesota North Stars
☐ 335 Curtis Leschyshyn............... .25 .11 .03
Quebec Nordiques
☐ 336 John McIntyre..................... .25 .11 .03
Los Angeles Kings
☐ 337 Stephane Quintal.................. .25 .11 .03
St. Louis Blues
☐ 338 Kelly Miller .... .25 .11 .03
Washington Capitals
☐ 339 Dave Manson .... .25 .11 .03
Edmonton Oilers
☐ 340 Stephane Matteau .... .25 .11 .03
Chicago Blackhawks
☐ 341 Christian Ruuttu.................. .25 .11 .03
Buffalo Sabres
☐ 342 Mike Donnelly .... .25 .11 .03
Los Angeles Kings
☐ 343 Eric Weinrich...................... .25 .11 .03
New Jersey Devils
☐ 344 Mats Sundin....................... 1.00 .45 .13
Quebec Nordiques
☐ 345 Geoff Courtnall................... .30 .14 .04
Vancouver Canucks
☐ 346 Stephan Lebeau .... .25 .11 .03
Montreal Canadiens
☐ 347 Jeff Beukeboom.................. .25 .11 .03
New York Rangers
☐ 348 Jeff Hackett....................... .25 .11 .03
San Jose Sharks

☐ 349 Uwe Krupp	.25	.11	.03
New York Islanders			
☐ 350 Igor Larionov	.30	.14	.04
Vancouver Canucks			
☐ 351 Ulf Samuelsson	.30	.14	.04
Pittsburgh Penguins			
☐ 352 Marty McInnis	.25	.11	.03
New York Islanders			
☐ 353 Peter Ahola	.25	.11	.03
Los Angeles Kings			
☐ 354 Mike Richter	1.75	.80	.22
New York Rangers			
☐ 355 Theoren Fleury	.50	.23	.06
Calgary Flames			
☐ 356 Dan Lambert	.25	.11	.03
Quebec Nordiques			
☐ 357 Brent Ashton	.25	.11	.03
Boston Bruins			
☐ 358 David Bruce	.25	.11	.03
San Jose Sharks			
☐ 359 Chris Dahlquist	.25	.11	.03
Minnesota North Stars			
☐ 360 Mike Ridley	.30	.14	.04
Washington Capitals			
☐ 361 Pat Falloon	.50	.23	.06
San Jose Sharks			
☐ 362 Doug Smail	.25	.11	.03
Quebec Nordiques			
☐ 363 Adrien Plavsic	.25	.11	.03
Vancouver Canucks			
☐ 364 Ron Wilson	.25	.11	.03
St. Louis Blues			
☐ 365 Derian Hatcher	.25	.11	.03
Minnesota North Stars			
☐ 366 Kevin Stevens	1.25	.55	.16
Pittsburgh Penguins			
☐ 367 Rob Blake	.60	.25	.08
Los Angeles Kings			
☐ 368 Curtis Joseph	1.25	.55	.16
St. Louis Blues			
☐ 369 Tom Fitzgerald	.25	.11	.03
New York Islanders			
☐ 370 Dave Lowry	.25	.11	.03
St. Louis Blues			
☐ 371 J.J. Daigneault	.25	.11	.03
Montreal Canadiens			
☐ 372 Jim Hrivnak	.25	.11	.03
Washington Capitals			
☐ 373 Adam Graves	1.75	.80	.22
New York Rangers			
☐ 374 Brad May	.25	.11	.03
Buffalo Sabres			
☐ 375 Todd Gill	.25	.11	.03
Toronto Maple Leafs			
☐ 376 Paul Ysebaert	.25	.11	.03
Detroit Red Wings			
☐ 377 David Williams	.35	.16	.04
San Jose Sharks			
☐ 378 Bob Bassen	.25	.11	.03
St. Louis Blues			
☐ 379 Brian Glynn	.25	.11	.03
Edmonton Oilers			
☐ 380 Kris King	.25	.11	.03
New York Rangers			
☐ 381 Rob Pearson	.25	.11	.03
Toronto Maple Leafs			
☐ 382 Marc Bureau	.25	.11	.03
Minnesota North Stars			
☐ 383 Jim Paek	.25	.11	.03
Pittsburgh Penguins			
☐ 384 Tomas Forslund	.25	.11	.03
Calgary Flames			
☐ 385 Darrin Shannon	.25	.11	.03
Toronto Maple Leafs			
☐ 386 Chris Terreri	.30	.14	.04
New Jersey Devils			
☐ 387 Andrew Cassels	.30	.14	.04
Hartford Whalers			
☐ 388 Jayson More	.25	.11	.03
San Jose Sharks			
☐ 389 Tony Amonte	.40	.18	.05
New York Rangers			
☐ 390 Mark Pederson	.25	.11	.03
Philadelphia Flyers			
☐ 391 Kevin Miller	.30	.14	.04
Detroit Red Wings			
☐ 392 Igor Ulanov	.25	.11	.03
Winnipeg Jets			
☐ 393 Kelly Buchberger	.25	.11	.03
Edmonton Oilers			
☐ 394 Mark Fitzpatrick	.30	.14	.04
New York Islanders			
☐ 395 Mikhail Tatarinov	.25	.11	.03

Quebec Nordiques			
☐ 396 Petr Nedved	.75	.35	.09
Vancouver Canucks			
☐ 397 Jeff Odgers	.25	.11	.03
San Jose Sharks			
☐ 398 Stephane Fiset	.40	.18	.05
Quebec Nordiques			
☐ 399 Mark Tinordi	.30	.14	.04
Minnesota North Stars			
☐ 400 Johan Garpenlov	.25	.11	.03
San Jose Sharks			
☐ 401 Robert Reichel	.50	.23	.06
Calgary Flames			
☐ 402 Don Sweeney UER	.25	.11	.03
(Back photo actually			
Bob Sweeney)			
Boston Bruins			
☐ 403 Rob DiMaio	.25	.11	.03
New York Islanders			
☐ 404 Bill Lindsay	.35	.16	.04
Quebec Nordiques			
☐ 405 Steph Beauregard	.25	.11	.03
Winnipeg Jets			
☐ 406 Mike Ricci	.50	.23	.06
Quebec Nordiques			
☐ 407 Bobby Holik	.25	.11	.03
Hartford Whalers			
☐ 408 Igor Kravchuk	.25	.11	.03
Chicago Blackhawks			
☐ 409 Murray Baron	.25	.11	.03
St. Louis Blues			
☐ 410 Troy Gamble	.25	.11	.03
Vancouver Canucks			
☐ 411 Cliff Ronning	.30	.14	.04
Vancouver Canucks			
☐ 412 Jeff Reese	.25	.11	.03
Calgary Flames			
☐ 413 Robert Kron	.25	.11	.03
Vancouver Canucks			
☐ 414 Benoit Brunet	.25	.11	.03
Montreal Canadiens			
☐ 415 Shawn McEachern	.40	.18	.05
Pittsburgh Penguins			
☐ 416 Sergei Fedorov	6.00	2.70	.75
Detroit Red Wings			
☐ 417 Joe Sacco	.25	.11	.03
Toronto Maple Leafs			
☐ 418 Bryan Marchment	.25	.11	.03
Chicago Blackhawks			
☐ 419 John LeBlanc	.25	.11	.03
Winnipeg Jets			
☐ 420 Tim Cheveldae	.30	.14	.04
Detroit Red Wings			
☐ 421 Claude LaPointe	.25	.11	.03
Quebec Nordiques			
☐ 422 Ken Sutton	.25	.11	.03
Buffalo Sabres			
☐ 423 Anatoli Semenov	.25	.11	.03
Toronto Maple Leafs			
☐ 424 Mike McNeil	.25	.11	.03
Quebec Nordiques			
☐ 425 Norm Maciver	.25	.11	.03
Edmonton Oilers			
☐ 426 Sergei Nemchinov	.30	.14	.04
New York Rangers			
☐ 427 Dimitri Khristich	.30	.14	.04
Washington Capitals			
☐ 428 Dominik Hasek	5.00	2.30	.60
Chicago Blackhawks			
☐ 429 Bob McGill	.25	.11	.03
Detroit Red Wings			
☐ 430 Valeri Zelepukin	.50	.23	.06
New Jersey Devils			
☐ 431 Vladimir Ruzicka	.25	.11	.03
Boston Bruins			
☐ 432 Valeri Kamensky	.40	.18	.05
Quebec Nordiques			
☐ 433 Pat MacLeod	.25	.11	.03
San Jose Sharks			
☐ 434 Glenn Healy	.30	.14	.04
New York Islanders			
☐ 435 Patrice Brisebois	.25	.11	.03
Montreal Canadiens			
☐ 436 James Baker	.25	.11	.03
Quebec Nordiques			
☐ 437 Michel Picard	.25	.11	.03
Hartford Whalers			
☐ 438 Scott Lachance UER	.25	.11	.03
(Back photo actually			
Brad Turner)			
New York Islanders			
☐ 439 Gilbert Dionne	.25	.11	.03
Montreal Canadiens			
☐ 440 Mario Lemieux FOIL	14.00	6.25	1.75

Conn Smythe Winner

		NRMT	VG-E	GOOD
☐ 441	Checklist 332-441	.25	.11	.03
☐ 442	Eric Lindros UER	25.00	11.50	3.10

(Acquired 6-30-92,
not 6-20-92 as in bio)
Philadelphia Flyers

1970-71 Bruins Team Issue

This set of 18 team-issue photos commemorates the Boston Bruins as 1970 Stanley Cup Champions. The set was issued in two different photo packs of nine photos each. The photos measure approximately 6" by 8" and feature a non-glossy posed head-and-shoulders shot of the player. The backs are blank. These unnumbered photos are listed below alphabetically by player's name within pack, i.e., 1-9 are from the first pack and 10-18 are found in the second pack.

		NRMT	VG-E	GOOD
COMPLETE SET (18)		40.00	16.00	4.00
COMMON PLAYER (1-9)		1.25	.50	.12
COMMON PLAYER (10-18)		1.25	.50	.12
☐ 1	Garnet Bailey	1.25	.50	.12
☐ 2	Johnny Bucyk	5.00	2.00	.50
☐ 3	Gary Doak	1.25	.50	.12
☐ 4	Phil Esposito	8.00	3.25	.80
☐ 5	Ed Johnston	2.00	.80	.20
☐ 6	Don Marcotte	1.25	.50	.12
☐ 7	Derek Sanderson	4.00	1.60	.40
☐ 8	Dallas Smith	2.00	.80	.20
☐ 9	Ed Westfall	2.00	.80	.20
☐ 10	Don Awrey	1.25	.50	.12
☐ 11	Wayne Carleton	1.25	.50	.12
☐ 12	Wayne Cashman	2.50	1.00	.25
☐ 13	Gerry Cheevers	5.00	2.00	.50
☐ 14	Ken Hodge	3.00	1.20	.30
☐ 15	John McKenzie	2.00	.80	.20
☐ 16	Bobby Orr	18.00	7.25	1.80
☐ 17	Rick Smith	1.25	.50	.12
☐ 18	Fred Stanfield	1.25	.50	.12

1971-72 Bruins Team Issue

Originally issued in booklet form, these 20 photo cards measure 3 1/2" by 5 1/2" and feature on their fronts borderless posed color shots of the 1971-72 Boston Bruins. The player's facsimile autograph appears near the bottom. The white back carries the player's name and uniform number at the top, followed by position, biography, and personal profile, all in blue lettering. The cards have perforated tops that allow them to be detached from the yellow booklet, which bears the Bruins logo and crossed hockey sticks on its front. The unnumbered cards are listed below as they are organized within the booklet.

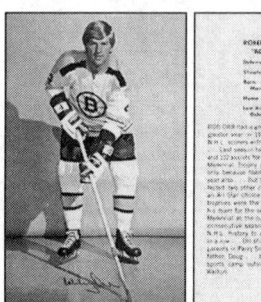

		NRMT	VG-E	GOOD
COMPLETE SET (20)		40.00	16.00	4.00
COMMON PLAYER (1-20)		1.00	.40	.10
☐ 1	Ed Johnston	2.00	.80	.20
☐ 2	Bobby Orr	18.00	7.25	1.80
☐ 3	Teddy Green	1.50	.60	.15
☐ 4	Phil Esposito	8.00	3.25	.80
☐ 5	Ken Hodge	3.00	1.20	.30
☐ 6	John Bucyk	5.00	2.00	.50
☐ 7	Rick Smith	1.00	.40	.10
☐ 8	Mike Walton	1.50	.60	.15
☐ 9	Wayne Cashman	2.50	1.00	.25
☐ 10	Ace Bailey	1.50	.60	.15
☐ 11	Derek Sanderson	4.00	1.60	.40
☐ 12	Fred Stanfield	1.00	.40	.10
☐ 13	Ed Westfall	2.00	.80	.20
☐ 14	John McKenzie	2.00	.80	.20
☐ 15	Dallas Smith	2.00	.80	.20
☐ 16	Donald Marcotte	1.00	.40	.10
☐ 17	Gary Peters	1.00	.40	.10
☐ 18	Don Awrey	1.00	.40	.10
☐ 19	Reggie Leach	3.00	1.20	.30
☐ 20	Gerry Cheevers	5.00	2.00	.50

1983-84 Bruins Team Issue

Ray Bourque

This 17-card set measures approximately 3 1/8" by 4 1/8" and features black and white action player photos with white borders. The pictures have irregular centering so that the bottom border is thicker than the top border. The player's name appears in the bottom border. The backs are blank. The cards are unnumbered and checklisted below alphabetically.

		MINT	EXC	G-VG
COMPLETE SET (17)		20.00	8.00	2.00
COMMON PLAYER (1-17)		1.00	.40	.10
☐ 1	Ray Bourque	7.00	2.80	.70
☐ 2	Bruce Crowder	1.00	.40	.10
☐ 3	Keith Crowder	1.00	.40	.10
☐ 4	Luc Dufour	1.00	.40	.10
☐ 5	Tom Fergus	1.00	.40	.10
☐ 6	Randy Hillier	1.00	.40	.10

		MINT	EXC	G-VG
☐ 7	Steve Kasper	1.50	.60	.15
☐ 8	Gord Kluzak	1.50	.60	.15
☐ 9	Mike Krushelnyski	2.00	.80	.20
☐ 10	Peter McNab	1.50	.60	.15
☐ 11	Rick Middleton	2.50	1.00	.25
☐ 12	Mike Milbury	1.50	.60	.15
☐ 13	Mike O'Connell	1.00	.40	.10
☐ 14	Terry O'Reilly	2.00	.80	.20
☐ 15	Brad Palmer	1.00	.40	.10
☐ 16	Barry Pederson	1.50	.60	.15
☐ 17	Pete Peeters	2.00	.80	.20

1988-89 Bruins Sports Action

RICK MIDDLETON
Left/Right Wing

Height: 5'10"   Weight: 185 lbs.

NY Rangers' first choice, 14th overall in 1973 Amateur Draft. Traded to Boston by NY Rangers for Ken Hodge, May 26, 1976. Scored a hat trick in his first game for Boston vs. Minnesota on October 7, 1976. Named a Second Team All-Star and won the Lady Byng Trophy in 1981-82. Became the first Bruin since Phil Esposito to hit the 50-goal mark with 51 in 1981-82. Named as Bruins co-captain on September 17, 1985. 1,000th NHL game was March 13, 1988 vs. Washington.

Rick Middleton #16

This 24-card set measures the standard 2 1/2" by 3 1/2". This set was issued by Sports Action and features members of the 1988-89 Boston Bruins. The fronts of these cards have the action photo of the player framed by the colors of the Bruins while the backs of the cards contain biographical information. The cards are unnumbered so we have checklisted them below in alphabetical order. The set features an early card of Craig Janney pre-dating his Rookie Cards by one year.

		MINT	EXC	G-VG
	COMPLETE SET (24)	15.00	6.00	1.50
	COMMON PLAYER (1-24)	.50	.20	.05
☐ 1	Ray Bourque	3.00	1.20	.30
☐ 2	Randy Burridge	.90	.36	.09
☐ 3	Lyndon Byers	.50	.20	.05
☐ 4	Keith Crowder	.50	.20	.05
☐ 5	Craig Janney	2.00	.80	.20
☐ 6	Bob Joyce	.75	.30	.07
☐ 7	Steve Kasper	.75	.30	.07
☐ 8	Gord Kluzak	.50	.20	.05
☐ 9	Reed Larson	.50	.20	.05
☐ 10	Rejean Lemelin	.90	.36	.09
☐ 11	Ken Linseman	.50	.20	.05
☐ 12	Tom McCarthy	.50	.20	.05
☐ 13	Rick Middleton	1.00	.40	.10
☐ 14	Jay Miller	.50	.20	.05
☐ 15	Andy Moog	1.50	.60	.15
☐ 16	Cam Neely	2.50	1.00	.25
☐ 17	Terry O'Reilly CO	.75	.30	.07
☐ 18	Allen Pedersen	.50	.20	.05
☐ 19	Willi Plett	.50	.20	.05
☐ 20	Bob Sweeney	.75	.30	.07
☐ 21	Michael Thelven	.50	.20	.05
☐ 22	Glen Wesley	1.00	.40	.10
☐ 23	Joyce and Janney	1.25	.50	.12
☐ 24	Dynamic Duo Ray Bourque Cam Neely	2.00	.80	.20

1989-90 Bruins Sports Action

This standard sized (2 1/2" by 3 1/2") 24-card set was issued by Sports Action and features members of the 1989-90 Boston Bruins. The fronts of the cards feature full-color

RANDY BURRIDGE
Left Wing

Height: 5'9"
Weight: 180 lbs.

Boston's eighth round choice in the 1985 Entry Draft. Had his finest NHL season in 1988-89 with career highs in goals (31), assists (30), and points (61). Scored six game winning goals and two hat tricks last year. Has twice been voted winner of the TV-38 Seventh Player Award by the fans.

borderless action shots of the Bruins while the backs of the cards have biographical information about the player. Since there is no numerical designation for these players, we have checklisted this set in alphabetical order.

		MINT	EXC	G-VG
	COMPLETE SET (24)	12.00	5.00	1.20
	COMMON PLAYER (1-24)	.50	.20	.05
☐ 1	Ray Bourque	2.50	1.00	.25
☐ 2	Andy Brickley	.60	.24	.06
☐ 3	Randy Burridge	.75	.30	.07
☐ 4	Lyndon Byers	.50	.20	.05
☐ 5	Bob Carpenter	.60	.24	.06
☐ 6	John Carter	.50	.20	.05
☐ 7	Rob Cimetta	.50	.20	.05
☐ 8	Garry Galley	.75	.30	.07
☐ 9	Bob Gould	.50	.20	.05
☐ 10	Greg Hawgood	.50	.20	.05
☐ 11	Craig Janney	1.25	.50	.12
☐ 12	Bob Joyce	.60	.24	.06
☐ 13	Rejean Lemelin	.60	.24	.06
☐ 14	Ken Linseman	.50	.20	.05
☐ 15	Andy Moog	1.25	.50	.12
☐ 16	Nevin Markwart	.50	.20	.05
☐ 17	Cam Neely	2.00	.80	.20
☐ 18	Allen Pedersen	.50	.20	.05
☐ 19	Stephane Quintal	.75	.30	.07
☐ 20	Bob Sweeney	.60	.24	.06
☐ 21	Michael Thelven	.50	.20	.05
☐ 22	Glen Wesley	.75	.30	.07
☐ 23	Bruins Top 10 Scorers	.75	.30	.07
☐ 24	Stanley Cup Champions	.75	.30	.07

1989-90 Bruins Sports Action Update

RAY BOURQUE
Defense

Height: 5'11"   Weight: 210 lbs.

1989-90 has been Ray's best all-around season ever. His play on defense has made him a leading candidate for the Norris Trophy. His overall play and leadership puts him among the top contenders for the Hart Trophy (MVP). Earlier this season he surpassed the 800 point mark, putting him close to Bobby Orr's career total of 915. A Stanley Cup Championship for Ray and the Bruins would be the perfect ending to an already memorable season.

This 12-card set which measures the standard size, 2 1/2" by 3 1/2", was issued by Sports Action to reflect the changes made by the Boston Bruins during the 1989-90 hockey season. The borderless fronts feature full-color action shots while the backs feature biographical information. Since the cards are unnumbered, they are checklisted in alphabetical order.

	MINT	EXC	G-VG
COMPLETE SET (12).......................	8.00	3.25	.80
COMMON PLAYER (1-12)................	.50	.20	.05
☐ 1 Ray Bourque	2.50	1.00	.25
☐ 2 Dave Christian........................	.75	.30	.07
☐ 3 Peter Douris	.50	.20	.05
☐ 4 Gord Kluzak...........................	.50	.20	.05
☐ 5 Brian Lawton..........................	.50	.20	.05
☐ 6 Mike Millar	.50	.20	.05
☐ 7 Dave Poulin...........................	.75	.30	.07
☐ 8 Brian Propp............................	.90	.36	.09
☐ 9 Don Sweeney	.50	.20	.05
☐ 10 Graeme Townshend	.50	.20	.05
☐ 11 Jim Wiemer...........................	.50	.20	.05
☐ 12 Bruins Leaders.....................	1.50	.60	.15
Ray Bourque			
Rejean Lemelin			
Cam Neely			

☐ 25 Glen Wesley	.75	.30	.07
☐ 26 Rejean Lemelin and................	.90	.36	.09
Andy Moog, William M.			
Jennings Trophy			

1991-92 Bruins Sports Action

This 24-card set was issued by Sports Action and features members of the 1991-92 Boston Bruins. The standard-size (2 1/2" by 3 1/2") cards are printed on thin card stock. The fronts feature full-bleed glossy color action photos. In a horizontal format, the backs carry brief biography, career summary, and the team logo. The cards are unnumbered and checklisted in alphabetical order.

	MINT	EXC	G-VG
COMPLETE SET (24).......................	12.00	5.00	1.20
COMMON PLAYER (1-24)................	.40	.16	.04
☐ 1 Brent Ashton	.40	.16	.04
☐ 2 Bob Beers	.50	.20	.05
☐ 3 Daniel Berthiaume...................	.50	.20	.05
☐ 4 Ray Bourque	2.00	.80	.20
☐ 5 Bob Carpenter.......................	.50	.20	.05
☐ 6 Peter Douris	.40	.16	.04
☐ 7 Glen Featherstone	.60	.24	.06
☐ 8 Ken Hodge Jr.	.50	.20	.05
☐ 9 Jeff Lazaro	.40	.16	.04
☐ 10 Stephen Leach	.50	.20	.05
☐ 11 Andy Moog...........................	1.25	.50	.12
☐ 12 Gord Murphy.........................	.40	.16	.04
☐ 13 Cam Neely............................	1.50	.60	.15
☐ 14 Adam Oates..........................	1.50	.60	.15
☐ 15 Dave Poulin..........................	.50	.20	.05
☐ 16 David Reid............................	.40	.16	.04
☐ 17 Vladimir Ruzicka	.60	.24	.06
☐ 18 Bob Sweeney	.40	.16	.04
☐ 19 Don Sweeney	.40	.16	.04
☐ 20 Jim Vesey.............................	.40	.16	.04
☐ 21 Glen Wesley	.60	.24	.06
☐ 22 Jim Wiemer..........................	.40	.16	.04
☐ 23 Chris Winnes........................	.40	.16	.04
☐ 24 The Big Three.......................	1.50	.60	.15
Andy Moog			
Ray Bourque			
Cam Neely			

1990-91 Bruins Sports Action

This 26-card standard size, 2 1/2" by 3 1/2", set features members of the 1990-91 Boston Bruins. This set features full-color borderless action shots of the Bruins. The back is in a horizontal format with biographical information about the player on the left side of the card and a black-and-white photo on the right. The Markwart and Quintal cards were reportedly only issued in the first print run of 400 24-card sets. In the second and larger print run, these cards were replaced by Byers and Hodge. Consequently, the Markwart and Quintal cards are more difficult to find than the Byers and Hodge cards. We have checklisted this set in alphabetical order below, with the multi-player card listed at the end.

	MINT	EXC	G-VG
COMPLETE SET (26).......................	18.00	7.25	1.80
COMMON PLAYER (1-26)................	.50	.20	.05
☐ 1 Bob Beers	.60	.24	.06
☐ 2 Ray Bourque	2.50	1.00	.25
☐ 3 Andy Brickley	.60	.24	.06
☐ 4 Randy Burridge	.75	.30	.07
☐ 5 John Byce..............................	.50	.20	.05
☐ 6 Lyndon Byers..........................	.75	.30	.07
☐ 7 Bob Carpenter........................	.60	.24	.06
☐ 8 John Carter............................	.50	.20	.05
☐ 9 Dave Christian........................	.60	.24	.06
☐ 10 Peter Douris	.50	.20	.05
☐ 11 Garry Galley	.75	.30	.07
☐ 12 Ken Hodge Jr.	.90	.36	.09
☐ 13 Craig Janney	1.25	.50	.12
☐ 14 Rejean Lemelin	.60	.24	.06
☐ 15 Nevin Markwart SP	3.00	1.20	.30
☐ 16 Andy Moog...........................	1.25	.50	.12
☐ 17 Cam Neely............................	2.00	.80	.20
☐ 18 Chris Nilan	.60	.24	.06
☐ 19 Allen Pedersen	.50	.20	.05
☐ 20 Dave Poulin..........................	.60	.24	.06
☐ 21 Stephane Quintal SP	3.00	1.20	.30
☐ 22 Bob Sweeney	.50	.20	.05
☐ 23 Don Sweeney	.50	.20	.05
☐ 24 Wes Walz.............................	.60	.24	.06

1991-92 Bruins
Sports Action Legends

The 1991-92 Bruins Legends hockey set features the outstanding players throughout the history of the Boston Bruins' franchise. The fronts of the standard-size (2 1/2" by 3 1/2") cards feature full-bleed black and white player photos. The backs present the player's name, position, biography, honors received, and career statistics. The cards of players with retired numbers have their number inside the

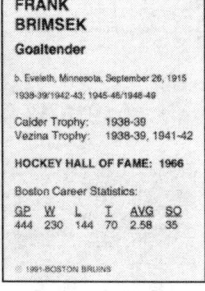

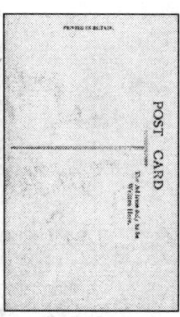

team logo in the upper right corner of the back. Though most of the cards feature one player, the set includes several multi-player cards with brief commentary on their backs. The cards are unnumbered and checklisted in alphabetical order.

	MINT	EXC	G-VG
COMPLETE SET (36)......................	12.00	5.00	1.20
COMMON PLAYER (1-36)...............	.25	.10	.02
☐ 1 Bob Armstrong	.25	.10	.02
☐ 2 Leo Boivin.............................	.50	.20	.05
☐ 3 Ray Bourque	1.50	.60	.15
☐ 4 Frank Brimsek	.75	.30	.07
☐ 5 Johnny Bucyk	1.00	.40	.10
☐ 6 Wayne Cashman	.35	.14	.03
☐ 7 Gerry Cheevers	1.00	.40	.10
☐ 8 Dit Clapper	.75	.30	.07
☐ 9 Bill Cowley	.25	.10	.02
☐ 10 Phil Esposito	1.25	.50	.12
☐ 11 Fernie Flaman	.50	.20	.05
☐ 12 Mel Hill.................................	.25	.10	.02
Bill Cowley			
Roy Conacher			
☐ 13 Lionel Hitchman	.25	.10	.02
☐ 14 Fleming Mackell	.25	.10	.02
☐ 15 Don Marcotte	.25	.10	.02
☐ 16 Don McKenney	.25	.10	.02
☐ 17 Rick Middleton	.50	.20	.05
☐ 18 Doug Mohns	.35	.14	.03
☐ 19 Terry O'Reilly	.35	.14	.03
☐ 20 Bobby Orr	3.00	1.20	.30
☐ 21 Brad Park..............................	1.00	.40	.10
☐ 22 John Pierson	.25	.10	.02
☐ 23 Bill Quackenbush	.50	.20	.05
☐ 24 Jean Ratelle...........................	1.00	.40	.10
☐ 25 Art Ross CO/GM.....................	.50	.20	.05
☐ 26 Ed Sandford	.25	.10	.02
☐ 27 Terry Sawchuk	1.50	.60	.15
☐ 28 Milt Schmidt	1.00	.40	.10
☐ 29 Milt Schmidt	.50	.20	.05
Cooney Weiland			
Bill Cowley			
☐ 30 Eddie Shore...........................	1.00	.40	.10
☐ 31 Harry Sinden CO/GM.............	.50	.20	.05
and President			
☐ 32 Tiny Thompson	.35	.14	.03
☐ 33 Cooney Weiland	.35	.14	.03
☐ 34 Ed Westfall............................	.35	.14	.03
☐ 35 Bruins Defense.......................	.35	.14	.03
1955-56			
Bill Quackenbush			
Fern Flaman			
Terry Sawchuk			
Bob Armstrong			
Leo Boivin			
☐ 36 The Kraut Line......................	.75	.30	.07
Milt Schmidt			
Woody Dumart			
Bobby Bauer			

1910-11 C55 Sweet Caporal Postcards

These black-and-white photo postcards apparently were used by the artists working on the C55 cards of the next

year, 1911-12. Printed by the British American Tobacco Co. in England, these cards were distributed by Imperial Tobacco of Canada. One card was reportedly packed in each 50-cigarette tin of Sweet Caporal cigarettes. The backs show the postcard design. The cards are checklisted below according to teams as follows: Quebec Bulldogs (1-8), Ottawa Senators (10-17), Renfrew Millionaires (18-26), Montreal Wanderers (27-36), and Montreal Canadiens (37-45).

	EX-MT	VG-E	GOOD
COMPLETE SET (45)......................	15000.	6000.	1500.
COMMON PLAYER (1-45)...............	150.00	60.00	15.00
☐ 1 Paddy Moran..........................	450.00	180.00	45.00
☐ 2 Joe Hall	300.00	120.00	30.00
☐ 3 Barney Holden.......................	150.00	60.00	15.00
☐ 4 Ed Oatman	750.00	300.00	75.00
☐ 5 Ed Oatman	150.00	60.00	15.00
☐ 6 Tom Dunderdale	300.00	120.00	30.00
☐ 7 Ken Mallen	150.00	60.00	15.00
☐ 8 Jack MacDonald.....................	150.00	60.00	15.00
☐ 9 Fred Lake	150.00	60.00	15.00
☐ 10 Albert Kerr............................	150.00	60.00	15.00
☐ 11 Marty Walsh..........................	300.00	120.00	30.00
☐ 12 Hamby Shore	150.00	60.00	15.00
☐ 13 Alex Currie	150.00	60.00	15.00
☐ 14 Bruce Ridpath........................	150.00	60.00	15.00
☐ 15 Bruce Stuart..........................	300.00	120.00	30.00
☐ 16 Percy Lesueur	300.00	120.00	30.00
☐ 17 Jack Darragh.........................	300.00	120.00	30.00
☐ 18 Steve Vair	150.00	60.00	15.00
☐ 19 Don Smith.............................	150.00	60.00	15.00
☐ 20 Fred Taylor...........................	900.00	360.00	90.00
☐ 21 Bert Lindsay..........................	200.00	80.00	20.00
☐ 22 H.L.(Larry) Gilmour..............	300.00	120.00	30.00
☐ 23 Bobby Rowe	150.00	60.00	15.00
☐ 24 Sprague Cleghorn	450.00	180.00	45.00
☐ 25 Odie Cleghorn	200.00	80.00	20.00
☐ 26 Skein Ronan..........................	150.00	60.00	15.00
☐ 27 Walter Smaill.........................	200.00	80.00	20.00
☐ 28 Ernest(Moose) Johnson........	350.00	140.00	35.00
☐ 29 Jack Marshall........................	300.00	120.00	30.00
☐ 30 Harry Hyland	300.00	120.00	30.00
☐ 31 Art Ross...............................	1000.00	400.00	100.00
☐ 32 Riley Hern	300.00	120.00	30.00
☐ 33 Gordon Roberts	300.00	120.00	30.00
☐ 34 Frank Glass	150.00	60.00	15.00
☐ 35 Ernest Russell	350.00	140.00	35.00
☐ 36 James Gardner.......................	300.00	120.00	30.00
☐ 37 Art Bernier............................	150.00	60.00	15.00
☐ 38 Georges Vezina	3000.00	1200.00	300.00
☐ 39 G.(Henri) Dallaire.................	150.00	60.00	15.00
☐ 40 R.(Rocket) Power...................	150.00	60.00	15.00
☐ 41 Didier(Pit) Pitre....................	300.00	120.00	30.00
☐ 42 Newsy Lalonde.......................	1000.00	400.00	100.00
☐ 43 Eugene Payan	150.00	60.00	15.00
☐ 44 George Poulin........................	150.00	60.00	15.00
☐ 45 Jack Laviolette	350.00	140.00	35.00

1911-12 C55 Hockey

The C55 Hockey set, probably issued during the 1911-12 season, contains 45 numbered cards. Being one of the early

☐ 42	Newsy Lalonde	750.00	300.00	75.00
☐ 43	Eugene Payan	100.00	40.00	10.00
☐ 44	George Poulin	100.00	40.00	10.00
☐ 45	Jack Laviolette	250.00	100.00	25.00

1910-11 C56 Hockey

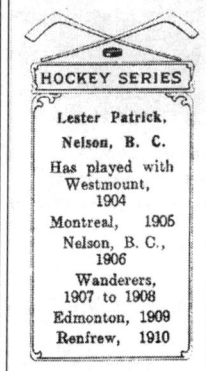

Canadian cigarette cards, the issuer of this set is anonymous, although there is speculation that it may have been Imperial Tobacco. These small cigarette cards measure approximately 1 1/2" by 2 1/2". The line drawing, color portrait on the front of the card is framed by two hockey sticks. The number of the card appears on both the front and back as does the player's name. The players in the set were members of the NHA: Quebec Bulldogs, Ottawa Senators, Montreal Canadiens, Montreal Wanderers, and Renfrew Millionaires. This set is prized highly by collectors but is the easiest of the three early sets (C55, C56, or C57) to find. The complete set price includes either variety of the Smaill variation.

	EX-MT	VG-E	GOOD
COMPLETE SET (45)	10000.	4000.	1000.
COMMON PLAYER (1-45)	100.00	40.00	10.00

☐ 1	Paddy Moran	300.00	120.00	30.00
☐ 2	Joe Hall	200.00	80.00	20.00
☐ 3	Barney Holden	100.00	40.00	10.00
☐ 4	Joe Malone	500.00	200.00	50.00
☐ 5	Ed Oatman	100.00	40.00	10.00
☐ 6	Tom Dunderdale	200.00	80.00	20.00
☐ 7	Ken Mallen	100.00	40.00	10.00
☐ 8	Jack MacDonald	100.00	40.00	10.00
☐ 9	Fred Lake	100.00	40.00	10.00
☐ 10	Albert Kerr	100.00	40.00	10.00
☐ 11	Marty Walsh	200.00	80.00	20.00
☐ 12	Hamby Shore	100.00	40.00	10.00
☐ 13	Alex Currie	100.00	40.00	10.00
☐ 14	Bruce Ridpath	100.00	40.00	10.00
☐ 15	Bruce Stuart	200.00	80.00	20.00
☐ 16	Percy Lesueur	200.00	80.00	20.00
☐ 17	Jack Darragh	200.00	80.00	20.00
☐ 18	Steve Vair	100.00	40.00	10.00
☐ 19	Don Smith	100.00	40.00	10.00
☐ 20	Fred Taylor	600.00	240.00	60.00
☐ 21	Bert Lindsay	150.00	60.00	15.00
☐ 22	H.L.(Larry) Gilmour	200.00	80.00	20.00
☐ 23	Bobby Rowe	100.00	40.00	10.00
☐ 24	Sprague Cleghorn	300.00	120.00	30.00
☐ 25	Odie Cleghorn	150.00	60.00	15.00
☐ 26	Skein Ronan	100.00	40.00	10.00
☐ 27A	Walter Smaill	300.00	120.00	30.00
	(Right hand on top of hockey stick)			
☐ 27B	Walter Smaill	300.00	120.00	30.00
	(Right hand on hip)			
☐ 28	Ernest(Moose) Johnson	250.00	100.00	25.00
☐ 29	Jack Marshall	200.00	80.00	20.00
☐ 30	Harry Hyland	200.00	80.00	20.00
☐ 31	Art Ross	750.00	300.00	75.00
☐ 32	Riley Hern	200.00	80.00	20.00
☐ 33	Gordon Roberts	200.00	80.00	20.00
☐ 34	Frank Kerr	100.00	40.00	10.00
☐ 35	Ernest Russell	250.00	100.00	25.00
☐ 36	James Gardner	200.00	80.00	20.00
☐ 37	Art Bernier	100.00	40.00	10.00
☐ 38	Georges Vezina	2500.00	1000.00	250.00
☐ 39	G.(Henri) Dallaire	100.00	40.00	10.00
☐ 40	R.(Rocket) Power	100.00	40.00	10.00
☐ 41	Didier(Pit) Pitre	200.00	80.00	20.00

One of the first hockey sets to appear (circa 1910-11), this full-color set of unknown origin (although there is speculation that the issuer was Imperial Tobacco) features 36 cards. The card numbering appears in the upper left part of the front of the card. These small cards measure approximately 1 1/2" by 2 5/8". The player's name and affiliation appear at the bottom within the border. The backs feature the player's name and career affiliations below crossed hockey sticks, a puck and the words "Hockey Series."

	EX-MT	VG-E	GOOD
COMPLETE SET (36)	8500.00	3750.00	850.00
COMMON PLAYER (1-36)	125.00	50.00	12.50

☐ 1	Frank Patrick	350.00	140.00	35.00
☐ 2	Percy Lesueur	225.00	90.00	22.00
☐ 3	Gordon Roberts	225.00	90.00	22.00
☐ 4	Barney Holden	125.00	50.00	12.50
☐ 5	Frank(Pud) Glass	125.00	50.00	12.50
☐ 6	Edgar Dey	125.00	50.00	12.50
☐ 7	Marty Walsh	225.00	90.00	22.00
☐ 8	Art Ross	800.00	320.00	80.00
☐ 9	Angus Campbell	225.00	90.00	22.00
☐ 10	Harry Hyland	225.00	90.00	22.00
☐ 11	Herb Clark	125.00	50.00	12.50
☐ 12	Art Ross	800.00	320.00	80.00
☐ 13	Ed Decary	125.00	50.00	12.50
☐ 14	Tom Dunderdale	225.00	90.00	22.00
☐ 15	Fred Taylor	650.00	260.00	65.00
☐ 16	Jos. Cattarinich	125.00	50.00	12.50
☐ 17	Bruce Stuart	225.00	90.00	22.00
☐ 18	Nick Bawlf	125.00	50.00	12.50
☐ 19	J.Jones	125.00	50.00	12.50
☐ 20	Ernest Russell	300.00	120.00	30.00
☐ 21	Jack Laviolette	225.00	90.00	22.00
☐ 22	Riley Hern	225.00	90.00	22.00
☐ 23	Didier(Pit) Pitre	225.00	90.00	22.00
☐ 24	Skinner Poulin	125.00	50.00	12.50
☐ 25	Art Bernier	125.00	50.00	12.50
☐ 26	Lester Patrick	500.00	200.00	50.00
☐ 27	Fred Lake	125.00	50.00	12.50
☐ 28	Paddy Moran	300.00	120.00	30.00
☐ 29	C.Toms	125.00	50.00	12.50
☐ 30	Ernest(Moose) Johnson	300.00	120.00	30.00
☐ 31	Horace Gaul	125.00	50.00	12.50
☐ 32	Harold McNamara	125.00	50.00	12.50
☐ 33	Jack Marshall	225.00	90.00	22.00
☐ 34	Bruce Ridpath	125.00	50.00	12.50
☐ 35	Jack Marshall	225.00	90.00	22.00
☐ 36	Newsy Lalonde	800.00	320.00	80.00

1912-13 C57 Hockey

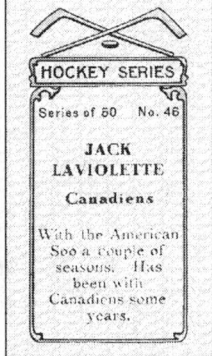

JACK LAVIOLETTE
Canadiens

This set of 50 black and white cards was produced circa 1912-13. These small cards measure approximately 1 1/2" by 2 5/8". The player's name and affiliation are printed on both the front and back. The card number appears on the back only with the words "Series of 50." Although the origin of the set is unknown, it is safe to assume that the same producer who issued the C56 series also issued this series, as the backs of the cards are quite similar. A brief career outline in English and French is contained on the back. This set is considered to be the toughest to find of the three early hockey sets.

		EX-MT	VG-E	GOOD
COMPLETE SET (50)		13500.	6000.	1350.
COMMON PLAYER (1-50)		175.00	70.00	18.00
☐ 1	Georges Vezina	1500.00	600.00	150.00
☐ 2	Punch Broadbent	500.00	200.00	50.00
☐ 3	Clint Benedict	400.00	160.00	40.00
☐ 4	A.Atchinson	175.00	70.00	18.00
☐ 5	Tom Dunderdale	300.00	120.00	30.00
☐ 6	Art Bernier	175.00	70.00	18.00
☐ 7	G.(Henri) Dallaire	175.00	70.00	18.00
☐ 8	George Poulin	175.00	70.00	18.00
☐ 9	Eugene Payan	175.00	70.00	18.00
☐ 10	Steve Vair	175.00	70.00	18.00
☐ 11	Bobby Rowe	175.00	70.00	18.00
☐ 12	Don Smith	175.00	70.00	18.00
☐ 13	Bert Lindsay	225.00	90.00	22.00
☐ 14	Skene Ronan	175.00	70.00	18.00
☐ 15	Sprague Cleghorn	350.00	140.00	35.00
☐ 16	Joe Hall	350.00	140.00	35.00
☐ 17	Jack MacDonald	175.00	70.00	18.00
☐ 18	Paddy Moran	350.00	140.00	35.00
☐ 19	Harry Hyland	300.00	120.00	30.00
☐ 20	Art Ross	900.00	360.00	90.00
☐ 21	Frank(Pud) Glass	175.00	70.00	18.00
☐ 22	Walter Smaill	175.00	70.00	18.00
☐ 23	Gordon Roberts	300.00	120.00	30.00
☐ 24	Jas. Gardner	300.00	120.00	30.00
☐ 25	Ernest(Moose) Johnson	350.00	140.00	35.00
☐ 26	Ernie Russell	350.00	140.00	35.00
☐ 27	Percy Lesueur	300.00	120.00	30.00
☐ 28	Bruce Ridpath	175.00	70.00	18.00
☐ 29	Jack Darragh	300.00	120.00	30.00
☐ 30	Hamby Shore	175.00	70.00	18.00
☐ 31	Fred Lake	175.00	70.00	18.00
☐ 32	Alex Currie	175.00	70.00	18.00
☐ 33	Albert Kerr	175.00	70.00	18.00
☐ 34	Eddie Gerard	300.00	120.00	30.00
☐ 35	C.Kendall	175.00	70.00	18.00
☐ 36	Jack Fournier	175.00	70.00	18.00
☐ 37	Goldie Prodgers	175.00	70.00	18.00
☐ 38	Jack Marks	175.00	70.00	18.00
☐ 39	G.Broughton	175.00	70.00	18.00
☐ 40	A.Boyce	175.00	70.00	18.00
☐ 41	Lester Patrick	600.00	240.00	60.00
☐ 42	Joe Dennison	175.00	70.00	18.00
☐ 43	Fred Taylor	700.00	280.00	70.00
☐ 44	Newsy Lalonde	900.00	360.00	90.00
☐ 45	Didier(Pit) Pitre	300.00	120.00	30.00
☐ 46	Jack Laviolette	300.00	120.00	30.00
☐ 47	Ed Oatman	175.00	70.00	18.00
☐ 48	Joe Malone	500.00	200.00	50.00
☐ 49	Marty Walsh	300.00	120.00	30.00
☐ 50	Odie Cleghorn	225.00	90.00	22.00

1924-25 C144 Champ's Cigarettes

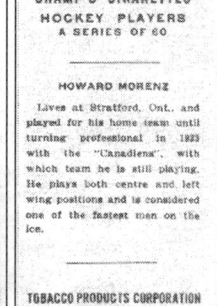

This unnumbered 60-card set was issued during the 1924-25 season by Champ's Cigarettes. There is a brief biography on the card back written in English. The cards are sepia tone and measure approximately 1 1/2" by 2 1/2". Since the cards are unnumbered, they are checklisted in alphabetical order by subject.

		EX-MT	VG-E	GOOD
COMPLETE SET (60)		15000.	6000.	1500.
COMMON PLAYER (1-60)		150.00	60.00	15.00
☐ 1	Jack Adams	300.00	120.00	30.00
☐ 2	Lloyd Andrews	150.00	60.00	15.00
☐ 3	Clint Benedict	300.00	120.00	30.00
☐ 4	Louis Berlinquette	150.00	60.00	15.00
☐ 5	Eddie Bouchard	150.00	60.00	15.00
☐ 6	Billy Boucher	150.00	60.00	15.00
☐ 7	Bob Boucher	150.00	60.00	15.00
☐ 8	Punch Broadbent	300.00	120.00	30.00
☐ 9	Billy Burch	300.00	120.00	30.00
☐ 10	Dutch Cain	150.00	60.00	15.00
☐ 11	Earl Campbell	150.00	60.00	15.00
☐ 12	George Carroll	150.00	60.00	15.00
☐ 13	King Clancy	1200.00	500.00	120.00
☐ 14	Odie Cleghorn	175.00	70.00	18.00
☐ 15	Sprague Cleghorn	300.00	120.00	30.00
☐ 16	Alex Connell	300.00	120.00	30.00
☐ 17	Carson Cooper	150.00	60.00	15.00
☐ 18	Bert Corbeau	150.00	60.00	15.00
☐ 19	Billy Coutu	150.00	60.00	15.00
☐ 20	Clarence(Hap) Day	350.00	140.00	35.00
☐ 21	Cy Denneny	300.00	120.00	30.00
☐ 22	Charles A. Dinsmore	150.00	60.00	15.00
☐ 23	C.A. Dye	300.00	120.00	30.00
☐ 24	Frank Finnigan	300.00	120.00	30.00
☐ 25	Vernon Forbes	150.00	60.00	15.00
☐ 26	Norman Fowler	150.00	60.00	15.00
☐ 27	Red Green	150.00	60.00	15.00
☐ 28	Shorty Green	300.00	120.00	30.00
☐ 29	Curly Headley	150.00	60.00	15.00
☐ 30	Jim Herberts	150.00	60.00	15.00
☐ 31	Fred Hitchman	150.00	60.00	15.00
☐ 32	Albert Holway	150.00	60.00	15.00
☐ 33	Stan Jackson	150.00	60.00	15.00
☐ 34	Aurel Joliat	1000.00	400.00	100.00
☐ 35	Louis C. Langlois	150.00	60.00	15.00
☐ 36	Fred(Frock) Lowrey	150.00	60.00	15.00
☐ 37	Sylvio Mantha	300.00	120.00	30.00
☐ 38	Albert McCaffrey	150.00	60.00	15.00
☐ 39	Robert McKinnon	150.00	60.00	15.00

☐ 40	Herbie Mitchell	150.00	60.00	15.00
☐ 41	Howie Morenz	2500.00	1000.00	250.00
☐ 42	Dunc Munro	150.00	60.00	15.00
☐ 43	Gerald J.M. Munro	150.00	60.00	15.00
☐ 44	Frank Nighbor	350.00	140.00	35.00
☐ 45	Reg Noble	300.00	120.00	30.00
☐ 46	Mickey O'Leary	150.00	60.00	15.00
☐ 47	Goldie Prodgers	150.00	60.00	15.00
☐ 48	Ken Randall	150.00	60.00	15.00
☐ 49	George Redding	150.00	60.00	15.00
☐ 50	John Ross Roach	150.00	60.00	15.00
☐ 51	Mickey Roach	150.00	60.00	15.00
☐ 52	Sam Rothschild	150.00	60.00	15.00
☐ 53	Werner Schnarr	150.00	60.00	15.00
☐ 54	Ganton Scott	150.00	60.00	15.00
☐ 55	Alf Skinner	150.00	60.00	15.00
☐ 56	Hooley Smith	300.00	120.00	30.00
☐ 57	Chris Speyers	150.00	60.00	15.00
☐ 58	Jesse Spring	150.00	60.00	15.00
☐ 59	The Stanley Cup	350.00	140.00	35.00
☐ 60	Georges Vezina	1200.00	500.00	120.00

1983 Canadian National Juniors

STEVE YZERMAN

This 21-card set features Canada's 1983 National Junior Team. The cards measure approximately 3 1/2" by 5" and feature on the fronts either color posed action shots or close-up photos, shot against a blue background. On a red card face, the photos are enclosed by white borders, and the upper right corner of the picture is cut off to allow space for the team logo. The backs are blank and the unnumbered cards are checklisted below in alphabetical order. The set includes early cards of Mario Lemieux and Steve Yzerman. Three other players on the team who were not at the photo session and therefore not represented in the set are Paul Boutillier, Marc Habscheid, and Brad Shaw. A large team card (approximately 5" by 10 1/4") featuring all the players (except Marc Habscheid) and coaches was also produced. A two-thirds size (measuring approximately 5" by 7 1/4") team card entitled, "Celebration '82" with Troy Murray holding the Memorial Cup as well as a (7 1/4" by 10 1/4") '82 team card were also produced. These special oversized cards are not typically included as part of the complete set as listed and valued below.

	MINT	EXC	G-VG
COMPLETE SET (21)	125.00	50.00	12.50
COMMON PLAYER (1-21)	1.00	.40	.10
☐ 1 Dave Andreychuk	12.00	5.00	1.20
☐ 2 Joe Cirella	1.50	.60	.15
☐ 3 Paul Cyr	1.00	.40	.10
☐ 4 Dale Derkatch	1.00	.40	.10
☐ 5 Mike Eagles	1.00	.40	.10
☐ 6 Pat Flatley UER	2.00	.80	.20
(Misspelled Flately)			
☐ 7 Mario Gosselin	2.00	.80	.20
☐ 8 Gary Leeman	2.00	.80	.20
☐ 9 Mario Lemieux	60.00	24.00	6.00
☐ 10 Mark Morrison	1.00	.40	.10
☐ 11 James Patrick	3.00	1.20	.30

☐ 12	Mike Sands	1.00	.40	.10
☐ 13	Gord Sherven	1.00	.40	.10
☐ 14	Tony Tanti	2.00	.80	.20
☐ 15	Larry Trader	1.00	.40	.10
☐ 16	Sylvain Turgeon	2.00	.80	.20
☐ 17	Pat Verbeek	6.00	2.40	.60
☐ 18	Mike Vernon	7.50	3.00	.75
☐ 19	Steve Yzerman	30.00	12.00	3.00
☐ 20	Checklist Card	3.00	1.20	.30
☐ 21	Title Card	3.00	1.20	.30
☐ x	Team Card	6.00	2.40	.60
	(Regular size)			
☐ x	Large Team Card	20.00	8.00	2.00
☐ x	Team Card '82	10.00	4.00	1.00
☐ x	Celebration '82	10.00	4.00	1.00
	(Troy Murray holding			
	Memorial Cup)			

1967-68 Canadiens IGA

8 DICK DUFF

The 1967-68 IGA Montreal Canadiens set includes 23 color cards measuring approximately 1 5/8" by 1 7/8". The cards are unnumbered other than by jersey number which is how they are listed below. The cards were part of a game involving numerous prizes. The card backs contain no personal information about the player (only information about the IGA game) and are written in French and English. The set features early cards of Jacques Lemaire and Rogatien Vachon in their Rookie Card year as well as Serge Savard two years prior to his Rookie Card year.

	NRMT	VG-E	GOOD
COMPLETE SET (23)	650.00	260.00	65.00
COMMON PLAYER	20.00	8.00	2.00
☐ 1 Gump Worsley	60.00	24.00	6.00
☐ 2 Jacques Laperriere	30.00	12.00	3.00
☐ 3 J.C. Tremblay	25.00	10.00	2.50
☐ 4 Jean Beliveau	75.00	30.00	7.50
☐ 5 Gilles Tremblay	20.00	8.00	2.00
☐ 6 Ralph Backstrom	20.00	8.00	2.00
☐ 8 Dick Duff	25.00	10.00	2.50
☐ 10 Ted Harris	20.00	8.00	2.00
☐ 11 Claude Larose	20.00	8.00	2.00
☐ 12 Yvan Cournoyer	40.00	16.00	4.00
☐ 14 Claude Provost	20.00	8.00	2.00
☐ 15 Bobby Rousseau	25.00	10.00	2.50
☐ 16 Henri Richard	50.00	20.00	5.00
☐ 17 Carol Vadnais	20.00	8.00	2.00
☐ 18 Serge Savard	50.00	20.00	5.00
☐ 19 Terry Harper	25.00	10.00	2.50
☐ 20 Garry Monahan	20.00	8.00	2.00
☐ 22 John Ferguson	25.00	10.00	2.50
☐ 23 Danny Grant	25.00	10.00	2.50
☐ 24 Mickey Redmond	30.00	12.00	3.00
☐ 25 Jacques Lemaire	50.00	20.00	5.00
☐ 30 Rogatien Vachon	50.00	20.00	5.00
☐ NNO Hector(Toe) Blake CO	30.00	12.00	3.00

1968-69 Canadiens IGA

The 1968-69 IGA Montreal Canadiens set includes 19 color cards measuring approximately 1 1/4" by 2 1/4". The cards

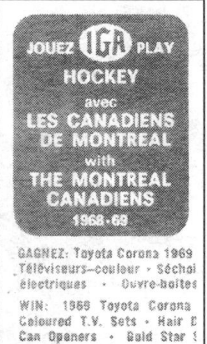

25. JACQUES LEMAIRE

are unnumbered other than by jersey number which is how they are listed below. The cards were part of a game involving numerous prizes. The card backs contain no personal information about the player (only information about the IGA game) and are written in French and English.

	NRMT	VG-E	GOOD
COMPLETE SET (19)	550.00	220.00	55.00
COMMON PLAYER	20.00	8.00	2.00
☐ 1 Gump Worsley	60.00	24.00	6.00
☐ 2 Jacques Laperriere	30.00	12.00	3.00
☐ 3 J.C. Tremblay	25.00	10.00	2.50
☐ 4 Jean Beliveau	75.00	30.00	7.50
☐ 5 Gilles Tremblay	20.00	8.00	2.00
☐ 6 Ralph Backstrom	25.00	10.00	2.50
☐ 8 Dick Duff	25.00	10.00	2.50
☐ 10 Ted Harris	20.00	8.00	2.00
☐ 12 Yvan Cournoyer	40.00	16.00	4.00
☐ 14 Claude Provost	20.00	8.00	2.00
☐ 15 Bobby Rousseau	25.00	10.00	2.50
☐ 16 Henri Richard	50.00	20.00	5.00
☐ 18 Serge Savard	40.00	16.00	4.00
☐ 19 Terry Harper	25.00	10.00	2.50
☐ 20 Garry Monahan	20.00	8.00	2.00
☐ 22 John Ferguson	25.00	10.00	2.50
☐ 24 Mickey Redmond	30.00	12.00	3.00
☐ 25 Jacques Lemaire	50.00	20.00	5.00
☐ 30 Rogatien Vachon	40.00	16.00	4.00

1968-69 Canadiens Postcards BW

This 20-card set of black and white postcards features full-bleed posed player photos with facsimile autographs in white. A row of Forum lights is noticeable in the background of the pictures. This set marks the last year the Canadiens' organization issued black and white postcards. The cards are unnumbered and checklisted below in alphabetical order. Serge Savard appears in this set prior to his Rookie Card year.

	NRMT	VG-E	GOOD
COMPLETE SET (20)	75.00	30.00	7.50
COMMON PLAYER (1-20)	2.50	1.00	.25
☐ 1 Ralph Backstrom	3.00	1.20	.30
☐ 2 Jean Beliveau	12.00	5.00	1.20
☐ 3 Yvan Cournoyer	8.00	3.25	.80
☐ 4 Dick Duff	3.00	1.20	.30
☐ 5 John Ferguson	3.00	1.20	.30
☐ 6 Terry Harper	3.00	1.20	.30
☐ 7 Ted Harris	2.50	1.00	.25
☐ 8 Jacques Laperriere	4.00	1.60	.40
☐ 9 Jacques Lemaire	6.00	2.40	.60
☐ 10 Garry Monahan	2.50	1.00	.25
☐ 11 Claude Provost	2.50	1.00	.25
☐ 12 Mickey Redmond	4.00	1.60	.40
☐ 13 Henri Richard	9.00	3.75	.90
☐ 14 Bobby Rousseau	3.00	1.20	.30

☐ 15 Claude Ruel CO	2.50	1.00	.25
☐ 16 Serge Savard	8.00	3.25	.80
☐ 17 Gilles Tremblay	2.50	1.00	.25
☐ 18 J.C. Tremblay	3.00	1.20	.30
☐ 19 Rogatien Vachon	8.00	3.25	.80
☐ 20 Gump Worsley	9.00	3.75	.90

1969-71 Canadiens Postcards Color

This 31-card set of postcards features full-bleed posed color player photos with facsimile autographs in black across the bottom of the pictures. These postcards were also issued without facsimile autographs. For the 1969-70, 1970-71, and 1971-72 seasons, many of the same postcards were issued. The cards are unnumbered and checklisted below in alphabetical order.

	NRMT	VG-E	GOOD
COMPLETE SET (31)	90.00	36.00	9.00
COMMON PLAYER (1-31)	2.50	1.00	.25
☐ 1 Ralph Backstrom	3.00	1.20	.30
☐ 2 Jean Beliveau	12.00	5.00	1.20
☐ 3 Chris Bordeleau	2.50	1.00	.25
☐ 4 Pierre Bouchard	2.50	1.00	.25
☐ 5 Guy Charron	2.50	1.00	.25
☐ 6 Bill Collins	2.50	1.00	.25
☐ 7 Yvan Cournoyer	8.00	3.25	.80
☐ 8 John Ferguson	3.00	1.20	.30
☐ 9 Terry Harper	3.00	1.20	.30
☐ 10 Ted Harris	2.50	1.00	.25
☐ 11 Rejean Houle	2.50	1.00	.25
☐ 12 Jacques Laperriere	4.00	1.60	.40
☐ 13 Guy Lapointe	6.00	2.40	.60
☐ 14 Claude Larose	2.50	1.00	.25
☐ 15 Jacques Lemaire	6.00	2.40	.60
☐ 16 Al MacNeil CO	2.50	1.00	.25
☐ 17 Frank Mahovlich	8.00	3.25	.80
☐ 18 Peter Mahovlich	6.00	2.40	.60
☐ 19 Phil Myre	3.00	1.20	.30
☐ 20 Larry Pleau	3.00	1.20	.30
☐ 21 Claude Provost	3.00	1.20	.30
☐ 22 Mickey Redmond	4.00	1.60	.40
☐ 23 Henri Richard	9.00	3.75	.90
☐ 24 Phil Roberto	2.50	1.00	.25
☐ 25 Jim Roberts	2.50	1.00	.25
☐ 26 Bobby Rousseau	3.00	1.20	.30
☐ 27 Claude Ruel CO	2.50	1.00	.25
☐ 28 Serge Savard	6.00	2.40	.60
☐ 29 Marc Tardif	3.00	1.20	.30
☐ 30 J.C. Tremblay	3.00	1.20	.30
☐ 31 Rogatien Vachon	8.00	3.25	.80

1970-72 Canadiens Pins

This 17-pin set features members of the Montreal Canadiens. Each pin measures approximately 1 3/4" in diameter and has a black and white picture of the player. With the exception of Guy Lafleur, Frank Mahovlich, and Claude Ruel, who are pictured from the waist up, the other pictures are full body shots. The player's name appears below the picture. The pins are made of metal and have a metal clasp on the back. We have checklisted the pins below in alphabetical order. The pins are undated; since Bobby Rousseau's last season with the Canadiens was 1969-70 and 1971-72 was Ken Dryden, Guy Lafleur, and Frank Mahovlich's first season with Montreal, we have assigned 1970-72 to the set, since the set was undoubtedly issued over a period of years.

	MINT	EXC	G-VG
COMPLETE SET (17)	100.00	40.00	10.00
COMMON PLAYER (1-17)	3.00	1.20	.30
☐ 1 Jean Beliveau	15.00	6.00	1.50
☐ 2 Yvan Cournoyer	7.50	3.00	.75
☐ 3 Ken Dryden	25.00	10.00	2.50
☐ 4 John Ferguson	4.00	1.60	.40
☐ 5 Terry Harper	4.00	1.60	.40
☐ 6 Guy Lafleur	25.00	10.00	2.50
☐ 7 Jacques Laperriere	5.00	2.00	.50
☐ 8 Guy Lapointe	5.00	2.00	.50
☐ 9 Jacques Lemaire	7.50	3.00	.75
☐ 10 Frank Mahovlich	10.00	4.00	1.00
☐ 11 Peter Mahovlich	5.00	2.00	.50
☐ 12 Henri Richard	7.50	3.00	.75
☐ 13 Bobby Rousseau	5.00	2.00	.50
☐ 14 Claude Ruel CO	3.00	1.20	.30
☐ 15 Serge Savard	5.00	2.00	.50
☐ 16 J.C. Tremblay	4.00	1.60	.40
☐ 17 Rogatien Vachon	6.00	2.40	.60

1971-72 Canadiens Postcards

This 25-card set of postcards features full-bleed posed color player photos with facsimile autographs in black across the pictures. For the 1969-70, 1970-71, and 1971-72 seasons, many of the same poses were issued. The cards are unnumbered and checklisted below in alphabetical order. The key cards in the set are Ken Dryden and Guy Lafleur appearing in their Rookie Card year. Also noteworthy is Coach Scotty Bowman's first card.

	NRMT	VG-E	GOOD
COMPLETE SET (25)	90.00	36.00	9.00
COMMON PLAYER (1-25)	2.00	.80	.20
☐ 1 Pierre Bouchard	2.00	.80	.20
☐ 2 Scotty Bowman CO	8.00	3.25	.80
☐ 3 Yvan Cournoyer	6.00	2.40	.60
☐ 4 Denis DeJordy	2.50	1.00	.25
☐ 5 Ken Dryden	25.00	10.00	2.50
☐ 6 Terry Harper	2.50	1.00	.25
☐ 7 Dale Hoganson	2.00	.80	.20
☐ 8 Rejean Houle	2.00	.80	.20
☐ 9 Guy Lafleur	25.00	10.00	2.50
☐ 10 Jacques Laperriere	4.00	1.60	.40
☐ 11 Guy Lapointe	4.00	1.60	.40
☐ 12 Claude Larose	2.00	.80	.20
☐ 13 Jacques Lemaire	5.00	2.00	.50
☐ 14 Frank Mahovlich	8.00	3.25	.80
☐ 15 Peter Mahovlich	4.00	1.60	.40
☐ 16 Phil Myre	2.50	1.00	.25
☐ 17 Larry Pleau	2.50	1.00	.25
☐ 18 Henri Richard	6.00	2.40	.60
☐ 19 Phil Roberto	2.00	.80	.20
☐ 20 Jim Roberts	2.00	.80	.20
☐ 21 Leon Rochefort	2.00	.80	.20
☐ 22 Serge Savard	4.00	1.60	.40
☐ 23 Marc Tardif	2.50	1.00	.25
☐ 24 J.C. Tremblay	2.50	1.00	.25
☐ 25 Rogatien Vachon	5.00	2.00	.50

1972-73 Canadiens Postcards

This 22-card set features white bordered posed color player photos with pale green backgrounds. A facsimile autograph appears across the picture. The words "Pro Star Promotions, Inc." are printed in the border at the bottom. The Scotty Bowman card is the same as in the 1971-72 set. The cards are unnumbered and checklisted below in alphabetical order. The card of Steve Shutt predates his Rookie Card by two years.

	NRMT	VG-E	GOOD
COMPLETE SET (22)	60.00	24.00	6.00
COMMON PLAYER (1-22)	1.50	.60	.15
☐ 1 Chuck Arnason	1.50	.60	.15
☐ 2 Pierre Bouchard	1.50	.60	.15
☐ 3 Scotty Bowman CO	7.50	3.00	.75
☐ 4 Yvan Cournoyer	5.00	2.00	.50
☐ 5 Ken Dryden	12.00	5.00	1.20
☐ 6 Rejean Houle	1.50	.60	.15
☐ 7 Guy Lafleur	12.00	5.00	1.20
☐ 8 Jacques Laperriere	3.00	1.20	.30
☐ 9 Guy Lapointe	3.50	1.40	.35
☐ 10 Claude Larose	1.50	.60	.15
☐ 11 Chuck Lefley	1.50	.60	.15
☐ 12 Jacques Lemaire	3.50	1.40	.35
☐ 13 Frank Mahovlich	6.00	2.40	.60
☐ 14 Peter Mahovlich	3.00	1.20	.30
☐ 15 Bob Murdoch	1.50	.60	.15
☐ 16 Michel Plasse	1.50	.60	.15
☐ 17 Henri Richard	5.00	2.00	.50
☐ 18 Jim Roberts	1.50	.60	.15
☐ 19 Serge Savard	3.00	1.20	.30
☐ 20 Steve Shutt	7.50	3.00	.75
☐ 21 Marc Tardif	2.00	.80	.20
☐ 22 Murray Wilson	1.50	.60	.15

1973-74 Canadiens Postcards

This 24-card set features full-bleed color action player photos. The player's name, number and a facsimile autograph are printed on the back. Reportedly distribution problems limited sales to the public. The cards are unnumbered and checklisted below in alphabetical order. The card of Bob Gainey predates his Rookie Card by one year.

	NRMT	VG-E	GOOD
COMPLETE SET (22)	75.00	30.00	7.50
COMMON PLAYER (1-22)	1.50	.60	.15

			NRMT	VG-E	GOOD
☐	1	Jean Beliveau (Portrait)	10.00	4.00	1.00
☐	2	Pierre Bouchard	1.50	.60	.15
☐	3	Scotty Bowman CO (At bench)	5.00	2.00	.50
☐	4	Yvan Cournoyer	5.00	2.00	.50
☐	5	Bob Gainey	7.50	3.00	.75
☐	6	Dave Gardner	1.50	.60	.15
☐	7	Guy Lafleur	10.00	4.00	1.00
☐	8	Yvon Lambert	1.50	.60	.15
☐	9	Jacques Laperriere	3.00	1.20	.30
☐	10	Guy Lapointe	3.50	1.40	.35
☐	11	Michel Larocque	3.00	1.20	.30
☐	12	Claude Larose SP	5.00	2.00	.50
☐	12	Chuck Lefley	1.50	.60	.15
☐	13	Jacques Lemaire	3.50	1.40	.35
☐	14	Frank Mahovlich	6.00	2.40	.60
☐	15	Peter Mahovlich	2.50	1.00	.25
☐	16	Michel Plasse SP	5.00	2.00	.50
☐	17	Henri Richard	5.00	2.00	.50
☐	18	Jim Roberts SP	5.00	2.00	.50
☐	19	Larry Robinson	10.00	4.00	1.00
☐	20	Serge Savard	3.00	1.20	.30
☐	21	Steve Shutt	5.00	2.00	.50
☐	22	Wayne Thomas	2.00	.80	.20
☐	24	Murray Wilson SP	5.00	2.00	.50

1974-75 Canadiens Postcards

This 27-card set features full-bleed color photos of players seated on a bench in the forum. The cards were issued with and without facsimile autographs. Claude Larose (13) and Chuck Lefley (14) went to St. Louis mid-season resulting in limited distribution of their cards. The Mario Tremblay card (25) was issued only without a facsimile autograph. The cards are unnumbered and checklisted below in alphabetical order.

			NRMT	VG-E	GOOD
		COMPLETE SET (27)	60.00	24.00	6.00
		COMMON PLAYER (1-27)	1.25	.50	.12
☐	1	Pierre Bouchard	1.25	.50	.12
☐	2	Scotty Bowman CO	4.00	1.60	.40
☐	3	Rick Chartraw	1.25	.50	.12
☐	4	Yvan Cournoyer	4.00	1.60	.40
☐	5	Ken Dryden	8.00	3.25	.80
☐	6	Bob Gainey	5.00	2.00	.50
☐	7	Glenn Goldup	1.25	.50	.12
☐	8	Guy Lafleur	8.00	3.25	.80
☐	9	Yvon Lambert	1.25	.50	.12
☐	10	Jacques Laperriere	2.50	1.00	.25
☐	11	Guy Lapointe	3.00	1.20	.30
☐	12	Michel Larocque	2.00	.80	.20
☐	13	Claude Larose SP	3.00	1.20	.30
☐	14	Chuck Lefley SP	3.00	1.20	.30
☐	15	Jacques Lemaire	3.00	1.20	.30
☐	16	Peter Mahovlich	2.00	.80	.20
☐	17	Henri Richard	4.00	1.60	.40
☐	18	Doug Risebrough	2.00	.80	.20
☐	19	Jim Roberts SP	3.00	1.20	.30
☐	20	Larry Robinson	6.00	2.40	.60
☐	21	Glen Sather	3.00	1.20	.30
☐	22	Serge Savard	2.50	1.00	.25
☐	23	Steve Shutt	4.00	1.60	.40
☐	24	Wayne Thomas	2.00	.80	.20
☐	25	Mario Tremblay	2.00	.80	.20
☐	26	John Van Boxmeer	1.25	.50	.12
☐	27	Murray Wilson SP	3.00	1.20	.30

1975-76 Canadiens Postcards

This 20-card set features posed color photos of players on ice. A facsimile autograph appears in a white bottom border. The cards are unnumbered and checklisted below in alphabetical order. The Doug Jarvis card predates his Rookie Card by one year.

			NRMT	VG-E	GOOD
		COMPLETE SET (20)	40.00	16.00	4.00
		COMMON PLAYER (1-20)	1.25	.50	.12
☐	1	Don Awrey	1.25	.50	.12
☐	2	Pierre Bouchard	1.25	.50	.12
☐	3	Scotty Bowman CO (Portrait)	4.00	1.60	.40
☐	4	Yvan Cournoyer	4.00	1.60	.40
☐	5	Ken Dryden	8.00	3.25	.80
☐	6	Bob Gainey	4.00	1.60	.40
☐	7	Doug Jarvis (White uniform)	3.00	1.20	.30
☐	8	Guy Lafleur	8.00	3.25	.80
☐	9	Yvon Lambert	1.25	.50	.12
☐	10	Guy Lapointe	3.00	1.20	.30
☐	11	Michel Larocque	2.00	.80	.20
☐	12	Jacques Lemaire	3.00	1.20	.30
☐	13	Peter Mahovlich	2.50	1.00	.25
☐	14	Doug Risebrough	1.25	.50	.12
☐	15	Jim Roberts	1.25	.50	.12
☐	16	Larry Robinson	5.00	2.00	.50
☐	17	Serge Savard	2.50	1.00	.25
☐	18	Steve Shutt	4.00	1.60	.40
☐	19	Mario Tremblay	2.00	.80	.20
☐	20	Murray Wilson	1.25	.50	.12

1976-77 Canadiens Postcards

This 23-card set features posed color photos of players seated in front of a light blue studio background. A facsimile autograph appears in a white bottom border. The cards are unnumbered and checklisted below in alphabetical order.

			NRMT	VG-E	GOOD
		COMPLETE SET (23)	40.00	16.00	4.00
		COMMON PLAYER (1-23)	1.25	.50	.12
☐	1	Pierre Bouchard	1.25	.50	.12
☐	2	Scotty Bowman CO	4.00	1.60	.40
☐	3	Rick Chartraw	1.25	.50	.12
☐	4	Yvan Cournoyer	4.00	1.60	.40
☐	5	Ken Dryden	8.00	3.25	.80

		NRMT	VG-E	GOOD
☐ 6	Bob Gainey	4.00	1.60	.40
☐ 7	Rejean Houle	1.25	.50	.12
☐ 8	Doug Jarvis	2.00	.80	.20
☐ 9	Guy Lafleur	8.00	3.25	.80
☐ 10	Yvon Lambert	1.25	.50	.12
☐ 11	Guy Lapointe	3.00	1.20	.30
☐ 12	Michel Larocque	2.00	.80	.20
☐ 13	Jacques Lemaire	3.00	1.20	.30
☐ 14	Peter Mahovlich	2.50	1.00	.25
☐ 15	Bill Nyrop	1.25	.50	.12
☐ 16	Doug Risebrough	1.25	.50	.12
☐ 17	Jim Roberts	1.25	.50	.12
☐ 18	Larry Robinson	5.00	2.00	.50
☐ 19	Claude Ruel	1.25	.50	.12
☐ 20	Serge Savard	2.50	1.00	.25
☐ 21	Steve Shutt	4.00	1.60	.40
☐ 22	Mario Tremblay	2.00	.80	.20
☐ 23	Murray Wilson	1.25	.50	.12

1977-78 Canadiens Postcards

This 25-card set features posed action color photos of players on the ice. A facsimile autograph appears in a white bottom bottom. New players were photographed from the shoulders up. Many of the cards are the same as in the 1975-76 set. The cards are unnumbered and checklisted below in alphabetical order.

		NRMT	VG-E	GOOD
COMPLETE SET (25)		35.00	14.00	3.50
COMMON PLAYER (1-25)		.90	.36	.09
☐ 1	Pierre Bouchard	.90	.36	.09
☐ 2	Scotty Bowman CO	3.00	1.20	.30
☐ 3	Rick Chartraw	.90	.36	.09
☐ 4	Yvan Cournoyer	3.00	1.20	.30
☐ 5	Ken Dryden	6.00	2.40	.60
☐ 6	Brian Engblom	.90	.36	.09
☐ 7	Bob Gainey	3.00	1.20	.30
☐ 8	Rejean Houle	.90	.36	.09
☐ 9	Doug Jarvis	1.50	.60	.15
☐ 10	Guy Lafleur	6.00	2.40	.60
☐ 11	Yvon Lambert	.90	.36	.09
☐ 12	Guy Lapointe	2.50	1.00	.25
☐ 13	Michel Larocque	1.50	.60	.15
☐ 14	Pierre Larouche	2.00	.80	.20
☐ 15	Jacques Lemaire	2.00	.80	.20
☐ 16	Gilles Lupien	.90	.36	.09
☐ 17	Pierre Mondou	.90	.36	.09
☐ 18	Bill Nyrop	.90	.36	.09
☐ 19	Doug Risebrough	.90	.36	.09
☐ 20	Larry Robinson	4.00	1.60	.40
☐ 21	Claude Ruel CO	.90	.36	.09
☐ 22	Serge Savard	2.00	.80	.20
☐ 23	Steve Shutt	3.00	1.20	.30
☐ 24	Mario Tremblay	1.50	.60	.15
☐ 25	Murray Wilson	.90	.36	.09

1978-79 Canadiens Postcards

This 26-card set features posed color player photos taken from the shoulders up. All the pictures have a red background except for Ruel and Cournoyer who are shown against blue. A facsimile autograph appears in a white bottom border. The cards are unnumbered and checklisted below in alphabetical order. The key card in the set is Rod Langway appearing two years before his Rookie Card.

		NRMT	VG-E	GOOD
COMPLETE SET (26)		35.00	14.00	3.50
COMMON PLAYER (1-26)		.90	.36	.09
☐ 1	Scotty Bowman CO	3.00	1.20	.30
☐ 2	Rick Chartraw	.90	.36	.09
☐ 3	Cam Connor	.90	.36	.09
☐ 4	Yvan Cournoyer	3.00	1.20	.30
☐ 5	Ken Dryden	6.00	2.40	.60
☐ 6	Brian Engblom	.90	.36	.09
☐ 7	Bob Gainey	3.00	1.20	.30
☐ 8	Rejean Houle	.90	.36	.09
☐ 9	Pat Hughes	.90	.36	.09
☐ 10	Doug Jarvis	1.50	.60	.15
☐ 11	Guy Lafleur	6.00	2.40	.60
☐ 12	Yvon Lambert	.90	.36	.09
☐ 13	Rod Langway	6.00	2.40	.60
☐ 14	Guy Lapointe	2.50	1.00	.25
☐ 15	Michel Larocque	1.50	.60	.15
☐ 16	Pierre Larouche	1.50	.60	.15
☐ 17	Jacques Lemaire	2.00	.80	.20
☐ 18	Gilles Lupien	.90	.36	.09
☐ 19	Pierre Mondou	.90	.36	.09
☐ 20	Mark Napier	.90	.36	.09
☐ 21	Doug Risebrough	.90	.36	.09
☐ 22	Larry Robinson	4.00	1.60	.40
☐ 23	Claude Ruel CO	.90	.36	.09
☐ 24	Serge Savard	2.00	.80	.20
☐ 25	Steve Shutt	3.00	1.20	.30
☐ 26	Mario Tremblay	1.50	.60	.15

1979-80 Canadiens Postcards

This 25-card set features posed color player photos taken from the waist up. All the pictures have a red background except for Ruel who is shown against blue. A facsimile autograph appears in a white bottom border. Several cards are the same as the 1978-79 issue. Bernie Geoffrion's card was not distributed after he resigned as coach on December 12, 1980. Richard Sevigny's card received limited distribution because of late issue. The cards are unnumbered and checklisted below in alphabetical order. The cards measure approximately 3 1/2" by 5 1/2" and the backs are blank.

		NRMT	VG-E	GOOD
COMPLETE SET (25)		30.00	12.00	3.00
COMMON PLAYER (1-25)		.75	.30	.07
☐ 1	Rick Chartraw	.75	.30	.07
☐ 2	Normand Dupont	.75	.30	.07
☐ 3	Brian Engblom	.75	.30	.07
☐ 4	Bob Gainey	2.00	.80	.20
☐ 5	B.Geoffrion CO SP	5.00	2.00	.50
☐ 6	Danny Geoffrion	1.00	.40	.10
☐ 7	Denis Herron	1.00	.40	.10

		MINT	EXC	G-VG
☐ 8	Rejean Houle	.75	.30	.07
☐ 9	Doug Jarvis	1.00	.40	.10
☐ 10	Guy Lafleur	4.00	1.60	.40
☐ 11	Yvon Lambert	.75	.30	.07
☐ 12	Rod Langway	2.00	.80	.20
☐ 13	Guy Lapointe	2.00	.80	.20
☐ 14	Michel Larocque	1.00	.40	.10
☐ 15	Pierre Larouche	1.00	.40	.10
☐ 16	Gilles Lupien	.75	.30	.07
☐ 17	Pierre Mondou	.75	.30	.07
☐ 18	Mark Napier	1.00	.40	.10
☐ 19	Doug Risebrough	1.00	.40	.10
☐ 20	Larry Robinson	3.00	1.20	.30
☐ 21	Claude Ruel CO	.75	.30	.07
☐ 22	Serge Savard	1.50	.60	.15
☐ 23	Richard Sevigny SP	5.00	2.00	.50
☐ 24	Steve Shutt	2.00	.80	.20
☐ 25	Mario Tremblay	1.00	.40	.10

1980-81 Canadiens Postcards

This 26-card set features posed color player photos taken from the waist up against a blue background. A facsimile autograph appears in a white bottom border. The cards are unnumbered and checklisted below in alphabetical order. The cards measure approximately 3 1/2" by 5 1/2" and the backs are blank.

		MINT	EXC	G-VG
COMPLETE SET (26)		25.00	10.00	2.50
COMMON PLAYER (1-26)		.75	.30	.07
☐ 1	Keith Acton	1.00	.40	.10
☐ 2	Bill Baker	.75	.30	.07
☐ 3	Rick Chartraw	.75	.30	.07
☐ 4	Brian Engblom	.75	.30	.07
☐ 5	Bob Gainey	2.00	.80	.20
☐ 6	Gaston Gingras	.75	.30	.07
☐ 7	Denis Herron	1.00	.40	.10
☐ 8	Rejean Houle	.75	.30	.07
☐ 9	Doug Jarvis	1.00	.40	.10
☐ 10	Guy Lafleur	4.00	1.60	.40
☐ 11	Yvon Lambert	.75	.30	.07
☐ 12	Rod Langway	1.50	.60	.15
☐ 13	Guy Lapointe	2.00	.80	.20
☐ 14	Michel Larocque	1.00	.40	.10
☐ 15	Pierre Larouche	1.00	.40	.10
☐ 16	Pierre Mondou	.75	.30	.07
☐ 17	Mark Napier	1.00	.40	.10
☐ 18	Chris Nilan	1.50	.60	.15
☐ 19	Doug Risebrough	.75	.30	.07
☐ 20	Larry Robinson	3.00	1.20	.30
☐ 21	Claude Ruel CO	.75	.30	.07
☐ 22	Serge Savard	1.50	.60	.15
☐ 23	Richard Sevigny	1.00	.40	.10
☐ 24	Steve Shutt	2.00	.80	.20
☐ 25	Mario Tremblay	1.00	.40	.10
☐ 26	Doug Wickenheiser	.75	.30	.07

1981-82 Canadiens Postcards

This 28-card set features posed color player photos taken from the waist up against a blue or blue-white background. A facsimile autograph appears in a white bottom border. Many cards are the same as in the 1980-81 set. The Gilbert Delorme card was not issued with the set. The cards are unnumbered and checklisted below in alphabetical order.

		MINT	EXC	G-VG
COMPLETE SET (28)		25.00	10.00	2.50
COMMON PLAYER (1-28)		.75	.30	.07
☐ 1	Team Photo	2.00	.80	.20
☐ 2	Keith Acton CO	1.00	.40	.10
☐ 3	Bob Berry	1.00	.40	.10
☐ 4	Jeff Brubaker	.75	.30	.07
☐ 5	Gilbert Delorme SP	3.00	1.20	.30
☐ 6	Brian Engblom	.75	.30	.07
☐ 7	Bob Gainey	2.00	.80	.20
☐ 8	Gaston Gingras	.75	.30	.07

		MINT	EXC	G-VG
☐ 9	Denis Herron	1.00	.40	.10
☐ 10	Rejean Houle	.75	.30	.07
☐ 11	Mark Hunter	1.00	.40	.10
☐ 12	Doug Jarvis	1.00	.40	.10
☐ 13	Guy Lafleur	4.00	1.60	.40
☐ 14	Rod Langway	1.50	.60	.15
☐ 15	Jacques Laperriere	1.50	.60	.15
☐ 16	Guy Lapointe	1.50	.60	.15
☐ 17	Craig Laughlin	.75	.30	.07
☐ 18	Pierre Mondou	.75	.30	.07
☐ 19	Mark Napier	1.00	.40	.10
☐ 20	Chris Nilan	1.00	.40	.10
☐ 21	Robert Picard	.75	.30	.07
☐ 22	Doug Risebrough	.75	.30	.07
☐ 23	Larry Robinson	3.00	1.20	.30
☐ 24	Richard Sevigny	.75	.30	.07
☐ 25	Steve Shutt	2.00	.80	.20
☐ 26	Mario Tremblay	1.00	.40	.10
☐ 27	Rick Wamsley	1.00	.40	.10
☐ 28	Doug Wickenheiser	.75	.30	.07

1982-83 Canadiens Postcards

This 28-card set features posed color player photos taken from the waist up against a blue background. A facsimile autograph appears in a white bottom panel. Many cards are the same as in the 1980-81 and 1981-82 sets. Player information, jersey number, and the team logo are on the back. The Richard card has the same style but it is not originally part of the set; it was issued in 1983. The Root card was issued late in the year and thus was limited in its distribution. Some color variation appears in the Gainey and Picard cards. The cards are unnumbered and checklisted below in alphabetical order. Notable cards in the set include Guy Carbonneau and Mats Naslund appearing the year before their Rookie Card.

		MINT	EXC	G-VG
COMPLETE SET (28)		25.00	10.00	2.50
COMMON PLAYER (1-28)		.75	.30	.07
☐ 1	Keith Acton	1.00	.40	.10
☐ 2	Bob Berry CO	1.00	.40	.10
☐ 3	Guy Carbonneau	3.00	1.20	.30
☐ 4	Dan Daoust	.75	.30	.07
☐ 5	Gilbert Delorme	.75	.30	.07
☐ 6	Bob Gainey	2.00	.80	.20
☐ 7	Gaston Gingras	.75	.30	.07
☐ 8	Rick Green	1.00	.40	.10
☐ 9	Rejean Houle	.75	.30	.07
☐ 10	Mark Hunter	.75	.30	.07
☐ 11	Guy Lafleur	4.00	1.60	.40
☐ 12	Jacques Laperriere	1.50	.60	.15
☐ 13	Craig Ludwig	1.00	.40	.10
☐ 14	Pierre Mondou	.75	.30	.07
☐ 15	Mark Napier	1.00	.40	.10
☐ 16	Mats Naslund	3.00	1.20	.30
☐ 17	Ric Nattress	.75	.30	.07
☐ 18	Chris Nilan	1.00	.40	.10
☐ 19	Robert Picard	.75	.30	.07
☐ 20	Henri Richard	3.00	1.20	.30
☐ 21	Larry Robinson	3.00	1.20	.30

			MINT	EXC	G-VG
☐	22	Bill Root SP	2.00	.80	.20
☐	23	Richard Sevigny	.75	.30	.07
☐	24	Steve Shutt	2.00	.80	.20
☐	25	Mario Tremblay	1.00	.40	.10
☐	26	Ryan Walter	1.00	.40	.10
☐	27	Rick Wamsley	1.00	.40	.10
☐	28	Doug Wickenheiser	.75	.30	.07

1982-83 Canadiens Steinberg

This 24-card set was sponsored by Steinberg and the Montreal Canadiens Hockey Club as the "Follow the Play" promotion. The cards were issued in a small vinyl photo album with one card per binder and measure approximately 3 1/2" by 4 15/16". A full color action photo of the player occupies the entire front of the card, and the player's facsimile signature is inscribed across the bottom of the picture. The back has a full-color posed (head and shoulders) photo of the player, uniform number, Steinberg logo, and basic biographical information. For a few of the players, the biography on the card back is written in French; those players are so noted in the checklist below. We have checklisted the cards below in alphabetical order, with sweater number to the right of the player's name. The cards are thin and glossy.

			MINT	EXC	G-VG
	COMPLETE SET (24)		15.00	6.00	1.50
	COMMON PLAYER (1-24)		.60	.24	.06
☐	1	Keith Acton 12	.75	.30	.07
☐	2	Guy Carbonneau 21	2.00	.80	.20
☐	3	Gilbert Delorme 27	.60	.24	.06
		(French bio)			
☐	4	Bob Gainey 23	1.50	.60	.15
☐	5	Rick Green 5	.75	.30	.07
☐	6	Mark Hunter 20	.60	.24	.06
☐	7	Rejean Houle 15	.60	.24	.06
☐	8	Guy Lafleur 10	4.00	1.60	.40
☐	9	Craig Ludwig 17	.75	.30	.07
☐	10	Pierre Mondou 14	.60	.24	.06
☐	11	Mark Napier 31	.75	.30	.07
☐	12	Mats Naslund 26	1.50	.60	.15
☐	13	Ric Nattress 3	.60	.24	.06
		(French bio)			
☐	14	Chris Nilan 30	.75	.30	.07
☐	15	Robert Picard 24	.60	.24	.06
☐	16	Larry Robinson 19	2.00	.80	.20
☐	17	Bill Root 18	.60	.24	.06
☐	18	Richard Sevigny 33	.60	.24	.06
☐	19	Steve Shutt 22	1.50	.60	.15
☐	20	Mario Tremblay 14	.75	.30	.07
☐	21	Ryan Walter 26	.75	.30	.07
☐	22	Rick Wamsley 1	.75	.30	.07
		(French bio)			
☐	23	Doug Wickenheiser 25	.60	.24	.06
☐	24	Title Card	1.25	.50	.12
		Team photo (Canadiens celebrating on ice)			
☐	xx	Vinyl Card Album	5.00	2.00	.50

1983-84 Canadiens Postcards

This 33-card set features color photos of players posed on the ice. A facsimile autograph appears at the bottom. Player information, jersey number, and the team logo are on the back. The team continued to issue cards throughout the season, so several card were distributed on a limited basis. The Laperriere card (number 14) is the same card as in the 1982-83 set. The Delorme and Wickenheiser cards were not issued as part of the set because of trade. Issued in 1984, the Beliveau card was not part of the team set but has the same style. The cards are unnumbered and checklisted below in alphabetical order. The key card in the set is Chris Chelios appearing the year before his Rookie Card.

			MINT	EXC	G-VG
	COMPLETE SET (33)		30.00	12.00	3.00
	COMMON PLAYER (1-33)		.75	.30	.07
☐	1	Jean Beliveau	2.50	1.00	.25
☐	2	Bob Berry	1.00	.40	.10
☐	3	Guy Carbonneau	1.50	.60	.15
☐	4	Kent Carlson	.75	.30	.07
☐	5	John Chabot	.75	.30	.07
☐	6	Chris Chelios	5.00	2.00	.50
☐	7	Gilbert Delorme SP	3.00	1.20	.30
☐	8	Bob Gainey	1.50	.60	.15
☐	9	Rick Green	.75	.30	.07
☐	10	Jean Hamel	.75	.30	.07
☐	11	Mark Hunter	.75	.30	.07
☐	12	Guy Lafleur	3.00	1.20	.30
☐	13	Jacques Lemaire	1.50	.60	.15
☐	14	Jacques Laperriere	1.25	.50	.12
		(Action shot)			
☐	15	Jacques Laperriere	1.25	.50	.12
		(Head shot)			
☐	16	Craig Ludwig	.75	.30	.07
☐	17	Pierre Mondou	.75	.30	.07
☐	18	Mats Naslund	1.25	.50	.12
☐	19	Ric Nattress	.75	.30	.07
☐	20	Chris Nilan	1.00	.40	.10
☐	21	Steve Penney	1.00	.40	.10
☐	22	Jacques Plante	2.50	1.00	.25
☐	23	Larry Robinson	2.00	.80	.20
☐	24	Bill Root	.75	.30	.07
☐	25	Richard Sevigny	.75	.30	.07
☐	26	Steve Shutt	1.50	.60	.15
☐	27	Bobby Smith	1.50	.60	.15
☐	28	Mario Tremblay	1.00	.40	.10
☐	29	Alfie Turcotte	.75	.30	.07
☐	30	Perry Turnbull	1.00	.40	.10
☐	31	Ryan Walter	1.00	.40	.10
☐	32	Rick Wamsley	1.00	.40	.10
☐	33	Doug Wickenheiser SP	3.00	1.20	.30

1984-85 Canadiens Postcards

This 31-card set features color photos of players posed on the ice. A facsimile autograph appears at the bottom. Player information, jersey number, and the team logo are on the

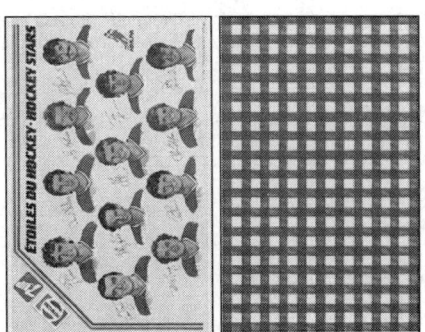

back. Many cards are the same as in the 1983-84 set. The cards are unnumbered and checklisted below in alphabetical order.

		MINT	EXC	G-VG
	COMPLETE SET (31)	25.00	10.00	2.50
	COMMON PLAYER (1-31)	.75	.30	.07
☐ 1	Guy Carbonneau	1.50	.60	.15
	(Action on ice, foot raised, with puck)			
☐ 2	Guy Carbonneau	1.50	.60	.15
	(Still, both feet on ice, no puck)			
☐ 3	Kent Carlson	1.00	.40	.10
☐ 4	Chris Chelios	3.00	1.20	.30
	(Same card as 1983-84, but with autograph on front)			
☐ 5	Lucien Deblois	.75	.30	.07
☐ 6	Ron Flockhart	1.00	.40	.10
☐ 7	Bob Gainey	1.50	.60	.15
☐ 8	Rick Green	.75	.30	.07
☐ 9	Jean Hamel	.75	.30	.07
☐ 10	Mark Hunter	.75	.30	.07
☐ 11	Tom Kurvers	1.25	.50	.12
☐ 12	Guy Lafleur	3.00	1.20	.30
☐ 13	Jacques Laperriere	1.25	.50	.12
☐ 14	Jacques Lemaire	1.50	.60	.15
☐ 15	Craig Ludwig	.75	.30	.07
☐ 16	Mike McPhee	1.50	.60	.15
☐ 17	Pierre Mondou	.75	.30	.07
☐ 18	Mats Naslund	1.25	.50	.12
☐ 19	Ric Nattress	.75	.30	.07
☐ 20	Chris Nilan	1.00	.40	.10
☐ 21	Steve Penney	1.00	.40	.10
	(Same card as 1983-84)			
☐ 22	Steve Penney	1.00	.40	.10
☐ 23	Jean Perron	.75	.30	.07
☐ 24	Larry Robinson	2.00	.80	.20
☐ 25	Bobby Smith	1.50	.60	.15
☐ 26	Doug Soetaert	.75	.30	.07
☐ 27	Petr Svoboda	1.25	.50	.12
☐ 28	Mario Tremblay	1.00	.40	.10
☐ 29	Alfie Turcotte	.75	.30	.07
	(Same card as 1983-84)			
☐ 30	Alfie Turcotte	.75	.30	.07
	(Autograph on front)			
☐ 31	Ryan Walter	1.00	.40	.10

1985-86 Canadiens Placemats

Sponsored by Pepsi-Cola and Seven-Up, this set of seven placemats was issued to commemorate the Montreal Canadiens as the 1984-85 Division Champions. Each placemat measures approximately 11" by 17". On an yellow-orange background with a white border, the front carries a painted portrait, action shot and a facsimile autograph of two different players. Player name, position, and number, date and place of birth, and career statistics in French and English are also found on the front. The sponsors' logos appear in the upper right corner. The backs feature a red-and-white plaid design. The placemats are unnumbered. One placemat shows portraits of all twelve players with their facsimile autographs.

		MINT	EXC	G-VG
	COMPLETE SET (7)	25.00	10.00	2.50
	COMMON PLAYER (1-7)	3.00	1.20	.30
☐ 1	Bob Gainey	5.00	2.00	.50
	Guy Carbonneau			
☐ 2	Mats Naslund	3.00	1.20	.30
	Tom Kurvers			
☐ 3	Chris Nilan	3.00	1.20	.30
	Petr Svoboda			
☐ 4	Steve Penney	5.00	2.00	.50
	Chris Chelios			
☐ 5	Larry Robinson	4.00	1.60	.40
	Serge Boisvert			
☐ 6	Mario Tremblay	3.00	1.20	.30
	Bobby Smith			
☐ 7	Hockey Stars	7.00	2.80	.70
	Steve Penney			
	Chris Chelios			
	Larry Robinson			
	Serge Boisvert			
	Mario Tremblay			
	Bobby Smith			
	Mats Naslund			
	Tom Kurvers			
	Bob Gainey			
	Guy Carbonneau			
	Chris Nilan			
	Petr Svoboda			

1985-86 Canadiens Postcards

This 40-card set features color photos of players posed in red uniforms against a white background. A facsimile autograph appears on a red diagonal line in the lower right corner on most cards. However, there is some variation in the autograph location. Player information and the team logo are on the back. Several cards (1, 2, 3, 11, 14, 17, 19) were issued late in the season. The cards are unnumbered and checklisted below in alphabetical order. Notable early cards include Claude Lemieux, Stephane Richer, and Patrick Roy.

	MINT	EXC	G-VG
COMPLETE SET (40)........................	40.00	16.00	4.00
COMMON PLAYER (1-40).................	.60	.24	.06
☐ 1 Serge Boisvert SP..................	1.50	.60	.15
(No red line or autograph)			
☐ 2 Serge Boisvert SP..................	1.50	.60	.15
(Portrait)			
☐ 3 Randy Bucyk SP....................	1.50	.60	.15
(No red line or autograph)			
☐ 4 Guy Carbonneau	1.25	.50	.12
☐ 5 Chris Chelios........................	2.50	1.00	.25
☐ 6 Kjell Dahlin..........................	.75	.30	.07
(J in autograph on stick)			
☐ 7 Kjell Dahlin..........................	.75	.30	.07
(E in autograph on stick)			
☐ 8 Lucien Deblois	.60	.24	.06
☐ 9 Bob Gainey...........................	1.50	.60	.15
(B in autograph on stick)			
☐ 10 Bob Gainey...........................	1.50	.60	.15
(G in autograph on stick)			
☐ 11 Gaston Gingras SP..............	1.50	.60	.15
☐ 12 Rick Green..........................	.60	.24	.06
(No letters on stick)			
☐ 13 Rick Green..........................	.60	.24	.06
(C in autograph on stick)			
☐ 14 John Kordic SP	1.50	.60	.15
(No red line or autograph)			
☐ 15 Tom Kurvers	.75	.30	.07
☐ 16 Mike Lalor...........................	.60	.24	.06
☐ 17 Claude Lemieux SP..............	6.00	2.40	.60
(No red line or autograph)			
☐ 18 Craig Ludwig.......................	.60	.24	.06
☐ 19 David Maley SP....................	1.50	.60	.15
(No red line or autograph)			
☐ 20 Mike McPhee	1.00	.40	.10
☐ 21 Sergio Momesso...................	1.00	.40	.10
☐ 22 Mats Naslund	.75	.30	.07
☐ 23 Chris Nilan	.75	.30	.07
(Dot from i in Nilan touching toe)			
☐ 24 Chris Nilan	.75	.30	.07
(Dot from i in Nilan away from toe)			
☐ 25 Steve Penney	.75	.30	.07
☐ 26 Jean Perron.........................	.60	.24	.06
(Portrait)			
☐ 27 Stephane Richer...................	3.00	1.20	.30
☐ 28 Larry Robinson	2.00	.80	.20
☐ 29 Steve Rooney	.60	.24	.06
(Loop in R through skate toe)			
☐ 30 Steve Rooney	.60	.24	.06
(Loop in R through skate laces)			
☐ 31 Patrick Roy	15.00	6.00	1.50
☐ 32 Brian Skrudland	.75	.30	.07
☐ 33 Bobby Smith........................	1.00	.40	.10
(B in autograph touching stick)			
☐ 34 Bobby Smith........................	1.00	40	.10
(O in autograph on stick)			
☐ 35 Doug Soetaert......................	.60	.24	.06
(T at end of name by pad)			
☐ 36 Doug Soetaert......................	.60	.24	.06
(T at end of name away from pad)			
☐ 37 Petr Svoboda	.75	.30	.07
☐ 38 Mario Tremblay....................	.75	.30	.07
(T in autograph touching blade)			
☐ 39 Mario Tremblay....................	.75	.30	.07
(T in autograph away from blade)			
☐ 40 Ryan Walter	.75	.30	.07

1985-86 Canadiens Provigo

This 25-sticker set of the Montreal Canadiens was produced by Provigo. The puffy (styrofoam-backed) stickers measure approximately 1 1/8" by 2 1/4" and feature a color head and shoulders photo of the player, with the player's number and name bordered by star-studded banners across the bottom of the picture. The Canadiens' logo is superimposed over the banner at its right end. The backs are blank. We have checklisted them below in alphabetical order, with the uniform number to the right of the player's name. The 25 stickers were to be attached to a cardboard poster. The poster measures approximately 20" by 11" and has 25 white spaces designated for the stickers on a red background. At the center is a picture of a goalie mask, with the Canadiens' logo above and slightly to the right. The back of the poster has a checklist, stripes in the team's colors, and two team logos. The set features early cards of Stephane Richer and Patrick Roy pre-dating their actual Rookie Cards.

	MINT	EXC	G-VG
COMPLETE SET (25)........................	25.00	10.00	2.50
COMMON PLAYER (1-25).................	.60	.24	.06
☐ 1 Guy Carbonneau 21	1.25	.50	.12
☐ 2 Chris Chelios 24....................	2.50	1.00	.25
☐ 3 Kjell Dahlin 20.......................	.75	.30	.07
☐ 4 Lucien DeGlois 27...................	.60	.24	.06
☐ 5 Bob Gainey 23.......................	1.50	.60	.15
☐ 6 Rick Green 5.........................	.60	.24	.06
☐ 7 Tom Kurvers 18......................	.75	.30	.07
☐ 8 Mike Lalor 38........................	.60	.24	.06
☐ 9 Craig Ludwig 17.....................	.75	.30	.07
☐ 10 Mike McPhee 35	1.00	.40	.10
☐ 11 Sergio Momesso 36...............	1.00	.40	.10
☐ 12 Mats Naslund 26...................	.75	.30	.07
☐ 13 Chris Nilan 30	.75	.30	.07
☐ 14 Steve Penney 37...................	.75	.30	.07
☐ 15 Jean Perron CO.....................	.60	.24	.06
☐ 16 Stephane Richer 44...............	3.00	1.20	.30
☐ 17 Larry Robinson 19.................	2.00	.80	.20
☐ 18 Steve Rooney 28...................	.60	.24	.06
☐ 19 Patrick Roy 33	12.50	5.00	1.25
☐ 20 Brian Skrudland 39	.75	.30	.07
☐ 21 Bobby Smith 15....................	1.00	.40	.10
☐ 22 Doug Soetaert 1	.60	.24	.06
☐ 23 Petr Svoboda 25...................	.75	.30	.07
☐ 24 Mario Tremblay 14................	.75	.30	.07
☐ 25 Ryan Walter 11	.75	.30	.07

1986-87 Canadiens Postcards

Each card of this 25-card set of Montreal Canadiens measures approximately 3 3/8" by 5 1/2". The front features a color posed photo (without borders) of the player. The information on the back has a diagonal orientation and is printed in the Canadiens' team colors read and blue. At the top are the back appears the Canadiens' logo, followed by the player's name, his signature, and brief biographical information (in French and English). The 1985-86 season is the only season Shayne Corson wore sweater 34.

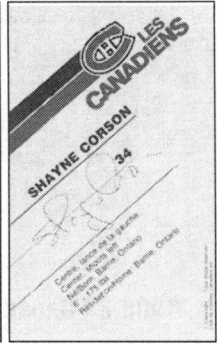

	MINT	EXC	G-VG
COMPLETE SET (25)	25.00	10.00	2.50
COMMON PLAYER (1-25)	.60	.24	.06
☐ 1 Guy Carbonneau 21	1.00	.40	.10
☐ 2 Chris Chelios 24	2.00	.80	.20
☐ 3 Shayne Corson 34	1.00	.40	.10
☐ 4 Kjell Dahlin 20	.60	.24	.06
☐ 5 Bob Gainey 23	1.25	.50	.12
☐ 6 Rick Green 5	.60	.24	.06
☐ 7 Brian Hayward 1	1.00	.40	.10
☐ 8 John Kordic 31	.75	.30	.07
☐ 9 Mike Lalor 38	.60	.24	.06
☐ 10 Jacques Laperriere ACO	.75	.30	.07
☐ 11 Claude Lemieux	1.50	.60	.15
☐ 12 Craig Ludwig 17	.75	.30	.07
☐ 13 Mike McPhee 35	.75	.30	.07
☐ 14 Sergio Momesso 36	.60	.24	.06
☐ 15 Mats Naslund 26	.75	.30	.07
☐ 16 Chris Nilan 30	.75	.30	.07
☐ 17 Jean Perron CO	.60	.24	.06
☐ 18 Stephane Richer 44	1.25	.50	.12
☐ 19 Larry Robinson 19	1.50	.60	.15
☐ 20 Patrick Roy 33	12.00	5.00	1.20
☐ 21 Scott Sandelin 3	.60	.24	.06
☐ 22 Brian Skrudland 39	.75	.30	.07
☐ 23 Bobby Smith 15	.75	.30	.07
☐ 24 Petr Svoboda 25	.60	.24	.06
☐ 25 Ryan Walter 11	.75	.30	.07

1987-88 Canadiens Postcards

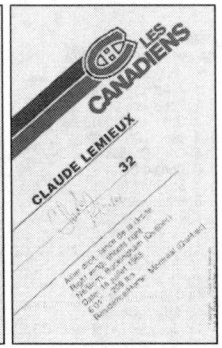

This 35-card set is in the postcard size format, with each card measuring approximately 3 1/2" by 5 1/2". The fronts feature full-bleed posed color action shots. In a diagonal format at the top of the back appears the team logo, followed by the player's name, his signature, and brief biographical information (in French and English). The cards are unnumbered and checklisted below in alphabetical order.

	MINT	EXC	G-VG
COMPLETE SET (35)	25.00	10.00	2.50
COMMON PLAYER (1-34)	.60	.24	.06
☐ 1 Francois Allaire ACO	.60	.24	.06
☐ 2 Guy Carbonneau	1.00	.40	.10
☐ 3 Jose Charbonneau	.60	.24	.06
☐ 4 Chris Chelios	1.50	.60	.15
☐ 5 Shayne Corson	.75	.30	.07
☐ 6 Kjell Dahlen	.60	.24	.06
☐ 7 Bob Gainey	1.25	.50	.12
☐ 8 Rick Green	.60	.24	.06
☐ 9 Gaston Gringras	.60	.24	.06
☐ 10 Brian Hayward	.75	.30	.07
☐ 11 John Kordic	.60	.24	.06
☐ 12 Mike Lalor	.60	.24	.06
☐ 13 Jacques Laperriere ACO	.75	.30	.07
☐ 14 Claude Lemieux	1.25	.50	.12
☐ 15 Craig Ludwig	.75	.30	.07
☐ 16 David Maley	.60	.24	.06
☐ 17 Mike McPhee	.75	.30	.07
☐ 18 Sergio Momesso	.75	.30	.07
☐ 19 Claude Mouton ANN	.60	.24	.06
☐ 20 Mats Naslund	.75	.30	.07
☐ 21 Chris Nilan	.75	.30	.07
☐ 22 Jean Perron	.60	.24	.06
☐ 23A Stephane Richer (With moustache)	1.25	.50	.12
☐ 23B Stephane Richer (No moustache)	1.25	.50	.12
☐ 24 Larry Robinson	1.50	.60	.15
☐ 25 Steve Rooney	.60	.24	.06
☐ 26 Patrick Roy	8.00	3.25	.80
☐ 27 Scott Sandelin	.60	.24	.06
☐ 28 Serge Savard DIR	.75	.30	.07
☐ 29 Brian Skrudland	.75	.30	.07
☐ 30 Bobby Smith	.75	.30	.07
☐ 31 Petr Svoboda	.60	.24	.06
☐ 32 Gilles Thibaudeau	.60	.24	.06
☐ 33 Larry Trader	.60	.24	.06
☐ 34 Ryan Walter	.75	.30	.07

1987-88 Canadiens Vachon Stickers

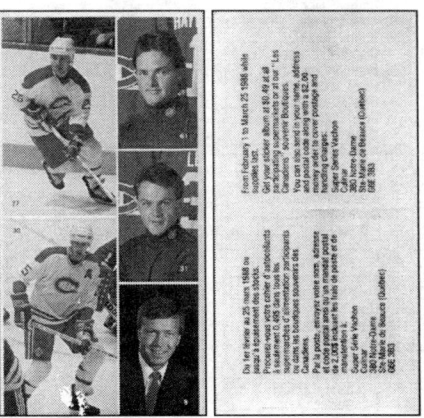

Featuring the Montreal Canadiens, this set consists of 28 panels, each measuring approximately 2 7/8" by 5 9/16". Each panel is made up of five stickers, two that measure approximately 1 1/2" by 2 5/8", and three that measure approximately 1" by 1 11/16". The larger stickers carry color action player photos or team pictures. The smaller ones are close-ups of players or action shots. The stickers appear in a variety of combinations on the panels, with one panel showing small player shots and another panel carrying the same player shots but with different action photos. All total, 88 different stickers were printed. The back of the panel explains in French and English that albums are available for 49 cents at participating supermarkets and at "Les

Canadiens" souvenir boutiques, and that collectors can send in 2.00 to Super Series Vachon and receive the album through the mail. The first seven stickers can be pieced together to form a composite team photo. The stickers are numbered on the front.

	MINT	EXC	G-VG
COMPLETE SET (88)	30.00	12.00	3.00
COMMON PLAYER (1-88)	.25	.10	.02
□ 1 Canadiens Team Photo (Top left)	.35	.14	.03
□ 2 Canadiens Team Photo (Top middle)	.35	.14	.03
□ 3 Canadiens Team Photo (Top right)	.35	.14	.03
□ 4 Canadiens Team Photo (Bottom left)	.35	.14	.03
□ 5 Canadiens Team Photo (Bottom middle)	.35	.14	.03
□ 6 Canadiens Team Photo (Bottom right)	.35	.14	.03
□ 7 Jean Perron CO	.25	.10	.02
□ 8 Jacques Laperriere ACO	.35	.14	.03
□ 9 Fracois Allaire Goaltending Instructor	.25	.10	.02
□ 10 Jean Perron CO	.25	.10	.02
□ 11 Jacques Laperriere	.35	.14	.03
□ 12 Bob Gainey	.50	.20	.05
□ 13 Bob Gainey	.50	.20	.05
□ 14 Guy Carbonneau	.35	.14	.03
□ 15 Guy Carbonneau	.35	.14	.03
□ 16 Guy Carbonneau	.35	.14	.03
□ 17 Michael McPhee	.35	.14	.03
□ 18 Bob Gainey	.50	.20	.05
□ 19 Chris Nilan	.35	.14	.03
□ 20 Chris Nilan	.35	.14	.03
□ 21 Guy Carbonneau	.35	.14	.03
□ 22 Mike Lalor	.25	.10	.02
□ 23 Patrick Roy and Guy Carbonneau	2.50	1.00	.25
□ 24 Ryan Walter	.25	.10	.02
□ 25 Ryan Walter	.25	.10	.02
□ 26 Bobby Smith	.35	.14	.03
□ 27 Mats Naslund	.35	.14	.03
□ 28 Bobby Smith	.35	.14	.03
□ 29 Mike McPhee	.35	.14	.03
□ 30 Bobby Smith	.35	.14	.03
□ 31 Claude Lemieux	1.00	.40	.10
□ 32 Brian Skrudland	.25	.10	.02
□ 33 Craig Ludwig	.25	.10	.02
□ 34 Brian Skrudland	.25	.10	.02
□ 35 Craig Ludwig	.25	.10	.02
□ 36 Brian Skrudland	.25	.10	.02
□ 37 Mike McPhee	.35	.14	.03
□ 38 Mike McPhee	.35	.14	.03
□ 39 Kjell Dahlin	.25	.10	.02
□ 40 Kjell Dahlin	.25	.10	.02
□ 41 Bobby Smith	.35	.14	.03
□ 42 Patrick Roy	2.50	1.00	.25
□ 43 Patrick Roy	2.50	1.00	.25
□ 44 Larry Trader	.25	.10	.02
□ 45 Mats Naslund	.35	.14	.03
□ 46 Mats Naslund	.35	.14	.03
□ 47 Mats Naslund	.35	.14	.03
□ 48 Mats Naslund	.35	.14	.03
□ 49 Shayne Corson	.35	.14	.03
□ 50 Shayne Corson	.35	.14	.03
□ 51 Stephane J.J. Richer	.50	.20	.05
□ 52 Stephane J.J. Richer	.50	.20	.05
□ 53 Bob Gainey	.50	.20	.05
□ 54 Stephane J.J. Richer	.50	.20	.05
□ 55 Sergio Momesso	.35	.14	.03
□ 56 Sergio Memesso	.35	.14	.03
□ 57 John Kordic	.35	.14	.03
□ 58 John Kordic	.35	.14	.03
□ 59 Mike Lalor	.25	.10	.02
□ 60 Mike Lalor	.25	.10	.02
□ 61 Brian Hayward	.35	.14	.03
□ 62 Guy Carbonneau	.35	.14	.03
□ 63 Guy Carbonneau	.35	.14	.03
□ 64 Brian Hayward	.35	.14	.03
□ 65 Rick Green	.25	.10	.02
□ 66 Rick Green	.25	.10	.02
□ 67 Brian Hayward	.35	.14	.03
□ 68 Rick Green	.25	.10	.02
□ 69 Patrick Roy	2.50	1.00	.25
□ 70 Rick Green	.25	.10	.02
□ 71 Patrick Roy	2.50	1.00	.25
□ 72 Larry Robinson	.75	.30	.07
□ 73 Larry Robinson	.75	.30	.07
□ 74 Patrick Roy	2.50	1.00	.25

	MINT	EXC	G-VG
□ 75 Petr Svoboda	.25	.10	.02
□ 76 Patrick Roy	2.50	1.00	.25
□ 77 Petr Svoboda	.25	.10	.02
□ 78 Chris Chelios	.75	.30	.07
□ 79 Chris Chelios	.75	.30	.07
□ 80 Craig Ludwig	.35	.14	.03
□ 81 Craig Ludwig	.35	.14	.03
□ 82 Chris Chelios	.75	.30	.07
□ 83 Chris Chelios	.75	.30	.07
□ 84 Brian Hayward	.35	.14	.03
□ 85 Craig Ludwig	.35	.14	.03
□ 86 Bobby Smith	.35	.14	.03
□ 87 Mats Naslund	.35	.14	.03
□ 88 Bob Gainey	.50	.20	.05
□ xx Sticker Album	5.00	2.00	.50

1988-89 Canadiens Postcards

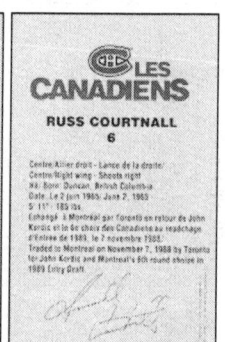

This 30-card, team-issued set measures approximately 3 1/2" by 5 1/2" and features full-bleed color player photos. The players are posed on the ice against a white background. The coaches' cards feature color portraits against a black background. The backs are white and show the team name and logo in large red letters at the top. The player's name, number, and biography are printed in blue. A facsimile autograph at the bottom rounds out the back. The cards are unnumbered and checklisted below in alphabetical order.

	MINT	EXC	G-VG
COMPLETE SET (30)	20.00	8.00	2.00
COMMON PLAYER (1-30)	.50	.20	.05
□ 1 Francois Allaire ACO	.50	.20	.05
□ 2 Pat Burns CO	.75	.30	.07
□ 3 Guy Carbonneau	1.00	.40	.10
□ 4 Jose Carbonneau	.75	.30	.07
□ 5 Chris Chelios	1.00	.40	.10
□ 6 Ronald Corey PRES	.50	.20	.05
□ 7 Shayne Corson	.75	.30	.07
□ 8 Russ Courtnall	1.00	.40	.10
□ 9 Eric Desjardins	.75	.30	.07
□ 10 Bob Gainey	1.00	.40	.10
□ 11 Brent Gilcrist	.75	.30	.07
□ 12 Rick Green	.50	.20	.05
□ 13 Brian Hayward	.75	.30	.07
□ 14 Mike Keane	.75	.30	.07
□ 15 Mike Lalor	.50	.20	.05
□ 16 Jacques Laperriere ACO	.75	.30	.07
□ 17 Claude Lemieux	1.00	.40	.10
□ 18 Craig Ludwig	.75	.30	.07
□ 19 Steven Martinson	.50	.20	.05
□ 20 Mike McPhee	.75	.30	.07
□ 21 Mats Naslund	.75	.30	.07
□ 22 Stephane Richer	1.00	.40	.10
□ 23 Larry Robinson	1.50	.60	.15
□ 24 Patrick Roy	6.00	2.40	.60
□ 25 Serge Savard DIR	.75	.30	.07
□ 26 Brian Skrudland	.75	.30	.07
□ 27 Bobby Smith	.75	.30	.07
□ 28 Petr Svoboda	.50	.20	.05
□ 29 Ryan Walter	.50	.20	.05
□ 39 Gilles Thibodeau	.50	.20	.05

1989-90 Canadiens Kraft

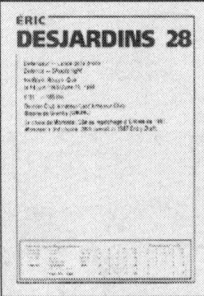

This 24-card set of Montreal Canadiens was sponsored by Le Journal de Montreal and Kraft Foods. The cards were issued as two four-card insert sheets in Les Canadiens magazine. The cards measure approximately 3 3/4" by 5 7/16". The front features a posed color photo of the player on white card stock. Thin red, white, and blue borders outline the card face, and the sponsors' logos appear in the lower corners. The upper right-hand corner of the border is formed by text rather than by the color lines. The card gives the player's name and number in large red print at the top. Brief biographical information is given (in French and English) below the player's name in black lettering. The card back is framed by a thin blue border. The red box at the bottom is filled with statistical information. The cards are unnumbered and hence are listed below in alphabetical order by player name with sweater number after the name.

	MINT	EXC	G-VG
COMPLETE SET (24)	25.00	10.00	2.50
COMMON PLAYER (1-24)	.75	.30	.07
☐ 1 Pat Burns CO	1.25	.50	.12
☐ 2 Guy Carbonneau 21	1.25	.50	.12
☐ 3 Chris Chelios 24	2.00	.80	.20
☐ 4 Shayne Corson 27	1.25	.50	.12
☐ 5 Russ Courtnall 6	1.50	.60	.15
☐ 6 J.J. Daigneault 48	1.00	.40	.10
☐ 7 Eric Desjardins 28	1.25	.50	.12
☐ 8 Todd Ewen 36	1.00	.40	.10
☐ 9 Brent Gilchrist 41	1.00	.40	.10
☐ 10 Brian Hayward 1	1.00	.40	.10
☐ 11 Mike Keane 12	1.25	.50	.12
☐ 12 Stephan Lebeau 47	2.00	.80	.20
☐ 13 Sylvain Lefebvre 3	1.00	.40	.10
☐ 14 Claude Lemieux 32	1.50	.60	.15
☐ 15 Craig Ludwig 17	1.00	.40	.10
☐ 16 Mike McPhee 35	1.25	.50	.12
☐ 17 Mats Naslund 26	1.25	.50	.12
☐ 18 Stephane Richer 44	1.50	.60	.15
☐ 19 Patrick Roy 33	6.00	2.40	.60
☐ 20 Mathieu Schneider 18	2.00	.80	.20
☐ 21 Brian Skrudland 39	.75	.30	.07
☐ 22 Bobby Smith 15	1.25	.50	.12
☐ 23 Petr Svoboda 25	.75	.30	.07
☐ 24 Ryan Walter 11	.75	.30	.07

1989-90 Canadiens Provigo Figurines

These 13 plastic figurines of the 1989-90 Canadiens are approximately 3" tall and show the players in their white home jerseys, wearing skates and holding white hockey sticks. The players' names and uniform numbers appear on their jersey backs. The figurines are numbered on the backs of the hockey sticks. The original issue price for these figurines was 1.99 Canadian. The figurines were distributed in a package with a coupon booklet.

	MINT	EXC	G-VG
COMPLETE SET (13)	35.00	14.00	3.50
COMMON PLAYER	3.00	1.20	.30
☐ 6 Russ Courtnall	4.00	1.60	.40
☐ 15 Bobby Smith	4.00	1.60	.40
☐ 17 Craig Ludwig	3.00	1.20	.30
☐ 21 Guy Carbonneau	4.00	1.60	.40
☐ 23 Bob Gainey	5.00	2.00	.50
☐ 24 Chris Chelios	6.00	2.40	.60
☐ 25 Petr Svoboda	3.00	1.20	.30
☐ 26 Mats Naslund	4.00	1.60	.40
☐ 27 Shayne Corson	3.00	1.20	.30
☐ 33 Patrick Roy	10.00	4.00	1.00
☐ 35 Mike McPhee	3.00	1.20	.30
☐ 39 Brian Skrudland	3.00	1.20	.30
☐ 44 Stephane Richer	4.00	1.60	.40

1991-92 Canadiens Postcards

This 31-card team-issued set measures approximately 3 1/2" by 5 1/2". The fronts feature full-bleed color photos, with the players posed in front of a white background. The backs are white and show the team name in large red letters at the top. The player's name, number, and biography (in French and English) are printed in blue. A facsimile autograph at the bottom rounds out the back. The cards are unnumbered and checklisted below in alphabetical order. This is Kirk Muller's first year in a Canadiens' uniform.

	MINT	EXC	G-VG
COMPLETE SET (31)	15.00	6.00	1.50
COMMON PLAYER (1-31)	.50	.20	.05
☐ 1 Francois Allaire ACO	.50	.20	.05
☐ 2 Patrice Brisebois	.75	.30	.07
☐ 3 Pat Burns CO	.75	.30	.07
☐ 4 Guy Carbonneau	.75	.30	.07
☐ 5 Ronald Corey PRES	.50	.20	.05
☐ 6 Shayne Corson	.75	.30	.07
☐ 7 Alain Cote	.50	.20	.05
☐ 8 Russ Courtnall	1.00	.40	.10
☐ 9 Jean-Jacques Daigneault	.50	.20	.05

☐ 10	Eric Desjardins	.75	.30	.07
☐ 11	Donald Dufresne	.50	.20	.05
☐ 12	Todd Ewen	.50	.20	.05
☐ 13	Brent Gilchrist	.75	.30	.07
☐ 14	Mike Keane	.75	.30	.07
☐ 15	Jacques Laperriere ACO	.75	.30	.07
☐ 16	Stephan Lebeau	1.00	.40	.10
☐ 17	John LeClair	1.00	.40	.10
☐ 18	Sylvain Lefebvre	.75	.30	.07
☐ 19	Mike McPhee	.75	.30	.07
☐ 20	Kirk Muller	1.50	.60	.15
☐ 21	Lyle Odelein	.75	.30	.07
☐ 22	Andre Racicot	.75	.30	.07
☐ 23	Mario Roberge	.50	.20	.05
☐ 24	Patrick Roy	3.00	1.20	.30
☐ 25	Denis Savard	1.00	.40	.10
☐ 26	Serge Savard DIR	.75	.30	.07
☐ 27	Mathieu Schneider	1.00	.40	.10
☐ 28	Brian Skrudland	.75	.30	.07
☐ 29	Petr Svoboda	.50	.20	.05
☐ 30	Charles Thiffault ACO	.50	.20	.05
☐ 31	Sylvain Turgeon	.50	.20	.05

☐ 24	Patrick Roy	2.50	1.00	.25
☐ 25	Denis Savard	1.00	.40	.10
☐ 26	Mathieu Schneider	.75	.30	.07
☐ 27	Brian Skrudland	.60	.24	.06

1993-94 Canadiens Molson

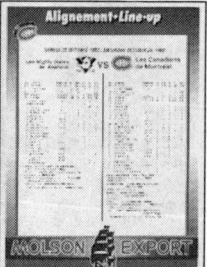

Measuring approximately 8" by 10 1/2", this ten-card set was sponsored by Molson and was apparently distributed in conjunction with certain games throughout the season. The fronts feature full-bleed posed color photos. The photos are accented by a red line on the top and each side; at the bottom, a blue stripe carries the player's name and his uniform number. Inside a white outer border and a fading team color-coded inner border, the backs present team line-ups in English and French for the Canadiens and the respective visiting team. The cards are unnumbered and checklisted below in alphabetical order.

	MINT	EXC	G-VG
COMPLETE SET (10)	20.00	8.00	2.00
COMMON PLAYER (1-10)	2.00	.80	.20

☐ 1	Brian Bellows	3.00	1.20	.30
☐ 2	Benoit Brunet	3.00	1.20	.30
☐ 3	Guy Carbonneau	3.00	1.20	.30
☐ 4	Vincent Damphousse	4.00	1.60	.40
☐ 5	Jean-Jacques Diagneault	2.00	.80	.20
☐ 6	Kevin Haller	2.00	.80	.20
☐ 7	Mike Keane	3.00	1.20	.30
☐ 8	Kirk Muller	4.00	1.60	.40
☐ 9	Peter Popovic	2.00	.80	.20
☐ 10	Mathieu Schneider	3.00	1.20	.30

1992-93 Canadiens Postcards

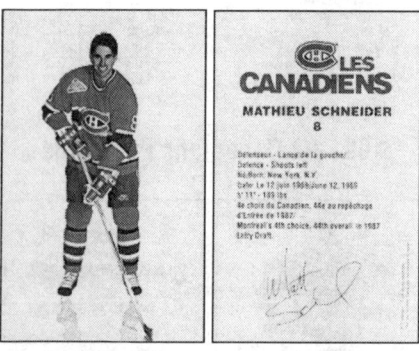

This 27-card team-issued set measures 3 1/2" by 5 1/2" and features full-bleed glossy color player photos. The players are posed on the ice against a white background. The backs are white and show the team name in large red letters at the top. The player's name, number, and biography are printed in blue. A facsimile autograph at the bottom rounds out the back. The cards are unnumbered and checklisted below in alphabetical order.

	MINT	EXC	G-VG
COMPLETE SET (27)	12.00	5.00	1.20
COMMON PLAYER (1-27)	.40	.16	.04

☐ 1	Brian Bellows	1.00	.40	.10
☐ 2	Patrice Brisebois	.75	.30	.07
☐ 3	Benoit Brunet	.60	.24	.06
☐ 4	Guy Carbonneau	.60	.24	.06
☐ 5	Jean-Jacques Daigneault	.40	.16	.04
☐ 6	Vincent Damphousse	1.25	.50	.12
☐ 7	Eric Dejardins	.60	.24	.06
☐ 8	Jacques Demers CO	1.00	.40	.10
☐ 9	Gilbert Dionne	.75	.30	.07
☐ 10	Donald Dufresne	.40	.16	.04
☐ 11	Todd Ewen	.40	.16	.04
☐ 12	Kevin Haller	.60	.24	.06
☐ 13	Sean Hill	.60	.24	.06
☐ 14	Mike Keane	.60	.24	.06
☐ 15	Patric Kjellberg	.60	.24	.06
☐ 16	Stephan Lebeau	1.00	.40	.10
☐ 17	John LeClair	.75	.30	.07
☐ 18	Kirk Muller	1.25	.50	.12
☐ 19	Lyle Odelein	.60	.24	.06
☐ 20	Oleg Petrov	.60	.24	.06
☐ 21	Andre Racicot	.60	.24	.06
☐ 22	Mario Roberge	.40	.16	.04
☐ 23	Ed Ronan	.60	.24	.06

1993-94 Canadiens Postcards

This 27-card, team-issued set measures approximately 3 1/2" by 5 1/2" and features full-bleed glossy color player photos. The players are posed on the ice against a white background. The bilingual (French and English) backs are white and show the team name in large red letters at the top. The player's name, number, and biography are printed in blue. A facsimile autograph at the bottom rounds out the back. The cards are unnumbered and checklisted below in alphabetical order.

	MINT	EXC	G-VG
COMPLETE SET (27)	12.00	5.00	1.20
COMMON PLAYER (1-27)	.40	.16	.04

☐ 1	Brian Bellows	.75	.30	.07
☐ 2	Patrice Brisebois	.60	.24	.06
☐ 3	Benoit Brunet	.60	.24	.06
☐ 4	Guy Carbonneau	.75	.30	.07
☐ 5	Jean-Jacques Daigneault	.60	.24	.06
☐ 6	Vincent Damphousse	1.00	.40	.10

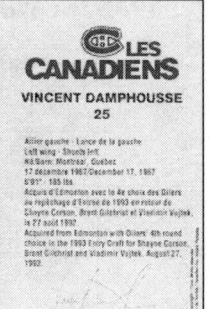

		NRMT	VG-E	GOOD
☐	4 Gary Doak	3.00	1.20	.30
☐	5 George Gardner	2.50	1.00	.25
☐	6 Murray Hall	2.50	1.00	.25
☐	7 Charlie Hodge	4.00	1.60	.40
☐	8 Danny Johnson	2.50	1.00	.25
☐	9 Orland Kurtenbach	3.50	1.40	.35
☐	10 Wayne Maki	3.00	1.20	.30
☐	11 Rosaire Paiement	2.50	1.00	.25
☐	12 Poul Popiel	3.00	1.20	.30
☐	13 Pat Quinn	5.00	2.00	.50
☐	14 Marc Reaume	2.50	1.00	.25
☐	15 Darryl Sly	2.50	1.00	.25
☐	16 Dale Tallon	3.00	1.20	.30
☐	17 Ted Taylor	3.00	1.20	.30
☐	18 Barry Wilkins	2.50	1.00	.25
☐	19 Dunc Wilson	3.00	1.20	.30
☐	20 Jim Wiste	2.50	1.00	.25

1971-72 Canucks Royal Bank

☐	7 Jacques Demers CO	.75	.30	.07
☐	8 Eric Desjardins	.60	.24	.06
☐	9 Gilbert Dionne	.75	.30	.07
☐	10 Paul Dipietro	.60	.24	.06
☐	11 Kevin Haller	.60	.24	.06
☐	12 Mike Keane	.60	.24	.06
☐	13 Stephan LeBeau	.75	.30	.07
☐	14 John LeClair	.75	.30	.07
☐	15 Gary Leeman	.60	.24	.06
☐	16 Kirk Muller	1.00	.40	.10
☐	17 Lyle Odelein	.60	.24	.06
☐	18 Peter Popovic	.40	.16	.04
☐	19 Andre Racicot	.60	.24	.06
☐	20 Rob Ramage	.60	.24	.06
☐	21 Mario Roberge	.40	.16	.04
☐	22 Ed Ronan	.60	.24	.06
☐	23 Patrick Roy	2.50	1.00	.25
☐	24 Mathieu Schneider	.75	.30	.07
☐	25 Pierre Sevigny	.40	.16	.04
☐	26 Ron Wilson	.40	.16	.04

1970-71 Canucks Royal Bank

This 20-card set of Vancouver Canucks was sponsored by Royal Bank, whose company logo appears at the lower left corner on the front. The set is subtitled Leo's Leaders Canucks Player of the Week. The black and white posed player photos measure approximately 5" by 7" and have white borders. The player's signature is inscribed across the bottom of the picture, and the backs are blank. The cards are unnumbered and checklisted below in alphabetical order.

		NRMT	VG-E	GOOD
COMPLETE SET (20)		40.00	16.00	4.00
COMMON PLAYER (1-20)		2.50	1.00	.25
☐	1 Andre Boudrias	2.50	1.00	.25
☐	2 Mike Corrigan	2.50	1.00	.25
☐	3 Ray Cullen	3.00	1.20	.30

This 20-card set of Vancouver Canucks was sponsored by Royal Bank, whose company logo appears at the lower left corner on the front. The set is subtitled Leo's Leaders Canucks Player of the Week. The black and white posed player photos measure approximately 5" by 7" and have white borders. The player's signature is inscribed across the bottom of the picture, and the backs are blank. The cards are numbered by week of issue. Card number 10 is unknown and may have never been issued.

		NRMT	VG-E	GOOD
COMPLETE SET (20)		40.00	16.00	4.00
COMMON PLAYER (1-21)		2.50	1.00	.25
☐	1 Bobby Lalonde	2.50	1.00	.25
☐	2 Mike Corrigan	2.50	1.00	.25
☐	3 Murray Hall	2.50	1.00	.25
☐	4 Jocelyn Guevremont	3.00	1.20	.30
☐	5 Pat Quinn	5.00	2.00	.50
☐	6 Orland Kurtenbach	3.50	1.40	.35
☐	7 Poul Popiel	3.00	1.20	.30
☐	8 Ron Ward	2.50	1.00	.25
☐	9 Rosaire Paiement	2.50	1.00	.25
☐	11 Dale Tallon	3.00	1.20	.30
☐	12 Bobby Schmautz	3.00	1.20	.30
☐	13 Dennis Kearns	2.50	1.00	.25
☐	14 Barry Wilkins	2.50	1.00	.25
☐	15 Dunc Wilson	3.00	1.20	.30
☐	16 Andre Boudrias	2.50	1.00	.25
☐	17 Ted Taylor	3.00	1.20	.30
☐	18 George Gardner	2.50	1.00	.25
☐	19 John Schella	2.50	1.00	.25
☐	20 Wayne Maki	3.00	1.20	.30
☐	21 Gary Doak	3.00	1.20	.30

1972-73 Canucks Nalley's

This six-card set was available on the backs of specially marked Nalley's Triple Pak Potato Chips boxes. The back

Wayne Maki — Forward

yellow panel has a 6 3/4" by 5 3/8" (approximately) action shot of a Canuck player beside the goalie and net. One player card is superimposed over the lower left corner of this large action photo. The card is framed by a thin perforated line; if the card were cut out, it would measure about 3" by 3 3/4". The front features a close-up posed color player photo (from the waste up) with white borders. The player's name and position appear in white bottom border. The backs are blank. At the bottom of each back panel are miniature blue-tinted versions of all six player cards. The cards are unnumbered and checklisted below in alphabetical order.

		MINT	EXC	G-VG
COMPLETE SET (6)		100.00	40.00	10.00
COMMON PLAYER (1-6)		20.00	8.00	2.00
☐ 1	Andre Boudrias	20.00	8.00	2.00
☐ 2	George Gardner	20.00	8.00	2.00
☐ 3	Wayne Maki	25.00	10.00	2.50
☐ 4	Rosaire Paiement	20.00	8.00	2.00
☐ 5	Pat Quinn	30.00	12.00	3.00
☐ 6	Barry Wilkins	20.00	8.00	2.00

1972-73 Canucks Royal Bank

This 21-card set of Vancouver Canucks was sponsored by Royal Bank, whose company logo appears at the lower left corner on the front. The set is subtitled Leo's Leaders Canucks Player of the Week. These colorful full body player photos measure approximately 5" by 7" and have white borders. The background of the photos ranges from light blue to royal blue. The player's facsimile signature is inscribed across the bottom of the picture, and the backs are blank. The cards are unnumbered on the front and checklisted below in alphabetical order.

		NRMT	VG-E	GOOD
COMPLETE SET (21)		35.00	14.00	3.50
COMMON PLAYER (1-21)		2.00	.80	.20
☐ 1	Dave Balon	2.00	.80	.20
☐ 2	Gregg Boddy	2.00	.80	.20
☐ 3	Larry Bolonchuk	2.00	.80	.20
☐ 4	Andro Boudrias	2.00	.80	.20
☐ 5	Ed Dyck	2.00	.80	.20
☐ 6	Jocelyn Guevremont	2.50	1.00	.25
☐ 7	James Hargreaves	2.00	.80	.20
☐ 8	Dennis Kearns	2.00	.80	.20
☐ 9	Orland Kurtenbach	3.00	1.20	.30
☐ 10	Bobby Lalonde	2.00	.80	.20
☐ 11	Richard Lemieux	2.00	.80	.20
☐ 12	Don Lever	2.50	1.00	.25
☐ 13	Wayne Maki	2.50	1.00	.25
☐ 14	Bryan McSceffrey	2.00	.80	.20
☐ 15	Gerry O'Flaherty	2.00	.80	.20
☐ 16	Bobby Schmautz	2.50	1.00	.25
☐ 17	Dale Tallon	2.50	1.00	.25
☐ 18	Don Tannahill	2.00	.80	.20
☐ 19	Barry Wilkins	2.00	.80	.20
☐ 20	Dunc Wilson	2.50	1.00	.25
☐ 21	John Wright	2.00	.80	.20

1973-74 Canucks Royal Bank

Royal Leaders
CANUCKS PLAYER OF THE WEEK

This 21-card set of Vancouver Canucks was sponsored by Royal Bank, whose company logo appears at the lower left corner on the front. The set is subtitled Royal Leaders Canucks Player of the Week. These colorful full body player photos measure approximately 5" by 7" and have white borders. The background of the photos ranges from yellowish green to green. The player's facsimile signature is inscribed across the bottom of the picture, and the backs are blank. The cards are unnumbered on the front and checklisted below in alphabetical order.

		NRMT	VG-E	GOOD
COMPLETE SET (21)		35.00	14.00	3.50
COMMON PLAYER (1-21)		2.00	.80	.20
☐ 1	Paulin Bordeleau	2.00	.80	.20
☐ 2	Andre Boudrias	2.00	.80	.20
☐ 3	Jacques Caron	2.00	.80	.20
☐ 4	Bob Dailey	2.00	.80	.20
☐ 5	Dave Dunn	2.00	.80	.20
☐ 6	Jocelyn Guevremont	2.50	1.00	.25
☐ 7	Dennis Kearns	2.00	.80	.20
☐ 8	Jerry Korab	2.00	.80	.20
☐ 9	Orland Kurtenbach	3.00	1.20	.30
☐ 10	Bobby Lalonde	2.00	.80	.20
☐ 11	Richard Lemieux	2.00	.80	.20
☐ 12	Don Lever	2.50	1.00	.25
☐ 13	Bill McCreary	2.00	.80	.20
☐ 14	Bryan McScheffrey	2.00	.80	.20
☐ 15	Gerry O'Flaherty	2.00	.80	.20
☐ 16	Bobby Schmautz	2.50	1.00	.25
☐ 17	Gary Smith	3.00	1.20	.30
☐ 18	Don Tannahill	2.00	.80	.20
☐ 19	Dennis Ververgaert	2.50	1.00	.25
☐ 20	Barry Wilkins	2.00	.80	.20
☐ 21	John Wright	2.00	.80	.20

1974-75 Canucks Royal Bank

Royal Leaders
PLAYER OF THE WEEK

This 20-card set of Vancouver Canucks was sponsored by Royal Bank, whose company logo appears at the lower left corner on the front. The set is subtitled Royal Leaders Player of the Week. These colorful head and shoulders player photos are presented on a white background with a thin black border. The cards measure approximately 5" by 7", have white borders, and are printed on glossy paper. The player's facsimile signature is inscribed across the bottom of the picture, and the backs are blank. The cards are unnumbered on the front and checklisted below in alphabetical order.

	NRMT	VG-E	GOOD
COMPLETE SET (20)	30.00	12.00	3.00
COMMON PLAYER (1-20)	2.00	.80	.20

		NRMT	VG-E	GOOD
☐ 1	Gregg Boddy	2.00	.80	.20
☐ 2	Paulin Bordeleau	2.00	.80	.20
☐ 3	Andre Boudrias	2.00	.80	.20
☐ 4	Bob Dailey	2.00	.80	.20
☐ 5	Ab DeMarco	2.00	.80	.20
☐ 6	John Gould	2.00	.80	.20
☐ 7	John Grisdale	2.00	.80	.20
☐ 8	Dennis Kearns	2.00	.80	.20
☐ 9	Bobby Lalonde	2.00	.80	.20
☐ 10	Don Lever	2.50	1.00	.25
☐ 11	Ken Lockett	2.00	.80	.20
☐ 12	Gerry Meehan	3.50	1.40	.35
☐ 13	Garry Monahan	2.00	.80	.20
☐ 14	Chris Oddleifson	2.00	.80	.20
☐ 15	Gerry O'Flaherty	2.00	.80	.20
☐ 16	Tracy Pratt	2.00	.80	.20
☐ 17	Mike Robitaille	2.00	.80	.20
☐ 18	Leon Rochefort	2.00	.80	.20
☐ 19	Gary Smith	3.00	1.20	.30
☐ 20	Dennis Ververgaert	2.50	1.00	.25

1975-76 Canucks Royal Bank

This 22-card set of Vancouver Canucks was sponsored by Royal Bank, whose company logo appears at the lower left corner on the front. The set is subtitled Royal Leaders Player of the Week. The cards measure approximately 4 3/4" by 7 1/4" and are printed on glossy paper. The fronts feature a color head and shoulders shot of the player on white background with a thin black border. The player's facsimile autograph appears below the picture. The backs are blank. The cards are unnumbered and we have checklisted them below in alphabetical order.

	NRMT	VG-E	GOOD
COMPLETE SET (22)	30.00	12.00	3.00
COMMON PLAYER (1-22)	1.50	.60	.15

☐ 1	Rick Blight	1.50	.60	.15
☐ 2	Gregg Boddy	1.50	.60	.15
☐ 3	Paulin Bordeleau	1.50	.60	.15
☐ 4	Andre Boudrias	1.50	.60	.15
☐ 5	Bob Dailey	1.50	.60	.15
☐ 6	Ab DeMarco	1.50	.60	.15
☐ 7	John Gould	1.50	.60	.15
☐ 8	John Grisdale	1.50	.60	.15
☐ 9	Dennis Kearns	1.50	.60	.15

☐ 10	Bobby Lalonde	1.50	.60	.15
☐ 11	Don Lever	2.00	.80	.20
☐ 12	Ken Lockett	1.50	.60	.15
☐ 13	Garry Monahan	1.50	.60	.15
☐ 14	Bob Murray	1.50	.60	.15
☐ 15	Chris Oddleifson	1.50	.60	.15
☐ 16	Gerry O'Flaherty	1.50	.60	.15
☐ 17	Tracy Pratt	1.50	.60	.15
☐ 18	Mike Robitaille	1.50	.60	.15
☐ 19	Ron Sedlbauer	1.50	.60	.15
☐ 20	Gary Smith	2.50	1.00	.25
☐ 21	Harold Snepsts	6.00	2.40	.60
☐ 22	Dennis Ververgaert	2.00	.80	.20

1976-77 Canucks Royal Bank

This 23-card set of Vancouver Canucks was sponsored by Royal Bank, whose company logo appears at the lower left corner on the front. The set is subtitled Royal Leaders Canucks Player of the Week. The cards measure approximately 4 3/4" by 7 1/4" and are printed on glossy paper. The fronts feature a color head and shoulders shot of the player on white background with a thin black border. The player's facsimile autograph appears below the picture. The backs are blank. The cards are unnumbered and we have checklisted them below in alphabetical order.

	NRMT	VG-E	GOOD
COMPLETE SET (23)	30.00	12.00	3.00
COMMON PLAYER (1-23)	1.50	.60	.15

☐ 1	Rick Blight	1.50	.60	.15
☐ 2	Bob Dailey	1.50	.60	.15
☐ 3	Dave Fortier	1.50	.60	.15
☐ 4	Brad Gassoff	1.50	.60	.15
☐ 5	John Gould	1.50	.60	.15
☐ 6	John Grisdale	1.50	.60	.15
☐ 7	Dennis Kearns	1.50	.60	.15
☐ 8	Bobby Lalonde	1.50	.60	.15
☐ 9	Don Lever	2.00	.80	.20
☐ 10	Cesare Maniago	3.50	1.40	.35
☐ 11	Garry Monahan	1.50	.60	.15
☐ 12	Bob Murray	1.50	.60	.15
☐ 13	Chris Oddleifson	1.50	.60	.15
☐ 14	Gerry O'Flaherty	1.50	.60	.15
☐ 15	Curt Ridley	1.50	.60	.15
☐ 16	Mike Robitaille	1.50	.60	.15
☐ 17	Ron Sedlbauer	1.50	.60	.15
☐ 18	Harold Snepsts	4.00	1.60	.40
☐ 19	Andy Spruce	1.50	.60	.15
☐ 20	Ralph Stewart	1.50	.60	.15
☐ 21	Dennis Ververgaert	2.00	.80	.20
☐ 22	Mike Walton	2.50	1.00	.25
☐ 23	Jim Wiley	1.50	.60	.15

1977-78 Canucks Royal Bank

This 21-card set of Vancouver Canucks was sponsored by Royal Bank, whose company logo appears at the lower left corner on the front. The set is subtitled Royal Leaders

Player of the Week. The cards measure approximately 4 1/4" by 5 1/2" and are printed on thin cardboard stock. The fronts feature a color head and shoulders shot of the player on white background with a thin black border. The player's facsimile autograph appears below the picture. The backs are blank. The cards are unnumbered; they are checklisted below in alphabetical order.

		NRMT	VG-E	GOOD
COMPLETE SET (21)		25.00	10.00	2.50
COMMON PLAYER (1-21)		1.50	.60	.15
☐ 1	Rick Blight	1.50	.60	.15
☐ 2	Larry Carriere	1.50	.60	.15
☐ 3	Rob Flockhart	1.50	.60	.15
☐ 4	Brad Gassoff	1.50	.60	.15
☐ 5	Jere Gillis	1.50	.60	.15
☐ 6	Larry Goodenough	1.50	.60	.15
☐ 7	Hilliard Graves	1.50	.60	.15
☐ 8	John Grisdale	1.50	.60	.15
☐ 9	Dennis Kearns	1.50	.60	.15
☐ 10	Don Lever	2.00	.80	.20
☐ 11	Cesare Maniago	3.00	1.20	.30
☐ 12	Bob Manno	1.50	.60	.15
☐ 13	Jack McIlhargey	1.50	.60	.15
☐ 14	Garry Monahan	1.50	.60	.15
☐ 15	Chris Oddleifson	1.50	.60	.15
☐ 16	Gerry O'Flaherty	1.50	.60	.15
☐ 17	Curt Ridley	1.50	.60	.15
☐ 18	Ron Sedlbauer	1.50	.60	.15
☐ 19	Harold Snepsts	3.00	1.20	.30
☐ 20	Dennis Ververgaert	2.00	.80	.20
☐ 21	Mike Walton	2.00	.80	.20

1978-79 Canucks Royal Bank

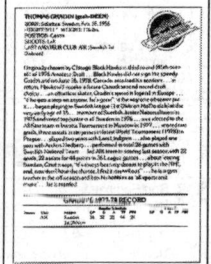

This 23-card set of Vancouver Canucks was sponsored by Royal Bank, whose company logo appears at the upper left corner on the front. The cards measure approximately 4 1/4" by 5 1/2" and are printed on thin cardboard stock. The fronts feature a color head and shoulders shot of the player on white background with a thin blue border. The player's

facsimile autograph and the team logo appear above the picture. The backs present biographical and statistical information. The cards are unnumbered; they are checklisted below in alphabetical order.

		NRMT	VG-E	GOOD
COMPLETE SET (23)		25.00	10.00	2.50
COMMON PLAYER (1-23)		1.50	.60	.15
☐ 1	Rick Blight	1.50	.60	.15
☐ 2	Gary Bromley	2.00	.80	.20
☐ 3	Bill Derlago	1.50	.60	.15
☐ 4	Roland Eriksson	1.50	.60	.15
☐ 5	Curt Fraser	2.00	.80	.20
☐ 6	Jere Gillis	1.50	.60	.15
☐ 7	Thomas Gradin	3.00	1.20	.30
☐ 8	Hilliard Graves	1.50	.60	.15
☐ 9	John Grisdale	1.50	.60	.15
☐ 10	Glen Hanlon	2.50	1.00	.25
☐ 11	Randy Holt	1.50	.60	.15
☐ 12	Dennis Kearns	1.50	.60	.15
☐ 13	Don Lever	2.00	.80	.20
☐ 14	Lars Lindgren	1.50	.60	.15
☐ 15	Bob Manno	1.50	.60	.15
☐ 16	Pit Martin	2.00	.80	.20
☐ 17	Jack McIlhargey	1.50	.60	.15
☐ 18	Chris Oddleifson	1.50	.60	.15
☐ 19	Ron Sedlbauer	1.50	.60	.15
☐ 20	Stan Smyl	3.50	1.40	.35
☐ 21	Harold Snepsts	3.00	1.20	.30
☐ 22	Dennis Ververgaert	2.00	.80	.20
☐ 23	Lars Zetterstrom	1.50	.60	.15

1979-80 Canucks Royal Bank

This 22-card set features posed color player photos from the shoulders up of the Vancouver Canucks. There are actually two different sets with the same value, a team-issued (no reference to Royal Bank) blank back set and a Royal Bank set; the card pictures are the same in both sets. The sponsor name appears in black print at the card top, with the words "Player of the Week 1979/80" immediately below. The cards measure approximately 4 1/4" by 5 1/2". The front features a color head shot with a blue background and black and white borders. The player's jersey number, facsimile autograph, and team logo appear in the bottom white border. Since this is an unnumbered set, the cards are listed alphabetically. The Royal Bank backs carry biography, career summary, and complete statistical information (season by season, regular schedule, and playoffs).

		MINT	EXC	G-VG
COMPLETE SET (22)		25.00	10.00	2.50
COMMON PLAYER (1-22)		1.50	.60	.15
☐ 1	Brent Ashton	2.00	.80	.20
☐ 2	Rick Blight	1.50	.60	.15
☐ 3	Gary Bromley	2.00	.80	.20
☐ 4	Drew Callander	1.50	.60	.15
☐ 5	Bill Derlago	1.50	.60	.15
☐ 6	Curt Fraser	2.00	.80	.20

		MINT	EXC	G-VG
☐ 7	Jere Gillis	1.50	.60	.15
☐ 8	Thomas Gradin	2.50	1.00	.25
☐ 9	Glen Hanlon	2.50	1.00	.25
☐ 10	John Hughes	1.50	.60	.15
☐ 11	Dennis Kearns	1.50	.60	.15
☐ 12	Don Lever	2.00	.80	.20
☐ 13	Lars Lindgren	1.50	.60	.15
☐ 14	Bob Manno	1.50	.60	.15
☐ 15	Kevin McCarthy	1.50	.60	.15
☐ 16	Jack McIlhargey	1.50	.60	.15
☐ 17	Chris Oddleifson	1.50	.60	.15
☐ 18	Curt Ridley	1.50	.60	.15
☐ 19	Ron Sedlbauer	1.50	.60	.15
☐ 20	Stan Smyl	2.50	1.00	.25
☐ 21	Harold Snepsts	3.00	1.20	.30
☐ 22	Rick Vaive	2.50	1.00	.25

		MINT	EXC	G-VG
☐ 9	Thomas Gradin	2.50	1.00	.25
☐ 10	Glen Hanlon	2.50	1.00	.25
☐ 11	Dennis Kearns	1.50	.60	.15
☐ 12	Rick Lanz	1.50	.60	.15
☐ 13	Lars Lindgren	1.50	.60	.15
☐ 14	Dave Logan	1.50	.60	.15
☐ 15	Gary Lupul	1.50	.60	.15
☐ 16	Kevin McCarthy	1.50	.60	.15
☐ 17	Gerry Minor	1.50	.60	.15
☐ 18	Darcy Rota	1.50	.60	.15
☐ 19	Bobby Schmautz	2.00	.80	.20
☐ 20	Stan Smyl	2.50	1.00	.25
☐ 21	Harold Snepsts	3.00	1.20	.30
☐ 22	Tiger Williams	3.00	1.20	.30

1980-81 Canucks Silverwood Dairy

This 24-card set of Vancouver Canucks was sponsored by Silverwood Dairy. The cards measure approximately 2 1/2" by 3 1/2" individually but were issued as perforated panels of three. The cards are checklisted below in alphabetical order, with the panel number after the player's name.

	MINT	EXC	G-VG
COMPLETE SET (24)	40.00	16.00	4.00
COMMON PLAYER (1-24)	1.50	.60	.15

		MINT	EXC	G-VG
☐ 1	Brent Ashton 6	2.00	.80	.20
☐ 2	Ivan Boldirev 4	2.00	.80	.20
☐ 3	Per-Olov Brasar 5	1.50	.60	.15
☐ 4	Richard Brodeur 3	4.00	1.60	.40
☐ 5	Gary Bromley 4	2.00	.80	.20
☐ 6	Jerry Butler 1	1.50	.60	.15
☐ 7	Colin Campbell 5	2.50	1.00	.25
☐ 8	Curt Fraser 8	2.00	.80	.20
☐ 9	Thomas Gradin 6	2.50	1.00	.25
☐ 10	Glen Hanlon 5	2.00	.80	.20
☐ 11	Dennis Kearns 6	1.50	.60	.15
☐ 12	Rick Lanz 2	1.50	.60	.15
☐ 13	Lars Lindgren 7	1.50	.60	.15
☐ 14	Dave Logan 8	1.50	.60	.15
☐ 15	Gary Lupul 3	1.50	.60	.15
☐ 16	Bob Manno 1	1.50	.60	.15
☐ 17	Kevin McCarthy 3	1.50	.60	.15
☐ 18	Garry Minor 2	1.50	.60	.15
☐ 19	Kevin Primeau 7	1.50	.60	.15
☐ 20	Darcy Rota 2	1.50	.60	.15
☐ 21	Stan Smyl 1	2.50	1.00	.25
☐ 22	Harold Snepsts 4	3.00	1.20	.30
☐ 23	Bobby Schmautz 8	2.00	.80	.20
☐ 24	Dave(Tiger) Williams 7	3.00	1.20	.30

1980-81 Canucks Team Issue

This 22-card set measures approximately 3 3/4" by 4 7/8" and features posed color head and shoulder player photos against a light blue-gray background. The pictures have rounded corners and are enclosed by thick black and thin red border stripes. The player's name, uniform number, position, and the team logo appear in the thicker bottom border. A facsimile autograph runs vertically to the left of the player's head. The backs are blank.

	MINT	EXC	G-VG
COMPLETE SET (22)	25.00	10.00	2.50
COMMON PLAYER (1-22)	1.50	.60	.15

		MINT	EXC	G-VG
☐ 1	Brent Ashton	2.00	.80	.20
☐ 2	Ivan Boldirev	2.00	.80	.20
☐ 3	Per-Olov Brasar	1.50	.60	.15
☐ 4	Richard Brodeur	3.00	1.20	.30
☐ 5	Gary Bromley	2.00	.80	.20
☐ 6	Jerry Butler	1.50	.60	.15
☐ 7	Colin Campbell	2.50	1.00	.25
☐ 8	Curt Fraser	2.00	.80	.20

1981-82 Canucks Silverwood Dairy

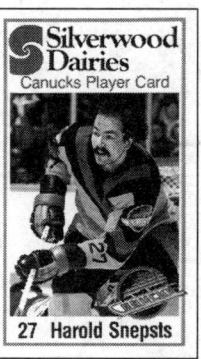 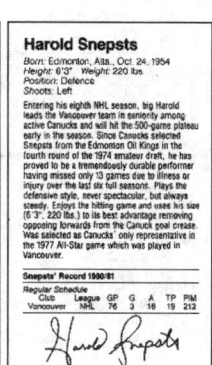

27 Harold Snepsts

This 24-card set of Vancouver Canucks was sponsored by Silverwood Dairy, and the sponsor's name and logo appear at the top of the card face. The cards measure approximately 2 7/16" by 4 1/16" and feature a color action player photo, with the team logo superimposed at the lower right corner of the picture. The sponsor information above and the player information below the photo are enframed by an orange border (on white cardboard stock). The backs have career summary and statistics, as well as a facsimile autograph of the player at the bottom of the card. The cards are unnumbered and are checklisted by the order they appear on the panels. The panel number is given after the name for each card in the checklist below.

	MINT	EXC	G-VG
COMPLETE SET (24)	20.00	8.00	2.00
COMMON PLAYER (1-24)	1.00	.40	.10

		MINT	EXC	G-VG
☐ 1	Rick Lanz 1	1.00	.40	.10
☐ 2	Curt Fraser 1	1.25	.50	.12
☐ 3	Marc Crawford 1	1.00	.40	.10
☐ 4	Ivan Hlinka 2	1.50	.60	.15
☐ 5	Jerry Butler 2	1.00	.40	.10
☐ 6	Doug Halward 2	1.00	.40	.10
☐ 7	Glen Hanlon 2	1.50	.60	.15
☐ 8	Harold Snepsts 3	2.50	1.00	.25
☐ 9	Gerry Minor 3	1.00	.40	.10
☐ 10	Richard Brodeur 4	2.50	1.00	.25
☐ 11	Lars Lindren 4	1.00	.40	.10
☐ 12	Darcy Rota 4	1.00	.40	.10
☐ 13	Stan Smyl 5	2.00	.80	.20
☐ 14	Colin Campbell 5	2.00	.80	.20
☐ 15	Per-Olov Brasar 5	1.00	.40	.10
☐ 16	Dave(Tiger) Williams 6	2.50	1.00	.25
☐ 17	Anders Eldebrink 6	1.00	.40	.10
☐ 18	Gary Lupul 6	1.00	.40	.10
☐ 19	Thomas Gradin 7	1.50	.60	.15
☐ 20	Jiri Bubla 7	1.00	.40	.10
☐ 21	Blair MacDonald 7	1.00	.40	.10
☐ 22	Kevin McCarthy 8	1.00	.40	.10
☐ 23	Ivan Boldirev 8	1.25	.50	.12
☐ 24	Lars Molin 8	1.00	.40	.10

1981-82 Canucks Team Issue

This 20-card set measures approximately 3 3/4" by 4 7/8" and features posed color head and shoulder player photos against a blue background. The pictures have rounded corners and are enclosed by thick black and thin red border stripes. The player's name, uniform number, position, and the team logo appear in the thicker bottom border. A facsimile autograph runs vertically to the left of the player's head. The backs are blank. The card of Richard Brodeur is the same one used in the 1980-81 team-issued set.

	MINT	EXC	G-VG
COMPLETE SET (20)	20.00	8.00	2.00
COMMON PLAYER (1-20)	1.00	.40	.10

		MINT	EXC	G-VG
☐	1 Ivan Boldirev	1.25	.50	.12
☐	2 Per-Olov Brasar	1.00	.40	.10
☐	3 Richard Brodeur	2.50	1.00	.25
☐	4 Jiri Bubla	1.00	.40	.10
☐	5 Jerry Butler	1.00	.40	.10
☐	6 Colin Campbell	2.00	.80	.20
☐	7 Anders Eldebrink	1.00	.40	.10
☐	8 Curt Fraser	1.25	.50	.12
☐	9 Thomas Gradin	2.00	.80	.20
☐	10 Doug Halward	1.00	.40	.10
☐	11 Glen Hanlon	1.50	.60	.15
☐	12 Rick Lanz	1.00	.40	.10
☐	13 Gary Lupul	1.00	.40	.10
☐	14 Blair MacDonald	1.00	.40	.10
☐	15 Kevin McCarthy	1.00	.40	.10
☐	16 Gerry Minor	1.00	.40	.10
☐	17 Lars Molin	1.00	.40	.10
☐	18 Darcy Rota	1.00	.40	.10
☐	19 Stan Smyl	1.50	.60	.15
☐	20 Tiger Williams	2.50	1.00	.25

1983-84 Canucks

 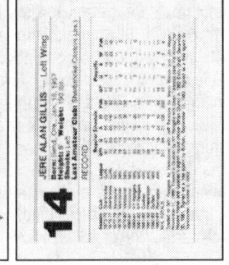

This 23-card set of Vancouver Canucks was issued in three panels of six cards each, with the fourth panel having 5 cards (the team photo card fills the space of two player cards). The player cards measure approximately 3 11/16" by 4 5/8". The front features a color posed photo (with rounded corners) of the player, surrounded by a thick black and a thin red border. The Canucks' logo and player information appear below the picture. The back has biographical and statistical information in a horizontal format. We have checklisted the names below in alphabetical order, with the uniform number to the right of the name.

	MINT	EXC	G-VG
COMPLETE SET (23)	20.00	8.00	2.00
COMMON PLAYER (1-23)	.75	.30	.07

		MINT	EXC	G-VG
☐	1 Richard Brodeur 35	2.00	.80	.20
☐	2 Jiri Bubla 29	.75	.30	.07
☐	3 Garth Butcher 5	2.00	.80	.20
☐	4 Marc Crawford 28	.75	.30	.07
☐	5 Ron Delorme 19	.75	.30	.07
☐	6 John Garrett 31	1.00	.40	.10
☐	7 Jere Gillis 4	.75	.30	.07

		MINT	EXC	G-VG
☐	8 Thomas Gradin 23	1.50	.60	.15
☐	9 Doug Halward 2	.75	.30	.07
☐	10 Mark Kirton 16	.75	.30	.07
☐	11 Rick Lanz 4	.75	.30	.07
☐	12 Gary Lupul 7	.75	.30	.07
☐	13 Kevin McCarthy 25	.75	.30	.07
☐	14 Lars Molin 26	.75	.30	.07
☐	15 Jim Nill 8	.75	.30	.07
☐	16 Michel Petit 3	1.00	.40	.10
☐	17 Darcy Rota 18	.75	.30	.07
☐	18 Stan Smyl 12	1.50	.60	.15
☐	19 Harold Snepsts 27	2.00	.80	.20
☐	20 Patrik Sundstrom 17	1.50	.60	.15
☐	21 Tony Tanti 9	1.50	.60	.15
☐	22 Dave(Tiger) Williams 22	2.00	.80	.20
☐	23 Team Photo	3.00	1.20	.30

1984-85 Canucks

This 26-card set of Vancouver Canucks was issued in four six-card panels plus a larger team photo card and a Air Canucks advertisement card (the latter two measure approximately 4 5/8" by 7"). The player cards measure 3 5/16" by 4 1/4". The key card in the set is Cam Neely appearing in his Rookie Card year. The cards are unnumbered and checklisted below in alphabetical order.

	MINT	EXC	G-VG
COMPLETE SET (26)	20.00	8.00	2.00
COMMON PLAYER (1-26)	.60	.24	.06

		MINT	EXC	G-VG
☐	1 Neil Belland	.60	.24	.06
☐	2 Richard Brodeur	1.25	.50	.12
☐	3 Jiri Bubla	.60	.24	.06
☐	4 Garth Butcher	1.00	.40	.10
☐	5 Frank Caprice	.75	.30	.07
☐	6 J.J. Daigneault	.75	.30	.07
☐	7 Ron Delorme	.60	.24	.06
☐	8 John Garrett	1.00	.40	.10
☐	9 Thomas Gradin	1.25	.50	.12
☐	10 Taylor Hall	.60	.24	.06
☐	11 Doug Halward	.60	.24	.06
☐	12 Rick Lanz	.60	.24	.06
☐	13 Moe Lemay	.60	.24	.06
☐	14 Gary Lidster	.75	.30	.07
☐	15 Gary Lupul	.60	.24	.06
☐	16 Al MacAdam	.60	.24	.06
☐	17 Peter McNab	.75	.30	.07
☐	18 Cam Neely	7.50	3.00	.75
☐	19 Michel Petit	.75	.30	.07
☐	20 Darcy Rota	.60	.24	.06
☐	21 Petri Skriko	1.00	.40	.10
☐	22 Stan Smyl	1.00	.40	.10
☐	23 Patrik Sundstrom	1.00	.40	.10
☐	24 Tony Tanti	1.00	.40	.10
☐	25 Team Photo (Large size)	3.00	1.20	.30
☐	26 Air Canuck. (Advertisement)	.75	.30	.07

1985-86 Canucks

This 25-card set of Vancouver Canucks was issued in four panels of six cards each, with a separate team photo card.

The player cards measure approximately 3 3/8" by 4 1/4". The team photo measures approximately 7" by 4 5/8". The fronts feature color posed player photos (with rounded corners) surrounded by thick black and thin red borders. The Canucks' logo and player information appear below the picture. The backs are blank. The cards are unnumbered and checklisted below in alphabetical order.

	MINT	EXC	G-VG
COMPLETE SET (25)	20.00	8.00	2.00
COMMON PLAYER (1-25)	.60	.24	.06
☐ 1 Richard Brodeur	1.25	.50	.12
☐ 2 Jiri Bubla	.60	.24	.06
☐ 3 Garth Butcher	1.00	.40	.10
☐ 4 Frank Caprice	.75	.30	.07
☐ 5 Glen Cochrane	.60	.24	.06
☐ 6 Craig Coxe	.60	.24	.06
☐ 7 J.J. Daigneault	.75	.30	.07
☐ 8 Thomas Gradin	1.00	.40	.10
☐ 9 Taylor Hall	.60	.24	.06
☐ 10 Doug Halward	.60	.24	.06
☐ 11 Jean-Marc Lanthier	.60	.24	.06
☐ 12 Rick Lanz	.60	.24	.06
☐ 13 Moe Lemay	.60	.24	.06
☐ 14 Doug Lidster	.75	.30	.07
☐ 15 Dave Lowry	.60	.24	.06
☐ 16 Gary Lupul	.60	.24	.06
☐ 17 Cam Neely	6.00	2.40	.60
☐ 18 Brent Peterson	.60	.24	.06
☐ 19 Jim Sandlak	1.00	.40	.10
☐ 20 Petri Skriko	1.00	.40	.10
☐ 21 Stan Smyl	1.00	.40	.10
☐ 22 Patrik Sundstrom	1.00	.40	.10
☐ 23 Steve Tambellini	.60	.24	.06
☐ 24 Tony Tanti	1.00	.40	.10
☐ 25 Team Photo	3.00	1.20	.30
(Large size)			

1986-87 Canucks

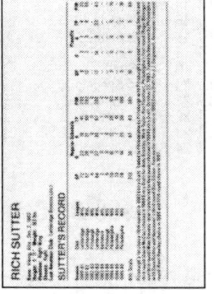

This 24-card set of Vancouver Canucks was issued in four panels of six cards each; after perforation, the cards measure the standard size (2 1/2" by 3 1/2"). The front design has color head and shoulder shots with white borders. Below the picture the player's name and number appear between two team logos. The horizontally oriented backs have biography and career statistics. The cards are unnumbered and checklisted below in alphabetical order, with the uniform number after the name.

	MINT	EXC	G-VG
COMPLETE SET (24)	12.00	5.00	1.20
COMMON PLAYER (1-24)	.60	.24	.06
☐ 1 Richard Brodeur 35	1.00	.40	.10
☐ 2 Garth Butcher 5	1.00	.40	.10
☐ 3 Frank Caprice 30	.75	.30	.07
☐ 4 Glen Cochrane 29	.60	.24	.06
☐ 5 Craig Coxe 32	.60	.24	.06
☐ 6 Taylor Hall 8	.60	.24	.06
☐ 7 Stu Kulak 16	.60	.24	.06
☐ 8 Moe Lemay 14	.60	.24	.06

☐ 9 Dave Lowry 22	.60	.24	.06
☐ 10 Brad Maxwell 27	.60	.24	.06
☐ 11 Petri Skriko 26	1.00	.40	.10
☐ 12 Barry Pederson 7	1.00	.40	.10
☐ 13 Rick Lanz 4	.60	.24	.06
☐ 14 Doug Lidster 3	.75	.30	.07
☐ 15 Brent Peterson 10	.60	.24	.06
☐ 16 Michel Petit 24	.75	.30	.07
☐ 17 Dave Richter 6	.60	.24	.06
☐ 18 Stan Smyl 12	1.00	.40	.10
☐ 19 Jim Sandlak 33	.75	.30	.07
☐ 20 Patrik Sundstrom 17	1.00	.40	.10
☐ 21 Rich Sutter 15	.75	.30	.07
☐ 22 Steve Tambellini 20	.60	.24	.06
☐ 23 Tony Tanti 9	1.00	.40	.10
☐ 24 Wendell Young 1	1.00	.40	.10

1987-88 Canucks Shell Oil

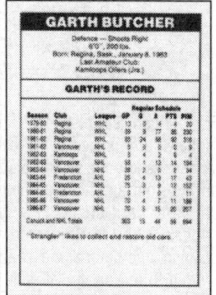

This 24-card set of Vancouver Canucks was sponsored by Shell Oil and released only in British Columbia. It was issued as eight different three-card panels, with the cards measuring the standard size, 2 1/2" by 3 1/2", after perforation. The cards were distributed as a promotion for Shell Oil, with one panel set per week given out at participating Shell stations. Included with the cards was a coupon offering a 5.00 discount on tickets to the Canucks games. The front features a color head and shoulders shot of the player, with the Canucks' logo superimposed at the upper left hand corner of the picture. The player's name, position, and the "Formula Shell" logo appear below the picture. The back has biographical and career information on the player. The cards are unnumbered and checklisted below in alphabetical order. Kirk McLean's card predates his Rookie Card by two years.

	MINT	EXC	G-VG
COMPLETE SET (24)	12.00	5.00	1.20
COMMON PLAYER (1-24)	.50	.20	.05
☐ 1 Greg Adams	1.25	.50	.12
☐ 2 Jim Benning	.60	.24	.06
☐ 3 Randy Boyd	.50	.20	.05
☐ 4 Richard Brodeur	1.00	.40	.10
☐ 5 David Bruce	.60	.24	.06
☐ 6 Garth Butcher	1.00	.40	.10
☐ 7 Frank Caprice	.50	.20	.05
☐ 8 Craig Coxe	.50	.20	.05
☐ 9 Willie Huber	.50	.20	.05
☐ 10 Doug Lidster	.60	.24	.06
☐ 11 Dave Lowry	.50	.20	.05
☐ 12 Kirk McLean	5.00	2.00	.50
☐ 13 Larry Melnyk	.50	.20	.05
☐ 14 Barry Pederson	.75	.30	.07
☐ 15 Dave Richter	.50	.20	.05
☐ 16 Jim Sandlak	.60	.24	.06
☐ 17 Dave Saunders	.50	.20	.05
☐ 18 Petri Skriko	.75	.30	.07
☐ 19 Stan Smyl	1.00	.40	.10
☐ 20 Daryl Stanley	.50	.20	.05
☐ 21 Rich Sutter	.75	.30	.07
☐ 22 Steve Tambellini	.50	.20	.05

☐	23 Tony Tanti	.75	.30	.07
☐	24 Doug Wickenheiser	.50	.20	.05

1988-89 Canucks Mohawk

"2" before it joining with the circular shape of the logo to suggest "20." The player's name, position, and number are given in black lettering running the bottom to top on the left side of the picture. The backs are blank. We have checklisted the cards below in alphabetical order, with the player's number to the right of his name.

This 24-card set of Vancouver Canucks was sponsored by Mohawk and issued in six panels of four cards each. The cards measure the standard size 2 1/2" by 3 1/2" and feature on the front a color head and shoulders shot of the player on white card stock. The Canucks' and Mohawk logos appear at the bottom of the card. The player's name, position, and number are given in black lettering running the bottom to top on the left side of the picture. The backs are blank. We have checklisted the cards below in alphabetical order, with the player's number to the right of his name. Trevor Linden and Kirk McLean's cards predate their Rookie Cards by one year.

	MINT	EXC	G-VG
COMPLETE SET (24)	15.00	6.00	1.50
COMMON PLAYER (1-24)	.50	.20	.05
☐ 1 Greg Adams 8	1.00	.40	.10
☐ 2 Jim Benning 4	.60	.24	.06
☐ 3 Ken Berry 18	.50	.20	.05
☐ 4 Randy Boyd 29	.50	.20	.05
☐ 5 Steve Bozek 14	.50	.20	.05
☐ 6 Brian Bradley 10	2.00	.80	.20
☐ 7 David Bruce 25	.60	.24	.06
☐ 8 Garth Butcher 5	1.00	.40	.10
☐ 9 Kevan Guy 2	.50	.20	.05
☐ 10 Doug Lidster 3	.60	.24	.06
☐ 11 Trevor Linden 16	5.00	2.00	.50
☐ 12 Kirk McLean 1	4.00	1.60	.40
☐ 13 Larry Melnyk 24	.50	.20	.05
☐ 14 Robert Nordmark 6	.50	.20	.05
☐ 15 Barry Pederson 7	.75	.30	.07
☐ 16 Paul Reinhart 23	1.00	.40	.10
☐ 17 Jim Sandlak 19	.60	.24	.06
☐ 18 Petri Skriko 26	.75	.30	.07
☐ 19 Stan Smyl 12	1.00	.40	.10
☐ 20 Harold Snepsts 27	1.50	.60	.15
☐ 21 Ronnie Stern 20	.60	.24	.06
☐ 22 Rich Sutter 15	.75	.30	.07
☐ 23 Tony Tanti 9	.75	.30	.07
☐ 24 Steve Weeks 31	.75	.30	.07

1989-90 Canucks Mohawk

This 24-card set was sponsored by Mohawk to commemorate the Vancouver Canucks' 20th year in the NHL and was issued in six panels of four cards each. The cards measure the standard size, 2 1/2" by 3 1/2", and feature a color head and shoulders shot of the player on white card stock. The Canucks' and Mohawk logos appear at the bottom of the card, and the Canucks' logo has the number

	MINT	EXC	G-VG
COMPLETE SET (24)	20.00	8.00	2.00
COMMON PLAYER (1-24)	.75	.30	.07
☐ 1 Greg Adams 8	1.00	.40	.10
☐ 2 Jim Benning 4	.75	.30	.07
☐ 3 Steve Bozek 14	.75	.30	.07
☐ 4 Brian Bradley 10	1.50	.60	.15
☐ 5 Garth Butcher 5	1.25	.50	.12
☐ 6 Craig Coxe 22	.75	.30	.07
☐ 7 Vladimir Krutov 17	1.00	.40	.10
☐ 8 Igor Larionov 18	2.00	.80	.20
☐ 9 Doug Lidster 3	.75	.30	.07
☐ 10 Trevor Linden 16	4.00	1.60	.40
☐ 11 Kirk McLean 1	3.00	1.20	.30
☐ 12 Larry Melnyk 24	.75	.30	.07
☐ 13 Robert Nordmark 6	.75	.30	.07
☐ 14 Barry Pederson 7	1.00	.40	.10
☐ 15 Paul Reinhart 23	1.00	.40	.10
☐ 16 Jim Sandlak 19	1.00	.40	.10
☐ 17 Petri Skriko 26	1.00	.40	.10
☐ 18 Doug Smith	.75	.30	.07
☐ 19 Stan Smyl 12	1.50	.60	.15
☐ 20 Harold Snepsts 27	2.00	.80	.20
☐ 21 Daryl Stanley 29	.75	.30	.07
☐ 22 Rich Sutter 15	1.00	.40	.10
☐ 23 Tony Tanti 9	1.00	.40	.10
☐ 24 Steve Weeks 31	1.00	.40	.10

1990-91 Canucks Mohawk

This 29-card set of Vancouver Canucks was sponsored by Mohawk and issued in panels. After perforation, the cards measure the standard size (2 1/2" by 3 1/2"). The front features color mugshots of the players, with thin red borders on a white card face. The player's name and position appear in black lettering above the picture, while the team logo in the lower right corner rounds out the card face. The horizontally oriented backs have biographical information and statistics (regular season and playoff). The cards are unnumbered and checklisted below in alphabetical order.

	MINT	EXC	G-VG
COMPLETE SET (29)	15.00	6.00	1.50
COMMON PLAYER (1-29)	.50	.20	.05
☐ 1 Greg Adams	.75	.30	.07
☐ 2 Jim Agnew	.50	.20	.05
☐ 3 Steve Bozek	.50	.20	.05
☐ 4 Garth Butcher	.75	.30	.07
☐ 5 Dave Capuano	.50	.20	.05
☐ 6 Craig Coxe	.50	.20	.05
☐ 7 Gerald Diduck	.50	.20	.05
☐ 8 Troy Gamble	.75	.30	.07
☐ 9 Don Gibson	.50	.20	.05

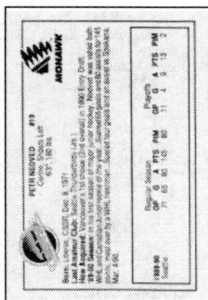

Petr Nedved   CENTRE

☐ 10	Kevan Guy	.50	.20	.05
☐ 11	Robert Kron	.75	.30	.07
☐ 12	Tom Kurvers	.60	.24	.06
☐ 13	Igor Larionov	1.00	.40	.10
☐ 14	Doug Lidster	.60	.24	.06
☐ 15	Trevor Linden	2.00	.80	.20
☐ 16	Jyrki Lumme	.75	.30	.07
☐ 17	Jay Mazur	.50	.20	.05
☐ 18	Andrew McBain	.50	.20	.05
☐ 19	Kirk McLean	2.00	.80	.20
☐ 20	Rob Murphy	.50	.20	.05
☐ 21	Petr Nedved	3.00	1.20	.30
☐ 22	Robert Nordmark	.50	.20	.05
☐ 23	Gino Odjick	1.00	.40	.10
☐ 24	Adrien Plavsic	.50	.20	.05
☐ 25	Dan Quinn	.50	.20	.05
☐ 26	Jim Sandlak	.60	.24	.06
☐ 27	Stan Smyl	.75	.30	.07
☐ 28	Ronnie Stern	.60	.24	.06
☐ 29	Garry Valk	.60	.24	.06

1990-91 Canucks Molson

This set features large (approximately 8" by 10") glossy color close-up photos of Canucks, who were honored as the Molson Canadian Player of the Month. The photos are enclosed by a gold border. The player's name appears in the bottom gold border. At the bottom center is a picture of the Molson Cup. The team logo and a Molson logo in the lower corners round out the front. The backs are blank, and the unnumbered photos are checklisted below in alphabetical order.

		MINT	EXC	G-VG
COMPLETE SET (6)		30.00	12.00	3.00
COMMON PLAYER (1-6)		4.00	1.60	.40
☐ 1	Brian Bradley	5.00	2.00	.50
☐ 2	Troy Gamble	4.00	1.60	.40
☐ 3	Doug Lidster	4.00	1.60	.40
☐ 4	Trevor Linden	8.00	3.25	.80
☐ 5	Kirk McLean (Facing right)	8.00	3.25	.80
☐ 6	Kirk McLean (Facing front)	8.00	3.25	.80

1991-92 Canucks Autograph Cards

These autograph cards, each measuring approximately 3 3/4" by 8 1/2", were issued by the team with a large white area at the bottom for the players to sign. The front features a glossy color close-up photo, with the year and the team logo in the white border above the picture. In cursive lettering, the player's name and number appear below the picture, with his position printed in block lettering. The unnumbered cards are blank on the back and checklisted below in alphabetical order.

		MINT	EXC	G-VG
COMPLETE SET (23)		25.00	10.00	2.50
COMMON PLAYER (1-23)		.75	.30	.07
☐ 1	Greg Adams	1.00	.40	.10
☐ 2	Pavel Bure	8.00	3.25	.80
☐ 3	Dave Babych	1.00	.40	.10
☐ 4	Geoff Courtnall	2.00	.80	.20
☐ 5	Gerald Diduck	.75	.30	.07
☐ 6	Robert Dirk	.75	.30	.07
☐ 7	Troy Gamble	1.00	.40	.10
☐ 8	Randy Gregg	1.00	.40	.10
☐ 9	Robert Kron	.75	.30	.07
☐ 10	Igor Larionov	1.00	.40	.10
☐ 11	Doug Lidster	.75	.30	.07
☐ 12	Trevor Linden	3.00	1.20	.30
☐ 13	Jyrki Lumme	1.00	.40	.10
☐ 14	Kirk McLean	3.00	1.20	.30
☐ 15	Sergio Momesso	1.00	.40	.10
☐ 16	Rob Murphy	.75	.30	.07
☐ 17	Dana Murzyn	.75	.30	.07
☐ 18	Petr Nedved	2.00	.80	.20
☐ 19	Gino Odjick	1.50	.60	.15
☐ 20	Adrien Plavsic	.75	.30	.07
☐ 21	Cliff Ronning	1.50	.60	.15
☐ 22	Jim Sandlak	1.00	.40	.10
☐ 23	Ryan Walter	.75	.30	.07

1991-92 Canucks Molson

This set features large (approximately 8" by 10") glossy color close-up photos of Canucks who were honored as the Molson Canadian Player of the Month or Player of the Year. The photos are enclosed by white, red, and blue border stripes. A gold leaf appear above the picture, while a gold plaque identifying the player appears below the picture. The

		MINT	EXC	G-VG
☐	10 Igor Larionov	2.00	.80	.20
☐	11 Doug Lidster	1.50	.60	.15
☐	12 Trevor Linden	5.00	2.00	.50
☐	13 Jyrki Lumme	1.50	.60	.15
☐	14 Kirk McLean	5.00	2.00	.50
☐	15 Sergio Momesso	1.50	.60	.15
☐	16 Rob Murphy	1.00	.40	.10
☐	17 Dana Murzyn	1.00	.40	.10
☐	18 Petr Nedved	3.00	1.20	.30
☐	19 Gino Odjick	2.00	.80	.20
☐	20 Adrien Plavsic	1.00	.40	.10
☐	21 Cliff Ronning	2.50	1.00	.25
☐	22 Jim Sandlak	1.50	.60	.15
☐	23 Ryan Walter	1.00	.40	.10

team logo and a Molson logo appear in the lower corners. The backs are blank, and the unnumbered photos are checklisted below in alphabetical order.

	MINT	EXC	G-VG
COMPLETE SET (7)	50.00	20.00	5.00
COMMON PLAYER (1-7)	4.00	1.60	.40

		MINT	EXC	G-VG
☐	1 Greg Adams	4.00	1.60	.40
☐	2 Pavel Bure	15.00	6.00	1.50
	(White uniform)			
☐	3 Pavel Bure POY	15.00	6.00	1.50
	(Black uniform)			
☐	4 Igor Larionov	5.00	2.00	.50
☐	5 Trevor Linden	8.00	3.25	.80
☐	6 Kirk McLean	8.00	3.25	.80
☐	7 Cliff Ronning	5.00	2.00	.50

1991-92 Canucks Team Issue 8x10

 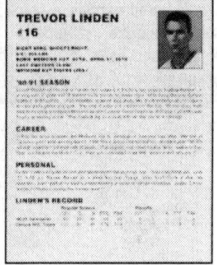

This set features 8" by 10" glossy color close-up photos of the Vancouver Canucks. The photos are enclosed by a thin black border. In cursive lettering, the player's name and number appear below the picture, with his position printed in block lettering. The team logo in the lower left corner completes the front. The backs carry a black and white head shot, biography, 1990-91 season summary, career highlights, personal information, and complete statistics. The cards are unnumbered and checklisted below in alphabetical order.

	MINT	EXC	G-VG
COMPLETE SET (23)	35.00	14.00	3.50
COMMON PLAYER (1-23)	1.00	.40	.10

		MINT	EXC	G-VG
☐	1 Greg Adams	1.50	.60	.15
☐	2 Pavel Bure	10.00	4.00	1.00
☐	3 Dave Babych	1.50	.60	.15
☐	4 Geoff Courtnall	2.50	1.00	.25
☐	5 Gerald Diduck	1.00	.40	.10
☐	6 Robert Dirk	1.00	.40	.10
☐	7 Troy Gamble	1.50	.60	.15
☐	8 Randy Gregg	1.50	.60	.15
☐	9 Robert Kron	1.50	.60	.15

1992-93 Canucks Road Trip Art

 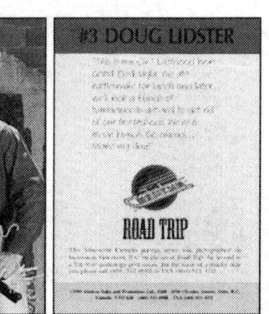

Dubbed "Road Trip Art Cards," this set of 25 approximately 4 3/4" by 7" player portraits was available only at Subway and Payless stores. Each week for six weeks, a set of four signed player portraits was released at a suggested price of 2.29 per pack. Also there was a tab inside each package and one could win a pair of 1993-94 season tickets, autographed Road Trip prints, limited edition Road Trip prints, Road Trip puzzles, and Road Trip coloring books. The photos are black-and-white and picture the Canuck players dressed in western garb. A gold foil facsimile autograph is printed near the bottom. The backs carry the player's name in a wide red stripe at the top. Humorous text in the form of player quotes rests against a white background along with the team logo and the words "Road Trip." A bright yellow stripe accents the bottom of the card and contains manufacturer information. The portraits are listed below in alphabetical order with the week issued denoted.

	MINT	EXC	G-VG
COMPLETE SET (25)	10.00	4.00	1.00
COMMON PLAYER (1-25)	.40	.16	.04

		MINT	EXC	G-VG
☐	1 Greg Adams W1	.60	.24	.06
☐	2 Shawn Antoski W5	.50	.20	.05
☐	3 Dave Babych W5	.60	.24	.06
☐	4 Pavel Bure W3	4.00	1.60	.40
☐	5 Geoff Courtnall W5	.75	.30	.07
☐	6 Gerald Diduck W3	.40	.16	.04
☐	7 Robert Dirk W5	.40	.16	.04
☐	8 Tom Fergus W3	.50	.20	.05
☐	9 Robert Kron W2	.50	.20	.05
☐	10 Doug Lidster W2	.50	.20	.05
☐	11 Trevor Linden W1	1.50	.60	.15
☐	12 Jyrki Lumme W1	.60	.24	.06
☐	13 Kirk McLean W2	1.50	.60	.15
☐	14 Sergio Momesso W2	.60	.24	.06
☐	15 Dana Murzyn W2	.40	.16	.04
☐	16 Petr Nedved W4	1.00	.40	.10
☐	17 Gino Odjick W4	.60	.24	.06
☐	18 Adrien Plavsic W6	.40	.16	.04
☐	19 Cliff Ronning W6	.75	.30	.07
☐	20 Jim Sandlak W6	.50	.20	.05
☐	21 Jiri Slegr W1	.50	.20	.05
☐	22 Garry Valk W4	.50	.20	.05

		MINT	EXC	G-VG
☐ 23	Ryan Walter W5	.40	.16	.04
☐ 24	Dixon Ward W3	.75	.30	.07
☐ 25	Kay Whitmore W6	.60	.24	.06

1984-85 Capitals Pizza Hut

These cards of Washington Capitals were given out to members of the Junior Capitals Club and measure approximately 4 1/2" by 6". The front features a color action photo of the player, with three blue stripes on the picture. The back has a small head shot of the player and his career statistics. The cards are unnumbered and hence are listed below alphabetically by player name.

		MINT	EXC	G-VG
COMPLETE SET (15)		35.00	14.00	3.50
COMMON PLAYER (1-15)		1.50	.60	.15
☐ 1	Bob Carpenter	2.00	.80	.20
☐ 2	Dave Christian	2.50	1.00	.25
☐ 3	Glen Currie	1.50	.60	.15
☐ 4	Gaetan Duchesne	1.50	.60	.15
☐ 5	Mike Gartner	7.50	3.00	.75
☐ 6	Bob Gould	1.50	.60	.15
☐ 7	Bengt Gustafsson	2.00	.80	.20
☐ 8	Alan Haworth	1.50	.60	.15
☐ 9	Doug Jarvis	2.00	.80	.20
☐ 10	Al Jensen	1.50	.60	.15
☐ 11	Rod Langway	3.00	1.20	.30
☐ 12	Craig Laughlin	1.50	.60	.15
☐ 13	Larry Murphy	4.00	1.60	.40
☐ 14	Pat Riggin	2.00	.80	.20
☐ 15	Scott Stevens	6.00	2.40	.60

1985-86 Capitals Pizza Hut

These cards of Washington Capitals were mailed three at a time to members of the Junior Capitals Club and measure approximately 4 1/2" by 6". The front features a color action photo of the player, with three red stripes on the picture. The back has a small head shot of the player and his career statistics. When Doug Jarvis, Pat Riggin, and Darren Veitch were traded, supposedly their cards were pulled and never mailed to club members. It is alleged that these cards were destroyed and only a few were kept. Consequently, these player cards are scarce.

		MINT	EXC	G-VG
COMPLETE SET (15)		35.00	14.00	3.50
COMMON PLAYER (1-15)		1.50	.60	.15
☐ 1	Bob Carpenter	2.00	.80	.20
☐ 2	Dave Christian	2.50	1.00	.25
☐ 3	Gaetan Duchesne	1.50	.60	.15
☐ 4	Mike Gartner	7.50	3.00	.75
☐ 5	Bob Gould	1.50	.60	.15
☐ 6	Bengt Gustafsson	1.50	.60	.15
☐ 7	Alan Haworth	1.50	.60	.15
☐ 8	Doug Jarvis SP	5.00	2.00	.50
☐ 9	Al Jensen	1.50	.60	.15
☐ 10	Rod Langway	3.00	1.20	.30
☐ 11	Craig Laughlin	1.50	.60	.15
☐ 12	Larry Murphy	3.50	1.40	.35
☐ 13	Pat Riggin SP	5.00	2.00	.50
☐ 14	Scott Stevens	5.00	2.00	.50
☐ 15	Darren Veitch SP	4.00	1.60	.40

1986-87 Capitals Kodak

The 1986-87 Washington Capitals Team Photo Album was sponsored by Kodak. It consists of three large sheets joined together to form one continuous sheet. The first panel has a team photo measuring approximately 10" by 8". The second and third panels consist of player cards; after perforation, they measure approximately 2" by 2 5/8". The cards feature color posed photos, with player information below. The cards are unnumbered and we have checklisted them below in alphabetical order. Kevin Hatcher's card predates his Rookie Card by one year.

		MINT	EXC	G-VG
COMPLETE SET (26)		35.00	14.00	3.50
COMMON PLAYER (1-26)		1.00	.40	.10
☐ 1	Greg Adams	1.50	.60	.15
☐ 2	John Barrett	1.00	.40	.10
☐ 3	John Blum	1.00	.40	.10
☐ 4	Dave Christian	1.50	.60	.15
☐ 5	Bob Crawford	1.00	.40	.10
☐ 6	Gaetan Duchesne	1.00	.40	.10
☐ 7	Lou Franceschetti	1.00	.40	.10
☐ 8	Mike Gartner	6.00	2.40	.60
☐ 9	Bob Gould	1.00	.40	.10
☐ 10	Jeff Greenlaw	1.00	.40	.10
☐ 11	Kevin Hatcher	7.50	3.00	.75
☐ 12	Alan Haworth	1.00	.40	.10
☐ 13	David A. Jensen	1.00	.40	.10
☐ 14	Rod Langway	2.50	1.00	.25
☐ 15	Craig Laughlin	1.00	.40	.10
☐ 16	Bob Mason	1.50	.60	.15
☐ 17	Kelly Miller	2.50	1.00	.25
☐ 18	Larry Murphy	3.00	1.20	.30
☐ 19	Bryan Murray CO	1.50	.60	.15
☐ 20	Pete Peeters	2.00	.80	.20
☐ 21	Michal Pivonka	3.00	1.20	.30
☐ 22	Mike Ridley	3.00	1.20	.30
☐ 23	Gary Sampson	1.00	.40	.10
☐ 24	Greg Smith	1.00	.40	.10
☐ 25	Scott Stevens	3.00	1.20	.30
☐ 26	Large Team Photo	4.00	1.60	.40

1986-87 Capitals Police

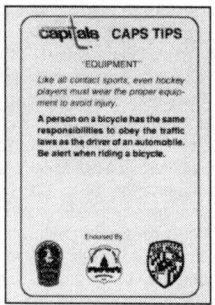

This 24-card police set features players of the Washington Capitals. The cards measure approximately 2 5/8" by 3 3/4" and were issued in two-card panels. The front has a color action photo on white card stock, with player information and the Capitals' logo below the picture. Inside a thin black border the back features a hockey tip ("Caps Tips"), an anti-crime tip, and logos of sponsoring police agenices. The cards are unnumbered and we have checklisted them below in alphabetical order, with the jersey number to the right of the player's name. Kevin Hatcher's card predates his Rookie Card by one year.

		MINT	EXC	G-VG
COMPLETE SET (24)		15.00	6.00	1.50
COMMON PLAYER (1-24)		.50	.20	.05
☐ 1	Greg Adams 22	.75	.30	.07
☐ 2	John Barrett 6	.50	.20	.05
☐ 3	Bob Carpenter 10	.75	.30	.07
☐ 4	Dave Christian 27	.75	.30	.07
☐ 5	Yvon Corriveau 26	.50	.20	.05
☐ 6	Gaetan Duchesne 14	.50	.20	.05

☐ 7	Lou Franceschetti 32	.50	.20	.05
☐ 8	Mike Gartner 11	3.00	1.20	.30
☐ 9	Bob Gould 23	.50	.20	.05
☐ 10	Kevin Hatcher 4	3.50	1.40	.35
☐ 11	Alan Haworth 15	.50	.20	.05
☐ 12	Al Jensen 35	.50	.20	.05
☐ 13	David A. Jensen 9	.50	.20	.05
☐ 14	Rod Langway 5	1.00	.40	.10
☐ 15	Craig Laughlin 18	.50	.20	.05
☐ 16	Stephen Leach 21	1.00	.40	.10
☐ 17	Larry Murphy 8	1.50	.60	.15
☐ 18	Bryan Murray CO	.75	.30	.07
☐ 19	Pete Peeters 1	1.00	.40	.10
☐ 20	Jorgen Pettersson 12	.50	.20	.05
☐ 21	Michal Pivonka 17	2.00	.80	.20
☐ 22	David Poile VP/GM	.50	.20	.05
☐ 23	Greg Smith 19	.50	.20	.05
☐ 24	Scott Stevens 3	2.00	.80	.20

1987-88 Capitals Kodak

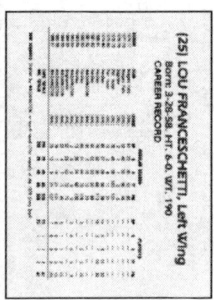

The 1987-88 Washington Capitals Team Photo Album was sponsored by Kodak. It consists of three large sheets, each measuring approximately 11" by 8 1/4" and joined together to form one continuous sheet. The first panel has a team photo, with the players' names listed according to rows below the picture. While the second panel presents three rows of five cards each, the third panel presents two rows of five cards, with five Kodak coupons completing the left over portion of the panel. After perforation, the cards measure approximately 2 3/16" by 2 15/16". They feature color-posed photos bordered in red, with player information below the picture. The Capitals' logo and a picture of a Kodak film box complete the card face. The back has biographical and statistical information in a horizontal format. The cards are checklisted below by sweater number.

		MINT	EXC	G-VG
COMPLETE SET (25)		25.00	10.00	2.50
COMMON PLAYER		.75	.30	.07
☐ 1	Pete Peeters	1.25	.50	.12
☐ 2	Garry Galley	1.50	.60	.15
☐ 3	Scott Stevens	2.00	.80	.20
☐ 4	Kevin Hatcher	3.50	1.40	.35
☐ 5	Rod Langway	1.60	.60	.15
☐ 6	John Barrett	1.00	.40	.10
☐ 8	Larry Murphy	2.00	.80	.20
☐ 10	Kelly Miller	1.50	.60	.15
☐ 11	Mike Gartner	3.50	1.40	.35
☐ 12	Peter Sundstrom	1.00	.40	.10
☐ 16	Bengt Gustafsson	.75	.30	.07
☐ 17	Mike Ridley	2.00	.80	.20
☐ 18	Craig Laughlin	.75	.30	.07
☐ 19	Greg Smith	.75	.30	.07
☐ 20	Michal Pivonka	2.00	.80	.20
☐ 22	Greg Adams	1.00	.40	.10
☐ 23	Bob Gould	.75	.30	.07
☐ 25	Lou Franceschetti	.75	.30	.07
☐ 27	Dave Christian	1.25	.50	.12
☐ 29	Ed Kastelic	.75	.30	.07
☐ 30	Clint Malarchuk	1.00	.40	.10
☐ 32	Dale Hunter	2.00	.80	.20

☐ 34	Bill Houlder	.75	.30	.07
☐ xx	Bryan Murray CO	1.00	.40	.10
☐ xx	David Poile VP/GM	.75	.30	.07

1988-89 Capitals Smokey

This 24-card safety set features players of the Washington Capitals. The cards measure 2 5/8" by 3 3/4" and were issued in two-card panels. The front has a color action photo on white card stock, with player information and logos below the picture. Inside a thin black border the back features a hockey tip ("Caps Tips") and a fire prevention cartoon starring Smokey. The cards are unnumbered and we have checklisted them below in alphabetical order, with the sweater number to the right of the player's name. Geoff Courtnall's card predates his Rookie card.

		MINT	EXC	G-VG
COMPLETE SET (24)		15.00	6.00	1.50
COMMON PLAYER (1-24)		.50	.20	.05
☐ 1	Dave Christian 27	.75	.30	.07
☐ 2	Yvon Corriveau 26	.50	.20	.05
☐ 3	Geoff Courtnall 14	3.00	1.20	.30
☐ 4	Lou Franceschetti 25	.50	.20	.05
☐ 5	Mike Gartner 11	3.00	1.20	.30
☐ 6	Bob Gould 23	.50	.20	.05
☐ 7	Bengt Gustafsson 16	.75	.30	.07
☐ 8	Kevin Hatcher 4	2.50	1.00	.25
☐ 9	Dale Hunter 32	1.00	.40	.10
☐ 10	Rod Langway 5	1.00	.40	.10
☐ 11	Stephen Leach 21	.75	.30	.07
☐ 12	Grant Ledyard 6	.50	.20	.05
☐ 13	Clint Malarchuk 30	.75	.30	.07
☐ 14	Kelly Miller 10	.75	.30	.07
☐ 15	Larry Murphy 8	1.25	.50	.12
☐ 16	Bryan Murray CO	.75	.30	.07
☐ 17	Pete Peeters 1	.75	.30	.07
☐ 18	Michal Pivonka 17	1.00	.40	.10
☐ 19	David Poile VP/GM	.50	.20	.05
☐ 20	Mike Ridley 17	1.00	.40	.10
☐ 21	Neil Sheehy 15	.50	.20	.05
☐ 22	Scott Stevens 3	1.50	.60	.15
☐ 23	Peter Sundstrom 12	.75	.30	.07
☐ 24	Title Card	.50	.20	.05
	Smokey the Bear			

1989-90 Capitals Kodak

The 1989-90 Washington Capitals Team Photo Album was co-sponsored by Kodak and W. Bell and Co. It consists of three large sheets, each measuring approximately 11" by 8 1/4" and joined together to form one continuous sheet. The first panel has a large blue square designated for autographs. While the second panel presents three rows of five cards each, the third panel presents two rows of five cards, with Kodak advertisements completing the left over portion of the panel. After perforation, the cards measure

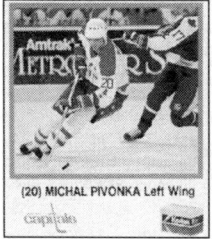
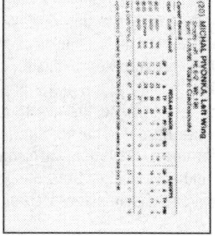

(20) MICHAL PIVONKA Left Wing

approximately 2 3/16" by 2 1/2". They feature color action photos bordered in red, with player information below the picture. The Capitals' logo and a picture of a Kodak film box complete the card face. The back has biographical and statistical information in a horizontal format. The cards are checklisted below by sweater number.

		MINT	EXC	G-VG
COMPLETE SET (25)		20.00	8.00	2.00
COMMON PLAYER		.75	.30	.07
☐ 1	Mike Liut	1.25	.50	.12
☐ 3	Scott Stevens	2.00	.80	.20
☐ 4	Kevin Hatcher	2.50	1.00	.25
☐ 5	Rod Langway	1.50	.60	.15
☐ 6	Calle Johansson	1.25	.50	.12
☐ 8	Bob Rouse	.75	.30	.07
☐ 10	Kelly Miller	1.25	.50	.12
☐ 11	Tim Bergland	.75	.30	.07
☐ 12	John Tucker	.75	.30	.07
☐ 14	Geoff Courtnall	2.00	.80	.20
☐ 15	Neil Sheehy	.75	.30	.07
☐ 16	Alan May	.75	.30	.07
☐ 17	Mike Ridley	1.25	.50	.12
☐ 19	John Druce	1.00	.40	.10
☐ 20	Michal Pivonka	1.25	.50	.12
☐ 21	Stephen Leach	1.00	.40	.10
☐ 22	Dino Ciccarelli	2.50	1.00	.25
☐ 26	Steve Maltais	.75	.30	.07
☐ 27	Bob Joyce	1.00	.40	.10
☐ 29	Scot Kleinendorst	.75	.30	.07
☐ 32	Dale Hunter	1.25	.50	.12
☐ 33	Don Beaupre	1.25	.50	.12
☐ xx	Rob Laird ACO	.75	.30	.07
☐ xx	Terry Murray CO	1.00	.40	.10
☐ xx	David Poile VP/GM	.75	.30	.07

1990-91 Capitals Kodak

The 1990-91 Washington Capitals Team Photo Album was sponsored by Kodak. It consists of three large sheets joined together to form one continuous sheet. The first panel has a team photo measuring approximately 10" by 8". The second and third panels consist of player cards; after perforation, they measure approximately 2" by 2 5/8". The cards feature color posed photos, with player information below. The cards are unnumbered and we have checklisted them below in alphabetical order.

		MINT	EXC	G-VG
COMPLETE SET (25)		12.00	5.00	1.20
COMMON PLAYER (1-25)		.50	.20	.05
☐ 1	Don Beaupre	1.00	.40	.10
☐ 2	Tim Bergland	.50	.20	.05
☐ 3	Peter Bondra	2.00	.80	.20
☐ 4	Dino Ciccarelli	1.50	.60	.15
☐ 5	John Druce	.75	.30	.07
☐ 6	Kevin Hatcher	1.50	.60	.15
☐ 7	Dale Hunter	.75	.30	.07
☐ 8	Al Iafrate	1.50	.60	.15
☐ 9	Calle Johansson	.75	.30	.07
☐ 10	Dimitri Khristich	1.00	.40	.10
☐ 11	Nick Kypreos	.50	.20	.05
☐ 12	Mike Lalor	.50	.20	.05
☐ 13	Rod Langway	1.00	.40	.10
☐ 14	Stephen Leach	.75	.30	.07

☐ 15	Mike Liut	.75	.30	.07
☐ 16	Alan May	.50	.20	.05
☐ 17	Kelly Miller	.75	.30	.07
☐ 18	Terry Murray CO	.75	.30	.07
☐ 19	John Perpich	.50	.20	.05
☐ 20	Michal Pivonka	1.00	.40	.10
☐ 21	David Poile VP/GM	.50	.20	.05
☐ 22	Mike Ridley	1.00	.40	.10
☐ 23	Ken Sabourin	.50	.20	.05
☐ 24	Mikhail Tatarinov	.75	.30	.07
☐ 25	Dave Tippett	.50	.20	.05

1990-91 Capitals Smokey

This fire safety set contains 22 cards and features members of the Washington Capitals. The cards measure approximately 2 1/2" by 3 3/4" and were issued in two-card panels. The front has a color action photo of the player, with player information below the picture between the Smokey the Bear and team logos. The back includes "Caps Tips" and a fire prevention message from Smokey.

		MINT	EXC	G-VG
COMPLETE SET (22)		10.00	4.00	1.00
COMMON PLAYER (1-22)		.40	.16	.04
☐ 1	Don Beaupre	.80	.32	.08
☐ 2	Tim Bergland	.40	.16	.04
☐ 3	Peter Bondra	1.50	.60	.15
☐ 4	Dino Ciccarelli	1.25	.50	.12
☐ 5	John Druce	.60	.24	.06
☐ 6	Kevin Hatcher	1.25	.50	.12
☐ 7	Jim Hrivnak	.80	.32	.08
☐ 8	Dale Hunter	.80	.32	.08
☐ 9	Calle Johansson	.60	.24	.06
☐ 10	Nick Kypreos	.40	.16	.04
☐ 11	Mike Lalor	.40	.16	.04
☐ 12	Rod Langway	.80	.32	.08
☐ 13	Stephen Leach	.60	.24	.06
☐ 14	Mike Liut	.80	.32	.08
☐ 15	Alan May	.40	.16	.04
☐ 16	Kelly Miller	.60	.24	.06
☐ 17	Rob Murray	.40	.16	.04
☐ 18	Michal Pivonka	1.00	.40	.10
☐ 19	Mike Ridley	.80	.32	.08
☐ 20	Neil Sheehy	.40	.16	.04
☐ 21	Mikhail Tatarinov	.60	.24	.06
☐ 22	Dave Tippett	.40	.16	.04

1991-92 Capitals Junior 5x7

This 25-card set measures approximately 5" by 7" and features full-bleed glossy action photos; in small black type across the bottom, the uniform number, name, and position are burned in. The backs are blank.

		MINT	EXC	G-VG
COMPLETE SET (25)		15.00	6.00	1.50
COMMON PLAYER (1-25)		.50	.20	.05
☐ 1	Don Beaupre	1.00	.40	.10
☐ 2	Tim Bergland	.50	.20	.05
☐ 3	Peter Bondra	2.00	.80	.20
☐ 4	Randy Burridge	1.00	.40	.10
☐ 5	Shawn Chambers	.50	.20	.05
☐ 6	Dino Ciccarelli	1.50	.60	.15
☐ 7	Sylvain Cote	.75	.30	.07
☐ 8	John Druce	.75	.30	.07
☐ 9	Jeff Greenlaw	.50	.20	.05
☐ 10	Kevin Hatcher	2.00	.80	.20
☐ 11	Dale Hunter	1.00	.40	.10
☐ 12	Al Iafrate	2.00	.80	.20
☐ 13	Calle Johansson	.75	.30	.07
☐ 14	Dimitri Khristich	1.50	.60	.15
☐ 15	Todd Krygier	.75	.30	.07
☐ 16	Nick Kypreos	.50	.20	.05
☐ 17	Mike Lalor	.50	.20	.05
☐ 18	Rod Langway	1.00	.40	.10
☐ 19	Mike Liut	1.00	.40	.10
☐ 20	Alan May	.50	.20	.05

☐ 21	Kelly Miller	.75	.30	.07
☐ 22	Michal Pivonka	1.25	.50	.12
☐ 23	Mike Ridley	1.00	.40	.10
☐ 24	Ken Sabourin	.50	.20	.05
☐ 25	Dave Tippett	.50	.20	.05

1991-92 Capitals Kodak

The 1991-92 Washington Capitals Team Photo Album was sponsored by Kodak. It consists of three large sheets joined together to form one continuous sheet. The first panel measures approximately 11" by 8," and it has blank space allotted for autographs. The second panel carries three rows with five player cards each; after perforation, they measure approximately 2 3/16" by 2 3/4." The third panel has two rows with five player cards each, and a final row consisting of two Kodak coupons. The cards feature color head shots, with player information, team logo, and a picture of a Kodak film below. In a horizontal format, the backs have biographical and statistical information. Though the cards are unnumbered, they are arranged in alphabetical order by players' last names and checklisted below accordingly.

	MINT	EXC	G-VG
COMPLETE SET (25)	12.00	5.00	1.20
COMMON PLAYER (1-25)	.40	.16	.04

☐ 1	Don Beaupre	.80	.32	.08
☐ 2	Tim Bergland	.40	.16	.04
☐ 3	Peter Bondra	1.25	.50	.12
☐ 4	Randy Burridge	.60	.24	.06
☐ 5	Shawn Chambers	.40	.16	.04
☐ 6	Dino Ciccarelli	1.25	.50	.12
☐ 7	Sylvain Cote	.60	.24	.06
☐ 8	John Druce	.60	.24	.06
☐ 9	Kevin Hatcher	1.25	.50	.12
☐ 10	Jim Hrivnak	.60	.24	.06
☐ 11	Dale Hunter	.80	.32	.08
☐ 12	Al Iafrate	1.25	.50	.12
☐ 13	Calle Johansson	.60	.24	.06
☐ 14	Dimitri Khristich	.80	.32	.08
☐ 15	Todd Krygier	.40	.16	.04
☐ 16	Nick Kypreos	.40	.16	.04
☐ 17	Rod Langway	.80	.32	.08
☐ 18	Mike Liut	.80	.32	.08
☐ 19	Paul MacDermid	.40	.16	.04
☐ 20	Alan May	.40	.16	.04
☐ 21	Kelly Miller	.60	.24	.06
☐ 22	Michal Pivonka	1.00	.40	.10
☐ 23	Mike Ridley	.80	.32	.08
☐ 24	Brad Schlegel	.60	.24	.06
☐ 25	Dave Tippett	.40	.16	.04

1992-93 Capitals Kodak

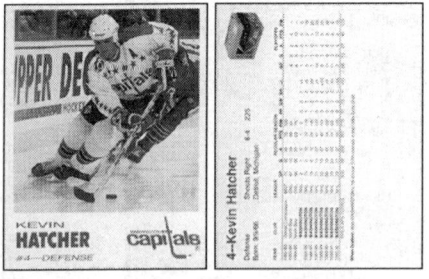

The 1992-93 Washington Capitals Team Photo Album was sponsored by Kodak. It consists of three 8 1/4" by 11"

sheets joined together to form one continuous sheet. The first panel has a slot for collecting autographs. The second and third panels consist of player cards; after perforation, they measure approximately 2 3/16" by 2 3/4". The fronts feature color action player photos with white borders. Player information and the team logo are printed in the bottom white border. The horizontal backs carry biography and complete statistical information. Though the cards are unnumbered, they are arranged alphabetically on the sheet and checklisted below accordingly.

	MINT	EXC	G-VG
COMPLETE SET (25)	12.00	5.00	1.20
COMMON PLAYER (1-25)	.40	.16	.04

☐ 1	Shawn Anderson	.40	.16	.04
☐ 2	Don Beaupre	.80	.32	.08
☐ 3	Peter Bondra	1.25	.50	.12
☐ 4	Randy Burridge	.60	.24	.06
☐ 5	Bobby Carpenter	.60	.24	.06
☐ 6	Paul Cavallini	.40	.16	.04
☐ 7	Sylvain Cote	.60	.24	.06
☐ 8	Pat Elynuik	.60	.24	.06
☐ 9	Kevin Hatcher	1.25	.50	.12
☐ 10	Jim Hrivnak	.60	.24	.06
☐ 11	Dale Hunter	.80	.32	.08
☐ 12	Al Iafrate	1.25	.50	.12
☐ 13	Calle Johansson	.60	.24	.06
☐ 14	Keith Jones	.40	.16	.04
☐ 15	Dimitri Khristich	.80	.32	.08
☐ 16	Steve Konowalchuk	.60	.24	.06
☐ 17	Todd Krygier	.40	.16	.04
☐ 18	Rod Langway	.80	.32	.08
☐ 19	Paul MacDermid	.40	.16	.04
☐ 20	Alan May	.40	.16	.04
☐ 21	Kelly Miller	.60	.24	.06
☐ 22	Michal Pivonka	1.00	.40	.10
☐ 23	Mike Ridley	.80	.32	.08
☐ 24	Reggie Savage	.60	.24	.06
☐ 25	Jason Woolley	.60	.24	.06

1936 Champion Postcards

The set is in the same format as the 1936 Triumph set and was issued in the same manner as the Triumph set, except as an insert in "Boys" magazine published weekly in Great Britain. Three cards were issued in the first week of the promotion in "The Champion" and then one per week in "Boys" magazine. The cards are sepia toned and are postcard size, measuring approximately 3 1/2" by 5 1/2". The set is subtitled "Stars of the Ice Rinks". The cards are unnumbered and hence presented in alphabetical order. The date mentioned below is the issue date as noted on the card back in Canadian style, day/month/year.

	EX-MT	VG-E	GOOD
COMPLETE SET (10)	1500.00	600.00	150.00
COMMON PLAYER (1-10)	75.00	30.00	7.50

☐ 1	Marty Barry Boston Bruins 18/1/36	75.00	30.00	7.50
☐ 2	Harold(Mush) March Chicago Blackhawks 8/2/36	75.00	30.00	7.50
☐ 3	Reg(Hooley) Smith Montreal Canadiens 18/1/36	150.00	60.00	15.00
☐ 4	Sweeney Schriner New York Americans 22/2/36	150.00	60.00	15.00
☐ 5	King Clancy Toronto Maple Leafs 18/1/36	450.00	180.00	45.00
☐ 6	Bill Cook New York Rangers 1/2/36	150.00	60.00	15.00
☐ 7	Pep Kelly Toronto Maple Leafs 25/1/36	75.00	30.00	7.50

		NRMT	VG-E	GOOD
☐ 8	Aurel Joliat	350.00	140.00	35.00
	Montreal Canadiens 15/2/36			
☐ 9	Charles Conacher	350.00	140.00	35.00
	Toronto Maple Leafs 29/2/36			
☐ 10	Fred(Bun) Cook	100.00	40.00	10.00
	New York Rangers 7/3/36			

1963-65 Chex Photos

The 1963-65 Chex Photos measure approximately 5" by 7". This unnumbered set depicts players from four NHL teams, Chicago Blackhawks, Detroit Red Wings, Toronto Maple Leafs, and Montreal Canadiens. These blank-backed, stiff-cardboard photos are thought to have been issued during the 1963-64 (Canadiens and Maple Leafs) and 1964-65 (Blackhawks, Red Wings, and Canadiens again) seasons. Since these photo cards are unnumbered, they are ordered and numbered below alphabetically according to the player's name. There is rumored to be a Denis DeJordy in this set. The complete set price below includes both varieties of Beliveau.

		NRMT	VG-E	GOOD
	COMPLETE SET (60)	2000.00	800.00	200.00
	COMMON PLAYER (1-58)	15.00	6.00	1.50
☐ 1	George Armstrong	35.00	14.00	3.50
☐ 2	Ralph Backstrom	18.00	7.25	1.80
☐ 3	Dave Balon	15.00	6.00	1.50
☐ 4	Bob Baun	20.00	8.00	2.00
☐ 5A	Jean Beliveau (Looking ahead)	75.00	30.00	7.50
☐ 5B	Jean Beliveau (Looking left)	75.00	30.00	7.50
☐ 6	Red Berenson	18.00	7.25	1.80
☐ 7	Hector(Toe) Blake CO	30.00	12.00	3.00
☐ 8	Johnny Bower	40.00	16.00	4.00
☐ 9	Alex Delvecchio	40.00	16.00	4.00
☐ 10	Kent Douglas	15.00	6.00	1.50
☐ 11	Dick Duff	15.00	6.00	1.50
☐ 12	Phil Esposito	100.00	40.00	10.00
☐ 13	John Ferguson	18.00	7.25	1.80
☐ 14	Bill Gadsby	30.00	12.00	3.00
☐ 15	Jean Gauthier	15.00	6.00	1.50
☐ 16	BoomBoom Geoffrion	60.00	24.00	6.00
☐ 17	Glenn Hall	50.00	20.00	5.00
☐ 18	Terry Harper	18.00	7.25	1.80
☐ 19	Billy Harris	15.00	6.00	1.50
☐ 20	Bill(Red) Hay	15.00	6.00	1.50
☐ 21	Paul Henderson	20.00	8.00	2.00
☐ 22	Bill Hicke	15.00	6.00	1.50
☐ 23	Wayne Hillman	15.00	6.00	1.50
☐ 24	Charlie Hodge	20.00	8.00	2.00
☐ 25	Tim Horton	50.00	20.00	5.00
☐ 26	Gordie Howe	200.00	80.00	20.00
☐ 27	Bobby Hull	125.00	50.00	12.50
☐ 28	Punch Imlach CO	18.00	7.25	1.80
☐ 29	Red Kelly	40.00	16.00	4.00
☐ 30	Dave Keon	40.00	16.00	4.00
☐ 31	Jacques Laperriere	30.00	12.00	3.00

☐ 32	Ed Litzenberger	15.00	6.00	1.50
☐ 33	Parker MacDonald	15.00	6.00	1.50
☐ 34	Bruce MacGregor	15.00	6.00	1.50
☐ 35	Frank Mahovlich	60.00	24.00	6.00
☐ 36	Chico Maki	18.00	7.25	1.80
☐ 37	Pit Martin	18.00	7.25	1.80
☐ 38	John MacMillan	15.00	6.00	1.50
☐ 39	Stan Mikita	60.00	24.00	6.00
☐ 40	Bob Nevin	15.00	6.00	1.50
☐ 41	Pierre Pilote	30.00	12.00	3.00
☐ 42	Marcel Pronovost	30.00	12.00	3.00
☐ 43	Claude Provost	15.00	6.00	1.50
☐ 44	Bob Pulford	30.00	12.00	3.00
☐ 45	Marc Reaume	15.00	6.00	1.50
☐ 46	Henri Richard	45.00	18.00	4.50
☐ 47A	Bobby Rousseau	20.00	8.00	2.00
☐ 47B	Bob Rousseau	30.00	12.00	3.00
☐ 48	Eddie Shack	30.00	12.00	3.00
☐ 49	Don Simmons	15.00	6.00	1.50
☐ 50	Allan Stanley	30.00	12.00	3.00
☐ 51	Ron Stewart	15.00	6.00	1.50
☐ 52	Jean-Guy Talbot	20.00	8.00	2.00
☐ 53	Gilles Tremblay	15.00	6.00	1.50
☐ 54	J.C. Tremblay	20.00	8.00	2.00
☐ 55	Norm Ullman	40.00	16.00	4.00
☐ 56	Elmer(Moose) Vasko	15.00	6.00	1.50
☐ 57	Ken Wharram	18.00	7.25	1.80
☐ 58	Gump Worsley	50.00	20.00	5.00

1992-93 Clark Candy Mario Lemieux

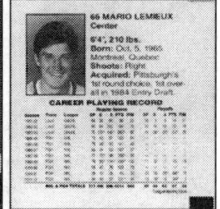

Issued by Clark Candy, this three-card set features three different color player photos of the Pittsburgh Penguins' Mario Lemieux. One card was inserted in each Bun candy bar pack. Each card measures approximately 3" by 3" and has a facsimile autograph in black inscribed across the picture. The pictures have black borders, and a gold stripe carrying the team logo cuts across the bottom of the card. The backs present biographical information, career summary, honors and awards, or career playing record. Only card number 3 listed below has a black-and-white close-up photo on its back. The cards are unnumbered and checklisted below in alphabetical order.

		MINT	EXC	G-VG
	COMPLETE SET (3)	4.00	1.60	.40
	COMMON PLAYER (1-3)	1.50	.60	.15
☐ 1	Mario Lemieux (Skating left)	1.50	.60	.15
☐ 2	Mario Lemieux (Close-up photo)	1.50	.60	.15
☐ 3	Mario Lemieux (Skating right)	1.50	.60	.15

1991 Classic Draft Promos

The two standard size (2 1/2" by 3 1/2") promo cards were issued by Classic to show collectors and dealers the style of their new hockey draft picks set.

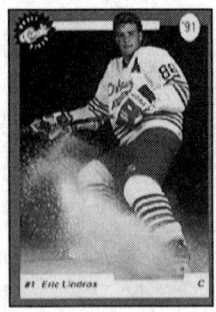

	MINT	EXC	G-VG
COMPLETE SET (2)	6.00	2.40	.60
COMMON PLAYER (1-2)	1.00	.40	.10
☐ 1 Eric Lindros	5.00	2.00	.50
☐ 2 Pat Falloon	1.00	.40	.10

1991 Classic Draft

The premier edition of Classic's 1991 Hockey Draft Pick set includes 50 standard-size (2 1/2" by 3 1/2") cards featuring 50 of the top 60 NHL draft picks. The set was issued in a limited edition run (360,000 factory sets) and included an individually numbered certificate of authenticity. The front has glossy color action player photos, with blue-green borders. The "Classic Draft Picks" logo appears in the upper left corner, and player information appears in a lemon yellow stripe below the picture. The backs have the player's current statistics and biography. Included in the set are Eric Lindros, Pat Falloon, and Scott Niedermayer, the top three picks respectively. The cards are numbered on the back roughly according to the order in which the players were drafted. The cards were issued in both English and French versions; the French version is valued from 1X to 1.25X the prices listed below.

	MINT	EXC	G-VG
COMPLETE SET (50)	7.00	2.80	.70
COMMON PLAYER (1-50)	.10	.04	.01
☐ 1 Eric Lindros	3.00	1.20	.30
☐ 2 Pat Falloon	.75	.30	.07
☐ 3 Scott Niedermayer	.75	.30	.07
☐ 4 Scott Lachance	.20	.08	.02
☐ 5 Peter Forsberg	1.00	.40	.10
☐ 6 Alek Stojanov	.10	.04	.01
☐ 7 Richard Matvichuk	.15	.06	.01
☐ 8 Patrick Poulin	.25	.10	.02
☐ 9 Martin Lapointe	.20	.08	.02
☐ 10 Tyler Wright	.15	.06	.01
☐ 11 Philippe Boucher	.15	.06	.01
☐ 12 Pat Peake	.40	.16	.04
☐ 13 Markus Naslund	.20	.08	.02
☐ 14 Brent Bilodeau	.10	.04	.01
☐ 15 Glen Murray	.30	.12	.03
☐ 16 Niklas Sundblad	.10	.04	.01
☐ 17 Martin Rucinsky	.20	.08	.02
☐ 18 Trevor Halverson	.10	.04	.01
☐ 19 Dean McAmmond	.15	.06	.01
☐ 20 Ray Whitney	.25	.10	.02
☐ 21 Rene Corbet	.15	.06	.01
☐ 22 Eric Lavigne	.10	.04	.01
☐ 23 Zigmund Palffy	.25	.10	.02
☐ 24 Steve Staios	.15	.06	.01
☐ 25 Jim Campbell	.15	.06	.01
☐ 26 Jassen Cullimore	.10	.04	.01
☐ 27 Martin Hamrlik	.10	.04	.01
☐ 28 Jamie Pushor	.10	.04	.01
☐ 29 Donevan Hextall	.10	.04	.01
☐ 30 Andrew Verner	.15	.06	.01
☐ 31 Jason Dawe	.15	.06	.01
☐ 32 Jeff Nelson	.15	.06	.01
☐ 33 Darcy Werenka	.10	.04	.01
☐ 34 Jozef Stumpel	.25	.10	.02
☐ 35 Francois Groleau	.10	.04	.01
☐ 36 Guy Leveque	.15	.06	.01
☐ 37 Jamie Matthews	.10	.04	.01
☐ 38 Dody Wood	.10	.04	.01
☐ 39 Yanic Perrault	.20	.08	.02
☐ 40 Jamie McLennan	.20	.08	.02
☐ 41 Yanic Dupre UER	.10	.04	.01
☐ 42 Sandy McCarthy	.15	.06	.01
☐ 43 Chris Osgood	.35	.14	.03
☐ 44 Fredrik Lindquist	.10	.04	.01
☐ 45 Jason Young	.10	.04	.01
☐ 46 Steve Konowalchuk	.15	.06	.01
☐ 47 Mikael Nylander UER	.25	.10	.02
☐ 48 Shane Peacock	.10	.04	.01
☐ 49 Yves Sarault	.10	.04	.01
☐ 50 Marcel Cousineau	.10	.04	.01
☐ B Raghib(Rocket) Ismail	.50	.20	.05
Rocket On Ice			
(Pictured on skates)			

1992 Classic Draft Promos

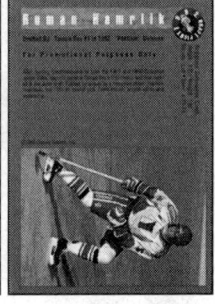

These three cards measure the standard size (2 1/2" by 3 1/2") and feature color action player photos with white borders, except for the Lemieux card, which has a black and white picture with the words "Flash Back 92" printed at the top. The player's name is printed in a gold stripe at the bottom, which intersects the Classic logo at the lower left corner. The gold backs have horizontally oriented player photos, again the Lemieux being black and white and the others color. The text on the back is vertically oriented, except for the biography, and includes draft information, career highlights, and the words "For Promotional Purposes Only". The cards are unnumbered and checklisted below in alphabetical order.

	MINT	EXC	G-VG
COMPLETE SET (3)	6.00	2.40	.60
COMMON PLAYER (1-3)	1.00	.40	.10

☐ 1 Roman Hamrlik	1.50	.60	.15
☐ 2 Mario Lemieux	5.00	2.00	.50
(Flash Back '92)			
☐ 3 Ray Whitney	1.00	.40	.10

1992 Classic Draft

The 1992 Classic Hockey Draft Picks set consists of 120 standard-size (2 1/2" by 3 1/2") cards. Mario Lemieux was featured on a special flashback card, an autograph card, and a special card individually numbered 1-10,000, all of which were randomly inserted throughout the production run. Also randomly inserted throughout the foil packs were 1,366 instant winner cards that entitled the holder to win autographed memorabilia from Mario Lemieux and other hockey stars. The production run for the regular issue cards was reportedly 9,966 ten-box cases. Classic also issued the 1992 Draft Pick set in a Gold version. The Gold factory sets were packaged in a walnut display case. The Gold sets also included an individually numbered card signed by Valeri and Pavel Bure.

	MINT	EXC	G-VG
COMPLETE SET (120)	10.00	4.00	1.00
COMMON PLAYER (1-120)	.10	.04	.01
☐ 1 Roman Hamrlik	.20	.08	.02
☐ 2 Alexei Yashin	1.00	.40	.10
☐ 3 Mike Rathje	.20	.08	.02
☐ 4 Darius Kasparaitis	.20	.08	.02
☐ 5 Cory Stillman	.15	.06	.01
☐ 6 Robert Petrovicky	.20	.08	.02
☐ 7 Andrei Nazarov	.20	.08	.02
☐ 8 Cory Stillman CL	.10	.04	.01
☐ 9 Jason Bowen	.15	.06	.01
☐ 10 Jason Smith	.15	.06	.01
☐ 11 David Wilkie	.10	.04	.01
☐ 12 Curtis Bowen	.15	.06	.01
☐ 13 Grant Marshall	.10	.04	.01
☐ 14 Valeri Bure	.75	.30	.07
☐ 15 Jeff Shantz	.15	.06	.01
☐ 16 Justin Hocking	.10	.04	.01
☐ 17 Mike Peca	.20	.08	.02
☐ 18 Marc Hussey	.10	.04	.01
☐ 19 Sandy Allan	.10	.04	.01
☐ 20 Kirk Maltby	.15	.06	.01
☐ 21 Cale Hulse	.10	.04	.01
☐ 22 Sylvain Cloutier	.10	.04	.01
☐ 23 Martin Gendron	.15	.06	.01
☐ 24 Kevin Smythe	.15	.06	.01
☐ 25 Jason McBain	.10	.04	.01
☐ 26 Lee J. Leslie	.10	.04	.01
☐ 27 Ralph Intranuovo	.15	.06	.01
☐ 28 Martin Reichel	.10	.04	.01
☐ 29 Stefan Ustorf	.10	.04	.01
☐ 30 Jarkko Varvio	.20	.08	.02
☐ 31 Jere Lehtinen	.15	.06	.01
☐ 32 Janne Gronvall	.10	.04	.01
☐ 33 Martin Straka	.75	.30	.07
☐ 34 Libor Polasek	.10	.04	.01
☐ 35 Jozef Cierny	.10	.04	.01
☐ 36 Jan Vopat	.15	.06	.01
☐ 37 Ondrej Steiner	.10	.04	.01
☐ 38 Jan Caloun	.15	.06	.01
☐ 39 Petr Hrbek	.10	.04	.01
☐ 40 Richard Smehlik	.20	.08	.02
☐ 41 Sergei Gonchar CL	.10	.04	.01
☐ 42 Sergei Krivokrasov	.20	.08	.02
☐ 43 Sergei Gonchar	.15	.06	.01
☐ 44 Boris Mironov	.20	.08	.02
☐ 45 Denis Metliuk	.10	.04	.01
☐ 46 Sergei Klimovich	.10	.04	.01
☐ 47 Sergei Brylin	.15	.06	.01
☐ 48 Andrei Nikolishin	.10	.04	.01
☐ 49 Alexander Cherbayev	.20	.08	.02
☐ 50 Sergei Zholtok	.15	.06	.01
☐ 51 Vitali Prokhorov	.15	.06	.01
☐ 52 Nikolai Borschevsky	.25	.10	.02
☐ 53 Vitali Tomilin	.10	.04	.01
☐ 54 Alexander Alexeyev	.15	.06	.01
☐ 55 Roman Zolotov	.10	.04	.01
☐ 56 Konstantin Korotkov	.15	.06	.01
☐ 57 Laperriere Family	.10	.04	.01
☐ 58 Lacroix Family	.10	.04	.01
☐ 59 Manon Rheaume	7.00	2.80	.70
☐ 60 Roman Hamrlik CL	.15	.06	.01
Alexei Yashin			
Mike Rathje			
☐ 61 Viktor Kozlov CL	.20	.08	.02
☐ 62 Viktor Kozlov	.50	.20	.05
☐ 63 Denny Felsner CL	.10	.04	.01
☐ 64 Denny Felsner	.15	.06	.01
☐ 65 Darrin Madeley	.15	.06	.01
☐ 66 Mario Lemieux FLB	1.00	.40	.10
☐ 67 Sandy Moger	.10	.04	.01
☐ 68 Dave Karpa	.15	.06	.01
☐ 69 Martin Jiranek	.10	.04	.01
☐ 70 Dwayne Norris	.15	.06	.01
☐ 71 Michael Stewart	.10	.04	.01
☐ 72 Joby Messier	.10	.04	.01
☐ 73 Mike Bales	.10	.04	.01
☐ 74 Scott Thomas	.10	.04	.01
☐ 75 Daniel Laperriere	.10	.04	.01
☐ 76 Mike Lappin	.10	.04	.01
☐ 77 Eric Lacroix	.10	.04	.01
☐ 78 Martin Lacroix	.10	.04	.01
☐ 79 Scott LaGrand	.15	.06	.01
☐ 80 Jean-Yves Roy	.15	.06	.01
☐ 81 Scott Pellerin	.10	.04	.01
☐ 82 Rob Gaudreau	.20	.08	.02
☐ 83 Mike Boback	.10	.04	.01
☐ 84 Dixon Ward	.15	.06	.01
☐ 85 Jeff McLean	.10	.04	.01
☐ 86 Dallas Drake	.20	.08	.02
☐ 87 Bret Hedican	.20	.08	.02
☐ 88 Doug Zmolek	.15	.06	.01
☐ 89 Trent Klatt	.20	.08	.02
☐ 90 Larry Olimb	.10	.04	.01
☐ 91 Duane Derksen	.10	.04	.01
☐ 92 Doug MacDonald	.10	.04	.01
☐ 93 Dmitri Kvartalnov CL	.10	.04	.01
☐ 94 Jim Cummins	.15	.06	.01
☐ 95 Lonnie Loach	.10	.04	.01
☐ 96 Keith Jones	.15	.06	.01
☐ 97 Jason Woolley	.10	.04	.01
☐ 98 Rob Zamuner	.15	.06	.01
☐ 99 Brad Werenka	.15	.06	.01
☐ 100 Brent Grieve	.15	.06	.01
☐ 101 Sean Hill	.15	.06	.01
☐ 102 Keith Carney	.10	.04	.01
☐ 103 Peter Ciavaglia	.10	.04	.01
☐ 104 David Littman	.10	.04	.01
☐ 105 Bill Guerin	.25	.10	.02
☐ 106 Mikhail Kravets	.10	.04	.01
☐ 107 J.F. Quintin	.10	.04	.01
☐ 108 Mike Needham	.15	.06	.01
☐ 109 Jason Ruff	.10	.04	.01
☐ 110 Mike Vukonich	.10	.04	.01
☐ 111 Shawn McCosh	.10	.04	.01
☐ 112 Dave Tretowicz	.10	.04	.01
☐ 113 Todd Harkins	.10	.04	.01
☐ 114 Jason Muzzatti	.15	.06	.01
☐ 115 Paul Kruse	.10	.04	.01
☐ 116 Kevin Wortman	.10	.04	.01
☐ 117 Sean Burke	.15	.06	.01
☐ 118 Keith Gretzky	.20	.08	.02
☐ 119 Ray Whitney	.20	.08	.02
☐ 120 Dmitri Kvartalnov	.20	.08	.02
☐ AU1 Mario Lemieux	200.00	80.00	20.00
AU/2000			
(Flashback '92;			
certified autograph)			
☐ SP1 Mario Lemieux	35.00	14.00	3.50
(Flashback '92)			

1992 Classic Draft Gold Promo

The front features a black-and-white action player photo bordered in white. The player's name is printed in a gold foil stripe beneath the picture, with the position given on a short black bar. On a gold background, the back has draft information, statistics, player profile, and a second black-and-white photo that is horizontally oriented. The card is unnumbered and has the disclaimer "For Promotional Purposes Only" printed on the back.

	MINT	EXC	G-VG
COMPLETE SET (1)	7.50	3.00	.75
COMMON CARD	7.50	3.00	.75
☐ NNO Mario Lemieux	7.50	3.00	.75

1992 Classic Draft Gold

Classic also issued the 1992 Draft Picks set in a Gold version which sells for between three and six times the corresponding regular cards. Reportedly only 6,000 sets and 7,500 uncut sheets were produced. The sets were packaged in a walnut display case. The fronts feature posed and action color player photos bordered in white. The player's name is printed in a gold stripe beneath the picture, with the position given on a short black bar. On a gold background, the backs have draft information, statistics, player profile, and a second color photo that is horizontally oriented. The Gold factory sets also included an individually numbered card signed by Valeri and Pavel Bure. Gold star cards are valued at three to six times the prices listed below.

	MINT	EXC	G-VG
COMPLETE SET (121)	100.00	40.00	10.00
COMMON PLAYER (1-120)	.25	.10	.02

		MINT	EXC	G-VG
☐ AU	Bure Brothers AU/6000	50.00	20.00	5.00
	Pavel Bure			
	Valeri Bure			
	(Only available in			
	Gold sets)			

1992 Classic Draft LPs

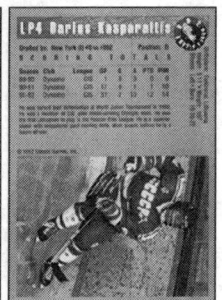

This ten-card set features hockey draft picks signed by Classic. The cards are standard size, 2 1/2" by 3 1/2", and are numbered on the back with an "LP" prefix. The cards were random inserts in packs of 1992 Classic Hockey Draft Picks.

	MINT	EXC	G-VG
COMPLETE SET (10)	30.00	12.00	3.00
COMMON PLAYER (LP1-LP10)	1.25	.50	.12
☐ LP1 Roman Hamrlik	4.00	1.60	.40
☐ LP2 Alexei Yashin	8.00	3.25	.80
☐ LP3 Mike Rathje	1.50	.60	.15
☐ LP4 Darius Kasparaitis	4.00	1.60	.40
☐ LP5 Cory Stillman	1.50	.60	.15
☐ LP6 Dmitri Kvartalnov	4.00	1.60	.40
☐ LP7 David Wilkie	1.25	.50	.12
☐ LP8 Curtis Bowen	1.25	.50	.12
☐ LP9 Valeri Bure	7.00	2.80	.70
☐ LP10 Joby Messier	1.25	.50	.12

1992-93 Classic Manon Rheaume C3 Presidential

This standard-size (2 1/2" by 3 1/2") card pictures Rheaume holding a hockey stick and carrying an equipment bag over her shoulder. The picture is bordered in white, and her name and position are printed on the wider right border. The Classic "C3 Presidential" logo is gold foil stamped across the top of the picture. The back has a color close-up photo and a player quote. Reportedly only 5,000 of these cards were produced. The card is numbered on the back.

	MINT	EXC	G-VG
COMPLETE SET (1)	10.00	4.00	1.00
COMMON CARD	10.00	4.00	1.00
☐ 1 Manon Rheaume	10.00	4.00	1.00

1992-93 Classic Manon Rheaume Promo

Manon Rheaume, professional hockey's first female player, signed her trading card for fans before the Atlanta Braves playoff game Wednesday, October 7, 1992. Sponsored by Power 99, a local radio station, this promotion was aimed at benefiting "Pennies from Heaven," an urban renewal movement championed by former President Jimmy Carter and Atlanta Braves third baseman Terry Pendleton. Fans who brought a jar of pennies or a 10.00 donation were given the autographed Rheaume promotional card; close to 1,000 cards were signed and about 2,500 promo bags were given away. The front of this standard size (2 1/2" by 3 1/2") card features a posed color player photo with white borders. Her name appears in a gold stripe across the bottom of the picture. The words "A Classic First" are printed in gold at the upper right corner of the picture. The center back shows the yellow and green Classic logo. The disclaimer "For Promotional Purposes Only" is printed in black at the top and bottom and in gray over the rest of the card back.

	MINT	EXC	G-VG
COMPLETE SET (1)	10.00	4.00	1.00
COMMON CARD	10.00	4.00	1.00
☐ NNO Manon Rheaume	10.00	4.00	1.00

1993 Classic Pro Prospects Previews

These five standard-size (2 1/2" by 3 1/2") cards were reportedly inserted on an average of three per case of 1993 Classic Basketball Draft Picks. The cards are unnumbered.

	MINT	EXC	G-VG
COMPLETE SET (5)	35.00	14.00	3.50
COMMON PLAYER (HK1-HK5)	4.00	1.60	..40
☐ HK1 Alexandre Daigle	6.00	2.40	.60
☐ HK2 Manon Rheaume	15.00	6.00	1.50
☐ HK3 Barry Richter	4.00	1.60	.40
☐ HK4 Teemu Selanne	7.00	2.80	.70
☐ HK5 Alexei Yashin	7.00	2.80	.70

1993 Classic Pro Prospects Prototypes

These three standard-size (2 1/2" by 3 1/2") promo cards were issued to show the design of the 1993 Classic Pro Hockey Prospects set. Inside white borders, the fronts display color action player photos. A color bar edges the top of each picture and carries the player's name, team, and position. Also a black bar edges the bottom of each picture. On a gray background, the backs feature a color close-up photo, logos, biographical information, statistics, and career summary. A black bar that accents the top carries the card number and the disclaimer "For Promotional Purposes Only".

	MINT	EXC	G-VG
COMPLETE SET (3)	8.00	3.25	.80
COMMON PLAYER (PR1-PR3)	1.50	.60	.15
☐ PR1 Steve King	1.50	.60	.15
Binghamton Rangers			
☐ PR2 Manon Rheaume	6.00	2.40	.60
The First Lady of			
Hockey			
☐ PR3 Rob Gaudreau	1.50	.60	.15
Kansas City Blades			

1993 Classic Pro Prospects

The 1993 Classic Pro Hockey Prospects set features 150 standard-size (2 1/2" by 3 1/2") cards. The production run was 6,500 sequentially numbered cases, and female hockey phenom Manon Rheaume autographed 6,500 cards for random insertion into the foil packs. Inside white borders, the fronts display color action player photos. A color bar edges the top of each picture and carries the player's name, team, and position. On the subset cards, a black bar edges the bottom of the picture. On a gray background, the backs feature a color close-up photo, logos, biographical information, statistics, and career summary. The set includes a Manon Rheaume subset (1-7), a Minor League Graduate subset (31-34), a 1993 Draft Prospect subset (93-98), and, scattered throughout the set, 24 cards of the

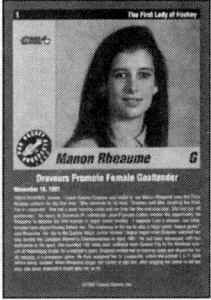

hottest AHL and IHL All-Stars of the 1992-93 season. The cards are numbered on the back.

		MINT	EXC	G-VG
	COMPLETE SET (150)	15.00	6.00	1.50
	COMMON PLAYER (1-150)	.10	.04	.01
☐ 1	Manon Rheaume Draveurs Promote Female Goaltender	3.00	1.20	.30
☐ 2	Manon Rheaume Quebec League Welcomes Female Netminder	3.00	1.20	.30
☐ 3	Manon Rheaume Woman Plays Preseason Game	3.00	1.20	.30
☐ 4	Manon Rheaume Atlanta Knights Sign Female Netminder	3.00	1.20	.30
☐ 5	Manon Rheaume Rheaume Makes Pro Hockey History	3.00	1.20	.30
☐ 6	Manon Rheaume Standing Ovation for Hockey Pioneer	3.00	1.20	.30
☐ 7	Manon Rheaume Rheaume Has Golden Touch in Finland	3.00	1.20	.30
☐ 8	Oleg Petrov Fredericton Canadiens	.25	.10	.02
☐ 9	Shjon Podein Cape Breton Oilers	.15	.06	.01
☐ 10	Alexei Kovalev AS Binghamton Rangers	.60	.24	.06
☐ 11	Roman Oksiuta Cape Breton Oilers	.15	.06	.01
☐ 12	Dave Tomlinson St. John's Maple Leafs	.10	.04	.01
☐ 13	Jason Miller Utica Devils	.15	.06	.01
☐ 14	Andrew McKim Providence Bruins	.10	.04	.01
☐ 15	Dallas Drake Fantastic Frosh	.20	.08	.02
☐ 16	Rob Gaudreau Kansas City Blades	.20	.08	.02
☐ 17	Darrin Madeley New Haven Senators	.15	.06	.01
☐ 18	Scott Pellerin Utica Devils	.10	.04	.01
☐ 19	Scott Thomas Rochester Americans	.10	.04	.01
☐ 20	Chris Tancill AS Adirondack Red Wings	.10	.04	.01
☐ 21	Patrick Kjellberg Fredericton Canadiens	.10	.04	.01
☐ 22	Jim Dowd Utica Devils	.15	.06	.01
☐ 23	Daniel Gauthier Cleveland Lumberjacks	.10	.04	.01
☐ 24	Mark Beaufait Kansas City Blades	.15	.06	.01
☐ 25	Milan Tichy AS Indianapolis Ice	.10	.04	.01
☐ 26	Chris Osgood Adirondack Red Wings	.40	.16	.04
☐ 27	Charles Poulin Fredericton Canadiens	.10	.04	.01
☐ 28	Patrick Lebeau Salt Lake Golden Eagles	.10	.04	.01
☐ 29	Chris Govedaris Springfield Indians	.10	.04	.01
☐ 30	Andrei Trefilov AS	.35	.14	.03
☐ 31	Kevin Stevens MLG Muskegon Lumberjacks	.25	.10	.02
☐ 32	Dmitri Kvartalnov MLG San Diego Gulls	.20	.08	.02
☐ 33	Patrick Roy MLG Sherbrooke Canadiens	.75	.30	.07
☐ 34	Mark Recchi MLG Muskegon Lumberjacks	.25	.10	.02
☐ 35	Adam Oates MLG Adirondack Red Wings	.25	.10	.02
☐ 36	Patrik Augusta St. John's Maple Leafs	.10	.04	.01
☐ 37	Gerry Fleming Fredericton Canadiens	.10	.04	.01
☐ 38	Sergei Krivokrasov Indianapolis Ice	.20	.08	.02
☐ 39	Mike O'Neill Moncton Hawks	.15	.06	.01
☐ 40	Darrin Madeley AS New Haven Senators	.15	.06	.01
☐ 41	Linsay Vallis Fredericton Canadiens	.10	.04	.01
☐ 42	Todd Nelson Cleveland Lumberjacks	.10	.04	.01
☐ 43	Keith Jones Baltimore Skipjacks	.10	.04	.01
☐ 44	Howie Rosenblatt Cincinnati Cyclones The Legend	.10	.04	.01
☐ 45	Jason Ruff AS Peoria Rivermen	.10	.04	.01
☐ 46	Robert Lang Phoenix Roadrunners	.20	.08	.02
☐ 47	Andre Faust Hershey Bears	.10	.04	.01
☐ 48	Steve Bancroft Indianapolis Ice	.10	.04	.01
☐ 49	Iain Fraser Capital District Islanders	.20	.08	.02
☐ 50	Roman Hamrlik AS Atlanta Knights	.20	.08	.02
☐ 51	Pierre Sevigny Fredericton Canadiens	.15	.06	.01
☐ 52	Jeff Levy Kalamazoo Wings	.10	.04	.01
☐ 53	Len Barrie Hershey Bears	.10	.04	.01
☐ 54	David Goverde Phoenix Roadrunners	.15	.06	.01
☐ 55	Vladimir Malakhov AS Capital District Islanders	.30	.12	.03
☐ 56	Scott White New Haven Senators	.10	.04	.01
☐ 57	Dmitri Motkov Adirondack Red Wings	.10	.04	.01
☐ 58	Jason Herter Hamilton Canucks	.10	.04	.01
☐ 59	Drake Berehowsky St. John's Maple Leafs	.15	.06	.01
☐ 60	Steve King AS Binghamton Rangers	.10	.04	.01
☐ 61	Doug Barrault Kalamazoo Wings	.10	.04	.01
☐ 62	Martin Hamrlik Springfield Indians	.10	.04	.01
☐ 63	Kevin Miehm Peoria Rivermen	.10	.04	.01
☐ 64	Shaun Van Allen Cape Breton Oilers	.10	.04	.01
☐ 65	Corey Hirsch AS Binghamton Rangers	.25	.10	.02
☐ 66	Dwayne Norris Halifax Citadels	.15	.06	.01
☐ 67	Petr Hrbek Adirondack Red Wings	.10	.04	.01
☐ 68	Philippe Boucher Rochester Americans	.10	.04	.01
☐ 69	Denis Chervyakov Providence Bruins	.10	.04	.01
☐ 70	Sergei Zubov AS Binghamton Rangers	.60	.24	.06
☐ 71	Geoff Sarjeant Peoria Rivermen	.10	.04	.01
☐ 72	Les Kuntar Fredericton Canadiens	.10	.04	.01
☐ 73	Byron Dafoe Baltimore Skipjacks	.10	.04	.01
☐ 74	Checklist Alexei Kovalev Sergei Zubov Steve King Corey Hirsch	.20	.08	.02
☐ 75	Alexandr Andrievski AS	.10	.04	.01

	Indianapolis Ice			
☐ 76	Checklist	.10	.04	.01
	Joby Messier			
	Mitch Messier			
☐ 77	Brian Sullivan	.10	.04	.01
	Utica Devils			
☐ 78	Steve Larouche	.10	.04	.01
	Fredericton Canadiens			
☐ 79	Denis Chasse	.15	.06	.01
	Halifax Citadels			
☐ 80	Felix Potvin AS	1.50	.60	.15
	St. John's Maple Leafs			
☐ 81	Josef Beranek	.20	.08	.02
	Cape Breton Oilers			
☐ 82	Ken Klee	.10	.04	.01
	Baltimore Skipjacks			
☐ 83	Jozef Stumpel	.20	.08	.02
	Providence Bruins			
☐ 84	Andrew Verner	.10	.04	.01
	Cape Breton Oilers			
☐ 85	Keith Osborne AS	.10	.04	.01
	Atlanta Knights			
☐ 86	Igor Malykhin	.10	.04	.01
	Adirondack Red Wings			
☐ 87	Gilbert Dionne	.15	.06	.01
	Fredericton Canadiens			
☐ 88	Viktor Gordijuk	.20	.08	.02
	Rochester Americans			
☐ 89	Glen Murray	.20	.08	.02
	Providence Bruins			
☐ 90	Scott Pellerin AS	.10	.04	.01
	Utica Devils			
☐ 91	Tommy Soderstrom	.20	.08	.02
	Hershey Bears			
☐ 92	Terry Chitaroni	.10	.04	.01
	St. John's Maple Leafs			
☐ 93	Viktor Kozlov	.50	.20	.05
	Russian National Team			
☐ 94	Mikhail Shtalenkov	.35	.14	.03
	Milwaukee Admirals			
☐ 95	Leonid Toropchenko	.10	.04	.01
	Springfield Indians			
☐ 96	Alex Galchenyuk	.10	.04	.01
	Milwaukee Admirals			
☐ 97	Anatoli Fedotov	.10	.04	.01
	Moncton Hawks			
☐ 98	Igor Chibirev	.15	.06	.01
	Fort Wayne Komets			
☐ 99	Keith Gretzky	.20	.08	.02
	San Diego Gulls			
☐ 100	Manon Rheaume	4.00	1.60	.40
	Atlanta Knights			
☐ 101	Sean Whyte	.10	.04	.01
	Phoenix Roadrunners			
☐ 102	Steve Konowalchuk	.15	.06	.01
	Baltimore Skipjacks			
☐ 103	Richard Borgo	.10	.04	.01
	Cape Breton Oilers			
☐ 104	Paul DiPietro	.15	.06	.01
	Fredericton Canadiens			
☐ 105	Patrik Carnback AS	.10	.04	.01
	Fredericton Canadiens			
☐ 106	Mike Fountain	.15	.06	.01
	Hamilton Canucks			
☐ 107	Jamie Heward	.10	.04	.01
	Cleveland Lumberjacks			
☐ 108	David St. Pierre	.10	.04	.01
	Salt Lake Golden Eagles			
☐ 109	Sean O'Donnell	.10	.04	.01
	Rochester Americans			
☐ 110	Greg Andrusak AS	.10	.04	.01
	Cleveland Lumberjacks			
☐ 111	Damian Rhodes	.25	.10	.02
	St. John's Maple Leafs			
☐ 112	Ted Crowley	.10	.04	.01
	St. John's Maple Leafs			
☐ 113	Chris Taylor	.10	.04	.01
	Capital District Islanders			
☐ 114	Terran Sandwith	.10	.04	.01
	Hershey Bears			
☐ 115	Jesse Belanger AS	.25	.10	.02
	Fredericton Canadiens			
☐ 116	Justin Duberman	.15	.06	.01
	Cleveland Lumberjacks			
☐ 117	Arturs Irbe	1.00	.40	.10
	Kansas City Blades			
☐ 118	Chris LiPuma	.10	.04	.01
	Atlanta Knights			
☐ 119	Mike Torchia	.10	.04	.01
	Kalamazoo Wings			
☐ 120	Niclas Andersson AS	.10	.04	.01
	Halifax Citadels			
☐ 121	Rick Knickle	.15	.06	.01
	San Diego Gulls			

☐ 122	Scott Gruhl	.10	.04	.01
	Fort Wayne Komets			
☐ 123	Dave Michayluk	.10	.04	.01
	Cleveland Lumberjacks			
☐ 124	Guy Leveque	.15	.06	.01
	Phoenix Roadrunners			
☐ 125	Scott Thomas AS	.10	.04	.01
	Rochester Americans			
☐ 126	Travis Green	.15	.06	.01
	Capital District Islanders			
☐ 127	Joby Messier	.10	.04	.01
	Binghamton Rangers			
☐ 128	Victor Ignatjev	.10	.04	.01
	Kansas City Blades			
☐ 129	Brad Tiley	.10	.04	.01
	Binghamton Rangers			
☐ 130	Grigori Panteleyev AS	.10	.04	.01
	Providence Bruins			
☐ 131	Vyatcheslav Butsayev	.15	.06	.01
	Hershey Bears			
☐ 132	Danny Lorenz	.10	.04	.01
	Capital District Islanders			
☐ 133	Marty McInnis	.15	.06	.01
	Capital District Islanders			
☐ 134	Ed Ronan	.10	.04	.01
	Fredericton Canadiens			
☐ 135	Vyacheslav Kozlov AS	.40	.16	.04
	Adirondack Red Wings			
☐ 136	Kevin St. Jacques	.10	.04	.01
	Indianapolis Ice			
☐ 137	Pavel Kostichkin	.10	.04	.01
	Moncton Hawks			
☐ 138	Mike Hurlbut	.10	.04	.01
	Binghamton Rangers			
☐ 139	Tomas Forslund	.10	.04	.01
	Salt Lake Golden Eagles			
☐ 140	Rob Gaudreau AS	.20	.08	.02
	Kansas City Blades			
☐ 141	Shawn Heaphy	.10	.04	.01
	Salt Lake Golden Eagles			
☐ 142	Radek Hamr	.15	.06	.01
	New Haven Senators			
☐ 143	Jaroslav Otevrel	.15	.06	.01
	Kansas City Blades			
☐ 144	Keith Redmond	.10	.04	.01
	Phoenix Roadrunners			
☐ 145	Tom Pederson AS	.15	.06	.01
	Kansas City Blades			
☐ 146	Jaroslav Modry	.15	.06	.01
	Utica Devils			
☐ 147	Darren McCarty	.20	.08	.02
	Adirondack Red Wings			
☐ 148	Terry Yake	.20	.08	.02
	Springfield Indians			
☐ 149	Ivan Droppa	.10	.04	.01
	Indianapolis Ice			
☐ 150	The VCR Line	.10	.04	.01
	Shaun Van Allen			
	Dan Currie			
	Steven Rice			
	Cape Breton Islanders			
☐ AU	Dmitri Kvartalnov	25.00	10.00	2.50
	AU/4000			
	(Certified autograph)			
☐ AU	Manon Rheaume	80.00	32.00	8.00
	AU/6500			
	(Certified autograph)			

1993 Classic Pro Prospects BCs

This 20-card set measures the standard size (2 1/2" by 3 1/2") and features full-bleed, color, action player photos. One BC card was inserted in each jumbo pack. A silver foil bar at the bottom contains the player's name, team, and position. According to the silver-foil print near the top of the photo, each card is one of 40,000 limited edition bonus cards. The backs are gray and display a player picture, biographical information, statistics, and career highlights. The cards are numbered on the back with a "BC" prefix.

	MINT	EXC	G-VG
COMPLETE SET (20)	30.00	12.00	3.00
COMMON PLAYER (BC1-BC20)	.50	.20	.05
☐ BC1 Alexei Kovalev	3.50	1.40	.35

☐ BC2	Andrei Trefilov	1.50	.60	.15
☐ BC3	Roman Hamrlik	1.50	.60	.15
☐ BC4	Vladimir Malakhov	2.00	.80	.20
☐ BC5	Corey Hirsch	1.50	.60	.15
☐ BC6	Sergei Zubov	3.00	1.20	.30
☐ BC7	Felix Potvin	6.00	2.40	.60
☐ BC8	Tommy Soderstrom	1.00	.40	.10
☐ BC9	Viktor Kozlov	2.00	.80	.20
☐ BC10	Manon Rheaume	15.00	6.00	1.50
☐ BC11	Jesse Belanger	2.00	.80	.20
☐ BC12	Rick Knickle	.50	.20	.05
☐ BC13	Joby Messier	.50	.20	.05
☐ BC14	Vyacheslav Butsayev	.50	.20	.05
☐ BC15	Tomas Forslund	.50	.20	.05
☐ BC16	Jozef Stumpel	2.00	.80	.20
☐ BC17	Dmitri Kvartalnov MLG	1.50	.60	.15
☐ BC18	Adam Oates MLG	2.00	.80	.20
☐ BC19	Dallas Drake	1.00	.40	.10
☐ BC20	Mark Recchi MLG	2.00	.80	.20

1993 Classic Pro Prospects LPs

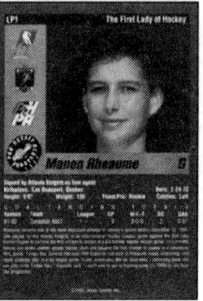

These five limited-print cards were randomly inserted throughout each case. The cards measure the standard size (2 1/2" by 3 1/2"). The fronts feature full-bleed, color, posed and action player photos. A metallic aqua stripe across the top carries the player's name, team, and position. The Classic logo overlaps this stripe and the photo. In a black stripe at the bottom are the words, "Limited Edition 1 of 26,000." The backs display a small player photo that is bordered on two sides by a light gray area containing hockey organizations logos and the player's name and position. Below the picture are statistics, biographical information, and career highlights. This information is printed in white against a dark gray background. The cards are numbered on the back with an "LP" prefix.

	MINT	EXC	G-VG
COMPLETE SET (5)	35.00	14.00	3.50
COMMON PLAYER (LP1-LP5)	4.00	1.60	.40
☐ LP1 Manon Rheaume	20.00	8.00	2.00

☐ LP2	Alexei Kovalev	8.00	3.25	.80
☐ LP3	Rob Gaudreau	4.00	1.60	.40
☐ LP4	Viktor Kozlov	5.00	2.00	.50
☐ LP5	Dallas Drake	4.00	1.60	.40

1993 Classic Draft Promos

These four standard-size (2 1/2" by 3 1/2") promo cards feature gray-bordered glossy color player action shots on the fronts. The player's name and position appears in blue lettering within the bottom border. The back carries another color player action shot, but bordered in white. The player's biography and draft status are printed in black lettering within the broad lower border. The unnumbered Paul Kariya card was distributed at the San Francisco Labor Day Sports Collectors Convention, held in September 1993. The cards are numbered on the back with a "PR" prefix.

	MINT	EXC	G-VG
COMPLETE SET (4)	20.00	8.00	2.00
COMMON PLAYER (1-3)	5.00	2.00	.50
☐ 1 Alexandre Daigle	5.00	2.00	.50
☐ 2 Jeff O'Neill	5.00	2.00	.50
Jason Bonsignore			
Jeff Friesen			
The Class of '94			
☐ 3 Pavel Bure	5.00	2.00	.50
☐ NNO Paul Kariya	5.00	2.00	.50

1993 Classic Draft Manon Rheaume Promo

This standard-size (2 1/2" by 3 1/2") promo card features the Atlanta Knights goaltender, Manon Rheaume. Inside a light gray border, the fronts features Rheaume in a sleeveless white blouse. The horizontal back has player information on the left and a second picture on the right with Rheaume dressed in black. The disclaimer "For Promotional Purposes Only" appears on the left beneath the text. The card is unnumbered.

	MINT	EXC	G-VG
COMPLETE SET (1)	7.50	3.00	.75
COMMON CARD	7.50	3.00	.75
☐ 1 Manon Rheaume	7.50	3.00	.75
Up Close and Personal			

1993 Classic Draft

 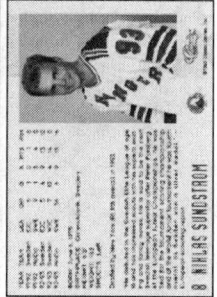

The 1993 Classic Hockey Draft set consists of 150 standard-size (2 1/2" by 3 1/2") cards. Production was limited to 14,500 sequentially-numbered ten-box cases. More than 15,000 autographed cards from Manon Rheaume, Doug Gilmour, Mark Recchi, Mike Bossy, Jeff O'Neill and other hockey stars were randomly inserted throughout the packs. Other randomly inserted limited-print cards were a ten-card Top Ten subset, a seven-card Team Canada subset, a 14-card Class of '94 subset, a seven-card Crash Numbered subset, and a special Manon Rheaume card. Reportedly 25,000 of each LP were produced. Topical subsets featuring foil-stamped cards are Top 10, The Class of '94, The Daigle File, Flashbacks, College Champions, Manon Rheaume, and Hockey Art. The cards are numbered on the back.

	MINT	EXC	G-VG
COMPLETE SET (150)	15.00	6.00	1.50
COMMON PLAYER (1-150)	.10	.04	.01
☐ 1 Alexandre Daigle	.50	.20	.05
☐ 2 Chris Pronger	.40	.16	.04
☐ 3 Chris Gratton	.40	.16	.04
☐ 4 Paul Kariya	.75	.30	.07
☐ 5 Rob Niedermayer	.40	.16	.04
☐ 6 Viktor Kozlov	.25	.10	.02
☐ 7 Jason Arnott	1.00	.40	.10
☐ 8 Niklas Sundstrom	.20	.08	.02
☐ 9 Todd Harvey	.25	.10	.02
☐ 10 Jocelyn Thibault	.25	.10	.02
☐ 11 Checklist 1	.10	.04	.01
Top Draft Picks			
☐ 12 Pat Peake	.20	.08	.02
1993 CHL POY			
☐ 13 Jason Allison	.25	.10	.02
☐ 14 Todd Bertuzzi	.15	.06	.01
☐ 15 Maxim Bets	.20	.08	.02
☐ 16 Curtis Bowen	.10	.04	.01
☐ 17 Kevin Brown	.10	.04	.01
☐ 18 Valeri Bure	.30	.12	.03
☐ 19 Jason Dawe	.10	.04	.01
☐ 20 Adam Deadmarsh	.15	.06	.01
☐ 21 Aaron Gavey	.20	.08	.02
☐ 22 Nathan Lafayette	.20	.08	.02
☐ 23 Eric Lecompte	.15	.06	.01
☐ 24 Manny Legace	.20	.08	.02
☐ 25 Mike Peca	.15	.06	.01
☐ 26 Denis Pederson	.15	.06	.01
☐ 27 Jeff Shantz	.10	.04	.01
☐ 28 Nick Stadjuhar	.15	.06	.01
☐ 29 Cory Stillman	.10	.04	.01
☐ 30 Michal Sykora	.15	.06	.01
☐ 31 Brent Tully	.10	.04	.01
☐ 32 Mike Wilson	.10	.04	.01
☐ 33 Junior Production Line	.10	.04	.01
Kevin Brown			
Pat Peake			
Bob Wren			
☐ 34 Checklist 2	.25	.10	.02
Dynamic Duo			
Alexandre Daigle			
Alexei Yashin			
☐ 35 Antti Aalto	.10	.04	.01
☐ 36 Radim Bicanek	.10	.04	.01
☐ 37 Vladimir Chebaturkin	.10	.04	.01
☐ 38 Alexander Cherbayev	.15	.06	.01
☐ 39 Markus Ketterer	.15	.06	.01
☐ 40 Saku Koivu	.35	.14	.03
☐ 41 Vladimir Krechin	.10	.04	.01
☐ 42 Alexei Kudashov	.15	.06	.01
☐ 43 Janne Laukkanen	.10	.04	.01
☐ 44 Janne Niinimaa	.10	.04	.01
☐ 45 Juha Riihijarvi	.10	.04	.01
☐ 46 Nikolai Tsulygin	.15	.06	.01
☐ 47 Vesa Viitakoski	.15	.06	.01
☐ 48 David Vyborny	.15	.06	.01
☐ 49 Nikolai Zavarukhin	.10	.04	.01
☐ 50 Alexandre Daigle	.50	.20	.05
1991 QMJHL Draft			
☐ 51 Alexandre Daigle	.50	.20	.05
1991-92 QMJHL Rookie			
☐ 52 Alexandre Daigle	.50	.20	.05
1992 CHL ROY			
☐ 53 Alexandre Daigle	.50	.20	.05
Emerging Superstar			
1992-93			
☐ 54 Alexandre Daigle	.50	.20	.05
First Draft Pick			
☐ 55 Jim Montgomery	.15	.06	.01
☐ 56 Mike Dunham	.15	.06	.01
☐ 57 Matt Martin	.15	.06	.01
☐ 58 Garth Snow	.15	.06	.01
☐ 59 Shawn Walsh	.10	.04	.01
☐ 60 Mark Bavis	.10	.04	.01
Mike Bavis			
☐ 61 Scott Chartier	.10	.04	.01
☐ 62 Craig Darby	.10	.04	.01
☐ 63 Ted Drury	.15	.06	.01
☐ 64 Steve Dubinsky	.15	.06	.01
☐ 65 Joe Frederick	.15	.06	.01
☐ 66 Cammi Granato	1.00	.40	.10
☐ 67 Brett Hauer	.10	.04	.01
☐ 68 Jon Hillebrandt	.15	.06	.01
☐ 69 Ryan Hughes	.10	.04	.01
☐ 70 Dean Hulett	.10	.04	.01
☐ 71 Kevin O'Sullivan	.10	.04	.01
☐ 72 Dan Plante	.10	.04	.01
☐ 73 Derek Plante	.40	.16	.04
☐ 74 Travis Richards	.10	.04	.01
☐ 75 Barry Richter	.15	.06	.01
☐ 76 David Roberts	.15	.06	.01
☐ 77 Chris Rogles	.15	.06	.01
☐ 78 Jon Rohloff	.10	.04	.01
☐ 79 Brian Rolston	.25	.10	.02
☐ 80 David Sacco	.15	.06	.01
☐ 81 Brian Savage	.15	.06	.01
☐ 82 Mike Smith	.10	.04	.01
☐ 83 Chris Tamer	.10	.04	.01
☐ 84 Chris Therien	.10	.04	.01
☐ 85 Aaron Ward	.15	.06	.01
☐ 86 Russian Celebration	.10	.04	.01
☐ 87 Vyacheslav Butsayev	.10	.04	.01
☐ 88 Jan Kaminsky	.15	.06	.01
☐ 89 Alexander Karpovtsev	.15	.06	.01
☐ 90 Valeri Karpov	.20	.08	.02
☐ 91 Sergei Petrenko	.15	.06	.01
☐ 92 Andrei Sapozhnikov	.10	.04	.01
☐ 93 Sergei Sorokin	.15	.06	.01
☐ 94 German Titov	.20	.08	.02
☐ 95 Vladimir Trefilov	.15	.06	.01
☐ 96 Alexei Yashin	.50	.20	.05
☐ 97 Dimitri Yushkevich	.10	.04	.01
☐ 98 Radek Bonk	1.00	.40	.10
☐ 99 Jason Bonsignore	.40	.16	.04
☐ 100 Brad Brown	.20	.08	.02
☐ 101 Chris Drury	.20	.08	.02
☐ 102 Jeff Friesen	.50	.20	.05
☐ 103 Sean Haggerty	.10	.04	.01
☐ 104 Jeff Kealty	.15	.06	.01
☐ 105 Alexandr Kharlamov	.30	.12	.03
☐ 106 Stanislav Neckar	.20	.08	.02
☐ 107 Tom O'Connor	.10	.04	.01

			MINT	EXC	G-VG
☐	108 Jeff O'Neill	.50	.20	.05
☐	109 Deron Quint	.15	.06	.01
☐	110 Vadim Sharifianov	.30	.12	.03
☐	111 Oleg Tverdovsky	.75	.30	.07
☐	112 Manon Rheaume COMIC	1.00	.40	.10
☐	113 Paul Kariya COMIC	.40	.16	.04
☐	114 Alexandre Daigle COMIC	.25	.10	.02
☐	115 Jeff O'Neill COMIC	.25	.10	.02
☐	116 Mike Bossy	.15	.06	.01
☐	117 Pavel Bure	.75	.30	.07
☐	118 Chris Chelios	.15	.06	.01
☒	119 Doug Gilmour	.25	.10	.02
☐	120 Roman Hamrlik	.15	.06	.01
☐	121 Jari Kurri	.15	.06	.01
☐	122 Alexander Mogilny	.20	.08	.02
☐	123 Felix Potvin	.75	.30	.07
☐	124 Teemu Selanne	.50	.20	.05
☐	125 Tommy Soderstrom	.15	.06	.01
☐	126 Mike Bales	.10	.04	.01
☐	127 Jozef Cierny	.10	.04	.01
☐	128 Ivan Droppa	.10	.04	.01
☐	129 Anders Eriksson	.10	.04	.01
☐	130 Anatoli Fedotov	.10	.04	.01
☐	131 Martin Gendron	.15	.06	.01
☐	132 Daniel Guerard	.10	.04	.01
☐	133 Corey Hirsch	.20	.08	.02
☐	134 Milos Holan	.10	.04	.01
☐	135 Kenny Jonsson	.25	.10	.02
☐	136 Steven King	.10	.04	.01
☐	137 Alexei Kovalev	.30	.12	.03
☐	138 Sergei Krivokrasov	.15	.06	.01
☐	139 Mats Lindgren	.15	.06	.01
☐	140 Grant Marshall	.10	.04	.01
☐	141 Jesper Mattsson	.15	.06	.01
☐	142 Sandy McCarthy	.15	.06	.01
☐	143 Dean Melanson	.10	.04	.01
☐	144 Robert Petrovicky	.15	.06	.01
☐	145 Mike Rathje	.10	.04	.01
☐	146 Manon Rheaume	2.50	1.00	.25
☐	147 Claude Savoie	.10	.04	.01
☐	148 Mikhail Shtalenkov	.20	.08	.02
☐	149 Manon Rheaume	2.50	1.00	.25
	A Season to Remember			
☐	150 Manon Rheaume	3.00	1.20	.30
	Up Close and Personnel			
☐	AU Mike Bossy AU/975	35.00	14.00	3.50
☐	AU Pavel Bure AU/900	90.00	36.00	9.00
☐	AU Chris Chelios AU/1800	35.00	14.00	3.50
☐	AU Doug Gilmour AU/1850	60.00	24.00	6.00
☐	AU Alex. Mogilny AU/950	60.00	24.00	6.00
☐	AU Jim Montgomery AU/975	20.00	8.00	2.00
☐	AU Rob Niedermayer AU/2500	35.00	14.00	3.50
☐	AU Jeff O'Neill AU/2225	35.00	14.00	3.50
☐	AU Pat Peake AU/790	30.00	12.00	3.00
☐	AU Mark Recchi AU/1725	35.00	14.00	3.50
☐	AU Manon Rheaume AU/1500	125.00	50.00	12.50
☐	AU Geoff Sanderson AU/975	50.00	20.00	5.00
☐	MR1 Manon Rheaume	35.00	14.00	3.50
	Acetate			

1993 Classic Draft Class of '94

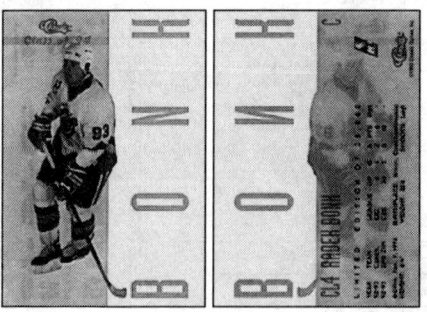

These standard size (2 1/2" by 3 1/2") cards were randomly inserted in foil packs. The cards are numbered on the back with a "CL" prefix.

	MINT	EXC	G-VG
COMPLETE SET (7)	40.00	16.00	4.00
COMMON PLAYER (CL1-CL7)	2.00	.80	.20
☐ CL1 Jeff O'Neill	7.00	2.80	.70
☐ CL2 Jason Bonsignore	7.00	2.80	.70
☐ CL3 Jeff Friesen	7.00	2.80	.70
☐ CL4 Radek Bonk	12.00	5.00	1.20
☐ CL5 Deron Quint	2.50	1.00	.25
☐ CL6 Vadim Sharifianov	5.00	2.00	.50
☐ CL7 Tom O'Connor	2.00	.80	.20

1993 Classic Draft Crash Numbered

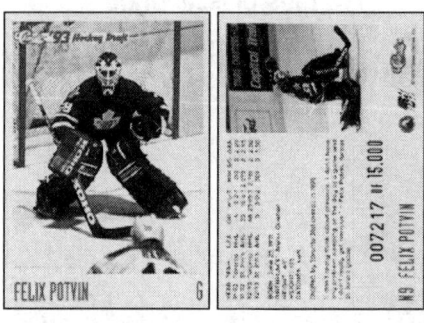

These standard size (2 1/2" by 3 1/2") cards were randomly inserted in foil packs. The cards are numbered on the back with a "N" prefix. These cards were individually numbered out of 10,000.

	MINT	EXC	G-VG
COMPLETE SET (10)	110.00	45.00	11.00
COMMON PLAYER (1-10)	10.00	4.00	1.00
☐ N1 Alexandre Daigle	10.00	4.00	1.00
☐ N2 Paul Kariya	12.00	5.00	1.20
☐ N3 Jeff O'Neill	10.00	4.00	1.00
☐ N4 Jason Bonsignore	10.00	4.00	1.00
☐ N5 Teemu Selanne	15.00	6.00	1.50
☐ N6 Pavel Bure	20.00	8.00	2.00
☐ N7 Alexander Mogilny	10.00	4.00	1.00
☐ N8 Manon Rheaume	40.00	16.00	4.00
☐ N9 Felix Potvin	18.00	7.25	1.80
☐ N10 Radek Bonk	18.00	7.25	1.80

1993 Classic Draft Team Canada

These standard size (2 1/2" by 3 1/2") cards were randomly inserted throughout the foil packs. The cards are numbered on the back with a "TC" prefix.

	MINT	EXC	G-VG
COMPLETE SET (7)	22.00	9.00	2.00
COMMON PLAYER (TC1-TC7)	2.50	1.00	.25

		MINT	EXC	G-VG
☐ TC1	Greg Johnson	2.50	1.00	.25
☐ TC2	Paul Kariya	7.00	2.80	.70
☐ TC3	Brian Savage	2.50	1.00	.25
☐ TC4	Bill Ranford	2.50	1.00	.25
☐ TC5	Mark Recchi	3.00	1.20	.30
☐ TC6	Geoff Sanderson	3.00	1.20	.30
☐ TC7	Adam Graves	4.00	1.60	.40

1993 Classic Draft Top Ten

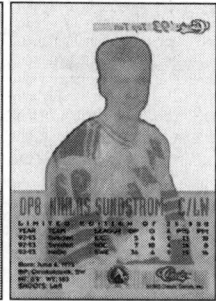

Measuring the standard-size (2 1/2" by 3 1/2"), these ten acetate cards were randomly inserted in foil packs. The cards are numbered on the back with a "DP" prefix.

		MINT	EXC	G-VG
COMPLETE SET (10)		40.00	16.00	4.00
COMMON PLAYER (DP1-DP10)		3.00	1.20	.30
☐ DP1	Alexandre Daigle	6.00	2.40	.60
☐ DP2	Chris Pronger	5.00	2.00	.50
☐ DP3	Chris Gratton	5.00	2.00	.50
☐ DP4	Paul Kariya	8.00	3.25	.80
☐ DP5	Rob Niedermayer	5.00	2.00	.50
☐ DP6	Viktor Kozlov	4.00	1.60	.40
☐ DP7	Jason Arnott	8.00	3.25	.80
☐ DP8	Niklas Sundstrom	3.00	1.20	.30
☐ DP9	Todd Harvey	4.00	1.60	.40
☐ DP10	Jocelyn Thibault	4.00	1.60	.40

1994 Classic Draft Day

Issued in a ten-card cello pack, these cards were issued on the occasion of the NHL draft, which took place on June 28-29, 1994. The cards measure the standard size (2 1/2" by 3 1/2"), and were available through a wrapper redemption offer. The fronts feature borderless color action player photos; the player's name is printed in a bar at the bottom that intersects the Classic logo at the lower left corner. The city (or state) of the teams likely to draft the player is printed

vertically in block lettering along the right edge. The backs carry the "Draft Day 94" logo superimposed over a color painting of a hockey player. A tagline at the bottom rounds out the back and gives the production figures "1 of 10,000". The cards are unnumbered and checklisted below in alphabetical order.

		MINT	EXC	G-VG
COMPLETE SET (10)		35.00	14.00	3.50
COMMON PLAYER (1-10)		4.00	1.60	.40
☐ 1	Radek Bonk	6.00	2.40	.60
	Anaheim Mighty Ducks			
☐ 2	Radek Bonk	6.00	2.40	.60
	Florida Panthers			
☐ 3	Radek Bonk	6.00	2.40	.60
	Ottawa Senators			
☐ 4	Jason Bonsignore	4.00	1.60	.40
	Edmonton Oilers			
☐ 5	Ed Jovanovski	6.00	2.40	.60
	Anaheim Mighty Ducks			
☐ 6	Ed Jovanovski	6.00	2.40	.60
	Florida Panthers			
☐ 7	Ed Jovanovski	6.00	2.40	.60
	Ottawa Senators			
☐ 8	Jeff O'Neill	4.00	1.60	.40
	Anaheim Mighty Ducks			
☐ 9	Jeff O'Neill	4.00	1.60	.40
	Florida Panthers			
☐ 10	Jeff O'Neill	4.00	1.60	.40
	Ottawa Senators			

1994 Classic Draft Previews

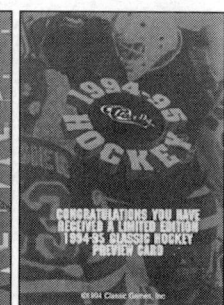

Randomly inserted in 1994 basketball packs, this 5-card set measures the standard-size (2 1/2" by 3 1/2"). The fronts feature full-bleed color action photos, except at the bottom where a color stripe carries the player's name. The word "PREVIEW" is printed vertically in large block letters running down the right edge. On a purple-tinted action photo, the backs display the Classic logo and a short congratulatory message. The cards are unnumbered and checklisted below in alphabetical order.

		MINT	EXC	G-VG
COMPLETE SET (5)		35.00	14.00	3.50
COMMON PLAYER (1-5)		5.00	2.00	.50
☐ HK1	Jason Allison	5.00	2.00	.50
☐ HK2	Radek Bonk	8.00	3.25	.80
☐ HK3	Xavier Majic	5.00	2.00	.50
☐ HK4	Manon Rheaume	15.00	6.00	1.50
☐ HK5	Oleg Tverdovsky	8.00	3.25	.80

1994 Classic Pro Prospects Promo

This standard-size (2 1/2" by 3 1/2") promo card was issued to show the design of the 1994 Classic Pro Hockey

Prospects set. Inside white borders, the front displays a color action player photo. The player's name, team, and position appear in a black bar at the bottom of the card. Also inside white borders, the back features another color player photo, logos, biographical information, and scoring totals. The disclaimer "For Promotional Purposes Only" are printed on the back. The card is unnumbered.

	MINT	EXC	G-VG
COMPLETE SET (1)	4.00	1.60	.40
COMMON CARD	4.00	1.60	.40
☐ 1 Radek Bonk	4.00	1.60	.40
Las Vegas Thunder			

1994 Classic Pro Prospects Prototype

Given away at the 1994 National Sports Convention in Houston, this prototype card measures the standard size (2 1/2" by 3 1/2"). The front features a borderless color action player photo, with the player's name on the bottom. The word "PROTOTYPE" is written vertically in red block lettering along the right edge. On a screened background, the back carries an advertisement for the convention in gold foil lettering. The card is unnumbered.

	MINT	EXC	G-VG
COMPLETE SET (1)	4.00	1.60	.40
COMMON CARD	4.00	1.60	.40
☐ 1 Jason Arnott	4.00	1.60	.40

1994 Classic Pro Prospects

This 250-card set includes more than 100 foil-stamped subset cards. Randomly inserted throughout the foil packs

were 25 limited print clear acetate cards and over 15,000 randomly inserted autographed cards of Radek Bonk, Alexei Yashin, Chris Pronger, Manon Rheaume, Joe Juneau, and more. Topical subsets featured were Class of '94, All-Rookie and The Women of Pro Hockey (248-250).

	MINT	EXC	G-VG
COMPLETE SET (250)	20.00	8.00	2.00
COMMON PLAYER (1-250)	.10	.04	.01
☐ 1 Radek Bonk	.75	.30	.07
☐ 2 Radek Bonk	.75	.30	.07
☐ 3 Radek Bonk	.75	.30	.07
☐ 4 Vlastimil Kroupa	.20	.08	.02
☐ 5 Mattias Norstrom	.10	.04	.01
☐ 6 Jaroslav Nedved	.10	.04	.01
☐ 7 Steve Dubinsky	.15	.06	.01
☐ 8 Christian Proulx	.10	.04	.01
☐ 9 Michal Grosek	.10	.04	.01
☐ 10 Pat Neaton	.15	.06	.01
☐ 11 Jason Arnott	1.00	.40	.10
☐ 12 Martin Brodeur	.50	.20	.05
☐ 13 Alexandre Daigle	.50	.20	.05
☐ 14 Ted Drury	.15	.06	.01
☐ 15 Iain Fraser	.15	.06	.01
☐ 16 Chris Gratton	.40	.16	.04
☐ 17 Greg Johnson	.15	.06	.01
☐ 18 Paul Kariya	.75	.30	.07
☐ 19 Alexander Karpovtsev	.15	.06	.01
☐ 20 Chris Lipuma	.10	.04	.01
☐ 21 Kirk Maltby	.15	.06	.01
☐ 22 Sandy McCarthy	.15	.06	.01
☐ 23 Darren McCarty	.15	.06	.01
☐ 24 Jaroslav Modry	.15	.06	.01
☐ 25 Jim Montgomery	.15	.06	.01
☐ 26 Markus Naslund	.15	.06	.01
☐ 27 Rob Niedermayer	.40	.16	.04
☐ 28 Chris Osgood	.30	.12	.03
☐ 29 Pat Peake	.20	.08	.02
☐ 30 Derek Plante	.40	.16	.04
☐ 31 Chris Pronger	.40	.16	.04
☐ 32 Mike Rathje	.10	.04	.01
☐ 33 Mikael Renberg	.50	.20	.05
☐ 34 Damian Rhodes	.20	.08	.02
☐ 35 Garth Snow	.15	.06	.01
☐ 36 Cam Stewart	.25	.10	.02
☐ 37 Jim Storm	.15	.06	.01
☐ 38 Michal Sykora	.15	.06	.01
☐ 39 Jocelyn Thibault	.25	.10	.02
☐ 40 Alexei Yashin	.50	.20	.05
☐ 41 Checklist 1	.10	.04	.01
☐ 42 Vesa Viitakoski	.15	.06	.01
☐ 43 Jake Grimes	.10	.04	.01
☐ 44 Jim Dowd	.15	.06	.01
☐ 45 Craig Ferguson	.10	.04	.01
☐ 46 Mike Boback	.10	.04	.01
☐ 47 Francois Groleau	.10	.04	.01
☐ 48 Juha Riihijarvi	.10	.04	.01
☐ 49 Mikhail Shtalenkov	.20	.08	.02
☐ 50 Zigmund Palffy	.15	.06	.01
☐ 51 Felix Potvin	.75	.30	.07
☐ 52 Alexei Kovalev	.30	.12	.03
☐ 53 Larry Robinson	.15	.06	.01
☐ 54 John LeClair	.15	.06	.01
☐ 55 Dominic Roussel	.15	.06	.01
☐ 56 Geoff Sanderson	.20	.08	.02
☐ 57 Greg Pankewicz	.10	.04	.01
☐ 58 Brent Bilodeau	.10	.04	.01
☐ 59 Brandon Convery	.15	.06	.01
☐ 60 Fred Knipscheer	.25	.10	.02
☐ 61 Igor Chibirev	.10	.04	.01

☐ 62	Anatoli Fedotov	.10	.04	.01
☐ 63	Bob Kellogg	.10	.04	.01
☐ 64	Mike Maurice	.10	.04	.01
☐ 65	Chad Penney	.10	.04	.01
☐ 66	Mike Bavis	.10	.04	.01
☐ 67	Eric Veilleux	.10	.04	.01
☐ 68	Parris Duffus	.15	.06	.01
☐ 69	Daniel Lacroix	.10	.04	.01
☐ 70	Milos Holan	.10	.04	.01
☐ 71	Mike Muller	.10	.04	.01
☐ 72	Micah Aivazoff	.15	.06	.01
☐ 73	Krzysztof Oliwa	.10	.04	.01
☐ 74	Ryan Hughes	.10	.04	.01
☐ 75	Christian Soucy	.15	.06	.01
☐ 76	Keith Redmond	.10	.04	.01
☐ 77	Mark De Santis	.10	.04	.01
☐ 78	Craig Martin	.15	.06	.01
☐ 79	Mike Kennedy	.10	.04	.01
☐ 80	Pauli Jaks	.15	.06	.01
☐ 81	Colin Chin	.10	.04	.01
☐ 82	Jody Gage	.15	.06	.01
☐ 83	Don Biggs	.10	.04	.01
☐ 84	Tim Tookey	.10	.04	.01
☐ 85	Clint Malarchuk	.10	.04	.01
☐ 86	Jozef Cierny	.10	.04	.01
☐ 87	Radek Hamr	.15	.06	.01
☐ 88	Jason Dawe	.10	.04	.01
☐ 89	Chris Longo	.10	.04	.01
☐ 90	Brian Rolston	.25	.10	.02
☐ 91	Mike McKee	.10	.04	.01
☐ 92	Vitali Prokhorov	.10	.04	.01
☐ 93	Chris Snell	.15	.06	.01
☐ 94	Martin Brochu	.15	.06	.01
☐ 95	Dan Plante	.10	.04	.01
☐ 96	Darcy Werenka	.15	.06	.01
☐ 97	Steffon Walby	.10	.04	.01
☐ 98	David Emma	.15	.06	.01
☐ 99	Dan Stiver	.10	.04	.01
☐ 100	Radek Bonk	1.00	.40	.10
☐ 101	Mark Visheau	.10	.04	.01
☐ 102	Dean Melanson	.10	.04	.01
☐ 103	Vladimir Tsyplakov	.10	.04	.01
☐ 104	Mikhail Volkov	.10	.04	.01
☐ 105	Aaron Miller	.10	.04	.01
☐ 106	Alexei Kudashov	.15	.06	.01
☐ 107	Shawn Rivers	.10	.04	.01
☐ 108	Ladislav Karabin	.15	.06	.01
☐ 109	Matt Mallgrave	.10	.04	.01
☐ 110	Craig Darby	.10	.04	.01
☐ 111	Marcel Cousineau	.15	.06	.01
☐ 112	Jamie McLennan	.15	.06	.01
☐ 113	Yanic Perreault	.15	.06	.01
☐ 114	Zac Boyer	.10	.04	.01
☐ 115	Sergei Zubov	.35	.14	.03
☐ 116	Dan Kesa	.10	.04	.01
☐ 117	Jim Hiller	.10	.04	.01
☐ 118	Dmitri Starostenko	.10	.04	.01
☐ 119	Chris Tamer	.10	.04	.01
☐ 120	Aaron Ward	.15	.06	.01
☐ 121	Claude Savoie	.10	.04	.01
☐ 122	Jamie Black	.10	.04	.01
☐ 123	Jean-Francois Jomphe	.10	.04	.01
☐ 124	Paxton Schulte	.10	.04	.01
☐ 125	Jarkko Varvio	.15	.06	.01
☐ 126	Jaroslav Otevrel	.15	.06	.01
☐ 127	Dane Jackson	.10	.04	.01
☐ 128	Brent Grieve	.15	.06	.01
☐ 129	Checklist 2	.75	.30	.07
	Pascal Rheaume			
	Manon Rheaume			
☐ 130	Rene Corbet	.15	.06	.01
☐ 131	Joe Frederick	.15	.06	.01
☐ 132	Martin Tanguay	.10	.04	.01
☐ 133	Fredrik Jax	.10	.04	.01
☐ 134	Jamie Linden	.10	.04	.01
☐ 135	Jason Smith	.15	.06	.01
☐ 136	Rick Kowalsky	.10	.04	.01
☐ 137	Dino Grossi	.10	.04	.01
☐ 138	Aris Brimanis	.10	.04	.01
☐ 139	Jeff McLean	.10	.04	.01
☐ 140	Tyler Wright	.15	.06	.01
☐ 141	Roman Gorev	.10	.04	.01
☐ 142	Dean Hulett	.10	.04	.01
☐ 143	Niklas Sundblad	.10	.04	.01
☐ 144	Jeff Bes	.15	.06	.01
☐ 145	Pascal Rheaume	.15	.06	.01
☐ 146	Donald Brashear	.15	.06	.01
☐ 147	Hugo Belanger	.10	.04	.01
☐ 148	Blair Scott	.10	.04	.01
☐ 149	Steve Staios	.10	.04	.01
☐ 150	Matt Martin	.15	.06	.01
☐ 151	Richard Matvichuk	.15	.06	.01
☐ 152	Paul Brousseau	.15	.06	.01
☐ 153	Evgeny Namestnikov	.15	.06	.01
☐ 154	Mike Peca	.15	.06	.01
☐ 155	Jeff Nelson	.15	.06	.01
☐ 156	Greg Andrusak	.10	.04	.01
☐ 157	Norm Batherson	.10	.04	.01
☐ 158	Martin Bakula	.10	.04	.01
☐ 159	Ed Patterson	.15	.06	.01
☐ 160	Steve Larouche	.10	.04	.01
☐ 161	Libor Polasek	.10	.04	.01
☐ 162	Jon Hillebrandt	.10	.04	.01
☐ 163	Guy Leveque	.15	.06	.01
☐ 164	Eric Lacroix	.10	.04	.01
☐ 165	Scott Walker	.10	.04	.01
☐ 166	Robert Burakovsky	.10	.04	.01
☐ 167	Markus Ketterer	.15	.06	.01
☐ 168	Mike Speer	.10	.04	.01
☐ 169	Martin Jiranek	.10	.04	.01
☐ 170	Andy Schneider	.10	.04	.01
☐ 171	Terry Hollinger	.10	.04	.01
☐ 172	Mark Lawrence	.10	.04	.01
☐ 173	Martin Lapointe	.10	.04	.01
☐ 174	Vaclav Prospal	.15	.06	.01
☐ 175	Mike Fountain	.15	.06	.01
☐ 176	Alexander Kerch	.10	.04	.01
☐ 177	Oleg Petrov	.25	.10	.02
☐ 178	Derek Armstrong	.15	.06	.01
☐ 179	Matthew Barnaby	.15	.06	.01
☐ 180	Andrei Nazarov	.15	.06	.01
☐ 181	Andrei Trefilov	.15	.06	.01
☐ 182	Jean-Yves Roy	.10	.04	.01
☐ 183	Boris Rousson	.15	.06	.01
☐ 184	Daniel Laperriere	.10	.04	.01
☐ 185	Yan Kaminsky	.15	.06	.01
☐ 186	Ralph Intranuovo	.15	.06	.01
☐ 187	Sandy Moger	.10	.04	.01
☐ 188	Grant Marshall	.10	.04	.01
☐ 189	Denny Felsner	.10	.04	.01
☐ 190	Cory Stillman	.10	.04	.01
☐ 191	Eric Lavigne	.10	.04	.01
☐ 192	Jarrod Skalde	.15	.06	.01
☐ 193	Steve Junker	.10	.04	.01
☐ 194	Alexander Cherbayev	.15	.06	.01
☐ 195	Nathan Lafayette	.20	.08	.02
☐ 196	Ed Ward	.10	.04	.01
☐ 197	Harijs Vitolinsh	.10	.04	.01
☐ 198	Jarmo Kekalainen	.10	.04	.01
☐ 199	Neil Eisenhut	.10	.04	.01
☐ 200	Radek Bonk	1.00	.40	.10
☐ 201	Jason Bonsignore	.50	.20	.05
☐ 202	Jeff Friesen	.50	.20	.05
☐ 203	Ed Jovanovski	1.25	.50	.12
☐ 204	Brett Lindros	1.50	.60	.15
☐ 205	Jeff O'Neill	.50	.20	.05
☐ 206	Deron Quint	.15	.06	.01
☐ 207	Vadim Sharifjanov	.30	.12	.03
☐ 208	Oleg Tverdovsky	.75	.30	.07
☐ 209	Checklist 3	.15	.06	.01
	Jeff O'Neill			
	Jeff Friesen			
☐ 210	David Cooper	.10	.04	.01
☐ 211	Doug McDonald	.10	.04	.01
☐ 212	Leonid Toropchenko	.10	.04	.01
☐ 213	Chris Rogles	.15	.06	.01
☐ 214	Vyacheslav Kozlov	.30	.12	.03
☐ 215	Dennis Metlyuk	.10	.04	.01
☐ 216	Scott McKay	.10	.04	.01
☐ 217	Brian Loney	.10	.04	.01
☐ 218	Kevin Hodson	.15	.06	.01
☐ 219	Bobby House	.10	.04	.01
☐ 220	Sergei Krivokrasov	.15	.06	.01
☐ 221	Brett Harkins	.10	.04	.01
☐ 222	Cale Hulse	.10	.04	.01
☐ 223	Marc Tardif	.10	.04	.01
☐ 224	Jon Rohloff	.10	.04	.01
☐ 225	Kevin Smyth	.10	.04	.01
☐ 226	Jason Young	.10	.04	.01
☐ 227	Sergei Zholtok	.10	.04	.01
☐ 228	Todd Simon	.10	.04	.01
☐ 229	Jerome Bechard	.10	.04	.01
☐ 230	Matt Robbins	.10	.04	.01
☐ 231	Joe Cook	.10	.04	.01
☐ 232	John Brill	.10	.04	.01
☐ 233	Dan Goldie	.10	.04	.01
☐ 234	Dan Gravelle	.10	.04	.01
☐ 235	Shawn Wheeler	.10	.04	.01
☐ 236	Brad Harrison	.10	.04	.01
☐ 237	Joe Dragon	.10	.04	.01
☐ 238	Jason Jennings	.10	.04	.01
☐ 239	Manon Rheaume	2.50	1.00	.25
☐ 240	Jamie Steer	.10	.04	.01
☐ 241	Scott Rogers	.10	.04	.01
☐ 242	Lyle Wildgoose	.10	.04	.01
☐ 243	Darren Colbourne	.10	.04	.01

☐ 244 Mike Smith	.10	.04	.01
☐ 245 Chris Bright	.10	.04	.01
☐ 246 Chirs Belanger	.10	.04	.01
☐ 247 Darren Schwartz	.10	.04	.01
☐ 248 Cammi Granato	1.00	.40	.10
☐ 249 Erin Whitten	1.00	.40	.10
☐ 250 Manon Rheaume	2.50	1.00	.25
☐ AU Radek Bonk AU/2400	75.00	30.00	7.50
☐ AU Jason Bonsignore	40.00	16.00	4.00
AU/2450			
☐ AU Chris Pronger AU/1400	40.00	16.00	4.00
☐ AU Alexei Kovalev AU/1900	50.00	20.00	5.00
☐ AU Manon Rheaume AU/1900	100.00	40.00	10.00
☐ AU Jeff Friesen AU/2450	35.00	14.00	3.50
☐ AU Erin Whitten AU/1800	50.00	20.00	5.00
☐ AU Alexei Yashin AU/1400	75.00	30.00	7.50
☐ AU Joe Juneau AU/1370	50.00	20.00	5.00

1994 Classic Pro Prospects
International Heroes

Randomly inserted through the foil packs, these 25 clear acetate cards predominantly feature the U.S. and Canadian National Teams. The cards measure the standard-size (2 1/2" by 3 1/2"). The cards are numbered on the back with an "LP" prefix. The nationalities of the players are as follows: U.S. (1-10); Canadian (11-20, 24); Czech (21); Russian (22, 25); and Finnish (23).

	MINT	EXC	G-VG
COMPLETE SET (25)	80.00	32.00	8.00
COMMON PLAYER (LP1-LP25)	3.00	1.20	.30
☐ LP1 Jim Campbell	3.00	1.20	.30
☐ LP2 Ted Drury	4.00	1.60	.40
☐ LP3 Mike Dunham	3.00	1.20	.30
☐ LP4 Chris Ferraro	3.00	1.20	.30
☐ LP5 Peter Ferraro	4.00	1.60	.40
☐ LP6 Darby Hendrickson	3.00	1.20	.30
☐ LP7 Craig Johnson	3.00	1.20	.30
☐ LP8 Todd Marchant	3.00	1.20	.30
☐ LP9 Matt Martin	3.00	1.20	.30
☐ LP10 Brian Rolston	4.00	1.60	.40
☐ LP11 Adrian Aucoin	3.00	1.20	.30
☐ LP12 Martin Gendron	3.00	1.20	.30
☐ LP13 David Harlock	3.00	1.20	.30
☐ LP14 Corey Hirsch	4.00	1.60	.40
☐ LP15 Paul Kariya	10.00	4.00	1.00
☐ LP16 Manny Legace	3.00	1.20	.30
☐ LP17 Drett Lindroc	12.00	5.00	1.20
☐ LP18 Brian Savage	3.00	1.20	.30
☐ LP19 Chris Therien	3.00	1.20	.30
☐ LP20 Todd Warriner	4.00	1.60	.40
☐ LP21 Radek Bonk	10.00	4.00	1.00
☐ LP22 Pavel Bure	10.00	4.00	1.00
☐ LP23 Teemu Selanne	6.00	2.40	.60
☐ LP24 Mark Recchi	4.00	1.60	.40
☐ LP25 Alexei Yashin	6.00	2.40	.60

1964-65 Coca-Cola Caps

The 1964-65 Coca-Cola Caps set contains 108 bottle caps measuring approximately 1 1/8" in diameter. The caps

feature a black and white picture on the tops, and are unnumbered except for uniform numbers (which is listed to the right of the player's name in the checklist below). These caps were issued with both Coke and Sprite. The set numbering below is by teams and numerically within teams as follows: Boston Bruins (1-18), Chicago Blackhawks (19-36), Detroit Red Wings (37-54), Montreal Canadiens (55-72), New York Rangers (73-90), and Toronto Maple Leafs (91-108). A plastic holder (in the shape of a rink) was also available for holding and displaying the caps; the holder is not included in the complete set price below.

	NRMT	VG-E	GOOD
COMPLETE SET (108)	350.00	140.00	35.00
COMMON PLAYER (1-108)	2.50	1.00	.25
☐ 1 Ed Johnston 1	3.50	1.40	.35
☐ 2 Bob McCord 4	2.50	1.00	.25
☐ 3 Ted Green 6	3.50	1.40	.35
☐ 4 Orland Kurtenbach 7	3.50	1.40	.35
☐ 5 Gary Dornhoefer 8	3.50	1.40	.35
☐ 6 Johnny Bucyk 9	7.50	3.00	.75
☐ 7 Tom Johnson 10	3.50	1.40	.35
☐ 8 Tom Williams 11	2.50	1.00	.25
☐ 9 Murray Balfour 12	2.50	1.00	.25
☐ 10 Forbes Kennedy 14	2.50	1.00	.25
☐ 11 Murray Oliver 16	2.50	1.00	.25
☐ 12 Dean Prentice 17	3.50	1.40	.35
☐ 13 Ed Westfall 18	3.50	1.40	.35
☐ 14 Reg Fleming 19	2.50	1.00	.25
☐ 15 Leo Boivin 20	3.50	1.40	.35
☐ 16 Ab McDonald 21	2.50	1.00	.25
☐ 17 Ron Schock 23	2.50	1.00	.25
☐ 18 Bob Leiter 24	2.50	1.00	.25
☐ 19 Glenn Hall 1	9.00	3.75	.90
☐ 20 Doug Mohns 2	2.50	1.00	.25
☐ 21 Pierre Pilote 3	3.50	1.40	.35
☐ 22 Elmer Vasko 4	2.50	1.00	.25
☐ 23 Fred Stanfield 6	2.50	1.00	.25
☐ 24 Phil Esposito 7	35.00	14.00	3.50
☐ 25 Bobby Hull 9	35.00	14.00	3.50
☐ 26 Bill(Red) Hay 11	2.50	1.00	.25
☐ 27 John Brenneman 12	2.50	1.00	.25
☐ 28 Doug Robinson 14	2.50	1.00	.25
☐ 29 Eric Nesterenko 15	3.50	1.40	.35
☐ 30 Chico Maki 16	3.50	1.40	.35
☐ 31 Ken Wharram 17	2.50	1.00	.25
☐ 32 John McKenzie 18	2.50	1.00	.25
☐ 33 Al MacNeil 19	2.50	1.00	.25
☐ 34 Wayne Hillman 20	2.50	1.00	.25
☐ 35 Stan Mikita 21	12.00	5.00	1.20
☐ 36 Denis DeJordy 30	3.50	1.40	.35
☐ 37 Roger Crozier 1	3.50	1.40	.35
☐ 38 Albert Langlois 2	2.50	1.00	.25
☐ 39 Marcel Pronovost 3	3.50	1.40	.35
☐ 40 Bill Gadsby 4	3.50	1.40	.35
☐ 41 Doug Barkley 5	2.50	1.00	.25
☐ 42 Norm Ullman 7	5.00	2.00	.50
☐ 43 Pit Martin 8	3.50	1.40	.35
☐ 44 Gordie Howe 9	50.00	20.00	5.00
☐ 45A Gordie Howe 10	60.00	24.00	6.00
☐ 45B Alex Delvecchio 10	30.00	12.00	3.00
☐ 46 Ron Murphy 12	2.50	1.00	.25
☐ 47 Larry Jeffrey 14	2.50	1.00	.25
☐ 48 Ted Lindsay 15	7.50	3.00	.75
☐ 49 Bruce MacGregor 16	2.50	1.00	.25
☐ 50 Floyd Smith 17	2.50	1.00	.25
☐ 51 Gary Bergman 18	2.50	1.00	.25
☐ 52 Paul Henderson 19	3.50	1.40	.35
☐ 53 Parker MacDonald 20	2.50	1.00	.25
☐ 54 Eddie Joyal 21	2.50	1.00	.25
☐ 55 Charlie Hodge 1	3.50	1.40	.35
☐ 56 Jacques Laperriere 2	3.50	1.40	.35
☐ 57 J.C. Tremblay 3	3.50	1.40	.35

		NRMT	VG-E	GOOD
☐ 58	Jean Beliveau 4	15.00	6.00	1.50
☐ 59	Ralph Backstrom 6	3.50	1.40	.35
☐ 60	Bill Hicke 8	2.50	1.00	.25
☐ 61	Ted Harris 10	2.50	1.00	.25
☐ 62	Claude Larose 11	2.50	1.00	.25
☐ 63	Yvan Cournoyer 12	15.00	6.00	1.50
☐ 64	Claude Provost 14	2.50	1.00	.25
☐ 65	Bobby Rousseau 15	3.50	1.40	.35
☐ 66	Henri Richard 16	6.00	2.40	.60
☐ 67	Jean-Guy Talbot 17	3.50	1.40	.35
☐ 68	Terry Harper 19	3.50	1.40	.35
☐ 69	Dave Balon 20	2.50	1.00	.25
☐ 70	Gilles Tremblay 21	2.50	1.00	.25
☐ 71	John Ferguson 22	3.50	1.40	.35
☐ 72	Jim Roberts 26	2.50	1.00	.25
☐ 73	Jacques Plante 1	15.00	6.00	1.50
☐ 74	Harry Howell 3	3.50	1.40	.35
☐ 75	Arnie Brown 4	2.50	1.00	.25
☐ 76	Don Johns 6	2.50	1.00	.25
☐ 77	Rod Gilbert 7	6.00	2.40	.60
☐ 78	Bob Nevin 8	2.50	1.00	.25
☐ 79	Dick Duff 9	3.50	1.40	.35
☐ 80	Earl Ingarfield 10	2.50	1.00	.25
☐ 81	Vic Hadfield 11	3.50	1.40	.35
☐ 82	Jim Mikol 12	2.50	1.00	.25
☐ 83	Val Fonteyne 14	2.50	1.00	.25
☐ 84	Jim Nielson 15	2.50	1.00	.25
☐ 85	Rod Seiling 16	2.50	1.00	.25
☐ 86	Lou Angotti 17	2.50	1.00	.25
☐ 87	Phil Goyette 20	2.50	1.00	.25
☐ 88	Camille Henry 21	3.50	1.40	.35
☐ 89	Don Marshall 22	2.50	1.00	.25
☐ 90	Marcel Paille 23	2.50	1.00	.25
☐ 91	Johnny Bower 1	6.00	2.40	.60
☐ 92	Carl Brewer 2	3.50	1.40	.35
☐ 93	Red Kelly 4	7.50	3.00	.75
☐ 94	Tim Horton 7	10.00	4.00	1.00
☐ 95	Andy Bathgate 9	6.00	2.40	.60
☐ 96	Andy Bathgate 10	6.00	2.40	.60
☐ 97	Ron Ellis 11	3.50	1.40	.35
☐ 98	Ralph Stewart 12	2.50	1.00	.25
☐ 99	Dave Keon 14	5.00	2.00	.50
☐ 100	Dickie Moore 16	6.00	2.40	.60
☐ 101	Don McKenney 17	2.50	1.00	.25
☐ 102	Kent Douglas 19	2.50	1.00	.25
☐ 103	Bob Pulford 20	3.50	1.40	.35
☐ 104	Bob Baun 21	3.50	1.40	.35
☐ 105	Eddie Shack 23	5.00	2.00	.50
☐ 106	Terry Sawchuk 24	15.00	6.00	1.50
☐ 107	Allan Stanley 26	3.50	1.40	.35
☐ 108	Frank Mahovlich	10.00	4.00	1.00
☐ xx	Cap Holder	75.00	30.00	7.50
	(Plastic Rink)			

1965-66 Coca-Cola

YVAN COURNOYER

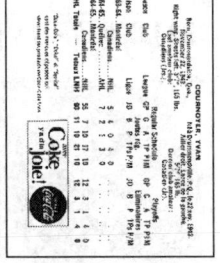

This set contains 108 unnumbered black and white cards featuring 18 players from each of the six NHL teams. The cards were issued in perforated team panels of 18 cards. The cards are priced below as perforated cards; the value of unperforated strips is approximately 20 percent more than the sum of the individual prices. The cards are approximately 2 3/4" by 3 1/2" and have bi-lingual (French and English) write-ups on the card backs. An album to hold the cards was available from the company on a mail-order basis. The set numbering below is by teams and numerically

within teams as follows: Boston Bruins (1-18), Chicago Blackhawks (19-36), Detroit Red Wings (37-54), Montreal Canadiens (55-72, New York Rangers (73-90), and Toronto Maple Leafs (91-108).

		NRMT	VG-E	GOOD
COMPLETE SET (108)		300.00	120.00	30.00
COMMON PLAYER (1-108)		1.50	.60	.15
☐ 1	Gerry Cheevers	15.00	6.00	1.50
☐ 2	Albert Langlois	1.50	.60	.15
☐ 3	Ted Green	2.00	.80	.20
☐ 4	Ron Stewart	1.50	.60	.15
☐ 5	Bob Woytowich	1.50	.60	.15
☐ 6	Johnny Bucyk	5.00	2.00	.50
☐ 7	Tom Williams	1.50	.60	.15
☐ 8	Forbes Kennedy	1.50	.60	.15
☐ 9	Murray Oliver	1.50	.60	.15
☐ 10	Dean Prentice	2.00	.80	.20
☐ 11	Ed Westfall	2.00	.80	.20
☐ 12	Reg Fleming	1.50	.60	.15
☐ 13	Leo Boivin	3.00	1.20	.30
☐ 14	Parker MacDonald	1.50	.60	.15
☐ 15	Bob Dillabough	1.50	.60	.15
☐ 16	Barry Ashbee	4.00	1.60	.40
☐ 17	Don Awrey	1.50	.60	.15
☐ 18	Bernie Parent	20.00	8.00	2.00
☐ 19	Glenn Hall	6.00	2.40	.60
☐ 20	Doug Mohns	2.00	.80	.20
☐ 21	Pierre Pilote	3.00	1.20	.30
☐ 22	Elmer Vasko	1.50	.60	.15
☐ 23	Matt Ravlich	1.50	.60	.15
☐ 24	Fred Stanfield	1.50	.60	.15
☐ 25	Phil Esposito	30.00	12.00	3.00
☐ 26	Bobby Hull	30.00	12.00	3.00
☐ 27	Dennis Hull	3.00	1.20	.30
☐ 28	Bill(Red) Hay	2.00	.80	.20
☐ 29	Ken Hodge	3.00	1.20	.30
☐ 30	Eric Nesterenko	2.00	.80	.20
☐ 31	Chico Maki	2.00	.80	.20
☐ 32	Ken Wharram	1.50	.60	.15
☐ 33	Al MacNeil	1.50	.60	.15
☐ 34	Doug Jarrett	1.50	.60	.15
☐ 35	Stan Mikita	10.00	4.00	1.00
☐ 36	Dave Dryden	2.00	.80	.20
☐ 37	Roger Crozier	2.00	.80	.20
☐ 38	Warren Godfrey	1.50	.60	.15
☐ 39	Bert Marshall	1.50	.60	.15
☐ 40	Bill Gadsby	3.00	1.20	.30
☐ 41	Doug Barkley	1.50	.60	.15
☐ 42	Norm Ullman	4.00	1.60	.40
☐ 43	Gordie Howe	50.00	20.00	5.00
☐ 44	Alex Delvecchio	5.00	2.00	.50
☐ 45	Val Fonteyne	1.50	.60	.15
☐ 46	Ron Murphy	1.50	.60	.15
☐ 47	Billy Harris	1.50	.60	.15
☐ 48	Bruce MacGregor	1.50	.60	.15
☐ 49	Floyd Smith	1.50	.60	.15
☐ 50	Paul Henderson	2.50	1.00	.25
☐ 51	Andy Bathgate	3.50	1.40	.35
☐ 52	Ab McDonald	1.50	.60	.15
☐ 53	Gary Bergman	1.50	.60	.15
☐ 54	Hank Bassen	1.50	.60	.15
☐ 55	Charlie Hodge	3.00	1.20	.30
☐ 56	Jacques Laperriere	3.00	1.20	.30
☐ 57	Jean-Claude Tremblay	2.00	.80	.20
☐ 58	Jean Beliveau	12.50	5.00	1.25
☐ 59	Ralph Backstrom	2.00	.80	.20
☐ 60	Dick Duff	2.00	.80	.20
☐ 61	Ted Harris	2.00	.80	.20
☐ 62	Claude Larose	1.50	.60	.15
☐ 63	Yvan Cournoyer	15.00	6.00	1.50
☐ 64	Claude Provost	1.50	.60	.15
☐ 65	Bobby Rousseau	2.00	.80	.20
☐ 66	Henri Richard	6.00	2.40	.60
☐ 67	Jean-Guy Talbot	2.50	1.00	.25
☐ 68	Terry Harper	2.00	.80	.20
☐ 69	Gilles Tremblay	1.50	.60	.15
☐ 70	John Ferguson	2.00	.80	.20
☐ 71	Jim Roberts	2.00	.80	.20
☐ 72	Gump Worsley	9.00	3.75	.90
☐ 73	Ed Giacomin	15.00	6.00	1.50
☐ 74	Wayne Hillman	1.50	.60	.15
☐ 75	Harry Howell	3.00	1.20	.30
☐ 76	Arnie Brown	1.50	.60	.15
☐ 77	Doug Robinson	1.50	.60	.15
☐ 78	Mike McMahon	1.50	.60	.15
☐ 79	Rod Gilbert	5.00	2.00	.50
☐ 80	Bob Nevin	1.50	.60	.15
☐ 81	Earl Ingarfield	1.50	.60	.15
☐ 82	Vic Hadfield	2.50	1.00	.25
☐ 83	Bill Hicke	1.50	.60	.15

☐ 84	John McKenzie	1.50	.60	.15
☐ 85	Jim Neilson	1.50	.60	.15
☐ 86	Jean Ratelle	5.00	2.00	.50
☐ 87	Phil Goyette	1.50	.60	.15
☐ 88	Garry Peters	1.50	.60	.15
☐ 89	Don Marshall	1.50	.60	.15
☐ 90	Don Simmons	1.50	.60	.15
☐ 91	Johnny Bower	5.00	2.00	.50
☐ 92	Marcel Pronovost	3.00	1.20	.30
☐ 93	Red Kelly	5.00	2.00	.50
☐ 94	Tim Horton	9.00	3.75	.90
☐ 95	Ron Ellis	2.00	.80	.20
☐ 96	George Armstrong	4.00	1.60	.40
☐ 97	Brit Selby	1.50	.60	.15
☐ 98	Pete Stemkowski	1.50	.60	.15
☐ 99	Dave Keon	4.00	1.60	.40
☐ 100	Mike Walton	2.00	.80	.20
☐ 101	Kent Douglas	1.50	.60	.15
☐ 102	Bob Pulford	3.00	1.20	.30
☐ 103	Bob Baun	2.00	.80	.20
☐ 104	Eddie Shack	3.00	1.20	.30
☐ 105	Orland Kurtenbach	2.00	.80	.20
☐ 106	Allan Stanley	3.00	1.20	.30
☐ 107	Frank Mahovlich	10.00	4.00	1.00
☐ 108	Terry Sawchuk	15.00	6.00	1.50

1965-66 Coca-Cola Booklets

These four "How To Play" booklets are illustrated with cartoon-like drawings, each measure approximately 4 7/8" by 3 1/2", and are printed on newsprint. Booklets A and B have yellow covers, while booklets C and D have blue covers. The 31-page booklets could be obtained through a mail-in offer. Under bottle caps of Coke or Sprite (marked with a hockey stick) were cork liners bearing the name of the player who wrote a booklet. To receive a booklet, the collector had to send in ten cork liners (with name of the player whose booklet was desired), ten cents, and the correct answer to a trivia question. Issued by Coca-Cola to promote hockey among the school-aged, they are designed in comic book fashion showing correct positions and moves for goalie, forward (both defensive and offensive), and defenseman. They are authored by the hockey players listed below. They are lettered rather than numbered and we have checklisted them below accordingly. The booklets were available in both English and French.

	NRMT	VG-E	GOOD
COMPLETE SET (4)	80.00	32.00	8.00
COMMON PLAYER (A-D)	15.00	6.00	1.50
☐ A Johnny Bower	25.00	10.00	2.50
How To Play Goal			
☐ B Dave Keon	25.00	10.00	2.50
How To Play Forward (Defensive)			
☐ C Jacques Laperriere	15.00	6.00	1.50
How To Play Defence			
☐ D Henri Richard	30.00	12.00	3.00
How To Play Forward (Offensive)			

1977-78 Coca-Cola

Each of these mini-cards measures approximately 1 3/8" by 1 3/8". The fronts feature a color "mug shot" of the player,

with his name given above the picture. Red and blue lines form the borders on the sides of the picture. The year 1978, the city from which the team hails, and the Coke logo appear below the picture. Inside a black border (with rounded corners) the back has basic biographical information. These unnumbered cards are listed alphabetically below.

	NRMT	VG-E	GOOD
COMPLETE SET (30)	75.00	30.00	7.50
COMMON PLAYER (1-30)	1.50	.60	.15
☐ 1 Syl Apps	1.50	.60	.15
☐ 2 Dave Burrows	1.50	.60	.15
☐ 3 Bobby Clarke	7.50	3.00	.75
☐ 4 Yvan Cournoyer	5.00	2.00	.50
☐ 5 John Davidson	2.00	.80	.20
☐ 6 Marcel Dionne	6.00	2.40	.60
☐ 7 Doug Favell	1.50	.60	.15
☐ 8 Rod Gilbert	3.00	1.20	.30
☐ 9 Brian Glennie	1.50	.60	.15
☐ 10 Butch Goring	2.00	.80	.20
☐ 11 Lorne Henning	1.50	.60	.15
☐ 12 Cliff Koroll	1.50	.60	.15
☐ 13 Guy Lapointe	3.00	1.20	.30
☐ 14 Dave Maloney	1.50	.60	.15
☐ 15 Pit Martin	1.50	.60	.15
☐ 16 Lou Nanne	1.50	.60	.15
☐ 17 Bobby Orr	35.00	14.00	3.50
☐ 18 Brad Park	5.00	2.00	.50
☐ 19 Craig Ramsey	1.50	.60	.15
☐ 20 Larry Robinson	6.00	2.40	.60
☐ 21 Jim Rutherford	2.00	.80	.20
☐ 22 Don Saleski	1.50	.60	.15
☐ 23 Steve Shutt	4.00	1.60	.40
☐ 24 Darryl Sittler	5.00	2.00	.50
☐ 25 Billy Smith	4.00	1.60	.40
☐ 26 Bob Stewart	1.50	.60	.15
☐ 27 Rogatien Vachon	3.00	1.20	.30
☐ 28 Jimmy Watson	1.50	.60	.15
☐ 29 Joe Watson	1.50	.60	.15
☐ 30 Ed Westfall	2.00	.80	.20

1994 Coke/Mac's Milk Gretzky POGs

This 18-disc set features POGs measuring approximately 1 5/8" in diameter. These cards were offered through Mac's Milk stores in Canada (primarily Ontario); they were available at the store counter with the purchase of any Coke bottled product from May through middle of June of 1994. Inside a gold-foil holographic border, the fronts feature action color player photos with the words "The Great One" printed in black letters above the photo and a Coca-Cola

Future Stars emblem at the bottom. The backs feature Gretzky's most prolific records and accomplishments. The discs are numbered on the back.

	MINT	EXC	G-VG
COMPLETE SET (18)	15.00	6.00	1.50
COMMON POG (1-18)	1.00	.40	.10
☐ 1 Wayne Gretzky	1.00	.40	.10
Most Assists, Career			
☐ 2 Wayne Gretzky	1.00	.40	.10
Most Points, Career			
☐ 3 Wayne Gretzky	1.00	.40	.10
Most 100 Point Seasons			
☐ 4 Wayne Gretzky	1.00	.40	.10
Most Three Goal			
Games, Career			
☐ 5 Wayne Gretzky	1.00	.40	.10
Most Goals, Season			
☐ 6 Wayne Gretzky	1.00	.40	.10
Most Points, Season			
☐ 7 Wayne Gretzky	1.00	.40	.10
Longest Consecutive			
Point Streak			
☐ 8 Wayne Gretzky	1.00	.40	.10
Most Assists, Game			
☐ 9 Wayne Gretzky	1.00	.40	.10
Most Goals, One Period			
☐ 10 Wayne Gretzky	1.00	.40	.10
Most Playoff			
Points, Career			
☐ 11 Wayne Gretzky	1.00	.40	.10
Most Points In			
One Playoff Year			
☐ 12 Wayne Gretzky	1.00	.40	.10
Most Goals			
All-Star Game, Career			
☐ 13 Wayne Gretzky	1.00	.40	.10
Most Goals, One			
Period, All-Star Game			
☐ 14 Wayne Gretzky	1.00	.40	.10
MVP (Hart Trophy)			
☐ 15 Wayne Gretzky	1.00	.40	.10
NHL Leading Scorer			
(Art Ross Trophy)			
☐ 16 Wayne Gretzky	1.00	.40	.10
MVP As Voted By Players			
(Lester B. Pearson			
Trophy)			
☐ 17 Wayne Gretzky	1.00	.40	.10
Most Game Winning Goals			
In Playoffs (Career)			
☐ 18 Wayne Gretzky	1.00	.40	.10
Most Goals			

1970-71 Colgate Stamps

The 1970-71 Colgate Stamps set includes 93 small color stamps measuring approximately 1" by 1 1/4". The set was distributed in three sheets of 31. Sheet one featured centers (numbered 1-31) and was available with the giant size of toothpaste, sheet two featured wings (numbered 32-62) and was available with the family size of toothpaste, and sheet three featured goalies and defensemen (numbered 63-93) and was available with king and super size toothpaste. The cards are priced below as individual stamps; the value of a complete sheet would be approximately 20 percent more than the sum of the individual stamp prices. Colgate also issued three calendars so that brushers could stick a stamp on each day for brushing regularly. The cards were numbered in a star in the upper left corner of the card face.

	NRMT	VG-E	GOOD
COMPLETE SET (93)	125.00	50.00	12.50
COMMON PLAYER (1-93)	.75	.30	.07
☐ 1 Walt McKechnie	.75	.30	.07
☐ 2 Bob Pulford	1.50	.60	.15
☐ 3 Mike Walton	1.00	.40	.10
☐ 4 Alex Delvecchio	2.50	1.00	.25
☐ 5 Tom Williams	.75	.30	.07
☐ 6 Derek Sanderson	2.00	.80	.20
☐ 7 Garry Unger	1.25	.50	.12
☐ 8 Lou Angotti	.75	.30	.07
☐ 9 Ted Hampson	.75	.30	.07
☐ 10 Phil Goyette	.75	.30	.07
☐ 11 Juha Widing	.75	.30	.07
☐ 12 Norm Ullman	2.00	.80	.20
☐ 13 Garry Monahan	.75	.30	.07
☐ 14 Henri Richard	3.00	1.20	.30
☐ 15 Ray Cullen	1.00	.40	.10
☐ 16 Danny O'Shea	.75	.30	.07
☐ 17 Marc Tardiff	1.00	.40	.10
☐ 18 Jude Drouin	.75	.30	.07
☐ 19 Charlie Burns	.75	.30	.07
☐ 20 Gerry Meehan	1.00	.40	.10
☐ 21 Ralph Backstrom	1.00	.40	.10
☐ 22 Frank St.Marseille	.75	.30	.07
☐ 23 Orland Kurtenbach	1.00	.40	.10
☐ 24 Red Berenson	1.00	.40	.10
☐ 25 Jean Ratelle	2.00	.80	.20
☐ 26 Syl Apps	1.00	.40	.10
☐ 27 Don Marshall	.75	.30	.07
☐ 28 Gilbert Perreault	6.00	2.40	.60
☐ 29 Andre Lacroix	1.00	.40	.10
☐ 30 Jacques Lemaire	2.00	.80	.20
☐ 31 Pit Martin	1.00	.40	.10
☐ 32 Dennis Hull	1.25	.50	.12
☐ 33 Dave Balon	.75	.30	.07
☐ 34 Keith McCreary	.75	.30	.07
☐ 35 Bobby Rousseau	1.00	.40	.10
☐ 36 Danny Grant	1.00	.40	.10
☐ 37 Brit Selby	.75	.30	.07
☐ 38 Bob Nevin	.75	.30	.07
☐ 39 Rosaire Paiement	.75	.30	.07
☐ 40 Gary Dornhoefer	1.00	.40	.10
☐ 41 Eddie Shack	1.50	.60	.15
☐ 42 Ron Schock	.75	.30	.07
☐ 43 Jim Pappin	1.00	.40	.10
☐ 44 Mickey Redmond	1.25	.50	.12
☐ 45 Vic Hadfield	1.25	.50	.12
☐ 46 Johnny Bucyk	2.50	1.00	.25
☐ 47 Gordie Howe	25.00	10.00	2.50
☐ 48 Ron Anderson	.75	.30	.07
☐ 49 Gary Jarrett	.75	.30	.07
☐ 50 Jean Pronovost	1.00	.40	.10
☐ 51 Simon Nolet	.75	.30	.07
☐ 52 Bill Goldsworthy	1.25	.50	.12
☐ 53 Rod Gilbert	2.00	.80	.20
☐ 54 Ron Ellis	1.00	.40	.10
☐ 55 Mike Byers	.75	.30	.07
☐ 56 Norm Ferguson	.75	.30	.07
☐ 57 Gary Sabourin	.75	.30	.07
☐ 58 Tim Ecclestone	.75	.30	.07
☐ 59 John McKenzie	.75	.30	.07
☐ 60 Yvan Cournoyer	2.50	1.00	.25
☐ 61 Ken Schinkel	.75	.30	.07
☐ 62 Ken Hodge	1.25	.50	.12
☐ 63 Cesare Maniago	1.00	.40	.10
☐ 64 J.C. Tremblay	1.00	.40	.10
☐ 65 Gilles Marotte	1.00	.40	.10
☐ 66 Bob Baun	1.00	.40	.10
☐ 67 Gerry Desjardins	1.00	.40	.10
☐ 68 Charlie Hodge	1.25	.50	.12
☐ 69 Matt Ravlich	.75	.30	.07
☐ 70 Ed Giacomin	2.00	.80	.20
☐ 71 Gerry Cheevers	2.50	1.00	.25
☐ 72 Pat Quinn	1.25	.50	.12
☐ 73 Gary Bergman	1.00	.40	.10
☐ 74 Serge Savard	2.00	.80	.20
☐ 75 Les Binkley	1.00	.40	.10
☐ 76 Arnie Brown	.75	.30	.07
☐ 77 Pat Stapleton	1.00	.40	.10
☐ 78 Ed Van Impe	.75	.30	.07
☐ 79 Jim Dorey	.75	.30	.07
☐ 80 Dave Dryden	1.00	.40	.10
☐ 81 Dale Tallon	1.00	.40	.10
☐ 82 Bruce Gamble	.75	.30	.07

☐	83	Roger Crozier	1.00	.40	.10
☐	84	Denis DeJordy	1.00	.40	.10
☐	85	Rogatien Vachon	2.00	.80	.20
☐	86	Carol Vadnais	.75	.30	.07
☐	87	Bobby Orr	30.00	12.00	3.00
☐	88	Noel Picard	.75	.30	.07
☐	89	Gilles Villemure	1.00	.40	.10
☐	90	Gary Smith	1.00	.40	.10
☐	91	Doug Favell	1.00	.40	.10
☐	92	Ernie Wakely	.75	.30	.07
☐	93	Bernie Parent	2.50	1.00	.25

1971-72 Colgate Heads

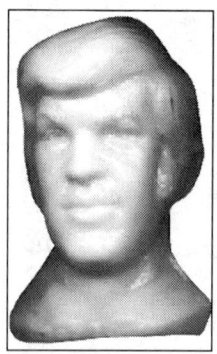

The 17 hockey collectibles in this set measure approximately 1 1/4" in height with a base of 7/8" and are made out of cream-colored or beige plastic. The promotion lasted approximately five months during the winter of 1972. The busts were issued in series of four in the various sizes of the product, Colgate Toothpaste. The player's last name is found only on the back of the base of the head. The Ullmann error is not included in the complete set price below. The heads are unnumbered and checklisted below in alphabetical order.

		NRMT	VG-E	GOOD
COMPLETE SET (16)		100.00	40.00	10.00
COMMON PLAYER (1-16)		3.00	1.20	.30
☐ 1	Yvon Cournoyer	7.50	3.00	.75
☐ 2	Marcel Dionne UER	15.00	6.00	1.50
	(Head actually Stan Mikita)			
☐ 3	Ken Dryden	20.00	8.00	2.00
☐ 4	Paul Henderson	4.00	1.60	.40
☐ 5	Guy Lafleur	20.00	8.00	2.00
☐ 6	Frank Mahovlich	10.00	4.00	1.00
☐ 7	Richard Martin	4.00	1.60	.40
☐ 8	Bobby Orr	40.00	16.00	4.00
☐ 9	Brad Park	10.00	4.00	1.00
☐ 10	Jacques Plante	10.00	4.00	1.00
☐ 11	Jean Ratelle	7.50	3.00	.75
☐ 12	Derek Sanderson	6.00	2.40	.60
☐ 13	Dale Tallon	3.00	1.20	.30
☐ 14	Walt Tkaczuk	3.00	1.20	.30
☐ 15A	Norm Ullman ERR	50.00	20.00	5.00
	(Misspelled Ullmann)			
☐ 15B	Norm Ullman COR	6.00	2.40	.60
☐ 16	Garry Unger	4.00	1.60	.40

1923-24 Crescent Selkirks

The 1923-24 Crescent Ice Cream set contains 14 cards measuring approximately 1 9/16" by 2 3/8". The set features the Selkirks hockey club. The front shows a black and white head and shoulders shot of the player, with the team name written in a crescent over the player's head. At the bottom of the picture, the player's name and position appear in white

lettering in a black stripe. The back has the card number (at the top) and two offers: 1) a brick of ice cream to any person bringing to the Crescent Ice Cream plant any 14 Crescent Hockey Pictures bearing consecutive numbers; and 2) a hockey stick to anyone bringing to the ice cream plant three sets of Crescent Hockey Pictures bearing consecutive numbers from 1-14. The complete set price below does not include the unknown card number 6.

		EX-MT	VG-E	GOOD
COMPLETE SET (13)		900.00	375.00	90.00
COMMON PLAYER (1-14)		75.00	30.00	7.50
☐ 1	Cliff O'Meara	75.00	30.00	7.50
☐ 2	Leo Benard	75.00	30.00	7.50
☐ 3	Pete Speirs	75.00	30.00	7.50
☐ 4	Howard Brandon	75.00	30.00	7.50
☐ 5	George Clark	75.00	30.00	7.50
☐ 7	Cecil Browne	75.00	30.00	7.50
☐ 8	Jack Connelly	75.00	30.00	7.50
☐ 9	Charlie Gardner	150.00	60.00	15.00
☐ 10	Ward Turvey	75.00	30.00	7.50
☐ 11	Connie Johanneson	75.00	30.00	7.50
☐ 12	Frank Woodall	75.00	30.00	7.50
☐ 13	Harold McMunn	75.00	30.00	7.50
☐ 14	Connie Neil	75.00	30.00	7.50

1924-25 Crescent Selkirks

The 1924-25 Crescent Ice Cream Selkirks set contains 14 black and white cards measuring approximately 1 9/16" by 2 3/8". The back has the card number (at the top) and two offers: 1) a brick of ice cream to any person bringing to the Crescent Ice Cream plant any 14 Crescent Hockey Pictures bearing consecutive numbers; and 2) a hockey stick to anyone bringing to the ice cream plant three sets of Crescent Hockey Pictures bearing consecutive numbers from 1-14. Card number 8 of the Selkirks team is perhaps the first hockey team card ever issued.

	EX-MT	VG-E	GOOD
COMPLETE SET (14)	1200.00	500.00	120.00
COMMON PLAYER (1-14)	75.00	30.00	7.50
☐ 1 Howard Brandon	75.00	30.00	7.50
☐ 2 Jack Hughes	75.00	30.00	7.50
☐ 3 Tony Baril	75.00	30.00	7.50
☐ 4 Bill Bowman	75.00	30.00	7.50
☐ 5 W. Roberts	75.00	30.00	7.50
☐ 6 Cecil Browne	250.00	100.00	25.00
☐ 7 Errol Gillis	75.00	30.00	7.50
☐ 8 Selkirks Team	150.00	60.00	15.00
☐ 9 Fred Comfort	75.00	30.00	7.50
☐ 10 Cliff O'Meara	75.00	30.00	7.50
☐ 11 Leo Benard	75.00	30.00	7.50
☐ 12 Pete Speirs	75.00	30.00	7.50
☐ 13 Peter Meurer	75.00	30.00	7.50
☐ 14 Bill Borland	75.00	30.00	7.50

1924-25 Crescent Tigers

The 1924-25 Crescent Ice Cream Tigers set contains 14 black and white cards measuring approximately 1 9/16" by 2 3/8". The back has the card number (at the top) and two offers: 1) a brick of ice cream to any person bringing to the Crescent Ice Cream plant any 14 Crescent Hockey Pictures bearing consecutive numbers; and 2) a hockey stick to anyone bringing to the ice cream plant three sets of Crescent Hockey Pictures bearing consecutive numbers from 1-14.

	EX-MT	VG-E	GOOD
COMPLETE SET (13)	1000.00	400.00	100.00
COMMON PLAYER (1-14)	100.00	40.00	10.00
☐ 1 Bill Cockburn	100.00	40.00	10.00
☐ 2 Wally Byron	100.00	40.00	10.00
☐ 3 Wally Fridfinson	100.00	40.00	10.00
☐ 4 Murray Murdoch	100.00	40.00	10.00
☐ 5 Oliver Redpath	100.00	40.00	10.00
☐ 7 Ward McVey	100.00	40.00	10.00
☐ 8 Tote Mitchell	100.00	40.00	10.00
☐ 9 Lorne Carrol	100.00	40.00	10.00
☐ 10 Tony Wise	100.00	40.00	10.00
☐ 11 Johnny Myres	100.00	40.00	10.00
☐ 12 Gordon McKenzie	100.00	40.00	10.00
☐ 13 Harry Neal	100.00	40.00	10.00
☐ 14 Blake Watson	100.00	40.00	10.00

1970-71 Dad's Cookies

The 1970-71 Dad's Cookies Hockey set contains 144 unnumbered color cards. Each card measures approximately 1 7/8" by 5 3/8"; this unusual size is one reason the set has never been very popular with collectors. Each player is pictured on the fronts dressed in a "NHL Players" emblazoned jersey. The fronts contain player statistics for the 1969-70 season and for his career. The backs, in both English and French, are the same for all cards. The backs contain an ad for these cards and Dad's Cookies, a special offer for an NHL Players Association decal and a 1969 NHL Players Association copyright line.

	NRMT	VG-E	GOOD
COMPLETE SET (144)	125.00	50.00	12.50
COMMON PLAYER (1-144)	.60	.24	.06
☐ 1 Lou Angotti	.60	.24	.06
☐ 2 Don Awrey	.60	.24	.06
☐ 3 Bob Baun	.75	.30	.07
☐ 4 Jean Beliveau	6.00	2.40	.60
☐ 5 Red Berenson	.75	.30	.07
☐ 6 Gary Bergman	.75	.30	.07
☐ 7 Les Binkley	.75	.30	.07
☐ 8 Andre Boudrias	.60	.24	.06
☐ 9 Wally Boyer	.60	.24	.06

PHIL ESPOSITO
BOSTON

Centre/Centre

	NHL Totals 69/70	LNH Totaux
GP/PJ	76	459
G/B	43	201
A/A	56	282
TP/PT	99	483

☐ 10 Arnie Brown	.60	.24	.06
☐ 11 Johnny Bucyk	2.50	1.00	.25
☐ 12 Charlie Burns	.60	.24	.06
☐ 13 Larry Cahan	.60	.24	.06
☐ 14 Gerry Cheevers	3.00	1.20	.30
☐ 15 Bobby Clarke	6.00	2.40	.60
☐ 16 Wayne Connelly	.60	.24	.06
☐ 17 Yvan Cournoyer	2.50	1.00	.25
☐ 18 Roger Crozier	.75	.30	.07
☐ 19 Ray Cullen	.75	.30	.07
☐ 20 Denis DeJordy	.75	.30	.07
☐ 21 Alex Delvecchio	2.50	1.00	.25
☐ 22 Bob Dillabough	.60	.24	.06
☐ 23 Gary Doak	.60	.24	.06
☐ 24 Gary Dornhoefer	.75	.30	.07
☐ 25 Dick Duff	.75	.30	.07
☐ 26 Tim Ecclestone	.60	.24	.06
☐ 27 Roy Edwards	.75	.30	.07
☐ 28 Gerry Ehman	.60	.24	.06
☐ 29 Ron Ellis	.75	.30	.07
☐ 30 Phil Esposito	6.00	2.40	.60
☐ 31 Tony Esposito	5.00	2.00	.50
☐ 32 Doug Favell	.75	.30	.07
☐ 33 John Ferguson	.75	.30	.07
☐ 34 Norm Ferguson	.60	.24	.06
☐ 35 Reg Fleming	.60	.24	.06
☐ 36 Bill Flett	.60	.24	.06
☐ 37 Bruce Gamble	.60	.24	.06
☐ 38 Jean-Guy Gendron	.60	.24	.06
☐ 39 Ed Giacomin	2.50	1.00	.25
☐ 40 Rod Gilbert	2.00	.80	.20
☐ 41 Bill Goldsworthy	.75	.30	.07
☐ 42 Phil Goyette	.60	.24	.06
☐ 43 Danny Grant	.75	.30	.07
☐ 44 Ted Green	.75	.30	.07
☐ 45 Vic Hadfield	.75	.30	.07
☐ 46 Al Hamilton	.60	.24	.06
☐ 47 Ted Hampson	.60	.24	.06
☐ 48 Terry Harper	.75	.30	.07
☐ 49 Ted Harris	.60	.24	.06
☐ 50 Paul Henderson	1.00	.40	.10
☐ 51 Bryan Hextall	.75	.30	.07
☐ 52 Bill Hicke	.60	.24	.06
☐ 53 Larry Hillman	.60	.24	.06
☐ 54 Wayne Hillman	.60	.24	.06
☐ 55 Charlie Hodge	1.00	.40	.10
☐ 56 Ken Hodge	1.00	.40	.10
☐ 57 Gordie Howe	20.00	8.00	2.00
☐ 58 Harry Howell	1.50	.60	.15
☐ 59 Bobby Hull	10.00	4.00	1.00
☐ 60 Dennis Hull	1.00	.40	.10
☐ 61 Earl Ingarfield	.60	.24	.06
☐ 62 Doug Jarrett	.60	.24	.06
☐ 63 Gary Jarrett	.60	.24	.06
☐ 64 Ed Johnston	1.00	.40	.10

☐	65	Dave Keon	1.50	.60	.15
☐	66	Skip Krake	.60	.24	.06
☐	67	Orland Kurtenbach	.75	.30	.07
☐	68	Andre Lacroix	.75	.30	.07
☐	69	Jacques Laperriere	1.00	.40	.10
☐	70	Jacques Lemaire	1.50	.60	.15
☐	71	Rick Ley	.75	.30	.07
☐	72	Bruce MacGregor	.60	.24	.06
☐	73	Keith Magnuson	.75	.30	.07
☐	74	Frank Mahovlich	4.00	1.60	.40
☐	75	Chico Maki	.75	.30	.07
☐	76	Gilles Marotte	.75	.30	.07
☐	77	Bert Marshall	.60	.24	.06
☐	78	Don Marshall	.60	.24	.06
☐	79	Pit Martin	.75	.30	.07
☐	80	Keith McCreary	.60	.24	.06
☐	81	Ab McDonald	.60	.24	.06
☐	82	Jim McKenny	.60	.24	.06
☐	83	John McKenzie	.75	.30	.07
☐	84	Mike McMahon	.60	.24	.06
☐	85	Larry Mickey	.60	.24	.06
☐	86	Stan Mikita	4.00	1.60	.40
☐	87	Doug Mohns	.75	.30	.07
☐	88	Wayne Muloin	.60	.24	.06
☐	89	Jim Neilson	.60	.24	.06
☐	90	Bob Nevin	.60	.24	.06
☐	91	Murray Oliver	.60	.24	.06
☐	92	Bobby Orr	20.00	8.00	2.00
☐	93	Danny O'Shea	.60	.24	.06
☐	94	Rosaire Paiement	.60	.24	.06
☐	95	Bernie Parent	3.00	1.20	.30
☐	96	Jean-Paul Parise	.75	.30	.07
☐	97	Brad Park	2.50	1.00	.25
☐	98	Mike Pelyk	.60	.24	.06
☐	99	Gilbert Perreault	4.00	1.60	.40
☐	100	Noel Picard	.60	.24	.06
☐	101	Barclay Plager	1.00	.40	.10
☐	102	Jacques Plante	4.00	1.60	.40
☐	103	Tracy Pratt	.60	.24	.06
☐	104	Dean Prentice	.75	.30	.07
☐	105	Jean Pronovost	.75	.30	.07
☐	106	Bob Pulford	1.00	.40	.10
☐	107	Pat Quinn	1.00	.40	.10
☐	108	Jean Ratelle	2.00	.80	.20
☐	109	Matt Ravlich	.60	.24	.06
☐	110	Mickey Redmond	1.00	.40	.10
☐	111	Henri Richard	3.00	1.20	.30
☐	112	Jim Roberts	.75	.30	.07
☐	113	Dale Rolfe	.60	.24	.06
☐	114	Bobby Rousseau	.75	.30	.07
☐	115	Gary Sabourin	.60	.24	.06
☐	116	Derek Sanderson	1.50	.60	.15
☐	117	Glen Sather	2.00	.80	.20
☐	118	Serge Savard	1.50	.60	.15
☐	119	Ken Schinkel	.60	.24	.06
☐	120	Ron Seiling	.60	.24	.06
☐	121	Brit Selby	.60	.24	.06
☐	122	Eddie Shack	1.50	.60	.15
☐	123	Floyd Smith	.60	.24	.06
☐	124	Fred Stanfield	.60	.24	.06
☐	125	Pat Stapleton	.75	.30	.07
☐	126	Frank St.Marseille	.60	.24	.06
☐	127	Dale Tallon	.75	.30	.07
☐	128	Walt Tkaczuk	.75	.30	.07
☐	129	J.C. Tremblay	.75	.30	.07
☐	130	Norm Ullman	1.50	.60	.15
☐	131	Garry Unger	1.00	.40	.10
☐	132	Rogatien Vachon	1.50	.60	.15
☐	133	Carol Vadnais	.60	.24	.06
☐	134	Ed Van Impe	.60	.24	.06
☐	135	Bob Wall	.60	.24	.06
☐	136	Mike Walton	.75	.30	.07
☐	137	Bryan Watson	.60	.24	.06
☐	138	Joe Watson	.60	.24	.06
☐	139	Tom Webster	.75	.30	.07
☐	140	Juha Widing	.60	.24	.06
☐	141	Tom Williams	.60	.24	.06
☐	142	Jim Wiste	.60	.24	.06
☐	143	Gump Worsley	3.00	1.20	.30
☐	144	Bob Woytowich	.60	.24	.06

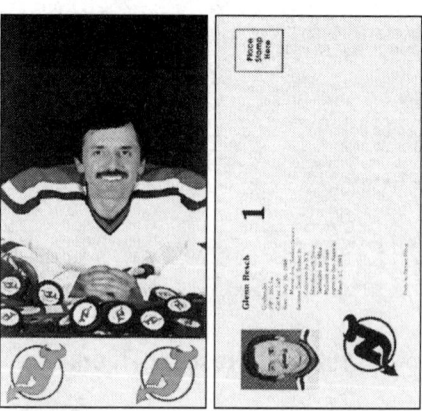

postcard type format. On the left half of the back appear a black and white head shot of the player, basic player information, and the Devils' team logo. The cards are checklisted below according to uniform number. The side panel of the package of Colgate Dental Cream listed the checklist of the complete set. Hannu Kamppuri only played during the 1984-85 season. The cards of John MacLean and Kirk Muller predate their Rookie Cards.

			MINT	EXC	G-VG
	COMPLETE SET (25)		20.00	8.00	2.00
	COMMON PLAYER		.50	.20	.05
☐	1	Glenn Resch	2.00	.80	.20
☐	2	Joe Cirella	.75	.30	.07
☐	4	Bob Lorimer	.50	.20	.05
☐	5	Phil Russell	.50	.20	.05
☐	8	Dave Pichette	.50	.20	.05
☐	9	Don Lever	.75	.30	.07
☐	10	Aaron Broten	.50	.20	.05
☐	12	Pat Verbeek	3.00	1.20	.30
☐	14	Rich Chernomaz	.60	.24	.06
☐	15	John MacLean	5.00	2.00	.50
☐	16	Rick Meagher	.75	.30	.07
☐	17	Paul Gagne	.50	.20	.05
☐	18	Mel Bridgman	.75	.30	.07
☐	19	Rich Preston	.50	.20	.05
☐	20	Tim Higgins	.50	.20	.05
☐	21	Bob Hoffmeyer	.50	.20	.05
☐	22	Doug Sulliman	.50	.20	.05
☐	23	Bruce Driver	.75	.30	.07
☐	25	Dave Lewis	.50	.20	.05
☐	27	Kirk Muller	7.50	3.00	.75
☐	28	Uli Hiemer	.50	.20	.05
☐	29	Jan Ludvig	.50	.20	.05
☐	30	Ron Low	.75	.30	.07
☐	33	Hannu Kamppuri	.50	.20	.05
☐	NNO	Doug Carpenter CO	.50	.20	.05

1985-86 Devils Postcards

This ten-card set of New Jersey Devils features on the front borderless color player photos. The cards measure approximately 3 5/8" by 5 1/2" and are in the postcard format. The horizontal backs are divided in half by a thin black line and have the year, biographical information, home town, and a career highlight at the upper left corner. The cards are unnumbered and checklisted below in alphabetical order. Key cards in the set are Kirk Muller in his Rookie Card year and Craig Billington prior to his Rookie Card year.

			MINT	EXC	G-VG
	COMPLETE SET (10)		15.00	6.00	1.50
	COMMON PLAYER (1-10)		1.00	.40	.10
☐	1	Greg Adams	1.25	.50	.12
☐	2	Perry Anderson	1.00	.40	.10

1984-85 Devils Postcards

This 25-card set of New Jersey Devils features on the front borderless color photos of the players, with two team logos (in green and red) in the white stripe below the picture. The cards measure approximately 3 1/4" by 6 1/8" and are in the

		MINT	EXC	G-VG
☐	10 Bruce Driver 23	1.50	.60	.15
☐	11 Uli Hiemer 28	1.25	.50	.12
☐	12 Mark Johnson 12	1.50	.60	.15
☐	13 Jan Ludvig 29	1.25	.50	.12
☐	14 John MacLean 15	5.00	2.00	.50
☐	15 Peter McNab 7	1.50	.60	.15
☐	16 Kirk Muller 9	7.50	3.00	.75
☐	17 Doug Sulliman 22	1.25	.50	.12
☐	18 Randy Velischek 27	1.25	.50	.12
☐	19 Pat Verbeek	3.00	1.20	.30
☐	20 Craig Wolanin 6	1.25	.50	.12

		MINT	EXC	G-VG
☐	3 Craig Billington	1.50	.60	.15
☐	4 Alain Chevrier	1.00	.40	.10
☐	5 Paul Gagne	1.00	.40	.10
☐	6 Mark Johnson	1.25	.50	.12
☐	7 Kirk Muller	7.50	3.00	.75
☐	8 Chico Resch	2.00	.80	.20
☐	9 Randy Velischek	1.00	.40	.10
☐	10 Craig Wolanin	1.00	.40	.10

1988-89 Devils Carretta

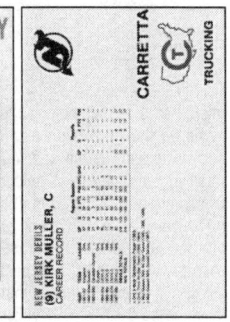

This 30-card set has color action photos of the New Jersey Devils on the front, with a thin black border on white card stock. The cards measure approximately 2 7/8" by 4 1/4". The team name and logo on the top are printed in green and red; the text below the picture, giving player name, uniform number, and position, is printed in black. The horizontally oriented back has career statistics, a team logo, and a Carretta Trucking logo. We have checklisted the cards below in alphabetical order. Brendan Shanahan appears in his Rookie Card year.

1986-87 Devils Police

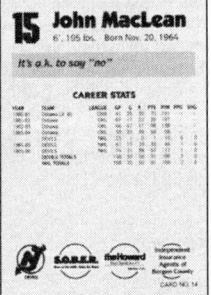

This 20-card set was jointly sponsored by the New Jersey Devils, S.O.B.E.R., Howard Bank, and Independent Insurance Agents of Bergen County. Logos for these sponsors appear on the bottom of the card back. The front features a color action photo of the player, with the Devils' and NHL logos superimposed over the top corners of the picture. A thin black line and a green line serves as the inner and outer borders respectively; the area in between is yellow, with printing in the team's colors red and black. In addition to sponsors' logos, the back has biographical information, an anti-drug message, and career statistics. We have checklisted the cards below in alphabetical order, with uniform number to the right of the player's name.

	MINT	EXC	G-VG
COMPLETE SET (30)	20.00	8.00	2.00
COMMON PLAYER (1-30)	.50	.20	.05

		MINT	EXC	G-VG
☐	1 Perry Anderson 25	.50	.20	.05
☐	2 Bob Bellemore CO	.50	.20	.05
☐	3 Aaron Broten 10	.50	.20	.05
☐	4 Doug Brown 24	.50	.20	.05
☐	5 Sean Burke 1	1.50	.60	.15
☐	6 Anders Carlsson 20	.50	.20	.05
☐	7 Joe Cirella 2	.75	.30	.07
☐	8 Pat Conacher 32	.50	.20	.05
☐	9 Ken Daneyko 3	.75	.30	.07
☐	10 Bruce Driver 23	.60	.24	.06
☐	11 Bob Hoffmeyer CO	.50	.20	.05
☐	12 Jamie Huscroft 4	.50	.20	.05
☐	13 Mark Johnson 12	.60	.24	.06
☐	14 Jim Korn 14	.50	.20	.05
☐	15 Tom Kurvers 5	.75	.30	.07
☐	16 Lou Lamoriello P/GM	.50	.20	.05
☐	17 Claude Loiselle 19	.50	.20	.05
☐	18 John MacLean 15	2.00	.80	.20
☐	19 David Maley 8	.60	.24	.06
☐	20 Doug McKay CO	.50	.20	.05
☐	21 Kirk Muller 9	3.00	1.20	.30
☐	22 Jack O'Callahan 7	.50	.20	.05
☐	23 Steve Rooney 18	.50	.20	.05
☐	24 Bob Sauve 28	.60	.24	.06
☐	25 Jim Schoenfeld CO	.75	.30	.07
☐	26 Brendan Shanahan 11	7.50	3.00	.75
☐	27 Patrik Sundstrom 17	.75	.30	.07
☐	28 Randy Velischek 27	.50	.20	.05
☐	29 Pat Verbeek 16	1.25	.50	.12
☐	30 Craig Wolanin 6	.50	.20	.05

	MINT	EXC	G-VG
COMPLETE SET (20)	30.00	12.00	3.00
COMMON PLAYER (1-20)	1.25	.50	.12

		MINT	EXC	G-VG
☐	1 Greg Adams 24	1.50	.60	.15
☐	2 Perry Anderson 25	1.25	.50	.12
☐	3 Timo Blomqvist 5	1.25	.50	.12
☐	4 Andy Brickley 26	1.50	.60	.15
☐	5 Mel Bridgman 18	1.50	.60	.15
☐	6 Aaron Broten 10	1.25	.50	.12
☐	7 Alain Chevrier 30	1.50	.60	.15
☐	8 Joe Cirella 2	1.50	.60	.15
☐	9 Ken Daneyko 3	1.50	.60	.15

1989-90 Devils

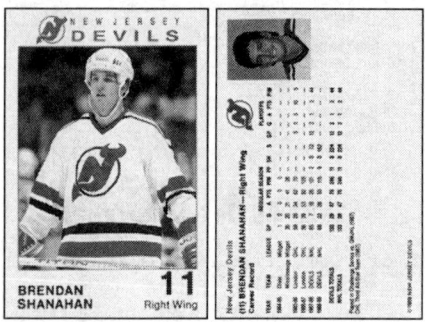

This 29-card set has color action photos of the New Jersey Devils on the front, with a thin red border on white card stock. The team name and logo on the top are printed in green and red; the text below the picture, giving player name, uniform number, and position, is printed in black. The horizontally oriented back provides brief biographical information and career statistics, as well as a black and white picture of the player in the upper right-hand corner. The cards measure approximately 2 7/8" by 4 1/4". These unnumbered cards are checklisted below alphabetically with sweater number noted to the right.

	MINT	EXC	G-VG
COMPLETE SET (29)	12.00	5.00	1.20
COMMON PLAYER (1-29)	.40	.16	.04
☐ 1 Tommy Albelin 26	.40	.16	.04
☐ 2 Bob Bellemore CO	.40	.16	.04
☐ 3 Neil Brady 11	.40	.16	.04
☐ 4 Aaron Broten 10	.40	.16	.04
☐ 5 Doug Brown 24	.40	.16	.04
☐ 6 Sean Burke 1	1.00	.40	.10
☐ 7 Pat Conacher 32	.40	.16	.04
☐ 8 John Cunniff CO	.40	.16	.04
☐ 9 Ken Daneyko 3	.60	.24	.06
☐ 10 Bruce Driver 23	.60	.24	.06
☐ 11 Viacheslav Fetisov 2	1.50	.60	.15
☐ 12 Mark Johnson 12	.40	.16	.04
☐ 13 Jim Korn 14	.40	.16	.04
☐ 14 Lou Lamoriello P/GM	.40	.16	.04
☐ 15 John MacLean 15	1.50	.60	.15
☐ 16 David Maley 8	.40	.16	.04
☐ 17 Kirk Muller 9	2.50	1.00	.25
☐ 18 Janne Ojanen 22	.40	.16	.04
☐ 19 Walt Poddubny 16	.60	.24	.06
☐ 20 Reijo Ruotsalainen 29	.60	.24	.06
☐ 21 Brendan Shanahan 11	4.00	1.60	.40
☐ 22 Sergei Starikov 4	.40	.16	.04
☐ 23 Patrik Sundstrom 17	.60	.24	.06
☐ 24 Peter Sundstrom 20	.40	.16	.04
☐ 25 Chris Terreri 31	1.50	.60	.15
☐ 26 Sylvain Turgeon 16	.60	.24	.06
☐ 27 Randy Velischek 27	.40	.16	.04
☐ 28 Eric Weinrich 7	.60	.24	.06
☐ 29 Craig Wolanin 6	.40	.16	.04

1990-91 Devils

This set contains 30 cards and features members of the New Jersey Devils. The cards measure the standard size, 2 1/2" by 3 1/2". The front has a color photo of the player, with the team logo in the upper left corner. The back has statistical information. These cards are unnumbered and are checklisted below in alphabetical order.

	MINT	EXC	G-VG
COMPLETE SET (30)	10.00	4.00	1.00
COMMON PLAYER (1-30)	.35	.14	.03

☐ 1 Tommy Albelin	.35	.14	.03
☐ 2 Laurie Boschman	.35	.14	.03
☐ 3 Doug Brown	.35	.14	.03
☐ 4 Sean Burke	.75	.30	.07
☐ 5 Tim Burke	.35	.14	.03
☐ 6 Zdeno Ciger	.75	.30	.07
☐ 7 Pat Conacher	.35	.14	.03
☐ 8 Troy Crowder	.50	.20	.05
☐ 9 John Cunniff CO	.35	.14	.03
☐ 10 Ken Daneyko	.50	.20	.05
☐ 11 Bruce Driver	.50	.20	.05
☐ 12 Viacheslav Fetisov	.75	.30	.07
☐ 13 Alexei Kasatonov	.60	.24	.06
☐ 14 Lou Lamoriello P/GM	.35	.14	.03
☐ 15 Claude Lemieux	.75	.30	.07
☐ 16 David Maley	.35	.14	.03
☐ 17 John MacLean	1.25	.50	.12
☐ 18 Jon Morris	.50	.20	.05
☐ 19 Kirk Muller	2.00	.80	.20
☐ 20 Lee Norwood	.35	.14	.03
☐ 21 Myles O'Connor	.35	.14	.03
☐ 22 Walt Poddubny	.50	.20	.05
☐ 23 Brendan Shanahan	3.00	1.20	.30
☐ 24 Peter Stastny	1.50	.60	.15
☐ 25 Alan Stewart	.35	.14	.03
☐ 26 Warren Strelow	.35	.14	.03
☐ 27 Doug Sulliman	.35	.14	.03
☐ 28 Patrik Sundstrom	.50	.20	.05
☐ 29 Chris Terreri	.75	.30	.07
☐ 30 Eric Weinrich	.60	.24	.06

1991-92 Devils Teams Carvel

This ten-card set features team photos of the ten Devils teams from 1982-83 through 1991-92. The cards have a coupon for Carvel Ice Cream with an entry form for the "Shoot to Win" contest. The backs list all the players who are pictured and the statistical leaders from that particular year. The cards are unnumbered and measure approximately 2 1/2" by 6" with coupon. One card was issued per spectator at certain home games during the 1991-92 season.

	MINT	EXC	G-VG
COMPLETE SET (10)	15.00	6.00	1.50
COMMON TEAM (1-10)	1.50	.60	.15
☐ 1 1982-83 Devils Team	1.50	.60	.15
☐ 2 1983-84 Devils Team	1.50	.60	.15
☐ 3 1984-85 Devils Team	1.50	.60	.15
☐ 4 1985-86 Devils Team	1.50	.60	.15
☐ 5 1986-87 Devils Team	1.50	.60	.15
☐ 6 1987-88 Devils Team	1.50	.60	.15
☐ 7 1988-89 Devils Team	1.50	.60	.15
☐ 8 1989-90 Devils Team	1.50	.60	.15
☐ 9 1990-91 Devils Team	1.50	.60	.15
☐ 10 1991-92 Devils Team	1.50	.60	.15

1992 Disney Mighty Ducks

Issued to promote the Walt Disney movie "The Mighty Ducks", this eight-card set measures approximately 3 1/2" by 6" and is designed in the postcard format. Each card is perforated; the left portion, measuring the standard size (2 1/2" by 3 1/2"), displays a full-bleed color photo, while the right portion is a solid neon color with a box for the stamp at the upper right. The back of the trading card portion has a brief player profile, while the other portion has an advertisement for the movie. The cards are unnumbered and checklisted below in alphabetical order. The character's name in the movie is given on the continuation line.

	MINT	EXC	G-VG
COMPLETE SET (8)	20.00	8.00	2.00
COMMON PLAYER (1-8)	2.00	.80	.20

		MINT	EXC	G-VG
☐ 1	Brandon Adams Jesse	2.00	.80	.20
☐ 2	Emilio Estevez Coach Bombay	6.00	2.40	.60
☐ 3	Joshua Jackson Charlie	2.00	.80	.20
☐ 4	Marguerite Moreau Connie	2.00	.80	.20
☐ 5	Elden Ratliff Fulton	2.00	.80	.20
☐ 6	Shaun Weiss Goldberg	2.00	.80	.20
☐ 7	Rollerblading in Shopping Mall	2.00	.80	.20
☐ 8	Team Photo	6.00	2.40	.60

1993-94 Donruss

These 510 standard-size (2 1/2" by 3 1/2") cards feature borderless color player action shots on their fronts. The player's name appears in gold foil within a team-color-coded stripe near the bottom. His team logo rests in a lower corner. The backs, some of which are horizontal, carry another borderless color player action shot. The player's name, team, position, and biography are shown within a black rectangle on the left. His statistics appear in ghosted strips below or alongside. The cards are numbered on the back. Ten Elite cards were random inserts in Series 1 packs. Also randomly inserted in first-series packs were Donruss Ice Kings and Rated Rookies. Production of the Update set (401-510) was limited to 4,000 cases issued to the hobby in the last week of April. Five Elite cards, each limited to 10,000 and individually numbered, were random inserts in Update foil packs. Also, a 45-card World Junior Championship insert set featuring 22 players from the U.S. Junior National Team and 22 from the Canada Junior National team were included one per pack.

	MINT	EXC	G-VG
COMPLETE SET (510)	42.00	19.00	5.25

COMPLETE SERIES 1 (400)	32.00	14.50	4.00
COMPLETE UPDATE SET (110)	10.00	4.50	1.25
COMMON PLAYER (1-400)	.10	.05	.01
COMMON PLAYER (401-510)	.10	.05	.01
☐ 1	Steven King Anaheim Mighty Ducks	.10	.05	.01
☐ 2	Joe Sacco Anaheim Mighty Ducks	.10	.05	.01
☐ 3	Anatoli Semenov Anaheim Mighty Ducks	.10	.05	.01
☐ 4	Terry Yake Anaheim Mighty Ducks	.10	.05	.01
☐ 5	Alexei Kasatonov Anaheim Mighty Ducks	.10	.05	.01
☐ 6	Patrik Carnback Anaheim Mighty Ducks	.15	.07	.02
☐ 7	Sean Hill Anaheim Mighty Ducks	.10	.05	.01
☐ 8	Bill Houlder Anaheim Mighty Ducks	.10	.05	.01
☐ 9	Todd Ewen Anaheim Mighty Ducks	.10	.05	.01
☐ 10	Bob Corkum Anaheim Mighty Ducks	.10	.05	.01
☐ 11	Tim Sweeney Anaheim Mighty Ducks	.10	.05	.01
☐ 12	Ron Tugnutt Anaheim Mighty Ducks	.10	.05	.01
☐ 13	Guy Hebert Anaheim Mighty Ducks	.25	.11	.03
☐ 14	Shaun Van Allen Anaheim Mighty Ducks	.10	.05	.01
☐ 15	Stu Grimson Anaheim Mighty Ducks	.10	.05	.01
☐ 16	Jon Casey Boston Bruins	.10	.05	.01
☐ 17	Dan Marois Boston Bruins	.10	.05	.01
☐ 18	Adam Oates Boston Bruins	.20	.09	.03
☐ 19	Glen Wesley Boston Bruins	.10	.05	.01
☐ 20	Cam Stewart Boston Bruins	.25	.11	.03
☐ 21	Don Sweeney Boston Bruins	.10	.05	.01
☐ 22	Glen Murray Boston Bruins	.10	.05	.01
☐ 23	Jozef Stumpel Boston Bruins	.10	.05	.01
☐ 24	Ray Bourque Boston Bruins	.25	.11	.03
☐ 25	Ted Donato Boston Bruins	.10	.05	.01
☐ 26	Joe Juneau Boston Bruins	.75	.35	.09
☐ 27	Dmitri Kvartalov Boston Bruins	.10	.05	.01
☐ 28	Steve Leach Boston Bruins	.10	.05	.01
☐ 29	Cam Neely Boston Bruins	.20	.09	.03
☐ 30	Bryan Smolinski Boston Bruins	.75	.35	.09
☐ 31	Craig Simpson Buffalo Sabres	.10	.05	.01
☐ 32	Donald Audette Buffalo Sabres	.10	.05	.01
☐ 33	Doug Bodger Buffalo Sabres	.10	.05	.01
☐ 34	Grant Fuhr Buffalo Sabres	.10	.05	.01
☐ 35	Dale Hawerchuk Buffalo Sabres	.10	.05	.01
☐ 36	Yuri Khmylev Buffalo Sabres	.10	.05	.01
☐ 37	Pat LaFontaine Buffalo Sabres	.30	.14	.04
☐ 38	Brad May Buffalo Sabres	.10	.05	.01
☐ 39	Alexander Mogilny Buffalo Sabres	.50	.23	.06
☐ 40	Richard Smehlik Buffalo Sabres	.10	.05	.01
☐ 41	Petr Svoboda Buffalo Sabres	.10	.05	.01
☐ 42	Matthew Barnaby Buffalo Sabres	.25	.11	.03
☐ 43	Sergei Petrenko Buffalo Sabres	.10	.05	.01
☐ 44	Mark Astley Buffalo Sabres	.20	.09	.03
☐ 45	Derek Plante	1.00	.45	.13

Buffalo Sabres				
☐ 46	Theoren Fleury	.10	.05	.01
Calgary Flames				
☐ 47	Al MacInnis	.20	.09	.03
Calgary Flames				
☐ 48	Joe Nieuwendyk	.15	.07	.02
Calgary Flames				
☐ 49	Joel Otto	.10	.05	.01
Calgary Flames				
☐ 50	Paul Ranheim	.10	.05	.01
Calgary Flames				
☐ 51	Robert Reichel	.15	.07	.02
Calgary Flames				
☐ 52	Gary Roberts	.15	.07	.02
Calgary Flames				
☐ 53	Gary Suter	.15	.07	.02
Calgary Flames				
☐ 54	Mike Vernon	.15	.07	.02
Calgary Flames				
☐ 55	Kelly Kisio	.10	.05	.01
Calgary Flames				
☐ 56	German Titov	.60	.25	.08
Calgary Flames				
☐ 57	Wes Walz	.10	.05	.01
Calgary Flames				
☐ 58	Ted Drury	.10	.05	.01
Calgary Flames				
☐ 59	Sandy McCarthy	.10	.05	.01
Calgary Flames				
☐ 60	Vesa Viitakoski	.25	.11	.03
Calgary Flames				
☐ 61	Jeff Hackett	.10	.05	.01
Chicago Blackhawks				
☐ 62	Neil Wilkinson	.10	.05	.01
Chicago Blackhawks				
☐ 63	Dirk Graham	.10	.05	.01
Chicago Blackhawks				
☐ 64	Ed Belfour	.30	.14	.04
Chicago Blackhawks				
☐ 65	Chris Chelios	.15	.07	.02
Chicago Blackhawks				
☐ 66	Joe Murphy	.10	.05	.01
Chicago Blackhawks				
☐ 67	Jeremy Roenick	.75	.35	.09
Chicago Blackhawks				
☐ 68	Steve Smith	.10	.05	.01
Chicago Blackhawks				
☐ 69	Brent Sutter	.15	.07	.02
Chicago Blackhawks				
☐ 70	Steve Dubinsky	.20	.09	.03
Chicago Blackhawks				
☐ 71	Michel Goulet	.15	.07	.02
Chicago Blackhawks				
☐ 72	Christian Ruuttu	.10	.05	.01
Chicago Blackhawks				
☐ 73	Bryan Marchment	.10	.05	.01
Hartford Whalers				
☐ 74	Sergei Krivokrasov	.10	.05	.01
Chicago Blackhawks				
☐ 75	Jeff Shantz	.25	.11	.03
Chicago Blackhawks				
☐ 76	Mike Modano	.35	.16	.04
Dallas Stars				
☐ 77	Derian Hatcher	.10	.05	.01
Dallas Stars				
☐ 78	Ulf Dahlen	.10	.05	.01
Dallas Stars				
☐ 79	Mark Tinordi	.10	.05	.01
Dallas Stars				
☐ 80	Russ Courtnall	.15	.07	.02
Dallas Stars				
☐ 81	Mike Craig	.10	.05	.01
Dallas Stars				
☐ 82	Trent Klatt	.10	.05	.01
Dallas Stars				
☐ 83	Dave Gagner	.15	.07	.02
Dallas Stars				
☐ 84	Chris Tancill	.10	.05	.01
Dallas Stars				
☐ 85	James Black	.10	.05	.01
Dallas Stars				
☐ 86	Dean Evason	.10	.05	.01
Dallas Stars				
☐ 87	Andy Moog	.15	.07	.02
Dallas Stars				
☐ 88	Paul Cavallini	.10	.05	.01
Dallas Stars				
☐ 89	Grant Ledyard	.10	.05	.01
Dallas Stars				
☐ 90	Jarkko Varvio	.25	.11	.03
Dallas Stars				
☐ 91	Vyacheslav Kozlov	1.00	.45	.13
Detroit Red Wings				
☐ 92	Mike Sillinger	.10	.05	.01
Detroit Red Wings				
☐ 93	Aaron Ward	.20	.09	.03
Detroit Red Wings				
☐ 94	Greg Johnson	.10	.05	.01
Detroit Red Wings				
☐ 95	Steve Yzerman	.40	.18	.05
Detroit Red Wings				
☐ 96	Tim Cheveldae	.15	.07	.02
Detroit Red Wings				
☐ 97	Steve Chiasson	.10	.05	.01
Detroit Red Wings				
☐ 98	Dino Ciccarelli	.15	.07	.02
Detroit Red Wings				
☐ 99	Paul Coffey	.25	.11	.03
Detroit Red Wings				
☐ 100	Dallas Drake	.30	.14	.04
Detroit Red Wings				
☐ 101	Sergei Fedorov	1.25	.55	.16
Detroit Red Wings				
☐ 102	Nicklas Lidstrom	.15	.07	.02
Detroit Red Wings				
☐ 103	Darren McCarty	.30	.14	.04
Detroit Red Wings				
☐ 104	Bob Probert	.10	.05	.01
Detroit Red Wings				
☐ 105	Ray Sheppard	.10	.05	.01
Detroit Red Wings				
☐ 106	Scott Pearson	.10	.05	.01
Edmonton Oilers				
☐ 107	Steven Rice	.10	.05	.01
Edmonton Oilers				
☐ 108	Louie DeBrusk	.10	.05	.01
Edmonton Oilers				
☐ 109	Dave Manson	.10	.05	.01
Edmonton Oilers				
☐ 110	Dean McAmmond	.10	.05	.01
Edmonton Oilers				
☐ 111	Roman Oksiuta	.20	.09	.03
Edmonton Oilers				
☐ 112	Geoff Smith	.10	.05	.01
Edmonton Oilers				
☐ 113	Zdeno Ciger	.10	.05	.01
Edmonton Oilers				
☐ 114	Shayne Corson	.10	.05	.01
Edmonton Oilers				
☐ 115	Luke Richardson	.10	.05	.01
Edmonton Oilers				
☐ 116	Igor Kravchuk	.10	.05	.01
Edmonton Oilers				
☐ 117	Bill Ranford	.15	.07	.02
Edmonton Oilers				
☐ 118	Doug Weight	.15	.07	.02
Edmonton Oilers				
☐ 119	Fred Brathwaite	.20	.09	.03
Edmonton Oilers				
☐ 120	Jason Arnott	2.50	1.15	.30
Edmonton Oilers				
☐ 121	Tom Fitzgerald	.10	.05	.01
Florida Panthers				
☐ 122	Mike Hough	.10	.05	.01
Florida Panthers				
☐ 123	Jesse Belanger	.25	.11	.03
Florida Panthers				
☐ 124	Brian Skrudland	.10	.05	.01
Florida Panthers				
☐ 125	Dave Lowry	.10	.05	.01
Florida Panthers				
☐ 126	Scott Mellanby	.10	.05	.01
Florida Panthers				
☐ 127	Evgeny Davydov	.10	.05	.01
Florida Panthers				
☐ 128	Andrei Lomakin	.10	.05	.01
Florida Panthers				
☐ 129	Brian Benning	.10	.05	.01
Florida Panthers				
☐ 130	Scott Levins	.25	.11	.03
Florida Panthers				
☐ 131	Gord Murphy	.10	.05	.01
Florida Panthers				
☐ 132	John Vanbiesbrouck	.25	.11	.03
Florida Panthers				
☐ 133	Mark Fitzpatrick	.10	.05	.01
Florida Panthers				
☐ 134	Rob Niedermayer	1.00	.45	.13
Florida Panthers				
☐ 135	Alexander Godynyuk	.10	.05	.01
Florida Panthers				
☐ 136	Eric Weinrich	.10	.05	.01
Chicago Blackhawks				
☐ 137	Mark Greig	.10	.05	.01
Hartford Whalers				
☐ 138	Jim Sandlak	.10	.05	.01
Hartford Whalers				
☐ 139	Adam Burt	.10	.05	.01

Hartford Whalers				
☐ 140 Nick Kypreos	.10	.05	.01	
New York Rangers				
☐ 141 Sean Burke	.15	.07	.02	
Hartford Whalers				
☐ 142 Andrew Cassels	.10	.05	.01	
Hartford Whalers				
☐ 143 Robert Kron	.10	.05	.01	
Hartford Whalers				
☐ 144 Mikael Nylander	.25	.11	.03	
Hartford Whalers				
☐ 145 Robert Petrovicky	.10	.05	.01	
Hartford Whalers				
☐ 146 Pat Poulin	.10	.05	.01	
Chicago Blackhawks				
☐ 147 Geoff Sanderson	.35	.16	.04	
Hartford Whalers				
☐ 148 Pat Verbeek	.15	.07	.02	
Hartford Whalers				
☐ 149 Zarley Zalapski	.10	.05	.01	
Hartford Whalers				
☐ 150 Chris Pronger	1.00	.45	.13	
Hartford Whalers				
☐ 151 Jari Kurri	.20	.09	.03	
Los Angeles Kings				
☐ 152 Wayne Gretzky	2.00	.90	.25	
Los Angeles Kings				
☐ 153 Pat Conacher	.10	.05	.01	
Los Angeles Kings				
☐ 154 Shawn McEachern	.20	.09	.03	
Los Angeles Kings				
☐ 155 Mike Donnelly	.10	.05	.01	
Los Angeles Kings				
☐ 156 Warren Rychel	.10	.05	.01	
Los Angeles Kings				
☐ 157 Gary Shuchuk	.10	.05	.01	
Los Angeles Kings				
☐ 158 Rob Blake	.15	.07	.02	
Los Angeles Kings				
☐ 159 Jimmy Carson	.10	.05	.01	
Los Angeles Kings				
☐ 160 Tony Granato	.10	.05	.01	
Los Angeles Kings				
☐ 161 Kelly Hrudley	.10	.05	.01	
Los Angeles Kings				
☐ 162 Luc Robitaille	.25	.11	.03	
Los Angeles Kings				
☐ 163 Tomas Sandstrom	.10	.05	.01	
Los Angeles Kings				
☐ 164 Darryl Sydor	.15	.07	.02	
Los Angeles Kings				
☐ 165 Alexei Zhitnik	.25	.11	.03	
Los Angeles Kings				
☐ 166 Benoit Brunet	.10	.05	.01	
Montreal Canadiens				
☐ 167 Lyle Odelein	.10	.05	.01	
Montreal Canadiens				
☐ 168 Kevin Haller	.10	.05	.01	
Montreal Canadiens				
☐ 169 Pierre Sevigny	.10	.05	.01	
Montreal Canadiens				
☐ 170 Brian Bellows	.15	.07	.02	
Montreal Canadiens				
☐ 171 Patrice Brisebois	.10	.05	.01	
Montreal Canadiens				
☐ 172 Vincent Damphousse	.15	.07	.02	
Montreal Canadiens				
☐ 173 Eric Desjardins	.10	.05	.01	
Montreal Canadiens				
☐ 174 Gilbert Dionne	.10	.05	.01	
Montreal Canadiens				
☐ 175 Stephan Lebeau	.10	.05	.01	
Montreal Canadiens				
☐ 176 John LeClair	.10	.05	.01	
Montreal Canadiens				
☐ 177 Kirk Muller	.15	.07	.02	
Montreal Canadiens				
☐ 178 Patrick Roy	1.00	.45	.13	
Montreal Canadiens				
☐ 179 Matt Schneider	.15	.07	.02	
Montreal Canadiens				
☐ 180 Peter Popovic	.20	.09	.03	
Montreal Canadiens				
☐ 181 Corey Millen	.10	.05	.01	
New Jersey Devils				
☐ 182 Jason Smith	.20	.09	.03	
New Jersey Devils				
☐ 183 Bobby Holik	.10	.05	.01	
New Jersey Devils				
☐ 184 John MacLean	.15	.07	.02	
New Jersey Devils				
☐ 185 Bruce Driver	.10	.05	.01	
New Jersey Devils				
☐ 186 Bill Guerin	.10	.05	.01	

New Jersey Devils				
☐ 187 Claude Lemieux	.15	.07	.02	
New Jersey Devils				
☐ 188 Bernie Nicholls	.15	.07	.02	
New Jersey Devils				
☐ 189 Scott Niedermayer	.25	.11	.03	
New Jersey Devils				
☐ 190 Stephane Richer	.15	.07	.02	
New Jersey Devils				
☐ 191 Alexander Semak	.10	.05	.01	
New Jersey Devils				
☐ 192 Scott Stevens	.15	.07	.02	
New Jersey Devils				
☐ 193 Valeri Zelepukin	.15	.07	.02	
New Jersey Devils				
☐ 194 Chris Terreri	.15	.07	.02	
New Jersey Devils				
☐ 195 Martin Brodeur	.75	.35	.09	
New Jersey Devils				
☐ 196 Ron Hextall	.15	.07	.02	
New York Islanders				
☐ 197 Brad Dalgarno	.10	.05	.01	
New York Islanders				
☐ 198 Ray Ferraro	.10	.05	.01	
New York Islanders				
☐ 199 Patrick Flatley	.10	.05	.01	
New York Islanders				
☐ 200 Travis Green	.10	.05	.01	
New York Islanders				
☐ 201 Benoit Hogue	.10	.05	.01	
New York Islanders				
☐ 202 Steve Junker	.20	.09	.03	
New York Islanders				
☐ 203 Darius Kasparaitis	.10	.05	.01	
New York Islanders				
☐ 204 Derek King	.10	.05	.01	
New York Islanders				
☐ 205 Uwe Krupp	.10	.05	.01	
New York Islanders				
☐ 206 Scott Lachance	.10	.05	.01	
New York Islanders				
☐ 207 Vladimir Malakhov	.25	.11	.03	
New York Islanders				
☐ 208 Steve Thomas	.15	.07	.02	
New York Islanders				
☐ 209 Pierre Turgeon	.35	.16	.04	
New York Islanders				
☐ 210 Scott Scissons	.10	.05	.01	
New York Islanders				
☐ 211 Glenn Healy	.10	.05	.01	
New York Islanders				
☐ 212 Alexander Karpovtsev	.15	.07	.02	
New York Rangers				
☐ 213 James Patrick	.10	.05	.01	
Hartford Whalers				
☐ 214 Sergei Nemchinov	.10	.05	.01	
New York Rangers				
☐ 215 Esa Tikkanen	.15	.07	.02	
New York Rangers				
☐ 216 Corey Hirsch	.25	.11	.03	
New York Rangers				
☐ 217 Tony Amonte	.15	.07	.02	
New York Rangers				
☐ 218 Mike Gartner	.20	.09	.03	
New York Rangers				
☐ 219 Adam Graves	.35	.16	.04	
New York Rangers				
☐ 220 Alexei Kovalev	.75	.35	.09	
New York Rangers				
☐ 221 Brian Leetch	.35	.16	.04	
New York Rangers				
☐ 222 Mark Messier	.25	.11	.03	
New York Rangers				
☐ 223 Mike Richter	.30	.14	.04	
New York Rangers				
☐ 224 Darren Turcotte	.10	.05	.01	
Hartford Whalers				
☐ 225 Sergei Zubov	.75	.35	.09	
New York Rangers				
☐ 226 Craig Billington	.10	.05	.01	
Ottawa Senators				
☐ 227 Troy Mallette	.10	.05	.01	
Ottawa Senators				
☐ 228 Vladimir Ruzicka	.10	.05	.01	
Ottawa Senators				
☐ 229 Darrin Madeley	.25	.11	.03	
Ottawa Senators				
☐ 230 Mark Lamb	.10	.05	.01	
Ottawa Senators				
☐ 231 Dave Archibald	.10	.05	.01	
Ottawa Senators				
☐ 232 Bob Kudelski	.15	.07	.02	
Ottawa Senators				
☐ 233 Norm Maciver	.10	.05	.01	

	Ottawa Senators					Quebec Nordiques			
☐ 234	Brad Shaw	.10	.05	.01	☐ 281	Martin Rucinsky	.10	.05	.01
	Ottawa Senators					Quebec Nordiques			
☐ 235	Sylvain Turgeon	.10	.05	.01	☐ 282	Joe Sakic	.30	.14	.04
	Ottawa Senators					Quebec Nordiques			
☐ 236	Brian Glynn	.10	.05	.01	☐ 283	Mats Sundin	.30	.14	.04
	Ottawa Senators					Quebec Nordiques			
☐ 237	Alexandre Daigle	1.00	.45	.13	☐ 284	Scott Young	.10	.05	.01
	Ottawa Senators					Quebec Nordiques			
☐ 238	Alexei Yashin	1.50	.65	.19	☐ 285	Claude Lapointe	.10	.05	.01
	Ottawa Senators					Quebec Nordiques			
☐ 239	Dimitri Filimonov	.10	.05	.01	☐ 286	Brett Hull	1.00	.45	.13
	Ottawa Senators					St. Louis Blues			
☐ 240	Pavol Demitra	.20	.09	.03	☐ 287	Vitali Karamnov	.10	.05	.01
	Ottawa Senators					St. Louis Blues			
☐ 241	Jason Bowen	.10	.05	.01	☐ 288	Ron Sutter	.10	.05	.01
	Philadelphia Flyers					St. Louis Blues			
☐ 242	Eric Lindros	3.50	1.55	.45	☐ 289	Garth Butcher	.10	.05	.01
	Philadelphia Flyers					St. Louis Blues			
☐ 243	Dominic Roussel	.20	.09	.03	☐ 290	Vitali Prokhorov	.10	.05	.01
	Philadelphia Flyers					St. Louis Blues			
☐ 244	Milos Holan	.15	.07	.02	☐ 291	Bret Hedican	.10	.05	.01
	Philadelphia Flyers					St. Louis Blues			
☐ 245	Greg Hawgood	.10	.05	.01	☐ 292	Tony Hrkac	.10	.05	.01
	Philadelphia Flyers					St. Louis Blues			
☐ 246	Yves Racine	.10	.05	.01	☐ 293	Jeff Brown	.15	.07	.02
	Philadelphia Flyers					St. Louis Blues			
☐ 247	Josef Beranek	.15	.07	.02	☐ 294	Phil Housley	.15	.07	.02
	Philadelphia Flyers					St. Louis Blues			
☐ 248	Rod Brind'Amour	.25	.11	.03	☐ 295	Craig Janney	.20	.09	.03
	Philadelphia Flyers					St. Louis Blues			
☐ 249	Kevin Dineen	.15	.07	.02	☐ 296	Curtis Joseph	.30	.14	.04
	Philadelphia Flyers					St. Louis Blues			
☐ 250	Pelle Eklund	.10	.05	.01	☐ 297	Igor Korolev	.10	.05	.01
	Philadelphia Flyers					St. Louis Blues			
☐ 251	Garry Galley	.10	.05	.01	☐ 298	Kevin Miller	.10	.05	.01
	Philadelphia Flyers					St. Louis Blues			
☐ 252	Mark Recchi	.30	.14	.04	☐ 299	Brendan Shanahan	.25	.11	.03
	Philadelphia Flyers					St. Louis Blues			
☐ 253	Tommy Soderstrom	.25	.11	.03	☐ 300	Jim Montgomery	.25	.11	.03
	Philadelphia Flyers					St. Louis Blues			
☐ 254	Dimitri Yushkevich	.10	.05	.01	☐ 301	Gaetan Duchesne	.10	.05	.01
	Philadelphia Flyers					San Jose Sharks			
☐ 255	Mikael Renberg	1.50	.65	.19	☐ 302	Jimmy Waite	.10	.05	.01
	Philadelphia Flyers					San Jose Sharks			
☐ 256	Marty McSorley	.15	.07	.02	☐ 303	Jeff Norton	.10	.05	.01
	Pittsburgh Penguins					San Jose Sharks			
☐ 257	Joe Mullen	.15	.07	.02	☐ 304	Sergei Makarov	.15	.07	.02
	Pittsburgh Penguins					San Jose Sharks			
☐ 258	Doug Brown	.10	.05	.01	☐ 305	Igor Larionov	.10	.05	.01
	Pittsburgh Penguins					San Jose Sharks			
☐ 259	Kjell Samuelsson	.10	.05	.01	☐ 306	Mike Lalor	.10	.05	.01
	Pittsburgh Penguins					San Jose Sharks			
☐ 260	Tom Barrasso	.15	.07	.02	☐ 307	Michal Sykora	.25	.11	.03
	Pittsburgh Penguins					San Jose Sharks			
☐ 261	Ron Francis	.15	.07	.02	☐ 308	Pat Falloon	.15	.07	.02
	Pittsburgh Penguins					San Jose Sharks			
☐ 262	Mario Lemieux	1.50	.65	.19	☐ 309	Johan Garpenlov	.10	.05	.01
	Pittsburgh Penguins					San Jose Sharks			
☐ 263	Larry Murphy	.15	.07	.02	☐ 310	Rob Gaudreau	.30	.14	.04
	Pittsburgh Penguins					San Jose Sharks			
☐ 264	Ulf Samuelsson	.15	.07	.02	☐ 311	Arturs Irbe	.60	.25	.08
	Pittsburgh Penguins					San Jose Sharks			
☐ 265	Kevin Stevens	.30	.14	.04	☐ 312	Sandis Ozolinsh	.30	.14	.04
	Pittsburgh Penguins					San Jose Sharks			
☐ 266	Martin Straka	.60	.25	.08	☐ 313	Doug Zmolek	.10	.05	.01
	Pittsburgh Penguins					San Jose Sharks			
☐ 267	Rick Tocchet	.15	.07	.02	☐ 314	Mike Rathje	.10	.05	.01
	Pittsburgh Penguins					San Jose Sharks			
☐ 268	Bryan Trottier	.15	.07	.02	☐ 315	Vlastimil Kroupa	.30	.14	.04
	Pittsburgh Penguins					San Jose Sharks			
☐ 269	Markus Naslund	.25	.11	.03	☐ 316	Daren Puppa	.15	.07	.02
	Pittsburgh Penguins					Tampa Bay Lightning			
☐ 270	Jaromir Jagr	.75	.35	.09	☐ 317	Petr Klima	.10	.05	.01
	Pittsburgh Penguins					Tampa Bay Lightning			
☐ 271	Martin Gelinas	.10	.05	.01	☐ 318	Brent Gretzky	.50	.23	.06
	Quebec Nordiques					Tampa Bay Lightning			
☐ 272	Adam Foote	.10	.05	.01	☐ 319	Denis Cavard	.20	.09	.03
	Quebec Nordiques					Tampa Bay Lightning			
☐ 273	Curtis Leschyshyn	.10	.05	.01	☐ 320	Garard Gallant	.10	.05	.01
	Quebec Nordiques					Tampa Bay Lightning			
☐ 274	Stephane Fiset	.10	.05	.01	☐ 321	Joe Reekie	.10	.05	.01
	Quebec Nordiques					Tampa Bay Lightning			
☐ 275	Jocelyn Thibault	1.00	.45	.13	☐ 322	Mikael Andersson	.10	.05	.01
	Quebec Nordiques					Tampa Bay Lightning			
☐ 276	Steve Duchesne	.15	.07	.02	☐ 323	Bill McDougall	.10	.05	.01
	Quebec Nordiques					Tampa Bay Lightning			
☐ 277	Valeri Kamensky	.25	.11	.03	☐ 324	Brian Bradley	.10	.05	.01
	Quebec Nordiques					Tampa Bay Lightning			
☐ 278	Andrei Kovalenko	.20	.09	.03	☐ 325	Shawn Chambers	.10	.05	.01
	Quebec Nordiques					Tampa Bay Lightning			
☐ 279	Owen Nolan	.15	.07	.02	☐ 326	Adam Creighton	.10	.05	.01
	Quebec Nordiques					Tampa Bay Lightning			
☐ 280	Mike Ricci	.15	.07	.02	☐ 327	Roman Hamrlik	.20	.09	.03

	Tampa Bay Lightning			
☐ 328	John Tucker	.10	.05	.01
	Tampa Bay Lightning			
☐ 329	Rob Zamuner	.10	.05	.01
	Tampa Bay Lightning			
☐ 330	Chris Gratton	1.00	.45	.13
	Tampa Bay Lightning			
☐ 331	Sylvain Lefebvre	.10	.05	.01
	Toronto Maple Leafs			
☐ 332	Nikolai Borschevsky	.25	.11	.03
	Toronto Maple Leafs			
☐ 333	Bob Rouse	.10	.05	.01
	Toronto Maple Leafs			
☐ 334	John Cullen	.10	.05	.01
	Toronto Maple Leafs			
☐ 335	Todd Gill	.10	.05	.01
	Toronto Maple Leafs			
☐ 336	Drake Berehowsky	.10	.05	.01
	Toronto Maple Leafs			
☐ 337	Wendel Clark	.20	.09	.03
	Toronto Maple Leafs			
☐ 338	Peter Zezel	.10	.05	.01
	Toronto Maple Leafs			
☐ 339	Rob Pearson	.10	.05	.01
	Toronto Maple Leafs			
☐ 340	Glenn Anderson	.15	.07	.02
	Toronto Maple Leafs			
☐ 341	Doug Gilmour	.50	.23	.06
	Toronto Maple Leafs			
☐ 342	Dave Andreychuk	.20	.09	.03
	Toronto Maple Leafs			
☐ 343	Felix Potvin	1.50	.65	.19
	Toronto Maple Leafs			
☐ 344	David Ellett	.10	.05	.01
	Toronto Maple Leafs			
☐ 345	Alexei Kudashov	.20	.09	.03
	Toronto Maple Leafs			
☐ 346	Gino Odjick	.10	.05	.01
	Vancouver Canucks			
☐ 347	Jyrki Lumme	.10	.05	.01
	Vancouver Canucks			
☐ 348	Dana Murzyn	.10	.05	.01
	Vancouver Canucks			
☐ 349	Sergio Momesso	.10	.05	.01
	Vancouver Canucks			
☐ 350	Greg Adams	.10	.05	.01
	Vancouver Canucks			
☐ 351	Pavel Bure	2.00	.90	.25
	Vancouver Canucks			
☐ 352	Geoff Courtnall	.10	.05	.01
	Vancouver Canucks			
☐ 353	Murray Craven	.10	.05	.01
	Vancouver Canucks			
☐ 354	Trevor Linden	.20	.09	.03
	Vancouver Canucks			
☐ 355	Kirk McLean	.20	.09	.03
	Vancouver Canucks			
☐ 356	Petr Nedved	.15	.07	.02
	Vancouver Canucks			
☐ 357	Cliff Ronning	.10	.05	.01
	Vancouver Canucks			
☐ 358	Jiri Slegr	.10	.05	.01
	Vancouver Canucks			
☐ 359	Kay Whitmore	.10	.05	.01
	Vancouver Canucks			
☐ 360	Gerald Diduck	.10	.05	.01
	Vancouver Canucks			
☐ 361	Pat Peake	.20	.09	.03
	Washington Capitals			
☐ 362	Dave Poulin	.10	.05	.01
	Washington Capitals			
☐ 363	Rick Tabaracci	.10	.05	.01
	Washington Capitals			
☐ 364	Jason Woolley	.10	.05	.01
	Washington Capitals			
☐ 365	Kelly Miller	.10	.05	.01
	Washington Capitals			
☐ 366	Peter Bondra	.15	.07	.02
	Washington Capitals			
☐ 367	Sylvain Cote	.10	.05	.01
	Washington Capitals			
☐ 368	Pat Elynuik	.10	.05	.01
	Tampa Bay Lightning			
☐ 369	Kevin Hatcher	.15	.07	.02
	Washington Capitals			
☐ 370	Dale Hunter	.15	.07	.02
	Washington Capitals			
☐ 371	Al Iafrate	.15	.07	.02
	Washington Capitals			
☐ 372	Calle Johansson	.10	.05	.01
	Washington Capitals			
☐ 373	Dimitri Khristich	.15	.07	.02
	Washington Capitals			
☐ 374	Michal Pivonka	.10	.05	.01

	Washington Capitals			
☐ 375	Mike Ridley	.15	.07	.02
	Washington Capitals			
☐ 376	Paul Ysebaert	.10	.05	.01
	Winnipeg Jets			
☐ 377	Stu Barnes	.10	.05	.01
	Winnipeg Jets			
☐ 378	Sergei Bautin	.10	.05	.01
	Winnipeg Jets			
☐ 379	Kris King	.10	.05	.01
	Winnipeg Jets			
☐ 380	Alexei Zhamnov	.50	.23	.06
	Winnipeg Jets			
☐ 381	Tie Domi	.10	.05	.01
	Winnipeg Jets			
☐ 382	Bob Essensa	.15	.07	.02
	Winnipeg Jets			
☐ 383	Nelson Emerson	.15	.07	.02
	Winnipeg Jets			
☐ 384	Boris Mironov	.10	.05	.01
	Winnipeg Jets			
☐ 385	Teppo Numminen	.10	.05	.01
	Winnipeg Jets			
☐ 386	Fredrik Olausson	.10	.05	.01
	Winnipeg Jets			
☐ 387	Teemu Selanne	1.50	.65	.19
	Winnipeg Jets			
☐ 388	Darrin Shannon	.10	.05	.01
	Winnipeg Jets			
☐ 389	Thomas Steen	.10	.05	.01
	Winnipeg Jets			
☐ 390	Keith Tkachuk	.30	.14	.04
	Winnipeg Jets			
☐ 391	Opening Night	1.00	.45	.13
	Panthers			
☐ 392	Opening Night-Ducks	1.00	.45	.13
☐ 393	NHL Top Draft Picks	.75	.35	.09
☐ 394	Rookie Record	.50	.23	.06
	Breakers			
☐ 395	Kings Record Breakers	.75	.35	.09
☐ 396	Inserts Checklist	.15	.07	.02
☐ 397	Atlantic Div. Checklist	.10	.05	.01
☐ 398	Northeast Div. Checklist	.10	.05	.01
☐ 399	Central Div. Checklist	.10	.05	.01
☐ 400	Pacific Div. Checklist	.10	.05	.01
☐ 401	Garry Valk	.10	.05	.01
	Anaheim Mighty Ducks			
☐ 402	Al Iarante	.10	.05	.01
	Boston Bruins			
☐ 403	Dave Reid	.10	.05	.01
	Boston Bruins			
☐ 404	Jason Dawe	.10	.05	.01
	Buffalo Sabres			
☐ 405	Craig Muni	.10	.05	.01
	Buffalo Sabres			
☐ 406	Dan Keczmer	.20	.09	.03
	Calgary Flames			
☐ 407	Mikael Nylander	.25	.11	.03
	Calgary Flames			
☐ 408	James Patrick	.10	.05	.01
	Calgary Flames			
☐ 409	Andreti Trefilov	.30	.14	.04
	Calgary Flames			
☐ 410	Zarley Zalapski	.10	.05	.01
	Calgary Flames			
☐ 411	Tony Amonte	.15	.07	.02
	Chicago Blackhawks			
☐ 412	Keith Carney	.10	.05	.01
	Chicago Blackhawks			
☐ 413	Randy Cunneyworth	.10	.05	.01
	Chicago Blackhawks			
☐ 414	Ivan Droppa	.20	.09	.03
	Chicago Blackhawks			
☐ 415	Gary Suter	.15	.07	.02
	Chicago Blackhawks			
☐ 416	Eric Weinrich	.10	.05	.01
	Chicago Blackhawks			
☐ 417	Paul Ysebaert	.10	.05	.01
	Chicago Blackhawks			
☐ 418	Richard Matvichuk	.10	.05	.01
	Dallas Stars			
☐ 419	Alan May	.10	.05	.01
	Dallas Stars			
☐ 420	Darcy Wakaluk	.10	.05	.01
	Dallas Stars			
☐ 421	Micah Aivazoff	.20	.09	.03
	Detroit Red Wings			
☐ 422	Terry Carkner	.10	.05	.01
	Detroit Red Wings			
☐ 423	Kris Draper	.10	.05	.01
	Detroit Red Wings			
☐ 424	Chris Osgood	1.00	.45	.13
	Detroit Red Wings			
☐ 425	Keith Primeau	.15	.07	.02

Detroit Red Wings			
☐ 426 Bob Beers	.10	.05	.01
Edmonton Oilers			
☐ 427 Ilya Byakin	.20	.09	.03
Edmonton Oilers			
☐ 428 Kirk Maltby	.20	.09	.03
Edmonton Oilers			
☐ 429 Boris Mironov	.10	.05	.01
Edmonton Oilers			
☐ 430 Fredrik Olausson	.10	.05	.01
Edmonton Oilers			
☐ 431 Peter White	.20	.09	.03
Edmonton Oilers			
☐ 432 Stu Barnes	.10	.05	.01
Florida Panthers			
☐ 433 Mike Foligno	.10	.05	.01
Florida Panthers			
☐ 434 Bob Kudelski	.15	.07	.02
Florida Panthers			
☐ 435 Geoff Smith	.10	.05	.01
Florida Panthers			
☐ 436 Igor Chibirev	.25	.11	.03
Hartford Whalers			
☐ 437 Ted Drury	.10	.05	.01
Hartford Whalers			
☐ 438 Alexander Godynyuk	.10	.05	.01
Hartford Whalers			
☐ 439 Frank Kucera	.10	.05	.01
Hartford Whalers			
☐ 440 Jocelyn Lemieux	.10	.05	.01
Hartford Whalers			
☐ 441 Brian Propp	.15	.07	.02
Hartford Whalers			
☐ 442 Paul Ranheim	.10	.05	.01
Hartford Whalers			
☐ 443 Jeff Reese	.10	.05	.01
Hartford Whalers			
☐ 444 Kevin Smyth	.15	.07	.02
Hartford Whalers			
☐ 445 Jim Storm	.25	.11	.03
Hartford Whalers			
☐ 446 Phil Crowe	.15	.07	.02
Los Angeles Kings			
☐ 447 Marty McSorley	.15	.07	.02
Los Angeles Kings			
☐ 448 Keith Redmond	.15	.07	.02
Los Angeles Kings			
☐ 449 Dixon Ward	.10	.05	.01
Los Angeles Kings			
☐ 450 Guy Carbonneau	.15	.07	.02
Montreal Canadiens			
☐ 451 Mike Keane	.10	.05	.01
Montreal Canadiens			
☐ 452 Oleg Petrov	.30	.14	.04
Montreal Canadiens			
☐ 453 Ron Tugnutt	.10	.05	.01
Montreal Canadiens			
☐ 454 Randy McKay	.10	.05	.01
New Jersey Devils			
☐ 455 Jaroslav Modry	.25	.11	.03
New Jersey Devils			
☐ 456 Yan Kaminsky	.10	.05	.01
New York Islanders			
☐ 457 Marty McInnis	.10	.05	.01
New York Islanders			
☐ 458 Jamie McLennan	.25	.11	.03
New York Islanders			
☐ 459 Zigmund Palffy	.10	.05	.01
New York Islanders			
☐ 460 Glenn Anderson	.15	.07	.02
New York Rangers			
☐ 461 Steve Larmer	.15	.07	.02
New York Rangers			
☐ 462 Craig MacTavish	.10	.05	.01
New York Rangers			
☐ 463 Stephane Matteau	.10	.05	.01
New York Rangers			
☐ 464 Brian Moonan	.10	.05	.01
New York Rangers			
☐ 465 Mattias Norstrom	.20	.09	.03
New York Rangers			
☐ 466 Scott Levins	.20	.09	.03
Ottawa Senators			
☐ 467 Derek Mayer	.20	.09	.03
Ottawa Senators			
☐ 468 Andy Schneider	.15	.07	.02
Ottawa Senators			
☐ 469 Todd Hlushko	.25	.11	.03
Philadelphia Flyers			
☐ 470 Stewart Malgunas	.20	.09	.03
Philadelphia Flyers			
☐ 471 Justin Duberman	.20	.09	.03
Pittsburgh Penguins			
☐ 472 Ladislav Karabin	.20	.09	.03

Pittsburgh Penguins			
☐ 473 Shawn McEachern	.15	.07	.02
Pittsburgh Penguins			
☐ 474 Ed Patterson	.20	.09	.03
Pittsburgh Penguins			
☐ 475 Tomas Sandstrom	.10	.05	.01
Pittsburgh Penguins			
☐ 476 Bob Bassen	.10	.05	.01
Quebec Nordiques			
☐ 477 Garth Butcher	.10	.05	.01
Quebec Nordiques			
☐ 478 Iain Fraser	.25	.11	.03
Quebec Nordiques			
☐ 479 Mike McKee	.15	.07	.02
Quebec Nordiques			
☐ 480 Dwayne Norris	.25	.11	.03
Quebec Nordiques			
☐ 481 Garth Snow	.30	.14	.04
Quebec Nordiques			
☐ 482 Ron Sutter	.10	.05	.01
Quebec Nordiques			
☐ 483 Kelly Chase	.10	.05	.01
St. Louis Blues			
☐ 484 Steve Duchesne	.15	.07	.02
St. Louis Blues			
☐ 485 Dan Laperrire	.10	.05	.01
St. Louis Blues			
☐ 486 Petr Nedved	.15	.07	.02
St. Louis Blues			
☐ 487 Peter Stastny	.15	.07	.02
St. Louis Blues			
☐ 488 Ulf Dahlen	.10	.05	.01
San Jose Sharks			
☐ 489 Todd Elik	.10	.05	.01
San Jose Sharks			
☐ 490 Andrei Nazarov	.25	.11	.03
San Jose Sharks			
☐ 491 Danton Cole	.10	.05	.01
Tampa Bay Lightning			
☐ 492 Chris Joseph	.10	.05	.01
Tampa Bay Lightning			
☐ 493 Chris LiPuma	.20	.09	.03
Tampa Bay Lightning			
☐ 494 Mike Gartner	.20	.09	.03
Toronto Maple Leafs			
☐ 495 Mark Greig	.10	.05	.01
Toronto Maple Leafs			
☐ 496 David Harlock	.10	.05	.01
Toronto Maple Leafs			
☐ 497 Matt Martin	.25	.11	.03
Toronto Maple Leafs			
☐ 498 Shawn Antoski	.10	.05	.01
Vancouver Canucks			
☐ 499 Jeff Brown	.15	.07	.02
Vancouver Canucks			
☐ 500 Jimmy Carson	.10	.05	.01
Vancouver Canucks			
☐ 501 Martin Gelinas	.10	.05	.01
Vancouver Canucks			
☐ 502 Yevgeny Namestnikov	.15	.07	.02
Vancouver Canucks			
☐ 503 Randy Burridge	.10	.05	.01
Washington Capitals			
☐ 504 Joe Juneau	1.00	.45	.13
Washington Capitals			
☐ 505 Kevin Kaminski	.20	.09	.03
Washington Capitals			
☐ 506 Arto Blomsten	.10	.05	.01
Winnipeg Jets			
☐ 507 Tim Cheveldae	.15	.07	.02
Winnipeg Jets			
☐ 508 Dallas Drake	.15	.07	.02
Winnipeg Jets			
☐ 509 Dave Manson	.10	.05	.01
Winnipeg Jets			
☐ 510 Update Checklist	.10	.05	.01

1993-94 Donruss Elite

These 15 standard-size (2 1/2" by 3 1/2") cards feature on their fronts color player photos framed by diamond-shaped starburst designs set within dark marbleized inner borders and prismatic foil outer borders. The player's name appears within the lower prismatic foil margin. The back carries the player's name, career highlights, and a color head shot, all set on a dark marbleized background framed by a silver

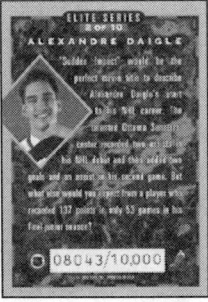

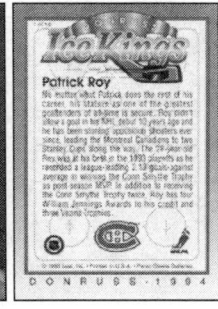

border. The cards are numbered on the back. The 10 first-series Elite cards (1-10) were random inserts in '93-94 Donruss Series 1 packs. The five Elite Update cards (U1-U5) were randomly inserted in Donruss Update packs. All Elite cards are individually numbered on the back and have a production limited to 10,000 of each.

	MINT	EXC	G-VG
COMPLETE SET (15)	700.00	325.00	90.00
COMPLETE SERIES 1 (10)	500.00	230.00	65.00
COMPLETE SERIES 2 (5)	200.00	90.00	25.00
COMMON PLAYER (1-10)	35.00	16.00	4.40
COMMON PLAYER (U1-U5)	35.00	16.00	4.40
☐ 1 Mario Lemieux	80.00	36.00	10.00
Pittsburgh Penguins			
☐ 2 Alexandre Daigle	35.00	16.00	4.40
Ottawa Senators			
☐ 3 Teemu Selanne	45.00	20.00	5.75
Winnipeg Jets			
☐ 4 Eric Lindros	100.00	45.00	12.50
Philadelphia Flyers			
☐ 5 Brett Hull	50.00	23.00	6.25
St. Louis Blues			
☐ 6 Jeremy Roenick	45.00	20.00	5.75
Chicago Blackhawks			
☐ 7 Doug Gilmour	55.00	25.00	7.00
Toronto Maple Leafs			
☐ 8 Alexander Mogilny	40.00	18.00	5.00
Buffalo Sabres			
☐ 9 Patrick Roy	75.00	34.00	9.50
Montreal Canadiens			
☐ 10 Wayne Gretzky	125.00	57.50	15.50
Los Angeles Kings			
☐ U1 Mikael Renberg	40.00	18.00	5.00
Philadelphia Flyers			
☐ U2 Sergei Fedorov	55.00	25.00	7.00
Detroit Red Wings			
☐ U3 Felix Potvin	50.00	23.00	6.25
Toronto Maple Leafs			
☐ U4 Cam Neely	35.00	16.00	4.40
Boston Bruins			
☐ U5 Alexei Yashin	40.00	18.00	5.00
Ottawa Senators			

1993-94 Donruss Ice Kings

Randomly inserted in Series 1 packs, these 10 standard-size (2 1/2" by 3 1/2") cards feature on their fronts borderless color player drawings by noted sports artist Dick Perez. The player's name, his team's logo, and the year, 1994, appear within a blue banner near the bottom. The blue-bordered back carries the player's career highlights via a ghosted representation of a hockey rink. The cards are numbered on the back as "X of 10."

	MINT	EXC	G-VG
COMPLETE SET (10)	40.00	18.00	5.00
COMMON PLAYER (1-10)	2.00	.90	.25
☐ 1 Patrick Roy	5.00	2.30	.60
Montreal Canadiens			
☐ 2 Pat LaFontaine	2.50	1.15	.30
Buffalo Sabres			

	MINT	EXC	G-VG
☐ 3 Jaromir Jagr	3.00	1.35	.40
Pittsburgh Penguins			
☐ 4 Wayne Gretzky	8.00	3.60	1.00
Los Angeles Kings			
☐ 5 Chris Chelios	2.00	.90	.25
Chicago Blackhawks			
☐ 6 Felix Potvin	5.00	2.30	.60
Toronto Maple Leafs			
☐ 7 Mario Lemieux	6.00	2.70	.75
Pittsburgh Penguins			
☐ 8 Pavel Bure	8.00	3.60	1.00
Vancouver Canucks			
☐ 9 Eric Lindros	8.00	3.60	1.00
Philadelphia Flyers			
☐ 10 Teemu Selanne	4.00	1.80	.50
Winnipeg Jets			

1993-94 Donruss Rated Rookies

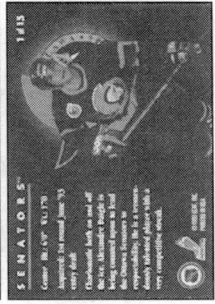

Randomly inserted in Series 1 packs, these 15 standard-size (2 1/2" by 3 1/2") cards have borderless fronts that feature color player action shots on motion streaked backgrounds. The player's name appears at the top. On its right side, the black horizontal back carries a color player action cutout superposed upon his team's logo. Biography and career highlights are shown alongside on the left. The cards are numbered on the back as "X of 15."

	MINT	EXC	G-VG
COMPLETE SET (15)	45.00	20.00	5.75
COMMON PLAYER (1-15)	2.50	1.15	.30
☐ 1 Alexandre Daigle	5.00	2.30	.60
Ottawa Senators			
☐ 2 Chris Gratton	4.00	1.80	.50
Tampa Bay Lightning			
☐ 3 Chris Pronger	4.00	1.80	.50
Hartford Whalers			
☐ 4 Rob Niedermayer	4.00	1.80	.50
Florida Panthers			
☐ 5 Mikael Renberg	6.00	2.70	.75
Philadelphia Flyers			
☐ 6 Jarkko Varvio	2.50	1.15	.30
Ottawa Senators			

☐ 7 Alexei Yashin	6.00	2.70	.75
Ottawa Senators			
☐ 8 Markus Naslund	2.50	1.15	.30
Pittsburgh Penguins			
☐ 9 Boris Mironov	2.50	1.15	.30
Winnipeg Jets			
☐ 10 Martin Brodeur	9.00	4.00	1.15
New Jersey Devils			
☐ 11 Jocelyn Thibault	5.00	2.30	.60
Quebec Nordiques			
☐ 12 Jason Arnott	10.00	4.50	1.25
Edmonton Oilers			
☐ 13 Jim Montgomery	2.50	1.15	.30
St. Louis Blues			
☐ 14 Ted Drury	2.50	1.15	.30
Calgary Flames			
☐ 15 Roman Oksiuta	2.50	1.15	.30
Edmonton Oilers			

☐ N Pierre Turgeon	6.00	2.70	.75
New York Islanders			
☐ O Mark Messier	6.00	2.70	.75
New York Rangers			
☐ P Alexandre Daigle	7.00	3.10	.85
Ottawa Senators			
☐ Q Eric Lindros	24.00	11.00	3.00
Philadelphia Flyers			
☐ R Mario Lemieux	18.00	8.00	2.30
Pittsburgh Penguins			
☐ S Mats Sundin	6.00	2.70	.75
Quebec Nordiques			
☐ T Pat Falloon	3.00	1.35	.40
San Jose Sharks			
☐ U Brett Hull	8.00	3.60	1.00
St. Louis Blues			
☐ V Chris Gratton	5.00	2.30	.60
Tampa Bay Lightning			
☐ W Felix Potvin	12.00	5.50	1.50
Toronto Maple Leafs			
☐ X Pavel Bure	16.00	7.25	2.00
Vancouver Canucks			
☐ Y Al Iafrate	3.00	1.35	.40
Washington Capitals			
☐ Z Teemu Selanne	9.00	4.00	1.15
Winnipeg Jets			
☐ NNO Luc Robitaille WC	25.00	11.50	3.10
Los Angeles Kings			
☐ NNO Mario Lemieux EC	50.00	23.00	6.25
Pittsburgh Penguins			

1993-94 Donruss Special Print

Randomly inserted in Series 1 packs, these 26 standard-size (2 1/2" by 3 1/2") cards feature on their fronts color player action shots that are borderless, except at the bottom, where the black edge carries the player's name in white cursive lettering. The prismatic foil set logo rests in a lower corner. The words "Special Print 1 of 20,000" appear in prismatic foil across the top. The backs, some of which are horizontal, carry another borderless color player action shot. The player's name, team, position, and biography are shown within a black rectangle on one side. His statistics appear in ghosted strips below or alongside. The cards are numbered, or rather lettered (A-Z), on the back.

	MINT	EXC	G-VG
COMPLETE SET (26)	175.00	80.00	22.00
COMMON PLAYER (A-Z)	3.00	1.35	.40
☐ A Ron Tugnutt	3.00	1.35	.40
Anaheim Mighty Ducks			
☐ B Adam Oates	4.00	1.80	.50
Boston Bruins			
☐ C Alexander Mogilny	6.00	2.70	.75
Buffalo Sabres			
☐ D Theoren Fleury	3.00	1.35	.40
Calgary Flames			
☐ E Jeremy Roenick	7.00	3.10	.85
Chicago Blackhawks			
☐ F Mike Modano	6.00	2.70	.75
Dallas Stars			
☐ G Steve Yzerman	8.00	3.60	1.00
Detroit Red Wings			
☐ H Jason Arnott	15.00	6.75	1.90
Edmonton Oilers			
☐ I Rob Niedermayer	5.00	2.30	.60
Florida Panthers			
☐ J Chris Pronger	5.00	2.30	.60
Hartford Whalers			
☐ K Wayne Gretzky	25.00	11.50	3.10
Los Angeles Kings			
☐ L Patrick Roy	12.00	5.50	1.50
Montreal Canadiens			
☐ M Scott Niedermayer	3.00	1.35	.40
New Jersey Devils			

1993-94 Donruss Team Canada

One of these 22 (or one of the 22 Team USA) standard-size (2 1/2" by 3 1/2") cards were inserted in every 1993-94 Donruss Update pack. The front of each card features a player action cutout set on a red metallic background highlighted by a world map. The player's name appears in the upper left. The horizontal back carries a color player action shot on the right side. Below the photo are the player's statistics from his 1994 World Junior Championships play. On the left side are the player's name, position, biography, and NHL status. The cards are numbered on the back as "X of 22." The unnumbered checklist carries the 22 Team Canada cards, as well as the 22 Team USA cards.

	MINT	EXC	G-VG
COMPLETE SET (22)	18.00	8.00	2.30
COMMON PLAYER (1-22)	.75	.35	.09
☐ 1 Jason Allison	2.00	.90	.25
☐ 2 Chris Armstrong	.75	.35	.09
☐ 3 Drew Bannister	.75	.35	.09
☐ 4 Jason Botterill	1.25	.55	.16
☐ 5 Joel Bouchard	.75	.35	.09
☐ 6 Curtis Bowen	.75	.35	.09
☐ 7 Anson Carter	1.00	.45	.13
☐ 8 Brandon Convery	1.00	.45	.13
☐ 9 Yannick Dube	1.25	.55	.16
☐ 10 Manny Fernandez	1.00	.45	.13
☐ 11 Jeff Friesen	3.50	1.55	.45
☐ 12 Aaron Gavey	1.50	.65	.19
☐ 13 Martin Gendron	.75	.35	.09

		MINT	EXC	G-VG
☐ 14	Rick Girard	1.00	.45	.13
☐ 15	Todd Harvey	2.00	.90	.25
☐ 16	Bryan McCabe	.75	.35	.09
☐ 17	Marty Murray	.75	.35	.09
☐ 18	Mike Peca	1.25	.55	.16
☐ 19	Nick Stajduhar	1.25	.55	.16
☐ 20	Jamie Storr	4.00	1.80	.50
☐ 21	Brent Tully	.75	.35	.09
☐ 22	Brendan Witt	1.25	.55	.16
☐ NNO	WJC Checklist	2.00	.90	.25

1993-94 Donruss Team USA

One of these 22 (or one of the 22 Team Canada) standard-size (2 1/2" by 3 1/2") cards were inserted in every 1993-94 Donruss Update pack. The front of each card features a player action cutout set on a blue metallic background highlighted by a world map. The player's name appears at the upper left. The horizontal back carries a color player action shot on the right side. Below the photo are the player's statistics from his 1994 World Junior Championships play. On the left side are the player's name, position, biography, and NHL status. The cards are numbered on the back as "X of 22." The unnumbered checklist carries the 22 Team Canada cards, as well as the 22 Team USA cards.

		MINT	EXC	G-VG
	COMPLETE SET (22)	14.00	6.25	1.75
	COMMON PLAYER (1-22)	.75	.35	.09
☐ 1	Kevyn Adams	1.50	.65	.19
☐ 2	Jason Bonsignore	2.50	1.15	.30
☐ 3	Andy Brink	.75	.35	.09
☐ 4	Jon Coleman	.75	.35	.09
☐ 5	Adam Deadmarsh	.75	.35	.09
☐ 6	Aaron Ellis	.75	.35	.09
☐ 7	John Emmons	.75	.35	.09
☐ 8	Ashlin Halfnight	.75	.35	.09
☐ 9	Kevin Hilton	.75	.35	.09
☐ 10	Jason Karmanos	.75	.35	.09
☐ 11	Toby Kvalevog	.75	.35	.09
☐ 12	Bob Lachance	.75	.35	.09
☐ 13	Jamie Langenbrunner	1.00	.45	.13
☐ 14	Jason McBain	.75	.35	.09
☐ 15	Chris O'Sullivan	.75	.35	.09
☐ 16	Jay Pandolfo	.75	.35	.09
☐ 17	Richard Park	1.25	.55	.16
☐ 18	Deron Quint	1.00	.45	.13
☐ 19	Ryan Sittler	.75	.35	.09
☐ 20	Blake Sloan	.75	.35	.09
☐ 21	John Varga	.75	.35	.09
☐ 22	David Wilkie	.75	.35	.09
☐ NNO	WJC Checklist	2.00	.90	.25

1993-94 Ducks Milk Caps

This set of six milk caps measures approximately 1 1/2" in diameter and features the Mighty Ducks of Anaheim. The

fronts show a color player headshot set against a teal green background with a neon yellow stripe. The player's name appears at the bottom, along with the production figures "One of 15,000". The backs are solid white. The milk caps are numbered on the front.

		MINT	EXC	G-VG
	COMPLETE SET (6)	5.00	2.00	.50
	COMMON PLAYER (1-5)	1.00	.40	.10
☐ 1	Tim Sweeney	1.00	.40	.10
☐ 2	Bobby Dollas	1.00	.40	.10
☐ 3	Stu Grimson	1.50	.60	.15
☐ 4	Terry Yake	1.00	.40	.10
☐ 5	Bob Corkum	1.00	.40	.10
☐ NNO	Inaugural Season First Win	1.00	.40	.10

1992-93 Durivage Panini

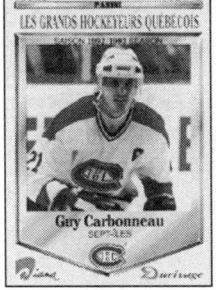
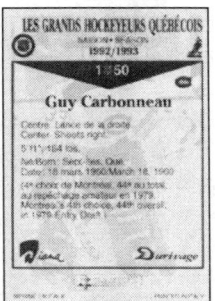

This 50-card set showcases hockey stars who were born in Quebec. The cards measure the standard size (2 1/2" by 3 1/2") and feature color, action player photos set on a gold plaque design. The player's name appears below the photo on the plaque. The words "Les Grands Hockeyeurs Quebecois" are printed in red at the top of the card. The backs have a ghosted black-and-white player photo with biography and career summary printed in French over the picture. The cards are numbered on the back.

		MINT	EXC	G-VG
	COMPLETE SET (50)	30.00	12.00	3.00
	COMMON PLAYER (1-50)	.50	.20	.05
☐ 1	Guy Carbonneau Montreal Canadiens	.75	.30	.07
☐ 2	Lucien DeGlois Winnipeg Jets	.50	.20	.05
☐ 3	Benoit Hogue New York Islanders	.60	.24	.06
☐ 4	Steve Kasper Philadelphia Flyers	.50	.20	.05
☐ 5	Mike Krushelnyski Toronto Maple Leafs	.60	.24	.06
☐ 6	Claude Lapointe Quebec Nordiques	.60	.24	.06
☐ 7	Stephan Lebeau Montreal Canadiens	.75	.30	.07
☐ 8	Mario Lemieux	5.00	2.00	.50

Pittsburgh Penguins
☐ 9	Stephane Morin	.50	.20	.05
	Quebec Nordiques			
☐ 10	Denis Savard	.75	.30	.07
	Montreal Canadiens			
☐ 11	Pierre Turgeon	1.50	.60	.15
	New York Islanders			
☐ 12	Kevin Dineen	.60	.24	.06
	Philadelphia Flyers			
☐ 13	Gord Donnelly	.50	.20	.05
	Buffalo Sabres			
☐ 14	Claude Lemieux	.75	.30	.07
	New Jersey Devils			
☐ 15	Jocelyn Lemieux	.50	.20	.05
	Chicago Blackhawks			
☐ 16	Daniel Marois	.50	.20	.05
	New York Islanders			
☐ 17	Scott Mellanby	.50	.20	.05
	Edmonton Oilers			
☐ 18	Stephane Richer	.75	.30	.07
	New Jersey Devils			
☐ 19	Benoit Brunet	.75	.30	.07
	Montreal Canadiens			
☐ 20	Vincent Damphousse	.75	.30	.07
	Montreal Canadiens			
☐ 21	Gilbert Dionne	.75	.30	.07
	Montreal Canadiens			
☐ 22	Gaetan Duchesne	.50	.20	.05
	Minnesota North Stars			
☐ 23	Bob Errey	.50	.20	.05
	Pittsburgh Penguins			
☐ 24	Michel Goulet	.75	.30	.07
	Chicago Blackhawks			
☐ 25	Mike Hough	.50	.20	.05
	Quebec Nordiques			
☐ 26	Sergio Momesso	.50	.20	.05
	Vancouver Canucks			
☐ 27	Mario Roberge	.50	.20	.05
	Montreal Canadiens			
☐ 28	Luc Robitaille	1.25	.50	.12
	Los Angeles Kings			
☐ 29	Sylvain Turgeon	.50	.20	.05
	Ottawa Senators			
☐ 30	Marc Bergevin	.50	.20	.05
	Tampa Bay Lightning			
☐ 31	Raymond Bourque	1.50	.60	.15
	Boston Bruins			
☐ 32	Patrice Brisebois	.75	.30	.07
	Montreal Canadiens			
☐ 33	Jeff Chychrun	.50	.20	.05
	Pittsburgh Penguins			
☐ 34	Sylvain Cote	.50	.20	.05
	Washington Capitals			
☐ 35	J.J. Daigneault	.50	.20	.05
	Montreal Canadiens			
☐ 36	Eric Desjardins	.75	.30	.07
	Montreal Canadiens			
☐ 37	Gord Dineen	.50	.20	.05
	Ottawa Senators			
☐ 38	Steve Duchesne	.60	.24	.06
	Quebec Nordiques			
☐ 39	Donald Dufresne	.50	.20	.05
	Montreal Canadiens			
☐ 40	Steven Finn	.50	.20	.05
	Quebec Nordiques			
☐ 41	Garry Galley	.60	.24	.06
	Philadelphia Flyers			
☐ 42	Kevin Lowe	.60	.24	.06
	Edmonton Oilers			
☐ 43	Michel Petit	.50	.20	.05
	Calgary Flames			
☐ 44	Normand Rochefort	.50	.20	.05
	New York Rangers			
☐ 45	Randy Velischek	.50	.20	.05
	Quebec Nordiques			
☐ 46	Jacques Cloutier	.50	.20	.05
	Quebec Nordiques			
☐ 47	Stephane Fiset	1.00	.40	.10
	Quebec Nordiques			
☐ 48	Rejean Lemelin	.60	.24	.06
	Boston Bruins			
☐ 49	Andre Racicot	.50	.20	.05
	Montreal Canadiens			
☐ 50	Patrick Roy	3.50	1.40	.35
	Montreal Canadiens			

1993-94 Durivage Score

These 50 standard-size (2 1/2" by 3 1/2") white-bordered cards feature color player action shots "mounted" on golden

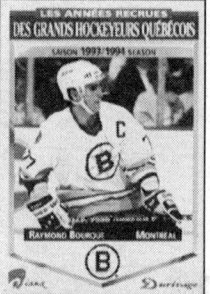

plaque designs. The player's name and hometown appear within a black stripe below the photo. All the players in the set are from the province of Quebec. His team's logo appears further below. The white-bordered back carries a color player action photo on the right and, on the left, bilingual biography and statistics. Cards 1-6 belong to a "Special Edition" subset and have gold-foil highlights on their fronts. The cards are numbered on the back as "X of 50."

		MINT	EXC	G-VG
COMPLETE SET (50)		25.00	10.00	2.50
COMMON PLAYER (1-50)		.50	.20	.05
☐ 1	Alexandre Daigle	3.00	1.20	.30
	Ottawa Senators			
☐ 2	Pierre Sevigny	.50	.20	.05
	Montreal Canadiens			
☐ 3	Jocelyn Thibault	1.50	.60	.15
	Quebec Nordiques			
☐ 4	Philippe Boucher	.50	.20	.05
	Buffalo Sabres			
☐ 5	Martin Brodeur	2.00	.80	.20
	New Jersey Devils			
☐ 6	Martin Lapointe	.75	.30	.07
	Detroit Red Wings			
☐ 7	Patrice Brisebois	.50	.20	.05
	Montreal Canadiens			
☐ 8	Benoit Brunet	.50	.20	.05
	Montreal Canadiens			
☐ 9	Guy Carbonneau	.75	.30	.07
	Montreal Canadiens			
☐ 10	Jean-Jacques Daigneault	.50	.20	.05
	Montreal Canadiens			
☐ 11	Vincent Damphousse	.75	.30	.07
	Montreal Canadiens			
☐ 12	Eric Desjardins	.50	.20	.05
	Montreal Canadiens			
☐ 13	Gilbert Dionne	.75	.30	.07
	Montreal Canadiens			
☐ 14	Stephan Lebeau	.75	.30	.07
	Montreal Canadiens			
☐ 15	Andre Racicot	.50	.20	.05
	Montreal Canadiens			
☐ 16	Mario Roberge	.50	.20	.05
	Montreal Canadiens			
☐ 17	Patrick Roy	5.00	2.00	.50
	Montreal Canadiens			
☐ 18	Jacques Cloutier	.50	.20	.05
	Quebec Nordiques			
☐ 19	Alain Cote	.50	.20	.05
	Quebec Nordiques			
☐ 20	Steven Finn	.50	.20	.05
	Quebec Nordiques			
☐ 21	Stephane Fiset	1.00	.40	.10
	Quebec Nordiques			
☐ 22	Martin Gelinas	.50	.20	.05
	Quebec Nordiques			
☐ 23	Reggie Savage	.50	.20	.05
	Quebec Nordiques			
☐ 24	Claude Lapointe	.50	.20	.05
	Quebec Nordiques			
☐ 25	Denis Savard	.75	.30	.07
	Tampa Bay Lightning			
☐ 26	Ray Bourque	1.25	.50	.12
	Boston Bruins			
☐ 27	Joe Juneau	2.00	.80	.20
	Boston Bruins			
☐ 28	Ron Stern	.50	.20	.05
	Calgary Flames			

		MINT	EXC	G-VG

☐ 29	Benoit Hogue .... New York Islanders	.75	.30	.07
☐ 30	Pierre Turgeon .... New York Islanders	1.50	.60	.15
☐ 31	Mike Krushelnyski............... Toronto Maple Leafs	.50	.20	.05
☐ 32	Felix Potvin .... Toronto Maple Leafs	4.00	1.60	.40
☐ 33	Sergio Momesso.................. Vancouver Canucks	.50	.20	.05
☐ 34	Yves Racine .... Philadelphia Flyers	.50	.20	.05
☐ 35	Sylvain Cote .... Washington Capitals	.50	.20	.05
☐ 36	Sylvain Turgeon .... Ottawa Senators	.50	.20	.05
☐ 37	Kevin Dineen........................ Philadelphia Flyers	.75	.30	.07
☐ 38	Garry Galley .... Philadelphia Flyers	.75	.30	.07
☐ 39	Dominic Roussel.................. Philadelphia Flyers	.75	.30	.07
☐ 40	Gaetan Duchesne .... San Jose Sharks	.50	.20	.05
☐ 41	Luc Robitaille....................... Los Angeles Kings	1.50	.60	.15
☐ 42	Michel Goulet....................... Chicago Blackhawks	.75	.30	.07
☐ 43	Jocelyn Lemieux .... Chicago Blackhawks	.50	.20	.05
☐ 44	Stephane Matteau .... Chicago Blackhawks	.50	.20	.05
☐ 45	Mike Hough.......................... Florida Panthers	.50	.20	.05
☐ 46	Scott Mellanby..................... Florida Panthers	.50	.20	.05
☐ 47	Claude Lemieux.................... New Jersey Devils	.75	.30	.07
☐ 48	Stephane Richer................... New Jersey Devils	.75	.30	.07
☐ 49	Jimmy Waite .... San Jose Sharks	.50	.20	.05
☐ 50	Patrick Poulin...................... Hartford Whalers	.75	.30	.07

1994 EA Sports

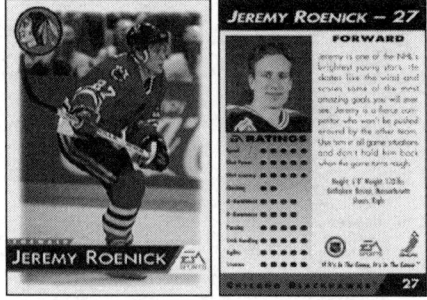

This 225-card boxed set was issued by Electronic Arts Sports as a premium within packages of its NHLPA '94 video game. Two cards were included with each game. In addition, an order form for a complete set was found inside the game box; the original price was 24.95 direct. The cards measure the standard size (2 1/2" by 3 1/2"). The fronts are white with action player photos that have airbrushed edges. The team logo appears in the upper left corner with the player's name printed on a black bar across the bottom edge. The player's position is on a team color-coded stripe above the player's name. The borderless backs display a head shot in the upper left corner with player performance rating below. A brief biography and career summary appear to the right. The Player Rating cards (1-156) are arranged below alphabetically according to teams as follows:

Anaheim Mighty Ducks (1-6), Boston Bruins (7-12), Buffalo Sabres (13-18), Calgary Flames (19-24), Chicago Blackhawks (25-30), Dallas Stars (31-36), Detroit Red Wings (37-42), Edmonton Oilers (43-48), Florida Panthers (49-54), Hartford Whalers (55-60), Los Angeles Kings (61-66), Montreal Canadiens (67-72), New Jersey Devils (73-78), New York Islanders (79-84), New York Rangers (85-87, 89-90), Ottawa Senators (91-96), Philadelphia Flyers (97-102), Pittsburgh Penguins (103-108), Quebec Nordiques (109-114), San Jose Sharks (115-120), St. Louis Blues (121-126), Tampa Bay Lightning (127-132), Toronto Maple Leafs (133-138), Vancouver Canucks (139-144), Winnipeg Jets (145-150) and Washington Capitals (151-156). The set closes with the following topical subsets: Team Rating Cards (157-184), Skill Leader Cards (185-192), New Feature Cards (193-212), and Designer Tips Cards (88, 213-225).

		MINT	EXC	G-VG
COMPLETE SET (225).....................		40.00	16.00	4.00
COMMON PLAYER (1-225)..............		.15	.06	.01
☐ 1	Alexei Kasatonov....................	.15	.06	.01
☐ 2	Randy Ladouceur...................	.15	.06	.01
☐ 3	Terry Yake.............................	.15	.06	.01
☐ 4	Troy Loney.............................	.15	.06	.01
☐ 5	Anatoli Semenov....................	.15	.06	.01
☐ 6	Guy Hebert............................	.15	.06	.01
☐ 7	Ray Bourque..........................	.75	.30	.07
☐ 8	Don Sweeney.........................	.15	.06	.01
☐ 9	Adam Oates...........................	.50	.20	.05
☐ 10	Joe Juneau............................	.75	.30	.07
☐ 11	Cam Neely.............................	.50	.20	.05
☐ 12	Andy Moog............................	.25	.10	.02
☐ 13	Doug Bodger.........................	.15	.06	.01
☐ 14	Petr Svoboda.........................	.15	.06	.01
☐ 15	Pat LaFontaine......................	.75	.30	.07
☐ 16	Dale Hawerchuk....................	.25	.10	.02
☐ 17	Alexander Mogilny	1.00	.40	.10
☐ 18	Grant Fuhr.............................	.25	.10	.02
☐ 19	Gary Suter	.15	.06	.01
☐ 20	Al MacInnis...........................	.35	.14	.03
☐ 21	Joe Nieuwendyk	.25	.10	.02
☐ 22	Gary Roberts.........................	.25	.10	.02
☐ 23	Theoren Fleury......................	.25	.10	.02
☐ 24	Mike Vernon..........................	.25	.10	.02
☐ 25	Chris Chelios.........................	.25	.10	.02
☐ 26	Steve Smith...........................	.15	.06	.01
☐ 27	Jeremy Roenick.....................	1.25	.50	.12
☐ 28	Michel Goulet........................	.25	.10	.02
☐ 29	Steve Larmer........................	.25	.10	.02
☐ 30	Ed Belfour.............................	1.00	.40	.10
☐ 31	Mark Tinordi.........................	.15	.06	.01
☐ 32	Tommy Sjodin........................	.15	.06	.01
☐ 33	Mike Modano.........................	.75	.30	.07
☐ 34	Dave Gagner.........................	.15	.06	.01
☐ 35	Russ Courtnall......................	.15	.06	.01
☐ 36	Jon Casey..............................	.15	.06	.01
☐ 37	Paul Coffey............................	.25	.10	.02
☐ 38	Steve Chiasson	.15	.06	.01
☐ 39	Steve Yzerman.......................	.75	.30	.07
☐ 40	Sergei Fedorov......................	1.50	.60	.15
☐ 41	Dino Ciccarelli.......................	.25	.10	.02
☐ 42	Tim Cheveldae.......................	.25	.10	.02
☐ 43	Dave Manson.........................	.15	.06	.01
☐ 44	Igor Kravchuk........................	.15	.06	.01
☐ 45	Doug Weight..........................	.15	.06	.01
☐ 46	Shayne Corson......................	.15	.06	.01
☐ 47	Petr Klima.............................	.15	.06	.01
☐ 48	Bill Ranford	.25	.10	.02
☐ 49	Joe Cirella.............................	.15	.06	.01
☐ 50	Gord Murphy.........................	.15	.06	.01
☐ 51	Brian Skrudland	.15	.06	.01
☐ 52	Andrei Lomakin.....................	.15	.06	.01
☐ 53	Scott Mellanby.......................	.15	.06	.01
☐ 54	John Vanbiesbrouck	.35	.14	.03
☐ 55	Zarley Zalapski......................	.15	.06	.01
☐ 56	Eric Weinrich.........................	.15	.06	.01
☐ 57	Andrew Cassels......................	.15	.06	.01
☐ 58	Geoff Sanderson	.35	.14	.03
☐ 59	Pat Verbeek...........................	.15	.06	.01
☐ 60	Sean Burke............................	.15	.06	.01
☐ 61	Rob Blake..............................	.25	.10	.02
☐ 62	Marty McSorley......................	.25	.10	.02
☐ 63	Wayne Gretzky.......................	4.00	1.60	.40
☐ 64	Luc Robitaille........................	.50	.20	.05
☐ 65	Tomas Sandstrom..................	.15	.06	.01
☐ 66	Kelly Hrudey..........................	.25	.10	.02
☐ 67	Eric Desjardins.....................	.15	.06	.01

☐ 68	Mathieu Schneider	.25	.10	.02
☐ 69	Kirk Muller	.25	.10	.02
☐ 70	Vincent Damphousse	.25	.10	.02
☐ 71	Brian Bellows	.25	.10	.02
☐ 72	Patrick Roy	2.50	1.00	.25
☐ 73	Scott Stevens	.25	.10	.02
☐ 74	Viacheslav Fetisov	.25	.10	.02
☐ 75	Alexander Semak	.25	.10	.02
☐ 76	Stephane Richer	.25	.10	.02
☐ 77	Claude Lemieux	.25	.10	.02
☐ 78	Chris Terreri	.25	.10	.02
☐ 79	Vladimir Malakhov	.15	.06	.01
☐ 80	Darius Kasparitis	.25	.10	.02
☐ 81	Pierre Turgeon	.50	.20	.05
☐ 82	Steve Thomas	.15	.06	.01
☐ 83	Benoit Hogue	.15	.06	.01
☐ 84	Glenn Healy	.15	.06	.01
☐ 85	Brian Leetch	.75	.30	.07
☐ 86	James Patrick	.15	.06	.01
☐ 87	Mark Messier	.75	.30	.07
☐ 88	Designer Tip The Wong One-Timer From Boards To Slot	.15	.06	.01
☐ 89	Mike Gartner	.35	.14	.03
☐ 90	Mike Richter	.75	.30	.07
☐ 91	Norm Maciver	.15	.06	.01
☐ 92	Brad Shaw	.15	.06	.01
☐ 93	Jamie Baker	.15	.06	.01
☐ 94	Sylvain Turgeon	.15	.06	.01
☐ 95	Bob Kudelski	.15	.06	.01
☐ 96	Peter Sidorkiewicz	.15	.06	.01
☐ 97	Garry Galley	.15	.06	.01
☐ 98	Dimitri Yushkevich	.15	.06	.01
☐ 99	Eric Lindros	4.00	1.60	.40
☐ 100	Rod Brind'Amour	.35	.14	.03
☐ 101	Mark Recchi	.35	.14	.03
☐ 102	Tommy Soderstrom	.25	.10	.02
☐ 103	Larry Murphy	.25	.10	.02
☐ 104	Ulf Samuelsson	.15	.06	.01
☐ 105	Mario Lemieux	3.00	1.20	.30
☐ 106	Kevin Stevens	.50	.20	.05
☐ 107	Jaromir Jagr	1.25	.50	.12
☐ 108	Tom Barrasso	.25	.10	.02
☐ 109	Steve Duchesne	.15	.06	.01
☐ 110	Curtis Leschyshyn	.15	.06	.01
☐ 111	Mats Sundin	.75	.30	.07
☐ 112	Joe Sakic	.50	.20	.05
☐ 113	Owen Nolan	.35	.14	.03
☐ 114	Ron Hextall	.25	.10	.02
☐ 115	Doug Wilson	.25	.10	.02
☐ 116	Neil Wilkinson	.15	.06	.01
☐ 117	Kelly Kisio	.15	.06	.01
☐ 118	Johan Garpenlov	.15	.06	.01
☐ 119	Pat Falloon	.35	.14	.03
☐ 120	Arturs Irbe	.75	.30	.07
☐ 121	Jeff Brown	.25	.10	.02
☐ 122	Garth Butcher UER (Ray Bourque photo on card back)	.25	.10	.02
☐ 123	Craig Janney	.35	.14	.03
☐ 124	Brendan Shanahan	.75	.30	.07
☐ 125	Brett Hull	1.25	.50	.12
☐ 126	Curtis Joseph	.75	.30	.07
☐ 127	Bob Beers	.15	.06	.01
☐ 128	Roman Hamrlik	.25	.10	.02
☐ 129	Brian Bradley	.25	.10	.02
☐ 130	Mikael Andersson	.15	.06	.01
☐ 131	Chris Kontos	.15	.06	.01
☐ 132	Wendell Young	.15	.06	.01
☐ 133	Todd Gill	.15	.06	.01
☐ 134	Dave Ellett	.15	.06	.01
☐ 135	Doug Gilmour	.75	.30	.07
☐ 136	Dave Andreychuk	.35	.14	.03
☐ 137	Nikolai Borschevsky	.25	.10	.02
☐ 138	Felix Potvin	1.25	.50	.12
☐ 139	Jyrki Lumme	.15	.06	.01
☐ 140	Doug Lidster	.15	.06	.01
☐ 141	Cliff Ronning	.25	.10	.02
☐ 142	Geoff Courtnall	.25	.10	.02
☐ 143	Pavel Bure	2.50	1.00	.25
☐ 144	Kirk McLean	.35	.14	.03
☐ 145	Phil Housley	.25	.10	.02
☐ 146	Teppo Numminen	.15	.06	.01
☐ 147	Alexei Zhamnov	.75	.30	.07
☐ 148	Thomas Steen	.15	.06	.01
☐ 149	Teemu Selanne	1.00	.40	.10
☐ 150	Bob Essensa	.15	.06	.01
☐ 151	Kevin Hatcher	.25	.10	.02
☐ 152	Al Iafrate	.25	.10	.02
☐ 153	Mike Ridley	.15	.06	.01
☐ 154	Dimitri Khristich	.15	.06	.01
☐ 155	Peter Bondra	.15	.06	.01
☐ 156	Don Beaupre	.15	.06	.01
☐ 157	All Stars East CL	.15	.06	.01
☐ 158	All Stars West CL	.15	.06	.01
☐ 159	Mighty Ducks Team CL	.25	.10	.02
☐ 160	Bruins Team CL	.15	.06	.01
☐ 161	Sabres Team CL	.15	.06	.01
☐ 162	Flames Team CL	.15	.06	.01
☐ 163	Blackhawks Team CL	.15	.06	.01
☐ 164	Red Wings Team CL	.15	.06	.01
☐ 165	Oilers Team CL	.15	.06	.01
☐ 166	Panthers Team CL	.15	.06	.01
☐ 167	Whalers Team CL	.15	.06	.01
☐ 168	Kings Team CL	.15	.06	.01
☐ 169	Stars Team CL	.15	.06	.01
☐ 170	Canadiens Team CL	.15	.06	.01
☐ 171	Devils Team CL	.15	.06	.01
☐ 172	Islanders Team CL	.15	.06	.01
☐ 173	Rangers Team CL	.15	.06	.01
☐ 174	Senators Team CL	.15	.06	.01
☐ 175	Flyers Team CL	.15	.06	.01
☐ 176	Penguins Team CL	.15	.06	.01
☐ 177	Nordiques Team CL	.15	.06	.01
☐ 178	Sharks Team CL	.15	.06	.01
☐ 179	Blues Team CL	.15	.06	.01
☐ 180	Lightning Team CL	.15	.06	.01
☐ 181	Leafs Team CL	.15	.06	.01
☐ 182	Canucks Team CL	.15	.06	.01
☐ 183	Capitals Team CL	.15	.06	.01
☐ 184	Jets Team CL	.15	.06	.01
☐ 185	Skill Leaders Checking Ray Bourque	.35	.14	.03
☐ 186	Skill Leaders Defense Chris Chelios	.25	.10	.02
☐ 187	Skill Leaders Goaltending Ed Belfour	.50	.20	.05
☐ 188	Skill Leaders Passing Adam Oates	.25	.10	.02
☐ 189	Skill Leaders Shot Accuracy Mario Lemieux	1.00	.40	.10
☐ 190	Skill Leaders Shot Power Al Iafrate	.25	.10	.02
☐ 191	Skill Leaders Skating Alexander Mogilny	.50	.20	.05
☐ 192	Skill Leaders Stickhandling Wayne Gretzky	2.00	.80	.20
☐ 193	New Feature 4 Way Play (Sega Genesis)	.15	.06	.01
☐ 194	New Feature Auto Line Changes Derian Hatcher	.15	.06	.01
☐ 195	New Feature Bench Checks Dmitri Kvartalnov	.15	.06	.01
☐ 196	New Feature Board Checks Randy Wood	.15	.06	.01
☐ 197	New Feature Clear Zone Gord Murphy	.15	.06	.01
☐ 198	New Feature Crowd Records (Crowd scene)	.15	.06	.01
☐ 199	New Feature Expansion Teams Ducks/Panthers Team Logo	.25	.10	.02
☐ 200	New Feature Goalie Control Luc Robittaille	.25	.10	.02
☐ 201	New Feature Hot/Cold Streaks Terry Yake	.15	.06	.01
☐ 202	New Feature Local Organ Music Mark Fitzpatrick	.15	.06	.01
☐ 203	New Feature More Stats Brad Shaw	.15	.06	.01
☐ 204	New Feature NHL Logos	.15	.06	.01
☐ 205	New Feature One Timers Jyrki Lumme	.15	.06	.01
☐ 206	New Feature	.15	.06	.01

	Penalty Shots			
	Peter Sidorkiewicz			
☐ 207	New Feature	.15	.06	.01
	Player Cards			
	Gord Murphy			
☐ 208	New Feature	.15	.06	.01
	Player Profiles			
	Viacheslav Fetisov			
☐ 209	New Feature	.15	.06	.01
	Player Records			
	Stephan LeBeau			
☐ 210	New Feature	.15	.06	.01
	Reverse Angle			
	Gord Murphy			
☐ 211	New Feature	.50	.20	.05
	Shootout Game			
	Dominik Hasek			
☐ 212	New Feature	.25	.10	.02
	User Records			
	Cam Neely			
☐ 213	Designer Tips	.15	.06	.01
	The Brook			
	Delayed Slap Shot			
☐ 214	Designer Tips	.15	.06	.01
	The Coast			
	Skate Away From Goal			
☐ 215	Designer Tips	.15	.06	.01
	The Hogan			
	Slide Into Goal			
☐ 216	Designer Tips	.15	.06	.01
	The Lange			
	Use Goalie To Take			
	Out Shooter			
☐ 217	Designer Tips	.15	.06	.01
	The Lesser			
	Create A Screen			
	With Defender			
☐ 218	Designer Tips	.15	.06	.01
	The Matulac			
	Fake Outside,			
	Shoot Inside			
☐ 219	Designer Tips	.15	.06	.01
	The Scott			
	Fake Inside,			
	Shoot Outside			
☐ 220	Designer Tips	.15	.06	.01
	The Probin			
	Set Up One-Timer			
	In The Slot			
☐ 221	Designer Tips	.15	.06	.01
	The Rogers			
	Set Up One-Sider			
	Across The Crease			
☐ 222	Designer Tips	.15	.06	.01
	The Rubinelli			
	Fake Outside,			
	Fake Inside,			
	Shoot Outside			
☐ 223	Designer Tips	.15	.06	.01
	The Shin			
	Wrap Around Goal,			
	Shoot Wide			
☐ 224	Designer Tips	.15	.06	.01
	The White			
	Deflection At			
	Goal Mouth			
☐ 225	Designer Tips	.15	.06	.01
	The Wike			
	Set Up One-Timer			
	From Behind The Goal			

1962-63 El Producto Discs

The six discs in this set measure approximately 3" in diameter. They were issued as a strip of six connected in a fragile manner and are in full color. The discs are unnumbered and checklisted below in alphabetical order. The set in unperforated form is valued 25 percent greater than the value below.

	NRMT	VG-E	GOOD
COMPLETE SET (6)	250.00	100.00	25.00
COMMON PLAYER (1-6)	30.00	12.00	3.00
☐ 1 Jean Beliveau	60.00	24.00	6.00
☐ 2 Glenn Hall	40.00	16.00	4.00
☐ 3 Gordie Howe	125.00	50.00	12.50

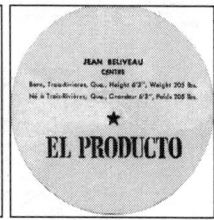

☐ 4	Dave Keon	30.00	12.00	3.00
☐ 5	Frank Mahovlich	50.00	20.00	5.00
☐ 6	Henri Richard	40.00	16.00	4.00

1992-93 Enor Mark Messier

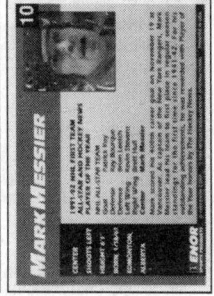

One card from this ten-card set was included in each specially marked package of Enor Progard Plus sportscard pages. The cards measure the standard size (2 1/2" by 3 1/2") and feature color player photos with silver borders. A red stripe that runs along the right edge and top of the photo accents the card face and provides a backdrop for the player's name, which is printed in white and blue. The horizontal back shows a close-up player photo that overlaps a red border stripe similar to the one on the front and a pale blue panel. The red stripe contains the player's name. The blue panel contains player information. A black vertical bar runs along the left edge of the panel and contains biographical information. The cards are numbered on the back.

	MINT	EXC	G-VG
COMPLETE SET (10)	7.50	3.00	.75
COMMON CARD (1-10)	1.00	.40	.10
☐ 1 Mark Messier	1.00	.40	.10
☐ 2 Mark Messier	1.00	.40	.10
☐ 3 Mark Messier	1.00	.40	.10
☐ 4 Mark Messier	1.00	.40	.10
☐ 5 Mark Messier	1.00	.40	.10
☐ 6 Mark Messier	1.00	.40	.10
☐ 7 Mark Messier	1.00	.40	.10
☐ 8 Mark Messier	1.00	.40	.10
☐ 9 Mark Messier	1.00	.40	.10
☐ 10 Mark Messier	1.00	.40	.10
(Close-up photo, helmet on)			

1970-71 Esso Power Players

The 1970-71 Esso Power Players set includes 252 color stamps measuring approximately 1 1/2" by 2". The stamps were issued in six-stamp sheets and given away free with a minimum purchase of 3.00 of Esso gasoline. There were 18

stamps for each of the 14 teams then in the NHL. The stamps are unnumbered except for jersey (uniform) number. The set was issued with an album, which can be found in either a soft or hard bound version. The hard cover album supposedly had extra pages with additional players. The stamps and albums are available in both French and English language versions. The set is numbered below numerically within each team as follows: Montreal Canadiens (1-18), Toronto Maple Leafs (19-36), Vancouver Canucks (37-54), Boston Bruins (55-72), Buffalo Sabres (73-90), California Golden Seals (91-108), Chicago Blackhawks (109-126), Detroit Red Wings (127-144), Los Angeles Kings (145-162), Minnesota North Stars (163-180), New York Rangers (181-198), Philadelphia Flyers (199-216), Pittsburgh Penguins (217-234), and St. Louis Blues (235-252). Supposedly there are 59 stamps which are tougher to find than the others. The short-printed stamps are apparently those players who were pre-printed into the soft-cover album and hence not included in the first stamp printing.

	NRMT	VG-E	GOOD
COMPLETE SET (252)	150.00	60.00	15.00
COMMON PLAYER (1-252)	.35	.14	.03
☐ 1 Rogatien Vachon 1	1.00	.40	.10
☐ 2 Jacques Laperriere 2	.75	.30	.07
☐ 3 J.C. Tremblay 3	.50	.20	.05
☐ 4 Jean Beliveau 4	5.00	2.00	.50
☐ 5 Guy Lapointe 5	1.00	.40	.10
☐ 6 Fran Huck 6	.35	.14	.03
☐ 7 Bill Collins 10	.35	.14	.03
☐ 8 Marc Tardif 11	.50	.20	.05
☐ 9 Yvan Cournoyer 12	1.50	.60	.15
☐ 10 Claude Larose 15	.35	.14	.03
☐ 11 Henri Richard 16	2.00	.80	.20
☐ 12 Serge Savard 18	1.50	.60	.15
☐ 13 Terry Harper 19	.50	.20	.05
☐ 14 Pete Mahovlich 20	.50	.20	.05
☐ 15 John Ferguson 22	.50	.20	.05
☐ 16 Mickey Redmond 24	.75	.30	.07
☐ 17 Jacques Lemaire 25	1.50	.60	.15
☐ 18 Phil Myre 30	.50	.20	.05
☐ 19 Jacques Plante 1	4.00	1.60	.40
☐ 20 Rick Ley 2	.50	.20	.05
☐ 21 Mike Pelyk 4	.35	.14	.03
☐ 22 Ron Ellis 6	.50	.20	.05
☐ 23 Jim Dorey 8	.35	.14	.03
☐ 24 Norm Ullman 9	1.50	.60	.15
☐ 25 Guy Trottier 11	.35	.14	.03
☐ 26 Jim Harrison 12	.35	.14	.03
☐ 27 Dave Keon 14	1.50	.60	.15
☐ 28 Mike Walton 16	.50	.20	.05
☐ 29 Jim McKenny 18	.35	.14	.03
☐ 30 Paul Henderson 19	.75	.30	.07
☐ 31 Garry Monahan 20 SP	.75	.30	.07
☐ 32 Bob Baun 21	.50	.20	.05
☐ 33 Bill MacMillan 23	.35	.14	.03
☐ 34 Brian Glennie 24	.35	.14	.03
☐ 35 Darryl Sittler 27	3.00	1.20	.30
☐ 36 Bruce Gamble 30	.35	.14	.03
☐ 37 Charlie Hodge 1	.75	.30	.07
☐ 38 Gary Doak 2	.50	.20	.05
☐ 39 Pat Quinn 3	.75	.30	.07
☐ 40 Barry Wilkins 4	.35	.14	.03
☐ 41 Darryl Sly 5 SP	.75	.30	.07
☐ 42 Marc Reaume 6	.35	.14	.03
☐ 43 Andre Boudrias 7	.35	.14	.03
☐ 44 Danny Johnson 8	.35	.14	.03
☐ 45 Ray Cullen 10 SP	.75	.30	.07
☐ 46 Wayne Maki 11	.35	.14	.03
☐ 47 Mike Corrigan 12	.35	.14	.03
☐ 48 Rosaire Paiement 15	.35	.14	.03
☐ 49 Poul Popeil 18 SP	.75	.30	.07
☐ 50 Dale Tallon 19	.50	.20	.05
☐ 51 Murray Hall 23 SP	.75	.30	.07
☐ 52 Len Lunde 24	.35	.14	.03
☐ 53 Orland Kurtenbach 25	.50	.20	.05
☐ 54 Dunc Wilson 30 SP	.75	.30	.07
☐ 55 Ed Johnston 1	.75	.30	.07
☐ 56 Bobby Orr 4	15.00	6.00	1.50
☐ 57 Ted Green 6	.50	.20	.05
☐ 58 Phil Esposito 7	5.00	2.00	.50
☐ 59 Ken Hodge 8	.75	.30	.07
☐ 60 Johnny Bucyk 9	2.00	.80	.20
☐ 61 Rick Smith 10 SP	.75	.30	.07
☐ 62 Wayne Carleton 11 SP	.75	.30	.07
☐ 63 Wayne Cashman 12 SP	1.00	.40	.10
☐ 64 Garnet Bailey 14	.35	.14	.03
☐ 65 Derek Sanderson 16	1.50	.60	.15
☐ 66 Fred Stanfield 17 SP	.75	.30	.07
☐ 67 Ed Westfall 18	.50	.20	.05
☐ 68 John McKenzie 19	.35	.14	.03
☐ 69 Dallas Smith 20	.50	.20	.05
☐ 70 Don Marcotte 21	.35	.14	.03
☐ 71 Don Awrey 26 SP	.75	.30	.07
☐ 72 Gerry Cheevers 30	2.50	1.00	.25
☐ 73 Roger Crozier 1	.50	.20	.05
☐ 74 Jim Watson 2	.50	.20	.05
☐ 75 Tracy Pratt 3	.35	.14	.03
☐ 76 Doug Barrie 5 SP	.75	.30	.07
☐ 77 Al Hamilton 6	.35	.14	.03
☐ 78 Cliff Schmautz 7 SP	.75	.30	.07
☐ 79 Reg Fleming 9	.35	.14	.03
☐ 80 Phil Goyette 10	.35	.14	.03
☐ 81 Gilbert Perreault 11	5.00	2.00	.50
☐ 82 Skip Krake 12	.35	.14	.03
☐ 83 Gerry Meehan 15	.50	.20	.05
☐ 84 Ron Anderson 16	.35	.14	.03
☐ 85 Floyd Smith 17 SP	.75	.30	.07
☐ 86 Steve Atkinson 19	.35	.14	.03
☐ 87 Paul Andrea 21 SP	.75	.30	.07
☐ 88 Don Marshall 22	.35	.14	.03
☐ 89 Eddie Shack 23 SP	2.00	.80	.20
☐ 90 Larry Keenan 26	.35	.14	.03
☐ 91 Gary Smith 1	.50	.20	.05
☐ 92 Doug Roberts 2	.35	.14	.03
☐ 93 Harry Howell 3	1.25	.50	.12
☐ 94 Wayne Muloin 4	.35	.14	.03
☐ 95 Carol Vadnais 5	.50	.20	.05
☐ 96 Dick Mattiussi 6	.35	.14	.03
☐ 97 Earl Ingarfield 7	.35	.14	.03
☐ 98 Gerry Ehman 8	.35	.14	.03
☐ 99 Bill Hicke 9	.35	.14	.03
☐ 100 Ted Hampson 10	.35	.14	.03
☐ 101 Gary Jarrett 12	.35	.14	.03
☐ 102 Joe Hardy 14 SP	.75	.30	.07
☐ 103 Tony Featherstone 16 SP	.75	.30	.07
☐ 104 Gary Croteau 18	.35	.14	.03
☐ 105 Ernie Hicke 20 SP	.75	.30	.07
☐ 106 Ron Stackhouse 21	.35	.14	.03
☐ 107 Dennis Hextall 22 SP	1.25	.50	.12
☐ 108 Bob Sneddon 30 SP	.75	.30	.07
☐ 109 Gerry Desjardins 1 SP	1.00	.40	.10
☐ 110 Bill White 2	.50	.20	.05
☐ 111 Keith Magnuson 3	.50	.20	.05
☐ 112 Doug Jarrett 4 SP	.75	.30	.07
☐ 113 Lou Angotti 6	.35	.14	.03
☐ 114 Pit Martin 7	.50	.20	.05
☐ 115 Jim Pappin 8	.35	.14	.03
☐ 116 Bobby Hull 9	9.00	3.75	.90
☐ 117 Dennis Hull 10 SP	1.50	.60	.15
☐ 118 Doug Mohns 11	.50	.20	.05
☐ 119 Pat Stapleton 12	.50	.20	.05
☐ 120 Bryan Campbell 14 SP	.75	.30	.07
☐ 121 Eric Nesterenko 15	.50	.20	.05
☐ 122 Chico Maki 16	.50	.20	.05
☐ 123 Gerry Pinder 18	.50	.20	.05
☐ 124 Cliff Koroll 20	.35	.14	.03
☐ 125 Stan Mikita 21	5.00	2.00	.50
☐ 126 Tony Esposito 35	5.00	2.00	.50
☐ 127 Jim Rutherford 1 SP	1.25	.50	.12
☐ 128 Gary Bergman 2	.50	.20	.05
☐ 129 Dale Rolfe 3	.35	.14	.03
☐ 130 Larry Brown 4 SP	.75	.30	.07
☐ 131 Serge Lajeunesse 5	.35	.14	.03
☐ 132 Garry Unger 7	.75	.30	.07
☐ 133 Tom Webster 8	.50	.20	.05

☐ 134	Gordie Howe 9	15.00	6.00	1.50
☐ 135	Alex Delvecchio 10	2.00	.80	.20
☐ 136	Don Luce 11 SP	.75	.30	.07
☐ 137	Bruce MacGregor 12	.35	.14	.03
☐ 138	Nick Libett 14	.50	.20	.05
☐ 139	Al Karlander 15	.35	.14	.03
☐ 140	Ron Harris 16	.35	.14	.03
☐ 141	Wayne Connelly 17 SP	.75	.30	.07
☐ 142	Billy Dea 21 SP	.75	.30	.07
☐ 143	Frank Mahovlich 27	5.00	2.00	.50
☐ 144	Roy Edwards 30	.50	.20	.05
☐ 145	Jack Norris 1	.35	.14	.03
☐ 146	Dale Hoganson 2	.35	.14	.03
☐ 147	Larry Cahan 3	.35	.14	.03
☐ 148	Gilles Marotte 4 SP	.75	.30	.07
☐ 149	Noel Price 5 SP	.75	.30	.07
☐ 150	Paul Curtis 6 SP	.75	.30	.07
☐ 151	Ross Lonsberry 8	.35	.14	.03
☐ 152	Gord Labossiere 9	.35	.14	.03
☐ 153	Doug Robinson 11 SP	.75	.30	.07
☐ 154	Larry Mickey 12	.35	.14	.03
☐ 155	Juha Widing 15	.35	.14	.03
☐ 156	Eddie Joyal 16	.35	.14	.03
☐ 157	Bill Flett 17	.35	.14	.03
☐ 158	Bob Berry 18	.50	.20	.05
☐ 159	Bob Pulford 20	1.00	.40	.10
☐ 160	Matt Ravlich 21	.35	.14	.03
☐ 161	Mike Byers 24 SP	.75	.30	.07
☐ 162	Denis DeJordy 30	.50	.20	.05
☐ 163	Gump Worsley 1	3.00	1.20	.30
☐ 164	Barry Gibbs 2 SP	.75	.30	.07
☐ 165	Fred Barrett 3	.35	.14	.03
☐ 166	Ted Harris 4	.35	.14	.03
☐ 167	Danny O'Shea 7	.35	.14	.03
☐ 168	Bill Goldsworthy 8	.50	.20	.05
☐ 169	Charlie Burns 9	.35	.14	.03
☐ 170	Murray Oliver 10	.35	.14	.03
☐ 171	Jean-Paul Parise 11	.35	.14	.03
☐ 172	Tom Williams 12 SP	.75	.30	.07
☐ 173	Bobby Rousseau 15	.50	.20	.05
☐ 174	Buster Harvey 18 SP	.75	.30	.07
☐ 175	Tom Reid 20 SP	.75	.30	.07
☐ 176	Danny Grant 21	.50	.20	.05
☐ 177	Walt McKechnie 22	.35	.14	.03
☐ 178	Lou Nanne 23	.50	.20	.05
☐ 179	Danny Lawson 24 SP	1.00	.40	.10
☐ 180	Cesare Maniago 30	.50	.20	.05
☐ 181	Ed Giacomin 1	2.50	1.00	.25
☐ 182	Brad Park 2	3.00	1.20	.30
☐ 183	Tim Horton 3	3.00	1.20	.30
☐ 184	Arnie Brown 4	.35	.14	.03
☐ 185	Rod Gilbert 7	2.00	.80	.20
☐ 186	Bob Nevin 8	.35	.14	.03
☐ 187	Bill Fairbairn 10 SP	.75	.30	.07
☐ 188	Vic Hadfield 11	.75	.30	.07
☐ 189	Ron Stewart 12	.35	.14	.03
☐ 190	Jim Neilson 15	.35	.14	.03
☐ 191	Rod Seiling 16 SP	.75	.30	.07
☐ 192	Dave Balon 17 SP	.75	.30	.07
☐ 193	Walt Tkaczuk 18	.50	.20	.05
☐ 194	Jean Ratelle 19	2.00	.80	.20
☐ 195	Jack Egers 20	.35	.14	.03
☐ 196	Pete Stemkowski 21 SP	1.00	.40	.10
☐ 197	Ted Irvine 27	.35	.14	.03
☐ 198	Gilles Villemure 30	.75	.30	.07
☐ 199	Doug Favell 1	.50	.20	.05
☐ 200	Ed Van Impe 2	.35	.14	.03
☐ 201	Larry Hillman 3	.35	.14	.03
☐ 202	Barry Ashbee 4	.75	.30	.07
☐ 203	Wayne Hillman 6 SP	.75	.30	.07
☐ 204	Andre Lacroix 7	.50	.20	.05
☐ 205	Lew Morrison 8	.35	.14	.03
☐ 206	Bob Kelly 9 SP	1.00	.40	.10
☐ 207	Jean-Guy Gendron 11	.35	.14	.03
☐ 208	Gary Dornhoefer 12	.50	.20	.05
☐ 209	Joe Watson 14	.35	.14	.03
☐ 210	Garry Peters 15 SP	.75	.30	.07
☐ 211	Bobby Clarke 16	5.00	2.00	.50
☐ 212	Earl Heiskala 19 SP	.75	.30	.07
☐ 213	Jim Johnson 20	.35	.14	.03
☐ 214	Serge Bernier 21	.35	.14	.03
☐ 215	Larry Hale 23 SP	.75	.30	.07
☐ 216	Bernie Parent 30	2.50	1.00	.25
☐ 217	Al Smith 1	.50	.20	.05
☐ 218	Duane Rupp 2	.35	.14	.03
☐ 219	Bob Woytowich 3	.35	.14	.03
☐ 220	Bob Blackburn 4	.35	.14	.03
☐ 221	Bryan Watson 5 SP	.75	.30	.07
☐ 222	Dunc McCallum 6	.50	.20	.05
☐ 223	Bryan Hextall 7	.50	.20	.05
☐ 224	Andy Bathgate 9 SP	2.00	.80	.20
☐ 225	Keith McCreary 10 SP	.75	.30	.07
☐ 226	Nick Harbaruk 11	.35	.14	.03

☐ 227	Ken Schinkel 12	.35	.14	.03
☐ 228	Glen Sather 16 SP	2.00	.80	.20
☐ 229	Ron Schock 17	.35	.14	.03
☐ 230	Wally Boyer 18	.35	.14	.03
☐ 231	Jean Pronovost 19	.50	.20	.05
☐ 232	Dean Prentice 20	.50	.20	.05
☐ 233	Jim Morrison 27	.35	.14	.03
☐ 234	Les Binkley 30 SP	1.00	.40	.10
☐ 235	Glenn Hall 1	3.00	1.20	.30
☐ 236	Bob Wall 2	.35	.14	.03
☐ 237	Noel Picard 4	.35	.14	.03
☐ 238	Bob Plager 5	.50	.20	.05
☐ 239	Jim Roberts 6	.50	.20	.05
☐ 240	Red Berenson 7	.50	.20	.05
☐ 241	Barclay Plager 8	.50	.20	.05
☐ 242	Frank St.Marseille 9	.35	.14	.03
☐ 243	George Morrison 10 SP	.75	.30	.07
☐ 244	Gary Sabourin 11	.35	.14	.03
☐ 245	Terry Crisp 12 SP	1.25	.50	.12
☐ 246	Tim Ecclestone 14	.35	.14	.03
☐ 247	Bill McCreary 15	.35	.14	.03
☐ 248	Brit Selby 18 SP	.75	.30	.07
☐ 249	Jim Lorentz 19 SP	.75	.30	.07
☐ 250	Ab McDonald 20	.35	.14	.03
☐ 251	Chris Bordeleau 21 SP	.75	.30	.07
☐ 252	Ernie Wakely 31	.35	.14	.03
☐ xx	Soft Cover Album	15.00	6.00	1.50
☐ xx	Hard Cover Album	50.00	20.00	5.00

1983-84 Esso

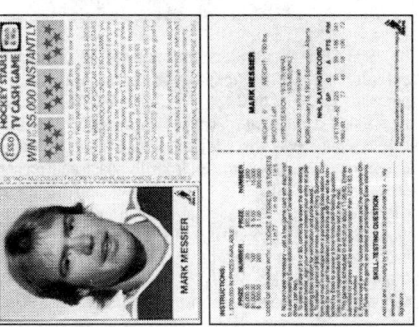

The 1983-84 Esso set contains 21 color cards measuring approximately 4 1/2" by 3" although the player photo portion of the card is only 2" by 3". There are actually two different sets, one in French and one in English. The cards are actually part of a lottery-type game where 5000.00 cash could be won instantly via a scratch-off. The card backs contain information about the contest on the back of the contest portion and player statistics on the back of the player photo portion of the card. The cards are unnumbered and hence they are checklisted below alphabetically. There is very little difference in availablility of the English set as opposed to the French set; however there seems to be a slight premium on the French set over the English set of about 20 percent over the prices listed below.

	MINT	EXC	G-VG
COMPLETE SET (21)	12.00	5.00	1.20
COMMON PLAYER (1-21)	.50	.20	.05

☐ 1	Glenn Anderson	1.00	.40	.10
☐ 2	John Anderson	.50	.20	.05
☐ 3	Dave Babych	.50	.20	.05
☐ 4	Richard Brodeur	.75	.30	.07
☐ 5	Paul Coffey	2.00	.80	.20
☐ 6	Bill Derlago	.50	.20	.05
☐ 7	Bob Gainey	1.25	.50	.12
☐ 8	Michel Goulet	1.00	.40	.10
☐ 9	Dale Hawerchuk	2.00	.80	.20
☐ 10	Dale Hunter	.75	.30	.07
☐ 11	Morris Lukowich	.50	.20	.05
☐ 12	Lanny McDonald	1.50	.60	.15
☐ 13	Mark Messier	2.50	1.00	.25

☐ 14 Jim Peplinski	.50	.20	.05
☐ 15 Paul Reinhart	.75	.30	.07
☐ 16 Larry Robinson	1.25	.50	.12
☐ 17 Stan Smyl	.75	.30	.07
☐ 18 Harold Snepsts	.75	.30	.07
☐ 19 Marc Tardif	.50	.20	.05
☐ 20 Mario Tremblay	.50	.20	.05
☐ 21 Rick Vaive	.75	.30	.07

1988-89 Esso All-Stars

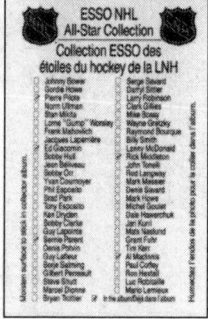

Wayne GRETZKY

The 1988-89 Esso All-Stars set contains 48 color cards (actually adhesive-backed "stickers") measuring approximately 2 1/8" by 3 1/4". The fronts feature borderless color action photos with facsimile autographs. The backs have complete checklists for the whole set. The players depicted include hockey greats from the past and present. The cards (stickers) are unnumbered and hence are checklisted below in alphabetical order. There is a 32-page album (8 1/2" by 11") available in either English or French, which was intended to hold the stickers. In fact each album already contains five pasted-in cards, Ed Giacomin, Al MacInnis, Rick Middleton, Bernie Parent, and Pierre Pilote. The cards were reportedly distributed in Canada in packs of six with a purchase of gasoline at participating Esso service stations. The complete price below includes the album.

	MINT	EXC	G-VG
COMPLETE SET (48)	15.00	6.00	1.50
COMMON PLAYER (1-48)	.25	.10	.02
☐ 1 Jean Beliveau	.75	.30	.07
☐ 2 Mike Bossy	.75	.30	.07
☐ 3 Ray Bourque	.75	.30	.07
☐ 4 Johnny Bower	.35	.14	.03
☐ 5 Bobby Clarke	.50	.20	.05
☐ 6 Paul Coffey	.75	.30	.07
☐ 7 Yvan Cournoyer	.35	.14	.03
☐ 8 Marcel Dionne	.50	.20	.05
☐ 9 Ken Dryden	.75	.30	.07
☐ 10 Phil Esposito	.75	.30	.07
☐ 11 Tony Esposito	.50	.20	.05
☐ 12 Grant Fuhr	.35	.14	.03
☐ 13 Clark Gillies	.25	.10	.02
☐ 14 Michel Goulet	.35	.14	.03
☐ 15 Wayne Gretzky	3.00	1.20	.30
☐ 16 Dale Hawerchuk	.35	.14	.03
☐ 17 Ron Hextall	.25	.10	.02
☐ 18 Gordie Howe	1.50	.60	.15
☐ 19 Mark Howe	.25	.10	.02
☐ 20 Bobby Hull	1.00	.40	.10
☐ 21 Tim Kerr	.25	.10	.02
☐ 22 Jari Kurri	.35	.14	.03
☐ 23 Guy Lafleur	.75	.30	.07
☐ 24 Rod Langway	.25	.10	.02
☐ 25 Jacques Laperriere	.25	.10	.02
☐ 26 Guy Lapointe	.35	.14	.03
☐ 27 Mario Lemieux	2.00	.80	.20
☐ 28 Frank Mahovlich	.50	.20	.05
☐ 29 Lanny McDonald	.35	.14	.03
☐ 30 Mark Messier	.75	.30	.07
☐ 31 Stan Mikita	.50	.20	.05

☐ 32 Mats Naslund	.25	.10	.02
☐ 33 Bobby Orr	2.00	.80	.20
☐ 34 Brad Park	.35	.14	.03
☐ 35 Gilbert Perreault	.35	.14	.03
☐ 36 Denis Potvin	.35	.14	.03
☐ 37 Larry Robinson	.35	.14	.03
☐ 38 Luc Robitaille	.75	.30	.07
☐ 39 Borje Salming	.25	.10	.02
☐ 40 Denis Savard	.35	.14	.03
☐ 41 Serge Savard	.35	.14	.03
☐ 42 Steve Shutt	.35	.14	.03
☐ 43 Darryl Sittler	.35	.14	.03
☐ 44 Billy Smith	.35	.14	.03
☐ 45 John Tonelli	.25	.10	.02
☐ 46 Bryan Trottier	.35	.14	.03
☐ 47 Norm Ullman	.35	.14	.03
☐ 48 Gump Worsley	.50	.20	.05
☐ xx Album	3.00	1.20	.30

1948-52 Exhibits Canadian

These cards measure approximately 3 1/4" by 5 1/4" and were issued on heavy cardboard stock. The cards show full-bleed photos with the player's name burned in toward the bottom. The hockey exhibit cards are generally considered more scarce than their baseball exhibit counterparts. Since the cards are unnumbered, the set is arranged below alphabetically within teams as follows: Montreal (1-27), Toronto (28-42), Detroit (43-46), Boston (47-48), Chicago (49-50), and New York (51). The set closes with an Action subset (52-65).

	NRMT	VG-E	GOOD
COMPLETE SET (65)	1250.00	500.00	125.00
COMMON PLAYER (1-65)	10.00	4.00	1.00
☐ 1 Reggie Abbott	10.00	4.00	1.00
☐ 2 Jean Beliveau	50.00	20.00	5.00
☐ 3 Jean Beliveau (As captain)	50.00	20.00	5.00
☐ 4 Toe Blake	25.00	10.00	2.50
☐ 5 Butch Bouchard	20.00	8.00	2.00
☐ 6 Bob Fillion	10.00	4.00	1.00
☐ 7 Dick Gamble	10.00	4.00	1.00
☐ 8 Bernie Geoffrion	40.00	16.00	4.00
☐ 9 Doug Harvey	30.00	12.00	3.00
☐ 10 Tom Johnson	20.00	8.00	2.00
☐ 11 Elmer Lach	25.00	10.00	2.50
☐ 12 Hal Laycoe	10.00	4.00	1.00
☐ 13 Jacques Locas	10.00	4.00	1.00
☐ 14 Bud McPherson	10.00	4.00	1.00
☐ 15 Paul Maznick	10.00	4.00	1.00
☐ 16 Gerry McNeil	15.00	6.00	1.50
☐ 17 Paul Meger	10.00	4.00	1.00
☐ 18 Dickie Moore	25.00	10.00	2.50
☐ 19 Ken Mosdell	10.00	4.00	1.00
☐ 20 Bert Olmstead	20.00	8.00	2.00
☐ 21 Ken Reardon	20.00	8.00	2.00
☐ 22 Billy Reay	15.00	6.00	1.50
☐ 23 Maurice Richard (Stick on ice)	60.00	24.00	6.00
☐ 24 Maurice Richard (Stairs in back ground)	60.00	24.00	6.00
☐ 25 Dollard St.Laurent	10.00	4.00	1.00
☐ 26 Grant Warwick	10.00	4.00	1.00
☐ 27 Floyd Curry	15.00	6.00	1.50
☐ 28 Bill Barilko	20.00	8.00	2.00
☐ 29 Turk Broda	30.00	12.00	3.00
☐ 30 Cal Gardner	20.00	8.00	2.00
☐ 31 Bill Judza	10.00	4.00	1.00
☐ 32 Ted Kennedy	30.00	12.00	3.00
☐ 33 Joe Klukay	10.00	4.00	1.00
☐ 34 Fleming Mackell	10.00	4.00	1.00
☐ 35 Howie Meeker	15.00	6.00	1.50
☐ 36 Gus Mortson	10.00	4.00	1.00
☐ 37 Al Rollins	15.00	6.00	1.50
☐ 38 Sid Smith	15.00	6.00	1.50
☐ 39 Tod Sloan	10.00	4.00	1.00
☐ 40 Ray Timgren	10.00	4.00	1.00
☐ 41 Jim Thomson	10.00	4.00	1.00
☐ 42 Max Bentley	25.00	10.00	2.50
☐ 43 Sid Abel	20.00	8.00	2.00
☐ 44 Gordie Howe	75.00	30.00	7.50
☐ 45 Ted Lindsay	30.00	12.00	3.00
☐ 46 Harry Lumley	30.00	12.00	3.00

☐	47 Jack Gelineau	10.00	4.00	1.00	☐	3 Lanny McDonald DP	8.00	3.25	.80
☐	48 Paul Ronty	10.00	4.00	1.00	☐	4 Kent Nilsson	5.00	2.00	.50
☐	49 Doug Bentley	25.00	10.00	2.50	☐	5 Jim Peplinski	4.00	1.60	.40
☐	50 Roy Conacher	15.00	6.00	1.50	☐	6 Paul Reinhart	4.00	1.60	.40
☐	51 Chuck Rayner	20.00	8.00	2.00					
☐	52 Boston vs. Montreal	20.00	8.00	2.00					

☐ 52 Boston vs. Montreal 20.00 8.00 2.00
(In front of net;
23 of Boston visible)
☐ 53 Detroit vs. New York 40.00 16.00 4.00
(Howe and Ranger on
goal line on ice)
☐ 54 Montreal vs. Toronto 30.00 12.00 3.00
(Richard shooting puck
past Toronto goalie)
☐ 55 New York vs. Montreal 30.00 12.00 3.00
(Richard is on
goalie)
☐ 56 New York vs. Montreal 20.00 8.00 2.00
(Open net; 9 of
Rangers on ice)
☐ 57 Montreal vs. Boston 20.00 8.00 2.00
(Ref and several
players in front of
Boston goal)
☐ 58 Detroit vs. Montreal 20.00 8.00 2.00
(Two Canadiens in
front of Detroit goalie)
☐ 59 Chicago vs. Montreal 20.00 8.00 2.00
(5 Blackhawks and 2
Canadiens on ice in
front of goalie)
☐ 60 New York vs. Montreal 20.00 8.00 2.00
(Richard and 16 of
Montreal in front of
Ranger and Rayner)
☐ 61 Chicago vs. Montreal 25.00 10.00 2.50
(5 Geoffrion
shooting at Chicago
goalie)
☐ 62 Detroit vs. Montreal 30.00 12.00 3.00
(Sawchuk saves
against 8)
☐ 63 Detroit vs. Montreal 20.00 8.00 2.00
(Canadiens score)
☐ 64 Toronto vs. Montreal 20.00 8.00 2.00
(Canadiens score)
☐ 65 Chicago vs. Montreal 20.00 8.00 2.00
(Canadiens score)

1982-83 Flames Dollars

These six cards, measuring approximately 3" by 5" and perforated on each end, were issued with "Hockey Dollars" or what may be better described as silver-colored coins. Each coin (measuring approximately 1 1/4" in diameter) displayed an engraving of the player's face on the obverse and the team logo on the reverse. The card fronts are gray with tan lettering. They have the player's name, number, year, team logo, and a picture of the coin. In a horizontal format, the backs carry biography, career highlights, and career statistics. The cards are numbered on the back in the upper right corner. The prices below refer to the coin-card combination intact.

	MINT	EXC	G-VG
COMPLETE SET (6)	25.00	10.00	2.50
COMMON PLAYER (1-6)	4.00	1.60	.40
☐ 1 Mel Bridgman	4.00	1.60	.40
☐ 2 Don Edwards	4.00	1.60	.40

1985-86 Flames Red Rooster Police

 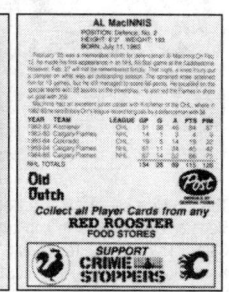

This 30-card set of Calgary Flames was sponsored by Red Rooster Food Stores, Old Dutch Potato Chips, and Post Cereals. The player cards could be collected from any Red Rooster Food Stores. The cards measure approximately 2 3/4" by 3 5/8" and feature on the front a color posed head shot (with rounded corners) of the player, with a facsimile autograph in white ink in the lower right-hand corner of the picture. The player's name, uniform number, the Calgary Flames' logo, and a hockey tip appear below the picture. The back has biographical and statistical information on the top portion, while the bottom has sponsor advertisements and the anti-crime slogan "Support Crime Stoppers." The set includes two different cards of Lanny McDonald and Doug Risebrough. Al MacInnis appears in his Rookie Card year whereas Mike Vernon's appearance predates his Rookie Card by two years.

	MINT	EXC	G-VG
COMPLETE SET (30)	12.00	5.00	1.20
COMMON PLAYER (1-30)	.35	.14	.03
☐ 1 Paul Baxter	.35	.14	.03
☐ 2 Ed Beers	.35	.14	.03
☐ 3 Perry Berezan	.35	.14	.03
☐ 4 Charlie Bourgeois	.35	.14	.03
☐ 5 Steve Bozek	.35	.14	.03
☐ 6 Gino Cavallini	.60	.24	.06
☐ 7 Marc D'Amour	.35	.14	.03
☐ 8 Tim Hunter	.60	.24	.06
☐ 9 Bob Johnson CO	2.00	.80	.20
☐ 10 Steve Konroyd	.35	.14	.03
☐ 11 Richard Kromm	.35	.14	.03
☐ 12 Rejean Lemelin	.60	.24	.06
☐ 13 Hakan Loob	.60	.24	.06
☐ 14 Lanny McDonald	1.50	.60	.15
☐ 15 Lanny McDonald	1.50	.60	.15
☐ 16 Al MacInnis	5.00	2.00	.50
☐ 17 Jamie Macoun	.60	.24	.06
☐ 18 Bob Murdoch CO	.35	.14	.03
☐ 19 Joel Otto	.60	.24	.06
☐ 20 Pierre Page CO	.60	.24	.06
☐ 21 Colin Patterson	.35	.14	.03
☐ 22 Jim Peplinski	.60	.24	.06
☐ 23 Dan Quinn	.35	.14	.03
☐ 24 Paul Reinhart	.60	.24	.06
☐ 25 Doug Risebrough	.35	.14	.03
☐ 26 Doug Risebrough	.35	.14	.03
☐ 27 Neil Sheehy	.35	.14	.03
☐ 28 Gary Suter	1.00	.40	.10
☐ 29 Mike Vernon	3.00	1.20	.30
(No facsimile autograph on card front)			
☐ 30 Carey Wilson	.35	.14	.03

1986-87 Flames Red Rooster Police

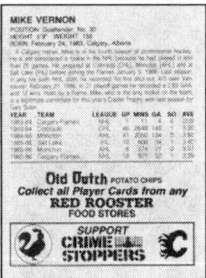

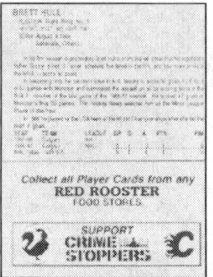

This 30-card set of Calgary Flames was sponsored by Red Rooster Food Stores in conjunction with Old Dutch Potato Chips. The player cards could be collected from any Red Rooster Food Stores. The cards measure approximately 2 3/4" by 3 5/8" and feature a color posed photo (with rounded corners) of the player, with a facsimile autograph in blue ink across the bottom of the picture. The player's name, uniform number, the Calgary Flames' logo, and a hockey tip appear below the picture. The back has biographical and statistical information on the top portion, while the bottom has sponsor advertisements and the anti-crime slogan "Support Crime Stoppers." The set includes two different cards of Lanny McDonald, Joe Mullen, and Paul Reinhart. Gary Roberts' card predates his Rookie Card year by three years.

	MINT	EXC	G-VG
COMPLETE SET (30)	12.00	5.00	1.20
COMMON PLAYER (1-30)	.35	.14	.03
☐ 1 Paul Baxter	.35	.14	.03
☐ 2 Perry Berezan	.35	.14	.03
☐ 3 Steve Bozek	.35	.14	.03
☐ 4 Brian Bradley	1.25	.50	.12
☐ 5 Brian Engblom	.35	.14	.03
☐ 6 Nick Fotiu	.60	.24	.06
☐ 7 Tim Hunter	.60	.24	.06
☐ 8 Bob Johnson CO	1.50	.60	.15
☐ 9 Rejean Lemelin	.60	.24	.06
☐ 10 Hakan Loob	.60	.24	.06
☐ 11 Al MacInnis	2.50	1.00	.25
☐ 12 Jamie Macoun	.60	.24	.06
☐ 13 Lanny McDonald	1.50	.60	.15
☐ 14 Lanny McDonald	1.50	.60	.15
☐ 15 Joe Mullen	1.25	.50	.12
☐ 16 Joe Mullen	1.25	.50	.12
☐ 17 Bob Murdoch CO	.35	.14	.03
☐ 18 Joel Otto	.60	.24	.06
☐ 19 Pierre Page CO	.60	.24	.06
☐ 20 Colin Patterson	.35	.14	.03
☐ 21 Jim Peplinski	.60	.24	.06
☐ 22 Paul Reinhart	.60	.24	.06
☐ 23 Paul Reinhart	.60	.24	.06
☐ 24 Doug Risebrough	.35	.14	.03
☐ 25 Gary Roberts	3.00	1.20	.30
☐ 26 Neil Sheehy	.35	.14	.03
☐ 27 Gary Suter	.75	.30	.07
☐ 28 John Tonelli	.60	.24	.06
☐ 29 Mike Vernon	1.50	.60	.15
☐ 30 Carey Wilson	.35	.14	.03

1987-88 Flames Red Rooster Police

This 30-card set of Calgary Flames was sponsored by Red Rooster Food Stores, and the player cards could be collected from any of these stores. The cards measure 2 11/16" by 3 9/16" and feature on the front a color posed head-and-shoulders shot (with rounded corners) of the

player, with a facsimile autograph in blue ink across the bottom of the picture. The player's name, uniform number, the Calgary Flames' logo, and a hockey tip appear below the picture. The back has biographical and statistical information on the top portion, while the bottom has a sponsor advertisement and the anti-crime slogan "Support Crime Stoppers." The set includes two different cards of Hakan Loob, Lanny McDonald, and Joe Nieuwendyk. The Brett Hull and Joe Nieuwendyk cards are the key cards in the set since they pre-date their O-Pee-Chee and Topps Rookie Cards by one year and are, arguably, their earliest NHL cards.

	MINT	EXC	G-VG
COMPLETE SET (30)	35.00	14.00	3.50
COMMON PLAYER (1-30)	.35	.14	.03
☐ 1 Perry Berezan	.35	.14	.03
☐ 2 Steve Bozek	.35	.14	.03
☐ 3 Mike Bullard	.60	.24	.06
☐ 4 Shane Churla	.75	.30	.07
☐ 5 Terry Crisp CO	.60	.24	.06
☐ 6 Doug Dadswell	.35	.14	.03
☐ 7 Brian Glynn	.35	.14	.03
☐ 8 Brett Hull	20.00	8.00	2.00
☐ 9 Tim Hunter	.60	.24	.06
☐ 10 Hakan Loob	.60	.24	.06
☐ 11 Hakan Loob	.60	.24	.06
☐ 12 Al MacInnis	2.00	.80	.20
☐ 13 Brad McCrimmon	.60	.24	.06
☐ 14 Lanny McDonald	1.25	.50	.12
☐ 15 Lanny McDonald	1.25	.50	.12
☐ 16 Joe Mullen	1.25	.50	.12
☐ 17 Dana Murzyn	.35	.14	.03
☐ 18 Ric Nattress	.35	.14	.03
☐ 19 Joe Nieuwendyk	5.00	2.00	.50
☐ 20 Joe Nieuwendyk	5.00	2.00	.50
☐ 21 Joel Otto	.60	.24	.06
☐ 22 Pierre Page CO	.60	.24	.06
☐ 23 Colin Patterson	.35	.14	.03
☐ 24 Jim Peplinski	.60	.24	.06
☐ 25 Paul Reinhart	.60	.24	.06
☐ 26 Doug Risebrough CO	.35	.14	.03
☐ 27 Gary Roberts	1.50	.60	.15
☐ 28 Gary Suter	.75	.30	.07
☐ 29 John Tonelli	.60	.24	.06
☐ 30 Mike Vernon	1.25	.50	.12

1990-91 Flames IGA/McGavin's

This 30-card set was sponsored by IGA food stores in conjunction with McGavin's, a distributor of bread and other products in Alberta. Protected by a cello pack, one card was inserted in bread loaves distributed by McGavin's to IGA stores in Calgary and Edmonton. Calgary consumers received a Flames' card, while Edmonton consumers received an Oilers' card. Checklist and coaches cards were not inserted in the loaves but were included on five hundred individually numbered and uncut sheets not offered to the general public. The cards measure the standard size (2 1/2" by 3 1/2") and are printed on thin card stock. The fronts have posed color player photos, with a border that shades

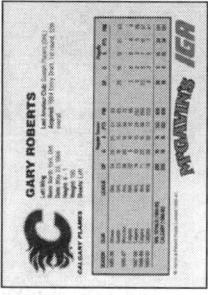

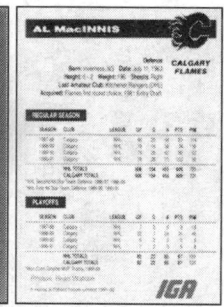

from red to orange and back to red. The player's name is printed in the bottom border, and his uniform number is printed in a circle in the upper left corner of each picture. The horizontally oriented backs feature biographical information, with year-by-year statistics presented in a pink rectangle. Sponsor logos at the bottom round out the back. The cards are unnumbered and checklisted below in alphabetical order.

		MINT	EXC	G-VG
	COMPLETE SET (30)	40.00	16.00	4.00
	COMMON PLAYER (1-30)	.75	.30	.07
☐ 1	Paul Baxter CO SP	3.00	1.20	.30
☐ 2	Guy Charron CO SP	3.00	1.20	.30
☐ 3	Theoren Fleury	3.00	1.20	.30
☐ 4	Doug Gilmour	5.00	2.00	.50
☐ 5	Jiri Hrdina	.75	.30	.07
☐ 6	Mark Hunter	.75	.30	.07
☐ 7	Tim Hunter	.75	.30	.07
☐ 8	Roger Johansson	.75	.30	.07
☐ 9	Al MacInnis	3.00	1.20	.30
☐ 10	Brian MacLellan	.75	.30	.07
☐ 11	Jamie Macoun	1.00	.40	.10
☐ 12	Sergei Makarov	2.00	.80	.20
☐ 13	Sergei Makarov (Calder Trophy Winner) and Al MacInnis (NHL First AS Team, Defence 1989-90)	1.50	.60	.15
☐ 14	Stephane Matteau	1.00	.40	.10
☐ 15	Dana Murzyn	.75	.30	.07
☐ 16	Frantisek Musil	.75	.30	.07
☐ 17	Ric Nattress	.75	.30	.07
☐ 18	Joe Nieuwendyk	3.00	1.20	.30
☐ 19	Joel Otto	1.00	.40	.10
☐ 20	Colin Patterson	.75	.30	.07
☐ 21	Sergei Priakin	.75	.30	.07
☐ 22	Paul Ranheim	1.00	.40	.10
☐ 23	Robert Reichel	2.50	1.00	.25
☐ 24	Doug Risebrough SP CO/GM	3.00	1.20	.30
☐ 25	Gary Roberts	2.00	.80	.20
☐ 26	Gary Suter	1.50	.60	.15
☐ 27	Tim Sweeney	1.00	.40	.10
☐ 28	Mike Vernon	1.50	.60	.15
☐ 29	Rick Wamsley	1.00	.40	.10
☐ 30	Checklist Card SP	3.00	1.20	.30

1991-92 Flames IGA

This 30-card set of Calgary Flames was sponsored by IGA food stores and included manufacturers' discount coupons. One pack of cards was distributed in Calgary and Edmonton IGA stores with any grocery purchase of 10.00 or more. The cards measure the standard size (2 1/2" by 3 1/2") and are printed on thin card stock. The fronts have posed color action photos bordered in red. The player's name is printed vertically in the wider left border, and his uniform number and the team name appear at the bottom of the picture. In black print on a white background, the backs present biography and statistics (regular season and playoff). Packs were kept under the cash drawer, and therefore many of the

cards were creased. Each pack contained three Oilers and two Flames cards. The checklist and coaches cards for both teams were not included in the packs but were available on a very limited basis through an uncut team sheet offer. Also the Osiecki card seemed to be in short supply, either because of short printing or short distribution. The cards are unnumbered and checklisted below in alphabetical order, with the coaches cards listed after the players.

		MINT	EXC	G-VG
	COMPLETE SET (30)	20.00	8.00	2.00
	COMMON PLAYER (1-30)	.40	.16	.04
☐ 1	Theoren Fleury	1.50	.60	.15
☐ 2	Tomas Forslund	1.00	.40	.10
☐ 3	Doug Gilmour	2.50	1.00	.25
☐ 4	Marc Habscheid	.40	.16	.04
☐ 5	Tim Hunter	.40	.16	.04
☐ 6	Jim Kyte	.40	.16	.04
☐ 7	Al MacInnis	1.25	.50	.12
☐ 8	Jamie Macoun	.40	.16	.04
☐ 9	Sergei Makarov	1.00	.40	.10
☐ 10	Stephane Matteau	.60	.24	.06
☐ 11	Frantisek Musil	.40	.16	.04
☐ 12	Ric Nattress	.40	.16	.04
☐ 13	Joe Nieuwendyk	1.50	.60	.15
☐ 14	Mark Osiecki	.60	.24	.06
☐ 15	Joel Otto	.60	.24	.06
☐ 16	Paul Ranheim	.60	.24	.06
☐ 17	Robert Reichel	1.25	.50	.12
☐ 18	Gary Roberts	1.25	.50	.12
☐ 19	Neil Sheehy	.40	.16	.04
☐ 20	Martin Simard	.40	.16	.04
☐ 21	Ronnie Stern	.60	.24	.06
☐ 22	Gary Suter	.75	.30	.07
☐ 23	Tim Sweeney	.40	.16	.04
☐ 24	Mike Vernon	1.00	.40	.10
☐ 25	Rick Wamsley	.60	.24	.06
☐ 26	Carey Wilson	.40	.16	.04
☐ 27	Paul Baxter CO SP	2.50	1.00	.25
☐ 28	Guy Charron CO SP	2.50	1.00	.25
☐ 29	Doug Risebrough CO SP	2.50	1.00	.25
☐ 30	Checklist Card SP	2.50	1.00	.25

1992-93 Flames IGA

Sponsored by IGA food stores, the 30 standard-size (2 1/2" by 3 1/2") cards comprising this Special Edition Collector Series set feature color player action shots on their fronts. Each photo is trimmed with a black line and offset flush with the thin white border on the right, which surrounds the card. On the remaining three sides, the picture is edged with a gray and white netlike pattern. The player's name appears in the upper right and the Flames logo rests in the lower left. The back carries the player's name at the top, with his position, uniform number, biography, and stat table set within a reddish-gray screened background. The Flames logo in the upper right rounds out the card. The cards are numbered on the back.

	MINT	EXC	G-VG
COMPLETE SET (30)	15.00	6.00	1.50
COMMON PLAYER (1-30)	.40	.16	.04

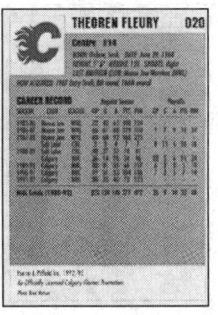

☐ 1	Checklist	1.00	.40	.10
☐ 2	Craig Berube	.40	.16	.04
☐ 3	Gary Leeman	.60	.24	.06
☐ 4	Joel Otto	.60	.24	.06
☐ 5	Robert Reichel	1.00	.40	.10
☐ 6	Gary Roberts	1.25	.50	.12
☐ 7	Greg Smyth	.40	.16	.04
☐ 8	Gary Suter	.75	.30	.07
☐ 9	Jeff Reese	.60	.24	.06
☐ 10	Mike Vernon	1.00	.40	.10
☐ 11	Carey Wilson	.40	.16	.04
☐ 12	Trent Yawney	.40	.16	.04
☐ 13	Michel Petit	.40	.16	.04
☐ 14	Paul Ranheim	.60	.24	.06
☐ 15	Sergei Makarov	1.00	.40	.10
☐ 16	Frantisek Musil	.40	.16	.04
☐ 17	Joe Nieuwendyk	1.50	.60	.15
☐ 18	Alexander Godynyuk	.60	.24	.06
☐ 19	Roger Johansson	.40	.16	.04
☐ 20	Theoren Fleury	1.25	.50	.12
☐ 21	Chris Lindberg	.60	.24	.06
☐ 22	Al MacInnis	1.50	.60	.15
☐ 23	Kevin Dahl	.40	.16	.04
☐ 24	Chris Dahlquist	.40	.16	.04
☐ 25	Ronnie Stern	.60	.24	.06
☐ 26	Dave King CO	.60	.24	.06
☐ 27	Guy Charron CO	.40	.16	.04
☐ 28	Slavomir Lener CO	.40	.16	.04
☐ 29	Jamie Hislop CO	.40	.16	.04
☐ 30	Franchise History	.40	.16	.04

1994 Fleury Hockey Tips

Titled "Theoren Fleury Hockey School Tip of the Week," this 14-card set measures the standard size (2 1/2" by 3 1/2"). The lavender-bordered fronts have color action photos illustrating each hockey tip. The backs carry the "Tip of the Week" in black lettering followed by discussion. The cards are numbered on the front and the back.

		MINT	EXC	G-VG
	COMPLETE SET (14)	5.00	2.00	.50
	COMMON PLAYER (1-14)	.50	.20	.05
☐ 1	Stickhandling	.50	.20	.05
☐ 2	An Explosive Start	.50	.20	.05

☐ 3	Shoot To Score	.50	.20	.05
☐ 4	Passing Accurately	.50	.20	.05
☐ 5	A Good Bodycheck	.50	.20	.05
☐ 6	The Backhand Shot	.50	.20	.05
☐ 7	Receiving A Pass	.50	.20	.05
☐ 8	Stopping	.50	.20	.05
☐ 9	At The Opponent's Net	.50	.20	.05
☐ 10	Protecting The Puck	.50	.20	.05
☐ 11	Playing In The Defensive Zone	.50	.20	.05
☐ 12	Supporting My Defenseman	.50	.20	.05
☐ 13	Winning The Face Off	.50	.20	.05
☐ 14	The One-Timer	.50	.20	.05

1972 Flyers Mighty Milk

These seven panels, which were issued on the sides of half gallon cartons of Mighty Milk, feature members of the Philadelphia Flyers. After cutting, the panels measure approximately 3 5/8" by 7 1/2". All lettering and the portrait itself are in blue. Inside a frame with rounded corners, each panel displays a portrait of the player and a player profile. The words "Philadelphia Hockey Star" and the player's name appear above the frame, while an advertisement for Mighty Milk and another for TV Channel 29 appear immediately below. The backs are blank. The panels are unnumbered and checklisted below in alphabetical order.

		NRMT	VG-E	GOOD
	COMPLETE SET (7)	100.00	40.00	10.00
	COMMON PLAYER (1-7)	12.00	5.00	1.20
☐ 1	Serge Bernier	12.00	5.00	1.20
☐ 2	Bobby Clarke	50.00	20.00	5.00
☐ 3	Gary Dornhoefer	15.00	0.00	1.50
☐ 4	Doug Favell	18.00	7.25	1.80
☐ 5	Jean-Guy Gendron	12.00	5.00	1.20
☐ 6	Bill Lesuk	12.00	5.00	1.20
☐ 7	Ed Van Impe	12.00	5.00	1.20

1983-84 Flyers J.C. Penney

Sponsored by J.C. Penney, this 22-card set measures approximately 4" by 6". The fronts feature color posed action shots of the players on ice. Beneath the picture are the team name, logo, player's name, and the phrase "Compliments of J.C. Penney Stores in the Delaware Valley." The backs are blank. The cards are unnumbered and checklisted below in alphabetical order.

	MINT	EXC	G-VG
COMPLETE SET (22)	25.00	10.00	2.50
COMMON PLAYER (1-22)	1.00	.40	.10
☐ 1 Ray Allison	1.00	.40	.10
☐ 2 Bill Barber	2.50	1.00	.25
☐ 3 Frank Bathe	1.00	.40	.10
☐ 4 Lindsay Carson	1.00	.40	.10
☐ 5 Bobby Clarke	4.00	1.60	.40
☐ 6 Glen Cochrane	1.00	.40	.10
☐ 7 Doug Crossman	1.50	.60	.15
☐ 8 Miroslav Dvorak	1.00	.40	.10
☐ 9 Thomas Eriksson	1.00	.40	.10
☐ 10 Bob Froese	1.50	.60	.15
☐ 11 Randy Holt	1.00	.40	.10
☐ 12 Mark Howe	2.00	.80	.20
☐ 13 Tim Kerr	2.00	.80	.20
☐ 14 Pelle Lindbergh	6.00	2.40	.60
☐ 15 Brad Marsh	1.50	.60	.15
☐ 16 Brad McCrimmon	1.50	.60	.15
☐ 17 Dave Poulin	1.50	.60	.15
☐ 18 Brian Propp	2.00	.80	.20
☐ 19 Ilkka Sinisalo	1.50	.60	.15
☐ 20 Darryl Sittler	4.00	1.60	.40
☐ 21 Rich Sutter	1.50	.60	.15
☐ 22 Ron Sutter	1.50	.60	.15

1986-87 Flyers Postcards

This 29-card set of Philadelphia Flyers features full-bleed, color action and posed photos. The cards measure approximately 4 1/8" by 6" and are in a postcard format. A player's autograph facsimile is printed on the front. A diagonal black stripe cuts across the lower portion of the picture. Within the black stripe appear narrow orange stripes, the Flyers logo, and player information. The horizontal white backs carry career statistics and biography on the left, and the postcard format mailing address space on the right. The cards are unnumbered and checklisted below in alphabetical order.

	MINT	EXC	G-VG
COMPLETE SET (29)	20.00	8.00	2.00
COMMON PLAYER (1-29)	.50	.20	.05
☐ 1 Bill Barber CO	1.00	.40	.10
☐ 2 Dave Brown	.75	.30	.07
☐ 3 Lindsay Carson	.50	.20	.05
☐ 4 Murray Craven	.75	.30	.07
☐ 5 Pat Croce CO	.50	.20	.05
☐ 6 Doug Crossman	.75	.30	.07
☐ 7 Jean-Jacques Daigneault	.75	.30	.07
☐ 8 Pelle Eklund	.75	.30	.07
☐ 9 Ron Hextall	2.50	1.00	.25
☐ 10 Paul Holmgren CO	1.00	.40	.10
☐ 11 Ed Hospodar	.75	.30	.07
☐ 12 Mark Howe	1.50	.60	.15
☐ 13 Mike Keenan CO	1.50	.60	.15

☐ 14 Tim Kerr	1.00	.40	.10
☐ 15 Brad Marsh	.75	.30	.07
☐ 16 Brad McCrimmon	.75	.30	.07
☐ 17 E.J. McGuire CO	.50	.20	.05
☐ 18 Scott Mellanby	.75	.30	.07
☐ 19 Bernie Parent CO	1.25	.50	.12
☐ 20 Dave Poulin	.75	.30	.07
☐ 21 Brian Propp	1.00	.40	.10
☐ 22 Glenn Resch	1.25	.50	.12
☐ 23 Ilkka Sinisalo	.75	.30	.07
☐ 24 Derrick Smith	.50	.20	.05
☐ 25 Daryl Stanley	.50	.20	.05
☐ 26 Ron Sutter	.75	.30	.07
☐ 27 Rick Tocchet	2.50	1.00	.25
☐ 28 Peter Zezel	1.00	.40	.10
☐ 29 Team Photo	1.50	.60	.15

1990-91 Flyers Postcards

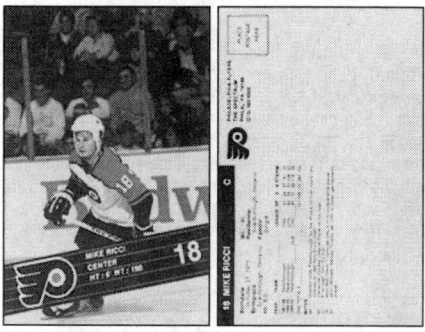

This 26-card set was issued by the Philadelphia Flyers. Each card measures approximately 4 1/8" by 6". The fronts display full-bleed color action photos. A team color-coded (black with thin orange stripes) diagonal stripe cuts across the bottom portion and carries the team logo, biographical information, and jersey number. The horizontal backs are postcard design and, on the left, present biography, statistics, and notes. The cards are unnumbered and checklisted below in alphabetical order.

	MINT	EXC	G-VG
COMPLETE SET (26)	15.00	6.00	1.50
COMMON PLAYER (1-26)	.50	.20	.05
☐ 1 Keith Acton	.75	.30	.07
☐ 2 Murray Baron	.50	.20	.05
☐ 3 Craig Berube	.50	.20	.05
☐ 4 Terry Carkner	.50	.20	.05
☐ 5 Jeff Chychrun	.50	.20	.05
☐ 6 Murray Craven	.75	.30	.07
☐ 7 Pelle Eklund	.75	.30	.07
☐ 8 Ron Hextall	1.00	.40	.10
☐ 9 Tony Horacek	.50	.20	.05
☐ 10 Martin Hostak	.50	.20	.05
☐ 11 Mark Howe	1.00	.40	.10
☐ 12 Kerry Huffman	.50	.20	.05
☐ 13 Tim Kerr	.75	.30	.07
☐ 14 Dale Kushner	.50	.20	.05
☐ 15 Norman Lacombe	.50	.20	.05
☐ 16 Jiri Latal	.50	.20	.05
☐ 17 Scott Mellanby	.75	.30	.07
☐ 18 Gord Murphy	.50	.20	.05
☐ 19 Pete Peeters	.75	.30	.07
☐ 20 Mike Ricci	2.00	.80	.20
☐ 21 Kjell Samuelsson	.75	.30	.07
☐ 22 Derrick Smith	.50	.20	.05
☐ 23 Ron Sutter	.75	.30	.07
☐ 24 Rick Tocchet	1.50	.60	.15
☐ 25 Ken Wregget	1.00	.40	.10
☐ 26 Team Photo	2.50	1.00	.25

1991-92 Flyers J.C. Penney

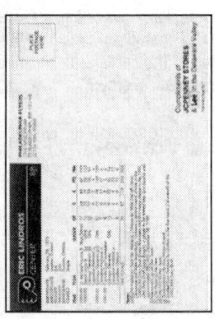

This 26-card set was issued by the Flyers in conjunction with J.C. Penney Stores and Lee. Each card measures approximately 4 1/8" by 6". The fronts display full-bleed color action photos. A team color-coded (black with thin orange stripes) diagonal stripe cuts across the bottom portion and carries the team logo, biographical information, and jersey number. The horizontal backs are postcard design and, on the left, present biography, statistics, and notes. The cards are unnumbered and checklisted below in alphabetical order.

		MINT	EXC	G-VG
COMPLETE SET (26)		15.00	6.00	1.50
COMMON PLAYER (1-26)		.50	.20	.05
☐ 1	Keith Acton	.75	.30	.07
☐ 2	Rod Brind'Amour	1.50	.60	.15
☐ 3	Dave Brown	.75	.30	.07
☐ 4	Terry Carkner	.75	.30	.07
☐ 5	Kimbi Daniels	.50	.20	.05
☐ 6	Kevin Dineen	1.00	.40	.10
☐ 7	Steve Duchesne	.75	.30	.07
☐ 8	Pelle Eklund	.75	.30	.07
☐ 9	Corey Foster	.50	.20	.05
☐ 10	Ron Hextall	1.00	.40	.10
☐ 11	Tony Horacek	.50	.20	.05
☐ 12	Mark Howe	1.00	.40	.10
☐ 13	Kerry Huffman	.50	.20	.05
☐ 14	Brad Jones	.50	.20	.05
☐ 15	Steve Kasper UER	.75	.30	.07
	(Misspelled Kaspar on front)			
☐ 16	Dan Kordic	.50	.20	.05
☐ 17	Jiri Latal	.50	.20	.05
☐ 18	Andrei Lomakin	.75	.30	.07
☐ 19	Gord Murphy	.50	.20	.05
☐ 20	Mark Pederson	.50	.20	.05
☐ 21	Dan Quinn	.50	.20	.05
☐ 22	Mike Ricci	1.50	.60	.15
☐ 23	Kjell Samuelsson	.50	.20	.05
☐ 24	Rick Tocchet	1.50	.60	.15
☐ 25	Ken Wregget	.75	.30	.07
☐ 26	Team Photo	2.50	1.00	.25

1992-93 Flyers J.C. Penney

This 23-card set was sponsored by J.C. Penney Stores and Lee in the Delaware Valley. The cards measure approximately 4 1/8" by 6" and feature color, action player photos with facsimile autographs near the bottom of each picture. A gray border stripe across the bottom carries the team logo, player's name, position, and jersey number. The horizontal backs display biographical information, statistics, and career notes within a postcard-type format. The cards are unnumbered and checklisted below in alphabetical order.

		MINT	EXC	G-VG
COMPLETE SET (23)		15.00	6.00	1.50
COMMON PLAYER (1-23)		.50	.20	.05
☐ 1	Keith Acton	.50	.20	.05
☐ 2	Stephane Beauregard	.50	.20	.05
☐ 3	Brian Benning	.50	.20	.05
☐ 4	Rod Brind'Amour	1.00	.40	.10
☐ 5	Claude Boivin	.50	.20	.05
☐ 6	Dave Brown	.75	.30	.07
☐ 7	Terry Carkner	.50	.20	.05
☐ 8	Shawn Cronin	.50	.20	.05
☐ 9	Kevin Dineen	.75	.30	.07
☐ 10	Pelle Eklund	.75	.30	.07
☐ 11	Doug Evans	.50	.20	.05
☐ 12	Brent Fedyk	.75	.30	.07
☐ 13	Garry Galley	.75	.30	.07
☐ 14	Gord Hynes	.50	.20	.05
☐ 15	Eric Lindros	7.50	3.00	.75
☐ 16	Andrei Lomakin	.75	.30	.07
☐ 17	Ryan McGill	.50	.20	.05
☐ 18	Ric Nattress	.50	.20	.05
☐ 19	Greg Paslawski	.50	.20	.05
☐ 20	Mark Recchi	2.50	1.00	.25
☐ 21	Dominic Roussel	1.00	.40	.10
☐ 22	Dimitri Yushkevich	.75	.30	.07
☐ 23	Team Photo	2.00	.80	.20

1971-72 Frito Lay

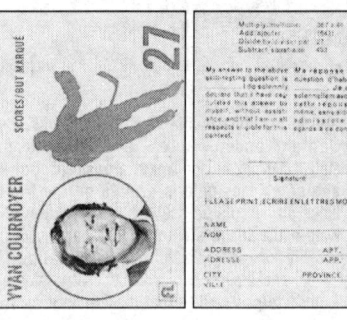

This ten-card set features members of the Toronto Maple Leafs and Montreal Canadiens. Since the cards are unnumbered, they have been listed below in alphabetical order within team, Montreal (1-5) and Toronto (6-10). The cards are paper thin, each measuring approximately 1 1/2" by 2".

		NRMT	VG-E	GOOD
COMPLETE SET (10)		60.00	24.00	6.00
COMMON PLAYER (1-10)		3.00	1.20	.30
☐ 1	Yvan Cournoyer	6.00	2.40	.60
☐ 2	Ken Dryden	25.00	10.00	2.50
☐ 3	Frank Mahovlich	7.50	3.00	.75
☐ 4	Henri Richard	6.00	2.40	.60
☐ 5	J.C. Tremblay	3.00	1.20	.30

		MINT	EXC	G-VG
☐ 6	Bobby Baun	3.00	1.20	.30
☐ 7	Ron Ellis	3.00	1.20	.30
☐ 8	Paul Henderson	4.00	1.60	.40
☐ 9	Jacques Plante	9.00	3.75	.90
☐ 10	Norm Ullman	6.00	2.40	.60

1988-89 Frito-Lay Stickers

19 Steve Yzerman

The 1988-89 Frito-Lay Hockey Stickers set includes 42 small (1 3/8" by 1 3/4") stickers. The fronts are dominated by color photos, but also have each player's name and uniform number. The stickers were distributed in sealed plastic, and packaged one per special Frito-Lay snack bag. Distribution was via 35 million bags of Ruffles, O'Gradys, Dulac, Lays, Doritos, Fritos, Tostitos, Cheetos, and Chester Popcorn -- each containing one of the 42 players in the set. Since they are actually stickers, there is very little information on the backing. The checklist below also gives the player's uniform number as listed on each card. A poster was also available from the company by sending in 2.00 and one UPC symbol from any Frito-Lay product.

		MINT	EXC	G-VG
COMPLETE SET (42)		25.00	10.00	2.50
COMMON PLAYER (1-42)		.35	.14	.03
☐ 1	Mario Lemieux 66	4.00	1.60	.40
☐ 2	Bryan Trottier 19	.75	.30	.07
☐ 3	Steve Yzerman 19	1.50	.60	.15
☐ 4	Bernie Federko 24	.35	.14	.03
☐ 5	Brian Bellows 23	.35	.14	.03
☐ 6	Denis Savard 18	.50	.20	.05
☐ 7	Neal Broten 7	.35	.14	.03
☐ 8	Doug Gilmour 9	2.00	.80	.20
☐ 9	Dale Hawerchuk 10	.50	.20	.05
☐ 10	Luc Robitaille 20	1.25	.50	.12
☐ 11	Ed Olczyk 16	.35	.14	.03
☐ 12	Andrew McBain 20	.35	.14	.03
☐ 13	Mike Gartner 11	.75	.30	.07
☐ 14	Pat LaFontaine 16	1.50	.60	.15
☐ 15	Scott Stevens 3	.50	.20	.05
☐ 16	Ray Bourque 77	1.25	.50	.12
☐ 17	Cam Neely 8	1.25	.50	.12
☐ 18	Mike Foligno 17	.35	.14	.03
☐ 19	Tom Barrasso 30	.50	.20	.05
☐ 20	Ron Francis 10	.50	.20	.05
☐ 21	Peter Stastny 26	.50	.20	.05
☐ 22	Michel Goulet 16	.50	.20	.05
☐ 23	Bernie Nicholls 9	.50	.20	.05
☐ 24	Paul Coffey 77	1.00	.40	.10
☐ 25	Mats Naslund 26	.35	.14	.03
☐ 26	Glenn Anderson 9	.50	.20	.05
☐ 27	Dave Poulin 20	.35	.14	.03
☐ 28	Kevin Dineen 11	.35	.14	.03
☐ 29	Wendel Clark 17	.75	.30	.07
☐ 30	James Patrick 3	.35	.14	.03
☐ 31	Al MacInnis 2	.75	.30	.07
☐ 32	Troy Murray 19	.35	.14	.03
☐ 33	Kirk Muller 9	.75	.30	.07
☐ 34	Marcel Dionne 16	.75	.30	.07
☐ 35	Mark Messier 11	1.25	.50	.12
☐ 36	Joe Nieuwendyk 25	1.25	.50	.12
☐ 37	Ron Hextall 27	.50	.20	.05
☐ 38	Sean Burke 1	.35	.14	.03
☐ 39	Barry Pederson 7	.35	.14	.03
☐ 40	Stephane Richer 44	.50	.20	.05

		MINT	EXC	G-VG
☐ 41	Bob Probert 24	1.00	.40	.10
☐ 42	Tony Tanti 9	.35	.14	.03
☐ xx	Set Poster	3.00	1.20	.30

1991-92 Future Trends Canada '72 Promos

This standard-size (2 1/2" by 3 1/2") three-card set was issued to promote the release of Future Trends' Team Canada '72 set. To commemorate Team Canada of 1972, 7200 of each promotional card were offered for sale at Canada's Hudson Bay Stores. The fronts feature full-bleed black-and-white action shots from a game between Team Canada and the Soviet team. The card title appears in white lettering within a red stripe across the bottom of the picture. The '72 Hockey Canada logo appears in the lower right. Except for their horizontal orientation, the backs are similar to the fronts, with full-bleed black-and-white photos, white lettering within a red stripe at the bottom, and logo in the lower right. The cards are unnumbered and checklisted below in alphabetical order by title. These promos were issued in English and French versions.

		MINT	EXC	G-VG
COMPLETE SET (3)		18.00	7.25	1.80
COMMON PLAYER (1-3)		6.00	2.40	.60
☐ 1	The Goal / The Scoreboard	7.50	3.00	.75
☐ 2	The Leader / Phil Esposito	9.00	3.75	.90
☐ 3	The Legend / The Kid	6.00	2.40	.60

1991-92 Future Trends Canada '72

Future Trends Experience Ltd. produced this 101-card set to celebrate the 20th anniversary of the 1972 Summit Series between the Soviets and the Canadians. The cards were available initially only at the Bay and were sold in ten-card foil packs with no factory sets. The 70 players of the Canadian and Russian teams are represented, and 30 additional special cards capture unforgettable moments from the series. Between one and two special cards, signed in gold paint pen by living Canadian players, were randomly inserted into each foil case. Only one non-Canadian, Vladislav Tretiak, signed cards. Supposedly each of the signers signed only 750 cards for insertion and distribution within the packs. The standard size (2 1/2" by 3 1/2") cards feature on the fronts borderless black-and-white, action or posed pictures. A white, red, and gold stripe cuts across the bottom of the card face and intersects the '72 Hockey Canada logo at the lower right corner. The backs carry

additional photos, biographical information, series statistics, sportswriters' editorial comments, and/or player quotes. Card number 40 features Phil Esposito's September 8, 1972, address to the nation. The card number appears in a blue oblong design within the bottom red stripe on both sides. The '72 Hockey Canada logo also appears in the lower right corner of the back. The set was issued in both an English and a French version. The production quantities were reportedly 9,000 English and 1,000 French 12-box cases. Also released were 1972 uncut sheet sets.

	MINT	EXC	G-VG
COMPLETE SET (101)	9.00	3.75	.90
COMMON CARD (1-101)	.10	.04	.01

		MINT	EXC	G-VG
☐ 1	In The Beginning	.20	.08	.02
☐ 2	The Backyard Rink	.10	.04	.01
☐ 3	It Didn't Take Long	.10	.04	.01
☐ 4	The Patriarch	.20	.08	.02
	Anatoli Tarasov			
☐ 5	More Hours a Day	.75	.30	.07
	Vladislav Tretiak			
☐ 6	Coming Out Party	.20	.08	.02
☐ 7	Never In Doubt	.10	.04	.01
☐ 8	Team Canada	.30	.12	.03
☐ 9	Pat Stapleton	.10	.04	.01
☐ 10	Vsevolod Bobrov	.10	.04	.01
☐ 11	Vladislav Tretiak	.75	.30	.07
☐ 12	Faceoff	.10	.04	.01
	Game 1, Montreal (9/2/72)			
☐ 13	30 Seconds	.10	.04	.01
	Game 1, Montreal (9/2/72)			
☐ 14	Yevgeny Zimin	.10	.04	.01
☐ 15	Bill White	.10	.04	.01
☐ 16	7-3	.10	.04	.01
	Game 1 Statistics			
☐ 17	Don Awrey	.10	.04	.01
☐ 18	Mickey Redmond	.20	.08	.02
☐ 19	Alexander Gusev	.20	.08	.02
☐ 20	Alexander Maltsev	.30	.12	.03
☐ 21	Rod Seiling	.10	.04	.01
☐ 22	Dale Tallon	.10	.04	.01
☐ 23	Coming Back	.10	.04	.01
	Game 2, Toronto (9/4/72)			
☐ 24	Unforgettable	.10	.04	.01
	Game 2 Statistics			
☐ 25	Wayne Cashman	.20	.08	.02
☐ 26	Frank Mahovlich	.30	.12	.03
☐ 27	Peter Mahovlich	.10	.04	.01
☐ 28	Vyacheslav Solodukhin	.20	.08	.02
	Alexander Sidelnikov			
☐ 29	Yuri Shatalov	.20	.08	.02
☐ 30	Brothers	.20	.08	.02
	Frank Mahovlich			
	Peter Mahovlich			
☐ 31	The Goalies	.30	.12	.03
☐ 32	Alexander Bodunov	.10	.04	.01
☐ 33	All Even	.10	.04	.01
	Game 3 Statistics			
☐ 34	Yuri Blinov	.10	.04	.01
☐ 35	Jocelyn Guevremont	.10	.04	.01
☐ 36	Vic Hadfield	.10	.04	.01
☐ 37	Yuri Lebedev	.10	.04	.01
☐ 38	Yevgeny Poladiev	.20	.08	.02
	Vyacheslav Starshinov			
☐ 39	Disaster	.10	.04	.01
	Game 4 Statistics			
☐ 40	Address to The Nation	.30	.12	.03
	Phil Esposito			

		MINT	EXC	G-VG
☐ 41	Victor Kuzkin	.10	.04	.01
☐ 42	Vladimir Lutchenko	.30	.12	.03
☐ 43	Boris Mikhailov	.40	.16	.04
☐ 44	Grace Under Pressure	.10	.04	.01
	Game 5, Moscow (9/22/72)			
☐ 45	Afraid to Lose	.10	.04	.01
☐ 46	Ready To Win	.10	.04	.01
	Game 5 Statistics			
☐ 47	Vladimir Vikulov	.10	.04	.01
☐ 48	Red Berenson	.10	.04	.01
☐ 49	Richard Martin	.10	.04	.01
☐ 50	Alexander Martynyuk	.10	.04	.01
☐ 51	Gilbert Perreault	.30	.12	.03
☐ 52	Vladimir Petrov	.50	.20	.05
☐ 53	Serge Savard	.20	.08	.02
☐ 54	Vladimir Shadrin	.10	.04	.01
☐ 55	DA DA KA-NA-DA	.10	.04	.01
	Game 6, Moscow (9/24/72)			
☐ 56	One Step Back	.10	.04	.01
	Game 6 Statistics			
☐ 57	Bobby Clarke	.40	.16	.04
☐ 58	Valeri Kharlamov	1.00	.40	.10
☐ 59	Alexander Volchkov	.20	.08	.02
☐ 60	Standing Guard	.20	.08	.02
☐ 61	Stan Mikita	.40	.16	.04
☐ 62	One More To Go	.10	.04	.01
	Game 7 Statistics			
	Moscow (9/26/72)			
☐ 63	The Winner	.10	.04	.01
☐ 64	The Fans Go Wild	.10	.04	.01
☐ 65	Alexander Ragulin	.20	.08	.02
☐ 66	Jean Ratelle	.20	.08	.02
☐ 67	Gennady Tsygankov	.20	.08	.02
☐ 68	Valeri Vasiliev	.40	.16	.04
☐ 69	International Dialogue	.10	.04	.01
☐ 70	Series Stars	.40	.16	.04
	Phil Esposito			
	Alexander Yakushev			
☐ 71	Series Stars	.40	.16	.04
	Paul Henderson			
	Vladislav Tretiak			
☐ 72	No Solitudes	.10	.04	.01
	Game 8, Moscow (9/28/72)			
	The Telegrams			
☐ 73	2-2	.10	.04	.01
	Game 8, Moscow (9/28/72)			
☐ 74	Rod Gilbert	.20	.08	.02
☐ 75	Yevgeny Mishokov	.20	.08	.02
☐ 76	Ron Ellis	.10	.04	.01
☐ 77	5-4	.10	.04	.01
☐ 78	Different Games	.10	.04	.01
	Game 8, Moscow (9/28/72)			
	Interlude			
☐ 79	Bill Goldsworthy	.10	.04	.01
☐ 80	The Huddle	.10	.04	.01
☐ 81	The Moment	.30	.12	.03
☐ 82	Yvan Cournoyer	.30	.12	.03
☐ 83	Yuri Liapkin	.10	.04	.01
☐ 84	Phil Esposito	.40	.16	.04
☐ 85	Ken Dryden	.50	.20	.05
☐ 86	Peace	.10	.04	.01
	Game 8 Statistics			
☐ 87	Gary Bergman	.10	.04	.01
☐ 88	Brian Glennie	.10	.04	.01
☐ 89	Dennis Hull	.10	.04	.01
☐ 90	Vyacheslav Anisin	.10	.04	.01
☐ 91	Marcel Dionne	.30	.12	.03
☐ 92	Guy Lapointe	.20	.08	.02
☐ 93	Ed Johnston	.10	.04	.01
☐ 94	Harry Sinden GM	.10	.04	.01
☐ 95	Brad Park	.30	.12	.03
☐ 96	Tony Esposito	.30	.12	.03
☐ 97	Alexander Yakushev	.40	.16	.04
☐ 98	Paul Henderson	.30	.12	.03
☐ 99	J.P. Parise	.10	.04	.01
☐ 100	V. Kharlamov	1.00	.40	.10
	1948-1981			
	(Alexander Kharlamov			
	featured on back)			
☐ 101	Checklist	.20	.08	.02

1992 Future Trends Promo Sheet

Produced by The Future Trends Experience Ltd., this limited edition sample sheet commemorates the 1976 U.S. Olympic Team. The front of this 11" by 8 1/2" sheet features a full-bleed ghosted team photo as the background for six Canada Cup cards. The cards are placed in two rows diagonally

across the sheet. Red and gold stripes form a border surrounding the cards and intersecting a white panel on the left side of the sheet. The panel has a thin red, gold, and blue border and contains an American flag icon, the Team USA emblem, text about the team, and a gold limited edition stamp with the production run total (10,000). The back is blank. The cards are unnumbered and checklisted below as they appear from left to right starting with the first row.

	MINT	EXC	G-VG
COMPLETE SET (1)	5.00	2.00	.50
COMMON SHEET	5.00	2.00	.50
☐ 1 Team USA Sheet	5.00	2.00	.50

Anticipation
Vladislav Tretiak
Gary Sargent
Defending the Crease
Maltsev vs. Milbury
Mike Curran

1992 Future Trends '76 Canada Cup

This 100-card, standard-size (2 1/2" by 3 1/2") set was produced by The Future Trends Experience Ltd. and licensed by Hockey Canada. Commemorating the 1976 Canada Cup, the card numbering picks up where the '72 Team Canada set left off by tracing the growth of international hockey. According to the company the production run was 50,000 numbered display boxes. Randomly inserted in the packs were 3,750 gold-foil stamped signature cards; five players (Bobby Orr, Bobby Hull, Rogatien Vachon, Darryl Sittler, and Bobby Clarke) signed 7,500 cards each. The cards feature vertical and horizontal color action and posed player and team photos. Some shots are of game action with several players pictured. The bottom of each is accented by red and gold border stripes with a red Canada Cup logo in the right corner. Most cards are bordered in white, but some are bordered on the top by the national flags of the various

teams in the set. The horizontal backs carry the same flag pattern ghosted behind information about the pictured player or team. A color photo of the players or player is displayed to the right of the copy. Red and gold border stripes similar to the front appear below. Topical subsets featured are '72 Retrospective (102-106), 1974 Russian team vs. WHA (107-110), a 6-card training camp subset (111-116), MVPs (184-190), and the first ever Canada Cup All-Star team (195-200). The cards are numbered on the back.

	MINT	EXC	G-VG
COMPLETE SET (100)	10.00	4.00	1.00
COMMON PLAYER (102-201)	.10	.04	.01
☐ 102 Phil Esposito Sergeant Pepper Retrospective	.40	.16	.04
☐ 103 Vladislav Tretiak Soviet Ambassador Retrospective	.50	.20	.05
☐ 104 Bobby Orr Impossible Retrospective	1.00	.40	.10
☐ 105 Paul Henderson The Goal Retrospective	.20	.08	.02
☐ 106 Alexander Yakushev If -- Retrospective	.20	.08	.02
☐ 107 Bobby Hull The Golden Jet Summit Series	.50	.20	.05
☐ 108 Valeri Kharlamov Soviet Superstar Summit Series	.50	.20	.05
☐ 109 Gerry Cheevers Vladislav Tretiak Great Goalies Summit Series	.30	.12	.03
☐ 110 Bobby Hull Vladislav Tretiak What If Series Summit Series	.50	.20	.05
☐ 111 Soviet on-ice workout A Soviet Surprise Canada Cup	.20	.08	.02
☐ 112 Czech on-ice workout World Champs Canada Cup	.10	.04	.01
☐ 113 Finn on-ice workout Tournament Underdogs Canada Cup	.10	.04	.01
☐ 114 Swedes take the ice Sweden's Best Ever Canada Cup	.10	.04	.01
☐ 115 USA on-ice workout Team USA Trains Canada Cup	.20	.08	.02
☐ 116 Darryl Sittler Canada Cup Camp Canada Cup	.30	.12	.03
☐ 117 Serge Savard Canada Cup	.20	.08	.02
☐ 118 Team Finland Canada Cup	.10	.04	.01
☐ 119 Team Sweden Canada Cup	.10	.04	.01
☐ 120 Team Czechoslavakia Canada Cup	.10	.04	.01
☐ 121 Soviets Canada Cup	.20	.08	.02
☐ 122 Team USA Canada Cup	.20	.08	.02
☐ 123 Team Canada Canada Cup	.20	.08	.02
☐ 124 The Opening Barrage Canada Cup	.10	.04	.01
☐ 125 Richard Martin Canada Cup	.10	.04	.01
☐ 126 Bobby Orr Canada Cup	.50	.20	.05
☐ 127 Sweden vs. USA Power Play Canada Cup	.10	.04	.01
☐ 128 Ivan Hlinka Canada Cup	.10	.04	.01
☐ 129 CSSR 5 - CCCP 3 Canada Cup	.10	.04	.01
☐ 130 Helmut Balderis Canada Cup	.20	.08	.02

☐ 131 Peter Stastny...................... .20 .08 .02
Canada Cup
☐ 132 Valeri Vasiliev...................... .20 .08 .02
Canada Cup
☐ 133 Out of Contention............... .10 .04 .01
Canada Cup
☐ 134 Standing Alone................... .10 .04 .01
Canada Cup
☐ 135 The Miracle On Ice.............. .10 .04 .01
Almost
Canada Cup
☐ 136 Josef Augusta .... .10 .04 .01
Canada Cup
☐ 137 A Soviet Rout...................... .10 .04 .01
Canada Cup
☐ 138 Vicktor Zhluktov.................. .20 .08 .02
Canada Cup
☐ 139 Bobby Hull .... .40 .16 .04
Phil Esposito
Marcel Dionne
Hull's a Hit
Canada Cup
☐ 140 Bob Gainey.......................... .20 .08 .02
Canada Cup
☐ 141 Anders Hedberg .... .20 .08 .02
Canada Cup
☐ 142 Bobby Hull .... .50 .20 .05
Canada Cup
☐ 143 Ulf Nilsson .... .20 .08 .02
Canada Cup
☐ 144 Sergei Kapustin .... .20 .08 .02
Canada Cup
☐ 145 Borje Salming .... .20 .08 .02
Canada Cup
☐ 146 Well Enough To Win .... .10 .04 .01
Canada Cup
☐ 147 Biggest Upset...................... .10 .04 .01
Canada Cup
☐ 148 Matti Hagman .... .10 .04 .01
Canada Cup
☐ 149 Unbeatable.......................... .10 .04 .01
Canada Cup
☐ 150 Boris Alexandrov.................. .20 .08 .02
Canada Cup
☐ 151 A Goal Tending Duel .... .10 .04 .01
Canada Cup
☐ 152 Vladimir Dzurilla.................. .10 .04 .01
Canada Cup
☐ 153 Phil Esposito .... .40 .16 .04
Canada Cup
☐ 154 Rogatien Vachon................. .20 .08 .02
Canada Cup
☐ 155 Milan Novy .... .10 .04 .01
Canada Cup
☐ 156 Vladimir Martinec................ .20 .08 .02
Canada Cup
☐ 157 Good For Hockey .... .10 .04 .01
Canada Cup
☐ 158 Bill Nyrop .... .10 .04 .01
Canada Cup
☐ 159 Pride .... .10 .04 .01
Canada Cup
☐ 160 Another Summit................... .10 .04 .01
Canada Cup
☐ 161 Alexander Maltsev............... .20 .08 .02
Canada Cup
☐ 162 Gilbert Perreault.................. .30 .12 .03
Canada Cup
☐ 163 Vladislav Tretiak.................. .50 .20 .05
Canada Cup
☐ 164 Vladimir Vikulov.................. .20 .08 .02
Canada Cup
☐ 165 Canada Cup Final .... .10 .04 .01
Game 1
☐ 166 Not There Yet .... .10 .04 .01
Canada Cup
☐ 167 Fast and Furious................. .10 .04 .01
Canada Cup
☐ 168 4 - 3 .... .10 .04 .01
Canada Cup
4 - 4 (on back)
☐ 169 Bill Barber .... .20 .08 .02
Canada Cup
☐ 170 The Grapevine..................... .10 .04 .01
Canada Cup
☐ 171 Guy Lapointe....................... .20 .08 .02
Canada Cup
☐ 172 Reggie Leach .... .10 .04 .01
Canada Cup
☐ 173 Sittler's Goal .... .30 .12 .03
Canada Cup
☐ 174 Lanny McDonald .... .30 .12 .03
Canada Cup

☐ 175 Darryl Sittler....................... .30 .12 .03
Canada Cup
☐ 176 The Canada Cup.................. .20 .08 .02
Canada Cup
☐ 177 Bobby Clarke...................... .30 .12 .03
Canada Cup
☐ 178 Last Time for No. 9 .... .30 .12 .03
Canada Cup
☐ 179 Marcel Dionne..................... .30 .12 .03
Canada Cup
☐ 180 Peter Mahovlich .... .10 .04 .01
Canada Cup
☐ 181 Denis Potvin........................ .30 .12 .03
Canada Cup
☐ 182 Larry Robinson .... .30 .12 .03
Canada Cup
☐ 183 Steve Shutt .... .20 .08 .02
Canada Cup
☐ 184 Bobby Orr .... .50 .20 .05
Tournament MVP
Canada Cup
☐ 185 Rogatien Vachon................. .20 .08 .02
MVP -- Canada Cup
Canada Cup
☐ 186 Milan Novy .... .20 .08 .02
MVP -- CSSR
Canada Cup
☐ 187 Matti Hagman .... .10 .04 .01
MVP -- Finland
Canada Cup
☐ 188 Borje Salming .... .20 .08 .02
MVP -- Sweden
Canada Cup
☐ 189 Robbie Ftorek...................... .10 .04 .01
MVP -- USA
Canada Cup
☐ 190 Alexander Maltsev............... .30 .12 .03
MVP -- USSR
Canada Cup
☐ 191 Canada Final Series............. .10 .04 .01
Totals
Canada Cup
☐ 192 Canada Series Totals........... .10 .04 .01
Canada Cup
☐ 193 CSSR Final Series .... .10 .04 .01
Totals
Canada Cup
☐ 194 CSSR Series Totals .... .10 .04 .01
Canada Cup
☐ 195 Rogatien Vachon AS .... .20 .08 .02
Canada Cup
☐ 196 Bobby Orr AS .... .50 .20 .05
Canada Cup
☐ 197 Borje Salming AS .... .20 .08 .02
Canada Cup
☐ 198 Milan Novy AS .... .10 .04 .01
Canada Cup
☐ 199 Darryl Sittler AS .... .20 .08 .02
Canada Cup
☐ 200 Alexander Maltsev AS .... .30 .12 .03
Canada Cup
☐ 201 Canada Cup Checklist.......... .20 .08 .02

1991-92 Gillette

This 48-card set, sponsored by Gillette and measuring the standard size (2 1/2" by 3 1/2"), features players in the four divisions of the NHL: Smythe (1-10), Norris (11-20), Adams (21-30), and Patrick (31-40). Each ten-card pack came with a trivia card and a checklist card. To receive one ten-card pack, collectors were required to send to Gillette of Canada one UPC symbol from any Canadian Gillette product, the dated receipt with purchase price circled, and 2.00 for shipping and handling. The entire set could be obtained by sending in three UPC symbols plus 5.00. Reportedly just 30,000 sets were produced, and the offer expired on August 28, 1992. On a black card face, the fronts carry a full-color action photo enclosed by a gold border. The title "Gillette Series" appears in gold lettering at the top, while the player's name appears at the bottom between the 75th NHL Anniversary logo and the team logo. Some of the cards have the words "Rookie Card" in the bottom gold border (numbers 3, 10, 20, 30, 40). In a horizontal format, the backs have biography and statistics (1987-91) in English and French, as well as a color head shot. The player cards are numbered on the back. Although the backs of the four unnumbered checklist cards are identical (each one lists all 40 cards), a different division name appears on the front of each checklist card: Smythe, Norris, Adams, and Patrick. The fronts of each of the four unnumbered trivia card are identical, while their backs features two different questions and answers.

		MINT	EXC	G-VG
	COMPLETE SET (48)	25.00	10.00	2.50
	COMMON PLAYER (1-48)	.35	.14	.03
☐ 1	Luc Robitaille	.75	.30	.07
☐ 2	Esa Tikkanen	.35	.14	.03
☐ 3	Pat Falloon	.75	.30	.07
☐ 4	Theoren Fleury	.50	.20	.05
☐ 5	Trevor Linden	1.00	.40	.10
☐ 6	Rob Blake	.75	.30	.07
☐ 7	Al MacInnis	.75	.30	.07
☐ 8	Bob Essensa	.35	.14	.03
☐ 9	Bill Ranford	.50	.20	.05
☐ 10	Pavel Bure	4.00	1.60	.40
☐ 11	Wendel Clark	.75	.30	.07
☐ 12	Sergei Fedorov	1.75	.70	.17
☐ 13	Jeremy Roenick	1.50	.60	.15
☐ 14	Brett Hull	1.50	.60	.15
☐ 15	Mike Modano	1.00	.40	.10
☐ 16	Chris Chelios	.75	.30	.07
☐ 17	Dave Ellett	.35	.14	.03
☐ 18	Ed Belfour	1.00	.40	.10
☐ 19	Grant Fuhr	.50	.20	.05
☐ 20	Martin Lapointe	.35	.14	.03
☐ 21	Kirk Muller	.50	.20	.05
☐ 22	Joe Sakic	.75	.30	.07
☐ 23	Pat LaFontaine	1.00	.40	.10
☐ 24	Pat Verbeek	.35	.14	.03
☐ 25	Owen Nolan	.75	.30	.07
☐ 26	Ray Bourque	.75	.30	.07
☐ 27	Eric Desjardins	.35	.14	.03
☐ 28	Patrick Roy	2.00	.80	.20
☐ 29	Andy Moog	.35	.14	.03
☐ 30	Valeri Kamensky	.50	.20	.05
☐ 31	Mark Messier	1.00	.40	.10
☐ 32	Mike Ricci	.75	.30	.07
☐ 33	Mario Lemieux	2.50	1.00	.25
☐ 34	Jaromir Jagr	1.50	.60	.15
☐ 35	Pierre Turgeon	1.00	.40	.10
☐ 36	Kevin Hatcher	.35	.14	.03
☐ 37	Paul Coffey	.75	.30	.07
☐ 38	Chris Terreri	.35	.14	.03
☐ 39	Mike Richter	.75	.30	.07
☐ 40	Kevin Todd	.35	.14	.03
☐ 41	Checklist 1-40 Smythe Division (Unnumbered)	.35	.14	.03
☐ 42	Gillette Series Trivia Smythe Division (Unnumbered)	.35	.14	.03
☐ 43	Checklist 1-40 Norris Division (Unnumbered)	.35	.14	.03
☐ 44	Gillette Series Trivia Norris Division (Unnumbered)	.35	.14	.03
☐ 45	Checklist 1-40 Adams Division (Unnumbered)	.35	.14	.03
☐ 46	Gillette Series Trivia Adams Division (Unnumbered)	.35	.14	.03
☐ 47	Checklist 1-40 Patrick Division (Unnumbered)	.35	.14	.03
☐ 48	Gillette Series Trivia Patrick Division (Unnumbered)	.35	.14	.03

1983 Hall of Fame Postcards

These postcard-sized (approximately 4" by 6") cards were distributed by complete sub-series. The set is complete at 15 series totalling 240 members of the Hockey Hall of Fame. Cards are listed alphabetically within each sub-series in the checklist below. The cards in this imperial postcard-sized set feature full-color art work by Carlton McDiarmid. The set was produced by the Hockey Hall of Fame, Carleton McDiarmid, and Cartophilium. The postcard backs contain the player's name and the year he was elected to the Hockey Hall of Fame. Career milestones or significant accomplishments of the player are listed in both French and English.

		MINT	EXC	G-VG
	COMPLETE SET (240)	225.00	100.00	20.00
	COMMON PLAYER	1.00	.40	.10
☐ A1	Sid Abel	1.50	.60	.15
☐ A2	Punch Broadbent	1.00	.40	.10
☐ A3	Clarence Campbell	1.25	.50	.12
☐ A4	Neil Colville	1.00	.40	.10
☐ A5	Charlie Conacher	2.50	1.00	.25
☐ A6	Mervyn(Red) Dutton	1.00	.40	.10
☐ A7	Foster Hewitt	1.50	.60	.15
☐ A8	Fred Hume	1.00	.40	.10
☐ A9	Mickey Ion	1.00	.40	.10
☐ A10	Ernest(Moose) Johnson	1.00	.40	.10
☐ A11	Bill Mosienko	1.00	.40	.10
☐ A12	Maurice Richard	6.00	2.40	.60
☐ A13	Barney Stanley	1.00	.40	.10
☐ A14	Lord Stanley	1.25	.50	.12
☐ A15	Cyclone Taylor	1.50	.60	.15
☐ A16	Tiny Thompson	1.00	.40	.10
☐ B1	Dan Bain	1.00	.40	.10
☐ B2	Hobey Baker	1.25	.50	.12
☐ B3	Frank Calder	1.25	.50	.12
☐ B4	Frank Foyston	1.00	.40	.10
☐ B5	James Hendy	1.00	.40	.10
☐ B6	Gordie Howe	7.50	3.00	.75
☐ B7	Harry Lumley	1.25	.50	.12
☐ B8	Reg Noble	1.00	.40	.10
☐ B9	Frank Patrick	1.25	.50	.12
☐ B10	Harvey Pulford	1.00	.40	.10
☐ B11	Ken Reardon	1.25	.50	.12
☐ B12	Bullet Joe Simpson	1.00	.40	.10
☐ B13	Conn Smythe	1.50	.60	.15
☐ B14	Red Storey	1.00	.40	.10
☐ B15	Lloyd Turner	1.00	.40	.10
☐ B16	Georges Vezina	4.00	1.60	.40
☐ C1	Jean Beliveau	4.00	1.60	.40
☐ C2	Max Bentley	1.25	.50	.12
☐ C3	King Clancy	2.50	1.00	.25
☐ C4	Babe Dye	1.00	.40	.10
☐ C5	Ebbie Goodfellow	1.00	.40	.10

☐	C6	Charles Hay	1.00	.40	.10
☐	C7	Percy Lesueur	1.00	.40	.10
☐	C8	Tommy Lockhart	1.00	.40	.10
☐	C9	Jack Marshall	1.00	.40	.10
☐	C10	Lester Patrick	2.00	.80	.20
☐	C11	Bill Quackenbush	1.00	.40	.10
☐	C12	Frank Selke	1.50	.60	.15
☐	C13	Cooper Smeaton	1.00	.40	.10
☐	C14	Hooley Smith	1.00	.40	.10
☐	C15	Capt.J.T.Sutherland	1.00	.40	.10
☐	C16	Fred Whitcroft	1.00	.40	.10
☐	D1	Charles F. Adams	1.00	.40	.10
☐	D2	Russell Bowie	1.00	.40	.10
☐	D3	Frank Frederickson	1.00	.40	.10
☐	D4	Billy Gilmour	1.00	.40	.10
☐	D5	Ivan(Ching) Johnson	1.25	.50	.12
☐	D6	Tom Johnson	1.25	.50	.12
☐	D7	Aurel Joliat	2.50	1.00	.25
☐	D8	Duke Keats	1.00	.40	.10
☐	D9	Red Kelly	1.50	.60	.15
☐	D10	Frank McGee	1.00	.40	.10
☐	D11	James D. Norris	1.25	.50	.12
☐	D12	Philip D. Ross	1.00	.40	.10
☐	D13	Terry Sawchuk	2.50	1.00	.25
☐	D14	Babe Siebert	1.50	.60	.15
☐	D15	Anatoli V. Tarasov	1.25	.50	.12
☐	D16	Roy Worters	1.25	.50	.12
☐	E1	T. Franklin Ahearn	1.00	.40	.10
☐	E2	Harold E. Ballard	2.50	1.00	.25
☐	E3	Billy Burch	1.00	.40	.10
☐	E4	Bill Chadwick	1.00	.40	.10
☐	E5	Sprague Cleghorn	1.25	.50	.12
☐	E6	Rusty Crawford	1.00	.40	.10
☐	E7	Alex Delvecchio	1.50	.60	.15
☐	E8	George S. Dudley	1.00	.40	.10
☐	E9	Ted Kennedy	1.50	.60	.15
☐	E10	Newsy Lalonde	2.00	.80	.20
☐	E11	Billy McGimsie	1.00	.40	.10
☐	E12	Frank Nighbor	1.00	.40	.10
☐	E13	Bobby Orr	6.00	2.40	.60
☐	E14	Sen. Donat Raymond	1.00	.40	.10
☐	E15	Art Ross	2.00	.80	.20
☐	E16	Jack Walker	1.00	.40	.10
☐	F1	Doug Bentley	1.25	.50	.12
☐	F2	Walter A. Brown	1.00	.40	.10
☐	F3	Dit Clapper	1.25	.50	.12
☐	F4	Hap Day	1.00	.40	.10
☐	F5	Frank Dilio	1.00	.40	.10
☐	F6	Bobby Hewitson	1.00	.40	.10
☐	F7	Harry Howell	1.00	.40	.10
☐	F8	Paul Loicq	1.00	.40	.10
☐	F9	Sylvio Mantha	1.00	.40	.10
☐	F10	Jacques Plante	2.50	1.00	.25
☐	F11	George Richardson	1.00	.40	.10
☐	F12	Nels Stewart	1.50	.60	.15
☐	F13	Hod Stuart	1.00	.40	.10
☐	F14	Harry Trihey	1.00	.40	.10
☐	F15	Marty Walsh	1.00	.40	.10
☐	F16	Arthur M. Wirtz	1.25	.50	.12
☐	G1	Toe Blake	1.50	.60	.15
☐	G2	Frank Boucher	1.00	.40	.10
☐	G3	Turk Broda	2.00	.80	.20
☐	G4	Harry Cameron	1.00	.40	.10
☐	G5	Leo Dandurand	1.00	.40	.10
☐	G6	Joe Hall	1.00	.40	.10
☐	G7	George Hay	1.00	.40	.10
☐	G8	William A. Hewitt	1.00	.40	.10
☐	G9	Bouse Hutton	1.00	.40	.10
☐	G10	Dick Irvin	1.25	.50	.12
☐	G11	Henri Richard	2.00	.80	.20
☐	G12	John Ross Robertson	1.00	.40	.10
☐	G13	Frank D. Smith	1.00	.40	.10
☐	G14	Allan Stanley	1.00	.40	.10
☐	G15	Norm Ullman	1.00	.40	.10
☐	G16	Harry Watson	1.00	.40	.10
☐	H1	Clint Benedict	1.50	.60	.15
☐	H2	Dickie Boon	1.00	.40	.10
☐	H3	Gordie Drillon	1.25	.50	.12
☐	H4	Bill Gadsby	1.00	.40	.10
☐	H5	Rod Gilbert	1.25	.50	.12
☐	H6	Moose Goheen	1.00	.40	.10
☐	H7	T.P. Gorman	1.00	.40	.10
☐	H8	Glenn Hall	1.50	.60	.15
☐	H9	Red Horner	1.00	.40	.10
☐	H10	Gen.J.R.Kilpatrick	1.00	.40	.10
☐	H11	Robert Lebel	1.00	.40	.10
☐	H12	Howie Morenz	4.00	1.60	.40
☐	H13	Fred Scanlan	1.00	.40	.10
☐	H14	Tommy Smith	1.00	.40	.10
☐	H15	Fred C. Waghorne	1.00	.40	.10
☐	H16	Cooney Weiland	1.00	.40	.10
☐	I1	Weston Adams	1.00	.40	.10
☐	I2	Sir Montagu Allan	1.00	.40	.10
☐	I3	Frank Brimsek	1.25	.50	.12
☐	I4	Angus Campbell	1.25	.50	.12
☐	I5	Bill Cook	1.00	.40	.10
☐	I6	Tom Dunderdale	1.00	.40	.10
☐	I7	Emile Francis	1.00	.40	.10
☐	I8	Charlie Gardiner	1.00	.40	.10
☐	I9	Elmer Lach	1.00	.40	.10
☐	I10	Frank Mahovlich	2.00	.80	.20
☐	I11	Didier Pitre	1.00	.40	.10
☐	I12	Joe Primeau	1.50	.60	.15
☐	I13	Frank Rankin	1.00	.40	.10
☐	I14	Ernie Russell	1.25	.50	.12
☐	I15	Thayer Tutt	1.00	.40	.10
☐	I16	Harry Westwick	1.00	.40	.10
☐	J1	Jack Adams	1.00	.40	.10
☐	J2	J.F.(Bunny) Ahearne	1.00	.40	.10
☐	J3	J.P. Bickell	1.00	.40	.10
☐	J4	Johnny Bucyk	1.50	.60	.15
☐	J5	Art Coulter	1.00	.40	.10
☐	J6	C.G. Drinkwater	1.00	.40	.10
☐	J7	George Hainsworth	1.25	.50	.12
☐	J8	Tim Horton	2.50	1.00	.25
☐	J9	Maj. F. McLaughlin	1.00	.40	.10
☐	J10	Dickie Moore	1.50	.60	.15
☐	J11	Pierre Pilote	1.00	.40	.10
☐	J12	Claude C. Robinson	1.00	.40	.10
☐	J13	Sweeney Schriner	1.00	.40	.10
☐	J14	Oliver Seibert	1.00	.40	.10
☐	J15	Alfred Smith	1.00	.40	.10
☐	J16	Phat Wilson	1.25	.50	.12
☐	K1	Yvan Cournoyer	1.25	.50	.12
☐	K2	Scotty Davidson	1.00	.40	.10
☐	K3	Cy Denneny	1.00	.40	.10
☐	K4	Bill Durnan	1.25	.50	.12
☐	K5	Shorty Green	1.00	.40	.10
☐	K6	Riley Hern	1.00	.40	.10
☐	K7	Bryan Hextall	1.00	.40	.10
☐	K8	W.M.(Bill) Jennings	1.00	.40	.10
☐	K9	Gordon W. Juckes	1.00	.40	.10
☐	K10	Paddy Moran	1.00	.40	.10
☐	K11	James Norris	1.00	.40	.10
☐	K12	Harry Oliver	1.00	.40	.10
☐	K13	Sam Pollock	1.00	.40	.10
☐	K14	Marcel Pronovost	1.00	.40	.10
☐	K15	Jack Ruttan	1.00	.40	.10
☐	K16	Earl Seibert	1.00	.40	.10
☐	L1	George(Buck) Boucher	1.00	.40	.10
☐	L2	George V. Brown	1.00	.40	.10
☐	L3	Arthur F. Farrell	1.00	.40	.10
☐	L4	Herb Gardiner	1.00	.40	.10
☐	L5	Si Griffis	1.00	.40	.10
☐	L6	Hap Holmes	1.00	.40	.10
☐	L7	Harry Hyland	1.00	.40	.10
☐	L8	Tommy Ivan	1.00	.40	.10
☐	L9	Jack Laviolette	1.00	.40	.10
☐	L10	Ted Lindsay	1.50	.60	.15
☐	L11	Francis Nelson	1.00	.40	.10
☐	L12	William M. Northey	1.00	.40	.10
☐	L13	Babe Pratt	1.00	.40	.10
☐	L14	Chuck Rayner	1.25	.50	.12
☐	L15	Milt Rodden	1.00	.40	.10
☐	L16	Milt Schmidt	1.50	.60	.15
☐	M1	Butch Bouchard	1.00	.40	.10
☐	M2	Jack Butterfield	1.00	.40	.10
☐	M3	Joseph Cattarinich	1.00	.40	.10
☐	M4	Alex Connell	1.25	.50	.12
☐	M5	Bill Cowley	1.00	.40	.10
☐	M6	Chaucer Elliott	1.00	.40	.10
☐	M7	Jimmy Gardner	1.00	.40	.10
☐	M8	BoomBoom Geoffrion	2.50	1.00	.25
☐	M9	Tom Hooper	1.00	.40	.10
☐	M10	Syd Howe	1.00	.40	.10
☐	M11	Harvey(Busher)Jackson	1.25	.50	.12
☐	M12	Al Leader	1.00	.40	.10
☐	M13	Steamer Maxwell	1.00	.40	.10
☐	M14	Blair Russell	1.00	.40	.10
☐	M15	William W. Wirtz	1.00	.40	.10
☐	M16	Gump Worsley	1.50	.60	.15
☐	N1	George Armstrong	1.25	.50	.12
☐	N2	Ace Bailey	1.25	.50	.12
☐	N3	Jack Darragh	1.00	.40	.10
☐	N4	Ken Dryden	2.50	1.00	.25
☐	N5	Eddie Gerard	1.00	.40	.10
☐	N6	Jack Gibson	1.00	.40	.10
☐	N7	Hugh Lehman	1.00	.40	.10
☐	N8	Mickey MacKay	1.00	.40	.10
☐	N9	Joe Malone	1.25	.50	.12
☐	N10	Bruce A. Norris	1.00	.40	.10
☐	N11	J. Ambrose O'Brien	1.00	.40	.10
☐	N12	Lynn Patrick	1.00	.40	.10
☐	N13	Tommy Phillips	1.00	.40	.10
☐	N14	Allan W. Pickard	1.00	.40	.10
☐	N15	Jack Stewart	1.00	.40	.10

			MINT	EXC	G-VG
☐	N16	Frank Udvari	1.00	.40	.10
☐	01	Syl Apps	1.25	.50	.12
☐	02	John G. Ashley	1.00	.40	.10
☐	03	Marty Barry	1.00	.40	.10
☐	04	Andy Bathgate	1.25	.50	.12
☐	05	Johnny Bower	1.25	.50	.12
☐	06	Frank Buckland	1.00	.40	.10
☐	07	Jimmy Dunn	1.00	.40	.10
☐	08	Michael Grant	1.00	.40	.10
☐	09	Doug Harvey	2.00	.80	.20
☐	010	George McNamara	1.00	.40	.10
☐	011	Stan Mikita	2.00	.80	.20
☐	012	Sen.H.de M. Molson	1.00	.40	.10
☐	013	Gordon Roberts	1.00	.40	.10
☐	014	Eddie Shore	3.00	1.20	.30
☐	015	Bruce Stuart	1.00	.40	.10
☐	016	Carl P. Voss	1.00	.40	.10

1985-87 Hall of Fame Cards

This 261-card set is basically two different sets but the second set is merely a reissue of the first Hall of Fame set done two years before, adding the new inductees since that time. The only difference in the first 240 cards in this later 1987 set and the prior set is the different copyright year at the bottom of each reverse in this set. Note however that the copyright line for the 1985 set confusingly shows a 1983 copyright date (apparently referring back to the post card set) vertically printed on the card back. One exception is Gordie Howe; his career was so long that his season-by-season statistics fill up the entire card back leaving no room for a copyright line. The cards are numbered and are standard size, 2 1/2" by 3 1/2". The set features members of the Hockey Hall of Fame portrayed by the artwork of Carlton McDiarmid. Backs are written in both French and English. The set was originally sold in the Canadian Sears 1985 Christmas Catalog.

		MINT	EXC	G-VG
COMPLETE SET (261)		60.00	24.00	6.00
COMMON PLAYER (1-240)		.35	.14	.03
COMMON PLAYER (241-261)		.60	.24	.06

			MINT	EXC	G-VG
☐	1	Maurice Richard	2.50	1.00	.25
☐	2	Sid Abel	.50	.20	.05
☐	3	Punch Broadbent	.35	.14	.03
☐	4	Clarence S. Campbell	.50	.20	.05
☐	5	Neil Colville	.35	.14	.03
☐	6	Charlie Conacher	1.25	.50	.12
☐	7	Mervyn(Red) Dutton	.35	.14	.03
☐	8	Foster W. Hewitt	.50	.20	.05
☐	9	F.J.(Mickey) Ion	.35	.14	.03
☐	10	Ernest(Moose) Johnson	.35	.14	.03
☐	11	Bill Mosienko	.35	.14	.03
☐	12	Russell Stanley (Barney)	.35	.14	.03
☐	13	Lord Stanley	.50	.20	.05
☐	14	Fred(Cyclone) Taylor	.50	.20	.05
☐	15	Cecil(Tiny) Thompson	.35	.14	.03
☐	16	Gordie Howe	3.00	1.20	.30
☐	17	Hobey Baker	.50	.20	.05
☐	18	Frank Calder	.35	.14	.03
☐	19	J.C.V.(Jim) Hendy	.35	.14	.03
☐	20	Frank Foyston	.35	.14	.03
☐	21	Harry Lumley	.35	.14	.03
☐	22	Reg Noble	.35	.14	.03
☐	23	Frank A. Patrick	.35	.14	.03
☐	24	Harvey Pulford	.35	.14	.03
☐	25	Ken Reardon	.50	.20	.05
☐	26	J.J. Simpson (Bullet Joe)	.35	.14	.03
☐	27	Conn Smythe	.50	.20	.05
☐	28	R.A.(Red) Storey	.35	.14	.03
☐	29	Lloyd Turner	.35	.14	.03
☐	30	Georges Vezina	1.50	.60	.15
☐	31	Jean Beliveau	1.25	.50	.12
☐	32	Max Bentley	.35	.14	.03
☐	33	King Clancy	1.25	.50	.12
☐	34	Cecil(Babe) Dye	.35	.14	.03
☐	35	Ebbie Goodfellow	.35	.14	.03
☐	36	Charles Hay	.35	.14	.03
☐	37	Percy Lesueur	.35	.14	.03
☐	38	T.F.(Tommy) Lockhart	.35	.14	.03
☐	39	J.C.(Jack) Marshall	.35	.14	.03
☐	40	Lester Patrick	.50	.20	.05
☐	41	Frank Selke	.50	.20	.05
☐	42	J. Cooper Smeaton	.35	.14	.03
☐	43	Hooley Smith	.35	.14	.03
☐	44	Capt.J.T. Sutherland	.35	.14	.03
☐	45	Fred Whitcroft	.35	.14	.03
☐	46	Terry Sawchuk	1.00	.40	.10
☐	47	Charles F. Adams	.35	.14	.03
☐	48	Russell Bowie	.35	.14	.03
☐	49	Frank Frederickson	.35	.14	.03
☐	50	H.L.(Billy) Gilmour	.35	.14	.03
☐	51	Ivan(Ching) Johnson	.35	.14	.03
☐	52	Tom Johnson	.35	.14	.03
☐	53	Aurel Joliat	.75	.30	.07
☐	54	G.B.(Duke) Keats	.35	.14	.03
☐	55	Red Kelly	.50	.20	.05
☐	56	Frank McGee	.35	.14	.03
☐	57	James D. Norris	.35	.14	.03
☐	58	Philip D. Ross	.35	.14	.03
☐	59	Albert(Babe) Siebert	.50	.20	.05
☐	60	Roy Worters	.35	.14	.03
☐	61	Bobby Orr	3.00	1.20	.30
☐	62	T. Franklin	.35	.14	.03
☐	63	Harold E. Ballard	.75	.30	.07
☐	64	Billy Burch	.35	.14	.03
☐	65	W.L.(Bill) Chadwick	.35	.14	.03
☐	66	Sprague Cleghorn	.35	.14	.03
☐	67	S.R.(Rusty) Crawford	.35	.14	.03
☐	68	George S. Dudley	.35	.14	.03
☐	69	Teeder Kennedy	.50	.20	.05
☐	70	Newsy Lalonde	.75	.30	.07
☐	71	W.G.(Billy) McGimsie	.35	.14	.03
☐	72	Frank Nighbor	.35	.14	.03
☐	73	Sen. Donat Raymond	.35	.14	.03
☐	74	Art Ross	.50	.20	.05
☐	75	J.P.(Jack) Walker	.35	.14	.03
☐	76	Jacques Plante	1.25	.50	.12
☐	77	Doug Bentley	.35	.14	.03
☐	78	Walter A. Brown	.35	.14	.03
☐	79	Dit Clapper	.50	.20	.05
☐	80	Clarence(Hap) Day	.35	.14	.03
☐	81	Frank Dilio	.35	.14	.03
☐	82	R.W.(Bobby) Hewitson	.35	.14	.03
☐	83	Harry Howell	.35	.14	.03
☐	84	Sylvio Mantha	.35	.14	.03
☐	85	George Richardson	.35	.14	.03
☐	86	Nels Stewart	.50	.20	.05
☐	87	W.H.(Hod) Stuart	.35	.14	.03
☐	88	H.J.(Harry) Trihey	.35	.14	.03
☐	89	Marty Walsh	.35	.14	.03
☐	90	Arthur M. Wirtz	.35	.14	.03
☐	91	J. Henri Rivard	.75	.30	.07
☐	92	Hector(Toe) Blake	.50	.20	.05
☐	93	Frank Boucher	.35	.14	.03
☐	94	Turk Broda	.75	.30	.07
☐	95	H.H.(Harry) Cameron	.35	.14	.03
☐	96	Leo J.V. Dandurand	.35	.14	.03
☐	97	J.H.(Joe) Hall	.35	.14	.03
☐	98	George W. Hay	.35	.14	.03
☐	99	William A. Hewitt	.35	.14	.03
☐	100	J.B.(Bouse) Hutton	.35	.14	.03
☐	101	J.D.(Dick) Irvin	.35	.14	.03
☐	102	John Ross Robertson	.35	.14	.03
☐	103	Frank D. Smith	.35	.14	.03
☐	104	Norm Ullman	.35	.14	.03
☐	105	H.E.(Moose) Watson	.35	.14	.03
☐	106	Howie Morenz	1.50	.60	.15
☐	107	Clint Benedict	.35	.14	.03
☐	108	Dickie Boon	.35	.14	.03
☐	109	Gordon Drillon	.50	.20	.05
☐	110	Bill Gadsby	.35	.14	.03

☐ 111	Rod Gilbert	.35	.14	.03
☐ 112	F.X.(Moose) Goheen	.35	.14	.03
☐ 113	T.P.(Tommy) Gorman	.35	.14	.03
☐ 114	Glenn Hall	.50	.20	.05
☐ 115	Red Horner	.35	.14	.03
☐ 116	Gen.J.R. Kilpatrick	.35	.14	.03
☐ 117	Robert Lebel	.35	.14	.03
☐ 118	Fred Scanlan	.35	.14	.03
☐ 119	Fred C. Waghorne	.35	.14	.03
☐ 120	Cooney Weiland	.35	.14	.03
☐ 121	Frank Mahovlich	.75	.30	.07
☐ 122	Weston W. Adams, Sr.	.35	.14	.03
☐ 123	Sir Montagu Allan	.35	.14	.03
☐ 124	Frank Brimsek	.50	.20	.05
☐ 125	Angus D. Campbell	.35	.14	.03
☐ 126	Bill Cook	.35	.14	.03
☐ 127	Tom Dunderdale	.35	.14	.03
☐ 128	G.R.(Chuck) Gardiner	.35	.14	.03
☐ 129	Elmer Lach	.35	.14	.03
☐ 130	Didier Pitre	.35	.14	.03
☐ 131	Joe Primeau	.35	.14	.03
☐ 132	Frank Rankin	.35	.14	.03
☐ 133	Ernie Russell	.35	.14	.03
☐ 134	W. Thayer Tutt	.35	.14	.03
☐ 135	Harry Westwick	.35	.14	.03
☐ 136	Yvan Cournoyer	.50	.20	.05
☐ 137	A.M.(Scotty) Davidson	.35	.14	.03
☐ 138	Cy Denneny	.35	.14	.03
☐ 139	Bill Durnan	.50	.20	.05
☐ 140	Shorty Green	.35	.14	.03
☐ 141	Bryan Hextall	.35	.14	.03
☐ 142	W.M.(Bill) Jennings	.35	.14	.03
☐ 143	Gordon W. Juckes	.35	.14	.03
☐ 144	Paddy Moran	.35	.14	.03
☐ 145	James Norris	.35	.14	.03
☐ 146	Harold Oliver	.35	.14	.03
☐ 147	Sam Pollock	.35	.14	.03
☐ 148	Marcel Pronovost	.35	.14	.03
☐ 149	J.D.(Jack) Ruttan	.35	.14	.03
☐ 150	Earl W. Seibert	.35	.14	.03
☐ 151	Ted Lindsay	.50	.20	.05
☐ 152	George V. Brown	.35	.14	.03
☐ 153	Arthur F. Farrell	.35	.14	.03
☐ 154	Herb Gardiner	.35	.14	.03
☐ 155	S.S.(Si) Griffis	.35	.14	.03
☐ 156	Harry(Hap) Holmes	.35	.14	.03
☐ 157	Harry Hyland	.35	.14	.03
☐ 158	T.H.(Tommy) Ivan	.35	.14	.03
☐ 159	Jack Laviolette	.35	.14	.03
☐ 160	Francis Nelson	.35	.14	.03
☐ 161	William M. Northey	.35	.14	.03
☐ 162	Walter(Babe) Pratt	.35	.14	.03
☐ 163	Chuck Rayner	.35	.14	.03
☐ 164	M.J.(Mike) Rodden	.35	.14	.03
☐ 165	Milt Schmidt	.50	.20	.05
☐ 166	Boom Boom Geoffrion	1.00	.40	.10
☐ 167	Jack Butterfield	.35	.14	.03
☐ 168	Joseph Cattarinich	.35	.14	.03
☐ 169	Alex Connell	.50	.20	.05
☐ 170	Bill Cowley	.35	.14	.03
☐ 171	E.S.(Chaucer) Eliott	.35	.14	.03
☐ 172	J.H.(Jimmy) Gardner	.35	.14	.03
☐ 173	C.T.(Tom) Hooper	.35	.14	.03
☐ 174	Syd Howe	.35	.14	.03
☐ 175	Harvey(Busher) Jackson	.50	.20	.05
☐ 176	G.A.(Al) Leader	.35	.14	.03
☐ 177	F.G. Maxwell (Steamer)	.35	.14	.03
☐ 178	Blair Russell	.35	.14	.03
☐ 179	William W. Wirtz	.35	.14	.03
☐ 180	Gump Worsley	.75	.30	.07
☐ 181	Johnny Bucyk	.50	.20	.05
☐ 182	Jack Adams	.35	.14	.03
☐ 183	J.F.(Bunny) Ahearne	.35	.14	.03
☐ 184	J.P. Bickell	.35	.14	.03
☐ 185	Art Coulter	.35	.14	.03
☐ 186	C.G. Drinkwater	.35	.14	.03
☐ 187	George Hainsworth	.50	.20	.05
☐ 188	Tim Horton	1.25	.50	.12
☐ 189	Maj.F. McLaughlin	.35	.14	.03
☐ 190	Dickie Moore	.50	.20	.05
☐ 191	Pierre Pilote	.35	.14	.03
☐ 192	Claude C. Robinson	.35	.14	.03
☐ 193	Oliver L. Seibert	.35	.14	.03
☐ 194	Alfred E. Smith	.35	.14	.03
☐ 195	A.G.(Phat) Wilson	.35	.14	.03
☐ 196	Ken Dryden	1.25	.50	.12
☐ 197	George Armstrong	.50	.20	.05
☐ 198	Ace Bailey	.75	.30	.07
☐ 199	Jack Darragh	.35	.14	.03
☐ 200	Eddie Gerard	.35	.14	.03
☐ 201	J.L.(Jack) Gibson	.35	.14	.03
☐ 202	F.H.(Hughie) Lehman	.35	.14	.03

☐ 203	D.(Mickey) MacKay	.35	.14	.03
☐ 204	M.J.(Joe) Malone	.50	.20	.05
☐ 205	Bruce A. Norris	.35	.14	.03
☐ 206	J.Ambroise O'Brien	.35	.14	.03
☐ 207	Lynn Patrick	.35	.14	.03
☐ 208	Tommy Phillips	.35	.14	.03
☐ 209	Allan W. Pickard	.35	.14	.03
☐ 210	J.S.(Jack) Stewart	.35	.14	.03
☐ 211	Johnny Bower	.50	.20	.05
☐ 212	Syl Apps	.35	.14	.03
☐ 213	John G. Ashley	.35	.14	.03
☐ 214	Marty Barry	.35	.14	.03
☐ 215	Andy Bathgate	.35	.14	.03
☐ 216	Frank Buckland	.35	.14	.03
☐ 217	J.A.(Jimmy) Dunn	.35	.14	.03
☐ 218	Michael Grant	.35	.14	.03
☐ 219	Doug Harvey	.75	.30	.07
☐ 220	George McNamara	.35	.14	.03
☐ 221	Sen.H.deM. Molson	.35	.14	.03
☐ 222	Gordon Roberts	.35	.14	.03
☐ 223	Eddie Shore	1.25	.50	.12
☐ 224	Bruce Stuart	.35	.14	.03
☐ 225	Carl P. Voss	.35	.14	.03
☐ 226	Stan Mikita	1.00	.40	.10
☐ 227	D.H.(Dan) Bain	.35	.14	.03
☐ 228	Butch Bouchard	.35	.14	.03
☐ 229	George(Buck) Boucher	.35	.14	.03
☐ 230	Alex Delvecchio	.50	.20	.05
☐ 231	Emile P. Francis	.35	.14	.03
☐ 232	W.M.(Riley) Hern	.35	.14	.03
☐ 233	Fred J. Hume	.35	.14	.03
☐ 234	Paul Loicq	.35	.14	.03
☐ 235	Bill Quackenbush	.35	.14	.03
☐ 236	Sweeney Schriner	.35	.14	.03
☐ 237	Thomas J. Smith	.35	.14	.03
☐ 238	Allan Stanley	.35	.14	.03
☐ 239	Anatoli V. Tarasov	.35	.14	.03
☐ 240	Frank Udvari	.35	.14	.03
☐ 241	Harry Sinden	.75	.30	.07
☐ 242	Bobby Hull	3.00	1.20	.30
☐ 243	Punch Imlach	.60	.24	.06
☐ 244	Phil Esposito	1.25	.50	.12
☐ 245	Jacques Lemaire	.75	.30	.07
☐ 246	Bernie Parent	1.00	.40	.10
☐ 247	Rudy Pilous	.60	.24	.06
☐ 248	Bert Olmstead	.60	.24	.06
☐ 249	Jean Ratelle	1.00	.40	.10
☐ 250	Gerry Cheevers	1.00	.40	.10
☐ 251	William Hanley	.60	.24	.06
☐ 252	Leo Boivin	.60	.24	.06
☐ 253	John C.(Jake) Milford	.60	.24	.06
☐ 254	John Mariucci	.60	.24	.06
☐ 255	Dave Keon	1.00	.40	.10
☐ 256	Serge Savard	.75	.30	.07
☐ 257	John A. Ziegler Jr.	.60	.24	.06
☐ 258	Bobby Clarke	1.50	.60	.15
☐ 259	Ed Giacomin	1.00	.40	.10
☐ 260	Jacques Laperriere	.60	.24	.06
☐ 261	Matt Pavelich	.60	.24	.06

1992-93 Hall of Fame Legends

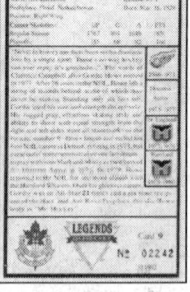

The Hockey Hall of Fame in association with the Diamond Connection and the Sports Gallery of Art produced this 18-card set as the first of three series to be released each year. Over a four year period, all members and builders of Hockey's Hall of Fame will be featured. Production was limited to 10,000 numbered sets, and buyers retained exclusive rights to their assigned number throughout the duration of the project. Issued in a cardboard box, the cards measure approximately 3 1/2" by 5 1/2" and feature the work of noted sports artist Doug West. The front displays a color reproduction of the artist's original painting. The back has a parchment background with navy blue borders and includes biographical information, a player profile, career statistics, each team played for, and the years played. A registration form and an ownership transfer form were included with each set. The card number and set serial number are in the lower right corner.

		MINT	EXC	G-VG
COMPLETE SET (36)		150.00	60.00	15.00
COMMON PLAYER (1-18)		4.00	1.60	.40
COMMON PLAYER (19-36)		4.00	1.60	.40
☐ 1	Harry Lumley	4.00	1.60	.40
☐ 2	Conn Smythe CO	4.00	1.60	.40
☐ 3	Maurice Richard	8.00	3.25	.80
☐ 4	Bobby Orr	10.00	4.00	1.00
☐ 5	Bernie Geoffrion	6.00	2.40	.60
☐ 6	Hobey Baker	5.00	2.00	.50
☐ 7	Phil Esposito	6.00	2.40	.60
☐ 8	King Clancy	6.00	2.40	.60
☐ 9	Gordie Howe	10.00	4.00	1.00
☐ 10	Emile Francis	4.00	1.60	.40
☐ 11	Jacques Plante	6.00	2.40	.60
☐ 12	Sid Abel	4.00	1.60	.40
☐ 13	Foster Hewitt	4.00	1.60	.40
☐ 14	Charlie Conacher	5.00	2.00	.50
☐ 15	Stan Mikita	6.00	2.40	.60
☐ 16	Bobby Clarke	5.00	2.00	.50
☐ 17	Norm Ullman	4.00	1.60	.40
☐ 18	Lord Stanley of Preston	5.00	2.00	.50
☐ 19	Ted Lindsay	5.00	2.00	.50
☐ 20	Duke Keats	4.00	1.60	.40
☐ 21	Jack Adams	4.00	1.60	.40
☐ 22	William Mosienko	4.00	1.60	.40
☐ 23	Johnny Bower	4.00	1.60	.40
☐ 24	Tim Horton	6.00	2.40	.60
☐ 25	Punch Imlach	4.00	1.60	.40
☐ 26	Georges Vezina	8.00	3.25	.80
☐ 27	Earl Seibert	4.00	1.60	.40
☐ 28	Bryan Hextall Sr.	4.00	1.60	.40
☐ 29	Babe Pratt	4.00	1.60	.40
☐ 30	Gump Worsley	5.00	2.00	.50
☐ 31	Ed Giacomin	5.00	2.00	.50
☐ 32	Ace Bailey	5.00	2.00	.50
☐ 33	Harry Sinden	4.00	1.60	.40
☐ 34	Lanny McDonald	5.00	2.00	.50
☐ 35	Tommy Ivan	4.00	1.60	.40
☐ 36	Frank Calder	4.00	1.60	.40

1975-76 Heroes Stand-Ups

These 31 "Hockey Heroes Autographed Pin-up/Stand-Up Sportrophies" feature NHL players from five different teams. The stand-ups come in two different sizes. The Bruins and Flyers stand-ups are approximately 15 1/2" by 8/3/4", while the Islanders stand-ups are approximately 13 1/2" by 7 1/2" and were issued three to a strip. The stand-ups are made of laminated cardboard, and the yellow frame is decorated with red stars. Each stand-up features a color action shot of the player. A facsimile autograph is inscribed across the bottom of the stand-up. The stand-ups are unnumbered and checklisted below alphabetically according to and within teams as follows: Boston Bruins (1-7), Montreal Canadiens (8-13), New York Islanders (14-19), Philadelphia Flyers (20-25), and Toronto Maple Leafs (26-31).

		NRMT	VG-E	GOOD
COMPLETE SET (31)		150.00	60.00	15.00
COMMON PLAYER (1-31)		4.00	1.60	.40
☐ 1	Gerry Cheevers	8.00	3.25	.80
☐ 2	Terry O'Reilly	5.00	2.00	.50
☐ 3	Bobby Orr	25.00	10.00	2.50
☐ 4	Brad Park	8.00	3.25	.80

☐ 5	Jean Ratelle	7.00	2.80	.70
☐ 6	Andre Savard	4.00	1.60	.40
☐ 7	Gregg Sheppard	4.00	1.60	.40
☐ 8	Yvan Cournoyer	7.00	2.80	.70
☐ 9	Guy Lafleur	15.00	6.00	1.50
☐ 10	Jacques Lemaire	6.00	2.40	.60
☐ 11	Peter Mahovlich	4.00	1.60	.40
☐ 12	Doug Risebourgh	4.00	1.60	.40
☐ 13	Larry Robinson	10.00	4.00	1.00
☐ 14	Billy Harris	4.00	1.60	.40
☐ 15	Gerry Hart	4.00	1.60	.40
☐ 16	Denis Potvin	7.00	2.80	.70
☐ 17	Glenn Resch	6.00	2.40	.60
☐ 18	Bryan Trottier	8.00	3.25	.80
☐ 19	Ed Westfall	4.00	1.60	.40
☐ 20	Bill Barber	6.00	2.40	.60
☐ 21	Bobby Clarke	10.00	4.00	1.00
☐ 22	Reggie Leach	5.00	2.00	.50
☐ 23	Rick MacLeish	6.00	2.40	.60
☐ 24	Bernie Parent	8.00	3.25	.80
☐ 25	Dave Schultz	6.00	2.40	.60
☐ 26	Lanny MacDonald	8.00	3.25	.80
☐ 27	Borje Salming	6.00	2.40	.60
☐ 28	Darryl Sittler	8.00	3.25	.80
☐ 29	Wayne Thomas	4.00	1.60	.40
☐ 30	Errol Thompson	4.00	1.60	.40
☐ 31	Dave(Tiger) Williams	5.00	2.00	.50

1992 High-5 Previews

These six cards measure the standard size (2 1/2" by 3 1/2"). On a black background, the fronts feature color action player photos with the player's name and position printed above the photo. The backs carry another color player photo, with the player's name and career highlights on a white panel. The words "Preview Sample" appear in the top left corner. The cards are numbered on the back with a "P" prefix. Bourque and Belfour were produced in larger quantities.

	MINT	EXC	G-VG
COMPLETE SET (6)	300.00	120.00	30.00
COMMON PLAYER (P1-P6)	10.00	4.00	1.00
☐ P1 Wayne Gretzky Los Angeles Kings	150.00	60.00	15.00
☐ P2 Mario Lemieux Pittsburgh Penguins	100.00	40.00	10.00
☐ P3 Brett Hull St. Louis Blues	50.00	20.00	5.00
☐ P4 Mark Messier Edmonton Oilers	40.00	16.00	4.00
☐ P5 Ray Bourque DP Boston Bruins	10.00	4.00	1.00
☐ P6 Ed Belfour DP Chicago Blackhawks	10.00	4.00	1.00

1992-93 High Liner Stanley Cup

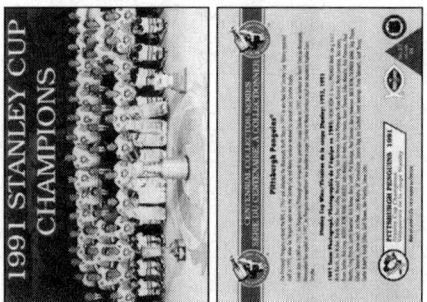

National Sea Products Ltd., producer and manufacturer of High Liner brand fish products, produced a 28-card, standard-size (2 1/2" by 3 1/2") set to celebrate the Centennial of the Stanley Cup (1893-1993). Specially marked packages of High Liner frozen fish products contained two cards. Collectors could also order additional cards by clipping the order form from the box, checking the cards desired, and sending it in with six UPC symbols from any High Liner brand product plus 3.99. The form limited requests to one card request per card number. The fronts feature full-bleed black-and-white and color team pictures of Stanley Cup champions. The pale blue, horizontal backs present a French and English summary of the championship season and a list of the players pictured. A darker blue stripe across the top displays the Stanley Cup logo and the set name in French and English. The team name and the year they won the Stanley Cup appear in the lower left corner. The cards are numbered on the back.

	MINT	EXC	G-VG
COMPLETE SET (28)	40.00	16.00	4.00
COMMON TEAM (1-28)	2.00	.80	.20
☐ 1 Montreal AAA	2.50	1.00	.25
☐ 2 Winnipeg Victorias	2.00	.80	.20
☐ 3 Montreal Victorias	2.50	1.00	.25
☐ 4 Montreal Shamrocks	2.50	1.00	.25
☐ 5 Ottawa Silver Seven	2.00	.80	.20
☐ 6 Kenora Thistles	2.00	.80	.20
☐ 7 Montreal Wanderers	2.50	1.00	.25
☐ 8 Quebec Bulldogs	2.00	.80	.20
☐ 9 Toronto Blueshirts	2.50	1.00	.25
☐ 10 Vancouver Millionaires	2.50	1.00	.25
☐ 11 Seattle Metropolitans	2.50	1.00	.25
☐ 12 Toronto Arenas	2.50	1.00	.25
☐ 13 Toronto St. Patricks	2.50	1.00	.25
☐ 14 Victoria Cougars	2.00	.80	.20
☐ 15 Ottawa Senators	2.00	.80	.20
☐ 16 Montreal Maroons	2.50	1.00	.25
☐ 17 New York Rangers	2.00	.80	.20
☐ 18 Detroit Red Wings	2.50	1.00	.25
☐ 19 Montreal Canadiens	2.50	1.00	.25
☐ 20 Chicago Blackhawks	2.00	.80	.20
☐ 21 Toronto Maple Leafs	2.50	1.00	.25
☐ 22 Boston Bruins	2.50	1.00	.25
☐ 23 Philadelphia Flyers	2.00	.80	.20
☐ 24 New York Islanders	2.00	.80	.20
☐ 25 Edmonton Oilers	2.00	.80	.20
☐ 26 Calgary Flames	2.00	.80	.20
☐ 27 Pittsburgh Penguins	2.00	.80	.20
☐ 28 Checklist Card	2.50	1.00	.25

1993-94 High Liner Greatest Goalies

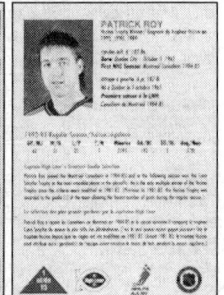

National Sea Products Ltd., producer and manufacturer of High Liner brand fish products, produced a 15-card, standard-size (2 1/2" by 3 1/2") set of the Greatest Goalies of the NHL, a follow-up to High Liner's 28-card 1992-93 Stanley Cup Centennial set. Specially marked packages of High Liner frozen fish products contained one card. Collectors could also order the complete set through a mail-in offer as outlined on the inside of the specially marked High Liner packages. The set is made from white card stock and is primarily devoted to goalies that have won the Vezina Trophy, the NHL's top annual award for goaltenders. The fronts feature white-bordered color player action shots, with the player's name, team and, season printed in white within a blue band at the bottom. The logo, with Greatest Goalies printed in French and English, appears in the lower left. The white back has a color posed player head shot in the upper left, with the player's name in orange lettering alongside to the right. A biography, stat table, and career highlights are printed in English and French. The High Liner, NHLPA, and NHL logos on the bottom round out the card. The cards are numbered on the back.

	MINT	EXC	G-VG
COMPLETE SET (15)	20.00	8.00	2.00
COMMON PLAYER (1-15)	1.00	.40	.10
☐ 1 Patrick Roy Montreal Canadiens	5.00	2.00	.50
☐ 2 Ed Belfour Chicago Blackhawks	2.50	1.00	.25
☐ 3 Grant Fuhr Buffalo Sabres	1.00	.40	.10
☐ 4 Ron Hextall Quebec Nordiques	1.00	.40	.10
☐ 5 John Vanbiesbrouck New York Rangers	1.25	.50	.12
☐ 6 Tom Barrasso Pittsburgh Penguins	1.00	.40	.10
☐ 7 Bernie Parent Philadelphia Flyers	1.25	.50	.12
☐ 8 Tony Esposito Chicago Blackhawks	1.50	.60	.15
☐ 9 Johnny Bower Toronto Maple Leafs	1.25	.50	.12
☐ 10 Jacques Plante Montreal Canadiens	2.50	1.00	.25
☐ 11 Terry Sawchuk Detroit Red Wings	2.50	1.00	.25
☐ 12 Bill Durnan Montreal Canadiens	1.25	.50	.12
☐ 13 Felix Potvin Toronto Maple Leafs	4.00	1.60	.40

		MINT	EXC	G-VG
☐ 14	The Evolution of the .... Goalie Mask	2.50	1.00	.25
☐ 15	Vezina Trophy Checklist	2.00	.80	.20

1994 Hockey Wit

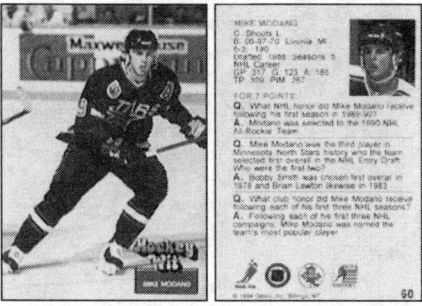

Seventh in a series of "WIT" trivia games, this Hockey Wit card set features 108 standard-size (2 1/2" by 3 1/2") cards and includes hockey players of the past and present. The fronts feature full-bleed color action player photos, with the player's name inside a blue box with a gold-foil border and the words "Hockey Wit". On a white background, the backs carry a small color headshot, player biography and trivia questions and answers. Inserted in each mastercase of 72 games was a bonus card which collectors could redeem for one of 500 limited edition sets of uncut flat sheets. The production run was reportedly limited to 30,000 sets, and a portion of the proceeds from the sale benefited amateur hockey in Canada and the United States. The set includes 21 Hall of Famers. The collector who answers all the questions on the backs achieved a perfect score of 801, the total number of goals scored in the NHL by Gordie Howe. The cards are numbered on the back at the lower right corner.

		MINT	EXC	G-VG
COMPLETE SET (108)		15.00	6.00	1.50
COMMON PLAYER (1-108)		.10	.04	.01
☐ 1	Mike Richter .... New York Rangers	.30	.12	.03
☐ 2	Tony Amonte .... New York Rangers	.10	.04	.01
☐ 3	Patrick Roy .... Montreal Canadiens	1.50	.60	.15
☐ 4	Craig Janney .... St. Louis Blues	.20	.08	.02
☐ 5	Adam Oates .... Boston Bruins	.30	.12	.03
☐ 6	Geoff Sanderson .... Hartford Whalers	.20	.08	.02
☐ 7	Pavel Bure .... Vancouver Canucks	2.00	.80	.20
☐ 8	Steve Duchesne .... Quebec Nordiques	.10	.04	.01
☐ 9	Gordie Howe .... Detroit Red Wings	1.00	.40	.10
☐ 10	Brad Park .... New York Rangers	.10	.04	.01
☐ 11	Brian Bellows .... Montreal Canadiens	.10	.04	.01
☐ 12	Chris Chelios .... Chicago Blackhawks	.20	.08	.02
☐ 13	Bill Barber .... Philadelphia Flyers	.10	.04	.01
☐ 14	Gump Worsley .... Montreal Canadiens	.20	.08	.02
☐ 15	The Stanley Cup	.20	.08	.02
☐ 16	Maurice Richard .... Montreal Canadiens	.50	.20	.05
☐ 17	Kevin Hatcher .... Washington Capitals	.10	.04	.01
☐ 18	Ed Belfour .... Chicago Blackhawks	.50	.20	.05
☐ 19	Kirk Muller .... Montreal Canadiens	.20	.08	.02
☐ 20	Kevin Stevens .... Pittsburgh Penguins	.30	.12	.03
☐ 21	Dave Taylor .... Los Angeles Kings	.10	.04	.01
☐ 22	Dale Hawerchuk .... Buffalo Sabres	.20	.08	.02
☐ 23	Jean Beliveau .... Montreal Canadiens	.40	.16	.04
☐ 24	Rogatien Vachon .... Los Angeles Kings	.20	.08	.02
☐ 25	Tom Barrasso .... Pittsburgh Penguins	.10	.04	.01
☐ 26	Rod Langway .... Washington Capitals	.10	.04	.01
☐ 27	Pierre Turgeon .... New York Islanders	.50	.20	.05
☐ 28	Derek King .... New York Islanders	.10	.04	.01
☐ 29	Brendan Shanahan .... St. Louis Blues	.30	.12	.03
☐ 30	Darren Turcotte .... New York Rangers	.10	.04	.01
☐ 31	Chris Terreri .... New Jersey Devils	.10	.04	.01
☐ 32	Tony Granato .... Los Angeles Kings	.10	.04	.01
☐ 33	Michel Goulet .... Chicago Blackhawks	.20	.08	.02
☐ 34	Felix Potvin .... Toronto Maple Leafs	1.25	.50	.12
☐ 35	Curtis Joseph .... St. Louis Blues	.40	.16	.04
☐ 36	Cam Neely .... Boston Bruins	.30	.12	.03
☐ 37	Borje Salming .... Toronto Maple Leafs	.10	.04	.01
☐ 38	Denis Savard .... Montreal Canadiens	.20	.08	.02
☐ 39	Stan Mikita .... Chicago Blackhawks	.30	.12	.03
☐ 40	Grant Fuhr .... Buffalo Sabres	.20	.08	.02
☐ 41	Gary Suter .... Calgary Flames	.10	.04	.01
☐ 42	Serge Savard .... Montreal Canadiens	.20	.08	.02
☐ 43	Steve Larmer .... Chicago Blackhawks	.20	.08	.02
☐ 44	Bryan Trottier .... Pittsburgh Penguins	.20	.08	.02
☐ 45	Mike Vernon .... Calgary Flames	.20	.08	.02
☐ 46	Paul Coffey .... Detroit Red Wings	.30	.12	.03
☐ 47	Bernie Federko .... St. Louis Blues	.10	.04	.01
☐ 48	Larry Murphy .... Pittsburgh Penguins	.10	.04	.01
☐ 49	Scotty Bowman CO .... Montreal Canadiens	.30	.12	.03
☐ 50	Glenn Anderson .... Toronto Maple Leafs	.10	.04	.01
☐ 51	Mats Sundin .... Quebec Nordiques	.40	.16	.04
☐ 52	Henri Richard .... Montreal Canadiens	.30	.12	.03
☐ 53	Ron Francis .... Pittsburgh Penguins	.20	.08	.02
☐ 54	Scott Niedermayer .... New Jersey Devils	.20	.08	.02
☐ 55	Teemu Selanne .... Winnipeg Jets	1.00	.40	.10
☐ 56	Frank Mahovlich .... Toronto Maple Leafs	.30	.12	.03
☐ 57	Owen Nolan .... Quebec Nordiques	.30	.12	.03
☐ 58	Rick Tocchet .... Pittsburgh Penguins	.20	.08	.02
☐ 59	Rod Brind'Amour .... Philadelphia Flyers	.20	.08	.02
☐ 60	Mike Modano .... Dallas Stars	.50	.20	.05
☐ 61	Doug Gilmour .... Toronto Maple Leafs	1.00	.40	.10
☐ 62	Jimmy Carson .... Los Angeles Kings	.10	.04	.01
☐ 63	Mike Keane .... Montreal Canadiens	.10	.04	.01
☐ 64	Bernie Nicholls .... New Jersey Devils	.20	.08	.02
☐ 65	Scott Stevens .... New Jersey Devils	.20	.08	.02
☐ 66	Mario Lemieux	1.50	.60	.15

	Pittsburgh Penguins			
☐ 67	Keith Primeau	.20	.08	.02
	Detroit Red Wings			
☐ 68	Bobby Carpenter	.10	.04	.01
	New Jersey Devils			
☐ 69	Sergei Fedorov	1.50	.60	.15
	Detroit Red Wings			
☐ 70	Peter Stastny	.20	.08	.02
	Quebec Nordiques			
☐ 71	Brian Leetch	.75	.30	.07
	New York Rangers			
☐ 72	Vincent Damphousse	.20	.08	.02
	Toronto Maple Leafs			
☐ 73	Darryl Sitter	.20	.08	.02
	Toronto Maple Leafs			
☐ 74	Al Iafrate	.20	.08	.02
	Washington Capitals			
☐ 75	Alexander Mogilny	.75	.30	.07
	Buffalo Sabres			
☐ 76	Bill Ranford	.20	.08	.02
	Edmonton Oilers			
☐ 77	Raymond Bourque	.40	.16	.04
	Boston Bruins			
☐ 78	Joey Mullen	.20	.08	.02
	Pittsburgh Penguins			
☐ 79	Mike Ricci	.30	.12	.03
	Quebec Nordiques			
☐ 80	Bobby Clarke	.30	.12	.03
	Philadelphia Flyers			
☐ 81	Gerry Cheevers	.20	.08	.02
	Boston Bruins			
☐ 82	Joe Nieuwendyk	.20	.08	.02
	Calgary Flames			
☐ 83	Terry Sawchuk	.40	.16	.04
	Detroit Red Wings			
☐ 84	Ray Ferraro	.10	.04	.01
	New York Islanders			
☐ 85	Lanny McDonald	.30	.12	.03
	Calgary Flames			
☐ 86	Adam Graves	.20	.08	.02
	New York Islanders			
☐ 87	Tomas Sandstrom	.20	.08	.02
	Los Angeles Kings			
☐ 88	Eric Lindros	2.50	1.00	.25
	Philadelphia Flyers			
☐ 89	Jari Kurri	.20	.08	.02
	Los Angeles Kings			
☐ 90	Al MacInnis	.20	.08	.02
	Calgary Flames			
☐ 91	Alexandre Daigle	.40	.16	.04
	Ottawa Senators			
☐ 92	Larry Robinson	.30	.12	.03
	Montreal Canadiens			
☐ 93	Kelly Hrudey	.20	.08	.02
	Los Angeles Kings			
☐ 94	Theoren Fleury	.20	.08	.02
	Calgary Flames			
☐ 95	Billy Smith	.20	.08	.02
	New York Islanders			
☐ 96	Luc Robitaille	.40	.16	.04
	Los Angeles Kings			
☐ 97	Brett Hull	1.00	.40	.10
	St. Louis Blues			
☐ 98	Pat Falloon	.30	.12	.03
	San Jose Sharks			
☐ 99	Wayne Gretzky	3.00	1.20	.30
	Los Angeles Kings			
☐ 100	Joe Sakic	.40	.16	.04
	Quebec Nordiques			
☐ 101	Phil Housley	.20	.08	.02
	Winnipeg Jets			
☐ 102	Mark Messier	.50	.20	.05
	New York Rangers			
☐ 103	Jeremy Roenick	1.50	.60	.15
	Chicago Blackhawks			
☐ 104	Mark Recchi	.30	.12	.03
	Philadelphia Flyers			
☐ 105	Pat LaFontaine	.75	.30	.07
	Buffalo Sabres			
☐ 106	Trevor Linden	.50	.20	.05
	Vancouver Canucks			
☐ 107	Jaromir Jagr	1.00	.40	.10
	Pittsburgh Penguins			
☐ 108	Steve Yzerman	1.00	.40	.10
	Detroit Red Wings			

1924-25 Holland Creameries

The 1924-25 Holland Creameries set contains ten black and white cards measuring approximately 1 1/2" by 3". The front

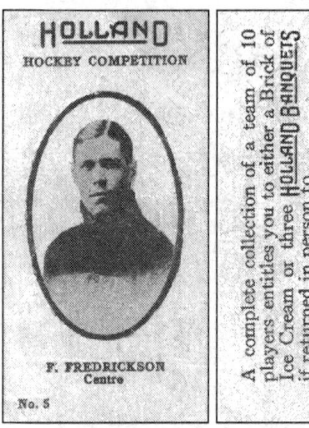

has a black and white head and shoulders shot of the player, in an oval-shaped black frame on white card stock. The words "Holland Hockey Competition" appear above the picture, with the player's name and position below. The cards are numbered in the lower left corner on the front. The horizontally formatted card back has an offer to exchange one complete collection of ten players for either a brick of ice cream or three Holland Banquets. Supposedly the difficult card in the set was C. Neil, marked as SP in the checklist below.

		EX-MT	VG-E	GOOD
COMPLETE SET (10)		750.00	300.00	75.00
COMMON PLAYER (1-10)		75.00	30.00	7.50
☐ 1	Wally Fridfinson	75.00	30.00	7.50
☐ 2	H. McMunn	75.00	30.00	7.50
☐ 3	A. Somers	75.00	30.00	7.50
☐ 4	F. Woodall	75.00	30.00	7.50
☐ 5	Frank Fredrickson	150.00	60.00	15.00
☐ 6	R.J. Benson	75.00	30.00	7.50
☐ 7	H. Neil	75.00	30.00	7.50
☐ 8	J.W. Byron	75.00	30.00	7.50
☐ 9	C. Neil SP	150.00	60.00	15.00
☐ 10	J. Austman	75.00	30.00	7.50

1990 Hull Collection UMD

This 12-card set (The Brett Hull Collection), which measures the standard, 2 1/2" by 3 1/2", was issued by University Minnesota-Duluth in conjunction with World Class Marketing and Collect-A-Sport. The cards have maroon and gold borders on the top and the bottom and are borderless on the side. The border colors are the school colors of

University Minnesota-Duluth. The horizontally formatted card back features his amateur statistics along with various biographical blurbs. Cards numbered 10 and 11 are in black and white while the rest of the set was issued with color photos. The set was issued in a special white box with a photo of Brett Hull on the front as well. The sets are numbered (out of 5,000) on the backs of the number 1 card.

	MINT	EXC	G-VG
COMPLETE SET (12)	15.00	6.00	1.50
COMMON HULL (1-12)	1.50	.60	.15
☐ 1 Hull Portrait	3.00	1.20	.30
☐ 2 Hull Behind the Net	1.50	.60	.15
☐ 3 Hull Skating	1.50	.60	.15
(8 in picture)			
☐ 4 Hull Shooting	1.50	.60	.15
☐ 5 Hull Stick under	1.50	.60	.15
right arm			
☐ 6 Hull Action stick	1.50	.60	.15
at waist			
☐ 7 Hull in front of	1.50	.60	.15
opponents bench			
☐ 8 Hull stickhandling	1.50	.60	.15
☐ 9 Hull Against	1.50	.60	.15
Providence			
☐ 10 Hull at the net	2.50	1.00	.25
(black and white; shown playing against the Russian Junior Red Army team in Leningrad)			
☐ 11 Hull Portrait	1.50	.60	.15
(black and white)			
☐ 12 1985-86 UMD	1.50	.60	.15

1992-93 Humpty Dumpty I

This 26-card set was sponsored by Humpty Dumpty Foods Ltd., a snack food company located in Eastern Canada and owned by Borden Inc. This promotion consisted of one cello-wrapped (approximately) 1 7/16" by 1 15/16" mini-hockey card, which was inserted into specially marked bags of Humpty Dumpty Chips and Snacks. Two series of cards were produced, and complete sets could be obtained only by collecting the cards through the promotion. The promotion lasted from October 1992 to March 1993. A total of 11,000,000 series I cards were produced, or 423,077 of each card, and they were evenly distributed between Ontario, Quebec, and the Atlantic provinces. The fronts display glossy color action photos, with the team logo superimposed toward the bottom of the picture. On a white panel framed by gray, the back presents 1991-92 season statistics and biography in French and English. The cards are unnumbered and checklisted below in alphabetical order.

	MINT	EXC	G-VG
COMPLETE SET (26)	15.00	6.00	1.50
COMMON PLAYER (1-26)	.35	.14	.03

☐ 1 Ray Bourque	.75	.30	.07
Boston Bruins			
☐ 2 Rod Brind'Amour	.50	.20	.05
Philadelphia Flyers			
☐ 3 Chris Chelios	.50	.20	.05
Chicago Blackhawks			
☐ 4 Wendel Clark	.75	.30	.07
Toronto Maple Leafs			
☐ 5 Gilbert Dionne	.35	.14	.03
Montreal Canadiens			
☐ 6 Pat Falloon	.50	.20	.05
San Jose Sharks			
☐ 7 Ray Ferraro	.35	.14	.03
New York Islanders			
☐ 8 Theoren Fleury	.50	.20	.05
Calgary Flames			
☐ 9 Grant Fuhr	.50	.20	.05
Toronto Maple Leafs			
☐ 10 Wayne Gretzky	4.00	1.60	.40
Los Angeles Kings			
☐ 11 Kevin Hatcher	.35	.14	.03
Washington Capitals			
☐ 12 Valeri Kamensky	.35	.14	.03
Quebec Nordiques			
☐ 13 Mike Keane	.35	.14	.03
Montreal Canadiens			
☐ 14 Brian Leetch	1.00	.40	.10
New York Rangers			
☐ 15 Kirk McLean	.75	.30	.07
Vancouver Canucks			
☐ 16 Alexander Mogilny	1.25	.50	.12
Buffalo Sabres			
☐ 17 Troy Murray	.35	.14	.03
Winnipeg Jets			
☐ 18 Patrick Roy	2.00	.80	.20
Montreal Canadiens			
☐ 19 Joe Sakic	.75	.30	.07
Quebec Nordiques			
☐ 20 Brendan Shanahan	1.00	.40	.10
St. Louis Blues			
☐ 21 Kevin Stevens	.75	.30	.07
Pittsburgh Penguins			
☐ 22 Scott Stevens	.50	.20	.05
New Jersey Devils			
☐ 23 Mark Tinordi	.35	.14	.03
Minnesota North Stars			
☐ 24 Steve Yzerman	1.25	.50	.12
Detroit Red Wings			
☐ 25 Zarley Zalapski	.35	.14	.03
Hartford Whalers			
☐ 26 Checklist	.35	.14	.03

1992-93 Humpty Dumpty II

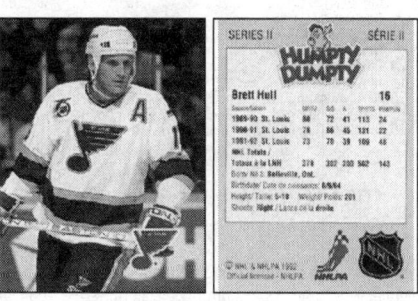

This 26-card set was sponsored by Humpty Dumpty Foods Ltd., a snack food company located in Eastern Canada and owned by Borden Inc. This promotion consisted of one cello-wrapped approximately 1 7/16" by 1 15/16" mini-hockey card randomly inserted into specially marked bags of Humpty Dumpty Chips and Snacks. Two series of cards were produced, and complete sets could be obtained only by collecting the cards through the promotion. The promotion lasted from October 1992 to March 1993. A total of 18,000,000 series II cards were produced, or 692,307 of each card, and they were evenly distributed between Ontario, Quebec, and the Atlantic provinces. The fronts display glossy color action photos, with the team logo superimposed toward the bottom of the picture. On a white panel framed by beige, the back presents 1991-92 season statistics and biography in French and English. The cards are unnumbered and checklisted below in alphabetical order.

	MINT	EXC	G-VG
COMPLETE SET (26)	15.00	6.00	1.50
COMMON PLAYER (1-26)	.35	.14	.03
☐ 1 Drake Berehowsky	.35	.14	.03
Toronto Maple Leafs			
☐ 2 Shayne Corson	.35	.14	.03
Edmonton Oilers			
☐ 3 Russ Courtnall	.50	.20	.05
Minnesota North Stars			
☐ 4 Dave Ellett	.35	.14	.03
Toronto Maple Leafs			
☐ 5 Sergei Fedorov	1.50	.60	.15
Detroit Red Wings			
☐ 6 Dave Gagner	.35	.14	.03
Minnesota North Stars			
☐ 7 Doug Gilmour	1.50	.60	.15
Toronto Maple Leafs			
☐ 8 Phil Housley	.50	.20	.05
Winnipeg Jets			
☐ 9 Brett Hull	2.00	.80	.20
St. Louis Blues			
☐ 10 Jaromir Jagr	1.50	.60	.15
Pittsburgh Penguins			
☐ 11 Pat LaFontaine	1.25	.50	.12
Buffalo Sabres			
☐ 12 Mario Lemieux	3.00	1.20	.30
Pittsburgh Penguins			
☐ 13 Trevor Linden	1.00	.40	.10
Vancouver Canucks			
☐ 14 Al MacInnis	.50	.20	.05
Calgary Flames			
☐ 15 Mark Messier	1.00	.40	.10
New York Rangers			
☐ 16 Cam Neely	.75	.30	.07
Boston Bruins			
☐ 17 Owen Nolan	.50	.20	.05
Quebec Nordiques			
☐ 18 Bill Ranford	.50	.20	.05
Edmonton Oilers			
☐ 19 Luc Robitaille	.75	.30	.07
Los Angeles Kings			
☐ 20 Jeremy Roenick	1.50	.60	.15
Chicago Blackhawks			
☐ 21 Mats Sundin	1.00	.40	.10
Quebec Nordiques			
☐ 22 Chris Terreri	.35	.14	.03
New Jersey Devils			
☐ 23 Steve Thomas	.35	.14	.03
New York Islanders			
☐ 24 Pat Verbeek	.35	.14	.03
Hartford Whalers			
☐ 25 Neil Wilkinson	.35	.14	.03
San Jose Sharks			
☐ 26 Checklist	.35	.14	.03

1984 Islanders Islander News

This 38-card set of New York Islanders was sponsored by Islander News and issued during the summer of 1984 to commemorate the Islanders' fourth consecutive Stanley Cup victory. The cards measure the standard size, 2 1/2" by 3 1/2". The color photo on the front is framed by a thin black border. Another thin black border (with rounded corners) outlines the card front, and the space in between is pale blue. The player's name is given below the picture and sandwiched between a trophy cup icon and the New York Islanders' logo. The back has biographical information and a career summary on the player.

	MINT	EXC	G-VG
COMPLETE SET (38)	25.00	10.00	2.50
COMMON PLAYER (1-38)	.60	.24	.06

☐ 1 Checklist Card	1.25	.50	.12
☐ 2 Mike Bossy	4.00	1.60	.40
☐ 3 Bob Bourne	.60	.24	.06
☐ 4 Billy Carroll	.60	.24	.06
☐ 5 Greg Gilbert	.60	.24	.06
☐ 6 Clark Gillies	1.00	.40	.10
☐ 7 Butch Goring	.75	.30	.07
☐ 8 Mats Hallin	.60	.24	.06
☐ 9 Anders Kallur	.60	.24	.06
☐ 10 Wayne Merrick	.60	.24	.06
☐ 11 Bob Nystrom	.75	.30	.07
☐ 12 Brent Sutter	1.00	.40	.10
☐ 13 Duane Sutter	1.00	.40	.10
☐ 14 John Tonelli	1.00	.40	.10
☐ 15 Bryan Trottier	3.00	1.20	.30
☐ 16 Tomas Jonsson	.60	.24	.06
☐ 17 Gordie Lane	.60	.24	.06
☐ 18 Dave Langevin	.60	.24	.06
☐ 19 Ken Morrow	.75	.30	.07
☐ 20 Stefan Persson	.75	.30	.07
☐ 21 Denis Potvin	2.00	.80	.20
☐ 22 Roland Melanson	.75	.30	.07
☐ 23 Billy Smith	2.00	.80	.20
☐ 24 Cup Number 1	.60	.24	.06
☐ 25 Cup Number 2	.60	.24	.06
☐ 26 Cup Number 4	.60	.24	.06
☐ 27 Lorne Henning CO	.60	.24	.06
☐ 28 Bill Torrey GM	.60	.24	.06
☐ 29 Al Arbour CO	1.00	.40	.10
☐ 30 Waske-Pickard	.60	.24	.06
Two Trainers			
☐ 31 1979-80 Team Photo	1.00	.40	.10
☐ 32 1980-81 Team Photo	1.00	.40	.10
☐ 33 1981-82 Team Photo	1.00	.40	.10
☐ 34 1982-83 Team Photo	1.00	.40	.10
☐ 35 Mike Bossy	2.00	.80	.20
'82 Conn Smythe Winner			
☐ 36 Billy Smith	1.25	.50	.12
'83 Conn Smythe Winner			
☐ 37 Bryan Trottier	1.50	.60	.15
'80 Conn Smythe Winner			
☐ 38 Butch Goring	.75	.30	.07
'81 Conn Smythe Winner			

1985 Islanders Islander News

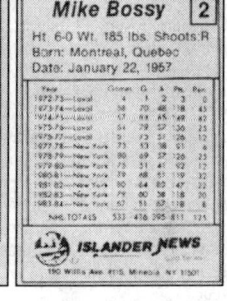

This 37-card set of New York Islanders was sponsored by Islander News and issued during the summer of 1985. The cards measure the standard size 2 1/2" by 3 1/2". The color photo on the front is enframed by a thin black border. A red and blue hockey stick forms the border on the left side of the picture, with the end of the stick below the picture. The words "Islander News" appears on the end of the stick, and the player's name is given to the right. The back has biographical information including a career summary on the player as well as the notation "Second Series". The key card in the set is the Pat LaFontaine card as it was issued concurrently with his O-Pee-Chee and Topps Rookie Cards.

		MINT	EXC	G-VG
COMPLETE SET (37)		30.00	12.00	3.00
COMMON PLAYER (1-37)		.60	.24	.06
☐ 1	Checklist Card	1.25	.50	.12
☐ 2	Mike Bossy	4.00	1.60	.40
☐ 3	Bob Bourne	.60	.24	.06
☐ 4	Pat Flatley	1.00	.40	.10
☐ 5	Greg Gilbert	.60	.24	.06
☐ 6	Clark Gillies	1.00	.40	.10
☐ 7	Mats Hallin	.60	.24	.06
☐ 8	Anders Kallur	.60	.24	.06
☐ 9	Alan Kerr	.60	.24	.06
☐ 10	Roger Kortko	.60	.24	.06
☐ 11	Pat LaFontaine	8.00	3.25	.80
☐ 12	Bob Nystrom	.75	.30	.07
☐ 13	Brent Sutter	1.00	.40	.10
☐ 14	Duane Sutter	1.00	.40	.10
☐ 15	John Tonelli	1.00	.40	.10
☐ 16	Bryan Trottier	3.00	1.20	.30
☐ 17	Paul Boutilier	.60	.24	.06
☐ 18	Gerald Diduck	.60	.24	.06
☐ 19	Gord Dineen	.60	.24	.06
☐ 20	Tomas Jonsson	.60	.24	.06
☐ 21	Gordie Lane	.60	.24	.06
☐ 22	Dave Langevin	.60	.24	.06
☐ 23	Ken Morrow	.75	.30	.07
☐ 24	Stefan Persson	.75	.30	.07
☐ 25	Denis Potvin	2.00	.80	.20
☐ 26	Kelly Hrudey	3.00	1.20	.30
☐ 27	Billy Smith	2.00	.80	.20
☐ 28	Bill Torrey GM/P.	.60	.24	.06
☐ 29	Al Arbour CO	1.00	.40	.10
☐ 30	Brian Kilrea CO	.60	.24	.06
☐ 31	Pickard/Smith Two Trainers	.60	.24	.06
☐ 32	Mike Bossy Milestone-400 Goals	2.00	.80	.20
☐ 33	Denis Potvin Milestone-600 Assists	1.25	.50	.12
☐ 34	Billy Smith Milestone-500 Games	1.25	.50	.12
☐ 35	Bryan Trottier Milestone-1000 Points	1.50	.60	.15
☐ 36	1984-85 Team	1.00	.40	.10
☐ 37	Wales Champs	.75	.30	.07

1985 Islanders Islander News Trottier

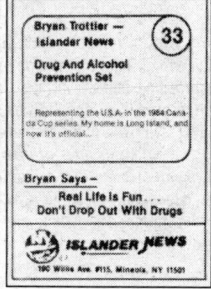

This 33-card set was sponsored by the New York Islander News and issued during the summer of 1985 supposedly by the Port Washington Police Department. It highlights the early career of then-Islander, Bryan Trottier, who is credited with writing the drug and alcohol prevention tips on the back of the cards. The cards measure the standard size, 2 1/2" by 3 1/2", and feature color or black and white photos of Trottier on the front. They are framed by a red border on two sides, and white border; the white border is in the shape of a hockey stick, with Trottier's signature across the bottom of the stick. The cards are numbered on both sides. In addition to the anti-drug or alcohol message, the back also has Trottier's own comments about each photo.

		MINT	EXC	G-VG
COMPLETE SET (33)		20.00	8.00	2.00
COMMON PLAYER (1-33)		.60	.24	.06
☐ 1	Bryan Trottier Penalty box	1.50	.60	.15
☐ 2	Bryan Trottier Swift Current Broncos	1.00	.40	.10
☐ 3	Bryan Trottier Three goals in first game at Nassau Coliseum	.60	.24	.06
☐ 4	Bryan Trottier All-Star game	.60	.24	.06
☐ 5	Bryan Trottier Four goals vs. Atlanta	.60	.24	.06
☐ 6	Bryan Trottier Ross and Hart Trophies	.75	.30	.07
☐ 7	Bryan Trottier Street hockey equipment	.60	.24	.06
☐ 8	Bryan Trottier Bearing down on the draw against Maruk	.75	.30	.07
☐ 9	Bryan Trottier Pleading with referee	.60	.24	.06
☐ 10	Bryan Trottier Trottier/Rangers action	.60	.24	.06
☐ 11	Bryan Trottier Trottier/Holmgren action	.75	.30	.07
☐ 12	Bryan Trottier Trottier/Canadiens action	.75	.30	.07
☐ 13	Bryan Trottier 1980 Boston playoff	.60	.24	.06
☐ 14	Bryan Trottier 1980 Final Game vs. Flyers	.60	.24	.06
☐ 15	Bryan Trottier NHL Awards Luncheon	.60	.24	.06
☐ 16	Bryan Trottier Trottier/Rangers action	.60	.24	.06
☐ 17	Bryan Trottier Watching action in resting area	.60	.24	.06
☐ 18	Bryan Trottier Warm-up time	.60	.24	.06
☐ 19	Bryan Trottier Debating with referee	.60	.24	.06
☐ 20	Bryan Trottier 1981 Playoff with Oilers	.60	.24	.06
☐ 21	Bryan Trottier Trottier/Gretzky action	5.00	2.00	.50
☐ 22	Bryan Trottier Trottier/North Stars action	.60	.24	.06
☐ 23	Bryan Trottier Congratulating Don Beaupre	.75	.30	.07
☐ 24	Bryan Trottier Second Stanley Cup Championship	.60	.24	.06
☐ 25	Bryan Trottier Trottier/Sutter celebrate	.60	.24	.06
☐ 26	Bryan Trottier Trottier psyching himself	.60	.24	.06
☐ 27	Bryan Trottier Trottier/Devils action	.60	.24	.06
☐ 28	Bryan Trottier 1983 All-Star	.75	.30	.07
☐ 29	Bryan Trottier Trottier defending goal	.60	.24	.06
☐ 30	Bryan Trottier Fourth Stanley Cup Championship	.60	.24	.06
☐ 31	Bryan Trottier Trottier and Denis	1.50	.60	.15

		MINT	EXC	G-VG
	Potvin celebrate			
☐ 32	Bryan Trottier.....................	2.00	.80	.20
	Trottier and Mike			
	Bossy celebrate			
☐ 33	Bryan Trottier.......................	1.00	.40	.10
	1984 Canada Cup Series			

1984-85 Jets Police

This 24-card set of Winnipeg Jets was sponsored by The Kinsmen Club of Winnipeg and all police forces in Manitoba. The cards measure approximately 2 5/8" by 3 11/16" and were issued in panels of two cards each. The front features a color posed photo of the player shot against a blue background. The borders are white, and the player information beneath the picture is sandwiched between the Jets' and the Kinsmen logos. The back has "Jets Tips" in the form of a hockey tip paralleled by an anti-crime or safety tip. We have checklisted the cards below in alphabetical order, with the uniform number to the right of the player's name.

		MINT	EXC	G-VG
COMPLETE SET (24).....................		8.00	3.25	.80
COMMON PLAYER (1-24)...............		.35	.14	.03
☐ 1	Scott Arniel 11	.35	.14	.03
☐ 2	Dave Babych 44	.50	.20	.05
☐ 3	Marc Behrend 29	.35	.14	.03
☐ 4	Laurie Boschman 16	.35	.14	.03
☐ 5	Randy Carlyle 8.....................	.50	.20	.05
☐ 6	Dave Ellett 2	.50	.20	.05
☐ 7	John B. Ferguson VP/GM........	.50	.20	.05
☐ 8	Dale Hawerchuk 10	1.50	.60	.15
☐ 9	Brian Hayward 1....................	.50	.20	.05
☐ 10	Jim Kyte 6	.35	.14	.03
☐ 11	Morris Lukowich 12	.35	.14	.03
☐ 12	Bengt Lundholm 22	.35	.14	.03
☐ 13	Paul MacLean 15	.50	.20	.05
☐ 14	Andrew McBain 20.................	.35	.14	.03
☐ 15	Brian Mullen 19....................	.50	.20	.05
☐ 16	Robert Picard 3	.35	.14	.03
☐ 17	Paul Pooley 23	.35	.14	.03
☐ 18	Doug Smail 9	.50	.20	.05
☐ 19	Thomas Steen 25	.75	.30	.07
☐ 20	Perry Turnbull 27	.35	.14	.03
☐ 21	Tim Watters 7	.35	.14	.03
☐ 22	Ron Wilson 24	.35	.14	.03
☐ 23	Assistant Coaches.................	.35	.14	.03
	Bill Sutherland			
	Barry Long			
	Rick Bowness			
☐ 24	Team Photo..........................	.75	.30	.07

1985-86 Jets Police

This 24-card set of Winnipeg Jets was sponsored by The Kinsmen Club of Winnipeg and all police forces in Manitoba. The cards measure approximately 2 5/8" by 3 3/4" and were issued in panels of two cards each. The front features a

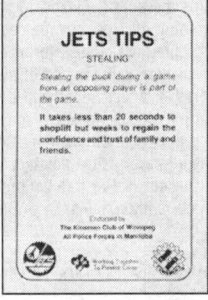

color action shot of the player. The borders are white, and the player information beneath the picture is sandwiched between the Jets' and the Kinsmen logos. The back has "Jets Tips" in the form of a hockey tip paralleled by an anti-crime or safety tip. We have checklisted the cards below in alphabetical order, with the uniform number to the right of the player's name.

		MINT	EXC	G-VG
COMPLETE SET (24).....................		8.00	3.25	.80
COMMON PLAYER (1-24)...............		.35	.14	.03
☐ 1	Scott Arniel 11	.35	.14	.03
☐ 2	Laurie Boschman 16	.35	.14	.03
☐ 3	Dan Bouchard 35	.35	.14	.03
☐ 4	Randy Carlyle 8.....................	.50	.20	.05
☐ 5	Dave Ellett 2	.50	.20	.05
☐ 6	John B. Ferguson VP/GM........	.50	.20	.05
☐ 7	Dale Hawerchuk 10	1.25	.50	.12
☐ 8	Brian Hayward 1....................	.50	.20	.05
☐ 9	Jim Kyte 6	.35	.14	.03
☐ 10	Paul MacLean 15	.50	.20	.05
☐ 11	Mario Marois 22....................	.35	.14	.03
☐ 12	Andrew McBain 20.................	.35	.14	.03
☐ 13	Anssi Melametsa 14	.35	.14	.03
☐ 14	Brian Mullen 19....................	.50	.20	.05
☐ 15	Ray Neufeld 28.....................	.35	.14	.03
☐ 16	Jim Nill 17	.35	.14	.03
☐ 17	Dave Silk 34	.35	.14	.03
☐ 18	Doug Smail 9	.50	.20	.05
☐ 19	Thomas Steen 25	.75	.30	.07
☐ 20	Perry Turnbull 27	.35	.14	.03
☐ 21	Tim Watters 7	.35	.14	.03
☐ 22	Ron Wilson 24	.35	.14	.03
☐ 23	Assistant Coaches.................	.35	.14	.03
	Bill Sutherland			
	Barry Long			
	Rick Bowness			
☐ 24	Team Photo..........................	.75	.30	.07

1985-86 Jets Silverwood Dairy

This six-panel set of Winnipeg Jets was issued by Silverwood Dairy on the side of half-gallon milk cartons. The picture and text are printed in blue. The top of the panel features an oval-shaped head and shoulders shot of the player, with his name immediately below the picture. The bottom of the panel presents the instructions for the Silverwood Game of the Month contest, in which ten lucky winners would win a pair of tickets to see the featured game of the month. The panels are unnumbered and checklisted below in alphabetical order.

		MINT	EXC	G-VG
COMPLETE SET (6)........................		60.00	24.00	6.00
COMMON PLAYER (1-6).................		10.00	4.00	1.00
☐ 1	Laurie Boschman	10.00	4.00	1.00
☐ 2	Randy Carlyle........................	12.00	5.00	1.20

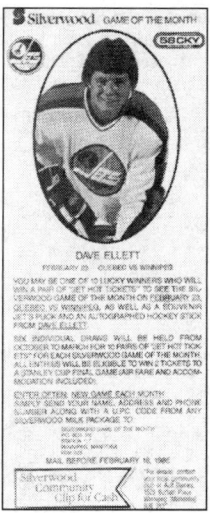

		MINT	EXC	G-VG
☐ 3	Dave Ellett	12.00	5.00	1.20
☐ 4	Dale Hawerchuk	20.00	8.00	2.00
☐ 5	Paul MacLean	10.00	4.00	1.00
☐ 6	Brian Mullen	12.00	5.00	1.20

1988-89 Jets Police

This 24-card set of Winnipeg Jets was sponsored by The Kinsmen Club of Winnipeg and all police forces in Manitoba. The cards measure approximately 2 5/8" by 3 3/4" and were issued as 12 panels of two cards each. By uniform numbers, the panel pairs are CO/TEAM, 39/ACO, 23/4, 6/10, 16/20, 25/32, 19/22, 8/7, 27/28, 2/34, 9/12, and 31/33. The front features a color action shot of the player. The borders are white, and the player information beneath the picture is sandwiched between the Jets' and the Kinsmen logos. The back has "Jets Tips" in the form of a hockey tip paralleled by an anti-crime or safety tip. We have checklisted the cards below in alphabetical order, with the uniform number to the right of the player's name.

		MINT	EXC	G-VG
COMPLETE SET (24)		8.00	3.25	.80
COMMON PLAYER (1-24)		.35	.14	.03
☐ 1	Brent Ashton 7	.35	.14	.03
☐ 2	Laurie Boschman 16	.35	.14	.03
☐ 3	Randy Carlyle 8	.50	.20	.05
☐ 4	Alain Chevrier 31	.50	.20	.05
☐ 5	Iain Duncan 19	.35	.14	.03

☐ 6	Dave Ellett 2	.50	.20	.05
☐ 7	Pat Elynuik 34	.75	.30	.07
☐ 8	Randy Gilhen 39	.35	.14	.03
☐ 9	Dale Hawerchuk 10	1.00	.40	.10
☐ 10	Dave Hunter 12	.35	.14	.03
☐ 11	Hannu Jarvenpaa 23	.35	.14	.03
☐ 12	Jim Kyte 6	.35	.14	.03
☐ 13	Dan Maloney CO	.35	.14	.03
☐ 14	Mario Marois 22	.35	.14	.03
☐ 15	Andrew McBain 20	.35	.14	.03
☐ 16	Ray Neufeld 28	.35	.14	.03
☐ 17	Teppo Numminen 27	.50	.20	.05
☐ 18	Fredrik Olausson 4	.75	.30	.07
☐ 19	Eldon Reddick 33	.75	.30	.07
☐ 20	Doug Smail 9	.50	.20	.05
☐ 21	Thomas Steen 25	.75	.30	.07
☐ 22	Peter Taglianetti 32	.35	.14	.03
☐ 23	Assistant Coaches	.35	.14	.03
	Bill Sutherland			
	Bruce Southern			
	Rick St.Croix			
☐ 24	Team Photo	.75	.30	.07

1989-90 Jets Safeway

This 30-card set was sponsored by Safeway Limited of Canada and features players from the Winnipeg Jets. The cards measure approximately 3 3/4" by 6 7/8". The front has a color action photo of the player, with his number and name above the picture between the Jets' and Safeway logos. The back is outlined in black boxes and includes player information as well as an oversized Safeway logo and advertisement. Since the cards are unnumbered, they are listed below in alphabetical order with the player's sweater number after the name.

		MINT	EXC	G-VG
COMPLETE SET (30)		12.00	5.00	1.20
COMMON PLAYER (1-30)		.35	.14	.03
☐ 1	Brent Ashton 7	.35	.14	.03
☐ 2	Stu Barnes 14	.50	.20	.05
☐ 3	Brad Berry 29	.35	.14	.03
☐ 4	Daniel Berthiaume 30	.50	.20	.05
☐ 5	Laurie Boschman 16	.35	.14	.03
☐ 6	Randy Carlyle 8	.50	.20	.05
☐ 7	Shawn Cronin 44	.35	.14	.03
☐ 8	Randy Cunneyworth 18	.50	.20	.05
☐ 9	Gord Donnelly 34	.50	.20	.05
☐ 10	Tom Draper 37	.75	.30	.07
☐ 11	Iain Duncan 19	.35	.14	.03
☐ 12	Dave Ellett 2	.50	.20	.05
☐ 13	Pat Elynuik 15	.60	.24	.06
☐ 14	Bob Essensa 35	1.00	.40	.10
☐ 15	Paul Fenton 11	.35	.14	.03
☐ 16	Dale Hawerchuk 10	1.00	.40	.10
☐ 17	Brent Hughes 46	.50	.20	.05
☐ 18	Mark Kumpel 21	.35	.14	.03
☐ 19	Moe Mantha 22	.35	.14	.03

☐ 20 Dave McLlwain 20	.35	.14	.03
☐ 21 Brian McReynolds 26	.50	.20	.05
☐ 22 Teppo Numminen 27	.50	.20	.05
☐ 23 Fredrik Olausson 4	.75	.30	.07
☐ 24 Greg Paslawski 28	.35	.14	.03
☐ 25 Doug Smail 12	.50	.20	.05
☐ 26 Thomas Steen 25	.75	.30	.07
☐ 27 Peter Taglianetti 32	.35	.14	.03
☐ 28 Benny 00 (Mascot)	.35	.14	.03
☐ 29 Coaches Card	.35	.14	.03
Alpo Suhonen			
Bob Murdoch			
Clare Drake			
☐ 30 Team Photo	.75	.30	.07

1990-91 Jets IGA

This 35-card set measures approximately 3 1/2" by 6 1/2" and features color action player photos with white borders. The team logo, sweater number, player's name, and sponsor logo appear at the card top between two thin purple stripes. The back is divided into two sections; in the upper appears player information, while in the lower appears a GreenCare advertisement (environmentally safe and carried in IGA stores). The cards are unnumbered and checklisted below in alphabetical order.

	MINT	EXC	G-VG
COMPLETE SET (35)	15.00	6.00	1.50
COMMON PLAYER (1-35)	.40	.16	.04
☐ 1 Scott Arniel	.40	.16	.04
☐ 2 Brent Ashton	.40	.16	.04
☐ 3 Don Barber	.40	.16	.04
☐ 4 Stephane Beauregard	.75	.30	.07
☐ 5 Randy Carlyle	.60	.24	.06
☐ 6 Danton Cole	.60	.24	.06
☐ 7 Shawn Cronin	.40	.16	.04
☐ 8 Gord Donnelly	.60	.24	.06
☐ 9 Clare Drake CO	.40	.16	.04
☐ 10 Kris Draper	.60	.24	.06
☐ 11 Iain Duncan	.40	.16	.04
☐ 12 Pat Elynuik	.75	.30	.07
☐ 13 Bob Essensa	1.00	.40	.10
☐ 14 Doug Evans	.40	.16	.04
☐ 15 Phil Housley	1.25	.50	.12
☐ 16 Sergei Kharin	.40	.16	.04
☐ 17 Mark Kumpel	.40	.16	.04
☐ 18 Guy Larose	.40	.16	.04
☐ 19 Paul MacDermid	.40	.16	.04
☐ 20 Moe Mantha	.40	.16	.04
☐ 21 Brian Marchment	.60	.24	.06
☐ 22 Dave McLlwain	.40	.16	.04
☐ 23 Bob Murdoch CO	.40	.16	.04
☐ 24 Teppo Numminen	.60	.24	.06
☐ 25 Fredrik Olausson	.75	.30	.07
☐ 26 Ed Olczyk	.75	.30	.07
☐ 27 Mark Osborne	.40	.16	.04
☐ 28 Greg Paslawski	.40	.16	.04
☐ 29 Terry Simpson CO	.40	.16	.04
☐ 30 Thomas Steen	.75	.30	.07
☐ 31 Phil Sykes	.40	.16	.04
☐ 32 Rick Tabaracci	.60	.24	.06
☐ 33 Simon Wheeldon	.40	.16	.04
☐ 34 Benny (Mascot)	.40	.16	.04
☐ 35 Team Photo	1.25	.50	.12

1991-92 Jets IGA

This 35-card set measures approximately 3 1/2" by 6 1/2" and features color action player photos with white borders. The IGA logo, sweater number, player's name, and a picture of Cadbury's Caramilk candy appear at the card bottom between two thin purple stripes. The back is divided into three sections; in the top appears player information; in the middle appears a Caramilk advertisement; while in the bottom appears a GreenCare advertisement (environ-

mentally safe and carried in IGA stores). The front of the Thomas Steen card shows (in lower right corner) another Cadbury candy bar/product, "Crunchie". The cards are unnumbered and checklisted below in alphabetical order.

	MINT	EXC	G-VG
COMPLETE SET (35)	15.00	6.00	1.50
COMMON PLAYER (1-35)	.40	.16	.04
☐ 1 Stu Barnes	.60	.24	.06
☐ 2 Stephane Beauregard	.75	.30	.07
☐ 3 Luciano Borsato	.40	.16	.04
☐ 4 Randy Carlyle	.60	.24	.06
☐ 5 Danton Cole	.60	.24	.06
☐ 6 Shawn Cronin	.40	.16	.04
☐ 7 Burton Cummings	.75	.30	.07
☐ 8 Mike Eagles	.40	.16	.04
☐ 9 Pat Elynuik	.60	.24	.06
☐ 10 Bryan Erickson	.40	.16	.04
☐ 11 Bob Essensa	.75	.30	.07
☐ 12 Doug Evans	.40	.16	.04
☐ 13 Mike Hartman	.40	.16	.04
☐ 14 Phil Housley	1.00	.40	.10
☐ 15 Dean Kennedy	.40	.16	.04
☐ 16 Paul MacDermid	.40	.16	.04
☐ 17 Moe Mantha	.40	.16	.04
☐ 18 Rob Murray	.40	.16	.04
☐ 19 Troy Murray	.75	.30	.07
☐ 20 Teppo Numminen	.60	.24	.06
☐ 21 Fredrik Olausson	.75	.30	.07
☐ 22 Ed Olczyk	.75	.30	.07
☐ 23 Mark Osborne	.40	.16	.04
☐ 24 John Paddock CO	.40	.16	.04
☐ 25 Kent Paynter	.40	.16	.04
☐ 26 Dave Prior	.40	.16	.04
☐ 27 Russ Romaniuk	.40	.16	.04
☐ 28 Darrin Shannon	.60	.24	.06
☐ 29 Terry Simpson CO	.40	.16	.04
☐ 30 Thomas Steen	.75	.30	.07
☐ 31 Phil Sykes	.40	.16	.04
☐ 32 Rick Tabaracci	.60	.24	.06
☐ 33 Glen Williamson CO	.40	.16	.04
☐ 34 Benny (Mascot)	.40	.16	.04
☐ 35 Team Photo UER	1.25	.50	.12
(Incorrectly marked 1990-91)			

1992 Jofa/Koho

 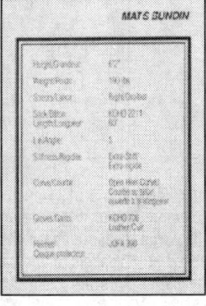

This six-card set was apparently sponsored by four major manufacturers of hockey equipment: Jofa, Koho, Titan, and Canadien. The set is also known as "The Endorsers" and features six famous current players who endorse their respective products. The cards measure the standard size (2 1/2" by 3 1/2") and are printed on thin card stock. The fronts feature color close-up player photos. The borders shade from one color to another and are studded with miniature stars. On various pastel-colored backs, biographical information is presented inside black border stripes. The cards are unnumbered and checklisted below in alphabetical order. The manufacturer's name that appears at the bottom of the card front is listed below beneath the player's name.

	MINT	EXC	G-VG
COMPLETE SET (6)	10.00	4.00	1.00
COMMON PLAYER (1-6)	1.00	.40	.10
☐ 1 Theoren Fleury	1.00	.40	.10
Jofa			
☐ 2 Jari Kurri	1.00	.40	.10
Koho			
☐ 3 Mario Lemieux	4.00	1.60	.40
Koho			
☐ 4 Eric Lindros	5.00	2.00	.50
Titan			
☐ 5 Denis Savard	1.00	.40	.10
Canadien			
☐ 6 Mats Sundin	1.50	.60	.15
Jofa			

1975-76 Kahn's Stingers

This set of 14 photos was issued on wrappers of Kahn's Wieners and Beef Franks and features players of the Cincinnati Stingers of the WHA. The wrappers are approximately 2 11/16" wide and 11 5/8" long. The wiener wrappers are predominantly yellow and carry a 2" by 1 1/4" black-and-white posed photo of the player with a facsimile autograph inscribed across the picture. The beef frank wrappers are identical in design but predominantly red in color. The wrappers are unnumbered and checklisted below in alphabetical order.

	NRMT	VG-E	GOOD
COMPLETE SET (14)	120.00	50.00	12.00
COMMON PLAYER (1-14)	10.00	4.00	1.00
☐ 1 Serge Aubry	10.00	4.00	1.00
☐ 2 Bryan Campbell	10.00	4.00	1.00
☐ 3 Rick Dudley	15.00	6.00	1.50
☐ 4 Pierre Guite	10.00	4.00	1.00
☐ 5 John Hughes	10.00	4.00	1.00
☐ 6 Claude Larose	12.00	5.00	1.20
☐ 7 Jacques Locas UER	10.00	4.00	1.00
(Misspelled Jacque)			
☐ 8 Bernie MacNeil	10.00	4.00	1.00
☐ 9 Mike Pelyk	10.00	4.00	1.00
☐ 10 Ron Plumb	10.00	4.00	1.00
☐ 11 Dave Smedsmo	10.00	4.00	1.00
☐ 12 Dennis Sobchuk	10.00	4.00	1.00
☐ 13 Gene Sobchuk	10.00	4.00	1.00
☐ 14 Gary Veneruzzo	10.00	4.00	1.00

1976-77 Kahn's Stingers

This set of six photos was issued on wrappers of Kahn's Wieners and features players of the Cincinnati Stingers of the WHA. The wrappers are approximately 2 11/16" wide and 11 5/8" long. On a predominantly yellow wrapper with red lettering, a 2" by 1 1/4" black and white player action photo appears, with a facsimile autograph inscribed across the picture. The wrappers are unnumbered and checklisted below in alphabetical order. This set is distinguished from the previous year by the fact that these card photo poses (for the players in both sets) appear to be taken in an action sequence compared to the posed photographs taken the previous year.

	NRMT	VG-E	GOOD
COMPLETE SET (6)	120.00	50.00	12.00
COMMON PLAYER (1-6)	20.00	8.00	2.00
☐ 1 Rick Dudley	30.00	12.00	3.00
(Action sequence photo)			
☐ 2 Dave Inkpen	25.00	10.00	2.50
☐ 3 Claude Larose	25.00	10.00	2.50
(Action sequence photo)			
☐ 4 Jacques Locas	20.00	8.00	2.00
(Action sequence photo)			
☐ 5 Ron Plumb	20.00	8.00	2.00
(Action sequence photo)			
☐ 6 Dennis Sobchuk	20.00	8.00	2.00
(Action sequence photo)			

1972 Kellogg's Iron-On Transfers

These six iron-on transfers each measure approximately 6 1/2" by 10". Each transfer consists of a cartoon drawing of the player's body with an oversized head. The puck is comically portrayed with human characteristics (face, arms, and legs). A facsimile player autograph appears below the drawing. At the bottom are instructions in English and French for applying the iron-on to clothing; these are to be cut off before application. These iron-on transfers are unnumbered and checklisted below in alphabetical order.

	NRMT	VG-E	GOOD
COMPLETE SET (6)	250.00	100.00	25.00
COMMON PLAYER (1-6)	25.00	10.00	2.50
☐ 1 Ron Ellis	25.00	10.00	2.50
☐ 2 Phil Esposito	60.00	24.00	6.00
☐ 3 Rod Gilbert	40.00	16.00	4.00
☐ 4 Bobby Hull	125.00	50.00	12.50
☐ 5 Frank Mahovlich	50.00	20.00	5.00
☐ 6 Stan Mikita	50.00	20.00	5.00

1984-85 Kelloggs Accordion Discs

The entire set consisted of eight picture pucks: six different pro hockey pucks each containing action shots and personal records for six NHL players, and two different sports pucks each featuring achievements of six famous female athletes. Each puck came with a stick-on NHL Team Emblem or Sports Crest. The pucks were inserted in specially marked packages of Kellogg's Cereals in Canada. By finding instant prize messages inside the picture pucks, one could win sports equipment, such as hockey jerseys, skates, sport bags, or hockey sticks. The promotion also included a mail-in offer for a plastic collector's shield that would hold all the picture pucks and be mounted on a wall. This set of thin cardboard discs measure approximately 2" in diameter. Six discs are joined together at their sides (like the bellows of an accordion) and were issued in a thin black plastic case. The front features a round-shaped color action photo with white border. The back provides biographical and statistical information in French and English, with the team logo at the top and a facsimile autograph at the bottom. The complete set price below includes only one of the variation pairs.

	MINT	EXC	G-VG
COMPLETE SET (8)	40.00	16.00	4.00
COMMON PANEL (1-8)	4.00	1.60	.40
☐ 1 Panel 1	5.00	2.00	.50

Dino Ciccarelli
Minnesota North Stars
Mike Bossy
New York Islanders
Richard Brodeur
Vancouver Canucks
Michel Goulet
Quebec Nordiques
Jari Kurri
Edmonton Oilers
Paul Reinhart
Calgary Flames

☐ 2 Panel 2	5.00	2.00	.50

Reed Larson
Detroit Red Wings
Marcel Dionne
Los Angeles Kings
Peter Stastny
Quebec Nordiques
Paul MacLean
Winnipeg Jets
Doug Risebrough
Calgary Flames
Larry Robinson
Montreal Canadiens

☐ 3A Panel 3A	5.00	2.00	.50

Stanley Cup
Gilbert Perreault
Buffalo Sabres
Rick Middleton
Boston Bruins
Bob Gainey
Montreal Canadiens
Kevin Lowe
Edmonton Oilers
Borje Salming
Toronto Maple Leafs

☐ 3B Panel 3B	5.00	2.00	.50

Stanley Cup
Gilbert Perreault
Buffalo Sabres
Rick Middleton
Boston Bruins
Guy Lafleur
Montreal Canadiens
Kevin Lowe
Edmonton Oilers
Borje Salming
Toronto Maple Leafs

☐ 4 Panel 4	5.00	2.00	.50

Bernie Federko
St. Louis Blues
Ron Francis
Hartford Whalers
Stan Smyl
Vancouver Canucks
Mike Gartner
Washington Capitals
Dave Babych
Winnipeg Jets
Lanny McDonald
Calgary Flames

☐ 5A Panel 5A	5.00	2.00	.50

Barry Beck
New York Rangers
Rick Kehoe
Pittsburgh Penguins
Dale Hawerchuk
Winnipeg Jets
John Anderson
Toronto Maple Leafs
Mario Tremblay
Montreal Canadiens
Paul Coffey
Edmonton Oilers

☐ 5B Panel 5B	5.00	2.00	.50

Barry Beck
New York Rangers
Denis Herron
Pittsburgh Penguins
Dale Hawerchuk
Winnipeg Jets
Dan Daoust
Toronto Maple Leafs
Mario Tremblay
Montreal Canadiens
Paul Coffey
Edmonton Oilers

☐ 6 Panel 6	4.00	1.60	.40

Thomas Gradin
Vancouver Canucks
Dale Hunter
Quebec Nordiques
Doug Wilson
Chicago Blackhawks
Darryl Sittler
Philadelphia Flyers
Glenn Resch
New Jersey Devils
Rick Vaive
Toronto Maple Leafs

☐ 7 Panel 7	5.00	2.00	.50

Tracy Austin
Tennis
Olga Korbut
Gymnastics
Kathy Kreiner
Alpine Skiing
Angela Taylor
Track and Field
Anne Ottenbrite
Swimming
Paul Martini and
Barbara Underhill
Skating

☐ 8 Panel 8	5.00	2.00	.50

Tatiana Kolpakova
Long Jump
Kay Thompson
Skating
Kornelia Ender
Swimming
Melanie Smith
Equestrianism
Nadia Comaneci
Gymnastics
Carling Bassett
Tennis

1992 Kellogg's Trophies

Protected by a clear plastic cello pack, these three cards were inserted into Kellogg's Rice Krispies cereal boxes in Canada. The cards measure approximately 2 3/8" by 3 1/4" and are printed on thin card stock. The fronts feature a color photo of the trophy inside a gold border on a turquoise card face. The name of the trophy appears in a red circle at the center of the top. The backs are red and carry text in white print about the trophy. All text on both sides is in English and French. The cards are numbered on the front at the bottom center.

	MINT	EXC	G-VG
COMPLETE SET (3)	6.00	2.40	.60
COMMON CARD (1-3)	2.00	.80	.20

 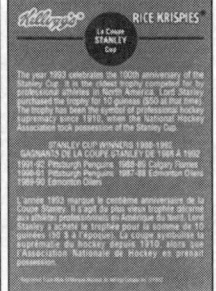  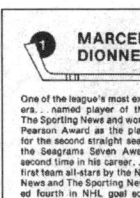

		MINT	EXC	G-VG
☐ 1	Stanley Cup	3.00	1.20	.30
☐ 2	Presidents' Trophy	2.00	.80	.20
☐ 3	Hart Memorial Trophy	2.00	.80	.20

1993 Kenner Starting Lineup

This was the first edition of Starting Lineup National Hockey League figurines. Each player's likeness was sculpted in an action pose featuring his authentic NHL team uniform. Two collector cards are included with each figurine. There is a 20 percent premium on the Canadian versions of these statues. The statues of Ed Belfour, Grant Fuhr, and Pat LaFontaine were produced in smaller quantities; in fact, the Grant Fuhr was only produced in one version. The values listed below refer to unopened packages.

	MINT	EXC	G-VG
COMPLETE SET (12)	325.00	125.00	25.00
COMMON PLAYER (1-12)	15.00	6.00	1.50

		MINT	EXC	G-VG
☐ 1	Ed Belfour SP Chicago Blackhawks	60.00	24.00	6.00
☐ 2	Ray Bourque Boston Bruins	15.00	6.00	1.50
☐ 3	Grant Fuhr SP Buffalo Sabres	90.00	36.00	9.00
☐ 4	Brett Hull St. Louis Blues	15.00	6.00	1.50
☐ 5	Jaromir Jagr Pittsburgh Penguins	15.00	6.00	1.50
☐ 6	Pat LaFontaine SP Buffalo Sabres	40.00	16.00	4.00
☐ 7	Mario Lemieux Pittsburgh Penguins	20.00	8.00	2.00
☐ 8	Eric Lindros Philadelphia Flyers	30.00	12.00	3.00
☐ 9	Mark Messier New York Rangers	15.00	6.00	1.50
☐ 10	Jeremy Roenick Chicago Blackhawks	15.00	6.00	1.50
☐ 11	Patrick Roy Montreal Canadiens	25.00	10.00	2.50
☐ 12	Steve Yzerman Detroit Red Wings	20.00	8.00	2.00

1980-81 Kings Card Night

The cards in this 14-card set are in color and are standard size, 2 1/2" by 3 1/2". The set was produced during the 1980-81 season by All-Star Cards Ltd. for the Los Angeles Kings at the request of owner Jerry Buss. Reportedly 5000 sets were produced, virtually all of which were given away at the Kings' "Card Night." The fronts feature color "mug shots" of the players; the backs provide career highlights and brief biographical information.

	MINT	EXC	G-VG
COMPLETE SET (14)	15.00	6.00	1.50
COMMON PLAYER (1-14)	1.00	.40	.10

		MINT	EXC	G-VG
☐ 1	Marcel Dionne	6.00	2.40	.60
☐ 2	Glenn Goldup	1.00	.40	.10
☐ 3	Doug Halward	1.00	.40	.10
☐ 4	Billy Harris	1.25	.50	.12
☐ 5	Steve Jensen	1.00	.40	.10
☐ 6	Jerry Korab	1.00	.40	.10
☐ 7	Mario Lessard	1.25	.50	.12
☐ 8	Dave Lewis	1.25	.50	.12
☐ 9	Mike Murphy	1.00	.40	.10
☐ 10	Rob Palmer	1.00	.40	.10
☐ 11	Charlie Simmer	2.00	.80	.20
☐ 12	Dave Taylor	3.00	1.20	.30
☐ 13	Garry Unger	1.50	.60	.15
☐ 14	Jay Wells	1.00	.40	.10

1984-85 Kings Smokey

This fire safety set contains 23 cards which are numbered on the back. Players in the set are members of the Los Angeles Kings hockey team. The cards measure approximately 2 15/16" by 4 3/8" and are numbered on the back in the upper right corner. Card backs contain a fire safety cartoon and minimal information about the player. The set was sponsored by the California Department of Forestry.

	MINT	EXC	G-VG
COMPLETE SET (23)	15.00	6.00	1.50
COMMON PLAYER (1-23)	.50	.20	.05

		MINT	EXC	G-VG
☐ 1	Russ Anderson	.50	.20	.05
☐ 2	Marcel Dionne	5.00	2.00	.50
☐ 3	Brian Engblom	.50	.20	.05
☐ 4	Daryl Evans	.50	.20	.05
☐ 5	Jim Fox	.50	.20	.05
☐ 6	Garry Galley	1.00	.40	.10
☐ 7	Anders Hakansson	.50	.20	.05
☐ 8	Mark Hardy	.50	.20	.05
☐ 9	Bob Janecyk	.75	.30	.07
☐ 10	John Paul Kelly	.50	.20	.05
☐ 11	Brian MacLellan	.50	.20	.05
☐ 12	Bernie Nicholls	2.00	.80	.20
☐ 13	Craig Redmond	.50	.20	.05
☐ 14	Terry Ruskowski	.75	.30	.07

		MINT	EXC	G-VG
☐ 15	Doug Smith	.50	.20	.05
☐ 16	Dave Taylor	1.50	.60	.15
☐ 17	Jay Wells	.50	.20	.05
☐ 18	Darren Eliot	.50	.20	.05
☐ 19	Rick Lapointe	.50	.20	.05
☐ 20	Bob Miller	.50	.20	.05
☐ 21	Steve Seguin	.50	.20	.05
☐ 22	Phil Sykes	.50	.20	.05
☐ 23	Pat Quinn CO	1.00	.40	.10

1987-88 Kings Team Issue 4x6

Luc Robitaille—LW

Issued to commemorate the Kings' 20th season, the 23 blank-backed photos comprising this set measure approximately 4" by 6 1/4" and feature white-bordered, black-and-white photos of Kings player's suited-up and posed on the ice. The player's name, along with the 20th Kings Season logo, appear in black lettering within the lower margin. The photos are unnumbered and checklisted below in alphabetical order. The set features early cards of Jimmy Carson, Steve Duchesne, and Luc Robitaille.

		MINT	EXC	G-VG
COMPLETE SET (23)		25.00	10.00	2.50
COMMON PLAYER (1-23)		.75	.30	.07
☐ 1	Bob Bourne	.75	.30	.07
☐ 2	Jimmy Carson	3.00	1.20	.30
☐ 3	Steve Duchesne	3.00	1.20	.30
☐ 4	Darren Eliot	.75	.30	.07
☐ 5	Bryan Erickson	.75	.30	.07
☐ 6	Jim Fox	.75	.30	.07
☐ 7	Garry Galley	1.50	.60	.15
☐ 8	Paul Guay	.75	.30	.07
☐ 9	Mark Hardy	.75	.30	.07
☐ 10	Bob Janecyk	1.00	.40	.10
☐ 11	Dean Kennedy	.75	.30	.07
☐ 12	Grant Ledyard	1.00	.40	.10
☐ 13	Morris Lukowich	.75	.30	.07
☐ 14	Sean McKenna	.75	.30	.07
☐ 15	Roland Melanson	1.00	.40	.10
☐ 16	Bernie Nicholls	2.50	1.00	.25
☐ 17	Joe Paterson	.75	.30	.07
☐ 18	Larry Playfair	.75	.30	.07
☐ 19	Luc Robitaille	9.00	3.75	.90
☐ 20	Phil Sykes	.75	.30	.07
☐ 21	Dave Taylor	1.50	.60	.15
☐ 22	Jay Wells	.75	.30	.07
☐ 23	Dave(Tiger) Williams	1.25	.50	.12

1988-89 Kings Smokey

This fire safety set contains 25 cards and features members of the Los Angeles Kings hockey team in their then-new silver and black colors. The cards are unnumbered; not even the player's uniform number is given on the card. The players are listed below alphabetically by name. The cards measure approximately 2 1/2" by 3 1/2". Card backs contain

a fire safety cartoon and minimal information about the player. The set was sponsored by the California Department of Forestry and Fire Protection.

		MINT	EXC	G-VG
COMPLETE SET (25)		25.00	10.00	2.50
COMMON PLAYER (1-25)		.40	.16	.04
☐ 1	Mike Allison	.40	.16	.04
☐ 2	Ken Baumgartner	.40	.16	.04
☐ 3	Bob Carpenter	.60	.24	.06
☐ 4	Doug Crossman	.60	.24	.06
☐ 5	Dale DeGray	.40	.16	.04
☐ 6	Steve Duchesne	1.25	.50	.12
☐ 7	Ron Duguay	.60	.24	.06
☐ 8	Mark Fitzpatrick	1.25	.50	.12
☐ 9	Jim Fox	.40	.16	.04
☐ 10	Robbie Ftorek CO	.60	.24	.06
☐ 11	Wayne Gretzky	12.00	5.00	1.20
☐ 12	Gilles Hamel	.40	.16	.04
☐ 13	Glenn Healy	1.25	.50	.12
☐ 14	Mike Krushelnyski	.60	.24	.06
☐ 15	Tom Laidlaw	.40	.16	.04
☐ 16	Bryan Maxwell CO	.40	.16	.04
☐ 17	Wayne McBean	.40	.16	.04
☐ 18	Marty McSorley	2.00	.80	.20
☐ 19	Bernie Nicholls	1.50	.60	.15
☐ 20	Cap Raeder CO	.40	.16	.04
☐ 21	Luc Robitaille	4.00	1.60	.40
☐ 22	Dave Taylor	1.25	.50	.12
☐ 23	John Tonelli	.75	.30	.07
☐ 24	Tim Watters	.40	.16	.04
☐ 25	Title Card	.60	.24	.06
	(Checklist on back)			

1989-90 Kings Smokey

This 24-card set of Los Angeles Kings was sponsored by the USDA Forest Service in cooperation with other agencies. The cards measure the standard size, 2 1/2" by 3 1/2". The front features a color action photo, banded above and below with gray stripes. The Smokey the Bear logo appears in the upper left-hand corner, and the Los Angeles Kings logo in the lower right-hand corner. A black border below and on the right of the picture creates the impression of a shadow.

The back provides player information, card number, and a fire prevention cartoon. The cards are numbered in the upper right corner of the reverse.

	MINT	EXC	G-VG
COMPLETE SET (24)	20.00	8.00	2.00
COMMON PLAYER (1-24)	.40	.16	.04
☐ 1 Wayne Gretzky	8.00	3.25	.80
☐ 2 Tim Watters	.40	.16	.04
☐ 3 Mikael Lindholm	.40	.16	.04
☐ 4 Mike Allison	.40	.16	.04
☐ 5 Steve Kasper	.60	.24	.06
☐ 6 Dave Taylor	1.25	.50	.12
☐ 7 Larry Robinson	2.00	.80	.20
☐ 8 Luc Robitaille	4.00	1.60	.40
☐ 9 Barry Beck	.60	.24	.06
☐ 10 Keith Crowder	.40	.16	.04
☐ 11 Petr Prajsler	.40	.16	.04
☐ 12 Mike Krushelnyski	.60	.24	.06
☐ 13 John Tonelli	.75	.30	.07
☐ 14 Steve Duchesne	1.00	.40	.10
☐ 15 Jay Miller	.40	.16	.04
☐ 16 Kelly Hrudey	1.25	.50	.12
☐ 17 Marty McSorley	2.00	.80	.20
☐ 18 Mario Gosselin	.60	.24	.06
☐ 19 Craig Duncanson	.40	.16	.04
☐ 20 Bob Kudelski	.75	.30	.07
☐ 21 Brian Benning	.40	.16	.04
☐ 22 Mikko Makela	.40	.16	.04
☐ 23 Tom Laidlaw	.40	.16	.04
☐ 24 Checklist Card	.60	.24	.06

1989-90 Kings Smokey Gretzky 8x10

This 8" by 10" blowup of Wayne Gretzky's regular Smokey issue features a white-bordered color action shot of him on the front. The team name appears at the top, and his name and position, along with the Kings and Smokey logos, are shown at the bottom. The black-and-white back has his name and biography in the upper left corner and features a cartoon of bears on skates scoring a goal against a wildfire goalie while Smokey looks on. The card is unnumbered.

	MINT	EXC	G-VG
COMPLETE SET (1)	15.00	6.00	1.50
COMMON CARD	15.00	6.00	1.50
☐ 1 Wayne Gretzky	15.00	6.00	1.50

1990-91 Kings Smokey

This 25-card set of Los Angeles Kings was sponsored by Royal Crown Cola in cooperation with the USDA Forest Service and other agencies and features members of the Los Angeles Kings. The cards measure the standard size (2 1/2" by 3 1/2"). The fronts feature color action player photos with

white borders. The player's name appears in a silver-gray stripe above the picture, while his position and several logos appear in a white rectangle below the picture. The backs have biographical information and a fire prevention cartoon starring Smokey, enframed by thin black borders. The cards are numbered on the back in the upper left corner. The mascot card has a checklist on its reverse.

	MINT	EXC	G-VG
COMPLETE SET (25)	15.00	6.00	1.50
COMMON PLAYER (1-24)	.35	.14	.03
☐ 1 Wayne Gretzky	7.00	2.80	.70
☐ 2 Brian Benning	.60	.24	.06
☐ 3 Rob Blake	2.00	.80	.20
☐ 4 Tim Watters	.35	.14	.03
☐ 5 Todd Elik	.75	.30	.07
☐ 6 Tomas Sandstrom	1.25	.50	.12
☐ 7 Steve Kasper	.60	.24	.06
☐ 8 Dave Taylor	1.00	.40	.10
☐ 9 Larry Robinson	1.50	.60	.15
☐ 10 Luc Robitaille	2.50	1.00	.25
☐ 11 Tony Granato	1.25	.50	.12
☐ 12 Tom Laidlaw	.35	.14	.03
☐ 13 Francois Breault	.35	.14	.03
☐ 14 John Tonelli	.60	.24	.06
☐ 15 Steve Duchesne	.75	.30	.07
☐ 16 Jay Miller	.35	.14	.03
☐ 17 Kelly Hrudey	1.25	.50	.12
☐ 18 Marty McSorley	1.50	.60	.15
☐ 19 Daniel Berthiaume	.60	.24	.06
☐ 20 Bob Kudelski	.75	.30	.07
☐ 21 Brad Jones	.35	.14	.03
☐ 22 John McIntyre	.35	.14	.03
☐ 23 Rod Buskas	.35	.14	.03
☐ 24 Kingston (Mascot)	.35	.14	.03
(Checklist on back)			
☐ NNO RC Cola Challenge	.35	.14	.03

1986-87 Kraft Drawings

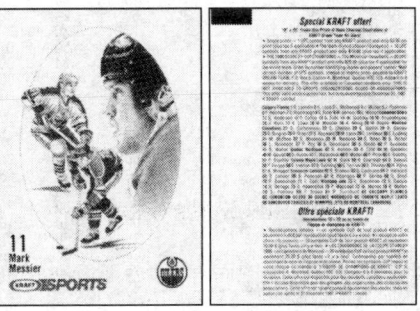

The 1986-87 Kraft Hockey Drawings set contains 81 standard-size (2 1/2" by 3 1/2") unnumbered cards featuring players from Canadian-based NHL teams. The fronts feature black and white drawings of the players in action, along with each player's team logo. Each back shows the entire checklist for the set. Noted sports artists Jerry Hersh and Carlton McDiarmid drew 42 and 30, respectively, of the 81 cards in the set. The cards are unnumbered and so they are presented below in alphabetical order. Prints of these cards were available through an offer detailed on the card backs. An album for the cards was also offered. The set features early cards of Wendel Clark, Stephane Richer, Patrick Roy, and Mike Vernon.

		MINT	EXC	G-VG
	COMPLETE SET (81)	75.00	30.00	7.50
	COMPLETE FACT.SET (82)	125.00	50.00	12.50
	COMMON PLAYER (1-81)	.60	.24	.06
☐ 1	Glenn Anderson	1.00	.40	.10
☐ 2	Brent Ashton	.60	.24	.06
☐ 3	Laurie Boschman	.60	.24	.06
☐ 4	Richard Brodeur	.75	.30	.07
☐ 5	Guy Carbonneau	1.00	.40	.10
☐ 6	Randy Carlyle	.75	.30	.07
☐ 7	Chris Chelios	1.50	.60	.15
☐ 8	Wendel Clark	4.00	1.60	.40
☐ 9	Glen Cochrane	.60	.24	.06
☐ 10	Paul Coffey	2.50	1.00	.25
☐ 11	Alain Cote	.60	.24	.06
☐ 12	Russ Courtnall	1.00	.40	.10
☐ 13	Kjell Dahlin	.60	.24	.06
☐ 14	Dan Daoust	.60	.24	.06
☐ 15	Bill Derlago	.60	.24	.06
☐ 16	Tom Fergus	.60	.24	.06
☐ 17	Grant Fuhr	1.00	.40	.10
☐ 18	Bob Gainey	1.00	.40	.10
☐ 19	Gaston Gingras	.60	.24	.06
☐ 20	Mario Gosselin	.75	.30	.07
☐ 21	Michel Goulet	1.00	.40	.10
☐ 22	Rick Green	.60	.24	.06
☐ 23	Wayne Gretzky	20.00	8.00	2.00
☐ 24	Doug Halward	.60	.24	.06
☐ 25	Dale Hawerchuk	1.00	.40	.10
☐ 26	Brian Hayward	.75	.30	.07
☐ 27	Dale Hunter	1.00	.40	.10
☐ 28	Mike Krushelnyski	.60	.24	.06
☐ 29	Jari Kurri	1.25	.50	.12
☐ 30	Mike Lalor	.60	.24	.06
☐ 31	Gary Leeman	.60	.24	.06
☐ 32	Rejean Lemelin	.75	.30	.07
☐ 33	Claude Lemieux	1.50	.60	.15
☐ 34	Doug Lidster	.60	.24	.06
☐ 35	Hakan Loob	.75	.30	.07
☐ 36	Kevin Lowe	1.00	.40	.10
☐ 37	Craig Ludwig	.60	.24	.06
☐ 38	Paul MacLean	.60	.24	.06
☐ 39	Clint Malarchuk	.75	.30	.07
☐ 40	Mario Marois	.60	.24	.06
☐ 41	Lanny McDonald	1.50	.60	.15
☐ 42	Mike McPhee	.75	.30	.07
☐ 43	Mark Messier	5.00	2.00	.50
☐ 44	Randy Moller	.60	.24	.06
☐ 45	Sergio Momesso	.75	.30	.07
☐ 46	Andy Moog	1.25	.50	.12
☐ 47	Brian Mullen	.75	.30	.07
☐ 48	Joe Mullen	1.25	.50	.12
☐ 49	Mark Napier	.60	.24	.06
☐ 50	Mats Naslund	.75	.30	.07
☐ 51	Chris Nilan	.75	.30	.07
☐ 52	Barry Pederson	.60	.24	.06
☐ 53	Steve Penney	.60	.24	.06
☐ 54	Jim Peplinski	.60	.24	.06
☐ 55	Brent Peterson	.60	.24	.06
☐ 56	Pat Price	.60	.24	.06
☐ 57	Paul Reinhart	.75	.30	.07
☐ 58	Stephane Richer	2.50	1.00	.25
☐ 59	Doug Risebrough	.60	.24	.06
☐ 60	Larry Robinson	1.25	.50	.12
☐ 61	Patrick Roy	12.00	5.00	1.20
☐ 62	Borje Salming	1.00	.40	.10
☐ 63	Petri Skriko	.75	.30	.07
☐ 64	Brian Skrudland	.60	.24	.06
☐ 65	Bobby Smith	.75	.30	.07
☐ 66	Stan Smyl UER	.75	.30	.07
	(Misspelled Syml on card front)			
☐ 67	Anton Stastny	.60	.24	.06
☐ 68	Peter Stastny	1.50	.60	.15
☐ 69	Thomas Steen	.75	.30	.07
☐ 70	Patrik Sundstrom	.75	.30	.07
☐ 71	Gary Suter	.75	.30	.07
☐ 72	Petr Svoboda	.60	.24	.06
☐ 73	Tony Tanti	.75	.30	.07
☐ 74	Greg Terrion	.60	.24	.06
☐ 75	Steve Thomas	1.00	.40	.10
☐ 76	Perry Turnbull	.60	.24	.06
☐ 77	Rick Vaive	.75	.30	.07
☐ 78	Mike Vernon	2.00	.80	.20
☐ 79	Ryan Walter	.60	.24	.06
☐ 80	Carey Wilson	.60	.24	.06
☐ 81	Ken Wregget	.75	.30	.07
☐ x	Album	35.00	14.00	3.50

1989-90 Kraft

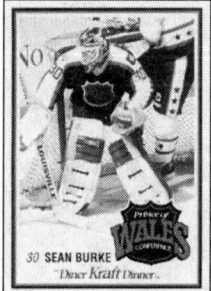
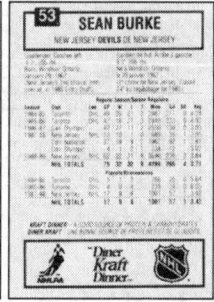

This set of 64 cards featuring players from Canadian-based NHL teams was available on the package backs of specially marked boxes of Kraft Dinner, Spirals, and Egg Noodles. Also specially marked boxes of Jello Puddings and Pie Fillings and Kraft Singles featured additional NHL hockey cards. Each card measures the standard size, 2 1/2" by 3 1/2", and featured a color action photo of the player, with his name, number, and team logo in different color strips running across the bottom of the picture. Kraft also issued a special album to house the cards. The cards were distributed in a variety of ways. There were 26 different Kraft boxes each with two cards on the package back. A sheet of six All-Star cards was packed in each unopened case of Kraft Dinners. Sticker sheets were found in specially marked 500g packages of Kraft Singles. Crads could also be obtained in exchange for UPCs and a small handling fee. The set numbering is listed below according to the company's checklist.

		MINT	EXC	G-VG
	COMPLETE SET (64)	75.00	30.00	7.50
	COMPLETE FACT.SET (65)	100.00	40.00	10.00
	COMMON PLAYER (1-51)	.60	.24	.06
	COMMON ALL-STARS (52-64)	1.00	.40	.10
☐ 1	Doug Gilmour	3.50	1.40	.35
	Calgary Flames			
☐ 2	Theoren Fleury	2.50	1.00	.25
	Calgary Flames			
☐ 3	Al MacInnis	1.50	.60	.15
	Calgary Flames			
☐ 4	Sergei Makarov	2.50	1.00	.25
	Calgary Flames			
☐ 5	Joe Nieuwendyk	1.50	.60	.15
	Calgary Flames			
☐ 6	Joel Otto	.75	.30	.07
	Calgary Flames			
☐ 7	Colin Patterson	.60	.24	.06
	Calgary Flames			
☐ 8	Sergei Priakin	.60	.24	.06
	Calgary Flames			
☐ 9	Paul Ranheim	.75	.30	.07
	Calgary Flames			
☐ 10	Glenn Anderson	1.00	.40	.10
	Edmonton Oilers			
☐ 11	Grant Fuhr	1.25	.50	.12
	Edmonton Oilers			
☐ 12	Charlie Huddy	.60	.24	.06

	Edmonton Oilers			
☐ 13	Jarl Kurri	1.25	.50	.12
	Edmonton Oilers			
☐ 14	Kevin Lowe	.75	.30	.07
	Edmonton Oilers			
☐ 15	Mark Messier	3.50	1.40	.35
	Edmonton Oilers			
☐ 16	Craig Simpson	.75	.30	.07
	Edmonton Oilers			
☐ 17	Steve Smith	.75	.30	.07
	Edmonton Oilers			
☐ 18	Esa Tikkanen	1.00	.40	.10
	Edmonton Oilers			
☐ 19	Guy Carbonneau	1.00	.40	.10
	Montreal Canadiens			
☐ 20	Chris Chelios	1.50	.60	.15
	Montreal Canadiens			
☐ 21	Shayne Corson	1.00	.40	.10
	Montreal Canadiens			
☐ 22	Russ Courtnall	1.00	.40	.10
	Montreal Canadiens			
☐ 23	Mats Naslund	.75	.30	.07
	Montreal Canadiens			
☐ 24	Stephane Richer	1.50	.60	.15
	Montreal Canadiens			
☐ 25	Patrick Roy	6.00	2.40	.60
	Montreal Canadiens			
☐ 26	Bobby Smith	.75	.30	.07
	Montreal Canadiens			
☐ 27	Petr Svoboda	.60	.24	.06
	Montreal Canadiens			
☐ 28	Jeff Brown	1.00	.40	.10
	Quebec Nordiques			
☐ 29	Paul Gillis	.60	.24	.06
	Quebec Nordiques			
☐ 30	Michel Goulet	1.00	.40	.10
	Quebec Nordiques			
☐ 31	Guy Lafleur	2.00	.80	.20
	Quebec Nordiques			
☐ 32	Joe Sakic	3.50	1.40	.35
	Quebec Nordiques			
☐ 33	Peter Stastny	1.50	.60	.15
	Quebec Nordiques			
☐ 34	Wendel Clark	1.50	.60	.15
	Toronto Maple Leafs			
☐ 35	Vincent Damphousse	1.50	.60	.15
	Toronto Maple Leafs			
☐ 36	Gary Leeman	.60	.24	.06
	Toronto Maple Leafs			
☐ 37	Daniel Marois	.60	.24	.06
	Toronto Maple Leafs			
☐ 38	Ed Olczyk	.60	.24	.06
	Toronto Maple Leafs			
☐ 39	Rob Ramage	.60	.24	.06
	Toronto Maple Leafs			
☐ 40	Vladimir Krutov	.60	.24	.06
	Vancouver Canucks			
☐ 41	Igor Larionov	1.00	.40	.10
	Vancouver Canucks			
☐ 42	Trevor Linden	3.50	1.40	.35
	Vancouver Canucks			
☐ 43	Kirk McLean	2.50	1.00	.25
	Vancouver Canucks			
☐ 44	Paul Reinhart	.60	.24	.06
	Vancouver Canucks			
☐ 45	Tony Tanti	.75	.30	.07
	Vancouver Canucks			
☐ 46	Brent Ashton	.60	.24	.06
	Winnipeg Jets			
☐ 47	Randy Carlyle	.60	.24	.06
	Winnipeg Jets			
☐ 48	Randy Cunneyworth	.60	.24	.06
	Winnipeg Jets			
☐ 49	Dave Ellett	.60	.24	.06
	Winnipeg Jets			
☐ 50	Dale Hawerchuk	1.25	.50	.12
	Winnipeg Jets			
☐ 51	Fredrik Olausson	1.00	.40	.10
	Winnipeg Jets			
☐ 52	Ray Bourque AS	2.50	1.00	.25
☐ 53	Sean Burke AS	1.00	.40	.10
☐ 54	Paul Coffey AS	2.50	1.00	.25
☐ 55	Mario Lemieux AS	6.00	2.40	.60
☐ 56	Cam Neely AS	3.00	1.20	.30
☐ 57	Rick Tocchet AS	2.00	.80	.20
☐ 58	Steve Duchesne AS	1.00	.40	.10
☐ 59	Wayne Gretzky AS	7.50	3.00	.75
☐ 60	Joe Mullen AS	1.25	.50	.12
☐ 61	Gary Suter AS	1.00	.40	.10
☐ 62	Mike Vernon AS	1.25	.50	.12
☐ 63	Steve Yzerman AS	3.00	1.20	.30
☐ 64	Checklist Card	1.00	.40	.10
☐ xx	Album	25.00	10.00	2.50

1989-90 Kraft All-Stars Stickers

Distributed by Kraft General Foods Canada in packages of Kraft Singles, these six bilingual sticker-sheets measure approximately 4 1/2" by 2 3/4" and each features stickers of two players in their NHL All-Star uniforms and four NHL team logo stickers. The sheets are white, with color player action shots and color team logos on the peel-away stickers. The white back of each sticker-sheet carries a bilingual order form for the Kraft NHL Hockey sticker/card album. The stickers are numbered on the front.

		MINT	EXC	G-VG
	COMPLETE SET (6)	12.00	5.00	1.20
	COMMON PANEL (1-6)	2.00	.80	.20
☐ 1	Mike McPhee	2.00	.80	.20
	and Paul Reinhart			
☐ 2	Wayne Gretzky	5.00	2.00	.50
	and Rick Tocchet			
☐ 3	Paul Coffey	3.00	1.20	.30
	and Steve Yzerman			
☐ 4	Mike Vernon	3.00	1.20	.30
	and Ray Bourque			
☐ 5	Jari Kurri	4.00	1.60	.40
	and Mario Lemieux			
☐ 6	Kevin Lowe	2.00	.80	.20
	and Sean Burke			

1990-91 Kraft

This 115-card set (standard size, 2 1/2" by 3 1/2") was issued by Kraft to honor some of the stars of the NHL. There was also a special album, which included advertisements for various Kraft products, issued to store all the cards. The set is divided into three parts: Cards 1-64 are NHL star players listed alphabetically while 65-91 are the Conference All-Stars

(Campbell 65-78 and Wales 79-91). Card numbers 92-115 are team photos along with three unnumbered team checklist cards. To complete the set, the consumer had to purchase items from eight different Kraft product groups. Only card number 66 (Wayne Gretzky) was available in two different product groups: Jello Instant Pudding (four servings) and Jello Lemon Pie Filling (tri-portion).

	MINT	EXC	G-VG
COMPLETE SET (115)	100.00	40.00	10.00
COMPLETE FACT.SET (116)	125.00	50.00	12.50
COMMON PLAYER (1-115)	.50	.20	.05

		MINT	EXC	G-VG
☐	1 Dave Babych	.50	.20	.05
☐	2 Brian Bellows	.75	.30	.07
☐	3 Ray Bourque	2.00	.80	.20
☐	4 Sean Burke	.50	.20	.05
☐	5 Jimmy Carson	.50	.20	.05
☐	6 Chris Chelios	1.00	.40	.10
☐	7 Dino Ciccarelli	.75	.30	.07
☐	8 Paul Coffey	1.50	.60	.15
☐	9 Geoff Courtnall	.75	.30	.07
☐	10 Doug Crossman	.50	.20	.05
☐	11 Kevin Dineen	.75	.30	.07
☐	12 Pat Elynuik	.50	.20	.05
☐	13 Ron Francis	.75	.30	.07
☐	14 Gerard Gallant	.50	.20	.05
☐	15 Wayne Gretzky	7.50	3.00	.75
☐	16 Dale Hawerchuk	1.00	.40	.10
☐	17 Ron Hextall	.75	.30	.07
☐	18 Phil Housley	1.00	.40	.10
☐	19 Mark Howe	.75	.30	.07
☐	20 Brett Hull	5.00	2.00	.50
☐	21 Al Iafrate	.75	.30	.07
☐	22 Guy Lafleur	1.50	.60	.15
☐	23 Pat LaFontaine	2.50	1.00	.25
☐	24 Rod Langway	.60	.24	.06
☐	25 Igor Larionov	.60	.24	.06
☐	26 Steve Larmer	.75	.30	.07
☐	27 Gary Leeman	.50	.20	.05
☐	28 Brian Leetch	2.50	1.00	.25
☐	29 Mario Lemieux	6.00	2.40	.60
☐	30 Trevor Linden	2.00	.80	.20
☐	31 Mike Liut	.60	.24	.06
☐	32 Mark Messier	3.00	1.20	.30
☐	33 Al MacInnis	1.25	.50	.12
☐	34 Mike Modano	2.00	.80	.20
☐	35 Andy Moog	1.25	.50	.12
☐	36 Joe Mullen	.75	.30	.07
☐	37 Kirk Muller	1.25	.50	.12
☐	38 Petr Nedved	2.00	.80	.20
☐	39 Cam Neely	2.50	1.00	.25
☐	40 Bernie Nicholls	.75	.30	.07
☐	41 Joe Nieuwendyk	1.00	.40	.10
☐	42 Mats Sundin	1.50	.60	.15
☐	43 Daren Puppa	.60	.24	.06
☐	44 Rob Ramage	.60	.24	.06
☐	45 Bill Ranford	1.00	.40	.10
☐	46 Stephane Richer	1.00	.40	.10
☐	47 Larry Robinson	1.00	.40	.10
☐	48 Luc Robitaille	2.50	1.00	.25
☐	49 Patrick Roy	5.00	2.00	.50
☐	50 Joe Sakic	2.50	1.00	.25
☐	51 Denis Savard	1.00	.40	.10
☐	52 Craig Simpson	.60	.24	.06
☐	53 Bobby Smith	.60	.24	.06
☐	54 Peter Stastny	1.25	.50	.12
☐	55 Thomas Steen	.60	.24	.06
☐	56 Scott Stevens	1.00	.40	.10
☐	57 Brent Sutter	.60	.24	.06
☐	58 Rick Tocchet	1.25	.50	.12
☐	59 Pierre Turgeon	2.50	1.00	.25
☐	60 John Vanbiesbrouck	1.25	.50	.12
☐	61 Mike Vernon	1.00	.40	.10
☐	62 Doug Wilson	.75	.30	.07
☐	63 Steve Yzerman	3.00	1.20	.30
☐	64 Checklist Card	.50	.20	.05
☐	65 Steve Duchesne AS	.50	.20	.05
☐	66 Wayne Gretzky AS	5.00	2.00	.50
☐	67 Brett Hull AS	3.00	1.20	.30
☐	68 Jari Kurri AS	.75	.30	.07
☐	69 Mike Gartner AS	1.00	.40	.10
☐	70 Kirk McLean AS	1.25	.50	.12
☐	71 Mark Messier AS	1.50	.60	.15
☐	72 Joe Mullen AS	.60	.24	.06
☐	73 Bernie Nicholls AS	.75	.30	.07
☐	74 Joe Nieuwendyk AS	.75	.30	.07
☐	75 Luc Robitaille AS	1.25	.50	.12
☐	76 Mike Vernon AS	.75	.30	.07
☐	77 Doug Wilson AS	.60	.24	.06
☐	78 Steve Yzerman AS	1.50	.60	.15

		MINT	EXC	G-VG
☐	79 Joe Sakic AS	2.00	.80	.20
☐	80 Ray Bourque AS	1.50	.60	.15
☐	81 Chris Chelios AS	1.00	.40	.10
☐	82 Paul Coffey AS	1.25	.50	.12
☐	83 Ron Francis AS	.60	.24	.06
☐	84 Cam Neely AS	1.50	.60	.15
☐	85 Phil Housley AS	.75	.30	.07
☐	86 Pat LaFontaine AS	1.50	.60	.15
☐	87 Mario Lemieux AS	4.00	1.60	.40
☐	88 Kirk Muller AS	1.00	.40	.10
☐	89 Stephane Richer AS	.75	.30	.07
☐	90 Patrick Roy AS	3.00	1.20	.30
☐	91 Pierre Turgeon AS	1.50	.60	.15
☐	92 Boston Bruins	.50	.20	.05
☐	93 Buffalo Sabres	.50	.20	.05
☐	94 Calgary Flames	.50	.20	.05
☐	95 Chicago Blackhawks	.50	.20	.05
☐	96 Detroit Red Wings	.50	.20	.05
☐	97 Edmonton Oilers	.50	.20	.05
☐	98 Hartford Whalers	.50	.20	.05
☐	99 Los Angeles Kings	.50	.20	.05
☐	100 Minnesota North Stars	.50	.20	.05
☐	101 Montreal Canadiens	.50	.20	.05
☐	102 New Jersey Devils	.50	.20	.05
☐	103 New York Islanders	.50	.20	.05
☐	104 New York Rangers	.50	.20	.05
☐	105 Philadelphia Flyers	.50	.20	.05
☐	106 Pittsburgh Penguins	.50	.20	.05
☐	107 Quebec Nordiques	.50	.20	.05
☐	108 St. Louis Blues	.50	.20	.05
☐	109 Toronto Maple Leafs	.50	.20	.05
☐	110 Vancouver Canucks	.50	.20	.05
☐	111 Washington Capitals	.50	.20	.05
☐	112 Winnipeg Jets	.50	.20	.05
☐	113 Unnumbered Checklist	.50	.20	.05
☐	114 Unnumbered Checklist	.50	.20	.05
☐	115 Unnumbered Checklist	.50	.20	.05
☐	xx Album	25.00	10.00	2.50

1991-92 Kraft

 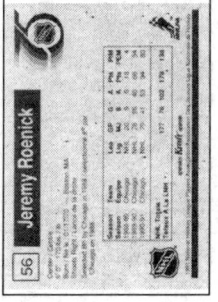

This set of 92 collectibles was sponsored by Kraft-General Foods Canada to commemorate the 75th anniversary of the NHL. It consists of 68 standard-size (2 1/2" by 3 1/2") cards and 24 discs. To store the set, a 75th Anniversary NHL hockey card album could be purchased. Kraft also provided the opportunity for the collector to purchase any combination of ten cards or discs through the mail to complete the set. Cards 1-40 were issued in Kraft Dinners, cards 41-56 in Kraft Spirals, and cards 57-64 in Kraft Noodles. An eight-card subset highlights "Great Moments" in NHL history. The fronts feature action player photos framed inside a team color border. The player's name is printed in black lettering across the top while the team name, team logo, and 75th NHL Anniversary logo appear below the picture. The horizontally oriented backs are light gray with red print and carry biography, career statistics, and logos. Measuring 2 3/4" in diameter, the discs (65-88) were available under the caps of Kraft Peanut Butter. They feature action cut-out photos of two players (superimposed on a blue background), pairing today's All-Stars with legends of the past. Players' names and their teams appear in a white semi-circular margin. The bilingual disc backs are bright yellow with black print and carry biographical and statistical information. Both discs and cards are numbered on the back.

	MINT	EXC	G-VG
COMPLETE SET (92)	100.00	40.00	10.00
COMPLETE FACT.SET (93)	125.00	50.00	12.50
COMMON PLAYER (1-64)	.50	.20	.05
COMMON DISC (65-88)	.75	.30	.07
COMMON LOGO (89-92)	.50	.20	.05

☐ 1	Mario Lemieux Pittsburgh Penguins	6.00	2.40	.60
☐ 2	Mark Recchi Pittsburgh Penguins	2.50	1.00	.25
☐ 3	Jaromir Jagr Pittsburgh Penguins	6.00	2.40	.60
☐ 4	Mats Sundin Quebec Nordiques	3.00	1.20	.30
☐ 5	Adam Oates St. Louis Blues	2.50	1.00	.25
☐ 6	Great Moments Canadien Dynasty Maurice Richard Jacques Plante	1.50	.60	.15
☐ 7	Brendan Shanahan St. Louis Blues	2.50	1.00	.25
☐ 8	Pat Falloon San Jose Sharks	1.50	.60	.15
☐ 9	Grant Fuhr Toronto Maple Leafs	1.00	.40	.10
☐ 10	Gary Leeman Toronto Maple Leafs	.50	.20	.05
☐ 11	Petr Nedved Vancouver Canucks	1.50	.60	.15
☐ 12	Kirk Muller Montreal Canadiens	1.00	.40	.10
☐ 13	Theoren Fleury Calgary Flames	1.00	.40	.10
☐ 14	Dino Ciccarelli Washington Capitals	.75	.30	.07
☐ 15	Geoff Courtnall Vancouver Canucks	.75	.30	.07
☐ 16	Mark Messier New York Rangers	3.00	1.20	.30
☐ 17	Ken Hodge Jr. Boston Bruins	.50	.20	.05
☐ 18	Chris Chelios Chicago Blackhawks	1.00	.40	.10
☐ 19	Mike Vernon Calgary Flames	1.00	.40	.10
☐ 20	Kevin Hatcher Washington Capitals	.75	.30	.07
☐ 21	Stephane Richer New Jersey Devils	1.00	.40	.10
☐ 22	Mark Tinordi Minnesota North Stars	.50	.20	.05
☐ 23	Pat Verbeek Hartford Whalers	.75	.30	.07
☐ 24	John Cullen Hartford Whalers	.50	.20	.05
☐ 25	Pat LaFontaine Buffalo Sabres	2.50	1.00	.25
☐ 26	Stephan Lebeau Montreal Canadiens	1.00	.40	.10
☐ 27	Mike Gartner New York Rangers	1.00	.40	.10
☐ 28	Great Moments Last Leaf Dynasty Bobby Baun	.75	.30	.07
☐ 29	Shayne Corson Montreal Canadiens	.60	.24	.06
☐ 30	Trevor Linden Vancouver Canucks	2.00	.80	.20
☐ 31	Craig Janney Boston Bruins	1.50	.60	.15
☐ 32	Al MacInnis Calgary Flames	1.25	.50	.12
☐ 33	Phil Housley Winnipeg Jets	1.00	.40	.10
☐ 34	Doug Wilson San Jose Sharks	.75	.30	.07
☐ 35	Tony Granato Los Angeles Kings	.50	.20	.05
☐ 36	Dale Hawerchuk Buffalo Sabres	.75	.30	.07
☐ 37	Great Moments Goaltending Greats Bill Durnan Turk Broda	.75	.30	.07
☐ 38	Brian Bellows Minnesota North Stars	.75	.30	.07
☐ 39	Great Moments Number 23 with number 23 Bob Gainey	.75	.30	.07
☐ 40	Great Moments A Night to Remember Darryl Sittler	.75	.30	.07
☐ 41	Joe Sakic Quebec Nordiques	1.25	.50	.12
☐ 42	Wendel Clark Toronto Maple Leafs	1.25	.50	.12
☐ 43	Brent Sutter Chicago Blackhawks	.60	.24	.06
☐ 44	Bill Ranford Edmonton Oilers	.75	.30	.07
☐ 45	Rick Tocchet Philadelphia Flyers	1.00	.40	.10
☐ 46	Paul Ysebaert Detroit Red Wings	.50	.20	.05
☐ 47	Adam Creighton New York Islanders	.50	.20	.05
☐ 48	Mike Modano Minnesota North Stars	1.50	.60	.15
☐ 49	Russ Courtnall Montreal Canadiens	.60	.24	.06
☐ 50	Great Moments Evolution of Stanley Cup Syl Apps	.50	.20	.05
☐ 51	Sergei Fedorov Detroit Red Wings	6.00	2.40	.60
☐ 52	Mike Ricci Philadelphia Flyers	1.50	.60	.15
☐ 53	Scott Stevens New Jersey Devils	1.00	.40	.10
☐ 54	Great Moments The Ultimate Expansion Bobby Clarke	1.25	.50	.12
☐ 55	Owen Nolan Quebec Nodiques	1.00	.40	.10
☐ 56	Jeremy Roenick Chicago Blackhawks	6.00	2.40	.60
☐ 57	Ray Bourque Boston Bruins	1.50	.60	.15
☐ 58	Gerard Gallant Detroit Red Wings	.50	.20	.05
☐ 59	Andy Moog Boston Bruins	1.00	.40	.10
☐ 60	Alexander Mogilny Buffalo Sabres	4.00	1.60	.40
☐ 61	Great Moments Islander Tradition Denis Potvin	.75	.30	.07
☐ 62	Ed Olczyk Winnipeg Jets	.60	.24	.06
☐ 63	Tomas Sandstrom Los Angeles Kings	.75	.30	.07
☐ 64	Checklist	.60	.24	.06
☐ 65	Wayne Gretzky Los Angeles Kings Maurice Richard Montreal Canadiens	8.00	3.25	.80
☐ 66	Brett Hull St. Louis Blues Guy Lafleur Montreal Canadiens	5.00	2.00	.50
☐ 67	Jari Kurri Los Angeles Kings Bobby Clarke Philadelphia Flyers	1.00	.40	.10
☐ 68	Steve Yzerman Detroit Red Wings Jean Beliveau Montreal Canadiens	3.00	1.20	.30
☐ 69	Steve Larmer Chicago Blackhawks Pat Stapleton Chicago Blackhawks	.75	.30	.07
☐ 70	Luc Robitaille Los Angeles Kings Ted Lindsay Detroit Red Wings	2.00	.80	.20
☐ 71	Larry Murphy Pittsburgh Penguins Doug Harvey Montreal Canadiens	1.00	.40	.10
☐ 72	Denis Potvin New York Islanders Gary Suter Calgary Flames	.75	.30	.07
☐ 73	Brian Leetch New York Rangers Harry Howell	1.50	.60	.15

	New York Rangers			
☐ 74	Paul Coffey	1.00	.40	.10
	Pittsburgh Penguins			
	Bill Gadsby			
	Detroit Red Wings			
☐ 75	Jon Casey	1.25	.50	.12
	Minnesota North Stars			
	Terry Sawchuk			
	Detroit Red Wings			
☐ 76	Patrick Roy	5.00	2.00	.50
	Montreal Canadiens			
	Jacques Plante			
	Montreal Canadiens			
☐ 77	Denis Savard	1.50	.60	.15
	Montreal Canadiens			
	Serge Savard			
	Montreal Canadiens			
☐ 78	Doug Gilmour	2.50	1.00	.25
	Calgary Flames			
	Bob Baun			
	Toronto Maple Leafs			
☐ 79	Guy Carbonneau	1.00	.40	.10
	Montreal Canadiens			
	Yvan Cournoyer			
	Montreal Canadiens			
☐ 80	Gilbert Perreault	1.25	.50	.12
	Buffalo Sabres			
	Larry Robinson			
	Los Angeles Kings			
☐ 81	Red Kelly	.75	.30	.07
	Toronto Maple Leafs			
	Craig Simpson			
	Edmonton Oilers			
☐ 82	Bobby Smith	.75	.30	.07
	Minnesota North Stars			
	Rod Gilbert			
	New York Rangers			
☐ 83	Syl Apps	.75	.30	.07
	Toronto Maple Leafs			
	Peter Stastny			
	New Jersey Devils			
☐ 84	BoomBoom Geoffrion	1.50	.60	.15
	Montreal Canadiens			
	Vincent Damphousse			
	Edmonton Oilers			
☐ 85	Marcel Dionne	.75	.30	.07
	Los Angeles Kings			
	Steve Smith			
	Chicago Blackhawks			
☐ 86	Tim Horton	.75	.30	.07
	Toronto Maple Leafs			
	Kevin Dineen			
	Hartford Whalers			
☐ 87	Michel Goulet	1.00	.40	.10
	Chicago Blackhawks			
	Frank Mahovlich			
	Toronto Maple Leafs			
☐ 88	Mike Richter........................	1.25	.50	.12
	New York Rangers			
	Henri Richard			
	Montreal Canadiens			
☐ 89	Boston Bruins logo	.50	.20	.05
	New York Rangers logo			
	Original Six			
	(Unnumbered)			
☐ 90	Montreal Canadiens logo	.50	.20	.05
	Toronto Maple Leafs logo			
	Original Six			
	(Unnumbered)			
☐ 91	Chicago Blackhawks logo......	.50	.20	.05
	Detroit Red Wings logo			
	Original Six			
	(Unnumbered)			
☐ 92	Stanley Cup........................	1.00	.40	.10
	(Unnumbered)			
☐ xx	Album.................................	25.00	10.00	2.50

1992-93 Kraft

This set of 48 collectibles was sponsored by Kraft General Foods Canada to commemorate the 100th anniversary of the Stanley Cup. It consists of 24 team cards, 12 discs, and 12 All-Star cards. To store the set, a Stanley Cup 100th anniversary album could be purchased by sending in three UPC symbols from Kraft Dinner, one UPC symbol from both Kraft Peanut Butter and Kraft Singles, and 12.99 along with

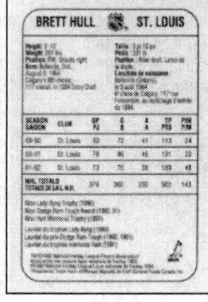

sales tax and shipping and handling charges. The album included special storage sheets for the cards, the history of the Stanley Cup, and team autographs. The team cards, which measure approximately 5 3/16" by 3 7/16" and were distributed on the back of Kraft Dinner boxes, show players in their centennial uniforms. The team name and logo appear in a team color-coded stripe at the bottom. The backs are plain cardboard with the team history in red print. The discs, which measure approximately 2 3/4" in diameter and were distributed under the lids of Kraft Peanut Butter jars, are double-sided and feature the 24 NHL goaltenders. The goalies are shown in action in a three-quarter-moon shaped picture against a team color-coded background. Statistics are included on the disc. The 12 All-Star cards, which measure approximately 1 3/4" by 2 1/2" and were distributed in groups of four in packages of Kraft Singles, carry color action player photos with white borders. A facsimile autograph is near the bottom of the picture. The player's name is printed in the wider bottom border between sponsor logos. The backs are white and include biographical information, statistics, and career highlights. Collectors who did not complete the series by purchasing the products could obtain any combination of eight cards or discs by sending the same UPC symbols, 3.00, plus shipping and handling charges. The cards are unnumbered and checklisted below in alphabetical order within each subset.

		MINT	EXC	G-VG
COMPLETE SET (48)........................		60.00	24.00	6.00
COMPLETE FACT.SET (49)		75.00	30.00	7.50
COMMON TEAM CARD (1-24)		1.00	.40	.10
COMMON DISC (25-36)...................		1.00	.40	.10
COMMON ALL-STAR (37-48)		.75	.30	.07

☐ 1	Boston Bruins	1.00	.40	.10
☐ 2	Buffalo Sabres.....................	1.00	.40	.10
☐ 3	Calgary Flames....................	1.00	.40	.10
☐ 4	Chicago Blackhawks	1.00	.40	.10
☐ 5	Detroit Red Wings	1.00	.40	.10
☐ 6	Edmonton Oilers	1.00	.40	.10
☐ 7	Hartford Whalers...................	1.00	.40	.10
☐ 8	Los Angeles Kings	1.00	.40	.10
☐ 9	Minnesota North Stars	1.00	.40	.10
☐ 10	Montreal Canadiens	1.00	.40	.10
☐ 11	New Jersey Devils	1.00	.40	.10
☐ 12	New York Islanders...............	1.00	.40	.10
☐ 13	New York Rangers	1.00	.40	.10
☐ 14	Ottawa Senators...................	1.00	.40	.10
☐ 15	Philadelphia Flyers	1.00	.40	.10
☐ 16	Pittsburgh Penguins..............	1.00	.40	.10
☐ 17	Quebec Nordiques.................	1.00	.40	.10
☐ 18	San Jose Sharks	1.00	.40	.10
☐ 19	St. Louis Blues....................	1.00	.40	.10
☐ 20	Tampa Bay Lightning	1.00	.40	.10
☐ 21	Toronto Maple Leafs	1.00	.40	.10
☐ 22	Vancouver Canucks...............	1.00	.40	.10
☐ 23	Washington Capitals	1.00	.40	.10
☐ 24	Winnipeg Jets	1.00	.40	.10
☐ 25	Tom Barrasso	1.00	.40	.10
	Wendell Young			
☐ 26	Don Beaupre	1.00	.40	.10
	Bob Essensa			

☐ 27	Jon Casey	1.00	.40	.10
	Dominic Roussel			
☐ 28	Tim Cheveldae	1.00	.40	.10
	Sean Burke			
☐ 29	Jeff Hackett	1.50	.60	.15
	Kirk McLean			
☐ 30	Dominik Hasek	1.50	.60	.15
	Chris Terreri			
☐ 31	Ron Hextall	1.50	.60	.15
	Curtis Joseph			
☐ 32	Andy Moog	1.00	.40	.10
	Mark Fitzpatrick			
☐ 33	Bill Ranford	1.50	.60	.15
	Kelly Hrudey			
☐ 34	Patrick Roy	5.00	2.00	.50
	John Vanbiesbrouck			
☐ 35	Peter Sidorkiewicz	1.00	.40	.10
	Grant Fuhr			
☐ 36	Mike Vernon	2.00	.80	.20
	Ed Belfour			
☐ 37	Ray Bourque AS	1.50	.60	.15
☐ 38	Chris Chelios AS	.75	.30	.07
☐ 39	Paul Coffey AS	1.25	.50	.12
☐ 40	Wayne Gretzky AS	6.00	2.40	.60
☐ 41	Brett Hull AS	3.00	1.20	.30
☐ 42	Jaromir Jagr AS	3.00	1.20	.30
☐ 43	Mario Lemieux AS	5.00	2.00	.50
☐ 44	Trevor Linden AS	1.50	.60	.15
☐ 45	Mark Messier AS	2.00	.80	.20
☐ 46	Jeremy Roenick AS	3.00	1.20	.30
☐ 47	Patrick Roy AS	3.00	1.20	.30
☐ 48	Steve Yzerman AS	2.00	.80	.20
☐ xx	Album	15.00	6.00	1.50

1993-94 Kraft

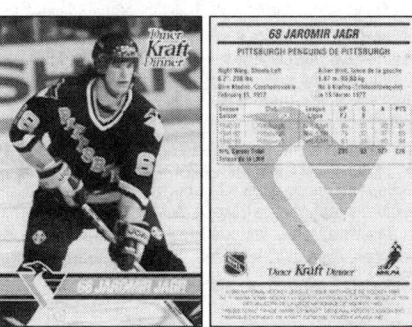

This set of 72 collectibles was sponsored by Kraft General Foods Canada. It consists of 26 team cards, 23 discs, 17 cut-outs, three Rookie cards, and three Trophy Winner cards. The album was available for purchase and contained special storage sheets for all the collectibles. It is organized by team and also includes information (both in French and English) and a picture of the teams' stadiums. The team cards measure approximately 3 1/2" by 5 1/8" and were distributed on the back of Kraft Dinner boxes. The fronts show a color action player photo with the player's name and number, and the team logo printed in a team color-coded stripe at the bottom. The backs have a ghosted light red team logo with biography (both in French and English) and statistics printed over the team logo. The discs, which measure approximately 3 3/4" in diameter and were distributed under the lids of Kraft Peanut Butter Jars, feature NHL captains and coaches. The captains' cards are double-sided and feature a blue border, while the double-sided coaches' cards have a gray border around the photo. The cut-outs, which were distributed in Jello boxes, feature color action poses. Also distributed in Kraft dinner boxes, the Rookie and Trophy Winner cards measure the same size as

the team cards. The Trophy Winner cards show the players with their respective trophies. The cards are unnumbered and checklisted below in alphabetical order within each subset.

	MINT	EXC	G-VG
COMPLETE SET (72)	100.00	40.00	10.00
COMPLETE FACT.SET (73)	125.00	50.00	12.50
COMMON PLAYER (1-26)	.50	.20	.05
COMMON DISC (27-49)	2.00	.80	.20
COMMON CUT-OUT (50-66)	.50	.20	.05
COMMON ROOKIE (67-69)	1.50	.60	.15
COMMON AWARD WINNER(70-72)	.75	.30	.07

☐ 1	Ed Belfour	1.50	.60	.15
	Chicago Blackhawks			
☐ 2	Brian Bradley	.50	.20	.05
	Tampa Bay Lightning			
☐ 3	Pavel Bure	4.00	1.60	.40
	Vancouver Canucks			
☐ 4	Paul Coffey	1.00	.40	.10
	Detroit Red Wings			
☐ 5	Russ Courtnall	.75	.30	.07
	Dallas Stars			
☐ 6	Alexander Daigle	2.50	1.00	.25
	Ottawa Senators			
☐ 7	Pat Falloon	1.00	.40	.10
	San Jose Sharks			
☐ 8	Theoren Fleury	.75	.30	.07
	Calgary Flames			
☐ 9	Doug Gilmour	1.50	.60	.15
	Toronto Maple Leafs			
☐ 10	Adam Graves	.75	.30	.07
	New York Rangers			
☐ 11	Stu Grimson	.50	.20	.05
	Anaheim Mighty Ducks			
☐ 12	Al Iafrate	.60	.24	.06
	Washington Capitals			
☐ 13	Jaromir Jagr	1.50	.60	.15
	Pittsburgh Penguins			
☐ 14	Joe Juneau	1.50	.60	.15
	Boston Bruins			
☐ 15	Eric Lindros	4.00	1.60	.40
	Philadelphia Flyers			
☐ 16	Alexander Mogilny	1.25	.50	.12
	Buffalo Sabres			
☐ 17	Kirk Muller	.60	.24	.06
	Montreal Canadiens			
☐ 18	Bill Ranford	.75	.30	.07
	Edmonton Oilers			
☐ 19	Mike Ricci	.75	.30	.07
	Quebec Nordiques			
☐ 20	Luc Robitaille	1.00	.40	.10
	Los Angeles Kings			
☐ 21	Geoff Sanderson	.75	.30	.07
	Hartford Whalers			
☐ 22	Teemu Selanne	2.00	.80	.20
	Winnipeg Jets			
☐ 23	Brendan Shanahan	1.00	.40	.10
	St. Louis Blues			
☐ 24	Pierre Turgeon	1.25	.50	.12
	New York Islanders			
☐ 25	John Vanbiesbrouck	1.00	.40	.10
	Florida Panthers			
☐ 26	Valeri Zelepukin	.50	.20	.05
	New Jersey Devils			
☐ 27	Al Arbour CO	2.00	.80	.20
	New York Islanders			
☐ 28	Bob Berry CO	2.00	.80	.20
	St. Louis Blues			
☐ 29	Ray Bourque	3.00	1.20	.30
	Boston Bruins			
	Patrick Flatley			
	New York Islanders			
☐ 30	Scott Bowman CO	3.00	1.20	.30
	Detroit Red Wings			
☐ 31	Pat Burns CO	2.50	1.00	.25
	Toronto Maple Leafs			
☐ 32	Jacques Demers CO	2.50	1.00	.25
	Montreal Canadiens			
☐ 33	Kevin Dineen	2.00	.80	.20
	Philadelphia Flyers			
	Kevin Hatcher			
	Washington Capitals			
☐ 34	Wayne Gretzky	7.00	2.80	.70
	Los Angeles Kings			
	Wendel Clark			
	Toronto Maple Leafs			
☐ 35	Brett Hull	3.00	1.20	.30
	St. Louis Blues			
	Brad Shaw			
	Ottawa Senators			

☐ 36	Eddie Johnston CO................ Pittsburgh Penguins	2.00	.80	.20
☐ 37	Dean Kennedy...................... Winnipeg Jets Denis Savard Tampa Bay Lightning	2.00	.80	.20
☐ 38	Dave King CO....................... Calgary Flames	2.00	.80	.20
☐ 39	Pat LaFontaine..................... Buffalo Sabres Pat Verbeek Hartford Whalers	3.50	1.40	.35
☐ 40	Mike Lalor........................... San Jose Sharks Mark Tinordi Dallas Stars	2.00	.80	.20
☐ 41	Trevor Linden....................... Vancouver Canucks Troy Loney Anaheim Mighty Ducks	3.00	1.20	.30
☐ 42	Barry Melrose CO.................. Los Angeles Kings	2.00	.80	.20
☐ 43	Mark Messier....................... Los Angeles Kings Mario Lemieux Pittsburgh Penguins	6.00	2.40	.60
☐ 44	John Muckler CO................... Buffalo Sabres	2.00	.80	.20
☐ 45	Joe Nieuwendyk................... Calgary Flames Joe Sakic Quebec Nordiques	3.00	1.20	.30
☐ 46	Pierre Page CO..................... Quebec Nordiques	2.00	.80	.20
☐ 47	Jeremy Roenick.................... Chicago Blackhawks Guy Carbonneau Montreal Canadiens	3.50	1.40	.35
☐ 48	Brian Skrudland.................... Florida Panthers Craig MacTavish Edmonton Oilers	2.00	.80	.20
☐ 49	Scott Stevens....................... New Jersey Devils Steve Yzerman Detroit Red Wings	3.50	1.40	.35
☐ 50	Tom Barrasso....................... Pittsburgh Penguins	.50	.20	.05
☐ 51	Pavel Bure........................... Vancouver Canucks	2.00	.80	.20
☐ 53	Stephane Fiset..................... Quebec Nordiques	.50	.20	.05
☐ 53	Doug Gilmour....................... Toronto Maple Leafs	1.00	.40	.10
☐ 54	Wayne Gretzky..................... Los Angeles Kings	5.00	2.00	.50
☐ 55	Kelly Hrudey........................ Los Angeles Kings	.50	.20	.05
☐ 56	Mario Lemieux...................... Pittsburgh Penguins	4.00	1.60	.40
☐ 57	Eric Lindros......................... Philadelphia Flyers	5.00	2.00	.50
☐ 58	Kirk McLean......................... Vancouver Canucks	1.00	.40	.10
☐ 59	Kirk Muller........................... Montreal Canadiens	.60	.24	.06
☐ 60	Joe Nieuwendyk................... Calgary Flames	.75	.30	.07
☐ 61	Felix Potvin......................... Toronto Maple Leafs	2.00	.80	.20
☐ 63	Dominic Roussel.................. Philadelphia Flyers	.75	.30	.07
☐ 64	Patrick Roy.......................... Montreal Canadiens	2.50	1.00	.25
☐ 65	Joe Sakic............................ Quebec Nordiques	1.00	.40	.10
☐ 66	Mike Vernon......................... Calgary Flames	.75	.30	.07
☐ 67	Jason Arnott........................ Edmonton Oilers	3.00	1.20	.30
☐ 68	Rob Niedermayer.................. Florida Panthers	1.50	.60	.15
☐ 69	Chris Pronger....................... Hartford Whalers	1.50	.60	.15
☐ 70	Chris Chelios....................... Chicago Blackhawks	.75	.30	.07
☐ 71	Mario Lemieux...................... Pittsburgh Penguins	3.00	1.20	.30
☐ 72	Patrick Roy.......................... Montreal Canadiens	2.50	1.00	.25
☐ xx	Album..................................	25.00	10.00	2.50

1993-94 Kraft Recipes

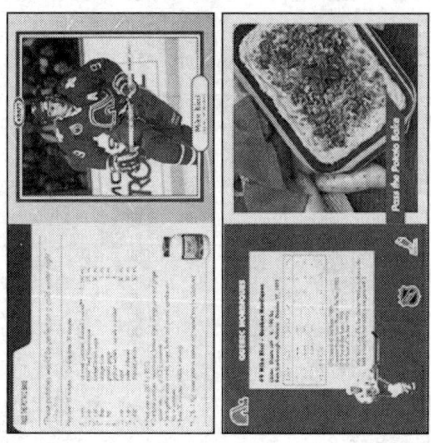

Packaged in a folding cardboard cover, this set of recipe cards features one card for each of the Canadian NHL teams. Each card features a favorite food of a Canadian hockey star. The cards measure approximately 4 3/4" by 4 3/4" and consist of two pages bound by a perforated hinge. The front page displays a color picture of the prepared food item, while its inside presents the recipe. On the page opposite the recipe appears a color action player photo with a white-and-red inner border and a ice-blue outer border. The back page carries in its center a color panel displaying biography, statistics, and career summary; the wide surrounding border is a bright color (blue, green, orange, or red) and carries a player cutout as well as team and league logos. The recipe cards are unnumbered and checklisted below in alphabetical order. A Manufacturer's Rebate Coupon was also included in the package but is not considered part of the card set.

		MINT	EXC	G-VG
COMPLETE SET (8).....................		5.00	2.00	.50
COMMON CARD (1-8)................		.50	.20	.05
☐ 1	Vincent Damphousse............. Montreal Canadiens	.75	.30	.07
☐ 2	Bob Essensa........................ Winnipeg Jets	.50	.20	.05
☐ 3	Doug Gilmour....................... Toronto Maple Leafs	1.25	.50	.12
☐ 4	Trevor Linden....................... Vancouver Canucks	.75	.30	.07
☐ 5	Al MacInnis......................... Calgary Flames	.75	.30	.07
☐ 6	Bill Ranford......................... Edmonton Oilers	.60	.24	.06
☐ 7	Mike Ricci........................... Quebec Nordiques	.60	.24	.06
☐ 8	Brad Shaw........................... Ottawa Senators	.50	.20	.05

1927-28 La Patrie

The 1927-28 La Patrie set contains 21 notebook paper-sized (approximately 8 1/2" by 11") photos. The front has a sepia-toned posed photo of the player, enframed by a thin black border. The words "La Patrie" appear above the picture, with the player's name below it. The photo number and year appear at the lower right corner of the picture. A patterned border completes the front. The back is blank.

	MINT	EXC	G-VG
COMPLETE SET (1)	15.00	6.00	1.50
COMMON CARD	15.00	6.00	1.50
☐ 1 Mario Lemieux	15.00	6.00	1.50

1993-94 Leaf

The 1993-94 Leaf hockey set consists of 440 standard-size (2 1/2" by 3 1/2") cards that were issued in two series of 220. The fronts display color action player photos that are full-bleed except at the bottom, where a red diagonal edges the picture. Below the diagonal are a black stripe carrying the player's name in gold foil lettering, and a team color-coded triangle displaying the team logo. Against the background of the home team's skyline or another prominent architectural landmark, the backs carry a color action player cut-out overprinted at the bottom with biographical and statistical information. A holographic team logo appears in the lower right corner. The cards are numbered on the back.

	MINT	EXC	G-VG
COMPLETE SET (440)	45.00	20.00	5.75
COMPLETE SERIES 1 (220)	20.00	9.00	2.50
COMPLETE SERIES 2 (220)	25.00	11.50	3.10
COMMON PLAYER (1-220)	.08	.04	.01
COMMON PLAYER (221-440)	.08	.04	.01
☐ 1 Mario Lemieux Pittsburgh Penguins	1.25	.55	.16
☐ 2 Curtis Joseph St. Louis Blues	.25	.11	.03
☐ 3 Steve Leach Boston Bruins	.08	.04	.01
☐ 4 Vincent Damphousse Montreal Canadiens	.10	.05	.01
☐ 5 Murray Craven Vancouver Canucks	.08	.04	.01
☐ 6 Pat Elynuik Washington Capitals	.08	.04	.01
☐ 7 Bill Guerin New Jersey Devils	.08	.04	.01
☐ 8 Zarley Zalapski Hartford Whalers	.08	.04	.01
☐ 9 Rob Gaudreau San Jose Sharks	.25	.11	.03
☐ 10 Pavel Bure Vancouver Canucks	1.25	.55	.16
☐ 11 Brad Shaw Ottawa Senators	.08	.04	.01
☐ 12 Pat LaFontaine Buffalo Sabres	.30	.14	.04
☐ 13 Teemu Selanne Winnipeg Jets	1.00	.45	.13
☐ 14 Trent Klatt Dallas Stars	.08	.04	.01
☐ 15 Kevin Todd Edmonton Oilers	.08	.04	.01
☐ 16 Larry Murphy Pittsburgh Penguins	.10	.05	.01
☐ 17 Tony Amonte New York Rangers	.10	.05	.01
☐ 18 Dino Ciccarelli	.10	.05	.01

	EX-MT	VG-E	GOOD
COMPLETE SET (21)	2000.00	800.00	200.00
COMMON PLAYER (1-21)	40.00	16.00	4.00
☐ 1 Sylvio Mantha	80.00	32.00	8.00
☐ 2 Art Gagne	40.00	16.00	4.00
☐ 3 Leo Lafrance	40.00	16.00	4.00
☐ 4 Aurel Joliat	200.00	80.00	20.00
☐ 5 Pit Lepine	40.00	16.00	4.00
☐ 6 Gizzy Hart	60.00	24.00	6.00
☐ 7 Wildor Larochelle	40.00	16.00	4.00
☐ 8 Georges Hainsworth	100.00	40.00	10.00
☐ 9 Herb Gardiner	80.00	32.00	8.00
☐ 10 Albert Leduc	40.00	16.00	4.00
☐ 11 Marty Burke	80.00	32.00	8.00
☐ 12 Charlie Langlois	40.00	16.00	4.00
☐ 13 Leonard Gaudreault	40.00	16.00	4.00
☐ 14 Howie Morenz	500.00	200.00	50.00
☐ 15 Cecil M. Hart	100.00	40.00	10.00
☐ 16 Leo Dandurand	40.00	16.00	4.00
☐ 17 Newsy Lalonde	200.00	80.00	20.00
☐ 18 Didier Pitre	40.00	16.00	4.00
☐ 19 Jack Laviolette	100.00	40.00	10.00
☐ 20 Georges Patterson	40.00	16.00	4.00
☐ 21 George Vezina	400.00	160.00	40.00

1993-94 Leaf Mario Lemieux Large Promo

Measuring approximately 8" by 11 3/8", this oversize card features on its front Leaf spokesman Mario Lemieux in a borderless color action shot. The lower right corner is truncated by a Penguin-yellow diagonal line, beneath which is a black area that contains Lemieux's name in gold foil and the Penguins' name and logo. The gold foil-stamped Leaf logo is in the upper left. The back features another action shot, but this time superimposed on the Pittsburgh skyline. The lower right corner is truncated by Lemieux's 1992-93 stats appearing at an angle. A holographic Penguins logo in the lower right corner rounds out the back. The card is unnumbered.

Detroit Red Wings
☐ 19	Doug Bodger	.08	.04	.01

Buffalo Sabres
| ☐ 20 | Luc Robitaille | .20 | .09 | .03 |

Los Angeles Kings
| ☐ 21 | John Tucker | .08 | .04 | .01 |

Tampa Bay Lightning
| ☐ 22 | Todd Gill | .08 | .04 | .01 |

Toronto Maple Leafs
| ☐ 23 | Mike Ricci | .10 | .05 | .01 |

Quebec Nordiques
| ☐ 24 | Evgeny Davydov | .08 | .04 | .01 |

Winnipeg Jets
| ☐ 25 | Pierre Turgeon | .30 | .14 | .04 |

New York Islanders
| ☐ 26 | Rod Brind'Amour | .20 | .09 | .03 |

Philadelphia Flyers
| ☐ 27 | Jeremy Roenick | .75 | .35 | .09 |

Chicago Blackhawks
| ☐ 28 | Joel Otto | .08 | .04 | .01 |

Calgary Flames
| ☐ 29 | Jeff Brown | .10 | .05 | .01 |

St. Louis Blues
| ☐ 30 | Brendan Shanahan | .25 | .11 | .03 |

St. Louis Blues
| ☐ 31 | Jiri Slegr | .08 | .04 | .01 |

Vancouver Canucks
| ☐ 32 | Vladimir Malakhov | .20 | .09 | .03 |

New York Islanders
| ☐ 33 | Patrick Roy | .75 | .35 | .09 |

Montreal Canadiens
| ☐ 34 | Kevin Hatcher | .10 | .05 | .01 |

Washington Capitals
| ☐ 35 | Alexander Semak | .08 | .04 | .01 |

New Jersey Devils
| ☐ 36 | Gary Roberts | .10 | .05 | .01 |

Calgary Flames
| ☐ 37 | Tommy Soderstrom | .20 | .09 | .03 |

Philadelphia Flyers
| ☐ 38 | Bob Essensa | .10 | .05 | .01 |

Winnipeg Jets
| ☐ 39 | Kelly Hrudey | .10 | .05 | .01 |

Los Angeles Kings
| ☐ 40 | Shawn Chambers | .08 | .04 | .01 |

Tampa Bay Lightning
| ☐ 41 | Glenn Anderson | .10 | .05 | .01 |

Toronto Maple Leafs
| ☐ 42 | Owen Nolan | .10 | .05 | .01 |

Quebec Nordiques
| ☐ 43 | Patrick Flatley | .08 | .04 | .01 |

New York Islanders
| ☐ 44 | Ray Sheppard | .08 | .04 | .01 |

Detroit Red Wings
| ☐ 45 | Darren Turcotte | .08 | .04 | .01 |

New York Rangers
| ☐ 46 | Shayne Corson | .08 | .04 | .01 |

Edmonton Oilers
| ☐ 47 | Brad May | .08 | .04 | .01 |

Buffalo Sabres
| ☐ 48 | Bob Kudelski | .10 | .05 | .01 |

Ottawa Senators
| ☐ 49 | Pat Falloon | .10 | .05 | .01 |

San Jose Sharks
| ☐ 50 | Andrew Cassels | .08 | .04 | .01 |

Hartford Whalers
| ☐ 51 | Chris Chelios | .10 | .05 | .01 |

Chicago Blackhawks
| ☐ 52 | Sylvain Cote | .08 | .04 | .01 |

Washington Capitals
| ☐ 53 | Matt Schneider | .10 | .05 | .01 |

Montreal Canadiens
| ☐ 54 | Ted Donato | .08 | .04 | .01 |

Boston Bruins
| ☐ 55 | Kirk McLean | .15 | .07 | .02 |

Vancouver Canucks
| ☐ 56 | Bruce Driver | .08 | .04 | .01 |

New Jersey Devils
| ☐ 57 | Uwe Krupp | .08 | .04 | .01 |

New York Islanders
| ☐ 58 | Brent Fedyk | .08 | .04 | .01 |

Philadelphia Flyers
| ☐ 59 | Robert Reichel | .10 | .05 | .01 |

Calgary Flames
| ☐ 60 | Scott Stevens | .10 | .05 | .01 |

New Jersey Devils
| ☐ 61 | Phil Housley | .10 | .05 | .01 |

Winnipeg Jets
| ☐ 62 | Ed Belfour | .25 | .11 | .03 |

Chicago Blackhawks
| ☐ 63 | Dave Andreychuk | .15 | .07 | .02 |

Toronto Maple Leafs
| ☐ 64 | Claude Lapointe | .08 | .04 | .01 |

Quebec Nordiques
| ☐ 65 | Russ Courtnall | .10 | .05 | .01 |

Dallas Stars
| ☐ 66 | Grant Fuhr | .10 | .05 | .01 |

Buffalo Sabres
| ☐ 67 | Paul Coffey | .20 | .09 | .03 |

Detroit Red Wings
| ☐ 68 | Bill Ranford | .10 | .05 | .01 |

Edmonton Oilers
| ☐ 69 | Kevin Stevens | .30 | .14 | .04 |

Pittsburgh Penguins
| ☐ 70 | Brian Leetch | .30 | .14 | .04 |

New York Rangers
| ☐ 71 | Dale Hawerchuk | .10 | .05 | .01 |

Buffalo Sabres
| ☐ 72 | Geoff Courtnall | .08 | .04 | .01 |

Vancouver Canucks
| ☐ 73 | Sandis Ozolinsh | .25 | .11 | .03 |

San Jose Sharks
| ☐ 74 | Sylvain Turgeon | .08 | .04 | .01 |

Ottawa Senators
| ☐ 75 | Nelson Emerson | .10 | .05 | .01 |

St. Louis Blues
| ☐ 76 | Brian Bellows | .10 | .05 | .01 |

Montreal Canadiens
| ☐ 77 | Geoff Sanderson | .25 | .11 | .03 |

Hartford Whalers
| ☐ 78 | Petr Nedved | .10 | .05 | .01 |

Vancouver Canucks
| ☐ 79 | Peter Bondra | .10 | .05 | .01 |

Washington Capitals
| ☐ 80 | Scott Niedermayer | .20 | .09 | .03 |

New Jersey Devils
| ☐ 81 | Steve Thomas | .10 | .05 | .01 |

New York Islanders
| ☐ 82 | Dimitri Yushkevich | .08 | .04 | .01 |

Philadelphia Flyers
| ☐ 83 | Mike Vernon | .10 | .05 | .01 |

Calgary Flames
| ☐ 84 | Alexei Zhamnov | .40 | .18 | .05 |

Winnipeg Jets
| ☐ 85 | Adam Creighton | .08 | .04 | .01 |

Tampa Bay Lightning
| ☐ 86 | Dave Ellett | .08 | .04 | .01 |

Toronto Maple Leafs
| ☐ 87 | Joe Sakic | .25 | .11 | .03 |

Quebec Nordiques
| ☐ 88 | Mike Craig | .08 | .04 | .01 |

Dallas Stars
| ☐ 89 | Nicklas Lidstrom | .10 | .05 | .01 |

Detroit Red Wings
| ☐ 90 | Ed Olczyk | .08 | .04 | .01 |

New York Rangers
| ☐ 91 | Alexander Mogilny | .50 | .23 | .06 |

Buffalo Sabres
| ☐ 92 | Ulf Samuelsson | .10 | .05 | .01 |

Pittsburgh Penguins
| ☐ 93 | Doug Gilmour | .40 | .18 | .05 |

Toronto Maple Leafs
| ☐ 94 | Mikael Nylander | .20 | .09 | .03 |

Hartford Whalers
| ☐ 95 | Steve Smith | .08 | .04 | .01 |

Chicago Blackhawks
| ☐ 96 | Igor Korolev | .08 | .04 | .01 |

St. Louis Blues
| ☐ 97 | Dixon Ward | .08 | .04 | .01 |

Vancouver Canucks
| ☐ 98 | John LeClair | .08 | .04 | .01 |

Montreal Canadiens
| ☐ 99 | Cam Neely | .10 | .05 | .01 |

Boston Bruins
| ☐ 100 | Stanley Cup Champs | .75 | .35 | .09 |

Montreal Canadiens
| ☐ 101 | Darius Kasparaitis | .08 | .04 | .01 |

New York Islanders
| ☐ 102 | Mike Ridley | .10 | .05 | .01 |

Washington Capitals
| ☐ 103 | Josef Beranek | .10 | .05 | .01 |

Philadelphia Flyers
| ☐ 104 | Valeri Zelepukin | .10 | .05 | .01 |

New Jersey Devils
| ☐ 105 | Keith Tkachuk | .25 | .11 | .03 |

Winnipeg Jets
| ☐ 106 | Tomas Sandstrom | .08 | .04 | .01 |

Los Angeles Kings
| ☐ 107 | Peter Zezel | .08 | .04 | .01 |

Toronto Maple Leafs
| ☐ 108 | Scott Young | .08 | .04 | .01 |

Quebec Nordiques
| ☐ 109 | Rick Tocchet | .10 | .05 | .01 |

Pittsburgh Penguins
| ☐ 110 | Checklist | .30 | .06 | .02 |

Teemu Selanne
| ☐ 111 | Steve Chiasson | .08 | .04 | .01 |

Detroit Red Wings
| ☐ 112 | Doug Zmolek | .08 | .04 | .01 |

San Jose Sharks			
☐ 113 Patrick Poulin	.08	.04	.01
Hartford Whalers			
☐ 114 Stephane Matteau	.08	.04	.01
Chicago Blackhawks			
☐ 115 Yves Racine	.08	.04	.01
Detroit Red Wings			
☐ 116 Steve Heinze	.08	.04	.01
Boston Bruins			
☐ 117 Gilbert Dionne	.08	.04	.01
Montreal Canadiens			
☐ 118 Dale Hunter	.10	.05	.01
Washington Capitals			
☐ 119 Derek King	.08	.04	.01
New York Islanders			
☐ 120 Garry Galley	.08	.04	.01
Philadelphia Flyers			
☐ 121 Ray Ferraro	.08	.04	.01
New York Islanders			
☐ 122 Andrei Kovalenko	.20	.09	.03
Quebec Nordiques			
☐ 123 Alexei Zhitnik	.20	.09	.03
Los Angeles Kings			
☐ 124 Fredrik Olausson	.08	.04	.01
Winnipeg Jets			
☐ 125 Claude Lemieux	.10	.05	.01
New Jersey Devils			
☐ 126 Joe Nieuwendyk	.10	.05	.01
Calgary Flames			
☐ 127 Travis Green	.08	.04	.01
New York Islanders			
☐ 128 Dave Gagner	.10	.05	.01
Dallas Stars			
☐ 129 Sergei Fedorov	1.00	.45	.13
Detroit Red Wings			
☐ 130 Adam Graves	.30	.14	.04
New York Rangers			
☐ 131 Petr Svoboda	.08	.04	.01
Buffalo Sabres			
☐ 132 Sean Burke	.10	.05	.01
Hartford Whalers			
☐ 133 Johan Garpenlov	.08	.04	.01
San Jose Sharks			
☐ 134 Jamie Baker	.08	.04	.01
Ottawa Senators			
☐ 135 Teppo Numminen	.08	.04	.01
Winnipeg Jets			
☐ 136 Mats Sundin	.25	.11	.03
Quebec Nordiques			
☐ 137 Nikolai Borschevsky	.20	.09	.03
Toronto Maple Leafs			
☐ 138 Stephane Richer	.10	.05	.01
New Jersey Devils			
☐ 139 Scott Lachance	.08	.04	.01
New York Islanders			
☐ 140 Gary Suter	.10	.05	.01
Calgary Flames			
☐ 141 Al Iafrate	.10	.05	.01
Washington Capitals			
☐ 142 Brent Sutter	.10	.05	.01
Chicago Blackhawks			
☐ 143 Dmitri Kvartalnov	.08	.04	.01
Boston Bruins			
☐ 144 Pat Verbeek	.10	.05	.01
Hartford Whalers			
☐ 145 Ed Courtenay	.08	.04	.01
San Jose Sharks			
☐ 146 Mark Tinordi	.08	.04	.01
Dallas Stars			
☐ 147 Alexei Kovalev	.60	.25	.08
New York Rangers			
☐ 148 Dallas Drake	.20	.09	.03
Detroit Red Wings			
☐ 149 Jimmy Carson	.08	.04	.01
Los Angeles Kings			
☐ 150 Florida Panthers Logo	1.00	.45	.13
☐ 151 Roman Hamrlik	.15	.07	.02
Tampa Bay Lightning			
☐ 152 Martin Rucinsky	.08	.04	.01
Quebec Nordiques			
☐ 153 Calle Johansson	.08	.04	.01
Washington Capitals			
☐ 154 Theoren Fleury	.15	.07	.02
Calgary Flames			
☐ 155 Benoit Hogue	.08	.04	.01
New York Islanders			
☐ 156 Kevin Dineen	.10	.05	.01
Philadelphia Flyers			
☐ 157 Jody Hull	.08	.04	.01
Ottawa Senators			
☐ 158 Mark Messier	.20	.09	.03
New York Rangers			
☐ 159 Dave Manson	.08	.04	.01
Edmonton Oilers			
☐ 160 Chris Kontos	.08	.04	.01
Tampa Bay Lightning			
☐ 161 Ron Francis	.10	.05	.01
Pittsburgh Penguins			
☐ 162 Steve Yzerman	.35	.16	.04
Detroit Red Wings			
☐ 163 Igor Kravchuk	.08	.04	.01
Edmonton Oilers			
☐ 164 Sergei Zubov	.60	.25	.08
New York Rangers			
☐ 165 Thomas Steen	.08	.04	.01
Winnipeg Jets			
☐ 166 Wendel Clark	.15	.07	.02
Toronto Maple Leafs			
☐ 167 Scott Pellerin	.20	.09	.03
New Jersey Devils			
☐ 168 Dimitri Khristich	.10	.05	.01
Washington Capitals			
☐ 169 Bernie Nicholls	.10	.05	.01
New Jersey Devils			
☐ 170 Paul Ranheim	.08	.04	.01
Calgary Flames			
☐ 171 Robert Kron	.08	.04	.01
Hartford Whalers			
☐ 172 Rob Blake	.10	.05	.01
Los Angeles Kings			
☐ 173 Rob Zamuner	.08	.04	.01
Tampa Bay Lightning			
☐ 174 Rob Pearson	.08	.04	.01
Toronto Maple Leafs			
☐ 175 Checklist	.15	.05	.01
Ed Belfour			
☐ 176 Steve Duchesne	.10	.05	.01
Quebec Nordiques			
☐ 177 Pelle Eklund	.08	.04	.01
Philadelphia Flyers			
☐ 178 Michal Pivonka	.10	.05	.01
Washington Capitals			
☐ 179 Joe Murphy	.08	.04	.01
Chicago Blackhawks			
☐ 180 Al MacInnis	.15	.07	.02
Calgary Flames			
☐ 181 Craig Janney	.15	.07	.02
St. Louis Blues			
☐ 182 Kirk Muller	.10	.05	.01
Montreal Canadiens			
☐ 183 Cliff Ronning	.08	.04	.01
Vancouver Canucks			
☐ 184 Doug Weight	.10	.05	.01
Edmonton Oilers			
☐ 185 Mike Richter	.25	.11	.03
New York Rangers			
☐ 186 Bob Probert	.08	.04	.01
Detroit Red Wings			
☐ 187 Robert Petrovicky	.08	.04	.01
Hartford Whalers			
☐ 188 Richard Smehlik	.10	.05	.01
Buffalo Sabres			
☐ 189 Norm Maciver	.08	.04	.01
Ottawa Senators			
☐ 190 Stephan Lebeau	.08	.04	.01
Montreal Canadiens			
☐ 191 Patrice Brisebois	.08	.04	.01
Montreal Canadiens			
☐ 192 Kevin Miller	.08	.04	.01
St. Louis Blues			
☐ 193 Trevor Linden	.15	.07	.02
Vancouver Canucks			
☐ 194 Darrin Shannon	.08	.04	.01
Winnipeg Jets			
☐ 195 Tim Cheveldae	.10	.05	.01
Detroit Red Wings			
☐ 196 Tom Barrasso	.10	.05	.01
Pittsburgh Penguins			
☐ 197 Zdeno Ciger	.08	.04	.01
Edmonton Oilers			
☐ 198 Ulf Dahlen	.08	.04	.01
Dallas Stars			
☐ 199 Arturs Irbe	.40	.18	.05
San Jose Sharks			
☐ 200 Anaheim Mighty Ducks Logo	1.00	.45	.13
☐ 201 Tony Granato	.08	.04	.01
Los Angeles Kings			
☐ 202 Mike Modano	.30	.14	.04
Dallas Stars			
☐ 203 Eric Desjardins	.08	.04	.01
Montreal Canadiens			
☐ 204 Bryan Smolinski	.60	.25	.08
Boston Bruins			
☐ 205 Mark Recchi	.25	.11	.03
Philadelphia Flyers			
☐ 206 Darryl Sydor	.10	.05	.01
Los Angeles Kings			

☐ 207 Valeri Kamensky	.20	.09	.03
Quebec Nordiques			
☐ 208 Kelly Kisio	.08	.04	.01
San Jose Sharks			
☐ 209 Brian Bradley	.08	.04	.01
Tampa Bay Lightning			
☐ 210 Checklist	.40	.08	.02
Mario Lemieux			
☐ 211 Yuri Khmylev	.10	.05	.01
Buffalo Sabres			
☐ 212 Derian Hatcher	.08	.04	.01
Dallas Stars			
☐ 213 Mike Gartner	.15	.07	.02
New York Rangers			
☐ 214 Mike Needham UER	.08	.04	.01
Pittsburgh Penguins			
(Grant Jennings on back)			
☐ 215 Ray Bourque	.20	.09	.03
Boston Bruins			
☐ 216 Tie Domi	.08	.04	.01
Winnipeg Jets			
☐ 217 Shawn McEachern	.15	.07	.02
Pittsburgh Penguins			
☐ 218 Joe Juneau	.60	.25	.08
Boston Bruins			
☐ 219 Greg Adams	.08	.04	.01
Vancouver Canucks			
☐ 220 Martin Straka	.50	.23	.06
Pittsburgh Penguins			
☐ 221 Tom Fitzgerald	.08	.04	.01
Florida Panthers			
☐ 222 Gary Shuchuk	.08	.04	.01
Los Angeles Kings			
☐ 223 Kevin Haller	.08	.04	.01
Montreal Canadiens			
☐ 224 Bryan Marchment	.08	.04	.01
Hartford Whalers			
☐ 225 Louie DeBrusk	.08	.04	.01
Edmonton Oilers			
☐ 226 Randy Wood	.08	.04	.01
Buffalo Sabres			
☐ 227 Bobby Holik	.08	.04	.01
New Jersey Devils			
☐ 228 Troy Mallette	.08	.04	.01
Ottawa Senators			
☐ 229 Adam Foote	.08	.04	.01
Quebec Nordiques			
☐ 230 Bob Rouse	.08	.04	.01
Toronto Maple Leafs			
☐ 231 Jyrki Lumme	.08	.04	.01
Vancouver Canucks			
☐ 232 James Patrick	.08	.04	.01
Hartford Whalers			
☐ 233 Eric Lindros	3.00	1.35	.40
Philadelphia Flyers			
☐ 234 Joe Reekie	.08	.04	.01
Tampa Bay Lightning			
☐ 235 Adam Oates	.20	.09	.03
Boston Bruins			
☐ 236 Frank Musil	.08	.04	.01
Calgary Flames			
☐ 237 Vladimir Konstantinov	.08	.04	.01
Detroit Red Wings			
☐ 238 Dave Lowry	.08	.04	.01
Florida Panthers			
☐ 239 Garth Butcher	.08	.04	.01
St. Louis Blues			
☐ 240 Jari Kurri	.15	.07	.02
Los Angeles Kings			
☐ 241 Rick Tabaracci	.08	.04	.01
Washington Capitals			
☐ 242 Sergei Bautin	.08	.04	.01
Winnipeg Jets			
☐ 243 Scott Scissons	.08	.04	.01
New York Islanders			
☐ 244 Dominic Roussel	.15	.07	.02
Philadelphia Flyers			
☐ 245 John Cullen	.08	.04	.01
Toronto Maple Leafs			
☐ 246 Sheldon Kennedy	.08	.04	.01
Detroit Red Wings			
☐ 247 Mike Hough	.08	.04	.01
Florida Panthers			
☐ 248 Paul DiPietro	.08	.04	.01
Montreal Canadiens			
☐ 249 David Shaw	.08	.04	.01
Boston Bruins			
☐ 250 Sergio Momesso	.08	.04	.01
Vancouver Canucks			
☐ 251 Jeff Daniels	.08	.04	.01
Pittsburgh Penguins			
☐ 252 Sergei Nemchinov	.08	.04	.01
New York Rangers			

☐ 253 Kris King	.08	.04	.01
Winnipeg Jets			
☐ 254 Kelly Miller	.08	.04	.01
Washington Capitals			
☐ 255 Brett Hull	.75	.35	.09
St. Louis Blues			
☐ 256 Dominik Hasek	.15	.07	.02
Buffalo Sabres			
☐ 257 Chris Pronger	.75	.35	.09
Hartford Whalers			
☐ 258 Derek Plante	.75	.35	.09
Buffalo Sabres			
☐ 259 Mark Howe	.10	.05	.01
Detroit Red Wings			
☐ 260 Oleg Petrov	.25	.11	.03
Montreal Canadiens			
☐ 261 Ronnie Stern	.08	.04	.01
Calgary Flames			
☐ 262 Scott Mellanby	.08	.04	.01
Florida Panthers			
☐ 263 Warren Rychel	.08	.04	.01
Los Angeles Kings			
☐ 264 John MacLean	.10	.05	.01
New Jersey Devils			
☐ 265 Radek Hamr	.20	.09	.03
Ottawa Senators			
☐ 266 Greg Hawgood	.08	.04	.01
Philidelphia Flyers			
☐ 267 Sylvain Lefebvre	.08	.04	.01
Toronto Maple Leafs			
☐ 268 Glen Wesley	.08	.04	.01
Boston Bruins			
☐ 269 Joe Cirella	.08	.04	.01
Florida Panthers			
☐ 270 Dirk Graham	.08	.04	.01
Chicago Blackhawks			
☐ 271 Eric Weinrich	.08	.04	.01
Hartford Whalers			
☐ 272 Donald Audette	.08	.04	.01
Buffalo Sabres			
☐ 273 Jason Woolley	.08	.04	.01
Washington Capitals			
☐ 274 Kjell Samuelsson	.08	.04	.01
Pittsburgh Penguins			
☐ 275 Ron Sutter	.08	.04	.01
St. Louis Blues			
☐ 276 Keith Primeau	.10	.05	.01
Detroit Red Wings			
☐ 277 Ron Tugnutt	.08	.04	.01
Anaheim Mighty Ducks			
☐ 278 Jesse Belanger	.20	.09	.03
Florida Panthers			
☐ 279 Mike Keane	.08	.04	.01
Montreal Canadiens			
☐ 280 Adam Burt	.08	.04	.01
Hartford Whalers			
☐ 281 Don Sweeney	.08	.04	.01
Boston Bruins			
☐ 282 Mike Donnelly	.08	.04	.01
Los Angeles Kings			
☐ 283 Lyle Odelein	.08	.04	.01
Montreal Canadiens			
☐ 284 Gord Murphy	.08	.04	.01
Florida Panthers			
☐ 285 Mikael Andersson	.08	.04	.01
Tampa Bay Lightning			
☐ 286 Bret Hedican	.08	.04	.01
St. Louis Blues			
☐ 287 Bill Berg	.08	.04	.01
Toronto Maple Leafs			
☐ 288 Esa Tikkanen	.08	.04	.01
New York Rangers			
☐ 289 Markus Naslund	.20	.09	.03
Pittsburgh Penguins			
☐ 290 Checklist	.08	.04	.01
☐ 291 Kerry Huffman	.08	.04	.01
Quebec Nordiques			
☐ 292 Dana Murzyn	.08	.04	.01
Vancouver Canucks			
☐ 293 Rob Niedermayer	.75	.35	.09
Florida Panthers			
☐ 294 Andre Racicot	.08	.04	.01
Montreal Canadiens			
☐ 295 Ken Sutton	.08	.04	.01
Buffalo Sabres			
☐ 296 Shawn Burr	.08	.04	.01
Detroit Red Wings			
☐ 297 Scott Pearson	.08	.04	.01
Edmonton Oilers			
☐ 298 Joby Messier	.15	.07	.02
New York Rangers			
☐ 299 Darrin Madeley	.20	.09	.03
Ottawa Senators			

☐ 300	Joe Mullen	.08	.04	.01	☐ 347	Tyler Wright	.08	.04	.01
	Pittsburgh Penguins					Edmonton Oilers			
☐ 301	Stephane Fiset	.08	.04	.01	☐ 348	Greg Gilbert	.08	.04	.01
	Quebec Nordiques					New York Rangers			
☐ 302	Geoff Smith	.08	.04	.01	☐ 349	Dave Tippett	.08	.04	.01
	Edmonton Oilers					Philadelphia Flyers			
☐ 303	Vyacheslav Kozlov	.75	.35	.09	☐ 350	Stu Barnes	.08	.04	.01
	Detroit Red Wings					Winnipeg Jets			
☐ 304	Wayne Gretzky	1.75	.80	.22	☐ 351	Daniel Lacroix	.15	.07	.02
	Los Angeles Kings					New York Rangers			
☐ 305	Curtis Leschyshyn	.08	.04	.01	☐ 352	Marty McSorley	.08	.04	.01
	Quebec Nordiques					Pittsburgh Penguins			
☐ 306	Mike Sillinger	.08	.04	.01	☐ 353	Sean Hill	.08	.04	.01
	Detroit Red Wings					Anaheim Mighty Ducks			
☐ 307	Vyacheslav Butsayev	.08	.04	.01	☐ 354	Craig Billington	.08	.04	.01
	Philadelphia Flyers					New Jersey Devils			
☐ 308	Mark Lamb	.08	.04	.01	☐ 355	Donald Dufresne	.08	.04	.01
	Edmonton Oilers					Tampa Bay Lightning			
☐ 309	German Titov	.50	.23	.06	☐ 356	Guy Hebert	.15	.07	.02
	Calgary Flames					Anaheim Mighty Ducks			
☐ 310	Gerard Gallant	.08	.04	.01	☐ 357	Neil Wilkinson	.08	.04	.01
	Tampa Bay Lightning					Chicago Blackhawks			
☐ 311	Alexandre Daigle	.75	.35	.09	☐ 358	Sandy McCarthy	.08	.04	.01
	Ottawa Senators					Calgary Flames			
☐ 312	Jim Hrivnak	.08	.04	.01	☐ 359	Aaron Ward	.15	.07	.02
	Washington Capitals					Detroit Red Wings			
☐ 313	Corey Hirsch	.25	.11	.03	☐ 360	Scott Thomas	.15	.07	.02
	New York Rangers					Buffalo Sabres			
☐ 314	Craig Berube	.08	.04	.01	☐ 361	Corey Millen	.08	.04	.01
	Toronto Maple Leafs					New Jersey Devils			
☐ 315	Bill Houlder	.08	.04	.01	☐ 362	Matthew Barnaby	.20	.09	.03
	Anaheim Mighty Ducks					Buffalo Sabres			
☐ 316	Ron Wilson	.08	.04	.01	☐ 363	Benoit Brunet	.08	.04	.01
	Montreal Canadiens					Montreal Canadiens			
☐ 317	Glen Murray	.08	.04	.01	☐ 364	Boris Mironov	.08	.04	.01
	Boston Bruins					Winnipeg Jets			
☐ 318	Bryan Trottier	.10	.05	.01	☐ 365	Doug Lidster	.08	.04	.01
	Pittsburgh Penguins					New York Rangers			
☐ 319	Jeff Hackett	.08	.04	.01	☐ 366	Pavol Demitra	.15	.07	.02
	Chicago Blackhawks					Ottawa Senators			
☐ 320	Brad Dalgarno	.08	.04	.01	☐ 367	Damian Rhodes	.30	.14	.04
	New York Islanders					Toronto Maple Leafs			
☐ 321	Petr Klima	.08	.04	.01	☐ 368	Shawn Antoski	.08	.04	.01
	Tampa Bay Lightning					Vancouver Canucks			
☐ 322	Jon Casey	.10	.05	.01	☐ 369	Andy Moog	.10	.05	.01
	Boston Bruins					Dallas Stars			
☐ 323	Mikael Renberg	.75	.35	.09	☐ 370	Greg Johnson	.08	.04	.01
	Philadelphia Flyers					Detroit Red Wings			
☐ 324	Jimmy Waite	.08	.04	.01	☐ 371	John Vanbiesbrouck	.20	.09	.03
	San Jose Sharks					Florida Panthers			
☐ 325	Brian Skrudland	.08	.04	.01	☐ 372	Denis Savard	.10	.05	.01
	Florida Panthers					Tampa Bay Lightning			
☐ 326	Vitali Prokhorov	.08	.04	.01	☐ 373	Michel Goulet	.10	.05	.01
	St. Louis Blues					Chicago Blackhawks			
☐ 327	Glenn Healy	.08	.04	.01	☐ 374	Dave Taylor	.10	.05	.01
	New York Rangers					Los Angeles Kings			
☐ 328	Brian Benning	.08	.04	.01	☐ 375	Enrico Ciccone	.08	.04	.01
	Florida Panthers					Washington Capitals			
☐ 329	Tony Hrkac	.08	.04	.01	☐ 376	Sergei Zholtok	.08	.04	.01
	St. Louis Blues					Boston Bruins			
☐ 330	Stu Grimson	.08	.04	.01	☐ 377	Bob Errey	.08	.04	.01
	Anaheim Mighty Ducks					San Jose Sharks			
☐ 331	Chris Gratton	.75	.35	.09	☐ 378	Doug Brown	.08	.04	.01
	Tampa Bay Lightning					Pittsburgh Penguins			
☐ 332	Dave Poulin	.08	.04	.01	☐ 379	Bill McDougall	.08	.04	.01
	Washington Capitals					Florida Panthers			
☐ 333	Jarrod Skalde	.08	.04	.01	☐ 380	Pat Conacher	.08	.04	.01
	Anaheim Mighty Ducks					Los Angeles Kings			
☐ 334	Christian Ruuttu	.08	.04	.01	☐ 381	Alexei Kasatonov	.08	.04	.01
	Chicago Blackhawks					Anaheim Mighty Ducks			
☐ 335	Mark Fitzpatrick	.08	.04	.01	☐ 382	Jason Arnott	2.00	.90	.25
	Florida Panthers					Edmonton Oilers			
☐ 336	Martin Lapointe	.08	.04	.01	☐ 383	Jarkko Varvio	.20	.09	.03
	Detroit Red Wings					Dallas Stars			
☐ 337	Cam Stewart	.20	.09	.03	☐ 384	Sergei Makarov	.10	.05	.01
	Boston Bruins					San Jose Sharks			
☐ 338	Anatoli Semenov	.08	.04	.01	☐ 385	Trevor Kidd	.10	.05	.01
	Anaheim Mighty Ducks					Calgary Flames			
☐ 339	Gaetan Duchesne	.08	.04	.01	☐ 386	Alexei Yashin	.75	.35	.09
	San Jose Sharks					Ottawa Senators			
☐ 340	Checklist	.08	.04	.01	☐ 387	Gerald Diduck	.08	.04	.01
☐ 341	Ron Hextall	.10	.05	.01		Vancouver Canucks			
	New York Islanders				☐ 388	Paul Ysebaert	.08	.04	.01
☐ 342	Mikhail Tatarinov	.08	.04	.01		Winnipeg Jets			
	Boston Bruins				☐ 389	Jason Smith	.15	.07	.02
☐ 343	Danny Lorenz	.08	.04	.01		New Jersey Devils			
	New York Islanders				☐ 390	Jeff Norton	.08	.04	.01
☐ 344	Craig Simpson	.08	.04	.01		San Jose Sharks			
	Edmonton Oilers				☐ 391	Igor Larionov	.08	.04	.01
☐ 345	Martin Brodeur	.15	.07	.02		San Jose Sharks			
	New Jersey Devils				☐ 392	Pierre Sevigny	.08	.04	.01
☐ 346	Jaromir Jagr	.75	.35	.09		Montreal Canadiens			
	Pittsburgh Penguins				☐ 393	Wes Walz	.08	.04	.01

	Calgary Flames			
☐ 394	Grant Ledyard	.08	.04	.01
	Dallas Stars			
☐ 395	Brad McCrimmon	.08	.04	.01
	Hartford Whalers			
☐ 396	Martin Gelinas	.08	.04	.01
	Quebec Nordiques			
☐ 397	Paul Cavallini	.08	.04	.01
	Dallas Stars			
☐ 398	Brian Noonan	.08	.04	.01
	Chicago Blackhawks			
☐ 399	Mike Lalor	.08	.04	.01
	San Jose Sharks			
☐ 400	Dimitri Filimonov	.08	.04	.01
	Ottawa Senators			
☐ 401	Andrei Lomakin	.08	.04	.01
	Florida Panthers			
☐ 402	Steve Junker	.15	.07	.02
	New York Islanders			
☐ 403	Daren Puppa	.10	.05	.01
	Tampa Bay Lightning			
☐ 404	Jozef Stumpel	.08	.04	.01
	Boston Bruins			
☐ 405	Jeff Shantz	.20	.09	.03
	Chicago Blackhawks			
☐ 406	Terry Yake	.08	.04	.01
	Anaheim Mighty Ducks			
☐ 407	Mike Peluso	.08	.04	.01
	New Jersey Devils			
☐ 408	Vitali Karamnov	.08	.04	.01
	St. Louis Blues			
☐ 409	Felix Potvin	1.00	.45	.13
	Toronto Maple Leafs			
☐ 410	Steven King	.08	.04	.01
	Anaheim Mighty Ducks			
☐ 411	Roman Oksiuta	.15	.07	.02
	Edmonton Oilers			
☐ 412	Mark Greig	.08	.04	.01
	Hartford Whalers			
☐ 413	Wayne McBean	.08	.04	.01
	New York Islanders			
☐ 414	Nick Kypreos	.08	.04	.01
	Hartford Whalers			
☐ 415	Dominic Lavoie	.08	.04	.01
	Los Angeles Kings			
☐ 416	Chris Simon	.20	.09	.03
	Quebec Nordiques			
☐ 417	Peter Popovic	.15	.07	.02
	Montreal Canadiens			
☐ 418	Gino Odjick	.08	.04	.01
	Vancouver Canucks			
☐ 419	Mike Rathje	.08	.04	.01
	San Jose Sharks			
☐ 420	Keith Acton	.08	.04	.01
	Philadelphia Flyers			
☐ 421	Bob Carpenter	.08	.04	.01
	Washington Capitals			
☐ 422	Steven Finn	.08	.04	.01
	Quebec Nordiques			
☐ 423	Ian Herbers	.15	.07	.02
	Edmonton Oilers			
☐ 424	Ted Drury	.08	.04	.01
	Calgary Flames			
☐ 425	Sergei Petrenko	.08	.04	.01
	Buffalo Sabres			
☐ 426	Mattias Norstrom	.15	.07	.02
	New York Rangers			
☐ 427	Todd Ewen	.08	.04	.01
	Anaheim Mighty Ducks			
☐ 428	Jocelyn Thibault	.75	.35	.09
	Quebec Nordiques			
☐ 429	Robert Burakovsky	.08	.04	.01
	Ottawa Senators			
☐ 430	Chris Terreri	.10	.05	.01
	New Jersey Devils			
☐ 431	Michal Sykora	.25	.11	.03
	San Jose Sharks			
☐ 432	Craig Ludwig	.08	.04	.01
	Dallas Stars			
☐ 433	Vesa Vitakoski	.20	.09	.03
	Calgary Flames			
☐ 434	Sergei Krivokrasov	.08	.04	.01
	Chicago Blackhawks			
☐ 435	Darren McCarty	.25	.11	.03
	Detroit Red Wings			
☐ 436	Dean McAmmond	.08	.04	.01
	Edmonton Oilers			
☐ 437	J.J. Daigneault	.08	.04	.01
	Montreal Canadiens			
☐ 438	Vladimir Ruzicka	.08	.04	.01
	Ottawa Senators			
☐ 439	Vlastimil Kroupa	.25	.11	.03
	San Jose Sharks			
☐ 440	Checklist	.08	.04	.01

1993-94 Leaf Freshman Phenoms

Randomly inserted in Series II packs, these 10 standard-size (2 1/2" by 3 1/2") cards feature borderless color player action shots on their fronts. The player's name appears in white lettering beneath the set's title in the darkened area at the bottom of the player photo. The horizontal back carries a color player action shot on one side, and player information within a black rectangle on the other. The cards are numbered on the back.

		MINT	EXC	G-VG
COMPLETE SET (10)		40.00	18.00	5.00
COMMON PLAYER (1-10)		2.00	.90	.25
☐ 1	Alexandre Daigle	5.00	2.30	.60
	Ottawa Senators			
☐ 2	Chris Pronger	4.00	1.80	.50
	Hartford Whalers			
☐ 3	Chris Gratton	4.00	1.80	.50
	Tampa Bay Lightning			
☐ 4	Markus Naslund	2.00	.90	.25
	Pittsburgh Penguins			
☐ 5	Mikael Renberg	7.00	3.10	.85
	Philadelphia Flyers			
☐ 6	Rob Niedermayer	4.00	1.80	.50
	Florida Panthers			
☐ 7	Jason Arnott	10.00	4.50	1.25
	Edmonton Oilers			
☐ 8	Jarkko Varvio	2.00	.90	.25
	Dallas Stars			
☐ 9	Alexei Yashin	7.00	3.10	.85
	Ottawa Senators			
☐ 10	Jocelyn Thibault	5.00	2.30	.60
	Quebec Nordiques			

1993-94 Leaf Mario Lemieux

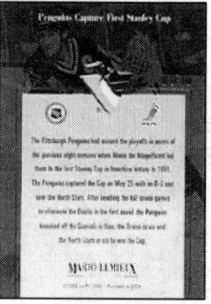

As part of a ten-card subset randomly inserted in first (1-5) and second (6-10) series foil packs, these standard-size (2 1/2" by 3 1/2") cards trace Lemieux's illustrious career. Mario Lemieux personally autographed 2,000 of his cards.

	MINT	EXC	G-VG
COMPLETE SET (10)..................	30.00	13.50	3.80
COMPLETE SERIES 1 (5).............	15.00	6.75	1.90
COMPLETE SERIES 2 (5).............	15.00	6.75	1.90
COMMON LEMIEUX (1-5).............	3.00	1.35	.40
COMMON LEMIEUX (6-10).............	3.00	1.35	.40
☐ 1 Mario Lemieux .... Title Card	3.00	1.35	.40
☐ 2 Mario Lemieux .... 1st Pick in 1984 NHL Draft	3.00	1.35	.40
☐ 3 Mario Lemieux .... 1984 QMJHL POY	3.00	1.35	.40
☐ 4 Mario Lemieux .... 1984-85 Calder Trophy Winner	3.00	1.35	.40
☐ 5 Mario Lemieux .... 1987-88 Hart Trophy and Art Ross Trophy Winner	3.00	1.35	.40
☐ 6 Two Time Conn Smythe .... Trophy Winner	3.00	1.35	.40
☐ 7 Six Time .... NHL All-Star	3.00	1.35	.40
☐ 8 Penguins Capture................... First Stanley Cup	3.00	1.35	.40
☐ 9 1992-93;.............................. Mario Lemieux Best Season Ever	3.00	1.35	.40
☐ 10 Mario's.............................. Magnificent Career	3.00	1.35	.40
☐ AU Mario Lemieux AU............... (Certified autograph)	300.00	135.00	38.00

1993-94 Leaf Gold All-Stars

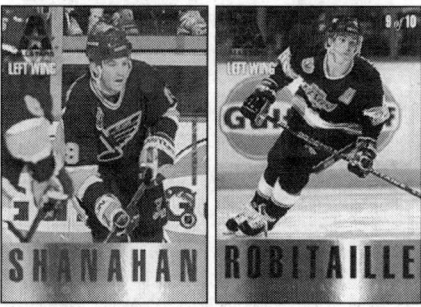

As part of a ten-card subset randomly inserted in first (1-5) and second (6-10) series foil packs, these standard-size (2 1/2" by 3 1/2") cards feature the the NHL's top players at each position, with one player portrayed on each card side.

	MINT	EXC	G-VG
COMPLETE SET (10)......................	90.00	40.00	11.50
COMPLETE SERIES 1 (5).................	45.00	20.00	5.75
COMPLETE SERIES 2 (5).................	45.00	20.00	5.75
COMMON PAIR (1-5).....................	5.00	2.30	.60
COMMON PAIR (6-10).....................	6.00	2.70	.75
☐ 1 Mario Lemieux .... Pittsburgh Penguins Pat LaFontaine Buffalo Sabres	18.00	8.00	2.30
☐ 2 Chris Chelios......................... Chicago Blackhawks Larry Murphy Pittsburgh Penguins	5.00	2.30	.60
☐ 3 Brett Hull............................. St. Louis Blues Teemu Selanne Winnipeg Jets	14.00	6.25	1.75
☐ 4 Kevin Stevens .... Pittsburgh Penguins Dave Andreychuk Toronto Maple Leafs	8.00	3.60	1.00
☐ 5 Patrick Roy .... Montreal Canadiens Tom Barrasso	15.00	6.75	1.90

	MINT	EXC	G-VG
Pittsburgh Penguins			
☐ 6 Wayne Gretzky .... Los Angeles Kings Doug Gilmour Toronto Maple Leafs	25.00	11.50	3.10
☐ 7 Ray Bourque .... Boston Bruins Paul Coffey Detroit Red Wings	6.00	2.70	.75
☐ 8 Alexander Mogilny .... Buffalo Sabres Pavel Bure Vancouver Canucks	16.00	7.25	2.00
☐ 9 Luc Robitaille .... Los Angeles Kings Brendan Shanahan St. Louis Blues	8.00	3.60	1.00
☐ 10 Ed Belfour .... Chicago Blackhawks Felix Potvin Toronto Maple Leafs	12.00	5.50	1.50

1993-94 Leaf Painted Warriors

As part of a ten-card subset randomly inserted in first (1-5) and second (6-10) series foil packs, these standard-size (2 1/2" by 3 1/2") cards feature up-close shots of NHL goalies with emphasis on mask design. The back has a small color photo, biography and career highlights.

	MINT	EXC	G-VG
COMPLETE SET (10)........................	32.00	14.50	4.00
COMPLETE SERIES 1 (5).................	18.00	8.00	2.30
COMPLETE SERIES 2 (5).................	14.00	6.25	1.75
COMMON PLAYER (1-5).................	3.00	1.35	.40
COMMON PLAYER (6-10).................	3.00	1.35	.40
☐ 1 Felix Potvin .... Toronto Maple Leafs	9.00	4.00	1.15
☐ 2 Curtis Joseph........................ St. Louis Blues	4.00	1.80	.50
☐ 3 Kirk McLean.......................... Vancouver Canucks	4.00	1.80	.50
☐ 4 Patrick Roy........................... Montreal Canadiens	9.00	4.00	1.15
☐ 5 Grant Fuhr............................ Buffalo Sabres	3.00	1.35	.40
☐ 6 Ed Belfour............................ Chicago Blackhawks	4.00	1.80	.50
☐ 7 Mike Vernon.......................... Calgary Flames	3.00	1.35	.40
☐ 8 John Vanbiesbrouck .... Florida Panthers	4.00	1.80	.50
☐ 9 Tom Barrasso .... Pittsburgh Penguins	3.00	1.35	.40
☐ 10 Bill Ranford .... Edmonton Oilers	3.00	1.35	.40

1993-94 Leaf Gold Rookies

Randomly inserted in first series foil packs, this 15-card standard-size (2 1/2" by 3 1/2") set showcases top rookies

from the 1992-93 season. Borderless horizontal fronts have a photo of the player along with "Gold Leaf Rookie 1992-93" prominent on the front. Red backs carry a player photo and rookie year highlights. The cards are numbered on back as "X of 15".

		MINT	EXC	G-VG
COMPLETE SET (15)		50.00	23.00	6.25
COMMON PLAYER (1-15)		2.00	.90	.25
☐ 1	Teemu Selanne	7.00	3.10	.85
	Winnipeg Jets			
☐ 2	Joe Juneau	5.00	2.30	.60
	Boston Bruins			
☐ 3	Eric Lindros	18.00	8.00	2.30
	Philadelphia Flyers			
☐ 4	Felix Potvin	10.00	4.50	1.25
	Toronto Maple Leafs			
☐ 5	Alexei Zhamnov	3.00	1.35	.40
	Winnipeg Jets			
☐ 6	Andrei Kovalenko	2.00	.90	.25
	Quebec Nordiques			
☐ 7	Shawn McEachern	2.00	.90	.25
	Pittsburgh Penguins			
☐ 8	Alexei Zhitnik	2.50	1.15	.30
	Los Angeles Kings			
☐ 9	Vladimir Malakhov	2.50	1.15	.30
	New York Islanders			
☐ 10	Patrick Poulin	2.00	.90	.25
	Hartford Whalers			
☐ 11	Keith Tkachuk	2.50	1.15	.30
	Winnipeg Jets			
☐ 12	Tommy Soderstrom	2.00	.90	.25
	Philadelphia Flyers			
☐ 13	Darius Kasparaitis	2.00	.90	.25
	New York Islanders			
☐ 14	Scott Niedermayer	2.50	1.15	.30
	New Jersey Devils			
☐ 15	Darryl Sydor	2.00	.90	.25
	Los Angeles Kings			

1993-94 Leaf Hat Trick Artists

As part of a ten-card subset randomly inserted in first (1-5) and second (6-10) series foil packs, these standard-size (2 1/2" by 3 1/2") cards honor players who score three or more hat tricks in a season. The cards were available in U.S. foil packs and magazine distribution packs.

		MINT	EXC	G-VG
COMPLETE SET (10)		28.00	12.50	3.50
COMPLETE SERIES 1 (5)		14.00	6.25	1.75
COMPLETE SERIES 2 (5)		14.00	6.25	1.75
COMMON PLAYER (1-5)		3.00	1.35	.40
COMMON PLAYER (6-10)		2.00	.90	.25
☐ 1	Title Card	4.00	1.80	.50
☐ 2	Alexander Mogilny	3.00	1.35	.40
	Buffalo Sabres			
☐ 3	Teemu Selanne	5.00	2.30	.60
	Winnipeg Jets			
☐ 4	Mario Lemieux	6.00	2.70	.75
	Pittsburgh Penguins			
☐ 5	Pierre Turgeon	3.00	1.35	.40
	New York Islanders			
☐ 6	Kevin Dineen	2.00	.90	.25
	Philadelphia Flyers			
☐ 7	Eric Lindros	9.00	4.00	1.15
	Philadelphia Flyers			
☐ 8	Adam Oates	3.00	1.35	.40
	Boston Bruins			
☐ 9	Kevin Stevens	3.00	1.35	.40
	Pittsburgh Penguins			
☐ 10	Steve Yzerman	4.00	1.80	.50
	Detroit Red Wings			

1993-94 Leaf Studio Signature

As part of a ten-card subset randomly inserted in first (1-5) and second (6-10) series foil packs, these standard-size (2 1/2" by 3 1/2") cards spotlight the NHL's top players. The cards were available in Canada and magazine distribution packs. Against a colorful background of the team's uniform, the fronts display a cut out player photo with his gold foil signature stamped across the bottom. The backs carry a full-bleed color close-up photo and text that defines the player's personal style. The cards are numbered on the back.

		MINT	EXC	G-VG
COMPLETE SET (10)		50.00	23.00	6.25
COMPLETE SERIES 1 (5)		25.00	11.50	3.10
COMPLETE SERIES 2 (5)		25.00	11.50	3.10
COMMON PLAYER (1-5)		4.00	1.80	.50
COMMON PLAYER (6-10)		5.00	2.30	.60
☐ 1	Doug Gilmour	6.00	2.70	.75
	Toronto Maple Leafs			
☐ 2	Pat Falloon	4.00	1.80	.50
	San Jose Sharks			
☐ 3	Pat LaFontaine	5.00	2.30	.60
	Buffalo Sabres			
☐ 4	Wayne Gretzky	15.00	6.75	1.90
	Los Angeles Kings			
☐ 5	Steve Yzerman	6.00	2.70	.75
	Detroit Red Wings			
☐ 6	Patrick Roy	9.00	4.00	1.15
	Montreal Canadiens			
☐ 7	Jeremy Roenick	6.00	2.70	.75
	Chicago Blackhawks			
☐ 8	Brett Hull	7.00	3.10	.85

St. Louis Blues
☐ 9 Alexandre Daigle .... 5.00 2.30 .60
Ottawa Senators
☐ 10 Eric Lindros.......................... 15.00 6.75 1.90
Philadelphia Flyers

1971-72 Letraset Action Replays

This set of 24 Hockey Action Replays was issued in Canada by Letraset. Printed on thin paper stock, each replay measures approximately 5 1/4" by 6 1/4" and is folded in the center. All replays have a common front consisting of a color photo of a faceoff between Danny O'Shea of the Hawks and Jean Ratelle of the Rangers. On the reverse side, a "Know Your Signals" series illustrates arm signals used by hockey referees. The inside unfolds to display a 5" by 4 1/2" color drawings of NHL action shots. Immediately above is a description of the play plus slots for photos of the players involved in the action. The center photos and some of the players needed to complete the play are missing and supplied on a separate run-on transfer sheet. The action scene could be completed by rubbing the players on the transfer sheet onto the action scene. The replays are numbered in the white panel that presents the referee arm signals, and checklisted below accordingly.

		NRMT	VG-E	GOOD
COMPLETE SET (24)......................		125.00	50.00	12.50
COMMON CARD (1-24)		4.00	1.60	.40
☐ 1	Rogatien Vachon....................	6.00	2.40	.60
	Los Angeles Kings			
	Dave Keon			
	Toronto Maple Leafs			
	Gilles Marotte			
	Los Angeles Kings			
☐ 2	Ken Dryden	12.00	5.00	1.20
	Montreal Canadiens			
	Chico Maki			
	Chicago Blackhawks			
	Jacques Laperriere			
	Montreal Canadiens			
☐ 3	Gary Dornhoefer	4.00	1.60	.40
	Philadelphia Flyers			
	Roger Crozier			
	Buffalo Sabres			
	Tracy Pratt			
	Buffalo Sabres			
☐ 4	Walt Tkaczuk........................	6.00	2.40	.60
	New York Rangers			
	Gump Worsley			
	Minnesota North Stars			
	Vic Hadfield			
	New York Rangers			
☐ 5	Dallas Smith..........................	20.00	8.00	2.00
	Boston Bruins			
	Bobby Orr			
	Boston Bruins			
	Walt McKechnie			
	California Golden Seals			
☐ 6	Ab MacDonald......................	4.00	1.60	.40
	Detroit Red Wings			

	Gary Sabourin			
	St. Louis Blues			
	Garry Unger			
	St. Louis Blues			
☐ 7	Jim Rutherford......................	4.00	1.60	.40
	Pittsburgh Penguins			
	Orland Kurtenbach			
	Vancouver Canucks			
	Bob Woytovich			
	Pittsburgh Penguins			
☐ 8	Gerry Cheevers	8.00	3.25	.80
	Boston Bruins			
	Frank Mahovlich			
	Montreal Canadiens			
	Don Awrey			
	Boston Bruins			
☐ 9	Tim Ecclestone......................	6.00	2.40	.60
	Detroit Red Wings			
	Bob Baun			
	Toronto Maple Leafs			
	Jacques Plante			
	Toronto Maple Leafs			
☐ 10	Stan Mikita...........................	8.00	3.25	.80
	Chicago Blackhawks			
	Ed Giacomin			
	New York Rangers			
	Jim Pappin			
	Chicago Blackhawks			
☐ 11	Doug Favell	4.00	1.60	.40
	Philadelphia Flyers			
	Danny Grant			
	Minnesota North Stars			
	Ed Van Impe			
	Philadelphia Flyers			
☐ 12	Ernie Wakely	4.00	1.60	.40
	St. Louis Blues			
	Barclay Plager			
	St. Louis Blues			
	Gary Croteau			
	California Golden Seals			
☐ 13	Bryan Hextall........................	6.00	2.40	.60
	Pittsburgh Penguins			
	Tony Esposito			
	Chicago Blackhawks			
	Pat Stapleton			
	Chicago Blackhawks			
☐ 14	Jean Ratelle..........................	6.00	2.40	.60
	Boston Bruins			
	Rod Gilbert			
	New York Rangers			
	Jim Roberts			
	St. Louis Blues			
☐ 15	Jacques Lemaire	10.00	4.00	1.00
	Montreal Canadiens			
	Henri Richard			
	Montreal Canadiens			
	Yvan Cournoyer			
	Montreal Canadiens			
☐ 16	George Gardiner.....................	4.00	1.60	.40
	Vancouver Canucks			
	Dennis Hull			
	Chicago Blackhawks			
	Lou Angotti			
	Chicago Blackhawks			
☐ 17	Ed Johnston..........................	25.00	10.00	2.50
	Boston Bruins			
	Norm Ullman			
	Toronto Maple Leafs			
	Bobby Orr			
	Boston Bruins			
☐ 18	Gilles Meloche.......................	4.00	1.60	.40
	California Golden Seals			
	Wayne Carleton			
	California Golden Seals			
	Dick Redmond			
	California Golden Seals			
☐ 19	Al Smith	4.00	1.60	.40
	Detroit Red Wings			
	Gary Bergman			
	Detroit Red Wings			
	Stan Gilbertson			
	California Golden Seals			
☐ 20	Dunc Wilson	6.00	2.40	.60
	Vancouver Canucks			
	Brad Park			
	New York Rangers			
	Dale Tallon			
	Vancouver Canucks			
☐ 21	Jude Drouin	4.00	1.60	.40
	Minnesota North Stars			
	Doug Favell			
	Philadelphia Flyers			
	Barry Ashbee			
	Philadelphia Flyers			

		MINT	EXC	G-VG
☐ 22	Ron Ellis....................	12.00	5.00	1.20
	Toronto Maple Leafs			
	Ken Dryden			
	Montreal Canadiens			
	Paul Henderson			
	Toronto Maple Leafs			
☐ 23	Gary Edwards...............	4.00	1.60	.40
	Los Angeles Kings			
	Jean Pronovost			
	Pittsburgh Penguins			
	Ron Shock			
	Pittsburgh Penguins			
☐ 24	Cesare Maniago	4.00	1.60	.40
	Minnesota North Stars			
	Chris Bordeleau			
	St. Louis Blues			
	Ted Harris			
	Minnesota North Stars			

		MINT	EXC	G-VG
☐ 21	Joe Reekie......................	.50	.20	.05
☐ 22	Thunderbug (Mascot)	.50	.20	.05
☐ 23	John Tucker.....................	.75	.30	.07
☐ 24	Wendell Young..................	.75	.30	.07
☐ 25	Rob Zamuner	.75	.30	.07
☐ 26	Title card	.75	.30	.07
☐ 27	Inaugural season card..........	.50	.20	.05
☐ 28	Sheraton logo card.............	.50	.20	.05

1993-94 Lightning Kash n'Karry

Sponsored by Kash n'Karry, this six-card set measures approximately 5" by 7". Inside gray borders, the fronts feature color action player photos. A blue bar on the left side carries the player's name and number. The sponsor's logo appears in the bottom gray border. The horizontal backs have a postcard design, with the player's name, position, a short biography, and career highlights on the left side. The cards are unnumbered and checklisted below in alphabetical order. The checklist below is incomplete.

	MINT	EXC	G-VG
COMPLETE SET (6)........................	7.50	3.00	.75
COMMON PLAYER (1-6).................	1.00	.40	.10

		MINT	EXC	G-VG
☐ 1	Brian Bradley...................	2.00	.80	.20
☐ 2	Shawn Chambers..................	1.50	.60	.15
☐ 3	Chris Gratton...................	4.00	1.60	.40
☐ 4	Adam Creighton..................	1.50	.60	.15
☐ 5	Rob DiMaio......................	1.00	.40	.10
☐ 6	Wendell Young...................	1.50	.60	.15

1992-93 Lightning Sheraton

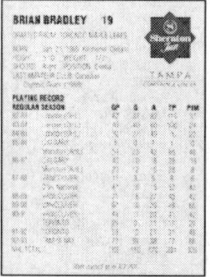

Sponsored by the Sheraton Inn Tampa Conference Center, this album and its 28 perforated cards commemorate the Tampa Bay Lightning's inaugural season. Folded closed, the album measures 10" by 13". The 28 standard-size (2 1/2" by 3 1/2") cards fold out and feature color player action shots on their fronts. These photos are borderless on their top and right sides, and white-bordered on the left and bottom edges. The player's name appears vertically in blue lettering in the margin on the left side, his position appears in blue in the bottom margin, and his uniform number is shown in silver, just above the Lightning logo in the lower left. The white backs display the player's name, uniform number, and biography in the upper left. Below are stats from the player's previous seasons. In the upper right, the Sheraton logo rounds out the card. The cards are unnumbered and checklisted below in alphabetical order.

	MINT	EXC	G-VG
COMPLETE SET (28)........................	15.00	6.00	1.50
COMMON PLAYER (1-28).................	.50	.20	.05

		MINT	EXC	G-VG
☐ 1	Mikael Andersson	.75	.30	.07
☐ 2	Bob Beers	.50	.20	.05
☐ 3	J.C. Bergeron....................	.75	.30	.07
☐ 4	Marc Bergevin....................	.50	.20	.05
☐ 5	Tim Bergland....................	.50	.20	.05
☐ 6	Brian Bradley....................	2.00	.80	.20
☐ 7	Marc Bureau	.75	.30	.07
☐ 8	Wayne Cashman CO...............	.75	.30	.07
☐ 9	Shawn Chambers..................	.75	.30	.07
☐ 10	Danton Cole	.50	.20	.05
☐ 11	Adam Creighton...................	.75	.30	.07
☐ 12	Terry Crisp CO...................	.75	.30	.07
☐ 13	Rob DiMaio......................	.50	.20	.05
☐ 14	Phil Esposito GM	2.50	1.00	.25
☐ 15	Tony Esposito DIR................	1.50	.60	.15
☐ 16	Roman Hamrlik...................	2.00	.80	.20
☐ 17	Pat Jablonski....................	.75	.30	.07
☐ 18	Steve Kasper....................	.75	.30	.07
☐ 19	Chris Kontos....................	1.50	.60	.15
☐ 20	Steve Maltais....................	.50	.20	.05

1993-94 Lightning Season in Review

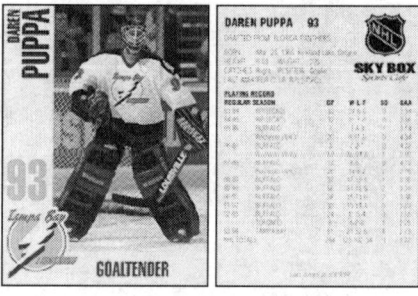

Subtitled "1993-94 Season in Review," the 28 cards comprising this set of the Tampa Bay Lightning were issued in a perforated sheet, which also included a 10" by 13" title page. Each card measures approximately 2 1/2" by 3 1/4" and features on its front a color player action shot, which is borderless at the top and right. The player's name appears vertically within the white margin to the left of the photo; his position appears within the white margin below. His unfiorm number and the team logo appear at the lower left. The white back carries the player's name and uniform number at the top, followed below by biography and statistics. Logos for the NHL and The Sky Box Sports Cafe at the upper right round out the card. The cards are unnumbered and checklisted below in alphabetical order.

	MINT	EXC	G-VG
COMPLETE SET (28)	12.00	5.00	1.20
COMMON PLAYER (1-28)	.35	.14	.03

		MINT	EXC	G-VG
☐ 1	Mikael Andersson	.50	.20	.05
☐ 2	Marc Bergevin	.35	.14	.03
☐ 3	Brian Bradley	.75	.30	.07
☐ 4	Marc Bureau	.35	.14	.03
☐ 5	Wayne Cashman ACO	.50	.20	.05
☐ 6	Shawn Chambers	.50	.20	.05
☐ 7	Enrico Ciccone	.35	.14	.03
☐ 8	Danton Cole	.50	.20	.05
☐ 9	Adam Creighton	.50	.20	.05
☐ 10	Terry Crisp CO	.50	.20	.05
☐ 11	Jim Cummins	.35	.14	.03
☐ 12	Pat Elynuik	.50	.20	.05
☐ 13	Phil Esposito GM	1.50	.60	.15
☐ 14	Tony Esposito DIR	1.00	.40	.10
☐ 15	Gerard Gallant	.35	.14	.03
☐ 16	Danny Gare ACO	.50	.20	.05
☐ 17	Chris Gratton	1.50	.60	.15
☐ 18	Roman Hamrlik	.75	.30	.07
☐ 19	Chris Joseph	.35	.14	.03
☐ 20	Petr Klima	.50	.20	.05
☐ 21	Chris LiPuma	.50	.20	.05
☐ 22	Rudy Poeschek	.35	.14	.03
☐ 23	Daren Puppa	.75	.30	.07
☐ 24	Denis Savard	1.00	.40	.10
☐ 25	Thunderbug MASCOT	.50	.20	.05
☐ 26	John Tucker	.50	.20	.05
☐ 27	Wendell Young	.50	.20	.05
☐ 28	Rob Zamuner	.50	.20	.05

☐ 8	Bobby Orr	60.00	24.00	6.00
☐ 9	Wayne Cashman	5.00	2.00	.50
☐ 10	Brad Park	8.00	3.25	.80
☐ 11	Serge Savard	8.00	3.25	.80
☐ 12	Walt Tkaczuk	5.00	2.00	.50
☐ 13	Yvan Cournoyer	8.00	3.25	.80
☐ 14	Andre Boudrias	4.00	1.60	.40
☐ 15	Gary Smith	4.00	1.60	.40
☐ 16	Guy Lapointe	8.00	3.25	.80
☐ 17	Dennis Hull	5.00	2.00	.50
☐ 18	Bernie Parent	10.00	4.00	1.00
☐ 19	Ken Dryden	25.00	10.00	2.50
☐ 20	Rick MacLeish	6.00	2.40	.60
☐ 21	Bobby Clarke	12.00	5.00	1.20
☐ 22	Dale Tallon	4.00	1.60	.40
☐ 23	Jim McKenny	4.00	1.60	.40
☐ 24	Rene Robert	5.00	2.00	.50
☐ 25	Red Berenson	5.00	2.00	.50
☐ 26	Ed Giacomin	8.00	3.25	.80
☐ 27	Cesare Maniago	5.00	2.00	.50
☐ 28	Ken Hodge	5.00	2.00	.50
☐ 29	Gregg Sheppard	4.00	1.60	.40
☐ 30	Dave Schultz	6.00	2.40	.60
☐ 31	Bill Barber	8.00	3.25	.80
☐ 32	Henry Boucha	4.00	1.60	.40
☐ 33	Richard Martin	5.00	2.00	.50
☐ 34	Steve Vickers	4.00	1.60	.40
☐ 35	Billy Harris	4.00	1.60	.40
☐ 36	Jim Pappin	4.00	1.60	.40
☐ 37	Pit Martin	4.00	1.60	.40
☐ 38	Jacques Lemaire	8.00	3.25	.80
☐ 39	Peter Mahovlich	5.00	2.00	.50
☐ 40	Rod Gilbert	8.00	3.25	.80
☐ 41A	Borje Salming (Horizontal pose)	10.00	4.00	1.00
☐ 41B	Borje Salming (Vertical pose)	10.00	4.00	1.00
☐ 42	Pete Stemkowski	4.00	1.60	.40
☐ 43	Ron Schock	4.00	1.60	.40
☐ 44	Dan Bouchard	4.00	1.60	.40
☐ 45	Tony Esposito	12.00	5.00	1.20
☐ 46	Craig Patrick	5.00	2.00	.50
☐ 47	Ed Westfall	5.00	2.00	.50
☐ 48	Jocelyn Guevremont	4.00	1.60	.40
☐ 49	Syl Apps	4.00	1.60	.40
☐ 50	Dave Keon	10.00	4.00	1.00l

1974-75 Lipton Soup

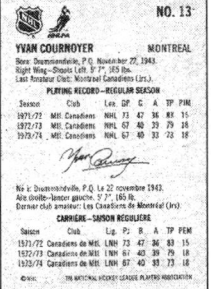

The 1974-75 Lipton Soup NHL set contains 50 color cards measuring approximately 2 1/4" by 3 1/4". The set was issued in two-card panels on the back of Lipton Soup packages. The backs feature statistics in French and English. Both varieties of Salming are included in the complete set below.

	NRMT	VG-E	GOOD
COMPLETE SET (51)	300.00	120.00	30.00
COMMON PLAYER (1-50)	4.00	1.60	.40

		NRMT	VG-E	GOOD
☐ 1	Norm Ullman	8.00	3.25	.80
☐ 2	Gilbert Perreault	10.00	4.00	1.00
☐ 3	Darryl Sittler	10.00	4.00	1.00
☐ 4	Jean-Paul Parise	4.00	1.60	.40
☐ 5	Garry Unger	5.00	2.00	.50
☐ 6	Ron Ellis	5.00	2.00	.50
☐ 7	Rogatien Vachon	8.00	3.25	.80

1973-74 Mac's Milk

The 1973-74 Mac's Milk set contains 30 unnumbered discs measuring approximately 3" in diameter. These round discs are actually cloth stickers with a peel-off back. They are unnumbered and feature popular players in the National Hockey League. There is no identiifying mark anywhere on the discs identifying the sponsor as Mac's Milk. They are checklisted below in alphabetical order by player's name.

	NRMT	VG-E	GOOD
COMPLETE SET (30)	165.00	70.00	15.00
COMMON PLAYER (1-30)	3.00	1.20	.30

		NRMT	VG-E	GOOD
☐ 1	Gary Bergman	3.00	1.20	.30
☐ 2	Johnny Bucyk	7.50	3.00	.75
☐ 3	Wayne Cashman	4.00	1.60	.40
☐ 4	Bobby Clarke	12.50	5.00	1.25
☐ 5	Yvan Cournoyer	9.00	3.75	.90
☐ 6	Ron Ellis	3.00	1.20	.30
☐ 7	Rod Gilbert	7.50	3.00	.75
☐ 8	Brian Glennie	3.00	1.20	.30
☐ 9	Paul Henderson	4.00	1.60	.40
☐ 10	Ed Johnston	5.00	2.00	.50

		NRMT	VG-E	GOOD
☐ 11	Rick Kehoe	3.00	1.20	.30
☐ 12	Orland Kurtenbach	3.00	1.20	.30
☐ 13	Guy Lapointe	7.50	3.00	.75
☐ 14	Jacques Lemaire	7.50	3.00	.75
☐ 15	Frank Mahovlich	12.50	5.00	1.25
☐ 16	Pete Mahovlich	5.00	2.00	.50
☐ 17	Richard Martin	4.00	1.60	.40
☐ 18	Jim McKenny	3.00	1.20	.30
☐ 19	Bobby Orr	40.00	16.00	4.00
☐ 20	Jean-Paul Parise	3.00	1.20	.30
☐ 21	Brad Park	7.50	3.00	.75
☐ 22	Jacques Plante	12.50	5.00	1.25
☐ 23	Jean Ratelle	7.50	3.00	.75
☐ 24	Mickey Redmond	5.00	2.00	.50
☐ 25	Serge Savard	7.50	3.00	.75
☐ 26	Darryl Sittler	9.00	3.75	.90
☐ 27	Pat Stapleton	3.00	1.20	.30
☐ 28	Dale Tallon	3.00	1.20	.30
☐ 29	Norm Ullman	7.50	3.00	.75
☐ 30	Bill White	4.00	1.60	.40

1963-64 Maple Leafs White Border

This 22-card 3 1/2" by 5 1/2" set of postcards features black and white action and posed player photos with white borders. The old Toronto Maple Leafs logo is in the bottom right corner. The player's name and position appear at the bottom. The backs are blank. The cards are unnumbered and checklisted below in alphabetical order.

		NRMT	VG-E	GOOD
	COMPLETE SET (22)	80.00	32.00	8.00
	COMMON PLAYER (1-22)	3.00	1.20	.30
☐ 1	Bob Baun (Posed)	5.00	2.00	.50
☐ 2	Bob Baun (Posed in white uniform, position not listed)	5.00	2.00	.50
☐ 3	Carl Brewer (White uniform)	5.00	2.00	.50
☐ 4	Carl Brewer (Dark uniform)	5.00	2.00	.50
☐ 5	Kent Douglas	3.00	1.20	.30
☐ 6	Dick Duff	4.00	1.60	.40
☐ 7	Ron Ellis	4.00	1.60	.40
☐ 8	Billy Harris (Portrait)	3.00	1.20	.30
☐ 9	Billy Harris (Action)	3.00	1.20	.30
☐ 10	Larry Hillman	3.00	1.20	.30
☐ 11	Red Kelly	7.50	3.00	.75
☐ 12	Dave Keon (No number)	9.00	3.75	.90
☐ 13	Dave Keon (Number 14)	9.00	3.75	.90
☐ 14	Frank Mahovlich (Dark uniform)	15.00	6.00	1.50
☐ 15	Frank Mahovlich (Dark uniform with added line NHL All-Star)	15.00	6.00	1.50
☐ 16	Don McKenney	3.00	1.20	.30
☐ 17	Dickie Moore	7.50	3.00	.75
☐ 18	Bob Nevin	4.00	1.60	.40
☐ 19	Bert Olmstead	5.00	2.00	.50
☐ 20	Eddie Shack	7.50	3.00	.75
☐ 21	Don Simmons	3.00	1.20	.30
☐ 22	Allan Stanley	6.00	2.40	.60

1965-66 Maple Leafs White Border

This 17-card 3 1/2" by 5 1/2" set of postcards features black and white portrait and full length photos with white borders. The Toronto Maple Leafs logo is printed in both bottom corners. A facsimile autograph appears at the bottom between the logos. The backs are blank. The cards are unnumbered and checklisted below in alphabetical order.

		NRMT	VG-E	GOOD
	COMPLETE SET (17)	50.00	20.00	5.00
	COMMON PLAYER (1-17)	2.50	1.00	.25
☐ 1	George Armstrong	6.00	2.40	.60
☐ 2	Bob Baun	3.50	1.40	.35
☐ 3	Johnny Bower	6.00	2.40	.60
☐ 4	John Brenneman	2.50	1.00	.25
☐ 5	Brian Conacher	2.50	1.00	.25
☐ 6	Ron Ellis (Portrait)	3.50	1.40	.35
☐ 7	Ron Ellis (Full length; name in print)	3.50	1.40	.35
☐ 8	Larry Hillman	2.50	1.00	.25
☐ 9	Larry Jeffrey	2.50	1.00	.25
☐ 10	Bruce Gamble	3.50	1.40	.35
☐ 11	Red Kelly	6.00	2.40	.60
☐ 12	Dave Keon	7.50	3.00	.75
☐ 13	Orland Kurtenbach	3.50	1.40	.35
☐ 14	Jim Pappin	2.50	1.00	.25
☐ 15	Marcel Pronovost	5.00	2.00	.50
☐ 16	Eddie Shack	6.00	2.40	.60
☐ 17	Allan Stanley	6.00	2.40	.60

1968-69 Maple Leafs White Border

This 11-card 3 1/2" by 5 1/2" set of postcards features black and white player photos with white borders. The Pelyk and Smith cards are portraits while the other cards have posed action shots. The Maple Leafs logo is at the bottom left corner. A facsimile autograph appears at the bottom. The backs are blank. The cards are unnumbered and checklisted below in alphabetical order.

		NRMT	VG-E	GOOD
	COMPLETE SET (11)	30.00	12.00	3.00
	COMMON PLAYER (1-11)	2.50	1.00	.25
☐ 1	Johnny Bower	6.00	2.40	.60
☐ 2	Jim Dorey	2.50	1.00	.25
☐ 3	Paul Henderson	3.50	1.40	.35
☐ 4	Tim Horton	7.50	3.00	.75
☐ 5	Rick Ley	2.50	1.00	.25
☐ 6	Murray Oliver	2.50	1.00	.25
☐ 7	Mike Pelyk	2.50	1.00	.25
☐ 8	Pierre Pilote	5.00	2.00	.50
☐ 9	Darryl Sly	2.50	1.00	.25
☐ 10	Floyd Smith	2.50	1.00	.25
☐ 11	Bill Sutherland	2.50	1.00	.25

1969-70 Maple Leafs White Border Glossy

This 40-card 3 1/2" by 5 1/2" set of postcards features glossy black and white player photos (posed action or portraits) with white borders. The Maple Leafs logo is printed in black in the bottom left corner. The player's name appears at the bottom in block letters. The backs are blank. The cards are unnumbered and checklisted below in alphabetical order.

	NRMT	VG-E	GOOD
COMPLETE SET (40)	80.00	32.00	8.00
COMMON PLAYER (1-40)	2.00	.80	.20
☐ 1 George Armstrong	5.00	2.00	.50
☐ 2 Johnny Bower	5.00	2.00	.50
☐ 3 Wayne Carleton	2.00	.80	.20
☐ 4 King Clancy	5.00	2.00	.50
☐ 5 Terry Clancy	2.00	.80	.20
☐ 6 Brian Conacher	2.00	.80	.20
☐ 7 Marv Edwards	2.00	.80	.20
☐ 8 Ron Ellis (Number 6)	2.50	1.00	.25
☐ 9 Ron Ellis (Number 8)	3.00	1.20	.30
☐ 10 Ron Ellis (No number)	3.00	1.20	.30
☐ 11 Bruce Gamble (Front view)	2.50	1.00	.25
☐ 12 Bruce Gamble (Side view)	2.50	1.00	.25
☐ 13 Brian Glennie (Portrait)	2.00	.80	.20
☐ 14 Brian Glennie (Full length)	2.00	.80	.20
☐ 15 Jim Harrison	2.00	.80	.20
☐ 16 Larry Hillman	2.00	.80	.20
☐ 17 Tim Horton	7.50	3.00	.75
☐ 18 Dave Keon ("A" on jersey)	6.00	2.40	.60
☐ 19 Dave Keon ("C" on jersey)	6.00	2.40	.60
☐ 20 Rick Ley	3.00	1.20	.30
☐ 21 Frank Mahovlich	9.00	3.75	.90
☐ 22 Jim McKenny	2.00	.80	.20
☐ 23 Larry Mickey	2.00	.80	.20
☐ 24 Murray Oliver	2.00	.80	.20
☐ 25 Jim Pappin	2.00	.80	.20
☐ 26 Mike Pelyk	2.00	.80	.20
☐ 27 Marcel Pronovost	4.00	1.60	.40
☐ 28 Bob Pulford (Number on gloves)	4.00	1.60	.40
☐ 29 Bob Pulford (No number on gloves)	4.00	1.60	.40
☐ 30 Pat Quinn	4.00	1.60	.40
☐ 31 Brit Selby	2.00	.80	.20
☐ 32 Al Smith	2.00	.80	.20
☐ 33 Floyd Smith	2.00	.80	.20
☐ 34 Allan Stanley	5.00	2.00	.50
☐ 35 Norm Ullman	5.00	2.00	.50
☐ 36 Mike Walton (Stick touching border)	3.00	1.20	.30
☐ 37 Mike Walton (Stick away from border)	3.00	1.20	.30
☐ 38 Ron Ward	2.00	.80	.20
☐ 39 Team Photo 1966-67	5.00	2.00	.50
☐ 40 Punch Imlach and King Clancy	5.00	2.00	.50

1969-70 Maple Leafs White Border Matte

This six-card 3 1/2" by 5 1/2" set of postcards features matte black and white player photos with white borders. The Toronto Maple Leafs logo is printed in black in the bottom left corner. The player's name appears at the bottom in block letters. The backs are blank. The cards are unnumbered and checklisted below in alphabetical order.

	NRMT	VG-E	GOOD
COMPLETE SET (6)	15.00	6.00	1.50
COMMON PLAYER (1-6)	2.00	.80	.20
☐ 1 Brian Glennie	2.00	.80	.20
☐ 2 Dave Keon	6.00	2.40	.60
☐ 3 Bill MacMillan	2.00	.80	.20
☐ 4 Larry McIntyre	2.00	.80	.20
☐ 5 Brian Spencer	3.00	1.20	.30
☐ 6 Norm Ullman	5.00	2.00	.50

1970-71 Maple Leafs Postcards

This 15-card 3 1/2" by 5 1/2" set features matte black and white player photos with white borders. The Maple Leafs logo is printed in the bottom left corner. The player's name appears in block letters, and a facsimile autograph is printed in black. The backs are blank. The cards are unnumbered and checklisted below in alphabetical order. Key card in the set is Darryl Sittler appearing in his Rookie Card year.

	NRMT	VG-E	GOOD
COMPLETE SET (15)	50.00	20.00	5.00
COMMON PLAYER (1-15)	2.00	.80	.20
☐ 1 Jim Dorey	2.00	.80	.20
☐ 2 Ron Ellis	3.00	1.20	.30
☐ 3 Bruce Gamble	2.50	1.00	.25
☐ 4 Jim Harrison	2.00	.80	.20
☐ 5 Paul Henderson	3.00	1.20	.30
☐ 6 Rick Ley	2.00	.80	.20
☐ 7 Bob Liddington	2.00	.80	.20
☐ 8 Jim McKenny	2.00	.80	.20
☐ 9 Garry Monahan	2.00	.80	.20
☐ 10 Mike Pelyk	2.00	.80	.20
☐ 11 Jacques Plante	10.00	4.00	1.00
☐ 12 Brad Selwood	2.00	.80	.20
☐ 13 Darryl Sittler	25.00	10.00	2.50
☐ 14 Guy Trottier	2.00	.80	.20
☐ 15 Mike Walton	3.00	1.20	.30

1971-72 Maple Leafs Postcards

This 21-card 3 1/2" by 5 1/2" set features posed color player photos with black backgrounds. (The sweaters have lace-style neck.) The cards feature a facsimile autograph. The backs are blank. The cards are unnumbered and checklisted below in alphabetical order.

	NRMT	VG-E	GOOD
COMPLETE SET (21)	50.00	20.00	5.00
COMMON PLAYER (1-21)	2.00	.80	.20
☐ 1 Bob Baun	3.00	1.20	.30
☐ 2 Jim Dorey	2.00	.80	.20
☐ 3 Denis Dupere	2.00	.80	.20
☐ 4 Ron Ellis	3.00	1.20	.30
☐ 5 Brian Glennie	2.00	.80	.20
☐ 6 Jim Harrison	2.00	.80	.20
☐ 7 Paul Henderson	3.00	1.20	.30
☐ 8 Dave Keon	5.00	2.00	.50
☐ 9 Rick Ley	2.00	.80	.20
☐ 10 Billy MacMillan	2.00	.80	.20
☐ 11 Don Marshall	2.00	.80	.20
☐ 12 Jim McKenny	2.00	.80	.20
☐ 13 Garry Monahan	2.00	.80	.20
☐ 14 Bernie Parent	6.00	2.40	.60
☐ 15 Mike Pelyk	2.00	.80	.20
☐ 16 Jacques Plante	8.00	3.25	.80
☐ 17 Brad Selwood	2.00	.80	.20
☐ 18 Darryl Sittler	8.00	3.25	.80
☐ 19 Brian Spencer	3.00	1.20	.30
☐ 20 Guy Trottier	2.00	.80	.20
☐ 21 Norm Ullman	4.00	1.60	.40

1972-73 Maple Leafs Postcards

This 30-card 3 1/2" by 5 1/2" set features posed color player photos with a black background. The players are pictured wearing "V-neck" sweaters. The cards feature a facsimile autograph. The backs are blank. The cards are unnumbered and checklisted below in alphabetical order.

	NRMT	VG-E	GOOD
COMPLETE SET (30)	50.00	20.00	5.00
COMMON PLAYER (1-30)	1.50	.60	.15
☐ 1 Bob Baun	2.50	1.00	.25
☐ 2 Terry Clancy	1.50	.60	.15
☐ 3 Denis Dupere	1.50	.60	.15
☐ 4 Ron Ellis	2.50	1.00	.25
(Dark print)			
☐ 5 Ron Ellis	2.50	1.00	.25
(Light print)			
☐ 6 George Ferguson	1.50	.60	.15
☐ 7 Brian Glennie	1.50	.60	.15
(Autograph touches stick)			
☐ 8 Brian Glennie	1.50	.60	.15
(Autograph away from stick)			
☐ 9 John Grisdale	1.50	.60	.15
☐ 10 Paul Henderson	2.50	1.00	.25
(Light print)			
☐ 11 Paul Henderson	2.50	1.00	.25
(Dark print)			
☐ 12 Pierre Jarry	1.50	.60	.15
☐ 13 Rick Kehoe	2.50	1.00	.25
☐ 14 Dave Keon	5.00	2.00	.50
(Autograph touches skate)			
☐ 15 Dave Keon	5.00	2.00	.50
(Autograph away from skate)			
☐ 16 Ron Low	2.50	1.00	.25
☐ 17 Joe Lundrigan	1.50	.60	.15
☐ 18 Larry McIntyre	1.50	.60	.15
☐ 19 Jim McKenny	1.50	.60	.15
(Blue tinge)			
☐ 20 Jim McKenny	1.50	.60	.15
(Red tinge)			
☐ 21 Garry Monahan	1.50	.60	.15
☐ 22 Randy Osburn	1.50	.60	.15
☐ 23 Mike Pelyk	1.50	.60	.15
☐ 24 Jacques Plante	6.00	2.40	.60
(Autograph through tape)			
☐ 25 Jacques Plante	6.00	2.40	.60
(Autograph under tape)			
☐ 26 Darryl Sittler	6.00	2.40	.60
(Autograph over stick)			
☐ 27 Darryl Sittler	6.00	2.40	.60
(Autograph away from stick)			
☐ 28 Errol Thompson	1.50	.60	.15
☐ 29 Norm Ullman	3.50	1.40	.35
(Best Wishes above blueline)			
☐ 30 Norm Ullman	3.50	1.40	.35
(Best Wishes across blueline)			

1973-74 Maple Leafs Postcards

This 29-card 3 1/2" by 5 1/2" set features posed color player photos with a blue-green background. The cards feature a facsimile autograph. The backs are blank. The cards are unnumbered and checklisted below in alphabetical order. The key card in the set is Lanny McDonald, whose card predates his Rookie Card.

	NRMT	VG-E	GOOD
COMPLETE SET (29)	50.00	20.00	5.00
COMMON PLAYER (1-29)	1.50	.60	.15
☐ 1 Johnny Bower	4.50	1.80	.45
☐ 2 Willie Brossart	1.50	.60	.15
☐ 3 Denis Dupere	1.50	.60	.15
☐ 4 Ron Ellis	2.50	1.00	.25
☐ 5 Doug Favell	2.50	1.00	.25
(Standing)			
☐ 6 Doug Favell	2.50	1.00	.25
(Bending)			
☐ 7 Brian Glennie	1.50	.60	.15
☐ 8 Jim Gregory	1.50	.60	.15
☐ 9 Inge Hammarstrom	1.50	.60	.15
☐ 10 Paul Henderson	2.50	1.00	.25
☐ 11 Eddie Johnston	2.50	1.00	.25
☐ 12 Rick Kehoe	2.50	1.00	.25
(Same as 1972-73 set)			
☐ 13 Rick Kehoe	2.50	1.00	.25
(Bending)			
☐ 14 Rick Kehoe	2.50	1.00	.25
(Standing)			
☐ 15 Red Kelly	4.50	1.80	.45
☐ 16 Dave Keon	4.50	1.80	.45
☐ 17 Lanny McDonald	10.00	4.00	1.00
☐ 18 Jim McKenny	1.50	.60	.15
☐ 19 Garry Monahan	1.50	.60	.15
☐ 20 Bob Neely	1.50	.60	.15
☐ 21 Mike Pelyk	1.50	.60	.15
☐ 22 Borje Salming	6.00	2.40	.60
☐ 23 Eddie Shack	3.50	1.40	.35
☐ 24 Darryl Sittler	4.50	1.80	.45
(Bending)			
☐ 25 Darryl Sittler	4.50	1.80	.45
(Standing)			
☐ 26 Errol Thompson	1.50	.60	.15
☐ 27 Ian Turnbull	1.50	.60	.15
☐ 28 Norm Ullman	3.50	1.40	.35
☐ 29 Dunc Wilson	2.50	1.00	.25

1974-75 Maple Leafs Postcards

This 27-card, 3 1/2" by 5 1/2" set features posed color player photos with a pale-blue background and a "venetian blind" effect. The cards feature facsimile autographs. The backs are blank. The cards are unnumbered and checklisted below in alphabetical

	NRMT	VG-E	GOOD
COMPLETE SET (27)	40.00	16.00	4.00
COMMON PLAYER (1-27)	1.25	.50	.12
☐ 1 Claire Alexander	1.25	.50	.12
☐ 2 Dave Dunn	1.25	.50	.12
☐ 3 Ron Ellis	1.75	.70	.17
☐ 4 George Ferguson	1.25	.50	.12
(Bending)			
☐ 5 George Ferguson	1.25	.50	.12
(Standing)			
☐ 6 Bill Flett	1.25	.50	.12
(Front view)			
☐ 7 Bill Flett	1.25	.50	.12
(Side view)			
☐ 8 Brian Glennie	1.25	.50	.12
☐ 9 Inge Hammarstrom	1.25	.50	.12
☐ 10 Dave Keon	3.50	1.40	.35
(Bending)			
☐ 11 Dave Keon	3.50	1.40	.35
(Standing)			
☐ 12 Lanny McDonald	5.00	2.00	.50
☐ 13 Jim McKenny	1.25	.50	.12
☐ 14 Gord McRae	1.25	.50	.12
☐ 15 Lyle Moffat	1.25	.50	.12
☐ 16 Bob Neely	1.25	.50	.12
☐ 17 Gary Sabourin	1.25	.50	.12
☐ 18 Borje Salming	3.00	1.20	.30
☐ 19 Rod Seiling	1.25	.50	.12
☐ 20 Eddie Shack	3.00	1.20	.30
☐ 21 Darryl Sittler	4.00	1.60	.40
☐ 22 Blaine Stoughton	1.75	.70	.17

			NRMT	VG-E	GOOD
☐	23	Errol Thompson	1.25	.50	.12
☐	24	Ian Turnbull	1.25	.50	.12
☐	25	Norm Ullman	3.00	1.20	.30
☐	26	Dave(Tiger) Williams	3.00	1.20	.30
☐	27	Dunc Williams	1.75	.70	.17

1975-76 Maple Leafs Postcards

This 30-card 3 1/2" by 5 1/2" set of postcards features posed color photos of players in blue uniforms. The Maple Leafs logo, the player's name, and number appear inn a white panel at the bottom. A facsimile autograph is inscribed across the picture. The backs have player information. The cards are unnumbered and checklisted below in alphabetical order.

WAYNE THOMAS

			NRMT	VG-E	GOOD
COMPLETE SET (30)			30.00	12.00	3.00
COMMON PLAYER (1-30)			1.00	.40	.10
☐	1	Claire Alexander	1.00	.40	.10
☐	2	Don Ashby (Bending)	1.00	.40	.10
☐	3	Don Ashby (Standing)	1.00	.40	.10
☐	4	Pat Boutette	1.00	.40	.10
☐	5	Dave Dunn	1.00	.40	.10
☐	6	Doug Favell	1.75	.70	.17
☐	7	George Ferguson	1.00	.40	.10
☐	8	Brian Glennie	1.00	.40	.10
☐	9	Inge Hammarstrom (Bending)	1.00	.40	.10
☐	10	Inge Hammarstrom (Standing)	1.00	.40	.10
☐	11	Greg Hubick	1.00	.40	.10
☐	12	Lanny McDonald	4.00	1.60	.40
☐	13	Jim McKenny	1.00	.40	.10
☐	14	Gord McRae	1.00	.40	.10
☐	15	Bob Neely	1.00	.40	.10
☐	16	Borje Salming (Side view)	3.00	1.20	.30
☐	17	Borje Salming (Front view)	3.00	1.20	.30
☐	18	Rod Seiling	1.00	.40	.10
☐	19	Darryl Sittler (Bending)	4.00	1.60	.40
☐	20	Darryl Sittler (Standing)	5.00	2.00	.50
☐	21	Blaine Stoughton	1.75	.70	.17
☐	22	Wayne Thomas (Crouching)	1.00	.40	.10
☐	23	Wayne Thomas (Standing)	1.00	.40	.10
☐	24	Errol Thompson	1.00	.40	.10
☐	25	Ian Turnbull (Bending)	1.00	.40	.10
☐	26	Ian Turnbull (Standing)	1.00	.40	.10
☐	27	Stan Weir	1.00	.40	.10
☐	28	Dave(Tiger) Williams (Bending)	2.50	1.00	.25
☐	29	Dave(Tiger) Williams (Standing)	2.50	1.00	.25
☐	30	Maple Leaf Gardens (Painting)	1.75	.70	.17

1976-77 Maple Leafs Postcards

This 24-card 3 1/2" by 5 1/2" set in the postcard format features posed color photos of players in blue uniforms. A white panel at the bottom contains the Maple Leafs logo in each corner, the player's name, and uniform number. A facsimile autograph is inscribed across the picture. The cards are unnumbered and checklisted below in alphabetical order. Key card in the set is Randy Carlyle appearing prior to his Rookie Card year.

			NRMT	VG-E	GOOD
COMPLETE SET (24)			25.00	10.00	2.50
COMMON PLAYER (1-24)			1.00	.40	.10
☐	1	Claire Alexander	1.00	.40	.10
☐	2	Don Ashby	1.00	.40	.10
☐	3	Pat Boutette	1.00	.40	.10
☐	4	Randy Carlyle	3.00	1.20	.30
☐	5	George Ferguson	1.00	.40	.10
☐	6	Scott Garland	1.00	.40	.10
☐	7	Brian Glennie	1.00	.40	.10
☐	8	Inge Hammarstrom	1.00	.40	.10
☐	9	Lanny McDonald	3.50	1.40	.35
☐	10	Jim McKenny	1.00	.40	.10
☐	11	Gord McRae	1.00	.40	.10
☐	12	Bob Neely	1.00	.40	.10
☐	13	Mike Palmateer	2.00	.80	.20
☐	14	Mike Pelyk	1.00	.40	.10
☐	15	Borje Salming	2.50	1.00	.25
☐	16	Darryl Sittler	3.50	1.40	.35
☐	17	Wayne Thomas	1.00	.40	.10
☐	18	Errol Thompson	1.00	.40	.10
☐	19	Ian Turnbull (Dark printing)	1.00	.40	.10
☐	20	Ian Turnbull (Light printing)	1.00	.40	.10
☐	21	Jack Valiquette	1.00	.40	.10
☐	22	Kurt Walker	1.00	.40	.10
☐	23	Stan Weir	1.00	.40	.10
☐	24	Dave(Tiger) Williams	2.00	.80	.20

1977-78 Maple Leafs Postcards

This 19-card 3 1/2" by 5 1/2" set features posed color photos of players in white uniforms. At the bottom are the Toronto Maple Leafs logo in each corner, the player's uniform number, and the player's name in blue print. The backs are blank. The cards are unnumbered and checklisted below in alphabetical order.

			NRMT	VG-E	GOOD
COMPLETE SET (19)			20.00	8.00	2.00
COMMON PLAYER (1-19)			1.00	.40	.10
☐	1	Pat Boutette	1.00	.40	.10
☐	2	Randy Carlyle	1.50	.60	.15
☐	3	Ron Ellis	1.50	.60	.15
☐	4	George Ferguson	1.00	.40	.10
☐	5	Brian Glennie	1.00	.40	.10
☐	6	Inge Hammarstrom	1.00	.40	.10
☐	7	Trevor Johansen	1.00	.40	.10
☐	8	Jim Jones	1.00	.40	.10
☐	9	Lanny McDonald	3.00	1.20	.30
☐	10	Jim McKenny	1.00	.40	.10
☐	11	Gord McRae	1.00	.40	.10
☐	12	Mike Palmateer	1.50	.60	.15
☐	13	Borje Salming	2.00	.80	.20
☐	14	Darryl Sittler	3.00	1.20	.30
☐	15	Errol Thompson	1.00	.40	.10
☐	16	Ian Turnbull	1.00	.40	.10
☐	17	Jack Valiquette	1.00	.40	.10
☐	18	Kurt Walker	1.00	.40	.10
☐	19	Dave(Tiger) Williams	2.00	.80	.20

1978-79 Maple Leafs Postcards

BORJE SALMING

LANNY McDONALD

This 25-card 3 1/2" by 5 1/2" set in the postcard format features posed color photos of players in blue uniforms. At the bottom are the Toronto Maple Leafs logo in each corner, the player's uniform number in the logo at the bottom right, and the player's name in blue print. The cards are unnumbered and checklisted below in alphabetical order.

	NRMT	VG-E	GOOD
COMPLETE SET (25)	20.00	8.00	2.00
COMMON PLAYER (1-25)	.75	.30	.07

		NRMT	VG-E	GOOD
☐ 1	John Anderson	1.25	.50	.12
☐ 2	Bruce Boudreau	.75	.30	.07
	(Black and white)			
☐ 3	Pat Boutette	.75	.30	.07
☐ 4	Pat Boutette	.75	.30	.07
☐ 5	Dave Burrows	.75	.30	.07
☐ 6	Jerry Butler	.75	.30	.07
☐ 7	Ron Ellis	1.00	.40	.10
☐ 8	Paul Harrison	.75	.30	.07
☐ 9	Dave Hutchison	.75	.30	.07
☐ 10	Trevor Johansen	.75	.30	.07
☐ 11	Jimmy Jones	.75	.30	.07
☐ 12	Dan Maloney	1.00	.40	.10
☐ 13	Lanny McDonald	3.00	1.20	.30
☐ 14	Walt McKechnie	.75	.30	.07
☐ 15	Garry Monahan	.75	.30	.07
☐ 16	Roger Neilson	1.50	.60	.15
☐ 17	Mike Palmateer	1.25	.50	.12
☐ 18	Borje Salming	1.50	.60	.15
☐ 19	Darryl Sittler	2.50	1.00	.25
☐ 20	Lorne Stamler	.75	.30	.07
☐ 21	Ian Turnbull	.75	.30	.07
☐ 22	Dave(Tiger) Williams	1.50	.60	.15
☐ 23	Ron Wilson	.75	.30	.07
☐ 24	Harold Ballard and King Clancy	2.00	.80	.20
☐ 25	Team Photo	2.00	.80	.20

1979-80 Maple Leafs Postcards

This 34-card 3 1/2" by 5 1/2" set in the postcard format features posed color photos of players in blue uniforms. The Toronto Maple Leafs logo is in each bottom corner. A blue panel across the bottom contains the player's name in white print. The player's uniform number is printed in the logo at the bottom right. Most of the pictures have a light blue tint and are taken against a studio background. These cards also feature facsimile autographs on the lower portion of the picture. The backs are printed with a light blue postcard design and carry the player's name and position. The cards are unnumbered and checklisted below in alphabetical order.

	NRMT	VG-E	GOOD
COMPLETE SET (34)	25.00	10.00	2.50
COMMON PLAYER (1-34)	.75	.30	.07

		NRMT	VG-E	GOOD
☐ 1	John Anderson	1.00	.40	.10
☐ 2	Harold Ballard	1.50	.60	.15
☐ 3	Laurie Boschman	1.00	.40	.10
☐ 4	Pat Boutette	.75	.30	.07
☐ 5	Carl Brewer	1.50	.60	.15
	(Action shot taken at rink; borderless; no facsimile autograph; black print on back)			
☐ 6	Dave Burrows	.75	.30	.07
☐ 7	Jerry Butler	.75	.30	.07
☐ 8	Jiri Crha	.75	.30	.07
☐ 9	Ron Ellis	1.00	.40	.10
☐ 10	Paul Gardner	.75	.30	.07
☐ 11	Paul Harrison	.75	.30	.07
☐ 12	Greg Hotham	.75	.30	.07
☐ 13	Dave Hutchison	.75	.30	.07
☐ 14	Punch Imlach CO	2.00	.80	.20
☐ 15	Jimmy Jones	.75	.30	.07
☐ 16	Mark Kirton	.75	.30	.07
☐ 17	Dan Maloney	1.00	.40	.10
☐ 18	Terry Martin	1.00	.40	.10
	(Action shot taken at rink; borderless; facsimile autograph; black print on back)			
☐ 19	Lanny McDonald	3.00	1.20	.30
☐ 20	Walt McKechnie	.75	.30	.07
☐ 21	Mike Palmateer	1.00	.40	.10
☐ 22	Mike Palmateer	1.00	.40	.10
	(Autograph at different angle)			
☐ 23	Joel Quenneville	.75	.30	.07
☐ 24	Rocky Saganiuk	.75	.30	.07
☐ 25	Borje Salming	1.50	.60	.15
	(Autograph touches blue panel)			
☐ 26	Borje Salming	1.50	.60	.15
	(Autograph away from blue panel)			
☐ 27	Darryl Sittler	3.00	1.20	.30
	(Autograph closer to blue panel)			
☐ 28	Darryl Sittler	3.00	1.20	.30
☐ 29	Floyd Smith	.75	.30	.07
☐ 30	Bob Stephenson	1.00	.40	.10
	(Action shot taken at rink; borderless; no facsimile autograph; black print on back)			
☐ 31	Ian Turnbull	.75	.30	.07
☐ 32	Dave(Tiger) Williams	1.50	.60	.15
☐ 33	Ron Wilson	.75	.30	.07
☐ 34	Faceoff with Cardinal Carter	1.00	.40	.10

1980-81 Maple Leafs Postcards

This 28-card 3 1/2" by 5 1/2" set features horizontally oriented color player photos on the left half of the card. The right half displays player information, blue logos, and a facsimile autograph printed in sky blue along with the team logo and a maple leaf carrying the player's jersey number. The backs are blank. The cards are unnumbered and checklisted below in alphabetical order.

	MINT	EXC	G-VG
COMPLETE SET (28)......................	20.00	8.00	2.00
COMMON PLAYER (1-28)................	.75	.30	.07
☐ 1 John Anderson..........................	1.00	.40	.10
☐ 2 Harold Ballard	1.50	.60	.15
☐ 3 Laurie Boschman	1.00	.40	.10
(Portrait)			
☐ 4 Laurie Boschman	1.00	.40	.10
(Action)			
☐ 5 Johnny Bower	2.00	.80	.20
☐ 6 King Clancy	2.00	.80	.20
☐ 7 Jiri Crha	.75	.30	.07
☐ 8 Joe Crozier CO	.75	.30	.07
☐ 9 Bill Derlago	.75	.30	.07
☐ 10 Dick Duff	1.00	.40	.10
☐ 11 Vitezslav Duris	.75	.30	.07
☐ 12 Dave Farrish	.75	.30	.07
☐ 13 Stewart Gavin	1.00	.40	.10
☐ 14 Paul Harrison	.75	.30	.07
☐ 15 Pat Hickey	1.00	.40	.10
☐ 16 Mark Kirton	.75	.30	.07
☐ 17 Terry Martin	.75	.30	.07
☐ 18 Gerry McNamara..................	.75	.30	.07
☐ 19 Wilf Paiement	1.00	.40	.10
☐ 20 Robert Picard	1.00	.40	.10
☐ 21 Curt Ridley	.75	.30	.07
☐ 22 Rocky Saganiuk	.75	.30	.07
☐ 23 Borje Salming	1.50	.60	.15
☐ 24 Dave Shand	.75	.30	.07
☐ 25 Darryl Sittler........................	3.00	1.20	.30
(Portrait)			
☐ 26 Darryl Sittler........................	3.00	1.20	.30
(Action)			
☐ 27 Ian Turnbull..........................	.75	.30	.07
☐ 28 Rick Vaive	1.25	.50	.12

1981-82 Maple Leafs Postcards

This 26-card 3 1/2" by 5 1/2" set in the postcard format features full-bleed color photos of players posed on the ice against a dark background. A white Maple Leafs logo appears in each top corner and the player's name in white between the logos. The player's number is printed in the right top logo. These cards also feature facsimile autographs. The backs are white and have a basic postcard design printed in light blue. The cards are unnumbered and checklisted below in alphabetical order.

	MINT	EXC	G-VG
COMPLETE SET (26)......................	20.00	8.00	2.00
COMMON PLAYER (1-26)................	.75	.30	.07
☐ 1 John Anderson..........................	1.00	.40	.10
☐ 2 Harold Ballard	2.00	.80	.20
(Painting)			
☐ 3 Jim Benning............................	.75	.30	.07
☐ 4 Fred Boimistruck....................	.75	.30	.07
☐ 5 Laurie Boschman	1.00	.40	.10
☐ 6 Bill Derlago	.75	.30	.07
☐ 7 Stewart Gavin........................	1.00	.40	.10
☐ 8 Bunny Larocque	1.00	.40	.10
☐ 9 Don Luce..............................	.75	.30	.07
☐ 10 Dan Maloney	1.00	.40	.10
☐ 11 Bob Manno	.75	.30	.07
☐ 12 Paul Marshall	.75	.30	.07
☐ 13 Terry Martin	.75	.30	.07
☐ 14 Bob McGill	1.00	.40	.10
☐ 15 Barry Melrose	1.50	.60	.15
☐ 16 Mike Nykoluk CO..................	.75	.30	.07
☐ 17 Wilf Paiement......................	1.00	.40	.10
☐ 18 Rene Robert	1.25	.50	.12
☐ 19 Rocky Saganiuk	.75	.30	.07
☐ 20 Borje Salming	1.50	.60	.15
☐ 21 Darryl Sittler........................	3.00	1.20	.30
☐ 22 Vincent Tremblay	.75	.30	.07
☐ 23 Rick Vaive	1.25	.50	.12
☐ 24 Gary Yaremchuk	.75	.30	.07
☐ 25 Ron Zanussi	.75	.30	.07
☐ 26 Frank J. Selke and................	1.50	.60	.15
Harold Ballard			
(Official Opening			
of the 1981-82			
Hockey Season)			

1982-83 Maple Leafs Postcards

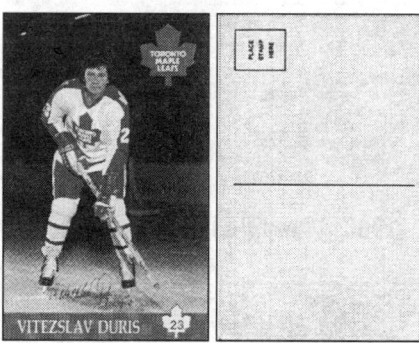

This 37-card, 3 1/2" by 5 1/2" set in the postcard format features color photos of players on the ice against a dark background. A white Maple Leafs logo, the sweater number, and the player's name appear in a blue panel at the bottom. A facsimile autograph appears near the bottom of the picture. A blue Maple Leafs logo is printed in one of the top corners. The postcard backs are printed in light blue, in contrast to the 1984-85 issue, which features black print on the back. The cards are unnumbered and checklisted below in alphabetical order.

	MINT	EXC	G-VG
COMPLETE SET (37)......................	20.00	8.00	2.00
COMMON PLAYER (1-37)................	.75	.30	.07
☐ 1 Russ Adam	.75	.30	.07
☐ 2 John Anderson........................	1.00	.40	.10
☐ 3 Normand Aubin	.75	.30	.07
☐ 4 Jim Benning	.75	.30	.07
☐ 5 Fred Boimistruck....................	.75	.30	.07
☐ 6 Serge Boisvert........................	.75	.30	.07
☐ 7 Dan Daoust	.75	.30	.07
☐ 8 Bill Derlago	.75	.30	.07
(Autograph 1/8"			

☐ 9 Bill Derlago .... (Autograph 1/4" from border)	.75	.30	.07
☐ 10 Vitezslav Duris	.75	.30	.07
☐ 11 Miroslav Frycer .... (Autograph touching skate blade)	.75	.30	.07
☐ 12 Miroslav Frycer .... (Autograph away from skate blade)	.75	.30	.07
☐ 13 Stewart Gavin......................	1.00	.40	.10
☐ 14 Gaston Gingras .... (Dark background)	.75	.30	.07
☐ 15 Gaston Gingras .... (Light background)	.75	.30	.07
☐ 16 Billy Harris	.75	.30	.07
☐ 17 Paul Higgins	.75	.30	.07
☐ 18 Peter Inhacak	.75	.30	.07
☐ 19 Jim Korn	.75	.30	.07
☐ 20 Bunny Larocque .... (Bunny touching stick)	1.00	.40	.10
☐ 21 Bunny Larocque.................... (Bunny touching goalie pad)	1.00	.40	.10
☐ 22 Dan Maloney	1.00	.40	.10
☐ 23 Terry Martin	.75	.30	.07
☐ 24 Bob McGill	1.00	.40	.10
☐ 25 Frank Nigro	.75	.30	.07
☐ 26 Mike Nykoluk CO...................	.75	.30	.07
☐ 27 Gary Nylund	1.00	.40	.10
☐ 28 Mike Palmateer	1.00	.40	.10
☐ 29 Walt Poddubny	1.00	.40	.10
☐ 30 Borje Salming .... (Autograph 1/8" from skate)	1.50	.60	.15
☐ 31 Borje Salming .... (Autograph 1/4" from skate)	1.50	.60	.15
☐ 32 Rick St. Croix	1.00	.40	.10
☐ 33 Greg Terrion........................ (Dark background)	.75	.30	.07
☐ 34 Greg Terrion........................ (Light background)	.75	.30	.07
☐ 35 Vincent Tremblay	.75	.30	.07
☐ 36 Rick Vaive .... (Autograph touching blade)	1.25	.50	.12
☐ 37 Rick Vaive .... (Autograph touching toe of skate)	1.25	.50	.12

1983-84 Maple Leafs Postcards

This 26-card 3 1/2" by 5 1/2" set in the postcard format features posed color photos of players on the ice. A pale blue border contains a blue Maple Leafs logo in the bottom right corner. The player's name and number is printed running up the left side and across the top in the left corner. A facsimile autograph is printed in black on the front near the bottom of the photo. The backs are white and carry a basic postcard design in light blue. The cards are unnumbered and checklisted below in alphabetical order.

		MINT	EXC	G-VG
COMPLETE SET (26)......................		15.00	6.00	1.50
COMMON PLAYER (1-26)................		.60	.24	.06
☐ 1 John Anderson......................		1.00	.40	.10
☐ 2 Jim Benning		.60	.24	.06
☐ 3 Dan Daoust		.60	.24	.06
☐ 4 Bill Derlago		.60	.24	.06
☐ 5 Dave Farrish........................		.60	.24	.06
☐ 6 Myroslav Frycer		.60	.24	.06
☐ 7 Stewart Gavin......................		1.00	.40	.10
☐ 8 Gaston Gingras		.60	.24	.06
☐ 9 Pat Graham		.60	.24	.06
☐ 10 Billy Harris		.60	.24	.06
☐ 11 Peter Inhacak		.60	.24	.06
☐ 12 Jim Korn		.60	.24	.06
☐ 13 Gary Leeman		1.00	.40	.10
☐ 14 Dan Maloney		1.00	.40	.10
☐ 15 Terry Martin		.60	.24	.06
☐ 16 Basil McRae		1.00	.40	.10
☐ 17 Frank Nigro		.60	.24	.06
☐ 18 Mike Nykoluk CO...................		.60	.24	.06
☐ 19 Gary Nylund		.60	.24	.06
☐ 20 Mike Palmateer		1.00	.40	.10
☐ 21 Walt Poddubny		1.00	.40	.10
☐ 22 Borje Salming		1.50	.60	.15
☐ 23 Bill Stewart.........................		.60	.24	.06
☐ 24 Rick St. Croix		1.00	.40	.10
☐ 25 Greg Terrion		.60	.24	.06
☐ 26 Rick Vaive		1.25	.50	.12

1984-85 Maple Leafs Postcards

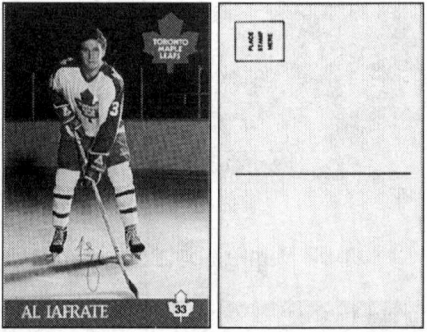

This 25-card 3 1/2" by 5 1/2" set in the postcard format features posed color photos of players on the ice with facsimile autographs. A blue panel at the bottom contains the player's name, sweater number, and a white Maple Leafs logo. A blue Toronto Maple Leafs logo appears in one of the top corners. The backs have a basic postcard design printed in black. The cards are unnumbered and checklisted below in alphabetical order. Both Russ Courtnall and Al Iafrate appear in this set prior to their Rookie Card year. This set can be distinguished from the similarly designed 1982-83 postcard set by the black jersey number and black outline around the team logo in the bottom border stripe.

		MINT	EXC	G-VG
COMPLETE SET (25)......................		20.00	8.00	2.00
COMMON PLAYER (1-25)................		.60	.24	.06
☐ 1 John Anderson......................		.75	.30	.07
☐ 2 Jim Benning		.60	.24	.06
☐ 3 Allan Bester		1.00	.40	.10
☐ 4 John Brophy		1.00	.40	.10
☐ 5 Jeff Brubaker		.60	.24	.06
☐ 6 Russ Courtnall		4.00	1.60	.40
☐ 7 Dan Daoust		.60	.24	.06
☐ 8 Bill Derlago		.60	.24	.06
☐ 9 Miroslav Frycer		.60	.24	.06

☐	10 Stewart Gavin	.75	.30	.07
☐	11 Al Iafrate	6.00	2.40	.60
☐	12 Peter Inhacak	.60	.24	.06
☐	13 Jeff Jackson	.60	.24	.06
☐	14 Jim Korn	.60	.24	.06
☐	15 Gary Leeman	.75	.30	.07
☐	16 Dan Maloney CO	.75	.30	.07
☐	17 Bob McGill	.75	.30	.07
☐	18 Gary Nylund	.75	.30	.07
☐	19 Walt Poddubny	.75	.30	.07
☐	20 Bill Root	.60	.24	.06
☐	21 Borje Salming	1.25	.50	.12
☐	22 Bill Stewart	.60	.24	.06
☐	23 Greg Terrion	.60	.24	.06
☐	24 Rick Vaive	.75	.30	.07
☐	25 Ken Wregget	1.00	.40	.10

1985-86 Maple Leafs Postcards

This 34-card 3 1/2" by 5 1/2" set in the postcard format features color action photos of players on the ice. A blue panel at the bottom contains the player's name, number, and a white Maple Leafs logo. The cards are unnumbered and checklisted below in alphabetical order. Wendel Clark appears in this set the year before his Rookie Card.

		MINT	EXC	G-VG
	COMPLETE SET (34)	20.00	8.00	2.00
	COMMON PLAYER (1-34)	.60	.24	.06
☐	1 Harold Ballard PR	1.00	.40	.10
☐	2 Jim Benning	.60	.24	.06
☐	3 Tim Bernhardt	.60	.24	.06
☐	4 Johnny Bower CO	1.50	.60	.15
☐	5 Jeff Brubaker	.60	.24	.06
☐	6 Wendel Clark	6.00	2.40	.60
☐	7 Russ Courtnall	2.00	.80	.20
	(Dark uniform)			
☐	8 Russ Courtnall	2.00	.80	.20
	(Light uniform)			
☐	9 Dan Daoust	.60	.24	.06
☐	10 Don Edwards	.60	.24	.06
☐	11 Tom Fergus	.60	.24	.06
☐	12 Miroslav Frycer	.60	.24	.06
☐	13 Dan Hodgson	.60	.24	.06
☐	14 Al Iafrate	4.00	1.60	.40
☐	15 Miroslav Inhacak	.60	.24	.06
☐	16 Peter Inhacak	.60	.24	.06
☐	17 Jim Korn	.60	.24	.06
☐	18 Chris Kotsopoulos	.60	.24	.06
☐	19 Gary Leeman	.75	.30	.07
☐	20 Brad Maxwell	.60	.24	.06
	(Dark uniform)			
☐	21 Brad Maxwell	.60	.24	.06
	(Light uniform)			
☐	22 Bob McGill	.75	.30	.07
☐	23 Gary Nylund	.75	.30	.07
☐	24 Walt Poddubny	.75	.30	.07
☐	25 Bill Root	.60	.24	.06
☐	26 Borje Salming	1.25	.50	.12
☐	27 Marion Stastny	.75	.30	.07
☐	28 Greg Terrion	.60	.24	.06
☐	29 Steve Thomas	2.50	1.00	.25
☐	30 Rick Vaive	.75	.30	.07
	(Taking slapshot, visor on helmet)			
☐	31 Rick Vaive	.75	.30	.07
	(Light uniform)			
☐	32 Blake Wesley	.50	.20	.05
☐	33 Ken Wregget	.75	.30	.07
☐	34 Team Photo	2.50	1.00	.25
	(5 1/2" by 8 1/2")			

1987-88 Maple Leafs Postcards

Measuring approximately 5" by 8", this set of oversized postcards features the Toronto Maple Leafs. The fronts have full-bleed color action player photos; the player's name, number, and team logo are printed in a blue-and-white bar at the bottom. The backs are white and show a postcard design. The cards are unnumbered and checklisted below in alphabetical order.

		MINT	EXC	G-VG
	COMPLETE SET (21)	20.00	8.00	2.00
	COMMON PLAYER (1-21)	.75	.30	.07
☐	1 Allan Bester	1.00	.40	.10
☐	2 Wendel Clark	4.00	1.60	.40
☐	3 Russ Courtnall	2.00	.80	.20
☐	4 Vincent Damphousse	4.00	1.60	.40
☐	5 Dan Daoust	.75	.30	.07
☐	6 Tom Fergus	.75	.30	.07
☐	7 Miroslav Frycer	.75	.30	.07
☐	8 Todd Gill	1.00	.40	.10
☐	9 Al Iafrate	2.00	.80	.20
☐	10 Peter Ihnacak	.75	.30	.07
☐	11 Chris Kotsopoulos	.75	.30	.07
☐	12 Rick Lanz	.75	.30	.07
☐	13 Gary Leeman	1.00	.40	.10
☐	14 Ed Olczyk	1.25	.50	.12
☐	15 Mark Osborne	.75	.30	.07
☐	16 Luke Richardson	1.00	.40	.10
☐	17 Borje Salming	1.50	.60	.15
☐	18 Al Secord	1.00	.40	.10
☐	19 Dave Semenko	1.00	.40	.10
☐	20 Ken Wregget	1.00	.40	.10
☐	21 Team Photo	2.50	1.00	.25

1987-88 Maple Leafs PLAY

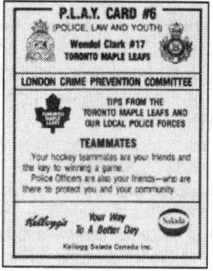

This set contains 30 P.L.A.Y. (Police, Law and Youth) cards, and it was sponsored by Kellogg Salada Canada Inc. in conjunction with the Toronto Maple Leafs and various police agencies. The cards could be collected from members of the London City Police and the Ontario Provincial Police, at a rate of three new cards per week. Three special "make-up" weeks" were held to acquire any cards that were missed. The cards measure approximately 2 3/4" by 3 1/4".

		MINT	EXC	G-VG
	COMPLETE SET (30)	18.00	7.25	1.80
	COMMON PLAYER (1-30)	.50	.20	.05

☐ 1 N.Laverne Shipley .... (Police Chief)	.50	.20	.05
☐ 2 Tom Gosnell (Mayor)	.50	.20	.05
☐ 3 Sponsor's Card .... Kellogg Salada Canada, Inc.	.50	.20	.05
☐ 4 Harold E. Ballard PR	1.25	.50	.12
☐ 5 D. Almond .... (Police Superintendent)	.50	.20	.05
☐ 6 Wendel Clark 17	4.00	1.60	.40
☐ 7 Tom Fergus 19	.75	.30	.07
☐ 8 Borje Salming 21	1.50	.60	.15
☐ 9 Ed Olczyk 16	1.00	.40	.10
☐ 10 Gary Leeman 11	.75	.30	.07
☐ 11 Rick Lanz 4	.50	.20	.05
☐ 12 Allan Bester 30	.75	.30	.07
☐ 13 Todd Gill 23	.75	.30	.07
☐ 14 Al Secord 20	.75	.30	.07
☐ 15 Miroslav Frycer 14	.50	.20	.05
☐ 16 Chris Kotsopoulos 26	.50	.20	.05
☐ 17 Vincent Damphousse 10	4.00	1.60	.40
☐ 18 Mike Allison 8	.50	.20	.05
☐ 19 Al Iafrate 33	2.00	.80	.20
☐ 20 Dan Daoust 24	.50	.20	.05
☐ 21 Greg Terrion 7	.50	.20	.05
☐ 22 Brad Smith 29	.75	.30	.07
☐ 23 Mark Osborne 12	.50	.20	.05
☐ 24 Peter Ihnacak 18	.50	.20	.05
☐ 25 Dale Degray 3	.50	.20	.05
☐ 26 Dave Semenko 27	.75	.30	.07
☐ 27 Luke Richardson 2	.75	.30	.07
☐ 28 John Brophy CO	.75	.30	.07
☐ 29 Ken Wregget 31	.75	.30	.07
☐ 30 Russ Courtnall 9	1.50	.60	.15

☐ 2 Wendel Clark 17	2.00	.80	.20
☐ 3 Tom Fergus 19	.60	.24	.06
☐ 4 D. Almond .... Superintendent	.50	.20	.05
☐ 5 Borje Salming 21	1.25	.50	.12
☐ 6 Ed Olczyk 16	.75	.30	.07
☐ 7 Sponsor's Card .... Kellogg Canada, Inc.	.50	.20	.05
☐ 8 Gary Leeman 11	.60	.24	.06
☐ 9 Rick Lanz 4	.50	.20	.05
☐ 10 N.LaVerne Shipley .... (Chief of Police)	.50	.20	.05
☐ 11 Allan Bester 30	.75	.30	.07
☐ 12 Todd Gill 23	.60	.24	.06
☐ 13 Harold E. Ballard PR	1.00	.40	.10
☐ 14 Al Secord 20	.75	.30	.07
☐ 15 Daniel Marois 32	.75	.30	.07
☐ 16 Chris Kotsopoulos 26	.50	.20	.05
☐ 17 Vincent Damphousse 10	2.00	.80	.20
☐ 18 Craig Laughlin 14	.50	.20	.05
☐ 19 Al Iafrate 33	1.25	.50	.12
☐ 20 Dan Daoust 24	.50	.20	.05
☐ 21 Derek Laxdal 35	.50	.20	.05
☐ 22 Darren Veitch 25	.50	.20	.05
☐ 23 Mark Osborne 12	.75	.30	.07
☐ 24 David Reid 34	.75	.30	.07
☐ 25 Brad Marsh 3	.75	.30	.07
☐ 26 Brian Curran 28	.50	.20	.05
☐ 27 Sean McKenna 8	.50	.20	.05
☐ 28 John Brophy CO	.60	.24	.06
☐ 29 Ken Wregget 31	.75	.30	.07
☐ 30 Russ Courtnall 9	1.25	.50	.12

1988-89 Maple Leafs PLAY

1974-75 Mariners San Diego WHA

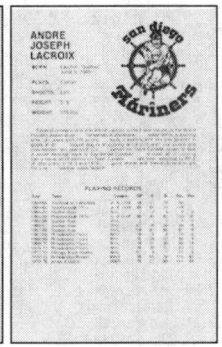

This set contains 30 P.L.A.Y. (Police, Law and Youth) cards, and it was sponsored by Kellogg's in conjunction with Toronto Maple Leafs and various police agencies. The cards could be collected from members of the London City Police and the Ontario Provincial Police, at a rate of three new cards per week. Three special "make-up weeks" were held to acquire any cards that were missed. After collecting the first 12 cards, they were to be brought to police stations in order to obtain the collector album, which measured approximately 7" by 10". The P.L.A.Y. cards measure 2 3/4" by 3 1/2" and the album has three slots per page in a horizontal format. Below each picture the album has the player's name, number, and a hockey tip paralleled by an anti-crime message. All children under 16 years of age who had completed their album received an entry form to qualify for the chance to attend the Toronto Maple Leafs vs. Detroit Red Wings hockey game on March 25, 1989.

	MINT	EXC	G-VG
COMPLETE SET (30)	15.00	6.00	1.50
COMMON PLAYER (1-30)	.50	.20	.05
☐ 1 Rules and Tips	.50	.20	.05

Sponsored by Dean's Photo Service Inc., this set of seven photos measures approximately 5 3/8" by 8 1/2" and features black-and-white action pictures against a white background on thin paper stock. The player's name appears in the white margin below the photo along with the team and sponsor logos. The backs feature biographical information, career highlights, and statistics. The cards came in a light blue paper "picture pack" with the team and sponsor logos and game dates suggested for acquiring autographs. The cards are unnumbered and checklisted below in alphabetical order. This set may be incomplete.

	NRMT	VG-E	GOOD
COMPLETE SET (7)	30.00	12.00	3.00
COMMON PLAYER (1-7)	5.00	2.00	.50
☐ 1 Andre Lacroix	7.50	3.00	.75
☐ 2 Mike Laughton	5.00	2.00	.50
☐ 3 Brian Morenz	5.00	2.00	.50
☐ 4 Kevin Morrison	5.00	2.00	.50
☐ 5 Gene Peacosh	5.00	2.00	.50
☐ 6 Ron Plumb	6.00	2.40	.60
☐ 7 Craig Reichmuth	5.00	2.00	.50

1982-83 McDonald's Stickers

This set consists of 36 full-color stickers measuring 2" by 2 1/2". A 12-page album was also available. The stickers were only issued in the province of Quebec. The stickers are numbered on the front and on the back. The sticker numbering is by position, i.e., goalies (1-5), right wings (6-10), left wings (11-15), all-stars (16-21), centers (22-26), and defensemen (27-36). The all-star stickers are gold foils; the other stickers all have a distinctive red border and show the McDonald's logo in the lower right corner.

		MINT	EXC	G-VG
COMPLETE SET (36)		25.00	10.00	2.50
COMMON PLAYER (1-36)		.40	.16	.04
☐ 1	Dan Bouchard	.40	.16	.04
☐ 2	Richard Brodeur	.60	.24	.06
☐ 3	Gilles Meloche	.40	.16	.04
☐ 4	Billy Smith	1.00	.40	.10
☐ 5	Rick Wamsley	.40	.16	.04
☐ 6	Mike Bossy	1.25	.50	.12
☐ 7	Dino Ciccarelli	.75	.30	.07
☐ 8	Guy Lafleur	1.25	.50	.12
☐ 9	Rick Middleton	.60	.24	.06
☐ 10	Marian Stastny	.40	.16	.04
☐ 11	Bill Barber	.60	.24	.06
☐ 12	Bob Gainey	.75	.30	.07
☐ 13	Clark Gillies	.60	.24	.06
☐ 14	Michel Goulet	.75	.30	.07
☐ 15	Mark Messier	2.50	1.00	.25
☐ 16	Billy Smith AS	.60	.24	.06
☐ 17	Larry Robinson AS	.60	.24	.06
☐ 18	Denis Potvin AS	.60	.24	.06
☐ 19	Michel Goulet AS	.60	.24	.06
☐ 20	Wayne Gretzky AS	3.00	1.20	.30
☐ 21	Mike Bossy AS	.75	.30	.07
☐ 22	Wayne Gretzky	6.00	2.40	.60
☐ 23	Denis Savard	.75	.30	.07
☐ 24	Peter Stastny	.75	.30	.07
☐ 25	Bryan Trottier	1.00	.40	.10
☐ 26	Doug Wickenheiser	.40	.16	.04
☐ 27	Barry Beck	.40	.16	.04
☐ 28	Ray Bourque	1.50	.60	.15
☐ 29	Brian Engblom	.40	.16	.04
☐ 30	Craig Hartsburg	.40	.16	.04
☐ 31	Mark Howe	.60	.24	.06
☐ 32	Rod Langway	.60	.24	.06
☐ 33	Denis Potvin	.75	.30	.07
☐ 34	Larry Robinson	1.00	.40	.10
☐ 35	Normand Rochefort	.40	.16	.04
☐ 36	Doug Wilson	.60	.24	.06
☐ xx	Album	5.00	2.00	.50

1972-73 Nationals Ottawa WHA

This 23-card set measures approximately 4 3/4" by 4 1/8" and features two black-and-white player photos on a white card face. The left side of the card shows a small, close-up picture above the team logo. The right side of the card is devoted to a full length posed action shot. The words "World Hockey Association" are printed in black at the lower left corner. The backs are blank. The cards are unnumbered and checklisted below in alphabetical order.

		MINT	EXC	G-VG
COMPLETE SET (23)		25.00	10.00	2.50
COMMON PLAYER (1-23)		1.25	.50	.12
☐ 1	Mike Amodeo	1.25	.50	.12
☐ 2	Les Binkley	2.50	1.00	.25
☐ 3	Mike Boland	1.25	.50	.12
☐ 4	Wayne Carleton	2.25	.90	.22
☐ 5	Bob Charlebois	1.25	.50	.12
☐ 6	Ron Climie	1.75	.70	.17
☐ 7	Brian Conacher	1.25	.50	.12
☐ 8	Rick Cunningham	1.25	.50	.12
☐ 9	John Donnelly	1.25	.50	.12
☐ 10	Brian Gibbons	1.25	.50	.12
☐ 11	Jack Gibson	1.25	.50	.12
☐ 12	Gilles Gratton	2.50	1.00	.25
☐ 13	Steve King	1.25	.50	.12
☐ 14	Gavin Kirk	1.25	.50	.12
☐ 15	Bob Leduc	1.75	.70	.17
☐ 16	Tom Martin	1.25	.50	.12
☐ 17	Chris Meloff	1.25	.50	.12
☐ 18	Ron Riley	1.25	.50	.12
☐ 19	Rick Sentes	1.25	.50	.12
☐ 20	Tom Simpson	1.25	.50	.12
☐ 21	Ken Stephanson	1.25	.50	.12
☐ 22	Guy Trottier	1.75	.70	.17
☐ 23	Steve Warr	1.25	.50	.12

1982-83 Neilson's Gretzky

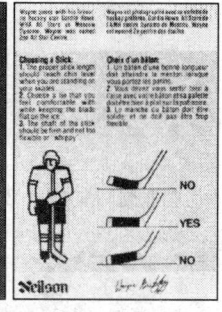

This 50-card set was issued to honor one of hockey's all-time great players, Wayne Gretzky. The cards measure 2 1/2" by 3 1/2". The first nine cards feature vintage black and white photos from Gretzky's childhood up to age 17. The rest of the cards feature color action photos highlighting Gretzky's pro career. All the pictures on the cards are framed by white and orange borders on a dark blue background. The card number appears in a star at the upper left hand corner of the card face. A facsimile autograph is inscribed across the bottom of each picture. The card backs have captions to the pictures and include a discussion of some aspect of the game. The card backs are bilingual, i.e., French and English. Many of these discussions are accompanied by illustrations. The cards were issued as inserts with Neilson's candy bars.

	MINT	EXC	G-VG
COMPLETE SET (50)........................	175.00	70.00	18.00
COMMON CARD (1-50)..................	4.00	1.60	.40
☐ 1 Discard Broken Stick............	8.00	3.25	.80
☐ 2 Handling the Puck.................	4.00	1.60	.40
☐ 3 Offsides...............................	4.00	1.60	.40
☐ 4 Penalty Shot.........................	4.00	1.60	.40
☐ 5 Icing the Puck......................	4.00	1.60	.40
☐ 6 Taping your Stick..................	4.00	1.60	.40
☐ 7 Skates................................	4.00	1.60	.40
☐ 8 The Helmet..........................	4.00	1.60	.40
☐ 9 Selecting Skates...................	4.00	1.60	.40
☐ 10 Choosing a Stick..................	25.00	10.00	2.50
(with Gordie Howe)			
☐ 11 General Equipment Care........	4.00	1.60	.40
☐ 12 The Hook Check...................	8.00	3.25	.80
(with Marcel Dionne)			
☐ 13 The Hip Check.....................	4.00	1.60	.40
☐ 14 Forward Skating...................	8.00	3.25	.80
(With Mike Gartner)			
☐ 15 Stopping	4.00	1.60	.40
☐ 16 Sharp Turning	4.00	1.60	.40
☐ 17 Fast Starts	4.00	1.60	.40
☐ 18 Backward Skating	4.00	1.60	.40
☐ 19 The Grip	4.00	1.60	.40
☐ 20 The Wrist Shot....................	4.00	1.60	.40
☐ 21 The Back Hand Shot.............	4.00	1.60	.40
☐ 22 The Slap Shot......................	4.00	1.60	.40
☐ 23 The Flip Shot.......................	4.00	1.60	.40
☐ 24 Pass Receiving.....................	4.00	1.60	.40
☐ 25 Faking................................	4.00	1.60	.40
☐ 26 Puck Handling......................	4.00	1.60	.40
☐ 27 Deflecting Shots...................	4.00	1.60	.40
☐ 28 One On One.........................	4.00	1.60	.40
☐ 29 Keep Your Head Up..............	4.00	1.60	.40
☐ 30 Passing to the Slot...............	4.00	1.60	.40
☐ 31 Winning Face-Offs................	10.00	4.00	1.00
(with Guy Lafleur			
and Mike Bossy)			
☐ 32 Forechecking.......................	4.00	1.60	.40
☐ 33 Body Checking.....................	4.00	1.60	.40
☐ 34 Breaking Out.......................	4.00	1.60	.40
☐ 35 The Drop Pass.....................	4.00	1.60	.40
☐ 36 Backchecking.......................	8.00	3.25	.80
(with Phil Esposito)			
☐ 37 Using the Boards..................	4.00	1.60	.40
☐ 38 The Power Play....................	6.00	2.40	.60
☐ 39 Passing the Puck..................	4.00	1.60	.40
☐ 40 Clear the Slot......................	4.00	1.60	.40
☐ 41 Leg Lifts.............................	4.00	1.60	.40
☐ 42 Balance Exercise	4.00	1.60	.40
☐ 43 Leg Stretches......................	4.00	1.60	.40
☐ 44 Hip and Groin Stretch	4.00	1.60	.40
☐ 45 Toe Touches	8.00	3.25	.80
(With Mark Messier)			
☐ 46 Goalie Warm Up Drill	4.00	1.60	.40
☐ 47 Leg Exercises......................	4.00	1.60	.40
☐ 48 Arm Exercises.....................	4.00	1.60	.40
☐ 49 Wrist Exercises....................	4.00	1.60	.40
☐ 50 Flip Pass............................	5.00	2.00	.50

1974-75 NHL Action Stamps

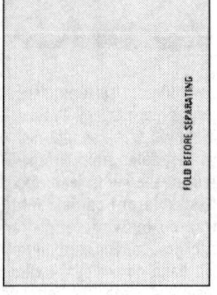

30 Rogie Vachon G
Los Angeles Kings

FOLD BEFORE SEPARATING

This set of NHL Action Stamps was distributed throughout North America in large grocery chains such as Loblaw's, IGA, A&P, and Acme. These small stickers (or stamps) do not mention the particular grocery store. A strip of seven player stamps was given out with a grocery purchase. The stamps measure approximately 1 5/8" by 2 1/8". These unnumbered stamps are ordered below by teams following the order presented in the album, Atlanta Flames (1-18), Boston Bruins (19-36), Buffalo Sabres (37-54), California Golden Seals (55-72), Chicago Blackhawks (73-90), Detroit Red Wings (91-108), Kansas City Scouts (109-126), Los Angeles Kings (127-144), Minnesota North Stars (145-162), Montreal Canadiens (163-180), New York Islanders (181-198), New York Rangers (199-216), Philadelphia Flyers (217-234), Pittsburgh Penguins (235-252), St. Louis Blues (253-270), Toronto Maple Leafs (271-288), Vancouver Canucks (289-306), and Washington Capitals (307-324). An album was available for this set which included 20 stamps in the back. Reportedly some of the stamps (29, 57, 94, and 164) were only available in the album. Intact strips would be valued at 50 percent more than the sum of the respective player prices listed below.

	NRMT	VG-E	GOOD
COMPLETE SET (324)...................	150.00	60.00	15.00
COMMON PLAYER (1-324)............	.40	.16	.04
☐ 1 Eric Vail.............................	.40	.16	.04
☐ 2 Jerry Byers.........................	.40	.16	.04
☐ 3 Rey Comeau.......................	.40	.16	.04
☐ 4 Curt Bennett.......................	.40	.16	.04
☐ 5 Bob Murray........................	.40	.16	.04
☐ 6 Don Bouchard	.60	.24	.06
☐ 7 Pat Quinn..........................	1.00	.40	.10
☐ 8 Larry Romanchych...............	.40	.16	.04
☐ 9 Randy Manery.....................	.40	.16	.04
☐ 10 Phil Myre..........................	.60	.24	.06
☐ 11 Buster Harvey....................	.40	.16	.04
☐ 12 Keith McCreary...................	.40	.16	.04
☐ 13 Jean Lemieux.....................	.40	.16	.04
☐ 14 Arnie Brown.......................	.40	.16	.04
☐ 15 Bob Leiter.........................	.40	.16	.04
☐ 16 Jacques Richard.................	.40	.16	.04
☐ 17 Noel Price.........................	.40	.16	.04
☐ 18 Tom Lysiak........................	.60	.24	.06
☐ 19 Bobby Orr.........................	15.00	6.00	1.50
☐ 20 Al Sims............................	.40	.16	.04
☐ 21 Don Marcotte.....................	.40	.16	.04
☐ 22 Terry O'Reilly.....................	.60	.24	.06
☐ 23 Carol Vadnais....................	.40	.16	.04
☐ 24 Gilles Gilbert.....................	.40	.16	.04
☐ 25 Bobby Schmautz.................	.60	.24	.06
☐ 26 Phil Esposito......................	4.00	1.60	.40
☐ 27 Walt McKechnie..................	.40	.16	.04
☐ 28 Ken Hodge.........................	.75	.30	.07
☐ 29 Dave Forbes......................	.40	.16	.04
☐ 30 Wayne Cashman..................	.60	.24	.06
☐ 31 Johnny Bucyk.....................	1.50	.60	.15
☐ 32 Ross Brooks.......................	.40	.16	.04
☐ 33 Dallas Smith.......................	.60	.24	.06
☐ 34 Darryl Edestrand.................	.40	.16	.04
☐ 35 Gregg Sheppard..................	.40	.16	.04
☐ 36 Andre Savard......................	.60	.24	.06
☐ 37 Jim Schoenfeld...................	.60	.24	.06
☐ 38 Brian Spencer.....................	.60	.24	.06
☐ 39 Rick Dudley........................	.60	.24	.06
☐ 40 Craig Ramsay.....................	.40	.16	.04
☐ 41 Gary Bromley......................	.40	.16	.04
☐ 42 Lee Fogolin........................	.40	.16	.04
☐ 43 Jerry Korab........................	.40	.16	.04
☐ 44 Larry Mickey.......................	.40	.16	.04
☐ 45 Roger Crozier......................	.60	.24	.06
☐ 46 Larry Carriere.....................	.40	.16	.04
☐ 47 Norm Gratton......................	.40	.16	.04
☐ 48 Jim Lorentz.........................	.40	.16	.04
☐ 49 Rene Robert.......................	.60	.24	.06
☐ 50 Gilbert Perreault..................	3.00	1.20	.30
(74/75 season on back)			
☐ 51 Mike Robitaille....................	.40	.16	.04
☐ 52 Don Luce...........................	.40	.16	.04
☐ 53 Richard Martin....................	.75	.30	.07
☐ 54 Gerry Meehan.....................	.60	.24	.06
☐ 55 Bruce Affleck......................	.40	.16	.04
☐ 56 Wayne King........................	.40	.16	.04
☐ 57 Joseph Johnston..................	.40	.16	.04
☐ 58 Ron Huston........................	.40	.16	.04
☐ 59 Dave Hrechkosy...................	.40	.16	.04
☐ 60 Stan Gilbertson...................	.40	.16	.04
☐ 61 Mike Christie.......................	.40	.16	.04
☐ 62 Larry Wright........................	.40	.16	.04
☐ 63 Stan Weir...........................	.40	.16	.04

☐	64	Larry Patey	.40	.16	.04	☐ 157	Claude Larose	.40	.16	.04
☐	65	Al MacAdam	.60	.24	.06	☐ 158	Ken Dryden	6.00	2.40	.60
☐	66	Ted McAneeley	.40	.16	.04	☐ 159	Pierre Bouchard	.40	.16	.04
☐	67	Jim Neilson	.40	.16	.04	☐ 160	Murray Wilson	.40	.16	.04
☐	68	Rick Hampton	.40	.16	.04	☐ 161	Jim Roberts	.60	.24	.06
☐	69	Len Frig	.40	.16	.04	☐ 162	Serge Savard	1.25	.50	.12
☐	70	Gilles Meloche	.60	.24	.06	☐ 163	Clark Gillies	.60	.24	.06
☐	71	Robert Stewart	.40	.16	.04	☐ 164	Garry Howatt	.40	.16	.04
☐	72	Craig Patrick	.60	.24	.06	☐ 165	Ernie Hicke	.40	.16	.04
☐	73	Dennis Hull	.75	.30	.07	☐ 166	Craig Cameron	.40	.16	.04
☐	74	Dale Tallon	.40	.16	.04	☐ 167	Ralph Stewart	.40	.16	.04
☐	75	Bill White	.60	.24	.06	☐ 168	Lorne Henning	.40	.16	.04
☐	76	Jim Pappin	.40	.16	.04	☐ 169	Glenn Resch	.75	.30	.07
☐	77	Cliff Koroll	.40	.16	.04	☐ 170	Bill MacMillan	.40	.16	.04
☐	78	Tony Esposito	4.00	1.60	.40	☐ 171	Doug Rombough	.40	.16	.04
☐	79	Doug Jarrett	.40	.16	.04	☐ 172	Jean Potvin	.60	.24	.06
☐	80	John Marks	.40	.16	.04	☐ 173	Gerry Hart	.40	.16	.04
☐	81	Stan Mikita	3.00	1.20	.30	☐ 174	Bert Marshall	.40	.16	.04
☐	82	Darcy Rota	.40	.16	.04	☐ 175	Billy Harris	.40	.16	.04
☐	83	J.P. Bordeleau	.40	.16	.04	☐ 176	Bob Nystrom	.60	.24	.06
☐	84	Ivan Boldirev	.40	.16	.04	☐ 177	Dave Lewis	.40	.16	.04
☐	85	Germaine Gagnon UER	.40	.16	.04	☐ 178	Billy Smith	2.00	.80	.20
☐	86	Dick Redmond	.40	.16	.04	☐ 179	Denis Potvin	2.00	.80	.20
☐	87	Pit Martin	.40	.16	.04	☐ 180	Ed Westfall	.60	.24	.06
☐	88	Keith Magnuson	.60	.24	.06	☐ 181	Jerry Butler	.40	.16	.04
☐	89	Phil Russell	.40	.16	.04	☐ 182	Bobby Rousseau	.60	.24	.06
☐	90	Chico Maki	.60	.24	.06	☐ 183	Ron Harris	.40	.16	.04
☐	91	Jean Hamel	.40	.16	.04	☐ 184	Bill Fairbairn	.40	.16	.04
☐	92	Nick Libett	.60	.24	.06	☐ 185	Derek Sanderson	1.50	.60	.15
☐	93	Hank Nowak	.40	.16	.04	☐ 186	Jean Ratelle	2.00	.80	.20
☐	94	Guy Charron	.40	.16	.04	☐ 187	Greg Polis	.40	.16	.04
☐	95	Bryan Watson	.40	.16	.04	☐ 188	Rod Gilbert	2.00	.80	.20
☐	96	Nelson Pyatt	.40	.16	.04	☐ 189	Ed Giacomin	2.00	.80	.20
☐	97	Billy Lochead	.40	.16	.04	☐ 190	Rod Seiling	.40	.16	.04
☐	98	Danny Grant	.60	.24	.06	☐ 191	Dale Rolfe	.40	.16	.04
☐	99	Bill Hogaboam	.40	.16	.04	☐ 192	Walt Tkaczuk	.60	.24	.06
☐	100	Jim Rutherford	.60	.24	.06	☐ 193	Pete Stemkowski	.60	.24	.06
☐	101	Doug Grant	.40	.16	.04	☐ 194	Gilles Villemure	.75	.30	.07
☐	102	Pierre Jarry	.40	.16	.04	☐ 195	Ted Irvine	.40	.16	.04
☐	103	Doug Roberts	.40	.16	.04	☐ 196	Brad Park	2.00	.80	.20
☐	104	Red Berenson	.60	.24	.06	☐ 197	Gilles Marotte	.60	.24	.06
☐	105	Marcel Dionne	3.00	1.20	.30	☐ 198	Steve Vickers	.40	.16	.04
☐	106	Mickey Redmond	.75	.30	.07	☐ 199	Ross Lonsberry	.40	.16	.04
☐	107	Jack Lynch	.40	.16	.04	☐ 200	Bob Kelly	.60	.24	.06
☐	108	Thommie Bergman	.40	.16	.04	☐ 201	Reggie Leach	.60	.24	.06
☐	109	Mike Corrigan	.40	.16	.04	☐ 202	Bernie Parent	2.00	.80	.20
☐	110	Frank St.Marseille	.40	.16	.04	☐ 203	Terry Crisp	.60	.24	.06
☐	111	Gene Carr	.40	.16	.04	☐ 204	Bill Clement	.75	.30	.07
☐	112	Neil Komadoski	.40	.16	.04	☐ 205	Bill Barber	1.50	.60	.15
☐	113	Gary Edwards	.60	.24	.06	☐ 206	Dave Schultz	.75	.30	.07
☐	114	Sheldon Kannegiesser	.40	.16	.04	☐ 207	Ed Van Impe	.40	.16	.04
☐	115	Bob Murdoch	.40	.16	.04	☐ 208	Jimmy Watson	.40	.16	.04
☐	116	Rogatien Vachon	2.00	.80	.20	☐ 209	Tom Bladon	.40	.16	.04
☐	117	Dave Hutchinson	.40	.16	.04	☐ 210	Rick MacLeish	1.00	.40	.10
☐	118	Tom Williams	.40	.16	.04	☐ 211	Andre Dupont	.60	.24	.06
☐	119	Butch Goring	.75	.30	.07	☐ 212	Orest Kindrachuk	.40	.16	.04
☐	120	Bob Berry	.60	.24	.06	☐ 213	Gary Dornhoefer	.60	.24	.06
☐	121	Dan Maloney	.60	.24	.06	☐ 214	Joe Watson	.40	.16	.04
☐	122	Mike Murphy	.40	.16	.04	☐ 215	Don Saleski	.40	.16	.04
☐	123	Juha Widing	.40	.16	.04	☐ 216	Bobby Clarke	3.00	1.20	.30
☐	124	Don Kozak	.40	.16	.04	☐ 217	Jean Pronovost	.60	.24	.06
☐	125	Bob Nevin	.40	.16	.04	☐ 218	Ab DeMarco	.40	.16	.04
☐	126	Terry Harper	.60	.24	.06	☐ 219	Wayne Bianchin	.40	.16	.04
☐	127	Bill Goldsworthy	.75	.30	.07	☐ 220	Dave Burrows	.40	.16	.04
☐	128	Dennis O'Brien	.40	.16	.04	☐ 221	Ron Lalonde	.40	.16	.04
☐	129	Dennis Hextall	.60	.24	.06	☐ 222	Syl Apps	.60	.24	.06
☐	130	Murray Oliver	.40	.16	.04	☐ 223	Bob Kelly	.40	.16	.04
☐	131	Lou Nanne	.60	.24	.06	☐ 224	Chuck Arnason	.40	.16	.04
☐	132	Fred Stanfield	.40	.16	.04	☐ 225	Steve Durbano	.40	.16	.04
☐	133	Jean-Paul Parise	.40	.16	.04	☐ 226	Ron Schock	.40	.16	.04
☐	134	Tom Reid	.40	.16	.04	☐ 227	Bob Paradise	.40	.16	.04
☐	135	Fred Barrett	.40	.16	.04	☐ 228	Ron Stackhouse	.40	.16	.04
☐	136	Gary Bergman	.40	.16	.04	☐ 229	Lowell MacDonald	.60	.24	.06
☐	137	Barry Gibbs	.40	.16	.04	☐ 230	Bob Johnson	1.00	.40	.10
☐	138	Cesare Maniago	.60	.24	.06	☐ 231	Rick Kehoe	.60	.24	.06
☐	139	Jude Drouin	.40	.16	.04	☐ 232	Nelson Debenedet	.40	.16	.04
☐	140	Blake Dunlop	.40	.16	.04	☐ 233	Vic Hadfield	.60	.24	.06
☐	141	Henry Boucha	.40	.16	.04	☐ 234	Denis Herron	.60	.24	.06
☐	142	Fern Rivard	.40	.16	.04	☐ 235	Phil Roberto	.40	.16	.04
☐	143	Chris Ahrens	.40	.16	.04	☐ 236	Floyd Thomson	.40	.16	.04
☐	144	Don Martineau	.40	.16	.04	☐ 237	Don Awrey	.40	.16	.04
☐	145	Jacques Lemaire	1.50	.60	.15	☐ 238	Rick Wilson	.40	.16	.04
☐	146	Peter Mahovlich	.75	.30	.07	☐ 239	John Davidson	.75	.30	.07
☐	147	Yvon Lambert	.40	.16	.04	☐ 240	Pierre Plante	.40	.16	.04
☐	148	Yvan Cournoyer	2.50	1.00	.25	☐ 241	Barclay Plager	.60	.24	.06
☐	149	Michel Larocque	.75	.30	.07	☐ 242	Larry Giroux	.40	.16	.04
☐	150	Guy Lapointe	1.50	.60	.15	☐ 243	Bob Gassoff	.60	.24	.06
☐	151	Steve Shutt	2.00	.80	.20	☐ 244	Dave Gardner	.40	.16	.04
☐	152	Guy Lafleur	6.00	2.40	.60	☐ 245	Brian Ogilvie	.40	.16	.04
☐	153	Larry Robinson	2.00	.80	.20	☐ 246	Ed Johnston	.75	.30	.07
☐	154	Jacques Laperriere	1.00	.40	.10	☐ 247	Bob Plager	.60	.24	.06
☐	155	Chuck Lefley	.40	.16	.04	☐ 248	Wayne Merrick	.40	.16	.04
☐	156	Henri Richard	2.00	.80	.20	☐ 249	Larry Sacharuk	.40	.16	.04

☐	250	Bill Collins	.40	.16	.04
☐	251	Garnet Bailey	.40	.16	.04
☐	252	Garry Unger	.75	.30	.07
☐	253	Gary Sabourin	.40	.16	.04
☐	254	Willie Brossart	.40	.16	.04
☐	255	Tim Ecclestone	.40	.16	.04
☐	256	Dave Keon	1.50	.60	.15
☐	257	Darryl Sittler	2.50	1.00	.25
☐	258	Inge Hammarstrom	.40	.16	.04
☐	259	Ian Turnbull	.40	.16	.04
☐	260	Jim McKenny	.40	.16	.04
☐	261	Norm Ullman	1.25	.50	.12
☐	262	Doug Favell	.60	.24	.06
☐	263	Bob Neely	.40	.16	.04
☐	264	Lanny McDonald	3.00	1.20	.30
☐	265	Dunc Wilson	.60	.24	.06
☐	266	Errol Thompson	.40	.16	.04
☐	267	Brian Glennie	.40	.16	.04
☐	268	Bill Flett	.40	.16	.04
☐	269	Borje Salming	1.50	.60	.15
☐	270	Ron Ellis	.60	.24	.06
☐	271	Dave Dunn	.40	.16	.04
☐	272	Chris Oddleifson	.40	.16	.04
☐	273	Barry Wilkins	.40	.16	.04
☐	274	Gary Smith	.60	.24	.06
☐	275	Dennis Ververgaert	.40	.16	.04
☐	276	Jocelyn Guevremont	.40	.16	.04
☐	277	Andre Boudrias	.40	.16	.04
☐	278	John Gould	.40	.16	.04
☐	279	Jim Wiley	.40	.16	.04
☐	280	Bob Dailey	.40	.16	.04
☐	281	Tracy Pratt	.40	.16	.04
☐	282	Ken Lockett	.40	.16	.04
☐	283	Paulin Bordeleau	.40	.16	.04
☐	284	Gerry O'Flaherty	.40	.16	.04
☐	285	Bryan McSheffrey	.40	.16	.04
☐	286	Gregg Boddy	.40	.16	.04
☐	287	Don Lever	.60	.24	.06
☐	288	Dennis Kearns	.40	.16	.04
☐	289	Robin Burns	.40	.16	.04
☐	290	Gary Coalter	.40	.16	.04
☐	291	John Wright	.40	.16	.04
☐	292	Peter McDuffe	.40	.16	.04
☐	293	Simon Nolet	.40	.16	.04
☐	294	Ted Snell	.40	.16	.04
☐	295	Gary Croteau	.40	.16	.04
☐	296	Lynn Powis	.40	.16	.04
☐	297	Dave Hudson	.40	.16	.04
☐	298	Richard Lemieux	.40	.16	.04
☐	299	Bryan Lefley	.40	.16	.04
☐	300	Doug Horbul	.40	.16	.04
☐	301	Brent Hughes	.40	.16	.04
☐	302	Ed Gilbert	.40	.16	.04
☐	303	Michel Plasse	.60	.24	.06
☐	304	Dennis Patterson	.40	.16	.04
☐	305	Randy Rota	.40	.16	.04
☐	306	Chris Evans	.40	.16	.04
☐	307	Bill Mikkelson	.40	.16	.04
☐	308	Ron Low	.60	.24	.06
☐	309	Doug Mohns	.60	.24	.06
☐	310	Joe Lundrigan	.40	.16	.04
☐	311	Steve Atkinson	.40	.16	.04
☐	312	Ron Anderson	.40	.16	.04
☐	313	Mike Marson	.40	.16	.04
☐	314	Lew Morrison	.40	.16	.04
☐	315	Jack Egers	.40	.16	.04
☐	316	Gordy Brooks	.40	.16	.04
☐	317	Pete Laframboise	.40	.16	.04
☐	318	Mike Bloom	.40	.16	.04
☐	319	Bob Collyard	.40	.16	.04
☐	320	Dave Kryskow	.40	.16	.04
☐	321	Greg Joly	.40	.16	.04
☐	322	Jim Hrycuik	.40	.16	.04
☐	323	Bob Gryp	.40	.16	.04
☐	324	Larry Fullan	.40	.16	.04
☐	xx	Album	20.00	8.00	2.00

1973-74 Nordiques Team Issue

This 21-card team issue set features the 1973-74 Quebec Nordiques of the World Hockey Association. The oversized cards measure approximately 3 1/2" by 5 1/2". The fronts feature glossy color posed action photos with white borders. The team and WHA logos are superimposed in the upper corners of the picture. A facsimile autograph is inscribed across the bottom of the picture. The backs are blank. The cards are unnumbered and checklisted below in alphabetical order.

		NRMT	VG-E	GOOD
COMPLETE SET (21)		25.00	10.00	2.50
COMMON PLAYER (1-21)		1.25	.50	.12

☐	1	Mike Archambault	1.25	.50	.12
☐	2	Serge Aubry	1.25	.50	.12
☐	3	Yves Bergeron	1.25	.50	.12
☐	4	Jacques Blain	1.25	.50	.12
☐	5	Richard Brodeur	2.50	1.00	.25
☐	6	Alain Caron	1.25	.50	.12
☐	7	Ken Desjardine	1.25	.50	.12
☐	8	Maurice Filion	1.25	.50	.12
☐	9	Andre Gaudette	1.25	.50	.12
☐	10	Jean-Guy Gendron	1.25	.50	.12
☐	11	Rejean Giroux	1.25	.50	.12
☐	12	Frank Golembrosky	1.25	.50	.12
☐	13	Bob Guindon	1.25	.50	.12
☐	14	Pierre Guite	1.25	.50	.12
☐	15	Frank Lacombe	1.25	.50	.12
☐	16	Paul Larose	1.25	.50	.12
☐	17	Michel Parizeau	1.25	.50	.12
☐	18	Jean Payette	1.25	.50	.12
☐	19	Michel Rouleau	1.25	.50	.12
☐	20	Pierre Roy	1.25	.50	.12
☐	21	J.C. Tremblay	2.50	1.00	.25

1983-84 Nordiques Postcards

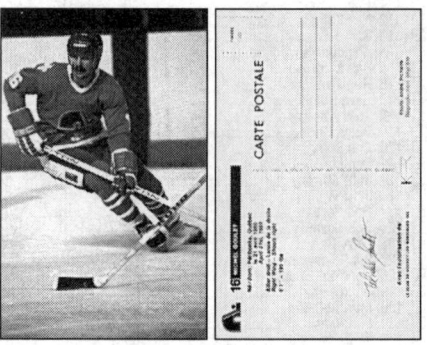

This 24-card set measures approximately 3 1/2" by 5 1/2" and features members of the 1983-84 Quebec Nordiques. This set features borderless full-color action shots on the front. The back is in postcard format with a brief identification of the player written in blue ink. This unnumbered set has been checklisted in alphabetical order.

		MINT	EXC	G-VG
COMPLETE SET (24)		15.00	6.00	1.50
COMMON PLAYER (1-24)		.50	.20	.05

☐	1	Pierre Aubry	.50	.20	.05
☐	2	Michel Bergeron CO	.75	.30	.07
☐	3	Dan Bouchard	.75	.30	.07
☐	4	Real Cloutier	.75	.30	.07
☐	5	Alain Cote	.50	.20	.05
☐	6	Andre Dupont	.50	.20	.05
☐	7	John Garrett	.75	.30	.07
☐	8	Michel Goulet	2.50	1.00	.25
☐	9	Jean Hamel	.50	.20	.05

☐	10	Dale Hunter	1.25	.50	.12
☐	11	Rick Lapointe	.50	.20	.05
☐	12	Clint Malarchuk	1.00	.40	.10
☐	13	Mario Marois	.75	.30	.07
☐	14	Randy Moller	.50	.20	.05
☐	15	Wilf Paiement	.75	.30	.07
☐	16	Dave Pichette	.50	.20	.05
☐	17	Jacques Richard	.50	.20	.05
☐	18	Normand Rochefort	.75	.30	.07
☐	19	Louis Sleigher	.50	.20	.05
☐	20	Anton Stastny	.75	.30	.07
☐	21	Marian Stastny	.75	.30	.07
☐	22	Peter Stastny	3.00	1.20	.30
☐	23	Marc Tardif	.75	.30	.07
☐	24	Wally Weir	.50	.20	.05

1985-86 Nordiques Provigo

This 25-sticker set of Quebec Nordiques was released through Provigo. The puffy (styrofoam) stickers measure approximately 1 1/8" by 2 1/4" and feature a color head and shoulders photo of the player, with the player's number and name bordered by star-studded banners across the bottom of the picture. The player's signature is inscribed just above the banner. The Nordiques' logo is superimposed over the banner at its right end. The backs are blank. The 25 styrofoam stickers were to be attached to a cardboard poster. The poster measures approximately 20" by 11" and has 25 white spaces (designated for the stickers) on blue background. At the center is a picture of a goalie mask, with the Nordiques' logo above and slightly to the right. The back of the poster has a checklist, stripes in the team's colors, and two team logos. We have checklisted them below in alphabetical order, with the uniform number to the right of the player's name.

		MINT	EXC	G-VG
COMPLETE SET (25)		15.00	6.00	1.50
COMMON PLAYER (1-25)		.60	.24	.06
☐	1 John Anderson 14	.75	.30	.07
☐	2 Brent Ashton 9	.60	.24	.06
☐	3 Wayne Babych 18	.75	.30	.07
☐	4 Michel Bergeron CO	1.00	.40	.10
☐	5 Alain Cote 19	.60	.24	.06
☐	6 Gilbert Delorme 6	.60	.24	.06
☐	7 Mike Eagles 11	.60	.24	.06
☐	8 Steven Finn 25	.60	.24	.06
☐	9 Paul Gillis 23	.60	.24	.06
☐	10 Mario Gosselin 33	1.00	.40	.10
☐	11 Michel Goulet 16	2.00	.80	.20
☐	12 Dale Hunter 32	1.25	.50	.12
☐	13 Mark Kumpel 17	.60	.24	.06
☐	14 Clint Malarchuck 30	1.00	.40	.10
☐	15 Jimmy Mann 10	.60	.24	.06
☐	16 Mario Marois 22	.75	.30	.07
☐	17 Randy Moller 21	.60	.24	.06
☐	18 Wilf Paiement 27	.75	.30	.07
☐	19 Pat Price 7	.60	.24	.06
☐	20 Normand Rochefort 5	.75	.30	.07
☐	21 J.F. Sauve 15	.60	.24	.06
☐	22 Richard Sevigny 1	.75	.30	.07
☐	23 David Shaw 4	.75	.30	.07
☐	24 Anton Stastny 20	.75	.30	.07
☐	25 Peter Stastny 26	2.50	1.00	.25

1986-87 Nordiques Yum-Yum

Each card in this ten-card set measures approximately 2" by 2 1/2". The fronts feature color action player photos with blue, white, and red borders. The player's name and number, along with sponsor and team logos, appear on the front. The backs carry a team checklist. The cards are unnumbered and checklisted below in alphabetical order.

		MINT	EXC	G-VG
COMPLETE SET (10)		20.00	8.00	2.00
COMMON PLAYER (1-10)		2.00	.80	.20
☐	1 Alain Cote	2.00	.80	.20
☐	2 Gilbert Delorme	2.00	.80	.20
☐	3 Paul Gillis	2.00	.80	.20
☐	4 Michel Goulet	5.00	2.00	.50
☐	5 Dale Hunter	4.00	1.60	.40
☐	6 Clint Malarchuk	3.00	1.20	.30
☐	7 Robert Picard	2.00	.80	.20
☐	8 Normand Rochefort	2.00	.80	.20
☐	9 Anton Stastny	2.00	.80	.20
☐	10 Peter Stastny	5.00	2.00	.50

1987-88 Nordiques

Each card in this 32-card set measures approximately 3 3/4" by 5 5/8". The fronts feature a full color action photo of the player, with the Quebec Nordiques' logo superimposed at the upper left-hand corner of the picture. At the bottom the player's number and name are given in the white triangle. The backs are blank.

		MINT	EXC	G-VG
COMPLETE SET (32)		15.00	6.00	1.50
COMMON PLAYER (1-32)		.50	.20	.05
☐	1 Tommy Albelin 28	.50	.20	.05
☐	2 Jeff Brown 22	2.00	.80	.20
☐	3 Mario Brunetta 30	.50	.20	.05
☐	4 Terry Carkner 4	.75	.30	.07
☐	5 Alain Cote 19	.50	.20	.05

		MINT	EXC	G-VG
☐ 6	Gord Donnelly 34	.75	.30	.07
☐ 7	Gaetan Duchesne 14	.75	.30	.07
☐ 8	Mike Eagles 11	.50	.20	.05
☐ 9	Steven Finn 29	.50	.20	.05
☐ 10	Paul Gillis 23	.75	.30	.07
☐ 11	Mario Gosselin 33	1.00	.40	.10
☐ 12	Michel Goulet 16	2.00	.80	.20
☐ 13	Stephane Guerard 46	.50	.20	.05
☐ 14	Alan Haworth 15	.50	.20	.05
☐ 15	Mike Hough 18	.50	.20	.05
☐ 16	Jeff Jackson 25	.50	.20	.05
☐ 17	Stu Kulak 17	.50	.20	.05
☐ 18	Jason Lafreniere 10	.75	.30	.07
☐ 19	Lane Lambert 7	.50	.20	.05
☐ 20	David Latta 27	.50	.20	.05
☐ 21	Max Middendorf 12	.50	.20	.05
☐ 22	Randy Moller 21	.50	.20	.05
☐ 23	Robert Picard 24	.50	.20	.05
☐ 24	Daniel Poudrier 2	.50	.20	.05
☐ 25	Ken Quinney 54	.50	.20	.05
☐ 26	Normand Rochefort 5	.50	.20	.05
☐ 27	Richard Sevigny 1	.75	.30	.07
☐ 28	Anton Stastny 20	.75	.30	.07
☐ 29	Peter Stastny 26	2.00	.80	.20
☐ 30	Ron Tugnutt 50	1.50	.60	.15
☐ 31	Alain Chainey, Andre Savard, Guy Lapointe	.75	.30	.07
☐ 32	Badaboum (Mascot)	.50	.20	.05

1987-88 Nordiques Yum-Yum

Each card in this ten-card set measures approximately 2" by 2 1/2". The front has a color action photo of the player, enframed by red, white, and blue borders. At the bottom the player's number and name are sandwiched between the Nordiques' logo and the Yum-Yum potato chips logo. The back is printed in red, white, and blue, and presents in two columns a checklist of the ten players. We have checklisted the cards below in alphabetical order, with the uniform number to the right of the player's name.

	MINT	EXC	G-VG
COMPLETE SET (10)	18.00	7.25	1.80
COMMON PLAYER (1-10)	1.50	.60	.15
☐ 1 Alain Cote 19	1.50	.60	.15
☐ 2 Paul Gillis 23	1.50	.60	.15
☐ 3A Mario Gosselin 33 ERR	3.00	1.20	.30
(Reverse has 83 for sweater number; three numbers messed up)			
☐ 3B Mario Gosselin 33 COR	3.00	1.20	.30
☐ 4 Michel Goulet 16	4.00	1.60	.40
☐ 5 Alan Haworth 15 UER	1.50	.60	.15
(Reverse has 35 for sweater number)			
☐ 6 Jason Lefreniere 10 UER	2.00	.80	.20
(Reverse has 30 for sweater number)			
☐ 7 Robert Picard 24	1.50	.60	.15
☐ 8 Normand Rochefort 5	1.50	.60	.15
☐ 9 Anton Stastny 20	2.00	.80	.20
☐ 10 Peter Stastny 26	4.00	1.60	.40

1988-89 Nordiques General Foods

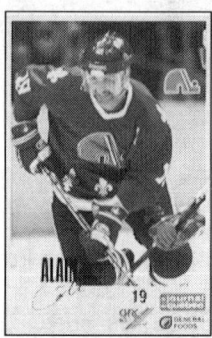

The 31 blank-backed cards comprising this set measure approximately 3 3/4" by 5 5/8" and feature white-bordered color action shots. The Nordiques logo is displayed at the upper right. The player's first name appears at the lower left of the photo. His last name appears in cursive lettering in the wide white margin below. The player's uniform number and the logos for General Foods, Le Journal de Quebec, and CHRC Sport Radio appear at the bottom right. The cards are unnumbered and checklisted below in alphabetical order. Joe Sakic's card predates his Rookie Card.

	MINT	EXC	G-VG
COMPLETE SET (31)	20.00	8.00	2.00
COMMON PLAYER (1-31)	.50	.20	.05
☐ 1 Tommy Albelin	.50	.20	.05
☐ 2 Joel Baillargeon	.50	.20	.05
☐ 3 Jeff Brown	1.25	.50	.12
☐ 4 Mario Brunetta	.50	.20	.05
☐ 5 Coaches	.50	.20	.05
Serge Aubry			
Ron Lapointe			
Guy Lapointe			
Alain Chainey			
☐ 6 Alain Cote	.50	.20	.05
☐ 7 Gord Donnelly	.75	.30	.07
☐ 8 Daniel Dore	.50	.20	.05
☐ 9 Gaetan Duchesne	.75	.30	.07
☐ 10 Steven Finn	.50	.20	.05
☐ 11 Marc Fortier	.50	.20	.05
☐ 12 Paul Gillis	.50	.20	.05
☐ 13 Mario Gosselin	.75	.30	.07
☐ 14 Michel Goulet	2.00	.80	.20
☐ 15 Jari Gronstrand	.50	.20	.05
☐ 16 Stephane Guerard	.50	.20	.05
☐ 17 Jeff Jackson	.50	.20	.05
☐ 18 Iiro Jarvi	.50	.20	.05
☐ 19 Lane Lambert	.50	.20	.05
☐ 20 David Latta	.50	.20	.05
☐ 21 Curtis Leschyshyn	.75	.30	.07
☐ 22 Bob Mason	.50	.20	.05
☐ 23 Randy Moller	.50	.20	.05
☐ 24 Robert Picard	.50	.20	.05
☐ 25 Walt Puddubny	.75	.30	.07
☐ 26 Joe Sakic	7.50	3.00	.75
☐ 27 Greg Smyth	.50	.20	.05
☐ 28 Anton Stastny	.75	.30	.07
☐ 29 Peter Stastny	2.50	1.00	.25
☐ 30 Trevor Stienberg	.50	.20	.05
☐ 31 Mark Vermette	.50	.20	.05

1989-90 Nordiques General Foods

This 30-card set of Quebec Nordiques printed on white card stock measures approximately 5 5/8" by 3 3/4" and features a borderless posed head shot of the player against a blue background. The team logo appears to the left of each picture while the General Foods logo appears in a reverse-

19. Joe SAKIC

GENERAL FOODS

out design in the lower left corner. Card backs are blank and unnumbered; thus the cards are listed below aphabetically. Joe Sakic's card appears during his Rookie Card year.

	MINT	EXC	G-VG
COMPLETE SET (30)	15.00	6.00	1.50
COMMON PLAYER (1-30)	.40	.16	.04
☐ 1 Michel Bergeron CO	.60	.24	.06
☐ 2 Jeff Brown	1.00	.40	.10
☐ 3 Joe Cirella	.60	.24	.06
☐ 4 Lucien DeBlois	.40	.16	.04
☐ 5 Daniel Dore	.40	.16	.04
☐ 6 Marc Fortier	.40	.16	.04
☐ 7 Steven Finn	.40	.16	.04
☐ 8 Stephane Fiset	1.25	.50	.12
☐ 9 Paul Gillis	.40	.16	.04
☐ 10 Michel Goulet	1.25	.50	.12
☐ 11 Jari Gronstrand	.40	.16	.04
☐ 12 Stephane Guerard	.40	.16	.04
☐ 13 Mike Hough	.40	.16	.04
☐ 14 Jeff Jackson	.40	.16	.04
☐ 15 Iiro Jarvi	.40	.16	.04
☐ 16 Kevin Kaminski	.40	.16	.04
☐ 17 Darin Kimble	.60	.24	.06
☐ 18 Guy Lafleur	2.00	.80	.20
☐ 19 David Latta	.40	.16	.04
☐ 20 Curtis Leschyshyn	.75	.30	.07
☐ 21 Claude Loiselle	.40	.16	.04
☐ 22 Mario Marois	.40	.16	.04
☐ 23 Ken McRae	.40	.16	.04
☐ 24 Sergei Mylnikov	.40	.16	.04
☐ 25 Michel Petit	.60	.24	.06
☐ 26 Robert Picard	.40	.16	.04
☐ 27 Joe Sakic	5.00	2.00	.50
☐ 28 Peter Stastny	1.50	.60	.15
☐ 29 Ron Tugnutt	1.00	.40	.10
☐ 30 Team Photo	1.25	.50	.12

1989-90 Nordiques Police

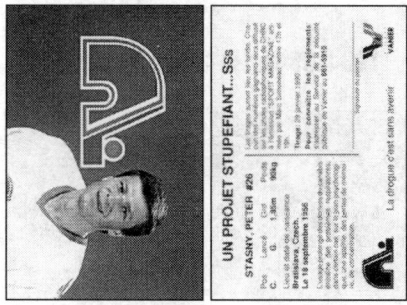

UN PROJET STUPEFIANT...Sss

STASNY, PETER #26

VANIER

La drogue c'est sains inverisf

This 27-card police set of Quebec Nordiques was sponsored by the city of Vanier. The cards measure approximately 4" by 2 3/4" and feature a borderless posed head and shoulders photo against a blue background. The team logo appears to the left of each player picture. The backs, which read "Un Project Stupefiant..Sss" across the top, are printed in French and present biography and an anti-drug or alcohol message on the left side. The right side has a local police number and

slot for a police officer's signature. The cards are unnumbered and checklisted below in alphabetical order. Joe Sakic's card appears during his Rookie Card year.

	MINT	EXC	G-VG
COMPLETE SET (27)	15.00	6.00	1.50
COMMON PLAYER (1-27)	.40	.16	.04
☐ 1 Jeff Brown	1.00	.40	.10
☐ 2 Joe Cirella	.60	.24	.06
☐ 3 Lucien DeBlois	.40	.16	.04
☐ 4 Daniel Dore	.40	.16	.04
☐ 5 Steven Finn	.40	.16	.04
☐ 6 Stephane Fiset	1.25	.50	.12
☐ 7 Marc Fortier	.40	.16	.04
☐ 8 Paul Gillis	.40	.16	.04
☐ 9 Michel Goulet	1.25	.50	.12
☐ 10 Stephane Guerard	.40	.16	.04
☐ 11 Mike Hough	.40	.16	.04
☐ 12 Jeff Jackson	.40	.16	.04
☐ 13 Iiro Jarvi	.40	.16	.04
☐ 14 Darin Kimble	.60	.24	.06
☐ 15 Guy Lafleur	2.00	.80	.20
☐ 16 David Latta	.40	.16	.04
☐ 17 Curtis Leschyshyn	.75	.30	.07
☐ 18 Claude Loiselle	.40	.16	.04
☐ 19 Mario Marois	.40	.16	.04
☐ 20 Ken McRae	.40	.16	.04
☐ 21 Sergei Mylnikov	.40	.16	.04
☐ 22 Michel Petit	.60	.24	.06
☐ 23 Robert Picard	.40	.16	.04
☐ 24 Jean-Marc Routhier	.40	.16	.04
☐ 25 Joe Sakic	5.00	2.00	.50
☐ 26 Peter Stastny	1.50	.60	.15
☐ 27 Ron Tugnutt	1.00	.40	.10

1990-91 Nordiques Team Issue

26. Peter STASTNY

The 25 blank-backed cards comprising this set measure approximately 5 5/8" by 3 3/4" and feature white-bordered posed color player head shots against blue backgrounds. The Quebec Nordiques logo is prominently displayed to the left of the player. The player's name and uniform number appear in white lettering below the logo. The cards are unnumbered and checklisted below in alphabetical order.

	MINT	EXC	G-VG
COMPLETE SET (25)	12.00	5.00	1.20
COMMON PLAYER (1-25)	.40	.16	.04
☐ 1 Joe Cirella	.60	.24	.06
☐ 2 Lucien DeBlois	.40	.16	.04
☐ 3 Daniel Dore	.40	.16	.04
☐ 4 Steven Finn	.40	.16	.04
☐ 5 Stephane Fiset	1.00	.40	.10
☐ 6 Bryan Fogarty	.60	.24	.06
☐ 7 Marc Fortier	.40	.16	.04
☐ 8 Paul Gillis	.40	.16	.04
☐ 9 Michel Goulet	1.25	.50	.12
☐ 10 Stephane Guerard	.40	.16	.04
☐ 11 Mike Hough	.40	.16	.04
☐ 12 Tony Hrkac	.60	.24	.06
☐ 13 Jeff Jackson	.40	.16	.04
☐ 14 Iiro Jarvi	.40	.16	.04

		NRMT	VG-E	GOOD
☐ 15	Kevin Kaminski	.40	.16	.04
☐ 16	Darin Kimble	.60	.24	.06
☐ 17	David Latta	.40	.16	.04
☐ 18	Curtis Leschyshyn	.60	.24	.06
☐ 19	Claude Loiselle	.40	.16	.04
☐ 20	Mario Marois	.40	.16	.04
☐ 21	Tony McKegney	.40	.16	.04
☐ 22	Ken McRae	.40	.16	.04
☐ 23	Michel Petit	.40	.16	.04
☐ 24	Peter Stastny	1.25	.50	.12
☐ 25	Ron Tugnutt	1.00	.40	.10

1972-73 North Stars Glossy Photos

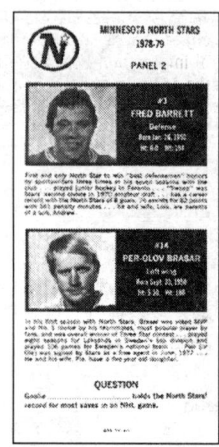

These 20 blank-backed approximately 8" by 10" glossy white-bordered black-and-white photo sheets feature a suited-up posed player photo on the right and, on the left, a posed player head shot. Below the head shot appears the player's name and the Minnesota North Stars name and logo. The photos are unnumbered and checklisted below in alphabetical order.

		NRMT	VG-E	GOOD
	COMPLETE SET (20)	20.00	8.00	2.00
	COMMON PLAYER (1-20)	1.00	.40	.10
☐ 1	Fred Barrett	1.00	.40	.10
☐ 2	Charlie Burns	1.00	.40	.10
☐ 3	Jude Drouin	1.00	.40	.10
☐ 4	Barry Gibbs	1.00	.40	.10
☐ 5	Bill Goldsworthy	2.50	1.00	.25
☐ 6	Danny Grant	1.50	.60	.15
☐ 7	Ted Harris	1.00	.40	.10
☐ 8	Fred(Buster) Harvey	1.00	.40	.10
☐ 9	Dennis Hextall	1.50	.60	.15
☐ 10	Cesare Maniago	2.00	.80	.20
☐ 11	Doug Mohns	1.50	.60	.15
☐ 12	Lou Nanne	1.50	.60	.15
☐ 13	Bob Nevin	1.00	.40	.10
☐ 14	Dennis O'Brien	1.00	.40	.10
☐ 15	Murray Oliver	1.00	.40	.10
☐ 16	J.P. Parise	1.00	.40	.10
☐ 17	Dean Prentice	1.50	.60	.15
☐ 18	Tom Reid	1.00	.40	.10
☐ 19	Gump Worsley	5.00	2.00	.50
☐ 20	Wren Blair GM	1.00	.40	.10
	Jack Gordon CO			

1978-79 North Stars Cloverleaf Dairy

This ten-panel set of Minnesota North Stars was issued on the side of half gallon milk cartons as part of a sweepstakes. The picture and text are printed in either red or purple. The panels measure approximately 3 3/4" by 7 5/8", with two players per panel. The North Stars' logo, the team name, year, and panel number appear at the top of each panel. Each panel features a "mug shot" and brief biographical information on two players. A North Stars question was included at the bottom of each panel. There were ten

questions in all: one per panel, and a tenth question on the final entry panel, which also included a list of all ten questions and gave complete entry information. The unnumbered panel describes the sweepstakes promotion and lists the prizes.

		NRMT	VG-E	GOOD
	COMPLETE SET (11)	125.00	50.00	12.50
	COMMON PLAYER (1-10)	12.00	5.00	1.20
☐ 1	Gilles Meloche and Gary Sargent	15.00	6.00	1.50
☐ 2	Fred Barrett and Per-Olov Brasar	12.00	5.00	1.20
☐ 3	Jean-Paul Parise and Greg Smith	12.00	5.00	1.20
☐ 4	Al MacAdam and Kent-Erik Andersson	12.00	5.00	1.20
☐ 5	Gary Edwards and Bobby Smith	25.00	10.00	2.50
☐ 6	Mike Polich and Brad Maxwell	12.00	5.00	1.20
☐ 7	Steve Payne and Glen Sharpley	12.00	5.00	1.20
☐ 8	Tim Young and Kris Manery	12.00	5.00	1.20
☐ 9	Ron Zanussi and Tom Younghans	12.00	5.00	1.20
☐ 10	Final Entry Panel	12.00	5.00	1.20
☐ NNO	Sweepstakes Promotion	12.00	5.00	1.20

1984-85 North Stars Postcards

This 25-card set measures approximately 3 1/2" by 5 1/2" and features full-bleed, posed, color player photos. The backs have a green postcard design. The North Stars' logo is printed in pale green on the left side. The player's name and biographical information appears in the upper left corner. The season and team name appear vertically in the middle, bisecting the cards. The cards are unnumbered and checklisted below in alphabetical order.

	MINT	EXC	G-VG
COMPLETE SET (25)	15.00	6.00	1.50
COMMON PLAYER (1-25)	.50	.20	.05
☐ 1 Keith Acton	.75	.30	.07
☐ 2 Don Beaupre	1.25	.50	.12
☐ 3 Brian Bellows	2.00	.80	.20
☐ 4 Scott Bjugstad	.50	.20	.05
☐ 5 Neal Broten	1.50	.60	.15
☐ 6 Dino Ciccarelli	2.00	.80	.20
☐ 7 Curt Giles	.50	.20	.05
☐ 8 Craig Hartsburg	.75	.30	.07
☐ 9 Tom Hirsch	.50	.20	.05
☐ 10 Paul Holmgren	1.00	.40	.10
☐ 11 Brian Lawton	.50	.20	.05
☐ 12 Dan Mandich	.50	.20	.05
☐ 13 Dennis Maruk	1.00	.40	.10
☐ 14 Brad Maxwell	.50	.20	.05
☐ 15 Tom McCarthy	.50	.20	.05
☐ 16 Roland Melanson	.75	.30	.07
☐ 17 Gilles Meloche	.75	.30	.07
☐ 18 Mark Napier	.75	.30	.07
☐ 19 Steve Payne	.75	.30	.07
☐ 20 Willi Plett	.75	.30	.07
☐ 21 Dave Richter	.50	.20	.05
☐ 22 Gordie Roberts	.50	.20	.05
☐ 23 Bob Rouse	.75	.30	.07
☐ 24 Harold Snepsts	1.00	.40	.10
☐ 25 Ken Solheim	.50	.20	.05

1984-85 North Stars 7-Eleven

 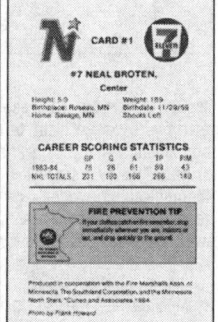

This 12-card safety set was sponsored by the Southland Corporation in cooperation with the Fire Marshalls Assn. of Minnesota and the Minnesota North Stars. The cards measure 2 5/8" by 4 1/8". The front has a color action photo enframed by a thin green border on white card stock. The green box below the picture gives the uniform number, player's name, position, the team name, and team logo. The card number on the back is sandwiched between the North Stars' and 7-Eleven logos. The back also has basic biographical information, career scoring statistics, and a fire prevention tip in a yellow box on the lower portion of the card back.

	MINT	EXC	G-VG
COMPLETE SET (12)	7.00	2.80	.70
COMMON PLAYER (1-12)	.50	.20	.05
☐ 1 Neal Broten	1.00	.40	.10
☐ 2 Willi Plett	.75	.30	.07
☐ 3 Craig Hartsburg	.75	.30	.07

	MINT	EXC	G-VG
☐ 4 Brian Bellows	2.00	.80	.20
☐ 5 Gordie Roberts	.50	.20	.05
☐ 6 Keith Acton	.75	.30	.07
☐ 7 Paul Holmgren	.75	.30	.07
☐ 8 Gilles Meloche	.75	.30	.07
☐ 9 Dennis Maruk	1.00	.40	.10
☐ 10 Tom McCarthy	.50	.20	.05
☐ 11 Steve Payne	.75	.30	.07
☐ 12 Dino Ciccarelli	2.00	.80	.20

1985-86 North Stars Postcards

This 27-card set measures 3 1/2" by 5 1/2" and features full-bleed, posed, color player photos on thin card stock. The backs have a green postcard design. The North Stars' logo is printed in pale green outline lettering on the left side. The player's name and biographical information appears in the upper left corner. The cards are unnumbered and checklisted below in alphabetical order. The year of the set is established by the Dave Langevin card; he played with the North Stars only during the 1985-86 season.

	MINT	EXC	G-VG
COMPLETE SET (27)	15.00	6.00	1.50
COMMON PLAYER (1-27)	.50	.20	.05
☐ 1 Keith Acton	.75	.30	.07
☐ 2 Don Beaupre	1.25	.50	.12
☐ 3 Brian Bellows	1.50	.60	.15
☐ 4 Bo Bergland	.50	.20	.05
☐ 5 Scott Bjugstad	.50	.20	.05
☐ 6 Neal Broten	1.25	.50	.12
☐ 7 Jon Casey	3.00	1.20	.30
☐ 8 Dino Ciccarelli	1.50	.60	.15
☐ 9 Tim Coulis	.50	.20	.05
☐ 10 Curt Giles	.50	.20	.05
☐ 11 Dirk Graham	1.00	.40	.10
☐ 12 Mats Hallin	.50	.20	.05
☐ 13 Craig Hartsburg	.75	.30	.07
☐ 14 Tom Hirsch	.50	.20	.05
☐ 15 Dave Langevin	.50	.20	.05
☐ 16 Brian Lawton	.50	.20	.05
☐ 17 Craig Levie	.50	.20	.05
☐ 18 Dan Mandich	.50	.20	.05
☐ 19 Dennis Maruk	1.00	.40	.10
☐ 20 Tom McCarthy	.50	.20	.05
☐ 21 Tony McKegney	.75	.30	.07
☐ 22 Roland Melanson	.75	.30	.07
☐ 23 Steve Payne	.70	.28	.07
☐ 24 Willi Plett	.75	.30	.07
☐ 25 Gordie Roberts	.50	.20	.05
☐ 26 Bob Rouse	.75	.30	.07
☐ 27 Gord Sherven	.50	.20	.05

1985-86 North Stars 7-Eleven

This 12-card safety set was sponsored by the Southland Corporation in cooperation with the Fire Marshalls Assn. of

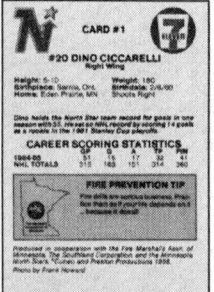

Minnesota and the Minnesota North Stars. The cards measure the standard size, 2 1/2" by 3 1/2". The front has a color action photo enframed by a thin green border on white card stock. The green box below the picture gives the uniform number, player's name, position, the team name, and team logo. The card number on the back is sandwiched between the North Stars' and 7-Eleven logos. The back also has basic biographical information, career scoring statistics, and a fire prevention tip in a yellow box on the lower portion of the card back.

	MINT	EXC	G-VG
COMPLETE SET (12)	7.00	2.80	.70
COMMON PLAYER (1-12)	.50	.20	.05
☐ 1 Dino Ciccarelli	1.50	.60	.15
☐ 2 Scott Bjugstad	.50	.20	.05
☐ 3 Curt Giles	.50	.20	.05
☐ 4 Don Beaupre	1.00	.40	.10
☐ 5 Tony McKegney	.75	.30	.07
☐ 6 Neal Broten	1.00	.40	.10
☐ 7 Willi Plett	.75	.30	.07
☐ 8 Craig Hartsburg	.75	.30	.07
☐ 9 Brian Bellows	1.50	.60	.15
☐ 10 Keith Acton	.75	.30	.07
☐ 11 Dave Langevin	.50	.20	.05
☐ 12 Dirk Graham	1.00	.40	.10

1986-87 North Stars 7-Eleven

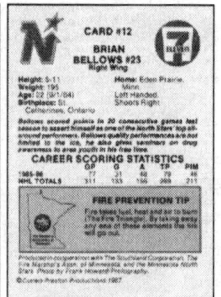

This 12-card safety set was sponsored by the Southland Corporation in cooperation with the Fire Marshalls Assn. of Minnesota and the Minnesota North Stars. The cards measure the standard size, 2 1/2" by 3 1/2". The front has a color action photo enframed by a thin green border on white card stock. The green box below the picture gives the uniform number, player's name, position, the team name, and team logo. The card number on the back is sandwiched between the North Stars' and 7-Eleven logos. The back also has basic biographical information, career scoring statistics,

and a fire prevention tip in a yellow box on the lower portion of the card back. The copyright notice on the back says 1987.

	MINT	EXC	G-VG
COMPLETE SET (12)	7.00	2.80	.70
COMMON PLAYER (1-12)	.50	.20	.05
☐ 1 Neal Broten	1.00	.40	.10
☐ 2 Brian MacLellan	.50	.20	.05
☐ 3 Willi Plett	.75	.30	.07
☐ 4 Scott Bjugstad	.50	.20	.05
☐ 5 Don Beaupre	1.00	.40	.10
☐ 6 Dino Ciccarelli	1.50	.60	.15
☐ 7 Craig Hartsburg	.75	.30	.07
☐ 8 Dennis Maruk	1.00	.40	.10
☐ 9 Bob Rouse	.75	.30	.07
☐ 10 Gordie Roberts	.50	.20	.05
☐ 11 Bob Brooke	.50	.20	.05
☐ 12 Brian Bellows	1.50	.60	.15

1987-88 North Stars Postcards

This 31-card set of Minnesota North Stars features color action photos without borders. The cards measure approximately 3 1/2" by 5 3/8" and are of the postcard type format. The backs are printed in green, provide brief biographical information, and have the North Stars' logo on the left-hand portion. These cards are unnumbered and we have checklisted them below in alphabetical order.

	MINT	EXC	G-VG
COMPLETE SET (31)	12.00	5.00	1.20
COMMON PLAYER (1-31)	.40	.16	.04
☐ 1 Keith Acton	.60	.24	.06
☐ 2 Dave Archibald	.40	.16	.04
☐ 3 Warren Babe	.40	.16	.04
☐ 4 Don Beaupre	1.00	.40	.10
☐ 5 Brian Bellows	1.50	.60	.15
☐ 6 Mike Berger	.40	.16	.04
☐ 7 Scott Bjugstad	.40	.16	.04
☐ 8 Bob Brooke	.40	.16	.04
☐ 9 Herb Brooks CO	.75	.30	.07
☐ 10 Neal Broten	1.00	.40	.10
☐ 11 Dino Ciccarelli	1.50	.60	.15
☐ 12 Larry DePalma	.40	.16	.04
☐ 13 Dave Gagner	2.50	1.00	.25
☐ 14 Curt Giles	.40	.16	.04
☐ 15 Dirk Graham	.75	.30	.07
☐ 16 Craig Hartsburg	.60	.24	.06
☐ 17 Tom Hirsch	.40	.16	.04
☐ 18 Brian Lawton	.40	.16	.04
☐ 19 Brian MacLellan	.40	.16	.04
☐ 20 Dennis Maruk	.75	.30	.07
☐ 21 Basil McRae	.60	.24	.06
☐ 22 Frantisek Musil	.75	.30	.07
☐ 23 Steve Payne	.60	.24	.06
☐ 24 Pat Price	.40	.16	.04
☐ 25 Chris Pryor	.40	.16	.04
☐ 26 Gordie Roberts	.40	.16	.04
☐ 27 Bob Rouse	.60	.24	.06
☐ 28 Terry Ruskowski	.60	.24	.06

			NRMT	VG-E	GOOD
☐	29	Kari Takko	.60	.24	.06
☐	30	Ron Wilson	.40	.16	.04
☐	31	Richard Zemlak	.40	.16	.04

1979-80 Oilers Postcards

Measuring approximately 3 1/2" by 5 1/4", this 24-card set features borderless posed-on-ice photos of the Edmonton Oilers on the fronts. The postcard format has each of the horizontal backs bisected by a vertical line, with the player's name, position, and biography on the left side, and the team logo on the right. The cards are unnumbered and checklisted below in alphabetical order. Early cards of Wayne Gretzky, Kevin Lowe, and Mark Messier are featured in this set. Set price includes both Mio variations.

		NRMT	VG-E	GOOD
COMPLETE SET (24)		50.00	20.00	5.00
COMMON PLAYER (1-23)		.75	.30	.07
☐ 1	Brett Callighen	.75	.30	.07
☐ 2	Colin Campbell	1.25	.50	.12
☐ 3	Ron Chipperfield	.75	.30	.07
☐ 4	Cam Connor	.75	.30	.07
☐ 5	Peter Driscoll	.75	.30	.07
☐ 6	Dave Dryden	.75	.30	.07
☐ 7	Bill Flett	.75	.30	.07
☐ 8	Lee Fogolin	.75	.30	.07
☐ 9	Wayne Gretzky	35.00	14.00	3.50
☐ 10	Al Hamilton	.75	.30	.07
☐ 11	Doug Hicks	.75	.30	.07
☐ 12	Dave Hunter	.75	.30	.07
☐ 13	Kevin Lowe	2.50	1.00	.25
☐ 14	Dave Lumley	.75	.30	.07
☐ 15	Blair MacDonald	.75	.30	.07
☐ 16	Kari Makkonen	.75	.30	.07
☐ 17	Mark Messier	12.50	5.00	1.25
☐ 18A	Ed Mio ERR	1.00	.40	.10
	(Back says DOB Jan. 31, 1979)			
☐ 18B	Ed Mio COR	1.00	.40	.10
	(Back says DOB Jan. 31, 1954)			
☐ 19	Pat Price	.75	.30	.07
☐ 20	Dave Semenko	.75	.30	.07
☐ 21	Bobby Schmautz	.75	.30	.07
☐ 22	Risto Siltanen	.75	.30	.07
☐ 23	Stan Weir	.75	.30	.07

1981-82 Oilers Red Rooster

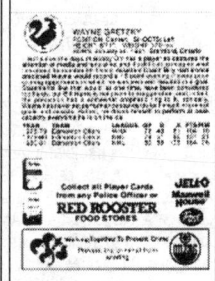

This 30-card set of Edmonton Oilers was sponsored by Red Rooster Food Stores in conjunction with Sun-Rype, Jello, Maxwell House, and Post. The player cards could be collected from any police officer or Red Rooster store. The cards measure approximately 2 3/4" by 3 9/16". The front has a color photo (with rounded corners) of the player, with the Oilers'logo and player's signature across the bottom of

the picture. The player's name, uniform number, and a hockey tip are given below the photo. The back has the Red Rooster logo at the upper left-hand corner as well as biographical and statistical information on the player. The bottom includes logos of the sponsors and an anti-crime message. The original printing included four "long-hair" Gretzky cards as well as coaches' cards of Billy Harris and Ted Green. Reportedly those involved didn't approve of the photos and thus most of the offending pictures were destroyed. Consequently, the new poses are much more common and the old ones more scarce. The mass-produced second printing produced six variations so that the total possible cards is 36. These (original) other six cards are very hard to find as they were apparently not released to the general collecting public. The set is checklisted below using sweater numbers for reference.

		MINT	EXC	G-VG
COMPLETE SET (30)		50.00	20.00	5.00
COMMON PLAYER		.50	.20	.05
☐ 1	Grant Fuhr	4.00	1.60	.40
☐ 2	Lee Fogolin	.50	.20	.05
☐ 4	Kevin Lowe	2.00	.80	.20
☐ 5	Doug Hicks	.50	.20	.05
☐ 6	Garry Lariviere	.50	.20	.05
☐ 7	Paul Coffey	5.00	2.00	.50
☐ 8	Risto Siltanen	.50	.20	.05
☐ 9	Glenn Anderson	3.00	1.20	.30
☐ 10	Matti Hagman	.50	.20	.05
☐ 11	Mark Messier	6.00	2.40	.60
☐ 12	Dave Hunter	.50	.20	.05
☐ 15	Curt Brackenbury	.50	.20	.05
☐ 16	Pat Hughes	.50	.20	.05
☐ 17	Jari Kurri	4.00	1.60	.40
☐ 18	Brett Callighen	.50	.20	.05
☐ 20	Dave Lumley	.50	.20	.05
☐ 21	Stan Weir	.50	.20	.05
☐ 26	Mike Forbes	.50	.20	.05
☐ 27	Dave Semenko	.60	.24	.06
☐ 30	Ron Low	.60	.24	.06
☐ 35	Andy Moog	4.00	1.60	.40
☐ 77	Garry Unger	.75	.30	.07
☐ 99	Wayne Gretzky	10.00	4.00	1.00
☐ 99	Wayne Gretzky	10.00	4.00	1.00
☐ 99	Wayne Gretzky	10.00	4.00	1.00
☐ 99	Wayne Gretzky	10.00	4.00	1.00
☐ xx	Team Autographs	1.00	.40	.10
☐ xx	Glen Sather CO	.75	.30	.07
☐ xx	Billy Harris CO	.50	.20	.05
☐ xx	Ted Green CO	.60	.24	.06

1981-82 Oilers West Edmonton Mall

These nine blank-backed photos measure approximately 5" by 7" and feature white-bordered black-and-white player head shots. The player's name and uniform number, along with the name and logo of the West Edmonton Mall, appear in the wide bottom white margin. The photos are unnumbered and checklisted below in alphabetical order.

	MINT	EXC	G-VG
COMPLETE SET (9).........................	60.00	24.00	6.00
COMMON PLAYER (1-9).................	3.00	1.20	.30
☐ 1 Lee Fogolin	3.00	1.20	.30
☐ 2 Grant Fuhr	7.50	3.00	.75
☐ 3 Wayne Gretzky	50.00	20.00	5.00
☐ 4 Billy Harris ACO	3.00	1.20	.30
☐ 5 Charlie Huddy	4.00	1.60	.40
☐ 6 Gary Lariviere.........................	3.00	1.20	.30
☐ 7 Dave Lumley	3.00	1.20	.30
☐ 8 Risto Siltanen..........................	3.00	1.20	.30
☐ 9 Stan Weir	3.00	1.20	.30

1982-83 Oilers Red Rooster

 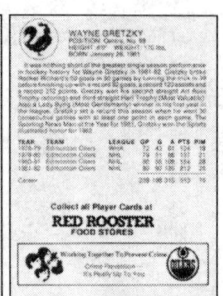

This 30-card set of Edmonton Oilers was sponsored by Red Rooster Food Stores, and the player cards could be collected at any of these stores. The cards measure approximately 2 3/4" by 3 9/16" and the set includes four different cards of Wayne Gretzky. The front has a color photo (with rounded corners) of the player, with the Oilers' logo and player's signature across the bottom of the picture. The player's name, uniform number, and a hockey tip are given below the photo. The back has the Red Rooster logo at the upper left-hand corner as well as biographical and statistical information on the player. The bottom has an anti-crime message. The set is checklisted below using sweater numbers for reference.

	MINT	EXC	G-VG
COMPLETE SET (30)........................	30.00	12.00	3.00
COMMON PLAYER..........................	.50	.20	.05
☐ 2 Lee Fogolin	.50	.20	.05
☐ 4 Kevin Lowe	1.00	.40	.10
☐ 6 Gary Lariviere	.50	.20	.05
☐ 7 Paul Coffey.............................	3.00	1.20	.30
☐ 9 Glenn Anderson	1.00	.40	.10
☐ 10 Jaroslav Pouzar......................	.50	.20	.05
☐ 11 Mark Messier	4.00	1.60	.40
☐ 12 Dave Hunter	.50	.20	.05
☐ 13 Ken Linseman	.60	.24	.06
☐ 14 Laurie Boschman	.60	.24	.06
☐ 16 Pat Hughes	.50	.20	.05
☐ 17 Jari Kurri	2.00	.80	.20
☐ 20 Dave Lumley	.50	.20	.05
☐ 21 Randy Gregg..........................	.60	.24	.06
☐ 22 Charlie Huddy	.75	.30	.07
☐ 23 Marc Habscheid	.50	.20	.05
☐ 24 Tom Roulston	.50	.20	.05
☐ 27 Dave Semenko	.60	.24	.06
☐ 29 Don Jackson	.50	.20	.05
☐ 30 Ron Low	.60	.24	.06
☐ 31 Grant Fuhr............................	2.00	.80	.20
☐ 35 Andy Moog	2.00	.80	.20
☐ 77 Gary Unger............................	.75	.30	.07
☐ 99 Wayne Gretzky	6.00	2.40	.60
☐ 99 Wayne Gretzky	6.00	2.40	.60
☐ 99 Wayne Gretzky	6.00	2.40	.60
☐ 99 Wayne Gretzky	6.00	2.40	.60
☐ NNO Glen Sather CO	.75	.30	.07
☐ NNO John Muckler ACO...............	.60	.24	.06
☐ NNO Ted Green ACO	.60	.24	.06

1983-84 Oilers Dollars

These seven cards, measuring approximately 3" by 5" and perforated on each end, were issued with "Hockey Dollars" or what may be better described as silver-colored coins. Each coin displayed an engraving of the player's face on the obverse and the team logo on the reverse. The card fronts are gray with tan lettering. They have the player's name, number, year, team logo, and a picture of the coin. In a horizontal format, the backs carry biography, career highlights, and career statistics. The cards are numbered on the back in the upper right corner. The prices below refer to the coin-card combination intact.

	MINT	EXC	G-VG
COMPLETE SET (7).........................	50.00	20.00	5.00
COMMON PLAYER (H14-H20)..........	3.00	1.20	.30
☐ H14 Wayne Gretzky.....................	15.00	6.00	1.50
☐ H15 Andy Moog	5.00	2.00	.50
☐ H16 Dave Hunter	3.00	1.20	.30
☐ H17 Ken Linseman SP	15.00	6.00	1.50
☐ H18 Lee Fogolin SP.....................	15.00	6.00	1.50
☐ H19 Dave Semenko......................	3.00	1.20	.30
☐ H20 Mark Messier........................	7.50	3.00	.75

1983-84 Oilers McDonald's

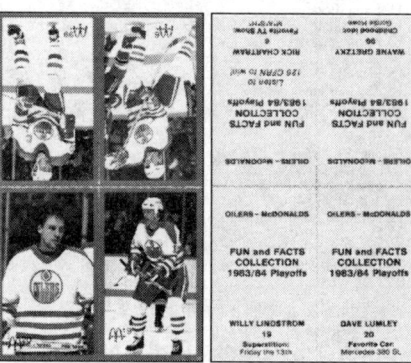

This 25-card set of Edmonton Oilers (entitled McDonald's Playoff Action Album) was issued in seven panels. After perforation, the standard issue cards measure 1 1/2" by 2 1/2" and number 22; three cards (3, 19, and 20) are oversized and measure 3" by 2 1/2". The card fronts feature color action photos with dark blue borders. The card backs give the player's name and number and often include a bit of trivia about player's career or preferences. Cards could be collected from participating McDonald's restaurants and pasted in a playoff album. An adhesive strip on the back could be used to stick the card in a special album. We have checklisted the names below according to the order of the album.

	MINT	EXC	G-VG
COMPLETE SET (25)........................	15.00	6.00	1.50
COMMON PLAYER (1-25).................	.35	.14	.03
☐ 1 Ken Linseman 13	.50	.20	.05
☐ 2 Dave Semenko 27	.35	.14	.03
☐ 3 Andy Moog 35	1.25	.50	.12
☐ 4 Raimo Summanen 25	.35	.14	.03
☐ 5 Jari Kurri 17	1.25	.50	.12
☐ 6 Rick Chartraw 6	.35	.14	.03
☐ 7 Don Jackson 29	.35	.14	.03

☐	8 Dave Hunter 12	.35	.14	.03
☐	9 Charlie Huddy 22	.50	.20	.05
☐	10 Emery Award	.50	.20	.05
☐	11 Pat Conacher 15	.35	.14	.03
☐	12 Lee Fogolin 2	.35	.14	.03
☐	13 Kevin Lowe 4	.75	.30	.07
☐	14 Randy Gregg 21	.50	.20	.05
☐	15 Pat Hughes 16	.35	.14	.03
☐	16 Kevin McClelland 24	.35	.14	.03
☐	17 Willy Lindstrom 19	.35	.14	.03
☐	18 Mark Messier 11	2.50	1.00	.25
☐	19 Grant Fuhr 31	1.25	.50	.12
☐	20 Coaches	.75	.30	.07
	Ted Green			
	Glen Sather			
	John Muckler			
☐	21 Wayne Gretzky 99	6.00	2.40	.60
☐	22 Dave Lumley 20	.35	.14	.03
☐	23 Jaroslav Pouzar 10	.35	.14	.03
☐	24 Glen Anderson 9	.75	.30	.07
☐	25 Paul Coffey 7	1.50	.60	.15
☐	xx Playoff Album	3.00	1.20	.30

1984-85 Oilers

Each of these collectibles measure approximately 4 1/2" by 6 1/2" and is printed on very thin glossy paper. The set was packaged in a plastic bag that included three small stickers. Two of the stickers ("Go 2 It Oilers" and "do it again Oilers") determine the date of the set as 1984-85, the season following the Oilers' 1983-84 championship. On the top half, the front features player information on the left and a color portrait with a light blue studio background on the right. On the bottom half, a white-bordered 4" by 3" color action player photo appears. The backs are blank. The photos are unnumbered and checklisted below in alphabetical order.

		MINT	EXC	G-VG
	COMPLETE SET (23)	20.00	8.00	2.00
	COMMON PLAYER (1-23)	.50	.20	.05
☐	1 Glenn Anderson	1.00	.40	.10
☐	2 Billy Carroll	.50	.20	.05
☐	3 Paul Coffey	2.00	.80	.20
☐	4 Lee Fogolin	.50	.20	.05
☐	5 Grant Fuhr	1.50	.60	.15
☐	6 Randy Gregg	.75	.30	.07
☐	7 Wayne Gretzky	7.50	3.00	.75
☐	8 Charlie Huddy	.75	.30	.07
☐	9 Pat Hughes	.50	.20	.05
☐	10 Dave Hunter	.50	.20	.05
☐	11 Don Jackson	.50	.20	.05
☐	12 Mike Krushelnyski	.75	.30	.07
☐	13 Jari Kurri	2.00	.80	.20
☐	14 Willy Lindstrom	.50	.20	.05
☐	15 Kevin Lowe	1.00	.40	.10
☐	16 Dave Lumley	.50	.20	.05
☐	17 Kevin McClelland	.50	.20	.05
☐	18 Larry Melnyk	.50	.20	.05
☐	19 Mark Messier	3.00	1.20	.30
☐	20 Andy Moog	1.25	.50	.12
☐	21 Mark Napier	.75	.30	.07
☐	22 Jaroslav Pouzar	.50	.20	.05
☐	23 Dave Semenko	.50	.20	.05

1984-85 Oilers Red Rooster

 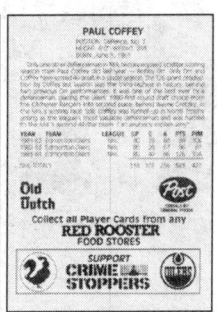

This 30-card set of Edmonton Oilers was sponsored by Red Rooster Food Stores in conjunction with Old Dutch Potato Chips and Post. The player cards could be collected at Red Rooster stores. The cards measure approximately 2 3/4" by 3 9/16" and the set includes four different cards of Wayne Gretzky. The front has a color photo of the player, with the Oilers' logo and player's signature across the bottom of the picture. The player's name, uniform number, and a hockey tip are given below the photo. The top half of the back has biographical and statistical information on the player, while the bottom half has company logos and an anti-crime message. There is a second print version of Glen Sather, which color corrects his first print card to reduce the redness in his face. The set is checklisted below using sweater numbers for reference.

		MINT	EXC	G-VG
	COMPLETE SET (30)	20.00	8.00	2.00
	COMMON PLAYER (1-30)	.35	.14	.03
☐	2 Lee Fogolin	.35	.14	.03
☐	4 Kevin Lowe	.75	.30	.07
☐	7 Paul Coffey	1.50	.60	.15
☐	8 Dave Lumley	.35	.14	.03
☐	9 Glenn Anderson	.75	.30	.07
☐	10 Jaroslav Pouzar	.35	.14	.03
☐	11 Mark Messier	2.50	1.00	.25
☐	12 Dave Hunter	.35	.14	.03
☐	16 Pat Hughes	.35	.14	.03
☐	17 Jari Kurri	1.25	.50	.12
☐	18 Mark Napier	.50	.20	.05
☐	19 Willi Lindstrom	.35	.14	.03
☐	20 Billy Carroll	.35	.14	.03
☐	21 Randy Gregg	.50	.20	.05
☐	22 Charlie Huddy	.50	.20	.05
☐	23 Marc Habscheid	.35	.14	.03
☐	24 Kevin McClelland	.35	.14	.03
☐	26 Mike Krushelnyski	.50	.20	.05
☐	27 Dave Semenko	.35	.14	.03
☐	28 Larry Melnyk	.35	.14	.03
☐	29 Don Jackson	.35	.14	.03
☐	31 Grant Fuhr	1.25	.50	.12
☐	35 Andy Moog	1.25	.50	.12
☐	99 Wayne Gretzky	4.00	1.60	.40
☐	99 Wayne Gretzky	4.00	1.60	.40
☐	99 Wayne Gretzky	4.00	1.60	.40
☐	99 Wayne Gretzky	4.00	1.60	.40
☐	NNO Ted Green ACO	.50	.20	.05
☐	NNO John Muckler ACO	.35	.14	.03
☐	NNO Glen Sather CO P1	.50	.20	.05
	(Facsimile autograph on			
	front, redness in face)			
☐	NNO Glen Sather CO P2	5.00	2.00	.50
	(No facsimile autograph			
	on front, softer colors)			

1985-86 Oilers Red Rooster

This 30-card set of Edmonton Oilers was sponsored by Red Rooster Food Stores in conjunction with Old Dutch Potato

 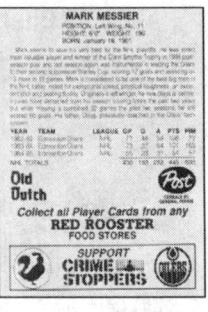

 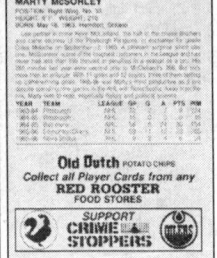

Chips and Post. The player cards could be collected from any Red Rooster stores. The cards measure approximately 2 3/4" by 3 9/16" and the set includes three different cards of Wayne Gretzky. The front has a color photo (with rounded corners) of the player, with the player's signature across the bottom of the picture. The player's name, uniform number, and a hockey tip are given below the photo. In contrast to earlier issues, the team logo now appears beneath the picture. The top half of the back has biographical and statistical information on the player, while the bottom half has company logos and an anti-crime message. The cards of Marty McSorley, Steve Smith, and Esa Tikkanen predate their O-Pee-Chee Rookie Cards by at least a year. The set is checklisted below using sweater numbers for reference.

	MINT	EXC	G-VG
COMPLETE SET (30)	20.00	8.00	2.00
COMMON PLAYER (1-30)	.35	.14	.03
☐ 2 Lee Fogolin	.35	.14	.03
☐ 4 Kevin Lowe	.75	.30	.07
☐ 5 Steve Smith	2.00	.80	.20
☐ 7 Paul Coffey	1.50	.60	.15
☐ 8 Gord Sherven	.35	.14	.03
☐ 9 Glenn Anderson	.75	.30	.07
☐ 10 Esa Tikkanen	2.50	1.00	.25
☐ 11 Mark Messier	2.50	1.00	.25
☐ 12 Dave Hunter	.35	.14	.03
☐ 14 Craig MacTavish	1.00	.40	.10
☐ 17 Jari Kurri	1.25	.50	.12
☐ 18 Mark Napier	.50	.20	.05
☐ 19 Mike Rogers	.50	.20	.05
☐ 20 Dave Lumley	.35	.14	.03
☐ 21 Randy Gregg	.50	.20	.05
☐ 22 Charlie Huddy	.50	.20	.05
☐ 24 Kevin McClelland	.35	.14	.03
☐ 25 Raimo Summanen	.35	.14	.03
☐ 26 Mike Krushelnyski	.50	.20	.05
☐ 27 Dave Semenko	.35	.14	.03
☐ 29 Don Jackson	.35	.14	.03
☐ 31 Grant Fuhr	1.25	.50	.12
☐ 33 Marty McSorley	2.50	1.00	.25
☐ 35 Andy Moog	1.25	.50	.12
☐ 99 Wayne Gretzky	4.00	1.60	.40
☐ 99 Wayne Gretzky	4.00	1.60	.40
☐ 99 Wayne Gretzky	4.00	1.60	.40
☐ NNO Bob McCammon ACO	.35	.14	.03
☐ NNO John Muckler ACO	.35	.14	.03
☐ NNO Glen Sather CO	.50	.20	.05

1986-87 Oilers Red Rooster

This 30-card set of Edmonton Oilers was sponsored by Red Rooster Food Stores in conjunction with Old Dutch Potato Chips. The player cards could be collected from any Red Rooster stores. The cards measure approximately 2 3/4" by 3 9/16" and the set includes two different cards of Wayne Gretzky and of Andy Moog. The front has a color photo (with rounded corners) of the player, with the player's signature across the bottom of the picture. The player's

name, uniform number, the team logo, and a safety tip are given below the photo. The top half of the back has biographical and statistical information on the player, while the bottom half has the sponsor's advertisements and the anti-crime slogan "Support Crime Stoppers." The set is checklisted below using sweater numbers for reference.

	MINT	EXC	G-VG
COMPLETE SET (30)	15.00	6.00	1.50
COMMON PLAYER (1-30)	.35	.14	.03
☐ 2 Lee Fogolin	.35	.14	.03
☐ 4 Kevin Lowe	.75	.30	.07
☐ 5 Steve Smith	1.00	.40	.10
☐ 6 Jeff Beukeboom	.50	.20	.05
☐ 7 Paul Coffey	1.25	.50	.12
☐ 8 Stu Kulak	.35	.14	.03
☐ 9 Glenn Anderson	.75	.30	.07
☐ 10 Esa Tikkanen	1.25	.50	.12
☐ 11 Mark Messier	2.00	.80	.20
☐ 12 Dave Hunter	.35	.14	.03
☐ 14 Craig MacTavish	.75	.30	.07
☐ 15 Steve Graves	.35	.14	.03
☐ 17 Jari Kurri	1.00	.40	.10
☐ 18 Danny Gare	.50	.20	.05
☐ 21 Randy Gregg	.50	.20	.05
☐ 22 Charlie Huddy	.50	.20	.05
☐ 24 Kevin McClelland	.35	.14	.03
☐ 25 Raimo Summanen	.35	.14	.03
☐ 26 Mike Krushelnyski	.50	.20	.05
☐ 28 Craig Muni	.35	.14	.03
☐ 31 Grant Fuhr	1.00	.40	.10
☐ 33 Marty McSorley	2.00	.80	.20
☐ 35 Andy Moog	1.00	.40	.10
☐ 35 Andy Moog	1.00	.40	.10
☐ 65 Mark Napier	.50	.20	.05
☐ 99 Wayne Gretzky	3.00	1.20	.30
☐ 99 Wayne Gretzky	3.00	1.20	.30
☐ NNO Ted Green ACO	.35	.14	.03
☐ NNO John Muckler ACO	.35	.14	.03
☐ NNO Glen Sather CO	.50	.20	.05

1986-87 Oilers Team Issue

This set of Edmonton Oilers consists of 24 cards, each measuring approximately 3 11/16" by 6 13/16". The front features a full color action shot of the player on white card stock, with a color "mug shot" superimposed for the most part at one of the lower corners of the picture. The player's uniform number, name, Oilers' logo, and brief biographical information are given above the photo. The back of each card is blank. The set is checklisted below using sweater numbers for reference.

	MINT	EXC	G-VG
COMPLETE SET (24)	25.00	10.00	2.50
COMMON PLAYER (1-24)	.60	.24	.06
☐ 2 Lee Fogolin	.60	.24	.06
☐ 4 Kevin Lowe	1.00	.40	.10
☐ 5 Steve Smith	1.25	.50	.12
☐ 6 Jeff Beukeboom	.75	.30	.07
☐ 7 Paul Coffey	2.00	.80	.20
☐ 8 Stu Kulak	.60	.24	.06
☐ 9 Glenn Anderson	1.00	.40	.10

☐ 10	Esa Tikkanen	1.50	.60	.15
☐ 11	Mark Messier	3.00	1.20	.30
☐ 12	Dave Hunter	.60	.24	.06
☐ 14	Craig MacTavish	1.00	.40	.10
☐ 17	Jari Kurri	1.50	.60	.15
☐ 20	Jaroslav Pouzar	.60	.24	.06
☐ 21	Randy Gregg	.75	.30	.07
☐ 22	Charlie Huddy	.75	.30	.07
☐ 24	Kevin McClelland	.60	.24	.06
☐ 25	Raimo Summanen	.60	.24	.06
☐ 26	Mike Krushelnyski	.75	.30	.07
☐ 28	Craig Muni	.60	.24	.06
☐ 31	Grant Fuhr	1.25	.50	.12
☐ 33	Marty McSorley	2.00	.80	.20
☐ 35	Andy Moog	1.25	.50	.12
☐ 65	Mark Napier	.75	.30	.07
☐ 99	Wayne Gretzky	8.00	3.25	.80

1987-88 Oilers Team Issue

This set of Edmonton Oilers consists of 22 cards, each measuring approximately 3 11/16" by 6 13/16". The front features a full color action shot of the player on white card stock, with a color "mug shot" superimposed for the most part at one of the lower corners of the picture. The player's uniform number, name, Oilers' logo, and brief biographical information are given above the photo. The back of each card is blank. The set is checklisted below using sweater numbers for reference.

	MINT	EXC	G-VG
COMPLETE SET (22)	25.00	10.00	2.50
COMMON PLAYER (1-22)	.60	.24	.06

☐ 4	Kevin Lowe	1.00	.40	.10
☐ 5	Steve Smith	1.25	.50	.12
☐ 6	Jeff Beukeboom	.75	.30	.07
☐ 9	Glenn Anderson	1.00	.40	.10
☐ 10	Esa Tikkanen	1.50	.60	.15
☐ 11	Mark Messier	3.00	1.20	.30
☐ 12	Dave Hannan	.60	.24	.06
☐ 14	Craig MacTavish	1.00	.40	.10
☐ 17	Jari Kurri	1.50	.60	.15
☐ 18	Craig Simpson	1.25	.50	.12
☐ 19	Normand Lacombe	.60	.24	.06
☐ 22	Charlie Huddy	.75	.30	.07
☐ 23	Keith Acton	.60	.24	.06
☐ 24	Kevin McClelland	.60	.24	.06
☐ 26	Mike Krushelnyski	.75	.30	.07
☐ 28	Craig Muni	.60	.24	.06
☐ 29	Daryl Reaugh	.75	.30	.07
☐ 30	Warren Skorodenski	.60	.24	.06
☐ 31	Grant Fuhr	1.25	.50	.12
☐ 33	Marty McSorley	1.50	.60	.15
☐ 36	Selmar Odelein	.60	.24	.06
☐ 99	Wayne Gretzky	8.00	3.25	.80

1988-89 Oilers Tenth Ann.

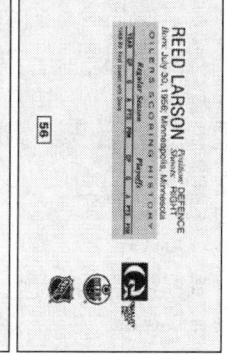

This set contains 164 cards and commemorates the tenth anniversary of the Edmonton Oilers. The cards were issued in four card panels, and each regular season edition of Action Magazine (Edmonton Oilers game program) contained one panel. The panels measured approximately 9 1/4 by 7 7/16", and the horizontally oriented cards were in between a gray stripe at the top and card information at the bottom. The cards were not perforated, but after cutting they measure approximately 2 9/16" by 4 5/16". The front features a color action photo of the player, with a thin black border on white card stock. The box below the picture has player identification and three logos. The back has biographical and statistical information in a horizontal format concerning the player's history with the Oilers.

	MINT	EXC	G-VG
COMPLETE SET (164)	100.00	40.00	10.00
COMMON PLAYER (1-164)	.50	.20	.05

☐ 1	Garry Unger	.75	.30	.07
☐ 2	Chris Joseph	.50	.20	.05
☐ 3	Raimo Summanen	.50	.20	.05
☐ 4	Mike Zanier	.50	.20	.05
☐ 5	Kevin Lowe	1.00	.40	.10
☐ 6	Dave Semenko	.75	.30	.07
☐ 7	Peter Driscoll	.50	.20	.05
☐ 8	Ken Solheim	.50	.20	.05
☐ 9	Glenn Anderson	2.00	.80	.20
☐ 10	Curt Brackenbury	.50	.20	.05
☐ 11	Ron Shudra	.50	.20	.05
☐ 12	Gord Sherven	.50	.20	.05
☐ 13	Randy Gregg	.60	.24	.06
☐ 14	Larry Melnyk	.50	.20	.05
☐ 15	Tom Roulston	.50	.20	.05
☐ 16	Billy Carroll	.50	.20	.05

☐	17	Jeff Beukeboom	.60	.24	.06
☐	18	Jaroslav Pouzar	.50	.20	.05
☐	19	Jeff Brubaker	.50	.20	.05
☐	20	Danny Gare	.60	.24	.06
☐	21	Craig MacTavish	.75	.30	.07
☐	22	Reijo Routsalainen	.50	.20	.05
☐	23	Willy Lindstrom	.50	.20	.05
☐	24	Pat Hughes	.50	.20	.05
☐	25	Jim Wiemer	.50	.20	.05
☐	26	Selmar Odelein	.50	.20	.05
☐	27	Kent Nilsson	.75	.30	.07
☐	28	Mark Napier	.60	.24	.06
☐	29	Esa Tikkanen	2.00	.80	.20
☐	30	John Miner	.50	.20	.05
☐	31	Tom McMurchy	.50	.20	.05
☐	32	Steve Graves	.50	.20	.05
☐	33	Craig Muni	.60	.24	.06
☐	34	Moe Mantha	.50	.20	.05
☐	35	Dave Lumley	.50	.20	.05
☐	36	Ron Low	.60	.24	.06
☐	37	Marty McSorley	2.00	.80	.20
☐	38	Steve Dykstra	.50	.20	.05
☐	39	Risto Jalo	.50	.20	.05
☐	40	Dave Hunter	.50	.20	.05
☐	41	Jari Kurri	3.00	1.20	.30
☐	42	Lee Fogolin	.50	.20	.05
☐	43	Moe Lemay	.50	.20	.05
☐	44	Stu Kulak	.50	.20	.05
☐	45	Charlie Huddy	.60	.24	.06
☐	46	Wayne Gretzky	12.00	5.00	1.20
☐	47	Ken Linseman	.60	.24	.06
☐	48	Risto Siltanen	.50	.20	.05
☐	49	Glen Sather	1.00	.40	.10
☐	50	Brett Callighen	.50	.20	.05
☐	51	Eddie Mio	.60	.24	.06
☐	52	Ken Hammond	.50	.20	.05
☐	53	Jimmy Carson	1.50	.60	.15
☐	54	Paul Coffey	3.00	1.20	.30
☐	55	Wayne Gretzky 1050th	5.00	2.00	.50
☐	56	Reed Larson	.75	.30	.07
☐	57	Ted Green	.60	.24	.06
☐	58	Matti Hagman	.50	.20	.05
☐	59	Marc Habscheid	.50	.20	.05
☐	60	Bill Ranford	3.00	1.20	.30
☐	61	Mark Lamb	.75	.30	.07
☐	62	Daryl Reaugh	.60	.24	.06
☐	63	Al Hamilton	.50	.20	.05
☐	64	Paul Coffey's 47th	1.00	.40	.10
☐	65	Grant Fuhr	2.50	1.00	.25
☐	66	Stan Weir	.50	.20	.05
☐	67	Ken Berry	.50	.20	.05
☐	68	John Muckler CO	.60	.24	.06
☐	69	Doug Smith	.50	.20	.05
☐	70	Lance Nethery	.50	.20	.05
☐	71	Bill Flett	.50	.20	.05
☐	72	Mike Forbes	.50	.20	.05
☐	73	Martin Gelinas	.75	.30	.07
☐	74	Ron Chipperfield	.50	.20	.05
☐	75	Reg Kerr	.50	.20	.05
☐	76	Don Jackson	.50	.20	.05
☐	77	Keith Acton	.50	.20	.05
☐	78	Gary Edwards	.60	.24	.06
☐	79	Mike Krushelnyski	.60	.24	.06
☐	80	Trainers	.50	.20	.05
		Lyle Kulchisky			
		Peter Millar			
		Barrie Stafford			
☐	81	Normand Lacombe	.50	.20	.05
☐	82	Pat Price	.50	.20	.05
☐	83	Dave Hannan	.50	.20	.05
☐	84	Garry Lariviere	.50	.20	.05
☐	85	Greg Adams	.60	.24	.06
☐	86	Poul Popiel	.60	.24	.06
☐	87	Tom Gorence	.50	.20	.05
☐	88	Geoff Courtnall	1.50	.60	.15
☐	89	Mark Messier	5.00	2.00	.50
☐	90	Dave Dryden	.60	.24	.06
☐	91	Andy Moog	2.50	1.00	.25
☐	92	Jim Ennis	.50	.20	.05
☐	93	Craig Simpson	1.00	.40	.10
☐	94	Laurie Boschman	.60	.24	.06
☐	95	Doug Hicks	.50	.20	.05
☐	96	Rick Chartraw	.50	.20	.05
☐	97	1984 Stanley Cup	.75	.30	.07
		Champs			
☐	98	Ron Carter	.50	.20	.05
☐	99	Blair MacDonald	.50	.20	.05
☐	100	Dean Clark	.50	.20	.05
☐	101	Glen Cochrane	.50	.20	.05
☐	102	Lindsay Middlebrook	.50	.20	.05
☐	103	Ron Areshenkoff	.50	.20	.05
☐	104	Billy Harris CO	.50	.20	.05
☐	105	Conn Smythe Trophy	.75	.30	.07

☐	106	John Blum	.50	.20	.05
☐	107	Wayne Bianchin	.50	.20	.05
☐	108	Tom Bladon	.60	.24	.06
☐	109	Kevin McClelland	.50	.20	.05
☐	110	Roy Sommer	.50	.20	.05
☐	111	Mike Toal	.50	.20	.05
☐	112	Don Ashby	.50	.20	.05
☐	113	Don Nachbaur	.50	.20	.05
☐	114	1985 Stanley Cup	.75	.30	.07
		Champions			
☐	115	Jim Corsi	.50	.20	.05
☐	116	John Hughes	.50	.20	.05
☐	117	Coach of the Year	.75	.30	.07
		Glen Sather			
☐	118	Bob Dupuis	.50	.20	.05
☐	119	Jim Harrison	.50	.20	.05
☐	120	Don Murdoch	.50	.20	.05
☐	121	Steve Smith	1.00	.40	.10
☐	122	Pete Lopresti	.50	.20	.05
☐	123	Colin Campbell	1.00	.40	.10
☐	124	Bryan Watson	.50	.20	.05
☐	125	John Bednarski	.50	.20	.05
☐	126	1987 Stanley Cup	.75	.30	.07
		Champions			
☐	127	Scott Metcalfe	.50	.20	.05
☐	128	Mike Rogers	.75	.30	.07
☐	129	Dan Newman	.50	.20	.05
☐	130	Fuhr's 75th	.75	.30	.07
☐	131	Warren Skorodenski	.60	.24	.06
☐	132	Todd Strueby	.50	.20	.05
☐	133	Kelly Buchberger	.75	.30	.07
☐	134	Cam Connor	.50	.20	.05
☐	135	Dean Hopkins	.50	.20	.05
☐	136	Mike Moller	.50	.20	.05
☐	137	1988 Stanley Cup	4.00	1.60	.40
		Champions			
		(Wayne Gretzky)			
☐	138	Bryon Baltimore	.50	.20	.05
☐	139	Pat Conacher	.60	.24	.06
☐	140	Ray Cote	.50	.20	.05
☐	141	Walt Poddubny	.60	.24	.06
☐	142	Jim Playfair	.50	.20	.05
☐	143	Nick Fotiu	.75	.30	.07
☐	144	Kari Makkonen	.50	.20	.05
☐	145	Dave Brown	.75	.30	.07
☐	146	Terry Martin	.50	.20	.05
☐	147	Francois Leroux	.50	.20	.05
☐	148	Kari Jalonen	.50	.20	.05
☐	149	Tomas Jonsson	.60	.24	.06
☐	150	Dave Donnelly	.50	.20	.05
☐	151	Mike Ware	.50	.20	.05
☐	152	Don Cutts	.50	.20	.05
☐	153	Miroslav Frycer	.50	.20	.05
☐	154	Bruce MacGregor GM	.50	.20	.05
☐	155	Kim Issel	.50	.20	.05
☐	156	Marco Baron	.50	.20	.05
☐	157	Doug Halward	.50	.20	.05
☐	158	Barry Fraser DIR	.50	.20	.05
☐	159	Alan May	.50	.20	.05
☐	160	Bobby Schmautz	.50	.20	.05
☐	161	Craig Redmond	.50	.20	.05
☐	162	Oilers Host '89	.60	.24	.06
		All-Star Game			
☐	163	Alex Tidey	.50	.20	.05
☐	164	Wayne Van Dorp	.50	.20	.05

1990-91 Oilers IGA

This 30-card set was sponsored by IGA food stores in conjunction with McGavin's, a distributor of bread and other products in Alberta. Protected by a cello pack, one card was inserted in bread loaves distributed by McGavin's to IGA stores in Calgary and Edmonton. Calgary consumers received a Flames' card, while Edmonton consumers received an Oilers' card. Checklist and coaches cards were not inserted in the loaves but were included on five hundred individually numbered and uncut sheets not offered to the general public. The cards measure the standard size (2 1/2" by 3 1/2") and are printed on thin card stock. The fronts have posed color player photos, with a border that shades from blue to orange and back to blue. Most of the photos are shot against the background of the equipment room or dressing room. The player's name is printed in the bottom

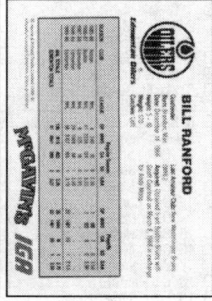

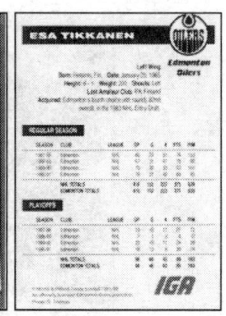

border, and his uniform number is printed in a circle in the upper left corner of each picture. The horizontally oriented backs feature biographical information, with year-by-year statistics presented in a pink rectangle. Sponsor logos at the bottom round out the back. The cards are unnumbered and checklisted below in alphabetical order. Adam Graves appears during his Rookie Card year.

	MINT	EXC	G-VG
COMPLETE SET (30)	35.00	14.00	3.50
COMMON PLAYER (1-30)	.75	.30	.07
☐ 1 Glenn Anderson	1.50	.60	.15
☐ 2 Jeff Beukeboom	1.00	.40	.10
☐ 3 Dave Brown	1.05	.00	.00
☐ 4 Kelly Buchberger	1.00	.40	.10
☐ 5 Martin Gelinas	1.25	.50	.12
☐ 6 Adam Graves	3.00	1.20	.30
☐ 7 Ted Green CO SP	3.00	1.20	.30
☐ 8 Charlie Huddy	1.00	.40	.10
☐ 9 Chris Joseph	.75	.30	.07
☐ 10 Petr Klima	1.25	.50	.12
☐ 11 Mark Lamb	1.00	.40	.10
☐ 12 Ken Linseman	1.00	.40	.10
☐ 13 Ron Low CO SP	3.00	1.20	.30
☐ 14 Kevin Lowe	1.25	.50	.12
☐ 15 Craig MacTavish	1.00	.40	.10
☐ 16 Mark Messier	5.00	2.00	.50
☐ 17 Joey Moss	.75	.30	.07
☐ 18 John Muckler CO SP	3.00	1.20	.30
☐ 19 Craig Muni	.75	.30	.07
☐ 20 Joe Murphy	1.50	.60	.15
☐ 21 Bill Ranford	2.50	1.00	.25
☐ 22 Anatoli Semenov	1.00	.40	.10
☐ 23 Craig Simpson	1.25	.50	.12
☐ 24 Geoff Smith	.75	.30	.07
☐ 25 Steve Smith	1.25	.50	.12
☐ 26 Kari Takko	.75	.30	.07
☐ 27 Esa Tikkanen	1.50	.60	.15
☐ 28 Training Staff SP	3.00	1.20	.30
Ken Low TR/THER			
Lyle Kulchisky TR			
Barrie Stafford TR			
Stewart Poirier THER			
☐ 29 Edmonton Oilers	.75	.30	.07
Year-by-Year Record			
☐ 30 Checklist Card SP	3.00	1.20	.30

1991-92 Oilers IGA

This 30-card set of Edmonton Oilers was sponsored by IGA food stores and included manufacturers' discount coupons. One pack of cards was distributed in Calgary and Edmonton IGA stores with any grocery purchase of 10.00 or more. The cards measure the standard size (2 1/2" by 3 1/2") and are printed on thin card stock. The fronts have posed color action photos bordered in dark blue. The player's name is printed vertically in the wider left border, and his uniform number and the team name appear at the bottom of the picture. In black print on a white background, the backs present biography and statistics (regular season

and playoff). Packs were kept under the cash till drawer, and therefore many of the cards were creased. Each pack contained three Oiler and two Flame cards. The checklist and coaches cards for both teams were not included in the packs but were available on a very limited basis through an uncut team sheet offer. The cards are unnumbered and checklisted below in alphabetical order, with the coaches cards listed after the players.

	MINT	EXC	G-VG
COMPLETE SET (30)	20.00	8.00	2.00
COMMON PLAYER (1-30)	.50	.20	.05
☐ 1 Josef Beranek	1.00	.40	.10
☐ 2 Kelly Buchberger	.75	.30	.07
☐ 3 Vincent Damphousse	1.25	.50	.12
☐ 4 Louie DeBrusk	.60	.24	.06
☐ 5 Martin Gelinas	.75	.30	.07
☐ 6 Peter Ing	.60	.24	.06
☐ 7 Petr Klima	.75	.30	.07
☐ 8 Mark Lamb	.60	.24	.06
☐ 9 Kevin Lowe	.75	.30	.07
☐ 10 Norm Maciver	.60	.24	.06
☐ 11 Craig MacTavish	.75	.30	.07
☐ 12 Troy Mallette	.50	.20	.05
☐ 13 Dave Manson	.75	.30	.07
☐ 14 Scott Mellanby	.60	.24	.06
☐ 15 Craig Muni	.50	.20	.05
☐ 16 Joe Murphy	1.00	.40	.10
☐ 17 Bill Ranford	1.50	.60	.15
☐ 18 Steven Rice	.75	.30	.07
☐ 19 Luke Richardson	.50	.20	.05
☐ 20 Anatoli Semenov	.60	.24	.06
☐ 21 David Shaw	.50	.20	.05
☐ 22 Craig Simpson	.75	.30	.07
☐ 23 Geoff Smith	.50	.20	.05
☐ 24 Scott Thornton	.50	.20	.05
☐ 25 Esa Tikkanen	1.00	.40	.10
☐ 26 Training Staff SP	2.50	1.00	.25
☐ 27 Ted Green CO SP	2.50	1.00	.25
☐ 28 Ron Low CO SP	2.50	1.00	.25
☐ 29 Kevin Primeau CO SP	2.50	1.00	.25
☐ 30 Checklist Card SP	2.50	1.00	.25

1992-93 Oilers

The 22 blank-backed cards comprising this set are printed on thin white card stock and measure approximately 3 3/4" by 6 7/8". They feature white-bordered color player action photos and display the Oilers logo, the player's name, jersey number, and brief biography within the broad white border at the top. The cards are unnumbered and checklisted below in alphabetical order.

	MINT	EXC	G-VG
COMPLETE SET (22)	12.00	5.00	1.20
COMMON PLAYER (1-22)	.50	.20	.05
☐ 1 Kelly Buchberger	.60	.24	.06
☐ 2 Zdeno Ciger	.60	.24	.06
☐ 3 Shayne Corson	.75	.30	.07
☐ 4 Louie DeBrusk	.60	.24	.06
☐ 5 Todd Elik	.75	.30	.07

☐ 6	Brian Glynn	.50	.20	.05
☐ 7	Mike Hudson	.60	.24	.06
☐ 8	Chris Joseph	.50	.20	.05
☐ 9	Igor Kravchuk	.75	.30	.07
☐ 10	Francois Leroux	.60	.24	.06
☐ 11	Craig MacTavish	.75	.30	.07
☐ 12	Dave Manson	.75	.30	.07
☐ 13	Shjon Podein	.60	.24	.06
☐ 14	Bill Ranford	1.00	.40	.10
☐ 15	Steve Rice	.75	.30	.07
☐ 16	Luke Richardson	.60	.24	.06
☐ 17	Craig Simpson	.75	.30	.07
☐ 18	Geoff Smith	.50	.20	.05
☐ 19	Kevin Todd	.60	.24	.06
☐ 20	Vladimir Vujtek	.60	.24	.06
☐ 21	Doug Weight	1.00	.40	.10
☐ 22	Brad Werenka	.60	.24	.06

1992-93 Oilers IGA

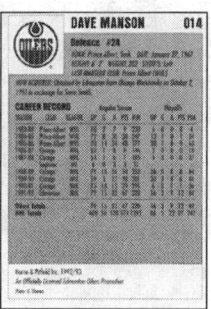

Sponsored by IGA food stores, the 30 standard-size (2 1/2" by 3 1/2") cards comprising this Special Edition Collector Series set feature color player action shots on their fronts. Each photo is trimmed with a black line and offset flush with the thin white border on the right, which surrounds the card. On the remaining three sides, the picture is edged with a gray and white netlike pattern. The player's name appears in the upper right and the Oilers logo rests in the lower left. The back carries the player's name at the top, with his position, uniform number, biography, and stat table set within a bluish-gray screened background. The Oilers logo in the upper right rounds out the card. The cards are numbered on the back.

	MINT	EXC	G-VG
COMPLETE SET (30)	15.00	6.00	1.50
COMMON PLAYER (1-30)	.50	.20	.05

☐ 1	Checklist	.50	.20	.05
☐ 2	Joseph Beranek	.75	.30	.07
☐ 3	Kelly Buchberger	.60	.24	.06
☐ 4	Shayne Corson	.75	.30	.07
☐ 5	Louie DeBrusk	.60	.24	.06
☐ 6	Martin Gelinas	.75	.30	.07
☐ 7	Brent Gilchrist	.60	.24	.06
☐ 8	Brian Glynn	.50	.20	.05
☐ 9	Greg Hawgood	.50	.20	.05
☐ 10	Petr Klima	.75	.30	.07
☐ 11	Chris Joseph	.50	.20	.05
☐ 12	Craig MacTavish	.75	.30	.07
☐ 13	Dan Currie	.60	.24	.06
☐ 14	Dave Manson	.75	.30	.07
☐ 15	Scott Mellanby	.60	.24	.06
☐ 16	Craig Muni	.50	.20	.05
☐ 17	Bernie Nicholls	1.00	.40	.10
☐ 18	Bill Ranford	1.25	.50	.12
☐ 19	Luke Richardson	.60	.24	.06
☐ 20	Craig Simpson	.75	.30	.07
☐ 21	Geoff Smith	.50	.20	.05
☐ 22	Vladimir Vujtek	.75	.30	.07
☐ 23	Esa Tikkanen	1.00	.40	.10
☐ 24	Ron Tugnutt	.75	.30	.07
☐ 25	Shaun Van Allen	.60	.24	.06
☐ 26	Glen Sather GM	.75	.30	.07
☐ 27	Ted Green CO	.50	.20	.05
☐ 28	Ron Low CO	.50	.20	.05
☐ 29	Kevin Primeau CO	.50	.20	.05
☐ 30	Oilers yearly record	.50	.20	.05

1932-33 O'Keefe Maple Leafs

This 20-card set was issued by O'Keefe's Beverages and features the Toronto Maples Leafs, 1931-32 Stanley Cup Champions. Each was designed for use as a coaster. The shape of each card is an eight-pointed star, which measures approximately 5" from one point across to its opposite. Inside a blue border, the front has a black and blue ink portrait or drawing of the player, which is surrounded by cartoons and captions presenting player information. The backs read "O'Keefe's Big 4" and "Each a Leader in its Class." The coasters are numbered on the front near the top and are checklisted below accordingly.

	EX-MT	VG-E	GOOD
COMPLETE SET (20)	6000.00	2500.00	600.00
COMMON PLAYER (1-20)	150.00	60.00	15.00

☐ 1	Lorne Chabot	175.00	70.00	18.00
☐ 2	Red Horner	300.00	120.00	30.00
☐ 3	Alex Levinsky	200.00	80.00	20.00
☐ 4	Hap Day	300.00	120.00	30.00
☐ 5	Andy Blair	150.00	60.00	15.00
☐ 6	Ace Bailey	400.00	160.00	40.00
☐ 7	King Clancy	750.00	300.00	75.00
☐ 8	Harold Cotton	300.00	120.00	30.00
☐ 9	Charlie Conacher	500.00	200.00	50.00
☐ 10	Joe Primeau	300.00	120.00	30.00
☐ 11	Harvey Jackson	500.00	200.00	50.00
☐ 12	Frank Finnegan	150.00	60.00	15.00
☐ 13	Unknown	.00	.00	.00
☐ 14	Bob Gracie	150.00	60.00	15.00
☐ 15	Unknown	.00	.00	.00
☐ 16	Harold Darragh	150.00	60.00	15.00
☐ 17	Benny Grant	150.00	60.00	15.00
☐ 18	Fred Robertson	150.00	60.00	15.00
☐ 19	Conn Smythe	500.00	200.00	50.00
☐ 20	Dick Irvin	300.00	120.00	30.00

☐ NNO	Ken Doraty	300.00	120.00	30.00
☐ NNO	Bill Thoms	300.00	120.00	30.00

1933-34 O-Pee-Chee V304A

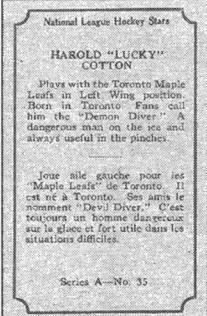

This first of five O-Pee-Chee 1930's hockey card issues features a black and white photo of the player portrayed on a colored field of stars. The cards in the set are approximately 2 5/16" by 3 9/16". The player's name appears in a rectangle at the bottom of the front of the card. Four possible color background fields exist, red, blue, orange and green. The cards are numbered on the back, and a short biography in both English and French is also contained on the back. The catalog designation for this set is V304A.

	EX-MT	VG-E	GOOD
COMPLETE SET (48)	9000.00	3750.00	900.00
COMMON PLAYER (1-48)	75.00	30.00	7.50

☐ 1	Danny Cox	150.00	50.00	10.00
☐ 2	Joe Lamb	75.00	30.00	7.50
☐ 3	Eddie Shore	1200.00	500.00	125.00
☐ 4	Ken Doraty	75.00	30.00	7.50
☐ 5	Fred Hitchman	75.00	30.00	7.50
☐ 6	Nels Stewart	500.00	200.00	50.00
☐ 7	Walter Galbraith	75.00	30.00	7.50
☐ 8	Dit Clapper	350.00	140.00	35.00
☐ 9	Harry Oliver	150.00	60.00	15.00
☐ 10	Red Horner	200.00	80.00	20.00
☐ 11	Alex Levinsky	75.00	30.00	7.50
☐ 12	Joe Primeau	350.00	140.00	35.00
☐ 13	Ace Bailey	350.00	140.00	35.00
☐ 14	George Patterson	75.00	30.00	7.50
☐ 15	George Hainsworth	200.00	80.00	20.00
☐ 16	Ott Heller	75.00	30.00	7.50
☐ 17	Art Somers	75.00	30.00	7.50
☐ 18	Lorne Chabot	125.00	50.00	12.50
☐ 19	Johnny Gagnon	75.00	30.00	7.50
☐ 20	Pit Lepine	75.00	30.00	7.50
☐ 21	Wildor Larochelle	75.00	30.00	7.50
☐ 22	Georges Mantha	75.00	30.00	7.50
☐ 23	Howie Morenz	1500.00	600.00	150.00
☐ 24	Syd Howe	200.00	80.00	20.00
☐ 25	Frank Finnigan	100.00	40.00	10.00
☐ 26	Bill Touhey	75.00	30.00	7.50
☐ 27	Cooney Weiland	150.00	60.00	15.00
☐ 28	Leo Bourgeault	75.00	30.00	7.50
☐ 29	Normie Himes	75.00	30.00	7.50
☐ 30	Johnny Sheppard	75.00	30.00	7.50
☐ 31	King Clancy	750.00	300.00	75.00
☐ 32	Clarence(Hap) Day	150.00	60.00	15.00
☐ 33	Harvey(Busher) Jackson	350.00	140.00	35.00
☐ 34	Charlie Conacher	600.00	240.00	60.00
☐ 35	Harold Cotton	75.00	30.00	7.50
☐ 36	Butch Keeling	75.00	30.00	7.50
☐ 37	Murray Murdoch	75.00	30.00	7.50
☐ 38	Bill Cook	150.00	60.00	15.00
☐ 39	Ivan(Ching) Johnson	200.00	80.00	20.00
☐ 40	Happy Emms	75.00	30.00	7.50
☐ 41	Bert McInenly	75.00	30.00	7.50
☐ 42	John Sorrell	75.00	30.00	7.50
☐ 43	Bill Phillips	75.00	30.00	7.50

☐ 44	Charley McVeigh	75.00	30.00	7.50
☐ 45	Roy Worters	200.00	80.00	20.00
☐ 46	Albert Leduc	75.00	30.00	7.50
☐ 47	Nick Wasnie	75.00	30.00	7.50
☐ 48	Armand Mondou	100.00	40.00	8.00

1933-34 O-Pee-Chee V304B

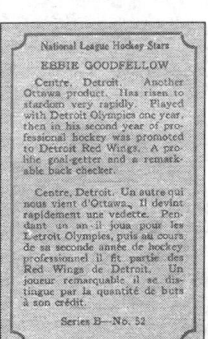

The second O-Pee-Chee hockey series of the 1930's contains 24 cards and continues the numbering sequence of the Series A cards. The format is exactly the same as the cards of Series A. The cards in the set measure approximately 2 5/16" by 3 9/16". The catalog designation for this set is V304B.

	EX-MT	VG-E	GOOD
COMPLETE SET (24)	3000.00	1250.00	300.00
COMMON PLAYER (49-72)	90.00	36.00	9.00

☐ 49	Babe Siebert	225.00	90.00	22.00
☐ 50	Aurel Joliat	600.00	240.00	60.00
☐ 51	Larry Aurie	125.00	50.00	12.50
☐ 52	Ebbie Goodfellow	175.00	70.00	18.00
☐ 53	John Ross Roach	90.00	36.00	9.00
☐ 54	Bill Beveridge	90.00	36.00	9.00
☐ 55	Earl Robinson	90.00	36.00	9.00
☐ 56	Jimmy Ward	90.00	36.00	9.00
☐ 57	Archie Wilcox	90.00	36.00	9.00
☐ 58	Lorne Duguid	90.00	36.00	9.00
☐ 59	Dave Kerr	125.00	50.00	12.50
☐ 60	Baldy Northcott	90.00	36.00	9.00
☐ 61	Marvin Wentworth	90.00	36.00	9.00
☐ 62	Dave Trottier	90.00	36.00	9.00
☐ 63	Wally Kilrea	90.00	36.00	9.00
☐ 64	Glen Brydson	90.00	36.00	9.00
☐ 65	Vernon Ayers	90.00	36.00	9.00
☐ 66	Bob Gracie	90.00	36.00	9.00
☐ 67	Vic Ripley	90.00	36.00	9.00
☐ 68	Tiny Thompson	175.00	70.00	18.00
☐ 69	Alex Smith	90.00	36.00	9.00
☐ 70	Andy Blair	90.00	36.00	9.00
☐ 71	Cecil Dillon	90.00	36.00	9.00
☐ 72	Bun Cook	175.00	70.00	18.00

1935-36 O-Pee-Chee V304C

While Series C in the O-Pee-Chee 1930's hockey card set continues the numbering sequence of the previous two years, this 24-card set differs significantly in both format and size. The cards in this set measure approximately 2 3/8" by 2 7/8". Each black and white photo portraying the player on the front can be found on four possible color fields, green, orange, maroon, or yellow. The field consists of a star in the center and cartooned hockey players flanking the center of the card. The backs contain the player's name, the

card number, and biographical data in both English and French. The catalog designation for this set is V304C.

	EX-MT	VG-E	GOOD
COMPLETE SET (24)	2500.00	1000.00	250.00
COMMON PLAYER (73-96)	90.00	36.00	9.00
☐ 73 Wilfred Cude	150.00	60.00	15.00
☐ 74 Jack McGill	90.00	36.00	9.00
☐ 75 Russ Blinco	90.00	36.00	9.00
☐ 76 Hooley Smith	175.00	70.00	18.00
☐ 77 Herb Cain	125.00	50.00	12.50
☐ 78 Gus Marker	90.00	36.00	9.00
☐ 79 Lynn Patrick	200.00	80.00	20.00
☐ 80 Johnny Gottselig	90.00	36.00	9.00
☐ 81 Marty Barry	175.00	70.00	18.00
☐ 82 Sylvio Mantha	175.00	70.00	18.00
☐ 83 Flash Hollett	90.00	36.00	9.00
☐ 84 Nick Metz	90.00	36.00	9.00
☐ 85 Bill Thoms	90.00	36.00	9.00
☐ 86 Hec Kilrea	90.00	36.00	9.00
☐ 87 Pep Kelly	90.00	36.00	9.00
☐ 88 Art Jackson	90.00	36.00	9.00
☐ 89 Allan Shields	90.00	36.00	9.00
☐ 90 Buzz Boll	90.00	36.00	9.00
☐ 91 Jean Pusie	90.00	36.00	9.00
☐ 92 Roger Jenkins	90.00	36.00	9.00
☐ 93 Arthur Coulter	175.00	70.00	18.00
☐ 94 Art Chapman	90.00	36.00	9.00
☐ 95 Paul Haynes	90.00	36.00	9.00
☐ 96 Leroy Goldsworthy	150.00	60.00	15.00

1936-37 O-Pee-Chee V304D

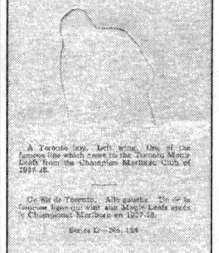

The most significant difference between Series D cards and cards from the previous three O-Pee-Chee sets is the fact that these cards are die-cut and may be folded to give a stand-up figure, like the 1934-36 Batter-Up baseball cards. The cards are in black and white with no colored background field. The cards in the set measure approximately 2 3/8" by 2 15/16". As these cards are difficult to find without the backs missing, this set is the most valuable of the 1930's O-Pee-Chee sets. The backs contain the card number and biographical data in English and French. The player's name is given on the front of the card only. The catalog designation for this set is V304D.

	EX-MT	VG-E	GOOD
COMPLETE SET (36)	10000.	4000.	1000.
COMMON PLAYER (97-132)	125.00	50.00	12.50
☐ 97 Turk Broda	900.00	300.00	60.00
☐ 98 Sweeney Schriner	300.00	120.00	30.00
☐ 99 Jack Shill	125.00	50.00	12.50
☐ 100 Bob Davidson	125.00	50.00	12.50
☐ 101 Syl Apps	500.00	200.00	50.00
☐ 102 Lionel Conacher	400.00	160.00	40.00
☐ 103 Jimmy Fowler	125.00	50.00	12.50
☐ 104 Al Murray	125.00	50.00	12.50
☐ 105 Neil Colville	200.00	80.00	20.00
☐ 106 Paul Runge	125.00	50.00	12.50
☐ 107 Mike Karakas	125.00	50.00	12.50
☐ 108 John Gallagher	125.00	50.00	12.50
☐ 109 Alex Shibicky	125.00	50.00	12.50
☐ 110 Herb Cain	150.00	60.00	15.00
☐ 111 Bill McKenzie	125.00	50.00	12.50
☐ 112 Harold Jackson	125.00	50.00	12.50
☐ 113 Art Wiebe	125.00	50.00	12.50
☐ 114 Joffre Desilets	125.00	50.00	12.50
☐ 115 Earl Robinson	125.00	50.00	12.50
☐ 116 Cy Wentworth	125.00	50.00	12.50
☐ 117 Ebbie Goodfellow	200.00	80.00	20.00
☐ 118 Eddie Shore	1200.00	500.00	125.00
☐ 119 Buzz Boll	125.00	50.00	12.50
☐ 120 Wilfred Cude	125.00	50.00	12.50
☐ 121 Howie Morenz	1500.00	600.00	150.00
☐ 122 Red Horner	250.00	100.00	25.00
☐ 123 Charlie Conacher	600.00	240.00	60.00
☐ 124 Harvey(Busher)Jackson	350.00	140.00	35.00
☐ 125 King Clancy	750.00	300.00	75.00
☐ 126 Dave Trottier	125.00	50.00	12.50
☐ 127 Russ Blinco	125.00	50.00	12.50
☐ 128 Lynn Patrick	250.00	100.00	25.00
☐ 129 Aurel Joliat	600.00	240.00	60.00
☐ 130 Baldy Northcott	125.00	50.00	12.50
☐ 131 Larry Aurie	125.00	50.00	12.50
☐ 132 Hooley Smith	300.00	100.00	20.00

1937-38 O-Pee-Chee V304E

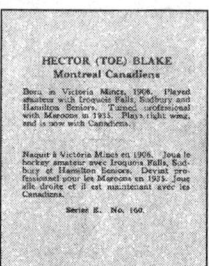

Series E cards continue the numerical series of the 1930's O-Pee-Chee sets and feature a black and white photo of the player within a serrated, colored (blue or purple) frame. A facsimile autograph and a cartooned hockey player appear on the front in the same color as the frame. The cards in the set measure approximately 2 3/8" by 2 7/8". The backs contain the card number, the player's name, and biographical data in both English and French. The catalog designation for this set is V304E.

	EX-MT	VG-E	GOOD
COMPLETE SET (48)	5000.00	2000.00	500.00
COMMON PLAYER (133-180)	75.00	30.00	7.50
☐ 133 Turk Broda	400.00	125.00	25.00
☐ 134 Red Horner	175.00	70.00	18.00
☐ 135 Jimmy Fowler	75.00	30.00	7.50
☐ 136 Bob Davidson	75.00	30.00	7.50
☐ 137 Reg. Hamilton	75.00	30.00	7.50
☐ 138 Charlie Conacher	400.00	160.00	40.00
☐ 139 Harvey(Busher)Jackson	200.00	80.00	20.00
☐ 140 Buzz Boll	75.00	30.00	7.50
☐ 141 Syl Apps	250.00	100.00	25.00

☐	142	Gordie Drillon	200.00	80.00	20.00

☐	#	Player	EX	VG	GOOD
☐	142	Gordie Drillon	200.00	80.00	20.00
☐	143	Bill Thoms	75.00	30.00	7.50
☐	144	Nick Metz	75.00	30.00	7.50
☐	145	Pep Kelly	75.00	30.00	7.50
☐	146	Murray Armstrong	75.00	30.00	7.50
☐	147	Murph Chamberlain	75.00	30.00	7.50
☐	148	Des Smith	75.00	30.00	7.50
☐	149	Wilfred Cude	75.00	30.00	7.50
☐	150	Babe Siebert	175.00	70.00	18.00
☐	151	Bill MacKenzie	75.00	30.00	7.50
☐	152	Aurel Joliat	400.00	160.00	40.00
☐	153	Georges Mantha	75.00	30.00	7.50
☐	154	Johnny Gagnon	75.00	30.00	7.50
☐	155	Paul Haynes	75.00	30.00	7.50
☐	156	Joffre Desilets	75.00	30.00	7.50
☐	157	George Allen Brown	75.00	30.00	7.50
☐	158	Paul Drouin	75.00	30.00	7.50
☐	159	Pit Lepine	75.00	30.00	7.50
☐	160	Toe Blake	600.00	240.00	60.00
☐	161	Bill Beveridge	75.00	30.00	7.50
☐	162	Allan Shields	75.00	30.00	7.50
☐	163	Cy Wentworth	75.00	30.00	7.50
☐	164	Stew Evans	75.00	30.00	7.50
☐	165	Earl Robinson	75.00	30.00	7.50
☐	166	Baldy Northcott	75.00	30.00	7.50
☐	167	Paul Runge	75.00	30.00	7.50
☐	168	Dave Trottier	75.00	30.00	7.50
☐	169	Russ Blinco	75.00	30.00	7.50
☐	170	Jimmy Ward	75.00	30.00	7.50
☐	171	Bob Gracie	75.00	30.00	7.50
☐	172	Herb Cain	90.00	36.00	9.00
☐	173	Gus Marker	75.00	30.00	7.50
☐	174	Walter Buswell	75.00	30.00	7.50
☐	175	Carl Voss	150.00	60.00	15.00
☐	176	Rod Lorraine	75.00	30.00	7.50
☐	177	Armand Mondou	75.00	30.00	7.50
☐	178	Cliff(Red) Goupille	75.00	30.00	7.50
☐	179	Jerry Shannon	75.00	30.00	7.50
☐	180	Tom Cook	150.00	60.00	15.00

1939-40 O-Pee-Chee V301-1

This O-Pee-Chee set of 100 large cards was apparently issued during the 1939-40 season. The catalog designation for this set is V301-1. The cards are black and white and measure approximately 5" by 7". The card backs are blank. The cards are numbered on the front in the lower right corner. Cards in the set are identified on the front by name, team, and position. These cards were premiums and were issued one per cello pack.

	EX-MT	VG-E	GOOD
COMPLETE SET (100)	4500.00	1800.00	450.00
COMMON PLAYER (1-100)	30.00	12.00	3.00

☐	1	Reg Hamilton	40.00	16.00	4.00
☐	2	Turk Broda	200.00	80.00	20.00
☐	3	Bingo Kampman	30.00	12.00	3.00
☐	4	Gordie Drillon	60.00	24.00	6.00
☐	5	Bob Davidson	30.00	12.00	3.00
☐	6	Syl Apps	150.00	60.00	15.00
☐	7	Pete Langelle	30.00	12.00	3.00
☐	8	Don Metz	30.00	12.00	3.00
☐	9	Pep Kelly	30.00	12.00	3.00

☐	10	Red Horner	75.00	30.00	7.50
☐	11	Wally Stanowsky	30.00	12.00	3.00
☐	12	Murph Chamberlain	30.00	12.00	3.00
☐	13	Bucko MacDonald	30.00	12.00	3.00
☐	14	Sweeney Schriner	75.00	30.00	7.50
☐	15	Billy Taylor	30.00	12.00	3.00
☐	16	Gus Marker	30.00	12.00	3.00
☐	17	Hooley Smith	75.00	30.00	7.50
☐	18	Art Chapman	30.00	12.00	3.00
☐	19	Murray Armstrong	30.00	12.00	3.00
☐	20	Harvey(Busher) Jackson	125.00	50.00	12.50
☐	21	Buzz Boll	30.00	12.00	3.00
☐	22	Cliff(Red) Goupille	30.00	12.00	3.00
☐	23	Rod Lorraine	30.00	12.00	3.00
☐	24	Paul Drouin	30.00	12.00	3.00
☐	25	Johnny Gagnon	30.00	12.00	3.00
☐	26	Georges Mantha	30.00	12.00	3.00
☐	27	Armand Mondou	30.00	12.00	3.00
☐	28	Claude Bourque	30.00	12.00	3.00
☐	29	Ray Getliffe	30.00	12.00	3.00
☐	30	Cy Wentworth	30.00	12.00	3.00
☐	31	Paul Haynes	30.00	12.00	3.00
☐	32	Walter Buswell	30.00	12.00	3.00
☐	33	Ott Heller	30.00	12.00	3.00
☐	34	Arthur Coulter	60.00	24.00	6.00
☐	35	Clint Smith	75.00	30.00	7.50
☐	36	Lynn Patrick	75.00	30.00	7.50
☐	37	Dave Kerr	40.00	16.00	4.00
☐	38	Murray Patrick	40.00	16.00	4.00
☐	39	Neil Colville	75.00	30.00	7.50
☐	40	Jack Portland	30.00	12.00	3.00
☐	41	Flash Hollett	30.00	12.00	3.00
☐	42	Herb Cain	40.00	16.00	4.00
☐	43	Mud Bruneteau	40.00	16.00	4.00
☐	44	Cully Dahlstrom	30.00	12.00	3.00
☐	45	Harold(Mush) March	30.00	12.00	3.00
☐	46	Cully Dahlstrom	30.00	12.00	3.00
☐	47	Mike Karakas	40.00	16.00	4.00
☐	48	Bill Thoms	30.00	12.00	3.00
☐	49	Art Wiebe	30.00	12.00	3.00
☐	50	Johnny Gottselig	30.00	12.00	3.00
☐	51	Nick Metz	30.00	12.00	3.00
☐	52	Jack Church	30.00	12.00	3.00
☐	53	Bob(Red) Heron	30.00	12.00	3.00
☐	54	Hank Goldup	30.00	12.00	3.00
☐	55	Jimmy Fowler	30.00	12.00	3.00
☐	56	Charlie Sands	30.00	12.00	3.00
☐	57	Marty Barry	60.00	24.00	6.00
☐	58	Doug Young	30.00	12.00	3.00
☐	59	Charlie Conacher	200.00	80.00	20.00
☐	60	John Sorrell	30.00	12.00	3.00
☐	61	Tommy Anderson	30.00	12.00	3.00
☐	62	Lorne Carr	30.00	12.00	3.00
☐	63	Earl Robertson	30.00	12.00	3.00
☐	64	Wilfy Field	30.00	12.00	3.00
☐	65	Jimmy Orlando	30.00	12.00	3.00
☐	66	Ebbie Goodfellow	60.00	24.00	6.00
☐	67	Jack Keating	30.00	12.00	3.00
☐	68	Sid Abel	300.00	120.00	30.00
☐	69	Gus Giesebrecht	30.00	12.00	3.00
☐	70	Don Deacon	30.00	12.00	3.00
☐	71	Hec Kilrea	30.00	12.00	3.00
☐	72	Syd Howe	75.00	30.00	7.50
☐	73	Eddie Wares	30.00	12.00	3.00
☐	74	Carl Liscombe	30.00	12.00	3.00
☐	75	Tiny Thompson	60.00	24.00	6.00
☐	76	Earl Seibert	60.00	24.00	6.00
☐	77	Des Smith	30.00	12.00	3.00
☐	78	Les Cunningham	30.00	12.00	3.00
☐	79	Geo.Allen	30.00	12.00	3.00
☐	80	Bill Carse	30.00	12.00	3.00
☐	81	Bill McKenzie	30.00	12.00	3.00
☐	82	Ab DeMarco	30.00	12.00	3.00
☐	83	Phil Watson	40.00	16.00	4.00
☐	84	Alf Pike	30.00	12.00	3.00
☐	85	Babe Pratt	60.00	24.00	6.00
☐	86	Bryan Hextall	50.00	20.00	5.00
☐	87	Kilby MacDonald	30.00	12.00	3.00
☐	88	Alex Shibicky	30.00	12.00	3.00
☐	89	Dutch Hiller	30.00	12.00	3.00
☐	90	Mac Colville	30.00	12.00	3.00
☐	91	Roy Conacher	60.00	24.00	6.00
☐	92	Cooney Weiland	60.00	24.00	6.00
☐	93	Art Jackson	30.00	12.00	3.00
☐	94	Porky Dumart	100.00	40.00	10.00
☐	95	Dit Clapper	125.00	50.00	12.50
☐	96	Mel Hill	30.00	12.00	3.00
☐	97	Frank Brimsek	200.00	80.00	20.00
☐	98	Bill Cowley	100.00	40.00	10.00
☐	99	Bobby Bauer	40.00	16.00	4.00
☐	100	Eddie Shore	250.00	100.00	25.00

1940-41 O-Pee-Chee V301-2

This O-Pee-Chee set is continuously numbered from the 1939-40 O-Pee-Chee set. These large cards were apparently issued during the 1940-41 season. The catalog designation for this set is V301-2. The cards are sepia and measure approximately 5" by 7". The second series numbers are somewhat larger than the numbers used for the first series. The card backs are blank. The cards are numbered on the front in the lower right corner. Cards in the set are identified on the front by name, team, and position. These cards were premiums and were issued one per cello pack.

	EX-MT	VG-E	GOOD
COMPLETE SET (50)	3500.00	1400.00	350.00
COMMON PLAYER (101-125)	40.00	16.00	4.00
COMMON PLAYER (126-150)	60.00	24.00	6.00
☐ 101 Toe Blake	150.00	60.00	15.00
☐ 102 Charlie Sands	40.00	16.00	4.00
☐ 103 Wally Stanowski	40.00	16.00	4.00
☐ 104 Jack Adams	80.00	32.00	8.00
☐ 105 Johnny Mowers	40.00	16.00	4.00
☐ 106 Johnny Quilty	40.00	16.00	4.00
☐ 107 Billy Taylor	40.00	16.00	4.00
☐ 108 Turk Broda	200.00	80.00	20.00
☐ 109 Bingo Kampman	40.00	16.00	4.00
☐ 110 Gordie Drillon	80.00	32.00	8.00
☐ 111 Don Metz	40.00	16.00	4.00
☐ 112 Paul Haynes	40.00	16.00	4.00
☐ 113 Gus Marker	40.00	16.00	4.00
☐ 114 Alex Singbush	40.00	16.00	4.00
☐ 115 Alex Motter	40.00	16.00	4.00
☐ 116 Ken Reardon	125.00	50.00	12.50
☐ 117 Pete Langelle	40.00	16.00	4.00
☐ 118 Syl Apps	100.00	40.00	10.00
☐ 119 Reg. Hamilton	40.00	16.00	4.00
☐ 120 Cliff(Red) Goupille	40.00	16.00	4.00
☐ 121 Joe Benoit	40.00	16.00	4.00
☐ 122 Dave Schriner	80.00	32.00	8.00
☐ 123 Joe Carveth	40.00	16.00	4.00
☐ 124 Jack Stewart	80.00	32.00	8.00
☐ 125 Elmer Lach	125.00	50.00	12.50
☐ 126 Jack Schewchuk	60.00	24.00	6.00
☐ 127 Norman Larson	60.00	24.00	6.00
☐ 128 Don Grosso	60.00	24.00	6.00
☐ 129 Lester Douglas	60.00	24.00	6.00
☐ 130 Turk Broda	200.00	80.00	20.00
☐ 131 Max Bentley	250.00	100.00	25.00
☐ 132 Milt Schmidt	250.00	100.00	25.00
☐ 133 Nick Metz	60.00	24.00	6.00
☐ 134 Jack Crawford	60.00	24.00	6.00
☐ 135 Bill Benson	60.00	24.00	6.00
☐ 136 Lynn Patrick	125.00	50.00	12.50
☐ 137 Cully Dahlstrom	60.00	24.00	6.00
☐ 138 Mud Bruneteau	80.00	32.00	8.00
☐ 139 Dave Kerr	80.00	32.00	8.00
☐ 140 Bob(Red) Heron	60.00	24.00	6.00
☐ 141 Nick Metz	60.00	24.00	6.00
☐ 142 Ott Heller	60.00	24.00	6.00
☐ 143 Phil Hergesheimer	60.00	24.00	6.00
☐ 144 Tony Demers	60.00	24.00	6.00
☐ 145 Archie Wilder	60.00	24.00	6.00
☐ 146 Syl Apps	200.00	80.00	20.00
☐ 147 Ray Getliffe	60.00	24.00	6.00
☐ 148 Lex Chisholm	60.00	24.00	6.00
☐ 149 Eddie Wiseman	60.00	24.00	6.00
☐ 150 Paul Goodman	80.00	32.00	8.00

1968-69 O-Pee-Chee

The 1968-69 O-Pee-Chee set contains 216 color cards. The cards measure the standard 2 1/2" by 3 1/2". The cards were originally sold in five-cent wax packs. The horizontally oriented fronts feature the player in the foreground with an artistically rendered hockey scene in the background. The bilingual backs are printed in red and black ink. The player's 1967-68 and career statistics, a short biography, and a cartoon-illustrated fact about the player are included on the back. The cards were printed in Canada and were issued by O-Pee-Chee; even though the Topps Gum copyright is found on the reverse. The O-Pee-Chee set features many different poses from the corresponding Topps cards. Card number 193 can be found either numbered or unnumbered. Rookie Cards in this set include Bernie Parent, Mickey Redmond and Gary Unger.

	NRMT	VG-E	GOOD
COMPLETE SET (216)	1500.00	700.00	190.00
COMMON PLAYER (1-216)	5.00	2.30	.60
☐ 1 Doug Harvey	25.00	6.25	2.00
☐ 2 Bobby Orr	350.00	160.00	45.00
☐ 3 Don Awrey UER	5.00	2.30	.60
(Photo actually Skip Krake)			
☐ 4 Ted Green	6.00	2.70	.75
☐ 5 Johnny Bucyk	10.00	4.50	1.25
☐ 6 Derek Sanderson	20.00	9.00	2.50
☐ 7 Phil Esposito	40.00	18.00	5.00
☐ 8 Ken Hodge	6.00	2.70	.75
☐ 9 John McKenzie	6.00	2.70	.75
☐ 10 Fred Stanfield	5.00	2.30	.60
☐ 11 Tom Williams	5.00	2.30	.60
☐ 12 Denis DeJordy	6.00	2.70	.75
☐ 13 Doug Jarrett	5.00	2.30	.60
☐ 14 Gilles Marotte	5.00	2.30	.60
☐ 15 Pat Stapleton	6.00	2.70	.75
☐ 16 Bobby Hull	80.00	36.00	10.00
☐ 17 Chico Maki	5.00	2.30	.60
☐ 18 Pit Martin	6.00	2.70	.75
☐ 19 Doug Mohns	5.00	2.30	.60
☐ 20 John Ferguson	6.00	2.70	.75
☐ 21 Jim Pappin	5.00	2.30	.60
☐ 22 Ken Wharram	5.00	2.30	.60
☐ 23 Roger Crozier	6.00	2.70	.75
☐ 24 Bob Baun	6.00	2.70	.75
☐ 25 Gary Bergman	5.00	2.30	.60
☐ 26 Kent Douglas	5.00	2.30	.60
☐ 27 Ron Harris	5.00	2.30	.60
☐ 28 Alex Delvecchio	9.00	4.00	1.15
☐ 29 Gordie Howe	100.00	45.00	12.50
☐ 30 Bruce MacGregor	5.00	2.30	.60
☐ 31 Frank Mahovlich	15.00	6.75	1.90
☐ 32 Dean Prentice	5.00	2.30	.60
☐ 33 Pete Stemkowski	5.00	2.30	.60
☐ 34 Terry Sawchuk	40.00	18.00	5.00
☐ 35 Larry Cahan	5.00	2.30	.60
☐ 36 Real Lemieux	5.00	2.30	.60

☐ 37	Bill White	7.00	3.10	.85
☐ 38	Gord Labossiere	5.00	2.30	.60
☐ 39	Ted Irvine	5.00	2.30	.60
☐ 40	Eddie Joyal	5.00	2.30	.60
☐ 41	Dale Rolfe	5.00	2.30	.60
☐ 42	Lowell MacDonald	7.00	3.10	.85
☐ 43	Skip Krake UER	5.00	2.30	.60
	(Photo actually			
	Don Awrey)			
☐ 44	Terry Gray	5.00	2.30	.60
☐ 45	Cesare Maniago	6.00	2.70	.75
☐ 46	Mike McMahon	5.00	2.30	.60
☐ 47	Wayne Hillman	5.00	2.30	.60
☐ 48	Larry Hillman	5.00	2.30	.60
☐ 49	Bob Woytowich	5.00	2.30	.60
☐ 50	Wayne Connelly	5.00	2.30	.60
☐ 51	Claude Larose	5.00	2.30	.60
☐ 52	Danny Grant	8.00	3.60	1.00
☐ 53	Andre Boudrias	5.00	2.30	.60
☐ 54	Ray Cullen	6.00	2.70	.75
☐ 55	Parker MacDonald	5.00	2.30	.60
☐ 56	Gump Worsley	10.00	4.50	1.25
☐ 57	Terry Harper	5.00	2.30	.60
☐ 58	Jacques Laperriere	6.00	2.70	.75
☐ 59	J.C. Tremblay	5.00	2.30	.60
☐ 60	Ralph Backstrom	6.00	2.70	.75
☐ 61	Checklist 2	125.00	12.50	2.50
☐ 62	Yvan Cournoyer	15.00	6.75	1.90
☐ 63	Jacques Lemaire	20.00	9.00	2.50
☐ 64	Mickey Redmond	25.00	11.50	3.10
☐ 65	Bobby Rousseau	5.00	2.30	.60
☐ 66	Gilles Tremblay	5.00	2.30	.60
☐ 67	Ed Giacomin	20.00	9.00	2.50
☐ 68	Arnie Brown	5.00	2.30	.60
☐ 69	Harry Howell	6.00	2.70	.75
☐ 70	Al Hamilton	5.00	2.30	.60
☐ 71	Rod Seiling	5.00	2.30	.60
☐ 72	Rod Gilbert	10.00	4.50	1.25
☐ 73	Phil Goyette	5.00	2.30	.60
☐ 74	Larry Jeffrey	5.00	2.30	.60
☐ 75	Don Marshall	5.00	2.30	.60
☐ 76	Bob Nevin	6.00	2.70	.75
☐ 77	Jean Ratelle	10.00	4.50	1.25
☐ 78	Charlie Hodge	6.00	2.70	.75
☐ 79	Bert Marshall	5.00	2.30	.60
☐ 80	Billy Harris	5.00	2.30	.60
☐ 81	Carol Vadnais	6.00	2.70	.75
☐ 82	Howie Young	5.00	2.30	.60
☐ 83	John Brenneman	5.00	2.30	.60
☐ 84	Gerry Ehman	5.00	2.30	.60
☐ 85	Ted Hampson	5.00	2.30	.60
☐ 86	Bill Hicke	5.00	2.30	.60
☐ 87	Gary Jarrett	5.00	2.30	.60
☐ 88	Doug Roberts	5.00	2.30	.60
☐ 89	Bernie Parent	100.00	45.00	12.50
☐ 90	Joe Watson	5.00	2.30	.60
☐ 91	Ed Van Impe	5.00	2.30	.60
☐ 92	Larry Zeidel	5.00	2.30	.60
☐ 93	John Miszuk	5.00	2.30	.60
☐ 94	Gary Dornhoefer	6.00	2.70	.75
☐ 95	Leon Rochefort	5.00	2.30	.60
☐ 96	Brit Selby	5.00	2.30	.60
☐ 97	Forbes Kennedy	5.00	2.30	.60
☐ 98	Ed Hoekstra	5.00	2.30	.60
☐ 99	Garry Peters	5.00	2.30	.60
☐ 100	Les Binkley	8.00	3.60	1.00
☐ 101	Leo Boivin	5.00	2.30	.60
☐ 102	Earl Ingarfield	5.00	2.30	.60
☐ 103	Lou Angotti	5.00	2.30	.60
☐ 104	Andy Bathgate	6.00	2.70	.75
☐ 105	Wally Boyer	5.00	2.30	.60
☐ 106	Ken Schinkel	5.00	2.30	.60
☐ 107	Ab McDonald	5.00	2.30	.60
☐ 108	Charlie Burns	5.00	2.30	.60
☐ 109	Val Fonteyne	5.00	2.30	.60
☐ 110	Noel Price	5.00	2.30	.60
☐ 111	Glenn Hall	12.00	5.50	1.50
☐ 112	Bob Plager	10.00	4.50	1.25
☐ 113	Jim Roberts	5.00	2.30	.60
☐ 114	Red Berenson	6.00	2.70	.75
☐ 115	Larry Keenan	5.00	2.30	.60
☐ 116	Camille Henry	5.00	2.30	.60
☐ 117	Gary Sabourin	5.00	2.30	.60
☐ 118	Ron Schock	5.00	2.30	.60
☐ 119	Gary Veneruzzo	5.00	2.30	.60
☐ 120	Gerry Melnyk	5.00	2.30	.60
☐ 121	Checklist Card	125.00	12.50	2.50
☐ 122	Johnny Bower	8.00	3.60	1.00
☐ 123	Tim Horton	15.00	6.75	1.90
☐ 124	Pierre Pilote	5.00	2.30	.60
☐ 125	Marcel Pronovost	5.00	2.30	.60
☐ 126	Ron Ellis	6.00	2.70	.75
☐ 127	Paul Henderson	6.00	2.70	.75
☐ 128	Al Arbour	7.00	3.10	.85
☐ 129	Bob Pulford	6.00	2.70	.75
☐ 130	Floyd Smith	5.00	2.30	.60
☐ 131	Norm Ullman	8.00	3.60	1.00
☐ 132	Mike Walton	6.00	2.70	.75
☐ 133	Ed Johnston	6.00	2.70	.75
☐ 134	Glen Sather	10.00	4.50	1.25
☐ 135	Ed Westfall	6.00	2.70	.75
☐ 136	Dallas Smith	5.00	2.30	.60
☐ 137	Eddie Shack	9.00	4.00	1.15
☐ 138	Gary Doak	5.00	2.30	.60
☐ 139	Ron Murphy	5.00	2.30	.60
☐ 140	Gerry Cheevers	20.00	9.00	2.50
☐ 141	Bob Falkenberg	5.00	2.30	.60
☐ 142	Garry Unger	15.00	6.75	1.90
☐ 143	Peter Mahovlich	6.00	2.70	.75
☐ 144	Roy Edwards	6.00	2.70	.75
☐ 145	Gary Bauman	6.00	2.70	.75
☐ 146	Bob McCord	5.00	2.30	.60
☐ 147	Elmer Vasko	5.00	2.30	.60
☐ 148	Bill Goldsworthy	10.00	4.50	1.25
☐ 149	Jean-Paul Parise	7.00	3.10	.85
☐ 150	Dave Dryden	6.00	2.70	.75
☐ 151	Howie Young	5.00	2.30	.60
☐ 152	Matt Ravlich	5.00	2.30	.60
☐ 153	Dennis Hull	6.00	2.70	.75
☐ 154	Eric Nesterenko	6.00	2.70	.75
☐ 155	Stan Mikita	30.00	13.50	3.80
☐ 156	Bob Wall	5.00	2.30	.60
☐ 157	Dave Amadio	5.00	2.30	.60
☐ 158	Howie Hughes	5.00	2.30	.60
☐ 159	Bill Flett	7.00	3.10	.85
☐ 160	Doug Robinson	5.00	2.30	.60
☐ 161	Dick Duff	6.00	2.70	.75
☐ 162	Ted Harris	5.00	2.30	.60
☐ 163	Claude Provost	5.00	2.30	.60
☐ 164	Rogatien Vachon	25.00	11.50	3.10
☐ 165	Henri Richard	12.00	5.50	1.50
☐ 166	Jean Beliveau	22.00	10.00	2.80
☐ 167	Reg Fleming	5.00	2.30	.60
☐ 168	Ron Stewart	5.00	2.30	.60
☐ 169	Dave Balon	5.00	2.30	.60
☐ 170	Orland Kurtenbach	5.00	2.30	.60
☐ 171	Vic Hadfield	6.00	2.70	.75
☐ 172	Jim Neilson	5.00	2.30	.60
☐ 173	Bryan Watson	5.00	2.30	.60
☐ 174	George Swarbrick	5.00	2.30	.60
☐ 175	Joe Szura	5.00	2.30	.60
☐ 176	Gary Smith	8.00	3.60	1.00
☐ 177	Barclay Plager UER	9.00	4.00	1.15
	(Photo actually			
	Bob Plager)			
☐ 178	Tim Ecclestone	5.00	2.30	.60
☐ 179	Jean-Guy Talbot	5.00	2.30	.60
☐ 180	Ab McDonald	5.00	2.30	.60
☐ 181	Jacques Plante	40.00	18.00	5.00
☐ 182	Bill McCreary	5.00	2.30	.60
☐ 183	Allan Stanley	6.00	2.70	.75
☐ 184	Andre Lacroix	10.00	4.50	1.25
☐ 185	Jean-Guy Gendron	5.00	2.30	.60
☐ 186	Jim Johnson	5.00	2.30	.60
☐ 187	Simon Nolet	7.00	3.10	.85
☐ 188	Joe Daley	9.00	4.00	1.15
☐ 189	John Arbour	5.00	2.30	.60
☐ 190	Billy Dea	5.00	2.30	.60
☐ 191	Bob Dillabough	5.00	2.30	.60
☐ 192	Bob Woytowich	5.00	2.30	.60
☐ 193A	Keith McCreary ERR	7.00	3.10	.85
	(No number)			
☐ 193B	Keith McCreary COR	5.00	2.30	.60
☐ 194	Murray Oliver	5.00	2.30	.60
☐ 195	Larry Mickey	5.00	2.30	.60
☐ 196	Bill Sutherland	5.00	2.30	.60
☐ 197	Bruce Gamble	6.00	2.70	.75
☐ 198	Dave Keon	9.00	4.00	1.15
☐ 199	Gump Worsley AS1	7.00	3.10	.85
☐ 200	Bobby Orr AS1	150.00	70.00	19.00
☐ 201	Tim Horton AS1	8.00	3.60	1.00
☐ 202	Stan Mikita AS1	15.00	6.75	1.90
☐ 203	Gordie Howe AS1	60.00	27.00	7.50
☐ 204	Bobby Hull AS1	50.00	23.00	6.25
☐ 205	Ed Giacomin AS2	10.00	4.50	1.25
☐ 206	J.C. Tremblay AS2	5.00	2.30	.60
☐ 207	Jim Neilson AS2	5.00	2.30	.60
☐ 208	Phil Esposito AS2	25.00	11.50	3.10
☐ 209	Rod Gilbert AS2	6.00	2.70	.75
☐ 210	Johnny Bucyk AS2	6.00	2.70	.75
☐ 211	Stan Mikita	15.00	6.75	1.90
	Hart Trophy			
	Ross Trophy			
	Lady Byng Trophy			
☐ 212	Worsley/Vachon	20.00	9.00	2.50
	Vezina Trophy			

		NRMT	VG-E	GOOD
☐ 213	Derek Sanderson.................	10.00	4.50	1.25
	Calder Trophy			
☐ 214	Bobby Orr	150.00	70.00	19.00
	Norris Trophy			
☐ 215	Glenn Hall	9.00	4.00	1.15
	Conn Smythe Trophy			
☐ 216	Claude Provost..................	10.00	2.50	.80
	Masterson Trophy			

1968-69 O-Pee-Chee Puck Stickers

No. 1 of 21

This set consists of 22 numbered (on the front), full-color stickers measuring 2 1/2" by 3 1/2". The card backs are blank and contain an adhesive. These stickers were printed in Canada and were inserted one per pack in 1968-69 O-Pee-Chee regular issue hockey packs. The pucks were perforated so that they could be punched out; this is obviously not recommended. Sticker card 22 is a special card honoring Gordie Howe's 700th goal.

	NRMT	VG-E	GOOD
COMPLETE SET (22)......................	250.00	100.00	25.00
COMMON PLAYER (1-22)...............	3.00	1.20	.30

		NRMT	VG-E	GOOD
☐ 1	Stan Mikita.........................	12.00	5.00	1.20
☐ 2	Frank Mahovlich..................	12.00	5.00	1.20
☐ 3	Bobby Hull	30.00	12.00	3.00
☐ 4	Bobby Orr	50.00	20.00	5.00
☐ 5	Phil Esposito	15.00	6.00	1.50
☐ 6	Gump Worsley	9.00	3.75	.90
☐ 7	Jean Beliveau	15.00	6.00	1.50
☐ 8	Elmer Vasko	3.00	1.20	.30
☐ 9	Rod Gilbert	7.50	3.00	.75
☐ 10	Roger Crozier......................	3.00	1.20	.30
☐ 11	Lou Angotti	3.00	1.20	.30
☐ 12	Charlie Hodge	4.00	1.60	.40
☐ 13	Glenn Hall	9.00	3.75	.90
☐ 14	Doug Harvey	9.00	3.75	.90
☐ 15	Jacques Plante	12.00	5.00	1.20
☐ 16	Allan Stanley	7.50	3.00	.75
☐ 17	Johnny Bower......................	7.50	3.00	.75
☐ 18	Tim Horton..........................	9.00	3.75	.90
☐ 19	Dave Keon	7.50	3.00	.75
☐ 20	Terry Sawchuk	15.00	6.00	1.50
☐ 21	Henri Richard	9.00	3.75	.90
☐ 22	Gordie Howe Special............	50.00	20.00	5.00
	(700th Goal)			

1969-70 O-Pee-Chee

The 1969-70 O-Pee-Chee set contains 231 color cards issued in two series. The cards measure the standard 2 1/2" by 3 1/2". Bilingual backs contain 1968-69 and career statistics, a short biography and a cartoon-illustrated fact about the player. The cards were printed in Canada with the Topps Gum Company copyright appearing on the reverse. Many player poses in this set are different from the corresponding player poses of the Topps set of this year.

HENRI RICHARD
CANADIENS   CENTER

Card 193 Gordie Howe "Mr. Hockey" exists with or without the card number. Wax packs from both series were originally sold for ten cents and contained an insert. The first series insert was a player stamp and the second series insert was a four-in-one standard size card panel. The stamps could be placed on the back of the regular issue cards in a space provided. A card with a stamp on the back is considered to be of less value than one without the stamp. Rookie Cards include Tony Esposito and Serge Savard.

	NRMT	VG-E	GOOD
COMPLETE SET (231).....................	1300.00	575.00	160.00
COMMON PLAYER (1-132)..............	3.50	1.55	.45
COMMON PLAYER (133-231)..........	3.50	1.55	.45

		NRMT	VG-E	GOOD
☐ 1	Gump Worsley	20.00	5.00	1.60
☐ 2	Ted Harris	3.50	1.55	.45
☐ 3	Jacques Laperriere.................	4.00	1.80	.50
☐ 4	Serge Savard	35.00	16.00	4.40
☐ 5	J.C. Tremblay	3.50	1.55	.45
☐ 6	Yvan Cournoyer	10.00	4.50	1.25
☐ 7	John Ferguson	4.00	1.80	.50
☐ 8	Jacques Lemaire..................	12.00	5.50	1.50
☐ 9	Bobby Rousseau	3.50	1.55	.45
☐ 10	Jean Beliveau	18.00	8.00	2.30
☐ 11	Dick Duff	4.00	1.80	.50
☐ 12	Glenn Hall	10.00	4.50	1.25
☐ 13	Bob Plager	4.00	1.80	.50
☐ 14	Ron Anderson	3.50	1.55	.45
☐ 15	Jean-Guy Talbot	3.50	1.55	.45
☐ 16	Andre Boudrias	3.50	1.55	.45
☐ 17	Camille Henry.....................	3.50	1.55	.45
☐ 18	Ab McDonald	3.50	1.55	.45
☐ 19	Gary Sabourin	3.50	1.55	.45
☐ 20	Red Berenson	4.00	1.80	.50
☐ 21	Phil Goyette........................	3.50	1.55	.45
☐ 22	Gerry Cheevers	15.00	6.75	1.90
☐ 23	Ted Green	4.00	1.80	.50
☐ 24	Bobby Orr	175.00	80.00	22.00
☐ 25	Dallas Smith	3.50	1.55	.45
☐ 26	Johnny Bucyk	6.00	2.70	.75
☐ 27	Ken Hodge	4.00	1.80	.50
☐ 28	John McKenzie	4.00	1.80	.50
☐ 29	Ed Westfall	4.00	1.80	.50
☐ 30	Phil Esposito	30.00	13.50	3.80
☐ 31	Checklist 2	90.00	9.00	1.80
☐ 32	Fred Stanfield	3.50	1.55	.45
☐ 33	Ed Giacomin........................	15.00	6.75	1.90
☐ 34	Arnie Brown	3.50	1.55	.45
☐ 35	Jim Neilson	3.50	1.55	.45
☐ 36	Rod Seiling	3.50	1.55	.45
☐ 37	Rod Gilbert.........................	7.50	3.40	.95
☐ 38	Vic Hadfield	4.00	1.80	.50
☐ 39	Don Marshall.......................	3.50	1.55	.45
☐ 40	Bob Nevin	4.00	1.80	.50
☐ 41	Ron Stewart	3.50	1.55	.45
☐ 42	Jean Ratelle........................	7.50	3.40	.95
☐ 43	Walt Tkaczuk.......................	7.00	3.10	.85
☐ 44	Bruce Gamble	4.00	1.80	.50
☐ 45	Jim Dorey	3.50	1.55	.45
☐ 46	Ron Ellis	4.00	1.80	.50
☐ 47	Paul Henderson....................	4.00	1.80	.50
☐ 48	Brit Selby	3.50	1.55	.45
☐ 49	Floyd Smith.........................	3.50	1.55	.45
☐ 50	Mike Walton	4.00	1.80	.50
☐ 51	Dave Keon	7.00	3.10	.85
☐ 52	Murray Oliver	3.50	1.55	.45
☐ 53	Bob Pulford.........................	4.00	1.80	.50
☐ 54	Norm Ullman	6.00	2.70	.75
☐ 55	Roger Crozier......................	4.00	1.80	.50

☐	56	Roy Edwards	4.00	1.80	.50	☐ 149	Gene Ubriaco	3.50	1.55	.45
☐	57	Bob Baun	4.00	1.80	.50	☐ 150	Bob Dillabough	3.50	1.55	.45
☐	58	Gary Bergman	3.50	1.55	.45	☐ 151	Bob Woytowich	3.50	1.55	.45
☐	59	Carl Brewer	4.00	1.80	.50	☐ 152	Joe Daley	4.00	1.80	.50
☐	60	Wayne Connelly	3.50	1.55	.45	☐ 153	Duane Rupp	3.50	1.55	.45
☐	61	Gordie Howe	80.00	36.00	10.00	☐ 154	Bryan Hextall	6.00	2.70	.75
☐	62	Frank Mahovlich	12.00	5.50	1.50	☐ 155	Jean Pronovost	5.00	2.30	.60
☐	63	Bruce MacGregor	3.50	1.55	.45	☐ 156	Jim Morrison	3.50	1.55	.45
☐	64	Ron Harris	3.50	1.55	.45	☐ 157	Alex Delvecchio	7.00	3.10	.85
☐	65	Pete Stemkowski	3.50	1.55	.45	☐ 158	Poul Popiel	3.50	1.55	.45
☐	66	Denis DeJordy	4.00	1.80	.50	☐ 159	Garry Unger	6.00	2.70	.75
☐	67	Doug Jarrett	3.50	1.55	.45	☐ 160	Garry Monahan	3.50	1.55	.45
☐	68	Gilles Marotte	3.50	1.55	.45	☐ 161	Matt Ravlich	3.50	1.55	.45
☐	69	Pat Stapleton	4.00	1.80	.50	☐ 162	Nick Libett	5.00	2.30	.60
☐	70	Bobby Hull	70.00	32.00	8.75	☐ 163	Henri Richard	10.00	4.50	1.25
☐	71	Dennis Hull	4.00	1.80	.50	☐ 164	Terry Harper	4.00	1.80	.50
☐	72	Doug Mohns	3.50	1.55	.45	☐ 165	Rogatien Vachon	12.00	5.50	1.50
☐	73	Howie Menard	3.50	1.55	.45	☐ 166	Ralph Backstrom	4.00	1.80	.50
☐	74	Ken Wharram	3.50	1.55	.45	☐ 167	Claude Provost	3.50	1.55	.45
☐	75	Pit Martin	4.00	1.80	.50	☐ 168	Gilles Tremblay	3.50	1.55	.45
☐	76	Stan Mikita	25.00	11.50	3.10	☐ 169	Jean-Guy Gendron	3.50	1.55	.45
☐	77	Charlie Hodge	4.00	1.80	.50	☐ 170	Earl Heiskala	3.50	1.55	.45
☐	78	Gary Smith	4.00	1.80	.50	☐ 171	Garry Peters	3.50	1.55	.45
☐	79	Harry Howell	4.00	1.80	.50	☐ 172	Bill Sutherland	3.50	1.55	.45
☐	80	Bert Marshall	3.50	1.55	.45	☐ 173	Dick Cherry	3.50	1.55	.45
☐	81	Doug Roberts	3.50	1.55	.45	☐ 174	Jim Roberts	4.00	1.80	.50
☐	82	Carol Vadnais	4.00	1.80	.50	☐ 175	Noel Picard	3.50	1.55	.45
☐	83	Gerry Ehman	3.50	1.55	.45	☐ 176	Barclay Plager	4.00	1.80	.50
☐	84	Brian Perry	3.50	1.55	.45	☐ 177	Frank St.Marseille	3.50	1.55	.45
☐	85	Gary Jarrett	3.50	1.55	.45	☐ 178	Al Arbour	5.00	2.30	.60
☐	86	Ted Hampson	3.50	1.55	.45	☐ 179	Tim Ecclestone	3.50	1.55	.45
☐	87	Earl Ingarfield	3.50	1.55	.45	☐ 180	Jacques Plante	30.00	13.50	3.80
☐	88	Doug Favell	10.00	4.50	1.25	☐ 181	Bill McCreary	3.50	1.55	.45
☐	89	Bernie Parent	40.00	18.00	5.00	☐ 182	Tim Horton	10.00	4.50	1.25
☐	90	Larry Hillman	3.50	1.55	.45	☐ 183	Rick Ley	5.00	2.30	.60
☐	91	Wayne Hillman	3.50	1.55	.45	☐ 184	Wayne Carleton	3.50	1.55	.45
☐	92	Ed Van Impe	3.50	1.55	.45	☐ 185	Marv Edwards	4.00	1.80	.50
☐	93	Joe Watson	3.50	1.55	.45	☐ 186	Pat Quinn	15.00	6.75	1.90
☐	94	Gary Dornhoefer	4.00	1.80	.50	☐ 187	Johnny Bower	6.00	2.70	.75
☐	95	Reg Fleming	3.50	1.55	.45	☐ 188	Orland Kurtenbach	3.50	1.55	.45
☐	96	Ralph McSweyn	3.50	1.55	.45	☐ 189	Terry Sawchuk	35.00	16.00	4.40
☐	97	Jim Johnson	3.50	1.55	.45	☐ 190	Real Lemieux	3.50	1.55	.45
☐	98	Andre Lacroix	5.00	2.30	.60	☐ 191	Dave Balon	3.50	1.55	.45
☐	99	Gerry Desjardins	6.00	2.70	.75	☐ 192	Al Hamilton	3.50	1.55	.45
☐	100	Dale Rolfe	3.50	1.55	.45	☐ 193A	Gordie Howe ERR	150.00	70.00	19.00
☐	101	Bill White	3.50	1.55	.45		"Mr. Hockey"			
☐	102	Bill Flett	3.50	1.55	.45		(No number)			
☐	103	Ted Irvine	3.50	1.55	.45	☐ 193B	Gordie Howe COR	175.00	80.00	22.00
☐	104	Ross Lonsberry	4.00	1.80	.50		"Mr. Hockey"			
☐	105	Leon Rochefort	3.50	1.55	.45	☐ 194	Claude Larose	3.50	1.55	.45
☐	106	Bryan Campbell	3.50	1.55	.45	☐ 195	Bill Goldsworthy	4.00	1.80	.50
☐	107	Dennis Hextall	5.00	2.30	.60	☐ 196	Bob Barlow	3.50	1.55	.45
☐	108	Eddie Joyal	3.50	1.55	.45	☐ 197	Ken Broderick	4.00	1.80	.50
☐	109	Gord Labossiere	3.50	1.55	.45	☐ 198	Lou Nanne	5.00	2.30	.60
☐	110	Les Binkley	4.00	1.80	.50	☐ 199	Tom Polonic	3.50	1.55	.45
☐	111	Tracy Pratt	3.50	1.55	.45	☐ 200	Ed Johnston	4.00	1.80	.50
☐	112	Bryan Watson	3.50	1.55	.45	☐ 201	Derek Sanderson	12.00	5.50	1.50
☐	113	Bob Blackburn	3.50	1.55	.45	☐ 202	Gary Doak	3.50	1.55	.45
☐	114	Keith McCreary	3.50	1.55	.45	☐ 203	Don Awrey	3.50	1.55	.45
☐	115	Dean Prentice	3.50	1.55	.45	☐ 204	Ron Murphy	3.50	1.55	.45
☐	116	Glen Sather	6.00	2.70	.75	☐ 205A	Phil Esposito	25.00	11.50	3.10
☐	117	Ken Schinkel	3.50	1.55	.45		Art Ross Trophy			
☐	118	Wally Boyer	3.50	1.55	.45		Hart Trophy			
☐	119	Val Fonteyne	3.50	1.55	.45		(214 on back and			
☐	120	Ron Schock	3.50	1.55	.45		no number on front)			
☐	121	Cesare Maniago	4.00	1.80	.50	☐ 205B	Phil Esposito	20.00	9.00	2.50
☐	122	Leo Boivin	3.50	1.55	.45		Art Ross Trophy			
☐	123	Bob McCord	3.50	1.55	.45		Hart Trophy			
☐	124	John Miszuk	3.50	1.55	.45		(214 on back and			
☐	125	Danny Grant	4.00	1.80	.50		205 on front)			
☐	126	Bill Collins	3.50	1.55	.45	☐ 206	Alex Delvecchio	5.00	2.30	.60
☐	127	Jean-Paul Parise	4.00	1.80	.50		Lady Byng			
☐	128	Tom Williams	3.50	1.55	.45	☐ 207	Vezina Trophy	30.00	13.50	3.80
☐	129	Charlie Burns	3.50	1.55	.45		Winners:			
☐	130	Ray Cullen	3.50	1.55	.45		Jacques Plante and			
☐	131	Danny O'Shea	3.50	1.55	.45		Glenn Hall			
☐	132	Checklist 1	90.00	9.00	1.80	☐ 208	Danny Grant	3.50	1.55	.45
☐	133	Jim Pappin	3.50	1.55	.45		Calder Trophy			
☐	134	Lou Angotti	3.50	1.55	.45	☐ 209	Bobby Orr	75.00	34.00	9.50
☐	135	Terry Cafery	3.50	1.55	.45		Norris Trophy			
☐	136	Eric Nesterenko	4.00	1.80	.50	☐ 210	Serge Savard	10.00	4.50	1.25
☐	137	Chico Maki	3.50	1.55	.45		Conn Smythe Trophy			
☐	138	Tony Esposito	135.00	60.00	17.00	☐ 211	Glenn Hall AS	7.00	3.10	.85
☐	139	Eddie Shack	6.00	2.70	.75	☐ 212	Bobby Orr AS	75.00	34.00	9.50
☐	140	Bob Wall	3.50	1.55	.45	☐ 213	Tim Horton AS	5.00	2.30	.60
☐	141	Skip Krake	3.50	1.55	.45	☐ 214	Phil Esposito AS	20.00	9.00	2.50
☐	142	Howie Hughes	3.50	1.55	.45	☐ 215	Gordie Howe AS	50.00	23.00	6.25
☐	143	Jimmy Peters	3.50	1.55	.45	☐ 216	Bobby Hull AS	35.00	16.00	4.40
☐	144	Brent Hughes	3.50	1.55	.45	☐ 217	Ed Giacomin AS	7.50	3.40	.95
☐	145	Bill Hicke	3.50	1.55	.45	☐ 218	Ted Green AS	4.00	1.80	.50
☐	146	Norm Ferguson	3.50	1.55	.45	☐ 219	Ted Harris AS	3.50	1.55	.45
☐	147	Dick Mattiussi	3.50	1.55	.45	☐ 220	Jean Beliveau AS	10.00	4.50	1.25
☐	148	Mike Laughton	3.50	1.55	.45	☐ 221	Yvan Cournoyer AS	5.00	2.30	.60

			NRMT	VG-E	GOOD
☐	222	Frank Mahovlich AS	8.00	3.60	1.00
☐	223	Art Ross Trophy	5.00	2.30	.60
☐	224	Hart Trophy	5.00	2.30	.60
☐	225	Lady Byng Trophy	5.00	2.30	.60
☐	226	Vezina Trophy	5.00	2.30	.60
☐	227	Calder Trophy	5.00	2.30	.60
☐	228	James Norris Trophy	5.00	2.30	.60
☐	229	Conn Smythe Trophy	5.00	2.30	.60
☐	230	Prince of Wales Trophy	5.00	2.30	.60
☐	231	The Stanley Cup	40.00	10.00	3.20

1969-70 O-Pee-Chee Stamps

The 1969-70 O-Pee-Chee Stamps set contains 26 black and white stamps measuring approximately 1 1/2" by 1 1/4". The stamps were distributed with the first series of regular 1969-70 O-Pee-Chee hockey cards and may also have been available in some of the Topps wax packs of that year as well. The stamps are unnumbered and hence are checklisted below alphabetically for convenience. Apparently the card company intended for the stamps to be stuck on the blank space provided on the backs of the corresponding regular card; collectors are strongly encouraged NOT to follow that procedure. The stamps were produced as pairs; intact pairs are now valued at double the sum of the individual player prices listed below.

		NRMT	VG-E	GOOD
COMPLETE SET (26)		125.00	50.00	12.50
COMMON PLAYER (1-26)		2.50	1.00	.25
☐ 1	Jean Beliveau	12.00	5.00	1.20
☐ 2	Red Berenson	3.50	1.40	.35
☐ 3	Les Binkley	2.50	1.00	.25
☐ 4	Yvan Cournoyer	7.50	3.00	.75
☐ 5	Ray Cullen	2.50	1.00	.25
☐ 6	Gerry Desjardins	2.50	1.00	.25
☐ 7	Phil Esposito	12.00	5.00	1.20
☐ 8	Ed Giacomin	7.50	3.00	.75
☐ 9	Rod Gilbert	7.50	3.00	.75
☐ 10	Danny Grant	2.50	1.00	.25
☐ 11	Glenn Hall	7.50	3.00	.75
☐ 12	Ted Hampson	2.50	1.00	.25
☐ 13	Ken Hodge	3.50	1.40	.35
☐ 14	Gordie Howe	25.00	10.00	2.50
☐ 15	Bobby Hull	15.00	6.00	1.50
☐ 16	Eddie Joyal	2.50	1.00	.25
☐ 17	Dave Keon	7.50	3.00	.75
☐ 18	Andre Lacroix	3.50	1.40	.35
☐ 19	Frank Mahovlich	10.00	4.00	1.00
☐ 20	Keith McCreary	2.50	1.00	.25
☐ 21	Stan Mikita	10.00	4.00	1.00
☐ 22	Bobby Orr	25.00	10.00	2.50
☐ 23	Bernie Parent	9.00	3.75	.90
☐ 24	Jean Ratelle	7.50	3.00	.75
☐ 25	Norm Ullman	6.00	2.40	.60
☐ 26	Carol Vadnais	2.50	1.00	.25

1969-70 O-Pee-Chee Four-in-One

The 1969-70 O-Pee-Chee Four-in-One set contains 18 four-player adhesive-backed color cards. The cards are standard size, 2 1/2" by 3 1/2", whereas the individual mini-cards are approximately 1" by 1 1/2". These small cards could be

separated and then stuck in a small team album/booklet that was also available that year from O-Pee-Chee. This set was distributed as an insert with the second series of regular 1969-70 O-Pee-Chee cards. Cards that have been separated into the mini-cards have very little value. The cards are unnumbered and so they are checklisted below alphabetically by the (upper left corner) player's name.

		NRMT	VG-E	GOOD
COMPLETE SET (18)		750.00	300.00	75.00
COMMON CARD (1-18)		25.00	10.00	2.50
☐ 1	Bob Baun Ken Schinkel Tim Horton Bernie Parent	35.00	14.00	3.50
☐ 2	Les Binkley Ken Hodge Reg Fleming Jacques Laperriere	25.00	10.00	2.50
☐ 3	Yvan Cournoyer Jim Neilson Gary Sabourin John Miszuk	25.00	10.00	2.50
☐ 4	Bruce Gamble Carol Vadnais Frank Mahovlich Larry Hillman	35.00	14.00	3.50
☐ 5	Ed Giacomin Jean Beliveau Eddie Joyal Leo Boivin	50.00	20.00	5.00
☐ 6	Phil Goyette Doug Jarrett Ted Green Bill Hicke	25.00	10.00	2.50
☐ 7	Ted Hampson Carl Brewer Denis DeJordy Leon Rochefort	25.00	10.00	2.50
☐ 8	Charlie Hodge Pat Quinn Derek Sanderson Duane Rupp	35.00	14.00	3.50
☐ 9	Earl Ingarfield Jim Roberts Gump Worsley Bobby Hull	90.00	36.00	9.00
☐ 10	Andre Lacroix Bob Wall Serge Savard Roger Crozier	25.00	10.00	2.50
☐ 11	Cesare Maniago Bobby Orr Dave Keon Jean-Guy Gendron	150.00	60.00	15.00
☐ 12	Keith McCreary Claude Larose Rod Gilbert Gerry Cheevers	35.00	14.00	3.50
☐ 13	Stan Mikita Al Arbour Rod Seiling Ron Schock	35.00	14.00	3.50
☐ 14	Doug Mohns Bob Woytowich Gordie Howe Gerry Desjardins	150.00	60.00	15.00
☐ 15	Bob Nevin Jacques Plante Mike Walton	35.00	14.00	3.50

	Ray Cullen			
☐ 16	Bob Pulford	60.00	24.00	6.00
	Henri Richard			
	Red Berenson			
	Eddie Shack			
☐ 17	Pat Stapleton	25.00	10.00	2.50
	Danny Grant			
	Bert Marshall			
	Jean Ratelle			
☐ 18	Ed Van Impe	50.00	20.00	5.00
	Dale Rolfe			
	Alex Delvecchio			
	Phil Esposito			

1969-70 O-Pee-Chee Team Booklets

The 1969-70 O-Pee-Chee Team Booklets were issued in order to hold the individual mini-cards of the four-in-one insert set. These small team albums/booklets measure approximately 2 1/2" by 3 1/2". There were 12 albums in the set, one album per team. The team booklets are light green in color. There were four pages in each little booklet with spaces for six stickers (two per page after the front title page) to be placed within.

		NRMT	VG-E	GOOD
	COMPLETE SET (12)	75.00	30.00	7.50
	COMMON CARD (1-12)	7.50	3.00	.75
☐ 1	Boston Bruins	10.00	4.00	1.00
☐ 2	Chicago Blackhawks	10.00	4.00	1.00
☐ 3	Detroit Red Wings	10.00	4.00	1.00
☐ 4	Los Angeles Kings	7.50	3.00	.75
☐ 5	Minnesota North Stars	7.50	3.00	.75
☐ 6	Montreal Canadiens	10.00	4.00	1.00
☐ 7	New York Rangers	10.00	4.00	1.00
☐ 8	Oakland Seals	7.50	3.00	.75
☐ 9	Philadelphia Flyers	10.00	4.00	1.00
☐ 10	Pittsburgh Penguins	7.50	3.00	.75
☐ 11	St. Louis Blues	7.50	3.00	.75
☐ 12	Toronto Maple Leafs	10.00	4.00	1.00

1970-71 O-Pee-Chee

The 1970-71 O-Pee-Chee set contains 264 color cards. The cards measure the standard, 2 1/2" by 3 1/2". Bilingual backs feature a short biography as well as the player's 1969-70 and career statistics. Printed in Canada, the O-Pee-Chee copyright, and not the Topps, appears on the back for the first time. Many player poses are different from the Topps set of this year. Card 231 is a special memorial to Terry Sawchuk who passed away earlier in the year. Rookie Cards include Bobby Clarke, Brad Park, Gilbert Perreault, Darryl Sittler, Wayne Cashman and Guy Lapointe.

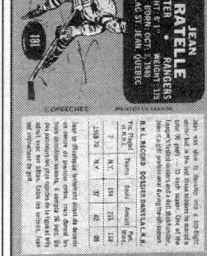

JEAN RATELLE   CENTER
N.Y. RANGERS

		NRMT	VG-E	GOOD
	COMPLETE SET (264)	1200.00	550.00	150.00
	COMMON PLAYER (1-264)	3.00	1.35	.40
☐ 1	Gerry Cheevers	20.00	5.00	1.60
☐ 2	Johnny Bucyk	6.00	2.70	.75
☐ 3	Bobby Orr	125.00	57.50	15.50
☐ 4	Don Awrey	3.00	1.35	.40
☐ 5	Fred Stanfield	3.00	1.35	.40
☐ 6	John McKenzie	3.50	1.55	.45
☐ 7	Wayne Cashman	12.00	5.50	1.50
☐ 8	Ken Hodge	3.50	1.55	.45
☐ 9	Wayne Carleton	3.00	1.35	.40
☐ 10	Garnet Bailey	3.00	1.35	.40
☐ 11	Phil Esposito	25.00	11.50	3.10
☐ 12	Lou Angotti	3.00	1.35	.40
☐ 13	Jim Pappin	3.00	1.35	.40
☐ 14	Dennis Hull	3.50	1.55	.45
☐ 15	Bobby Hull	50.00	23.00	6.25
☐ 16	Doug Mohns	3.00	1.35	.40
☐ 17	Pat Stapleton	3.50	1.55	.45
☐ 18	Pit Martin	3.50	1.55	.45
☐ 19	Eric Nesterenko	3.50	1.55	.45
☐ 20	Stan Mikita	20.00	9.00	2.50
☐ 21	Roy Edwards	3.50	1.55	.45
☐ 22	Frank Mahovlich	10.00	4.50	1.25
☐ 23	Ron Harris	3.00	1.35	.40
☐ 24	Checklist 1	80.00	8.00	1.60
☐ 25	Pete Stemkowski	3.00	1.35	.40
☐ 26	Garry Unger	4.00	1.80	.50
☐ 27	Bruce MacGregor	3.00	1.35	.40
☐ 28	Larry Jeffrey	3.00	1.35	.40
☐ 29	Gordie Howe	70.00	32.00	8.75
☐ 30	Billy Dea	3.00	1.35	.40
☐ 31	Denis DeJordy	3.50	1.55	.45
☐ 32	Matt Ravlich	3.00	1.35	.40
☐ 33	Dave Amadio	3.00	1.35	.40
☐ 34	Gilles Marotte	3.00	1.35	.40
☐ 35	Eddie Shack	5.00	2.30	.60
☐ 36	Bob Pulford	3.50	1.55	.45
☐ 37	Ross Lonsberry	3.50	1.55	.45
☐ 38	Gord Labossiere	3.00	1.35	.40
☐ 39	Eddie Joyal	3.00	1.35	.40
☐ 40	Gump Worsley	8.00	3.60	1.00
☐ 41	Bob McCord	3.00	1.35	.40
☐ 42	Leo Boivin	3.00	1.35	.40
☐ 43	Tom Reid	3.00	1.35	.40
☐ 44	Charlie Burns	3.00	1.35	.40
☐ 45	Bob Barlow	3.00	1.35	.40
☐ 46	Bill Goldsworthy	3.50	1.55	.45
☐ 47	Danny Grant	3.50	1.55	.45
☐ 48	Norm Beaudin	3.00	1.35	.40
☐ 49	Rogatien Vachon	9.00	4.00	1.15
☐ 50	Yvan Cournoyer	8.00	3.60	1.00
☐ 51	Serge Savard	10.00	4.50	1.25
☐ 52	Jacques Laperriere	3.50	1.55	.45
☐ 53	Terry Harper	3.00	1.35	.40
☐ 54	Ralph Backstrom	3.50	1.55	.45
☐ 55	Jean Beliveau	15.00	6.75	1.90
☐ 56	Claude Larose	3.00	1.35	.40
☐ 57	Jacques Lemaire	7.00	3.10	.85
☐ 58	Peter Mahovlich	3.50	1.55	.45
☐ 59	Tim Horton	8.00	3.60	1.00
☐ 60	Bob Nevin	3.00	1.35	.40
☐ 61	Dave Balon	3.00	1.35	.40
☐ 62	Vic Hadfield	3.50	1.55	.45
☐ 63	Rod Gilbert	6.00	2.70	.75
☐ 64	Ron Stewart	3.00	1.35	.40
☐ 65	Ted Irvine	3.00	1.35	.40
☐ 66	Arnie Brown	3.00	1.35	.40
☐ 67	Brad Park	50.00	23.00	6.25
☐ 68	Ed Giacomin	10.00	4.50	1.25

☐ 69	Gary Smith	3.50	1.55	.45
☐ 70	Carol Vadnais	3.50	1.55	.45
☐ 71	Doug Roberts	3.00	1.35	.40
☐ 72	Harry Howell	3.50	1.55	.45
☐ 73	Joe Szura	3.00	1.35	.40
☐ 74	Mike Laughton	3.00	1.35	.40
☐ 75	Gary Jarrett	3.00	1.35	.40
☐ 76	Bill Hicke	3.00	1.35	.40
☐ 77	Paul Andrea	3.00	1.35	.40
☐ 78	Bernie Parent	20.00	9.00	2.50
☐ 79	Joe Watson	3.00	1.35	.40
☐ 80	Ed Van Impe	3.00	1.35	.40
☐ 81	Larry Hillman	3.00	1.35	.40
☐ 82	George Swarbrick	3.00	1.35	.40
☐ 83	Bill Sutherland	3.00	1.35	.40
☐ 84	Andre Lacroix	3.50	1.55	.45
☐ 85	Gary Dornhoefer	3.00	1.35	.40
☐ 86	Jean-Guy Gendron	3.00	1.35	.40
☐ 87	Al Smith	3.50	1.55	.45
☐ 88	Bob Woytowich	3.00	1.35	.40
☐ 89	Duane Rupp	3.00	1.35	.40
☐ 90	Jim Morrison	3.00	1.35	.40
☐ 91	Ron Schock	3.00	1.35	.40
☐ 92	Ken Schinkel	3.00	1.35	.40
☐ 93	Keith McCreary	3.00	1.35	.40
☐ 94	Bryan Hextall	3.50	1.55	.45
☐ 95	Wayne Hicks	3.00	1.35	.40
☐ 96	Gary Sabourin	3.00	1.35	.40
☐ 97	Ernie Wakely	3.00	1.35	.40
☐ 98	Bob Wall	3.00	1.35	.40
☐ 99	Barclay Plager	3.50	1.55	.45
☐ 100	Jean-Guy Talbot	3.00	1.35	.40
☐ 101	Gary Veneruzzo	3.00	1.35	.40
☐ 102	Tim Ecclestone	3.00	1.35	.40
☐ 103	Red Berenson	3.50	1.55	.45
☐ 104	Larry Keenan	3.00	1.35	.40
☐ 105	Bruce Gamble	3.50	1.55	.45
☐ 106	Jim Dorey	3.00	1.35	.40
☐ 107	Mike Pelyk	3.00	1.35	.40
☐ 108	Rick Ley	3.00	1.35	.40
☐ 109	Mike Walton	3.00	1.35	.40
☐ 110	Norm Ullman	5.00	2.30	.60
☐ 111A	Brit Selby (No mention of trade)	3.00	1.35	.40
☐ 111B	Brit Selby (Trade noted)	7.50	3.40	.95
☐ 112	Garry Monahan	3.00	1.35	.40
☐ 113	George Armstrong	3.50	1.55	.45
☐ 114	Gary Doak	3.00	1.35	.40
☐ 115	Darryl Sly	3.00	1.35	.40
☐ 116	Wayne Maki	3.00	1.35	.40
☐ 117	Orland Kurtenbach	3.00	1.35	.40
☐ 118	Murray Hall	3.00	1.35	.40
☐ 119	Marc Reaume	3.00	1.35	.40
☐ 120	Pat Quinn	4.00	1.80	.50
☐ 121	Andre Boudrias	3.00	1.35	.40
☐ 122	Poul Popiel	3.00	1.35	.40
☐ 123	Paul Terbenche	3.00	1.35	.40
☐ 124	Howie Menard	3.00	1.35	.40
☐ 125	Gerry Meehan	4.00	1.80	.50
☐ 126	Skip Krake	3.00	1.35	.40
☐ 127	Phil Goyette	3.00	1.35	.40
☐ 128	Reg Fleming	3.00	1.35	.40
☐ 129	Don Marshall	3.00	1.35	.40
☐ 130	Bill Inglis	3.00	1.35	.40
☐ 131	Gilbert Perreault	90.00	40.00	11.50
☐ 132	Checklist 2	80.00	8.00	1.60
☐ 133	Ed Johnston	3.50	1.55	.45
☐ 134	Ted Green	3.50	1.55	.45
☐ 135	Rick Smith	3.00	1.35	.40
☐ 136	Derek Sanderson	7.00	3.10	.85
☐ 137	Dallas Smith	3.00	1.35	.40
☐ 138	Don Marcotte	4.00	1.80	.50
☐ 139	Ed Westfall	3.50	1.55	.45
☐ 140	Floyd Smith	3.00	1.35	.40
☐ 141	Randy Wyrozub	3.00	1.35	.40
☐ 142	Cliff Schmautz	3.00	1.35	.40
☐ 143	Mike McMahon	3.00	1.35	.40
☐ 144	Jim Watson	3.00	1.35	.40
☐ 145	Roger Crozier	3.50	1.55	.45
☐ 146	Tracy Pratt	3.00	1.35	.40
☐ 147	Cliff Koroll	4.00	1.80	.50
☐ 148	Gerry Pinder	4.00	1.80	.50
☐ 149	Chico Maki	3.00	1.35	.40
☐ 150	Doug Jarrett	3.00	1.35	.40
☐ 151	Keith Magnuson	8.00	3.60	1.00
☐ 152	Gerry Desjardins	3.50	1.55	.45
☐ 153	Tony Esposito	50.00	23.00	6.25
☐ 154	Gary Bergman	3.00	1.35	.40
☐ 155	Tom Webster	4.00	1.80	.50
☐ 156	Dale Rolfe	3.00	1.35	.40
☐ 157	Alex Delvecchio	6.00	2.70	.75
☐ 158	Nick Libett	3.00	1.35	.40
☐ 159	Wayne Connelly	3.00	1.35	.40
☐ 160	Mike Byers	3.00	1.35	.40
☐ 161	Bill Flett	3.00	1.35	.40
☐ 162	Larry Mickey	3.00	1.35	.40
☐ 163	Noel Price	3.00	1.35	.40
☐ 164	Larry Cahan	3.00	1.35	.40
☐ 165	Jack Norris	3.00	1.35	.40
☐ 166	Ted Harris	3.00	1.35	.40
☐ 167	Murray Oliver	3.00	1.35	.40
☐ 168	Jean-Paul Parise	3.50	1.55	.45
☐ 169	Tom Williams	3.00	1.35	.40
☐ 170	Bobby Rousseau	3.00	1.35	.40
☐ 171	Jude Drouin	4.00	1.80	.50
☐ 172	Walt McKechnie	4.00	1.80	.50
☐ 173	Cesare Maniago	3.50	1.55	.45
☐ 174	Rejean Houle	5.00	2.30	.60
☐ 175A	Mickey Redmond (No mention of trade)	7.00	3.10	.85
☐ 175B	Mickey Redmond (Trade noted)	12.00	5.50	1.50
☐ 176	Henri Richard	7.50	3.40	.95
☐ 177	Guy Lapointe	20.00	9.00	2.50
☐ 178	J.C. Tremblay	3.00	1.35	.40
☐ 179	Marc Tardif	6.00	2.70	.75
☐ 180	Walt Tkaczuk	3.50	1.55	.45
☐ 181	Jean Ratelle	6.00	2.70	.75
☐ 182	Pete Stemkowski	3.00	1.35	.40
☐ 183	Gilles Villemure	3.50	1.55	.45
☐ 184	Rod Seiling	3.00	1.35	.40
☐ 185	Jim Neilson	3.00	1.35	.40
☐ 186	Dennis Hextall	3.50	1.55	.45
☐ 187	Gerry Ehman	3.00	1.35	.40
☐ 188	Bert Marshall	3.00	1.35	.40
☐ 189	Gary Croteau	3.00	1.35	.40
☐ 190	Ted Hampson	3.00	1.35	.40
☐ 191	Earl Ingarfield	3.00	1.35	.40
☐ 192	Dick Mattiussi	3.00	1.35	.40
☐ 193	Earl Heiskala	3.00	1.35	.40
☐ 194	Simon Nolet	3.00	1.35	.40
☐ 195	Bobby Clarke	125.00	57.50	15.50
☐ 196	Garry Peters	3.00	1.35	.40
☐ 197	Lew Morrison	3.00	1.35	.40
☐ 198	Wayne Hillman	3.00	1.35	.40
☐ 199	Doug Favell	3.50	1.55	.45
☐ 200	Les Binkley	3.50	1.55	.45
☐ 201	Dean Prentice	3.00	1.35	.40
☐ 202	Jean Pronovost	3.50	1.55	.45
☐ 203	Wally Boyer	3.00	1.35	.40
☐ 204	Bryan Watson	3.00	1.35	.40
☐ 205	Glen Sather	5.00	2.30	.60
☐ 206	Lowell MacDonald	3.50	1.55	.45
☐ 207	Andy Bathgate	3.50	1.55	.45
☐ 208	Val Fonteyne	3.00	1.35	.40
☐ 209	Jim Lorentz	3.00	1.35	.40
☐ 210	Glenn Hall	8.00	3.60	1.00
☐ 211	Bob Plager	3.50	1.55	.45
☐ 212	Noel Picard	3.00	1.35	.40
☐ 213	Jim Roberts	3.50	1.55	.45
☐ 214	Frank St.Marseille	3.00	1.35	.40
☐ 215	Ab McDonald	3.00	1.35	.40
☐ 216	Brian Glennie	3.00	1.35	.40
☐ 217	Paul Henderson	3.50	1.55	.45
☐ 218	Darryl Sittler	115.00	52.50	14.50
☐ 219	Dave Keon	5.00	2.30	.60
☐ 220	Jim Harrison	3.00	1.35	.40
☐ 221	Ron Ellis	3.50	1.55	.45
☐ 222	Jacques Plante	25.00	11.50	3.10
☐ 223	Bob Baun	3.50	1.55	.45
☐ 224	George Gardner	3.00	1.35	.40
☐ 225	Dale Tallon	5.00	2.30	.60
☐ 226	Rosaire Paiement	3.00	1.35	.40
☐ 227	Mike Corrigan	3.00	1.35	.40
☐ 228	Ray Cullen	3.00	1.35	.40
☐ 229	Charlie Hodge	3.50	1.55	.45
☐ 230	Len Lunde	3.00	1.35	.40
☐ 231	Terry Sawchuk Memorial	50.00	23.00	6.25
☐ 232	Boston Bruins Team Stanley Cup Champs	10.00	4.50	1.25
☐ 233	Esposito line: Cashman/Hodge	20.00	9.00	2.50
☐ 234	Tony Esposito AS1	20.00	9.00	2.50
☐ 235	Bobby Hull AS1	27.00	12.00	3.40
☐ 236	Bobby Orr AS1	50.00	23.00	6.25
☐ 237	Phil Esposito AS1	15.00	6.75	1.90
☐ 238	Gordie Howe AS1	40.00	18.00	5.00
☐ 239	Brad Park AS1	18.00	8.00	2.30
☐ 240	Stan Mikita AS2	9.00	4.00	1.15
☐ 241	John McKenzie AS2	3.50	1.55	.45
☐ 242	Frank Mahovlich AS2	6.00	2.70	.75
☐ 243	Carl Brewer AS2	3.00	1.35	.40
☐ 244	Ed Giacomin AS2	5.00	2.30	.60
☐ 245	Jacques Laperriere AS2	3.00	1.35	.40

		NRMT	VG-E	GOOD
☐ 246	Bobby Orr	50.00	23.00	6.25
	Hart Trophy			
☐ 247	Tony Esposito	20.00	9.00	2.50
	Calder Trophy			
☐ 248A	Bobby Orr	50.00	23.00	6.25
	Norris Trophy			
	(No mention of Howe			
	as NHL all-time			
	leading scorer)			
☐ 248B	Bobby Orr	50.00	23.00	6.25
	Norris Trophy			
	(Mentions Howe			
	as NHL all-time			
	leading scorer)			
☐ 249	Bobby Orr	50.00	23.00	6.25
	Art Ross Trophy			
☐ 250	Tony Esposito	20.00	9.00	2.50
	Vezina Trophy			
☐ 251	Phil Goyette	3.00	1.35	.40
	Lady Byng Trophy			
☐ 252	Bobby Orr	50.00	23.00	6.25
	Conn Smythe			
☐ 253	Pit Martin	3.00	1.35	.40
	Bill Masterton			
	Memorial Trophy)			
☐ 254	The Stanley Cup	12.00	5.50	1.50
☐ 255	Prince of Wales	3.50	1.55	.45
	Trophy			
☐ 256	Conn Smythe Trophy	3.50	1.55	.45
☐ 257	James Norris Trophy	3.50	1.55	.45
☐ 258	Calder Trophy	3.50	1.55	.45
☐ 259	Vezina Trophy	3.50	1.55	.45
☐ 260	Lady Byng Trophy	3.50	1.55	.45
☐ 261	Hart Trophy	3.50	1.55	.45
☐ 262	Art Ross Trophy	3.50	1.55	.45
☐ 263	Clarence S. Campbell	3.50	1.55	.45
	Bowl			
☐ 264	John Ferguson	10.00	2.00	.60

1970-71 O-Pee-Chee Deckle

GORDIE HOWE
No. 18 of 48 photos

This set consists of 48 numbered black and white deckle edge cards measuring approximately 2 1/8" by 3 1/8". The set was issued as an insert with the second series regular issue of the same year. The cards are numbered on the backs. The set was printed in Canada.

		NRMT	VG-E	GOOD
COMPLETE SET (48)		250.00	100.00	25.00
COMMON PLAYER (1-48)		2.00	.80	.20
☐ 1	Pat Quinn	3.00	1.20	.30
☐ 2	Eddie Shack	4.00	1.60	.40
☐ 3	Eddie Joyal	2.00	.80	.20
☐ 4	Bobby Orr	50.00	20.00	5.00
☐ 5	Derek Sanderson	4.00	1.60	.40
☐ 6	Phil Esposito	12.50	5.00	1.25
☐ 7	Fred Stanfield	2.00	.80	.20
☐ 8	Bob Woytowich	2.00	.80	.20
☐ 9	Ron Schock	2.00	.80	.20
☐ 10	Les Binkley	2.00	.80	.20
☐ 11	Roger Crozier	3.00	1.20	.30
☐ 12	Reg Fleming	2.00	.80	.20
☐ 13	Charlie Burns	2.00	.80	.20

☐ 14	Bobby Rousseau	2.00	.80	.20
☐ 15	Leo Boivin	3.00	1.20	.30
☐ 16	Garry Unger	3.00	1.20	.30
☐ 17	Frank Mahovlich	10.00	4.00	1.00
☐ 18	Gordie Howe	50.00	20.00	5.00
☐ 19	Jacques Lemaire	5.00	2.00	.50
☐ 20	Jacques Laperriere	3.00	1.20	.30
☐ 21	Jean Beliveau	12.50	5.00	1.25
☐ 22	Rogatien Vachon	5.00	2.00	.50
☐ 23	Yvon Cournoyer	4.00	1.60	.40
☐ 24	Henri Richard	5.00	2.00	.50
☐ 25	Red Berenson	3.00	1.20	.30
☐ 26	Frank St.Marseille	2.00	.80	.20
☐ 27	Glenn Hall	6.00	2.40	.60
☐ 28	Gary Sabourin	2.00	.80	.20
☐ 29	Doug Mohns	2.00	.80	.20
☐ 30	Bobby Hull	30.00	12.00	3.00
☐ 31	Ray Cullen	2.00	.80	.20
☐ 32	Tony Esposito	10.00	4.00	1.00
☐ 33	Gary Dornhoefer	2.00	.80	.20
☐ 34	Ed Van Impe	2.00	.80	.20
☐ 35	Doug Favell	2.00	.80	.20
☐ 36	Carol Vadnais	2.00	.80	.20
☐ 37	Harry Howell	3.00	1.20	.30
☐ 38	Bill Hicke	2.00	.80	.20
☐ 39	Rod Gilbert	4.00	1.60	.40
☐ 40	Jean Ratelle	4.00	1.60	.40
☐ 41	Walt Tkaczuk	3.00	1.20	.30
☐ 42	Ed Giacomin	5.00	2.00	.50
☐ 43	Brad Park	7.50	3.00	.75
☐ 44	Bruce Gamble	2.00	.80	.20
☐ 45	Orland Kurtenbach	3.00	1.20	.30
☐ 46	Ron Ellis	3.00	1.20	.30
☐ 47	Dave Keon	5.00	2.00	.50
☐ 48	Norm Ullman	4.00	1.60	.40

1971-72 O-Pee-Chee

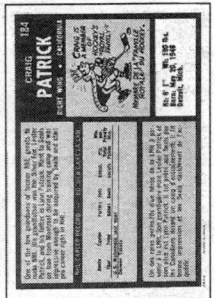

The 1971-72 O-Pee-Chee set contains 264 color cards. Player photos are framed in an oval. The cards were originally sold in ten-cent wax packs which contained eight cards with gum. The cards in the set measure 2 1/2" by 3 1/2". Bilingual backs feature a short biography, year by year statistics and a cartoon-illustrated fact about the player. The O.P.C. copyright appears on the backs of these cards, which were printed in Canada. Cards 262 and 263 are special cards honoring "retiring" legends Gordie Howe and Jean Beliveau. Rookie Cards in this set include Marcel Dionne, Ken Dryden, Guy Lafleur, Rick MacLeish, Richard Martin, Butch Goring and Reggie Leach.

		NRMT	VG-E	GOOD
COMPLETE SET (264)		1400.00	650.00	180.00
COMMON PLAYER (1-132)		2.50	1.15	.30
COMMON PLAYER (133-264)		3.00	1.35	.40
☐ 1	Poul Popiel	5.00	1.40	.45
☐ 2	Pierre Bouchard	3.50	1.55	.45
☐ 3	Don Awrey	2.50	1.15	.30
☐ 4	Paul Curtis	2.50	1.15	.30
☐ 5	Guy Trottier	2.50	1.15	.30
☐ 6	Paul Shmyr	3.00	1.35	.40

☐	7	Fred Stanfield	2.50	1.15	.30			
☐	8	Mike Robitaille	2.50	1.15	.30			
☐	9	Vic Hadfield	3.00	1.35	.40			
☐	10	Jim Harrison	2.50	1.15	.30			
☐	11	Bill White	2.50	1.15	.30			
☐	12	Andre Boudrias	2.50	1.15	.30			
☐	13	Gary Sabourin	2.50	1.15	.30			
☐	14	Arnie Brown	2.50	1.15	.30			
☐	15	Yvan Cournoyer	6.00	2.70	.75			
☐	16	Bryan Hextall	3.00	1.35	.40			
☐	17	Gary Croteau	2.50	1.15	.30			
☐	18	Gilles Villemure	3.00	1.35	.40			
☐	19	Serge Bernier	3.00	1.35	.40			
☐	20	Phil Esposito	20.00	9.00	2.50			
☐	21	Tom Reid	2.50	1.15	.30			
☐	22	Doug Barrie	2.50	1.15	.30			
☐	23	Eddie Joyal	2.50	1.15	.30			
☐	24	Dunc Wilson	3.50	1.55	.45			
☐	25	Pat Stapleton	3.00	1.35	.40			
☐	26	Garry Unger	3.00	1.35	.40			
☐	27	Al Smith	3.00	1.35	.40			
☐	28	Bob Woytowich	2.50	1.15	.30			
☐	29	Marc Tardif	3.00	1.35	.40			
☐	30	Norm Ullman	5.00	2.30	.60			
☐	31	Tom Williams	2.50	1.15	.30			
☐	32	Ted Harris	2.50	1.15	.30			
☐	33	Andre Lacroix	3.00	1.35	.40			
☐	34	Mike Byers	2.50	1.15	.30			
☐	35	Johnny Bucyk	5.00	2.30	.60			
☐	36	Roger Crozier	3.00	1.35	.40			
☐	37	Alex Delvecchio	5.00	2.30	.60			
☐	38	Frank St.Marseille	2.50	1.15	.30			
☐	39	Pit Martin	3.00	1.35	.40			
☐	40	Brad Park	18.00	8.00	2.30			
☐	41	Greg Polis	2.50	1.15	.30			
☐	42	Orland Kurtenbach	2.50	1.15	.30			
☐	43	Jim McKenny	2.50	1.15	.30			
☐	44	Bob Nevin	2.50	1.15	.30			
☐	45	Ken Dryden	300.00	135.00	38.00			
☐	46	Carol Vadnais	3.00	1.35	.40			
☐	47	Bill Flett	2.50	1.15	.30			
☐	48	Jim Johnson	2.50	1.15	.30			
☐	49	Al Hamilton	2.50	1.15	.30			
☐	50	Bobby Hull	40.00	18.00	5.00			
☐	51	Chris Bordeleau	2.50	1.15	.30			
☐	52	Tim Ecclestone	2.50	1.15	.30			
☐	53	Rod Seiling	2.50	1.15	.30			
☐	54	Gerry Cheevers	8.00	3.60	1.00			
☐	55	Bill Goldsworthy	3.00	1.35	.40			
☐	56	Ron Schock	2.50	1.15	.30			
☐	57	Jim Dorey	2.50	1.15	.30			
☐	58	Wayne Maki	2.50	1.15	.30			
☐	59	Terry Harper	2.50	1.15	.30			
☐	60	Gilbert Perreault	30.00	13.50	3.80			
☐	61	Ernie Hicke	2.50	1.15	.30			
☐	62	Wayne Hillman	2.50	1.15	.30			
☐	63	Denis DeJordy	3.00	1.35	.40			
☐	64	Ken Schinkel	2.50	1.15	.30			
☐	65	Derek Sanderson	6.00	2.70	.75			
☐	66	Barclay Plager	3.00	1.35	.40			
☐	67	Paul Henderson	3.00	1.35	.40			
☐	68	Jude Drouin	2.50	1.15	.30			
☐	69	Keith Magnuson	3.00	1.35	.40			
☐	70	Ron Harris	2.50	1.15	.30			
☐	71	Jacques Lemaire	6.00	2.70	.75			
☐	72	Doug Favell	3.00	1.35	.40			
☐	73	Bert Marshall	2.50	1.15	.30			
☐	74	Ted Irvine	2.50	1.15	.30			
☐	75	Walt Tkaczuk	3.00	1.35	.40			
☐	76	Bob Berry	4.00	1.80	.50			
☐	77	Syl Apps	4.00	1.80	.50			
☐	78	Tom Webster	3.00	1.35	.40			
☐	79	Danny Grant	3.00	1.35	.40			
☐	80	Dave Keon	4.00	1.80	.50			
☐	81	Ernie Wakely	2.50	1.15	.30			
☐	82	John McKenzie	3.00	1.35	.40			
☐	83	Ron Stackhouse	2.50	1.15	.30			
☐	84	Peter Mahovlich	3.00	1.35	.40			
☐	85	Dennis Hull	3.00	1.35	.40			
☐	86	Juha Widing	2.50	1.15	.30			
☐	87	Gary Doak	2.50	1.15	.30			
☐	88	Phil Goyette	2.50	1.15	.30			
☐	89	Lew Morrison	2.50	1.15	.30			
☐	90	Ab DeMarco	2.50	1.15	.30			
☐	91	Red Berenson	3.00	1.35	.40			
☐	92	Mike Pelyk	2.50	1.15	.30			
☐	93	Gary Jarrett	2.50	1.15	.30			
☐	94	Bob Pulford	3.00	1.35	.40			
☐	95	Dan Johnson	2.50	1.15	.30			
☐	96	Eddie Shack	3.00	1.35	.40			
☐	97	Jean Ratelle	5.00	2.30	.60			
☐	98	Jim Pappin	2.50	1.15	.30			
☐	99	Roy Edwards	3.00	1.35	.40			
☐	100	Bobby Orr	80.00	36.00	10.00			
☐	101	Ted Hampson	2.50	1.15	.30			
☐	102	Mickey Redmond	5.00	2.30	.60			
☐	103	Bob Plager	3.00	1.35	.40			
☐	104	Barry Ashbee	5.00	2.30	.60			
☐	105	Frank Mahovlich	9.00	4.00	1.15			
☐	106	Dick Redmond	2.50	1.15	.30			
☐	107	Tracy Pratt	2.50	1.15	.30			
☐	108	Ralph Backstrom	3.00	1.35	.40			
☐	109	Murray Hall	2.50	1.15	.30			
☐	110	Tony Esposito	35.00	16.00	4.40			
☐	111	Checklist Card	300.00	30.00	6.00			
☐	112	Jim Neilson	2.50	1.15	.30			
☐	113	Ron Ellis	3.00	1.35	.40			
☐	114	Bobby Clarke	45.00	20.00	5.75			
☐	115	Ken Hodge	3.00	1.35	.40			
☐	116	Jim Roberts	3.00	1.35	.40			
☐	117	Cesare Maniago	3.00	1.35	.40			
☐	118	Jean Pronovost	3.00	1.35	.40			
☐	119	Gary Bergman	2.50	1.15	.30			
☐	120	Henri Richard	6.00	2.70	.75			
☐	121	Ross Lonsberry	2.50	1.15	.30			
☐	122	Pat Quinn	3.00	1.35	.40			
☐	123	Rod Gilbert	5.00	2.30	.60			
☐	124	Walt McKechnie	3.00	1.35	.40			
☐	125	Stan Mikita	15.00	6.75	1.90			
☐	126	Ed Van Impe	2.50	1.15	.30			
☐	127	Terry Crisp	7.00	3.10	.85			
☐	128	Fred Barrett	2.50	1.15	.30			
☐	129	Wayne Cashman	4.00	1.80	.50			
☐	130	J.C. Tremblay	2.50	1.15	.30			
☐	131	Bernie Parent	15.00	6.75	1.90			
☐	132	Bryan Watson	4.00	1.80	.50			
☐	133	Marcel Dionne	125.00	57.50	15.50			
☐	134	Ab McDonald	3.00	1.35	.40			
☐	135	Leon Rochefort	3.00	1.35	.40			
☐	136	Serge Lajeunesse	3.00	1.35	.40			
☐	137	Joe Daley	3.50	1.55	.45			
☐	138	Brian Conacher	3.00	1.35	.40			
☐	139	Bill Collins	3.00	1.35	.40			
☐	140	Nick Libett	3.00	1.35	.40			
☐	141	Bill Sutherland	3.00	1.35	.40			
☐	142	Bill Hicke	3.00	1.35	.40			
☐	143	Serge Savard	5.00	2.30	.60			
☐	144	Jacques Laperriere	3.50	1.55	.45			
☐	145	Guy Lapointe	6.00	2.70	.75			
☐	146	Claude Larose UER	3.00	1.35	.40			
		(Misspelled La Rose on both sides)						
☐	147	Rejean Houle	3.00	1.35	.40			
☐	148	Guy Lafleur UER	225.00	100.00	28.00			
		(Misspelled La Fleur on both sides)						
☐	149	Dale Hoganson	3.00	1.35	.40			
☐	150	Al McDonough	3.00	1.35	.40			
☐	151	Gilles Marotte	3.00	1.35	.40			
☐	152	Butch Goring	10.00	4.50	1.25			
☐	153	Harry Howell	3.50	1.55	.45			
☐	154	Real Lemieux	3.00	1.35	.40			
☐	155	Gary Edwards	3.50	1.55	.45			
☐	156	Rogatien Vachon	5.00	2.30	.60			
☐	157	Mike Corrigan	3.00	1.35	.40			
☐	158	Floyd Smith	3.00	1.35	.40			
☐	159	Dave Dryden	3.50	1.55	.45			
☐	160	Gerry Meehan	3.50	1.55	.45			
☐	161	Richard Martin	15.00	6.75	1.90			
☐	162	Steve Atkinson	3.00	1.35	.40			
☐	163	Ron Anderson	3.00	1.35	.40			
☐	164	Dick Duff	3.50	1.55	.45			
☐	165	Jim Watson	3.00	1.35	.40			
☐	166	Don Luce	4.00	1.80	.50			
☐	167	Larry Mickey	3.00	1.35	.40			
☐	168	Larry Hillman	3.00	1.35	.40			
☐	169	Ed Westfall	3.50	1.55	.45			
☐	170	Dallas Smith	3.00	1.35	.40			
☐	171	Mike Walton	3.00	1.35	.40			
☐	172	Ed Johnston	3.50	1.55	.45			
☐	173	Ted Green	3.50	1.55	.45			
☐	174	Rick Smith	3.00	1.35	.40			
☐	175	Reggie Leach	10.00	4.50	1.25			
☐	176	Don Marcotte	3.00	1.35	.40			
☐	177	Bobby Sheehan	3.00	1.35	.40			
☐	178	Wayne Carleton	3.00	1.35	.40			
☐	179	Norm Ferguson	3.00	1.35	.40			
☐	180	Don O'Donoghue	3.00	1.35	.40			
☐	181	Gary Kurt	3.00	1.35	.40			
☐	182	Joey Johnston	3.00	1.35	.40			
☐	183	Stan Gilbertson	3.00	1.35	.40			
☐	184	Craig Patrick	8.00	3.60	1.00			
☐	185	Gerry Pinder	3.00	1.35	.40			
☐	186	Tim Horton	7.00	3.10	.85			
☐	187	Darryl Edestrand	3.00	1.35	.40			
☐	188	Keith McCreary	3.00	1.35	.40			

☐	189	Val Fonteyne	3.00	1.35	.40

#	Player	NRMT	VG-E	GOOD
☐ 189	Val Fonteyne	3.00	1.35	.40
☐ 190	Sheldon Kannegiesser	3.00	1.35	.40
☐ 191	Nick Harbaruk	3.00	1.35	.40
☐ 192	Les Binkley	3.50	1.55	.45
☐ 193	Darryl Sittler	40.00	18.00	5.00
☐ 194	Rick Ley	3.00	1.35	.40
☐ 195	Jacques Plante	20.00	9.00	2.50
☐ 196	Bob Baun	3.50	1.55	.45
☐ 197	Brian Glennie	3.00	1.35	.40
☐ 198	Brian Spencer	5.00	2.30	.60
☐ 199	Don Marshall	3.00	1.35	.40
☐ 200	Denis Dupere	3.00	1.35	.40
☐ 201	Bruce Gamble	3.50	1.55	.45
☐ 202	Gary Dornhoefer	3.00	1.35	.40
☐ 203	Bob Kelly	5.00	2.30	.60
☐ 204	Jean-Guy Gendron	3.00	1.35	.40
☐ 205	Brent Hughes	3.00	1.35	.40
☐ 206	Simon Nolet	3.00	1.35	.40
☐ 207	Rick MacLeish	15.00	6.75	1.90
☐ 208	Doug Jarrett	3.00	1.35	.40
☐ 209	Cliff Koroll	3.00	1.35	.40
☐ 210	Chico Maki	3.00	1.35	.40
☐ 211	Danny O'Shea	3.00	1.35	.40
☐ 212	Lou Angotti	3.00	1.35	.40
☐ 213	Eric Nesterenko	3.50	1.55	.45
☐ 214	Bryan Campbell	3.00	1.35	.40
☐ 215	Bill Fairbairn	3.00	1.35	.40
☐ 216	Bruce MacGregor	3.00	1.35	.40
☐ 217	Pete Stemkowski	3.00	1.35	.40
☐ 218	Bobby Rousseau	3.00	1.35	.40
☐ 219	Dale Rolfe	3.00	1.35	.40
☐ 220	Ed Giacomin	8.00	3.60	1.00
☐ 221	Glen Sather	3.50	1.55	.45
☐ 222	Carl Brewer	3.50	1.55	.45
☐ 223	George Morrison	3.00	1.35	.40
☐ 224	Noel Picard	3.00	1.35	.40
☐ 225	Peter McDuffe	3.50	1.55	.45
☐ 226	Brit Selby	3.00	1.35	.40
☐ 227	Jim Lorentz	3.00	1.35	.40
☐ 228	Phil Roberto	3.00	1.35	.40
☐ 229	Dave Balon	3.00	1.35	.40
☐ 230	Barry Wilkins	3.00	1.35	.40
☐ 231	Dennis Kearns	3.00	1.35	.40
☐ 232	Jocelyn Guevremont	3.50	1.55	.45
☐ 233	Rosaire Paiement	3.00	1.35	.40
☐ 234	Dale Tallon	3.50	1.55	.45
☐ 235	George Gardner	3.00	1.35	.40
☐ 236	Ron Stewart	3.00	1.35	.40
☐ 237	Wayne Connelly	3.00	1.35	.40
☐ 238	Charlie Burns	3.00	1.35	.40
☐ 239	Murray Oliver	3.00	1.35	.40
☐ 240	Lou Nanne	3.50	1.55	.45
☐ 241	Gump Worsley	6.00	2.70	.75
☐ 242	Doug Mohns	3.00	1.35	.40
☐ 243	Jean-Paul Parise	3.00	1.35	.40
☐ 244	Dennis Hextall	3.50	1.55	.45
☐ 245	Bobby Orr	50.00	23.00	6.25
	Hart Trophy			
	Norris Trophy			
☐ 246	Gilbert Perreault	15.00	6.75	1.90
	Calder Trophy			
☐ 247	Phil Esposito	10.00	4.50	1.25
	Ross Trophy			
☐ 248	Ed Giacomin and	5.00	2.30	.60
	Gilles Villemure			
	Vezina Trophy			
☐ 249	Johnny Bucyk	4.00	1.80	.50
	Lady Byng Trophy			
☐ 250	Ed Giacomin AS1	5.00	2.30	.60
☐ 251	Bobby Orr AS1	50.00	23.00	6.25
☐ 252	J.C. Tremblay AS1	2.50	1.15	.30
☐ 253	Phil Esposito AS1 UER	10.00	4.50	1.25
	(Back reads Phil.,			
	shouldn't be a			
	period after Phil)			
☐ 254	Ken Hodge AS1	2.50	1.15	.30
☐ 255	Johnny Bucyk AS1	4.00	1.80	.50
☐ 256	Jacques Plante AS2 UER	12.00	5.50	1.50
	(63 shutouts, should			
	be 77 shutouts)			
☐ 257	Brad Park AS2	7.00	3.10	.85
☐ 258	Pat Stapleton AS2	2.50	1.15	.30
☐ 259	Dave Keon AS2	3.50	1.55	.45
☐ 260	Yvan Cournoyer AS2	4.00	1.80	.50
☐ 261	Bobby Hull AS2	25.00	11.50	3.10
☐ 262	Gordie Howe	75.00	34.00	9.50
	(Retirement Special)			
☐ 263	Jean Beliveau	35.00	16.00	4.40
	(Retirement Special)			
☐ 264	Checklist Card	100.00	10.00	2.00

1971-72 O-Pee-Chee/Topps Booklets

 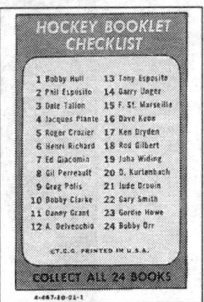

This set consists of 24 colorful comic booklets (eight pages in format) each measuring 2 1/2" by 3 1/2". The booklets were included as an insert with the regular issue of the same year and give a mini-biography of the player. These booklets were also put out by Topps and were printed in the United States. They can be found in either French or English language versions. The booklets are numbered on the fronts with a complete set checklist on the backs. The prices below are valid as well for the 1971-72 Topps version of these booklets although the English version is probably a little easier to find.

	NRMT	VG-E	GOOD
COMPLETE SET (24)	75.00	30.00	7.50
COMMON PLAYER (1-24)	.75	.30	.07

#	Player	NRMT	VG-E	GOOD
☐ 1	Bobby Hull	12.00	5.00	1.20
☐ 2	Phil Esposito	5.00	2.00	.50
☐ 3	Dale Tallon	.75	.30	.07
☐ 4	Jacques Plante	4.00	1.60	.40
☐ 5	Roger Crozier	1.00	.40	.10
☐ 6	Henri Richard	2.50	1.00	.25
☐ 7	Ed Giacomin	2.00	.80	.20
☐ 8	Gilbert Perreault	2.50	1.00	.25
☐ 9	Greg Polis	.75	.30	.07
☐ 10	Bobby Clarke	3.00	1.20	.30
☐ 11	Danny Grant	1.00	.40	.10
☐ 12	Alex Delvecchio	2.00	.80	.20
☐ 13	Tony Esposito	3.00	1.20	.30
☐ 14	Garry Unger	1.00	.40	.10
☐ 15	Frank St.Marseille	.75	.30	.07
☐ 16	Dave Keon	2.00	.80	.20
☐ 17	Ken Dryden	9.00	3.75	.90
☐ 18	Rod Gilbert	2.00	.80	.20
☐ 19	Juha Widing	.75	.30	.07
☐ 20	Orland Kurtenbach	1.00	.40	.10
☐ 21	Jude Drouin	.75	.30	.07
☐ 22	Gary Smith	.75	.30	.07
☐ 23	Gordie Howe	20.00	8.00	2.00
☐ 24	Bobby Orr	20.00	8.00	2.00

1971-72 O-Pee-Chee Posters

The 1971-72 O-Pee-Chee Posters set contains 24 color pictures measuring approximately 10" by 18". They were originally issued (as a separate issue) in folded form, two to a wax pack. Attached pairs are still sometimes found; these pairs are valued at 25 percent greater than the sum of the individual players included in the pair. The current scarcity of these posters suggests that they may have been a test issue. These posters are numbered and blank backed.

	NRMT	VG-E	GOOD
COMPLETE SET (24)	800.00	320.00	80.00
COMMON PLAYER (1-24)	12.00	5.00	1.20

#	Player	NRMT	VG-E	GOOD
☐ 1	Bobby Orr	200.00	80.00	20.00

printed in lesser quantities, features players from the newly formed WHA. There are apparently 22 double-printed cards in the first series (1-110), but the identity of these 22 is not known at this time except for Johnny Bucyk (No.1). There are also 22 known double-printed cards in the second series (111-209). These cards are identified by DP in the checklist below. There are no major Rookie Cards in this set.

		NRMT	VG-E	GOOD
COMPLETE SET (341)...............		1200.00	550.00	150.00
COMMON PLAYER (1-110).............		1.25	.55	.16
COMMON PLAYER (111-209)..........		1.50	.65	.19
COMMON PLAYER (210-289)..........		4.00	1.80	.50
COMMON PLAYER (290-341)..........		8.00	3.60	1.00
☐ 1	Johnny Bucyk DP.................	7.00	1.75	.55
☐ 2	Rene Robert........................	5.00	2.30	.60
☐ 3	Gary Croteau.......................	1.25	.55	.16
☐ 4	Pat Stapleton......................	1.50	.65	.19
☐ 5	Ron Harris..........................	1.25	.55	.16
☐ 6	Checklist 1	25.00	2.50	.50
☐ 7	Playoff Game 1....................	1.50	.65	.19
☐ 8	Marcel Dionne......................	30.00	13.50	3.80
☐ 9	Bob Berry............................	1.50	.65	.19
☐ 10	Lou Nanne..........................	1.50	.65	.19
☐ 11	Marc Tardif........................	1.25	.55	.16
☐ 12	Jean Ratelle.......................	4.00	1.80	.50
☐ 13	Craig Cameron	1.25	.55	.16
☐ 14	Bobby Clarke.......................	30.00	13.50	3.80
☐ 15	Jim Rutherford....................	6.00	2.70	.75
☐ 16	Andre Dupont.......................	4.00	1.80	.50
☐ 17	Mike Pelyk..........................	1.25	.55	.16
☐ 18	Dunc Wilson........................	1.50	.65	.19
☐ 19	Checklist 2	25.00	2.50	.50
	(See also card 190;			
	160 is Bill Harris)			
☐ 20	Playoff Game 2....................	1.50	.65	.19
	Bruins 2,			
	Rangers 1			
☐ 21	Dallas Smith.......................	1.25	.55	.16
☐ 22	Gerry Meehan	1.50	.65	.19
☐ 23	Rick Smith UER	1.25	.55	.16
	(Wrong total games,			
	should be 262, not 265)			
☐ 24	Pit Martin..........................	1.50	.65	.19
☐ 25	Keith McCreary	1.25	.55	.16
☐ 26	Alex Delvecchio...................	4.00	1.80	.50
☐ 27	Gilles Marotte.....................	1.25	.55	.16
☐ 28	Gump Worsley	5.00	2.30	.60
☐ 29	Yvan Cournoyer	5.00	2.30	.60
☐ 30	Playoff Game 3....................	1.50	.65	.19
	Rangers 5,			
	Bruins 2			
☐ 31	Vic Hadfield........................	1.50	.65	.19
☐ 32	Tom Miller..........................	1.25	.55	.16
☐ 33	Ed Van Impe........................	1.25	.55	.16
☐ 34	Greg Polis..........................	1.25	.55	.16
☐ 35	Barclay Plager.....................	1.50	.65	.19
☐ 36	Ron Ellis...........................	1.50	.65	.19
☐ 37	Jocelyn Guevremont..............	1.25	.55	.16
☐ 38	Playoff Game 4....................	1.50	.65	.19
	Bruins 3,			
	Rangers 2			
☐ 39	Carol Vadnais.....................	1.25	.55	.16
☐ 40	Steve Atkinson	1.25	.55	.16
☐ 41	Ivan Boldirev	3.50	1.55	.45
☐ 42	Jim Pappin.........................	1.25	.55	.16
☐ 43	Phil Myre...........................	5.00	2.30	.60
☐ 44	Yvan Cournoyer IA	3.00	1.35	.40
☐ 45	Nick Libett.........................	1.25	.55	.16
☐ 46	Juha Widing........................	1.25	.55	.16
☐ 47	Jude Drouin........................	1.25	.55	.16
☐ 48A	Jean Ratelle IA ERR	5.00	2.30	.60
	(Defense on back)			
☐ 48B	Jean Ratelle IA COR	3.00	1.35	.40
	(Center on back)			
☐ 49	Ken Hodge	1.50	.65	.19
☐ 50	Roger Crozier......................	1.50	.65	.19
☐ 51	Reggie Leach	4.00	1.80	.50
☐ 52	Dennis Hull.........................	1.50	.65	.19
☐ 53	Larry Hale..........................	1.25	.55	.16
☐ 54	Playoff Game 5....................	1.50	.65	.19
	Rangers 3,			
	Bruins 2			
☐ 55	Tim Ecclestone....................	1.25	.55	.16
☐ 56	Butch Goring.......................	4.00	1.80	.50
☐ 57	Danny Grant........................	1.50	.65	.19
☐ 58	Bobby Orr IA	25.00	11.50	3.10
☐ 59	Guy Lafleur........................	50.00	23.00	6.25
☐ 60	Jim Neilson........................	1.25	.55	.16
☐ 61	Brian Spencer	1.50	.65	.19

☐ 2	Bob Pulford........................	25.00	10.00	2.50
☐ 3	Dave Keon..........................	30.00	12.00	3.00
☐ 4	Yvan Cournoyer	35.00	14.00	3.50
☐ 5	Dale Tallon........................	12.00	5.00	1.20
☐ 6	Richard Martin.....................	15.00	6.00	1.50
☐ 7	Rod Gilbert........................	30.00	12.00	3.00
☐ 8	Tony Esposito......................	40.00	16.00	4.00
☐ 9	Bobby Hull..........................	75.00	30.00	7.50
☐ 10	Red Berenson......................	15.00	6.00	1.50
☐ 11	Norm Ullman........................	30.00	12.00	3.00
☐ 12	Orland Kurtenbach	15.00	6.00	1.50
☐ 13	Guy Lafleur........................	90.00	36.00	9.00
☐ 14	Gilbert Perreault.................	40.00	16.00	4.00
☐ 15	Jacques Plante.....................	40.00	16.00	4.00
☐ 16	Bruce Gamble	12.00	5.00	1.20
☐ 17	Walt McKechnie	12.00	5.00	1.20
☐ 18	Tim Horton..........................	40.00	16.00	4.00
☐ 19	Jean Ratelle.......................	30.00	12.00	3.00
☐ 20	Garry Unger........................	15.00	6.00	1.50
☐ 21	Phil Esposito......................	50.00	20.00	5.00
☐ 22	Ken Dryden..........................	100.00	40.00	10.00
☐ 23	Gump Worsley	35.00	14.00	3.50
☐ 24	Montreal Canadiens	20.00	8.00	2.00
	Team Photo			

1972-73 O-Pee-Chee

The 1972-73 O-Pee-Chee set features 341 standard size (2 1/2" by 3 1/2") cards that were printed in Canada. Tan borders on the front include the team name on the lefthand side. Bilingual backs feature a year-by-year record of the player's career, a short biography and a cartoon-illustrated fact about the player. There are a number of In-Action (IA) cards of popular players distributed throughout the set. Card number 208 was never issued. The last series, which was

☐ 62	Joe Watson	1.25	.55	.16	☐ 148	Art Ross Trophy	1.50	.65	.19
☐ 63	Playoff Game 6	1.50	.65	.19		Winners
	Bruins 3,				☐ 149	Orland Kurtenbach IA	1.50	.65	.19
	Rangers 0				☐ 150	Fred Stanfield	1.50	.65	.19
☐ 64	Jean Pronovost	1.50	.65	.19	☐ 151	Dick Redmond DP	1.00	.45	.13
☐ 65	Frank St.Marseille	1.25	.55	.16	☐ 152	Serge Bernier	1.75	.80	.22
☐ 66	Bob Baun	1.50	.65	.19	☐ 153	Rod Gilbert	4.00	1.80	.50
☐ 67	Poul Popiel	1.25	.55	.16	☐ 154	Duane Rupp	1.50	.65	.19
☐ 68	Wayne Cashman	2.00	.90	.25	☐ 155	Vezina Trophy Winners	2.00	.90	.25
☐ 69	Tracy Pratt	1.25	.55	.16	☐ 156	Stan Mikita IA	5.00	2.30	.60
☐ 70	Stan Gilbertson	1.25	.55	.16	☐ 157	Richard Martin DP	5.00	2.30	.60
☐ 71	Keith Magnuson	1.50	.65	.19	☐ 158	Bill White DP	1.50	.65	.19
☐ 72	Ernie Hicke	1.25	.55	.16	☐ 159	Bill Goldsworthy DP	1.25	.55	.16
☐ 73	Gary Doak	1.25	.55	.16	☐ 160	Jack Lynch	1.50	.65	.19
☐ 74	Mike Corrigan	1.25	.55	.16	☐ 161	Bob Plager DP	1.25	.55	.16
☐ 75	Doug Mohns	1.25	.55	.16	☐ 162	Dave Balon UER	1.50	.65	.19
☐ 76	Phil Esposito IA	7.00	3.10	.85		(Misspelled Ballon
☐ 77	Jacques Lemaire	4.00	1.80	.50		on card back)
☐ 78	Pete Stemkowski	1.25	.55	.16	☐ 163	Noel Price	1.50	.65	.19
☐ 79	Bill Mikkelson	1.25	.55	.16	☐ 164	Gary Bergman DP	1.00	.45	.13
☐ 80	Rick Foley	1.25	.55	.16	☐ 165	Pierre Bouchard	1.75	.80	.22
☐ 81	Ron Schock	1.25	.55	.16	☐ 166	Ross Lonsberry	1.50	.65	.19
☐ 82	Phil Roberto	1.25	.55	.16	☐ 167	Denis Dupere	1.50	.65	.19
☐ 83	Jim McKenny	1.25	.55	.16	☐ 168	Byng Trophy Winners DP	2.00	.90	.25
☐ 84	Wayne Maki	1.25	.55	.16	☐ 169	Ken Hodge	1.75	.80	.22
☐ 85A	Brad Park IA ERR	7.00	3.10	.85	☐ 170	Don Awrey DP	1.00	.45	.13
	(Center on back)				☐ 171	Marshall Johnston DP	1.00	.45	.13
☐ 85B	Brad Park IA COR	5.00	2.30	.60	☐ 172	Terry Harper	1.50	.65	.19
	(Defense on back)				☐ 173	Ed Giacomin	5.00	2.30	.60
☐ 86	Guy Lapointe	3.00	1.35	.40	☐ 174	Bryan Hextall DP	1.00	.45	.13
☐ 87	Bill Fairbairn	1.25	.55	.16	☐ 175	Conn Smythe	2.00	.90	.25
☐ 88	Terry Crisp	2.50	1.15	.30		Trophy Winners
☐ 89	Doug Favell	1.50	.65	.19	☐ 176	Larry Hillman	1.50	.65	.19
☐ 90	Bryan Watson	1.25	.55	.16	☐ 177	Stan Mikita DP	8.00	3.60	1.00
☐ 91	Gary Sabourin	1.25	.55	.16	☐ 178	Charlie Burns	1.50	.65	.19
☐ 92	Jacques Plante	15.00	6.75	1.90	☐ 179	Brian Marchinko	1.50	.65	.19
☐ 93	Andre Boudrias	1.25	.55	.16	☐ 180	Noel Picard DP	1.00	.45	.13
☐ 94	Mike Walton	1.25	.55	.16	☐ 181	Bobby Schmautz	3.50	1.55	.45
☐ 95	Don Luce	1.50	.65	.19	☐ 182	Richard Martin IA UER	3.50	1.55	.45
☐ 96	Joey Johnston	1.25	.55	.16		(Photo actually
☐ 97	Doug Jarrett	1.25	.55	.16		Gilbert Perreault)
☐ 98	Bill MacMillan	1.25	.55	.16	☐ 183	Pat Quinn	1.75	.80	.22
☐ 99	Mickey Redmond	3.00	1.35	.40	☐ 184	Denis DeJordy UER	1.75	.80	.22
☐ 100	Rogatien Vachon UER	4.00	1.80	.50		(Back says plays for
	(Misspelled Ragatien					Flames, should be
	on card back)					Red Wings)
☐ 101	Barry Gibbs	1.25	.55	.16	☐ 185	Serge Savard	3.00	1.35	.40
☐ 102	Frank Mahovlich DP	6.00	2.70	.75	☐ 186	Eddie Shack	1.75	.80	.22
☐ 103	Bruce MacGregor	1.25	.55	.16	☐ 187	Bill Flett	1.50	.65	.19
☐ 104	Ed Westfall	1.50	.65	.19	☐ 188	Darryl Sittler	25.00	11.50	3.10
☐ 105	Rick MacLeish	6.00	2.70	.75	☐ 189	Gump Worsley IA	4.00	1.80	.50
☐ 106	Nick Harbaruk	1.25	.55	.16	☐ 190	Checklist 2	35.00	3.50	.70
☐ 107	Jack Egers	1.25	.55	.16		(See also card 19;
☐ 108	Dave Keon	3.00	1.35	.40		160 is Jack Lynch)
☐ 109	Barry Wilkins	1.25	.55	.16	☐ 191	Garnet Bailey DP	1.00	.45	.13
☐ 110	Walt Tkaczuk	1.50	.65	.19	☐ 192	Walt McKechnie	1.75	.80	.22
☐ 111	Phil Esposito	15.00	6.75	1.90	☐ 193	Harry Howell	1.75	.80	.22
☐ 112	Gilles Meloche	7.00	3.10	.85	☐ 194	Rod Seiling	1.50	.65	.19
☐ 113	Gary Edwards	1.75	.80	.22	☐ 195	Darryl Edestrand	1.50	.65	.19
☐ 114	Brad Park	10.00	4.50	1.25	☐ 196	Tony Esposito IA	8.00	3.60	1.00
☐ 115	Syl Apps DP	1.25	.55	.16	☐ 197	Tim Horton	5.00	2.30	.60
☐ 116	Jim Lorentz	1.50	.65	.19	☐ 198	Chico Maki DP	1.00	.45	.13
☐ 117	Gary Smith	1.75	.80	.22	☐ 199	Jean-Paul Parise	1.50	.65	.19
☐ 118	Ted Harris	1.50	.65	.19	☐ 200	Germaine Gagnon UER	1.50	.65	.19
☐ 119	Gerry Desjardins DP	1.25	.55	.16	☐ 201	Danny O'Shea	1.50	.65	.19
☐ 120	Garry Unger	1.75	.80	.22	☐ 202	Richard Lemieux	1.50	.65	.19
☐ 121	Dale Tallon	1.50	.65	.19	☐ 203	Dan Bouchard	6.00	2.70	.75
☐ 122	Bill Plager	2.50	1.15	.30	☐ 204	Leon Rochefort	1.50	.65	.19
☐ 123	Red Berenson DP	1.25	.55	.16	☐ 205	Jacques Laperriere	1.75	.80	.22
☐ 124	Peter Mahovlich DP	1.25	.55	.16	☐ 206	Barry Ashbee	2.00	.90	.25
☐ 125	Simon Nolet	1.50	.65	.19	☐ 207	Garry Monahan	1.50	.65	.19
☐ 126	Paul Henderson	1.75	.80	.22	☐ 208	Never Issued	.00	.00	.00
☐ 127	Hart Trophy Winners	2.00	.90	.25	☐ 209	Dave Keon IA	2.50	1.15	.30
☐ 128	Frank Mahovlich IA	4.00	1.80	.50	☐ 210	Rejean Houle	4.00	1.80	.50
☐ 129	Bobby Orr	50.00	23.00	6.25	☐ 211	Dave Hudson	4.00	1.80	.50
☐ 130	Bert Marshall	1.50	.65	.19	☐ 212	Ted Irvine	4.00	1.80	.50
☐ 131	Ralph Backstrom	1.75	.80	.22	☐ 213	Don Saleski	5.00	2.30	.60
☐ 132	Gilles Villemure	1.75	.80	.22	☐ 214	Lowell MacDonald	4.00	1.80	.50
☐ 133	Dave Burrows	1.50	.65	.19	☐ 215	Mike Murphy	4.50	2.00	.55
☐ 134	Calder Trophy Winners	2.00	.90	.25	☐ 216	Brian Glennie	4.00	1.80	.50
☐ 135	Dallas Smith IA	1.50	.65	.19	☐ 217	Bobby Lalonde	4.00	1.80	.50
☐ 136	Gilbert Perreault DP	14.00	6.25	1.75	☐ 218	Bob Leiter	4.00	1.80	.50
☐ 137	Tony Esposito DP	20.00	9.00	2.50	☐ 219	Don Marcotte	4.00	1.80	.50
☐ 138	Cesare Maniago DP	1.25	.55	.16	☐ 220	Jim Schoenfeld	10.00	4.50	1.25
☐ 139	Gerry Hart	1.50	.65	.19	☐ 221	Craig Patrick	5.00	2.30	.60
☐ 140	Jacques Caron	1.50	.65	.19	☐ 222	Cliff Koroll	4.00	1.80	.50
☐ 141	Orland Kurtenbach	1.50	.65	.19	☐ 223	Guy Charron	4.50	2.00	.55
☐ 142	Norris Trophy Winners	2.00	.90	.25	☐ 224	Jim Peters	4.00	1.80	.50
☐ 143	Lew Morrison	1.50	.65	.19	☐ 225	Dennis Hextall	4.00	1.80	.50
☐ 144	Arnie Brown	1.50	.65	.19	☐ 226	Tony Esposito AS1	10.00	4.50	1.25
☐ 145	Ken Dryden DP	40.00	18.00	5.00	☐ 227	Orr/Park AS1	35.00	16.00	4.40
☐ 146	Gary Dornhoefer	1.50	.65	.19	☐ 228	Bobby Hull AS1	25.00	11.50	3.10
☐ 147	Norm Ullman	3.50	1.55	.45	☐ 229	Rod Gilbert AS1	5.00	2.30	.60

☐ 230	Phil Esposito AS1................	9.00	4.00	1.15
	(Brother Tony pictured in background)			
☐ 231	Claude Larose UER	4.00	1.80	.50
	(Misspelled La Rose on both sides)			
☐ 232	Jim Mair........................	4.00	1.80	.50
☐ 233	Bobby Rousseau	4.00	1.80	.50
☐ 234	Brent Hughes	4.00	1.80	.50
☐ 235	Al McDonough	4.00	1.80	.50
☐ 236	Chris Evans	4.00	1.80	.50
☐ 237	Pierre Jarry.....................	4.00	1.80	.50
☐ 238	Don Tannahill...................	4.00	1.80	.50
☐ 239	Rey Comeau.....................	4.00	1.80	.50
☐ 240	Gregg Sheppard UER	4.00	1.80	.50
	(Misspelled Shepherd on card front)			
☐ 241	Dave Dryden	4.50	2.00	.55
☐ 242	Ted McAneeley..................	4.00	1.80	.50
☐ 243	Lou Angotti	4.00	1.80	.50
☐ 244	Len Fontaine	4.00	1.80	.50
☐ 245	Bill Lesuk	4.00	1.80	.50
☐ 246	Fred Harvey	4.00	1.80	.50
☐ 247	Ken Dryden AS2	25.00	11.50	3.10
☐ 248	Bill White AS2	4.00	1.80	.50
☐ 249	Pat Stapleton AS2	4.00	1.80	.50
☐ 250	Ratelle/Cournoyer/	6.00	2.70	.75
	Hadfield AS2			
☐ 251	Henri Richard	5.00	2.30	.60
☐ 252	Bryan Lefley	4.00	1.80	.50
☐ 253	Stanley Cup Trophy............	8.00	3.60	1.00
☐ 254	Steve Vickers	7.00	3.10	.85
☐ 255	Wayne Hillman	4.00	1.80	.50
☐ 256	Ken Schinkel UER	4.00	1.80	.50
	(Misspelled Shinkel on card front)			
☐ 257	Kevin O'Shea....................	4.00	1.80	.50
☐ 258	Ron Low	5.00	2.30	.60
☐ 259	Don Lever	5.00	2.30	.60
☐ 260	Randy Manery	4.00	1.80	.50
☐ 261	Ed Johnston.....................	4.50	2.00	.55
☐ 262	Craig Ramsay	6.00	2.70	.75
☐ 263	Pete Laframboise	4.00	1.80	.50
☐ 264	Dan Maloney	5.00	2.30	.60
☐ 265	Bill Collins	4.00	1.80	.50
☐ 266	Paul Curtis	4.00	1.80	.50
☐ 267	Bob Nevin	4.00	1.80	.50
☐ 268	Penalty Min. Leaders..........	4.00	1.80	.50
	Bryan Watson			
	Keith Magnuson			
	Gary Dornhoefer			
☐ 269	Jim Roberts	4.00	1.80	.50
☐ 270	Brian Lavender	4.00	1.80	.50
☐ 271	Dale Rolfe	4.00	1.80	.50
☐ 272	Goals Leaders	18.00	8.00	2.30
	Phil Esposito			
	Vic Hadfield			
	Bobby Hull			
☐ 273	Michel Belhumeur	5.00	2.30	.60
☐ 274	Eddie Shack	4.50	2.00	.55
☐ 275	Wayne Stephenson UER	6.00	2.70	.75
	(Back has Forward stats instead of Goalie stats)			
☐ 276	Stanley Cup Winner	6.00	2.70	.75
	Boston Bruins Team			
☐ 277	Rick Kehoe......................	8.00	3.60	1.00
☐ 278	Gerry O'Flaherty	4.00	1.80	.50
☐ 279	Jacques Richard	4.00	1.80	.50
☐ 280	Scoring Leaders................	25.00	11.50	3.10
	Phil Esposito			
	Bobby Orr			
	Jean Ratelle			
☐ 281	Nick Beverley	5.00	2.30	.60
☐ 282	Larry Carriere	4.00	1.80	.50
☐ 283	Assists Leaders................	25.00	11.50	3.10
	Bobby Orr			
	Phil Esposito			
	Jean Ratelle			
☐ 284	Rick Smith IA	4.00	1.80	.50
☐ 285	Jerry Korab	5.00	2.30	.60
☐ 286	Goals Against	10.00	4.50	1.25
	Average Leaders			
	Tony Esposito			
	Gilles Villemure			
	Gump Worsley			
☐ 287	Ron Stackhouse	4.00	1.80	.50
☐ 288	Barry Long	4.00	1.80	.50
☐ 289	Dean Prentice	4.00	1.80	.50
☐ 290	Norm Beaudin	8.00	3.60	1.00
☐ 291	Mike Amodeo	8.00	3.60	1.00
☐ 292	Jim Harrison	8.00	3.60	1.00
☐ 293	J.C. Tremblay...................	8.00	3.60	1.00
☐ 294	Murray Hall	8.00	3.60	1.00

☐ 295	Bart Crashley...................	8.50	3.80	1.05
☐ 296	Wayne Connelly	8.50	3.80	1.05
☐ 297	Bobby Sheehan	8.00	3.60	1.00
☐ 298	Ron Anderson	8.00	3.60	1.00
☐ 299	Chris Bordeleau................	8.00	3.60	1.00
☐ 300	Les Binkley......................	8.50	3.80	1.05
☐ 301	Ron Walters	8.00	3.60	1.00
☐ 302	Jean-Guy Gendron	8.00	3.60	1.00
☐ 303	Gord Labossiere................	8.00	3.60	1.00
☐ 304	Gerry Odrowski	8.00	3.60	1.00
☐ 305	Mike McMahon	8.00	3.60	1.00
☐ 306	Gary Kurt........................	8.00	3.60	1.00
☐ 307	Larry Cahan.....................	8.00	3.60	1.00
☐ 308	Wally Boyer	8.00	3.60	1.00
☐ 309	Bob Charlebois.................	8.00	3.60	1.00
☐ 310	Bob Falkenberg	8.00	3.60	1.00
☐ 311	Jean Payette	8.00	3.60	1.00
☐ 312	Ted Taylor	8.00	3.60	1.00
☐ 313	Joe Szura	8.00	3.60	1.00
☐ 314	George Morrison	8.00	3.60	1.00
☐ 315	Wayne Rivers....................	8.00	3.60	1.00
☐ 316	Reg Fleming	8.00	3.60	1.00
☐ 317	Larry Hornung..................	8.00	3.60	1.00
☐ 318	Ron Climie	8.00	3.60	1.00
☐ 319	Val Fonteyne	8.00	3.60	1.00
☐ 320	Michel Archambault	8.00	3.60	1.00
☐ 321	Ab McDonald	8.00	3.60	1.00
☐ 322	Bob Leduc	8.00	3.60	1.00
☐ 323	Bob Wall	8.00	3.60	1.00
☐ 324	Alain Caron	8.00	3.60	1.00
☐ 325	Bob Woytowich..................	8.00	3.60	1.00
☐ 326	Guy Trottier.....................	8.00	3.60	1.00
☐ 327	Bill Hicke	8.00	3.60	1.00
☐ 328	Guy Dufour	8.00	3.60	1.00
☐ 329	Wayne Rutledge................	8.00	3.60	1.00
☐ 330	Gary Veneruzzo	8.00	3.60	1.00
☐ 331	Fred Speck	8.00	3.60	1.00
☐ 332	Ron Ward........................	8.00	3.60	1.00
☐ 333	Rosaire Paiement..............	8.50	3.80	1.05
☐ 334A	Checklist 3	65.00	6.50	1.30
	(Numbers 335-341 listed as More WHA Stars)			
☐ 334B	Checklist 3	55.00	5.50	1.10
	(Numbers 335-341 listed correctly)			
☐ 335	Michel Parizeau................	8.00	3.60	1.00
☐ 336	Bobby Hull	50.00	23.00	6.25
☐ 337	Wayne Carleton.................	8.00	3.60	1.00
☐ 338	John McKenzie..................	8.50	3.80	1.05
☐ 339	Jim Dorey........................	8.00	3.60	1.00
☐ 340	Gerry Cheevers	30.00	13.50	3.80
☐ 341	Gerry Pinder....................	20.00	5.00	1.60

1972-73 O-Pee-Chee Player Crests

This set consists of 22 full-color cardboard stickers measuring 2 1/2" by 3 1/2". The set was issued as an insert with the regular issue of the same year in with the first series wax packs. Cards are numbered on the front and have a blank adhesive back. Although the cards were designed so that the crest could be popped out, this is strongly discouraged. These stickers were printed in Canada.

	NRMT	VG-E	GOOD
COMPLETE SET (22)	100.00	40.00	10.00
COMMON PLAYER (1-22)	2.00	.80	.20
☐ 1 Pat Quinn	3.00	1.20	.30
☐ 2 Phil Esposito	10.00	4.00	1.00
☐ 3 Bobby Orr	40.00	16.00	4.00
☐ 4 Richard Martin	3.00	1.20	.30
☐ 5 Stan Mikita	8.00	3.25	.80
☐ 6 Bill White	3.00	1.20	.30
☐ 7 Red Berenson	3.00	1.20	.30
☐ 8 Gary Bergman	2.00	.80	.20
☐ 9 Gary Edwards	2.00	.80	.20
☐ 10 Bill Goldsworthy	3.00	1.20	.30
☐ 11 Jacques Laperriere	3.00	1.20	.30
☐ 12 Ken Dryden	15.00	6.00	1.50
☐ 13 Ed Westfall	3.00	1.20	.30
☐ 14 Walt Tkaczuk	3.00	1.20	.30
☐ 15 Brad Park	6.00	2.40	.60
☐ 16 Doug Favell	2.00	.80	.20
☐ 17 Eddie Shack	4.00	1.60	.40
☐ 18 Jacques Caron	2.00	.80	.20
☐ 19 Paul Henderson	3.00	1.20	.30
☐ 20 Jim Harrison	2.00	.80	.20
☐ 21 Dale Tallon	2.00	.80	.20
☐ 22 Orland Kurtenbach	3.00	1.20	.30

1972-73 O-Pee-Chee Team Canada

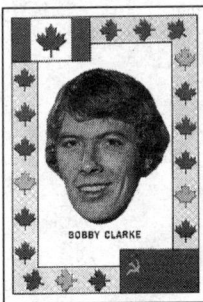 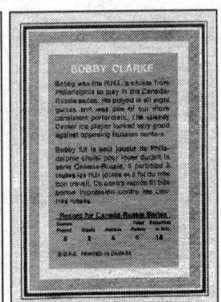

BOBBY CLARKE

This attractive set consists of 28 unnumbered color cards measuring 2 1/2" by 3 1/2". The 28 players are those who represented Team Canada against Russia in the 1972 Summit Series. Only the players' heads are shown surrounded by a border of maple leaves with a Canadian and Russian flag in each corner. The card back provides a summary of that player's performance in the eight-game series. The set was issued as an insert with the second series of the 1972-73 O-Pee-Chee regular issue. Backs are written in both French and English. The cards were printed in Canada.

	NRMT	VG-E	GOOD
COMPLETE SET (28)	175.00	70.00	18.00
COMMON PLAYER (1-28)	3.00	1.20	.30
☐ 1 Don Awrey	3.00	1.20	.30
☐ 2 Red Berenson	3.50	1.40	.35
☐ 3 Gary Bergman	3.00	1.20	.30
☐ 4 Wayne Cashman	3.50	1.40	.35
☐ 5 Bobby Clarke	15.00	6.00	1.50
☐ 6 Yvan Cournoyer	10.00	4.00	1.00
☐ 7 Ken Dryden	30.00	12.00	3.00
☐ 8 Ron Ellis	3.50	1.40	.35
☐ 9 Phil Esposito	25.00	10.00	2.50
☐ 10 Tony Esposito	15.00	6.00	1.50
☐ 11 Rod Gilbert	8.00	3.25	.80
☐ 12 Bill Goldsworthy	3.50	1.40	.35
☐ 13 Vic Hadfield	3.50	1.40	.35
☐ 14 Paul Henderson	5.00	2.00	.50
☐ 15 Dennis Hull	3.50	1.40	.35
☐ 16 Guy Lapointe	8.00	3.25	.80
☐ 17 Frank Mahovlich	15.00	6.00	1.50
☐ 18 Pete Mahovlich	3.50	1.40	.35
☐ 19 Stan Mikita	12.00	5.00	1.20
☐ 20 Jean-Paul Parise	3.00	1.20	.30

	NRMT	VG-E	GOOD
☐ 21 Brad Park	10.00	4.00	1.00
☐ 22 Gilbert Perreault	10.00	4.00	1.00
☐ 23 Jean Ratelle	8.00	3.25	.80
☐ 24 Mickey Redmond	5.00	2.00	.50
☐ 25 Serge Savard	8.00	3.25	.80
☐ 26 Rod Seiling	3.00	1.20	.30
☐ 27 Pat Stapleton	3.00	1.20	.30
☐ 28 Bill White	3.00	1.20	.30

1972-73 O-Pee-Chee Team Logos

This set of 30 team logo pushouts include logos for the 15 NHL established teams as well as the two new NHL teams, the 12 WHA teams, and the WHA League emblem. The cards are die-cut and adhesive backed. They were inserted in with the third series of the 1972-73 O-Pee-Chee wax packs. The expansion and WHA emblems are more difficult to find and are listed as SP in the checklist below. These inserts are standard size, 2 1/2" by 3 1/2".

	NRMT	VG-E	GOOD
COMPLETE SET (30)	100.00	40.00	10.00
COMMON LOGO (1-30)	2.00	.80	.20
COMMON LOGO SP	6.00	2.40	.60
☐ 1 NHL Logo	5.00	2.00	.50
☐ 2 Atlanta Flames SP	10.00	4.00	1.00
☐ 3 Boston Bruins	3.00	1.20	.30
☐ 4 Buffalo Sabres	2.00	.80	.20
☐ 5 California Seals	3.00	1.20	.30
☐ 6 Chicago Blackhawks	3.00	1.20	.30
☐ 7 Detroit Red Wings	3.00	1.20	.30
☐ 8 Los Angeles Kings	2.00	.80	.20
☐ 9 Minnesota North Stars	2.00	.80	.20
☐ 10 Montreal Canadiens	3.00	1.20	.30
☐ 11 New York Islanders SP	10.00	4.00	1.00
☐ 12 New York Rangers	3.00	1.20	.30
☐ 13 Philadelphia Flyers	3.00	1.20	.30
☐ 14 Pittsburgh Penguins	2.00	.80	.20
☐ 15 St. Louis Blues	2.00	.80	.20
☐ 16 Toronto Maple Leafs	3.00	1.20	.30
☐ 17 Vancouver Canucks	3.00	1.20	.30
☐ 18 WHA Logo SP	10.00	4.00	1.00
☐ 19 Chicago Cougars SP	6.00	2.40	.60
☐ 20 Cleveland Crusaders SP	6.00	2.40	.60
☐ 21 Edmonton Oilers SP	10.00	4.00	1.00
☐ 22 Houston Aeros SP	6.00	2.40	.60
☐ 23 Los Angeles Sharks SP	10.00	4.00	1.00
☐ 24 Minnesota Fighting Saints SP	6.00	2.40	.60
☐ 25 New England Whalers SP	6.00	2.40	.60
☐ 26 New York Raiders SP	6.00	2.40	.60
☐ 27 Ottawa Nationals SP	6.00	2.40	.60
☐ 28 Phila. Blazers SP	6.00	2.40	.60
☐ 29 Quebec Nordiques SP	10.00	4.00	1.00
☐ 30 Winnipeg Jets SP	10.00	4.00	1.00

1973-74 O-Pee-Chee

The 1973-74 O-Pee-Chee NHL set features 264 NHL players in color. The cards measure 2 1/2" by 3 1/2". The border

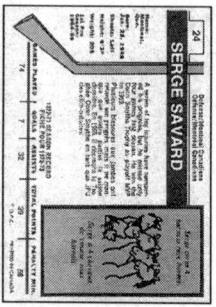

SERGE SAVARD   defense

color on the fronts differs from the Topps set. All the first series O-Pee-Chee cards have a red border whereas the second series cards have a green border. Topps cards are a mix of blue and green. Bilingual backs contain 1972-73 and career statistics, a short biography and a cartoon-illustrated fact about the player. Team cards (92-107) contain team and player records on the back. The cards were printed in Canada on cream or gray card stock. Rookie Cards in this set include Bill Barber, Larry Robinson, Billy Smith, Terry O'Reilly and Dave Schultz.

		NRMT	VG-E	GOOD
	COMPLETE SET (264)	400.00	180.00	50.00
	COMMON PLAYER (1-264)	1.00	.45	.13
☐ 1	Alex Delvecchio	5.00	1.00	.30
☐ 2	Gilles Meloche	1.25	.55	.16
☐ 3	Phil Roberto	1.00	.45	.13
☐ 4	Orland Kurtenbach	1.00	.45	.13
☐ 5	Gilles Marotte	1.00	.45	.13
☐ 6	Stan Mikita	8.00	3.60	1.00
☐ 7	Paul Henderson	1.25	.55	.16
☐ 8	Gregg Sheppard	1.00	.45	.13
☐ 9	Rod Seiling	1.00	.45	.13
☐ 10	Red Berenson	1.25	.55	.16
☐ 11	Jean Pronovost	1.25	.55	.16
☐ 12	Dick Redmond	1.00	.45	.13
☐ 13	Keith McCreary	1.00	.45	.13
☐ 14	Bryan Watson	1.00	.45	.13
☐ 15	Garry Unger	1.25	.55	.16
☐ 16	Neil Komadoski	1.00	.45	.13
☐ 17	Marcel Dionne	18.00	8.00	2.30
☐ 18	Ernie Hicke	1.00	.45	.13
☐ 19	Andre Boudrias	1.00	.45	.13
☐ 20	Bill Flett	1.00	.45	.13
☐ 21	Marshall Johnston	1.00	.45	.13
☐ 22	Gerry Meehan	1.25	.55	.16
☐ 23	Ed Johnston	1.25	.55	.16
☐ 24	Serge Savard	2.00	.90	.25
☐ 25	Walt Tkaczuk	1.25	.55	.16
☐ 26	Ken Hodge	1.25	.55	.16
☐ 27	Norm Ullman	3.00	1.35	.40
☐ 28	Cliff Koroll	1.00	.45	.13
☐ 29	Rey Comeau	1.00	.45	.13
☐ 30	Bobby Orr	40.00	18.00	5.00
☐ 31	Wayne Stephenson	1.25	.55	.16
☐ 32	Dan Maloney	1.25	.55	.16
☐ 33	Henry Boucha	1.00	.45	.13
☐ 34	Gerry Hart	1.00	.45	.13
☐ 35	Bobby Schmautz	1.00	.45	.13
☐ 36	Ross Lonsberry	1.00	.45	.13
☐ 37	Ted McAneeley	1.00	.45	.13
☐ 38	Don Luce	1.00	.45	.13
☐ 39	Jim McKenny	1.00	.45	.13
☐ 40	Jacques Laperriere	1.25	.55	.16
☐ 41	Bill Fairbairn	1.00	.45	.13
☐ 42	Craig Cameron	1.00	.45	.13
☐ 43	Bryan Hextall	1.00	.45	.13
☐ 44	Chuck Lefley	1.00	.45	.13
☐ 45	Dan Bouchard	1.25	.55	.16
☐ 46	Jean-Paul Parise	1.00	.45	.13
☐ 47	Barclay Plager	1.25	.55	.16
☐ 48	Mike Corrigan	1.00	.45	.13
☐ 49	Nick Libett	1.00	.45	.13
☐ 50	Bobby Clarke	20.00	9.00	2.50
☐ 51	Bert Marshall	1.00	.45	.13
☐ 52	Craig Patrick	1.25	.55	.16
☐ 53	Richard Lemieux	1.00	.45	.13
☐ 54	Tracy Pratt	1.00	.45	.13
☐ 55	Ron Ellis	1.25	.55	.16
☐ 56	Jacques Lemaire	3.50	1.55	.45
☐ 57	Steve Vickers	1.25	.55	.16
☐ 58	Carol Vadnais	1.00	.45	.13
☐ 59	Jim Rutherford	1.25	.55	.16
☐ 60	Rick Kehoe	1.25	.55	.16
☐ 61	Pat Quinn	1.25	.55	.16
☐ 62	Bill Goldsworthy	1.25	.55	.16
☐ 63	Dave Dryden	1.25	.55	.16
☐ 64	Rogatien Vachon	3.00	1.35	.40
☐ 65	Gary Bergman	1.00	.45	.13
☐ 66	Bernie Parent	7.00	3.10	.85
☐ 67	Ed Westfall	1.25	.55	.16
☐ 68	Ivan Boldirev	1.25	.55	.16
☐ 69	Don Tannahill	1.00	.45	.13
☐ 70	Gilbert Perreault	10.00	4.50	1.25
☐ 71	Mike Pelyk	1.00	.45	.13
☐ 72	Guy Lafleur	25.00	11.50	3.10
☐ 73	Pit Martin	1.25	.55	.16
☐ 74	Gilles Gilbert	5.00	2.30	.60
☐ 75	Jim Lorentz	1.00	.45	.13
☐ 76	Syl Apps	1.25	.55	.16
☐ 77	Phil Myre	1.25	.55	.16
☐ 78	Bill White	1.00	.45	.13
☐ 79	Jack Egers	1.00	.45	.13
☐ 80	Terry Harper	1.00	.45	.13
☐ 81	Bill Barber	25.00	11.50	3.10
☐ 82	Roy Edwards	1.25	.55	.16
☐ 83	Brian Spencer	1.25	.55	.16
☐ 84	Reggie Leach	2.50	1.15	.30
☐ 85	Wayne Cashman	1.25	.55	.16
☐ 86	Jim Schoenfeld	3.50	1.55	.45
☐ 87	Henri Richard	3.50	1.55	.45
☐ 88	Dennis O'Brien	1.00	.45	.13
☐ 89	Al McDonough	1.00	.45	.13
☐ 90	Tony Esposito	10.00	4.50	1.25
☐ 91	Joe Watson	1.00	.45	.13
☐ 92	Flames Team	2.50	1.15	.30
☐ 93	Bruins Team	2.75	1.25	.35
☐ 94	Sabres Team	2.50	1.15	.30
☐ 95	Golden Seals Team	2.50	1.15	.30
☐ 96	Blackhawks Team	2.50	1.15	.30
☐ 97	Red Wings Team	2.50	1.15	.30
☐ 98	Kings Team	2.50	1.15	.30
☐ 99	North Stars Team	2.50	1.15	.30
☐ 100	Canadiens Team	2.75	1.25	.35
☐ 101	Islanders Team	2.50	1.15	.30
☐ 102	Rangers Team	2.50	1.15	.30
☐ 103	Flyers Team	2.75	1.25	.35
☐ 104	Penguins Team	2.50	1.15	.30
☐ 105	Blues Team	2.50	1.15	.30
☐ 106	Maple Leafs Team	2.75	1.25	.35
☐ 107	Canucks Team	2.50	1.15	.30
☐ 108	Vic Hadfield	1.25	.55	.16
☐ 109	Tom Reid	1.00	.45	.13
☐ 110	Hilliard Graves	1.00	.45	.13
☐ 111	Don Lever	1.25	.55	.16
☐ 112	Jim Pappin	1.00	.45	.13
☐ 113	Andre Dupont	1.00	.45	.13
☐ 114	Guy Lapointe	1.50	.65	.19
☐ 115	Dennis Hextall	1.00	.45	.13
☐ 116	Checklist 1	35.00	3.50	.70
☐ 117	Bob Leiter	1.00	.45	.13
☐ 118	Ab DeMarco	1.00	.45	.13
☐ 119	Gilles Villemure	1.25	.55	.16
☐ 120	Phil Esposito	10.00	4.50	1.25
☐ 121	Mike Robitaille	1.00	.45	.13
☐ 122	Real Lemieux	1.00	.45	.13
☐ 123	Jim Neilson	1.00	.45	.13
☐ 124	Steve Durbano	1.00	.45	.13
☐ 125	Jude Drouin	1.00	.45	.13
☐ 126	Gary Smith	1.25	.55	.16
☐ 127	Cesare Maniago	1.25	.55	.16
☐ 128	Lowell MacDonald	1.00	.45	.13
☐ 129	Checklist 2	35.00	3.50	.70
☐ 130	Billy Harris	1.25	.55	.16
☐ 131	Randy Manery	1.00	.45	.13
☐ 132	Darryl Sittler	18.00	8.00	2.30
☐ 133	Goals Leaders	4.00	1.80	.50
	Phil Esposito			
	Rick MacLeish			
☐ 134	Assists Leaders	7.00	3.10	.85
	Phil Esposito			
	Bobby Clarke			
☐ 135	Scoring Leaders	7.00	3.10	.85
	Phil Esposito			
	Bobby Clarke			
☐ 136	Goals Against	10.00	4.50	1.25
	Average Leaders			
	Ken Dryden			
	Tony Esposito			
☐ 137	Penalty Min. Leaders	3.00	1.35	.40
	Jim Schoenfeld			

Dave Schultz
☐ 138	Power Play Goal	4.00	1.80	.50

Leaders
Phil Esposito
Rick MacLeish

☐ 139	Rene Robert	1.25	.55	.16
☐ 140	Dave Burrows	1.00	.45	.13
☐ 141	Jean Ratelle	3.50	1.55	.45
☐ 142	Billy Smith	35.00	16.00	4.40
☐ 143	Jocelyn Guevremont	1.00	.45	.13
☐ 144	Tim Ecclestone	1.00	.45	.13
☐ 145	Frank Mahovlich	6.00	2.70	.75
☐ 146	Rick MacLeish	3.50	1.55	.45
☐ 147	Johnny Bucyk	3.00	1.35	.40
☐ 148	Bob Plager	1.25	.55	.16
☐ 149	Curt Bennett	1.00	.45	.13
☐ 150	Dave Keon	2.50	1.15	.30
☐ 151	Keith Magnuson	1.25	.55	.16
☐ 152	Walt McKechnie	1.00	.45	.13
☐ 153	Roger Crozier	1.25	.55	.16
☐ 154	Ted Harris	1.00	.45	.13
☐ 155	Butch Goring	2.00	.90	.25
☐ 156	Rod Gilbert	3.50	1.55	.45
☐ 157	Yvan Cournoyer	4.00	1.80	.50
☐ 158	Doug Favell	1.25	.55	.16
☐ 159	Juha Widing	1.00	.45	.13
☐ 160	Ed Giacomin	4.00	1.80	.50
☐ 161	Germaine Gagnon UER	1.00	.45	.13
☐ 162	Dennis Kearns	1.00	.45	.13
☐ 163	Bill Collins	1.00	.45	.13
☐ 164	Peter Mahovlich	1.25	.55	.16
☐ 165	Brad Park	6.00	2.70	.75
☐ 166	Dave Schultz	10.00	4.50	1.25
☐ 167	Dallas Smith	1.00	.45	.13
☐ 168	Gary Sabourin	1.00	.45	.13
☐ 169	Jacques Richard	1.00	.45	.13
☐ 170	Brian Glennie	1.00	.45	.13
☐ 171	Dennis Hull	1.25	.55	.16
☐ 172	Joey Johnston	1.00	.45	.13
☐ 173	Richard Martin	3.50	1.55	.45
☐ 174	Barry Gibbs	1.00	.45	.13
☐ 175	Bob Berry	1.00	.45	.13
☐ 176	Greg Polis	1.00	.45	.13
☐ 177	Dale Rolfe	1.00	.45	.13
☐ 178	Gerry Desjardins	1.25	.55	.16
☐ 179	Bobby Lalonde	1.00	.45	.13
☐ 180	Mickey Redmond	1.25	.55	.16
☐ 181	Jim Roberts	1.00	.45	.13
☐ 182	Gary Dornhoefer	1.00	.45	.13
☐ 183	Derek Sanderson	3.50	1.55	.45
☐ 184	Brent Hughes	1.00	.45	.13
☐ 185	Larry Romanchych	1.00	.45	.13
☐ 186	Pierre Jarry	1.00	.45	.13
☐ 187	Doug Jarrett	1.00	.45	.13
☐ 188	Bob Stewart	1.00	.45	.13
☐ 189	Tim Horton	4.00	1.80	.50
☐ 190	Fred Harvey	1.00	.45	.13
☐ 191	Series A	1.50	.65	.19

Canadiens 4,
Sabres 2
☐ 192	Series B	1.50	.65	.19

Flyers 4,
North Stars 2
☐ 193	Series C	1.50	.65	.19

Blackhawks 4,
Blues 1
☐ 194	Series D	1.50	.65	.19

Rangers 4
Bruins
☐ 195	Series E	1.50	.65	.19

Canadiens 4,
Flyers 1
☐ 196	Series F	1.50	.65	.19

Blackhawks 4,
Rangers 1
☐ 197	Series G	1.50	.65	.19

Canadiens 4,
Blackhawks 2
☐ 198	Stanley Cup Champs	3.50	1.55	.45

Montreal Canadiens
☐ 199	Gary Edwards	1.25	.55	.16
☐ 200	Ron Schock	1.00	.45	.13
☐ 201	Bruce MacGregor	1.00	.45	.13
☐ 202	Bob Nystrom	8.00	3.60	1.00
☐ 203	Jerry Korab	1.00	.45	.13
☐ 204	Thommie Bergman	1.00	.45	.13
☐ 205	Bill Lesuk	1.00	.45	.13
☐ 206	Ed Van Impe	1.00	.45	.13
☐ 207	Doug Roberts	1.00	.45	.13
☐ 208	Chris Evans	1.00	.45	.13
☐ 209	Lynn Powis	1.00	.45	.13
☐ 210	Denis Dupere	1.00	.45	.13
☐ 211	Dale Tallon	1.00	.45	.13
☐ 212	Stan Gilbertson	1.00	.45	.13

☐ 213	Craig Ramsay	1.25	.55	.16
☐ 214	Danny Grant	1.25	.55	.16
☐ 215	Doug Volmar	1.00	.45	.13
☐ 216	Darryl Edestrand	1.00	.45	.13
☐ 217	Pete Stemkowski	1.00	.45	.13
☐ 218	Lorne Henning	1.00	.45	.13
☐ 219	Bryan McSheffrey	1.00	.45	.13
☐ 220	Guy Charron	1.25	.55	.16
☐ 221	Wayne Thomas	3.00	1.35	.40
☐ 222	Simon Nolet	1.00	.45	.13
☐ 223	Fred O'Donnell	1.00	.45	.13
☐ 224	Lou Angotti	1.00	.45	.13
☐ 225	Arnie Brown	1.00	.45	.13
☐ 226	Garry Monahan	1.00	.45	.13
☐ 227	Chico Maki	1.00	.45	.13
☐ 228	Gary Croteau	1.00	.45	.13
☐ 229	Paul Terbenche	1.00	.45	.13
☐ 230	Gump Worsley	4.00	1.80	.50
☐ 231	Jim Peters	1.00	.45	.13
☐ 232	Jack Lynch	1.00	.45	.13
☐ 233	Bobby Rousseau	1.00	.45	.13
☐ 234	Dave Hudson	1.00	.45	.13
☐ 235	Gregg Boddy	1.00	.45	.13
☐ 236	Ron Stackhouse	1.00	.45	.13
☐ 237	Larry Robinson	50.00	23.00	6.25
☐ 238	Bobby Taylor	2.00	.90	.25
☐ 239	Nick Beverley	1.00	.45	.13
☐ 240	Don Awrey	1.00	.45	.13
☐ 241	Doug Mohns	1.00	.45	.13
☐ 242	Eddie Shack	1.25	.55	.16
☐ 243	Phil Russell	2.00	.90	.25
☐ 244	Pete Laframboise	1.00	.45	.13
☐ 245	Steve Atkinson	1.00	.45	.13
☐ 246	Lou Nanne	1.25	.55	.16
☐ 247	Yvon Labre	1.00	.45	.13
☐ 248	Ted Irvine	1.00	.45	.13
☐ 249	Tom Miller	1.00	.45	.13
☐ 250	Gerry O'Flaherty	1.00	.45	.13
☐ 251	Larry Johnston	1.00	.45	.13
☐ 252	Michel Plasse	3.00	1.35	.40
☐ 253	Bob Kelly	1.00	.45	.13
☐ 254	Terry O'Reilly	10.00	4.50	1.25
☐ 255	Pierre Plante	1.00	.45	.13
☐ 256	Noel Price	1.00	.45	.13
☐ 257	Dunc Wilson	1.25	.55	.16
☐ 258	J.P. Bordeleau	1.00	.45	.13
☐ 259	Terry Murray	2.00	.90	.25
☐ 260	Larry Carriere	1.00	.45	.13
☐ 261	Pierre Bouchard	1.25	.55	.16
☐ 262	Frank St.Marseille	1.00	.45	.13
☐ 263	Checklist 3	35.00	3.50	.70
☐ 264	Fred Barrett	2.50	.45	.13

1973-74 O-Pee-Chee Rings

The 1973-74 O-Pee-Chee Rings set contains 17 standard-size (2 1/2" by 3 1/2") cards, featuring the NHL league and team logos. The fronts have a push-out cardboard ring and instructions in English and French. The rings are yellow-colored and feature a NHL team logo in the team's colors. The cards are numbered on the front and the backs are blank.

	NRMT	VG-E	GOOD
COMPLETE SET (17)	60.00	24.00	6.00
COMMON RING CARD (1-17)	5.00	2.00	.50

☐ 1	Vancouver Canucks	6.00	2.40	.60
☐ 2	Montreal Canadiens	6.00	2.40	.60
☐ 3	Toronto Maple Leafs	6.00	2.40	.60
☐ 4	NHL Logo	6.00	2.40	.60
☐ 5	Minnesota North Stars	5.00	2.00	.50
☐ 6	New York Rangers	6.00	2.40	.60
☐ 7	California Seals	6.00	2.40	.60
☐ 8	Pittsburgh Penguins	5.00	2.00	.50
☐ 9	Philadelphia Flyers	6.00	2.40	.60
☐ 10	Chicago Blackhawks	6.00	2.40	.60
☐ 11	Boston Bruins	6.00	2.40	.60
☐ 12	Los Angeles Kings	5.00	2.00	.50
☐ 13	Detroit Red Wings	6.00	2.40	.60
☐ 14	St. Louis Blues	5.00	2.00	.50
☐ 15	Buffalo Sabres	5.00	2.00	.50
☐ 16	Atlanta Flames	5.00	2.00	.50
☐ 17	New York Islanders	6.00	2.40	.60

1973-74 O-Pee-Chee Team Logos

The 1973-74 O-Pee-Chee Team Logos set contains 17 unnumbered, standard-size (2 1/2" by 3 1/2") color stickers, featuring the NHL league and team logos. The cards are die-cut and adhesive backed. After the NHL logo, they are ordered below alphabetically by team city/location. This set is distinguished from the similar set of the previous year by the presence of written instructions on the fronts.

		NRMT	VG-E	GOOD
COMPLETE SET (17)		25.00	10.00	2.50
COMMON CARD (1-17)		2.00	.80	.20
☐ 1	NHL Logo	3.00	1.20	.30
☐ 2	Atlanta Flames	2.00	.80	.20
☐ 3	Boston Bruins	3.00	1.20	.30
☐ 4	Buffalo Sabres	2.00	.80	.20
☐ 5	California Seals	2.00	.80	.20
☐ 6	Chicago Blackhawks	3.00	1.20	.30
☐ 7	Detroit Red Wings	3.00	1.20	.30
☐ 8	Los Angeles Kings	2.00	.80	.20
☐ 9	Minnesota North Stars	2.00	.80	.20
☐ 10	Montreal Canadiens	3.00	1.20	.30
☐ 11	New York Islanders	3.00	1.20	.30
☐ 12	New York Rangers	3.00	1.20	.30
☐ 13	Philadelphia Flyers	3.00	1.20	.30
☐ 14	Pittsburgh Penguins	2.00	.80	.20
☐ 15	St. Louis Blues	2.00	.80	.20
☐ 16	Toronto Maple Leafs	3.00	1.20	.30
☐ 17	Vancouver Canucks	3.00	1.20	.30

1973-74 O-Pee-Chee WHA Posters

Players featured in this set are from the World Hockey Association (WHA). The set consists of 20 large posters each measuring approximately 7 1/2" by 13 3/4" and was a separate issue in its own wax packs. The packs contained two posters and gum; gum stains are frequently seen. Posters are numbered on the front and were issued folded. As a result, folded copies are accepted as NRMT. The posters are blank backed.

		NRMT	VG-E	GOOD
COMPLETE SET (20)		60.00	24.00	6.00
COMMON PLAYER (1-20)		1.25	.50	.12
☐ 1	Al Smith	1.50	.60	.15
☐ 2	J.C. Tremblay	1.50	.60	.15
☐ 3	Guy Dufour	1.25	.50	.12
☐ 4	Pat Stapleton	1.50	.60	.15
☐ 5	Rosaire Paiement	1.25	.50	.12
☐ 6	Gerry Cheevers	6.00	2.40	.60
☐ 7	Gerry Pinder	1.50	.60	.15
☐ 8	Wayne Carleton	1.25	.50	.12
☐ 9	Bob Leduc	1.25	.50	.12
☐ 10	Andre Lacroix	1.50	.60	.15
☐ 11	Jim Harrison	1.25	.50	.12
☐ 12	Ron Climie	1.25	.50	.12
☐ 13	Gordie Howe	25.00	10.00	2.50
☐ 14	The Howe Family	15.00	6.00	1.50
	Gordie/Mark/Marty			
☐ 15	Mike Walton	1.50	.60	.15
☐ 16	Bobby Hull	12.50	5.00	1.25
☐ 17	Chris Bordeleau	1.25	.50	.12
☐ 18	Claude St.Sauveur	1.25	.50	.12
☐ 19	Bryan Campbell	1.25	.50	.12
☐ 20	Marc Tardif	1.50	.60	.15

1974-75 O-Pee-Chee NHL

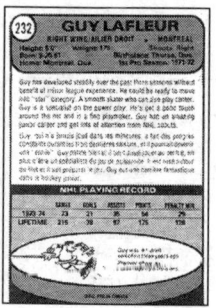

The 1974-75 O-Pee-Chee NHL set contains 396 color cards. The first 264 cards are identical to that of Topps in terms of numbering and photos. Bilingual backs feature the player's 1973-74 and career statistics, a short biography and a cartoon-illustrated fact about the player. The first six cards in the set (1-6) feature league leaders of the previous season. Cards measure 2 1/2" by 3 1/2" and were printed in Canada. The set marks the return of coach cards, including Rookie Cards of Don Cherry and Scotty Bowman. Other Rookie Cards include Bob Gainey, Lanny McDonald, Rick Middleton, Denis Potvin, Glenn Resch, Steve Shutt and Borje Salming.

	NRMT	VG-E	GOOD
COMPLETE SET (396)......	450.00	200.00	57.50
COMMON PLAYER (1-396)......	.75	.35	.09
☐ 1 Goal Leaders	5.00	1.50	.50
Phil Esposito			
Bill Goldsworthy			
☐ 2 Assists Leaders	8.00	3.60	1.00
Bobby Orr			
Dennis Hextall			
☐ 3 Scoring Leaders	6.00	2.70	.75
Phil Esposito			
Bobby Clarke			
☐ 4 Goals Against Leaders	2.50	1.15	.30
Doug Favell			
Bernie Parent			
☐ 5 Penalty Min. Leaders......	1.00	.45	.13
Bryan Watson			
Dave Schultz			
☐ 6 Power Play Goal	1.00	.45	.13
Leaders			
Mickey Redmond			
Rick MacLeish			
☐ 7 Gary Bromley	.90	.40	.11
☐ 8 Bill Barber	8.00	3.60	1.00
☐ 9 Emile Francis CO	1.50	.65	.19
☐ 10 Gilles Gilbert	.90	.40	.11
☐ 11 John Davidson	7.50	3.40	.95
☐ 12 Ron Ellis	.90	.40	.11
☐ 13 Syl Apps	.75	.35	.09
☐ 14 Flames Leaders	1.25	.55	.16
Jacques Richard			
Tom Lysiak			
Tom Lysiak			
Keith McCreary			
☐ 15 Dan Bouchard	.90	.40	.11
☐ 16 Ivan Boldirev	.90	.40	.11
☐ 17 Gary Coalter	.75	.35	.09
☐ 18 Bob Berry	.75	.35	.09
☐ 19 Red Berenson	.90	.40	.11
☐ 20 Stan Mikita	7.00	3.10	.85
☐ 21 Fred Shero CO	3.50	1.55	.45
☐ 22 Gary Smith	.90	.40	.11
☐ 23 Bill Mikkelson	.75	.35	.09
☐ 24 Jacques Lemaire UER	3.50	1.55	.45
(Pictured in			
Sabres sweater)			
☐ 25 Gilbert Perreault	7.00	3.10	.85
☐ 26 Cesare Maniago	.90	.40	.11
☐ 27 Bobby Schmautz	.75	.35	.09
☐ 28 Bruins Leaders	10.00	4.50	1.25
Phil Esposito			
Bobby Orr			
Phil Esposito			
Johnny Bucyk			
☐ 29 Steve Vickers	.90	.40	.11
☐ 30 Lowell MacDonald UER......	.75	.35	.09
(Home: Thornburn,			
should be Thorburn)			
☐ 31 Fred Stanfield	.75	.35	.09
☐ 32 Ed Westfall	.90	.40	.11
☐ 33 Curt Bennett	.75	.35	.09
☐ 34 Bep Guidolin CO	.75	.35	.09
☐ 35 Cliff Koroll	.75	.35	.09
☐ 36 Gary Croteau	.75	.35	.09
☐ 37 Mike Corrigan	.75	.35	.09
☐ 38 Henry Boucha	.75	.35	.09
☐ 39 Ron Low	.90	.40	.11
☐ 40 Darryl Sittler	9.00	4.00	1.15
☐ 41 Tracy Pratt	.75	.35	.09
☐ 42 Sabres Leaders	1.25	.55	.16
Richard Martin			
Rene Robert			
Richard Martin			
Richard Martin			
☐ 43 Larry Carriere	.75	.35	.09
☐ 44 Gary Dornhoefer	.75	.35	.09
☐ 45 Denis Herron......	5.00	2.30	.60
☐ 46 Doug Favell	.90	.40	.11
☐ 47 Dave Gardner	.75	.35	.09
☐ 48 Morris Mott	.75	.35	.09
☐ 49 Marc Boileau CO	.75	.35	.09
☐ 50 Brad Park	5.00	2.30	.60
☐ 51 Bob Leiter	.75	.35	.09
☐ 52 Tom Reid	.75	.35	.09
☐ 53 Serge Savard	1.50	.65	.19
☐ 54 Checklist 1-132 UER	20.00	2.00	.40
(73 Brent Hughes, should			
be 73 Butch Deadmarsh)			
☐ 55 Terry Harper	.75	.35	.09
☐ 56 Golden Seals	1.00	.45	.13
Leaders			
Joey Johnston			
Joey Johnston			
Joey Johnston			
Walt McKechnie			
☐ 57 Guy Charron......	.90	.40	.11
☐ 58 Pit Martin	.75	.35	.09
☐ 59 Chris Evans	.75	.35	.09
☐ 60 Bernie Parent	5.00	2.30	.60
☐ 61 Jim Lorentz	.75	.35	.09
☐ 62 Dave Kryskow	.75	.35	.09
☐ 63 Lou Angotti CO......	.75	.35	.09
☐ 64 Bill Flett......	.75	.35	.09
☐ 65 Vic Hadfield......	.90	.40	.11
☐ 66 Wayne Merrick	.75	.35	.09
☐ 67 Andre Dupont......	.75	.35	.09
☐ 68 Tom Lysiak	2.50	1.15	.30
☐ 69 Blackhawks Leaders......	1.50	.65	.19
Jim Pappin			
Stan Mikita			
J.P. Bordeleau			
☐ 70 Guy Lapointe	1.00	.45	.13
☐ 71 Gerry O'Flaherty	.75	.35	.09
☐ 72 Marcel Dionne	12.00	5.50	1.50
☐ 73 Butch Deadmarsh	.75	.35	.09
☐ 74 Butch Goring......	.90	.40	.11
☐ 75 Keith Magnuson	.75	.35	.09
☐ 76 Red Kelly CO	1.50	.65	.19
☐ 77 Pete Stemkowski......	.75	.35	.09
☐ 78 Jim Roberts	.75	.35	.09
Montreal Canadiens			
☐ 79 Don Luce......	.75	.35	.09
☐ 80 Don Awrey	.75	.35	.09
☐ 81 Rick Kehoe	.90	.40	.11
☐ 82 Billy Smith......	10.00	4.50	1.25
☐ 83 Jean-Paul Parise	.75	.35	.09
☐ 84 Red Wings Leaders......	2.50	1.15	.30
Mickey Redmond			
Marcel Dionne			
Marcel Dionne			
Bill Hogaboam			
☐ 85 Ed Van Impe......	.75	.35	.09
☐ 86 Randy Manery	.75	.35	.09
☐ 87 Barclay Plager	.90	.40	.11
☐ 88 Inge Hammarstrom	.75	.35	.09
☐ 89 Ab DeMarco	.75	.35	.09
☐ 90 Bill White......	.75	.35	.09
☐ 91 Al Arbour CO	2.50	1.15	.30
☐ 92 Bob Stewart	.75	.35	.09
☐ 93 Jack Egers......	.75	.35	.09
☐ 94 Don Lever......	.90	.40	.11
☐ 95 Reggie Leach	1.50	.65	.19
☐ 96 Dennis O'Brien	.75	.35	.09
☐ 97 Peter Mahovlich......	.90	.40	.11
☐ 98 Kings Leaders	1.00	.45	.13
Butch Goring			
Frank St.Marseille			
Butch Goring			
Don Kozak			
☐ 99 Gerry Meehan	.90	.40	.11
☐ 100 Bobby Orr	35.00	16.00	4.40
☐ 101 Jean Potvin	1.00	.45	.13
☐ 102 Rod Seiling	.75	.35	.09
☐ 103 Keith McCreary	.75	.35	.09
☐ 104 Phil Maloney CO	.75	.35	.09
☐ 105 Denis Dupere	.75	.35	.09
☐ 106 Steve Durbano	.75	.35	.09
☐ 107 Bob Plager UER	.90	.40	.11
(Photo actually			
Barclay Plager)			
☐ 108 Chris Oddleifson	.75	.35	.09
☐ 109 Jim Neilson	.75	.35	.09
☐ 110 Jean Pronovost	.90	.40	.11
☐ 111 Don Kozak	.75	.35	.09
☐ 112 North Stars Leaders	1.00	.45	.13
Bill Goldsworthy			
Dennis Hextall			
Dennis Hextall			
Danny Grant			
☐ 113 Jim Pappin	.75	.35	.09
☐ 114 Richard Lemieux	.75	.35	.09
☐ 115 Dennis Hextall	.75	.35	.09
☐ 116 Bill Hogaboam......	.75	.35	.09
☐ 117 Canucks Leaders	1.00	.45	.13
Dennis Ververgaert			
Bobby Schmautz			
Andre Boudrias			
Andre Boudrias			
Don Tannahill			
☐ 118 Jimmy Anderson CO	.75	.35	.09
☐ 119 Walt Tkaczuk	.90	.40	.11
☐ 120 Mickey Redmond	.90	.40	.11
☐ 121 Jim Schoenfeld	1.50	.65	.19
☐ 122 Jocelyn Guevremont	.75	.35	.09
☐ 123 Bob Nystrom	2.50	1.15	.30
☐ 124 Canadiens Leaders	2.50	1.15	.30
Yvan Cournoyer			

Frank Mahovlich
Frank Mahovlich
Claude Larose

☐ 125	Lew Morrison	.75	.35	.09
☐ 126	Terry Murray	.90	.40	.11
☐ 127	Richard Martin AS	1.00	.45	.13
☐ 128	Ken Hodge AS	1.00	.45	.13
☐ 129	Phil Esposito AS	4.00	1.80	.50
☐ 130	Bobby Orr AS	18.00	8.00	2.30
☐ 131	Brad Park AS	2.50	1.15	.30
☐ 132	Gilles Gilbert AS	1.00	.45	.13
☐ 133	Lowell MacDonald AS	1.00	.45	.13
☐ 134	Bill Goldsworthy AS	1.00	.45	.13
☐ 135	Bobby Clarke AS	6.00	2.70	.75
☐ 136	Bill White AS	1.00	.45	.13
☐ 137	Dave Burrows AS	1.00	.45	.13
☐ 138	Bernie Parent AS	2.50	1.15	.30
☐ 139	Jacques Richard	.75	.35	.09
☐ 140	Yvan Cournoyer	3.50	1.55	.45
☐ 141	Rangers Leaders	2.50	1.15	.30

Rod Gilbert
Brad Park
Brad Park
Rod Gilbert

☐ 142	Rene Robert	.90	.40	.11
☐ 143	J. Bob Kelly	.75	.35	.09
☐ 144	Ross Lonsberry	.75	.35	.09
☐ 145	Jean Ratelle	2.50	1.15	.30
☐ 146	Dallas Smith	.75	.35	.09
☐ 147	Boom Boom Geoffrion CO	3.50	1.55	.45
☐ 148	Ted McAneeley	.75	.35	.09
☐ 149	Pierre Plante	.75	.35	.09
☐ 150	Dennis Hull	.90	.40	.11
☐ 151	Dave Keon	2.00	.90	.25
☐ 152	Dave Dunn	.75	.35	.09
☐ 153	Michel Belhumeur	.90	.40	.11
☐ 154	Flyers Leaders	3.00	1.35	.40

Bobby Clarke
Bobby Clarke
Bobby Clarke
Dave Schultz

☐ 155	Ken Dryden	22.00	10.00	2.80
☐ 156	John Wright	.75	.35	.09
☐ 157	Larry Romanchych	.75	.35	.09
☐ 158	Ralph Stewart	.75	.35	.09
☐ 159	Mike Robitaille	.75	.35	.09
☐ 160	Ed Giacomin	3.00	1.35	.40
☐ 161	Don Cherry CO	25.00	11.50	3.10
☐ 162	Checklist 133-264	20.00	2.00	.40
☐ 163	Rick MacLeish	2.00	.90	.25
☐ 164	Greg Polis	.75	.35	.09
☐ 165	Carol Vadnais	.75	.35	.09
☐ 166	Pete Laframboise	.75	.35	.09
☐ 167	Ron Schock	.75	.35	.09
☐ 168	Jack McDonald	30.00	13.50	3.80
☐ 169	Scouts Emblem	2.00	.90	.25

Draft Selections
on back

☐ 170	Tony Esposito	7.50	3.40	.95
☐ 171	Pierre Jarry	.75	.35	.09
☐ 172	Dan Maloney	.90	.40	.11
☐ 173	Peter McDuffe	.90	.40	.11
☐ 174	Danny Grant	.90	.40	.11
☐ 175	John Stewart	.75	.35	.09
☐ 176	Floyd Smith CO	.75	.35	.09
☐ 177	Bert Marshall	.75	.35	.09
☐ 178	Chuck Lefley UER	.75	.35	.09

(Photo actually
Pierre Bouchard)

☐ 179	Gilles Villemure	.90	.40	.11
☐ 180	Borje Salming	14.00	6.25	1.75
☐ 181	Doug Mohns	.75	.35	.09
☐ 182	Barry Wilkins	.75	.35	.09
☐ 183	Penguins Leaders	1.00	.45	.13

Lowell MacDonald
Syl Apps
Syl Apps
Lowell MacDonald

☐ 184	Gregg Sheppard	.75	.35	.09
☐ 185	Joey Johnston	.75	.35	.09
☐ 186	Dick Redmond	.75	.35	.09
☐ 187	Simon Nolet	.75	.35	.09
☐ 188	Ron Stackhouse	.75	.35	.09
☐ 189	Marshall Johnston	.75	.35	.09
☐ 190	Richard Martin	2.00	.90	.25
☐ 191	Andre Boudrias	.75	.35	.09
☐ 192	Steve Atkinson	.75	.35	.09
☐ 193	Nick Libett	.75	.35	.09
☐ 194	Bob Murdoch	.75	.35	.09

Los Angeles Kings

☐ 195	Denis Potvin	40.00	18.00	5.00
☐ 196	Dave Schultz	3.50	1.55	.45
☐ 197	Blues Leaders	1.25	.55	.16

Garry Unger
Garry Unger
Garry Unger
Pierre Plante

☐ 198	Jim McKenny	.75	.35	.09
☐ 199	Gerry Hart	.75	.35	.09
☐ 200	Phil Esposito	7.00	3.10	.85
☐ 201	Rod Gilbert	2.50	1.15	.30
☐ 202	Jacques Laperriere	.90	.40	.11
☐ 203	Barry Gibbs	.75	.35	.09
☐ 204	Billy Reay CO	.90	.40	.11
☐ 205	Gilles Meloche	.90	.40	.11
☐ 206	Wayne Cashman	.90	.40	.11
☐ 207	Dennis Ververgaert	.75	.35	.09
☐ 208	Phil Roberto	.75	.35	.09
☐ 209	Quarter Finals	1.00	.45	.13

Flyers sweep
Flames

☐ 210	Quarter Finals	1.00	.45	.13

Rangers over
Canadiens

☐ 211	Quarter Finals	1.00	.45	.13

Bruins sweep
Maple Leafs

☐ 212	Quarter Finals	1.00	.45	.13

Blackhawks over
L.A. Kings

☐ 213	Semi-Finals	1.00	.45	.13

Flyers over Rangers

☐ 214	Semi-Finals	1.00	.45	.13

Bruins over
Blackhawks

☐ 215	'73-'74 Finals	1.00	.45	.13

Flyers over Bruins

☐ 216	Cup Champions	1.50	.65	.19

Philadelphia Flyers

☐ 217	Joe Watson	.75	.35	.09
☐ 218	Wayne Stephenson	.90	.40	.11
☐ 219	Maple Leaf Leaders	2.00	.90	.25

Darryl Sittler
Norm Ullman
Darryl Sittler
Paul Henderson
Denis Dupere

☐ 220	Bill Goldsworthy	.90	.40	.11
☐ 221	Don Marcotte	.75	.35	.09
☐ 222	Alex Delvecchio CO	1.50	.65	.19
☐ 223	Stan Gilbertson	.75	.35	.09
☐ 224	Mike Murphy	.75	.35	.09
☐ 225	Jim Rutherford	.90	.40	.11
☐ 226	Phil Russell	.75	.35	.09
☐ 227	Lynn Powis	.75	.35	.09
☐ 228	Billy Harris	.75	.35	.09
☐ 229	Bob Pulford CO	.90	.40	.11

L.A. Kings Coach

☐ 230	Ken Hodge	.90	.40	.11
☐ 231	Bill Fairbairn	.75	.35	.09
☐ 232	Guy Lafleur	18.00	8.00	2.30
☐ 233	Islanders Leaders UER	3.50	1.55	.45

Billy Harris
Ralph Stewart
Denis Potvin
Denis Potvin
Ralph Stewart
(Steward on front)

☐ 234	Fred Barrett	.75	.35	.09
☐ 235	Rogatien Vachon	2.50	1.15	.30
☐ 236	Norm Ullman	2.00	.90	.25
☐ 237	Garry Unger	.90	.40	.11
☐ 238	Jack Gordon CO	.75	.35	.09
☐ 239	Johnny Bucyk	2.50	1.15	.30
☐ 240	Bob Dailey	.75	.35	.09
☐ 241	Dave Burrows	.75	.35	.09
☐ 242	Len Frig	.75	.35	.09
☐ 243	Masterson Trophy	2.00	.90	.25

Henri Richard

☐ 244	Hart Trophy	4.00	1.80	.50

Phil Esposito

☐ 245	Byng Trophy	1.50	.65	.19

Johnny Bucyk

☐ 246	Ross Trophy	4.00	1.80	.50

Phil Esposito

☐ 247	Prince of Wales	1.00	.45	.13

Trophy
Boston Bruins

☐ 248	Norris Trophy	18.00	8.00	2.30

Bobby Orr

☐ 249	Vezina Trophy	2.00	.90	.25

Bernie Parent

☐ 250	Stanley Cup	1.00	.45	.13

Philadelphia Flyers

☐ 251	Smythe Trophy	2.00	.90	.25

Bernie Parent

☐ 252	Calder Trophy	10.00	4.50	1.25

Denis Potvin

☐ 253	Campbell Trophy	1.00	.45	.13
	Philadelphia Flyers			
☐ 254	Pierre Bouchard	.75	.35	.09
☐ 255	Jude Drouin	.75	.35	.09
☐ 256	Capitals Emblem	2.00	.90	.25
	(Draft Selections on back)			
☐ 257	Michel Plasse	.90	.40	.11
☐ 258	Juha Widing	.75	.35	.09
☐ 259	Bryan Watson	.75	.35	.09
☐ 260	Bobby Clarke UER	12.00	5.50	1.50
	Back mentions Art Ross Trophy. Should be Hart Trophy			
☐ 261	Scotty Bowman CO	18.00	8.00	2.30
☐ 262	Craig Patrick	.90	.40	.11
☐ 263	Craig Cameron	.75	.35	.09
☐ 264	Ted Irvine	.75	.35	.09
☐ 265	Ed Johnston	.90	.40	.11
☐ 266	Dave Forbes	.75	.35	.09
☐ 267	Detroit Red Wings	2.00	.90	.25
	Team Card (checklist back)			
☐ 268	Rick Dudley	1.00	.45	.13
☐ 269	Darcy Rota	.90	.40	.11
☐ 270	Phil Myre	.90	.40	.11
☐ 271	Larry Brown	.75	.35	.09
☐ 272	Bob Neely	.75	.35	.09
☐ 273	Jerry Byers	.75	.35	.09
☐ 274	Pittsburgh Penguins	2.00	.90	.25
	Team Card (checklist back)			
☐ 275	Glenn Goldup	.75	.35	.09
☐ 276	Ron Harris	.75	.35	.09
☐ 277	Joe Lundrigan	.75	.35	.09
☐ 278	Mike Christie	.75	.35	.09
☐ 279	Doug Rombough	.75	.35	.09
☐ 280	Larry Robinson	20.00	9.00	2.50
☐ 281	St. Louis Blues	2.00	.90	.25
	Team Card (checklist back)			
☐ 282	John Marks	.75	.35	.09
☐ 283	Don Saleski	.90	.40	.11
☐ 284	Rick Wilson	.75	.35	.09
☐ 285	Andre Savard	.75	.35	.09
☐ 286	Pat Quinn	.90	.40	.11
☐ 287	Los Angeles Kings	2.00	.90	.25
	Team Card (checklist back)			
☐ 288	Norm Gratton	.75	.35	.09
☐ 289	Ian Turnbull	1.00	.45	.13
☐ 290	Derek Sanderson	2.50	1.15	.30
☐ 291	Murray Oliver	.75	.35	.09
☐ 292	Wilf Paiement UER	2.50	1.15	.30
	(Misspelled Paiemont on card front)			
☐ 293	Nelson Debenedet	.75	.35	.09
☐ 294	Greg Joly	.75	.35	.09
☐ 295	Terry O'Reilly	3.50	1.55	.45
☐ 296	Rey Comeau	.75	.35	.09
☐ 297	Michel Larocque	5.00	2.30	.60
☐ 298	Floyd Thomson	.75	.35	.09
☐ 299	Jean-Guy Lagace	.75	.35	.09
☐ 300	Philadelphia Flyers	2.25	1.00	.30
	Team Card (checklist back)			
☐ 301	Al MacAdam	3.00	1.35	.40
☐ 302	George Ferguson	.75	.35	.09
☐ 303	Jim Watson	2.50	1.15	.30
☐ 304	Rick Middleton	18.00	8.00	2.30
☐ 305	Craig Ramsay UER	.75	.35	.09
	(Name on front is "Graig")			
☐ 306	Hilliard Graves	.75	.35	.09
☐ 307	New York Islanders	2.00	.90	.25
	Team Card (checklist back)			
☐ 308	Blake Dunlop	.75	.35	.09
☐ 309	J.P. Bordeleau	.75	.35	.09
☐ 310	Brian Glennie	.75	.35	.09
☐ 311	Checklist 265-396 UER	20.00	2.00	.40
	(373 Gilies Marotte, should be Gilles)			
☐ 312	Doug Roberts	.75	.35	.09
☐ 313	Darryl Edestrand	.75	.35	.09
☐ 314	Ron Anderson	.75	.35	.09
☐ 315	Chicago Blackhawks	2.00	.90	.25
	Team Card (checklist back)			
☐ 316	Steve Shutt	18.00	8.00	2.30
☐ 317	Doug Horbul	.75	.35	.09
☐ 318	Billy Lochead	.75	.35	.09
☐ 319	Fred Harvey	.75	.35	.09
☐ 320	Gene Carr	.75	.35	.09
☐ 321	Henri Richard	2.50	1.15	.30
☐ 322	Vancouver Canucks	2.00	.90	.25
	Team Card (checklist back)			
☐ 323	Tim Ecclestone	.75	.35	.09
☐ 324	Dave Lewis	1.00	.45	.13
☐ 325	Lou Nanne	.90	.40	.11
☐ 326	Bobby Rousseau	.75	.35	.09
☐ 327	Dunc Wilson	.90	.40	.11
☐ 328	Brian Spencer	.75	.35	.09
☐ 329	Rick Hampton	.75	.35	.09
☐ 330	Montreal Canadiens	2.25	1.00	.30
	Team Card UER (checklist back; 275 Glen Holdup, should be Goldup)			
☐ 331	Jack Lynch	.75	.35	.09
☐ 332	Garnet Bailey	.75	.35	.09
☐ 333	Al Sims	.75	.35	.09
☐ 334	Orest Kindrachuk	2.00	.90	.25
☐ 335	Dave Hudson	.75	.35	.09
☐ 336	Bob Murray	.90	.40	.11
☐ 337	Buffalo Sabres	2.00	.90	.25
	Team Card (checklist back)			
☐ 338	Sheldon Kannegiesser	.75	.35	.09
☐ 339	Bill MacMillan	.75	.35	.09
☐ 340	Paulin Bordeleau	.75	.35	.09
☐ 341	Dale Rolfe	.75	.35	.09
☐ 342	Yvon Lambert	2.00	.90	.25
☐ 343	Bob Paradise	.75	.35	.09
☐ 344	Germaine Gagnon UER	.75	.35	.09
☐ 345	Yvon Labre	.75	.35	.09
☐ 346	Chris Ahrens	.75	.35	.09
☐ 347	Doug Grant	.75	.35	.09
☐ 348	Blaine Stoughton	4.00	1.80	.50
☐ 349	Gregg Boddy	.75	.35	.09
☐ 350	Boston Bruins	2.25	1.00	.30
	Team Card (checklist back)			
☐ 351	Doug Jarrett	.75	.35	.09
☐ 352	Terry Crisp	.75	.35	.09
☐ 353	Glenn Resch	15.00	6.75	1.90
☐ 354	Jerry Korab	.75	.35	.09
☐ 355	Stan Weir	.75	.35	.09
☐ 356	Noel Price	.75	.35	.09
☐ 357	Bill Clement	7.50	3.40	.95
☐ 358	Neil Komadoski	.75	.35	.09
☐ 359	Murray Wilson	.75	.35	.09
☐ 360	Dale Tallon UER	.75	.35	.09
	(Misspelled Talon on card front)			
☐ 361	Gary Doak	.75	.35	.09
☐ 362	Randy Rota	.75	.35	.09
☐ 363	Minnesota North Stars	2.00	.90	.25
	Team Card (checklist back)			
☐ 364	Bill Collins	.75	.35	.09
☐ 365	Thommie Bergman UER	.75	.35	.09
	(Misspelled Tommie on card front)			
☐ 366	Dennis Kearns	.75	.35	.09
☐ 367	Lorne Henning	.75	.35	.09
☐ 368	Gary Sabourin	.75	.35	.09
☐ 369	Mike Bloom	.75	.35	.09
☐ 370	New York Rangers	2.00	.90	.25
	Team Card (checklist back)			
☐ 371	Gary Simmons	2.50	1.15	.30
☐ 372	Dwight Bialowas	.75	.35	.09
☐ 373	Gilles Marotte	.75	.35	.09
☐ 374	Frank St.Marseille	.75	.35	.09
☐ 375	Garry Howatt	1.00	.45	.13
☐ 376	Ross Brooks	.75	.35	.09
☐ 377	Atlanta Flames	2.00	.90	.25
	Team Card (checklist back)			
☐ 378	Bob Nevin	.75	.35	.09
☐ 379	Lyle Moffat	.75	.35	.09
☐ 380	Bob Kelly	.75	.35	.09
☐ 381	John Gould	.75	.35	.09
☐ 382	Dave Fortier	.75	.35	.09
☐ 383	Jean Hamel	.75	.35	.09
☐ 384	Bert Wilson	.75	.35	.09
☐ 385	Chuck Arnason	.75	.35	.09
☐ 386	Bruce Cowick	.75	.35	.09
☐ 387	Ernie Hicke	.75	.35	.09
☐ 388	Bob Gainey	20.00	9.00	2.50
☐ 389	Vic Venasky	.75	.35	.09
☐ 390	Toronto Maple Leafs	2.25	1.00	.30
	Team Card (checklist back)			
☐ 391	Eric Vail	2.00	.90	.25

			NRMT	VG-E	GOOD
☐	392	Bobby Lalonde	.75	.35	.09
☐	393	Jerry Butler	.75	.35	.09
☐	394	Tom Williams	.75	.35	.09
☐	395	Chico Maki	.75	.35	.09
☐	396	Tom Bladon	4.00	.80	.20

1974-75 O-Pee-Chee WHA

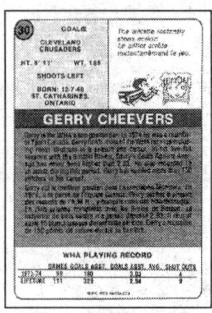

The 1974-75 O-Pee-Chee WHA set consists of 66 color cards. The cards were originally sold in ten-cent wax packs. Printed in Canada, the cards measure 2 1/2" by 3 1/2". Bilingual backs feature a short biography, the player's 1973-74 and career WHA statistics as well as a cartoon-illustrated hockey fact or interpretation of a referee's signal. Rookie Cards in this set include Anders Hedberg and Ulf Nilsson, although some collectors and dealers consider the Howe Family card to be the Rookie Card for Mark and Marty Howe.

			NRMT	VG-E	GOOD
	COMPLETE SET (66)		175.00	80.00	22.00
	COMMON PLAYER (1-66)		2.50	1.15	.30
☐	1	The Howes Gordie Howe Mark Howe Marty Howe	75.00	19.00	3.80
☐	2	Bruce MacGregor	2.50	1.15	.30
☐	3	Wayne Dillon	2.50	1.15	.30
☐	4	Ulf Nilsson	9.00	4.00	1.15
☐	5	Serge Bernier	3.00	1.35	.40
☐	6	Bryan Campbell	2.50	1.15	.30
☐	7	Rosaire Paiement	2.50	1.15	.30
☐	8	Tom Webster	3.00	1.35	.40
☐	9	Gerry Pinder	2.50	1.15	.30
☐	10	Mike Walton	2.50	1.15	.30
☐	11	Norm Beaudin	2.50	1.15	.30
☐	12	Bob Whitlock	2.50	1.15	.30
☐	13	Wayne Rivers	2.50	1.15	.30
☐	14	Gerry Odrowski	2.50	1.15	.30
☐	15	Ron Climie	2.50	1.15	.30
☐	16	Tom Simpson	2.50	1.15	.30
☐	17	Anders Hedberg	9.00	4.00	1.15
☐	18	J.C. Tremblay	2.50	1.15	.30
☐	19	Mike Pelyk	2.50	1.15	.30
☐	20	Dave Dryden	3.00	1.35	.40
☐	21	Ron Ward	2.50	1.15	.30
☐	22	Larry Lund	2.50	1.15	.30
☐	23	Ron Buchanan	2.50	1.15	.30
☐	24	Pat Hickey	4.00	1.80	.50
☐	25	Danny Lawson	3.00	1.35	.40
☐	26	Bob Guindon	2.50	1.15	.30
☐	27	Gene Peacosh	2.50	1.15	.30
☐	28	Fran Huck	2.50	1.15	.30
☐	29	Al Hamilton	2.50	1.15	.30
☐	30	Gerry Cheevers	12.00	5.50	1.50
☐	31	Heikki Riihiranta	2.50	1.15	.30
☐	32	Don Burgess	2.50	1.15	.30
☐	33	John French	2.50	1.15	.30
☐	34	Jim Wiste	2.50	1.15	.30
☐	35	Pat Stapleton	3.00	1.35	.40
☐	36	J.P. LeBlanc	2.50	1.15	.30
☐	37	Mike Antonovich	2.50	1.15	.30
☐	38	Joe Daley	3.00	1.35	.40
☐	39	Ross Perkins	2.50	1.15	.30
☐	40	Frank Mahovlich	10.00	4.50	1.25
☐	41	Rejean Houle	2.50	1.15	.30
☐	42	Ron Chipperfield	2.50	1.15	.30
☐	43	Marc Tardif	2.50	1.15	.30
☐	44	Murray Keogan	2.50	1.15	.30
☐	45	Wayne Carleton	2.50	1.15	.30
☐	46	Andre Gaudette	2.50	1.15	.30
☐	47	Ralph Backstrom	3.00	1.35	.40
☐	48	Don McLeod	2.50	1.15	.30
☐	49	Vaclav Nedomansky	4.00	1.80	.50
☐	50	Bobby Hull	35.00	16.00	4.40
☐	51	Rusty Patenaude	2.50	1.15	.30
☐	52	Michel Parizeau	2.50	1.15	.30
☐	53	Checklist	20.00	2.00	.30
☐	54	Wayne Connelly	3.00	1.35	.40
☐	55	Gary Veneruzzo	2.50	1.15	.30
☐	56	Dennis Sobchuk	2.50	1.15	.30
☐	57	Paul Henderson	3.00	1.35	.40
☐	58	Andy Brown	3.00	1.35	.40
☐	59	Poul Popiel	2.50	1.15	.30
☐	60	Andre Lacroix	3.00	1.35	.40
☐	61	Gary Jarrett	2.50	1.15	.30
☐	62	Claude St.Sauveur	2.50	1.15	.30
☐	63	Real Cloutier	4.00	1.80	.50
☐	64	Jacques Plante	35.00	16.00	4.40
☐	65	Gilles Gratton	6.00	2.70	.75
☐	66	Lars-Erik Sjoberg	5.00	1.15	.30

1975-76 O-Pee-Chee NHL

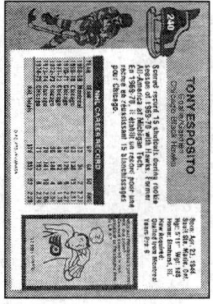

The 1975-76 O-Pee-Chee NHL set consists of 396 color cards. The cards were originally sold in ten-cent wax packs. The first 330 cards have identical fronts (except perhaps for a short traded line) as the Topps set of this year. Printed in Canada, the cards measure 2 1/2" by 3 1/2". Number 395 was not issued; however, the set contains two of number 267 which are checklist cards. Cards 26, 27, 200, 236, 243, 260, and 359 come with or without a traded line. Team cards (81-98) have a team checklist on the back. Bilingual backs contain year by year and career statistics, a short biography and a cartoon-illustrated NHL fact or interpretation of a referee's signal. The key Rookie Cards in this set are Clark Gillies, Pierre Larouche, and Harold Snepsts. Snepsts, the last card in the set, is considered very difficult to find in top grades.

			NRMT	VG-E	GOOD
	COMPLETE SET (396)		275.00	125.00	34.00
	COMMON PLAYER (1-396)		.50	.23	.06
☐	1	Stanley Cup Finals Philadelphia 4, Buffalo 2	2.00	.50	.10
☐	2	Semi-Finals Philadelphia 4, N.Y. Islanders 3	.75	.35	.09
☐	3	Semi-Finals Buffalo 4, Montreal	.75	.35	.09
☐	4	Quarter Finals N.Y. Islanders 4, Pittsburgh 2	.75	.35	.09
☐	5	Quarter Finals Montreal 4,	.75	.35	.09

	Vancouver 1				
☐ 6	Quarter Finals	.75	.35	.09	
	Buffalo 4,				
	Chicago 1				
☐ 7	Quarter Finals	.75	.35	.09	
	Philadelphia 4,				
	Toronto 0				
☐ 8	Curt Bennett	.50	.23	.06	
☐ 9	Johnny Bucyk	2.00	.90	.25	
☐ 10	Gilbert Perreault	5.00	2.30	.60	
☐ 11	Darryl Edestrand	.50	.23	.06	
☐ 12	Ivan Boldirev	.50	.23	.06	
☐ 13	Nick Libett	.50	.23	.06	
☐ 14	Jim McElmury	.50	.23	.06	
☐ 15	Frank St.Marseille	.50	.23	.06	
☐ 16	Blake Dunlop	.50	.23	.06	
☐ 17	Yvon Lambert	.60	.25	.08	
☐ 18	Gerry Hart	.50	.23	.06	
☐ 19	Steve Vickers	.50	.23	.06	
☐ 20	Rick MacLeish	.60	.25	.08	
☐ 21	Bob Paradise	.50	.23	.06	
☐ 22	Red Berenson	.60	.25	.08	
☐ 23	Lanny McDonald	10.00	4.50	1.25	
☐ 24	Mike Robitaille	.50	.23	.06	
☐ 25	Ron Low	.60	.25	.08	
☐ 26A	Bryan Hextall	1.00	.45	.13	
	(No mention of trade)				
☐ 26B	Bryan Hextall	.75	.35	.09	
	(Trade noted)				
☐ 27A	Carol Vadnais	1.00	.45	.13	
	(No mention of trade)				
☐ 27B	Carol Vadnais	.75	.35	.09	
	(Trade noted)				
☐ 28	Jim Lorentz	.50	.23	.06	
☐ 29	Gary Simmons	.60	.25	.08	
☐ 30	Stan Mikita	5.00	2.30	.60	
☐ 31	Bryan Watson	.50	.23	.06	
☐ 32	Guy Charron	.50	.23	.06	
☐ 33	Bob Murdoch	.50	.23	.06	
	Los Angeles Kings				
☐ 34	Norm Gratton	.50	.23	.06	
☐ 35	Ken Dryden	18.00	8.00	2.30	
☐ 36	Jean Potvin	.50	.23	.06	
☐ 37	Rick Middleton	5.00	2.30	.60	
☐ 38	Ed Van Impe	.50	.23	.06	
☐ 39	Rick Kehoe	.60	.25	.08	
☐ 40	Garry Unger	.60	.25	.08	
☐ 41	Ian Turnbull	.60	.25	.08	
☐ 42	Dennis Ververgaert	.50	.23	.06	
☐ 43	Mike Marson	.50	.23	.06	
☐ 44	Randy Manery	.50	.23	.06	
☐ 45	Gilles Gilbert	.60	.25	.08	
☐ 46	Rene Robert	.60	.25	.08	
☐ 47	Bob Stewart	.50	.23	.06	
☐ 48	Pit Martin	.50	.23	.06	
☐ 49	Danny Grant	.60	.25	.08	
☐ 50	Peter Mahovlich	.60	.25	.08	
☐ 51	Dennis Patterson	.50	.23	.06	
☐ 52	Mike Murphy	.50	.23	.06	
☐ 53	Dennis O'Brien	.50	.23	.06	
☐ 54	Garry Howatt	.50	.23	.06	
☐ 55	Ed Giacomin	2.50	1.15	.30	
☐ 56	Andre Dupont	.50	.23	.06	
☐ 57	Chuck Arnason	.50	.23	.06	
☐ 58	Bob Gassoff	.50	.23	.06	
☐ 59	Ron Ellis	.60	.25	.08	
☐ 60	Andre Boudrias	.50	.23	.06	
☐ 61	Yvon Labre	.50	.23	.06	
☐ 62	Hilliard Graves	.50	.23	.06	
☐ 63	Wayne Cashman	.60	.25	.08	
☐ 64	Danny Gare	3.00	1.35	.40	
☐ 65	Rick Hampton	.50	.23	.06	
☐ 66	Darcy Rota	.50	.23	.06	
☐ 67	Bill Hogaboam	.50	.23	.06	
☐ 68	Denis Herron	.60	.25	.08	
☐ 69	Sheldon Kannegiesser	.50	.23	.06	
☐ 70	Yvan Cournoyer	2.50	1.15	.30	
☐ 71	Ernie Hicke	.50	.23	.06	
☐ 72	Bert Marshall	.50	.23	.06	
☐ 73	Derek Sanderson	2.00	.90	.25	
☐ 74	Tom Bladon	.60	.25	.08	
☐ 75	Ron Schock	.50	.23	.06	
☐ 76	Larry Sacharuk	.50	.23	.06	
☐ 77	George Ferguson	.50	.23	.06	
☐ 78	Ab DeMarco	.50	.23	.06	
☐ 79	Tom Williams	.50	.23	.06	
☐ 80	Phil Roberto	.50	.23	.06	
☐ 81	Bruins Team	2.00	.90	.25	
	(checklist back)				
☐ 82	Seals Team	1.50	.65	.19	
	(checklist back)				
☐ 83	Sabres Team	1.50	.65	.19	
	(checklist back)				
☐ 84	Blackhawks Team	1.50	.65	.19	

	(checklist back)				
☐ 85	Flames Team	1.50	.65	.19	
	(checklist back)				
☐ 86	Kings Team	1.50	.65	.19	
	(checklist back)				
☐ 87	Red Wings Team	1.50	.65	.19	
	(checklist back)				
☐ 88	Scouts Team	1.50	.65	.19	
	(checklist back)				
☐ 89	North Stars Team	1.50	.65	.19	
	(checklist back)				
☐ 90	Canadiens Team	2.00	.90	.25	
	(checklist back)				
☐ 91	Maple Leafs Team	2.00	.90	.25	
	(checklist back)				
☐ 92	Islanders Team	1.50	.65	.19	
	(checklist back)				
☐ 93	Penguins Team	1.50	.65	.19	
	(checklist back)				
☐ 94	Rangers Team	1.50	.65	.19	
	(checklist back)				
☐ 95	Flyers Team	1.50	.65	.19	
	(checklist back)				
☐ 96	Blues Team	1.50	.65	.19	
	(checklist back)				
☐ 97	Canucks Team	1.50	.65	.19	
	(checklist back)				
☐ 98	Capitals Team	1.50	.65	.19	
	(checklist back)				
☐ 99	Checklist 1-110	14.00	1.40	.30	
☐ 100	Bobby Orr	30.00	13.50	3.80	
☐ 101	Germaine Gagnon UER	.50	.23	.06	
☐ 102	Phil Russell	.50	.23	.06	
☐ 103	Billy Lochead	.50	.23	.06	
☐ 104	Robin Burns	.50	.23	.06	
☐ 105	Gary Edwards	.60	.25	.08	
☐ 106	Dwight Bialowas	.50	.23	.06	
☐ 107	Doug Risebrough UER	3.50	1.55	.45	
	(Photo actually				
	Bob Gainey)				
☐ 108	Dave Lewis	.50	.23	.06	
☐ 109	Bill Fairbairn	.50	.23	.06	
☐ 110	Ross Lonsberry	.50	.23	.06	
☐ 111	Ron Stackhouse	.50	.23	.06	
☐ 112	Claude Larose	.50	.23	.06	
☐ 113	Don Luce	.50	.23	.06	
☐ 114	Errol Thompson	.50	.23	.06	
☐ 115	Gary Smith	.60	.25	.08	
☐ 116	Jack Lynch	.50	.23	.06	
☐ 117	Jacques Richard	.50	.23	.06	
☐ 118	Dallas Smith	.50	.23	.06	
☐ 119	Dave Gardner	.50	.23	.06	
☐ 120	Mickey Redmond	.60	.25	.08	
☐ 121	John Marks	.50	.23	.06	
☐ 122	Dave Hudson	.50	.23	.06	
☐ 123	Bob Nevin	.50	.23	.06	
☐ 124	Fred Barrett	.50	.23	.06	
☐ 125	Gerry Desjardins	.60	.25	.08	
☐ 126	Guy Lafleur UER	15.00	6.75	1.90	
	(Shown as Defenseman				
	on card front)				
☐ 127	Jean-Paul Parise	.50	.23	.06	
☐ 128	Walt Tkaczuk	.60	.25	.08	
☐ 129	Gary Dornhoefer	.50	.23	.06	
☐ 130	Syl Apps	.50	.23	.06	
☐ 131	Bob Plager	.60	.25	.08	
☐ 132	Stan Weir	.50	.23	.06	
☐ 133	Tracy Pratt	.50	.23	.06	
☐ 134	Jack Egers	.50	.23	.06	
☐ 135	Eric Vail	.50	.23	.06	
☐ 136	Al Sims	.50	.23	.06	
☐ 137	Larry Patey	.50	.23	.06	
☐ 138	Jim Schoenfeld	.60	.25	.08	
☐ 139	Cliff Koroll	.50	.23	.06	
☐ 140	Marcel Dionne	9.00	4.00	1.15	
☐ 141	Jean-Guy Lagace	.50	.23	.06	
☐ 142	Juha Widing	.50	.23	.06	
☐ 143	Lou Nanne	.60	.25	.08	
☐ 144	Serge Savard	1.00	.45	.13	
☐ 145	Glenn Resch	5.00	2.30	.60	
☐ 146	Ron Greschner	4.00	1.80	.50	
☐ 147	Dave Schultz	2.00	.90	.25	
☐ 148	Barry Wilkins	.50	.23	.06	
☐ 149	Floyd Thomson	.50	.23	.06	
☐ 150	Darryl Sittler	7.50	3.40	.95	
☐ 151	Paulin Bordeleau	.50	.23	.06	
☐ 152	Ron Lalonde	.50	.23	.06	
☐ 153	Larry Romanchych	.50	.23	.06	
☐ 154	Larry Carriere	.50	.23	.06	
☐ 155	Andre Savard	.50	.23	.06	
☐ 156	Dave Hrechkosy	.50	.23	.06	
☐ 157	Bill White	.50	.23	.06	
☐ 158	Dave Kryskow	.50	.23	.06	
☐ 159	Denis Dupere	.50	.23	.06	

☐ 160	Rogatien Vachon	2.00	.90	.25
☐ 161	Doug Rombough	.50	.23	.06
☐ 162	Murray Wilson	.50	.23	.06
☐ 163	Bob Bourne	3.00	1.35	.40
☐ 164	Gilles Marotte	.50	.23	.06
☐ 165	Vic Hadfield	.60	.25	.08
☐ 166	Reggie Leach	.60	.25	.08
☐ 167	Jerry Butler	.50	.23	.06
☐ 168	Inge Hammarstrom	.50	.23	.06
☐ 169	Chris Oddleifson	.50	.23	.06
☐ 170	Greg Joly	.50	.23	.06
☐ 171	Checklist 111-220	14.00	1.40	.30
☐ 172	Pat Quinn	.60	.25	.08
☐ 173	Dave Forbes	.50	.23	.06
☐ 174	Len Frig	.50	.23	.06
☐ 175	Richard Martin	.60	.25	.08
☐ 176	Keith Magnuson	.50	.23	.06
☐ 177	Dan Maloney	.50	.23	.06
☐ 178	Craig Patrick	.60	.25	.08
☐ 179	Tom Williams	.50	.23	.06
☐ 180	Bill Goldsworthy	.60	.25	.08
☐ 181	Steve Shutt	5.00	2.30	.60
☐ 182	Ralph Stewart	.50	.23	.06
☐ 183	John Davidson	2.50	1.15	.30
☐ 184	Bob Kelly	.50	.23	.06
☐ 185	Ed Johnston	.60	.25	.08
☐ 186	Dave Burrows	.50	.23	.06
☐ 187	Dave Dunn	.50	.23	.06
☐ 188	Dennis Kearns	.50	.23	.06
☐ 189	Bill Clement	2.00	.90	.25
☐ 190	Gilles Meloche	.60	.25	.08
☐ 191	Bob Leiter	.50	.23	.06
☐ 192	Jerry Korab	.50	.23	.06
☐ 193	Joey Johnston	.50	.23	.06
☐ 194	Walt McKechnie	.50	.23	.06
☐ 195	Wilf Paiement	.60	.25	.08
☐ 196	Bob Berry	.50	.23	.06
☐ 197	Dean Talafous	.50	.23	.06
☐ 198	Guy Lapointe	.60	.25	.08
☐ 199	Clark Gillies	7.00	3.10	.85
☐ 200A	Phil Esposito	7.50	3.40	.95
	(No mention of trade)			
☐ 200B	Phil Esposito	5.00	2.30	.60
	(Trade noted)			
☐ 201	Greg Polis	.50	.23	.06
☐ 202	Jim Watson	.60	.25	.08
☐ 203	Gord McRae	.60	.25	.08
☐ 204	Lowell MacDonald	.50	.23	.06
☐ 205	Barclay Plager	.60	.25	.08
☐ 206	Don Lever	.50	.23	.06
☐ 207	Bill Mikkelson	.50	.23	.06
☐ 208	Goals Leaders	5.00	2.30	.60
	Phil Esposito			
	Guy Lafleur			
	Richard Martin			
☐ 209	Assists Leaders	7.00	3.10	.85
	Bobby Clarke			
	Bobby Orr			
	Pete Mahovlich			
☐ 210	Scoring Leaders	8.00	3.60	1.00
	Bobby Orr			
	Phil Esposito			
	Marcel Dionne			
☐ 211	Penalty Min. Leaders	.75	.35	.09
	Dave Schultz			
	Andre Dupont			
	Phil Russell			
☐ 212	Power Play	3.00	1.35	.40
	Goal Leaders			
	Phil Esposito			
	Richard Martin			
	Danny Grant			
☐ 213	Goals Against	7.00	3.10	.85
	Average Leaders			
	Bernie Parent			
	Rogatien Vachon			
	Ken Dryden			
☐ 214	Barry Gibbs	.50	.23	.06
☐ 215	Ken Hodge	.60	.25	.08
☐ 216	Jocelyn Guevremont	.50	.23	.06
☐ 217	Warren Williams	.50	.23	.06
☐ 218	Dick Redmond	.50	.23	.06
☐ 219	Jim Rutherford	.60	.25	.08
☐ 220	Simon Nolet	.50	.23	.06
☐ 221	Butch Goring	.60	.25	.08
☐ 222	Glen Sather	1.00	.45	.13
☐ 223	Mario Tremblay UER	3.00	1.35	.40
	(Photo not him)			
☐ 224	Jude Drouin	.50	.23	.06
☐ 225	Rod Gilbert	2.00	.90	.25
☐ 226	Bill Barber	5.00	2.30	.60
☐ 227	Gary Inness	.60	.25	.08
☐ 228	Wayne Merrick	.50	.23	.06
☐ 229	Rod Seiling	.50	.23	.06
☐ 230	Tom Lysiak	.60	.25	.08
☐ 231	Bob Dailey	.50	.23	.06
☐ 232	Michel Belhumeur	.60	.25	.08
☐ 233	Bill Hajt	.50	.23	.06
☐ 234	Jim Pappin	.50	.23	.06
☐ 235	Gregg Sheppard	.50	.23	.06
☐ 236A	Gary Bergman	1.00	.45	.13
	(No mention of trade)			
☐ 236B	Gary Bergman	.75	.35	.09
	(Trade noted)			
☐ 237	Randy Rota	.50	.23	.06
☐ 238	Neil Komadoski	.50	.23	.06
☐ 239	Craig Cameron	.50	.23	.06
☐ 240	Tony Esposito	5.00	2.30	.60
☐ 241	Larry Robinson	12.00	5.50	1.50
☐ 242	Billy Harris	.50	.23	.06
☐ 243A	Jean Ratelle	3.00	1.35	.40
	(No mention of trade)			
☐ 243B	Jean Ratelle	2.00	.90	.25
	(Trade noted)			
☐ 244	Ted Irvine UER	.50	.23	.06
	(Photo actually			
	Ted Harris)			
☐ 245	Bob Kelly	.50	.23	.06
☐ 246	Bobby Lalonde	.50	.23	.06
☐ 247	Ron Jones	.50	.23	.06
☐ 248	Rey Comeau	.50	.23	.06
☐ 249	Michel Plasse	.60	.25	.08
☐ 250	Bobby Clarke	10.00	4.50	1.25
☐ 251	Bobby Schmautz	.50	.23	.06
☐ 252	Peter McNab	3.50	1.55	.45
☐ 253	Al MacAdam	.50	.23	.06
☐ 254	Dennis Hull	.60	.25	.08
☐ 255	Terry Harper	.50	.23	.06
☐ 256	Peter McDuffe	.60	.25	.08
☐ 257	Jean Hamel	.50	.23	.06
☐ 258	Jacques Lemaire	2.00	.90	.25
☐ 259	Bob Nystrom	.60	.25	.08
☐ 260A	Brad Park	4.00	1.80	.50
	(No mention of trade)			
☐ 260B	Brad Park	3.00	1.35	.40
	(Trade noted)			
☐ 261	Cesare Maniago	.60	.25	.08
☐ 262	Don Saleski	.50	.23	.06
☐ 263	J. Bob Kelly	.50	.23	.06
☐ 264	Bob Hess	.50	.23	.06
☐ 265	Blaine Stoughton	1.00	.45	.13
☐ 266	John Gould	.50	.23	.06
☐ 267A	Checklist 221-330	16.00	1.60	.30
	(See number 395)			
☐ 267B	Checklist 331-396	16.00	1.60	.30
☐ 268	Dan Bouchard	.60	.25	.08
☐ 269	Don Marcotte	.50	.23	.06
☐ 270	Jim Neilson	.50	.23	.06
☐ 271	Craig Ramsay	.50	.23	.06
☐ 272	Grant Mulvey	1.50	.65	.19
☐ 273	Larry Giroux	.50	.23	.06
☐ 274	Real Lemieux	.50	.23	.06
☐ 275	Denis Potvin	15.00	6.75	1.90
☐ 276	Don Kozak	.50	.23	.06
☐ 277	Tom Reid	.50	.23	.06
☐ 278	Bob Gainey	7.00	3.10	.85
☐ 279	Nick Beverley	.50	.23	.06
☐ 280	Jean Pronovost	.60	.25	.08
☐ 281	Joe Watson	.50	.23	.06
☐ 282	Chuck Lefley	.50	.23	.06
☐ 283	Borje Salming	5.00	2.30	.60
☐ 284	Garnet Bailey	.50	.23	.06
☐ 285	Gregg Boddy	.50	.23	.06
☐ 286	Bobby Clarke AS1	4.00	1.80	.50
☐ 287	Denis Potvin AS1	5.00	2.30	.60
☐ 288	Bobby Orr AS1	15.00	6.75	1.90
☐ 289	Richard Martin AS1	.75	.35	.09
☐ 290	Guy Lafleur AS1	5.00	2.30	.60
☐ 291	Bernie Parent AS1	2.00	.90	.25
☐ 292	Phil Esposito AS2	3.50	1.55	.45
☐ 293	Guy Lapointe AS2	.75	.35	.09
☐ 294	Borje Salming AS2	2.00	.90	.25
☐ 295	Steve Vickers AS2	.75	.35	.09
☐ 296	Rene Robert AS2	.75	.35	.09
☐ 297	Rogatien Vachon AS2	1.00	.45	.13
☐ 298	Buster Harvey	.50	.23	.06
☐ 299	Gary Sabourin	.50	.23	.06
☐ 300	Bernie Parent	4.00	1.80	.50
☐ 301	Terry O'Reilly	2.00	.90	.25
☐ 302	Ed Westfall	.60	.25	.08
☐ 303	Pete Stemkowski	.50	.23	.06
☐ 304	Pierre Bouchard	.50	.23	.06
☐ 305	Pierre Larouche	7.00	3.10	.85
☐ 306	Lee Fogolin	.50	.23	.06
☐ 307	Gerry O'Flaherty	.50	.23	.06
☐ 308	Phil Myre	.60	.25	.08

☐ 309	Pierre Plante	.50	.23	.06
☐ 310	Dennis Hextall	.50	.23	.06
☐ 311	Jim McKenny	.50	.23	.06
☐ 312	Vic Venasky	.50	.23	.06
☐ 313	Flames Leaders	.75	.35	.09
	Eric Vail			
	Tom Lysiak			
	Tom Lysiak			
	Tom Lysiak			
☐ 314	Bruins Leaders	8.00	3.60	1.00
	Phil Esposito			
	Bobby Orr			
	Phil Esposito			
	Johnny Bucyk			
☐ 315	Sabres Leaders	.75	.35	.09
	Richard Martin			
	Rene Robert			
	Rene Robert			
	Richard Martin			
☐ 316	Seals Leaders	.75	.35	.09
	Dave Hrechkosy			
	Larry Patey			
	Stan Weir			
	Stan Weir			
	Larry Patey			
	Dave Hrechkosy			
☐ 317	Blackhawks Leaders	1.50	.65	.19
	Stan Mikita			
	Jim Pappin			
	Stan Mikita			
	Stan Mikita			
	Stan Mikita			
☐ 318	Red Wings Leaders	1.50	.65	.19
	Danny Grant			
	Marcel Dionne			
	Marcel Dionne			
	Danny Grant			
☐ 319	Scouts Leaders	.75	.35	.09
	Simon Nolet			
	Wilf Paiement			
	Simon Nolet			
	Guy Charron			
	Simon Nolet			
☐ 320	Kings Leaders	.75	.35	.09
	Bob Nevin			
	Bob Nevin			
	Bob Nevin			
	Bob Nevin			
	Juha Widing			
	Bob Berry			
☐ 321	North Stars Leaders	.75	.35	.09
	Bill Goldsworthy			
	Dennis Hextall			
	Dennis Hextall			
	Bill Goldsworthy			
☐ 322	Canadiens Leaders	3.00	1.35	.40
	Guy Lafleur			
	Pete Mahovlich			
	Guy Lafleur			
	Guy Lafleur			
☐ 323	Islanders Leaders	2.50	1.15	.30
	Bob Nystrom			
	Denis Potvin			
	Denis Potvin			
	Clark Gillies			
☐ 324	Rangers Leaders	1.50	.65	.19
	Steve Vickers			
	Steve Vickers			
	Rod Gilbert			
	Rod Gilbert			
	Jean Ratelle			
☐ 325	Flyers Leaders	2.00	.90	.25
	Reggie Leach			
	Bobby Clarke			
	Bobby Clarke			
	Reggie Leach			
☐ 326	Penguins Leaders	.75	.35	.09
	Jean Pronovost			
	Ron Schock			
	Ron Schock			
	Jean Pronovost			
☐ 327	Blues Leaders	.75	.35	.09
	Garry Unger			
	Garry Unger			
	Garry Unger			
	Garry Unger			
	Larry Sacharuk			
☐ 328	Maple Leafs Leaders	2.50	1.15	.30
	Darryl Sittler			
	Darryl Sittler			
	Darryl Sittler			
	Darryl Sittler			
☐ 329	Canucks Leaders	.75	.35	.09

	Don Lever			
	Don Lever			
	Andre Boudrias			
	Andre Boudrias			
☐ 330	Capitals Leaders	.75	.35	.09
	Tommy Williams			
	Garnet Bailey			
	Tommy Williams			
	Garnet Bailey			
	Tommy Williams			
☐ 331	Noel Price	.50	.23	.06
☐ 332	Fred Stanfield	.50	.23	.06
☐ 333	Doug Jarrett	.50	.23	.06
☐ 334	Gary Coalter	.50	.23	.06
☐ 335	Murray Oliver	.50	.23	.06
☐ 336	Dave Fortier	.50	.23	.06
☐ 337	Terry Crisp UER	.50	.23	.06
	(Photo actually			
	Don Saleski)			
☐ 338	Bert Wilson	.50	.23	.06
☐ 339	John Grisdale	.50	.23	.06
☐ 340	Ken Broderick	.60	.25	.08
☐ 341	Frank Spring	.50	.23	.06
☐ 342	Mike Korney	.50	.23	.06
☐ 343	Gene Carr	.50	.23	.06
☐ 344	Don Awrey	.50	.23	.06
☐ 345	Pat Hickey	.50	.23	.06
☐ 346	Colin Campbell	1.25	.55	.16
☐ 347	Wayne Thomas	.60	.25	.08
☐ 348	Bob Gryp	.50	.23	.06
☐ 349	Bill Flett	.50	.23	.06
☐ 350	Roger Crozier	.60	.25	.08
☐ 351	Dale Tallon	.50	.23	.06
☐ 352	Larry Johnston	.50	.23	.06
☐ 353	John Flesch	.50	.23	.06
☐ 354	Lorne Henning	.50	.23	.06
☐ 355	Wayne Stephenson	.60	.25	.08
☐ 356	Rick Wilson	.50	.23	.06
☐ 357	Garry Monahan	.50	.23	.06
☐ 358	Gary Doak	.50	.23	.06
☐ 359A	Pierre Jarry	1.00	.45	.13
	(No mention of trade)			
☐ 359B	Pierre Jarry	.75	.35	.09
	(Trade noted)			
☐ 360	George Pesut	.50	.23	.06
☐ 361	Mike Corrigan	.50	.23	.06
☐ 362	Michel Larocque	1.25	.55	.16
☐ 363	Wayne Dillon	.50	.23	.06
☐ 364	Pete Laframboise	.50	.23	.06
☐ 365	Brian Glennie	.50	.23	.06
☐ 366	Mike Christie	.50	.23	.06
☐ 367	Jean Lemieux	.50	.23	.06
☐ 368	Gary Bromley	.60	.25	.08
☐ 369	J.P. Bordeleau	.50	.23	.06
☐ 370	Ed Gilbert	.50	.23	.06
☐ 371	Chris Ahrens	.50	.23	.06
☐ 372	Billy Smith	7.00	3.10	.85
☐ 373	Larry Goodenough	.50	.23	.06
☐ 374	Leon Rochefort	.50	.23	.06
☐ 375	Doug Gibson	.50	.23	.06
☐ 376	Mike Bloom	.50	.23	.06
☐ 377	Larry Brown	.50	.23	.06
☐ 378	Jim Roberts	.50	.23	.06
	Montreal Canadiens			
☐ 379	Gilles Villemure	.60	.25	.08
☐ 380	Dennis Owchar	.50	.23	.06
☐ 381	Doug Favell	.60	.25	.08
☐ 382	Stan Gilbertson UER	.50	.23	.06
	(Photo actually			
	Denis Dupere)			
☐ 383	Ed Kea	.50	.23	.06
☐ 384	Brian Spencer	.50	.23	.06
☐ 385	Mike Veisor	.60	.25	.08
☐ 386	Bob Murray	.60	.25	.08
☐ 387	Andre St.Laurent	.50	.23	.06
☐ 388	Rick Chartraw	.50	.23	.06
☐ 389	Orest Kindrachuk	.50	.23	.06
☐ 390	Dave Hutchinson	.50	.23	.06
☐ 391	Glenn Goldup	.50	.23	.06
☐ 392	Jerry Holland	.50	.23	.06
☐ 393	Peter Sturgeon	.50	.23	.06
☐ 394	Alain Daigle	.50	.23	.06
☐ 395	Never Issued	.00	.00	.00
	(Checklist 330-396,			
	numbered as 267			
	and listed as 267B)			
☐ 396	Harold Snepsts	20.00	5.00	1.00

1975-76 O-Pee-Chee WHA

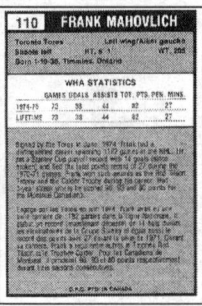

The 1975-76 O-Pee-Chee WHA set consists of 132 color cards. Printed in Canada, the cards measure 2 1/2" by 3 1/2". Bilingual backs feature 1974-75 and career WHA statistics as well as a short biography. Rookie Cards include Richard Brodeur, Nick Fotiu, Robbie Ftorek, John Garrett, Mark Howe, and Mike Rogers.

	NRMT	VG-E	GOOD
COMPLETE SET (132)	450.00	200.00	57.50
COMMON PLAYER (1-132)	2.50	1.15	.30

		NRMT	VG-E	GOOD
☐	1 Bobby Hull	60.00	18.00	6.00
☐	2 Dale Hoganson	2.50	1.15	.30
☐	3 Serge Aubry	2.50	1.15	.30
☐	4 Ron Chipperfield	2.50	1.15	.30
☐	5 Paul Shmyr	2.50	1.15	.30
☐	6 Perry Miller	2.50	1.15	.30
☐	7 Mark Howe	35.00	16.00	4.40
☐	8 Mike Rogers	6.00	2.70	.75
☐	9 Bryon Baltimore	2.50	1.15	.30
☐	10 Andre Lacroix	2.75	1.25	.35
☐	11 Nick Harbaruk	2.50	1.15	.30
☐	12 John Garrett	5.00	2.30	.60
☐	13 Lou Nistico	2.50	1.15	.30
☐	14 Rick Ley	2.50	1.15	.30
☐	15 Veli Pekka Ketola	2.50	1.15	.30
☐	16 Real Cloutier	2.75	1.25	.35
☐	17 Pierre Guite	2.50	1.15	.30
☐	18 Duane Rupp	2.50	1.15	.30
☐	19 Robbie Ftorek	5.00	2.30	.60
☐	20 Gerry Cheevers	15.00	6.75	1.90
☐	21 John Schella	2.50	1.15	.30
☐	22 Bruce MacGregor	2.50	1.15	.30
☐	23 Ralph Backstrom	2.75	1.25	.35
☐	24 Gene Peacosh	2.50	1.15	.30
☐	25 Pierre Roy	2.50	1.15	.30
☐	26 Mike Walton	2.50	1.15	.30
☐	27 Vaclav Nedomansky	2.75	1.25	.35
☐	28 Christer Abrahamsson	2.50	1.15	.30
☐	29 Thommie Bergman	2.50	1.15	.30
☐	30 Marc Tardif	2.50	1.15	.30
☐	31 Bryan Campbell	2.50	1.15	.30
☐	32 Don McLeod	2.75	1.25	.35
☐	33 Al McDonough	2.50	1.15	.30
☐	34 Jacques Plante	35.00	16.00	4.40
☐	35 Andre Hinse	2.50	1.15	.30
☐	36 Eddie Joyal	2.50	1.15	.30
☐	37 Ken Baird	2.50	1.15	.30
☐	38 Wayne Rivers	2.50	1.15	.30
☐	39 Ron Buchanan	2.50	1.15	.30
☐	40 Anders Hedberg	5.00	2.30	.60
☐	41 Rick Smith	2.50	1.15	.30
☐	42 Paul Henderson	2.75	1.25	.35
☐	43 Wayne Carleton	2.75	1.25	.35
☐	44 Richard Brodeur	10.00	4.50	1.25
☐	45 John Hughes	2.50	1.15	.30
☐	46 Larry Israelson	2.50	1.15	.30
☐	47 Jim Harrison	2.50	1.15	.30
☐	48 Cam Connor	3.00	1.35	.40
☐	49 Al Hamilton	2.50	1.15	.30
☐	50 Ron Grahame	2.75	1.25	.35
☐	51 Frank Rochon	2.50	1.15	.30
☐	52 Ron Climie	2.50	1.15	.30
☐	53 Murray Heatley	2.50	1.15	.30
☐	54 John Arbour	2.50	1.15	.30
☐	55 Jim Shaw	2.50	1.15	.30
☐	56 Larry Pleau	3.00	1.35	.40
☐	57 Ted Green	5.00	2.30	.60
☐	58 Rick Dudley	2.50	1.15	.30
☐	59 Butch Deadmarsh	2.50	1.15	.30
☐	60 Serge Bernier	2.75	1.25	.35
☐	61 Ron Grahame AS	3.00	1.35	.40
☐	62 J.C. Tremblay AS	3.00	1.35	.40
☐	63 Kevin Morrison AS	3.00	1.35	.40
☐	64 Andre Lacroix AS	3.50	1.55	.45
☐	65 Bobby Hull AS	30.00	13.50	3.80
☐	66 Gordie Howe AS	35.00	16.00	4.40
☐	67 Gerry Cheevers AS	8.00	3.60	1.00
☐	68 Poul Popiel AS	3.00	1.35	.40
☐	69 Barry Long AS	3.00	1.35	.40
☐	70 Serge Bernier AS	3.00	1.35	.40
☐	71 Marc Tardif AS	3.00	1.35	.40
☐	72 Anders Hedberg AS	3.50	1.55	.45
☐	73 Ron Ward	2.50	1.15	.30
☐	74 Michel Cormier	2.50	1.15	.30
☐	75 Marty Howe	5.00	2.30	.60
☐	76 Rusty Patenaude	2.50	1.15	.30
☐	77 John McKenzie	2.75	1.25	.35
☐	78 Mark Napier	5.00	2.30	.60
☐	79 Henry Boucha	2.50	1.15	.30
☐	80 Kevin Morrison	2.50	1.15	.30
☐	81 Tom Simpson	2.50	1.15	.30
☐	82 Brad Selwood	2.50	1.15	.30
☐	83 Ulf Nilsson	5.00	2.30	.60
☐	84 Rejean Houle	2.50	1.15	.30
☐	85 Normand Lapointe UER	2.50	1.15	.30
	(Misspelled Lapoint on card back)			
☐	86 Danny Lawson	2.75	1.25	.35
☐	87 Gary Jarrett	2.50	1.15	.30
☐	88 Al McLeod	2.50	1.15	.30
☐	89 Gord Labossiere	2.50	1.15	.30
☐	90 Barry Long	2.75	1.25	.35
☐	91 Rick Morris	2.50	1.15	.30
☐	92 Norm Ferguson	2.50	1.15	.30
☐	93 Bob Whitlock	2.50	1.15	.30
☐	94 Jim Dorey	2.50	1.15	.30
☐	95 Tom Webster	2.75	1.25	.35
☐	96 Gordie Gallant	2.50	1.15	.30
☐	97 Dave Keon	5.00	2.30	.60
☐	98 Ron Plumb	3.00	1.35	.40
☐	99 Rick Jodzio	2.50	1.15	.30
☐	100 Gordie Howe	50.00	23.00	6.25
☐	101 Joe Daley	2.75	1.25	.35
☐	102 Wayne Muloin	2.50	1.15	.30
☐	103 Gavin Kirk	2.50	1.15	.30
☐	104 Dave Dryden	2.75	1.25	.35
☐	105 Bob Liddington	2.50	1.15	.30
☐	106 Rosaire Paiement	2.50	1.15	.30
☐	107 John Sheridan	2.50	1.15	.30
☐	108 Nick Fotiu	10.00	4.50	1.25
☐	109 Lars-Erik Sjoberg	2.50	1.15	.30
☐	110 Frank Mahovlich	12.00	5.50	1.50
☐	111 Mike Antonovich	2.50	1.15	.30
☐	112 Paul Terbenche	2.50	1.15	.30
☐	113 Rich Leduc	2.50	1.15	.30
☐	114 Jack Norris	2.50	1.15	.30
☐	115 Dennis Sobchuk	2.50	1.15	.30
☐	116 Chris Bordeleau	2.50	1.15	.30
☐	117 Doug Barrie	2.50	1.15	.30
☐	118 Hugh Harris	2.50	1.15	.30
☐	119 Cam Newton	2.50	1.15	.30
☐	120 Poul Popiel	2.50	1.15	.30
☐	121 Fran Huck	2.50	1.15	.30
☐	122 Tony Featherstone	2.50	1.15	.30
☐	123 Bob Woytowich	2.50	1.15	.30
☐	124 Claude St.Sauveur	2.50	1.15	.30
☐	125 Heikki Riihiranta	2.50	1.15	.30
☐	126 Gary Kurt	2.75	1.25	.35
☐	127 Thommy Abrahamsson	2.50	1.15	.30
☐	128 Danny Gruen	2.50	1.15	.30
☐	129 Jacques Locas	2.50	1.15	.30
☐	130 J.C. Tremblay	2.50	1.15	.30
☐	131 Checklist Card	30.00	3.00	.60
☐	132 Ernie Wakely	5.00	1.50	.50

1976-77 O-Pee-Chee NHL

The 1976-77 O-Pee-Chee NHL set consists of 396 color cards. Printed in Canada, the cards measure 2 1/2" by 3 1/2" and contain both the O-Pee-Chee and the NHL Players Association copyright. Several Record Breaker (RB) cards feature achievements from the previous season. Team cards (132-149) have a team checklist on the back.

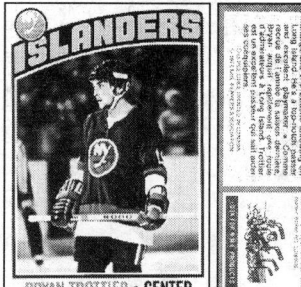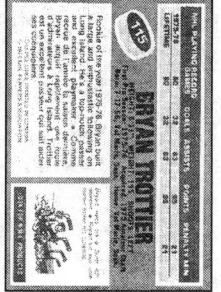

BRYAN TROTTIER • CENTER

Bilingual backs contain the player's statistics from the 1975-76 season, career numbers, a short biography and a cartoon-illustrated fact about the player. Cards that feature California players in the 1976-77 Topps set have been updated in this set to show them with the Cleveland Barons. Rookie Cards include Bryan Trottier and Tiger Williams.

	NRMT	VG-E	GOOD
COMPLETE SET (396)	200.00	90.00	25.00
COMMON PLAYER (1-396)	.40	.18	.05

		NRMT	VG-E	GOOD
☐ 1	Goals Leaders	3.00	1.00	.30
	Reggie Leach			
	Guy Lafleur			
	Pierre Larouche			
☐ 2	Assists Leaders	3.00	1.35	.40
	Bobby Clarke			
	Peter Mahovlich			
	Guy Lafleur			
	Gilbert Perrault			
	Jean Ratelle			
☐ 3	Scoring Leaders	3.00	1.35	.40
	Guy Lafleur			
	Bobby Clarke			
	Gilbert Perreault			
☐ 4	Penalty Min. Leaders	.50	.23	.06
	Steve Durbano			
	Bryan Watson			
	Dave Schultz			
☐ 5	Power Play Goals Leaders	3.00	1.35	.40
	Phil Esposito			
	Guy Lafleur			
	Richard Martin			
	Pierre Larouche			
	Denis Potvin			
☐ 6	Goals Against Average Leaders	3.00	1.35	.40
	Ken Dryden			
	Glenn Resch			
	Michel Larocque			
☐ 7	Gary Doak	.40	.18	.05
☐ 8	Jacques Richard	.40	.18	.05
☐ 9	Wayne Dillon	.40	.18	.05
☐ 10	Bernie Parent	3.00	1.35	.40
☐ 11	Ed Westfall	.50	.23	.06
☐ 12	Dick Redmond	.40	.18	.05
☐ 13	Bryan Hextall	.40	.18	.05
☐ 14	Jean Pronovost	.50	.23	.06
☐ 15	Peter Mahovlich	.50	.23	.06
☐ 16	Danny Grant	.50	.23	.06
☐ 17	Phil Myre	.50	.23	.06
☐ 18	Wayne Merrick	.40	.18	.05
☐ 19	Steve Durbano	.40	.18	.05
☐ 20	Derek Sanderson	1.50	.65	.19
☐ 21	Mike Murphy	.40	.18	.05
☐ 22	Borje Salming	2.00	.90	.25
☐ 23	Mike Walton	.40	.18	.05
☐ 24	Randy Manery	.40	.18	.05
☐ 25	Ken Hodge	.50	.23	.06
☐ 26	Mel Bridgman	2.00	.90	.25
☐ 27	Jerry Korab	.40	.18	.05
☐ 28	Gilles Gratton	.50	.23	.06
☐ 29	Andre St.Laurent	.40	.18	.05
☐ 30	Yvan Cournoyer	2.00	.90	.25
☐ 31	Phil Russell	.40	.18	.05
☐ 32	Dennis Hextall	.40	.18	.05
☐ 33	Lowell MacDonald	.40	.18	.05
☐ 34	Dennis O'Brien	.40	.18	.05
☐ 35	Gerry Meehan	.50	.23	.06
☐ 36	Gilles Meloche	.50	.23	.06

		NRMT	VG-E	GOOD
☐ 37	Wilf Paiement	.50	.23	.06
☐ 38	Bob MacMillan	1.00	.45	.13
☐ 39	Ian Turnbull	.50	.23	.06
☐ 40	Rogatien Vachon	1.50	.65	.19
☐ 41	Nick Beverley	.40	.18	.05
☐ 42	Rene Robert	.50	.23	.06
☐ 43	Andre Savard	.40	.18	.05
☐ 44	Bob Gainey	3.50	1.55	.45
☐ 45	Joe Watson	.40	.18	.05
☐ 46	Billy Smith	4.00	1.80	.50
☐ 47	Darcy Rota	.40	.18	.05
☐ 48	Rick Lapointe	.40	.18	.05
☐ 49	Pierre Jarry	.40	.18	.05
☐ 50	Syl Apps	.40	.18	.05
☐ 51	Eric Vail	.40	.18	.05
☐ 52	Greg Joly	.40	.18	.05
☐ 53	Don Lever	.40	.18	.05
☐ 54	Bob Murdoch	.40	.18	.05
	Seals Right Wing			
☐ 55	Denis Herron	.50	.23	.06
☐ 56	Mike Bloom	.40	.18	.05
☐ 57	Bill Fairbairn	.40	.18	.05
☐ 58	Fred Stanfield	.40	.18	.05
☐ 59	Steve Shutt	3.00	1.35	.40
☐ 60	Brad Park	2.50	1.15	.30
☐ 61	Gilles Villemure	.50	.23	.06
☐ 62	Bert Marshall	.40	.18	.05
☐ 63	Chuck Lefley	.40	.18	.05
☐ 64	Simon Nolet	.40	.18	.05
☐ 65	Reggie Leach RB	.50	.23	.06
	Most Goals, Playoffs			
☐ 66	Darryl Sittler RB	1.50	.65	.19
	Most Points, Game			
☐ 67	Bryan Trottier RB	7.00	3.10	.85
	Most Points, Season, Rookie			
☐ 68	Garry Unger RB	.50	.23	.06
	Most Consecutive Games, Lifetime			
☐ 69	Ron Low	.50	.23	.06
☐ 70	Bobby Clarke	7.00	3.10	.85
☐ 71	Michel Bergeron	.40	.18	.05
☐ 72	Ron Stackhouse	.40	.18	.05
☐ 73	Bill Hogaboam	.40	.18	.05
☐ 74	Bob Murdoch	.40	.18	.05
	Kings Defenseman			
☐ 75	Steve Vickers	.40	.18	.05
☐ 76	Pit Martin	.40	.18	.05
☐ 77	Gerry Hart	.40	.18	.05
☐ 78	Craig Ramsay	.40	.18	.05
☐ 79	Michel Larocque	.50	.23	.06
☐ 80	Jean Ratelle	1.50	.65	.19
☐ 81	Don Saleski	.40	.18	.05
☐ 82	Bill Clement	1.00	.45	.13
☐ 83	Dave Burrows	.40	.18	.05
☐ 84	Wayne Thomas	.50	.23	.06
☐ 85	John Gould	.40	.18	.05
☐ 86	Dennis Maruk	4.00	1.80	.50
☐ 87	Ernie Hicke	.40	.18	.05
☐ 88	Jim Rutherford	.50	.23	.06
☐ 89	Dale Tallon	.40	.18	.05
☐ 90	Rod Gilbert	1.50	.65	.19
☐ 91	Marcel Dionne	7.00	3.10	.85
☐ 92	Chuck Arnason	.40	.18	.05
☐ 93	Jean Potvin	.40	.18	.05
☐ 94	Don Luce	.40	.18	.05
☐ 95	Johnny Bucyk	1.50	.65	.19
☐ 96	Larry Goodenough	.40	.18	.05
☐ 97	Mario Tremblay	.50	.23	.06
☐ 98	Nelson Pyatt	.40	.18	.05
☐ 99	Brian Glennie	.40	.18	.05
☐ 100	Tony Esposito	3.50	1.55	.45
☐ 101	Dan Maloney	.40	.18	.05
☐ 102	Dunc Wilson	.50	.23	.06
☐ 103	Dean Talafous	.40	.18	.05
☐ 104	Ed Staniowski	.50	.23	.06
☐ 105	Dallas Smith	.40	.18	.05
☐ 106	Jude Drouin	.40	.18	.05
☐ 107	Pat Hickey	.40	.18	.05
☐ 108	Jocelyn Guevremont	.40	.18	.05
☐ 109	Doug Risebrough	1.00	.45	.13
☐ 110	Reggie Leach	.50	.23	.06
☐ 111	Dan Bouchard	.50	.23	.06
☐ 112	Chris Oddleifson	.40	.18	.05
☐ 113	Rick Hampton	.40	.18	.05
☐ 114	John Marks	.40	.18	.05
☐ 115	Bryan Trottier	50.00	23.00	6.25
☐ 116	Checklist 1-132	10.00	1.00	.20
☐ 117	Greg Polis	.40	.18	.05
☐ 118	Peter McNab	1.00	.45	.13
☐ 119	Jim Roberts	.40	.18	.05
	Montreal Canadiens			
☐ 120	Gerry Cheevers	3.00	1.35	.40

☐ 121	Rick MacLeish	.50	.23	.06
☐ 122	Billy Lochead	.40	.18	.05
☐ 123	Tom Reid	.40	.18	.05
☐ 124	Rick Kehoe	.50	.23	.06
☐ 125	Keith Magnuson	.40	.18	.05
☐ 126	Clark Gillies	2.00	.90	.25
☐ 127	Rick Middleton	3.00	1.35	.40
☐ 128	Bill Hajt	.40	.18	.05
☐ 129	Jacques Lemaire	1.50	.65	.19
☐ 130	Terry O'Reilly	1.00	.45	.13
☐ 131	Andre Dupont	.40	.18	.05
☐ 132	Flames Team	1.50	.65	.19
	(checklist back)			
☐ 133	Bruins Team	1.75	.80	.22
	(checklist back)			
☐ 134	Sabres Team	1.50	.65	.19
	(checklist back)			
☐ 135	Seals Team	1.50	.65	.19
	(checklist back)			
☐ 136	Blackhawks Team	1.50	.65	.19
	(checklist back)			
☐ 137	Red Wings Team	1.50	.65	.19
	(checklist back)			
☐ 138	Scouts Team	1.50	.65	.19
	(checklist back)			
☐ 139	Kings Team	1.50	.65	.19
	(checklist back)			
☐ 140	North Stars Team	1.50	.65	.19
	(checklist back)			
☐ 141	Canadiens Team	1.75	.80	.22
	(checklist back)			
☐ 142	Islanders Team	1.50	.65	.19
	(checklist back)			
☐ 143	Rangers Team	1.50	.65	.19
	(checklist back)			
☐ 144	Flyers Team	1.50	.65	.19
	(checklist back)			
☐ 145	Penguins Team	1.50	.65	.19
	(checklist back)			
☐ 146	Blues Team	1.50	.65	.19
	(checklist back)			
☐ 147	Maple Leafs Team	1.75	.80	.22
	(checklist back)			
☐ 148	Canucks Team	1.50	.65	.19
	(checklist back)			
☐ 149	Capitals Team	1.50	.65	.19
	(checklist back)			
☐ 150	Dave Schultz	1.00	.45	.13
☐ 151	Larry Robinson	7.00	3.10	.85
☐ 152	Al Smith	.50	.23	.06
☐ 153	Bob Nystrom	.50	.23	.06
☐ 154	Ron Greschner	1.00	.45	.13
☐ 155	Gregg Sheppard	.40	.18	.05
☐ 156	Alain Daigle	.40	.18	.05
☐ 157	Ed Van Impe	.40	.18	.05
☐ 158	Tim Young	.75	.35	.09
☐ 159	Bryan Lefley	.40	.18	.05
☐ 160	Ed Giacomin	2.00	.90	.25
☐ 161	Yvon Labre	.40	.18	.05
☐ 162	Jim Lorentz	.40	.18	.05
☐ 163	Guy Lafleur	12.00	5.50	1.50
☐ 164	Tom Bladon	.50	.23	.06
☐ 165	Wayne Cashman	.50	.23	.06
☐ 166	Pete Stemkowski	.40	.18	.05
☐ 167	Grant Mulvey	.40	.18	.05
☐ 168	Yves Belanger	.50	.23	.06
☐ 169	Bill Goldsworthy	.50	.23	.06
☐ 170	Denis Potvin	8.00	3.60	1.00
☐ 171	Nick Libett	.40	.18	.05
☐ 172	Michel Plasse	.50	.23	.06
☐ 173	Lou Nanne	.40	.18	.05
☐ 174	Tom Lysiak	.50	.23	.06
☐ 175	Dennis Ververgaert	.40	.18	.05
☐ 176	Gary Simmons	.50	.23	.06
☐ 177	Pierre Bouchard	.40	.18	.05
☐ 178	Bill Barber	2.50	1.15	.30
☐ 179	Darryl Edestrand	.40	.18	.05
☐ 180	Gilbert Perreault	3.00	1.35	.40
☐ 181	Dave Maloney	1.00	.45	.13
☐ 182	Jean-Paul Parise	.40	.18	.05
☐ 183	Jim Harrison	.40	.18	.05
☐ 184	Pete Lopresti	.50	.23	.06
☐ 185	Don Kozak	.40	.18	.05
☐ 186	Guy Charron	.40	.18	.05
☐ 187	Stan Gilbertson	.40	.18	.05
☐ 188	Bill Nyrop	.40	.18	.05
☐ 189	Bobby Schmautz	.40	.18	.05
☐ 190	Wayne Stephenson	.50	.23	.06
☐ 191	Brian Spencer	.40	.18	.05
☐ 192	Gilles Marotte	.40	.18	.05
☐ 193	Lorne Henning	.40	.18	.05
☐ 194	Bob Neely	.40	.18	.05
☐ 195	Dennis Hull	.50	.23	.06

☐ 196	Walt McKechnie	.40	.18	.05
☐ 197	Curt Ridley	.50	.23	.06
☐ 198	Dwight Bialowas	.40	.18	.05
☐ 199	Pierre Larouche	2.00	.90	.25
☐ 200	Ken Dryden	15.00	6.75	1.90
☐ 201	Ross Lonsberry	.40	.18	.05
☐ 202	Curt Bennett	.40	.18	.05
☐ 203	Hartland Monahan	.40	.18	.05
☐ 204	John Davidson	1.00	.45	.13
☐ 205	Serge Savard	.40	.18	.05
☐ 206	Garry Howatt	.40	.18	.05
☐ 207	Darryl Sittler	5.00	2.30	.60
☐ 208	J.P. Bordeleau	.40	.18	.05
☐ 209	Henry Boucha	.40	.18	.05
☐ 210	Richard Martin	.50	.23	.06
☐ 211	Vic Venasky	.40	.18	.05
☐ 212	Buster Harvey	.40	.18	.05
☐ 213	Bobby Orr	25.00	11.50	3.10
☐ 214	French Connection	3.00	1.35	.40
	Richard Martin			
	Gilbert Perreault			
	Rene Robert			
☐ 215	LCB Line	3.50	1.55	.45
	Reggie Leach			
	Bobby Clarke			
	Bill Barber			
☐ 216	Long Island Lightning	5.00	2.30	.60
	Clark Gillies			
	Bryan Trottier			
	Billy Harris			
☐ 217	Checking Line	1.00	.45	.13
	Bob Gainey			
	Doug Jarvis			
	Jim Roberts			
☐ 218	Bicentennial Line	.50	.23	.06
	Lowell MacDonald			
	Syl Apps			
	Jean Pronovost			
☐ 219	Bob Kelly	.40	.18	.05
☐ 220	Walt Tkaczuk	.50	.23	.06
☐ 221	Dave Lewis	.40	.18	.05
☐ 222	Danny Gare	1.00	.45	.13
☐ 223	Guy Lapointe	.50	.23	.06
☐ 224	Hank Nowak	.40	.18	.05
☐ 225	Stan Mikita	4.00	1.80	.50
☐ 226	Vic Hadfield	.50	.23	.06
☐ 227	Bernie Wolfe	.50	.23	.06
☐ 228	Bryan Watson	.40	.18	.05
☐ 229	Ralph Stewart	.40	.18	.05
☐ 230	Gerry Desjardins	.50	.23	.06
☐ 231	John Bednarski	.40	.18	.05
☐ 232	Yvon Lambert	.40	.18	.05
☐ 233	Orest Kindrachuk	.40	.18	.05
☐ 234	Don Marcotte	.40	.18	.05
☐ 235	Bill White	.40	.18	.05
☐ 236	Red Berenson	.50	.23	.06
☐ 237	Al MacAdam	.40	.18	.05
☐ 238	Rick Blight	.40	.18	.05
☐ 239	Butch Goring	.50	.23	.06
☐ 240	Cesare Maniago	.50	.23	.06
☐ 241	Jim Schoenfeld	.50	.23	.06
☐ 242	Cliff Koroll	.40	.18	.05
☐ 243	Scott Garland	.40	.18	.05
☐ 244	Rick Chartraw	.40	.18	.05
☐ 245	Phil Esposito	4.00	1.80	.50
☐ 246	Dave Forbes	.40	.18	.05
☐ 247	Joe Watson	.40	.18	.05
☐ 248	Ron Schock	.40	.18	.05
☐ 249	Fred Barrett	.40	.18	.05
☐ 250	Glenn Resch	2.00	.90	.25
☐ 251	Ivan Boldirev	.40	.18	.05
☐ 252	Billy Harris	.40	.18	.05
☐ 253	Lee Fogolin	.40	.18	.05
☐ 254	Murray Wilson	.40	.18	.05
☐ 255	Gilles Gilbert	.50	.23	.06
☐ 256	Gary Dornhoefer	.40	.18	.05
☐ 257	Carol Vadnais	.40	.18	.05
☐ 258	Checklist 133-264	10.00	1.00	.20
☐ 259	Errol Thompson	.40	.18	.05
☐ 260	Garry Unger	.50	.23	.06
☐ 261	J. Bob Kelly	.40	.18	.05
☐ 262	Terry Harper	.40	.18	.05
☐ 263	Blake Dunlop	.40	.18	.05
☐ 264	Stanley Cup Champs	1.50	.65	.19
	Montreal Canadiens			
☐ 265	Richard Mulhern	.40	.18	.05
☐ 266	Gary Sabourin	.40	.18	.05
☐ 267	Bill McKenzie	.50	.23	.06
☐ 268	Mike Corrigan	.40	.18	.05
☐ 269	Rick Smith	.40	.18	.05
☐ 270	Stan Weir	.40	.18	.05
☐ 271	Ron Sedlbauer	.40	.18	.05
☐ 272	Jean Lemieux	.40	.18	.05

☐ 273	Hilliard Graves	.40	.18	.05
☐ 274	Dave Gardner	.40	.18	.05
☐ 275	Tracy Pratt	.40	.18	.05
☐ 276	Frank St.Marseille	.40	.18	.05
☐ 277	Bob Hess	.40	.18	.05
☐ 278	Bobby Lalonde	.40	.18	.05
☐ 279	Tony White	.40	.18	.06
☐ 280	Rod Seiling	.40	.18	.05
☐ 281	Larry Romanchych	.40	.18	.05
☐ 282	Ralph Klassen	.40	.18	.05
☐ 283	Gary Croteau	.40	.18	.05
☐ 284	Neil Komadoski	.40	.18	.05
☐ 285	Ed Johnston	.50	.23	.06
☐ 286	George Ferguson	.40	.18	.05
☐ 287	Gerry O'Flaherty	.40	.18	.05
☐ 288	Jack Lynch	.40	.18	.05
☐ 289	Pat Quinn	.50	.23	.06
☐ 290	Gene Carr	.40	.18	.05
☐ 291	Bob Stewart	.40	.18	.05
☐ 292	Doug Favell	.50	.23	.06
☐ 293	Rick Wilson	.40	.18	.05
☐ 294	Jack Valiquette	.40	.18	.05
☐ 295	Garry Monahan	.40	.18	.05
☐ 296	Michel Belhumeur	.50	.23	.06
☐ 297	Larry Carriere	.40	.18	.05
☐ 298	Fred Ahern	.40	.18	.05
☐ 299	Dave Hudson	.40	.18	.05
☐ 300	Bob Berry	.40	.18	.05
☐ 301	Bob Gassoff	.40	.18	.05
☐ 302	Jim McKenny	.40	.18	.05
☐ 303	Gord Smith	.40	.18	.05
☐ 304	Garnet Bailey	.40	.18	.05
☐ 305	Bruce Affleck	.40	.18	.05
☐ 306	Doug Halward	.40	.18	.05
☐ 307	Lew Morrison	.40	.18	.05
☐ 308	Bob Sauve	2.00	.90	.25
☐ 309	Bob Murray (Chicago)	.60	.25	.08
☐ 310	Claude Larose	.40	.18	.05
☐ 311	Don Awrey	.40	.18	.05
☐ 312	Bill MacMillan	.40	.18	.05
☐ 313	Doug Jarvis	2.50	1.15	.30
☐ 314	Dennis Owchar	.40	.18	.05
☐ 315	Jerry Holland	.40	.18	.05
☐ 316	Guy Chouinard	1.00	.45	.13
☐ 317	Gary Smith	.50	.23	.06
☐ 318	Pat Price	.40	.18	.05
☐ 319	Tom Williams	.40	.18	.05
☐ 320	Larry Patey	.40	.18	.05
☐ 321	Claire Alexander	.40	.18	.05
☐ 322	Larry Bolonchuk	.40	.18	.05
☐ 323	Bob Sirois	.40	.18	.05
☐ 324	Joe Zanussi	.40	.18	.05
☐ 325	Joey Johnston	.40	.18	.05
☐ 326	J.P. LeBlanc	.40	.18	.05
☐ 327	Craig Cameron	.40	.18	.05
☐ 328	Dave Fortier	.40	.18	.05
☐ 329	Ed Gilbert	.40	.18	.05
☐ 330	John Van Boxmeer	.50	.23	.06
☐ 331	Gary Inness	.50	.23	.06
☐ 332	Bill Flett	.40	.18	.05
☐ 333	Mike Christie	.40	.18	.05
☐ 334	Denis Dupere	.40	.18	.05
☐ 335	Sheldon Kannegiesser	.40	.18	.05
☐ 336	Jerry Butler	.40	.18	.05
☐ 337	Gord McRae	.50	.23	.06
☐ 338	Dennis Kearns	.40	.18	.05
☐ 339	Ron Lalonde	.40	.18	.05
☐ 340	Jean Hamel	.40	.18	.05
☐ 341	Barry Gibbs	.40	.18	.05
☐ 342	Mike Pelyk	.40	.18	.05
☐ 343	Rey Comeau	.40	.18	.05
☐ 344	Jim Neilson	.40	.18	.05
☐ 345	Phil Roberto	.40	.18	.05
☐ 346	Dave Hutchinson	.40	.18	.05
☐ 347	Ted Irvine	.40	.18	.05
☐ 348	Lanny McDonald	5.00	2.30	.60
☐ 349	Jim Moxey	.40	.18	.05
☐ 350	Bob Dailey	.40	.18	.05
☐ 351	Tim Ecclestone	.40	.18	.05
☐ 352	Len Frig	.40	.18	.05
☐ 353	Randy Rota	.40	.18	.05
☐ 354	Juha Widing	.40	.18	.05
☐ 355	Larry Brown	.40	.18	.05
☐ 356	Floyd Thomson	.40	.18	.05
☐ 357	Richard Nantais	.40	.18	.05
☐ 358	Inge Hammarstrom	.40	.18	.05
☐ 359	Mike Robitaille	.40	.18	.05
☐ 360	Rejean Houle	.40	.18	.05
☐ 361	Ed Kea	.40	.18	.05
☐ 362	Bob Girard	.40	.18	.05
☐ 363	Bob Murray (Vancouver)	.40	.18	.05
☐ 364	Dave Hrechkosy	.40	.18	.05
☐ 365	Gary Edwards	.50	.23	.06
☐ 366	Harold Snepsts	3.00	1.35	.40
☐ 367	Pat Boutette	1.00	.45	.13
☐ 368	Bob Paradise	.40	.18	.05
☐ 369	Bob Plager	.50	.23	.06
☐ 370	Tim Jacobs	.40	.18	.05
☐ 371	Pierre Plante	.40	.18	.05
☐ 372	Colin Campbell	.50	.23	.06
☐ 373	Dave(Tiger) Williams	10.00	4.50	1.25
☐ 374	Ab Demarco	.40	.18	.05
☐ 375	Mike Lampman	.40	.18	.05
☐ 376	Mark Heaslip	.40	.18	.05
☐ 377	Checklist Card	10.00	1.00	.20
☐ 378	Bert Wilson	.40	.18	.05
☐ 379	Flames Leaders	.50	.23	.06
	Curt Bennett			
	Tom Lysiak			
	Pat Quinn			
	Claude St.Sauveur			
☐ 380	Sabres Leaders	.75	.35	.09
	Danny Gare			
	Gilbert Perreault			
	Danny Gare			
	Richard Martin			
☐ 381	Bruins Leaders	1.75	.80	.22
	Johnny Bucyk			
	Jean Ratelle			
	Jean Ratelle			
	Terry O'Reilly			
	Jean Ratelle			
☐ 382	Blackhawks Leaders	.50	.23	.06
	Pit Martin			
	Dale Tallon			
	Phil Russell			
	Cliff Koroll			
☐ 383	Seals Leaders	.50	.23	.06
	Wayne Merrick			
	Al MacAdam			
	Rick Hampton			
	Mike Christie			
	Bob Murdoch			
☐ 384	Scouts Leaders	.50	.23	.06
	Guy Charron			
	Guy Charron			
	Steve Durbano			
	Guy Charron			
☐ 385	Red Wings Leaders	.50	.23	.06
	Michel Bergeron			
	Walt McKechnie			
	Bryan Watson			
	Michel Bergeron			
☐ 386	Kings Leaders	1.00	.45	.13
	Marcel Dionne			
	Marcel Dionne			
	Dave Hutchison			
	Mike Corrigan			
☐ 387	North Stars Leaders	.50	.23	.06
	Bill Hogaboam			
	Tim Young			
	Dennis O'Brien			
	Bill Hogaboam			
☐ 388	Canadiens Leaders	2.00	.90	.25
	Guy Lafleur			
	Pete Mahovlich			
	Doug Risebrough			
	Guy Lafleur			
☐ 389	Islanders Leaders	1.50	.65	.19
	Clark Gillies			
	Denis Potvin			
	Garry Howatt			
	Denis Potvin			
☐ 390	Rangers Leaders	1.75	.80	.22
	Rod Gilbert			
	Steve Vickers			
	Carol Vadnais			
	Phil Esposito			
☐ 391	Flyers Leaders	2.00	.90	.25
	Reggie Leach			
	Bobby Clarke			
	Dave Schultz			
	Bill Barber			
☐ 392	Penguins Leaders	.75	.35	.09
	Pierre Larouche			
	Syl Apps			
	Ron Schock			
	Pierre Larouche			
☐ 393	Blues Leaders	.50	.23	.06
	Chuck Lefley			
	Garry Unger			
	Bob Gassoff			
	Garry Unger			
☐ 394	Maple Leafs Leaders	.50	.23	.06
	Errol Thompson			
	Darryl Sittler			

Dave(Tiger) Williams
Errol Thompson
☐ 395 Canucks Leaders................ .50 .23 .06
Dennis Ververgaert
Chris Oddleifson
Dennis Kearns
Harold Snepsts
Dennis Ververgaert
☐ 396 Capitals Leaders................ .75 .23 .06
Nelson Pyatt
Gerry Meehan
Yvon Labre
Tony White

1976-77 O-Pee-Chee WHA

The 1976-77 O-Pee-Chee WHA set consists of 132 color cards featuring WHA players. Cards are 2 1/2" by 3 1/2". The cards were originally sold in ten-cent wax packs. The backs, in both French and English, feature the card number, a short biography of the player, and career statistics. The cards were printed in Canada. Cards 1-6 feature the league leaders from the previous season in various statistical categories. The backs of cards 62-65, 67, and 71 form a puzzle of Gordie Howe. A puzzle of Bobby Hull is derived from the backs of cards 61, 66, 68-70 and 72. These cards (61-72) comprise the All-Star subset.

	NRMT	VG-E	GOOD
COMPLETE SET (132).....................	175.00	80.00	22.00
COMMON PLAYER (1-132)...............	1.50	.65	.19

☐ 1	Goals Leaders	4.00	1.00	.20
	Marc Tardif			
	Real Cloutier			
	Vaclav Nedomansky			
☐ 2	Assists Leaders	3.00	1.35	.40
	J.C. Tremblay			
	Marc Tardif			
	Ulf Nilsson			
☐ 3	Scoring Leaders	7.00	3.10	.85
	Marc Tardif			
	Bobby Hull			
	Real Cloutier			
	Ulf Nilsson			
☐ 4	Penalties Leaders	2.00	.90	.25
	Curt Brackenbury			
	Gord Gallant			
☐ 5	Points Leaders	7.00	3.10	.85
	Marc Tardif			
	Bobby Hull			
	Ulf Nilsson			
☐ 6	Goals Against........................	2.00	.90	.25
	Average Leaders			
	Michel Dion			
	Joe Daley			
	Wayne Rutledge			
☐ 7	Barry Long	1.50	.65	.19
☐ 8	Danny Lawson	1.50	.65	.19
☐ 9	Ulf Nilsson	2.50	1.15	.30
☐ 10	Kevin Morrison	1.50	.65	.19
☐ 11	Gerry Pinder	1.50	.65	.19
☐ 12	Richard Brodeur......................	5.00	2.30	.60
☐ 13	Robbie Ftorek.........................	2.00	.90	.25
☐ 14	Tom Webster	1.75	.80	.22

☐ 15	Marty Howe..........................	2.00	.90	.25
☐ 16	Bryan Campbell	1.50	.65	.19
☐ 17	Rick Dudley	1.50	.65	.19
☐ 18	Jim Turkiewicz	1.50	.65	.19
☐ 19	Rusty Patenaude	1.50	.65	.19
☐ 20	Joe Daley	1.75	.80	.22
☐ 21	Gary Veneruzzo	1.50	.65	.19
☐ 22	Chris Evans	1.50	.65	.19
☐ 23	Mike Antonovich	1.50	.65	.19
☐ 24	Jim Dorey	1.50	.65	.19
☐ 25	John Gray	1.50	.65	.19
☐ 26	Larry Pleau	1.50	.65	.19
☐ 27	Poul Popiel	1.50	.65	.19
☐ 28	Renald Leclerc ..,....................	1.50	.65	.19
☐ 29	Dennis Sobchuk	1.50	.65	.19
☐ 30	Lars-Erik Sjoberg	1.50	.65	.19
☐ 31	Wayne Wood..........................	2.00	.90	.25
☐ 32	Ron Chipperfield	1.50	.65	.19
☐ 33	Tim Sheehy	1.50	.65	.19
☐ 34	Brent Hughes	1.50	.65	.19
☐ 35	Ron Ward	1.50	.65	.19
☐ 36	Ron Huston	1.50	.65	.19
☐ 37	Rosaire Paiement....................	1.50	.65	.19
☐ 38	Terry Ruskowski	3.50	1.55	.45
☐ 39	Hugh Harris	1.50	.65	.19
☐ 40	J.C. Tremblay	1.50	.65	.19
☐ 41	Rich Leduc	1.50	.65	.19
☐ 42	Peter Sullivan	1.50	.65	.19
☐ 43	Jerry Rollins	1.50	.65	.19
☐ 44	Ken Broderick	1.75	.80	.22
☐ 45	Peter Driscoll	1.50	.65	.19
☐ 46	Joe Noris...............................	2.00	.90	.25
☐ 47	Al McLeod	1.50	.65	.19
☐ 48	Bruce Landon	1.50	.65	.19
☐ 49	Chris Bordeleau......................	1.50	.65	.19
☐ 50	Gordie Howe	35.00	16.00	4.40
☐ 51	Thommie Bergman	1.50	.65	.19
☐ 52	Dave Keon	4.00	1.80	.50
☐ 53	Butch Deadmarsh	1.50	.65	.19
☐ 54	Bryan Maxwell	1.50	.65	.19
☐ 55	John Garrett..........................	1.75	.80	.22
☐ 56	Glen Sather	3.00	1.35	.40
☐ 57	John Miszuk..........................	1.50	.65	.19
☐ 58	Heikki Riihiranta....................	1.50	.65	.19
☐ 59	Richard Grenier	1.50	.65	.19
☐ 60	Gene Peacosh	1.50	.65	.19
☐ 61	Joe Daley AS	2.00	.90	.25
☐ 62	J.C. Tremblay AS	2.00	.90	.25
☐ 63	Lars-Erik Sjoberg AS	2.00	.90	.25
☐ 64	Vaclav Nedomansky AS	2.00	.90	.25
☐ 65	Bobby Hull AS........................	20.00	9.00	2.50
☐ 66	Anders Hedberg AS.................	2.50	1.15	.30
☐ 67	Chr. Abrahamsson AS..............	2.00	.90	.25
☐ 68	Kevin Morrison AS...................	2.00	.90	.25
☐ 69	Paul Shmyr AS	2.00	.90	.25
☐ 70	Andre Lacroix AS	2.50	1.15	.30
☐ 71	Gene Peacosh AS....................	2.00	.90	.25
☐ 72	Gordie Howe AS......................	25.00	11.50	3.10
☐ 73	Bob Nevin	1.50	.65	.19
☐ 74	Richard Lemieux	1.50	.65	.19
☐ 75	Mike Ford	1.50	.65	.19
☐ 76	Real Cloutier	1.75	.80	.22
☐ 77	Al McDonough	1.50	.65	.19
☐ 78	Del Hall	1.50	.65	.19
☐ 79	Thommy Abrahamsson...........	1.50	.65	.19
☐ 80	Andre Lacroix.........................	1.75	.80	.22
☐ 81	Frank Hughes	1.50	.65	.19
☐ 82	Reg Thomas...........................	1.50	.65	.19
☐ 83	Dave Inkpen	1.50	.65	.19
☐ 84	Paul Henderson......................	1.75	.80	.22
☐ 85	Dave Dryden	1.75	.80	.22
☐ 86	Lynn Powis	1.50	.65	.19
☐ 87	Andre Boudrias	1.50	.65	.19
☐ 88	Veli Pekka Ketola	1.50	.65	.19
☐ 89	Cam Connor	1.50	.65	.19
☐ 90	Claude St.Sauveur	1.50	.65	.19
☐ 91	Garry Swain	1.50	.65	.19
☐ 92	Ernie Wakely	2.00	.90	.25
☐ 93	Blair MacDonald	1.50	.65	.19
☐ 94	Ron Plumb	1.50	.65	.19
☐ 95	Mark Howe	9.00	4.00	1.15
☐ 96	Peter Marrin	1.50	.65	.19
☐ 97	Al Hamilton	1.50	.65	.19
☐ 98	Paulin Bordeleau	1.50	.65	.19
☐ 99	Gavin Kirk	1.50	.65	.19
☐ 100	Bobby Hull	30.00	13.50	3.80
☐ 101	Rick Ley	1.50	.65	.19
☐ 102	Gary Kurt..............................	1.50	.65	.19
☐ 103	John McKenzie	1.75	.80	.22
☐ 104	Al Karlander	1.50	.65	.19
☐ 105	John French	1.50	.65	.19
☐ 106	John Hughes	1.50	.65	.19
☐ 107	Ron Grahame	1.75	.80	.22

		NRMT	VG-E	GOOD
☐ 108	Mark Napier	2.00	.90	.25
☐ 109	Serge Bernier	1.75	.80	.22
☐ 110	Christer Abrahamsson	1.50	.65	.19
☐ 111	Frank Mahovlich	5.00	2.30	.60
☐ 112	Ted Green	1.75	.80	.22
☐ 113	Rick Jodzio	1.50	.65	.19
☐ 114	Michel Dion	4.00	1.80	.50
☐ 115	Rich Preston	1.50	.65	.19
☐ 116	Pekka Rautakallio	1.50	.65	.19
☐ 117	Checklist Card	18.00	1.80	.35
☐ 118	Marc Tardif	1.50	.65	.19
☐ 119	Doug Barrie	1.50	.65	.19
☐ 120	Vaclav Nedomansky	1.75	.80	.22
☐ 121	Bill Lesuk	1.50	.65	.19
☐ 122	Wayne Connelly	1.50	.65	.19
☐ 123	Pierre Guite	1.50	.65	.19
☐ 124	Ralph Backstrom	1.75	.80	.22
☐ 125	Anders Hedberg	2.50	1.15	.30
☐ 126	Norm Ullman	3.00	1.35	.40
☐ 127	Steve Sutherland	1.50	.65	.19
☐ 128	John Schella	1.50	.65	.19
☐ 129	Don McLeod	1.50	.65	.19
☐ 130	Canadian Finals	2.00	.90	.25
☐ 131	U.S. Finals	2.00	.90	.25
☐ 132	World Trophy Final	5.00	1.50	.50

1977-78 O-Pee-Chee NHL

 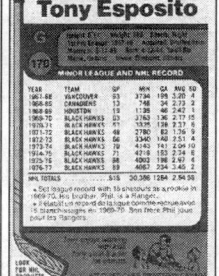

The 1977-78 O-Pee-Chee NHL set consists of 396 color cards. Cards 203 and 255 feature different players than corresponding Topps cards. Printed in Canada, the cards measure the standard 2 1/2" by 3 1/2". Bilingual backs contain yearly statistics and a cartoon-illustrated fact about the player. Cards 322-339 have a team logo on the front with team records on the back. There are no key Rookie Cards in this set, although the Rick Bourbonnais card (312) actually depicts Bernie Federko, predating his Rookie Card by one year.

	NRMT	VG-E	GOOD
COMPLETE SET (396)	150.00	70.00	19.00
COMMON PLAYER (1-396)	.35	.16	.04

		NRMT	VG-E	GOOD
☐ 1	Goals Leaders	3.00	.90	3.00
	Steve Shutt			
	Guy Lafleur			
	Marcel Dionne			
☐ 2	Assists Leaders	2.00	.90	.25
	Guy Lafleur			
	Marcel Dionne			
	Larry Robinson			
	Borje Salming			
	Tim Young			
☐ 3	Scoring Leaders	2.50	1.15	.30
	Guy Lafleur			
	Marcel Dionne			
	Steve Shutt			
☐ 4	Penalty Min. Leaders	.50	.23	.06
	Dave(Tiger) Williams			
	Dennis Polonich			
	Bob Gassoff			
☐ 5	Power Play Goals	1.00	.45	.13
	Leaders			
	Lanny McDonald			

		NRMT	VG-E	GOOD
	Phil Esposito			
	Tom Williams			
☐ 6	Goals Against	2.00	.90	.25
	Average Leaders			
	Michel Larocque			
	Ken Dryden			
	Glenn Resch			
☐ 7	Game Winning	2.50	1.15	.30
	Goals Leaders			
	Gilbert Perreault			
	Steve Shutt			
	Guy Lafleur			
	Rick MacLeish			
	Peter McNab			
☐ 8	Shutouts Leaders	3.00	1.35	.40
	Ken Dryden			
	Rogatien Vachon			
	Bernie Parent			
	Dunc Wilson			
☐ 9	Brian Spencer	.35	.16	.04
☐ 10	Denis Potvin AS2	5.00	2.30	.60
☐ 11	Nick Fotiu	1.00	.45	.13
☐ 12	Bob Murray	.35	.16	.04
☐ 13	Pete Lopresti	.50	.23	.06
☐ 14	J. Bob Kelly	.35	.16	.04
☐ 15	Rick MacLeish	.50	.23	.06
☐ 16	Terry Harper	.35	.16	.04
☐ 17	Willi Plett	3.00	1.35	.40
☐ 18	Peter McNab	.50	.23	.06
☐ 19	Wayne Thomas	.50	.23	.06
☐ 20	Pierre Bouchard	.35	.16	.04
☐ 21	Dennis Maruk	1.00	.45	.13
☐ 22	Mike Murphy	.35	.16	.04
☐ 23	Cesare Maniago	.50	.23	.06
☐ 24	Paul Gardner	.50	.23	.06
☐ 25	Rod Gilbert	1.25	.55	.16
☐ 26	Orest Kindrachuk	.35	.16	.04
☐ 27	Bill Hajt	.35	.16	.04
☐ 28	John Davidson	.50	.23	.06
☐ 29	Jean-Paul Parise	.35	.16	.04
☐ 30	Larry Robinson AS1	5.00	2.30	.60
☐ 31	Yvon Labre	.35	.16	.04
☐ 32	Walt McKechnie	.35	.16	.04
☐ 33	Rick Kehoe	.50	.23	.06
☐ 34	Randy Holt	.35	.16	.04
☐ 35	Garry Unger	.50	.23	.06
☐ 36	Lou Nanne	.35	.16	.04
☐ 37	Dan Bouchard	.50	.23	.06
☐ 38	Darryl Sittler	3.50	1.55	.45
☐ 39	Bob Murdoch	.35	.16	.04
☐ 40	Jean Ratelle	1.25	.55	.16
☐ 41	Dave Maloney	.35	.16	.04
☐ 42	Danny Gare	.50	.23	.06
☐ 43	Jim Watson	.35	.16	.04
☐ 44	Tom Williams	.35	.16	.04
☐ 45	Serge Savard	.35	.16	.04
☐ 46	Derek Sanderson	.50	.23	.06
☐ 47	John Marks	.35	.16	.04
☐ 48	Al Cameron	.35	.16	.04
☐ 49	Dean Talafous	.35	.16	.04
☐ 50	Glenn Resch	1.00	.45	.13
☐ 51	Ron Schock	.35	.16	.04
☐ 52	Gary Croteau	.35	.16	.04
☐ 53	Gerry Meehan	.50	.23	.06
☐ 54	Ed Staniowski	.50	.23	.06
☐ 55	Phil Esposito UER	3.50	1.55	.45
	(Goal total reads 78,			
	should be 55)			
☐ 56	Dennis Ververgaert	.35	.16	.04
☐ 57	Rick Wilson	.35	.16	.04
☐ 58	Jim Lorentz	.35	.16	.04
☐ 59	Bobby Schmautz	.35	.16	.04
☐ 60	Guy Lapointe AS2	.50	.23	.06
☐ 61	Ivan Boldirev	.35	.16	.04
☐ 62	Bob Nystrom	.50	.23	.06
☐ 63	Rick Hampton	.35	.16	.04
☐ 64	Jack Valiquette	.35	.16	.04
☐ 65	Bernie Parent	2.00	.90	.25
☐ 66	Dave Burrows	.35	.16	.04
☐ 67	Butch Goring	.50	.23	.06
☐ 68	Checklist 1-132	8.00	.80	.16
☐ 69	Murray Wilson	.35	.16	.04
☐ 70	Ed Giacomin	1.50	.65	.19
☐ 71	Flames Team	1.00	.45	.13
☐ 72	Bruins Team	1.15	.50	.14
☐ 73	Sabres Team	1.00	.45	.13
☐ 74	Blackhawks Team	1.00	.45	.13
☐ 75	Barons Team	1.00	.45	.13
☐ 76	Rockies Team	1.00	.45	.13
☐ 77	Red Wings Team	1.00	.45	.13
☐ 78	Kings Team	1.00	.45	.13
☐ 79	North Stars Team	1.00	.45	.13
☐ 80	Canadiens Team	1.15	.50	.14
☐ 81	Islanders Team	1.00	.45	.13

☐	82 Rangers Team	1.00	.45	.13
☐	83 Flyers Team	1.00	.45	.13
☐	84 Penguins Team	1.00	.45	.13
☐	85 Blues Team	1.00	.45	.13
☐	86 Maple Leafs Team	1.15	.50	.14
☐	87 Canucks Team	1.00	.45	.13
☐	88 Capitals Team	1.00	.45	.13
☐	89 Keith Magnuson	.35	.16	.04
☐	90 Walt Tkaczuk	.50	.23	.06
☐	91 Bill Nyrop	.35	.16	.04
☐	92 Michel Plasse	.50	.23	.06
☐	93 Bob Bourne	.50	.23	.06
☐	94 Lee Fogolin	.35	.16	.04
☐	95 Gregg Sheppard	.35	.16	.04
☐	96 Hartland Monahan	.35	.16	.04
☐	97 Curt Bennett	.35	.16	.04
☐	98 Bob Dailey	.35	.16	.04
☐	99 Bill Goldsworthy	.50	.23	.06
☐	100 Ken Dryden AS1	10.00	4.50	1.25
☐	101 Grant Mulvey	.35	.16	.04
☐	102 Pierre Larouche	.75	.35	.09
☐	103 Nick Libett	.35	.16	.04
☐	104 Rick Smith	.35	.16	.04
☐	105 Bryan Trottier	20.00	9.00	2.50
☐	106 Pierre Jarry	.35	.16	.04
☐	107 Red Berenson	.50	.23	.06
☐	108 Jim Schoenfeld	.50	.23	.06
☐	109 Gilles Meloche	.50	.23	.06
☐	110 Lanny McDonald AS2	3.00	1.35	.40
☐	111 Don Lever	.35	.16	.04
☐	112 Greg Polis	.35	.16	.04
☐	113 Gary Sargent	.40	.18	.05
☐	114 Earl Anderson	.35	.16	.04
☐	115 Bobby Clarke	5.00	2.30	.60
☐	116 Dave Lewis	.35	.16	.04
☐	117 Darcy Rota	.35	.16	.04
☐	118 Andre Savard	.35	.16	.04
☐	119 Denis Herron	.50	.23	.06
☐	120 Steve Shutt AS1	2.00	.90	.25
☐	121 Mel Bridgman	1.00	.45	.13
☐	122 Buster Harvey	.35	.16	.04
☐	123 Roland Eriksson	.35	.16	.04
☐	124 Dale Tallon	.35	.16	.04
☐	125 Gilles Gilbert	.50	.23	.06
☐	126 Billy Harris	.35	.16	.04
☐	127 Tom Lysiak	.50	.23	.06
☐	128 Jerry Korab	.35	.16	.04
☐	129 Bob Gainey	2.00	.90	.25
☐	130 Wilf Paiement	.50	.23	.06
☐	131 Tom Bladon	.35	.16	.04
☐	132 Ernie Hicke	.35	.16	.04
☐	133 J.P. LeBlanc	.35	.16	.04
☐	134 Mike Milbury	2.50	1.15	.30
☐	135 Pit Martin	.35	.16	.04
☐	136 Steve Vickers	.35	.16	.04
☐	137 Don Awrey	.35	.16	.04
☐	138 Bernie Wolfe	.50	.23	.06
☐	139 Doug Jarvis	.60	.25	.08
☐	140 Borje Salming AS1	1.50	.65	.19
☐	141 Bob MacMillan	.35	.16	.04
☐	142 Wayne Stephenson	.50	.23	.06
☐	143 Dave Forbes	.35	.16	.04
☐	144 Jean Potvin	.35	.16	.04
☐	145 Guy Charron	.35	.16	.04
☐	146 Cliff Koroll	.35	.16	.04
☐	147 Danny Grant	.50	.23	.06
☐	148 Bill Hogaboam	.35	.16	.04
☐	149 Al MacAdam	.35	.16	.04
☐	150 Gerry Desjardins	.50	.23	.06
☐	151 Yvon Lambert	.35	.16	.04
☐	152 Rick Lapointe	.35	.16	.04
☐	153 Ed Westfall	.50	.23	.06
☐	154 Carol Vadnais	.35	.16	.04
☐	155 Johnny Bucyk	1.00	.45	.13
☐	156 J.P. Bordeleau	.35	.16	.04
☐	157 Ron Stackhouse	.35	.16	.04
☐	158 Glen Sharpley	.35	.16	.04
☐	159 Michel Bergeron	.35	.16	.04
☐	160 Rogatien Vachon AS2	1.00	.45	.13
☐	161 Fred Stanfield	.35	.16	.04
☐	162 Gerry Hart	.35	.16	.04
☐	163 Mario Tremblay	.50	.23	.06
☐	164 Andre Dupont	.35	.16	.04
☐	165 Don Marcotte	.35	.16	.04
☐	166 Wayne Dillon	.35	.16	.04
☐	167 Claude Larose	.35	.16	.04
☐	168 Eric Vail	.35	.16	.04
☐	169 Tom Edur	.35	.16	.04
☐	170 Tony Esposito	2.50	1.15	.30
☐	171 Andre St.Laurent	.35	.16	.04
☐	172 Dan Maloney	.35	.16	.04
☐	173 Dennis O'Brien	.35	.16	.04
☐	174 Blair Chapman	.35	.16	.04
☐	175 Dennis Kearns	.35	.16	.04
☐	176 Wayne Merrick	.35	.16	.04
☐	177 Michel Larocque	.50	.23	.06
☐	178 Bob Kelly	.35	.16	.04
☐	179 Dave Farrish	.35	.16	.04
☐	180 Richard Martin AS2	.50	.23	.06
☐	181 Gary Doak	.35	.16	.04
☐	182 Jude Drouin	.35	.16	.04
☐	183 Barry Dean	.35	.16	.04
☐	184 Gary Smith	.50	.23	.06
☐	185 Reggie Leach	.50	.23	.06
☐	186 Ian Turnbull	.50	.23	.06
☐	187 Vic Venasky	.35	.16	.04
☐	188 Wayne Bianchin	.35	.16	.04
☐	189 Doug Risebrough	.50	.23	.06
☐	190 Brad Park	2.00	.90	.25
☐	191 Craig Ramsay	.35	.16	.04
☐	192 Ken Hodge	.50	.23	.06
☐	193 Phil Myre	.50	.23	.06
☐	194 Garry Howatt	.35	.16	.04
☐	195 Stan Mikita	3.50	1.55	.45
☐	196 Garnet Bailey	.35	.16	.04
☐	197 Dennis Hextall	.35	.16	.04
☐	198 Nick Beverley	.35	.16	.04
☐	199 Larry Patey	.35	.16	.04
☐	200 Guy Lafleur AS1	8.00	3.60	1.00
☐	201 Don Edwards	3.00	1.35	.40
☐	202 Gary Dornhoefer	.35	.16	.04
☐	203 Bob Paradise	.35	.16	.04
☐	204 Alex Pirus	.35	.16	.04
☐	205 Peter Mahovlich	.50	.23	.06
☐	206 Bert Marshall	.35	.16	.04
☐	207 Gilles Gratton	.50	.23	.06
☐	208 Alain Daigle	.35	.16	.04
☐	209 Chris Oddleifson	.35	.16	.04
☐	210 Gilbert Perreault AS2	2.50	1.15	.30
☐	211 Mike Palmateer	4.00	1.80	.50
☐	212 Billy Lochead	.35	.16	.04
☐	213 Dick Redmond	.35	.16	.04
☐	214 Guy Lafleur RB	2.50	1.15	.30
	Most Points,			
	RW, Season			
☐	215 Ian Turnbull RB	.35	.16	.04
	Most Goals,			
	Defenseman, Game			
☐	216 Guy Lafleur RB	2.50	1.15	.30
	Longest Point			
	Scoring Streak			
☐	217 Steve Shutt RB	.50	.23	.06
	Most Goals,			
	LW, Season			
☐	218 Guy Lafleur RB	2.50	1.15	.30
	Most Assists,			
	RW, Season			
☐	219 Lorne Henning	.35	.16	.04
☐	220 Terry O'Reilly	.50	.23	.06
☐	221 Pat Hickey	.35	.16	.04
☐	222 Rene Robert	.50	.23	.06
☐	223 Tim Young	.35	.16	.04
☐	224 Dunc Wilson	.50	.23	.06
☐	225 Dennis Hull	.50	.23	.06
☐	226 Rod Seiling	.35	.16	.04
☐	227 Bill Barber	1.25	.55	.16
☐	228 Dennis Polonich	.35	.16	.04
☐	229 Billy Smith	2.00	.90	.25
☐	230 Yvan Cournoyer	1.50	.65	.19
☐	231 Don Luce	.35	.16	.04
☐	232 Mike McEwen	.50	.23	.06
☐	233 Don Saleski	.35	.16	.04
☐	234 Wayne Cashman	.50	.23	.06
☐	235 Phil Russell	.35	.16	.04
☐	236 Mike Corrigan	.35	.16	.04
☐	237 Guy Chouinard	.50	.23	.06
☐	238 Steve Jensen	.35	.16	.04
☐	239 Jim Rutherford	.50	.23	.06
☐	240 Marcel Dionne AS1	5.00	2.30	.60
☐	241 Rejean Houle	.35	.16	.04
☐	242 Jocelyn Guevremont	.35	.16	.04
☐	243 Jim Harrison	.35	.16	.04
☐	244 Don Murdoch	.35	.16	.04
☐	245 Rick Green	1.00	.45	.13
☐	246 Rick Middleton	2.00	.90	.25
☐	247 Joe Watson	.35	.16	.04
☐	248 Syl Apps	.50	.23	.06
☐	249 Checklist 133-264	8.00	.80	.16
☐	250 Clark Gillies	.75	.35	.09
☐	251 Bobby Orr	20.00	9.00	2.50
☐	252 Nelson Pyatt	.35	.16	.04
☐	253 Gary McAdam	.35	.16	.04
☐	254 Jacques Lemaire	1.00	.45	.13
☐	255 Bob Girard	.35	.16	.04
☐	256 Ron Greschner	.50	.23	.06
☐	257 Ross Lonsberry	.35	.16	.04

☐	258	Dave Gardner	.35	.16	.04	☐	332	Islanders Records and Team Logo	2.00	.90	.25
☐	259	Rick Blight	.35	.16	.04	☐	333	Rangers Records and Team Logo	2.00	.90	.25
☐	260	Gerry Cheevers	2.00	.90	.25	☐	334	Flyers Records and Team Logo	2.00	.90	.25
☐	261	Jean Pronovost	.50	.23	.06	☐	335	Penguins Records and Team Logo	2.00	.90	.25
☐	262	Cup Semi-Finals Canadiens skate Past Islanders	.50	.23	.06	☐	336	Blues Records and Team Logo	2.00	.90	.25
☐	263	Cup Semi-Finals Bruins Advance to Finals	.50	.23	.06	☐	337	Leafs Records and Team Logo	2.50	1.15	.30
☐	264	Stanley Cup Finals Canadiens Win 20th Stanley Cup	1.00	.45	.13	☐	338	Canucks Records and Team Logo	2.00	.90	.25
☐	265	Rick Bowness	1.00	.45	.13	☐	339	Capitals Records and Team Logo	2.00	.90	.25
☐	266	George Ferguson	.35	.16	.04	☐	340	Chuck Lefley	.35	.16	.04
☐	267	Mike Kitchen	.35	.16	.04	☐	341	Garry Monahan	.35	.16	.04
☐	268	Bob Berry	.35	.16	.04	☐	342	Bryan Watson	.35	.16	.04
☐	269	Greg Smith	.35	.16	.04	☐	343	Dave Hudson	.35	.16	.04
☐	270	Stan Jonathan	2.50	1.15	.30	☐	344	Neil Komadoski	.35	.16	.04
☐	271	Dwight Bialowas	.35	.16	.04	☐	345	Gary Edwards	.50	.23	.06
☐	272	Pete Stemkowski	.35	.16	.04	☐	346	Rey Comeau	.35	.16	.04
☐	273	Greg Joly	.35	.16	.04	☐	347	Bob Neely	.35	.16	.04
☐	274	Ken Houston	.35	.16	.04	☐	348	Jean Hamel	.35	.16	.04
☐	275	Brian Glennie	.35	.16	.04	☐	349	Jerry Butler	.35	.16	.04
☐	276	Ed Johnston	.50	.23	.06	☐	350	Mike Walton	.35	.16	.04
☐	277	John Grisdale	.35	.16	.04	☐	351	Bob Sirois	.35	.16	.04
☐	278	Craig Patrick	.50	.23	.06	☐	352	Jim McElmury	.35	.16	.04
☐	279	Ken Breitenbach	.35	.16	.04	☐	353	Dave Schultz	.50	.23	.06
☐	280	Fred Ahern	.35	.16	.04	☐	354	Doug Palazzari	.35	.16	.04
☐	281	Jim Roberts St. Louis Blues	.35	.16	.04	☐	355	David Shand	.35	.16	.04
☐	282	Harvey Bennett	.35	.16	.04	☐	356	Stan Weir	.35	.16	.04
☐	283	Ab DeMarco	.35	.16	.04	☐	357	Mike Christie	.35	.16	.04
☐	284	Pat Boutette	.35	.16	.04	☐	358	Floyd Thomson	.35	.16	.04
☐	285	Bob Plager	.50	.23	.06	☐	359	Larry Goodenough	.35	.16	.04
☐	286	Hilliard Graves	.35	.16	.04	☐	360	Bill Riley	.35	.16	.04
☐	287	Gordie Lane	.35	.16	.04	☐	361	Doug Hicks	.35	.16	.04
☐	288	Ron Andruff	.35	.16	.04	☐	362	Dan Newman	.35	.16	.04
☐	289	Larry Brown	.35	.16	.04	☐	363	Rick Chartraw	.35	.16	.04
☐	290	Mike Fidler	.35	.16	.04	☐	364	Tim Ecclestone	.35	.16	.04
☐	291	Fred Barrett	.35	.16	.04	☐	365	Don Ashby	.35	.16	.04
☐	292	Bill Clement	.50	.23	.06	☐	366	Jacques Richard	.35	.16	.04
☐	293	Errol Thompson	.35	.16	.04	☐	367	Yves Belanger	.50	.23	.06
☐	294	Doug Grant	.50	.23	.06	☐	368	Ron Sedlbauer	.35	.16	.04
☐	295	Harold Snepts	1.50	.65	.19	☐	369	Jack Lynch UER (Photo actually Bill Collins)	.35	.16	.04
☐	296	Rick Bragnalo	.35	.16	.04						
☐	297	Bryan Lefley	.35	.16	.04						
☐	298	Gene Carr	.35	.16	.04						
☐	299	Bob Stewart	.35	.16	.04	☐	370	Doug Favell	.50	.23	.06
☐	300	Lew Morrison	.35	.16	.04	☐	371	Bob Murdoch	.35	.16	.04
☐	301	Ed Kea	.35	.16	.04	☐	372	Ralph Klassen	.35	.16	.04
☐	302	Scott Garland	.35	.16	.04	☐	373	Richard Mulhern	.35	.16	.04
☐	303	Bill Fairbairn	.35	.16	.04	☐	374	Jim McKenny	.35	.16	.04
☐	304	Larry Carriere	.35	.16	.04	☐	375	Mike Bloom	.35	.16	.04
☐	305	Ron Low	.50	.23	.06	☐	376	Bruce Affleck	.35	.16	.04
☐	306	Tom Reid	.35	.16	.04	☐	377	Gerry O'Flaherty	.35	.16	.04
☐	307	Paul Holmgren	2.50	1.15	.30	☐	378	Ron Lalonde	.35	.16	.04
☐	308	Pat Price	.35	.16	.04	☐	379	Chuck Arnason	.35	.16	.04
☐	309	Kirk Bowman	.35	.16	.04	☐	380	Dave Hutchinson	.35	.16	.04
☐	310	Bobby Simpson	.35	.16	.04	☐	381A	Checklist ERR (Topps heading)	8.00	.80	.16
☐	311	Ron Ellis	.50	.23	.06						
☐	312	Rick Bourbonnais UER (Photo actually Bernie Federko)	1.00	.45	.13	☐	381B	Checklist COR (No Topps heading)	8.00	.80	.16
						☐	382	John Gould	.35	.16	.04
☐	313	Bobby Lalonde	.35	.16	.04	☐	383	Dave(Tiger) Williams	3.00	1.35	.40
☐	314	Tony White	.35	.16	.04	☐	384	Len Frig	.35	.16	.04
☐	315	John Van Boxmeer	.50	.23	.06	☐	385	Pierre Plante	.35	.16	.04
☐	316	Don Kozak	.35	.16	.04	☐	386	Ralph Stewart	.35	.16	.04
☐	317	Jim Neilson	.35	.16	.04	☐	387	Gord Smith	.35	.16	.04
☐	318	Terry Martin	.35	.16	.04	☐	388	Denis Dupere	.35	.16	.04
☐	319	Barry Gibbs	.35	.16	.04	☐	389	Randy Manery	.35	.16	.04
☐	320	Inge Hammarstrom	.35	.16	.04	☐	390	Lowell MacDonald	.35	.16	.04
☐	321	Darryl Edestrand	.35	.16	.04	☐	391	Dennis Owchar	.35	.16	.04
☐	322	Flames Records and Team Logo	2.00	.90	.25	☐	392	Jim Roberts Minnesota North Stars	.35	.16	.04
☐	323	Bruins Records and Team Logo	2.50	1.15	.30	☐	393	Mike Veisor	.50	.23	.06
☐	324	Sabres Records and Team Logo	2.00	.90	.25	☐	394	Bob Hess	.35	.16	.04
☐	325	Blackhawks Records and Team Logo	2.00	.90	.25	☐	395	Curt Ridley	.50	.23	.06
☐	326	Barons Records and Team Logo	2.00	.90	.25	☐	396	Mike Lampman	1.00	.25	.08
☐	327	Rockies Records and Team Logo	2.00	.90	.25						
☐	328	Red Wings Records and Team Logo	2.00	.90	.25						
☐	329	Kings Records and Team Logo	2.00	.90	.25						
☐	330	North Stars Records and Team Logo	2.00	.90	.25						
☐	331	Canadiens Records and Team Logo	2.50	1.15	.30						

1977-78 O-Pee-Chee WHA

The 1977-78 O-Pee-Chee WHA set consists of 66 color cards. Printed in Canada, the cards were originally sold in 15-cent wax packs containing 12 cards and gum. Cards measure 2 1/2" by 3 1/2". Bilingual backs feature player statistics and a short biography. Card number 1 features

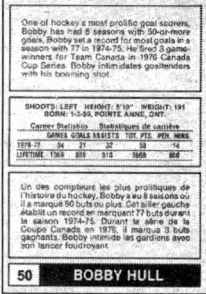

Gordie Howe's 1000th career goal. There are no key Rookie Cards in this set. This was the final WHA set. The league disbanded following the 1978-79 season with the four surviving teams (Edmonton, New England/Hartford, Quebec and Winnipeg) merging with the NHL.

	NRMT	VG-E	GOOD
COMPLETE SET (66)	80.00	36.00	10.00
COMMON PLAYER (1-66)	.75	.35	.09

		NRMT	VG-E	GOOD
☐ 1	Gordie Howe	35.00	10.50	3.50
☐ 2	Jean Bernier	.75	.35	.09
☐ 3	Anders Hedberg	1.75	.80	.22
☐ 4	Ken Broderick	1.00	.45	.13
☐ 5	Joe Noris	.75	.35	.09
☐ 6	Blaine Stoughton	1.00	.45	.13
☐ 7	Claude St.Sauveur	.75	.35	.09
☐ 8	Real Cloutier	1.00	.45	.13
☐ 9	Joe Daley	1.00	.45	.13
☐ 10	Ron Chipperfield	.75	.35	.09
☐ 11	Wayne Rutledge	.75	.35	.09
☐ 12	Mark Napier	1.00	.45	.13
☐ 13	Rich Leduc	.75	.35	.09
☐ 14	Don McLeod	.75	.35	.09
☐ 15	Ulf Nilsson	1.75	.80	.22
☐ 16	Blair MacDonald	.75	.35	.09
☐ 17	Mike Rogers	1.00	.45	.13
☐ 18	Gary Inness	1.00	.45	.13
☐ 19	Larry Lund	.75	.35	.09
☐ 20	Marc Tardif	.75	.35	.09
☐ 21	Lars-Erik Sjoberg	.75	.35	.09
☐ 22	Bryan Campbell	.75	.35	.09
☐ 23	John Garrett	1.00	.45	.13
☐ 24	Ron Plumb	.75	.35	.09
☐ 25	Mark Howe	6.00	2.70	.75
☐ 26	Garry Lariviere	.75	.35	.09
☐ 27	Peter Sullivan	.75	.35	.09
☐ 28	Dave Dryden	1.00	.45	.13
☐ 29	Reg Thomas	.75	.35	.09
☐ 30	Andre Lacroix	1.00	.45	.13
☐ 31	Paul Henderson	1.00	.45	.13
☐ 32	Paulin Bordeleau	.75	.35	.09
☐ 33	Juha Widing	.75	.35	.09
☐ 34	Mike Antonovich	.75	.35	.09
☐ 35	Robbie Ftorek	1.00	.45	.13
☐ 36	Rosaire Paiement	.75	.35	.09
☐ 37	Terry Ruskowski	1.00	.45	.13
☐ 38	Richard Brodeur	3.00	1.35	.40
☐ 39	Willy Lindstrom	1.50	.65	.19
☐ 40	Al Hamilton	.75	.35	.09
☐ 41	John McKenzie	1.00	.45	.13
☐ 42	Wayne Wood	.75	.35	.09
☐ 43	Claude Larose	.75	.35	.09
☐ 44	J.C. Tremblay	.75	.35	.09
☐ 45	Gary Bromley	1.00	.45	.13
☐ 46	Ken Baird	.75	.35	.09
☐ 47	Bobby Sheehan	.75	.35	.09
☐ 48	Don Larway	.75	.35	.09
☐ 49	Al Smith	1.00	.45	.13
☐ 50	Bobby Hull	20.00	9.00	2.50
☐ 51	Peter Marrin	.75	.35	.09
☐ 52	Norm Ferguson	.75	.35	.09
☐ 53	Dennis Sobchuk	.75	.35	.09
☐ 54	Norm Dube	.75	.35	.09
☐ 55	Tom Webster	1.00	.45	.13
☐ 56	Jim Park	.75	.35	.09
☐ 57	Dan Labraaten	1.00	.45	.13
☐ 58	Checklist Card	8.00	.80	.16
☐ 59	Paul Shmyr	.75	.35	.09
☐ 60	Serge Bernier	1.00	.45	.13
☐ 61	Frank Mahovlich	4.00	1.80	.50
☐ 62	Michel Dion	.75	.35	.09
☐ 63	Poul Popiel	.75	.35	.09
☐ 64	Lyle Moffat	.75	.35	.09
☐ 65	Marty Howe	1.00	.45	.13
☐ 66	Don Burgess	2.00	.50	.16

1978-79 O-Pee-Chee

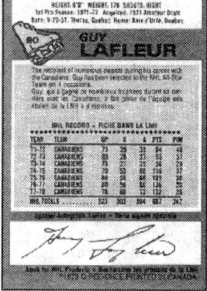

The 1978-79 O-Pee-Chee set consists of 396 cards. Cards measure the standard 2 1/2" by 3 1/2". Bilingual backs feature the card number (pictured in a hockey skate), year-by-year player statistics, a short biography and a facsimile autograph. Card number 300 honors Bobby Orr's retirement early in the season. Rookie Cards include Mike Bossy, Bernie Federko, Dave Taylor, Doug Wilson, Ron Duguay, Brian Sutter and Randy Carlyle.

	NRMT	VG-E	GOOD
COMPLETE SET (396)	175.00	80.00	22.00
COMMON PLAYER (1-396)	.25	.11	.03

		NRMT	VG-E	GOOD
☐ 1	Mike Bossy HL Goals by Rookie	7.50	1.90	7.50
☐ 2	Phil Esposito HL 29th Hat Trick	1.25	.55	.16
☐ 3	Guy Lafleur HL Scores against Every Team	1.50	.65	.19
☐ 4	Darryl Sittler HL Goals In Nine Straight Games	.75	.35	.09
☐ 5	Garry Unger HL 803 Consec. Games	.30	.14	.04
☐ 6	Gary Edwards	.30	.14	.04
☐ 7	Rick Blight	.25	.11	.03
☐ 8	Larry Patey	.25	.11	.03
☐ 9	Craig Ramsay	.25	.11	.03
☐ 10	Bryan Trottier	10.00	4.50	1.25
☐ 11	Don Murdoch	.25	.11	.03
☐ 12	Phil Russell	.25	.11	.03
☐ 13	Doug Jarvis	.30	.14	.04
☐ 14	Gene Carr	.25	.11	.03
☐ 15	Bernie Parent	1.50	.65	.19
☐ 16	Perry Miller	.25	.11	.03
☐ 17	Kent-Erik Andersson	.25	.11	.03
☐ 18	Gregg Sheppard	.25	.11	.03
☐ 19	Dennis Owchar	.25	.11	.03
☐ 20	Rogatien Vachon	.75	.35	.09
☐ 21	Dan Maloney	.25	.11	.03
☐ 22	Guy Charron	.25	.11	.03
☐ 23	Dick Redmond	.25	.11	.03
☐ 24	Checklist 1-132	4.50	.45	.09
☐ 25	Anders Hedberg	.30	.14	.04
☐ 26	Mel Bridgman	.30	.14	.04
☐ 27	Lee Fogolin	.25	.11	.03
☐ 28	Gilles Meloche	.30	.14	.04
☐ 29	Garry Howatt	.25	.11	.03
☐ 30	Darryl Sittler	2.50	1.15	.30
☐ 31	Curt Bennett	.25	.11	.03
☐ 32	Andre St.Laurent	.25	.11	.03
☐ 33	Blair Chapman	.25	.11	.03
☐ 34	Keith Magnuson	.25	.11	.03
☐ 35	Pierre Larouche	.30	.14	.04
☐ 36	Michel Plasse	.30	.14	.04
☐ 37	Gary Sargent	.25	.11	.03
☐ 38	Mike Walton	.25	.11	.03

☐ 39	Robert Picard	.40	.18	.05
☐ 40	Terry O'Reilly	.40	.18	.05
☐ 41	Dave Farrish	.25	.11	.03
☐ 42	Gary McAdam	.25	.11	.03
☐ 43	Joe Watson	.25	.11	.03
☐ 44	Yves Belanger	.30	.14	.04
☐ 45	Steve Jensen	.25	.11	.03
☐ 46	Bob Stewart	.25	.11	.03
☐ 47	Darcy Rota	.25	.11	.03
☐ 48	Dennis Hextall	.25	.11	.03
☐ 49	Bert Marshall	.25	.11	.03
☐ 50	Ken Dryden	7.00	3.10	.85
☐ 51	Peter Mahovlich	.30	.14	.04
☐ 52	Dennis Ververgaert	.25	.11	.03
☐ 53	Inge Hammarstrom	.25	.11	.03
☐ 54	Doug Favell	.30	.14	.04
☐ 55	Steve Vickers	.25	.11	.03
☐ 56	Syl Apps	.25	.11	.03
☐ 57	Errol Thompson	.25	.11	.03
☐ 58	Don Luce	.25	.11	.03
☐ 59	Mike Milbury	.50	.23	.06
☐ 60	Yvan Cournoyer	1.25	.55	.16
☐ 61	Kirk Bowman	.25	.11	.03
☐ 62	Billy Smith	1.25	.55	.16
☐ 63	Goal Leaders Guy Lafleur Mike Bossy Steve Shutt	3.50	1.55	.45
☐ 64	Assist Leaders Bryan Trottier Guy Lafleur Darryl Sittler	2.50	1.15	.30
☐ 65	Scoring Leaders Guy Lafleur Bryan Trottier Darryl Sittler	2.50	1.15	.30
☐ 66	Penalty Minutes Leaders Dave Schultz Dave(Tiger) Williams Dennis Polonich	.50	.23	.06
☐ 67	Power Play Goal Leaders Mike Bossy Phil Esposito Steve Shutt	3.50	1.55	.45
☐ 68	Goals Against Average Leaders Ken Dryden Bernie Parent Gilles Gilbert	3.00	1.35	.40
☐ 69	Game Winning Goal Leaders Guy Lafleur Bill Barber Darryl Sittler Bob Bourne	2.00	.90	.25
☐ 70	Shutout Leaders Bernie Parent Ken Dryden Don Edwards Tony Esposito Mike Palmateer	4.00	1.80	.50
☐ 71	Bob Kelly	.25	.11	.03
☐ 72	Ron Stackhouse	.25	.11	.03
☐ 73	Wayne Dillon	.25	.11	.03
☐ 74	Jim Rutherford	.30	.14	.04
☐ 75	Stan Mikita	2.50	1.15	.30
☐ 76	Bob Gainey	1.50	.65	.19
☐ 77	Gerry Hart	.25	.11	.03
☐ 78	Lanny McDonald	1.50	.65	.19
☐ 79	Brad Park	1.50	.65	.19
☐ 80	Richard Martin	.30	.14	.04
☐ 81	Bernie Wolfe	.30	.14	.04
☐ 82	Bob MacMillan	.25	.11	.03
☐ 83	Brad Maxwell	.25	.11	.03
☐ 84	Mike Fidler	.25	.11	.03
☐ 85	Carol Vadnais	.25	.11	.03
☐ 86	Don Lever	.25	.11	.03
☐ 87	Phil Myre	.30	.14	.04
☐ 88	Paul Gardner	.25	.11	.03
☐ 89	Bob Murray	.25	.11	.03
☐ 90	Guy Lafleur	6.00	2.70	.75
☐ 91	Bob Murdoch	.25	.11	.03
☐ 92	Ron Ellis	.30	.14	.04
☐ 93	Jude Drouin	.25	.11	.03
☐ 94	Jocelyn Guevremont	.25	.11	.03
☐ 95	Gilles Gilbert	.30	.14	.04
☐ 96	Bob Sirois	.25	.11	.03
☐ 97	Tom Lysiak	.30	.14	.04
☐ 98	Andre Dupont	.25	.11	.03
☐ 99	Per-Olov Brasar	.25	.11	.03
☐ 100	Phil Esposito	3.00	1.35	.40
☐ 101	J.P. Bordeleau	.25	.11	.03
☐ 102	Pierre Mondou	1.00	.45	.13
☐ 103	Wayne Bianchin	.25	.11	.03
☐ 104	Dennis O'Brien	.25	.11	.03
☐ 105	Glenn Resch	.75	.35	.09
☐ 106	Dennis Polonich	.25	.11	.03
☐ 107	Kris Manery	.25	.11	.03
☐ 108	Bill Hajt	.25	.11	.03
☐ 109	Jere Gillis	.25	.11	.03
☐ 110	Garry Unger	.30	.14	.04
☐ 111	Nick Beverley	.25	.11	.03
☐ 112	Pat Hickey	.25	.11	.03
☐ 113	Rick Middleton	1.25	.55	.16
☐ 114	Orest Kindrachuk	.25	.11	.03
☐ 115	Mike Bossy	45.00	20.00	5.75
☐ 116	Pierre Bouchard	.25	.11	.03
☐ 117	Alain Daigle	.25	.11	.03
☐ 118	Terry Martin	.25	.11	.03
☐ 119	Tom Edur	.25	.11	.03
☐ 120	Marcel Dionne	4.00	1.80	.50
☐ 121	Barry Beck	2.00	.90	.25
☐ 122	Billy Lochead	.25	.11	.03
☐ 123	Paul Harrison	.30	.14	.04
☐ 124	Wayne Cashman	.30	.14	.04
☐ 125	Rick MacLeish	.30	.14	.04
☐ 126	Bob Bourne	.30	.14	.04
☐ 127	Ian Turnbull	.25	.11	.03
☐ 128	Gerry Meehan	.30	.14	.04
☐ 129	Eric Vail	.25	.11	.03
☐ 130	Gilbert Perreault	1.50	.65	.19
☐ 131	Bob Dailey	.25	.11	.03
☐ 132	Dale McCourt	.50	.23	.06
☐ 133	John Wensink	1.00	.45	.13
☐ 134	Bill Nyrop	.25	.11	.03
☐ 135	Ivan Boldirev	.25	.11	.03
☐ 136	Lucien Deblois	.50	.23	.06
☐ 137	Brian Spencer	.25	.11	.03
☐ 138	Tim Young	.25	.11	.03
☐ 139	Ron Sedlbauer	.25	.11	.03
☐ 140	Gerry Cheevers	1.50	.65	.19
☐ 141	Dennis Maruk	.30	.14	.04
☐ 142	Barry Dean	.25	.11	.03
☐ 143	Bernie Federko	14.00	6.25	1.75
☐ 144	Stefan Persson	.50	.23	.06
☐ 145	Wilf Paiement	.30	.14	.04
☐ 146	Dale Tallon	.25	.11	.03
☐ 147	Yvon Lambert	.25	.11	.03
☐ 148	Greg Joly	.25	.11	.03
☐ 149	Dean Talafous	.25	.11	.03
☐ 150	Don Edwards	.30	.14	.04
☐ 151	Butch Goring	.30	.14	.04
☐ 152	Tom Bladon	.25	.11	.03
☐ 153	Bob Nystrom	.30	.14	.04
☐ 154	Ron Greschner	.30	.14	.04
☐ 155	Jean Ratelle	1.00	.45	.13
☐ 156	Russ Anderson	.25	.11	.03
☐ 157	John Marks	.25	.11	.03
☐ 158	Michel Larocque	.30	.14	.04
☐ 159	Paul Woods	.25	.11	.03
☐ 160	Mike Palmateer	.30	.14	.04
☐ 161	Jim Lorentz	.25	.11	.03
☐ 162	Dave Lewis	.25	.11	.03
☐ 163	Harvey Bennett	.25	.11	.03
☐ 164	Rick Smith	.25	.11	.03
☐ 165	Reggie Leach	.30	.14	.04
☐ 166	Wayne Thomas	.30	.14	.04
☐ 167	Dave Forbes	.25	.11	.03
☐ 168	Doug Wilson	14.00	6.25	1.75
☐ 169	Dan Bouchard	.30	.14	.04
☐ 170	Steve Shutt	1.25	.55	.16
☐ 171	Mike Kaszycki	.25	.11	.03
☐ 172	Denis Herron	.30	.14	.04
☐ 173	Rick Bowness	.30	.14	.04
☐ 174	Rick Hampton	.25	.11	.03
☐ 175	Glen Sharpley	.25	.11	.03
☐ 176	Bill Barber	1.00	.45	.13
☐ 177	Ron Duguay	3.00	1.35	.40
☐ 178	Jim Schoenfeld	.30	.14	.04
☐ 179	Pierre Plante	.25	.11	.03
☐ 180	Jacques Lemaire	.75	.35	.09
☐ 181	Stan Jonathan	.25	.11	.03
☐ 182	Billy Harris	.25	.11	.03
☐ 183	Chris Oddleifson	.25	.11	.03
☐ 184	Jean Pronovost	.30	.14	.04
☐ 185	Fred Barrett	.25	.11	.03
☐ 186	Ross Lonsberry	.25	.11	.03
☐ 187	Mike McEwen	.25	.11	.03
☐ 188	Rene Robert	.30	.14	.04
☐ 189	J. Bob Kelly	.25	.11	.03
☐ 190	Serge Savard	.25	.11	.03
☐ 191	Dennis Kearns	.25	.11	.03
☐ 192	Flames Team	.50	.23	.06
☐ 193	Bruins Team	.60	.25	.08

☐ 194	Sabres Team	.50	.23	.06
☐ 195	Blackhawks Team	.50	.23	.06
☐ 196	Rockies Team	.50	.23	.06
☐ 197	Red Wings Team	.50	.23	.06
☐ 198	Kings Team	.50	.23	.06
☐ 199	North Stars Team	.50	.23	.06
☐ 200	Canadiens Team	.60	.25	.08
☐ 201	Islanders Team	.50	.23	.06
☐ 202	Rangers Team	.50	.23	.06
☐ 203	Flyers Team	.50	.23	.06
☐ 204	Penguins Team	.50	.23	.06
☐ 205	Blues Team	.50	.23	.06
☐ 206	Maple Leafs Team	.60	.25	.08
☐ 207	Canucks Team	.50	.23	.06
☐ 208	Capitals Team	.50	.23	.06
☐ 209	Danny Gare	.30	.14	.04
☐ 210	Larry Robinson	2.00	.90	.25
☐ 211	John Davidson	.30	.14	.04
☐ 212	Peter McNab	.30	.14	.04
☐ 213	Rick Kehoe	.30	.14	.04
☐ 214	Terry Harper	.25	.11	.03
☐ 215	Bobby Clarke	3.50	1.55	.45
☐ 216	Bryan Maxwell UER (Photo actually Brad Maxwell)	.25	.11	.03
☐ 217	Ted Bulley	.25	.11	.03
☐ 218	Red Berenson	.30	.14	.04
☐ 219	Ron Grahame	.30	.14	.04
☐ 220	Clark Gillies	.30	.14	.04
☐ 221	Dave Maloney	.25	.11	.03
☐ 222	Derek Smith	.25	.11	.03
☐ 223	Wayne Stephenson	.30	.14	.04
☐ 224	John Van Boxmeer	.25	.11	.03
☐ 225	Dave Schultz	.40	.18	.05
☐ 226	Reed Larson	1.00	.45	.13
☐ 227	Rejean Houle	.25	.11	.03
☐ 228	Doug Hicks	.25	.11	.03
☐ 229	Mike Murphy	.25	.11	.03
☐ 230	Pete Lopresti	.30	.14	.04
☐ 231	Jerry Korab	.25	.11	.03
☐ 232	Ed Westfall	.30	.14	.04
☐ 233	Greg Malone	.25	.11	.03
☐ 234	Paul Holmgren	.50	.23	.06
☐ 235	Walt Tkaczuk	.30	.14	.04
☐ 236	Don Marcotte	.25	.11	.03
☐ 237	Ron Low	.30	.14	.04
☐ 238	Rick Chartraw	.25	.11	.03
☐ 239	Cliff Koroll	.25	.11	.03
☐ 240	Borje Salming	1.00	.45	.13
☐ 241	Roland Eriksson	.25	.11	.03
☐ 242	Ric Seiling	.25	.11	.03
☐ 243	Jim Bedard	.30	.14	.04
☐ 244	Peter Lee	.30	.14	.04
☐ 245	Denis Potvin	3.50	1.55	.45
☐ 246	Greg Polis	.25	.11	.03
☐ 247	Jim Watson	.25	.11	.03
☐ 248	Bobby Schmautz	.25	.11	.03
☐ 249	Doug Risebrough	.30	.14	.04
☐ 250	Tony Esposito	2.00	.90	.25
☐ 251	Nick Libett	.25	.11	.03
☐ 252	Ron Zanussi	.25	.11	.03
☐ 253	Andre Savard	.25	.11	.03
☐ 254	Dave Burrows	.25	.11	.03
☐ 255	Ulf Nilsson	.50	.23	.06
☐ 256	Richard Mulhern	.25	.11	.03
☐ 257	Don Saleski	.25	.11	.03
☐ 258	Wayne Merrick	.25	.11	.03
☐ 259	Checklist 133-264	4.50	.45	.09
☐ 260	Guy Lapointe	.30	.14	.04
☐ 261	Grant Mulvey	.25	.11	.03
☐ 262	Stanley Cup Semifinals Canadiens Sweep Maple Leafs	.50	.23	.06
☐ 263	Stanley Cup Semifinals Bruins Skate Past Flyers	.50	.23	.06
☐ 264	Stanley Cup Finals Canadiens Win Third Straight Cup	.75	.35	.09
☐ 265	Bob Sauve	.30	.14	.04
☐ 266	Randy Manery	.25	.11	.03
☐ 267	Bill Fairbairn	.25	.11	.03
☐ 268	Garry Monahan	.25	.11	.03
☐ 269	Colin Campbell	.30	.14	.04
☐ 270	Dan Newman	.25	.11	.03
☐ 271	Dwight Foster	.25	.11	.03
☐ 272	Larry Carriere	.25	.11	.03
☐ 273	Michel Bergeron	.25	.11	.03
☐ 274	Scott Garland	.25	.11	.03
☐ 275	Bill McKenzie	.30	.14	.04
☐ 276	Garnet Bailey	.25	.11	.03
☐ 277	Ed Kea	.25	.11	.03
☐ 278	Dave Gardner	.25	.11	.03
☐ 279	Bruce Affleck	.25	.11	.03
☐ 280	Bruce Boudreau	.25	.11	.03
☐ 281	Jean Hamel	.25	.11	.03
☐ 282	Kurt Walker	.25	.11	.03
☐ 283	Denis Dupere	.25	.11	.03
☐ 284	Gordie Lane	.25	.11	.03
☐ 285	Bobby Lalonde	.25	.11	.03
☐ 286	Pit Martin	.25	.11	.03
☐ 287	Jean Potvin	.25	.11	.03
☐ 288	Jimmy Jones	.25	.11	.03
☐ 289	Dave Hutchinson	.25	.11	.03
☐ 290	Pete Stemkowski	.25	.11	.03
☐ 291	Mike Christie	.25	.11	.03
☐ 292	Bill Riley	.25	.11	.03
☐ 293	Rey Comeau	.25	.11	.03
☐ 294	Jack McIlhargey	.25	.11	.03
☐ 295	Tom Younghans	.25	.11	.03
☐ 296	Mario Faubert	.25	.11	.03
☐ 297	Checklist Card	4.50	.45	.09
☐ 298	Rob Palmer	.25	.11	.03
☐ 299	Dave Hudson	.25	.11	.03
☐ 300	Bobby Orr	35.00	16.00	4.40
☐ 301	Lorne Stamler	.25	.11	.03
☐ 302	Curt Ridley	.30	.14	.04
☐ 303	Greg Smith	.25	.11	.03
☐ 304	Jerry Butler	.25	.11	.03
☐ 305	Gary Doak	.25	.11	.03
☐ 306	Danny Grant	.30	.14	.04
☐ 307	Mark Suzor	.25	.11	.03
☐ 308	Rick Bragnalo	.25	.11	.03
☐ 309	John Gould	.25	.11	.03
☐ 310	Sheldon Kannegiesser	.25	.11	.03
☐ 311	Bobby Sheehan	.25	.11	.03
☐ 312	Randy Carlyle	5.00	2.30	.60
☐ 313	Lorne Henning	.25	.11	.03
☐ 314	Tom Williams	.25	.11	.03
☐ 315	Ron Andruff	.25	.11	.03
☐ 316	Bryan Watson	.25	.11	.03
☐ 317	Willi Plett	.30	.14	.04
☐ 318	John Grisdale	.25	.11	.03
☐ 319	Brian Sutter	12.00	5.50	1.50
☐ 320	Trevor Johansen	.25	.11	.03
☐ 321	Vic Venasky	.25	.11	.03
☐ 322	Rick Lapointe	.25	.11	.03
☐ 323	Ron Delorme	.25	.11	.03
☐ 324	Yvon Labre	.25	.11	.03
☐ 325	Bryan Trottier AS UER (Misspelled Brian on card front)	4.00	1.80	.50
☐ 326	Guy Lafleur AS	2.50	1.15	.30
☐ 327	Clark Gillies AS	.25	.11	.03
☐ 328	Borje Salming AS	.30	.14	.04
☐ 329	Larry Robinson AS	1.00	.45	.13
☐ 330	Ken Dryden AS	3.00	1.35	.40
☐ 331	Darryl Sittler AS	1.00	.45	.13
☐ 332	Terry O'Reilly AS	.25	.11	.03
☐ 333	Steve Shutt AS	.30	.14	.04
☐ 334	Denis Potvin AS	1.50	.65	.19
☐ 335	Serge Savard AS	.25	.11	.03
☐ 336	Don Edwards AS	.25	.11	.03
☐ 337	Glenn Goldup	.25	.11	.03
☐ 338	Mike Kitchen	.25	.11	.03
☐ 339	Bob Girard	.25	.11	.03
☐ 340	Guy Chouinard	.30	.14	.04
☐ 341	Randy Holt	.25	.11	.03
☐ 342	Jim Roberts	.25	.11	.03
☐ 343	Dave Logan	.25	.11	.03
☐ 344	Walt McKechnie	.25	.11	.03
☐ 345	Brian Glennie	.25	.11	.03
☐ 346	Ralph Klassen	.25	.11	.03
☐ 347	Gord Smith	.25	.11	.03
☐ 348	Ken Houston	.25	.11	.03
☐ 349	Bob Manno	.25	.11	.03
☐ 350	Jean Paul Parise	.25	.11	.03
☐ 351	Don Ashby	.25	.11	.03
☐ 352	Fred Stanfield	.25	.11	.03
☐ 353	Dave Taylor	20.00	9.00	2.50
☐ 354	Nelson Pyatt	.25	.11	.03
☐ 355	Blair Stewart	.25	.11	.03
☐ 356	David Shand	.25	.11	.03
☐ 357	Hilliard Graves	.25	.11	.03
☐ 358	Bob Hess	.25	.11	.03
☐ 359	Dave(Tiger) Williams	1.25	.55	.16
☐ 360	Larry Wright	.25	.11	.03
☐ 361	Larry Brown	.25	.11	.03
☐ 362	Gary Croteau	.25	.11	.03
☐ 363	Rick Green	.30	.14	.04
☐ 364	Bill Clement	.30	.14	.04
☐ 365	Gerry O'Flaherty	.25	.11	.03
☐ 366	John Baby	.25	.11	.03
☐ 367	Nick Fotiu	.30	.14	.04
☐ 368	Pat Price	.25	.11	.03
☐ 369	Bert Wilson	.25	.11	.03

☐ 370	Bryan Lefley	.25	.11	.03
☐ 371	Ron Lalonde	.25	.11	.03
☐ 372	Bobby Simpson	.25	.11	.03
☐ 373	Doug Grant	.30	.14	.04
☐ 374	Pat Boutette	.25	.11	.03
☐ 375	Bob Paradise	.25	.11	.03
☐ 376	Mario Tremblay	.30	.14	.04
☐ 377	Darryl Edestrand	.25	.11	.03
☐ 378	Andy Spruce	.25	.11	.03
☐ 379	Jack Brownschidle	.25	.11	.03
☐ 380	Harold Snepsts	1.00	.45	.13
☐ 381	Al MacAdam	.25	.11	.03
☐ 382	Neil Komadoski	.25	.11	.03
☐ 383	Don Awrey	.25	.11	.03
☐ 384	Ron Schock	.25	.11	.03
☐ 385	Gary Simmons	.30	.14	.04
☐ 386	Fred Ahern	.25	.11	.03
☐ 387	Larry Bolonchuk	.25	.11	.03
☐ 388	Brad Gassoff	.25	.11	.03
☐ 389	Chuck Arnason	.25	.11	.03
☐ 390	Barry Gibbs	.25	.11	.03
☐ 391	Jack Valiquette	.25	.11	.03
☐ 392	Doug Halward	.25	.11	.03
☐ 393	Hartland Monahan	.25	.11	.03
☐ 394	Rod Seiling	.25	.11	.03
☐ 395	George Ferguson	.25	.11	.03
☐ 396	Al Cameron	.50	.11	.03

1979-80 O-Pee-Chee

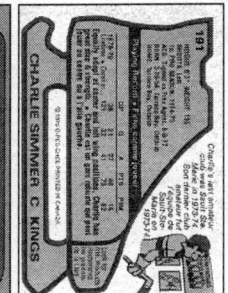

The 1979-80 O-Pee-Chee set consists of 396 cards. Cards 81, 82, 141, 163, and 263 differ from that of the corresponding Topps issue. Printed in Canada the cards measure 2 1/2" by 3 1/2". The fronts feature distinctive blue borders (that are prone to chipping), while bilingual backs feature 1978-79 and career stats, a short biography and a cartoon-illustrated fact about the player. The Rookie Card of Wayne Gretzky (No. 18) has been illegally reprinted. Most of the reprints were discovered and then destroyed or clearly marked as reprints. However some still exist in the market. The reprint is difficult to distinguish from the real card, hence, collectors and dealers should be careful. The set also marks the last active card appearance of Ken Dryden, Gordie Howe, Bobby Hull, and Stan Mikita. In addition to Gretzky, Rookie Cards include John Tonelli, Charlie Simmer, Bobby Smith and Barry Melrose.

	MINT	EXC	G-VG
COMPLETE SET (396)	900.00	400.00	115.00
COMMON PLAYER (1-396)	.40	.18	.05

☐ 1	Goal Leaders	4.00	1.40	.40
	Mike Bossy			
	Marcel Dionne			
	Guy Lafleur			
☐ 2	Assist Leaders	3.00	1.35	.40
	Bryan Trottier			
	Guy Lafleur			
	Marcel Dionne			
	Bob MacMillan			
☐ 3	Scoring Leaders	3.00	1.35	.40
	Bryan Trottier			

	Marcel Dionne			
	Guy Lafleur			
☐ 4	Penalty Minute	.60	.25	.08
	Leaders			
	Dave(Tiger) Williams			
	Randy Holt			
	Dave Schultz			
☐ 5	Power Play	2.50	1.15	.30
	Goal Leaders			
	Mike Bossy			
	Marcel Dionne			
	Paul Gardner			
	Lanny McDonald			
☐ 6	Goals Against	2.50	1.15	.30
	Average Leaders			
	Ken Dryden			
	Glenn Resch			
	Bernie Parent			
☐ 7	Game Winning	3.00	1.35	.40
	Goals Leaders			
	Guy Lafleur			
	Mike Bossy			
	Bryan Trottier			
	Jean Pronovost			
	Ted Bulley			
☐ 8	Shutout Leaders	3.00	1.35	.40
	Ken Dryden			
	Tony Esposito			
	Mario Lessard			
	Mike Palmateer			
	Bernie Parent			
☐ 9	Greg Malone	.40	.18	.05
☐ 10	Rick Middleton	1.00	.45	.13
☐ 11	Greg Smith	.40	.18	.05
☐ 12	Rene Robert	.50	.23	.06
☐ 13	Doug Risebrough	.50	.23	.06
☐ 14	Bob Kelly	.40	.18	.05
☐ 15	Walt Tkaczuk	.50	.23	.06
☐ 16	John Marks	.40	.18	.05
☐ 17	Willie Huber	.40	.18	.05
☐ 18	Wayne Gretzky	750.00	350.00	95.00
☐ 19	Ron Sedlbauer	.40	.18	.05
☐ 20	Glenn Resch AS2	.60	.25	.08
☐ 21	Blair Chapman	.40	.18	.05
☐ 22	Ron Zanussi	.40	.18	.05
☐ 23	Brad Park	1.00	.45	.13
☐ 24	Yvon Lambert	.40	.18	.05
☐ 25	Andre Savard	.40	.18	.05
☐ 26	Jim Watson	.40	.18	.05
☐ 27	Hal Philipoff	.40	.18	.05
☐ 28	Dan Bouchard	.50	.23	.06
☐ 29	Bob Sirois	.40	.18	.05
☐ 30	Ulf Nilsson	.50	.23	.06
☐ 31	Mike Murphy	.40	.18	.05
☐ 32	Stefan Persson	.40	.18	.05
☐ 33	Garry Unger	.50	.23	.06
☐ 34	Rejean Houle	.40	.18	.05
☐ 35	Barry Beck	.50	.23	.06
☐ 36	Tim Young	.40	.18	.05
☐ 37	Rick Dudley	.40	.18	.05
☐ 38	Wayne Stephenson	.50	.23	.06
☐ 39	Peter McNab	.50	.23	.06
☐ 40	Borje Salming AS2	.75	.35	.09
☐ 41	Tom Lysiak	.40	.18	.05
☐ 42	Don Maloney	1.00	.45	.13
☐ 43	Mike Rogers	.50	.23	.06
☐ 44	Dave Lewis	.40	.18	.05
☐ 45	Peter Lee	.40	.18	.05
☐ 46	Marty Howe	.50	.23	.06
☐ 47	Serge Bernier	.40	.18	.05
☐ 48	Paul Woods	.40	.18	.05
☐ 49	Bob Sauve	.50	.23	.06
☐ 50	Larry Robinson AS1	2.00	.90	.25
☐ 51	Tom Gorence	.40	.18	.05
☐ 52	Gary Sargent	.40	.18	.05
☐ 53	Thomas Gradin	2.00	.90	.25
☐ 54	Dean Talafous	.40	.18	.05
☐ 55	Bob Murray	.40	.18	.05
☐ 56	Bob Bourne	.50	.23	.06
☐ 57	Larry Patey	.40	.18	.05
☐ 58	Ross Lonsberry	.40	.18	.05
☐ 59	Rick Smith UER	.40	.18	.05
	(Born Kinston,			
	should be Kingston)			
☐ 60	Guy Chouinard	.50	.23	.06
☐ 61	Danny Gare	.50	.23	.06
☐ 62	Jim Bedard	.50	.23	.06
☐ 63	Dale McCourt UER	.40	.18	.05
	(Pictured in Kings'			
	sweater, but he never			
	played for the Kings)			
☐ 64	Steve Payne	.50	.23	.06
☐ 65	Pat Hughes	.40	.18	.05
☐ 66	Mike McEwen	.40	.18	.05

☐ 67	Reg Kerr	.40	.18	.05
☐ 68	Walt McKechnie	.40	.18	.05
☐ 69	Michel Plasse	.50	.23	.06
☐ 70	Denis Potvin AS1	2.00	.90	.25
☐ 71	Dave Dryden	.50	.23	.06
☐ 72	Gary McAdam	.40	.18	.05
☐ 73	Andre St.Laurent	.40	.18	.05
☐ 74	Jerry Korab	.40	.18	.05
☐ 75	Rick MacLeish	.50	.23	.06
☐ 76	Dennis Kearns	.40	.18	.05
☐ 77	Jean Pronovost	.50	.23	.06
☐ 78	Ron Greschner	.50	.23	.06
☐ 79	Wayne Cashman	.50	.23	.06
☐ 80	Tony Esposito	2.00	.90	.25
☐ 81	Jets Team Emblem	6.00	2.70	.75
☐ 82	Oilers Team Emblem	8.00	3.60	1.00
☐ 83	Stanley Cup Finals	.75	.35	.09
	Canadiens Make It			
	Four Straight Cups			
☐ 84	Brian Sutter	4.00	1.80	.50
☐ 85	Gerry Cheevers	1.00	.45	.13
☐ 86	Pat Hickey	.40	.18	.05
☐ 87	Mike Kaszycki	.40	.18	.05
☐ 88	Grant Mulvey	.40	.18	.05
☐ 89	Derek Smith	.40	.18	.05
☐ 90	Steve Shutt	1.00	.45	.13
☐ 91	Robert Picard	.40	.18	.05
☐ 92	Dan Labraaten	.40	.18	.05
☐ 93	Glen Sharpley	.40	.18	.05
☐ 94	Denis Herron	.50	.23	.06
☐ 95	Reggie Leach	.50	.23	.06
☐ 96	John Van Boxmeer	.40	.18	.05
☐ 97	Dave(Tiger) Williams	.50	.23	.06
☐ 98	Butch Goring	.50	.23	.06
☐ 99	Don Marcotte	.40	.18	.05
☐ 100	Bryan Trottier AS1	4.00	1.80	.50
☐ 101	Serge Savard AS2	.50	.23	.06
☐ 102	Cliff Koroll	.40	.18	.05
☐ 103	Gary Smith	.50	.23	.06
☐ 104	Al MacAdam	.40	.18	.05
☐ 105	Don Edwards	.50	.23	.06
☐ 106	Errol Thompson	.40	.18	.05
☐ 107	Andre Lacroix	.50	.23	.06
☐ 108	Marc Tardif	.40	.18	.05
☐ 109	Rick Kehoe	.50	.23	.06
☐ 110	John Davidson	.50	.23	.06
☐ 111	Behn Wilson	.50	.23	.06
☐ 112	Doug Jarvis	.50	.23	.06
☐ 113	Tom Rowe	.40	.18	.05
☐ 114	Mike Milbury	.50	.23	.06
☐ 115	Billy Harris	.40	.18	.05
☐ 116	Greg Fox	.40	.18	.05
☐ 117	Curt Fraser	.50	.23	.06
☐ 118	Jean-Paul Parise	.40	.18	.05
☐ 119	Ric Seiling	.40	.18	.05
☐ 120	Darryl Sittler	1.75	.80	.22
☐ 121	Rick Lapointe	.40	.18	.05
☐ 122	Jim Rutherford	.50	.23	.06
☐ 123	Mario Tremblay	.50	.23	.06
☐ 124	Randy Carlyle	1.50	.65	.19
☐ 125	Bobby Clarke	2.00	.90	.25
☐ 126	Wayne Thomas	.50	.23	.06
☐ 127	Ivan Boldirev	.40	.18	.05
☐ 128	Ted Bulley	.40	.18	.05
☐ 129	Dick Redmond	.40	.18	.05
☐ 130	Clark Gillies AS1	.50	.23	.06
☐ 131	Checklist 1-132	6.00	.60	.12
☐ 132	Vaclav Nedomansky	.40	.18	.05
☐ 133	Richard Mulhern	.40	.18	.05
☐ 134	Dave Schultz	.50	.23	.06
☐ 135	Guy Lapointe	.50	.23	.06
☐ 136	Gilles Meloche	.50	.23	.06
☐ 137	Randy Pierce UER	.40	.18	.05
	(Photo actually			
	Ron Delorme)			
☐ 138	Cam Connor	.40	.18	.05
☐ 139	George Ferguson	.40	.18	.05
☐ 140	Bill Barber	.75	.35	.09
☐ 141	Terry Ruskowski UER	.50	.23	.06
	(Misspelled Ruskouski			
	on both sides)			
☐ 142	Wayne Babych	1.00	.45	.13
☐ 143	Phil Russell	.40	.18	.05
☐ 144	Bobby Schmautz	.40	.18	.05
☐ 145	Carol Vadnais	.40	.18	.05
☐ 146	John Tonelli	7.00	3.10	.85
☐ 147	Peter Marsh	.40	.18	.05
☐ 148	Thommie Bergman	.40	.18	.05
☐ 149	Richard Martin	.50	.23	.06
☐ 150	Ken Dryden AS1	6.00	2.70	.75
☐ 151	Kris Manery	.40	.18	.05
☐ 152	Guy Charron	.40	.18	.05
☐ 153	Lanny McDonald	1.50	.65	.19
☐ 154	Ron Stackhouse	.40	.18	.05
☐ 155	Stan Mikita	2.50	1.15	.30
☐ 156	Paul Holmgren	.50	.23	.06
☐ 157	Perry Miller	.40	.18	.05
☐ 158	Gary Croteau	.40	.18	.05
☐ 159	Dave Maloney	.40	.18	.05
☐ 160	Marcel Dionne AS2	3.00	1.35	.40
☐ 161	Mike Bossy RB	3.00	1.35	.40
	Most Goals,			
	RW Season			
☐ 162	Don Maloney RB	.60	.25	.08
	Rookie, Most Points,			
	Playoff Series			
☐ 163	Whalers Team Emblem	6.00	2.70	.75
☐ 164	Brad Park RB	.60	.25	.08
	Most Career Playoff			
	Goals, Defenseman			
☐ 165	Bryan Trottier RB	1.50	.65	.19
	Most Points, Period			
☐ 166	Al Hill	.40	.18	.05
☐ 167	Gary Bromley UER	.50	.23	.06
	(Photo actually			
	Glen Hanlon)			
☐ 168	Don Murdoch	.40	.18	.05
☐ 169	Wayne Merrick	.40	.18	.05
☐ 170	Bob Gainey	1.00	.45	.13
☐ 171	Jim Schoenfeld	.40	.18	.05
☐ 172	Gregg Sheppard	.40	.18	.05
☐ 173	Dan Bolduc	.40	.18	.05
☐ 174	Blake Dunlop	.40	.18	.05
☐ 175	Gordie Howe	30.00	13.50	3.80
☐ 176	Richard Brodeur	1.00	.45	.13
☐ 177	Tom Younghans	.40	.18	.05
☐ 178	Andre Dupont	.40	.18	.05
☐ 179	Ed Johnstone	.40	.18	.05
☐ 180	Gilbert Perreault	1.50	.65	.19
☐ 181	Bob Lorimer	.40	.18	.05
☐ 182	John Wensink	.40	.18	.05
☐ 183	Lee Fogolin	.40	.18	.05
☐ 184	Greg Carroll	.40	.18	.05
☐ 185	Bobby Hull	25.00	11.50	3.10
☐ 186	Harold Snepsts	.50	.23	.06
☐ 187	Peter Mahovlich	.50	.23	.06
☐ 188	Eric Vail	.40	.18	.05
☐ 189	Phil Myre	.50	.23	.06
☐ 190	Wilf Paiement	.50	.23	.06
☐ 191	Charlie Simmer	6.00	2.70	.75
☐ 192	Per-Olov Brasar	.40	.18	.05
☐ 193	Lorne Henning	.40	.18	.05
☐ 194	Don Luce	.40	.18	.05
☐ 195	Steve Vickers	.40	.18	.05
☐ 196	Bob Miller	.40	.18	.05
☐ 197	Mike Palmateer	.50	.23	.06
☐ 198	Nick Libett	.40	.18	.05
☐ 199	Pat Ribble	.40	.18	.05
☐ 200	Guy Lafleur AS1	5.00	2.30	.60
☐ 201	Mel Bridgman	.50	.23	.06
☐ 202	Morris Lukowich	.50	.23	.06
☐ 203	Don Lever	.40	.18	.05
☐ 204	Tom Bladon	.40	.18	.05
☐ 205	Garry Howatt	.40	.18	.05
☐ 206	Bobby Smith	7.00	3.10	.85
☐ 207	Craig Ramsay	.40	.18	.05
☐ 208	Ron Duguay	.50	.23	.06
☐ 209	Gilles Gilbert	.50	.23	.06
☐ 210	Bob MacMillan	.40	.18	.05
☐ 211	Pierre Mondou	.40	.18	.05
☐ 212	J.P. Bordeleau	.40	.18	.05
☐ 213	Reed Larson	.50	.23	.06
☐ 214	Dennis Ververgaert	.40	.18	.05
☐ 215	Bernie Federko	4.00	1.80	.50
☐ 216	Mark Howe	2.50	1.15	.30
☐ 217	Bob Nystrom	.50	.23	.06
☐ 218	Orest Kindrachuk	.40	.18	.05
☐ 219	Mike Fidler	.40	.18	.05
☐ 220	Phil Esposito	3.00	1.35	.40
☐ 221	Bill Hajt	.40	.18	.05
☐ 222	Mark Napier	.50	.23	.06
☐ 223	Dennis Maruk	.50	.23	.06
☐ 224	Dennis Polonich	.40	.18	.05
☐ 225	Jean Ratelle	1.00	.45	.13
☐ 226	Bob Dailey	.40	.18	.05
☐ 227	Alain Daigle	.40	.18	.05
☐ 228	Ian Turnbull	.40	.18	.05
☐ 229	Jack Valiquette	.40	.18	.05
☐ 230	Mike Bossy AS2	15.00	6.75	1.90
☐ 231	Brad Maxwell	.40	.18	.05
☐ 232	Dave Taylor	7.00	3.10	.85
☐ 233	Pierre Larouche	.50	.23	.06
☐ 234	Rod Schutt	.40	.18	.05
☐ 235	Rogatien Vachon	.75	.35	.09
☐ 236	Ryan Walter	1.50	.65	.19
☐ 237	Checklist 133-264 UER	6.00	.60	.12

(245 Buins, should
be Bruins)

☐	238	Terry O'Reilly	.50	.23	.06
☐	239	Real Cloutier	.50	.23	.06
☐	240	Anders Hedberg	.50	.23	.06
☐	241	Ken Linseman	4.00	1.80	.50
☐	242	Billy Smith	1.00	.45	.13
☐	243	Rick Chartraw	.40	.18	.05
☐	244	Flames Team	1.50	.65	.19
☐	245	Bruins Team	2.00	.90	.25
☐	246	Sabres Team	1.50	.65	.19
☐	247	Blackhawks Team	1.50	.65	.19
☐	248	Rockies Team	1.50	.65	.19
☐	249	Red Wings Team	1.50	.65	.19
☐	250	Kings Team	1.50	.65	.19
☐	251	North Stars Team	1.50	.65	.19
☐	252	Canadiens Team	2.00	.90	.25
☐	253	Islanders Team	2.00	.90	.25
☐	254	Rangers Team	1.50	.65	.19
☐	255	Flyers Team	1.50	.65	.19
☐	256	Penguins Team	1.50	.65	.19
☐	257	Blues Team	1.50	.65	.19
☐	258	Maple Leafs Team	2.00	.90	.25
☐	259	Canucks Team	1.50	.65	.19
☐	260	Capitals Team	1.50	.65	.19
☐	261	Nordiques Team	5.00	2.30	.60
☐	262	Jean Hamel	.40	.18	.05
☐	263	Stan Jonathan	.40	.18	.05
☐	264	Russ Anderson	.40	.18	.05
☐	265	Gordie Roberts	2.00	.90	.25
☐	266	Bill Flett	.40	.18	.05
☐	267	Robbie Ftorek	.50	.23	.06
☐	268	Mike Amodeo	.40	.18	.05
☐	269	Vic Venasky	.40	.18	.05
☐	270	Bob Manno	.40	.18	.05
☐	271	Dan Maloney	.40	.18	.05
☐	272	Al Sims	.40	.18	.05
☐	273	Greg Polis	.40	.18	.05
☐	274	Doug Favell	.50	.23	.06
☐	275	Pierre Plante	.40	.18	.05
☐	276	Bob Murdoch	.40	.18	.05

Atlanta Flames

☐	277	Lyle Moffat	.40	.18	.05
☐	278	Jack Brownschidle	.40	.18	.05
☐	279	Dave Keon	.75	.35	.09
☐	280	Darryl Edestrand	.40	.18	.05
☐	281	Greg Millen	3.00	1.35	.40
☐	282	John Gould	.40	.18	.05
☐	283	Rich Leduc	.40	.18	.05
☐	284	Ron Delorme	.40	.18	.05
☐	285	Gord Smith	.40	.18	.05
☐	286	Nick Fotiu	.50	.23	.06
☐	287	Kevin McCarthy	.40	.18	.05
☐	288	Jimmy Jones	.40	.18	.05
☐	289	Pierre Bouchard	.40	.18	.05
☐	290	Wayne Bianchin	.40	.18	.05
☐	291	Garry Lariviere	.40	.18	.05
☐	292	Steve Jensen	.40	.18	.05
☐	293	John Garrett	.50	.23	.06
☐	294	Hilliard Graves	.40	.18	.05
☐	295	Bill Clement	.50	.23	.06
☐	296	Michel Larocque	.50	.23	.06
☐	297	Bob Stewart	.40	.18	.05
☐	298	Doug Patey	.40	.18	.05
☐	299	Dave Farrish	.40	.18	.05
☐	300	Al Smith	.50	.23	.06
☐	301	Billy Lochead	.40	.18	.05
☐	302	Dave Hutchinson	.40	.18	.05
☐	303	Bill Riley	.40	.18	.05
☐	304	Barry Gibbs	.40	.18	.05
☐	305	Chris Oddleifson	.40	.18	.05
☐	306	J. Bob Kelly UER	.40	.18	.05

(Photo actually
Bob Kelly)

☐	307	Al Hangsleben	.40	.18	.05
☐	308	Curt Brackenbury	.40	.18	.05
☐	309	Rick Green	.50	.23	.06
☐	310	Ken Houston	.40	.18	.05
☐	311	Greg Joly	.40	.18	.05
☐	312	Bill Lesuk	.40	.18	.05
☐	313	Bill Stewart	.40	.18	.05
☐	314	Rick Ley	.40	.18	.05
☐	315	Brett Callighen	.40	.18	.05
☐	316	Michel Dion	.40	.18	.05
☐	317	Randy Manery	.40	.18	.05
☐	318	Barry Dean	.40	.18	.05
☐	319	Pat Boutette	.40	.18	.05
☐	320	Mark Heaslip	.40	.18	.05
☐	321	Dave Inkpen	.40	.18	.05
☐	322	Jere Gillis	.40	.18	.05
☐	323	Larry Brown	.40	.18	.05
☐	324	Alain Cote	.40	.18	.05
☐	325	Gordie Lane	.40	.18	.05
☐	326	Bobby Lalonde	.40	.18	.05

☐	327	Ed Staniowski	.50	.23	.06
☐	328	Ron Plumb	.40	.18	.05
☐	329	Jude Drouin	.40	.18	.05
☐	330	Rick Hampton	.40	.18	.05
☐	331	Stan Weir	.40	.18	.05
☐	332	Blair Stewart	.40	.18	.05
☐	333	Mike Polich	.40	.18	.05
☐	334	Jean Potvin	.40	.18	.05
☐	335	Jordy Douglas	.40	.18	.05
☐	336	Joel Quenneville	.40	.18	.05
☐	337	Glen Hanlon	2.00	.90	.25
☐	338	Dave Hoyda	.40	.18	.05
☐	339	Colin Campbell	.40	.18	.05
☐	340	John Smrke	.40	.18	.05
☐	341	Brian Glennie	.40	.18	.05
☐	342	Don Kozak	.40	.18	.05
☐	343	Yvon Labre	.40	.18	.05
☐	344	Curt Bennett	.40	.18	.05
☐	345	Mike Christie	.40	.18	.05
☐	346	Checklist 265-396	6.00	.60	.12
☐	347	Pat Price	.40	.18	.05
☐	348	Ron Low	.50	.23	.06
☐	349	Mike Antonovich	.40	.18	.05
☐	350	Roland Eriksson	.40	.18	.05
☐	351	Bob Murdoch	.40	.18	.05

St. Louis Blues

☐	352	Rob Palmer	.40	.18	.05
☐	353	Brad Gassoff	.40	.18	.05
☐	354	Bruce Boudreau	.40	.18	.05
☐	355	Al Hamilton	.40	.18	.05
☐	356	Blaine Stoughton	.50	.23	.06
☐	357	John Baby	.40	.18	.05
☐	358	Gary Inness	.50	.23	.06
☐	359	Wayne Dillon	.40	.18	.05
☐	360	Darcy Rota	.40	.18	.05
☐	361	Brian Engblom	.50	.23	.06
☐	362	Bill Hogaboam	.40	.18	.05
☐	363	Dave Debol	.40	.18	.05
☐	364	Pete Lopresti	.50	.23	.06
☐	365	Gerry Hart	.40	.18	.05
☐	366	Syl Apps	.40	.18	.05
☐	367	Jack McIlhargey	.40	.18	.05
☐	368	Willy Lindstrom	.40	.18	.05
☐	369	Don Laurence	.40	.18	.05
☐	370	Chuck Luksa	.40	.18	.05
☐	371	Dave Semenko	3.00	1.35	.40
☐	372	Paul Baxter	.50	.23	.06
☐	373	Ron Ellis	.50	.23	.06
☐	374	Leif Svensson	.40	.18	.05
☐	375	Dennis O'Brien	.40	.18	.05
☐	376	Glenn Goldup	.40	.18	.05
☐	377	Terry Richardson	.40	.18	.05
☐	378	Peter Sullivan	.40	.18	.05
☐	379	Doug Hicks	.40	.18	.05
☐	380	Jamie Hislop	.40	.18	.05
☐	381	Jocelyn Guevremont	.40	.18	.05
☐	382	Willi Plett	.50	.23	.06
☐	383	Larry Goodenough	.40	.18	.05
☐	384	Jim Warner	.40	.18	.05
☐	385	Rey Comeau	.40	.18	.05
☐	386	Barry Melrose	3.50	1.55	.45
☐	387	Dave Hunter	1.00	.45	.13
☐	388	Wally Weir	.40	.18	.05
☐	389	Mario Lessard	.60	.25	.08
☐	390	Ed Kea	.40	.18	.05
☐	391	Bob Stephenson	.40	.18	.05
☐	392	Dennis Hextall	.40	.18	.05
☐	393	Jerry Butler	.40	.18	.05
☐	394	David Shand	.40	.18	.05
☐	395	Rick Blight	.40	.18	.05
☐	396	Lars-Erik Sjoberg	1.00	.30	.10

1980-81 O-Pee-Chee

Card fronts of this 396-card set contain the player's name and position (bilingual text) in a hockey puck on the lower right of the front. Unlike the Topps set of this year, the puck was not issued with a black scratch-off covering. The team name is listed to the left of the puck. The cards were originally sold in 20-cent wax packs and measure the standard 2 1/2" by 3 1/2". Bilingual backs feature a short list of career milestones, 1979-80 season and career statistics along with short trivia comments. Members of the U.S. Olympic hockey team (USA in checklist below) are honored

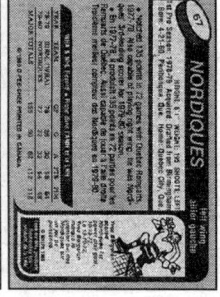

with the USA hockey emblem on the card front. A great crop of Rookie Cards includes Ray Bourque, Mike Gartner, Michel Goulet, Rod Langway, Mike Liut, Brad Marsh, Mark Messier, John Ogrodnick, Pete Peeters, Brian Propp, Rick Vaive, Dave Christian, Mike Ramsey, Mike Foligno, Kent Nilsson and Rob Ramage. Beware when purchasing the cards of Ray Bourque and Mark Messier as they have been counterfeited.

	MINT	EXC	G-VG
COMPLETE SET (396)	650.00	300.00	80.00
COMMON PLAYER (1-264)	.35	.16	.04
COMMON PLAYER (265-396)	.40	.18	.05

☐ 1	Flyers Streak to 35 RB Longest in Sports History	.75	.35	.09
☐ 2	Ray Bourque RB 65 Pts., Record for Rookie Defenseman	10.00	4.50	1.25
☐ 3	Wayne Gretzky RB Youngest Ever 50-goal Scorer	35.00	16.00	4.40
☐ 4	Charlie Simmer RB Scores 13th Straight Game, NHL Record	.50	.23	.06
☐ 5	Billy Smith RB First Goalie to Score a Goal	.50	.23	.06
☐ 6	Jean Ratelle	.75	.35	.09
☐ 7	Dave Maloney	.35	.16	.04
☐ 8	Phil Myre	.35	.16	.04
☐ 9	Ken Morrow USA	1.50	.65	.19
☐ 10	Guy Lafleur	3.50	1.55	.45
☐ 11	Bill Derlago	.40	.18	.05
☐ 12	Doug Wilson	3.00	1.35	.40
☐ 13	Craig Ramsay	.35	.16	.04
☐ 14	Pat Boutette	.35	.16	.04
☐ 15	Eric Vail	.35	.16	.04
☐ 16	Red Wings Leaders Mike Foligno	.60	.25	.08
☐ 17	Bobby Smith	2.00	.90	.25
☐ 18	Rick Kehoe	.40	.18	.05
☐ 19	Joel Quenneville	.35	.16	.04
☐ 20	Marcel Dionne	2.00	.90	.25
☐ 21	Kevin McCarthy	.35	.16	.04
☐ 22	Jim Craig USA	1.00	.45	.13
☐ 23	Steve Vickers	.35	.16	.04
☐ 24	Ken Linseman	1.00	.45	.13
☐ 25	Mike Bossy	8.00	3.60	1.00
☐ 26	Serge Savard	.40	.18	.05
☐ 27	Blackhawks Leaders Grant Mulvey	.50	.23	.06
☐ 28	Pat Hickey	.35	.16	.04
☐ 29	Peter Sullivan	.35	.16	.04
☐ 30	Blaine Stoughton	.40	.18	.05
☐ 31	Mike Liut	8.00	3.60	1.00
☐ 32	Blair MacDonald	.35	.16	.04
☐ 33	Rick Green	.35	.16	.04
☐ 34	Al MacAdam	.35	.16	.04
☐ 35	Robbie Ftorek	.40	.18	.05
☐ 36	Dick Redmond	.35	.16	.04
☐ 37	Ron Duguay	.40	.18	.05
☐ 38	Sabres Leaders Danny Gare	.50	.23	.06
☐ 39	Brian Propp	7.00	3.10	.85
☐ 40	Bryan Trottier	2.50	1.15	.30
☐ 41	Rich Preston	.35	.16	.04
☐ 42	Pierre Mondou	.35	.16	.04
☐ 43	Reed Larson	.40	.18	.05
☐ 44	George Ferguson	.35	.16	.04
☐ 45	Guy Chouinard	.40	.18	.05

☐ 46	Billy Harris	.35	.16	.04
☐ 47	Gilles Meloche	.40	.18	.05
☐ 48	Blair Chapman	.35	.16	.04
☐ 49	Capitals Leaders Mike Gartner	6.00	2.70	.75
☐ 50	Darryl Sittler	1.25	.55	.16
☐ 51	Richard Martin	.40	.18	.05
☐ 52	Ivan Boldirev	.35	.16	.04
☐ 53	Craig Norwich	.35	.16	.04
☐ 54	Dennis Polonich	.35	.16	.04
☐ 55	Bobby Clarke	1.50	.65	.19
☐ 56	Terry O'Reilly	.40	.18	.05
☐ 57	Carol Vadnais	.35	.16	.04
☐ 58	Bob Gainey	.75	.35	.09
☐ 59	Whalers Leaders Blaine Stoughton	.50	.23	.06
☐ 60	Billy Smith	.75	.35	.09
☐ 61	Mike O'Connell	.60	.25	.08
☐ 62	Lanny McDonald	1.00	.45	.13
☐ 63	Lee Fogolin	.35	.16	.04
☐ 64	Rocky Saganiuk	.35	.16	.04
☐ 65	Rolf Edberg	.35	.16	.04
☐ 66	Paul Shmyr	.35	.16	.04
☐ 67	Michel Goulet	25.00	11.50	3.10
☐ 68	Dan Bouchard	.40	.18	.05
☐ 69	Mark Johnson USA	.75	.35	.09
☐ 70	Reggie Leach	.40	.18	.05
☐ 71	Blues Leaders Bernie Federko	.60	.25	.08
☐ 72	Peter Mahovlich	.40	.18	.05
☐ 73	Anders Hedberg	.40	.18	.05
☐ 74	Brad Park	.75	.35	.09
☐ 75	Clark Gillies	.40	.18	.05
☐ 76	Doug Jarvis	.40	.18	.05
☐ 77	John Garrett	.35	.16	.04
☐ 78	Dave Hutchinson	.35	.16	.04
☐ 79	John Anderson	.50	.23	.06
☐ 80	Gilbert Perreault	1.00	.45	.13
☐ 81	Marcel Dionne ASI	1.00	.45	.13
☐ 82	Guy Lafleur AS1	1.50	.65	.19
☐ 83	Charlie Simmer AS1	.55	.25	.07
☐ 84	Larry Robinson AS1	.50	.23	.06
☐ 85	Borje Salming AS1	.55	.25	.07
☐ 86	Tony Esposito AS1	.75	.35	.09
☐ 87	Wayne Gretzky AS2	50.00	23.00	6.25
☐ 88	Danny Gare AS2	.50	.23	.06
☐ 89	Steve Shutt AS2	.50	.23	.06
☐ 90	Barry Beck AS2	.50	.23	.06
☐ 91	Mark Howe AS2	.55	.25	.07
☐ 92	Don Edwards AS2	.50	.23	.06
☐ 93	Tom McCarthy	.50	.23	.06
☐ 94	Bruins Leaders Peter McNab Rick Middleton	.50	.23	.06
☐ 95	Mike Palmateer	.35	.16	.04
☐ 96	Jim Schoenfeld	.35	.16	.04
☐ 97	Jordy Douglas	.35	.16	.04
☐ 98	Keith Brown	.60	.25	.08
☐ 99	Dennis Ververgaert	.35	.16	.04
☐ 100	Phil Esposito	2.00	.90	.25
☐ 101	Jack Brownschidle	.35	.16	.04
☐ 102	Bob Nystrom	.35	.16	.04
☐ 103	Steve Christoff USA	.50	.23	.06
☐ 104	Rob Palmer	.35	.16	.04
☐ 105	Dave(Tiger) Williams	.40	.18	.05
☐ 106	Flames Leaders Kent Nilsson	.60	.25	.08
☐ 107	Morris Lukowich	.40	.18	.05
☐ 108	Jack Valiquette	.35	.16	.04
☐ 109	Richie Dunn	.35	.16	.04
☐ 110	Rogatien Vachon	.50	.23	.06
☐ 111	Mark Napier	.35	.16	.04
☐ 112	Gordie Roberts	.40	.18	.05
☐ 113	Stan Jonathan	.35	.16	.04
☐ 114	Brett Callighen	.35	.16	.04
☐ 115	Rick MacLeish	.40	.18	.05
☐ 116	Ulf Nilsson	.40	.18	.05
☐ 117	Penguins Leaders Rick Kehoe	.50	.23	.06
☐ 118	Dan Maloney	.35	.16	.04
☐ 119	Terry Ruskowski	.35	.16	.04
☐ 120	Denis Potvin	1.50	.65	.19
☐ 121	Wayne Stephenson	.35	.16	.04
☐ 122	Rich Leduc	.35	.16	.04
☐ 123	Checklist 1-132	5.00	.50	.10
☐ 124	Don Lever	.35	.16	.04
☐ 125	Jim Rutherford	.35	.16	.04
☐ 126	Ray Allison	.35	.16	.04
☐ 127	Mike Ramsey USA	3.00	1.35	.40
☐ 128	Canucks Leaders Stan Smyl	.50	.23	.06
☐ 129	Al Secord	3.00	1.35	.40
☐ 130	Denis Herron	.35	.16	.04

131	Bob Dailey	.35	.16	.04
132	Dean Talafous	.35	.16	.04
133	Ian Turnbull	.35	.16	.04
134	Ron Sedlbauer	.35	.16	.04
135	Tom Bladon	.35	.16	.04
136	Bernie Federko	2.50	1.15	.30
137	Dave Taylor	3.50	1.55	.45
138	Bob Lorimer	.35	.16	.04
139	North Stars Leaders Al MacAdam Steve Payne	.50	.23	.06
140	Ray Bourque	140.00	65.00	17.50
141	Glen Hanlon	.50	.23	.06
142	Willy Lindstrom	.35	.16	.04
143	Mike Rogers	.40	.18	.05
144	Tony McKegney	.75	.35	.09
145	Behn Wilson	.35	.16	.04
146	Lucien Deblois	.35	.16	.04
147	Dave Burrows	.35	.16	.04
148	Paul Woods	.35	.16	.04
149	Rangers Leaders Phil Esposito	.60	.25	.08
150	Tony Esposito	1.50	.65	.19
151	Pierre Larouche	.40	.18	.05
152	Brad Maxwell	.35	.16	.04
153	Stan Weir	.35	.16	.04
154	Ryan Walter	.40	.18	.05
155	Dale Hoganson	.35	.16	.04
156	Anders Kallur	.35	.16	.04
157	Paul Reinhart	1.50	.65	.19
158	Greg Millen	1.00	.45	.13
159	Ric Seiling	.35	.16	.04
160	Mark Howe	1.00	.45	.13
161	Goals Leaders Danny Gare (1) Charlie Simmer (1) B. Stoughton (1)	.50	.23	.06
162	Assists Leaders Wayne Gretzky (1) Marcel Dionne (2) Guy Lafleur (3)	15.00	6.75	1.90
163	Scoring Leaders Marcel Dionne (1) Wayne Gretzky (1) Guy Lafleur (3)	15.00	6.75	1.90
164	Penalty Minutes Leaders Jimmy Mann (1) Dave(Tiger) Williams (2) Paul Holmgren (3)	.50	.23	.06
165	Power Play Goals Leaders Charlie Simmer (1) Marcel Dionne (2) Danny Gare (2) Steve Shutt (2) Darryl Sittler (2)	.75	.35	.09
166	Goals Against Avg. Leaders Bob Sauve (1) Denis Herron (2) Don Edwards (3)	.50	.23	.06
167	Game-Winning Goals Leaders Danny Gare (1) Peter McNab (1) Blaine Stoughton (2)	.50	.23	.06
168	Shutout Leaders Tony Esposito (1) Gerry Cheevers (2) Bob Sauve (2) Rogatien Vachon (2)	1.50	.65	.19
169	Perry Turnbull	.50	.23	.06
170	Barry Beck	.40	.18	.05
171	Kings Leaders Charlie Simmer	.60	.25	.08
172	Paul Holmgren	.40	.18	.05
173	Willie Huber	.35	.16	.04
174	Tim Young	.35	.16	.04
175	Gilles Gilbert	.35	.16	.04
176	Dave Christian USA	3.50	1.55	.45
177	Lars Lindgren	.35	.16	.04
178	Real Cloutier	.35	.16	.04
179	Laurie Boschman	.75	.35	.09
180	Steve Shutt	.60	.25	.08
181	Bob Murray	.35	.16	.04
182	Oilers Leaders Wayne Gretzky	20.00	9.00	2.50
183	John Van Boxmeer	.35	.16	.04
184	Nick Fotiu	.40	.18	.05
185	Mike McEwen	.35	.16	.04
186	Greg Malone	.35	.16	.04
187	Mike Foligno	5.00	2.30	.60
188	Dave Langevin	.50	.23	.06
189	Mel Bridgman	.35	.16	.04
190	John Davidson	.40	.18	.05
191	Mike Milbury	.40	.18	.05
192	Ron Zanussi	.35	.16	.04
193	Maple Leafs Leader Darryl Sittler	.50	.23	.06
194	John Marks	.35	.16	.04
195	Mike Gartner	80.00	36.00	10.00
196	Dave Lewis	.35	.16	.04
197	Kent Nilsson	3.00	1.35	.40
198	Rick Ley	.35	.16	.04
199	Derek Smith	.35	.16	.04
200	Bill Barber	.50	.23	.06
201	Guy Lapointe	.40	.18	.05
202	Vaclav Nedomansky	.35	.16	.04
203	Don Murdoch	.35	.16	.04
204	Islanders Leaders Mike Bossy	1.50	.65	.19
205	Pierre Hamel	.35	.16	.04
206	Mike Eaves	.35	.16	.04
207	Doug Halward	.35	.16	.04
208	Stan Smyl	1.50	.65	.19
209	Mike Zuke	.35	.16	.04
210	Borje Salming	.35	.16	.04
211	Walt Tkaczuk	.40	.18	.05
212	Grant Mulvey	.35	.16	.04
213	Rob Ramage	3.00	1.35	.40
214	Tom Rowe	.35	.16	.04
215	Don Edwards	.35	.16	.04
216	Canadiens Leaders Guy Lafleur Pierre Larouche	1.50	.65	.19
217	Dan Labraaten	.35	.16	.04
218	Glen Sharpley	.35	.16	.04
219	Stefan Persson	.35	.16	.04
220	Peter McNab	.40	.18	.05
221	Doug Hicks	.35	.16	.04
222	Bengt Gustafsson	.50	.23	.06
223	Michel Dion	.35	.16	.04
224	Jim Watson	.35	.16	.04
225	Wilf Paiement	.40	.18	.05
226	Phil Russell	.35	.16	.04
227	Jets Leaders Morris Lukowich	.50	.23	.06
228	Ron Stackhouse	.35	.16	.04
229	Ted Bulley	.35	.16	.04
230	Larry Robinson	1.00	.45	.13
231	Don Maloney	.40	.18	.05
232	Rob McClanahan USA	.50	.23	.06
233	Al Sims	.35	.16	.04
234	Errol Thompson	.35	.16	.04
235	Glenn Resch	.40	.18	.05
236	Bob Miller	.35	.16	.04
237	Gary Sargent	.35	.16	.04
238	Nordiques Leaders Real Cloutier	.50	.23	.06
239	Rene Robert	.40	.18	.05
240	Charlie Simmer	2.00	.90	.25
241	Thomas Gradin	.50	.23	.06
242	Rick Vaive	3.00	1.35	.40
243	Ron Wilson	.75	.35	.09
244	Brian Sutter	2.00	.90	.25
245	Dale McCourt	.35	.16	.04
246	Yvon Lambert	.35	.16	.04
247	Tom Lysiak	.35	.16	.04
248	Ron Greschner	.35	.16	.04
249	Flyers Leaders Reggie Leach	.50	.23	.06
250	Wayne Gretzky	150.00	70.00	19.00
251	Rick Middleton	.60	.25	.08
252	Al Smith	.35	.16	.04
253	Fred Barrett	.35	.16	.04
254	Butch Goring	.40	.18	.05
255	Robert Picard	.35	.16	.04
256	Marc Tardif	.35	.16	.04
257	Checklist 133-264	5.00	.50	.10
258	Barry Long	.35	.16	.04
259	Rockies Leaders Rene Robert	.50	.23	.06
260	Danny Gare	.40	.18	.05
261	Rejean Houle	.35	.16	.04
262	Stanley Cup Semifinals Islanders-Sabres	.50	.23	.06
263	Stanley Cup Semifinals Flyers-North Stars	.50	.23	.06
264	Stanley Cup Finals Islanders win 1st	.60	.25	.08
265	Bobby Lalonde	.40	.18	.05
266	Bob Sauve	.40	.18	.05
267	Bob MacMillan	.40	.18	.05
268	Greg Fox	.40	.18	.05
269	Hardy Astrom	.50	.23	.06

☐	270	Greg Joly	.40	.18	.05
☐	271	Dave Lumley	.40	.18	.05
☐	272	Dave Keon	.50	.23	.06
☐	273	Garry Unger	.50	.23	.06
☐	274	Steve Payne	.40	.18	.05
☐	275	Doug Risebrough UER	.50	.23	.06
		(Photo actually			
		Serge Savard)			
☐	276	Bob Bourne	.40	.18	.05
☐	277	Ed Johnstone	.40	.18	.05
☐	278	Peter Lee	.40	.18	.05
☐	279	Pete Peeters	5.00	2.30	.60
☐	280	Ron Chipperfield	.40	.18	.05
☐	281	Wayne Babych	.50	.23	.06
☐	282	David Shand	.40	.18	.05
☐	283	Jere Gillis	.40	.18	.05
☐	284	Dennis Maruk	.50	.23	.06
☐	285	Jude Drouin	.40	.18	.05
☐	286	Mike Murphy	.40	.18	.05
☐	287	Curt Fraser	.40	.18	.05
☐	288	Gary McAdam	.40	.18	.05
☐	289	Mark Messier UER	175.00	80.00	22.00
		(Back says shoots right)			
☐	290	Vic Venasky	.40	.18	.05
☐	291	Per-Olov Brasar	.40	.18	.05
☐	292	Orest Kindrachuk	.40	.18	.05
☐	293	Dave Hunter	.40	.18	.05
☐	294	Steve Jensen	.40	.18	.05
☐	295	Chris Oddleifson	.40	.18	.05
☐	296	Larry Playfair	.40	.18	.05
☐	297	Mario Tremblay	.50	.23	.06
☐	298	Gilles Lupien	.40	.18	.05
☐	299	Pat Price	.40	.18	.05
☐	300	Jerry Korab	.40	.18	.05
☐	301	Darcy Rota	.40	.18	.05
☐	302	Don Luce	.40	.18	.05
☐	303	Ken Houston	.40	.18	.05
☐	304	Brian Engblom	.40	.18	.05
☐	305	John Tonelli	1.50	.65	.19
☐	306	Doug Sulliman	.40	.18	.05
☐	307	Rod Schutt	.40	.18	.05
☐	308	Norm Barnes	.40	.18	.05
☐	309	Serge Bernier	.40	.18	.05
☐	310	Larry Patey	.40	.18	.05
☐	311	Dave Farrish	.40	.18	.05
☐	312	Harold Snepsts	.50	.23	.06
☐	313	Bob Sirois	.40	.18	.05
☐	314	Peter Marsh	.40	.18	.05
☐	315	Risto Siltanen	.50	.23	.06
☐	316	Andre St.Laurent	.40	.18	.05
☐	317	Craig Hartsburg	.75	.35	.09
☐	318	Wayne Cashman	.50	.23	.06
☐	319	Lindy Ruff	.50	.23	.06
☐	320	Willi Plett	.50	.23	.06
☐	321	Ron Delorme	.40	.18	.05
☐	322	Gaston Gingras	.40	.18	.05
☐	323	Gordie Lane	.40	.18	.05
☐	324	Doug Soetaert	.60	.25	.08
☐	325	Gregg Sheppard	.40	.18	.05
☐	326	Mike Busniuk	.40	.18	.05
☐	327	Jamie Hislop	.40	.18	.05
☐	328	Ed Staniowski	.40	.18	.05
☐	329	Ron Ellis	.50	.23	.06
☐	330	Gary Bromley UER	.40	.18	.05
		(Photo actually			
		Curt Ridley)			
☐	331	Mark Lofthouse	.40	.18	.05
☐	332	Dave Hoyda	.40	.18	.05
☐	333	Ron Low	.40	.18	.05
☐	334	Barry Gibbs	.40	.18	.05
☐	335	Gary Edwards	.40	.18	.05
☐	336	Don Marcotte	.40	.18	.05
☐	337	Bill Hajt	.40	.18	.05
☐	338	Brad Marsh	4.00	1.80	.50
☐	339	J.P. Bordeleau	.40	.18	.05
☐	340	Randy Pierce	.40	.18	.05
☐	341	Eddie Mio	.60	.25	.08
☐	342	Randy Manery	.40	.18	.05
☐	343	Tom Younghans	.40	.18	.05
☐	344	Rod Langway	12.00	5.50	1.50
☐	345	Wayne Merrick	.40	.18	.05
☐	346	Steve Baker	.40	.18	.05
☐	347	Pat Hughes	.40	.18	.05
☐	348	Al Hill	.40	.18	.05
☐	349	Gerry Hart	.40	.18	.05
☐	350	Richard Mulhern	.40	.18	.05
☐	351	Jerry Butler	.40	.18	.05
☐	352	Guy Charron	.40	.18	.05
☐	353	Jimmy Mann	.50	.23	.06
☐	354	Brad McCrimmon	3.00	1.35	.40
☐	355	Rick Dudley	.40	.18	.05
☐	356	Pekka Rautakallio	.40	.18	.05
☐	357	Tim Trimper	.40	.18	.05

☐	358	Mike Christie	.40	.18	.05
☐	359	John Ogrodnick	3.00	1.35	.40
☐	360	Dave Semenko	.50	.23	.06
☐	361	Mike Veisor	.40	.18	.05
☐	362	Syl Apps	.40	.18	.05
☐	363	Mike Polich	.40	.18	.05
☐	364	Rick Chartraw	.40	.18	.05
☐	365	Steve Tambellini	.50	.23	.06
☐	366	Ed Hospodar	.40	.18	.05
☐	367	Randy Carlyle	.50	.23	.06
☐	368	Tom Gorence	.40	.18	.05
☐	369	Pierre Plante	.40	.18	.05
☐	370	Blake Dunlop	.40	.18	.05
☐	371	Mike Kaszycki	.40	.18	.05
☐	372	Rick Blight	.40	.18	.05
☐	373	Pierre Bouchard	.40	.18	.05
☐	374	Gary Doak	.40	.18	.05
☐	375	Andre Savard	.40	.18	.05
☐	376	Bill Clement	.50	.23	.06
☐	377	Reg Kerr	.40	.18	.05
☐	378	Walt McKechnie	.40	.18	.05
☐	379	George Lyle	.40	.18	.05
☐	380	Colin Campbell	.40	.18	.05
☐	381	Dave Debol	.40	.18	.05
☐	382	Glenn Goldup	.40	.18	.05
☐	383	Kent-Erik Andersson	.40	.18	.05
☐	384	Tony Currie	.40	.18	.05
☐	385	Richard Sevigny	.75	.35	.09
☐	386	Garry Howatt	.40	.18	.05
☐	387	Cam Connor	.40	.18	.05
☐	388	Ross Lonsberry	.40	.18	.05
☐	389	Frank Bathe	.40	.18	.05
☐	390	John Wensink	.40	.18	.05
☐	391	Paul Harrison	.40	.18	.05
☐	392	Dennis Kearns	.40	.18	.05
☐	393	Pat Ribble	.40	.18	.05
☐	394	Markus Mattsson	.40	.18	.05
☐	395	Chuck Lefley	.40	.18	.05
☐	396	Checklist 265-396	8.00	.80	.16

1980-81 O-Pee-Chee Super

These large (approximately 5" by 7") full-color photos are numbered on the back. They are made of thicker cardboard stock. They were a separate issue rather than an insert. Player information on the card back is sparse.

		MINT	EXC	G-VG
COMPLETE SET (24)		40.00	16.00	4.00
COMMON PLAYER (1-24)		.50	.20	.05
☐ 1	Brad Park	1.50	.60	.15
☐ 2	Gilbert Perreault	1.50	.60	.15
☐ 3	Kent Nilsson	.60	.24	.06
☐ 4	Tony Esposito	2.00	.80	.20
☐ 5	Lanny McDonald	2.00	.80	.20
☐ 6	Pete Mahovlich	.75	.30	.07
☐ 7	Wayne Gretzky	20.00	8.00	2.00
☐ 8	Marcel Dionne	2.50	1.00	.25
☐ 9	Bob Gainey	1.50	.60	.15
☐ 10	Guy Lafleur	3.50	1.40	.35
☐ 11	Larry Robinson	2.00	.80	.20
☐ 12	Mike Bossy	3.00	1.20	.30
☐ 13	Denis Potvin	1.50	.60	.15
☐ 14	Phil Esposito	3.00	1.20	.30
☐ 15	Anders Hedberg	.60	.24	.06
☐ 16	Bobby Clarke	2.00	.80	.20

☐ 17	Marc Tardif	.50	.20	.05
☐ 18	Bernie Federko	.75	.30	.07
☐ 19	Borje Salming	1.00	.40	.10
☐ 20	Darryl Sittler	2.50	1.00	.25
☐ 21	Ian Turnbull	.50	.20	.05
☐ 22	Glen Hanlon	.60	.24	.06
☐ 23	Mike Palmateer	.60	.24	.06
☐ 24	Morris Lukowich	.50	.20	.05

1981-82 O-Pee-Chee

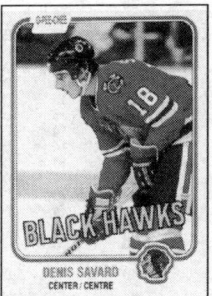 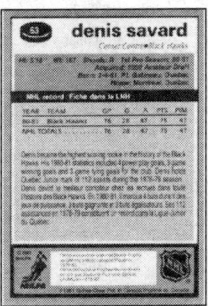

The 396 cards in this set feature the player's name, position and team logo along the front bottom border. The team name appears in bold letters across the lower portion of the photo. Cards in the set measure 2 1/2" by 3 1/2". Bilingual backs feature yearly and career statistics and biographical data. Super Action (SA) cards are designated in the list below. The set is essentially numbered in team order with the team leader (TL) card typically portraying the team's leading scorer. Rookie Cards in this set include Glenn Anderson, Don Beaupre, Dino Ciccarelli, Paul Coffey, Dale Hunter, Tim Kerr, Jari Kurri, Rejean Lemelin, Kevin Lowe, Andy Moog, Larry Murphy, Denis Savard and Peter Stastny. Beware when purchasing the Rookie Card of Paul Coffey as it has been counterfeited.

	MINT	EXC	G-VG
COMPLETE SET (396)	450.00	200.00	57.50
COMMON PLAYER (1-396)	.30	.14	.04

☐ 1	Ray Bourque	30.00	13.50	3.80
☐ 2	Rick Middleton	.40	.18	.05
☐ 3	Dwight Foster	.30	.14	.04
☐ 4	Steve Kasper	1.50	.65	.19
☐ 5	Peter McNab	.35	.16	.04
☐ 6	Mike O'Connell	.35	.16	.04
☐ 7	Terry O'Reilly	.35	.16	.04
☐ 8	Brad Park	.50	.23	.06
☐ 9	Dick Redmond	.30	.14	.04
☐ 10	Rogatien Vachon	.40	.18	.05
☐ 11	Wayne Cashman	.35	.16	.04
☐ 12	Mike Gillis	.30	.14	.04
☐ 13	Stan Jonathan	.30	.14	.04
☐ 14	Don Marcotte	.30	.14	.04
☐ 15	Brad McCrimmon	.75	.35	.09
☐ 16	Mike Milbury	.30	.14	.04
☐ 17	Ray Bourque SA	7.00	3.10	.85
☐ 18	Rick Middleton SA	.35	.16	.04
☐ 19	Boston Bruins TL	.40	.18	.05
	Rick Middleton			
☐ 20	Danny Gare	.30	.14	.04
☐ 21	Don Edwards	.30	.14	.04
☐ 22	Tony McKegney	.35	.16	.04
☐ 23	Bob Sauve	.30	.14	.04
☐ 24	Andre Savard	.30	.14	.04
☐ 25	Derek Smith	.30	.14	.04
☐ 26	John Van Boxmeer	.30	.14	.04
☐ 27	Danny Gare SA	.30	.14	.04
☐ 28	Buffalo Sabres TL	.40	.18	.05
	Danny Gare			
☐ 29	Richie Dunn	.30	.14	.04
☐ 30	Gilbert Perreault	.75	.35	.09
☐ 31	Craig Ramsay	.30	.14	.04

☐ 32	Ric Seiling	.30	.14	.04
☐ 33	Guy Chouinard	.30	.14	.04
☐ 34	Kent Nilsson	.35	.16	.04
☐ 35	Willi Plett	.30	.14	.04
☐ 36	Paul Reinhart	.35	.16	.04
☐ 37	Pat Riggin	.50	.23	.06
☐ 38	Eric Vail	.30	.14	.04
☐ 39	Bill Clement	.35	.16	.04
☐ 40	Jamie Hislop	.30	.14	.04
☐ 41	Randy Holt	.30	.14	.04
☐ 42	Dan Labraaten	.30	.14	.04
☐ 43	Kevin Lavallee	.30	.14	.04
☐ 44	Rejean Lemelin	4.00	1.80	.50
☐ 45	Don Lever	.30	.14	.04
☐ 46	Bob MacMillan	.30	.14	.04
☐ 47	Brad Marsh	.75	.35	.09
☐ 48	Bob Murdoch	.30	.14	.04
☐ 49	Jim Peplinski	2.50	1.15	.30
☐ 50	Pekka Rautakallio	.30	.14	.04
☐ 51	Phil Russell	.30	.14	.04
☐ 52	Kent Nilsson SA	.35	.16	.04
☐ 53	Calgary Flames TL	.50	.23	.06
	Kent Nilsson			
☐ 54	Tony Esposito	1.00	.45	.13
☐ 55	Keith Brown	.30	.14	.04
☐ 56	Ted Bulley	.30	.14	.04
☐ 57	Tim Higgins	.30	.14	.04
☐ 58	Reg Kerr	.30	.14	.04
☐ 59	Tom Lysiak	.30	.14	.04
☐ 60	Grant Mulvey	.30	.14	.04
☐ 61	Bob Murray	.30	.14	.04
☐ 62	Terry Ruskowski	.30	.14	.04
☐ 63	Denis Savard	20.00	9.00	2.50
☐ 64	Glen Sharpley	.30	.14	.04
☐ 65	Darryl Sutter	1.50	.65	.19
☐ 66	Doug Wilson	1.75	.80	.22
☐ 67	Tony Esposito SA	.50	.23	.06
☐ 68	Murray Bannerman	.50	.23	.06
☐ 69	Greg Fox	.30	.14	.04
☐ 70	John Marks	.30	.14	.04
☐ 71	Peter Marsh	.30	.14	.04
☐ 72	Al Secord	.75	.35	.09
☐ 73	Chicago Blackhawks TL	.40	.18	.05
	Tom Lysiak			
☐ 74	Lucien Deblois	.30	.14	.04
☐ 75	Paul Gagne	.30	.14	.04
☐ 76	Merlin Malinowski	.30	.14	.04
☐ 77	Lanny McDonald	.75	.35	.09
☐ 78	Joel Quenneville	.30	.14	.04
☐ 79	Rob Ramage	.50	.23	.06
☐ 80	Glenn Resch	.35	.16	.04
☐ 81	Steve Tambellini	.30	.14	.04
☐ 82	Ron Delorme	.30	.14	.04
☐ 83	Mike Kitchen	.30	.14	.04
☐ 84	Yvon Vautour	.30	.14	.04
☐ 85	Colorado Rockies TL	.50	.23	.06
	Lanny McDonald			
☐ 86	Dale McCourt	.30	.14	.04
☐ 87	Mike Foligno	.75	.35	.09
☐ 88	Gilles Gilbert	.30	.14	.04
☐ 89	Willie Huber	.30	.14	.04
☐ 90	Mark Kirton	.30	.14	.04
☐ 91	Jim Korn	.30	.14	.04
☐ 92	Reed Larson	.35	.16	.04
☐ 93	Gary McAdam	.30	.14	.04
☐ 94	Vaclav Nedomansky	.30	.14	.04
☐ 95	John Ogrodnick	.75	.35	.09
☐ 96	Dale McCourt SA	.30	.14	.04
☐ 97	Jean Hamel	.30	.14	.04
☐ 98	Glen Hicks	.30	.14	.04
☐ 99	Larry Lozinski	.30	.14	.04
☐ 100	George Lyle	.30	.14	.04
☐ 101	Perry Miller	.30	.14	.04
☐ 102	Brad Maxwell	.30	.14	.04
☐ 103	Brad Smith	.30	.14	.04
☐ 104	Paul Woods	.30	.14	.04
☐ 105	Detroit Red Wings TL	.40	.18	.05
	Dale McCourt			
☐ 106	Wayne Gretzky	55.00	25.00	7.00
☐ 107	Jari Kurri	45.00	20.00	5.75
☐ 108	Glenn Anderson	20.00	9.00	2.50
☐ 109	Curt Brackenbury	.30	.14	.04
☐ 110	Brett Callighen	.30	.14	.04
☐ 111	Paul Coffey	90.00	40.00	11.50
☐ 112	Lee Fogolin	.30	.14	.04
☐ 113	Matti Hagman	.30	.14	.04
☐ 114	Doug Hicks	.30	.14	.04
☐ 115	Dave Hunter	.30	.14	.04
☐ 116	Garry Lariviere	.30	.14	.04
☐ 117	Kevin Lowe	12.00	5.50	1.50
☐ 118	Mark Messier	50.00	23.00	6.25
☐ 119	Eddie Mio	.30	.14	.04
☐ 120	Andy Moog	30.00	13.50	3.80

☐ 121	Dave Semenko	.35	.16	.04
☐ 122	Risto Siltanen	.30	.14	.04
☐ 123	Garry Unger	.35	.16	.04
☐ 124	Stan Weir	.30	.14	.04
☐ 125	Wayne Gretzky SA	25.00	11.50	3.10
☐ 126	Edmonton Oilers TL	10.00	4.50	1.25
	Wayne Gretzky			
☐ 127	Mike Rogers	.35	.16	.04
☐ 128	Mark Howe	.75	.35	.09
☐ 129	Dave Keon	.50	.23	.06
☐ 130	Warren Miller	.30	.14	.04
☐ 131	Al Sims	.30	.14	.04
☐ 132	Blaine Stoughton	.35	.16	.04
☐ 133	Rick MacLeish	.35	.16	.04
☐ 134	Greg Millen	.35	.16	.04
☐ 135	Mike Rogers SA	.30	.14	.04
☐ 136	Mike Fidler	.30	.14	.04
☐ 137	John Garrett	.30	.14	.04
☐ 138	Don Nachbaur	.30	.14	.04
☐ 139	Tom Rowe	.30	.14	.04
☐ 140	Hartford Whalers TL	.40	.18	.05
	Mike Rogers			
☐ 141	Marcel Dionne	1.50	.65	.19
☐ 142	Charlie Simmer	1.00	.45	.13
☐ 143	Dave Taylor	1.75	.80	.22
☐ 144	Billy Harris	.30	.14	.04
☐ 145	Jerry Korab	.30	.14	.04
☐ 146	Mario Lessard	.30	.14	.04
☐ 147	Don Luce	.30	.14	.04
☐ 148	Larry Murphy	15.00	6.75	1.90
☐ 149	Mike Murphy	.30	.14	.04
☐ 150	Marcel Dionne SA	.75	.35	.09
☐ 151	Charlie Simmer SA	.35	.16	.04
☐ 152	Dave Taylor SA	.50	.23	.06
☐ 153	Jim Fox	.50	.23	.06
☐ 154	Steve Jensen	.30	.14	.04
☐ 155	Greg Terrion	.30	.14	.04
☐ 156	Los Angeles Kings TL	.50	.23	.06
	Marcel Dionne			
☐ 157	Bobby Smith	.75	.35	.09
☐ 158	Kent-Erik Andersson	.30	.14	.04
☐ 159	Don Beaupre	6.00	2.70	.75
☐ 160	Steve Christoff	.30	.14	.04
☐ 161	Dino Ciccarelli	20.00	9.00	2.50
☐ 162	Craig Hartsburg	.35	.16	.04
☐ 163	Al MacAdam	.30	.14	.04
☐ 164	Tom McCarthy	.35	.16	.04
☐ 165	Gilles Meloche	.35	.16	.04
☐ 166	Steve Payne	.30	.14	.04
☐ 167	Gordie Roberts	.35	.16	.04
☐ 168	Greg Smith	.30	.14	.04
☐ 169	Tim Young	.30	.14	.04
☐ 170	Bobby Smith SA	.40	.18	.05
☐ 171	Mike Eaves	.30	.14	.04
☐ 172	Mike Polich	.30	.14	.04
☐ 173	Tom Younghans	.30	.14	.04
☐ 174	Minn. North Stars TL	.50	.23	.06
	Bobby Smith			
☐ 175	Brian Engblom	.30	.14	.04
☐ 176	Bob Gainey	.50	.23	.06
☐ 177	Guy Lafleur	2.50	1.15	.30
☐ 178	Mark Napier	.30	.14	.04
☐ 179	Larry Robinson	.75	.35	.09
☐ 180	Steve Shutt	.40	.18	.05
☐ 181	Keith Acton	1.00	.45	.13
☐ 182	Gaston Gingras	.30	.14	.04
☐ 183	Rejean Houle	.30	.14	.04
☐ 184	Doug Jarvis	.30	.14	.04
☐ 185	Yvon Lambert	.30	.14	.04
☐ 186	Rod Langway	2.50	1.15	.30
☐ 187	Pierre Larouche	.35	.16	.04
☐ 188	Pierre Mondou	.30	.14	.04
☐ 189	Robert Picard	.30	.14	.04
☐ 190	Doug Risebrough	.35	.16	.04
☐ 191	Richard Sevigny	.30	.14	.04
☐ 192	Mario Tremblay	.35	.16	.04
☐ 193	Doug Wickenheiser	.40	.18	.05
☐ 194	Bob Gainey SA	.35	.16	.04
☐ 195	Guy Lafleur SA	1.00	.45	.13
☐ 196	Larry Robinson SA	.40	.18	.05
☐ 197	Montreal Canadiens TL	.40	.18	.05
	Steve Shutt			
☐ 198	Mike Bossy	4.00	1.80	.50
☐ 199	Denis Potvin	1.00	.45	.13
☐ 200	Bryan Trottier	2.00	.90	.25
☐ 201	Bob Bourne	.30	.14	.04
☐ 202	Clark Gillies	.35	.16	.04
☐ 203	Butch Goring	.35	.16	.04
☐ 204	Anders Kallur	.30	.14	.04
☐ 205	Ken Morrow	.35	.16	.04
☐ 206	Stefan Persson	.30	.14	.04
☐ 207	Billy Smith	.50	.23	.06
☐ 208	Mike Bossy SA	1.50	.65	.19
☐ 209	Denis Potvin SA	.50	.23	.06
☐ 210	Bryan Trottier SA	.75	.35	.09
☐ 211	Duane Sutter	1.00	.45	.13
☐ 212	Gordie Lane	.30	.14	.04
☐ 213	Dave Langevin	.30	.14	.04
☐ 214	Bob Lorimer	.30	.14	.04
☐ 215	Mike McEwen	.30	.14	.04
☐ 216	Wayne Merrick	.30	.14	.04
☐ 217	Bob Nystrom	.30	.14	.04
☐ 218	John Tonelli	1.00	.45	.13
☐ 219	New York Islanders TL	.75	.35	.09
	Mike Bossy			
☐ 220	Barry Beck	.35	.16	.04
☐ 221	Mike Allison	.30	.14	.04
☐ 222	John Davidson	.35	.16	.04
☐ 223	Ron Duguay	.35	.16	.04
☐ 224	Ron Greschner	.30	.14	.04
☐ 225	Anders Hedberg	.35	.16	.04
☐ 226	Ed Johnstone	.30	.14	.04
☐ 227	Dave Maloney	.30	.14	.04
☐ 228	Don Maloney	.35	.16	.04
☐ 229	Ulf Nilsson	.35	.16	.04
☐ 230	Barry Beck SA	.30	.14	.04
☐ 231	Steve Baker	.30	.14	.04
☐ 232	Jere Gillis	.30	.14	.04
☐ 233	Ed Hospodar	.30	.14	.04
☐ 234	Tom Laidlaw	.35	.16	.04
☐ 235	Dean Talafous	.30	.14	.04
☐ 236	Carol Vadnais	.30	.14	.04
☐ 237	New York Rangers TL	.40	.18	.05
	Anders Hedberg			
☐ 238	Bill Barber	.40	.18	.05
☐ 239	Behn Wilson	.30	.14	.04
☐ 240	Bobby Clarke	1.25	.55	.16
☐ 241	Bob Dailey	.30	.14	.04
☐ 242	Paul Holmgren	.30	.14	.04
☐ 243	Reggie Leach	.35	.16	.04
☐ 244	Ken Linseman	.35	.16	.04
☐ 245	Pete Peeters	1.25	.55	.16
☐ 246	Brian Propp	2.00	.90	.25
☐ 247	Bill Barber SA	.35	.16	.04
☐ 248	Mel Bridgman	.30	.14	.04
☐ 249	Mike Busniuk	.30	.14	.04
☐ 250	Tom Gorence	.30	.14	.04
☐ 251	Tim Kerr	4.50	2.00	.55
☐ 252	Rick St.Croix	.30	.14	.04
☐ 253	Philadelphia Flyers TL	.50	.23	.06
	Bill Barber			
☐ 254	Rick Kehoe	.30	.14	.04
☐ 255	Pat Boutette	.30	.14	.04
☐ 256	Randy Carlyle	.35	.16	.04
☐ 257	Paul Gardner	.30	.14	.04
☐ 258	Peter Lee	.30	.14	.04
☐ 259	Rod Schutt	.30	.14	.04
☐ 260	Rick Kehoe SA	.30	.14	.04
☐ 261	Mario Faubert	.30	.14	.04
☐ 262	George Ferguson	.30	.14	.04
☐ 263	Ross Lonsberry	.30	.14	.04
☐ 264	Greg Malone	.30	.14	.04
☐ 265	Pat Price	.30	.14	.04
☐ 266	Ron Stackhouse	.30	.14	.04
☐ 267	Pittsburgh Penguins TL	.40	.18	.05
	Rick Kehoe			
☐ 268	Jacques Richard	.30	.14	.04
☐ 269	Peter Stastny	25.00	11.50	3.10
☐ 270	Dan Bouchard	.35	.16	.04
☐ 271	Kim Clackson	.30	.14	.04
☐ 272	Alain Cote	.30	.14	.04
☐ 273	Andre Dupont	.30	.14	.04
☐ 274	Robbie Ftorek	.35	.16	.04
☐ 275	Michel Goulet	7.00	3.10	.85
☐ 276	Dale Hoganson	.30	.14	.04
☐ 277	Dale Hunter	10.00	4.50	1.25
☐ 278	Pierre Lacroix	.30	.14	.04
☐ 279	Mario Marois	.40	.18	.05
☐ 280	Dave Pichette	.30	.14	.04
☐ 281	Michel Plasse	.30	.14	.04
☐ 282	Anton Stastny	.75	.35	.09
☐ 283	Marc Tardif	.30	.14	.04
☐ 284	Wally Weir	.30	.14	.04
☐ 285	Jacques Richard SA	.30	.14	.04
☐ 286	Peter Stastny SA	5.00	2.30	.60
☐ 287	Quebec Nordiques TL	3.00	1.35	.40
	Peter Stastny			
☐ 288	Bernie Federko	1.50	.65	.19
☐ 289	Mike Liut	2.00	.90	.25
☐ 290	Wayne Babych	.30	.14	.04
☐ 291	Blair Chapman	.30	.14	.04
☐ 292	Tony Currie	.30	.14	.04
☐ 293	Blake Dunlop	.30	.14	.04
☐ 294	Ed Kea	.30	.14	.04
☐ 295	Rick Lapointe	.30	.14	.04
☐ 296	Jorgen Pettersson	.30	.14	.04

☐ 297	Brian Sutter	1.00	.45	.13
☐ 298	Perry Turnbull	.30	.14	.04
☐ 299	Mike Zuke	.30	.14	.04
☐ 300	Bernie Federko SA	.50	.23	.06
☐ 301	Mike Liut SA	.35	.16	.04
☐ 302	Jack Brownschidle	.30	.14	.04
☐ 303	Larry Patey	.30	.14	.04
☐ 304	St. Louis Blues TL	.50	.23	.06
	Bernie Federko			
☐ 305	Bill Derlago	.30	.14	.04
☐ 306	Wilf Paiement	.35	.16	.04
☐ 307	Borje Salming	.35	.16	.04
☐ 308	Darryl Sittler	1.00	.45	.13
☐ 309	Ian Turnbull	.30	.14	.04
☐ 310	Rick Vaive	.75	.35	.09
☐ 311	Wilf Paiement SA	.30	.14	.04
☐ 312	Darryl Sittler SA	.35	.16	.04
☐ 313	John Anderson	.30	.14	.04
☐ 314	Laurie Boschman	.35	.16	.04
☐ 315	Jiri Crha	.30	.14	.04
☐ 316	Vitezslav Duris	.30	.14	.04
☐ 317	Dave Farrish	.30	.14	.04
☐ 318	Pat Hickey	.30	.14	.04
☐ 319	Michel Larocque	.35	.16	.04
☐ 320	Dan Maloney	.30	.14	.04
☐ 321	Terry Martin	.30	.14	.04
☐ 322	Rene Robert	.35	.16	.04
☐ 323	Rocky Saganiuk	.30	.14	.04
☐ 324	Ron Sedlbauer	.30	.14	.04
☐ 325	Ron Zanussi	.30	.14	.04
☐ 326	Toronto Maple Leafs TL	.40	.18	.05
	Wilf Paiement			
☐ 327	Thomas Gradin	.35	.16	.04
☐ 328	Stan Smyl	.35	.16	.04
☐ 329	Ivan Boldirev	.30	.14	.04
☐ 330	Per-Olov Brasar UER	.30	.14	.04
	(Photo actually			
	Brent Ashton)			
☐ 331	Richard Brodeur	.35	.16	.04
☐ 332	Jerry Butler	.30	.14	.04
☐ 333	Colin Campbell	.30	.14	.04
☐ 334	Curt Fraser	.30	.14	.04
☐ 335	Doug Halward	.30	.14	.04
☐ 336	Glen Hanlon	.35	.16	.04
☐ 337	Dennis Kearns	.30	.14	.04
☐ 338	Rick Lanz UER	.30	.14	.04
	(Photo actually			
	Thomas Gradin)			
☐ 339	Pat Ribble	.30	.14	.04
☐ 340	Blair MacDonald	.30	.14	.04
☐ 341	Kevin McCarthy	.30	.14	.04
☐ 342	Gerry Minor	.30	.14	.04
☐ 343	Darcy Rota	.30	.14	.04
☐ 344	Harold Snepsts	.35	.16	.04
☐ 345	Dave(Tiger) Williams	.35	.16	.04
☐ 346	Vancouver Canucks TL	.40	.18	.05
	Thomas Gradin			
☐ 347	Mike Gartner	20.00	9.00	2.50
☐ 348	Rick Green	.30	.14	.04
☐ 349	Bob Kelly	.30	.14	.04
☐ 350	Dennis Maruk	.35	.16	.04
☐ 351	Mike Palmateer	.30	.14	.04
☐ 352	Ryan Walter	.35	.16	.04
☐ 353	Bengt Gustafsson	.35	.16	.04
☐ 354	Al Hangsleben	.30	.14	.04
☐ 355	Jean Pronovost	.35	.16	.04
☐ 356	Dennis Ververgaert	.30	.14	.04
☐ 357	Washington Capitols TL	.40	.18	.05
	Dennis Maruk			
☐ 358	Dave Babych	1.25	.55	.16
☐ 359	Dave Christian	1.00	.45	.13
☐ 360	Dave Christian SA	.40	.18	.05
☐ 361	Rick Bowness	.35	.16	.04
☐ 362	Rick Dudley	.30	.14	.04
☐ 363	Norm Dupont	.30	.14	.04
☐ 364	Dan Geoffrion	.30	.14	.04
☐ 365	Pierre Hamel	.30	.14	.04
☐ 366	Dave Hoyda UER	.30	.14	.04
	(Photo actually			
	Doug Lecuyer)			
☐ 367	Doug Lecuyer	.30	.14	.04
☐ 368	Willy Lindstrom	.30	.14	.04
☐ 369	Barry Long	.30	.14	.04
☐ 370	Morris Lukowich	.30	.14	.04
☐ 371	Kris Manery	.30	.14	.04
☐ 372	Jimmy Mann	.35	.16	.04
☐ 373	Moe Mantha	.50	.23	.06
☐ 374	Markus Mattsson	.30	.14	.04
☐ 375	Don Spring	.30	.14	.04
☐ 376	Tim Trimper	.30	.14	.04
☐ 377	Ron Wilson	.30	.14	.04
☐ 378	Winnipeg Jets TL	.50	.23	.06
	Dave Christian			

☐ 379	Checklist 1-132	4.00	.40	.08
☐ 380	Checklist 133-264	4.00	.40	.08
☐ 381	Checklist 265-396	4.00	.40	.08
☐ 382	Goal Leader	1.00	.45	.13
	Mike Bossy			
☐ 383	Assist Leader	10.00	4.50	1.25
	Wayne Gretzky			
☐ 384	Scoring Leader	10.00	4.50	1.25
	Wayne Gretzky			
☐ 385	Penalty Leader	.40	.18	.05
	Dave(Tiger) Williams			
☐ 386	Power Play Leader	1.00	.45	.13
	Mike Bossy			
☐ 387	Goals Against Leader	.40	.18	.05
	Richard Sevigny			
☐ 388	Game Winning Goal	1.00	.45	.13
	Leader			
	Mike Bossy			
☐ 389	Shutout Leaders	.40	.18	.05
	Don Edwards			
	Glenn Resch			
☐ 390	Mike Bossy RB	1.00	.45	.13
	Eight hat tricks			
	in one season			
☐ 391	Marcel Dionne,	3.00	1.35	.40
	Charlie Simmer,			
	Dave Taylor RB			
	100 points each			
☐ 392	Wayne Gretzky RB	10.00	4.50	1.25
	Season scoring record			
☐ 393	Larry Murphy RB	3.00	1.35	.40
	Highest scoring			
	rookie defenseman			
☐ 394	Mike Palmateer RB	.40	.18	.05
	Seventh assist,			
	new goalie record			
☐ 395	Peter Stastny RB	4.00	1.80	.50
	Rookie scoring record			
☐ 396	Bob Manno	.35	.16	.04

1982-83 O-Pee-Chee

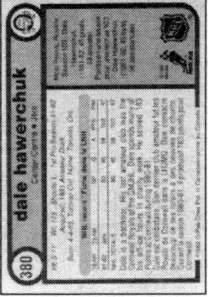

Because Topps did not issue a set for a two year period, this 396-card set marks the first time since the pre-war era that O-Pee-Chee manufactured hockey cards without competition. Card fronts display the player's name, team and position at the top. A team logo appears at the bottom. The cards were originally sold in 25-cent wax packs. Cards measure 2 1/2" by 3 1/2". Highlight cards, team scoring leaders cards, league leaders cards and In Action cards are contained within the set. Rookie Cards in this set include Neal Broten, Ron Francis, Grant Fuhr, Dale Hawerchuk, Joe Mullen, Brent Sutter and Thomas Steen.

	MINT	EXC	G-VG
COMPLETE SET (396)	140.00	65.00	17.50
COMMON PLAYER (1-396)	.20	.09	.03
☐ 1 Wayne Gretzky HL	10.00	4.50	1.25
More Records			
☐ 2 Mike Bossy HL	.75	.35	.09
Record 147 Points			
☐ 3 Dale Hawerchuk HL	5.00	2.30	.60
Rookie Record			

☐ 4 Mikko Leinonen HL	.20	.09	.03
Six Assists One Game			
☐ 5 Bryan Trottier HL	.40	.18	.05
Sets Assist Mark			
☐ 6 Boston Bruins	.25	.11	.03
Scoring Leaders:			
Rick Middleton			
☐ 7 Ray Bourque	7.50	3.40	.95
☐ 8 Wayne Cashman	.25	.11	.03
☐ 9 Bruce Crowder	.20	.09	.03
☐ 10 Keith Crowder	.25	.11	.03
☐ 11 Tom Fergus	1.50	.65	.19
☐ 12 Steve Kasper	.25	.11	.03
☐ 13 Normand Leveille	.50	.23	.06
☐ 14 Don Marcotte	.20	.09	.03
☐ 15 Rick Middleton	.30	.14	.04
☐ 16 Peter McNab	.25	.11	.03
☐ 17 Mike O'Connell	.25	.11	.03
☐ 18 Terry O'Reilly	.25	.11	.03
☐ 19 Brad Park	.40	.18	.05
☐ 20 Barry Pederson	1.00	.45	.13
☐ 21 Brad Palmer	.20	.09	.03
☐ 22 Pete Peeters	.50	.23	.06
☐ 23 Rogatien Vachon	.20	.09	.03
☐ 24 Ray Bourque IA	2.50	1.15	.30
☐ 25 Buffalo Sabres	.25	.11	.03
Scoring Leaders:			
Gilbert Perreault			
☐ 26 Mike Foligno	.30	.14	.04
☐ 27 Yvon Lambert	.20	.09	.03
☐ 28 Dale McCourt	.20	.09	.03
☐ 29 Tony McKegney	.20	.09	.03
☐ 30 Gilbert Perreault	.50	.23	.06
☐ 31 Lindy Ruff	.20	.09	.03
☐ 32 Mike Ramsey	.50	.23	.06
☐ 33 J.F. Sauve	.20	.09	.03
☐ 34 Bob Sauve	.20	.09	.03
☐ 35 Ric Seiling	.20	.09	.03
☐ 36 John Van Boxmeer	.20	.09	.03
☐ 37 John Van Boxmeer IA	.20	.09	.03
☐ 38 Calgary Flames	.25	.11	.03
Scoring Leaders:			
Lanny McDonald			
☐ 39 Mel Bridgman	.20	.09	.03
☐ 40 Mel Bridgman IA	.20	.09	.03
☐ 41 Guy Chouinard	.20	.09	.03
☐ 42 Steve Christoff	.20	.09	.03
☐ 43 Denis Cyr	.20	.09	.03
☐ 44 Bill Clement	.25	.11	.03
☐ 45 Richie Dunn	.20	.09	.03
☐ 46 Don Edwards	.20	.09	.03
☐ 47 Jamie Hislop	.20	.09	.03
☐ 48 Steve Konroyd	.35	.16	.04
☐ 49 Kevin Lavallee	.20	.09	.03
☐ 50 Rejean Lemelin	.75	.35	.09
☐ 51 Lanny McDonald	.50	.23	.06
☐ 52 Lanny McDonald IA	.25	.11	.03
☐ 53 Bob Murdoch	.20	.09	.03
☐ 54 Kent Nilsson	.30	.14	.04
☐ 55 Jim Peplinski	.25	.11	.03
☐ 56 Paul Reinhart	.25	.11	.03
☐ 57 Doug Risebrough	.20	.09	.03
☐ 58 Phil Russell	.20	.09	.03
☐ 59 Howard Walker	.20	.09	.03
☐ 60 Chicago Blackhawks	.20	.09	.03
Scoring Leaders:			
Al Secord			
☐ 61 Murray Bannerman	.25	.11	.03
☐ 62 Keith Brown	.20	.09	.03
☐ 63 Doug Crossman	1.00	.45	.13
☐ 64 Tony Esposito	.75	.35	.09
☐ 65 Greg Fox	.20	.09	.03
☐ 66 Tim Higgins	.20	.09	.03
☐ 67 Reg Kerr	.20	.09	.03
☐ 68 Tom Lysiak	.20	.09	.03
☐ 69 Grant Mulvey	.20	.09	.03
☐ 70 Bob Murray	.20	.09	.03
☐ 71 Rich Preston	.20	.09	.03
☐ 72 Terry Ruskowski	.20	.09	.03
☐ 73 Denis Savard	4.00	1.80	.50
☐ 74 Al Secord	.25	.11	.03
☐ 75 Glen Sharpley	.20	.09	.03
☐ 76 Darryl Sutter	.25	.11	.03
☐ 77 Doug Wilson	.75	.35	.09
☐ 78 Doug Wilson IA	.25	.11	.03
☐ 79 Detroit Red Wings	.25	.11	.03
Scoring Leaders:			
John Ogrodnick			
☐ 80 John Barrett	.20	.09	.03
☐ 81 Mike Blaisdell	.20	.09	.03
☐ 82 Colin Campbell	.20	.09	.03
☐ 83 Danny Gare	.20	.09	.03
☐ 84 Gilles Gilbert	.20	.09	.03
☐ 85 Willie Huber	.20	.09	.03
☐ 86 Greg Joly	.20	.09	.03
☐ 87 Mark Kirton	.20	.09	.03
☐ 88 Reed Larson	.25	.11	.03
☐ 89 Reed Larson IA	.20	.09	.03
☐ 90 Reggie Leach	.25	.11	.03
☐ 91 Walt McKechnie	.20	.09	.03
☐ 92 John Ogrodnick	.25	.11	.03
☐ 93 Mark Osborne	.75	.35	.09
☐ 94 Jim Schoenfeld	.20	.09	.03
☐ 95 Derek Smith	.20	.09	.03
☐ 96 Greg Smith	.20	.09	.03
☐ 97 Eric Vail	.20	.09	.03
☐ 98 Paul Woods	.20	.09	.03
☐ 99 Edmonton Oilers	6.00	2.70	.75
Scoring Leaders:			
Wayne Gretzky			
☐ 100 Glenn Anderson	5.00	2.30	.60
☐ 101 Paul Coffey	18.00	8.00	2.30
☐ 102 Paul Coffey IA	6.00	2.70	.75
☐ 103 Brett Callighen	.20	.09	.03
☐ 104 Lee Fogolin	.20	.09	.03
☐ 105 Grant Fuhr	20.00	9.00	2.50
☐ 106 Wayne Gretzky	40.00	18.00	5.00
☐ 107 Wayne Gretzky IA	15.00	6.75	1.90
☐ 108 Matti Hagman	.20	.09	.03
☐ 109 Pat Hughes	.20	.09	.03
☐ 110 Dave Hunter	.20	.09	.03
☐ 111 Jari Kurri	7.50	3.40	.95
☐ 112 Ron Low	.20	.09	.03
☐ 113 Kevin Lowe	3.00	1.35	.40
☐ 114 Dave Lumley	.20	.09	.03
☐ 115 Ken Linseman	.25	.11	.03
☐ 116 Garry Lariviere	.20	.09	.03
☐ 117 Mark Messier	20.00	9.00	2.50
☐ 118 Tom Roulston	.20	.09	.03
☐ 119 Dave Semenko	.25	.11	.03
☐ 120 Garry Unger	.25	.11	.03
☐ 121 Checklist 1-132	2.50	.25	.05
☐ 122 Hartford Whalers	.20	.09	.03
Scoring Leaders:			
Blaine Stoughton			
☐ 123 Ron Francis	15.00	6.75	1.90
☐ 124 Chris Kotsopoulos	.20	.09	.03
☐ 125 Pierre Larouche	.25	.11	.03
☐ 126 Greg Millen	.25	.11	.03
☐ 127 Warren Miller	.20	.09	.03
☐ 128 Merlin Malinowski	.20	.09	.03
☐ 129 Risto Siltanen	.20	.09	.03
☐ 130 Blaine Stoughton	.25	.11	.03
☐ 131 Blaine Stoughton IA	.20	.09	.03
☐ 132 Doug Sulliman	.20	.09	.03
☐ 133 Blake Wesley	.20	.09	.03
☐ 134 New Jersey Devils	.20	.09	.03
Scoring Leaders:			
Steve Tambellini			
☐ 135 Brent Ashton	.40	.18	.05
☐ 136 Aaron Broten	.25	.11	.03
☐ 137 Joe Cirella	.40	.18	.05
☐ 138 Dwight Foster	.20	.09	.03
☐ 139 Paul Gagne	.20	.09	.03
☐ 140 Garry Howatt	.20	.09	.03
☐ 141 Don Lever	.20	.09	.03
☐ 142 Bob Lorimer	.20	.09	.03
☐ 143 Bob MacMillan	.20	.09	.03
☐ 144 Rick Meagher	.75	.35	.09
☐ 145 Glenn Resch	.30	.14	.04
☐ 146 Glenn Resch IA	.20	.09	.03
☐ 147 Steve Tambellini	.20	.09	.03
☐ 148 Carol Vadnais	.20	.09	.03
☐ 149 Los Angeles Kings	.35	.16	.04
Scoring Leaders:			
Marcel Dionne			
☐ 150 Dan Bonar	.20	.09	.03
☐ 151 Steve Bozek	.20	.09	.03
☐ 152 Marcel Dionne	1.00	.45	.13
☐ 153 Marcel Dionne IA	.40	.18	.05
☐ 154 Jim Fox	.20	.09	.03
☐ 155 Mark Hardy	.25	.11	.03
☐ 156 Mario Lessard	.20	.09	.03
☐ 157 Dave Lewis	.20	.09	.03
☐ 158 Larry Murphy	4.00	1.80	.50
☐ 159 Charlie Simmer	.50	.23	.06
☐ 160 Doug Smith	.20	.09	.03
☐ 161 Dave Taylor	.60	.25	.08
☐ 162 Minnesota North Stars	.50	.23	.06
Scoring Leaders:			
Dino Ciccarelli			
☐ 163 Don Beaupre	1.00	.45	.13
☐ 164 Neal Broten	6.00	2.70	.75
☐ 165 Dino Ciccarelli	4.00	1.80	.50
☐ 166 Curt Giles	.50	.23	.06
☐ 167 Craig Hartsburg	.25	.11	.03

168	Brad Maxwell	.20	.09	.03
169	Tom McCarthy	.20	.09	.03
170	Gilles Meloche	.25	.11	.03
171	Al MacAdam	.20	.09	.03
172	Steve Payne	.20	.09	.03
173	Willi Plett	.20	.09	.03
174	Gordie Roberts	.20	.09	.03
175	Bobby Smith	.50	.23	.06
176	Bobby Smith IA	.30	.14	.04
177	Tim Young	.20	.09	.03
178	Montreal Canadiens	.20	.09	.03

Scoring Leaders: Mark Napier

179	Keith Acton	.25	.11	.03
180	Keith Acton IA	.20	.09	.03
181	Bob Gainey	.35	.16	.04
182	Gaston Gingras	.20	.09	.03
183	Rick Green	.20	.09	.03
184	Rejean Houle	.20	.09	.03
185	Mark Hunter	.50	.23	.06
186	Guy Lafleur	1.50	.65	.19
187	Guy Lafleur IA	.50	.23	.06
188	Pierre Mondou	.20	.09	.03
189	Mark Napier	.20	.09	.03
190	Robert Picard	.20	.09	.03
191	Larry Robinson	.50	.23	.06
192	Steve Shutt	.20	.09	.03
193	Mario Tremblay	.20	.09	.03
194	Ryan Walter	.25	.11	.03
195	Rick Wamsley	1.00	.45	.13
196	Doug Wickenheiser	.20	.09	.03
197	New York Islanders	.50	.23	.06

Scoring Leaders: Mike Bossy

198	Bob Bourne	.20	.09	.03
199	Mike Bossy	2.00	.90	.25
200	Butch Goring	.25	.11	.03
201	Clark Gillies	.25	.11	.03
202	Tomas Jonsson	.20	.09	.03
203	Anders Kallur	.20	.09	.03
204	Dave Langevin	.20	.09	.03
205	Wayne Merrick	.20	.09	.03
206	Ken Morrow	.25	.11	.03
207	Mike McEwen	.20	.09	.03
208	Bob Nystrom	.20	.09	.03
209	Stefan Persson	.20	.09	.03
210	Denis Potvin	.75	.35	.09
211	Billy Smith	.30	.14	.04
212	Duane Sutter	.25	.11	.03
213	John Tonelli	.75	.35	.09
214	Bryan Trottier	1.00	.45	.13
215	Bryan Trottier IA	.40	.18	.05
216	Brent Sutter	3.00	1.35	.40
217	New York Rangers	.20	.09	.03

Scoring Leaders: Ron Duguay

218	Kent-Erik Andersson	.20	.09	.03
219	Barry Beck	.25	.11	.03
220	Barry Beck IA	.20	.09	.03
221	Ron Duguay	.25	.11	.03
222	Nick Fotiu	.25	.11	.03
223	Robbie Ftorek	.25	.11	.03
224	Ron Greschner	.20	.09	.03
225	Anders Hedberg	.25	.11	.03
226	Ed Johnstone	.20	.09	.03
227	Tom Laidlaw	.20	.09	.03
228	Dave Maloney	.20	.09	.03
229	Don Maloney	.20	.09	.03
230	Eddie Mio	.20	.09	.03
231	Mark Pavelich	.25	.11	.03
232	Mike Rogers	.25	.11	.03
233	Reijo Ruotsalainen	.40	.18	.05
234	Steve Weeks	.50	.23	.06
235	Goals Leader (Wayne Gretzky)	6.00	2.70	.75
236	Power Play Leader (Paul Gardner)	.25	.11	.03
237	Shorthanded Goal Leader (Wayne Gretzky and Michel Goulet)	6.00	2.70	.75
238	Penalty Minutes Leader (Paul Baxter)	.25	.11	.03
239	Goals Against Leader (Denis Herron)	.25	.11	.03
240	Assist Leader (Wayne Gretzky)	6.00	2.70	.75
241	Shutout Leader (Denis Herron)	.25	.11	.03
242	Winning Goal Leader (Wayne Gretzky)	6.00	2.70	.75
243	Scoring Leader (Wayne Gretzky)	6.00	2.70	.75
244	Philadelphia Flyers	.25	.11	.03

Scoring Leaders: Bill Barber

245	Fred Arthur	.20	.09	.03
246	Bill Barber	.30	.14	.04
247	Bill Barber IA	.25	.11	.03
248	Bobby Clarke	1.00	.45	.13
249	Ron Flockhart	.40	.18	.05
250	Tom Gorence	.20	.09	.03
251	Paul Holmgren	.20	.09	.03
252	Mark Howe	.50	.23	.06
253	Tim Kerr	1.00	.45	.13
254	Brad Marsh	.25	.11	.03
255	Brad McCrimmon	.25	.11	.03
256	Brian Propp	1.00	.45	.13
257	Darryl Sittler	.60	.25	.08
258	Rick St.Croix	.20	.09	.03
259	Jim Watson	.20	.09	.03
260	Behn Wilson	.20	.09	.03
261	Checklist 133-264	2.50	.25	.05
262	Pittsburgh Penguins	.20	.09	.03

Scoring Leaders: Mike Bullard

263	Pat Boutette	.20	.09	.03
264	Mike Bullard	1.00	.45	.13
265	Randy Carlyle	.25	.11	.03
266	Randy Carlyle IA	.20	.09	.03
267	Michel Dion	.20	.09	.03
268	George Ferguson	.20	.09	.03
269	Paul Gardner	.20	.09	.03
270	Denis Herron	.20	.09	.03
271	Rick Kehoe	.20	.09	.03
272	Greg Malone	.20	.09	.03
273	Rick MacLeish	.25	.11	.03
274	Pat Price	.20	.09	.03
275	Ron Stackhouse	.20	.09	.03
276	Quebec Nordiques	.60	.25	.08

Scoring Leaders: Peter Stastny

277	Pierre Aubry	.20	.09	.03
278	Dan Bouchard	.25	.11	.03
279	Real Cloutier	.20	.09	.03
280	Real Cloutier IA	.20	.09	.03
281	Alain Cote	.20	.09	.03
282	Andre Dupont	.20	.09	.03
283	John Garrett	.20	.09	.03
284	Michel Goulet	3.50	1.55	.45
285	Dale Hunter	2.50	1.15	.30
286	Pierre Lacroix	.20	.09	.03
287	Mario Marois	.20	.09	.03
288	Wilf Paiement	.25	.11	.03
289	Dave Pichette	.20	.09	.03
290	Jacques Richard	.20	.09	.03
291	Normand Rochefort	.20	.09	.03
292	Peter Stastny	5.00	2.30	.60
293	Peter Stastny IA	1.50	.65	.19
294	Anton Stastny	.25	.11	.03
295	Marian Stastny	.25	.11	.03
296	Marc Tardif	.20	.09	.03
297	Wally Weir	.20	.09	.03
298	St. Louis Blues	.25	.11	.03

Scoring Leaders: Brian Sutter

299	Wayne Babych	.20	.09	.03
300	Jack Brownschidle	.20	.09	.03
301	Blake Dunlop	.20	.09	.03
302	Bernie Federko	.50	.23	.06
303	Bernie Federko IA	.30	.14	.04
304	Pat Hickey	.20	.09	.03
305	Guy Lapointe	.25	.11	.03
306	Mike Liut	1.00	.45	.13
307	Joe Mullen	15.00	6.75	1.90
308	Larry Patey	.20	.09	.03
309	Jorgen Pettersson	.20	.09	.03
310	Rob Ramage	.25	.11	.03
311	Brian Sutter	.50	.23	.06
312	Perry Turnbull	.20	.09	.03
313	Mike Zuke	.20	.09	.03
314	Toronto Maple Leafs	.25	.11	.03

Scoring Leaders: Rick Vaive

315	John Anderson	.20	.09	.03
316	Normand Aubin	.20	.09	.03
317	Jim Benning	.20	.09	.03
318	Fred Boimistruck	.20	.09	.03
319	Bill Derlago	.20	.09	.03
320	Bill Derlago IA	.20	.09	.03
321	Miroslav Frycer	.20	.09	.03
322	Billy Harris	.20	.09	.03
323	Jim Korn	.20	.09	.03
324	Michel Larocque	.25	.11	.03
325	Bob Manno	.20	.09	.03
326	Dan Maloney	.20	.09	.03
327	Bob McGill	.40	.18	.05
328	Barry Melrose	.40	.18	.05

☐	329	Terry Martin	.20	.09	.03
☐	330	Rene Robert	.25	.11	.03
☐	331	Rocky Saganiuk	.20	.09	.03
☐	332	Borje Salming	.30	.14	.04
☐	333	Greg Terrion	.20	.09	.03
☐	334	Vincent Tremblay	.20	.09	.03
☐	335	Rick Vaive	.25	.11	.03
☐	336	Rick Vaive IA	.20	.09	.03
☐	337	Vancouver Canucks	.20	.09	.03
		Scoring Leaders:			
		Thomas Gradin			
☐	338	Ivan Boldirev	.20	.09	.03
☐	339	Richard Brodeur	.25	.11	.03
☐	340	Richard Brodeur IA	.20	.09	.03
☐	341	Tony Currie	.20	.09	.03
☐	342	Marc Crawford	.20	.09	.03
☐	343	Curt Fraser	.20	.09	.03
☐	344	Thomas Gradin	.25	.11	.03
☐	345	Thomas Gradin IA	.20	.09	.03
☐	346	Ivan Hlinka UER	.20	.09	.03
		(Photo actually			
		Jiri Bubla)			
☐	347	Ron Delorme	.20	.09	.03
☐	348	Rick Lanz	.20	.09	.03
☐	349	Lars Lindgren	.20	.09	.03
☐	350	Blair MacDonald	.20	.09	.03
☐	351	Kevin McCarthy	.20	.09	.03
☐	352	Gerry Minor	.20	.09	.03
☐	353	Lars Molin	.20	.09	.03
☐	354	Gary Lupul	.20	.09	.03
☐	355	Darcy Rota	.20	.09	.03
☐	356	Stan Smyl	.25	.11	.03
☐	357	Harold Snepsts	.25	.11	.03
☐	358	Dave(Tiger) Williams	.25	.11	.03
☐	359	Washington Capitals	.20	.09	.03
		Scoring Leaders:			
		Dennis Maruk			
☐	360	Ted Bulley	.20	.09	.03
☐	361	Bob Carpenter	1.50	.65	.19
☐	362	Brian Engblom	.20	.09	.03
☐	363	Mike Gartner	9.00	4.00	1.15
☐	364	Bengt Gustafsson	.25	.11	.03
☐	365	Doug Hicks	.20	.09	.03
☐	366	Ken Houston	.20	.09	.03
☐	367	Doug Jarvis	.20	.09	.03
☐	368	Rod Langway	1.00	.45	.13
☐	369	Dennis Maruk	.25	.11	.03
☐	370	Dennis Maruk IA	.20	.09	.03
☐	371	Dave Parro	.20	.09	.03
☐	372	Pat Riggin	.25	.11	.03
☐	373	Chris Valentine	.20	.09	.03
☐	374	Winnipeg Jets	3.00	1.35	.40
		Scoring Leaders:			
		Dale Hawerchuk			
☐	375	Dave Babych	.25	.11	.03
☐	376	Dave Babych IA	.20	.09	.03
☐	377	Dave Christian	.35	.16	.04
☐	378	Norm Dupont	.20	.09	.03
☐	379	Lucien Deblois	.20	.09	.03
☐	380	Dale Hawerchuk	20.00	9.00	2.50
☐	381	Dale Hawerchuk IA	4.00	1.80	.50
☐	382	Craig Levie	.20	.09	.03
☐	383	Morris Lukowich	.20	.09	.03
☐	384	Willy Lindstrom	.20	.09	.03
☐	385	Bengt Lundholm	.20	.09	.03
☐	386	Paul MacLean UER	.75	.35	.09
		Photo of Larry Hopkins			
☐	387	Bryan Maxwell	.20	.09	.03
☐	388	Doug Smail	.75	.35	.09
☐	389	Doug Soetaert	.20	.09	.03
☐	390	Serge Savard	.30	.14	.04
☐	391	Thomas Steen	4.00	1.80	.50
☐	392	Don Spring	.20	.09	.03
☐	393	Ed Staniowski	.20	.09	.03
☐	394	Tim Trimper	.20	.09	.03
☐	395	Tim Watters	.25	.11	.03
☐	396	Checklist 265-396	2.50	.25	.05

1983-84 O-Pee-Chee

This 396-card set features card fronts that contain player name, position, team name and team logo at the top. The player's position appears within an area that resembles a hockey stick blade with the team logo fronting the blade as if to be a puck. Cards measure 2 1/2" by 3 1/2". Bilingual backs contain yearly and career statistics. Each team has a

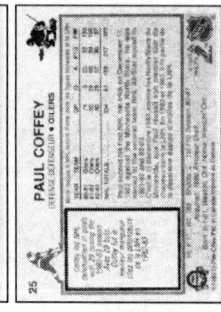

Highlight (HL) card featuring one or two players. Rookie Cards include Brian Bellows, Guy Carbonneau, Phil Housley, Steve Larmer, Pelle Lindbergh, Steve Ludzik (photo of Larmer), Brian Mullen, Mats Naslund, Bernie Nicholls, and Scott Stevens. For the second straight year, Topps did not produce a set.

			MINT	EXC	G-VG
	COMPLETE SET (396)		140.00	65.00	17.50
	COMMON PLAYER (1-396)		.20	.09	.03
☐	1	Islanders Leaders:	.75	.35	.09
		Mike Bossy			
☐	2	Islanders HL:	.25	.11	.03
		Denis Potvin			
☐	3	Mike Bossy	1.50	.65	.19
☐	4	Bob Bourne	.20	.09	.03
☐	5	Billy Carroll	.20	.09	.03
☐	6	Clark Gillies	.20	.09	.03
☐	7	Butch Goring	.25	.11	.03
☐	8	Mats Hallin	.20	.09	.03
☐	9	Tomas Jonsson	.20	.09	.03
☐	10	Gordie Lane	.20	.09	.03
☐	11	Dave Langevin	.20	.09	.03
☐	12	Rollie Melanson	.50	.23	.06
☐	13	Ken Morrow	.20	.09	.03
☐	14	Bob Nystrom	.20	.09	.03
☐	15	Stefan Persson	.20	.09	.03
☐	16	Denis Potvin	.50	.23	.06
☐	17	Billy Smith	.25	.11	.03
☐	18	Brent Sutter	.75	.35	.09
☐	19	Duane Sutter	.25	.11	.03
☐	20	John Tonelli	.35	.16	.04
☐	21	Bryan Trottier	.75	.35	.09
☐	22	Oilers Leaders:	6.00	2.70	.75
		Wayne Gretzky			
☐	23	Oilers HL:	22.00	10.00	2.80
		Mark Messier			
		Wayne Gretzky			
☐	24	Glenn Anderson	2.50	1.15	.30
☐	25	Paul Coffey	10.00	4.50	1.25
☐	26	Lee Fogolin	.20	.09	.03
☐	27	Grant Fuhr	6.00	2.70	.75
☐	28	Randy Gregg	.50	.23	.06
☐	29	Wayne Gretzky	30.00	13.50	3.80
☐	30	Charlie Huddy	1.50	.65	.19
☐	31	Pat Hughes	.20	.09	.03
☐	32	Dave Hunter	.20	.09	.03
☐	33	Don Jackson	.20	.09	.03
☐	34	Jari Kurri	5.00	2.30	.60
☐	35	Willy Lindstrom	.20	.09	.03
☐	36	Ken Linseman	.25	.11	.03
☐	37	Kevin Lowe	1.25	.55	.16
☐	38	Dave Lumley	.20	.09	.03
☐	39	Mark Messier	14.00	6.25	1.75
☐	40	Andy Moog	6.00	2.70	.75
☐	41	Jaroslav Pouzar	.20	.09	.03
☐	42	Tom Roulston	.20	.09	.03
☐	43	Bruins Leaders:	.25	.11	.03
		Rick Middleton			
☐	44	Bruins HL:	.25	.11	.03
		Pete Peeters			
☐	45	Ray Bourque	6.00	2.70	.75
☐	46	Bruce Crowder	.20	.09	.03
☐	47	Keith Crowder	.25	.11	.03
☐	48	Luc Dufour	.25	.11	.03
☐	49	Tom Fergus	.25	.11	.03
☐	50	Steve Kasper	.25	.11	.03
☐	51	Gord Kluzak	.50	.23	.06
☐	52	Mike Krushelnyski	1.00	.45	.13
☐	53	Peter McNab	.25	.11	.03

☐ 54	Rick Middleton	.30	.14	.04
☐ 55	Mike Milbury	.20	.09	.03
☐ 56	Mike O'Connell	.20	.09	.03
☐ 57	Barry Pederson	.25	.11	.03
☐ 58	Pete Peeters	.25	.11	.03
☐ 59	Jim Schoenfeld	.20	.09	.03
☐ 60	Sabres Leaders: Tony McKegney	.20	.09	.03
☐ 61	Sabres HL: Bob Sauve	.20	.09	.03
☐ 62	Real Cloutier	.20	.09	.03
☐ 63	Mike Foligno	.30	.14	.04
☐ 64	Bill Hajt	.20	.09	.03
☐ 65	Phil Housley	9.00	4.00	1.15
☐ 66	Dale McCourt	.20	.09	.03
☐ 67	Gilbert Perreault	.40	.18	.05
☐ 68	Brent Peterson	.20	.09	.03
☐ 69	Craig Ramsay	.20	.09	.03
☐ 70	Mike Ramsey	.25	.11	.03
☐ 71	Bob Sauve	.20	.09	.03
☐ 72	Ric Seiling	.20	.09	.03
☐ 73	John Van Boxmeer	.20	.09	.03
☐ 74	Flames Leaders: Lanny McDonald	.30	.14	.04
☐ 75	Flames HL: Lanny McDonald	.30	.14	.04
☐ 76	Ed Beers	.20	.09	.03
☐ 77	Steve Bozek	.20	.09	.03
☐ 78	Guy Chouinard	.20	.09	.03
☐ 79	Mike Eaves	.20	.09	.03
☐ 80	Don Edwards	.20	.09	.03
☐ 81	Kari Eloranta	.20	.09	.03
☐ 82	Dave Hindmarch	.20	.09	.03
☐ 83	Jamie Hislop	.20	.09	.03
☐ 84	Jim Jackson	.20	.09	.03
☐ 85	Steve Konroyd	.20	.09	.03
☐ 86	Rejean Lemelin	.35	.16	.04
☐ 87	Lanny McDonald	.35	.16	.04
☐ 88	Greg Meredith	.20	.09	.03
☐ 89	Kent Nilsson	.30	.14	.04
☐ 90	Jim Peplinski	.25	.11	.03
☐ 91	Paul Reinhart	.20	.09	.03
☐ 92	Doug Risebrough	.20	.09	.03
☐ 93	Steve Tambellini	.20	.09	.03
☐ 94	Mickey Volcan	.20	.09	.03
☐ 95	Blackhawks Leaders: Al Secord	.20	.09	.03
☐ 96	Blackhawks HL: Denis Savard	.40	.18	.05
☐ 97	Murray Bannerman	.20	.09	.03
☐ 98	Keith Brown	.20	.09	.03
☐ 99	Tony Esposito	.50	.23	.06
☐ 100	Dave Feamster	.20	.09	.03
☐ 101	Greg Fox	.20	.09	.03
☐ 102	Curt Fraser	.20	.09	.03
☐ 103	Bill Gardner	.20	.09	.03
☐ 104	Tim Higgins	.20	.09	.03
☐ 105	Steve Larmer UER (Photo actually Steve Ludzik)	20.00	9.00	2.50
☐ 106	Steve Ludzik UER (Photo actually Steve Larmer)	5.00	2.30	.60
☐ 107	Tom Lysiak	.20	.09	.03
☐ 108	Bob Murray	.20	.09	.03
☐ 109	Rick Paterson	.20	.09	.03
☐ 110	Rich Preston	.20	.09	.03
☐ 111	Denis Savard	2.50	1.15	.30
☐ 112	Al Secord	.25	.11	.03
☐ 113	Darryl Sutter	.25	.11	.03
☐ 114	Doug Wilson	.50	.23	.06
☐ 115	Red Wings Leaders: John Ogrodnick	.25	.11	.03
☐ 116	Red Wings HL: Corrado Micalef	.20	.09	.03
☐ 117	John Barrett	.20	.09	.03
☐ 118	Ivan Boldirev	.20	.09	.03
☐ 119	Colin Campbell	.20	.09	.03
☐ 120	Murray Craven	2.00	.90	.25
☐ 121	Ron Duguay	.25	.11	.03
☐ 122	Dwight Foster	.20	.09	.03
☐ 123	Danny Gare	.20	.09	.03
☐ 124	Ed Johnstone	.20	.09	.03
☐ 125	Reed Larson	.25	.11	.03
☐ 126	Corrado Micalef	.20	.09	.03
☐ 127	Eddie Mio	.20	.09	.03
☐ 128	John Ogrodnick	.25	.11	.03
☐ 129	Brad Park	.20	.09	.03
☐ 130	Greg Smith	.20	.09	.03
☐ 131	Ken Solheim	.20	.09	.03
☐ 132	Bob Manno	.20	.09	.03
☐ 133	Paul Woods	.20	.09	.03
☐ 134	Checklist 1-132	2.50	.25	.05
☐ 135	Whalers Leaders: Blaine Stoughton	.20	.09	.03
☐ 136	Whalers HL: Blaine Stoughton	.20	.09	.03
☐ 137	Richie Dunn	.20	.09	.03
☐ 138	Ron Francis	5.00	2.30	.60
☐ 139	Marty Howe	.25	.11	.03
☐ 140	Mark Johnson	.25	.11	.03
☐ 141	Paul Lawless	.20	.09	.03
☐ 142	Merlin Malinowski	.20	.09	.03
☐ 143	Greg Millen	.25	.11	.03
☐ 144	Ray Neufeld	.20	.09	.03
☐ 145	Joel Quenneville	.20	.09	.03
☐ 146	Risto Siltanen	.20	.09	.03
☐ 147	Blaine Stoughton	.20	.09	.03
☐ 148	Doug Sulliman	.20	.09	.03
☐ 149	Bob Sullivan	.20	.09	.03
☐ 150	Kings Leaders: Marcel Dionne	.25	.11	.03
☐ 151	Kings HL: Marcel Dionne	.25	.11	.03
☐ 152	Marcel Dionne	.75	.35	.09
☐ 153	Daryl Evans	.20	.09	.03
☐ 154	Jim Fox	.20	.09	.03
☐ 155	Mark Hardy	.20	.09	.03
☐ 156	Gary Laskoski	.20	.09	.03
☐ 157	Kevin Lavallee	.20	.09	.03
☐ 158	Dave Lewis	.20	.09	.03
☐ 159	Larry Murphy	1.75	.80	.22
☐ 160	Bernie Nicholls	9.00	4.00	1.15
☐ 161	Terry Ruskowski	.20	.09	.03
☐ 162	Charlie Simmer	.35	.16	.04
☐ 163	Dave Taylor	.50	.23	.06
☐ 164	North Stars Leaders: Dino Ciccarelli	.40	.18	.05
☐ 165	North Stars HL: Brian Bellows	2.00	.90	.25
☐ 166	Don Beaupre	.40	.18	.05
☐ 167	Brian Bellows	9.00	4.00	1.15
☐ 168	Neal Broten	1.50	.65	.19
☐ 169	Steve Christoff	.20	.09	.03
☐ 170	Dino Ciccarelli	2.50	1.15	.30
☐ 171	George Ferguson	.20	.09	.03
☐ 172	Craig Hartsburg	.20	.09	.03
☐ 173	Al MacAdam	.20	.09	.03
☐ 174	Dennis Maruk	.25	.11	.03
☐ 175	Brad Maxwell	.20	.09	.03
☐ 176	Tom McCarthy	.20	.09	.03
☐ 177	Gilles Meloche	.25	.11	.03
☐ 178	Steve Payne	.20	.09	.03
☐ 179	Willi Plett	.20	.09	.03
☐ 180	Gordie Roberts	.20	.09	.03
☐ 181	Bobby Smith	.30	.14	.04
☐ 182	Canadiens Leaders: Mark Napier	.20	.09	.03
☐ 183	Canadiens HL: Guy Lafleur	.50	.23	.06
☐ 184	Keith Acton	.25	.11	.03
☐ 185	Guy Carbonneau	6.00	2.70	.75
☐ 186	Gilbert Delorme	.20	.09	.03
☐ 187	Bob Gainey	.25	.11	.03
☐ 188	Rick Green	.20	.09	.03
☐ 189	Guy Lafleur	1.25	.55	.16
☐ 190	Craig Ludwig	.50	.23	.06
☐ 191	Pierre Mondou	.20	.09	.03
☐ 192	Mark Napier	.20	.09	.03
☐ 193	Mats Naslund	2.50	1.15	.30
☐ 194	Chris Nilan	1.50	.65	.19
☐ 195	Larry Robinson	.40	.18	.05
☐ 196	Bill Root	.20	.09	.03
☐ 197	Richard Sevigny	.50	.23	.06
☐ 198	Steve Shutt	.20	.09	.03
☐ 199	Mario Tremblay	.20	.09	.03
☐ 200	Ryan Walter	.20	.09	.03
☐ 201	Rick Wamsley	.25	.11	.03
☐ 202	Doug Wickenheiser	.20	.09	.03
☐ 203	Hart Trophy (Wayne Gretzky)	6.00	2.70	.75
☐ 204	Ross Trophy (Wayne Gretzky)	6.00	2.70	.75
☐ 205	Lady Byng Trophy (Mike Bossy)	.50	.23	.06
☐ 206	Calder Trophy (Steve Larmer)	3.00	1.35	.40
☐ 207	Norris Trophy (Rod Langway)	.25	.11	.03
☐ 208	Masterton Trophy (Lanny McDonald)	.25	.11	.03
☐ 209	Vezina Trophy (Pete Peeters)	.25	.11	.03
☐ 210	Mike Bossy RB Scores 50 goals, first six seasons	.50	.23	.06

☐ 211	Marcel Dionne RB	.25	.11	.03
	Scores 100 points			
	in seven seasons			
☐ 212	Wayne Gretzky RB	6.00	2.70	.75
	Scores in 30			
	consecutive games			
☐ 213	Pat Hughes RB	.20	.09	.03
	Two short-handed goals			
	within 25 seconds			
☐ 214	Rick Middleton RB	.25	.11	.03
	19 points in one			
	playoff series			
☐ 215	Goal Leaders	6.00	2.70	.75
	Wayne Gretzky			
☐ 216	Assists Leaders	6.00	2.70	.75
	Wayne Gretzky			
☐ 217	Scoring Leaders	6.00	2.70	.75
	Wayne Gretzky			
☐ 218	Game Winning	.20	.09	.03
	Goal Leaders			
	Brian Propp			
☐ 219	Power Play	.20	.09	.03
	Goal Leaders			
	Paul Gardner			
	Al Secord			
☐ 220	Penalty Min. Leaders	.20	.09	.03
	Randy Holt			
☐ 221	Goals Against	.20	.09	.03
	Average Leaders			
	Pete Peeters			
☐ 222	Shutout Leaders	.20	.09	.03
	Pete Peeters			
☐ 223	Devils Leaders:	.20	.09	.03
	Steve Tambellini			
☐ 224	Devils HL:	.20	.09	.03
	Don Lever			
☐ 225	Brent Ashton	.25	.11	.03
☐ 226	Mel Bridgman	.20	.09	.03
☐ 227	Aaron Broten	.20	.09	.03
☐ 228	Murray Brumwell	.20	.09	.03
☐ 229	Garry Howatt	.20	.09	.03
☐ 230	Jeff Larmer	.20	.09	.03
☐ 231	Don Lever	.20	.09	.03
☐ 232	Bob Lorimer	.20	.09	.03
☐ 233	Ron Low	.20	.09	.03
☐ 234	Bob MacMillan	.20	.09	.03
☐ 235	Hector Marini	.20	.09	.03
☐ 236	Glenn Resch	.30	.14	.04
☐ 237	Phil Russell	.20	.09	.03
☐ 238	Rangers Leaders:	.20	.09	.03
	Mark Pavelich			
☐ 239	Rangers HL:	.20	.09	.03
	Mark Pavelich			
☐ 240	Bill Baker	.20	.09	.03
☐ 241	Barry Beck	.25	.11	.03
☐ 242	Mike Blaisdell	.20	.09	.03
☐ 243	Nick Fotiu	.25	.11	.03
☐ 244	Robbie Ftorek	.25	.11	.03
☐ 245	Anders Hedberg	.25	.11	.03
☐ 246	Willie Huber	.20	.09	.03
☐ 247	Tom Laidlaw	.20	.09	.03
☐ 248	Mikko Leinonen	.20	.09	.03
☐ 249	Dave Maloney	.20	.09	.03
☐ 250	Don Maloney	.20	.09	.03
☐ 251	Rob McClanahan	.20	.09	.03
☐ 252	Mark Osborne	.20	.09	.03
☐ 253	Mark Pavelich	.25	.11	.03
☐ 254	Mike Rogers	.25	.11	.03
☐ 255	Reijo Ruotsalainen	.25	.11	.03
☐ 256	Checklist 133-264	2.50	.25	.05
☐ 257	Flyers Leaders:	.30	.14	.04
	Darryl Sittler			
☐ 258	Flyers HL:	.30	.14	.04
	Darryl Sittler			
☐ 259	Ray Allison	.20	.09	.03
☐ 260	Bill Barber	.30	.14	.04
☐ 261	Lindsay Carson	.20	.09	.03
☐ 262	Bobby Clarke	.75	.35	.09
☐ 263	Doug Crossman	.25	.11	.03
☐ 264	Ron Flockhart	.20	.09	.03
☐ 265	Bob Froese	1.00	.45	.13
☐ 266	Paul Holmgren	.20	.09	.03
☐ 267	Mark Howe	.30	.14	.04
☐ 268	Pelle Lindbergh	15.00	6.75	1.90
☐ 269	Brad Marsh	.25	.11	.03
☐ 270	Brad McCrimmon	.25	.11	.03
☐ 271	Brian Propp	.50	.23	.06
☐ 272	Darryl Sittler	.50	.23	.06
☐ 273	Mark Taylor	.20	.09	.03
☐ 274	Penguins Leaders:	.20	.09	.03
	Rick Kehoe			
☐ 275	Penguins HL:	.20	.09	.03
	Paul Gardner			

☐ 276	Pat Boutette	.20	.09	.03
☐ 277	Mike Bullard	.25	.11	.03
☐ 278	Randy Carlyle	.25	.11	.03
☐ 279	Michel Dion	.20	.09	.03
☐ 280	Paul Gardner	.20	.09	.03
☐ 281	Dave Hannan	.50	.23	.06
☐ 282	Rick Kehoe	.20	.09	.03
☐ 283	Randy Boyd	.20	.09	.03
☐ 284	Greg Malone	.20	.09	.03
☐ 285	Doug Shedden	.25	.11	.03
☐ 286	Andre St.Laurent	.20	.09	.03
☐ 287	Nordiques Leaders:	.50	.23	.06
	Michel Goulet			
☐ 288	Nordiques HL:	.50	.23	.06
	Michel Goulet			
☐ 289	Pierre Aubry	.20	.09	.03
☐ 290	Dan Bouchard	.25	.11	.03
☐ 291	Alain Cote	.20	.09	.03
☐ 292	Michel Goulet	1.50	.65	.19
☐ 293	Dale Hunter	1.00	.45	.13
☐ 294	Rick Lapointe	.20	.09	.03
☐ 295	Mario Marois	.20	.09	.03
☐ 296	Tony McKegney	.20	.09	.03
☐ 297	Randy Moller	.25	.11	.03
☐ 298	Wilf Paiement	.25	.11	.03
☐ 299	Dave Pichette	.20	.09	.03
☐ 300	Normand Rochefort	.20	.09	.03
☐ 301	Louis Sleigher	.20	.09	.03
☐ 302	Anton Stastny	.25	.11	.03
☐ 303	Marian Stastny	.25	.11	.03
☐ 304	Peter Stastny	3.00	1.35	.40
☐ 305	Marc Tardif	.20	.09	.03
☐ 306	Wally Weir	.20	.09	.03
☐ 307	Blake Wesley	.20	.09	.03
☐ 308	Blues Leaders:	.25	.11	.03
	Brian Sutter			
☐ 309	Blues HL:	.25	.11	.03
	Mike Liut			
☐ 310	Wayne Babych	.20	.09	.03
☐ 311	Jack Brownschidle	.20	.09	.03
☐ 312	Mike Crombeen	.20	.09	.03
☐ 313	Andre Dore	.20	.09	.03
☐ 314	Blake Dunlop	.20	.09	.03
☐ 315	Bernie Federko	.40	.18	.05
☐ 316	Mike Liut	.50	.23	.06
☐ 317	Joe Mullen	5.00	2.30	.60
☐ 318	Jorgen Pettersson	.20	.09	.03
☐ 319	Rob Ramage	.20	.09	.03
☐ 320	Brian Sutter	.30	.14	.04
☐ 321	Perry Turnbull	.20	.09	.03
☐ 322	Mike Zuke	.20	.09	.03
☐ 323	Maple Leafs Leaders:	.20	.09	.03
	Rick Vaive			
☐ 324	Maple Leafs HL:	.20	.09	.03
	Rick Vaive			
☐ 325	John Anderson	.20	.09	.03
☐ 326	Jim Benning	.20	.09	.03
☐ 327	Bill Derlago	.20	.09	.03
☐ 328	Dan Daoust	.20	.09	.03
☐ 329	Dave Farrish	.20	.09	.03
☐ 330	Miroslav Frycer	.20	.09	.03
☐ 331	Stewart Gavin	.40	.18	.05
☐ 332	Gaston Gingras	.20	.09	.03
☐ 333	Billy Harris	.20	.09	.03
☐ 334	Peter Inhacak	.20	.09	.03
☐ 335	Jim Korn	.20	.09	.03
☐ 336	Terry Martin	.20	.09	.03
☐ 337	Frank Nigro	.20	.09	.03
☐ 338	Mike Palmateer	.20	.09	.03
☐ 339	Walt Poddubny	.75	.35	.09
☐ 340	Rick St.Croix	.20	.09	.03
☐ 341	Borje Salming	.30	.14	.04
☐ 342	Greg Terrion	.20	.09	.03
☐ 343	Riok Vaive	.25	.11	.03
☐ 344	Canucks Leaders:	.20	.09	.03
	Darcy Rota			
☐ 345	Canucks HL:	.20	.09	.03
	Darcy Rota			
☐ 346	Richard Brodeur	.25	.11	.03
☐ 347	Jiri Bubla	.20	.09	.03
☐ 348	Ron Delorme	.20	.09	.03
☐ 349	John Garrett	.20	.09	.03
☐ 350	Thomas Gradin	.25	.11	.03
☐ 351	Doug Halward	.20	.09	.03
☐ 352	Mark Kirton	.20	.09	.03
☐ 353	Rick Lanz	.20	.09	.03
☐ 354	Lars Lindgren	.20	.09	.03
☐ 355	Gary Lupul	.20	.09	.03
☐ 356	Kevin McCarthy	.20	.09	.03
☐ 357	Jim Nill	.20	.09	.03
☐ 358	Darcy Rota	.20	.09	.03
☐ 359	Stan Smyl	.25	.11	.03
☐ 360	Harold Snepsts	.25	.11	.03

☐ 361	Patrik Sundstrom	.60	.25	.08
☐ 362	Tony Tanti	1.00	.45	.13
☐ 363	Dave(Tiger) Williams	.25	.11	.03
☐ 364	Capitals Leaders:	1.00	.45	.13
	Mike Gartner			
☐ 365	Capitals HL:	.20	.09	.03
	Rod Langway			
☐ 366	Bob Carpenter	.40	.18	.05
☐ 367	Dave Christian	.25	.11	.03
☐ 368	Brian Engblom	.20	.09	.03
☐ 369	Mike Gartner	5.00	2.30	.60
☐ 370	Bengt Gustafsson	.20	.09	.03
☐ 371	Ken Houston	.20	.09	.03
☐ 372	Doug Jarvis	.20	.09	.03
☐ 373	Al Jensen	.25	.11	.03
☐ 374	Rod Langway	.50	.23	.06
☐ 375	Craig Laughlin	.20	.09	.03
☐ 376	Scott Stevens	15.00	6.75	1.90
☐ 377	Jets Leaders:	1.00	.45	.13
	Dale Hawerchuk			
☐ 378	Jets HL:	.20	.09	.03
	Lucien Deblois			
☐ 379	Scott Arniel	.25	.11	.03
☐ 380	Dave Babych	.25	.11	.03
☐ 381	Laurie Boschman	.25	.11	.03
☐ 382	Wade Campbell	.20	.09	.03
☐ 383	Lucien DeBlois	.20	.09	.03
☐ 384	Murray Eaves	.20	.09	.03
☐ 385	Dale Hawerchuk	5.00	2.30	.60
☐ 386	Morris Lukowich	.20	.09	.03
☐ 387	Bengt Lundholm	.20	.09	.03
☐ 388	Paul MacLean	.20	.09	.03
☐ 389	Brian Mullen	2.00	.90	.25
☐ 390	Doug Smail	.20	.09	.03
☐ 391	Doug Soetaert	.20	.09	.03
☐ 392	Don Spring	.20	.09	.03
☐ 393	Thomas Steen	.75	.35	.09
☐ 394	Tim Watters	.20	.09	.03
☐ 395	Tim Young	.20	.09	.03
☐ 396	Checklist 265-396	2.50	.25	.05

1984-85 O-Pee-Chee

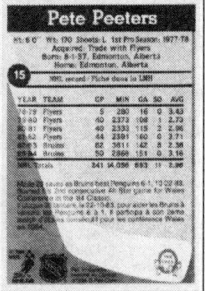

This 396-card set two player photos on the front. A small head shot appears in a circle toward the bottom of the card. Cards measure 2 1/2" by 3 1/2". Bilingual backs contain yearly and career statistics and career highlights. All-Stars are featured on cards 207-218. Cards 352-372 feature each team's leading goal scorer on the front and team individual scoring statistics on the back. A healthy selection of Rookie Cards includes Dave Andreychuk, Tom Barrasso, Chris Chelios, Doug Gilmour, Pat LaFontaine, Cam Neely, Pat Verbeek, and Steve Yzerman.

	MINT	EXC	G-VG
COMPLETE SET (396)	240.00	110.00	30.00
COMMON PLAYER (1-396)	.20	.09	.03

☐ 1	Ray Bourque	5.00	1.65	.50
☐ 2	Keith Crowder	.20	.09	.03
☐ 3	Luc Dufour	.20	.09	.03
☐ 4	Tom Fergus	.25	.11	.03
☐ 5	Doug Keans	.20	.09	.03
☐ 6	Gord Kluzak	.20	.09	.03
☐ 7	Ken Linseman	.20	.09	.03

☐ 8	Nevin Markwart	.20	.09	.03
☐ 9	Rick Middleton	.30	.14	.04
☐ 10	Mike Milbury	.20	.09	.03
☐ 11	Jim Nill	.20	.09	.03
☐ 12	Mike O'Connell	.20	.09	.03
☐ 13	Terry O'Reilly	.25	.11	.03
☐ 14	Barry Pederson	.25	.11	.03
☐ 15	Pete Peeters	.25	.11	.03
☐ 16	Dave Silk	.25	.11	.03
☐ 17	Dave Andreychuk	28.00	12.50	3.50
☐ 18	Tom Barrasso	10.00	4.50	1.25
☐ 19	Real Cloutier	.20	.09	.03
☐ 20	Mike Foligno	.25	.11	.03
☐ 21	Bill Hajt	.20	.09	.03
☐ 22	Gilles Hamel	.20	.09	.03
☐ 23	Phil Housley	2.00	.90	.25
☐ 24	Gilbert Perreault	.35	.16	.04
☐ 25	Brent Peterson	.20	.09	.03
☐ 26	Larry Playfair	.20	.09	.03
☐ 27	Craig Ramsay	.20	.09	.03
☐ 28	Mike Ramsey	.25	.11	.03
☐ 29	Lindy Ruff	.20	.09	.03
☐ 30	Bob Sauve	.20	.09	.03
☐ 31	Ric Seiling	.20	.09	.03
☐ 32	Murray Bannerman	.20	.09	.03
☐ 33	Keith Brown	.20	.09	.03
☐ 34	Curt Fraser	.20	.09	.03
☐ 35	Bill Gardner	.20	.09	.03
☐ 36	Jeff Larmer	.20	.09	.03
☐ 37	Steve Larmer	5.00	2.30	.60
☐ 38	Steve Ludzik	.20	.09	.03
☐ 39	Tom Lysiak	.20	.09	.03
☐ 40	Bob MacMillan	.20	.09	.03
☐ 41	Bob Murray	.20	.09	.03
☐ 42	Troy Murray	1.00	.45	.13
☐ 43	Jack O'Callahan	.20	.09	.03
☐ 44	Rick Paterson	.20	.09	.03
☐ 45	Denis Savard	1.50	.65	.19
☐ 46	Al Secord	.25	.11	.03
☐ 47	Darryl Sutter	.20	.09	.03
☐ 48	Doug Wilson	.25	.11	.03
☐ 49	John Barrett	.20	.09	.03
☐ 50	Ivan Boldirev	.20	.09	.03
☐ 51	Colin Campbell	.20	.09	.03
☐ 52	Ron Duguay	.25	.11	.03
☐ 53	Dwight Foster	.20	.09	.03
☐ 54	Danny Gare	.20	.09	.03
☐ 55	Ed Johnstone	.20	.09	.03
☐ 56	Kelly Kisio	1.50	.65	.19
☐ 57	Lane Lambert	.20	.09	.03
☐ 58	Reed Larson	.25	.11	.03
☐ 59	Bob Manno	.20	.09	.03
☐ 60	Randy Ladouceur	.20	.09	.03
☐ 61	Eddie Mio	.20	.09	.03
☐ 62	John Ogrodnick	.25	.11	.03
☐ 63	Brad Park	.20	.09	.03
☐ 64	Greg Smith	.20	.09	.03
☐ 65	Greg Stefan	.25	.11	.03
☐ 66	Paul Woods	.20	.09	.03
☐ 67	Steve Yzerman	55.00	25.00	7.00
☐ 68	Bob Crawford	.20	.09	.03
☐ 69	Richie Dunn	.20	.09	.03
☐ 70	Ron Francis	2.50	1.15	.30
☐ 71	Marty Howe	.25	.11	.03
☐ 72	Mark Johnson	.20	.09	.03
☐ 73	Chris Kotsopoulos	.20	.09	.03
☐ 74	Greg Malone	.20	.09	.03
☐ 75	Greg Millen	.25	.11	.03
☐ 76	Ray Neufeld	.20	.09	.03
☐ 77	Joel Quenneville	.20	.09	.03
☐ 78	Risto Siltanen	.20	.09	.03
☐ 79	Sylvain Turgeon	1.00	.45	.13
☐ 80	Mike Zuke	.20	.09	.03
☐ 81	Steve Christoff	.20	.09	.03
☐ 82	Marcel Dionne	.50	.23	.06
☐ 83	Brian Engblom	.20	.09	.03
☐ 84	Jim Fox	.20	.09	.03
☐ 85	Anders Hakansson	.20	.09	.03
☐ 86	Mark Hardy	.20	.09	.03
☐ 87	Brian MacLellan	.25	.11	.03
☐ 88	Bernie Nicholls	2.00	.90	.25
☐ 89	Terry Ruskowski	.20	.09	.03
☐ 90	Charlie Simmer	.30	.14	.04
☐ 91	Doug Smith	.20	.09	.03
☐ 92	Dave Taylor	.40	.18	.05
☐ 93	Keith Acton	.20	.09	.03
☐ 94	Don Beaupre	.25	.11	.03
☐ 95	Brian Bellows	2.00	.90	.25
☐ 96	Neal Broten	.50	.23	.06
☐ 97	Dino Ciccarelli	1.25	.55	.16
☐ 98	Craig Hartsburg	.20	.09	.03
☐ 99	Tom Hirsch	.20	.09	.03
☐ 100	Paul Holmgren	.20	.09	.03

☐	101	Dennis Maruk	.25	.11	.03
☐	102	Brad Maxwell	.20	.09	.03
☐	103	Tom McCarthy	.20	.09	.03
☐	104	Gilles Meloche	.20	.09	.03
☐	105	Mark Napier	.20	.09	.03
☐	106	Steve Payne	.20	.09	.03
☐	107	Gordie Roberts	.20	.09	.03
☐	108	Harold Snepsts	.25	.11	.03
☐	109	Mel Bridgman	.20	.09	.03
☐	110	Joe Cirella	.20	.09	.03
☐	111	Tim Higgins	.20	.09	.03
☐	112	Don Lever	.20	.09	.03
☐	113	Dave Lewis	.20	.09	.03
☐	114	Bob Lorimer	.20	.09	.03
☐	115	Ron Low	.20	.09	.03
☐	116	Jan Ludvig	.20	.09	.03
☐	117	Gary McAdam	.20	.09	.03
☐	118	Rich Preston	.20	.09	.03
☐	119	Glenn Resch	.30	.14	.04
☐	120	Phil Russell	.20	.09	.03
☐	121	Pat Verbeek	4.00	1.80	.50
☐	122	Mike Bossy	1.00	.45	.13
☐	123	Bob Bourne	.20	.09	.03
☐	124	Pat Flatley	1.50	.65	.19
☐	125	Greg Gilbert	.50	.23	.06
☐	126	Clark Gillies	.20	.09	.03
☐	127	Butch Goring	.25	.11	.03
☐	128	Tomas Jonsson	.20	.09	.03
☐	129	Pat LaFontaine	45.00	20.00	5.75
☐	130	Rollie Melanson	.20	.09	.03
☐	131	Ken Morrow	.20	.09	.03
☐	132	Bob Nystrom	.20	.09	.03
☐	133	Stefan Persson	.20	.09	.03
☐	134	Denis Potvin	.40	.18	.05
☐	135	Billy Smith	.25	.11	.03
☐	136	Brent Sutter	.50	.23	.06
☐	137	Duane Sutter	.25	.11	.03
☐	138	John Tonelli	.25	.11	.03
☐	139	Bryan Trottier	.60	.25	.08
☐	140	Barry Beck	.25	.11	.03
☐	141	Ron Greschner	.20	.09	.03
☐	142	Glen Hanlon	.25	.11	.03
☐	143	Anders Hedberg	.25	.11	.03
☐	144	Tom Laidlaw	.20	.09	.03
☐	145	Pierre Larouche	.25	.11	.03
☐	146	Dave Maloney	.20	.09	.03
☐	147	Don Maloney	.20	.09	.03
☐	148	Mark Osborne	.20	.09	.03
☐	149	Larry Patey	.20	.09	.03
☐	150	James Patrick	2.00	.90	.25
☐	151	Mark Pavelich	.20	.09	.03
☐	152	Mike Rogers	.25	.11	.03
☐	153	Reijo Ruotsalainen	.20	.09	.03
☐	154	Blaine Stoughton	.20	.09	.03
☐	155	Peter Sundstrom	.20	.09	.03
☐	156	Bill Barber	.30	.14	.04
☐	157	Doug Crossman	.20	.09	.03
☐	158	Thomas Eriksson	.20	.09	.03
☐	159	Bob Froese	.25	.11	.03
☐	160	Paul Guay	.20	.09	.03
☐	161	Mark Howe	.25	.11	.03
☐	162	Tim Kerr	.25	.11	.03
☐	163	Brad Marsh	.25	.11	.03
☐	164	Brad McCrimmon	.20	.09	.03
☐	165	Dave Poulin	2.00	.90	.25
☐	166	Brian Propp	.35	.16	.04
☐	167	Ilkka Sinisalo	.25	.11	.03
☐	168	Darryl Sittler	.30	.14	.04
☐	169	Rich Sutter	1.00	.45	.13
☐	170	Ron Sutter	1.00	.45	.13
☐	171	Pat Boutette	.20	.09	.03
☐	172	Mike Bullard	.25	.11	.03
☐	173	Michel Dion	.20	.09	.03
☐	174	Ron Flockhart	.20	.09	.03
☐	175	Greg Fox	.20	.09	.03
☐	176	Denis Herron	.20	.09	.03
☐	177	Rick Kehoe	.20	.09	.03
☐	178	Kevin McCarthy	.20	.09	.03
☐	179	Tom Roulston	.20	.09	.03
☐	180	Mark Taylor	.20	.09	.03
☐	181	Wayne Babych	.20	.09	.03
☐	182	Tim Bothwell	.20	.09	.03
☐	183	Kevin Lavallee	.20	.09	.03
☐	184	Bernie Federko	.30	.14	.04
☐	185	Doug Gilmour	55.00	25.00	7.00
☐	186	Terry Johnson	.20	.09	.03
☐	187	Mike Liut	.30	.14	.04
☐	188	Joe Mullen	2.00	.90	.25
☐	189	Jorgen Pettersson	.20	.09	.03
☐	190	Rob Ramage	.20	.09	.03
☐	191	Dwight Schofield	.20	.09	.03
☐	192	Brian Sutter	.30	.14	.04
☐	193	Doug Wickenheiser	.20	.09	.03
☐	194	Bob Carpenter	.25	.11	.03
☐	195	Dave Christian	.25	.11	.03
☐	196	Bob Gould	.20	.09	.03
☐	197	Mike Gartner	2.50	1.15	.30
☐	198	Bengt Gustafsson	.20	.09	.03
☐	199	Alan Haworth	.20	.09	.03
☐	200	Doug Jarvis	.20	.09	.03
☐	201	Al Jensen	.20	.09	.03
☐	202	Rod Langway	.30	.14	.04
☐	203	Craig Laughlin	.20	.09	.03
☐	204	Larry Murphy	1.00	.45	.13
☐	205	Pat Riggin	.20	.09	.03
☐	206	Scott Stevens	4.00	1.80	.50
☐	207	Michel Goulet AS	.35	.16	.04
☐	208	Wayne Gretzky AS	5.00	2.30	.60
☐	209	Mike Bossy AS	.40	.18	.05
☐	210	Rod Langway AS	.20	.09	.03
☐	211	Ray Bourque AS	1.50	.65	.19
☐	212	Tom Barrasso AS	2.00	.90	.25
☐	213	Mark Messier AS	2.00	.90	.25
☐	214	Bryan Trottier AS	.30	.14	.04
☐	215	Jari Kurri AS	.75	.35	.09
☐	216	Denis Potvin AS	.25	.11	.03
☐	217	Paul Coffey AS	1.50	.65	.19
☐	218	Pat Riggin AS	.20	.09	.03
☐	219	Ed Beers	.20	.09	.03
☐	220	Steve Bozek	.20	.09	.03
☐	221	Mike Eaves	.20	.09	.03
☐	222	Don Edwards	.20	.09	.03
☐	223	Kari Eloranta	.20	.09	.03
☐	224	Dave Hindmarch	.20	.09	.03
☐	225	Jim Jackson	.20	.09	.03
☐	226	Steve Konroyd	.20	.09	.03
☐	227	Richard Kromm	.20	.09	.03
☐	228	Rejean Lemelin	.25	.11	.03
☐	229	Hakan Loob	1.50	.65	.19
☐	230	Jamie Macoun	1.00	.45	.13
☐	231	Lanny McDonald	.30	.14	.04
☐	232	Kent Nilsson	.25	.11	.03
☐	233	Jim Peplinski	.20	.09	.03
☐	234	Dan Quinn	.50	.23	.06
☐	235	Paul Reinhart	.20	.09	.03
☐	236	Doug Risebrough	.20	.09	.03
☐	237	Steve Tambellini	.20	.09	.03
☐	238	Glenn Anderson	1.50	.65	.19
☐	239	Paul Coffey	4.00	1.80	.50
☐	240	Lee Fogolin	.20	.09	.03
☐	241	Grant Fuhr	4.00	1.80	.50
☐	242	Randy Gregg	.25	.11	.03
☐	243	Wayne Gretzky	20.00	9.00	2.50
☐	244	Charlie Huddy	.25	.11	.03
☐	245	Pat Hughes	.20	.09	.03
☐	246	Dave Hunter	.20	.09	.03
☐	247	Don Jackson	.20	.09	.03
☐	248	Mike Krushelnyski	.30	.14	.04
☐	249	Jari Kurri	3.00	1.35	.40
☐	250	Willy Lindstrom	.20	.09	.03
☐	251	Kevin Lowe	.60	.25	.08
☐	252	Dave Lumley	.20	.09	.03
☐	253	Kevin McClelland	.20	.09	.03
☐	254	Mark Messier	8.00	3.60	1.00
☐	255	Andy Moog	4.00	1.80	.50
☐	256	Jaroslav Pouzar	.20	.09	.03
☐	257	Guy Carbonneau	2.00	.90	.25
☐	258	John Chabot	.20	.09	.03
☐	259	Chris Chelios	15.00	6.75	1.90
☐	260	Lucien Deblois	.20	.09	.03
☐	261	Bob Gainey	.25	.11	.03
☐	262	Rick Green	.20	.09	.03
☐	263	Jean Hamel	.20	.09	.03
☐	264	Guy Lafleur	1.00	.45	.13
☐	265	Craig Ludwig	.20	.09	.03
☐	266	Pierre Mondou	.20	.09	.03
☐	267	Mats Naslund	.50	.23	.06
☐	268	Chris Nilan	.35	.16	.04
☐	269	Steve Penney	.25	.11	.03
☐	270	Larry Robinson	.30	.14	.04
☐	271	Bill Root	.20	.09	.03
☐	272	Steve Shutt	.30	.14	.04
☐	273	Bobby Smith	.30	.14	.04
☐	274	Mario Tremblay	.20	.09	.03
☐	275	Ryan Walter	.20	.09	.03
☐	276	Bo Berglund	.20	.09	.03
☐	277	Dan Bouchard	.25	.11	.03
☐	278	Alain Cote	.20	.09	.03
☐	279	Andre Dore	.20	.09	.03
☐	280	Michel Goulet	1.00	.45	.13
☐	281	Dale Hunter	.50	.23	.06
☐	282	Mario Marois	.20	.09	.03
☐	283	Tony McKegney	.20	.09	.03
☐	284	Randy Moller	.20	.09	.03
☐	285	Wilf Paiement	.25	.11	.03
☐	286	Pat Price	.20	.09	.03

☐	287	Normand Rochefort	.20	.09	.03
☐	288	Andre Savard	.20	.09	.03
☐	289	Richard Sevigny	.20	.09	.03
☐	290	Louis Sleigher	.20	.09	.03
☐	291	Anton Stastny	.25	.11	.03
☐	292	Marian Stastny	.25	.11	.03
☐	293	Peter Stastny	2.00	.90	.25
☐	294	Blake Wesley	.20	.09	.03
☐	295	John Anderson	.20	.09	.03
☐	296	Jim Benning	.20	.09	.03
☐	297	Allan Bester UER	.35	.16	.04
		(Name misspelled Alan on both sides)			
☐	298	Rich Costello	.20	.09	.03
☐	299	Dan Daoust	.20	.09	.03
☐	300	Bill Derlago	.20	.09	.03
☐	301	Dave Farrish	.20	.09	.03
☐	302	Stewart Gavin	.20	.09	.03
☐	303	Gaston Gingras	.20	.09	.03
☐	304	Jim Korn	.20	.09	.03
☐	305	Gary Leeman	.75	.35	.09
☐	306	Terry Martin	.20	.09	.03
☐	307	Gary Nylund	.30	.14	.04
☐	308	Mike Palmateer	.20	.09	.03
☐	309	Walt Poddubny	.25	.11	.03
☐	310	Rick St.Croix	.20	.09	.03
☐	311	Borje Salming	.30	.14	.04
☐	312	Greg Terrion	.20	.09	.03
☐	313	Rick Vaive	.25	.11	.03
☐	314	Richard Brodeur	.25	.11	.03
☐	315	Jiri Bubla	.20	.09	.03
☐	316	Ron Delorme	.20	.09	.03
☐	317	John Garrett	.20	.09	.03
☐	318	Jere Gillis	.20	.09	.03
☐	319	Thomas Gradin	.20	.09	.03
☐	320	Doug Halward	.20	.09	.03
☐	321	Rick Lanz	.20	.09	.03
☐	322	Moe Lemay	.20	.09	.03
☐	323	Gary Lupul	.20	.09	.03
☐	324	Al MacAdam	.20	.09	.03
☐	325	Rob McClanahan	.20	.09	.03
☐	326	Peter McNab	.25	.11	.03
☐	327	Cam Neely	40.00	18.00	5.00
☐	328	Darcy Rota	.20	.09	.03
☐	329	Andy Schliebener	.20	.09	.03
☐	330	Stan Smyl	.25	.11	.03
☐	331	Patrik Sundstrom	.25	.11	.03
☐	332	Tony Tanti	.25	.11	.03
☐	333	Scott Arniel	.20	.09	.03
☐	334	Dave Babych	.25	.11	.03
☐	335	Laurie Boschman	.20	.09	.03
☐	336	Wade Campbell	.20	.09	.03
☐	337	Randy Carlyle	.25	.11	.03
☐	338	Jordy Douglas	.20	.09	.03
☐	339	Dale Hawerchuk	3.50	1.55	.45
☐	340	Morris Lukowich	.20	.09	.03
☐	341	Bengt Lundholm	.20	.09	.03
☐	342	Paul MacLean	.25	.11	.03
☐	343	Andrew McBain	.20	.09	.03
☐	344	Brian Mullen	.35	.16	.04
☐	345	Robert Picard	.20	.09	.03
☐	346	Doug Smail	.20	.09	.03
☐	347	Doug Soetaert	.20	.09	.03
☐	348	Thomas Steen	.25	.11	.03
☐	349	Perry Turnbull	.20	.09	.03
☐	350	Tim Watters	.20	.09	.03
☐	351	Tim Young	.20	.09	.03
☐	352	Boston Bruins	.25	.11	.03
		Rick Middleton			
☐	353	Buffalo Sabres	3.00	1.35	.40
		Dave Andreychuk			
☐	354	Calgary Flames	.20	.09	.03
		Ed Beers			
☐	355	Chicago Blackhawks	.35	.16	.04
		Denis Savard			
☐	356	Detroit Red Wings	.20	.09	.03
		John Ogrodnick			
☐	357	Edmonton Oilers	5.00	2.30	.60
		Wayne Gretzky			
☐	358	Los Angeles Kings	.25	.11	.03
		Charlie Simmer			
☐	359	Minnesota North Stars	.50	.23	.06
		Brian Bellows			
☐	360	Montreal Canadiens	.40	.18	.05
		Guy Lafleur			
☐	361	New Jersey Devils	.20	.09	.03
		Mel Bridgman			
☐	362	New York Islanders	.40	.18	.05
		Mike Bossy			
☐	363	New York Rangers	.25	.11	.03
		Pierre Larouche			
☐	364	Philadelphia Flyers	.25	.11	.03
		Tim Kerr			
☐	365	Pittsburgh Penguins	.20	.09	.03
		Mike Bullard			
☐	366	Quebec Nordiques	.35	.16	.04
		Michel Goulet			
☐	367	St. Louis Blues UER	.50	.23	.06
		Bernie Federko			
		Joe Mullen			
		(Names reversed)			
☐	368	Toronto Maple Leafs	.20	.09	.03
		Rick Vaive			
☐	369	Vancouver Canucks	.20	.09	.03
		Tony Tanti			
☐	370	Washington Capitals	.60	.25	.08
		Mike Gartner			
☐	371	Winnipeg Jets	.20	.09	.03
		Paul MacLean			
☐	372	Hartford Whalers	.20	.09	.03
		Sylvain Turgeon			
☐	373	Art Ross Trophy	5.00	2.30	.60
		Wayne Gretzky			
☐	374	Hart Trophy	5.00	2.30	.60
		Wayne Gretzky			
☐	375	Calder Trophy	2.00	.90	.25
		Tom Barasso			
☐	376	Lady Byng Trophy	.40	.18	.05
		Mike Bossy			
☐	377	Norris Trophy	.20	.09	.03
		Rod Langway			
☐	378	Masterton Trophy	.20	.09	.03
		Brad Park			
☐	379	Vezina Trophy	2.00	.90	.25
		Tom Barasso			
☐	380	Scoring Leaders	5.00	2.30	.60
		Wayne Gretzky			
☐	381	Goals Leaders	5.00	2.30	.60
		Wayne Gretzky			
☐	382	Assists Leaders	5.00	2.30	.60
		Wayne Gretzky			
☐	383	Power Play	5.00	2.30	.60
		Goal Leaders			
		Wayne Gretzky			
☐	384	Game Winning	.35	.16	.04
		Goal Leaders			
		Michel Goulet			
☐	385	Rookie Scoring	7.00	3.10	.85
		Leaders UER			
		Steve Yzerman			
		(Gilmour misspelled as Gilmore on reverse)			
☐	386	Goals Against	.20	.09	.03
		Average Leaders			
		Pat Riggin			
☐	387	Save Percentage	.20	.09	.03
		Leaders			
		Rollie Melanson			
☐	388	Wayne Gretzky RB	5.00	2.30	.60
		Scores in 51			
		Straight Games			
☐	389	Denis Potvin RB	.20	.09	.03
		20 Goals, Eight			
		Seasons, Defenseman			
☐	390	Brad Park RB	.20	.09	.03
		Most Career Assists,			
		Defenseman			
☐	391	Michel Goulet RB	.35	.16	.04
		Most Points, Season,			
		Left Wing			
☐	392	Pat LaFontaine RB	5.00	2.30	.60
		Rookie Scoring Mark			
☐	393	Dale Hawerchuk RB	.75	.35	.09
		Five Assists, Period			
☐	394	Checklist 1-132	2.00	.20	.04
☐	395	Checklist 133-264 UER	2.00	.20	.04
		(185 Gilmore)			
☐	396	Checklist 265-396	2.00	.20	.04

1985-86 O-Pee-Chee

The 1985-86 O-Pee-Chee set contains 264-cards. Cards measure 2 1/2" by 3 1/2". The fronts have player name and position at the bottom with team logo at the top right or left. Bilingual backs contain yealy and career stats and highlights. Wax boxes had cards printed on the bottom with four players per box. These wax box cards are "lettered" A-P rather than numbered. The set is considered complete without these wax box cards. The key Rookie Card in this

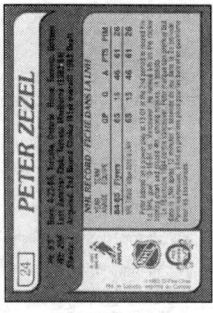

set is that of Mario Lemieux. Other Rookie Cards include Kevin Dineen, Dave Ellett, Kelly Hrudey, Al Iafrate, Al MacInnis, Kirk Muller, Tomas Sandstrom and Peter Zezel. Printed later than Topps, O-Pee-Chee was able to issue a memorial card to the late Pelle Lindbergh. Beware when purchasing the Rookie Card of Mario Lemieux as it has been counterfeited.

		MINT	EXC	G-VG
	COMPLETE SET (264)	650.00	300.00	80.00
	COMMON PLAYER (1-264)	.30	.14	.04
☐ 1	Lanny McDonald	.60	.25	.08
☐ 2	Mike O'Connell	.30	.14	.04
☐ 3	Curt Fraser	.30	.14	.04
☐ 4	Steve Penney	.30	.14	.04
☐ 5	Brian Engblom	.30	.14	.04
☐ 6	Ron Sutter	.35	.16	.04
☐ 7	Joe Mullen	1.75	.80	.22
☐ 8	Rod Langway	.35	.16	.04
☐ 9	Mario Lemieux	400.00	180.00	50.00
☐ 10	Dave Babych	.30	.14	.04
☐ 11	Bob Nystrom	.30	.14	.04
☐ 12	Andy Moog	3.00	1.35	.40
☐ 13	Dino Ciccarelli	1.00	.45	.13
☐ 14	Dwight Foster	.30	.14	.04
☐ 15	James Patrick	.35	.16	.04
☐ 16	Thomas Gradin	.30	.14	.04
☐ 17	Mike Foligno	.35	.16	.04
☐ 18	Mario Gosselin	.40	.18	.05
☐ 19	Mike Zuke	.30	.14	.04
☐ 20	John Anderson	.30	.14	.04
☐ 21	Dave Pichette	.30	.14	.04
☐ 22	Nick Fotiu	.35	.16	.04
☐ 23	Tom Lysiak	.30	.14	.04
☐ 24	Peter Zezel	3.00	1.35	.40
☐ 25	Denis Potvin	.50	.23	.06
☐ 26	Bob Carpenter	.35	.16	.04
☐ 27	Murray Bannerman	.30	.14	.04
☐ 28	Gordie Roberts	.30	.14	.04
☐ 29	Steve Yzerman	25.00	11.50	3.10
☐ 30	Phil Russell	.30	.14	.04
☐ 31	Peter Stastny	1.50	.65	.19
☐ 32	Craig Ramsay	.30	.14	.04
☐ 33	Terry Ruskowski	.30	.14	.04
☐ 34	Kevin Dineen	7.00	3.10	.85
☐ 35	Mark Howe	.35	.16	.04
☐ 36	Glenn Resch	.35	.16	.04
☐ 37	Danny Gare	.30	.14	.04
☐ 38	Doug Bodger	1.00	.45	.13
☐ 39	Mike Rogers	.35	.16	.04
☐ 40	Ray Bourque	4.00	1.80	.50
☐ 41	John Tonelli	.35	.16	.04
☐ 42	Mel Bridgman	.30	.14	.04
☐ 43	Sylvain Turgeon	.35	.16	.04
☐ 44	Mark Johnson	.30	.14	.04
☐ 45	Doug Wilson	.35	.16	.04
☐ 46	Mike Gartner	3.00	1.35	.40
☐ 47	Brent Peterson	.30	.14	.04
☐ 48	Paul Reinhart	.30	.14	.04
☐ 49	Mike Krushelnyski	.35	.16	.04
☐ 50	Brian Bellows	2.00	.90	.25
☐ 51	Chris Chelios	5.00	2.30	.60
☐ 52	Barry Pederson	.30	.14	.04
☐ 53	Murray Craven	.35	.16	.04
☐ 54	Pierre Larouche	.35	.16	.04
☐ 55	Reed Larson	.35	.16	.04
☐ 56	Pat Verbeek	1.50	.65	.19
☐ 57	Randy Carlyle	.35	.16	.04
☐ 58	Ray Neufeld	.30	.14	.04
☐ 59	Keith Brown	.30	.14	.04
☐ 60	Bryan Trottier	.50	.23	.06
☐ 61	Jim Fox	.30	.14	.04
☐ 62	Scott Stevens	4.00	1.80	.50
☐ 63	Phil Housley	2.00	.90	.25
☐ 64	Rick Middleton	.35	.16	.04
☐ 65	Steve Payne	.30	.14	.04
☐ 66	Dave Lewis	.30	.14	.04
☐ 67	Mike Bullard	.35	.16	.04
☐ 68	Stan Smyl	.35	.16	.04
☐ 69	Mark Pavelich	.30	.14	.04
☐ 70	John Ogrodnick	.35	.16	.04
☐ 71	Bill Derlago	.30	.14	.04
☐ 72	Brad Marsh	.35	.16	.04
☐ 73	Denis Savard	1.00	.45	.13
☐ 74	Mark Fusco	.30	.14	.04
☐ 75	Pete Peeters	.35	.16	.04
☐ 76	Doug Gilmour	25.00	11.50	3.10
☐ 77	Mike Ramsey	.30	.14	.04
☐ 78	Anton Stastny	.30	.14	.04
☐ 79	Steve Kasper	.30	.14	.04
☐ 80	Bryan Erickson	.30	.14	.04
☐ 81	Clark Gillies	.30	.14	.04
☐ 82	Keith Acton	.30	.14	.04
☐ 83	Pat Flatley	.35	.16	.04
☐ 84	Kirk Muller	15.00	6.75	1.90
☐ 85	Paul Coffey	3.50	1.55	.45
☐ 86	Ed Olczyk	1.50	.65	.19
☐ 87	Charlie Simmer	.35	.16	.04
☐ 88	Mike Liut	.35	.16	.04
☐ 89	Dave Maloney	.30	.14	.04
☐ 90	Marcel Dionne	.50	.23	.06
☐ 91	Tim Kerr	.35	.16	.04
☐ 92	Ivan Boldirev	.30	.14	.04
☐ 93	Ken Morrow	.30	.14	.04
☐ 94	Don Maloney	.30	.14	.04
☐ 95	Rejean Lemelin	.35	.16	.04
☐ 96	Curt Giles	.30	.14	.04
☐ 97	Bob Bourne	.30	.14	.04
☐ 98	Joe Cirella	.30	.14	.04
☐ 99	Dave Christian	.35	.16	.04
☐ 100	Darryl Sutter	.30	.14	.04
☐ 101	Kelly Kisio	.50	.23	.06
☐ 102	Mats Naslund	.35	.16	.04
☐ 103	Joel Quenneville	.30	.14	.04
☐ 104	Bernie Federko	.40	.18	.05
☐ 105	Tom Barrasso	3.50	1.55	.45
☐ 106	Rick Vaive	.35	.16	.04
☐ 107	Brent Sutter	.50	.23	.06
☐ 108	Wayne Babych	.30	.14	.04
☐ 109	Dale Hawerchuk	3.00	1.35	.40
☐ 110	Pelle Lindbergh (Memorial)	15.00	6.75	1.90
☐ 111	Dennis Maruk	.35	.16	.04
☐ 112	Reijo Ruotsalainen	.30	.14	.04
☐ 113	Tom Fergus	.35	.16	.04
☐ 114	Bob Murray	.30	.14	.04
☐ 115	Patrik Sundstrom	.30	.14	.04
☐ 116	Ron Duguay	.35	.16	.04
☐ 117	Alan Haworth	.30	.14	.04
☐ 118	Greg Malone	.30	.14	.04
☐ 119	Bill Hajt	.30	.14	.04
☐ 120	Wayne Gretzky	25.00	11.50	3.10
☐ 121	Craig Redmond	.30	.14	.04
☐ 122	Kelly Hrudey	7.00	3.10	.85
☐ 123	Tomas Sandstrom	8.00	3.60	1.00
☐ 124	Neal Broten	.35	.16	.04
☐ 125	Moe Mantha	.30	.14	.04
☐ 126	Greg Gilbert	.30	.14	.04
☐ 127	Bruce Driver	1.50	.65	.19
☐ 128	Dave Poulin	.35	.16	.04
☐ 129	Morris Lukowich	.30	.14	.04
☐ 130	Mike Bossy	1.00	.45	.13
☐ 131	Larry Playfair	.30	.14	.04
☐ 132	Steve Larmer	3.50	1.55	.45
☐ 133	Doug Keans	.30	.14	.04
☐ 134	Bob Manno	.30	.14	.04
☐ 135	Brian Sutter	.40	.18	.05
☐ 136	Pat Riggin	.30	.14	.04
☐ 137	Pat LaFontaine	18.00	8.00	2.30
☐ 138	Barry Beck	.35	.16	.04
☐ 139	Rich Preston	.30	.14	.04
☐ 140	Ron Francis	2.00	.90	.25
☐ 141	Brian Propp	.40	.18	.05
☐ 142	Don Beaupre	.35	.16	.04
☐ 143	Dave Andreychuk	10.00	4.50	1.25
☐ 144	Ed Beers	.30	.14	.04
☐ 145	Paul MacLean	.35	.16	.04
☐ 146	Troy Murray	.60	.25	.08
☐ 147	Larry Robinson	.40	.18	.05
☐ 148	Bernie Nicholls	1.50	.65	.19
☐ 149	Glen Hanlon	.35	.16	.04
☐ 150	Michel Goulet	1.00	.45	.13
☐ 151	Doug Jarvis	.30	.14	.04

☐	152	Warren Young	.30	.14	.04
☐	153	Tony Tanti	.35	.16	.04
☐	154	Tomas Jonsson	.30	.14	.04
☐	155	Jari Kurri	2.50	1.15	.30
☐	156	Tony McKegney	.30	.14	.04
☐	157	Greg Stefan	.30	.14	.04
☐	158	Brad McCrimmon	.30	.14	.04
☐	159	Keith Crowder	.30	.14	.04
☐	160	Gilbert Perreault	.30	.14	.04
☐	161	Tim Bothwell	.30	.14	.04
☐	162	Bob Crawford	.30	.14	.04
☐	163	Paul Gagne	.30	.14	.04
☐	164	Dan Daoust	.30	.14	.04
☐	165	Checklist 1-132	4.00	.40	.08
☐	166	Tim Bernhardt	.30	.14	.04
☐	167	Gord Kluzak	.30	.14	.04
☐	168	Glenn Anderson	1.50	.65	.19
☐	169	Bob Gainey	.35	.16	.04
☐	170	Brent Ashton	.35	.16	.04
☐	171	Ron Flockhart	.30	.14	.04
☐	172	Gary Nylund	.30	.14	.04
☐	173	Moe Lemay	.30	.14	.04
☐	174	Bob Sauve	.30	.14	.04
☐	175	Doug Smail	.30	.14	.04
☐	176	Dan Quinn	.35	.16	.04
☐	177	Mark Messier	8.00	3.60	1.00
☐	178	Jay Wells	.75	.35	.09
☐	179	Dale Hunter	.50	.23	.06
☐	180	Richard Brodeur	.35	.16	.04
☐	181	Bobby Smith	.35	.16	.04
☐	182	Ron Greschner	.30	.14	.04
☐	183	Don Edwards	.30	.14	.04
☐	184	Hakan Loob	.30	.14	.04
☐	185	Dave Ellett	6.00	2.70	.75
☐	186	Denis Herron	.30	.14	.04
☐	187	Charlie Huddy	.35	.16	.04
☐	188	Ilkka Sinisalo	.30	.14	.04
☐	189	Doug Halward	.30	.14	.04
☐	190	Craig Laughlin	.30	.14	.04
☐	191	Carey Wilson	.50	.23	.06
☐	192	Craig Ludwig	.30	.14	.04
☐	193	Bob MacMillan	.30	.14	.04
☐	194	Mario Marois	.30	.14	.04
☐	195	Brian Mullen	.35	.16	.04
☐	196	Rob Ramage	.30	.14	.04
☐	197	Rick Lanz	.30	.14	.04
☐	198	Miroslav Frycer	.30	.14	.04
☐	199	Randy Gregg	.30	.14	.04
☐	200	Corrado Micalef	.30	.14	.04
☐	201	Jamie Macoun	.35	.16	.04
☐	202	Bob Brooke	.30	.14	.04
☐	203	Billy Carroll	.30	.14	.04
☐	204	Brian MacLellan	.30	.14	.04
☐	205	Alain Cote	.35	.16	.04
☐	206	Thomas Steen	.35	.16	.04
☐	207	Grant Fuhr	3.00	1.35	.40
☐	208	Rich Sutter	.35	.16	.04
☐	209	Al MacAdam	.30	.14	.04
☐	210	Al Iafrate	20.00	9.00	2.50
☐	211	Pierre Mondou	.30	.14	.04
☐	212	Randy Hillier	.30	.14	.04
☐	213	Mike Eaves	.30	.14	.04
☐	214	Dave Taylor	.40	.18	.05
☐	215	Robert Picard	.30	.14	.04
☐	216	Randy Ladouceur	.30	.14	.04
☐	217	Willy Lindstrom	.30	.14	.04
☐	218	Torrie Robertson	.30	.14	.04
☐	219	Tom Kurvers	1.00	.45	.13
☐	220	John Garrett	.30	.14	.04
☐	221	Greg Millen	.30	.14	.04
☐	222	Richard Kromm	.30	.14	.04
☐	223	Bob Janecyk	.30	.14	.04
☐	224	Brad Maxwell	.30	.14	.04
☐	225	Mike McPhee	2.00	.90	.25
☐	226	Brian Hayward	1.75	.80	.22
☐	227	Duane Sutter	.30	.14	.04
☐	228	Cam Neely	15.00	6.75	1.90
☐	229	Doug Wickenheiser	.30	.14	.04
☐	230	Rollie Melanson	.30	.14	.04
☐	231	Bruce Bell	.30	.14	.04
☐	232	Harold Snepsts	.35	.16	.04
☐	233	Guy Carbonneau	1.00	.45	.13
☐	234	Doug Sulliman	.30	.14	.04
☐	235	Lee Fogolin	.30	.14	.04
☐	236	Larry Murphy	1.00	.45	.13
☐	237	Al MacInnis	40.00	18.00	5.00
☐	238	Don Lever	.30	.14	.04
☐	239	Kevin Lowe	.75	.35	.09
☐	240	Randy Moller	.30	.14	.04
☐	241	Doug Lidster	1.00	.45	.13
☐	242	Craig Hartsburg	.30	.14	.04
☐	243	Doug Risebrough	.30	.14	.04
☐	244	John Chabot	.30	.14	.04
☐	245	Mario Tremblay	.30	.14	.04
☐	246	Dan Bouchard	.35	.16	.04
☐	247	Doug Shedden	.30	.14	.04
☐	248	Borje Salming	.35	.16	.04
☐	249	Aaron Broten	.30	.14	.04
☐	250	Jim Benning	.30	.14	.04
☐	251	Laurie Boschman	.30	.14	.04
☐	252	George McPhee	.30	.14	.04
☐	253	Mark Napier	.30	.14	.04
☐	254	Perry Turnbull	.30	.14	.04
☐	255	Warren Skorodenski	.30	.14	.04
☐	256	Checklist 133-264	4.00	.40	.08
☐	257	Goal Leaders Wayne Gretzky	6.00	2.70	.75
☐	258	Assist Leaders Wayne Gretzky	6.00	2.70	.75
☐	259	Scoring Leaders Wayne Gretzky	6.00	2.70	.75
☐	260	Power Play Goals Leaders Tim Kerr	.40	.18	.05
☐	261	Game Winning Goals Leaders Jari Kurri	.75	.35	.09
☐	262	Rookie Scoring Leaders Mario Lemieux	45.00	20.00	5.75
☐	263	Goals Against Average Leaders Tom Barrasso	1.50	.65	.19
☐	264	Save Percent Leaders Warren Skorodenski	.40	.18	.05

1985-86 O-Pee-Chee/Topps Box Bottoms

 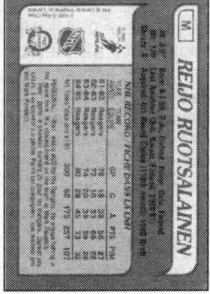

This sixteen-card set measures the standard card size, 2 1/2" by 3 1/2", and was issued in sets of four on the bottom of the 1985-86 O-Pee-Chee and Topps wax pack boxes. Complete box bottom panels are valued at a 25 percent premium above the prices listed below. The card back includes statistical information and is written in English and French for the O-Pee-Chee cards but English only for the Topps cards. The cards are lettered rather than numbered. The key card in the set is obviously Mario Lemieux, pictured in his Rookie Card year.

			MINT	EXC	G-VG
	COMPLETE SET (16)		80.00	32.00	8.00
	COMMON PLAYER (A-P)		.50	.20	.05
☐	A	Brian Bellows	1.00	.40	.10
☐	B	Ray Bourque	2.50	1.00	.25
☐	C	Bob Carpenter	.75	.30	.07
☐	D	Chris Chelios	2.50	1.00	.25
☐	E	Marcel Dionne	2.00	.80	.20
☐	F	Ron Francis	1.50	.60	.15
☐	G	Wayne Gretzky	20.00	8.00	2.00
☐	H	Tim Kerr	.75	.30	.07
☐	I	Mario Lemieux	50.00	20.00	5.00
☐	J	John Ogrodnick	.50	.20	.05
☐	K	Gilbert Perreault	1.25	.50	.12
☐	L	Glenn Resch	1.00	.40	.10
☐	M	Reijo Ruotsalainen	.50	.20	.05

☐ N	Brian Sutter	1.00	.40	.10
☐ O	John Tonelli	.50	.20	.05
☐ P	Doug Wilson	1.00	.40	.10

1986-87 O-Pee-Chee

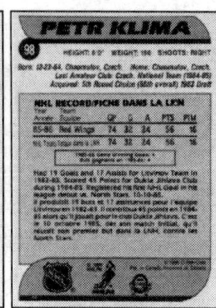

This 1986-87 O-Pee-Chee set consists of 264 cards. Cards measure 2 1/2" by 3 1/2". Card fronts feature player name, team, team logo and position at the bottom. Bilingual backs feature yearly and career statistics as well as the number of game winning goals scored in 1985-86. There were also 16 cards printed on the bottom of the wax pack boxes with four to a box. These cards are "lettered" A-P rather than numbered and are not considered part of the complete set. The key Rookie Card in this set is Patrick Roy. Other Rookie Cards include Wendel Clark, Russ Courtnall, Ray Ferraro, Dirk Graham, John MacLean, Craig MacTavish, Mike Ridley, Gary Suter, Steve Thomas, and John Vanbiesbrouck. Beware when purchasing the Wayne Gretzky card from this set as it has been counterfeited.

		MINT	EXC	G-VG
	COMPLETE SET (264)	250.00	115.00	31.00
	COMMON PLAYER (1-264)	.20	.09	.03
☐ 1	Ray Bourque	3.00	1.00	.30
☐ 2	Pat LaFontaine	8.00	3.60	1.00
☐ 3	Wayne Gretzky	20.00	9.00	2.50
☐ 4	Lindy Ruff	.20	.09	.03
☐ 5	Brad McCrimmon	.20	.09	.03
☐ 6	Dave(Tiger) Williams	.25	.11	.03
☐ 7	Denis Savard	.75	.35	.09
☐ 8	Lanny McDonald	.25	.11	.03
☐ 9	John Vanbiesbrouck	14.00	6.25	1.75
☐ 10	Greg Adams	3.00	1.35	.40
	New Jersey Devils			
☐ 11	Steve Yzerman	12.00	5.50	1.50
☐ 12	Craig Hartsburg	.20	.09	.03
☐ 13	John Anderson	.20	.09	.03
☐ 14	Bob Bourne	.20	.09	.03
☐ 15	Kjell Dahlin	.25	.11	.03
☐ 16	Dave Andreychuk	6.00	2.70	.75
☐ 17	Rob Ramage	.20	.09	.03
☐ 18	Ron Greschner	.20	.09	.03
☐ 19	Bruce Driver	.25	.11	.03
☐ 20	Peter Stastny	1.00	.45	.13
☐ 21	Dave Christian	.25	.11	.03
☐ 22	Doug Keans	.20	.09	.03
☐ 23	Scott Bjugstad	.20	.09	.03
☐ 24	Doug Bodger	.25	.11	.03
☐ 25	Troy Murray	.25	.11	.03
☐ 26	Al Iafrate	5.00	2.30	.60
☐ 27	Kelly Hrudey	2.00	.90	.25
☐ 28	Doug Jarvis	.20	.09	.03
☐ 29	Rich Sutter	.20	.09	.03
☐ 30	Marcel Dionne	.40	.18	.05
☐ 31	Curt Fraser	.20	.09	.03
☐ 32	Doug Lidster	.25	.11	.03
☐ 33	Brian MacLellan	.20	.09	.03
☐ 34	Barry Pederson	.20	.09	.03
☐ 35	Craig Laughlin	.20	.09	.03
☐ 36	Ilkka Sinisalo	.20	.09	.03
☐ 37	John MacLean	7.00	3.10	.85

☐ 38	Brian Mullen	.25	.11	.03
☐ 39	Duane Sutter	.20	.09	.03
☐ 40	Brian Engblom	.20	.09	.03
☐ 41	Chris Cichocki	.20	.09	.03
☐ 42	Gordie Roberts	.20	.09	.03
☐ 43	Ron Francis	1.00	.45	.13
☐ 44	Joe Mullen	.75	.35	.09
☐ 45	Moe Mantha	.20	.09	.03
☐ 46	Pat Verbeek	.50	.23	.06
☐ 47	Clint Malarchuk	1.00	.45	.13
☐ 48	Bob Brooke	.20	.09	.03
☐ 49	Darryl Sutter	.20	.09	.03
☐ 50	Stan Smyl	.25	.11	.03
☐ 51	Greg Stefan	.20	.09	.03
☐ 52	Bill Hajt	.20	.09	.03
☐ 53	Patrick Roy	140.00	65.00	17.50
☐ 54	Gord Kluzak	.20	.09	.03
☐ 55	Bob Froese	.20	.09	.03
☐ 56	Grant Fuhr	2.00	.90	.25
☐ 57	Mark Hunter	.20	.09	.03
☐ 58	Dana Murzyn	.30	.14	.04
☐ 59	Mike Gartner	1.25	.55	.16
☐ 60	Dennis Maruk	.25	.11	.03
☐ 61	Rich Preston	.20	.09	.03
☐ 62	Larry Robinson	.30	.14	.04
☐ 63	Dave Taylor	.30	.14	.04
☐ 64	Bob Murray	.20	.09	.03
☐ 65	Ken Morrow	.20	.09	.03
☐ 66	Mike Ridley	4.00	1.80	.50
☐ 67	John Tucker	.50	.23	.06
☐ 68	Miroslav Frycer	.20	.09	.03
☐ 69	Danny Gare	.20	.09	.03
☐ 70	Randy Burridge	1.50	.65	.19
☐ 71	Dave Poulin	.25	.11	.03
☐ 72	Brian Sutter	.30	.14	.04
☐ 73	Dave Babych	.20	.09	.03
☐ 74	Dale Hawerchuk	1.50	.65	.19
☐ 75	Brian Bellows	1.25	.55	.16
☐ 76	Dave Pasin	.20	.09	.03
☐ 77	Pete Peeters	.25	.11	.03
☐ 78	Tomas Jonsson	.20	.09	.03
☐ 79	Gilbert Perreault	.20	.09	.03
☐ 80	Glenn Anderson	1.00	.45	.13
☐ 81	Don Maloney	.20	.09	.03
☐ 82	Ed Olczyk	.35	.16	.04
☐ 83	Mike Bullard	.25	.11	.03
☐ 84	Tom Fergus	.20	.09	.03
☐ 85	Dave Lewis	.20	.09	.03
☐ 86	Brian Propp	.30	.14	.04
☐ 87	John Ogrodnick	.25	.11	.03
☐ 88	Kevin Dineen	1.50	.65	.19
☐ 89	Don Beaupre	.25	.11	.03
☐ 90	Mike Bossy	.75	.35	.09
☐ 91	Tom Barrasso	2.00	.90	.25
☐ 92	Michel Goulet	.50	.23	.06
☐ 93	Doug Gilmour	12.00	5.50	1.50
☐ 94	Kirk Muller	3.50	1.55	.45
☐ 95	Larry Melnyk	.20	.09	.03
☐ 96	Bob Gainey	.25	.11	.03
☐ 97	Steve Kasper	.20	.09	.03
☐ 98	Petr Klima	2.00	.90	.25
☐ 99	Neal Broten	.25	.11	.03
☐ 100	Al Secord	.25	.11	.03
☐ 101	Bryan Erickson	.20	.09	.03
☐ 102	Rejean Lemelin	.25	.11	.03
☐ 103	Sylvain Turgeon	.20	.09	.03
☐ 104	Bob Nystrom	.20	.09	.03
☐ 105	Bernie Federko	.30	.14	.04
☐ 106	Doug Wilson	.25	.11	.03
☐ 107	Alan Haworth	.20	.09	.03
☐ 108	Jari Kurri	1.50	.65	.19
☐ 109	Ron Sutter	.25	.11	.03
☐ 110	Reed Larson	.20	.09	.03
☐ 111	Terry Ruskowski	.20	.09	.03
☐ 112	Mark Johnson	.20	.09	.03
☐ 113	James Patrick	.25	.11	.03
☐ 114	Paul MacLean	.25	.11	.03
☐ 115	Mike Ramsey	.20	.09	.03
☐ 116	Kelly Kisio	.25	.11	.03
☐ 117	Brent Sutter	.25	.11	.03
☐ 118	Joel Quenneville	.20	.09	.03
☐ 119	Curt Giles	.20	.09	.03
☐ 120	Tony Tanti	.20	.09	.03
☐ 121	Doug Sulliman	.20	.09	.03
☐ 122	Mario Lemieux	80.00	36.00	10.00
☐ 123	Mark Howe	.25	.11	.03
☐ 124	Bob Sauve	.20	.09	.03
☐ 125	Anton Stastny	.20	.09	.03
☐ 126	Scott Stevens	2.50	1.15	.30
☐ 127	Mike Foligno	.25	.11	.03
☐ 128	Reijo Ruotsalainen	.20	.09	.03
☐ 129	Denis Potvin	.35	.16	.04
☐ 130	Keith Crowder	.20	.09	.03

□	131	Bob Janecyk	.20	.09	.03
□	132	John Tonelli	.25	.11	.03
□	133	Mike Liut	.25	.11	.03
□	134	Tim Kerr	.25	.11	.03
□	135	Al Jensen	.20	.09	.03
□	136	Mel Bridgman	.20	.09	.03
□	137	Paul Coffey	2.50	1.15	.30
□	138	Dino Ciccarelli	.75	.35	.09
□	139	Steve Larmer	1.50	.65	.19
□	140	Mike O'Connell	.20	.09	.03
□	141	Clark Gillies	.20	.09	.03
□	142	Phil Russell	.20	.09	.03
□	143	Dirk Graham	2.50	1.15	.30
□	144	Randy Carlyle	.25	.11	.03
□	145	Charlie Simmer	.25	.11	.03
□	146	Ron Flockhart	.20	.09	.03
□	147	Tom Laidlaw	.20	.09	.03
□	148	Dave Tippett	.50	.23	.06
□	149	Wendel Clark	30.00	13.50	3.80
□	150	Bob Carpenter	.25	.11	.03
□	151	Bill Watson	.20	.09	.03
□	152	Roberto Romano	.35	.16	.04
□	153	Doug Shedden	.20	.09	.03
□	154	Phil Housley	.75	.35	.09
□	155	Bryan Trottier	.35	.16	.04
□	156	Patrik Sundstrom	.20	.09	.03
□	157	Rick Middleton	.25	.11	.03
□	158	Glenn Resch	.25	.11	.03
□	159	Bernie Nicholls	1.00	.45	.13
□	160	Ray Ferraro	3.00	1.35	.40
□	161	Mats Naslund	.25	.11	.03
□	162	Pat Flatley	.20	.09	.03
□	163	Joe Cirella	.20	.09	.03
□	164	Rod Langway	.25	.11	.03
□	165	Checklist 1-132	2.00	.20	.04
□	166	Carey Wilson	.20	.09	.03
□	167	Murray Craven	.25	.11	.03
□	168	Paul Gillis	.20	.09	.03
□	169	Borje Salming	.25	.11	.03
□	170	Perry Turnbull	.20	.09	.03
□	171	Chris Chelios	3.00	1.35	.40
□	172	Keith Acton	.20	.09	.03
□	173	Al MacInnis	10.00	4.50	1.25
□	174	Russ Courtnall	7.00	3.10	.85
□	175	Brad Marsh	.25	.11	.03
□	176	Guy Carbonneau	.50	.23	.06
□	177	Ray Neufeld	.20	.09	.03
□	178	Craig MacTavish	2.50	1.15	.30
□	179	Rick Lanz	.20	.09	.03
□	180	Murray Bannerman	.20	.09	.03
□	181	Brent Ashton	.20	.09	.03
□	182	Jim Peplinski	.20	.09	.03
□	183	Mark Napier	.20	.09	.03
□	184	Laurie Boschman	.20	.09	.03
□	185	Larry Murphy	.75	.35	.09
□	186	Mark Messier	5.00	2.30	.60
□	187	Risto Siltanen	.20	.09	.03
□	188	Bobby Smith	.25	.11	.03
□	189	Gary Suter	3.00	1.35	.40
□	190	Peter Zezel	.60	.25	.08
□	191	Rick Vaive	.25	.11	.03
□	192	Dale Hunter	.25	.11	.03
□	193	Mike Krushelnyski	.25	.11	.03
□	194	Scott Arniel	.20	.09	.03
□	195	Larry Playfair	.20	.09	.03
□	196	Doug Risebrough	.20	.09	.03
□	197	Kevin Lowe	.50	.23	.06
□	198	Checklist 133-264	2.00	.20	.04
□	199	Chris Nilan	.25	.11	.03
□	200	Paul Cyr	.20	.09	.03
□	201	Ric Seiling	.20	.09	.03
□	202	Doug Smith	.20	.09	.03
□	203	Jamie Macoun	.20	.09	.03
□	204	Dan Quinn	.20	.09	.03
□	205	Paul Reinhart	.20	.09	.03
□	206	Keith Brown	.20	.09	.03
□	207	Jack O'Callahan	.20	.09	.03
□	208	Steve Richmond	.20	.09	.03
□	209	Warren Young	.20	.09	.03
□	210	Lee Fogolin	.20	.09	.03
□	211	Charlie Huddy	.20	.09	.03
□	212	Andy Moog	2.00	.90	.25
□	213	Wayne Babych	.20	.09	.03
□	214	Torrie Robertson	.20	.09	.03
□	215	Jim Fox	.20	.09	.03
□	216	Phil Sykes	.20	.09	.03
□	217	Jay Wells	.20	.09	.03
□	218	Dave Langevin	.20	.09	.03
□	219	Steve Payne	.20	.09	.03
□	220	Craig Ludwig	.20	.09	.03
□	221	Mike McPhee	.50	.23	.06
□	222	Steve Penney	.20	.09	.03
□	223	Mario Tremblay	.20	.09	.03

□	224	Ryan Walter	.20	.09	.03
□	225	Alain Chevrier	.20	.09	.03
□	226	Uli Hiemer	.20	.09	.03
□	227	Tim Higgins	.20	.09	.03
□	228	Billy Smith	.25	.11	.03
□	229	Richard Kromm	.20	.09	.03
□	230	Tomas Sandstrom	2.00	.90	.25
□	231	Jim Johnson	.35	.16	.04
□	232	Willy Lindstrom	.20	.09	.03
□	233	Alain Cote	.20	.09	.03
□	234	Gilbert Delorme	.20	.09	.03
□	235	Mario Gosselin	.20	.09	.03
□	236	David Shaw	.35	.16	.04
□	237	Dave Barr	.30	.14	.04
□	238	Ed Beers	.20	.09	.03
□	239	Charlie Bourgeois	.20	.09	.03
□	240	Rick Wamsley	.25	.11	.03
□	241	Dan Daoust	.20	.09	.03
□	242	Brad Maxwell	.20	.09	.03
□	243	Gary Nylund	.20	.09	.03
□	244	Greg Terrion	.20	.09	.03
□	245	Steve Thomas	5.00	2.30	.60
□	246	Richard Brodeur	.25	.11	.03
□	247	Joel Otto UER	1.50	.65	.19
		(Photo actually			
		Moe Lemay)			
□	248	Doug Halward	.20	.09	.03
□	249	Moe Lemay UER	.35	.16	.04
		(Photo actually			
		Joel Otto)			
□	250	Cam Neely	8.00	3.60	1.00
□	251	Brent Peterson	.20	.09	.03
□	252	Petri Skriko	.30	.14	.04
□	253	Greg C. Adams	.20	.09	.03
		Washington Capitals			
□	254	Bill Derlago	.20	.09	.03
□	255	Brian Hayward	.50	.23	.06
□	256	Doug Smail	.20	.09	.03
□	257	Thomas Steen	.25	.11	.03
□	258	Goals Leaders	.50	.23	.06
		Jari Kurri			
□	259	Assists Leaders	5.00	2.30	.60
		Wayne Gretzky			
□	260	Points Leaders	5.00	2.30	.60
		Wayne Gretzky			
□	261	Power Play	.30	.14	.04
		Goal Leaders			
		Tim Kerr			
□	262	Rookie Leaders	.30	.14	.04
		Kjell Dahlin			
□	263	Goals Against	.30	.14	.04
		Average Leaders			
		Bob Froese			
□	264	Save Pct. Leaders	.30	.14	.04
		Bob Froese			

1986-87 O-Pee-Chee/Topps
Box Bottoms

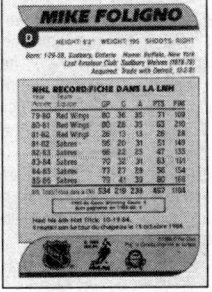

This sixteen-card set measures the standard card size 2 1/2"
by 3 1/2" and was issued in sets of four on the bottom of the
1986-87 O-Pee-Chee and Topps wax pack boxes. Complete
box bottom panels are valued at a 25 percent premium
above the prices listed below. This set features some of the
leading NHL players including Mike Bossy, Wayne Gretzky,

Mario Lemieux, and Bryan Trottier. The front presents a color action photo with various color borders, with the team's logo in the lower right hand corner. The back includes statistical information, is written in English and French (for the O-Pee-Chee cards and English only for the Topps cards), and is printed in blue with black ink. The cards are lettered rather than numbered.

	MINT	EXC	G-VG
COMPLETE SET (16)	35.00	14.00	3.50
COMMON PLAYER (A-P)	.40	.16	.04

		MINT	EXC	G-VG
☐	A Greg Adams	.60	.24	.06
☐	B Mike Bossy	1.50	.60	.15
☐	C Dave Christian	.60	.24	.06
☐	D Mike Foligno	.40	.16	.04
☐	E Michel Goulet	1.00	.40	.10
☐	F Wayne Gretzky	15.00	6.00	1.50
☐	G Tim Kerr	.60	.24	.06
☐	H Jari Kurri	1.00	.40	.10
☐	I Mario Lemieux	15.00	6.00	1.50
☐	J Lanny McDonald	1.00	.40	.10
☐	K Bernie Nicholls	.75	.30	.07
☐	L Mike Ridley	1.00	.40	.10
☐	M Larry Robinson	1.00	.40	.10
☐	N Denis Savard	.75	.30	.07
☐	O Brian Sutter	.50	.20	.05
☐	P Bryan Trottier	1.25	.50	.12

1987-88 O-Pee-Chee

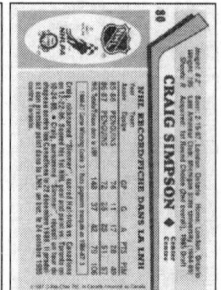

Card fronts in this 264-card set feature a bottom border that contains the design of a hockey stick with which the player's name appears. Also, the team name appears within a puck. Cards measure the standard 2 1/2" by 3 1/2". Bilingual backs contain yearly, career statistics and highlights. Wax boxes have four cards on the bottom. These cards are similar to the regular issue cards but are "lettered" A-P rather than numbered. The set is considered complete without the wax box cards. Rookie Cards in this set include Jimmy Carson, Vincent Damphousse, Kevin Hatcher, Ron Hextall, Claude Lemieux, Marty McSorley, Adam Oates, Bill Ranford, Stephane Richer, Luc Robitaille, Ulf Samuelsson, Craig Simpson, Esa Tikkanen, Rick Tocchet, and Mike Vernon. Beware when purchasing the cards of Wayne Gretzky, Adam Oates and Luc Robitaille from this set as they have been counterfeited.

	MINT	EXC	G-VG
COMPLETE SET (264)	250.00	115.00	31.00
COMPLETE FACT.SET (264)	275.00	125.00	34.00
COMMON PLAYER (1-264)	.15	.07	.02

		MINT	EXC	G-VG
☐	1 Denis Potvin	.40	.18	.05
☐	2 Rick Tocchet	14.00	6.25	1.75
☐	3 Dave Andreychuk	3.00	1.35	.40
☐	4 Stan Smyl	.20	.09	.03
☐	5 Dave Babych	.15	.07	.02
☐	6 Pat Verbeek	.35	.16	.04
☐	7 Esa Tikkanen	10.00	4.50	1.25

		MINT	EXC	G-VG
☐	8 Mike Ridley	.60	.25	.08
☐	9 Randy Carlyle UER	.20	.09	.03
	(Misspelled Calryle on card front)			
☐	10 Greg Paslawski	.35	.16	.04
☐	11 Neal Broten	.20	.09	.03
☐	12 Wendel Clark	6.00	2.70	.75
☐	13 Bill Ranford	12.00	5.50	1.50
☐	14 Doug Wilson	.20	.09	.03
☐	15 Mario Lemieux	40.00	18.00	5.00
☐	16 Mats Naslund	.20	.09	.03
☐	17 Mel Bridgman	.15	.07	.02
☐	18 James Patrick	.15	.07	.02
☐	19 Rollie Melanson	.15	.07	.02
☐	20 Lanny McDonald	.25	.11	.03
☐	21 Peter Stastny	.75	.35	.09
☐	22 Murray Craven	.15	.07	.02
☐	23 Ulf Samuelsson	5.00	2.30	.60
☐	24 Michael Thelven	.15	.07	.02
☐	25 Scott Stevens	1.25	.55	.16
☐	26 Petr Klima	.50	.23	.06
☐	27 Brent Sutter	.20	.09	.03
☐	28 Tomas Sandstrom	1.25	.55	.16
☐	29 Tim Bothwell	.15	.07	.02
☐	30 Bob Carpenter	.20	.09	.03
☐	31 Brian MacLellan	.15	.07	.02
☐	32 John Chabot	.15	.07	.02
☐	33 Phil Housley	.50	.23	.06
☐	34 Patrik Sundstrom	.15	.07	.02
☐	35 Dave Ellett	1.00	.45	.13
☐	36 John Vanbiesbrouck	4.00	1.80	.50
☐	37 Dave Lewis	.15	.07	.02
☐	38 Tom McCarthy	.15	.07	.02
☐	39 Dave Poulin	.20	.09	.03
☐	40 Mike Foligno	.20	.09	.03
☐	41 Gordie Roberts	.15	.07	.02
☐	42 Luc Robitaille	50.00	23.00	6.25
☐	43 Duane Sutter	.15	.07	.02
☐	44 Pete Peeters	.20	.09	.03
☐	45 John Anderson	.15	.07	.02
☐	46 Aaron Broten	.15	.07	.02
☐	47 Keith Brown	.15	.07	.02
☐	48 Bobby Smith	.20	.09	.03
☐	49 Don Maloney	.15	.07	.02
☐	50 Mark Hunter	.15	.07	.02
☐	51 Moe Mantha	.15	.07	.02
☐	52 Charlie Simmer	.20	.09	.03
☐	53 Wayne Gretzky	18.00	8.00	2.30
☐	54 Mark Howe	.20	.09	.03
☐	55 Bob Gould	.15	.07	.02
☐	56 Steve Yzerman	7.00	3.10	.85
☐	57 Larry Playfair	.15	.07	.02
☐	58 Alain Chevrier	.15	.07	.02
☐	59 Steve Larmer	1.00	.45	.13
☐	60 Bryan Trottier	.25	.11	.03
☐	61 Stewart Gavin	.15	.07	.02
☐	62 Russ Courtnall	1.50	.65	.19
☐	63 Mike Ramsey	.15	.07	.02
☐	64 Bob Brooke	.15	.07	.02
☐	65 Rick Wamsley	.15	.07	.02
☐	66 Ken Morrow	.15	.07	.02
☐	67 Gerard Gallant UER	.50	.23	.06
	(Misspelled Gerald on both sides)			
☐	68 Kevin Hatcher	9.00	4.00	1.15
☐	69 Cam Neely	5.00	2.30	.60
☐	70 Sylvain Turgeon	.15	.07	.02
☐	71 Peter Zezel	.20	.09	.03
☐	72 Al MacInnis	4.00	1.80	.50
☐	73 Terry Ruskowski	.15	.07	.02
☐	74 Troy Murray	.15	.07	.02
☐	75 Jim Fox	.15	.07	.02
☐	76 Kelly Kisio	.20	.09	.03
☐	77 Michel Goulet	.35	.16	.04
☐	78 Tom Barrasco	.75	.35	.09
☐	79 Bruce Driver	.20	.09	.03
☐	80 Craig Simpson	2.00	.90	.25
☐	81 Dino Ciccarelli	.50	.23	.06
☐	82 Gary Nylund	.15	.07	.02
☐	83 Bernie Federko	.25	.11	.03
☐	84 John Tonelli	.20	.09	.03
☐	85 Brad McCrimmon	.15	.07	.02
☐	86 Dave Tippett	.15	.07	.02
☐	87 Ray Bourque	2.00	.90	.25
☐	88 Dave Christian	.20	.09	.03
☐	89 Glen Hanlon	.20	.09	.03
☐	90 Brian Curran	.15	.07	.02
☐	91 Paul MacLean	.20	.09	.03
☐	92 Jimmy Carson	2.00	.90	.25
☐	93 Willie Huber	.15	.07	.02
☐	94 Brian Bellows	.50	.23	.06
☐	95 Doug Jarvis	.15	.07	.02
☐	96 Clark Gillies	.15	.07	.02

☐	97	Tony Tanti	.15	.07	.02	☐	185	Anton Stastny	.15	.07	.02

☐ 97 Tony Tanti	.15	.07	.02
☐ 98 Pelle Eklund	.75	.35	.09
☐ 99 Paul Coffey	1.50	.65	.19
☐ 100 Brent Ashton	.15	.07	.02
☐ 101 Mark Johnson	.15	.07	.02
☐ 102 Greg Johnston	.15	.07	.02
☐ 103 Ron Flockhart	.15	.07	.02
☐ 104 Ed Olczyk	.15	.07	.02
☐ 105 Mike Bossy	.60	.25	.08
☐ 106 Chris Chelios	1.50	.65	.19
☐ 107 Gilles Meloche	.15	.07	.02
☐ 108 Rod Langway	.20	.09	.03
☐ 109 Ray Ferraro	1.00	.45	.13
☐ 110 Ron Duguay	.20	.09	.03
☐ 111 Al Secord	.15	.07	.02
☐ 112 Mark Messier	3.00	1.35	.40
☐ 113 Ron Sutter	.15	.07	.02
☐ 114 Darren Veitch	.15	.07	.02
☐ 115 Rick Middleton	.20	.09	.03
☐ 116 Doug Sulliman	.15	.07	.02
☐ 117 Dennis Maruk	.20	.09	.03
☐ 118 Dave Taylor	.25	.11	.03
☐ 119 Kelly Hrudey	1.00	.45	.13
☐ 120 Tom Fergus	.15	.07	.02
☐ 121 Christian Ruuttu	.75	.35	.09
☐ 122 Brian Benning	.40	.18	.05
☐ 123 Adam Oates	40.00	18.00	5.00
☐ 124 Kevin Dineen	.75	.35	.09
☐ 125 Doug Bodger	.15	.07	.02
☐ 126 Joe Mullen	.50	.23	.06
☐ 127 Denis Savard	.50	.23	.06
☐ 128 Brad Marsh	.20	.09	.03
☐ 129 Marcel Dionne	.35	.16	.04
☐ 130 Bryan Erickson	.15	.07	.02
☐ 131 Reed Larson	.15	.07	.02
☐ 132 Don Beaupre	.20	.09	.03
☐ 133 Larry Murphy	.35	.16	.04
☐ 134 John Ogrodnick	.20	.09	.03
☐ 135 Greg Adams	.20	.09	.03
New Jersey Devils			
☐ 136 Pat Flatley	.15	.07	.02
☐ 137 Scott Arniel	.15	.07	.02
☐ 138 Dana Murzyn	.15	.07	.02
☐ 139 Greg C. Adams	.15	.07	.02
Washington Capitals			
☐ 140 Bob Sauve	.15	.07	.02
☐ 141 Mike O'Connell	.15	.07	.02
☐ 142 Walt Poddubny	.20	.09	.03
☐ 143 Paul Reinhart	.15	.07	.02
☐ 144 Tim Kerr	.20	.09	.03
☐ 145 Brian Lawton	.15	.07	.02
☐ 146 Gino Cavallini	.35	.16	.04
☐ 147 Doug Keans	.15	.07	.02
☐ 148 Jari Kurri	1.00	.45	.13
☐ 149 Dale Hawerchuk	1.00	.45	.13
☐ 150 Randy Cunneyworth	.35	.16	.04
☐ 151 Jay Wells	.15	.07	.02
☐ 152 Mike Liut	.20	.09	.03
☐ 153 Steve Konroyd	.15	.07	.02
☐ 154 John Tucker	.15	.07	.02
☐ 155 Rick Vaive	.20	.09	.03
☐ 156 Bob Murray	.15	.07	.02
☐ 157 Kirk Muller	2.00	.90	.25
☐ 158 Brian Propp	.25	.11	.03
☐ 159 Ron Greschner	.15	.07	.02
☐ 160 Rob Ramage	.15	.07	.02
☐ 161 Craig Laughlin	.15	.07	.02
☐ 162 Steve Kasper	.15	.07	.02
☐ 163 Patrick Roy	38.00	17.00	4.70
☐ 164 Shawn Burr	.50	.23	.06
☐ 165 Craig Hartsburg	.15	.07	.02
☐ 166 Dean Evason	.40	.18	.05
☐ 167 Bob Bourne	.15	.07	.02
☐ 168 Mike Gartner	.75	.35	.09
☐ 169 Ron Hextall	6.00	2.70	.75
☐ 170 Joe Cirella	.15	.07	.02
☐ 171 Dan Quinn	.15	.07	.02
☐ 172 Tony McKegney	.15	.07	.02
☐ 173 Pat LaFontaine	5.00	2.30	.60
☐ 174 Allen Pedersen	.15	.07	.02
☐ 175 Doug Gilmour	7.00	3.10	.85
☐ 176 Gary Suter	.50	.23	.06
☐ 177 Barry Pederson	.15	.07	.02
☐ 178 Grant Fuhr	1.00	.45	.13
☐ 179 Wayne Presley	.50	.23	.06
☐ 180 Wilf Paiement	.20	.09	.03
☐ 181 Doug Smail	.15	.07	.02
☐ 182 Doug Crossman	.15	.07	.02
☐ 183 Bernie Nicholls UER	.50	.23	.06
(Misspelled Nichols on both sides)			
☐ 184 Dirk Graham UER	.40	.18	.05
(Misspelled Dick)			

☐ 185 Anton Stastny	.15	.07	.02
☐ 186 Greg Stefan	.15	.07	.02
☐ 187 Ron Francis	.60	.25	.08
☐ 188 Steve Thomas	1.00	.45	.13
☐ 189 Kelly Miller	1.00	.45	.13
☐ 190 Tomas Jonsson	.15	.07	.02
☐ 191 John MacLean	1.50	.65	.19
☐ 192 Larry Robinson	.25	.11	.03
☐ 193 Doug Wickenheiser	.15	.07	.02
☐ 194 Keith Crowder	.15	.07	.02
☐ 195 Bob Froese	.15	.07	.02
☐ 196 Jim Johnson	.15	.07	.02
☐ 197 Checklist 1-132	1.50	.15	.03
☐ 198 Checklist 133-264	1.50	.15	.03
☐ 199 Glenn Anderson	.75	.35	.09
☐ 200 Kevin Lowe	.20	.09	.03
☐ 201 Kevin McClelland	.15	.07	.02
☐ 202 Mike Krushelnyski	.20	.09	.03
☐ 203 Craig MacTavish	.50	.23	.06
☐ 204 Andy Moog	1.00	.45	.13
☐ 205 Marty McSorley	8.00	3.60	1.00
☐ 206 Craig Muni	.35	.16	.04
☐ 207 Charlie Huddy	.15	.07	.02
☐ 208 Hakan Loob	.15	.07	.02
☐ 209 Jim Peplinski	.15	.07	.02
☐ 210 Mike Bullard	.20	.09	.03
☐ 211 Carey Wilson	.15	.07	.02
☐ 212 Joel Otto	.20	.09	.03
☐ 213 Neil Sheehy	.15	.07	.02
☐ 214 Jamie Macoun	.15	.07	.02
☐ 215 Mike Vernon	7.50	3.40	.95
☐ 216 Steve Bozek	.15	.07	.02
☐ 217 Daniel Berthiaume	.35	.16	.04
☐ 218 Gilles Hamel	.15	.07	.02
☐ 219 Tim Watters	.15	.07	.02
☐ 220 Mario Marois	.15	.07	.02
☐ 221 Thomas Steen	.20	.09	.03
☐ 222 Laurie Boschman	.15	.07	.02
☐ 223 Steve Rooney	.15	.07	.02
☐ 224 Ron Wilson	.15	.07	.02
☐ 225 Fredrik Olausson	1.00	.45	.13
☐ 226 Jim Kyte	.15	.07	.02
☐ 227 Claude Lemieux	9.00	4.00	1.15
☐ 228 Bob Gainey	.20	.09	.03
☐ 229 Gaston Gingras	.15	.07	.02
☐ 230 Brian Hayward	.20	.09	.03
☐ 231 Ryan Walter	.15	.07	.02
☐ 232 Guy Carbonneau	.25	.11	.03
☐ 233 Stephane Richer	9.00	4.00	1.15
☐ 234 Rick Green	.15	.07	.02
☐ 235 Brian Skrudland	1.00	.45	.13
☐ 236 Allan Bester	.15	.07	.02
☐ 237 Borje Salming	.20	.09	.03
☐ 238 Al Iafrate	2.50	1.15	.30
☐ 239 Rick Lanz	.15	.07	.02
☐ 240 Gary Leeman	.20	.09	.03
☐ 241 Greg Terrion	.15	.07	.02
☐ 242 Ken Wregget	1.50	.65	.19
☐ 243 Vincent Damphousse	14.00	6.25	1.75
☐ 244 Chris Kotsopoulos	.15	.07	.02
☐ 245 Dale Hunter	.20	.09	.03
☐ 246 Clint Malarchuk	.20	.09	.03
☐ 247 Paul Gillis	.15	.07	.02
☐ 248 Robert Picard	.15	.07	.02
☐ 249 Doug Shedden	.15	.07	.02
☐ 250 Mario Gosselin	.15	.07	.02
☐ 251 Randy Moller	.15	.07	.02
☐ 252 David Shaw	.15	.07	.02
☐ 253 Mike Eagles	.30	.14	.04
☐ 254 Alain Cote	.15	.07	.02
☐ 255 Petri Skriko	.15	.07	.02
☐ 256 Doug Lidster	.15	.07	.02
☐ 257 Richard Brodeur UER	.20	.09	.03
(Photo actually Frank Caprice)			
☐ 258 Rich Sutter	.15	.07	.02
☐ 259 Steve Tambellini	.15	.07	.02
☐ 260 Jim Benning	.15	.07	.02
☐ 261 Dave Richter	.15	.07	.02
☐ 262 Michel Petit	.35	.16	.04
☐ 263 Brent Peterson	.15	.07	.02
☐ 264 Jim Sandlak	.60	.15	.06

1987-88 O-Pee-Chee/Topps
Box Bottoms

This sixteen-card set was issued in sets of four on the bottom of the 1987-88 O-Pee-Chee and Topps wax pack

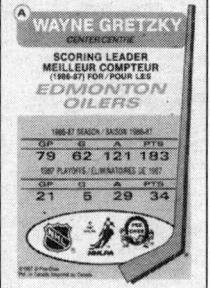

	MINT	EXC	G-VG
COMPLETE SET (42).........................	15.00	6.00	1.50
COMMON PLAYER (1-42)................	.10	.04	.01
☐ 1 Glenn Anderson	.30	.12	.03
☐ 2 Brian Benning	.10	.04	.01
☐ 3 Daniel Berthiaume...................	.10	.04	.01
☐ 4 Ray Bourque	.75	.30	.07
☐ 5 Shawn Burr............................	.10	.04	.01
☐ 6 Jimmy Carson	.50	.20	.05
☐ 7 Dino Ciccarelli	.30	.12	.03
☐ 8 Paul Coffey...........................	.75	.30	.07
☐ 9 Pelle Eklund	.20	.08	.02
☐ 10 Ron Francis	.30	.12	.03
☐ 11 Doug Gilmour	1.25	.50	.12
☐ 12 Michel Goulet........................	.30	.12	.03
☐ 13 Wayne Gretzky	5.00	2.00	.50
☐ 14 Glen Hanlon	.10	.04	.01
☐ 15 Brian Hayward........................	.15	.06	.01
☐ 16 Ron Hextall	.50	.20	.05
☐ 17 Phil Housley..........................	.50	.20	.05
☐ 18 Mark Howe............................	.15	.06	.01
☐ 19 Doug Jarvis	.10	.04	.01
☐ 20 Tim Kerr...............................	.15	.06	.01
☐ 21 Jari Kurri..............................	.30	.12	.03
☐ 22 Pat LaFontaine	1.00	.40	.10
☐ 23 Mario Lemieux	5.00	2.00	.50
☐ 24 Mike Liut.............................	.15	.06	.01
☐ 25 Kevin Lowe	.15	.06	.01
☐ 26 Al MacInnis...........................	.50	.20	.05
☐ 27 Brad McCrimmon.....................	.10	.04	.01
☐ 28 Mark Messier	1.25	.50	.12
☐ 29 Joe Mullen	.30	.12	.03
☐ 30 Craig Muni	.10	.04	.01
☐ 31 Larry Murphy	.30	.12	.03
☐ 32 Dave Poulin..........................	.10	.04	.01
☐ 33 Brian Propp...........................	.15	.06	.01
☐ 34 Paul Reinhart	.15	.06	.01
☐ 35 Luc Robitaille	4.00	1.60	.40
☐ 36 Patrick Roy...........................	3.00	1.20	.30
☐ 37 Christian Ruuttu	.15	.06	.01
☐ 38 Tomas Sandstrom...................	.30	.12	.03
☐ 39 Denis Savard	.30	.12	.03
☐ 40 Petri Skriko	.10	.04	.01
☐ 41 Bryan Trottier........................	.40	.16	.04
☐ 42 Checklist 1-42	.10	.04	.01

boxes. The cards measure the standard 2 1/2" by 3 1/2" and feature team scoring leaders. Complete box bottom panels are valued at a 25 percent premium above the prices listed below. The cards are in the same design as the 1987-88 O-Pee-Chee (and Topps) regular issues except they are bordered in yellow. The backs are printed in red and black ink and give statistical information. The cards are lettered rather than numbered. This set features NHL luminaries such as Ray Bourque, Wayne Gretzky, and Steve Yzerman. The key card in the set is Luc Robitaille, appearing in the same year as his Rookie Card.

	MINT	EXC	G-VG
COMPLETE SET (16).......................	25.00	10.00	2.50
COMMON PLAYER (A-P)	.35	.14	.03
☐ A Wayne Gretzky........................	10.00	4.00	1.00
☐ B Tim Kerr.................................	.35	.14	.03
☐ C Steve Yzerman	2.50	1.00	.25
☐ D Luc Robitaille	10.00	4.00	1.00
☐ E Doug Gilmour	2.50	1.00	.25
☐ F Ray Bourque	1.50	.60	.15
☐ G Joe Mullen	.75	.30	.07
☐ H Larry Murphy..........................	.75	.30	.07
☐ I Dale Hawerchuk.......................	.75	.30	.07
☐ J Ron Francis	.75	.30	.07
☐ K Walt Poddubny	.35	.14	.03
☐ L Mats Naslund	.50	.20	.05
☐ M Michel Goulet.........................	.75	.30	.07
☐ N Denis Savard	.75	.30	.07
☐ O Bryan Trottier.........................	1.00	.40	.10
☐ P Russ Courtnall........................	1.00	.40	.10

1987-88 O-Pee-Chee Minis

PATRICK ROY

The 1987-88 O-Pee-Chee Minis set contains 42 cards measuring approximately 2 1/8" by 3". The fronts are white with vignette-style color photos and player names in navy blue. The backs are pale pink and blue, and show 1986-87 stats. The cards were distributed packed five per cello pack at a suggested retail price of 25 cents.

1988-89 O-Pee-Chee

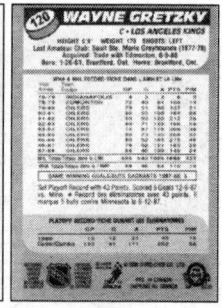

The 1988-89 O-Pee-Chee set consists of 264 cards that measure the standard 2 1/2" by 3 1/2". The card fronts contain the player's name within a team colored banner, position and team logo at the top. Bilingual backs have yearly and career statistics, number of game winning goals from previous season, playoff scoring records and highlights. There were cards printed on the bottoms of the wax boxes that are similar to the regular issue cards but are "lettered" A-P rather than numbered. The set is considered complete without these wax box cards. The Wayne Gretzky card (120) differs from that of Topps which shows Wayne posing with his Kings uniform on in an arena setting. Rookie Cards in this set include Jeff Brown, Sean Burke, Ulf Dahlen, Steve Duchesne, Dave Gagner, Brett Hull, Joe

Nieuwendyk, Bob Probert, Brendan Shanahan, Ray Sheppard, Steve Smith, Pierre Turgeon, and Glen Wesley. Beware when purchasing the Wayne Gretzky, Brett Hull, Mario Lemieux, Joe Nieuwendyk, and Pierre Turgeon cards from this set as they have been counterfeited.

		MINT	EXC	G-VG
	COMPLETE SET (264)	175.00	80.00	22.00
	COMPLETE FACT.SET (264)	200.00	90.00	25.00
	COMMON PLAYER (1-264)	.12	.05	.02
☐ 1	Mario Lemieux	10.00	4.50	1.25
☐ 2	Bob Joyce	.12	.05	.02
☐ 3	Joel Quenneville	.12	.05	.02
☐ 4	Tony McKegney	.12	.05	.02
☐ 5	Stephane Richer	2.00	.90	.25
☐ 6	Mark Howe	.15	.07	.02
☐ 7	Brent Sutter	.15	.07	.02
☐ 8	Gilles Meloche	.12	.05	.02
☐ 9	Jimmy Carson	.50	.23	.06
☐ 10	John MacLean	.50	.23	.06
☐ 11	Gary Leeman	.12	.05	.02
☐ 12	Gerard Gallant	.15	.07	.02
☐ 13	Marcel Dionne	.25	.11	.03
☐ 14	Dave Christian	.15	.07	.02
☐ 15	Gary Nylund	.12	.05	.02
☐ 16	Joe Nieuwendyk	12.00	5.50	1.50
☐ 17	Billy Smith	.20	.09	.03
☐ 18	Christian Ruuttu	.12	.05	.02
☐ 19	Randy Cunneyworth	.12	.05	.02
☐ 20	Brian Lawton	.12	.05	.02
☐ 21	Scott Mellanby	.75	.35	.09
☐ 22	Peter Stastny	.50	.23	.06
☐ 23	Gord Kluzak	.12	.05	.02
☐ 24	Sylvain Turgeon	.12	.05	.02
☐ 25	Clint Malarchuk	.15	.07	.02
☐ 26	Denis Savard	.40	.18	.05
☐ 27	Craig Simpson	.40	.18	.05
☐ 28	Petr Klima	.15	.07	.02
☐ 29	Pat Verbeek	.25	.11	.03
☐ 30	Moe Mantha	.12	.05	.02
☐ 31	Chris Nilan	.15	.07	.02
☐ 32	Barry Pederson	.12	.05	.02
☐ 33	Randy Burridge	.25	.11	.03
☐ 34	Ron Hextall	1.50	.65	.19
☐ 35	Gaston Gingras	.12	.05	.02
☐ 36	Kevin Dineen	.35	.16	.04
☐ 37	Tom Laidlaw	.12	.05	.02
☐ 38	Paul MacLean	.12	.05	.02
☐ 39	John Chabot	.12	.05	.02
☐ 40	Lindy Ruff	.12	.05	.02
☐ 41	Dan Quinn	.12	.05	.02
☐ 42	Don Beaupre	.15	.07	.02
☐ 43	Gary Suter	.30	.14	.04
☐ 44	Mikko Makela	.12	.05	.02
☐ 45	Mark Johnson	.12	.05	.02
☐ 46	Dave Taylor	.20	.09	.03
☐ 47	Ulf Dahlen	2.00	.90	.25
☐ 48	Jeff Sharples	.12	.05	.02
☐ 49	Chris Chelios	.50	.23	.06
☐ 50	Mike Gartner	.40	.18	.05
☐ 51	Darren Pang	.30	.14	.04
☐ 52	Ron Francis	.40	.18	.05
☐ 53	Ken Morrow	.12	.05	.02
☐ 54	Michel Goulet	.20	.09	.03
☐ 55	Ray Sheppard	7.00	3.10	.85
☒ 56	Doug Gilmour	4.00	1.80	.50
☐ 57	David Shaw	.12	.05	.02
☐ 58	Cam Neely	2.50	1.15	.30
☐ 59	Grant Fuhr	.60	.25	.08
☐ 60	Scott Stevens	.50	.23	.06
☐ 61	Bob Brooke	.12	.05	.02
☐ 62	Dave Hunter	.12	.05	.02
☐ 63	Alan Kerr	.12	.05	.02
☐ 64	Brad Marsh	.15	.07	.02
☐ 65	Dale Hawerchuk	.60	.25	.08
☐ 66	Brett Hull	60.00	27.00	7.50
☐ 67	Patrik Sundstrom	.12	.05	.02
☐ 68	Greg Stefan	.12	.05	.02
☐ 69	James Patrick	.12	.05	.02
☐ 70	Dale Hunter	.15	.07	.02
☐ 71	Al Iafrate	.60	.25	.08
☐ 72	Bob Carpenter	.15	.07	.02
☐ 73	Ray Bourque	1.00	.45	.13
☐ 74	John Tucker	.12	.05	.02
☐ 75	Carey Wilson	.12	.05	.02
☐ 76	Joe Mullen	.35	.16	.04
☐ 77	Rick Vaive	.12	.05	.02
☐ 78	Shawn Burr	.12	.05	.02
☐ 79	Murray Craven	.12	.05	.02
☐ 80	Clark Gillies	.12	.05	.02
☐ 81	Bernie Federko	.15	.07	.02
☐ 82	Tony Tanti	.12	.05	.02
☐ 83	Greg Gilbert	.12	.05	.02
☐ 84	Kirk Muller	1.00	.45	.13
☐ 85	Dave Tippett	.12	.05	.02
☐ 86	Kevin Hatcher	2.00	.90	.25
☐ 87	Rick Middleton	.15	.07	.02
☐ 88	Bobby Smith	.15	.07	.02
☐ 89	Doug Wilson	.15	.07	.02
☐ 90	Scott Arniel	.12	.05	.02
☐ 91	Brian Mullen	.15	.07	.02
☐ 92	Mike O'Connell	.12	.05	.02
☐ 93	Mark Messier	1.50	.65	.19
☐ 94	Sean Burke	1.50	.65	.19
☐ 95	Brian Bellows	.35	.16	.04
☐ 96	Doug Bodger	.12	.05	.02
☐ 97	Bryan Trottier	.20	.09	.03
☐ 98	Anton Stastny	.12	.05	.02
☐ 99A	Checklist 1-99	.75	.11	.02
	(found in vending cases)			
☐ 99B	Checklist 1-132	.75	.11	.02
	(found in wax cases)			
☐ 100	Dave Poulin	.15	.07	.02
☐ 101	Bob Bourne	.12	.05	.02
☐ 102	John Vanbiesbrouck	1.25	.55	.16
☐ 103	Allen Pedersen	.12	.05	.02
☐ 104	Mike Ridley	.15	.07	.02
☐ 105	Andrew McBain	.12	.05	.02
☐ 106	Troy Murray	.12	.05	.02
☐ 107	Tom Barrasso	.40	.18	.05
☐ 108	Tomas Jonsson	.12	.05	.02
☐ 109	Rob Brown	.60	.25	.08
☐ 110	Hakan Loob	.12	.05	.02
☐ 111	Ilkka Sinisalo	.12	.05	.02
☐ 112	Dave Archibald	.12	.05	.02
☐ 113	Doug Halward	.12	.05	.02
☐ 114	Ray Ferraro	.15	.07	.02
☐ 115	Doug Brown	.50	.23	.06
☐ 116	Patrick Roy	10.00	4.50	1.25
☐ 117	Greg Millen	.12	.05	.02
☐ 118	Ken Linseman	.12	.05	.02
☐ 119	Phil Housley	.35	.16	.04
☐ 120	Wayne Gretzky UER	18.00	8.00	2.30
	(No position on front)			
☐ 121	Tomas Sandstrom	.50	.23	.06
☐ 122	Brendan Shanahan	20.00	9.00	2.50
☐ 123	Pat LaFontaine	2.50	1.15	.30
☐ 124	Luc Robitaille	8.00	3.60	1.00
☐ 125	Ed Olczyk	.12	.05	.02
☐ 126	Ron Sutter	.12	.05	.02
☐ 127	Mike Liut	.15	.07	.02
☐ 128	Brent Ashton	.12	.05	.02
☐ 129	Tony Hrkac	.30	.14	.04
☐ 130	Kelly Miller	.15	.07	.02
☐ 131	Alan Haworth	.12	.05	.02
☐ 132	Dave McLlwain	.30	.14	.04
☐ 133	Mike Ramsey	.12	.05	.02
☐ 134	Bob Sweeney	.40	.18	.05
☐ 135	Dirk Graham	.15	.07	.02
☐ 136	Ulf Samuelsson	1.00	.45	.13
☐ 137	Petri Skriko	.12	.05	.02
☐ 138	Aaron Broten	.12	.05	.02
☐ 139	Jim Fox	.12	.05	.02
☐ 140	Randy Wood	.50	.23	.06
☐ 141	Larry Murphy	.20	.09	.03
☐ 142	Daniel Berthiaume	.12	.05	.02
☐ 143	Kelly Kisio	.12	.05	.02
☐ 144	Neal Broten	.15	.07	.02
☐ 145	Reed Larson	.12	.05	.02
☐ 146	Peter Zezel	.15	.07	.02
☐ 147	Jari Kurri	.60	.25	.08
☐ 148	Jim Johnson	.12	.05	.02
☐ 149	Gino Cavallini	.12	.05	.02
☐ 150	Glen Hanlon	.12	.05	.02
☐ 151	Bengt Gustafsson	.12	.05	.02
☐ 152	Mike Bullard	.12	.05	.02
☐ 153	John Ogrodnick	.15	.07	.02
☐ 154	Steve Larmer	.50	.23	.06
☐ 155	Kelly Hrudey	.35	.16	.04
☐ 156	Mats Naslund	.15	.07	.02
☐ 157	Bruce Driver	.12	.05	.02
☐ 158	Randy Hillier	.12	.05	.02
☐ 159	Craig Hartsburg	.12	.05	.02
☐ 160	Rollie Melanson	.12	.05	.02
☐ 161	Adam Oates	7.00	3.10	.85
☐ 162	Greg Adams	.15	.07	.02
	Vancouver Canucks			
☐ 163	Dave Andreychuk	1.25	.55	.16
☐ 164	Dave Babych	.12	.05	.02
☐ 165	Brian Noonan	1.00	.45	.13
☐ 166	Glen Wesley	1.50	.65	.19
☐ 167	Dave Ellett	.15	.07	.02
☐ 168	Brian Propp	.15	.07	.02
☐ 169	Bernie Nicholls	.35	.16	.04

☐ 170	Walt Poddubny	.12	.05	.02
☐ 171	Steve Konroyd	.12	.05	.02
☐ 172	Doug Sulliman	.12	.05	.02
☐ 173	Mario Gosselin	.12	.05	.02
☐ 174	Brian Benning	.12	.05	.02
☐ 175	Dino Ciccarelli	.20	.09	.03
☐ 176	Steve Kasper	.12	.05	.02
☐ 177	Rick Tocchet	3.00	1.35	.40
☐ 178	Brad McCrimmon	.12	.05	.02
☐ 179	Paul Coffey	1.00	.45	.13
☐ 180	Pete Peeters	.15	.07	.02
☐ 181	Bob Probert	4.00	1.80	.50
☐ 182	Steve Duchesne	4.00	1.80	.50
☐ 183	Russ Courtnall	.50	.23	.06
☐ 184	Mike Foligno	.15	.07	.02
☐ 185	Wayne Presley	.12	.05	.02
☐ 186	Rejean Lemelin	.15	.07	.02
☐ 187	Mark Hunter	.12	.05	.02
☐ 188	Joe Cirella	.12	.05	.02
☐ 189	Glenn Anderson	.50	.23	.06
☐ 190	John Anderson	.12	.05	.02
☐ 191	Pat Flatley	.12	.05	.02
☐ 192	Rod Langway	.15	.07	.02
☐ 193	Brian MacLellan	.12	.05	.02
☐ 194	Pierre Turgeon	30.00	13.50	3.80
☐ 195	Brian Hayward	.12	.05	.02
☐ 196	Steve Yzerman	4.00	1.80	.50
☐ 197	Doug Crossman	.12	.05	.02
☐ 198A	Checklist 100-198	.75	.11	.02
	(Found in vending cases)			
☐ 198B	Checklist 133-264 UER	.75	.11	.02
	(Found in wax cases; 233 Mario Marios)			
☐ 199	Greg C. Adams	.12	.05	.02
	Edmonton Oilers			
☐ 200	Laurie Boschman	.12	.05	.02
☐ 201	Jeff Brown	6.00	2.70	.75
☐ 202	Garth Butcher	.75	.35	.09
☐ 203	Guy Carbonneau	.20	.09	.03
☐ 204	Randy Carlyle	.15	.07	.02
☐ 205	Alain Cote	.12	.05	.02
☐ 206	Keith Crowder	.12	.05	.02
☐ 207	Vincent Damphousse	4.00	1.80	.50
☐ 208	Gaetan Duchesne	.50	.23	.06
☐ 209	Iain Duncan	.12	.05	.02
☐ 210	Tommy Albelin	.12	.05	.02
☐ 211	Pelle Eklund	.12	.05	.02
☐ 212	Jan Erixon	.25	.11	.03
☐ 213	Paul Fenton	.12	.05	.02
☐ 214	Tom Fergus	.12	.05	.02
☐ 215	Dave Gagner	3.00	1.35	.40
☐ 216	Bob Gainey	.15	.07	.02
☐ 217	Stewart Gavin	.12	.05	.02
☐ 218	Charlie Huddy	.12	.05	.02
☐ 219	Jeff Jackson	.12	.05	.02
☐ 220	Uwe Krupp	.75	.35	.09
☐ 221	Mike Krushelnyski	.12	.05	.02
☐ 222	Tom Kurvers	.15	.07	.02
☐ 223	Jason Lafreniere	.12	.05	.02
☐ 224	Lane Lambert	.12	.05	.02
☐ 225	Rick Lanz	.12	.05	.02
☐ 226	Brad Lauer	.12	.05	.02
☐ 227	Claude Lemieux	2.00	.90	.25
☐ 228	Doug Lidster	.12	.05	.02
☐ 229	Kevin Lowe UER	.15	.07	.02
	(Has Gretzky's stats)			
☐ 230	Craig Ludwig	.12	.05	.02
☐ 231	Al MacInnis	2.50	1.15	.30
☐ 232	Craig MacTavish	.15	.07	.02
☐ 233	Mario Marois	.12	.05	.02
	(misspelled Marios on checklist 198)			
☐ 234	Lanny McDonald	.15	.07	.02
☐ 235	Rick Meagher	.15	.07	.02
☐ 236	Craig Muni	.12	.05	.02
☐ 237	Mike McPhee	.15	.07	.02
☐ 238	Ric Nattress	.12	.05	.02
☐ 239	Ray Neufeld	.12	.05	.02
☐ 240	Lee Norwood	.25	.11	.03
☐ 241	Mark Osborne UER	.12	.05	.02
	(Misspelled Osbourne on both sides)			
☐ 242	Joel Otto	.15	.07	.02
☐ 243	Jim Peplinski	.12	.05	.02
☐ 244	Rob Ramage	.12	.05	.02
☐ 245	Luke Richardson	.25	.11	.03
☐ 246	Larry Robinson	.20	.09	.03
☐ 247	Borje Salming	.15	.07	.02
☐ 248	David Saunders	.12	.05	.02
☐ 249	Al Secord	.12	.05	.02
☐ 250	Charlie Simmer	.15	.07	.02
☐ 251	Doug Smail	.12	.05	.02
☐ 252	Steve Smith UER	3.50	1.55	.45

	(Now with Sabres 10-3-88 on front)			
☐ 253	Stan Smyl	.15	.07	.02
☐ 254	Thomas Steen	.15	.07	.02
☐ 255	Rich Sutter	.12	.05	.02
☐ 256	Petr Svoboda	.50	.23	.06
☐ 257	Peter Taglianetti	.12	.05	.02
☐ 258	Steve Tambellini	.12	.05	.02
☐ 259	Steve Thomas	.50	.23	.06
☐ 260	Esa Tikkanen	3.00	1.35	.40
☐ 261	Mike Vernon	2.00	.90	.25
☐ 262	Ryan Walter	.12	.05	.02
☐ 263	Doug Wickenheiser	.12	.05	.02
☐ 264	Ken Wregget	.35	.16	.04

1988-89 O-Pee-Chee/Topps Box Bottoms

 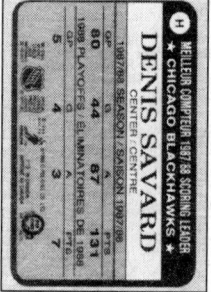

This sixteen-card set was issued in sets of four on the bottom of the 1988-89 O-Pee-Chee and Topps wax pack boxes. The cards measure the standard 2 1/2" by 3 1/2" and feature team scoring leaders. Complete box bottom panels are valued at a 25 percent premium above the prices listed below. The O-Pee-Chee cards are in the same design as the 1988-89 O-Pee-Chee regular issues. The Topps cards are in the same design as the 1988-89 Topps regular issues except they are bordered only in gray. The backs are printed in purple on orange background and give statistical information. The cards are lettered rather than numbered and include stars such as Ray Bourque, Wayne Gretzky, Pat LaFontaine, Luc Robitaille, and Steve Yzerman.

		MINT	EXC	G-VG
COMPLETE SET (16)		15.00	6.00	1.50
COMMON PLAYER (A-P)		.25	.10	.02
☐ A	Ron Francis	.50	.20	.05
☐ B	Wayne Gretzky	7.50	3.00	.75
☐ C	Pat LaFontaine	1.50	.60	.15
☐ D	Bobby Smith	.50	.20	.05
☐ E	Bernie Federko	.35	.14	.03
☐ F	Kirk Muller	1.00	.40	.10
☐ G	Ed Olczyk	.25	.10	.02
☐ H	Denis Savard	.75	.30	.07
☐ I	Ray Bourque	1.00	.40	.10
☐ J	Murray Craven and Brian Propp	.35	.14	.03
☐ K	Dale Hawerchuk	.75	.30	.07
☐ L	Steve Yzerman	1.50	.60	.15
☐ M	Dave Andreychuk	.75	.30	.07
☐ N	Mike Gartner	.75	.30	.07
☐ O	Hakan Loob	.25	.10	.02
☐ P	Luc Robitaille	1.50	.60	.15

1988-89 O-Pee-Chee Minis

The 1988-89 O-Pee-Chee Minis set contains 46 numbered cards measuring approximately 2 1/8" by 3". The fronts are

CAM NEELY

white with vignette-style color photos and player names in navy blue. The backs are pale pink and blue, and show 1987-88 stats. The key card in the set is Brett Hull, appearing in his Rookie Card year. The set numbering is alphabetical by player's name.

	MINT	EXC	G-VG
COMPLETE SET (46)	18.00	7.25	1.80
COMMON PLAYER (1-46)	.10	.04	.01
☐ 1 Tom Barrasso	.30	.12	.03
☐ 2 Bob Bourne	.10	.04	.01
☐ 3 Ray Bourque	.75	.30	.07
☐ 4 Guy Carbonneau	.20	.08	.02
☐ 5 Jimmy Carson	.30	.12	.03
☐ 6 Paul Coffey	.75	.30	.07
☐ 7 Ulf Dahlen	.25	.10	.02
☐ 8 Marcel Dionne	.50	.20	.05
☐ 9 Grant Fuhr	.40	.16	.04
☐ 10 Michel Goulet	.25	.10	.02
☐ 11 Wayne Gretzky	5.00	2.00	.50
☐ 12 Dale Hawerchuk	.30	.12	.03
☐ 13 Brian Hayward	.15	.06	.01
☐ 14 Ron Hextall	.25	.10	.02
☐ 15 Tony Hrkac	.15	.06	.01
☐ 16 Brett Hull	6.00	2.40	.60
☐ 17 Steve Larmer	.30	.12	.03
☐ 18 Rejean Lemelin	.15	.06	.01
☐ 19 Mario Lemieux	5.00	2.00	.50
☐ 20 Mike Liut	.15	.06	.01
☐ 21 Hakan Loob	.10	.04	.01
☐ 22 Al MacInnis	.30	.12	.03
☐ 23 Paul MacLean	.10	.04	.01
☐ 24 Brad McCrimmon	.10	.04	.01
☐ 25 Mark Messier	1.25	.50	.12
☐ 26 Mats Naslund	.15	.06	.01
☐ 27 Cam Neely	.75	.30	.07
☐ 28 Bernie Nicholls	.30	.12	.03
☐ 29 Joe Nieuwendyk	2.00	.80	.20
☐ 30 Pete Peeters	.15	.06	.01
☐ 31 Stephane Richer	.75	.30	.07
☐ 32 Luc Robitaille	1.00	.40	.10
☐ 33 Patrick Roy	2.50	1.00	.25
☐ 34 Denis Savard	.35	.14	.03
☐ 35 Ray Sheppard	.50	.20	.05
☐ 36 Craig Simpson	.30	.12	.03
☐ 37 Peter Stastny	.35	.14	.03
☐ 38 Greg Stefan	.15	.06	.01
☐ 39 Scott Stevens	.40	.16	.04
☐ 40 Gary Suter	.20	.08	.02
☐ 41 Petr Svoboda	.10	.04	.01
☐ 42 John Vanbiesbrouck	.75	.30	.07
☐ 43 Pat Verbeek	.20	.08	.02
☐ 44 Mike Vernon	.40	.16	.04
☐ 45 Carey Wilson	.10	.04	.01
☐ 46 Checklist Card	.10	.04	.01

1988-89 O-Pee-Chee
Sticker Back Cards

This 22-card set is actually a subset of the 1988-89 O-Pee-Chee sticker set. The cards are numbered on the front (although the numbering is essentially in alphabetical order) and have a distinctive bright orange background. The set is subtitled "Future Stars" and features many young prospects. The cards measure approximately 2 1/8" by 3". The two key cards in the set are Brett Hull, appearing in his rookie year for cards, and Brian Leetch, predating his Rookie Card by one year.

	MINT	EXC	G-VG
COMPLETE SET (22)	12.00	5.00	1.20
COMMON PLAYER (1-22)	.10	.04	.01
☐ 1 Dave Archibald	.10	.04	.01
☐ 2 Doug Brown	.10	.04	.01
☐ 3 Rob Brown	.20	.08	.02
☐ 4 Sean Burke	.30	.12	.03
☐ 5 Ulf Dahlen	.25	.10	.02
☐ 6 Iain Duncan	.10	.04	.01
☐ 7 Glenn Healy	.15	.06	.01
☐ 8 Tony Hrkac	.15	.06	.01
☐ 9 Brett Hull	4.00	1.60	.40
☐ 10 Craig Janney	1.25	.50	.12
☐ 11 Calle Johansson	.15	.06	.01
☐ 12 Brian Leetch	3.00	1.20	.30
☐ 13 Kirk McLean	1.25	.50	.12
☐ 14 Joe Nieuwendyk	1.50	.60	.15
☐ 15 Brian Noonan	.15	.06	.01
☐ 16 Darren Pang	.15	.06	.01
☐ 17 Jeff Sharples	.10	.04	.01
☐ 18 Ray Sheppard	.50	.20	.05
☐ 19 Bob Sweeney	.15	.06	.01
☐ 20 Pierre Turgeon	2.50	1.00	.25
☐ 21 Glen Wesley	.30	.12	.03
☐ 22 Randy Wood	.15	.06	.01

1989-90 O-Pee-Chee

 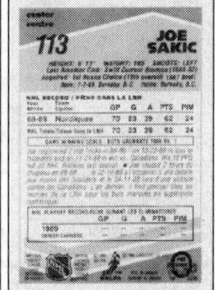

This 330-card set is O-Pee-Chee's largest issue since 1984-85. The cards measure standard size 2 1/2" by 3 1/2". The fronts feature color action photos with "blue ice" borders and player name and team logo at the lower right hand corner. Solid blue borders appear at the top and bottom on the card face. Bilingual backs are tinted red with black lettering and provide career and playoff statistics as well as highlights. The team cards in the set (298-318) are actually action scenes with no players explicitly identified. The team card backs provide power play stats from the previous season. This set was produced in mass quantity as O-Pee-Chee gave dealers the option to order vending cases following the initial printing. A second printing allowed for these orders to be filled, saturating the market. Most dealers believe that this O-Pee-Chee set was produced in an amount much greater than the Topps production of this year. Rookie Cards in this set include Brian Bradley, Jon Casey, Geoff Courtnall, Theoren Fleury, Tony Granato, Craig Janney, Derek King, Brian Leetch, Trevor Linden, Kirk McLean, Daren Puppa, Gary Roberts, Cliff Ronning and Joe Sakic.

		MINT	EXC	G-VG
	COMPLETE SET (330)	20.00	9.00	2.50
	COMPLETE FACT.SET (330)	35.00	16.00	4.40
	COMMON PLAYER (1-330)	.05	.02	.01

	#	Player	MINT	EXC	G-VG
☐	1	Mario Lemieux	1.00	.45	.13
☐	2	Ulf Dahlen	.08	.04	.01
☐	3	Terry Carkner	.10	.05	.01
☐	4	Tony McKegney	.05	.02	.01
☐	5	Denis Savard	.10	.05	.01
☐	6	Derek King	.50	.23	.06
☐	7	Lanny McDonald	.08	.04	.01
☐	8	John Tonelli	.08	.04	.01
☐	9	Tom Kurvers	.05	.02	.01
☐	10	Dave Archibald	.05	.02	.01
☐	11	Peter Sidorkiewicz	.15	.07	.02
☐	12	Esa Tikkanen	.15	.07	.02
☐	13	Dave Barr	.05	.02	.01
☐	14	Brent Sutter	.08	.04	.01
☐	15	Cam Neely	.30	.14	.04
☐	16	Calle Johansson	.15	.07	.02
☐	17	Patrick Roy	1.00	.45	.13
☐	18	Dale DeGray	.05	.02	.01
☐	19	Phil Bourque	.15	.07	.02
☐	20	Kevin Dineen	.08	.04	.01
☐	21	Mike Bullard	.05	.02	.01
☐	22	Gary Leeman	.05	.02	.01
☐	23	Greg Stefan	.05	.02	.01
☐	24	Brian Mullen	.08	.04	.01
☐	25	Pierre Turgeon	.75	.35	.09
☐	26	Bob Rouse	.05	.02	.01
☐	27	Peter Zezel	.08	.04	.01
☐	28	Jeff Brown	.35	.16	.04
☐	29	Andy Brickley	.10	.05	.01
☐	30	Mike Gartner	.15	.07	.02
☐	31	Darren Pang	.05	.02	.01
☐	32	Pat Verbeek	.10	.05	.01
☐	33	Petri Skriko	.05	.02	.01
☐	34	Tom Laidlaw	.05	.02	.01
☐	35	Randy Wood	.05	.02	.01
☐	36	Tom Barrasso	.05	.02	.01
☐	37	John Tucker	.05	.02	.01
☐	38	Andrew McBain	.05	.02	.01
☐	39	David Shaw	.05	.02	.01
☐	40	Rejean Lemelin	.08	.04	.01
☐	41	Dino Ciccarelli	.08	.04	.01
☐	42	Jeff Sharples	.05	.02	.01
☐	43	Jari Kurri	.15	.07	.02
☐	44	Murray Craven	.05	.02	.01
☐	45	Cliff Ronning	.75	.35	.09
☐	46	Dave Babych	.05	.02	.01
☐	47	Bernie Nicholls	.10	.05	.01
☐	48	Jon Casey	.50	.23	.06
☐	49	Al MacInnis	.15	.07	.02
☐	50	Bob Errey	.20	.09	.03
☐	51	Glen Wesley	.08	.04	.01
☐	52	Dirk Graham	.08	.04	.01
☐	53	Guy Carbonneau	.08	.04	.01
☐	54	Tomas Sandstrom	.08	.04	.01
☐	55	Rod Langway	.05	.02	.01
☐	56	Patrik Sundstrom	.05	.02	.01
☐	57	Michel Goulet	.08	.04	.01
☐	58	Dave Taylor	.08	.04	.01
☐	59	Phil Housley	.08	.04	.01
☐	60	Pat LaFontaine	.35	.16	.04
☐	61	Kirk McLean	1.50	.65	.19
☐	62	Ken Leiter	.05	.02	.01
☐	63	Randy Cunneyworth	.05	.02	.01
☐	64	Tony Hrkac	.05	.02	.01
☐	65	Mark Messier	.50	.23	.06
☐	66	Carey Wilson	.05	.02	.01
☐	67	Stephen Leach	.25	.11	.03
☐	68	Christian Ruuttu	.05	.02	.01
☐	69	Dave Ellett	.08	.04	.01
☐	70	Ray Ferraro	.08	.04	.01
☐	71	Colin Patterson	.05	.02	.01
☐	72	Tim Kerr	.08	.04	.01
☐	73	Bob Joyce	.05	.02	.01
☑	74	Doug Gilmour	.50	.23	.06
☐	75	Lee Norwood	.05	.02	.01
☐	76	Dale Hunter	.08	.04	.01
☐	77	Jim Johnson	.05	.02	.01
☐	78	Mike Foligno	.08	.04	.01
☐	79	Al Iafrate	.15	.07	.02
☐	80	Rick Tocchet	.20	.09	.03
☐	81	Greg Hawgood	.15	.07	.02
☐	82	Steve Thomas	.08	.04	.01
☐	83	Steve Yzerman	.50	.23	.06
☐	84	Mike McPhee	.08	.04	.01
☐	85	David Volek	.15	.07	.02
☐	86	Brian Benning	.05	.02	.01
☐	87	Neal Broten	.08	.04	.01
☐	88	Luc Robitaille	.75	.35	.09
☐	89	Trevor Linden	2.00	.90	.25
☐	90	James Patrick	.05	.02	.01
☐	91	Brian Lawton	.05	.02	.01
☐	92	Sean Burke	.08	.04	.01
☐	93	Scott Stevens	.10	.05	.01
☐	94	Pat Elynuik	.20	.09	.03
☐	95	Paul Coffey	.25	.11	.03
☐	96	Jan Erixon	.05	.02	.01
☐	97	Mike Liut	.08	.04	.01
☐	98	Wayne Presley	.05	.02	.01
☐	99	Craig Simpson	.08	.04	.01
☐	100	Kjell Samuelsson	.20	.09	.03
☐	101	Shawn Burr	.05	.02	.01
☐	102	John MacLean	.08	.04	.01
☐	103	Tom Fergus	.05	.02	.01
☐	104	Mike Krushelnyski	.05	.02	.01
☐	105	Gary Nylund	.05	.02	.01
☐	106	Dave Andreychuk	.25	.11	.03
☐	107	Bernie Federko	.08	.04	.01
☐	108	Gary Suter	.08	.04	.01
☐	109	Dave Gagner	.15	.07	.02
☐	110	Ray Bourque	.25	.11	.03
☐	111	Geoff Courtnall	.75	.35	.09
☐	112	Doug Wilson	.08	.04	.01
☐	113	Joe Sakic	4.00	1.80	.50
☐	114	John Vanbiesbrouck	.25	.11	.03
☐	115	Dave Poulin	.08	.04	.01
☐	116	Rick Meagher	.05	.02	.01
☐	117	Kirk Muller	.15	.07	.02
☐	118	Mats Naslund	.08	.04	.01
☐	119	Ray Sheppard	.25	.11	.03
☐	120	Jeff Norton	.20	.09	.03
☐	121	Randy Burridge	.08	.04	.01
☐	122	Dale Hawerchuk	.15	.07	.02
☐	123	Steve Duchesne	.15	.07	.02
☐	124	John Anderson	.05	.02	.01
☐	125	Rick Vaive	.08	.04	.01
☐	126	Randy Hillier	.05	.02	.01
☐	127	Jimmy Carson	.08	.04	.01
☐	128	Larry Murphy	.08	.04	.01
☐	129	Paul MacLean	.05	.02	.01
☐	130	Joe Cirella	.05	.02	.01
☐	131	Kelly Miller	.08	.04	.01
☐	132	Alain Chevrier	.05	.02	.01
☐	133	Ed Olczyk	.05	.02	.01
☐	134	Dave Tippett	.05	.02	.01
☐	135	Bob Sweeney	.05	.02	.01
☐	136	Brian Leetch	5.00	2.30	.60
☐	137	Greg Millen	.05	.02	.01
☐	138	Joe Nieuwendyk	.25	.11	.03
☐	139	Brian Propp	.08	.04	.01
☐	140	Mike Ramsey	.05	.02	.01
☐	141	Mike Allison	.05	.02	.01
☐	142	Shawn Chambers	.10	.05	.01
☐	143	Peter Stastny	.08	.04	.01
☐	144	Glen Hanlon	.05	.02	.01
☐	145	John Cullen	.35	.16	.04
☐	146	Kevin Hatcher	.15	.07	.02
☐	147	Brendan Shanahan	.75	.35	.09
☐	148	Paul Reinhart	.05	.02	.01
☐	149	Bryan Trottier	.08	.04	.01
☐	150	Dave Manson	.35	.16	.04
☐	151	Marc Habscheid	.05	.02	.01
☐	152	Dan Quinn	.05	.02	.01
☐	153	Stephane Richer	.15	.07	.02
☐	154	Doug Bodger	.05	.02	.01
☐	155	Ron Hextall	.15	.07	.02
☐	156	Wayne Gretzky	1.50	.65	.19
☐	157	Steve Tuttle	.05	.02	.01
☐	158	Charlie Huddy	.05	.02	.01
☐	159	Dave Christian	.08	.04	.01
☐	160	Andy Moog	.15	.07	.02
☐	161	Tony Granato	.40	.18	.05
☐	162	Sylvain Cote	.08	.04	.01
☐	163	Mike Vernon	.20	.09	.03
☐	164	Steve Chiasson	.25	.11	.03

165	Mike Ridley	.08	.04	.01
166	Kelly Hrudey	.08	.04	.01
167	Bob Carpenter	.05	.02	.01
168	Zarley Zalapski	.25	.11	.03
169	Derek Laxdal	.05	.02	.01
170	Clint Malarchuk	.08	.04	.01
171	Kelly Kisio	.05	.02	.01
172	Gerard Gallant	.05	.02	.01
173	Ron Sutter	.05	.02	.01
174	Chris Chelios	.10	.05	.01
175	Ron Francis	.15	.07	.02
176	Gino Cavallini	.05	.02	.01
177	Brian Bellows	.08	.04	.01
178	Greg C. Adams	.05	.02	.01
	Vancouver Canucks			
179	Steve Larmer	.15	.07	.02
180	Aaron Broten	.05	.02	.01
181	Brent Ashton	.05	.02	.01
182	Gerald Diduck	.05	.02	.01
183	Paul MacDermid	.05	.02	.01
184	Walt Poddubny	.05	.02	.01
185	Adam Oates	.50	.23	.06
186	Brett Hull	3.00	1.35	.40
187	Scott Arniel	.05	.02	.01
188	Bobby Smith	.08	.04	.01
189	Guy Lafleur	.15	.07	.02
190	Craig Janney	1.50	.65	.19
191	Mark Howe	.08	.04	.01
192	Grant Fuhr	.15	.07	.02
193	Rob Brown	.05	.02	.01
194	Steve Kasper	.05	.02	.01
195	Pete Peeters	.08	.04	.01
196	Joe Mullen	.15	.07	.02
197	Checklist 1-110	.10	.02	.01
198	Checklist 111-220	.10	.02	.01
199	Keith Crowder	.05	.02	.01
200	Daren Puppa	.60	.25	.08
201	Benoit Hogue	.50	.23	.06
202	Gary Roberts	1.50	.65	.19
203	Brad McCrimmon	.05	.02	.01
204	Rick Wamsley	.05	.02	.01
205	Joel Otto	.08	.04	.01
206	Jim Peplinski	.05	.02	.01
207	Jamie Macoun	.05	.02	.01
208	Brian MacLellan	.05	.02	.01
209	Scott Young	.25	.11	.03
210	Ulf Samuelsson	.08	.04	.01
211	Joel Quenneville UER	.05	.02	.01
	(Misspelled Quennville on card back)			
212	Tim Watters	.05	.02	.01
213	Curt Giles	.05	.02	.01
214	Stewart Gavin	.05	.02	.01
215	Bob Brooke	.05	.02	.01
216	Basil McRae	.20	.09	.03
217	Frantisek Musil	.15	.07	.02
218	Adam Creighton	.20	.09	.03
219	Troy Murray	.05	.02	.01
220	Steve Konroyd	.05	.02	.01
221	Duane Sutter	.05	.02	.01
222	Trent Yawney	.10	.05	.01
223	Mike O'Connell	.05	.02	.01
224	Jim Nill	.05	.02	.01
225	John Chabot	.05	.02	.01
226	Glenn Anderson	.10	.05	.01
227	Kevin Lowe	.08	.04	.01
228	Steve Smith	.25	.11	.03
229	Randy Gregg	.05	.02	.01
230	Craig MacTavish	.08	.04	.01
231	Craig Muni	.05	.02	.01
232	Theoren Fleury	3.00	1.35	.40
233	Bill Ranford	.50	.23	.06
234	Claude Lemieux	.25	.11	.03
235	Larry Robinson	.08	.04	.01
236	Craig Ludwig	.05	.02	.01
237	Brian Hayward	.05	.02	.01
238	Petr Svoboda	.05	.02	.01
239	Russ Courtnall	.15	.07	.02
240	Ryan Walter	.05	.02	.01
241	Tommy Albelin	.05	.02	.01
242	Doug Brown	.05	.02	.01
243	Ken Daneyko	.20	.09	.03
244	Mark Johnson	.05	.02	.01
245	Randy Velischek	.05	.02	.01
246	Brad Dalgarno	.05	.02	.01
247	Mikko Makela	.05	.02	.01
248	Shayne Corson	.40	.18	.05
249	Marc Bergevin	.05	.02	.01
250	Pat Flatley	.05	.02	.01
251	Michel Petit	.05	.02	.01
252	Mark Hardy	.05	.02	.01
253	Scott Mellanby	.08	.04	.01
254	Keith Acton	.05	.02	.01
255	Ken Wregget	.08	.04	.01
256	Gord Dineen	.05	.02	.01
257	Dave Hannan	.05	.02	.01
258	Mario Gosselin	.05	.02	.01
259	Randy Moller	.05	.02	.01
260	Mario Marois	.05	.02	.01
261	Robert Picard	.05	.02	.01
262	Marc Fortier	.05	.02	.01
263	Ron Tugnutt	.35	.16	.04
264	Iiro Jarvi	.05	.02	.01
265	Paul Gillis	.05	.02	.01
266	Mike Hough	.10	.05	.01
267	Jim Sandlak	.05	.02	.01
268	Greg Paslawski	.05	.02	.01
269	Paul Cavallini	.25	.11	.03
270	Gaston Gingras	.05	.02	.01
271	Allan Bester	.05	.02	.01
272	Vincent Damphousse	.35	.16	.04
273	Daniel Marois	.20	.09	.03
274	Mark Osborne UER	.05	.02	.01
	(Misspelled Osbourne on card front)			
275	Craig Laughlin	.05	.02	.01
276	Brad Marsh	.08	.04	.01
277	Dan Daoust	.05	.02	.01
278	Borje Salming	.08	.04	.01
279	Chris Kotsopoulos	.05	.02	.01
280	Tony Tanti	.05	.02	.01
281	Barry Pederson	.05	.02	.01
282	Rich Sutter	.05	.02	.01
283	Stan Smyl	.05	.02	.01
284	Doug Lidster	.05	.02	.01
285	Steve Weeks	.05	.02	.01
286	Harold Snepsts	.05	.02	.01
287	Brian Bradley	.75	.35	.09
288	Larry Melnyk	.05	.02	.01
289	Bob Gould	.05	.02	.01
290	Thomas Steen	.08	.04	.01
291	Randy Carlyle	.05	.02	.01
292	Hannu Jarvenpaa UER	.05	.02	.01
	(Misspelled Jaryenpaa on card front)			
293	Iain Duncan	.05	.02	.01
294	Doug Smail	.05	.02	.01
295	Jim Kyte	.05	.02	.01
296	Daniel Berthiaume	.05	.02	.01
297	Peter Taglianetti	.05	.02	.01
298	Boston Bruins Action Scene (Craig Janney)	.15	.07	.02
299	Buffalo Sabres Action Scene (Dave Andreychuk)	.06	.03	.01
300	Calgary Flames Action Scene (Mike Vernon)	.06	.03	.01
301	Chicago Blackhawks Action Scene (Dirk Graham)	.06	.03	.01
302	Detroit Red Wings Action Scene (Gerard Gallant)	.06	.03	.01
303	Edmonton Oilers Action Scene (Glenn Anderson)	.06	.03	.01
304	Hartford Whalers Action Scene (Kevin Dineen)	.06	.03	.01
305	Los Angeles Kings Action Scene (Kelly Hrudey)	.06	.03	.01
306	Minnesota North Stars Action Scene (Neal Broten)	.06	.03	.01
307	Montreal Canadiens Action Scene (Chris Chelios)	.06	.03	.01
308	New Jersey Devils Action Scene (Aaron Broten)	.06	.03	.01
309	New York Islanders Action Scene (David Volek)	.06	.03	.01
310	New York Rangers Action Scene (Tony Granato)	.06	.03	.01
311	Philadelphia Flyers Action Scene (Ron Hextall)	.06	.03	.01
312	Pittsburgh Penguins Action Scene (Mario Lemieux)	.35	.16	.04
313	Quebec Nordiques	.25	.11	.03

	Action Scene (Joe Sakic)			
☐ 314	St. Louis Blues	.06	.03	.01
	Action Scene (Greg Millen)			
☐ 315	Toronto Maple Leafs	.06	.03	.01
	Action Scene (Brian Bradley)			
☐ 316	Vancouver Canucks	.06	.03	.01
	Action Scene (Jim Sandlak, Ray Bourque defending)			
☐ 317	Washington Capitals	.06	.03	.01
	Action Scene (Mike Liut)			
☐ 318	Winnipeg Jets	.06	.03	.01
	Action Scene			
☐ 319	Art Ross Trophy	.35	.16	.04
	Mario Lemieux			
☐ 320	Hart Trophy	.50	.23	.06
	Wayne Gretzky			
☐ 321	Calder Trophy	.50	.23	.06
	Brian Leetch			
☐ 322	Vezina Trophy	.40	.18	.05
	Patrick Roy			
☐ 323	Norris Trophy	.05	.02	.01
	Chris Chelios			
☐ 324	Lady Byng Trophy	.05	.02	.01
	Joe Mullen			
☐ 325	1988-89 Highlight	.50	.23	.06
	Wayne Gretzky			
☐ 326	1988-89 Highlight	.50	.23	.06
	Brian Leetch UER (Photo actually David Shaw)			
☐ 327	1988-89 Highlight	.35	.16	.04
	Mario Lemieux			
☐ 328	1988-89 Highlight	.06	.03	.01
	Esa Tikkanen			
☐ 329	Coupe Stanley Cup	.06	.03	.01
	Calgary Flames			
☐ 330	Checklist 221-330	.10	.02	.01

☐ A	Mario Lemieux	2.00	.80	.20
☐ B	Mike Ridley	.25	.10	.02
☐ C	Tomas Sandstrom	.25	.10	.02
☐ D	Petri Skriko	.15	.06	.01
☐ E	Wayne Gretzky	2.00	.80	.20
☐ F	Brett Hull	1.25	.50	.12
☐ G	Tim Kerr	.15	.06	.01
☐ H	Mats Naslund	.15	.06	.01
☐ I	Jari Kurri	.35	.14	.03
☐ J	Steve Larmer	.25	.10	.02
☐ K	Cam Neely	.75	.30	.07
☐ L	Steve Yzerman	1.00	.40	.10
☐ M	Kevin Dineen	.25	.10	.02
☐ N	Dave Gagner	.35	.14	.03
☐ O	Joe Mullen	.25	.10	.02
☐ P	Pierre Turgeon	.75	.30	.07

1989-90 O-Pee-Chee Sticker Back Cards

This 34-card set is a subset of the 1989-90 O-Pee-Chee sticker set. It is similar to the previous year's issue except that this issue also features All-Stars. The cards measure approximately 2 1/8" by 3". The backs of the cards are actually the fronts of the stickers; color action player photos have been cut out and superimposed on solid color backgrounds (red, orange, or green). The player's name, position, and team appear next to the cut-out picture. The stickers are numbered on the back and checklisted below accordingly.

		MINT	EXC	G-VG
COMPLETE SET (34)		12.00	5.00	1.20
COMMON PLAYER (1-34)		.10	.04	.01
☐ 1	Greg Hawgood	.10	.04	.01
☐ 2	Craig Janney	.75	.30	.07
☐ 3	Bob Joyce	.10	.04	.01
☐ 4	Benoit Hogue	.20	.08	.02
☐ 5	Jiri Hrdina	.10	.04	.01
☐ 6	Peter Sidorkiewicz	.20	.08	.02
☐ 7	Scott Young	.20	.08	.02
☐ 8	Sean Burke	.25	.10	.02
☐ 9	Dave Volek	.20	.08	.02
☐ 10	Tony Granato	.20	.08	.02
☐ 11	Brian Leetch	2.00	.80	.20
☐ 12	Gord Murphy	.10	.04	.01
☐ 13	John Cullen	.50	.20	.05
☐ 14	Zarley Zalapski	.25	.10	.02
☐ 15	Iiro Jarvi	.10	.04	.01
☐ 16	Joe Sakic	2.00	.80	.20
☐ 17	Vincent Riendeau	.40	.16	.04
☐ 18	Dan Marois	.20	.08	.02
☐ 19	Trevor Linden	1.50	.60	.15
☐ 20	Pat Elynuik	.20	.08	.02
☐ 21	Bob Essensa	.50	.20	.05
☐ 22	Checklist	.10	.04	.01
☐ 23	Joe Mullen	.20	.08	.02
☐ 24	Mario Lemieux	2.00	.80	.20
☐ 25	Gerard Gallant	.10	.04	.01
☐ 26	Chris Chelios	.30	.12	.03
☐ 27	Al MacInnis	.30	.12	.03
☐ 28	Patrick Roy	1.25	.50	.12

1989-90 O-Pee-Chee/Topps Box Bottoms

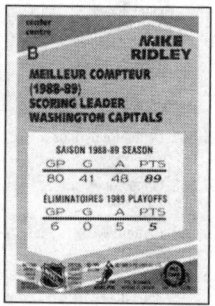

This sixteen-card set measures the standard size, 2 1/2" by 3 1/2", and was issued in sets of four on the bottom of the 1989-90 O-Pee-Chee and Topps wax pack boxes. Complete box bottom panels are valued at a 25 percent premium above the prices listed below. The cards feature sixteen NHL star players who were scoring leaders on their teams. A color action photo appears on the front and the player's name, team, and team logo at the bottom of the picture. The back is printed in red and black ink and gives the player's position and statistical information. The cards are lettered rather than numbered. The set features such NHL stars as Wayne Gretzky, Brett Hull, and Mario Lemieux.

	MINT	EXC	G-VG
COMPLETE SET (16)	6.00	2.40	.60
COMMON PLAYER (A-P)	.15	.06	.01

		MINT	EXC	G-VG
☐ 29	Geoff Courtnall	.30	.12	.03
☐ 30	Wayne Gretzky	2.00	.80	.20
☐ 31	Rob Brown	.20	.08	.02
☐ 32	Steve Duchesne	.30	.12	.03
☐ 33	Ray Bourque	.50	.20	.05
☐ 34	Mike Vernon	.30	.12	.03

1990-91 O-Pee-Chee

 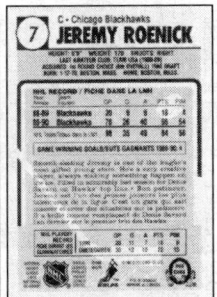

At 528 cards, this is the largest set ever issued by O-Pee-Chee. Cards measure the standard 2 1/2" by 3 1/2". The fronts feature color photos bordered by team colors. A hockey stick is superimposed over the picture at the top border. Bilingual backs have blue lettering on a pale green background and have biographical information and career statistics. Stats include game winning goals and playoff scoring. Team cards feature action scenes with the team's previous season standings and power play stats on the card back. The latter part of the set includes a heavy emphasis on Russian players who toured the NHL in 1989-90 as part of the Super Series. Rookie Cards in this set include Rod Brind'Amour, Tim Cheveldae, Bob Essensa, Garry Galley, Adam Graves, Arturs Irbe, Curtis Joseph, Bob Kudelski, Sergei Makarov, Mike Modano, Alexander Mogilny, Sergei Nemchinov, Mark Recchi, Jeremy Roenick, Kevin Stevens, Chris Terreri and Darren Turcotte.

		MINT	EXC	G-VG
COMPLETE SET (528)		20.00	9.00	2.50
COMPLETE FACT.SET (528)		20.00	9.00	2.50
COMMON PLAYER (1-528)		.05	.02	.01
☐ 1	Gretzky Tribute	.40	.18	.05
	Indianapolis Racers			
☐ 2	Gretzky Tribute	.35	.16	.04
	Edmonton Oilers			
☐ 3	Gretzky Tribute	.35	.16	.04
	Los Angeles Kings			
☐ 4	Brett Hull HL	.20	.09	.03
☐ 5	Jari Kurri HL UER	.08	.04	.01
	(Misspelled Jarri)			
☐ 6	Bryan Trottier HL	.05	.02	.01
☐ 7	Jeremy Roenick	1.50	.65	.19
☐ 8	Brian Propp	.08	.04	.01
☐ 9	Jim Hrivnak	.15	.07	.02
☐ 10	Mick Vukota	.05	.02	.01
☐ 11	Tom Kurvers	.05	.02	.01
☐ 12	Ulf Dahlen	.08	.04	.01
☐ 13	Bernie Nicholls	.10	.05	.01
☐ 14	Peter Sidorkiewicz	.05	.02	.01
☐ 15	Peter Zezel	.05	.02	.01
☐ 16	Mike Hartman	.05	.02	.01
☐ 17	Kings Team	.05	.02	.01
☐ 18	Jim Sandlak	.05	.02	.01
☐ 19	Rob Brown	.05	.02	.01
☐ 20	Paul Ranheim	.15	.07	.02
☐ 21	Rick Zombo	.05	.02	.01
☐ 22	Paul Gillis	.05	.02	.01
☐ 23	Brian Hayward	.05	.02	.01
☐ 24	Brent Ashton	.05	.02	.01
☐ 25	Mark Lamb	.05	.02	.01
☐ 26	Rick Tocchet	.08	.04	.01

		MINT	EXC	G-VG
☐ 27	Viacheslav Fetisov	.15	.07	.02
☐ 28	Denis Savard	.08	.04	.01
☐ 29	Chris Chelios	.08	.04	.01
☐ 30	Janne Ojanen	.05	.02	.01
☐ 31	Don Maloney	.05	.02	.01
☐ 32	Allan Bester	.05	.02	.01
☐ 33	Geoff Smith	.05	.02	.01
☐ 34	Daniel Shank	.05	.02	.01
☐ 35	Mikael Andersson	.10	.05	.01
☐ 36	Gino Cavallini	.05	.02	.01
☐ 37	Rob Murphy	.05	.02	.01
☐ 38	Flames Team	.05	.02	.01
☐ 39	Laurie Boschman	.05	.02	.01
☐ 40	Craig Wolanin	.05	.02	.01
☐ 41	Phil Bourque	.05	.02	.01
☐ 42	Alexander Mogilny	1.00	.45	.13
☐ 43	Ray Bourque	.20	.09	.03
☐ 44	Mike Liut	.08	.04	.01
☐ 45	Ron Sutter	.05	.02	.01
☐ 46	Bob Kudelski	.40	.18	.05
☐ 47	Larry Murphy	.08	.04	.01
☐ 48	Darren Turcotte	.25	.11	.03
☐ 49	Paul Ysebaert	.15	.07	.02
☐ 50	Alan Kerr	.05	.02	.01
☐ 51	Randy Carlyle	.05	.02	.01
☐ 52	Iiro Jarvi	.05	.02	.01
☐ 53	Don Barber	.05	.02	.01
☐ 54	Carey Wilson UER	.05	.02	.01
	(Misspelled Cary on both sides)			
☐ 55	Joey Kocur	.05	.02	.01
☐ 56	Steve Larmer	.08	.04	.01
☐ 57	Paul Cavallini	.05	.02	.01
☐ 58	Shayne Corson	.08	.04	.01
☐ 59	Canucks Team	.05	.02	.01
☐ 60	Sergei Makarov	.40	.18	.05
☐ 61	Kjell Samuelsson	.05	.02	.01
☐ 62	Tony Granato	.08	.04	.01
☐ 63	Tom Fergus	.05	.02	.01
☐ 64	Martin Gelinas	.15	.07	.02
☐ 65	Tom Barrasso	.10	.05	.01
☐ 66	Pierre Turgeon	.30	.14	.04
☐ 67	Randy Cunneyworth	.05	.02	.01
☐ 68	Michal Pivonka	.25	.11	.03
☐ 69	Cam Neely	.25	.11	.03
☐ 70	Brian Bellows	.08	.04	.01
☐ 71	Pat Elynuik	.05	.02	.01
☐ 72	Doug Crossman	.05	.02	.01
☐ 73	Sylvain Turgeon	.05	.02	.01
☐ 74	Shawn Burr	.05	.02	.01
☐ 75	John Vanbiesbrouck	.15	.07	.02
☐ 76	Steve Bozek	.05	.02	.01
☐ 77	Brett Hull	.75	.35	.09
☐ 78	Zarley Zalapski	.08	.04	.01
☐ 79	Wendel Clark	.25	.11	.03
☐ 80	Flyers Team	.05	.02	.01
☐ 81	Kelly Miller	.05	.02	.01
☐ 82	Mark Pederson	.05	.02	.01
☐ 83	Adam Creighton	.05	.02	.01
☐ 84	Scott Young	.05	.02	.01
☐ 85	Petr Klima	.08	.04	.01
☐ 86	Steve Duchesne	.08	.04	.01
☐ 87	Joe Nieuwendyk	.15	.07	.02
☐ 88	Andy Brickley	.05	.02	.01
☐ 89	Phil Housley	.08	.04	.01
☐ 90	Neal Broten	.08	.04	.01
☐ 91	Al Iafrate	.08	.04	.01
☐ 92	Steve Thomas	.08	.04	.01
☐ 93	Guy Carbonneau	.08	.04	.01
☐ 94	Steve Chiasson	.08	.04	.01
☐ 95	Mike Tomlak	.05	.02	.01
☐ 96	Roger Johansson	.05	.02	.01
☐ 97	Randy Wood	.05	.02	.01
☐ 98	Jim Johnson	.05	.02	.01
☐ 99	Bob Sweeney	.05	.02	.01
☐ 100	Dino Ciccarelli	.08	.04	.01
☐ 101	Rangers Team	.05	.02	.01
☐ 102	Mike Ramsey	.05	.02	.01
☐ 103	Kelly Hrudey	.08	.04	.01
☐ 104	Dave Ellett	.05	.02	.01
☐ 105	Bob Brooke	.05	.02	.01
☐ 106	Greg Adams	.05	.02	.01
	Vancouver Canucks			
☐ 107	Joe Cirella	.05	.02	.01
☐ 108	Jari Kurri	.10	.05	.01
☐ 109	Pete Peeters	.08	.04	.01
☐ 110	Paul MacLean	.05	.02	.01
☐ 111	Doug Wilson	.08	.04	.01
☐ 112	Pat Verbeek	.08	.04	.01
☐ 113	Bob Beers	.10	.05	.01
☐ 114	Mike O'Connell	.05	.02	.01
☐ 115	Brian Bradley	.08	.04	.01
☐ 116	Paul Coffey	.15	.07	.02

☐ 117 Doug Brown	.05	.02	.01
☐ 118 Aaron Broten	.05	.02	.01
☐ 119 Bob Essensa	.25	.11	.03
☐ 120 Wayne Gretzky UER	1.25	.55	.16
(1302 career assists, not 13102)			
☐ 121 Vincent Damphousse	.08	.04	.01
☐ 122 Nordiques Team	.05	.02	.01
☐ 123 Mike Foligno	.08	.04	.01
☐ 124 Russ Courtnall	.08	.04	.01
☐ 125 Rick Meagher	.05	.02	.01
☐ 126 Craig Fisher	.05	.02	.01
☐ 127 Al MacInnis	.10	.04	.01
☐ 128 Derek King	.08	.04	.01
☐ 129 Dale Hunter	.08	.04	.01
☐ 130 Mark Messier UER	.35	.16	.04
(Position LW, should be C)			
☐ 131 James Patrick UER	.05	.02	.01
(Blue border, should be orange)			
☐ 132 Checklist 1-132 UER	.05	.02	.01
(132 Cary Wilson, should be Carey)			
☐ 133 Red Wings Team	.05	.02	.01
☐ 134 Barry Pederson	.05	.02	.01
☐ 135 Gary Leeman	.05	.02	.01
☒ 136 Doug Gilmour	.35	.16	.04
☐ 137 Mike McPhee	.05	.02	.01
☐ 138 Bob Murray	.05	.02	.01
☐ 139 Bob Carpenter	.05	.02	.01
☐ 140 Sean Burke	.08	.04	.01
☐ 141 Dale Hawerchuk	.08	.04	.01
☐ 142 Guy Lafleur	.05	.02	.01
☐ 143 Lindy Ruff	.05	.02	.01
☐ 144 Whalers Team	.05	.02	.01
☐ 145 Glenn Anderson	.10	.05	.01
☐ 146 Dave Chyzowski	.05	.02	.01
☐ 147 Kevin Hatcher	.08	.04	.01
☐ 148 Rick Vaive	.05	.02	.01
☐ 149 Adam Oates	.20	.09	.03
☐ 150 Garth Butcher	.08	.04	.01
☐ 151 Basil McRae	.08	.04	.01
☐ 152 Ilkka Sinisalo	.05	.02	.01
☐ 153 Steve Kasper	.05	.02	.01
☐ 154 Greg Paslawski	.05	.02	.01
☐ 155 Brad Marsh	.08	.04	.01
☐ 156 Esa Tikkanen	.08	.04	.01
☐ 157 Tony Tanti	.05	.02	.01
☐ 158 Mario Marois UER	.05	.02	.01
(On front, "oi" in Marois is out of line)			
☐ 159 Sylvain Lefebvre	.05	.02	.01
☐ 160 Troy Murray	.05	.02	.01
☐ 161 Gary Roberts	.20	.09	.03
☐ 162 Randy Ladouceur	.05	.02	.01
☐ 163 John Chabot	.05	.02	.01
☐ 164 Calle Johansson	.05	.02	.01
☐ 165 Bruins Team	.05	.02	.01
☐ 166 Jeff Norton	.05	.02	.01
☐ 167 Mike Krushelnyski	.05	.02	.01
☐ 168 Dave Gagner	.08	.04	.01
☐ 169 Dave Andreychuk	.25	.11	.03
☐ 170 Dave Capuano	.05	.02	.01
☐ 171 Curtis Joseph	1.00	.45	.13
☐ 172 Bruce Driver	.05	.02	.01
☐ 173 Scott Mellanby	.08	.04	.01
☐ 174 John Ogrodnick	.05	.02	.01
☐ 175 Mario Lemieux	1.00	.45	.13
☐ 176 Marc Fortier	.05	.02	.01
☐ 177 Vincent Riendeau	.15	.07	.02
☐ 178 Mark Johnson	.05	.02	.01
☐ 179 Dirk Graham	.08	.04	.01
☐ 180 Jets Team	.05	.02	.01
☐ 181 Robb Stauber	.25	.11	.03
☐ 182 Christian Ruuttu	.05	.02	.01
☐ 183 Dave Tippett	.05	.02	.01
☐ 184 Pat LaFontaine	.30	.14	.04
☐ 185 Mark Howe	.08	.04	.01
☐ 186 Stephane Richer	.08	.04	.01
☐ 187 Jan Erixon	.05	.02	.01
☐ 188 Neil Sheehy	.05	.02	.01
☐ 189 Craig MacTavish	.08	.04	.01
☐ 190 Randy Burridge	.05	.02	.01
☐ 191 Bernie Federko	.08	.04	.01
☐ 192 Shawn Chambers	.05	.02	.01
☐ 193 Mark Messier AS1	.05	.02	.01
☐ 194 Luc Robitaille AS1	.05	.02	.01
☐ 195 Brett Hull AS1	.25	.11	.03
☐ 196 Ray Bourque AS1	.05	.02	.01
☐ 197 Al MacInnis AS1	.08	.04	.01
☐ 198 Patrick Roy AS1	.40	.18	.05
☐ 199 Wayne Gretzky AS2	.50	.23	.06
☐ 200 Brian Bellows AS2	.05	.02	.01
☐ 201 Cam Neely AS2	.10	.05	.01
☐ 202 Paul Coffey AS2	.08	.04	.01
☐ 203 Doug Wilson AS2	.05	.02	.01
☐ 204 Daren Puppa AS2 UER	.05	.02	.01
(Misspelled Darren)			
☐ 205 Gary Suter	.08	.04	.01
☐ 206 Ed Olczyk	.05	.02	.01
☐ 207 Doug Lidster	.05	.02	.01
☐ 208 John Cullen	.08	.04	.01
☐ 209 Luc Robitaille	.30	.14	.04
☐ 210 Tim Kerr	.08	.04	.01
☐ 211 Scott Stevens	.10	.05	.01
☐ 212 Craig Janney	.25	.11	.03
☐ 213 Kevin Dineen	.08	.04	.01
☐ 214 Jimmy Waite	.25	.11	.03
☐ 215 Benoit Hogue	.08	.04	.01
☐ 216 Curtis Leschyshyn	.05	.02	.01
☐ 217 Brad Lauer	.05	.02	.01
☐ 218 Joe Mullen	.10	.05	.01
☐ 219 Patrick Roy	1.00	.45	.13
☐ 220 Blues Team	.05	.02	.01
☐ 221 Brian Leetch	.50	.23	.06
☐ 222 Steve Yzerman	.35	.16	.04
☐ 223 Stephane Beauregard	.10	.05	.01
☐ 224 John MacLean	.08	.04	.01
☐ 225 Trevor Linden	.30	.14	.04
☐ 226 Bill Ranford	.10	.05	.01
☐ 227 Mark Osborne	.05	.02	.01
☐ 228 Curt Giles	.05	.02	.01
☐ 229 Mikko Makela	.05	.02	.01
☐ 230 Bob Errey	.05	.02	.01
☐ 231 Jimmy Carson	.08	.04	.01
☐ 232 Kay Whitmore	.20	.09	.03
☐ 233 Gary Nylund	.05	.02	.01
☐ 234 Jiri Hrdina	.05	.02	.01
☐ 235 Stephen Leach	.05	.02	.01
☐ 236 Greg Hawgood UER	.05	.02	.01
(Photo actually Don Sweeney)			
☐ 237 Jocelyn Lemieux	.05	.02	.01
☐ 238 Daren Puppa	.08	.04	.01
☐ 239 Kelly Kisio	.05	.02	.01
☐ 240 Craig Simpson	.08	.04	.01
☐ 241 Maple Leafs Team	.05	.02	.01
☐ 242 Fredrik Olausson	.08	.04	.01
☐ 243 Ron Hextall	.08	.04	.01
☐ 244 Sergio Momesso	.15	.07	.02
☐ 245 Kirk Muller	.08	.04	.01
☐ 246 Petr Svoboda	.05	.02	.01
☐ 247 Daniel Berthiaume	.05	.02	.01
☐ 248 Andrew McBain	.05	.02	.01
☐ 249 Jeff Jackson UER	.05	.02	.01
('89-90 stats should be 65, not 0)			
☐ 250 Randy Gilhen	.05	.02	.01
☐ 251 Oilers Team	.15	.07	.02
☐ 252 Rick Bennett	.08	.04	.01
☐ 253 Don Beaupre	.08	.04	.01
☐ 254 Pelle Eklund	.05	.02	.01
☐ 255 Greg Gilbert	.05	.02	.01
☐ 256 Gordie Roberts	.05	.02	.01
☐ 257 Kirk McLean	.25	.11	.03
☐ 258 Brent Sutter	.08	.04	.01
☐ 259 Brendan Shanahan	.30	.14	.04
☐ 260 Todd Krygier	.05	.02	.01
☐ 261 Larry Robinson UER	.08	.04	.01
('80-81 season stats missing making career totals wrong)			
☐ 262 Sabres Team	.05	.02	.01
☐ 263 Dave Christian	.05	.02	.01
☐ 264 Checklist 133-264	.05	.02	.01
☐ 265 Jamie Macoun	.05	.02	.01
☐ 266 Glen Hanlon	.05	.02	.01
☐ 267 Daniel Marois	.05	.02	.01
☐ 268 Doug Smail	.05	.02	.01
☐ 269 Jon Casey	.08	.04	.01
☐ 270 Brian Skrudland	.05	.02	.01
☐ 271 Michel Petit	.05	.02	.01
☐ 272 Dan Quinn	.05	.02	.01
☐ 273 Geoff Courtnall	.08	.04	.01
☐ 274 Mike Bullard	.05	.02	.01
☐ 275 Randy Gregg	.05	.02	.01
☐ 276 Keith Brown	.05	.02	.01
☐ 277 Troy Mallette	.05	.02	.01
☐ 278 Steve Tuttle	.05	.02	.01
☐ 279 Brad Shaw	.05	.02	.01
☐ 280 Mark Recchi	1.00	.45	.13
☐ 281 John Tonelli	.08	.04	.01
☐ 282 Doug Bodger	.05	.02	.01
☐ 283 Thomas Steen	.08	.04	.01
☐ 284 Devils Team	.05	.02	.01

☐ 285	Lee Norwood	.05	.02	.01
☐ 286	Brian MacLellan	.05	.02	.01
☐ 287	Bobby Smith	.08	.04	.01
☐ 288	Rob Cimetta	.05	.02	.01
☐ 289	Rob Zettler	.05	.02	.01
☐ 290	David Reid	.05	.02	.01
☐ 291	Bryan Trottier	.08	.04	.01
☐ 292	Brian Mullen	.08	.04	.01
☐ 293	Paul Reinhart	.05	.02	.01
☐ 294	Andy Moog	.10	.05	.01
☐ 295	Jeff Brown	.08	.04	.01
☐ 296	Ryan Walter	.05	.02	.01
☐ 297	Trent Yawney	.05	.02	.01
☐ 298	John Druce	.05	.02	.01
☐ 299	Dave McLlwain	.05	.02	.01
☐ 300	David Volek	.05	.02	.01
☐ 301	Tomas Sandstrom	.08	.04	.01
☐ 302	Gord Murphy	.05	.02	.01
☐ 303	Lou Franceschetti	.05	.02	.01
☐ 304	Dana Murzyn	.05	.02	.01
☐ 305	North Stars Team	.05	.02	.01
☐ 306	Patrik Sundstrom	.05	.02	.01
☐ 307	Kevin Lowe	.08	.04	.01
☐ 308	Dave Barr	.05	.02	.01
☐ 309	Wendell Young	.05	.02	.01
☐ 310	Darrin Shannon	.15	.07	.02
☐ 311	Ron Francis	.10	.05	.01
☐ 312	Stephane Fiset	.25	.11	.03
☐ 313	Paul Fenton	.05	.02	.01
☐ 314	Dave Taylor	.08	.04	.01
☐ 315	Islanders Team	.05	.02	.01
☐ 316	Petri Skriko	.05	.02	.01
☐ 317	Rob Ramage	.05	.02	.01
☐ 318	Murray Craven	.05	.02	.01
☐ 319	Gaetan Duchesne	.05	.02	.01
☐ 320	Brad McCrimmon	.05	.02	.01
☐ 321	Grant Fuhr	.10	.05	.01
☐ 322	Gerard Gallant	.05	.02	.01
☐ 323	Tommy Albelin	.05	.02	.01
☐ 324	Scott Arniel	.05	.02	.01
☐ 325	Mike Keane	.20	.09	.03
☐ 326	Penguins Team	.05	.02	.01
☐ 327	Mike Ridley	.08	.04	.01
☐ 328	Dave Babych	.05	.02	.01
☐ 329	Michel Goulet	.08	.04	.01
☐ 330	Mike Richter	1.00	.45	.13
☐ 331	Garry Galley	.20	.09	.03
☐ 332	Rod Brind'Amour	.60	.25	.08
☐ 333	Tony McKegney	.05	.02	.01
☐ 334	Peter Stastny	.08	.04	.01
☐ 335	Greg Millen	.05	.02	.01
☐ 336	Ray Ferraro	.08	.04	.01
☐ 337	Miloslav Horava	.05	.02	.01
☐ 338	Paul MacDermid	.05	.02	.01
☐ 339	Craig Coxe	.05	.02	.01
☐ 340	Dave Snuggerud	.05	.02	.01
☐ 341	Mike Lalor	.05	.02	.01
☐ 342	Marc Habscheid	.05	.02	.01
☐ 343	Rejean Lemelin	.08	.04	.01
☐ 344	Charlie Huddy	.05	.02	.01
☐ 345	Ken Linseman	.05	.02	.01
☐ 346	Canadiens Team	.05	.02	.01
☐ 347	Troy Loney	.05	.02	.01
☐ 348	Mike Modano	1.00	.45	.13
☐ 349	Jeff Reese	.15	.07	.02
☐ 350	Pat Flatley	.05	.02	.01
☐ 351	Mike Vernon	.08	.04	.01
☐ 352	Todd Elik	.25	.11	.03
☐ 353	Rod Langway	.05	.02	.01
☐ 354	Moe Mantha	.05	.02	.01
☐ 355	Keith Acton	.05	.02	.01
☐ 356	Scott Pearson	.05	.02	.01
☐ 357	Perry Berezan	.05	.02	.01
☐ 358	Alexei Kasatonov	.15	.07	.02
☐ 359	Igor Larionov	.35	.16	.04
☐ 360	Kevin Stevens	1.00	.45	.13
☐ 361	Yves Racine	.15	.07	.02
☐ 362	Dave Poulin	.08	.04	.01
☐ 363	Blackhawks Team	.05	.02	.01
☐ 364	Yvon Corriveau	.05	.02	.01
☐ 365	Brian Benning	.05	.02	.01
☐ 366	Hubie McDonough	.05	.02	.01
☐ 367	Ron Tugnutt	.08	.04	.01
☐ 368	Steve Smith	.08	.04	.01
☐ 369	Joel Otto	.05	.02	.01
☐ 370	Dave Lowry	.05	.02	.01
☐ 371	Clint Malarchuk	.08	.04	.01
☐ 372	Mathieu Schneider	.25	.11	.03
☐ 373	Mike Gartner	.10	.05	.01
☐ 374	John Tucker	.05	.02	.01
☐ 375	Chris Terreri	.30	.14	.04
☐ 376	Dean Evason	.05	.02	.01
☐ 377	Jamie Leach	.05	.02	.01
☐ 378	Jacques Cloutier	.05	.02	.01
☐ 379	Glen Wesley	.08	.04	.01
☐ 380	Vladimir Krutov	.05	.02	.01
☐ 381	Terry Carkner	.05	.02	.01
☐ 382	John McIntyre	.05	.02	.01
☐ 383	Ville Siren	.05	.02	.01
☐ 384	Joe Sakic	.50	.23	.06
☐ 385	Teppo Numminen	.15	.07	.02
☐ 386	Theoren Fleury	.30	.14	.04
☐ 387	Glen Featherstone	.05	.02	.01
☐ 388	Stephan Lebeau	.35	.16	.04
☐ 389	Kevin McClelland	.05	.02	.01
☐ 390	Uwe Krupp	.08	.04	.01
☐ 391	Mark Janssens	.05	.02	.01
☐ 392	Marty McSorley	.08	.04	.01
☐ 393	Vladimir Ruzicka	.15	.07	.02
☐ 394	Capitals Team	.05	.02	.01
☐ 395	Mark Fitzpatrick	.15	.07	.02
☐ 396	Checklist 265-396	.05	.02	.01
☐ 397	Dave Manson	.08	.04	.01
☐ 398	Bob Gould	.05	.02	.01
☐ 399	Bill Houlder	.20	.09	.03
☐ 400	Glenn Healy	.25	.11	.03
☐ 401	John Kordic UER	.15	.07	.02
	(Listed as Defence, should be LW)			
☐ 402	Stewart Gavin	.05	.02	.01
☐ 403	David Shaw	.05	.02	.01
☐ 404	Ed Kastelic	.05	.02	.01
☐ 405	Rich Sutter	.05	.02	.01
☐ 406	Grant Ledyard	.15	.07	.02
☐ 407	Steve Weeks	.05	.02	.01
☐ 408	Randy Hillier	.05	.02	.01
☐ 409	Rick Wamsley	.05	.02	.01
☐ 410	Doug Houda	.05	.02	.01
☐ 411	Ken McRae	.05	.02	.01
☐ 412	Craig Ludwig	.05	.02	.01
☐ 413	Doug Evans	.05	.02	.01
☐ 414	Ken Baumgartner	.05	.02	.01
☐ 415	Ken Wregget	.05	.02	.01
☐ 416	Eric Weinrich	.15	.07	.02
☐ 417	Mike Allison	.05	.02	.01
☐ 418	Joel Quenneville	.05	.02	.01
☐ 419	Larry Melnyk	.05	.02	.01
☐ 420	Colin Patterson	.05	.02	.01
☐ 421	Gerald Diduck	.05	.02	.01
☐ 422	Brent Gilchrist	.15	.07	.02
☐ 423	Craig Muni	.05	.02	.01
☐ 424	Mike Hudson	.15	.07	.02
☐ 425	Eric Desjardins	.25	.11	.03
☐ 426	Walt Poddubny	.05	.02	.01
☐ 427	Mike Hough	.05	.02	.01
☐ 428	Luke Richardson	.05	.02	.01
☐ 429	Joe Murphy	.30	.14	.04
☐ 430	Tim Cheveldae	.25	.11	.03
☐ 431	Adam Burt	.05	.02	.01
☐ 432	Kelly Chase	.05	.02	.01
☐ 433	Robert Nordmark	.05	.02	.01
☐ 434	Tim Hunter	.15	.07	.02
☐ 435	Peter Taglianetti	.05	.02	.01
☐ 436	Alain Chevrier	.05	.02	.01
☐ 437	Darin Kimble	.10	.05	.01
☐ 438	David Maley	.05	.02	.01
☐ 439	Jim Wiemer	.05	.02	.01
☐ 440	Nick Kypreos	.05	.02	.01
☐ 441	Lucien Deblois	.05	.02	.01
☐ 442	Mario Gosselin	.05	.02	.01
☐ 443	Neil Wilkinson	.15	.07	.02
☐ 444	Mark Kumpel	.05	.02	.01
☐ 445	Sergei Mylnikov UER	.05	.02	.01
	(Misspelled Sergi)			
☐ 446	Ray Sheppard	.15	.07	.02
☐ 447	Ron Greschner	.05	.02	.01
☐ 448	Craig Berube	.05	.02	.01
☐ 449	Dave Hannan	.05	.02	.01
☐ 450	Jim Korn UER	.05	.02	.01
	(Photo actually Paul Ranheim)			
☐ 451	Claude Lemieux	.08	.04	.01
☐ 452	Eldon Reddick	.05	.02	.01
☐ 453	Randy Velischek	.05	.02	.01
☐ 454	Chris Nilan	.08	.04	.01
☐ 455	Jim Benning	.05	.02	.01
☐ 456	Wayne Presley	.05	.02	.01
☐ 457	Jon Morris	.05	.02	.01
☐ 458	Clark Donatelli	.05	.02	.01
☐ 459	Ric Nattress	.05	.02	.01
☐ 460	Rob Murray	.05	.02	.01
☐ 461	Tim Watters	.05	.02	.01
☐ 462	Checklist 397-528	.05	.02	.01
☐ 463	Derrick Smith	.05	.02	.01
☐ 464	Lyndon Byers	.05	.02	.01
☐ 465	Jeff Chychrun	.05	.02	.01

☐	466 Duane Sutter	.05	.02	.01
☐	467 Conn Smythe Trophy	.05	.02	.01
	Bill Ranford			
☐	468 Anatoli Semenov	.20	.09	.03
☐	469 Konstantin Kurashov	.05	.02	.01
☐	470 Gord Dineen	.05	.02	.01
☐	471 Jeff Beukeboom	.20	.09	.03
☐	472 Andrei Lomakin	.25	.11	.03
☐	473 Doug Sulliman	.05	.02	.01
☐	474 Alexander Kerch	.05	.02	.01
☐	475 Norris Trophy	.08	.04	.01
	Ray Bourque			
☐	476 Keith Crowder	.05	.02	.01
☐	477 Oleg Znarok	.05	.02	.01
☐	478 Dimitri Zinovyev	.05	.02	.01
☐	479 Igor Esmantovich	.05	.02	.01
☐	480 Adam Graves	1.25	.55	.16
☐	481 Petr Prajsler	.05	.02	.01
☐	482 Sergei Yashin	.05	.02	.01
☐	483 Jeff Bloemberg	.05	.02	.01
☐	484 Yuri Strakhov	.05	.02	.01
☐	485 Sergei B. Makarov	.05	.02	.01
☐	486 Jennings Trophy	.05	.02	.01
	Rejean Lemelin,			
	Andy Moog			
☐	487 Sergei Zaltsev	.05	.02	.01
☐	488 Selke Trophy	.05	.02	.01
	Rick Meagher			
☐	489 Yuri Kusnetsov	.05	.02	.01
☐	490 Tom Chorske	.05	.02	.01
☐	491 Igor Akulinin	.05	.02	.01
☐	492 Mikhail Panin	.05	.02	.01
☐	493 Sergei Nemchinov	.40	.18	.05
☐	494 Vladimir Yurzinov	.05	.02	.01
☐	495 Gord Kluzak	.05	.02	.01
☐	496 Sergei Skosyrev	.05	.02	.01
☐	497 Jeff Parker	.05	.02	.01
☐	498 Tom Tilley	.05	.02	.01
☐	499 Alexander Smirnov	.05	.02	.01
☐	500 Alexander Lysenko	.05	.02	.01
☐	501 Arturs Irbe UER	4.00	1.80	.50
	(Misspelled Artur;			
	played in 7 games of			
	Dynamo Riga's tour)			
☐	502 Alexei Frolikov	.05	.02	.01
☐	503 Calder Trophy	.20	.09	.03
	Sergei Makarov			
☐	504 Nikolai Varjanov	.05	.02	.01
☐	505 Allen Pedersen	.05	.02	.01
☐	506 Vladimir Shashov	.05	.02	.01
☐	507 Tim Bergland	.05	.02	.01
☐	508 Gennady Lebedev	.05	.02	.01
☐	509 Rod Buskas	.05	.02	.01
☐	510 Grant Jennings	.05	.02	.01
☐	511 Ulf Samuelsson	.08	.04	.01
☐	512 Vezina Trophy	.40	.18	.05
	Patrick Roy			
☐	513 Lady Byng Trophy	.25	.11	.03
	Brett Hull			
☐	514 Dimitri Mironov	.40	.18	.05
☐	515 Randy Moller	.05	.02	.01
☐	516 Kerry Huffman	.10	.05	.01
☐	517 Gilbert Delorme	.05	.02	.01
☐	518 Greg C. Adams	.05	.02	.01
☐	519 Hart Trophy	.08	.04	.01
	Mark Messier			
☐	520 Sheldon Kennedy	.20	.09	.03
☐	521 Harijs Vitolins	.05	.02	.01
☐	522 Art Ross Trophy	.50	.23	.06
	Wayne Gretzky			
☐	523 Dmitri Frolov	.05	.02	.01
☐	524 Tom Laidlaw	.05	.02	.01
☐	525 Oleg Bratash UER	.05	.02	.01
	(Played in 2 games of			
	Wings' 1990 NHL tour)			
☐	526 Kris King	.10	.05	.01
☐	527 Wayne Van Dorp	.05	.02	.01
☐	528 Chris Dahlquist	.05	.02	.01

1990-91 O-Pee-Chee/Topps Box Bottoms

This sixteen-card set measures the standard size, 2 1/2" by 3 1/2", and was issued in sets of four on the bottom of the 1990-91 O-Pee-Chee and Topps wax pack boxes. Complete box bottom panels are valued at a 25 percent premium

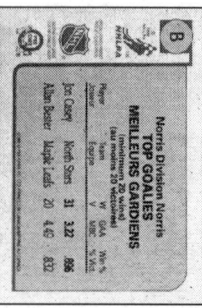

above the prices listed below. The cards are lettered rather than numbered. This set features NHL stars such as Wayne Gretzky, Mario Lemieux, and Patrick Roy. The front design of these cards is essentially the same as the regular issue cards. The horizontally oriented backs have special statistics in blue lettering on a pale green background. The checklist does not agree with the actual grouping of the players in the four panels.

		MINT	EXC	G-VG
COMPLETE SET (16)		5.00	2.00	.50
COMMON PLAYER (A-P)		.15	.06	.01
☐ A	Alexander Mogilny	1.25	.50	.12
	Buffalo Sabres			
☐ B	Jon Casey	.25	.10	.02
	Minnesota North Stars			
☐ C	Paul Coffey	.35	.14	.03
	Pittsburgh Penguins			
☐ D	Wayne Gretzky	1.50	.60	.15
	Los Angeles Kings			
☐ E	Patrick Roy	1.00	.40	.10
	Montreal Canadiens			
☐ F	Mike Modano	1.25	.50	.12
	Minnesota North Stars			
☐ G	Mario Lemieux	1.25	.50	.12
	Pittsburgh Penguins			
☐ H	Al MacInnis	.35	.14	.03
	Calgary Flames			
☐ I	Ray Bourque	.50	.20	.05
	Boston Bruins			
☐ J	Steve Yzerman	.75	.30	.07
	Detroit Red Wings			
☐ K	Darren Turcotte	.35	.14	.03
	New York Rangers			
☐ L	Mike Vernon	.25	.10	.02
	Calgary Flames			
☐ M	Pierre Turgeon	.60	.24	.06
	Buffalo Sabres			
☐ N	Doug Wilson	.25	.10	.02
	Chicago Blackhawks			
☐ O	Don Beaupre	.15	.06	.01
	Washington Capitals			
☐ P	Sergei Makarov	.50	.20	.05
	Calgary Flames			

1990-91 O-Pee-Chee Red Army

This 22-card set was distributed one card per 1990-91 O-Pee-Chee wax pack. Measuring the standard 2 1/2" by 3 1/2" the fronts feature color action photos surrounded by red borders. The words "Central Red Army" appear above the photos in the red border. The horizontally designed backs contain the player's statistics compiled from the Super Series tour against the NHL. The statistical information on the back is superimposed over a white Soviet star and a "hammer and sickle" insignia. The card number is followed by an R suffix. Parts of the first print run suffered from pin punctures and other quality control flaws. First cards of Sergei Fedorov and Arturs Irbe are a part of this set. Because this is an insert set, these cards are not considered Rookie Cards.

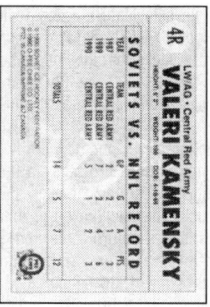

	MINT	EXC	G-VG
COMPLETE SET (22)	9.00	4.00	1.15
COMMON PLAYER (1R-22R)	.25	.11	.03

		MINT	EXC	G-VG
☐ 1R	Ilya Byalsin	.25	.11	.03
☐ 2R	Vladimir Malakhov	.75	.35	.09
☐ 3R	Andrei Khomutov	.40	.18	.05
☐ 4R	Valeri Kamensky	1.00	.45	.13
☐ 5R	Dimitri Motkov	.35	.16	.04
☐ 6R	Evgeny Shastin	.25	.11	.03
☐ 7R	Arturs Irbe UER	3.00	1.35	.40
	(Misspelled Artur; played in 3 games in Red Army's NHL tour)			
☐ 8R	Igor Chibirev	.40	.18	.05
☐ 9R	Maxim Mikhailovsky UER	.25	.11	.03
	(Played one game not one minute on 1990 NHL tour)			
☐ 10R	Viacheslav Bykov	.40	.18	.05
☐ 11R	Central Red Army Team	.30	.14	.04
	(Igor Kravchuk)			
☐ 12R	Central Red Army Team	.25	.11	.03
☐ 13R	Valeri Shirjaev	.25	.11	.03
☐ 14R	Igor Maslennikov	.25	.11	.03
☐ 15R	Igor Malykhin	.25	.11	.03
☐ 16R	Dimitri Khristich	1.00	.45	.13
☐ 17R	Viktor Tikhonov (Coach)	.30	.14	.04
☐ 18R	Eugeny Davydov	.50	.23	.06
☐ 19R	Sergei Fedorov	5.00	2.30	.60
☐ 20R	Pavel Kostichkin	.25	.11	.03
☐ 21R	Vladimir Konstantinov	.75	.35	.09
☐ 22R	Checklist Card	.20	.09	.03

1990-91 O-Pee-Chee Premier

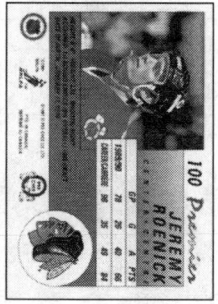

The 1990-91 O-Pee-Chee Premier hockey set contains 132 cards measuring the standard size (2 1/2" by 3 1/2"). The fronts feature color action photos of the players and have the words "O-Pee-Chee Premier" in a gold border above the picture. Border colors according to team frame the photo. Horizontal backs contain 1989-90 and career statistics. A player photo appears in the upper left hand corner. The checklist is numbered alphabetically. Rookie Cards include Rob Blake, Sergei Fedorov, Jaromir Jagr, Curtis Joseph,

Mike Modano, Alexander Mogilny, Petr Nedved, Owen Nolan, Mike Ricci, Robert Reichel, Jeremy Roenick, Kevin Stevens, and Mats Sundin.

	MINT	EXC	G-VG
COMPLETE SET (132)	90.00	40.00	11.50
COMPLETE FACT.SET (132)	120.00	55.00	15.00
COMMON PLAYER (1-132)	.20	.09	.03

		MINT	EXC	G-VG
☐ 1	Scott Arniel	.20	.09	.03
☐ 2	Jergus Baca	.20	.09	.03
☐ 3	Brian Bellows	.25	.11	.03
☐ 4	Jean-Claude Bergeron	.20	.09	.03
☐ 5	Daniel Berthiaume	.20	.09	.03
☐ 6	Rob Blake	2.00	.90	.25
☐ 7	Peter Bondra	1.50	.65	.19
☐ 8	Laurie Boschman	.20	.09	.03
☐ 9	Ray Bourque	.60	.25	.08
☐ 10	Aaron Broten	.20	.09	.03
☐ 11	Greg Brown	.20	.09	.03
☐ 12	Jimmy Carson	.20	.09	.03
☐ 13	Chris Chelios	.40	.18	.05
☐ 14	Dino Ciccarelli	.25	.11	.03
☐ 15	Zdeno Ciger	.50	.23	.06
☐ 16	Paul Coffey	.50	.23	.06
☐ 17	Danton Cole	.25	.11	.03
☐ 18	Geoff Courtnall	.25	.11	.03
☐ 19	Mike Craig UER	.40	.18	.05
	(Played Juniors at Oshawa, not Minors)			
☐ 20	John Cullen	.25	.11	.03
☐ 21	Vincent Damphousse	.50	.23	.06
☐ 22	Gerald Diduck	.20	.09	.03
☐ 23	Kevin Dineen	.25	.11	.03
☐ 24	Per-Olav Djoos UER	.20	.09	.03
	(Photo shoots right, back says shoots left)			
☐ 25	Tie Domi	1.00	.45	.13
☐ 26	Peter Douris	.25	.11	.03
☐ 27	Rob DiMaio	.20	.09	.03
☐ 28	Pat Elynuik	.20	.09	.03
☐ 29	Bob Essensa	.60	.25	.08
☐ 30	Sergei Fedorov	18.00	8.00	2.30
☐ 31	Brent Fedyk	.50	.23	.06
☐ 32	Ron Francis	.30	.14	.04
☐ 33	Link Gaetz	.20	.09	.03
☐ 34	Troy Gamble	.20	.09	.03
☐ 35	Johan Garpenlov	.75	.35	.09
☐ 36	Mike Gartner	.50	.23	.06
☐ 37	Rick Green	.20	.09	.03
☐ 38	Wayne Gretzky	5.00	2.30	.60
☐ 39	Jeff Hackett	.40	.18	.05
☐ 40	Dale Hawerchuk UER	.30	.14	.04
	(Misspelled Hawerchuck)			
☐ 41	Ron Hextall	.30	.14	.04
☐ 42	Bruce Hoffort	.20	.09	.03
☐ 43	Bobby Holik	1.00	.45	.13
☐ 44	Martin Hostak	.20	.09	.03
☐ 45	Phil Housley	.25	.11	.03
☐ 46	Jody Hull	.20	.09	.03
☐ 47	Brett Hull	3.00	1.35	.40
☐ 48	Al Iafrate	.50	.23	.06
☐ 49	Peter Ing	.20	.09	.03
☐ 50	Jaromir Jagr	12.00	5.50	1.50
☐ 51	Curtis Joseph	6.00	2.70	.75
☐ 52	Robert Kron	.20	.09	.03
☐ 53	Frantisek Kucera	.20	.09	.03
☐ 54	Dale Kushner	.20	.09	.03
☐ 55	Guy Lafleur	.20	.09	.03
☐ 56	Pat LaFontaine	1.25	.55	.16
☐ 57	Mike Lalor	.20	.09	.03
☐ 58	Steve Larmer	.30	.14	.04
☐ 59	Jiri Latal	.20	.09	.03
☐ 60	Jamie Leach	.20	.09	.03
☐ 61	Brian Leetch	2.00	.90	.25
☐ 62	Claude Lemieux	.25	.11	.03
☐ 63	Mario Lemieux	4.00	1.80	.50
☐ 64	Craig Ludwig	.20	.09	.03
☐ 65	Al MacInnis	.50	.23	.06
☐ 66	Mikko Makela	.20	.09	.03
☐ 67	David Marcinyshyn	.20	.09	.03
☐ 68	Stephane Matteau	.75	.35	.09
☐ 69	Brad McCrimmon	.20	.09	.03
☐ 70	Kirk McLean	2.00	.90	.25
☐ 71	Mark Messier	1.00	.45	.13
☐ 72	Kelly Miller	.20	.09	.03
☐ 73	Kevin Miller	1.00	.45	.13
☐ 74	Mike Modano	7.50	3.40	.95
☐ 75	Alexander Mogilny	9.00	4.00	1.15
☐ 76	Andy Moog	.50	.23	.06
☐ 77	Joe Mullen	.30	.14	.04
☐ 78	Kirk Muller	.25	.11	.03
☐ 79	Pat Murray	.20	.09	.03

☐	80 Jarmo Myllys	.20	.09	.03
☐	81 Petr Nedved	3.50	1.55	.45
☐	82 Cam Neely	.75	.35	.09
☐	83 Bernie Nicholls	.30	.14	.04
☐	84 Joe Nieuwendyk	.50	.23	.06
☐	85 Chris Nilan	.20	.09	.03
☐	86 Owen Nolan	2.50	1.15	.30
☐	87 Brian Noonan UER	.20	.09	.03
	(Photo actually Dan Vincelette)			
☐	88 Adam Oates	.75	.35	.09
☐	89 Greg Parks UER	.20	.09	.03
	(Back photo actually Scott Arniel)			
☐	90 Adrien Plavsic	.20	.09	.03
☐	91 Keith Primeau	1.50	.65	.19
☐	92 Brian Propp	.25	.11	.03
☐	93 Dan Quinn	.20	.09	.03
☐	94 Bill Ranford	.50	.23	.06
☐	95 Robert Reichel	2.50	1.15	.30
☐	96 Mike Ricci UER	2.00	.90	.25
	(Born 11/27/71, should be October)			
☐	97 Steven Rice UER	.30	.14	.04
	(Played Juniors at Kitchener, not Minors)			
☐	98 Stephane Richer	.30	.14	.04
☐	99 Luc Robitaille	1.00	.45	.13
☐	100 Jeremy Roenick	14.00	6.25	1.75
☐	101 Patrick Roy	2.50	1.15	.30
☐	102 Joe Sakic	1.50	.65	.19
☐	103 Denis Savard	.30	.14	.04
☐	104 Anatoli Semenov	.50	.23	.06
☐	105 Brendan Shanahan	1.25	.55	.16
☐	106 Ray Sheppard	.50	.23	.06
☐	107 Mike Sillinger UER	.35	.16	.04
	(Played Juniors at Regina, not Minors)			
☐	108 Ilkka Sinisalo	.20	.09	.03
☐	109 Bobby Smith	.25	.11	.03
☐	110 Paul Stanton	.20	.09	.03
☐	111 Kevin Stevens	4.00	1.80	.50
☐	112 Scott Stevens	.30	.14	.04
☐	113 Alan Stewart	.20	.09	.03
☐	114 Mats Sundin	6.50	2.90	.80
☐	115 Brent Sutter	.25	.11	.03
☐	116 Tim Sweeney	.25	.11	.03
☐	117 Peter Taglianetti	.20	.09	.03
☐	118 John Tanner	.20	.09	.03
☐	119 Dave Tippett	.20	.09	.03
☐	120 Rick Tocchet	.30	.14	.04
☐	121 Bryan Trottier	.30	.14	.04
☐	122 John Tucker	.20	.09	.03
☐	123 Darren Turcotte	.50	.23	.06
☐	124 Pierre Turgeon	1.25	.55	.16
☐	125 Randy Velischek	.20	.09	.03
☐	126 Mike Vernon	.25	.11	.03
☐	127 Wes Walz	.30	.14	.04
☐	128 Carey Wilson	.20	.09	.03
☐	129 Doug Wilson	.25	.11	.03
☐	130 Steve Yzerman	1.50	.65	.19
☐	131 Peter Zezel	.25	.11	.03
☐	132 Checklist 1-132	.25	.09	.03

1991-92 O-Pee-Chee and Topps

 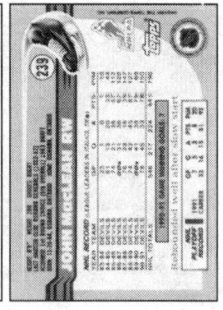

The 1991-92 O-Pee-Chee and Topps hockey sets contain 528 cards measuring the standard size (2 1/2" by 3 1/2").

Both sets feature a Guy Lafleur Tribute (1-3) and a Super Rookie (4-13) subset. Topps hockey cards were sold in 15-card packs that included a bonus team scoring leader card, whereas the O-Pee-Chee cards were sold in nine-card wax packs that included a stick of gum plus one insert card from a special 66-card insert set. The fronts have glossy color action player photos, with two different color border stripes and a white card face. In the lower right corner, the team logo appears as a hockey puck superimposed on a hockey stick. The backs are horizontally oriented and printed in a variety of colors (blue, red, yellow, pink, and white). They present full player information, including biography, statistics, 1990-91 game winning goals, and NHL playoff record (the OPC cards present player information in French as well as English). The card number appears next to a hockey skate in the upper right corner of the back. Rookie Cards in this set include Tony Amonte, Valeri Kamensky, John LeClair, Corey Millen and Dmitri Mironov.

		MINT	EXC	G-VG
COMPLETE SET (528)		10.00	4.50	1.25
COMPLETE FACT.SET (528)		15.00	6.75	1.90
COMMON PLAYER (1-528)		.05	.02	.01
*TOPPS: SAME PRICE AS OPC				

☐	1 Lafleur Tribute	.10	.05	.01
	Goodbye Guy			
☐	2 Lafleur Tribute	.10	.05	.01
	Gueeey's Last Hoorah			
☐	3 Lafleur Tribute	.10	.05	.01
	Guy Bids Farewell			
☐	4 Ed Belfour SR	.15	.07	.02
	Chicago Blackhawks			
☐	5 Ken Hodge Jr. SR	.10	.05	.01
	Boston Bruins			
☐	6 Rob Blake SR UER	.10	.05	.01
	Los Angeles Kings (Center on back, should say Defense)			
☐	7 Bobby Holik SR	.10	.05	.01
	Hartford Whalers			
☐	8 Sergei Fedorov SR UER	.25	.11	.03
	Detroit Red Wings (Name misspelled on front and in stats)			
☐	9 Jaromir Jagr SR	.25	.11	.03
	Pittsburgh Penguins			
☐	10 Eric Weinrich SR	.10	.05	.01
	New Jersey Devils			
☐	11 Mike Richter SR	.15	.07	.02
	New York Rangers			
☐	12 Mats Sundin SR	.15	.07	.02
	Quebec Nordiques			
☐	13 Mike Ricci SR	.10	.05	.01
	Philadelphia Flyers			
☐	14 Eric Desjardins	.08	.04	.01
	Montreal Canadiens			
☐	15 Paul Ranheim	.05	.02	.01
	Calgary Flames			
☐	16 Joe Sakic	.25	.11	.03
	Quebec Nordiques			
☐	17 Curt Giles	.05	.02	.01
	Minnesota North Stars			
☐	18 Mike Foligno	.05	.02	.01
	Buffalo Sabres			
☐	19 Brad Marsh	.08	.04	.01
	Detroit Red Wings			
☐	20 Ed Belfour	.25	.11	.03
	Chicago Blackhawks			
☐	21 Steve Smith	.08	.04	.01
	Edmonton Oilers			
☐	22 Kirk Muller	.08	.04	.01
	New Jersey Devils			
☐	23 Kelly Chase	.05	.02	.01
	St. Louis Blues			
☐	24 Jim McKenzie	.05	.02	.01
	Hartford Whalers			
☐	25 Mick Vukota	.05	.02	.01
	New York Islanders			
☐	26 Tony Amonte	.30	.14	.04
	New York Rangers			
☐	27 Danton Cole	.05	.02	.01
	Winnipeg Jets			
☐	28 Jay Mazur	.05	.02	.01
	Vancouver Canucks			
☐	29 Pete Peeters	.08	.04	.01
	Philadelphia Flyers			

☐ 30	Petri Skriko — Boston Bruins	.05	.02	.01
☐ 31	Steve Duchesne — Los Angeles Kings	.08	.04	.01
☐ 32	Sabres Team	.05	.02	.01
☐ 33	Phil Bourque UER — Pittsburgh Penguins (Born Chelmford, should be Chelmsford)	.05	.02	.01
☐ 34	Tim Bergland — Washington Capitals	.05	.02	.01
☐ 35	Tim Cheveldae — Detroit Red Wings	.08	.04	.01
☐ 36	Bill Armstrong — Philadelphia Flyers	.05	.02	.01
☐ 37	John McIntyre — Los Angeles Kings	.05	.02	.01
☐ 38	Dave Andreychuk — Buffalo Sabres	.15	.07	.02
☐ 39	Curtis Leschyshyn — Quebec Nordiques	.05	.02	.01
☐ 40	Jaromir Jagr — Pittsburgh Penguins	.50	.23	.06
☐ 41	Craig Janney — Boston Bruins	.15	.07	.02
☐ 42	Doug Brown — New Jersey Devils	.05	.02	.01
☐ 43	Ken Sabourin — Washington Capitals	.05	.02	.01
☐ 44	North Stars Team	.05	.02	.01
☐ 45	Fredrik Olausson UER — Winnipeg Jets (Misspelled Clausson on card front)	.08	.04	.01
☐ 46	Mike Gartner UER — New York Rangers (No italics or diamond 81-82 GP)	.10	.05	.01
☐ 47	Mark Fitzpatrick — New York Islanders	.08	.04	.01
☐ 48	Joe Murphy — Edmonton Oilers	.08	.04	.01
☐ 49	Doug Wilson — Chicago Blackhawks	.08	.04	.01
☐ 50	Brian MacLellan — Calgary Flames	.05	.02	.01
☐ 51	Bob Bassen — St. Louis Blues	.05	.02	.01
☐ 52	Robert Kron — Vancouver Canucks	.05	.02	.01
☐ 53	Roger Johansson — Calgary Flames	.05	.02	.01
☐ 54	Guy Carbonneau UER — Montreal Canadiens (No italics or diamond 85-86 GP)	.08	.04	.01
☐ 55	Rob Ramage — Toronto Maple Leafs	.05	.02	.01
☐ 56	Bobby Holik — Hartford Whalers	.08	.04	.01
☐ 57	Alan May — Washington Capitals	.05	.02	.01
☐ 58	Rick Meagher — St. Louis Blues	.05	.02	.01
☐ 59	Cliff Ronning — Vancouver Canucks	.08	.04	.01
☐ 60	Red Wings Team	.05	.02	.01
☐ 61	Bob Kudelski — Los Angeles Kings	.08	.04	.01
☐ 62	Wayne McBean — New York Islanders	.05	.02	.01
☐ 63	Craig MacTavish — Edmonton Oilers	.05	.02	.01
☐ 64	Owen Nolan — Quebec Nordiques	.15	.07	.02
☐ 65	Dale Hawerchuk — Winnipeg Jets	.08	.04	.01
☐ 66	Ray Bourque — Boston Bruins	.15	.07	.02
☐ 67	Sean Burke — New Jersey Devils	.08	.04	.01
☐ 68	Frantisek Musil — Calgary Flames	.05	.02	.01
☐ 69	Joe Mullen — Calgary Flames	.10	.05	.01
☐ 70	Drake Berehowsky — Toronto Maple Leafs	.05	.02	.01
☐ 71	Darren Turcotte — New York Rangers	.05	.02	.01
☐ 72	Randy Carlyle — Winnipeg Jets	.05	.02	.01
☐ 73	Paul Cyr — Hartford Whalers	.05	.02	.01
☐ 74	Dave Gagner — Minnesota North Stars	.08	.04	.01
☐ 75	Steve Larmer — Chicago Blackhawks	.08	.04	.01
☐ 76	Petr Svoboda — Montreal Canadiens	.05	.02	.01
☐ 77	Keith Acton — Philadelphia Flyers	.05	.02	.01
☐ 78	Dimitri Khristich — Washington Capitals	.08	.04	.01
☐ 79	Brad McCrimmon — Detroit Red Wings	.05	.02	.01
☐ 80	Pat LaFontaine UER — New York Islanders (Should be lower case a in name, not d)	.20	.09	.03
☐ 81	Jeff Reese — Toronto Maple Leafs	.05	.02	.01
☐ 82	Mario Marois — St. Louis Blues	.05	.02	.01
☐ 83	Rob Brown — Hartford Whalers	.05	.02	.01
☐ 84	Grant Fuhr — Edmonton Oilers	.08	.04	.01
☐ 85	Carey Wilson — Calgary Flames	.05	.02	.01
☐ 86	Garry Galley — Boston Bruins	.08	.04	.01
☐ 87	Troy Murray — Chicago Blackhawks	.05	.02	.01
☐ 88	Tony Granato — Los Angeles Kings	.08	.04	.01
☐ 89	Gord Murphy UER — Philadelphia Flyers (No italics or diamond 90-91 GP)	.05	.02	.01
☐ 90	Brent Gilchrist — Montreal Canadiens	.05	.02	.01
☐ 91	Mike Richter — New York Rangers	.25	.11	.03
☐ 92	Eric Weinrich — New Jersey Devils	.05	.02	.01
☐ 93	Marc Bureau — Minnesota North Stars	.05	.02	.01
☐ 94	Bob Errey — Pittsburgh Penguins	.05	.02	.01
☐ 95	Dave McLlwain — Winnipeg Jets	.05	.02	.01
☐ 96	Nordiques Team	.05	.02	.01
☐ 97	Clint Malarchuk UER — Buffalo Sabres (Center on front)	.08	.04	.01
☐ 98	Shawn Antoski UER — Vancouver Canucks (Admirals are in IHL, not AHL)	.05	.02	.01
☐ 99	Bob Sweeney — Boston Bruins	.05	.02	.01
☐ 100	Stephen Leach — Washington Capitals	.05	.02	.01
☐ 101	Gary Nylund — New York Islanders	.05	.02	.01
☐ 102	Lucien Deblois — Toronto Maple Leafs	.05	.02	.01
☐ 103	Oilers Team	.05	.02	.01
☐ 104	Jimmy Carson — Detroit Red Wings	.08	.04	.01
☐ 105	Rod Langway — Washington Capitals	.05	.02	.01
☐ 106	Jeremy Roenick — Chicago Blackhawks	.50	.23	.06
☐ 107	Mike Vernon — Calgary Flames	.08	.04	.01
☐ 108	Brian Leetch — New York Rangers	.35	.16	.04
☐ 109	Mark Hunter — Hartford Whalers	.05	.02	.01
☐ 110	Brian Bellows — Minnesota North Stars	.08	.04	.01
☐ 111	Pelle Eklund — Philadelphia Flyers	.05	.02	.01
☐ 112	Rob Blake — Los Angeles Kings	.15	.07	.02
☐ 113	Mike Hough — Quebec Nordiques	.05	.02	.01
☐ 114	Frank Pietrangelo — Pittsburgh Penguins	.05	.02	.01
☐ 115	Christian Ruuttu — Buffalo Sabres	.05	.02	.01
☐ 116	Bryan Marchment — Winnipeg Jets	.10	.05	.01
☐ 117	Garry Valk — Vancouver Canucks	.05	.02	.01

☐ 118 Ken Daneyko UER	.05	.02	.01
New Jersey Devils			
(No italics or diamond			
90-91 GP)			
☐ 119 Russ Courtnall	.08	.04	.01
Montreal Canadiens			
☐ 120 Ron Wilson	.05	.02	.01
St. Louis Blues			
☐ 121 Shayne Stevenson	.05	.02	.01
Boston Bruins			
☐ 122 Bill Berg	.05	.02	.01
New York Islanders			
☐ 123 Maple Leafs Team	.05	.02	.01
☐ 124 Glenn Anderson	.08	.04	.01
Edmonton Oilers			
☐ 125 Kevin Miller	.08	.04	.01
Detroit Red Wings			
☐ 126 Calle Johansson	.05	.02	.01
Washington Capitals			
☐ 127 Jimmy Waite	.08	.04	.01
Chicago Blackhawks			
☐ 128 Allen Pedersen	.05	.02	.01
Boston Bruins			
☐ 129 Brian Mullen	.08	.04	.01
New York Rangers			
☐ 130 Ron Francis	.08	.04	.01
Pittsburgh Penguins			
☐ 131 Jergus Baca	.05	.02	.01
Hartford Whalers			
☐ 132 Checklist 1-132	.05	.02	.01
☐ 133 Tony Tanti	.05	.02	.01
Buffalo Sabres			
☐ 134 Wes Walz	.05	.02	.01
Boston Bruins			
☐ 135 Stephan Lebeau	.15	.07	.02
Montreal Canadiens			
☐ 136 Ken Wregget	.05	.02	.01
Philadelphia Flyers			
☐ 137 Scott Arniel UER	.05	.02	.01
Winnipeg Jets			
(No italics or diamond			
85-86 GP)			
☐ 138 Dave Taylor	.08	.04	.01
Los Angeles Kings			
☐ 139 Steven Finn	.05	.02	.01
Quebec Nordiques			
☐ 140 Brendan Shanahan	.25	.11	.03
New Jersey Devils			
☐ 141 Petr Nedved	.25	.11	.03
Vancouver Canucks			
☐ 142 Chris Dahlquist	.05	.02	.01
Minnesota North Stars			
☐ 143 Rich Sutter	.05	.02	.01
St. Louis Blues			
☐ 144 Joe Reekie	.05	.02	.01
New York Islanders			
☐ 145 Peter Ing	.05	.02	.01
Toronto Maple Leafs			
☐ 146 Ken Linseman	.05	.02	.01
Edmonton Oilers			
☐ 147 Dave Barr	.05	.02	.01
Detroit Red Wings			
☐ 148 Al Iafrate	.08	.04	.01
Washington Capitals			
☐ 149 Greg Gilbert	.05	.02	.01
Chicago Blackhawks			
☐ 150 Craig Ludwig	.05	.02	.01
New York Islanders			
☐ 151 Gary Suter	.08	.04	.01
Calgary Flames			
☐ 152 Jan Erixon	.05	.02	.01
New York Rangers			
☐ 153 Mario Lemieux	.75	.35	.09
Pittsburgh Penguins			
☐ 154 Mike Liut UER	.08	.04	.01
Washington Capitals			
(In stats 84-85 repeats			
for 85-86 thru 89-90)			
☐ 155 Uwe Krupp	.05	.02	.01
Buffalo Sabres			
☐ 156 Darin Kimble	.05	.02	.01
St. Louis Blues			
☐ 157 Shayne Corson	.08	.04	.01
Montreal Canadiens			
☐ 158 Jets Team	.05	.02	.01
☐ 159 Stephane Morin UER	.05	.02	.01
Quebec Nordiques			
(Photo actually			
Jeff Jackson)			
☐ 160 Rick Tocchet	.08	.04	.01
Philadelphia Flyers			
☐ 161 John Tonelli UER	.08	.04	.01
Los Angeles Kings			
(No italics or diamond			
81-82 GP)			
☐ 162 Adrien Plavsic	.05	.02	.01
Vancouver Canucks			
☐ 163 Jason Miller	.05	.02	.01
New Jersey Devils			
☐ 164 Tim Kerr	.08	.04	.01
Philadelphia Flyers			
☐ 165 Brent Sutter	.08	.04	.01
New York Islanders			
☐ 166 Michel Petit	.05	.02	.01
Toronto Maple Leafs			
☐ 167 Adam Graves	.25	.11	.03
Edmonton Oilers			
☐ 168 Jamie Macoun	.05	.02	.01
Calgary Flames			
☐ 169 Terry Yake	.08	.04	.01
Hartford Whalers			
☐ 170 Bruins Team	.05	.02	.01
☐ 171 Alexander Mogilny	.40	.18	.05
Buffalo Sabres			
☐ 172 Karl Dykhuis	.05	.02	.01
Top Prospect			
☐ 173 Tomas Sandstrom	.08	.04	.01
Los Angeles Kings			
☐ 174 Bernie Nicholls	.08	.04	.01
New York Rangers			
☐ 175 Viacheslav Fetisov	.08	.04	.01
New Jersey Devils			
☐ 176 Andrew Cassels	.08	.04	.01
Montreal Canadiens			
☐ 177 Ulf Dahlen	.08	.04	.01
Minnesota North Stars			
☐ 178 Brian Hayward	.05	.02	.01
Minnesota North Stars			
☐ 179 Doug Lidster	.05	.02	.01
Vancouver Canucks			
☐ 180 Dave Lowry	.05	.02	.01
St. Louis Blues			
☐ 181 Ron Tugnutt UER	.05	.02	.01
Quebec Nordiques			
(Birthplace and home			
should be Ontario,			
not Quebec)			
☐ 182 Ed Olczyk	.05	.02	.01
Winnipeg Jets			
☐ 183 Paul Coffey	.15	.07	.02
Pittsburgh Penguins			
☐ 184 Shawn Burr UER	.05	.02	.01
Detroit Red Wings			
(No italics or diamond			
90-91 GP)			
☐ 185 Whalers Team	.05	.02	.01
☐ 186 Mark Janssens	.05	.02	.01
New York Rangers			
☐ 187 Mike Craig	.05	.02	.01
Minnesota North Stars			
☐ 188 Gary Leeman	.05	.02	.01
Toronto Maple Leafs			
☐ 189 Phil Sykes	.05	.02	.01
Winnipeg Jets			
☐ 190 Brett Hull LL	.20	.09	.03
St. Louis Blues			
☐ 191 Devils Team	.05	.02	.01
☐ 192 Cam Neely	.15	.07	.02
Boston Bruins			
☐ 193 Petr Klima	.05	.02	.01
Edmonton Oilers			
☐ 194 Mike Ricci	.15	.07	.02
Philadelphia Flyers			
☐ 195 Kelly Hrudey	.08	.04	.01
Los Angeles Kings			
☐ 196 Mark Recchi	.30	.14	.04
Pittsburgh Penguins			
☐ 197 Mikael Andersson	.05	.02	.01
Hartford Whalers			
☐ 198 Bob Probert	.08	.04	.01
Detroit Red Wings			
☐ 199 Craig Wolanin	.05	.02	.01
Quebec Nordiques			
☐ 200 Scott Mellanby	.05	.02	.01
Philadelphia Flyers			
☐ 201 Wayne Gretzky HL UER	.35	.16	.04
(Thomas Sandstrom			
mentioned on back)			
Los Angeles Kings			
☐ 202 Laurie Boschman	.05	.02	.01
New Jersey Devils			
☐ 203 Gino Odjick	.08	.04	.01
Vancouver Canucks			
☐ 204 Garth Butcher	.05	.02	.01
St. Louis Blues			
☐ 205 Randy Wood	.05	.02	.01
New York Islanders			

☐ 206 John Druce	.05	.02	.01
Washington Capitals			
☐ 207 Doug Bodger	.05	.02	.01
Buffalo Sabres			
☒ 208 Doug Gilmour	.25	.11	.03
Calgary Flames			
☐ 209 John LeClair	.20	.09	.03
Montreal Canadiens			
☐ 210 Steve Thomas	.08	.04	.01
Chicago Blackhawks			
☐ 211 Kjell Samuelsson	.05	.02	.01
Philadelphia Flyers			
☐ 212 Daniel Marois	.05	.02	.01
Toronto Maple Leafs			
☐ 213 Jiri Hrdina	.05	.02	.01
Pittsburgh Penguins			
☐ 214 Darrin Shannon	.05	.02	.01
Buffalo Sabres			
☐ 215 Rangers Team	.05	.02	.01
☐ 216 Bob McGill	.05	.02	.01
Chicago Blackhawks			
☐ 217 Dirk Graham UER	.05	.02	.01
Chicago Blackhawks			
(No italics or diamond			
85-86 or 90-91 GP)			
☐ 218 Thomas Steen	.05	.02	.01
Winnipeg Jets			
☐ 219 Mats Sundin	.25	.11	.03
Quebec Nordiques			
☐ 220 Kevin Lowe UER	.08	.04	.01
Edmonton Oilers			
(No italics or diamond			
81-82 GP)			
☐ 221 Kirk McLean	.25	.11	.03
Vancouver Canucks			
☐ 222 Jeff Brown	.08	.04	.01
St. Louis Blues			
☐ 223 Joe Nieuwendyk	.10	.05	.01
Calgary Flames			
☐ 224 Wayne Gretzky LL	.35	.16	.04
Los Angeles Kings			
☐ 225 Marty McSorley	.08	.04	.01
Los Angeles Kings			
☐ 226 John Cullen	.05	.02	.01
Hartford Whalers			
☐ 227 Brian Propp UER	.08	.04	.01
Minnesota North Stars			
(No italics or diamond			
81-82 GP)			
☐ 228 Yves Racine	.05	.02	.01
Detroit Red Wings			
☐ 229 Dale Hunter	.08	.04	.01
Washington Capitals			
☐ 230 Dennis Vaske	.05	.02	.01
New York Islanders			
☐ 231 Sylvain Turgeon	.05	.02	.01
Montreal Canadiens			
☐ 232 Ron Sutter	.05	.02	.01
Philadelphia Flyers			
☐ 233 Chris Chelios	.08	.04	.01
Chicago Blackhawks			
☐ 234 Brian Bradley	.08	.04	.01
Toronto Maple Leafs			
☐ 235 Scott Young	.05	.02	.01
Pittsburgh Penguins			
☐ 236 Mike Ramsey UER	.05	.02	.01
Buffalo Sabres			
(No italics or diamond			
81-82 GP)			
☐ 237 Jon Casey	.08	.04	.01
Minnesota North Stars			
☐ 238 Nevin Markwart	.05	.02	.01
Boston Bruins			
☐ 239 John MacLean	.08	.04	.01
New Jersey Devils			
☐ 240 Brent Ashton	.05	.02	.01
Winnipeg Jets			
☐ 241 Tony Hrkac	.05	.02	.01
Quebec Nordiques			
☐ 242 Canucks Team	.05	.02	.01
☐ 243 Jeff Norton	.05	.02	.01
New York Islanders			
☐ 244 Martin Gelinas	.05	.02	.01
Edmonton Oilers			
☐ 245 Mike Ridley	.08	.04	.01
Washington Capitals			
☐ 246 Pat Jablonski	.10	.05	.01
St. Louis Blues			
☐ 247 Flames Team	.05	.02	.01
☐ 248 Paul Ysebaert	.05	.02	.01
Detroit Red Wings			
☐ 249 Sylvain Cote	.05	.02	.01
Hartford Whalers			

☐ 250 Marc Habscheid	.05	.02	.01
Detroit Red Wings			
☐ 251 Todd Elik	.05	.02	.01
Los Angeles Kings			
☐ 252 Mike McPhee	.05	.02	.01
Montreal Canadiens			
☐ 253 James Patrick	.05	.02	.01
New York Rangers			
☐ 254 Murray Craven	.05	.02	.01
Philadelphia Flyers			
☐ 255 Trent Yawney	.05	.02	.01
Chicago Blackhawks			
☐ 256 Rob Cimetta	.05	.02	.01
Toronto Maple Leafs			
☐ 257 Wayne Gretzky LL	.35	.16	.04
Los Angeles Kings			
☐ 258 Wayne Gretzky AS	.35	.16	.04
Los Angeles Kings			
☐ 259 Brett Hull AS	.20	.09	.03
St. Louis Blues			
☐ 260 Luc Robitaille AS	.13	.06	.02
Los Angeles Kings			
☐ 261 Ray Bourque AS	.13	.06	.02
Boston Bruins			
☐ 262 Al MacInnis AS	.13	.06	.02
Calgary Flames			
☐ 263 Ed Belfour AS	.10	.05	.01
Chicago Blackhawks			
☐ 264 Checklist 133-264	.05	.02	.01
☐ 265 Adam Oates AS	.13	.06	.02
St. Louis Blues			
☐ 266 Cam Neely AS	.10	.05	.01
Boston Bruins			
☐ 267 Kevin Stevens AS	.10	.05	.01
Pittsburgh Penguins			
☐ 268 Chris Chelios AS	.10	.05	.01
Chicago Blackhawks			
☐ 269 Brian Leetch AS	.15	.07	.02
New York Rangers			
☐ 270 Patrick Roy AS	.25	.11	.03
Montreal Canadiens			
☐ 271 Ed Belfour LL	.05	.02	.01
Chicago Blackhawks			
☐ 272 Rob Zettler	.05	.02	.01
Minnesota North Stars			
☐ 273 Donald Audette	.05	.02	.01
Buffalo Sabres			
☐ 274 Teppo Numminen	.05	.02	.01
Winnipeg Jets			
☐ 275 Peter Stastny UER	.08	.04	.01
New Jersey Devils			
(No italics or diamond			
81-82 GP)			
☐ 276 Dave Christian	.05	.02	.01
Boston Bruins			
☐ 277 Larry Murphy	.08	.04	.01
Pittsburgh Penguins			
☐ 278 Johan Garpenlov	.05	.02	.01
Detroit Red Wings			
☐ 279 Tom Fitzgerald	.05	.02	.01
New York Islanders			
☐ 280 Gerald Diduck	.05	.02	.01
Vancouver Canucks			
☐ 281 Gino Cavallini	.05	.02	.01
St. Louis Blues			
☐ 282 Theoren Fleury	.15	.07	.02
Calgary Flames			
☐ 283 Kings Team	.05	.02	.01
Los Angeles Kings			
☐ 284 Jeff Beukeboom	.05	.02	.01
Edmonton Oilers			
☐ 285 Kevin Dineen	.08	.04	.01
Hartford Whalers			
☐ 286 Jacques Cloutier	.05	.02	.01
Quebec Nordiques			
☐ 287 Tom Chorske	.05	.02	.01
Montreal Canadiens			
☐ 288 Ed Belfour LL	.05	.02	.01
Chicago Blackhawks			
☐ 289 Ray Sheppard	.08	.04	.01
New York Rangers			
☐ 290 Olaf Kolzig Washington Capitals	.05	.02	.01
☐ 291 Terry Carkner	.05	.02	.01
Philadelphia Flyers			
☐ 292 Benoit Hogue	.05	.02	.01
Buffalo Sabres			
☐ 293 Mike Peluso	.05	.02	.01
Chicago Blackhawks			
☐ 294 Bruce Driver	.05	.02	.01
New Jersey Devils			
☐ 295 Jari Kurri	.10	.05	.01
Edmonton Oilers			
☐ 296 Peter Sidorkiewicz	.05	.02	.01

Hartford Whalers			
☐ 297 Scott Pearson	.05	.02	.01
Quebec Nordiques			
☐ 298 Canadiens Team	.05	.02	.01
☐ 299 Vincent Damphousse	.08	.04	.01
Toronto Maple Leafs			
☐ 300 John Carter	.05	.02	.01
Boston Bruins			
☐ 301 Geoff Smith........................	.05	.02	.01
Edmonton Oilers			
☐ 302 Steve Kasper UER	.05	.02	.01
Los Angeles Kings			
(No italics or diamond			
85-86 GP)			
☐ 303 Brett Hull...........................	.50	.23	.06
St. Louis Blues			
☐ 304 Ray Ferraro	.08	.04	.01
New York Islanders			
☐ 305 Geoff Courtnall	.08	.04	.01
Vancouver Canucks			
☐ 306 David Shaw	.05	.02	.01
New York Rangers			
☐ 307 Bob Essensa	.08	.04	.01
Winnipeg Jets			
☐ 308 Mark Tinordi	.08	.04	.01
Minnesota North Stars			
☐ 309 Keith Primeau	.15	.07	.02
Detroit Red Wings			
☐ 310 Kevin Hatcher.....................	.08	.04	.01
Washington Capitals			
☐ 311 Chris Nilan	.08	.04	.01
Boston Bruins			
☐ 312 Trevor Kidd	.08	.04	.01
Top Prospect			
☐ 313 Daniel Berthiaume	.05	.02	.01
Los Angeles Kings			
☐ 314 Adam Creighton	.05	.02	.01
Chicago Blackhawks			
☐ 315 Everett Sanipass	.05	.02	.01
Quebec Nordiques			
☐ 316 Ken Baumgartner	.05	.02	.01
New York Islanders			
☐ 317 Sheldon Kennedy	.05	.02	.01
Detroit Red Wings			
☐ 318 Dave Capuano	.05	.02	.01
Vancouver Canucks			
☐ 319 Don Sweeney	.05	.02	.01
Boston Bruins			
☐ 320 Gary Roberts	.08	.04	.01
Calgary Flames			
☐ 321 Wayne Gretzky	1.00	.45	.13
Los Angeles Kings			
☐ 322 Theoren Fleury and	.08	.04	.01
Marty McSorley UER			
(Name misspelled			
McSorely on both			
sides of card)			
☐ 323 Ulf Samuelsson..................	.08	.04	.01
Pittsburgh Penguins			
☐ 324 Mike Krushelnyski..............	.05	.02	.01
Toronto Maple Leafs			
☐ 325 Dan Evason	.05	.02	.01
Hartford Whalers			
☐ 326 Pat Elynuik........................	.05	.02	.01
Winnipeg Jets			
☐ 327 Michal Pivonka...................	.08	.04	.01
Washington Capitals			
☐ 328 Paul Cavallini.....................	.05	.02	.01
St. Louis Blues			
☐ 329 Flyers Team.......................	.05	.02	.01
☐ 330 Denis Savard......................	.08	.04	.01
Montreal Canadiens			
☐ 331 Paul Fenton	.05	.02	.01
Calgary Flames			
☐ 332 Jon Morris	.05	.02	.01
New Jersey Devils			
☐ 333 Daren Puppa	.08	.04	.01
Buffalo Sabres			
☐ 334 Doug Smail	.05	.02	.01
Minnesota North Stars			
☐ 335 Kelly Kisio	.05	.02	.01
New York Rangers			
☐ 336 Michel Goulet UER	.08	.04	.01
Chicago Blackhawks			
(No italics or diamond			
81-82 GP)			
☐ 337 Mike Sillinger	.05	.02	.01
Detroit Red Wings			
☐ 338 Andy Moog	.10	.05	.01
Boston Bruins			
☐ 339 Paul Stanton	.05	.02	.01
Pittsburgh Penguins			
☐ 340 Greg Adams	.05	.02	.01
Vancouver Canucks			

☐ 341 Doug Crossman UER	.05	.02	.01
Detroit Red Wings			
(No italics or diamond			
85-86 GP)			
☐ 342 Kelly Miller........................	.05	.02	.01
Washington Capitals			
☐ 343 Pat Flatley.........................	.05	.02	.01
New York Islanders			
☐ 344 Zarley Zalapski...................	.05	.02	.01
Hartford Whalers			
☐ 345 Mark Osborne UER	.05	.02	.01
Winnipeg Jets			
(No italics or diamond			
81-82 GP)			
☐ 346 Mark Messier	.25	.11	.03
Edmonton Oilers			
☐ 347 Blues Team........................	.05	.02	.01
☐ 348 Neil Wilkinson....................	.05	.02	.01
Minnesota North Stars			
☐ 349 Brian Skrudland	.05	.02	.01
Montreal Canadiens			
☐ 350 Lyle Odelein	.05	.02	.01
Montreal Canadiens			
☐ 351 Luke Richardson	.05	.02	.01
Toronto Maple Leafs			
☐ 352 Zdeno Ciger.......................	.05	.02	.01
New Jersey Devils			
☐ 353 John Vanbiesbrouck	.10	.05	.01
New York Rangers			
☐ 354 Lou Franceschetti...............	.05	.02	.01
Buffalo Sabres			
☐ 355 Alexei Gusarov	.10	.05	.01
Quebec Nordiques			
☐ 356 Bill Ranford........................	.08	.04	.01
Edmonton Oilers			
☐ 357 Normand Lacombe	.05	.02	.01
Philadelphia Flyers			
☐ 358 Randy Burridge	.05	.02	.01
Boston Bruins			
☐ 359 Brian Benning	.05	.02	.01
Los Angeles Kings			
☐ 360 Dave Hannan	.05	.02	.01
Toronto Maple Leafs			
☐ 361 Todd Gill	.05	.02	.01
Toronto Maple Leafs			
☐ 362 Peter Bondra	.08	.04	.01
Washington Capitals			
☐ 363 Mike Hartman	.05	.02	.01
Buffalo Sabres			
☐ 364 Trevor Linden.....................	.25	.11	.03
Vancouver Canucks			
☐ 365 John Ogrodnick..................	.05	.02	.01
New York Rangers			
☐ 366 Steve Konroyd....................	.05	.02	.01
Chicago Blackhawks			
☐ 367 Mike Modano......................	.30	.14	.04
Minnesota North Stars			
☐ 368 Glenn Healy	.08	.04	.01
New York Islanders			
☐ 369 Stephane Richer..................	.08	.04	.01
Montreal Canadiens			
☐ 370 Vincent Riendeau	.05	.02	.01
St. Louis Blues			
☐ 371 Randy Moller......................	.05	.02	.01
New York Rangers			
☐ 372 Penguins Team	.05	.02	.01
☐ 373 Murray Baron	.05	.02	.01
Philadelphia Flyers			
☐ 374 Troy Crowder	.05	.02	.01
New Jersey Devils			
☐ 375 Rick Tabaracci....................	.05	.02	.01
Winnipeg Jets			
☐ 376 Brent Fedyk	.08	.04	.01
Detroit Red Wings			
☐ 377 Randy Velischek..................	.05	.02	.01
Quebec Nordiques			
☐ 378 Esa Tikkanen	.08	.04	.01
Edmonton Oilers			
☐ 379 Richard Pilon	.05	.02	.01
New York Islanders			
☐ 380 Jeff Lazaro	.05	.02	.01
Boston Bruins			
☐ 381 Dave Ellett.........................	.05	.02	.01
Toronto Maple Leafs			
☐ 382 Jeff Hackett........................	.05	.02	.01
New York Islanders			
☐ 383 Stephane Matteau	.05	.02	.01
Calgary Flames			
☐ 384 Capitals Team	.05	.02	.01
☐ 385 Wayne Presley	.05	.02	.01
Chicago Blackhawks			
☐ 386 Grant Ledyard	.05	.02	.01
Buffalo Sabres			

☐ 387 Kip Miller	.05	.02	.01
Quebec Nordiques			
☐ 388 Dean Kennedy	.05	.02	.01
Buffalo Sabres			
☐ 389 Hubie McDonough	.05	.02	.01
New York Islanders			
☐ 390 Anatoli Semenov	.05	.02	.01
Edmonton Oilers			
☐ 391 Daryl Reaugh	.05	.02	.01
Hartford Whalers			
☐ 392 Mathieu Schneider	.08	.04	.01
Montreal Canadiens			
☐ 393 Dan Quinn	.05	.02	.01
St. Louis Blues			
☐ 394 Claude Lemieux	.08	.04	.01
New Jersey Devils			
☐ 395 Phil Housley	.08	.04	.01
Winnipeg Jets			
☐ 396 Checklist 265-396	.05	.02	.01
☐ 397 Steve Bozek	.05	.02	.01
Vancouver Canucks			
☐ 398 Bobby Smith	.08	.04	.01
Minnesota North Stars			
☐ 399 Mark Pederson	.05	.02	.01
Philadelphia Flyers			
☐ 400 Kevin Todd	.15	.07	.02
New Jersey Devils			
☐ 401 Sergei Fedorov	.60	.25	.08
Detroit Red Wings			
☐ 402 Tom Barrasso	.08	.04	.01
Pittsburgh Penguins			
☐ 403 Brett Hull HL	.20	.09	.03
St. Louis Blues			
☐ 404 Bob Carpenter UER	.05	.02	.01
Boston Bruins			
(No italics or diamond			
85-86 or 90-91 GP)			
☐ 405 Luc Robitaille	.15	.07	.02
Los Angeles Kings			
☐ 406 Mark Hardy	.05	.02	.01
New York Rangers			
☐ 407 Neil Sheehy	.05	.02	.01
Washington Capitals			
☐ 408 Mike McNeil	.05	.02	.01
Quebec Nordiques			
☐ 409 Dave Manson	.08	.04	.01
Chicago Blackhawks			
☐ 410 Mike Tomlak	.05	.02	.01
Hartford Whalers			
☐ 411 Robert Reichel	.15	.07	.02
Calgary Flames			
☐ 412 Islanders Team	.05	.02	.01
☐ 413 Patrick Roy	.50	.23	.06
Montreal Canadiens			
☐ 414 Shaun Van Allen	.10	.05	.01
Edmonton Oilers			
☐ 415 Dale Kushner	.05	.02	.01
Philadelphia Flyers			
☐ 416 Pierre Turgeon	.20	.09	.03
Buffalo Sabres			
☐ 417 Curtis Joseph	.25	.11	.03
St. Louis Blues			
☐ 418 Randy Gilhen	.05	.02	.01
Pittsburgh Penguins			
☐ 419 Jyrki Lumme	.05	.02	.01
Vancouver Canucks			
☐ 420 Neal Broten	.08	.04	.01
Minnesota North Stars			
☐ 421 Kevin Stevens	.30	.14	.04
Pittsburgh Penguins			
☐ 422 Chris Terreri	.08	.04	.01
New Jersey Devils			
☐ 423 David Reid	.05	.02	.01
Toronto Maple Leafs			
☐ 424 Steve Yzerman	.25	.11	.03
Detroit Red Wings			
☐ 425 Ed Belfour LL	.05	.02	.01
Chicago Blackhawks			
☐ 426 Jim Johnson	.05	.02	.01
Minnesota North Stars			
☐ 427 Joey Kocur	.05	.02	.01
New York Rangers			
☐ 428 Joel Otto	.05	.02	.01
Calgary Flames			
☐ 429 Dino Ciccarelli	.08	.04	.01
Washington Capitals			
☐ 430 Blackhawks Team	.05	.02	.01
☐ 431 Claude Lapointe	.10	.05	.01
Quebec Nordiques			
☐ 432 Chris Joseph	.05	.02	.01
Edmonton Oilers			
☐ 433 Gaetan Duchesne	.05	.02	.01
Minnesota North Stars			
☐ 434 Mike Keane	.05	.02	.01
Montreal Canadiens			
☐ 435 Dave Chyzowski	.05	.02	.01
New York Islanders			
☐ 436 Glen Featherstone	.05	.02	.01
St. Louis Blues			
☐ 437 Jim Paek	.10	.05	.01
Pittsburgh Penguins			
☐ 438 Doug Evans	.05	.02	.01
Winnipeg Jets			
☐ 439 Alexei Kasatonov UER	.05	.02	.01
New Jersey Devils			
(Misspelled Alexi			
on card back)			
☐ 440 Ken Hodge Jr.	.05	.02	.01
Boston Bruins			
☐ 441 Dave Snuggerud	.05	.02	.01
Buffalo Sabres			
☐ 442 Brad Shaw	.05	.02	.01
Hartford Whalers			
☐ 443 Gerard Gallant	.05	.02	.01
Detroit Red Wings			
☐ 444 Jiri Latal	.05	.02	.01
Philadelphia Flyers			
☐ 445 Peter Zezel	.05	.02	.01
Toronto Maple Leafs			
☐ 446 Troy Gamble	.05	.02	.01
Vancouver Canucks			
☐ 447 Craig Coxe	.05	.02	.01
Vancouver Canucks			
☐ 448 Adam Oates	.20	.09	.03
St. Louis Blues			
☐ 449 Todd Krygier	.05	.02	.01
Hartford Whalers			
☐ 450 Andre Racicot	.10	.05	.01
Montreal Canadiens			
☐ 451 Patrik Sundstrom	.05	.02	.01
New Jersey Devils			
☐ 452 Glen Wesley UER	.05	.02	.01
Boston Bruins			
(No italics or diamond			
90-91 GP)			
☐ 453 Jocelyn Lemieux	.05	.02	.01
Chicago Blackhawks			
☐ 454 Rick Zombo	.05	.02	.01
Detroit Red Wings			
☐ 455 Derek King	.08	.04	.01
New York Islanders			
☐ 456 J.J. Daigneault	.05	.02	.01
Montreal Canadiens			
☐ 457 Rick Vaive	.05	.02	.01
Buffalo Sabres			
☐ 458 Larry Robinson	.08	.04	.01
Los Angeles Kings			
☐ 459 Rick Wamsley	.05	.02	.01
Calgary Flames			
☐ 460 Craig Simpson	.08	.04	.01
Edmonton Oilers			
☐ 461 Corey Millen	.20	.09	.03
New York Rangers			
☐ 462 Sergio Momesso	.05	.02	.01
Vancouver Canucks			
☐ 463 Paul MacDermid	.05	.02	.01
Winnipeg Jets			
☐ 464 Wendel Clark	.20	.09	.03
Toronto Maple Leafs			
☐ 465 Mikhail Tatarinov	.05	.02	.01
Washington Capitals			
☐ 466 Mark Howe	.08	.04	.01
Philadelphia Flyers			
☐ 467 Jay Miller	.05	.02	.01
Los Angeles Kings			
☐ 468 Grant Jennings	.05	.02	.01
Pittsburgh Penguins			
☐ 469 Paul Gillis	.05	.02	.01
Chicago Blackhawks			
☐ 470 Ron Hextall	.08	.04	.01
Philadelphia Flyers			
☐ 471 Alexander Godynyuk	.05	.02	.01
Toronto Maple Leafs			
☐ 472 Bryan Trottier	.08	.04	.01
Pittsburgh Penguins			
☐ 473 Kevin Haller	.15	.07	.02
Buffalo Sabres			
☐ 474 Troy Mallette	.05	.02	.01
New York Rangers			
☐ 475 Jim Wiemer	.05	.02	.01
Boston Bruins			
☐ 476 David Maley	.05	.02	.01
New Jersey Devils			
☐ 477 Moe Mantha UER	.05	.02	.01
Winnipeg Jets			
(Photo actually			

Paul MacDermid)
- [ ] 478 Brad Jones .... .05 .02 .01
  Los Angeles Kings
- [ ] 479 Craig Muni .... .05 .02 .01
  Edmonton Oilers
- [ ] 480 Igor Larionov .... .08 .04 .01
  Vancouver Canucks
- [ ] 481 Scott Stevens .... .10 .05 .01
  St. Louis Blues
- [ ] 482 Sergei Makarov .... .08 .04 .01
  Calgary Flames
- [ ] 483 Mike Lalor .... .05 .02 .01
  Washington Capitals
- [ ] 484 Tony McKegney .... .05 .02 .01
  Chicago Blackhawks
- [ ] 485 Perry Berezan .... .05 .02 .01
  Minnesota North Stars
- [ ] 486 Derrick Smith .... .05 .02 .01
  Philadelphia Flyers
- [ ] 487 Jim Hrivnak .... .05 .02 .01
  Washington Capitals
- [ ] 488 David Volek .... .05 .02 .01
  New York Islanders
- [ ] 489 Sylvain Lefebvre .... .05 .02 .01
  Montreal Canadiens
- [ ] 490 Rod Brind'Amour .... .15 .07 .02
  St. Louis Blues
- [ ] 491 Al MacInnis .... .10 .05 .01
  Calgary Flames
- [ ] 492 Jamie Leach .... .05 .02 .01
  Pittsburgh Penguins
- [ ] 493 Robert Dirk .... .05 .02 .01
  Vancouver Canucks
- [ ] 494 Gordie Roberts .... .05 .02 .01
  Pittsburgh Penguins
- [ ] 495 Mike Hudson .... .05 .02 .01
  Chicago Blackhawks
- [ ] 496 Frank Breault .... .05 .02 .01
  Los Angeles Kings
- [ ] 497 Rejean Lemelin .... .08 .04 .01
  Boston Bruins
- [ ] 498 Kris King .... .05 .02 .01
  New York Rangers
- [ ] 499 Pat Verbeek .... .08 .04 .01
  Hartford Whalers
- [ ] 500 Bryan Fogarty .... .05 .02 .01
  Quebec Nordiques
- [ ] 501 Perry Anderson .... .05 .02 .01
  New Jersey Devils
- [ ] 502 Joe Cirella .... .05 .02 .01
  New York Rangers
- [ ] 503 Mikko Makela .... .05 .02 .01
  Buffalo Sabres
- [ ] 504 Paul Coffey HL UER .... .08 .04 .01
  (Misspelled Coffee and
  Dennis Potvin on card
  back; date 12/22/90 in
  English, but 12/23/90
  in French)
- [ ] 505 Don Beaupre .... .08 .04 .01
  Washington Capitals
- [ ] 506 Brian Glynn .... .05 .02 .01
  Minnesota North Stars
- [ ] 507 Dave Poulin .... .08 .04 .01
  Boston Bruins
- [ ] 508 Steve Chiasson .... .05 .02 .01
  Detroit Red Wings
- [ ] 509 Myles O'Connor .... .05 .02 .01
  New Jersey Devils
- [ ] 510 Ilkka Sinisalo .... .05 .02 .01
  Los Angeles Kings
- [ ] 511 Nick Kypreos .... .05 .02 .01
  Washington Capitals
- [ ] 512 Doug Houda UER .... .05 .02 .01
  Hartford Whalers
  (No position after
  name on back)
- [ ] 513 Valeri Kamensky .... .35 .16 .04
  Quebec Nordiques
- [ ] 514 Sergei Nemchinov .... .15 .07 .02
  New York Rangers
- [ ] 515 Dimitri Mironov .... .15 .07 .02
  Toronto Maple Leafs
- [ ] 516 Brett Hull Hart .... .20 .09 .03
  St. Louis Blues
- [ ] 517 Ray Bourque Norris .... .13 .06 .02
  Boston Bruins
- [ ] 518 Ed Belfour Calder .... .10 .05 .01
  Chicago Blackhawks
- [ ] 519 Ed Belfour UER .... .10 .05 .01
  Chicago Blackhawks
  Vezina Trophy
  (Georges misspelled as
  George)

- [ ] 520 Wayne Gretzky Byng .... .35 .16 .04
  Los Angeles Kings
- [ ] 521 Dirk Graham Selke .... .10 .05 .01
  Chicago Blackhawks
- [ ] 522 Wayne Gretzky Ross .... .35 .16 .04
  Los Angeles Kings
- [ ] 523 Mario Lemieux Smythe ...... .25 .11 .03
  Pittsburgh Penguins
- [ ] 524 Wayne Gretzky HL.............. .35 .16 .04
  Los Angeles Kings
- [ ] 525 Sharks Team .... .30 .14 .04
- [ ] 526 Lightning Team UER .... .25 .11 .03
  (Team name on back in
  white, should be yellow)
- [ ] 527 Senators Team .... .25 .11 .03
- [ ] 528 Checklist 397-528 .... .05 .02 .01

1991-92 O-Pee-Chee Inserts

Inserted one per 1991-92 O-Pee-Chee nine-card wax pack, this 66-card set features 10 cards of San Jose Sharks (1S-10S) and 56 Russian hockey players (11R-66R). Among the 56 Russian player cards are those from Central Red Army (11R-30R), Dynamo Moscow (31R-48R), and Khimik (49R-66R). Cards measure the standard 2 1/2" by 3 1/2". The Sharks' cards have either posed or action player photos with gray and teal border stripes. The player's name appears in the bottom teal border stripe, while the team logo is superimposed over a hockey stick at the lower right corner. Card backs present biography and statistics. The Russian player cards have color action player photos enclosed by yellow and red borders. On a red and white background, the backs carry a blue hammer and sickle emblem, a blue Russian star, biography, and statistics versus NHL clubs while touring. The cards are numbered on the back. Sergei Zubov and Alexei Zhamnov are part of this set.

	MINT	EXC	G-VG
COMPLETE SET (66).........................	12.00	5.50	1.50
COMMON PLAYER (1S-10S)..........	.10	.05	.01
COMMON PLAYER (11R-66R)..........	.15	.07	.02
[ ] 1S Link Gaetz	.10	.05	.01
[ ] 2S Bengt Gustafsson	.10	.05	.01
[ ] 3S Dan Keczmer	.15	.07	.02
[ ] 4S Dean Kolstad........................	.10	.05	.01
[ ] 5S Peter Lappin	.10	.05	.01
[ ] 6S Jeff Madill	.10	.05	.01
[ ] 7S Mike McHugh	.10	.05	.01
[ ] 8S Jarmo Myllys UER	.10	.05	.01
(Stat line is for			
Offense/Defense)			
[ ] 9S Doug Zmolek	.15	.07	.02
[ ] 10S Sharks Checklist	.15	.07	.02
[ ] 11R Vadim Brezgunov	.15	.07	.02
[ ] 12R Vyacheslav Butsayev	.40	.18	.05
[ ] 13R Ilya Byakin	.25	.11	.03
[ ] 14R Igor Chibirev......................	.25	.11	.03
[ ] 15R Victor Gordijuk	.25	.11	.03
[ ] 16R Yuri Khmiliov	.40	.18	.05
[ ] 17R Pavel Kostichkin	.15	.07	.02
[ ] 18R Andrei Kovalenko................	.40	.18	.05

☐ 19R Igor Kravchuk	.40	.18	.05
☐ 20R Igor Malykhin	.20	.09	.03
☐ 21R Igor Maslennikov	.15	.07	.02
☐ 22R Maxim Mikhailovsky	.20	.09	.03
☐ 23R Dimitri Mironov	.40	.18	.05
☐ 24R Sergei Nemchinov	.40	.18	.05
☐ 25R Alexander Prokopjev	.15	.07	.02
☐ 26R Igor Stelnov	.15	.07	.02
☐ 27R Sergei Vostrikov	.15	.07	.02
☐ 28R Sergei Zubov	2.50	1.15	.30
☐ 29R Central Red Army Team	.15	.07	.02
☐ 30R Central Red Army Team	.50	.23	.06
☐ 31R Alexander Andreivsky	.20	.09	.03
☐ 32R Igor Dorofeyev	.15	.07	.02
☐ 33R Alexander Galchenyuk	.15	.07	.02
☐ 34R Roman Ilyin	.15	.07	.02
☐ 35R Alexander Karpovtsev	.35	.16	.04
☐ 36R Ravil Khaidarov	.15	.07	.02
☐ 37R Igor Korolytov	.25	.11	.03
☐ 38R Andrei Kovalyov	.15	.07	.02
☐ 39R Yuri Leonov	.15	.07	.02
☐ 40R Andrei Lomakin UER	.25	.11	.03
(Misspelled Adrei on card front)			
☐ 41R Evgeny Popikhin	.15	.07	.02
☐ 42R Alexander Semak	.60	.25	.08
☐ 43R Mikhail Shtalenkov	.50	.23	.06
☐ 44R Serguei Sorokin	.15	.07	.02
☐ 45R Andrei Trefilov	.60	.25	.08
☐ 46R Ravil Yakubov	.15	.07	.02
☐ 47R Alexander Yudin	.15	.07	.02
☐ 48R Alexei Zhamnov	1.75	.80	.22
☐ 49R Andrei Basalgin	.15	.07	.02
☐ 50R Lev Berdichevsky	.15	.07	.02
☐ 51R Konstantin Kapkaikin	.15	.07	.02
☐ 52R Konstantin Kurashov	.15	.07	.02
☐ 53R Andrei Kvartalnov	.30	.14	.04
☐ 54R Albert Malgin	.15	.07	.02
☐ 55R Nikolai Maslov	.15	.07	.02
☐ 56R Anatoli Naida	.15	.07	.02
☐ 57R Roman Oksyuta	.25	.11	.03
☐ 58R Sergei Selyanin	.15	.07	.02
☐ 59R Valeri Shiryev	.15	.07	.02
☐ 60R Alexander Smirnov	.15	.07	.02
☐ 61R Leonid Trukhno	.15	.07	.02
☐ 62R Igor Ulanov UER	.25	.11	.03
(Misspelled Vlanov on card front)			
☐ 63R Andrei Yakovenko	.20	.09	.03
☐ 64R Oleg Yashin	.15	.07	.02
☐ 65R Valeri Zelepukin	.75	.35	.09
☐ 66R Russian Checklist	.15	.07	.02

1991-92 O-Pee-Chee Premier

NICKLAS LIDSTROM DEFENSE • DÉFENSEUR

The 1991-92 O-Pee-Chee Premier hockey set contains 198 cards measuring the standard size (2 1/2" by 3 1/2"). Color player photos are bordered above and below in gold. Player name, team and position appear at the bottom. The backs have a small color player photo, biography, team logo and statistics. Rookie Cards in this set include Tony Amonte, Josef Beranek, Vladimir Konstantinov, Nicklas Lidstrom, and Doug Weight. A Konstantinov variation can be found with Lidstrom's photo on the back. Very few of these variations have been located.

	MINT	EXC	G-VG
COMPLETE SET (198)	10.00	4.50	1.25
COMPLETE FACT.SET (198)	15.00	6.75	1.90
COMMON PLAYER (1-198)	.05	.02	.01
☐ 1 Dale Hawerchuk	.08	.04	.01
Buffalo Sabres			
☐ 2 Ray Sheppard	.08	.04	.01
Detroit Red Wings			
☐ 3 Wayne Gretzky UER	1.00	.45	.13
(Canada Cup stats incorrect)			
Los Angeles Kings			
☐ 4 John MacLean	.08	.04	.01
New Jersey Devils			
☐ 5 Pat Verbeek	.08	.04	.01
Hartford Whalers			
☐ 6 Doug Wilson	.08	.04	.01
San Jose Sharks			
☐ 7 Adam Oates	.20	.09	.03
St. Louis Blues			
☐ 8 Bob McGill	.05	.02	.01
San Jose Sharks			
☐ 9 Mike Vernon	.08	.04	.01
Calgary Flames			
☐ 10 Glenn Anderson	.10	.05	.01
Toronto Maple Leafs			
☐ 11 Tony Amonte	.40	.18	.05
New York Rangers			
☐ 12 Stephen Leach	.05	.02	.01
Boston Bruins			
☐ 13 Steve Duchesne	.08	.04	.01
Philadelphia Flyers			
☐ 14 Patrick Roy	.60	.25	.08
Montreal Canadiens			
☐ 15 Jarmo Myllys	.05	.02	.01
San Jose Sharks			
☐ 16 Yanic Dupre	.05	.02	.01
Philadelphia Flyers			
☐ 17 Chris Chelios	.08	.04	.01
Chicago Blackhawks			
☐ 18 Bill Ranford	.08	.04	.01
Edmonton Oilers			
☐ 19 Ed Belfour	.30	.14	.04
Chicago Blackhawks			
☐ 20 Michel Picard	.05	.02	.01
Hartford Whalers			
☐ 21 Rob Zettler	.05	.02	.01
San Jose Sharks			
☐ 22 Kevin Todd	.15	.07	.02
New Jersey Devils			
☐ 23 Mike Ricci	.15	.07	.02
Philadelphia Flyers			
☐ 24 Jaromir Jagr	.75	.35	.09
Pittsburgh Penguins			
☐ 25 Sergei Nemchinov	.15	.07	.02
New York Rangers			
☐ 26 Kevin Stevens	.35	.16	.04
Pittsburgh Penguins			
☐ 27 Dan Quinn	.05	.02	.01
Philadelphia Flyers			
☐ 28 Adam Graves	.30	.14	.04
Edmonton Oilers			
☐ 29 Pat Jablonski	.10	.05	.01
St. Louis Blues			
☐ 30 Scott Mellanby	.05	.02	.01
Edmonton Oilers			
☐ 31 Tomas Forslund	.05	.02	.01
Calgary Flames			
☐ 32 Doug Weight	.25	.11	.03
New York Rangers			
☐ 33 Peter Ing	.05	.02	.01
Edmonton Oilers			
☐ 34 Luc Robitaille	.20	.09	.03
Los Angeles Kings			
☐ 35 Scott Niedermayer	.50	.23	.06
New Jersey Devils			
☐ 36 Dean Evason	.05	.02	.01
San Jose Sharks			
☐ 37 John Tonelli	.08	.04	.01
Chicago Blackhawks			
☐ 38 Ron Hextall	.08	.04	.01
Philadelphia Flyers			
☐ 39 Troy Mallette	.05	.02	.01
Edmonton Oilers			
☐ 40 Tony Hrkac	.05	.02	.01
San Jose Sharks			
☐ 41 Ken Hodge Jr.	.05	.02	.01
Boston Bruins			
☐ 42 Kip Miller	.05	.02	.01
Quebec Nordiques			
☐ 43 Randy Burridge	.05	.02	.01
Washington Capitals			
☐ 44 Rob Blake	.15	.07	.02

Los Angeles Kings
- ☐ 45 Sergei Makarov .08 .04 .01

Calgary Flames
- ☐ 46 Luke Richardson .05 .02 .01

Toronto Maple Leafs
- ☐ 47 Craig Berube .05 .02 .01

Philadelphia Flyers
- ☐ 48 Joe Nieuwendyk .10 .05 .01

Calgary Flames
- ☐ 49 Brett Hull .60 .25 .08

St. Louis Blues
- ☐ 50 Phil Housley .08 .04 .01

Winnipeg Jets
- ☐ 51 Mark Messier .30 .14 .04

New York Rangers
- ☐ 52 Jeremy Roenick .75 .35 .09

Chicago Blackhawks
- ☐ 53 Dave Christian .05 .02 .01

St. Louis Blues
- ☐ 54 Dave Barr .05 .02 .01

Detroit Red Wings
- ☐ 55 Sergio Momesso .05 .02 .01

Vancouver Canucks
- ☐ 56 Pat Falloon .35 .16 .04

San Jose Sharks
- ☐ 57 Brian Leetch .35 .16 .04

New York Rangers
- ☐ 58 Russ Courtnall .08 .04 .01

Toronto Maple Leafs
- ☐ 59 Pierre Turgeon .30 .14 .04

New York Islanders
- ☐ 60 Steve Larmer .08 .04 .01

Chicago Blackhawks
- ☐ 61 Petr Klima .05 .02 .01

Edmonton Oilers
- ☐ 62 Mikhail Tatarinov .05 .02 .01

Washington Capitals
- ☐ 63 Rick Tocchet .08 .04 .01

Philadelphia Flyers
- ☐ 64 Pat LaFontaine .30 .14 .04

Buffalo Sabres
- ☐ 65 Rob Pearson .25 .11 .03

Toronto Maple Leafs
- ☐ 66 Glen Featherstone .05 .02 .01

Boston Bruins
- ☐ 67 Pavel Bure 2.00 .90 .25

Vancouver Canucks
- ☐ 68 Sergei Fedorov 1.50 .65 .19

Detroit Red Wings
- ☐ 69 Kelly Kisio .05 .02 .01

San Jose Sharks
- ☐ 70 Joe Sakic .30 .14 .04

Quebec Nordiques
- ☐ 71 Denis Savard .08 .04 .01

Montreal Canadiens
- ☐ 72 Andrew Cassels .08 .04 .01

Montreal Canadiens
- ☐ 73 Steve Yzerman .35 .16 .04

Detroit Red Wings
- ☐ 74 Todd Elik .05 .02 .01

Toronto Maple Leafs
- ☐ 75 Troy Murray .05 .02 .01

Winnipeg Jets
- ☐ 76 Rob Ramage .05 .02 .01

Buffalo Sabres
- ☐ 77 Trevor Linden .25 .11 .03

Vancouver Canucks
- ☐ 78 Mike Richter .25 .11 .03

New York Rangers
- ☐ 79 Paul Coffey .15 .07 .02

Pittsburgh Penguins
- ☐ 80 Craig Ludwig .05 .02 .01

New York Islanders
- ☐ 81 Al MacInnis .10 .05 .01

Calgary Flames
- ☐ 82 Tomas Sandstrom .08 .04 .01

Los Angeles Kings
- ☐ 83 Tim Kerr .08 .04 .01

New York Rangers
- ☐ 84 Scott Stevens .10 .05 .01

New Jersey Devils
- ☐ 85 Steve Kasper .05 .02 .01

Philadelphia Flyers
- ☐ 86 Kirk Muller .08 .04 .01

Montreal Canadiens
- ☐ 87 Pat MacLeod .05 .02 .01

San Jose Sharks
- ☐ 88 Kevin Hatcher .08 .04 .01

Washington Capitals
- ☐ 89 Wayne Presley .05 .02 .01

San Jose Sharks
- ☐ 90 Daryl Sydor .08 .04 .01

Los Angeles Kings
- ☐ 91 Tom Chorske .05 .02 .01

Montreal Canadiens
- ☐ 92 Theoren Fleury .15 .07 .02

Calgary Flames
- ☐ 93 Craig Janney .15 .07 .02

Boston Bruins
- ☐ 94 Rod Brind'Amour .25 .11 .03

Philadelphia Flyers
- ☐ 95 Ron Sutter .05 .02 .01

St. Louis Blues
- ☐ 96 Matt DelGuidice .05 .02 .01

Boston Bruins
- ☐ 97 Rollie Melanson .05 .02 .01

Montreal Canadiens
- ☐ 98 Tom Kurvers .05 .02 .01

New Jersey Devils
- ☐ 99 Bryan Marchment .10 .05 .01

Chicago Blackhawks
- ☐ 100 Grant Fuhr .08 .04 .01

Toronto Maple Leafs
- ☐ 101 Geoff Courtnall .08 .04 .01

Vancouver Canucks
- ☐ 102 Joel Otto .05 .02 .01

Calgary Flames
- ☐ 103 Tom Barrasso .08 .04 .01

Buffalo Sabres
- ☐ 104 Vincent Damphousse .08 .04 .01

Edmonton Oilers
- ☐ 105 John LeClair .20 .09 .03

Montreal Canadiens
- ☐ 106 Gary Leeman .05 .02 .01

Toronto Maple Leafs
- ☐ 107 Cam Neely .15 .07 .02

Boston Bruins
- ☐ 108 Jeff Hackett .05 .02 .01

San Jose Sharks
- ☐ 109 Stu Barnes .08 .04 .01

Winnipeg Jets
- ☐ 110 Neil Wilkinson .05 .02 .01

San Jose Sharks
- ☐ 111 Jari Kurri .10 .05 .01

Los Angeles Kings
- ☐ 112 Jon Casey .08 .04 .01

Minnesota North Stars
- ☐ 113 Stephane Richer .08 .04 .01

New Jersey Devils
- ☐ 114 Mario Lemieux 1.00 .45 .13

Pittsburgh Penguins
- ☐ 115 Brad Jones .05 .02 .01

Philadelphia Flyers
- ☐ 116 Wendel Clark .20 .09 .03

Toronto Maple Leafs
- ☐ 117 Nicklas Lidstrom .50 .23 .06

Detroit Red Wings
- ☐ 118A Vladimir Konstantinov 10.00 4.50 1.25

Detroit Red Wings ERR
(Lidstrom photo on back)
- ☐ 118B Vladimir Konstantinov COR .35 .16 .04

Detroit Red Wings
- ☐ 119 Ray Bourque .15 .07 .02

Boston Bruins
- ☐ 120 Ron Francis .08 .04 .01

Hartford Whalers
- ☐ 121 Esa Tikkanen .08 .04 .01

Edmonton Oilers
- ☐ 122 Randy Hillier .05 .02 .01

Pittsburgh Penguins
- ☐ 123 Randy Gilhen .05 .02 .01

Los Angeles Kings
- ☐ 124 Barry Pederson .05 .02 .01

Vancouver Canucks
- ☐ 125 Charlie Huddy .05 .02 .01

Los Angeles Kings
- ☐ 126 Gary Roberts .05 .02 .01

Calgary Flames
- ☐ 127 John Cullen .05 .02 .01

Hartford Whalers
- ☐ 128 Dave Gagner .08 .04 .01

Minnesota North Stars
- ☐ 129 Bob Kudelski .08 .04 .01

Los Angeles Kings
- ☐ 130 Brendan Shanahan .25 .11 .03

St. Louis Blues
- ☐ 131 Dirk Graham .05 .02 .01

Chicago Blackhawks
- ☐ 132 Checklist 1-99 .05 .02 .01
- ☐ 133 Andy Moog .10 .05 .01

Boston Bruins
- ☐ 134 Original Six Toronto .05 .02 .01
  Gary Leeman
- ☐ 135 Original Six Chicago .05 .02 .01
  Steve Larmer
- ☐ 136 Steve Smith .08 .04 .01

Chicago Blackhawks
- ☐ 137 Dave Manson .08 .04 .01

Edmonton Oilers
☐ 138 Nelson Emerson .... .25 .11 .03
St. Louis Blues
☐ 139 Original Six New York .... .05 .02 .01
Doug Weight
☐ 140 Uwe Krupp .... .05 .02 .01
New York Islanders
☐ 141 Original Six Boston .... .05 .02 .01
Peter Douris
☐ 142 Original Six Detroit .... .15 .07 .02
Steve Yzerman
☐ 143 Derian Hatcher .... .08 .04 .01
Minnesota North Stars
☐ 144 Original Six Boston .... .05 .02 .01
Vladimir Ruzicka
☐ 145 Original Six Montreal .... .08 .04 .01
Kirk Muller
☐ 146 Darrin Shannon.................. .05 .02 .01
Winnipeg Jets
☐ 147 Original Six New York .... .08 .04 .01
Mike Gartner
☐ 148 Original Six Boston .... .05 .02 .01
Bob Carpenter
☐ 149 Josef Beranek .... .25 .11 .03
Edmonton Oilers
☐ 150 Original Six Chicago........... .08 .04 .01
Chris Chelios
☐ 151 Original Six Toronto .... .05 .02 .01
Bob Rouse
☐ 152 Original Six Montreal .... .05 .02 .01
Guy Carbonneau
☐ 153 Joe Mullen .... .10 .05 .01
Pittsburgh Penguins
☐ 154 Ken Hodge Jr. .... .05 .02 .01
Original Six Boston
☐ 155 Original Six Detroit .... .15 .07 .02
Vladimir Konstantinov
☐ 156 Brent Sutter...................... .08 .04 .01
Chicago Blackhawks
☐ 157 Original Six Montreal .... .05 .02 .01
Eric Desjardins
☐ 158 Kirk McLean UER .... .25 .11 .03
(Photo on back act-
ually Frank Caprice)
Vancouver Canucks
☐ 159 Original Six Chicago........... .05 .02 .01
John Tonelli
☐ 160 Original Six Toronto .... .05 .02 .01
Rob Cimetta
☐ 161 Shayne Corson.................. .08 .04 .01
Montreal Canadiens
☐ 162 Russ Romaniuk................. .10 .05 .01
Winnipeg Jets
☐ 163 Original Six Detroit .... .20 .09 .03
Nicklas Lidstrom
☐ 164 Mike Gartner .... .10 .05 .01
New York Rangers
☐ 165 Curtis Joseph .... .30 .14 .04
St. Louis Blues
☐ 166 Brian Mullen...................... .08 .04 .01
San Jose Sharks
☐ 167 Jimmy Carson.................... .08 .04 .01
Detroit Red Wings
☐ 168 Original Six Montreal .... .05 .02 .01
Petr Svoboda
☐ 169 Troy Crowder .... .05 .02 .01
Detroit Red Wings
☐ 170 Original Six Montreal .... .35 .16 .04
Patrick Roy
☐ 171 Adam Creighton .... .05 .02 .01
New York Islanders
☐ 172 Original Six New York .... .05 .02 .01
James Patrick
☐ 173 Original Six Detroit .... .50 .23 .06
Sergei Fedorov
☐ 174 Original Six Chicago........... .50 .23 .06
Jeremy Roenick
☐ 175 Original Six Detroit .... .05 .02 .01
Tim Cheveldae
☐ 176 Dimitri Khristich................. .08 .04 .01
Washington Capitals
☐ 177 Original Six Toronto .... .08 .04 .01
Wendel Clark
☐ 178 Andrei Lomakin.................. .05 .02 .01
Philadelphia Flyers
☐ 179 Benoit Hogue .... .05 .02 .01
New York Islanders
☐ 180 Original Six Toronto .... .05 .02 .01
Dave Ellett
☐ 181 Original Six Montreal .... .05 .02 .01
Mathieu Schneider
☐ 182 Kay Whitmore .... .05 .02 .01
Hartford Whalers
☐ 183 Original Six New York .... .15 .07 .02

Brian Leetch
☐ 184 Original Six Montreal .... .05 .02 .01
Sylvain Turgeon
☐ 185 Original Six Toronto .... .05 .02 .01
Brian Bradley
☐ 186 Original Six Montreal .... .05 .02 .01
John LeClair
☐ 187 Paul Fenton....................... .05 .02 .01
San Jose Sharks
☐ 188 Original Six Montreal .... .05 .02 .01
Alain Cote
☐ 189 Original Six Toronto .... .05 .02 .01
Mike Krushelnyski UER
(Misspelled on back
as Krushelnynski)
☐ 190 Brian Bradley..................... .08 .04 .01
Vancouver Canucks
☐ 191 Original Six Toronto .... .08 .04 .01
Grant Fuhr
☐ 192 Original Six Boston .... .08 .04 .01
Ray Bourque
☐ 193 Owen Nolan....................... .15 .07 .02
Quebec Nordiques
☐ 194 Original Six Montreal .... .08 .04 .01
Russ Courtnall
☐ 195 Steve Thomas.................... .08 .04 .01
New York Islanders
☐ 196 Ed Olczyk .... .05 .02 .01
Winnipeg Jets
☐ 197 Chris Terreri...................... .08 .04 .01
New Jersey Devils
☐ 198 Checklist 100-198.............. .05 .02 .01

1992-93 O-Pee-Chee

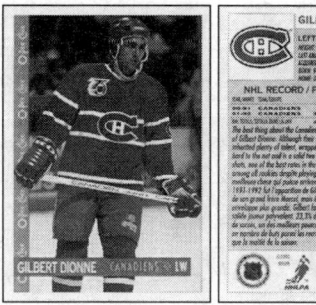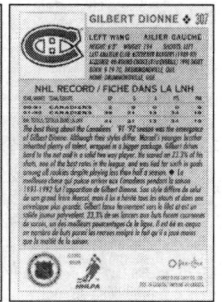

The 1992-93 set marks O-Pee-Chee's 25th consecutive year of manufacturing hockey cards. The set contains 396 standard-size (2 1/2" by 3 1/2") cards. The set includes 25 special 25th Anniversary Tribute cards. The same 25 players are featured in a 25th Anniversary wax pack insert set. O-Pee-Chee produced 12,000 Special Anniversary Collector sets which included the complete 396-card set and the 26-card (including checklist) anniversary insert set. Also, 750 additional factory sets were allocated across Canada for confectionary customers and O-Pee-Chee employees to purchase. Card fronts feature color player photos bordered by a metallic blue stripe on the left and full-bleed on the other three sides. The player's name, team name, and position appear in a gray stripe toward the bottom of the card. The bilingual backs carry the team logo, biography, complete statistics, and player profile.

	MINT	EXC	G-VG
COMPLETE SET (396)......................	20.00	9.00	2.50
COMPLETE FACT.SET (396)...........	28.00	12.50	3.50
COMP.ANNIV.FACT.SET (422).........	75.00	34.00	9.50
COMMON PLAYER (1-396)...............	.05	.02	.01

☐ 1 Kevin Todd........................ .05 .02 .01
New Jersey Devils
☐ 2 Robert Kron .... .05 .02 .01
Vancouver Canucks
☐ 3 David Volek .... .05 .02 .01

New York Islanders
☐ 4	Teppo Numminen	.05	.02	.01

Winnipeg Jets
☐ 5	Paul Coffey	.15	.07	.02

Los Angeles Kings
☐ 6	Luc Robitaille	.15	.07	.02

Los Angeles Kings
☐ 7	Steven Finn	.05	.02	.01

Quebec Nordiques
☐ 8	Gord Hynes	.05	.02	.01

Boston Bruins
☐ 9	Dave Ellett	.05	.02	.01

Toronto Maple Leafs
☐ 10	Alexander Godynyuk	.05	.02	.01

Calgary Flames
☐ 11	Darryl Sydor	.08	.04	.01

Los Angeles Kings
☐ 12	Randy Carlyle	.05	.02	.01

Winnipeg Jets
☐ 13	Chris Chelios	.08	.04	.01

Chicago Blackhawks
☐ 14	Kent Manderville	.05	.02	.01

Toronto Maple Leafs
☐ 15	Wayne Gretzky	1.00	.45	.13

Los Angeles Kings
☐ 16	Jon Casey	.08	.04	.01

Minnesota North Stars
☐ 17	Mark Tinordi	.08	.04	.01

Minnesota North Stars
☐ 18	Dale Hunter	.08	.04	.01

Washington Capitals
☐ 19	Martin Gelinas UER	.05	.02	.01

(Trade was 8-9-88,
not 8-9-89)
Edmonton Oilers
☐ 20	Todd Elik	.05	.02	.01

Minnesota North Stars
☐ 21	Bob Sweeney	.05	.02	.01

Boston Bruins
☐ 22	Chris Dahlquist	.05	.02	.01

Minnesota North Stars
☐ 23	Joe Mullen	.08	.04	.01

Pittsburgh Penguins
☐ 24	Shawn Burr	.05	.02	.01

Detroit Red Wings
☐ 25	Pavel Bure	1.00	.45	.13

Vancouver Canucks
☐ 26	Randy Gilhen	.05	.02	.01

New York Rangers
☐ 27	Brian Bradley	.05	.02	.01

Tampa Bay Lightning
☐ 28	Don Beaupre	.08	.04	.01

Washington Capitals
☐ 29	Kevin Stevens	.20	.09	.03

Pittsburgh Penguins
☐ 30	Michal Pivonka	.08	.04	.01

Washington Capitals
☐ 31	Grant Fuhr	.08	.04	.01

Toronto Maple Leafs
☐ 32	Steve Larmer	.08	.04	.01

Chicago Blackhawks
☐ 33	Gary Leeman	.05	.02	.01

Calgary Flames
☐ 34	Tony Tanti	.05	.02	.01

Buffalo Sabres
☐ 35	Denis Savard	.08	.04	.01

Montreal Canadiens
☐ 36	Paul Ranheim	.05	.02	.01

Calgary Flames
☐ 37	Andrei Lomakin	.05	.02	.01

Philadelphia Flyers
☐ 38	Perry Anderson	.05	.02	.01

San Jose Sharks
☐ 39	Stu Barnes	.05	.02	.01

Winnipeg Jets
☐ 40	Don Sweeney	.05	.02	.01

Boston Bruins
☐ 41	Jamie Baker	.05	.02	.01

Quebec Nordiques
☐ 42	Ray Ferraro	.05	.02	.01

New York Islanders
☐ 43	Bobby Clarke 70-71	.30	.14	.04

Philadelphia Flyers
☐ 44	Kelly Hrudey	.08	.04	.01

Los Angeles Kings
☐ 45	Brian Skrudland	.05	.02	.01

Montreal Canadiens
☐ 46	Paul Ysebaert	.05	.02	.01

Detroit Red Wings
☐ 47	Pierre Turgeon	.15	.07	.02

New York Islanders
☐ 48	Keith Brown	.05	.02	.01

Chicago Blackhawks
☐ 49	Rod Brind'Amour	.15	.07	.02

Philadelphia Flyers
☐ 50	Wayne McBean	.05	.02	.01

New York Islanders
☐ 51	Doug Lidster	.05	.02	.01

Vancouver Canucks
☐ 52	Bernie Nicholls	.08	.04	.01

Edmonton Oilers
☐ 53	Daren Puppa	.08	.04	.01

Buffalo Sabres
☐ 54	Joe Sakic	.20	.09	.03

Quebec Nordiques
☐ 55	Joe Sakic 89-90	.15	.07	.02

Quebec Nordiques
☐ 56	Dave Manson	.05	.02	.01

Edmonton Oilers
☐ 57	Denis Potvin 74-75	.25	.11	.03

New York Islanders
☐ 58	Daniel Marois	.05	.02	.01

New York Islanders
☐ 59	Martin Brodeur	.50	.23	.06

New Jersey Devils
☐ 60	Brent Sutter	.08	.04	.01

Chicago Blackhawks
☐ 61	Steve Yzerman	.25	.11	.03

Detroit Red Wings
☐ 62	Neal Broten	.08	.04	.01

Minnesota North Stars
☐ 63	Darcy Wakaluk	.08	.04	.01

Minnesota North Stars
☐ 64	Troy Murray	.05	.02	.01

Winnipeg Jets
☐ 65	Tony Granato	.05	.02	.01

Los Angeles Kings
☐ 66	Frantisek Musil	.05	.02	.01

Calgary Flames
☐ 67	Claude Lemieux	.08	.04	.01

New Jersey Devils
☐ 68	Brian Benning	.05	.02	.01

Philadelphia Flyers
☐ 69	Stephane Matteau	.05	.02	.01

Chicago Blackhawks
☐ 70	Tomas Forslund	.05	.02	.01

Calgary Flames
☐ 71	Dmitri Mironov	.08	.04	.01

Toronto Maple Leafs
☐ 72	Gary Roberts	.08	.04	.01

Calgary Flames
☐ 73	Felix Potvin	1.00	.45	.13

Toronto Maple Leafs
☐ 74	Glen Murray UER	.05	.02	.01

(Misspelled Glenn
on both sides)
Boston Bruins
☐ 75	Stephane Fiset	.08	.04	.01

Quebec Nordiques
☐ 76	Stephane Richer	.08	.04	.01

New Jersey Devils
☐ 77	Jeff Reese	.05	.02	.01

Calgary Flames
☐ 78	Marc Bureau	.05	.02	.01

Minnesota North Stars
☐ 79	Derek King	.05	.02	.01

New York Islanders
☐ 80	Dave Gagner	.08	.04	.01

Minnesota North Stars
☐ 81	Ed Belfour	.25	.11	.03

Chicago Blackhawks
☐ 82	Joel Otto	.05	.02	.01

Calgary Flames
☐ 83	Anatoli Semenov	.05	.02	.01

Tampa Bay Lightning
☐ 84	Ron Hextall	.08	.04	.01

Quebec Nordiques
☐ 85	Adam Creighton	.05	.02	.01

New York Islanders
☐ 86	Kris King	.05	.02	.01

New York Rangers
☐ 87	Brett Hull	.50	.23	.06

St. Louis Blues
☐ 88	Zdeno Ciger	.05	.02	.01

New Jersey Devils
☐ 89	Petr Nedved	.10	.05	.01

Vancouver Canucks
☐ 90	Sergei Makarov	.08	.04	.01

Calgary Flames
☐ 91	Tomas Sandstrom	.05	.02	.01

Los Angeles Kings
☐ 92	Steve Heinze	.05	.02	.01

Boston Bruins
☐ 93	Robert Reichel	.08	.04	.01

Calgary Flames
☐ 94	Cliff Ronning	.05	.02	.01

Vancouver Canucks
☐ 95	Eric Weinrich	.05	.02	.01

	New Jersey Devils			
☐ 96	Wendel Clark	.10	.05	.01
	Toronto Maple Leafs			
☐ 97	Rick Zombo	.05	.02	.01
	St. Louis Blues			
☐ 98	Ric Nattress	.05	.02	.01
	Toronto Maple Leafs			
☐ 99	Theoren Fleury	.10	.05	.01
	Calgary Flames			
☐ 100	Joe Murphy	.05	.02	.01
	Edmonton Oilers			
☐ 101	Gord Murphy	.05	.02	.01
	Boston Bruins			
☐ 102	Jaromir Jagr	.50	.23	.06
	Pittsburgh Penguins			
☐ 103	Mike Craig	.05	.02	.01
	Minnesota North Stars			
☐ 104	John Cullen	.05	.02	.01
	Hartford Whalers			
☐ 105	John Druce	.05	.02	.01
	Washington Capitals			
☐ 106	Peter Bondra	.08	.04	.01
	Washington Capitals			
☐ 107	Bryan Trottier 76-77	.25	.11	.03
	New York Islanders			
☐ 108	Steve Smith	.08	.04	.01
	Chicago Blackhawks			
☐ 109	Petr Svoboda	.05	.02	.01
	Buffalo Sabres			
☐ 110	Mats Sundin	.20	.09	.03
	Quebec Nordiques			
☐ 111	Patrick Roy 86-87	1.50	.65	.19
	Montreal Canadiens			
☐ 112	Steve Leach	.05	.02	.01
	Boston Bruins			
☐ 113	Jacques Cloutier	.05	.02	.01
	Quebec Nordiques			
☐ 114	Doug Weight	.08	.04	.01
	New York Rangers			
☐ 115	Frank Pietrangelo	.05	.02	.01
	Hartford Whalers			
☐ 116	Guy Hebert	.40	.18	.05
	St. Louis Blues			
☐ 117	Donald Audette	.05	.02	.01
	Buffalo Sabres			
☐ 118	Craig MacTavish	.05	.02	.01
	Edmonton Oilers			
☐ 119	Grant Fuhr 82-83	.25	.11	.03
	Edmonton Oilers			
☐ 120	Trevor Linden	.20	.09	.03
	Vancouver Canucks			
☐ 121	Fredrik Olausson	.05	.02	.01
	Winnipeg Jets			
☐ 122	Geoff Sanderson	.30	.14	.04
	Hartford Whalers			
☐ 123	Derian Hatcher	.05	.02	.01
	Minnesota North Stars			
☐ 124	Brett Hull 88-89	.75	.35	.09
	St. Louis Blues			
☐ 125	Kelly Buchberger	.05	.02	.01
	Edmonton Oilers			
☐ 126	Ray Bourque	.15	.07	.02
	Boston Bruins			
☐ 127	Murray Craven	.05	.02	.01
	Hartford Whalers			
☐ 128	Tim Cheveldae	.08	.04	.01
	Detroit Red Wings			
☐ 129	Ulf Dahlen	.05	.02	.01
	Minnesota North Stars			
☐ 130	Bryan Trottier	.08	.04	.01
	Pittsburgh Penguins			
☐ 131	Bob Carpenter	.05	.02	.01
	Washington Capitals			
☐ 132	Benoit Hogue	.05	.02	.01
	New York Islanders			
☐ 133	Claude Vilgrain	.05	.02	.01
	New Jersey Devils			
☐ 134	Glenn Anderson	.08	.04	.01
	Toronto Maple Leafs			
☐ 135	Marty McInnis	.05	.02	.01
	New York Islanders			
☐ 136	Rob Pearson	.05	.02	.01
	Toronto Maple Leafs			
☐ 137	Bill Ranford	.08	.04	.01
	Edmonton Oilers			
☐ 138	Mario Lemieux	.75	.35	.09
	Pittsburgh Penguins			
☐ 139	Bob Bassen	.05	.02	.01
	St. Louis Blues			
☐ 140	Scott Mellanby	.05	.02	.01
	Edmonton Oilers			
☐ 141	Dave Andreychuk	.05	.02	.01
	Buffalo Sabres			
☐ 142	Kelly Miller	.05	.02	.01
	Washington Capitals			
☐ 143	Gaetan Duchesne	.05	.02	.01
	Minnesota North Stars			
☐ 144	Mike Sullivan	.05	.02	.01
	San Jose Sharks			
☐ 145	Kevin Hatcher	.08	.04	.01
	Washington Capitals			
☐ 146	Doug Bodger	.05	.02	.01
	Buffalo Sabres			
☐ 147	Craig Berube	.05	.02	.01
	Calgary Flames			
☐ 148	Rick Tocchet	.08	.04	.01
	Pittsburgh Penguins			
☐ 149	Luciano Borsato	.05	.02	.01
	Winnipeg Jets			
☐ 150	Glen Wesley	.05	.02	.01
	Boston Bruins			
☐ 151	Mike Donnelly	.05	.02	.01
	Los Angeles Kings			
☐ 152	Jimmy Carson	.05	.02	.01
	Detroit Red Wings			
☐ 153	Jocelyn Lemieux	.05	.02	.01
	Chicago Blackhawks			
☐ 154	Ray Sheppard	.08	.04	.01
	Detroit Red Wings			
☐ 155	Tony Amonte	.20	.09	.03
	New York Rangers			
☐ 156	Adrien Plavsic	.05	.02	.01
	Vancouver Canucks			
☐ 157	Mark Pederson	.05	.02	.01
	Philadelphia Flyers			
☐ 158	Adam Graves	.25	.11	.03
	New York Rangers			
☐ 159	Igor Larionov	.08	.04	.01
	Vancouver Canucks			
☐ 160	Steve Chiasson	.05	.02	.01
	Detroit Red Wings			
☐ 161	Igor Kravchuk	.05	.02	.01
	Chicago Blackhawks			
☐ 162	Viacheslav Fetisov	.05	.02	.01
	New Jersey Devils			
☐ 163	Gerard Gallant	.05	.02	.01
	Detroit Red Wings			
☐ 164	Patrick Roy	.50	.23	.06
	Montreal Canadiens			
☐ 165	Ken Sutton	.05	.02	.01
	Buffalo Sabres			
☐ 166	Mathieu Schneider	.08	.04	.01
	Montreal Canadiens			
☐ 167	Larry Robinson 73-74	.20	.09	.03
	Montreal Canadiens			
☐ 168	Jim Sandlak	.05	.02	.01
	Vancouver Canucks			
☐ 169	Joey Kocur	.05	.02	.01
	New York Rangers			
☐ 170	Rob Brown	.05	.02	.01
	Chicago Blackhawks			
☐ 171	Luke Richardson	.05	.02	.01
	Edmonton Oilers			
☐ 172	Adam Oates 87-88	.15	.07	.02
	Detroit Red Wings			
☐ 173	Uwe Krupp	.05	.02	.01
	New York Islanders			
☐ 174	Cam Neely	.15	.07	.02
	Boston Bruins			
☐ 175	Peter Sidorkiewicz	.05	.02	.01
	Ottawa Senators			
☐ 176	Geoff Courtnall	.05	.02	.01
	Vancouver Canucks			
☒ 177	Doug Gilmour	.25	.11	.03
	Toronto Maple Leafs			
☐ 178	Josef Beranek	.15	.07	.02
	Edmonton Oilers			
☐ 179	Michel Picard	.05	.02	.01
	Hartford Whalers			
☐ 180	Terry Carkner	.05	.02	.01
	Philadelphia Flyers			
☐ 181	Nelson Emerson	.15	.07	.02
	St. Louis Blues			
☐ 182	Perry Berezan	.05	.02	.01
	San Jose Sharks			
☐ 183	Checklist C	.05	.02	.01
☐ 184	Andy Moog	.08	.04	.01
	Boston Bruins			
☐ 185	Michel Petit	.05	.02	.01
	Calgary Flames			
☐ 186	Mark Greig	.05	.02	.01
	Hartford Whalers			
☐ 187	Paul Coffey 81-82	.30	.14	.04
	Edmonton Oilers			
☐ 188	Ron Francis	.08	.04	.01
	Pittsburgh Penguins			
☐ 189	Joe Juneau	1.00	.45	.13
	Boston Bruins			

☐ 190 Jeff Odgers	.05	.02	.01
San Jose Sharks			
☐ 191 Darryl Sittler 75-76	.25	.11	.03
Toronto Maple Leafs			
☐ 192 Vincent Damphousse	.08	.04	.01
Edmonton Oilers			
☐ 193 Greg Paslawski	.05	.02	.01
Quebec Nordiques			
☐ 194 Tony Esposito 69-70	.30	.14	.04
Chicago Blackhawks			
☐ 195 Sergei Fedorov	.75	.35	.09
Detroit Red Wings			
☐ 196 Doug Smail	.05	.02	.01
Quebec Nordiques			
☐ 197 Pat Verbeek	.08	.04	.01
Hartford Whalers			
☐ 198 Dominic Roussel	.15	.07	.02
Philadelphia Flyers			
☐ 199 Mike McPhee	.05	.02	.01
Montreal Canadiens			
☐ 200 Kevin Dineen	.08	.04	.01
Philadelphia Flyers			
☐ 201 Pat Elynuik	.05	.02	.01
Winnipeg Jets			
☐ 202 Tom Kurvers	.05	.02	.01
New York Islanders			
☐ 203 Chris Joseph	.05	.02	.01
Edmonton Oilers			
☐ 204 Mark Fitzpatrick	.08	.04	.01
New York Islanders			
☐ 205 Jari Kurri	.10	.05	.01
Los Angeles Kings			
☐ 206 Guy Carbonneau	.08	.04	.01
Montreal Canadiens			
☐ 207 Jan Erixon	.05	.02	.01
New York Rangers			
☐ 208 Mark Messier	.20	.09	.03
New York Rangers			
☐ 209 Larry Murphy	.08	.04	.01
Pittsburgh Penguins			
☐ 210 Dirk Graham	.05	.02	.01
Chicago Blackhawks			
☐ 211 Ron Tugnutt	.05	.02	.01
Edmonton Oilers			
☐ 212 Dale Hawerchuk	.08	.04	.01
Buffalo Sabres			
☐ 213 Dave Babych	.05	.02	.01
Vancouver Canucks			
☐ 214 Mikael Andersson	.05	.02	.01
Hartford Whalers			
☐ 215 James Patrick	.05	.02	.01
New York Rangers			
☐ 216 Peter Stastny	.08	.04	.01
New Jersey Devils			
☐ 217 Bernie Parent 68-69	.25	.11	.03
Philadelphia Flyers			
☐ 218 Jeff Hackett	.05	.02	.01
San Jose Sharks			
☐ 219 Dave Lowry	.05	.02	.01
St. Louis Blues			
☐ 220 Wayne Gretzky 79-80	3.00	1.35	.40
Edmonton Oilers			
☐ 221 Brent Gilchrist	.05	.02	.01
Montreal Canadiens			
☐ 222 Andrew Cassels	.05	.02	.01
Hartford Whalers			
☐ 223 Calle Johansson	.05	.02	.01
Washington Capitals			
☐ 224 Joe Reekie	.05	.02	.01
Tampa Bay Lightning			
☐ 225 Craig Simpson	.05	.02	.01
Edmonton Oilers			
☐ 226 Bob Essensa	.08	.04	.01
Winnipeg Jets			
☐ 227 Pat Falloon	.15	.07	.02
San Jose Sharks			
☐ 228 Vladimir Ruzicka	.05	.02	.01
Boston Bruins			
☐ 229 Igor Ulanov	.05	.02	.01
Winnipeg Jets			
☐ 230 Kjell Samuelsson	.05	.02	.01
Pittsburgh Penguins			
☐ 231 Shayne Corson	.08	.04	.01
Montreal Canadiens			
☐ 232 Kelly Kisio	.05	.02	.01
San Jose Sharks			
☐ 233 Gordie Roberts	.05	.02	.01
Boston Bruins			
☐ 234 Brian Noonan	.05	.02	.01
Chicago Blackhawks			
☐ 235 Vyacheslav Kozlov UER	.60	.25	.08
(Misspelled Viacheslav			
on both sides)			
Detroit Red Wings			
☐ 236 Checklist B	.05	.02	.01
☐ 237 Jeff Beukeboom	.05	.02	.01
New York Rangers			
☐ 238 Steve Konroyd	.05	.02	.01
Hartford Whalers			
☐ 239 Patrice Brisebois	.05	.02	.01
Montreal Canadiens			
☐ 240 Mario Lemieux	.25	.11	.03
Pittsburgh Penguins			
Playoff MVP			
☐ 241 Dana Murzyn	.05	.02	.01
Vancouver Canucks			
☐ 242 Pelle Eklund	.05	.02	.01
Philadelphia Flyers			
☐ 243 Rob Blake	.10	.05	.01
Los Angeles Kings			
☐ 244 Brendan Shanahan	.25	.11	.03
St. Louis Blues			
☐ 245 Mike Gartner HL	.10	.05	.01
New York Rangers			
☐ 246 David Bruce	.05	.02	.01
San Jose Sharks			
☐ 247 Mike Vernon	.08	.04	.01
Calgary Flames			
☐ 248 Zarley Zalapski	.05	.02	.01
Hartford Whalers			
☐ 249 Dino Ciccarelli	.08	.04	.01
Detroit Red Wings			
☐ 250 David Williams	.10	.05	.01
San Jose Sharks			
☐ 251 Scott Stevens 83-84	.15	.07	.02
Washington Capitals			
☐ 252 Bob Probert	.05	.02	.01
Detroit Red Wings			
☐ 253 Mikhail Tatarinov	.05	.02	.01
Quebec Nordiques			
☐ 254 Bobby Holik	.05	.02	.01
Hartford Whalers			
☐ 255 Tony Amonte 91-92	.05	.02	.01
New York Rangers			
☐ 256 Brad May	.05	.02	.01
Buffalo Sabres			
☐ 257 Philippe Bozon	.05	.02	.01
St. Louis Blues			
☐ 258 Mark Messier 80-81	.60	.25	.08
Edmonton Oilers			
☐ 259 Mike Richter	.25	.11	.03
New York Rangers			
☐ 260 Brian Mullen	.08	.04	.01
San Jose Sharks			
☐ 261 Marty McSorley	.08	.04	.01
Los Angeles Kings			
☐ 262 Glenn Healy	.08	.04	.01
New York Islanders			
☐ 263 Russ Romaniuk	.05	.02	.01
Winnipeg Jets			
☐ 264 Dan Quinn	.05	.02	.01
Philadelphia Flyers			
☐ 265 Jyrki Lumme	.05	.02	.01
Vancouver Canucks			
☐ 266 Valeri Kamensky	.15	.07	.02
Quebec Nordiques			
☐ 267 Vladimir Konstantinov	.05	.02	.01
Detroit Red Wings			
☐ 268 Peter Ahola	.05	.02	.01
Los Angeles Kings			
☐ 269 Guy Larose	.05	.02	.01
Toronto Maple Leafs			
☐ 270 Ulf Samuelsson	.08	.04	.01
Pittsburgh Penguins			
☐ 271 Dale Craigwell	.05	.02	.01
San Jose Sharks			
☐ 272 Adam Oates	.15	.07	.02
Boston Bruins			
☐ 273 Pat MacLeod	.05	.02	.01
San Jose Sharks			
☐ 274 Mike Keane	.05	.02	.01
Montreal Canadiens			
☐ 275 John Vanbiesbrouck	.10	.05	.01
New York Rangers			
☐ 276 Brian Lawton	.05	.02	.01
San Jose Sharks			
☐ 277 Sylvain Cote	.05	.02	.01
Washington Capitals			
☐ 278 Gary Suter	.08	.04	.01
Calgary Flames			
☐ 279 Alexander Mogilny	.40	.18	.05
Buffalo Sabres			
☐ 280 Garth Butcher	.05	.02	.01
St. Louis Blues			
☐ 281 Doug Wilson	.08	.04	.01
San Jose Sharks			
☐ 282 Chris Terreri	.08	.04	.01

New Jersey Devils
☐ 283 Phil Esposito 77-78............	.25	.11	.03

New York Rangers
☐ 284 Russ Courtnall	.08	.04	.01

Montreal Canadiens
☐ 285 Pat LaFontaine	.15	.07	.02

Buffalo Sabres
☐ 286 Dimitri Khristich	.08	.04	.01

Washington Capitals
☐ 287 John LeBlanc	.05	.02	.01

Winnipeg Jets
☐ 288 Randy Velischek...............	.05	.02	.01

Quebec Nordiques
☐ 289 Dave Christian..................	.05	.02	.01

St. Louis Blues
☐ 290 Kevin Haller.....................	.05	.02	.01

Montreal Canadiens
☐ 291 Kevin Miller......................	.08	.04	.01

Washington Capitals
☐ 292 Mario Lemieux 85-86.........	2.00	.90	.25

Pittsburgh Penguins
☐ 293 Stephan Lebeau	.05	.02	.01

Montreal Canadiens
☐ 294 Marcel Dionne 71-72	.25	.11	.03

Detroit Red Wings
☐ 295 Barry Pederson	.05	.02	.01

Boston Bruins
☐ 296 Steve Duchesne	.08	.04	.01

Quebec Nordiques
☐ 297 Yves Racine	.05	.02	.01

Detroit Red Wings
☐ 298 Phil Housley	.08	.04	.01

Winnipeg Jets
☐ 299 Randy Ladouceur..............	.05	.02	.01

Hartford Whalers
☐ 300 Mike Gartner	.10	.05	.01

New York Rangers
☐ 301 Dominik Hasek...................	.40	.18	.05

Chicago Blackhawks
☐ 302 Kevin Lowe	.05	.02	.01

Edmonton Oilers
☐ 303 Sylvain Lefebvre................	.05	.02	.01

Montreal Canadiens
☐ 304 J.J. Daigneault	.05	.02	.01

Montreal Canadiens
☐ 305 Mike Ridley	.08	.04	.01

Washington Capitals
☐ 306 Curtis Leschyshyn.............	.05	.02	.01

Quebec Nordiques
☐ 307 Gilbert Dionne	.05	.02	.01

Montreal Canadiens
☐ 308 Bill Guerin	.20	.09	.03

New Jersey Devils
☐ 309 Gerald Diduck	.05	.02	.01

Vancouver Canucks
☐ 310 Rick Wamsley	.05	.02	.01

Toronto Maple Leafs
☐ 311 Pat Jablonski UER.............	.05	.02	.01

(Listed as Ottawa Senator
on both sides, should
be Tampa Bay Lightning)
Tampa Bay Lightning
☐ 312 Jayson More	.05	.02	.01

San Jose Sharks
☐ 313 Mike Modano	.25	.11	.03

Minnesota North Stars
☐ 314 Checklist A	.05	.02	.01
☐ 315 Slyvain Turgeon	.05	.02	.01

Ottawa Senators
☐ 316 Sergei Nemchinov..............	.08	.04	.01

New York Rangers
☐ 317 Garry Galley	.05	.02	.01

Philadelphia Flyers
☐ 318 Paul Coffey HL	.08	.04	.01

Los Angeles Kings
☐ 319 Esa Tikkanen	.08	.04	.01

Edmonton Oilers
☐ 320 Claude LaPointe	.05	.02	.01

Quebec Nordiques
☐ 321 Steve Yzerman 84-85.........	.40	.18	.05

Detroit Red Wings
☐ 322 Mark Lamb	.05	.02	.01

Ottawa Senators
☐ 323 Bob Errey	.05	.02	.01

Pittsburgh Penguins
☐ 324 Pavel Bure 92-93	.50	.23	.06

Vancouver Canucks
☐ 325 Craig Janney	.10	.05	.01

St. Louis Blues
☐ 326 Bob Kudelski	.08	.04	.01

Los Angeles Kings
☐ 327 Kirk Muller	.08	.04	.01

Montreal Canadiens
☐ 328 Jim Paek	.05	.02	.01

Pittsburgh Penguins
☐ 329 Mike Ricci	.08	.04	.01

Quebec Nordiques
☐ 330 Al MacInnis........................	.10	.05	.01

Calgary Flames
☐ 331 Mike Hudson......................	.05	.02	.01

Chicago Blackhawks
☐ 332 Darrin Shannon..................	.05	.02	.01

Winnipeg Jets
☐ 333 Doug Brown......................	.05	.02	.01

New Jersey Devils
☐ 334 Corey Millen	.08	.04	.01

Los Angeles Kings
☐ 335 Mike Krushelnyski..............	.05	.02	.01

Toronto Maple Leafs
☐ 336 Scott Stevens.....................	.10	.05	.01

New Jersey Devils
☐ 337 Peter Zezel	.05	.02	.01

Toronto Maple Leafs
☐ 338 Geoff Smith........................	.05	.02	.01

Edmonton Oilers
☐ 339 Curtis Joseph.....................	.25	.11	.03

St. Louis Blues
☐ 340 Tom Barrasso	.08	.04	.01

Pittsburgh Penguins
☐ 341 Al Iafrate	.08	.04	.01

Washington Capitals
☐ 342 Patrick Flatley....................	.05	.02	.01

New York Islanders
☐ 343 Gerry Cheevers 72-73	.25	.11	.03

Cleveland Crusaders
☐ 344 Norm Maciver	.05	.02	.01

Edmonton Oilers
☐ 345 Jeremy Roenick	.50	.23	.06

Chicago Blackhawks
☐ 346 Keith Tkachuk UER.............	.30	.14	.04

(Photo actually
Petri Skriko)
Winnipeg Jets
☐ 347 Rod Langway	.05	.02	.01

Washington Capitals
☐ 348 Ray Bourque HL.................	.08	.04	.01

Boston Bruins
☐ 349 Kirk McLean	.20	.09	.03

Vancouver Canucks
☐ 350 Brian Propp	.08	.04	.01

Minnesota North Stars
☐ 351 John Ogrodnick..................	.05	.02	.01

New York Rangers
☐ 352 Benoit Brunet	.05	.02	.01

Montreal Canadiens
☐ 353 Alexei Kasatonov................	.05	.02	.01

New Jersey Devils
☐ 354 Joe Nieuwendyk	.08	.04	.01

Calgary Flames
☐ 355 Joe Sacco	.05	.02	.01

Toronto Maple Leafs
☐ 356 Tom Fergus.......................	.05	.02	.01

Vancouver Canucks
☐ 357 Dan Lambert	.05	.02	.01

Quebec Nordiques
☐ 358 Michel Goulet.....................	.08	.04	.01

Chicago Blackhawks
☐ 359 Shawn McEachern	.15	.07	.02

Pittsburgh Penguins
☐ 360 Eric Desjardins...................	.05	.02	.01

Montreal Canadiens
☐ 361 Paul Stanton	.05	.02	.01

Pittsburgh Penguins
☐ 362 Ron Sutter..........................	.05	.02	.01

St. Louis Blues
☐ 363 Derrick Smith......................	.05	.02	.01

Minnesota North Stars
☐ 364 Paul Broten	.05	.02	.01

Pittsburgh Penguins
☐ 365 Greg Adams	.05	.02	.01

Vancouver Canucks
☐ 366 Rob Zettler	.05	.02	.01

San Jose Sharks
☐ 367 Dave Poulin........................	.05	.02	.01

Boston Bruins
☐ 368 Keith Acton	.05	.02	.01

Philadelphia Flyers
☐ 369 Nicklas Lidstrom..................	.08	.04	.01

Detroit Red Wings
☐ 370 Randy Burridge	.05	.02	.01

Washington Capitals
☐ 371 Jamie Macoun	.05	.02	.01

Toronto Maple Leafs
☐ 372 Craig Billington	.05	.02	.01

New Jersey Devils
☐ 373 Mark Recchi........................	.25	.11	.03

Philadelphia Flyers
☐ 374 Kris Draper	.05	.02	.01

		MINT	EXC	G-VG
	Winnipeg Jets			
☐ 375	Ed Olczyk	.05	.02	.01
	Winnipeg Jets			
☐ 376	Tom Draper	.05	.02	.01
	Buffalo Sabres			
☐ 377	Sergio Momesso	.05	.02	.01
	Vancouver Canucks			
☐ 378	Brian Leetch	.25	.11	.03
	New York Rangers			
☐ 379	Paul Cavallini	.05	.02	.01
	St. Louis Blues			
☐ 380	Paul Fenton	.05	.02	.01
	San Jose Sharks			
☐ 381	Dean Evason	.05	.02	.01
	San Jose Sharks			
☐ 382	Owen Nolan	.08	.04	.01
	Quebec Nordiques			
☐ 383	Jeremy Roenick 90-91	.25	.11	.03
	Chicago Blackhawks			
☐ 384	Brian Bellows	.08	.04	.01
	Minnesota North Stars			
☐ 385	Thomas Steen	.05	.02	.01
	Winnipeg Jets			
☐ 386	John LeClair	.05	.02	.01
	Montreal Canadiens			
☐ 387	Darren Turcotte	.05	.02	.01
	New York Rangers			
☐ 388	James Black	.05	.02	.01
	Hartford Whalers			
☐ 389	Alexei Gusarov	.05	.02	.01
	Quebec Nordiques			
☐ 390	Scott Lachance	.05	.02	.01
	New York Islanders			
☐ 391	Mike Bossy 78-79	.25	.11	.03
	New York Islanders			
☐ 392	Mike Hough	.05	.02	.01
	Quebec Nordiques			
☐ 393	Grant Ledyard	.05	.02	.01
	Buffalo Sabres			
☐ 394	Tom Fitzgerald	.05	.02	.01
	New York Islanders			
☐ 395	Steve Thomas	.08	.04	.01
	New York Islanders			
☐ 396	Bobby Smith	.08	.04	.01
	Minnesota North Stars			

1992-93 O-Pee-Chee Trophy Winners

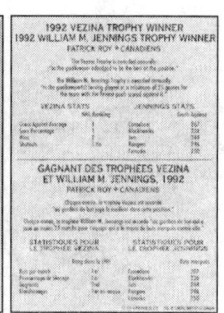

These four oversized cards measure approximately 4 7/8" by 6 3/4" and were bottoms from 1992-93 O-Pee-Chee pack boxes. Each features on its front a white-bordered color shot of the player in a tuxedo, holding his trophy and standing in front of an NHL backdrop. The player's name, team, and the trophy name appear in a dark gray stripe near the bottom. O-Pee-Chee appears vertically in a blue stripe along the left edge of the photo. In both French and English, the back has the trophy name, player name and team, and stats in blue lettering. The cards are unnumbered and checklisted below in alphabetical order.

	MINT	EXC	G-VG
COMPLETE SET (4)	5.00	2.00	.50
COMMON PLAYER (1-4)	1.25	.50	.12
☐ 1 Pavel Bure	2.00	.80	.20

		MINT	EXC	G-VG
	Vancouver Canucks			
	Calder Trophy			
☐ 2	Brian Leetch	1.25	.50	.12
	New York Rangers			
	James Norris Trophy			
☐ 3	Mark Messier	1.25	.50	.12
	New York Rangers			
	Hart Trophy			
☐ 4	Patrick Roy	1.50	.60	.15
	Montreal Canadiens			
	Vezina Trophy			

1992-93 O-Pee-Chee 25th Anniv. Inserts

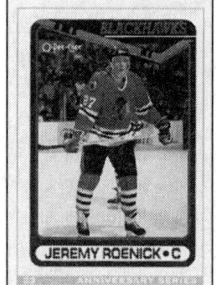

This insert subset was featured in 1992-93 O-Pee-Chee wax packs. The first 25 cards commemorate each of the past 25 years, beginning with the 1968-69 series. The cards measure the standard size (2 1/2" by 3 1/2"), and each one is a reproduction of the actual card design from each of the past 25 years; the front is bordered in silver metallic ink with a "watermark" mat varnish logo to commemorate the 25th Anniversary. The cards are numbered on the back as originally issued; however, the set has been renumbered on the front at the lower left and are checklisted below accordingly. Cards can be found with and without the 25th Anniversary emblem embossed on the front.

		MINT	EXC	G-VG
COMPLETE SET (26)		9.00	3.75	.90
COMMON PLAYER (1-25)		.15	.06	.01
☐ 1	Bernie Parent	.25	.10	.02
	1968-69			
☐ 2	Tony Esposito	.35	.14	.03
	1969-70			
☐ 3	Bobby Clarke	.25	.10	.02
	1970-71			
☐ 4	Marcel Dionne	.35	.14	.03
	1971-72			
☐ 5	Gerry Cheevers	.35	.14	.03
	1972-73			
☐ 6	Larry Robinson	.35	.14	.03
	1973-74			
☐ 7	Denis Potvin	.25	.10	.02
	1974-75			
☐ 8	Darryl Sittler	.35	.14	.03
	1975-76			
☐ 9	Bryan Trottier	.35	.14	.03
	1976-77			
☐ 10	Phil Esposito	.50	.20	.05
	1977-78			
☐ 11	Mike Bossy	.35	.14	.03
	1978-79			
☐ 12	Wayne Gretzky	2.00	.80	.20
	1979-80			
☐ 13	Mark Messier	.50	.20	.05
	1980-81			
☐ 14	Paul Coffey	.35	.14	.03
	1981-82			
☐ 15	Grant Fuhr	.25	.10	.02
	1982-83			
☐ 16	Scott Stevens	.25	.10	.02

		MINT	EXC	G-VG
	1983-84			
☐ 17	Steve Yzerman	.50	.20	.05
	1984-85			
☐ 18	Mario Lemieux	1.50	.60	.15
	1985-86			
☐ 19	Patrick Roy	1.00	.40	.10
	1986-87			
☐ 20	Adam Oates	.35	.14	.03
	1987-88			
☐ 21	Brett Hull	.75	.30	.07
	1988-89			
☐ 22	Joe Sakic	.25	.10	.02
	1989-90			
☐ 23	Jeremy Roenick	.50	.20	.05
	1990-91			
☐ 24	Tony Amonte	.15	.06	.01
	1991-92			
☐ 25	Pavel Bure	.75	.30	.07
	1992			
☐ NNO	Checklist	.15	.06	.01

1992-93 O-Pee-Chee Premier

DMITRI KVARTALNOV • LW

The 1992-93 O-Pee-Chee Premier hockey set consists of 132 cards, each measuring the standard size (2 1/2" by 3 1/2"). The fronts feature action color player photos with white borders. A team color-coded stripe accents the top edge of each picture. The O-Pee-Chee logo overlaps the picture at the lower right corner. The player's name and position appear in the bottom border. The backs show a slightly offset, pale, team color-coded panel which carries a close-up photo and biographical data. A darker team color-coded bar with a speckled effect presents statistics and appears at the bottom. The team logo overlaps the picture panel at the lower left corner of the photo. Rookie Cards in the set include Nikolai Borschevsky, Roman Hamrlik, Guy Hebert, Andrei Kovalenko, Mikael Nylander and Martin Straka. Each pack contained an insert from either the Top Rookie set or the 22-card Star Performers set. According to O-Pee-Chee, every ninth pack contained a Top Rookie card as its insert with the other packs containing a Star Performers card. The production quantity was reportedly 7,500 20-box wax cases.

		MINT	EXC	G-VG
	COMPLETE SET (132)	15.00	6.75	1.90
	COMMON PLAYER (1-132)	.05	.02	.01
☐ 1	Dave Christian	.05	.02	.01
	Chicago Blackhawks			
☐ 2	Christian Ruuttu	.05	.02	.01
	Chicago Blackhawks			
☐ 3	Vin Damphousse	.08	.04	.01
	Montreal Canadiens			
☐ 4	Chris Lindberg	.05	.02	.01
	Calgary Flames			
☐ 5	Bill Lindsay	.10	.05	.01
	Quebec Nordiques			
☐ 6	Dmitri Kvartalnov	.25	.11	.03
	Boston Bruins			
☐ 7	Darcy Loewen	.05	.02	.01
	Ottawa Senators			
☐ 8	Ed Courtenay	.05	.02	.01
	San Jose Sharks			
☐ 9	Sergei Krivokrasov	.20	.09	.03
	Chicago Blackhawks			
☐ 10	Shawn Antoski	.05	.02	.01
	Vancouver Canucks			
☐ 11	Andre Racicot	.05	.02	.01
	Montreal Canadiens			
☐ 12	Marty McInnis	.05	.02	.01
	New York Islanders			
☐ 13	Alexei Zhamnov	.50	.23	.06
	Winnipeg Jets			
☐ 14	Keith Jones	.15	.07	.02
	Washington Capitals			
☐ 15	Steve Konowalchuk	.15	.07	.02
	Washington Capitals			
☐ 16	Darryl Sydor	.08	.04	.01
	Los Angeles Kings			
☐ 17	Janne Ojanen	.05	.02	.01
	New Jersey Devils			
☐ 18	Doug Zmolek	.15	.07	.02
	San Jose Sharks			
☐ 19	Mikael Nylander	.30	.14	.04
	Hartford Whalers			
☐ 20	Russ Courtnall	.08	.04	.01
	Minnesota North Stars			
☐ 21	Martin Straka	1.00	.45	.13
	Pittsburgh Penguins			
☐ 22	Kevin Dahl	.05	.02	.01
	Calgary Flames			
☐ 23	Kent Manderville	.05	.02	.01
	Toronto Maple Leafs			
☐ 24	Steve Heinze	.05	.02	.01
	Boston Bruins			
☐ 25	Philippe Bozon	.05	.02	.01
	St. Louis Blues			
☐ 26	Brent Fedyk	.05	.02	.01
	Philadelphia Flyers			
☐ 27	Kris Draper	.05	.02	.01
	Winnipeg Jets			
☐ 28	Brad Schlegel	.05	.02	.01
	Washington Capitals			
☐ 29	Patric Kjellberg	.05	.02	.01
	Montreal Canadiens			
☐ 30	Ted Donato	.05	.02	.01
	Boston Bruins			
☐ 31	Vyatcheslav Butsayev	.20	.09	.03
	Philadelphia Flyers			
☐ 32	Tyler Wright	.05	.02	.01
	Edmonton Oilers			
☐ 33	Tom Pederson	.15	.07	.02
	San Jose Sharks			
☐ 34	Jim Hiller	.10	.05	.01
	Los Angeles Kings			
☐ 35	Chris Luongo	.05	.02	.01
	Ottawa Senators			
☐ 36	Robert Petrovicky	.20	.09	.03
	Hartford Whalers			
☐ 37	Jean-Francois Quintin	.05	.02	.01
	San Jose Sharks			
☐ 38	Chris Dahlquist	.05	.02	.01
	Calgary Flames			
☐ 39	Daniel LaPerriere	.15	.07	.02
	St. Louis Blues			
☐ 40	Guy Hebert	.50	.23	.06
	St. Louis Blues			
☐ 41	Ed Ronan	.10	.05	.01
	Montreal Canadiens			
☐ 42	Shawn Cronin	.05	.02	.01
	Philadelphia Flyers			
☐ 43	Keith Tkachuk	.30	.14	.04
	Winnipeg Jets			
☐ 44	Dino Ciccarelli	.08	.04	.01
	Detroit Red Wings			
☐ 45	Doug Evans	.05	.02	.01
	Philadelphia Flyers			
☐ 46	Roman Hamrlik	.50	.23	.06
	Tampa Bay Lightning			
☐ 47	Robert Lang	.20	.09	.03
	Los Angeles Kings			
☐ 48	Kerry Huffman	.05	.02	.01
	Quebec Nordiques			
☐ 49	Pat Conacher	.05	.02	.01
	Los Angeles Kings			
☐ 50	Dominik Hasek	.50	.23	.06
	Buffalo Sabres			
☐ 51	Dominic Roussel	.20	.09	.03
	Philadelphia Flyers			
☐ 52	Glen Murray	.05	.02	.01
	Boston Bruins			
☐ 53	Igor Korolev	.15	.07	.02
	St. Louis Blues			
☐ 54	Jiri Slegr	.05	.02	.01

Vancouver Canucks				
☐ 55	Mikael Andersson	.05	.02	.01
Tampa Bay Lightning				
☐ 56	Bob Babcock	.05	.02	.01
Washington Capitals				
☐ 57	Ron Hextall	.08	.04	.01
Quebec Nordiques				
☐ 58	Jeff Daniels	.05	.02	.01
Pittsburgh Penguins				
☐ 59	Doug Crossman	.05	.02	.01
Tampa Bay Lightning				
☐ 60	Viktor Gordijuk	.20	.09	.03
Buffalo Sabres				
☐ 61	Adam Creighton	.05	.02	.01
Tampa Bay Lightning				
☐ 62	Rob DiMaio	.05	.02	.01
Tampa Bay Lightning				
☐ 63	Eric Weinrich	.05	.02	.01
Hartford Whalers				
☐ 64	Vitali Prokhorov	.15	.07	.02
St. Louis Blues				
☐ 65	Dimitri Yushkevich	.20	.09	.03
Philadelphia Flyers				
☐ 66	Evgeny Davydov	.05	.02	.01
Winnipeg Jets				
☐ 67	Dixon Ward	.15	.07	.02
Vancouver Canucks				
☐ 68	Teemu Selanne	1.75	.80	.22
Winnipeg Jets				
☐ 69	Rob Zamuner	.10	.05	.01
Tampa Bay Lightning				
☐ 70	Joe Reekie	.05	.02	.01
Tampa Bay Lightning				
☐ 71	Vyacheslav Kozlov	1.00	.45	.13
Detroit Red Wings				
☐ 72	Philippe Boucher	.05	.02	.01
Buffalo Sabres				
☐ 73	Phil Bourque	.05	.02	.01
New York Rangers				
☐ 74	Yvon Corriveau	.05	.02	.01
San Jose Sharks				
☐ 75	Brian Bellows	.08	.04	.01
Montreal Canadiens				
☐ 76	Wendell Young	.05	.02	.01
Tampa Bay Lightning				
☐ 77	Bobby Holik	.05	.02	.01
New Jersey Devils				
☐ 78	Bob Carpenter	.05	.02	.01
Washington Capitals				
☐ 79	Scott Lachance	.05	.02	.01
New York Islanders				
☐ 80	John Druce	.05	.02	.01
Winnipeg Jets				
☐ 81	Keith Carney	.10	.05	.01
Buffalo Sabres				
☐ 82	Neil Brady	.05	.02	.01
Ottawa Senators				
☐ 83	Richard Matvichuk	.15	.07	.02
Minnesota North Stars				
☐ 84	Sergei Bautin	.15	.07	.02
Winnipeg Jets				
☐ 85	Patrick Poulin	.05	.02	.01
Hartford Whalers				
☐ 86	Gordie Roberts	.05	.02	.01
Boston Bruins				
☐ 87	Kay Whitmore	.05	.02	.01
Vancouver Canucks				
☐ 88	Steph Beauregard	.05	.02	.01
Philadelphia Flyers				
☐ 89	Vladimir Malakhov	.25	.11	.03
New York Islanders				
☐ 90	Richard Smehlik	.20	.09	.03
Buffalo Sabres				
☐ 91	Mike Ricci	.08	.04	.01
Quebec Nordiques				
☐ 92	Sean Burke	.08	.04	.01
Hartford Whalers				
☐ 93	Andrei Kovalenko	.30	.14	.04
Quebec Nordiques				
☐ 94	Shawn McEachern	.20	.09	.03
Pittsburgh Penguins				
☐ 95	Pat Jablonski	.05	.02	.01
Tampa Bay Lightning				
☐ 96	Oleg Petrov	.30	.14	.04
Montreal Canadiens				
☐ 97	Glenn Mulvenna	.05	.02	.01
Philadelphia Flyers				
☐ 98	Jason Woolley	.10	.05	.01
Washington Capitals				
☐ 99	Mark Greig	.05	.02	.01
Hartford Whalers				
☐ 100	Nikolai Borschevsky	.40	.18	.05
Toronto Maple Leafs				
☐ 101	Joe Juneau	1.50	.65	.19

Boston Bruins				
☐ 102	Eric Lindros	4.50	2.00	.55
Philadelphia Flyers				
☐ 103	Darius Kasparaitis	.15	.07	.02
New York Islanders				
☐ 104	Sandis Ozolinsh	.50	.23	.06
San Jose Sharks				
☐ 105	Stan Drulia	.05	.02	.01
Tampa Bay Lightning				
☐ 106	Mike Needham	.15	.07	.02
Pittsburgh Penguins				
☐ 107	Norm Maciver	.05	.02	.01
Ottawa Senators				
☐ 108	Sylvain Lefebvre	.05	.02	.01
Toronto Maple Leafs				
☐ 109	Tommy Sjodin	.10	.05	.01
Minnesota North Stars				
☐ 110	Bob Sweeney	.05	.02	.01
Buffalo Sabres				
☐ 111	Brian Mullen	.08	.04	.01
New York Islanders				
☐ 112	Peter Sidorkiewicz	.05	.02	.01
Ottawa Senators				
☐ 113	Scott Niedermayer	.35	.16	.04
New Jersey Devils				
☐ 114	Felix Potvin	1.50	.65	.19
Toronto Maple Leafs				
☐ 115	Robb Stauber	.05	.02	.01
Los Angeles Kings				
☐ 116	Sylvain Turgeon	.05	.02	.01
Ottawa Senators				
☐ 117	Mark Janssens	.05	.02	.01
Hartford Whalers				
☐ 118	Darren Banks	.05	.02	.01
Boston Bruins				
☐ 119	Pat Elynuik	.05	.02	.01
Washington Capitals				
☐ 120	Bill Guerin	.20	.09	.03
New Jersey Devils				
☐ 121	Reggie Savage	.05	.02	.01
Washington Capitals				
☐ 122	Enrico Ciccone	.05	.02	.01
Minnesota North Stars				
☐ 123	Chris Kontos	.15	.07	.02
Tampa Bay Lightning				
☐ 124	Martin Rucinsky	.15	.07	.02
Quebec Nordiques				
☐ 125	Alexei Zhitnik	.25	.11	.03
Los Angeles Kings				
☐ 126	Alexei Kovalev	1.00	.45	.13
New York Rangers				
☐ 127	Tim Kerr	.08	.04	.01
Hartford Whalers				
☐ 128	Guy Larose	.05	.02	.01
Toronto Maple Leafs				
☐ 129	Brent Gilchrist	.05	.02	.01
Edmonton Oilers				
☐ 130	Steve Duchesne	.08	.04	.01
Quebec Nordiques				
☐ 131	Drake Berehowsky	.05	.02	.01
Toronto Maple Leafs				
☐ 132	Checklist 1-132	.05	.02	.01

1992-93 OPC Premier Star Performers

 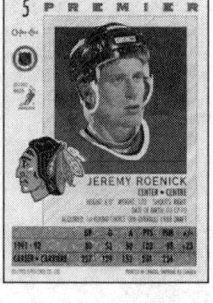

This 22-card standard-size (2 1/2" by 3 1/2") set was randomly inserted in 1992-93 O-Pee-Chee Premier foil packs. According to O-Pee-Chee, the insertion rate was eight out of every nine packs. The other packs contained Top Rookie inserts. Card fronts are similar to the basic Premier issue. The difference being a red "Star Performers" stripe at the top. The backs are also like those of Premier with a small player photo and team logo included.

	MINT	EXC	G-VG
COMPLETE SET (22)	10.00	4.50	1.25
COMMON PLAYER (1-22)	.15	.07	.02
☐ 1 Ray Ferraro New York Islanders	.15	.07	.02
☐ 2 Dale Hunter Washington Capitals	.20	.09	.03
☐ 3 Murray Craven Hartford Whalers	.15	.07	.02
☐ 4 Paul Coffey Los Angeles Kings	.20	.09	.03
☐ 5 Jeremy Roenick Chicago Blackhawks	1.00	.45	.13
☐ 6 Denis Savard Montreal Canadiens	.20	.09	.03
☐ 7 Jon Casey Minnesota North Stars	.15	.07	.02
☒ 8 Doug Gilmour Toronto Maple Leafs	.60	.25	.08
☐ 9 Rod Brind'Amour Philadelphia Flyers	.20	.09	.03
☐ 10 Pavel Bure Vancouver Canucks	3.00	1.35	.40
☐ 11 Joe Sakic Quebec Nordiques	.30	.14	.04
☐ 12 Pat Falloon San Jose Sharks	.25	.11	.03
☐ 13 Adam Oates Boston Bruins	.25	.11	.03
☐ 14 Gary Roberts Calgary Flames	.20	.09	.03
☐ 15 Mark Messier New York Rangers	.40	.18	.05
☐ 16 Phil Housley Winnipeg Jets	.20	.09	.03
☐ 17 Pat LaFontaine Buffalo Sabres	.25	.11	.03
☐ 18 Stephane Richer New Jersey Devils	.20	.09	.03
☐ 19 Bill Ranford Edmonton Oilers	.20	.09	.03
☐ 20 Sergei Fedorov Detroit Red Wings	1.50	.65	.19
☐ 21 Brett Hull St. Louis Blues	1.00	.45	.13
☐ 22 Mario Lemieux Pittsburgh Penguins	2.00	.90	.25

1992-93 OPC Premier Top Rookies

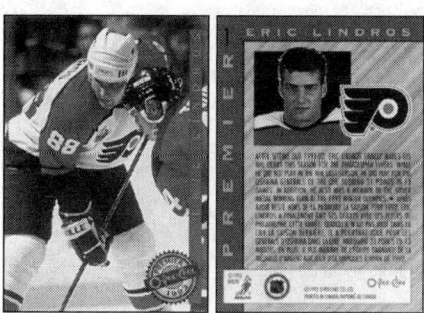

This four-card Top Rookies insert set was randomly inserted in 1992-93 O-Pee-Chee Premier foil packs. According to O-Pee-Chee, eight out of nine packs contained a Star Performer insert card, while the ninth pack contained a Top Rookie card as its insert. Measuring the standard-size (2 1/2" by 3 1/2"), the fronts feature full-bleed color action

player photos. A color bar carrying the player's name runs down the right side and intersects the 1993 O-Pee-Chee Premier logo at the lower right corner. Inside red border stripes on the top and left, the backs present a close-up photo, team logo, and player profile (in French and English) on a gradated rose panel. The cards are numbered on the back at the upper left corner.

	MINT	EXC	G-VG
COMPLETE SET (4)	12.00	5.50	1.50
COMMON PLAYER (1-4)	2.00	.90	.25
☐ 1 Eric Lindros Philadelphia Flyers	7.00	3.10	.85
☐ 2 Roman Hamrlik Tampa Bay Lightning	2.00	.90	.25
☐ 3 Dominic Roussel Philadelphia Flyers	2.00	.90	.25
☐ 4 Felix Potvin Toronto Maple Leafs	5.00	2.30	.60

1993 O-Pee-Chee Canadiens Panel

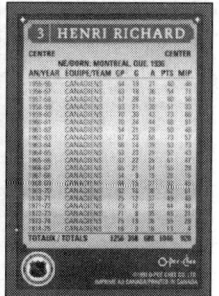

This approximately 5" by 7" panel displays samples of the O-Pee-Chee Canadiens Hockey Fest cards. If the cards were cut, they would measure the standard size (2 1/2" by 3 1/2"). The front features three cards with posed color player photos with red borders, and one sepia-tone action player photo with red borders. The cards are printed on a white card face. The back show variegated pale blue panels containing statistics. The panels are bordered in dark blue and set on a red background. The cards are numbered on the back.

	MINT	EXC	G-VG
COMPLETE SET (1)	10.00	4.00	1.00
COMMON PANEL	10.00	4.00	1.00
☐ 1 Canadiens Panel 3 Henri Richard 14 Jean Beliveau 23 Yvan Cournoyer 29 Maurice Richard	10.00	4.00	1.00

1993 O-Pee-Chee Canadiens Hockey Fest

Sold initially only at Hockey Fest '93 (February 4-7, 1993) and the Montreal Forum, this 66-card set features tribute cards to the Stanley Cup, the Montreal Forum, and past and present stars of the Montreal Canadiens. The production run was 5,000 sets, and each set came in a puck-shaped display

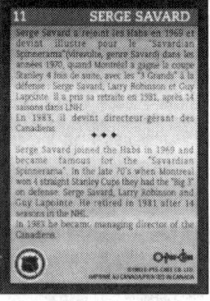

box that bore the set serial number. A portion of the proceeds went to the Montreal Canadiens Old Timers Association. The cards measure the standard size (2 1/2" by 3 1/2"). Current players are shown in color action photos with white borders and a red stripe at the top. Cards showing former players and people associated with the team have either color or sepia-tone photos framed by red borders on a white card face. The backs of all cards display a variegated pale blue card panel containing text or statistics. The current player cards also carry a close-up player photo on the back. Former player cards have a red border around the panel. All the cards have a royal blue outer border. The cards are numbered on the back.

	MINT	EXC	G-VG
COMPLETE SET (66)	60.00	24.00	6.00
COMMON PLAYER (1-66)	.50	.20	.05
☐ 1 Montreal Forum 1924	1.00	.40	.10
☐ 2 Emile Bouchard	.50	.20	.05
☐ 3 Henri Richard	1.25	.50	.12
☐ 4 Serge Savard	.75	.30	.07
☐ 5 Toe Blake CO HL	1.00	.40	.10
☐ 6 Maurice Richard HL	3.00	1.20	.30
☐ 7 Stephan Lebeau	.75	.30	.07
☐ 8 Kevin Haller	.50	.20	.05
☐ 9 Guy Carbonneau	.75	.30	.07
☐ 10 Jacques Demers CO	1.00	.40	.10
☐ 11 Serge Savard	1.00	.40	.10
☐ 12 Montreal Forum 1968	.50	.20	.05
☐ 13 Howie Morenz	2.00	.80	.20
☐ 14 Jean Beliveau	3.00	1.20	.30
☐ 15 Jacques Laperriere	.75	.30	.07
☐ 16 Bob Gainey	1.00	.40	.10
☐ 17 Guy Lafleur HL	1.50	.60	.15
☐ 18 Jacques Raymond	.50	.20	.05
☐ 19 Sean Hill	.50	.20	.05
☐ 20 Eric Desjardins	.75	.30	.07
☐ 21 Aurel Joliat	1.25	.50	.12
☐ 22 Doug Harvey	1.25	.50	.12
☐ 23 Yvan Cournoyer	1.00	.40	.10
☐ 24 Frank Mahovlich HL	1.25	.50	.12
☐ 25 J.J. Daigneault	.50	.20	.05
☐ 26 Kirk Muller	1.00	.40	.10
☐ 27 Jean Beliveau	3.00	1.20	.30
☐ 28 Georges Vezina	3.00	1.20	.30
☐ 29 Maurice Richard	4.00	1.60	.40
☐ 30 Patrick Roy	4.00	1.60	.40
☐ 31 Benoit Brunet	.60	.24	.06
☐ 32 Jacques Plante HL	1.25	.50	.12
☐ 33 Ralph Backstrom	.50	.20	.05
☐ 34 Elmer Lach	1.00	.40	.10
☐ 35 Stanley Cup Champions	.60	.24	.06
☐ 36 Jacques Laperriere	.75	.30	.07
☐ 37 Montreal Individual Records--Playoffs	.50	.20	.05
☐ 38 Vincent Damphousse	1.00	.40	.10
☐ 39 Frank Mahovlich	1.50	.60	.15
☐ 40 Jacques Plante	2.00	.80	.20
☐ 41 Stanley Cup Champions Montreal	.60	.24	.06
☐ 42 Kenny Reardon	1.00	.40	.10
☐ 43 Claude Provost	.50	.20	.05
☐ 44 Jean Beliveau HL	2.50	1.00	.25
☐ 45 Edward Ronan	.50	.20	.05
☐ 46 Canadiens NHL Individual Records	.50	.20	.05
☐ 47 Bill Durnan	1.00	.40	.10
☐ 48 Stanley Cup	.75	.30	.07
☐ 49 Patrice Brisebois	.60	.24	.06
☐ 50 Denis Savard	.75	.30	.07
☐ 51 Ken Dryden	3.00	1.20	.30
☐ 52 Lou Fontinato	.50	.20	.05
☐ 53 Jean-Guy Talbot	.75	.30	.07
☐ 54 BoomBoom Geoffrion	1.50	.60	.15
☐ 55 Joe Malone	.75	.30	.07
☐ 56 Oleg Petrov	.75	.30	.07
☐ 57 Guy Lafleur	2.00	.80	.20
☐ 58 Bert Olmstead	.75	.30	.07
☐ 59 The Dream Team Jacques Plante Larry Robinson Toe Blake CO Jean Beliveau Dickie Moore Doug Harvey Maurice Richard Aurel Joliat Bob Gainey	1.50	.60	.15
☐ 60 Brian Bellows	1.00	.40	.10
☐ 61 Henri Richard HL	1.00	.40	.10
☐ 62 Jacques Lemaire	1.00	.40	.10
☐ 63 Dickie Moore	1.25	.50	.12
☐ 64 Lorne Worsley	1.50	.60	.15
☐ 65 Toe Blake	1.25	.50	.12
☐ 66 Checklist Card	.50	.20	.05
☐ NNO Advertisement Card	.50	.20	.05

1993-94 OPC Premier Black Gold

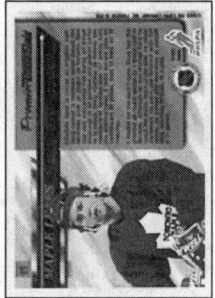

These 24 standard-size (2 1/2" by 3 1/2") Black Gold cards were randomly inserted in O-Pee-Chee packs. The white-bordered fronts feature color player action shots with darkened backgrounds. Gold-foil stripes above and below the photo carry multiple set logos. The player's name appears in white lettering within a black stripe through the lower gold-foil stripe. The white-bordered and horizontal back carries a color player cutout on one side, and career highlights in French and English within a purple rectangle on the other. The cards are numbered on the back.

	MINT	EXC	G-VG
COMPLETE SET (24)	265.00	120.00	33.00
COMPLETE SERIES 1 (12)	140.00	65.00	17.50
COMPLETE SERIES 2 (12)	125.00	57.50	15.50
COMMON PLAYER (1-12)	7.00	3.10	.85
COMMON PLAYER (13-24)	7.00	3.10	.85
☐ 1 Wayne Gretzky Los Angeles Kings	40.00	18.00	5.00
☐ 2 Vincent Damphousse Montreal Canadiens	7.00	3.10	.85
☐ 3 Adam Oates Boston Bruins	9.00	4.00	1.15
☐ 4 Phil Housley Winnipeg Jets	7.00	3.10	.85
☐ 5 Mike Vernon Calgary Flames	7.00	3.10	.85
☐ 6 Mats Sundin Quebec Nordiques	10.00	4.50	1.25
☐ 7 Pavel Bure Vancouver Canucks	28.00	12.50	3.50

☐ 8 Patrick Roy Montreal Canadiens	25.00	11.50	3.10
☐ 9 Tom Barrasso Pittsburgh Penguins	7.00	3.10	.85
☐ 10 Alexander Mogilny Buffalo Sabres	14.00	6.25	1.75
☐ 11 Doug Gilmour Toronto Maple Leafs	18.00	8.00	2.30
☐ 12 Eric Lindros Philadelphia Flyers	40.00	18.00	5.00
☐ 13 Theoren Fleury Calgary Flames	7.00	3.10	.85
☐ 14 Pat LaFontaine Buffalo Sabres	10.00	4.50	1.25
☐ 15 Joe Sakic Quebec Nordiques	9.00	4.00	1.15
☐ 16 Ed Belfour Chicago Blackhawks	12.00	5.50	1.50
☐ 17 Felix Potvin Toronto Maple Leafs	20.00	9.00	2.50
☐ 18 Mario Lemieux Pittsburgh Penguins	25.00	11.50	3.10
☐ 19 Jaromir Jagr Pittsburgh Penguins	15.00	6.75	1.90
☐ 20 Teemu Selanne Winnipeg Jets	15.00	6.75	1.90
☐ 21 Ray Bourque Boston Bruins	9.00	4.00	1.15
☐ 22 Brett Hull St. Louis Blues	15.00	6.75	1.90
☐ 23 Steve Yzerman Detroit Red Wings	18.00	8.00	2.30
☐ 24 Kirk Muller Montreal Canadiens	7.00	3.10	.85

1993-94 OPC Premier Team Canada

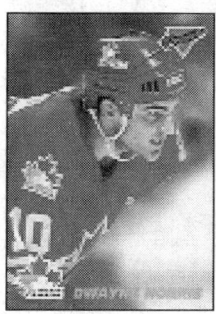

Randomly inserted in second-series OPC Premier packs, these 19 standard-size (2 1/2" by 3 1/2") cards feature borderless color player action shots on their fronts. The player's name and the Hockey Canada logo appear at the bottom. The red back carries the player's name and position at the top, followed below by biography, player photo, career highlights in English and French, and statistics. The cards are numbered on the back as "X of 19."

	MINT	EXC	G-VG
COMPLETE SET (19)	55.00	25.00	7.00
COMMON PLAYER (1-19)	2.00	.90	.25
☐ 1 Brett Lindros	12.00	5.50	1.50
☐ 2 Manny Legace	3.00	1.35	.40
☐ 3 Adrian Aucoin	2.00	.90	.25
☐ 4 Ken Lovsin	2.00	.90	.25
☐ 5 Craig Woodcroft	2.00	.90	.25
☐ 6 Derek Mayer	2.00	.90	.25
☐ 7 Fabian Joseph	2.00	.90	.25
☐ 8 Todd Brost	2.00	.90	.25
☐ 9 Chris Therien	2.00	.90	.25
☐ 10 Brad Turner	2.00	.90	.25
☐ 11 Trevor Sim	2.00	.90	.25
☐ 12 Todd Hlushko	2.50	1.15	.30
☐ 13 Dwayne Norris	2.50	1.15	.30
☐ 14 Chris Kontos	2.50	1.15	.30
☐ 15 Petr Nedved	5.00	2.30	.60
☐ 16 Brian Savage	4.00	1.80	.50

☐ 17 Paul Kariya	10.00	4.50	1.25
☐ 18 Corey Hirsch	5.00	2.30	.60
☐ 19 Todd Warriner	7.00	3.10	.85

1951-52 Parkhurst

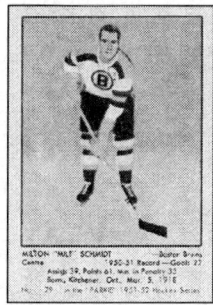

The 1951-52 Parkhurst set contains 105 small cards in crude color. Cards are 1 3/4" by 2 1/2". The player's name, team, card number, and 1950-51 statistics all appear on the front of the card. The backs of the cards are blank. The cards feature players from each of the six NHL teams. The set numbering is basically according to teams, i.e., Montreal Canadiens (1-18), Boston Bruins (19-35), Chicago Blackhawks (36-51 and 53), Detroit Red Wings (54-69), Toronto Maple Leafs (70-88), and New York Rangers (89-105). The set features the first cards of hockey greats Gordie Howe and Maurice Richard. Other notable Rookie Cards in this set are Alex Delvecchio, Boom Boom Geoffrion, Doug Harvey, Red Kelly, Ted Lindsay, and Terry Sawchuk.

	NRMT	VG-E	GOOD
COMPLETE SET (105)	10000.	4500.	1250.
COMMON PLAYER (1-105)	40.00	18.00	5.00
☐ 1 Elmer Lach	350.00	90.00	28.00
☐ 2 Paul Meger	40.00	18.00	5.00
☐ 3 Butch Bouchard	75.00	34.00	9.50
☐ 4 Maurice Richard	1500.00	700.00	190.00
☐ 5 Bert Olmstead	80.00	36.00	10.00
☐ 6 Bud MacPherson	40.00	18.00	5.00
☐ 7 Tom Johnson	80.00	36.00	10.00
☐ 8 Paul Masnick	40.00	18.00	5.00
☐ 9 Calum Mackay	40.00	18.00	5.00
☐ 10 Doug Harvey	350.00	160.00	45.00
☐ 11 Ken Mosdell	45.00	20.00	5.75
☐ 12 Floyd(Busher) Curry	50.00	23.00	6.25
☐ 13 Billy Reay	50.00	23.00	6.25
☐ 14 Boom Boom Geoffrion	400.00	180.00	50.00
☐ 15 Gerry McNeil	80.00	36.00	10.00
☐ 16 Dick Gamble	40.00	18.00	5.00
☐ 17 Gerry Couture	40.00	18.00	5.00
☐ 18 Ross Robert Lowe	40.00	18.00	5.00
☐ 19 Jim Henry	75.00	34.00	9.50
☐ 20 Victor Ivan Lynn	40.00	18.00	5.00
☐ 21 Walter(Gus) Kyle	40.00	18.00	5.00
☐ 22 Ed Sandford	40.00	18.00	5.00
☐ 23 John Henderson	40.00	18.00	5.00
☐ 24 Dunc Fisher	40.00	18.00	5.00
☐ 25 Hal Laycoe	42.50	19.00	5.25
☐ 26 Bill Quackenbush	75.00	34.00	9.50
☐ 27 George Sullivan	42.50	19.00	5.25
☐ 28 Woody Dumart	60.00	27.00	7.50
☐ 29 Milt Schmidt	100.00	45.00	12.50
☐ 30 Adam Brown	40.00	18.00	5.00
☐ 31 Pentti Lund	40.00	18.00	5.00
☐ 32 Ray Barry	40.00	18.00	5.00
☐ 33 Ed Kryznowski UER (Misspelled Kryzanowski on card)	40.00	18.00	5.00
☐ 34 Johnny Pierson	40.00	18.00	5.00
☐ 35 Lorne Ferguson	40.00	18.00	5.00
☐ 36 Clare(Rags) Raglan	40.00	18.00	5.00
☐ 37 Bill Gadsby	80.00	36.00	10.00
☐ 38 Al Dewsbury	40.00	18.00	5.00

☐ 39	George Clare Martin	40.00	18.00	5.00
☐ 40	Gus Bodnar	42.50	19.00	5.25
☐ 41	Jim Peters	40.00	18.00	5.00
☐ 42	Bep Guidolin	42.50	19.00	5.25
☐ 43	George Gee	40.00	18.00	5.00
☐ 44	Jim McFadden	40.00	18.00	5.00
☐ 45	Fred Hucul	40.00	18.00	5.00
☐ 46	John Lee Fogolin	40.00	18.00	5.00
☐ 47	Harry Lumley	100.00	45.00	12.50
☐ 48	Doug Bentley	75.00	34.00	9.50
☐ 49	Bill Mosienko	80.00	36.00	10.00
☐ 50	Roy Conacher	50.00	23.00	6.25
☐ 51	Pete Babando	40.00	18.00	5.00
☐ 52	The Winning Goal	135.00	60.00	17.00
	(Bill Barilko against			
	Gerry McNeil)			
☐ 53	Jack Stewart	45.00	20.00	5.75
☐ 54	Marty Pavelich	40.00	18.00	5.00
☐ 55	Red Kelly	250.00	115.00	31.00
☐ 56	Ted Lindsay	250.00	115.00	31.00
☐ 57	Glen Skov	40.00	18.00	5.00
☐ 58	Benny Woit	40.00	18.00	5.00
☐ 59	Tony Leswick	42.50	19.00	5.25
☐ 60	Fred Glover	40.00	18.00	5.00
☐ 61	Terry Sawchuk	1000.00	450.00	125.00
☐ 62	Vic Stasiuk	45.00	20.00	5.75
☐ 63	Alex Delvecchio	250.00	115.00	31.00
☐ 64	Sid Abel	75.00	34.00	9.50
☐ 65	Metro Prystai	40.00	18.00	5.00
☐ 66	Gordie Howe	3000.00	1350.00	375.00
☐ 67	Bob Goldham	40.00	18.00	5.00
☐ 68	Marcel Pronovost	75.00	34.00	9.50
☐ 69	Leo Reise	40.00	18.00	5.00
☐ 70	Harry Watson	60.00	27.00	7.50
☐ 71	Danny Lewicki	40.00	18.00	5.00
☐ 72	Howie Meeker	100.00	45.00	12.50
☐ 73	Gus Mortson	42.50	19.00	5.25
☐ 74	Joe Klukay	40.00	18.00	5.00
☐ 75	Turk Broda	135.00	60.00	17.00
☐ 76	Al Rollins	75.00	34.00	9.50
☐ 77	Bill Juzda	40.00	18.00	5.00
☐ 78	Ray Timgren	40.00	18.00	5.00
☐ 79	Hugh Bolton	40.00	18.00	5.00
☐ 80	Fern Flaman	75.00	34.00	9.50
☐ 81	Max Bentley	75.00	34.00	9.50
☐ 82	Jim Thomson	40.00	18.00	5.00
☐ 83	Fleming Mackell	42.50	19.00	5.25
☐ 84	Sid Smith	50.00	23.00	6.25
☐ 85	Cal Gardner	42.50	19.00	5.25
☐ 86	Teeder Kennedy	125.00	57.50	15.50
☐ 87	Tod Sloan	45.00	20.00	5.75
☐ 88	Bob Solinger	40.00	18.00	5.00
☐ 89	Frank Eddolls	40.00	18.00	5.00
☐ 90	Jack Evans	42.50	19.00	5.25
☐ 91	Hy Buller	40.00	18.00	5.00
☐ 92	Steve Kraftcheck	40.00	18.00	5.00
☐ 93	Don(Bones) Raleigh	40.00	18.00	5.00
☐ 94	Allan Stanley	125.00	57.50	15.50
☐ 95	Paul Ronty	40.00	18.00	5.00
☐ 96	Edgar Laprade	60.00	27.00	7.50
☐ 97	Nick Mickoski	40.00	18.00	5.00
☐ 98	Jack McLeod	40.00	18.00	5.00
☐ 99	Gaye Stewart	42.50	19.00	5.00
☐ 100	Wally Hergesheimer	42.50	19.00	5.25
☐ 101	Ed Kullman	40.00	18.00	5.00
☐ 102	Ed Slowinski	40.00	18.00	5.00
☐ 103	Reg Sinclair	40.00	18.00	5.00
☐ 104	Chuck Rayner	75.00	34.00	9.50
☐ 105	Jim Conacher	125.00	25.00	7.50

1952-53 Parkhurst

The 1952-53 Parkhurst set contains 105 color, line-drawing cards. Cards are approximately 1 15/16" by 2 15/16". The obverse contains a facsimile autograph of the player pictured while the backs contain a short biography in English and 1951-52 statistics. The backs also contain the card number and a special album (for holding a set of cards) offer. The cards feature players from each of the Original Six NHL teams. The set numbering is roughly according to teams, i.e., Montreal Canadiens (1-15, 52, 93), Boston Bruins (68-85), Chicago Blackhawks (16-17, 26-27, 29-33, 35-41, 55-56), Detroit Red Wings (53, 60-67, 86-92, 104), Toronto Maple Leafs (28, 34, 42-48, 50-51, 54, 58-59, 94-

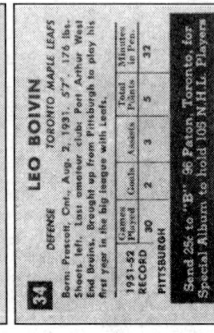

96, 105), and New York Rangers (18-25, 49, 57, 97-103). The key Rookie Cards in this set are George Armstrong, Tim Horton, and Dickie Moore.

		NRMT	VG-E	GOOD
COMPLETE SET (105)		6500.00	2900.00	800.00
COMMON PLAYER (1-105)		30.00	13.50	3.80
☐ 1	Maurice Richard	1000.00	300.00	100.00
☐ 2	Billy Reay	32.00	14.50	4.00
☐ 3	Boom Boom Geoffrion	200.00	90.00	25.00
	UER (Misspelled			
	Gioffrion on back)			
☐ 4	Paul Meger	30.00	13.50	3.80
☐ 5	Dick Gamble	30.00	13.50	3.80
☐ 6	Elmer Lach	60.00	27.00	7.50
☐ 7	Floyd(Busher) Curry	32.00	14.50	4.00
☐ 8	Ken Mosdell	32.00	14.50	4.00
☐ 9	Tom Johnson	45.00	20.00	5.75
☐ 10	Dickie Moore	150.00	70.00	19.00
☐ 11	Bud MacPherson	30.00	13.50	3.80
☐ 12	Gerry McNeil	45.00	20.00	5.75
☐ 13	Butch Bouchard	40.00	18.00	5.00
☐ 14	Doug Harvey	150.00	70.00	19.00
☐ 15	John McCormack	30.00	13.50	3.80
☐ 16	Pete Babando	30.00	13.50	3.80
☐ 17	Al Dewsbury	30.00	13.50	3.80
☐ 18	Ed Kullman	30.00	13.50	3.80
☐ 19	Ed Slowinski	30.00	13.50	3.80
☐ 20	Wally Hergesheimer	32.00	14.50	4.00
☐ 21	Allan Stanley	65.00	29.00	8.25
☐ 22	Chuck Rayner	40.00	18.00	5.00
☐ 23	Steve Kraftcheck	30.00	13.50	3.80
☐ 24	Paul Ronty	30.00	13.50	3.80
☐ 25	Gaye Stewart	30.00	13.50	3.80
☐ 26	Fred Hucul	30.00	13.50	3.80
☐ 27	Bill Mosienko	45.00	20.00	5.75
☐ 28	Jim Morrison	30.00	13.50	3.80
☐ 29	Ed Kryznowski	30.00	13.50	3.80
☐ 30	Cal Gardner	32.00	14.50	4.00
☐ 31	Al Rollins	40.00	18.00	5.00
☐ 32	Enio Sclisizzi	30.00	13.50	3.80
☐ 33	Pete Conacher	32.00	14.50	4.00
☐ 34	Leo Boivin	50.00	23.00	6.25
☐ 35	Jim Peters	30.00	13.50	3.80
☐ 36	George Gee	30.00	13.50	3.80
☐ 37	Gus Bodnar	32.00	14.50	4.00
☐ 38	Jim McFadden	30.00	13.50	3.80
☐ 39	Gus Mortson	32.00	14.50	4.00
☐ 40	Fred Glover	30.00	13.50	3.80
☐ 41	Gerry Couture	30.00	13.50	3.80
☐ 42	Howie Meeker	60.00	27.00	7.50
☐ 43	Jim Thomson	30.00	13.50	3.80
☐ 44	Teeder Kennedy	65.00	29.00	8.25
☐ 45	Sid Smith	32.00	14.50	4.00
☐ 46	Harry Watson	35.00	16.00	4.40
☐ 47	Fern Flaman	40.00	18.00	5.00
☐ 48	Tod Sloan	32.00	14.50	4.00
☐ 49	Leo Reise	30.00	13.50	3.80
☐ 50	Bob Solinger	30.00	13.50	3.80
☐ 51	George Armstrong	150.00	70.00	19.00
☐ 52	Dollard St.Laurent	32.00	14.50	4.00
☐ 53	Alex Delvecchio	125.00	57.50	15.50
☐ 54	Gord Hannigan	30.00	13.50	3.80
☐ 55	Lee Fogolin	30.00	13.50	3.80
☐ 56	Bill Gadsby	45.00	20.00	5.75
☐ 57	Herb Dickenson	30.00	13.50	3.80
☐ 58	Tim Horton	450.00	200.00	57.50
☐ 59	Harry Lumley	60.00	27.00	7.50
☐ 60	Metro Prystai	30.00	13.50	3.80
☐ 61	Marcel Pronovost	40.00	18.00	5.00

☐ 62	Benny Woit	30.00	13.50	3.80
☐ 63	Glen Skov	30.00	13.50	3.80
☐ 64	Bob Goldham	30.00	13.50	3.80
☐ 65	Tony Leswick	30.00	13.50	3.80
☐ 66	Marty Pavelich	30.00	13.50	3.80
☐ 67	Red Kelly	125.00	57.50	15.50
☐ 68	Bill Quackenbush	40.00	18.00	5.00
☐ 69	Ed Sandford	30.00	13.50	3.80
☐ 70	Milt Schmidt	60.00	27.00	7.50
☐ 71	Hal Laycoe	32.00	14.50	4.00
☐ 72	Woody Dumart	35.00	16.00	4.40
☐ 73	Zellio Toppazzini	30.00	13.50	3.80
☐ 74	Jim Henry	40.00	18.00	5.00
☐ 75	Joe Klukay	30.00	13.50	3.80
☐ 76	Dave Creighton	35.00	16.00	4.40
☐ 77	Jack McIntyre	30.00	13.50	3.80
☐ 78	Johnny Pierson	30.00	13.50	3.80
☐ 79	George Sullivan	32.00	14.50	4.00
☐ 80	Real Chevrefils	35.00	16.00	4.40
☐ 81	Leo Labine	32.00	14.50	4.00
☐ 82	Fleming Mackell	32.00	14.50	4.00
☐ 83	Pentti Lund	30.00	13.50	3.80
☐ 84	Bob Armstrong	30.00	13.50	3.80
☐ 85	Warren Godfrey	30.00	13.50	3.80
☐ 86	Terry Sawchuk	500.00	230.00	65.00
☐ 87	Ted Lindsay	125.00	57.50	15.50
☐ 88	Gordie Howe	1400.00	650.00	180.00
☐ 89	Johnny Wilson	30.00	13.50	3.80
☐ 90	Vic Stasiuk	32.00	14.50	4.00
☐ 91	Larry Zeidel	30.00	13.50	3.80
☐ 92	Larry Wilson	30.00	13.50	3.80
☐ 93	Bert Olmstead	45.00	20.00	5.75
☐ 94	Ron Stewart	45.00	20.00	5.75
☐ 95	Max Bentley	40.00	18.00	5.00
☐ 96	Rudy Migay	30.00	13.50	3.80
☐ 97	Jack Stoddard	30.00	13.50	3.80
☐ 98	Hy Buller	30.00	13.50	3.80
☐ 99	Don(Bones) Raleigh	30.00	13.50	3.80
	UER (James on back)			
☐ 100	Edgar Laprade	35.00	16.00	4.40
☐ 101	Nick Mickoski	30.00	13.50	3.80
☐ 102	Jack McLeod UER	30.00	13.50	3.80
	(Robert on back)			
☐ 103	Jim Conacher	32.00	14.50	4.00
☐ 104	Reg Sinclair	30.00	13.50	3.80
☐ 105	Bob Hassard	75.00	15.00	4.50

1953-54 Parkhurst

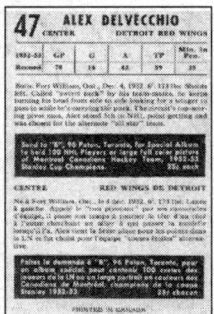

The 1953-54 Parkhurst set contains 100 cards in full color. Cards measure approximately 2 1/2" by 3 5/8". The cards were sold in five-cent wax packs each containing four cards and gum. The size of the card increased from the previous year and the picture and color show marked improvement. A facsimile autograph of the player is found on the front. The backs contain the card number, 1952-53 statistics, a short biography, and an album offer. The back data is presented in both English and French. The cards feature players from each of the six NHL teams. The set numbering is basically according to teams, i.e., Toronto Maple Leafs (1-17), Montreal Canadiens (18-35), Detroit Red Wings (36-52),

New York Rangers (53-68), Chicago Blackhawks (69-84), and Boston Bruins (85-100). The key Rookie Cards in this set are Al Arbour, Andy Bathgate, Jean Beliveau, Harry Howell, and Gump Worsley.

		NRMT	VG-E	GOOD
	COMPLETE SET (100)	4300.00	1900.00	550.00
	COMMON PLAYER (1-100)	22.00	10.00	2.80
☐ 1	Harry Lumley	100.00	30.00	10.00
☐ 2	Sid Smith	22.00	10.00	2.80
☐ 3	Gord Hannigan	22.00	10.00	2.80
☐ 4	Bob Hassard	22.00	10.00	2.80
☐ 5	Tod Sloan	25.00	11.50	3.10
☐ 6	Leo Boivin	25.00	11.50	3.10
☐ 7	Teeder Kennedy	50.00	23.00	6.25
☐ 8	Jim Thomson	22.00	10.00	2.80
☐ 9	Ron Stewart	25.00	11.50	3.10
☐ 10	Eric Nesterenko	35.00	16.00	4.40
☐ 11	George Armstrong	75.00	34.00	9.50
☐ 12	Harry Watson	25.00	11.50	3.10
☐ 13	Tim Horton	200.00	90.00	25.00
☐ 14	Fern Flaman	30.00	13.50	3.80
☐ 15	Jim Morrison	22.00	10.00	2.80
☐ 16	Bob Solinger	22.00	10.00	2.80
☐ 17	Rudy Migay	22.00	10.00	2.80
☐ 18	Dick Gamble	22.00	10.00	2.80
☐ 19	Bert Olmstead	35.00	16.00	4.40
☐ 20	Eddie Mazur	22.00	10.00	2.80
☐ 21	Paul Meger	22.00	10.00	2.80
☐ 22	Bud MacPherson	22.00	10.00	2.80
☐ 23	Dollard St.Laurent	22.00	10.00	2.80
☐ 24	Maurice Richard	450.00	200.00	57.50
☐ 25	Gerry McNeil	35.00	16.00	4.40
☐ 26	Doug Harvey	100.00	45.00	12.50
☐ 27	Jean Beliveau	600.00	275.00	75.00
☐ 28	Dickie Moore UER	100.00	45.00	12.50
	(Photo actually			
	Jean Beliveau)			
☐ 29	Boom Boom Geoffrion	125.00	57.50	15.50
☐ 30	Lach/Richard	175.00	80.00	22.00
	Elmer Lach and			
	Maurice Richard			
☐ 31	Elmer Lach	50.00	23.00	6.25
☐ 32	Butch Bouchard	30.00	13.50	3.80
☐ 33	Ken Mosdell	25.00	11.50	3.10
☐ 34	John McCormack	22.00	10.00	2.80
☐ 35	Floyd(Busher) Curry	25.00	11.50	3.10
☐ 36	Earl Reibel	25.00	11.50	3.10
☐ 37	Bill Dineen UER	45.00	20.00	5.75
	(Photo actually			
	Al Arbour)			
☐ 38	Al Arbour UER	60.00	27.00	7.50
	(Photo actually			
	Bill Dineen)			
☐ 39	Vic Stasiuk	22.00	10.00	2.80
☐ 40	Red Kelly	70.00	32.00	8.75
☐ 41	Marcel Pronovost	30.00	13.50	3.80
☐ 42	Metro Prystai	22.00	10.00	2.80
☐ 43	Tony Leswick	22.00	10.00	2.80
☐ 44	Marty Pavelich	22.00	10.00	2.80
☐ 45	Benny Woit	22.00	10.00	2.80
☐ 46	Terry Sawchuk	250.00	115.00	31.00
☐ 47	Alex Delvecchio	70.00	32.00	8.75
☐ 48	Glen Skov	22.00	10.00	2.80
☐ 49	Bob Goldham	22.00	10.00	2.80
☐ 50	Gordie Howe	800.00	350.00	100.00
☐ 51	Johnny Wilson	22.00	10.00	2.80
☐ 52	Ted Lindsay	75.00	34.00	9.50
☐ 53	Gump Worsley	300.00	135.00	38.00
☐ 54	Jack Evans	25.00	11.50	3.10
☐ 55	Max Bentley	30.00	13.50	3.80
☐ 56	Andy Bathgate	125.00	57.50	15.50
☐ 57	Harry Howell	125.00	57.50	15.50
☐ 58	Hy Buller	22.00	10.00	2.80
☐ 59	Chuck Rayner	30.00	13.50	3.80
☐ 60	Jack Stoddard	22.00	10.00	2.80
☐ 61	Ed Kullman	22.00	10.00	2.80
☐ 62	Nick Mickoski	22.00	10.00	2.80
☐ 63	Paul Ronty	22.00	10.00	2.80
☐ 64	Allan Stanley	50.00	23.00	6.25
☐ 65	Leo Reise	22.00	10.00	2.80
☐ 66	Aldo Guidolin	22.00	10.00	2.80
☐ 67	Wally Hergesheimer	22.00	10.00	2.80
☐ 68	Don Raleigh	22.00	10.00	2.80
☐ 69	Jim Peters	22.00	10.00	2.80
☐ 70	Pete Conacher	25.00	11.50	3.10
☐ 71	Fred Hucul	22.00	10.00	2.80
☐ 72	Lee Fogolin	22.00	10.00	2.80
☐ 73	Larry Zeidel	22.00	10.00	2.80
☐ 74	Larry Wilson	22.00	10.00	2.80
☐ 75	Gus Bodnar	25.00	11.50	3.10

☐ 76	Bill Gadsby	35.00	16.00	4.40
☐ 77	Jim McFadden	22.00	10.00	2.80
☐ 78	Al Dewsbury	22.00	10.00	2.80
☐ 79	Clare Raglan	22.00	10.00	2.80
☐ 80	Bill Mosienko	35.00	16.00	4.40
☐ 81	Gus Mortson	25.00	11.50	3.10
☐ 82	Al Rollins	30.00	13.50	3.80
☐ 83	George Gee	22.00	10.00	2.80
☐ 84	Gerry Couture	22.00	10.00	2.80
☐ 85	Dave Creighton	22.00	10.00	2.80
☐ 86	Jim Henry	30.00	13.50	3.80
☐ 87	Hal Laycoe	22.00	10.00	2.80
☐ 88	Johnny Peirson UER	22.00	10.00	2.80
	(Misspelled Pierson on card back)			
☐ 89	Real Chevrefils	22.00	10.00	2.80
☐ 90	Ed Sandford	22.00	10.00	2.80
☐ 91A	Fleming Mackell ERR	30.00	13.50	3.80
	(No bio)			
☐ 91B	Fleming Mackell COR	30.00	13.50	3.80
☐ 92	Milt Schmidt	45.00	20.00	5.75
☐ 93	Leo Labine	25.00	11.50	3.10
☐ 94	Joe Klukay	22.00	10.00	2.80
☐ 95	Warren Godfrey	22.00	10.00	2.80
☐ 96	Woody Dumart	25.00	11.50	3.10
☐ 97	Frank Martin	22.00	10.00	2.80
☐ 98	Jerry Toppazzini	25.00	11.50	3.10
☐ 99	Cal Gardner	25.00	11.50	3.10
☐ 100	Bill Quackenbush	60.00	18.00	6.00

1954-55 Parkhurst

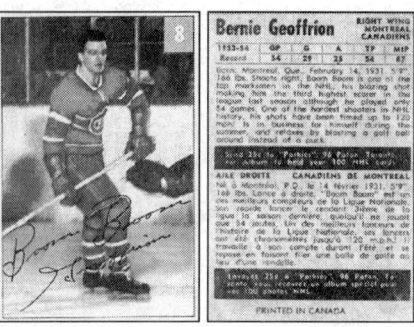

The 1954-55 Parkhurst set contains 100 cards in full color with both the card number and a facsimile autograph on the fronts. Cards in the set measure approximately 2 1/2" by 3 5/8". The backs, in both English and French, contain 1953-54 statistics, a short player biography, and an album offer (contained only on cards 1-88). Cards 1-88 feature players from each of the six NHL teams and the remaining cards are action scenes. Cards 1-88 were available with either a stat or a premium back; the cards with the statistics on the back are the more desirable of the two. The player/set numbering is basically according to teams, i.e., Montreal Canadiens (1-15), Toronto Maple Leafs (16-32), Detroit Red Wings (33-48), Boston Bruins (49-64), New York Rangers (65-76), and Chicago Blackhawks (77-88), and All-Star selections from the previous season are denoted discreetly on the card front by a red star (first team selection) or blue star (second team). The key Rookie Card in this set is Johnny Bower, although there are several Action Scene cards featuring Jacques Plante in the year before his regular Rookie Card.

	NRMT	VG-E	GOOD
COMPLETE SET (100)	4000.00	1800.00	500.00
COMMON PLAYER (1-100)	18.00	8.00	2.30
*PREMIUM BACKS 1-88: SAME VALUE			

☐ 1	Gerry McNeil	50.00	12.50	4.00

☐ 2	Dickie Moore	50.00	23.00	6.25
☐ 3	Jean Beliveau	300.00	135.00	38.00
☐ 4	Eddie Mazur	18.00	8.00	2.30
☐ 5	Bert Olmstead	30.00	13.50	3.80
☐ 6	Butch Bouchard	25.00	11.50	3.10
☐ 7	Maurice Richard	400.00	180.00	50.00
☐ 8	Boom Boom Geoffrion	100.00	45.00	12.50
☐ 9	John McCormack	18.00	8.00	2.30
☐ 10	Tom Johnson	30.00	13.50	3.80
☐ 11	Calum Mackay	18.00	8.00	2.30
☐ 12	Ken Mosdell	20.00	9.00	2.50
☐ 13	Paul Masnick	18.00	8.00	2.30
☐ 14	Doug Harvey	80.00	36.00	10.00
☐ 15	Floyd(Busher) Curry	20.00	9.00	2.50
☐ 16	Harry Lumley	35.00	16.00	4.40
☐ 17	Harry Watson	20.00	9.00	2.50
☐ 18	Jim Morrison	18.00	8.00	2.30
☐ 19	Eric Nesterenko	20.00	9.00	2.50
☐ 20	Fern Flaman	25.00	11.50	3.10
☐ 21	Rudy Migay	18.00	8.00	2.30
☐ 22	Sid Smith	20.00	9.00	2.50
☐ 23	Ron Stewart	20.00	9.00	2.50
☐ 24	George Armstrong	50.00	23.00	6.25
☐ 25	Earl Balfour	18.00	8.00	2.30
☐ 26	Leo Boivin	18.00	8.00	2.30
☐ 27	Gord Hannigan	18.00	8.00	2.30
☐ 28	Bob Bailey	18.00	8.00	2.30
☐ 29	Teeder Kennedy	40.00	18.00	5.00
☐ 30	Tod Sloan	18.00	8.00	2.30
☐ 31	Tim Horton	125.00	57.50	15.50
☐ 32	Jim Thomson	18.00	8.00	2.30
☐ 33	Terry Sawchuk	200.00	90.00	25.00
☐ 34	Marcel Pronovost	25.00	11.50	3.10
☐ 35	Metro Prystai	18.00	8.00	2.30
☐ 36	Alex Delvecchio	50.00	23.00	6.25
☐ 37	Earl Reibel	18.00	8.00	2.30
☐ 38	Benny Woit	18.00	8.00	2.30
☐ 39	Bob Goldham	18.00	8.00	2.30
☐ 40	Glen Skov	18.00	8.00	2.30
☐ 41	Gordie Howe	600.00	275.00	75.00
☐ 42	Red Kelly	50.00	23.00	6.25
☐ 43	Marty Pavelich	18.00	8.00	2.30
☐ 44	Johnny Wilson	18.00	8.00	2.30
☐ 45	Tony Leswick	18.00	8.00	2.30
☐ 46	Ted Lindsay	55.00	25.00	7.00
☐ 47	Keith Allen	25.00	11.50	3.10
☐ 48	Bill Dineen	20.00	9.00	2.50
☐ 49	Jim Henry	25.00	11.50	3.10
☐ 50	Fleming Mackell	18.00	8.00	2.30
☐ 51	Bill Quackenbush	25.00	11.50	3.10
☐ 52	Hal Laycoe	18.00	8.00	2.30
☐ 53	Cal Gardner	20.00	9.00	2.50
☐ 54	Joe Klukay	18.00	8.00	2.30
☐ 55	Bob Armstrong	18.00	8.00	2.30
☐ 56	Warren Godfrey	18.00	8.00	2.30
☐ 57	Doug Mohns	30.00	13.50	3.80
☐ 58	Dave Creighton	20.00	9.00	2.50
☐ 59	Milt Schmidt	30.00	13.50	3.80
☐ 60	Johnny Pierson	18.00	8.00	2.30
☐ 61	Leo Labine	20.00	9.00	2.50
☐ 62	Gus Bodnar	20.00	9.00	2.50
☐ 63	Real Chevrefils	18.00	8.00	2.30
☐ 64	Ed Sandford	18.00	8.00	2.30
☐ 65	Johnny Bower UER	250.00	115.00	31.00
	(Misspelled Bowers)			
☐ 66	Paul Ronty	18.00	8.00	2.30
☐ 67	Leo Reise	18.00	8.00	2.30
☐ 68	Don Raleigh	18.00	8.00	2.30
☐ 69	Bob Chrystal	18.00	8.00	2.30
☐ 70	Harry Howell	60.00	27.00	7.50
☐ 71	Wally Hergesheimer	18.00	8.00	2.30
☐ 72	Jack Evans	18.00	8.00	2.30
☐ 73	Camille Henry	30.00	13.50	3.80
☐ 74	Dean Prentice	30.00	13.50	3.80
☐ 75	Nick Mickoski	18.00	8.00	2.30
☐ 76	Ron Murphy	18.00	8.00	2.30
☐ 77	Al Rollins	25.00	11.50	3.10
☐ 78	Al Dewsbury	18.00	8.00	2.30
☐ 79	Lou Jankowski	18.00	8.00	2.30
☐ 80	George Gee	18.00	8.00	2.30
☐ 81	Gus Mortson	18.00	8.00	2.30
☐ 82	Fred Sasakamoose	20.00	9.00	2.50
☐ 83	Ike Hildebrand	18.00	8.00	2.30
☐ 84	Lee Fogolin	18.00	8.00	2.30
☐ 85	Larry Wilson	18.00	8.00	2.30
☐ 86	Pete Conacher	20.00	9.00	2.50
☐ 87	Bill Gadsby	30.00	13.50	3.80
☐ 88	Jack McIntyre	18.00	8.00	2.30
☐ 89	Busher Curry goes up and over	20.00	9.00	2.50
☐ 90	Delvecchio finds Leaf defense hard to crack	25.00	11.50	3.10

☐ 91	(Tim Horton) Battle of All-Stars	30.00	13.50	3.80
☐ 92	(Red Kelly and Harry Lumley) Lum stops Howe	85.00	38.00	10.50
☐ 93	With help of Stewart's stick Net-minders nightmare	20.00	9.00	2.50
☐ 94	(Harry Lumley and others) Meger goes down	20.00	9.00	2.50
☐ 95	and under (Jim Morrison) Harvey takes nosedive	35.00	16.00	4.40
☐ 96	(Eric Nesterenko) Terry boots out	70.00	32.00	8.75
☐ 97	Teeder's blast (Terry Sawchuk and Teeder Kennedy) Reibel tests Habs	85.00	38.00	10.50
☐ 98	Rookie "Mr. Zero" (Jacques Plante and Butch Bouchard) Plante protects	85.00	38.00	10.50
☐ 99	against slippery Sloan (Doug Harvey) Placid Plante foils	85.00	38.00	10.50
☐ 100	tireless Teeder Sawchuck stops Boom Boom	125.00	38.00	10.50

1955-56 Parkhurst

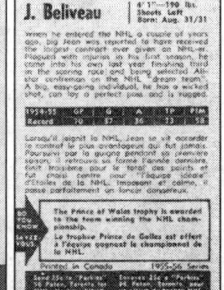

The 1955-56 Parkhurst set contains 79 cards in full color with the number and team insignia on the fronts. Cards in the set measure approximately 2 1/2" by 3 9/16". The set features players from Montreal and Toronto as well as Old-Time Greats. The Old-Time Great selections are numbers 21-32 and 55-66. The backs, printed in red ink, in both English and French, contain 1954-55 statistics, a short biography, a "Do You Know" information section, and an album offer. The key Rookie Card in this set is Jacques Plante. The same 79 cards can also be found with Quaker Oats backs, i.e., green printing on back. The Quaker Oats version is much tougher to locate and the values are approximately three to four times the value of the corresponding Parkhurst player's card.

	NRMT	VG-E	GOOD
COMPLETE SET (79)	3200.00	1450.00	400.00
COMMON PLAYER (1-79)	20.00	9.00	2.50
*QUAKER OATS: 3X to 4X			

☐ 1	Harry Lumley	80.00	20.00	6.50
☐ 2	Sid Smith	22.00	10.00	2.80
☐ 3	Tim Horton	125.00	57.50	15.50
☐ 4	George Armstrong	50.00	23.00	6.25
☐ 5	Ron Stewart	22.00	10.00	2.80

☐ 6	Joe Klukay	20.00	9.00	2.50
☐ 7	Marc Reaume	20.00	9.00	2.50
☐ 8	Jim Morrison	20.00	9.00	2.50
☐ 9	Parker MacDonald	20.00	9.00	2.50
☐ 10	Tod Sloan	20.00	9.00	2.50
☐ 11	Jim Thomson	20.00	9.00	2.50
☐ 12	Rudy Migay	20.00	9.00	2.50
☐ 13	Brian Cullen	25.00	11.50	3.10
☐ 14	Hugh Bolton	20.00	9.00	2.50
☐ 15	Eric Nesterenko	22.00	10.00	2.80
☐ 16	Larry Cahan	20.00	9.00	2.50
☐ 17	Willie Marshall	20.00	9.00	2.50
☐ 18	Dick Duff	45.00	20.00	5.75
☐ 19	Jack Caffery	20.00	9.00	2.50
☐ 20	Billy Harris	25.00	11.50	3.10
☐ 21	Lorne Chabot OTG	24.00	11.00	3.00
☐ 22	Harvey(Busher) Jackson OTG	30.00	13.50	3.80
☐ 23	Turk Broda OTG	40.00	18.00	5.00
☐ 24	Joe Primeau OTG	28.00	12.50	3.50
☐ 25	Gordie Drillon OTG	20.00	9.00	2.50
☐ 26	Chuck Conacher OTG	25.00	11.50	3.10
☐ 27	Sweeney Schriner OTG	20.00	9.00	2.50
☐ 28	Syl Apps OTG	25.00	11.50	3.10
☐ 29	Teeder Kennedy OTG	30.00	13.50	3.80
☐ 30	Ace Bailey OTG	40.00	18.00	5.00
☐ 31	Babe Pratt OTG	20.00	9.00	2.50
☐ 32	Harold Cotton OTG	20.00	9.00	2.50
☐ 33	King Clancy	40.00	18.00	5.00
☐ 34	Hap Day	24.00	11.00	3.00
☐ 35	Don Marshall	25.00	11.50	3.10
☐ 36	Jackie LeClair	22.00	10.00	2.80
☐ 37	Maurice Richard	350.00	160.00	45.00
☐ 38	Dickie Moore	50.00	23.00	6.25
☐ 39	Ken Mosdell	22.00	10.00	2.80
☐ 40	Floyd(Busher) Curry	20.00	9.00	2.50
☐ 41	Calum Mackay	20.00	9.00	2.50
☐ 42	Bert Olmstead	30.00	13.50	3.80
☐ 43	Boom Boom Geoffrion	100.00	45.00	12.50
☐ 44	Jean Beliveau	250.00	115.00	31.00
☐ 45	Doug Harvey	75.00	34.00	9.50
☐ 46	Butch Bouchard	25.00	11.50	3.10
☐ 47	Bud MacPherson	20.00	9.00	2.50
☐ 48	Dollard St.Laurent	20.00	9.00	2.50
☐ 49	Tom Johnson	30.00	13.50	3.80
☐ 50	Jacques Plante	700.00	325.00	90.00
☐ 51	Paul Meger	20.00	9.00	2.50
☐ 52	Gerry McNeil	30.00	13.50	3.80
☐ 53	Jean-Guy Talbot	25.00	11.50	3.10
☐ 54	Bob Turner	20.00	9.00	2.50
☐ 55	Newsy Lalonde OTG	40.00	18.00	5.00
☐ 56	Georges Vezina OTG	75.00	34.00	9.50
☐ 57	Howie Morenz OTG	75.00	34.00	9.50
☐ 58	Aurel Joliat OTG	35.00	16.00	4.40
☐ 59	George Hainsworth OTG	40.00	18.00	5.00
☐ 60	Sylvio Mantha OTG	20.00	9.00	2.50
☐ 61	Battleship Leduc OTG	20.00	9.00	2.50
☐ 62	Babe Siebert OTG UER	20.00	9.00	2.50
☐ 63	(Misspelled Seibert on both sides) Bill Durnan OTG	30.00	13.50	3.80
☐ 64	Ken Reardon OTG	25.00	11.50	3.10
☐ 65	Johnny Gagnon OTG	20.00	9.00	2.50
☐ 66	Billy Reay OTG	22.00	10.00	2.80
☐ 67	Toe Blake CO	25.00	11.50	3.10
☐ 68	Frank Selke MG	28.00	12.50	3.50
☐ 69	Hugh beats Hodge	20.00	9.00	2.50
☐ 70	(Hugh Bolton and Charlie Hodge) Lum stops Boom Boom	45.00	20.00	5.75
☐ 71	(Harry Lumley) Plante is protected	60.00	27.00	7.50
☐ 72	(Butch Bouchard and Tom Johnson) Rocket roars through	75.00	34.00	9.50
☐ 73	(Maurice Richard) Richard tests Lumley	75.00	34.00	9.50
☐ 74	(Maurice Richard) Beliveau bats puck	50.00	23.00	6.25
☐ 75	(Harry Lumley) Leaf speedsters attack	60.00	27.00	7.50
☐ 76	(Eric Nesterenko, Sid Smith, and Jacques Plante) Curry scores again	20.00	9.00	2.50
☐ 77	(Harry Lumley and Jim Morrison) Jammed on the boards	60.00	27.00	7.50
☐ 78	(Tod Sloan, Parker MacDonald, Doug Harvey, and Jean Beliveau) The Montreal Forum	150.00	70.00	19.00
☐ 79	Maple Leaf Gardens	175.00	70.00	19.00

1957-58 Parkhurst

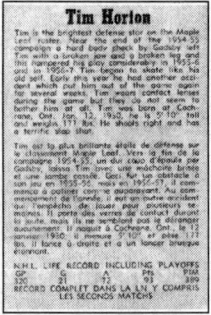

The 1957-58 Parkhurst set contains 50 color cards featuring Montreal and Toronto players. Cards are approximately 2 7/16" by 3 5/8". There are card numbers 1 to 25 for Montreal (M prefix in checklist) and card numbers 1 to 25 for Toronto (T prefix in checklist). The cards are numbered on the fronts and the backs feature resumes in both French and English. The card number, the player's name, and his position appear in a red rectangle on the front. The backs are printed in blue ink. The key Rookie Cards in this set are Frank Mahovlich and Henri Richard. There was no Parkhurst hockey set in 1956-57 reportedly due to market re-evaluation.

	NRMT	VG-E	GOOD
COMPLETE SET (50)	2000.00	900.00	250.00
COMMON MONTREAL (M1-M20)	18.00	8.00	2.30
COMMON TORONTO (T1-T25)	18.00	8.00	2.30
☐ M1 Doug Harvey	90.00	23.00	7.25
☐ M2 Boom Boom Geoffrion	80.00	36.00	10.00
☐ M3 Jean Beliveau	200.00	90.00	25.00
☐ M4 Henri Richard	350.00	160.00	45.00
☐ M5 Maurice Richard	350.00	160.00	45.00
☐ M6 Tom Johnson	22.00	10.00	2.80
☐ M7 Andre Pronovost	22.00	10.00	2.80
☐ M8 Don Marshall	18.00	8.00	2.30
☐ M9 Jean-Guy Talbot	20.00	9.00	2.50
☐ M10 Dollard St.Laurent	18.00	8.00	2.30
☐ M11 Phil Goyette	25.00	11.50	3.10
☐ M12 Claude Provost	30.00	13.50	3.80
☐ M13 Bob Turner	18.00	8.00	2.30
☐ M14 Dickie Moore	35.00	16.00	4.40
☐ M15 Jacques Plante	350.00	160.00	45.00
☐ M16 Toe Blake CO	22.00	10.00	2.80
☐ M17 Charlie Hodge	50.00	23.00	6.25
☐ M18 Marcel Bonin	18.00	8.00	2.30
☐ M19 Bert Olmstead	22.00	10.00	2.80
☐ M20 Floyd(Busher) Curry	20.00	9.00	2.50
☐ M21 Canadiens on guard	20.00	9.00	2.50
(Len Broderick)			
☐ M22 Brian Cullen scores	20.00	9.00	2.50
☐ M23 Puck and sticks high	25.00	11.50	3.10
(Len Broderick and			
Doug Harvey)			
☐ M24 Geoffrion side-	30.00	13.50	3.80
steps Chadwick			
☐ M25 Olmstead beats	25.00	11.50	3.10
Chadwick			
☐ T1 George Armstrong	40.00	18.00	5.00
☐ T2 Ed Chadwick	35.00	16.00	4.40
☐ T3 Dick Duff	25.00	11.50	3.10
☐ T4 Bob Pulford	50.00	23.00	6.25
☐ T5 Tod Sloan	18.00	8.00	2.30
☐ T6 Rudy Migay	18.00	8.00	2.30
☐ T7 Ron Stewart	20.00	9.00	2.50
☐ T8 Gerry James	20.00	9.00	2.50
☐ T9 Brian Cullen	18.00	8.00	2.30
☐ T10 Sid Smith	20.00	9.00	2.50
☐ T11 Jim Morrison	18.00	8.00	2.30
☐ T12 Marc Reaume	18.00	8.00	2.30
☐ T13 Hugh Bolton	18.00	8.00	2.30
☐ T14 Pete Conacher	20.00	9.00	2.50
☐ T15 Billy Harris	20.00	9.00	2.50
☐ T16 Mike Nykoluk	20.00	9.00	2.50
☐ T17 Frank Mahovlich	400.00	180.00	50.00
☐ T18 Ken Girard	18.00	8.00	2.30
☐ T19 Al MacNeil	18.00	8.00	2.30
☐ T20 Bob Baun	50.00	23.00	6.25
☐ T21 Barry Cullen	20.00	9.00	2.50
☐ T22 Tim Horton	100.00	45.00	12.50
☐ T23 Gary Collins	18.00	8.00	2.30
☐ T24 Gary Aldcorn	18.00	8.00	2.30
☐ T25 Billy Reay CO	28.00	8.00	2.30

1958-59 Parkhurst

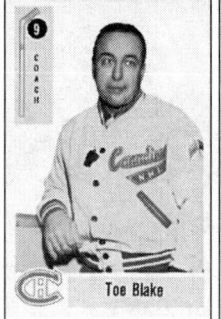
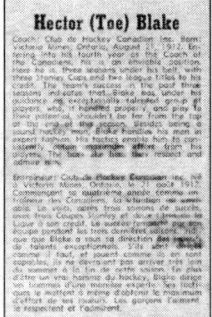

The 1958-59 Parkhurst set contains 50 color cards of Montreal and Toronto players. Cards are approximately 2 7/16" by 3 5/8". In contrast to the 1957-58 Parkhurst set, the cards, numbered on the fronts, are numbered continuously from 1 to 50. Resumes on the backs of the cards are in both French and English. The player's name and the team logo appears in a yellow rectangle at the bottom on the front. The number, position, and (usually) a hockey stick appear on the front at the upper left. The backs are printed in black ink. The key Rookie Card in this set is Ralph Backstrom.

	NRMT	VG-E	GOOD
COMPLETE SET (50)	1500.00	700.00	190.00
COMMON PLAYER (1-50)	16.00	7.25	2.00
☐ 1 Pulford Comes Close	40.00	10.00	3.20
☐ 2 Henri Richard	150.00	70.00	19.00
☐ 3 Andre Pronovost	16.00	7.25	2.00
☐ 4 Billy Harris	17.00	7.75	2.10
☐ 5 Albert Langlois	16.00	7.25	2.00
☐ 6 Noel Price	16.00	7.25	2.00
☐ 7 Armstrong Breaks	20.00	9.00	2.50
Through			
(Tom Johnson)			
☐ 8 Dickie Moore	28.00	12.50	3.50
☐ 9 Toe Blake CO	20.00	9.00	2.50
☐ 10 Tom Johnson	20.00	9.00	2.50
☐ 11 An Object of Interest	45.00	20.00	5.75
(Jacques Plante and			
George Armstrong)			
☐ 12 Ed Chadwick	17.00	7.75	2.10
☐ 13 Bob Nevin	20.00	9.00	2.50
☐ 14 Ron Stewart	17.00	7.75	2.10
☐ 15 Bob Baun	30.00	13.50	3.80
☐ 16 Ralph Backstrom	30.00	13.50	3.80
☐ 17 Charlie Hodge	30.00	13.50	3.80
☐ 18 Gary Aldcorn	16.00	7.25	2.00
☐ 19 Willie Marshall	16.00	7.25	2.00
☐ 20 Marc Reaume	16.00	7.25	2.00
☐ 21 All Eyes on Puck	40.00	18.00	5.00
(Jacques Plante			
and others)			
☐ 22 Jacques Plante	250.00	115.00	31.00
☐ 23 Allan Stanley	25.00	11.50	3.10
☐ 24 Ian Cushenan	16.00	7.25	2.00
☐ 25 Billy Reay CO	17.00	7.75	2.10
☐ 26 Plante Catches a Shot	40.00	18.00	5.00
☐ 27 Bert Olmstead	20.00	9.00	2.50
☐ 28 Boom Boom Geoffrion	70.00	32.00	8.75
☐ 29 Dick Duff	18.00	8.00	2.30
☐ 30 Ab McDonald	16.00	7.25	2.00

			NRMT	VG-E	GOOD
☐	31	Barry Cullen	16.00	7.25	2.00
☐	32	Marcel Bonin	16.00	7.25	2.00
☐	33	Frank Mahovlich	200.00	90.00	25.00
☐	34	Jean Beliveau	125.00	57.50	15.50
☐	35	Canadiens on Guard	45.00	20.00	5.75
		(Jacques Plante			
		and others)			
☐	36	Brian Cullen Shoots	18.00	8.00	2.30
☐	37	Steve Kraftcheck	16.00	7.25	2.00
☐	38	Maurice Richard	300.00	135.00	38.00
☐	39	Action Around the Net	40.00	18.00	5.00
		(Jacques Plante			
		and others)			
☐	40	Bob Turner	16.00	7.25	2.00
☐	41	Jean-Guy Talbot	17.00	7.75	2.10
☐	42	Tim Horton	75.00	34.00	9.50
☐	43	Claude Provost	17.00	7.75	2.10
☐	44	Don Marshall	17.00	7.75	2.10
☐	45	Bob Pulford	30.00	13.50	3.80
☐	46	Johnny Bower UER	90.00	40.00	11.50
		(Misspelled Bowers			
		on card front)			
☐	47	Phil Goyette	17.00	7.75	2.10
☐	48	George Armstrong	28.00	12.50	3.50
☐	49	Doug Harvey	40.00	18.00	5.00
☐	50	Brian Cullen	30.00	9.00	3.00

			NRMT	VG-E	GOOD
☐	25	Johnny Bower IA	25.00	11.50	3.10
☐	26	Ron Stewart	15.00	6.75	1.90
☐	27	Toe Blake CO	18.00	8.00	2.30
☐	28	Bob Pulford	20.00	9.00	2.50
☐	29	Ralph Backstrom	18.00	8.00	2.30
☐	30	Action Around the Net	16.00	7.25	2.00
		(Canadiens vs. Leafs)			
☐	31	Bill Hicke	18.00	8.00	2.30
☐	32	Johnny Bower	60.00	27.00	7.50
☐	33	Boom Boom Geoffrion	60.00	27.00	7.50
☐	34	Ted Hampson	15.00	6.75	1.90
☐	35	Andre Pronovost	15.00	6.75	1.90
☐	36	Stafford Smythe CHC	20.00	9.00	2.50
☐	37	Don Marshall	16.00	7.25	2.00
☐	38	Dick Duff	17.00	7.75	2.10
☐	39	Henri Richard	90.00	40.00	11.50
☐	40	Bert Olmstead	18.00	8.00	2.30
☐	41	Jacques Plante	150.00	70.00	19.00
☐	42	Noel Price	15.00	6.75	1.90
☐	43	Bob Turner	15.00	6.75	1.90
☐	44	Allan Stanley	22.00	10.00	2.80
☐	45	Albert Langlois	15.00	6.75	1.90
☐	46	Officials Intervene	16.00	7.25	2.00
		(Canadiens vs. Leafs)			
☐	47	Frank Selke MD	20.00	9.00	2.50
☐	48	Gary Edmundson	15.00	6.75	1.90
☐	49	Jean-Guy Talbot	16.00	7.25	2.00
☐	50	King Clancy AGM	50.00	12.50	4.00

1959-60 Parkhurst

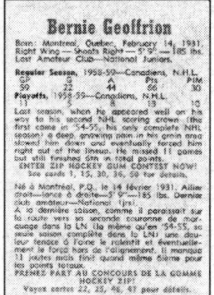

Bernie Geoffrion

The 1959-60 Parkhurst set contains 50 color cards of Montreal and Toronto players. Cards are approximately 2 7/16" by 3 5/8". The cards are numbered on the fronts. The backs, which contain 1958-59 statistics, a short biography, and a Hockey Gum contest ad, are written in both French and English. The key Rookie Cards in this set are Carl Brewer and Punch Imlach.

			NRMT	VG-E	GOOD
	COMPLETE SET (50)		1200.00	550.00	150.00
	COMMON PLAYER (1-50)		15.00	6.75	1.90
☐	1	Canadiens on Guard	50.00	12.50	4.00
		(Versus Maple Leafs)			
☐	2	Maurice Richard	250.00	115.00	31.00
☐	3	Carl Brewer	30.00	13.50	3.80
☐	4	Phil Goyette	16.00	7.25	2.00
☐	5	Ed Chadwick	16.00	7.25	2.00
☐	6	Jean Beliveau	100.00	45.00	12.50
☐	7	George Armstrong	25.00	11.50	3.10
☐	8	Doug Harvey	35.00	16.00	4.40
☐	9	Billy Harris	15.00	6.75	1.90
☐	10	Tom Johnson	18.00	8.00	2.30
☐	11	Marc Reaume	15.00	6.75	1.90
☐	12	Marcel Bonin	15.00	6.75	1.90
☐	13	Johnny Wilson	15.00	6.75	1.90
☐	14	Dickie Moore	25.00	11.50	3.10
☐	15	Punch Imlach CO/MG	25.00	11.50	3.10
☐	16	Charlie Hodge	20.00	9.00	2.50
☐	17	Larry Regan	15.00	6.75	1.90
☐	18	Claude Provost	16.00	7.25	2.00
☐	19	Gerry Ehman	15.00	6.75	1.90
☐	20	Ab McDonald	15.00	6.75	1.90
☐	21	Bob Baun	20.00	9.00	2.50
☐	22	Ken Reardon VP	18.00	8.00	2.30
☐	23	Tim Horton	60.00	27.00	7.50
☐	24	Frank Mahovlich	125.00	57.50	15.50

1960-61 Parkhurst

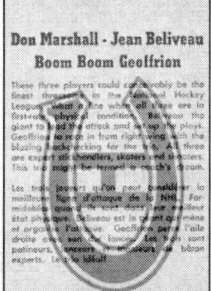

The 1960-61 Parkhurst set of 61 color cards, numbered on the fronts, contains players from Montreal, Toronto, and Detroit. The numbering of the players in the set is basically by teams, i.e., Toronto Maple Leafs (1-19), Detroit Red Wings (20-37), and Montreal Canadiens (38-55). Cards in the set are 2 7/16" by 3 5/8". The backs, in both French and English, are printed in blue ink and contain NHL lifetime records, vital statistics, and biographical data of the player. This set contains the last card of Maurice "Rocket" Richard. The key Rookie Card in this set is John McKenzie.

			NRMT	VG-E	GOOD
	COMPLETE SET (61)		1600.00	700.00	200.00
	COMMON PLAYER (1-61)		14.00	6.25	1.75
☐	1	Tim Horton	80.00	24.00	8.00
☐	2	Frank Mahovlich	100.00	45.00	12.50
☐	3	Johnny Bower	40.00	18.00	5.00
☐	4	Bert Olmstead	16.00	7.25	2.00
☐	5	Gary Edmundson	14.00	6.25	1.75
☐	6	Ron Stewart	15.00	6.75	1.90
☐	7	Gerry James	15.00	6.75	1.90
☐	8	Gerry Ehman	14.00	6.25	1.75
☐	9	Red Kelly	25.00	11.50	3.10
☐	10	Dave Creighton	14.00	6.25	1.75
☐	11	Bob Baun	18.00	8.00	2.30
☐	12	Dick Duff	16.00	7.25	2.00
☐	13	Larry Regan	14.00	6.25	1.75
☐	14	Johnny Wilson	14.00	6.25	1.75
☐	15	Billy Harris	15.00	6.25	1.75
☐	16	Allan Stanley	20.00	9.00	2.50
☐	17	George Armstrong	20.00	9.00	2.50

☐ 18	Carl Brewer	18.00	8.00	2.30
☐ 19	Bob Pulford	18.00	8.00	2.30
☐ 20	Gordie Howe	400.00	180.00	50.00
☐ 21	Val Fonteyne	15.00	6.75	1.90
☐ 22	Murray Oliver	16.00	7.25	2.00
☐ 23	Sid Abel CO	16.00	7.25	2.00
☐ 24	Jack McIntyre	14.00	6.25	1.75
☐ 25	Marc Reaume	14.00	6.25	1.75
☐ 26	Norm Ullman	40.00	18.00	5.00
☐ 27	Brian Smith	14.00	6.25	1.75
☐ 28	Gerry Melnyk UER	14.00	6.25	1.75
	(Misspelled Jerry on both sides)			
☐ 29	Marcel Pronovost	16.00	7.25	2.00
☐ 30	Warren Godfrey	14.00	6.25	1.75
☐ 31	Terry Sawchuk	125.00	57.50	15.50
☐ 32	Barry Cullen	14.00	6.25	1.75
☐ 33	Gary Aldcorn	14.00	6.25	1.75
☐ 34	Pete Goegan	14.00	6.25	1.75
☐ 35	Len Lunde	14.00	6.25	1.75
☐ 36	Alex Delvecchio	25.00	11.50	3.10
☐ 37	John McKenzie	25.00	11.50	3.10
☐ 38	Dickie Moore	20.00	9.00	2.50
☐ 39	Albert Langlois	14.00	6.25	1.75
☐ 40	Bill Hicke	14.00	6.25	1.75
☐ 41	Ralph Backstrom	15.00	6.75	1.90
☐ 42	Don Marshall	15.00	6.75	1.90
☐ 43	Bob Turner	14.00	6.25	1.75
☐ 44	Tom Johnson	16.00	7.25	2.00
☐ 45	Maurice Richard	200.00	90.00	25.00
☐ 46	Boom Boom Geoffrion	55.00	25.00	7.00
☐ 47	Henri Richard	65.00	29.00	8.25
☐ 48	Doug Harvey	30.00	13.50	3.80
☐ 49	Jean Beliveau	90.00	40.00	11.50
☐ 50	Phil Goyette	15.00	6.75	1.90
☐ 51	Marcel Bonin	14.00	6.25	1.75
☐ 52	Jean-Guy Talbot	15.00	6.75	1.90
☐ 53	Jacques Plante	125.00	57.50	15.50
☐ 54	Claude Provost	15.00	6.75	1.90
☐ 55	Andre Pronovost	14.00	6.25	1.75
☐ 56	Linemates: Hicke, McDonald, Backstrom	15.00	6.75	1.90
☐ 57	Linemates: Marshall, Moore, H.Richard	40.00	18.00	5.00
☐ 58	Linemates: Provost, Pronovost, Goyette	15.00	6.75	1.90
☐ 59	Linemates: Geoffrion, Marshall, Beliveau	70.00	32.00	8.75
☐ 60	Ab McDonald	14.00	6.25	1.75
☐ 61	Jim Morrison	60.00	15.00	4.80

1961-62 Parkhurst

Jean Beliveau

The 1961-62 Parkhurst set contains 51 cards in full color, numbered on the fronts. Cards are 2 7/16" by 3 5/8". The backs contain 1960-61 statistics and a cartoon; the punch line for which could be seen by rubbing the card with a coin. The cards contain players from Montreal, Toronto, and Detroit. The numbering of the players in the set is basically by teams, i.e., Toronto Maple Leafs (1-18), Detroit Red Wings (19-34), and Montreal Canadiens (35-51). The backs are in both French and English. The key Rookie Card in this set is Dave Keon.

		NRMT	VG-E	GOOD
COMPLETE SET (51)		1250.00	575.00	160.00
COMMON PLAYER (1-51)		12.00	5.50	1.50
☐ 1	Tim Horton	70.00	21.00	7.00
☐ 2	Frank Mahovlich	80.00	36.00	10.00
☐ 3	Johnny Bower	30.00	13.50	3.80
☐ 4	Bert Olmstead	15.00	6.75	1.90
☐ 5	Dave Keon	200.00	90.00	25.00
☐ 6	Ron Stewart	13.00	5.75	1.65
☐ 7	Eddie Shack	35.00	16.00	4.40
☐ 8	Bob Pulford	16.00	7.25	2.00
☐ 9	Red Kelly	22.00	10.00	2.80
☐ 10	Bob Nevin	13.00	5.75	1.65
☐ 11	Bob Baun	15.00	6.75	1.90
☐ 12	Dick Duff	15.00	6.75	1.90
☐ 13	Larry Keenan	12.00	5.50	1.50
☐ 14	Larry Hillman	13.00	5.75	1.65
☐ 15	Billy Harris	12.00	5.50	1.50
☐ 16	Allan Stanley	18.00	8.00	2.30
☐ 17	George Armstrong	18.00	8.00	2.30
☐ 18	Carl Brewer	13.00	5.75	1.65
☐ 19	Howie Glover	12.00	5.50	1.50
☐ 20	Gordie Howe	350.00	160.00	45.00
☐ 21	Val Fonteyne	12.00	5.50	1.50
☐ 22	Al Johnson	12.00	5.50	1.50
☐ 23	Pete Goegan	12.00	5.50	1.50
☐ 24	Len Lunde	12.00	5.50	1.50
☐ 25	Alex Delvecchio	22.00	10.00	2.80
☐ 26	Norm Ullman	32.00	14.50	4.00
☐ 27	Bill Gadsby	15.00	6.75	1.90
☐ 28	Ed Litzenberger	12.00	5.50	1.50
☐ 29	Marcel Pronovost	15.00	6.75	1.90
☐ 30	Warren Godfrey	12.00	5.50	1.50
☐ 31	Terry Sawchuk	100.00	45.00	12.50
☐ 32	Vic Stasiuk	12.00	5.50	1.50
☐ 33	Leo Labine	12.00	5.50	1.50
☐ 34	John McKenzie	15.00	6.75	1.90
☐ 35	Boom Boom Geoffrion	45.00	20.00	5.75
☐ 36	Dickie Moore	18.00	8.00	2.30
☐ 37	Albert Langlois	12.00	5.50	1.50
☐ 38	Bill Hicke	12.00	5.50	1.50
☐ 39	Ralph Backstrom	13.00	5.75	1.65
☐ 40	Don Marshall	12.00	5.50	1.50
☐ 41	Bob Turner	12.00	5.50	1.50
☐ 42	Tom Johnson	15.00	6.75	1.90
☐ 43	Henri Richard	50.00	23.00	6.25
☐ 44	Wayne Connelly UER	15.00	6.75	1.90
	(Misspelled Conolly on both sides)			
☐ 45	Jean Beliveau	75.00	34.00	9.50
☐ 46	Phil Goyette	12.00	5.50	1.50
☐ 47	Marcel Bonin	12.00	5.50	1.50
☐ 48	Jean-Guy Talbot	13.00	5.75	1.65
☐ 49	Jacques Plante	100.00	45.00	12.50
☐ 50	Claude Provost	13.00	5.75	1.65
☐ 51	Andre Pronovost UER	30.00	9.00	3.00
	(Shown as Montreal, should be Boston)			

1962-63 Parkhurst

Horton, Myles Gilbert (Tim)

The 1962-63 Parkhurst set contains 54 cards in full color, with the card number and, on some cards, a facsimile autograph on the front. Cards are approximately 2 7/16" by 3 5/8". The backs, in both French and English, contain player lifetime statistics and player vital statistics in paragraph form. An unnumbered checklist card was issued as well as an unnumbered game or tally card, which is also referred to as the "Zip" card. Both of these are considered rather difficult to obtain. There are several different styles or designs within this set depending on card number, e.g., some cards have a giant puck as background for their photo on the front. Other cards have the player's team logo as background. The numbering of the players in the set is basically by teams, i.e., Toronto Maple Leafs (1-18), Detroit Red Wings (19-36), and Montreal Canadiens (37-54). The notable Rookie Cards in this set are Bobby Rousseau, Gilles Trembley, and J.C.Trembley.

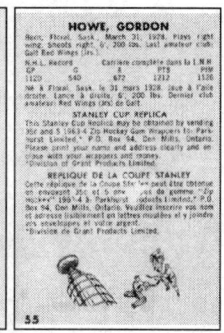

		NRMT	VG-E	GOOD
	COMPLETE SET (55)	1500.00	700.00	190.00
	COMMON PLAYER (1-54)	12.00	5.50	1.50
☐ 1	Billy Harris	25.00	6.25	2.00
☐ 2	Dick Duff	14.00	6.25	1.75
☐ 3	Bob Baun	14.00	6.25	1.75
☐ 4	Frank Mahovlich	70.00	32.00	8.75
☐ 5	Red Kelly	20.00	9.00	2.50
☐ 6	Ron Stewart	12.00	5.50	1.50
☐ 7	Tim Horton	50.00	23.00	6.25
☐ 8	Carl Brewer	13.00	5.75	1.65
☐ 9	Allan Stanley	15.00	6.75	1.90
☐ 10	Bob Nevin	13.00	5.75	1.65
☐ 11	Bob Pulford	15.00	6.75	1.90
☐ 12	Ed Litzenberger	12.00	5.50	1.50
☐ 13	George Armstrong	15.00	6.75	1.90
☐ 14	Eddie Shack	27.00	12.00	3.40
☐ 15	Dave Keon	75.00	34.00	9.50
☐ 16	Johnny Bower	25.00	11.50	3.10
☐ 17	Larry Hillman	13.00	5.75	1.65
☐ 18	Frank Mahovlich	70.00	32.00	8.75
☐ 19	Hank Bassen	13.00	5.75	1.65
☐ 20	Gerry Odrowski	12.00	5.50	1.50
☐ 21	Norm Ullman	27.00	12.00	3.40
☐ 22	Vic Stasiuk	12.00	5.50	1.50
☐ 23	Bruce MacGregor	12.00	5.50	1.50
☐ 24	Claude Laforge	12.00	5.50	1.50
☐ 25	Bill Gadsby	12.00	5.50	1.50
☐ 26	Leo Labine	12.00	5.50	1.50
☐ 27	Val Fonteyne	12.00	5.50	1.50
☐ 28	Howie Glover	12.00	5.50	1.50
☐ 29	Marc Boileau	12.00	5.50	1.50
☐ 30	Gordie Howe	300.00	135.00	38.00
☐ 31	Gordie Howe	300.00	135.00	38.00
☐ 32	Alex Delvecchio	20.00	9.00	2.50
☐ 33	Marcel Pronovost	12.00	5.50	1.50
☐ 34	Sid Abel CO	14.00	6.25	1.75
☐ 35	Len Lunde	12.00	5.50	1.50
☐ 36	Warren Godfrey	12.00	5.50	1.50
☐ 37	Phil Goyette	12.00	5.50	1.50
☐ 38	Henri Richard	40.00	18.00	5.00
☐ 39	Jean Beliveau	70.00	32.00	8.75
☐ 40	Bill Hicke	12.00	5.50	1.50
☐ 41	Claude Provost	12.00	5.50	1.50
☐ 42	Dickie Moore	15.00	6.75	1.90
☐ 43	Don Marshall	12.00	5.50	1.50
☐ 44	Ralph Backstrom	13.00	5.75	1.65
☐ 45	Marcel Bonin	12.00	5.50	1.50
☐ 46	Gilles Tremblay	25.00	11.50	3.10
☐ 47	Bobby Rousseau	20.00	9.00	2.50
☐ 48	Boom Boom Geoffrion	40.00	18.00	5.00
☐ 49	Jacques Plante	90.00	40.00	11.50
☐ 50	Tom Johnson	14.00	6.25	1.75
☐ 51	Jean-Guy Talbot	13.00	5.75	1.65
☐ 52	Lou Fontinato	12.00	5.50	1.50
☐ 53	Boom Boom Geoffrion	40.00	18.00	5.00
☐ 54	J.C. Tremblay	40.00	10.00	3.20
☐ NNO1	Checklist Card	125.00	31.00	6.25
☐ NNO2	Tally Game Card	200.00	80.00	16.00

1963-64 Parkhurst

The 1963-64 Parkhurst set contains 99 color cards. Cards measure approximately 2 7/16" by 3 5/8". The fronts of the cards feature the player with a background of either thin stripes or the Canadian or American flag, depending upon whether the player is on the Detroit (American flag), Toronto (Canadian flag), or Montreal (multi-color striped

background) team. The numbering of the players in the set is basically by teams, i.e., Toronto Maple Leafs (1-20 and 61-79), Detroit Red Wings (41-60), and Montreal Canadiens (21-40 and 80-99). The backs, in both French and English, contain the card number, player lifetime NHL statistics, player biography, and a Stanley Cup replica offer. The set includes two different cards of each Montreal and Toronto player and only one of each Detroit player (with the following exceptions, numbers 15, 20, and 75 (single card Maple Leafs). Each Toronto player's double is obtained by adding 60, e.g., 1 and 61, 2 and 62, 3 and 63, etc., are the same player. Each Montreal player's double is obtained by adding 59, e.g., 21 and 80, 22 and 81, 23 and 82, etc., are the same player. The key Rookie Cards in the set are Red Berenson, John Ferguson, Jacques Laperriere, and Cesare Maniago.

		NRMT	VG-E	GOOD
	COMPLETE SET (99)	1800.00	800.00	230.00
	COMMON PLAYER (1-99)	12.00	5.50	1.50
☐ 1	Allan Stanley	30.00	9.00	3.00
☐ 2	Don Simmons	13.00	5.75	1.65
☐ 3	Red Kelly	20.00	9.00	2.50
☐ 4	Dick Duff	14.00	6.25	1.75
☐ 5	Johnny Bower	25.00	11.50	3.10
☐ 6	Ed Litzenberger	12.00	5.50	1.50
☐ 7	Kent Douglas	12.00	5.50	1.50
☐ 8	Carl Brewer	13.00	5.75	1.65
☐ 9	Eddie Shack	27.00	12.00	3.40
☐ 10	Bob Nevin	13.00	5.75	1.65
☐ 11	Billy Harris	12.00	5.50	1.50
☐ 12	Bob Pulford	15.00	6.75	1.90
☐ 13	George Armstrong	15.00	6.75	1.90
☐ 14	Ron Stewart	12.00	5.50	1.50
☐ 15	John McMillan	12.00	5.50	1.50
☐ 16	Tim Horton	50.00	23.00	6.25
☐ 17	Frank Mahovlich	70.00	32.00	8.75
☐ 18	Bob Baun	14.00	6.25	1.75
☐ 19	Punch Imlach ACO/GM	15.00	6.75	1.90
☐ 20	King Clancy ACO	18.00	8.00	2.30
☐ 21	Gilles Tremblay	13.00	5.75	1.65
☐ 22	Jean-Guy Talbot	13.00	5.75	1.65
☐ 23	Henri Richard	40.00	18.00	5.00
☐ 24	Ralph Backstrom	13.00	5.75	1.65
☐ 25	Bill Hicke	12.00	5.50	1.50
☐ 26	Red Berenson	30.00	13.50	3.80
☐ 27	Jacques Laperriere	40.00	18.00	5.00
☐ 28	Jean Gauthier	12.00	5.50	1.50
☐ 29	Boom Boom Geoffrion	40.00	18.00	5.00
☐ 30	Jean Beliveau	70.00	32.00	8.75
☐ 31	J.C. Tremblay	15.00	6.75	1.90
☐ 32	Terry Harper	25.00	11.50	3.10
☐ 33	John Ferguson	40.00	18.00	5.00
☐ 34	Toe Blake CO	15.00	6.75	1.90
☐ 35	Bobby Rousseau	13.00	5.75	1.65
☐ 36	Claude Provost	12.00	5.50	1.50
☐ 37	Marc Reaume	12.00	5.50	1.50
☐ 38	Dave Balon	12.00	5.50	1.50
☐ 39	Gump Worsley	30.00	13.50	3.80
☐ 40	Cesare Maniago	30.00	13.50	3.80
☐ 41	Bruce MacGregor	12.00	5.50	1.50
☐ 42	Alex Faulkner	12.00	5.50	1.50
☐ 43	Pete Goegan	12.00	5.50	1.50
☐ 44	Parker MacDonald	12.00	5.50	1.50

☐ 45	Andre Pronovost	12.00	5.50	1.50
☐ 46	Marcel Pronovost	12.00	5.50	1.50
☐ 47	Bob Dillabough	12.00	5.50	1.50
☐ 48	Larry Jeffrey	12.00	5.50	1.50
☐ 49	Ian Cushenan	12.00	5.50	1.50
☐ 50	Alex Delvecchio	20.00	9.00	2.50
☐ 51	Hank Ciesla	12.00	5.50	1.50
☐ 52	Norm Ullman	27.00	12.00	3.40
☐ 53	Terry Sawchuk	100.00	45.00	12.50
☐ 54	Ron Ingram	12.00	5.50	1.50
☐ 55	Gordie Howe	350.00	160.00	45.00
☐ 56	Billy McNeil	12.00	5.50	1.50
☐ 57	Floyd Smith	12.00	5.50	1.50
☐ 58	Vic Stasiuk	12.00	5.50	1.50
☐ 59	Bill Gadsby	12.00	5.50	1.50
☐ 60	Doug Barkley	12.00	5.50	1.50
☐ 61	Allan Stanley	15.00	6.75	1.90
☐ 62	Don Simmons	13.00	5.75	1.65
☐ 63	Red Kelly	20.00	9.00	2.50
☐ 64	Dick Duff	14.00	6.25	1.75
☐ 65	Johnny Bower	25.00	11.50	3.10
☐ 66	Ed Litzenberger	12.00	5.50	1.50
☐ 67	Kent Douglas	12.00	5.50	1.50
☐ 68	Carl Brewer	13.00	5.75	1.65
☐ 69	Eddie Shack	27.00	12.00	3.40
☐ 70	Bob Nevin	13.00	5.75	1.65
☐ 71	Billy Harris	12.00	5.50	1.50
☐ 72	Bob Pulford	15.00	6.75	1.90
☐ 73	George Armstrong	15.00	6.75	1.90
☐ 74	Ron Stewart	12.00	5.50	1.50
☐ 75	Dave Keon	75.00	34.00	9.50
☐ 76	Tim Horton	50.00	23.00	6.25
☐ 77	Frank Mahovlich	70.00	32.00	8.75
☐ 78	Bob Baun	14.00	6.25	1.75
☐ 79	Punch Imlach ACO/GM	15.00	6.75	1.90
☐ 80	Gilles Tremblay	13.00	5.75	1.65
☐ 81	Jean-Guy Talbot	12.00	5.50	1.50
☐ 82	Henri Richard	40.00	18.00	5.00
☐ 83	Ralph Backstrom	13.00	5.75	1.65
☐ 84	Bill Hicke	12.00	5.50	1.50
☐ 85	Red Berenson	30.00	13.50	3.80
☐ 86	Jacques Laperriere	40.00	18.00	5.00
☐ 87	Jean Gauthier	12.00	5.50	1.50
☐ 88	Boom Boom Geoffrion	40.00	18.00	5.00
☐ 89	Jean Beliveau	70.00	32.00	8.75
☐ 90	J.C. Tremblay	15.00	6.75	1.90
☐ 91	Terry Harper	25.00	11.50	3.10
☐ 92	John Ferguson	40.00	18.00	5.00
☐ 93	Toe Blake CO	15.00	6.75	1.90
☐ 94	Bobby Rousseau	13.00	5.75	1.65
☐ 95	Claude Provost	12.00	5.50	1.50
☐ 96	Marc Reaume	12.00	5.50	1.50
☐ 97	Dave Balon	12.00	5.50	1.50
☐ 98	Gump Worsley	35.00	16.00	4.40
☐ 99	Cesare Maniago	60.00	18.00	6.00

1991-92 Parkhurst

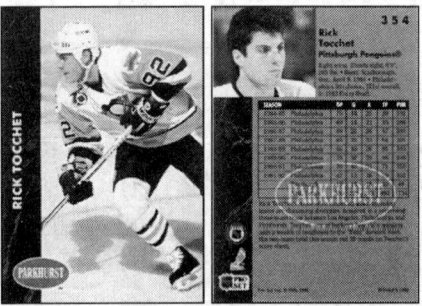

Parkhurst hockey cards were issued for 13 years beginning in the early 1950's, and the 1991-92 Parkhurst hockey set marks Pro Set's resurrection of this venerable hockey card brand. The set was primarily released in two series. Both series contain 225 standard-size (2 1/2" by 3 1/2") cards and five (four in the second series) special PHC collectible cards randomly inserted into foil packs. First and second series production quantities were each reported to be 15,000

numbered ten-box foil cases, including 2,500 cases that were translated into French and distributed predominately to French-speaking Canadian provinces. The fronts feature full-bleed glossy color photos, bordered on the left by a dark brown marbled border stripe. The player's name appears in the stripe; Parkhurst's teal oval-shaped logo in the lower left corner rounds out the card face. The backs carry a color head shot, with biography, career statistics, and player profile all on a bronze background. The cards are numbered on the back and checklisted below alphabetically according to teams as follows: Boston Bruins (1-9), Buffalo Sabres (10-19), Calgary Flames (20-28), Chicago Blackhawks (29-36), Detroit Red Wings (37-46), Edmonton Oilers (47-55), Hartford Whalers (56-64), Los Angeles Kings (65-74), Minnesota North Stars (75-83), Montreal Canadiens (84-93), New Jersey Devils (94-103), New York Islanders (104-113), New York Rangers (114-122), Philadelphia Flyers (123-131), Pittsburgh Penguins (132-141), Quebec Nordiques (142-150), St. Louis Blues (151-159), San Jose Sharks (160-168), Toronto Maple Leafs (169-177), Vancouver Canucks (178-187), Washington Capitals (188-197), Winnipeg Jets (198-206), 1,000 Point Club (207-217), League Leaders (218-219), Frequent All-Stars (220-225), Boston Bruins (226-235), Buffalo Sabres (236-244), Calgary Flames (245-254), Chicago Blackhawks (255-264), Detroit Red Wings (265-273), Edmonton Oilers (274-283), Hartford Whalers (284-291), Los Angeles Kings (292-299), Minnesota North Stars (300-306), Montreal Canadiens (307-315), New Jersey Devils (316-324), New York Islanders (325-332), New York Rangers (333-341), Philadelphia Flyers (342-351), Pittsburgh Penguins (352-361), Quebec Nordiques (362-371), St. Louis Blues (372-380), San Jose Sharks (381-389), Toronto Maple Leafs (390-399), Vancouver Canucks (400-407), Washington Capitals (408-417), Winnipeg Jets (418-427), 500-Goal Club (428-431), Leaders (432-442), and Rookie Leaders (443-450). The NNO Santa Claus card was randomly inserted in first series packs. The key Rookie Cards in the set are Tony Amonte, Gilbert Dionne, Dominik Hasek, Joe Juneau, Valeri Kamensky, Vladimir Konstantinov, Vyacheslav Kozlov, Nicklas Lidstrom, Shawn McEachern, Geoff Sanderson, Keith Tkachuk, and Doug Weight. A special promotion offer for a 25-card Final Update set was included on Parkhurst Series II packs. It is estimated less than 15,000 sets exist.

	MINT	EXC	G-VG
COMPLETE SET (475)	100.00	45.00	12.50
COMPLETE SERIES 1 (225)	20.00	9.00	2.50
COMPLETE SERIES 2 (225)	20.00	9.00	2.50
COMPLETE FIN.UPDATE (25)	60.00	27.00	7.50
COMMON PLAYER (1-225)	.05	.02	.01
COMMON PLAYER (226-450)	.05	.02	.01
COMMON PLAYER (451-475)	1.00	.45	.13
*FRENCH VERSION: 1X to 1.2X			

☐ 1	Matt DelGuidice	.05	.02	.01
☐ 2	Ken Hodge Jr.	.05	.02	.01
☐ 3	Vladimir Ruzicka UER	.05	.02	.01
	(Misspelled Vladimar Ruzika on card front)			
☐ 4	Craig Janney	.20	.09	.03
☐ 5	Glen Wesley	.05	.02	.01
☐ 6	Stephen Leach	.05	.02	.01
☐ 7	Garry Galley	.08	.04	.01
☐ 8	Andy Moog	.10	.05	.01
☐ 9	Ray Bourque	.25	.11	.03
☐ 10	Brad May	.08	.04	.01
☐ 11	Donald Audette	.05	.02	.01
☐ 12	Alexander Mogilny	.75	.35	.09
☐ 13	Randy Wood	.05	.02	.01
☐ 14	Daren Puppa	.08	.04	.01
☐ 15	Doug Bodger	.05	.02	.01
☐ 16	Pat LaFontaine	.30	.14	.04
☐ 17	Dave Andreychuk	.20	.09	.03
☐ 18	Dale Hawerchuk	.08	.04	.01
☐ 19	Mike Ramsey	.05	.02	.01

☐ 20	Tomas Forslund UER	.05	.02	.01
	(Misspelled Thomas on card back)			
☐ 21	Robert Reichel	.25	.11	.03
☐ 22	Theoren Fleury	.25	.11	.03
☐ 23	Joe Nieuwendyk	.10	.05	.01
☐ 24	Gary Roberts	.08	.04	.01
☐ 25	Gary Suter	.08	.04	.01
☒ 26	Doug Gilmour	.35	.16	.04
☐ 27	Mike Vernon	.08	.04	.01
☐ 28	Al MacInnis	.10	.05	.01
☐ 29	Jeremy Roenick	1.25	.55	.16
☐ 30	Ed Belfour	.60	.25	.08
☐ 31	Steve Smith	.08	.04	.01
☐ 32	Chris Chelios	.08	.04	.01
☐ 33	Dirk Graham	.05	.02	.01
☐ 34	Steve Larmer	.08	.04	.01
☐ 35	Brent Sutter	.08	.04	.01
☐ 36	Michel Goulet	.08	.04	.01
☐ 37	Nicklas Lidstrom UER	.75	.35	.09
	(Misspelled Niklas on card front)			
☐ 38	Sergei Fedorov	1.50	.65	.19
☐ 39	Tim Cheveldae	.08	.04	.01
☐ 40	Kevin Miller	.08	.04	.01
☐ 41	Ray Sheppard	.08	.04	.01
☐ 42	Paul Ysebaert	.05	.02	.01
☐ 43	Jimmy Carson	.08	.04	.01
☐ 44	Steve Yzerman	.50	.23	.06
☐ 45	Shawn Burr	.05	.02	.01
☐ 46	Vladimir Konstantinov	.35	.16	.04
☐ 47	Josef Beranek	.40	.18	.05
☐ 48	Vincent Damphousse	.08	.04	.01
☐ 49	Dave Manson	.08	.04	.01
☐ 50	Scott Mellanby	.05	.02	.01
☐ 51	Kevin Lowe	.08	.04	.01
☐ 52	Joe Murphy	.08	.04	.01
☐ 53	Bill Ranford	.08	.04	.01
☐ 54	Craig Simpson	.08	.04	.01
☐ 55	Esa Tikkanen	.08	.04	.01
☐ 56	Michel Picard	.05	.02	.01
☐ 57	Geoff Sanderson	2.00	.90	.25
☐ 58	Kay Whitmore	.05	.02	.01
☐ 59	John Cullen	.05	.02	.01
☐ 60	Rob Brown	.05	.02	.01
☐ 61	Zarley Zalapski	.05	.02	.01
☐ 62	Brad Shaw	.05	.02	.01
☐ 63	Mikael Anderson	.05	.02	.01
☐ 64	Pat Verbeek	.08	.04	.01
☐ 65	Peter Ahola	.05	.02	.01
☐ 66	Tony Granato	.08	.04	.01
☐ 67	Dave Taylor	.08	.04	.01
☐ 68	Luc Robitaille	.30	.14	.04
☐ 69	Marty McSorley	.08	.04	.01
☐ 70	Tomas Sandstrom	.08	.04	.01
☐ 71	Kelly Hrudey	.08	.04	.01
☐ 72	Jari Kurri	.10	.05	.01
☐ 73	Wayne Gretzky	1.50	.65	.19
☐ 74	Larry Robinson	.08	.04	.01
☐ 75	Derian Hatcher	.08	.04	.01
☐ 76	Ulf Dahlen	.08	.04	.01
☐ 77	Jon Casey	.08	.04	.01
☐ 78	Dave Gagner	.08	.04	.01
☐ 79	Brian Bellows	.08	.04	.01
☐ 80	Neal Broten	.08	.04	.01
☐ 81	Mike Modano	.50	.23	.06
☐ 82	Brian Propp	.08	.04	.01
☐ 83	Bobby Smith	.08	.04	.01
☐ 84	John LeClair	.25	.11	.03
☐ 85	Eric Desjardins	.08	.04	.01
☐ 86	Shayne Corson	.08	.04	.01
☐ 87	Stephan Lebeau	.15	.07	.02
☐ 88	Mathieu Schneider	.08	.04	.01
☐ 89	Kirk Muller	.08	.04	.01
☐ 90	Patrick Roy	.75	.35	.09
☐ 91	Sylvain Turgeon	.05	.02	.01
☐ 92	Guy Carbonneau	.08	.04	.01
☐ 93	Denis Savard	.08	.04	.01
☐ 94	Scott Niedermayer	.60	.25	.08
☐ 95	Tom Chorske	.05	.02	.01
☐ 96	Viacheslav Fetisov	.08	.04	.01
☐ 97	Kevin Todd	.20	.09	.03
☐ 98	Chris Terreri	.08	.04	.01
☐ 99	David Maley	.05	.02	.01
☐ 100	Stephane Richer	.08	.04	.01
☐ 101	Claude Lemieux	.08	.04	.01
☐ 102	Scott Stevens	.10	.05	.01
☐ 103	Peter Stastny	.08	.04	.01
☐ 104	David Volek	.05	.02	.01
☐ 105	Steve Thomas	.08	.04	.01
☐ 106	Pierre Turgeon	.40	.18	.05
☐ 107	Glenn Healy UER	.08	.04	.01
	(Misspelled Healey on card back)			
☐ 108	Derek King	.08	.04	.01
☐ 109	Uwe Krupp	.05	.02	.01
☐ 110	Ray Ferraro	.08	.04	.01
☐ 111	Pat Flatley	.05	.02	.01
☐ 112	Tom Kurvers	.05	.02	.01
☐ 113	Adam Creighton	.05	.02	.01
☐ 114	Tony Amonte UER	.60	.25	.08
	(Back says shoots right)			
☐ 115	John Ogrodnick	.05	.02	.01
☐ 116	Doug Weight	.50	.23	.06
☐ 117	Mike Richter	.50	.23	.06
☐ 118	Darren Turcotte	.05	.02	.01
☐ 119	Brian Leetch	.50	.23	.06
☐ 120	James Patrick	.05	.02	.01
☐ 121	Mark Messier	.35	.16	.04
☐ 122	Mike Gartner	.10	.05	.01
☐ 123	Mike Ricci	.20	.09	.03
☐ 124	Rod Brind'Amour	.30	.14	.04
☐ 125	Steve Duchesne	.08	.04	.01
☐ 126	Ron Hextall	.08	.04	.01
☐ 127	Brad Jones	.05	.02	.01
☐ 128	Pelle Eklund	.05	.02	.01
☐ 129	Rick Tocchet	.08	.04	.01
☐ 130	Mark Howe	.08	.04	.01
☐ 131	Andrei Lomakin	.05	.02	.01
☐ 132	Jaromir Jagr	1.00	.45	.13
☐ 133	Jim Paek	.15	.07	.02
☐ 134	Mark Recchi	.75	.35	.09
☐ 135	Kevin Stevens	.60	.25	.08
☐ 136	Phil Bourque	.05	.02	.01
☐ 137	Mario Lemieux	1.25	.55	.16
☐ 138	Bob Errey	.05	.02	.01
☐ 139	Tom Barrasso	.08	.04	.01
☐ 140	Paul Coffey	.20	.09	.03
☐ 141	Joe Mullen	.10	.05	.01
☐ 142	Kip Miller	.05	.02	.01
☐ 143	Owen Nolan	.20	.09	.03
☐ 144	Mats Sundin	.50	.23	.06
☐ 145	Mikhail Tatarinov	.05	.02	.01
☐ 146	Bryan Fogarty	.05	.02	.01
☐ 147	Stephane Morin	.05	.02	.01
☐ 148	Joe Sakic	.50	.23	.06
☐ 149	Ron Tugnutt	.05	.02	.01
☐ 150	Mike Hough	.05	.02	.01
☐ 151	Nelson Emerson	.40	.18	.05
☐ 152	Curtis Joseph	.40	.18	.05
☐ 153	Brendan Shanahan	.35	.16	.04
☐ 154	Paul Cavallini	.05	.02	.01
☐ 155	Adam Oates	.25	.11	.03
☐ 156	Jeff Brown	.08	.04	.01
☐ 157	Brett Hull	1.00	.45	.13
☐ 158	Ron Sutter	.05	.02	.01
☐ 159	Dave Christian	.05	.02	.01
☐ 160	Pat Falloon	.40	.18	.05
☐ 161	Pat MacLeod	.05	.02	.01
☐ 162	Jarmo Myllys	.05	.02	.01
☐ 163	Wayne Presley	.05	.02	.01
☐ 164	Perry Anderson	.05	.02	.01
☐ 165	Kelly Kisio	.05	.02	.01
☐ 166	Brian Mullen	.08	.04	.01
☐ 167	Brian Lawton	.05	.02	.01
☐ 168	Doug Wilson	.08	.04	.01
☐ 169	Rob Pearson	.30	.14	.04
☐ 170	Wendel Clark	.25	.11	.03
☐ 171	Brian Bradley	.08	.04	.01
☐ 172	Dave Ellett	.05	.02	.01
☐ 173	Gary Leeman	.05	.02	.01
☐ 174	Peter Zezel	.05	.02	.01
☐ 175	Grant Fuhr	.08	.04	.01
☐ 176	Bob Rouse	.05	.02	.01
☐ 177	Glenn Anderson	.08	.04	.01
☐ 178	Petr Nedved	.25	.11	.03
☐ 179	Trevor Linden	.30	.14	.04
☐ 180	Jyrki Lumme	.05	.02	.01
☐ 181	Kirk McLean	.30	.14	.04
☐ 182	Cliff Ronning	.08	.04	.01
☐ 183	Greg Adams	.05	.02	.01
☐ 184	Doug Lidster	.05	.02	.01
☐ 185	Sergio Momesso	.05	.02	.01
☐ 186	Geoff Courtnall	.08	.04	.01
☐ 187	Dave Babych	.05	.02	.01
☐ 188	Peter Bondra	.08	.04	.01
☐ 189	Dimitri Khristich	.08	.04	.01
☐ 190	Randy Burridge	.05	.02	.01
☐ 191	Kevin Hatcher	.08	.04	.01
☐ 192	Mike Ridley	.08	.04	.01
☐ 193	Dino Ciccarelli	.08	.04	.01
☐ 194	Al Iafrate	.08	.04	.01
☐ 195	Dale Hunter	.08	.04	.01
☐ 196	Mike Liut	.08	.04	.01
☐ 197	Rod Langway	.05	.02	.01
☐ 198	Russell Romaniuk	.10	.05	.01
☐ 199	Bob Essensa	.08	.04	.01

☐ 200	Teppo Numminen	.05	.02	.01
☐ 201	Darrin Shannon	.05	.02	.01
☐ 202	Pat Elynuik	.05	.02	.01
☐ 203	Fredrik Olausson	.08	.04	.01
☐ 204	Ed Olczyk	.05	.02	.01
☐ 205	Phil Housley	.08	.04	.01
☐ 206	Troy Murray	.05	.02	.01
☐ 207	Wayne Gretzky 1000	.60	.25	.08
☐ 208	Bryan Trottier 1000	.08	.04	.01
☐ 209	Peter Stastny 1000	.08	.04	.01
☐ 210	Jari Kurri 1000	.12	.05	.02
☐ 211	Denis Savard 1000	.08	.04	.01
☐ 212	Paul Coffey 1000	.12	.05	.02
☐ 213	Mark Messier 1000	.20	.09	.03
☐ 214	Dave Taylor 1000	.08	.04	.01
☐ 215	Michel Goulet 1000	.08	.04	.01
☐ 216	Dale Hawerchuk 1000	.08	.04	.01
☐ 217	Bobby Smith 1000	.08	.04	.01
☐ 218	Ed Belfour LL	.20	.09	.03
☐ 219	Brett Hull LL	.25	.11	.03
☐ 220	Patrick Roy AS	.40	.18	.05
☐ 221	Ray Bourque AS	.11	.05	.01
☐ 222	Wayne Gretzky AS	.60	.25	.08
☐ 223	Jari Kurri AS	.11	.05	.01
☐ 224	Luc Robitaille AS	.15	.07	.02
☐ 225	Paul Coffey AS	.11	.05	.01
☐ 226	Bob Carpenter	.05	.02	.01
☐ 227	Gord Murphy	.05	.02	.01
☐ 228	Don Sweeney	.05	.02	.01
☐ 229	Glen Murray	.35	.16	.04
☐ 230	Ted Donato	.25	.11	.03
☐ 231	Jozef Stumpel	.30	.14	.04
☐ 232	Stephen Heinze	.25	.11	.03
☐ 233	Adam Oates	.25	.11	.03
☐ 234	Joe Juneau	4.00	1.80	.50
☐ 235	Gord Hynes	.05	.02	.01
☐ 236	Tony Tanti	.05	.02	.01
☐ 237	Petr Svoboda	.05	.02	.01
☐ 238	Bob Corkum	.05	.02	.01
☐ 239	Ken Sutton	.10	.05	.01
☐ 240	Tom Draper	.10	.05	.01
☐ 241	Grant Ledyard	.05	.02	.01
☐ 242	Christian Ruuttu	.05	.02	.01
☐ 243	Brad Miller	.05	.02	.01
☐ 244	Clint Malarchuk	.08	.04	.01
☐ 245	Trent Yawney	.05	.02	.01
☐ 246	Craig Berube	.05	.02	.01
☐ 247	Sergei Makarov	.08	.04	.01
☐ 248	Alexander Godynyuk	.05	.02	.01
☐ 249	Paul Ranheim	.05	.02	.01
☐ 250	Jeff Reese	.05	.02	.01
☐ 251	Chris Lindberg	.05	.02	.01
☐ 252	Michel Petit	.05	.02	.01
☐ 253	Joel Otto	.05	.02	.01
☐ 254	Gary Leeman	.05	.02	.01
☐ 255	Ray LeBlanc	.15	.07	.02
☐ 256	Jocelyn Lemieux	.05	.02	.01
☐ 257	Igor Kravchuk	.25	.11	.03
☐ 258	Rob Brown	.05	.02	.01
☐ 259	Stephane Matteau	.05	.02	.01
☐ 260	Mike Hudson	.05	.02	.01
☐ 261	Keith Brown	.05	.02	.01
☐ 262	Karl Dykhuis	.05	.02	.01
☐ 263	Dominik Hasek	3.50	1.55	.45
☐ 264	Brian Noonan	.05	.02	.01
☐ 265	Yves Racine	.05	.02	.01
☐ 266	Viacheslav Kozlov	2.00	.90	.25
☐ 267	Martin Lapointe	.15	.07	.02
☐ 268	Steve Chiasson	.05	.02	.01
☐ 269	Gerard Gallant	.05	.02	.01
☐ 270	Brent Fedyk	.08	.04	.01
☐ 271	Brad McCrimmon	.05	.02	.01
☐ 272	Bob Probert	.08	.04	.01
☐ 273	Alan Kerr	.05	.02	.01
☐ 274	Luke Richardson	.05	.02	.01
☐ 275	Kelly Buchberger	.05	.02	.01
☐ 276	Craig MacTavish	.05	.02	.01
☐ 277	Ron Tugnutt	.05	.02	.01
☐ 278	Bernie Nicholls	.08	.04	.01
☐ 279	Anatoli Semenov	.05	.02	.01
☐ 280	Petr Klima	.05	.02	.01
☐ 281	Louie DeBrusk	.05	.02	.01
☐ 282	Norm MacIver	.25	.11	.03
☐ 283	Martin Gelinas	.05	.02	.01
☐ 284	Randy Cunneyworth	.05	.02	.01
☐ 285	Andrew Cassels	.08	.04	.01
☐ 286	Peter Sidorkiewicz	.05	.02	.01
☐ 287	Steve Konroyd	.05	.02	.01
☐ 288	Murray Craven	.05	.02	.01
☐ 289	Randy Ladouceur	.05	.02	.01
☐ 290	Bobby Holik	.08	.04	.01
☐ 291	Adam Burt	.05	.02	.01
☐ 292	Corey Millen	.35	.16	.04
☐ 293	Rob Blake	.25	.11	.03
☐ 294	Mike Donnelly	.20	.09	.03
☐ 295	Kyosti Karjalainen	.05	.02	.01
☐ 296	John McIntyre	.05	.02	.01
☐ 297	Paul Coffey	.20	.09	.03
☐ 298	Charlie Huddy	.05	.02	.01
☐ 299	Bob Kudelski	.20	.09	.03
☐ 300	Todd Elik	.05	.02	.01
☐ 301	Mike Craig	.05	.02	.01
☐ 302	Marc Bureau	.05	.02	.01
☐ 303	Jim Johnson	.05	.02	.01
☐ 304	Mark Tinordi	.08	.04	.01
☐ 305	Gaetan Duchesne	.05	.02	.01
☐ 306	Darcy Wakaluk	.40	.18	.05
☐ 307	Sylvain Lefebvre	.05	.02	.01
☐ 308	Russ Courtnall	.08	.04	.01
☐ 309	Patrice Brisebois	.20	.09	.03
☐ 310	Mike McPhee	.05	.02	.01
☐ 311	Mike Keane	.05	.02	.01
☐ 312	J.J. Daigneault	.05	.02	.01
☐ 313	Gilbert Dionne	.35	.16	.04
☐ 314	Brian Skrudland	.05	.02	.01
☐ 315	Brent Gilchrist	.05	.02	.01
☐ 316	Laurie Boschman	.05	.02	.01
☐ 317	Ken Daneyko	.05	.02	.01
☐ 318	Eric Weinrich	.05	.02	.01
☐ 319	Alexei Kasatonov	.08	.04	.01
☐ 320	Craig Billington	.25	.11	.03
☐ 321	Claude Vilgrain	.05	.02	.01
☐ 322	Bruce Driver	.05	.02	.01
☐ 323	Alexander Semak	.40	.18	.05
☐ 324	Valeri Zelepukin	.60	.25	.08
☐ 325	Rob DiMaio	.05	.02	.01
☐ 326	Scott Lachance	.30	.14	.04
☐ 327	Marty McInnis	.25	.11	.03
☐ 328	Joe Reekie	.05	.02	.01
☐ 329	Daniel Marois	.05	.02	.01
☐ 330	Wayne McBean	.05	.02	.01
☐ 331	Jeff Norton	.05	.02	.01
☐ 332	Benoit Hogue	.05	.02	.01
☐ 333	Tie Domi	.08	.04	.01
☐ 334	Sergei Nemchinov	.20	.09	.03
☐ 335	Randy Gilhen	.05	.02	.01
☐ 336	Paul Broten	.05	.02	.01
☐ 337	Kris King	.05	.02	.01
☐ 338	John Vanbiesbrouck	.25	.11	.03
☐ 339	Adam Graves	.50	.23	.06
☐ 340	Joe Cirella	.05	.02	.01
☐ 341	Jeff Beukeboom	.05	.02	.01
☐ 342	Terry Carkner	.05	.02	.01
☐ 343	Mark Freer	.05	.02	.01
☐ 344	Corey Foster	.05	.02	.01
☐ 345	Mark Pederson	.05	.02	.01
☐ 346	Kimbi Daniels	.05	.02	.01
☐ 347	Mark Recchi	.75	.35	.09
☐ 348	Kevin Dineen	.08	.04	.01
☐ 349	Kerry Huffman	.05	.02	.01
☐ 350	Garry Galley	.08	.04	.01
☐ 351	Dan Quinn	.05	.02	.01
☐ 352	Troy Loney	.05	.02	.01
☐ 353	Ron Francis	.08	.04	.01
☐ 354	Rick Tocchet	.08	.04	.01
☐ 355	Shawn McEachern	.75	.35	.09
☐ 356	Kjell Samuelsson	.05	.02	.01
☐ 357	Ken Wregget	.05	.02	.01
☐ 358	Larry Murphy	.08	.04	.01
☐ 359	Ken Priestlay	.05	.02	.01
☐ 360	Bryan Trottier	.08	.04	.01
☐ 361	Ulf Samuelsson	.08	.04	.01
☐ 362	Valeri Kamensky	.50	.23	.06
☐ 363	Stephane Fiset	.20	.09	.03
☐ 364	Alexei Gusarov	.10	.05	.01
☐ 365	Greg Paslawski	.05	.02	.01
☐ 366	Martin Rucinsky	.25	.11	.03
☐ 367	Curtis Leschyshyn	.05	.02	.01
☐ 368	Jacques Cloutier	.05	.02	.01
☐ 369	Craig Wolanin	.05	.02	.01
☐ 370	Claude Lapointe	.10	.05	.01
☐ 371	Adam Foote	.10	.05	.01
☐ 372	Rich Sutter	.05	.02	.01
☐ 373	Lee Norwood	.05	.02	.01
☐ 374	Garth Butcher	.05	.02	.01
☐ 375	Philippe Bozon	.15	.07	.02
☐ 376	Dave Lowry	.05	.02	.01
☐ 377	Darin Kimble	.05	.02	.01
☐ 378	Craig Janney	.15	.07	.02
☐ 379	Bob Bassen	.05	.02	.01
☐ 380	Rick Zombo	.05	.02	.01
☐ 381	Perry Berezan	.05	.02	.01
☐ 382	Neil Wilkinson	.05	.02	.01
☐ 383	Mike Sullivan	.05	.02	.01
☐ 384	David Bruce	.05	.02	.01
☐ 385	Johan Garpenlov	.05	.02	.01

☐ 386	Jeff Odgers	.15	.07	.02
☐ 387	Jayson More	.15	.07	.02
☐ 388	Dean Evason	.05	.02	.01
☐ 389	Dale Craigwell	.05	.02	.01
☐ 390	Darryl Shannon	.05	.02	.01
☐ 391	Dimitri Mironov	.20	.09	.03
☐ 392	Kent Manderville	.05	.02	.01
☐ 393	Todd Gill	.05	.02	.01
☐ 394	Rick Wamsley	.05	.02	.01
☐ 395	Joe Sacco	.20	.09	.03
☒ 396	Doug Gilmour	.50	.23	.06
☐ 397	Mike Bullard	.05	.02	.01
☐ 398	Felix Potvin	2.50	1.15	.30
☐ 399	Guy Larose	.05	.02	.01
☐ 400	Tom Fergus	.05	.02	.01
☐ 401	Ryan Walter	.05	.02	.01
☐ 402	Troy Gamble	.05	.02	.01
☐ 403	Robert Dirk	.05	.02	.01
☐ 404	Pavel Bure	2.50	1.15	.30
☐ 405	Jim Sandlak	.05	.02	.01
☐ 406	Igor Larionov	.08	.04	.01
☐ 407	Gerald Diduck	.05	.02	.01
☐ 408	Todd Krygier	.05	.02	.01
☐ 409	Tim Bergland	.05	.02	.01
☐ 410	Calle Johansson	.05	.02	.01
☐ 411	Nick Kypreos	.05	.02	.01
☐ 412	Michal Pivonka	.08	.04	.01
☐ 413	Brad Schlegel	.05	.02	.01
☐ 414	Kelly Miller	.05	.02	.01
☐ 415	John Druce	.05	.02	.01
☐ 416	Don Beaupre	.08	.04	.01
☐ 417	Alan May	.05	.02	.01
☐ 418	Randy Carlyle	.05	.02	.01
☐ 419	Stu Barnes	.08	.04	.01
☐ 420	Mike Eagles	.05	.02	.01
☐ 421	Igor Ulanov	.15	.07	.02
☐ 422	Evgeny Davydov	.20	.09	.03
☐ 423	Shawn Cronin	.05	.02	.01
☐ 424	Keith Tkachuk	2.00	.90	.25
☐ 425	Luciano Borsato	.15	.07	.02
☐ 426	Stephane Beauregard	.05	.02	.01
☐ 427	Mike Lalor	.05	.02	.01
☐ 428	Michel Goulet 500	.08	.04	.01
	Chicago Blackhawks			
☐ 429	Wayne Gretzky 500	.60	.25	.08
	Los Angeles Kings			
☐ 430	Mike Gartner 500	.12	.05	.02
	New York Rangers			
☐ 431	Bryan Trottier 500	.08	.04	.01
	Pittsburgh Penguins			
☐ 432	Brett Hull LL	.25	.11	.03
	St. Louis Blues			
☐ 433	Wayne Gretzky LL	.60	.25	.08
	Los Angeles Kings			
☐ 434	Steve Yzerman LL	.20	.09	.03
	Detroit Red Wings			
☐ 435	Paul Ysebaert LL	.08	.04	.01
	Detroit Red Wings			
☐ 436	Gary Roberts LL	.08	.04	.01
	Calgary Flames			
☐ 437	Dave Andreychuk LL	.12	.05	.02
	Buffalo Sabres			
☐ 438	Brian Leetch LL	.20	.09	.03
	New York Rangers			
☐ 439	Jeremy Roenick LL	.25	.11	.03
	Chicago Blackhawks			
☐ 440	Kirk McLean LL	.12	.05	.02
	Vancouver Canucks			
☐ 441	Tim Cheveldae LL	.08	.04	.01
	Detroit Red Wings			
☐ 442	Patrick Roy LL	.40	.18	.05
	Montreal Canadiens			
☐ 443	Tony Amonte RL	.25	.11	.03
	New York Rangers			
☐ 444	Kevin Todd RL	.06	.03	.01
	New Jersey Devils			
☐ 445	Nicklas Lidstrom RL	.20	.09	.03
	Detroit Red Wings			
☐ 446	Pavel Bure RL	.75	.35	.09
	Vancouver Canucks			
☐ 447	Gilbert Dionne RL	.15	.07	.02
	Montreal Canadiens			
☐ 448	Tom Draper RL	.06	.03	.01
	Buffalo Sabres			
☐ 449	Dominik Hasek RL	.75	.35	.09
	Chicago Blackhawks			
☐ 450	Dominic Roussel RL	.50	.23	.06
☐ 451	Header/Checklist	1.00	.45	.13
☐ 452	Trent Klatt	2.50	1.15	.30
☐ 453	Bill Guerin	2.50	1.15	.30
☐ 454	Ray Whitney	3.00	1.35	.40
☐ 455	Boston Bruins	1.00	.45	.13
	Adams Winner			

☐ 456	Pittsburgh Penguins	1.50	.65	.19
	Patrick Winner			
☐ 457	Chicago Blackhawks	1.00	.45	.13
	Norris Winner			
☐ 458	Edmonton Oilers	1.00	.45	.13
	Smythe Winner			
☐ 459	Pittsburgh Penguins	2.00	.90	.25
	Wales Winner			
☐ 460	Chicago Blackhawks	1.00	.45	.13
	Campbell Winner			
☐ 461	Pittsburgh Penguins	1.50	.65	.19
	Stanley Cup Winner			
☐ 462	Pavel Bure	14.00	6.25	1.75
	Calder Winner			
☐ 463	Patrick Roy	12.00	5.50	1.50
	Vezina Winner			
☐ 464	Brian Leetch	5.00	2.30	.60
	Norris Winner			
☐ 465	Wayne Gretzky	15.00	6.75	1.90
	Lady Byng Winner			
☐ 466	Guy Carbonneau	1.00	.45	.13
	Selke Winner			
☐ 467	Mario Lemieux	10.00	4.50	1.25
	Smythe Winner			
☐ 468	Mark Messier	3.50	1.55	.45
	Pearson Winner			
☐ 469	Ray Bourque	2.50	1.15	.30
	Clancy Winner			
☐ 470	Patrick Roy AS	12.00	5.50	1.50
☐ 471	Brian Leetch AS	5.00	2.30	.60
☐ 472	Ray Bourque AS	2.50	1.15	.30
☐ 473	Kevin Stevens AS	2.50	1.15	.30
☐ 474	Brett Hull AS	6.00	2.70	.75
☐ 475	Mark Messier AS	3.50	1.55	.45
☐ NNO	Santa Claus	2.00	.90	.25

1991-92 Parkhurst PHC

This nine-card set was randomly inserted in packs of 1991-92 Parkhurst hockey cards with the first five being in the first series and the last four in the second series. PHC stands for Parkhurst Collectibles. The second series PHC cards are four special "Award Winner" collectibles. The cards are standard size (2 1/2" by 3 1/2") and are numnbered with a "PHC" prefix.

	MINT	EXC	G-VG
COMPLETE SET (9)	18.00	8.00	2.30
COMMON PLAYER (PHC1-PHC9)	1.25	.55	.16

☐ PHC1	Gordie Howe	5.00	2.30	.60
	Detroit Red Wings			
☐ PHC2	Alex Delvecchio	1.25	.55	.16
	Detroit Red Wings			
☐ PHC3	Ken Hodge Jr.	1.25	.55	.16
	Boston Bruins			
☐ PHC4	Robert Kron	1.25	.55	.16
	Vancouver Canucks			
☐ PHC5	Sergei Fedorov	5.00	2.30	.60
	Detroit Red Wings			
☐ PHC6	Brett Hull	4.00	1.80	.50
	St. Louis Blues			
☐ PHC7	Mario Lemieux	5.00	2.30	.60
	Pittsburgh Penguins			
☐ PHC8	New York Rangers	3.00	1.35	.40
	(Brian Leetch/Mark Messier/			
	John Ziegler)			
☐ PHC9	Terry Sawchuk	2.00	.90	.25
	Detroit Red Wings			

1992-93 Parkhurst Previews

Randomly inserted in 1992-93 Pro Set foil packs, these five preview cards were issued to show the design of the 1992-93 Parkhurst issue. The cards measure the standard size (2 1/2") by 3 1/2"). The fronts feature color action player photos that are full-bleed except for one edge that is bordered by a dark blue-green marbleized stripe. The player's name is

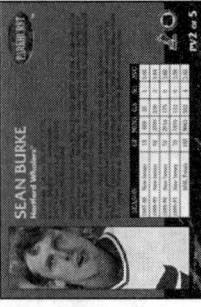

printed vertically in this stripe. The Parkhurst logo overlays the stripe. The backs have a bluish-green background and carry small close-up shots, biography, statistics, and career highlights in French and English. The cards are numbered on the back with a "PV" prefix.

	MINT	EXC	G-VG
COMPLETE SET (5)	7.50	3.40	.95
COMMON PLAYER (PV1-PV5)	1.50	.65	.19
☐ PV1 Paul Ysebaert	1.50	.65	.19
Detroit Red Wings			
☐ PV2 Sean Burke	1.50	.65	.19
Hartford Whalers			
☐ PV3 Gilbert Dionne	1.50	.65	.19
Montreal Canadiens			
☐ PV4 Ken Hammond	1.50	.65	.19
Ottawa Senators			
☐ PV5 Grant Fuhr	1.50	.65	.19
Toronto Maple Leafs			

1992-93 Parkhurst

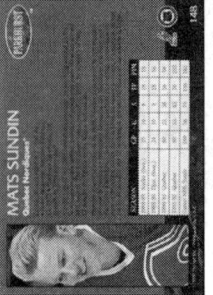

The 1992-93 Parkhurst set consists of 510 cards, measuring the standard size (2 1/2" by 3 1/2"). The set was released in three series with 240, 240, and 30 cards, respectively. The first series production run was reportedly 7,000 numbered 20-box foil cases with a nine-card insert set of Parkie Reprint cards randomly inserted into first series foil packs. Also reportedly produced were 3,000 five-box cases of jumbo packs distributed along with another nine-card random insert set of Parkie Reprint cards of defensemen. Each pack also includes one Emerald Ice card distinguished by a foil-stamped and embossed Parkhurst logo. Since a limited number of every card in the set was foil-stamped and embossed, an entire 240-card Emerald Ice set was achievable. The fronts feature color action player photos that are full-bleed except for one edge that is bordered by a dark blue-green marbleized stripe. The Parkhurst logo overlays the stripe. The backs have a bluish green background and carry small close-up shots,

biographies, statistics, and career highlights in French and English. The second series featured traded players in their new uniforms as well as 35 Calder Candidates. As in the first series, one Emerald Ice card was inserted in each foil pack. Randomly inserted throughout the foil packs were a nine-card Parkie Reprint set and a 21-card Don Cherry "Cherry Picks" set. All cases included one Parkie Reprint commemorative sheet and one Parkhurst poster; Canadian cases only also included a newly created 1954-55 Don Cherry Parkhurst card. The cards are numbered on the back and checklisted below alphabetically according to teams as follows: Boston Bruins (1-9), Buffalo Sabres (10-18), Calgary Flames (19-27), Chicago Blackhawks (28-36), Detroit Red Wings (37-45), Edmonton Oilers (46-54), Hartford Whalers (55-62), Los Angeles Kings (63-71), Minnesota North Stars (72-79), Montreal Canadiens (80-88), New Jersey Devils (89-97), New York Islanders (98-106), New York Rangers (107-115), Ottawa Senators (116-124), Philadelphia Flyers (125-133), Pittsburgh Penguins (134-142), Quebec Nordiques (143-151), St. Louis Blues (152-159), San Jose Sharks (160-168), Tampa Bay Lightning (169-177), Toronto Maple Leafs (178-187), Vancouver Canucks (188-196), Washington Capitals (197-205), Winnipeg Jets (206-214), International Rising Stars (215-227), Sensational Sophomores (228-240), Boston Bruins (241-249), Buffalo Sabres (250-257), Calgary Flames (258-266), Chicago Blackhawks (267-275), Detroit Red Wings (276-283), Edmonton Oilers (284-292), Hartford Whalers (293-300), Los Angeles Kings (301-309), Minnesota North Stars (310-317), Montreal Canadiens (318-326), New Jersey Devils (327-334), New York Islanders (335-343), New York Rangers (344-351), Ottawa Senators (352-359), Philadelphia Flyers (360-367), Pittsburgh Penguins (368-375), Quebec Nordiques (376-383), St. Louis Blues (384-391), San Jose Sharks (392-399), Tampa Bay Lightning (400-408), Toronto Maple Leafs (409-417), Vancouver Canucks (418-425), Washington Capitals (426-433), Winnipeg Jets (434-442), International Rising Stars (443-455), Campbell All-Stars (456-461), Wales All-Stars (462-467), and Philadelphia Flyers Dynasty (468-480). An update set was issued in set form only. Like the first two series, these cards were also available in Emerald Ice form. The update set is cards numbers 481-510. Rookie Cards in the set include Nikolai Borschevsky, Roman Hamrlik, Andrei Kovalenko, Tommy Soderstrom and Sergei Zubov.

	MINT	EXC	G-VG
COMPLETE SET (510)	45.00	20.00	5.75
COMPLETE SERIES 1 (240)	18.00	8.00	2.30
COMPLETE SERIES 2 (240)	15.00	6.75	1.90
COMPLETE FIN.UPDATE (30)	12.00	5.50	1.50
COMMON PLAYER (1-240)	.05	.02	.01
COMMON PLAYER (241-480)	.05	.02	.01
COMMON PLAYER (481-510)	.15	.07	.02
☐ 1 Ray Bourque	.20	.09	.03
☐ 2 Joe Juneau	1.50	.65	.19
☐ 3 Andy Moog	.08	.04	.01
☐ 4 Adam Oates	.20	.09	.03
☐ 5 Vladimir Ruzicka	.05	.02	.01
☐ 6 Glen Wesley	.05	.02	.01
☐ 7 Dmitri Kvartalnov	.25	.11	.03
☐ 8 Ted Donato	.05	.02	.01
☐ 9 Glen Murray	.05	.02	.01
☐ 10 Dave Andreychuk	.20	.09	.03
☐ 11 Dale Hawerchuk	.08	.04	.01
☐ 12 Pat LaFontaine	.30	.14	.04
☐ 13 Alexander Mogilny	.50	.23	.06
☐ 14 Richard Smehlik	.25	.11	.03
☐ 15 Keith Carney	.15	.07	.02
☐ 16 Philippe Boucher	.05	.02	.01
☐ 17 Viktor Gordijuk	.25	.11	.03
☐ 18 Donald Audette	.05	.02	.01
☐ 19 Theoren Fleury	.10	.05	.01
☐ 20 Al MacInnis	.10	.05	.01
☐ 21 Joe Nieuwendyk	.08	.04	.01

☐	22	Gary Roberts	.08	.04	.01
☐	23	Gary Suter	.08	.04	.01
☐	24	Mike Vernon	.08	.04	.01
☐	25	Sergei Makarov	.08	.04	.01
☐	26	Robert Reichel	.08	.04	.01
☐	27	Chris Lindberg	.05	.02	.01
☐	28	Ed Belfour	.30	.14	.04
☐	29	Chris Chelios	.08	.04	.01
☐	30	Steve Larmer	.08	.04	.01
☐	31	Jeremy Roenick	.75	.35	.09
☐	32	Steve Smith	.08	.04	.01
☐	33	Brent Sutter	.08	.04	.01
☐	34	Christian Ruuttu	.05	.02	.01
☐	35	Igor Kravchuk	.05	.02	.01
☐	36	Sergei Krivokasov	.20	.09	.03
☐	37	Tim Cheveldae	.08	.04	.01
☐	38	Mike Sillinger	.05	.02	.01
☐	39	Sergei Fedorov	1.00	.45	.13
☐	40	Viacheslav Kozlov	1.00	.45	.13
☐	41	Bob Probert	.05	.02	.01
☐	42	Nicklas Lidstrom	.20	.09	.03
☐	43	Paul Ysebaert	.05	.02	.01
☐	44	Steve Yzerman	.35	.16	.04
☐	45	Dino Ciccarelli	.08	.04	.01
☐	46	Esa Tikkanen	.08	.04	.01
☐	47	Dave Manson	.05	.02	.01
☐	48	Craig MacTavish	.05	.02	.01
☐	49	Bernie Nicholls	.08	.04	.01
☐	50	Bill Ranford	.08	.04	.01
☐	51	Craig Simpson	.05	.02	.01
☐	52	Scott Mellanby	.05	.02	.01
☐	53	Shayne Corson	.08	.04	.01
☐	54	Petr Klima	.05	.02	.01
☐	55	Murray Craven	.05	.02	.01
☐	56	Eric Weinrich	.05	.02	.01
☐	57	Sean Burke	.08	.04	.01
☐	58	Pat Verbeek	.08	.04	.01
☐	59	Zarley Zalapski	.05	.02	.01
☐	60	Patrick Poulin	.05	.02	.01
☐	61	Robert Petrovicky	.20	.09	.03
☐	62	Geoff Sanderson	.40	.18	.05
☐	63	Paul Coffey	.20	.09	.03
☐	64	Robert Lang	.25	.11	.03
☐	65	Wayne Gretzky	1.50	.65	.19
☐	66	Kelly Hrudey	.08	.04	.01
☐	67	Jari Kurri	.10	.05	.01
☐	68	Luc Robitaille	.25	.11	.03
☐	69	Darryl Sydor	.08	.04	.01
☐	70	Jim Hiller	.10	.05	.01
☐	71	Alexei Zhitnik	.25	.11	.03
☐	72	Derian Hatcher	.05	.02	.01
☐	73	Jon Casey	.08	.04	.01
☐	74	Richard Matvichuk	.15	.07	.02
☐	75	Mike Modano	.35	.16	.04
☐	76	Mark Tinordi	.08	.04	.01
☐	77	Todd Elik	.05	.02	.01
☐	78	Russ Courtnall	.08	.04	.01
☐	79	Tommy Sjodin	.10	.05	.01
☐	80	Eric Desjardins	.05	.02	.01
☐	81	Gilbert Dionne	.05	.02	.01
☐	82	Stephan Lebeau	.05	.02	.01
☐	83	Kirk Muller	.08	.04	.01
☐	84	Patrick Roy	.75	.35	.09
☐	85	Denis Savard	.08	.04	.01
☐	86	Vin Damphousse	.08	.04	.01
☐	87	Brian Bellows	.08	.04	.01
☐	88	Ed Ronan	.15	.07	.02
☐	89	Claude Lemieux	.08	.04	.01
☐	90	John MacLean	.08	.04	.01
☐	91	Stephane Richer	.08	.04	.01
☐	92	Scott Stevens	.10	.05	.01
☐	93	Chris Terreri	.08	.04	.01
☐	94	Kevin Todd	.05	.02	.01
☐	95	Scott Niedermayer	.40	.18	.05
☐	96	Bobby Holik	.05	.02	.01
☐	97	Bill Guerin	.25	.11	.03
☐	98	Ray Ferraro	.05	.02	.01
☐	99	Mark Fitzpatrick	.08	.04	.01
☐	100	Derek King	.05	.02	.01
☐	101	Uwe Krupp	.05	.02	.01
☐	102	Darius Kasparaitis	.15	.07	.02
☐	103	Pierre Turgeon	.30	.14	.04
☐	104	Benoit Hogue	.05	.02	.01
☐	105	Scott Lachance	.05	.02	.01
☐	106	Marty McInnis	.05	.02	.01
☐	107	Tony Amonte	.20	.09	.03
☐	108	Mike Gartner	.10	.05	.01
☐	109	Alexei Kovalev	1.00	.45	.13
☐	110	Brian Leetch	.35	.16	.04
☐	111	Mark Messier	.25	.11	.03
☐	112	Mike Richter	.30	.14	.04
☐	113	James Patrick	.05	.02	.01
☐	114	Sergei Nemchinov	.08	.04	.01
☐	115	Doug Weight	.08	.04	.01
☐	116	Mark Lamb	.05	.02	.01
☐	117	Norm MacIver	.05	.02	.01
☐	118	Mike Peluso	.05	.02	.01
☐	119	Jody Hull	.05	.02	.01
☐	120	Peter Sidorkiewicz	.05	.02	.01
☐	121	Sylvain Turgeon	.05	.02	.01
☐	122	Laurie Boschman	.05	.02	.01
☐	123	Brad Marsh	.08	.04	.01
☐	124	Neil Brady	.05	.02	.01
☐	125	Brian Benning	.05	.02	.01
☐	126	Rod BrindAmour	.20	.09	.03
☐	127	Kevin Dineen	.08	.04	.01
☐	128	Eric Lindros	5.00	2.30	.60
☐	129	Dominic Roussel	.20	.09	.03
☐	130	Mark Recchi	.30	.14	.04
☐	131	Brent Fedyk	.05	.02	.01
☐	132	Greg Paslawski	.05	.02	.01
☐	133	Dimitri Yushkevich	.20	.09	.03
☐	134	Tom Barrasso	.08	.04	.01
☐	135	Jaromir Jagr	.60	.25	.08
☐	136	Mario Lemieux	1.25	.55	.16
☐	137	Larry Murphy	.08	.04	.01
☐	138	Kevin Stevens	.30	.14	.04
☐	139	Rick Tocchet	.08	.04	.01
☐	140	Martin Straka	1.00	.45	.13
☐	141	Ron Francis	.08	.04	.01
☐	142	Shawn McEachern	.20	.09	.03
☐	143	Steve Duchesne	.08	.04	.01
☐	144	Ron Hextall	.08	.04	.01
☐	145	Owen Nolan	.08	.04	.01
☐	146	Mike Ricci	.08	.04	.01
☐	147	Joe Sakic	.25	.11	.03
☐	148	Mats Sundin	.25	.11	.03
☐	149	Martin Rucinsky	.05	.02	.01
☐	150	Andrei Kovalenko	.40	.18	.05
☐	151	Dave Karpa	.10	.05	.01
☐	152	Nelson Emerson	.20	.09	.03
☐	153	Brett Hull	.75	.35	.09
☐	154	Craig Janney	.15	.07	.02
☐	155	Curtis Joseph	.30	.14	.04
☐	156	Brendan Shanahan	.30	.14	.04
☐	157	Vitali Prokhorov	.15	.07	.02
☐	158	Igor Korolev	.15	.07	.02
☐	159	Philippe Bozon	.05	.02	.01
☐	160	Ray Whitney	.25	.11	.03
☐	161	Pat Falloon	.20	.09	.03
☐	162	Jeff Hackett	.05	.02	.01
☐	163	Brian Lawton	.05	.02	.01
☐	164	Sandis Ozolinsh	.50	.23	.06
☐	165	Neil Wilkinson	.05	.02	.01
☐	166	Kelly Kisio	.05	.02	.01
☐	167	Doug Wilson	.08	.04	.01
☐	168	Dale Craigwell	.05	.02	.01
☐	169	Mikael Andersson	.05	.02	.01
☐	170	Wendell Young	.05	.02	.01
☐	171	Rob Zamuner	.15	.07	.02
☐	172	Adam Creighton	.05	.02	.01
☐	173	Roman Hamrlik	.50	.23	.06
☐	174	Brian Bradley	.05	.02	.01
☐	175	Rob Ramage	.05	.02	.01
☐	176	Chris Kontos	.15	.07	.02
☐	177	Stan Drulia	.05	.02	.01
☐	178	Glenn Anderson	.08	.04	.01
☐	179	Wendel Clark	.10	.05	.01
☐	180	John Cullen	.05	.02	.01
☐	181	Dave Ellett	.05	.02	.01
☐	182	Grant Fuhr	.08	.04	.01
☐	183	Doug Gilmour	.35	.16	.04
☐	184	Kent Manderville	.05	.02	.01
☐	185	Joe Sacco	.05	.02	.01
☐	186	Nikolai Borschevsky	.40	.18	.05
☐	187	Felix Potvin	2.00	.90	.25
☐	188	Pavel Bure	2.50	1.15	.30
☐	189	Geoff Courtnall	.05	.02	.01
☐	190	Trevor Linden	.25	.11	.03
☐	191	Jyrki Lumme	.05	.02	.01
☐	192	Kirk McLean	.25	.11	.03
☐	193	Cliff Ronning	.05	.02	.01
☐	194	Dixon Ward	.15	.07	.02
☐	195	Greg Adams	.05	.02	.01
☐	196	Jiri Slegr	.05	.02	.01
☐	197	Don Beaupre	.08	.04	.01
☐	198	Kevin Hatcher	.08	.04	.01
☐	199	Brad Schlegel	.05	.02	.01
☐	200	Mike Ridley	.08	.04	.01
☐	201	Calle Johansson	.05	.02	.01
☐	202	Steve Konowalchuk	.15	.07	.02
☐	203	Al Iafrate	.08	.04	.01
☐	204	Peter Bondra	.20	.09	.03
☐	205	Pat Elynuik	.05	.02	.01
☐	206	Keith Tkachuk	.35	.16	.04
☐	207	Bob Essensa	.08	.04	.01

☐ 208	Phil Housley	.08	.04	.01
☐ 209	Teemu Selanne	2.00	.90	.25
☐ 210	Alexei Zhamnov	.50	.23	.06
☐ 211	Evgeny Davydov	.05	.02	.01
☐ 212	Fredrik Olausson	.05	.02	.01
☐ 213	Ed Olczyk	.05	.02	.01
☐ 214	Thomas Steen	.05	.02	.01
☐ 215	Darius Kasparaitis New York Islanders	.08	.04	.01
☐ 216	Nikolai Borschevsky Toronto Maple Leafs	.20	.09	.03
☐ 217	Teemu Selanne Winnipeg Jets	1.00	.45	.13
☐ 218	Alexander Mogilny Buffalo Sabres	.25	.11	.03
☐ 219	Sergei Fedorov Detroit Red Wings	.40	.18	.05
☐ 220	Jaromir Jagr Pittsburgh Penguins	.30	.14	.04
☐ 221	Mats Sundin Quebec Nordiques	.20	.09	.03
☐ 222	Dimitri Kvartalnov Boston Bruins	.15	.07	.02
☐ 223	Andrei Kovalenko Quebec Nordiques	.15	.07	.02
☐ 224	Tommy Sjodin Minnesota North Stars	.08	.04	.01
☐ 225	Alexei Kovalev New York Rangers	.50	.23	.06
☐ 226	Evgeny Davydov Winnipeg Jets	.08	.04	.01
☐ 227	Robert Lang Los Angeles Kings	.15	.07	.02
☐ 228	Valeri Zelepukin New Jersey Devils	.15	.07	.02
☐ 229	Doug Weight New York Rangers	.08	.04	.01
☐ 230	Valeri Kamensky Quebec Nordiques	.15	.07	.02
☐ 231	Donald Audette Buffalo Sabres	.08	.04	.01
☐ 232	Nelson Emerson St. Louis Blues	.15	.07	.02
☐ 233	Pat Falloon San Jose Sharks	.15	.07	.02
☐ 234	Pavel Bure Vancouver Canucks	1.00	.45	.13
☐ 235	Tony Amonte New York Rangers	.15	.07	.02
☐ 236	Sergei Nemchinov New York Rangers	.08	.04	.01
☐ 237	Gilbert Dionne Montreal Canadiens	.08	.04	.01
☐ 238	Kevin Todd New Jersey Devils	.08	.04	.01
☐ 239	Nicklas Lidstrom Detroit Red Wings	.11	.05	.01
☐ 240	Brad May Buffalo Sabres	.08	.04	.01
☐ 241	Stephen Leach	.05	.02	.01
☐ 242	Dave Poulin	.05	.02	.01
☐ 243	Grigori Panteleyev	.10	.05	.01
☐ 244	Don Sweeney	.05	.02	.01
☐ 245	John Blue	.25	.11	.03
☐ 246	C.J. Young	.15	.07	.02
☐ 247	Stephen Heinze	.05	.02	.01
☐ 248	Cam Neely	.20	.09	.03
☐ 249	Dave Reid	.05	.02	.01
☐ 250	Grant Fuhr	.08	.04	.01
☐ 251	Bob Sweeney	.05	.02	.01
☐ 252	Rob Ray	.05	.02	.01
☐ 253	Doug Bodger	.05	.02	.01
☐ 254	Ken Sutton	.05	.02	.01
☐ 255	Yuri Khmylev	.35	.16	.04
☐ 256	Mike Ramsey	.05	.02	.01
☐ 257	Brad May	.05	.02	.01
☐ 258	Brent Ashton	.05	.02	.01
☐ 259	Joel Otto	.05	.02	.01
☐ 260	Paul Ranheim	.05	.02	.01
☐ 261	Kevin Dahl	.05	.02	.01
☐ 262	Trent Yawney	.05	.02	.01
☐ 263	Roger Johansson	.05	.02	.01
☐ 264	Jeff Reese	.05	.02	.01
☐ 265	Ron Stern	.05	.02	.01
☐ 266	Brian Skrudland	.05	.02	.01
☐ 267	Bryan Marchment	.05	.02	.01
☐ 268	Stephane Matteau	.05	.02	.01
☐ 269	Frantisek Kucera	.05	.02	.01
☐ 270	Jim Waite	.05	.02	.01
☐ 271	Dirk Graham	.05	.02	.01
☐ 272	Michel Goulet	.08	.04	.01
☐ 273	Joe Murphy	.05	.02	.01
☐ 274	Keith Brown	.05	.02	.01
☐ 275	Jocelyn Lemieux	.05	.02	.01
☐ 276	Paul Coffey	.20	.09	.03
☐ 277	Keith Primeau	.08	.04	.01
☐ 278	Vincent Riendeau	.05	.02	.01
☐ 279	Mark Howe	.08	.04	.01
☐ 280	Ray Sheppard	.08	.04	.01
☐ 281	Jim Hiller	.10	.05	.01
☐ 282	Steve Chiasson	.05	.02	.01
☐ 283	Vladimir Konstantinov	.05	.02	.01
☐ 284	Brian Benning	.05	.02	.01
☐ 285	Kevin Todd	.05	.02	.01
☐ 286	Zdeno Ciger	.05	.02	.01
☐ 287	Brian Glynn	.05	.02	.01
☐ 288	Shaun Van Allen	.05	.02	.01
☐ 289	Brad Werenka	.15	.07	.02
☐ 290	Ron Tugnutt	.05	.02	.01
☐ 291	Igor Kravchuk	.05	.02	.01
☐ 292	Todd Elik	.05	.02	.01
☐ 293	Terry Yake	.05	.02	.01
☐ 294	Michael Nylander	.40	.18	.05
☐ 295	Yvon Corriveau	.05	.02	.01
☐ 296	Frank Pietrangelo	.05	.02	.01
☐ 297	Nick Kypreos	.05	.02	.01
☐ 298	Andrew Cassels	.05	.02	.01
☐ 299	Steve Konroyd	.05	.02	.01
☐ 300	Allen Pedersen	.05	.02	.01
☐ 301	Tony Granato	.05	.02	.01
☐ 302	Rob Blake	.10	.05	.01
☐ 303	Robb Stauber	.05	.02	.01
☐ 304	Marty McSorley	.08	.04	.01
☐ 305	Lonnie Loach	.05	.02	.01
☐ 306	Corey Millen	.08	.04	.01
☐ 307	Dave Taylor	.08	.04	.01
☐ 308	Jimmy Carson	.05	.02	.01
☐ 309	Warren Rychel	.15	.07	.02
☐ 310	Ulf Dahlen	.05	.02	.01
☐ 311	Dave Gagner	.08	.04	.01
☐ 312	Brad Berry	.05	.02	.01
☐ 313	Neal Broten	.08	.04	.01
☐ 314	Mike Craig	.05	.02	.01
☐ 315	Darcy Wakaluk	.08	.04	.01
☐ 316	Shane Churla	.05	.02	.01
☐ 317	Trent Klatt	.20	.09	.03
☐ 318	Mike Keane	.05	.02	.01
☐ 319	Mathieu Schneider	.08	.04	.01
☐ 320	Patrice Brisebois	.05	.02	.01
☐ 321	Andre Racicot	.05	.02	.01
☐ 322	Mario Roberge	.05	.02	.01
☐ 323	Gary Leeman	.05	.02	.01
☐ 324	Jean-Jacques Daigneault	.05	.02	.01
☐ 325	Lyle Odelein	.05	.02	.01
☐ 326	John LeClair	.05	.02	.01
☐ 327	Valeri Zelepukin	.20	.09	.03
☐ 328	Bernie Nicholls	.08	.04	.01
☐ 329	Alexander Semak	.05	.02	.01
☐ 330	Craig Billington	.05	.02	.01
☐ 331	Randy McKay	.05	.02	.01
☐ 332	Ken Daneyko	.05	.02	.01
☐ 333	Bruce Driver	.05	.02	.01
☐ 334	Viacheslav Fetisov	.05	.02	.01
☐ 335	Dennis Vaske	.05	.02	.01
☐ 336	Brad Dalgarno	.05	.02	.01
☐ 337	Jeff Norton	.05	.02	.01
☐ 338	Steve Thomas	.08	.04	.01
☐ 339	Vladimir Malakhov	.25	.11	.03
☐ 340	David Volek	.05	.02	.01
☐ 341	Glenn Healy	.08	.04	.01
☐ 342	Patrick Flatley	.05	.02	.01
☐ 343	Travis Green	.15	.07	.02
☐ 344	Corey Hirsch	.50	.23	.06
☐ 345	Darren Turcotte	.05	.02	.01
☐ 346	Adam Graves	.35	.16	.04
☐ 347	Steve King	.15	.07	.02
☐ 348	Kevin Lowe	.05	.02	.01
☐ 349	John Vanbiesbrouck	.10	.05	.01
☐ 350	Ed Olczyk	.05	.02	.01
☐ 351	Sergei Zubov	2.50	1.15	.30
☐ 352	Brad Shaw	.05	.02	.01
☐ 353	Jamie Baker	.05	.02	.01
☐ 354	Mark Freer	.05	.02	.01
☐ 355	Darcy Loewen	.05	.02	.01
☐ 356	Darren Rumble	.10	.05	.01
☐ 357	Bob Kudelski	.08	.04	.01
☐ 358	Ken Hammond	.05	.02	.01
☐ 359	Daniel Berthiaume	.05	.02	.01
☐ 360	Josef Beranek	.20	.09	.03
☐ 361	Greg Hawgood	.05	.02	.01
☐ 362	Terry Carkner	.05	.02	.01
☐ 363	Vyacheslav Butsayev	.20	.09	.03
☐ 364	Garry Galley	.05	.02	.01
☐ 365	Andre Faust	.10	.05	.01
☐ 366	Ryan McGill	.10	.05	.01

☐	367	Tommy Soderstrom	.40	.18	.05
☐	368	Joe Mullen	.08	.04	.01
☐	369	Ulf Samuelsson	.08	.04	.01
☐	370	Mike Needham	.15	.07	.02
☐	371	Ken Wregget	.05	.02	.01
☐	372	Dave Tippett	.05	.02	.01
☐	373	Kjell Samuelsson	.05	.02	.01
☐	374	Bob Errey	.05	.02	.01
☐	375	Jim Paek	.05	.02	.01
☐	376	Bill Lindsay	.15	.07	.02
☐	377	Valeri Kamensky	.20	.09	.03
☐	378	Stephane Fiset	.08	.04	.01
☐	379	Steven Finn	.05	.02	.01
☐	380	Mike Hough	.05	.02	.01
☐	381	Scott Pearson	.05	.02	.01
☐	382	Kerry Huffman	.05	.02	.01
☐	383	Scott Young	.05	.02	.01
☐	384	Stephane Quintal	.05	.02	.01
☐	385	Bret Hedican	.20	.09	.03
☐	386	Guy Hebert	.50	.23	.06
☐	387	Vitali Karamnov	.15	.07	.02
☐	388	Doug Crossman	.05	.02	.01
☐	389	Ron Sutter	.05	.02	.01
☐	390	Garth Butcher	.05	.02	.01
☐	391	Basil McRae	.05	.02	.01
☐	392	Dean Evason	.05	.02	.01
☐	393	Doug Zmolek	.15	.07	.02
☐	394	Jay More	.05	.02	.01
☐	395	Mike Sullivan	.05	.02	.01
☐	396	Arturs Irbe	.50	.23	.06
☐	397	Johan Garpenlov	.05	.02	.01
☐	398	Jeff Odgers	.05	.02	.01
☐	399	Jaroslav Otevrel	.15	.07	.02
☐	400	Marc Bureau	.05	.02	.01
☐	401	Bob Beers	.05	.02	.01
☐	402	Rob DiMaio	.05	.02	.01
☐	403	Steve Kasper	.05	.02	.01
☐	404	Pat Jablonski	.05	.02	.01
☐	405	John Tucker	.05	.02	.01
☐	406	Shawn Chambers	.05	.02	.01
☐	407	Mike Hartman	.05	.02	.01
☐	408	Danton Cole	.05	.02	.01
☐	409	Dave Andreychuk	.20	.09	.03
☐	410	Peter Zezel	.05	.02	.01
☐	411	Mike Krushelnyski	.05	.02	.01
☐	412	Daren Puppa	.08	.04	.01
☐	413	Ken Baumgartner	.05	.02	.01
☐	414	Rob Pearson	.05	.02	.01
☐	415	Mike Foligno	.05	.02	.01
☐	416	Sylvain Lefebvre	.05	.02	.01
☐	417	Dimitri Mironov	.08	.04	.01
☐	418	Petr Nedved	.25	.11	.03
☐	419	Gerald Diduck	.05	.02	.01
☐	420	Anatoli Semenov	.05	.02	.01
☐	421	Sergio Momesso	.05	.02	.01
☐	422	Gino Odjick	.05	.02	.01
☐	423	Kay Whitmore	.05	.02	.01
☐	424	Dave Babych	.05	.02	.01
☐	425	Robert Dirk	.05	.02	.01
☐	426	Reggie Savage	.05	.02	.01
☐	427	Keith Jones	.15	.07	.02
☐	428	Dimitri Khristich	.08	.04	.01
☐	429	Jason Woolley	.10	.05	.01
☐	430	Jim Hrivnak	.05	.02	.01
☐	431	Sylvain Cote	.05	.02	.01
☐	432	Michal Pivonka	.08	.04	.01
☐	433	Rod Langway	.05	.02	.01
☐	434	Tie Domi	.05	.02	.01
☐	435	Sergei Bautin	.15	.07	.02
☐	436	Darrin Shannon	.05	.02	.01
☐	437	John Druce	.05	.02	.01
☐	438	Teppo Numminen	.05	.02	.01
☐	439	Luciano Borsato	.05	.02	.01
☐	440	Igor Ulanov	.05	.02	.01
☐	441	Mike O'Neill	.15	.07	.02
☐	442	Kris King	.05	.02	.01
☐	443	Roman Hamrlik	.20	.09	.03
		Tampa Bay Lightning			
☐	444	Steve Smith	.08	.04	.01
		Chicago Blackhawks			
☐	445	Jari Kurri	.10	.05	.01
		Los Angeles Kings			
☐	446	Ulf Samuelsson	.08	.04	.01
		Pittsburgh Penguins			
☐	447	Sergei Nemchinov	.08	.04	.01
		New York Rangers			
☐	448	Tommy Soderstrom	.20	.09	.03
		Philadelphia Flyers			
☐	449	Petr Nedved	.10	.05	.01
		Vancouver Canucks			
☐	450	Peter Sidorkiewicz	.08	.04	.01
		Ottawa Senators			
☐	451	Nicklas Lidstrom	.10	.05	.01
		Detroit Red Wings			
☐	452	Philippe Bozon	.08	.04	.01
		St. Louis Blues			
☐	453	Uwe Krupp	.08	.04	.01
		New York Islanders			
☐	454	Steve Thomas	.08	.04	.01
		New York Islanders			
☐	455	Owen Nolan	.08	.04	.01
		Quebec Nordiques			
☐	456	Steve Yzerman	.20	.09	.03
		Detroit Red Wings			
☐	457	Chris Chelios	.10	.05	.01
		Chicago Blackhawks			
☐	458	Paul Coffey	.15	.07	.02
		Detroit Red Wings			
☐	459	Brett Hull	.40	.18	.05
		St. Louis Blues			
☐	460	Pavel Bure	1.00	.45	.13
		Vancouver Canucks			
☐	461	Ed Belfour	.20	.09	.03
		Chicago Blackhawks			
☐	462	Mario Lemieux	.75	.35	.09
		Pittsburgh Penguins			
☐	463	Patrick Roy	.35	.16	.04
		Montreal Canadiens			
☐	464	Ray Bourque	.15	.07	.02
		Boston Bruins			
☐	465	Jaromir Jagr	.25	.11	.03
		Pittsburgh Penguins			
☐	466	Kevin Stevens	.15	.07	.02
		Pittsburgh Penguins			
☐	467	Brian Leetch	.15	.07	.02
		New York Rangers			
☐	468	Bobby Clarke	.25	.11	.03
☐	469	Bill Barber	.08	.04	.01
☐	470	Bernie Parent	.15	.07	.02
☐	471	Reggie Leach	.08	.04	.01
☐	472	Rick MacLeish	.08	.04	.01
☐	473	Dave Schultz	.08	.04	.01
☐	474	Joe Watson	.08	.04	.01
☐	475	Bob Taylor	.08	.04	.01
☐	476	Orest Kindrachuk	.08	.04	.01
☐	477	Bob Kelly	.08	.04	.01
☐	478	Bill Clement	.08	.04	.01
☐	479	Ed Van Impe	.08	.04	.01
☐	480	Fred Shero	.08	.04	.01
☐	481	Bryan Smolinski	2.00	.90	.25
		Boston Bruins			
☐	482	Sergei Zholtok	.25	.11	.03
		Boston Bruins			
☐	483	Matthew Barnaby	.50	.23	.06
		Buffalo Sabres			
☐	484	Gary Shuchuk	.15	.07	.02
		Los Angeles Kings			
☐	485	Guy Carbonneau	.18	.08	.02
		Montreal Canadiens			
☐	486	Oleg Petrov	.75	.35	.09
		Montreal Canadiens			
☐	487	Sean Hill	.15	.07	.02
		Montreal Canadiens			
☐	488	Jesse Belanger	1.00	.45	.13
		Montreal Canadiens			
☐	489	Paul DiPietro	.15	.07	.02
		Montreal Canadiens			
☐	490	Rich Pilon	.15	.07	.02
		New York Islanders			
☐	491	Greg Parks	.15	.07	.02
		New York Islanders			
☐	492	Jeff Daniels	.15	.07	.02
		Pittsburgh Penguins			
☐	493	Denny Felsner	.20	.09	.03
		St. Louis Blues			
☐	494	Mike Eastwood	.25	.11	.03
		Toronto Maple Leafs			
☐	495	Murray Craven	.15	.07	.02
		Vancouver Canucks			
☐	496	Vin Damphousse	.20	.09	.03
		Montreal Canadiens			
☐	497	Grant Fuhr	.15	.07	.02
		Buffalo Sabres			
☐	498	Mario Lemieux	2.00	.90	.25
		Pittsburgh Penguins			
☐	499	Ray Ferraro	.15	.07	.02
		New York Islanders			
☐	500	Teemu Selanne	2.50	1.15	.30
		Winnipeg Jets			
☐	501	Luc Robitaille	.60	.25	.08
		Los Angeles Kings			
☐	502	Doug Gilmour	1.00	.45	.13
		Toronto Maple Leafs			
☐	503	Curtis Joseph	.75	.35	.09
		St. Louis Blues			
☐	504	Kirk Muller	.20	.09	.03
		Montreal Canadiens			

☐ 505 Glenn Healy.............	.15	.07	.02
New York Islanders			
☐ 506 Pavel Bure...............	3.50	1.55	.45
Vancouver Canucks			
☐ 507 Felix Potvin.............	3.00	1.35	.40
Toronto Maple Leafs			
☐ 508 Guy Carbonneau........	.15	.07	.02
Montreal Canadiens			
☐ 509 Wayne Gretzky..........	3.50	1.55	.45
Los Angeles Kings			
☐ 510 Patrick Roy..............	2.50	1.15	.30
Montreal Canadiens			

1992-93 Parkhurst Cherry Picks

☐ CP13 Owen Nolan............	8.00	3.60	1.00
Quebec Nordiques			
☐ CP14 Cam Neely............	15.00	6.75	1.90
Boston Bruins			
☐ CP15 Dave Manson..........	8.00	3.60	1.00
Edmonton Oilers			
☐ CP16 Chris Chelios..........	8.00	3.60	1.00
Chicago Blackhawks			
☐ CP17 Marty McSorley.......	8.00	3.60	1.00
Los Angeles Kings			
☐ CP18 Scott Stevens.........	8.00	3.60	1.00
New Jersey Devils			
☐ CP19 John Blue.............	8.00	3.60	1.00
Boston Bruins			
☐ CP20 Ron Hextall...........	8.00	3.60	1.00
Quebec Nordiques			
☐ CP1993 Doug Gilmour.......	25.00	11.50	3.10
Cherry Pick of the Year			
Toronto Maple Leafs			
☐ NNO Don Cherry AU.........	200.00	90.00	25.00
☐ NNO Don Cherry...........	25.00	11.50	3.10
(Checklist back)			
☐ NNO Don Cherry...........	15.00	6.75	1.90
Redemption			

1992-93 Parkhurst Cherry Picks Sheet

Randomly inserted in second series Parkhurst foil packs on a limited basis, this 21-card set features Don Cherry's "Cherry Picks" as selected by the ex-coach and host of "Coach's Corner" on Hockey Night in Canada. Only Canadian cases included a newly created 1954-55 Don Cherry Parkhurst card (101). Measuring the standard size (2 1/2" by 3 1/2"), the cards feature full-bleed, color action player photos. The player's name is printed in gold foil near the bottom of the card along with the Cherry Picks logo. The backs have a dark blue-gray and black stripe background. Set at an angle on this background is a hockey arena graphic design that carries comments from Don Cherry in French and English. Overlapping the arena design is a small, action player photo. The cards are numbered on the backs with a "CP" prefix. The cover card carries a message from Don Cherry. The Doug Gilmour card (CP 1993) was randomly inserted in Final Update sets.

	MINT	EXC	G-VG
COMPLETE SET (21)............	200.00	90.00	25.00
COMMON PLAYER (CP1-CP20).......	8.00	3.60	1.00
☐ CP1 Doug Gilmour..........	20.00	9.00	2.50
Toronto Maple Leafs			
☐ CP2 Jeremy Roenick........	20.00	9.00	2.50
Chicago Blackhawks			
☐ CP3 Brent Sutter...........	8.00	3.60	1.00
Chicago Blackhawks			
☐ CP4 Mark Messier..........	15.00	6.75	1.90
New York Rangers			
☐ CP5 Kirk Muller............	8.00	3.60	1.00
Montreal Canadiens			
☐ CP6 Eric Lindros...........	50.00	23.00	6.25
Philadelphia Flyers			
☐ CP7 Dale Hunter............	8.00	3.60	1.00
Washington Capitals			
☐ CP8 Gary Roberts..........	8.00	3.60	1.00
Calgary Flames			
☐ CP9 Bob Probert...........	8.00	3.60	1.00
Detroit Red Wings			
☐ CP10 Brendan Shanahan..........	15.00	6.75	1.90
St. Louis Blues			
☐ CP11 Wendel Clark..........	15.00	6.75	1.90
Toronto Maple Leafs			
☐ CP12 Rick Tocchet..........	8.00	3.60	1.00
Pittsburgh Penguins			

This approximately 11" by 8 1/2" sheet presents the 1992-93 Parkhurst Cherry Picks insert set. The sheet could be obtained by collectors in exchange for four Don Cherry redemption cards, which were randomly inserted in 1992-93 Parkhurst series II packs. The sheet pictures the fronts of the cards from the 1992-93 Cherry Picks set with Don Cherry's card in the middle. The words "1993 Cherry Picks Promo" are printed in a pink to purple shaded bar at the top of the sheet. The back is blank and the sheet is unnumbered.

	MINT	EXC	G-VG
COMPLETE SET (1)............	75.00	30.00	7.50
COMMON SHEET.............	75.00	30.00	7.50
☐ 1 Dale Hunter.............	75.00	30.00	7.50
Dave Manson			
Doug Gilmour			
Gary Roberts			
Chris Chelios			
Jeremy Roenick			
Bob Probert			
Marty McSorley			
Brent Sutter			
Brendan Shanahan			
Don Cherry			
Mark Messier			
Wendel Clark			
Kirk Muller			
Rick Tocchet			
Scott Stevens			
Eric Lindros			
Owen Nolan			
John Blue			
Ron Hextall			
Cam Neely			

1992-93 Parkhurst Emerald Ice

A premium variation on the regular '92-93 Parkhurst set theme, these Emerald Ice cards measure the standard size (2 1/2" by 3 1/2") and all have their regular-issue counterparts. Each '92-93 Parkhurst regular foil pack contained one Emerald Ice card; each jumbo pack contained two. The fronts feature color player action shots that are borderless, except on the left, where a dark green marbleized stripe carries the player's name in white lettering. The special green foil-stamped and embossed Parkhurst logo appears at the lower left. The blue-green horizontal back carries a small color player closeup on the left, and on the right, the player's name, team, position, biography, statistics, and career highlights in French and English. The cards are numbered on the back.

	MINT	EXC	G-VG
COMPLETE SET (510)	300.00	135.00	38.00
COMPLETE SERIES 1 (240)	135.00	60.00	17.00
COMPLETE SERIES 2 (240)	135.00	60.00	17.00
COMPLETE FIN.UPDATE (30)	30.00	13.50	3.80
COMMON PLAYER (1-240)	.25	.11	.03
COMMON PLAYER (241-480)	.25	.11	.03
COMMON PLAYER (481-510)	.50	.23	.06

*VETERAN STARS: 3X to 6X VALUE
*YOUNG STARS 3X to 6X
*RCs: 2X to 4X
*UPDATE VETERAN STARS: 2X to 4X
*UPDATE YOUNG STARS: 2X to 4X
*UPDATE RCs: 2X to 3X

1992-93 Parkhurst Parkie Reprints

The cards are reprints of cards from the 1950s. This set of 36 cards was issued in four separate series. Capturing eight goalies from the 1950's Parkhurst collections, the first set was undercollated into first series 12-card foil packs. The second eight cards showcase defensemen; these cards were randomly inserted in series 1 jumbo packs. Forwards (17-24) were inserted in second series foil with the remaining forwards (25-32) inserted in second series jumbo packs. The cover cards, which reproduce Parkhurst wrappers on their fronts (1953-54 and 1955-56), have a checklist on their backs. The fronts vary in design but all carry a color shot of the featured player. The players' names are on the fronts, some in print, some in signature form. The backs carry the information from the original card. The print varies from red to black to a combination. The Turk Broda and Terry Sawchuk cards are blank on the back as the originals are. The cards are numbered on the back with a "PR" prefix.

		MINT	EXC	G-VG
	COMPLETE SET (36)	475.00	210.00	60.00
	COMPLETE SERIES 1 (9)	125.00	57.50	15.50
	COMPLETE SERIES 2 (9)	125.00	57.50	15.50
	COMPLETE SERIES 3 (9)	100.00	45.00	12.50
	COMPLETE SERIES 4 (9)	125.00	57.50	15.50
	COMMON GOALIES (1-8)	12.00	5.50	1.50
	COMMON DEFENSEMEN (9-16)	12.00	5.50	1.50
	COMMON FORWARDS (17-24)	12.00	5.50	1.50
	COMMON FORWARDS (25-32)	12.00	5.50	1.50
☐ 1	Jacques Plante Montreal Canadiens	25.00	11.50	3.10
☐ 2	Terry Sawchuk Detroit Red Wings	25.00	11.50	3.10
☐ 3	Johnny Bower Toronto Maple Leafs	12.00	5.50	1.50
☐ 4	Gump Worsley New York Rangers	20.00	9.00	2.50
☐ 5	Harry Lumley Toronto Maple Leafs	12.00	5.50	1.50
☐ 6	Turk Broda Toronto Maple Leafs	12.00	5.50	1.50
☐ 7	Jim Henry Boston Bruins	12.00	5.50	1.50
☐ 8	Al Rollins Chicago Blackhawks	12.00	5.50	1.50
☐ 9	Bill Gadsby Chicago Blackhawks	12.00	5.50	1.50
☐ 10	Red Kelly Detroit Red Wings	15.00	6.75	1.90
☐ 11	Allan Stanley New York Rangers	12.00	5.50	1.50
☐ 12	Bob Baun Toronto Maple Leafs	12.00	5.50	1.50
☐ 13	Carl Brewer Toronto Maple Leafs	12.00	5.50	1.50
☐ 14	Doug Harvey Montreal Canadiens	20.00	9.00	2.50
☐ 15	Harry Howell New York Rangers	12.00	5.50	1.50
☐ 16	Tim Horton Toronto Maple Leafs	25.00	11.50	3.10
☐ 17	George Armstrong	12.00	5.50	1.50
☐ 18	Ralph Backstrom	12.00	5.50	1.50
☐ 19	Alex Delvecchio	15.00	6.75	1.90
☐ 20	Bill Mosienko	12.00	5.50	1.50
☐ 21	Dave Keon	15.00	6.75	1.90
☐ 22	Andy Bathgate	12.00	5.50	1.50
☐ 23	Milt Schmidt	15.00	6.75	1.90
☐ 24	Dick Duff	12.00	5.50	1.50
☐ 25	Norm Ullman	15.00	6.75	1.90
☐ 26	Dickie Moore	12.00	5.50	1.50
☐ 27	Jerry Toppazzini	12.00	5.50	1.50
☐ 28	Henri Richard	15.00	6.75	1.90
☐ 29	Frank Mahovlich	15.00	6.75	1.90
☐ 30	Jean Beliveau	25.00	11.50	3.10
☐ 31	Ted Lindsay	15.00	6.75	1.90
☐ 32	Bernie Geoffrion	20.00	9.00	2.50
☐ CL1	Parkies Checklist 1 (Repro of 1955-56 Parkie Wrapper)	35.00	16.00	4.40
☐ CL2	Parkies Checklist 2 (Repro of 1953-54 Parkie Wrapper)	35.00	16.00	4.40
☐ CL3	Parkies Checklist 3 (Repro of 1958-59 Parkie Wrapper)	35.00	16.00	4.40
☐ CL4	Parkies Checklist 4 (Repro of 1954-55 Parkie Wrapper)	35.00	16.00	4.40

1992-93 Parkhurst Parkie Sheets

These five commemorative sheets measure approximately 8 1/2" by 11". The sheets are individually numbered; the production quantities are listed in the checklist below. The sheets were distributed one per case as an insert with the various series of 1992-93 Parkhurst hockey cards. The players pictured are the players in that respective Parkie reprint series. The Stanley Cup Commemorative Update sheet was issued one per case of Final Update. These unnumbered sheets are numbered chronologically below for convenience in reference.

	MINT	EXC	G-VG
COMPLETE SET (5).........................	100.00	40.00	10.00
COMMON SHEET (1-5).....................	20.00	8.00	2.00
☐ 1 Goalies..................................	20.00	8.00	2.00
(7000 sheets issued)			
☐ 2 Defensemen........................	25.00	10.00	2.50
(3000 sheets issued)			
☐ 3 Forwards/Wingers.................	20.00	8.00	2.00
(7000 sheets issued)			
☐ 4 Forwards/Centers....................	25.00	10.00	2.50
(3000 sheets issued)			
☐ 5 Stanley Cup Update................	35.00	14.00	3.50
(1000 sheets issued)			

1992-93 Parkhurst Arena Tour Sheets

Each sheet in this set of eight measures approximately 11" by 8 1/2" and commemorates a stop on the Canadian Arena Tour. The fronts feature color photos of 1992-93 Parkhurst hockey cards against a blue-green background that shades from dark to light. A thin metallic gold line frames the cards, and the word "Commemorative" is printed in large white letters on this line at the top of the sheet. Near the center are the words "Canadian Arena Tour" and a specific arena name along with the date the sheet was distributed. The team logo is printed above this text. Each sheet carries a serial number and the production run. The backs are blank. The sheets are unnumbered and checklisted below in chronological order. The Montreal sheet was not distributed at the Forum; reportedly because the sheet was not bilingual.

	MINT	EXC	G-VG
COMPLETE SET (8).........................	100.00	40.00	10.00
COMMON SHEET (1-8).....................	15.00	6.00	1.50
☐ 1 Calgary Flames........................	15.00	6.00	1.50
Olympic Saddledome			
April 1, 1993 (22,000)			
Mike Vernon			
Theoren Fleury			
Trent Yawney			
Brian Skrudland			
Joel Otto			
Al MacInnis			
☐ 2 Edmonton Oilers....................	15.00	6.00	1.50
Northlands Coliseum			

	MINT	EXC	G-VG
April 3, 1993 (22,000)			
Zdeno Ciger			
Bill Ranford			
Todd Elik			
Igor Kravchuk			
Craig MacTavish			
Shayne Corson			
☐ 3 Quebec Nordiques...................	15.00	6.00	1.50
Colisee de Quebec			
April 6, 1993 (22,000)			
Bill Lindsay			
Ron Hextall			
Valeri Kamensky			
Kerry Huffman			
Mats Sundin			
Joe Sakic			
☐ 4 Vancouver Canucks................	20.00	8.00	2.00
Pacific Coliseum			
April 11, 1993 (22,000)			
Dave Babych			
Pavel Bure			
Petr Nedved			
Anatoli Semenov			
Kirk McLean			
Trevor Linden			
☐ 5 Montreal Canadiens	30.00	12.00	3.00
The Forum			
April 12, 1993 (22,000)			
Denis Savard			
Kirk Muller			
J.J. Daigneault			
Patrice Brisebois			
Mathieu Schneider			
Patrick Roy			
☐ 6 Toronto Maple Leafs	20.00	8.00	2.00
Maple Leaf Gardens			
April 13, 1993 (22,000)			
Felix Potvin			
Dave Andreychuk			
Wendel Clark			
Peter Zezel			
Doug Gilmour			
Sylvain Lefebvre			
☐ 7 Ottawa Senators....................	15.00	6.00	1.50
Ottawa Civic Centre			
April 14, 1993 (22,000)			
Brad Marsh			
Ken Hammond			
Bob Kudelski			
Peter Sidorkiewicz			
Sylvain Turgeon			
Mark Freer			
☐ 8 Winnipeg Jets	15.00	6.00	1.50
Winnipeg Arena			
April 15, 1993 (22,000)			
Phil Housley			
John Druce			
Sergei Bautin			
Tie Domi			
Evgeny Davydov			
Teemu Selanne			

1993-94 Parkhurst

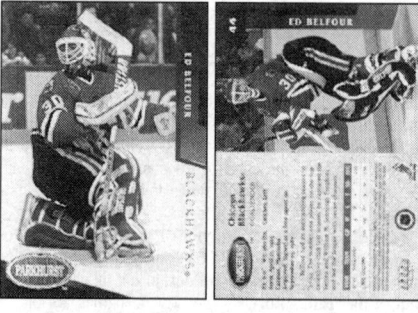

Issued in two series, these 540 standard-size (2 1/2" by 3 1/2") cards feature color player action shots on their fronts. They are borderless, except on the right, where black and green stripes set off by a silver-foil line carry the player's name in white lettering; and at the lower left, where a black and green corner backs up the silver foil-stamped Parkhurst logo. The player's team name appears near the right edge in vertical silver-foil lettering. The horizontal back carries another color player action shot on the right. On the left are the player's team name, position, biography, career highlights, and statistics. The cards are numbered on the back and checklisted below alphabetically according to teams as follows for Series 1 and 2: Anaheim Mighty Ducks (1-9) and (271-279), Boston Bruins (10-18) and (280-288), Buffalo Sabres (19-27) and (289-297), Calgary Flames (28-36) and (298-306), Chicago Blackhawks (37-45) and (307-315), Detroit Red Wings (46-54) and (325-333), Dallas Stars (55-63) and (316-324), Edmonton Oilers (64-72) and (334-342), Florida Panthers (73-81) and (343-351), Hartford Whalers (82-90) and (352-360), Los Angeles Kings (91-99) and (361-369), Montreal Canadiens (100-108) and (370-378), New Jersey Devils (109-117) and (379-387), New York Islanders (118-126) and (388-397), New York Rangers (127-135) and (398-405), Ottawa Senators (136-144) and (406-414), Philadelphia Flyers (145-153) and (415-423), Pittsburgh Penguins (154-162) and (424-432), Quebec Nordiques (163-171) and (433-441), St. Louis Blues (172-180) and (442-450), San Jose Sharks (181-189) and (451-459), Tampa Bay Lightning (190-198) and (460-468), Toronto Maple Leafs (199-207) and (469-477), Vancouver Canucks (208-216) and (478-486), Washington Capitals (217-225) and (487-495), and Winnipeg Jets (226-234) and (496-504). The first series closes with subsets Sensational Sophomores (235-243) and Parkie Prospects (244-270). Two topical subsets conclude the second series: World Junior Best (505-513) and Euro-Juniors (514-540) broken by nation as follows: Czech Republic (515-519), Finland (520-525), Russia (526-533), and Sweden (534-540). Card numbers 398 and 498 were not issued. The silver trade card (series 2 insert) was redeemable for the Calder Candidates insert set; the gold trade card was redeemable for a gold edition of the same insert set. A hobby exclusive Parkie Reprints bonus pack was included in every first- or second-series case.

	MINT	EXC	G-VG
COMPLETE SET (540)	50.00	23.00	6.25
COMPLETE SERIES 1 (270)	25.00	11.50	3.10
COMPLETE SERIES 2 (270)	25.00	11.50	3.10
COMMON PLAYER (1-270)	.08	.04	.01
COMMON PLAYER (271-540)	.08	.04	.01

☐	1 Steven King	.08	.04	.01
☐	2 Sean Hill	.08	.04	.01
☐	3 Anatoli Semenov	.08	.04	.01
☐	4 Garry Valk	.08	.04	.01
☐	5 Todd Ewen	.08	.04	.01
☐	6 Bob Corkum	.08	.04	.01
☐	7 Tim Sweeney	.08	.04	.01
☐	8 Patrick Carnback	.15	.07	.02
☐	9 Troy Loney	.08	.04	.01
☐	10 Cam Neely	.10	.05	.01
☐	11 Adam Oates	.20	.09	.03
☐	12 Jon Casey	.10	.05	.01
☐	13 Don Sweeney	.08	.04	.01
☐	14 Ray Bourque	.20	.09	.03
☐	15 Jozef Stumpel	.08	.04	.01
☐	16 Glen Murray	.08	.04	.01
☐	17 Glen Wesley	.08	.04	.01
☐	18 Fred Knipscheer	.25	.11	.03
☐	19 Craig Simpson	.08	.04	.01
☐	20 Richard Smehlik	.10	.05	.01
☐	21 Alexander Mogilny	.50	.23	.06
☐	22 Grant Fuhr	.10	.05	.01
☐	23 Dale Hawerchuk	.10	.05	.01
☐	24 Philippe Boucher	.08	.04	.01
☐	25 Scott Thomas	.15	.07	.02
☐	26 Donald Audette	.08	.04	.01
☐	27 Brad May	.08	.04	.01
☐	28 Theoren Fleury	.15	.07	.01
☐	29 Andrei Trefilov	.25	.11	.03
☐	30 Sandy McCarthy	.08	.04	.01
☐	31 Joe Nieuwendyk	.10	.05	.01

☐	32 Paul Ranheim	.08	.04	.01
☐	33 Kelly Kisio	.08	.04	.01
☐	34 Joel Otto	.08	.04	.01
☐	35 Ted Drury	.08	.04	.01
☐	36 Al MacInnis	.15	.07	.01
☐	37 Kevin Todd	.08	.04	.01
☐	38 Joe Murphy	.08	.04	.01
☐	39 Christian Ruuttu	.08	.04	.01
☐	40 Steve Dubinsky	.20	.09	.03
☐	41 Stephane Matteau	.08	.04	.01
☐	42 Ivan Droppa	.15	.07	.02
☐	43 Jocelyn Lemieux	.08	.04	.01
☐	44 Ed Belfour	.25	.11	.03
☐	45 Chris Chelios	.10	.05	.01
☐	46 Derian Hatcher	.08	.04	.01
☐	47 Andy Moog	.10	.05	.01
☐	48 Trent Klatt	.08	.04	.01
☐	49 Mike Modano	.30	.14	.04
☐	50 Paul Cavallini	.08	.04	.01
☐	51 Mike McPhee	.08	.04	.01
☐	52 Brent Gilchrist	.08	.04	.01
☐	53 Russ Courtnall	.10	.05	.01
☐	54 Neal Broten	.10	.05	.01
☐	55 Steve Chiasson	.08	.04	.01
☐	56 Paul Coffey	.08	.04	.01
☐	57 Vyacheslav Kozlov	.75	.35	.09
☐	58 Sergei Fedorov	1.00	.45	.13
☐	59 Tim Cheveldae	.10	.05	.01
☐	60 Dino Ciccarelli	.10	.05	.01
☐	61 Dallas Drake	.20	.09	.03
☐	62 Niklas Lidstrom	.10	.05	.01
☐	63 Martin Lapointe	.08	.04	.01
☐	64 Dean McAmmond	.08	.04	.01
☐	65 Igor Kravchuk	.08	.04	.01
☐	66 Shjon Podein	.20	.09	.03
☐	67 Bill Ranford	.10	.05	.01
☐	68 Brad Werenka	.08	.04	.01
☐	69 Doug Weight	.10	.05	.01
☐	70 Ian Herbers	.15	.07	.02
☐	71 Todd Elik	.08	.04	.01
☐	72 Steven Rice	.08	.04	.01
☐	73 John Vanbiesbrouck	.20	.09	.03
☐	74 Alexander Godynyuk	.08	.04	.01
☐	75 Brian Skrudland	.08	.04	.01
☐	76 Jody Hull	.08	.04	.01
☐	77 Brent Severyn	.15	.07	.02
☐	78 Evgeny Davydov	.08	.04	.01
☐	79 Dave Lowry	.08	.04	.01
☐	80 Scott Levins	.20	.09	.03
☐	81 Scott Mellanby	.08	.04	.01
☐	82 Dan Keczmer	.08	.04	.01
☐	83 Michael Nylander	.20	.09	.03
☐	84 Jim Sandlak	.08	.04	.01
☐	85 Brian Propp	.10	.05	.01
☐	86 Geoff Sanderson	.25	.11	.03
☐	87 Mike Lenarduzzi	.15	.07	.02
☐	88 Zarley Zalapski	.08	.04	.01
☐	89 Robert Petrovicky	.08	.04	.01
☐	90 Robert Kron	.08	.04	.01
☐	91 Luc Robitaille	.20	.09	.03
☐	92 Alexei Zhitnik	.20	.09	.03
☐	93 Tony Granato	.08	.04	.01
☐	94 Rob Blake	.10	.05	.01
☐	95 Gary Shuchuk	.08	.04	.01
☐	96 Darryl Sydor	.10	.05	.01
☐	97 Kelly Hrudey	.10	.05	.01
☐	98 Warren Rychel	.08	.04	.01
☐	99 Wayne Gretzky	1.75	.80	.22
☐	100 Patrick Roy	.75	.35	.09
☐	101 Gilbert Dionne	.08	.04	.01
☐	102 Eric Desjardins	.08	.04	.01
☐	103 Peter Popovic	.15	.07	.02
☐	104 Vincent Damphousse	.10	.05	.01
☐	105 Patrice Brisebois	.08	.04	.01
☐	106 Pierre Sevigny	.08	.04	.01
☐	107 John Leclair	.08	.04	.01
☐	108 Paul DiPietro	.08	.04	.01
☐	109 Alexander Semak	.08	.04	.01
☐	110 Claude Lemieux	.10	.05	.01
☐	111 Scott Niedermayer	.20	.09	.03
☐	112 Chris Terreri	.10	.05	.01
☐	113 Stephane Richer	.10	.05	.01
☐	114 Scott Stevens	.10	.05	.01
☐	115 John MacLean	.10	.05	.01
☐	116 Scott Pellerin	.20	.09	.03
☐	117 Bernie Nicholls	.10	.05	.01
☐	118 Derek King	.08	.04	.01
☐	119 Scott Lachance	.08	.04	.01
☐	120 Scott Scissons	.08	.04	.01
☐	121 Darius Kasparaitis	.08	.04	.01
☐	122 Ray Ferraro	.08	.04	.01
☐	123 Steve Thomas	.10	.05	.01

☐ 125	Vladimir Malakhov	.15	.07	.02
☐ 126	Travis Green	.08	.04	.01
☐ 127	Mark Messier	.08	.04	.01
☐ 128	Sergei Nemchinov	.08	.04	.01
☐ 129	Mike Richter	.20	.09	.03
☐ 130	Alexei Kovalev	.60	.25	.08
☐ 131	Brian Leetch	.30	.14	.04
☐ 132	Tony Amonte	.25	.11	.03
☐ 133	Sergei Zubov	.60	.25	.08
☐ 134	Adam Graves	.30	.14	.04
☐ 135	Esa Tikkanen	.10	.05	.01
☐ 136	Sylvain Turgeon	.08	.04	.01
☐ 137	Norm Maciver	.08	.04	.01
☐ 138	Craig Billington	.08	.04	.01
☐ 139	Dmitri Filiminov	.08	.04	.01
☐ 140	Pavel Demitra	.15	.07	.02
☐ 141	Brian Glynn	.08	.04	.01
☐ 142	Darrin Madeley	.20	.09	.03
☐ 143	Radek Hamr	.20	.09	.03
☐ 144	Robert Burakovsky	.08	.04	.01
☐ 145	Dimitri Yushkevich	.08	.04	.01
☐ 146	Claude Boivin	.08	.04	.01
☐ 147	Pelle Eklund	.08	.04	.01
☐ 148	Brent Fedyk	.08	.04	.01
☐ 149	Mark Recchi	.25	.11	.03
☐ 150	Tommy Soderstrom	.15	.07	.02
☐ 151	Vyacheslav Butsayev	.08	.04	.01
☐ 152	Rod Brind'Amour	.20	.09	.03
☐ 153	Josef Beranek	.10	.05	.01
☐ 154	Jaromir Jagr	.50	.23	.06
☐ 155	Ulf Samuelsson	.10	.05	.01
☐ 156	Martin Straka	.50	.23	.06
☐ 157	Tom Barrasso	.10	.05	.01
☐ 158	Kevin Stevens	.25	.11	.03
☐ 159	Joe Mullen	.10	.05	.01
☐ 160	Ron Francis	.10	.05	.01
☐ 161	Marty McSorley	.10	.05	.01
☐ 162	Larry Murphy	.10	.05	.01
☐ 163	Owen Nolan	.10	.05	.01
☐ 164	Stephane Fiset	.08	.04	.01
☐ 165	Dave Karpa	.08	.04	.01
☐ 166	Martin Gelinas	.08	.04	.01
☐ 167	Andrei Kovalenko	.15	.07	.02
☐ 168	Steve Duchesne	.10	.05	.01
☐ 169	Joe Sakic	.25	.11	.03
☐ 170	Martin Rucinsky	.08	.04	.01
☐ 171	Chris Simon	.20	.09	.03
☐ 172	Brendan Shanahan	.25	.11	.03
☐ 173	Jeff Brown	.10	.05	.01
☐ 174	Phil Housley	.10	.05	.01
☐ 175	Curtis Joseph	.25	.11	.03
☐ 176	Jim Montgomery	.20	.09	.03
☐ 177	Bret Hedican	.08	.04	.01
☐ 178	Kevin Miller	.08	.04	.01
☐ 179	Philippe Bozon	.08	.04	.01
☐ 180	Brett Hull	.75	.35	.09
☐ 181	Jimmy Waite	.08	.04	.01
☐ 182	Ray Whitney	.10	.05	.01
☐ 183	Pat Falloon	.10	.05	.01
☐ 184	Tom Pederson	.08	.04	.01
☐ 185	Igor Larionov	.08	.04	.01
☐ 186	Dody Wood	.15	.07	.02
☐ 187	Sandis Ozolinsh	.25	.11	.03
☐ 188	Sergei Makarov	.10	.05	.01
☐ 189	Rob Gaudreau	.25	.11	.03
☐ 190	Roman Hamrlik	.15	.07	.02
☐ 191	Stan Drulia	.08	.04	.01
☐ 192	Pat Jablonski	.08	.04	.01
☐ 193	Denis Savard	.15	.07	.02
☐ 194	Rob Zamuner	.08	.04	.01
☐ 195	Petr Klima	.08	.04	.01
☐ 196	Rob Dimiao	.08	.04	.01
☐ 197	Chris Kontos	.08	.04	.01
☐ 198	Mikael Andersson	.08	.04	.01
☐ 199	Drake Berehowsky	.08	.04	.01
☐ 200	Dave Andreychuk	.15	.07	.02
☐ 201	Glenn Anderson	.10	.05	.01
☐ 202	Felix Potvin	1.00	.45	.13
☐ 203	Nikolai Borschevsky	.20	.09	.03
☐ 204	Kent Manderville	.08	.04	.01
☐ 205	Dave Ellett	.08	.04	.01
☐ 206	Peter Zezel	.08	.04	.01
☐ 207	Ken Baumgartner	.08	.04	.01
☐ 208	Murray Craven	.08	.04	.01
☐ 209	Dixon Ward	.08	.04	.01
☐ 210	Cliff Ronning	.08	.04	.01
☐ 211	Pavel Bure	1.25	.55	.16
☐ 212	Sergio Momesso	.08	.04	.01
☐ 213	Kirk McLean	.15	.07	.02
☐ 214	Jiri Slegr	.08	.04	.01
☐ 215	Trevor Linden	.15	.07	.02
☐ 216	Geoff Courtnall	.08	.04	.01
☐ 217	Al Iafrate	.10	.05	.01

☐ 218	Mike Ridley	.10	.05	.01
☐ 219	Enrico Ciccone	.08	.04	.01
☐ 220	Dimitri Khristich	.10	.05	.01
☐ 221	Kevin Hatcher	.10	.05	.01
☐ 222	Peter Bondra	.10	.05	.01
☐ 223	Steve Konowalchuk	.08	.04	.01
☐ 224	Pat Elynuik	.08	.04	.01
☐ 225	Don Beaupre	.10	.05	.01
☐ 226	Stu Barnes	.08	.04	.01
☐ 227	Fredrik Olausson	.08	.04	.01
☐ 228	Keith Thachuk	.25	.11	.03
☐ 229	Mike Eagles	.08	.04	.01
☐ 230	Tie Domi	.08	.04	.01
☐ 231	Teppo Numminen	.08	.04	.01
☐ 232	Arto Blomsten	.08	.04	.01
☐ 233	Teemu Selanne	1.00	.45	.13
☐ 234	Bob Essensa	.10	.05	.01
☐ 235	Teemu Selanne SPH	.60	.25	.08
	Winnipeg Jets			
☐ 236	Eric Lindros SPH	2.00	.90	.25
	Philadelphia Flyers			
☐ 237	Felix Potvin SPH	.50	.23	.06
	Toronto Maple Leafs			
☐ 238	Alexei Kovalev SPH	.35	.16	.04
	New York Rangers			
☐ 239	Vladimir Malakhov SPH	.10	.05	.01
	New York Islanders			
☐ 240	Scott Niedermayer SPH	.10	.05	.01
	New Jersey Devils			
☐ 241	Joe Juneau SPH	.40	.18	.05
	Boston Bruins			
☐ 242	Shawn McEachern SPH	.10	.05	.01
	Los Angeles Kings			
☐ 243	Alexei Zhamnov SPH	.25	.11	.03
	Winnipeg Jets			
☐ 244	Alexandre Daigle PKP	.75	.35	.09
	Ottawa Senators			
☐ 245	Markus Naslund PKP	.20	.09	.03
	Pittsburgh Penguins			
☐ 246	Rob Niedermayer PKP	.75	.35	.09
	Florida Panthers			
☐ 247	Jocelyn Thibault PKP	.75	.35	.09
	Quebec Nordiques			
☐ 248	Brent Gretzky PKP	.40	.18	.05
	Tampa Bay Lightning			
☐ 249	Chris Pronger PKP	.75	.35	.09
	Hartford Whalers			
☐ 250	Chris Gratton PKP	.75	.35	.09
	Tampa Bay Lightning			
☐ 251	Mikael Renberg PKP	.75	.35	.09
	Philadelphia Flyers			
☐ 252	Jarkko Varvio PKP	.20	.09	.03
	Dallas Stars			
☐ 253	Micah Aivazoff PKP	.20	.09	.03
	Detroit Red Wings			
☐ 254	Alexei Yashin PKP	.75	.35	.09
	Ottawa Senators			
☐ 255	German Titov PKP	.50	.23	.06
	Calgary Flames			
☐ 256	Mattias Norstrom PKP	.15	.07	.02
	New York Rangers			
☐ 257	Michal Sykora PKP	.25	.11	.03
	San Jose Sharks			
☐ 258	Roman Oksyuta PKP	.15	.07	.02
	Edmonton Oilers			
☐ 259	Bryan Smolinski PKP	.60	.25	.08
	Boston Bruins			
☐ 260	Alexei Kudashov PKP	.20	.09	.03
	Toronto Maple Leafs			
☐ 261	Jason Arnott PKP	2.00	.90	.25
	Edmonton Oilers			
☐ 262	Aaron Ward PKP	.15	.07	.02
	Detroit Red Wings			
☐ 263	Vesa Vitakoski PKP	.20	.09	.03
	Calgary Flames			
☐ 264	Boris Mironov PKP	.10	.05	.01
	Winnipeg Jets			
☐ 265	Darren McCarty PKP	.25	.11	.03
	Detroit Red Wings			
☐ 266	Vlastimil Kroupa PKP	.25	.11	.03
	San Jose Sharks			
☐ 267	Denny Felsner PKP	.10	.05	.01
	St. Louis Blues			
☐ 268	Milos Holan PKP	.10	.05	.01
	Philadelphia Flyers			
☐ 269	Alexander Karpovtsev PKP	.12	.05	.02
	New York Rangers			
☐ 270	Greg Johnson PKP	.10	.05	.01
	Detroit Red Wings			
☐ 271	Terry Yake	.08	.04	.01
☐ 272	Bill Houlder	.08	.04	.01
☐ 273	Joe Sacco	.08	.04	.01
☐ 274	Myles O'Connor	.08	.04	.01

☐ 275	Mark Ferner	.10	.05	.01
☐ 276	Alexei Kasatanov	.08	.04	.01
☐ 277	Stu Grimson	.08	.04	.01
☐ 278	Shaun Van Allen	.08	.04	.01
☐ 279	Guy Hebert	.15	.07	.02
☐ 280	Joe Juneau	.60	.25	.08
☐ 281	Sergei Zholtok	.08	.04	.01
☐ 282	Daniel Marois	.08	.04	.01
☐ 283	Ted Donato	.08	.04	.01
☐ 284	Cam Stewart	.20	.09	.03
☐ 285	Stephen Leach	.08	.04	.01
☐ 286	Darren Banks	.08	.04	.01
☐ 287	Dmitri Kvartalnov	.08	.04	.01
☐ 288	Paul Stanton	.08	.04	.01
☐ 289	Pat LaFontaine	.30	.14	.04
☐ 290	Bob Sweeney	.08	.04	.01
☐ 291	Craig Muni	.08	.04	.01
☐ 292	Sergei Petrenko	.08	.04	.01
☐ 293	Derek Plante	.75	.35	.09
☐ 294	Wayne Presley	.08	.04	.01
☐ 295	Mark Astley	.15	.07	.02
☐ 296	Matthew Barnaby	.20	.09	.03
☐ 297	Randy Wood	.08	.04	.01
☐ 298	Kevin Dahl	.08	.04	.01
☐ 299	Gary Suter	.10	.05	.01
☐ 300	Robert Reichel	.10	.05	.01
☐ 301	Mike Vernon	.10	.05	.01
☐ 302	Gary Roberts	.10	.05	.01
☐ 303	Ronnie Stern	.08	.04	.01
☐ 304	Michel Petit	.08	.04	.01
☐ 305	Wes Walz	.08	.04	.01
☐ 306	Brad Miller	.08	.04	.01
☐ 307	Patrick Poulin	.08	.04	.01
☐ 308	Brent Sutter	.10	.05	.01
☐ 309	Jeremy Roenick	.75	.35	.09
☐ 310	Steve Smith	.08	.04	.01
☐ 311	Eric Weinrich	.08	.04	.01
☐ 312	Jeff Hackett	.08	.04	.01
☐ 313	Michel Goulet	.10	.05	.01
☐ 314	Jeff Shantz	.20	.09	.03
☐ 315	Neil Wilkinson	.08	.04	.01
☐ 316	Shane Churla	.08	.04	.01
☐ 317	Dave Gagner	.10	.05	.01
☐ 318	Chris Tancill	.08	.04	.01
☐ 319	Dean Evason	.08	.04	.01
☐ 320	Mark Tinordi	.08	.04	.01
☐ 321	Grant Ledyard	.08	.04	.01
☐ 322	Ulf Dahlen	.08	.04	.01
☐ 323	Mike Craig	.08	.04	.01
☐ 324	Paul Broten	.08	.04	.01
☐ 325	Vladimir Konstantinov	.08	.04	.01
☐ 326	Steve Yzerman	.40	.18	.05
☐ 327	Keith Primeau	.10	.05	.01
☐ 328	Shawn Burr	.08	.04	.01
☐ 329	Chris Osgood	.75	.35	.09
☐ 330	Ray Sheppard	.08	.04	.01
☐ 331	Mike Sillinger	.08	.04	.01
☐ 332	Terry Carkner	.08	.04	.01
☐ 333	Bob Probert	.08	.04	.01
☐ 334	Adam Bennett	.08	.04	.01
☐ 335	Dave Manson	.08	.04	.01
☐ 336	Zdeno Ciger	.08	.04	.01
☐ 337	Louie DeBrusk	.08	.04	.01
☐ 338	Shayne Corson	.08	.04	.01
☐ 339	Vladimir Vujtek	.08	.04	.01
☐ 340	Tyler Wright	.08	.04	.01
☐ 341	Ilya Byakin	.15	.07	.02
☐ 342	Craig MacTavish	.08	.04	.01
☐ 343	Brian Benning	.08	.04	.01
☐ 344	Mark Fitzpatrick	.08	.04	.01
☐ 345	Gord Murphy	.08	.04	.01
☐ 346	Jesse Belanger	.20	.09	.03
☐ 347	Joe Cirella	.08	.04	.01
☐ 348	Tom Fitzgerald	.08	.04	.01
☐ 349	Andrei Lomakin	.08	.04	.01
☐ 350	Bill Lindsay	.08	.04	.01
☐ 351	Len Barrie	.08	.04	.01
☐ 352	Frank Pietrangelo	.08	.04	.01
☐ 353	Pat Verbeek	.10	.05	.01
☐ 354	Jim Storm	.08	.04	.01
☐ 355	Mark Janssens	.08	.04	.01
☐ 356	Darren Turcotte	.08	.04	.01
☐ 357	Jim McKenzie	.08	.04	.01
☐ 358	Brad McCrimmon	.08	.04	.01
☐ 359	Andrew Cassels	.08	.04	.01
☐ 360	James Patrick	.08	.04	.01
☐ 361	Bob Jay	.15	.07	.02
☐ 362	Tomas Sandstrom	.08	.04	.01
☐ 363	Pat Conacher	.08	.04	.01
☐ 364	Shawn McEachern	.08	.04	.01
☐ 365	Jari Kurri	.15	.07	.02
☐ 366	Dominic Lavoie	.08	.04	.01
☐ 367	Dave Taylor	.10	.05	.01
☐ 368	Jimmy Carson	.08	.04	.01
☐ 369	Mike Donnelly	.08	.04	.01
☐ 370	Lyle Odelein	.08	.04	.01
☐ 371	Brian Bellows	.10	.05	.01
☐ 372	Guy Carbonneau	.10	.05	.01
☐ 373	Matt Schneider	.10	.05	.01
☐ 374	Stephan Lebeau	.08	.04	.01
☐ 375	Benoit Brunet	.08	.04	.01
☐ 376	Kevin Haller	.08	.04	.01
☐ 377	J.J. Daigneault	.08	.04	.01
☐ 378	Kirk Muller	.10	.05	.01
☐ 379	Jason Smith	.15	.07	.02
☐ 380	Martin Brodeur	.50	.23	.06
☐ 381	Corey Millen	.08	.04	.01
☐ 382	Bill Guerin	.08	.04	.01
☐ 383	Valeri Zelepukin	.10	.05	.01
☐ 384	Tom Chorske	.08	.04	.01
☐ 385	Bobby Holik	.08	.04	.01
☐ 386	Jaroslav Modry	.20	.09	.03
☐ 387	Ken Daneyko	.08	.04	.01
☐ 388	Uwe Krupp	.08	.04	.01
☐ 389	Pierre Turgeon	.30	.14	.04
☐ 390	Marty McInnis	.08	.04	.01
☐ 391	Patrick Flatley	.08	.04	.01
☐ 392	Tom Kurvers	.08	.04	.01
☐ 393	Brad Dalgarno	.08	.04	.01
☐ 394	Steve Junker	.15	.07	.02
☐ 395	David Volek	.08	.04	.01
☐ 396	Benoit Hogue	.08	.04	.01
☐ 397	Zigmund Palffy	.08	.04	.01
☐ 399	Joby Messier	.15	.07	.02
☐ 400	Mike Gartner	.15	.07	.02
☐ 401	Joey Kocur	.08	.04	.01
☐ 402	Ed Olczyk	.08	.04	.01
☐ 403	Doug Lidster	.08	.04	.01
☐ 404A	Greg Gilbert	.08	.04	.01
☐ 404B	Steve Larmer UER	.10	.05	.01
	(Issued as card 404)			
☐ 405	Glenn Healy	.08	.04	.01
☐ 406	Dennis Vial	.08	.04	.01
☐ 407	Darcy Loewen	.08	.04	.01
☐ 408	Bob Kudelski	.10	.05	.01
☐ 409	Hank Lammens	.10	.05	.01
☐ 410	Jarmo Kekalainen	.08	.04	.01
☐ 411	Darren Rumble	.08	.04	.01
☐ 412	Francois Leroux	.08	.04	.01
☐ 413	Troy Mallette	.08	.04	.01
☐ 414	Bill Huard	.15	.07	.02
☐ 415	Ryan McGill	.08	.04	.01
☐ 416	Eric Lindros	3.00	1.35	.40
☐ 417	Dominic Roussel	.15	.07	.02
☐ 418	Jason Bowen	.15	.07	.02
☐ 419	Andre Faust	.08	.04	.01
☐ 420	Stewart Malgunas	.15	.07	.02
☐ 421	Kevin Dineen	.10	.05	.01
☐ 422	Yves Racine	.08	.04	.01
☐ 423	Garry Galley	.08	.04	.01
☐ 424	Doug Brown	.08	.04	.01
☐ 425	Mario Lemieux	1.25	.55	.16
☐ 426	Ladislav Karabin	.15	.07	.02
☐ 427	Grant Jennings	.08	.04	.01
☐ 428	Rick Tocchet	.10	.05	.01
☐ 429	Jeff Daniels	.08	.04	.01
☐ 430	Peter Taglianetti	.08	.04	.01
☐ 431	Bryan Trottier	.10	.05	.01
☐ 432	Kjell Samuelsson	.08	.04	.01
☐ 433	Rene Corbet	.25	.11	.03
☐ 434	Iain Fraser	.20	.09	.03
☐ 435	Mats Sundin	.25	.11	.03
☐ 436	Curtis Leschyshyn	.08	.04	.01
☐ 437	Claude LaPointe	.08	.04	.01
☐ 438	Valeri Kamensky	.20	.09	.03
☐ 439	Mike Ricci	.10	.05	.01
☐ 440	Chris Lindberg	.08	.04	.01
☐ 441	Alexei Gusarov	.08	.04	.01
☐ 442	Tom Tilley	.08	.04	.01
☐ 443	Craig Janney	.15	.07	.02
☐ 444	Vitali Karamnov	.08	.04	.01
☐ 445	Bob Bassen	.08	.04	.01
☐ 446	Igor Korolev	.08	.04	.01
☐ 447	Kevin Miehm	.08	.04	.01
☐ 448	Tony Hrkac	.08	.04	.01
☐ 449	Garth Butcher	.08	.04	.01
☐ 450	Vitali Prokhorov	.08	.04	.01
☐ 451	Arturs Irbe	.40	.18	.05
☐ 452	Jayson More	.08	.04	.01
☐ 453	Bob Errey	.08	.04	.01
☐ 454	Mike Sullivan	.08	.04	.01
☐ 455	Jeff Norton	.08	.04	.01
☐ 456	Gaeten Duchesne	.08	.04	.01
☐ 457	Doug Zmolek	.08	.04	.01
☐ 458	Mike Rathje	.08	.04	.01
☐ 459	Jamie Baker	.08	.04	.01

☐	460	Joe Reekie	.08	.04	.01
☐	461	Mark Bureau	.08	.04	.01
☐	462	John Tucker	.08	.04	.01
☐	463	Bill McDougall	.08	.04	.01
☐	464	Danton Cole	.08	.04	.01
☐	465	Brian Bradley	.08	.04	.01
☐	466	Jason Lafreniere	.08	.04	.01
☐	467	Donald Dufresne	.08	.04	.01
☐	468	Daren Puppa	.10	.05	.01
☐	469	Doug Gilmour	.40	.18	.05
☐	470	Damian Rhodes	.30	.14	.04
☐	471	Matt Martin	.20	.09	.03
☐	472	Bill Berg	.08	.04	.01
☐	473	John Cullen	.08	.04	.01
☐	474	Rob Pearson	.08	.04	.01
☐	475	Wendel Clark	.15	.07	.02
☐	476	Mark Osborne	.08	.04	.01
☐	477	Dmitri Mironov	.08	.04	.01
☐	478A	Kay Whitmore	.08	.04	.01
☐	478B	Kris King	.08	.04	.01
		(Card issued as 478)			
☐	479	Shawn Antoski	.08	.04	.01
☐	480	Greg Adams	.08	.04	.01
☐	481	Dave Babych	.08	.04	.01
☐	482	John McIntyre	.08	.04	.01
☐	483	Jyrki Lumme	.08	.04	.01
☐	484	Jose Charbonneau	.15	.07	.02
☐	485	Gino Odjick	.08	.04	.01
☐	486	Dana Murzyn	.08	.04	.01
☐	487	Michal Pivonka	.08	.04	.01
☐	488	Dave Poulin	.08	.04	.01
☐	489	Sylvain Cote	.08	.04	.01
☐	490	Jason Woolley	.08	.04	.01
☐	491	Kelly Miller	.08	.04	.01
☐	492	Randy Burridge	.08	.04	.01
☐	493	Kevin Kaminski	.20	.09	.03
☐	494	John Slaney	.08	.04	.01
☐	495	Keith Jones	.08	.04	.01
☐	496	Harijs Vitolinsh	.08	.04	.01
☐	497	Nelson Emerson	.10	.05	.01
☐	499	Darrin Shannon	.08	.04	.01
☐	500	Stephane Quintal	.08	.04	.01
☐	501	Luciano Borsato	.08	.04	.01
☐	502	Thomas Steen	.08	.04	.01
☐	503	Alexei Zhamnov	.35	.16	.04
☐	504	Paul Ysebaert	.08	.04	.01
☐	505	Jeff Friesen	1.50	.65	.19
		Canada			
☐	506	Niklas Sundstrom	.40	.18	.05
		Sweden			
☐	507	Nick Stajduhar	.40	.18	.05
		Canada			
☐	508	Jamie Storr	2.00	.90	.25
		Canada			
☐	509	Valeri Bure	1.00	.45	.13
		Russia			
☐	510	Jason Bonsignore	1.50	.65	.19
		USA			
☐	511	Mats Lindgren	.35	.16	.04
		Sweden			
☐	512	Yanick Dube	.60	.25	.08
		Canada			
☐	513	Todd Harvey	.75	.35	.09
		Canada			
☐	514	Ladislav Prokupek	.20	.09	.03
☐	515	Tomas Vlasak	.20	.09	.03
☐	516	Josef Marha	.20	.09	.03
☐	517	Tomas Blazek	.20	.09	.03
☐	518	Zdenek Nedved	.25	.11	.03
☐	519	Jaroslav Miklenda	.25	.11	.03
☐	520	Janne Niinimaa	.25	.11	.03
☐	521	Saku Koivu	.50	.23	.06
☐	522	Tommi Miettinen	.15	.07	.02
☐	523	Tuomas Gronman	.15	.07	.02
☐	524	Jani Nikko	.15	.07	.02
☐	525	Jonni Vaukonen	.15	.07	.02
☐	526	Nikolai Tsulygin	.15	.07	.02
☐	527	Vadim Sharifjanov	.35	.16	.04
☐	528	Valeri Bure	1.00	.45	.13
☐	529	Alezander Kharlamov	.75	.35	.09
☐	530	Nikolai Zavarukhin	.20	.09	.03
☐	531	Oleg Tverdovsky	1.25	.55	.16
☐	532	Sergei Kondrashkin	.20	.09	.03
☐	533	Evgeni Ryabchikov	.40	.18	.05
☐	534	Mats Lindgren	.35	.16	.04
☐	535	Kenny Jonsson	.30	.14	.04
☐	536	Edvin Frylen	.25	.11	.03
☐	537	Mathias Johansson	.15	.07	.02
☐	538	Johan Davidsson	.15	.07	.02
☐	539	Mikael Hakansson	.15	.07	.02
☐	540	Anders Eriksson	.25	.11	.03

1993-94 Parkhurst Emerald Ice

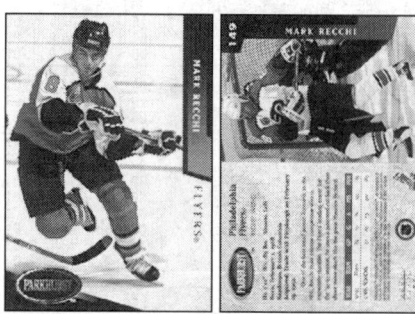

Like the previous year, each '93-94 Parkhurst regular foil pack contained one Emerald Ice card; each jumbo pack contained two. The 540 standard-size (2 1/2" by 3 1/2") cards feature color player action shots on their fronts. They are borderless, except on the right, where black and green stripes set off by a green-foil line carry the player's name in white lettering; and at the lower left, where a black and green corner backs up the green foil-stamped Parkhurst logo. The player's team name appears near the right edge in vertical green-foil lettering. The horizontal back carries another color player action shot on the right. On the left are the player's team name, position, biography, career highlights, and statistics. The cards are numbered on the back.

	MINT	EXC	G-VG
COMPLETE SET (540)	300.00	135.00	38.00
COMPLETE SERIES 1 (270)	150.00	70.00	19.00
COMPLETE SERIES 2 (270)	150.00	70.00	19.00
COMMON PLAYER (1-270)	.25	.11	.03
COMMON PLAYER (271-540)	.25	.11	.03
*VETERAN STARS: 3X to 6X VALUE			
*YOUNG STARS: 3X to 5X VALUE			
*RCs: 2X to 4X VALUE			

1993-94 Parkhurst Calder Candidates

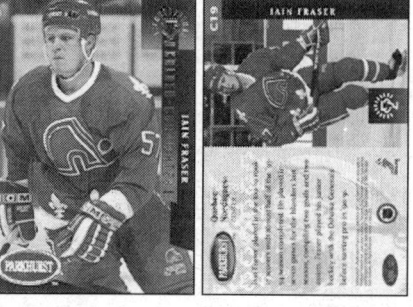

Randomly inserted in U.S. second-series retail foil packs, these 20 standard-size (2 1/2" by 3 1/2") cards feature color player action shots of some of the NHL's top rookies on their fronts. They are borderless, except on the right, where black and green stripes carry the player's name and the set's title and logo in silver foil; and at the lower left, where a black and green corner backs up the silver foil-stamped Parkhurst logo. The horizontal back carries another color player action shot on the right, edged by a black stripe that carries the player's name in vertical white lettering. On the left are the player's team name, position, and career highlights, all set on a ghosted and green color-screened image of the Calder Trophy. The cards are numbered on the back with a "C" prefix. The silver trade card randomly inserted in '93-94 Parkhurst packs was redeemable for this Calder Candidates insert set; the gold trade card was redeemable for a gold edition, which is valued up to 1.5 times the values listed below.

	MINT	EXC	G-VG
COMPLETE SET (20)	125.00	57.50	15.50
COMMON PLAYER (C1-C20)	5.00	2.30	.60
*GOLD REDEEMED CARDS: 1X to 1.5X VALUE.			
☐ C1 Alexandre Daigle	10.00	4.50	1.25
Ottawa Senators			
☐ C2 Chris Pronger	10.00	4.50	1.25
Hartford Whalers			
☐ C3 Chris Gratton	10.00	4.50	1.25
Tampa Bay Lightning			
☐ C4 Rob Niedermayer	10.00	4.50	1.25
Florida Panthers			
☐ C5 Markus Naslund	5.00	2.30	.60
Pittsburgh Penguins			
☐ C6 Jason Arnott	20.00	9.00	2.50
Edmonton Oilers			
☐ C7 Pierre Sevigny	5.00	2.30	.60
Montreal Canadiens			
☐ C8 Jarkko Varvio	5.00	2.30	.60
Dallas Stars			
☐ C9 Dean McAmmond	5.00	2.30	.60
Edmonton Oilers			
☐ C10 Alexei Yashin	15.00	6.75	1.90
Ottawa Senators			
☐ C11 Philippe Boucher	5.00	2.30	.60
Buffalo Sabres			
☐ C12 Mikael Renberg	15.00	6.75	1.90
Philadelphia Flyers			
☐ C13 Chris Simon	5.00	2.30	.60
Quebec Nordiques			
☐ C14 Brent Gretzky	6.00	2.70	.75
Tampa Bay Lightning			
☐ C15 Jesse Belanger	6.00	2.70	.75
Florida Panthers			
☐ C16 Jocelyn Thibault	8.00	3.60	1.00
Quebec Nordiques			
☐ C17 Chris Osgood	8.00	3.60	1.00
Detroit Red Wings			
☐ C18 Derek Plante	8.00	3.60	1.00
Buffalo Sabres			
☐ C19 Iain Fraser	5.00	2.30	.60
Quebec Nordiques			
☐ C20 Vesa Viitakoski	5.00	2.30	.60
Calgary Flames			
☐ NNO Silver Trade Card	6.00	2.70	.75
☐ NNO Gold Trade Card	4.00	1.80	.50

1993-94 Parkhurst East/West Stars

Randomly inserted in U.S. second-series hobby packs, these 20 standard-size (2 1/2" by 3 1/2") cards feature color player action shots on their fronts. They are borderless, except on the right, where a blue stripe carries the player's name in vertical white lettering highlighted by white stars. The set's gold-foil logo appears at the upper right; the gold foil-stamped Parkhurst logo rests at the lower left. The horizontal back carries a color player action cutout on the right, edged by a wide blue stripe that carries the player's name in vertical white lettering. On the left are the player's team name, position, and career highlights. The first ten cards feature Eastern Stars, numbered with an "E" prefix, while the last ten cards present Western Stars, numbered with a "W" prefix.

	MINT	EXC	G-VG
COMPLETE SET (20)	350.00	160.00	45.00
COMP.EAST SERIES (10)	150.00	70.00	19.00
COMP.WEST SERIES (10)	200.00	90.00	25.00
COMMON EAST (E1-E10)	12.00	5.50	1.50
COMMON WEST (W1-W10)	16.00	7.25	2.00
☐ E1 Eric Lindros	45.00	20.00	5.75
Philadelphia Flyers			
☐ E2 Mario Lemieux	30.00	13.50	3.80
Pittsburgh Penguins			
☐ E3 Alexandre Daigle	12.00	5.50	1.50
Ottawa Senators			
☐ E4 Patrick Roy	25.00	11.50	3.10
Montreal Canadiens			
☐ E5 Rob Niedermayer	12.00	5.50	1.50
Florida Panthers			
☐ E6 Chris Gratton	12.00	5.50	1.50
Tampa Bay Lightning			
☐ E7 Alexei Yashin	15.00	6.75	1.90
Ottawa Senators			
☐ E8 Pat LaFontaine	12.00	5.50	1.50
Buffalo Sabres			
☐ E9 Joe Sakic	12.00	5.50	1.50
Quebec Nordiques			
☐ E10 Pierre Turgeon	14.00	6.25	1.75
New York Islanders			
☐ W1 Wayne Gretzky	45.00	20.00	5.75
Los Angeles Kings			
☐ W2 Pavel Bure	30.00	13.50	3.80
Vancouver Canucks			
☐ W3 Teemu Selanne	16.00	7.25	2.00
Winnipeg Jets			
☐ W4 Doug Gilmour	16.00	7.25	2.00
Toronto Maple Leafs			
☐ W5 Steve Yzerman	16.00	7.25	2.00
Detroit Red Wings			
☐ W6 Jeremy Roenick	16.00	7.25	2.00
Chicago Blackhawks			
☐ W7 Brett Hull	16.00	7.25	2.00
St. Louis Blues			
☐ W8 Jason Arnott	22.00	10.00	2.80
Edmonton Oilers			
☐ W9 Felix Potvin	20.00	9.00	2.50
Toronto Maple Leafs			
☐ W10 Sergei Fedorov	20.00	9.00	2.50
Detroit Red Wings			

1993-94 Parkhurst Cherry's Playoff Heroes

Randomly inserted in Canadian second-series retail foil packs, these 20 standard-size (2 1/2" by 3 1/2") cards feature color player action shots on their fronts. They are borderless, except on the left, where a red-foil stripe carries the Parkhurst name, and a black bar carries the player's name in vertical white lettering. The red-foil set logo rests at the lower right. The horizontal back carries a color player action cutout on the right, edged by a red stripe that carries the player's name in vertical white lettering. On the left are the player's team name, position, career highlights, and a

photo of Don Cherry. The cards are numbered on the back with a "D" prefix.

	MINT	EXC	G-VG
COMPLETE SET (20)	500.00	230.00	65.00
COMMON PLAYER (D1-D20)	12.00	5.50	1.50
☐ D1 Wayne Gretzky Los Angeles Kings	85.00	38.00	10.50
☐ D2 Mario Lemieux Pittsburgh Penguins	65.00	29.00	8.25
☐ D3 Al MacInnis Calgary Flames	15.00	6.75	1.90
☐ D4 Mark Messier New York Rangers	20.00	9.00	2.50
☐ D5 Dino Ciccarelli Detroit Red Wings	12.00	5.50	1.50
☐ D6 Dale Hunter Washington Capitals	12.00	5.50	1.50
☐ D7 Grant Fuhr Buffalo Sabres	14.00	6.25	1.75
☐ D8 Paul Coffey Detroit Red Wings	15.00	6.75	1.90
☐ D9 Doug Gilmour Toronto Maple Leafs	35.00	16.00	4.40
☐ D10 Patrick Roy Montreal Canadiens	60.00	27.00	7.50
☐ D11 Alexandre Daigle Ottawa Senators	20.00	9.00	2.50
☐ D12 Chris Gratton Tampa Bay Lightning	20.00	9.00	2.50
☐ D13 Chris Pronger Hartford Whalers	20.00	9.00	2.50
☐ D14 Felix Potvin Toronto Maple Leafs	45.00	20.00	5.75
☐ D15 Eric Lindros Philadelphia Flyers	80.00	36.00	10.00
☐ D16 Maurice Richard Montreal Canadiens	28.00	12.50	3.50
☐ D17 Gordie Howe Detroit Red Wings	35.00	16.00	4.40
☐ D18 Henri Richard Montreal Canadiens	15.00	6.75	1.90
☐ D19 Reggie Leach Philadelphia Flyers	12.00	5.50	1.50
☐ D20 Checklist Don Cherry and Blue	30.00	13.50	3.80

1993-94 Parkhurst First Overall

Randomly inserted in Canadian first-series retail foil packs, these ten standard-size (2 1/2" by 3 1/2") cards feature on their fronts color action shots of players drafted first overall in the annual NHL Entry Draft over the past decade. They are borderless, except on the left, where a copper-foil stripe carries the Parkhurst name, and a bar that shades from green to black carries the player's name in vertical white lettering. The copper-foil set logo at the lower right carries the year that the player was "First Overall" in the NHL draft. The horizontal back carries a color player action cutout on the right. On the left are the player's team name, position, career highlights, and chart showing the Top-10 NHL draft

picks the year the featured player was the first. The cards are numbered on the back with an "F" prefix.

	MINT	EXC	G-VG
COMPLETE SET (10)	100.00	45.00	12.50
COMMON PLAYER (F1-F10)	5.00	2.30	.60
☐ F1 Alexandre Daigle Ottawa Senators	10.00	4.50	1.25
☐ F2 Roman Hamrlik Tampa Bay Lightning	5.00	2.30	.60
☐ F3 Eric Lindros Philadelphia Flyers	40.00	18.00	5.00
☐ F4 Owen Nolan Quebec Nordiques	5.00	2.30	.60
☐ F5 Mats Sundin Quebec Nordiques	10.00	4.50	1.25
☐ F6 Mike Modano Dallas Stars	10.00	4.50	1.25
☐ F7 Pierre Turgeon New York Islanders	9.00	4.00	1.15
☐ F8 Joe Murphy Chicago Blackhawks	5.00	2.30	.60
☐ F9 Wendel Clark Toronto Maple Leafs	8.00	3.60	1.00
☐ F10 Mario Lemieux Pittsburgh Penguins	30.00	13.50	3.80

1993-94 Parkhurst Parkie Reprints

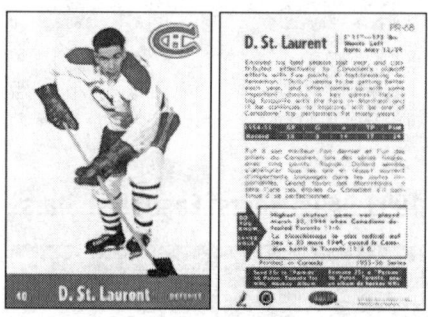

A continuation of the '92-93 Parkie Reprints set, these 40 (numbered 33-68, plus four checklists) cards measure the standard-size (2 1/2" by 3 1/2"). The first ten cards (33-41, plus checklist 5) were randomly inserted in '93-94 Parkhurst series foil packs. The second series (42-50, plus checklist 6) were random inserts in Parkhurst series one jumbo packs only. The third series (51-59, plus checklist 7) were random inserts in all series two Parkhurst packs. The fourth Parkie Reprints series (60-68, plus checklist 8) were random inserts in Parkhurst series two jumbo packs. The fronts are that of 1951-64 Parkhurst styles, but all carry a color player photo. The backs carry the information from the original card. The print varies from red to black to a combination. The cards are numbered on the back with a "PR" prefix. A hobby exclusive Parkie Reprints bonus pack was included in every series one and series two case.

		MINT	EXC	G-VG
COMPLETE SET (40)		575.00	250.00	70.00
COMPLETE SERIES 1 (10)		150.00	70.00	19.00
COMPLETE SERIES 2 (10)		150.00	70.00	19.00
COMPLETE SERIES 3 (10)		125.00	57.50	15.50
COMPLETE SERIES 4 (10)		150.00	70.00	19.00
COMMON PLAYER (33-41)		10.00	4.50	1.25
COMMON PLAYER (42-50)		12.00	5.50	1.50
COMMON PLAYER (51-59)		10.00	4.50	1.25
COMMON PLAYER (60-68)		12.00	5.50	1.50
☐ 33	Gordie Howe Detroit Red Wings	35.00	16.00	4.40
☐ 34	Tim Horton Toronto Maple Leafs	20.00	9.00	2.50
☐ 35	Bill Barilko Toronto Maple Leafs	18.00	8.00	2.30
☐ 36	Elmer Lach Maurice Richard Montreal Canadiens	20.00	9.00	2.50
☐ 37	Terry Sawchuk Detroit Red Wings	20.00	9.00	2.50
☐ 38	George Armstrong Toronto Maple Leafs	10.00	4.50	1.25
☐ 39	William Harris Toronto Maple Leafs	10.00	4.50	1.25
☐ 40	Doug Harvey Montreal Canadiens	18.00	8.00	2.30
☐ 41	Gump Worsley Montreal Canadiens	18.00	8.00	2.30
☐ 42	Gordie Howe Detroit Red Wings	35.00	16.00	4.40
☐ 43	Jacques Plante Montreal Canadiens	20.00	9.00	2.50
☐ 44	Frank Mahovlich Toronto Maple Leafs	18.00	8.00	2.30
☐ 45	Fern Flaman Toronto Maple Leafs	12.00	5.50	1.50
☐ 46	Boom Boom Geoffrion Montreal Canadiens	18.00	8.00	2.30
☐ 47	Toe Blake CO Montreal Canadiens	12.00	5.50	1.50
☐ 48	Maurice Richard Montreal Canadiens	20.00	9.00	2.50
☐ 49	Ted Lindsay Detroit Red Wings	15.00	6.75	1.90
☐ 50	Camille Henry New York Rangers	12.00	5.50	1.50
☐ 51	Gordie Howe Detroit Red Wings	30.00	13.50	3.80
☐ 52	Jean-Guy Talbot Montreal Canadiens	10.00	4.50	1.25
☐ 53	Terry Sawchuk Detroit Red Wings	20.00	9.00	2.50
☐ 54	Warren Godfrey Boston Bruins	10.00	4.50	1.25
☐ 55	Tom Johnson Montreal Canadiens	10.00	4.50	1.25
☐ 56	Bert Olmstead Toronto Maple Leafs	10.00	4.50	1.25
☐ 57	Cal Gardner Boston Bruins	10.00	4.50	1.25
☐ 58	Red Kelly Toronto Maple Leafs	15.00	6.75	1.90
☐ 59	Phil Goyette Montreal Canadiens	10.00	4.50	1.25
☐ 60	Gordie Howe Detroit Red Wings	30.00	13.50	3.80
☐ 61	Lou Fontinato Montreal Canadiens	12.00	5.50	1.50
☐ 62	Bill Dineen Detroit Red Wings	12.00	5.50	1.50
☐ 63	Maurice Richard Montreal Canadiens	20.00	9.00	2.50
☐ 64	Vic Stasiuk Detroit Red Wings	12.00	5.50	1.50
☐ 65	Marcel Pronovost Detroit Red Wings	12.00	5.50	1.50
☐ 66	Ed Litzenberger Toronto Maple Leafs	12.00	5.50	1.50
☐ 67	Dave Keon Toronto Maple Leafs	15.00	6.75	1.90
☐ 68	Dollard St. Laurent Montreal Canadiens	12.00	5.50	1.50
☐ CL5	Parkies Checklist 5	25.00	11.50	3.10
☐ CL6	Parkies Checklist 6	25.00	11.50	3.10
☐ CL7	Parkies Checklist 7	25.00	11.50	3.10
☐ CL8	Parkies Checklist 8	25.00	11.50	3.10

1993-94 Parkhurst Parkie Reprints Case Inserts

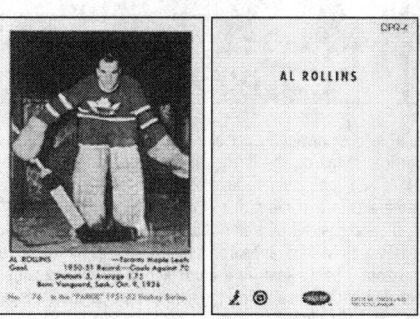

This set was inserted one per series one (1-6) and series 2 (7-12) hobby case. Parkhurst selected vintage cards from its past to reprint in this 12-card standard-size (2 1/2" by 3 1/2") set. The cards are coated on both sides and are easily recognizable as reprints. The cards are numbered on the back with the prefix "DPR".

		MINT	EXC	G-VG
COMP.SERIES I SET (6)		40.00	18.00	5.00
COMP.SERIES II SET (6)		35.00	16.00	4.40
COMMON PLAYER (1-6)		6.00	2.70	.75
COMMON PLAYER (7-12)		6.00	2.70	.75
☐ 1	Gordie Howe Detroit Red Wings	20.00	9.00	2.50
☐ 2	Milt Schmidt Boston Bruins	6.00	2.70	.75
☐ 3	Tim Horton Toronto Maple Leafs	12.00	5.50	1.50
☐ 4	Al Rollins Toronto Maple Leafs	6.00	2.70	.75
☐ 5	Maurice Richard Montreal Canadiens	12.00	5.50	1.50
☐ 6	Harry Howell New York Rangers	6.00	2.70	.75
☐ 7	Gordie Howe Detroit Red Wings	20.00	9.00	2.50
☐ 8	Johnny Bower Toronto Maple Leafs	10.00	4.50	1.25
☐ 9	Dean Prentice New York Rangers	6.00	2.70	.75
☐ 10	Leo Labine Boston Bruins	6.00	2.70	.75
☐ 11	Harry Watson Toronto Maple Leafs	7.00	3.10	.85
☐ 12	Dickie Moore Montreal Canadiens	7.00	3.10	.85

1993-94 Parkhurst USA/Canada Gold

Randomly inserted in U.S. first-series foil packs, Upper Deck selected the top five players from NHL teams based in the United States and the top five players from NHL teams based in Canada for this 10-card standard-size (2 1/2" by 3 1/2") set. Accordingly, cards 1-5 are USA Gold while cards 6-10 are Canadian Gold. The fronts of the USA cards feature

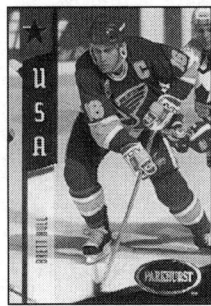

full-bleed color action player photos with a gold and blue vertical stripe on the left featuring a gold star, the word "USA" and the player's name. The Canadian version is the same except that the stripe is gold and red and features a maple leaf instead of a star and the word "Canada". A gold-foil Parkhurst logo appears in the lower right corner. The horizontal backs feature a color action cutout on a gold blended background using the same stripe as the front but on the right side. The player profile is to the left of the cutout. The cards are numbered on the back with a "G" prefix.

	MINT	EXC	G-VG
COMPLETE SET (10)	140.00	65.00	17.50
COMMON PLAYER (G1-G10)	10.00	4.50	1.25
☐ G1 Wayne Gretzky	40.00	18.00	5.00
Los Angeles Kings			
☐ G2 Mario Lemieux	30.00	13.50	3.80
Pittsburgh Penguins			
☐ G3 Eric Lindros	35.00	16.00	4.40
Philadelphia Flyers			
☐ G4 Brett Hull	14.00	6.25	1.75
St. Louis Blues			
☐ G5 Rob Niedermayer	10.00	4.50	1.25
Florida Panthers			
☐ G6 Alexandre Daigle	12.00	5.50	1.50
Ottawa Senators			
☐ G7 Pavel Bure	25.00	11.50	3.10
Vancouver Canucks			
☐ G8 Teemu Selanne	14.00	6.25	1.75
Winnipeg Jets			
☐ G9 Patrick Roy	20.00	9.00	2.50
Montreal Canadiens			
☐ G10 Doug Gilmour	15.00	6.75	1.90
Toronto Maple Leafs			

1994 Parkhurst Missing Link

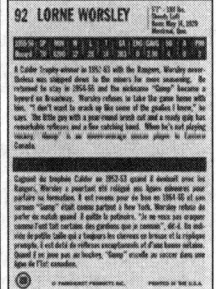

The Upper Deck Company and Parkhurst Products Inc. produced this "Missing Link" set. Parkhurst produced hockey cards from the 1951-52 season until the 1963-64 season. No cards were made by Parkhurst or any other

manufacturer for the 1956-57 season, until this set was produced. This "Missing Link" set was limited to 1,956 numbered cases for the U.S. distributed by Upper Deck and the same amount distributed in Canada by PHC Sports Card Distribution. These standard-size (2 1/2" by 3 1/2") cards were made of card stock similar to that used in the early Parkhurst days and came in ten-card wax packs that were intended to be retailed for about 1.99. Cards from three different insert sets were randomly inserted throughout the packs: a six-card Future Stars set; a six-card Autographed set of Hall of Famers; and 12 "Pop-Ups" (i.e., die-cut cards) of Canadian (1-6) and American (7-12) NHL greats of the 1930s. One thousand of each die-cut card were produced. The cards are numbered on the back and checklisted below alphabetically according to teams as follows: Boston Bruins (1-21), Chicago Blackhawks (22-42), Detroit Red Wings (43-63), Montreal Canadiens (64-85), New York Rangers (86-108), and Toronto Maple Leafs (109-134). The set closes with All-Stars (135-146), Award Winners (147-152), Action Shots (153-168), Scoring Leaders (169-174), Stanley Cup (175-178), and checklists (179-180).

	MINT	EXC	G-VG
COMPLETE SET (180)	40.00	18.00	5.00
COMMON PLAYER (1-180)	.25	.11	.03
☐ 1 Jerry Toppazzini	.25	.11	.03
☐ 2 Fern Flaman	.25	.11	.03
☐ 3 Fleming MacKell	.25	.11	.03
☐ 4 Leo Labine	.25	.11	.03
☐ 5 John Peirson	.25	.11	.03
☐ 6 Don McKenney	.25	.11	.03
☐ 7 Bob Armstrong	.25	.11	.03
☐ 8 Real Chevrefils	.25	.11	.03
☐ 9 Vic Stasiuk	.25	.11	.03
☐ 10 Cal Gardner	.25	.11	.03
☐ 11 Leo Boivin	.25	.11	.03
☐ 12 Jack Caffery	.25	.11	.03
☐ 13 Bob Beckett	.25	.11	.03
☐ 14 Jack Bionda	.25	.11	.03
☐ 15 Claude Pronovost	.25	.11	.03
☐ 16 Larry Regan	.25	.11	.03
☐ 17 Terry Sawchuk	2.00	.90	.25
☐ 18 Doug Mohns	.25	.11	.03
☐ 19 Marcel Bonin	.25	.11	.03
☐ 20 Allan Stanley	.50	.23	.06
☐ 21 Milt Schmidt CO	.40	.18	.05
☐ 22 Al Dewsbury	.25	.11	.03
☐ 23 Glen Skov	.25	.11	.03
☐ 24 Ed Litzenberger	.25	.11	.03
☐ 25 Nick Mickoski	.25	.11	.03
☐ 26 Walter Hergesheimer	.25	.11	.03
☐ 27 Jack McIntyre	.25	.11	.03
☐ 28 Al Rollins	.25	.11	.03
☐ 29 Hank Ciesla	.25	.11	.03
☐ 30 Gus Mortson	.25	.11	.03
☐ 31 Elmer Vasko	.25	.11	.03
☐ 32 Pierre Pilote	.50	.23	.06
☐ 33 Ron Ingram	.25	.11	.03
☐ 34 Frank Martin	.25	.11	.03
☐ 35 Forbes Kennedy	.25	.11	.03
☐ 36 Harry Watson	.25	.11	.03
☐ 37 Eddie Kachur	.25	.11	.03
☐ 38 Hec Lalande	.25	.11	.03
☐ 39 Eric Nesterenko	.25	.11	.03
☐ 40 Ben Woit	.25	.11	.03
☐ 41 Ken Mosdell	.25	.11	.03
☐ 42 Tommy Ivan CO	.25	.11	.03
☐ 43 Gordie Howe	4.00	1.80	.50
☐ 44 Ted Lindsay	.75	.35	.09
☐ 45 Norm Ullman	.25	.11	.03
☐ 46 Glenn Hall	1.00	.45	.13
☐ 47 Billy Dea	.25	.11	.03
☐ 48 Bill McNeill	.25	.11	.03
☐ 49 Earl Reibel	.25	.11	.03
☐ 50 Bill Dineen	.25	.11	.03
☐ 51 Warren Godfrey	.25	.11	.03
☐ 52 Red Kelly	.75	.35	.09
☐ 53 Marty Pavelich	.25	.11	.03
☐ 54 Lorne Ferguson	.25	.11	.03
☐ 55 Larry Hillman	.25	.11	.03
☐ 56 John Bucyk	.50	.23	.06
☐ 57 Metro Prystai	.25	.11	.03
☐ 58 Marcel Pronovost	.40	.18	.05
☐ 59 Alex Delvecchio	.75	.35	.09
☐ 60 Murray Costello	.25	.11	.03

☐	61 Al Arbour	.50	.23	.06
☐	62 Bucky Hollingworth	.25	.11	.03
☐	63 Jim Skinner CO	.25	.11	.03
☐	64 Jean Beliveau	2.00	.90	.25
☐	65 Maurice Richard	2.50	1.15	.30
☐	66 Henri Richard	.50	.23	.06
☐	67 Doug Harvey	.50	.23	.06
☐	68 Bernie Geoffrion	.60	.25	.08
☐	69 Dollard St. Laurent	.25	.11	.03
☐	70 Dickie Moore	.50	.23	.06
☐	71 Bert Olmstead	.40	.18	.05
☐	72 Jacques Plante	2.50	1.15	.30
☐	73 Claude Provost	.25	.11	.03
☐	74 Phil Goyette	.25	.11	.03
☐	75 Andre Pronovost	.25	.11	.03
☐	76 Don Marshall	.25	.11	.03
☐	77 Ralph Backstrom	.25	.11	.03
☐	78 Floyd Curry	.25	.11	.03
☐	79 Tom Johnson	.50	.23	.06
☐	80 Jean Guy Talbot	.25	.11	.03
☐	81 Bob Turner	.25	.11	.03
☐	82 Connie Broden	.25	.11	.03
☐	83 Jackie Leclair	.25	.11	.03
☐	84 Toe Blake CO	.25	.11	.03
☐	85 Frank Selke MD	.25	.11	.03
☐	86 George Sullivan	.25	.11	.03
☐	87 Larry Cahan	.25	.11	.03
☐	88 Jean Guy Gendron	.25	.11	.03
☐	89 Bill Gadsby	.50	.23	.06
☐	90 Andy Bathgate	.50	.23	.06
☐	91 Dean Prentice	.25	.11	.03
☐	92 Gump Worsley	1.00	.45	.13
☐	93 Lou Fontinato	.25	.11	.03
☐	94 Gerry Foley	.25	.11	.03
☐	95 Larry Popein	.25	.11	.03
☐	96 Harry Howell	.50	.23	.06
☐	97 Andy Hebenton	.25	.11	.03
☐	98 Danny Lewicki	.25	.11	.03
☐	99 Dave Creighton	.25	.11	.03
☐	100 Camille Henry	.25	.11	.03
☐	101 Jack Evans	.25	.11	.03
☐	102 Ron Murphy	.25	.11	.03
☐	103 Johnny Bower	.75	.35	.09
☐	104 Parker MacDonald	.25	.11	.03
☐	105 Bronco Horvath	.25	.11	.03
☐	106 Bruce Cline	.25	.11	.03
☐	107 Ivan Irwin	.25	.11	.03
☐	108 Phil Watson CO	.25	.11	.03
☐	109 Sid Smith	.25	.11	.03
☐	110 Ron Stewart	.25	.11	.03
☐	111 Rudy Migay	.25	.11	.03
☐	112 Tod Sloan	.25	.11	.03
☐	113 Bob Pulford	.25	.11	.03
☐	114 Marc Reaume	.25	.11	.03
☐	115 Jim Morrison	.25	.11	.03
☐	116 Ted Kennedy	.50	.23	.06
☐	117 Gerry James	.25	.11	.03
☐	118 Brian Cullen	.25	.11	.03
☐	119 Jim Thomson	.25	.11	.03
☐	120 Barry Cullen	.25	.11	.03
☐	121 Al MacNeil	.25	.11	.03
☐	122 Gary Aldcorn	.25	.11	.03
☐	123 Bob Baun	.25	.11	.03
☐	124 Hugh Bolton	.25	.11	.03
☐	125 George Armstrong	.50	.23	.06
☐	126 Dick Duff	.25	.11	.03
☐	127 Tim Horton	1.50	.65	.19
☐	128 Ed Chadwick	.25	.11	.03
☐	129 Billy Harris	.25	.11	.03
☐	130 Mike Nykoluk	.25	.11	.03
☐	131 Noel Price	.25	.11	.03
☐	132 Ken Girard	.25	.11	.03
☐	133 Howie Meeker	.50	.23	.06
☐	134 Hap Day CO	.25	.11	.03
☐	135 Jacques Plante AS	1.00	.45	.13
☐	136 Doug Harvey AS	.25	.11	.03
☐	137 Bill Gadsby AS	.25	.11	.03
☐	138 Jean Beliveau AS	.75	.35	.09
☐	139 Maurice Richard AS	1.00	.45	.13
☐	140 Ted Lindsay AS	.25	.11	.03
☐	141 Glenn Hall AS	.50	.23	.06
☐	142 Red Kelly AS	.25	.11	.03
☐	143 Tom Johnson AS	.25	.11	.03
☐	144 Tod Sloan AS	.25	.11	.03
☐	145 Gordie Howe AS	1.50	.65	.19
☐	146 Bert Olmstead AS	.25	.11	.03
☐	147 Earl Reibel AW	.25	.11	.03
	Lady Byng			
☐	148 Doug Harvey AW	.25	.11	.03
	Norris			
☐	149 Jean Beliveau AW	.75	.35	.09
	Hart			
☐	150 Jean Beliveau AW	.75	.35	.09
	Art Ross			
☐	151 Jacques Plante AW	1.00	.45	.13
	Vezina			
☐	152 Glenn Hall AW	.50	.23	.06
	Calder			
☐	153 Action Shot	.75	.35	.09
	All-Star			
☐	154 Action Shot	.25	.11	.03
	Toronto Maple Leafs			
☐	155 Action Shot	.25	.11	.03
	Toronto Maple Leafs			
☐	156 Action Shot	.75	.35	.09
	Toronto Maple Leafs			
☐	157 Action Shot	.75	.35	.09
	Toronto Maple Leafs			
☐	158 Action Shot	.50	.23	.06
	Detroit Red Wings			
☐	159 Action Shot	.50	.23	.06
	Detroit Red Wings			
☐	160 Action Shot	1.50	.65	.19
	Detroit Red Wings			
☐	161 Action Shot	1.00	.45	.13
	Montreal Canadiens			
☐	162 Action Shot	1.50	.65	.19
	Montreal Canadiens			
☐	163 Action Shot	1.00	.45	.13
	Montreal Canadiens			
☐	164 Action Shot	.50	.23	.06
	Montreal Canadiens			
☐	165 Action Shot	.50	.23	.06
	New York Rangers			
☐	166 Action Shot	.25	.11	.03
	Chicago Blackhawks			
☐	167 Action Shot	.75	.35	.09
	Boston Bruins			
☐	168 Action Shot	.75	.35	.09
	Boston Bruins			
☐	169 Vic Stasiuk SL	.25	.11	.03
☐	170 George Sullivan SL	.25	.11	.03
☐	171 Gordie Howe SL	1.50	.65	.19
☐	172 Jean Beliveau SL	.75	.35	.09
☐	173 Andy Bathgate SL	.25	.11	.03
☐	174 Tod Sloan SL	.25	.11	.03
☐	175 Stanley Cup	.25	.11	.03
☐	176 Stanley Cup	.25	.11	.03
☐	177 Stanley Cup	.25	.11	.03
☐	178 Stanley Cup	.25	.11	.03
☐	179 Checklist 1	.25	.11	.03
☐	180 Checklist 2	.25	.11	.03

1994 Parkhurst Missing Link Autograph

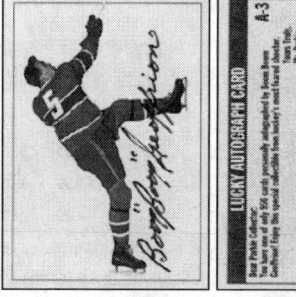

The 1994 Parkhurst Missing Link set comprises six Hall of Famers. Randomly inserted in Missing Link packs, the cards are autographed on the front and numbered "X of 956" on the back. The cards are also numbered for set purposes A1-A6. The design is different from those found in the Missing Link issue. Card fronts are color, but do not contain the player's name (except for autograph) or team name. The backs provide a congratulatory note to the collector

	MINT	EXC	G-VG
COMPLETE SET (6)	800.00	350.00	100.00
COMMON PLAYER (1-6)	125.00	57.50	15.50
☐ 1 Gordie Howe	250.00	115.00	31.00
Detroit Red Wings			
☐ 2 Maurice Richard	200.00	90.00	25.00
Montreal Canadiens			
☐ 3 Bernie Geoffrion	125.00	57.50	15.50
Montreal Canadiens			
☐ 4 Gump Worsley	125.00	57.50	15.50
Montreal Canadiens			
☐ 5 Jean Beliveau	175.00	80.00	22.00
Montreal Canadiens			
☐ 6 Frank Mahovlich	150.00	70.00	19.00
Toronto Maple Leafs			

1994 Parkhurst Missing Link Future Stars

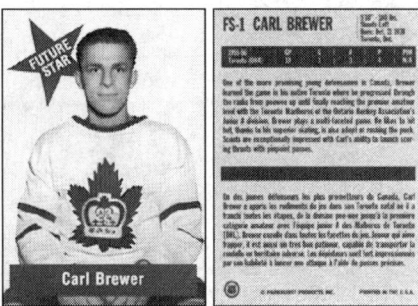

Randomly inserted in wax packs of 1994 Parkhurst Missing Link, this six-card standard-size (2 1/2" by 3 1/2") set features the best six players in the Canadian junior hockey leagues in 1956. On the fronts, the players are shown in their junior team uniforms in posed or action color player cutouts on white backgrounds. The player's name appears in a colored stripe near the bottom. In black lettering, the plain cardboard back carries the player's name, biography, and statistics at the top, followed below by career highlights in both English and French. The cards are numbered on the back with a "FS" prefix.

	MINT	EXC	G-VG
COMPLETE SET (6)	100.00	45.00	12.50
COMMON PLAYER (FS1-FS6)	15.00	6.75	1.90
☐ FS1 Carl Brewer	15.00	6.75	1.90
Toronto Maple Leafs			
☐ FS2 Dave Keon	25.00	11.50	3.10
Toronto Maple Leafs			
☐ FS3 Stan Mikita	25.00	11.50	3.10
Chicago Blackhawks			
☐ FS4 Eddie Shack	20.00	9.00	2.50
New York Rangers			
☐ FS5 Frank Mahovlich	25.00	11.50	3.10
Toronto Maple Leafs			
☐ FS6 Charlie Hodge	15.00	6.75	1.90
Montreal Canadiens			

1994 Parkhurst Missing Link Pop-Ups

This set of 12 die-cut inserts features cards of Canadian (1-6) and American (7-12) NHL greats of the 1930s, randomly inserted in Canadian only and American only packs, respectively. Just 1,000 cards of each player were produced. The borderless fronts feature sepiatone player shots superposed upon a drawing of hockey action. The player's name last name appears in a simulated plaque near the bottom. The plain cardboard back carries in its bottom half the player's name, biography, and statistics. The cards are numbered on the back with a "P" prefix.

	MINT	EXC	G-VG
COMPLETE SET (12)	500.00	230.00	65.00
COMP.CANADIAN SERIES (6)	275.00	125.00	34.00
COMP.AMERICAN SERIES (6)	225.00	100.00	28.00
COMMON PLAYER (P1-P6)	40.00	18.00	5.00
COMMON PLAYER (P7-P12)	30.00	13.50	3.80
☐ P1 Howie Morenz	65.00	29.00	8.25
Montreal Canadiens			
☐ P2 George Hainsworth	40.00	18.00	5.00
Montreal Canadiens			
☐ P3 Georges Vezina	65.00	29.00	8.25
Montreal Canadiens			
☐ P4 King Clancy	45.00	20.00	5.75
Toronto Maple Leafs			
☐ P5 Syl Apps	40.00	18.00	5.00
Toronto Maple Leafs			
☐ P6 Turk Broda	45.00	20.00	5.75
Toronto Maple Leafs			
☐ P7 Eddie Shore	65.00	29.00	8.25
Boston Bruins			
☐ P8 Bill Cook	30.00	13.50	3.80
New York Rangers			
☐ P9 Woody Dumart	30.00	13.50	3.80
Boston Bruins			
☐ P10 Lester Patrick	50.00	23.00	6.25
New York Rangers			
☐ P11 Doug Bentley	30.00	13.50	3.80
Chicago Blackhawks			
☐ P12 Earl Seibert	30.00	13.50	3.80
New York Rangers			

1994-95 Parkhurst

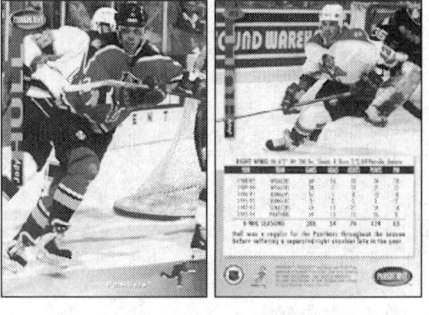

The 315 standard-size (2 1/2" by 3 1/2") cards comprising the first series of '94-95 Parkhurst feature borderless color player action shots on their fronts. The player's name appears in vertical lettering within a purplish strip at the upper left. His team name, along with a silver-foil icon of a player taking a slap shot, appears at the lower right. The back carries another color player action shot, and biography, statistics, and career highlights. The cards are numbered on the back.

		MINT	EXC	G-VG
COMPLETE SERIES 1 (315)		25.00	11.50	3.10
COMMON PLAYER (1-315)		.05	.02	.01
☐	1 Anatoli Semenov	.05	.02	.01
☐	2 Stephan Lebeau	.05	.02	.01
☐	3 Stu Grimson	.05	.02	.01
☐	4 Mikhail Shtalenkov	.15	.07	.02
☐	5 Troy Loney	.05	.02	.01
☐	6 Sean Hill	.05	.02	.01
☐	7 Patrik Carnback	.05	.02	.01
☐	8 John Lilley	.05	.02	.01
☐	9 Tim Sweeney	.05	.02	.01
☐	10 Maxim Bets	.15	.07	.02
☐	11 Cam Neely	.15	.07	.02
☐	12 Bryan Smolinski	.30	.14	.04
☐	13 Ray Bourque	.15	.07	.02
☐	14 Vincent Riendeau	.05	.02	.01
☐	15 Al Iafrate	.08	.04	.01
☐	16 Andrew McKim	.10	.05	.01
☐	17 Glen Wesley	.05	.02	.01
☐	18 Daniel Marois	.05	.02	.01
☐	19 Josef Stumpel	.05	.02	.01
☐	20 Mariusz Czerkawski	.25	.11	.03
☐	21 Alexander Mogilny	.30	.14	.04
☐	22 Yuri Khmylev	.08	.04	.01
☐	23 Donald Audette	.05	.02	.01
☐	24 Dominik Hasek	.10	.05	.01
☐	25 Randy Wood	.05	.02	.01
☐	26 Brad May	.05	.02	.01
☐	27 Wayne Presley	.05	.02	.01
☐	28 Richard Smehlik	.08	.04	.01
☐	29 Dale Hawerchuk	.08	.04	.01
☐	30 Rob Ray	.05	.02	.01
☐	31 Zarley Zalapski	.05	.02	.01
☐	32 Michael Nylander	.08	.04	.01
☐	33 Joe Nieuwendyk	.08	.04	.01
☐	34 Robert Reichel	.08	.04	.01
☐	35 Al MacInnis	.10	.05	.01
☐	36 Andrei Trefilov	.08	.04	.01
☐	37 Leonard Esau	.05	.02	.01
☐	38 Wes Walz	.05	.02	.01
☐	39 Michel Petit	.05	.02	.01
☐	40 James Patrick	.05	.02	.01
☐	41 Ed Belfour	.15	.07	.02
☐	42 Christian Ruuttu	.05	.02	.01
☐	43 Eric Weinrich	.05	.02	.01
☐	44 Joe Murphy	.05	.02	.01
☐	45 Chris Chelios	.08	.04	.01
☐	46 Jeff Shantz	.05	.02	.01
☐	47 Gary Suter	.08	.04	.01
☐	48 Paul Ysebaert	.05	.02	.01
☐	49 Ivan Droppa	.05	.02	.01
☐	50 Keith Carney	.05	.02	.01
☐	51 Andy Moog	.08	.04	.01
☐	52 Russ Courtnall	.08	.04	.01
☐	53 Neal Broten	.08	.04	.01
☐	54 Mike Craig	.05	.02	.01
☐	55 Brent Gilchrist	.05	.02	.01
☐	56 Pelle Eklund	.05	.02	.01
☐	57 Richard Matvichuk	.05	.02	.01
☐	58 Dave Gagner	.08	.04	.01
☐	59 Mark Tinordi	.05	.02	.01
☐	60 Paul Broten	.05	.02	.01
☐	61 Nicklas Lidstrom	.08	.04	.01
☐	62 Shawn Burr	.05	.02	.01
☐	63 Paul Coffey	.08	.04	.01
☐	64 Bob Essensa	.08	.04	.01
☐	65 Dino Ciccarelli	.08	.04	.01
☐	66 Slava Kozlov	.25	.11	.03
☐	67 Keith Primeau	.08	.04	.01
☐	68 Steve Chiasson	.05	.02	.01
☐	69 Terry Carkner	.05	.02	.01
☐	70 Martin Lapointe	.05	.02	.01
☐	71 Bob Probert	.05	.02	.01
☐	72 Bill Ranford	.08	.04	.01
☐	73 Scott Thornton	.05	.02	.01
☐	74 Doug Weight	.08	.04	.01
☐	75 Shayne Corson	.05	.02	.01
☐	76 Zdeno Ciger	.05	.02	.01
☐	77 Adam Bennett	.05	.02	.01
☐	78 Scott Pearson	.05	.02	.01
☐	79 Brent Grieve	.15	.07	.02
☐	80 Gordon Mark	.10	.05	.01
☐	81 Shjon Podein	.05	.02	.01
☐	82 Geoff Smith	.05	.02	.01
☐	83 Bob Kudelski	.08	.04	.01
☐	84 Andrei Lomakin	.05	.02	.01
☐	85 Scott Mellanby	.05	.02	.01
☐	86 Jesse Belanger	.05	.02	.01
☐	87 Mark Fitzpatrick	.05	.02	.01
☐	88 Peter Andersson	.05	.02	.01
☐	89 Jody Hull	.05	.02	.01
☐	90 Brent Severyn	.05	.02	.01
☐	91 Jim Sandlak	.05	.02	.01
☐	92 Pat Verbeek	.08	.04	.01
☐	93 Ted Crowley	.05	.02	.01
☐	94 Robert Petrovicky	.05	.02	.01
☐	95 Geoff Sanderson	.05	.02	.01
☐	96 Ted Drury	.05	.02	.01
☐	97 Andrew Cassels	.05	.02	.01
☐	98 Igor Chibirev	.05	.02	.01
☐	99 Kevin Smyth	.05	.02	.01
☐	100 Alexander Godynyuk	.05	.02	.01
☐	101 Alexei Zhitnik	.08	.04	.01
☐	102 Dixon Ward	.05	.02	.01
☐	103 Wayne Gretzky	1.50	.65	.19
☐	104 Jari Kurri	.10	.05	.01
☐	105 Rob Blake	.08	.04	.01
☐	106 Marty McSorley	.08	.04	.01
☐	107 Pat Conacher	.05	.02	.01
☐	108 Kevin Todd	.05	.02	.01
☐	109 Robb Stauber	.05	.02	.01
☐	110 Keith Redmond	.05	.02	.01
☐	111 John LeClair	.05	.02	.01
☐	112 Brian Bellows	.08	.04	.01
☐	113 Patrick Roy	.50	.23	.06
☐	114 Les Kuntar	.15	.07	.02
☐	115 Vincent Damphousse	.08	.04	.01
☐	116 Patrice Brisebois	.05	.02	.01
☐	117 Pierre Sevigny	.05	.02	.01
☐	118 Eric Desjardins	.05	.02	.01
☐	119 Oleg Petrov	.05	.02	.01
☐	120 Kevin Haller	.05	.02	.01
☐	121 Christian Proulx	.10	.05	.01
☐	122 Corey Millen	.05	.02	.01
☐	123 Jaroslav Modry	.05	.02	.01
☐	124 Valeri Zelepukin	.08	.04	.01
☐	125 John MacLean	.08	.04	.01
☐	126 Martin Brodeur	.30	.14	.04
☐	127 Bill Guerin	.05	.02	.01
☐	128 Bobby Holik	.05	.02	.01
☐	129 Claude Lemieux	.08	.04	.01
☐	130 Jason Smith	.05	.02	.01
☐	131 Ken Daneyko	.05	.02	.01
☐	132 Derek King	.05	.02	.01
☐	133 Darius Kasparaitis	.05	.02	.01
☐	134 Ray Ferraro	.05	.02	.01
☐	135 Pierre Turgeon	.20	.09	.03
☐	136 Ron Hextall	.08	.04	.01
☐	137 Travis Green	.05	.02	.01
☐	138 Joe Day	.05	.02	.01
☐	139 David Volek	.05	.02	.01
☐	140 Scott Lachance	.05	.02	.01
☐	141 Dennis Vaske	.05	.02	.01
☐	142 Alexei Kovalev	.30	.14	.04
☐	143 Brian Noonan	.05	.02	.01
☐	144 Sergei Zubov	.20	.09	.03
☐	145 Craig MacTavish	.05	.02	.01
☐	146 Steve Larmer	.08	.04	.01
☐	147 Adam Graves	.20	.09	.03
☐	148 Jeff Beukeboom	.05	.02	.01
☐	149 Corey Hirsch	.05	.02	.01
☐	150 Stephane Matteau	.05	.02	.01
☐	151 Brian Leetch	.20	.09	.03
☐	152 Mattias Norstrom	.05	.02	.01
☐	153 Sylvain Turgeon	.05	.02	.01
☐	154 Norm Maciver	.05	.02	.01
☐	155 Scott Levins	.05	.02	.01
☐	156 Derek Mayer	.05	.02	.01
☐	157 Dave McLlwain	.05	.02	.01
☐	158 Craig Billington	.05	.02	.01
☐	159 Claude Boivin	.05	.02	.01
☐	160 Troy Mallette	.05	.02	.01
☐	161 Evgeny Davydov	.05	.02	.01
☐	162 Dimitri Filimonov	.05	.02	.01
☐	163 Dimitri Yushkevich	.05	.02	.01
☐	164 Rob Zettler	.05	.02	.01
☐	165 Mark Recchi	.20	.09	.03
☐	166 Josef Beranek	.05	.02	.01
☐	167 Rod Brind'Amour	.10	.05	.01
☐	168 Yves Racine	.05	.02	.01
☐	169 Dominic Roussel	.05	.02	.01
☐	170 Brent Fedyk	.05	.02	.01
☐	171 Bob Wilkie	.10	.05	.01
☐	172 Kevin Dineen	.08	.04	.01

☐	173	Shawn McEachern	.05	.02	.01
☐	174	Jaromir Jagr	.30	.14	.04
☐	175	Tomas Sandstrom	.05	.02	.01
☐	176	Ron Francis	.08	.04	.01
☐	177	Kevin Stevens	.20	.09	.03
☐	178	Jim McKenzie	.05	.02	.01
☐	179	Larry Murphy	.08	.04	.01
☐	180	Joe Mullen	.08	.04	.01
☐	181	Greg Hawgood	.05	.02	.01
☐	182	Tom Barrasso	.08	.04	.01
☐	183	Ulf Samuelsson	.08	.04	.01
☐	184	Bob Bassen	.05	.02	.01
☐	185	Mats Sundin	.20	.09	.03
☐	186	Mike Ricci	.08	.04	.01
☐	187	Iain Fraser	.05	.02	.01
☐	188	Garth Butcher	.05	.02	.01
☐	189	Jocelyn Thibault	.25	.11	.03
☐	190	Valeri Kamensky	.05	.02	.01
☐	191	Martin Rucinsky	.05	.02	.01
☐	192	Ron Sutter	.05	.02	.01
☐	193	Rene Corbet	.05	.02	.01
☐	194	Reggie Savage	.05	.02	.01
☐	195	Alexei Kasatonov	.05	.02	.01
☐	196	Brendan Shanahan	.25	.11	.03
☐	197	Phil Housley	.08	.04	.01
☐	198	Jim Montgomery	.05	.02	.01
☐	199	Curtis Joseph	.10	.05	.01
☐	200	Craig Janney	.10	.05	.01
☐	201	David Roberts	.05	.02	.01
☐	202	Dave Mackey	.05	.02	.01
☐	203	Peter Stastny	.08	.04	.01
☐	204	Terry Hollinger	.10	.05	.01
☐	205	Steve Duchesne	.08	.04	.01
☐	206	Vitali Prokhorov	.05	.02	.01
☐	207	Rob Gaudreau	.05	.02	.01
☐	208	Sandis Ozolinsh	.10	.05	.01
☐	209	Johan Garpenlov	.05	.02	.01
☐	210	Todd Elik	.05	.02	.01
☐	211	Sergei Makarov	.08	.04	.01
☐	212	Jean-Francois Quintin	.05	.02	.01
☐	213	Vyacheslav Butsayev	.05	.02	.01
☐	214	Jimmy Waite	.05	.02	.01
☐	215	Ulf Dahlen	.05	.02	.01
☐	216	Andrei Nazarov	.05	.02	.01
☐	217	Denis Savard	.10	.05	.01
☐	218	Brent Gretzky	.20	.09	.03
☐	219	Petr Klima	.05	.02	.01
☐	220	Chris Gratton	.25	.11	.03
☐	221	Brian Bradley	.05	.02	.01
☐	222	Adam Creighton	.05	.02	.01
☐	223	Shawn Chambers	.05	.02	.01
☐	224	Rob Zamuner	.05	.02	.01
☐	225	Daren Puppa	.08	.04	.01
☐	226	Mikael Andersson	.05	.02	.01
☐	227	Dave Ellett	.05	.02	.01
☐	228	Mike Gartner	.10	.05	.01
☐	229	Felix Potvin	.50	.23	.06
☐	230	Yanic Perreault	.05	.02	.01
☐	231	Nikolai Borschevsky	.05	.02	.01
☐	232	Dmitri Mironov	.05	.02	.01
☐	233	Todd Gill	.05	.02	.01
☐	234	Eric Lacroix	.10	.05	.01
☐	235	Kent Manderville	.05	.02	.01
☐	236	Chris Govedaris	.05	.02	.01
☐	237	Frank Bialowas	.10	.05	.01
☐	238	Kirk McLean	.10	.05	.01
☐	239	Jimmy Carson	.05	.02	.01
☐	240	Geoff Courtnall	.05	.02	.01
☐	241	Trevor Linden	.10	.05	.01
☐	242	Murray Craven	.05	.02	.01
☐	243	Bret Hedican	.05	.02	.01
☐	244	Jeff Brown	.08	.04	.01
☐	245	Mike Peca	.20	.09	.03
☐	246	Yevgeny Namestnikov	.05	.02	.01
☐	247	Nathan Lafayette	.05	.02	.01
☐	248	Shawn Antoski	.06	.02	.01
☐	249	Sergio Momesso	.05	.02	.01
☐	250	Mike Ridley	.08	.04	.01
☐	251	Peter Bondra	.08	.04	.01
☐	252	Dimitri Khristich	.08	.04	.01
☐	253	Dave Poulin	.05	.02	.01
☐	254	Dale Hunter	.08	.04	.01
☐	255	Rick Tabaracci	.05	.02	.01
☐	256	Kelly Miller	.05	.02	.01
☐	257	John Slaney	.05	.02	.01
☐	258	Todd Krygier	.05	.02	.01
☐	259	Kevin Hatcher	.05	.02	.01
☐	260	Alexei Zhamnov	.20	.09	.03
☐	261	Dallas Drake	.05	.02	.01
☐	262	Dave Manson	.05	.02	.01
☐	263	Thomas Steen	.05	.02	.01
☐	264	Keith Tkachuk	.05	.02	.01
☐	265	Russ Romaniuk	.05	.02	.01
☐	266	Michal Grosek	.10	.05	.01
☐	267	Nelson Emerson	.08	.04	.01
☐	268	Michael O'Neill	.15	.07	.02
☐	269	Kris King	.05	.02	.01
☐	270	Teppo Numminen	.05	.02	.01
☐	271	Jason Arnott	.75	.35	.09
		Edmonton Oilers			
☐	272	Mikael Renberg	.25	.11	.03
		Philadelphia Flyers			
☐	273	Alexei Yashin	.30	.14	.04
		Ottawa Senators			
☐	274	Chris Pronger	.25	.11	.03
		Hartford Whalers			
☐	275	Jocelyn Thibault	.15	.07	.02
		Quebec Nordiques			
☐	276	Bryan Smolinski	.20	.09	.03
		Boston Bruins			
☐	277	Derek Plante	.20	.09	.03
		Buffalo Sabres			
☐	278	Martin Brodeur	.20	.09	.03
		New Jersey Devils			
☐	279	Jim Dowd	.05	.02	.01
		New Jersey Devils			
☐	280	Iain Fraser	.05	.02	.01
		Quebec Nordiques			
☐	281	Pat Peake	.05	.02	.01
		Washington Capitals			
☐	282	Chris Gratton	.20	.09	.03
		Tampa Bay Lightning			
☐	283	Chris Osgood	.15	.07	.02
		Detroit Red Wings			
☐	284	Jesse Belanger	.05	.02	.01
		Florida Panthers			
☐	285	Alexandre Daigle	.30	.14	.04
		Ottawa Senators			
☐	286	Robert Lang	.05	.02	.01
		Los Angeles Kings			
☐	287	Markus Naslund	.05	.02	.01
		Pittsburgh Penguins			
☐	288	Trevor Kidd	.08	.04	.01
		Calgary Flames			
☐	289	Jeff Shantz	.05	.02	.01
		Chicago Blackhawks			
☐	290	Jaroslav Modry	.05	.02	.01
		New Jersey Devils			
☐	291	Oleg Petrov	.05	.02	.01
		Montreal Canadiens			
☐	292	Scott Levins	.05	.02	.01
		Ottawa Senators			
☐	293	Josef Stumpel	.05	.02	.01
		Boston Bruins			
☐	294	Rob Niedermayer	.25	.11	.03
		Florida Panthers			
☐	295	Brent Gretzky	.15	.07	.02
		Tampa Bay Lightning			
☐	296	Mario Lemieux	.50	.23	.06
		Pittsburgh Penguins			
☐	297	Pavel Bure	.75	.35	.09
		Vancouver Canucks			
☐	298	Brendan Shanahan	.10	.05	.01
		St. Louis Blues			
☐	299	Steve Yzerman	.15	.07	.02
		Detroit Red Wings			
☐	300	Teemu Selanne	.30	.14	.04
		Winnipeg Jets			
☐	301	Eric Lindros	1.50	.65	.19
		Philadelphia Flyers			
☐	302	Jeremy Roenick	.35	.16	.04
		Chicago Blackhawks			
☐	303	Dave Andreychuk	.10	.05	.01
		Toronto Maple Leafs			
☐	304	Ray Bourque	.10	.05	.01
		Boston Bruins			
☐	305	Sergei Fedorov	.25	.11	.03
		Detroit Red Wings			
☐	306	Wayne Gretzky	.75	.35	.09
		Los Angeles Kings			
☐	307	Adam Graves	.10	.05	.01
		New York Rangers			
☐	308	Mike Modano	.10	.05	.01
		Dallas Stars			
☐	309	Brett Hull	.20	.09	.03
		St. Louis Blues			
☐	310	Pat LaFontaine	.10	.05	.01
		Buffalo Sabres			
☐	311	Adam Oates	.10	.05	.01
		Boston Bruins			
☐	312	Patrick Roy	.35	.16	.04
		Montreal Canadiens			
☐	313	Doug Gilmour	.15	.07	.02
		Toronto Maple Leafs			
☐	314	Jaromir Jagr	.20	.09	.03
		Pittsburgh Penguins			

☐ 315 Mark Recchi......................... .10   .05   .01
        Philadelphia Flyers

1971-72 Penguins Postcards

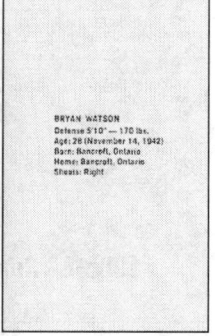

This 22-card set (measuring approximately 3 1/2" by 5 1/2")
features full-bleed posed action color player photos. The top
edges of the card show signs of perforation. The backs carry
the player's name and biography in blue print on a white
background. Only the Red Kelly card has a career summary
on its back. The cards are unnumbered and checklisted
below in alphabetical order. The set is dated by the inclusion
of Roy Edwards, whose only season with the Penguins was
1971-72.

	MINT	EXC	G-VG
COMPLETE SET (22)........................	25.00	10.00	2.50
COMMON CARD (1-22)	1.00	.40	.10
☐ 1 Syl Apps.................................	2.50	1.00	.25
☐ 2 Les Binkley............................	2.50	1.00	.25
☐ 3 Dave Burrows	1.50	.60	.15
☐ 4 Darryl Edestrand	1.00	.40	.10
☐ 5 Roy Edwards..........................	1.75	.70	.17
☐ 6 Val Fonteyne	1.00	.40	.10
☐ 7 Nick Harbaruk	1.00	.40	.10
☐ 8 Bryan Hextall..........................	2.50	1.00	.25
☐ 9 Sheldon Kannegiesser............	1.00	.40	.10
☐ 10 Red Kelly CO	2.50	1.00	.25
☐ 11 Bob Leiter	1.00	.40	.10
☐ 12 Keith McCreary	1.00	.40	.10
☐ 13 Joe Noris.............................	1.00	.40	.10
☐ 14 Greg Polis	1.00	.40	.10
☐ 15 Jean Pronovost	2.00	.80	.20
☐ 16 Rene Robert..........................	2.50	1.00	.25
☐ 17 Jim Rutherford......................	2.50	1.00	.25
☐ 18 Ken Schinkel	1.00	.40	.10
☐ 19 Ron Schock..........................	1.00	.40	.10
☐ 20 Bryan Watson	1.75	.70	.17
☐ 21 Bob Woytowich	1.00	.40	.10
☐ 22 Title Card.............................	1.00	.40	.10

1974-75 Penguins Postcards

This 22-card set features full-bleed black and white action
pictures by photographer Paul Salva. The player's autograph
is inscribed across the bottom of the picture. The cards are
in the postcard format and measure approximately 3 1/2" by
5 1/2". The horizontal backs are blank. The cards are
unnumbered and checklisted below in alphabetical order.
The set is dated by the fact that Nelson Debenedet was only
with the Penguins during the 1974-75 season. Pierre
Larouche appears in this set prior to his Rookie Card
appearance.

	MINT	EXC	G-VG
COMPLETE SET (22)........................	25.00	10.00	2.50
COMMON PLAYER (1-22)................	1.00	.40	.10
☐ 1 Syl Apps...............................	2.50	1.00	.25
☐ 2 Chuck Arnason.......................	1.00	.40	.10
☐ 3 Dave Burrows	1.50	.60	.15
☐ 4 Colin Campbell.......................	2.50	1.00	.25
☐ 5 Nelson Debenedet..................	1.75	.70	.17
☐ 6 Steve Durbano	1.00	.40	.10
☐ 7 Vic Hadfield...........................	1.75	.70	.17
☐ 8 Gary Inness...........................	1.75	.70	.17
☐ 9 Bob(B.J.) Johnson	1.00	.40	.10
☐ 10 Rick Kehoe..........................	2.50	1.00	.25
☐ 11 Bob Kelly.............................	1.75	.70	.17
☐ 12 Jean-Guy LaGacle	1.00	.40	.10
☐ 13 Ron Lalonde.........................	1.00	.40	.10
☐ 14 Pierre Larouche	5.00	2.00	.50
☐ 15 Lowell MacDonald.................	1.75	.70	.17
☐ 16 Dennis Owchar......................	1.00	.40	.10
☐ 17 Bob Paradise........................	1.00	.40	.10
☐ 18 Kelly Pratt	1.00	.40	.10
☐ 19 Jean Pronovost	1.75	.70	.17
☐ 20 Ron Schock..........................	1.00	.40	.10
☐ 21 Ron Stackhouse	1.00	.40	.10
☐ 22 Barry Williams.......................	1.00	.40	.10

1977-78 Penguins Puck Bucks

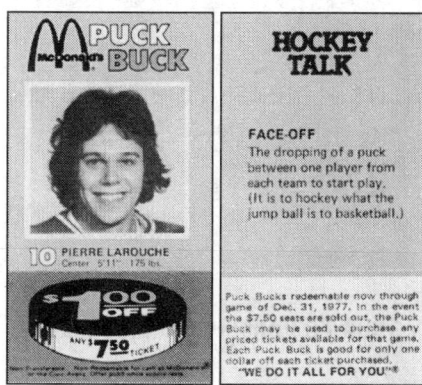

This 18-card set of Pittsburgh Penguins was sponsored by
McDonald's restaurants, whose company logo appears at
the top of the card face. The cards measure approximately 1
15/16" by 3 1/2" and are perforated so that the bottom tab
(measuring 1 15/16" by 1") may be removed. The front of

the top portion features a color head shot of the player, with a white border on a mustard-colored background. The back of the top portion has "Hockey Talk," in which a hockey term is explained. The front side of the tab portion shows a hockey puck on an orange background. Its back states that the "puck bucks" are coupons worth 1.00 toward the purchase of any 7.50 Penguins game ticket. These coupons had to be redeemed no later than December 31, 1977.

	NRMT	VG-E	GOOD
COMPLETE SET (18)	20.00	8.00	2.00
COMMON PLAYER	1.00	.40	.10

☐ 1	Denis Herron	2.00	.80	.20
☐ 3	Ron Stackhouse	1.00	.40	.10
☐ 4	Dave Burrows	1.50	.60	.15
☐ 6	Colin Campbell	2.50	1.00	.25
☐ 7	Russ Anderson	1.00	.40	.10
☐ 9	Blair Chapman	1.00	.40	.10
☐ 10	Pierre Larouche	3.00	1.20	.30
☐ 12	Greg Malone	2.00	.80	.20
☐ 14	Wayne Bianchin	1.00	.40	.10
☐ 17	Rick Kehoe	2.50	1.00	.25
☐ 18	Lowell MacDonald	2.00	.80	.20
☐ 19	Jean Pronovost	2.00	.80	.20
☐ 23	Jim Hamilton	1.00	.40	.10
☐ 25	Dennis Owchar	1.00	.40	.10
☐ 26	Syl Apps	2.00	.80	.20
☐ 27	Mike Corrigan	1.00	.40	.10
☐ 29	Dunc Wilson	2.00	.80	.20
☐ NNO	Johnny Wilson CO	1.00	.40	.10

1983-84 Penguins Heinz Photos

This Pittsburgh Penguins "Photo Pak" was sponsored by Heinz. The cards are unnumbered and checklisted below in alphabetical order. They were giveaways at Pittsburgh Penguins home games. Each photo measures approximately 6" by 9" and they were produced on one large folded sheet.

	MINT	EXC	G-VG
COMPLETE SET (22)	25.00	10.00	2.50
COMMON PLAYER (1-22)	1.00	.40	.10

☐ 1	Paul Baxter	1.50	.60	.15
☐ 2	Pat Boutette	1.50	.60	.15
☐ 3	Randy Boyd	1.00	.40	.10
☐ 4	Mike Bullard	2.00	.80	.20
☐ 5	Randy Carlyle	2.00	.80	.20
☐ 6	Marc Chorney	1.00	.40	.10
☐ 7	Michel Dion	2.00	.80	.20
☐ 8	Bill Gardner	1.00	.40	.10
☐ 9	Pat Graham	1.00	.40	.10
☐ 10	Anders Hakansson	1.00	.40	.10
☐ 11	Dave Hannan	1.00	.40	.10
☐ 12	Denis Herron	2.00	.80	.20
☐ 13	Greg Hotham	1.00	.40	.10
☐ 14	Stan Jonathan	1.50	.60	.15
☐ 15	Rick Kehoe	2.00	.80	.20
☐ 16	Peter Lee	1.50	.60	.15
☐ 17	Greg Malone	1.50	.60	.15
☐ 18	Kevin McClelland	1.00	.40	.10
☐ 19	Ron Meighan	1.00	.40	.10
☐ 20	Doug Shedden	1.00	.40	.10
☐ 21	Andre St. Laurent	1.00	.40	.10
☐ 22	Rich Sutter	2.00	.80	.20

1984-85 Penguins Heinz Photos

This Pittsburgh Penguins "Photo Pak" was sponsored by Heinz. The cards are unnumbered and checklisted below in alphabetical order. They were giveaways at Pittsburgh Penguins home games. Each photo measures approximately 6" by 9" and they were produced on one large folded sheet.

	MINT	EXC	G-VG
COMPLETE SET (22)	25.00	10.00	2.50
COMMON PLAYER (1-22)	1.00	.40	.10

☐ 1	Pat Boutette	1.50	.60	.15
☐ 2	Andy Brickley	2.00	.80	.20
☐ 3	Mike Bullard	2.00	.80	.20
☐ 4	Rod Buskas	1.00	.40	.10
☐ 5	Randy Carlyle	2.00	.80	.20
☐ 6	Michel Dion	2.00	.80	.20
☐ 7	Bob Errey	1.50	.60	.15
☐ 8	Ron Flockhart	1.00	.40	.10
☐ 9	Greg Fox	1.00	.40	.10
☐ 10	Steve Gatzos	1.00	.40	.10
☐ 11	Denis Herron	2.00	.80	.20
☐ 12	Greg Hotham	1.00	.40	.10
☐ 13	Rick Kehoe	2.00	.80	.20
☐ 14	Bryan Maxwell	1.50	.60	.15
☐ 15	Marty McSorley	5.00	2.00	.50
☐ 16	Tom O'Regan	1.00	.40	.10
☐ 17	Gary Rissling	1.00	.40	.10
☐ 18	Roberto Romano	1.50	.60	.15
☐ 19	Tom Roulston	1.00	.40	.10
☐ 20	Rocky Saganiuk	1.00	.40	.10
☐ 21	Doug Shedden	1.00	.40	.10
☐ 22	Mark Taylor	1.00	.40	.10

1986-87 Penguins Kodak

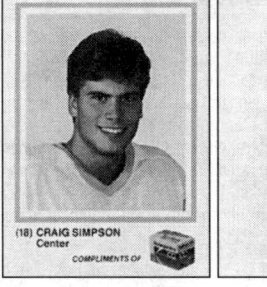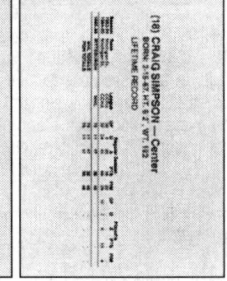

The 1986-87 Pittsburgh Penguins Team Photo Album was sponsored by Kodak and commemorates the team's 20 years in the NHL. It consists of three large sheets, each measuring approximately 11" by 8 1/4", joined together to form one continuous sheet. The first panel has a team photo of the 1967 Pittsburgh Penguins. The second panel presents three rows of five cards each. The third panel presents two rows of five cards, with five Kodak coupons completing the left over portion of the panel. After perforation, the cards measure approximately 2 3/16" by 2 1/2". They feature color posed photos bordered in yellow, with player information below the picture. A Kodak film box serving as a logo completes the card face. The back has biographical and statistical information in a horizontal format. We have checklisted the names below in alphabetical order, with the uniform number to the right of the name.

	MINT	EXC	G-VG
COMPLETE SET (26)	40.00	16.00	4.00
COMMON PLAYER (1-25)	.75	.30	.07

☐ 1	Bob Berry CO	1.00	.40	.10
☐ 2	Mike Blaisdell 26	1.00	.40	.10
☐ 3	Doug Bodger 3	1.25	.50	.12
☐ 4	Rod Buskas 7	.75	.30	.07
☐ 5	John Chabot 9	.75	.30	.07
☐ 6	Randy Cunneyworth 15	1.00	.40	.10
☐ 7	Ron Duguay 10	1.25	.50	.12
☐ 8	Bob Errey 12	1.00	.40	.10
☐ 9	Dan Frawley 26	.75	.30	.07
☐ 10	Dave Hannan 32	.75	.30	.07
☐ 11	Randy Hillier 23	.75	.30	.07
☐ 12	Jim Johnson 6	.75	.30	.07
☐ 13	Kevin Lavalle 16	.75	.30	.07
☐ 14	Mario Lemieux 66	20.00	8.00	2.00
☐ 15	Willy Lindstrom 19	.75	.30	.07
☐ 16	Moe Mantha 20	.75	.30	.07

		MINT	EXC	G-VG
☐ 17	Gilles Meloche 27	1.00	.40	.10
☐ 18	Dan Quinn 14	1.00	.40	.10
☐ 19	Jim Roberts CO	1.00	.40	.10
☐ 20	Roberto Romano 30	.75	.30	.07
☐ 21	Terry Ruskowski 8	1.00	.40	.10
☐ 22	Norm Schmidt 25	.75	.30	.07
☐ 23	Craig Simpson 18	2.50	1.00	.25
☐ 24	Ville Siren 5	.75	.30	.07
☐ 25	Warren Young 35	1.00	.40	.10
☐ xx	Team Photo	5.00	2.00	.50

1987-88 Penguins Kodak

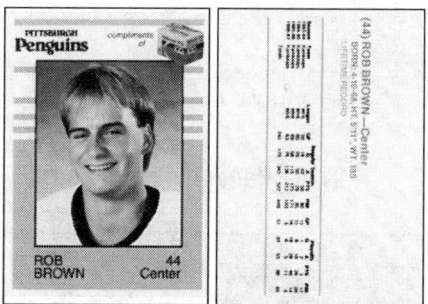

The 1987-88 Pittsburgh Penguins Team Photo Album was sponsored by Kodak. It consists of three large sheets, each measuring approximately 11" by 8 1/4", joined together to form one continuous sheet. The first panel has a team photo, with the players' names listed according to rows below the picture. The second panel presents three rows of five cards each. The third panel presents two rows of five cards, with five Kodak coupons completing the left over portion of the panel. After perforation, the cards measure approximately 2 3/16" by 2 1/2". A Kodak film box serves as a logo in the upper right hand corner of the card face. The front features a color head shot inside a thin black border. The picture is set on a Kodak "yellow" background, with white stripes traversing the top of the card. The player's name, number, and position are printed in black lettering below the picture. The back has biographical information and career statistics in a horizontal format. We have checklisted the cards below in alphabetical order, with the player's number to the right of his name.

		MINT	EXC	G-VG
COMPLETE SET (26)		30.00	12.00	3.00
COMMON PLAYER (1-25)		.75	.30	.07
☐ 1	Doug Bodger 3	1.00	.40	.10
☐ 2	Rob Brown 44	1.50	.60	.15
☐ 3	Rod Buskas 7	.75	.30	.07
☐ 4	Jock Callander 36	.75	.30	.07
☐ 5	Paul Coffey 77	2.50	1.00	.25
☐ 6	Randy Cunneyworth 15	1.00	.40	.10
☐ 7	Chris Dahlquist 4	.75	.30	.07
☐ 8	Bob Errey 12	.75	.30	.07
☐ 9	Dan Frawley 28	.75	.30	.07
☐ 10	Steve Guenette 30	.75	.30	.07
☐ 11	Randy Hillier 23	.75	.30	.07
☐ 12	Dave Hunter 20	.75	.30	.07
☐ 13	Jim Johnson 6	.75	.30	.07
☐ 14	Mark Kachowski 26	.75	.30	.07
☐ 15	Chris Kontos 14	1.50	.60	.15
☐ 16	Mario Lemieux 66	15.00	6.00	1.50
☐ 17	Troy Loney 24	1.00	.40	.10
☐ 18	Dwight Mathiasen 34	.75	.30	.07
☐ 19	Dave McLlwain 19	.75	.30	.07
☐ 20	Gilles Meloche 27	1.00	.40	.10
☐ 21	Dan Quinn 10	1.00	.40	.10
☐ 22	Pat Riggin 1	1.00	.40	.10
☐ 23	Charlie Simmer 16	1.25	.50	.12
☐ 24	Ville Siren 5	.75	.30	.07

☐ 25	Wayne Van Dorp	.75	.30	.07
☐ NNO	Large Team Photo	4.00	1.60	.40

1989-90 Penguins Foodland

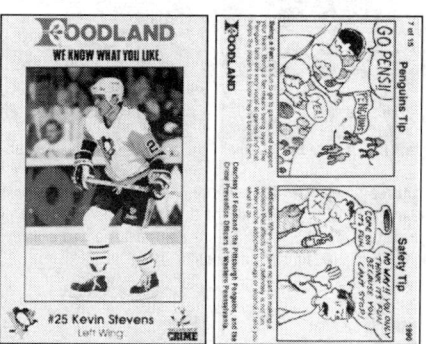

This 15-card set was sponsored by Foodland in conjunction with the Pittsburgh Penguins and the Crime Prevention Officers of Western Pennsylvania. The Foodland company logo appears on the top and back of each card. The cards measure approximately 2 9/16" by 4 1/8" and could be collected from police officers. The front features a color action photo with a thin black border on white card stock. The player information below the picture is sandwiched between the Penguin and the Crime Dog McGruff logos. The back is dated and presents a Penguins tip and a safety tip (both illustrated with cartoons) in a horizontal format. There were two late issue cards distributed after trades although they are rather scarce and not usually considered part of the complete set.

		MINT	EXC	G-VG
COMPLETE SET (15)		20.00	8.00	2.00
COMMON PLAYER (1-15)		.60	.24	.06
☐ 1	Rob Brown	1.00	.40	.10
☐ 2	Jim Johnson	.60	.24	.06
☐ 3	Zarley Zalapski	1.00	.40	.10
☐ 4	Paul Coffey	2.00	.80	.20
☐ 5	Phil Bourque	.75	.30	.07
☐ 6A	Dan Quinn	.75	.30	.07
☐ 6B	Gilbert Delorme SP	5.00	2.00	.50
☐ 7	Kevin Stevens	5.00	2.00	.50
☐ 8	Bob Errey	.60	.24	.06
☐ 9	John Cullen	1.50	.60	.15
☐ 10	Mario Lemieux	8.00	3.25	.80
☐ 11	Randy Hillier	.60	.24	.06
☐ 12	Jay Caufield	.60	.24	.06
☐ 13A	Andrew McBain	.60	.24	.06
☐ 13B	Troy Loney SP	5.00	2.00	.50
☐ 14	Wendell Young	.75	.30	.07
☐ 15	Tom Barrasso	1.50	.60	.15

1990-91 Penguins Foodland

This 15-card set was sponsored by Foodland in conjunction with the Pittsburgh Penguins and the Crime Prevention Officers of Western Pennsylvania. The Foodland company logo appears at the bottom of the card front and the top of the horizontally oriented back. The cards measure approximately 2 11/16" by 4 1/8" and could be collected from police officers. The front features a color action photo with a thin black border surrounded by wide yellow margins

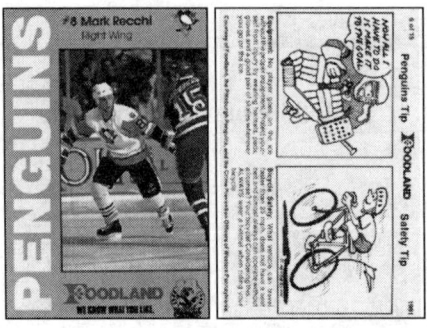

on three sides. The team name is printed in white block lettering, running the length of the card on the left side of the picture. The back presents a Penguins tip and a safety tip (both illustrated with cartoons).

	MINT	EXC	G-VG
COMPLETE SET (15)	20.00	8.00	2.00
COMMON PLAYER (1-15)	.60	.24	.06
☐ 1 Phil Bourque 29	.75	.30	.07
☐ 2 Paul Coffey 77	1.50	.60	.15
☐ 3 Randy Hillier 23	.60	.24	.06
☐ 4 Barry Pederson 10	.75	.30	.07
☐ 5 Tom Barrasso 35	1.50	.60	.15
☐ 6 Mark Recchi 8	4.00	1.60	.40
☐ 7 Bob Johnson CO	2.00	.80	.20
☐ 8 Joe Mullen 7	1.00	.40	.10
☐ 9 Kevin Stevens 25	3.00	1.20	.30
☐ 10 John Cullen 11	1.00	.40	.10
☐ 11 Jaromir Jagr 68	6.00	2.40	.60
☐ 12 Zarley Zalapski 33	.75	.30	.07
☐ 13 Mario Lemieux 66	6.00	2.40	.60
☐ 14 Tony Tanti 9	.75	.30	.07
☐ 15 Bryan Trottier 19	1.25	.50	.12

1991-92 Penguins Coke/Elby's

This 24-card set was sponsored by Cola-Cola in conjunction with Elby's Big Boy restaurants. The cards measure approximately 4" by 6" and are printed on thin card stock. The headline "1990-91 Stanley Cup Champions" adorns the top of each front. Immediately below appears the uniform number, player's name, and a twenty-fifth anniversary team logo. The color action player photos are bordered in white, with the two sponsor logos appearing in the bottom white border. The backs are blank. The cards are skip-numbered by uniform number and checklisted below accordingly.

	MINT	EXC	G-VG
COMPLETE SET (24)	20.00	8.00	2.00
COMMON PLAYER	.50	.20	.05

☐ 1	Wendell Young	.60	.24	.06
☐ 2	Jim Paek	.75	.30	.07
☐ 3	Grant Jennings	.60	.24	.06
☐ 5	Ulf Samuelsson	1.00	.40	.10
☐ 7	Joe Mullen	1.00	.40	.10
☐ 8	Mark Recchi	2.00	.80	.20
☐ 10	Ron Francis	1.25	.50	.12
☐ 16	Jay Caufield	.50	.20	.05
☐ 18	Ken Priestlay	.50	.20	.05
☐ 19	Bryan Trottier	1.00	.40	.10
☐ 20	Jamie Leach	.50	.20	.05
☐ 22	Paul Stanton	.50	.20	.05
☐ 24	Troy Loney	.60	.24	.06
☐ 25	Kevin Stevens	2.00	.80	.20
☐ 28	Gord Roberts	.50	.20	.05
☐ 29	Phil Bourque	.60	.24	.06
☐ 32	Peter Taglianetti	.50	.20	.05
☐ 40	Frank Pietrangelo	.75	.30	.07
☐ 43	Jeff Daniels	.50	.20	.05
☐ 55	Larry Murphy	1.00	.40	.10
☐ 66	Mario Lemieux	5.00	2.00	.50
☐ 68	Jaromir Jagr	3.50	1.40	.35
☐ NNO	Scotty Bowman CO	1.25	.50	.12

1991-92 Penguins Foodland

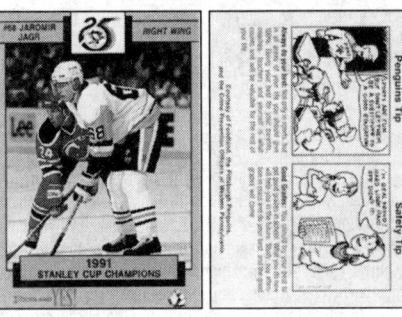

This 15-card set was sponsored by Foodland in conjunction with the Pittsburgh Penguins and the Crime Prevention Officers of Western Pennsylvania. The cards measure the standard size (2 1/2" by 3 1/2"). The Foodland logo and McGruff the Crime Dog appear at the bottom of the card face, while a 25th year anniversary emblem appears at the top center. The fronts feature color action player photos on an orangish-yellow card face. The player's name, uniform number, and his position appear in the top silver stripe; the words "1991 Stanley Cup Champions" appears in another silver stripe beneath the picture. The horizontally oriented backs have a "Penguins Tip" and a "Safety Tip," each of which is illustrated by a cartoon. The cards are numbered on the back.

	MINT	EXC	G-VG
COMPLETE SET (15)	15.00	6.00	1.50
COMMON PLAYER (1-15)	.50	.20	.05
☐ 1 Jim Paek	.75	.30	.07
☐ 2 Ulf Samuelsson	1.00	.40	.10
☐ 3 Ron Francis	1.25	.50	.12
☐ 4 Mario Lemieux	5.00	2.00	.50
☐ 5 Rick Tocchet	1.25	.50	.12
☐ 6 Joe Mullen	1.00	.40	.10
☐ 7 Troy Loney	.50	.20	.05
☐ 8 Kevin Stevens	2.00	.80	.20
☐ 9 Tom Barrasso	1.25	.50	.12
☐ 10 Larry Murphy	1.00	.40	.10
☐ 11 Jaromir Jagr	3.00	1.20	.30
☐ 12 Bryan Trottier	1.25	.50	.12
☐ 13 Paul Stanton	.50	.20	.05
☐ 14 Peter Taglianetti	.50	.20	.05
☐ 15 Phil Bourque	.60	.24	.06

1992-93 Penguins Coke/Clark

This 26-card set was sponsored by Cola-Cola and Clark. These cards followed the same concept as Coke/Elby's sets of the previous years, i.e., large autograph cards issued to the players for use in personal appearances. The cards measure approximately 4" by 6" and were printed on thin card stock. The backs are blank. The cards are unnumbered and checklisted below in alphabetical order.

	MINT	EXC	G-VG
COMPLETE SET (26)	20.00	8.00	2.00
COMMON PLAYER (1-26)	.50	.20	.05
☐ 1 Tom Barrasso	1.25	.50	.12
☐ 2 Scotty Bowman	1.00	.40	.10
☐ 3 Jay Caulfield	.50	.20	.05
☐ 4 Jeff Daniels	.50	.20	.05
☐ 5 Bob Errey	.50	.20	.05
☐ 6 Bryan Fogarty	.60	.24	.06
☐ 7 Ron Francis	1.25	.50	.12
☐ 8 Jaromir Jagr	3.00	1.20	.30
☐ 9 Grant Jennings	.60	.24	.06
☐ 10 Mario Lemieux	5.00	2.00	.50
☐ 11 Troy Loney	.50	.20	.05
☐ 12 Shawn McEachern	1.00	.40	.10
☐ 13 Joe Mullen	1.00	.40	.10
☐ 14 Larry Murphy	1.00	.40	.10
☐ 15 Mike Needham	.50	.20	.05
☐ 16 Jim Paek	.75	.30	.07
☐ 17 Kjell Samuelsson	.60	.24	.06
☐ 18 Ulf Samuelsson	1.00	.40	.10
☐ 19 Paul Stanton	.50	.20	.05
☐ 20 Mike Stapleton	.50	.20	.05
☐ 21 Keven Stevens	2.00	.80	.20
☐ 22 Martin Straka	2.00	.80	.20
☐ 23 Dave Tippett	.50	.20	.05
☐ 24 Rick Tocchet	1.25	.50	.12
☐ 25 Ken Wregget	.75	.30	.07
☐ 26 Penguins Mascot	.50	.20	.05

	MINT	EXC	G-VG
COMPLETE SET (18)	12.00	5.00	1.20
COMMON PLAYER (1-18)	.50	.20	.05
☐ 1 Mario Lemieux	4.00	1.60	.40
☐ 2 Bob Errey	.50	.20	.05
☐ 3 Jaromir Jagr	2.50	1.00	.25
☐ 4 Rick Tocchet	1.25	.50	.12
☐ 5 Tom Barrasso	1.25	.50	.12
☐ 6 Joe Mullen	1.00	.40	.10
☐ 7 Ron Francis	1.00	.40	.10
☐ 8 Troy Loney	.50	.20	.05
☐ 9 Shawn McEachern	1.50	.60	.15
☐ 10 Larry Murphy	1.00	.40	.10
☐ 11 Jim Paek	.75	.30	.07
☐ 12 Ulf Samuelsson	1.00	.40	.10
☐ 13 Paul Stanton	.50	.20	.05
☐ 14 Kjell Samuelsson	.60	.24	.06
☐ 15 Kevin Stevens	2.00	.80	.20
☐ 16 Dave Tippett	.50	.20	.05
☐ 17 Martin Straka	2.00	.80	.20
☐ 18 Penguins Mascot	.50	.20	.05

1993-94 Penguins Foodland

1992-93 Penguins Foodland

This 18-card standard-size (2 1/2" by 3 1/2") set was sponsored by Foodland in conjunction with the Pittsburgh Penguins and the Crime Prevention Officers of Western Pennsylvania. The cards feature color action player photos with orange-yellow borders on a black card face. The player's name is printed in an orange-yellow stripe below the photo. The words "1991 and 1992 Stanley Cup Champions" are on an orange-yellow bar that overlaps the top of the picture. The Foodland logo and McGruff the Crime Dog appear at the bottom. The horizontal backs have a "Penguins Tip" and a "Safety Tip," each illustrated with a cartoon. The cards are numbered on the back.

Sponsored by Foodland, this 25-card standard-size (2 1/2" by 3 1/2") set features the 1993-94 Pittsburgh Penguins. The fronts have color action player photos with black borders on gray backgrounds. The team name appears in the top part of the card, while the player's name, number and position are printed under the photo. The sponsor's logo on the bottom rounds out the front. The horizontal backs have a "Penguin Tip" and a "Safety Tip," each illustrated with a cartoon. The cards are numbered on the back.

	MINT	EXC	G-VG
COMPLETE SET (25)	12.00	5.00	1.20
COMMON PLAYER (1-25)	.50	.20	.05
☐ 1 Mario Lemieux	3.50	1.40	.35
☐ 2 Grant Jennings	.60	.24	.06
☐ 3 Ulf Samuelsson	.75	.30	.07
☐ 4 Rick Tocchet	1.00	.40	.10
☐ 5 Marty McSorley	1.00	.40	.10
☐ 6 Rick Kehoe ACO	.60	.24	.06
☐ 7 Doug Brown	.50	.20	.05
☐ 8 Martin Straka	1.25	.50	.12
☐ 9 Jim Paek	.75	.30	.07
☐ 10 Ken Wregget	.75	.30	.07
☐ 11 Jeff Daniels	.50	.20	.05
☐ 12 Bryan Trottier	1.00	.40	.10
☐ 13 Larry Murphy	.75	.30	.07
☐ 14 Ron Francis	1.00	.40	.10
☐ 15 Mike Needham	.50	.20	.05
☐ 16 Mike Ramsey	.50	.20	.05
☐ 17 Kevin Stevens	1.50	.60	.15
☐ 18 Kjell Samuelsson	.60	.24	.06
☐ 19 Ed Johnston	.60	.24	.06
☐ 20 Markus Naslund	1.00	.40	.10
☐ 21 Mike Stapleton	.50	.20	.05
☐ 22 Peter Taglianetti	.50	.20	.05
☐ 23 Jaromir Jagr	2.00	.80	.20
☐ 24 Tom Barrasso	1.00	.40	.10
☐ 25 Joe Mullen	1.00	.40	.10

1980-81 Pepsi-Cola Caps

This set of 140 bottle caps features 20 players from each of the seven Canadian hockey teams. The bottle caps are written in French and English. There are two sizes of caps depending on whether the cap was from a small or large bottle. The top of the cap displays the Pepsi logo in the familiar red, white, and blue. The sides of the cap were done in blue and white lettering on a pink background. On the inside of the cap is a "black and aluminum" head shot of the player, with his name and the city (from which the team hails) below. We have checklisted the caps in alphabetical order of the teams as follows: Calgary Flames (1-20), Edmonton Oilers (21-40), Montreal Canadiens (41-60), Quebec Nordiques (61-80), Toronto Maple Leafs (81-100), Vancouver Canucks (101-120), and Winnipeg Jets (121-140). Also the players' names have been alphabetized within their teams. Also available through a mail-in offer was a white plastic circular display plaque (approximately 24" by 24") for the caps.

	MINT	EXC	G-VG
COMPLETE SET (140)	200.00	80.00	20.00
COMMON PLAYER (1-140)	1.50	.60	.15

		MINT	EXC	G-VG
☐ 1	Dan Bouchard	2.00	.80	.20
☐ 2	Guy Chouinard	2.00	.80	.20
☐ 3	Bill Clement	2.50	1.00	.25
☐ 4	Randy Holt	1.50	.60	.15
☐ 5	Ken Houston	1.50	.60	.15
☐ 6	Kevin Lavallee	1.50	.60	.15
☐ 7	Don Lever	1.50	.60	.15
☐ 8	Bob MacMillan	2.00	.80	.20
☐ 9	Brad Marsh	2.50	1.00	.25
☐ 10	Bob Murdoch	1.50	.60	.15
☐ 11	Kent Nilsson	2.00	.80	.20
☐ 12	Willi Plett	1.50	.60	.15
☐ 13	Jim Peplinski	2.00	.80	.20
☐ 14	Pekka Rautakallio	1.50	.60	.15
☐ 15	Paul Reinhart	2.00	.80	.20
☐ 16	Pat Riggin	2.00	.80	.20
☐ 17	Phil Russell	1.50	.60	.15
☐ 18	Brad Smith	1.50	.60	.15
☐ 19	Eric Vail	1.50	.60	.15
☐ 20	Bert Wilson	1.50	.60	.15
☐ 21	Glenn Anderson	4.00	1.60	.40
☐ 22	Curt Brackenbury	1.50	.60	.15
☐ 23	Brett Callighen	1.50	.60	.15
☐ 24	Paul Coffey	9.00	3.75	.90
☐ 25	Lee Fogolin	1.50	.60	.15
☐ 26	Matti Hagman	1.50	.60	.15
☐ 27	John Hughes	1.50	.60	.15
☐ 28	Dave Hunter	1.50	.60	.15
☐ 29	Jari Kurri	7.50	3.00	.75
☐ 30	Ron Low	2.00	.80	.20
☐ 31	Kevin Lowe	2.50	1.00	.25
☐ 32	Dave Lumley	1.50	.60	.15
☐ 33	Blair MacDonald	1.50	.60	.15
☐ 34	Mark Messier	15.00	6.00	1.50
☐ 35	Ed Mio	2.00	.80	.20
☐ 36	Don Murdoch	1.50	.60	.15
☐ 37	Pat Price	1.50	.60	.15
☐ 38	Dave Semenko	2.00	.80	.20
☐ 39	Risto Siltanen	1.50	.60	.15
☐ 40	Stan Weir	1.50	.60	.15
☐ 41	Keith Acton	1.50	.60	.15
☐ 42	Brian Engblom	1.50	.60	.15

		MINT	EXC	G-VG
☐ 43	Bob Gainey	3.00	1.20	.30
☐ 44	Gaston Gingras	1.50	.60	.15
☐ 45	Denis Herron	2.00	.80	.20
☐ 46	Rejean Houle	1.50	.60	.15
☐ 47	Doug Jarvis	2.00	.80	.20
☐ 48	Yvon Lambert	1.50	.60	.15
☐ 49	Rod Langway	3.00	1.20	.30
☐ 50	Guy Lapointe	3.00	1.20	.30
☐ 51	Pierre Larouche	2.50	1.00	.25
☐ 52	Pierre Mondou	1.50	.60	.15
☐ 53	Mark Napier	2.00	.80	.20
☐ 54	Chris Nilan	2.00	.80	.20
☐ 55	Doug Risebrough	2.00	.80	.20
☐ 56	Larry Robinson	4.00	1.60	.40
☐ 57	Serge Savard	3.00	1.20	.30
☐ 58	Steve Shutt	3.00	1.20	.30
☐ 59	Mario Tremblay	2.00	.80	.20
☐ 60	Doug Wickenheiser	1.50	.60	.15
☐ 61	Serge Bernier	1.50	.60	.15
☐ 62	Kim Clackson	1.50	.60	.15
☐ 63	Real Cloutier	1.50	.60	.15
☐ 64	Andre Dupont	1.50	.60	.15
☐ 65	Robbie Ftorek	2.00	.80	.20
☐ 66	Michel Goulet	7.50	3.00	.75
☐ 67	Jamie Hislop	1.50	.60	.15
☐ 68	Dale Hoganson	1.50	.60	.15
☐ 69	Dale Hunter	3.00	1.20	.30
☐ 70	Pierre Lacroix	1.50	.60	.15
☐ 71	Garry Lariviere	1.50	.60	.15
☐ 72	Rich Leduc	1.50	.60	.15
☐ 73	John Paddock	2.00	.80	.20
☐ 74	Michel Plasse	2.00	.80	.20
☐ 75	Jacques Richard	1.50	.60	.15
☐ 76	Anton Stastny	2.00	.80	.20
☐ 77	Peter Stastny	7.50	3.00	.75
☐ 78	Mark Tardif	2.00	.80	.20
☐ 79	Wally Weir	1.50	.60	.15
☐ 80	John Wensink	1.50	.60	.15
☐ 81	John Anderson	1.50	.60	.15
☐ 82	Laurie Boschman	1.50	.60	.15
☐ 83	Jiri Crha	1.50	.60	.15
☐ 84	Bill Derlago	1.50	.60	.15
☐ 85	Vitezslav Duris	1.50	.60	.15
☐ 86	Ron Ellis	2.00	.80	.20
☐ 87	Dave Farrish	1.50	.60	.15
☐ 88	Stewart Gavin	2.00	.80	.20
☐ 89	Pat Hickey	1.50	.60	.15
☐ 90	Dan Maloney	2.00	.80	.20
☐ 91	Terry Martin	1.50	.60	.15
☐ 92	Barry Melrose	2.50	1.00	.25
☐ 93	Wilf Paiement	2.00	.80	.20
☐ 94	Robert Picard	1.50	.60	.15
☐ 95	Jim Rutherford	2.50	1.00	.25
☐ 96	Rocky Saganiuk	1.50	.60	.15
☐ 97	Borje Salming	3.00	1.20	.30
☐ 98	David Shand	1.50	.60	.15
☐ 99	Ian Turnbull	1.50	.60	.15
☐ 100	Rick Vaive	2.50	1.00	.25
☐ 101	Brent Ashton	2.00	.80	.20
☐ 102	Ivan Boldirev	1.50	.60	.15
☐ 103	Per-Olov Brasar	1.50	.60	.15
☐ 104	Richard Brodeur	2.00	.80	.20
☐ 105	Jerry Butler	1.50	.60	.15
☐ 106	Colin Campbell	2.50	1.00	.25
☐ 107	Curt Fraser	1.50	.60	.15
☐ 108	Thomas Gradin	2.00	.80	.20
☐ 109	Dennis Kearns	1.50	.60	.15
☐ 110	Rick Lanz	1.50	.60	.15
☐ 111	Lars Lindgren	1.50	.60	.15
☐ 112	Dave Logan	1.50	.60	.15
☐ 113	Mario Marois	1.50	.60	.15
☐ 114	Kevin McCarthy	1.50	.60	.15
☐ 115	Gerald Minor	1.50	.60	.15
☐ 116	Darcy Rota	1.50	.60	.15
☐ 117	Bobby Schmautz	1.50	.60	.15
☐ 118	Stan Smyl	2.00	.80	.20
☐ 119	Harold Snepsts	2.50	1.00	.25
☐ 120	Dave(Tiger) Williams	2.50	1.00	.25
☐ 121	Dave Babych	2.00	.80	.20
☐ 122	Al Cameron	1.50	.60	.15
☐ 123	Scott Campbell	1.50	.60	.15
☐ 124	Dave Christian	2.00	.80	.20
☐ 125	Jude Drouin	1.50	.60	.15
☐ 126	Norm Dupont	1.50	.60	.15
☐ 127	Dan Geoffrion	1.50	.60	.15
☐ 128	Pierre Hamel	1.50	.60	.15
☐ 129	Barry Legge	1.50	.60	.15
☐ 130	Willy Lindstrom	1.50	.60	.15
☐ 131	Barry Long	1.50	.60	.15
☐ 132	Kris Manery	1.50	.60	.15
☐ 133	Jimmy Mann	1.50	.60	.15
☐ 134	Moe Mantha	1.50	.60	.15
☐ 135	Markus Mattsson	1.50	.60	.15

			MINT	EXC	G-VG
☐	136	Doug Smail	2.00	.80	.20
☐	137	Don Spring	1.50	.60	.15
☐	138	Anders Steen	2.00	.80	.20
☐	139	Peter Sullivan	1.50	.60	.15
☐	140	Ron Wilson	1.50	.60	.15
☐	xx	Plastic Circular Display	75.00	30.00	7.50

1991-92 Pinnacle

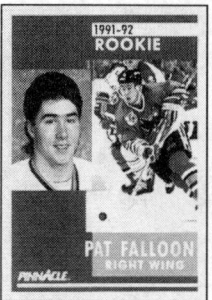

The 1991-92 (Score) Pinnacle Hockey set was issued in English and French editions; each set consists of 420 standard-size (2 1/2" by 3 1/2") cards. The front design of the veteran player cards features two color photos, an action photo and a head shot, on a black background with white borders. The card backs have a color action shot silhouetted against a black background. The rookie cards have the same design, except with green background on the front, and black and white head shots rather than action shots on the back. The backs of the veteran player cards include biography, player profile, and statistics, while those of the rookie cards only have a player profile. Subsets include 55 rookies (301-355). Special subsets featured are Gamewinners (356-360), Good Guys (366-375, with portraits by sports artist Christopher Greco), Technicians (376-380), Idols (381-395), and Sidelines (396-418). A French version of this set commands a slight premium of up to 1.25 times the values below. The cards are numbered on the back. The notable Rookie Cards in the set are Tony Amonte, Valeri Kamensky, and Geoff Sanderson.

			MINT	EXC	G-VG
	COMPLETE SET (420)		40.00	18.00	5.00
	COMMON PLAYER (1-420)		.07	.03	.01
	*FRENCH VERSION: 1X to 1.25X VALUE				
☐	1	Mario Lemieux Pittsburgh Penguins	1.75	.80	.22
☐	2	Trevor Linden Vancouver Canucks	.40	.18	.05
☐	3	Kirk Muller Montreal Canadiens	.10	.05	.01
☐	4	Phil Housley Winnipeg Jets	.10	.05	.01
☐	5	Mike Modano Minnesota North Stars	.75	.35	.09
☐	6	Adam Oates St. Louis Blues	.30	.14	.04
☐	7	Tom Kurvers New York Islanders	.07	.03	.01
☐	8	Doug Bodger Buffalo Sabres	.07	.03	.01
☐	9	Rod Brind'Amour Philadelphia Flyers	.40	.18	.05
☐	10	Mats Sundin Quebec Nordiques	.75	.35	.09
☐	11	Gary Suter Calgary Flames	.10	.05	.01
☐	12	Glenn Anderson Toronto Maple Leafs	.10	.05	.01
☐	13	Doug Wilson San Jose Sharks	.10	.05	.01
☐	14	Stephane Richer New Jersey Devils	.10	.05	.01
☐	15	Ray Bourque Boston Bruins	.30	.14	.04
☐	16	Adam Graves New York Rangers	.75	.35	.09
☐	17	Luc Robitaille Los Angeles Kings	.40	.18	.05
☐	18	Steve Smith Chicago Blackhawks	.10	.05	.01
☐	19	Uwe Krupp New York Islanders	.07	.03	.01
☐	20	Rick Tocchet Philadelphia Flyers	.10	.05	.01
☐	21	Tim Cheveldae Detroit Red Wings	.10	.05	.01
☐	22	Kay Whitmore Hartford Whalers	.07	.03	.01
☐	23	Kelly Miller Washington Capitals	.07	.03	.01
☐	24	Esa Tikkanen Edmonton Oilers	.10	.05	.01
☐	25	Pat LaFontaine Buffalo Sabres	.50	.23	.06
☐	26	James Patrick New York Rangers	.07	.03	.01
☐	27	Daniel Marois Toronto Maple Leafs	.07	.03	.01
☐	28	Denis Savard Montreal Canadiens	.10	.05	.01
☐	29	Steve Larmer Chicago Blackhawks	.10	.05	.01
☐	30	Pierre Turgeon New York Islanders	.50	.23	.06
☐	31	Gary Leeman Toronto Maple Leafs	.07	.03	.01
☐	32	Mike Ricci Philadelphia Flyers	.30	.14	.04
☐	33	Troy Murray Winnipeg Jets	.07	.03	.01
☐	34	Sergio Momesso Vancouver Canucks	.07	.03	.01
☐	35	Marty McSorley Los Angeles Kings	.10	.05	.01
☐	36	Paul Ysebaert Detroit Red Wings	.07	.03	.01
☐	37	Gary Roberts Calgary Flames	.10	.05	.01
☐	38	Mike Hudson Chicago Blackhawks	.07	.03	.01
☐	39	Kelly Hrudey Los Angeles Kings	.10	.05	.01
☐	40	Dale Hunter Washington Capitals	.10	.05	.01
☐	41	Brendan Shanahan St. Louis Blues	.60	.25	.08
☐	42	Steve Duchesne Philadelphia Flyers	.10	.05	.01
☐	43	Pat Verbeek Hartford Whalers	.10	.05	.01
☐	44	Tom Barrasso Pittsburgh Penguins	.10	.05	.01
☐	45	Scott Mellanby Edmonton Oilers	.07	.03	.01
☐	46	Stephen Leach Boston Bruins	.07	.03	.01
☐	47	Darren Turcotte New York Rangers	.07	.03	.01
☐	48	Jari Kurri Los Angeles Kings	.15	.07	.02
☐	49	Michel Petit Toronto Maple Leafs	.07	.03	.01
☐	50	Mark Messier New York Rangers	.50	.23	.06
☐	51	Terry Carkner Philadelphia Flyers	.07	.03	.01
☐	52	Tim Kerr New York Rangers	.10	.05	.01
☐	53	Jaromir Jagr Pittsburgh Penguins	1.25	.55	.16
☐	54	Joe Nieuwendyk Calgary Flames	.15	.07	.02
☐	55	Randy Burridge Washington Capitals	.07	.03	.01
☐	56	Robert Reichel Calgary Flames	.30	.14	.04
☐	57	Craig Janney Boston Bruins	.25	.11	.03
☐	58	Chris Chelios Chicago Blackhawks	.10	.05	.01
☐	59	Bryan Fogarty	.07	.03	.01

Quebec Nordiques				
☐ 60 Christian Ruuttu	.07	.03	.01
Buffalo Sabres				
☐ 61 Steve Bozek	.07	.03	.01
San Jose Sharks				
☐ 62 Dave Manson	.10	.05	.01
Edmonton Oilers				
☐ 63 Bruce Driver	.07	.03	.01
New Jersey Devils				
☐ 64 Mike Ramsey	.07	.03	.01
Buffalo Sabres				
☐ 65 Bobby Holik	.10	.05	.01
Hartford Whalers				
☐ 66 Bob Essensa	.10	.05	.01
Winnipeg Jets				
☐ 67 Pat Flatley	.07	.03	.01
New York Islanders				
☐ 68 Wayne Presley	.07	.03	.01
San Jose Sharks				
☐ 69 Mike Bullard	.07	.03	.01
Toronto Maple Leafs				
☐ 70 Claude Lemieux	.10	.05	.01
New Jersey Devils				
☐ 71 Dave Gagner	.10	.05	.01
Minnesota North Stars				
☐ 72 Jeff Brown	.10	.05	.01
St. Louis Blues				
☐ 73 Eric Desjardins	.10	.05	.01
Montreal Canadiens				
☐ 74 Fredrik Olausson	.10	.05	.01
Winnipeg Jets				
☐ 75 Steve Yzerman	.60	.25	.08
Detroit Red Wings				
☐ 76 Tony Granato	.10	.05	.01
Los Angeles Kings				
☐ 77 Adam Burt	.07	.03	.01
Hartford Whalers				
☐ 78 Cam Neely	.25	.11	.03
Boston Bruins				
☐ 79 Brent Sutter	.10	.05	.01
Chicago Blackhawks				
☐ 80 Dale Hawerchuk	.10	.05	.01
Buffalo Sabres				
☐ 81 Scott Stevens	.15	.07	.02
New Jersey Devils				
☐ 82 Adam Creighton	.07	.03	.01
New York Islanders				
☐ 83 Brian Hayward	.07	.03	.01
San Jose Sharks				
☐ 84 Dan Quinn	.07	.03	.01
Philadelphia Flyers				
☐ 85 Garth Butcher	.07	.03	.01
St. Louis Blues				
☐ 86 Shawn Burr	.07	.03	.01
Detroit Red Wings				
☐ 87 Peter Bondra	.10	.05	.01
Washington Capitals				
☐ 88 Brad Shaw	.07	.03	.01
Hartford Whalers				
☐ 89 Eric Weinrich	.07	.03	.01
New Jersey Devils				
☐ 90 Brian Bradley	.10	.05	.01
Toronto Maple Leafs				
☐ 91 Vincent Damphousse	.10	.05	.01
Edmonton Oilers				
☐ 92 Doug Gilmour	.60	.25	.08
Calgary Flames				
☐ 93 Martin Gelinas	.07	.03	.01
Edmonton Oilers				
☐ 94 Mike Ridley	.10	.05	.01
Washington Capitals				
☐ 95 Ron Sutter	.07	.03	.01
St. Louis Blues				
☐ 96 Mark Osborne	.07	.03	.01
Winnipeg Jets				
☐ 97 Mikhail Tatarinov	.07	.03	.01
Quebec Nordiques				
☐ 98 Bob McGill	.07	.03	.01
San Jose Sharks				
☐ 99 Bob Carpenter	.07	.03	.01
Boston Bruins				
☐ 100 Wayne Gretzky	2.00	.90	.25
Los Angeles Kings				
☐ 101 Viacheslav Fetisov	.10	.05	.01
New Jersey Devils				
☐ 102 Shayne Corson	.10	.05	.01
Montreal Canadiens				
☐ 103 Clint Malarchuk	.10	.05	.01
Buffalo Sabres				
☐ 104 Randy Wood	.07	.03	.01
Buffalo Sabres				
☐ 105 Curtis Joseph	.50	.23	.06
St. Louis Blues				
☐ 106 Cliff Ronning	.10	.05	.01

Vancouver Canucks				
☐ 107 Derek King	.10	.05	.01
New York Islanders				
☐ 108 Neil Wilkinson	.07	.03	.01
San Jose Sharks				
☐ 109 Michel Goulet	.10	.05	.01
Chicago Blackhawks				
☐ 110 Zarley Zalapski	.07	.03	.01
Hartford Whalers				
☐ 111 Dave Ellett	.07	.03	.01
Toronto Maple Leafs				
☐ 112 Glen Wesley	.07	.03	.01
Boston Bruins				
☐ 113 Bob Kudelski	.25	.11	.03
Los Angeles Kings				
☐ 114 Jamie Macoun	.07	.03	.01
Calgary Flames				
☐ 115 John MacLean	.10	.05	.01
New Jersey Devils				
☐ 116 Steve Thomas	.10	.05	.01
New York Islanders				
☐ 117 Pat Elynuik	.07	.03	.01
Winnipeg Jets				
☐ 118 Ron Hextall	.10	.05	.01
Philadelphia Flyers				
☐ 119 Jeff Hackett	.07	.03	.01
San Jose Sharks				
☐ 120 Jeremy Roenick	1.50	.65	.19
Chicago Blackhawks				
☐ 121 John Vanbiesbrouck	.30	.14	.04
New York Rangers				
☐ 122 Dave Andreychuk	.30	.14	.04
Buffalo Sabres				
☐ 123 Ray Ferraro	.10	.05	.01
New York Islanders				
☐ 124 Ron Tugnutt	.07	.03	.01
Quebec Nordiques				
☐ 125 John Cullen	.07	.03	.01
Hartford Whalers				
☐ 126 Andy Moog	.15	.07	.02
Boston Bruins				
☐ 127 Ed Belfour	.75	.35	.09
Chicago Blackhawks				
☐ 128 Dino Ciccarelli	.10	.05	.01
Washington Capitals				
☐ 129 Brian Bellows	.10	.05	.01
Minnesota North Stars				
☐ 130 Guy Carbonneau	.10	.05	.01
Montreal Canadiens				
☐ 131 Kevin Hatcher	.10	.05	.01
Washington Capitals				
☐ 132 Mike Vernon	.10	.05	.01
Calgary Flames				
☐ 133 Kevin Miller	.10	.05	.01
Detroit Red Wings				
☐ 134 Pelle Eklund	.07	.03	.01
Philadelphia Flyers				
☐ 135 Brian Mullen	.10	.05	.01
San Jose Sharks				
☐ 136 Brian Leetch	.75	.35	.09
New York Rangers				
☐ 137 Daren Puppa	.10	.05	.01
Buffalo Sabres				
☐ 138 Steven Finn	.07	.03	.01
Quebec Nordiques				
☐ 139 Stephan Lebeau	.20	.09	.03
Montreal Canadiens				
☐ 140 Gord Murphy	.07	.03	.01
Philadelphia Flyers				
☐ 141 Rob Brown	.07	.03	.01
Hartford Whalers				
☐ 142 Ken Daneyko	.07	.03	.01
New Jersey Devils				
☐ 143 Larry Murphy	.10	.05	.01
Pittsburgh Penguins				
☐ 144 Jon Casey	.10	.05	.01
Minnesota North Stars				
☐ 145 John Ogrodnick	.07	.03	.01
New York Rangers				
☐ 146 Benoit Hogue	.07	.03	.01
New York Islanders				
☐ 147 Mike McPhee	.07	.03	.01
Montreal Canadiens				
☐ 148 Don Beaupre	.10	.05	.01
Washington Capitals				
☐ 149 Kjell Samuelsson	.07	.03	.01
Philadelphia Flyers				
☐ 150 Joe Sakic	.60	.25	.08
Quebec Nordiques				
☐ 151 Mark Recchi	.75	.35	.09
Pittsburgh Penguins				
☐ 152 Ulf Dahlen	.10	.05	.01
Minnesota North Stars				
☐ 153 Dean Evason	.07	.03	.01

	San Jose Sharks			
☐ 154	Keith Brown	.07	.03	.01
	Chicago Blackhawks			
☐ 155	Ray Sheppard	.10	.05	.01
	Detroit Red Wings			
☐ 156	Owen Nolan	.25	.11	.03
	Quebec Nordiques			
☐ 157	Sergei Fedorov	2.00	.90	.25
	Detroit Red Wings			
☐ 158	Kirk McLean	.35	.16	.04
	Vancouver Canucks			
☐ 159	Petr Klima	.07	.03	.01
	Edmonton Oilers			
☐ 160	Brian Skrudland	.07	.03	.01
	Montreal Canadiens			
☐ 161	Neal Broten	.10	.05	.01
	Minnesota North Stars			
☐ 162	Dimitri Khristich	.10	.05	.01
	Washington Capitals			
☐ 163	Alexander Mogilny	1.00	.45	.13
	Buffalo Sabres			
☐ 164	Mike Richter	.60	.25	.08
	New York Rangers			
☐ 165	Daniel Berthiaume	.07	.03	.01
	Los Angeles Kings			
☐ 166	Teppo Numminen	.07	.03	.01
	Winnipeg Jets			
☐ 167	Ron Francis	.10	.05	.01
	Pittsburgh Penguins			
☐ 168	Grant Fuhr	.10	.05	.01
	Toronto Maple Leafs			
☐ 169	Mike Liut	.10	.05	.01
	Washington Capitals			
☐ 170	Bill Ranford	.10	.05	.01
	Edmonton Oilers			
☐ 171	Garry Galley	.10	.05	.01
	Boston Bruins			
☐ 172	Jeff Norton	.07	.03	.01
	New York Islanders			
☐ 173	Jimmy Carson	.10	.05	.01
	Detroit Red Wings			
☐ 174	Peter Zezel	.07	.03	.01
	Toronto Maple Leafs			
☐ 175	Patrick Roy	1.50	.65	.19
	Montreal Canadiens			
☐ 176	Joe Mullen	.15	.07	.02
	Pittsburgh Penguins			
☐ 177	Murray Craven	.07	.03	.01
	Hartford Whalers			
☐ 178	Tomas Sandstrom	.10	.05	.01
	Los Angeles Kings			
☐ 179	Joel Otto	.07	.03	.01
	Calgary Flames			
☐ 180	Steve Konroyd	.07	.03	.01
	Chicago Blackhawks			
☐ 181	Vladimir Ruzicka	.07	.03	.01
	Boston Bruins			
☐ 182	Paul Cavallini	.07	.03	.01
	St. Louis Blues			
☐ 183	Bob Probert	.10	.05	.01
	Detroit Red Wings			
☐ 184	Brian Propp	.10	.05	.01
	Minnesota North Stars			
☐ 185	Glenn Healy	.10	.05	.01
	New York Islanders			
☐ 186	Paul Coffey	.25	.11	.03
	Pittsburgh Penguins			
☐ 187	Jan Erixon	.07	.03	.01
	New York Rangers			
☐ 188	Kevin Lowe	.10	.05	.01
	Edmonton Oilers			
☐ 189	Doug Lidster	.07	.03	.01
	Vancouver Canucks			
☐ 190	Theoren Fleury	.30	.14	.04
	Calgary Flames			
☐ 191	Kevin Stevens	.60	.25	.08
	Pittsburgh Penguins			
☐ 192	Petr Nedved	.40	.18	.05
	Vancouver Canucks			
☐ 193	Ed Olczyk	.07	.03	.01
	Winnipeg Jets			
☐ 194	Mike Hough	.07	.03	.01
	Quebec Nordiques			
☐ 195	Rod Langway	.07	.03	.01
	Washington Capitals			
☐ 196	Craig Simpson	.10	.05	.01
	Edmonton Oilers			
☐ 197	Petr Svoboda	.07	.03	.01
	Montreal Canadiens			
☐ 198	David Volek	.07	.03	.01
	New York Islanders			
☐ 199	Mark Tinordi	.10	.05	.01
	Minnesota North Stars			
☐ 200	Brett Hull	1.50	.65	.19

	St. Louis Blues			
☐ 201	Rob Blake	.30	.14	.04
	Los Angeles Kings			
☐ 202	Mike Gartner	.15	.07	.02
	New York Rangers			
☐ 203	Ken Hodge Jr.	.07	.03	.01
	Boston Bruins			
☐ 204	Murray Baron	.07	.03	.01
	St. Louis Blues			
☐ 205	Gerard Gallant	.07	.03	.01
	Detroit Red Wings			
☐ 206	Joe Murphy	.10	.05	.01
	Edmonton Oilers			
☐ 207	Al Iafrate	.10	.05	.01
	Washington Capitals			
☐ 208	Larry Robinson	.10	.05	.01
	Los Angeles Kings			
☐ 209	Mathieu Schneider	.10	.05	.01
	Montreal Canadiens			
☐ 210	Bobby Smith	.10	.05	.01
	Minnesota North Stars			
☐ 211	Gerald Diduck	.07	.03	.01
	Vancouver Canucks			
☐ 212	Luke Richardson	.07	.03	.01
	Edmonton Oilers			
☐ 213	Rob Zettler	.07	.03	.01
	San Jose Sharks			
☐ 214	Brad McCrimmon	.07	.03	.01
	Detroit Red Wings			
☐ 215	Craig MacTavish	.07	.03	.01
	Edmonton Oilers			
☐ 216	Gino Cavallini	.07	.03	.01
	St. Louis Blues			
☐ 217	Craig Wolanin	.07	.03	.01
	Quebec Nordiques			
☐ 218	Greg Adams	.07	.03	.01
	Vancouver Canucks			
☐ 219	Mike Craig	.07	.03	.01
	Minnesota North Stars			
☐ 220	Al MacInnis	.15	.07	.02
	Calgary Flames			
☐ 221	Sylvain Cote	.07	.03	.01
	Washington Capitals			
☐ 222	Bob Sweeney	.07	.03	.01
	Boston Bruins			
☐ 223	Dave Snuggerud	.07	.03	.01
	Buffalo Sabres			
☐ 224	Randy Ladouceur	.07	.03	.01
	Hartford Whalers			
☐ 225	Charlie Huddy	.07	.03	.01
	Los Angeles Kings			
☐ 226	Sylvain Turgeon	.07	.03	.01
	Montreal Canadiens			
☐ 227	Phil Bourque	.07	.03	.01
	Pittsburgh Penguins			
☐ 228	Rob Ramage	.07	.03	.01
	Minnesota North Stars			
☐ 229	Jeff Beukeboom	.07	.03	.01
	New York Rangers			
☐ 230	Alexei Gusarov	.15	.07	.02
	Quebec Nordiques			
☐ 231	Kelly Kisio	.07	.03	.01
	San Jose Sharks			
☐ 232	Calle Johansson	.07	.03	.01
	Washington Capitals			
☐ 233	Yves Racine	.07	.03	.01
	Detroit Red Wings			
☐ 234	Peter Sidorkiewicz	.07	.03	.01
	Hartford Whalers			
☐ 235	Jim Johnson	.07	.03	.01
	Minnesota North Stars			
☐ 236	Brent Gilchrist	.07	.03	.01
	Montreal Canadiens			
☐ 237	Jyrki Lumme	.07	.03	.01
	Vancouver Canucks			
☐ 238	Randy Gilhen	.07	.03	.01
	Los Angeles Kings			
☐ 239	Ken Baumgartner	.07	.03	.01
	New York Islanders			
☐ 240	Joey Kocur	.07	.03	.01
	New York Rangers			
☐ 241	Bryan Trottier	.10	.05	.01
	Pittsburgh Penguins			
☐ 242	Todd Krygier	.07	.03	.01
	Washington Capitals			
☐ 243	Darrin Shannon	.07	.03	.01
	Winnipeg Jets			
☐ 244	Dave Christian	.07	.03	.01
	St. Louis Blues			
☐ 245	Stephane Morin	.07	.03	.01
	Quebec Nordiques			
☐ 246	Kevin Dineen	.10	.05	.01
	Philadelphia Flyers			
☐ 247	Chris Terreri	.10	.05	.01

New Jersey Devils			
☐ 248 Craig Ludwig	.07	.03	.01
Minnesota North Stars			
☐ 249 Dave Taylor	.10	.05	.01
Los Angeles Kings			
☐ 250 Wendel Clark	.25	.11	.03
Toronto Maple Leafs			
☐ 251 David Shaw	.07	.03	.01
Edmonton Oilers			
☐ 252 Paul Ranheim	.07	.03	.01
Calgary Flames			
☐ 253 Mark Hunter	.07	.03	.01
Hartford Whalers			
☐ 254 Russ Courtnall	.10	.05	.01
Montreal Canadiens			
☐ 255 Alexei Kasatonov	.10	.05	.01
New Jersey Devils			
☐ 256 Randy Moller	.07	.03	.01
New York Rangers			
☐ 257 Bob Errey	.07	.03	.01
Pittsburgh Penguins			
☐ 258 Curtis Leschyshyn	.07	.03	.01
Quebec Nordiques			
☐ 259 Rick Zombo	.07	.03	.01
St. Louis Blues			
☐ 260 Dana Murzyn	.07	.03	.01
Vancouver Canucks			
☐ 261 Dirk Graham	.07	.03	.01
Chicago Blackhawks			
☐ 262 Craig Muni	.07	.03	.01
Edmonton Oilers			
☐ 263 Geoff Courtnall	.10	.05	.01
Vancouver Canucks			
☐ 264 Todd Elik	.07	.03	.01
Minnesota North Stars			
☐ 265 Mike Keane	.07	.03	.01
Montreal Canadiens			
☐ 266 Peter Stastny	.10	.05	.01
New Jersey Devils			
☐ 267 Ulf Samuelsson	.10	.05	.01
Pittsburgh Penguins			
☐ 268 Rich Sutter	.07	.03	.01
St. Louis Blues			
☐ 269 Mike Krushelnyski	.07	.03	.01
Toronto Maple Leafs			
☐ 270 Dave Babych	.07	.03	.01
Vancouver Canucks			
☐ 271 Sergei Makarov	.25	.11	.03
Calgary Flames			
☐ 272 David Maley	.07	.03	.01
New Jersey Devils			
☐ 273 Normand Rochefort	.07	.03	.01
New York Rangers			
☐ 274 Gordie Roberts	.07	.03	.01
Pittsburgh Penguins			
☐ 275 Thomas Steen	.07	.03	.01
Winnipeg Jets			
☐ 276 Dave Lowry	.07	.03	.01
St. Louis Blues			
☐ 277 Michal Pivonka	.10	.05	.01
Washington Capitals			
☐ 278 Todd Gill	.07	.03	.01
Toronto Maple Leafs			
☐ 279 Paul MacDermid	.07	.03	.01
Winnipeg Jets			
☐ 280 Brent Ashton	.07	.03	.01
Boston Bruins			
☐ 281 Randy Hillier	.07	.03	.01
Buffalo Sabres			
☐ 282 Frantisek Musil	.07	.03	.01
Calgary Flames			
☐ 283 Geoff Smith	.07	.03	.01
Edmonton Oilers			
☐ 284 John Tonelli	.10	.05	.01
Chicago Blackhawks			
☐ 285 Joe Reekie	.07	.03	.01
New York Islanders			
☐ 286 Greg Paslawski	.07	.03	.01
Quebec Nordiques			
☐ 287 Perry Berezan	.07	.03	.01
San Jose Sharks			
☐ 288 Randy Carlyle	.07	.03	.01
Winnipeg Jets			
☐ 289 Chris Nilan	.10	.05	.01
Boston Bruins			
☐ 290 Patrik Sundstrom	.07	.03	.01
New Jersey Devils			
☐ 291 Garry Valk	.07	.03	.01
Vancouver Canucks			
☐ 292 Mike Foligno	.07	.03	.01
Toronto Maple Leafs			
☐ 293 Igor Larionov	.10	.05	.01
Vancouver Canucks			
☐ 294 Jim Sandlak	.07	.03	.01
Vancouver Canucks			
☐ 295 Tom Chorske	.07	.03	.01
New Jersey Devils			
☐ 296 Claude Loiselle	.07	.03	.01
Toronto Maple Leafs			
☐ 297 Mark Howe	.10	.05	.01
Philadelphia Flyers			
☐ 298 Steve Chiasson	.07	.03	.01
Detroit Red Wings			
☐ 299 Mike Donnelly	.25	.11	.03
Los Angeles Kings			
☐ 300 Bernie Nicholls	.10	.05	.01
Edmonton Oilers			
☐ 301 Tony Amonte	.60	.25	.08
New York Rangers			
☐ 302 Brad May	.10	.05	.01
Buffalo Sabres			
☐ 303 Josef Beranek	.60	.25	.08
Edmonton Oilers			
☐ 304 Rob Pearson	.30	.14	.04
Toronto Maple Leafs			
☐ 305 Andrei Lomakin	.07	.03	.01
Philadelphia Flyers			
☐ 306 Kip Miller	.07	.03	.01
Quebec Nordiques			
☐ 307 Kevin Haller	.20	.09	.03
Buffalo Sabres			
☐ 308 Kevin Todd	.20	.09	.03
New Jersey Devils			
☐ 309 Geoff Sanderson	2.50	1.15	.30
Hartford Whalers			
☐ 310 Doug Weight	.60	.25	.08
New York Rangers			
☐ 311 Vladimir Konstantinov	.40	.18	.05
Detroit Red Wings			
☐ 312 Peter Ahola	.07	.03	.01
Los Angeles Kings			
☐ 313 Claude Lapointe	.15	.07	.02
Quebec Nordiques			
☐ 314 Nelson Emerson	.50	.23	.06
St. Louis Blues			
☐ 315 Pavel Bure	3.50	1.55	.45
Vancouver Canucks			
☐ 316 Jimmy Waite	.10	.05	.01
Chicago Blackhawks			
☐ 317 Sergei Nemchinov	.25	.11	.03
New York Rangers			
☐ 318 Alexander Godynyuk	.07	.03	.01
Toronto Maple Leafs			
☐ 319 Stu Barnes	.10	.05	.01
Winnipeg Jets			
☐ 320 Niklas Lidstrom	.75	.35	.09
Detroit Red Wings			
☐ 321 Daryl Sydor	.10	.05	.01
Los Angeles Kings			
☐ 322 John LeClair	.30	.14	.04
Montreal Canadiens			
☐ 323 Arturs Irbe	1.00	.45	.13
San Jose Sharks			
☐ 324 Russ Romaniuk	.15	.07	.02
Winnipeg Jets			
☐ 325 Ken Sutton	.15	.07	.02
Buffalo Sabres			
☐ 326 Bob Beers	.07	.03	.01
Boston Bruins			
☐ 327 Michel Picard	.07	.03	.01
Hartford Whalers			
☐ 328 Derian Hatcher	.10	.05	.01
Minnesota North Stars			
☐ 329 Pat Falloon	.50	.23	.06
San Jose Sharks			
☐ 330 Donald Audette	.07	.03	.01
Buffalo Sabres			
☐ 331 Pat Jablonski	.20	.09	.03
St. Louis Blues			
☐ 332 Corey Foster	.07	.03	.01
Philadelphia Flyers			
☐ 333 Tomas Forslund	.07	.03	.01
Calgary Flames			
☐ 334 Steven Rice	.07	.03	.01
Edmonton Oilers			
☐ 335 Marc Bureau	.07	.03	.01
Minnesota North Stars			
☐ 336 Kimbi Daniels	.07	.03	.01
Philadelphia Flyers			
☐ 337 Adam Foote	.07	.03	.01
Quebec Nordiques			
☐ 338 Dan Kordic	.07	.03	.01
Philadelphia Flyers			
☐ 339 Link Gaetz	.07	.03	.01
San Jose Sharks			
☐ 340 Valeri Kamensky	.60	.25	.08
Quebec Nordiques			
☐ 341 Tom Draper	.15	.07	.02

Buffalo Sabres
☐ 342 Jayson More	.20	.09	.03
San Jose Sharks			
☐ 343 Dominic Roussel	.60	.25	.08
Philadelphia Flyers			
☐ 344 Jim Paek	.15	.07	.02
Pittsburgh Penguins			
☐ 345 Felix Potvin	3.50	1.55	.45
Toronto Maple Leafs			
☐ 346 Dan Lambert	.07	.03	.01
Quebec Nordiques			
☐ 347 Louie DeBrusk	.07	.03	.01
Edmonton Oilers			
☐ 348 Jamie Baker	.20	.09	.03
Quebec Nordiques			
☐ 349 Scott Niedermayer	.75	.35	.09
New Jersey Devils			
☐ 350 Paul DiPietro	.25	.11	.03
Montreal Canadiens			
☐ 351 Chris Winnes	.07	.03	.01
Boston Bruins			
☐ 352 Mark Greig	.07	.03	.01
Hartford Whalers			
☐ 353 Luciano Borsato	.15	.07	.02
Winnipeg Jets			
☐ 354 Valeri Zelepukin	.75	.35	.09
New Jersey Devils			
☐ 355 Martin Lapointe	.20	.09	.03
Detroit Red Wings			
☐ 356 Brett Hull GW	.30	.14	.04
St. Louis Blues			
☐ 357 Steve Larmer GW	.10	.05	.01
Chicago Blackhawks			
☐ 358 Theoren Fleury GW	.10	.05	.01
Calgary Flames			
☐ 359 Jeremy Roenick GW	.40	.18	.05
Chicago Blackhawks			
☐ 360 Mark Recchi GW	.25	.11	.03
Pittsburgh Penguins			
☐ 361 Brad Marsh	.10	.05	.01
Detroit Red Wings			
☐ 362 Kris King	.07	.03	.01
New York Rangers			
☐ 363 Doug Brown	.07	.03	.01
New Jersey Devils			
☐ 364 Carey Wilson	.07	.03	.01
Calgary Flames			
☐ 365 Eric Lindros	7.50	3.40	.95
Canadian National Team			
☐ 366 Kevin Dineen GG	.07	.03	.01
Philadelphia Flyers			
☐ 367 John Vanbiesbrouck GG	.15	.07	.02
New York Rangers			
☐ 368 Ray Bourque GG	.10	.05	.01
Boston Bruins			
☐ 369 Doug Wilson GG	.07	.03	.01
San Jose Sharks			
☐ 370 Keith Brown GG	.07	.03	.01
Chicago Blackhawks			
☐ 371 Kevin Lowe GG	.07	.03	.01
Edmonton Oilers			
☐ 372 Kelly Miller GG	.07	.03	.01
Washington Capitals			
☐ 373 Dave Taylor GG	.07	.03	.01
Los Angeles Kings			
☐ 374 Guy Carbonneau GG	.07	.03	.01
Montreal Canadiens			
☐ 375 Tim Hunter GG	.07	.03	.01
Calgary Flames			
☐ 376 Brett Hull TECH	.30	.14	.04
St. Louis Blues			
☐ 377 Paul Coffey TECH	.12	.05	.02
Pittsburgh Penguins			
☐ 378 Adam Oates TECH	.15	.07	.02
St. Louis Blues			
☐ 379 Andy Moog TECH	.12	.05	.02
Boston Bruins			
☐ 380 Mario Lemieux TECH	.50	.23	.06
Pittsburgh Penguins			
☐ 381 Joe Sakic IDOL	.75	.35	.09
Quebec Nordiques			
(Wayne Gretzky)			
☐ 382 Rob Blake IDOL	.12	.05	.02
Los Angeles Kings			
(Larry Robinson)			
☐ 383 Doug Weight IDOL	.25	.11	.03
New York Rangers			
(Steve Yzerman)			
☐ 384 Mike Richter	.30	.14	.04
New York Rangers			
IDOL (Bernie Parent)			
☐ 385 Luc Robitaille IDOL	.20	.09	.03
Los Angeles Kings			
(Marcel Dionne)			

☐ 386 Ed Olczyk IDOL	.10	.05	.01
Winnipeg Jets			
(Bobby Clarke)			
☐ 387 Patrick Roy IDOL	.50	.23	.06
Montreal Canadiens			
(Rogatien Vachon)			
☐ 388 Ed Belfour IDOL	.25	.11	.03
Chicago Blackhawks			
(Tony Esposito)			
☐ 389 Mats Sundin IDOL	.15	.07	.02
Quebec Nordiques			
(Mats Naslund)			
☐ 390 Tony Amonte IDOL	.25	.11	.03
New York Rangers			
(Mark Messier)			
☐ 391 John Cullen IDOL	.10	.05	.01
Hartford Whalers			
(Ray Cullen)			
☐ 392 Gary Suter IDOL	.50	.23	.06
Calgary Flames			
(Bobby Orr)			
☐ 393 Rick Zombo IDOL	.10	.05	.01
St. Louis Blues			
(Glenn Resch)			
☐ 394 Todd Krygier IDOL	.10	.05	.01
Washington Capitals			
(Gilbert Perreault)			
☐ 395 John Druce IDOL	.10	.05	.01
Washington Capitals			
(Bob Gainey)			
☐ 396 Bob Carpenter SL	.07	.03	.01
Boston Bruins			
☐ 397 Clint Malarchuk SL	.07	.03	.01
Buffalo Sabres			
☐ 398 Jim Kyte SL	.07	.03	.01
Calgary Flames			
☐ 399 Al MacInnis SL	.10	.05	.01
Calgary Flames			
☐ 400 Ed Belfour SL	.25	.11	.03
Chicago Blackhawks			
☐ 401 Brad Marsh SL	.07	.03	.01
Detroit Red Wings			
☐ 402 Brian Benning SL	.07	.03	.01
Los Angeles Kings			
☐ 403 Larry Robinson SL	.10	.05	.01
Los Angeles Kings			
☐ 404 Craig Ludwig SL	.07	.03	.01
Minnesota North Stars			
☐ 405 Pat Flatley SL	.07	.03	.01
New York Islanders			
☐ 406 Gary Nylund SL	.07	.03	.01
New York Islanders			
☐ 407 Kjell Samuelsson SL	.07	.03	.01
Philadelphia Flyers			
☐ 408 Dan Quinn SL	.07	.03	.01
Philadelphia Flyers			
☐ 409 Garth Butcher SL	.07	.03	.01
St. Louis Blues			
☐ 410 Rick Zombo SL	.07	.03	.01
St. Louis Blues			
☐ 411 Paul Cavallini SL	.07	.03	.01
St. Louis Blues			
☐ 412 Link Gaetz SL	.07	.03	.01
San Jose Sharks			
☐ 413 Dave Hannan SL	.07	.03	.01
Toronto Maple Leafs			
☐ 414 Peter Zezel SL	.07	.03	.01
Toronto Maple Leafs			
☐ 415 Randy Gregg SL	.07	.03	.01
Vancouver Canucks			
☐ 416 Pat Elynuik SL	.07	.03	.01
Winnipeg Jets			
☐ 417 Rod Buskas SL	.07	.03	.01
Chicago Blackhawks			
☐ 418 Mark Howe SL	.10	.05	.01
Philadelphia Flyers			
☐ 419 Don Sweeney	.07	.03	.01
Boston Bruins			
☐ 420 Mark Hardy	.07	.03	.01
New York Rangers			

1991-92 Pinnacle B

This 12-card set presents the starting lineup from the 1991 All-Star Game. It features six players each from the Wales Conference (B1-B6) and the Campbell Conference (B7-B12). The cards were inserted into Pinnacle French and English

 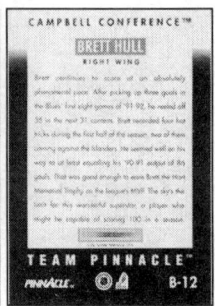

foil packs. The French version has a red name plate, while the English version has a blue name plate. The fronts of these standard-size (2 1/2" by 3 1/2") cards feature black and white head shots, with black borders on three sides and a thicker white border at the bottom. The words "Team Pinnacle" appear in the top black border, while the player's name and team affiliation are listed in the bottom white border. The border design on the back is similar and frames a player profile. The cards are numbered on the back with a "B" prefix.

	MINT	EXC	G-VG
COMPLETE SET (12)........................	500.00	230.00	65.00
COMMON PLAYER (B1-B12)...........	30.00	13.50	3.80
☐ B1 Patrick Roy........................ Montreal Canadiens	90.00	40.00	11.50
☐ B2 Ray Bourque..................... Boston Bruins	40.00	18.00	5.00
☐ B3 Brian Leetch..................... New York Rangers	50.00	23.00	6.25
☐ B4 Kevin Stevens.................... Pittsburgh Penguins	40.00	18.00	5.00
☐ B5 Mario Lemieux................... Pittsburgh Penguins	90.00	40.00	11.50
☐ B6 Cam Neely......................... Boston Bruins	40.00	18.00	5.00
☐ B7 Bill Ranford....................... Edmonton Oilers	30.00	13.50	3.80
☐ B8 Al MacInnis....................... Calgary Flames	30.00	13.50	3.80
☐ B9 Chris Chelios..................... Chicago Blackhawks	30.00	13.50	3.80
☐ B10 Luc Robitaille.................. Los Angeles Kings	40.00	18.00	5.00
☐ B11 Wayne Gretzky................. Los Angeles Kings	110.00	50.00	14.00
☐ B12 Brett Hull......................... St. Louis Blues	65.00	29.00	8.25

1992-93 Pinnacle

The 1992-93 (Score) Pinnacle Hockey set was issued in U.S. and Canadian bilingual editions; each set consists of 420 standard-size (2 1/2" by 3 1/2") cards. While card numbers 1-220 and 271-390 have different front photography in the U.S. and Canadian versions, the subset cards (221-270) depict the same photos. The color action player photos on the fronts are off-center and bordered in black. The player's name appears in a gradated team color-coded stripe that cuts across the bottom of the picture, and the team name is given immediately below. On the black, horizontal backs, the player's name appears in a turquoise stripe at the top, with biography, a color head shot, and player profile below. Topical subsets featured include Rookies (221-230, 391-420), Sidelines (231-240), Idols (241-250), Good Guys

(251-255), Gamewinners (256-262), and Masks (263-270). Except for the expansion clubs, Ottawa Senators (371-380) and Tampa Bay Lightning (381-390), the cards are not arranged by team. The cards are numbered on the back. Rookie Cards in the set include Nikolai Borschevsky, Roman Hamrlik, Andrei Kovalenko, Dmitri Kvartalnov, Tommy Soderstrom, and Martin Straka.

	MINT	EXC	G-VG
COMPLETE SET (420).....................	35.00	16.00	4.40
COMMON PLAYER (1-420)...............	.07	.03	.01
*FRENCH VERSION: 1X to 1.2X VALUE			
☐ 1 Mark Messier....................... New York Rangers	.30	.14	.04
☐ 2 Ray Bourque........................ Boston Bruins	.25	.11	.03
☐ 3 Gary Roberts........................ Calgary Flames	.07	.03	.01
☐ 4 Bill Ranford......................... Edmonton Oilers	.07	.03	.01
☐ 5 Gilbert Dionne..................... Montreal Canadiens	.07	.03	.01
☐ 6 Owen Nolan......................... Quebec Nordiques	.20	.09	.03
☐ 7 Pat LaFontaine..................... Buffalo Sabres	.30	.14	.04
☐ 8 Nicklas Lidstrom................... Detroit Red Wings	.20	.09	.03
☐ 9 Pat Falloon......................... San Jose Sharks	.25	.11	.03
☐ 10 Jeremy Roenick.................. Chicago Blackhawks	1.00	.45	.13
☐ 11 Kevin Hatcher..................... Washington Capitals	.07	.03	.01
☐ 12 Cliff Ronning...................... Vancouver Canucks	.07	.03	.01
☐ 13 Jeff Brown......................... St. Louis Blues	.07	.03	.01
☐ 14 Kevin Dineen...................... Philadelphia Flyers	.10	.05	.01
☐ 15 Brian Leetch....................... New York Rangers	.40	.18	.05
☐ 16 Eric Desjardins................... Montreal Canadiens	.07	.03	.01
☐ 17 Derek King......................... New York Islanders	.07	.03	.01
☐ 18 Mark Tinordi...................... Minnesota North Stars	.10	.05	.01
☐ 19 Kelly Hrudey....................... Los Angeles Kings	.10	.05	.01
☐ 20 Sergei Fedorov.................... Detroit Red Wings	1.25	.55	.16
☐ 21 Mike Ramsey...................... Buffalo Sabres	.07	.03	.01
☐ 22 Michel Goulet..................... Chicago Blackhawks	.10	.05	.01
☐ 23 Joe Murphy......................... Edmonton Oilers	.07	.03	.01
☐ 24 Mark Fitzpatrick.................. New York Islanders	.10	.05	.01
☐ 25 Cam Neely......................... Boston Bruins	.25	.11	.03
☐ 26 Rod Brind'Amour................. Philadelphia Flyers	.20	.09	.03
☐ 27 Neil Wilkinson..................... San Jose Sharks	.07	.03	.01
☐ 28 Greg Adams........................ Vancouver Canucks	.07	.03	.01
☐ 29 Thomas Steen..................... Winnipeg Jets	.07	.03	.01
☐ 30 Calle Johansson.................. Washington Capitals	.07	.03	.01
☐ 31 Joe Nieuwendyk................. Calgary Flames	.10	.05	.01
☐ 32 Rob Blake......................... Los Angeles Kings	.15	.07	.02
☐ 33 Darren Turcotte.................. New York Rangers	.07	.03	.01
☐ 34 Derian Hatcher.................... Minnesota North Stars	.07	.03	.01
☐ 35 Mikhail Tatarinov................ Quebec Nordiques	.07	.03	.01
☐ 36 Nelson Emerson................... St. Louis Blues	.20	.09	.03
☐ 37 Tim Cheveldae.................... Detroit Red Wings	.10	.05	.01
☐ 38 Donald Audette.................... Buffalo Sabres	.07	.03	.01
☐ 39 Brent Sutter....................... Chicago Blackhawks	.10	.05	.01

□	#	Player			
□	40	Adam Oates — Boston Bruins	.25	.11	.03
□	41	Luke Richardson — Toronto Maple Leafs	.07	.03	.01
□	42	Jon Casey — Minnesota North Stars	.10	.05	.01
□	43	Guy Carbonneau — Montreal Canadiens	.10	.05	.01
□	44	Patrick Flatley — New York Islanders	.07	.03	.01
□	45	Brian Benning — Philadelphia Flyers	.07	.03	.01
□	46	Curtis Leschyshyn — Quebec Nordiques	.07	.03	.01
□	47	Trevor Linden — Vancouver Canucks	.30	.14	.04
□	48	Don Beaupre — Washington Capitals	.10	.05	.01
□	49	Troy Murray — Winnipeg Jets	.07	.03	.01
□	50	Paul Coffey — Los Angeles Kings	.25	.11	.03
□	51	Frantisek Musil — Calgary Flames	.07	.03	.01
□	52	Doug Wilson — San Jose Sharks	.10	.05	.01
□	53	Pat Elynuik — Washington Capitals	.07	.03	.01
□	54	Curtis Joseph — St. Louis Blues	.40	.18	.05
□	55	Tony Amonte — New York Rangers	.20	.09	.03
□	56	Bob Probert — Detroit Red Wings	.07	.03	.01
□	57	Steve Smith — Chicago Blackhawks	.10	.05	.01
□	58	Dave Andreychuk — Buffalo Sabres	.25	.11	.03
□	59	Vladimir Ruzicka — Boston Bruins	.07	.03	.01
□	60	Jari Kurri — Los Angeles Kings	.15	.07	.02
□	61	Denis Savard — Montreal Canadiens	.10	.05	.01
□	62	Benoit Hogue — New York Islanders	.07	.03	.01
□	63	Terry Carkner — Philadelphia Flyers	.07	.03	.01
□	64	Valeri Kamensky — Quebec Nordiques	.25	.11	.03
□	65	Jyrki Lumme — Vancouver Canucks	.07	.03	.01
□	66	Al Iafrate — Washington Capitals	.10	.05	.01
□	67	Paul Ranheim — Calgary Flames	.07	.03	.01
□	68	Ulf Dahlen — Minnesota North Stars	.07	.03	.01
□	69	Tony Granato — Los Angeles Kings	.07	.03	.01
□	70	Phil Housley — Winnipeg Jets	.10	.05	.01
□	71	Brian Lawton — San Jose Sharks	.07	.03	.01
□	72	Garth Butcher — St. Louis Blues	.07	.03	.01
□	73	Steve Leach — Boston Bruins	.07	.03	.01
□	74	Steve Larmer — Chicago Blackhawks	.10	.05	.01
□	75	Mike Richter — New York Rangers	.35	.16	.04
□	76	Vladimir Konstantinov — Detroit Red Wings	.07	.03	.01
□	77	Alexander Mogilny — Buffalo Sabres	.75	.35	.09
□	78	Craig MacTavish — Edmonton Oilers	.07	.03	.01
□	79	Mathieu Schneider — Montreal Canadiens	.10	.05	.01
□	80	Mark Recchi — Pittsburgh Penguins	.35	.16	.04
□	81	Gerald Diduck — Vancouver Canucks	.07	.03	.01
□	82	Peter Bondra — Washington Capitals	.10	.05	.01
□	83	Al MacInnis — Calgary Flames	.15	.07	.02
□	84	Bob Kudelski — Los Angeles Kings	.10	.05	.01
□	85	Dave Gagner — Minnesota North Stars	.10	.05	.01
□	86	Uwe Krupp — New York Islanders	.07	.03	.01
□	87	Randy Carlyle — Winnipeg Jets	.07	.03	.01
□	88	Eric Lindros — Philadelphia Flyers	6.00	2.70	.75
□	89	Rob Zettler — San Jose Sharks	.07	.03	.01
□	90	Mats Sundin — Quebec Nordiques	.35	.16	.04
□	91	Andy Moog — Boston Bruins	.10	.05	.01
□	92	Keith Brown — Chicago Blackhawks	.07	.03	.01
□	93	Paul Ysebaert — Detroit Red Wings	.07	.03	.01
□	94	Mike Gartner — New York Rangers	.15	.07	.02
□	95	Kelly Buchberger — Edmonton Oilers	.07	.03	.01
□	96	Dominic Roussel — Philadelphia Flyers	.25	.11	.03
□	97	Doug Bodger — Buffalo Sabres	.07	.03	.01
□	98	Mike Donnelly — Los Angeles Kings	.07	.03	.01
□	99	Mike Craig — Minnesota North Stars	.07	.03	.01
□	100	Brett Hull — St. Louis Blues	1.00	.45	.13
□	101	Robert Reichel — Calgary Flames	.10	.05	.01
□	102	Jeff Norton — New York Islanders	.07	.03	.01
□	103	Garry Galley — Boston Bruins	.07	.03	.01
□	104	Dale Hunter — Washington Capitals	.10	.05	.01
□	105	Jeff Hackett — San Jose Sharks	.07	.03	.01
□	106	Darrin Shannon — Winnipeg Jets	.07	.03	.01
□	107	Craig Wolanin — Quebec Nordiques	.07	.03	.01
□	108	Adam Graves — New York Rangers	.40	.18	.05
□	109	Chris Chelios — Chicago Blackhawks	.10	.05	.01
□	110	Pavel Bure — Vancouver Canucks	3.00	1.35	.40
□	111	Kirk Muller — Montreal Canadiens	.10	.05	.01
□	112	Jeff Beukeboom — New York Rangers	.07	.03	.01
□	113	Mike Hough — Quebec Nordiques	.07	.03	.01
□	114	Brendan Shanahan — St. Louis Blues	.35	.16	.04
□	115	Randy Burridge — Washington Capitals	.07	.03	.01
□	116	Dave Poulin — Boston Bruins	.07	.03	.01
□	117	Petr Svoboda — Buffalo Sabres	.07	.03	.01
□	118	Ed Belfour — Chicago Blackhawks	.40	.18	.05
□	119	Ray Sheppard — Detroit Red Wings	.10	.05	.01
□	120	Bernie Nicholls — Edmonton Oilers	.10	.05	.01
□	121	Glenn Healy — New York Islanders	.10	.05	.01
□	122	Johan Garpenlov — San Jose Sharks	.07	.03	.01
□	123	Mike Lalor — Winnipeg Jets	.07	.03	.01
□	124	Brad McCrimmon — Detroit Red Wings	.07	.03	.01
□	125	Theoren Fleury — Calgary Flames	.15	.07	.02
□	126	Randy Gilhen — New York Rangers	.07	.03	.01
□	127	Petr Nedved — Vancouver Canucks	.30	.14	.04
□	128	Steve Thomas — New York Islanders	.10	.05	.01
□	129	Rick Zombo — St. Louis Blues	.07	.03	.01
□	130	Patrick Roy — Montreal Canadiens	1.00	.45	.13
□	131	Rod Langway — Washington Capitals	.07	.03	.01
□	132	Gord Murphy — Philadelphia Flyers	.07	.03	.01
□	133	Randy Wood	.07	.03	.01

Buffalo Sabres			
☐ 134 Mike Hudson	.07	.03	.01
Chicago Blackhawks			
☐ 135 Gerard Gallant	.07	.03	.01
Detroit Red Wings			
☐ 136 Brian Glynn	.07	.03	.01
Edmonton Oilers			
☐ 137 Jim Johnson	.07	.03	.01
Minnesota North Stars			
☐ 138 Corey Millen	.10	.05	.01
Los Angeles Kings			
☐ 139 Daniel Marois	.07	.03	.01
New York Islanders			
☐ 140 James Patrick	.07	.03	.01
New York Rangers			
☐ 141 Claude Lapointe	.07	.03	.01
Quebec Nordiques			
☐ 142 Bobby Smith	.10	.05	.01
Minnesota North Stars			
☐ 143 Charlie Huddy	.07	.03	.01
Los Angeles Kings			
☐ 144 Murray Baron	.07	.03	.01
St. Louis Blues			
☐ 145 Ed Olczyk	.07	.03	.01
Winnipeg Jets			
☐ 146 Dimitri Khristich	.10	.05	.01
Washington Capitals			
☐ 147 Doug Lidster	.07	.03	.01
Vancouver Canucks			
☐ 148 Perry Berezan	.07	.03	.01
San Jose Sharks			
☐ 149 Pelle Eklund	.07	.03	.01
Philadelphia Flyers			
☐ 150 Joe Sakic	.30	.14	.04
Quebec Nordiques			
☐ 151 Michal Pivonka	.10	.05	.01
Washington Capitals			
☐ 152 Joe Kocur	.07	.03	.01
New York Rangers			
☐ 153 Patrice Brisebois	.07	.03	.01
Montreal Canadiens			
☐ 154 Ray Ferraro	.07	.03	.01
New York Islanders			
☐ 155 Mike Modano	.40	.18	.05
Minnesota North Stars			
☐ 156 Marty McSorley	.10	.05	.01
Los Angeles Kings			
☐ 157 Norm Maciver	.07	.03	.01
Ottawa Senators			
☐ 158 Sergei Nemchinov	.10	.05	.01
New York Rangers			
☐ 159 David Bruce	.07	.03	.01
San Jose Sharks			
☐ 160 Kelly Miller	.07	.03	.01
Detroit Red Wings			
☐ 161 Alexei Gusarov	.07	.03	.01
Quebec Nordiques			
☐ 162 Andrei Lomakin	.07	.03	.01
Philadelphia Flyers			
☐ 163 Sergio Momesso	.07	.03	.01
Vancouver Canucks			
☐ 164 Mike Keane	.07	.03	.01
Montreal Canadiens			
☐ 165 Pierre Turgeon	.35	.16	.04
New York Islanders			
☐ 166 Martin Gelinas	.07	.03	.01
Edmonton Oilers			
☐ 167 Chris Dahlquist	.07	.03	.01
Calgary Flames			
☐ 168 Kris King	.07	.03	.01
New York Islanders			
☐ 169 Dean Evason	.07	.03	.01
San Jose Sharks			
☐ 170 Mike Ridley	.10	.05	.01
Washington Capitals			
☐ 171 Shawn Burr	.07	.03	.01
Detroit Red Wings			
☐ 172 Dana Murzyn	.07	.03	.01
Vancouver Canucks			
☐ 173 Dirk Graham	.07	.03	.01
Chicago Blackhawks			
☐ 174 Trent Yawney	.07	.03	.01
Calgary Flames			
☐ 175 Luc Robitaille	.30	.14	.04
Los Angeles Kings			
☐ 176 Randy Moller	.07	.03	.01
Buffalo Sabres			
☐ 177 Vincent Riendeau	.07	.03	.01
Detroit Red Wings			
☐ 178 Brian Propp	.10	.05	.01
Minnesota North Stars			
☐ 179 Don Sweeney	.07	.03	.01
Buffalo Sabres			
☐ 180 Stephane Matteau	.07	.03	.01
Chicago Blackhawks			
☐ 181 Garry Valk	.07	.03	.01
Vancouver Canucks			
☐ 182 Sylvain Cote	.07	.03	.01
Washington Capitals			
☐ 183 Dave Snuggerud	.07	.03	.01
San Jose Sharks			
☐ 184 Gary Leeman	.07	.03	.01
Calgary Flames			
☐ 185 John Druce	.07	.03	.01
Washington Capitals			
☐ 186 John Vanbiesbrouck	.15	.07	.02
New York Rangers			
☐ 187 Geoff Courtnall	.07	.03	.01
Vancouver Canucks			
☐ 188 David Volek	.07	.03	.01
New York Islanders			
☐ 189 Doug Weight	.10	.05	.01
New York Rangers			
☐ 190 Bob Essensa	.10	.05	.01
Winnipeg Jets			
☐ 191 Jan Erixon	.07	.03	.01
New York Rangers			
☐ 192 Geoff Smith	.07	.03	.01
Edmonton Oilers			
☐ 193 Dave Christian	.07	.03	.01
Chicago Blackhawks			
☐ 194 Brian Noonan	.07	.03	.01
Chicago Blackhawks			
☐ 195 Gary Suter	.10	.05	.01
Calgary Flames			
☐ 196 Craig Janney	.20	.09	.03
St. Louis Blues			
☐ 197 Brad May	.07	.03	.01
Buffalo Sabres			
☐ 198 Gaetan Duchesne	.07	.03	.01
Minnesota North Stars			
☐ 199 Adam Creighton	.07	.03	.01
Tampa Bay Lightning			
☐ 200 Wayne Gretzky	1.50	.65	.19
Los Angeles Kings			
☐ 201 Dave Babych	.07	.03	.01
Vancouver Canucks			
☐ 202 Fredrik Olausson	.07	.03	.01
Winnipeg Jets			
☐ 203 Bob Bassen	.07	.03	.01
St. Louis Blues			
☐ 204 Todd Krygier	.07	.03	.01
Washington Capitals			
☐ 205 Grant Ledyard	.07	.03	.01
Buffalo Sabres			
☐ 206 Michel Petit	.07	.03	.01
Calgary Flames			
☐ 207 Todd Elik	.07	.03	.01
Minnesota North Stars			
☐ 208 Josef Beranek	.25	.11	.03
Edmonton Oilers			
☐ 209 Neal Broten	.10	.05	.01
Minnesota North Stars			
☐ 210 Jim Sandlak	.07	.03	.01
Vancouver Canucks			
☐ 211 Kevin Haller	.07	.03	.01
Montreal Canadiens			
☐ 212 Paul Broten	.07	.03	.01
New York Rangers			
☐ 213 Mark Pederson	.07	.03	.01
Philadelphia Flyers			
☐ 214 John McIntyre	.07	.03	.01
Los Angeles Kings			
☐ 215 Teppo Numminen	.07	.03	.01
Winnipeg Jets			
☐ 216 Ken Sutton	.07	.03	.01
Buffalo Sabres			
☐ 217 Ronnie Stern	.07	.03	.01
Calgary Flames			
☐ 218 Luciano Borsato	.07	.03	.01
Winnipeg Jets			
☐ 219 Claude Loiselle	.07	.03	.01
New York Islanders			
☐ 220 Mark Hardy	.07	.03	.01
New York Rangers			
☐ 221 Joe Juneau RK	1.75	.80	.22
Boston Bruins			
☐ 222 Keith Tkachuk RK	.40	.18	.05
Winnipeg Jets			
☐ 223 Scott Lachance RK	.07	.03	.01
New York Islanders			
☐ 224 Glen Murray RK	.07	.03	.01
Boston Bruins			
☐ 225 Igor Kravchuk RK	.07	.03	.01
Chicago Blackhawks			
☐ 226 Evgeny Davydov RK	.07	.03	.01
Winnipeg Jets			
☐ 227 Ray Whitney RK	.35	.16	.04

San Jose Sharks			
☐ 228 Bret Hedican RK	.25	.11	.03
St. Louis Blues			
☐ 229 Keith Carney RK	.20	.09	.03
Buffalo Sabres			
☐ 230 Viacheslav Kozlov RK	1.25	.55	.16
Detroit Red Wings			
☐ 231 Mario Lemieux SL	.07	.03	.01
Pittsburgh Penguins			
☐ 232 Cam Neely SL	.10	.05	.01
Boston Bruins			
☐ 233 Al Iafrate SL	.10	.05	.01
Washington Capitals			
☐ 234 Randy Wood SL	.07	.03	.01
New York Islanders			
☐ 235 Luke Richardson SL	.07	.03	.01
Toronto Maple Leafs			
☐ 236 Eric Lindros SL	1.50	.65	.19
Philadelphia Flyers			
☐ 237 Dale Hunter SL	.07	.03	.01
Washington Capitals			
☐ 238 Pat Falloon SL	.15	.07	.02
San Jose Sharks			
☐ 239 Dean Kennedy SL	.07	.03	.01
Winnipeg Jets			
☐ 240 Uwe Krupp SL	.07	.03	.01
New York Islanders			
☐ 241 Scott Niedermayer Idol	.30	.14	.04
New Jersey Devils			
(Steve Yzerman)			
☐ 242 Gary Roberts Idol	.10	.05	.01
Calgary Flames			
(Lanny McDonald)			
☐ 243 Peter Ahola Idol	.07	.03	.01
Los Angeles Kings			
(Jari Kurri)			
☐ 244 Scott Lachance Idol	.07	.03	.01
New York Islanders			
(Mark Howe)			
☐ 245 Rob Pearson Idol	.15	.07	.02
Toronto Maple Leafs			
(Mike Bossy)			
☐ 246 Kirk McLean Idol	.10	.05	.01
Vancouver Canucks			
(Bernie Parent)			
☐ 247 Dmitri Mironov Idol	.10	.05	.01
Toronto Maple Leafs			
(Viacheslav Fetisov)			
☐ 248 Brendan Shanahan Idol	.20	.09	.03
St. Louis Blues			
(Darryl Sittler)			
☐ 249 Petr Nedved Idol	.60	.25	.08
Vancouver Canucks			
(Wayne Gretzky)			
☐ 250 Todd Ewen Idol	.07	.03	.01
Montreal Canadiens			
(Clark Gillies)			
☐ 251 Luc Robitaille GG	.10	.05	.01
Los Angeles Kings			
☐ 252 Mark Tinordi GG	.07	.03	.01
Minnesota North Stars			
☐ 253 Kris King GG	.07	.03	.01
New York Islanders			
☐ 254 Pat LaFontaine GG	.15	.07	.02
Buffalo Sabres			
☐ 255 Ryan Walter GG	.07	.03	.01
Vancouver Canucks			
☐ 256 Jeremy Roenick GW	.25	.11	.03
Chicago Blackhawks			
☐ 257 Brett Hull GW	.25	.11	.03
St. Louis Blues			
☐ 258 Steve Yzerman GW	.20	.09	.03
Detroit Red Wings			
☐ 259 Claude Lemieux GW	.07	.03	.01
New Jersey Devils			
☐ 260 Mike Modano GW	.07	.03	.01
Minnesota North Stars			
☐ 261 Vincent Damphousse GW	.10	.05	.01
Montreal Canadiens			
☐ 262 Tony Granato GW	.07	.03	.01
Los Angeles Kings			
☐ 263 Andy Moog Mask	2.00	.90	.25
Boston Bruins			
☐ 264 Curtis Joseph Mask	2.50	1.15	.30
St. Louis Blues			
☐ 265 Ed Belfour Mask	2.50	1.15	.30
Chicago Blackhawks			
☐ 266 Brian Hayward Mask	3.00	1.35	.40
San Jose Sharks			
☐ 267 Grant Fuhr Mask	1.00	.45	.13
Toronto Maple Leafs			
☐ 268 Don Beaupre Mask	1.00	.45	.13
Washington Capitals			
☐ 269 Tim Cheveldae Mask	1.00	.45	.13
Detroit Red Wings			
☐ 270 Mike Richter Mask	2.50	1.15	.30
New York Rangers			
☐ 271 Zarley Zalapski	.07	.03	.01
Hartford Whalers			
☐ 272 Kevin Todd	.07	.03	.01
New Jersey Devils			
☐ 273 Dave Ellett	.07	.03	.01
Toronto Maple Leafs			
☐ 274 Chris Terreri	.10	.05	.01
New Jersey Devils			
☐ 275 Jaromir Jagr	1.00	.45	.13
Pittsburgh Penguins			
☐ 276 Wendel Clark	.15	.07	.02
Toronto Maple Leafs			
☐ 277 Bobby Holik	.07	.03	.01
New Jersey Devils			
☐ 278 Bruce Driver	.07	.03	.01
New Jersey Devils			
☒ 279 Doug Gilmour	.40	.18	.05
Toronto Maple Leafs			
☐ 280 Scott Stevens	.15	.07	.02
New Jersey Devils			
☐ 281 Murray Craven	.07	.03	.01
Hartford Whalers			
☐ 282 Rick Tocchet	.10	.05	.01
Pittsburgh Penguins			
☐ 283 Peter Zezel	.07	.03	.01
Toronto Maple Leafs			
☐ 284 Claude Lemieux	.10	.05	.01
New Jersey Devils			
☐ 285 John Cullen	.07	.03	.01
Hartford Whalers			
☐ 286 Valeri Zelepukin	.25	.11	.03
New Jersey Devils			
☐ 287 Rob Pearson	.07	.03	.01
Toronto Maple Leafs			
☐ 288 Kevin Stevens	.35	.16	.04
Pittsburgh Penguins			
☐ 289 Alexei Kasatonov	.07	.03	.01
New Jersey Devils			
☐ 290 Todd Gill	.07	.03	.01
Toronto Maple Leafs			
☐ 291 Randy Ladouceur	.07	.03	.01
Hartford Whalers			
☐ 292 Larry Murphy	.10	.05	.01
Pittsburgh Penguins			
☐ 293 Tom Chorske	.07	.03	.01
New Jersey Devils			
☐ 294 Jamie Macoun	.07	.03	.01
Toronto Maple Leafs			
☐ 295 Sean Burke	.10	.05	.01
Hartford Whalers			
☐ 296 Ulf Samuelsson	.10	.05	.01
Pittsburgh Penguins			
☐ 297 Eric Weinrich	.07	.03	.01
Hartford Whalers			
☐ 298 Tom Barrasso	.10	.05	.01
Pittsburgh Penguins			
☐ 299 Viacheslav Fetisov	.07	.03	.01
New Jersey Devils			
☐ 300 Mario Lemieux	1.25	.55	.16
Pittsburgh Penguins			
☐ 301 Grant Fuhr	.10	.05	.01
Toronto Maple Leafs			
☐ 302 Zdeno Ciger	.07	.03	.01
New Jersey Devils			
☐ 303 Ron Francis	.10	.05	.01
Pittsburgh Penguins			
☐ 304 Scott Niedermayer	.50	.23	.06
New Jersey Devils			
☐ 305 Mark Osborne	.07	.03	.01
Toronto Maple Leafs			
☐ 306 Kjell Samuelsson	.07	.03	.01
Pittsburgh Penguins			
☐ 307 Geoff Sanderson	.50	.23	.06
Hartford Whalers			
☐ 308 Paul Stanton	.07	.03	.01
Pittsburgh Penguins			
☐ 309 Frank Pietrangelo	.07	.03	.01
Hartford Whalers			
☐ 310 Bob Errey	.07	.03	.01
Pittsburgh Penguins			
☐ 311 Dino Ciccarelli	.10	.05	.01
Washington Capitals			
☐ 312 Gordie Roberts	.07	.03	.01
Pittsburgh Penguins			
☐ 313 Kevin Miller	.10	.05	.01
Washington Capitals			
☐ 314 Mike Ricci	.20	.09	.03
Quebec Nordiques			
☐ 315 Bob Carpenter	.07	.03	.01
Boston Bruins			
☐ 316 Dale Hawerchuk	.10	.05	.01

Buffalo Sabres				
☐ 317 Christian Ruuttu	.07	.03	.01	
Chicago Blackhawks				
☐ 318 Mike Vernon	.10	.05	.01	
Calgary Flames				
☐ 319 Paul Cavallini	.07	.03	.01	
St. Louis Blues				
☐ 320 Steve Duchesne	.10	.05	.01	
Quebec Nordiques				
☐ 321 Craig Simpson	.07	.03	.01	
Edmonton Oilers				
☐ 322 Mark Howe	.10	.05	.01	
Detroit Red Wings				
☐ 323 Shayne Corson	.10	.05	.01	
Montreal Canadiens				
☐ 324 Tom Kurvers	.07	.03	.01	
New York Islanders				
☐ 325 Brian Bellows	.10	.05	.01	
Montreal Canadiens				
☐ 326 Glen Wesley	.07	.03	.01	
Boston Bruins				
☐ 327 Daren Puppa	.10	.05	.01	
Buffalo Sabres				
☐ 328 Joel Otto	.07	.03	.01	
Calgary Flames				
☐ 329 Jimmy Carson	.07	.03	.01	
Detroit Red Wings				
☐ 330 Kirk McLean	.30	.14	.04	
Vancouver Canucks				
☐ 331 Rob Brown	.07	.03	.01	
Chicago Blackhawks				
☐ 332 Yves Racine	.07	.03	.01	
Detroit Red Wings				
☐ 333 Brian Mullen	.10	.05	.01	
San Jose Sharks				
☐ 334 Dave Manson	.07	.03	.01	
Edmonton Oilers				
☐ 335 Sergei Makarov	.10	.05	.01	
Calgary Flames				
☐ 336 Esa Tikkanen	.10	.05	.01	
Edmonton Oilers				
☐ 337 Russ Courtnall	.10	.05	.01	
Minnesota North Stars				
☐ 338 Kevin Lowe	.07	.03	.01	
Edmonton Oilers				
☐ 339 Steve Chiasson	.07	.03	.01	
Detroit Red Wings				
☐ 340 Ron Hextall	.10	.05	.01	
Quebec Nordiques				
☐ 341 Stephen Lebeau	.07	.03	.01	
Montreal Canadiens				
☐ 342 Mike McPhee	.07	.03	.01	
Montreal Canadiens				
☐ 343 David Shaw	.07	.03	.01	
Boston Bruins				
☐ 344 Petr Klima	.07	.03	.01	
Edmonton Oilers				
☐ 345 Tomas Sandstrom	.07	.03	.01	
Los Angeles Kings				
☐ 346 Scott Mellanby	.07	.03	.01	
Edmonton Oilers				
☐ 347 Brian Skrudland	.07	.03	.01	
Montreal Canadiens				
☐ 348 Pat Verbeek	.10	.05	.01	
Hartford Whalers				
☐ 349 Vincent Damphousse	.10	.05	.01	
Montreal Canadiens				
☐ 350 Steve Yzerman	.40	.18	.05	
Detroit Red Wings				
☐ 351 John MacLean	.10	.05	.01	
New Jersey Devils				
☐ 352 Steve Konroyd	.07	.03	.01	
Hartford Whalers				
☐ 353 Phil Bourque	.07	.03	.01	
Pittsburgh Penguins				
☐ 354 Ken Daneyko	.07	.03	.01	
New Jersey Devils				
☐ 355 Glenn Anderson	.10	.05	.01	
Toronto Maple Leafs				
☐ 356 Ken Wregget	.07	.03	.01	
Pittsburgh Penguins				
☐ 357 Brent Gilchrist	.07	.03	.01	
Montreal Canadiens				
☐ 358 Bob Rouse	.07	.03	.01	
Toronto Maple Leafs				
☐ 359 Peter Stastny	.10	.05	.01	
New Jersey Devils				
☐ 360 Joe Mullen	.10	.05	.01	
Pittsburgh Penguins				
☐ 361 Stephane Richer	.10	.05	.01	
New Jersey Devils				
☐ 362 Kelly Kisio	.07	.03	.01	
San Jose Sharks				
☐ 363 Keith Acton	.07	.03	.01	
Philadelphia Flyers				
☐ 364 Felix Potvin	2.50	1.15	.30	
Toronto Maple Leafs				
☐ 365 Martin Lapointe	.07	.03	.01	
Detroit Red Wings				
☐ 366 Ron Tugnutt	.07	.03	.01	
Edmonton Oilers				
☐ 367 Dave Taylor	.10	.05	.01	
Los Angeles Kings				
☐ 368 Tim Kerr	.10	.05	.01	
Hartford Whalers				
☐ 369 Carey Wilson	.07	.03	.01	
Calgary Flames				
☐ 370 Greg Paslawski	.07	.03	.01	
Philadelphia Flyers				
☐ 371 Peter Sidorkiewicz	.07	.03	.01	
Ottawa Senators				
☐ 372 Brad Shaw	.07	.03	.01	
Ottawa Senators				
☐ 373 Sylvain Turgeon	.07	.03	.01	
Ottawa Senators				
☐ 374 Mark Lamb	.07	.03	.01	
Ottawa Senators				
☐ 375 Laurie Boschman	.07	.03	.01	
Ottawa Senators				
☐ 376 Mark Osiecki	.07	.03	.01	
Ottawa Senators				
☐ 377 Doug Smail	.07	.03	.01	
Ottawa Senators				
☐ 378 Brad Marsh	.10	.05	.01	
Ottawa Senators				
☐ 379 Mike Peluso	.07	.03	.01	
Ottawa Senators				
☐ 380 Steve Weeks	.07	.03	.01	
Ottawa Senators				
☐ 381 Wendell Young	.07	.03	.01	
Tampa Bay Lightning				
☐ 382 Joe Reekie	.07	.03	.01	
Tampa Bay Lightning				
☐ 383 Peter Taglianetti	.07	.03	.01	
Tampa Bay Lightning				
☐ 384 Mikael Andersson	.07	.03	.01	
Tampa Bay Lightning				
☐ 385 Marc Bergevin	.07	.03	.01	
Tampa Bay Lightning				
☐ 386 Anatoli Semenov	.07	.03	.01	
Tampa Bay Lightning				
☐ 387 Brian Bradley	.07	.03	.01	
Tampa Bay Lightning				
☐ 388 Michel Mongeau	.07	.03	.01	
Tampa Bay Lightning				
☐ 389 Rob Ramage	.07	.03	.01	
Tampa Bay Lightning				
☐ 390 Ken Hodge Jr.	.07	.03	.01	
Tampa Bay Lightning				
☐ 391 Richard Matvichuk RK	.20	.09	.03	
Minnesota North Stars				
☐ 392 Alexei Zhitnik RK UER	.30	.14	.04	
Los Angeles Kings (Drafted in fourth round, not third as bio indicates)				
☐ 393 Dallas Drake RK	.30	.14	.04	
Detroit Red Wings				
☐ 394 Dimitri Yushkevich RK	.25	.11	.03	
Philadelphia Flyers				
☐ 395 Andrei Kovalenko RK	.50	.23	.06	
Quebec Nordiques				
☐ 396 Vladimir Vujtek RK	.20	.09	.03	
Edmonton Oilers				
☐ 397 Nikolai Borschevsky RK	.50	.23	.06	
Toronto Maple Leafs				
☐ 398 Vitali Karamnov RK	.20	.09	.03	
St. Louis Blues				
☐ 399 Jim Hiller RK	.15	.07	.02	
Los Angeles Kings				
☐ 400 Michael Nylander RK	.50	.23	.06	
Hartford Whalers				
☐ 401 Tommy Sjodin RK	.15	.07	.02	
Minnesota North Stars				
☐ 402 Martin Straka RK	.25	.11	.03	
Pittsburgh Penguins				
☐ 403 Alexei Kovalev RK	1.25	.55	.16	
New York Rangers				
☐ 404 Vitali Prokhorov RK	.20	.09	.03	
St. Louis Blues				
☐ 405 Dmitri Kvartalnov RK	.30	.14	.04	
Boston Bruins				
☐ 406 Teemu Selanne RK	2.00	.90	.25	
Winnipeg Jets				
☐ 407 Darius Kasparaitis RK	.15	.07	.02	
New York Islanders				
☐ 408 Roman Hamrlik RK	.60	.25	.08	
Tampa Bay Lightning				
☐ 409 Vladimir Malakhov RK	.30	.14	.04	

		MINT	EXC	G-VG
	New York Islanders			
☐ 410	Sergei Krivokrasov RK	.25	.11	.03
	Chicago Blackhawks			
☐ 411	Robert Lang RK	.30	.14	.04
	Los Angeles Kings			
☐ 412	Jozef Stumpel RK..............	.07	.03	.01
	Boston Bruins			
☐ 413	Denny Felsner RK..............	.25	.11	.03
	St. Louis Blues			
☐ 414	Rob Zamuner RK	.20	.09	.03
	Tampa Bay Lightning			
☐ 415	Jason Woolley RK	.15	.07	.02
	Washington Capitals			
☐ 416	Alexei Zhamnov RK............	.75	.35	.09
	Winnipeg Jets			
☐ 417	Igor Korolev RK	.20	.09	.03
	St. Louis Blues			
☐ 418	Patrick Poulin RK	.07	.03	.01
	Hartford Whalers			
☐ 419	Dmitri Mironov RK	.10	.05	.01
	Toronto Maple Leafs			
☐ 420	Shawn McEachern RK........	.25	.11	.03
	Pittsburgh Penguins			

		MINT	EXC	G-VG
	Pavel Bure			
	Vancouver Canucks			
☐ 5	Eric Lindros...............	45.00	20.00	5.75
	Philadelphia Flyers			
	Wayen Gretzky			
	Los Angeles Kings			
☐ 6	Jaromir Jagr	25.00	11.50	3.10
	Pittsburgh Penguins			
	Brett Hull			
	St. Louis Blues			

1992-93 Pinnacle Team 2000

 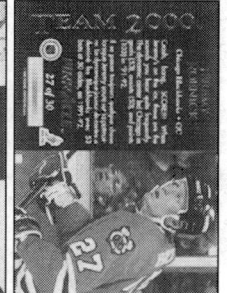

Inserted two per 27-card super pack, these 30 cards feature players who Score predicts will be stars in the NHL in the year 2000. The cards measure the standard size (2 1/2" by 3 1/2"). The U.S. features glossy color action photos are full-bleed on the top and right and edged by black wedged-shaped borders on the left and bottom. In a gold-foil edged circle, the team logo appears in the lower left corner at the intersection of these two stripes. In gold-foil lettering, the words "Team 2000" are printed vertically in the left stripe while the player's name appears in the bottom stripe. The Canadian version offers artists renditions on front instead of player photos and has a maple leaf following the Team 2000 insignia.The horizontal backs have a black panel with bilingual player profile on the left half and a full-bleed color close-up photo on the right.

1992-93 Pinnacle Team Pinnacle

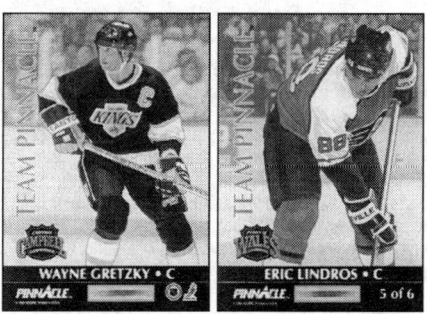

Randomly inserted in 1992-93 Score Pinnacle foil packs, these six double-sided cards feature a top player from the Campbell Conference with his Wales Conference counterpart on the other side. According to Score, the odds of finding a card are not less than one in 125 packs. Painted by Score artist Christopher Greco, the pictures on the U.S. versions (photos appear on the Canadian versions) are full-bleed on three sides but edged on the bottom by a gold-foil stripe that features the player's name and position. A black stripe immediately below completes the card face. The words "Team Pinnacle" are printed in turquoise (pink in the Canadian version) vertically near the left edge of both sides of the card, and the conference logo appears below it. The backs of these cards may be distinguished from the fronts by the card number in the lower right corner.

		MINT	EXC	G-VG
COMPLETE SET (6)........................		90.00	40.00	11.50
COMMON PLAYER (1-6)................		15.00	6.75	1.90
*FRENCH VERSION: 1X to 1.2X VALUE				
☐ 1	Mike Richter............................	18.00	8.00	2.30
	New York Rangers			
	Ed Belfour			
	Chicago Blackhawks			
☐ 2	Ray Bourque	15.00	6.75	1.90
	Boston Bruins			
	Chris Chelios			
	Chicago Blackhawks			
☐ 3	Brian Leetch..........................	18.00	8.00	2.30
	New York Rangers			
	Paul Coffey			
	Los Angeles Kings			
☐ 4	Kevin Stevens	30.00	13.50	3.80
	Pittsburgh Penguins			

		MINT	EXC	G-VG
COMPLETE SET (30)........................		35.00	16.00	4.40
COMMON PLAYER (1-30)...............		.50	.23	.06
*FRENCH VERSION: 1X to 1.2X VALUE				
☐ 1	Eric Lindros...........................	8.00	3.60	1.00
	Philadelphia Flyers			
☐ 2	Mike Modano	2.00	.90	.25
	Minnesota North Stars			
☐ 3	Nicklas Lidstrom....................	.50	.23	.06
	Detroit Red Wings			
☐ 4	Tony Amonte...........................	.60	.25	.08
	New York Rangers			
☐ 5	Felix Potvin	6.00	2.70	.75
	Toronto Maple Leafs			
☐ 6	Scott Lachance	.50	.23	.06
	New York Islanders			
☐ 7	Mats Sundin	1.25	.55	.16
	Quebec Nordiques			
☐ 8	Pavel Bure.............................	7.00	3.10	.85
	Vancouver Canucks			
☐ 9	Eric Desjardins......................	.50	.23	.06
	Montreal Canadiens			
☐ 10	Owen Nolan...........................	.60	.25	.08
	Quebec Nordiques			
☐ 11	Dominic Roussel....................	.60	.25	.08
	Philadelphia Flyers			
☐ 12	Scott Niedermayer	1.00	.45	.13
	New Jersey Devils			
☐ 13	Viacheslav Kozlov	2.50	1.15	.30
	Detroit Red Wings			
☐ 14	Patrick Poulin.......................	.50	.23	.06

		MINT	EXC	G-VG
Hartford Whalers				
☐ 15	Jaromir Jagr	2.50	1.15	.30
Pittsburgh Penguins				
☐ 16	Rob Blake	.60	.25	.08
Los Angeles Kings				
☐ 17	Pierre Turgeon	1.25	.55	.16
New York Islanders				
☐ 18	Rod Brind'Amour	.60	.25	.08
Philadelphia Flyers				
☐ 19	Joe Juneau	3.00	1.35	.40
Boston Bruins				
☐ 20	Tim Cheveldae	.60	.25	.08
Detroit Red Wings				
☐ 21	Joe Sakic	1.25	.55	.16
Quebec Nordiques				
☐ 22	Kevin Todd	.50	.23	.06
New Jersey Devils				
☐ 23	Rob Pearson	.50	.23	.06
Toronto Maple Leafs				
☐ 24	Trevor Linden	1.00	.45	.13
Vancouver Canucks				
☐ 25	Dimitri Khristich	.50	.23	.06
Washington Capitals				
☐ 26	Pat Falloon	.60	.25	.08
San Jose Sharks				
☐ 27	Jeremy Roenick	3.00	1.35	.40
Chicago Blackhawks				
☐ 28	Alexander Mogilny	2.00	.90	.25
Buffalo Sabres				
☐ 29	Gilbert Dionne	.50	.23	.06
Montreal Canadiens				
☐ 30	Sergei Fedorov	4.00	1.80	.50
Detroit Red Wings				

1992-93 Pinnacle Promo Sheet

This promo sheet features six cards measuring the standard size (2 1/2" by 3 1/2"). The cards feature color action photos with the players extending beyond the picture background. The card face is black and a thin white line forms a frame around the picture. The player's name appears in a gradated bar at the bottom that matches the team colors. The horizontal backs feature the player's name in a gradated turquoise bar at the top. Close-up player photos are surrounded by biography, statistics, and career highlights on a black background. The backs have white borders. This sheet was intended to remain uncut and the disclaimers "Not For Resale" and "For Promotional Use Only" are printed in the white borders between the rows of cards. The cards are numbered on the back and listed as they appear on the sheet from left to right.

		MINT	EXC	G-VG
COMPLETE SET (1)		3.00	1.20	.30
COMMON PANEL		3.00	1.20	.30
☐ 1	Promo Sheet	3.00	1.20	.30
	91 Andy Moog			
	Boston Bruins			
	36 Nelson Emerson			
	St. Louis Blues			
	61 Denis Savard			
	Montreal Canadiens			
	6 Owen Nolan			
	Quebec Nordiques			
	22 Michel Goulet			

Chicago Blackhawks
88 Eric Lindros
Philadelphia Flyers

1992-93 Pinnacle Eric Lindros

This 30-card boxed set measures the standard size (2 1/2" by 3 1/2") and features posed and action color photos of Eric Lindros as he has progressed from the junior leagues to the NHL. The set begins when Eric Lindros first received attention as a 14-year-old with the St. Michael's Buzzers and ends with his playing for the Philadelphia Flyers. According to Score, only 3,750 numbered cases were produced. The cards have black borders, and his name is printed in gold foil at the top. The backs display a vertical, color photo and Eric's comments about a particular phase of his career. The cards are numbered on the back.

		MINT	EXC	G-VG
COMPLETE SET (30)		12.00	5.00	1.20
COMMON PLAYER (1-30)		.60	.24	.06
☐ 1	St. Michael's Buzzers	1.00	.40	.10
☐ 2	Detroit Compuware	.60	.24	.06
☐ 3	Oshawa Generals	.60	.24	.06
	(Skating, white jersey)			
☐ 4	Oshawa Generals	.60	.24	.06
	(Red jersey)			
☐ 5	Oshawa Generals	.60	.24	.06
	(Passing, white jersey)			
☐ 6	Oshawa Generals	.60	.24	.06
	(Sliding to stop)			
☐ 7	Memorial Cup	.60	.24	.06
☐ 8	World Junior	.60	.24	.06
	Championship (Portrait in red jersey)			
☐ 9	World Junior	.60	.24	.06
	Championship (Portrait in tux)			
☐ 10	World Junior Champ-ionship (In action)	1.00	.40	.10
☐ 11	Canada Cup	1.00	.40	.10
	(In action)			
☐ 12	Canada Cup	.60	.24	.06
	(In jeans)			
☐ 13	Canadian National	1.00	.40	.10
	Team (In action, black eye visible)			
☐ 14	Canadian National	1.00	.40	.10
	Team (White jersey, arms raised)			
☐ 15	Canadian National	.60	.24	.06
	Team (Skating with stick in air)			
☐ 16	Canadian National	.60	.24	.06
	Team (Shaking hands)			
☐ 17	First-Round Draft Pick	.60	.24	.06
☐ 18	Trade To Philadelphia	.60	.24	.06
☐ 19	Happy Flyer	.60	.24	.06
☐ 20	Preseason Action	.60	.24	.06
	(White helmet)			
☐ 21	Preseason Action	.60	.24	.06
	(Black helmet)			

☐ 22	Regular Season Debut	.60	.24	.06
☐ 23	First NHL Goal	.60	.24	.06
☐ 24	Winning Home Debut	.60	.24	.06
☐ 25	First NHL Hat Trick	.60	.24	.06
☐ 26	Playing Golf	.60	.24	.06
☐ 27	Backyard Fun	.60	.24	.06
☐ 28	Fan Favorite	.60	.24	.06
☐ 29	Welcome To Philly	.60	.24	.06
☐ 30	Philly Hero	1.00	.40	.10

1993 Pinnacle Power *

This card was given to dealers who attended the Pinnacle Brands factory tour at the 1993 SCAI Convention. It measures approximately 3 1/2" by 5", and came in a hard plastic holder with a black velvet case that carries the word "Pinnacle" in yellow letters. According to Score, only 200 cards exist, the remainder of the print run having been shredded following distribution of the gift. The horizontal front features color head shots of Alexander Daigle, Franco Harris, and Eric Lindros on a red background with a thin gold border, and a slightly thicker black border around it. The words "Pinnacle Power" on a red bar on the bottom of the card complete the front. On a shaded red to black background, the horizontal back carries biographical information about all three players. The cards are sequentially numbered on the back.

	MINT	EXC	G-VG
COMPLETE SET (1)	250.00	100.00	25.00
COMMON CARD	250.00	100.00	25.00
☐ 1 Alexandre Daigle Franco Harris Eric Lindros	250.00	100.00	25.00

1993-94 Pinnacle Daigle Entry Draft

To commemorate Daigle's signing with Score as a spokesperson, Score issued this standard-size card (2 1/2" by 3 1/2") and distributed it to the news media and others who attended the 1993 NHL Draft in Quebec on June 26. The card was also distributed to media at the 1993 National Sports Collectors Convention in Chicago. The front features a color close-up photo with white borders. Daigle is pictured wearing a jersey with "Score" emblazoned across it. The back has a full-bleed action shot with Daigle wearing a "Pinnacle" jersey. A black stripe at the bottom carries the player's name and the anti-counterfeiting device. The card is unnumbered.

	MINT	EXC	G-VG
COMPLETE SET (1)	30.00	12.00	3.00
COMMON CARD	30.00	12.00	3.00
☐ 1 Alexandre Daigle	30.00	12.00	3.00

1993-94 Pinnacle I Samples

These six cards were distributed to dealers and media during the summer of 1993 to show the style of the upcoming Pinnacle hockey cards for the 1993-94 season. The cards are standard size, 2 1/2" by 3 1/2" and unnumbered.

	MINT	EXC	G-VG
COMPLETE SET (6)	15.00	6.00	1.50
COMMON PLAYER (1-6)	.75	.30	.07
☐ 1 Tony Amonte	.75	.30	.07
☐ 2 Tom Barrasso	.75	.30	.07
☐ 3 Joe Juneau	3.00	1.20	.30
☐ 4 Eric Lindros	7.50	3.00	.75
☐ 5 Teemu Selanne	5.00	2.00	.50
☐ 6 Mats Sundin	1.50	.60	.15

1993-94 Pinnacle II Hobby Samples

This 11-card hobby sample set was enclosed in a cello pack. The cards measure the standard-size (2 1/2" by 3 1/2") and, with the exception of the Mogilny "Nifty 50" card, the top right corners of each card have been cut off, apparently to

Issued in a first and second series of 236 and 275 cards, respectively, the 1993-94 Score Pinnacle hockey set consists of 511 standard-size (2 1/2" by 3 1/2") cards. On a black background with a thin white border, the fronts feature color action player photos. The team's name in white letters appears above the photo, while the player's name, also in white letters, and Pinnacle's logo in gold foil are printed at the bottom. On a black background, the horizontal backs carry a color head shot in the center with the player's biography and the team logo on the left, while his profile is on the right. The player's name and stats appear at the bottom. Both series were offered in both a U.S. version as well as a Canadian, bilingual version. A card honoring Wayne Gretzky's 802 career goal was included in second series jumbo packs. Because of this distribution, the card (#512) is not considered part of the complete set. The set features the following subsets: Rookie (206-220 and 236), Award Winners (221-230), Hometown Heroes (231-235), Now , Then (237-241), Rookies (427-456), Canadian World Junior (457-478), USA World Junior (479-500), and Russian World Junior (501-511). The cards are numbered on the back.

indicate that these are promo cards. The disclaimer "SAMPLE" is stamped across the photo on the back of the Mogilny, WJC card, and the Lindros redemption card. The fronts feature glossy color action player photos inside a white picture frame and a black outer border. The team name is printed above the picture, while the player's name is printed below it. On a black background, the horizontal backs carry biography, team logo, a color head shot, player profile, and statistics. Most of the cards are numbered on the back; they are arranged below with the regular issue cards listed before the other cards. The clipped corner cards hold little value due to the fact that they may be reproduced by mutilating the regular issue cards.

	MINT	EXC	G-VG
COMPLETE SET (11)	8.00	3.25	.80
COMMON PLAYER	.10	.04	.01
☐ 0 Player Unnamed (World Jr. Championships)	.50	.20	.05
☐ 275 Brian Leetch New York Rangers	.15	.06	.01
☐ 280 Guy Carbonneau Montreal Canadiens	.10	.04	.01
☐ 300 Pat LaFontaine Buffalo Sabres	.15	.06	.01
☐ 320 Pavel Bure Vancouver Canucks	.50	.20	.05
☐ 340 Terry Yake Anaheim Mighty Ducks	.10	.04	.01
☐ 341 Brian Benning Florida Panthers	.10	.04	.01
☐ NF9 Alexander Mogilny Nifty 50	4.00	1.60	.40
☐ NNO Ad Card	.25	.10	.02
☐ NNO You're A Winner (Lindros Instant Winner Game)	4.00	1.60	.40
☐ SR1 Alexandre Daigle Super Rookie	1.50	.60	.15

1993-94 Pinnacle

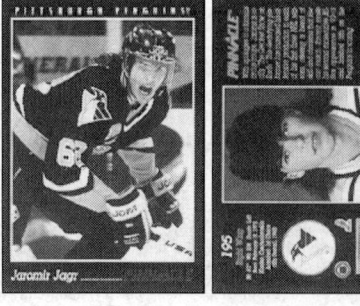

	MINT	EXC	G-VG
COMPLETE SET (511)	40.00	18.00	5.00
COMPLETE SERIES 1 (236)	20.00	9.00	2.50
COMPLETE SERIES 2 (275)	20.00	9.00	2.50
COMMON PLAYER (1-236)	.08	.04	.01
COMMON PLAYER (237-511)	.08	.04	.01
*AMERICAN AND CANADIAN: SAME VALUE			
☐ 1 Eric Lindros Philadelphia Flyers	3.00	1.35	.40
☐ 2 Mats Sundin Quebec Nordiques	.25	.11	.03
☐ 3 Tom Barrasso Pittsburgh Penguins	.10	.05	.01
☐ 4 Teemu Selanne Winnipeg Jets	1.00	.45	.13
☐ 5 Joe Juneau Boston Bruins	.60	.25	.08
☐ 6 Tony Amonte New York Rangers	.10	.05	.01
☐ 7 Bob Probert Detroit Red Wings	.08	.04	.01
☐ 8 Chris Kontos Tampa Bay Lightning	.08	.04	.01
☐ 9 Geoff Sanderson Hartford Whalers	.25	.11	.03
☐ 10 Alexander Mogilny Buffalo Sabres	.50	.23	.06
☐ 11 Kevin Lowe New York Rangers	.08	.04	.01
☐ 12 Nikolai Borschevsky Toronto Maple Leafs	.20	.09	.03
☐ 13 Dale Hunter Washington Capitals	.10	.05	.01
☐ 14 Gary Suter Calgary Flames	.10	.05	.01
☐ 15 Curtis Joseph St. Louis Blues	.20	.09	.03
☐ 16 Mark Tinordi Dallas Stars	.08	.04	.01
☐ 17 Doug Weight Edmonton Oilers	.10	.05	.01
☐ 18 Benoit Hogue New York Islanders	.08	.04	.01
☐ 19 Tommy Soderstrom Philadelphia Flyers	.15	.07	.02
☐ 20 Pat Falloon San Jose Sharks	.10	.05	.01
☐ 21 Jyrki Lumme Vancouver Canucks	.08	.04	.01
☐ 22 Brian Bellows Montreal Canadiens	.10	.05	.01
☐ 23 Alexei Zhitnik Los Angeles Kings	.20	.09	.03
☐ 24 Dirk Graham Chicago Blackhawks	.08	.04	.01
☐ 25 Scott Stevens New Jersey Devils	.10	.05	.01
☐ 26 Adam Foote Quebec Nordiques	.08	.04	.01
☐ 27 Mike Gartner New York Rangers	.15	.07	.02

☐ 28	Dallas Drake	.20	.09	.03	Detroit Red Wings
☐ 29	Uff Samuelsson	.08	.04	.01	Pittsburgh Penguins
☐ 30	Cam Neely	.10	.05	.01	Boston Bruins
☐ 31	Sean Burke	.10	.05	.01	Hartford Whalers
☐ 32	Petr Svoboda	.08	.04	.01	Buffalo Sabres
☐ 33	Keith Tkachuk	.25	.11	.03	Winnipeg Jets
☐ 34	Roman Hamrlik	.15	.07	.02	Tampa Bay Lightning
☐ 35	Robert Reichel	.10	.05	.01	Calgary Flames
☐ 36	Igor Kravchuk	.08	.04	.01	Edmonton Oilers
☐ 37	Mathieu Schneider	.10	.05	.01	Montreal Canadiens
☐ 38	Bob Kudelski	.10	.05	.01	Ottawa Senators
☐ 39	Jeff Brown	.10	.05	.01	St. Louis Blues
☐ 40	Mike Modano	.30	.14	.04	Dallas Stars
☐ 41	Rob Gaudreau	.25	.11	.03	San Jose Sharks
☐ 42	Dave Andreychuk	.15	.07	.02	Toronto Maple Leafs
☐ 43	Trevor Linden	.15	.07	.02	Vancouver Canucks
☐ 44	Dimitri Khristich	.10	.05	.01	Washington Capitals
☐ 45	Joe Murphy	.08	.04	.01	Chicago Blackhawks
☐ 46	Rob Blake	.10	.05	.01	Los Angeles Kings
☐ 47	Alexander Semak	.08	.04	.01	New Jersey Devils
☐ 48	Ray Ferraro	.08	.04	.01	New York Islanders
☐ 49	Curtis Leschyshyn	.08	.04	.01	Quebec Nordiques
☐ 50	Mark Recchi	.25	.11	.03	Philadelphia Flyers
☐ 51	Sergei Nemchinov	.08	.04	.01	New York Rangers
☐ 52	Larry Murphy	.10	.05	.01	Pittsburgh Penguins
☐ 53	Steve Heinze	.08	.04	.01	Boston Bruins
☐ 54	Sergei Fedorov	1.00	.45	.13	Detroit Red Wings
☐ 55	Gary Roberts	.10	.05	.01	Calgary Flames
☐ 56	Alexei Zhamnov	.35	.16	.04	Winnipeg Jets
☐ 57	Derian Hatcher	.08	.04	.01	Dallas Stars
☐ 58	Kelly Buchberger	.08	.04	.01	Edmonton Oilers
☐ 59	Eric Desjardins	.08	.04	.01	Montreal Canadiens
☐ 60	Brian Bradley	.08	.04	.01	Tampa Bay Lightning
☐ 61	Patrick Poulin	.08	.04	.01	Hartford Whalers
☐ 62	Scott Lachance	.08	.04	.01	New York Islanders
☐ 63	Johan Garpenlov	.08	.04	.01	San Jose Sharks
☐ 64	Sylvain Turgeon	.08	.04	.01	Ottawa Senators
☐ 65	Grant Fuhr	.10	.05	.01	Buffalo Sabres
☐ 66	Garth Butcher	.08	.04	.01	St. Louis Blues
☐ 67	Michal Pivonka	.08	.04	.01	Washington Capitals
☐ 68	Todd Gill	.08	.04	.01	Toronto Maple Leafs
☐ 69	Cliff Ronning	.08	.04	.01	Vancouver Canucks
☐ 70	Steve Smith	.08	.04	.01	Chicago Blackhawks
☐ 71	Bobby Holik	.08	.04	.01	Hartford Whalers
☐ 72	Garry Galley	.08	.04	.01	Philadelphia Flyers
☐ 73	Steve Leach	.08	.04	.01	Boston Bruins
☐ 74	Ron Francis	.10	.05	.01	Pittsburgh Penguins
☐ 75	Jari Kurri	.15	.07	.02	Los Angeles Kings
☐ 76	Alexei Kovalev	.60	.25	.08	New York Rangers
☐ 77	Dave Gagner	.10	.05	.01	Dallas Stars
☐ 78	Steve Duchesne	.10	.05	.01	Quebec Nordiques
☐ 79	Theoren Fleury	.15	.07	.02	Calgary Flames
☐ 80	Paul Coffey	.20	.09	.03	Detroit Red Wings
☐ 81	Bill Ranford	.10	.05	.01	Edmonton Oilers
☐ 82	Doug Bodger	.08	.04	.01	Buffalo Sabres
☐ 83	Nick Kypreos	.08	.04	.01	Hartford Whalers
☐ 84	Darius Kasparaitis	.08	.04	.01	New York Islanders
☐ 85	Vincent Damphousse	.10	.05	.01	Montreal Canadiens
☐ 86	Arturs Irbe	.40	.18	.05	San Jose Sharks
☐ 87	Shawn Chambers	.08	.04	.01	Tampa Bay Lightning
☐ 88	Murray Craven	.08	.04	.01	Vancouver Canucks
☐ 89	Rob Pearson	.08	.04	.01	Toronto Maple Leafs
☐ 90	Kevin Hatcher	.10	.05	.01	Washington Capitals
☐ 91	Brent Sutter	.10	.05	.01	New York Islanders
☐ 92	Teppo Numminen	.08	.04	.01	Winnipeg Jets
☐ 93	Shawn Burr	.08	.04	.01	Detroit Red Wings
☐ 94	Valeri Zelepukin	.10	.05	.01	New Jersey Devils
☐ 95	Ron Sutter	.08	.04	.01	St. Louis Blues
☐ 96	Craig MacTavish	.08	.04	.01	Edmonton Oilers
☐ 97	Dominic Roussel	.15	.07	.02	Philadelphia Flyers
☐ 98	Nicklas Lidstrom	.10	.05	.01	Detroit Red Wings
☐ 99	Adam Graves	.35	.16	.04	New York Rangers
☐ 100	Doug Gilmour	.40	.18	.05	Toronto Maple Leafs
☐ 101	Frantisek Musil	.08	.04	.01	Calgary Flames
☐ 102	Ted Donato	.08	.04	.01	Boston Bruins
☐ 103	Andrew Cassels	.08	.04	.01	Hartford Whalers
☐ 104	Vladimir Malakhov	.15	.07	.02	New York Islanders
☐ 105	Shawn McEachern	.15	.07	.02	Los Angeles Kings
☐ 106	Petr Nedved	.10	.05	.01	Vancouver Canucks
☐ 107	Calle Johansson	.08	.04	.01	Washington Capitals
☐ 108	Rich Sutter	.08	.04	.01	St. Louis Blues
☐ 109	Evgeny Davydov	.08	.04	.01	Winnipeg Jets
☐ 110	Mike Ricci	.10	.05	.01	Quebec Nordiques
☐ 111	Scott Niedermayer	.20	.09	.03	New Jersey Devils
☐ 112	John LeClair	.08	.04	.01	Montreal Canadiens
☐ 113	Darryl Sydor	.10	.05	.01	Los Angeles Kings
☐ 114	Paul DiPietro	.08	.04	.01	Montreal Canadiens
☐ 115	Stephane Fiset	.08	.04	.01	Quebec Nordiques
☐ 116	Christian Ruuttu	.08	.04	.01	Chicago Blackhawks
☐ 117	Doug Zmolek	.08	.04	.01	San Jose Sharks
☐ 118	Bob Sweeney	.08	.04	.01	Buffalo Sabres
☐ 119	Brent Fedyk	.08	.04	.01	Philadelphia Flyers
☐ 120	Norm Maciver	.08	.04	.01	Ottawa Senators
☐ 121	Rob Zamuner	.08	.04	.01	

Tampa Bay Lightning				
☐ 122 Joe Mullen	.10	.05	.01
New York Islanders			
☐ 123 Trent Yawney	.08	.04	.01
Chicago Blackhawks			
☐ 124 David Shaw	.08	.04	.01
Boston Bruins			
☐ 125 Mark Messier	.20	.09	.03
New York Rangers			
☐ 126 Kevin Miller	.08	.04	.01
Washington Capitals			
☐ 127 Dino Ciccarelli	.10	.05	.01
Detroit Red Wings			
☐ 128 Derek King	.08	.04	.01
New York Islanders			
☐ 129 Scott Young	.08	.04	.01
Quebec Nordiques			
☐ 130 Craig Janney	.15	.07	.02
St. Louis Blues			
☐ 131 Jamie Macoun	.08	.04	.01
Toronto Maple Leafs			
☐ 132 Geoff Courtnall	.08	.04	.01
Vancouver Canucks			
☐ 133 Bob Essensa	.10	.05	.01
Winnipeg Jets			
☐ 134 Ken Daneyko	.08	.04	.01
New Jersey Devils			
☐ 135 Mike Ridley	.10	.05	.01
Washington Capitals			
☐ 136 Stephan Lebeau	.08	.04	.01
Montreal Canadiens			
☐ 137 Tony Granato	.08	.04	.01
Los Angeles Kings			
☐ 138 Kay Whitmore	.08	.04	.01
Vancouver Canucks			
☐ 139 Luke Richardson	.08	.04	.01
Edmonton Oilers			
☐ 140 Jeremy Roenick	.75	.35	.09
Chicago Blackhawks			
☐ 141 Brad May	.08	.04	.01
Buffalo Sabres			
☐ 142 Sandis Ozolinsh	.25	.11	.03
San Jose Sharks			
☐ 143 Stephane Richer	.10	.05	.01
New Jersey Devils			
☐ 144 John Tucker	.08	.04	.01
Tampa Bay Lightning			
☐ 145 Luc Robitaille	.20	.09	.03
Los Angeles Kings			
☐ 146 Dimitri Yushkevich	.08	.04	.01
Philadelphia Flyers			
☐ 147 Sean Hill	.08	.04	.01
Anaheim Mighty Ducks			
☐ 148 John Vanbiesbrouck	.20	.09	.03
Florida Panthers			
☐ 149 Kevin Stevens	.30	.14	.04
Pittsburgh Penguins			
☐ 150 Patrick Roy	.75	.35	.09
Montreal Canadiens			
☐ 151 Owen Nolan	.10	.05	.01
Quebec Nordiques			
☐ 152 Richard Smehlik	.10	.05	.01
Buffalo Sabres			
☐ 153 Ray Sheppard	.08	.04	.01
Detroit Red Wings			
☐ 154 Ed Olczyk	.08	.04	.01
New York Rangers			
☐ 155 Al MacInnis	.15	.07	.02
Calgary Flames			
☐ 156 Sergei Zubov	.60	.25	.08
New York Rangers			
☐ 157 Wendel Clark	.15	.07	.02
Toronto Maple Leafs			
☐ 158 Kirk McLean	.15	.07	.02
Vancouver Canucks			
☐ 159 Thomas Steen	.08	.04	.01
Winnipeg Jets			
☐ 160 Pierre Turgeon	.30	.14	.04
New York Islanders			
☐ 161 Dmitri Kvartalnov	.08	.04	.01
Boston Bruins			
☐ 162 Brian Noonan	.08	.04	.01
Chicago Blackhawks			
☐ 163 Mike McPhee	.08	.04	.01
Dallas Stars			
☐ 164 Peter Bondra	.10	.05	.01
Washington Capitals			
☐ 165 Bernie Nicholls	.10	.05	.01
New Jersey Devils			
☐ 166 Michael Nylander	.20	.09	.03
Hartford Whalers			
☐ 167 Guy Hebert	.20	.09	.03
Anaheim Mighty Ducks			
☐ 168 Scott Mellanby	.08	.04	.01

Florida Panthers				
☐ 169 Bob Bassen	.08	.04	.01
St. Louis Blues			
☐ 170 Rod Brind'Amour	.20	.09	.03
Philadelphia Flyers			
☐ 171 Andrei Kovalenko	.15	.07	.02
Quebec Nordiques			
☐ 172 Mike Donnelly	.08	.04	.01
Los Angeles Kings			
☐ 173 Steve Thomas	.10	.05	.01
New York Islanders			
☐ 174 Rick Tocchet	.10	.05	.01
Pittsburgh Penguins			
☐ 175 Steve Yzerman	.40	.18	.05
Detroit Red Wings			
☐ 176 Dixon Ward	.08	.04	.01
Vancouver Canucks			
☐ 177 Randy Wood	.08	.04	.01
Buffalo Sabres			
☐ 178 Dean Kennedy	.08	.04	.01
Winnipeg Jets			
☐ 179 Joel Otto	.08	.04	.01
Calgary Flames			
☐ 180 Kirk Muller	.10	.05	.01
Montreal Canadiens			
☐ 181 Chris Chelios	.10	.05	.01
Chicago Blackhawks			
☐ 182 Richard Matvichuk	.08	.04	.01
Dallas Stars			
☐ 183 John MacLean	.10	.05	.01
New Jersey Devils			
☐ 184 Joe Kocur	.08	.04	.01
New York Rangers			
☐ 185 Adam Oates	.20	.09	.03
Boston Bruins			
☐ 186 Bob Beers	.08	.04	.01
Tampa Bay Lightning			
☐ 187 Ron Tugnutt	.08	.04	.01
Anaheim Mighty Ducks			
☐ 188 Brian Skrudland	.08	.04	.01
Florida Panthers			
☐ 189 Al Iafrate	.10	.05	.01
Washington Capitals			
☐ 190 Felix Potvin	1.00	.45	.13
Toronto Maple Leafs			
☐ 191 Dave Reid	.08	.04	.01
Boston Bruins			
☐ 192 Jim Johnson	.08	.04	.01
Dallas Stars			
☐ 193 Kevin Haller	.08	.04	.01
Buffalo Sabres			
☐ 194 Steve Chiasson	.08	.04	.01
Detroit Red Wings			
☐ 195 Jaromir Jagr	.60	.25	.08
Pittsburgh Penguins			
☐ 196 Martin Rucinsky	.08	.04	.01
Quebec Nordiques			
☐ 197 Sergei Bautin	.08	.04	.01
Winnipeg Jets			
☐ 198 Joe Nieuwendyk	.10	.05	.01
Calgary Flames			
☐ 199 Gilbert Dionne	.08	.04	.01
Montreal Canadiens			
☐ 200 Brett Hull	.75	.35	.09
St. Louis Blues			
☐ 201 Yuri Khmylev	.10	.05	.01
Buffalo Sabres			
☐ 202 Todd Elik	.08	.04	.01
Edmonton Oilers			
☐ 203 Patrick Flatley	.08	.04	.01
New York Islanders			
☐ 204 Martin Straka	.50	.23	.06
Pittsburgh Penguins			
☐ 205 Brendan Shanahan	.25	.11	.03
St. Louis Blues			
☐ 206 Mark Beaufait	.15	.07	.02
San Jose Sharks			
☐ 207 Mike Lenarduzzi	.15	.07	.02
Hartford Whalers			
☐ 208 Chris LiPuma	.08	.04	.01
Tampa Bay Lightning			
☐ 209 Andre Faust	.08	.04	.01
Philadelphia Flyers			
☐ 210 Ben Hankinson	.15	.07	.02
New Jersey Devils			
☐ 211 Darrin Madeley	.20	.09	.03
Ottawa Senators			
☐ 212 Oleg Petrov	.25	.11	.03
Montreal Canadiens			
☐ 213 Philippe Boucher	.08	.04	.01
Buffalo Sabres			
☐ 214 Tyler Wright	.08	.04	.01
Edmonton Oilers			
☐ 215 Jason Bowen	.15	.07	.02

Philadelphia Flyers			
☐ 216 Matthew Barnaby	.20	.09	.03
Buffalo Sabres			
☐ 217 Bryan Smolinski	.60	.25	.08
Boston Bruins			
☐ 218 Dan Keczmer	.08	.04	.01
Hartford Whalers			
☐ 219 Chris Simon	.20	.09	.03
Quebec Nordiques			
☐ 220 Corey Hirsch AW	.25	.11	.03
New York Rangers			
☐ 221 Mario Lemieux AW	.35	.16	.04
Pittsburgh Penguins			
☐ 222 Teemu Selanne AW	.35	.16	.04
Winnipeg Jets			
☐ 223 Chris Chelios AW	.10	.05	.01
Chicago Blackhawks			
☐ 224 Ed Belfour AW	.15	.07	.02
Chicago Blackhawks			
☐ 225 Pierre Turgeon AW	.15	.07	.02
New York Islanders			
☐ 226 Doug Gilmour AW	.20	.09	.03
Toronto Maple Leafs			
☐ 227 Ed Belfour AW	.15	.07	.02
Chicago Blackhawks			
☐ 228 Patrick Roy AW	.30	.14	.04
Montreal Canadiens			
☐ 229 Dave Poulin AW	.10	.05	.01
Boston Bruins			
☐ 230 Mario Lemieux AW	.35	.16	.04
Pittsburgh Penguins			
☐ 231 Mike Vernon HH	.08	.04	.01
Calgary Flames			
☐ 232 Vincent Damphousse HH	.08	.04	.01
Montreal Canadiens			
☐ 233 Chris Chelios HH	.08	.04	.01
Chicago Blackhawks			
☐ 234 Cliff Ronning HH	.08	.04	.01
Vancouver Canucks			
☐ 235 Mark Howe HH	.08	.04	.01
Detroit Red Wings			
☐ 236 Alexandre Daigle	.75	.35	.09
Ottawa Senators			
☐ 237 Wayne Gretzky	1.00	.45	.13
Los Angeles Kings			
☐ 238 Mark Messier	.25	.11	.03
New York Rangers			
☐ 239 Dino Ciccarelli	.08	.04	.01
Detroit Red Wings			
☐ 240 Joe Mullen	.10	.05	.01
Pittsburgh Penguins			
☐ 241 Mike Gartner	.15	.07	.02
New York Rangers			
☐ 242 Mike Richter	.25	.11	.03
New York Rangers			
☐ 243 Pat Verbeek	.10	.05	.01
Hartford Whalers			
☐ 244 Valeri Kamensky	.20	.09	.03
Quebec Nordiques			
☐ 245 Nelson Emerson	.10	.05	.01
Winnipeg Jets			
☐ 246 James Patrick	.08	.04	.01
Hartford Whalers			
☐ 247 Greg Adams	.08	.04	.01
Vancouver Canucks			
☐ 248 Ulf Dahlen	.08	.04	.01
Dallas Stars			
☐ 249 Shayne Corson	.08	.04	.01
Edmonton Oilers			
☐ 250 Ray Bourque	.20	.09	.03
Boston Bruins			
☐ 251 Claude Lemieux	.10	.05	.01
New Jersey Devils			
☐ 252 Kelly Hrudey	.10	.05	.01
Los Angeles Kings			
☐ 253 Patrice Brisebois	.08	.04	.01
Montreal Canadiens			
☐ 254 Mark Howe	.10	.05	.01
Detroit Red Wings			
☐ 255 Ed Belfour	.25	.11	.03
Chicago Blackhawks			
☐ 256 Pelle Eklund	.08	.04	.01
Philadelphia Flyers			
☐ 257 Zarley Zalapski	.08	.04	.01
Hartford Whalers			
☐ 258 Sylvain Cote	.08	.04	.01
Washington Capitals			
☐ 259 Uwe Krupp	.08	.04	.01
New York Islanders			
☐ 260 Dale Hawerchuk	.10	.05	.01
Toronto Maple Leafs			
☐ 261 Alexei Gusarov	.08	.04	.01
Quebec Nordiques			
☐ 262 Dave Ellett	.08	.04	.01
Toronto Maple Leafs			
☐ 263 Tomas Sandstrom	.08	.04	.01
Los Angeles Kings			
☐ 264 Vladimir Konstantinov	.08	.04	.01
Detroit Red Wings			
☐ 265 Paul Ranheim	.08	.04	.01
Calgary Flames			
☐ 266 Darrin Shannon	.08	.04	.01
Winnipeg Jets			
☐ 267 Chris Terreri	.10	.05	.01
New Jersey Devils			
☐ 268 Russ Courtnall	.10	.05	.01
Dallas Stars			
☐ 269 Don Sweeney	.08	.04	.01
Boston Bruins			
☐ 270 Kevin Todd	.08	.04	.01
Chicago Blackhawks			
☐ 271 Brad Shaw	.08	.04	.01
Ottawa Senators			
☐ 272 Adam Creighton	.08	.04	.01
Tampa Bay Lightning			
☐ 273 Dana Murzyn	.08	.04	.01
Hartford Whalers			
☐ 274 Donald Audette	.08	.04	.01
Buffalo Sabres			
☐ 275 Brian Leetch	.30	.14	.04
New York Rangers			
☐ 276 Kevin Dineen	.10	.05	.01
Philadelphia Flyers			
☐ 277 Bruce Driver	.08	.04	.01
New Jersey Devils			
☐ 278 Jim Paek	.08	.04	.01
Pittsburgh Penguins			
☐ 279 Esa Tikkanen	.10	.05	.01
New York Rangers			
☐ 280 Guy Carbonneau	.10	.05	.01
Montreal Canadiens			
☐ 281 Eric Weinrich	.08	.04	.01
Chicago Blackhawks			
☐ 282 Tim Cheveldae	.10	.05	.01
Detroit Red Wings			
☐ 283 Bryan Marchment	.08	.04	.01
Chicago Blackhawks			
☐ 284 Kelly Miller	.08	.04	.01
Washington Capitals			
☐ 285 Jimmy Carson	.08	.04	.01
Los Angeles Kings			
☐ 286 Terry Carkner	.08	.04	.01
Detroit Red Wings			
☐ 287 Mike Sullivan	.08	.04	.01
San Jose Sharks			
☐ 288 Joe Reekie	.08	.04	.01
Tampa Bay Lightning			
☐ 289 Bob Rouse	.08	.04	.01
Toronto Maple Leafs			
☐ 290 Joe Sakic	.25	.11	.03
Quebec Nordiques			
☐ 291 Gerald Diduck	.08	.04	.01
Vancouver Canucks			
☐ 292 Don Beaupre	.10	.05	.01
Washington Capitals			
☐ 293 Kjell Samuelsson	.08	.04	.01
Pittsburgh Penguins			
☐ 294 Claude Lapointe	.08	.04	.01
Quebec Nordiques			
☐ 295 Tie Domi	.08	.04	.01
Winnipeg Jets			
☐ 296 Charlie Huddy	.08	.04	.01
Los Angeles Kings			
☐ 297 Peter Zezel	.08	.04	.01
Toronto Maple Leafs			
☐ 298 Craig Muni	.08	.04	.01
Dallas Stars			
☐ 299 Rick Tabaracci	.08	.04	.01
Washington Capitals			
☐ 300 Pat LaFontaine	.30	.14	.04
Buffalo Sabres			
☐ 301 Lyle Odelein	.08	.04	.01
Montreal Canadiens			
☐ 302 Jocelyn Lemieux	.08	.04	.01
Chicago Blackhawks			
☐ 303 Craig Ludwig	.08	.04	.01
Dallas Stars			
☐ 304 Marc Bergevin	.08	.04	.01
Tampa Bay Lightning			
☐ 305 Bill Guerin	.08	.04	.01
New Jersey Devils			
☐ 306 Rick Zombo	.08	.04	.01
St. Louis Blues			
☐ 307 Steven Finn	.08	.04	.01
Quebec Nordiques			
☐ 308 Gino Odjick	.08	.04	.01
Vancouver Canucks			
☐ 309 Jeff Beukeboom	.08	.04	.01

	New York Rangers			
☐ 310	Mario Lemieux	1.25	.55	.16
	Pittsburgh Penguins			
☐ 311	J.J. Daigneault	.08	.04	.01
	Montreal Canadiens			
☐ 312	Vincent Riendeau	.08	.04	.01
	Detroit Red Wings			
☐ 313	Adam Burt	.08	.04	.01
	Hartford Whalers			
☐ 314	Mike Craig	.08	.04	.01
	Dallas Stars			
☐ 315	Bret Hedican	.08	.04	.01
	St. Louis Blues			
☐ 316	Kris King	.08	.04	.01
	Winnipeg Jets			
☐ 317	Sylvain Lefebvre	.08	.04	.01
	Toronto Maple Leafs			
☐ 318	Troy Murray	.08	.04	.01
	Chicago Blackhawks			
☐ 319	Gordie Roberts	.08	.04	.01
	Boston Bruins			
☐ 320	Pavel Bure	1.25	.55	.16
	Vancouver Canucks			
☐ 321	Marc Bureau	.08	.04	.01
	Tampa Bay Lightning			
☐ 322	Randy McKay	.08	.04	.01
	New Jersey Devils			
☐ 323	Mark Lamb	.08	.04	.01
	Ottawa Senators			
☐ 324	Brian Mullen	.10	.05	.01
	New York Islanders			
☐ 325	Ken Wregget	.08	.04	.01
	Pittsburgh Penguins			
☐ 326	Stephane Quintal	.08	.04	.01
	Winnipeg Jets			
☐ 327	Robert Dirk	.08	.04	.01
	Vancouver Canucks			
☐ 328	Mike Krushelnyski	.08	.04	.01
	Toronto Maple Leafs			
☐ 329	Mikael Andersson	.08	.04	.01
	Tampa Bay Lightning			
☐ 330	Paul Stanton	.08	.04	.01
	Boston Bruins			
☐ 331	Phil Bourque	.08	.04	.01
	New York Rangers			
☐ 332	Andre Racicot	.08	.04	.01
	Montreal Canadiens			
☐ 333	Brad Dalgarno	.08	.04	.01
	New York Islanders			
☐ 334	Neal Broten	.10	.05	.01
	Dallas Stars			
☐ 335	John Blue	.08	.04	.01
	Boston Bruins			
☐ 336	Ken Sutton	.08	.04	.01
	Buffalo Sabres			
☐ 337	Greg Paslawski	.08	.04	.01
	Ottawa Senators			
☐ 338	Robb Stauber	.08	.04	.01
	Los Angeles Kings			
☐ 339	Mike Keane	.08	.04	.01
	Montreal Canadiens			
☐ 340	Terry Yake	.08	.04	.01
	Anaheim Mighty Ducks			
☐ 341	Brian Benning	.08	.04	.01
	Florida Panthers			
☐ 342	Brian Propp	.10	.05	.01
	Hartford Whalers			
☐ 343	Frank Pietrangelo	.08	.04	.01
	Hartford Whalers			
☐ 344	Stephane Matteau	.08	.04	.01
	Chicago Blackhawks			
☐ 345	Steven King	.08	.04	.01
	Anaheim Mighty Ducks			
☐ 346	Joe Cirella	.08	.04	.01
	Florida Panthers			
☐ 347	Andy Moog	.10	.05	.01
	Dallas Stars			
☐ 348	Paul Ysebaert	.08	.04	.01
	Winnipeg Jets			
☐ 349	Petr Klima	.08	.04	.01
	Tampa Bay Lightning			
☐ 350	Corey Millen	.08	.04	.01
	New Jersey Devils			
☐ 351	Phil Housley	.10	.05	.01
	St. Louis Blues			
☐ 352	Craig Billington	.08	.04	.01
	Ottawa Senators			
☐ 353	Jeff Norton	.08	.04	.01
	New York Islanders			
☐ 354	Neil Wilkinson	.08	.04	.01
	Chicago Blackhawks			
☐ 355	Doug Lidster	.08	.04	.01
	New York Rangers			
☐ 356	Steve Larmer	.10	.05	.01
	New York Rangers			
☐ 357	Jon Casey	.10	.05	.01
	Boston Bruins			
☐ 358	Brad McCrimmon	.08	.04	.01
	Detroit Red Wings			
☐ 359	Alexei Kasatonov	.08	.04	.01
	Anaheim Mighty Ducks			
☐ 360	Andrei Lomakin	.08	.04	.01
	Florida Panthers			
☐ 361	Daren Puppa	.10	.05	.01
	Tampa Bay Lightning			
☐ 362	Sergei Makarov	.10	.05	.01
	San Jose Sharks			
☐ 363	Dave Manson	.08	.04	.01
	Edmonton Oilers			
☐ 364	Jim Sandlak	.08	.04	.01
	Vancouver Canucks			
☐ 365	Glenn Healy	.08	.04	.01
	New York Rangers			
☐ 366	Martin Gelinas	.08	.04	.01
	Quebec Nordiques			
☐ 367	Igor Larionov	.08	.04	.01
	San Jose Sharks			
☐ 368	Anatoli Semenov	.08	.04	.01
	Anaheim Mighty Ducks			
☐ 369	Mark Fitzpatrick	.08	.04	.01
	Florida Panthers			
☐ 370	Paul Cavallini	.08	.04	.01
	Dallas Stars			
☐ 371	Jimmy Waite	.08	.04	.01
	San Jose Sharks			
☐ 372	Yves Racine	.08	.04	.01
	Philadelphia Flyers			
☐ 373	Jeff Hackett	.08	.04	.01
	New York Islanders			
☐ 374	Marty McSorley	.10	.05	.01
	Pittsburgh Penguins			
☐ 375	Scott Pearson	.08	.04	.01
	Edmonton Oilers			
☐ 376	Ron Hextall	.10	.05	.01
	New York Islanders			
☐ 377	Gaetan Duchesne	.08	.04	.01
	San Jose Sharks			
☐ 378	Jamie Baker	.08	.04	.01
	San Jose Sharks			
☐ 379	Troy Loney	.08	.04	.01
	Anaheim Mighty Ducks			
☐ 380	Gord Murphy	.08	.04	.01
	Florida Panthers			
☐ 381	Peter Sidorkiewicz	.08	.04	.01
	New Jersey Devils			
☐ 382	Pat Elynuik	.08	.04	.01
	Tampa Bay Lightning			
☐ 383	Glen Wesley	.08	.04	.01
	Boston Bruins			
☐ 384	Dean Evason	.08	.04	.01
	Dallas Stars			
☐ 385	Mike Peluso	.08	.04	.01
	New Jersey Devils			
☐ 386	Darren Turcotte	.08	.04	.01
	Hartford Whalers			
☐ 387	Dave Poulin	.08	.04	.01
	Washington Capitals			
☐ 388	John Cullen	.08	.04	.01
	Toronto Maple Leafs			
☐ 389	Randy Ladouceur	.08	.04	.01
	Anaheim Mighty Ducks			
☐ 390	Tom Fitzgerald	.08	.04	.01
	Florida Panthers			
☐ 391	Denis Savard	.15	.07	.02
	Tampa Bay Lightning			
☐ 392	Fredrik Olausson	.08	.04	.01
	Edmonton Oilers			
☐ 393	Sergio Momesso	.08	.04	.01
	Vancouver Canucks			
☐ 394	Mike Ramsey	.08	.04	.01
	Pittsburgh Penguins			
☐ 395	Kelly Kisio	.08	.04	.01
	Calgary Flames			
☐ 396	Craig Simpson	.08	.04	.01
	Buffalo Sabres			
☐ 397	Viacheslav Fetisov	.08	.04	.01
	New Jersey Devils			
☐ 398	Glenn Anderson	.10	.05	.01
	Toronto Maple Leafs			
☐ 399	Michel Goulet	.10	.05	.01
	Chicago Blackhawks			
☐ 400	Wayne Gretzky	1.75	.80	.22
	Los Angeles Kings			
☐ 401	Stu Grimson	.08	.04	.01
	Anaheim Mighty Ducks			
☐ 402	Mike Hough	.08	.04	.01
	Florida Panthers			
☐ 403	Dominik Hasek	.15	.07	.02

Buffalo Sabres			
☐ 404 Gerard Gallant	.08	.04	.01
Tampa Bay Lightning			
☐ 405 Greg Gilbert	.08	.04	.01
New York Rangers			
☐ 406 Vladimir Ruzicka	.08	.04	.01
Ottawa Senators			
☐ 407 Jim Hrivnak	.08	.04	.01
Washington Capitals			
☐ 408 Dave Lowry	.08	.04	.01
Florida Panthers			
☐ 409 Todd Ewen	.08	.04	.01
Anaheim Mighty Ducks			
☐ 410 Bob Errey	.08	.04	.01
San Jose Sharks			
☐ 411 Bryan Trottier	.10	.05	.01
Pittsburgh Penguins			
☐ 412 Dave Taylor	.10	.05	.01
Los Angeles Kings			
☐ 413 Grant Ledyard	.08	.04	.01
Dallas Stars			
☐ 414 Chris Dahlquist	.08	.04	.01
Calgary Flames			
☐ 415 Brent Gilchrist	.08	.04	.01
Dallas Stars			
☐ 416 Geoff Smith	.08	.04	.01
Edmonton Oilers			
☐ 417 Jiri Slegr	.08	.04	.01
Vancouver Canucks			
☐ 418 Randy Burridge	.08	.04	.01
Washington Capitals			
☐ 419 Sergei Krivokrasov	.08	.04	.01
Chicago Blackhawks			
☐ 420 Keith Primeau	.10	.05	.01
Detroit Red Wings			
☐ 421 Robert Kron	.08	.04	.01
Hartford Whalers			
☐ 422 Keith Brown	.08	.04	.01
Florida Panthers			
☐ 423 David Volek	.08	.04	.01
New York Islanders			
☐ 424 Josef Beranek	.10	.05	.01
Philadelphia Flyers			
☐ 425 Wayne Presley	.08	.04	.01
Buffalo Sabres			
☐ 426 Stu Barnes	.08	.04	.01
Florida Panthers			
☐ 427 Milos Holan	.15	.07	.02
Philadelphia Flyers			
☐ 428 Jeff Shantz	.08	.04	.01
Chicago Blackhawks			
☐ 429 Brent Gretzky	.35	.16	.04
Tampa Bay Lightning			
☐ 430 Jarkko Varvio	.20	.09	.03
Dallas Stars			
☐ 431 Chris Osgood	.75	.35	.09
Detroit Red Wings			
☐ 432 Aaron Ward	.15	.07	.02
Detroit Red Wings			
☐ 433 Jason Smith	.15	.07	.02
New Jersey Devils			
☐ 434 Cam Stewart	.20	.09	.03
Boston Bruins			
☐ 435 Derek Plante	.75	.35	.09
Buffalo Sabres			
☐ 436 Pat Peake	.15	.07	.02
Washington Capitals			
☐ 437 Alexander Karpovtsev	.10	.05	.01
New York Rangers			
☐ 438 Jim Montgomery	.20	.09	.03
St. Louis Blues			
☐ 439 Rob Niedermayer	.75	.35	.09
Florida Panthers			
☐ 440 Jocelyn Thibault	.75	.35	.09
Quebec Nordiques			
☐ 441 Jason Arnott	2.00	.90	.25
Edmonton Oilers			
☐ 442 Mike Rathje	.08	.04	.01
San Jose Sharks			
☐ 443 Chris Gratton	.75	.35	.09
Tampa Bay Lightning			
☐ 444 Vesa Vitakoski	.20	.09	.03
Calgary Flames			
☐ 445 Alexei Kudashov	.20	.09	.03
Toronto Maple Leafs			
☐ 446 Pavol Demitra	.15	.07	.02
Ottawa Senators			
☐ 447 Ted Drury	.08	.04	.01
Calgary Flames			
☐ 448 Rene Corbet	.25	.11	.03
Quebec Nordiques			
☐ 449 Markus Naslund	.20	.09	.03
Pittsburgh Penguins			
☐ 450 Dmitri Filimonov	.08	.04	.01

Ottawa Senators			
☐ 451 Roman Oksiuta	.15	.07	.02
Edmonton Oilers			
☐ 452 Michal Sykora	.20	.09	.03
San Jose Sharks			
☐ 453 Greg Johnson	.08	.04	.01
Detroit Red Wings			
☐ 454 Mikael Renberg	.75	.35	.09
Philadelphia Flyers			
☐ 455 Alexei Yashin	.75	.35	.09
Ottawa Senators			
☐ 456 Chris Pronger	.75	.35	.09
Hartford Whalers			
☐ 457 Emmanuel Fernandez	.60	.25	.08
☐ 458 Jamie Storr	2.50	1.15	.30
☐ 459 Chris Armstrong	.25	.11	.03
☐ 460 Drew Bannister	.40	.18	.05
☐ 461 Joel Bouchard	.25	.11	.03
☐ 462 Bryan McCabe	.30	.14	.04
☐ 463 Nick Stajduhar	.50	.23	.06
☐ 464 Brent Tully	.20	.09	.03
☐ 465 Brendan Witt	.60	.25	.08
☐ 466 Jason Allison	1.25	.55	.16
☐ 467 Jason Botterill	.75	.35	.09
☐ 468 Curtis Bowen	.50	.23	.06
☐ 469 Anson Carter	.35	.16	.04
☐ 470 Brandon Convery	.50	.23	.06
☐ 471 Yanick Dube	.75	.35	.09
☐ 472 Jeff Friesen	1.50	.65	.19
☐ 473 Aaron Gavey	1.00	.45	.13
☐ 474 Martin Gendron	.40	.18	.05
☐ 475 Rick Girard	.50	.23	.06
☐ 476 Todd Harvey	1.00	.45	.13
☐ 477 Marty Murray	.40	.18	.05
☐ 478 Mike Peca	.60	.25	.08
☐ 479 Aaron Ellis	.20	.09	.03
☐ 480 Toby Kvalevog	.25	.11	.03
☐ 481 Jon Coleman	.25	.11	.03
☐ 482 Ashlin Halfnight	.25	.11	.03
☐ 483 Jason McBain	.25	.11	.03
☐ 484 Chris O'Sullivan	.25	.11	.03
☐ 485 Deron Quint	.40	.18	.05
☐ 486 Blake Sloan	.25	.11	.03
☐ 487 David Wilkie	.25	.11	.03
☐ 488 Kevyn Adams	.60	.25	.08
☐ 489 Jason Bonsignore	1.50	.65	.19
☐ 490 Andy Brink	.20	.09	.03
☐ 491 Adam Deadmarsh	.25	.11	.03
☐ 492 John Emmons	.15	.07	.02
☐ 493 Kevin Hilton	.25	.11	.03
☐ 494 Jason Karmanos	.20	.09	.03
☐ 495 Bob Lachance	.20	.09	.03
☐ 496 Jamie Langenbrunner	.40	.18	.05
☐ 497 Jay Pandolfo	.25	.11	.03
☐ 498 Richard Park	.75	.35	.09
☐ 499 Ryan Sittler	.15	.07	.02
☐ 500 John Varga	.40	.18	.05
☐ 501 Valeri Bure	1.25	.55	.16
☐ 502 Maxim Bets	.75	.35	.09
☐ 503 Vadim Sharifjanov	.40	.18	.05
☐ 504 Alexander Kharlamov	.75	.35	.09
☐ 505 Pavel Desyatkov	.20	.09	.03
☐ 506 Oleg Tverdovsky	1.50	.65	.19
☐ 507 Nikolai Tsulygin	.15	.07	.02
☐ 508 Evgeni Ryabchikov	.50	.23	.06
☐ 509 Sergei Brylin	.30	.14	.04
☐ 510 Maxim Sushinski	.20	.09	.03
☐ 511 Sergei Kondrashkin	.20	.09	.03
☐ 512 Wayne Gretzky HL SP	10.00	4.50	1.25
☐ AU1 Alexandre Daigle AU	125.00	57.50	15.50
☐ AU2 Eric Lindros AU	200.00	90.00	25.00
☐ NNO Brett Lindros CDN	30.00	13.50	3.80
Eric Lindros			
☐ NNO Eric Lindros US	30.00	13.50	3.80
Brett Lindros			
☐ NNO Lindros Redempt.Expired	10.00	4.50	1.25

1993-94 Pinnacle All-Stars

One Bonus Pinnacle All-Star card was inserted in every U.S. and Canadian pack of Score hockey cards. The wrappers from those packs carried a mail-away offer for cards 46-50. These standard-size (2 1/2" by 3 1/2") cards feature on their fronts color action shots of players in their All-Star uniforms. The photos of Canadian and U.S. cards differ, but

there is no way of discerning the two. The left side is edged with a stripe that shades from orange-red at the bottom to black at the top and carries the player's name, team, and position vertically in gold foil. The 44th NHL All-Star Game logo appears near the bottom. On a background that shades from light brown at the bottom to black at the top, the horizontal back sports an orange-bordered posed color player head shot on the left. On the right, the player's name and team appear in yellow ocher lettering and the All-Star Game logo is displayed beneath. At the bottom, a table carries the player's 1992-93 All-Star game stats. The cards are numbered on the back.

	MINT	EXC	G-VG
COMPLETE SET (50)	20.00	9.00	2.50
COMPLETE INS.SERIES (45)	10.00	4.50	1.25
COMPLETE MAIL SERIES (5)	10.00	4.50	1.25
COMMON PLAYER (1-45)	.15	.07	.02
COMMON PLAYER (46-50)	2.50	1.15	.30
*AMERICAN AND CANADIAN: SAME VALUE			

☐ 1	Craig Billington	.15	.07	.02
	Ottawa Senators			
☐ 2	Zarley Zalapski	.15	.07	.02
	Hartford Whalers			
☐ 3	Kevin Lowe	.15	.07	.02
	New York Rangers			
☐ 4	Scott Stevens	.20	.09	.03
	New Jersey Devils			
☐ 5	Pierre Turgeon	.30	.14	.04
	New York Islanders			
☐ 6	Mark Recchi	.25	.11	.03
	Philadelphia Flyers			
☐ 7	Kirk Muller	.20	.09	.03
	Montreal Canadiens			
☐ 8	Mike Gartner	.20	.09	.03
	New York Rangers			
☐ 9	Adam Oates	.25	.11	.03
	Boston Bruins			
☐ 10	Brad Marsh	.15	.07	.02
	Ottawa Senators			
☐ 11	Pat LaFontaine	.30	.14	.04
	Buffalo Sabres			
☐ 12	Peter Bondra	.15	.07	.02
	Washington Capitals			
☐ 13	Joe Sakic	.25	.11	.03
	Quebec Nordiques			
☐ 14	Rick Tocchet	.20	.09	.03
	Pittsburgh Penguins			
☐ 15	Kevin Stevens	.25	.11	.03
	Pittsburgh Penguins			
☐ 16	Steve Duchesne	.15	.07	.02
	Quebec Nordiques			
☐ 17	Peter Sidorkiewicz	.15	.07	.02
	Ottawa Senators			
☐ 18	Patrick Roy	.75	.35	.09
	Montreal Canadiens			
☐ 19	Al Iafrate	.15	.07	.02
	Washington Capitals			
☐ 20	Jaromir Jagr	.50	.23	.06
	Pittsburgh Penguins			
☐ 21	Ray Bourque	.25	.11	.03
	Boston Bruins			
☐ 22	Alexander Mogilny	.40	.18	.05
	Buffalo Sabres			
☐ 23	Steve Chiasson	.15	.07	.02
	Detroit Red Wings			
☐ 24	Garth Butcher	.15	.07	.02
	St. Louis Blues			
☐ 25	Phil Housley	.15	.07	.02
	Winnipeg Jets			
☐ 26	Chris Chelios	.20	.09	.03
	Chicago Blackhawks			
☐ 27	Randy Carlyle	.15	.07	.02
	Winnipeg Jets			
☐ 28	Mike Modano	.30	.14	.04
	Dallas Stars			
☐ 29	Gary Roberts	.20	.09	.03
	Calgary Flames			
☐ 30	Kelly Kisio	.15	.07	.02
	Calgary Flames			
☐ 31	Pavel Bure	1.00	.45	.13
	Vancouver Canucks			
☐ 32	Teemu Selanne	.75	.35	.09
	Winnipeg Jets			
☐ 33	Brian Bradley	.15	.07	.02
	Tampa Bay Lightning			
☐ 34	Brett Hull	.75	.35	.09
	St. Louis Blues			
☐ 35	Jari Kurri	.20	.09	.03
	Los Angeles Kings			
☐ 36	Steve Yzerman	.50	.23	.06
	Detroit Red Wings			
☐ 37	Luc Robitaille	.30	.14	.04
	Los Angeles Kings			
☐ 38	Dave Manson	.15	.07	.02
	Edmonton Oilers			
☐ 39	Jeremy Roenick	.50	.23	.06
	Chicago Blackhawks			
☐ 40	Mike Vernon	.20	.09	.03
	Calgary Flames			
☐ 41	Jon Casey	.15	.07	.02
	Minnesota North Stars			
☐ 42	Ed Belfour	.35	.16	.04
	Chicago Blackhawks			
☐ 43	Paul Coffey	.20	.09	.03
	Detroit Red Wings			
☒ 44	Doug Gilmour	.50	.23	.06
	Toronto Maple Leafs			
☐ 45	Wayne Gretzky	1.50	.65	.19
	Los Angeles Kings			
☐ 46	Mike Gartner	2.50	1.15	.30
	New York Rangers			
☐ 47	Al Iafrate	2.50	1.15	.30
	Washington Capitals			
☐ 48	Ray Bourque	3.50	1.55	.45
	Boston Bruins			
☐ 49	Jon Casey	2.50	1.15	.30
	Minnesota North Stars			
☐ 50	Campbell Conference	2.50	1.15	.30

1993-94 Pinnacle Captains

Randomly inserted in second-series jumbo packs, these 27 standard-size (2 1/2" by 3 1/2") cards feature on their fronts two photos of each NHL team captain. The photos of the Canadian and U.S. versions differ. The large borderless photo is a ghosted color action shot; the smaller image in the center overlays the larger and is a full-contrast color head shot. The player's name in gold-foil lettering appears above the smaller photo. The grayish back carries a color action cutout on the left and a player profile in English and French on the right. The cards are numbered on the back with a "CA" prefix.

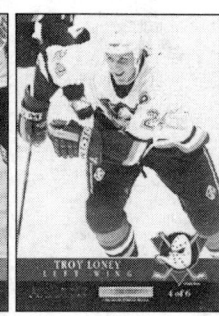

	MINT	EXC	G-VG
COMPLETE SET (27)	150.00	70.00	19.00
COMMON PLAYER (1-27)	4.00	1.80	.50

*CANADIAN VERSION: 1X to 1.25X VALUE

	MINT	EXC	G-VG
☐ 1 Troy Loney Anaheim Mighty Ducks	4.00	1.80	.50
☐ 2 Ray Bourque Boston Bruins	6.00	2.70	.75
☐ 3 Pat LaFontaine Buffalo Sabres	7.00	3.10	.85
☐ 4 Joe Nieuwendyk Calgary Flames	5.00	2.30	.60
☐ 5 Dirk Graham Chicago Blackhawks	4.00	1.80	.50
☐ 6 Mark Tinordi Dallas Stars	4.00	1.80	.50
☐ 7 Steve Yzerman Detroit Red Wings	12.00	5.50	1.50
☐ 8 Craig MacTavish Edmonton Oilers	4.00	1.80	.50
☐ 9 Brian Skrudland Florida Panthers	4.00	1.80	.50
☐ 10 Pat Verbeek Hartford Whalers	5.00	2.30	.60
☐ 11 Wayne Gretzky Los Angeles Kings	35.00	16.00	4.40
☐ 12 Guy Carbonneau Montreal Canadiens	5.00	2.30	.60
☐ 13 Scott Stevens New Jersey Devils	5.00	2.30	.60
☐ 14 Pat Flatley New York Islanders	4.00	1.80	.50
☐ 15 Mark Messier New York Rangers	10.00	4.50	1.25
☐ 16 Mark Lamb Dallas Stars Brad Shaw Ottawa Senators	4.00	1.80	.50
☐ 17 Kevin Dineen Philadelphia Flyers	4.00	1.80	.50
☐ 18 Mario Lemieux Pittsburgh Penguins	22.00	10.00	2.80
☐ 19 Joe Sakic Quebec Nordiques	6.00	2.70	.75
☐ 20 Brett Hull St. Louis Blues	12.00	5.50	1.50
☐ 21 Bob Errey San Jose Sharks	4.00	1.80	.50
☐ 22 Marc Bergevin Tampa Bay Lightning Denis Savard Tampa Bay Lightning John Tucker Tampa Bay Lightning	4.00	1.80	.50
☐ 23 Wendel Clark Toronto Maple Leafs	6.00	2.70	.75
☐ 24 Trevor Linden Vancouver Canucks	6.00	2.70	.75
☐ 25 Kevin Hatcher Washington Capitals	5.00	2.30	.60
☐ 26 Keith Tkachuk Winnipeg Jets	5.00	2.30	.60
☐ 27 Checklist	15.00	6.75	1.90

	MINT	EXC	G-VG
☐ 1 John Vanbiesbrouck Florida Panthers Guy Hebert Anaheim Mighty Ducks	5.00	2.30	.60
☐ 2 Gord Murphy Florida Panthers Randy Ladouceur Anaheim Mighty Ducks	3.00	1.35	.40
☐ 3 Joe Cirella Florida Panthers Sean Hill Anaheim Mighty Ducks	3.00	1.35	.40
☐ 4 Dave Lowry Florida Panthers Troy Loney Anaheim Mighty Ducks	3.00	1.35	.40
☐ 5 Brian Skrudland Florida Panthers Terry Yake Anaheim Mighty Ducks	3.00	1.35	.40
☐ 6 Scott Mellanby Florida Panthers Steven King Anaheim Mighty Ducks	3.00	1.35	.40

1993-94 Pinnacle Masks

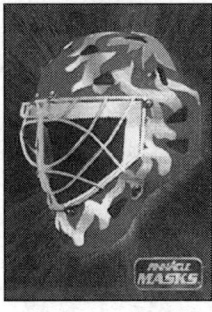
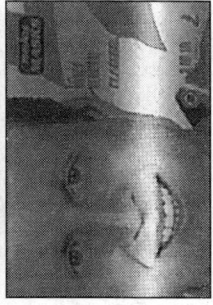

Randomly inserted in first-series packs, this 10-card standard-size (2 1/2" by 3 1/2") set showcases some of the elaborate masks NHL goalies wear. Each metallic front features a colorful rendering of a goalie mask on a dark background highlighted by radial lines. The metallic, borderless, and horizontal backs carry a color player head shot on the left with his name and team name appearing alongside on the right. The cards are numbered on the back as "X of 10."

	MINT	EXC	G-VG
COMPLETE SET (10)	200.00	90.00	25.00
COMMON PLAYER (1-10)	20.00	9.00	2.50
☐ 1 Grant Fuhr Buffalo Sabres	25.00	11.50	3.10
☐ 2 Mike Vernon	25.00	11.50	3.10

1993-94 Pinnacle Expansion

Inserted one per series one hobby box, this six-card set measures the standard size (2 1/2" by 3 1/2"). One side features a color action shot of a player from the Anaheim Mighty Ducks; the other, his counterpart at that position from the Florida Panthers. Each player's name and position, along with his team's logo, appear in a team color-coded bar below the photo. The cards are numbered on both sides as "X of 6."

	MINT	EXC	G-VG
COMPLETE SET (6)	16.00	7.25	2.00
COMMON PAIR (1-6)	3.00	1.35	.40

	MINT	EXC	G-VG
Calgary Flames			
☐ 3 Robb Stauber........................	20.00	9.00	2.50
Los Angeles Kings			
☐ 4 Dominic Roussel...................	25.00	11.50	3.10
Philadelphia Flyers			
☐ 5 Pat Jablonski.......................	20.00	9.00	2.50
Tampa Bay Lightning			
☐ 6 Stephane Fiset.....................	20.00	9.00	2.50
Quebec Nordiques			
☐ 7 Wendell Young.....................	20.00	9.00	2.50
Tampa Bay Lightning			
☐ 8 Ron Hextall.........................	28.00	12.50	3.50
Quebec Nordiques			
☐ 9 John Vanbiesbrouck.............	30.00	13.50	3.80
New York Rangers			
☐ 10 Peter Sidorkiewicz.............	20.00	9.00	2.50
Ottawa Senators			

1993-94 Pinnacle Nifty Fifty

Randomly inserted in second-series foil packs, and featuring Pinnacle's Dufex process, this 15-card standard-size (2 1/2" by 3 1/2") set spotlights players who scored 50 or more goals. The borderless fronts feature metallic color head shots with a gold-foil Nifty Fifty logo at the lower left. The player's name and team name appear in a black bar next to the logo. The metallic backs carry a color action shot on the left side, with statistics and player profile appearing on a black background to the right. The cards are numbered on the back as "X of 15."

	MINT	EXC	G-VG
COMPLETE SET (15)...................	225.00	100.00	28.00
COMMON PLAYER (1-15).............	15.00	6.75	1.90
☐ 1 Introductory CL Card............	40.00	18.00	5.00
☐ 2 Alexander Mogilny................	17.00	7.75	2.10
Buffalo Sabres			
☐ 3 Teemu Selanne....................	20.00	9.00	2.50
Winnipeg Jets			
☐ 4 Mario Lemieux.....................	35.00	16.00	4.40
Pittsburgh Penguins			
☐ 5 Luc Robitaille......................	15.00	6.75	1.90
Los Angeles Kings			
☐ 6 Pavel Bure..........................	35.00	16.00	4.40
Vancouver Canucks			
☐ 7 Pierre Turgeon....................	15.00	6.75	1.90
New York Islanders			
☐ 8 Steve Yzerman.....................	22.00	10.00	2.80
Detroit Red Wings			
☐ 9 Kevin Stevens......................	15.00	6.75	1.90
Pittsburgh Penguins			
☐ 10 Brett Hull...........................	22.00	10.00	2.80
St. Louis Blues			
☐ 11 Dave Andreychuk................	15.00	6.75	1.90
Toronto Maple Leafs			
☐ 12 Pat LaFontaine...................	15.00	6.75	1.90
Buffalo Sabres			
☐ 13 Mark Recchi.......................	15.00	6.75	1.90
Philadelphia Flyers			
☐ 14 Brendan Shanahan..............	20.00	9.00	2.50
St. Louis Blues			
☐ 15 Jeremy Roenick..................	22.00	10.00	2.80
Chicago Blackhawks			

1993-94 Pinnacle Super Rookies

Randomly inserted in second-series hobby foil packs, this nine-card standard-size (2 1/2" by 3 1/2") set spotlights players who were rookies in 1993-94. The fronts feature color action player shots on darkened backgrounds. The player's name in gold-foil lettering appears at the lower right. On a dark red background, the horizontal backs carry a color player cutout on the left, with career highlights to the right. The set was issued in Canadian and U.S. versions. Each version carries its own front photos; the Canadian backs are bilingual. The Canadian cards are valued 1X-1.25X times their U.S. counterparts. The cards are numbered on the back with an "SR" prefix.

	MINT	EXC	G-VG
COMPLETE SET (9)......................	70.00	32.00	8.75
COMMON PLAYER (1-9)................	4.00	1.80	.50
*CANADIAN VERSION: 1X to 1.25X .VALUE			
☐ 1 Alexandre Daigle..................	8.00	3.60	1.00
Ottawa Senators			
☐ 2 Chris Pronger......................	7.00	3.10	.85
Hartford Whalers			
☐ 3 Chris Gratton.......................	7.00	3.10	.85
Tampa Bay Lightning			
☐ 4 Rob Niedermayer..................	7.00	3.10	.85
Florida Panthers			
☐ 5 Alexei Yashin.......................	12.00	5.50	1.50
Ottawa Senators			
☐ 6 Mikael Renberg....................	12.00	5.50	1.50
Philadelphia Flyers			
☐ 7 Jason Arnott........................	18.00	8.00	2.30
Edmonton Oilers			
☐ 8 Markus Naslund....................	4.00	1.80	.50
Pittsburgh Penguins			
☐ 9 Pat Peake............................	4.00	1.80	.50
Washington Capitals			

1993-94 Pinnacle Team Pinnacle

Randomly inserted in packs, this 12-card set measures the standard size (2 1/2" by 3 1/2"). One side features a black-bordered color action photo of a player from the Eastern Conference, the other, one of a player from the Western Conference. The player's name and position appear below. The Canadian version carries color player drawings instead of photos. The Canadian cards are valued at 1X-1.25X times their U.S. counterparts. The cards are numbered on both sides as "X of 12."

	MINT	EXC	G-VG
COMPLETE SET (12).....................	425.00	190.00	52.50
COMPLETE SERIES 1 (6)...............	250.00	115.00	31.00
COMPLETE SERIES 2 (6)...............	175.00	80.00	22.00
COMMON PAIR (1-6)....................	25.00	11.50	3.10
COMMON PAIR (7-12)...................	20.00	9.00	2.50
*CANADIAN VERSION: 1X to 1.25X .VALUE			

		MINT	EXC	G-VG
☐ 1	Patrick Roy	70.00	32.00	8.75
	Montreal Canadiens			
	Ed Belfour			
	Chicago Blackhawks			
☐ 2	Brian Leetch	25.00	11.50	3.10
	New York Rangers			
	Chris Chelios			
	Chicago Blackhawks			
☐ 3	Scott Stevens	25.00	11.50	3.10
	New Jersey Devils			
	Al MacInnis			
	Calgary Flames			
☐ 4	Kevin Stevens	25.00	11.50	3.10
	Pittsburgh Penguins			
	Luc Robitaille			
	Los Angeles Kings			
☐ 5	Mario Lemieux	100.00	45.00	12.50
	Pittsburgh Penguins			
	Wayne Gretzky			
	Los Angeles Kings			
☐ 6	Jaromir Jagr	35.00	16.00	4.40
	Pittsburgh Penguins			
	Brett Hull			
	St. Louis Blues			
☐ 7	Tom Barrasso	25.00	11.50	3.10
	Pittsburgh Penguins			
	Kirk McLean			
	Vancouver Canucks			
☐ 8	Ray Bourque	25.00	11.50	3.10
	Boston Bruins			
	Paul Coffey			
	Detroit Red Wings			
☐ 9	Al Iafrate	20.00	9.00	2.50
	Washington Capitals			
	Phil Housley			
	St. Louis Blues			
☐ 10	Vincent Damphousse	45.00	20.00	5.75
	Montreal Canadiens			
	Pavel Bure			
	Vancouver Canucks			
☐ 11	Eric Lindros	75.00	34.00	9.50
	Philadelphia Flyers			
	Jeremy Roenick			
	Chicago Blackhawks			
☐ 12	Alexander Mogilny	35.00	16.00	4.40
	Buffalo Sabres			
	Teemu Selanne			
	Winnipeg Jets			

1993-94 Pinnacle Team 2001

Inserted one per first-series jumbo pack, this 30-card set measures the standard size (2 1/2" by 3 1/2"). The fronts feature color action player photos. The words "Team 2001" are printed in gold foil inside a black bar on the left, while the player's name in gold foil appears in a black bar on the bottom, along with the team logo. The horizontal backs carry a color head shot on the right. On a black background to the left of the photo are the player's name in gold foil and career highlights. The Canadian version carries color player drawings instead of photos. The Canadian cards are valued at 1X-1.25X times their U.S. counterparts. The cards are numbered on the back as "X of 30."

		MINT	EXC	G-VG
COMPLETE SET (30)		40.00	18.00	5.00
COMMON PLAYER (1-30)		.60	.25	.08
*CANADIAN VERSION: 1X to 1.25X .VALUE				
☐ 1	Eric Lindros	8.00	3.60	1.00
	Philadelphia Flyers			
☐ 2	Alexander Mogilny	2.00	.90	.25
	Buffalo Sabres			
☐ 3	Pavel Bure	6.00	2.70	.75
	Vancouver Canucks			
☐ 4	Joe Juneau	2.50	1.15	.30
	Boston Bruins			
☐ 5	Felix Potvin	5.00	2.30	.60
	Toronto Maple Leafs			
☐ 6	Nicklas Lidstrom	.60	.25	.08
	Detroit Red Wings			
☐ 7	Alexei Kovalev	2.50	1.15	.30
	New York Rangers			
☐ 8	Patrick Poulin	.60	.25	.08
	Hartford Whalers			
☐ 9	Shawn McEachern	.60	.25	.08
	Los Angeles Kings			
☐ 10	Teemu Selanne	3.00	1.35	.40
	Winnipeg Jets			
☐ 11	Rod Brind'Amour	.75	.35	.09
	Philadelphia Flyers			
☐ 12	Jaromir Jagr	2.50	1.15	.30
	Pittsburgh Penguins			
☐ 13	Pierre Turgeon	1.25	.55	.16
	New York Islanders			
☐ 14	Scott Niedermayer	.75	.35	.09
	New Jersey Devils			
☐ 15	Mats Sundin	1.50	.65	.19
	Quebec Nordiques			
☐ 16	Trevor Linden	.75	.35	.09
	Vancouver Canucks			
☐ 17	Mike Modano	1.50	.65	.19
	Dallas Stars			
☐ 18	Roman Hamrlik	.60	.25	.08
	Tampa Bay Lightning			
☐ 19	Tony Amonte	.60	.25	.08
	New York Rangers			
☐ 20	Jeremy Roenick	3.00	1.35	.40
	Chicago Blackhawks			
☐ 21	Scott Lachance	.60	.25	.08
	New York Islanders			
☐ 22	Mike Ricci	.60	.25	.08
	Quebec Nordiques			
☐ 23	Dimitri Khristich	.60	.25	.08
	Washington Capitals			
☐ 24	Sergei Fedorov	4.00	1.80	.50
	Detroit Red Wings			
☐ 25	Joe Sakic	.75	.35	.09
	Quebec Nordiques			
☐ 26	Pat Falloon	.60	.25	.08
	San Jose Sharks			
☐ 27	Mathieu Schneider	.75	.35	.09
	Montreal Canadiens			
☐ 28	Owen Nolan	.75	.35	.09
	Quebec Nordiques			
☐ 29	Brendan Shanahan	2.00	.90	.25
	St. Louis Blues			
☐ 30	Mark Recchi	1.00	.45	.13
	Philadelphia Flyers			

1975-76 Popsicle

This 18-card set presents the teams of the NHL. The cards measure approximately 3 3/8" by 2 1/8" and are printed in

the "credit card format", only slightly thinner than an actual credit card. The front has the NHL logo in the upper left hand corner, and the city and team names in the black bar across the top. A colorful team logo appears on the left side of the card face, while a color action shot of the teams' players appears on the right side. The back provides a brief history of the team. We have checklisted the cards below in alphabetical order of the team nicknames.

	NRMT	VG-E	GOOD
COMPLETE SET (18)	25.00	10.00	2.50
COMMON TEAM (1-18)	1.50	.60	.15
☐ 1 Chicago Blackhawks	2.00	.80	.20
☐ 2 St. Louis Blues	1.50	.60	.15
☐ 3 Boston Bruins	2.00	.80	.20
☐ 4 Montreal Canadiens	2.50	1.00	.25
☐ 5 Vancouver Canucks	2.00	.80	.20
☐ 6 Washington Capitals	1.50	.60	.15
☐ 7 Atlanta Flames	1.50	.60	.15
☐ 8 Philadelphia Flyers	2.00	.80	.20
☐ 9 California Golden Seals	3.00	1.20	.30
☐ 10 New York Islanders	2.00	.80	.20
☐ 11 Los Angeles Kings	2.00	.80	.20
☐ 12 Toronto Maple Leafs	2.00	.80	.20
☐ 13 Minnesota North Stars	1.50	.60	.15
☐ 14 Pittsburgh Penguins	2.00	.80	.20
☐ 15 New York Rangers	2.00	.80	.20
☐ 16 Detroit Red Wings	2.00	.80	.20
☐ 17 Buffalo Sabres	1.50	.60	.15
☐ 18 Kansas City Scouts	3.00	1.20	.30

1976-77 Popsicle

This 18-card set presents the teams of the NHL. The cards measure approximately 3 3/8" by 2 1/8" and are printed in the "credit card format", only slightly thinner than an actual credit card. The front has the NHL logo in the upper left hand corner, and the city and team names in the black bar

across the top. A colorful team logo appears on the left side of the card face, while a color action shot of the teams' players appears on the right side. The back provides a brief history of the team. We have checklisted the cards below in alphabetical order of the team nicknames.

	NRMT	VG-E	GOOD
COMPLETE SET (18)	25.00	10.00	2.50
COMMON TEAM (1-18)	1.50	.60	.15
☐ 1 Cleveland Barons	3.00	1.20	.30
☐ 2 Chicago Blackhawks	2.00	.80	.20
☐ 3 St. Louis Blues	1.50	.60	.15
☐ 4 Boston Bruins	2.00	.80	.20
☐ 5 Montreal Canadiens	2.50	1.00	.25
☐ 6 Vancouver Canucks	2.00	.80	.20
☐ 7 Washington Capitals	1.50	.60	.15
☐ 8 Atlanta Flames	1.50	.60	.15
☐ 9 Philadelphia Flyers	2.00	.80	.20
☐ 10 New York Islanders	2.00	.80	.20
☐ 11 Los Angeles Kings	2.00	.80	.20
☐ 12 Toronto Maple Leafs	2.00	.80	.20
☐ 13 Minnesota North Stars	1.50	.60	.15
☐ 14 Pittsburgh Penguins	2.00	.80	.20
☐ 15 New York Rangers	2.00	.80	.20
☐ 16 Detroit Red Wings	2.00	.80	.20
☐ 17 Colorado Rockies	3.00	1.20	.30
☐ 18 Buffalo Sabres	1.50	.60	.15

1968-69 Post Cereal Marbles

This set of 30 marbles was issued by Post Cereal in Canada and features players of the Montreal Canadiens (MC) and the Toronto Maple Leafs (TML). Also produced was an attractive game board which is rather difficult to find and not included in the complete set price below.

	NRMT	VG-E	GOOD
COMPLETE SET (30)	150.00	60.00	15.00
COMMON PLAYER (1-30)	3.50	1.40	.35
☐ 1 Ralph Backstrom MC	3.50	1.40	.35
☐ 2 Jean Beliveau MC	15.00	6.00	1.50
☐ 3 Johnny Bower TML	9.00	3.75	.90
☐ 4 Wayne Carleton TML	3.50	1.40	.35
☐ 5 Yvan Cournoyer MC	9.00	3.75	.90
☐ 6 Ron Ellis TML	3.50	1.40	.35
☐ 7 John Ferguson MC	3.50	1.40	.35
☐ 8 Bruce Gamble TML	3.50	1.40	.35
☐ 9 Terry Harper MC	3.50	1.40	.35
☐ 10 Ted Harris MC	3.50	1.40	.35
☐ 11 Paul Henderson TML	5.00	2.00	.50
☐ 12 Tim Horton TML	10.00	4.00	1.00
☐ 13 Dave Keon TML	8.00	3.25	.80
☐ 14 Jacques Laperriere MC	6.00	2.40	.60
☐ 15 Jacques Lemaire MC	8.00	3.25	.80
☐ 16 Murray Oliver TML	3.50	1.40	.35
☐ 17 Mike Pelyk TML	3.50	1.40	.35
☐ 18 Pierre Pilote TML	6.00	2.40	.60
☐ 19 Marcel Pronovost TML	6.00	2.40	.60
☐ 20 Bob Pulford TML	6.00	2.40	.60
☐ 21 Henri Richard MC	10.00	4.00	1.00
☐ 22 Bobby Rousseau MC	3.50	1.40	.35
☐ 23 Serge Savard MC	7.00	2.80	.70
☐ 24 Floyd Smith TML	3.50	1.40	.35
☐ 25 Gilles Tremblay MC	3.50	1.40	.35
☐ 26 J.C. Tremblay MC	5.00	2.00	.50
☐ 27 Norm Ullman TML	9.00	3.75	.90
☐ 28 Rogatien Vachon MC	7.00	2.80	.70
☐ 29 Mike Walton TML	3.50	1.40	.35

☐ 30 Gump Worsley MC	10.00	4.00	1.00
☐ xx Game Board	125.00	50.00	12.50

1970-71 Post Cereal Shooters

This set of 16 shooters was intended to be used with the hockey game that Post had advertised as a premium. The shooter consists of a plastic figure with a colorful adhesive decal sheet, with stickers that could be applied to the shooter for identification. All players come with home and away, i.e., red or blue shoulders. The figures measure approximately 3 1/2" by 4 1/2". Players are featured in their NHLPA uniform. They are unnumbered and hence are listed below in alphabetical order.

	NRMT	VG-E	GOOD
COMPLETE SET (16)	200.00	80.00	20.00
COMMON PLAYER (1-16)	8.00	3.25	.80
☐ 1 Johnny Bucyk	15.00	6.00	1.50
☐ 2 Ron Ellis	8.00	3.25	.80
☐ 3 Ed Giacomin	15.00	6.00	1.50
☐ 4 Paul Henderson	10.00	4.00	1.00
☐ 5 Ken Hodge	10.00	4.00	1.00
☐ 6 Dennis Hull	10.00	4.00	1.00
☐ 7 Orland Kurtenbach	8.00	3.25	.80
☐ 8 Jacques Laperriere	10.00	4.00	1.00
☐ 9 Jacques Lemaire	12.00	5.00	1.20
☐ 10 Frank Mahovlich	20.00	8.00	2.00
☐ 11 Peter Mahovlich	10.00	4.00	1.00
☐ 12 Bobby Orr	75.00	30.00	7.50
☐ 13 Jacques Plante	25.00	10.00	2.50
☐ 14 Jean Ratelle	15.00	6.00	1.50
☐ 15 Dale Tallon	8.00	3.25	.80
☐ 16 J.C. Tremblay	10.00	4.00	1.00

1981-82 Post Standups

Each thick card in this 28-card set measures approximately 2 13/16" by 3 3/4" and consists of three panels joined together at one end. The front of the first panel has the logos of Post, the NHL, the NHLPA, and a NHL team, with the title NHL Stars in Action in English and French. The back

of the first panel has a full color action photo of a player from the NHL team featured on the card. The second panel is blank backed and features a standup of the player, with his signature at the bottom of the standup. The front of the third panel has the player's name and statistics (from the 1980-81 regular season) in English and French for that player as well as for his entire team, with instructions on the card back in both languages for creating the standup. These three dimensional cards were issued in cellophane packs with one card per specially marked box of Post Sugar-Crisp, Honeycomb, or Alpha-Bits. The set is composed of two players from each Canadian team and one player from each American NHL team. The promotion included a mail-in offer for an official NHL fact chart, which featured the new NHL divisional alignment. Also available, but hard to find, is a two-piece display box; the cover has logos of all NHL teams with two slots inside for cards and space to display one "opened" card.

	MINT	EXC	G-VG
COMPLETE SET (28)	40.00	16.00	4.00
COMMON PLAYER (1-28)	1.00	.40	.10
☐ 1 Ray Bourque	6.00	2.40	.60
☐ 2 Gilbert Perreault	3.00	1.20	.30
☐ 3 Denis Savard	3.00	1.20	.30
☐ 4 Dale McCourt	1.00	.40	.10
☐ 5 Bobby Smith	1.00	.40	.10
☐ 6 Mike Bossy	4.00	1.60	.40
☐ 7 Bobby Clarke	3.00	1.20	.30
☐ 8 Randy Carlyle	1.00	.40	.10
☐ 9 Mike Palmateer	1.00	.40	.10
☐ 10 Dave(Tiger) Williams	1.00	.40	.10
☐ 11 Mark Howe	1.25	.50	.12
☐ 12 Marcel Dionne	3.00	1.20	.30
☐ 13 Mike Liut	1.25	.50	.12
☐ 14 Barry Beck	1.00	.40	.10
☐ 15 Mark Messier	7.50	3.00	.75
☐ 16 Larry Robinson	3.00	1.20	.30
☐ 17 Real Cloutier	1.00	.40	.10
☐ 18 Borje Salming	1.50	.60	.15
☐ 19 Morris Lukowich	1.00	.40	.10
☐ 20 Brett Callighen	1.00	.40	.10
☐ 21 Rob Ramage	1.00	.40	.10
☐ 22 Wilf Paiement	1.00	.40	.10
☐ 23 Mario Tremblay	1.00	.40	.10
☐ 24 Robbie Ftorek	1.00	.40	.10
☐ 25 Stan Smyl	1.00	.40	.10
☐ 26 Dave Babych	1.00	.40	.10
☐ 27 Willi Plett	1.00	.40	.10
☐ 28 Kent Nilsson	1.00	.40	.10
☐ xx Display Box	20.00	8.00	2.00

1982-83 Post Cereal

This set is composed of panels of 16 mini playing cards, each measuring approximately 1 1/4" by 2" after perforation. The cards were issued in panel form in a cellophane wrapper inside specially marked packages of Post Cereal. The front of each individual card has an action color photo of the player, with uniform number in the upper left-hand corner, and the player's name and uniform number beneath the picture. The back is done in the team's colors and includes the logos of the team, the sponsor (Post), the NHL, and the NHLPA. There were 21 panels produced, one for each NHL team. Game instructions were included in each box so that one could play Shut-out, Face Off, or Hockey Match with the set of 16 hockey playing cards. By mailing in the UPC code or a reasonable hand drawn facsimile, one could enter the sweepstakes for the grand prize of a trip for two to a Stanley Cup Final playoff game. The sweepstakes was only open to residents of Canada. The complete set was available for a limited time through a mail-in offer.

	MINT	EXC	G-VG
COMPLETE SET (21)	60.00	24.00	6.00
COMMON PANEL (1-21)	2.50	1.00	.25

		MINT	EXC	G-VG
☐ 1	Boston Bruins	5.00	2.00	.50
	1 Rogie Vachon			
	7 Ray Bourque			
	8 Peter McNab			
	11 Steve Kasper			
	12 Wayne Cashman			
	14 Mike Gillis			
	16 Rick Middleton			
	17 Stan Jonathan			
	20 Mike O'Connell			
	22 Brad Park			
	24 Terry O'Reilly			
	26 Mike Milbury			
	28 Tom Fergus			
	29 Brad McCrimmon			
	32 Bruce Crowder			
	33 Larry Melynk			
☐ 2	Buffalo Sabres	3.50	1.40	.35
	1 Don Edwards			
	3 Richie Dunn			
	4 John Van Boxmeer			
	5 Mike Ramsey			
	7 Dale McCourt			
	8 Tony McKegney			
	10 Craig Ramsey			
	11 Gilbert Perreault			
	12 Andre Savard			
	15 Yvon Lambert			
	16 Ric Seiling			
	17 Mike Foligno			
	21 J. Francois Sauve			
	22 Lindy Ruff			
	24 Bill Hajt			
	27 Larry Playfair			
☐ 3	Calgary Flames	3.50	1.40	.35
	1 Pat Riggin			
	4 Pekka Rautakallio			
	5 Phil Russell			
	6 Ken Houston			
	9 Lanny McDonald			
	12 Dennis Cyr			
	14 Kent Nilsson			
	15 Kevin Lavalle			
	16 Guy Chouinard			
	17 Jamie Hislop			
	20 Bob Murdoch			
	23 Paul Reinhart			
	24 Jim Peplinski			
	25 Willi Plett			
	26 Mel Bridgeman			
	28 Gary McAdam			
☐ 4	Chicago Blackhawks	5.00	2.00	.50
	2 Greg Fox			
	5 Dave Hutchison			
	8 Terry Ruskowski			
	10 Reg Kerr			
	12 Tom Lysiak			
	14 Bill Gardner			
	15 Tom Higgins			
	16 Rich Preston			
	18 Denis Savard			
	20 Al Secord			
	22 Grant Mulvey			
	23 Doug Crossman			
	24 Doug Wilson			
	26 Rick Paterson			
	29 Ted Bulley			
	35 Tony Esposito			
☐ 5	Detroit Red Wings	2.50	1.00	.25
	2 Jim Schoenfeld			
	3 John Barrett			
	5 Greg Smith			
	7 Willie Huber			
	11 Walt McKechnie			
	15 Paul Woods			
	16 Mark Kirton			
	18 Danny Gare			
	20 Vaclav Nedomansky			
	21 Mike Blaisdell			
	22 Greg Joly			
	23 Mark Osborne			
	24 Derrek Smith			
	25 John Ogrodnick			
	28 Reed Larsen			
	31 Bob Sauve			
☐ 6	Edmonton Oilers	20.00	8.00	2.00
	1 Grant Fuhr			
	2 Lee Fogolin			
	4 Kevin Lowe			
	6 Garry Lariviere			
	7 Paul Coffey			
	8 Risto Siltanen			
	9 Glenn Anderson			
	10 Matti Hagman			
	11 Mark Messier			
	12 Dave Hunter			
	16 Pat Hughes			
	17 Jari Kurri			
	18 Brett Callighen			
	20 Dave Lumley			
	27 Dave Semenko			
	99 Wayne Gretzky			
☐ 7	Hartford Whalers	3.50	1.40	.35
	3 Paul Shmyr			
	4 Ron Francis			
	5 Mark Howe			
	6 Blake Wesley			
	8 Garry Howatt			
	11 Jordy Douglas			
	14 Dave Keon			
	16 George Lyle			
	21 Blaine Stoughton			
	22 Doug Sulliman			
	24 Chris Kotsopoulos			
	26 Don Nachbaur			
	27 Warren Miller			
	28 Pierre Larouche			
	30 Greg Millen			
☐ 8	Los Angeles Kings	3.50	1.40	.35
	1 Mario Lessard			
	2 Rick Chartraw			
	4 Jerry Korab			
	5 Larry Murphy			
	11 Charlie Simmer			
	12 Dean Hopkins			
	16 Marcel Dionne			
	17 John P. Kelly			
	18 Dave Taylor			
	19 Jim Fox			
	20 Mark Hardy			
	22 Steve Jensen			
	23 Doug Smith			
	24 Jay Wells			
	25 Dave Lewis			
	26 Steve Bozek			
☐ 9	Minnesota North Stars	2.50	1.00	.25
	2 Curt Giles			
	3 Fred Barrett			
	4 Craig Hartsburg			
	5 Brad Maxwell			
	8 K.E. Anderson			
	10 Gord Roberts			
	11 Tom McCarthy			
	14 Brad Palmer			
	15 Dobby Smith			
	17 Tim Young			
	20 Dino Ciccarelli			
	22 Gary Sargent			
	25 Al MacAdam			
	26 Steve Payne			
	27 Gilles Meloche			
	28 Steve Christoff			
☐ 10	Montreal Canadiens	7.50	3.00	.75
	3 Brian Engblom			
	6 Pierre Mondou			
	8 Doug Risebrough			
	10 Guy Lafleur			
	12 Keith Acton			
	14 Mario Tremblay			
	17 Rod Langway			
	19 Larry Robinson			

20 Mark Hunter
21 Doug Jarvis
22 Steve Shutt
23 Bob Gainey
24 Robert Picard
26 Craig Laughlin
31 Mark Napier
33 Richard Sevigny
☐ 11 New Jersey Devils .... 2.50 1.00 .25
(Colorado Rockies)
1 Glenn Resch
2 Joe Cirella
4 Bob Lorimer
5 Rob Ramage
6 Joe Micheletti
9 Don Lever
10 Dave Cameron
12 Bob MacMillan
14 Steve Tambellini
15 Brent Ashton
16 Merlin Malinowski
18 Bobby Miller
20 Dwight Foster
21 Kevin Maxwell
26 Mike Kitchen
27 John Wensink
☐ 12 New York Islanders .... 7.50 3.00 .75
2 Mike McEwen
3 Tomas Jonsson
5 Denis Potvin
6 Ken Morrow
7 Stefan Persson
9 Clark Gillies
11 Wayne Merrick
14 Bob Bourne
19 Bryan Trottier
22 Mike Bossy
23 Bob Nystrom
26 Dave Langevin
27 John Tonelli
28 Anders Kallur
31 Billy Smith
91 Butch Goring
☐ 13 New York Rangers .... 2.50 1.00 .25
2 Tom Laidlaw
3 Barry Beck
4 Ron Greschner
8 Steve Vickers
10 Ron Duguay
12 Don Maloney
14 Mike Allison
17 Ed Johnstone
22 Nick Fotiu
26 Dave Maloney
27 Mike Rogers
29 R. Ruotsalainen
31 Steve Weeks
33 Andre Dore
38 Robbie Ftorek
40 Mark Pavelich
☐ 14 Philadelphia Flyers .... 5.00 2.00 .50
3 Behn Wilson
6 Fred Arthur
7 Bill Barber
8 Brad Marsh
9 Reid Bailey
9 Darryl Sittler
12 Tim Kerr
14 Kenny Linseman
16 Bobby Clarke
17 Paul Holmgren
20 Jimmy Watson
23 Ilkka Sinisalo
26 Brian Propp
27 Reggie Leach
29 Glen Cochrane
33 Pete Peeters
☐ 15 Pittsburgh Penguins .... 2.50 1.00 .25
2 Pat Price
3 Ron Stackhouse
4 Paul Baxter
10 Peter Lee
11 George Ferguson
12 Greg Malone
14 Doug Shedden
15 Pat Boutette
16 Marc Chorney
17 Rick Kehoe
19 Gregg Sheppard
20 Paul Gardner
22 Mike Bullard
24 Pat Graham
25 Randy Carlyle
29 Michel Dion

☐ 16 Quebec Nordiques .... 3.50 1.40 .35
1 John Garrett
2 Wally Weir
5 Normand Rochefort
8 Marc Tardif
9 Real Cloutier
12 Jere Gillis
16 Michel Goulet
18 Marion Stastny
19 Alain Cote
20 Anton Stastny
22 Mario Marois
23 Jacques Richard
26 Peter Stastny
27 Wilf Paiement
28 Andre Dupont
32 Dale Hunter
☐ 17 St. Louis Blues .... 2.50 1.00 .25
1 Mike Liut
5 Guy Lapointe
6 Larry Patey
9 Perry Turnbull
10 Wayne Babych
11 Brian Sutter
16 J. Brownschidle
17 Ed Kea
18 Rick Lapointe
19 Blake Dunlop
21 Mike Zuke
22 Jorgen Pettersson
24 Bernie Federko
25 Bill Baker
26 Mike Crombeen
35 Jim Pavese
☐ 18 Toronto Maple Leafs .... 3.50 1.40 .35
1 Michel Larocque
3 Bob Manno
4 Bob McGill
7 Rocky Saganiuk
10 John Anderson
11 F. Boimistruck
12 Walt Poddubny
14 Miroslav Frycer
15 Jim Benning
17 Stewart Gavin
19 Bill Derlago
21 Borje Salming
22 Rick Vaive
24 Normand Aubin
25 Terry Martin
26 Barry Melrose
☐ 19 Vancouver Canucks .... 2.50 1.00 .25
2 Doug Halward
7 Gary Lupul
9 Ivan Boldirev
12 Stan Smyl
13 Lars Lindgren
18 Darcy Rota
19 Ron Delorme
21 Ivan Hlinka
22 Dave(Tiger) Williams
23 Thomas Gradin
24 Curt Fraser
25 Kevin McCarthy
26 Lars Molin
27 Harold Snepsts
28 Marc Crawford
35 Richard Brodeur
☐ 20 Washington Capitals .... 3.50 1.40 .35
2 Doug Hicks
4 Randy Holt
5 Rick Green
6 Darren Veitch
9 Ryan Walter
10 Bob Carpenter
11 Mike Gartner
12 Glen Currie
14 Gaetan Duchesne
16 Bengt Gustafsson
20 Greg Theberge
21 Dennis Maruk
23 Bob Gould
25 Terry Murray
28 Chris Valentine
35 Al Jensen
☐ 21 Winnipeg Jets .... 3.50 1.40 .35
3 Bryan Maxwell
7 Tim Watters
10 Dale Hawerchuk
11 Scott Arniel
12 Morris Lukowich
13 Dave Christian
14 Tim Trimper

15 Paul MacLean
18 Serge Savard
20 Willy Lindstrom
22 Bengt Lundholm
23 Lucien DeBlois
27 Don Spring
28 Norm Dupont
31 Ed Staniowski
44 Dave Babych

1993-94 PowerPlay

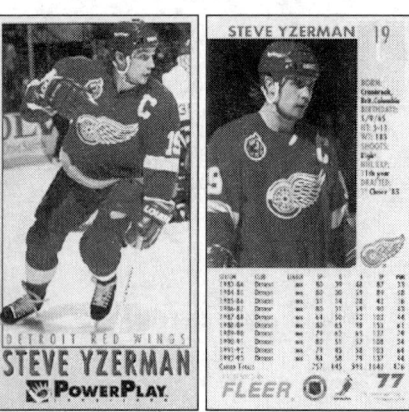

This 520-card set measures 2 1/2" by 4 3/4". The fronts feature color action shots set within a blended team-colored border. The team name and the player's name appear in team-colored lettering below the photo. The backs carry color player photos at the upper left. The player's name appears above; his number, position, and a short biography are displayed alongside. Statistics are shown below. The cards are numbered on the back and checklisted below alphabetically within and according to teams as follows: Anaheim Mighty Ducks (1-15), Boston Bruins (16-25), Buffalo Sabres (26-35), Calgary Flames (36-45), Chicago Blackhawks (46-56), Dallas Stars (57-66), Detroit Red Wings (67-77), Edmonton Oilers (78-87), Florida Panthers (88-102), Hartford Whalers (103-112), Los Angeles Kings (113-123), Montreal Canadiens (124-134), New Jersey Devils (135-145), New York Islanders (146-155), New York Rangers (156-167), Ottawa Senators (168-176), Philadelphia Flyers (177-186), Pittsburgh Penguins (187-196), Quebec Nordiques (197-206), St. Louis Blues (207-216), San Jose Sharks (217-226), Tampa Bay Lightning (227-236), Toronto Maple Leafs (237-246), Vancouver Canucks (247-257), Washington Capitals (258-267), and Winnipeg Jets (268-278). The second series cards are also grouped alphabetically within teams, and checklisted below alphabetically according to teams as follows: Anaheim Mighty Ducks (281-286), Boston Bruins (287-294), Buffalo Sabres (295-302), Calgary Flames (303-311), Chicago Blackhawks (312-319), Dallas Stars (320-327), Detroit Red Wings (328-336), Edmonton Oilers (337-344), Florida Panthers (345-349), Hartford Whalers (350-357), Los Angeles Kings (358-365), Montreal Canadiens (366-373), New Jersey Devils (374-381), New York Islanders (382-388), New York Rangers (389-395), Ottawa Senators (396-403), Philadelphia Flyers (404-410), Pittsburgh Penguins (411-417), Quebec Nordiques (418-426), St. Louis Blues (427-432), San Jose Sharks (433-439), Tampa Bay Lightning (440-447), Toronto Maple Leafs (448-455),

Vancouver Canucks (456-462), Washington Capitals (463-470), and Winnipeg Jets (471-477). The set closes with the following subsets: Team Canada (478-497), Team USA (498-517), and checklists (518-520). One insert card was included in every series 2 pack.

	MINT	EXC	G-VG
COMPLETE SET (520)	55.00	25.00	7.00
COMPLETE SERIES 1 (280)	25.00	11.50	3.10
COMPLETE SERIES 2 (240)	30.00	13.50	3.80
COMMON PLAYER (1-280)	.08	.04	.01
COMMON PLAYER (281-520)	.08	.04	.01

		MINT	EXC	G-VG
☐	1 Stu Grimson	.08	.04	.01
☐	2 Guy Hebert	.20	.09	.03
☐	3 Sean Hill	.08	.04	.01
☐	4 Bill Houlder	.08	.04	.01
☐	5 Alexei Kasatonov	.08	.04	.01
☐	6 Steven King	.08	.04	.01
☐	7 Lonnie Loach	.08	.04	.01
☐	8 Troy Loney	.08	.04	.01
☐	9 Joe Sacco	.08	.04	.01
☐	10 Anatoli Semenov	.08	.04	.01
☐	11 Jarrod Skalde	.08	.04	.01
☐	12 Tim Sweeney	.08	.04	.01
☐	13 Ron Tugnutt	.08	.04	.01
☐	14 Terry Yake	.08	.04	.01
☐	15 Shaun Van Allen	.08	.04	.01
☐	16 Ray Bourque	.20	.09	.03
☐	17 Jon Casey	.10	.05	.01
☐	18 Ted Donato	.08	.04	.01
☐	19 Joe Juneau	.60	.25	.08
☐	20 Dmitri Kvartalnov	.08	.04	.01
☐	21 Steve Leach	.08	.04	.01
☐	22 Cam Neely	.10	.05	.01
☐	23 Adam Oates	.20	.09	.03
☐	24 Don Sweeney	.08	.04	.01
☐	25 Glen Wesley	.08	.04	.01
☐	26 Doug Bodger	.08	.04	.01
☐	27 Grant Fuhr	.10	.05	.01
☐	28 Viktor Gordiouk	.08	.04	.01
☐	29 Dale Hawerchuk	.10	.05	.01
☐	30 Yuri Khmylev	.10	.05	.01
☐	31 Pat LaFontaine	.30	.14	.04
☐	32 Alexander Mogilny	.50	.23	.06
☐	33 Richard Smehlik	.10	.05	.01
☐	34 Bob Sweeney	.08	.04	.01
☐	35 Randy Wood	.08	.04	.01
☐	36 Theoren Fleury	.15	.07	.02
☐	37 Kelly Kisio	.08	.04	.01
☐	38 Al MacInnis	.15	.07	.02
☐	39 Joe Nieuwendyk	.10	.05	.01
☐	40 Joel Otto	.08	.04	.01
☐	41 Robert Reichel	.10	.05	.01
☐	42 Gary Roberts	.10	.05	.01
☐	43 Ronnie Stern	.08	.04	.01
☐	44 Gary Suter	.10	.05	.01
☐	45 Mike Vernon	.10	.05	.01
☐	46 Ed Belfour	.25	.11	.03
☐	47 Chris Chelios	.10	.05	.01
☐	48 Karl Dykhuis	.08	.04	.01
☐	49 Michel Goulet	.10	.05	.01
☐	50 Dirk Graham	.08	.04	.01
☐	51 Sergei Krivokrasov	.08	.04	.01
☐	52 Steve Larmer	.10	.05	.01
☐	53 Joe Murphy	.08	.04	.01
☐	54 Jeremy Roenick	.75	.35	.09
☐	55 Steve Smith	.08	.04	.01
☐	56 Brent Sutter	.10	.05	.01
☐	57 Neal Broten	.10	.05	.01
☐	58 Russ Courtnall	.10	.05	.01
☐	59 Ulf Dahlen	.08	.04	.01
☐	60 Dave Gagner	.10	.05	.01
☐	61 Derian Hatcher	.08	.04	.01
☐	62 Trent Klatt	.08	.04	.01
☐	63 Mike Modano	.30	.14	.04
☐	64 Andy Moog	.10	.05	.01
☐	65 Tommy Sjodin	.08	.04	.01
☐	66 Mark Tinordi	.08	.04	.01
☐	67 Tim Cheveldae	.10	.05	.01
☐	68 Steve Chiasson	.08	.04	.01
☐	69 Dino Ciccarelli	.10	.05	.01
☐	70 Paul Coffey	.20	.09	.03
☐	71 Dallas Drake	.20	.09	.03
☐	72 Sergei Fedorov	1.25	.55	.16
☐	73 Vladimir Konstantinov	.08	.04	.01
☐	74 Nicklas Lidstrom	.10	.05	.01
☐	75 Keith Primeau	.10	.05	.01
☐	76 Ray Sheppard	.08	.04	.01
☐	77 Steve Yzerman	.50	.23	.06
☐	78 Zdeno Ciger	.08	.04	.01
☐	79 Shayne Corson	.08	.04	.01

☐ 80	Todd Elik	.08	.04	.01
☐ 81	Igor Kravchuk	.08	.04	.01
☐ 82	Craig MacTavish	.08	.04	.01
☐ 83	Dave Manson	.08	.04	.01
☐ 84	Shjon Podein	.20	.09	.03
☐ 85	Bill Ranford	.10	.05	.01
☐ 86	Steven Rice	.08	.04	.01
☐ 87	Doug Weight	.10	.05	.01
☐ 88	Doug Barrault	.20	.09	.03
☐ 89	Jesse Belanger	.20	.09	.03
☐ 90	Brian Benning	.08	.04	.01
☐ 91	Joe Cirella	.08	.04	.01
☐ 92	Mark Fitzpatrick	.08	.04	.01
☐ 93	Randy Gilhen	.08	.04	.01
☐ 94	Mike Hough	.08	.04	.01
☐ 95	Bill Lindsay	.08	.04	.01
☐ 96	Andrei Lomakin	.08	.04	.01
☐ 97	Dave Lowry	.08	.04	.01
☐ 98	Scott Mellanby	.08	.04	.01
☐ 99	Gord Murphy	.08	.04	.01
☐ 100	Brian Skrudland	.08	.04	.01
☐ 101	Milan Tichy	.20	.09	.03
☐ 102	John Vanbiesbrouck	.20	.09	.03
☐ 103	Sean Burke	.10	.05	.01
☐ 104	Andrew Cassels	.08	.04	.01
☐ 105	Nick Kypreos	.08	.04	.01
☐ 106	Michael Nylander	.20	.09	.03
☐ 107	Robert Petrovicky	.08	.04	.01
☐ 108	Patrick Poulin	.08	.04	.01
☐ 109	Geoff Sanderson	.25	.11	.03
☐ 110	Pat Verbeek	.10	.05	.01
☐ 111	Eric Weinrich	.08	.04	.01
☐ 112	Zarley Zalapski	.08	.04	.01
☐ 113	Rob Blake	.10	.05	.01
☐ 114	Jimmy Carson	.08	.04	.01
☐ 115	Tony Granato	.08	.04	.01
☐ 116	Wayne Gretzky	2.00	.90	.25
☐ 117	Kelly Hrudey	.10	.05	.01
☐ 118	Jari Kurri	.15	.07	.02
☐ 119	Shawn McEachern	.15	.07	.02
☐ 120	Luc Robitaille	.20	.09	.03
☐ 121	Tomas Sandstrom	.08	.04	.01
☐ 122	Darryl Sydor	.10	.05	.01
☐ 123	Alexei Zhitnik	.20	.09	.03
☐ 124	Brian Bellows	.10	.05	.01
☐ 125	Patrice Brisebois	.08	.04	.01
☐ 126	Guy Carbonneau	.10	.05	.01
☐ 127	Vincent Damphousse	.10	.05	.01
☐ 128	Eric Desjardins	.08	.04	.01
☐ 129	Mike Keane	.08	.04	.01
☐ 130	Stephan Lebeau	.08	.04	.01
☐ 131	Kirk Muller	.10	.05	.01
☐ 132	Lyle Odelein	.08	.04	.01
☐ 133	Patrick Roy	1.00	.45	.13
☐ 134	Mathieu Schneider	.10	.05	.01
☐ 135	Bruce Driver	.08	.04	.01
☐ 136	Viacheslav Fetisov	.08	.04	.01
☐ 137	Claude Lemieux	.10	.05	.01
☐ 138	John MacLean	.10	.05	.01
☐ 139	Bernie Nicholls	.10	.05	.01
☐ 140	Scott Niedermayer	.20	.09	.03
☐ 141	Stephane Richer	.10	.05	.01
☐ 142	Alexander Semak	.08	.04	.01
☐ 143	Scott Stevens	.10	.05	.01
☐ 144	Chris Terreri	.10	.05	.01
☐ 145	Valeri Zelepukin	.10	.05	.01
☐ 146	Patrick Flatley	.08	.04	.01
☐ 147	Ron Hextall	.10	.05	.01
☐ 148	Benoit Hogue	.08	.04	.01
☐ 149	Darius Kasparaitis	.08	.04	.01
☐ 150	Derek King	.08	.04	.01
☐ 151	Uwe Krupp	.08	.04	.01
☐ 152	Scott Lachance	.08	.04	.01
☐ 153	Vladimir Malakhov	.15	.07	.02
☐ 154	Steve Thomas	.10	.05	.01
☐ 155	Pierre Turgeon	.30	.14	.04
☐ 156	Tony Amonte	.10	.05	.01
☐ 157	Mike Gartner	.08	.04	.01
☐ 158	Adam Graves	.30	.14	.04
☐ 159	Alexei Kovalev	.60	.25	.08
☐ 160	Brian Leetch	.30	.14	.04
☐ 161	Joby Messier	.15	.07	.02
☐ 162	Mark Messier	.25	.11	.03
☐ 163	Sergei Nemchinov	.08	.04	.01
☐ 164	James Patrick	.08	.04	.01
☐ 165	Mike Richter	.25	.11	.03
☐ 166	Darren Turcotte	.08	.04	.01
☐ 167	Sergei Zubov	.60	.25	.08
☐ 168	Dave Archibald	.08	.04	.01
☐ 169	Craig Billington	.08	.04	.01
☐ 170	Bob Kudelski	.10	.05	.01
☐ 171	Mark Lamb	.08	.04	.01
☐ 172	Norm MacIver	.08	.04	.01
☐ 173	Darren Rumble	.08	.04	.01
☐ 174	Vladimir Ruzicka	.08	.04	.01
☐ 175	Brad Shaw	.08	.04	.01
☐ 176	Sylvain Turgeon	.08	.04	.01
☐ 177	Josef Beranek	.10	.05	.01
☐ 178	Rod Brind'Amour	.20	.09	.03
☐ 179	Kevin Dineen	.10	.05	.01
☐ 180	Pelle Eklund	.08	.04	.01
☐ 181	Brent Fedyk	.08	.04	.01
☐ 182	Garry Galley	.08	.04	.01
☐ 183	Eric Lindros	3.50	1.55	.45
☐ 184	Mark Recchi	.25	.11	.03
☐ 185	Tommy Soderstrom	.15	.07	.02
☐ 186	Dimitri Yushkevich	.08	.04	.01
☐ 187	Tom Barrasso	.10	.05	.01
☐ 188	Ron Francis	.10	.05	.01
☐ 189	Jaromir Jagr	.60	.25	.08
☐ 190	Mario Lemieux	1.25	.55	.16
☐ 191	Marty McSorley	.10	.05	.01
☐ 192	Joe Mullen	.10	.05	.01
☐ 193	Larry Murphy	.10	.05	.01
☐ 194	Ulf Samuelsson	.10	.05	.01
☐ 195	Kevin Stevens	.25	.11	.03
☐ 196	Rick Tocchet	.10	.05	.01
☐ 197	Steve Duchesne	.10	.05	.01
☐ 198	Stephane Fiset	.08	.04	.01
☐ 199	Valeri Kamensky	.20	.09	.03
☐ 200	Andrei Kovalenko	.15	.07	.02
☐ 201	Owen Nolan	.10	.05	.01
☐ 202	Mike Ricci	.10	.05	.01
☐ 203	Martin Rucinsky	.08	.04	.01
☐ 204	Joe Sakic	.25	.11	.03
☐ 205	Mats Sundin	.25	.11	.03
☐ 206	Scott Young	.08	.04	.01
☐ 207	Jeff Brown	.10	.05	.01
☐ 208	Garth Butcher	.08	.04	.01
☐ 209	Nelson Emerson	.10	.05	.01
☐ 210	Bret Hedican	.08	.04	.01
☐ 211	Brett Hull	1.00	.45	.13
☐ 212	Craig Janney	.15	.07	.02
☐ 213	Curtis Joseph	.25	.11	.03
☐ 214	Igor Korolev	.08	.04	.01
☐ 215	Kevin Miller	.08	.04	.01
☐ 216	Brendan Shanahan	.25	.11	.03
☐ 217	Ed Courtenay	.08	.04	.01
☐ 218	Pat Falloon	.10	.05	.01
☐ 219	Johan Garpenlov	.08	.04	.01
☐ 220	Rob Gaudreau	.25	.11	.03
☐ 221	Artus Irbe	.50	.23	.06
☐ 222	Sergei Makarov	.10	.05	.01
☐ 223	Jeff Norton	.08	.04	.01
☐ 224	Jeff Odgers	.08	.04	.01
☐ 225	Sandis Ozolinsh	.25	.11	.03
☐ 226	Tom Pederson	.08	.04	.01
☐ 227	Bob Beers	.08	.04	.01
☐ 228	Brian Bradley	.08	.04	.01
☐ 229	Shawn Chambers	.08	.04	.01
☐ 230	Gerard Gallant	.08	.04	.01
☐ 231	Roman Hamrlik	.15	.07	.02
☐ 232	Petr Klima	.08	.04	.01
☐ 233	Chris Kontos	.08	.04	.01
☐ 234	Daren Puppa	.10	.05	.01
☐ 235	John Tucker	.08	.04	.01
☐ 236	Rob Zamuner	.08	.04	.01
☐ 237	Glenn Anderson	.10	.05	.01
☐ 238	Dave Andreychuk	.15	.07	.02
☐ 239	Drake Berehowsky	.08	.04	.01
☐ 240	Nikolai Borschevsky	.20	.09	.03
☐ 241	Wendel Clark	.15	.07	.02
☐ 242	John Cullen	.08	.04	.01
☐ 243	Dave Ellett	.08	.04	.01
☐ 244	Doug Gilmour	.50	.23	.06
☐ 245	Dimitri Mironov	.08	.04	.01
☐ 246	Felix Potvin	1.25	.55	.16
☐ 247	Greg Adams	.08	.04	.01
☐ 248	Pavel Bure	1.50	.65	.19
☐ 249	Geoff Courtnall	.08	.04	.01
☐ 250	Gerald Diduck	.08	.04	.01
☐ 251	Trevor Linden	.15	.07	.02
☐ 252	Jyrki Lumme	.08	.04	.01
☐ 253	Kirk McLean	.15	.07	.02
☐ 254	Petr Nedved	.10	.05	.01
☐ 255	Cliff Ronning	.08	.04	.01
☐ 256	Jiri Slegr	.08	.04	.01
☐ 257	Dixon Ward	.08	.04	.01
☐ 258	Peter Bondra	.10	.05	.01
☐ 259	Sylvain Cote	.08	.04	.01
☐ 260	Pat Elynuik	.08	.04	.01
☐ 261	Kevin Hatcher	.10	.05	.01
☐ 262	Dale Hunter	.10	.05	.01
☐ 263	Al Iafrate	.10	.05	.01
☐ 264	Dimitri Khristich	.10	.05	.01
☐ 265	Michal Pivonka	.08	.04	.01

☐ 266	Mike Ridley	.10	.05	.01
☐ 267	Rick Tabaracci	.08	.04	.01
☐ 268	Sergei Bautin	.08	.04	.01
☐ 269	Evgeny Davydov	.08	.04	.01
☐ 270	Bob Essensa	.10	.05	.01
☐ 271	Phil Housley	.10	.05	.01
☐ 272	Teppo Numminen	.08	.04	.01
☐ 273	Fredrik Olausson	.08	.04	.01
☐ 274	Teemu Selanne	1.00	.45	.13
☐ 275	Thomas Steen	.08	.04	.01
☐ 276	Keith Tkachuk	.25	.11	.03
☐ 277	Paul Ysebaert	.08	.04	.01
☐ 278	Alexei Zhamnov	.35	.16	.04
☐ 279	Checklist	.08	.04	.01
☐ 280	Checklist	.08	.04	.01
☐ 281	Patrick Carnback	.15	.07	.02
☐ 282	Bob Corkum	.08	.04	.01
☐ 283	Bobby Dollas	.08	.04	.01
☐ 284	Peter Douris	.08	.04	.01
☐ 285	Todd Ewen	.08	.04	.01
☐ 286	Garry Valk	.08	.04	.01
☐ 287	John Blue	.08	.04	.01
☐ 288	Glen Featherstone	.08	.04	.01
☐ 289	Steve Heinze	.08	.04	.01
☐ 290	Dave Reid	.08	.04	.01
☐ 291	Bryan Smolinski	.60	.25	.08
☐ 292	Cam Stewart	.20	.09	.03
☐ 293	Jozef Stumpel	.08	.04	.01
☐ 294	Sergei Zholtok	.08	.04	.01
☐ 295	Donald Audette	.08	.04	.01
☐ 296	Philippe Boucher	.08	.04	.01
☐ 297	Dominik Hasek	.15	.07	.02
☐ 298	Brad May	.08	.04	.01
☐ 299	Craig Muni	.08	.04	.01
☐ 300	Derek Plante	.75	.35	.09
☐ 301	Craig Simpson	.08	.04	.01
☐ 302	Scott Thomas	.15	.07	.02
☐ 303	Ted Drury	.08	.04	.01
☐ 304	Dan Keezmer	.15	.07	.02
☐ 305	Trevor Kidd	.10	.05	.01
☐ 306	Sandy McCarthy	.08	.04	.01
☐ 307	Frank Musil	.08	.04	.01
☐ 308	Michel Petit	.08	.04	.01
☐ 309	Paul Ranheim	.08	.04	.01
☐ 310	German Titov	.50	.23	.06
☐ 311	Andrei Trefilov	.25	.11	.03
☐ 312	Jeff Hackett	.08	.04	.01
☐ 313	Stephane Matteau	.08	.04	.01
☐ 314	Brian Noonan	.08	.04	.01
☐ 315	Patrick Poulin	.08	.04	.01
☐ 316	Jeff Shantz	.20	.09	.03
☐ 317	Rich Sutter	.08	.04	.01
☐ 318	Kevin Todd	.08	.04	.01
☐ 319	Eric Weinrich	.08	.04	.01
☐ 320	Dave Barr	.08	.04	.01
☐ 321	Paul Cavallini	.08	.04	.01
☐ 322	Mike Craig	.08	.04	.01
☐ 323	Dean Evason	.08	.04	.01
☐ 324	Brent Gilchrist	.08	.04	.01
☐ 325	Grant Ledyard	.08	.04	.01
☐ 326	Mike McPhee	.08	.04	.01
☐ 327	Darcy Wakaluk	.08	.04	.01
☐ 328	Terry Carkner	.08	.04	.01
☐ 329	Mark Howe	.10	.05	.01
☐ 330	Greg Johnson	.08	.04	.01
☐ 331	Vyacheslav Kozlov	.75	.35	.09
☐ 332	Martin Lapointe	.08	.04	.01
☐ 333	Darren McCarty	.20	.09	.03
☐ 334	Chris Osgood	.75	.35	.09
☐ 335	Bob Probert	.08	.04	.01
☐ 336	Mike Sillinger	.08	.04	.01
☐ 337	Jason Arnott	2.50	1.15	.30
☐ 338	Bob Beers	.08	.04	.01
☐ 339	Fred Brathwaite	.15	.07	.02
☐ 340	Kelly Buchberger	.08	.04	.01
☐ 341	Ilya Byakin	.15	.07	.02
☐ 342	Fredrik Olausson	.08	.04	.01
☐ 343	Vladimir Vujtek	.08	.04	.01
☐ 344	Peter White	.15	.07	.02
☐ 345	Stu Barnes	.08	.04	.01
☐ 346	Mike Foligno	.08	.04	.01
☐ 347	Greg Hawgood	.08	.04	.01
☐ 348	Bob Kudelski	.10	.05	.01
☐ 349	Rob Niedermayer	.75	.35	.09
☐ 350	Igor Chibirev	.20	.09	.03
☐ 351	Robert Kron	.08	.04	.01
☐ 352	Bryan Marchment	.08	.04	.01
☐ 353	James Patrick	.08	.04	.01
☐ 354	Chris Pronger	.75	.35	.09
☐ 355	Jeff Reese	.08	.04	.01
☐ 356	Jim Storm	.20	.09	.03
☐ 357	Darren Turcotte	.08	.04	.01
☐ 358	Pat Conacher	.08	.04	.01
☐ 359	Mike Donnelly	.08	.04	.01
☐ 360	John Druce	.08	.04	.01
☐ 361	Charlie Huddy	.08	.04	.01
☐ 362	Warren Rychel	.08	.04	.01
☐ 363	Robb Stauber	.08	.04	.01
☐ 364	Dave Taylor	.10	.05	.01
☐ 365	Dixon Ward	.08	.04	.01
☐ 366	Benoit Brunet	.08	.04	.01
☐ 367	J.J. Daigneault	.08	.04	.01
☐ 368	Gilbert Dionne	.08	.04	.01
☐ 369	Paul DiPietro	.08	.04	.01
☐ 370	Kevin Haller	.08	.04	.01
☐ 371	Oleg Petrov	.25	.11	.03
☐ 372	Peter Popovic	.15	.07	.02
☐ 373	Ron Wilson	.08	.04	.01
☐ 374	Martin Brodeur	.75	.35	.09
☐ 375	Tom Chorske	.08	.04	.01
☐ 376	Jim Dowd	.25	.11	.03
☐ 377	David Emma	.08	.04	.01
☐ 378	Bobby Holik	.08	.04	.01
☐ 379	Corey Millen	.08	.04	.01
☐ 380	Jaroslav Modry	.20	.09	.03
☐ 381	Jason Smith	.15	.07	.02
☐ 382	Ray Ferraro	.08	.04	.01
☐ 383	Travis Green	.08	.04	.01
☐ 384	Tom Kurvers	.08	.04	.01
☐ 385	Marty McInnis	.08	.04	.01
☐ 386	Jamie McLennan	.20	.09	.03
☐ 387	Dennis Vaske	.08	.04	.01
☐ 388	Dave Volek	.08	.04	.01
☐ 389	Jeff Beukeboom	.08	.04	.01
☐ 390	Glenn Healy	.08	.04	.01
☐ 391	Alexander Karpovtsev	.10	.05	.01
☐ 392	Steve Larmer	.10	.05	.01
☐ 393	Kevin Lowe	.08	.04	.01
☐ 394	Ed Olczyk	.08	.04	.01
☐ 395	Esa Tikkanen	.10	.05	.01
☐ 396	Alexandre Daigle	.75	.35	.09
☐ 397	Evgeny Davydov	.08	.04	.01
☐ 398	Dmitri Filimonov	.08	.04	.01
☐ 399	Brian Glynn	.08	.04	.01
☐ 400	Darrin Madeley	.20	.09	.03
☐ 401	Troy Mallette	.08	.04	.01
☐ 402	Dave McIlwain	.08	.04	.01
☐ 403	Alexei Yashin	.75	.35	.09
☐ 404	Jason Bowen	.15	.07	.02
☐ 405	Jeff Finley	.08	.04	.01
☐ 406	Yves Racine	.08	.04	.01
☐ 407	Rob Ramage	.08	.04	.01
☐ 408	Mikael Renberg	.75	.35	.09
☐ 409	Dominic Roussel	.15	.07	.02
☐ 410	Dave Tippett	.08	.04	.01
☐ 411	Doug Brown	.08	.04	.01
☐ 412	Markus Naslund	.15	.07	.02
☐ 413	Pat Neaton	.20	.09	.03
☐ 414	Kjell Samuelsson	.08	.04	.01
☐ 415	Martin Straka	.50	.23	.06
☐ 416	Bryan Trottier	.10	.05	.01
☐ 417	Ken Wregget	.08	.04	.01
☐ 418	Adam Foote	.08	.04	.01
☐ 419	Iain Fraser	.20	.09	.03
☐ 420	Alexei Gusarov	.08	.04	.01
☐ 421	Dave Karpa	.08	.04	.01
☐ 422	Claude Lapointe	.08	.04	.01
☐ 423	Curtis Leschyshyn	.08	.04	.01
☐ 424	Mike McKee	.15	.07	.02
☐ 425	Garth Snow	.25	.11	.03
☐ 426	Jocelyn Thibault	.75	.35	.09
☐ 427	Phil Housley	.10	.05	.01
☐ 428	Jim Hrivnak	.08	.04	.01
☐ 429	Vitali Karamnov	.08	.04	.01
☐ 430	Basil McRae	.08	.04	.01
☐ 431	Jim Montgomery	.20	.09	.03
☐ 432	Vitali Prokhorov	.08	.04	.01
☐ 433	Gaetan Duchesne	.08	.04	.01
☐ 434	Todd Elik	.08	.04	.01
☐ 435	Bob Errey	.08	.04	.01
☐ 436	Igor Larionov	.08	.04	.01
☐ 437	Mike Rathje	.08	.04	.01
☐ 438	Jim Waite	.08	.04	.01
☐ 439	Ray Whitney	.10	.05	.01
☐ 440	Mikael Anderson	.08	.04	.01
☐ 441	Danton Cole	.08	.04	.01
☐ 442	Pat Elynuik	.08	.04	.01
☐ 443	Chris Gratton	.75	.35	.09
☐ 444	Pat Jablonski	.08	.04	.01
☐ 445	Chris Joseph	.08	.04	.01
☐ 446	Chris LiPuma	.15	.07	.02
☐ 447	Denis Savard	.15	.07	.02
☐ 448	Ken Baumgartner	.08	.04	.01
☐ 449	Todd Gill	.08	.04	.01
☐ 450	Sylvain Lefebvre	.08	.04	.01
☐ 451	Jamie Macoun	.08	.04	.01

☐	452	Mark Osborne	.08	.04	.01
☐	453	Rob Pearson	.08	.04	.01
☐	454	Damian Rhodes	.30	.14	.04
☐	455	Peter Zezel	.08	.04	.01
☐	456	Dave Babych	.08	.04	.01
☐	457	Jose Charbonneau	.15	.07	.02
☐	458	Murray Craven	.08	.04	.01
☐	459	Neil Eisenhut	.15	.07	.02
☐	460	Dan Kesa	.15	.07	.02
☐	461	Gino Odjick	.08	.04	.01
☐	462	Kay Whitmore	.08	.04	.01
☐	463	Don Beaupre	.10	.05	.01
☐	464	Randy Burridge	.08	.04	.01
☐	465	Calle Johansson	.08	.04	.01
☐	466	Keith Jones	.08	.04	.01
☐	467	Todd Krygier	.08	.04	.01
☐	468	Kelly Miller	.08	.04	.01
☐	469	Pat Peake	.15	.07	.02
☐	470	Dave Poulin	.08	.04	.01
☐	471	Luciano Borsato	.08	.04	.01
☐	472	Nelson Emerson	.10	.05	.01
☐	473	Randy Gilhen	.08	.04	.01
☐	474	Boris Mironov	.08	.04	.01
☐	475	Stephane Quintal	.08	.04	.01
☐	476	Thomas Steen	.08	.04	.01
☐	477	Igor Ulanov	.08	.04	.01
☐	478	Adrian Aucoin	.25	.11	.03
☐	479	Todd Brost	.15	.07	.02
☐	480	Martin Gendron	.35	.16	.04
☐	481	David Harlock	.08	.04	.01
☐	482	Corey Hirsch	.25	.11	.03
☐	483	Todd Hlushko	.20	.09	.03
☐	484	Fabian Joseph	.20	.09	.03
☐	485	Paul Kariya	4.00	1.80	.50
☐	486	Brett Lindros	6.00	2.70	.75
☐	487	Ken Lovsin	.15	.07	.02
☐	488	Jason Marshall	.08	.04	.01
☐	489	Derek Mayer	.15	.07	.02
☐	490	Petr Nedved	.10	.05	.01
☐	491	Dwayne Norris	.20	.09	.03
☐	492	Russ Romaniuk	.08	.04	.01
☐	493	Brian Savage	.30	.14	.04
☐	494	Trevor Sim	.15	.07	.02
☐	495	Chris Therien	.15	.07	.02
☐	496	Todd Warriner	.60	.25	.08
☐	497	Craig Woodcroft	.15	.07	.02
☐	498	Mark Beaufait	.15	.07	.02
☐	499	Jim Campbell	.20	.09	.03
☐	500	Ted Crowley	.20	.09	.03
☐	501	Mike Dunham	.25	.11	.03
☐	502	Chris Ferraro	.20	.09	.03
☐	503	Peter Ferraro	.25	.11	.03
☐	504	Brett Hauer	.08	.04	.01
☐	505	Darby Hendrickson	.20	.09	.03
☐	506	Chris Imes	.15	.07	.02
☐	507	Craig Johnson	.20	.09	.03
☐	508	Peter Laviolette	.15	.07	.02
☐	509	Jeff Lazaro	.08	.04	.01
☐	510	John Lilley	.25	.11	.03
☐	511	Todd Marchant	.20	.09	.03
☐	512	Ian Moran	.15	.07	.02
☐	513	Travis Richards	.20	.09	.03
☐	514	Barry Richter	.25	.11	.03
☐	515	David Roberts	.25	.11	.03
☐	516	Brian Rolston	.50	.23	.06
☐	517	David Sacco	.25	.11	.03
☐	518	Checklist	.08	.04	.01
☐	519	Checklist	.08	.04	.01
☐	520	Checklist	.08	.04	.01

1993-94 PowerPlay Gamebreakers

Randomly inserted in series two packs, this ten-card set measurs 2 1/2" by 4 3/4". The fronts feature color action cutouts on a borderless marbleized background. The player's name in gold foil appears at the lower right, while the word "Gamebreakers" is printed vertically in pastel-colored lettering on the left side. On the same marbleized background, the backs carry another color photo, with the player's name displayed above and career highlights shown below. The cards are numbered on the back as "X of 10."

	MINT	EXC	G-VG
COMPLETE SET (10)	28.00	12.50	3.50
COMMON PLAYER (1-10)	2.00	.90	.25
☐ 1 Sergei Fedorov	3.50	1.55	.45
Detroit Red Wings			

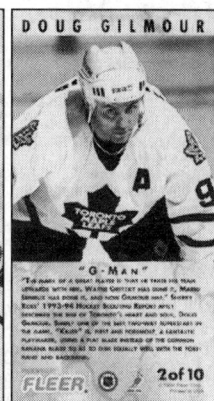

		MINT	EXC	G-VG
☐ 2	Doug Gilmour	2.50	1.15	.30
	Toronto Maple Leafs			
☐ 3	Wayne Gretzky	5.00	2.30	.60
	Los Angeles Kings			
☐ 4	Curtis Joseph	2.00	.90	.25
	St. Louis Blues			
☐ 5	Mario Lemieux	4.00	1.80	.50
	Pittsburgh Penguins			
☐ 6	Eric Lindros	5.00	2.30	.60
	Philadelphia Flyers			
☐ 7	Felix Potvin	3.50	1.55	.45
	Toronto Maple Leafs			
☐ 8	Jeremy Roenick	2.50	1.15	.30
	Chicago Blackhawks			
☐ 9	Patrick Roy	4.00	1.80	.50
	Montreal Canadiens			
☐ 10	Steve Yzerman	2.50	1.15	.30
	Detroit Red Wings			

1993-94 PowerPlay Global Greats

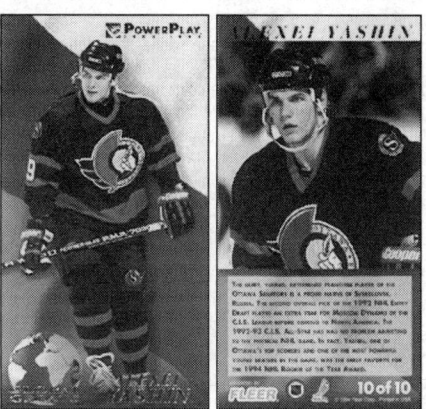

Randomly inserted in series two packs, this 10-card set measures 2 1/2" by 4 3/4". The borderless fronts feature color action cutouts superimposed on the player's national flag. The player's name and the Global Greats logo in gold foil appear at the bottom. On the same national flag background, the backs carry another color photo with the player's name above and career highlights below. The cards are numbered on the back as "X of 10."

	MINT	EXC	G-VG
COMPLETE SET (10)	20.00	9.00	2.50
COMMON PLAYER (1-10)	.50	.23	.06

		MINT	EXC	G-VG
☐ 1	Pavel Bure	6.00	2.70	.75
	Vancouver Canucks			
☐ 2	Sergei Federov	3.50	1.55	.45
	Detroit Red Wings			
☐ 3	Jaromir Jagr	2.00	.90	.25
	Pittsburgh Penguins			
☐ 4	Jari Kurri	.50	.23	.06
	Los Angeles Kings			
☐ 5	Alexander Mogilny	1.50	.65	.19
	Buffalo Sabres			
☐ 6	Mikael Renberg	3.00	1.35	.40
	Philadelphia Flyers			
☐ 7	Teemu Selanne	3.00	1.35	.40
	Winnipeg Jets			
☐ 8	Mats Sundin	1.00	.45	.13
	Quebec Nordiques			
☐ 9	Esa Tikkanen	.50	.23	.06
	New York Rangers			
☐ 10	Alexei Yashin	3.00	1.35	.40
	Ottawa Senators			

1993-94 PowerPlay Netminders

Randomly inserted in series one packs, this eight-card set measures 2 1/2" by 4 3/4". On a blue marbleized background, the fronts feature color action photos with the goalie's name in blue-foil lettering under the photo. On a lighter blue marbleized background, the backs carry another color photo, with the player's name displayed above and career highlights shown below. The cards are numbered on the back as "X of 8."

		MINT	EXC	G-VG
COMPLETE SET (8)		45.00	20.00	5.75
COMMON PLAYER (1-8)		3.00	1.35	.40
☐ 1	Tom Barrasso	3.00	1.35	.40
	Pittsburgh Penguins			
☐ 2	Ed Belfour	7.00	3.10	.85
	Chicago Blackhawks			
☐ 3	Grant Fuhr	3.00	1.35	.40
	Buffalo Sabres			
☐ 4	Curtis Joseph	7.00	3.10	.85
	St. Louis Blues			
☐ 5	Felix Potvin	14.00	6.25	1.75
	Toronto Maple Leafs			
☐ 6	Bill Ranford	3.00	1.35	.40
	Edmonton Oilers			
☐ 7	Patrick Roy	14.00	6.25	1.75
	Montreal Canadiens			
☐ 8	Tommy Soderstrom	5.00	2.30	.60
	Philadelphia Flyers			

1993-94 PowerPlay Point Leaders

Randomly inserted in series one packs, this 20-card set measures 2 1/2" by 4 3/4". The yellow-bordered fronts

feature color action cutouts against a yellow-tinted background. The player's name in silver foil appears under the photo. On a yellow background, the backs carry another color photo with the player's name in silver foil above the photo, and career highlights below. The cards are numbered on the back as "X of 20."

		MINT	EXC	G-VG
COMPLETE SET (20)		25.00	11.50	3.10
COMMON PLAYER (1-20)		.60	.25	.08
☐ 1	Pavel Bure	4.00	1.80	.50
	Vancouver Canucks			
☐ 2	Doug Gilmour	2.00	.90	.25
	Toronto Maple Leafs			
☐ 3	Wayne Gretzky	5.00	2.30	.60
	Los Angeles Kings			
☐ 4	Brett Hull	2.00	.90	.25
	St. Louis Blues			
☐ 5	Jaromir Jagr	1.50	.65	.19
	Pittsburgh Penguins			
☐ 6	Joe Juneau	1.50	.65	.19
	Boston Bruins			
☐ 7	Pat LaFontaine	1.00	.45	.13
	Buffalo Sabres			
☐ 8	Mario Lemieux	4.00	1.80	.50
	Pittsburgh Penguins			
☐ 9	Mark Messier	1.00	.45	.13
	New York Rangers			
☐ 10	Alexander Mogilny	1.00	.45	.13
	Buffalo Sabres			
☐ 11	Adam Oates	.60	.25	.08
	Boston Bruins			
☐ 12	Mark Recchi	1.00	.45	.13
	Philadelphia Flyers			
☐ 13	Luc Robitaille	.60	.25	.08
	Los Angeles Kings			
☐ 14	Jeremy Roenick	2.00	.90	.25
	Chicago Blackhawks			
☐ 15	Joe Sakic	1.00	.45	.13
	Quebec Nordiques			
☐ 16	Teemu Selanne	2.50	1.15	.30
	Winnipeg Jets			
☐ 17	Kevin Stevens	1.00	.45	.13
	Pittsburgh Penguins			
☐ 18	Mats Sundin	1.00	.45	.13
	Quebec Nordiques			
☐ 19	Pierre Turgeon	1.25	.55	.16
	New York Islanders			
☐ 20	Steve Yzerman	2.00	.90	.25
	Detroit Red Wings			

1993-94 PowerPlay Rising Stars

Randomly inserted in series two packs, this ten-card set measures 2 1/2" by 4 3/4". Each borderless front features a color action cutout, highlighted with a yellow "aura" and yellow radial lines, set on a stellar background. The player's name and the words "Rising Star" in silver foil appear in a

color player action shots on grainy and ghosted backgrounds. The player's name and the words "Rookie Standouts" in gold foil are printed atop ghosted bars to the right of the player. The backs carry a color player close-up, with the player's name above and career highlights below. The cards are numbered on the back as "X of 16."

	MINT	EXC	G-VG
COMPLETE SET (16)........................	30.00	13.50	3.80
COMMON PLAYER (1-16)................	.50	.23	.06
☐ 1 Jason Arnott............................	6.00	2.70	.75
Edmonton Oilers			
☐ 2 Jesse Belanger........................	.75	.35	.09
Florida Panthers			
☐ 3 Alexandre Daigle	3.00	1.35	.40
Ottawa Senators			
☐ 4 Iain Fraser..............................	.50	.23	.06
Quebec Nordiques			
☐ 5 Chris Gratton..........................	2.00	.90	.25
Tampa Bay Lightning			
☐ 6 Boris Mironov	.50	.23	.06
Winnipeg Jets			
☐ 7 Jaroslav Modry	.50	.23	.06
New Jersey Devils			
☐ 8 Rob Niedermayer......................	2.00	.90	.25
Florida Panthers			
☐ 9 Chris Osgood	1.50	.65	.19
Detroit Red Wings			
☐ 10 Pat Peake..............................	.75	.35	.09
Washington Capitals			
☐ 11 Derek Plante..........................	1.50	.65	.19
Buffalo Sabres			
☐ 12 Chris Pronger.........................	2.00	.90	.25
Hartford Whalers			
☐ 13 Mikael Renberg	3.00	1.35	.40
Philadelphia Flyers			
☐ 14 Bryan Smolinski......................	2.50	1.15	.30
Boston Bruins			
☐ 15 Jocelyn Thibault.....................	1.50	.65	.19
Quebec Nordiques			
☐ 16 Alexei Yashin........................	3.00	1.35	.40
Ottawa Senators			

top corner. On a similar background, the borderless horizontal back carries another color cutout on the left, with the player's name and career highlights to the right. The cards are numbered on the back as "X of 10."

	MINT	EXC	G-VG
COMPLETE SET (10)........................	25.00	11.50	3.10
COMMON PLAYER (1-10)................	1.50	.65	.19
☐ 1 Arturs Irbe..............................	5.00	2.30	.60
San Jose Sharks			
☐ 2 Vyacheslav Kozlov...................	4.00	1.80	.50
Detroit Red Wings			
☐ 3 Alexandre Daigle	3.50	1.55	.45
Ottawa Senators			
☐ 4 Felix Potvin	7.00	3.10	.85
Toronto Maple Leafs			
☐ 5 Robert Reichel	1.50	.65	.19
Calgary Flames			
☐ 6 Geoff Sanderson	2.00	.90	.25
Hartford Whalers			
☐ 7 Martin Straka	2.00	.90	.25
Pittsburgh Penguins			
☐ 8 Keith Tkachuk	2.50	1.15	.30
Winnipeg Jets			
☐ 9 Alexei Zhamnov.......................	2.50	1.15	.30
Winnipeg Jets			
☐ 10 Sergei Zubov.........................	3.50	1.55	.45
New York Rangers			

1993-94 PowerPlay Rookie Standouts

Randomly inserted in series two packs, this 16-card set measures 2 1/2" by 4 3/4". The borderless fronts feature

1993-94 PowerPlay Second Year Stars

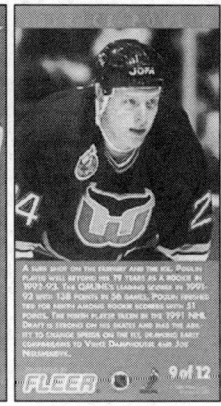

Randomly inserted in series one packs, this 12-card set measures 2 1/2" by 4 3/4". The fronts feature color action photos with light blue metallic borders. The player's name in gold foil appears on the bottom, while the words "2nd Year Stars" are printed in gold foil in an upper corner. On the same light blue metallic background, the backs carry another color player photo with the player's name above and career highlights below. The cards are numbered on the back as "X of 12."

	MINT	EXC	G-VG
COMPLETE SET (12)........................	15.00	6.75	1.90
COMMON PLAYER (1-12)................	.50	.23	.06

		MINT	EXC	G-VG
☐ 1	Rob Gaudreau San Jose Sharks	.50	.23	.06
☐ 2	Joe Juneau Boston Bruins	1.50	.65	.19
☐ 3	Darius Kasparaitis New York Islanders	.50	.23	.06
☐ 4	Felix Potvin Toronto Maple Leafs	4.00	1.80	.50
☐ 5	Eric Lindros Philadelphia Flyers	5.00	2.30	.60
☐ 6	Vladimir Malakhov New York Islanders	.50	.23	.06
☐ 7	Shawn McEachern Los Angeles Kings	.50	.23	.06
☐ 8	Felix Potvin Toronto Maple Leafs	.50	.23	.06
☐ 9	Patrick Poulin Hartford Whalers	.50	.23	.06
☐ 10	Teemu Selanne Winnipeg Jets	2.50	1.15	.30
☐ 11	Tommy Soderstrom Philadelphia Flyers	.50	.23	.06
☐ 12	Alexei Zhamnov Winnipeg Jets	1.50	.65	.19

1993-94 PowerPlay Slapshot Artists

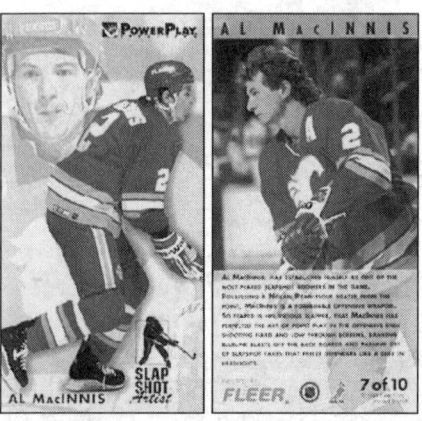

Randomly inserted in series two packs, this ten-card set measures 2 1/2" by 4 3/4". On a team-colored tinted background, the fronts feature color action cutouts with a smaller tinted head shot in an upper corner. The player's name and the Slapshot Artist logo in gold foil appear at the bottom. The bottom portion of the back's color player action photo is ghosted and team color-screened, and carries the player's career highlights. His name appears in black lettering in the team-colored margin above the photo. The cards are numbered on the back as "X of 10."

		MINT	EXC	G-VG
COMPLETE SET (10)		18.00	8.00	2.30
COMMON PLAYER (1-10)		1.00	.45	.13
☐ 1	Dave Andreychuk Toronto Maple Leafs	1.00	.45	.13
☐ 2	Ray Bourque Boston Bruins	1.50	.65	.19
☐ 3	Sergei Federov Detroit Red Wings	5.00	2.30	.60
☐ 4	Brett Hull St. Louis Blues	3.00	1.35	.40
☐ 5	Al Iafrate Washington Capitals	1.00	.45	.13
☐ 6	Brian Leetch New York Rangers	1.50	.65	.19
☐ 7	Al MacInnis Calgary Flames	1.00	.45	.13
☐ 8	Mike Modano Dallas Stars	2.00	.90	.25
☐ 9	Teemu Selanne Winnipeg Jets	4.00	1.80	.50

		MINT	EXC	G-VG
☐ 10	Brendan Shanahan St. Louis Blues	2.00	.90	.25

1990-91 Pro Set

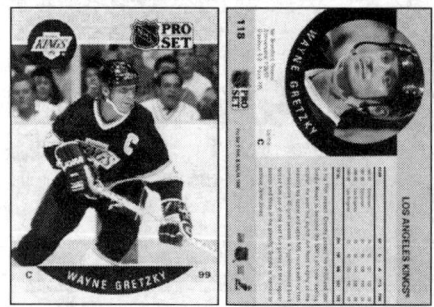

The first series of 1990-91 Pro Set contains 405 cards measuring the standard size (2 1/2" by 3 1/2"). The fronts feature a color action photo, banded above and below in the team's colors. The horizontally oriented backs have a head shot of each player and player information sandwiched between color stripes in the team's colors. Included in this set are 337 player cards, 40 NHL All-Star cards, 12 HOF player cards, and 17 NHL Trophy Collectibles. The set is numbered below alphabetically according to team names as follows: Boston Bruins (1-16), Buffalo Sabres (17-32), Calgary Flames (33-48), Chicago Blackhawks (49-64), Detroit Red Wings (65-80), Edmonton Oilers (81-97), Hartford Whalers (98-113), Los Angeles Kings (114-129), Minnesota North Stars (130-145), Montreal Canadiens (146-161), New Jersey Devils (162-177), New York Islanders (178-194), New York Rangers (195-210), Philadelphia Flyers (211-226), Pittsburgh Penguins (227-242), Quebec Nordiques (243-258), St. Louis Blues (259-274), Toronto Maple Leafs (275-290), Vancouver Canucks (291-306), Washington Capitals (307-322), and Winnipeg Jets (323-336). Also the players' names are alphabetized within their teams. The set is further subdivided as follows: Campbell Conference All-Stars (337-356), Wales Conference All-Stars (357-376), Trophy Collectibles (377-393), and Statistical Leaders (394-405). Pro Set consistently misspelled Massachusetts and Connecticut as Massachussetts and Conneticut for players born in those states; those errors were never corrected. The set as a whole was laden with errors. Randomly inserted in first series packs were numbered Stanley Cup hologram cards. The second series of Pro Set was released in February, 1991 about six months after Pro Set's first release. The second series contains 300 cards measuring the standard size (2 1/2" by 3 1/2"). The fronts and backs are styled the same as the first series. The series is again numbered alphabetically according to team names as follows: Boston Bruins (406-413), Buffalo Sabres (414-420), Calgary Flames (421-426), Chicago Blackhawks (427-434), Detroit Red Wings (435-438), Edmonton Oilers (439-446), Hartford Whalers (447-453), Los Angeles Kings (454-458), Minnesota North Stars (459-465), Montreal Canadiens (466-475), New Jersey Devils (476-481), New York Islanders (482-488), New York Rangers (489-496), Philadelphia Flyers (497-503), Pittsburgh Penguins (504-512), Quebec Nordiques (513-519), St. Louis Blues (520-529), Toronto Maple Leafs (530-542), Vancouver Canucks (543-549), Washington Capitals (550-556), and Winnipeg Jets (557-565). Also the players' names are alphabetized within their teams. The series is further subdivided as follows: teams (566-586), rookies (587-649), career point leaders (650-656), Hall of Fame (657-660), Coaches (661-680), and Referees (681-702). The key Rookie Cards in the set are Ed Belfour, Sergei Fedorov, Jaromir Jagr, Alexander Mogilny, Owen Nolan, Mike Ricci, Jeremy Roenick, and Kevin Stevens.

		MINT	EXC	G-VG
	COMPLETE SET (705)	17.00	7.75	2.10
	COMPLETE SERIES 1 (405)	7.00	3.10	.85
	COMPLETE SERIES 2 (300)	10.00	4.50	1.25
	COMMON PLAYER (1-405)	.05	.02	.01
	COMMON PLAYER (406-705)	.05	.02	.01
☐	1A Brett Hull Promo UER	2.50	1.15	.30
	(Born 9/9/64, 85 games in '87-88, height 6-0, TM under Pro Set logos, aqua blue team color)			
☐	1B Ray Bourque ERR	.30	.14	.04
	(Misspelled Borque on card front)			
☐	1C Ray Bourque COR	.15	.07	.02
☐	2 Randy Burridge	.05	.02	.01
☐	3 Lyndon Byers	.05	.02	.01
☐	4 Bob Carpenter UER	.05	.02	.01
	(Front LW, back C)			
☐	5 John Carter	.05	.02	.01
☐	6 Dave Christian UER	.05	.02	.01
	(28 games with Washington, 50 with Boston)			
☐	7A Garry Galley UER	.10	.05	.01
	(Misspelled Gary on card back)			
☐	7B Garry Galley COR	.10	.05	.01
☐	8 Craig Janney	.15	.07	.02
☐	9 Rejean Lemelin UER	.08	.04	.01
	(Wrong headings, not for goalie; '89-90 stats are Andy Moog's)			
☐	10 Andy Moog UER	.10	.05	.01
	('89-90 stats are Reggie Lemelin's; he was 3rd, not 2nd in Vezina voting)			
☐	11 Cam Neely UER	.15	.07	.02
	(Bruins not capitalized in text)			
☐	12 Allen Pedersen	.05	.02	.01
☐	13 Dave Poulin UER	.08	.04	.01
	(Flyers' stats missing from '89-90)			
☐	14 Brian Propp UER	.08	.04	.01
	(No Flyer stats, only Boston)			
☐	15 Bob Sweeney	.05	.02	.01
☐	16 Glen Wesley	.08	.04	.01
☐	17A Dave Andreychuk ERR	.25	.11	.03
	(Photo actually Scott Arniel on back)			
☐	17B Dave Andreychuk COR	.15	.07	.02
☐	18A Scott Arniel ERR	.05	.02	.01
	(Photo actually Dave Andreychuk on back)			
☐	18B Scott Arniel COR	.05	.02	.01
☐	19 Doug Bodger	.05	.02	.01
☐	20 Mike Foligno	.08	.04	.01
☐	21A Phil Housley ERR	.08	.04	.01
	(No traded stripe)			
☐	21B Phil Housley COR	.08	.04	.01
	(Traded stripe on card front)			
☐	22 Dean Kennedy UER	.05	.02	.01
	(Born Redvers, not Redver)			
☐	23 Uwe Krupp	.08	.04	.01
☐	24 Grant Ledyard	.05	.02	.01
☐	25 Clint Malarchuk UER	.08	.04	.01
	(Back in action 11 days after hurt, not 2 as said on card)			
☐	26 Alexander Mogilny	.50	.23	.06
☐	27 Daren Puppa UER	.08	.04	.01
	(Born 3/23/65, not 3/23/63)			
☐	28 Mike Ramsey	.05	.02	.01
☐	29 Christian Ruuttu UER	.05	.02	.01
	(Misspelled Ruutu)			
☐	30 Dave Snuggerud	.05	.02	.01
☐	31 Pierre Turgeon	.20	.09	.03
☐	32 Rick Vaive UER	.05	.02	.01
	(Sweater 22, not 12)			
☐	33 Theoren Fleury	.15	.07	.02
☒	34 Doug Gilmour	.25	.11	.03
☐	35 Al MacInnis UER	.10	.05	.01
	(Misspelled Allan on card back)			
☐	36 Brian MacLellan	.05	.02	.01
☐	37 Jamie Macoun UER	.05	.02	.01
	(Born 8/17/61, not 8/7/61)			
☐	38 Sergei Makarov	.25	.11	.03
☐	39A Brad McCrimmon	.05	.02	.01
	(No traded stripe, 39 on front)			
☐	39B Brad McCrimmon	.05	.02	.01
	(Traded stripe, 4 on front)			
☐	40A Joe Mullen	.10	.05	.01
	(No traded stripe)			
☐	40B Joe Mullen	.10	.05	.01
	(Traded stripe on card front)			
☐	41 Dana Murzyn	.05	.02	.01
☐	42A Joe Nieuwendyk ERR	1.50	.65	.19
	(Misspelled Niewendyk on card front)			
☐	42B Joe Nieuwendyk COR	.15	.07	.02
☐	43 Joel Otto	.05	.02	.01
☐	44 Paul Ranheim UER	.10	.05	.01
	(Front LW, Back C)			
☐	45 Gary Roberts	.15	.07	.02
☐	46 Gary Suter UER	.08	.04	.01
	(No space between sentences)			
☐	47 Mike Vernon	.08	.04	.01
☐	48 Rick Wamsley	.05	.02	.01
	(Misspelled Rich in bio on card back)			
☐	49 Keith Brown	.05	.02	.01
☐	50 Adam Creighton	.05	.02	.01
☐	51 Dirk Graham UER	.08	.04	.01
	(Sparking, should be sparkling; season was '88-89, not '89-90)			
☐	52 Steve Konroyd UER	.05	.02	.01
	(Front D, back LW)			
☐	53A Steve Larmer ERR	.08	.04	.01
	(Position and sweater number in white, should be black)			
☐	53B Steve Larmer COR	.08	.04	.01
☐	54A Dave Manson ERR	.08	.04	.01
	(Both photos actually Steve Konroyd)			
☐	54B Dave Manson COR	.08	.04	.01
☐	55A Bob McGill ERR	.05	.02	.01
	(No PIM totals on back)			
☐	55B Bob McGill COR	.05	.02	.01
☐	56 Greg Millen	.05	.02	.01
☐	57A Troy Murray	.05	.02	.01
	(Position and sweater number are white)			
☐	57B Troy Murray	.05	.02	.01
	(Position and sweater number are black)			
☐	58 Jeremy Roenick	.75	.35	.09
☐	59A Denis Savard	.08	.04	.01
	(No traded stripe; played 70 games in '86-87)			
☐	59B Denis Savard	.08	.04	.01
	(Traded stripe; played 70 games in '86-87)			
☐	60A Al Secord	.05	.02	.01
	(Called Alan on back)			
☐	60B Al Secord	.05	.02	.01
	(Called Al on back)			
☐	61A Duane Sutter	.05	.02	.01
	(No retired stripe)			
☐	61B Duane Sutter	.05	.02	.01
	(Retired stripe on front)			
☐	62 Steve Thomas	.08	.04	.01
☐	63A Doug Wilson	.05	.02	.01
	(Position and sweater number are white)			
☐	63B Doug Wilson	.08	.04	.01
	(Position and sweater number are black)			
☐	64 Trent Yawney	.05	.02	.01
☐	65 Dave Barr	.05	.02	.01
☐	66 Shawn Burr	.05	.02	.01
☐	67 Jimmy Carson	.08	.04	.01
☐	68 John Chabot	.05	.02	.01

☐ 69 Steve Chiasson	.08	.04	.01
☐ 70 Bernie Federko UER	.08	.04	.01
(Says only player from			
Foam Lake, but			
Elynuik was too)			
☐ 71 Gerard Gallant	.05	.02	.01
☐ 72 Glen Hanlon	.05	.02	.01
☐ 73 Joey Kocur	.05	.02	.01
☐ 74 Lee Norwood	.05	.02	.01
☐ 75 Mike O'Connell	.05	.02	.01
(No retired stripe)			
☐ 76 Bob Probert	.08	.04	.01
☐ 77 Torrie Robertson	.05	.02	.01
☐ 78 Daniel Shank	.05	.02	.01
☐ 79 Steve Yzerman	.25	.11	.03
☐ 80 Rick Zombo	.05	.02	.01
☐ 81 Glenn Anderson	.10	.05	.01
☐ 82 Grant Fuhr	.10	.05	.01
☐ 83 Martin Gelinas UER	.10	.05	.01
(Back photo actually			
Joe Murphy)			
☐ 84 Adam Graves UER	.50	.23	.06
(Stats missing '89-90			
Detroit info)			
☐ 85 Charlie Huddy UER	.05	.02	.01
(No accent in 1st e			
in Defenseur)			
☐ 86 Petr Klima UER	.08	.04	.01
(Born Chomulov, should			
be Chaomutov)			
☐ 87A Jari Kurri	.10	.05	.01
(No signed stripe)			
☐ 87B Jari Kurri	.10	.05	.01
(Signed with Milan)			
☐ 88 Mark Lamb	.05	.02	.01
☐ 89 Kevin Lowe UER	.08	.04	.01
(No accent in 1st e			
in Defenseur)			
☐ 90 Craig MacTavish	.08	.04	.01
☐ 91 Mark Messier	.25	.11	.03
☐ 92 Craig Muni	.05	.02	.01
☐ 93 Joe Murphy	.15	.07	.02
☐ 94 Bill Ranford	.10	.05	.01
☐ 95 Craig Simpson UER	.08	.04	.01
(Should be LW, not C)			
☐ 96 Steve Smith UER	.08	.04	.01
(No accent in 1st e			
in Defenseur)			
☐ 97 Esa Tikkanen	.08	.04	.01
☐ 98 Mikael Andersson	.05	.02	.01
☐ 99 Dave Babych UER	.05	.02	.01
(Extra space included			
after Forum)			
☐ 100 Yvon Corriveau UER	.05	.02	.01
(Washington and Hartford			
games not separate)			
☐ 101 Randy Cunneyworth UER	.05	.02	.01
(Front LW, back C)			
☐ 102 Kevin Dineen	.08	.04	.01
☐ 103 Dean Evason	.05	.02	.01
☐ 104 Ray Ferraro	.08	.04	.01
☐ 105 Ron Francis	.10	.05	.01
☐ 106 Grant Jennings	.05	.02	.01
☐ 107 Todd Krygier	.05	.02	.01
☐ 108 Randy Ladouceur	.05	.02	.01
☐ 109 Ulf Samuelsson	.08	.04	.01
☐ 110 Brad Shaw	.05	.02	.01
☐ 111 Dave Tippett UER	.05	.02	.01
(Front LW, back C)			
☐ 112 Pat Verbeek	.08	.04	.01
☐ 113 Scott Young	.05	.02	.01
☐ 114 Brian Benning UER	.05	.02	.01
(St.Louis and Los Angeles			
stats not separate)			
☐ 115 Steve Duchesne UER	.08	.04	.01
(Kings, should be Kings')			
☐ 116 Todd Elik	.15	.07	.02
☐ 117 Tony Granato UER	.08	.04	.01
(Plays RW, not C)			
☐ 118 Wayne Gretzky	.75	.35	.09
☐ 119 Kelly Hrudey	.08	.04	.01
☐ 120 Steve Kasper	.05	.02	.01
☐ 121A Mike Kushelnyski ERR	.05	.02	.01
(No position and number			
on card front)			
☐ 121B Mike Kushelnyski COR	.05	.02	.01
☐ 122 Bob Kudelski UER	.25	.11	.03
(Born Springfield, not			
Feeding Hills)			
☐ 123 Tom Laidlaw	.05	.02	.01
☐ 124 Marty McSorley	.08	.04	.01
☐ 125 Larry Robinson	.08	.04	.01
☐ 126 Luc Robitaille UER	.20	.09	.03

(Kings, should be Kings')			
☐ 127 Tomas Sandstrom UER......	.08	.04	.01
('89-90 Rangers stats			
not printed)			
☐ 128 Dave Taylor.......................	.08	.04	.01
☐ 129A John Tonelli ERR	.08	.04	.01
(Misspelled Tonnelli			
on card front)			
☐ 129B John Tonelli COR	1.00	.45	.13
☐ 130A Brian Bellows ERR...........	.08	.04	.01
(Back photo actually Dave			
Gagner; front LW, back RW)			
☐ 130B Brian Bellows COR/ERR....	1.00	.45	.13
(Back photo correct,			
facing forward;			
front LW, back RW)			
☐ 131 Aaron Broten UER	.05	.02	.01
(New Jersey and Minnesota			
stats not separate)			
☐ 132 Neal Broten	.08	.04	.01
☐ 133 Jon Casey UER	.08	.04	.01
(GAA 3.22, not 3122)			
☐ 134 Shawn Chambers UER	.05	.02	.01
(Back photo reversed)			
☐ 135 Shane Churla.....................	.25	.11	.03
☐ 136 Ulf Dahlen UER	.05	.02	.01
(Rangers and Minnesota			
stats not separate)			
☐ 137 Gaetan Duchesne	.05	.02	.01
☐ 138 Dave Gagner	.08	.04	.01
☐ 139 Stewart Gavin	.05	.02	.01
☐ 140 Curt Giles	.05	.02	.01
☐ 141 Basil McRae	.08	.04	.01
☐ 142 Mike Modano	.60	.25	.08
☐ 143 Larry Murphy	.08	.04	.01
☐ 144 Ville Siren	.05	.02	.01
☐ 145 Mark Tinordi	.10	.05	.01
☐ 146 Guy Carbonneau UER.........	.08	.04	.01
(Sep Iles should be			
Sept-Iles)			
☐ 147A Chris Chelios...................	.08	.04	.01
(No traded stripe)			
☐ 147B Chris Chelios...................	.08	.04	.01
(Traded stripe)			
☐ 148 Shayne Corson	.08	.04	.01
☐ 149 Russ Courtnall UER	.08	.04	.01
(Front RW, back C)			
☐ 150 Brian Hayward...................	.05	.02	.01
☐ 151 Mike Keane	.10	.05	.01
☐ 152 Stephan Lebeau	.20	.09	.03
☐ 153 Claude Lemieux UER..........	.08	.04	.01
(Reason is misspelled			
as reson)			
☐ 154 Craig Ludwig	.05	.02	.01
☐ 155 Mike McPhee	.05	.02	.01
☐ 156 Stephane Richer	.08	.04	.01
☐ 157 Patrick Roy	.50	.23	.06
☐ 158 Mathieu Schneider	.15	.07	.02
☐ 159 Brian Skrudland	.05	.02	.01
☐ 160 Bobby Smith UER	.08	.04	.01
(No mention of trade from			
Montreal to Minnesota)			
☐ 161 Petr Svoboda	.05	.02	.01
☐ 162 Tommy Albelin	.05	.02	.01
☐ 163 Doug Brown UER	.05	.02	.01
(Born 6/12/64,			
not 7/12/64)			
☐ 164 Sean Burke.......................	.08	.04	.01
☐ 165 Ken Daneyko	.05	.02	.01
☐ 166 Bruce Driver	.05	.02	.01
☐ 167A Viacheslav Fetisov...........	.10	.05	.01
ERR (Misspelled			
Vlacheslav on front)			
☐ 167B Viacheslav Fetisov...........	.10	.05	.01
COR			
☐ 168 Mark Johnson....................	.05	.02	.01
☐ 169 Alexei Kasatonov UER........	.10	.05	.01
(Stats should indicate			
either Soviet or NHL)			
☐ 170 John MacLean UER	.08	.04	.01
(Should have apostrophe			
after Devils)			
☐ 171A David Maley ERR	.05	.02	.01
(Front LW, back C)			
☐ 171B David Maley COR	.05	.02	.01
(LW on both sides)			
☐ 172 Kirk Muller	.08	.04	.01
☐ 173 Janne Ojanen	.05	.02	.01
☐ 174 Brendan Shanahan	.20	.09	.03
☐ 175A Peter Stastny ERR	.08	.04	.01
(Front photo actually			
Patrik Sundstrom)			
☐ 175B Peter Stastny COR	.08	.04	.01
☐ 176A Patrik Sundstrom ERR......	.05	.02	.01

(Front photo actually Peter Stastny)

☐ 176B Patrik Sundstrom COR.....	.05	.02	.01
☐ 177 Sylvain Turgeon	.05	.02	.01
☐ 178 Ken Baumgartner	.05	.02	.01
☐ 179 Doug Crossman UER	.05	.02	.01

(Born 6/30/60, not 5/30/60)

☐ 180 Gerald Diduck	.05	.02	.01
☐ 181 Mark Fitzpatrick.................	.10	.05	.01
☐ 182 Pat Flatley UER.................	.05	.02	.01

(Front C, back RW)

☐ 183 Glen Healy UER	.15	.07	.02

(Misspelled Glenn on card back)

☐ 184 Alan Kerr	.05	.02	.01
☐ 185 Derek King	.08	.04	.01
☐ 186 Pat LaFontaine	.20	.09	.03
☐ 187 Don Maloney	.05	.02	.01
☐ 188 Hubie McDonough UER	.05	.02	.01

(Kings and Islanders stats not separate)

☐ 189 Jeff Norton UER	.05	.02	.01

(Born Cambridge, Mass., not Acton)

☐ 190 Gary Nylund	.05	.02	.01
☐ 191 Brent Sutter......................	.08	.04	.01
☐ 192 Bryan Trottier UER	.08	.04	.01

(Finish the season, not finished)

☐ 193 David Volek UER	.05	.02	.01

(Front LW, back RW)

☐ 194 Randy Wood	.05	.02	.01
☐ 195 Jan Erixon	.05	.02	.01
☐ 196 Mike Gartner UER	.10	.05	.01

(Minnesota and Rangers stats not separate)

☐ 197 Ron Greschner...................	.05	.02	.01
☐ 198A Miloslav Horava ERR	.05	.02	.01

(Mispelled Miroslav)

☐ 198B Miloslav Horava COR	.05	.02	.01
☐ 199 Mark Janssens	.05	.02	.01
☐ 200 Kelly Kisio	.05	.02	.01
☐ 201 Brian Leetch	.25	.11	.03
☐ 202 Randy Moller......................	.05	.02	.01
☐ 203 Brian Mullen......................	.08	.04	.01
☐ 204 Bernie Nicholls UER	.10	.05	.01

(Kings and Rangers stats not separate)

☐ 205A Chris Nilan	.08	.04	.01

(No traded stripe)

☐ 205B Chris Nilan	.08	.04	.01

(Traded stripe on front)

☐ 206 John Ogrodnick..................	.05	.02	.01
☐ 207 James Patrick....................	.05	.02	.01
☐ 208 Darren Turcotte UER	.15	.07	.02

(GP total says 97, should be 96)

☐ 209 John Vanbiesbrouck UER....	.15	.07	.02

(Front C, back G)

☐ 210 Carey Wilson	.05	.02	.01
☐ 211 Mike Bullard......................	.05	.02	.01
☐ 212 Terry Carkner	.05	.02	.01
☐ 213 Jeff Chychrun....................	.05	.02	.01
☐ 214 Murray Craven	.05	.02	.01
☐ 215 Pelle Eklund UER	.05	.02	.01

(Centre and previous, not Center and previously)

☐ 216 Ron Hextall UER................	.08	.04	.01

(Born 5/3/64, not 3/3/64)

☐ 217 Mark Howe	.08	.04	.01
☐ 218 Tim Kerr...........................	.08	.04	.01
☐ 219 Ken Linseman UER	.05	.02	.01

(Bruins and Flyers stats not separate)

☐ 220 Scott Mellanby	.08	.04	.01
☐ 221 Gord Murphy......................	.05	.02	.01
☐ 222 Kjell Samuelsson UER........	.05	.02	.01

(Born 10/18/58, not 10/18/56)

☐ 223 Ilkka Sinisalo....................	.05	.02	.01
☐ 224 Ron Sutter........................	.05	.02	.01
☐ 225 Rick Tocchet	.08	.04	.01
☐ 226 Ken Wregget	.05	.02	.01
☐ 227 Tom Barrasso	.10	.05	.01
☐ 228A Phil Bourque ERR	.05	.02	.01

(Misspelled Borque on both sides)

☐ 228B Phil Bourque COR	.05	.02	.01
☐ 229 Rob Brown UER	.05	.02	.01

(Front RW, back C; actual position is LW)

☐ 230 Alain Chevrier UER.............	.05	.02	.01

(Chicago and Pittsburgh stats not separate)

☐ 231 Paul Coffey........................	.15	.07	.02
☐ 232 John Cullen........................	.08	.04	.01
☐ 233 Gord Dineen UER	.05	.02	.01

(Born Toronto, not Quebec City)

☐ 234 Bob Errey	.05	.02	.01
☐ 235 Jim Johnson UER	.05	.02	.01

(Born Minnesota, not Michigan)

☐ 236 Mario Lemieux UER	.75	.35	.09

(Missed 21 games, not 11)

☐ 237 Troy Loney	.05	.02	.01
☐ 238 Barry Pederson UER	.05	.02	.01

(No Vancouver stats included)

☐ 239 Mark Recchi......................	.50	.23	.06
☐ 240 Kevin Stevens UER............	.50	.23	.06

(Front LW, back C)

☐ 241 Tony Tanti UER	.05	.02	.01

(No Vancouver stats included)

☐ 242 Zarley Zalapski UER	.08	.04	.01

(Pittsburgh misspelled as Pittsburg)

☐ 243 Joe Cirella	.05	.02	.01
☐ 244 Lucien DeBlois UER	.05	.02	.01

(Front C, back RW; misspelled Deblois in bio on card back)

☐ 245A Marc Fortier ERR	.05	.02	.01

(Misspelled Mark on both sides)

☐ 245B Marc Fortier COR	1.00	.45	.13
☐ 246 Paul Gillis..........................	.05	.02	.01
☐ 247 Mike Hough........................	.05	.02	.01
☐ 248 Tony Hrkac UER	.05	.02	.01

(Blues and Nordiques stats not separate)

☐ 249 Jeff Johnson	.05	.02	.01
☐ 250 Guy Lafleur	.10	.05	.01
☐ 251 Curtis Leschyshyn..............	.05	.02	.01
☐ 252 Claude Loiselle..................	.05	.02	.01
☐ 253 Mario Marois......................	.05	.02	.01
☐ 254 Tony McKegney UER	.05	.02	.01

(Red Wings and Nordiques stats not separate)

☐ 255 Ken McRae........................	.05	.02	.01
☐ 256A Michel Petit ERR..............	.05	.02	.01

(Front 21, back 24)

☐ 256B Michel Petit COR..............	.05	.02	.01
☐ 257 Joe Sakic UER...................	.25	.11	.03

(Front 88, back 19)

☐ 258 Ron Tugnutt.......................	.08	.04	.01
☐ 259 Rod Brind'Amour UER	.35	.16	.04

(Misspelled Rob on card back)

☐ 260 Jeff Brown UER	.08	.04	.01

(Nordiques and Blues stats not separate)

☐ 261 Gino Cavallini UER	.05	.02	.01

(On back Meagher is mis-spelled as Meager)

☐ 262 Paul Cavallini.....................	.05	.02	.01
☐ 263 Brett Hull..........................	.50	.23	.06
☐ 264 Mike Lalor UER	.05	.02	.01

(No mention of trade to Washington)

☐ 265 Dave Lowry........................	.05	.02	.01
☐ 266 Paul MacLean	.05	.02	.01
☐ 267 Rick Meagher.....................	.05	.02	.01
☐ 268 Sergio Momesso UER	.10	.05	.01

(Text has 55 pts. in '89-90, stats 56)

☐ 269 Adam Oates........................	.15	.07	.02
☐ 270 Vincent Riendeau	.10	.05	.01
☐ 271 Gordie Roberts...................	.05	.02	.01
☐ 272 Rich Sutter UER	.05	.02	.01

(Canucks and Blues stats not separate)

☐ 273 Steve Tuttle	.05	.02	.01
☐ 274 Peter Zezel UER	.05	.02	.01

(No traded stripe)

☐ 275A Allan Bester ERR	.05	.02	.01

(Misspelled Alan on card front)

☐ 275B Allan Bester COR	.05	.02	.01
☐ 276 Wendel Clark.....................	.15	.07	.02
☐ 277 Brian Curran UER...............	.05	.02	.01

(Plays, not played)

☐ 278 Vincent Damphousse	.08	.04	.01

(Name not listed on

one line)

☐ 279A	Tom Fergus ERR	.05	.02	.01

(Fourth line in bio has
TI, should be that)

☐ 279B	Tom Fergus COR	.05	.02	.01
☐ 280	Lou Franceschetti	.05	.02	.01
☐ 281	Al Iafrate	.08	.04	.01
☐ 282	Tom Kurvers UER	.05	.02	.01

(Played for Toronto
in 71, not 70)

☐ 283	Gary Leeman	.05	.02	.01
☐ 284	Daniel Marois	.05	.02	.01
☐ 285	Brad Marsh	.08	.04	.01
☐ 286	Ed Olczyk UER	.05	.02	.01

(Front C, back RW)

☐ 287	Mark Osborne	.05	.02	.01
☐ 288	Rob Ramage	.05	.02	.01
☐ 289	Luke Richardson	.05	.02	.01
☐ 290	Gilles Thibaudeau UER	.05	.02	.01

(Islanders and Leafs
stats not separate)

☐ 291	Greg Adams UER	.05	.02	.01

(Front LW, back C)

☐ 292	Jim Benning	.05	.02	.01
☐ 293	Steve Bozek	.05	.02	.01
☐ 294	Brian Bradley	.08	.04	.01
☐ 295	Garth Butcher	.08	.04	.01
☐ 296	Vladimir Krutov	.05	.02	.01
☐ 297	Igor Larionov UER	.20	.09	.03

(Stats should indicate
either Soviet or NHL)

☐ 298	Doug Lidster	.05	.02	.01
☐ 299	Trevor Linden	.20	.09	.03
☐ 300	Jyrki Lumme UER	.10	.05	.01

('89-90 Canadiens and
Canucks stats
not separate)

☐ 301A	Andrew McBain ERR	.20	.09	.03

(Back photo actually
Jim Sandlak)

☐ 301B	Andrew McBain COR	.05	.02	.01
☐ 302	Kirk McLean UER	.15	.07	.02

(Career GAA should
be 3.46, not 6.50)

☐ 303	Dan Quinn UER	.05	.02	.01

(Penguins and Canucks
stats not separate)

☐ 304	Paul Reinhart UER	.05	.02	.01

(Born 1/8/60, not 1/6/60)

☐ 305	Jim Sandlak	.05	.02	.01
☐ 306	Petri Skriko	.05	.02	.01
☐ 307	Don Beaupre	.08	.04	.01
☐ 308	Dino Ciccarelli	.08	.04	.01
☐ 309	Geoff Courtnall UER	.08	.04	.01

(Trade stripe missing)

☐ 310	John Druce	.05	.02	.01
☐ 311	Kevin Hatcher	.08	.04	.01
☐ 312	Dale Hunter UER	.08	.04	.01

(Text has rougish,
should be roguish)

☐ 313	Calle Johansson UER	.05	.02	.01

(No accent in first e
in Defenseur)

☐ 314	Rod Langway	.05	.02	.01
☐ 315	Stephen Leach	.05	.02	.01
☐ 316	Mike Liut UER	.08	.04	.01

(Capitals and Whalers
stats not separate)

☐ 317	Alan May	.05	.02	.01
☐ 318	Kelly Miller UER	.05	.02	.01

(Front LW, back C)

☐ 319	Michal Pivonka UER	.10	.05	.01

(1988-89 Goals should
be 8, not 38)

☐ 320A	Mike Ridley ERR	.08	.04	.01

(Errant text reads
points.s)

☐ 320B	Mike Ridley COR	.08	.04	.01
☐ 321	Scott Stevens UER	.10	.05	.01

(No accent in first e
in Defenseur;
1987-886)

☐ 322	John Tucker UER	.05	.02	.01

(1989-90 Buffalo Sabres
team affiliation and
stats missing 8 games;
Ottawa misspelled Ottowa)

☐ 323	Brent Ashton	.05	.02	.01
☐ 324	Laurie Boschman	.05	.02	.01
☐ 325	Randy Carlyle	.05	.02	.01
☐ 326	Dave Ellett	.05	.02	.01
☐ 327	Pat Elynuik	.05	.02	.01
☐ 328	Bob Essensa	.15	.07	.02
☐ 329	Paul Fenton UER	.05	.02	.01

(Front LW, back C)

☐ 330A	Dale Hawerchuk	.08	.04	.01

(No traded stripe;
19089-90; Center
should be Centre)

☐ 330B	Dale Hawerchuk	.08	.04	.01

(Traded stripe on
front; 19089-90; Center
should be Centre)

☐ 331	Paul MacDermid	.05	.02	.01
☐ 332	Moe Mantha	.05	.02	.01
☐ 333	Dave McLlwain UER	.05	.02	.01

(Born 1/9/67, not 6/9/67)

☐ 334	Teppo Numminen	.10	.05	.01
☐ 335A	Fredrik Olausson ERR	.08	.04	.01

(Misspelled Frederik
on both sides)

☐ 335B	Fredrik Olausson COR	.08	.04	.01
☐ 336	Greg Paslawski	.05	.02	.01

(TM after Jets is larger
than other TM symbols)

☐ 337	Al MacInnis AS	.08	.04	.01
☐ 338	Mike Vernon AS	.05	.02	.01
☐ 339	Kevin Lowe AS	.05	.02	.01
☐ 340	Wayne Gretzky AS	.25	.11	.03
☐ 341	Luc Robitaille AS UER	.08	.04	.01

(Fewest shots by Eastern
AS's, not Boston)

☐ 342	Brett Hull AS	.20	.09	.03
☐ 343	Joe Mullen AS	.08	.04	.01
☐ 344	Joe Nieuwendyk AS UER	.08	.04	.01

(Front 26, should be 25)

☐ 345	Steve Larmer AS	.05	.02	.01
☐ 346	Doug Wilson AS UER	.05	.02	.01

(Premier is spelled
premiere)

☐ 347	Steve Yzerman AS	.08	.04	.01
☐ 348A	Jari Kurri AS	.08	.04	.01

(No signed stripe)

☐ 348B	Jari Kurri AS	.08	.04	.01

(Signed stripe on front)

☐ 349	Mark Messier AS	.08	.04	.01
☐ 350	Steve Duchesne AS UER	.05	.02	.01

(Shot record held by
Boston, not East)

☐ 351	Mike Gartner AS UER	.08	.04	.01

(Front 12, should be 11)

☐ 352	Bernie Nicholls AS	.05	.02	.01
☐ 353	Paul Cavallini AS	.05	.02	.01
☐ 354	Al Iafrate AS	.05	.02	.01
☐ 355	Kirk McLean AS	.08	.04	.01
☐ 356	Thomas Steen AS UER	.05	.02	.01

(Should be Doug Smail)

☐ 357	Ray Bourque AS	.08	.04	.01
☐ 358	Cam Neely AS	.10	.05	.01
☐ 359	Patrick Roy AS	.25	.11	.03
☐ 360	Brian Propp AS UER	.05	.02	.01

(Games misspelled
as gamies)

☐ 361	Paul Coffey AS UER	.08	.04	.01

(Front 7, should be 77)

☐ 362	Mario Lemieux AS	.25	.11	.03
☐ 363	Dave Andreychuk AS	.08	.04	.01
☐ 364	Phil Housley AS	.05	.02	.01
☐ 365	Daren Puppa AS	.05	.02	.01
☐ 366	Pierre Turgeon AS	.08	.04	.01
☐ 367	Ron Francis AS	.08	.04	.01
☐ 368	Chris Chelios AS	.05	.02	.01
☐ 369A	Shayne Corson AS ERR	.05	.02	.01

(Misspelled Shane)

☐ 369B	Shayne Corson AS COR	.05	.02	.01
☐ 370	Stephane Richer AS	.05	.02	.01
☐ 371	Kevin Muller AS	.08	.04	.01
☐ 372	Pat LaFontaine AS	.08	.04	.01
☐ 373	Brian Leetch AS	.08	.04	.01
☐ 374	Rick Tocchet AS	.08	.04	.01
☐ 376	Joo Sakic AS	.08	.04	.01
☐ 376	Kevin Hatcher AS	.05	.02	.01
☐ 377	Bob Murdoch Adams UER	.05	.02	.01

(One tie in 1989-90,
should be 11 ties)

☐ 378	Brett Hull Byng UER	.20	.09	.03

(Should be Lady Byng
Memorial Trophy)

☐ 379	Sergei Makarov Calder	.08	.04	.01
☐ 380	Kevin Lowe Clancy	.05	.02	.01
☐ 381	Mark Messier Hart	.08	.04	.01
☐ 382	Moog/Lemelin Jennings	.05	.02	.01
☐ 383	Gord Kluzak Mast UER	.05	.02	.01

(Should be Bill Masterton
Memorial Trophy)

☐ 384	Ray Bourque Norris	.08	.04	.01
☐ 385A	Len Ceglarski Patrick	.20	.09	.03

ERR (No number on back)

385B	Len Ceglarski Patrick COR	.05	.02	.01
386	Mark Messier Pearson	.08	.04	.01
387	Boston Bruins	.05	.02	.01
388	Wayne Gretzky Ross UER	.25	.11	.03
	(Gretzky has won eight Art Ross Trophies)			
389	Rick Meagher Selke	.05	.02	.01
390	Bill Ranford Smythe	.08	.04	.01
391	Patrick Roy Vezina	.25	.11	.03
392	Edmonton Oilers UER	.05	.02	.01
	(Should be Clarence S. Campbell Bowl)			
393	Boston Bruins	.05	.02	.01
394	Wayne Gretzky LL UER	.25	.11	.03
	(Lemieux and Dionne, should read Lemieux only)			
395	Brett Hull LL UER	.20	.09	.03
	(Born 8/9/64, not 9/9/64)			
396	Sergei Makarov ROY	.08	.04	.01
397	Mark Messier MVP	.08	.04	.01
398	Mike Richter RLL UER	.20	.09	.03
	(Plays, not lays)			
399	Patrick Roy LL	.25	.11	.03
400	Darren Turcotte RLL UER (Front RW, back C)	.08	.04	.01
401	Owen Nolan FDP	.40	.18	.05
402	Petr Nedved FDP	.50	.23	.06
403	Phil Esposito HOF	.05	.02	.01
404	Darryl Sittler HOF UER	.05	.02	.01
	(Career: 15 seasons, not stats)			
405	Stan Mikita HOF	.05	.02	.01
406	Andy Brickley UER	.05	.02	.01
	(Front LW, back C/LW)			
407	Peter Douris	.05	.02	.01
408	Nevin Markwart	.05	.02	.01
409	Chris Nilan	.08	.04	.01
410	Stephane Quintal	.10	.05	.01
411	Bruce Shoebottom	.05	.02	.01
412	Don Sweeney	.05	.02	.01
413	Jim Wiemer	.05	.02	.01
414	Mike Hartman	.05	.02	.01
415	Dale Hawerchuk	.08	.04	.01
416	Benoit Hogue	.08	.04	.01
417	Bill Houlder	.10	.05	.01
418	Mikko Makela	.05	.02	.01
419	Robert Ray	.05	.02	.01
420	John Tucker	.05	.02	.01
421	Jiri Hrdina UER	.05	.02	.01
	(Calgary logo on front, should be Pittsburgh)			
422	Mark Hunter	.05	.02	.01
423	Tim Hunter	.10	.05	.01
424	Roger Johansson	.05	.02	.01
425	Frantisek Musil	.05	.02	.01
426	Ric Nattress	.05	.02	.01
427	Chris Chelios	.08	.04	.01
428	Jacques Cloutier	.05	.02	.01
	(White position and number on front, not black)			
429	Greg Gilbert	.05	.02	.01
430	Michel Goulet	.08	.04	.01
	(White position and number on front, not black)			
431	Mike Hudson	.05	.02	.01
432	Jocelyn Lemieux	.05	.02	.01
433	Brian Noonan	.05	.02	.01
434	Wayne Presley	.05	.02	.01
435	Brent Fedyk	.15	.07	.02
436	Rick Green	.05	.02	.01
437	Marc Habscheid	.05	.02	.01
438	Brad McCrimmon	.05	.02	.01
439	Jeff Beukeboom	.15	.07	.02
440	Dave Brown	.10	.05	.01
441	Kelly Buchberger	.05	.02	.01
442	Greg Hawgood	.05	.02	.01
443	Chris Joseph	.05	.02	.01
444	Ken Linseman	.05	.02	.01
445	Eldon Reddick	.05	.02	.01
	(G on back in smaller type)			
446	Geoff Smith	.05	.02	.01
447	Adam Burt	.05	.02	.01
448	Sylvain Cote	.05	.02	.01
449	Paul Cyr	.05	.02	.01
450	Ed Kastelic	.05	.02	.01
451	Peter Sidorkiewicz	.05	.02	.01
452	Mike Tomlak	.05	.02	.01
453	Carey Wilson	.05	.02	.01
454	Daniel Berthiaume	.05	.02	.01
455	Scott Bjugstad	.05	.02	.01
456	Rod Buskas	.05	.02	.01
457	John McIntyre	.05	.02	.01
458	Tim Watters	.05	.02	.01
459	Perry Berezan	.05	.02	.01
460	Brian Propp	.08	.04	.01
461	Ilkka Sinisalo	.05	.02	.01
462	Doug Smail	.05	.02	.01
463	Bobby Smith	.08	.04	.01
464	Chris Dahlquist	.05	.02	.01
465	Neil Wilkinson	.05	.02	.01
466	J.J. Daigneault UER	.05	.02	.01
	(Front Jean Jacques, back J.J.)			
467	Eric Desjardins	.15	.07	.02
468	Gerald Diduck	.05	.02	.01
469	Donald Dufresne	.05	.02	.01
470A	Todd Ewen ERR	.05	.02	.01
	(Photo on back actually Eric Desjardins)			
470B	Todd Ewen COR	1.00	.45	.13
	(Photo on back facing forward)			
471	Brent Gilchrist	.10	.05	.01
472	Sylvain Lefebvre	.05	.02	.01
473	Denis Savard	.08	.04	.01
474	Sylvain Turgeon	.05	.02	.01
475	Ryan Walter UER	.05	.02	.01
	(Front C, back C/LW)			
476	Laurie Boschman	.05	.02	.01
477	Pat Conacher	.10	.05	.01
478	Claude Lemieux	.08	.04	.01
479	Walt Poddubny	.05	.02	.01
480	Alan Stewart	.05	.02	.01
481	Chris Terreri	.15	.07	.02
482	Brad Dalgarno	.05	.02	.01
483	Dave Chyzowski	.05	.02	.01
484	Craig Ludwig	.05	.02	.01
485	Wayne McBean	.05	.02	.01
486	Richard Pilon	.05	.02	.01
487	Joe Reekie	.05	.02	.01
488	Mick Vukota	.05	.02	.01
489	Mark Hardy	.05	.02	.01
490	Jody Hull	.05	.02	.01
491	Kris King	.05	.02	.01
492	Troy Mallette	.05	.02	.01
493	Kevin Miller	.15	.07	.02
494	Normand Rochefort	.05	.02	.01
495	David Shaw	.05	.02	.01
496	Ray Sheppard	.08	.04	.01
497	Keith Acton	.05	.02	.01
498	Craig Berube	.05	.02	.01
499	Tony Horacek	.05	.02	.01
500	Normand Lacombe	.05	.02	.01
501	Jiri Latal	.05	.02	.01
502	Pete Peeters	.08	.04	.01
503	Derrick Smith	.05	.02	.01
504	Jay Caufield	.05	.02	.01
505	Peter Taglianetti UER	.05	.02	.01
	(Front Pete, back Peter)			
506	Randy Gilhen	.05	.02	.01
507	Randy Hillier	.05	.02	.01
508	Joe Mullen	.10	.05	.01
509	Frank Pietrangelo	.05	.02	.01
510	Gordie Roberts	.05	.02	.01
511	Bryan Trottier	.08	.04	.01
512	Wendell Young	.05	.02	.01
513	Shawn Anderson	.05	.02	.01
514	Steven Finn	.05	.02	.01
515	Bryan Fogarty	.05	.02	.01
516	Mike Hough UER	.05	.02	.01
	(Front RW, back LW)			
517	Darin Kimble	.05	.02	.01
518	Randy Velischek	.05	.02	.01
519	Craig Wolanin	.05	.02	.01
520	Bob Bassen	.05	.02	.01
521	Geoff Courtnall	.08	.04	.01
522	Robert Dirk	.05	.02	.01
523	Glen Featherstone	.05	.02	.01
524	Mario Marois	.05	.02	.01
525	Herb Raglan	.05	.02	.01
526	Cliff Ronning	.08	.04	.01
527	Harold Snepsts	.05	.02	.01
528	Scott Stevens	.10	.05	.01
529	Ron Wilson	.05	.02	.01
530	Aaron Broten	.05	.02	.01
531	Lucien DeBlois	.05	.02	.01
532	Dave Ellett	.05	.02	.01
533A	Paul Fenton ERR	.05	.02	.01
	(Trademark on front next to name)			
533B	Paul Fenton COR	.05	.02	.01
534	Todd Gill	.10	.05	.01
535	Dave Hannan	.05	.02	.01

☐ 536	John Kordic	.05	.02	.01
☐ 537	Mike Krushelnyski	.05	.02	.01
☐ 538	Kevin Maguire	.05	.02	.01
☐ 539	Michel Petit	.05	.02	.01
☐ 540	Jeff Reese	.05	.02	.01
☐ 541	David Reid	.05	.02	.01
☐ 542	Doug Shedden	.05	.02	.01
☐ 543	Dave Capuano	.05	.02	.01
☐ 544	Craig Coxe	.05	.02	.01
☐ 545	Kevan Guy	.05	.02	.01
☐ 546	Rob Murphy	.05	.02	.01
☐ 547	Robert Nordmark	.05	.02	.01
☐ 548	Stan Smyl	.05	.02	.01
☐ 549	Ronnie Stern	.05	.02	.01
☐ 550	Tim Bergland	.05	.02	.01
☐ 551	Nick Kypreos	.05	.02	.01
☐ 552	Mike Lalor	.05	.02	.01
☐ 553	Rob Murray	.05	.02	.01
☐ 554	Bob Rouse	.05	.02	.01
☐ 555	Dave Tippett	.05	.02	.01
☐ 556	Peter Zezel UER	.05	.02	.01
	(Card says number 25, sweater shows 9)			
☐ 557	Scott Arniel	.05	.02	.01
☐ 558	Don Barber	.05	.02	.01
☐ 559	Shawn Cronin	.05	.02	.01
☐ 560	Gord Donnelly	.05	.02	.01
☐ 561	Doug Evans	.05	.02	.01
☐ 562	Phil Housley	.08	.04	.01
☐ 563	Ed Olczyk	.05	.02	.01
☐ 564	Mark Osborne	.05	.02	.01
☐ 565	Thomas Steen	.08	.04	.01
☐ 566	Boston Bruins Logo	.05	.02	.01
☐ 567	Buffalo Sabres Logo	.05	.02	.01
☐ 568	Calgary Flames Logo	.05	.02	.01
☐ 569	Chicago Blackhawks Logo	.05	.02	.01
☐ 570	Detroit Red Wings Logo	.05	.02	.01
☐ 571	Edmonton Oilers Logo	.05	.02	.01
☐ 572	Hartford Whalers Logo	.05	.02	.01
☐ 573A	Los Angeles Kings Logo ERR	.05	.02	.01
	(Registration mark missing from Kings on card front)			
☐ 573B	Los Angeles Kings Logo COR	.05	.02	.01
☐ 574	Minn. North Stars Logo	.05	.02	.01
☐ 575	Montreal Canadiens Logo	.05	.02	.01
☐ 576	New Jersey Devils Logo	.05	.02	.01
☐ 577	New York Islanders Logo	.05	.02	.01
☐ 578	New York Rangers Logo	.05	.02	.01
☐ 579	Philadelphia Flyers Logo	.05	.02	.01
☐ 580	Pittsburgh Penguins Logo	.05	.02	.01
☐ 581	Quebec Nordiques Logo	.05	.02	.01
☐ 582	St. Louis Blues Logo	.05	.02	.01
☐ 583	Toronto Maple Leafs Logo	.05	.02	.01
☐ 584	Vancouver Canucks Logo	.05	.02	.01
☐ 585	Washington Capitals Logo	.05	.02	.01
☐ 586	Winnipeg Jets Logo	.05	.02	.01
☐ 587	Ken Hodge Jr.	.05	.02	.01
☐ 588	Vladimir Ruzicka	.10	.05	.01
☐ 589	Wes Walz	.10	.05	.01
☐ 590	Greg Brown	.05	.02	.01
☐ 591	Brad Miller	.05	.02	.01
☐ 592	Darrin Shannon	.10	.05	.01
☐ 593	Stephane Matteau UER	.15	.07	.02
	(Front RW, back LW)			
☐ 594	Sergei Priakin	.05	.02	.01
☐ 595	Robert Reichel	.30	.14	.04
☐ 596	Ken Sabourin UER	.05	.02	.01
	(Front LW, back D; actual position is C)			
☐ 597	Tim Sweeney	.05	.02	.01
☐ 598	Ed Belfour UER	.60	.25	.08
	(Born Carmen, should be Carman)			
☐ 599	Frantisek Kucera	.05	.02	.01
☐ 600	Mike McNeil UER	.05	.02	.01
	(Front C, back LW)			
☐ 601	Mike Peluso	.05	.02	.01
☐ 602	Tim Cheveldae	.20	.09	.03
☐ 603	Per Djoos	.05	.02	.01
☐ 604	Sergei Fedorov	1.00	.45	.13
☐ 605	Johan Garpenlov	.15	.07	.02
☐ 606	Keith Primeau	.25	.11	.03
☐ 607	Paul Ysebaert	.10	.05	.01
☐ 608	Anatoli Semenov	.10	.05	.01
☐ 609	Bobby Holik	.25	.11	.03
☐ 610	Kay Whitmore	.10	.05	.01
☐ 611	Rob Blake	.25	.11	.03
☐ 612	Francois Breault	.05	.02	.01
☐ 613	Mike Craig UER	.10	.05	.01
	(Wearing 50, card says 20)			
☐ 614	J.C. Bergeron UER	.05	.02	.01
	(Front J.C., back Jean Claude)			
☐ 615	Andrew Cassels	.10	.05	.01
☐ 616	Tom Chorske	.05	.02	.01
☐ 617	Lyle Odelein	.20	.09	.03
☐ 618	Mark Pederson	.05	.02	.01
☐ 619	Zdeno Ciger	.05	.02	.01
☐ 620	Troy Crowder	.05	.02	.01
☐ 621	Jon Morris	.05	.02	.01
☐ 622	Eric Weinrich	.05	.02	.01
☐ 623	David Marcinyshyn	.05	.02	.01
	(Card number smaller than other cards in set)			
☐ 624	Jeff Hackett	.10	.05	.01
☐ 625	Rob DiMaio	.05	.02	.01
☐ 626	Steven Rice	.10	.05	.01
☐ 627	Mike Richter	.60	.25	.08
☐ 628	Dennis Vial	.05	.02	.01
☐ 629	Martin Hostak	.05	.02	.01
☐ 630	Pat Murray	.05	.02	.01
☐ 631	Mike Ricci UER	.25	.11	.03
	(Born October, not November)			
☐ 632A	Jaromir Jagr ERR	.75	.35	.09
	(Stat header not lined up with stats on back)			
☐ 632B	Jaromir Jagr COR	.75	.35	.09
	(Stat header lined up with stats on back)			
☐ 633	Paul Stanton	.05	.02	.01
☐ 634	Scott Gordon	.05	.02	.01
☐ 635	Owen Nolan	.30	.14	.04
☐ 636	Mats Sundin	.60	.25	.08
☐ 637	John Tanner	.05	.02	.01
☐ 638	Curtis Joseph	.50	.23	.06
☐ 639	Peter Ing	.05	.02	.01
☐ 640	Scott Thornton	.05	.02	.01
☐ 641	Troy Gamble	.05	.02	.01
☐ 642	Robert Kron	.05	.02	.01
☐ 643	Petr Nedved	.40	.18	.05
☐ 644	Adrien Plavsic	.05	.02	.01
☐ 645	Peter Bondra	.25	.11	.03
☐ 646	Jim Hrivnak	.10	.05	.01
☐ 647	Mikhail Tatarinov	.10	.05	.01
☐ 648	Stephane Beauregard	.10	.05	.01
☐ 649	Rick Tabaracci	.05	.02	.01
☐ 650	Mike Bossy CPL	.05	.02	.01
☐ 651	Bobby Clarke CPL	.05	.02	.01
☐ 652	Alex Delvecchio CPL	.05	.02	.01
☐ 653	Marcel Dionne CPL	.05	.02	.01
☐ 654	Gordie Howe CPL	.25	.11	.03
☐ 655	Stan Mikita CPL	.05	.02	.01
☐ 656	Denis Potvin CPL	.05	.02	.01
☐ 657	Bobby Clarke HOF	.05	.02	.01
☐ 658	Alex Delvecchio HOF	.05	.02	.01
☐ 659	Tony Esposito HOF	.05	.02	.01
☐ 660	Gordie Howe HOF	.25	.11	.03
☐ 661	Mike Milbury CO	.08	.04	.01
☐ 662	Rick Dudley CO	.05	.02	.01
☐ 663	Doug Risebrough CO	.05	.02	.01
☐ 664	Bryan Murray CO	.05	.02	.01
☐ 665	John Muckler CO	.05	.02	.01
☐ 666	Rick Ley CO	.05	.02	.01
☐ 667	Tom Webster CO	.05	.02	.01
☐ 668	Bob Gainey CO UER	.08	.04	.01
	(Stats and bio are Bob McCammon's)			
☐ 669	Pat Burns CO	.08	.04	.01
☐ 670	John Cunniff CO	.05	.02	.01
☐ 671	Al Arbour CO	.08	.04	.01
☐ 672	Roger Neilson CO	.05	.02	.01
☐ 673	Paul Holmgren CO	.05	.02	.01
☐ 674	Bob Johnson CO	.25	.11	.03
☐ 675	Dave Chambers CO	.05	.02	.01
☐ 676	Brian Sutter CO UER	.08	.04	.01
	(Coaching totals say 0-69-21, should be 70-69-21)			
☐ 677	Tom Watt CO	.05	.02	.01
☐ 678	Bob McCammon CO UER	.05	.02	.01

		MINT	EXC	G-VG
(Stats and bio are Bob Gainey's)				
☐ 679	Terry Murray CO	.05	.02	.01
☐ 680	Bob Murdoch CO	.05	.02	.01
☐ 681	Ron Asselstine REF	.05	.02	.01
☐ 682	Wayne Bonney REF	.05	.02	.01
☐ 683	Kevin Collins REF	.05	.02	.01
☐ 684	Pat Dapuzzo REF	.05	.02	.01
☐ 685	Ron Finn REF	.05	.02	.01
☐ 686	Kerry Fraser REF	.05	.02	.01
☐ 687	Gerard Gauthier REF	.05	.02	.01
☐ 688	Terry Gregson REF	.05	.02	.01
☐ 689	Bob Hodges REF	.05	.02	.01
☐ 690	Ron Hoggarth REF	.05	.02	.01
☐ 691	Don Koharski REF	.08	.04	.01
☐ 692	Dan Marouelli REF	.05	.02	.01
☐ 693	Danny McCourt REF UER	.05	.02	.01
(Front Dan, back Danny)				
☐ 694	Bill McCreary REF	.05	.02	.01
☐ 695	Denis Morel REF	.05	.02	.01
☐ 696	Jerry Pateman REF	.05	.02	.01
☐ 697	Ray Scapinello REF	.05	.02	.01
☐ 698	Rob Shick REF	.05	.02	.01
☐ 699	Paul Stewart REF	.05	.02	.01
☐ 700	Leon Stickle REF	.05	.02	.01
☐ 701	Andy van Hellemond REF	.08	.04	.01
☐ 702	Mark Vines REF	.05	.02	.01
☐ 703	Wayne Gretzky 2000th	.50	.23	.06
(2.33 goals per game, should be points) UER				
☐ 704	Stanley Cup Champs	.08	.04	.01
☐ 705	The Puck-La Rondelle	.05	.02	.01
☐ NNO	Stanley Cup Hologram	125.00	57.50	15.50

1990-91 Pro Set Player of the Month

This four-card set features the NHL player of the month for four consecutive months (the month for which the player won the award is listed below his name). The cards measure the standard size, 2 1/2" by 3 1/2". The front has an action photo of the player, bordered above and below in the team's colors. The team logo and "NHL Pro Set" logo overlay the top of the picture. All cards feature the basic 1990-91 Pro Set design, and say NHL Pro Set Player of the Month and the date at the bottom of each obverse. The back presents biographical information and career summary in a horizontal format, again bordered by stripes in the team's colors. The cards are numbered on the back; note that the Peeters card has no number. The cards were issued in the home rink of the winner each month after announcement of the winner. Pro Set sponsors the Player of the Week/Month/Year Awards for the NHL. The first POM was John Vanbiesbrouck, but no card was issued of him. The final POM was Kelly Hrudey, but no card was issued of him. Reportedly less than 25,000 of each POM card were produced.

	MINT	EXC	G-VG
COMPLETE SET (4)	30.00	12.00	3.00
COMMON PLAYER	6.00	2.40	.60

		MINT	EXC	G-VG
☐ NNO	Pete Peeters	6.00	2.40	.60
	POM November 1990			
☐ P1	Tom Barrasso	6.00	2.40	.60
	POM December 1990			
☐ P2	Wayne Gretzky	15.00	6.00	1.50
	POM January 1991			
☐ P3	Brett Hull	9.00	3.75	.90
	POM February 1991			

1991-92 Pro Set NHL Awards Special

This 17-card set features NHL players who were All-Stars, nominees, or winners of prestigious trophies. The cards measure the standard size, 2 1/2" by 3 1/2". The fronts feature a borderless color action photo, with the team logo in the lower left corner, and the player's name in the black wedge below the logo. The backs present player information and the award which the player won or was nominated for, on a white and gray hockey puck background. The cards are numbered on the back and also have a star logo with the words "A Celebration of Excellence". The cards have the 1991-92 Pro Set style of design.

		MINT	EXC	G-VG
COMPLETE SET (17)		150.00	60.00	15.00
COMMON PLAYER (AC1-AC16)		3.50	1.40	.35
☐ AC1	Ed Belfour	12.00	5.00	1.20
☐ AC2	Mike Richter	7.50	3.00	.75
☐ AC3	Patrick Roy	35.00	14.00	3.50
☐ AC4	Wayne Gretzky	60.00	24.00	6.00
☐ AC5	Joe Sakic	12.00	5.00	1.20
☐ AC6	Brett Hull	25.00	10.00	2.50
☐ AC7	Ray Bourque	7.50	3.00	.75
☐ AC8	Al MacInnis	6.00	2.40	.60
☐ AC9	Luc Robitaille	12.00	5.00	1.20
☐ AC10	Sergei Fedorov	25.00	10.00	2.50
☐ AC11	Ken Hodge Jr.	3.50	1.40	.35
☐ AC12	Dirk Graham	3.50	1.40	.35
☐ AC13	Steve Larmer	5.00	2.00	.50
☐ AC14	Esa Tikkanen	3.50	1.40	.35
☐ AC15	Chris Chelios	5.00	2.00	.50
☐ AC16	Dave Taylor	3.50	1.40	.35
☐ NNO	Title Card	3.50	1.40	.35

1991-92 Pro Set NHL Sponsor Awards

This eight-card set is numbered as an extension of the 1991-92 Pro Set NHL Awards Special. The cards are standard size (2 1/2" by 3 1/2") and feature the same glossy color player photos as does the regular issue. The fronts differ in having the name of the award inscribed across the bottom of the card face. Also the backs differ in that they omit the head and shoulders photo and have only a player

profile. The cards were distributed at The Hockey News Sponsor Awards luncheon in Toronto on June 6, 1991. The cards are numbered on the back.

	MINT	EXC	G-VG
COMPLETE SET (8).........................	75.00	30.00	7.50
COMMON PLAYER (AC17-AC23)......	6.00	2.40	.60
☐ AC17 Kevin Dineen..................... Bud Light/NHL Man of the Year Award	7.50	3.00	.75
☐ AC18 Brett Hull .... NHL Pro Set Player of the Year Award	25.00	10.00	2.50
☐ AC19 Ed Belfour......................... Trico Goaltender Award	15.00	6.00	1.50
☐ AC20 Theoren Fleury.................. Alka-Seltzer Plus Award	10.00	4.00	1.00
☐ AC21 Marty McSorley .... Alka-Seltzer Plus Award	7.50	3.00	.75
☐ AC22 Mike Ilitch........................ Detroit Red Wings OWN Lester Patrick Award	6.00	2.40	.60
☐ AC23 Rod Gilbert .... Lester Patrick Award	7.50	3.00	.75
☐ NNO Title Card .... 1990-91 NHL Sponsor Awards	6.00	2.40	.60

1991-92 Pro Set HOF Induction

This 14-card set was issued by Pro Set to commemorate the 1991 Hockey Hall of Fame Induction Dinner and Ceremonies in September, 1991 held in Ottawa. The standard-size (2 1/2" by 3 1/2") cards feature borderless glossy sepia-toned player or team photos on the fronts. A colorful insignia with the words "Hockey Hall of Fame and Museum" appears on the front of each card. The horizontally oriented backs have a facial drawing of the player (circular format) and career

summary; the team cards have no drawings on the back. The team cards represent the past Ottawa Stanley Cup winning teams. The cards are numbered on the back.

	MINT	EXC	G-VG
COMPLETE SET (14).......................	75.00	30.00	7.50
COMMON PLAYER (1-14)................	3.50	1.40	.35
☐ 1 Mike Bossy .... 1991 HOF Inductee	15.00	6.00	1.50
☐ 2 Denis Potvin........................... 1991 HOF Inductee	12.00	5.00	1.20
☐ 3 Bob Pulford .... 1991 HOF Inductee	9.00	3.75	.90
☐ 4 William Scott Bowman........... 1991 HOF Inductee	10.00	4.00	1.00
☐ 5 Neil P. Armstrong .... 1991 HOF Inductee	6.00	2.40	.60
☐ 6 Clint Smith .... 1991 HOF Inductee	6.00	2.40	.60
☐ 7 1903-04 Ottawa Silver .... Seven	3.50	1.40	.35
☐ 8 1905 Ottawa Silver................. Seven	3.50	1.40	.35
☐ 9 1909 Ottawa Senators............	3.50	1.40	.35
☐ 10 1911 Ottawa Senators..........	3.50	1.40	.35
☐ 11 1920-21 Ottawa .... Senators	3.50	1.40	.35
☐ 12 1923 Ottawa Senators..........	3.50	1.40	.35
☐ 13 1927 Ottawa Senators..........	3.50	1.40	.35
☐ 14 Title Card............................. 1991 Hockey Hall of Fame Dinner and Ceremonies	3.50	1.40	.35

1991-92 Pro Set Preview

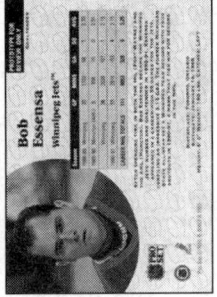

This six-card set was given to dealers to show what the 1991-92 Pro Set hockey set would look like. The cards are standard size, 2 1/2" by 3 1/2". There is really not that much interest in the set due to the relatively poor player selection, i.e., no superstars in the set. The setup of the text on the card backs of these preview cards is different from the regular issue cards; cards are labelled "Promo" on the back where the card number is in the regular issue cards. The David Reid card has an entirely different photo. Even though the cards are unnumbered, they are assigned reference numbers below according to their numbers in the 1991-92 Pro Set regular issue.

	MINT	EXC	G-VG
COMPLETE SET (6)..........................	5.00	2.00	.50
COMMON PLAYER..........................	1.00	.40	.10
☐ 151 Randy Wood NNO..............	1.00	.40	.10
☐ 171 Gord Murphy NNO	1.00	.40	.10
☐ 203 Craig Wolanin NNO	1.00	.40	.10
☐ 229 David Reid NNO	1.00	.40	.10
☐ 266 Bob Essensa NNO	1.50	.60	.15
☐ NNO Title Card	1.00	.40	.10

1991-92 Pro Set

 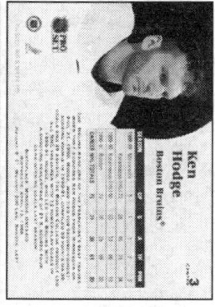

The Pro Set hockey issue contains 615 numbered cards measuring the standard size, 2 1/2" by 3 1/2". The set was released in two series of 345 and 270 cards, respectively. The fronts feature a borderless color action photo, with the team logo in the lower left corner, and the player's name in a black wedge below the logo. The backs have a color head and shoulders shot of the player (circular format) in the upper left corner, as well as biographical and statistical information on a white and gray hockey puck background. The cards are numbered on the back and they are checklisted alphabetically according to teams as follows: Boston Bruins (1-13), Buffalo Sabres (14-26), Calgary Flames (27-39), Chicago Blackhawks (40-52), Detroit Red Wings (53-65), Edmonton Oilers (66-78), Hartford Whalers (79-91), Los Angeles Kings (92-104), Minnesota North Stars (105-117), Montreal Canadiens (118-130), New Jersey Devils (131-143), New York Islanders (144-156), New York Rangers (157-169), Philadelphia Flyers (170-182), Pittsburgh Penguins (183-195), Quebec Nordiques (196-208), St. Louis Blues (209-221), Toronto Maple Leafs (222-234), Vancouver Canucks (235-247), Washington Capitals (248-260), Winnipeg Jets (261-273), Campbell Conference All-Stars (274-295), Wales Conference All-Stars (296-317), Stanley Cup Collectibles (318-319), Trophy Collectibles (320-326), San Jose Sharks (327-331), Historic Cards (332-344), Play Smart (345), Boston Bruins (346-353), Buffalo Sabres (354-360), Calgary Flames (361-368), Chicago Blackhawks (369-375), Detroit Red Wings (376-380), Edmonton Oilers (381-389), Hartford Whalers (390-397), Los Angeles Kings (398-403), Minnesota North Stars (404-411), Montreal Canadiens (412-419), New Jersey Devils (420-427), New York Islanders (428-438), New York Rangers (439-447), Philadelphia Flyers (448-456), Pittsburgh Penguins (457-461), Quebec Nordiques (462-470), San Jose Sharks (471-477), St. Louis Blues (478-488), Toronto Maple Leafs (489-496), Vancouver Canucks (497-505), Washington Capitals (506-513), Winnipeg Jets (514-519), Rookies (520-566), Captains (567-588), Historic Cards (589-598), Mid-Season Goals-Against Average Leaders (599-603), Mid-Season Power Play Goal Leaders (604-607), Mid-Season Plus/Minus Leaders (608-611), and Play Smart (612-615). Pro Set also issued a French version. French wax boxes also contained randomly inserted Patrick Roy personally autographed cards signed and numbered on the back; 1,000 of card number 125 (first series) and 1,000 of card number 599 numbered 1001 to 2000 (second series). Randomly inserted in U.S. packs were a limited quantity of Kirk McLean autographed cards. Membership applications for the Rink Rat Fan Club were inserted into wax packs and entitle those who join to receive an exclusive collectible card twice a year. Ten thousand hand-numbered 3-D hologram cards were inserted in second series foil packs to commemorate the NHL's Diamond Anniversary. The key Rookie Cards in the second series are Tony Amonte, Nicklas Lidstrom, Geoff Sanderson, and Doug Weight.

		MINT	EXC	G-VG
	COMPLETE SET (615)	15.00	6.75	1.90
	COMPLETE SERIES 1 (345)	7.50	3.40	.95
	COMPLETE SERIES 2 (270)	7.50	3.40	.95
	COMMON PLAYER (1-345)	.05	.02	.01
	COMMON PLAYER (346-615)	.05	.02	.01
	*FRENCH VERSION: SAME VALUE...			
☐ 1	Glen Wesley	.05	.02	.01
☐ 2	Craig Janney	.15	.07	.02
☐ 3	Ken Hodge Jr.	.05	.02	.01
☐ 4	Randy Burridge	.05	.02	.01
☐ 5	Cam Neely	.15	.07	.02
☐ 6	Bob Sweeney	.05	.02	.01
☐ 7	Garry Galley	.05	.02	.01
☐ 8	Petri Skriko	.05	.02	.01
☐ 9	Ray Bourque	.15	.07	.02
☐ 10	Andy Moog UER	.05	.02	.01
	(4.0 record, should be 4-0)			
☐ 11	Dave Christian	.05	.02	.01
☐ 12	Dave Poulin	.08	.04	.01
☐ 13	Jeff Lazaro	.05	.02	.01
☐ 14	Darrin Shannon	.05	.02	.01
☐ 15	Pierre Turgeon UER	.25	.11	.03
	(Born 8/29, not 8/28)			
☐ 16	Alexander Mogilny	.40	.18	.05
☐ 17	Benoit Hogue UER	.05	.02	.01
	(Stats show two seasons with Winnipeg, should say Buffalo)			
☐ 18	Dave Snuggerud	.05	.02	.01
☐ 19	Doug Bodger UER	.05	.02	.01
	(Second highest offensive total of his career, should say third highest)			
☐ 20	Uwe Krupp	.05	.02	.01
	(Phil and Joan Spector visible in stands)			
☐ 21	Daren Puppa	.08	.04	.01
☐ 22	Christian Ruuttu	.05	.02	.01
☐ 23	Dave Andreychuk	.15	.07	.02
☐ 24	Dale Hawerchuk	.08	.04	.01
☐ 25	Mike Ramsey	.05	.02	.01
☐ 26	Rick Vaive	.05	.02	.01
☐ 27	Stephane Matteau	.05	.02	.01
☐ 28	Theoren Fleury	.15	.07	.02
☐ 29	Joe Nieuwendyk	.10	.05	.01
☐ 30	Gary Roberts	.08	.04	.01
☐ 31	Paul Ranheim	.05	.02	.01
☐ 32	Gary Suter	.08	.04	.01
☐ 33	Al MacInnis	.10	.05	.01
☒ 34	Doug Gilmour	.25	.11	.03
☐ 35	Mike Vernon	.08	.04	.01
☐ 36	Carey Wilson	.05	.02	.01
☐ 37	Joel Otto UER	.05	.02	.01
	(Flame's has a tick mark instead of an apostrophe)			
☐ 38	Jamie Macoun	.05	.02	.01
☐ 39	Sergei Makarov	.08	.04	.01
☐ 40	Jeremy Roenick	.50	.23	.06
☐ 41	Dave Manson	.08	.04	.01
☐ 42	Adam Creighton	.05	.02	.01
☐ 43	Ed Belfour	.25	.11	.03
☐ 44	Wayne Presley	.05	.02	.01
☐ 45	Steve Thomas	.08	.04	.01
☐ 46	Troy Murray	.05	.02	.01
☐ 47	Bob McGill	.05	.02	.01
☐ 48	Chris Chelios	.08	.04	.01
☐ 49	Steve Larmer	.08	.04	.01
☐ 50	Michel Goulet	.08	.04	.01
☐ 51	Dirk Graham	.05	.02	.01
☐ 52	Doug Wilson	.08	.04	.01
☐ 53	Sergei Fedorov	.60	.25	.08
☐ 54	Yves Racine	.05	.02	.01
☐ 55	Jimmy Carson	.08	.04	.01
☐ 56	Johan Garpenlov	.05	.02	.01
☐ 57	Tim Cheveldae	.08	.04	.01
☐ 58	Shawn Burr	.05	.02	.01
☐ 59	Paul Ysebaert	.05	.02	.01
☐ 60	Kevin Miller	.08	.04	.01
☐ 61	Bob Probert	.08	.04	.01
☐ 62	Steve Yzerman	.25	.11	.03
☐ 63	Gerard Gallant	.05	.02	.01

☐ 64	Rick Zombo	.05	.02	.01
☐ 65	Dave Barr	.05	.02	.01
☐ 66	Martin Gelinas	.05	.02	.01
☐ 67	Adam Graves UER	.25	.11	.03
	(Kid Line included Gelinas, not Simpson)			
☐ 68	Joe Murphy	.08	.04	.01
☐ 69	Craig Simpson	.08	.04	.01
☐ 70	Bill Ranford	.08	.04	.01
☐ 71	Esa Tikkanen	.08	.04	.01
☐ 72	Petr Klima	.05	.02	.01
☐ 73	Steve Smith	.08	.04	.01
☐ 74	Mark Messier	.25	.11	.03
☐ 75	Glenn Anderson	.08	.04	.01
☐ 76	Kevin Lowe	.08	.04	.01
☐ 77	Craig MacTavish	.05	.02	.01
☐ 78	Grant Fuhr	.08	.04	.01
☐ 79	Bobby Holik	.08	.04	.01
☐ 80	Rob Brown	.05	.02	.01
☐ 81	Doug Houda	.05	.02	.01
☐ 82	Sylvain Cote	.05	.02	.01
☐ 83	Todd Krygier	.05	.02	.01
☐ 84	Dean Evason	.05	.02	.01
☐ 85	John Cullen	.05	.02	.01
☐ 86	Pat Verbeek	.08	.04	.01
☐ 87	Brad Shaw	.05	.02	.01
☐ 88	Paul Cyr UER	.05	.02	.01
	(Stats show New York, should say NY Rangers)			
☐ 89	Kevin Dineen	.08	.04	.01
☐ 90	Peter Sidorkiewicz	.05	.02	.01
☐ 91	Zarley Zalapski	.05	.02	.01
☐ 92	Rob Blake	.15	.07	.02
☐ 93	Jari Kurri UER	.10	.05	.01
	(No transaction line on front, although back says Kings)			
☐ 94	Todd Elik	.05	.02	.01
☐ 95	Luc Robitaille	.15	.07	.02
☐ 96	Steve Duchesne	.08	.04	.01
☐ 97	Tomas Sandstrom	.08	.04	.01
☐ 98	Tony Granato	.08	.04	.01
☐ 99	Bob Kudelski	.08	.04	.01
☐ 100	Marty McSorley	.08	.04	.01
☐ 101	Wayne Gretzky	1.00	.45	.13
☐ 102	Kelly Hrudey	.08	.04	.01
☐ 103	Dave Taylor	.08	.04	.01
☐ 104	Larry Robinson	.08	.04	.01
☐ 105	Mike Modano	.30	.14	.04
☐ 106	Ulf Dahlen	.08	.04	.01
☐ 107	Mark Tinordi	.08	.04	.01
☐ 108	Dave Gagner	.08	.04	.01
☐ 109	Brian Bellows	.08	.04	.01
☐ 110	Gaetan Duchesne	.05	.02	.01
☐ 111	Jon Casey	.08	.04	.01
☐ 112	Neal Broten	.08	.04	.01
☐ 113	Brian Propp	.08	.04	.01
☐ 114	Curt Giles	.05	.02	.01
☐ 115	Bobby Smith	.08	.04	.01
☐ 116	Jim Johnson	.05	.02	.01
☐ 117	Doug Smail	.05	.02	.01
☐ 118	Eric Desjardins	.08	.04	.01
☐ 119	Mathieu Schneider	.08	.04	.01
☐ 120	Stephan Lebeau	.15	.07	.02
☐ 121	Mike Keane	.05	.02	.01
☐ 122	Stephane Richer	.08	.04	.01
☐ 123	Petr Svoboda	.05	.02	.01
☐ 124	J.J. Daigneault	.05	.02	.01
☐ 125	Patrick Roy	.50	.23	.06
☐ 126	Russ Courtnall	.08	.04	.01
☐ 127	Brian Skrudland	.05	.02	.01
☐ 128	Denis Savard	.08	.04	.01
☐ 129	Mike McPhee	.05	.02	.01
☐ 130	Guy Carbonneau	.08	.04	.01
☐ 131	Brendan Shanahan	.25	.11	.03
☐ 132	Sean Burke	.08	.04	.01
☐ 133	Eric Weinrich	.05	.02	.01
☐ 134	Kirk Muller	.08	.04	.01
☐ 135	Claude Lemieux	.08	.04	.01
☐ 136	John MacLean	.08	.04	.01
☐ 137	Chris Terreri	.08	.04	.01
☐ 138	Doug Brown	.05	.02	.01
☐ 139	Ken Daneyko	.05	.02	.01
☐ 140	Bruce Driver	.05	.02	.01
☐ 141	Patrik Sundstrom	.05	.02	.01
☐ 142	Viacheslav Fetisov	.08	.04	.01
☐ 143	Peter Stastny	.08	.04	.01
☐ 144	Wayne McBean	.05	.02	.01
☐ 145	Bill Berg	.05	.02	.01
☐ 146	Derek King	.08	.04	.01
☐ 147	David Volek	.05	.02	.01
☐ 148	Jeff Norton	.05	.02	.01
☐ 149	Pat LaFontaine	.20	.09	.03

☐ 150	Gary Nylund	.05	.02	.01
☐ 151	Randy Wood	.05	.02	.01
☐ 152	Pat Flatley	.05	.02	.01
☐ 153	Glenn Healy	.08	.04	.01
☐ 154	Brent Sutter	.08	.04	.01
☐ 155	Craig Ludwig	.05	.02	.01
☐ 156	Ray Ferraro	.08	.04	.01
☐ 157	Troy Mallette	.05	.02	.01
☐ 158	Mark Janssens	.05	.02	.01
☐ 159	Brian Leetch UER	.30	.14	.04
	(Career points total 329, should be 229)			
☐ 160	Darren Turcotte	.05	.02	.01
☐ 161	Mike Richter	.25	.11	.03
☐ 162	Ray Sheppard	.08	.04	.01
☐ 163	Randy Moller	.05	.02	.01
☐ 164	James Patrick	.05	.02	.01
☐ 165	Brian Mullen UER	.08	.04	.01
	(Transaction says drafted by San Jose, was actually traded)			
☐ 166	Bernie Nicholls	.08	.04	.01
☐ 167	Mike Gartner	.10	.05	.01
☐ 168	Kelly Kisio UER	.05	.02	.01
	(Transaction says drafted by Minnesota, was actually traded to San Jose)			
☐ 169	John Ogrodnick	.05	.02	.01
☐ 170	Mike Ricci	.15	.07	.02
☐ 171	Gord Murphy	.05	.02	.01
☐ 172	Scott Mellanby	.05	.02	.01
☐ 173	Terry Carkner	.05	.02	.01
☐ 174	Derrick Smith	.05	.02	.01
☐ 175	Murray Craven	.05	.02	.01
☐ 176	Ron Hextall	.08	.04	.01
☐ 177	Rick Tocchet	.08	.04	.01
☐ 178	Ron Sutter	.05	.02	.01
☐ 179	Pelle Eklund	.05	.02	.01
☐ 180	Tim Kerr UER	.08	.04	.01
	(Only transaction line to show a date)			
☐ 181	Kjell Samuelsson	.05	.02	.01
☐ 182	Mark Howe	.08	.04	.01
☐ 183	Jaromir Jagr	.50	.23	.06
☐ 184	Mark Recchi	.30	.14	.04
☐ 185	Kevin Stevens	.25	.11	.03
☐ 186	Tom Barrasso	.08	.04	.01
☐ 187	Bob Errey	.05	.02	.01
☐ 188	Ron Francis	.08	.04	.01
☐ 189	Phil Bourque	.05	.02	.01
☐ 190	Paul Coffey	.15	.07	.02
☐ 191	Joe Mullen	.10	.05	.01
☐ 192	Bryan Trottier	.08	.04	.01
☐ 193	Larry Murphy	.08	.04	.01
☐ 194	Mario Lemieux	.75	.35	.09
☐ 195	Scott Young	.05	.02	.01
☐ 196	Owen Nolan	.15	.07	.02
☐ 197	Mats Sundin	.25	.11	.03
☐ 198	Curtis Leschyshyn	.05	.02	.01
☐ 199	Joe Sakic	.25	.11	.03
☐ 200	Bryan Fogarty	.05	.02	.01
☐ 201	Stephane Morin	.05	.02	.01
☐ 202	Ron Tugnutt	.05	.02	.01
☐ 203	Craig Wolanin	.05	.02	.01
☐ 204	Steven Finn	.05	.02	.01
☐ 205	Tony Hrkac	.05	.02	.01
☐ 206	Randy Velischek	.05	.02	.01
☐ 207	Alexei Gusarov	.10	.05	.01
☐ 208	Scott Pearson	.05	.02	.01
☐ 209	Dan Quinn	.05	.02	.01
☐ 210	Garth Butcher	.05	.02	.01
☐ 211	Rod Brind'Amour UER	.15	.07	.02
	(Type in stat box is smaller than others)			
☐ 212	Jeff Brown	.08	.04	.01
☐ 213	Vincent Riendeau	.05	.02	.01
☐ 214	Paul Cavallini	.05	.02	.01
☐ 215	Brett Hull	.50	.23	.06
☐ 216	Scott Stevens	.10	.05	.01
☐ 217	Rich Sutter	.05	.02	.01
☐ 218	Gino Cavallini	.05	.02	.01
☐ 219	Adam Oates UER	.15	.07	.02
	(Stats are off-line from top to bottom)			
☐ 220	Ron Wilson	.05	.02	.01
☐ 221	Bob Bassen	.05	.02	.01
☐ 222	Peter Ing	.05	.02	.01
☐ 223	Daniel Marois	.05	.02	.01
☐ 224	Vincent Damphousse	.08	.04	.01
☐ 225	Wendel Clark UER	.15	.07	.02
	(Connecticut not capitalized in last line)			

☐ 226 Todd Gill	.05	.02	.01
☐ 227 Peter Zezel	.05	.02	.01
☐ 228 Bob Rouse	.05	.02	.01
☐ 229 David Reid	.05	.02	.01
☐ 230 Dave Ellett	.05	.02	.01
☐ 231 Gary Leeman	.05	.02	.01
☐ 232 Rob Ramage	.05	.02	.01
☐ 233 Mike Krushelnyski	.05	.02	.01
☐ 234 Tom Fergus	.05	.02	.01
☐ 235 Petr Nedved	.20	.09	.03
☐ 236 Trevor Linden	.25	.11	.03
☐ 237 Dave Capuano	.05	.02	.01
☐ 238 Troy Gamble	.05	.02	.01
☐ 239 Robert Kron UER	.05	.02	.01
(Type in stat box is			
smaller than others)			
☐ 240 Jyrki Lumme	.05	.02	.01
☐ 241 Cliff Ronning	.08	.04	.01
☐ 242 Sergio Momesso	.05	.02	.01
☐ 243 Greg Adams	.05	.02	.01
☐ 244 Tom Kurvers	.05	.02	.01
☐ 245 Geoff Courtnall	.08	.04	.01
☐ 246 Igor Larionov	.08	.04	.01
☐ 247 Doug Lidster UER	.05	.02	.01
(No space between 51			
and assist in last			
line of text)			
☐ 248 Calle Johansson	.05	.02	.01
☐ 249 Kevin Hatcher	.08	.04	.01
☐ 250 Al Iafrate	.08	.04	.01
☐ 251 John Druce	.05	.02	.01
☐ 252 Michal Pivonka	.08	.04	.01
☐ 253 Stephen Leach	.05	.02	.01
☐ 254 Mike Ridley	.08	.04	.01
☐ 255 Mike Lalor	.05	.02	.01
☐ 256 Kelly Miller	.05	.02	.01
☐ 257 Don Beaupre	.08	.04	.01
☐ 258 Dino Ciccarelli	.08	.04	.01
☐ 259 Rod Langway	.05	.02	.01
☐ 260 Dimitri Khristich	.08	.04	.01
☐ 261 Teppo Numminen	.05	.02	.01
☐ 262 Pat Elynuik	.05	.02	.01
☐ 263 Danton Cole	.05	.02	.01
☐ 264 Fredrik Olausson UER	.08	.04	.01
(Fifth line of text,			
the word the is missing			
between in and 10th)			
☐ 265 Ed Olczyk	.05	.02	.01
☐ 266 Bob Essensa	.08	.04	.01
☐ 267 Phil Housley	.08	.04	.01
☐ 268 Shawn Cronin	.05	.02	.01
☐ 269 Paul MacDermid	.05	.02	.01
☐ 270 Mark Osborne	.05	.02	.01
☐ 271 Thomas Steen	.05	.02	.01
☐ 272 Brent Ashton	.05	.02	.01
☐ 273 Randy Carlyle	.05	.02	.01
☐ 274 Theoren Fleury AS	.12	.05	.02
☐ 275 Al MacInnis AS	.12	.05	.02
☐ 276 Gary Suter AS	.10	.05	.01
☐ 277 Mike Vernon AS	.12	.05	.02
☐ 278 Chris Chelios AS	.12	.05	.02
☐ 279 Steve Larmer AS	.10	.05	.01
☐ 280 Jeremy Roenick AS UER	.20	.09	.03
(Player's has tick mark			
instead of apostrophe)			
☐ 281 Steve Yzerman AS	.15	.07	.02
☐ 282 Mark Messier AS	.12	.05	.02
☐ 283 Bill Ranford AS	.10	.05	.01
☐ 284 Steve Smith AS	.10	.05	.01
☐ 285 Wayne Gretzky AS	.35	.16	.04
☐ 286 Luc Robitaille AS	.12	.05	.02
☐ 287 Tomas Sandstrom AS	.10	.05	.01
☐ 288 Dave Gagner AS	.10	.05	.01
☐ 289 Bobby Smith AS	.10	.05	.01
☐ 290 Brett Hull AS	.20	.09	.03
☐ 291 Adam Oates AS	.12	.05	.02
☐ 292 Scott Stevens AS	.12	.05	.02
☐ 293 Vincent Damphousse AS	.12	.05	.02
☐ 294 Trevor Linden AS	.12	.05	.02
☐ 295 Phil Housley AS	.10	.05	.01
☐ 296 Ray Bourque AS	.12	.05	.02
☐ 297 Dave Christian AS	.10	.05	.01
☐ 298 Garry Galley AS	.10	.05	.01
☐ 299 Andy Moog AS	.12	.05	.02
☐ 300 Cam Neely AS	.12	.05	.02
☐ 301 Uwe Krupp AS	.10	.05	.01
☐ 302 John Cullen AS	.10	.05	.01
☐ 303 Pat Verbeek AS	.10	.05	.01
☐ 304 Patrick Roy AS	.25	.11	.03
☐ 305 Denis Savard AS	.12	.05	.02
☐ 306 Brian Skrudland AS	.10	.05	.01
☐ 307 John MacLean AS	.10	.05	.01
☐ 308 Pat LaFontaine AS	.12	.05	.02
☐ 309 Brian Leetch AS	.15	.07	.02
☐ 310 Darren Turcotte AS	.10	.05	.01
☐ 311 Rick Tocchet AS	.12	.05	.02
☐ 312 Paul Coffey AS	.12	.05	.02
☐ 313 Mark Recchi AS	.12	.05	.02
☐ 314 Kevin Stevens AS	.12	.05	.02
☐ 315 Joe Sakic AS	.12	.05	.02
☐ 316 Kevin Hatcher AS	.12	.05	.02
☐ 317 Guy Lafleur AS	.12	.05	.02
☐ 318 Mario Lemieux UER	.25	.11	.03
Conn Smythe			
(Should be holding			
Smythe, not Stanley Cup)			
☐ 319 Pittsburgh Penguins	.10	.05	.01
Stanley Cup Champs UER			
(On fourth line, says			
won in 5 games, should			
say 6 games)			
☐ 320 Brett Hull	.20	.09	.03
Hart Trophy			
☐ 321 Ed Belfour	.12	.05	.02
Vezina/Jennings			
☐ 322 Ray Bourque	.12	.05	.02
Norris			
☐ 323 Dirk Graham	.10	.05	.01
Selke			
☐ 324 Wayne Gretzky UER	.35	.16	.04
Ross/Lady Byng			
(Year's has tick mark,			
instead of apostrophe)			
☐ 325 Dave Taylor	.10	.05	.01
King Clancy Trophy			
☐ 326 Brett Hull	.20	.09	.03
PS Player of the Year			
☐ 327 Brian Hayward	.05	.02	.01
☐ 328 Neil Wilkinson UER	.05	.02	.01
(Born Manitoba,			
not Minnesota)			
☐ 329 Craig Coxe UER	.05	.02	.01
(Jose's has tick mark,			
instead of apostrophe)			
☐ 330 Rob Zettler	.05	.02	.01
☐ 331 Jeff Hackett	.05	.02	.01
☐ 332 Joe Malone	.08	.04	.01
☐ 333 Georges Vezina	.15	.07	.02
☐ 334 The Modern Arena	.08	.04	.01
☐ 335 Ace Bailey Benefit	.08	.04	.01
☐ 336 Howie Morenz	.15	.07	.02
☐ 337 The Punch Line	.08	.04	.01
☐ 338 The Kid Line	.08	.04	.01
☐ 339 Before the Zamboni	.08	.04	.01
☐ 340 Bill Barilko	.25	.11	.03
☐ 341 Jacques Plante	.15	.07	.02
☐ 342 Arena Designs	.08	.04	.01
☐ 343 Terry Sawchuk	.15	.07	.02
☐ 344 Gordie Howe	.20	.09	.03
☐ 345 Guy Carbonneau UER	.08	.04	.01
Play Smart			
(Driver's has tick mark,			
instead of apostrophe)			
☐ 346 Stephen Leach	.05	.02	.01
☐ 347 Peter Douris	.05	.02	.01
☐ 348 David Reid	.05	.02	.01
☐ 349 Bob Carpenter	.05	.02	.01
☐ 350 Stephane Quintal	.05	.02	.01
☐ 351 Barry Pederson	.05	.02	.01
☐ 352 Brent Ashton	.05	.02	.01
☐ 353 Vladimir Ruzicka	.05	.02	.01
☐ 354 Brad Miller	.05	.02	.01
☐ 355 Robert Ray	.05	.02	.01
☐ 356 Colin Patterson	.05	.02	.01
☐ 357 Gord Donnelly	.05	.02	.01
☐ 358 Pat LaFontaine	.20	.09	.03
☐ 359 Randy Wood	.05	.02	.01
☐ 360 Randy Hillier	.05	.02	.01
☐ 361 Robert Reichel	.15	.07	.02
☐ 362 Ronnie Stern	.05	.02	.01
☐ 363 Ric Nattress	.05	.02	.01
☐ 364 Tim Sweeney	.05	.02	.01
☐ 365 Marc Habscheid	.05	.02	.01
☐ 366 Tim Hunter	.05	.02	.01
☐ 367 Rick Wamsley	.05	.02	.01
☐ 368 Frantisek Musil	.05	.02	.01
☐ 369 Mike Hudson	.05	.02	.01
☐ 370 Steve Smith	.08	.04	.01
☐ 371 Keith Brown	.05	.02	.01
☐ 372 Greg Gilbert	.05	.02	.01
☐ 373 John Tonelli	.08	.04	.01
☐ 374 Brent Sutter	.08	.04	.01
☐ 375 Brad Lauer	.05	.02	.01
☐ 376 Alan Kerr	.05	.02	.01
☐ 377 Brad McCrimmon	.05	.02	.01
☐ 378 Brad Marsh	.08	.04	.01

#	Player			
☐ 379	Brent Fedyk	.08	.04	.01
☐ 380	Ray Sheppard	.08	.04	.01
☐ 381	Vincent Damphousse	.08	.04	.01
☐ 382	Craig Muni	.05	.02	.01
☐ 383	Scott Mellanby	.05	.02	.01
☐ 384	Geoff Smith	.05	.02	.01
☐ 385	Kelly Buchberger	.05	.02	.01
☐ 386	Bernie Nicholls	.08	.04	.01
☐ 387	Luke Richardson	.05	.02	.01
☐ 388	Peter Ing	.05	.02	.01
☐ 389	Dave Manson	.08	.04	.01
☐ 390	Mark Hunter	.05	.02	.01
☐ 391	Jim McKenzie	.05	.02	.01
☐ 392	Randy Cunneyworth	.05	.02	.01
☐ 393	Murray Craven	.05	.02	.01
☐ 394	Mikael Andersson	.05	.02	.01
☐ 395	Andrew Cassels	.08	.04	.01
☐ 396	Randy Ladouceur	.05	.02	.01
☐ 397	Marc Bergevin	.05	.02	.01
☐ 398	Brian Benning	.05	.02	.01
☐ 399	Mike Donnelly	.15	.07	.02
☐ 400	Charlie Huddy	.05	.02	.01
☐ 401	John McIntyre	.05	.02	.01
☐ 402	Jay Miller	.05	.02	.01
☐ 403	Randy Gilhen	.05	.02	.01
☐ 404	Stewart Gavin	.05	.02	.01
☐ 405	Mike Craig	.05	.02	.01
☐ 406	Brian Glynn	.05	.02	.01
☐ 407	Rob Ramage	.05	.02	.01
☐ 408	Chris Dahlquist	.05	.02	.01
☐ 409	Basil McRae	.05	.02	.01
☐ 410	Todd Elik	.05	.02	.01
☐ 411	Craig Ludwig	.05	.02	.01
☐ 412	Kirk Muller	.08	.04	.01
☐ 413	Shayne Corson	.08	.04	.01
☐ 414	Brent Gilchrist	.05	.02	.01
☐ 415	Mario Roberge	.05	.02	.01
☐ 416	Sylvain Turgeon	.05	.02	.01
☐ 417	Alain Cote	.05	.02	.01
☐ 418	Donald Dufresne	.05	.02	.01
☐ 419	Todd Ewen	.05	.02	.01
☐ 420	Stephane Richer	.08	.04	.01
☐ 421	David Maley	.05	.02	.01
☐ 422	Randy McKay	.05	.02	.01
☐ 423	Scott Stevens	.10	.05	.01
☐ 424	Jon Morris	.05	.02	.01
☐ 425	Claude Vilgrain	.05	.02	.01
☐ 426	Laurie Boschman	.05	.02	.01
☐ 427	Pat Conacher	.05	.02	.01
☐ 428	Tom Kurvers	.05	.02	.01
☐ 429	Joe Reekie	.05	.02	.01
☐ 430	Rob DiMaio	.05	.02	.01
☐ 431	Tom Fitzgerald	.05	.02	.01
☐ 432	Ken Baumgartner	.05	.02	.01
☐ 433	Pierre Turgeon	.20	.09	.03
☐ 434	Dave McLlwain	.05	.02	.01
☐ 435	Benoit Hogue	.05	.02	.01
☐ 436	Uwe Krupp	.05	.02	.01
☐ 437	Adam Creighton	.05	.02	.01
☐ 438	Steve Thomas	.08	.04	.01
☐ 439	Mark Messier	.25	.11	.03
☐ 440	Tie Domi	.08	.04	.01
☐ 441	Sergei Nemchinov	.15	.07	.02
☐ 442	Mark Hardy	.05	.02	.01
☐ 443	Adam Graves	.25	.11	.03
☐ 444	Jeff Beukeboom	.05	.02	.01
☐ 445	Kris King	.05	.02	.01
☐ 446	Tim Kerr	.08	.04	.01
☐ 447	John Vanbiesbrouck	.10	.05	.01
☐ 448	Steve Duchesne	.08	.04	.01
☐ 449	Steve Kasper	.05	.02	.01
☐ 450	Ken Wregget	.05	.02	.01
☐ 451	Kevin Dineen	.08	.04	.01
☐ 452	Dave Brown	.05	.02	.01
☐ 453	Rod Brind'Amour	.15	.07	.02
☐ 454	Jiri Latal	.05	.02	.01
☐ 455	Tony Horacek	.05	.02	.01
☐ 456	Brad Jones	.05	.02	.01
☐ 457	Paul Stanton	.05	.02	.01
☐ 458	Gordie Roberts	.05	.02	.01
☐ 459	Ulf Samuelsson	.08	.04	.01
☐ 460	Ken Priestlay	.05	.02	.01
☐ 461	Jiri Hrdina	.05	.02	.01
☐ 462	Mikhail Tatarinov	.05	.02	.01
☐ 463	Mike Hough	.05	.02	.01
☐ 464	Don Barber	.05	.02	.01
☐ 465	Greg Smyth	.05	.02	.01
☐ 466	Doug Smail	.05	.02	.01
☐ 467	Mike McNeill	.05	.02	.01
☐ 468	John Kordic	.05	.02	.01
☐ 469	Greg Paslawski	.05	.02	.01
☐ 470	Herb Raglan	.05	.02	.01
☐ 471	Dave Christian	.05	.02	.01
☐ 472	Murray Baron	.05	.02	.01
☐ 473	Curtis Joseph	.25	.11	.03
☐ 474	Rick Zombo	.05	.02	.01
☐ 475	Brendan Shanahan	.25	.11	.03
☐ 476	Ron Sutter	.05	.02	.01
☐ 477	Mario Marois	.05	.02	.01
☐ 478	Doug Wilson	.08	.04	.01
☐ 479	Kelly Kisio	.05	.02	.01
☐ 480	Bob McGill	.05	.02	.01
☐ 481	Perry Anderson	.05	.02	.01
☐ 482	Brian Lawton	.05	.02	.01
☐ 483	Neil Wilkinson	.05	.02	.01
☐ 484	Ken Hammond	.05	.02	.01
☐ 485	David Bruce	.05	.02	.01
☐ 486	Steve Bozek	.05	.02	.01
☐ 487	Perry Berezan	.05	.02	.01
☐ 488	Wayne Presley	.05	.02	.01
☐ 489	Brian Bradley	.08	.04	.01
☐ 490	Darryl Shannon	.05	.02	.01
☐ 491	Lucien DeBlois	.05	.02	.01
☐ 492	Michel Petit	.05	.02	.01
☐ 493	Claude Loiselle	.05	.02	.01
☐ 494	Grant Fuhr	.08	.04	.01
☐ 495	Craig Berube	.05	.02	.01
☐ 496	Mike Bullard	.05	.02	.01
☐ 497	Jim Sandlak	.05	.02	.01
☐ 498	Dana Murzyn	.05	.02	.01
☐ 499	Garry Valk	.05	.02	.01
☐ 500	Andrew McBain	.05	.02	.01
☐ 501	Kirk McLean	.20	.09	.03
☐ 502	Gerald Diduck	.05	.02	.01
☐ 503	Dave Babych	.05	.02	.01
☐ 504	Ryan Walter	.05	.02	.01
☐ 505	Gino Odjick	.08	.04	.01
☐ 506	Dale Hunter	.08	.04	.01
☐ 507	Tim Bergland	.05	.02	.01
☐ 508	Alan May	.05	.02	.01
☐ 509	Jim Hrivnak	.05	.02	.01
☐ 510	Randy Burridge	.05	.02	.01
☐ 511	Peter Bondra	.08	.04	.01
☐ 512	Sylvain Cote	.05	.02	.01
☐ 513	Nick Kypreos	.05	.02	.01
☐ 514	Troy Murray	.05	.02	.01
☐ 515	Darrin Shannon	.05	.02	.01
☐ 516	Bryan Erickson	.05	.02	.01
☐ 517	Petri Skriko	.05	.02	.01
☐ 518	Mike Eagles	.05	.02	.01
☐ 519	Mike Hartman	.05	.02	.01
☐ 520	Bob Beers	.05	.02	.01
	Boston Bruins			
☐ 521	Matt DelGuidice	.05	.02	.01
	Boston Bruins			
☐ 522	Chris Winnes	.05	.02	.01
	Boston Bruins			
☐ 523	Brad May	.08	.04	.01
	Buffalo Sabres			
☐ 524	Donald Audette	.05	.02	.01
	Buffalo Sabres			
☐ 525	Kevin Haller	.10	.05	.01
	Buffalo Sabres			
☐ 526	Martin Simard	.05	.02	.01
	Calgary Flames			
☐ 527	Tomas Forslund	.05	.02	.01
	Calgary Flames			
☐ 528	Mark Osiecki	.05	.02	.01
	Calgary Flames			
☐ 529	Dominik Hasek	1.00	.45	.13
	Chicago Blackhawks			
☐ 530	Jimmy Waite	.08	.04	.01
	Chicago Blackhawks			
☐ 531	Nicklas Lidstrom UER	.35	.16	.04
	(Misspelled Niklas on card front)			
	Detroit Red Wings			
☐ 532	Martin Lapointe	.05	.02	.01
	Detroit Red Wings			
☐ 533	Vladimir Konstantinov	.15	.07	.02
	Detroit Red Wings			
☐ 534	Josef Beranek	.25	.11	.03
	Edmonton Oilers			
☐ 535	Louie DeBrusk	.05	.02	.01
	Edmonton Oilers			
☐ 536	Geoff Sanderson	.75	.35	.09
	Hartford Whalers			
☐ 537	Mark Greig	.05	.02	.01
	Hartford Whalers			
☐ 538	Michel Picard	.05	.02	.01
	Hartford Whalers			
☐ 539	Chris Tancill	.05	.02	.01
	Hartford Whalers			
☐ 540	Peter Ahola	.05	.02	.01
	Los Angeles Kings			
☐ 541	Francois Breault	.05	.02	.01

	Los Angeles Kings			
☐ 542	Daryl Sydor	.08	.04	.01
	Los Angeles Kings			
☐ 543	Derian Hatcher	.08	.04	.01
	Minnesota North Stars			
☐ 544	Marc Bureau	.05	.02	.01
	Minnesota North Stars			
☐ 545	John LeClair	.15	.07	.02
	Montreal Canadiens			
☐ 546	Paul DiPietro	.10	.05	.01
	Montreal Canadiens			
☐ 547	Scott Niedermayer UER	.25	.11	.03
	(Misspelled on front			
	as Neidermayer)			
	New Jersey Devils			
☐ 548	Kevin Todd	.15	.07	.02
	New Jersey Devils			
☐ 549	Doug Weight	.25	.11	.03
	New York Rangers			
☐ 550	Tony Amonte	.30	.14	.04
	New York Rangers			
☐ 551	Corey Foster	.05	.02	.01
	Philadelphia Flyers			
☐ 552	Dominic Roussel	.25	.11	.03
	Philadelphia Flyers			
☐ 553	Dan Kordic	.05	.02	.01
	Philadelphia Flyers			
☐ 554	Jim Paek	.10	.05	.01
	Pittsburgh Penguins			
☐ 555	Kip Miller	.05	.02	.01
	Quebec Nordiques			
☐ 556	Claude Lapointe	.10	.05	.01
	Quebec Nordiques			
☐ 557	Nelson Emerson	.20	.09	.03
	St. Louis Blues			
☐ 558	Pat Falloon	.35	.16	.04
	San Jose Sharks			
☐ 559	Pat MacLeod	.05	.02	.01
	San Jose Sharks			
☐ 560	Rick Lessard	.05	.02	.01
	San Jose Sharks			
☐ 561	Link Gaetz	.05	.02	.01
	San Jose Sharks			
☐ 562	Rob Pearson	.20	.09	.03
	Toronto Maple Leafs			
☐ 563	Alexander Godynyuk	.05	.02	.01
	Toronto Maple Leafs			
☐ 564	Pavel Bure	2.00	.90	.25
	Vancouver Canucks			
☐ 565	Russell Romaniuk	.10	.05	.01
	Winnipeg Jets			
☐ 566	Stu Barnes	.08	.04	.01
	Winnipeg Jets			
☐ 567	Ray Bourque CAP	.10	.05	.01
	Boston Bruins			
☐ 568	Mike Ramsey CAP	.08	.04	.01
	Buffalo Sabres			
☐ 569	Joe Nieuwendyk CAP	.10	.05	.01
	Calgary Flames			
☐ 570	Dirk Graham CAP	.08	.04	.01
	Chicago Blackhawks			
☐ 571	Steve Yzerman CAP	.15	.07	.02
	Detroit Red Wings			
☐ 572	Kevin Lowe CAP	.08	.04	.01
	Edmonton Oilers			
☐ 573	Randy Ladouceur CAP	.08	.04	.01
	Hartford Whalers			
☐ 574	Wayne Gretzky CAP	.35	.16	.04
	Los Angeles Kings			
☐ 575	Mark Tinordi CAP	.08	.04	.01
	Minnesota North Stars			
☐ 576	Guy Carbonneau CAP	.10	.05	.01
	Montreal Canadiens			
☐ 577	Bruce Driver CAP	.08	.04	.01
	New Jersey Devils			
☐ 578	Pat Flatley CAP	.08	.04	.01
	New York Islanders			
☐ 579	Mark Messier CAP	.10	.05	.01
	New York Rangers			
☐ 580	Rick Tocchet CAP	.10	.05	.01
	Philadelphia Flyers			
☐ 581	Mario Lemieux CAP	.25	.11	.03
	Pittsburgh Penguins			
☐ 582	Mike Hough CAP	.08	.04	.01
	Quebec Nordiques			
☐ 583	Garth Butcher CAP	.08	.04	.01
	St. Louis Blues			
☐ 584	Doug Wilson CAP	.08	.04	.01
	San Jose Sharks			
☐ 585	Wendel Clark CAP	.10	.05	.01
	Toronto Maple Leafs			
☐ 586	Trevor Linden CAP	.10	.05	.01
	Vancouver Canucks			
☐ 587	Rod Langway CAP	.08	.04	.01

	Washington Capitals			
☐ 588	Troy Murray CAP	.08	.04	.01
	Winnipeg Jets			
☐ 589	Practicing Outdoors	.08	.04	.01
☐ 590	Shape Up	.08	.04	.01
☐ 591	Boston Bruins Cartoon	.08	.04	.01
☐ 592	Opening Night	.08	.04	.01
☐ 593	Rod Gilbert	.08	.04	.01
	New York Rangers			
☐ 594	Phil Esposito	.10	.05	.01
	Boston Bruins			
☐ 595	Dale Tallon	.08	.04	.01
	Vancouver Canucks			
☐ 596	Gilbert Perreault	.08	.04	.01
	Buffalo Sabres			
☐ 597	Bernie Federko	.10	.05	.01
	St. Louis Blues			
☐ 598	All-Star Game	.08	.04	.01
☐ 599	Patrick Roy LL	.25	.11	.03
	Montreal Canadiens			
☐ 600	Ed Belfour LL	.12	.05	.02
	Chicago Blackhawks			
☐ 601	Don Beaupre LL	.10	.05	.01
	Washington Capitals			
☐ 602	Bob Essensa LL	.10	.05	.01
	Winnipeg Jets			
☐ 603	Kirk McLean UER LL	.12	.05	.02
	(Leader logo shows			
	PPG, should be GAA)			
	Vancouver Canucks			
☐ 604	Mike Gartner LL	.12	.05	.02
	New York Rangers			
☐ 605	Jeremy Roenick LL	.20	.09	.03
	Chicago Blackhawks			
☐ 606	Rob Brown LL	.10	.05	.01
	Hartford Whalers			
☐ 607	Ulf Dahlen LL	.10	.05	.01
	Minnesota North Stars			
☐ 608	Paul Ysebaert LL	.10	.05	.01
	Detroit Red Wings			
☐ 609	Brad McCrimmon LL	.10	.05	.01
	Detroit Red Wings			
☐ 610	Niklas Lidstrom LL	.15	.07	.02
	Detroit Red Wings			
☐ 611	Kelly Miller LL	.10	.05	.01
	Washington Capitals			
☐ 612	Jim Kyte SMART	.05	.02	.01
	Calgary Flames			
☐ 613	Patrick Roy SMART	.25	.11	.03
	Montreal Canadiens			
☐ 614	Alan May SMART	.05	.02	.01
	Washington Capitals			
☐ 615	Kelly Miller SMART	.05	.02	.01
	Washington Capitals			
☐ AU125	Patrick Roy Auto	250.00	115.00	31.00
	(Certified autograph)			
	Montreal Canadiens			
☐ AU501	Kirk McLean Auto	100.00	45.00	12.50
	(Certified autograph)			
	Vancouver Canucks			
☐ AU599	Patrick Roy LL Auto	250.00	115.00	31.00
	(Certified autograph)			
	Montreal Canadiens			
☐ NNO	Anniversary Hologram	100.00	45.00	12.50
	75th Anniversary			

1991-92 Pro Set CC

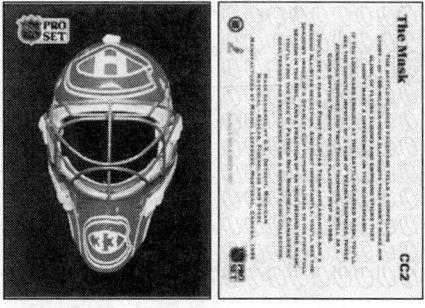

These standard-size (2 1/2" by 3 1/2") cards were issued as random inserts in French and English Pro Set 15-card foil packs. The first four were in the first series and the last five were inserted in with the second series. The Pat Falloon and Scott Niedermeyer cards were withdrawn early in the first series print run. This was due to the cards being released prior to the players having appeard in an NHL game; a contravention of licensing regulations. The cards are numbered on the back with a "CC" prefix.

	MINT	EXC	G-VG
COMPLETE SET (9)	50.00	23.00	6.25
COMMON CARD (CC1-CC4)	3.00	1.35	.40
COMMON CARD (CC5-CC9)	2.00	.90	.25
☐ CC1 Entry Draft	3.00	1.35	.40
☐ CC2 The Mask	5.00	2.30	.60
☐ CC3 Pat Falloon UER SP	15.00	6.75	1.90
(Born Birtle, not Foxwarren)			
☐ CC4 Scott Niedermeyer SP	18.00	8.00	2.30
☐ CC5 Wayne Gretzky	5.00	2.30	.60
Los Angeles Kings			
☐ CC6 Brett Hull	4.00	1.80	.50
St. Louis Blues			
☐ CC7 Adam Oates	2.50	1.15	.30
St. Louis Blues			
☐ CC8 Mark Recchi	2.50	1.15	.30
Pittsburgh Penguins			
☐ CC9 John Cullen	2.00	.90	.25
Hartford Whalers			

1991-92 Pro Set St. Louis Midwest

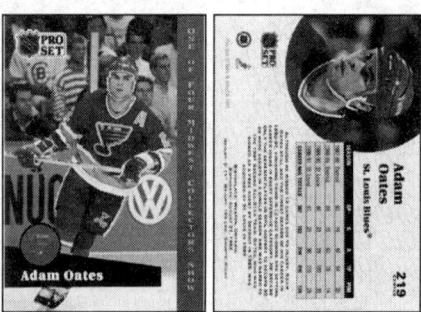

This four-card (standard-size, 2 1/2" by 3 1/2") set was available at the Midwest Sports Collectors Show in St. Louis in November 1991. The cards were a special issue for the card show; in fact, Pro Set did not even issue a Meagher card in its regular set. All four cards show explicitly on the front that they were a special issue from this show. The fronts of these cards differ from the regular issue in two respects: 1) a royal blue border stripe runs the length of the card on the right side; and 2) the cards are numbered in the stripe "X of Four Midwest Collectors Show".

	MINT	EXC	G-VG
COMPLETE SET (4)	12.00	5.00	1.20
COMMON PLAYER (1-4)	1.00	.40	.10
☐ 1 Adam Oates	5.00	2.00	.50
☐ 2 Paul Cavallini	1.00	.40	.10
☐ 3 Rick Meagher	1.50	.60	.15
☐ 4 Brett Hull	7.50	3.00	.75

1991-92 Pro Set Player of the Month

This six-card set was issued by Pro Set to honor hockey players for their outstanding performances during the season. The print run was limited to not more than 20,000

of each card. The cards were distributed to all ticket holders at home games the evening of the presentation. Another feature of the presentation was a 1,200.00 donation on behalf of the winning player to the youth hockey organization of his choice. Measuring the standard 2 1/2" by 3 1/2", card fronts feature borderless four-color action photographs. The player's team emblem appears in the lower left corner while the player's name is reversed-out white in a black wedge. On a screened hockey puck design, the horizontally oriented backs have a head shot in a circular format, biography, career statistics, and a summary of the outstanding achievement. The card number and team position appears in the upper right corner.

	MINT	EXC	G-VG
COMPLETE SET (6)	75.00	30.00	7.50
COMMON PLAYER (P1-P6)	10.00	4.00	1.00
☐ P1 Kirk McLean	20.00	8.00	2.00
Vancouver Canucks			
POM October 1991			
(Issued 11/19/91)			
☐ P2 Kevin Stevens	15.00	6.00	1.50
Pittsburgh Penguins			
POM November 1991			
(Issued 12/26/91)			
☐ P3 Mario Lemieux	18.00	7.25	1.80
Pittsburgh Penguins			
POM December 1991			
(Issued 1/28/92)			
☐ P4 Andy Moog	10.00	4.00	1.00
Boston Bruins			
POM January 1991			
☐ P5 Pat LaFontaine	15.00	6.00	1.50
Buffalo Sabres			
POM January 1991			
☐ P6 Luc Robitaille	12.00	5.00	1.20
Los Angeles Kings			
POM February 1991			

1991-92 Pro Set Platinum

The 1991-92 Pro Set Platinum hockey set contains 300 cards all measuring the standard-size (2 1/2" by 3 1/2"). The set was released in two series of 150 cards each. The front design features full-bleed glossy color action player photos, with the Pro Set Platinum icon superimposed at the lower right corner. Player names do not appear on the front.the backs have different glossy color player photos on the top portion, with brief player profiles beneath the pictures. The cards are numbered on the back and checklisted below alphabetically according to teams as follows: Boston Bruins (1-7), Buffalo Sabres (8-14), Calgary Flames (15-21), Chicago Blackhawks (22-28), Detroit Red Wings (29-34), Edmonton Oilers (35-41), Hartford Whalers (42-47), Los Angeles Kings (48-54), Minnesota North Stars (55-60), Montreal Canadiens (61-66), New Jersey Devils (67-72), New York Islanders (73-78), New York Rangers (79-84), Philadelphia Flyers (85-90), Pittsburgh Penguins (91-97), Quebec Nordiques (98-103), San Jose Sharks (104-107), St. Louis Blues (108-114), Toronto Maple Leafs (115-120), Vancouver Canucks (121-126), Washington Capitals (127-132), and Winnipeg Jets (133-138). Special subsets included in the first series are Platinum Performances (139-144) and NHL's "Original Six" Franchises (145-150). The second series production run was reported to be 15,000 individually numbered cases. To celebrate the NHL's 75th Anniversary, each NHL team chose a "Celebrity Captain" to represent them during the 1991-92 season. The Captains attended several games, were honored by their team at special ceremonies, and received a team jersey bearing their name. Twelve special cards of these Captains are featured in a special subset in the second series, and Pro Set donated a total of 12,000 dollars to three charities (Childrens Miracle Network, Grace Hospital Foundation, and American Liver Foundation) on behalf of these Celebrity Captains. Card numbers 151-248 feature Platinum Performers, and they are checklisted below alphabetically according to teams as follows: Boston Bruins (151-156), Buffalo Sabres (157-160), Calgary Flames (161-163), Chicago Blackhawks (164-166), Detroit Red Wings (167-170), Edmonton Oilers (171-174), Hartford Whalers (175-180), Los Angeles Kings (181-185), Minnesota North Stars (186-189), Montreal Canadiens (190-193), New Jersey Devils (194-199), New York Islanders (200-203), New York Rangers (204-207), Philadelphia Flyers (208-212), Pittsburgh Penguins (213-216), Quebec Nordiques (217-221), St. Louis Blues (222-225), San Jose Sharks (226-230), Toronto Maple Leafs (231-235), Vancouver Canucks (236-240), Washington Capitals (241-245), and Winnipeg Jets (246-248). Subsets included are Platinum Prospects (also listed alphabetically according to teams on cards 249-275), Platinum All-Stars (276-281), Platinum Performances (282-288), and Celebrity Captains (289-300). All cards are numbered on the back. The key Rookie Cards in the set are Tony Amonte, Nicklas Lidstrom, Geoff Sanderson, and Valeri Zelepukin.

	MINT	EXC	G-VG
COMPLETE SET (300)	15.00	6.75	1.90
COMPLETE SERIES 1 (150)	7.50	3.40	.95
COMPLETE SERIES 2 (150)	7.50	3.40	.95
COMMON PLAYER (1-150)	.05	.02	.01
COMMON PLAYER (151-300)	.05	.02	.01

☐	1	Cam Neely	.15	.07	.02
☐	2	Ray Bourque	.15	.07	.02
☐	3	Craig Janney	.15	.07	.02
☐	4	Andy Moog	.10	.05	.01
☐	5	Dave Poulin	.08	.04	.01
☐	6	Ken Hodge Jr.	.05	.02	.01
☐	7	Glen Wesley	.05	.02	.01
☐	8	Dave Andreychuk	.15	.07	.02
☐	9	Daren Puppa	.08	.04	.01
☐	10	Pierre Turgeon	.25	.11	.03
☐	11	Dale Hawerchuk	.08	.04	.01
☐	12	Doug Bodger	.05	.02	.01
☐	13	Mike Ramsey	.05	.02	.01
☐	14	Alexander Mogilny	.50	.23	.06
☐	15	Sergei Makarov	.08	.04	.01
☐	16	Theoren Fleury	.15	.07	.02
☐	17	Joel Otto	.05	.02	.01
☐	18	Joe Nieuwendyk	.10	.05	.01
☐	19	Al MacInnis	.10	.05	.01
☐	20	Gary Suter	.08	.04	.01
☐	21	Mike Vernon	.08	.04	.01
☐	22	John Tonelli	.08	.04	.01
☐	23	Dirk Graham	.05	.02	.01
☐	24	Jeremy Roenick	.60	.25	.08
☐	25	Chris Chelios	.08	.04	.01
☐	26	Ed Belfour	.30	.14	.04
☐	27	Steve Smith	.08	.04	.01
☐	28	Steve Larmer	.08	.04	.01
☐	29	Johan Garpenlov	.05	.02	.01
☐	30	Sergei Fedorov	.75	.35	.09
☐	31	Tim Cheveldae	.08	.04	.01
☐	32	Steve Yzerman	.30	.14	.04
☐	33	Jimmy Carson	.08	.04	.01
☐	34	Bob Probert	.08	.04	.01
☐	35	Vincent Damphousse	.08	.04	.01
☐	36	Bill Ranford	.08	.04	.01
☐	37	Petr Klima	.05	.02	.01
☐	38	Kevin Lowe	.08	.04	.01
☐	39	Esa Tikkanen	.08	.04	.01
☐	40	Craig Simpson	.08	.04	.01
☐	41	Peter Ing	.05	.02	.01
☐	42	Rob Brown	.05	.02	.01
☐	43	Bobby Holik	.08	.04	.01
☐	44	Pat Verbeek	.08	.04	.01
☐	45	Brad Shaw	.05	.02	.01
☐	46	Kevin Dineen	.08	.04	.01
☐	47	Zarley Zalapski	.05	.02	.01
☐	48	Jari Kurri	.10	.05	.01
☐	49	Tony Granato	.08	.04	.01
☐	50	Luc Robitaille	.15	.07	.02
☐	51	Rob Blake	.15	.07	.02
☐	52	Wayne Gretzky	1.25	.55	.16
☐	53	Tomas Sandstrom	.08	.04	.01
☐	54	Kelly Hrudey	.08	.04	.01
☐	55	Mike Modano	.30	.14	.04
☐	56	Jon Casey	.08	.04	.01
☐	57	Todd Elik	.05	.02	.01
☐	58	Mark Tinordi	.08	.04	.01
☐	59	Brian Bellows	.08	.04	.01
☐	60	Dave Gagner	.08	.04	.01
☐	61	Patrick Roy	.50	.23	.06
☐	62	Russ Courtnall	.08	.04	.01
☐	63	Guy Carbonneau	.08	.04	.01
☐	64	Denis Savard	.08	.04	.01
☐	65	Petr Svoboda	.05	.02	.01
☐	66	Kirk Muller	.08	.04	.01
☐	67	Stephane Richer	.08	.04	.01
☐	68	Chris Terreri	.08	.04	.01
☐	69	Bruce Driver	.05	.02	.01
☐	70	John MacLean	.08	.04	.01
☐	71	Patrik Sundstrom	.05	.02	.01
☐	72	Scott Stevens	.10	.05	.01
☐	73	Glenn Healy	.08	.04	.01
☐	74	Brent Sutter	.08	.04	.01
☐	75	David Volek	.05	.02	.01
☐	76	Ray Ferraro	.08	.04	.01
☐	77	Pat Flatley	.05	.02	.01
☐	78	Jeff Norton	.05	.02	.01
☐	79	Brian Leetch	.35	.16	.04
☐	80	Tim Kerr	.08	.04	.01
☐	81	Mark Messier	.25	.11	.03
☐	82	James Patrick	.05	.02	.01
☐	83	Mike Richter	.30	.14	.04
☐	84	Mike Gartner	.10	.05	.01
☐	85	Mike Ricci	.15	.07	.02
☐	86	Steve Duchesne	.08	.04	.01
☐	87	Ron Hextall	.08	.04	.01
☐	88	Rick Tocchet	.08	.04	.01
☐	89	Pelle Eklund	.05	.02	.01
☐	90	Rod Brind'Amour	.20	.09	.03
☐	91	Mario Lemieux	.75	.35	.09
☐	92	Jaromir Jagr	.60	.25	.08
☐	93	Kevin Stevens	.30	.14	.04
☐	94	Paul Coffey	.15	.07	.02
☐	95	Ulf Samuelsson	.08	.04	.01
☐	96	Tom Barrasso	.08	.04	.01
☐	97	Mark Recchi	.30	.14	.04
☐	98	Ron Tugnutt	.05	.02	.01
☐	99	Mats Sundin	.30	.14	.04
☐	100	Stephane Morin	.05	.02	.01
☐	101	Owen Nolan	.15	.07	.02
☐	102	Joe Sakic	.25	.11	.03
☐	103	Bryan Fogarty	.05	.02	.01
☐	104	Kelly Kisio	.05	.02	.01
☐	105	Tony Hrkac	.05	.02	.01
☐	106	Brian Mullen	.08	.04	.01

☐ 107	Doug Wilson	.08	.04	.01
☐ 108	Rich Sutter	.05	.02	.01
☐ 109	Brett Hull	.50	.23	.06
☐ 110	Dave Christian	.05	.02	.01
☐ 111	Brendan Shanahan	.30	.14	.04
☐ 112	Vincent Riendeau	.05	.02	.01
☐ 113	Adam Oates	.20	.09	.03
☐ 114	Jeff Brown	.08	.04	.01
☐ 115	Gary Leeman	.05	.02	.01
☐ 116	Dave Ellett	.05	.02	.01
☐ 117	Grant Fuhr	.08	.04	.01
☐ 118	Daniel Marois	.05	.02	.01
☐ 119	Mike Krushelnyski	.05	.02	.01
☐ 120	Wendel Clark	.15	.07	.02
☐ 121	Troy Gamble	.05	.02	.01
☐ 122	Robert Kron	.05	.02	.01
☐ 123	Geoff Courtnall	.08	.04	.01
☐ 124	Trevor Linden	.25	.11	.03
☐ 125	Greg Adams	.05	.02	.01
☐ 126	Igor Larionov	.08	.04	.01
☐ 127	Kevin Hatcher	.08	.04	.01
☐ 128	Mike Ridley	.08	.04	.01
☐ 129	John Druce	.05	.02	.01
☐ 130	Al Iafrate	.08	.04	.01
☐ 131	Dino Ciccarelli	.08	.04	.01
☐ 132	Michal Pivonka	.08	.04	.01
☐ 133	Fredrik Olausson	.08	.04	.01
☐ 134	Ed Olczyk	.05	.02	.01
☐ 135	Bob Essensa	.08	.04	.01
☐ 136	Pat Elynuik	.05	.02	.01
☐ 137	Phil Housley	.08	.04	.01
☐ 138	Thomas Steen	.05	.02	.01
☐ 139	Don Beaupre	.08	.04	.01
☐ 140	Boston Bruins	.05	.02	.01
☐ 141	Chicago Blackhawks	.05	.02	.01
☐ 142	Los Angeles Kings	.05	.02	.01
☐ 143	Minnesota North Stars	.05	.02	.01
☐ 144	Pittsburgh Penguins	.05	.02	.01
☐ 145	Boston Bruins	.05	.02	.01
☐ 146	Chicago Blackhawks	.05	.02	.01
☐ 147	Detroit Red Wings	.05	.02	.01
☐ 148	Montreal Canadiens	.05	.02	.01
☐ 149	New York Rangers	.05	.02	.01
☐ 150	Toronto Maple Leafs	.05	.02	.01
☐ 151	Stephen Leach	.05	.02	.01
☐ 152	Vladimir Ruzicka	.05	.02	.01
☐ 153	Don Sweeney	.05	.02	.01
☐ 154	Bob Carpenter	.05	.02	.01
☐ 155	Brent Ashton	.05	.02	.01
☐ 156	Gord Murphy	.05	.02	.01
☐ 157	Pat LaFontaine	.25	.11	.03
☐ 158	Randy Hillier	.05	.02	.01
☐ 159	Clint Malarchuk	.08	.04	.01
☐ 160	Randy Wood	.05	.02	.01
☐ 161	Gary Roberts	.08	.04	.01
☐ 162	Gary Leeman	.05	.02	.01
☐ 163	Robert Reichel	.15	.07	.02
☐ 164	Brent Sutter	.08	.04	.01
☐ 165	Brian Noonan	.05	.02	.01
☐ 166	Michel Goulet UER	.08	.04	.01
	(Prospect on front)			
☐ 167	Paul Ysebaert	.05	.02	.01
☐ 168	Kevin Miller	.08	.04	.01
☐ 169	Ray Sheppard	.08	.04	.01
☐ 170	Brad McCrimmon	.05	.02	.01
☐ 171	Joe Murphy	.08	.04	.01
☐ 172	Dave Manson	.08	.04	.01
☐ 173	Scott Mellanby	.05	.02	.01
☐ 174	Bernie Nicholls	.08	.04	.01
☐ 175	John Cullen	.08	.04	.01
☐ 176	Marc Bergevin	.05	.02	.01
☐ 177	Steve Konroyd	.05	.02	.01
☐ 178	Kay Whitmore	.05	.02	.01
☐ 179	Murray Craven	.05	.02	.01
☐ 180	Mikael Andersson	.05	.02	.01
☐ 181	Bob Kudelski	.08	.04	.01
☐ 182	Brian Benning	.05	.02	.01
☐ 183	Mike Donnelly	.05	.02	.01
☐ 184	Marty McSorley	.08	.04	.01
☐ 185	Corey Millen	.20	.09	.03
☐ 186	Ulf Dahlen	.08	.04	.01
☐ 187	Brian Propp	.08	.04	.01
☐ 188	Neal Broten	.08	.04	.01
☐ 189	Mike Craig	.05	.02	.01
☐ 190	Stephan Lebeau	.15	.07	.02
☐ 191	Mike Keane	.05	.02	.01
☐ 192	Brent Gilchrist	.05	.02	.01
☐ 193	Eric Desjardins	.08	.04	.01
☐ 194	Peter Stastny	.08	.04	.01
☐ 195	Claude Vilgrain	.05	.02	.01
☐ 196	Claude Lemieux	.08	.04	.01
☐ 197	Craig Billington UER	.15	.07	.02
	(Front photo act-			

	ually Chris Terreri)			
☐ 198	Alexei Kasatonov	.05	.02	.01
☐ 199	Viacheslav Fetisov	.08	.04	.01
☐ 200	Benoit Hogue	.05	.02	.01
☐ 201	Derek King	.08	.04	.01
☐ 202	Uwe Krupp	.05	.02	.01
☐ 203	Steve Thomas	.08	.04	.01
☐ 204	John Ogrodnick	.05	.02	.01
☐ 205	Sergei Nemchinov	.15	.07	.02
☐ 206	Jeff Beukeboom	.05	.02	.01
☐ 207	Adam Graves	.30	.14	.04
☐ 208	Andrei Lomakin	.05	.02	.01
☐ 209	Dan Quinn	.05	.02	.01
☐ 210	Ken Wreggett	.05	.02	.01
☐ 211	Garry Galley	.05	.02	.01
☐ 212	Terry Carkner	.05	.02	.01
☐ 213	Larry Murphy	.08	.04	.01
☐ 214	Ron Francis	.08	.04	.01
☐ 215	Bob Errey	.05	.02	.01
☐ 216	Bryan Trottier	.08	.04	.01
☐ 217	Mike Hough	.05	.02	.01
☐ 218	Mikhail Tatarinov	.05	.02	.01
☐ 219	Jacques Cloutier	.05	.02	.01
☐ 220	Greg Paslawski	.05	.02	.01
☐ 221	Alexei Gusarov	.10	.05	.01
☐ 222	Ron Sutter	.05	.02	.01
☐ 223	Garth Butcher	.05	.02	.01
☐ 224	Paul Cavallini	.05	.02	.01
☐ 225	Curtis Joseph	.30	.14	.04
☐ 226	Jeff Hackett	.05	.02	.01
☐ 227	David Bruce	.05	.02	.01
☐ 228	Wayne Presley	.05	.02	.01
☐ 229	Neil Wilkinson	.05	.02	.01
☐ 230	Dean Evason	.05	.02	.01
☐ 231	Brian Bradley	.08	.04	.01
☐ 232	Peter Zezel	.05	.02	.01
☐ 233	Mike Bullard	.05	.02	.01
☐ 234	Doug Gilmour	.30	.14	.04
☐ 235	Jamie Macoun	.05	.02	.01
☐ 236	Cliff Ronning	.08	.04	.01
☐ 237	Jyrki Lumme	.05	.02	.01
☐ 238	Tom Fergus	.05	.02	.01
☐ 239	Kirk McLean	.20	.09	.03
☐ 240	Sergio Momesso	.05	.02	.01
☐ 241	Randy Burridge	.05	.02	.01
☐ 242	Dimitri Khristich	.08	.04	.01
☐ 243	Calle Johansson	.05	.02	.01
☐ 244	Peter Bondra	.08	.04	.01
☐ 245	Dale Hunter	.08	.04	.01
☐ 246	Darrin Shannon	.05	.02	.01
☐ 247	Troy Murray	.05	.02	.01
☐ 248	Teppo Numminen	.05	.02	.01
☐ 249	Donald Audette	.05	.02	.01
	Buffalo Sabres			
☐ 250	Kevin Haller	.10	.05	.01
	Buffalo Sabres			
☐ 251	Alexander Godynyuk	.05	.02	.01
	Calgary Flames			
☐ 252	Dominik Hasek	1.00	.45	.13
	Chicago Blackhawks			
☐ 253	Nicklas Lidstrom	.40	.18	.05
	Detroit Red Wings			
☐ 254	Vladimir Konstantinov	.20	.09	.03
	Detroit Red Wings			
☐ 255	Josef Beranek	.30	.14	.04
	Edmonton Oilers			
☐ 256	Geoff Sanderson	1.00	.45	.13
	Hartford Whalers			
☐ 257	Peter Ahola	.05	.02	.01
	Los Angeles Kings			
☐ 258	Derian Hatcher	.08	.04	.01
	Minnesota North Stars			
☐ 259	John LeClair	.20	.09	.03
	Montreal Canadiens			
☐ 260	Kevin Todd	.15	.07	.02
	New Jersey Devils			
☐ 261	Valeri Zelepukin	.50	.23	.06
	New Jersey Devils			
☐ 262	Tony Amonte	.40	.18	.05
	New York Rangers			
☐ 263	Doug Weight	.25	.11	.03
	New York Rangers			
☐ 264	Claude Boivin	.10	.05	.01
	Philadelphia Flyers			
☐ 265	Corey Foster	.05	.02	.01
	Philadelphia Flyers			
☐ 266	Jim Paek	.10	.05	.01
	Pittsburgh Penguins			
☐ 267	Claude Lapointe	.10	.05	.01
	Quebec Nordiques			
☐ 268	Adam Foote	.05	.02	.01
	Quebec Nordiques			
☐ 269	Nelson Emerson	.20	.09	.03
	St. Louis Blues			

		MINT	EXC	G-VG
☐ 270	Arturs Irbe	.75	.35	.09
	San Jose Sharks			
☐ 271	Pat Falloon	.30	.14	.04
	San Jose Sharks			
☐ 272	Pavel Bure	2.00	.90	.25
	Vancouver Canucks			
☐ 273	Stu Barnes	.08	.04	.01
	Winnipeg Jets			
☐ 274	Russ Romaniuk	.10	.05	.01
	Winnipeg Jets			
☐ 275	Luciano Borsato	.10	.05	.01
	Winnipeg Jets			
☐ 276	Al MacInnis AS	.08	.04	.01
	Calgary Flames			
☐ 277	Sergei Fedorov AS	.25	.11	.03
	Detroit Red Wings			
☐ 278	Ray Bourque AS	.08	.04	.01
	Boston Bruins			
☐ 279	Mike Richter AS	.08	.04	.01
	New York Rangers			
☐ 280	Campbell Conference	.08	.04	.01
☐ 281	Wales Conference	.08	.04	.01
☐ 282	Brett Hull PP	.20	.09	.03
	St. Louis Blues			
☐ 283	Alexander Mogilny PP	.20	.09	.03
	Buffalo Sabres			
☐ 284	Brian Leetch PP	.15	.07	.02
	New York Rangers			
☐ 285	Bob Essensa PP	.05	.02	.01
	Winnipeg Jets			
☐ 286	Derek King PP	.05	.02	.01
	New York Islanders			
☐ 287	Steve Larmer PP	.05	.02	.01
	Chicago Blackhawks			
☐ 288	Chris Terreri PP	.05	.02	.01
	New Jersey Devils			
☐ 289	Terry O'Reilly CAP	.05	.02	.01
	Boston Bruins			
☐ 290	Burton Cummings CAP	.05	.02	.01
	Winnipeg Jets			
☐ 291	Marv Albert CAP	.15	.07	.02
	New York Rangers			
☐ 292	Larry King CAP	.15	.07	.02
	Washington Capitals			
☐ 293	Jim Kelly CAP	.50	.23	.06
	Buffalo Sabres			
☐ 294	David Wheaton CAP	.05	.02	.01
	Minnesota North Stars			
☐ 295	Ralph Macchio CAP	.05	.02	.01
	New York Islanders			
☐ 296	Rick Hansen CAP	.05	.02	.01
	Vancouver Canucks			
☐ 297	Fred Rogers CAP	.15	.07	.02
	Pittsburgh Penguins			
☐ 298	Gaetan Boucher CAP	.05	.02	.01
	Quebec Nordiques			
☐ 299	Susan Saint James CAP	.15	.07	.02
	Hartford Whalers			
☐ 300	James Belushi CAP	.15	.07	.02
	Chicago Blackhawks			

1991-92 Pro Set Platinum PC

The 1991-92 Pro Set Platinum PC set consists of 20 standard size (2 1/2" by 3 1/2") cards randomly inserted in Platinum foil packs. The first series inserts were a ten-card Platinum Collectibles subset featuring Players of the Month (PC1-PC6) and Sensational Sophomores (PC7-PC10). The second series inserts were subtitled Platinum Milestones (PC11-PC20).

	MINT	EXC	G-VG
COMPLETE SET (20)	28.00	12.50	3.50
COMMON POM (PC1-PC6)	1.25	.55	.16
COMMON SOPHS (PC7-PC10)	1.25	.55	.16
COMMON MILESTONES (PC11-PC20)	1.50	.65	.19

		MINT	EXC	G-VG
☐ PC1	John Vanbiesbrouck	2.00	.90	.25
	New York Rangers			
☐ PC2	Pete Peeters	1.25	.55	.16
	Philadelphia Flyers			
☐ PC3	Tom Barrasso	1.25	.55	.16
	Pittsburgh Penguins			
☐ PC4	Wayne Gretzky	6.00	2.70	.75
	Los Angeles Kings			

		MINT	EXC	G-VG
☐ PC5	Brett Hull	4.00	1.80	.50
	St. Louis Blues			
☐ PC6	Kelly Hrudey	1.25	.55	.16
	Los Angeles Kings			
☐ PC7	Sergei Fedorov	5.00	2.30	.60
	Detroit Red Wings			
☐ PC8	Rob Blake	1.25	.55	.16
	Los Angeles Kings			
☐ PC9	Ken Hodge Jr.	1.25	.55	.16
	Boston Bruins			
☐ PC10	Eric Weinrich	1.25	.55	.16
	New Jersey Devils			
☐ PC11	Mike Gartner	1.50	.65	.19
	New York Rangers			
☐ PC12	Paul Coffey	2.00	.90	.25
	Pittsburgh Penguins			
☐ PC13	Bobby Smith	1.50	.65	.19
	Minnesota North Stars			
☐ PC14	Wayne Gretzky	6.00	2.70	.75
	Los Angeles Kings			
☐ PC15	Michel Goulet	1.50	.65	.19
	Chicago Blackhawks			
☐ PC16	Mike Liut	1.50	.65	.19
	Washington Capitals			
☐ PC17	Brian Propp	1.50	.65	.19
	Minnesota North Stars			
☐ PC18	Denis Savard	1.50	.65	.19
	Montreal Canadiens			
☐ PC19	Bryan Trottier	1.50	.65	.19
	Pittsburgh Penguins			
☐ PC20	Mark Messier	3.50	1.55	.45
	New York Rangers			

1991-92 Pro Set Platinum HOF 75th

This eight-card set was issued in a cello pack to pay tribute to the NHL's 75th Anniversary. The cards measure the standard size (2 1/2" by 3 1/2"), and the set includes the Original Six team cards (indistinguishable from cards 145-150 in the regular set) from the 1991-92 Pro Set Platinum hockey set and two special cards. The Hockey Hall of Fame Collectible features on the front a full-bleed sepia-toned picture of Exhibition Place, where the Hockey Hall of Fame has been located since 1961. In addition to commentary, the back features a small color picture of BCE Place, its new location beginning in the fall of 1992. On a black background, the title card features the Hockey Hall of Fame and Museum logo at the top as well as the NHL and Pro Set logos at the bottom. The title card has a blank back. The actual numbering of the cards is reflected in the listing below.

	MINT	EXC	G-VG
COMPLETE SET (8)	10.00	4.00	1.00
COMMON CARD	.10	.04	.01

		MINT	EXC	G-VG
☐ 145	Boston Bruins	.10	.04	.01
☐ 146	Chicago Blackhawks	.10	.04	.01
☐ 147	Detroit Red Wings	.10	.04	.01
☐ 148	Montreal Canadiens	.10	.04	.01
☐ 149	New York Rangers	.10	.04	.01
☐ 150	Toronto Maple Leafs	.10	.04	.01

	MINT	EXC	G-VG
☐ HHOF1 Hockey Hall of Fame	6.00	2.40	.60
Collectible;			
Excellence, Education,			
Entertainment			
(Pictures the opening			
of the Hall of Fame			
in 1961 in Toronto)			
☐ xx Title Card	4.00	1.60	.40
(Blank back)			

1991-92 Pro Set Puck Candy Promos

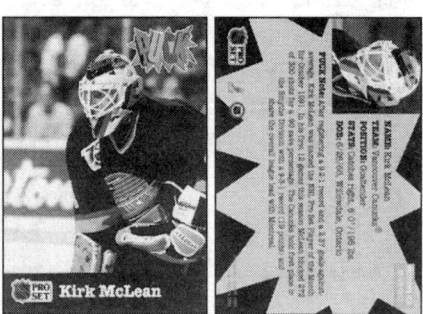

This set of three standard-size (2 1/2" by 3 1/2") hockey cards was distributed in a cello pack to show the design of the upcoming Puck cards. The fronts of the promos are identical to the regular issue. Their backs differ in two respects: 1) instead of a card number, the promos have the words "Prototype For Review Only" in an aqua box; and 2) The "Puck Note" on the promos differs from that found on the regular cards. The cards are unnumbered and checklisted below in alphabetical order.

	MINT	EXC	G-VG
COMPLETE SET (3)........................	5.00	2.00	.50
COMMON PLAYER (1-3).................	1.50	.60	.15
☐ 1 Kirk McLean	2.50	1.00	.25
Vancouver Canucks			
☐ 2 Andy Moog	2.50	1.00	.25
Boston Bruins			
☐ 3 Pat Verbeek............................	1.50	.60	.15
Hartford Whalers			

1991-92 Pro Set Puck Candy

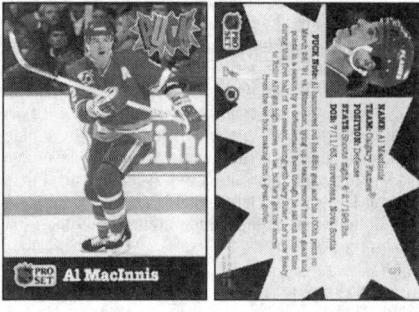

This set of thirty standard-size (2 1/2" by 3 1/2") hockey cards was created for a new product, the NHL Pro Set Puck, a combination chocolate, peanut vanilla nougat, and caramel confection. This test product was available in all U.S. NHL

and Northeast markets, and each candy package contained three Puck hockey cards. The fronts feature a borderless four-color action player photo with the Pro Set logo and player's name in the bottom border. The horizontally oriented backs have a head shot, biography, and a "Puck Note" that consists of personal information about the player. Pro Set advertised this 30-card set as Series 1.

	MINT	EXC	G-VG
COMPLETE SET (30)........................	30.00	12.00	3.00
COMMON PLAYER (1-30).................	.50	.20	.05
☐ 1 Ray Bourque	1.50	.60	.15
☐ 2 Andy Moog	.75	.30	.07
☐ 3 Doug Bodger	.50	.20	.05
☐ 4 Theoren Fleury	.75	.30	.07
☐ 5 Al MacInnis	1.00	.40	.10
☐ 6 Jeremy Roenick	3.50	1.40	.35
☐ 7 Tim Cheveldae.......................	.75	.30	.07
☐ 8 Steve Yzerman	2.00	.80	.20
☐ 9 Craig Simpson	.50	.20	.05
☐ 10 Pat Verbeek..........................	.50	.20	.05
☐ 11 Wayne Gretzky	7.50	3.00	.75
☐ 12 Luc Robitaille	1.50	.60	.15
☐ 13 Brian Bellows	.50	.20	.05
☐ 14 Patrick Roy	3.50	1.40	.35
☐ 15 Guy Carbonneau	.50	.20	.05
☐ 16 Peter Stastny........................	.75	.30	.07
☐ 17 Adam Creighton	.50	.20	.05
☐ 18 Glenn Healy	.50	.20	.05
☐ 19 Mark Messier	2.50	1.00	.25
☐ 20 Rod Brind'Amour....................	1.00	.40	.10
☐ 21 Paul Coffey	1.25	.50	.12
☐ 22 Tom Barasso.........................	.75	.30	.07
☐ 23 Joe Sakic.............................	1.50	.60	.15
☐ 24 Brett Hull	3.50	1.40	.35
☐ 25 Adam Oates	1.50	.60	.15
☐ 26 Kelly Kisio	.50	.20	.05
☐ 27 Grant Fuhr............................	.75	.30	.07
☐ 28 Kirk McLean	.75	.30	.07
☐ 29 Kevin Hatcher........................	.50	.20	.05
☐ 30 Phil Housley..........................	.75	.30	.07

1991-92 Pro Set Gazette

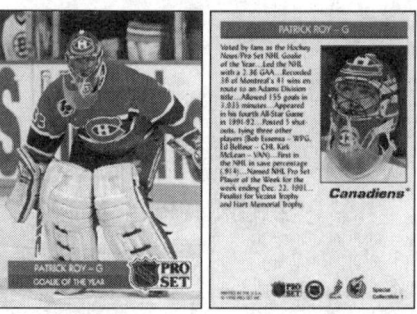

These standard-size (2 1/2" by 3 1/2") cards were issued in a cello pack and featured a mix of cards from several of Pro Set's sport and non-sport card issues, e.g., hockey, football (Emmitt Smith), golf, Guiness, Beauty and the Beast, Young Indiana Jones. Only the hockey cards are included below. The front of the Patrick Roy card (number 2) features a full-bleed color player photo, with the words "Pro Set Gazette" in the upper left corner and the player's name in a blue stripe near the bottom of the card. To the left of the number of the Roy card, it reads "Pro Set Gazette Collectible". The horizontally oriented back has a color close-up photo and summarizes some of Roy's activities off the ice. The SC1 Roy card has his name appearing in a red stripe at the bottom with the words "Goalie of the Year" in a blue stripe.

The back shows a red stripe across the top with the player's name. A close-up color player photo and career highlights appear below the red stripe on a white background. The card is numbered "Special Collectible 1" on the back.

	MINT	EXC	G-VG
COMPLETE SET (2)	5.00	2.00	.50
COMMON CARD	3.00	1.20	.30
☐ 2 Patrick Roy	3.00	1.20	.30
(Gazette Collectible) Montreal Canadiens			
☐ SC1 Patrick Roy	3.00	1.20	.30
(Special Collectible 1) Montreal Canadiens			

1991-92 Pro Set Opening Night

This six-card promo set was issued by Pro Set to commemorate the opening night of the 1991-92 NHL season. The standard-size (2 1/2" by 3 1/2") player cards are the same as the regular issue, with borderless glossy color player photos on the fronts, and a color headshot and player information on the backs. The cards are numbered on the back. Four (different each time) regular issue cards were included in each promo pack.

	MINT	EXC	G-VG
COMPLETE SET (2)	7.00	2.80	.70
COMMON CARD	3.50	1.40	.35
☐ NNO NHL 75th Anniversary	3.50	1.40	.35
Opening Night			
☐ NNO 1991-92 Opening Night	3.50	1.40	.35

1991-92 Pro Set Rink Rat

 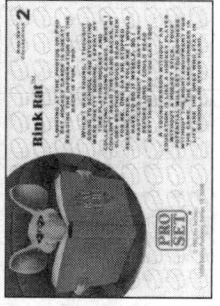

These standard-size (2 1/2" by 3 1/2") cards were produced by Pro Set to promote education. On card number 2 the

front cartoon portrays the Rink Rat shooting the puck through a defenseman's legs right toward the viewer of the card; on a screen design with miniature hockey pucks, the horizontally oriented back has another circular-shaped cartoon picture of the Rink Rat reading and a "stay in school/study hard" message. The cards are numbered on the back.

	MINT	EXC	G-VG
COMPLETE SET (2)	10.00	4.00	1.00
COMMON CARD (RR1-RR2)	5.00	2.00	.50
☐ RR1 Rink Rat	5.00	2.00	.50
(Holding stick over head; copyright 1991)			
☐ RR2 Rink Rat	5.00	2.00	.50
(Shooting puck)			

1992-93 Pro Set

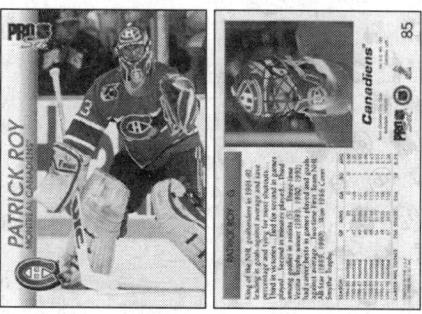

The 1992-93 Pro Set hockey set consists of 270 cards, each measuring the standard size (2 1/2" by 3 1/2"). The production run was 8,000 numbered 20-box foil cases and 2,000 20-box jumbo cases. Randomly inserted into foil packs were a five-card special collectible award winners set, a five-card Parkhurst Preview set, a 12-card Rookie Goal Leader set, and 1,000 Kirk McLean autographed cards. The McLean cards have number 239 on the back and does not relate to the checklist. The standard card fronts feature full-bleed color action player photos except for a gray and white vertical border stripe on the left edge. This border contains the player's name printed in team colors and the team name. The team logo overlays this stripe and the picture at the lower left corner. Cards belonging to topical subsets do not have this border stripe, but rather have the player's name and team name or achievement in a bar design at the bottom of the picture. The horizontal backs display close-up player photos along side statistics and career highlights. The cards are numbered on the back and checklisted below alphabetically according to teams as follows: Boston Bruins (3-11), Buffalo Sabres (12-20), Calgary Flames (21-29), Chicago Blackhawks (30-38), Detroit Red Wings (39-47), Edmonton Oilers (48-56), Hartford Whalers (57-65), Los Angeles Kings (66-74), Minnesota North Stars (75-83), Montreal Canadiens (84-92), New Jersey Devils (93-101), New York Islanders (102-110), New York Rangers (111-119), Ottawa Senators (120-128), Philadelphia Flyers (129-137), Pittsburgh Penguins (138-146), Quebec Nordiques (147-155), St. Louis Blues (156-164), San Jose Sharks (165-173), Tampa Bay Lightning (174-182), Toronto Maple Leafs (183-191), Vancouver Canucks (192-200), Washington Capitals (201-209), and Winnipeg Jets (210-218). Admittedly, this team ordering is slightly disturbed by a few trades (61, 65, 89, 90, 103, 129, 133, 136, 137, 214). The set closes with the following topical subsets: Statistical Leader (245-252), Newsreel (253-255), 1991-92 Milestone (256-265), and Play Smart (266-270). The most noteworthy Rookie Card in the set is Ray Whitney.

	MINT	EXC	G-VG
COMPLETE SET (270)	30.00	13.50	3.80
COMMON PLAYER (1-270)	.06	.03	.01
☐ 1 Mario Lemieux	.60	.25	.08
Pro Set POY			
☐ 2 Patrick Roy	.35	.16	.04
Hockey News POY			
☐ 3 Adam Oates	.15	.07	.02
☐ 4 Ray Bourque	.20	.09	.03
☐ 5 Vladimir Ruzicka	.06	.03	.01
☐ 6 Stephen Leach	.06	.03	.01
☐ 7 Andy Moog	.08	.04	.01
☐ 8 Cam Neely	.15	.07	.02
☐ 9 Dave Poulin	.06	.03	.01
☐ 10 Glen Wesley	.06	.03	.01
☐ 11 Gord Murphy	.06	.03	.01
☐ 12 Dale Hawerchuk	.08	.04	.01
☐ 13 Pat LaFontaine	.20	.09	.03
☐ 14 Tom Draper	.06	.03	.01
☐ 15 Dave Andreychuk	.06	.03	.01
☐ 16 Petr Svoboda	.06	.03	.01
☐ 17 Doug Bodger	.20	.09	.03
☐ 18 Donald Audette	.06	.03	.01
☐ 19 Alexander Mogilny	.50	.23	.06
☐ 20 Randy Wood	.06	.03	.01
☐ 21 Gary Roberts	.08	.04	.01
☐ 22 Al MacInnis	.10	.05	.01
☐ 23 Theoren Fleury	.10	.05	.01
☐ 24 Sergei Makarov	.08	.04	.01
☐ 25 Mike Vernon	.08	.04	.01
☐ 26 Joe Nieuwendyk	.08	.04	.01
☐ 27 Gary Suter	.08	.04	.01
☐ 28 Joel Otto	.06	.03	.01
☐ 29 Paul Ranheim	.06	.03	.01
☐ 30 Jeremy Roenick	.75	.35	.09
☐ 31 Steve Larmer	.08	.04	.01
☐ 32 Michel Goulet	.08	.04	.01
☐ 33 Ed Belfour	.30	.14	.04
☐ 34 Chris Chelios	.08	.04	.01
☐ 35 Igor Kravchuk	.06	.03	.01
☐ 36 Brent Sutter	.08	.04	.01
☐ 37 Steve Smith	.08	.04	.01
☐ 38 Dirk Graham	.06	.03	.01
☐ 39 Steve Yzerman	.30	.14	.04
☐ 40 Sergei Fedorov	1.00	.45	.13
☐ 41 Paul Ysebaert	.06	.03	.01
☐ 42 Nicklas Lidstrom	.20	.09	.03
☐ 43 Tim Cheveldae	.08	.04	.01
☐ 44 Vladimir Konstantinov	.06	.03	.01
☐ 45 Shawn Burr	.06	.03	.01
☐ 46 Bob Probert	.06	.03	.01
☐ 47 Ray Sheppard	.08	.04	.01
☐ 48 Kelly Buchberger	.06	.03	.01
☐ 49 Joe Murphy	.06	.03	.01
☐ 50 Norm MacIver	.06	.03	.01
☐ 51 Bill Ranford	.08	.04	.01
☐ 52 Bernie Nicholls	.08	.04	.01
☐ 53 Esa Tikkanen	.08	.04	.01
☐ 54 Scott Mellanby	.06	.03	.01
☐ 55 Dave Manson	.06	.03	.01
☐ 56 Craig Simpson	.06	.03	.01
☐ 57 John Cullen	.06	.03	.01
☐ 58 Pat Verbeek	.08	.04	.01
☐ 59 Zarley Zalapski	.06	.03	.01
☐ 60 Murray Craven	.06	.03	.01
☐ 61 Bobby Holik	.06	.03	.01
☐ 62 Steve Konroyd	.06	.03	.01
☐ 63 Geoff Sanderson	.40	.10	.05
☐ 64 Frank Pietrangelo	.06	.03	.01
☐ 65 Mikael Andersson UER	.06	.03	.01
(Front notes traded,			
actually he was signed			
as free agent)			
☐ 66 Wayne Gretzky	2.00	.90	.25
☐ 67 Rob Blake	.10	.05	.01
☐ 68 Jari Kurri	.10	.05	.01
☐ 69 Marty McSorley	.08	.04	.01
☐ 70 Kelly Hrudey	.08	.04	.01
☐ 71 Paul Coffey	.15	.07	.02
☐ 72 Luc Robitaille	.20	.09	.03
☐ 73 Peter Ahola	.06	.03	.01
☐ 74 Tony Granato	.06	.03	.01
☐ 75 Derian Hatcher	.06	.03	.01
☐ 76 Mike Modano	.35	.16	.04
☐ 77 Dave Gagner	.08	.04	.01
☐ 78 Mark Tinordi	.08	.04	.01
☐ 79 Craig Ludwig	.06	.03	.01
☐ 80 Ulf Dahlen	.06	.03	.01
☐ 81 Bobby Smith	.08	.04	.01
☐ 82 Jon Casey	.08	.04	.01
☐ 83 Jim Johnson	.06	.03	.01
☐ 84 Denis Savard	.08	.04	.01
☐ 85 Patrick Roy	.75	.35	.09
☐ 86 Eric Desjardins	.06	.03	.01
☐ 87 Kirk Muller	.08	.04	.01
☐ 88 Guy Carbonneau	.08	.04	.01
☐ 89 Shayne Corson	.08	.04	.01
☐ 90 Brent Gilchrist	.06	.03	.01
☐ 91 Mathieu Schneider UER	.08	.04	.01
(Back photo actually			
Stephan Lebeau)			
☐ 92 Gilbert Dionne	.06	.03	.01
☐ 93 Stephane Richer	.08	.04	.01
☐ 94 Kevin Todd	.06	.03	.01
☐ 95 Scott Stevens	.10	.05	.01
☐ 96 Viacheslav Fetisov	.06	.03	.01
☐ 97 Chris Terreri	.08	.04	.01
☐ 98 Claude Lemieux	.08	.04	.01
☐ 99 Bruce Driver	.06	.03	.01
☐ 100 Peter Stastny	.08	.04	.01
☐ 101 Alexei Kasatonov	.06	.03	.01
☐ 102 Patrick Flatley	.06	.03	.01
☐ 103 Adam Creighton UER	.06	.03	.01
(Front notes traded,			
actually he was			
claimed via waivers)			
☐ 104 Pierre Turgeon	.25	.11	.03
☐ 105 Ray Ferraro	.06	.03	.01
☐ 106 Steve Thomas	.08	.04	.01
☐ 107 Mark Fitzpatrick	.08	.04	.01
☐ 108 Benoit Hogue	.06	.03	.01
☐ 109 Uwe Krupp	.06	.03	.01
☐ 110 Derek King	.06	.03	.01
☐ 111 Mark Messier	.25	.11	.03
☐ 112 Brian Leetch	.35	.16	.04
☐ 113 Mike Gartner	.10	.05	.01
☐ 114 Darren Turcotte	.06	.03	.01
☐ 115 Adam Graves	.35	.16	.04
☐ 116 Mike Richter	.30	.14	.04
☐ 117 Sergei Nemchinov	.08	.04	.01
☐ 118 Tony Amonte	.20	.09	.03
☐ 119 James Patrick	.06	.03	.01
☐ 120 Andrew McBain	.06	.03	.01
☐ 121 Rob Murphy	.06	.03	.01
☐ 122 Mike Peluso	.06	.03	.01
☐ 123 Sylvain Turgeon	.06	.03	.01
☐ 124 Brad Shaw	.06	.03	.01
☐ 125 Peter Sidorkiewicz	.06	.03	.01
☐ 126 Brad Marsh	.08	.04	.01
☐ 127 Mark Freer	.06	.03	.01
☐ 128 Marc Fortier	.06	.03	.01
☐ 129 Ron Hextall	.08	.04	.01
☐ 130 Claude Boivin	.06	.03	.01
☐ 131 Mark Recchi	.30	.14	.04
☐ 132 Rod Brind'Amour	.15	.07	.02
☐ 133 Mike Ricci	.08	.04	.01
☐ 134 Kevin Dineen	.08	.04	.01
☐ 135 Brian Benning	.06	.03	.01
☐ 136 Kerry Huffman	.06	.03	.01
☐ 137 Steve Duchesne	.08	.04	.01
☐ 138 Rick Tocchet	.08	.04	.01
☐ 139 Mario Lemieux	1.25	.55	.16
☐ 140 Kevin Stevens	.30	.14	.04
☐ 141 Jaromir Jagr	.75	.35	.09
☐ 142 Joe Mullen	.08	.04	.01
☐ 143 Ulf Samuelsson	.08	.04	.01
☐ 144 Ron Francis	.08	.04	.01
☐ 145 Tom Barrasso	.08	.04	.01
☐ 146 Larry Murphy	.08	.04	.01
☐ 147 Alexei Gusarov	.06	.03	.01
☐ 148 Valeri Kamensky	.20	.09	.03
☐ 149 Mats Sundin	.30	.14	.04
☐ 150 Joe Sakic	.25	.11	.03
☐ 151 Claude Lapointe	.06	.03	.01
☐ 152 Stephane Fiset	.08	.04	.01
☐ 153 Nolan Owen	.06	.03	.01
☐ 154 Mike Hough	.06	.03	.01
☐ 155 Greg Paslawski	.06	.03	.01
☐ 156 Brett Hull	.75	.35	.09
☐ 157 Craig Janney	.15	.07	.02
☐ 158 Jeff Brown	.08	.04	.01
☐ 159 Paul Cavallini	.06	.03	.01
☐ 160 Garth Butcher	.06	.03	.01
☐ 161 Nelson Emerson	.15	.07	.02
☐ 162 Ron Sutter	.06	.03	.01
☐ 163 Brendan Shanahan	.25	.11	.03
☐ 164 Curtis Joseph	.30	.14	.04
☐ 165 Doug Wilson	.08	.04	.01

☐ 166 Pat Falloon	.20	.09	.03
☐ 167 Kelly Kisio	.06	.03	.01
☐ 168 Neil Wilkinson	.06	.03	.01
☐ 169 Jay More	.06	.03	.01
☐ 170 David Bruce	.06	.03	.01
☐ 171 Jeff Hackett	.06	.03	.01
☐ 172 David Williams	.10	.05	.01
☐ 173 Brian Lawton	.06	.03	.01
☐ 174 Brian Bradley	.06	.03	.01
☐ 175 Jock Callander	.06	.03	.01
☐ 176 Basil McRae	.06	.03	.01
☐ 177 Rob Ramage	.06	.03	.01
☐ 178 Pat Jablonski	.06	.03	.01
☐ 179 Joe Reekie	.06	.03	.01
☐ 180 Doug Crossman	.06	.03	.01
☐ 181 Jim Benning	.06	.03	.01
☐ 182 Ken Hodge Jr.	.06	.03	.01
☐ 183 Grant Fuhr	.08	.04	.01
☑ 184 Doug Gilmour	.30	.14	.04
☐ 185 Glenn Anderson	.08	.04	.01
☐ 186 Dave Ellett	.06	.03	.01
☐ 187 Peter Zezel	.06	.03	.01
☐ 188 Jamie Macoun	.06	.03	.01
☐ 189 Wendel Clark	.10	.05	.01
☐ 190 Bob Halkidis	.06	.03	.01
☐ 191 Rob Pearson	.06	.03	.01
☐ 192 Pavel Bure	2.00	.90	.25
☐ 193 Kirk McLean	.25	.11	.03
☐ 194 Sergio Momesso	.06	.03	.01
☐ 195 Cliff Ronning	.06	.03	.01
☐ 196 Jyrki Lumme	.06	.03	.01
☐ 197 Trevor Linden	.20	.09	.03
☐ 198 Geoff Courtnall	.06	.03	.01
☐ 199 Doug Lidster	.06	.03	.01
☐ 200 Dave Babych	.06	.03	.01
☐ 201 Michal Pivonka	.08	.04	.01
☐ 202 Dale Hunter	.08	.04	.01
☐ 203 Calle Johansson	.06	.03	.01
☐ 204 Kevin Hatcher	.08	.04	.01
☐ 205 Al Iafrate	.08	.04	.01
☐ 206 Don Beaupre	.08	.04	.01
☐ 207 Randy Burridge	.06	.03	.01
☐ 208 Dimitri Khristich	.08	.04	.01
☐ 209 Peter Bondra	.08	.04	.01
☐ 210 Teppo Numminen	.06	.03	.01
☐ 211 Bob Essensa	.08	.04	.01
☐ 212 Phil Housley	.08	.04	.01
☐ 213 Ed Olczyk	.06	.03	.01
☐ 214 Pat Elynuik	.06	.03	.01
☐ 215 Troy Murray	.06	.03	.01
☐ 216 Igor Ulanov	.06	.03	.01
☐ 217 Thomas Steen	.06	.03	.01
☐ 218 Darrin Shannon	.06	.03	.01
☐ 219 Joe Juneau UER (Back says shoots right, should be left) Boston Bruins	1.25	.55	.16
☐ 220 Stephen Heinze Boston Bruins	.06	.03	.01
☐ 221 Ted Donato Boston Bruins	.06	.03	.01
☐ 222 Glen Murray Boston Bruins	.06	.03	.01
☐ 223 Keith Carney Buffalo Sabres	.15	.07	.02
☐ 224 Dean McAmmond Chicago Blackhawks	.15	.07	.02
☐ 225 Slava Kozlov Detroit Red Wings	.75	.35	.09
☐ 226 Martin Lapointe Detroit Red Wings	.06	.03	.01
☐ 227 Patrick Poulin Hartford Whalers	.06	.03	.01
☐ 228 Darryl Sydor Los Angeles Kings	.08	.04	.01
☐ 229 Trent Klatt Minnesota North Stars	.25	.11	.03
☐ 230 Bill Guerin New Jersey Devils	.25	.11	.03
☐ 231 Jarrod Skalde New Jersey Devils	.06	.03	.01
☐ 232 Scott Niedermayer New Jersey Devils	.40	.18	.05
☐ 233 Marty McInnis New York Islanders	.06	.03	.01
☐ 234 Scott LaChance New York Islanders	.06	.03	.01
☐ 235 Dominic Roussel Philadelphia Flyers	.20	.09	.03
☐ 236 Eric Lindros Philadelphia Flyers	5.00	2.30	.60
☐ 237 Shawn McEachern Pittsburgh Penguins	.15	.07	.02
☐ 238 Martin Rucinsky Quebec Nordiques	.15	.07	.02
☐ 239 Bill Lindsay Quebec Nordiques	.15	.07	.02
☐ 240 Bret Hedican St. Louis Blues	.20	.09	.03
☐ 241 Ray Whitney San Jose Sharks	.25	.11	.03
☐ 242 Felix Potvin Toronto Maple Leafs	1.50	.65	.19
☐ 243 Keith Tkachuk Winnipeg Jets	.35	.16	.04
☐ 244 Evgeny Davydov Winnipeg Jets	.06	.03	.01
☐ 245 Brett Hull SL St. Louis Blues	.25	.11	.03
☐ 246 Wayne Gretzky SL Los Angeles Kings	.75	.35	.09
☐ 247 Steve Yzerman SL Detroit Red Wings	.20	.09	.03
☐ 248 Paul Ysebaert SL Detroit Red Wings	.06	.03	.01
☐ 249 Dave Andreychuk SL Buffalo Sabres	.08	.04	.01
☐ 250 Kirk McLean SL Vancouver Canucks	.15	.07	.02
☐ 251 Tim Cheveldae SL Detroit Red Wings	.06	.03	.01
☐ 252 Jeremy Roenick SL Chicago Blackhawks	.25	.11	.03
☐ 253 NHL Pro Set NR Youth Parade	.06	.03	.01
☐ 254 NHL Pro Set NR Youth Clinics	.06	.03	.01
☐ 255 NHL Pro Set NR All-Time Team	.06	.03	.01
☐ 256 Mike Gartner MS New York Rangers	.10	.05	.01
☐ 257 Brian Propp MS Minnesota North Stars	.08	.04	.01
☐ 258 Dave Taylor MS Los Angeles Kings	.06	.03	.01
☐ 259 Bobby Smith MS Minnesota North Stars	.06	.03	.01
☐ 260 Denis Savard MS Montreal Canadiens	.08	.04	.01
☐ 261 Ray Bourque MS Boston Bruins	.08	.04	.01
☐ 262 Joe Mullen MS Pittsburgh Penguins	.08	.04	.01
☐ 263 John Tonelli MS Quebec Nordiques	.06	.03	.01
☐ 264 Brad Marsh MS Ottawa Senators	.06	.03	.01
☐ 265 Randy Carlyle MS Winnipeg Jets	.06	.03	.01
☐ 266 Mike Hough PS Quebec Nordiques Power	.06	.03	.01
☐ 267 Bob Essensa PS Winnipeg Jets Achieve	.06	.03	.01
☐ 268 Mike Lalor PS Winnipeg Jets Motivate	.06	.03	.01
☐ 269 Terry Carkner PS Philadelphia Flyers Attitude	.06	.03	.01
☐ 270 Todd Krygier PS Washington Capitals Responsibility	.06	.03	.01

1992-93 Pro Set Award Winners

Randomly inserted in 1992-93 Pro Set series I foil packs, these five standard-size (2 1/2" by 3 1/2") cards capture five NHL players who were honored with trophies for their outstanding play. The fronts feature full-bleed color action player photos. A gold-foil stamped "Award Winner" emblem is superimposed at the upper right corner. The player's name, team name, and trophy awarded appear in two bars toward the bottom of the picture. The backs carry a color headshot and a career summary. The cards are numbered on the back.

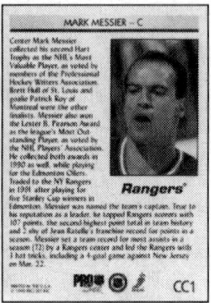

	MINT	EXC	G-VG
COMPLETE SET (5)	30.00	13.50	3.80
COMMON PLAYER (CC1-CC5)	2.00	.90	.25
☐ CC1 Mark Messier New York Rangers Hart/Pearson Trophies	5.00	2.30	.60
☐ CC2 Patrick Roy Montreal Canadiens Vezina/Jennings Trophies	12.00	5.50	1.50
☐ CC3 Pavel Bure Vancouver Canucks Calder Trophy	15.00	6.75	1.90
☐ CC4 Brian Leetch New York Rangers Norris Trophy	4.00	1.80	.50
☐ CC5 Guy Carbonneau Montreal Canadiens Selke Trophy	2.00	.90	.25

1992-93 Pro Set Gold Team Leaders

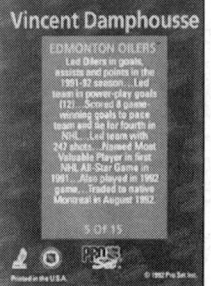

Randomly inserted in foil packs, this 15-card standard-size (2 1/2" by 3 1/2") set spotlights team scoring leaders from the Campbell Conference. The color action player photos on the fronts are full-bleed with "1991-92 Team Leader" gold foil stamped on the picture at the upper right corner. Toward the bottom of the picture the player's name appears on a rust-colored bar that overlays a jagged design. Bordered by a dark brown screened background with Campbell Conference logos, the back carries career summary on a rust-colored panel. The cards are numbered on the back "X of 15."

	MINT	EXC	G-VG
COMPLETE SET (15)	45.00	20.00	5.75
COMMON PLAYER (1-15)	1.25	.55	.16
☐ 1 Gary Roberts Calgary Flames	1.50	.65	.19
☐ 2 Jeremy Roenick Chicago Blackhawks	6.00	2.70	.75
☐ 3 Steve Yzerman Detroit Red Wings	6.00	2.70	.75
☐ 4 Nicklas Lidstrom Detroit Red Wings	1.50	.65	.19

☐ 5 Vin Damphousse Edmonton Oilers	1.50	.65	.19
☐ 6 Wayne Gretzky Los Angeles Kings	14.00	6.25	1.75
☐ 7 Mike Modano Minnesota North Stars	3.50	1.55	.45
☐ 8 Brett Hull St. Louis Blues	6.00	2.70	.75
☐ 9 Nelson Emerson St. Louis Blues	1.50	.65	.19
☐ 10 Pat Falloon San Jose Sharks	1.50	.65	.19
☐ 11 Doug Gilmour Toronto Maple Leafs	6.00	2.70	.75
☐ 12 Trevor Linden Vancouver Canucks	2.50	1.15	.30
☐ 13 Pavel Bure Vancouver Canucks	12.00	5.50	1.50
☐ 14 Phil Housley Winnipeg Jets	1.50	.65	.19
☐ 15 Luciano Borsato Winnipeg Jets	1.25	.55	.16

1992-93 Pro Set Rookie Goal Leaders

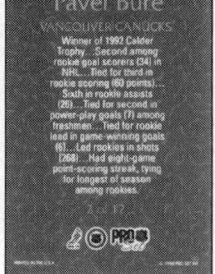

This 12-card Rookie Goal Leader set features the top rookie goal scorers from the 1991-92 season. The cards measure the standard size (2 1/2" by 3 1/2") and were randomly inserted one per 1992-93 Pro Set I jumbo packs. On a variegated purple card face, the fronts display color action player photos that are accented by gold drop borders. The player's name appears in a white bar above the picture, while the words "1991-92 Rookie Goal Leader" are gold foil-stamped across the bottom of the picture. On the same variegated purple background as the fronts, the backs present career summary. The cards are numbered on the back.

	MINT	EXC	G-VG
COMPLETE SET (12)	40.00	18.00	5.00
COMMON PLAYER (1-12)	3.00	1.35	.40
☐ 1 Tony Amonte New York Rangers	3.50	1.55	.45
☐ 2 Pavel Bure Vancouver Canucks	15.00	6.75	1.90
☐ 3 Donald Audette Buffalo Sabres	3.00	1.35	.40
☐ 4 Pat Falloon San Jose Sharks	4.00	1.80	.50
☐ 5 Nelson Emerson St. Louis Blues	4.00	1.80	.50
☐ 6 Gilbert Dionne Montreal Canadiens	3.00	1.35	.40
☐ 7 Kevin Todd New Jersey Devils	3.00	1.35	.40
☐ 8 Luciano Borsato Winnipeg Jets	3.00	1.35	.40
☐ 9 Rob Pearson Toronto Maple Leafs	3.00	1.35	.40
☐ 10 Valeri Zelepukin New Jersey Devils	3.50	1.55	.45
☐ 11 Geoff Sanderson	6.00	2.70	.75

Hartford Whalers
☐ 12 Claude Lapointe .... 3.00 1.35 .40
Quebec Nordiques

1987 Pro-Sport All-Stars

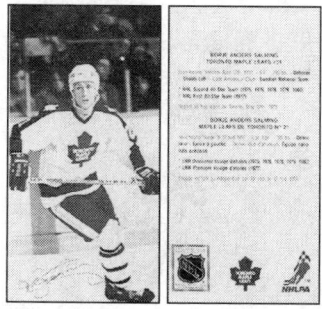

Issued in Canadian retail packs that included an LCD quartz watch, each of these red, white, and blue oversized cards measures approximately 11 3/4" by 10 1/2" when unfolded and features a color player action shot at the lower right. The player's name, along with his career highlights in English and French, are shown at the lower left. A middle section is cut away to accommodate the watch. The cards are numbered on the front with a "CW" prefix. These cards are priced below without the watches. Number 4 was apparently not issued.

	MINT	EXC	G-VG
COMPLETE SET (17)	50.00	20.00	5.00
COMMON PLAYER (1-18)	2.00	.80	.20
☐ 1 Larry Robinson	4.00	1.60	.40
Montreal Canadiens			
☐ 2 Guy Carbonneau	2.00	.80	.20
Montreal Canadiens			
☐ 3 Chris Chelios	3.00	1.20	.30
Montreal Candiens			
☐ 5 Mario Lemieux	10.00	4.00	1.00
Pittsburgh Penguins			
☐ 6 Mike Bossy	4.00	1.60	.40
New York Islanders			
☐ 7 Dale Hawerchuk	2.00	.80	.20
Winnipeg Jets			
☐ 8 Joe Mullen	2.00	.80	.20
Calgary Flames			
☐ 9 Rick Vaive	2.00	.80	.20
Toronto Maple Leafs			
☐ 10 Wendel Clark	5.00	2.00	.50
Toronto Maple Leafs			
☐ 11 Michel Goulet	3.00	1.20	.30
Quebec Nordiques			
☐ 12 Peter Stastny	3.00	1.20	.30
Quebec Nordiques			
☐ 13 Mark Messier	6.00	2.40	.60
Edmonton Oilers			
☐ 14 Paul Coffey	4.00	1.60	.40
Edmonton Oilers			
☐ 15 Tony Tanti	2.00	.80	.20
Vancouver Canucks			
☐ 16 Borje Salming	2.00	.80	.20
Toronto Maple Leafs			
☐ 17 Chris Nilan	2.00	.80	.20
Montreal Canadiens			
☐ 18 Mats Naslund	2.00	.80	.20
Montreal Canadiens			

1983-84 Puffy Stickers

This set of 150 puffy stickers was issued in panels of six stickers each. The panels measure approximately 3 1/2" by 6". There are 21 player panels and four logo panels. The

NHL and NHLPA logos appear in the center of each panel. The stickers are oval-shaped and measure approximately 1 1/4" by 1 3/4". In the top portion of the oval they feature a color head shot of the player, with the team name above the head and the player name below the picture in a white box. The sticker background is wood-grain in design. The 21 player panels are numbered and we have checklisted them below accordingly. The logo panels are unnumbered and they are listed after the player panels. The backs are blank. There was also an album produced for this set; the album is not included in the complete set price below.

	MINT	EXC	G-VG
COMPLETE SET (25)	60.00	24.00	6.00
COMMON PANEL (1-21)	1.50	.60	.15
COMMON PANEL (22-25)	2.50	1.00	.25
☐ 1 Doug Risebrough	15.00	6.00	1.50
Wayne Gretzky			
Mats Naslund			
Bill Derlago			
Richard Brodeur			
Dave Babych			
☐ 2 Glenn Anderson	2.50	1.00	.25
Larry Robinson			
Rick Vaive			
Stan Smyl			
Scott Arniel			
Don Edwards			
☐ 3 Ryan Walter	2.50	1.00	.25
Peter Ihnacak			
Thomas Gradin			
Morris Lukowich			
Kent Nilsson			
Paul Coffey			
☐ 4 John Anderson	6.00	2.40	.60
Dave(Tiger) Williams			
Brian Mullen			
Steve Tambellini			
Mark Messier			
Guy Lafleur			
☐ 5 Darcy Rota	2.50	1.00	.25
Dale Hawerchuk			
Paul Reinhart			
Jari Kurri			
Mario Tremblay			
Mike Palmateer			
☐ 6 Paul MacLean	3.50	1.40	.35
Lanny McDonald			
Ken Linseman			
Steve Shutt			
Borje Salming			
Kevin McCarthy			
☐ 7 Barry Pederson	2.50	1.00	.25
Mike Foligno			
Jim Fox			
Don Lever			
Bobby Clarke			
Greg Malone			
☐ 8 Gilbert Perreault	2.50	1.00	.25
Charlie Simmer			
Hector Marini			
Mark Howe			
Rick Kehoe			
Jim Schoenfeld			
☐ 9 Larry Murphy	2.50	1.00	.25
Phil Russell			
Bill Barber			
Mike Bullard			
Pete Peeters			

John Van Boxmeer
☐ 10 Tapio Levo .... 3.50 1.40 .35
Darryl Sittler
Paul Gardner
Rick Middleton
Real Cloutier
Bernie Nicholls
☐ 11 Brian Propp........................ 3.50 1.40 .35
Michel Dion
Ray Bourque
Dale McCourt
Marcel Dionne
Bob MacMillan
☐ 12 Randy Carlyle...................... 2.50 1.00 .25
Terry O'Reilly
Phil Housley
Dave Taylor
Glenn Resch
Behn Wilson
☐ 13 Tony Esposito .... 3.50 1.40 .35
Ron Duguay
Pierre Larouche
Neal Broten
Peter Stastny
Blake Dunlop
☐ 14 Walt McKechnie .... 1.50 .60 .15
Risto Siltanen
Bobby Smith
Anton Stastny
Mike Liut
Doug Wilson
☐ 15 Blaine Stoughton.................. 2.50 1.00 .25
Dino Ciccarelli
Michel Goulet
Jorgen Pettersson
Tom Lysiak
Brad Park
☐ 16 Craig Hartsburg.................... 1.50 .60 .15
Marian Stastny
Rob Ramage
Al Secord
John Ogrodnick
Greg Millen
☐ 17 Tony McKegney .... 2.50 1.00 .25
Brian Sutter
Steve Larmer
Danny Gare
Mark Johnson
Brian Bellows
☐ 18 Bernie Federko .... 2.50 1.00 .25
Denis Savard
Reed Larson
Ron Francis
Dennis Maruk
Dan Bouchard
☐ 19 Mike Bossy .... 3.50 1.40 .35
Anders Hedberg
Rod Langway
Billy Smith
Reijo Ruotsalainen
Milan Novy
☐ 20 Barry Beck.......................... 2.50 1.00 .25
Bob Carpenter
Clark Gillies
Rob McClanahan
Brian Engblom
Denis Potvin
☐ 21 Mike Gartner .... 3.50 1.40 .35
John Tonelli
Willie Huber
Pat Riggin
Bryan Trottier
Don Maloney
☐ 22 Norris Division .... 2.50 1.00 .25
Blackhawks logo
Red Wings logo
North Stars logo
Blues logo
Maple Leafs logo
NHL logo
☐ 23 Patrick Division .... 2.50 1.00 .25
Devils logo
Islanders logo
Rangers logo
Flyers logo
Penguins logo
Capitals logo
☐ 24 Adams Division .... 2.50 1.00 .25
Bruins logo
Sabres logo
Whalers logo
Canadiens logo
Nordiques logo
NHL logo

☐ 25 Smythe Division.................... 2.50 1.00 .25
Flames logo
Oilers logo
Kings logo
Canucks logo
Jets logo
NHL logo
☐ xx Album................................. 20.00 8.00 2.00

1938-39 Quaker Oats Photos

This 30-card set of Toronto Maple Leafs (TML) and
Montreal Canadiens (MC) was sponsored by Quaker Oats.
These oversized cards (approximately 6 1/4" by 7 3/8") are
unnumbered and hence are listed below alphabetically.
Facsimile autographs are printed in white on the fronts of
these blank-backed cards.

	EX-MT	VG-E	GOOD
COMPLETE SET (30)........................	1250.00	550.00	125.00
COMMON PLAYER (1-30)................	35.00	14.00	3.50
☐ 1 Syl Apps TML...........................	100.00	40.00	10.00
☐ 2 Toe Blake MC	150.00	60.00	15.00
☐ 3 Buzz Boll TML	35.00	14.00	3.50
☐ 4 Turk Broda TML.........................	125.00	50.00	12.50
☐ 5 Walter Buswell MC	35.00	14.00	3.50
☐ 6 Herb Cain MC...........................	45.00	18.00	4.50
☐ 7 Murph Chamberlain TML	35.00	14.00	3.50
☐ 8 Wilf Cude MC	35.00	14.00	3.50
☐ 9 Bob Davidson TML....................	35.00	14.00	3.50
☐ 10 Gordie Drillon TML................	65.00	26.00	6.50
☐ 11 Paul Drouin MC.....................	35.00	14.00	3.50
☐ 12 Stew Evans MC......................	35.00	14.00	3.50
☐ 13 James Fowler TML.................	35.00	14.00	3.50
☐ 14 Johnny Gagnon MC	35.00	14.00	3.50
☐ 15 Robert Gracie MC..................	35.00	14.00	3.50
☐ 16 Reg Hamilton TML.................	35.00	14.00	3.50
☐ 17 Paul Haynes MC....................	35.00	14.00	3.50
☐ 18 Foster Hewitt TML.................	65.00	26.00	6.50
☐ 19 Red Horner TML	65.00	26.00	6.50
☐ 20 Harvey(Busher) Jackson .... TML	100.00	40.00	10.00
☐ 21 R. Kampman TML	35.00	14.00	3.50
☐ 22 Pep Kelly TML........................	35.00	14.00	3.50
☐ 23 Rod Lorrain MC	35.00	14.00	3.50
☐ 24 George Mantha MC	35.00	14.00	3.50
☐ 25 Nick Metz TML.......................	35.00	14.00	3.50
☐ 26 George Parsons TML.............	35.00	14.00	3.50
☐ 27 Babe Siebert MC	65.00	26.00	6.50
☐ 28 W.D. Thoms TML....................	35.00	14.00	3.50
☐ 29 James Ward MC.....................	35.00	14.00	3.50
☐ 30 Marvin Wentworth MC	35.00	14.00	3.50

1973-74 Quaker Oats WHA

This set of 50 cards features players of the World Hockey
Association. The cards were issued in strips (panels) of five
in Quaker Oats products. The cards measure approximately
2 1/4" by 3 1/4" and are numbered on the back. The
information on the card backs is written in English and
French. The value of unseparated panels would be

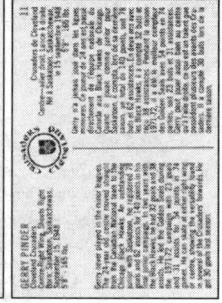

GERRY PINDER - CLEVELAND

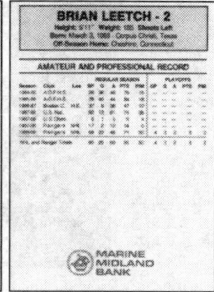

approximately 20 percent greater than the sum of the individual values listed below.

	NRMT	VG-E	GOOD
COMPLETE SET (50)	250.00	100.00	25.00
COMMON PLAYER (1-50)	4.00	1.60	.40
☐ 1 Jim Wiste	4.00	1.60	.40
☐ 2 Al Smith	6.00	2.40	.60
☐ 3 Rosaire Paiement	4.00	1.60	.40
☐ 4 Ted Hampson	4.00	1.60	.40
☐ 5 Gavin Kirk	4.00	1.60	.40
☐ 6 Andre Lacroix	6.00	2.40	.60
☐ 7 John Schella	4.00	1.60	.40
☐ 8 Gerry Cheevers	20.00	8.00	2.00
☐ 9 Norm Beaudin	4.00	1.60	.40
☐ 10 Jim Harrison	4.00	1.60	.40
☐ 11 Gerry Pinder	6.00	2.40	.60
☐ 12 Bob Sicinski	4.00	1.60	.40
☐ 13 Bryan Campbell	4.00	1.60	.40
☐ 14 Murray Hall	4.00	1.60	.40
☐ 15 Chris Bordeleau	6.00	2.40	.60
☐ 16 Al Hamilton	4.00	1.60	.40
☐ 17 Jimmy McLeod	4.00	1.60	.40
☐ 18 Larry Pleau	6.00	2.40	.60
☐ 19 Larry Lund	4.00	1.60	.40
☐ 20 Bobby Sheehan	4.00	1.60	.40
☐ 21 Jan Popiel	4.00	1.60	.40
☐ 22 Andre Guadette	4.00	1.60	.40
☐ 23 Bob Charlebois	4.00	1.60	.40
☐ 24 Gene Peacosh	4.00	1.60	.40
☐ 25 Rick Ley	6.00	2.40	.60
☐ 26 Larry Hornung	4.00	1.60	.40
☐ 27 Gary Jarrett	4.00	1.60	.40
☐ 28 Ted Taylor	6.00	2.40	.60
☐ 29 Pete Donnelly	4.00	1.60	.40
☐ 30 J.C. Tremblay	6.00	2.40	.60
☐ 31 Jim Cardiff	4.00	1.60	.40
☐ 32 Gary Veneruzzo	4.00	1.60	.40
☐ 33 John French	4.00	1.60	.40
☐ 34 Ron Ward	6.00	2.40	.60
☐ 35 Wayne Connelly	4.00	1.60	.40
☐ 36 Ron Buchanan	4.00	1.60	.40
☐ 37 Ken Block	4.00	1.60	.40
☐ 38 Alain Caron	4.00	1.60	.40
☐ 39 Brit Selby	6.00	2.40	.60
☐ 40 Guy Trottier	4.00	1.60	.40
☐ 41 Ernie Wakely	4.00	1.60	.40
☐ 42 J.P. LeBlanc	4.00	1.60	.40
☐ 43 Michel Parizeau	4.00	1.60	.40
☐ 44 Wayne Rivers	4.00	1.60	.40
☐ 45 Reg Fleming	4.00	1.60	.40
☐ 46 Don Herriman	4.00	1.60	.40
☐ 47 Jim Dorey	4.00	1.60	.40
☐ 48 Danny Lawson	6.00	2.40	.60
☐ 49 Dick Paradise	4.00	1.60	.40
☐ 50 Bobby Hull	60.00	24.00	6.00

1989-90 Rangers Marine Midland Bank

This 30-card set of New York Rangers was sponsored by Marine Midland Bank; the card backs have the bank's logo and name at the bottom. The cards measure 2 5/8" by 3 5/8". The fronts feature color action photos of the players, with a thin red border on the left and bottom of the picture. Outside the red border appears a blue margin, with the player's name, position, and jersey number printed at right angles to one another. The Rangers' logo in the lower right hand corner completes the face of the card. The back has biographical information and career statistics. The cards have been listed below according to sweater number. The key cards in the set are early cards of Brian Leetch and Mike Richter.

	MINT	EXC	G-VG
COMPLETE SET (30)	30.00	12.00	3.00
COMMON PLAYER	.75	.30	.07
☐ 2 Brian Leetch	7.50	3.00	.75
☐ 3 James Patrick	1.00	.40	.10
☐ 4 Ron Greschner	1.00	.40	.10
☐ 5 Normand Rochefort	.75	.30	.07
☐ 6 Miloslav Horava	.75	.30	.07
☐ 8 Darren Turcotte	1.25	.50	.12
☐ 9 Bernie Nicholls	1.25	.50	.12
☐ 11 Kelly Kisio	1.00	.40	.10
☐ 12 Kris King	.75	.30	.07
☐ 14 Mark Hardy	.75	.30	.07
☐ 15 Mark Janssens	.75	.30	.07
☐ 16 Ulf Dahlen	1.00	.40	.10
☐ 17 Carey Wilson	.75	.30	.07
☐ 19 Brian Mullen	1.00	.40	.10
☐ 20 Jan Erixon	.75	.30	.07
☐ 21 David Shaw	.75	.30	.07
☐ 23 Corey Millen	1.25	.50	.12
☐ 24 Randy Moller	.75	.30	.07
☐ 25 John Ogrodnick	1.00	.40	.10
☐ 26 Troy Mallette	.75	.30	.07
☐ 29 Rudy Poeschek	.75	.30	.07
☐ 30 Chris Nilan	1.00	.40	.10
☐ 33 Bob Froese	1.00	.40	.10
☐ 34 John Vanbiesbrouck	3.00	1.20	.30
☐ 35 Mike Richter	5.00	2.00	.50
☐ 37 Paul Broten	.75	.30	.07
☐ 38 Jeff Bloemberg	.75	.30	.07
☐ 44 Lindy Ruff	.75	.30	.07
☐ xx Roger Neilson CO	.75	.30	.07
☐ xx Rangers MasterCard	.75	.30	.07

1970-71 Red Wings Marathon

This 11-card (artistic) portrait set of Detroit Red Wings was part of a (Pro Star Portraits) promotion by Marathon Oil. The cards measure approximately 7 1/2" by 14"; the bottom portion, which measures 7 1/2" by 4 1/16", was a tear-off postcard in the form of a credit card application. The front features a full color portrait by Nicholas Volpe, with a facsimile autograph of the player inscribed across the bottom of the painting. The back included an offer for other sports memorabilia on the upper portion.

	NRMT	VG-E	GOOD
COMPLETE SET (11)	60.00	24.00	6.00
COMMON PLAYER (1-11)	3.50	1.40	.35

☐	1	Gary Bergman	5.00	2.00	.50
☐	2	Wayne Connelly	3.50	1.40	.35
☐	3	Alex Delvecchio	9.00	3.75	.90
☐	4	Roy Edwards	3.50	1.40	.35
☐	5	Gordie Howe	30.00	12.00	3.00
☐	6	Bruce MacGregor	3.50	1.40	.35
☐	7	Frank Mahovlich	10.00	4.00	1.00
☐	8	Dale Rolfe	3.50	1.40	.35
☐	9	Jim Rutherford	6.00	2.40	.60
☐	10	Garry Unger	5.00	2.00	.50
☐	11	Tom Webster	5.00	2.00	.50

1991-92 Red Wings Little Caesars

Sponsored by Little Caesars, this 15-card set measures approximately 8 1/2" by 3 5/8" and features a color, action player photo on the left half of the card. The right half displays the player's name, position, biographical information, early career history, and jersey number, along with a close-up player photo. The backs are blank. The cards are unnumbered and checklisted below in alphabetical order.

			MINT	EXC	G-VG
	COMPLETE SET (15)		30.00	12.00	3.00
	COMMON PLAYER (1-15)		1.00	.40	.10
☐	1	Shawn Burr	1.00	.40	.10
☐	2	Jimmy Carson	2.50	1.00	.25
☐	3	Sergei Fedorov	7.50	3.00	.75
☐	4	Johan Garpenlov	1.50	.60	.15
☐	5	Rick Green	1.00	.40	.10
☐	6	Marc Habscheid	1.00	.40	.10
☐	7	Martin Lapointe	2.00	.80	.20
☐	8	Nicklas Lidstrom	2.00	.80	.20
☐	9	Brad McCrimmon	1.50	.60	.15
☐	10	Bryan Murray CO/MG	1.50	.60	.15
☐	11	Keith Primeau	3.00	1.20	.30
☐	12	Bob Probert	3.00	1.20	.30
☐	13	Paul Ysebaert	2.00	.80	.20
☐	14	Steve Yzerman	6.00	2.40	.60
☐	15	Team Card	3.00	1.20	.30

1975-76 Roadrunners Phoenix WHA

This 22-card set features players of the WHA Phoenix Roadrunners. The cards measure approximately 3" by 4" and the backs are blank. The front features a poor quality black and white head-and-shoulders shot of the player with a white border. The cards are numbered by the uniform number on the front and we have checklisted them below accordingly. The player's position and weight are also given.

			NRMT	VG-E	GOOD
	COMPLETE SET (22)		15.00	6.00	1.50
	COMMON PLAYER		1.00	.40	.10
☐	1	Gary Kurt	1.50	.60	.15
☐	2	Jim Niekamp	1.00	.40	.10
☐	3	Al McLeod	1.50	.60	.15
☐	4	Garry Lariviere	1.50	.60	.15
☐	5	Serge Beaudoin	1.00	.40	.10
☐	6	Ron Serafini	1.00	.40	.10
☐	7	Peter McNamee	1.00	.40	.10
☐	8	Robbie Ftorek	3.00	1.20	.30
☐	9	Del Hall	1.00	.40	.10
☐	10	Dave Gorman	1.00	.40	.10
☐	11	Murray Keogan	1.00	.40	.10
☐	12	Ron Huston	1.00	.40	.10
☐	14	Jim Boyd	1.00	.40	.10
☐	15	John Gray	1.00	.40	.10
☐	16	Michel Cormier	1.00	.40	.10
☐	17	Cam Connor	1.50	.60	.15
☐	18	John Migneault	1.00	.40	.10
☐	19	Pekka Rautakallio	1.50	.60	.15
☐	21	Barry Dean	1.00	.40	.10
☐	24	Lauri Mononen	1.00	.40	.10
☐	26	Jim Clarke	1.00	.40	.10
☐	30	Jack Norris	1.00	.40	.10

1976-77 Roadrunners Phoenix WHA

This 18-card set features players of the WHA Phoenix Roadrunners. Each card measures approximately 3 3/8" by 4 5/16". The front features a black and white head shot of the player, enframed by an aqua blue border on white card stock. The top and bottom inner borders are curved, creating space for the basic biographical information as well as the team and league logos that surround the picture. The backs are blank. The cards are unnumbered and we have checklisted them below in alphabetical order.

	NRMT	VG-E	GOOD
COMPLETE SET (18)	20.00	8.00	2.00
COMMON PLAYER (1-18)	1.00	.40	.10
☐ 1 Serge Beaudoin	1.00	.40	.10
☐ 2 Michel Cormier	1.00	.40	.10
☐ 3 Robbie Ftorek	3.00	1.20	.30
☐ 4 Del Hall	1.00	.40	.10
☐ 5 Clay Hebenton	1.00	.40	.10
☐ 6 Andre Hinse	1.00	.40	.10
☐ 7 Mike Hobin	1.00	.40	.10
☐ 8 Frank Hughes	1.00	.40	.10
☐ 9 Ron Huston	1.00	.40	.10
☐ 10 Gary Kurt	1.50	.60	.15
☐ 11 Garry Lariviere	1.50	.60	.15
☐ 12 Bob Liddington	1.00	.40	.10
☐ 13 Lauri Mononen	1.00	.40	.10
☐ 14 Jim Niekamp	1.00	.40	.10
☐ 15 Pekka Rautakallio	1.50	.60	.15
☐ 16 Seppo Repo	1.00	.40	.10
☐ 17 Jerry Rollins	1.00	.40	.10
☐ 18 Juhani Tamminen	1.00	.40	.10

1976-77 Rockies Puck Bucks

This 20-card set measures approximately 2 9/16" by 2 1/8" (after perforation) and features members of the then-expansion Colorado Rockies team. The set was issued in the Greater Denver area as part of a regional promotion for the Rockies. The cards feature a horizontal format on the front which has the player's photo. The cards were issued two to a panel (they could be separated, but then one couldn't compete in contest). Left side and right side in the rules refers to the two different cards that were joined: an action scene on the left side and a posed head shot in a circle on the right side). If the same player appeared in the action scene and in the circle, and if the ticket values and the color bars below both pictures matched, the contestant became an instant winner of two Colorado Rockies' hockey tickets, whose value is shown in the color bar. One could also save all player pictures until one had the same player appearing in the action scene and in the circle both with matching ticket values and matching color bars. The color bars at the bottom appeared in four different colors (yellow, blue, green, or orange). The cards feature either a "Play Puck Bucks" logo on the back, which also features a skeletal-like picture of a player, or a rules definition. Winners had to claim prizes by February 20, 1977. Since there is no numerical designation for the cards, they are checklisted alphabetically below.

	MINT	EXC	G-VG
COMPLETE SET (20)	50.00	20.00	5.00
COMMON PLAYER (1-20)	3.00	1.20	.30
☐ 1 Ron Andruff	3.00	1.20	.30
☐ 2 Chuck Arnason	3.00	1.20	.30
☐ 3 Henry Boucha	4.00	1.60	.40
☐ 4 Colin Campbell	5.00	2.00	.50
☐ 5 Gary Croteau	3.00	1.20	.30
☐ 6 Guy Delparte	3.00	1.20	.30
☐ 7 Steve Durbano	4.00	1.60	.40
☐ 8 Tom Edur	3.00	1.20	.30
☐ 9 Doug Favell	4.00	1.60	.40
☐ 10 Dave Hudson	3.00	1.20	.30
☐ 11 Bryan Lefley	3.00	1.20	.30
☐ 12 Roger Lemelin	3.00	1.20	.30
☐ 13 Simon Nolet	3.00	1.20	.30
☐ 14 Wilf Paiement	4.00	1.60	.40
☐ 15 Michel Plasse	4.00	1.60	.40
☐ 16 Tracy Pratt	3.00	1.20	.30
☐ 17 Nelson Pyatt	3.00	1.20	.30
☐ 18 Phil Roberto	3.00	1.20	.30
☐ 19 Sean Shanahan	3.00	1.20	.30
☐ 20 Larry Skinner	3.00	1.20	.30

1981-82 Rockies Postcards

This 30-card postcard set measures 3 1/2" by 5 1/2" and features borderless black-and-white action player photos of the Colorado Rockies. The backs have the standard white postcard design with the player's name and biographical information in the upper left corner. The team emblem is printed in light gray on the left side. The cards are unnumbered and checklisted below in alphabetical order.

	MINT	EXC	G-VG
COMPLETE SET (30)	30.00	12.00	3.00
COMMON PLAYER (1-30)	1.25	.50	.12
☐ 1 Brent Ashton	1.50	.60	.15
☐ 2 Aaron Broten	2.00	.80	.20
☐ 3 Dave Cameron	1.25	.50	.12
☐ 4 Joe Cirella	2.00	.80	.20
☐ 5 Dwight Foster	1.25	.50	.12
☐ 6 Paul Gagne	1.25	.50	.12
☐ 7 Marshall Johnston CO	1.25	.50	.12
☐ 8 Veli-Pekka Ketola	1.25	.50	.12
☐ 9 Mike Kitchen	1.25	.50	.12
☐ 10 Rick Laferriere	1.25	.50	.12
☐ 11 Don Lever	1.50	.60	.15
☐ 12 Tapio Levo	1.25	.50	.12
☐ 13 Bob Lorimer	1.25	.50	.12
☐ 14 Bill MacMillan	1.25	.50	.12
☐ 15 Bob MacMillan VP	1.50	.60	.15
☐ 16 Merlin Malinowski	1.25	.50	.12
☐ 17 Bert Marshall GM	1.25	.50	.12
☐ 18 Kevin Maxwell	1.25	.50	.12
☐ 19 Joe Micheletti	1.25	.50	.12
☐ 20 Bobby Miller	1.25	.50	.12
☐ 21 Phil Myre	2.00	.80	.20
☐ 22 Graeme Nicolson	1.25	.50	.12
☐ 23 Jukka Porvari	1.25	.50	.12
☐ 24 Joel Quenneville	1.25	.50	.12
☐ 25 Rob Ramage	2.50	1.00	.25

☐	26 Glenn Resch	3.00	1.20	.30
☐	27 Steve Tambellini	1.50	.60	.15
☐	28 Yvon Vautour	1.25	.50	.12
☐	29 John Wensink	1.50	.60	.15
☐	30 Title Card	2.00	.80	.20
	(Team logo)			

1952 Royal Desserts Hockey

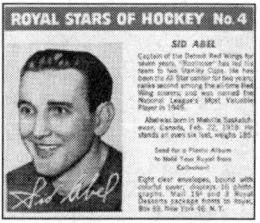

The 1952 Royal Desserts Hockey set contains eight cards. The cards measure approximately 2 5/8" by 3 1/4". The set is cataloged as F219-2. The cards formed the backs of Royal Desserts packages of the period; consequently many cards are found with uneven edges stemming from the method of cutting the cards off the box. Each card has its number and the statement "Royal Stars of Hockey" in a red rectangle at the top. The blue tinted picture also features a facsimile autograph of the player. An album was presumably available as it is advertised on the card. The exact year (or years) of issue of these cards is not verified at this time.

		NRMT	VG-E	GOOD
	COMPLETE SET (8)	4000.00	1600.00	400.00
	COMMON PLAYER (1-8)	250.00	100.00	25.00
☐	1 Tony Leswick	250.00	100.00	25.00
☐	2 Chuck Rayner	300.00	120.00	30.00
☐	3 Edgar Laprade	300.00	120.00	30.00
☐	4 Sid Abel	400.00	160.00	40.00
☐	5 Ted Lindsey	400.00	160.00	40.00
☐	6 Leo Reise	250.00	100.00	25.00
☐	7 Red Kelly	400.00	160.00	40.00
☐	8 Gordie Howe	2000.00	800.00	200.00

1983 Russian National Team

This 23-card set presents Russian hockey players. The cards were packaged in a cardboard sleeve that displays a photo of the 1983 Russian national team. The cards measure approximately 5 1/2" by 7" and feature full-bleed head and shoulders shots of the players dressed in civilian clothing. On the left portion, the backs carry three action shots in a filmstrip format while the right portion has player

information in Russian. The cards are unnumbered and checklisted below in alphabetical order.

		MINT	EXC	G-VG
	COMPLETE SET (23)	75.00	30.00	7.50
	COMMON PLAYER (1-23)	2.50	1.00	.25
☐	1 Sergei Babinov	2.50	1.00	.25
☐	2 Helmut Balderis	3.50	1.40	.35
☐	3 Zinetula Bilyaletinov	2.50	1.00	.25
☐	4 Vyacheslav Bykov	5.00	2.00	.50
☐	5 Vyacheslav Fetisov	8.00	3.25	.80
☐	6 Irek Gimaev	2.50	1.00	.25
☐	7 Sergei Kapustin	2.50	1.00	.25
☐	8 Alexei Kasatonov	6.00	2.40	.60
☐	9 Andrei Khomotov	5.00	2.00	.50
☐	10 Vladimir Krutov	5.00	2.00	.50
☐	11 Igor Larionov	8.00	3.25	.80
☐	12 Sergei Makarov	10.00	4.00	1.00
☐	13 Alexander Maltsev	5.00	2.00	.50
☐	14 Vasily Pervukhin	2.50	1.00	.25
☐	15 Sergei Shepelev	2.50	1.00	.25
☐	16 Alexander Skvorstsov	2.50	1.00	.25
☐	17 Sergei Starikov	3.50	1.40	.35
☐	18 Victor Tikhonov CO	5.00	2.00	.50
☐	19 Vladislav Tretiak	12.00	5.00	1.20
☐	20 Mikhael Vasiliev	3.50	1.40	.35
☐	21 Vladimir Yurzinov CO	3.50	1.40	.35
☐	22 Victor Zhluktov	2.50	1.00	.25
☐	23 Vladimir Zubkov	2.50	1.00	.25

1987 Russian National Team

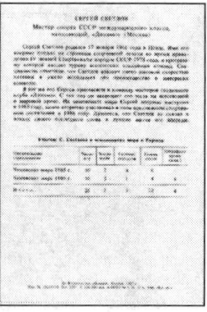

This 24-card set presents Russian hockey players and is subtitled "The USSR 1987 National Hockey Team." This 24-card set was printed in the USSR, released by Panorama Publishers (USSR), and distributed in North America by Tri-Globe International, Inc. The production run was reportedly 25,000 sets. The cards were packaged in a cardboard sleeve that displays a team photo from the world championships. The cards measure approximately 4 1/8" by 5 13/16" and feature full-bleed head and shoulders shots of the players dressed in coat and tie. The player's autograph and uniform number are printed on the lower portion of the picture in gold lettering. The backs are in Russian and present player profile and statistics. The cards are unnumbered and checklisted below in alphabetical order.

		MINT	EXC	G-VG
	COMPLETE SET (24)	35.00	14.00	3.50
	COMMON PLAYER (1-24)	1.00	.40	.10
☐	1 Sergei Ageikin	1.00	.40	.10
☐	2 Evgeny Belosheikin	1.50	.60	.15
☐	3 Zinetula Belyaletdinov	1.00	.40	.10
☐	4 Viacheslav Bykov	2.50	1.00	.25
☐	5 Viacheslav Fetisov	3.00	1.20	.30
☐	6 Alexei Gusarov	1.50	.60	.15
☐	7 Valeri Kamensky	4.00	1.60	.40
☐	8 Alexei Kasatonov	2.50	1.00	.25
☐	9 Yuri Khmylev	3.00	1.20	.30
☐	10 Andrei Khomotov	2.50	1.00	.25
☐	11 Vladimir Konstantinov	3.00	1.20	.30

		MINT	EXC	G-VG
☐	12 Vladimir Krutov	2.50	1.00	.25
☐	13 Igor Larionov	4.00	1.60	.40
☐	14 Sergei Makarov	5.00	2.00	.50
☐	15 Sergei Mylnikov	1.50	.60	.15
☐	16 Vasili Pervukhin	1.00	.40	.10
☐	17 Sergei Starikov	1.50	.60	.15
☐	18 Igor Stelnov	1.00	.40	.10
☐	19 Sergei Svetlov	1.00	.40	.10
☐	20 Victor Tikhonov CO	2.50	1.00	.25
☐	21 Victor Tjumenev	1.00	.40	.10
☐	22 Michael Varnakov	1.00	.40	.10
☐	23 Sergei Yashin	1.50	.60	.15
☐	24 Vladimir Yursinov CO	1.25	.50	.12

1989 Russian National Team

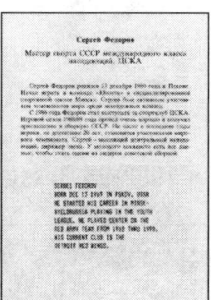

This set of 24 postcards was released by Plakat Publishers, USSR. The cards measure approximately 4 1/8" by 5 13/16" and features some of the best Russian players of modern years. The set features 22 player cards and two coach cards. The cards were packaged in a cardboard sleeve that displays an action photo of Valeri Kamensky. Reportedly 100,000 sets were printed but most were sold in the USSR and fewer sets made it to the U.S. and Canada. The fronts have head and shoulder shots of Russian Team players in coat and tie (street clothes) with a superimposed facsimile autograph while the backs contain biographical information in Russian. An unauthorized reprint of the set was issued in 1991, but the size was reduced to 2 1/2" by 3 1/2". The players in the reprint set who had since played in the NHL were given English biographies on labels added to the back. The cards are listed below alphabetically since they are unnumbered.

		MINT	EXC	G-VG
	COMPLETE SET (24)	35.00	14.00	3.50
	COMMON PLAYER (1-24)	1.00	.40	.10
☐	1 Ilya Byakin	1.50	.60	.15
☐	2 Viacheslav Bykov	2.00	.80	.20
☐	3 Alexandr Chernik	1.00	.40	.10
☐	4 Igor Dmitriev CO	1.00	.40	.10
☐	5 Sergei Fedorov	10.00	4.00	1.00
☐	6 Viacheslav Fetisov	2.50	1.00	.25
☐	7 Alexei Gusarov	1.50	.60	.15
☐	8 Arturs Irbe	5.00	2.00	.50
☐	9 Valeri Kamensky	3.00	1.20	.30
☐	10 Alexei Kasatonov	2.00	.80	.20
☐	11 Svatoslav Khalizov	1.00	.40	.10
☐	12 Yuri Khmylev	1.50	.60	.15
☐	13 Andrei Khomutov	1.50	.60	.15
☐	14 Vladimir Konstantinov	1.50	.60	.15
☐	15 Vladimir Krutov	1.50	.60	.15
☐	16 Dimitri Kvartalnov	2.00	.80	.20
☐	17 Igor Larionov	2.50	1.00	.25
☐	18 Sergei Makarov	3.00	1.20	.30
☐	19 Vladimir Mishkin	1.50	.60	.15
☐	20 Sergei Mylnikov	1.50	.60	.15
☐	21 Sergei Nemchinov	2.00	.80	.20
☐	22 Valeri Shirjaev	1.00	.40	.10
☐	23 Victor Tikhonov CO	2.00	.80	.20
☐	24 Sergei Yashin	1.50	.60	.15

1991 Russians Stars in NHL

This 11-card set was reportedly printed in Leningrad by Ivan Fiodorov Press as a special limited edition; it is claimed that there were only 50,000 sets issued. The cards measure the standard size, 2 1/2" by 3 1/2", and feature Russian players in the NHL. The front has a full-color player photo, bordered on the two sides by hockey sticks (with hockey gloves below). A red banner is draped across the top of the picture, with the player's name in between USSR (sickle and hammer) and USA (US flag) emblems. In contrast to the dark purple background, the bottom is light purple and presents the message "Sports Unites Hearts" in English and Russian. The horizontally-oriented back provide player information in two colored panels (English and Russian) and has a head shot of the player as well.

		MINT	EXC	G-VG
	COMPLETE SET (11)	8.00	3.25	.80
	COMMON PLAYER (1-11)	.75	.30	.07
☐	1 Sergei Fedorov	3.00	1.20	.30
☐	2 Viacheslav Fetisov	1.00	.40	.10
☐	3 Alexei Gusarov	.75	.30	.07
☐	4 Alexei Kasatonov	1.00	.40	.10
☐	5 Vladimir Konstantinov	1.00	.40	.10
☐	6 Igor Larionov	1.25	.50	.12
☐	7 Sergei Makarov	1.50	.60	.15
☐	8 Alexander Mogilny	2.50	1.00	.25
☐	9 Mikhail Tatarinov	.75	.30	.07
☐	10 Vladislav Tretiak	1.50	.60	.15
☐	11 Team Photo	.75	.30	.07
	USSR National Team			

1991-92 Russian Stars Red Ace

This 17-card set, featuring Russian stars in the NHL, was produced by Red Ace. The cards measure 2 1/2" by 3 1/2" and were packaged in a box, on which it is claimed that the production run was limited to 50,000 sets. The fronts feature borderless action shots with the player's name. Printed on white cover stock, the horizontal backs feature a close-up photograph as well as biographical and statistical information in Russian and English. The cards are unnumbered and checklisted below in alphabetical order.

		MINT	EXC	G-VG
	COMPLETE SET (17)	12.00	5.00	1.20
	COMMON PLAYER (1-17)	.50	.20	.05
☐	1 Pavel Bure	4.00	1.60	.40
☐	2 Evgeny Davydov	.75	.30	.07
☐	3 Sergei Fedorov	2.00	.80	.20
☐	4 Viacheslav Fetisov	1.00	.40	.10
☐	5 Alexei Gusarov	.50	.20	.05
☐	6 Valeri Kamensky	1.00	.40	.10

Kravchuk
Igor

		MINT	EXC	G-VG
☐ 7	Alexei Kasatonov	.75	.30	.07
☐ 8	Ravil Khaidarov	.50	.20	.05
☐ 9	Vladimir Konstantinov	.75	.30	.07
☐ 10	Igor Kravchuk	.75	.30	.07
☐ 11	Igor Larionov	1.00	.40	.10
☐ 12	Andrei Lomakin	.75	.30	.07
☐ 13	Sergei Makarov	1.25	.50	.12
☐ 14	Alexander Mogilny	1.50	.60	.15
☐ 15	Sergei Nemchinov	1.00	.40	.10
☐ 16	Anatoli Semenov	.60	.24	.06
☐ 17	Mikhail Tatarinov	.50	.20	.05

1992 Russian Stars Red Ace

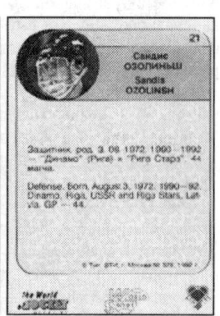

The 1992 Red Ace Russian Hockey Stars boxed set was co-sponsored by the World of Hockey Magazine and World Sport. The cards were sold in a light blue box with production limited to 25,000 sets. The cards are printed on thin card stock and measure approximately 2 1/2" by 3 3/8". The light blue bordered fronts feature color action player photos. The player's name appears on a light green diagonal stripe in an upper corner, accented with a red triangle containing a white star. The Red Ace logo is printed in a lower corner of the picture. The white backs display a small head shot next to the player's name on a green bar. In a pale pink panel below is the player's biography and career highlights in Russian and English. The cards are numbered on the back.

		MINT	EXC	G-VG
	COMPLETE SET (36)	12.00	5.00	1.20
	COMMON PLAYER (1-36)	.35	.14	.03
☐ 1	Darius Kasparajtis	.50	.20	.05
☐ 2	Alexei Zhamnov	1.00	.40	.10
☐ 3	Dmitri Khristich	.50	.20	.05
☐ 4	Andrei Trefilov	.50	.20	.05
☐ 5	Vitali Prokhorov	.35	.14	.03
☐ 6	Dmitri Filimonov	.35	.14	.03
☐ 7	Valeri Zelepukin	.50	.20	.05
☐ 8	Alexei Kovalev	2.50	1.00	.25
☐ 9	Dmitri Kvartalnov	.50	.20	.05
☐ 10	Igor Korolev	.35	.14	.03
☐ 11	Nikolai Borschevsky	.50	.20	.05

		MINT	EXC	G-VG
☐ 12	Igor Boldin	.35	.14	.03
☐ 13	Arturs Irbe	1.00	.40	.10
☐ 14	Viacheslav Butsayev	.50	.20	.05
☐ 15	Boris Mironov	.50	.20	.05
☐ 16	Sergei Bautin	.35	.14	.03
☐ 17	Alexander Kharlamov	1.00	.40	.10
☐ 18	Viacheslav Kozlov	1.50	.60	.15
☐ 19	Mikhail Shtalenkov	.50	.20	.05
☐ 20	Roman Oksyuta	.35	.14	.03
☐ 21	Sandis Ozolinsh	.75	.30	.07
☐ 22	Dmitri Mironov	.50	.20	.05
☐ 23	Sergei Brylin	.35	.14	.03
☐ 24	Vladimit Grachev	.35	.14	.03
☐ 25	Dmitri Starostenko	.35	.14	.03
☐ 26	Andrei Nazarov	.50	.20	.05
☐ 27	Alexei Yashin	2.00	.80	.20
☐ 28	Vladimir Malakhov	.50	.20	.05
☐ 29	Ravil Jakubov	.35	.14	.03
☐ 30	Sergei Klimovich	.35	.14	.03
☐ 31	Artur Oktjabrev	.35	.14	.03
☐ 32	Lev Berdichevski	.35	.14	.03
☐ 33	Ian Kaminski	.50	.20	.05
☐ 34	Andrei Kovalenko	.50	.20	.05
☐ 35	Dmitri Yushkevich	.50	.20	.05
☐ 36	Checklist	.35	.14	.03

1992-93 Russian Stars Red Ace

Dmitri
KVARTALNOV

This 37-card, standard-size (2 1/2" by 3 1/2") set features action color player photos bordered in white. The player's name and the Red Ace logo appear in a gradated violet stripe at the bottom. A red triangle at the upper left corner of the picture carries a white star outline. In a red box with rounded corners, the back provides biography in Cyrillic (Russian) and English. The top portion of the back has a yellow background and displays a close-up photo in a circular format and the player's name in Russian and English. The cards are numbered on the back essentially alphabetically.

		MINT	EXC	G-VG
	COMPLETE SET (37)	12.00	5.00	1.20
	COMMON PLAYER (1-36)	.35	.14	.03
☐ 1	Alexander Barkov	.35	.14	.03
☐ 2	Sergei Bautin	.35	.14	.03
☐ 3	Igor Boldin	.35	.14	.03
☐ 4	Nikolai Borchevsky	.50	.20	.05
☐ 5	Sergei Brylin	.35	.14	.03
☐ 6	Viacheslav Butsayev	.50	.20	.05
☐ 7	Alexander Cherbajev	.50	.20	.05
☐ 8	Evgeny Garanin	.35	.14	.03
☐ 9	Sergei Gonchar	.50	.20	.05
☐ 10	Alexander Karpovtsev	.50	.20	.05
☐ 11	Darius Kasparaitis	.50	.20	.05
☐ 12	Alexander Kharlamov	1.00	.40	.10
☐ 13	Yuri Khmylev	.75	.30	.07
☐ 14	Sergei Klimovich	.35	.14	.03
☐ 15	Igor Korolev	.35	.14	.03
☐ 16	Andrei Kovalenko	.50	.20	.05
☐ 17	Alexei Kovalev UER	2.50	1.00	.25
	(Back photo is Igor Korolev)			
☐ 18	Dmitri Kvartalnov	.50	.20	.05

☐ 19	Vladimir Malakhov	.50	.20	.05
☐ 20	Maxim Mikhailovsky	.35	.14	.03
☐ 21	Boris Mironov	.35	.14	.03
☐ 22	Dmitri Mironov	.50	.20	.05
☐ 23	Andrei Nazarov	.50	.20	.05
☐ 24	Roman Oksyuta	.35	.14	.03
☐ 25	Artur Oktyabrev	.35	.14	.03
☐ 26	Sergei Petrenko	.50	.20	.05
☐ 27	Oleg Petrov	.50	.20	.05
☐ 28	Andrei Potaichuk	.35	.14	.03
☐ 29	Vitali Prokhorov	.35	.14	.03
☐ 30	Alexander Semak	.75	.30	.07
☐ 31	Dmitri Starostenko	.35	.14	.03
☐ 32	Ravil Yakubov	.35	.14	.03
☐ 33	Alexei Yashin	2.00	.80	.20
☐ 34	Dmitri Yushkevich	.50	.20	.05
☐ 35	Alexei Zhamnov	1.00	.40	.10
☐ 36	Alexei Zhitnik	.75	.30	.07
☐ NNO	Checklist Card	.35	.14	.03

1973-74 Sabres Bells

This set of four photos of Buffalo Sabres players was sponsored by Bells Markets. The photos measure approximately 3 15/16" by 5 1/2". The front has a color action photo. These blank-backed cards are unnumbered and listed alphabetically in the checklist below.

		NRMT	VG-E	GOOD
COMPLETE SET (4)		25.00	10.00	2.50
COMMON PLAYER (1-4)		5.00	2.00	.50
☐ 1	Roger Crozier	6.00	2.40	.60
☐ 2	Jim Lorentz	5.00	2.00	.50
☐ 3	Richard Martin	7.50	3.00	.75
☐ 4	Gilbert Perreault	12.00	5.00	1.20

1979-80 Sabres Bells

This set of nine photos of Buffalo Sabres players was sponsored by Bells Markets. The photos measure approximately 7 5/8" by 10". The front has a color action photo, with the player's name and team name in the white border at the lower right hand corner. The back is printed in blue and has the Sabres' logo, a head shot of the player, biographical information, and career statistics.

		MINT	EXC	G-VG
COMPLETE SET (9)		20.00	8.00	2.00
COMMON PLAYER (1-9)		2.00	.80	.20
☐ 1	Don Edwards	2.50	1.00	.25
☐ 2	Danny Gare	2.50	1.00	.25
☐ 3	Jerry Korab	2.00	.80	.20
☐ 4	Richard Martin	4.00	1.60	.40
☐ 5	Tony McKegney	2.50	1.00	.25
☐ 6	Craig Ramsay	2.00	.80	.20
☐ 7	Bob Sauve	2.50	1.00	.25

☐ 8	Jim Schoenfeld	3.00	1.20	.30
☐ 9	John Van Boxmeer	2.00	.80	.20

1980-81 Sabres Milk Panels

This set of Buffalo Sabres was issued on the side of half gallon milk cartons. After cutting, the panels measure approximately 3 3/4" by 7 1/2", with two players per panel. The picture and text of the player panels are printed in red; the set can also be found in blue print. The top of the panel reads "Kids, Collect a Complete Set of Buffalo Sabres Players". Arranged alongside each other, the panel features for each player a head shot, biographical information, and player profile. The panels are subtly dated and numbered below the photo area in the following way, Perreault/Seiling is M325-80-4H (M325 is the product code, the number 80 gives the last two digits of the year, and 4 is the card number perhaps also indicating release week).

		MINT	EXC	G-VG
COMPLETE SET (2)		30.00	12.00	3.00
COMMON PANEL		12.00	5.00	1.20
☐ 4	Gilbert Perreault and Ric Seiling	20.00	8.00	2.00
☐ 8	Bob Sauve and Richard Martin	12.00	5.00	1.20

1981-82 Sabres Milk Panels

This sixteen-panel set of Buffalo Sabres was issued by Wilson Farms Dairy on the side of 2 percent milkfat and homogenized Vitamin D half gallon milk cartons. After cutting, the panels measure approximately 3 3/4" by 7 1/2". Although the 2 percent milk fat cartons have some lime green lettering and a lime green stripe, the picture and text of the player panels are printed in red on both cartons. The top of the panel reads "Kids, Collect Action Photos of the 1981-82 Buffalo Sabres." Inside a red broken border, the panel has a action player photo, with player information and career summary beneath the picture. The panels are subtly dated and numbered below the photo area in the following way, Gilbert Perreault is M325-81-4H (M325 is the product code, the number 81 gives the last two digits of year, and 4 is the card number perhaps also indicating release week). The set can also be found in blue print.

	MINT	EXC	G-VG
COMPLETE SET (16)	150.00	60.00	15.00
COMMON PLAYER (1-17)	10.00	4.00	1.00
☐ 1 Craig Ramsay	10.00	4.00	1.00
☐ 2 John Van Boxmeer	10.00	4.00	1.00
☐ 3 Don Edwards	12.00	5.00	1.20
☐ 4 Gilbert Perreault	20.00	8.00	2.00
☐ 5 Alan Haworth	10.00	4.00	1.00
☐ 6 Jim Schoenfeld	15.00	6.00	1.50
☐ 7 Richie Dunn	10.00	4.00	1.00
☐ 8 Bob Sauve	12.00	5.00	1.20
☐ 9 Bill Hajt	10.00	4.00	1.00
☐ 10 Larry Playfair	10.00	4.00	1.00
☐ 11 Tony McKegney	12.00	5.00	1.20
☐ 12 Mike Ramsey	12.00	5.00	1.20
☐ 13 Andre Savard	10.00	4.00	1.00
☐ 15 Ric Seiling	10.00	4.00	1.00
☐ 16 Yvon Lambert	10.00	4.00	1.00
☐ 17 Dale McCourt	12.00	5.00	1.20

1982-83 Sabres Milk Panels

This seventeen-panel set of Buffalo Sabres was issued on the side of half gallon milk cartons. After cutting, the panels measure approximately 3 3/4" by 7 1/2". The picture and text of the player panels are printed in blue. The top of the panel reads "Kids, Clip and Save Exciting Tips and Pictures of Buffalo Sabres." Inside a blue broken border, the panel has a posed head and shoulders shot, with the player's name, position, and a hockey tip beneath the picture. The panels are subtly dated and numbered below the photo area in the following way, Gilbert Perreault is M325-82-7H. Phil Housley's card predates his Rookie Card.

	MINT	EXC	G-VG
COMPLETE SET (17)	150.00	60.00	15.00
COMMON PLAYER (2-18)	9.00	3.75	.90
☐ 2 1982-83 Home Schedule	15.00	6.00	1.50
☐ 3 Craig Ramsay	9.00	3.75	.90
☐ 4 John Van Boxmeer	9.00	3.75	.90
☐ 5 Lindy Ruff	9.00	3.75	.90
☐ 6 Bob Sauve	10.00	4.00	1.00
☐ 7 Gilbert Perreault	20.00	8.00	2.00
☐ 8 Ric Seiling	9.00	3.75	.90
☐ 9 Jacques Cloutier	10.00	4.00	1.00
☐ 10 Larry Playfair	9.00	3.75	.90
☐ 11 Phil Housley	25.00	10.00	2.50
☐ 12 Mike Foligno	10.00	4.00	1.00
☐ 13 Tony McKegney	10.00	4.00	1.00
☐ 14 Dale McCourt	10.00	4.00	1.00
☐ 15 Mike Ramsey	10.00	4.00	1.00
☐ 16 Hannu Virta	9.00	3.75	.90
☐ 17 Brent Peterson	9.00	3.75	.90
☐ 18 Scott Bowman GM	20.00	8.00	2.00

1984-85 Sabres Blue Shield

This 21-card set was issued by the Buffalo Sabres in conjunction with Blue Shield of Western New York. The cards measure approximately 2 1/2" by 3 3/4". It has been reported that only 500 sets were printed as a test for future issues. The fronts feature a head and shoulders color photo with player information below the picture. The card backs have the Blue Shield logo and the words "The Caring Card -- The Blue Shield of Western New York, Inc." We have checklisted the cards below in alphabetical order. Dave Andreychuk and Tom Barrasso appear in their Rookie Card year.

	MINT	EXC	G-VG
COMPLETE SET (21)	120.00	50.00	12.00
COMMON PLAYER (1-21)	4.00	1.60	.40
☐ 1 Dave Andreychuk	25.00	10.00	2.50
☐ 2 Tom Barrasso	15.00	6.00	1.50
☐ 3 Adam Creighton	6.00	2.40	.60
☐ 4 Paul Cyr	4.00	1.60	.40
☐ 5 Malcolm Davis	4.00	1.60	.40
☐ 6 Mike Foligno	6.00	2.40	.60
☐ 7 Bill Hajt	4.00	1.60	.40
☐ 8 Gilles Hamel	4.00	1.60	.40
☐ 9 Phil Housley	20.00	8.00	2.00
☐ 10 Sean McKenna	4.00	1.60	.40
☐ 11 Mike Moller	4.00	1.60	.40
☐ 12 Gilbert Perreault	15.00	6.00	1.50
☐ 13 Brent Peterson	4.00	1.60	.40
☐ 14 Larry Playfair	4.00	1.60	.40
☐ 15 Craig Ramsay	4.00	1.60	.40
☐ 16 Mike Ramsey	5.00	2.00	.50
☐ 17 Lindy Ruff	4.00	1.60	.40
☐ 18 Bob Sauve	5.00	2.00	.50
☐ 19 Ric Seiling	4.00	1.60	.40
☐ 20 John Tucker	5.00	2.00	.50
☐ 21 Hannu Virta	4.00	1.60	.40

1985-86 Sabres Blue Shield

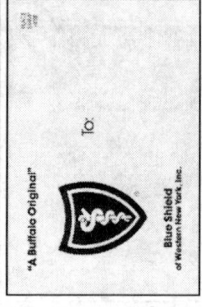

This 28-card set was issued by the Buffalo Sabres in conjunction with Blue Shield of Western New York. The cards were printed in two different sizes: large (4" by 6" with postcard backs) and small (2 1/2" by 3 1/2"). Both sizes have the Blue Shield logo on the backs. Though both sizes are scarce, the small cards are considered harder to obtain. The front of the large card features a color action photo of the player, with his name as well as biographical and statistical information below the picture. The front of the small card is identical except for the omission of the statistical information. The firing of Sabres' coach Jim Schoenfeld at the time the cards were issued makes his card rare as he was removed from the set. The set is priced below as complete without the Schoenfeld card. Daren Puppa's card predates his Rookie Card by three years.

	MINT	EXC	G-VG
COMPLETE SET (27)	35.00	14.00	3.50
COMMON PLAYER (1-28)	1.00	.40	.10

		MINT	EXC	G-VG
☐ 1	Mikael Andersson	1.25	.50	.12
☐ 2	Dave Andreychuk	7.50	3.00	.75
☐ 3	Tom Barrasso	5.00	2.00	.50
☐ 4	Adam Creighton	1.50	.60	.15
☐ 5	Paul Cyr	1.00	.40	.10
☐ 6	Malcolm Davis	1.00	.40	.10
☐ 7	Steve Dykstra	1.00	.40	.10
☐ 8	Dave Fenyves	1.00	.40	.10
☐ 9	Mike Foligno	1.25	.50	.12
☐ 10	Bill Hajt	1.00	.40	.10
☐ 11	Bob Halkidis	1.00	.40	.10
☐ 12	Gilles Hamel	1.00	.40	.10
☐ 13	Phil Housley	6.00	2.40	.60
☐ 14	Pat Hughes	1.00	.40	.10
☐ 15	Normand Lacombe	1.00	.40	.10
☐ 16	Chris Langevin	1.00	.40	.10
☐ 17	Sean McKenna	1.00	.40	.10
☐ 18	Gates Orlando	1.00	.40	.10
☐ 19	Gilbert Perreault	6.00	2.40	.60
☐ 20	Larry Playfair	1.00	.40	.10
☐ 21	Daren Puppa	5.00	2.00	.50
☐ 22	Craig Ramsay ACO	1.25	.50	.12
☐ 23	Mike Ramsey	1.50	.60	.15
☐ 24	Lindy Ruff	1.00	.40	.10
☐ 25	Jim Schoenfeld CO SP	25.00	10.00	2.50
☐ 26	Ric Seiling	1.00	.40	.10
☐ 27	John Tucker	1.25	.50	.12
☐ 28	Hannu Virta	1.00	.40	.10

1986-87 Sabres Blue Shield

 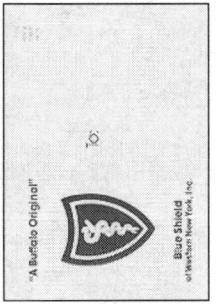

This 28-card set was issued by the Buffalo Sabres in conjunction with Blue Shield of Western New York. In contrast to the previous year's issue, the cards were printed only in one size, the approximately 4" by 6" postcard type with the Blue Shield logo on the backs. The front of the cards can be distinguished from the previous year's issue by the addition of the player's uniform number (inadvertently omitted on the Creighton and Fenyves cards) and updated statistics.

		MINT	EXC	G-VG
COMPLETE SET (28)		25.00	10.00	2.50
COMMON PLAYER (1-28)		1.00	.40	.10
☐ 1	Shawn Anderson 37	1.00	.40	.10
☐ 2	Dave Andreychuk 25	6.00	2.40	.60
☐ 3	Scott Arniel 9	1.00	.40	.10
☐ 4	Tom Barrasso 30	4.00	1.60	.40
☐ 5	Jacques Cloutier 1	1.25	.50	.12
☐ 6	Adam Creighton	1.25	.50	.12
☐ 7	Paul Cyr 18	1.00	.40	.10
☐ 8	Steve Dykstra 42	1.00	.40	.10
☐ 9	Dave Fenyves	1.00	.40	.10
☐ 10	Mike Foligno 17	1.25	.50	.12
☐ 11	Clark Gillies 39	2.00	.80	.20
☐ 12	Bill Hajt 24	1.00	.40	.10
☐ 13	Bob Halkidis 19	1.00	.40	.10
☐ 14	Jim Hofford 3	1.00	.40	.10
☐ 15	Phil Housley 6	4.00	1.60	.40
☐ 16	Jim Korn 4	1.00	.40	.10
☐ 17	Uwe Krupp 40	1.25	.50	.12
☐ 18	Tom Kurvers 28	1.25	.50	.12
☐ 19	Norm Lacombe 32	1.00	.40	.10
☐ 20	Gates Orlando 23	1.00	.40	.10
☐ 21	Wilf Paiement 27	1.25	.50	.12
☐ 22	Gilbert Perreault 11	5.00	2.00	.50
☐ 23	Daren Puppa 35	2.50	1.00	.25

		MINT	EXC	G-VG
☐ 24	Mike Ramsey 5	1.25	.50	.12
☐ 25	Lindy Ruff 22	1.00	.40	.10
☐ 26	Christian Ruuttu 21	1.50	.60	.15
☐ 27	Doug Smith 15	1.00	.40	.10
☐ 28	John Tucker 7	1.25	.50	.12

1987-88 Sabres Blue Shield

This 28-card set was issued by the Buffalo Sabres in conjunction with Blue Shield of Western New York. In contrast to the previous year's issue, the cards are a different size, approximately 4" by 5", again in the postcard format with the Blue Shield logo on the backs. The front of the cards feature a color action photo of the player, with the player's name, team name, and team logo in a yellow stripe at the top. The player's number and a facsimile autograph appear in blue at the bottom on the front. Supposedly there exists a rare variation on the Phil Housley card which has his last name misspelled "Housely". The card of Pierre Turgeon predates his Rookie Card by one year.

		MINT	EXC	G-VG
COMPLETE SET (28)		25.00	10.00	2.50
COMMON PLAYER (1-28)		.75	.30	.07
☐ 1	Mikael Andersson 14	1.00	.40	.10
☐ 2	Dave Andreychuk 25	3.50	1.40	.35
☐ 3	Scott Arniel 9	.75	.30	.07
☐ 4	Tom Barrasso 30	2.50	1.00	.25
☐ 5	Jacques Cloutier 1	1.00	.40	.10
☐ 6	Adam Creighton 38	1.00	.40	.10
☐ 7	Mike Donnelly 16	1.25	.50	.12
☐ 8	Mike Foligno 17	1.00	.40	.10
☐ 9	Clark Gillies 90	1.25	.50	.12
☐ 10	Bob Halkidis 18	.75	.30	.07
☐ 11	Mike Hartman 20	.75	.30	.07
☐ 12	Ed Hospodar 24	.75	.30	.07
☐ 13	Phil Housley 6	2.50	1.00	.25
☐ 14	Calle Johansson 3	1.00	.40	.10
☐ 15	Uwe Krupp 40	1.00	.40	.10
☐ 16	Jan Ludvig 36	.75	.30	.07
☐ 17	Kevin Maguire 19	.75	.30	.07
☐ 18	Mark Napier 65	1.00	.40	.10
☐ 19	Ken Priestlay 12	.75	.30	.07
☐ 20	Daren Puppa 35	1.50	.60	.15
☐ 21	Mike Ramsey 5	1.00	.40	.10
☐ 22	Joe Reekie 27	1.00	.40	.10
☐ 23	Lindy Ruff 22	.75	.30	.07
☐ 24	Christian Ruuttu 21	1.00	.40	.10
☐ 25	Ray Sheppard 23	2.00	.80	.20
☐ 26	Doug Smith 15	.75	.30	.07
☐ 27	John Tucker 7	1.00	.40	.10
☐ 28	Pierre Turgeon 77	12.50	5.00	1.25

1987-88 Sabres Wonder Bread/Hostess

The 1987-88 Buffalo Sabres Team Photo Album was sponsored by Wonder Bread and Hostess Cakes. It consists of three large sheets, each measuring approximately 13 1/2"

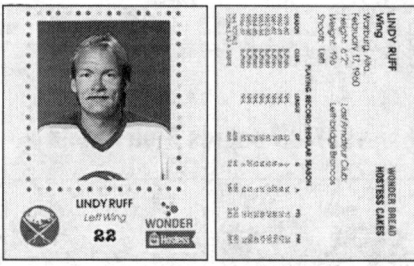

by 10 1/4" and joined together to form one continuous sheet. The first panel has a team photo of the Buffalo Sabres. The second and third panels present three rows of five cards each. After perforation, the cards measure approximately 2 5/8" by 3 3/8". They feature color posed photos bordered in various color dots, with player information below the picture sandwiched between the Sabres' and sponsors' logos. The back has biographical and statistical information in a horizontal format. We have checklisted the names below in alphabetical order, with the uniform number to the right of the name. The set features an early card of Pierre Turgeon pre-dating his Rookie Cards by one year.

	MINT	EXC	G-VG
COMPLETE SET (31)	20.00	8.00	2.00
COMMON PLAYER (1-30)	.75	.30	.07

		MINT	EXC	G-VG
☐ 1	Mikael Andersson 14	.75	.30	.07
☐ 2	Shawn Anderson 37	.60	.24	.06
☐ 3	Dave Andreychuk 25	3.00	1.20	.30
☐ 4	Scott Arniel 9	.60	.24	.06
☐ 5	Tom Barrasso 30	2.00	.80	.20
☐ 6	Jacques Cloutier 1	.75	.30	.07
☐ 7	Adam Creighton 38	.75	.30	.07
☐ 8	Steve Dykstra 4	.60	.24	.06
☐ 9	Mike Foligno 17	.75	.30	.07
☐ 10	Clark Gillies 90	1.00	.40	.10
☐ 11	Ed Hospodar 24	.60	.24	.06
☐ 12	Phil Housley 6	2.00	.80	.20
☐ 13	Calle Johannsson 3	.75	.30	.07
☐ 14	Uwe Krupp 40	.75	.30	.07
☐ 15	Don Lever CO	.60	.24	.06
☐ 16	Bob Logan 26	.60	.24	.06
☐ 17	Jan Ludvig 36	.60	.24	.06
☐ 18	Kevin Maguire 19	.60	.24	.06
☐ 19	Mark Napier 65	.75	.30	.07
☐ 20	Daren Puppa 31	1.25	.50	.12
☐ 21	Mike Ramsey 5	.75	.30	.07
☐ 22	Joe Reekie 27	.75	.30	.07
☐ 23	Lindy Ruff 22	.60	.24	.06
☐ 24	Christian Ruuttu 21	.75	.30	.07
☐ 25	Ted Sator CO	.60	.24	.06
☐ 26	Ray Sheppard 23	1.50	.60	.15
☐ 27	Barry Smith CO	.60	.24	.06
☐ 28	Doug Smith 15	.60	.24	.06
☐ 29	John Tucker 7	.75	.30	.07
☐ 30	Pierre Turgeon 77	8.00	3.25	.80
☐ xx	Large Team Photo	3.00	1.20	.30

1988-89 Sabres Blue Shield

This 28-card set was issued by the Buffalo Sabres in conjunction with Blue Shield of Western New York. The cards measure approximately 4" by 6" and are in the postcard format, with the Blue Shield logo on the backs. The fronts feature a color action photo of the player. The picture is sandwiched between yellow stripes, with team logo and player's name above, and player information below. The cards are unnumbered and we have checklisted them below in alphabetical order, with the uniform number next to the player's name. The cards of Benoit Hogue, Jan Ludvig, Mark

Napier, and Joe Reekie were apparently late additions to the set; they are marked as SP in the checklist below.

	MINT	EXC	G-VG
COMPLETE SET (28)	20.00	8.00	2.00
COMMON PLAYER (1-28)	.50	.20	.05

		MINT	EXC	G-VG
☐ 1	Mikael Andersson 14	.60	.24	.06
☐ 2	Dave Andreychuk 25	2.50	1.00	.25
☐ 3	Scott Arniel 9	.50	.20	.05
☐ 4	Doug Bodger 8	.75	.30	.07
☐ 5	Jacques Cloutier 1	.75	.30	.07
☐ 6	Mike Donnelly 16	.75	.30	.07
☐ 7	Mike Foligno 17	.60	.24	.06
☐ 8	Bob Halkidis 18	.50	.20	.05
☐ 9	Mike Hartman 20	.50	.20	.05
☐ 10	Benoit Hogue 33 SP	3.00	1.20	.30
☐ 11	Phil Housley 6	2.00	.80	.20
☐ 12	Calle Johansson 3	.75	.30	.07
☐ 13	Uwe Krupp 4	.75	.30	.07
☐ 14	Jan Ludvig 36 SP	2.00	.80	.20
☐ 15	Kevin Maguire 19	.50	.20	.05
☐ 16	Mark Napier 65 SP	2.50	1.00	.25
☐ 17	Jeff Parker 29	.50	.20	.05
☐ 18	Larry Playfair 27	.50	.20	.05
☐ 19	Daren Puppa 31	1.00	.40	.10
☐ 20	Mike Ramsey 5	.60	.24	.06
☐ 21	Joe Reekie 55 SP	2.50	1.00	.25
☐ 22	Lindy Ruff 22	.50	.20	.05
☐ 23	Christian Ruuttu 21	.75	.30	.07
☐ 24	Sabertooth Mascot	.50	.20	.05
☐ 25	Ray Sheppard 23	1.25	.50	.12
☐ 26	John Tucker 7	.60	.24	.06
☐ 27	Pierre Turgeon 77	6.00	2.40	.60
☐ 28	Rick Vaive 12	1.00	.40	.10

1988-89 Sabres Wonder Bread/Hostess

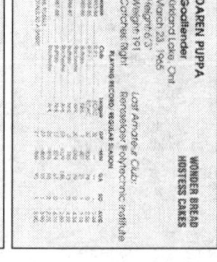

The 1988-89 Buffalo Sabres Team Photo Album was sponsored by Wonder Bread and Hostess Cakes. It consists of three large sheets, each measuring approximately 13 1/2" by 10 1/4" and joined together to form one continuous sheet. The first panel has a team photo of the Sabres in civilian clothing. The second and third panels present three rows of five cards each. After perforation, the cards measure approximately 2 5/8" by 3 3/8". They feature color posed photos on white card stock. The top half has thin diagonal blue lines traversing the white background. Player information appears below the picture, between the Sabres' and sponsors' logos. The back has biographical and statistical information in a horizontal format. The cards are unnumbered and we have checklisted them below in alphabetical order, with the uniform number to the right of the player's name.

	MINT	EXC	G-VG
COMPLETE SET (31)	15.00	6.00	1.50
COMMON PLAYER (1-30)	.50	.20	.05
☐ 1 Mikael Andersson 14	.60	.24	.06
☐ 2 Dave Andreychuk 25	2.00	.80	.20
☐ 3 Scott Arniel 9	.50	.20	.05
☐ 4 Doug Bodger 8	.75	.30	.07
☐ 5 Jacques Cloutier 1	.75	.30	.07
☐ 6 Adam Creighton 38	.60	.24	.06
☐ 7 Mike Foligno 17	.60	.24	.06
☐ 8 Bob Halkidis 18	.50	.20	.05
☐ 9 Mike Hartman 20	.50	.20	.05
☐ 10 Benoit Hogue 33	1.25	.50	.12
☐ 11 Phil Housley 6	1.50	.60	.15
☐ 12 Calle Johansson 3	.75	.30	.07
☐ 13 Uwe Krupp 4	.75	.30	.07
☐ 14 Don Lever CO	.60	.24	.06
☐ 15 Jan Ludvig 36	.50	.20	.05
☐ 16 Kevin Maguire 19	.50	.20	.05
☐ 17 Brad Miller 44	.50	.20	.05
☐ 18 Mark Napier 65	.60	.24	.06
☐ 19 Jeff Parker 29	.50	.20	.05
☐ 20 Larry Playfair 27	.50	.20	.05
☐ 21 Daren Puppa 31	1.00	.40	.10
☐ 22 Mike Ramsey 5	.60	.24	.06
☐ 23 Joe Reekie 55	.60	.24	.06
☐ 24 Lindy Ruff 22	.50	.20	.05
☐ 25 Christian Ruuttu 21	.75	.30	.07
☐ 26 Ted Sator CO	.50	.20	.05
☐ 27 Ray Sheppard 23	1.25	.50	.12
☐ 28 Barry Smith CO	.50	.20	.05
☐ 29 John Tucker 7	.60	.24	.06
☐ 30 Pierre Turgeon 77	6.00	2.40	.60
☐ xx Large Team Photo	3.00	1.20	.30

1989-90 Sabres Blue Shield

This 24-card set was issued by the Buffalo Sabres in conjunction with Blue Shield of Western New York. The cards measure approximately 4" by 6" and are in the postcard format, with the Blue Shield logo on the backs. The fronts feature a color action photo of the player. The picture is sandwiched between yellow stripes, with team logo and player's name above, and player information below. The cards are unnumbered and we have checklisted them below in alphabetical order, with the uniform number next to the player's name. The card of Alexander Mogilny predates his Rookie Card by one year.

	MINT	EXC	G-VG
COMPLETE SET (24)	15.00	6.00	1.50
COMMON PLAYER (1-24)	.50	.20	.05
☐ 1 Dave Andreychuk 25	2.00	.80	.20
☐ 2 Scott Arniel 9	.50	.20	.05
☐ 3 Doug Bodger 8	.75	.30	.07
☐ 4 Mike Foligno 17	.60	.24	.06
☐ 5 Mike Hartman 20	.50	.20	.05
☐ 6 Benoit Hogue 33	1.00	.40	.10
☐ 7 Phil Housley 6	1.50	.60	.15
☐ 8 Dean Kennedy 26	.50	.20	.05
☐ 9 Uwe Krupp 4	.75	.30	.07
☐ 10 Grant Ledyard 3	.60	.24	.06
☐ 11 Kevin Maguire 19	.50	.20	.05
☐ 12 Clint Malarchuk 30	.75	.30	.07
☐ 13 Alexander Mogilny 89	5.00	2.00	.50
☐ 14 Jeff Parker 29	.50	.20	.05
☐ 15 Larry Playfair 27	.50	.20	.05
☐ 16 Ken Priestlay 56	.50	.20	.05
☐ 17 Daren Puppa 31	1.00	.40	.10
☐ 18 Mike Ramsey 5	.60	.24	.06
☐ 19 Christian Ruuttu 21	.75	.30	.07
☐ 20 Ray Sheppard 23	1.00	.40	.10
☐ 21 Dave Snuggerud 18	.50	.20	.05
☐ 22 Sabretooth Mascot	.50	.20	.05
☐ 23 Pierre Turgeon 77	4.00	1.60	.40
☐ 24 Rick Vaive 22	.75	.30	.07

1989-90 Sabres Campbell's

The 1989-90 Buffalo Sabres Team Photo Album was sponsored by Campbell's and commemorates 20 years in the NHL. It consists of three large sheets (the first two measuring approximately 10" by 13 1/2" and the third smaller), all joined together to form one continuous sheet. The first panel has three color action shots superimposed on a large black and white picture of the Sabres. While the second panel presents four rows of four cards each (16 player cards), the third panel presents four rows of three cards each (11 player cards and a 20th year card). After perforation, the cards measure approximately 2 1/2" by 3 3/8". They feature color posed photos bordered in yellow (on three sides), on a dark blue background interspersed with Sabres' logos in light blue. Player information appears below the picture in a yellow diamond, sandwiched between the Sabres' and the Franco-American logos. The back has biographical and statistical information in a horizontal format. We have checklisted the names below in alphabetical order, with the uniform number to the right of the name. The card of Alexander Mogilny predates his Rookie Card by one year.

	MINT	EXC	G-VG
COMPLETE SET (28)	15.00	6.00	1.50
COMMON PLAYER (1-27)	.50	.20	.05
☐ 1 Shawn Anderson 37	.50	.20	.05
☐ 2 Dave Andreychuk 25	2.00	.80	.20
☐ 3 Scott Arniel 9	.50	.20	.05
☐ 4 Doug Bodger 8	.75	.30	.07

		MINT	EXC	G-VG
☐ 5	Rick Dudley CO	.75	.30	.07
☐ 6	Mike Foligno 17	.60	.24	.06
☐ 7	Mike Hartman 20	.50	.20	.05
☐ 8	Benoit Hogue 33	1.00	.40	.10
☐ 9	Phil Housley 6	1.50	.60	.15
☐ 10	Dean Kennedy 26	.50	.20	.05
☐ 11	Uwe Krupp 4	.75	.30	.07
☐ 12	Grant Ledyard 3	.60	.24	.06
☐ 13	Kevin Maguire 19	.50	.20	.05
☐ 14	Clint Malarchuk 39	.75	.30	.07
☐ 15	Alexander Mogilny 89	5.00	2.00	.50
☐ 16	Mark Napier 65	.60	.24	.06
☐ 17	Jeff Parker 29	.50	.20	.05
☐ 18	Larry Playfair 27	.50	.20	.05
☐ 19	Daren Puppa 31	1.00	.40	.10
☐ 20	Mike Ramsey 5	.60	.24	.06
☐ 21	Robert Ray 32	.75	.30	.07
☐ 22	Christian Ruuttu 21	.75	.30	.07
☐ 23	Ray Sheppard 23	1.00	.40	.10
☐ 24	Dave Snuggerud 18	.50	.20	.05
☐ 25	John Tortorella CO	.50	.20	.05
☐ 26	Pierre Turgeon 77	4.00	1.60	.40
☐ 27	Rick Vaive 22	.75	.30	.07
☐ xx	Large Team Photo	2.50	1.00	.25

		MINT	EXC	G-VG
☐ 21	Jiri Sejba 23	.50	.20	.05
☐ 22	Dave Snuggerud 18	.50	.20	.05
☐ 23	John Tucker 7	.60	.24	.06
☐ 24	Pierre Turgeon 77	3.00	1.20	.30
☐ 25	Rick Vaive 22	.75	.30	.07
☐ 26	Jay Wells 24	.50	.20	.05

1990-91 Sabres Campbell's

1990-91 Sabres Blue Shield

This 26-card set was issued by the Buffalo Sabres in conjunction with Blue Shield of Western New York. The cards measure approximately 4" by 6" and are in the postcard format, with the Blue Shield logo on the backs. The fronts feature a color action photo of the player. The picture is sandwiched between yellow stripes, with team logo and player's name above, and player information below. These cards may be distinguished from the previous year's issue by the "medical shield logo" in the upper right corner. The cards are unnumbered and we have checklisted them below in alphabetical order, with the uniform number next to the player's name.

		MINT	EXC	G-VG
	COMPLETE SET (26)	15.00	6.00	1.50
	COMMON PLAYER (1-26)	.50	.20	.05
☐ 1	Dave Andreychuk 25	1.50	.60	.15
☐ 2	Donald Audette 28	1.25	.50	.12
☐ 3	Doug Bodger 8	.75	.30	.07
☐ 4	Greg Brown 9	.60	.24	.06
☐ 5	Brian Curran 39	.50	.20	.05
☐ 6	Lou Franceschetti 15	.50	.20	.05
☐ 7	Mike Hartman 20	.50	.20	.05
☐ 8	Dale Hawerchuk 10	1.00	.40	.10
☐ 9	Benoit Hogue 33	1.00	.40	.10
☐ 10	Dean Kennedy 26	.50	.20	.05
☐ 11	Uwe Krupp 4	.75	.30	.07
☐ 12	Grant Ledyard 3	.60	.24	.06
☐ 13	Mikko Makela 42	.50	.20	.05
☐ 14	Clint Malarchuk 30	.75	.30	.07
☐ 15	Alexander Mogilny 89	3.00	1.20	.30
☐ 16	Daren Puppa 31	1.00	.40	.10
☐ 17	Mike Ramsey 5	.60	.24	.06
☐ 18	Robert Ray 32	.60	.24	.06
☐ 19	Christian Ruuttu 21	.75	.30	.07
☐ 20	Sabretooth Mascot	.50	.20	.05

The 1990-91 Buffalo Sabres Team Photo Album was sponsored by Campbell's. It consists of three large sheets, each measuring approximately 10" by 13 1/2" and joined together to form one continuous sheet. The first panel has a team photo of the Sabres in street clothing. The second and third panels present four rows of four cards each (31 player cards plus a Sabres' logo card). After perforation, the cards measure approximately 2 1/2" by 3 3/8". They feature color posed photos bordered in white, on a dark blue background. The player's name is given above the picture, with the Sabres' logo, uniform number, and Franco-American logo below the picture. The back has biographical and statistical information in a horizontal format. We have checklisted the names below in alphabetical order, with the uniform number to the right of the name.

		MINT	EXC	G-VG
	COMPLETE SET (32)	15.00	6.00	1.50
	COMMON PLAYER (1-31)	.50	.20	.05
☐ 1	Dave Andreychuk 25	1.50	.60	.15
☐ 2	Donald Audette 28	1.25	.50	.12
☐ 3	Doug Bodger 8	.75	.30	.07
☐ 4	Greg Brown 9	.60	.24	.06
☐ 5	Bob Corkum 19	.50	.20	.05
☐ 6	Rick Dudley CO	.75	.30	.07
☐ 7	Mike Foligno 17	.50	.20	.05
☐ 8	Mike Hartman 20	.50	.20	.05
☐ 9	Dale Hawerchuk 10	1.00	.40	.10
☐ 10	Benoit Hogue 33	1.00	.40	.10
☐ 11	Dean Kennedy 26	.50	.20	.05
☐ 12	Uwe Krupp 4	.75	.30	.07
☐ 13	Grant Ledyard 3	.60	.24	.06
☐ 14	Darcy Loewen 36	.50	.20	.05
☐ 15	Mikko Makela 42	.50	.20	.05
☐ 16	Clint Malarchuk 30	.75	.30	.07
☐ 17	Brad Miller 44	.50	.20	.05
☐ 18	Alexander Mogilny 89	3.00	1.20	.30
☐ 19	Daren Puppa 31	1.00	.40	.10
☐ 20	Mike Ramsey 5	.60	.24	.06
☐ 21	Robert Ray 32	.60	.24	.06
☐ 22	Christian Ruuttu 21	.75	.30	.07
☐ 23	Jiri Sejba 23	.50	.20	.05
☐ 24	Darrin Shannon 16	.75	.30	.07
☐ 25	Dave Snuggerud 18	.50	.20	.05
☐ 26	John Tortorella CO	.50	.20	.05
☐ 27	John Tucker 7	.60	.24	.06
☐ 28	Pierre Turgeon 77	3.00	1.20	.30
☐ 29	Rick Vaive 22	.75	.30	.07
☐ 30	John Van Boxmeer CO	.50	.20	.05
☐ 31	Jay Wells 24	.50	.20	.05
☐ xx	Large Team Photo	2.50	1.00	.25
	(In civilian clothes)			

1991-92 Sabres Blue Shield

This 26-card postcard set of Buffalo Sabres measuring approximately 4" by 6" features an action photograph enclosed in white and blue borders. The player's name, date, and team name appear in blue lettering on a gold background and are flanked on the right and left by the team logo and Blue Shield of Western New York's logo. Biographical information and the player's jersey number appear in blue over gold within a blue border at the bottom. Card backs carry a large Blue Shield logo and motto on the left side. The cards are unnumbered and checklisted below in alphabetical order, with the jersey number to the right of the name.

		MINT	EXC	G-VG
COMPLETE SET (26)		15.00	6.00	1.50
COMMON PLAYER (1-26)		.50	.20	.05
☐ 1	Dave Andreychuk 25	1.50	.60	.15
☐ 2	Donald Audette 28	1.00	.40	.10
☐ 3	Doug Bodger 8	.75	.30	.07
☐ 4	Gord Donnelly 34	.50	.20	.05
☐ 5	Tom Draper 35	1.00	.40	.10
☐ 6	Kevin Haller 7	1.00	.40	.10
☐ 7	Dale Hawerchuk 10	1.00	.40	.10
☐ 8	Randy Hillier 23	.50	.20	.05
☐ 9	Pat LaFontaine 16	4.00	1.60	.40
☐ 10	Grant Ledyard 3	.50	.20	.05
☐ 11	Clint Malarchuk 30	.75	.30	.07
☐ 12	Brad May 27	1.25	.50	.12
☐ 13	Brad Miller 44	.50	.20	.05
☐ 14	Alexander Mogilny 89	2.50	1.00	.25
☐ 15	Colin Patterson 17	.50	.20	.05
☐ 16	Daren Puppa 31	1.00	.40	.10
☐ 17	Mike Ramsey 5	.60	.24	.06
☐ 18	Robert Ray 32	.60	.24	.06
☐ 19	Christian Ruuttu 21	.60	.24	.06
☐ 20	Dave Snuggerud 18	.50	.20	.05
☐ 21	Ken Sutton 41	.60	.24	.06
☐ 22	Tony Tanti 19	.60	.24	.06
☐ 23	Rick Vaive 22	.75	.30	.07
☐ 24	Jay Wells 24	.50	.20	.05
☐ 25	Randy Wood 15	.50	.20	.05
☐ 26	Sabretooth (Mascot)	.50	.20	.05

1991-92 Sabres Pepsi/Campbell's

The 1991-92 Buffalo Sabres Team Photo Album was sponsored in two different varieties. One version was sponsored by Pepsi in conjunction with the Sheriff's Office of Erie County. The Pepsi logo appears on both sides of each card. A second version was sponsored by Campbell's; the card fronts have the Campbell's Chunky soup logo and the flipside carries the Franco-American emblem. The set consists of three large sheets, joined together to form one continuous sheet. The first panel has a team photo of the Sabres in street clothing, superimposed over lightning

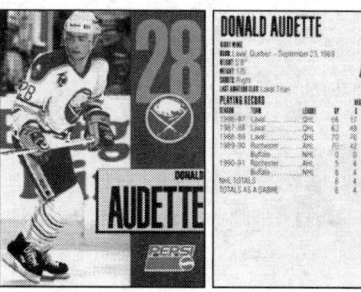

streaks on the left side. The second (10" by 13") and third (7 1/2" by 13") panels present 28 cards; after perforation, the cards measure 2 1/2" by 3 1/4". The color action photos are full-bleed on three sides; the blue border running down their right side carries the jersey number, team logo, player's name (on a gold band which jets out into the photo), and the Pepsi logo. The backs list biographical and statistical information. The cards are unnumbered and checklisted below in alphabetical order, with the jersey number to the right of the name.

		MINT	EXC	G-VG
COMPLETE SET (29)		15.00	6.00	1.50
COMMON PLAYER (1-28)		.50	.20	.05
☐ 1	Dave Andreychuk 25	1.50	.60	.15
☐ 2	Donald Audette 28	1.00	.40	.10
☐ 3	Doug Bodger 8	.75	.30	.07
☐ 4	Gord Donnelly 34	.50	.20	.05
☐ 5	Tom Draper 35	1.00	.40	.10
☐ 6	Kevin Haller 7	1.00	.40	.10
☐ 7	Dale Hawerchuk 10	1.00	.40	.10
☐ 8	Randy Hillier 23	.50	.20	.05
☐ 9	Pat LaFontaine 16	4.00	1.60	.40
☐ 10	Grant Ledyard 3	.50	.20	.05
☐ 11	Clint Malarchuk 30	.75	.30	.07
☐ 12	Brad May 27	1.25	.50	.12
☐ 13	Brad Miller 44	.50	.20	.05
☐ 14	Alexander Mogilny 89	2.50	1.00	.25
☐ 15	Colin Patterson 17	.50	.20	.05
☐ 16	Daren Puppa 31	1.00	.40	.10
☐ 17	Mike Ramsey 5	.60	.24	.06
☐ 18	Robert Ray 32	.60	.24	.06
☐ 19	Christian Ruuttu 21	.60	.24	.06
☐ 20	Dave Snuggerud 18	.50	.20	.05
☐ 21	Ken Sutton 41	.60	.24	.06
☐ 22	Tony Tanti 19	.60	.24	.06
☐ 23	Rick Vaive 22	.75	.30	.07
☐ 24	Jay Wells 24	.50	.20	.05
☐ 25	Randy Wood 15	.50	.20	.05
☐ 26	Sabretooth (Mascot)	.50	.20	.05
☐ 27	Team Logo	.50	.20	.05
☐ 28	NHL Logo	.50	.20	.05
☐ xx	Large Team Photo	2.50	1.00	.25
	(In civilian clothes)			

1992-93 Sabres Blue Shield

Sponsored by Blue Shield of Western New York, this 26-card postcard set measures approximately 4" by 6" and features color action player photos. In a mustard-colored box at the top are printed the player's name, the year and team name, and the team and sponsor logos. In a mustard-colored box at the bottom is biographical information. These boxes and the photo are outlined by a thin royal blue line. The horizontal backs have a light blue postcard design with the sponsor logo and a "Wellness Goal." The cards are unnumbered and checklisted below in alphabetical order.

	MINT	EXC	G-VG
COMPLETE SET (26)	15.00	6.00	1.50
COMMON PLAYER (1-26)	.50	.20	.05

		MINT	EXC	G-VG
☐ 1	Dave Andreychuk	1.50	.60	.15
☐ 2	Donald Audette	.75	.30	.07
☐ 3	Doug Bodger	.75	.30	.07
☐ 4	Bob Corkum	.50	.20	.05
☐ 5	Gord Donnelly	.50	.20	.05
☐ 6	Dave Hannan	.50	.20	.05
☐ 7	Dominik Hasek	2.50	1.00	.25
☐ 8	Dale Hawerchuk	1.00	.40	.10
☐ 9	Yuri Khmylev	1.50	.60	.15
☐ 10	Pat LaFontaine	4.00	1.60	.40
☐ 11	Grant Ledyard	.60	.24	.06
☐ 12	Brad May	1.00	.40	.10
☐ 13	Alexander Mogilny	2.50	1.00	.25
☐ 14	Randy Moller	.50	.20	.05
☐ 15	John Muckler CO	.60	.24	.06
☐ 16	Colin Patterson	.50	.20	.05
☐ 17	Wayne Presley	.50	.20	.05
☐ 18	Daren Puppa	1.00	.40	.10
☐ 19	Mike Ramsey	.60	.24	.06
☐ 20	Rob Ray	.60	.24	.06
☐ 21	Richard Smehlik	.75	.30	.07
☐ 22	Ken Sutton	.50	.20	.05
☐ 23	Petr Svoboda	.60	.24	.06
☐ 24	Bob Sweeney	.50	.20	.05
☐ 25	Randy Wood	.50	.20	.05
☐ 26	Sabretooth (Mascot)	.50	.20	.05

1992-93 Sabres Jubilee Foods

 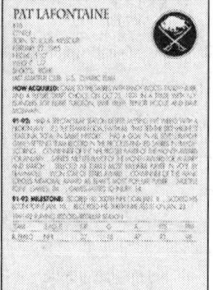

Printed on thin white stock, the cards of this set, which are subtitled "Junior Fan Club," measure approximately 4" by 7" and feature color action shots of Sabres players on their fronts. These photos are borderless, except across the bottom, where a half-inch wide, mustard-colored stripe carries the sponsor's name. A thin blue stripe edges the card at the very bottom. The player's name appears vertically in blue lettering down one side. The Junior Fan Club logo in the lower left straddles the bottom of the photo and the two stripes. The backs have the player's name and biography in the upper left and the Sabres logo in the upper right. Beneath are highlights and stats from the 1991-92 season. The Stanley Cup logo at the bottom rounds out the

card. The cards are unnumbered and checklisted below in alphabetical order.

		MINT	EXC	G-VG
COMPLETE SET (16)		12.00	5.00	1.20
COMMON PLAYER (1-16)		.50	.20	.05
☐ 1	Dave Andreychuk	1.50	.60	.15
☐ 2	Doug Bodger	.75	.30	.07
☐ 3	Gord Donnelly	.60	.24	.06
	Rob Ray			
☐ 4	Dominik Hasek	2.00	.80	.20
	Daren Puppa			
☐ 5	Dale Hawerchuk	1.00	.40	.10
☐ 6	Yuri Khmylev	1.25	.50	.12
	Viktor Gordijuk			
☐ 7	Pat LaFontaine	3.00	1.20	.30
☐ 8	Brad May	1.00	.40	.10
☐ 9	Alexander Mogilny	2.00	.80	.20
☐ 10	Randy Moller	.60	.24	.06
	Ken Sutton			
☐ 11	Wayne Presley	.75	.30	.07
	Donald Audette			
☐ 12	Mike Ramsey	.60	.24	.06
☐ 13	Richard Smehlik	.60	.24	.06
	Bob Corkum			
☐ 14	Petr Svoboda	.60	.24	.06
☐ 15	Bob Sweeney	.50	.20	.05
☐ 16	Randy Wood	.50	.20	.05

1993-94 Sabres Noco

 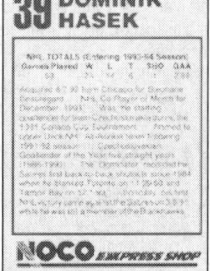

Subtitled Sabres Stars and issued in five-card perforated strips, these 20 standard-size (2 1/2" by 3 1/2") cards feature on their fronts white-bordered color player action shots framed by a yellow line. The player's name and the team logo appear in the white margin below the photo. The white back carries the player's name and number at the top, followed below by statistics and career highlights. The logo for the set's sponsor, Noco Express Shop, rounds out the card at the bottom. The cards are unnumbered and checklisted below in alphabetical order.

		MINT	EXC	G-VG
COMPLETE SET (20)		12.00	5.00	1.20
COMMON PLAYER (1-20)		.50	.20	.05
☐ 1	Roger Crozier	.60	.24	.06
☐ 2	Rick Dudley	.60	.24	.06
☐ 3	Mike Foligno	.50	.20	.05
☐ 4	Grant Fuhr	.75	.30	.07
☐ 5	Danny Gare	.60	.24	.06
☐ 6	Dominik Hasek	1.50	.60	.15
☐ 7	Dale Hawerchuk	1.00	.40	.10
☐ 8	Tim Horton	1.25	.50	.12
☐ 9	Pat LaFontaine	2.00	.80	.20
☐ 10	Don Luce	.50	.20	.05
☐ 11	Rick Martin	.75	.30	.07
☐ 12	Brad May	.60	.24	.06
☐ 13	Alexander Mogilny	2.00	.80	.20
☐ 14	Gilbert Perreault	1.25	.50	.12
☐ 15	Craig Ramsay	.50	.20	.05
☐ 16	Mike Ramsey	.60	.24	.06
☐ 17	Rene Robert	.60	.24	.06
☐ 18	Sabretooth MASCOT	.50	.20	.05

		NRMT	VG-E	GOOD
☐ 19	Jim Schoenfeld	.75	.30	.07
☐ 20	Knoxes Unveil	.50	.20	.05
	Sabres Uniform			
	Northrup Knox			
	Punch Imlach			
	Seymour Knox			

1970-71 Sargent Promotions Stamps

This set consists of 224 total stamps, 16 for each NHL team. Individual stamps measure approximately 2" by 2 1/2". The set could be put into a album featuring Bobby Orr on the cover. Stamp fronts feature a full-color head shot of the player, player's name, and team. The stamp number is located in the upper left corner. The 1970-71 set features one-time appearances in Eddie Sargent Promotions sets by Hall of Famers Gordie Howe, Jean Beliveau, and Andy Bathgate. The set also features first appearances of Gil Perreault, Brad Park, and Bobby Clarke. The three have Rookie Cards in both Topps and O-Pee-Chee for the same year.

		NRMT	VG-E	GOOD
COMPLETE SET (224)		550.00	220.00	55.00
COMMON PLAYER (1-224)		1.00	.40	.10
☐ 1	Bobby Orr	100.00	40.00	10.00
☐ 2	Don Awrey	1.00	.40	.10
☐ 3	Derek Sanderson	4.00	1.60	.40
☐ 4	Ted Green	1.25	.50	.12
☐ 5	Eddie Johnston	1.50	.60	.15
☐ 6	Wayne Carleton	1.00	.40	.10
☐ 7	Ed Westfall	1.50	.60	.15
☐ 8	Johnny Bucyk	7.50	3.00	.75
☐ 9	John McKenzie	1.00	.40	.10
☐ 10	Ken Hodge	2.00	.80	.20
☐ 11	Rick Smith	1.00	.40	.10
☐ 12	Fred Stanfield	1.00	.40	.10
☐ 13	Garnet Bailey	1.00	.40	.10
☐ 14	Phil Esposito	15.00	6.00	1.50
☐ 15	Gerry Cheevers	7.50	3.00	.75
☐ 16	Dallas Smith	1.25	.50	.12
☐ 17	Joe Daley	1.25	.50	.12
☐ 18	Ron Anderson	1.00	.40	.10
☐ 19	Tracy Pratt	1.00	.40	.10
☐ 20	Gerry Meehan	1.50	.60	.15
☐ 21	Reg Fleming	1.00	.40	.10
☐ 22	Al Hamilton	1.00	.40	.10
☐ 23	Gil Perreault	15.00	6.00	1.50
☐ 24	Skip Krake	1.00	.40	.10
☐ 25	Kevin O'Shea	1.00	.40	.10
☐ 26	Roger Crozier	1.50	.60	.15
☐ 27	Bill Inglis	1.00	.40	.10
☐ 28	Mike McMahon	1.00	.40	.10
☐ 29	Cliff Schmautz	1.00	.40	.10
☐ 30	Floyd Smith	1.00	.40	.10
☐ 31	Randy Wyrozub	1.00	.40	.10
☐ 32	Jim Watson	1.00	.40	.10
☐ 33	Tony Esposito	10.00	4.00	1.00
☐ 34	Doug Jarrett	1.00	.40	.10
☐ 35	Keith Magnuson	1.25	.50	.12
☐ 36	Dennis Hull	2.00	.80	.20
☐ 37	Cliff Koroll	1.00	.40	.10
☐ 38	Eric Nesterenko	1.50	.60	.15
☐ 39	Pit Martin	1.25	.50	.12
☐ 40	Lou Angotti	1.00	.40	.10
☐ 41	Jim Pappin	1.25	.50	.12
☐ 42	Gerry Pinder	1.25	.50	.12
☐ 43	Bobby Hull	35.00	14.00	3.50
☐ 44	Pat Stapleton	1.25	.50	.12
☐ 45	Gerry Desjardins	1.25	.50	.12
☐ 46	Chico Maki	1.25	.50	.12
☐ 47	Doug Mohns	1.25	.50	.12
☐ 48	Stan Mikita	15.00	6.00	1.50
☐ 49	Gary Bergman	1.25	.50	.12
☐ 50	Pete Stemkowski	1.25	.50	.12
☐ 51	Bruce MacGregor	1.00	.40	.10
☐ 52	Ron Harris	1.00	.40	.10
☐ 53	Billy Dea	1.00	.40	.10
☐ 54	Wayne Connelly	1.00	.40	.10
☐ 55	Dale Rolfe	1.00	.40	.10
☐ 56	Gordie Howe	75.00	30.00	7.50
☐ 57	Tom Webster	1.25	.50	.12
☐ 58	Al Karlander	1.00	.40	.10
☐ 59	Alex Delvecchio	6.00	2.40	.60
☐ 60	Nick Libett	1.25	.50	.12
☐ 61	Garry Unger	2.00	.80	.20
☐ 62	Roy Edwards	1.25	.50	.12
☐ 63	Frank Mahovlich	12.00	5.00	1.20
☐ 64	Bob Baun	1.50	.60	.15
☐ 65	Dick Duff	1.50	.60	.15
☐ 66	Ross Lonsberry	1.00	.40	.10
☐ 67	Ed Joyal	1.00	.40	.10
☐ 68	Dale Hoganson	1.00	.40	.10
☐ 69	Eddie Shack	3.00	1.20	.30
☐ 70	Real Lemieux	1.00	.40	.10
☐ 71	Matt Ravlich	1.00	.40	.10
☐ 72	Bob Pulford	3.00	1.20	.30
☐ 73	Denis DeJordy	1.50	.60	.15
☐ 74	Larry Mickey	1.00	.40	.10
☐ 75	Bill Flett	1.00	.40	.10
☐ 76	Juha Widing	1.00	.40	.10
☐ 77	Jim Peters	1.00	.40	.10
☐ 78	Gillies Marotte	1.25	.50	.12
☐ 79	Larry Cahan	1.00	.40	.10
☐ 80	Howie Hughes	1.00	.40	.10
☐ 81	Cesare Maniago	1.50	.60	.15
☐ 82	Ted Harris	1.00	.40	.10
☐ 83	Tom Williams	1.00	.40	.10
☐ 84	Gump Worsley	9.00	3.75	.90
☐ 85	Tom Reid	1.00	.40	.10
☐ 86	Murray Oliver	1.00	.40	.10
☐ 87	Charlie Burns	1.00	.40	.10
☐ 88	Jude Drouin	1.00	.40	.10
☐ 89	Walt McKechnie	1.00	.40	.10
☐ 90	Danny O'Shea	1.00	.40	.10
☐ 91	Barry Gibbs	1.00	.40	.10
☐ 92	Danny Grant	1.25	.50	.12
☐ 93	Bob Barlow	1.00	.40	.10
☐ 94	J.P. Parise	1.25	.50	.12
☐ 95	Bill Goldsworthy	1.50	.60	.15
☐ 96	Bobby Rousseau	1.25	.50	.12
☐ 97	Jacques Laperriere	3.00	1.20	.30
☐ 98	Henri Richard	9.00	3.75	.90
☐ 99	J.C. Tremblay	1.50	.60	.15
☐ 100	Rogie Vachon	3.00	1.20	.30
☐ 101	Claude Larose	1.25	.50	.12
☐ 102	Pete Mahovlich	1.50	.60	.15
☐ 103	Jacques Lemaire	4.00	1.60	.40
☐ 104	Bill Collins	1.00	.40	.10
☐ 105	Guy Lapointe	4.00	1.60	.40
☐ 106	Mickey Redmond	2.00	.80	.20
☐ 107	Larry Pleau	1.25	.50	.12
☐ 108	Jean Beliveau	20.00	8.00	2.00
☐ 109	Yvan Cournoyer	6.00	2.40	.60
☐ 110	Serge Savard	4.00	1.60	.40
☐ 111	Terry Harper	1.25	.50	.12
☐ 112	Phil Myre	1.25	.50	.12
☐ 113	Syl Apps	1.25	.50	.12
☐ 114	Ted Irvine	1.00	.40	.10
☐ 115	Ed Giacomin	6.00	2.40	.60
☐ 116	Arnie Brown	1.00	.40	.10
☐ 117	Walt Tkaczuk	1.25	.50	.12
☐ 118	Jean Ratelle	6.00	2.40	.60
☐ 119	Dave Balon	1.00	.40	.10
☐ 120	Ron Stewart	1.00	.40	.10
☐ 121	Jim Neilson	1.00	.40	.10
☐ 122	Rod Gilbert	6.00	2.40	.60
☐ 123	Bill Faibairn	1.00	.40	.10
☐ 124	Brad Park	7.50	3.00	.75
☐ 125	Tim Horton	9.00	3.75	.90
☐ 126	Vic Hadfield	1.25	.50	.12
☐ 127	Bob Nevin	1.25	.50	.12
☐ 128	Rod Seiling	1.00	.40	.10
☐ 129	Gary Smith	1.25	.50	.12
☐ 130	Carol Vadnais	1.25	.50	.12
☐ 131	Bert Marshall	1.00	.40	.10
☐ 132	Earl Ingarfield	1.00	.40	.10
☐ 133	Dennis Hextall	1.25	.50	.12
☐ 134	Harry Howell	3.00	1.20	.30
☐ 135	Wayne Muloin	1.00	.40	.10
☐ 136	Mike Laughton	1.00	.40	.10
☐ 137	Ted Hampson	1.00	.40	.10
☐ 138	Doug Roberts	1.00	.40	.10
☐ 139	Dick Mattiussi	1.00	.40	.10
☐ 140	Garry Jarrett	1.00	.40	.10
☐ 141	Gary Croteau	1.00	.40	.10
☐ 142	Norm Ferguson	1.00	.40	.10
☐ 143	Bill Hicke	1.00	.40	.10
☐ 144	Gerry Ehman	1.00	.40	.10
☐ 145	Ralph McSweyn	1.00	.40	.10
☐ 146	Bernie Parent	6.00	2.40	.60
☐ 147	Brent Hughes	1.00	.40	.10
☐ 148	Bobby Clarke	20.00	8.00	2.00
☐ 149	Gary Dornhoefer	1.25	.50	.12
☐ 150	Simon Nolet	1.00	.40	.10
☐ 151	Gary Peters	1.00	.40	.10
☐ 152	Doug Favell	1.25	.50	.12

☐ 153	Jim Johnson	1.00	.40	.10
☐ 154	Andre Lacroix	1.25	.50	.12
☐ 155	Larry Hale	1.00	.40	.10
☐ 156	Joe Watson	1.00	.40	.10
☐ 157	Jean Guy Gendron	1.00	.40	.10
☐ 158	Larry Hillman	1.00	.40	.10
☐ 159	Ed Van Impe	1.00	.40	.10
☐ 160	Wayne Hillman	1.00	.40	.10
☐ 161	Al Smith	1.25	.50	.12
☐ 162	Jean Pronovost	1.25	.50	.12
☐ 163	Bob Woytowich	1.00	.40	.10
☐ 164	Bryan Watson	1.25	.50	.12
☐ 165	Dean Prentice	1.50	.60	.15
☐ 166	Duane Rupp	1.00	.40	.10
☐ 167	Glen Sather	2.00	.80	.20
☐ 168	Keith McCreary	1.00	.40	.10
☐ 169	Jim Morrison	1.00	.40	.10
☐ 170	Ron Schock	1.00	.40	.10
☐ 171	Wally Boyer	1.00	.40	.10
☐ 172	Nick Harbaruk	1.00	.40	.10
☐ 173	Andy Bathgate	4.00	1.60	.40
☐ 174	Ken Schinkel	1.00	.40	.10
☐ 175	Les Binkley	1.25	.50	.12
☐ 176	Val Fonteyne	1.00	.40	.10
☐ 177	Red Berenson	1.50	.60	.15
☐ 178	Ab MacDonald	1.00	.40	.10
☐ 179	Jim Roberts	1.00	.40	.10
☐ 180	Frank St. Marseille	1.00	.40	.10
☐ 181	Ernie Wakely	1.00	.40	.10
☐ 182	Terry Crisp	1.25	.50	.12
☐ 183	Bob Plager	1.50	.60	.15
☐ 184	Barclay Plager	1.50	.60	.15
☐ 185	Chris Bordeleau	1.00	.40	.10
☐ 186	Gary Sabourin	1.00	.40	.10
☐ 187	Bill Plager	1.25	.50	.12
☐ 188	Tim Ecclestone	1.00	.40	.10
☐ 189	Jean Guy Talbot	1.50	.60	.15
☐ 190	Noel Picard	1.00	.40	.10
☐ 191	Bob Wall	1.00	.40	.10
☐ 192	Jim Lorentz	1.00	.40	.10
☐ 193	Bruce Gamble	1.00	.40	.10
☐ 194	Jim Harrison	1.00	.40	.10
☐ 195	Paul Henderson	2.00	.80	.20
☐ 196	Brian Glennie	1.25	.50	.12
☐ 197	Jim Dorey	1.00	.40	.10
☐ 198	Rick Ley	1.25	.50	.12
☐ 199	Jacques Plante	15.00	6.00	1.50
☐ 200	Ron Ellis	1.25	.50	.12
☐ 201	Jim McKenney	1.00	.40	.10
☐ 202	Brit Selby	1.00	.40	.10
☐ 203	Mike Pelyk	1.00	.40	.10
☐ 204	Norm Ullman	6.00	2.40	.60
☐ 205	Bill MacMillan	1.00	.40	.10
☐ 206	Mike Walton	1.25	.50	.12
☐ 207	Garry Monahan	1.00	.40	.10
☐ 208	Dave Keon	6.00	2.40	.60
☐ 209	Pat Quinn	2.00	.80	.20
☐ 210	Wayne Maki	1.00	.40	.10
☐ 211	Charlie Hodge	1.50	.60	.15
☐ 212	Orland Kurtenbach	1.25	.50	.12
☐ 213	Paul Popiel	1.25	.50	.12
☐ 214	Dan Johnson	1.00	.40	.10
☐ 215	Dale Tallon	1.25	.50	.12
☐ 216	Ray Cullen	1.25	.50	.12
☐ 217	Bob Dillabough	1.00	.40	.10
☐ 218	Gary Doak	1.25	.50	.12
☐ 219	Andre Boudrias	1.00	.40	.10
☐ 220	Rosaire Paiement	1.25	.50	.12
☐ 221	Darryl Sly	1.00	.40	.10
☐ 222	George Gardner	1.00	.40	.10
☐ 223	Jim Wiste	1.00	.40	.10
☐ 224	Murray Hall	1.00	.40	.10
☐ xx	Stamp Album	25.00	10.00	2.50
	(Bobby Orr on cover)			

1971-72 Sargent Promotions Stamps

Issued by Eddie Sargent Promotions in a series of 16 ten-cent sheets of 14 NHL players each, this 224-stamp set featured posed color photos of players in their NHLPA jerseys. The pictures are framed on their tops and sides in different color borders with the players' names and teams appearing along the bottom. Each sheet measured approximately 7 7/8" by 10" and was divided into four rows, with four 2" by 2 1/2" stamps per row. Two of these 16 sections gave the series number (e.g., Series 1), resulting in

a total of 14 players per sheet. The sections are perforated and the backs are blank. There was a stamp album (approximately 9 1/2" by 13") which featured information on the team history and individual players. The stamps are numbered in the upper left corner and they are grouped into 14 teams of 16 players each as follows: Boston Bruins (1-16), Buffalo Sabres (17-32), Chicago Blackhawks (33-48), Detroit Red Wings (49-64), Los Angeles Kings (65-80), Minnesota North Stars (81-96), Montreal Canadiens (97-112), New York Rangers (113-128), California Golden Seals (129-144), Philadelphia Flyers (145-160), Pittsburgh Penguins (161-176), St. Louis Blues (177-192), Toronto Maple Leafs (193-208), and Vancouver Canucks (209-224).

		NRMT	VG-E	GOOD
COMPLETE SET (224)		450.00	180.00	45.00
COMMON PLAYER (1-224)		1.00	.40	.10
☐ 1	Fred Stanfield	1.00	.40	.10
☐ 2	Ed Westfall	1.50	.60	.15
☐ 3	John McKenzie	1.25	.50	.12
☐ 4	Derek Sanderson	4.00	1.60	.40
☐ 5	Rick Smith	1.00	.40	.10
☐ 6	Teddy Green	1.25	.50	.12
☐ 7	Phil Esposito	15.00	6.00	1.50
☐ 8	Ken Hodge	2.00	.80	.20
☐ 9	Johnny Bucyk	7.50	3.00	.75
☐ 10	Bobby Orr	90.00	36.00	9.00
☐ 11	Dallas Smith	1.25	.50	.12
☐ 12	Mike Walton	1.25	.50	.12
☐ 13	Don Awrey	1.00	.40	.10
☐ 14	Unknown	1.00	.40	.10
☐ 15	Eddie Johnston	1.50	.60	.15
☐ 16	Gerry Cheevers	6.00	2.40	.60
☐ 17	Gerry Meehan	1.50	.60	.15
☐ 18	Ron Anderson	1.00	.40	.10
☐ 19	Gilbert Perreault	10.00	4.00	1.00
☐ 20	Eddie Shack	3.00	1.20	.30
☐ 21	Jim Watson	1.00	.40	.10
☐ 22	Kevin O'Shea	1.00	.40	.10
☐ 23	Al Hamilton	1.00	.40	.10
☐ 24	Dick Duff	1.50	.60	.15
☐ 25	Tracy Pratt	1.00	.40	.10
☐ 26	Don Luce	1.00	.40	.10
☐ 27	Roger Crozier	1.25	.50	.12
☐ 28	Doug Barrie	1.00	.40	.10
☐ 29	Mike Robitaille	1.00	.40	.10
☐ 30	Phil Goyette	1.00	.40	.10
☐ 31	Larry Keenan	1.00	.40	.10
☐ 32	Dave Dryden	1.25	.50	.12
☐ 33	Stan Mikita	12.00	5.00	1.20
☐ 34	Bobby Hull	30.00	12.00	3.00
☐ 35	Cliff Koroll	1.00	.40	.10
☐ 36	Chico Maki	1.25	.50	.12
☐ 37	Danny O'Shea	1.00	.40	.10
☐ 38	Lou Angotti	1.00	.40	.10
☐ 39	Andre Lacroix	1.25	.50	.12
☐ 40	Jim Pappin	1.25	.50	.12
☐ 41	Doug Jarrett	1.00	.40	.10
☐ 42	Pit Martin	1.25	.50	.12
☐ 43	Gary Smith	1.25	.50	.12
☐ 44	Tony Esposito	7.50	3.00	.75
☐ 45	Pat Stapleton	1.25	.50	.12
☐ 46	Dennis Hull	2.00	.80	.20
☐ 47	Bill White	1.25	.50	.12
☐ 48	Keith Magnuson	1.25	.50	.12
☐ 49	Bill Collins	1.00	.40	.10
☐ 50	Bob Wall	1.00	.40	.10
☐ 51	Red Berenson	1.50	.60	.15
☐ 52	Mickey Redmond	2.00	.80	.20
☐ 53	Nick Libett	1.25	.50	.12
☐ 54	Gary Bergman	1.25	.50	.12
☐ 55	Alex Delvecchio	5.00	2.00	.50
☐ 56	Tim Ecclestone	1.00	.40	.10
☐ 57	Arnie Brown	1.00	.40	.10
☐ 58	Ron Harris	1.00	.40	.10
☐ 59	Ab McDonald	1.00	.40	.10
☐ 60	Guy Charron	1.00	.40	.10
☐ 61	Al Smith	1.25	.50	.12
☐ 62	Joe Daley	1.25	.50	.12
☐ 63	Leon Rochefort	1.00	.40	.10
☐ 64	Ron Stackhouse	1.00	.40	.10
☐ 65A	Larry Johnston	1.50	.60	.15
☐ 65B	Juha Widing	1.50	.60	.15
☐ 66	Bob Pulford	3.00	1.20	.30
☐ 67	Bill Flett	1.00	.40	.10
☐ 68	Rogie Vachon	4.00	1.60	.40
☐ 69	Ross Lonsberry	1.00	.40	.10
☐ 70	Gilles Marotte	1.25	.50	.12

☐ 71	Harry Howell	3.00	1.20	.30
☐ 72	Real Lemieux	1.00	.40	.10
☐ 73	Butch Goring	1.50	.60	.15
☐ 74	Ed Joyal	1.00	.40	.10
☐ 75	Larry Hillman	1.00	.40	.10
☐ 76	Lucien Grenier	1.00	.40	.10
☐ 77	Paul Curtis	1.00	.40	.10
☐ 78	Unknown	1.00	.40	.10
☐ 79	Unknown	1.00	.40	.10
☐ 80	Unknown	1.00	.40	.10
☐ 81	Jude Drouin	1.00	.40	.10
☐ 82	Tom Reid	1.25	.50	.12
☐ 83	J.P. Parise	1.00	.40	.10
☐ 84	Doug Mohns	1.25	.50	.12
☐ 85	Danny Grant	1.25	.50	.12
☐ 86	Bill Goldsworthy	1.50	.60	.15
☐ 87	Charlie Burns	1.00	.40	.10
☐ 88	Murray Oliver	1.00	.40	.10
☐ 89	Dean Prentice	1.50	.60	.15
☐ 90	Bob Nevin	1.25	.50	.12
☐ 91	Ted Harris	1.25	.50	.12
☐ 92	Cesare Maniago	1.25	.50	.12
☐ 93	Lou Nanne	1.25	.50	.12
☐ 94	Ted Hampton	1.00	.40	.10
☐ 95	Barry Gibbs	1.00	.40	.10
☐ 96	Gump Worsley	7.50	3.00	.75
☐ 97	J.C. Tremblay	1.50	.60	.15
☐ 98	Guy Lapointe	3.00	1.20	.30
☐ 99	Pete Mahovlich	1.50	.60	.15
☐ 100	Larry Pleau	1.25	.50	.12
☐ 101	Phil Myre	1.25	.50	.12
☐ 102	Yvan Cournoyer	5.00	2.00	.50
☐ 103	Henri Richard	7.50	3.00	.75
☐ 104	Frank Mahovlich	10.00	4.00	1.00
☐ 105	Jacques Lemaire	4.00	1.60	.40
☐ 106	Claude Larose	1.25	.50	.12
☐ 107	Terry Harper	1.25	.50	.12
☐ 108	Jacques Laperriere	3.00	1.20	.30
☐ 109	Phil Roberto	1.00	.40	.10
☐ 110	Serge Savard	4.00	1.60	.40
☐ 111	Marc Tardif	1.25	.50	.12
☐ 112	Pierre Bouchard	1.25	.50	.12
☐ 113	Rod Gilbert	5.00	2.00	.50
☐ 114	Jean Ratelle	5.00	2.00	.50
☐ 115	Pete Stemkowski	1.25	.50	.12
☐ 116	Brad Park	6.00	2.40	.60
☐ 117	Bobby Rousseau	1.25	.50	.12
☐ 118	Dale Rolfe	1.00	.40	.10
☐ 119	Rod Seiling	1.00	.40	.10
☐ 120	Walt Tkaczuk	1.25	.50	.12
☐ 121	Vic Hadfield	1.25	.50	.12
☐ 122	Jim Neilson	1.00	.40	.10
☐ 123	Bill Fairbairn	1.00	.40	.10
☐ 124	Bruce MacGregor	1.00	.40	.10
☐ 125	Dave Balon	1.00	.40	.10
☐ 126	Ted Irvine	1.00	.40	.10
☐ 127	Gilles Villemure	1.50	.60	.15
☐ 128	Ed Giacomin	5.00	2.00	.50
☐ 129	Walt McKechnie	1.00	.40	.10
☐ 130	Tom Williams	1.00	.40	.10
☐ 131	Wayne Carleton	1.25	.50	.12
☐ 132	Gerry Pinder	1.25	.50	.12
☐ 133	Gary Croteau	1.00	.40	.10
☐ 134	Bert Marshall	1.00	.40	.10
☐ 135	Tom Webster	1.50	.60	.15
☐ 136	Norm Ferguson	1.00	.40	.10
☐ 137	Carol Vadnais	1.25	.50	.12
☐ 138	Garry Jarrett	1.00	.40	.10
☐ 139	Ernie Hicke	1.00	.40	.10
☐ 140	Paul Shmyr	1.00	.40	.10
☐ 141	Marshall Johnston	1.00	.40	.10
☐ 142	Don O'Donoghue	1.00	.40	.10
☐ 143	Joey Johnston	1.00	.40	.10
☐ 144	Dick Redmond	1.00	.40	.10
☐ 145	Simon Nolet	1.00	.40	.10
☐ 146	Wayne Hillman	1.00	.40	.10
☐ 147	Brent Hughes	1.00	.40	.10
☐ 148	Jim Johnson	1.00	.40	.10
☐ 149	Larry Mickey	1.00	.40	.10
☐ 150	Ed Van Impe	1.00	.40	.10
☐ 151	Gary Dornhoefer	1.25	.50	.12
☐ 152	Bobby Clarke	10.00	4.00	1.00
☐ 153	Jean Guy Gendron	1.00	.40	.10
☐ 154	Larry Hale	1.00	.40	.10
☐ 155	Serge Bernier	1.00	.40	.10
☐ 156	Doug Favell	1.25	.50	.12
☐ 157	Bob Kelly	1.25	.50	.12
☐ 158	Joe Watson	1.00	.40	.10
☐ 159	Larry Brown	1.00	.40	.10
☐ 160	Bruce Gamble	1.00	.40	.10
☐ 161	Syl Apps	1.25	.50	.12
☐ 162	Ken Schinkel	1.00	.40	.10
☐ 163	Val Fonteyne	1.00	.40	.10
☐ 164	Bryan Watson	1.25	.50	.12
☐ 165	Bob Woytowich	1.00	.40	.10
☐ 166	Les Binkley	1.25	.50	.12
☐ 167	Roy Edwards	1.25	.50	.12
☐ 168	Jean Pronovost	1.25	.50	.12
☐ 169	Tim Horton	9.00	3.75	.90
☐ 170	Ron Schock	1.00	.40	.10
☐ 171	Nick Harbaruk	1.00	.40	.10
☐ 172	Greg Polis	1.00	.40	.10
☐ 173	Bryan Hextall	1.25	.50	.12
☐ 174	Keith McCreary	1.00	.40	.10
☐ 175	Bill Hicke	1.00	.40	.10
☐ 176	Jim Rutherford	2.00	.80	.20
☐ 177	Gary Sabourin	1.00	.40	.10
☐ 178	Gary Unger	2.00	.80	.20
☐ 179	Terry Crisp	1.25	.50	.12
☐ 180	Noel Picard	1.00	.40	.10
☐ 181	Jim Roberts	1.00	.40	.10
☐ 182	Barclay Plager	1.50	.60	.15
☐ 183	Brit Selby	1.00	.40	.10
☐ 184	Frank St. Marseille	1.00	.40	.10
☐ 185	Ernie Wakely	1.00	.40	.10
☐ 186	Wayne Connelly	1.00	.40	.10
☐ 187	Chris Bordeleau	1.00	.40	.10
☐ 188	Bill Sutherland	1.00	.40	.10
☐ 189	Bob Plager	1.50	.60	.15
☐ 190	Bill Plager	1.25	.50	.12
☐ 191	George Morrison	1.00	.40	.10
☐ 192	Jim Lorentz	1.00	.40	.10
☐ 193	Norm Ullman	5.00	2.00	.50
☐ 194	Jim McKenney	1.00	.40	.10
☐ 195	Rick Ley	1.25	.50	.12
☐ 196	Bob Baun	1.50	.60	.15
☐ 197	Mike Pelyk	1.00	.40	.10
☐ 198	Bill MacMillan	1.00	.40	.10
☐ 199	Garry Monahan	1.00	.40	.10
☐ 200	Paul Henderson	2.00	.80	.20
☐ 201	Jim Dorey	1.00	.40	.10
☐ 202	Jim Harrison	1.00	.40	.10
☐ 203	Ron Ellis	1.25	.50	.12
☐ 204	Darryl Sittler	6.00	2.40	.60
☐ 205	Bernie Parent	5.00	2.00	.50
☐ 206	Dave Keon	5.00	2.00	.50
☐ 207	Brad Selwood	1.00	.40	.10
☐ 208	Don Marshall	1.00	.40	.10
☐ 209	Dale Tallon	1.25	.50	.12
☐ 210	Dan Johnson	1.00	.40	.10
☐ 211	Murray Hall	1.00	.40	.10
☐ 212	Paul Popiel	1.25	.50	.12
☐ 213	George Gardner	1.00	.40	.10
☐ 214	Gary Doak	1.25	.50	.12
☐ 215	Andre Boudrias	1.00	.40	.10
☐ 216	Orland Kurtenbach	1.25	.50	.12
☐ 217	Wayne Maki	1.00	.40	.10
☐ 218	Rosaire Paiement	1.25	.50	.12
☐ 219	Pat Quinn	2.00	.80	.20
☐ 220	Fred Speck	1.00	.40	.10
☐ 221	Barry Wilkins	1.00	.40	.10
☐ 222	Dunc Wilson	1.25	.50	.12
☐ 223	Ted Taylor	1.25	.50	.12
☐ 224	Mike Corrigan	1.00	.40	.10
☐ xx	Stamp Album	25.00	10.00	2.50
	(Bobby Orr on cover)			

1972-73 Sargent Promotions Stamps

During the 1972-73 hockey season, Eddie Sargent
Promotions produced a set of 224 stamps. They were

issued in cello packages in a series of 16 sheets and, at that time, sold for ten cents per sheet with one sheet being available each week of the promotion. Each sheet measures approximately 7 7/8" by 10" and was divided into four rows, with four 2" by 2 1/2" sections per row. Since two of the 16 sections gave the series number (e.g., Series 1), color photos of fourteen NHL players were featured in each series. The set features 224 players from sixteen NHL teams. The pictures were numbered in the upper left hand corner and are checklisted below accordingly. The pictures are framed on their top and sides in different color borders, with the player's name and the team's city name given below. The sections are perforated and the backs are blank. There are two sticker albums (approximately 11 1/4" by 12") available for the set, both of which are bilingual. After a general introduction, the album is divided into team sections, with two pages devoted to each team. A brief history of each team is presented, followed by 14 numbered sticker slots. Biographical information and career summary appear below each stamp slot on the page itself. The typically found album has Bobby Orr on the cover; the tougher album has a Paul Henderson Team Canada cover. The stamps are numbered on the front and checklisted below alphabetically according to teams as follows: Atlanta Flames (1-14), Boston Bruins (15-28), Buffalo Sabres (29-42), California Seals (43-56), Chicago Blackhawks (57-70), Detroit Red Wings (71-84), Los Angeles Kings (85-98), Minnesota North Stars (99-112), Montreal Canadiens (113-126), New York Islanders (127-140), New York Rangers (141-154), Philadelphia Flyers (155-168), Pittsburgh Penguins (169-182), St. Louis Blues (183-196), Toronto Maple Leafs (197-210), and Vancouver Canucks (211-224).

	NRMT	VG-E	GOOD
COMPLETE SET (224)	150.00	60.00	15.00
COMMON PLAYER (1-224)	.50	.20	.05

☐	1 Lucien Grenier	.50	.20	.05
☐	2 Phil Myre	.60	.24	.06
☐	3 Ernie Hicke	.50	.20	.05
☐	4 Keith McCreary	.50	.20	.05
☐	5 Bill MacMillan	.60	.24	.06
☐	6 Pat Quinn	1.00	.40	.10
☐	7 Bill Plager	.60	.24	.06
☐	8 Noel Price	.50	.20	.05
☐	9 Bob Leiter	.50	.20	.05
☐	10 Randy Manery	.50	.20	.05
☐	11 Bob Paradise	.50	.20	.05
☐	12 Larry Romanchych	.50	.20	.05
☐	13 Lew Morrison	.50	.20	.05
☐	14 Dan Bouchard	.60	.24	.06
☐	15 Fred Stanfield	.50	.20	.05
☐	16 Johnny Bucyk	3.50	1.40	.35
☐	17 Bobby Orr	30.00	12.00	3.00
☐	18 Wayne Cashman	.60	.24	.06
☐	19 Dallas Smith	.60	.24	.06
☐	20 Ed Johnston	.75	.30	.07
☐	21 Phil Esposito	6.00	2.40	.60
☐	22 Ken Hodge	1.00	.40	.10
☐	23 Don Awrey	.50	.20	.05
☐	24 Mike Walton	.60	.24	.06
☐	25 Carol Vadnais	.60	.24	.06
☐	26 Doug Roberts	.50	.20	.05
☐	27 Don Marcotte	.50	.20	.05
☐	28 Garnet Bailey	.50	.20	.05
☐	29 Gerry Meehan	.60	.24	.06
☐	30 Tracy Pratt	.50	.20	.05
☐	31 Gilbert Perreault	3.50	1.40	.35
☐	32 Roger Crozier	.60	.24	.06
☐	33 Don Luce	.50	.20	.05
☐	34 Dave Dryden	.60	.24	.06
☐	35 Richard Martin	1.00	.40	.10
☐	36 Jim Lorentz	.50	.20	.05
☐	37 Tim Horton	4.00	1.60	.40
☐	38 Craig Ramsey	.50	.20	.05
☐	39 Larry Hillman	.50	.20	.05
☐	40 Steve Atkinson	.50	.20	.05
☐	41 Jim Schoenfeld	.75	.30	.07
☐	42 Rene Robert	.75	.30	.07
☐	43 Walt McKechnie	.50	.20	.05
☐	44 Marshall Johnston	.50	.20	.05
☐	45 Joey Johnston	.50	.20	.05
☐	46 Dick Redmond	.50	.20	.05
☐	47 Bert Marshall	.50	.20	.05
☐	48 Gary Croteau	.50	.20	.05
☐	49 Marv Edwards	.50	.20	.05
☐	50 Gilles Meloche	.60	.24	.06
☐	51 Ivan Boldirev	.50	.20	.05
☐	52 Stan Gilbertson	.50	.20	.05
☐	53 Peter Laframboise	.50	.20	.05
☐	54 Reggie Leach	1.00	.40	.10
☐	55 Craig Patrick	1.00	.40	.10
☐	56 Bob Stewart	.50	.20	.05
☐	57 Keith Magnuson	.75	.30	.07
☐	58 Doug Jarrett	.50	.20	.05
☐	59 Cliff Koroll	.50	.20	.05
☐	60 Chico Maki	.60	.24	.06
☐	61 Gary Smith	.60	.24	.06
☐	62 Bill White	.60	.24	.06
☐	63 Stan Mikita	6.00	2.40	.60
☐	64 Jim Pappin	.60	.24	.06
☐	65 Lou Angotti	.50	.20	.05
☐	66 Tony Esposito	3.50	1.40	.35
☐	67 Dennis Hull	1.00	.40	.10
☐	68 Pit Martin	.60	.24	.06
☐	69 Pat Stapleton	.60	.24	.06
☐	70 Dan Maloney	.60	.24	.06
☐	71 Bill Collins	.50	.20	.05
☐	72 Arnie Brown	.50	.20	.05
☐	73 Red Berenson	.75	.30	.07
☐	74 Mickey Redmond	1.00	.40	.10
☐	75 Nick Libett	.60	.24	.06
☐	76 Alex Delvecchio	2.50	1.00	.25
☐	77 Ron Stackhouse	.50	.20	.05
☐	78 Tim Ecclestone	.50	.20	.05
☐	79 Gary Bergman	.60	.24	.06
☐	80 Guy Charron	.50	.20	.05
☐	81 Leon Rochefort	.50	.20	.05
☐	82 Larry Johnston	.50	.20	.05
☐	83 Andy Brown	.50	.20	.05
☐	84 Henry Boucha	.60	.24	.06
☐	85 Paul Curtis	.50	.20	.05
☐	86 Jim Stanfield	.50	.20	.05
☐	87 Rogatien Vachon	2.00	.80	.20
☐	88 Ralph Backstrom	.60	.24	.06
☐	89 Gilles Marotte	.60	.24	.06
☐	90 Harry Howell	1.50	.60	.15
☐	91 Real Lemieux	.50	.20	.05
☐	92 Butch Goring	.75	.30	.07
☐	93 Juha Widing	.50	.20	.05
☐	94 Mike Corrigan	.50	.20	.05
☐	95 Larry Brown	.50	.20	.05
☐	96 Terry Harper	.60	.24	.06
☐	97 Serge Bernier	.50	.20	.05
☐	98 Bob Berry	.60	.24	.06
☐	99 Tom Reid	.60	.24	.06
☐	100 Jude Drouin	.50	.20	.05
☐	101 Jean-Paul Parise	.60	.24	.06
☐	102 Doug Mohns	.60	.24	.06
☐	103 Danny Grant	.60	.24	.06
☐	104 Bill Goldsworthy	.75	.30	.07
☐	105 Gump Worsley	3.50	1.40	.35
☐	106 Charlie Burns	.50	.20	.05
☐	107 Murray Oliver	.50	.20	.05
☐	108 Barry Gibbs	.50	.20	.05
☐	109 Ted Harris	.60	.24	.06
☐	110 Cesare Maniago	.60	.24	.06
☐	111 Lou Nanne	.60	.24	.06
☐	112 Bob Nevin	.60	.24	.06
☐	113 Guy Lapointe	1.50	.60	.15
☐	114 Peter Mahovlich	.75	.30	.07
☐	115 Jacques Lemaire	2.00	.80	.20
☐	116 Pierre Bouchard	.60	.24	.06
☐	117 Yvan Cournoyer	2.50	1.00	.25
☐	118 Marc Tardif	.60	.24	.06
☐	119 Henri Richard	3.50	1.40	.35
☐	120 Frank Mahovlich	5.00	2.00	.50
☐	121 Jacques Laperriere	1.50	.60	.15
☐	122 Claude Larose	.60	.24	.06
☐	123 Serge Savard	2.00	.80	.20
☐	124 Ken Dryden	10.00	4.00	1.00
☐	125 Rejean Houle	.60	.24	.06
☐	126 Jim Roberts	.60	.24	.06
☐	127 Ed Westfall	.75	.30	.07
☐	128 Terry Crisp	.60	.24	.06
☐	129 Gerry Desjardins	.60	.24	.06
☐	130 Denis DeJordy	.75	.30	.07
☐	131 Billy Harris	.60	.24	.06
☐	132 Brian Spencer	.75	.30	.07
☐	133 Germaine Gagnon UER	.50	.20	.05
☐	134 David Hedson	.50	.20	.05
☐	135 Lorne Henning	.60	.24	.06
☐	136 Brian Marchinko	.50	.20	.05
☐	137 Tom Miller	.50	.20	.05

☐	138	Gerry Hart	.50	.20	.05
☐	139	Bryan Lefley	.50	.20	.05
☐	140	James Mair	.50	.20	.05
☐	141	Rod Gilbert	2.50	1.00	.25
☐	142	Jean Ratelle	2.50	1.00	.25
☐	143	Pete Stemkowski	.60	.24	.06
☐	144	Brad Park	3.00	1.20	.30
☐	145	Bobby Rousseau	.60	.24	.06
☐	146	Dale Rolfe	.60	.24	.06
☐	147	Ed Giacomin	2.50	1.00	.25
☐	148	Rod Seiling	.50	.20	.05
☐	149	Walt Tkaczuk	.60	.24	.06
☐	150	Bill Fairbairn	.50	.20	.05
☐	151	Vic Hadfield	.60	.24	.06
☐	152	Ted Irvine	.50	.20	.05
☐	153	Bruce MacGregor	.50	.20	.05
☐	154	Jim Neilson	.50	.20	.05
☐	155	Brent Hughes	.50	.20	.05
☐	156	Wayne Hillman	.50	.20	.05
☐	157	Doug Favell	.60	.24	.06
☐	158	Simon Nolet	.50	.20	.05
☐	159	Joe Watson	.50	.20	.05
☐	160	Ed Van Impe	.50	.20	.05
☐	161	Gary Dornhoefer	.60	.24	.06
☐	162	Bobby Clarke	4.00	1.60	.40
☐	163	Bob Kelly	.60	.24	.06
☐	164	Bill Flett	.50	.20	.05
☐	165	Rick Foley	.50	.20	.05
☐	166	Ross Lonsberry	.50	.20	.05
☐	167	Rick MacLeish	1.00	.40	.10
☐	168	Bill Clement	.75	.30	.07
☐	169	Syl Apps	.60	.24	.06
☐	170	Ken Schinkel	.50	.20	.05
☐	171	Nick Harbaruk	.50	.20	.05
☐	172	Bryan Watson	.60	.24	.06
☐	173	Bryan Hextall	.60	.24	.06
☐	174	Roy Edwards	.50	.20	.05
☐	175	Jim Rutherford	1.00	.40	.10
☐	176	Jean Provonost	.60	.24	.06
☐	177	Rick Kessell	.50	.20	.05
☐	178	Greg Polis	.50	.20	.05
☐	179	Ron Schock	.50	.20	.05
☐	180	Duane Rupp	.50	.20	.05
☐	181	Darryl Edestrand	.50	.20	.05
☐	182	Dave Burrows	.50	.20	.05
☐	183	Gary Sabourin	.50	.20	.05
☐	184	Garry Unger	1.00	.40	.10
☐	185	Noel Picard	.50	.20	.05
☐	186	Bob Plager	.75	.30	.07
☐	187	Barclay Plager	.75	.30	.07
☐	188	Frank St. Marseille	.50	.20	.05
☐	189	Danny O'Shea	.50	.20	.05
☐	190	Kevin O'Shea	.50	.20	.05
☐	191	Wayne Stephenson	.60	.24	.06
☐	192	Chris Evans	.50	.20	.05
☐	193	Jacques Caron	.50	.20	.05
☐	194	Andre Dupont	.60	.24	.06
☐	195	Mike Murphy	.50	.20	.05
☐	196	Jack Egers	.50	.20	.05
☐	197	Norm Ullman	2.50	1.00	.25
☐	198	Jim McKenny	.50	.20	.05
☐	199	Bob Baun	.75	.30	.07
☐	200	Mike Pelyk	.50	.20	.05
☐	201	Ron Ellis	.60	.24	.06
☐	202	Garry Monahan	.50	.20	.05
☐	203	Paul Henderson	1.00	.40	.10
☐	204	Darryl Sittler	3.00	1.20	.30
☐	205	Brian Glennie	.50	.20	.05
☐	206	Dave Keon	2.50	1.00	.25
☐	207	Jacques Plante	6.00	2.40	.60
☐	208	Pierre Jarry	.50	.20	.05
☐	209	Rick Kehoe	.75	.30	.07
☐	210	Denis Dupere	.50	.20	.05
☐	211	Dale Tallon	.60	.24	.06
☐	212	Murray Hall	.50	.20	.05
☐	213	Dunc Wilson	.60	.24	.06
☐	214	Andre Boudrias	.50	.20	.05
☐	215	Orland Kurtenbach	.60	.24	.06
☐	216	Wayne Maki	.50	.20	.05
☐	217	Barry Wilkins	.50	.20	.05
☐	218	Richard Lemieux	.50	.20	.05
☐	219	Bobby Schmautz	.50	.20	.05
☐	220	Dave Balon	.50	.20	.05
☐	221	Robert Lalonde	.50	.20	.05
☐	222	Jocelyn Guevremont	.60	.24	.06
☐	223	Gregg Boddy	.50	.20	.05
☐	224	Dennis Kearns	.50	.20	.05
☐	xx	Stamp Album	15.00	6.00	1.50
		(Bobby Orr on cover)			
☐	xx	Stamp Album	30.00	12.00	3.00
		(Paul Henderson on cover)			

1990-91 Score Promos

 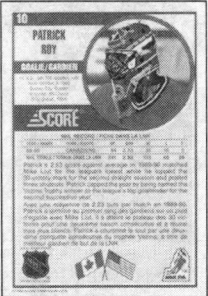

PATRICK ROY

The 1990-91 Score Promo set contains six different player cards, each measuring the standard size, 2 1/2" by 3 1/2". The promos were issued in both a Canadian and an American version. Three (10 Patrick Roy, 40 Gary Leeman, and 100 Mark Messier) were distributed as Canadian promos and the other three were given to U.S. card dealer accounts. Though all these promo versions have the same numbering as the regular issues, several of them are easily distinguished from their regular issue counterparts. The Roy and Messier promos have different player photos on their fronts (Roy promo also has a different photo on its back). The photo on the front of the Roenick promo is cropped differently, and the blurb on its back is also slightly different. Even for those promos that appear to be otherwise identical with the regular cards, close inspection reveals the following distinguishing marks: 1) on the backs, the promos have the registered mark (circle R) by the Score logo, whereas the regular issues have instead the trademark (TM); and 2) on the back, the NHL logo is slightly larger on the promos and the text around it is only in English (the regular issues also have a French translation).

			MINT	EXC	G-VG
COMPLETE SET (8)			125.00	50.00	12.50
COMMON PLAYER			2.00	.80	.20
☐	1A	Wayne Gretzky ERR	75.00	30.00	7.50
		(Catches Left)			
☐	1B	Wayne Gretzky COR	15.00	6.00	1.50
		(Shoots Left)			
☐	10	Patrick Roy	15.00	6.00	1.50
☐	40	Gary Leeman	2.00	.80	.20
☐	100A	Mark Messier ERR	20.00	8.00	2.00
		(Won Smythe in 1990)			
☐	100B	Mark Messier COR	10.00	4.00	1.00
		(Won Smythe in 1984)			
☐	179	Jeremy Roenick	20.00	8.00	2.00
☐	200	Ray Bourque	6.00	2.40	.60

1990-91 Score

The 1990-91 Score hockey set contains 440 cards, each measuring the standard size, 2 1/2" by 3 1/2". The fronts feature a color action photo, superimposed over blue and red stripes on a white background. The team logo appears in the upper left hand corner, while an image of a hockey player (in various colors) appears in the lower right hand corner. The backs are outlined in a blue border and show a head shot of the player on the upper half. The career statistics and highlights on the lower half are printed on a pale yellow background. The complete factory set price includes the five Eric Lindros bonus cards (B1-B5) that were

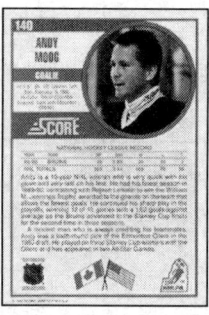

only available in the factory sets sold to hobby dealers. The few card numbers that are different in the Canadian and U.S. versions are labeled with an A (American) or C (Canadian) suffix after the card number. The key Rookie Cards in this set are Martin Brodeur, Nelson Emerson, Jaromir Jagr, Eric Lindros, Alexander Mogilny, Owen Nolan, Mark Recchi, Mike Ricci, Jeremy Roenick, Kevin Stevens, and Mats Sundin.

	MINT	EXC	G-VG
COMPLETE SET (440)	18.00	8.00	2.30
COMPLETE FACT.SET (445)	22.00	10.00	2.80
COMMON PLAYER (1-440)	.05	.02	.01
COMMON LINDROS (B1-B5)	2.00	.90	.25
*CANADIAN VERSION: 1X TO 1.3X VALUE			

☐	1 Wayne Gretzky	1.00	.45	.13
☐	2 Mario Lemieux	.75	.35	.09
☐	3 Steve Yzerman	.35	.16	.04
☐	4 Cam Neely	.20	.09	.03
☐	5 Al MacInnis	.10	.05	.01
☐	6 Paul Coffey	.15	.07	.02
☐	7 Brian Bellows	.08	.04	.01
☐	8 Joe Sakic	.40	.18	.05
☐	9 Bernie Nicholls	.10	.05	.01
☐	10 Patrick Roy	.75	.35	.09
☐	11 Doug Houda	.05	.02	.01
☐	12 David Volek	.05	.02	.01
☐	13 Esa Tikkanen	.08	.04	.01
☐	14 Thomas Steen	.08	.04	.01
☐	15 Chris Chelios	.08	.04	.01
☐	16 Bob Carpenter	.05	.02	.01
☐	17 Dirk Graham	.08	.04	.01
☐	18 Garth Butcher	.08	.04	.01
☐	19 Patrik Sundstrom	.05	.02	.01
☐	20 Rod Langway	.05	.02	.01
☐	21 Scott Young	.05	.02	.01
☐	22 Ulf Dahlen	.08	.04	.01
☐	23 Mike Ramsey	.05	.02	.01
☐	24 Peter Zezel	.05	.02	.01
☐	25 Ron Hextall	.08	.04	.01
☐	26 Steve Duchesne	.08	.04	.01
☐	27 Allan Bester	.05	.02	.01
☐	28 Everett Sanipass	.05	.02	.01
☐	29 Steve Konroyd	.05	.02	.01
☐	30A Joe Nieuwendyk ERR	.50	.23	.06
	(Text says, now I fell, should say feel)			
☐	30B Joe Nieuwendyk COR	.15	.07	.02
☐	31A Brent Ashton ERR	.15	.07	.02
	(No position on card front)			
☐	31A Brent Ashton COR	.15	.07	.02
	(LW on card front)			
☐	32 Trevor Linden	.25	.11	.03
☐	33 Mike Ridley	.08	.04	.01
☐	34 Sean Burke	.08	.04	.01
☐	35 Pat Verbeek	.08	.04	.01
☐	36 Rob Ramage	.05	.02	.01
☐	37 Kelly Kisio	.05	.02	.01
☐	38A Craig Muni ERR	.15	.07	.02
	(Back photo actually Craig Simpson)			
☐	38B Craig Muni COR	.05	.02	.01
☐	39 Brent Sutter	.08	.04	.01
☐	40 Gary Leeman	.05	.02	.01
☐	41 Jeff Brown	.08	.04	.01
☐	42 Greg Millen	.05	.02	.01
☐	43 Alexander Mogilny	.75	.35	.09
☐	44 Dale Hunter	.08	.04	.01
☐	45 Randy Moller	.05	.02	.01
☐	46 Peter Sidorkiewicz	.05	.02	.01
☐	47 Terry Carkner	.05	.02	.01

☐	48 Tony Granato	.08	.04	.01
☐	49 Shawn Burr	.05	.02	.01
☐	50 Dale Hawerchuk	.08	.04	.01
☐	51A Don Sweeney ERR	.15	.07	.02
	(Two black boxes at bottom of card)			
☐	51B Don Sweeney COR	.05	.02	.01
	(Three black boxes at bottom of card)			
☐	52 Mike Vernon UER	.08	.04	.01
	(Text says won WHL MVP twice, should be once)			
☐	53 Kevin Stevens	.60	.25	.08
☐	54 Bryan Fogarty	.05	.02	.01
☐	55 Dan Quinn	.05	.02	.01
☐	56 Murray Craven	.05	.02	.01
☐	57 Shawn Chambers	.05	.02	.01
☐	58 Craig Simpson	.08	.04	.01
☐	59 Doug Crossman	.05	.02	.01
☐	60 Daren Puppa	.08	.04	.01
☐	61 Bobby Smith	.08	.04	.01
☐	62 Viacheslav Fetisov	.10	.05	.01
☐	63 Gino Cavallini	.05	.02	.01
☐	64 Jimmy Carson	.08	.04	.01
☐	65 Dave Ellett	.05	.02	.01
☐	66 Steve Thomas	.08	.04	.01
☐	67 Mike Lalor	.05	.02	.01
☐	68 Mike Liut	.08	.04	.01
☐	69 Tom Laidlaw	.05	.02	.01
☐	70 Ron Francis	.10	.05	.01
☐	71 Sergei Makarov	.30	.14	.04
☐	72 Randy Burridge	.05	.02	.01
☐	73 Doug Lidster	.05	.02	.01
☐	74 Mike Richter	.75	.35	.09
☐	75 Stephane Richer	.08	.04	.01
☐	76 Randy Hillier	.05	.02	.01
☐	77 Christian Ruuttu	.05	.02	.01
☐	78 Marc Fortier	.05	.02	.01
☐	79 Bill Ranford	.10	.05	.01
☐	80 Rick Tocchet	.08	.04	.01
☐	81 Fredrik Olausson	.08	.04	.01
☐	82 Adam Creighton	.05	.02	.01
☐	83 Sylvain Cote	.05	.02	.01
☐	84 Brian Mullen	.08	.04	.01
☐	85 Adam Oates	.15	.07	.02
☐	86 Gary Nylund	.05	.02	.01
☐	87 Tim Cheveldae	.25	.11	.03
☐	88 Gary Suter	.08	.04	.01
☐	89 John Tonelli	.08	.04	.01
☐	90 Kevin Hatcher	.08	.04	.01
☐	91 Guy Carbonneau	.08	.04	.01
☐	92 Curtis Leschyshyn	.05	.02	.01
☐	93 Kirk McLean	.20	.09	.03
☐	94 Curt Giles	.05	.02	.01
☐	95 Vincent Damphousse	.08	.04	.01
☐	96 Peter Stastny	.08	.04	.01
☐	97 Glen Wesley	.08	.04	.01
☐	98 David Shaw	.05	.02	.01
☐	99 Brad Shaw	.05	.02	.01
☐	100 Mark Messier	.25	.11	.03
☐	101 Rick Zombo	.05	.02	.01
☐	102A Mark Fitzpatrick ERR	.25	.11	.03
	(Catches right)			
☐	102B Mark Fitzpatrick COR	.15	.07	.02
	(Catches left)			
☐	103 Rick Vaive	.05	.02	.01
☐	104 Mark Osborne	.05	.02	.01
☐	105 Rob Brown	.05	.02	.01
☐	106 Gary Roberts	.15	.07	.02
☐	107 Vincent Riendeau	.15	.07	.02
☐	108 Dave Gagner	.08	.04	.01
☐	109 Bruce Driver	.05	.02	.01
☐	110 Pierre Turgeon	.25	.11	.03
☐	111 Claude Lemieux	.08	.04	.01
☐	112 Bob Essensa	.20	.09	.03
☐	113 John Ogrodnick	.05	.02	.01
☐	114 Glenn Anderson	.10	.06	.01
☐	115 Kelly Hrudey	.08	.04	.01
☐	116 Sylvain Turgeon	.05	.02	.01
☐	117 Gord Murphy	.05	.02	.01
☐	118 Craig Janney	.20	.09	.03
☐	119 Randy Wood	.05	.02	.01
☐	120 Mike Modano	.75	.35	.09
☐	121 Tom Barrasso	.10	.05	.01
☐	122 Daniel Marois	.05	.02	.01
☐	123 Igor Larionov	.30	.14	.04
☐	124 Geoff Courtnall	.08	.04	.01
☐	125 Denis Savard	.08	.04	.01
☐	126 Ron Tugnutt	.08	.04	.01
☐	127 Mathieu Schneider	.20	.09	.03
☐	128 Joel Otto	.05	.02	.01
☐	129 Steve Smith	.08	.04	.01
☐	130 Mike Gartner	.10	.05	.01
☐	131 Rod Brind'Amour	.50	.23	.06

☐	132	Jyrki Lumme	.15	.07	.02
☐	133	Mike Foligno	.08	.04	.01
☐	134	Ray Ferraro	.08	.04	.01
☐	135	Steve Larmer	.08	.04	.01
☐	136	Randy Carlyle	.05	.02	.01
☐	137	Tony Tanti	.05	.02	.01
☐	138	Jeff Chychrun	.05	.02	.01
☐	139	Gerald Diduck	.05	.02	.01
☐	140	Andy Moog	.10	.05	.01
☐	141	Paul Gillis	.05	.02	.01
☐	142	Tom Kurvers	.05	.02	.01
☐	143	Bob Probert	.08	.04	.01
☐	144	Neal Broten	.08	.04	.01
☐	145	Phil Housley	.08	.04	.01
☐	146	Brendan Shanahan	.25	.11	.03
☐	147	Bob Rouse	.05	.02	.01
☐	148	Russ Courtnall	.08	.04	.01
☐	149	Normand Rochefort UER (RW, should be D)	.05	.02	.01
☐	150	Luc Robitaille	.25	.11	.03
☐	151	Curtis Joseph	.75	.35	.09
☐	152	Ulf Samuelsson	.08	.04	.01
☐	153	Ron Sutter	.05	.02	.01
☐	154	Petri Skriko	.05	.02	.01
☒	155	Doug Gilmour	.35	.16	.04
☐	156	Paul Fenton	.05	.02	.01
☐	157	Jeff Norton	.05	.02	.01
☐	158	Jari Kurri	.10	.05	.01
☐	159	Rejean Lemelin	.08	.04	.01
☐	160	Kirk Muller	.08	.04	.01
☐	161	Keith Brown	.05	.02	.01
☐	162	Aaron Broten UER (Photo actually Dave Archibald)	.05	.02	.01
☐	163	Adam Graves	.75	.35	.09
☐	164	John Cullen UER (Birthdate 1/6/6, should be 1/9/64)	.08	.04	.01
☐	165	Craig Ludwig	.05	.02	.01
☐	166	Dave Taylor	.08	.04	.01
☐	167	Craig Wolanin	.05	.02	.01
☐	168	Kelly Miller	.05	.02	.01
☐	169	Uwe Krupp	.08	.04	.01
☐	170	Kevin Lowe	.08	.04	.01
☐	171	Wendel Clark	.15	.07	.02
☐	172	Dave Babych	.05	.02	.01
☐	173	Paul Reinhart	.05	.02	.01
☐	174	Pat Flatley	.05	.02	.01
☐	175	John Vanbiesbrouck	.15	.07	.02
☐	176	Teppo Numminen	.15	.07	.02
☐	177	Tim Kerr	.08	.04	.01
☐	178	Ken Daneyko	.05	.02	.01
☐	179	Jeremy Roenick	1.25	.55	.16
☐	180	Gerard Gallant	.05	.02	.01
☐	181	Allen Pederson	.05	.02	.01
☐	182	Jon Casey	.08	.04	.01
☐	183	Tomas Sandstrom	.08	.04	.01
☐	184	Brad McCrimmon	.05	.02	.01
☐	185	Paul Cavallini	.05	.02	.01
☐	186	Mark Recchi	.60	.25	.08
☐	187	Michel Petit	.05	.02	.01
☐	188	Scott Stevens	.10	.05	.01
☐	189	Dave Andreychuk	.20	.09	.03
☐	190	John MacLean	.08	.04	.01
☐	191	Petr Svoboda	.05	.02	.01
☐	192	Dave Tippett	.05	.02	.01
☐	193	Dave Manson	.08	.04	.01
☐	194	James Patrick	.05	.02	.01
☐	195	Al Iafrate	.08	.04	.01
☐	196	Doug Smail	.05	.02	.01
☐	197	Kjell Samuelsson	.05	.02	.01
☐	198	Brian Bradley	.08	.04	.01
☐	199	Charlie Huddy	.05	.02	.01
☐	200	Ray Bourque	.20	.09	.03
☐	201	Joey Kocur	.05	.02	.01
☐	202	Jim Johnson UER (Born Michigan, not Minnesota)	.05	.02	.01
☐	203	Paul MacLean	.05	.02	.01
☐	204	Tim Watters	.05	.02	.01
☐	205	Pat Elynuik	.05	.02	.01
☐	206	Larry Murphy	.08	.04	.01
☐	207	Claude Loiselle	.05	.02	.01
☐	208	Joe Mullen	.10	.05	.01
☐	209	Alexei Kasatonov	.15	.07	.02
☐	210	Ed Olczyk	.05	.02	.01
☐	211	Doug Bodger	.05	.02	.01
☐	212	Kevin Dineen	.08	.04	.01
☐	213	Shayne Corson	.08	.04	.01
☐	214	Steve Chiasson	.08	.04	.01
☐	215	Don Beaupre	.08	.04	.01
☐	216	Jamie Macoun	.05	.02	.01
☐	217	Dave Poulin	.08	.04	.01
☐	218	Zarley Zalapski	.08	.04	.01
☐	219	Brad Marsh	.08	.04	.01
☐	220	Mark Howe	.08	.04	.01
☐	221	Michel Goulet	.08	.04	.01
☐	222	Hubie McDonough	.05	.02	.01
☐	223	Frantisek Musil	.05	.02	.01
☐	224	Sergio Momesso	.10	.05	.01
☐	225	Brian Leetch	.50	.23	.06
☐	226	Theoren Fleury	.25	.11	.03
☐	227	Mike Krushelnyski	.05	.02	.01
☐	228	Glen Hanlon	.05	.02	.01
☐	229	Mario Marois	.05	.02	.01
☐	230	Dino Ciccarelli	.08	.04	.01
☐	231A	Dave McLlwain ERR (Shoots right)	.15	.07	.02
☐	231B	Dave McLlwain COR (Shoots left)	.05	.02	.01
☐	232	Petr Klima	.08	.04	.01
☐	233	Grant Ledyard	.05	.02	.01
☐	234	Phil Bourque	.05	.02	.01
☐	235	Rob Sweeney	.05	.02	.01
☐	236	Luke Richardson	.05	.02	.01
☐	237	Todd Krygier	.05	.02	.01
☐	238	Brian Skrudland	.05	.02	.01
☐	239	Chris Terreri	.25	.11	.03
☐	240	Greg Adams	.05	.02	.01
☐	241	Darren Turcotte	.20	.09	.03
☐	242	Scott Mellanby	.08	.04	.01
☐	243	Troy Murray	.05	.02	.01
☐	244	Stewart Gavin	.05	.02	.01
☐	245	Gordie Roberts	.05	.02	.01
☐	246	John Druce	.05	.02	.01
☐	247	Steve Kasper	.05	.02	.01
☐	248	Paul Ranheim	.10	.05	.01
☐	249	Greg Paslawski	.05	.02	.01
☐	250	Pat LaFontaine	.25	.11	.03
☐	251	Scott Arniel	.05	.02	.01
☐	252	Bernie Federko	.08	.04	.01
☐	253	Garry Galley	.15	.07	.02
☐	254	Carey Wilson	.05	.02	.01
☐	255	Bob Errey	.05	.02	.01
☐	256	Tony Hrkac	.05	.02	.01
☐	257	Andrew McBain	.05	.02	.01
☐	258	Craig MacTavish	.08	.04	.01
☐	259A	Dean Evason ERR (Reversed negative)	.15	.07	.02
☐	259B	Dean Evason COR	.05	.02	.01
☐	260	Larry Robinson	.08	.04	.01
☐	261	Basil McRae	.08	.04	.01
☐	262	Stephan Lebeau	.30	.14	.04
☐	263	Ken Wregget	.05	.02	.01
☐	264	Greg Gilbert	.05	.02	.01
☐	265	Ken Baumgartner	.05	.02	.01
☐	266	Lou Franceschetti	.05	.02	.01
☐	267	Rick Meagher	.05	.02	.01
☐	268	Michal Pivonka	.25	.11	.03
☐	269	Brian Propp	.08	.04	.01
☐	270	Bryan Trottier	.08	.04	.01
☐	271	Marty McSorley	.08	.04	.01
☐	272	Jan Erixon	.05	.02	.01
☐	273	Vladimir Krutov	.05	.02	.01
☐	274	Dana Murzyn	.05	.02	.01
☐	275	Grant Fuhr	.10	.05	.01
☐	276	Randy Cunneyworth	.05	.02	.01
☐	277	John Chabot	.05	.02	.01
☐	278	Walt Poddubny	.05	.02	.01
☐	279	Stephen Leach	.05	.02	.01
☐	280	Doug Wilson	.08	.04	.01
☐	281	Rich Sutter	.05	.02	.01
☐	282	Stephane Beauregard (Played at Ft. Wayne, not Ft. Worth) UER	.10	.05	.01
☐	283	John Carter	.05	.02	.01
☐	284	Don Barber	.05	.02	.01
☐	285	Tom Fergus	.05	.02	.01
☐	286	Ilkka Sinisalo	.05	.02	.01
☐	287	Kevin McClelland UER (Back has shoots, but no side indicated)	.05	.02	.01
☐	288	Troy Mallette	.05	.02	.01
☐	289	Clint Malarchuk UER (Photo actually Tom Barrasso)	.08	.04	.01
☐	290	Guy Lafleur	.05	.02	.01
☐	291	Bob Joyce	.05	.02	.01
☐	292	Trent Yawney	.05	.02	.01
☐	293	Joe Murphy	.25	.11	.03
☐	294	Glenn Healy	.20	.09	.03
☐	295	Dave Christian	.05	.02	.01
☐	296	Paul MacDermid	.05	.02	.01
☐	297	Todd Elik	.20	.09	.03
☐	298	Wendell Young	.05	.02	.01
☐	299	Dean Kennedy	.05	.02	.01

☐ 300	Brett Hull	.75	.35	.09
☐ 301A	Keith Acton	.05	.02	.01
☐ 301C	Martin Gelinas	.15	.07	.02
☐ 302A	Yvon Corriveau	.05	.02	.01
☐ 302C	Ric Nattress	.05	.02	.01
☐ 303A	Don Maloney	.05	.02	.01
☐ 303C	Jim Sandlak	.05	.02	.01
☐ 304A	Mark Tinordi	.15	.07	.02
☐ 304C	Brian Hayward	.05	.02	.01
☐ 305A	Bob Kudelski	.35	.16	.04
☐ 305C	Joe Cirella	.05	.02	.01
☐ 306A	Brian Benning	.05	.02	.01
☐ 306C	Randy Gregg	.05	.02	.01
☐ 307A	Alan Kerr	.05	.02	.01
☐ 307C	Sylvain Lefebvre	.05	.02	.01
☐ 308A	Pelle Eklund	.05	.02	.01
☐ 308C	Mark Lamb	.05	.02	.01
☐ 309A	Calle Johansson	.05	.02	.01
☐ 309C	Rick Wamsley	.05	.02	.01
☐ 310A	David Maley	.05	.02	.01
☐ 310C	Moe Mantha	.05	.02	.01
☐ 311A	Chris Nilan	.08	.04	.01
☐ 311C	Tony McKegney	.05	.02	.01
☐ 312	Patrick Roy AS1	.25	.11	.03
☐ 313	Ray Bourque AS1	.08	.04	.01
☐ 314	Al MacInnis AS1	.08	.04	.01
☐ 315	Mark Messier AS1	.08	.04	.01
☐ 316	Luc Robitaille AS1	.08	.04	.01
☐ 317	Brett Hull AS1	.25	.11	.03
☐ 318	Daren Puppa AS2	.05	.02	.01
☐ 319	Paul Coffey AS2	.08	.04	.01
☐ 320	Doug Wilson AS2	.05	.02	.01
☐ 321	Wayne Gretzky AS2	.30	.14	.04
☐ 322	Brian Bellows AS2	.05	.02	.01
☐ 323	Cam Neely AS2	.08	.04	.01
☐ 324	Bob Essensa ART	.05	.02	.01
☐ 325	Brad Shaw ART	.05	.02	.01
☐ 326	Geoff Smith ART	.05	.02	.01
☐ 327	Mike Modano ART	.20	.09	.03
☐ 328	Rod Brind'Amour ART	.15	.07	.02
☐ 329	Sergei Makarov ART	.08	.04	.01
☐ 330A	Kip Miller Hobey ERR (No Score logo on card front)	.30	.14	.04
☐ 330B	Kip Miller Hobey COR	.05	.02	.01
☐ 330C	Memorial Cup	.50	.23	.06
☐ 331	Edmonton Oilers Champs	.05	.02	.01
☐ 332	Paul Coffey Speed	.08	.04	.01
☐ 333	Mike Gartner Speed	.08	.04	.01
☐ 334	Al Iafrate Blaster	.05	.02	.01
☐ 335	Al MacInnis Blaster	.08	.04	.01
☐ 336	Wayne Gretzky Sniper	.30	.14	.04
☐ 337	Mario Lemieux Sniper	.25	.11	.03
☐ 338	Wayne Gretzky Magic	.30	.14	.04
☐ 339	Steve Yzerman Magic	.08	.04	.01
☐ 340	Cam Neely Banger	.08	.04	.01
☐ 341	Scott Stevens Banger	.08	.04	.01
☐ 342	Esa Tikkanen Shadow	.05	.02	.01
☐ 343	Jan Erixon Shadow	.05	.02	.01
☐ 344	Patrick Roy Stopper	.25	.11	.03
☐ 345	Bill Ranford Stopper	.08	.04	.01
☐ 346	Brett Hull RB	.25	.11	.03
☐ 347	Wayne Gretzky RB	.30	.14	.04
☐ 348	Jari Kurri LL	.08	.04	.01
☐ 349	Paul Cavallini LL	.05	.02	.01
☐ 350	Sergei Makarov RLL	.08	.04	.01
☐ 351	Brett Hull LL	.25	.11	.03
☐ 352	Wayne Gretzky LL	.30	.14	.04
☐ 353	Wayne Gretzky LL	.30	.14	.04
☐ 354	P.Roy/Liut LL	.15	.07	.02
☐ 355	Gilbert Perreault HOF	.05	.02	.01
☐ 356	Bill Barber HOF	.05	.02	.01
☐ 357	Fern Flaman HOF	.05	.02	.01
☐ 358	Bill Ranford Smythe	.08	.04	.01
☐ 359	Rick Meagher Selke	.05	.02	.01
☐ 360	Mark Messier Hart	.08	.04	.01
☐ 361	Wayne Gretzky Ross	.30	.14	.04
☐ 362	Sergei Makarov Calder	.08	.04	.01
☐ 363	Ray Bourque Norris	.08	.04	.01
☐ 364	Patrick Roy Vezina	.25	.11	.03
☐ 365	Moog/Lemelin Jennings	.05	.02	.01
☐ 366	Brett Hull Byng	.25	.11	.03
☐ 367	Gord Kluzak Mast	.05	.02	.01
☐ 368	Boston/Washington UER (Line 11, Janney misspelled as Janny)	.05	.02	.01
☐ 369	Edmonton/Chicago	.05	.02	.01
☐ 370	Adam Burt	.05	.02	.01
☐ 371	Troy Loney	.05	.02	.01
☐ 372	Dave Chyzowski	.05	.02	.01
☐ 373	Geoff Smith	.05	.02	.01
☐ 374	Stan Smyl	.05	.02	.01
☐ 375	Gaetan Duchesne	.05	.02	.01
☐ 376	Bob Murray	.05	.02	.01
☐ 377	Daniel Shank	.05	.02	.01
☐ 378	Tommy Albelin	.05	.02	.01
☐ 379	Perry Berezan	.05	.02	.01
☐ 380	Ken Linseman	.05	.02	.01
☐ 381	Stephane Matteau	.20	.09	.03
☐ 382	Mario Thyer	.05	.02	.01
☐ 383	Nelson Emerson	.50	.23	.06
☐ 384	Kory Kocur	.05	.02	.01
☐ 385	Bob Beers	.10	.05	.01
☐ 386	Jim Hrivnak	.15	.07	.02
☐ 387	Mark Pederson	.05	.02	.01
☐ 388	Jeff Hackett	.15	.07	.02
☐ 389	Eric Weinrich	.15	.07	.02
☐ 390	Steven Rice	.10	.05	.01
☐ 391	Stu Barnes	.15	.07	.02
☐ 392	Olaf Kolzig	.15	.07	.02
☐ 393	Francois Leroux	.05	.02	.01
☐ 394	Adrien Plavsic	.05	.02	.01
☐ 395	Michel Mongeau	.05	.02	.01
☐ 396	Rick Corriveau	.05	.02	.01
☐ 397	Wayne Doucet	.05	.02	.01
☐ 398	Mats Sundin	.75	.35	.09
☐ 399	Murray Baron	.05	.02	.01
☐ 400	Rick Bennett	.05	.02	.01
☐ 401	Jon Morris	.05	.02	.01
☐ 402	Kay Whitmore	.15	.07	.02
☐ 403	Peter Lappin	.05	.02	.01
☐ 404	Kris Draper	.15	.07	.02
☐ 405	Shayne Stevenson	.05	.02	.01
☐ 406	Paul Ysebaert	.15	.07	.02
☐ 407A	Jimmy Waite ERR (Catches right)	.40	.18	.05
☐ 407B	Jimmy Waite COR (Catches left)	.25	.11	.03
☐ 408	Cam Russell	.05	.02	.01
☐ 409	Kim Issel UER (Photo shoots left, text has right)	.05	.02	.01
☐ 410	Darrin Shannon	.15	.07	.02
☐ 411	Link Gaetz	.05	.02	.01
☐ 412	Craig Fisher	.05	.02	.01
☐ 413	Bruce Hoffort	.05	.02	.01
☐ 414	Peter Ing	.05	.02	.01
☐ 415	Stephane Fiset	.20	.09	.03
☐ 416	Dominic Lavoie	.05	.02	.01
☐ 417	Steve Maltais	.05	.02	.01
☐ 418	Wes Walz	.15	.07	.02
☐ 419	Terry Yake	.25	.11	.03
☐ 420	Jamie Leach	.05	.02	.01
☐ 421	Rob Blake	.50	.23	.06
☐ 422	Andrew Cassels	.25	.11	.03
☐ 423	Marc Bureau	.05	.02	.01
☐ 424	Scott Allison	.05	.02	.01
☐ 425	Daryl Sydor	.25	.11	.03
☐ 426	Turner Stevenson	.15	.07	.02
☐ 427	Brad May	.20	.09	.03
☐ 428	Jaromir Jagr	1.00	.45	.13
☐ 429	Shawn Antoski	.10	.05	.01
☐ 430	Derian Hatcher	.20	.09	.03
☐ 431	Mark Greig UER (No indication of how he shoots on card back)	.05	.02	.01
☐ 432	Scott Scissons	.05	.02	.01
☐ 433	Mike Ricci UER (Born October, not November)	.35	.16	.04
☐ 434	Drake Berehowsky	.20	.09	.03
☐ 435	Owen Nolan	.50	.23	.06
☐ 436	Keith Primeau	.30	.14	.04
☐ 437	Karl Dykhuis	.10	.05	.01
☐ 438	Trevor Kidd	.30	.14	.04
☐ 439	Martin Brodeur	2.50	1.15	.30
☐ 440A	Eric Lindros	10.00	4.50	1.25
☐ 440C	Eric Lindros	18.00	8.00	2.30
☐ B1	Eric Lindros Junior B Team	2.00	.90	.25
☐ B2	Eric Lindros Regular Junior OHL	2.00	.90	.25
☐ B3	Eric Lindros OHL All-Star	2.00	.90	.25
☐ B4	Eric Lindros Oshawa Generals (Non-action pose; head shot with his gloves over his mouth)	2.00	.90	.25
☐ B5	Eric Lindros Oshawa Generals (Non-action pose; shot from waist up, arms draped over hockey stick across his back)	2.00	.90	.25

1990-91 Score Traded

 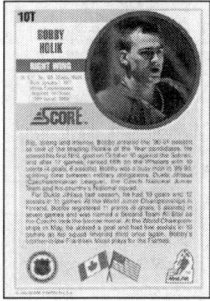

The 1990-91 Score Rookie and Traded hockey set contains 110 cards measuring the standard size, 2 1/2" by 3 1/2". The cards were issued as a complete set in a factory box. The fronts feature a color action photo, superimposed over blue and red stripes on a white background. The team logo appears in the upper left hand corner, while an image of a hockey player (in various colors) appears in the lower right hand corner. Yellow strips appear at the top and bottom of the card front. The backs are outlined in a yellow border and show a head shot of the player on the upper half. The career statistics and highlights on the lower half are printed on a pale blue background. Rookie Cards in this set are Ed Belfour, Peter Bondra, Sergei Fedorov, Bobby Holik, Robert Reichel, and Vladimir Ruzicka. The back of the set's custom box contains the set checklist. The cards are numbered with a "T" suffix.

	MINT	EXC	G-VG
COMPLETE SET (110)	20.00	9.00	2.50
COMMON PLAYER (1T-110T)	.05	.02	.01

		MINT	EXC	G-VG
☐	1T Denis Savard	.05	.02	.01
☐	2T Dale Hawerchuk	.08	.04	.01
☐	3T Phil Housley	.08	.04	.01
☐	4T Chris Chelios	.08	.04	.01
☐	5T Geoff Courtnall	.08	.04	.01
☐	6T Peter Zezel	.05	.02	.01
☐	7T Joe Mullen	.10	.05	.01
☐	8T Craig Ludwig	.05	.02	.01
☐	9T Claude Lemieux	.08	.04	.01
☐	10T Bobby Holik	.40	.18	.05
☐	11T Peter Ing	.05	.02	.01
☐	12T Rod Buskas	.05	.02	.01
☐	13T Tim Sweeney	.10	.05	.01
☐	14T Don Barber	.05	.02	.01
☐	15T Ray Ferraro	.08	.04	.01
☐	16T Peter Taglianetti	.05	.02	.01
☐	17T Johan Garpenlov	.25	.11	.03
☐	18T Kevin Miller	.30	.14	.04
☐	19T Frantisek Musil	.05	.02	.01
☐	20T Sergei Fedorov	3.50	1.55	.45
☐	21T Aaron Broten	.05	.02	.01
☐	22T Chris Nilan	.08	.04	.01
☐	23T Gerald Diduck	.05	.02	.01
☐	24T Marc Habscheid	.05	.02	.01
☐	25T Glen Featherstone	.05	.02	.01
☐	26T Mikko Makela	.05	.02	.01
☐	27T Paul Stanton	.05	.02	.01
☐	28T Mark Osborne	.05	.02	.01
☐	29T Dave Tippett	.05	.02	.01
☐	30T Robert Reichel	1.00	.45	.13
☐	31T Grant Jennings	.05	.02	.01
☐	32T Troy Gamble	.05	.02	.01
☐	33T Mark Janssens	.05	.02	.01
☐	34T Brian Propp	.08	.04	.01
☐	35T Donald Dufresne	.05	.02	.01
☐	36T Martin Hostak	.05	.02	.01
☐	37T Brad McCrimmon	.05	.02	.01
☐	38T Dave Lowry	.05	.02	.01
☐	39T Anatoli Semenov	.20	.09	.03
☐	40T Scott Stevens	.10	.05	.01
☐	41T Paul Broten	.05	.02	.01
☐	42T Carey Wilson	.05	.02	.01
☐	43T Troy Crowder	.05	.02	.01
☐	44T Vladimir Ruzicka	.15	.07	.02
☐	45T Richard Pilon	.05	.02	.01
☐	46T John McIntyre	.05	.02	.01
☐	47T Mike Krushelnyski	.05	.02	.01
☐	48T Dave Snuggerud	.05	.02	.01
☐	49T Bob McGill	.05	.02	.01
☐	50T Petr Nedved	.75	.35	.09
☐	51T Ed Olczyk	.05	.02	.01
☐	52T Doug Crossman	.05	.02	.01
☐	53T Mikhail Tatarinov	.10	.05	.01
☐	54T Michel Petit	.05	.02	.01
☐	55T Frank Pietrangelo	.05	.02	.01
☐	56T Brian MacLellan	.05	.02	.01
☐	57T Paul Fenton	.05	.02	.01
☐	58T Eric Desjardins	.25	.11	.03
☐	59T Mike Craig	.20	.09	.03
☐	60T Mike Ricci	.60	.25	.08
☐	61T Harold Snepsts	.05	.02	.01
☐	62T John Byce	.05	.02	.01
☐	63T Laurie Boschman	.05	.02	.01
☐	64T Randy Velischek	.05	.02	.01
☐	65T Robert Kron	.05	.02	.01
☐	66T Jocelyn Lemieux	.05	.02	.01
☐	67T Dave Ellett	.05	.02	.01
☐	68T Scott Arniel	.05	.02	.01
☐	69T Doug Small	.05	.02	.01
☐	70T Jaromir Jagr	2.00	.90	.25
☐	71T Peter Bondra	.40	.18	.05
☐	72T Paul Cyr	.05	.02	.01
☐	73T Daniel Berthiaume	.05	.02	.01
☐	74T Lee Norwood	.05	.02	.01
☐	75T Bobby Smith	.08	.04	.01
☐	76T Kris King	.05	.02	.01
☐	77T Mark Hunter	.05	.02	.01
☐	78T Brian Hayward	.05	.02	.01
☐	79T Greg Hawgood	.05	.02	.01
☐	80T Owen Nolan	.60	.25	.08
☐	81T Cliff Ronning	.08	.04	.01
☐	82T Zdeno Ciger	.25	.11	.03
☐	83T Gordie Roberts	.05	.02	.01
☐	84T Rick Green	.05	.02	.01
☐	85T Ken Hodge Jr. UER	.05	.02	.01
	(No Jr. on card front)			
☐	86T Derek King	.08	.04	.01
☐	87T Brent Gilchrist	.15	.07	.02
☐	88T Eric Lindros	12.00	5.50	1.50
☐	89T Steve Bozek	.05	.02	.01
☐	90T Keith Primeau	.50	.23	.06
☐	91T Roger Johansson	.05	.02	.01
☐	92T Wayne Presley	.05	.02	.01
☐	93T Ilkka Sinisalo	.05	.02	.01
☐	94T Mario Marois	.05	.02	.01
☐	95T Ken Linseman	.05	.02	.01
☐	96T Greg Brown	.05	.02	.01
☐	97T Ray Sheppard	.08	.04	.01
☐	98T Mike Lalor	.05	.02	.01
☐	99T Normand Lacombe	.05	.02	.01
☐	100T Mats Sundin	1.50	.65	.19
☐	101T Jergus Baca	.05	.02	.01
☐	102T Mike Keane	.20	.09	.03
☐	103T Ed Belfour	2.00	.90	.25
☐	104T Mark Hardy	.05	.02	.01
☐	105T Dave Capuano	.05	.02	.01
☐	106T Bryan Trottier	.08	.04	.01
☐	107T Per Djoos	.05	.02	.01
☐	108T Sylvain Turgeon	.05	.02	.01
☐	109T David Reid	.05	.02	.01
☐	110T Gretzky's 2000th Point	1.00	.45	.13

1990-91 Score Hottest/Rising Stars

This 100-card set which measures the standard size of 2 1/2" by 3 1/2" was released by Score along with a special book giving more biographical information about the players to honor some of the leading stars of the NHL. The fronts of the cards have the same photos as the regular Score issue but the numbers are different on the back.

	MINT	EXC	G-VG
COMPLETE SET (100)	10.00	4.00	1.00
COMMON PLAYER (1-100)	.10	.04	.01

		MINT	EXC	G-VG
☐	1 Wayne Gretzky	2.00	.80	.20
☐	2 Craig Simpson	.10	.04	.01
☐	3 Brian Bellows	.15	.06	.01

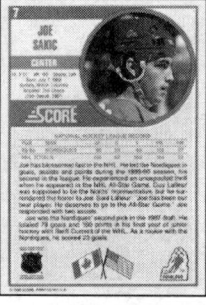

☐ 77 Tim Kerr	.10	.04	.01
☐ 78 Gerard Gallant	.10	.04	.01
☐ 79 Tomas Sandstrom	.15	.06	.01
☐ 80 Jon Casey	.15	.06	.01
☐ 81 Mark Recchi	.75	.30	.07
☐ 82 Scott Stevens	.25	.10	.02
☐ 83 John MacLean	.20	.08	.02
☐ 84 James Patrick	.10	.04	.01
☐ 85 Al Iafrate	.15	.06	.01
☐ 86 Pat Elyniuk	.10	.04	.01
☐ 87 Dave Andreychuk	.35	.14	.03
☐ 88 Joe Mullen	.20	.08	.02
☐ 89 Ed Olczyk	.15	.06	.01
☐ 90 Kevin Dineen	.15	.06	.01
☐ 91 Shayne Corson	.10	.04	.01
☐ 92 Mark Howe	.15	.06	.01
☐ 93 Brian Leetch	.60	.24	.06
☐ 94 Dino Ciccarelli	.20	.08	.02
☐ 95 Pat LaFontaine	.50	.20	.05
☐ 96 Guy Lafleur	.30	.12	.03
☐ 97 Mike Modano	.75	.30	.07
☐ 98 Rod Brind'Amour	.50	.20	.05
☐ 99 Sergei Makarov	.40	.16	.04
☐ 100 Brett Hull	1.00	.40	.10

1990-91 Score Young Superstars

This 40-card set which measures the standard 2 1/2" by 3 1/2" was issued by Score to honor some of the leading young players active in hockey. The set has a glossy sheen to it with an action shot of the player, while the back of the card has a portrait color shot on the back along with biographical and statistical information. The set comes in a special box and was available directly to dealers through the Score network of hobby dealers. The set was also available direct to collectors through an offer detailed on certain wax wrappers.

	MINT	EXC	G-VG
COMPLETE SET (40)	15.00	6.00	1.50
COMMON PLAYER (1-40)	.10	.04	.01

☐ 1 Pierre Turgeon	.60	.24	.06
☐ 2 Brian Leetch	.75	.30	.07
☐ 3 Daniel Marois	.10	.04	.01
☐ 4 Peter Sidorkiewicz	.10	.04	.01
☐ 5 Rob Brown	.10	.04	.01
☐ 6 Theoren Fleury	.50	.20	.05
☐ 7 Mats Sundin	1.00	.40	.10
☐ 8 Glen Wesley	.15	.06	.01
☐ 9 Sergei Fedorov	3.00	1.20	.30
☐ 10 Joe Sakic	.75	.30	.07
☐ 11 Sean Burke	.10	.04	.01
☐ 12 Dave Chyzowski	.10	.04	.01
☐ 13 Gord Murphy	.10	.04	.01
☐ 14 Scott Young	.10	.04	.01
☐ 15 Curtis Joseph	.75	.30	.07
☐ 16 Darren Turcotte	.25	.10	.02
☐ 17 Kevin Stevens	1.50	.60	.15
☐ 18 Mathieu Schneider	.50	.20	.05
☐ 19 Trevor Linden	.60	.24	.06
☐ 20 Mike Modano	1.00	.40	.10
☐ 21 Martin Gelinas	.30	.12	.03
☐ 22 Stephane Fiset	.40	.16	.04

☐ 4 Steve Yzerman	.50	.20	.05
☐ 5 Bernie Nicholls	.15	.06	.01
☐ 6 Esa Tikkanen	.15	.06	.01
☐ 7 Joe Sakic	.50	.20	.05
☐ 8 Thomas Steen	.10	.04	.01
☐ 9 Chris Chelios	.20	.08	.02
☐ 10 Patrik Sundstrom	.10	.04	.01
☐ 11 Rod Langway	.10	.04	.01
☐ 12 Scott Young	.10	.04	.01
☐ 13 Mike Ramsey	.10	.04	.01
☐ 14 Ron Hextall	.15	.06	.01
☐ 15 Steve Duchesne	.15	.06	.01
☐ 16 Trevor Linden	.35	.14	.03
☐ 17 Sean Burke	.15	.06	.01
☐ 18 Pat Verbeek	.10	.04	.01
☐ 19 Brent Sutter	.10	.04	.01
☐ 20 Gary Leeman	.10	.04	.01
☐ 21 Shawn Burr	.10	.04	.01
☐ 22 Dale Hawerchuk	.15	.06	.01
☐ 23 Mike Vernon	.15	.06	.01
☐ 24 Dan Quinn	.10	.04	.01
☐ 25 Patrick Roy	1.00	.40	.10
☐ 26 Daren Puppa	.15	.06	.01
☐ 27 Gino Cavallini	.10	.04	.01
☐ 28 Jimmy Carson	.10	.04	.01
☐ 29 Dave Ellett	.10	.04	.01
☐ 30 Steve Thomas	.10	.04	.01
☐ 31 Jeremy Roenick	1.50	.60	.15
☐ 32 Mike Liut	.15	.06	.01
☐ 33 Mark Messier	.50	.20	.05
☐ 34 Mario Lemieux	1.50	.60	.15
☐ 35 Ray Bourque	.40	.16	.04
☐ 36 Al MacInnis	.30	.12	.03
☐ 37 Ron Francis	.20	.08	.02
☐ 38 Stephane Richer	.20	.08	.02
☐ 39 Bill Ranford	.20	.08	.02
☐ 40 Rick Tocchet	.20	.08	.02
☐ 41 Adam Oates	.50	.20	.05
☐ 42 Kevin Hatcher	.20	.08	.02
☐ 43 Guy Carbonneau	.10	.04	.01
☐ 44 Curtis Leschyshyn	.10	.04	.01
☐ 45 Joe Nieuwendyk	.35	.14	.03
☐ 46 Kirk McLean	.35	.14	.03
☐ 47 Vincent Damphousse	.25	.10	.02
☐ 48 Peter Stastny	.20	.08	.02
☐ 49 Rick Zombo	.10	.04	.01
☐ 50 Mark Fitzpatrick	.20	.08	.02
☐ 51 Rob Brown	.10	.04	.01
☐ 52 Dave Gagner	.15	.06	.01
☐ 53 Pierre Turgeon	.50	.20	.05
☐ 54 Glenn Anderson	.20	.08	.02
☐ 55 Kelly Hrudey	.15	.06	.01
☐ 56 Gord Murphy	.10	.04	.01
☐ 57 Glen Wesley	.15	.06	.01
☐ 58 Craig Janney	.30	.12	.03
☐ 59 Denis Savard	.25	.10	.02
☐ 60 Mike Gartner	.35	.14	.03
☐ 61 Steve Larmer	.20	.08	.02
☐ 62 Andy Moog	.20	.08	.02
☐ 63 Phil Housley	.20	.08	.02
☐ 64 Ulf Samuelsson	.15	.06	.01
☐ 65 Paul Coffey	.40	.16	.04
☐ 66 Luc Robitaille	.50	.20	.05
☐ 67 Cam Neely	.40	.16	.04
☐ 68 Doug Wilson	.15	.06	.01
☐ 69 Doug Gilmour	.50	.20	.05
☐ 70 Jeff Norton	.10	.04	.01
☐ 71 Kirk Muller	.25	.10	.02
☐ 72 Aaron Broten	.10	.04	.01
☐ 73 John Cullen	.15	.06	.01
☐ 74 Craig Ludwig	.10	.04	.01
☐ 75 Kevin Lowe	.15	.06	.01
☐ 76 John Vanbiesbrouck	.25	.10	.02

☐ 23	Brendan Shanahan	.75	.30	.07
☐ 24	Jeremy Roenick	3.00	1.20	.30
☐ 25	John Druce	.10	.04	.01
☐ 26	Alexander Mogilny	2.00	.80	.20
☐ 27	Mike Richter	1.00	.40	.10
☐ 28	Pat Elyniuk	.10	.04	.01
☐ 29	Robert Reichel	.60	.24	.06
☐ 30	Craig Janney	.50	.20	.05
☐ 31	Rod Brind'Amour	.60	.24	.06
☐ 32	Mark Fitzpatrick	.20	.08	.02
☐ 33	Tony Granato	.20	.08	.02
☐ 34	Bobby Holik	.40	.16	.04
☐ 35	Mark Recchi	1.50	.60	.15
☐ 36	Owen Nolan	.75	.30	.07
☐ 37	Petr Nedved	1.25	.50	.12
☐ 38	Keith Primeau	.60	.24	.06
☐ 39	Mike Ricci	.75	.30	.07
☐ 40	Eric Lindros	6.00	2.40	.60

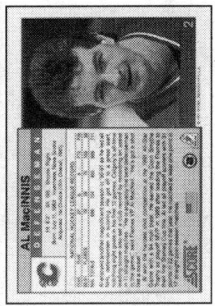

1991 Score National/FanFest

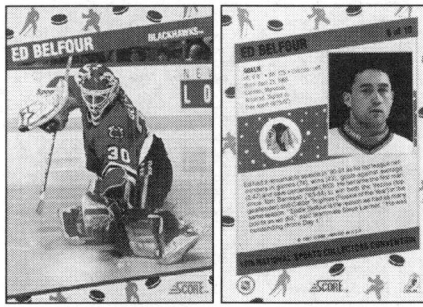

This ten-card set features outstanding hockey players and measures the standard size, 2 1/2" by 3 1/2". The cards were given out as a cello-wrapped complete set by Score at the National Sports Collectors Convention in Anaheim, at the Fanfest in Toronto, and at the National Candy Wholesalers Convention in St. Louis. The front has an action photo of the player, bounded by diagonal green borders above and below the picture. The player's name and team name appear in the top green border. The light blue background shows through above and below the green borders, and it is decorated with hockey pucks and player icons. The back presents player information and career summary in a diagonal format similar to the design of the front.

	MINT	EXC	G-VG
COMPLETE SET (10)	25.00	10.00	2.50
COMMON PLAYER (1-10)	1.50	.60	.15

☐ 1	Wayne Gretzky	9.00	3.75	.90
☐ 2	Brett Hull	5.00	2.00	.50
☐ 3	Ray Bourque	2.50	1.00	.25
☐ 4	Al MacInnis	1.50	.60	.15
☐ 5	Luc Robitaille	2.50	1.00	.25
☐ 6	Ed Belfour	3.50	1.40	.35
☐ 7	Steve Yzerman	3.50	1.40	.35
☐ 8	Cam Neely	3.50	1.40	.35
☐ 9	Paul Coffey	2.50	1.00	.25
☐ 10	Patrick Roy	5.00	2.00	.50

1991-92 Score American

The 1991-92 Score American hockey set features 440 cards measuring the standard size (2 1/2" by 3 1/2"). As one moves down the card face, the fronts shade from purple to white. The color action player photo is enclosed by an thin red border, with a shadow border on the right and below. At the card top, the player's name is written over a hockey puck, and the team name is printed below the picture in the lower right corner. A purple border stripe at the bottom completes the front. In a horizontal format, the backs have biography, statistics, player profile, and a color close-up photo. Subsets featured include Crunch Crew (301-305), NHL Brothers (306-309, 377-380), Top Prospect (310-329, 381-400), The Franchise (331-341, 415-424), Dream Team (342-347), All-Rookie Team (348-353), Eric Lindros (354-356), Thousand Point Club (372-376), Guy Lafleur (401-403), Season Leader (404-411), and players who were awarded trophies (426-435). The cards are numbered on the back. The key Rookie Cards in this set are Tony Amonte, Geoff Sanderson, and Doug Weight.

	MINT	EXC	G-VG
COMPLETE SET (440)	12.00	5.50	1.50
COMPLETE FACT.SET (440)	12.00	5.50	1.50
COMMON PLAYER (1-440)	.05	.02	.01

☐ 1	Brett Hull	.50	.23	.06
	St. Louis Blues			
☐ 2	Al MacInnis	.10	.05	.01
	Calgary Flames			
☐ 3	Luc Robitaille	.15	.07	.02
	Los Angeles Kings			
☐ 4	Pierre Turgeon	.20	.09	.03
	Buffalo Sabres			
☐ 5	Brian Leetch	.30	.14	.04
	New York Rangers			
☐ 6	Cam Neely	.15	.07	.02
	Boston Bruins			
☐ 7	John Cullen	.05	.02	.01
	Hartford Whalers			
☐ 8	Trevor Linden	.25	.11	.03
	Vancouver Canucks			
☐ 9	Rick Tocchet	.08	.04	.01
	Philadelphia Flyers			
☐ 10	John Vanbiesbrouck	.10	.05	.01
	New York Rangers			
☐ 11	Steve Smith	.08	.04	.01
	Edmonton Oilers			
☐ 12	Doug Smail	.05	.02	.01
	Minnesota North Stars			
☐ 13	Craig Ludwig	.05	.02	.01
	New York Islanders			
☐ 14	Paul Fenton	.05	.02	.01
	Calgary Flames			
☐ 15	Dirk Graham	.05	.02	.01
	Chicago Blackhawks			
☐ 16	Brad McCrimmon	.05	.02	.01
	Detroit Red Wings			
☐ 17	Dean Evason	.05	.02	.01
	Hartford Whalers			
☐ 18	Fredrik Olausson	.08	.04	.01
	Winnipeg Jets			
☐ 19	Guy Carbonneau	.08	.04	.01
	Montreal Canadiens			
☐ 20	Kevin Hatcher	.08	.04	.01
	Washington Capitals			
☐ 21	Paul Ranheim	.05	.02	.01
	Calgary Flames			
☐ 22	Claude Lemieux	.08	.04	.01
	New Jersey Devils			
☐ 23	Vincent Riendeau	.05	.02	.01
	St. Louis Blues			
☐ 24	Garth Butcher	.05	.02	.01

St. Louis Blues
☐ 25	Joe Sakic	.25	.11	.03

Quebec Nordiques
| ☐ 26 | Rick Vaive | .05 | .02 | .01 |

Buffalo Sabres
| ☐ 27 | Rob Blake | .15 | .07 | .02 |

Los Angeles Kings
| ☐ 28 | Mike Ricci | .15 | .07 | .02 |

Philadelphia Flyers
| ☐ 29 | Pat Flatley | .05 | .02 | .01 |

New York Islanders
| ☐ 30 | Bill Ranford | .08 | .04 | .01 |

Edmonton Oilers
| ☐ 31 | Larry Murphy | .08 | .04 | .01 |

Pittsburgh Penguins
| ☐ 32 | Bobby Smith | .08 | .04 | .01 |

Minnesota North Stars
| ☐ 33 | Mike Krushelnyski | .05 | .02 | .01 |

Toronto Maple Leafs
| ☐ 34 | Gerard Gallant | .05 | .02 | .01 |

Detroit Red Wings
| ☐ 35 | Doug Wilson | .08 | .04 | .01 |

Chicago Blackhawks
| ☐ 36 | John Ogrodnick | .05 | .02 | .01 |

New York Rangers
| ☐ 37 | Mikhail Tatarinov | .05 | .02 | .01 |

Washington Capitals
| ☐ 38 | Doug Crossman | .05 | .02 | .01 |

Detroit Red Wings
| ☐ 39 | Mark Osborne | .05 | .02 | .01 |

Winnipeg Jets
| ☐ 40 | Scott Stevens | .10 | .05 | .01 |

St. Louis Blues
| ☐ 41 | Ron Tugnutt | .05 | .02 | .01 |

Quebec Nordiques
| ☐ 42 | Russ Courtnall | .08 | .04 | .01 |

Montreal Canadiens
| ☐ 43 | Gord Murphy | .05 | .02 | .01 |

Philadelphia Flyers
| ☐ 44 | Greg Adams | .05 | .02 | .01 |

Vancouver Canucks
| ☐ 45 | Christian Ruuttu | .05 | .02 | .01 |

Buffalo Sabres
| ☐ 46 | Ken Daneyko | .05 | .02 | .01 |

New Jersey Devils
| ☐ 47 | Glenn Anderson | .08 | .04 | .01 |

Edmonton Oilers
| ☐ 48 | Ray Ferraro | .08 | .04 | .01 |

New York Islanders
| ☐ 49 | Tony Tanti | .05 | .02 | .01 |

Buffalo Sabres
| ☐ 50 | Ray Bourque | .15 | .07 | .02 |

Boston Bruins
| ☐ 51 | Sergei Makarov | .08 | .04 | .01 |

Calgary Flames
| ☐ 52 | Jim Johnson | .05 | .02 | .01 |

Minnesota North Stars
| ☐ 53 | Troy Murray | .05 | .02 | .01 |

Chicago Blackhawks
| ☐ 54 | Shawn Burr | .05 | .02 | .01 |

Detroit Red Wings
| ☐ 55 | Peter Ing | .05 | .02 | .01 |

Toronto Maple Leafs
| ☐ 56 | Dale Hunter | .08 | .04 | .01 |

Washington Capitals
| ☐ 57 | Tony Granato | .08 | .04 | .01 |

Los Angeles Kings
| ☐ 58 | Curtis Leschyshyn | .05 | .02 | .01 |

Quebec Nordiques
| ☐ 59 | Brian Mullen | .08 | .04 | .01 |

New York Rangers
| ☐ 60 | Ed Olczyk | .05 | .02 | .01 |

Winnipeg Jets
| ☐ 61 | Mike Ramsey | .05 | .02 | .01 |

Buffalo Sabres
| ☐ 62 | Dan Quinn | .05 | .02 | .01 |

St. Louis Blues
| ☐ 63 | Rich Sutter | .05 | .02 | .01 |

St. Louis Blues
| ☐ 64 | Terry Carkner | .05 | .02 | .01 |

Philadelphia Flyers
| ☐ 65 | Shayne Corson | .08 | .04 | .01 |

Montreal Canadiens
| ☐ 66 | Peter Stastny | .08 | .04 | .01 |

New Jersey Devils
| ☐ 67 | Craig Muni | .05 | .02 | .01 |

Edmonton Oilers
| ☐ 68 | Glenn Healy | .08 | .04 | .01 |

New York Islanders
| ☐ 69 | Phil Bourque | .05 | .02 | .01 |

Pittsburgh Penguins
| ☐ 70 | Pat Verbeek | .08 | .04 | .01 |

Hartford Whalers
| ☐ 71 | Garry Galley | .08 | .04 | .01 |

Boston Bruins
| ☐ 72 | Dave Gagner | .08 | .04 | .01 |

Minnesota North Stars
| ☐ 73 | Bob Probert | .08 | .04 | .01 |

Detroit Red Wings
| ☐ 74 | Craig Wolanin | .05 | .02 | .01 |

Quebec Nordiques
| ☐ 75 | Patrick Roy | .50 | .23 | .06 |

Montreal Canadiens
| ☐ 76 | Keith Brown | .05 | .02 | .01 |

Chicago Blackhawks
| ☐ 77 | Gary Leeman | .05 | .02 | .01 |

Toronto Maple Leafs
| ☐ 78 | Brent Ashton | .05 | .02 | .01 |

Winnipeg Jets
| ☐ 79 | Randy Moller | .05 | .02 | .01 |

New York Rangers
| ☐ 80 | Mike Vernon | .08 | .04 | .01 |

Calgary Flames
| ☐ 81 | Kelly Miller | .05 | .02 | .01 |

Washington Capitals
| ☐ 82 | Ulf Samuelsson | .08 | .04 | .01 |

Pittsburgh Penguins
| ☐ 83 | Todd Elik | .05 | .02 | .01 |

Los Angeles Kings
| ☐ 84 | Uwe Krupp | .05 | .02 | .01 |

Buffalo Sabres
| ☐ 85 | Rod Brind'Amour | .15 | .07 | .02 |

St. Louis Blues
| ☐ 86 | Dave Capuano | .05 | .02 | .01 |

Vancouver Canucks
| ☐ 87 | Geoff Smith | .05 | .02 | .01 |

Edmonton Oilers
| ☐ 88 | David Volek | .05 | .02 | .01 |

New York Islanders
| ☐ 89 | Bruce Driver | .05 | .02 | .01 |

New Jersey Devils
| ☐ 90 | Andy Moog | .10 | .05 | .01 |

Boston Bruins
| ☐ 91 | Pelle Eklund | .05 | .02 | .01 |

Philadelphia Flyers
| ☐ 92 | Joey Kocur | .05 | .02 | .01 |

New York Rangers
| ☐ 93 | Mark Tinordi | .08 | .04 | .01 |

Minnesota North Stars
| ☐ 94 | Steve Thomas | .08 | .04 | .01 |

Chicago Blackhawks
| ☐ 95 | Petr Svoboda | .05 | .02 | .01 |

Montreal Canadiens
| ☐ 96 | Joel Otto | .05 | .02 | .01 |

Calgary Flames
| ☐ 97 | Todd Krygier | .05 | .02 | .01 |

Hartford Whalers
| ☐ 98 | Jaromir Jagr | .50 | .23 | .06 |

Pittsburgh Penguins
| ☐ 99 | Mike Liut | .08 | .04 | .01 |

Washington Capitals
| ☐ 100 | Wayne Gretzky | 1.00 | .45 | .13 |

Los Angeles Kings
| ☐ 101 | Teppo Numminen | .05 | .02 | .01 |

Winnipeg Jets
| ☐ 102 | Randy Burridge | .05 | .02 | .01 |

Boston Bruins
| ☐ 103 | Michel Petit | .05 | .02 | .01 |

Toronto Maple Leafs
| ☐ 104 | Tony McKegney | .05 | .02 | .01 |

Chicago Blackhawks
| ☐ 105 | Mathieu Schneider | .08 | .04 | .01 |

Montreal Canadiens
| ☐ 106 | Daren Puppa | .08 | .04 | .01 |

Buffalo Sabres
| ☐ 107 | Paul Cavallini | .05 | .02 | .01 |

St. Louis Blues
| ☐ 108 | Tim Kerr | .08 | .04 | .01 |

Philadelphia Flyers
| ☐ 109 | Kevin Lowe | .08 | .04 | .01 |

Edmonton Oilers
| ☐ 110 | Kirk Muller | .08 | .04 | .01 |

New Jersey Devils
| ☐ 111 | Zarley Zalapski | .05 | .02 | .01 |

Hartford Whalers
| ☐ 112 | Mike Hough | .05 | .02 | .01 |

Quebec Nordiques
| ☐ 113 | Ken Hodge Jr. | .05 | .02 | .01 |

Boston Bruins
| ☐ 114 | Grant Fuhr | .08 | .04 | .01 |

Edmonton Oilers
| ☐ 115 | Paul Coffey | .15 | .07 | .02 |

Pittsburgh Penguins
| ☐ 116 | Wendel Clark | .15 | .07 | .02 |

Toronto Maple Leafs
| ☐ 117 | Patrik Sundstrom | .05 | .02 | .01 |

New Jersey Devils
| ☐ 118 | Kevin Dineen | .08 | .04 | .01 |

Hartford Whalers			
☐ 119 Eric Desjardins	.08	.04	.01
Montreal Canadiens			
☐ 120 Mike Richter	.25	.11	.03
New York Rangers			
☐ 121 Sergio Momesso	.05	.02	.01
Vancouver Canucks			
☐ 122 Tony Hrkac	.05	.02	.01
Quebec Nordiques			
☐ 123 Joe Reekie	.05	.02	.01
New York Rangers			
☐ 124 Petr Nedved	.20	.09	.03
Vancouver Canucks			
☐ 125 Randy Carlyle	.05	.02	.01
Winnipeg Jets			
☐ 126 Kevin Miller	.08	.04	.01
Detroit Red Wings			
☐ 127 Rejean Lemelin	.08	.04	.01
Boston Bruins			
☐ 128 Dino Ciccarelli	.08	.04	.01
Washington Capitals			
☐ 129 Sylvain Cote	.05	.02	.01
Hartford Whalers			
☐ 130 Mats Sundin	.25	.11	.03
Quebec Nordiques			
☐ 131 Eric Weinrich	.05	.02	.01
New Jersey Devils			
☐ 132 Daniel Berthiaume	.05	.02	.01
Los Angeles Kings			
☐ 133 Keith Acton	.05	.02	.01
Philadelphia Flyers			
☐ 134 Benoit Hogue	.05	.02	.01
Buffalo Sabres			
☐ 135 Mike Gartner	.10	.05	.01
New York Rangers			
☐ 136 Petr Klima	.05	.02	.01
Edmonton Oilers			
☐ 137 Curt Giles	.05	.02	.01
Minnesota North Stars			
☐ 138 Scott Pearson	.05	.02	.01
Quebec Nordiques			
☐ 139 Luke Richardson	.05	.02	.01
Toronto Maple Leafs			
☐ 140 Steve Larmer	.08	.04	.01
Chicago Blackhawks			
☐ 141 Ken Wregget	.05	.02	.01
Philadelphia Flyers			
☐ 142 Frantisek Musil	.05	.02	.01
Calgary Flames			
☐ 143 Owen Nolan	.15	.07	.02
Quebec Nordiques			
☐ 144 Keith Primeau	.15	.07	.02
Detroit Red Wings			
☐ 145 Mark Recchi	.30	.14	.04
Pittsburgh Penguins			
☐ 146 Don Sweeney	.05	.02	.01
Boston Bruins			
☐ 147 Mike McPhee	.05	.02	.01
Montreal Canadiens			
☐ 148 Ken Baumgartner	.05	.02	.01
New York Islanders			
☐ 149 Dave Lowry	.05	.02	.01
St. Louis Blues			
☐ 150 Geoff Courtnall	.08	.04	.01
Vancouver Canucks			
☐ 151 Chris Terreri	.08	.04	.01
New Jersey Devils			
☐ 152 Dave Manson	.08	.04	.01
Chicago Blackhawks			
☐ 153 Bobby Holik	.08	.04	.01
Hartford Whalers			
☐ 154 Bob Kudelski	.08	.04	.01
Los Angeles Kings			
☐ 155 Calle Johansson	.05	.02	.01
Washington Capitals			
☐ 156 Mark Hunter	.05	.02	.01
Hartford Whalers			
☐ 157 Randy Gilhen	.05	.02	.01
Pittsburgh Penguins			
☐ 158 Yves Racine	.05	.02	.01
Detroit Red Wings			
☐ 159 Martin Gelinas	.05	.02	.01
Edmonton Oilers			
☐ 160 Brian Bellows	.08	.04	.01
Minnesota North Stars			
☐ 161 David Shaw	.05	.02	.01
New York Rangers			
☐ 162 Bob Carpenter	.05	.02	.01
Boston Bruins			
☐ 163 Doug Brown	.05	.02	.01
New Jersey Devils			
☐ 164 Ulf Dahlen	.08	.04	.01
Minnesota North Stars			
☐ 165 Denis Savard	.08	.04	.01
Montreal Canadiens			
☐ 166 Paul Ysebaert	.05	.02	.01
Detroit Red Wings			
☐ 167 Derek King	.08	.04	.01
New York Islanders			
☐ 168 Igor Larionov	.08	.04	.01
Vancouver Canucks			
☐ 169 Bob Errey	.05	.02	.01
Pittsburgh Penguins			
☐ 170 Joe Nieuwendyk	.10	.05	.01
Calgary Flames			
☐ 171 Normand Rochefort	.05	.02	.01
New York Rangers			
☐ 172 John Tonelli	.08	.04	.01
Los Angeles Kings			
☐ 173 David Reid	.05	.02	.01
Toronto Maple Leafs			
☐ 174 Tom Kurvers	.05	.02	.01
Vancouver Canucks			
☐ 175 Dimitri Khristich	.08	.04	.01
Washington Capitals			
☐ 176 Bob Sweeney	.05	.02	.01
Boston Bruins			
☐ 177 Rick Zombo	.05	.02	.01
Detroit Red Wings			
☐ 178 Troy Mallette	.05	.02	.01
New York Rangers			
☐ 179 Bob Bassen	.05	.02	.01
St. Louis Blues			
☐ 180 John Druce	.05	.02	.01
Washington Capitals			
☐ 181 Mike Craig	.05	.02	.01
Minnesota North Stars			
☐ 182 John McIntyre	.05	.02	.01
Los Angeles Kings			
☐ 183 Murray Baron	.05	.02	.01
Philadelphia Flyers			
☐ 184 Viacheslav Fetisov	.08	.04	.01
New Jersey Devils			
☐ 185 Don Beaupre	.08	.04	.01
Washington Capitals			
☐ 186 Brian Benning	.05	.02	.01
Los Angeles Kings			
☐ 187 Dave Barr	.05	.02	.01
Detroit Red Wings			
☐ 188 Petri Skriko	.05	.02	.01
Boston Bruins			
☐ 189 Steve Konroyd	.05	.02	.01
Chicago Blackhawks			
☐ 190 Steve Yzerman	.25	.11	.03
Detroit Red Wings			
☐ 191 Jon Casey	.08	.04	.01
Minnesota North Stars			
☐ 192 Gary Nylund	.05	.02	.01
New York Islanders			
☐ 193 Michal Pivonka	.08	.04	.01
Washington Capitals			
☐ 194 Alexei Kasatonov	.05	.02	.01
New Jersey Devils			
☐ 195 Garry Valk	.05	.02	.01
Vancouver Canucks			
☐ 196 Darren Turcotte	.05	.02	.01
New York Rangers			
☐ 197 Chris Nilan	.06	.04	.01
Boston Bruins			
☐ 198 Thomas Steen	.05	.02	.01
Winnipeg Jets			
☐ 199 Gary Roberts	.08	.04	.01
Calgary Flames			
☐ 200 Mario Lemieux	.75	.35	.09
Pittsburgh Penguins			
☐ 201 Michel Goulet	.08	.04	.01
Chicago Blackhawks			
☐ 202 Craig MacTavish	.05	.02	.01
Edmonton Oilers			
☐ 203 Peter Sidorkiewicz	.05	.02	.01
Hartford Whalers			
☐ 204 Johan Garpenlov	.05	.02	.01
Detroit Red Wings			
☐ 205 Steve Duchesne	.08	.04	.01
Los Angeles Kings			
☐ 206 Dave Snuggerud	.05	.02	.01
Buffalo Sabres			
☐ 207 Kjell Samuelsson	.05	.02	.01
Philadelphia Flyers			
☐ 208 Sylvain Turgeon	.05	.02	.01
Montreal Canadiens			
☐ 209 Al Iafrate	.08	.04	.01
Washington Capitals			
☐ 210 John MacLean	.08	.04	.01
New Jersey Devils			
☐ 211 Brian Hayward	.05	.02	.01
Minnesota North Stars			
☐ 212 Cliff Ronning	.08	.04	.01

Vancouver Canucks			
☐ 213 Ray Sheppard	.08	.04	.01
New York Rangers			
☐ 214 Dave Taylor.........................	.08	.04	.01
Los Angeles Kings			
☐ 215 Doug Lidster	.05	.02	.01
Vancouver Canucks			
☐ 216 Peter Bondra........................	.08	.04	.01
Washington Capitals			
☐ 217 Marty McSorley..................	.08	.04	.01
Los Angeles Kings			
☐ 218 Doug Gilmour	.25	.11	.03
Calgary Flames			
☐ 219 Paul MacDermid	.05	.02	.01
Winnipeg Jets			
☐ 220 Jeremy Roenick	.50	.23	.06
Chicago Blackhawks			
☐ 221 Wayne Presley.....................	.05	.02	.01
Chicago Blackhawks			
☐ 222 Jeff Norton..........................	.05	.02	.01
New York Islanders			
☐ 223 Brian Propp.........................	.08	.04	.01
Minnesota North Stars			
☐ 224 Jimmy Carson	.08	.04	.01
Detroit Red Wings			
☐ 225 Tom Barrasso	.08	.04	.01
Pittsburgh Penguins			
☐ 226 Theoren Fleury	.15	.07	.02
Calgary Flames			
☐ 227 Carey Wilson........................	.05	.02	.01
Calgary Flames			
☐ 228 Rod Langway	.05	.02	.01
Washington Capitals			
☐ 229 Bryan Trottier	.08	.04	.01
Pittsburgh Penguins			
☐ 230 James Patrick	.05	.02	.01
New York Rangers			
☐ 231 Kelly Hrudey.........................	.08	.04	.01
Los Angeles Kings			
☐ 232 Dave Poulin.........................	.08	.04	.01
Boston Bruins			
☐ 233 Rob Ramage	.05	.02	.01
Toronto Maple Leafs			
☐ 234 Stephane Richer..................	.08	.04	.01
Montreal Canadiens			
☐ 235 Chris Chelios.......................	.08	.04	.01
Chicago Blackhawks			
☐ 236 Alexander Mogilny	.40	.18	.05
Buffalo Sabres			
☐ 237 Bryan Fogarty......................	.05	.02	.01
Quebec Nordiques			
☐ 238 Adam Oates.........................	.20	.09	.03
St. Louis Blues			
☐ 239 Ron Hextall	.08	.04	.01
Philadelphia Flyers			
☐ 240 Bernie Nichols......................	.08	.04	.01
New York Rangers			
☐ 241 Esa Tikkanen	.08	.04	.01
Edmonton Oilers			
☐ 242 Jyrki Lumme........................	.05	.02	.01
Vancouver Canucks			
☐ 243 Brent Sutter.........................	.08	.04	.01
New York Islanders			
☐ 244 Gary Suter............................	.08	.04	.01
Calgary Flames			
☐ 245 Sean Burke	.08	.04	.01
New Jersey Devils			
☐ 246 Rob Brown	.05	.02	.01
Hartford Whalers			
☐ 247 Mike Modano	.25	.11	.03
Minnesota North Stars			
☐ 248 Kevin Stevens	.25	.11	.03
Pittsburgh Penguins			
☐ 249 Mike Lalor	.05	.02	.01
Washington Capitals			
☐ 250 Sergei Fedorov.....................	.60	.25	.08
Detroit Red Wings			
☐ 251 Bob Essensa	.08	.04	.01
Winnipeg Jets			
☐ 252 Mark Howe	.08	.04	.01
Philadelphia Flyers			
☐ 253 Craig Janney	.15	.07	.02
Boston Bruins			
☐ 254 Daniel Marois	.05	.02	.01
Toronto Maple Leafs			
☐ 255 Craig Simpson	.08	.04	.01
Edmonton Oilers			
☐ 256 Steve Kasper	.05	.02	.01
Los Angeles Kings			
☐ 257 Randy Velischek....................	.05	.02	.01
Quebec Nordiques			
☐ 258 Gino Cavallini	.05	.02	.01
St. Louis Blues			
☐ 259 Dale Hawerchuk	.08	.04	.01

Buffalo Sabres			
☐ 260 Pat LaFontaine	.20	.09	.03
New York Islanders			
☐ 261 Kirk McLean	.20	.09	.03
Vancouver Canucks			
☐ 262 Murray Craven	.05	.02	.01
Philadelphia Flyers			
☐ 263 Robert Reichel	.15	.07	.02
Calgary Flames			
☐ 264 Jan Erixon	.05	.02	.01
New York Rangers			
☐ 265 Adam Creighton	.05	.02	.01
Chicago Blackhawks			
☐ 266 Mark Fitzpatrick..................	.08	.04	.01
New York Islanders			
☐ 267 Ron Francis	.08	.04	.01
Pittsburgh Penguins			
☐ 268 Joe Mullen	.10	.05	.01
Pittsburgh Penguins			
☐ 269 Peter Zezel	.05	.02	.01
Toronto Maple Leafs			
☐ 270 Tomas Sandstrom...............	.08	.04	.01
Los Angeles Kings			
☐ 271 Phil Housley	.08	.04	.01
Winnipeg Jets			
☐ 272 Tim Cheveldae	.08	.04	.01
Detroit Red Wings			
☐ 273 Glen Wesley	.05	.02	.01
Boston Bruins			
☐ 274 Stephan Lebeau	.15	.07	.02
Montreal Canadiens			
☐ 275 Dave Ellett	.05	.02	.01
Toronto Maple Leafs			
☐ 276 Jeff Brown............................	.08	.04	.01
St. Louis Blues			
☐ 277 Dave Andreychuk	.15	.07	.02
Buffalo Sabres			
☐ 278 Steven Finn	.05	.02	.01
Quebec Nordiques			
☐ 279 Scott Mellanby	.05	.02	.01
Philadelphia Flyers			
☐ 280 Neal Broten	.08	.04	.01
Minnesota North Stars			
☐ 281 Randy Wood	.05	.02	.01
New York Islanders			
☐ 282 Troy Gamble	.05	.02	.01
Vancouver Canucks			
☐ 283 Mike Ridley	.08	.04	.01
Washington Capitals			
☐ 284 Jamie Macoun......................	.05	.02	.01
Calgary Flames			
☐ 285 Mark Messier	.25	.11	.03
Edmonton Oilers			
☐ 286 Brendan Shanahan.............	.25	.11	.03
New Jersey Devils			
☐ 287 Scott Young	.05	.02	.01
Pittsburgh Penguins			
☐ 288 Kelly Kisio	.05	.02	.01
New York Rangers			
☐ 289 Brad Shaw	.05	.02	.01
Hartford Whalers			
☐ 290 Ed Belfour	.25	.11	.03
Chicago Blackhawks			
☐ 291 Larry Robinson	.08	.04	.01
Los Angeles Kings			
☐ 292 Dave Christian......................	.05	.02	.01
Boston Bruins			
☐ 293 Steve Chiasson	.05	.02	.01
Detroit Red Wings			
☐ 294 Brian Skrudland	.05	.02	.01
Montreal Canadiens			
☐ 295 Pat Elynuik	.05	.02	.01
Winnipeg Jets			
☐ 296 Curtis Joseph.......................	.25	.11	.03
St. Louis Blues			
☐ 297 Doug Bodger	.05	.02	.01
Buffalo Sabres			
☐ 298 Ron Sutter...........................	.05	.02	.01
Philadelphia Flyers			
☐ 299 Joe Murphy	.08	.04	.01
Edmonton Oilers			
☐ 300 Vincent Damphousse	.08	.04	.01
Toronto Maple Leafs			
☐ 301 Cam Neely CC	.08	.04	.01
Boston Bruins			
☐ 302 Rick Tocchet CC....................	.05	.02	.01
Philadelphia Flyers			
☐ 303 Scott Stevens CC	.08	.04	.01
St. Louis Blues			
☐ 304 Ulf Samuelsson CC	.05	.02	.01
Pittsburgh Penguins			
☐ 305 Jeremy Roenick CC	.15	.07	.02
Chicago Blackhawks			
☐ 306 The Hunter Brothers............	.05	.02	.01

Dale Hunter
Mark Hunter
☐ 307 The Broten Brothers .... .05 .02 .01
Aaron Broten
Neal Broten
☐ 308 The Cavallini Brothers .... .05 .02 .01
Gino Cavallini
Paul Cavallini
☐ 309 The Miller Brothers .... .05 .02 .01
Kelly Miller
Kevin Miller
☐ 310 Dennis Vaske TP .... .05 .02 .01
New York Islanders
☐ 311 Rob Pearson TP .... .20 .09 .03
Toronto Maple Leafs
☐ 312 Jason Miller TP .... .05 .02 .01
New Jersey Devils
☐ 313 John LeClair TP .... .15 .07 .02
Montreal Canadiens
☐ 314 Bryan Marchment TP .... .10 .05 .01
Winnipeg Jets
☐ 315 Gary Shuchuk TP .... .05 .02 .01
Detroit Red Wings
☐ 316 Dominik Hasek TP UER ...... 1.00 .45 .13
Chicago Blackhawks
(Misspelled Dominic
on both sides)
☐ 317 Michel Picard TP .... .05 .02 .01
Hartford Whalers
☐ 318 Corey Millen TP .... .20 .09 .03
New York Rangers
☐ 319 Joe Sacco TP .... .10 .05 .01
Toronto Maple Leafs
☐ 320 Reggie Savage TP .... .05 .02 .01
Washington Capitals
☐ 321 Pat Murray TP .... .05 .02 .01
Philadelphia Flyers
☐ 322 Myles O'Connor TP .... .05 .02 .01
New Jersey Devils
☐ 323 Shawn Antoski TP .... .05 .02 .01
Vancouver Canucks
☐ 324 Geoff Sanderson TP .... .75 .35 .09
Hartford Whalers
☐ 325 Chris Govedaris TP .... .05 .02 .01
Hartford Whalers
☐ 326 Alexei Gusarov TP .... .10 .05 .01
Quebec Nordiques
☐ 327 Mike Sillinger TP .... .05 .02 .01
Detroit Red Wings
☐ 328 Bob Wilkie TP .... .05 .02 .01
Detroit Red Wings
☐ 329 Pat Jablonski TP .... .10 .05 .01
St. Louis Blues
☐ 330 David Emma .... .20 .09 .03
Hobey Baker Award
☐ 331 Kirk Muller FP .... .08 .04 .01
New Jersey Devils
☐ 332 Pat LaFontaine FP .... .08 .04 .01
New York Islanders
☐ 333 Brian Leetch FP .... .15 .07 .02
New York Rangers
☐ 334 Rick Tocchet FP .... .08 .04 .01
Philadelphia Flyers
☐ 335 Mario Lemieux FP .... .25 .11 .03
Pittsburgh Penguins
☐ 336 Joe Sakic FP .... .08 .04 .01
Quebec Nordiques
☐ 337 Brett Hull FP .... .20 .09 .03
St. Louis Blues
☐ 338 Vincent Damphousse FP ..... .08 .04 .01
Toronto Maple Leafs
☐ 339 Trevor Linden FP .... .08 .04 .01
Vancouver Canucks
☐ 340 Kevin Hatcher FP .... .05 .02 .01
Washington Capitals
☐ 341 Pat Elynuik FP .... .05 .02 .01
Winnipeg Jets
☐ 342 Patrick Roy DT .... .30 .14 .04
Montreal Canadiens
☐ 343 Brian Leetch DT .... .15 .07 .02
New York Rangers
☐ 344 Ray Bourque DT .... .08 .04 .01
Boston Bruins
☐ 345 Luc Robitaille DT .... .08 .04 .01
Los Angeles Kings
☐ 346 Wayne Gretzky DT .... .35 .16 .04
Los Angeles Kings
☐ 347 Brett Hull DT .... .20 .09 .03
St. Louis Blues
☐ 348 Ed Belfour ART .... .08 .04 .01
Chicago Blackhawks
☐ 349 Rob Blake ART .... .08 .04 .01
Los Angeles Kings
☐ 350 Eric Weinrich ART .... .05 .02 .01

New Jersey Devils
☐ 351 Jaromir Jagr ART .... .20 .09 .03
Pittsburgh Penguins
☐ 352 Sergei Fedorov ART .... .25 .11 .03
Detroit Red Wings
☐ 353 Ken Hodge Jr. ART .... .05 .02 .01
Boston Bruins
☐ 354 Eric Lindros Art .... 1.00 .45 .13
☐ 355 Eric Lindros .... 1.00 .45 .13
Awards and Honors
☐ 356 Eric Lindros .... 1.00 .45 .13
'91 1st Rd Draft Choice
☐ 357 Dana Murzyn .... .05 .02 .01
Vancouver Canucks
☐ 358 Adam Graves .... .25 .11 .03
Edmonton Oilers
☐ 359 Ken Linseman .... .05 .02 .01
Edmonton Oilers
☐ 360 Mike Keane .... .05 .02 .01
Montreal Canadiens
☐ 361 Stephane Morin .... .05 .02 .01
Quebec Nordiques
☐ 362 Grant Ledyard .... .05 .02 .01
Buffalo Sabres
☐ 363 Kris King .... .05 .02 .01
New York Rangers
☐ 364 Paul Gillis .... .05 .02 .01
Chicago Blackhawks
☐ 365 Chris Dahlquist .... .05 .02 .01
Minnesota North Stars
☐ 366 Paul Stanton .... .05 .02 .01
Pittsburgh Penguins
☐ 367 Jeff Hackett .... .05 .02 .01
San Jose Sharks
☐ 368 Bob McGill .... .05 .02 .01
San Jose Sharks
☐ 369 Neil Wilkinson .... .05 .02 .01
San Jose Sharks
☐ 370 Rob Zettler .... .05 .02 .01
San Jose Sharks
☐ 371 Brett Hull MOY .... .20 .09 .03
☐ 372 Paul Coffey 1000 .... .08 .04 .01
☐ 373 Mark Messier 1000 .... .08 .04 .01
☐ 374 Dave Taylor 1000 .... .05 .02 .01
☐ 375 Michel Goulet 1000 .... .05 .02 .01
☐ 376 Dale Hawerchuk 1000 .... .05 .02 .01
☐ 377 The Turgeon Brothers .... .08 .04 .01
Pierre Turgeon
Sylvain Turgeon
☐ 378 The Sutter Brothers .... .05 .02 .01
Rich Sutter
Brian Sutter
Ron Sutter
☐ 379 The Mullen Brothers .... .05 .02 .01
Brian Mullen
Joe Mullen
☐ 380 The Courtnall Brothers .... .05 .02 .01
Geoff Courtnall
Russ Courtnall
☐ 381 Trevor Kidd TP .... .08 .04 .01
Calgary Flames
☐ 382 Patrice Brisebois TP .... .15 .07 .02
Montreal Canadiens
☐ 383 Mark Greig TP .... .05 .02 .01
Hartford Whalers
☐ 384 Kip Miller TP .... .05 .02 .01
Quebec Nordiques
☐ 385 Drake Berehowsky TP .... .05 .02 .01
Toronto Maple Leafs
☐ 386 Kevin Haller TP .... .10 .05 .01
Buffalo Sabres
☐ 387 Dave Gagnon TP .... .05 .02 .01
Detroit Red Wings
☐ 388 Jason Marshall TP .... .05 .02 .01
St. Louis Blues
☐ 389 Donald Audette TP .... .05 .02 .01
Buffalo Sabres
☐ 390 Patrick Lebeau TP .... .10 .05 .01
Montreal Canadiens
☐ 391 Alexander Godynyuk TP ...... .05 .02 .01
Toronto Maple Leafs
☐ 392 Jarrod Skalde TP .... .15 .07 .02
New Jersey Devils
☐ 393 Ken Sutton TP .... .10 .05 .01
Buffalo Sabres
☐ 394 Sergei Kharin TP .... .05 .02 .01
Winnipeg Jets
☐ 395 Andre Racicot TP .... .10 .05 .01
Montreal Canadiens
☐ 396 Doug Weight TP .... .25 .11 .03
New York Rangers
☐ 397 Kevin Todd TP .... .15 .07 .02
New Jersey Devils
☐ 398 Tony Amonte TP .... .30 .14 .04

New York Rangers
- ☐ 399 Kimbi Daniels TP .... .05 .02 .01
  Philadelphia Flyers
- ☐ 400 Jeff Daniels TP .... .05 .02 .01
  Pittsburgh Penguins
- ☐ 401 Guy Lafleur .... .05 .02 .01
  Speed and Grace
- ☐ 402 Guy Lafleur .... .05 .02 .01
  Awards and Achievements
- ☐ 403 Guy Lafleur .... .05 .02 .01
  A Hall of Famer
- ☐ 404 Brett Hull SL .... .20 .09 .03
  St. Louis Blues
- ☐ 405 Wayne Gretzky SL .... .35 .16 .04
  Los Angeles Kings
- ☐ 406 Wayne Gretzky SL .... .35 .16 .04
  Los Angeles Kings
- ☐ 407 Theoren Fleury SL and .... .08 .04 .01
  Marty McSorley SL
- ☐ 408 Sergei Fedorov SL .... .25 .11 .03
  Detroit Red Wings
- ☐ 409 Al MacInnis SL .... .08 .04 .01
  Calgary Flames
- ☐ 410 Ed Belfour SL .... .08 .04 .01
  Chicago Blackhawks
- ☐ 411 Ed Belfour SL .... .08 .04 .01
  Chicago Blackhawks
- ☐ 412 Brett Hull HL .... .20 .09 .03
  St. Louis Blues
- ☐ 413 Wayne Gretzky HL .... .35 .16 .04
  Los Angeles Kings
- ☐ 414 San Jose Sharks .... .30 .14 .04
- ☐ 415 Ray Bourque FP .... .08 .04 .01
  Boston Bruins
- ☐ 416 Pierre Turgeon FP .... .08 .04 .01
  Buffalo Sabres
- ☐ 417 Al MacInnis FP .... .08 .04 .01
  Calgary Flames
- ☐ 418 Jeremy Roenick FP .... .20 .09 .03
  Chicago Blackhawks
- ☐ 419 Steve Yzerman FP .... .15 .07 .02
  Detroit Red Wings
- ☐ 420 Mark Messier FP .... .08 .04 .01
  Edmonton Oilers
- ☐ 421 John Cullen FP .... .05 .02 .01
  Hartford Whalers
- ☐ 422 Wayne Gretzky FP .... .35 .16 .04
  Los Angeles Kings
- ☐ 423 Mike Modano FP .... .15 .07 .02
  Minnesota North Stars
- ☐ 424 Patrick Roy FP .... .25 .11 .03
  Montreal Canadiens
- ☐ 425 Stanley Cup Champs .... .05 .02 .01
  Pittsburgh Penguins
- ☐ 426 Mario Lemieux .... .25 .11 .03
  Conn Smythe Trophy
- ☐ 427 Wayne Gretzky .... .35 .16 .04
  Art Ross Trophy
- ☐ 428 Brett Hull .... .20 .09 .03
  Hart Memorial Trophy
- ☐ 429 Ray Bourque .... .08 .04 .01
  Norris Trophy
- ☐ 430 Ed Belfour .... .08 .04 .01
  Calder Trophy
- ☐ 431 Ed Belfour .... .08 .04 .01
  Vezina Trophy
- ☐ 432 Dirk Graham .... .05 .02 .01
  Frank J. Selke Trophy
- ☐ 433 Ed Belfour .... .08 .04 .01
  Jennings Trophy
- ☐ 434 Wayne Gretzky .... .35 .16 .04
  Lady Byng Trophy
- ☐ 435 Dave Taylor .... .08 .04 .01
  Bill Masterton Trophy
- ☐ 436 Randy Ladouceur .... .05 .02 .01
  Hartford Whalers
- ☐ 437 Dave Tippett .... .05 .02 .01
  Washington Capitals
- ☐ 438 Clint Malarchuk .... .08 .04 .01
  Buffalo Sabres
- ☐ 439 Gordie Roberts .... .05 .02 .01
  Pittsburgh Penguins
- ☐ 440 Frank Pietrangelo .... .05 .02 .01
  Pittsburgh Penguins

1991-92 Score Canadian

 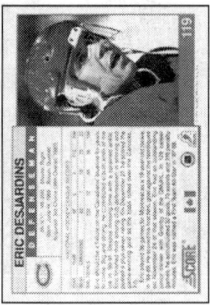

The 1991-92 Score Canadian hockey set features 660 cards measuring the standard size (2 1/2" by 3 1/2"). The set was released in two series of 330 cards each. As one moves down the card face, the fronts shade from red to white. The color action player photo is enclosed by a thin purple border, with a shadow border on the right and below. At the card top, the player's name is written over a hockey puck, and the team name is printed below the picture in the lower right corner. A red border stripe at the bottom completes the front. In a horizontal format, the bilingual backs have biography, statistics, player profile, and a color close-up photo. Subsets include Thousand Point Club (262-266), NHL Brothers (267-270), Top Prospect (271-290), Guy Lafleur (291-293), Season Leader (294-301), Crunch Crew (305-309), The Franchise (310-314), and players who were awarded trophies (316-325). Two additional Bobby Orr cards were inserted into second series packs. In contrast to the first series, the fronts of the second series cards shade from bright blue to white as one moves down the card face. The color action player photo is enclosed by a thin red border, with a shadow border on the right and below. At the card top, the player's name is written over a hockey puck, and the team name is printed below the picture in the lower right corner. A bright blue border stripe at the bottom completes the front. Subsets include The Franchise (331-335, 361-371), NHL Brothers (336-339), Top Prospect (340-359), Dream Team (372-377), and All-Rookie Team (378-383). The cards are numbered on the back. The key Rookie Cards in the set are Tony Amonte, Nicklas Lidstrom, Rob Pearson, Geoff Sanderson and Doug Weight.

	MINT	EXC	G-VG
COMPLETE SET (660)	16.00	7.25	2.00
COMPLETE FACT.SET (660)	16.00	7.25	2.00
COMPLETE SERIES 1 (330)	8.00	3.60	1.00
COMPLETE SERIES 2 (330)	8.00	3.60	1.00
COMMON PLAYER (1-330)	.05	.02	.01
COMMON PLAYER (331-660)	.05	.02	.01

- ☐ 1 Brett Hull .... .50 .23 .06
  St. Louis Blues
- ☐ 2 Al MacInnis .... .10 .05 .01
  Calgary Flames
- ☐ 3 Luc Robitaille .... .15 .07 .02
  Los Angeles Kings
- ☐ 4 Pierre Turgeon .... .20 .09 .03
  Buffalo Sabres
- ☐ 5 Brian Leetch .... .30 .14 .04
  New York Rangers
- ☐ 6 Cam Neely .... .15 .07 .02
  Boston Bruins
- ☐ 7 John Cullen .... .05 .02 .01
  Hartford Whalers
- ☐ 8 Trevor Linden .... .25 .11 .03
  Vancouver Canucks
- ☐ 9 Rick Tocchet .... .08 .04 .01
  Philadelphia Flyers

☐ 10	John Vanbiesbrouck	.10	.05	.01	
	New York Rangers				
☐ 11	Steve Smith.........................	.08	.04	.01	
	Edmonton Oilers				
☐ 12	Doug Smail.........................	.05	.02	.01	
	Minnesota North Stars				
☐ 13	Craig Ludwig.......................	.05	.02	.01	
	New York Islanders				
☐ 14	Paul Fenton	.05	.02	.01	
	Calgary Flames				
☐ 15	Dirk Graham........................	.05	.02	.01	
	Chicago Blackhawks				
☐ 16	Brad McCrimmon.................	.05	.02	.01	
	Detroit Red Wings				
☐ 17	Dean Evason	.05	.02	.01	
	Hartford Whalers				
☐ 18	Fredrik Olausson	.08	.04	.01	
	Winnipeg Jets				
☐ 19	Guy Carbonneau	.08	.04	.01	
	Montreal Canadiens				
☐ 20	Kevin Hatcher......................	.08	.04	.01	
	Washington Capitals				
☐ 21	Paul Ranheim.......................	.05	.02	.01	
	Calgary Flames				
☐ 22	Claude Lemieux...................	.08	.04	.01	
	New Jersey Devils				
☐ 23	Vincent Riendeau	.05	.02	.01	
	St. Louis Blues				
☐ 24	Garth Butcher......................	.05	.02	.01	
	St. Louis Blues				
☐ 25	Joe Sakic............................	.25	.11	.03	
	Quebec Nordiques				
☐ 26	Rick Vaive	.05	.02	.01	
	Buffalo Sabres				
☐ 27	Rob Blake...........................	.15	.07	.02	
	Los Angeles Kings				
☐ 28	Mike Ricci	.15	.07	.02	
	Philadelphia Flyers				
☐ 29	Pat Flatley	.05	.02	.01	
	New York Islanders				
☐ 30	Bill Ranford	.08	.04	.01	
	Edmonton Oilers				
☐ 31	Larry Murphy	.08	.04	.01	
	Pittsburgh Penguins				
☐ 32	Bobby Smith	.08	.04	.01	
	Minnesota North Stars				
☐ 33	Mike Krushelnyski...............	.05	.02	.01	
	Toronto Maple Leafs				
☐ 34	Gerard Gallant	.05	.02	.01	
	Detroit Red Wings				
☐ 35	Doug Wilson	.08	.04	.01	
	Chicago Blackhawks				
☐ 36	John Ogrodnick...................	.05	.02	.01	
	New York Rangers				
☐ 37	Mikhail Tatarinov.................	.05	.02	.01	
	Washington Capitals				
☐ 38	Doug Crossman	.05	.02	.01	
	Detroit Red Wings				
☐ 39	Mark Osborne	.05	.02	.01	
	Winnipeg Jets				
☐ 40	Scott Stevens	.10	.05	.01	
	St. Louis Blues				
☐ 41	Ron Tugnutt........................	.05	.02	.01	
	Quebec Nordiques				
☐ 42	Russ Courtnall	.08	.04	.01	
	Montreal Canadiens				
☐ 43	Gord Murphy.......................	.05	.02	.01	
	Philadelphia Flyers				
☐ 44	Greg Adams	.05	.02	.01	
	Vancouver Canucks				
☐ 45	Christian Ruuttu	.05	.02	.01	
	Buffalo Sabres				
☐ 46	Ken Daneyko	.05	.02	.01	
	New Jersey Devils				
☐ 47	Glenn Anderson	.08	.04	.01	
	Edmonton Oilers				
☐ 48	Ray Ferraro	.08	.04	.01	
	New York Islanders				
☐ 49	Tony Tanti	.05	.02	.01	
	Buffalo Sabres				
☐ 50	Ray Bourque	.15	.07	.02	
	Boston Bruins				
☐ 51	Sergei Makarov	.08	.04	.01	
	Calgary Flames				
☐ 52	Jim Johnson	.05	.02	.01	
	Minnesota North Stars				
☐ 53	Troy Murray	.05	.02	.01	
	Chicago Blackhawks				
☐ 54	Shawn Burr	.05	.02	.01	
	Detroit Red Wings				
☐ 55	Peter Ing	.05	.02	.01	
	Toronto Maple Leafs				
☐ 56	Dale Hunter	.08	.04	.01	

	Washington Capitals			
☐ 57	Tony Granato	.08	.04	.01
	Los Angeles Kings			
☐ 58	Curtis Leschyshyn...............	.05	.02	.01
	Quebec Nordiques			
☐ 59	Brian Mullen.......................	.08	.04	.01
	New York Rangers			
☐ 60	Ed Olczyk	.05	.02	.01
	Winnipeg Jets			
☐ 61	Mike Ramsey	.05	.02	.01
	Buffalo Sabres			
☐ 62	Dan Quinn	.05	.02	.01
	St. Louis Blues			
☐ 63	Rich Sutter.........................	.05	.02	.01
	St. Louis Blues			
☐ 64	Terry Carkner	.05	.02	.01
	Philadelphia Flyers			
☐ 65	Shayne Corson....................	.08	.04	.01
	Montreal Canadiens			
☐ 66	Peter Stastny......................	.08	.04	.01
	New Jersey Devils			
☐ 67	Craig Muni	.05	.02	.01
	Edmonton Oilers			
☐ 68	Glenn Healy	.08	.04	.01
	New York Islanders			
☐ 69	Phil Bourque	.05	.02	.01
	Pittsburgh Penguins			
☐ 70	Pat Verbeek........................	.08	.04	.01
	Hartford Whalers			
☐ 71	Garry Galley	.08	.04	.01
	Boston Bruins			
☐ 72	Dave Gagner	.08	.04	.01
	Minnesota North Stars			
☐ 73	Bob Probert........................	.08	.04	.01
	Detroit Red Wings			
☐ 74	Craig Wolanin	.05	.02	.01
	Quebec Nordiques			
☐ 75	Patrick Roy	.50	.23	.06
	Montreal Canadiens			
☐ 76	Keith Brown	.05	.02	.01
	Chicago Blackhawks			
☐ 77	Gary Leeman	.05	.02	.01
	Toronto Maple Leafs			
☐ 78	Brent Ashton	.05	.02	.01
	Winnipeg Jets			
☐ 79	Randy Moller.......................	.05	.02	.01
	New York Rangers			
☐ 80	Mike Vernon.......................	.08	.04	.01
	Calgary Flames			
☐ 81	Kelly Miller	.05	.02	.01
	Washington Capitals			
☐ 82	Ulf Samuelsson...................	.08	.04	.01
	Pittsburgh Penguins			
☐ 83	Todd Elik	.05	.02	.01
	Los Angeles Kings			
☐ 84	Uwe Krupp	.05	.02	.01
	Buffalo Sabres			
☐ 85	Rod Brind'Amour	.15	.07	.02
	St. Louis Blues			
☐ 86	Dave Capuano	.05	.02	.01
	Vancouver Canucks			
☐ 87	Geoff Smith........................	.05	.02	.01
	Edmonton Oilers			
☐ 88	David Volek	.05	.02	.01
	New York Islanders			
☐ 89	Bruce Driver	.05	.02	.01
	New Jersey Devils			
☐ 90	Andy Moog	.10	.05	.01
	Boston Bruins			
☐ 91	Pelle Eklund	.05	.02	.01
	Philadelphia Flyers			
☐ 92	Joey Kocur	.05	.02	.01
	New York Rangers			
☐ 93	Mark Tinordi	.08	.04	.01
	Minnesota North Stars			
☐ 94	Steve Thomas	.08	.04	.01
	Chicago Blackhawks			
☐ 95	Petr Svoboda	.05	.02	.01
	Montreal Canadiens			
☐ 96	Joel Otto	.05	.02	.01
	Calgary Flames			
☐ 97	Todd Krygier	.05	.02	.01
	Hartford Whalers			
☐ 98	Jaromir Jagr	.50	.23	.06
	Pittsburgh Penguins			
☐ 99	Mike Liut	.08	.04	.01
	Washington Capitals			
☐ 100	Wayne Gretzky	1.00	.45	.13
	Los Angeles Kings			
☐ 101	Teppo Numminen	.05	.02	.01
	Winnipeg Jets			
☐ 102	Randy Burridge...................	.05	.02	.01
	Boston Bruins			
☐ 103	Michel Petit........................	.05	.02	.01

Toronto Maple Leafs
- [ ] 104 Tony McKegney .... .05 .02 .01
Chicago Blackhawks
- [ ] 105 Mathieu Schneider .... .08 .04 .01
Montreal Canadiens
- [ ] 106 Daren Puppa .... .08 .04 .01
Buffalo Sabres
- [ ] 107 Paul Cavallini.................... .05 .02 .01
St. Louis Blues
- [ ] 108 Tim Kerr............................ .08 .04 .01
Philadelphia Flyers
- [ ] 109 Kevin Lowe .... .08 .04 .01
Edmonton Oilers
- [ ] 110 Kirk Muller .... .08 .04 .01
New Jersey Devils
- [ ] 111 Zarley Zalapski .... .05 .02 .01
Edmonton Oilers
- [ ] 112 Mike Hough........................ .05 .02 .01
Quebec Nordiques
- [ ] 113 Ken Hodge Jr. .... .05 .02 .01
Boston Bruins
- [ ] 114 Grant Fuhr.......................... .08 .04 .01
Edmonton Oilers
- [ ] 115 Paul Coffey........................ .15 .07 .02
Pittsburgh Penguins
- [ ] 116 Wendel Clark....................... .15 .07 .02
Toronto Maple Leafs
- [ ] 117 Patrik Sundstrom............... .05 .02 .01
New Jersey Devils
- [ ] 118 Kevin Dineen .... .08 .04 .01
Edmonton Oilers
- [ ] 119 Eric Desjardins.................. .08 .04 .01
Montreal Canadiens
- [ ] 120 Mike Richter....................... .25 .11 .03
New York Rangers
- [ ] 121 Sergio Momesso................ .05 .02 .01
Vancouver Canucks
- [ ] 122 Tony Hrkac........................ .05 .02 .01
Quebec Nordiques
- [ ] 123 Joe Reekie.......................... .05 .02 .01
New York Islanders
- [ ] 124 Petr Nedved .... .20 .09 .03
Vancouver Canucks
- [ ] 125 Randy Carlyle .... .05 .02 .01
Winnipeg Jets
- [ ] 126 Kevin Miller .... .08 .04 .01
Detroit Red Wings
- [ ] 127 Rejean Lemelin .... .08 .04 .01
Boston Bruins
- [ ] 128 Dino Ciccarelli................... .08 .04 .01
Washington Capitals
- [ ] 129 Sylvain Cote .... .05 .02 .01
Edmonton Oilers
- [ ] 130 Mats Sundin....................... .25 .11 .03
Quebec Nordiques
- [ ] 131 Eric Weinrich...................... .05 .02 .01
New Jersey Devils
- [ ] 132 Daniel Berthiaume............. .05 .02 .01
Los Angeles Kings
- [ ] 133 Keith Acton .... .05 .02 .01
Philadelphia Flyers
- [ ] 134 Benoit Hogue .... .05 .02 .01
Buffalo Sabres
- [ ] 135 Mike Gartner...................... .10 .05 .01
New York Rangers
- [ ] 136 Petr Klima .... .05 .02 .01
Edmonton Oilers
- [ ] 137 Curt Giles .... .05 .02 .01
Minnesota North Stars
- [ ] 138 Scott Pearson .... .05 .02 .01
Quebec Nordiques
- [ ] 139 Luke Richardson .... .05 .02 .01
Toronto Maple Leafs
- [ ] 140 Steve Larmer...................... .08 .04 .01
Chicago Blackhawks
- [ ] 141 Kon Wroggot .... .06 .02 .01
Philadelphia Flyers
- [ ] 142 Frantisek Musil.................. .05 .02 .01
Calgary Flames
- [ ] 143 Owen Nolan........................ .15 .07 .02
Quebec Nordiques
- [ ] 144 Keith Primeau .... .15 .07 .02
Detroit Red Wings
- [ ] 145 Mark Recchi .... .30 .14 .04
Pittsburgh Penguins
- [ ] 146 Don Sweeney .... .05 .02 .01
Boston Bruins
- [ ] 147 Mike McPhee .... .05 .02 .01
Montreal Canadiens
- [ ] 148 Ken Baumgartner .... .05 .02 .01
New York Islanders
- [ ] 149 Dave Lowry......................... .05 .02 .01
St. Louis Blues
- [ ] 150 Geoff Courtnall................... .08 .04 .01

Vancouver Canucks
- [ ] 151 Chris Terreri .... .08 .04 .01
New Jersey Devils
- [ ] 152 Dave Manson .... .08 .04 .01
Chicago Blackhawks
- [ ] 153 Bobby Holik........................ .08 .04 .01
Hartford Whalers
- [ ] 154 Bob Kudelski .... .08 .04 .01
Los Angeles Kings
- [ ] 155 Calle Johansson .... .05 .02 .01
Washington Capitals
- [ ] 156 Mark Hunter........................ .05 .02 .01
Hartford Whalers
- [ ] 157 Randy Gilhen....................... .05 .02 .01
Pittsburgh Penguins
- [ ] 158 Yves Racine .... .05 .02 .01
Detroit Red Wings
- [ ] 159 Martin Gelinas.................... .05 .02 .01
Edmonton Oilers
- [ ] 160 Brian Bellows .... .08 .04 .01
Minnesota North Stars
- [ ] 161 David Shaw .... .05 .02 .01
New York Rangers
- [ ] 162 Bob Carpenter .... .05 .02 .01
Boston Bruins
- [ ] 163 Doug Brown .... .05 .02 .01
New Jersey Devils
- [ ] 164 Ulf Dahlen .... .08 .04 .01
Minnesota North Stars
- [ ] 165 Denis Savard .... .08 .04 .01
Montreal Canadiens
- [ ] 166 Paul Ysebaert...................... .05 .02 .01
Detroit Red Wings
- [ ] 167 Derek King .... .08 .04 .01
New York Islanders
- [ ] 168 Igor Larionov .... .08 .04 .01
Vancouver Canucks
- [ ] 169 Bob Errey .... .05 .02 .01
Pittsburgh Penguins
- [ ] 170 Joe Nieuwendyk.................. .10 .05 .01
Calgary Flames
- [ ] 171 Normand Rochefort .... .05 .02 .01
New York Rangers
- [ ] 172 John Tonelli .... .08 .04 .01
Los Angeles Kings
- [ ] 173 David Reid........................... .05 .02 .01
Toronto Maple Leafs
- [ ] 174 Tom Kurvers .... .05 .02 .01
Vancouver Canucks
- [ ] 175 Dimitri Khristich.................. .08 .04 .01
Washington Capitals
- [ ] 176 Bob Sweeney .... .05 .02 .01
Boston Bruins
- [ ] 177 Rick Zombo......................... .05 .02 .01
Detroit Red Wings
- [ ] 178 Troy Mallette....................... .05 .02 .01
New York Rangers
- [ ] 179 Bob Bassen .... .05 .02 .01
St. Louis Blues
- [ ] 180 John Druce .... .05 .02 .01
Washington Capitals
- [ ] 181 Mike Craig .... .05 .02 .01
Minnesota North Stars
- [ ] 182 John McIntyre...................... .05 .02 .01
Los Angeles Kings
- [ ] 183 Murray Baron .... .05 .02 .01
Philadelphia Flyers
- [ ] 184 Viacheslav Fetisov.............. .08 .04 .01
New Jersey Devils
- [ ] 185 Don Beaupre .... .08 .04 .01
Washington Capitals
- [ ] 186 Brian Benning .... .05 .02 .01
Los Angeles Kings
- [ ] 187 Dave Barr .... .05 .02 .01
Detroit Red Wings
- [ ] 188 Petri Skriko .... .06 .02 .01
Boston Bruins
- [ ] 189 Steve Konroyd..................... .05 .02 .01
Chicago Blackhawks
- [ ] 190 Steve Yzerman .... .25 .11 .03
Detroit Red Wings
- [ ] 191 Jon Casey........................... .08 .04 .01
Minnesota North Stars
- [ ] 192 Gary Nylund .... .05 .02 .01
New York Islanders
- [ ] 193 Michal Pivonka.................... .08 .04 .01
Washington Capitals
- [ ] 194 Alexei Kasatonov .... .05 .02 .01
New Jersey Devils
- [ ] 195 Garry Valk .... .05 .02 .01
Vancouver Canucks
- [ ] 196 Darren Turcotte................... .05 .02 .01
New York Rangers
- [ ] 197 Chris Nilan .... .08 .04 .01

Boston Bruins			
☐ 198 Thomas Steen	.05	.02	.01
Winnipeg Jets			
☐ 199 Gary Roberts	.08	.04	.01
Calgary Flames			
☐ 200 Mario Lemieux	.75	.35	.09
Pittsburgh Penguins			
☐ 201 Michel Goulet	.08	.04	.01
Chicago Blackhawks			
☐ 202 Craig MacTavish	.05	.02	.01
Edmonton Oilers			
☐ 203 Peter Sidorkiewicz	.05	.02	.01
Hartford Whalers			
☐ 204 Johan Garpenlov	.05	.02	.01
Detroit Red Wings			
☐ 205 Steve Duchesne	.08	.04	.01
Los Angeles Kings			
☐ 206 Dave Snuggerud	.05	.02	.01
Buffalo Sabres			
☐ 207 Kjell Samuelsson	.05	.02	.01
Philadelphia Flyers			
☐ 208 Sylvain Turgeon	.05	.02	.01
Montreal Canadiens			
☐ 209 Al Iafrate	.08	.04	.01
Washington Capitals			
☐ 210 John MacLean	.08	.04	.01
New Jersey Devils			
☐ 211 Brian Hayward	.05	.02	.01
Minnesota North Stars			
☐ 212 Cliff Ronning	.08	.04	.01
Vancouver Canucks			
☐ 213 Ray Sheppard	.08	.04	.01
New York Rangers			
☐ 214 Dave Taylor	.08	.04	.01
Los Angeles Kings			
☐ 215 Doug Lidster	.05	.02	.01
Vancouver Canucks			
☐ 216 Peter Bondra	.08	.04	.01
Washington Capitals			
☐ 217 Marty McSorley	.08	.04	.01
Los Angeles Kings			
☒ 218 Doug Gilmour	.25	.11	.03
Calgary Flames			
☐ 219 Paul MacDermid	.05	.02	.01
Winnipeg Jets			
☐ 220 Jeremy Roenick	.50	.23	.06
Chicago Blackhawks			
☐ 221 Wayne Presley	.05	.02	.01
Chicago Blackhawks			
☐ 222 Jeff Norton	.05	.02	.01
New York Islanders			
☐ 223 Brian Propp	.08	.04	.01
Minnesota North Stars			
☐ 224 Jimmy Carson	.08	.04	.01
Detroit Red Wings			
☐ 225 Tom Barrasso	.08	.04	.01
Pittsburgh Penguins			
☐ 226 Theoren Fleury	.15	.07	.02
Calgary Flames			
☐ 227 Carey Wilson	.05	.02	.01
Calgary Flames			
☐ 228 Rod Langway	.05	.02	.01
Washington Capitals			
☐ 229 Bryan Trottier	.08	.04	.01
Pittsburgh Penguins			
☐ 230 James Patrick	.05	.02	.01
New York Rangers			
☐ 231 Dana Murzyn	.05	.02	.01
Vancouver Canucks			
☐ 232 Rick Wamsley	.05	.02	.01
Calgary Flames			
☐ 233 Dave McLlwain	.05	.02	.01
Winnipeg Jets			
☐ 234 Tom Fergus	.05	.02	.01
Toronto Maple Leafs			
☐ 235 Adam Graves	.25	.11	.03
Edmonton Oilers			
☐ 236 Jacques Cloutier	.05	.02	.01
Quebec Nordiques			
☐ 237 Gino Odjick	.08	.04	.01
Vancouver Canucks			
☐ 238 Andrew Cassels	.08	.04	.01
Montreal Canadiens			
☐ 239 Ken Linseman	.05	.02	.01
Edmonton Oilers			
☐ 240 Danton Cole	.05	.02	.01
Winnipeg Jets			
☐ 241 Dave Hannan	.05	.02	.01
Toronto Maple Leafs			
☐ 242 Stephane Matteau	.05	.02	.01
Calgary Flames			
☐ 243 Gerald Diduck	.05	.02	.01
Vancouver Canucks			
☐ 244 Rick Tabaracci	.05	.02	.01

Winnipeg Jets			
☐ 245 Sylvain Lefebvre	.05	.02	.01
Montreal Canadiens			
☐ 246 Bob Rouse	.05	.02	.01
Toronto Maple Leafs			
☐ 247 Charlie Huddy	.05	.02	.01
Edmonton Oilers			
☐ 248 Mike Foligno	.05	.02	.01
Toronto Maple Leafs			
☐ 249 Ric Nattress	.05	.02	.01
Calgary Flames			
☐ 250 Aaron Broten	.05	.02	.01
Toronto Maple Leafs			
☐ 251 Mike Keane	.05	.02	.01
Montreal Canadiens			
☐ 252 Steve Bozek	.05	.02	.01
Vancouver Canucks			
☐ 253 Jeff Beukeboom	.05	.02	.01
Edmonton Oilers			
☐ 254 Stephane Morin	.05	.02	.01
Quebec Nordiques			
☐ 255 Brian Bradley	.08	.04	.01
Toronto Maple Leafs			
☐ 256 Scott Arniel	.05	.02	.01
Winnipeg Jets			
☐ 257 Robert Kron	.05	.02	.01
Vancouver Canucks			
☐ 258 Anatoli Semenov	.05	.02	.01
Edmonton Oilers			
☐ 259 Brent Gilchrist	.05	.02	.01
Montreal Canadiens			
☐ 260 Jim Sandlak	.05	.02	.01
Vancouver Canucks			
☐ 261 Brett Hull (Man of the Year)	.20	.09	.03
☐ 262 Paul Coffey 1000 Points	.08	.04	.01
☐ 263 Mark Messier 1000 Points	.08	.04	.01
☐ 264 Dave Taylor 1000 Points	.05	.02	.01
☐ 265 Michel Goulet 1000 Points	.05	.02	.01
☐ 266 Dale Hawerchuk 1000 Points	.05	.02	.01
☐ 267 The Turgeon Brothers	.08	.04	.01
Pierre Turgeon			
Sylvain Turgeon			
☐ 268 The Sutter Brothers	.05	.02	.01
Rich Sutter			
Brian Sutter			
Ron Sutter			
☐ 269 The Mullen Brothers	.05	.02	.01
Brian Mullen			
Joe Mullen			
☐ 270 The Courtnall Brothers	.05	.02	.01
Geoff Courtnall			
Russ Courtnall			
☐ 271 Trevor Kidd TP	.08	.04	.01
Calgary Flames			
☐ 272 Patrice Brisebois TP	.15	.07	.02
Montreal Canadiens			
☐ 273 Mark Greig TP	.05	.02	.01
Hartford Whalers			
☐ 274 Kip Miller TP	.05	.02	.01
Quebec Nordiques			
☐ 275 Drake Berehowsky TP	.05	.02	.01
Toronto Maple Leafs			
☐ 276 Kevin Haller TP	.10	.05	.01
Buffalo Sabres			
☐ 277 Dave Gagnon TP	.05	.02	.01
Detroit Red Wings			
☐ 278 Jason Marshall TP	.05	.02	.01
St. Louis Blues			
☐ 279 Donald Audette TP	.05	.02	.01
Buffalo Sabres			
☐ 280 Patrick Lebeau TP	.10	.05	.01
Montreal Canadiens			
☐ 281 Alexander Godynyuk TP	.05	.02	.01
Toronto Maple Leafs			
☐ 282 Jarrod Skalde TP	.15	.07	.02
New Jersey Devils			
☐ 283 Ken Sutton TP	.10	.05	.01
Buffalo Sabres			
☐ 284 Sergei Kharin TP	.05	.02	.01
Winnipeg Jets			
☐ 285 Andre Racicot TP	.10	.05	.01
Montreal Canadiens			
☐ 286 Doug Weight TP	.25	.11	.03
New York Rangers			
☐ 287 Kevin Todd TP	.15	.07	.02
New Jersey Devils			
☐ 288 Tony Amonte TP	.30	.14	.04
New York Rangers			
☐ 289 Kimbi Daniels TP	.05	.02	.01
Philadelphia Flyers			
☐ 290 Jeff Daniels TP	.05	.02	.01
Pittsburgh Penguins			
☐ 291 Guy Lafleur	.05	.02	.01
Speed and Grace			

☐ 292	Guy Lafleur	.05	.02	.01
	Awards and Achievements			
☐ 293	Guy Lafleur	.05	.02	.01
	A Hall of Famer			
☐ 294	Brett Hull SL	.20	.09	.03
	St. Louis Blues			
☐ 295	Wayne Gretzky SL	.35	.16	.04
	Los Angeles Kings			
☐ 296	Wayne Gretzky SL	.35	.16	.04
	Los Angeles Kings			
☐ 297	Theoren Fleury and	.08	.04	.01
	Marty McSorley SL			
☐ 298	Sergei Fedorov SL	.25	.11	.03
	Detroit Red Wings			
☐ 299	Al MacInnis SL	.08	.04	.01
	Calgary Flames			
☐ 300	Ed Belfour SL	.08	.04	.01
	Chicago Blackhawks			
☐ 301	Ed Belfour SL	.08	.04	.01
	Chicago Blackhawks			
☐ 302	Brett Hull 50/50	.20	.09	.03
☐ 303	Wayne Gretzky	.35	.16	.04
	700th Career Goal			
☐ 304	San Jose Sharks Logo	.30	.14	.04
☐ 305	Cam Neely Crunch Crew	.08	.04	.01
☐ 306	Rick Tocchet Crunch Crew	.08	.04	.01
☐ 307	Scott Stevens Crunch Crew	.08	.04	.01
☐ 308	Ulf Samuelsson Crunch Crew	.05	.02	.01
☐ 309	Jeremy Roenick Crunch Crew	.15	.07	.02
☐ 310	Mark Messier FRAN	.08	.04	.01
	Edmonton Oilers			
☐ 311	John Cullen FRAN	.05	.02	.01
	Hartford Whalers			
☐ 312	Wayne Gretzky FRAN	.35	.16	.04
	Los Angeles Kings			
☐ 313	Mike Modano FRAN	.15	.07	.02
	Minnesota North Stars			
☐ 314	Patrick Roy FRAN	.25	.11	.03
	Montreal Canadiens			
☐ 315	Stanley Cup Champs	.05	.02	.01
	Pittsburgh Penguins			
☐ 316	Mario Lemieux	.25	.11	.03
	Pittsburgh Penguins			
	Conn Smythe Trophy			
☐ 317	Wayne Gretzky	.35	.16	.04
	Los Angeles Kings			
	Art Ross Trophy			
☐ 318	Brett Hull	.20	.09	.03
	St. Louis Blues			
	Hart Memorial Trophy			
☐ 319	Ray Bourque	.08	.04	.01
	Boston Bruins			
	Norris Trophy			
☐ 320	Ed Belfour	.08	.04	.01
	Chicago Blackhawks			
	Calder Trophy			
☐ 321	Ed Belfour	.08	.04	.01
	Chicago Blackhawks			
	Vezina Trophy			
☐ 322	Dirk Graham	.05	.02	.01
	Chicago Blackhawks			
	Frank J. Selke Trophy			
☐ 323	Ed Belfour	.08	.04	.01
	Chicago Blackhawks			
	Jennings Trophy			
☐ 324	Wayne Gretzky	.35	.16	.04
	Los Angeles Kings			
	Lady Byng Trophy			
☐ 325	Dave Taylor	.08	.04	.01
	Los Angeles Kings			
	Bill Masterton Trophy			
☐ 326	Jeff Hackett	.05	.02	.01
	San Jose Sharks			
☐ 327	Bob McGill	.05	.02	.01
	San Jose Sharks			
☐ 328	Noil Wilkinson	.05	.02	.01
	San Jose Sharks			
☐ 329	Eric Lindros	1.00	.45	.13
	1st Rd Draft Choice			
☐ 330	Eric Lindros	1.00	.45	.13
	Awards and Honors			
☐ 331	Ray Bourque FP	.08	.04	.01
	Boston Bruins			
☐ 332	Pierre Turgeon FP	.08	.04	.01
	Buffalo Sabres			
☐ 333	Al MacInnis FP	.08	.04	.01
	Calgary Flames			
☐ 334	Jeremy Roenick FP	.20	.09	.03
	Chicago Blackhawks			
☐ 335	Steve Yzerman FP	.15	.07	.02
	Detroit Red Wings			
☐ 336	The Hunter Brothers	.05	.02	.01
	Dale Hunter			
	Mark Hunter			
☐ 337	The Broten Brothers	.05	.02	.01
	Neal Broten			
	Aaron Broten			
☐ 338	The Cavallini Brothers	.05	.02	.01
	Gino Cavallini			
	Paul Cavallini			
☐ 339	The Miller Brothers	.05	.02	.01
	Kelly Miller			
	Kevin Miller			
☐ 340	Dennis Vaske TP	.05	.02	.01
	New York Islanders			
☐ 341	Rob Pearson TP	.20	.09	.03
	Toronto Maple Leafs			
☐ 342	Jason Miller TP	.05	.02	.01
	New Jersey Devils			
☐ 343	John LeClair TP	.15	.07	.02
	Montreal Canadiens			
☐ 344	Bryan Marchment TP	.10	.05	.01
	Winnipeg Jets			
☐ 345	Gary Shuchuk TP	.05	.02	.01
	Detroit Red Wings			
☐ 346	Dominik Hasek TP	1.00	.45	.13
	Chicago Blackhawks			
☐ 347	Michel Picard TP	.05	.02	.01
	Hartford Whalers			
☐ 348	Corey Millen TP	.20	.09	.03
	New York Rangers			
☐ 349	Joe Sacco TP	.10	.05	.01
	Toronto Maple Leafs			
☐ 350	Reggie Savage TP	.05	.02	.01
	Washington Capitals			
☐ 351	Pat Murray TP	.05	.02	.01
	Philadelphia Flyers			
☐ 352	Myles O'Connor TP	.05	.02	.01
	New Jersey Devils			
☐ 353	Shawn Antoski TP	.05	.02	.01
	Vancouver Canucks			
☐ 354	Geoff Sanderson TP	.75	.35	.09
	Hartford Whalers			
☐ 355	Chris Govedaris TP	.05	.02	.01
	Hartford Whalers			
☐ 356	Alexei Gusarov TP	.10	.05	.01
	Quebec Nordiques			
☐ 357	Mike Sillinger TP	.05	.02	.01
	Detroit Red Wings			
☐ 358	Bob Wilkie TP	.05	.02	.01
	Detroit Red Wings			
☐ 359	Pat Jablonski TP	.10	.05	.01
	St. Louis Blues			
☐ 360	Memorial Cup	.05	.02	.01
	Spokane Chiefs			
☐ 361	Kirk Muller FP	.08	.04	.01
	New Jersey Devils			
☐ 362	Pat LaFontaine FP	.08	.04	.01
	New York Islanders			
☐ 363	Brian Leetch FP	.15	.07	.02
	New York Rangers			
☐ 364	Rick Tocchet FP	.08	.04	.01
	Philadelphia Flyers			
☐ 365	Mario Lemieux FP	.25	.11	.03
	Pittsburgh Penguins			
☐ 366	Joe Sakic FP	.08	.04	.01
	Quebec Nordiques			
☐ 367	Brett Hull FP	.20	.09	.03
	St. Louis Blues			
☐ 368	Vincent Damphousse FP	.08	.04	.01
	Toronto Maple Leafs			
☐ 369	Trevor Linden FP	.08	.04	.01
	Vancouver Canucks			
☐ 370	Kevin Hatcher FP	.05	.02	.01
	Washington Capitals			
☐ 371	Pat Elynuik FP	.05	.02	.01
	Winnipeg Jets			
☐ 372	Patrick Roy DT	.30	.14	.04
	Montreal Canadiens			
☐ 373	Brian Leetch DT	.15	.07	.02
	New York Rangers			
☐ 374	Ray Bourque DT	.08	.04	.01
	Boston Bruins			
☐ 375	Luc Robitaille DT	.10	.05	.01
	Los Angeles Kings			
☐ 376	Wayne Gretzky DT	.35	.16	.04
	Los Angeles Kings			
☐ 377	Brett Hull DT	.20	.09	.03
	St. Louis Blues			
☐ 378	Ed Belfour ART	.08	.04	.01
	Chicago Blackhawks			
☐ 379	Rob Blake ART	.08	.04	.01
	Los Angeles Kings			
☐ 380	Eric Weinrich ART	.05	.02	.01
	New Jersey Devils			
☐ 381	Jaromir Jagr ART	.20	.09	.03
	Pittsburgh Penguins			

□				
382	Sergei Fedorov ART	.25	.11	.03
	Detroit Red Wings			
383	Ken Hodge Jr. ART	.05	.02	.01
	Boston Bruins			
384	Eric Lindros	1.00	.45	.13
	Art			
385	Eric Lindros	1.00	.45	.13
	with Rob Pearson			
386	Ottawa/Tampa Bay	.25	.11	.03
	Logo Card			
387	Mick Vukota	.05	.02	.01
	New York Islanders			
388	Lou Franceschetti	.05	.02	.01
	Buffalo Sabres			
389	Mike Hudson	.05	.02	.01
	Chicago Blackhawks			
390	Frantisek Kucera	.05	.02	.01
	Chicago Blackhawks			
391	Basil McRae	.05	.02	.01
	Minnesota North Stars			
392	Donald Dufresne	.05	.02	.01
	Montreal Canadiens			
393	Tommy Albelin	.05	.02	.01
	New Jersey Devils			
394	Normand Lacombe	.05	.02	.01
	Philadelphia Flyers			
395	Lucien DeBlois	.05	.02	.01
	Toronto Maple Leafs			
396	Tony Twist	.05	.02	.01
	Quebec Nordiques			
397	Rob Murphy	.05	.02	.01
	Vancouver Canucks			
398	Ken Sabourin	.05	.02	.01
	Washington Capitals			
399	Doug Evans	.05	.02	.01
	Winnipeg Jets			
400	Walt Poddubny	.05	.02	.01
	New Jersey Devils			
401	Grant Ledyard	.05	.02	.01
	Buffalo Sabres			
402	Kris King	.05	.02	.01
	New York Rangers			
403	Paul Gillis	.05	.02	.01
	Chicago Blackhawks			
404	Chris Dahlquist	.05	.02	.01
	Minnesota North Stars			
405	Zdeno Ciger	.05	.02	.01
	New Jersey Devils			
406	Paul Stanton	.05	.02	.01
	Pittsburgh Penguins			
407	Randy Ladouceur	.05	.02	.01
	Hartford Whalers			
408	Ronnie Stern	.05	.02	.01
	Calgary Flames			
409	Dave Tippett	.05	.02	.01
	Washington Capitals			
410	Jeff Reese	.05	.02	.01
	Toronto Maple Leafs			
411	Vladimir Ruzicka	.05	.02	.01
	Boston Bruins			
412	Brent Fedyk	.08	.04	.01
	Detroit Red Wings			
413	Paul Cyr	.05	.02	.01
	Hartford Whalers			
414	Mike Eagles	.05	.02	.01
	Winnipeg Jets			
415	Chris Joseph	.05	.02	.01
	Edmonton Oilers			
416	Brad Marsh	.08	.04	.01
	Detroit Red Wings			
417	Richard Pilon	.05	.02	.01
	New York Islanders			
418	Jiri Hrdina	.05	.02	.01
	Pittsburgh Penguins			
419	Clint Malarchuk	.08	.04	.01
	Buffalo Sabres			
420	Steven Rice	.05	.02	.01
	New York Rangers			
421	Mark Janssens	.05	.02	.01
	New York Rangers			
422	Gordie Roberts	.05	.02	.01
	Pittsburgh Penguins			
423	Shawn Cronin	.05	.02	.01
	Winnipeg Jets			
424	Randy Cunneyworth	.05	.02	.01
	Hartford Whalers			
425	Frank Pietrangelo	.05	.02	.01
	Pittsburgh Penguins			
426	David Maley	.05	.02	.01
	New Jersey Devils			
427	Rod Buskas	.05	.02	.01
	Los Angeles Kings			
428	Dennis Vial	.05	.02	.01

□				
	Detroit Red Wings			
429	Kelly Buchberger	.05	.02	.01
	Edmonton Oilers			
430	Wes Walz	.05	.02	.01
	Boston Bruins			
431	Dean Kennedy	.05	.02	.01
	Buffalo Sabres			
432	Nick Kypreos	.05	.02	.01
	Washington Capitals			
433	Stewart Gavin	.05	.02	.01
	Minnesota North Stars			
434	Norm Maciver	.15	.07	.02
	Edmonton Oilers			
435	Mark Pederson	.05	.02	.01
	Philadelphia Flyers			
436	Laurie Boschman	.05	.02	.01
	New Jersey Devils			
437	Stephane Quintal	.05	.02	.01
	Boston Bruins			
438	Darrin Shannon	.05	.02	.01
	Buffalo Sabres			
439	Trent Yawney	.05	.02	.01
	Chicago Blackhawks			
440	Gaetan Duchesne	.05	.02	.01
	Minnesota North Stars			
441	Joe Cirella	.05	.02	.01
	New York Rangers			
442	Doug Houda	.05	.02	.01
	Hartford Whalers			
443	Dave Chyzowski	.05	.02	.01
	New York Islanders			
444	Derrick Smith	.05	.02	.01
	Philadelphia Flyers			
445	Jeff Lazaro	.05	.02	.01
	Boston Bruins			
446	Brian Glynn	.05	.02	.01
	Minnesota North Stars			
447	Jocelyn Lemieux	.05	.02	.01
	Chicago Blackhawks			
448	Peter Taglianetti	.05	.02	.01
	Pittsburgh Penguins			
449	Adam Burt	.05	.02	.01
	Hartford Whalers			
450	Hubie McDonough	.05	.02	.01
	New York Islanders			
451	Kelly Hrudey	.08	.04	.01
	Los Angeles Kings			
452	Dave Poulin	.08	.04	.01
	Boston Bruins			
453	Mark Hardy	.05	.02	.01
	New York Rangers			
454	Mike Hartman	.05	.02	.01
	Buffalo Sabres			
455	Chris Chelios	.08	.04	.01
	Chicago Blackhawks			
456	Alexander Mogilny	.40	.18	.05
	Buffalo Sabres			
457	Bryan Fogarty	.05	.02	.01
	Quebec Nordiques			
458	Adam Oates	.20	.09	.03
	St. Louis Blues			
459	Ron Hextall	.08	.04	.01
	Philadelphia Flyers			
460	Bernie Nicholls	.08	.04	.01
	New York Rangers			
461	Esa Tikkanen	.08	.04	.01
	Edmonton Oilers			
462	Jyrki Lumme	.05	.02	.01
	Vancouver Canucks			
463	Brent Sutter	.08	.04	.01
	New York Islanders			
464	Gary Suter	.08	.04	.01
	Calgary Flames			
465	Sean Burke	.08	.04	.01
	New Jersey Devils			
466	Rob Brown	.05	.02	.01
	Hartford Whalers			
467	Mike Modano	.25	.11	.03
	Minnesota North Stars			
468	Kevin Stevens	.30	.14	.04
	Pittsburgh Penguins			
469	Mike Lalor	.05	.02	.01
	Washington Capitals			
470	Sergei Fedorov	.50	.23	.06
	Detroit Red Wings			
471	Bob Essensa	.08	.04	.01
	Winnipeg Jets			
472	Mark Howe	.08	.04	.01
	Philadelphia Flyers			
473	Craig Janney	.15	.07	.02
	Boston Bruins			
474	Daniel Marois	.05	.02	.01
	Toronto Maple Leafs			
475	Craig Simpson	.08	.04	.01

Edmonton Oilers
☐ 476 Marc Bureau	.05	.02	.01

Minnesota North Stars
☐ 477 Randy Velischek	.05	.02	.01

Quebec Nordiques
☐ 478 Gino Cavallini	.05	.02	.01

St. Louis Blues
☐ 479 Dale Hawerchuk	.08	.04	.01

Buffalo Sabres
☐ 480 Pat LaFontaine	.20	.09	.03

New York Islanders
☐ 481 Kirk McLean	.20	.09	.03

Vancouver Canucks
☐ 482 Murray Craven	.05	.02	.01

Philadelphia Flyers
☐ 483 Robert Reichel	.15	.07	.02

Calgary Flames
☐ 484 Jan Erixon	.05	.02	.01

New York Rangers
☐ 485 Adam Creighton	.05	.02	.01

Chicago Blackhawks
☐ 486 Mark Fitzpatrick	.08	.04	.01

New York Islanders
☐ 487 Ron Francis	.08	.04	.01

Pittsburgh Penguins
☐ 488 Joe Mullen	.10	.05	.01

Pittsburgh Penguins
☐ 489 Peter Zezel	.05	.02	.01

Toronto Maple Leafs
☐ 490 Tomas Sandstrom	.08	.04	.01

Los Angeles Kings
☐ 491 Phil Housley	.08	.04	.01

Winnipeg Jets
☐ 492 Tim Cheveldae	.08	.04	.01

Detroit Red Wings
☐ 493 Glen Wesley	.05	.02	.01

Boston Bruins
☐ 494 Stephan Lebeau	.15	.07	.02

Montreal Canadiens
☐ 495 Dave Ellett	.05	.02	.01

Toronto Maple Leafs
☐ 496 Jeff Brown	.08	.04	.01

St. Louis Blues
☐ 497 Dave Andreychuk	.15	.07	.02

Buffalo Sabres
☐ 498 Steven Finn	.05	.02	.01

Quebec Nordiques
☐ 499 Mike Donnelly	.15	.07	.02

Los Angeles Kings
☐ 500 Neal Broten	.08	.04	.01

Minnesota North Stars
☐ 501 Randy Wood	.05	.02	.01

New York Islanders
☐ 502 Troy Gamble	.05	.02	.01

Vancouver Canucks
☐ 503 Mike Ridley	.08	.04	.01

Washington Capitals
☐ 504 Jamie Macoun	.05	.02	.01

Calgary Flames
☐ 505 Mark Messier	.25	.11	.03

Edmonton Oilers
☐ 506 Moe Mantha	.05	.02	.01

Winnipeg Jets
☐ 507 Scott Young	.05	.02	.01

Pittsburgh Penguins
☐ 508 Robert Dirk	.05	.02	.01

Vancouver Canucks
☐ 509 Brad Shaw	.05	.02	.01

Hartford Whalers
☐ 510 Ed Belfour	.25	.11	.03

Chicago Blackhawks
☐ 511 Larry Robinson	.08	.04	.01

Los Angeles Kings
☐ 512 Dale Kushner	.05	.02	.01

Philadelphia Flyers
☐ 513 Steve Chiasson	.05	.02	.01

Detroit Red Wings
☐ 514 Brian Skrudland	.05	.02	.01

Montreal Canadiens
☐ 515 Pat Elynuik	.05	.02	.01

Winnipeg Jets
☐ 516 Curtis Joseph	.25	.11	.03

St. Louis Blues
☐ 517 Doug Bodger	.05	.02	.01

Buffalo Sabres
☐ 518 Greg Brown	.05	.02	.01

Buffalo Sabres
☐ 519 Joe Murphy	.08	.04	.01

Edmonton Oilers
☐ 520 J.J. Daigneault	.05	.02	.01

Montreal Canadiens
☐ 521 Todd Gill	.05	.02	.01

Toronto Maple Leafs
☐ 522 Troy Loney	.05	.02	.01

Pittsburgh Penguins
☐ 523 Tim Watters	.05	.02	.01

Los Angeles Kings
☐ 524 Jody Hull	.05	.02	.01

New York Rangers
☐ 525 Colin Patterson	.05	.02	.01

Calgary Flames
☐ 526 Darin Kimble	.05	.02	.01

St. Louis Blues
☐ 527 Perry Berezan	.05	.02	.01

Minnesota North Stars
☐ 528 Lee Norwood	.05	.02	.01

New Jersey Devils
☐ 529 Mike Peluso	.05	.02	.01

Chicago Blackhawks
☐ 530 Wayne McBean	.05	.02	.01

New York Islanders
☐ 531 Grant Jennings	.05	.02	.01

Pittsburgh Penguins
☐ 532 Claude Loiselle	.05	.02	.01

Toronto Maple Leafs
☐ 533 Ron Wilson	.05	.02	.01

St. Louis Blues
☐ 534 Phil Sykes	.05	.02	.01

Winnipeg Jets
☐ 535 Jim Wiemer	.05	.02	.01

Boston Bruins
☐ 536 Herb Raglan	.05	.02	.01

Quebec Nordiques
☐ 537 Tim Hunter	.05	.02	.01

Calgary Flames
☐ 538 Mike Tomlak	.05	.02	.01

Hartford Whalers
☐ 539 Greg Gilbert	.05	.02	.01

Chicago Blackhawks
☐ 540 Jiri Latal	.05	.02	.01

Philadelphia Flyers
☐ 541 Bill Berg	.05	.02	.01

New York Islanders
☐ 542 Shane Churla	.05	.02	.01

Minnesota North Stars
☐ 543 Jay Miller	.05	.02	.01

Los Angeles Kings
☐ 544 Pete Peeters	.08	.04	.01

Philadelphia Flyers
☐ 545 Alan May	.05	.02	.01

Washington Capitals
☐ 546 Mario Marois	.05	.02	.01

St. Louis Blues
☐ 547 Jim Kyte	.05	.02	.01

Calgary Flames
☐ 548 Jon Morris	.05	.02	.01

New Jersey Devils
☐ 549 Mikko Makela	.05	.02	.01

Buffalo Sabres
☐ 550 Nelson Emerson	.15	.07	.02

St. Louis Blues
☐ 551 Doug Wilson	.08	.04	.01

San Jose Sharks
☐ 552 Brian Mullen	.08	.04	.01

San Jose Sharks
☐ 553 Kelly Kisio	.05	.02	.01

San Jose Sharks
☐ 554 Brian Hayward	.05	.02	.01

San Jose Sharks
☐ 555 Tony Hrkac	.05	.02	.01

San Jose Sharks
☐ 556 Steve Bozek	.05	.02	.01

San Jose Sharks
☐ 557 John Carter	.05	.02	.01

San Jose Sharks
☐ 558 Neil Wilkinson	.05	.02	.01

San Jose Sharks
☐ 559 Wayne Presley	.05	.02	.01

San Jose Sharks
☐ 560 Bob McGill	.05	.02	.01

San Jose Sharks
☐ 561 Craig Ludwig	.05	.02	.01

Minnesota North Stars
☐ 562 Mikhail Tatarinov	.05	.02	.01

Quebec Nordiques
☐ 563 Todd Elik	.05	.02	.01

Minnesota North Stars
☐ 564 Randy Burridge	.05	.02	.01

Washington Capitals
☐ 565 Tim Kerr	.08	.04	.01

New York Rangers
☐ 566 Randy Gilhen	.05	.02	.01

Los Angeles Kings
☐ 567 John Tonelli	.08	.04	.01

Chicago Blackhawks
☐ 568 Tom Kurvers	.05	.02	.01

New York Islanders
☐ 569 Steve Duchesne	.08	.04	.01

Philadelphia Flyers			
☐ 570 Charlie Huddy	.05	.02	.01
Los Angeles Kings			
☐ 571 Alan Kerr	.05	.02	.01
Detroit Red Wings			
☐ 572 Shawn Chambers	.05	.02	.01
Washington Capitals			
☐ 573 Rob Ramage	.05	.02	.01
Minnesota North Stars			
☐ 574 Steve Kasper	.05	.02	.01
Philadelphia Flyers			
☐ 575 Scott Mellanby	.05	.02	.01
Edmonton Oilers			
☐ 576 Stephen Leach	.05	.02	.01
Boston Bruins			
☐ 577 Scott Niedermayer	.25	.11	.03
New Jersey Devils			
☐ 578 Craig Berube	.05	.02	.01
Toronto Maple Leafs			
☐ 579 Greg Paslawski	.05	.02	.01
Quebec Nordiques			
☐ 580 Randy Hillier	.05	.02	.01
New York Islanders			
☐ 581 Stephane Richer	.08	.04	.01
New Jersey Devils			
☐ 582 Brian MacLellan	.05	.02	.01
Detroit Red Wings			
☐ 583 Marc Habscheid	.05	.02	.01
Calgary Flames			
☐ 584 Dave Babych	.05	.02	.01
Vancouver Canucks			
☐ 585 Troy Murray	.05	.02	.01
Winnipeg Jets			
☐ 586 Ray Sheppard	.08	.04	.01
Detroit Red Wings			
☐ 587 Glen Featherstone	.05	.02	.01
Boston Bruins			
☐ 588 Brendan Shanahan	.25	.11	.03
St. Louis Blues			
☐ 589 Dave Christian	.05	.02	.01
St. Louis Blues			
☐ 590 Mike Bullard	.05	.02	.01
Toronto Maple Leafs			
☐ 591 Ryan Walter	.05	.02	.01
Vancouver Canucks			
☐ 592 Doug Smail	.05	.02	.01
Quebec Nordiques			
☐ 593 Paul Fenton	.05	.02	.01
Hartford Whalers			
☐ 594 Adam Graves	.25	.11	.03
New York Rangers			
☐ 595 Scott Stevens	.10	.05	.01
New Jersey Devils			
☐ 596 Sylvain Cote	.05	.02	.01
Washington Capitals			
☐ 597 Dave Barr	.05	.02	.01
New Jersey Devils			
☐ 598 Randy Gregg	.05	.02	.01
Vancouver Canucks			
☐ 599 Allen Pedersen	.05	.02	.01
Minnesota North Stars			
☐ 600 Jari Kurri	.10	.05	.01
Los Angeles Kings			
☐ 601 Troy Mallette	.05	.02	.01
Edmonton Oilers			
☐ 602 Troy Crowder	.05	.02	.01
Detroit Red Wings			
☐ 603 Brad Jones	.05	.02	.01
Philadelphia Flyers			
☐ 604 Randy McKay	.05	.02	.01
New Jersey Devils			
☐ 605 Scott Thornton	.05	.02	.01
Edmonton Oilers			
☐ 606 Bryan Marchment	.10	.05	.01
Chicago Blackhawks			
☐ 607 Andrew Cassels	.08	.04	.01
Hartford Whalers			
☐ 608 Grant Fuhr	.08	.04	.01
Toronto Maple Leafs			
☐ 609 Vincent Damphousse	.08	.04	.01
Edmonton Oilers			
☐ 610 Robert Ray	.05	.02	.01
Buffalo Sabres			
☐ 611 Glenn Anderson	.08	.04	.01
Toronto Maple Leafs			
☐ 612 Peter Ing	.05	.02	.01
Edmonton Oilers			
☐ 613 Tom Chorske	.05	.02	.01
New Jersey Devils			
☐ 614 Kirk Muller	.08	.04	.01
Montreal Canadiens			
☐ 615 Dan Quinn	.05	.02	.01
Philadelphia Flyers			
☐ 616 Murray Baron	.05	.02	.01

St. Louis Blues			
☐ 617 Sergei Nemchinov	.15	.07	.02
New York Rangers			
☐ 618 Rod Brind'Amour	.15	.07	.02
Philadelphia Flyers			
☐ 619 Ron Sutter	.05	.02	.01
St. Louis Blues			
☐ 620 Luke Richardson	.05	.02	.01
Edmonton Oilers			
☐ 621 Nicklas Lidstrom	.35	.16	.04
Detroit Red Wings			
☐ 622 Ken Linseman	.05	.02	.01
Toronto Maple Leafs			
☐ 623 Steve Smith	.08	.04	.01
Chicago Blackhawks			
☐ 624 Dave Manson	.08	.04	.01
Edmonton Oilers			
☐ 625 Kay Whitmore	.05	.02	.01
Hartford Whalers			
☐ 626 Jeff Chychrun	.05	.02	.01
Los Angeles Kings			
☐ 627 Russ Romaniuk	.10	.05	.01
Winnipeg Jets			
☐ 628 Brad May	.08	.04	.01
Buffalo Sabres			
☐ 629 Tomas Forslund	.05	.02	.01
Calgary Flames			
☐ 630 Stu Barnes	.08	.04	.01
Winnipeg Jets			
☐ 631 Daryl Sydor	.08	.04	.01
Los Angeles Kings			
☐ 632 Jimmy Waite	.08	.04	.01
Chicago Blackhawks			
☐ 633 Peter Douris	.05	.02	.01
Boston Bruins			
☐ 634 Dave Brown	.05	.02	.01
Philadelphia Flyers			
☐ 635 Mark Messier	.25	.11	.03
New York Rangers			
☐ 636 Neil Sheehy	.05	.02	.01
Calgary Flames			
☐ 637 Todd Krygier	.05	.02	.01
Washington Capitals			
☐ 638 Stephane Beauregard	.05	.02	.01
Winnipeg Jets			
☐ 639 Barry Pederson	.05	.02	.01
Hartford Whalers			
☐ 640 Pat Falloon	.35	.16	.04
San Jose Sharks			
☐ 641 Dean Evason	.05	.02	.01
San Jose Sharks			
☐ 642 Jeff Hackett	.05	.02	.01
San Jose Sharks			
☐ 643 Rob Zettler	.05	.02	.01
San Jose Sharks			
☐ 644 David Bruce	.05	.02	.01
San Jose Sharks			
☐ 645 Pat MacLeod	.05	.02	.01
San Jose Sharks			
☐ 646 Craig Coxe	.05	.02	.01
San Jose Sharks			
☐ 647 Ken Hammond	.05	.02	.01
San Jose Sharks			
☐ 648 Brian Lawton	.05	.02	.01
San Jose Sharks			
☐ 649 Perry Anderson	.05	.02	.01
San Jose Sharks			
☐ 650 Kevin Evans	.05	.02	.01
San Jose Sharks			
☐ 651 Mike McHugh	.05	.02	.01
San Jose Sharks			
☐ 652 Mark Lamb	.05	.02	.01
Edmonton Oilers			
☐ 653 Darcy Wakaluk	.30	.14	.04
Minnesota North Stars			
☐ 654 Pat Conacher	.05	.02	.01
New Jersey Devils			
☐ 655 Martin Lapointe	.05	.02	.01
Detroit Red Wings			
☐ 656 Derian Hatcher	.08	.04	.01
Minnesota North Stars			
☐ 657 Bryan Erickson	.05	.02	.01
Winnipeg Jets			
☐ 658 Ken Priestlay	.05	.02	.01
Pittsburgh Penguins			
☐ 659 Vladimir Konstantinov	.15	.07	.02
Detroit Red Wings			
☐ 660 Andrei Lomakin	.05	.02	.01
Philadelphia Flyers			

1991-92 Score Bobby Orr

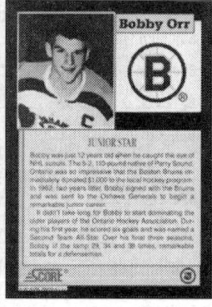

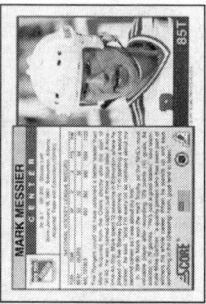

This six-card set highlights the career of Bobby Orr, one of hockey's all-time greats. The cards measure the standard size (2 1/2" by 3 1/2") and were inserted in 1991-92 Score hockey poly packs. Cards 1 and 2 were inserted in both American and Canadian editions. Cards 3 and 4 were inserted in Canadian packs, while cards 5 and 6 were inserted in American packs. On a black card face, the fronts feature color player photos enclosed by a thin red border and accented by yellow borders on three sides. The backs carry a close-up color photo and biographical comments on Orr's career. The cards are not numbered on the back. It is claimed that 270,000 of these Orr cards were produced, and that Orr personally signed 2,500 of each of these cards. The personally autographed cards are autographed on the card back and not individually numbered or certified. They are slightly different in design.

	MINT	EXC	G-VG
COMPLETE SET (6)	50.00	23.00	6.25
COMMON BOBBY ORR (1-6)	9.00	4.00	1.15
☐ 1 Bobby Orr	9.00	4.00	1.15
Junior Star			
☐ 2 Bobby Orr	9.00	4.00	1.15
Scoring Leader			
☐ 3 Bobby Orr	9.00	4.00	1.15
Hall of Famer			
(Issued in Canadian			
Bilingual packs)			
☐ 4 Bobby Orr	9.00	4.00	1.15
Hall of Famer			
(Issued in Canadian			
Bilingual packs)			
☐ 5 Bobby Orr	9.00	4.00	1.15
The Rookie			
(Found only in			
American English packs)			
☐ 6 Bobby Orr	9.00	4.00	1.15
Award Winner			
(Found only in			
American English packs)			
☐ AU Bobby Orr	300.00	135.00	38.00
(Autographed card)			

1991-92 Score Rookie/Traded

The 1991-92 Score Rookie and Traded hockey set contains 110 standard-size (2 1/2" by 3 1/2") cards. It was issued only as a factory set. As one moves down the card face, the fronts shade from dark green to white. The color action player photo is enclosed by an thin red border, with a shadow border on the right and below. At the card top, the player's name is written over a hockey puck, and the team name is printed below the picture in the lower right corner. A dark green border stripe at the bottom rounds out the

front. In a horizontal format, the backs present biography, statistics, player profile, and a color close-up photo. The cards are numbered on the back with a "T" suffix. The set includes Eric Lindros pictured in his World Junior uniform. The back of the set's custom box contains the set checklist. The key Rookie Cards in this set are Valeri Kamensky and Nicklas Lidstrom.

	MINT	EXC	G-VG
COMPLETE SET (110)	7.00	3.10	.85
COMMON PLAYER (1T-110T)	.05	.02	.01
☐ 1T Doug Wilson	.08	.04	.01
San Jose Sharks			
☐ 2T Brian Mullen	.08	.04	.01
San Jose Sharks			
☐ 3T Kelly Kisio	.05	.02	.01
San Jose Sharks			
☐ 4T Brian Hayward	.05	.02	.01
San Jose Sharks			
☐ 5T Tony Hrkac	.05	.02	.01
San Jose Sharks			
☐ 6T Steve Bozek	.05	.02	.01
San Jose Sharks			
☐ 7T John Carter	.05	.02	.01
San Jose Sharks			
☐ 8T Neil Wilkinson	.05	.02	.01
San Jose Sharks			
☐ 9T Wayne Presley	.05	.02	.01
San Jose Sharks			
☐ 10T Bob McGill	.05	.02	.01
San Jose Sharks			
☐ 11T Craig Ludwig	.05	.02	.01
Minnesota North Stars			
☐ 12T Mikhail Tatarinov	.05	.02	.01
Quebec Nordiques			
☐ 13T Todd Elik	.05	.02	.01
Minnesota North Stars			
☐ 14T Randy Burridge	.05	.02	.01
Washington Capitals			
☐ 15T Tim Kerr	.08	.04	.01
New York Rangers			
☐ 16T Randy Gilhen	.05	.02	.01
Los Angeles Kings			
☐ 17T John Tonelli	.08	.04	.01
Chicago Blackhawks			
☐ 18T Tom Kurvers	.05	.02	.01
New York Islanders			
☐ 19T Steve Duchesne	.08	.04	.01
Philadelphia Flyers			
☐ 20T Charlie Huddy	.05	.02	.01
Los Angeles Kings			
☐ 21T Adam Creighton	.05	.02	.01
New York Islanders			
☐ 22T Brent Ashton	.05	.02	.01
Boston Bruins			
☐ 23T Rob Ramage	.05	.02	.01
Minnesota North Stars			
☐ 24T Steve Kasper	.05	.02	.01
Philadelphia Flyers			
☐ 25T Scott Mellanby	.05	.02	.01
Edmonton Oilers			
☐ 26T Stephen Leach	.05	.02	.01
Boston Bruins			
☐ 27T Scott Niedermayer	.25	.11	.03
New Jersey Devils			
☐ 28T Craig Berube	.05	.02	.01
Toronto Maple Leafs			
☐ 29T Greg Paslawski	.05	.02	.01
Quebec Nordiques			
☐ 30T Randy Hillier	.05	.02	.01

Buffalo Sabres
☐ 31T Stephane Richer..............	.08	.04	.01

New Jersey Devils
☐ 32T Brian MacLellan	.05	.02	.01

Detroit Red Wings
☐ 33T Marc Habscheid	.05	.02	.01

Calgary Flames
☐ 34T Dave Babych	.05	.02	.01

Vancouver Canucks
☐ 35T Troy Murray	.05	.02	.01

Winnipeg Jets
☐ 36T Ray Sheppard	.08	.04	.01

Detroit Red Wings
☐ 37T Glen Featherstone	.05	.02	.01

Boston Bruins
☐ 38T Brendan Shanahan	.25	.11	.03

St. Louis Blues
☐ 39T Dave Christian..................	.05	.02	.01

St. Louis Blues
☐ 40T Mike Bullard	.05	.02	.01

Toronto Maple Leafs
☐ 41T Ryan Walter	.05	.02	.01

Vancouver Canucks
☐ 42T Randy Wood	.05	.02	.01

Buffalo Sabres
☐ 43T Vincent Riendeau	.05	.02	.01

Detroit Red Wings
☐ 44T Adam Graves...................	.25	.11	.03

New York Rangers
☐ 45T Scott Stevens....................	.10	.05	.01

New Jersey Devils
☐ 46T Sylvain Cote	.05	.02	.01

Washington Capitals
☐ 47T Dave Barr	.05	.02	.01

New Jersey Devils
☐ 48T Randy Gregg	.05	.02	.01

Vancouver Canucks
☐ 49T Pavel Bure	2.50	1.15	.30

Vancouver Canucks
☐ 50T Jari Kurri	.10	.05	.01

Los Angeles Kings
☐ 51T Steve Thomas	.08	.04	.01

New York Islanders
☐ 52T Troy Crowder	.05	.02	.01

Detroit Red Wings
☐ 53T Brad Jones	.05	.02	.01

Philadelphia Flyers
☐ 54T Randy McKay	.05	.02	.01

New Jersey Devils
☐ 55T Scott Thornton	.05	.02	.01

Edmonton Oilers
☐ 56T Bryan Marchment	.05	.02	.01

Chicago Blackhawks
☐ 57T Andrew Cassels.................	.08	.04	.01

Hartford Whalers
☐ 58T Grant Fuhr.......................	.08	.04	.01

Toronto Maple Leafs
☐ 59T Vincent Damphousse	.08	.04	.01

Edmonton Oilers
☐ 60T Rick Zombo......................	.05	.02	.01

St. Louis Blues
☐ 61T Glenn Anderson	.08	.04	.01

Toronto Maple Leafs
☐ 62T Peter Ing	.05	.02	.01

Edmonton Oilers
☐ 63T Tom Chorske....................	.05	.02	.01

New Jersey Devils
☐ 64T Kirk Muller	.08	.04	.01

Montreal Canadiens
☐ 65T Dan Quinn........................	.05	.02	.01

Philadelphia Flyers
☐ 66T Murray Baron	.05	.02	.01

St. Louis Blues
☐ 67T Sergei Nemchinov.............	.15	.07	.02

New York Rangers
☐ 68T Rod Brind'Amour	.15	.07	.02

Philadelphia Flyers
☐ 69T Ron Sutter.......................	.05	.02	.01

St. Louis Blues
☐ 70T Luke Richardson	.05	.02	.01

Edmonton Oilers
☐ 71T Nicklas Lidstrom	.35	.16	.04

Detroit Red Wings
☐ 72T Petri Skriko	.05	.02	.01

Winnipeg Jets
☐ 73T Steve Smith.....................	.08	.04	.01

Chicago Blackhawks
☐ 74T Dave Manson	.08	.04	.01

Edmonton Oilers
☐ 75T Kay Whitmore	.05	.02	.01

Hartford Whalers
☐ 76T Valeri Kamensky	.35	.16	.04

Quebec Nordiques
☐ 77T Russ Romaniuk..................	.10	.05	.01

Winnipeg Jets
☐ 78T Brad May...........................	.08	.04	.01

Buffalo Sabres
☐ 79T Tomas Forslund	.05	.02	.01

Calgary Flames
☐ 80T Stu Barnes	.08	.04	.01

Winnipeg Jets
☐ 81T Daryl Sydor.......................	.08	.04	.01

Los Angeles Kings
☐ 82T Jimmy Waite	.08	.04	.01

Chicago Blackhawks
☐ 83T Vladimir Ruzicka	.05	.02	.01

Boston Bruins
☐ 84T Dave Brown.......................	.05	.02	.01

Philadelphia Flyers
☐ 85T Mark Messier	.30	.14	.04

New York Rangers
☐ 86T Neil Sheehy......................	.05	.02	.01

Calgary Flames
☐ 87T Todd Krygier	.05	.02	.01

Washington Capitals
☐ 88T Eric Lindros......................	3.00	1.35	.40

Team Canada
☐ 89T Nelson Emerson................	.20	.09	.03

St. Louis Blues
☐ 90T Pat Falloon	.35	.16	.04

San Jose Sharks
☐ 91T Dean Evason	.05	.02	.01

San Jose Sharks
☐ 92T Jeff Hackett......................	.05	.02	.01

San Jose Sharks
☐ 93T Rob Zettler.......................	.05	.02	.01

San Jose Sharks
☐ 94T Perry Berezan....................	.05	.02	.01

San Jose Sharks
☐ 95T Pat MacLeod	.05	.02	.01

San Jose Sharks
☐ 96T Craig Coxe.......................	.05	.02	.01

San Jose Sharks
☐ 97T Ken Hammond	.05	.02	.01

San Jose Sharks
☐ 98T Brian Lawton.....................	.05	.02	.01

San Jose Sharks
☐ 99T Perry Anderson	.05	.02	.01

San Jose Sharks
☐ 100T Pat LaFontaine	.20	.09	.03

Buffalo Sabres
☐ 101T Pierre Turgeon	.20	.09	.03

New York Islanders
☐ 102T Dave McLlwain.................	.05	.02	.01

New York Islanders
☐ 103T Brent Sutter.....................	.08	.04	.01

Chicago Blackhawks
☐ 104T Uwe Krupp	.05	.02	.01

New York Islanders
☐ 105T Martin Lapointe................	.05	.02	.01

Detroit Red Wings
☐ 106T Derian Hatcher	.08	.04	.01

Minnesota North Stars
☐ 107T Darrin Shannon	.05	.02	.01

Winnipeg Jets
☐ 108T Benoit Hogue	.05	.02	.01

New York Islanders
☐ 109T Vladimir Konstantinov.......	.15	.07	.02

Detroit Red Wings
☐ 110T Andrei Lomakin................	.05	.02	.01

Philadelphia Flyers

1991-92 Score Eric Lindros

This three-card set was produced by Score and distributed in a cello pack with the first printing of Eric Lindros' autobiography "Fire on Ice". The standard-size (2 1/2" by 3 1/2") cards feature on the fronts color photos that capture three different moments in Lindros' life (childhood, adolescence, and NHL Entry Draft). The pictures are bordered on all sides by light blue, with the player's name in block lettering between two red stripes at the card top. A red stripe at the bottom separates the picture from its title line. The backs have relevant biographical comments as well as a second color photo. The cards are unnumbered and checklisted below in chronological order.

	MINT	EXC	G-VG
COMPLETE SET (3)..........................	15.00	6.00	1.50
COMMON LINDROS (1-3).................	6.00	2.40	.60
☐ 1 Eric Lindros.............................	6.00	2.40	.60
A Real Corker			
(Baby on skates)			
☐ 2 Eric Lindros.............................	7.50	3.00	.75
A Little Bit of Heaven			
(With brother Brett in			
Minor hockey sweaters)			
☐ 3 Eric Lindros.............................	6.00	2.40	.60
Graduation Day			
(Nordique sweater			
in background)			

1991-92 Score Hot Cards

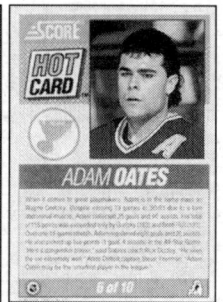

The 1991-92 Score Hot cards were inserted in American and Canadian English 100-card blister packs at a rate of one per pack. The standard size (2 1/2" by 3 1/2") cards feature on the fronts color action player photos bordered in bright red. Thin yellow stripes accent the photos, and the player's name appears beneath the picture in a purple stripe. The back design reflects the same three colors as the front and features a color head shot, team logo, and player profile. The cards are numbered on the back. Hot Cards differ in design, photos, and text from the regular issues.

	MINT	EXC	G-VG
COMPLETE SET (10).......................	30.00	13.50	3.80
COMMON PLAYER (1-10)................	1.50	.65	.19
☐ 1 Eric Lindros.............................	15.00	6.75	1.90
☐ 2 Wayne Gretzky	10.00	4.50	1.25
☐ 3 Brett Hull	3.50	1.55	.45
☐ 4 Sergei Fedorov	6.00	2.70	.75
☐ 5 Mario Lemieux	6.00	2.70	.75
☐ 6 Adam Oates.............................	2.00	.90	.25
☐ 7 Theoren Fleury	1.50	.65	.19
☐ 8 Jaromir Jagr	3.50	1.55	.45
☐ 9 Ed Belfour	2.00	.90	.25
☐ 10 Jeremy Roenick	4.00	1.80	.50

1991-92 Score Young Superstars

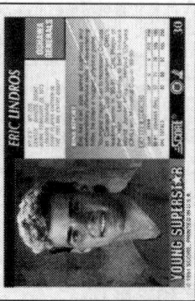

This 40-card standard-size (2 1/2" by 3 1/2") set was issued by Score to showcase some of the leading young hockey players. The color action player photos on the fronts are framed in green on a card face consisting of blended diagonal taupe stripes. In a horizontal format, the backs have a color head shot on the left half while the right half carries biography, "Rink Report," and career statistics. The cards are numbered on the back.

	MINT	EXC	G-VG
COMPLETE SET (40).......................	7.50	3.00	.75
COMMON PLAYER (1-40)................	.10	.04	.01
☐ 1 Sergei Fedorov	1.00	.40	.10
Detroit Red Wings			
☐ 2 Mike Richter............................	.35	.14	.03
New York Rangers			
☐ 3 Mats Sundin............................	.40	.16	.04
Quebec Nordiques			
☐ 4 Theoren Fleury	.20	.08	.02
Calgary Flames			
☐ 5 John Cullen.............................	.15	.06	.01
Hartford Whalers			
☐ 6 Dimitri Khristich......................	.20	.08	.02
Washington Capitals			
☐ 7 Stephan Lebeau	.25	.10	.02
Montreal Canadiens			
☐ 8 Rob Blake	.25	.10	.02
Los Angeles Kings			
☐ 9 Ken Hodge Jr.	.10	.04	.01
Boston Bruins			
☐ 10 Mike Ricci	.25	.10	.02
Philadelphia Flyers			
☐ 11 Trevor Linden........................	.35	.14	.03
Vancouver Canucks			
☐ 12 Peter Ing..............................	.10	.04	.01
Edmonton Oilers			
☐ 13 Alexander Mogilny	.75	.30	.07
Buffalo Sabres			
☐ 14 Martin Gelinas......................	.15	.06	.01
Edmonton Oilers			
☐ 15 Chris Terreri	.25	.10	.02
New Jersey Devils			
☐ 16 Jeff Norton...........................	.10	.04	.01
New York Islanders			
☐ 17 Bob Essensa	.15	.06	.01
Winnipeg Jets			
☐ 18 Mark Tinordi	.10	.04	.01
Minnesota North Stars			
☐ 19 Curtis Joseph.......................	.50	.20	.05
St. Louis Blues			
☐ 20 Joe Sakic.............................	.40	.16	.04
Quebec Nordiques			
☐ 21 Jeremy Roenick	1.00	.40	.10
Chicago Blackhawks			
☐ 22 Mark Recchi	.50	.20	.05
Pittsburgh Penguins			
☐ 23 Eric Desjardins......................	.15	.06	.01
Montreal Canadiens			
☐ 24 Robert Reichel	.35	.14	.03
Calgary Flames			
☐ 25 Tim Cheveldae.......................	.25	.10	.02
Detroit Red Wings			
☐ 26 Eric Weinrich........................	.10	.04	.01
New Jersey Devils			
☐ 27 Murray Baron........................	.10	.04	.01

	St. Louis Blues			
☐ 28	Darren Turcotte	.15	.06	.01
	New York Rangers			
☐ 29	Troy Gamble	.15	.06	.01
	Vancouver Canucks			
☐ 30	Eric Lindros	3.00	1.20	.30
	Oshawa Generals			
☐ 31	Benoit Hogue	.20	.08	.02
	Buffalo Sabres			
☐ 32	Ed Belfour	.60	.24	.06
	Chicago Blackhawks			
☐ 33	Ron Tugnutt	.20	.08	.02
	Quebec Nordiques			
☐ 34	Pat Elynuik	.15	.06	.01
	Winnipeg Jets			
☐ 35	Mike Modano	.50	.20	.05
	Minnesota North Stars			
☐ 36	Bobby Holik	.25	.10	.02
	Hartford Whalers			
☐ 37	Yves Racine	.10	.04	.01
	Detroit Red Wings			
☐ 38	Jaromir Jagr	1.00	.40	.10
	Pittsburgh Penguins			
☐ 39	Stephane Morin	.10	.04	.01
	Quebec Nordiques			
☐ 40	Kevin Miller	.15	.06	.01
	Detroit Red Wings			

☐ 17	Petr Klima	.75	.30	.07
☐ 18	Ed Olczyk	.75	.30	.07
☐ 19	Doug Wilson	.75	.30	.07
☐ 20	Trevor Linden	1.50	.60	.15
☐ 21	Brett Hull	3.00	1.20	.30
☐ 22	Rob Blake	1.00	.40	.10
☐ 23	Dave Ellett	.75	.30	.07
☐ 24	Cornelius Rooster SP	5.00	2.00	.50
	Kellogg's Corn Flakes Rooster			
☐ xx	Card Binder	3.00	1.20	.30

1992-93 Score

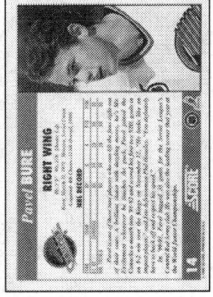

1991-92 Score Kellogg's

This 24-card standard-size (2 1/2" by 3 1/2") set was produced by Score as a promotion for Kellogg's Canada. Two-card foil packs were inserted in specially marked 675-gram Kellogg's Corn Flakes cereals. The side panel of the cereal boxes presented a mail-in offer for the complete set and a card binder for 5.99 plus three proof of purchase tokens (one token featured per side panel). Card fronts have player action photos enclosed in a small red border, player's name in white reverse-out lettering, and team logo in bottom portion of the purple border. Card backs, also in purple, red, and white, carry the card number, Kellogg's Limited Edition Collector's Set logo, biography, statistics, and player profile in English and French.

	MINT	EXC	G-VG
COMPLETE SET (24)	30.00	12.00	3.00
COMMON PLAYER (1-24)	.75	.30	.07

☐ 1	Patrick Roy	4.00	1.60	.40
☐ 2	Rick Tocchet	1.25	.50	.12
☐ 3	Wendel Clark	1.50	.60	.15
☐ 4	Mike Modano	1.50	.60	.15
☐ 5	Jeremy Roenick	3.00	1.20	.30
☐ 6	Pierre Turgeon	1.50	.60	.15
☐ 7	Kevin Hatcher	.75	.30	.07
☐ 8	Brian Leetch	1.50	.60	.15
☐ 9	Mark Recchi	1.50	.60	.15
☐ 10	Andy Moog	1.00	.40	.10
☐ 11	Kevin Dineen	.75	.30	.07
☐ 12	Joe Sakic	1.25	.50	.12
☐ 13	John MacLean	.75	.30	.07
☐ 14	Steve Yzerman	2.00	.80	.20
☐ 15	Pat LaFontaine	1.50	.60	.15
☐ 16	Al MacInnis	1.25	.50	.12

The 1992-93 Score hockey set contains 550 cards measuring the standard size (2 1/2" by 3 1/2"). The American and Canadian sets are identical in terms of player selection (except for card numbers 548-549) but feature different insert subsets (USA Greats in the American and Canadian Olympic Heroes in the Canadian). Moreover, the player photos and card design differ in each set. In the American set, the color action photos on the fronts have two-toned borders on three sides (icy gray diagonal stripes accented by either red, blue, or black); in the Canadian, the front borders are metallic blue with diagonally varnished stripes. The American backs are horizontally oriented and include biography, statistics, career summary, and a close-up photo; the Canadian backs are vertically oriented, bilingual, and have the same features in a different layout. Special subsets featured include Season Leaders (411-418), Franchise Players (419-440), Season Highlights (441-448), Top Prospects (449-488), Dream Team (489-500), Rookie Dream Team (501-506), Tampa Bay Lightning (507-511), Ottawa Senators (512-516), and Award Winners (519-527). The cards are numbered on the back. The notable Rookie Card in the set is Guy Hebert. A special Eric Lindros card, unnumbered and featuring his first photo in a Philadelphia Flyers uniform, was randomly inserted into packs. Reportedly more than 500 of these special Lindros "Press Conference" cards were given away to news media, members of the Flyers organization, and other guests attending the July 15 news conference which marked Lindros' signing with the Flyers. It is claimed that the odds of finding one of these cards are no less than one in 500 packs.

	MINT	EXC	G-VG
COMPLETE SET (550)	20.00	9.00	2.50
COMMON PLAYER (1-550)	.05	.02	.01
*AMERICAN AND CANADIAN: SAME VALUE			

☐ 1	Wayne Gretzky	1.00	.45	.13
	Los Angeles Kings			
☐ 2	Chris Chelios	.08	.04	.01
	Chicago Blackhawks			

☐ 3	Joe Mullen	.08	.04	.01
	Pittsburgh Penguins			
☐ 4	Russ Courtnall	.08	.04	.01
	Montreal Canadiens			
☐ 5	Mike Richter	.25	.11	.03
	New York Rangers			
☐ 6	Pat LaFontaine	.20	.09	.03
	Buffalo Sabres			
☐ 7	Mark Tinordi	.08	.04	.01
	Minnesota North Stars			
☐ 8	Claude Lemieux	.08	.04	.01
	New Jersey Devils			
☐ 9	Jimmy Carson	.05	.02	.01
	Detroit Red Wings			
☐ 10	Cam Neely	.08	.04	.01
	Boston Bruins			
☐ 11	Al Iafrate	.08	.04	.01
	Washington Capitals			
☐ 12	Steve Thomas	.08	.04	.01
	New York Islanders			
☐ 13	Fredrik Olausson	.05	.02	.01
	Winnipeg Jets			
☐ 14	Pavel Bure	1.00	.45	.13
	Vancouver Canucks			
☐ 15	Doug Wilson	.08	.04	.01
	San Jose Sharks			
☐ 16	Esa Tikkanen	.08	.04	.01
	Edmonton Oilers			
☐ 17	Gary Suter	.08	.04	.01
	Calgary Flames			
☐ 18	Murray Craven	.05	.02	.01
	Hartford Whalers			
☐ 19	Garry Galley	.05	.02	.01
	Philadelphia Flyers			
☐ 20	Grant Fuhr	.08	.04	.01
	Toronto Maple Leafs			
☐ 21	Craig Wolanin	.05	.02	.01
	Quebec Nordiques			
☐ 22	Paul Cavallini	.05	.02	.01
	St. Louis Blues			
☐ 23	Eric Desjardins	.05	.02	.01
	Montreal Canadiens			
☐ 24	Joe Kocur	.05	.02	.01
	New York Rangers			
☐ 25	Kevin Stevens	.20	.09	.03
	Pittsburgh Penguins			
☐ 26	Marty McSorley	.08	.04	.01
	Los Angeles Kings			
☐ 27	Dirk Graham	.05	.02	.01
	Chicago Blackhawks			
☐ 28	Mike Ramsey	.05	.02	.01
	Buffalo Sabres			
☐ 29	Gord Murphy	.05	.02	.01
	Boston Bruins			
☐ 30	John MacLean	.08	.04	.01
	New Jersey Devils			
☐ 31	Vladimir Konstantinov	.05	.02	.01
	Detroit Red Wings			
☐ 32	Neal Broten	.08	.04	.01
	Minnesota North Stars			
☐ 33	Dimitri Khristich	.08	.04	.01
	Washington Capitals			
☐ 34	Gerald Diduck	.05	.02	.01
	Vancouver Canucks			
☐ 35	Ken Baumgartner	.05	.02	.01
	Toronto Maple Leafs			
☐ 36	Darrin Shannon	.05	.02	.01
	Winnipeg Jets			
☐ 37	Steve Bozek	.05	.02	.01
	San Jose Sharks			
☐ 38	Michel Petit	.05	.02	.01
	Calgary Flames			
☐ 39	Kevin Lowe	.05	.02	.01
	Edmonton Oilers			
☒ 40	Doug Gilmour	.08	.04	.01
	Toronto Maple Leafs			
☐ 41	Peter Sidorkiewicz	.05	.02	.01
	Hartford Whalers			
☐ 42	Gino Cavallini	.05	.02	.01
	Quebec Nordiques			
☐ 43	Dan Quinn	.25	.11	.03
	Philadelphia Flyers			
☐ 44	Steven Finn	.05	.02	.01
	Quebec Nordiques			
☐ 45	Larry Murphy	.08	.04	.01
	Pittsburgh Penguins			
☐ 46	Brent Gilchrist	.05	.02	.01
	Montreal Canadiens			
☐ 47	Daren Puppa	.08	.04	.01
	Buffalo Sabres			
☐ 48	Steve Smith	.08	.04	.01
	Chicago Blackhawks			
☐ 49	Dave Taylor	.08	.04	.01

	Los Angeles Kings			
☐ 50	Mike Gartner	.10	.05	.01
	New York Rangers			
☐ 51	Derian Hatcher	.05	.02	.01
	Minnesota North Stars			
☐ 52	Bob Probert	.05	.02	.01
	Detroit Red Wings			
☐ 53	Ken Daneyko	.05	.02	.01
	New Jersey Devils			
☐ 54	Steve Leach	.05	.02	.01
	Boston Bruins			
☐ 55	Kelly Miller	.05	.02	.01
	Washington Capitals			
☐ 56	Jeff Norton	.05	.02	.01
	New York Islanders			
☐ 57	Kelly Kisio	.05	.02	.01
	San Jose Sharks			
☐ 58	Igor Larionov	.08	.04	.01
	Vancouver Canucks			
☐ 59	Paul MacDermid	.05	.02	.01
	Washington Capitals			
☐ 60	Mike Vernon	.08	.04	.01
	Calgary Flames			
☐ 61	Randy Ladouceur	.05	.02	.01
	Hartford Whalers			
☐ 62	Luke Richardson	.05	.02	.01
	Edmonton Oilers			
☐ 63	Daniel Marois	.05	.02	.01
	New York Islanders			
☐ 64	Mike Hough	.05	.02	.01
	Quebec Nordiques			
☐ 65	Garth Butcher	.05	.02	.01
	St. Louis Blues			
☐ 66	Terry Carkner	.05	.02	.01
	Philadelphia Flyers			
☐ 67	Mike Donnelly	.05	.02	.01
	Los Angeles Kings			
☐ 68	Keith Brown	.05	.02	.01
	Chicago Blackhawks			
☐ 69	Mathieu Schneider	.08	.04	.01
	Montreal Canadiens			
☐ 70	Tom Barrasso	.08	.04	.01
	Pittsburgh Penguins			
☐ 71	Adam Graves	.05	.02	.01
	New York Rangers			
☐ 72	Brian Propp	.08	.04	.01
	Minnesota North Stars			
☐ 73	Randy Wood	.05	.02	.01
	Buffalo Sabres			
☐ 74	Yves Racine	.05	.02	.01
	Detroit Red Wings			
☐ 75	Scott Stevens	.25	.11	.03
	New Jersey Devils			
☐ 76	Chris Nilan	.08	.04	.01
	Montreal Canadiens			
☐ 77	Uwe Krupp	.05	.02	.01
	New York Islanders			
☐ 78	Sylvain Cote	.05	.02	.01
	Washington Capitals			
☐ 79	Sergio Momesso	.05	.02	.01
	Vancouver Canucks			
☐ 80	Thomas Steen	.05	.02	.01
	Winnipeg Jets			
☐ 81	Craig Muni	.05	.02	.01
	Edmonton Oilers			
☐ 82	Jeff Hackett	.05	.02	.01
	San Jose Sharks			
☐ 83	Frantisek Musil	.05	.02	.01
	Calgary Flames			
☐ 84	Mike Ricci	.08	.04	.01
	Philadelphia Flyers			
☐ 85	Brad Shaw	.05	.02	.01
	Hartford Whalers			
☐ 86	Ron Sutter	.05	.02	.01
	St. Louis Blues			
☐ 87	Curtis Leschyshyn	.05	.02	.01
	Quebec Nordiques			
☐ 88	Jamie Macoun	.05	.02	.01
	Toronto Maple Leafs			
☐ 89	Brian Noonan	.05	.02	.01
	Chicago Blackhawks			
☐ 90	Ulf Samuelsson	.08	.04	.01
	Pittsburgh Penguins			
☐ 91	Mike McPhee	.05	.02	.01
	Montreal Canadiens			
☐ 92	Charlie Huddy	.05	.02	.01
	Los Angeles Kings			
☐ 93	Tim Kerr	.08	.04	.01
	New York Rangers			
☐ 94	Craig Ludwig	.05	.02	.01
	Minnesota North Stars			
☐ 95	Paul Ysebaert	.05	.02	.01
	Detroit Red Wings			
☐ 96	Brad May	.05	.02	.01

Buffalo Sabres				
☐ 97 Viacheslav Fetisov	.05	.02	.01
New Jersey Devils				
☐ 98 Todd Krygier	.05	.02	.01
Washington Capitals				
☐ 99 Patrick Flatley	.05	.02	.01
New York Islanders				
☐ 100 Ray Bourque	.15	.07	.02
Boston Bruins				
☐ 101 Petr Nedved	.10	.05	.01
Vancouver Canucks				
☐ 102 Teppo Numminen	.05	.02	.01
Winnipeg Jets				
☐ 103 Dean Evason	.05	.02	.01
San Jose Sharks				
☐ 104 Ron Hextall	.08	.04	.01
Philadelphia Flyers				
☐ 105 Josef Beranek	.15	.07	.02
Edmonton Oilers				
☐ 106 Robert Reichel	.08	.04	.01
Calgary Flames				
☐ 107 Mikhail Tatarinov	.05	.02	.01
Quebec Nordiques				
☐ 108 Geoff Sanderson	.30	.14	.04
Hartford Whalers				
☐ 109 Dave Lowry	.05	.02	.01
St. Louis Blues				
☐ 110 Wendel Clark	.10	.05	.01
Toronto Maple Leafs				
☐ 111 Corey Millen UER	.08	.04	.01
Los Angeles Kings				
(Mike Donnelly pictured on front)				
☐ 112 Brent Sutter	.08	.04	.01
Chicago Blackhawks				
☐ 113 Jaromir Jagr	.50	.23	.06
Pittsburgh Penguins				
☐ 114 Petr Svoboda	.05	.02	.01
Buffalo Sabres				
☐ 115 Sergei Nemchinov	.08	.04	.01
New York Rangers				
☐ 116 Tony Tanti	.05	.02	.01
Buffalo Sabres				
☐ 117 Stewart Gavin	.05	.02	.01
Minnesota North Stars				
☐ 118 Doug Brown	.05	.02	.01
New Jersey Devils				
☐ 119 Gerard Gallant	.05	.02	.01
Detroit Red Wings				
☐ 120 Andy Moog	.08	.04	.01
Boston Bruins				
☐ 121 John Druce	.05	.02	.01
Washington Capitals				
☐ 122 Dave McLlwain	.05	.02	.01
Toronto Maple Leafs				
☐ 123 Bob Essensa	.08	.04	.01
Winnipeg Jets				
☐ 124 Doug Lidster	.05	.02	.01
Vancouver Canucks				
☐ 125 Pat Falloon	.15	.07	.02
San Jose Sharks				
☐ 126 Kelly Buchberger	.05	.02	.01
Edmonton Oilers				
☐ 127 Carey Wilson	.05	.02	.01
Calgary Flames				
☐ 128 Bobby Holik	.05	.02	.01
Hartford Whalers				
☐ 129 Andrei Lomakin	.05	.02	.01
Philadelphia Flyers				
☐ 130 Bob Rouse	.05	.02	.01
Toronto Maple Leafs				
☐ 131 Adam Foote	.05	.02	.01
Quebec Nordiques				
☐ 132 Bob Bassen	.05	.02	.01
St. Louis Blues				
☐ 133 Brian Benning	.05	.02	.01
Philadelphia Flyers				
☐ 134 Greg Gilbert	.05	.02	.01
Chicago Blackhawks				
☐ 135 Paul Stanton	.05	.02	.01
Pittsburgh Penguins				
☐ 136 Brian Skrudland	.05	.02	.01
Montreal Canadiens				
☐ 137 Jeff Beukeboom	.05	.02	.01
New York Islanders				
☐ 138 Clint Malarchuk	.08	.04	.01
Buffalo Sabres				
☐ 139 Mike Modano	.25	.11	.03
Minnesota North Stars				
☐ 140 Stephane Richer	.08	.04	.01
New Jersey Devils				
☐ 141 Brad McCrimmon	.05	.02	.01
Detroit Red Wings				
☐ 142 Bob Carpenter	.05	.02	.01
Boston Bruins				
☐ 143 Rod Langway	.05	.02	.01
Washington Capitals				
☐ 144 Adam Creighton	.05	.02	.01
New York Islanders				
☐ 145 Ed Olczyk	.05	.02	.01
Winnipeg Jets				
☐ 146 Greg Adams	.05	.02	.01
Vancouver Canucks				
☐ 147 Jayson More	.05	.02	.01
San Jose Sharks				
☐ 148 Scott Mellanby	.05	.02	.01
Edmonton Oilers				
☐ 149 Paul Ranheim	.05	.02	.01
Calgary Flames				
☐ 150 John Cullen	.05	.02	.01
Hartford Whalers				
☐ 151 Steve Duchesne	.08	.04	.01
Philadelphia Flyers				
☐ 152 Dave Ellett	.05	.02	.01
Toronto Maple Leafs				
☐ 153 Mats Sundin	.20	.09	.03
Quebec Nordiques				
☐ 154 Rick Zombo	.05	.02	.01
St. Louis Blues				
☐ 155 Kelly Hrudey	.08	.04	.01
Los Angeles Kings				
☐ 156 Mike Hudson	.05	.02	.01
Chicago Blackhawks				
☐ 157 Bryan Trottier	.08	.04	.01
Pittsburgh Penguins				
☐ 158 Shayne Corson	.08	.04	.01
Montreal Canadiens				
☐ 159 Kevin Haller	.05	.02	.01
Montreal Canadiens				
☐ 160 John Vanbiesbrouck	.10	.05	.01
New York Rangers				
☐ 161 Jim Johnson	.05	.02	.01
Minnesota North Stars				
☐ 162 Kevin Todd	.05	.02	.01
New Jersey Devils				
☐ 163 Ray Sheppard	.08	.04	.01
Detroit Red Wings				
☐ 164 Brent Ashton	.05	.02	.01
Boston Bruins				
☐ 165 Peter Bondra	.08	.04	.01
Washington Capitals				
☐ 166 David Volek	.05	.02	.01
New York Islanders				
☐ 167 Randy Carlyle	.05	.02	.01
Winnipeg Jets				
☐ 168 Dana Murzyn	.05	.02	.01
Vancouver Canucks				
☐ 169 Perry Berezan	.05	.02	.01
San Jose Sharks				
☐ 170 Vin Damphousse	.08	.04	.01
Edmonton Oilers				
☐ 171 Gary Leeman	.05	.02	.01
Calgary Flames				
☐ 172 Steve Konroyd	.05	.02	.01
Hartford Whalers				
☐ 173 Pelle Eklund	.05	.02	.01
Philadelphia Flyers				
☐ 174 Peter Zezel	.05	.02	.01
Toronto Maple Leafs				
☐ 175 Greg Paslawski	.05	.02	.01
Quebec Nordiques				
☐ 176 Murray Baron	.05	.02	.01
St. Louis Blues				
☐ 177 Rob Blake	.10	.05	.01
Los Angeles Kings				
☐ 178 Ed Belfour	.25	.11	.03
Chicago Blackhawks				
☐ 179 Mike Keane	.05	.02	.01
Montreal Canadiens				
☐ 180 Mark Recchi	.25	.11	.03
Philadelphia Flyers				
☐ 181 Kris King	.05	.02	.01
New York Rangers				
☐ 182 Dave Snuggerud	.05	.02	.01
San Jose Sharks				
☐ 183 David Shaw	.05	.02	.01
Minnesota North Stars				
☐ 184 Tom Chorske	.05	.02	.01
New Jersey Devils				
☐ 185 Steve Chiasson	.05	.02	.01
Detroit Red Wings				
☐ 186 Don Sweeney	.05	.02	.01
Boston Bruins				
☐ 187 Mike Ridley	.08	.04	.01
Washington Capitals				
☐ 188 Glenn Healy	.08	.04	.01
New York Islanders				
☐ 189 Troy Murray	.05	.02	.01

Winnipeg Jets

☐ 190 Tom Fergus..............	.05	.02	.01

Vancouver Canucks

☐ 191 Rob Zettler..............	.05	.02	.01

San Jose Sharks

☐ 192 Geoff Smith..............	.05	.02	.01

Edmonton Oilers

☐ 193 Joe Nieuwendyk..............	.08	.04	.01

Calgary Flames

☐ 194 Mark Hunter..............	.05	.02	.01

Hartford Whalers

☐ 195 Kjell Samuelsson..............	.05	.02	.01

Pittsburgh Penguins

☐ 196 Todd Gill..............	.05	.02	.01

Toronto Maple Leafs

☐ 197 Doug Smail..............	.05	.02	.01

Quebec Nordiques

☐ 198 Dave Christian..............	.05	.02	.01

St. Louis Blues

☐ 199 Tomas Sandstrom..............	.05	.02	.01

Los Angeles Kings

☐ 200 Jeremy Roenick..............	.50	.23	.06

Chicago Blackhawks

☐ 201 Gordie Roberts..............	.05	.02	.01

Pittsburgh Penguins

☐ 202 Denis Savard..............	.08	.04	.01

Montreal Canadiens

☐ 203 James Patrick..............	.05	.02	.01

New York Rangers

☐ 204 Dave Andreychuk..............	.05	.02	.01

Buffalo Sabres

☐ 205 Bobby Smith..............	.08	.04	.01

Minnesota North Stars

☐ 206 Valeri Zelepukin..............	.15	.07	.02

New Jersey Devils

☐ 207 Shawn Burr..............	.05	.02	.01

Detroit Red Wings

☐ 208 Vladimir Ruzicka..............	.05	.02	.01

Boston Bruins

☐ 209 Calle Johansson..............	.05	.02	.01

Washington Capitals

☐ 210 Mark Fitzpatrick..............	.08	.04	.01

New York Islanders

☐ 211 Dean Kennedy..............	.05	.02	.01

Winnipeg Jets

☐ 212 Dave Babych..............	.05	.02	.01

Vancouver Canucks

☐ 213 Wayne Presley..............	.05	.02	.01

Buffalo Sabres

☐ 214 Dave Manson..............	.05	.02	.01

Edmonton Oilers

☐ 215 Mikael Andersson..............	.05	.02	.01

Hartford Whalers

☐ 216 Trent Yawney..............	.05	.02	.01

Calgary Flames

☐ 217 Mark Howe..............	.08	.04	.01

Philadelphia Flyers

☐ 218 Mike Bullard..............	.05	.02	.01

Toronto Maple Leafs

☐ 219 Claude Lapointe..............	.05	.02	.01

Quebec Nordiques

☐ 220 Jeff Brown..............	.08	.04	.01

St. Louis Blues

☐ 221 Bob Kudelski..............	.08	.04	.01

Los Angeles Kings

☐ 222 Michel Goulet..............	.08	.04	.01

Chicago Blackhawks

☐ 223 Phil Bourque..............	.05	.02	.01

Pittsburgh Penguins

☐ 224 Darren Turcotte..............	.05	.02	.01

New York Rangers

☐ 225 Kirk Muller..............	.08	.04	.01

Montreal Canadiens

☐ 226 Doug Bodger..............	.05	.02	.01

Buffalo Sabres

☐ 227 Dave Gagner..............	.08	.04	.01

Minnesota North Stars

☐ 228 Craig Billington..............	.05	.02	.01

New Jersey Devils

☐ 229 Kevin Miller..............	.08	.04	.01

Detroit Red Wings

☐ 230 Glen Wesley..............	.05	.02	.01

Boston Bruins

☐ 231 Dale Hunter..............	.08	.04	.01

Washington Capitals

☐ 232 Tom Kurvers..............	.05	.02	.01

New York Islanders

☐ 233 Pat Elynuik..............	.05	.02	.01

Winnipeg Jets

☐ 234 Geoff Courtnall..............	.05	.02	.01

Vancouver Canucks

☐ 235 Neil Wilkinson..............	.05	.02	.01

San Jose Sharks

☐ 236 Bill Ranford..............	.08	.04	.01

Edmonton Oilers

☐ 237 Ronnie Stern..............	.05	.02	.01

Calgary Flames

☐ 238 Zarley Zalapski..............	.05	.02	.01

Hartford Whalers

☐ 239 Kerry Huffman..............	.05	.02	.01

Philadelphia Flyers

☐ 240 Joe Sakic..............	.20	.09	.03

Quebec Nordiques

☐ 241 Glenn Anderson..............	.08	.04	.01

Toronto Maple Leafs

☐ 242 Stephane Quintal..............	.05	.02	.01

St. Louis Blues

☐ 243 Tony Granato..............	.05	.02	.01

Los Angeles Kings

☐ 244 Rob Brown..............	.05	.02	.01

Chicago Blackhawks

☐ 245 Rick Tocchet..............	.08	.04	.01

Pittsburgh Penguins

☐ 246 Stephan Lebeau..............	.05	.02	.01

Montreal Canadiens

☐ 247 Mark Hardy..............	.05	.02	.01

New York Rangers

☐ 248 Alexander Mogilny..............	.40	.18	.05

Buffalo Sabres

☐ 249 Jon Casey..............	.08	.04	.01

Minnesota North Stars

☐ 250 Adam Oates..............	.15	.07	.02

Boston Bruins

☐ 251 Bruce Driver..............	.05	.02	.01

New Jersey Devils

☐ 252 Sergei Fedorov..............	.75	.35	.09

Detroit Red Wings

☐ 253 Michal Pivonka..............	.08	.04	.01

Washington Capitals

☐ 254 Cliff Ronning..............	.05	.02	.01

Vancouver Canucks

☐ 255 Derek King..............	.05	.02	.01

New York Islanders

☐ 256 Luciano Borsato..............	.05	.02	.01

Winnipeg Jets

☐ 257 Paul Fenton..............	.05	.02	.01

San Jose Sharks

☐ 258 Craig Berube..............	.05	.02	.01

Calgary Flames

☐ 259 Brian Bradley..............	.05	.02	.01

Toronto Maple Leafs

☐ 260 Craig Simpson..............	.05	.02	.01

Edmonton Oilers

☐ 261 Adam Burt..............	.05	.02	.01

Hartford Whalers

☐ 262 Curtis Joseph..............	.25	.11	.03

St. Louis Blues

☐ 263 Mark Pederson..............	.05	.02	.01

Philadelphia Flyers

☐ 264 Alexei Gusarov..............	.05	.02	.01

Quebec Nordiques

☐ 265 Paul Coffey..............	.15	.07	.02

Los Angeles Kings

☐ 266 Steve Larmer..............	.08	.04	.01

Chicago Blackhawks

☐ 267 Ron Francis..............	.08	.04	.01

Pittsburgh Penguins

☐ 268 Randy Gilhen..............	.05	.02	.01

New York Rangers

☐ 269 Guy Carbonneau..............	.08	.04	.01

Montreal Canadiens

☐ 270 Chris Terreri..............	.08	.04	.01

New Jersey Devils

☐ 271 Mike Craig..............	.05	.02	.01

Minnesota North Stars

☐ 272 Dale Hawerchuk..............	.08	.04	.01

Buffalo Sabres

☐ 273 Kevin Hatcher..............	.08	.04	.01

Washington Capitals

☐ 274 Ken Hodge Jr,..............	.05	.02	.01

Boston Bruins

☐ 275 Tim Cheveldae..............	.08	.04	.01

Detroit Red Wings

☐ 276 Benoit Hogue..............	.05	.02	.01

New York Islanders

☐ 277 Mark Osborne..............	.05	.02	.01

Toronto Maple Leafs

☐ 278 Brian Mullen..............	.08	.04	.01

San Jose Sharks

☐ 279 Robert Dirk..............	.05	.02	.01

Vancouver Canucks

☐ 280 Theoren Fleury..............	.10	.05	.01

Calgary Flames

☐ 281 Martin Gelinas..............	.05	.02	.01

Edmonton Oilers

☐ 282 Pat Verbeek..............	.08	.04	.01

Hartford Whalers

☐ 283 Mike Krushelnyski..............	.05	.02	.01

284	Kevin Dineen	Toronto Maple Leafs	.08	.04	.01
285	Craig Janney	Philadelphia Flyers	.10	.05	.01
286	Owen Nolan	St. Louis Blues	.08	.04	.01
287	Bob Errey	Quebec Nordiques	.05	.02	.01
288	Bryan Marchment	Pittsburgh Penguins	.05	.02	.01
289	Randy Moller	Chicago Blackhawks	.05	.02	.01
290	Luc Robitaille	Buffalo Sabres	.15	.07	.02
291	Peter Stastny	Los Angeles Kings	.08	.04	.01
292	Ken Sutton	New Jersey Devils	.05	.02	.01
293	Brad Marsh	Buffalo Sabres	.08	.04	.01
294	Chris Dahlquist	Detroit Red Wings	.05	.02	.01
295	Patrick Roy	Minnesota North Stars	.50	.23	.06
296	Andy Brickley	Montreal Canadiens	.05	.02	.01
297	Randy Burridge	Boston Bruins	.05	.02	.01
298	Ray Ferraro	Washington Capitals	.05	.02	.01
299	Phil Housley	New York Islanders	.08	.04	.01
300	Mark Messier	Winnipeg Jets	.20	.09	.03
301	David Bruce	New York Rangers	.05	.02	.01
302	Al MacInnis	San Jose Sharks	.10	.05	.01
303	Craig MacTavish	Calgary Flames	.05	.02	.01
304	Kay Whitmore	Edmonton Oilers	.05	.02	.01
305	Trevor Linden	Hartford Whalers	.15	.07	.02
306	Steve Kasper	Vancouver Canucks	.05	.02	.01
307	Todd Elik	Philadelphia Flyers	.05	.02	.01
308	Eric Weinrich	Minnesota North Stars	.05	.02	.01
309	Jocelyn Lemieux	New Jersey Devils	.05	.02	.01
310	Peter Ahola	Chicago Blackhawks	.05	.02	.01
311	J.J. Daigneault	Los Angeles Kings	.05	.02	.01
312	Colin Patterson	Montreal Canadiens	.05	.02	.01
313	Darcy Wakaluk	Buffalo Sabres	.08	.04	.01
314	Doug Weight	Minnesota North Stars	.08	.04	.01
315	Dave Barr	New York Rangers	.05	.02	.01
316	Keith Primeau	New Jersey Devils	.08	.04	.01
317	Bob Sweeney	Detroit Red Wings	.05	.02	.01
318	Jyrki Lumme	Boston Bruins	.05	.02	.01
319	Stu Barnes	Vancouver Canucks	.05	.02	.01
320	Don Beaupre	Winnipeg Jets	.08	.04	.01
321	Joe Murphy	Washington Capitals	.05	.02	.01
322	Gary Roberts	Edmonton Oilers	.08	.04	.01
323	Andrew Cassels	Calgary Flames	.05	.02	.01
324	Rod Brind'Amour	Hartford Whalers	.15	.07	.02
325	Pierre Turgeon	Philadelphia Flyers	.20	.09	.03
326	Claude Vilgrain	New York Islanders	.05	.02	.01
327	Rich Sutter	New Jersey Devils	.05	.02	.01
328	Claude Loiselle	St. Louis Blues	.05	.02	.01
329	John Ogrodnick	New York Islanders	.05	.02	.01
330	Ulf Dahlen	New York Rangers	.05	.02	.01
331	Gilbert Dionne	Minnesota North Stars	.05	.02	.01
332	Joel Otto	Montreal Canadiens	.05	.02	.01
333	Rob Pearson	Calgary Flames	.05	.02	.01
334	Christian Ruuttu	Toronto Maple Leafs	.05	.02	.01
335	Brian Bellows	Buffalo Sabres	.08	.04	.01
336	Anatoli Semenov	Minnesota North Stars	.05	.02	.01
337	Brent Fedyk	Edmonton Oilers	.05	.02	.01
338	Gaetan Duchesne	Detroit Red Wings	.05	.02	.01
339	Randy McKay	Minnesota North Stars	.05	.02	.01
340	Bernie Nicholls	New Jersey Devils	.08	.04	.01
341	Keith Acton	Edmonton Oilers	.05	.02	.01
342	John Tonelli	Philadelphia Flyers	.08	.04	.01
343	Brian Lawton	Quebec Nordiques	.05	.02	.01
344	Ric Nattress	San Jose Sharks	.05	.02	.01
345	Mike Eagles	Toronto Maple Leafs	.05	.02	.01
346	Frantisek Kucera	Winnipeg Jets	.05	.02	.01
347	John McIntyre	Chicago Blackhawks	.05	.02	.01
348	Troy Loney	Los Angeles Kings	.05	.02	.01
349	Norm Maciver	Pittsburgh Penguins	.05	.02	.01
350	Brett Hull	Edmonton Oilers	.50	.23	.06
351	Rob Ramage	St. Louis Blues	.05	.02	.01
352	Claude Boivin	Minnesota North Stars	.05	.02	.01
353	Paul Broten	Philadelphia Flyers	.05	.02	.01
354	Stephane Fiset	New York Rangers	.08	.04	.01
355	Garry Valk	Quebec Nordiques	.05	.02	.01
356	Basil McRae	Vancouver Canucks	.05	.02	.01
357	Alan May	Minnesota North Stars	.05	.02	.01
358	Grant Ledyard	Washington Capitals	.05	.02	.01
359	Dave Poulin	Buffalo Sabres	.05	.02	.01
360	Valeri Kamensky	Boston Bruins	.15	.07	.02
361	Brian Glynn	Quebec Nordiques	.05	.02	.01
362	Jan Erixon	Edmonton Oilers	.05	.02	.01
363	Mike Lalor	New York Rangers	.05	.02	.01
364	Jeff Chychrun	Winnipeg Jets	.05	.02	.01
365	Ron Wilson	Pittsburgh Penguins	.05	.02	.01
366	Shawn Cronin	St. Louis Blues	.05	.02	.01
367	Sylvain Turgeon	Winnipeg Jets	.05	.02	.01
368	Mike Liut	Montreal Canadiens	.08	.04	.01
369	Joe Cirella	Washington Capitals	.05	.02	.01
370	David Maley	New York Rangers	.05	.02	.01
371	Lucien DeBlois	Edmonton Oilers	.05	.02	.01
372	Per Djoos	Winnipeg Jets	.05	.02	.01
373	Dominik Hasek	New York Rangers	.35	.16	.04
374	Laurie Boschman	Chicago Blackhawks	.05	.02	.01
375	Brian Leetch	New Jersey Devils	.30	.14	.04
376	Nelson Emerson	New York Rangers	.15	.07	.02
377	Normand Rochefort	St. Louis Blues	.05	.02	.01

New York Rangers
☐ 378	Jacques Cloutier	.05	.02	.01

Quebec Nordiques
| ☐ 379 | Jim Sandlak | .05 | .02 | .01 |

Vancouver Canucks
| ☐ 380 | Dave Reid | .05 | .02 | .01 |

Boston Bruins
| ☐ 381 | Gary Nylund | .05 | .02 | .01 |

New York Islanders
| ☐ 382 | Sergei Makarov | .08 | .04 | .01 |

Calgary Flames
| ☐ 383 | Petr Klima | .05 | .02 | .01 |

Edmonton Oilers
| ☐ 384 | Peter Douris | .05 | .02 | .01 |

Boston Bruins
| ☐ 385 | Kirk McLean | .20 | .09 | .03 |

Vancouver Canucks
| ☐ 386 | Bob McGill | .05 | .02 | .01 |

Detroit Red Wings
| ☐ 387 | Ron Tugnutt | .05 | .02 | .01 |

Edmonton Oilers
| ☐ 388 | Patrice Brisebois | .05 | .02 | .01 |

Montreal Canadiens
| ☐ 389 | Tony Amonte | .20 | .09 | .03 |

New York Rangers
| ☐ 390 | Mario Lemieux | .75 | .35 | .09 |

Pittsburgh Penguins
| ☐ 391 | Nicklas Lidstrom | .15 | .07 | .02 |

Detroit Red Wings
| ☐ 392 | Brendan Shanahan | .20 | .09 | .03 |

St. Louis Blues
| ☐ 393 | Donald Audette | .05 | .02 | .01 |

Buffalo Sabres
| ☐ 394 | Alexei Kasatonov | .05 | .02 | .01 |

New Jersey Devils
| ☐ 395 | Dino Ciccarelli | .08 | .04 | .01 |

Washington Capitals
| ☐ 396 | Vincent Riendeau | .05 | .02 | .01 |

Detroit Red Wings
| ☐ 397 | Joe Reekie | .05 | .02 | .01 |

New York Islanders
| ☐ 398 | Jari Kurri | .10 | .05 | .01 |

Edmonton Oilers
| ☐ 399 | Ken Wregget | .05 | .02 | .01 |

Pittsburgh Penguins
| ☐ 400 | Steve Yzerman | .25 | .11 | .03 |

Detroit Red Wings
| ☐ 401 | Scott Niedermayer | .25 | .11 | .03 |

New Jersey Devils
| ☐ 402 | Stephane Beauregard | .05 | .02 | .01 |

Winnipeg Jets
| ☐ 403 | Tim Hunter | .05 | .02 | .01 |

Calgary Flames
| ☐ 404 | Marc Bergevin | .05 | .02 | .01 |

Hartford Whalers
| ☐ 405 | Sylvain Lefebvre | .05 | .02 | .01 |

Montreal Canadiens
| ☐ 406 | Johan Garpenlov | .05 | .02 | .01 |

San Jose Sharks
| ☐ 407 | Tony Hrkac | .05 | .02 | .01 |

Chicago Blackhawks
| ☐ 408 | Tie Domi | .05 | .02 | .01 |

New York Rangers
| ☐ 409 | Martin Lapointe | .05 | .02 | .01 |

Detroit Red Wings
| ☐ 410 | Darryl Sydor | .08 | .04 | .01 |

Los Angeles Kings
| ☐ 411 | Brett Hull SL | .20 | .09 | .03 |

St. Louis Blues
| ☐ 412 | Wayne Gretzky SL | .35 | .16 | .04 |

Los Angeles Kings
| ☐ 413 | Mario Lemieux SL | .25 | .11 | .03 |

Pittsburgh Penguins
| ☐ 414 | Paul Ysebaert SL | .08 | .04 | .01 |

Detroit Red Wings
| ☐ 415 | Tony Amonte SL | .10 | .05 | .01 |

New York Rangers
| ☐ 416 | Brian Leetch SL | .15 | .07 | .02 |

New York Rangers
| ☐ 417 | Tim Cheveldae SL | .08 | .04 | .01 |

Detroit Red Wings
Kirk McLean SL
Vancouver Canucks
| ☐ 418 | Patrick Roy SL | .25 | .11 | .03 |

Montreal Canadiens
| ☐ 419 | Ray Bourque FP | .10 | .05 | .01 |

Boston Bruins
| ☐ 420 | Pat LaFontaine FP | .10 | .05 | .01 |

Buffalo Sabres
| ☐ 421 | Al MacInnis FP | .10 | .05 | .01 |

Calgary Flames
| ☐ 422 | Jeremy Roenick FP | .20 | .09 | .03 |

Chicago Blackhawks
| ☐ 423 | Steve Yzerman FP | .15 | .07 | .02 |

Detroit Red Wings
| ☐ 424 | Bill Ranford FP | .10 | .05 | .01 |

Edmonton Oilers
| ☐ 425 | John Cullen FP | .08 | .04 | .01 |

Hartford Whalers
| ☐ 426 | Wayne Gretzky FP | .35 | .16 | .04 |

Los Angeles Kings
| ☐ 427 | Mike Modano FP | .10 | .05 | .01 |

Minnesota North Stars
| ☐ 428 | Patrick Roy FP | .25 | .11 | .03 |

Montreal Canadiens
| ☐ 429 | Scott Stevens FP | .10 | .05 | .01 |

New Jersey Devils
| ☐ 430 | Pierre Turgeon FP | .10 | .05 | .01 |

New York Islanders
| ☐ 431 | Mark Messier FP | .15 | .07 | .02 |

New York Rangers
| ☐ 432 | Eric Lindros FP | 1.50 | .65 | .19 |

Philadelphia Flyers
| ☐ 433 | Mario Lemieux FP | .25 | .11 | .03 |

Pittsburgh Penguins
| ☐ 434 | Joe Sakic FP | .10 | .05 | .01 |

Quebec Nordiques
| ☐ 435 | Brett Hull FP | .20 | .09 | .03 |

St. Louis Blues
| ☐ 436 | Pat Falloon FP | .15 | .07 | .02 |

San Jose Sharks
| ☐ 437 | Grant Fuhr FP | .10 | .05 | .01 |

Toronto Maple Leafs
| ☐ 438 | Trevor Linden FP | .10 | .05 | .01 |

Vancouver Canucks
| ☐ 439 | Kevin Hatcher FP | .08 | .04 | .01 |

Washington Capitals
| ☐ 440 | Phil Housley FP | .08 | .04 | .01 |

Winnipeg Jets
| ☐ 441 | Paul Coffey SH | .08 | .04 | .01 |

Los Angeles Kings
| ☐ 442 | Brett Hull SH | .20 | .09 | .03 |

St. Louis Blues
| ☐ 443 | Mike Gartner SH | .08 | .04 | .01 |

New York Rangers
| ☐ 444 | Michel Goulet SH | .05 | .02 | .01 |

Chicago Blackhawks
| ☐ 445 | Mike Gartner SH | .08 | .04 | .01 |

New York Rangers
| ☐ 446 | Bobby Smith SH | .05 | .02 | .01 |

Minnesota North Stars
| ☐ 447 | Ray Bourque SH | .08 | .04 | .01 |

Boston Bruins
| ☐ 448 | Mario Lemieux SH | .25 | .11 | .03 |

Pittsburgh Penguins
| ☐ 449 | Scott Lachance TP | .05 | .02 | .01 |

New Jersey Devils
| ☐ 450 | Keith Tkachuk TP | .25 | .11 | .03 |

Winnipeg Jets
| ☐ 451 | Alexander Semak TP | .05 | .02 | .01 |

New Jersey Devils
| ☐ 452 | John Tanner TP | .05 | .02 | .01 |

Quebec Nordiques
| ☐ 453 | Joe Juneau TP | .75 | .35 | .09 |

Boston Bruins
| ☐ 454 | Igor Kravchuk TP | .05 | .02 | .01 |

Chicago Blackhawks
| ☐ 455 | Brent Thompson TP | .05 | .02 | .01 |

Los Angeles Kings
| ☐ 456 | Evgeny Davydov TP | .05 | .02 | .01 |

Winnipeg Jets
| ☐ 457 | Arturs Irbe TP | .35 | .16 | .04 |

San Jose Sharks
| ☐ 458 | Kent Manderville TP | .05 | .02 | .01 |

Toronto Maple Leafs
| ☐ 459 | Shawn McEachern TP | .15 | .07 | .02 |

Pittsburgh Penguins
| ☐ 460 | Guy Hebert TP | .40 | .18 | .05 |

St. Louis Blues
| ☐ 461 | Keith Carney TP | .10 | .05 | .01 |

Buffalo Sabres
| ☐ 462 | Karl Dykhuis TP | .05 | .02 | .01 |

Chicago Blackhawks
| ☐ 463 | Bill Lindsay TP | .10 | .05 | .01 |

Quebec Nordiques
| ☐ 464 | Dominic Roussel TP | .15 | .07 | .02 |

Philadelphia Flyers
| ☐ 465 | Marty McInnis TP | .05 | .02 | .01 |

New York Islanders
| ☐ 466 | Dale Craigwell TP | .05 | .02 | .01 |

San Jose Sharks
| ☐ 467 | Igor Ulanov TP | .05 | .02 | .01 |

Winnipeg Jets
| ☐ 468 | Dmitri Mironov TP | .08 | .04 | .01 |

Toronto Maple Leafs
| ☐ 469 | Dean McAmmond TP | .15 | .07 | .02 |

Chicago Blackhawks
| ☐ 470 | Bill Guerin TP | .20 | .09 | .03 |

	New Jersey Devils			
☐ 471	Bret Hedican TP	.15	.07	.02
	St. Louis Blues			
☐ 472	Felix Potvin TP	1.00	.45	.13
	Toronto Maple Leafs			
☐ 473	Vyacheslav Kozlov TP	.50	.23	.06
	UER (Misspelled Viaches-			
	lov on both sides)			
	Detroit Red Wings			
☐ 474	Martin Rucinsky TP	.05	.02	.01
	Quebec Nordiques			
☐ 475	Ray Whitney TP	.15	.07	.02
	San Jose Sharks			
☐ 476	Stephen Heinze TP	.05	.02	.01
	Boston Bruins			
☐ 477	Brad Schlegel TP	.05	.02	.01
	Washington Capitals			
☐ 478	Patrick Poulin TP	.05	.02	.01
	Hartford Whalers			
☐ 479	Ted Donato TP	.05	.02	.01
	Boston Bruins			
☐ 480	Martin Brodeur TP	.40	.18	.05
	New Jersey Devils			
☐ 481	Denny Felsner TP	.15	.07	.02
	St. Louis Blues			
☐ 482	Trent Klatt TP	.15	.07	.02
	Minnesota North Stars			
☐ 483	Gord Hynes TP	.05	.02	.01
	Boston Bruins			
☐ 484	Glen Murray TP	.05	.02	.01
	Boston Bruins			
☐ 485	Chris Lindberg TP	.05	.02	.01
	Calgary Flames			
☐ 486	Ray LeBlanc TP	.05	.02	.01
	Chicago Blackhawks			
☐ 487	Yanic Perreault TP	.20	.09	.03
	Toronto Maple Leafs			
☐ 488	J.F. Quintin TP	.05	.02	.01
	San Jose Sharks			
☐ 489	Patrick Roy DT	.30	.14	.04
	Montreal Canadiens			
☐ 490	Ray Bourque DT	.10	.05	.01
	Boston Bruins			
☐ 491	Brian Leetch DT	.15	.07	.02
	New York Rangers			
☐ 492	Kevin Stevens DT	.15	.07	.02
	Pittsburgh Penguins			
☐ 493	Mark Messier DT	.15	.07	.02
	New York Rangers			
☐ 494	Jaromir Jagr DT	.20	.09	.03
	Pittsburgh Penguins			
☐ 495	Bill Ranford DT	.08	.04	.01
	Edmonton Oilers			
☐ 496	Al MacInnis DT	.10	.05	.01
	Calgary Flames			
☐ 497	Chris Chelios DT	.08	.04	.01
	Chicago Blackhawks			
☐ 498	Luc Robitaille DT	.10	.05	.01
	Los Angeles Kings			
☐ 499	Jeremy Roenick DT	.20	.09	.03
	Chicago Blackhawks			
☐ 500	Brett Hull DT	.20	.09	.03
	St. Louis Blues			
☐ 501	Felix Potvin RDT	.60	.25	.08
	Toronto Maple Leafs			
☐ 502	Nicklas Lidstrom RDT	.08	.04	.01
	Detroit Red Wings			
☐ 503	Vladimir Konstantinov	.06	.03	.01
	RDT			
	Detroit Red Wings			
☐ 504	Pavel Bure RDT	.60	.25	.08
	Vancouver Canucks			
☐ 505	Nelson Emerson RDT	.08	.04	.01
	St. Louis Blues			
☐ 506	Tony Amonte RDT	.08	.04	.01
	New York Rangers			
☐ 507	Tampa Bay Lightning	.25	.11	.03
	Logo			
☐ 508	Shawn Chambers	.05	.02	.01
	Tampa Bay Lightning			
☐ 509	Basil McRae	.05	.02	.01
	Tampa Bay Lightning			
☐ 510	Joe Reekie	.05	.02	.01
	Tampa Bay Lightning			
☐ 511	Wendell Young	.05	.02	.01
	Tampa Bay Lightning			
☐ 512	Ottawa Senators Logo	.25	.11	.03
	Ottawa Senators			
☐ 513	Laurie Boschman	.05	.02	.01
	Ottawa Senators			
☐ 514	Mark Lamb	.05	.02	.01
	Ottawa Senators			
☐ 515	Peter Sidorkiewicz	.05	.02	.01
	Ottawa Senators			

☐ 516	Sylvain Turgeon	.05	.02	.01
	Ottawa Senators			
☐ 517	Bill Dineen	.05	.02	.01
	Kevin Dineen			
☐ 518	Stanley Cup	.05	.02	.01
	Champions			
☐ 519	Mario Lemieux AW	.25	.11	.03
	Pittsburgh Penguins			
	Conn Smythe			
☐ 520	Ray Bourque AW	.10	.05	.01
	Boston Bruins			
	King Clancy			
☐ 521	Mark Messier AW	.15	.07	.02
	New York Rangers			
	Hart Trophy			
☐ 522	Brian Leetch AW	.15	.07	.02
	New York Rangers			
	Norris Trophy			
☐ 523	Pavel Bure AW	.50	.23	.06
	Vancouver Canucks			
	Calder Trophy			
☐ 524	Guy Carbonneau AW	.08	.04	.01
	Montreal Canadiens			
	Selke Trophy			
☐ 525	Wayne Gretzky AW	.35	.16	.04
	Los Angeles Kings			
	Lady Byng Trophy			
☐ 526	Mark Fitzpatrick AW	.08	.04	.01
	New York Islanders			
	Masterton Trophy			
☐ 527	Patrick Roy AW	.25	.11	.03
	Montreal Canadiens			
	Vezina Trophy			
☐ 528	Memorial Cup	.05	.02	.01
	Kamloops Blazers			
☐ 529	Rick Tabaracci	.05	.02	.01
	Winnipeg Jets			
☐ 530	Tom Draper	.05	.02	.01
	Buffalo Sabres			
☐ 531	Adrien Plavsic	.05	.02	.01
	Vancouver Canucks			
☐ 532	Joe Sacco	.05	.02	.01
	Toronto Maple Leafs			
☐ 533	Mike Sullivan	.05	.02	.01
	San Jose Sharks			
☐ 534	Zdeno Ciger	.05	.02	.01
	New Jersey Devils			
☐ 535	Frank Pietrangelo	.05	.02	.01
	Hartford Whalers			
☐ 536	Mike Peluso	.05	.02	.01
	Chicago Blackhawks			
☐ 537	Jim Paek	.05	.02	.01
	Pittsburgh Penguins			
☐ 538	Dave Hannan	.05	.02	.01
	Buffalo Sabres			
☐ 539	David Williams	.10	.05	.01
	San Jose Sharks			
☐ 540	Gino Odjick	.05	.02	.01
	Vancouver Canucks			
☐ 541	Yvon Corriveau	.05	.02	.01
	Hartford Whalers			
☐ 542	Grant Jennings	.05	.02	.01
	Pittsburgh Penguins			
☐ 543	Stephane Matteau	.05	.02	.01
	Chicago Blackhawks			
☐ 544	Pat Conacher	.05	.02	.01
	New Jersey Devils			
☐ 545	Steven Rice	.05	.02	.01
	Edmonton Oilers			
☐ 546	Marc Habscheid	.05	.02	.01
	Calgary Flames			
☐ 547	Steve Weeks	.05	.02	.01
	Los Angeles Kings			
☐ 548A	Jay Wells USA	.05	.02	.01
	New York Rangers			
☐ 548C	Maurice Richard CAN	.25	.11	.03
	Montreal Canadiens			
☐ 549A	Mick Vukota USA	.05	.02	.01
	New York Islanders			
☐ 549C	Maurice Richard CAN	.25	.11	.03
	Montreal Canadiens			
☐ 550	Eric Lindros UER	4.00	1.80	.50
	(Acquired 6-30-92,			
	not 6-20-92)			
☐ NNO	Eric Lindros Press	50.00	23.00	6.25
	Conference Card			

1992-93 Score Canadian Promo Sheets

These two 5" by 7" promotional sheets each feature four uncut cards. If the cards were cut, they would measure the standard size (2 1/2" by 3 1/2"). The fronts feature color action player photos bordered at the top and bottom by black stripes containing the player's name and position. The outer borders are metallic-blue with diagonal stripes formed by an alternating matte and glossy finish. The backs have the disclaimers "For Promotional Purposes Only" and "Not For Resale"overprinted in magenta They show a white background with a narrow color player photo running along the left edge. Biography and career highlights are contained in a graded blue panel with black borders. Statistical information appears at the bottom. The cards are numbered on the back and are listed below as the appear on the sheets from left to right starting with the top row.

	MINT	EXC	G-VG
COMPLETE SET (2)	7.50	3.00	.75
COMMON PANEL (1-2)	2.50	1.00	.25
☐ 1 Promo Sheet 1	2.50	1.00	.25
6 Pat LaFontaine			
25 Kevin Stevens			
2 Chris Chelios			
16 Esa Tikkanen			
☐ 2 Promo Sheet 2	5.00	2.00	.50
5 Mike Richter			
14 Pavel Bure			
6 Pat LaFontaine			
25 Kevin Stevens			

1992-93 Score Canadian Olympians

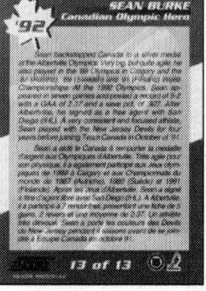

This 13-card set showcases Canadian hockey players who participated in the '92 Olympics in Albertville, France. The

standard-size (2 1/2" by 3 1/2") cards were randomly inserted in 1992-93 Score Canadian hockey packs. The color action photos on the fronts are highlighted by a red border with a diagonal white stripe. The year appears in a maple leaf at the upper left. The player's name and position are printed in the borders above and below the picture respectively. The backs feature the same red border design as the front with a player profile printed on a ghosted photo of the Canadian flag. The cards are numbered on the back. Not part of the set, but inserted in Canadian foil packs are two Maurice Richard cards and one autographed card of The Rocket.

	MINT	EXC	G-VG
COMPLETE SET (13)	100.00	45.00	12.50
COMMON PLAYER (1-13)	4.00	1.80	.50
☐ 1 Eric Lindros	45.00	20.00	5.75
☐ 2 Joe Juneau	30.00	13.50	3.80
☐ 3 Dave Archibald	4.00	1.80	.50
☐ 4 Randy Smith	4.00	1.80	.50
☐ 5 Gord Hynes	4.00	1.80	.50
☐ 6 Chris Lindberg	4.00	1.80	.50
☐ 7 Jason Woolley	4.00	1.80	.50
☐ 8 Fabian Joseph	4.00	1.80	.50
☐ 9 Brad Schlegel	4.00	1.80	.50
☐ 10 Kent Manderville	4.00	1.80	.50
☐ 11 Adrien Plavsic	4.00	1.80	.50
☐ 12 Trevor Kidd	4.00	1.80	.50
☐ 13 Sean Burke	5.00	2.30	.60
☐ AU Maurice Richard	200.00	90.00	25.00
(Certified autograph)			
☐ NNO1 Maurice Richard	15.00	6.75	1.90
The Rocket			
☐ NNO2 Maurice Richard	15.00	6.75	1.90
Stanley Cup Hero			

1992-93 Score Sharpshooters

This 30-card set showcases the most accurate shooters during the 1991-92 season. Two cards were inserted in each 1992-93 Score jumbo pack. The cards measures the standard size (2 1/2" by 3 1/2") and feature full-bleed color action photos. A black border at the bottom contains the player's name in red and the words "Sharp Shooters" in gold foil lettering. A puck and target icon fills out the card front at the lower left corner. The horizontal backs carry close-up player photos with statistics and the team logo on either side against a gray background. A black border, nearly identical to the front, runs across the bottom. The cards are numbered on the back and arranged in descending order of 1991-92 shooting percentage ranking.

	MINT	EXC	G-VG
COMPLETE SET (30)	12.00	5.50	1.50
COMMON PLAYER (1-30)	.40	.18	.05
*AMERICAN AND CANADIAN: SAME VALUE			

☐ 1	Gary Roberts	.60	.25	.08
	Calgary Flames			
☐ 2	Sergei Makarov	.60	.25	.08
	Calgary Flames			
☐ 3	Ray Ferraro	.40	.18	.05
	New York Islanders			
☐ 4	Dale Hunter	.60	.25	.08
	Washington Capitals			
☐ 5	Sergei Nemchinov	.40	.18	.05
	New York Rangers			
☐ 6	Mike Ridley	.60	.25	.08
	Washington Capitals			
☐ 7	Gilbert Dionne	.40	.18	.05
	Montreal Canadiens			
☐ 8	Pat LaFontaine	1.50	.65	.19
	Buffalo Sabres			
☐ 9	Jimmy Carson	.40	.18	.05
	Detroit Red Wings			
☐ 10	Jeremy Roenick	2.00	.90	.25
	Chicago Blackhawks			
☐ 11	Kelly Buchberger	.40	.18	.05
	Edmonton Oilers			
☐ 12	Owen Nolan	.60	.25	.08
	Quebec Nordiques			
☐ 13	Igor Larionov	.40	.18	.05
	Vancouver Canucks			
☐ 14	Claude Vilgrain	.40	.18	.05
	New Jersey Devils			
☐ 15	Derek King	.40	.18	.05
	New York Islanders			
☐ 16	Greg Paslawski	.40	.18	.05
	Quebec Nordiques			
☐ 17	Bob Probert	.40	.18	.05
	Detroit Red Wings			
☐ 18	Mark Recchi	1.00	.45	.13
	Philadelphia Flyers			
☐ 19	Donald Audette	.40	.18	.05
	Buffalo Sabres			
☐ 20	Ray Sheppard	.60	.25	.08
	Detroit Red Wings			
☐ 21	Benoit Hogue	.40	.18	.05
	New York Islanders			
☐ 22	Rob Brown	.40	.18	.05
	Chicago Blackhawks			
☐ 23	Pat Elynuik	.40	.18	.05
	Winnipeg Jets			
☐ 24	Petr Klima	.40	.18	.05
	Edmonton Oilers			
☐ 25	Pierre Turgeon	1.50	.65	.19
	New York Islanders			
☐ 26	Corey Millen	.40	.18	.05
	Los Angeles Kings			
☐ 27	Dimitri Khristich	.40	.18	.05
	Washington Capitals			
☐ 28	Anatoli Semenov	.40	.18	.05
	Edmonton Oilers			
☐ 29	Kirk Muller	.60	.25	.08
	Montreal Canadiens			
☐ 30	Craig Simpson	.40	.18	.05
	Edmonton Oilers			

1992-93 Score USA Greats

This 15-card set showcases outstanding United States-born players. The standard-size (2 1/2" by 3 1/2") cards were randomly inserted in 1992-93 Score American hockey packs. The color action photos on the fronts are full-bleed on the right side only and framed on the other three sides by a red foil stripe and a blue outer border. The backs feature a close-up photo and a player profile. Score estimates the odds of finding one of these cards are no less than one in 36 packs. The cards are numbered on the back.

		MINT	EXC	G-VG
COMPLETE SET (15)		60.00	27.00	7.50
COMMON PLAYER (1-15)		4.00	1.80	.50
☐ 1	Pat LaFontaine	6.00	2.70	.75
	Buffalo Sabres			
☐ 2	Chris Chelios	4.00	1.80	.50
	Chicago Blackhawks			
☐ 3	Jeremy Roenick	8.00	3.60	1.00
	Chicago Blackhawks			
☐ 4	Tony Granato	4.00	1.80	.50
	Los Angeles Kings			
☐ 5	Mike Modano	7.00	3.10	.85
	Minnesota North Stars			
☐ 6	Mike Richter	7.00	3.10	.85
	New York Rangers			
☐ 7	John Vanbiesbrouck	6.00	2.70	.75
	New York Rangers			
☐ 8	Brian Leetch	7.00	3.10	.85
	New York Rangers			
☐ 9	Joe Mullen	4.00	1.80	.50
	Pittsburgh Penguins			
☐ 10	Kevin Stevens	5.00	2.30	.60
	Pittsburgh Penguins			
☐ 11	Craig Janney	5.00	2.30	.60
	St. Louis Blues			
☐ 12	Brian Mullen	4.00	1.80	.50
	San Jose Sharks			
☐ 13	Kevin Hatcher	4.00	1.80	.50
	Washington Capitals			
☐ 14	Kelly Miller	4.00	1.80	.50
	Washington Capitals			
☐ 15	Ed Olczyk	4.00	1.80	.50
	Winnipeg Jets			

1992-93 Score Young Superstars

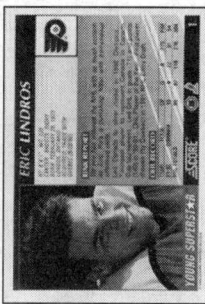

This 40-card, boxed set was issued to showcase some of the leading young hockey players. The cards measure the standard size (2 1/2" by 3 1/2"). The fronts feature glossy color player photos with white and bluish-gray streaked borders. The player's team name is printed in the top border, while the player's name is printed in the bottom border. The horizontal backs carry a close-up color photo, biography, "Rink Report," and statistics. The cards are numbered on the back.

		MINT	EXC	G-VG
COMPLETE SET (40)		7.50	3.00	.75
COMMON PLAYER (1-40)		.10	.04	.01
☐ 1	Eric Lindros	2.50	1.00	.25
	Philadelphia Flyers			
☐ 2	Tony Amonte	.20	.08	.02
	New York Rangers			
☐ 3	Mats Sundin	.40	.16	.04
	Quebec Nordiques			
☐ 4	Jaromir Jagr	1.00	.40	.10

Pittsburgh Penguins
☐ 5	Sergei Fedorov	1.50	.60	.15
	Detroit Red Wings			
☐ 6	Gilbert Dionne	.20	.08	.02
	Montreal Canadiens			
☐ 7	Mark Recchi	.50	.20	.05
	Philadelphia Flyers			
☐ 8	Alexander Mogilny	.75	.30	.07
	Buffalo Sabres			
☐ 9	Mike Richter	.30	.12	.03
	New York Rangers			
☐ 10	Jeremy Roenick	1.00	.40	.10
	Chicago Blackhawks			
☐ 11	Nicklas Lidstrom	.15	.06	.01
	Detroit Red Wings			
☐ 12	Scott Lachance	.10	.04	.01
	New York Islanders			
☐ 13	Nelson Emerson	.15	.06	.01
	St. Louis Blues			
☐ 14	Pat Falloon	.30	.12	.03
	San Jose Sharks			
☐ 15	Dimitri Khristich	.15	.06	.01
	Washington Capitals			
☐ 16	Trevor Linden	.30	.12	.03
	Vancouver Canucks			
☐ 17	Curtis Joseph	.35	.14	.03
	St. Louis Blues			
☐ 18	Rob Pearson	.15	.06	.01
	Toronto Maple Leafs			
☐ 19	Kevin Todd	.10	.04	.01
	New Jersey Devils			
☐ 20	Joe Sakic	.35	.14	.03
	Quebec Nordiques			
☐ 21	Tim Cheveldae	.20	.08	.02
	Detroit Red Wings			
☐ 22	Joe Juneau	.75	.30	.07
	Boston Bruins			
☐ 23	Vladimir Konstantinov	.15	.06	.01
	Detroit Red Wings			
☐ 24	Valeri Kamensky	.20	.08	.02
	Quebec Nordiques			
☐ 25	Ed Belfour	.50	.20	.05
	Chicago Blackhawks			
☐ 26	Rod Brind'Amour	.30	.12	.03
	Philadelphia Flyers			
☐ 27	Pierre Turgeon	.50	.20	.05
	New York Islanders			
☐ 28	Eric Desjardins	.15	.06	.01
	Montreal Canadiens			
☐ 29	Keith Tkachuk	.35	.14	.03
	Winnipeg Jets			
☐ 30	Pavel Bure	2.00	.80	.20
	Vancouver Canucks			
☐ 31	Patrick Poulin	.25	.10	.02
	Hartford Whalers			
☐ 32	Viacheslav Kozlov	.50	.20	.05
	Detroit Red Wings			
☐ 33	Scott Niedermayer	.25	.10	.02
	New Jersey Devils			
☐ 34	Jyrki Lumme	.10	.04	.01
	Vancouver Canucks			
☐ 35	Paul Ysebaert	.10	.04	.01
	Detroit Red Wings			
☐ 36	Dominic Roussel	.20	.08	.02
	Philadelphia Flyers			
☐ 37	Owen Nolan	.25	.10	.02
	Quebec Nordiques			
☐ 38	Rob Blake	.20	.08	.02
	Los Angeles Kings			
☐ 39	Felix Potvin	1.00	.40	.10
	Toronto Maple Leafs			
☐ 40	Mike Modano	.40	.16	.04
	Minnesota North Stars			

1993-94 Score Samples

This six-card set was issued by Score as a preview of the design of the 1993-94 Score set. The cards measure the standard size (2 1/2" by 3 1/2"). The fronts display color action shots within a white border. The team name is printed on a team color-coded stripe along the left side. The player's position and name is printed across the bottom of the picture. The backs have team color-coded backgrounds with a head shot on the upper half and biography, statistics, and player profile. The words "sample card" are printed in the lower right corner. The cards are numbered on the back.

	MINT	EXC	G-VG
COMPLETE SET (6)	8.00	3.25	.80
COMMON PLAYER (1-6)	.35	.14	.03
☐ 1 Eric Lindros	5.00	2.00	.50
Philadelphia Flyers			
☐ 2 Mike Gartner	.50	.20	.05
New York Rangers			
☐ 3 Steve Larmer	.35	.14	.03
Chicago Blackhawks			
☐ 4 Brian Bellows	.35	.14	.03
Montreal Canadiens			
☐ 5 Felix Potvin	2.50	1.00	.25
Toronto Maple Leafs			
☐ 6 Pierre Turgeon	.75	.30	.07
New York Islanders			

1993-94 Score

The 1993-94 Score hockey set consists of 661 cards standard-size cards. The first series contains 495 cards and the second series 166. The fronts of the first series feature white-bordered color player action shots. The player's name and position appear at the bottom, with his team name displayed vertically on the left within a team color-coded stripe. The back carries the player's name in team color-coded lettering at the top, with a head shot beneath and to the right. The player's biography and team logo appear alongside within a team color-coded rectangle. The team name appears vertically in a team color-coded stripe, this time on the right. The player's stat table in the middle portion of the card and his career highlights at the bottom round out the card. The second series was redesigned and consists of traded players in new uniforms, rookies and individual highlights. Blue borders surround the card with player name and team logo at the bottom. In addition to highlights and statistics, the backs contain another photo. The cards are numbered on the back. Several subsets grace the checklist: Little Big Men (441-445), Highlights (446-

452), Top Rookies (453-476), and Season Leaders (477-485). Card 496, Alexandre Daigle, is the card received after mailing in the unnumbered Daigle redemption card. The set is considered complete without card 496. The redemption card was randomly inserted in first series packs. An Eric Lindros All-Star card was the SP insert in second series packs.

	MINT	EXC	G-VG
COMPLETE SET (661)	27.00	12.00	3.40
COMPLETE SERIES 1 (495)	18.00	8.00	2.30
COMPLETE SERIES 2 (166)	9.00	4.00	1.15
COMMON PLAYER (1-495)	.05	.02	.01
COMMON PLAYER (497-662)	.05	.02	.01

☐ 1	Eric Lindros	1.50	.65	.19
	Philadelphia Flyers			
☐ 2	Mike Gartner	.10	.05	.01
	New York Rangers			
☐ 3	Steve Larmer	.08	.04	.01
	Chicago Blackhawks			
☐ 4	Brian Bellows	.08	.04	.01
	Montreal Canadiens			
☐ 5	Felix Potvin	.60	.25	.08
	Toronto Maple Leafs			
☐ 6	Pierre Turgeon	.20	.09	.03
	New York Islanders			
☐ 7	Joe Mullen	.08	.04	.01
	Pittsburgh Penguins			
☐ 8	Craig MacTavish	.05	.02	.01
	Edmonton Oilers			
☐ 9	Mats Sundin	.15	.07	.02
	Quebec Nordiques			
☐ 10	Pat Verbeek	.08	.04	.01
	Hartford Whalers			
☐ 11	Andy Moog	.08	.04	.01
	Boston Bruins			
☐ 12	Dirk Graham	.05	.02	.01
	Chicago Blackhawks			
☐ 13	Gary Suter	.08	.04	.01
	Calgary Flames			
☐ 14	Brent Fedyk	.05	.02	.01
	Philadelphia Flyers			
☐ 15	Brad Shaw	.05	.02	.01
	Ottawa Senators			
☐ 16	Benoit Hogue	.05	.02	.01
	New York Islanders			
☐ 17	Cliff Ronning	.05	.02	.01
	Vancouver Canucks			
☐ 18	Mathieu Schneider	.08	.04	.01
	Montreal Canadiens			
☐ 19	Bernie Nicholls	.08	.04	.01
	New Jersey Devils			
☐ 20	Vladimir Konstantinov	.05	.02	.01
	Detroit Red Wings			
☐ 21	Doug Bodger	.05	.02	.01
	Buffalo Sabres			
☐ 22	Peter Stastny	.08	.04	.01
	New Jersey Devils			
☐ 23	Larry Murphy	.08	.04	.01
	Pittsburgh Penguins			
☐ 24	Darren Turcotte	.05	.02	.01
	New York Rangers			
☐ 25	Doug Crossman	.05	.02	.01
	St. Louis Blues			
☐ 26	Bob Essensa	.08	.04	.01
	Winnipeg Jets			
☐ 27	Kelly Kisio	.05	.02	.01
	San Jose Sharks			
☐ 28	Nelson Emerson	.08	.04	.01
	St. Louis Blues			
☐ 29	Ray Bourque	.15	.07	.02
	Boston Bruins			
☐ 30	Kelly Miller	.05	.02	.01
	Washington Capitals			
☐ 31	Peter Zezel	.05	.02	.01
	Toronto Maple Leafs			
☐ 32	Owen Nolan	.08	.04	.01
	Quebec Nordiques			
☐ 33	Sergei Makarov	.08	.04	.01
	Calgary Flames			
☐ 34	Stephane Richer	.08	.04	.01
	New Jersey Devils			
☐ 35	Adam Graves	.20	.09	.03
	New York Rangers			
☐ 36	Rob Ramage	.05	.02	.01
	Montreal Canadiens			
☐ 37	Ed Olczyk	.05	.02	.01
	New York Rangers			
☐ 38	Jeff Hackett	.05	.02	.01
	San Jose Sharks			
☐ 39	Ron Sutter	.05	.02	.01
	St. Louis Blues			
☐ 40	Dale Hunter	.08	.04	.01
	Washington Capitals			
☐ 41	Nikolai Borschevsky	.15	.07	.02
	Toronto Maple Leafs			
☐ 42	Curtis Leschyshyn	.05	.02	.01
	Quebec Nordiques			
☐ 43	Mike Vernon	.08	.04	.01
	Calgary Flames			
☐ 44	Brent Sutter	.08	.04	.01
	Chicago Blackhawks			
☐ 45	Rod Brind'Amour	.08	.04	.01
	Philadelphia Flyers			
☐ 46	Sylvain Turgeon	.05	.02	.01
	Ottawa Senators			
☐ 47	Kirk McLean	.10	.05	.01
	Vancouver Canucks			
☐ 48	Derek King	.05	.02	.01
	New York Islanders			
☐ 49	Murray Craven	.05	.02	.01
	Vancouver Canucks			
☐ 50	Jaromir Jagr	.35	.16	.04
	Pittsburgh Penguins			
☐ 51	Guy Carbonneau	.08	.04	.01
	Montreal Canadiens			
☐ 52	Tony Granato	.05	.02	.01
	Los Angeles Kings			
☐ 53	Mark Tinordi	.05	.02	.01
	Dallas Stars			
☐ 54	Brad McCrimmon	.05	.02	.01
	Detroit Red Wings			
☐ 55	Randy Wood	.05	.02	.01
	Buffalo Sabres			
☐ 56	Scott Young	.05	.02	.01
	Quebec Nordiques			
☐ 57	Jamie Baker	.05	.02	.01
	Ottawa Senators			
☐ 58	Don Beaupre	.08	.04	.01
	Washington Capitals			
☐ 59	Bob Probert	.05	.02	.01
	Detroit Red Wings			
☐ 60	Ray Ferraro	.05	.02	.01
	New York Islanders			
☐ 61	Alexei Kasatonov	.05	.02	.01
	Anaheim Mighty Ducks			
☐ 62	Corey Millen	.05	.02	.01
	Los Angeles Kings			
☐ 63	Scott Mellanby	.05	.02	.01
	Edmonton Oilers			
☐ 64	Brian Benning	.05	.02	.01
	Florida Panthers			
☐ 65	Doug Lidster	.05	.02	.01
	Vancouver Canucks			
☒ 66	Doug Gilmour	.25	.11	.03
	Toronto Maple Leafs			
☐ 67	Shawn McEachern	.05	.02	.01
	Pittsburgh Penguins			
☐ 68	Tim Cheveldae	.08	.04	.01
	Detroit Red Wings			
☐ 69	Jeff Norton	.05	.02	.01
	New York Islanders			
☐ 70	Ed Belfour	.15	.07	.02
	Chicago Blackhawks			
☐ 71	Thomas Steen	.05	.02	.01
	Winnipeg Jets			
☐ 72	Stephan Lebeau	.05	.02	.01
	Montreal Canadiens			
☐ 73	James Patrick	.05	.02	.01
	New York Rangers			
☐ 74	Joel Otto	.05	.02	.01
	Calgary Flames			
☐ 75	Grant Fuhr	.08	.04	.01
	Buffalo Sabres			
☐ 76	Calle Johansson	.05	.02	.01
	Washington Capitals			
☐ 77	Donald Audette	.05	.02	.01
	Buffalo Sabres			
☐ 78	Geoff Courtnall	.05	.02	.01
	Vancouver Canucks			
☐ 79	Fredrik Olausson	.05	.02	.01
	Winnipeg Jets			
☐ 80	Dimitri Khristich	.08	.04	.01
	Washington Capitals			
☐ 81	John MacLean	.08	.04	.01
	New Jersey Devils			
☐ 82	Dominic Roussel	.15	.07	.02
	Philadelphia Flyers			
☐ 83	Ray Sheppard	.05	.02	.01
	Detroit Red Wings			
☐ 84	Christian Ruuttu	.05	.02	.01
	Chicago Blackhawks			
☐ 85	Mike McPhee	.05	.02	.01

	Dallas Stars			
☐ 86	Adam Creighton	.05	.02	.01
	Tampa Bay Lightning			
☐ 87	Uwe Krupp	.05	.02	.01
	New York Islanders			
☐ 88	Steve Leach	.05	.02	.01
	Boston Bruins			
☐ 89	Kevin Miller	.05	.02	.01
	St. Louis Blues			
☐ 90	Charlie Huddy	.05	.02	.01
	Los Angeles Kings			
☐ 91	Mark Howe	.08	.04	.01
	Detroit Red Wings			
☐ 92	Sylvain Cote	.05	.02	.01
	Washington Capitals			
☐ 93	Anatoli Semenov	.05	.02	.01
	Vancouver Canucks			
☐ 94	Jeff Beukeboom	.05	.02	.01
	New York Rangers			
☐ 95	Gord Murphy	.05	.02	.01
	Boston Bruins			
☐ 96	Rob Pearson	.05	.02	.01
	Toronto Maple Leafs			
☐ 97	Esa Tikkanen	.08	.04	.01
	New York Rangers			
☐ 98	Dave Gagner	.08	.04	.01
	Dallas Stars			
☐ 99	Mike Richter	.15	.07	.02
	New York Rangers			
☐ 100	Jari Kurri	.10	.05	.01
	Los Angeles Kings			
☐ 101	Chris Chelios	.08	.04	.01
	Chicago Blackhawks			
☐ 102	Peter Sidorkiewicz	.05	.02	.01
	Ottawa Senators			
☐ 103	Scott Lachance	.05	.02	.01
	New York Islanders			
☐ 104	Zarley Zalapski	.05	.02	.01
	Hartford Whalers			
☐ 105	Denis Savard	.08	.04	.01
	Montreal Canadiens			
☐ 106	Paul Coffey	.15	.07	.02
	Detroit Red Wings			
☐ 107	Ulf Dahlen	.05	.02	.01
	Dallas Stars			
☐ 108	Shayne Corson	.05	.02	.01
	Edmonton Oilers			
☐ 109	Jimmy Carson	.05	.02	.01
	Los Angeles Kings			
☐ 110	Petr Svoboda	.05	.02	.01
	Buffalo Sabres			
☐ 111	Scott Stevens	.08	.04	.01
	New Jersey Devils			
☐ 112	Kevin Lowe	.05	.02	.01
	New York Rangers			
☐ 113	Chris Kontos	.05	.02	.01
	Tampa Bay Lightning			
☐ 114	Evgeny Davydov	.05	.02	.01
	Winnipeg Jets			
☐ 115	Doug Wilson	.08	.04	.01
	San Jose Sharks			
☐ 116	Curtis Joseph	.15	.07	.02
	St. Louis Blues			
☐ 117	Trevor Linden	.10	.05	.01
	Vancouver Canucks			
☐ 118	Michal Pivonka	.08	.04	.01
	Washington Capitals			
☐ 119	Dave Ellett	.05	.02	.01
	Toronto Maple Leafs			
☐ 120	Mike Ricci	.08	.04	.01
	Quebec Nordiques			
☐ 121	Al MacInnis	.10	.05	.01
	Calgary Flames			
☐ 122	Kevin Dineen	.08	.04	.01
	Philadelphia Flyers			
☐ 123	Norm Maciver	.05	.02	.01
	Ottawa Senators			
☐ 124	Darius Kasparaitis	.05	.02	.01
	New York Islanders			
☐ 125	Adam Oates	.15	.07	.02
	Boston Bruins			
☐ 126	Sean Burke	.08	.04	.01
	Hartford Whalers			
☐ 127	Dave Manson	.05	.02	.01
	Edmonton Oilers			
☐ 128	Eric Desjardins	.05	.02	.01
	Montreal Canadiens			
☐ 129	Tomas Sandstrom	.05	.02	.01
	Los Angeles Kings			
☐ 130	Russ Courtnall	.08	.04	.01
	Dallas Stars			
☐ 131	Roman Hamrlik	.15	.07	.02
	Tampa Bay Lightning			
☐ 132	Teppo Numminen	.05	.02	.01
	Winnipeg Jets			
☐ 133	Pat Falloon	.08	.04	.01
	San Jose Sharks			
☐ 134	Jyrki Lumme	.05	.02	.01
	Vancouver Canucks			
☐ 135	Joe Sakic	.15	.07	.02
	Quebec Nordiques			
☐ 136	Kevin Hatcher	.08	.04	.01
	Washington Capitals			
☐ 137	Wendel Clark	.10	.05	.01
	Toronto Maple Leafs			
☐ 138	Neil Wilkinson	.05	.02	.01
	San Jose Sharks			
☐ 139	Craig Simpson	.05	.02	.01
	Edmonton Oilers			
☐ 140	Kelly Hrudey	.08	.04	.01
	Los Angeles Kings			
☐ 141	Steve Thomas	.08	.04	.01
	New York Islanders			
☐ 142	Mike Modano	.20	.09	.03
	Dallas Stars			
☐ 143	Garry Galley	.05	.02	.01
	Philadelphia Flyers			
☐ 144	Jim Johnson	.05	.02	.01
	Dallas Stars			
☐ 145	Rod Langway	.05	.02	.01
	Washington Capitals			
☐ 146	Bob Sweeney	.05	.02	.01
	Buffalo Sabres			
☐ 147	Gary Leeman	.05	.02	.01
	Montreal Canadiens			
☐ 148	Alexei Zhitnik	.05	.02	.01
	Los Angeles Kings			
☐ 149	Adam Foote	.05	.02	.01
	Quebec Nordiques			
☐ 150	Mark Recchi	.15	.07	.02
	Philadelphia Flyers			
☐ 151	Ron Francis	.08	.04	.01
	Pittsburgh Penguins			
☐ 152	Ron Hextall	.08	.04	.01
	Quebec Nordiques			
☐ 153	Michel Goulet	.08	.04	.01
	Chicago Blackhawks			
☐ 154	Vladimir Ruzicka	.05	.02	.01
	Boston Bruins			
☐ 155	Bill Ranford	.08	.04	.01
	Edmonton Oilers			
☐ 156	Mike Craig	.05	.02	.01
	Dallas Stars			
☐ 157	Vladimir Malakhov	.15	.07	.02
	New York Islanders			
☐ 158	Nicklas Lidstrom	.08	.04	.01
	Detroit Red Wings			
☐ 159	Dale Hawerchuk	.08	.04	.01
	Buffalo Sabres			
☐ 160	Claude Lemieux	.08	.04	.01
	New Jersey Devils			
☐ 161	Ulf Samuelsson	.08	.04	.01
	Pittsburgh Penguins			
☐ 162	John Vanbiesbrouck	.10	.05	.01
	New York Rangers			
☐ 163	Patrice Brisebois	.05	.02	.01
	Montreal Canadiens			
☐ 164	Andrew Cassels	.05	.02	.01
	Hartford Whalers			
☐ 165	Paul Ranheim	.05	.02	.01
	Calgary Flames			
☐ 166	Neal Broten	.08	.04	.01
	Dallas Stars			
☐ 167	Joe Reekie	.05	.02	.01
	Tampa Bay Lightning			
☐ 168	Derian Hatcher	.05	.02	.01
	Dallas Stars			
☐ 169	Don Sweeney	.05	.02	.01
	Boston Bruins			
☐ 170	Mike Keane	.05	.02	.01
	Montreal Canadiens			
☐ 171	Mark Fitzpatrick	.08	.04	.01
	Florida Panthers			
☐ 172	Paul Cavallini	.05	.02	.01
	Washington Capitals			
☐ 173	Garth Butcher	.05	.02	.01
	St. Louis Blues			
☐ 174	Andrei Kovalenko	.05	.02	.01
	Quebec Nordiques			
☐ 175	Shawn Burr	.05	.02	.01
	Detroit Red Wings			
☐ 176	Mike Donnelly	.05	.02	.01
	Los Angeles Kings			
☐ 177	Glenn Healy	.05	.02	.01
	New York Islanders			
☐ 178	Gilbert Dionne	.05	.02	.01
	Montreal Canadiens			
☐ 179	Mike Ramsey	.05	.02	.01

Pittsburgh Penguins				
☐ 180 Glenn Anderson	.08	.04	.01
Toronto Maple Leafs			
☐ 181 Pelle Eklund	.05	.02	.01
Philadelphia Flyers			
☐ 182 Kerry Huffman	.05	.02	.01
Quebec Nordiques			
☐ 183 Johan Garpenlov	.05	.02	.01
San Jose Sharks			
☐ 184 Kjell Samuelsson	.05	.02	.01
Pittsburgh Penguins			
☐ 185 Todd Elik	.05	.02	.01
Edmonton Oilers			
☐ 186 Craig Janney	.10	.05	.01
St. Louis Blues			
☐ 187 Dmitri Kvartalnov	.05	.02	.01
Boston Bruins			
☐ 188 Al Iafrate	.08	.04	.01
Washington Capitals			
☐ 189 John Cullen	.05	.02	.01
Toronto Maple Leafs			
☐ 190 Steve Duchesne	.08	.04	.01
Quebec Nordiques			
☐ 191 Theoren Fleury	.10	.05	.01
Calgary Flames			
☐ 192 Steve Smith	.05	.02	.01
Chicago Blackhawks			
☐ 193 Jon Casey	.08	.04	.01
Dallas Stars			
☐ 194 Jeff Brown	.08	.04	.01
St. Louis Blues			
☐ 195 Keith Tkachuk	.15	.07	.02
Winnipeg Jets			
☐ 196 Greg Adams	.05	.02	.01
Vancouver Canucks			
☐ 197 Mike Ridley	.08	.04	.01
Washington Capitals			
☐ 198 Bobby Holik	.05	.02	.01
New Jersey Devils			
☐ 199 Joe Nieuwendyk	.08	.04	.01
Calgary Flames			
☐ 200 Mark Messier	.15	.07	.02
New York Rangers			
☐ 201 Jim Hrivnak	.05	.02	.01
Winnipeg jets			
☐ 202 Patrick Poulin	.05	.02	.01
Hartford Whalers			
☐ 203 Alexei Kovalev	.30	.14	.04
New York Rangers			
☐ 204 Robert Reichel	.08	.04	.01
Calgary Flames			
☐ 205 David Shaw	.05	.02	.01
Boston Bruins			
☐ 206 Brent Gilchrist	.05	.02	.01
Dallas Stars			
☐ 207 Craig Billington	.05	.02	.01
New Jersey Devils			
☐ 208 Bob Errey	.05	.02	.01
San Jose Sharks			
☐ 209 Dmitri Mironov	.05	.02	.01
Toronto Maple Leafs			
☐ 210 Dixon Ward	.05	.02	.01
Vancouver Canucks			
☐ 211 Rick Zombo	.05	.02	.01
St. Louis Blues			
☐ 212 Marty McSorley	.08	.04	.01
Los Angeles Kings			
☐ 213 Geoff Sanderson	.15	.07	.02
Hartford Whalers			
☐ 214 Dino Ciccarelli	.08	.04	.01
Detroit Red Wings			
☐ 215 Tony Amonte	.08	.04	.01
New York Rangers			
☐ 216 Dimitri Yushkevich	.05	.02	.01
Philadelphia Flyers			
☐ 217 Scott Niedermayer	.15	.07	.02
New Jersey Devils			
☐ 218 Sergei Nemchinov	.05	.02	.01
New York Rangers			
☐ 219 Steve Konroyd	.05	.02	.01
Detroit Red Wings			
☐ 220 Patrick Flatley	.05	.02	.01
New York Islanders			
☐ 221 Steve Chiasson	.05	.02	.01
Detroit Red Wings			
☐ 222 Alexander Mogilny	.30	.14	.04
Buffalo Sabres			
☐ 223 Pat Elynuik	.05	.02	.01
Washington Capitals			
☐ 224 Jamie Macoun	.05	.02	.01
Toronto Maple Leafs			
☐ 225 Tom Barrasso	.08	.04	.01
Pittsburgh Penguins			
☐ 226 Gaetan Duchesne	.05	.02	.01
San Jose Sharks			
☐ 227 Eric Weinrich	.05	.02	.01
Hartford Whalers			
☐ 228 Dave Poulin	.05	.02	.01
Boston Bruins			
☐ 229 Viacheslav Fetisov	.05	.02	.01
New Jersey Devils			
☐ 230 Brian Bradley	.05	.02	.01
Tampa Bay Lightning			
☐ 231 Petr Nedved	.08	.04	.01
Vancouver Canucks			
☐ 232 Phil Housley	.08	.04	.01
Winnipeg Jets			
☐ 233 Terry Carkner	.05	.02	.01
Philadelphia Flyers			
☐ 234 Kirk Muller	.08	.04	.01
Montreal Canadiens			
☐ 235 Brian Leetch	.20	.09	.03
New York Rangers			
☐ 236 Rob Blake	.08	.04	.01
Los Angeles Kings			
☐ 237 Chris Terreri	.08	.04	.01
New Jersey Devils			
☐ 238 Brendan Shanahan	.15	.07	.02
St. Louis Blues			
☐ 239 Paul Ysebaert	.05	.02	.01
Detroit Red Wings			
☐ 240 Jeremy Roenick	.40	.18	.05
Chicago Blackhawks			
☐ 241 Gary Roberts	.08	.04	.01
Calgary Flames			
☐ 242 Petr Klima	.05	.02	.01
Edmonton Oilers			
☐ 243 Glen Wesley	.05	.02	.01
Boston Bruins			
☐ 244 Vincent Damphousse	.08	.04	.01
Montreal Canadiens			
☐ 245 Luc Robitaille	.15	.07	.02
Los Angeles Kings			
☐ 246 Dallas Drake	.15	.07	.02
Detroit Red Wings			
☐ 247 Rob Gaudreau	.15	.07	.02
San Jose Sharks			
☐ 248 Tommy Sjodin	.05	.02	.01
Dallas Stars			
☐ 249 Richard Smehlik	.08	.04	.01
Buffalo Sabres			
☐ 250 Sergei Fedorov	.50	.23	.06
Detroit Red Wings			
☐ 251 Steve Heinze	.05	.02	.01
Boston Bruins			
☐ 252 Luke Richardson	.05	.02	.01
Edmonton Oilers			
☐ 253 Doug Weight	.08	.04	.01
Edmonton Oilers			
☐ 254 Martin Rucinsky	.05	.02	.01
Quebec Nordiques			
☐ 255 Sergio Momesso	.05	.02	.01
Vancouver Canucks			
☐ 256 Alexei Zhamnov	.25	.11	.03
Winnipeg Jets			
☐ 257 Bob Kudelski	.08	.04	.01
Ottawa Senators			
☐ 258 Brian Skrudland	.05	.02	.01
Calgary Flames			
☐ 259 Terry Yake	.05	.02	.01
Anaheim Mighty Ducks			
☐ 260 Alexei Gusarov	.05	.02	.01
Quebec Nordiques			
☐ 261 Sandis Ozolinsh	.05	.02	.01
San Jose Sharks			
☐ 262 Ted Donato	.05	.02	.01
Boston Bruins			
☐ 263 Bruce Driver	.05	.02	.01
New Jersey Devils			
☐ 264 Yves Racine	.05	.02	.01
Detroit Red Wings			
☐ 265 Mike Peluso	.05	.02	.01
New Jersey Devils			
☐ 266 Craig Muni	.05	.02	.01
Chicago Blackhawks			
☐ 267 Bob Carpenter	.05	.02	.01
Washington Capitals			
☐ 268 Kevin Haller	.05	.02	.01
Montreal Canadiens			
☐ 269 Brad May	.05	.02	.01
Buffalo Sabres			
☐ 270 Joe Kocur	.05	.02	.01
New York Rangers			
☐ 271 Igor Korolev	.05	.02	.01
St. Louis Blues			
☐ 272 Troy Murray	.05	.02	.01
Chicago Blackhawks			
☐ 273 Daren Puppa	.08	.04	.01

Toronto Maple Leafs			
☐ 274 Gordie Roberts..................	.05	.02	.01
Boston Bruins			
☐ 275 Michel Petit......................	.05	.02	.01
Calgary Flames			
☐ 276 Vincent Riendeau	.05	.02	.01
Detroit Red Wings			
☐ 277 Robert Petrovicky	.05	.02	.01
Hartford Whalers			
☐ 278 Valeri Zelepukin.................	.08	.04	.01
New Jersey Devils			
☐ 279 Bob Bassen	.05	.02	.01
St. Louis Blues			
☐ 280 Darrin Shannon.................	.05	.02	.01
Winnipeg Jets			
☐ 281 Dominik Hasek..................	.10	.05	.01
Buffalo Sabres			
☐ 282 Craig Ludwig.....................	.05	.02	.01
Dallas Stars			
☐ 283 Lyle Odelein	.05	.02	.01
Montreal Canadiens			
☐ 284 Alexander Semak	.05	.02	.01
New Jersey Devils			
☐ 285 Richard Matvichuk	.05	.02	.01
Dallas Stars			
☐ 286 Ken Daneyko.....................	.05	.02	.01
New Jersey Devils			
☐ 287 Jan Erixon........................	.05	.02	.01
New York Rangers			
☐ 288 Robert Dirk	.05	.02	.01
Vancouver Canucks			
☐ 289 Laurie Boschman	.05	.02	.01
Ottawa Senators			
☐ 290 Greg Paslawski	.05	.02	.01
Calgary Flames			
☐ 291 Rob Zamuner	.05	.02	.01
Tampa Bay Lightning			
☐ 292 Todd Gill	.05	.02	.01
Toronto Maple Leafs			
☐ 293 Neil Brady	.05	.02	.01
Ottawa Senators			
☐ 294 Murray Baron....................	.05	.02	.01
St. Louis Blues			
☐ 295 Peter Taglianetti	.05	.02	.01
Pittsburgh Penguins			
☐ 296 Wayne Presley	.05	.02	.01
Buffalo Sabres			
☐ 297 Paul Broten	.05	.02	.01
New York Rangers			
☐ 298 Dana Murzyn.....................	.05	.02	.01
Vancouver Canucks			
☐ 299 J.J. Daigneault	.05	.02	.01
Montreal Canadiens			
☐ 300 Wayne Gretzky	.75	.35	.09
Los Angeles Kings			
☐ 301 Keith Acton	.05	.02	.01
Philadelphia Flyers			
☐ 302 Yuri Khmylev.....................	.08	.04	.01
Buffalo Sabres			
☐ 303 Frantisek Musil..................	.05	.02	.01
Calgary Flames			
☐ 304 Bob Rouse	.05	.02	.01
Toronto Maple Leafs			
☐ 305 Greg Gilbert......................	.05	.02	.01
New York Rangers			
☐ 306 Geoff Smith......................	.05	.02	.01
Edmonton Oilers			
☐ 307 Adam Burt........................	.05	.02	.01
Hartford Whalers			
☐ 308 Phil Bourque	.05	.02	.01
New York Rangers			
☐ 309 Igor Kravchuk	.05	.02	.01
Edmonton Oilers			
☐ 310 Steve Yzerman..................	.25	.11	.03
Detroit Red Wings			
☐ 311 Darryl Sydor.....................	.08	.04	.01
Los Angeles Kings			
☐ 312 Tie Domi	.05	.02	.01
Winnipeg Jets			
☐ 313 Sergei Zubov....................	.35	.16	.04
New York Rangers			
☐ 314 Chris Dahlquist	.05	.02	.01
Calgary Flames			
☐ 315 Patrick Roy	.50	.23	.06
Montreal Canadiens			
☐ 316 Mark Osborne	.05	.02	.01
Toronto Maple Leafs			
☐ 317 Kelly Buchberger...............	.05	.02	.01
Edmonton Oilers			
☐ 318 John LeClair.....................	.05	.02	.01
Montreal Canadiens			
☐ 319 Randy McKay....................	.05	.02	.01
New Jersey Devils			
☐ 320 Jody Hull.........................	.05	.02	.01
Ottawa Senators			
☐ 321 Paul Stanton	.05	.02	.01
Pittsburgh Penguins			
☐ 322 Steven Finn	.05	.02	.01
Quebec Nordiques			
☐ 323 Rich Sutter.......................	.05	.02	.01
St. Louis Blues			
☐ 324 Ray Whitney......................	.08	.04	.01
San Jose Sharks			
☐ 325 Kevin Stevens	.20	.09	.03
Pittsburgh Penguins			
☐ 326 Valeri Kamensky	.15	.07	.02
Quebec Nordiques			
☐ 327 Doug Zmolek.....................	.05	.02	.01
San Jose Sharks			
☐ 328 Mikhail Tatarinov................	.05	.02	.01
Quebec Nordiques			
☐ 329 Ken Wregget	.05	.02	.01
Pittsburgh Penguins			
☐ 330 Joe Juneau.......................	.50	.23	.06
Boston Bruins			
☐ 331 Teemu Selanne	.60	.25	.08
Winnipeg Jets			
☐ 332 Trent Yawney	.05	.02	.01
Calgary Flames			
☐ 333 Pavel Bure........................	.75	.35	.09
Vancouver Canucks			
☐ 334 Jim Paek	.05	.02	.01
Pittsburgh Penguins			
☐ 335 Brett Hull.........................	.40	.18	.05
St. Louis Blues			
☐ 336 Tommy Soderstrom	.15	.07	.02
Philadelphia Flyers			
☐ 337 Grigori Panteleyev..............	.05	.02	.01
Boston Bruins			
☐ 338 Kevin Todd	.05	.02	.01
Edmonton Oilers			
☐ 339 Mark Janssens...................	.05	.02	.01
Hartford Whalers			
☐ 340 Rick Tocchet	.08	.04	.01
Pittsburgh Penguins			
☐ 341 Wendell Young...................	.05	.02	.01
Tampa Bay Lightning			
☐ 342 Cam Neely	.08	.04	.01
Boston Bruins			
☐ 343 Dave Andreychuk	.10	.05	.01
Toronto Maple Leafs			
☐ 344 Peter Bondra.....................	.08	.04	.01
Washington Capitals			
☐ 345 Pat LaFontaine	.20	.09	.03
Buffalo Sabres			
☐ 346 Robb Stauber.....................	.05	.02	.01
Los Angeles Kings			
☐ 347 Brian Mullen.....................	.08	.04	.01
New York Islanders			
☐ 348 Joe Murphy.......................	.05	.02	.01
Chicago Blackhawks			
☐ 349 Pat Jablonski....................	.05	.02	.01
Tampa Bay Lightning			
☐ 350 Mario Lemieux...................	.75	.35	.09
Pittsburgh Penguins			
☐ 351 Sergei Bautin....................	.05	.02	.01
Winnipeg Jets			
☐ 352 Claude Lapointe	.05	.02	.01
Quebec Nordiques			
☐ 353 Dean Evason	.05	.02	.01
Dallas Stars			
☐ 354 John Tucker......................	.05	.02	.01
Tampa Bay Lightning			
☐ 355 Drake Berehowsky	.05	.02	.01
Toronto Maple Leafs			
☐ 356 Gerald Diduck	.05	.02	.01
Vancouver Canucks			
☐ 357 Todd Krygier	.05	.02	.01
Washington Capitals			
☐ 358 Adrien Plavsic	.05	.02	.01
Vancouver Canucks			
☐ 359 Sylvain Lefebvre................	.05	.02	.01
Toronto Maple Leafs			
☐ 360 Kay Whitmore	.05	.02	.01
Vancouver Canucks			
☐ 361 Sheldon Kennedy	.05	.02	.01
Detroit Red Wings			
☐ 362 Kris King	.05	.02	.01
Winnipeg Jets			
☐ 363 Marc Bergevin...................	.05	.02	.01
Tampa Bay Lightning			
☐ 364 Keith Primeau	.08	.04	.01
Detroit Red Wings			
☐ 365 Jimmy Waite.....................	.05	.02	.01
Chicago Blackhawks			
☐ 366 Dean Kennedy...................	.05	.02	.01
Winnipeg Jets			
☐ 367 Mike Krushelnyski...............	.05	.02	.01

Toronto Maple Leafs			
☐ 368 Ron Tugnutt	.05	.02	.01
Edmonton Oilers			
☐ 369 Bob Beers	.05	.02	.01
Tampa Bay Lightning			
☐ 370 Randy Burridge	.05	.02	.01
Washington Capitals			
☐ 371 Dave Reid	.05	.02	.01
Boston Bruins			
☐ 372 Frantisek Kucera	.05	.02	.01
Chicago Blackhawks			
☐ 373 Scott Pellerin	.10	.05	.01
New Jersey Devils			
☐ 374 Brad Dalgarno	.05	.02	.01
New York Islanders			
☐ 375 Martin Straka	.25	.11	.03
Pittsburgh Penguins			
☐ 376 Scott Pearson	.05	.02	.01
Edmonton Oilers			
☐ 377 Arturs Irbe	.25	.11	.03
San Jose Sharks			
☐ 378 Jiri Slegr	.05	.02	.01
Vancouver Canucks			
☐ 379 Stephane Fiset	.05	.02	.01
Quebec Nordiques			
☐ 380 Stu Barnes	.05	.02	.01
Winnipeg Jets			
☐ 381 Ric Nattress	.05	.02	.01
Philadelphia Flyers			
☐ 382 Steven King	.05	.02	.01
New York Rangers			
☐ 383 Michael Nylander	.15	.07	.02
Hartford Whalers			
☐ 384 Keith Brown	.05	.02	.01
Chicago Blackhawks			
☐ 385 Gino Odjick	.05	.02	.01
Vancouver Canucks			
☐ 386 Bryan Marchment	.05	.02	.01
Chicago Blackhawks			
☐ 387 Mike Foligno	.05	.02	.01
Toronto Maple Leafs			
☐ 388 Zdeno Ciger	.05	.02	.01
Edmonton Oilers			
☐ 389 Dave Taylor	.08	.04	.01
Los Angeles Kings			
☐ 390 Mike Sullivan	.05	.02	.01
San Jose Sharks			
☐ 391 Shawn Chambers	.05	.02	.01
Tampa Bay Lightning			
☐ 392 Brad Marsh	.08	.04	.01
Ottawa Senators			
☐ 393 Mike Hough	.05	.02	.01
Quebec Nordiques			
☐ 394 Jeff Reese	.05	.02	.01
Calgary Flames			
☐ 395 Bill Guerin	.05	.02	.01
New Jersey Devils			
☐ 396 Greg Hawgood	.05	.02	.01
Philadelphia Flyers			
☐ 397 Jim Sandlak	.05	.02	.01
Hartford Whalers			
☐ 398 Stephane Matteau	.05	.02	.01
Chicago Blackhawks			
☐ 399 John Blue	.05	.02	.01
Boston Bruins			
☐ 400 Tony Twist	.05	.02	.01
Quebec Nordiques			
☐ 401 Luciano Borsato	.05	.02	.01
Winnipeg Jets			
☐ 402 Gerard Gallant	.05	.02	.01
Tampa Bay Lightning			
☐ 403 Rick Tabaracci	.05	.02	.01
Washington Capitals			
☐ 404 Nick Kypreos	.05	.02	.01
Hartford Whalers			
☐ 405 Marty McInnis	.05	.02	.01
New York Islanders			
☐ 406 Craig Wolanin	.05	.02	.01
Quebec Nordiques			
☐ 407 Mark Lamb	.05	.02	.01
Ottawa Senators			
☐ 408 Martin Gelinas	.05	.02	.01
Quebec Nordiques			
☐ 409 Ronnie Stern	.05	.02	.01
Calgary Flames			
☐ 410 Ken Sutton	.05	.02	.01
Buffalo Sabres			
☐ 411 Brian Noonan	.05	.02	.01
Chicago Blackhawks			
☐ 412 Stephane Quintal	.05	.02	.01
St. Louis Blues			
☐ 413 Rob Zettler	.05	.02	.01
San Jose Sharks			
☐ 414 Gino Cavallini	.05	.02	.01
Quebec Nordiques			
☐ 415 Mark Hardy	.05	.02	.01
Los Angeles Kings			
☐ 416 Jay Wells	.05	.02	.01
New York Rangers			
☐ 417 Keith Jones	.05	.02	.01
Washington Capitals			
☐ 418 Dave McLlwain	.05	.02	.01
Toronto Maple Leafs			
☐ 419 Frank Pietrangelo	.05	.02	.01
Hartford Whalers			
☐ 420 Jocelyn Lemieux	.05	.02	.01
Chicago Blackhawks			
☐ 421 Vyacheslav Kozlov	.35	.16	.04
Detroit Red Wings			
☐ 422 Randy Moller	.05	.02	.01
Buffalo Sabres			
☐ 423 Kevin Dahl	.05	.02	.01
Calgary Flames			
☐ 424 Shjon Podein	.10	.05	.01
Edmonton Oilers			
☐ 425 Shane Churla	.05	.02	.01
Dallas Stars			
☐ 426 Guy Hebert	.15	.07	.02
St. Louis Blues			
☐ 427 Mikael Andersson	.05	.02	.01
Tampa Bay Lightning			
☐ 428 Robert Kron	.05	.02	.01
Hartford Whalers			
☐ 429 Mike Eagles	.05	.02	.01
Winnipeg Jets			
☐ 430 Alan May	.05	.02	.01
Washington Capitals			
☐ 431 Ron Wilson	.05	.02	.01
St. Louis Blues			
☐ 432 Darcy Wakaluk	.05	.02	.01
Dallas Stars			
☐ 433 Rob Ray	.05	.02	.01
Buffalo Sabres			
☐ 434 Brent Ashton	.05	.02	.01
Calgary Flames			
☐ 435 Jason Woolley	.05	.02	.01
Washington Capitals			
☐ 436 Basil McRae	.05	.02	.01
St. Louis Blues			
☐ 437 Andre Racicot	.05	.02	.01
Montreal Canadiens			
☐ 438 Brad Werenka	.05	.02	.01
Edmonton Oilers			
☐ 439 Josef Beranek	.08	.04	.01
Philadelphia Flyers			
☐ 440 Dave Christian	.05	.02	.01
Chicago Blackhawks			
☐ 441 Theoren Fleury LBM	.08	.04	.01
Calgary Flames			
☐ 442 Mark Recchi LBM	.08	.04	.01
Philadelphia Flyers			
☐ 443 Cliff Ronning LBM	.05	.02	.01
Vancouver Canucks			
☐ 444 Tony Granato LBM	.05	.02	.01
Los Angeles Kings			
☐ 445 John Vanbiesbrouck LBM	.08	.04	.01
New York Rangers			
☐ 446 Jari Kurri HL	.08	.04	.01
Los Angeles Kings			
500th goal			
☐ 447 Mike Gartner HL	.10	.05	.01
New York Rangers			
14th Straight			
30-goal season			
☐ 448 Steve Yzerman HL	.08	.04	.01
Detroit Red Wings			
1,000th Point			
☐ 449 Glenn Anderson HL	.05	.02	.01
Toronto Maple Leafs			
1,000th Point			
☐ 450 Washington Caps HL	.05	.02	.01
Al Iafrate			
Sylvain Cote			
Kevin Hatcher			
Highest Scoring Defense			
in NHL History			
☐ 451 Luc Robitaille HL	.08	.04	.01
Los Angeles Kings			
Most Goals by			
left winger			
☐ 452 Pittsburgh Penguins HL	.05	.02	.01
17-Game Winning Streak			
☐ 453 Corey Hirsch	.15	.07	.02
New York Rangers			
☐ 454 Jesse Belanger	.15	.07	.02
Montreal Canadiens			
☐ 455 Philippe Boucher	.06	.03	.01
Buffalo Sabres			

☐ 456 Robert Lang .... Los Angeles Kings	.06	.03	.01
☐ 457 Doug Barrault .... Dallas Stars	.15	.07	.02
☐ 458 Steve Konowalchuk .... Washington Capitals	.06	.03	.01
☐ 459 Oleg Petrov .... Montreal Canadiens	.15	.07	.02
☐ 460 Niclas Andersson .... Quebec Nordiques	.06	.03	.01
☐ 461 Milan Tichy .... Chicago Blackhawks	.10	.05	.01
☐ 462 Darrin Madeley .... Ottawa Senators	.20	.09	.03
☐ 463 Tyler Wright .... Edmonton Oilers	.06	.03	.01
☐ 464 Sergei Krivokrasov .... Chicago Blackhawks	.06	.03	.01
☐ 465 Vladimir Vujtek .... Edmonton Oilers	.06	.03	.01
☐ 466 Rick Knickle .... Los Angeles Kings	.15	.07	.02
☐ 467 Gord Kruppke .... Detroit Red Wings	.10	.05	.01
☐ 468 David Emma .... New Jersey Devils	.06	.03	.01
☐ 469 Scott Thomas .... Buffalo Sabres	.10	.05	.01
☐ 470 Shawn Rivers .... Tampa Bay Lightning	.10	.05	.01
☐ 471 Jason Bowen .... Philadelphia Flyers	.10	.05	.01
☐ 472 Bryan Smolinski .... Boston Bruins	.25	.11	.03
☐ 473 Chris Simon .... Quebec Nordiques	.15	.07	.02
☐ 474 Peter Ciavaglia .... Buffalo Sabres	.10	.05	.01
☐ 475 Sergei Zholtok .... Boston Bruins	.06	.03	.01
☐ 476 Radek Hamr .... Ottawa Senators	.10	.05	.01
☐ 477 Teemu Selanne SL .... Winnipeg Jets Alexander Mogilny Buffalo Sabres Goals	.25	.11	.03
☐ 478 Adam Oates SL .... Boston Bruins Assists	.08	.04	.01
☐ 479 Mario Lemieux SL .... Pittsburgh Penguins Points	.20	.09	.03
☐ 480 Mario Lemieux SL .... Pittsburgh Penguins Plus/Minus	.20	.09	.03
☐ 481 Dave Andreychuk SL .... Toronto Maple Leafs Power-Play Goals	.08	.04	.01
☐ 482 Phil Housley SL .... Winnipeg Jets Defenseman Scoring	.05	.02	.01
☐ 483 Tom Barrasso SL .... Pittsburgh Penguins Wins	.05	.02	.01
☐ 484 Felix Potvin SL .... Toronto Maple Leafs GAA	.35	.16	.04
☐ 485 Ed Belfour SL .... Chicago Blackhawks	.08	.04	.01
☐ 486 Sault Ste. Marie .... Greyhounds Memorial Cup Champions	.05	.02	.01
☐ 487 Montreal Canadiens .... Stanley Cup Champions	.05	.02	.01
☐ 488 Anaheim Mighty Ducks .... Logo	.50	.23	.06
☐ 489 Guy Hebert .... Anaheim Mighty Ducks	.15	.07	.02
☐ 490 Sean Hill .... Anaheim Mighty Ducks	.05	.02	.01
☐ 491 Florida Panthers Logo	.50	.23	.06
☐ 492 John Vanbiesbrouck .... Florida Panthers	.10	.05	.01
☐ 493 Tom Fitzgerald .... Florida Panthers	.05	.02	.01
☐ 494 Paul DiPietro .... Montreal Canadiens	.05	.02	.01
☐ 495 David Volek .... New York Islanders	.05	.02	.01
☐ 496 Alexander Daigle .... Ottawa Senators (Mail-in)	8.00	3.60	1.00
☐ 497 Shawn McEachern .... Pittsburgh Penguins	.05	.02	.01
☐ 498 Rich Sutter .... Chicago Blackhawks	.05	.02	.01
☐ 499 Evgeny Davydov .... Ottawa Senators	.05	.02	.01
☐ 500 Sean Hill .... Anaheim Mighty Ducks	.05	.02	.01
☐ 501 John Vanbiesbrouck .... Florida Panthers	.15	.07	.02
☐ 502 Guy Hebert .... Anaheim Mighty Ducks	.15	.07	.02
☐ 503 Scott Mellanby .... Florida Panthers	.05	.02	.01
☐ 504 Ron Tugnutt .... Anaheim Mighty Ducks	.05	.02	.01
☐ 505 Brian Skrudland .... Florida Panthers	.05	.02	.01
☐ 506 Nelson Emerson .... Winnipeg Jets	.08	.04	.01
☐ 507 Kevin Todd .... Chicago Blackhawks	.05	.02	.01
☐ 508 Terry Carkner .... Detroit Red Wings	.05	.02	.01
☐ 509 Stephane Quintal .... Winnipeg Jets	.05	.02	.01
☐ 510 Paul Stanton .... Boston Bruins	.05	.02	.01
☐ 511 Terry Yake .... Anaheim Mighty Ducks	.05	.02	.01
☐ 512 Brian Benning .... Florida Panthers	.05	.02	.01
☐ 513 Brian Propp .... Hartford Whalers	.08	.04	.01
☐ 514 Steven King .... Anaheim Mighty Ducks	.05	.02	.01
☐ 515 Joe Cirella .... Florida Panthers	.05	.02	.01
☐ 516 Andy Moog .... Dallas Stars	.08	.04	.01
☐ 517 Paul Ysebaert .... Winnipeg Jets	.05	.02	.01
☐ 518 Petr Klima .... Tampa Bay Lightning	.05	.02	.01
☐ 519 Corey Millen .... New Jersey Devils	.05	.02	.01
☐ 520 Phil Housley .... St. Louis Blues	.08	.04	.01
☐ 521 Craig Billington .... Ottawa Senators	.05	.02	.01
☐ 522 Jeff Norton .... San Jose Sharks	.05	.02	.01
☐ 523 Neil Wilkinson .... Chicago Blackhawks	.05	.02	.01
☐ 524 Doug Lidster .... New York Rangers	.05	.02	.01
☐ 525 Steve Larmer .... New York Rangers	.08	.04	.01
☐ 526 Jon Casey .... Boston Bruins	.08	.04	.01
☐ 527 Brad McCrimmon .... Detroit Red Wings	.05	.02	.01
☐ 528 Alexei Kasatonov .... Anaheim Mighty Ducks	.05	.02	.01
☐ 529 Andrei Lomakin .... Florida Panthers	.05	.02	.01
☐ 530 Daren Puppa .... Tampa Bay Lightning	.08	.04	.01
☐ 531 Sergei Makarov .... San Jose Sharks	.08	.04	.01
☐ 532 Jim Sandlak .... Hartford Whalers	.05	.02	.01
☐ 533 Glenn Healy .... New York Rangers	.05	.02	.01
☐ 534 Martin Gelinas .... Quebec Nordiques	.05	.02	.01
☐ 535 Igor Larionov .... San Jose Sharks	.05	.02	.01
☐ 536 Anatoli Semenov .... Anaheim Mighty Ducks	.05	.02	.01
☐ 537 Mark Fitzpatrick .... Florida Panthers	.05	.02	.01
☐ 538 Paul Cavallini .... Dallas Stars	.05	.02	.01
☐ 539 Jimmy Waite .... San Jose Sharks	.05	.02	.01
☐ 540 Yves Racine .... Philadelphia Flyers	.05	.02	.01
☐ 541 Jeff Hackett .... Chicago Blackhawks	.05	.02	.01
☐ 542 Marty McSorley .... Los Angeles Kings	.05	.02	.01
☐ 543 Scott Pearson	.05	.02	.01

Quebec Nordiques			
☐ 544 Ron Hextall	.08	.04	.01
New York Islanders			
☐ 545 Gaetan Duchesne	.05	.02	.01
San Jose Sharks			
☐ 546 Jamie Baker	.05	.02	.01
San Jose Sharks			
☐ 547 Troy Loney	.05	.02	.01
Anaheim Mighty Ducks			
☐ 548 Gord Murphy	.05	.02	.01
Florida Panthers			
☐ 549 Bob Kudelski	.08	.04	.01
Florida Panthers			
☐ 550 Dean Evason	.05	.02	.01
Dallas Stars			
☐ 551 Mike Peluso	.05	.02	.01
New Jersey Devils			
☐ 552 Dave Poulin	.05	.02	.01
Washington Capitals			
☐ 553 Randy Ladouceur	.05	.02	.01
Anaheim Mighty Ducks			
☐ 554 Tom Fitzgerald	.05	.02	.01
Florida Panthers			
☐ 555 Denis Savard	.08	.04	.01
Tampa Bay Lightning			
☐ 556 Kelly Kisio	.05	.02	.01
Calgary Flames			
☐ 557 Craig Simpson	.05	.02	.01
Buffalo Sabres			
☐ 558 Stu Grimson	.05	.02	.01
Anaheim Mighty Ducks			
☐ 559 Mike Hough	.05	.02	.01
Florida Panthers			
☐ 560 Gerard Gallant	.05	.02	.01
Tampa Bay Lightning			
☐ 561 Greg Gilbert	.05	.02	.01
New York Rangers			
☐ 562 Vladimir Ruzicka	.05	.02	.01
Ottawa Senators			
☐ 563 Jim Hrivnak	.05	.02	.01
Washington Capitals			
☐ 564 Dave Lowry	.05	.02	.01
Florida Panthers			
☐ 565 Todd Ewen	.05	.02	.01
Anaheim Mighty Ducks			
☐ 566 Bob Errey	.05	.02	.01
San Jose Sharks			
☐ 567 Bryan Trottier	.08	.04	.01
Pittsburgh Penguins			
☐ 568 Grant Ledyard	.05	.02	.01
Dallas Stars			
☐ 569 Keith Brown	.05	.02	.01
Florida Panthers			
☐ 570 Darren Turcotte	.05	.02	.01
Hartford Whalers			
☐ 571 Patrick Poulin	.05	.02	.01
Chicago Blackhawks			
☐ 572 Jimmy Carson	.05	.02	.01
Vancouver Canucks			
☐ 573 Eric Weinrich	.05	.02	.01
Chicago Blackhawks			
☐ 574 James Patrick	.05	.02	.01
Hartford Whalers			
☐ 575 Bob Beers	.05	.02	.01
Edmonton Oilers			
☐ 576 Chris Joseph	.05	.02	.01
Tampa Bay Lightning			
☐ 577 Bryan Marchment	.05	.02	.01
Chicago Blackhawks			
☐ 578 Bob Carpenter	.05	.02	.01
Washington Capitals			
☐ 579 Craig Muni	.05	.02	.01
Chicago Blackhawks			
☐ 580 Pat Elynuik	.05	.02	.01
Tampa Bay Lightning			
☐ 581 Todd Elik	.05	.02	.01
San Jose Sharks			
☐ 582 Doug Brown	.05	.02	.01
Pittsburgh Penguins			
☐ 583 Dave McIlwain	.05	.02	.01
Toronto Maple Leafs			
☐ 584 Dave Tippett	.05	.02	.01
Philadelphia Flyers			
☐ 585 Jesse Belanger	.15	.07	.02
Florida Panthers			
☐ 586 Chris Pronger	.35	.16	.04
Hartford Whalers			
☐ 587 Alexandre Daigle	.40	.18	.05
Ottawa Senators			
☐ 588 Cam Stewart	.10	.05	.01
Boston Bruins			
☐ 589 Derek Plante	.40	.18	.05
Buffalo Sabres			
☐ 590 Pat Peake	.10	.05	.01
Washington Capitals			
☐ 591 Alexander Karpovtsev	.05	.02	.01
New York Rangers			
☐ 592 Rob Niedermayer	.35	.16	.04
Florida Panthers			
☐ 593 Jocelyn Thibault	.40	.18	.05
Quebec Nordiques			
☐ 594 Jason Arnott	1.50	.65	.19
Edmonton Oilers			
☐ 595 Mike Rathje	.05	.02	.01
San Jose Sharks			
☐ 596 Chris Gratton	.35	.16	.04
Tampa Bay Lightning			
☐ 597 Markus Naslund	.10	.05	.01
Pittsburgh Penguins			
☐ 598 Dmitri Filimonov	.05	.02	.01
Ottawa Senators			
☐ 599 Andrei Trefilov	.20	.09	.03
Calgary Flames			
☐ 600 Michal Sykora	.15	.07	.02
San Jose Sharks			
☐ 601 Greg Johnson	.05	.02	.01
Detroit Red Wings			
☐ 602 Mikael Renberg	.40	.18	.05
Philadelphia Flyers			
☐ 603 Alexei Yashin	.50	.23	.06
Ottawa Senators			
☐ 604 Damian Rhodes	.15	.07	.02
Toronto Maple Leafs			
☐ 605 Jeff Shantz	.10	.05	.01
Chicago Blackhawks			
☐ 606 Brent Gretzky	.20	.09	.03
Tampa Bay Lightning			
☐ 607 Boris Mironov	.05	.02	.01
Winnipeg Jets			
☐ 608 Ted Drury	.05	.02	.01
Calgary Flames			
☐ 609 Chris Osgood	.40	.18	.05
Detroit Red Wings			
☐ 610 Jim Storm	.15	.07	.02
Hartford Whalers			
☐ 611 Dave Karpa	.05	.02	.01
Quebec Nordiques			
☐ 612 Stewart Malgunas	.10	.05	.01
Philadelphia Flyers			
☐ 613 Jason Smith	.10	.05	.01
New Jersey Devils			
☐ 614 German Titov	.20	.09	.03
Calgary Flames			
☐ 615 Patrick Carnback	.10	.05	.01
Anaheim Mighty Ducks			
☐ 616 Jaroslav Modry	.10	.05	.01
New Jersey Devils			
☐ 617 Scott Levins	.10	.05	.01
Ottawa Senators			
☐ 618 Fred Brathwaite	.15	.07	.02
Edmonton Oilers			
☐ 619 Ilya Byakin	.10	.05	.01
Edmonton Oilers			
☐ 620 Jarkko Varvio	.05	.02	.01
Dallas Stars			
☐ 621 Jim Montgomery	.10	.05	.01
St. Louis Blues			
☐ 622 Vesa Viitakoski	.10	.05	.01
Calgary Flames			
☐ 623 Alexei Kudashov	.10	.05	.01
Toronto Maple Leafs			
☐ 624 Pavol Demitra	.10	.05	.01
Ottawa Senators			
☐ 625 Iain Fraser	.10	.05	.01
Quebec Nordiques			
☐ 626 Peter Popovic	.10	.05	.01
Montreal Canadiens			
☐ 627 Kirk Maltby	.10	.05	.01
Edmonton Oilers			
☐ 628 Garth Snow	.15	.07	.02
Quebec Nordiques			
☐ 629 Peter White	.10	.05	.01
Edmonton Oilers			
☐ 630 Mike McKee	.10	.05	.01
Quebec Nordiques			
☐ 631 Darren McCarty	.10	.05	.01
Detroit Red Wings			
☐ 632 Pat Neaton	.10	.05	.01
Pittsburgh Penguins			
☐ 633 Sandy McCarthy	.05	.02	.01
Calgary Flames			
☐ 634 Pierre Sevigny	.05	.02	.01
Montreal Canadiens			
☐ 635 Matt Martin	.10	.05	.01
Toronto Maple Leafs			
☐ 636 John Slaney	.05	.02	.01
Washington Capitals			
☐ 637 Bob Corkum	.05	.02	.01

Anaheim Mighty Ducks			
☐ 638 Jose Charbonneau	.10	.05	.01
Vancouver Canucks			
☐ 639 Bill Houlder	.05	.02	.01
Anaheim Mighty Ducks			
☐ 640 Warren Rychel	.05	.02	.01
Los Angeles Kings			
☐ 641 Garry Valk	.05	.02	.01
Anaheim Mighty Ducks			
☐ 642 Greg Hawgood	.05	.02	.01
Florida Panthers			
☐ 643 Randy Gilhen	.05	.02	.01
Florida Panthers			
☐ 644 Stu Barnes	.05	.02	.01
Florida Panthers			
☐ 645 Fredrik Olausson	.05	.02	.01
Edmonton Oilers			
☐ 646 Geoff Smith	.05	.02	.01
Florida Panthers			
☐ 647 Mike Foligno	.05	.02	.01
Florida Panthers			
☐ 648 Martin Brodeur..................	.30	.14	.04
New Jersey Devils			
☐ 649 Ryan McGill.......................	.05	.02	.01
Philadelphia Flyers			
☐ 650 Jeff Reese	.05	.02	.01
Hartford Whalers			
☐ 651 Mike Sillinger	.05	.02	.01
Detroit Red Wings			
☐ 652 Brent Severyn	.10	.05	.01
Florida Panthers			
☐ 653 Rob Ramage	.05	.02	.01
Florida Panthers			
☐ 654 Dixon Ward.......................	.05	.02	.01
Los Angeles Kings			
☐ 655 Danton Cole	.05	.02	.01
Florida Panthers			
☐ 656 Viacheslav Butsayev...........	.05	.02	.01
Philadelphia Flyers			
☐ 657 Ron Wilson	.05	.02	.01
Montreal Canadiens			
☐ 658 Paul Broten	.05	.02	.01
Dallas Stars			
☐ 659 Mike Hudson......................	.05	.02	.01
New York Rangers			
☐ 660 Trevor Kidd.......................	.05	.02	.01
Calgary Flames			
☐ 661 Travis Green.......................	.05	.02	.01
New York Islanders			
☐ 662 Wayne Gretzky	2.00	.90	.25
Los Angeles Kings			
☐ NNO Alexandre Daigle...............	5.00	2.30	.60
Ottawa Senators			
Redemption card			
☐ NNO Eric Lindros AS SP	50.00	23.00	6.25
Philadelphia Flyers			

gently bending the card to pop up the player's head and then pulling a tab at the top to stand the player up. The fronts have an white outer border with a wider purple inner border overlaid with a thin red and purple line. The words "Collector's Edition" are printed in white at the top of the picture. The logo for Black's Photography is printed in the upper left vertical side. Player identification appears under the action photo. The purple backs have a white border with a second player portrait and biography. The Black's Photography logo is printed in the upper left corner. The cards are numbered on the front. There was also an album available for this set; it is not included in the complete set price below.

	MINT	EXC	G-VG
COMPLETE SET (24)......................	25.00	10.00	2.50
COMMON PLAYER (1-24)...............	.75	.30	.07

			MINT	EXC	G-VG
☐	1	Wendel Clark.........................	3.00	1.20	.30
☐	2	Doug Gilmour	5.00	2.00	.50
☐	3	Glenn Anderson	1.50	.60	.15
☐	4	Peter Zezel	1.00	.40	.10
☐	5	Bob Rouse	.75	.30	.07
☐	6	Rob Pearson	1.25	.50	.12
☐	7	Mark Osborne	.75	.30	.07
☐	8	Dmitri Mironov.....................	1.25	.50	.12
☐	9	Dave McLlwain.....................	.75	.30	.07
☐	10	Kent Manderville	1.00	.40	.10
☐	11	Jamie Macoun.......................	.75	.30	.07
☐	12	Sylvain Lefebvre	1.00	.40	.10
☐	13	Dave Andreychuk	2.50	1.00	.25
☐	14	Drake Berehowsky	1.00	.40	.10
☐	15	Bill Berg	.75	.30	.07
☐	16	John Cullen..........................	1.00	.40	.10
☐	17	Ken Baumgartner	.75	.30	.07
☐	18	Nikolai Borschevsky..............	1.25	.50	.12
☐	19	Mike Eastwood.....................	.75	.30	.07
☐	20	Dave Ellett	1.00	.40	.10
☐	21	Mike Foligno	1.00	.40	.10
☐	22	Todd Gill	.75	.30	.07
☐	23	Mike Krushelnyski................	1.00	.40	.10
☐	24	Felix Potvin	5.00	2.00	.50
☐	xx	Album	5.00	2.00	.50

1993-94 Score Gold Rush

Fredrik Olausson

The 1993-94 Score Gold Rush set consists of 166 standard-size (2 1/2" by 3 1/2") cards. The fronts are identical in design with the regular second-series Score cards, except for the metallic finish and gold marbleized borders. The backs are nearly identical to the regular issue cards, the Gold Rush logo at the top being the only difference. The cards are numbered on the back.

	MINT	EXC	G-VG
COMPLETE SET (166)......................	65.00	29.00	8.25
COMMON PLAYER (497-662)..........	.25	.11	.03
*VETERAN STARS: 3X to 6X VALUE.			
*YOUNG STARS: 2.5X to 5X VALUE.			
*RCs: 2X to 4X VALUE......................			

1993-94 Score Black's

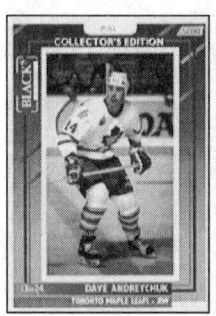

This 24-card, standard-size (2 1/2" by 3 1/2") Toronto Maple Leafs team set was produced by Score and sponsored by Black's Photography. The cards were distributed free in four-card packs, when a customer brought in film for developing, or with a second order of prints, or when purchasing two rolls of Black's P.I. film. The fronts feature a pop-up photo cut-out. The pop-up is accomplished by

1993-94 Score Dream Team

Randomly inserted in first series Canadian packs, this 24-card standard-size (2 1/2" by 3 1/2") set features Score's Dream Team selections. Horizontal fronts feature an action photo and a head shot at lower right. The player's name and position appear in beneath the large photo. The backs contain career highlights and are numbered "X of 24".

		MINT	EXC	G-VG
COMPLETE SET (24)		210.00	95.00	26.00
COMMON PLAYER (1-24)		4.00	1.80	.50
☐ 1	Tom Barrasso	4.00	1.80	.50
	Pittsburgh Penguins			
☐ 2	Patrick Roy	22.00	10.00	2.80
	Montreal Canadiens			
☐ 3	Chris Chelios	4.00	1.80	.50
	Chicago Blackhawks			
☐ 4	Al MacInnis	5.00	2.30	.60
	Calgary Flames			
☐ 5	Scott Stevens	4.00	1.80	.50
	New Jersey Devils			
☐ 6	Brian Leetch	12.00	5.50	1.50
	New York Rangers			
☐ 7	Ray Bourque	7.00	3.10	.85
	Boston Bruins			
☐ 8	Paul Coffey	5.00	2.30	.60
	Detroit Red wings			
☐ 9	Al Iafrate	4.00	1.80	.50
	Washington Capitals			
☐ 10	Mario Lemieux	25.00	11.50	3.10
	Pittsburgh Penguins			
☐ 11	Wayne Gretzky	35.00	16.00	4.40
	Los Angeles Kings			
☐ 12	Eric Lindros	35.00	16.00	4.40
	Philadelphia Flyers			
☐ 13	Pat LaFontaine	8.00	3.60	1.00
	Buffalo Sabres			
☐ 14	Joe Sakic	7.00	3.10	.85
	Quebec Nordiques			
☐ 15	Pierre Turgeon	8.00	3.60	1.00
	New York Islanders			
☐ 16	Steve Yzerman	12.00	5.50	1.50
	Detroit Red Wings			
☐ 17	Adam Oates	7.00	3.10	.85
	Boston Bruins			
☐ 18	Brett Hull	12.00	5.50	1.50
	St. Louis Blues			
☐ 19	Pavel Bure	25.00	11.50	3.10
	Vancouver Canucks			
☐ 20	Alexander Mogilny	8.00	3.60	1.00
	Buffalo Sabres			
☐ 21	Teemu Selanne	15.00	6.75	1.90
	Winnipeg Jets			
☐ 22	Steve Larmer	4.00	1.80	.50
	Chicago Blackhawks			
☐ 23	Kevin Stevens	6.00	2.70	.75
	Pittsburgh Penguins			
☐ 24	Luc Robitaille	6.00	2.70	.75
	Los Angeles Kings			

1993-94 Score Dynamic Duos Canadian

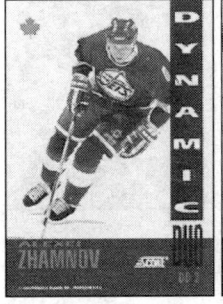

Randomly inserted in Canadian second-series packs, this nine-card standard-size (2 1/2" by 3 1/2") set highlights two team members on each card. Both the front and back of each card features a color player action shot. The player's name appears in red lettering within the team-colored bottom margin. The words "Dynamic Duos" appears in gold foil along the right side. A red maple leaf is placed at the upper left. A statement in English and French about the players begins on one side and is completed on the other. The cards are numbered on both the front and back with a "DD" prefix.

		MINT	EXC	G-VG
COMPLETE SET (9)		100.00	45.00	12.50
COMMON PAIR (1-9)		8.00	3.60	1.00
☐ 1	Doug Gilmour	20.00	9.00	2.50
	Dave Andreychuk			
	Toronto Maple Leafs			
☐ 2	Teemu Selanne/Alexei Zhamnov	15.00	6.75	1.90
	Winnipeg Jets			
☐ 3	Alexandre Daigle	15.00	6.75	1.90
	Alexei Yashin			
	Ottawa Senators			
☐ 4	Gary Roberts	8.00	3.60	1.00
	Joe Nieuwendyk			
	Calgary Flames			
☐ 5	Joe Sakic	10.00	4.50	1.25
	Mats Sundin			
	Quebec Nordiques			
☐ 6	Brian Bellows	8.00	3.60	1.00
	Kirk Muller			
	Montreal Canadiens			
☐ 7	Shayne Corson	20.00	9.00	2.50
	Jason Arnott			
	Edmonton Oilers			
☐ 8	Mario Lemieux	30.00	13.50	3.80
	Kevin Stevens			
	Pittsburgh Penguins			
☐ 9	Pierre Turgeon	10.00	4.50	1.25
	Derek King			
	New York Islanders			

1993-94 Score Dynamic Duos U.S.

Randomly inserted in American second-series packs, this nine-card standard-size (2 1/2" by 3 1/2") set highlights two team members on each card. Both the front and back of each card features a color player action shot. The player's name appears in red lettering within the team-colored bottom margin. The words "Dynamic Duos" appears in gold foil along the right side. A blue star is placed at the upper left. A statement about the players begins on one side and is completed on the other. The cards are numbered on both the front and back with a "DD" prefix.

	MINT	EXC	G-VG
COMPLETE SET (9)	125.00	57.50	15.50
COMMON PAIR (1-9)	8.00	3.60	1.00
☐ 1 Mark Recchi Eric Lindros Philadelphia Flyers	40.00	18.00	5.00
☐ 2 Pat LaFontaine Alexander Mogilny Buffalo Sabres	12.00	5.50	1.50
☐ 3 Adam Oates Joe Juneau Boston Bruins	10.00	4.50	1.25
☐ 4 Brett Hull Craig Janney St. Louis Blues	15.00	6.75	1.90
☐ 5 Mark Messier Adam Graves New York Rangers	15.00	6.75	1.90
☐ 6 Jeremy Roenick Joe Murphy Chicago Blackhawks	12.00	5.50	1.50
☐ 7 Jari Kurri Wayne Gretzky Los Angeles Kings	40.00	18.00	5.00
☐ 8 Sergei Makarov Igor Larionov San Jose Sharks	8.00	3.60	1.00
☐ 9 Steve Yzerman Sergei Fedorov Detroit Red Wings	22.00	10.00	2.80

	MINT	EXC	G-VG
COMPLETE SET (24)	225.00	100.00	28.00
COMMON PLAYER (1-24)	4.00	1.80	.50
☐ 1 Ray Bourque Boston Bruins	7.00	3.10	.85
☐ 2 Pat LaFontaine Buffalo Sabres	8.00	3.60	1.00
☐ 3 Al MacInnis Calgary Flames	5.00	2.30	.60
☐ 4 Jeremy Roenick Chicago Blackhawks	12.00	5.50	1.50
☐ 5 Mike Modano Dallas Stars	9.00	4.00	1.15
☐ 6 Steve Yzerman Detroit Red Wings	12.00	5.50	1.50
☐ 7 Bill Ranford Edmonton Oilers	4.00	1.80	.50
☐ 8 Sean Burke Hartford Whalers	4.00	1.80	.50
☐ 9 Wayne Gretzky Los Angeles Kings	35.00	16.00	4.40
☐ 10 Patrick Roy Montreal Canadiens	22.00	10.00	2.80
☐ 11 Scott Stevens New Jersey Devils	4.00	1.80	.50
☐ 12 Pierre Turgeon New York Islanders	8.00	3.60	1.00
☐ 13 Brian Leetch New York Rangers	12.00	5.50	1.50
☐ 14 Peter Sidorkiewicz Ottawa Senators	4.00	1.80	.50
☐ 15 Eric Lindros Philadelphia Flyers	35.00	16.00	4.40
☐ 16 Mario Lemieux Pittsburgh Penguins	25.00	11.50	3.10
☐ 17 Joe Sakic Quebec Nordiques	7.00	3.10	.85
☐ 18 Brett Hull St. Louis Blues	12.00	5.50	1.50
☐ 19 Pat Falloon San Jose Sharks	4.00	1.80	.50
☐ 20 Brian Bradley Tampa Bay Lightning	4.00	1.80	.50
☐ 21 Doug Gilmour Toronto Maple Leafs	12.00	5.50	1.50
☐ 22 Pavel Bure Vancouver Canucks	25.00	11.50	3.10
☐ 23 Kevin Hatcher Washington Capitals	4.00	1.80	.50
☐ 24 Teemu Selanne Winnipeg Jets	15.00	6.75	1.90

1993-94 Score Franchise

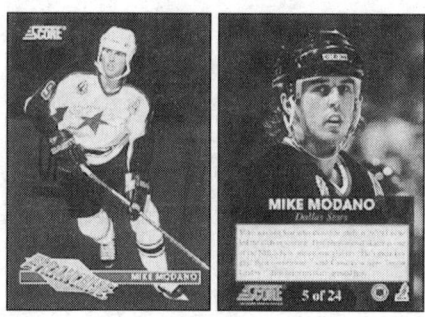

Randomly inserted in U.S. first-series packs, this 24-card standard-size (2 1/2" by 3 1/2") set features borderless color player action shots on the fronts, the backgrounds of which are ghosted and darkened. The player's name appears in a team color-coded stripe near the bottom. The Franchise logo is displayed in the lower left. The back sports another full-bleed color player shot, with his name and team shown within a darkened and ghosted rectangle near the bottom. Within this rectangle, a smaller white rectangle carries the player's career highlights. The cards are numbered on the back.

1993-94 Score International Stars

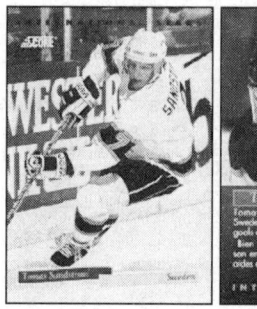

Inserted one per series one jumbo pack, this 22-card standard-size (2 1/2" by 3 1/2") set highlights some of the NHL's hottest international stars. The fronts feature full-bleed color action shots, with the player's name and nationality appearing in a banner at the bottom that bears the colors of his national flag. The words "International Stars" in gold foil are printed at the top. On purplish backgrounds, the backs carry a color headshot at the upper left, with the player's national flag to the right and his name and country in his flag's colors below. Career highlights in

English and French at the bottom round out the card. The cards are numbered on the back as "X of 22."

	MINT	EXC	G-VG
COMPLETE SET (22)	25.00	11.50	3.10
COMMON PLAYER (1-22)	.75	.35	.09
☐ 1 Pavel Bure	7.00	3.10	.85
Vancouver Canucks			
☐ 2 Teemu Selanne	3.00	1.35	.40
Winnipeg Jets			
☐ 3 Sergei Fedorov	4.00	1.80	.50
Detroit Red Wings			
☐ 4 Peter Bondra	.75	.35	.09
Washington Capitals			
☐ 5 Tommy Soderstrom	.75	.35	.09
Philadelphia Flyers			
☐ 6 Robert Reichel	1.00	.45	.13
Calgary Flames			
☐ 7 Jari Kurri	1.00	.45	.13
Los Angeles Kings			
☐ 8 Alexander Mogilny	2.00	.90	.25
Buffalo Sabres			
☐ 9 Jaromir Jagr	2.50	1.15	.30
Pittsburgh Penguins			
☐ 10 Mats Sundin	1.75	.80	.22
Quebec Nordiques			
☐ 11 Uwe Krupp	.75	.35	.09
New York Islanders			
☐ 12 Nikolai Borschevsky	.75	.35	.09
Toronto Maple Leafs			
☐ 13 Ulf Dahlen	.75	.35	.09
Dallas Stars			
☐ 14 Alexander Semak	.75	.35	.09
New Jersey Devils			
☐ 15 Michal Pivonka	.75	.35	.09
Washington Capitals			
☐ 16 Sergei Nemchinov	.75	.35	.09
New York Rangers			
☐ 17 Darius Kasparaitis	.75	.35	.09
New York Islanders			
☐ 18 Sandis Ozolinsh	1.25	.55	.16
San Jose Sharks			
☐ 19 Alexei Kovalev	1.75	.80	.22
New York Rangers			
☐ 20 Dimitri Khristich	.75	.35	.09
Washington Capitals			
☐ 21 Tomas Sandstrom	.75	.35	.09
Los Angeles Kings			
☐ 22 Petr Nedved	1.00	.45	.13
Vancouver Canucks			

1994-95 Score Hobby Samples

Issued in packs of 12, the 1994 Score hockey Hobby Sample cards measure standard-size (2 1/2" by 3 1/2") and preview the 1994 Score hockey issue. The top right and left corners have been cut off of some cards. The fronts feature color action player photos with white borders, and a small headshot in the left bottom corner. The player's name appears in colorful letters at the bottom of the picture. The horizontal backs carry another player photo on the left, along with the player's name, biography, career highlights and stats on the right. The cards are numbered on the back.

	MINT	EXC	G-VG
COMPLETE SET (12)	7.00	2.80	.70
COMMON PLAYER	.10	.04	.01
☐ 1 Eric Lindros	1.00	.40	.10
Philadelphia Flyers			
☐ 2 Pat LaFontaine	.30	.12	.03
Buffalo Sabres			
☐ 3 Wendel Clark	.20	.08	.02
Toronto Maple Leafs			
☐ 4 Cam Neely	.25	.10	.02
Boston Bruins			
☐ 5 Larry Murphy	.10	.04	.01
Pittsburgh Penguins			
☐ 6 Patrick Poulin	.10	.04	.01
Chicago Blackhawks			
☐ 7 Bob Beers	.10	.04	.01
Edmonton Oilers			
☐ 254 Jason Arnott	.75	.30	.07
Edmonton Oilers			
Young Stars			
☐ C13 Darius Kasparaitis	1.00	.40	.10
New York Islanders			
Check-It			
☐ NNO Pro Debut Rookie	2.00	.80	.20
Redemption Card			
☐ NNO Title Card	1.50	.60	.15
☐ TF16 Alexandre Daigle	2.00	.80	.20
Ottawa Senators			
The Franchise			

1994-95 Score

The 275 standard-size (2 1/2" by 3 1/2") cards that comprise the first series of '94-95 Score feature white-bordered color player action shots on their fronts. The player's name appears at the lower right. A triangular team color-screened head shot rests at the lower left, with the team logo set on a hockey puck icon. Five spheres highlight the upper left corner. The horizontal back carries a color player action shot set on a blue background on the left, with the player's name, biography, career highlights, and statistics appearing alongside on the right. The cards are numbered on the back.

	MINT	EXC	G-VG
COMPLETE SERIES 1 (275)	18.00	8.00	2.30
COMMON PLAYER (1-275)	.05	.02	.01
☐ 1 Eric Lindros	1.00	.45	.13
Philadelphia Flyers			
☐ 2 Pat LaFontaine	.15	.07	.02
Buffalo Sabres			
☐ 3 Wendel Clark	.10	.05	.01
Toronto Maple Leafs			
☐ 4 Cam Neely	.15	.07	.02
Boston Bruins			
☐ 5 Larry Murphy	.08	.04	.01
Pittsburgh Penguins			
☐ 6 Patrick Poulin	.05	.02	.01
Chicago Blackhawks			
☐ 7 Bob Beers	.05	.02	.01
Edmonton Oilers			
☐ 8 James Patrick	.05	.02	.01
Calgary Flames			
☐ 9 Gino Odjick	.05	.02	.01
Vancouver Canucks			

☐ 10	Arturs Irbe	.15	.07	.02
	San Jose Sharks			
☐ 11	Darius Kasparaitis	.05	.02	.01
	New York Islanders			
☐ 12	Peter Bondra	.08	.04	.01
	Washington Capitals			
☐ 13	Garth Butcher	.05	.02	.01
	Quebec Nordiques			
☐ 14	Sergei Nemchinov	.05	.02	.01
	New York Rangers			
☐ 15	Doug Brown	.05	.02	.01
	Pittsburgh Penguins			
☐ 16	Anatoli Semenov	.05	.02	.01
	Anaheim Mighty Ducks			
☐ 17	Mike McPhee	.05	.02	.01
	Dallas Stars			
☐ 18	Joel Otto	.05	.02	.01
	Calgary Flames			
☐ 19	Dino Ciccarelli	.08	.04	.01
	Detroit Red Wings			
☐ 20	Marty McSorley	.08	.04	.01
	Los Angeles Kings			
☐ 21	Ron Tugnutt	.05	.02	.01
	Montreal Canadiens			
☐ 22	Scott Niedermayer	.05	.02	.01
	New Jersey Devils			
☐ 23	John Tucker	.05	.02	.01
	Tampa Bay Lightning			
☐ 24	Norm Maciver	.05	.02	.01
	Ottawa Senators			
☐ 25	Kevin Miller	.05	.02	.01
	St. Louis Blues			
☐ 26	Garry Galley	.05	.02	.01
	Philadelphia Flyers			
☐ 27	Ted Donato	.05	.02	.01
	Boston Bruins			
☐ 28	Bob Kudelski	.08	.04	.01
	Florida Panthers			
☐ 29	Craig Muni	.05	.02	.01
	Buffalo Sabres			
☐ 30	Nikolai Borschevsky	.05	.02	.01
	Toronto Maple Leafs			
☐ 31	Tom Barrasso	.08	.04	.01
	Pittsburgh Penguins			
☐ 32	Brent Sutter	.08	.04	.01
	Chicago Blackhawks			
☐ 33	Igor Kravchuk	.05	.02	.01
	Edmonton Oilers			
☐ 34	Andrew Cassels	.05	.02	.01
	Hartford Whalers			
☐ 35	Jyrki Lumme	.05	.02	.01
	Vancouver Canucks			
☐ 36	Sandis Ozolinsh	.10	.05	.01
	San Jose Sharks			
☐ 37	Steve Thomas	.08	.04	.01
	New York Islanders			
☐ 38	Dave Poulin	.05	.02	.01
	Washington Capitals			
☐ 39	Andrei Kovalenko	.05	.02	.01
	Quebec Nordiques			
☐ 40	Steve Larmer	.08	.04	.01
	New York Rangers			
☐ 41	Nelson Emerson	.08	.04	.01
	Winnipeg Jets			
☐ 42	Guy Hebert	.08	.04	.01
	Anaheim Mighty Ducks			
☐ 43	Russ Courtnall	.08	.04	.01
	Dallas Stars			
☐ 44	Gary Suter	.08	.04	.01
	Chicago Blackhawks			
☐ 45	Steve Chiasson	.05	.02	.01
	Detroit Red Wings			
☐ 46	Guy Carbonneau	.08	.04	.01
	Montreal Canadiens			
☐ 47	Rob Blake	.08	.04	.01
	Los Angeles Kings			
☐ 48	Roman Hamrlik	.05	.02	.01
	Tampa Bay Lightning			
☐ 49	Valeri Zelepukin	.08	.04	.01
	New Jersey Devils			
☐ 50	Mark Recchi	.15	.07	.02
	Philadelphia Flyers			
☐ 51	Darrin Madeley	.05	.02	.01
	Ottawa Senators			
☐ 52	Steve Duchesne	.08	.04	.01
	St. Louis Blues			
☐ 53	Brian Skrudland	.05	.02	.01
	Florida Panthers			
☐ 54	Craig Simpson	.05	.02	.01
	Buffalo Sabres			
☐ 55	Todd Gill	.05	.02	.01
	Toronto Maple Leafs			
☐ 56	Dirk Graham	.05	.02	.01
	Chicago Blackhawks			
☐ 57	Joe Mullen	.08	.04	.01
	Pittsburgh Penguins			
☐ 58	Doug Weight	.08	.04	.01
	Edmonton Oilers			
☐ 59	Michael Nylander	.08	.04	.01
	Calgary Flames			
☐ 60	Kirk McLean	.10	.05	.01
	Vancouver Canucks			
☐ 61	Igor Larionov	.05	.02	.01
	San Jose Sharks			
☐ 62	Vladimir Malakhov	.08	.04	.01
	New York Islanders			
☐ 63	Kelly Miller	.05	.02	.01
	Washington Capitals			
☐ 64	Curtis Leschyshyn	.05	.02	.01
	Quebec Nordiques			
☐ 65	Thomas Steen	.05	.02	.01
	Winnipeg Jets			
☐ 66	Jeff Beukeboom	.05	.02	.01
	New York Rangers			
☐ 67	Troy Loney	.05	.02	.01
	Anaheim Mighty Ducks			
☐ 68	Mark Tinordi	.05	.02	.01
	Dallas Stars			
☐ 69	Theoren Fleury	.10	.05	.01
	Calgary Flames			
☐ 70	Slava Kozlov	.20	.09	.03
	Detroit Red Wings			
☐ 71	Tony Granato	.05	.02	.01
	Los Angeles Kings			
☐ 72	Daren Puppa	.08	.04	.01
	Tampa Bay Lightning			
☐ 73	Brian Bellows	.08	.04	.01
	Montreal Canadiens			
☐ 74	Bernie Nicholls	.08	.04	.01
	New Jersey Devils			
☐ 75	Rick Zombo	.05	.02	.01
	St. Louis Blues			
☐ 76	Brad Shaw	.05	.02	.01
	Ottawa Senators			
☐ 77	Josef Beranek	.05	.02	.01
	Philadelphia Flyers			
☐ 78	Dominik Hasek	.10	.05	.01
	Buffalo Sabres			
☐ 79	Steve Leach	.05	.02	.01
	Boston Bruins			
☐ 80	Dave Reid	.05	.02	.01
	Boston Bruins			
☐ 81	Dave Lowry	.05	.02	.01
	Florida Panthers			
☐ 82	Martin Straka	.15	.07	.02
	Pittsburgh Penguins			
☐ 83	Dave Ellett	.05	.02	.01
	Toronto Maple Leafs			
☐ 84	Sean Burke	.08	.04	.01
	Hartford Whalers			
☐ 85	Craig MacTavish	.05	.02	.01
	New York Rangers			
☐ 86	Cliff Ronning	.05	.02	.01
	Vancouver Canucks			
☐ 87	Bob Errey	.05	.02	.01
	San Jose Sharks			
☐ 88	Marty McInnis	.05	.02	.01
	New York Islanders			
☐ 89	Mats Sundin	.15	.07	.02
	Quebec Nordiques			
☐ 90	Randy Burridge	.05	.02	.01
	Washington Capitals			
☐ 91	Teppo Numminen	.05	.02	.01
	Winnipeg Jets			
☐ 92	Tony Amonte	.08	.04	.01
	Chicago Blackhawks			
☐ 93	Terry Yake	.05	.02	.01
	Anaheim Mighty Ducks			
☐ 94	Paul Cavallini	.05	.02	.01
	Dallas Stars			
☐ 95	German Titov	.08	.04	.01
	Calgary Flames			
☐ 96	Vladimir Konstantinov	.05	.02	.01
	Detroit Red Wings			
☐ 97	Darryl Sydor	.08	.04	.01
	Los Angeles Kings			
☐ 98	Chris Joseph	.05	.02	.01
	Tampa Bay Lightning			
☐ 99	Corey Millen	.05	.02	.01
	New Jersey Devils			
☐ 100	Brett Hull	.30	.14	.04
	St. Louis Blues			
☐ 101	Don Sweeney	.05	.02	.01
	Boston Bruins			
☐ 102	Scott Mellanby	.05	.02	.01
	Florida Panthers			
☐ 103	Mathieu Schneider	.08	.04	.01

Montreal Canadiens				
☐ 104 Brad May	.05	.02	.01
Buffalo Sabres				
☐ 105 Dominic Roussel	.08	.04	.01
Philadelphia Flyers				
☐ 106 Jamie Macoun	.05	.02	.01
Toronto Maple Leafs				
☐ 107 Bryan Marchment	.05	.02	.01
Hartford Whalers				
☐ 108 Shawn McEachern	.05	.02	.01
Pittsburgh Penguins				
☐ 109 Murray Craven	.05	.02	.01
Vancouver Canucks				
☐ 110 Eric Desjardins	.05	.02	.01
Montreal Canadiens				
☐ 111 Jon Casey	.08	.04	.01
Boston Bruins				
☐ 112 Mike Gartner	.10	.05	.01
Toronto Maple Leafs				
☐ 113 Neal Broten	.08	.04	.01
Dallas Stars				
☐ 114 Jari Kurri	.10	.05	.01
Los Angeles Kings				
☐ 115 Bruce Driver	.05	.02	.01
New Jersey Devils				
☐ 116 Patrick Flatley	.05	.02	.01
New York Islanders				
☐ 117 Gord Murphy	.05	.02	.01
Florida Panthers				
☐ 118 Dimitri Khristich	.08	.04	.01
Washington Capitals				
☐ 119 Nicklas Lidstrom	.08	.04	.01
Detroit Red Wings				
☐ 120 Al MacInnis	.10	.05	.01
Calgary Flames				
☐ 121 Steve Smith	.05	.02	.01
Chicago Blackhawks				
☐ 122 Zdeno Ciger	.05	.02	.01
Edmonton Oilers				
☐ 123 Tie Domi	.05	.02	.01
Winnipeg Jets				
☐ 124 Joe Juneau	.25	.11	.03
Washington Capitals				
☐ 125 Todd Elik	.05	.02	.01
San Jose Sharks				
☐ 126 Stephane Fiset	.05	.02	.01
Quebec Nordiques				
☐ 127 Craig Janney	.10	.05	.01
St. Louis Blues				
☐ 128 Stephan Lebeau	.05	.02	.01
Anaheim Mighty Ducks				
☐ 129 Richard Smehlik	.08	.04	.01
Buffalo Sabres				
☐ 130 Mike Richter	.15	.07	.02
New York Rangers				
☐ 131 Danton Cole	.05	.02	.01
Tampa Bay Lightning				
☐ 132 Rod Brind'Amour	.10	.05	.01
Philadelphia Flyers				
☐ 133 Dave Archibald	.05	.02	.01
Ottawa Senators				
☐ 134 Dana Murzyn	.05	.02	.01
Vancouver Canucks				
☐ 135 Jaromir Jagr	.25	.11	.03
Pittsburgh Penguins				
☐ 136 Esa Tikkanen	.08	.04	.01
New York Rangers				
☐ 137 Rob Pearson	.05	.02	.01
Toronto Maple Leafs				
☐ 138 Stu Barnes	.05	.02	.01
Florida Panthers				
☐ 139 Frank Musil	.05	.02	.01
Calgary Flames				
☐ 140 Ron Hextall	.08	.04	.01
New York Islanders				
☐ 141 Adam Oates	.15	.07	.02
Boston Bruins				
☐ 142 Ken Daneyko	.05	.02	.01
New Jersey Devils				
☐ 143 Dale Hunter	.08	.04	.01
Washington Capitals				
☐ 144 Geoff Sanderson	.05	.02	.01
Hartford Whalers				
☐ 145 Kelly Hrudey	.08	.04	.01
Los Angeles Kings				
☐ 146 Kirk Muller	.08	.04	.01
Montreal Canadiens				
☐ 147 Fredrik Olausson	.05	.02	.01
Edmonton Oilers				
☐ 148 Derian Hatcher	.05	.02	.01
Dallas Stars				
☐ 149 Ed Belfour	.15	.07	.02
Chicago Blackhawks				
☐ 150 Steve Yzerman	.20	.09	.03
Detroit Red Wings				
☐ 151 Adam Foote	.05	.02	.01
Quebec Nordiques				
☐ 152 Pat Falloon	.08	.04	.01
San Jose Sharks				
☐ 153 Shawn Chambers	.05	.02	.01
Tampa Bay Lightning				
☐ 154 Alexei Zhamnov	.15	.07	.02
Winnipeg Jets				
☐ 155 Brendan Shanahan	.15	.07	.02
St. Louis Blues				
☐ 156 Ulf Samuelsson	.08	.04	.01
Pittsburgh Penguins				
☐ 157 Donald Audette	.05	.02	.01
Buffalo Sabres				
☐ 158 Bob Corkum	.05	.02	.01
Anaheim Mighty Ducks				
☐ 159 Joe Nieuwendyk	.08	.04	.01
Calgary Flames				
☐ 160 Felix Potvin	.40	.18	.05
Toronto Maple Leafs				
☐ 161 Geoff Courtnall	.05	.02	.01
Vancouver Canucks				
☐ 162 Yves Racine	.05	.02	.01
Philadelphia Flyers				
☐ 163 Tom Fitzgerald	.05	.02	.01
Florida Panthers				
☐ 164 Adam Graves	.15	.07	.02
New York Rangers				
☐ 165 Vincent Damphousse	.08	.04	.01
Montreal Canadiens				
☐ 166 Pierre Turgeon	.15	.07	.02
New York Islanders				
☐ 167 Craig Billington	.05	.02	.01
Ottawa Senators				
☐ 168 Al Iafrate	.08	.04	.01
Boston Bruins				
☐ 169 Darren Turcotte	.05	.02	.01
Hartford Whalers				
☐ 170 Joe Murphy	.05	.02	.01
Chicago Blackhawks				
☐ 171 Alexei Zhitnik	.08	.04	.01
Los Angeles Kings				
☐ 172 John MacLean	.08	.04	.01
New Jersey Devils				
☐ 173 Andy Moog	.08	.04	.01
Dallas Stars				
☐ 174 Shayne Corson	.05	.02	.01
Edmonton Oilers				
☐ 175 Ray Sheppard	.05	.02	.01
Detroit Red Wings				
☐ 176 Johan Garpenlov	.05	.02	.01
San Jose Sharks				
☐ 177 Ron Sutter	.05	.02	.01
Quebec Nordiques				
☐ 178 Teemu Selanne	.40	.18	.05
Winnipeg Jets				
☐ 179 Brian Bradley	.05	.02	.01
Tampa Bay Lightning				
☐ 180 Ray Bourque	.15	.07	.02
Boston Bruins				
☐ 181 Curtis Joseph	.15	.07	.02
St. Louis Blues				
☐ 182 Kevin Stevens	.15	.07	.02
Pittsburgh Penguins				
☐ 183 Alexei Kasatonov	.05	.02	.01
St. Louis Blues				
☐ 184 Brian Leetch	.15	.07	.02
New York Rangers				
☐ 185 Doug Gilmour	.20	.09	.03
Toronto Maple Leafs				
☐ 186 Gary Roberts	.08	.04	.01
Calgary Flames				
☐ 187 Mike Keane	.05	.02	.01
Montreal Canadiens				
☐ 188 Mike Modano	.15	.07	.02
Dallas Stars				
☐ 189 Chris Chelios	.08	.04	.01
Chicago Blackhawks				
☐ 190 Pavel Bure	.75	.35	.09
Vancouver Canucks				
☐ 191 Bob Essensa	.08	.04	.01
Detroit Red Wings				
☐ 192 Dale Hawerchuk	.08	.04	.01
Buffalo Sabres				
☐ 193 Scott Stevens	.08	.04	.01
New Jersey Devils				
☐ 194 Claude Lapointe	.05	.02	.01
Quebec Nordiques				
☐ 195 Scott Lachance	.05	.02	.01
New York Islanders				
☐ 196 Gaetan Duchesne	.05	.02	.01
San Jose Sharks				
☐ 197 Kevin Dineen	.08	.04	.01

Philadelphia Flyers
☐ 198	Doug Bodger	.05	.02	.01

Buffalo Sabres
☐ 199	Mike Ridley	.08	.04	.01

Washington Capitals
☐ 200	Alexander Mogilny	.25	.11	.03

Buffalo Sabres
☐ 201	Jamie Storr	.50	.23	.06

Canada
☐ 202	Jason Botterill	.15	.07	.02

Canada
☐ 203	Jeff Friesen	.40	.18	.05

Canada
☐ 204	Todd Harvey	.25	.11	.03

Canada
☐ 205	Brendan Witt	.15	.07	.02

Canada
☐ 206	Jason Allison	.25	.11	.03

Canada
☐ 207	Aaron Gavey	.25	.11	.03

Canada
☐ 208	Deron Quint	.10	.05	.01

United States
☐ 209	Jason Bonsignore	.40	.18	.05

United States
☐ 210	Richard Park	.20	.09	.03

United States
☐ 211	Jamie Langenbrunner	.15	.07	.02

United States
☐ 212	Vadim Sharifjanov	.15	.07	.02

Russia
☐ 213	Alexander Kharlamov	.25	.11	.03

Russia
☐ 214	Oleg Tverdovsky	.40	.18	.05

Russia
☐ 215	Valeri Bure	.40	.18	.05

Russia
☐ 216	Dane Jackson	.15	.07	.02

Vancouver Canucks
☐ 217	Josef Cierny	.10	.05	.01

Edmonton Oilers
☐ 218	Yevgeny Namestnikov	.05	.02	.01

Vancouver Canucks
☐ 219	Daniel Laperriere	.15	.07	.02

St. Louis Blues
☐ 220	Fred Knipscheer	.05	.02	.01

Boston Bruins
☐ 221	Yan Kaminsky	.05	.02	.01

New York Islanders
☐ 222	David Roberts	.05	.02	.01

St. Louis Blues
☐ 223	Derek Mayer	.05	.02	.01

Ottawa Senators
☐ 224	Jamie McLennan	.05	.02	.01

New York Islanders
☐ 225	Kevin Smyth	.05	.02	.01

Hartford Whalers
☐ 226	Todd Marchant	.05	.02	.01

Edmonton Oilers
☐ 227	Mariusz Czerkawski	.20	.09	.03

Boston Bruins
☐ 228	John Lilley	.05	.02	.01

Anaheim Mighty Ducks
☐ 229	Aaron Ward	.05	.02	.01

Detroit Red Wings
☐ 230	Brian Savage	.05	.02	.01

Montreal Canadiens
☐ 231	Jason Allison	.25	.11	.03

Washington Capitals
☐ 232	Maxim Bets	.15	.07	.02

Anaheim Mighty Ducks
☐ 233	Ted Crowley	.05	.02	.01

Hartford Whalers
☐ 234	Todd Simon	.10	.05	.01

Buffalo Sabres
☐ 235	Zigmund Palffy	.05	.02	.01

New York Islanders
☐ 236	Rene Corbet	.05	.02	.01

Quebec Nordiques
☐ 237	Mike Peca	.15	.07	.02

Vancouver Canucks
☐ 238	Dwayne Norris	.05	.02	.01

Quebec Nordiques
☐ 239	Andrei Nazarov	.05	.02	.01

San Jose Sharks
☐ 240	David Sacco	.05	.02	.01

Toronto Maple Leafs
☐ 241	Wayne Gretzky	.50	.23	.06

Los Angeles Kings
☐ 242	Mike Gartner	.05	.02	.01

Toronto Maple Leafs
☐ 243	Dino Ciccarelli	.05	.02	.01

Detroit Red Wings
☐ 244	Ron Francis	.08	.04	.01

Pittsburgh Penguins
☐ 245	Bernie Nicholls	.05	.02	.01

New Jersey Devils
☐ 246	Dino Ciccarelli	.05	.02	.01

Detroit Red Wings
☐ 247	Brian Propp	.08	.04	.01

Hartford Whalers
☐ 248	Alexandre Daigle	.25	.11	.03

Ottawa Senators
☐ 249	Mikael Renberg	.25	.11	.03

Philadelphia Flyers
☐ 250	Jocelyn Thibault	.15	.07	.02

Quebec Nordiques
☐ 251	Derek Plante	.15	.07	.02

Buffalo Sabres
☐ 252	Chris Pronger	.20	.09	.03

Hartford Whalers
☐ 253	Alexei Yashin	.25	.11	.03

Ottawa Senators
☐ 254	Jason Arnott	.60	.25	.08

Edmonton Oilers
☐ 255	Boris Mironov	.05	.02	.01

Edmonton Oilers
☐ 256	Chris Osgood	.15	.07	.02

Detroit Red Wings
☐ 257	Jesse Belanger	.05	.02	.01

Florida Panthers
☐ 258	Darren McCarty	.05	.02	.01

Detroit Red Wings
☐ 259	Trevor Kidd	.08	.04	.01

Calgary Flames
☐ 260	Oleg Petrov	.05	.02	.01

Montreal Canadiens
☐ 261	Mike Rathje	.05	.02	.01

San Jose Sharks
☐ 262	John Slaney	.05	.02	.01

Washington Capitals
☐ 263	Anaheim Mighty Ducks CL	.05	.02	.01

Boston Bruins
☐ 264	Buffalo Sabres CL	.05	.02	.01

Calgary Flames
☐ 265	Chicago Blackhawks CL	.05	.02	.01

Dallas Stars
☐ 266	Detroit Red Wings CL	.05	.02	.01

Edmonton Oilers
☐ 267	Florida Panthers CL	.05	.02	.01

Hartford Whalers
☐ 268	Los Angeles Kings CL	.05	.02	.01

Montreal Canadiens
☐ 269	New Jersey Devils CL	.05	.02	.01

New York Islanders
☐ 270	New York Rangers CL	.05	.02	.01

Ottawa Senators
☐ 271	Philadelphia Flyers CL	.05	.02	.01

Pittsburgh Penguins
☐ 272	Quebec Nordiques CL	.05	.02	.01

St.Louis Blues
☐ 273	San Jose Sharks CL	.05	.02	.01

Tampa Bay Lightning
☐ 274	Toronto Maple Leafs CL	.05	.02	.01

Vancouver Canucks
☐ 275	Washington Capitals CL	.05	.02	.01

Winnipeg Jets

1994-95 Score Gold Line

Common to both USA and Canadian versions, the 1994-95 Score Gold Line hockey set consists of all-foil renditions of each of the 275 common cards. Each pack consisted of 13

regular cards plus one all-foil Gold Line card. The Gold Line cards have the same design as the regular series cards but are distinguished on their fronts by a mustard, teal, and silver foil background. The only distinguishing feature of the backs is a "Gold Line" emblem superposed on the player photo. The cards are numbered on the back. Complete team sets could be redeemed for platinum team sets. There were 1,994 of each platinum set produced.

	MINT	EXC	G-VG
COMPLETE SERIES 1 (275)	80.00	36.00	10.00
COMMON PLAYER (1-275)	.25	.11	.03
*UNLISTED VETERAN STARS: 5X to 10X			
*UNLISTED YOUNG STARS: 4X to 8X			
*UNLISTED RCs: 2X to 4X			
☐ 1 Eric Lindros	8.00	3.60	1.00
Philadelphia Flyers			
☐ 190 Pavel Bure	6.00	2.70	.75
Vancouver Canucks			
☐ 241 Wayne Gretzky	5.00	2.30	.60
Los Angeles Kings			

1994-95 Score Check It

Randomly inserted in Canadian first-series packs, these 18 standard-size (2 1/2" by 3 1/2") cards feature borderless color player action shots on their fronts. The player's name, along with the set title and logo, appear in red-foil lettering at the bottom. The back carries a vertically distorted color player close-up on the left, with career highlights in white lettering over the red and black checkerboard design on the right. The cards are numbered on the back with a "CI" prefix.

	MINT	EXC	G-VG
COMPLETE SET (18)	140.00	65.00	17.50
COMMON PLAYER (CI1-CI18)	6.00	2.70	.75
☐ CI1 Eric Lindros	40.00	18.00	5.00
Philadelphia Flyers			
☐ CI2 Scott Stevens	6.00	2.70	.75
New Jersey Devils			
☐ CI3 Darius Kasparaitis	6.00	2.70	.75
New York Islanders			
☐ CI4 Kevin Stevens	8.00	3.60	1.00
Pittsburgh Penguins			
☐ CI5 Brendan Shanahan	12.00	5.50	1.50
St. Louis Blues			
☐ CI6 Jeremy Roenick	14.00	6.25	1.75
Chicago Blackhawks			
☐ CI7 Ulf Samuelsson	6.00	2.70	.75
Pittsburgh Penguins			
☐ CI8 Cam Neely	8.00	3.60	1.00
Boston Bruins			
☐ CI9 Adam Graves	8.00	3.60	1.00
New York Rangers			
☐ CI10 Kirk Muller	6.00	2.70	.75
Montreal Canadiens			
☐ CI11 Rick Tocchet	6.00	2.70	.75
Pittsburgh Penguins			
☐ CI12 Gary Roberts	6.00	2.70	.75
Calgary Flames			
☐ CI13 Wendel Clark	8.00	3.60	1.00
Toronto Maple Leafs			
☐ CI14 Keith Tkachuk	8.00	3.60	1.00
Winnipeg Jets			
☐ CI15 Theoren Fleury	6.00	2.70	.75
Calgary Flames			
☐ CI16 Claude Lemieux	6.00	2.70	.75
New Jersey Devils			
☐ CI17 Chris Chelios	6.00	2.70	.75
Chicago Blackhawks			
☐ CI18 Pat Verbeek	6.00	2.70	.75
Hartford Whalers			

1994-95 Score Dream Team

Randomly inserted in American first-series packs, these 24 standard-size (2 1/2" by 3 1/2") holographic cards feature multi-hued player action shots on their borderless fronts. A holographic head shot appears at the upper left when the card is held at the proper angle. The player's name appears above the head shot. The back carries a regular borderless color player photo. Career highlights appear within the ghosted area accented by simulated goal netting at the bottom. The cards are numbered on the back with a "DT" prefix.

	MINT	EXC	G-VG
COMPLETE SET (24)	200.00	90.00	25.00
COMMON PLAYER (DT1-DT24)	6.00	2.70	.75
☐ DT1 Patrick Roy	18.00	8.00	2.30
Montreal Canadiens			
☐ DT2 Felix Potvin	15.00	6.75	1.90
Toronto Maple Leafs			
☐ DT3 Ray Bourque	7.00	3.10	.85
Boston Bruins			
☐ DT4 Brian Leetch	8.00	3.60	1.00
New York Rangers			
☐ DT5 Scott Stevens	6.00	2.70	.75
New Jersey Devils			
☐ DT6 Paul Coffey	6.00	2.70	.75
Detroit Red Wings			
☐ DT7 Al MacInnis	6.00	2.70	.75
Calgary Flames			
☐ DT8 Chris Chelios	6.00	2.70	.75
Chicago Blackhawks			
☐ DT9 Adam Graves	7.00	3.10	.85
New York Rangers			
☐ DT10 Luc Robitaille	7.00	3.10	.85
Los Angeles Kings			
☐ DT11 Dave Andreychuk	6.00	2.70	.75
Toronto Maple Leafs			
☐ DT12 Sergei Fedorov	15.00	6.75	1.90
Detroit Red Wings			
☐ DT13 Doug Gilmour	10.00	4.50	1.25
Toronto Maple Leafs			
☐ DT14 Wayne Gretzky	30.00	13.50	3.80
Los Angeles Kings			
☐ DT15 Mario Lemieux	20.00	9.00	2.50
Pittsburgh Penguins			
☐ DT16 Mark Messier	9.00	4.00	1.15
New York Rangers			
☐ DT17 Mike Modano	8.00	3.60	1.00
Dallas Stars			
☐ DT18 Jeremy Roenick	10.00	4.50	1.25
Chicago Blackhawks			
☐ DT19 Eric Lindros	25.00	11.50	3.10

		MINT	EXC	G-VG
☐	DT20 Steve Yzerman	10.00	4.50	1.25
	Detroit Red Wings			
☐	DT21 Alexandre Daigle	8.00	3.60	1.00
	Ottawa Senators			
☐	DT22 Brett Hull	10.00	4.50	1.25
	St. Louis Blues			
☐	DT23 Cam Neely	7.00	3.10	.85
	Boston Bruins			
☐	DT24 Pavel Bure	20.00	9.00	2.50
	Vancouver Canucks			

1994-95 Score Franchise

Randomly inserted in American first-series packs, these 26 standard-size (2 1/2" by 3 1/2") cards feature on their fronts borderless black-and-white action shots, with the head and shoulders of the player shown in a reduced scale color area framed by a white line. The player's name appears in red lettering just below this color area. His team name appears in red lettering at the bottom. The back carries another black-and-white photo with a color area framed by a white line. Career highlights appear in white lettering near the bottom. The cards are numbered on the back with a "TF" prefix.

		MINT	EXC	G-VG
	COMPLETE SET (26)	400.00	180.00	50.00
	COMMON PLAYER (TF1-TF26)	8.00	3.60	1.00
☐	TF1 Guy Hebert	8.00	3.60	1.00
	Anaheim Mighty Ducks			
☐	TF2 Cam Neely	10.00	4.50	1.25
	Boston Bruins			
☐	TF3 Pat LaFontaine	10.00	4.50	1.25
	Buffalo Sabres			
☐	TF4 Theoren Fleury	8.00	3.60	1.00
	Calgary Flames			
☐	TF5 Jeremy Roenick	15.00	6.75	1.90
	Chicago Blackhawks			
☐	TF6 Mike Modano	12.00	5.50	1.50
	Dallas Stars			
☐	TF7 Sergei Fedorov	30.00	13.50	3.80
	Detroit Red Wings			
☐	TF8 Jason Arnott	20.00	9.00	2.50
	Edmonton Oilers			
☐	TF9 John Vanbiesbrouck	8.00	3.60	1.00
	Florida Panthers			
☐	TF10 Geoff Sanderson	8.00	3.60	1.00
	Hartford Whalers			
☐	TF11 Wayne Gretzky	60.00	27.00	7.50
	Los Angeles Kings			
☐	TF12 Patrick Roy	30.00	13.50	3.80
	Montreal Canadiens			
☐	TF13 Scott Stevens	8.00	3.60	1.00
	New Jersey Devils			
☐	TF14 Pierre Turgeon	10.00	4.50	1.25
	New York Islanders			
☐	TF15 Mark Messier	12.00	5.50	1.50
	New York Rangers			
☐	TF16 Alexandre Daigle	12.00	5.50	1.50
	Ottawa Senators			
☐	TF17 Eric Lindros	50.00	23.00	6.25
	Philadelphia Flyers			
☐	TF18 Mario Lemieux	40.00	18.00	5.00
	Pittsburgh Penguins			
☐	TF19 Joe Sakic	10.00	4.50	1.25
	Quebec Nordiques			
☐	TF20 Brett Hull	15.00	6.75	1.90
	St. Louis Blues			
☐	TF21 Arturs Irbe	10.00	4.50	1.25
	San Jose Sharks			
☐	TF22 Daren Puppa	8.00	3.60	1.00
	Tampa Bay Lightning			
☐	TF23 Doug Gilmour	15.00	6.75	1.90
	Toronto Maple Leafs			
☐	TF24 Pavel Bure	40.00	18.00	5.00
	Vancouver Canucks			
☐	TF25 Joe Juneau	12.00	5.50	1.50
	Washington Capitals			
☐	TF26 Teemu Selanne	20.00	9.00	2.50
	Winnipeg Jets			

1994-95 Score Team Canada

Randomly inserted in Canadian first-series packs, these 24 standard-size (2 1/2" by 3 1/2") holographic cards feature multi-hued player action shots on their borderless fronts. Maple leafs and the word "Lillehammer" alternately appear in the background as the hologram is tilted. The player's name appears at the bottom. The horizontal back carries a color player head shot set within a red maple leaf in the center, set on a mountainous background photo. The player's name and career highlights appear within a brownish area on the right. The cards are numbered on the back with a "CT" prefix.

		MINT	EXC	G-VG
	COMPLETE SET (24)	130.00	57.50	16.50
	COMMON PLAYER (CT1-CT24)	5.00	2.30	.60
☐	CT1 Paul Kariya	15.00	6.75	1.90
☐	CT2 Petr Nedved	8.00	3.60	1.00
☐	CT3 Todd Warriner	6.00	2.70	.75
☐	CT4 Corey Hirsch	6.00	2.70	.75
☐	CT5 Greg Johnson	5.00	2.30	.80
☐	CT6 Chris Kontos	5.00	2.30	.60
☐	CT7 Dwayne Norris	5.00	2.30	.60
☐	CT8 Brian Savage	6.00	2.70	.75
☐	CT9 Todd Hlushko	5.00	2.30	.60
☐	CT10 Fabian Joseph	5.00	2.30	.60
☐	CT11 Greg Parks	5.00	2.30	.60
☐	CT12 Jean-Yves Roy	5.00	2.30	.60
☐	CT13 Mark Astley	5.00	2.30	.60
☐	CT14 Adrian Aucoin	5.00	2.30	.60
☐	CT15 David Harlock	5.00	2.30	.60
☐	CT16 Ken Lovsin	5.00	2.30	.60
☐	CT17 Derek Mayer	5.00	2.30	.60
☐	CT18 Brad Schlegel	5.00	2.30	.60
☐	CT19 Chris Therien	5.00	2.30	.60
☐	CT20 Manny Legace	6.00	2.70	.75
☐	CT21 Brad Werenka	5.00	2.30	.60
☐	CT22 Wally Schreiber	5.00	2.30	.60
☐	CT23 Allain Roy	6.00	2.70	.75
☐	CT24 Brett Lindros	18.00	8.00	2.30

1992-93 Seasons Patches

Each measuring approximately 3 1/8" by 4 1/4", these 70 patches were licensed by the NHL/NHLPA and feature color action player photos on black fabric. The player's team appears above the photo and his name, position, and sweater number are below. An embroidered border in the team color edges the patch. The patches come in a poly-wrap sleeve attached to a teal cardboard rack display. These displays were pegged on team customized counter display easels, showcasing four different players (six patches per player), for a total of 24 patches per team display. Two versions are available. The bilingual version has both French and English printed on the package. The other version is printed in English only. A checklist of 71 patches is printed on the back of the display. In the checklist, patch 22, an unnamed prototype, features ex-NHL star and Seasons President Grant Mulvey. Mulvey's patch was only available through him as a handout and could not be purchased by the public; it is not considered part of the complete set.

	MINT	EXC	G-VG
COMPLETE SET (70)	225.00	90.00	22.00
COMMON PLAYER (1-71)	3.00	1.20	.30

		MINT	EXC	G-VG
☐ 1	Jeremy Roenick	5.00	2.00	.50
	Chicago Blackhawks			
☐ 2	Steve Larmer	3.00	1.20	.30
	Chicago Blackhawks			
☐ 3	Ed Belfour	4.00	1.60	.40
	Chicago Blackhawks			
☐ 4	Chris Chelios	3.00	1.20	.30
	Chicago Blackhawks			
☐ 5	Sergei Fedorov	5.00	2.00	.50
	Detroit Red Wings			
☐ 6	Steve Yzerman	4.00	1.60	.40
	Detroit Red Wings			
☐ 7	Tim Cheveldae	3.00	1.20	.30
	Detroit Red Wings			
☐ 8	Bob Probert	3.00	1.20	.30
	Detroit Red Wings			
☐ 9	Wayne Gretzky	8.00	3.25	.80
	Los Angeles Kings			
☐ 10	Luc Robitaille	4.00	1.60	.40
	Los Angeles Kings			
☐ 11	Tony Granato	3.00	1.20	.30
	Los Angeles Kings			
☐ 12	Kelly Hrudey	3.00	1.20	.30
	Los Angeles Kings			
☐ 13	Brett Hull	5.00	2.00	.50
	St. Louis Blues			
☐ 14	Curtis Joseph	4.00	1.60	.40
	St. Louis Blues			
☐ 15	Brendon Shanahan	4.00	1.60	.40
	St. Louis Blues			
☐ 16	Nelson Emerson	3.00	1.20	.30
	St. Louis Blues			
☐ 17	Ray Bourque	4.00	1.60	.40
	Boston Bruins			
☐ 18	Joe Juneau	4.00	1.60	.40
	Boston Bruins			
☐ 19	Andy Moog	3.00	1.20	.30
	Boston Bruins			
☐ 20	Adam Oates	4.00	1.60	.40
	Boston Bruins			
☐ 21	Patrick Roy	6.00	2.40	.60
	Montreal Canadiens			
☐ 22	Grant Mulvey	20.00	8.00	2.00
	Chicago Blackhawks (Prototype)			
☐ 23	Denis Savard	3.00	1.20	.30
	Montreal Canadiens			
☐ 24	Gilbert Dionne	3.00	1.20	.30
	Montreal Canadiens			
☐ 25	Kirk Muller	3.00	1.20	.30
	Montreal Canadiens			
☐ 26	Mark Messier	5.00	2.00	.50
	New York Rangers			
☐ 27	Tony Amonte	3.00	1.20	.30
	New York Rangers			
☐ 28	Brian Leetch	4.00	1.60	.40
	New York Rangers			
☐ 29	Mike Richter	4.00	1.60	.40
	New York Rangers			
☐ 30	Trevor Linden	4.00	1.60	.40
	Vancouver Canucks			
☐ 31	Pavel Bure	6.00	2.40	.60
	Vancouver Canucks			
☐ 32	Cliff Ronning	3.00	1.20	.30
	Vancouver Canucks			
☐ 33	Russ Courtnall	3.00	1.20	.30
	Vancouver Canucks			
☐ 34	Mario Lemieux	6.00	2.40	.60
	Pittsburgh Penguins			
☐ 35	Jaromir Jagr	5.00	2.00	.50
	Pittsburgh Penguins			
☐ 36	Tom Barrasso	3.00	1.20	.30
	Pittsburgh Penguins			
☐ 37	Rick Tocchet	3.00	1.20	.30
	Pittsburgh Penguins			
☐ 38	Eric Lindros	8.00	3.25	.80
	Philadelphia Flyers			
☐ 39	Rod Brind'Amour	3.00	1.20	.30
	Philadelphia Flyers			
☐ 40	Dominic Roussel	3.00	1.20	.30
	Philadelphia Flyers			
☐ 41	Mark Recchi	4.00	1.60	.40
	Philadelphia Flyers			
☐ 42	Pat LaFontaine	4.00	1.60	.40
	Buffalo Sabres			
☐ 43	Donald Audette	3.00	1.20	.30
	Buffalo Sabres			
☐ 44	Pat Verbeek	3.00	1.20	.30
	Hartford Whalers			
☐ 45	John Cullen	3.00	1.20	.30
	Hartford Whalers			
☐ 46	Owen Nolan	3.00	1.20	.30
	Quebec Nordiques			
☐ 47	Joe Sakic	4.00	1.60	.40
	Quebec Nordiques			
☐ 48	Kevin Hatcher	3.00	1.20	.30
	Washington Capitals			
☐ 49	Don Beaupre	3.00	1.20	.30
	Washington Capitals			
☐ 50	Scott Stevens	3.00	1.20	.30
	New Jersey Devils			
☐ 51	Chris Terreri	3.00	1.20	.30
	New Jersey Devils			
☐ 52	Scott Lachance	3.00	1.20	.30
	New York Islanders			
☐ 53	Pierre Turgeon	4.00	1.60	.40
	New York Islanders			
☐ 54	Grant Fuhr	3.00	1.20	.30
	Toronto Maple Leafs			
☐ 55	Doug Gilmour	5.00	2.00	.50
	Toronto Maple Leafs			
☐ 56	Dave Manson	3.00	1.20	.30
	Edmonton Oilers			
☐ 57	Bill Ranford	3.00	1.20	.30
	Edmonton Oilers			
☐ 58	Troy Murray	3.00	1.20	.30
	Winnipeg Jets			
☐ 59	Phil Housley	3.00	1.20	.30
	Winnipeg Jets			
☐ 60	Al MacInnis	4.00	1.60	.40
	Calgary Flames			
☐ 61	Mike Vernon	3.00	1.20	.30
	Calgary Flames			
☐ 62	Pat Falloon	4.00	1.60	.40
	San Jose Sharks			
☐ 63	Doug Wilson	3.00	1.20	.30
	San Jose Sharks			
☐ 64	Jon Casey	3.00	1.20	.30
	Minnesota North Stars			
☐ 65	Mike Modano	4.00	1.60	.40
	Minnesota North Stars			
☐ 66	Kevin Stevens	4.00	1.60	.40
	Pittsburgh Penguins			

			MINT	EXC	G-VG
☐	67	Al Iafrate	3.00	1.20	.30
		Washington Capitals			
☐	68	Dale Hawerchuk	3.00	1.20	.30
		Buffalo Sabres			
☐	69	Igor Kravchuk	3.00	1.20	.30
		Chicago Blackhawks			
☐	70	Wendel Clark	4.00	1.60	.40
		Toronto Maple Leafs			
☐	71	Kirk McLean	4.00	1.60	.40
		Vancouver Canucks			

1993-94 Seasons Patches

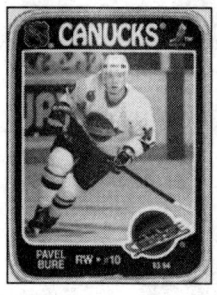

Each measuring approximately 3 1/8" by 4 1/4", these 20 patches were licensed by the NHL/NHLPA and feature color action player photos on black fabric. The player's team appears above the photo and his name, position, and jersey number are below. An embroidered border in the team color edges the patch. The team logo and year of issue in the lower right corner round out the front. The patches were encased in a hard plastic sleeve attached to a black cardboard rack display. A checklist was printed on the back of the display. The patches are unnumbered but are checklisted below according to the numbering of the checklist card.

			MINT	EXC	G-VG
		COMPLETE SET (20)	60.00	24.00	6.00
		COMMON PLAYER (1-20)	3.00	1.20	.30
☐	1	Ed Belfour	3.00	1.20	.30
		Chicago Blackhawks			
☐	2	Pavel Bure	5.00	2.00	.50
		Vancouver Canucks			
☐	3	Paul Coffey	3.00	1.20	.30
		Detroit Red Wings			
☐	4	Doug Gilmour	4.00	1.60	.40
		Toronto Maple Leafs			
☐	5	Wayne Gretzky	7.50	3.00	.75
		Los Angeles Kings			
☐	6	Brett Hull	5.00	2.00	.50
		St. Louis Blues			
☐	7	Jaromir Jagr	4.00	1.60	.40
		Pittsburgh Penguins			
☐	8	Joe Juneau	4.00	1.60	.40
		Boston Bruins			
☐	9	Mario Lemieux	6.00	2.40	.60
		Pittsburgh Penguins			
☐	10	Eric Lindros	7.50	0.00	.75
		Philadelphia Flyers			
☐	11	Shawn McEachern	3.00	1.20	.30
		Pittsburgh Penguins			
☐	12	Alexander Mogilny	4.00	1.60	.40
		Buffalo Sabres			
☐	13	Adam Oates	4.00	1.60	.40
		Boston Bruins			
☐	14	Felix Potvin	5.00	2.00	.50
		Toronto Maple Leafs			
☐	15	Jeremy Roenick	4.00	1.60	.40
		Chicago Blackhawks			
☐	16	Patrick Roy	5.00	2.00	.50
		Montreal Canadiens			
☐	17	Joe Sakic	3.00	1.20	.30
		Quebec Nordiques			
☐	18	Teemu Selanne	5.00	2.00	.50
		Winnipeg Jets			
☐	19	Kevin Stevens	3.00	1.20	.30

			MINT	EXC	G-VG
		Pittsburgh Penguins			
☐	20	Steve Yzerman	4.00	1.60	.40
		Detroit Red Wings			

1993-94 Senators Kraft Sheets

These 27 blank-backed photo sheets of the 1993-94 Ottawa Senators measure approximately 8 1/2" by 11" and feature color player action shots bordered in team colors (red, white, and gold). The player's name and uniform number, along with the Senators' logo, appear near the top. The logo for Kraft appears at the lower right; the logo for Loeb appears at the lower left. The production number out of the total produced for each sheet is shown within the white rectangle immediately above the Kraft logo. The sheets were produced in differing quantities. These production figures are shown in the checklist below. A special storage album was also available for the sheets. The sheets are unnumbered and checklisted below in alphabetical order.

			MINT	EXC	G-VG
		COMPLETE SET (27)	100.00	40.00	10.00
		COMMON PLAYER (1-27)	4.00	1.60	.40
☐	1	Dave Archibald	4.00	1.60	.40
		3,500			
☐	2	Craig Billington	4.00	1.60	.40
		6,500			
☐	3	Rick Bowness CO	4.00	1.60	.40
		6,500			
☐	4	Robert Burakovsky	5.00	2.00	.50
		1,500			
☐	5	Alexandre Daigle	9.00	3.75	.90
		6,500			
☐	6	Pavol Demitra	6.00	2.40	.60
		1,500			
☐	7	Gord Dineen	4.00	1.60	.40
		3,500			
☐	8	Dmitri Filimonov	5.00	2.00	.50
		1,500			
☐	9	Brian Glynn	5.00	2.00	.50
		1,500			
☐	10	Bill Huard	5.00	2.00	.50
		1,500			
☐	11	Jarmo Kekalainen	5.00	2.00	.50
		1,500			
☐	12	Bob Kudelski	5.00	2.00	.50
		1,500			
☐	13	Mark Lamb	5.00	2.00	.50
		1,500			
☐	14	Darcy Loewen	4.00	1.60	.40
		3,500			
☐	15	Norm Maciver	4.00	1.60	.40
		3,500			
☐	16	Darrin Madeley	5.00	2.00	.50
		1,500			
☐	17	Troy Mallette	4.00	1.60	.40
		3,500			
☐	18	Brad Marsh	5.00	2.00	.50
		6,500			
☐	19	Dave McIlwain	4.00	1.60	.40
		1,500			
☐	20	Darren Rumble	5.00	2.00	.50
		1,500			
☐	21	Vladimir Ruzicka	6.00	2.40	.60

			1,500			
☐	22	Brad Shaw		4.00	1.60	.40
			6,500			
☐	23	Graeme Townshend		5.00	2.00	.50
			1,500			
☐	24	Sylvain Turgeon		4.00	1.60	.40
			6,500			
☐	25	Dennis Vial		5.00	2.00	.50
			1,500			
☐	26	Alexei Yashin		10.00	4.00	1.00
			6,500			
☐	27	Team Photo		4.00	1.60	.40
			12,500			
☐	NNO	Team Photo		4.00	1.60	.40
☐	xx	Album		15.00	6.00	1.50

1984-85 7-Eleven Discs

This set of 60 discs was sponsored by 7-Eleven. Each disc or coin measures approximately 2" in diameter and features an alternating portrait of the player and the team's logo. The coins are quite colorful and have adhesive backing. We have checklisted the coins below in alphabetical order of team name as follows: Boston Bruins (1-2), Buffalo Sabres (3-4), Calgary Flames (5-8), Chicago Blackhawks (9-10), Detroit Red Wings (11-12), Edmonton Oilers (13-21), Hartford Whalers (22-23), Los Angeles Kings (24-25), Minnesota North Stars (26-28), Montreal Canadiens (29-30), New Jersey Devils (31-32), New York Islanders (33-34), New York Rangers (35-36), Philadelphia Flyers (37-38), Pittsburgh Penguins (39-40), Quebec Nordiques (41), St. Louis Blues (42-43), Toronto Maple Leaps (44-47), Vancouver Canucks (48-52), Washington Capitals (53-54), and Winnipeg Jets (55-60). Also the player's names have been alphabetized within their teams, and their uniform numbers placed to the right of their names. In addition, 7-Eleven also issued a large 4 1/2" diameter Wayne Gretzky disc which is not considered an essential part of the complete set. There is also a paper checklist sheet produced which pictured (in red, white, and blue) some of the coins and listed the players in the set.

		MINT	EXC	G-VG
COMPLETE SET (60)		75.00	30.00	7.50
COMMON PLAYER (1-60)		1.00	.40	.10

				MINT	EXC	G-VG
☐	1	Ray Bourque 7		5.00	2.00	.50
☐	2	Rick Middleton 16		1.50	.60	.15
☐	3	Tom Barrasso 30		3.00	1.20	.30
☐	4	Gilbert Perreault 11		2.00	.80	.20
☐	5	Rejean Lemelin 31		1.00	.40	.10
☐	6	Lanny McDonald 9		2.50	1.00	.25
☐	7	Paul Reinhart 23		1.00	.40	.10
☐	8	Doug Risebrough 8		1.00	.40	.10
☐	9	Denis Savard 18		2.50	1.00	.25
☐	10	Al Secord 20		1.00	.40	.10
☐	11	Steve Yzerman 19		6.00	2.40	.60
☐	12	Dave(Tiger) Williams 55		1.25	.50	.12
☐	13	Glenn Anderson 9		1.50	.60	.15
☐	14	Paul Coffey 7		5.00	2.00	.50
☐	15	Michel Goulet 16		2.50	1.00	.25
☐	16	Wayne Gretzky 99		12.00	5.00	1.20
☐	17	Charlie Huddy 22		1.00	.40	.10
☐	18	Pat Hughes 16		1.00	.40	.10

				MINT	EXC	G-VG
☐	19	Jari Kurri 17		3.00	1.20	.30
☐	20	Kevin Lowe 4		1.25	.50	.12
☐	21	Mark Messier 11		5.00	2.00	.50
☐	22	Ron Francis 10		2.00	.80	.20
☐	23	Sylvain Turgeon 16		1.25	.50	.12
☐	24	Marcel Dionne 16		2.00	.80	.20
☐	25	Dave Taylor 18		1.25	.50	.12
☐	26	Brian Bellows 23		1.50	.60	.15
☐	27	Dino Ciccarelli 20		1.50	.60	.15
☐	28	Harold Snepsts 28		1.25	.50	.12
☐	29	Bob Gainey 23		2.00	.80	.20
☐	30	Larry Robinson 19		2.50	1.00	.25
☐	31	Mel Bridgman 18		1.00	.40	.10
☐	32	Chico Resch 1		1.50	.60	.15
☐	33	Mike Bossy 22		3.50	1.40	.35
☐	34	Bryan Trottier 19		2.50	1.00	.25
☐	35	Barry Beck 5		1.00	.40	.10
☐	36	Don Maloney 12		1.00	.40	.10
☐	37	Tim Kerr 12		1.25	.50	.12
☐	38	Darryl Sittler 27		2.50	1.00	.25
☐	39	Mike Bullard 22		1.00	.40	.10
☐	40	Rick Kehoe 17		1.25	.50	.12
☐	41	Peter Stastny 26		3.00	1.20	.30
☐	42	Bernie Federko 24		1.50	.60	.15
☐	43	Rob Ramage 5		1.25	.50	.12
☐	44	John Anderson 10		1.00	.40	.10
☐	45	Bill Derlago 19		1.00	.40	.10
☐	46	Gary Nylund 2		1.00	.40	.10
☐	47	Rick Vaive 22		1.25	.50	.12
☐	48	Richard Brodeur 35		1.25	.50	.12
☐	49	Gary Lupul 7		1.00	.40	.10
☐	50	Darcy Rota 18		1.00	.40	.10
☐	51	Stan Smyl 12		1.25	.50	.12
☐	52	Tony Tanti 9		1.25	.50	.12
☐	53	Mike Gartner 11		3.00	1.20	.30
☐	54	Rod Langway 5		1.50	.60	.15
☐	55	Scott Arniel 11		1.00	.40	.10
☐	56	Dave Babych 44		1.25	.50	.12
☐	57	Laurie Boschman 16		1.00	.40	.10
☐	58	Dale Hawerchuk 10		2.50	1.00	.25
☐	59	Paul MacLean 15		1.00	.40	.10
☐	60	Brian Mullen 19		1.25	.50	.12
☐	xx	Wayne Gretzky Large		20.00	8.00	2.00
☐	xx	Paper Checklist Sheet		5.00	2.00	.50

1985-86 7-Eleven Credit Cards

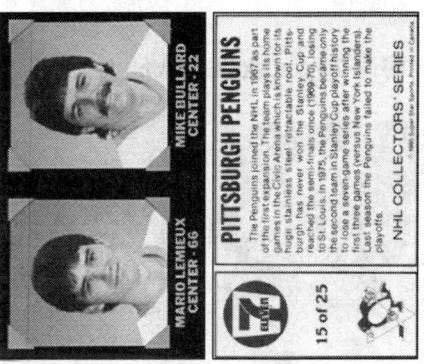

This 25-card set was sponsored by 7-Eleven. The cards measure approximately 3 3/8" by 2 1/8" and were issued in the "credit card" format. The front features color head and shoulder shots of two players from the same NHL team. These pictures are enframed by a black background, with the player's name, position, and uniform number in blue lettering below the photo. The information on the card back is framed in red boxes. In the smaller box on the left appears the 7-Eleven logo, card number, and the team logo. The right-hand box gives a brief history of the team. The key card in the set is Mario Lemieux, shown during his Rookie Card year.

	MINT	EXC	G-VG
COMPLETE SET (25)	35.00	14.00	3.50
COMMON CARD (1-25)	.75	.30	.07
☐ 1 Ray Bourque and Rick Middleton	1.50	.60	.15
☐ 2 Tom Barrasso and Gilbert Perreault	1.25	.50	.12
☐ 3 Paul Reinhart and Lanny McDonald	1.00	.40	.10
☐ 4 Denis Savard and Doug Wilson	1.25	.50	.12
☐ 5 Ron Duguay and Steve Yzerman	2.50	1.00	.25
☐ 6 Paul Coffey and Jari Kurri	2.50	1.00	.25
☐ 7 Ron Francis and Mike Liut	1.00	.40	.10
☐ 8 Marcel Dionne and Dave Taylor	1.25	.50	.12
☐ 9 Brian Bellows and Dino Ciccarelli	1.00	.40	.10
☐ 10 Larry Robinson and Guy Carbonneau	1.25	.50	.12
☐ 11 Mel Bridgman and Chico Resch	.75	.30	.07
☐ 12 Mike Bossy and Bryan Trottier	2.50	1.00	.25
☐ 13 Reijo Ruotsalainen and Barry Beck	.75	.30	.07
☐ 14 Tim Kerr and Mark Howe	.75	.30	.07
☐ 15 Mario Lemieux and Mike Bullard	20.00	8.00	2.00
☐ 16 Peter Stastny and Michel Goulet	2.50	1.00	.25
☐ 17 Rob Ramage and Brian Sutter	.75	.30	.07
☐ 18 Rick Vaive and Borje Salming	.75	.30	.07
☐ 19 Patrik Sundstrom and Stan Smyl	.75	.30	.07
☐ 20 Rod Langway and Mike Gartner	1.25	.50	.12
☐ 21 Dale Hawerchuk and Paul MacLean	1.00	.40	.10
☐ 22 Stanley Cup Winners	.75	.30	.07
☐ 23 Prince of Wales Trophy Winners	.75	.30	.07
☐ 24 Clarence S. Campbell Bowl Winners	.75	.30	.07
☐ 25 Title Card	.75	.30	.07

1972-73 Sharks Los Angeles WHA

This 19-card set features on the front black and white posed player photos, surrounded by a white border. The cards measure the standard size (2 1/2" by 3 1/2"), and the player's name is given in black lettering below the picture. The backs read "The Original Los Angeles Sharks, 1972-73" and have the Sharks' logo in the center.

	NRMT	VG-E	GOOD
COMPLETE SET (19)	40.00	16.00	4.00
COMMON PLAYER (1-19)	2.50	1.00	.25
☐ 1 Mike Byers	2.50	1.00	.25
☐ 2 Bart Crashley	3.50	1.40	.35

☐ 3 George Gardner	2.50	1.00	.25
☐ 4 Russ Gillow	2.50	1.00	.25
☐ 5 Tom Gilmore	2.50	1.00	.25
☐ 6 Earl Heiskala	2.50	1.00	.25
☐ 7 J.P. LeBlanc	3.00	1.20	.30
☐ 8 Ralph McSweyn	2.50	1.00	.25
☐ 9 Ted McCaskill	2.50	1.00	.25
☐ 10 Jim Niekamp	2.50	1.00	.25
☐ 11 Gerry Odrowski	3.00	1.20	.30
☐ 12 Tom Serviss	2.50	1.00	.25
☐ 13 Peter Slater	2.50	1.00	.25
☐ 14 Steve Sutherland	2.50	1.00	.25
☐ 15 Joe Szura	3.00	1.20	.30
☐ 16 Gary Veneruzzo	2.50	1.00	.25
☐ 17 Jim Watson	2.50	1.00	.25
☐ 18 Alton White	2.50	1.00	.25
☐ 19 Bill Young	2.50	1.00	.25

1991-92 Sharks San Jose Sports Action

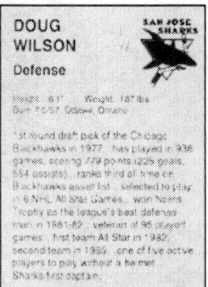

This 22-card set was issued by Sports Action and features members of the 1991-92 San Jose Sharks. The standard-size (2 1/2" by 3 1/2") cards are printed on thin card stock. The fronts feature full-bleed glossy color action photos. The backs carry brief biography, career summary, and the team logo. The cards are unnumbered and checklisted below in alphabetical order.

	MINT	EXC	G-VG
COMPLETE SET (22)	15.00	6.00	1.50
COMMON PLAYER (1-22)	.50	.20	.05
☐ 1 Perry Anderson	.50	.20	.05
☐ 2 Perry Berezan	.50	.20	.05
☐ 3 Steve Bozek	.50	.20	.05
☐ 4 Dean Evason	.75	.30	.07
☐ 5 Pat Falloon	2.00	.80	.20
☐ 6 Paul Fenton	.50	.20	.05
☐ 7 Link Gaetz	.75	.30	.07
☐ 8 Jeff Hackett	.75	.30	.07
☐ 9 Ken Hammond	.50	.20	.05
☐ 10 Brian Hayward	1.00	.40	.10
☐ 11 Tony Hrkac	.75	.30	.07
☐ 12 Kelly Kisio	.75	.30	.07
☐ 13 Brian Lawton	.50	.20	.05
☐ 14 Pat MacLeod	.75	.30	.07
☐ 15 Bob McGill	.50	.20	.05
☐ 16 Brian Mullen	.75	.30	.07
☐ 17 Jarmo Myllys	.75	.30	.07
☐ 18 Wayne Presley	.50	.20	.05
☐ 19 Neil Wilkinson	.75	.30	.07
☐ 20 Doug Wilson	1.00	.40	.10
☐ 21 Rob Zettler	.60	.24	.06
☐ 22 San Jose Sharks Game action	.75	.30	.07

1960-61 Shirriff Coins

This set of 120 coins (each measuring approximately 1 3/8" in diameter) features players from all six NHL teams. These plastic coins are in color and numbered on the front. The

coins are checklisted below according to teams as follows: Toronto Maple Leafs (1-20), Montreal Canadiens (21-40), Detroit Red Wings (41-60), Chicago Blackhawks (61-80), New York Rangers (81-100), and Boston Bruins (101-120). The set was also issued on a limited basis as a factory set in a black presentation box.

	NRMT	VG-E	GOOD
COMPLETE SET (120)	450.00	180.00	45.00
COMMON PLAYER (1-120)	2.50	1.00	.25

		NRMT	VG-E	GOOD
☐	1 Johnny Bower	7.50	3.00	.75
☐	2 Dick Duff	3.50	1.40	.35
☐	3 Carl Brewer	3.50	1.40	.35
☐	4 Red Kelly	7.50	3.00	.75
☐	5 Tim Horton	9.00	3.75	.90
☐	6 Allan Stanley	5.00	2.00	.50
☐	7 Bob Baun	3.50	1.40	.35
☐	8 Billy Harris	2.50	1.00	.25
☐	9 George Armstrong	6.00	2.40	.60
☐	10 Ron Stewart	2.50	1.00	.25
☐	11 Bert Olmstead	5.00	2.00	.50
☐	12 Frank Mahovlich	10.00	4.00	1.00
☐	13 Bob Pulford	5.00	2.00	.50
☐	14 Gary Edmundson	2.50	1.00	.25
☐	15 Johnny Wilson	2.50	1.00	.25
☐	16 Larry Regan	2.50	1.00	.25
☐	17 Gerry James	3.50	1.40	.35
☐	18 Rudy Migay	2.50	1.00	.25
☐	19 Gerry Ehman	2.50	1.00	.25
☐	20 Punch Imlach CO	3.50	1.40	.35
☐	21 Jacques Plante	12.00	5.00	1.20
☐	22 Dickie Moore	7.50	3.00	.75
☐	23 Don Marshall	2.50	1.00	.25
☐	24 Albert Langlois	2.50	1.00	.25
☐	25 Tom Johnson	5.00	2.00	.50
☐	26 Doug Harvey	9.00	3.75	.90
☐	27 Phil Goyette	2.50	1.00	.25
☐	28 Boom Boom Geoffrion	12.00	5.00	1.20
☐	29 Marcel Bonin	2.50	1.00	.25
☐	30 Jean Beliveau	15.00	6.00	1.50
☐	31 Ralph Backstrom	3.50	1.40	.35
☐	32 Andre Pronovost	2.50	1.00	.25
☐	33 Claude Provost	3.50	1.40	.35
☐	34 Henri Richard	9.00	3.75	.90
☐	35 Jean-Guy Talbot	3.50	1.40	.35
☐	36 J.C. Tremblay	3.50	1.40	.35
☐	37 Bob Turner	2.50	1.00	.25
☐	38 Bill Hicke	2.50	1.00	.25
☐	39 Charlie Hodge	3.50	1.40	.35
☐	40 Toe Blake CO	5.00	2.00	.50
☐	41 Terry Sawchuk	15.00	6.00	1.50
☐	42 Gordie Howe	40.00	16.00	4.00
☐	43 John McKenzie	2.50	1.00	.25
☐	44 Alex Delvecchio	7.50	3.00	.75
☐	45 Norm Ullman	6.00	2.40	.60
☐	46 Jack McIntyre	2.50	1.00	.25
☐	47 Barry Cullen	3.50	1.40	.35
☐	48 Val Fonteyne	2.50	1.00	.25
☐	49 Warren Godfrey	2.50	1.00	.25
☐	50 Pete Goegan	2.50	1.00	.25
☐	51 Gerry Melnyk	2.50	1.00	.25
☐	52 Mark Reaume	2.50	1.00	.25
☐	53 Gary Aldcorn	2.50	1.00	.25
☐	54 Len Lunde	2.50	1.00	.25
☐	55 Murray Oliver	2.50	1.00	.25
☐	56 Marcel Pronovost	5.00	2.00	.50
☐	57 Howie Glover	2.50	1.00	.25
☐	58 Gerry Odrowski	2.50	1.00	.25
☐	59 Parker MacDonald	2.50	1.00	.25
☐	60 Sid Abel CO	5.00	2.00	.50
☐	61 Glenn Hall	9.00	3.75	.90
☐	62 Ed Litzenberger	2.50	1.00	.25
☐	63 Bobby Hull	25.00	10.00	2.50
☐	64 Tod Sloan	2.50	1.00	.25
☐	65 Murray Balfour	2.50	1.00	.25

☐	66 Pierre Pilote	5.00	2.00	.50
☐	67 Al Arbour	5.00	2.00	.50
☐	68 Earl Balfour	2.50	1.00	.25
☐	69 Eric Nesterenko	3.50	1.40	.35
☐	70 Ken Wharram	3.50	1.40	.35
☐	71 Stan Mikita	12.00	5.00	1.20
☐	72 Ab McDonald	2.50	1.00	.25
☐	73 Elmer Vasko	2.50	1.00	.25
☐	74 Dollard St.Laurent	2.50	1.00	.25
☐	75 Ron Murphy	2.50	1.00	.25
☐	76 Jack Evans	2.50	1.00	.25
☐	77 Bill(Red) Hay	2.50	1.00	.25
☐	78 Reg Fleming	2.50	1.00	.25
☐	79 Cecil Hoekstra	2.50	1.00	.25
☐	80 Tommy Ivan CO	3.50	1.40	.35
☐	81 Jack McCartan	3.50	1.40	.35
☐	82 Red Sullivan	2.50	1.00	.25
☐	83 Camille Henry	3.50	1.40	.35
☐	84 Larry Popein	2.50	1.00	.25
☐	85 John Hanna	2.50	1.00	.25
☐	86 Harry Howell	5.00	2.00	.50
☐	87 Eddie Shack	6.00	2.40	.60
☐	88 Irv Spencer	2.50	1.00	.25
☐	89 Andy Bathgate	6.00	2.40	.60
☐	90 Bill Gadsby	5.00	2.00	.50
☐	91 Andy Hebenton	2.50	1.00	.25
☐	92 Earl Ingarfield	2.50	1.00	.25
☐	93 Don Johns	2.50	1.00	.25
☐	94 Dave Balon	2.50	1.00	.25
☐	95 Jim Morrison	2.50	1.00	.25
☐	96 Ken Schinkel	2.50	1.00	.25
☐	97 Lou Fontinato	2.50	1.00	.25
☐	98 Ted Hampson	2.50	1.00	.25
☐	99 Brian Cullen	3.50	1.40	.35
☐	100 Alf Pike CO	2.50	1.00	.25
☐	101 Don Simmons	2.50	1.00	.25
☐	102 Fern Flaman	5.00	2.00	.50
☐	103 Vic Stasiuk	2.50	1.00	.25
☐	104 Johnny Bucyk	7.50	3.00	.75
☐	105 Bronco Horvath	2.50	1.00	.25
☐	106 Doug Mohns	3.50	1.40	.35
☐	107 Leo Boivin	5.00	2.00	.50
☐	108 Don McKenney	2.50	1.00	.25
☐	109 Jean-Guy Gendron	2.50	1.00	.25
☐	110 Jerry Toppazzini	2.50	1.00	.25
☐	111 Dick Meissner	2.50	1.00	.25
☐	112 Autry Erickson	2.50	1.00	.25
☐	113 Jim Bartlett	2.50	1.00	.25
☐	114 Orval Tessier	3.50	1.40	.35
☐	115 Billy Carter	2.50	1.00	.25
☐	116 Dallas Smith	3.50	1.40	.35
☐	117 Leo Labine	2.50	1.00	.25
☐	118 Bob Armstrong	2.50	1.00	.25
☐	119 Bruce Gamble	2.50	1.00	.25
☐	120 Milt Schmidt CO	6.00	2.40	.60

1961-62 Shirriff/Salada Coins

This set of 120 coins (each measuring approximately 1 3/8" in diameter) features players of the NHL, all six teams. These plastic coins are in color and numbered on the front. The coins are numbered according to teams as follows: Boston Bruins (1-20), Chicago Blackhawks (21-40), Toronto Maple Leafs (41-60), Detroit Red Wings (61-80), New York Rangers (81-100), and Montreal Canadiens (101-120). The coins were also produced in identical fashion for Salada with a Salada imprint; the Salada version has the same values as listed below. This was the only year of Shirriff coins where collectors could obtain plastic shields for displaying their collection. These shields are not considered part of the complete set.

	NRMT	VG-E	GOOD
COMPLETE SET (120)	400.00	160.00	40.00
COMMON PLAYER (1-120)	2.50	1.00	.25
☐ 1 Cliff Pennington	2.50	1.00	.25
☐ 2 Dallas Smith	3.50	1.40	.35
☐ 3 Andre Pronovost	2.50	1.00	.25
☐ 4 Charlie Burns	2.50	1.00	.25
☐ 5 Leo Boivin	5.00	2.00	.50
☐ 6 Don McKenney	2.50	1.00	.25
☐ 7 Johnny Bucyk	7.50	3.00	.75
☐ 8 Murray Oliver	2.50	1.00	.25
☐ 9 Jerry Toppazinni	2.50	1.00	.25
☐ 10 Doug Mohns	3.50	1.40	.35
☐ 11 Don Head	2.50	1.00	.25
☐ 12 Bob Armstrong	2.50	1.00	.25
☐ 13 Pat Stapleton	3.50	1.40	.35
☐ 14 Orland Kurtenbach	3.50	1.40	.35
☐ 15 Dick Meissner	2.50	1.00	.25
☐ 16 Ted Green	3.50	1.40	.35
☐ 17 Tom Williams	2.50	1.00	.25
☐ 18 Autry Erickson	2.50	1.00	.25
☐ 19 Phil Watson CO	5.00	2.00	.50
☐ 20 Ed Chadwick	3.50	1.40	.35
☐ 21 Wayne Hillman	2.50	1.00	.25
☐ 22 Stan Mikita	12.00	5.00	1.20
☐ 23 Eric Nesterenko	3.50	1.40	.35
☐ 24 Reg Fleming	2.50	1.00	.25
☐ 25 Bobby Hull	25.00	10.00	2.50
☐ 26 Elmer Vasko	2.50	1.00	.25
☐ 27 Pierre Pilote	5.00	2.00	.50
☐ 28 Chico Maki	3.50	1.40	.35
☐ 29 Glenn Hall	9.00	3.75	.90
☐ 30 Murray Balfour	2.50	1.00	.25
☐ 31 Bronco Horvath	2.50	1.00	.25
☐ 32 Ken Wharram	3.50	1.40	.35
☐ 33 Ab McDonald	2.50	1.00	.25
☐ 34 Bill(Red) Hay	2.50	1.00	.25
☐ 35 Dollard St.Laurent	2.50	1.00	.25
☐ 36 Ron Murphy	2.50	1.00	.25
☐ 37 Bob Turner	2.50	1.00	.25
☐ 38 Gerry Melnyk	2.50	1.00	.25
☐ 39 Jack Evans	2.50	1.00	.25
☐ 40 Rudy Pilous CO	5.00	2.00	.50
☐ 41 Johnny Bower	7.50	3.00	.75
☐ 42 Allan Stanley	6.00	2.40	.60
☐ 43 Frank Mahovlich	10.00	4.00	1.00
☐ 44 Tim Horton	9.00	3.75	.90
☐ 45 Carl Brewer	3.50	1.40	.35
☐ 46 Bob Pulford	5.00	2.00	.50
☐ 47 Bob Nevin	3.50	1.40	.35
☐ 48 Eddie Shack	6.00	2.40	.60
☐ 49 Red Kelly	7.50	3.00	.75
☐ 50 Bob Baun	3.50	1.40	.35
☐ 51 George Armstrong	6.00	2.40	.60
☐ 52 Bert Olmstead	5.00	2.00	.50
☐ 53 Dick Duff	3.50	1.40	.35
☐ 54 Billy Harris	3.50	1.40	.35
☐ 55 Larry Keenan	2.50	1.00	.25
☐ 56 Johnny MacMillan	2.50	1.00	.25
☐ 57 Punch Imlach CO	3.50	1.40	.35
☐ 58 Dave Keon	6.00	2.40	.60
☐ 59 Larry Hillman	2.50	1.00	.25
☐ 60 Al Arbour	5.00	2.00	.50
☐ 61 Sid Abel CO	5.00	2.00	.50
☐ 62 Warren Godfrey	2.50	1.00	.25
☐ 63 Vic Stasiuk	2.50	1.00	.25
☐ 64 Leo Labine	2.50	1.00	.25
☐ 65 Howie Glover	2.50	1.00	.25
☐ 66 Gordie Howe	40.00	16.00	4.00
☐ 67 Val Fonteyne	2.50	1.00	.25
☐ 68 Marcel Pronovost	5.00	2.00	.50
☐ 69 Parker MacDonald	2.50	1.00	.25
☐ 70 Alex Delvecchio	7.50	3.00	.75
☐ 71 Ed Litzenberger	2.50	1.00	.25
☐ 72 Al Johnson	2.50	1.00	.25
☐ 73 Bruce MacGregor	2.50	1.00	.25
☐ 74 Howie Young	2.50	1.00	.25
☐ 75 Pete Goegan	2.50	1.00	.25
☐ 76 Norm Ullman	6.00	2.40	.60
☐ 77 Terry Sawchuk	15.00	6.00	1.50
☐ 78 Gerry Odrowski	2.50	1.00	.25
☐ 79 Bill Gadsby	5.00	2.00	.50
☐ 80 Hank Bassen	2.50	1.00	.25
☐ 81 Doug Harvey	9.00	3.75	.90
☐ 82 Earl Ingarfield	2.50	1.00	.25
☐ 83 Pat Hannigan	2.50	1.00	.25
☐ 84 Dean Prentice	3.50	1.40	.35
☐ 85 Gump Worsley	9.00	3.75	.90
☐ 86 Irv Spencer	2.50	1.00	.25
☐ 87 Camille Henry	3.50	1.40	.35
☐ 88 Andy Bathgate	6.00	2.40	.60
☐ 89 Harry Howell	5.00	2.00	.50
☐ 90 Andy Hebenton	2.50	1.00	.25
☐ 91 Red Sullivan	2.50	1.00	.25
☐ 92 Ted Hampson	2.50	1.00	.25
☐ 93 Jean-Guy Gendron	2.50	1.00	.25
☐ 94 Albert Langlois	2.50	1.00	.25
☐ 95 Larry Cahan	2.50	1.00	.25
☐ 96 Bob Cunningham	2.50	1.00	.25
☐ 97 Vic Hadfield	3.50	1.40	.35
☐ 98 Jean Ratelle	9.00	3.75	.90
☐ 99 Ken Schinkel	2.50	1.00	.25
☐ 100 Johnny Wilson	2.50	1.00	.25
☐ 101 Toe Blake CO	5.00	2.00	.50
☐ 102 Jean Beliveau	15.00	6.00	1.50
☐ 103 Don Marshall	2.50	1.00	.25
☐ 104 Boom Boom Geoffrion	12.00	5.00	1.20
☐ 105 Claude Provost	3.50	1.40	.35
☐ 106 Tom Johnson	5.00	2.00	.50
☐ 107 Dickie Moore	7.50	3.00	.75
☐ 108 Bill Hicke	2.50	1.00	.25
☐ 109 Jean-Guy Talbot	3.50	1.40	.35
☐ 110 Henri Richard	9.00	3.75	.90
☐ 111 Lou Fontinato	2.50	1.00	.25
☐ 112 Gilles Tremblay	2.50	1.00	.25
☐ 113 Jacques Plante	12.00	5.00	1.20
☐ 114 Ralph Backstrom	3.50	1.40	.35
☐ 115 Marcel Bonin	2.50	1.00	.25
☐ 116 Phil Goyette	2.50	1.00	.25
☐ 117 Bobby Rousseau	3.50	1.40	.35
☐ 118 J.C. Tremblay	3.50	1.40	.35
☐ 119 Al MacNeil	2.50	1.00	.25
☐ 120 Jean Gauthier	2.50	1.00	.25
☐ S1 Boston Bruins Shield	50.00	20.00	5.00
☐ S2 Chicago Blackhawks Shield	50.00	20.00	5.00
☐ S3 Detroit Red Wings Shield	50.00	20.00	5.00
☐ S4 Montreal Canadiens Shield	50.00	20.00	5.00
☐ S5 New York Rangers Shield	50.00	20.00	5.00
☐ S6 Toronto Maple Leafs Shield	50.00	20.00	5.00

1962-63 Shirriff Metal Coins

This set of 60 coins (each measuring approximately 1 1/2" in diameter) features 12 All-Stars, six Trophy winners, and players from Montreal (20) and Toronto (22). The four American teams in the NHL were not included in this set except where they appeared as All-Stars or Trophy winners. These metal coins are in color and numbered on the front. The backs are written in French and English.

	NRMT	VG-E	GOOD
COMPLETE SET (60)	350.00	140.00	35.00
COMMON PLAYER (1-60)	3.50	1.40	.35
☐ 1 Johnny Bower	10.00	4.00	1.00
☐ 2 Allan Stanley	7.50	3.00	.75
☐ 3 Frank Mahovlich	15.00	6.00	1.50
☐ 4 Tim Horton	12.00	5.00	1.20
☐ 5 Carl Brewer	6.00	2.40	.60
☐ 6 Bob Pulford	7.50	3.00	.75
☐ 7 Bob Nevin	4.50	1.80	.45
☐ 8 Eddie Shack	7.50	3.00	.75
☐ 9 Red Kelly	9.00	3.75	.90
☐ 10 George Armstrong	7.50	3.00	.75
☐ 11 Bert Olmstead	6.00	2.40	.60
☐ 12 Dick Duff	4.50	1.80	.45
☐ 13 Billy Harris	3.50	1.40	.35
☐ 14 Johnny MacMillan	3.50	1.40	.35

☐	15 Punch Imlach CO	4.50	1.80	.45
☐	16 Dave Keon	7.50	3.00	.75
☐	17 Larry Hillman	3.50	1.40	.35
☐	18 Ed Litzenberger	3.50	1.40	.35
☐	19 Bob Baun	4.50	1.80	.45
☐	20 Al Arbour	7.50	3.00	.75
☐	21 Ron Stewart	3.50	1.40	.35
☐	22 Don Simmons	3.50	1.40	.35
☐	23 Lou Fontinato	3.50	1.40	.35
☐	24 Gilles Tremblay	3.50	1.40	.35
☐	25 Jacques Plante	15.00	6.00	1.50
☐	26 Ralph Backstrom	4.50	1.80	.45
☐	27 Marcel Bonin	3.50	1.40	.35
☐	28 Phil Goyette	3.50	1.40	.35
☐	29 Bobby Rousseau	4.50	1.80	.45
☐	30 J.C. Tremblay	4.50	1.80	.45
☐	31 Toe Blake CO	7.50	3.00	.75
☐	32 Jean Beliveau	20.00	8.00	2.00
☐	33 Don Marshall	3.50	1.40	.35
☐	34 Boom Boom Geoffrion	15.00	6.00	1.50
☐	35 Claude Provost	4.50	1.80	.45
☐	36 Tom Johnson	7.50	3.00	.75
☐	37 Dickie Moore	9.00	3.75	.90
☐	38 Bill Hicke	3.50	1.40	.35
☐	39 Jean-Guy Talbot	4.50	1.80	.45
☐	40 Al MacNeil	3.50	1.40	.35
☐	41 Henri Richard	10.00	4.00	1.00
☐	42 Red Berenson	4.50	1.80	.45
☐	43 Jacques Plante AS	12.00	5.00	1.20
☐	44 Jean-Guy Talbot AS	4.50	1.80	.45
☐	45 Doug Harvey AS	7.50	3.00	.75
☐	46 Stan Mikita AS	9.00	3.75	.90
☐	47 Bobby Hull AS	20.00	8.00	2.00
☐	48 Andy Bathgate AS	7.50	3.00	.75
☐	49 Glenn Hall AS	9.00	3.75	.90
☐	50 Pierre Pilote AS	7.50	3.00	.75
☐	51 Carl Brewer AS	6.00	2.40	.60
☐	52 Dave Keon AS	7.50	3.00	.75
☐	53 Frank Mahovlich AS	9.00	3.75	.90
☐	54 Gordie Howe AS	30.00	12.00	3.00
☐	55 Dave Keon Byng	6.00	2.40	.60
☐	56 Bobby Rousseau Calder	4.50	1.80	.45
☐	57 Bobby Hull Ross	20.00	8.00	2.00
☐	58 Jacques Plante Vezina	12.00	5.00	1.20
☐	59 Jacques Plante Hart	12.00	5.00	1.20
☐	60 Doug Harvey Norris	7.50	3.00	.75

1968-69 Shirriff Coins

This set of 176 coins (each measuring approximately 1 3/8" in diameter) features players from all of the teams in the NHL. These plastic coins are in color and numbered on the front. However the coins are numbered by Shirriff within each team and not for the whole set. The correspondence between the actual coin numbers and the numbers assigned below should be apparent. For those few situations where two coins from the same team have the same number, that number is listed in the checklist below next to the name. The coins are checklisted below according to teams as follows: Boston Bruins (1-16), Chicago Blackhawks (17-33), Detroit Red Wings (34-49), Los Angeles Kings (50-61), Minnesota North Stars (62-74), Montreal Canadiens (75-92), New York Rangers (93-108), Oakland Seals (109-121), Philadelphia Flyers (122-134), Pittsburgh Penguins (135-146), St. Louis Blues (147-158), and Toronto Maple Leafs (159-176). Some of the coins are quite challenging to find. It seems the

higher numbers within each team and the coins from the players on the expansion teams are more difficult to find; these are marked by SP in the list below.

		NRMT	VG-E	GOOD
COMPLETE SET (176)		5000.00	2000.00	500.00
COMMON PLAYER (1-176)		4.00	1.60	.40
☐ 1	Eddie Shack	8.00	3.25	.80
☐ 2	Ed Westfall	5.00	2.00	.50
☐ 3	Don Awrey	4.00	1.60	.40
☐ 4	Gerry Cheevers	10.00	4.00	1.00
☐ 5	Bobby Orr	100.00	40.00	10.00
☐ 6	Johnny Bucyk	10.00	4.00	1.00
☐ 7	Derek Sanderson	8.00	3.25	.80
☐ 8	Phil Esposito	20.00	8.00	2.00
☐ 9	Fred Stanfield	4.00	1.60	.40
☐ 10	Ken Hodge	6.00	2.40	.60
☐ 11	John McKenzie	4.00	1.60	.40
☐ 12	Ted Green	5.00	2.00	.50
☐ 13	Dallas Smith SP	75.00	30.00	7.50
☐ 14	Gary Doak SP	75.00	30.00	7.50
☐ 15	Glen Sather SP	100.00	40.00	10.00
☐ 16	Tom Williams SP	75.00	30.00	7.50
☐ 17	Bobby Hull	50.00	20.00	5.00
☐ 18	Pat Stapleton	4.00	1.60	.40
☐ 19	Wayne Maki	4.00	1.60	.40
☐ 20	Denis DeJordy	6.00	2.40	.60
☐ 21	Ken Wharram	4.00	1.60	.40
☐ 22	Pit Martin	4.00	1.60	.40
☐ 23	Chico Maki	4.00	1.60	.40
☐ 24	Doug Mohns	5.00	2.00	.50
☐ 25	Stan Mikita	15.00	6.00	1.50
☐ 26	Doug Jarrett	4.00	1.60	.40
☐ 27	Dennis Hull 11 SP (small portrait)	100.00	40.00	10.00
☐ 28	Dennis Hull 11 SP (large portrait)	25.00	10.00	2.50
☐ 29	Matt Ravlich	4.00	1.60	.40
☐ 30	Dave Dryden SP	75.00	30.00	7.50
☐ 31	Eric Nesterenko SP	75.00	30.00	7.50
☐ 32	Gilles Marotte SP	75.00	30.00	7.50
☐ 33	Jim Pappin SP	75.00	30.00	7.50
☐ 34	Gary Bergman	4.00	1.60	.40
☐ 35	Roger Crozier	5.00	2.00	.50
☐ 36	Peter Mahovlich	6.00	2.40	.60
☐ 37	Alex Delvecchio	8.00	3.25	.80
☐ 38	Dean Prentice	5.00	2.00	.50
☐ 39	Kent Douglas	4.00	1.60	.40
☐ 40	Roy Edwards	4.00	1.60	.40
☐ 41	Bruce MacGregor	4.00	1.60	.40
☐ 42	Garry Unger	5.00	2.00	.50
☐ 43	Pete Stemkowski	4.00	1.60	.40
☐ 44	Gordie Howe	75.00	30.00	7.50
☐ 45	Frank Mahovlich	15.00	6.00	1.50
☐ 46	Bob Baun SP	75.00	30.00	7.50
☐ 47	Brian Conacher SP	75.00	30.00	7.50
☐ 48	Jim Watson SP	75.00	30.00	7.50
☐ 49	Nick Libett SP	75.00	30.00	7.50
☐ 50	Real Lemieux	5.00	2.00	.50
☐ 51	Ted Irvine	5.00	2.00	.50
☐ 52	Bob Wall	5.00	2.00	.50
☐ 53	Bill White	5.00	2.00	.50
☐ 54	Gord Labossiere	5.00	2.00	.50
☐ 55	Eddie Joyal	5.00	2.00	.50
☐ 56	Lowell MacDonald	5.00	2.00	.50
☐ 57	Bill Flett	5.00	2.00	.50
☐ 58	Wayne Rutledge	5.00	2.00	.50
☐ 59	Dave Amadio	5.00	2.00	.50
☐ 60	Skip Krake SP	50.00	20.00	5.00
☐ 61	Doug Robinson SP	50.00	20.00	5.00
☐ 62	Wayne Connelly	5.00	2.00	.50
☐ 63	Bob Woytowich	5.00	2.00	.50
☐ 64	Andre Boudrias	5.00	2.00	.50
☐ 65	Bill Goldsworthy	6.00	2.40	.60
☐ 66	Cesare Maniago	6.00	2.40	.60
☐ 67	Milan Marcetta	5.00	2.00	.50
☐ 68	Bill Collins SP 7	25.00	10.00	2.50
☐ 69	Claude Larose SP 7	90.00	36.00	9.00
☐ 70	Parker MacDonald	5.00	2.00	.50
☐ 71	Ray Cullen	5.00	2.00	.50
☐ 72	Mike McMahon	5.00	2.00	.50
☐ 73	Bob McCord SP	50.00	20.00	5.00
☐ 74	Larry Hillman SP	50.00	20.00	5.00
☐ 75	Gump Worsley	10.00	4.00	1.00
☐ 76	Rogatien Vachon	8.00	3.25	.80
☐ 77	Ted Harris	4.00	1.60	.40
☐ 78	Jacques Laperriere	6.00	2.40	.60
☐ 79	J.C. Tremblay	5.00	2.00	.50
☐ 80	Jean Beliveau	25.00	10.00	2.50
☐ 81	Gilles Tremblay	4.00	1.60	.40
☐ 82	Ralph Backstrom	4.00	1.60	.40
☐ 83	Bobby Rousseau	4.00	1.60	.40

☐ 84	John Ferguson	5.00	2.00	.50
☐ 85	Dick Duff	5.00	2.00	.50
☐ 86	Terry Harper	5.00	2.00	.50
☐ 87	Yvan Cournoyer	8.00	3.25	.80
☐ 88	Jacques Lemaire	8.00	3.25	.80
☐ 89	Henri Richard	10.00	4.00	1.00
☐ 90	Claude Provost SP	100.00	40.00	10.00
☐ 91	Serge Savard SP	125.00	50.00	12.50
☐ 92	Mickey Redmond SP	125.00	50.00	12.50
☐ 93	Rod Seiling	4.00	1.60	.40
☐ 94	Jean Ratelle	8.00	3.25	.80
☐ 95	Ed Giacomin	8.00	3.25	.80
☐ 96	Reg Fleming	4.00	1.60	.40
☐ 97	Phil Goyette	4.00	1.60	.40
☐ 98	Arnie Brown	4.00	1.60	.40
☐ 99	Don Marshall	4.00	1.60	.40
☐ 100	Orland Kurtenbach	5.00	2.00	.50
☐ 101	Bob Nevin	4.00	1.60	.40
☐ 102	Rod Gilbert	8.00	3.25	.80
☐ 103	Harry Howell	6.00	2.40	.60
☐ 104	Jim Neilson	4.00	1.60	.40
☐ 105	Vic Hadfield SP	125.00	50.00	12.50
☐ 106	Larry Jeffrey SP	175.00	70.00	18.00
☐ 107	Dave Balon SP	125.00	50.00	12.50
☐ 108	Ron Stewart SP	125.00	50.00	12.50
☐ 109	Gerry Ehman	5.00	2.00	.50
☐ 110	John Brenneman	5.00	2.00	.50
☐ 111	Ted Hampson	5.00	2.00	.50
☐ 112	Billy Harris	5.00	2.00	.50
☐ 113	George Swarbrick SP 5	25.00	10.00	2.50
☐ 114	Carol Vadnais SP 5	350.00	140.00	35.00
☐ 115	Gary Smith	6.00	2.40	.60
☐ 116	Charlie Hodge	6.00	2.40	.60
☐ 117	Bert Marshall	5.00	2.00	.50
☐ 118	Bill Hicke	5.00	2.00	.50
☐ 119	Tracy Pratt	5.00	2.00	.50
☐ 120	Garry Jarrett SP	450.00	180.00	45.00
☐ 121	Howie Young SP	400.00	160.00	40.00
☐ 122	Bernie Parent	12.00	5.00	1.20
☐ 123	John Miszuk	5.00	2.00	.50
☐ 124	Ed Hoekstra SP 3	25.00	10.00	2.50
☐ 125	Allan Stanley SP 3	100.00	40.00	10.00
☐ 126	Gary Dornhoefer	6.00	2.40	.60
☐ 127	Doug Favell	6.00	2.40	.60
☐ 128	Andre Lacroix	6.00	2.40	.60
☐ 129	Brit Selby	5.00	2.00	.50
☐ 130	Don Blackburn	5.00	2.00	.50
☐ 131	Leon Rochefort	5.00	2.00	.50
☐ 132	Forbes Kennedy	5.00	2.00	.50
☐ 133	Claude Laforge SP	75.00	30.00	7.50
☐ 134	Pat Hannigan SP	75.00	30.00	7.50
☐ 135	Ken Schinkel	5.00	2.00	.50
☐ 136	Earl Ingarfield	5.00	2.00	.50
☐ 137	Val Fonteyne	5.00	2.00	.50
☐ 138	Noel Price	5.00	2.00	.50
☐ 139	Andy Bathgate	8.00	3.25	.80
☐ 140	Les Binkley	6.00	2.40	.60
☐ 141	Leo Boivin	6.00	2.40	.60
☐ 142	Paul Andrea	5.00	2.00	.50
☐ 143	Dunc McCallum	5.00	2.00	.50
☐ 144	Keith McCreary	5.00	2.00	.50
☐ 145	Lou Angotti SP	75.00	30.00	7.50
☐ 146	Wally Boyer SP	75.00	30.00	7.50
☐ 147	Ron Schock	5.00	2.00	.50
☐ 148	Bob Plager	6.00	2.40	.60
☐ 149	Al Arbour	8.00	3.25	.80
☐ 150	Red Berenson	6.00	2.40	.60
☐ 151	Glenn Hall	12.00	5.00	1.20
☐ 152	Jim Roberts	6.00	2.40	.60
☐ 153	Noel Picard	5.00	2.00	.50
☐ 154	Barclay Plager	6.00	2.40	.60
☐ 155	Larry Keenan	5.00	2.00	.50
☐ 156	Terry Crisp	6.00	2.40	.60
☐ 157	Gary Sabourin SP	75.00	30.00	7.50
☐ 158	Ab McDonald SP	75.00	30.00	7.50
☐ 159	George Armstrong	8.00	3.25	.80
☐ 160	Wayne Carleton	4.00	1.60	.40
☐ 161	Paul Henderson	6.00	2.40	.60
☐ 162	Bob Pulford	6.00	2.40	.60
☐ 163	Mike Walton	5.00	2.00	.50
☐ 164	Johnny Bower	9.00	3.75	.90
☐ 165	Ron Ellis	5.00	2.00	.50
☐ 166	Mike Pelyk	4.00	1.60	.40
☐ 167	Murray Oliver	4.00	1.60	.40
☐ 168	Norm Ullman	9.00	3.75	.90
☐ 169	Dave Keon	9.00	3.75	.90
☐ 170	Floyd Smith	4.00	1.60	.40
☐ 171	Marcel Pronovost	6.00	2.40	.60
☐ 172	Tim Horton	10.00	4.00	1.00
☐ 173	Bruce Gamble	4.00	1.60	.40
☐ 174	Jim McKenny SP	100.00	40.00	10.00
☐ 175	Mike Byers SP	100.00	40.00	10.00
☐ 176	Pierre Pilote SP	125.00	50.00	12.50

1992 Sport-Flash

 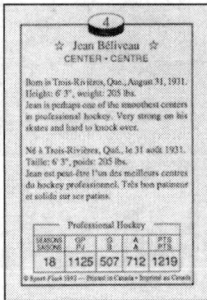

This 15-card standard-size (2 1/2" by 3 1/2") set was produced by Sport-Flash as the first series of "Hockey Stars since 1940". The accompanying certification of limited edition claims that the production run was 200,000 sets. Each set contained one autographed hockey card signed by the player. On a bright yellow card face, the fronts display close-up color photos enclosed by blue and black border stripes. The player's name appears in the bottom yellow border. The backs are bilingual and present biography, player profile, and career statistics. The cards are numbered on both sides.

	MINT	EXC	G-VG
COMPLETE SET (15)	15.00	6.00	1.50
COMMON PLAYER (1-15)	1.00	.40	.10

☐ 1	Jacques Laperriere	1.50	.60	.15
☐ 2	Larry Carriere	1.00	.40	.10
☐ 3	Chuck Rayner	1.50	.60	.15
☐ 4	Jean Beliveau	4.00	1.60	.40
☐ 5	BoomBoom Geoffrion	3.00	1.20	.30
☐ 6	Gilles Gilbert	1.00	.40	.10
☐ 7	Marcel Bonin	1.00	.40	.10
☐ 8	Leon Rochefort	1.00	.40	.10
☐ 9	Maurice Richard	5.00	2.00	.50
☐ 10	Rejean Houle	1.00	.40	.10
☐ 11	Pierre Mondou	1.00	.40	.10
☐ 12	Yvan Cournoyer	2.00	.80	.20
☐ 13	Henri Richard	2.50	1.00	.25
☐ 14	Checklist Card	1.00	.40	.10
☐ 15	Certification of Limited Edition	1.00	.40	.10

1991-92 Stadium Club

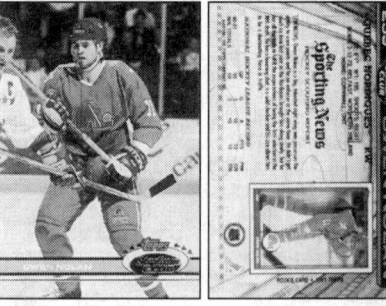

The 1991-92 Topps Stadium Club hockey set contains 400 cards measuring the standard size (2 1/2" by 3 1/2"). The fronts feature full-bleed glossy color player photos. At the bottom, the player's name appears in an aqua stripe that is bordered in gold. In the lower left or right corner the Stadium Club logo overlays the stripe. Against the background of a colorful drawing of a hockey rink, the horizontally oriented backs have a biography, The Sporting News Hockey Scouting Report (which consists of strengths and evaluative comments), statistics (last season and career totals), and a miniature photo of the player's first Topps card. The cards are numbered on the back. Corey Millen is the only Rookie Card of note. There are many cards in the set that can be found with or without "The Sporting News" on the card back; these variations (no added premium) are 13, 16, 22, 46, 50, 60, 68, 149, 190, 204, 230, 249, 264, 276, 297, 298, 307, 320, 332, 339, 341, 342, 348, 351, and 362.

		MINT	EXC	G-VG
	COMPLETE SET (400)	30.00	13.50	3.80
	COMMON PLAYER (1-400)	.07	.03	.01
☐ 1	Wayne Gretzky	3.00	1.35	.40
	Los Angeles Kings			
☐ 2	Randy Moller	.07	.03	.01
	New York Rangers			
☐ 3	Ray Ferraro	.10	.05	.01
	New York Islanders			
☐ 4	Craig Wolanin	.07	.03	.01
	Quebec Nordiques			
☐ 5	Shayne Corson	.10	.05	.01
	Montreal Canadiens			
☐ 6	Chris Chelios	.10	.05	.01
	Chicago Blackhawks			
☐ 7	Joe Mullen	.15	.07	.02
	Pittsburgh Penguins			
☐ 8	Ken Wregget	.07	.03	.01
	Philadelphia Flyers			
☐ 9	Rob Cimetta	.07	.03	.01
	Toronto Maple Leafs			
☐ 10	Mike Liut	.10	.05	.01
	Washington Capitals			
☐ 11	Martin Gelinas	.07	.03	.01
	Edmonton Oilers			
☐ 12	Mario Marois	.07	.03	.01
	St. Louis Blues			
☐ 13	Rick Vaive	.07	.03	.01
	Buffalo Sabres			
☐ 14	Brad McCrimmon	.07	.03	.01
	Detroit Red Wings			
☐ 15	Mark Hunter	.07	.03	.01
	Hartford Whalers			
☐ 16	Jim Wiemer	.07	.03	.01
	Boston Bruins			
☐ 17	Sergio Momesso	.07	.03	.01
	Vancouver Canucks			
☐ 18	Claude Lemieux	.10	.05	.01
	New Jersey Devils			
☐ 19	Brian Hayward	.07	.03	.01
	San Jose Sharks			
☐ 20	Pat Flatley	.07	.03	.01
	New York Islanders			
☐ 21	Mark Osborne	.07	.03	.01
	Winnipeg Jets			
☐ 22	Mike Hudson	.07	.03	.01
	Chicago Blackhawks			
☐ 23	Rejean Lemelin	.10	.05	.01
	Boston Bruins			
☐ 24	Viacheslav Fetisov	.10	.05	.01
	New Jersey Devils			
☐ 25	Bobby Smith	.10	.05	.01
	Minnesota North Stars			
☐ 26	Kris King	.07	.03	.01
	New York Rangers			
☐ 27	Randy Velischek	.07	.03	.01
	Quebec Nordiques			
☐ 28	Steve Bozek	.07	.03	.01
	San Jose Sharks			
☐ 29	Mike Foligno	.10	.05	.01
	Toronto Maple Leafs			
☐ 30	Scott Arniel	.07	.03	.01
	Winnipeg Jets			
☐ 31	Sergei Makarov	.30	.14	.04
	Calgary Flames			
☐ 32	Rick Zombo	.07	.03	.01
	Detroit Red Wings			
☐ 33	Christian Ruuttu	.10	.05	.01
	Buffalo Sabres			
☐ 34	Gino Cavallini	.07	.03	.01
	St. Louis Blues			
☐ 35	Rick Tocchet	.10	.05	.01
	Philadelphia Flyers			
☐ 36	Jiri Hrdina	.07	.03	.01
	Pittsburgh Penguins			
☐ 37	Peter Bondra	.25	.11	.03
	Washington Capitals			
☐ 38	Craig Ludwig	.07	.03	.01
	Minnesota North Stars			
☐ 39	Mikael Andersson	.07	.03	.01
	Hartford Whalers			
☐ 40	Bob Kudelski	.25	.11	.03
	Los Angeles Kings			
☐ 41	Guy Carbonneau	.10	.05	.01
	Montreal Canadiens			
☐ 42	Geoff Smith	.07	.03	.01
	Edmonton Oilers			
☐ 43	Russ Courtnall	.10	.05	.01
	Montreal Canadiens			
☐ 44	Michal Pivonka	.10	.05	.01
	Washington Capitals			
☐ 45	Todd Krygier	.07	.03	.01
	Hartford Whalers			
☐ 46	Jeremy Roenick	2.00	.90	.25
	Chicago Blackhawks			
☐ 47	Doug Brown	.07	.03	.01
	New Jersey Devils			
☐ 48	Paul Cavallini	.07	.03	.01
	St. Louis Blues			
☐ 49	Ron Sutter	.07	.03	.01
	Philadelphia Flyers			
☐ 50	Paul Ranheim	.07	.03	.01
	Calgary Flames			
☐ 51	Mike Gartner	.15	.07	.02
	New York Rangers			
☐ 52	Greg Adams	.07	.03	.01
	Vancouver Canucks			
☐ 53	Dave Capuano	.07	.03	.01
	Vancouver Canucks			
☐ 54	Mike Krushelnyski	.07	.03	.01
	Toronto Maple Leafs			
☐ 55	Ulf Dahlen	.10	.05	.01
	Minnesota North Stars			
☐ 56	Steven Finn	.07	.03	.01
	Quebec Nordiques			
☐ 57	Ed Olczyk	.07	.03	.01
	Winnipeg Jets			
☐ 58	Steve Duchesne	.10	.05	.01
	Philadelphia Flyers			
☐ 59	Bob Probert	.10	.05	.01
	Detroit Red Wings			
☐ 60	Joe Nieuwendyk	.15	.07	.02
	Calgary Flames			
☐ 61	Petr Klima	.10	.05	.01
	Edmonton Oilers			
☐ 62	Uwe Krupp	.07	.03	.01
	Buffalo Sabres			
☐ 63	Jay Miller	.07	.03	.01
	Los Angeles Kings			
☐ 64	Cam Neely	.30	.14	.04
	Boston Bruins			
☐ 65	Phil Housley	.10	.05	.01
	Winnipeg Jets			
☐ 66	Michel Goulet	.10	.05	.01
	Chicago Blackhawks			
☐ 67	Brett Hull	2.00	.90	.25
	St. Louis Blues			
☐ 68	Mike Ridley	.10	.05	.01
	Washington Capitals			
☐ 69	Esa Tikkanen	.10	.05	.01
	Edmonton Oilers			
☐ 70	Kjell Samuelsson	.07	.03	.01
	Philadelphia Flyers			
☐ 71	Corey Millen	.40	.18	.05
	New York Rangers			
☐ 72	Doug Lidster	.07	.03	.01
	Vancouver Canucks			
☐ 73	Ron Francis	.15	.07	.02
	Pittsburgh Penguins			
☐ 74	Scott Young	.07	.03	.01
	Pittsburgh Penguins			
☐ 75	Bob Sweeney	.07	.03	.01
	Boston Bruins			
☐ 76	Sean Burke	.10	.05	.01
	New Jersey Devils			
☐ 77	Pierre Turgeon	.75	.35	.09
	New York Islanders			
☐ 78	David Reid	.07	.03	.01
	Toronto Maple Leafs			
☐ 79	Al MacInnis	.15	.07	.02
	Calgary Flames			
☐ 80	Mike Hough	.07	.03	.01
	Quebec Nordiques			
☐ 81	Steve Yzerman	1.00	.45	.13
	Detroit Red Wings			
☐ 82	Derek King	.10	.05	.01

New York Islanders			
☐ 83 Brad Shaw	.07	.03	.01
Hartford Whalers			
☐ 84 Trevor Linden	.50	.23	.06
Vancouver Canucks			
☐ 85 Rick Meagher	.07	.03	.01
St. Louis Blues			
☐ 86 Stephane Richer	.10	.05	.01
Montreal Canadiens			
☐ 87 Brian Bellows	.10	.05	.01
Minnesota North Stars			
☐ 88 Pete Peeters	.10	.05	.01
Philadelphia Flyers			
☐ 89 Adam Creighton	.07	.03	.01
Chicago Blackhawks			
☐ 90 Brent Ashton	.07	.03	.01
Winnipeg Jets			
☐ 91 Bryan Trottier	.15	.07	.02
Pittsburgh Penguins			
☐ 92 Mike Richter	.75	.35	.09
New York Rangers			
☐ 93 Dave Andreychuk	.30	.14	.04
Buffalo Sabres			
☐ 94 Randy Carlyle	.07	.03	.01
Winnipeg Jets			
☐ 95 Dave Christian	.07	.03	.01
St. Louis Blues			
☐ 96 Doug Gilmour	1.00	.45	.13
Calgary Flames			
☐ 97 Tony Granato	.10	.05	.01
Los Angeles Kings			
☐ 98 Jeff Norton	.07	.03	.01
New York Islanders			
☐ 99 Neal Broten	.10	.05	.01
Minnesota North Stars			
☐ 100 Jody Hull	.07	.03	.01
New York Rangers			
☐ 101 Shawn Burr	.07	.03	.01
Detroit Red Wings			
☐ 102 Pat Verbeek	.15	.07	.02
Hartford Whalers			
☐ 103 Ken Daneyko	.07	.03	.01
New Jersey Devils			
☐ 104 Peter Zezel	.07	.03	.01
Toronto Maple Leafs			
☐ 105 Kirk McLean	.35	.16	.04
Vancouver Canucks			
☐ 106 Kelly Miller	.07	.03	.01
Washington Capitals			
☐ 107 Patrick Roy	2.00	.90	.25
Montreal Canadiens			
☐ 108 Adam Oates	.35	.16	.04
St. Louis Blues			
☐ 109 Steve Thomas	.10	.05	.01
Chicago Blackhawks			
☐ 110 Scott Mellanby	.07	.03	.01
Edmonton Oilers			
☐ 111 Mark Messier	.75	.35	.09
Edmonton Oilers			
☐ 112 Larry Murphy	.10	.05	.01
Pittsburgh Penguins			
☐ 113 Mark Janssens	.07	.03	.01
New York Rangers			
☐ 114 Doug Bodger	.07	.03	.01
Buffalo Sabres			
☐ 115 Ron Tugnutt	.07	.03	.01
Quebec Nordiques			
☐ 116 Glenn Anderson	.10	.05	.01
Edmonton Oilers			
☐ 117 Dave Gagner	.10	.05	.01
Minnesota North Stars			
☐ 118 Dino Ciccarelli	.10	.05	.01
Washington Capitals			
☐ 119 Randy Burridge	.07	.03	.01
Washington Capitals			
☐ 120 Kelly Hrudey	.10	.05	.01
Los Angeles Kings			
☐ 121 Jimmy Carson	.10	.05	.01
Detroit Red Wings			
☐ 122 Bruce Driver	.07	.03	.01
New Jersey Devils			
☐ 123 Pat LaFontaine	.75	.35	.09
New York Islanders			
☐ 124 Wendel Clark	.30	.14	.04
Toronto Maple Leafs			
☐ 125 Peter Sidorkiewicz	.07	.03	.01
Hartford Whalers			
☐ 126 Gary Roberts	.10	.05	.01
Calgary Flames			
☐ 127 Petr Svoboda	.07	.03	.01
Montreal Canadiens			
☐ 128 Vincent Riendeau	.07	.03	.01
St. Louis Blues			
☐ 129 Brian Skrudland	.07	.03	.01

Montreal Canadiens			
☐ 130 Tim Kerr	.10	.05	.01
New York Rangers			
☐ 131 Doug Wilson	.10	.05	.01
San Jose Sharks			
☐ 132 Pat Elynuik	.07	.03	.01
Winnipeg Jets			
☐ 133 Craig MacTavish	.10	.05	.01
Edmonton Oilers			
☐ 134 Troy Mallette	.07	.03	.01
New York Rangers			
☐ 135 Mike Ramsey	.07	.03	.01
Buffalo Sabres			
☐ 136 Tony Hrkac	.07	.03	.01
San Jose Sharks			
☐ 137 Craig Simpson	.10	.05	.01
Edmonton Oilers			
☐ 138 Jon Casey	.10	.05	.01
Minnesota North Stars			
☐ 139 Steve Kasper	.07	.03	.01
Philadelphia Flyers			
☐ 140 Kevin Hatcher	.10	.05	.01
Washington Capitals			
☐ 141 Dave Barr	.07	.03	.01
New Jersey Devils			
☐ 142 Brad Lauer	.07	.03	.01
New York Islanders			
☐ 143 Gary Suter	.10	.05	.01
Calgary Flames			
☐ 144 John MacLean	.10	.05	.01
New Jersey Devils			
☐ 145 Dean Evason	.07	.03	.01
Hartford Whalers			
☐ 146 Vincent Damphousse	.10	.05	.01
Toronto Maple Leafs			
☐ 147 Craig Janney	.25	.11	.03
Boston Bruins			
☐ 148 Jeff Brown	.10	.05	.01
St. Louis Blues			
☐ 149 Geoff Courtnall	.10	.05	.01
Vancouver Canucks			
☐ 150 Igor Larionov	.15	.07	.02
Vancouver Canucks			
☐ 151 Jan Erixon	.07	.03	.01
New York Rangers			
☐ 152 Bob Essensa	.10	.05	.01
Winnipeg Jets			
☐ 153 Gaetan Duchesne	.07	.03	.01
Minnesota North Stars			
☐ 154 Jyrki Lumme	.07	.03	.01
Vancouver Canucks			
☐ 155 Tom Barrasso	.15	.07	.02
Pittsburgh Penguins			
☐ 156 Curtis Leschyshyn	.07	.03	.01
Quebec Nordiques			
☐ 157 Benoit Hogue	.07	.03	.01
Buffalo Sabres			
☐ 158 Gary Leeman	.07	.03	.01
Toronto Maple Leafs			
☐ 159 Luc Robitaille	.50	.23	.06
Los Angeles Kings			
☐ 160 Jamie Macoun	.07	.03	.01
Calgary Flames			
☐ 161 Bob Carpenter	.07	.03	.01
Boston Bruins			
☐ 162 Kevin Dineen	.10	.05	.01
Hartford Whalers			
☐ 163 Gary Nylund	.07	.03	.01
New York Islanders			
☐ 164 Dale Hunter	.10	.05	.01
Washington Capitals			
☐ 165 Gerard Gallant	.07	.03	.01
Detroit Red Wings			
☐ 166 Jacques Cloutier	.07	.03	.01
Quebec Nordiques			
☐ 167 Troy Murray	.07	.03	.01
Winnipeg Jets			
☐ 168 Phil Bourque	.07	.03	.01
Pittsburgh Penguins			
☐ 169 Grant Ledyard	.07	.03	.01
Buffalo Sabres			
☐ 170 Joel Otto	.07	.03	.01
Calgary Flames			
☐ 171 Paul Ysebaert UER	.07	.03	.01
Detroit Red Wings			
(Photo actually			
Mike Sillinger)			
☐ 172 Luke Richardson	.07	.03	.01
Toronto Maple Leafs			
☐ 173 Ron Hextall	.15	.07	.02
Philadelphia Flyers			
☐ 174 Mario Lemieux	2.50	1.15	.30
Pittsburgh Penguins			
☐ 175 Garry Galley	.10	.05	.01

Boston Bruins
176 Murray Craven	.07	.03	.01

Philadelphia Flyers
177 Walt Poddubny — .07 .03 .01
New Jersey Devils
178 Scott Pearson — .07 .03 .01
Quebec Nordiques
179 Kevin Lowe — .10 .05 .01
Edmonton Oilers
180 Brent Sutter — .10 .05 .01
New York Islanders
181 Dirk Graham — .07 .03 .01
Chicago Blackhawks
182 Pelle Eklund — .07 .03 .01
Philadelphia Flyers
183 Sylvain Cote — .07 .03 .01
Washington Capitals
184 Rod Brind'Amour — .50 .23 .06
St. Louis Blues
185 Fredrik Olausson — .10 .05 .01
Winnipeg Jets
186 Kelly Kisio — .07 .03 .01
San Jose Sharks
187 Mike Modano — 1.00 .45 .13
Minnesota North Stars
188 Calle Johansson — .07 .03 .01
Washington Capitals
189 John Tonelli — .10 .05 .01
Chicago Blackhawks
190 Glen Wesley — .07 .03 .01
Boston Bruins
191 Bob Errey — .07 .03 .01
Pittsburgh Penguins
192 Rich Sutter — .07 .03 .01
St. Louis Blues
193 Kirk Muller — .10 .05 .01
New Jersey Devils
194 Rob Zettler — .07 .03 .01
San Jose Sharks
195 Alexander Mogilny — 1.25 .55 .16
Buffalo Sabres
196 Adrien Plavsic — .07 .03 .01
Vancouver Canucks
197 Daniel Marois — .07 .03 .01
Toronto Maple Leafs
198 Yves Racine — .07 .03 .01
Detroit Red Wings
199 Brendan Shanahan — .60 .25 .08
St. Louis Blues
200 Rob Brown — .07 .03 .01
Hartford Whalers
201 Brian Leetch — 1.00 .45 .13
New York Rangers
202 Dave McLlwain — .07 .03 .01
Buffalo Sabres
203 Charlie Huddy — .07 .03 .01
Los Angeles Kings
204 David Volek — .07 .03 .01
New York Islanders
205 Trent Yawney — .07 .03 .01
Chicago Blackhawks
206 Brian MacLellan — .07 .03 .01
Detroit Red Wings
207 Thomas Steen — .10 .05 .01
Winnipeg Jets
208 Sylvain Lefebvre — .07 .03 .01
Montreal Canadiens
209 Tomas Sandstrom — .10 .05 .01
Los Angeles Kings
210 Mike McPhee — .07 .03 .01
Montreal Canadiens
211 Andy Moog — .15 .07 .02
Boston Bruins
212 Paul Coffey — .35 .16 .04
Pittsburgh Penguins
213 Denis Savard — .15 .07 .02
Montreal Canadiens
214 Eric Desjardins — .10 .05 .01
Montreal Canadiens
215 Wayne Presley — .07 .03 .01
Chicago Blackhawks
216 Stephane Morin UER — .07 .03 .01
Quebec Nordiques
(Photo actually
Jeff Jackson)
217 Ric Nattress — .07 .03 .01
Calgary Flames
218 Troy Gamble — .07 .03 .01
Vancouver Canucks
219 Terry Carkner — .07 .03 .01
Philadelphia Flyers
220 Dave Hannan — .07 .03 .01
Toronto Maple Leafs
221 Randy Wood — .07 .03 .01

New York Islanders
222 Brian Mullen — .10 .05 .01
San Jose Sharks
223 Garth Butcher — .07 .03 .01
St. Louis Blues
224 Tim Cheveldae — .10 .05 .01
Detroit Red Wings
225 Rod Langway — .07 .03 .01
Washington Capitals
226 Stephen Leach — .07 .03 .01
Boston Bruins
227 Perry Berezan — .07 .03 .01
Minnesota North Stars
228 Zarley Zalapski — .07 .03 .01
Hartford Whalers
229 Patrik Sundstrom — .07 .03 .01
New Jersey Devils
230 Steve Smith — .10 .05 .01
Edmonton Oilers
231 Daren Puppa — .10 .05 .01
Buffalo Sabres
232 Dave Taylor — .10 .05 .01
Los Angeles Kings
233 Ray Bourque — .35 .16 .04
Boston Bruins
234 Kevin Stevens — .75 .35 .09
Pittsburgh Penguins
235 Frantisek Musil — .07 .03 .01
Calgary Flames
236 Mike Keane — .07 .03 .01
Montreal Canadiens
237 Brian Propp — .10 .05 .01
Minnesota North Stars
238 Brent Fedyk — .07 .03 .01
Detroit Red Wings
239 Rob Ramage — .07 .03 .01
Minnesota North Stars
240 Robert Kron — .07 .03 .01
Vancouver Canucks
241 Mike McNeil — .07 .03 .01
Quebec Nordiques
242 Greg Gilbert — .07 .03 .01
Chicago Blackhawks
243 Dan Quinn — .07 .03 .01
St. Louis Blues
244 Chris Nilan — .10 .05 .01
Boston Bruins
245 Bernie Nicholls — .15 .07 .02
New York Rangers
246 Don Beaupre — .10 .05 .01
Washington Capitals
247 Keith Acton — .07 .03 .01
Philadelphia Flyers
248 Gord Murphy — .07 .03 .01
Philadelphia Flyers
249 Bill Ranford — .15 .07 .02
Edmonton Oilers
250 Dave Chyzowski — .07 .03 .01
New York Islanders
251 Clint Malarchuk — .10 .05 .01
Buffalo Sabres
252 Larry Robinson — .10 .05 .01
Los Angeles Kings
253 Dave Poulin — .10 .05 .01
Boston Bruins
254 Paul MacDermid — .07 .03 .01
Winnipeg Jets
255 Doug Smail — .07 .03 .01
Quebec Nordiques
256 Mark Recchi — 1.00 .45 .13
Pittsburgh Penguins
257 Brian Bradley — .10 .05 .01
Toronto Maple Leafs
258 Grant Fuhr — .15 .07 .02
Edmonton Oilers
259 Owen Nolan — .30 .14 .04
Quebec Nordiques
260 Hubie McDonough — .07 .03 .01
New York Islanders
261 Mikko Makela — .07 .03 .01
Buffalo Sabres
262 Mathieu Schneider — .10 .05 .01
Montreal Canadiens
263 Peter Stastny — .10 .05 .01
New Jersey Devils
264 Jim Hrivnak — .07 .03 .01
Washington Capitals
265 Scott Stevens — .15 .07 .02
St. Louis Blues
266 Mike Tomlak — .07 .03 .01
Hartford Whalers
267 Marty McSorley — .10 .05 .01
Los Angeles Kings
268 Johan Garpenlov — .10 .05 .01

Detroit Red Wings				
☐ 269 Mike Vernon	.10	.05	.01	
Calgary Flames				
☐ 270 Steve Larmer	.15	.07	.02	
Chicago Blackhawks				
☐ 271 Phil Sykes	.07	.03	.01	
Winnipeg Jets				
☐ 272 Jay Mazur	.07	.03	.01	
Vancouver Canucks				
☐ 273 John Ogrodnick	.07	.03	.01	
New York Rangers				
☐ 274 Dave Ellett	.07	.03	.01	
Toronto Maple Leafs				
☐ 275 Randy Gilhen	.07	.03	.01	
Los Angeles Kings				
☐ 276 Tom Chorske	.07	.03	.01	
Montreal Canadiens				
☐ 277 James Patrick	.07	.03	.01	
New York Rangers				
☐ 278 Darin Kimble	.07	.03	.01	
St. Louis Blues				
☐ 279 Paul Cyr	.07	.03	.01	
Hartford Whalers				
☐ 280 Petr Nedved	.40	.18	.05	
Vancouver Canucks				
☐ 281 Tony McKegney	.07	.03	.01	
Chicago Blackhawks				
☐ 282 Alexei Kasatonov	.10	.05	.01	
New Jersey Devils				
☐ 283 Stephen Lebeau	.20	.09	.03	
Montreal Canadiens				
☐ 284 Everett Sanipass	.07	.03	.01	
Quebec Nordiques				
☐ 285 Tony Tanti	.07	.03	.01	
Buffalo Sabres				
☐ 286 Kevin Miller	.10	.05	.01	
Detroit Red Wings				
☐ 287 Moe Mantha	.07	.03	.01	
Winnipeg Jets				
☐ 288 Alan May	.07	.03	.01	
Washington Capitals				
☐ 289 John Cullen	.07	.03	.01	
Hartford Whalers				
☐ 290 Daniel Berthiaume	.07	.03	.01	
Los Angeles Kings				
☐ 291 Mark Pederson	.07	.03	.01	
Philadelphia Flyers				
☐ 292 Laurie Boschman	.07	.03	.01	
New Jersey Devils				
☐ 293 Neil Wilkinson	.07	.03	.01	
San Jose Sharks				
☐ 294 Rick Wamsley	.07	.03	.01	
Calgary Flames				
☐ 295 Ken Linseman	.07	.03	.01	
Edmonton Oilers				
☐ 296 Jamie Leach	.07	.03	.01	
Pittsburgh Penguins				
☐ 297 Chris Terreri	.10	.05	.01	
New Jersey Devils				
☐ 298 Cliff Ronning	.10	.05	.01	
Vancouver Canucks				
☐ 299 Bobby Holik	.10	.05	.01	
Hartford Whalers				
☐ 300 Mats Sundin	.75	.35	.09	
Quebec Nordiques				
☐ 301 Carey Wilson	.07	.03	.01	
Calgary Flames				
☐ 302 Teppo Numminen	.07	.03	.01	
Winnipeg Jets				
☐ 303 Dave Lowry	.07	.03	.01	
St. Louis Blues				
☐ 304 Joe Reekie	.07	.03	.01	
New York Rangers				
☐ 305 Keith Primeau	.40	.18	.05	
Detroit Red Wings				
☐ 306 David Shaw	.07	.03	.01	
New York Rangers				
☐ 307 Nick Kypreos	.07	.03	.01	
Washington Capitals				
☐ 308 Dave Manson	.10	.05	.01	
Chicago Blackhawks				
☐ 309 Mick Vukota	.07	.03	.01	
New York Islanders				
☐ 310 Todd Elik	.07	.03	.01	
Minnesota North Stars				
☐ 311 Michel Petit	.07	.03	.01	
Toronto Maple Leafs				
☐ 312 Dale Hawerchuk	.15	.07	.02	
Buffalo Sabres				
☐ 313 Joe Murphy	.10	.05	.01	
Edmonton Oilers				
☐ 314 Chris Dahlquist	.07	.03	.01	
Minnesota North Stars				
☐ 315 Petri Skriko	.07	.03	.01	
Boston Bruins				
☐ 316 Sergei Fedorov	3.00	1.35	.40	
Detroit Red Wings				
☐ 317 Lee Norwood	.07	.03	.01	
New Jersey Devils				
☐ 318 Garry Valk	.07	.03	.01	
Vancouver Canucks				
☐ 319 Glen Featherstone	.07	.03	.01	
Boston Bruins				
☐ 320 Dave Snuggerud	.07	.03	.01	
Buffalo Sabres				
☐ 321 Doug Evans	.07	.03	.01	
Winnipeg Jets				
☐ 322 Marc Bureau	.07	.03	.01	
Minnesota North Stars				
☐ 323 John Vanbiesbrouck	.30	.14	.04	
New York Rangers				
☐ 324 John McIntyre	.07	.03	.01	
Los Angeles Kings				
☐ 325 Wes Walz	.07	.03	.01	
Boston Bruins				
☐ 326 Daryl Reaugh	.07	.03	.01	
Hartford Whalers				
☐ 327 Paul Fenton	.07	.03	.01	
Hartford Whalers				
☐ 328 Ulf Samuelsson	.10	.05	.01	
Pittsburgh Penguins				
☐ 329 Andrew Cassels	.10	.05	.01	
Montreal Canadiens				
☐ 330 Alexei Gusarov	.15	.07	.02	
Quebec Nordiques				
☐ 331 John Druce	.07	.03	.01	
Washington Capitals				
☐ 332 Adam Graves	.75	.35	.09	
New York Rangers				
☐ 333 Ed Belfour	.75	.35	.09	
Chicago Blackhawks				
☐ 334 Murray Baron	.07	.03	.01	
Philadelphia Flyers				
☐ 335 John Tucker	.07	.03	.01	
New York Islanders				
☐ 336 Todd Gill	.07	.03	.01	
Toronto Maple Leafs				
☐ 337 Martin Hostak	.07	.03	.01	
Philadelphia Flyers				
☐ 338 Gino Odjick	.10	.05	.01	
Vancouver Canucks				
☐ 339 Eric Weinrich	.07	.03	.01	
New Jersey Devils				
☐ 340 Todd Ewen	.07	.03	.01	
Montreal Canadiens				
☐ 341 Mike Hartman	.07	.03	.01	
Buffalo Sabres				
☐ 342 Danton Cole	.07	.03	.01	
Winnipeg Jets				
☐ 343 Jaromir Jagr	2.00	.90	.25	
Pittsburgh Penguins				
☐ 344 Mike Craig	.07	.03	.01	
Minnesota North Stars				
☐ 345 Mark Fitzpatrick	.10	.05	.01	
New York Islanders				
☐ 346 Darren Turcotte	.07	.03	.01	
New York Rangers				
☐ 347 Ron Wilson	.07	.03	.01	
St. Louis Blues				
☐ 348 Rob Blake	.40	.18	.05	
Los Angeles Kings				
☐ 349 Dale Kushner	.07	.03	.01	
Philadelphia Flyers				
☐ 350 Jeff Beukeboom	.07	.03	.01	
Edmonton Oilers				
☐ 351 Tim Bergland	.07	.03	.01	
Washington Capitals				
☐ 352 Peter Ing	.07	.03	.01	
Toronto Maple Leafs				
☐ 353 Wayne McDean	.07	.03	.01	
New York Islanders				
☐ 354 Jim McKenzie	.07	.03	.01	
Hartford Whalers				
☐ 355 Theoren Fleury	.35	.16	.04	
Calgary Flames				
☐ 356 Jocelyn Lemieux	.07	.03	.01	
Chicago Blackhawks				
☐ 357 Ken Hodge Jr.	.07	.03	.01	
Boston Bruins				
☐ 358 Shawn Anderson	.07	.03	.01	
Quebec Nordiques				
☐ 359 Dimitri Khristich	.10	.05	.01	
Washington Capitals				
☐ 360 Jon Morris	.07	.03	.01	
New Jersey Devils				
☐ 361 Darrin Shannon	.07	.03	.01	
Buffalo Sabres				
☐ 362 Chris Joseph	.07	.03	.01	

Edmonton Oilers
- ☐ 363 Normand Lacombe .... .07 .03 .01
Philadelphia Flyers
- ☐ 364 Frank Pietrangelo .... .07 .03 .01
Pittsburgh Penguins
- ☐ 365 Joey Kocur .... .07 .03 .01
New York Rangers
- ☐ 366 Anatoli Semenov .... .07 .03 .01
Edmonton Oilers
- ☐ 367 Bob Bassen .... .07 .03 .01
St. Louis Blues
- ☐ 368 Brad Jones .... .07 .03 .01
Philadelphia Flyers
- ☐ 369 Glenn Healy........................ .10 .05 .01
New York Islanders
- ☐ 370 Don Sweeney .... .07 .03 .01
Boston Bruins
- ☐ 371 Brad Dalgarno .... .07 .03 .01
New York Islanders
- ☐ 372 Al Iafrate .... .10 .05 .01
Washington Capitals
- ☐ 373 Patrick Lebeau UER .... .15 .07 .02
Montreal Canadiens
(Photo actually
Brent Gilchrist)
- ☐ 374 Terry Yake......................... .10 .05 .01
Hartford Whalers
- ☐ 375 Roger Johansson .... .07 .03 .01
Calgary Flames
- ☐ 376 Paul Broten .... .07 .03 .01
New York Rangers
- ☐ 377 Andre Racicot .... .15 .07 .02
Montreal Canadiens
- ☐ 378 Scott Thornton.................. .07 .03 .01
Toronto Maple Leafs
- ☐ 379 Zdeno Ciger....................... .07 .03 .01
New Jersey Devils
- ☐ 380 Paul Stanton .... .07 .03 .01
Pittsburgh Penguins
- ☐ 381 Ray Sheppard .... .15 .07 .02
Detroit Red Wings
- ☐ 382 Kevin Haller....................... .15 .07 .02
Buffalo Sabres
- ☐ 383 Vladimir Ruzicka .... .07 .03 .01
Boston Bruins
- ☐ 384 Bryan Marchment .... .15 .07 .02
Chicago Blackhawks
- ☐ 385 Bill Berg .... .07 .03 .01
New York Islanders
- ☐ 386 Mike Ricci .... .30 .14 .04
Philadelphia Flyers
- ☐ 387 Pat Conacher...................... .07 .03 .01
New Jersey Devils
- ☐ 388 Brian Glynn .... .07 .03 .01
Minnesota North Stars
- ☐ 389 Joe Sakic........................... .75 .35 .09
Quebec Nordiques
- ☐ 390 Mikhail Tatarinov............... .07 .03 .01
Quebec Nordiques
- ☐ 391 Stephane Matteau .... .07 .03 .01
Calgary Flames
- ☐ 392 Mark Tinordi .... .10 .05 .01
Minnesota North Stars
- ☐ 393 Robert Reichel .... .35 .16 .04
Calgary Flames
- ☐ 394 Tim Sweeney...................... .07 .03 .01
Calgary Flames
- ☐ 395 Rick Tabaracci................... .07 .03 .01
Winnipeg Jets
- ☐ 396 Ken Sabourin .... .07 .03 .01
Washington Capitals
- ☐ 397 Jeff Lazaro .... .07 .03 .01
Boston Bruins
- ☐ 398 Checklist 1-133 .... .07 .03 .01
- ☐ 399 Checklist 134-266 .... .07 .03 .01
- ☐ 400 Checklist 267-400 .... .07 .03 .01

1992-93 Stadium Club

This 501-card set measures the standard size (2 1/2" by 3 1/2") and features full-bleed color action player photos. The Stadium Club logo appears at the bottom and intersects a gold foil double stripe carrying the team name. The horizontal backs show an artist's rendering of a hockey rink as the background. A mini-reproduction of the player's first Topps card is shown as well as biography, statistics, and

The Sporting News Skills Rating System. The Members Choice (241-250 and 251-260) subsets, showing full-bleed color photos, closes the first series and opens the second series. These backs have the same art work background with 1991-92 season statistics. The cards are numbered on the back. The notable Rookie Cards in the set are Bill Guerin, Bret Hedican, and Ray Whitney.

	MINT	EXC	G-VG
COMPLETE SET (501)......................	40.00	18.00	5.00
COMPLETE SERIES 1 (250)............	20.00	9.00	2.50
COMPLETE SERIES 2 (251).............	20.00	9.00	2.50
COMMON PLAYER (1-250).............	.05	.02	.01
COMMON PLAYER (251-501)...........	.05	.02	.01

- ☐ 1 Brett Hull.............. .75 .35 .09
St. Louis Blues
- ☐ 2 Theoren Fleury........... .10 .05 .01
Calgary Flames
- ☐ 3 Joe Sakic............... .25 .11 .03
Quebec Nordiques
- ☐ 4 Mike Modano............ .35 .16 .04
Minnesota North Stars
- ☐ 5 Dmitri Mironov.......... .08 .04 .01
Toronto Maple Leafs
- ☐ 6 Yves Racine............. .05 .02 .01
Detroit Red Wings
- ☐ 7 Igor Kravchuk .... .05 .02 .01
Chicago Blackhawks
- ☐ 8 Philippe Bozon .... .05 .02 .01
St. Louis Blues
- ☐ 9 Stephane Richer......... .08 .04 .01
New Jersey Devils
- ☐ 10 Dave Lowry............. .05 .02 .01
St. Louis Blues
- ☐ 11 Dean Evason .... .05 .02 .01
San Jose Sharks
- ☐ 12 Mark Fitzpatrick.......... .08 .04 .01
New York Islanders
- ☐ 13 Dave Poulin............. .05 .02 .01
Boston Bruins
- ☐ 14 Phil Housley............ .08 .04 .01
Winnipeg Jets
- ☐ 15 Adrien Plavsic .... .05 .02 .01
Vancouver Canucks
- ☐ 16 Claude Boivin.......... .05 .02 .01
Philadelphia Flyers
- ☐ 17 Bill Guerin............. .25 .11 .03
New Jersey Devils
- ☐ 18 Wayne Gretzky.......... 1.50 .65 .19
Los Angeles Kings
- ☐ 19 Steve Yzerman.......... .40 .18 .05
Detroit Red Wings
- ☐ 20 Joe Mullen............. .08 .04 .01
Pittsburgh Penguins
- ☐ 21 Brad McCrimmon.......... .05 .02 .01
Detroit Red Wings
- ☐ 22 Dan Quinn............. .05 .02 .01
Philadelphia Flyers
- ☐ 23 Rob Blake.............. .10 .05 .01
Los Angeles Kings
- ☐ 24 Wayne Presley .... .05 .02 .01
Buffalo Sabres
- ☐ 25 Zarley Zalapski .... .05 .02 .01
Hartford Whalers
- ☐ 26 Bryan Trottier.......... .08 .04 .01
Pittsburgh Penguins
- ☐ 27 Peter Sidorkiewicz....... .05 .02 .01
Hartford Whalers
- ☐ 28 John MacLean......... .08 .04 .01
New Jersey Devils

☐ 29	Brad Schlegel	.05	.02	.01
	Washington Capitals			
☐ 30	Marc Bureau	.05	.02	.01
	Minnesota North Stars			
☐ 31	Troy Murray	.05	.02	.01
	Winnipeg Jets			
☐ 32	Tony Amonte	.20	.09	.03
	New York Rangers			
☐ 33	Rob DiMaio	.05	.02	.01
	New York Islanders			
☐ 34	Joe Murphy	.05	.02	.01
	Edmonton Oilers			
☐ 35	Jim Waite	.05	.02	.01
	Chicago Blackhawks			
☐ 36	Ron Sutter	.05	.02	.01
	St. Louis Blues			
☐ 37	Joe Nieuwendyk	.08	.04	.01
	Calgary Flames			
☐ 38	Kevin Haller	.05	.02	.01
	Montreal Canadiens			
☐ 39	Andrew Cassels	.05	.02	.01
	Hartford Whalers			
☐ 40	Dale Hunter	.08	.04	.01
	Washington Capitals			
☐ 41	Craig Janney	.15	.07	.02
	St. Louis Blues			
☐ 42	Sergio Momesso	.05	.02	.01
	Vancouver Canucks			
☐ 43	Nicklas Lidstrom	.20	.09	.03
	Detroit Red Wings			
☐ 44	Luc Robitaille	.25	.11	.03
	Los Angeles Kings			
☐ 45	Adam Creighton	.05	.02	.01
	New York Islanders			
☐ 46	Norm Maciver	.05	.02	.01
	Edmonton Oilers			
☐ 47	Mikhail Tatarinov	.05	.02	.01
	Quebec Nordiques			
☐ 48	Gary Roberts	.08	.04	.01
	Calgary Flames			
☐ 49	Gord Hynes	.05	.02	.01
	Boston Bruins			
☐ 50	Claude Lemieux	.08	.04	.01
	New Jersey Devils			
☐ 51	Brad May	.05	.02	.01
	Buffalo Sabres			
☐ 52	Paul Stanton	.05	.02	.01
	Pittsburgh Penguins			
☐ 53	Rick Wamsley	.05	.02	.01
	Toronto Maple Leafs			
☐ 54	Steve Larmer	.08	.04	.01
	Chicago Blackhawks			
☐ 55	Darrin Shannon	.05	.02	.01
	Winnipeg Jets			
☐ 56	Pat Falloon	.20	.09	.03
	San Jose Sharks			
☐ 57	Chris Dahlquist	.05	.02	.01
	Minnesota North Stars			
☐ 58	John Vanbiesbrouck	.10	.05	.01
	New York Rangers			
☐ 59	Sylvain Turgeon	.05	.02	.01
	Montreal Canadiens			
☐ 60	Jayson More	.05	.02	.01
	San Jose Sharks			
☐ 61	Randy Burridge	.05	.02	.01
	Washington Capitals			
☐ 62	Vyacheslav Kozlov	1.00	.45	.13
	Detroit Red Wings			
☐ 63	Daniel Marois	.05	.02	.01
	New York Islanders			
☐ 64	Curt Giles	.05	.02	.01
	St. Louis Blues			
☐ 65	Brad Shaw	.05	.02	.01
	Hartford Whalers			
☐ 66	Bill Ranford	.08	.04	.01
	Edmonton Oilers			
☐ 67	Frantisek Musil	.05	.02	.01
	Calgary Flames			
☐ 68	Steve Leach	.05	.02	.01
	Boston Bruins			
☐ 69	Michel Goulet	.08	.04	.01
	Chicago Blackhawks			
☐ 70	Mathieu Schneider	.08	.04	.01
	Montreal Canadiens			
☐ 71	Steve Kasper	.05	.02	.01
	Philadelphia Flyers			
☐ 72	Darryl Sydor	.08	.04	.01
	Los Angeles Kings			
☐ 73	Brian Leetch	.35	.16	.04
	New York Rangers			
☐ 74	Chris Terreri	.08	.04	.01
	New Jersey Devils			
☐ 75	Jim Johnson	.05	.02	.01
	Minnesota North Stars			
☐ 76	Rick Tocchet	.08	.04	.01
	Pittsburgh Penguins			
☐ 77	Teppo Numminen	.05	.02	.01
	Winnipeg Jets			
☐ 78	Owen Nolan	.08	.04	.01
	Quebec Nordiques			
☐ 79	Grant Ledyard	.05	.02	.01
	Buffalo Sabres			
☐ 80	Trevor Linden	.25	.11	.03
	Vancouver Canucks			
☐ 81	Luciano Borsato	.05	.02	.01
	Winnipeg Jets			
☐ 82	Derek King	.05	.02	.01
	New York Islanders			
☐ 83	Robert Cimetta	.05	.02	.01
	Toronto Maple Leafs			
☐ 84	Geoff Smith	.05	.02	.01
	Edmonton Oilers			
☐ 85	Ray Sheppard	.08	.04	.01
	Detroit Red Wings			
☐ 86	Dimitri Khristich	.08	.04	.01
	Washington Capitals			
☐ 87	Chris Chelios	.08	.04	.01
	Chicago Blackhawks			
☐ 88	Alexander Godynyuk	.05	.02	.01
	Calgary Flames			
☐ 89	Perry Anderson	.05	.02	.01
	San Jose Sharks			
☐ 90	Neal Broten	.08	.04	.01
	Minnesota North Stars			
☐ 91	Brian Benning	.05	.02	.01
	Philadelphia Flyers			
☐ 92	Brent Thompson	.05	.02	.01
	Los Angeles Kings			
☐ 93	Claude LaPointe	.05	.02	.01
	Quebec Nordiques			
☐ 94	Mario Lemieux	1.25	.55	.16
	Pittsburgh Penguins			
☐ 95	Pat LaFontaine	.30	.14	.04
	Buffalo Sabres			
☐ 96	Frank Pietrangelo	.05	.02	.01
	Hartford Whalers			
☐ 97	Gerald Diduck	.05	.02	.01
	Vancouver Canucks			
☐ 98	Paul DiPietro	.05	.02	.01
	Montreal Canadiens			
☐ 99	Valeri Zelepukin	.20	.09	.03
	New Jersey Devils			
☐ 100	Rick Zombo	.05	.02	.01
	St. Louis Blues			
☐ 101	Daniel Berthiaume	.05	.02	.01
	Boston Bruins			
☐ 102	Tom Fitzgerald	.05	.02	.01
	New York Islanders			
☐ 103	Ken Baumgartner	.05	.02	.01
	Toronto Maple Leafs			
☐ 104	Esa Tikkanen	.08	.04	.01
	Edmonton Oilers			
☐ 105	Steve Chiasson	.05	.02	.01
	Detroit Red Wings			
☐ 106	Bobby Holik	.05	.02	.01
	Hartford Whalers			
☐ 107	Dominik Hasek	.60	.25	.08
	Chicago Blackhawks			
☐ 108	Jeff Hackett	.05	.02	.01
	San Jose Sharks			
☐ 109	Paul Broten	.05	.02	.01
	New York Rangers			
☐ 110	Kevin Stevens	.30	.14	.04
	Pittsburgh Penguins			
☐ 111	Geoff Sanderson	.40	.18	.05
	Hartford Whalers			
☐ 112	Donald Audette	.05	.02	.01
	Buffalo Sabres			
☐ 113	Jarmo Myllys	.05	.02	.01
	Toronto Maple Leafs			
☐ 114	Brian Skrudland	.05	.02	.01
	Montreal Canadiens			
☐ 115	Andrei Lomakin	.05	.02	.01
	Philadelphia Flyers			
☐ 116	Keith Tkachuk	.35	.16	.04
	Winnipeg Jets			
☐ 117	John McIntyre	.05	.02	.01
	Los Angeles Kings			
☐ 118	Jacques Cloutier	.05	.02	.01
	Quebec Nordiques			
☐ 119	Michel Picard	.05	.02	.01
	Hartford Whalers			
☐ 120	Dave Babych	.05	.02	.01
	Vancouver Canucks			
☐ 121	Dave Gagner	.08	.04	.01
	Minnesota North Stars			
☐ 122	Bob Carpenter	.05	.02	.01

Boston Bruins				
☐ 123 Ray Ferraro	.05	.02	.01	
New York Islanders				
☐ 124 Glenn Anderson	.10	.05	.01	
Toronto Maple Leafs				
☐ 125 Craig MacTavish	.05	.02	.01	
Edmonton Oilers				
☐ 126 Shawn Burr	.05	.02	.01	
Detroit Red Wings				
☐ 127 Tim Bergland	.05	.02	.01	
Washington Capitals				
☐ 128 Al MacInnis	.10	.05	.01	
Calgary Flames				
☐ 129 Jeff Beukeboom	.05	.02	.01	
New York Rangers				
☐ 130 Ken Wregget	.05	.02	.01	
Pittsburgh Penguins				
☐ 131 Arturs Irbe	.60	.25	.08	
San Jose Sharks				
☐ 132 Dave Andreychuk	.20	.09	.03	
Buffalo Sabres				
☐ 133 Patrick Roy	.75	.35	.09	
Montreal Canadiens				
☐ 134 Benoit Brunet	.05	.02	.01	
Montreal Canadiens				
☐ 135 Rick Tabaracci	.05	.02	.01	
Winnipeg Jets				
☐ 136 Jamie Baker	.05	.02	.01	
Quebec Nordiques				
☐ 137 Yanic Dupre	.05	.02	.01	
Philadelphia Flyers				
☐ 138 Jari Kurri	.10	.05	.01	
Los Angeles Kings				
☐ 139 Adam Burt	.05	.02	.01	
Hartford Whalers				
☐ 140 Peter Stastny	.08	.04	.01	
New Jersey Devils				
☐ 141 Brad Jones	.05	.02	.01	
Philadelphia Flyers				
☐ 142 Jeff Odgers	.05	.02	.01	
San Jose Sharks				
☐ 143 Anatoli Semenov UER	.05	.02	.01	
(Goalie stat headings)				
Edmonton Oilers				
☐ 144 Paul Ranheim	.05	.02	.01	
Calgary Flames				
☐ 145 Sylvain Cote	.05	.02	.01	
Washington Capitals				
☐ 146 Brent Ashton	.05	.02	.01	
Boston Bruins				
☐ 147 Doug Bodger	.05	.02	.01	
Buffalo Sabres				
☐ 148 Bryan Marchment	.05	.02	.01	
Chicago Blackhawks				
☐ 149 Bob Kudelski	.08	.04	.01	
Los Angeles Kings				
☐ 150 Adam Graves	.35	.16	.04	
New York Rangers				
☐ 151 Scott Stevens	.10	.05	.01	
New Jersey Devils				
☐ 152 Russ Courtnall	.08	.04	.01	
Montreal Canadiens				
☐ 153 Darcy Wakaluk	.08	.04	.01	
Minnesota North Stars				
☐ 154 Pelle Eklund	.05	.02	.01	
Philadelphia Flyers				
☐ 155 Robert Kron	.05	.02	.01	
Vancouver Canucks				
☐ 156 Randy Ladouceur	.05	.02	.01	
Hartford Whalers				
☐ 157 Ed Olczyk	.05	.02	.01	
Winnipeg Jets				
☐ 158 Jiri Hrdina	.05	.02	.01	
Pittsburgh Penguins				
☐ 159 John Tonelli	.08	.04	.01	
Quebec Nordiques				
☐ 160 John Cullen	.05	.02	.01	
Hartford Whalers				
☐ 161 Jan Erixon	.05	.02	.01	
New York Rangers				
☐ 162 David Shaw	.05	.02	.01	
Minnesota North Stars				
☐ 163 Brian Bradley	.05	.02	.01	
Toronto Maple Leafs				
☐ 164 Russ Romaniuk	.05	.02	.01	
Winnipeg Jets				
☐ 165 Eric Weinrich	.05	.02	.01	
New Jersey Devils				
☐ 166 Steve Heinze	.05	.02	.01	
Boston Bruins				
☐ 167 Jeremy Roenick	.75	.35	.09	
Chicago Blackhawks				
☐ 168 Mark Pederson	.05	.02	.01	
Philadelphia Flyers				

☐ 169 Paul Coffey	.20	.09	.03	
Los Angeles Kings				
☐ 170 Bob Errey	.05	.02	.01	
Pittsburgh Penguins				
☐ 171 Brian Lawton	.05	.02	.01	
San Jose Sharks				
☐ 172 Vincent Riendeau	.05	.02	.01	
Detroit Red Wings				
☐ 173 Marc Fortier	.05	.02	.01	
Quebec Nordiques				
☐ 174 Marc Bergevin	.05	.02	.01	
Hartford Whalers				
☐ 175 Jim Sandlak	.05	.02	.01	
Vancouver Canucks				
☐ 176 Bob Bassen	.05	.02	.01	
St. Louis Blues				
☐ 177 Uwe Krupp	.05	.02	.01	
New York Islanders				
☐ 178 Paul MacDermid	.05	.02	.01	
Washington Capitals				
☐ 179 Bob Corkum	.05	.02	.01	
Buffalo Sabres				
☐ 180 Robert Reichel	.08	.04	.01	
Calgary Flames				
☐ 181 John LeClair	.05	.02	.01	
Montreal Canadiens				
☐ 182 Mike Hudson	.05	.02	.01	
Chicago Blackhawks				
☐ 183 Mark Recchi	.30	.14	.04	
Philadelphia Flyers				
☐ 184 Rollie Melanson	.05	.02	.01	
Montreal Canadiens				
☐ 185 Gordie Roberts	.05	.02	.01	
Pittsburgh Penguins				
☐ 186 Clint Malarchuk	.08	.04	.01	
Buffalo Sabres				
☐ 187 Kris King	.05	.02	.01	
New York Rangers				
☐ 188 Adam Oates	.20	.09	.03	
Boston Bruins				
☐ 189 Jarrod Skalde	.05	.02	.01	
New Jersey Devils				
☐ 190 Mike Lalor	.05	.02	.01	
Winnipeg Jets				
☐ 191 Vincent Damphousse	.08	.04	.01	
Edmonton Oilers				
☐ 192 Peter Ahola	.05	.02	.01	
Los Angeles Kings				
☐ 193 Kirk McLean	.25	.11	.03	
Vancouver Canucks				
☐ 194 Murray Baron	.05	.02	.01	
St. Louis Blues				
☐ 195 Michel Petit	.05	.02	.01	
Calgary Flames				
☐ 196 Stephane Fiset	.08	.04	.01	
Quebec Nordiques				
☐ 197 Pat Verbeek	.08	.04	.01	
Hartford Whalers				
☐ 198 Jon Casey	.08	.04	.01	
Minnesota North Stars				
☐ 199 Tim Cheveldae	.08	.04	.01	
Detroit Red Wings				
☐ 200 Mike Ridley	.08	.04	.01	
Washington Capitals				
☐ 201 Scott Lachance	.05	.02	.01	
New York Islanders				
☐ 202 Rod Brind'Amour	.20	.09	.03	
Philadelphia Flyers				
☐ 203 Bret Hedican UER	.20	.09	.03	
(Misspelled Brett				
on both sides)				
St. Louis Blues				
☐ 204 Wendel Clark	.10	.05	.01	
Toronto Maple Leafs				
☐ 205 Shawn McEachern	.20	.09	.03	
Pittsburgh Penguins				
☐ 206 Randy Wood	.05	.02	.01	
Buffalo Sabres				
☐ 207 Ulf Dahlen	.05	.02	.01	
Minnesota North Stars				
☐ 208 Andy Brickley	.05	.02	.01	
Boston Bruins				
☐ 209 Scott Niedermayer	.40	.18	.05	
New Jersey Devils				
☐ 210 Bob Essensa	.08	.04	.01	
Winnipeg Jets				
☐ 211 Patrick Poulin	.05	.02	.01	
Hartford Whalers				
☐ 212 Johan Garpenlov	.05	.02	.01	
San Jose Sharks				
☐ 213 Marty McInnis	.05	.02	.01	
New York Islanders				
☐ 214 Josef Beranek	.20	.09	.03	

Edmonton Oilers
☐ 215 Rod Langway .... .05 .02 .01
Washington Capitals
☐ 216 Dave Christian.................... .05 .02 .01
St. Louis Blues
☐ 217 Sergei Makarov .... .08 .04 .01
Calgary Flames
☐ 218 Gerard Gallant.................... .05 .02 .01
Detroit Red Wings
☐ 219 Neil Wilkinson .... .05 .02 .01
San Jose Sharks
☐ 220 Tomas Sandstrom.............. .05 .02 .01
Los Angeles Kings
☐ 221 Shane Corson.................... .08 .04 .01
Montreal Canadiens
☐ 222 John Ogrodnick.................. .05 .02 .01
New York Rangers
☐ 223 Keith Acton .... .05 .02 .01
Philadelphia Flyers
☐ 224 Paul Fenton .... .05 .02 .01
San Jose Sharks
☐ 225 Rob Zettler .... .05 .02 .01
San Jose Sharks
☐ 226 Todd Elik .... .05 .02 .01
Minnesota North Stars
☐ 227 Petr Svoboda .... .05 .02 .01
Buffalo Sabres
☐ 228 Zdeno Ciger....................... .05 .02 .01
New Jersey Devils
☐ 229 Kevin Miller....................... .08 .04 .01
Detroit Red Wings
☐ 230 Rich Pilon .... .05 .02 .01
New York Islanders
☐ 231 Pat Jablonski..................... .05 .02 .01
St. Louis Blues
☐ 232 Greg Adams .... .05 .02 .01
Vancouver Canucks
☐ 233 Martin Brodeur................... .75 .35 .09
New Jersey Devils
☐ 234 Dave Taylor....................... .08 .04 .01
Los Angeles Kings
☐ 235 Kelly Buchberger................ .05 .02 .01
Edmonton Oilers
☐ 236 Steve Konroyd................... .05 .02 .01
Hartford Whalers
☐ 237 Guy Larose........................ .05 .02 .01
Toronto Maple Leafs
☐ 238 Patrice Brisebois .... .05 .02 .01
Montreal Canadiens
☐ 239 Checklist 1-125................. .05 .02 .01
☐ 240 Checklist 126-250............. .05 .02 .01
☐ 241 Mark Messier MC............... .25 .11 .03
New York Rangers
☐ 242 Mike Richter MC................ .20 .09 .03
New York Rangers
☐ 243 Ed Belfour MC................... .25 .11 .03
Chicago Blackhawks
☐ 244 Sergei Fedorov MC............ .75 .35 .09
Detroit Red Wings
☐ 245 Adam Oates MC................. .20 .09 .03
Boston Bruins
☐ 246 Pavel Bure MC .... 1.50 .65 .19
Vancouver Canucks
☐ 247 Luc Robitaille MC............... .20 .09 .03
Los Angeles Kings
☐ 248 Brian Leetch MC................ .25 .11 .03
New York Rangers
☐ 249 Ray Bourque MC................ .10 .05 .01
Boston Bruins
☐ 250 Tony Amonte MC .... .15 .07 .02
New York Rangers
☐ 251 Mario Lemieux MC............. .75 .35 .09
Pittsburgh Penguins
☐ 252 Patrick Roy MC................. .50 .23 .06
Montreal Canadiens
☐ 253 Nicklas Lidstrom MC.......... .15 .07 .02
Detroit Red Wings
☐ 254 Steve Yzerman MC............ .30 .14 .04
Detroit Red Wings
☐ 255 Jeremy Roenick MC........... .60 .25 .08
Chicago Blackhawks
☐ 256 Wayne Gretzky MC............ 1.00 .45 .13
Los Angeles Kings
☐ 257 Kevin Stevens MC .... .20 .09 .03
Pittsburgh Penguins
☐ 258 Brett Hull MC.................... .50 .23 .06
St. Louis Blues
☐ 259 Pat Falloon MC.................. .20 .09 .03
San Jose Sharks
☐ 260 Guy Carbonneau MC .... .10 .05 .01
Montreal Canadiens
☐ 261 Todd Gill .... .05 .02 .01
Toronto Maple Leafs
☐ 262 Mike Sullivan..................... .05 .02 .01

San Jose Sharks
☐ 263 Jeff Brown......................... .08 .04 .01
St. Louis Blues
☐ 264 Joe Reekie......................... .05 .02 .01
Tampa Bay Lightning
☐ 265 Geoff Courtnall.................. .05 .02 .01
Vancouver Canucks
☐ 266 Mike Richter .... .30 .14 .04
New York Rangers
☐ 267 Ray Bourque .... .20 .09 .03
Boston Bruins
☐ 268 Mike Craig .... .05 .02 .01
Minnesota North Stars
☐ 269 Scott King .... .05 .02 .01
Detroit Red Wings
☐ 270 Don Beaupre .... .08 .04 .01
Washington Capitals
☐ 271 Ted Donato .... .05 .02 .01
Boston Bruins
☐ 272 Gary Leeman .... .05 .02 .01
Calgary Flames
☐ 273 Steve Weeks .... .05 .02 .01
Ottawa Senators
☐ 274 Keith Brown .... .05 .02 .01
Chicago Blackhawks
☐ 275 Greg Paslawski .... .05 .02 .01
Philadelphia Flyers
☐ 276 Pierre Turgeon .... .30 .14 .04
New York Islanders
☐ 277 Jimmy Carson.................... .05 .02 .01
Detroit Red Wings
☐ 278 Tom Fergus .... .05 .02 .01
Vancouver Canucks
☐ 279 Glen Wesley .... .05 .02 .01
Boston Bruins
☐ 280 Tomas Forslund .... .05 .02 .01
Calgary Flames
☐ 281 Tony Granato .... .05 .02 .01
Los Angeles Kings
☐ 282 Phil Bourque .... .05 .02 .01
New York Rangers
☐ 283 Dave Ellett........................ .05 .02 .01
Toronto Maple Leafs
☐ 284 David Bruce....................... .05 .02 .01
San Jose Sharks
☐ 285 Stu Barnes .... .05 .02 .01
Winnipeg Jets
☐ 286 Peter Bondra .... .08 .04 .01
Washington Capitals
☐ 287 Garth Butcher .... .05 .02 .01
St. Louis Blues
☐ 288 Ron Hextall .... .08 .04 .01
Quebec Nordiques
☐ 289 Guy Carbonneau .... .08 .04 .01
Montreal Canadiens
☐ 290 Louie DeBrusk................... .05 .02 .01
Edmonton Oilers
☐ 291 Dave Barr .... .05 .02 .01
New Jersey Devils
☐ 292 Ken Sutton .... .05 .02 .01
Buffalo Sabres
☐ 293 Brian Bellows .... .08 .04 .01
Montreal Canadiens
☐ 294 Mike McNeill .... .05 .02 .01
Quebec Nordiques
☐ 295 Rob Brown .... .05 .02 .01
Chicago Blackhawks
☐ 296 Corey Millen...................... .08 .04 .01
Los Angeles Kings
☐ 297 Joe Juneau UER................ 1.25 .55 .16
(Shoots left, not right)
Boston Bruins
☐ 298 Jeff Chychrun UER............ .05 .02 .01
(Misspelled Chychurn
on card front)
Pittsburgh Penguins
☐ 299 Igor Larionov .... .08 .04 .01
Vancouver Canucks
☐ 300 Sergei Fedorov .... 1.00 .45 .13
Detroit Red Wings
☐ 301 Kevin Hatcher.................... .08 .04 .01
Washington Capitals
☐ 302 Al Iafrate .... .08 .04 .01
Washington Capitals
☐ 303 James Black....................... .05 .02 .01
Hartford Whalers
☐ 304 Steph Beauregard .... .05 .02 .01
Philadelphia Flyers
☐ 305 Joel Otto .... .05 .02 .01
Calgary Flames
☐ 306 Nelson Emerson.................. .20 .09 .03
St. Louis Blues
☐ 307 Gaetan Duchesne .... .05 .02 .01
Minnesota North Stars

308	J.J. Daigneault	Montreal Canadiens	.05	.02	.01
309	Jamie Macoun	Toronto Maple Leafs	.05	.02	.01
310	Laurie Boschman	Ottawa Senators	.05	.02	.01
311	Mike Gartner	New York Rangers	.10	.05	.01
312	Tony Tanti	Buffalo Sabres	.05	.02	.01
313	Steve Duchesne	Quebec Nordiques	.08	.04	.01
314	Martin Gelinas	Edmonton Oilers	.05	.02	.01
315	Dominic Roussel	Philadelphia Flyers	.20	.09	.03
316	Cam Neely	Boston Bruins	.20	.09	.03
317	Craig Wolanin	Quebec Nordiques	.05	.02	.01
318	Randy Gilhen	New York Rangers	.05	.02	.01
319	David Volek	New York Islanders	.05	.02	.01
320	Alexander Mogilny	Buffalo Sabres	.50	.23	.06
321	Jyrki Lumme	Vancouver Canucks	.05	.02	.01
322	Jeff Reese	Calgary Flames	.05	.02	.01
323	Greg Gilbert	Chicago Blackhawks	.05	.02	.01
324	Jeff Norton	New York Islanders	.05	.02	.01
325	Jim Hrivnak	Washington Capitals	.05	.02	.01
326	Eric Desjardins	Montreal Canadiens	.05	.02	.01
327	Curtis Joseph	St. Louis Blues	.35	.16	.04
328	Ric Nattress	Philadelphia Flyers	.05	.02	.01
329	Jamie Leach	Pittsburgh Penguins	.05	.02	.01
330	Christian Ruuttu	Chicago Blackhawks	.05	.02	.01
331	Doug Brown	New Jersey Devils	.05	.02	.01
332	Randy Carlyle	Winnipeg Jets	.05	.02	.01
333	Ed Belfour	Chicago Blackhawks	.30	.14	.04
334	Doug Smail	Ottawa Senators	.05	.02	.01
335	Hubie McDonough	New York Islanders	.05	.02	.01
336	Pat MacLeod	San Jose Sharks	.05	.02	.01
337	Don Sweeney	Boston Bruins	.05	.02	.01
338	Felix Potvin	Toronto Maple Leafs	2.00	.90	.25
339	Kent Manderville	Toronto Maple Leafs	.05	.02	.01
340	Sergei Nemchinov	New York Rangers	.08	.04	.01
341	Calle Johansson	Washington Capitals	.05	.02	.01
342	Dirk Graham	Chicago Blackhawks	.05	.02	.01
343	Craig Billington	New Jersey Devils	.05	.02	.01
344	Valeri Kamensky	Quebec Nordiques	.20	.09	.03
345	Mike Vernon	Calgary Flames	.08	.04	.01
346	Fredrik Olausson	Winnipeg Jets	.05	.02	.01
347	Peter Ing	Edmonton Oilers	.05	.02	.01
348	Mikael Andersson	Tampa Bay Lightning	.05	.02	.01
349	Mike Keane	Montreal Canadiens	.05	.02	.01
350	Stephane Quintal	St. Louis Blues	.05	.02	.01
351	Tom Chorske	New Jersey Devils	.05	.02	.01
352	Ron Francis	Pittsburgh Penguins	.08	.04	.01
353	Dana Murzyn	Vancouver Canucks	.05	.02	.01
354	Craig Ludwig	Minnesota North Stars	.05	.02	.01
355	Bob Probert	Detroit Red Wings	.05	.02	.01
356	Glenn Healy	New York Islanders	.08	.04	.01
357	Troy Loney	Pittsburgh Penguins	.05	.02	.01
358	Vladimir Ruzicka	Boston Bruins	.05	.02	.01
359	Doug Gilmour	Toronto Maple Leafs	.40	.18	.05
360	Darren Turcotte	New York Rangers	.05	.02	.01
361	Kelly Miller	Washington Capitals	.05	.02	.01
362	Dennis Vaske	New York Islanders	.05	.02	.01
363	Stephane Matteau	Chicago Blackhawks	.05	.02	.01
364	Brian Hayward	San Jose Sharks	.05	.02	.01
365	Kevin Dineen	Philadelphia Flyers	.08	.04	.01
366	Igor Ulanov	Winnipeg Jets	.05	.02	.01
367	Sylvain Lefebvre	Montreal Canadiens	.05	.02	.01
368	Petr Klima	Edmonton Oilers	.05	.02	.01
369	Steve Thomas	New York Islanders	.08	.04	.01
370	Daren Puppa	Buffalo Sabres	.08	.04	.01
371	Brendan Shanahan	St. Louis Blues	.30	.14	.04
372	Charlie Huddy	Los Angeles Kings	.05	.02	.01
373	Cliff Ronning	Vancouver Canucks	.05	.02	.01
374	Brian Propp	Minnesota North Stars	.08	.04	.01
375	Larry Murphy	Pittsburgh Penguins	.08	.04	.01
376	Bruce Driver	New Jersey Devils	.05	.02	.01
377	Rob Pearson	Toronto Maple Leafs	.05	.02	.01
378	Paul Ysebaert	Detroit Red Wings	.05	.02	.01
379	Mark Osborne	Toronto Maple Leafs	.05	.02	.01
380	Doug Weight	New York Rangers	.08	.04	.01
381	Kerry Huffman UER (Team name on front is Flyers)	Quebec Nordiques	.05	.02	.01
382	Michal Pivonka	Washington Capitals	.08	.04	.01
383	Steve Smith	Chicago Blackhawks	.08	.04	.01
384	Steven Finn	Quebec Nordiques	.05	.02	.01
385	Kevin Lowe	Edmonton Oilers	.05	.02	.01
386	Mike Ramsey	Buffalo Sabres	.05	.02	.01
387	Kirk Muller	Montreal Canadiens	.08	.04	.01
388	John LeBlanc	Winnipeg Jets	.05	.02	.01
389	Rich Sutter	St. Louis Blues	.05	.02	.01
390	Brent Fedyk	Philadelphia Flyers	.05	.02	.01
391	Kelly Hrudey	Los Angeles Kings	.08	.04	.01
392	Viacheslav Fetisov	New Jersey Devils	.05	.02	.01
393	Glen Murray UER (Misspelled Glenn on both sides)	Boston Bruins	.05	.02	.01
394	James Patrick	New York Rangers	.05	.02	.01
395	Tom Draper	Buffalo Sabres	.05	.02	.01
396	Mark Hunter	Washington Capitals	.05	.02	.01
397	Wayne McBean	New York Islanders	.05	.02	.01
398	Joe Sacco	Toronto Maple Leafs	.05	.02	.01
399	Dino Ciccarelli		.08	.04	.01

Detroit Red Wings
- [ ] 400 Brian Noonan .... .05 .02 .01

Chicago Blackhawks
- [ ] 401 Guy Hebert .... .50 .23 .06

St. Louis Blues
- [ ] 402 Peter Douris .... .05 .02 .01

Boston Bruins
- [ ] 403 Gilbert Dionne .... .05 .02 .01

Montreal Canadiens
- [ ] 404 Doug Lidster .... .05 .02 .01

Vancouver Canucks
- [ ] 405 John Druce .... .05 .02 .01

Winnipeg Jets
- [ ] 406 Alexei Kasatonov .... .05 .02 .01

New Jersey Devils
- [ ] 407 Chris Lindberg .... .05 .02 .01

Calgary Flames
- [ ] 408 Mike Ricci .... .08 .04 .01

Quebec Nordiques
- [ ] 409 Tom Kurvers .... .05 .02 .01

New York Islanders
- [ ] 410 Pat Elynuik .... .05 .02 .01

Washington Capitals
- [ ] 411 Mike Donnelly .... .05 .02 .01

Los Angeles Kings
- [ ] 412 Grant Fuhr .... .08 .04 .01

Toronto Maple Leafs
- [ ] 413 Curtis Leschyshyn .... .05 .02 .01

Quebec Nordiques
- [ ] 414 Derian Hatcher .... .05 .02 .01

Minnesota North Stars
- [ ] 415 Michel Mongeau .... .05 .02 .01

Tampa Bay Lightning
- [ ] 416 Tom Barrasso .... .08 .04 .01

Pittsburgh Penguins
- [ ] 417 Joey Kocur .... .05 .02 .01

New York Rangers
- [ ] 418 Vladimir Konstantinov .... .05 .02 .01

Detroit Red Wings
- [ ] 419 Dale Hawerchuk .... .08 .04 .01

Buffalo Sabres
- [ ] 420 Brian Mullen .... .08 .04 .01

New York Islanders
- [ ] 421 Mark Greig .... .05 .02 .01

Hartford Whalers
- [ ] 422 Claude Vilgrain .... .05 .02 .01

New Jersey Devils
- [ ] 423 Gary Suter .... .08 .04 .01

Calgary Flames
- [ ] 424 Garry Galley .... .05 .02 .01

Philadelphia Flyers
- [ ] 425 Benoit Hogue .... .05 .02 .01

New York Islanders
- [ ] 426 Jeff Finley .... .05 .02 .01

New York Islanders
- [ ] 427 Bobby Smith .... .08 .04 .01

Minnesota North Stars
- [ ] 428 Brent Sutter .... .08 .04 .01

Chicago Blackhawks
- [ ] 429 Ron Wilson .... .05 .02 .01

St. Louis Blues
- [ ] 430 Andy Moog .... .08 .04 .01

Boston Bruins
- [ ] 431 Stephan Lebeau .... .05 .02 .01

Montreal Canadiens
- [ ] 432 Troy Mallette .... .05 .02 .01

New Jersey Devils
- [ ] 433 Peter Zezel .... .05 .02 .01

Toronto Maple Leafs
- [ ] 434 Mike Hough .... .05 .02 .01

Quebec Nordiques
- [ ] 435 Mark Tinordi .... .08 .04 .01

Minnesota North Stars
- [ ] 436 Dave Manson .... .05 .02 .01

Edmonton Oilers
- [ ] 437 Jim Paek .... .05 .02 .01

Pittsburgh Penguins
- [ ] 438 Frantisek Kucera .... .05 .02 .01

Chicago Blackhawks
- [ ] 439 Rob Zamuner .... .10 .05 .01

Tampa Bay Lightning
- [ ] 440 Ulf Samuelsson .... .08 .04 .01

Pittsburgh Penguins
- [ ] 441 Perry Berezan .... .05 .02 .01

San Jose Sharks
- [ ] 442 Murray Craven .... .05 .02 .01

Hartford Whalers
- [ ] 443 Mark Messier .... .25 .11 .03

New York Rangers
- [ ] 444 Alexander Semak .... .05 .02 .01

New Jersey Devils
- [ ] 445 Gord Murphy .... .05 .02 .01

Boston Bruins
- [ ] 446 Jocelyn Lemieux .... .05 .02 .01

Chicago Blackhawks
- [ ] 447 Paul Cavallini .... .05 .02 .01

St. Louis Blues
- [ ] 448 Bernie Nicholls .... .08 .04 .01

Edmonton Oilers
- [ ] 449 Brent Gilchrist .... .05 .02 .01

Montreal Canadiens
- [ ] 450 Randy McKay .... .05 .02 .01

New Jersey Devils
- [ ] 451 Alexei Gusarov .... .05 .02 .01

Quebec Nordiques
- [ ] 452 Mike McPhee .... .05 .02 .01

Minnesota North Stars
- [ ] 453 Kimbi Daniels .... .05 .02 .01

Philadelphia Flyers
- [ ] 454 Kelly Kisio .... .05 .02 .01

San Jose Sharks
- [ ] 455 Bob Sweeney .... .05 .02 .01

Buffalo Sabres
- [ ] 456 Luke Richardson .... .05 .02 .01

Edmonton Oilers
- [ ] 457 Petr Nedved .... .25 .11 .03

Vancouver Canucks
- [ ] 458 Craig Berube .... .05 .02 .01

Toronto Maple Leafs
- [ ] 459 Kay Whitmore .... .05 .02 .01

Vancouver Canucks
- [ ] 460 Randy Velischek .... .05 .02 .01

Quebec Nordiques
- [ ] 461 David Williams .... .10 .05 .01

San Jose Sharks
- [ ] 462 Scott Mellanby .... .05 .02 .01

Edmonton Oilers
- [ ] 463 Terry Carkner .... .05 .02 .01

Philadelphia Flyers
- [ ] 464 Dale Craigwell .... .05 .02 .01

San Jose Sharks
- [ ] 465 Kevin Todd .... .05 .02 .01

New Jersey Devils
- [ ] 466 Kjell Samuelsson .... .05 .02 .01

Pittsburgh Penguins
- [ ] 467 Denis Savard .... .08 .04 .01

Montreal Canadiens
- [ ] 468 Adam Foote .... .05 .02 .01

Quebec Nordiques
- [ ] 469 Stephane Morin .... .05 .02 .01

Quebec Nordiques
- [ ] 470 Doug Wilson .... .08 .04 .01

San Jose Sharks
- [ ] 471 Shawn Cronin .... .05 .02 .01

Philadelphia Flyers
- [ ] 472 Brian Glynn .... .05 .02 .01

Edmonton Oilers
- [ ] 473 Craig Simpson .... .05 .02 .01

Edmonton Oilers
- [ ] 474 Todd Krygier .... .05 .02 .01

Washington Capitals
- [ ] 475 Brad Miller .... .05 .02 .01

Buffalo Sabres
- [ ] 476 Yvon Corriveau .... .05 .02 .01

San Jose Sharks
- [ ] 477 Patrick Flatley .... .05 .02 .01

New York Islanders
- [ ] 478 Mats Sundin .... .25 .11 .03

Quebec Nordiques
- [ ] 479 Joe Cirella .... .05 .02 .01

New York Rangers
- [ ] 480 Gino Cavallini .... .05 .02 .01

Quebec Nordiques
- [ ] 481 Marty McSorley .... .08 .04 .01

Los Angeles Kings
- [ ] 482 Brad Marsh .... .08 .04 .01

Ottawa Senators
- [ ] 483 Bob McGill .... .05 .02 .01

Tampa Bay Lightning
- [ ] 484 Randy Moller .... .05 .02 .01

Buffalo Sabres
- [ ] 485 Keith Primeau .... .08 .04 .01

Detroit Red Wings
- [ ] 486 Darin Kimble .... .05 .02 .01

St. Louis Blues
- [ ] 487 Mike Krushelnyski .... .05 .02 .01

Toronto Maple Leafs
- [ ] 488 Sutter Brothers .... .08 .04 .01
- [ ] 489 Pavel Bure .... 2.50 1.15 .30

Vancouver Canucks
- [ ] 490 Ray Whitney .... .25 .11 .03

San Jose Sharks
- [ ] 491 Dave McIlwain .... .05 .02 .01

Toronto Maple Leafs
- [ ] 492 Per Djoos .... .05 .02 .01

New York Rangers
- [ ] 493 Garry Valk .... .05 .02 .01

Vancouver Canucks

			MINT	EXC	G-VG
☐	494	Mike Bullard	.05	.02	.01
		Toronto Maple Leafs			
☐	495	Greg Hawgood	.05	.02	.01
		Edmonton Oilers			
☐	496	Terry Yake	.05	.02	.01
		Hartford Whalers			
☐	497	Mike Hartman	.05	.02	.01
		Tampa Bay Lightning			
☐	498	Jaromir Jagr	.75	.35	.09
		Pittsburgh Penguins			
☐	499	Checklist 251-384	.05	.02	.01
☐	500	Checklist 385-500	.05	.02	.01
☐	501	Eric Lindros	5.00	2.30	.60
		Philadelphia Flyers			

1993-94 Stadium Club

This 500-card standard-size (2 1/2" by 3 1/2") set features borderless color player action shots on the card fronts. The set was issued in two series of 250 cards each. Cards were printed for both the Canadian and U.S. markets and do not differ. The O-Pee-Chee version has a U.S.A. copyright on back.The player's name appears in gold foil at the bottom, atop blue and gold foil stripes. Using an out-of-focus photo of the ice and sideboards for background, the back features a color player photo at the upper left. His name, position, and team, along with a player skills rating, are displayed alongside. At the bottom, the player's career highlights and stats, and the NHL and NHLPA logos, round out the card. Included is a ten-card Award Winners subset (141-150) that features the 1992-93 NHL Trophy winners. Randomly inserted in every 24 packs are NHL All-Star cards and Master Photo winner cards. The cards are numbered on the back.

	MINT	EXC	G-VG
COMPLETE SET (500)	35.00	16.00	4.40
COMPLETE SERIES 1 (250)	17.00	7.75	2.10
COMPLETE SERIES 2 (250)	18.00	8.00	2.30
COMMON PLAYER (1-250)	.05	.02	.01
COMMON PLAYER (251-500)	.05	.02	.01
*OPC VERSION: SAME VALUE			

☐	1	Guy Carbonneau	.08	.04	.01
		Montreal Canadiens			
☐	2	Joe Cirella	.05	.02	.01
		New York Rangers			
☐	3	Laurie Boschman	.05	.02	.01
		Ottawa Senators			
☐	4	Arturs Irbe	.40	.18	.05
		San Jose Sharks			
☐	5	Adam Creighton	.05	.02	.01
		Tampa Bay Lightning			
☐	6	Mike McPhee	.05	.02	.01
		Dallas Stars			
☐	7	Jeff Beukeboom	.05	.02	.01
		New York Rangers			
☐	8	Kevin Todd	.05	.02	.01
		Edmonton Oilers			
☐	9	Yvon Corriveau	.05	.02	.01
		Hartford Whalers			
☐	10	Eric Lindros	2.00	.90	.25

		Philadelphia Flyers			
☐	11	Martin Rucinsky	.05	.02	.01
		Quebec Nordiques			
☐	12	Michel Goulet	.08	.04	.01
		Chicago Blackhawks			
☐	13	Scott Pellerin	.15	.07	.02
		New Jersey Devils			
☐	14	Mike Eagles	.05	.02	.01
		Winnipeg Jets			
☐	15	Steve Heinze	.05	.02	.01
		Boston Bruins			
☐	16	Gerard Gallant	.05	.02	.01
		Detroit Red Wings			
☐	17	Kelly Miller	.05	.02	.01
		Washington Capitals			
☐	18	Petr Nedved	.08	.04	.01
		Vancouver Canucks			
☐	19	Joe Mullen	.08	.04	.01
		Pittsburgh Penguins			
☐	20	Pat LaFontaine	.25	.11	.03
		Buffalo Sabres			
☐	21	Garth Butcher	.05	.02	.01
		St. Louis Blues			
☐	22	Jeff Reese	.05	.02	.01
		Calgary Flames			
☐	23	Dave Andreychuk	.10	.05	.01
		Toronto Maple Leafs			
☐	24	Patrick Flatley	.05	.02	.01
		New York Islanders			
☐	25	Tomas Sandstrom	.05	.02	.01
		Los Angeles Kings			
☐	26	Andre Racicot	.05	.02	.01
		Montreal Canadiens			
☐	27	Patrice Brisebois	.05	.02	.01
		Montreal Canadiens			
☐	28	Neal Broten	.08	.04	.01
		Dallas Stars			
☐	29	Mark Freer	.05	.02	.01
		Ottawa Senators			
☐	30	Kelly Kisio	.05	.02	.01
		San Jose Sharks			
☐	31	Scott Mellanby	.05	.02	.01
		Edmonton Oilers			
☐	32	Joe Sakic	.20	.09	.03
		Quebec Nordiques			
☐	33	Kerry Huffman	.05	.02	.01
		Quebec Nordiques			
☐	34	Evgeny Davydov	.05	.02	.01
		Winnipeg Jets			
☐	35	Mark Messier	.20	.09	.03
		New York Rangers			
☐	36	Pat Verbeek	.08	.04	.01
		Hartford Whalers			
☐	37	Greg Gilbert	.05	.02	.01
		Chicago Blackhawks			
☐	38	John Tucker	.05	.02	.01
		Tampa Bay Lightning			
☐	39	Claude Lemieux	.08	.04	.01
		New Jersey Devils			
☐	40	Shayne Corson	.05	.02	.01
		Edmonton Oilers			
☐	41	Gordie Roberts	.05	.02	.01
		Boston Bruins			
☐	42	Jiri Slegr	.05	.02	.01
		Vancouver Canucks			
☐	43	Kevin Dineen	.08	.04	.01
		Philadelphia Flyers			
☐	44	Johan Garpenlov	.05	.02	.01
		San Jose Sharks			
☐	45	Sergei Fedorov	.75	.35	.09
		Detroit Red Wings			
☐	46	Rich Sutter	.05	.02	.01
		St. Louis Blues			
☐	47	Dave Hannan	.05	.02	.01
		Buffalo Sabres			
☐	48	Sylvain Lefebvre	.05	.02	.01
		Toronto Maple Leafs			
☐	49	Pat Elynuik	.05	.02	.01
		Washington Capitals			
☐	50	Ray Ferraro	.05	.02	.01
		New York Islanders			
☐	51	Brent Ashton	.05	.02	.01
		Calgary Flames			
☐	52	Paul Stanton	.05	.02	.01
		Pittsburgh Penguins			
☐	53	Kevin Haller	.05	.02	.01
		Buffalo Sabres			
☐	54	Kelly Hrudey	.08	.04	.01
		Los Angeles Kings			
☐	55	Russ Courtnall	.08	.04	.01
		Dallas Stars			
☐	56	Alexei Zhamnov	.35	.16	.04
		Winnipeg Jets			
☐	57	Andrei Lomakin	.05	.02	.01

Philadelphia Flyers				
☐ 58 Keith Brown	.05	.02	.01
Chicago Blackhawks				
☐ 59 Glenn Murray	.05	.02	.01
Boston Bruins				
☐ 60 Kay Whitmore	.05	.02	.01
Vancouver Canucks				
☐ 61 Stephane Richer	.08	.04	.01
New Jersey Devils				
☐ 62 Todd Gill	.05	.02	.01
Toronto Maple Leafs				
☐ 63 Bob Sweeney	.05	.02	.01
Buffalo Sabres				
☐ 64 Mike Richter	.20	.09	.03
New York Rangers				
☐ 65 Brett Hull	.60	.25	.08
St. Louis Blues				
☐ 66 Sylvain Cote	.05	.02	.01
Washington Capitals				
☐ 67 Kirk Muller	.08	.04	.01
Montreal Canadiens				
☐ 68 Ronnie Stern	.05	.02	.01
Vancouver Canucks				
☐ 69 Josef Beranek	.08	.04	.01
Philadelphia Flyers				
☐ 70 Steve Yzerman	.35	.16	.04
Detroit Red Wings				
☐ 71 Don Deaupre	.05	.02	.01
Washington Capitals				
☐ 72 Ed Courtenay	.05	.02	.01
San Jose Sharks				
☐ 73 Zdeno Ciger	.05	.02	.01
New Jersey Devils				
☐ 74 Andrew Cassels	.05	.02	.01
Hartford Whalers				
☐ 75 Roman Hamrlik	.15	.07	.02
Tampa Bay Lightning				
☐ 76 Benoit Hogue	.05	.02	.01
New York Islanders				
☐ 77 Andrei Kovalenko	.15	.07	.02
Quebec Nordiques				
☐ 78 Rod Brind'Amour	.20	.09	.03
Philadelphia Flyers				
☐ 79 Tom Barrasso	.08	.04	.01
Pittsburgh Penguins				
☐ 80 Al Iafrate	.08	.04	.01
Washington Capitals				
☐ 81 Brett Hedican	.05	.02	.01
St. Louis Blues				
☐ 82 Peter Bondra	.08	.04	.01
Washington Capitals				
☐ 83 Ted Donato	.05	.02	.01
Boston Bruins				
☐ 84 Chris Lindberg	.05	.02	.01
Calgary Flames				
☐ 85 John Vanbiesbrouck	.10	.05	.01
New York Rangers				
☐ 86 Ron Sutter	.05	.02	.01
St. Louis Blues				
☐ 87 Luc Robitaille	.20	.09	.03
Los Angeles Kings				
☐ 88 Brian Leetch	.25	.11	.03
New York Rangers				
☐ 89 Randy Wood	.05	.02	.01
Buffalo Sabres				
☐ 90 Dirk Graham	.05	.02	.01
Chicago Blackhawks				
☐ 91 Alexander Mogilny	.40	.18	.05
Buffalo Sabres				
☐ 92 Mike Keane	.05	.02	.01
Montreal Canadiens				
☐ 93 Adam Oates	.15	.07	.02
Boston Bruins				
☐ 94 Viacheslav Butsayev	.05	.02	.01
Philadelphia Flyers				
☐ 95 John LeClair	.05	.02	.01
Montreal Canadiens				
☐ 96 Joe Nieuwendyk	.08	.04	.01
Calgary Flames				
☐ 97 Mikael Andersson	.05	.02	.01
Tampa Bay Lightning				
☐ 98 Jaromir Jagr	.50	.23	.06
Pittsburgh Penguins				
☐ 99 Ed Belfour	.20	.09	.03
Chicago Blackhawks				
☐ 100 Dave Reid	.05	.02	.01
Boston Bruins				
☐ 101 Darius Kasparaitis	.05	.02	.01
New York Islanders				
☐ 102 Zarley Zalapski	.05	.02	.01
Hartford Whalers				
☐ 103 Christian Ruuttu	.05	.02	.01
Chicago Blackhawks				
☐ 104 Phil Housley	.08	.04	.01

Winnipeg Jets				
☐ 105 Al MacInnis	.10	.05	.01
Calgary Flames				
☐ 106 Tommy Sjodin	.05	.02	.01
Dallas Stars				
☐ 107 Richard Smehlik	.08	.04	.01
Buffalo Sabres				
☐ 108 Jyrki Lumme	.05	.02	.01
Vancouver Canucks				
☐ 109 Dominic Roussel	.15	.07	.02
Philadelphia Flyers				
☐ 110 Mike Gartner	.10	.05	.01
New York Rangers				
☐ 111 Bernie Nicholls	.08	.04	.01
New Jersey Devils				
☐ 112 Mark Howe	.08	.04	.01
Detroit Red Wings				
☐ 113 Rich Pilon	.05	.02	.01
New York Islanders				
☐ 114 Jeff Odgers	.05	.02	.01
San Jose Sharks				
☐ 115 Gilbert Dionne	.05	.02	.01
Montreal Canadiens				
☐ 116 Peter Zezel	.05	.02	.01
Toronto Maple Leafs				
☐ 117 Don Sweeney	.05	.02	.01
Boston Bruins				
☐ 118 Jimmy Carson	.05	.02	.01
Los Angeles Kings				
☐ 119 Igor Korolev	.05	.02	.01
St. Louis Blues				
☐ 120 Bob Kudelski	.08	.04	.01
Los Angeles Kings				
☐ 121 Dave Lowry	.05	.02	.01
Vancouver Canucks				
☐ 122 Steve Kasper	.05	.02	.01
Tampa Bay Lightning				
☐ 123 Mike Ridley	.08	.04	.01
Washington Capitals				
☐ 124 Dave Tippett	.05	.02	.01
Pittsburgh Penguins				
☐ 125 Cliff Ronning	.05	.02	.01
Vancouver Canucks				
☐ 126 Bruce Driver	.05	.02	.01
New Jersey Devils				
☐ 127 Stephane Matteau	.05	.02	.01
Chicago Blackhawks				
☐ 128 Joel Otto	.05	.02	.01
Calgary Flames				
☐ 129 Alexei Kovalev	.50	.23	.06
New York Rangers				
☐ 130 Mike Modano	.25	.11	.03
Dallas Stars				
☐ 131 Bill Ranford	.08	.04	.01
Edmonton Oilers				
☐ 132 Petr Svoboda	.05	.02	.01
Buffalo Sabres				
☐ 133 Roger Johansson	.05	.02	.01
Calgary Flames				
☐ 134 Marc Bureau	.05	.02	.01
Tampa Bay Lightning				
☐ 135 Keith Tkachuk	.20	.09	.03
Winnipeg Jets				
☐ 136 Mark Recchi	.25	.11	.03
Philadelphia Flyers				
☐ 137 Bob Probert	.05	.02	.01
Detroit Red Wings				
☐ 138 Uwe Krupp	.05	.02	.01
New York Islanders				
☐ 139 Mike Sullivan	.05	.02	.01
San Jose Sharks				
✈ 140 Doug Gilmour	.35	.16	.04
Toronto Maple Leafs				
☐ 141 Calder Trophy Winner	.30	.14	.04
Teemu Selanne				
Winnipeg Jets				
☐ 142 Clancy Trophy Winner	.05	.02	.01
Dave Poulin				
Boston Bruins				
☐ 143 Hart Trophy Winner	.30	.14	.04
Mario Lemieux				
Pittsburgh Penguins				
☐ 144 Jennings Trophy Winner	.15	.07	.02
Ed Belfour				
Chicago Blackhawks				
☐ 145 Pierre Turgeon	.15	.07	.02
New York Islanders				
Lady Byng Trophy				
Winner				
☐ 146 Mario Lemieux	.30	.14	.04
Pittsburgh Penguins				
Masterton Trophy				
Winner				
☐ 147 Chris Chelios	.05	.02	.01

Chicago Blackhawks					Toronto Maple Leafs			
Norris Trophy Winner				☐ 193 Kevin Miller	.05	.02	.01
☐ 148 Mario Lemieux	.30	.14	.04		St. Louis Blues			
Pittsburgh Penguins				☐ 194 Paul DiPietro	.05	.02	.01
Art Ross Trophy Winner					Montreal Canadiens			
☒ 149 Doug Gilmour	.20	.09	.03	☐ 195 Steve Thomas	.08	.04	.01
Toronto Maple Leafs					New York Islanders			
Selke Trophy Winner				☐ 196 Nicklas Lidstrom	.08	.04	.01
☐ 150 Ed Belfour	.15	.07	.02		Detroit Red Wings			
Chicago Blackhawks				☐ 197 Ed Olczyk	.05	.02	.01
Vezina Trophy Winner					New York Rangers			
☐ 151 Paul Ranheim	.05	.02	.01	☐ 198 Robert Reichel	.08	.04	.01
Calgary Flames					Calgary Flames			
☐ 152 Gino Cavallini	.05	.02	.01	☐ 199 Neil Brady	.05	.02	.01
Quebec Nordiques					Ottawa Senators			
☐ 153 Kevin Hatcher	.08	.04	.01	☐ 200 Wayne Gretzky	1.50	.65	.19
Washington Capitals					Los Angeles Kings			
☐ 154 Marc Bergevin	.05	.02	.01	☐ 201 Adrien Plavsic	.05	.02	.01
Tampa Bay Lightning					Vancouver Canucks			
☐ 155 Marty McSorley	.08	.04	.01	☐ 202 Joe Juneau	.60	.25	.08
Los Angeles Kings					Boston Bruins			
☐ 156 Brian Bellows	.08	.04	.01	☐ 203 Brad May	.05	.02	.01
Montreal Canadiens					Buffalo Sabres			
☐ 157 Patrick Poulin	.05	.02	.01	☐ 204 Igor Kravchuk	.05	.02	.01
Hartford Whalers					Edmonton Oilers			
☐ 158 Kevin Stevens	.25	.11	.03	☐ 205 Keith Acton	.05	.02	.01
Pittsburgh Penguins					Philadelphia Flyers			
☐ 159 Bobby Holik	.05	.02	.01	☐ 206 Ken Daneyko	.05	.02	.01
New Jersey Devils					New Jersey Devils			
☐ 160 Ray Bourque	.20	.09	.03	☐ 207 Sean Burke	.08	.04	.01
Boston Bruins					Hartford Whalers			
☐ 161 Bryan Marchment	.05	.02	.01	☐ 208 Jayson More	.05	.02	.01
Chicago Blackhawks					San Jose Sharks			
☐ 162 Curtis Joseph	.20	.09	.03	☐ 209 John Cullen	.05	.02	.01
St. Louis Blues					Toronto Maple Leafs			
☐ 163 Kirk McLean	.10	.05	.01	☐ 210 Teemu Selanne	.75	.35	.09
Vancouver Canucks					Winnipeg Jets			
☐ 164 Teppo Numminen	.05	.02	.01	☐ 211 Brent Sutter	.08	.04	.01
Winnipeg Jets					Chicago Blackhawks			
☐ 165 Kevin Lowe	.05	.02	.01	☐ 212 Brian Bradley	.05	.02	.01
New York Rangers					Tampa Bay Lightning			
☐ 166 Tim Cheveldae	.08	.04	.01	☐ 213 Donald Audette	.05	.02	.01
Detroit Red Wings					Buffalo Sabres			
☐ 167 Brad Dalgarno	.05	.02	.01	☐ 214 Philippe Bozon	.05	.02	.01
New York Islanders					St. Louis Blues			
☐ 168 Glenn Anderson	.08	.04	.01	☐ 215 Derek King	.05	.02	.01
Toronto Maple Leafs					New York Islanders			
☐ 169 Frantisek Musil	.05	.02	.01	☐ 216 Cam Neely	.08	.04	.01
Calgary Flames					Boston Bruins			
☐ 170 Eric Desjardins	.05	.02	.01	☐ 217 Keith Primeau	.08	.04	.01
Montreal Canadiens					Detroit Red Wings			
☐ 171 Doug Zmolek	.05	.02	.01	☐ 218 Steve Smith	.05	.02	.01
San Jose Sharks					Chicago Blackhawks			
☐ 172 Mark Lamb	.05	.02	.01	☐ 219 Ken Sutton	.05	.02	.01
Edmonton Oilers					Buffalo Sabres			
☐ 173 Craig Ludwig	.05	.02	.01	☐ 220 Dale Hawerchuk	.08	.04	.01
Dallas Stars					Buffalo Sabres			
☐ 174 Rob Gaudreau	.20	.09	.03	☐ 221 Alexei Zhitnik	.15	.07	.02
San Jose Sharks					Los Angeles Kings			
☐ 175 Bob Carpenter	.05	.02	.01	☐ 222 Glen Wesley	.05	.02	.01
Washington Capitals					Boston Bruins			
☐ 176 Mike Ricci	.08	.04	.01	☐ 223 Nelson Emerson	.08	.04	.01
Quebec Nordiques					St. Louis Blues			
☐ 177 Brian Skrudland	.05	.02	.01	☐ 224 Pat Falloon	.08	.04	.01
Calgary Flames					San Jose Sharks			
☐ 178 Dominik Hasek	.10	.05	.01	☐ 225 Darryl Sydor	.08	.04	.01
Buffalo Sabres					Los Angeles Kings			
☐ 179 Pat Conacher	.05	.02	.01	☐ 226 Tony Amonte	.08	.04	.01
Los Angeles Kings					New York Rangers			
☐ 180 Mark Janssens	.05	.02	.01	☐ 227 Brian Mullen	.08	.04	.01
Hartford Whalers					New York Islanders			
☐ 181 Brent Fedyk	.05	.02	.01	☐ 228 Gary Suter	.08	.04	.01
Philadelphia Flyers					Calgary Flames			
☐ 182 Rob DiMaio	.05	.02	.01	☐ 229 David Shaw	.05	.02	.01
Tampa Bay Lightning					Boston Bruins			
☐ 183 Dave Manson	.05	.02	.01	☐ 230 Troy Murray	.05	.02	.01
Edmonton Oilers					Chicago Blackhawks			
☐ 184 Janne Ojanen	.05	.02	.01	☐ 231 Patrick Roy	.60	.25	.08
New Jersey Devils					Montreal Canadiens			
☐ 185 Ryan Walter	.05	.02	.01	☐ 232 Mitchel Petit	.05	.02	.01
Vancouver Canucks					Calgary Flames			
☐ 186 Mikael Nylander	.15	.07	.02	☐ 233 Wayne Presley	.05	.02	.01
Hartford Whalers					San Jose Sharks			
☐ 187 Steve Leach	.05	.02	.01	☐ 234 Keith Jones	.05	.02	.01
Boston Bruins					Washington Capitals			
☐ 188 Jeff Brown	.08	.04	.01	☐ 235 Gary Roberts	.08	.04	.01
St. Louis Blues					Calgary Flames			
☐ 189 Shawn McEachern	.15	.07	.02	☐ 236 Steve Larmer	.08	.04	.01
Pittsburgh Penguins					Chicago Blackhawks			
☐ 190 Jeremy Roenick	.50	.23	.06	☐ 237 Valeri Kamensky	.20	.09	.03
Chicago Blackhawks					Quebec Nordiques			
☐ 191 Darrin Shannon	.05	.02	.01	☐ 238 Ulf Dahlen	.05	.02	.01
Winnipeg Jets					Dallas Stars			
☐ 192 Wendel Clark	.10	.05	.01	☐ 239 Danton Cole	.05	.02	.01

Tampa Bay Lightning
☐ 240 Vincent Damphousse	.08	.04	.01

Montreal Canadiens
☐ 241 Yuri Khmylev......................	.08	.04	.01

Buffalo Sabres
☐ 242 Stephane Quintal.................	.05	.02	.01

St. Louis Blues
☐ 243 Peter Taglianetti	.05	.02	.01

Pittsburgh Penguins
☐ 244 Gary Leeman	.05	.02	.01

Montreal Canadiens
☐ 245 Sergei Nemchinov	.05	.02	.01

New York Rangers
☐ 246 Rob Blake	.08	.04	.01

Los Angeles Kings
☐ 247 Steve Chiasson	.05	.02	.01

Detroit Red Wings
☐ 248 Vladimir Malakhov	.15	.07	.02

New York Islanders
☐ 249 Checklist 1-125	.05	.02	.01
☐ 250 Checklist 126-250	.05	.02	.01
☐ 251 Kjell Samuelsson.................	.05	.02	.01

Pittsburgh Penguins
☐ 252 Terry Carkner	.05	.02	.01

Detroit Red Wings
☐ 253 Bill Lindsay	.05	.02	.01

Florida Panthers
☐ 254 Bob Essensa	.08	.04	.01

Winnipeg Jets
☐ 255 Jocelyn Lemieux	.05	.02	.01

Chicago Blackhawks
☐ 256 Joe Sacco	.05	.02	.01

Anaheim Mighty Ducks
☐ 257 Marty McInnis....................	.05	.02	.01

New York Islanders
☐ 258 Warren Rychel	.05	.02	.01

Los Angeles Kings
☐ 259 David Maley	.05	.02	.01

San Jose Sharks
☐ 260 Grant Fuhr	.08	.04	.01

Buffalo Sabres
☐ 261 Scott Young	.05	.02	.01

Quebec Nordiques
☐ 262 Ed Ronan	.05	.02	.01

Montreal Canadiens
☐ 263 Micah Aivazoff....................	.15	.07	.02

Detroit Red Wings
☐ 264 Murray Craven	.05	.02	.01

Vancouver Canucks
☐ 265 Viacheslav Fetisov..............	.05	.02	.01

New Jersey Devils
☐ 266 Chris Dahlquist	.05	.02	.01

Calgary Flames
☐ 267 Norm Maciver	.05	.02	.01

Ottawa Senators
☐ 268 Alexander Godynyuk	.05	.02	.01

Hartford Whalers
☐ 269 Mikael Renberg	.60	.25	.08

Philadelphia Flyers
☐ 270 Adam Graves	.25	.11	.03

New York Rangers
☐ 271 Randy Ladouceur	.05	.02	.01

Anaheim Mighty Ducks
☐ 272 Frank Pietrangelo	.05	.02	.01

Hartford Whalers
☐ 273 Basil McRae	.05	.02	.01

St. Louis Blues
☐ 274 Bryan Smolinski	.50	.23	.06

Boston Bruins
☐ 275 Daren Puppa	.08	.04	.01

Tampa Bay Lightning
☐ 276 Darcy Wakaluk...................	.05	.02	.01

Dallas Stars
☐ 277 Dimitri Khristich	.08	.04	.01

Washington Capitals
☐ 278 Vladimir Vujtek.....................	.05	.02	.01

Edmonton Oilers
☐ 279 Tom Kurvers	.05	.02	.01

New York Islanders
☐ 280 Felix Potvin	.75	.35	.09

Toronto Maple Leafs
☐ 281 Keith Brown	.05	.02	.01

Florida Panthers
☐ 282 Thomas Steen	.05	.02	.01

Winnipeg Jets
☐ 283 Larry Murphy	.08	.04	.01

Pittsburgh Penguins
☐ 284 Bob Corkum	.05	.02	.01

Anaheim Mighty Ducks
☐ 285 Tony Granato	.05	.02	.01

Los Angeles Kings
☐ 286 Cam Russell	.05	.02	.01

Chicago Blackhawks
☐ 287 John MacLean....................	.08	.04	.01

New Jersey Devils
☐ 288 Shawn Antoski	.05	.02	.01

Vancouver Canucks
☐ 289 Pelle Eklund	.05	.02	.01

Philadelphia Flyers
☐ 290 Chris Pronger......................	.60	.25	.08

Hartford Whalers
☐ 291 Alexander Karpovtsev	.08	.04	.01

New York Rangers
☐ 292 Paul Laus...........................	.15	.07	.02

Florida Panthers
☐ 293 Jaroslav Otevrel	.05	.02	.01

San Jose Sharks
☐ 294 Dino Ciccarelli	.08	.04	.01

Detroit Red Wings
☐ 295 Guy Hebert.........................	.15	.07	.02

Anaheim Mighty Ducks
☐ 296 Dave Karpa.........................	.05	.02	.01

Quebec Nordiques
☐ 297 Denis Savard	.10	.05	.01

Tampa Bay Lightning
☐ 298 Jim Johnson	.05	.02	.01

Dallas Stars
☐ 299 Kirk Maltby..........................	.15	.07	.02

Edmonton Oilers
☐ 300 Alexandre Daigle	.60	.25	.08

Ottawa Senators
☐ 301 Dave Poulin	.05	.02	.01

Washington Capitals
☐ 302 James Patrick	.05	.02	.01

New York Rangers
☐ 303 Jon Casey	.08	.04	.01

Boston Bruins
☐ 304 Yves Racine	.05	.02	.01

Philadelphia Flyers
☐ 305 Craig Simpson	.05	.02	.01

Buffalo Sabres
☐ 306 Mike Krushelnyski...............	.05	.02	.01

Toronto Maple Leafs
☐ 307 Mark Fitzpatrick...................	.05	.02	.01

Florida Panters
☐ 308 Charlie Huddy	.05	.02	.01

Los Angeles Kings
☐ 309 Todd Ewen	.05	.02	.01

Anaheim Mighty Ducks
☐ 310 Mario Lemieux	1.00	.45	.13

Pittsburgh Penguins
☐ 311 Dan Keczmer.......................	.15	.07	.02

Calgary Flames
☐ 312 Sergei Zubov.......................	.50	.23	.06

New York Rangers
☐ 313 Shawn Burr	.05	.02	.01

Detroit Red Wings
☐ 314 Valeri Zelepukin	.08	.04	.01

New Jersey Devils
☐ 315 Stephane Fiset....................	.05	.02	.01

Quebec Nordiques
☐ 316 C.J. Young	.05	.02	.01

Florida Panthers
☐ 317 Luciano Borsato	.05	.02	.01

Winnipeg Jets
☐ 318 Darcy Loewen	.05	.02	.01

Ottawa Senators
☐ 319 Mike Vernon	.08	.04	.01

Calgary Flames
☐ 320 Chris Gratton.......................	.60	.25	.08

Tampa Bay Lightning
☐ 321 Matthew Barnaby	.15	.07	.02

Buffalo Sabres
☐ 322 Mike Rathje	.05	.02	.01

San Jose Sharks
☐ 323 Sergio Momesso	.05	.02	.01

Vancouver Canucks
☐ 324 David Volek	.05	.02	.01

New York Islanders
☐ 325 Ron Tugnutt........................	.05	.02	.01

Anaheim Mighty Ducks
☐ 326 Jeff Hackett	.05	.02	.01

Chicago Blackhawks
☐ 327 Robb Stauber	.05	.02	.01

Los Angeles Kings
☐ 328 Chris Terreri	.08	.04	.01

New Jersey Devils
☐ 329 Rick Tocchet	.08	.04	.01

Pittsburgh Penguins
☐ 330 John Vanbiesbrouck	.20	.09	.03

Florida Panthers
☐ 331 Drake Berehowsky	.05	.02	.01

Toronto Maple Leafs
☐ 332 Alexei Kasatonov................	.05	.02	.01

Anaheim Mighty Ducks
☐ 333 Vladimir Konstantinov.........	.05	.02	.01

Detroit Red Wings
☐ 334 John Blue............................	.05	.02	.01

Boston Bruins				
☐ 335 Craig Janney	.10	.05	.01	
St. Louis Blues				
☐ 336 Curtis Leschyshyn	.05	.02	.01	
Quebec Nordiques				
☐ 337 Todd Krygier	.05	.02	.01	
Hartford Whalers				
☐ 338 Boris Mironov	.05	.02	.01	
Winnipeg Jets				
☐ 339 Joby Messier	.15	.07	.02	
New York Rangers				
☐ 340 Tommy Soderstrom	.15	.07	.02	
Philadelphia Flyers				
☐ 341 Randy Cunneyworth	.05	.02	.01	
Hartford Whalers				
☐ 342 Mark Ferner	.15	.07	.02	
Anaheim Mighty Ducks				
☐ 343 Stephan Lebeau	.05	.02	.01	
Montreal Canadiens				
☐ 344 Jody Hull	.05	.02	.01	
Florida Panthers				
☐ 345 Jason Arnott	2.00	.90	.25	
Edmonton Oilers				
☐ 346 Gerard Gallant	.05	.02	.01	
Tampa Bay Lightning				
☐ 347 Stephane Richer	.08	.04	.01	
New Jersey Devils				
☐ 348 Jeff Shantz	.20	.09	.03	
Chicago Blackhawks				
☐ 349 Brian Skrudland	.05	.02	.01	
Florida Panthers				
☐ 350 Chris Osgood	.60	.25	.08	
Detroit Red Wings				
☐ 351 Gary Shuchuk	.05	.02	.01	
Los Angeles Kings				
☐ 352 Martin Brodeur	.40	.18	.05	
New Jersey Devils				
☐ 353 Bob Rouse	.05	.02	.01	
Toronto Maple Leafs				
☐ 354 Doug Bodger	.05	.02	.01	
Buffalo Sabres				
☐ 355 Mike Craig	.05	.02	.01	
Dallas Stars				
☐ 356 Ulf Samuelsson	.08	.04	.01	
Pittsburgh Penguins				
☐ 357 Trevor Linden	.10	.05	.01	
Vancouver Canucks				
☐ 358 Dennis Vaske	.05	.02	.01	
New York Islanders				
☐ 359 Alexei Yashin	.75	.35	.09	
Ottawa Senators				
☐ 360 Paul Ysebaert	.05	.02	.01	
Winnipeg Jets				
☐ 361 Shaun Van Allen	.05	.02	.01	
Edmonton Oilers				
☐ 362 Sandis Ozolinsh	.20	.09	.03	
San Jose Sharks				
☐ 363 Todd Elik	.05	.02	.01	
San Jose Sharks				
☐ 364 German Titov	.40	.18	.05	
Calgary Flames				
☐ 365 Alexander Semak	.05	.02	.01	
New Jersey Devils				
☐ 366 Allen Pedersen	.05	.02	.01	
Hartford Whalers				
☐ 367 Greg Johnson	.05	.02	.01	
Detroit Red Wings				
☐ 368 Anatoli Semenov	.05	.02	.01	
Anaheim Mighty Ducks				
☐ 369 Scott Mellanby	.05	.02	.01	
Florida Panthers				
☐ 370 Mats Sundin	.20	.09	.03	
Quebec Nordiques				
☐ 371 Mattias Norstrom	.10	.05	.01	
New York Rangers				
☐ 372 Glen Featherstone	.05	.02	.01	
Boston Bruins				
☐ 373 Sergei Petrenko	.05	.02	.01	
Buffalo Sabres				
☐ 374 Mike Donnelly	.05	.02	.01	
Los Angeles Kings				
☐ 375 Nikolai Borschevsky	.15	.07	.02	
Toronto Maple Leafs				
☐ 376 Rob Zamuner	.05	.02	.01	
Tampa Bay Lightning				
☐ 377 Steven King	.05	.02	.01	
Anaheim Mighty Ducks				
☐ 378 Rick Tabaracci	.05	.02	.01	
Washington Capitals				
☐ 379 Dave Lowry	.05	.02	.01	
Florida Panthers				
☐ 380 Pierre Turgeon	.20	.09	.03	
New York Islanders				
☐ 381 Garry Galley	.05	.02	.01	
Philadelphia Flyers				
☐ 382 Doug Weight	.08	.04	.01	
Edmonton Oilers				
☐ 383 Scott Stevens	.08	.04	.01	
New Jersey Devils				
☐ 384 Mark Tinordi	.05	.02	.01	
Dallas Stars				
☐ 385 Ron Francis	.08	.04	.01	
Pittsburgh Penguins				
☐ 386 Mark Greig	.05	.02	.01	
Hartford Whalers				
☐ 387 Sean Hill	.05	.02	.01	
Anaheim Mighty Ducks				
☐ 388 Vyacheslav Kozlov	.50	.23	.06	
Detroit Red Wings				
☐ 389 Brendan Shanahan	.20	.09	.03	
St. Louis Blues				
☐ 390 Theoren Fleury	.10	.05	.01	
Chicago Blackhawks				
☐ 391 Mathieu Schneider	.08	.04	.01	
Montreal Canadiens				
☐ 392 Tom Fitzgerald	.05	.02	.01	
Florida Panthers				
☐ 393 Markus Naslund	.15	.07	.02	
Pittsburgh Penguins				
☐ 394 Travis Green	.05	.02	.01	
New York Islanders				
☐ 395 Troy Loney	.05	.02	.01	
Anaheim Mighty Ducks				
☐ 396 Gord Donnelly	.05	.02	.01	
Dallas Stars				
☐ 397 Owen Nolan	.08	.04	.01	
Quebec Nordiques				
☐ 398 Steve Larmer	.08	.04	.01	
New York Rangers				
☐ 399 Dave Archibald	.05	.02	.01	
Ottawa Senators				
☐ 400 Jari Kurri	.10	.05	.01	
Los Angeles Kings				
☐ 401 Jim Paek	.05	.02	.01	
Pittsburgh Penguins				
☐ 402 Andrei Lomakin	.05	.02	.01	
Florida Panthers				
☐ 403 Scott Niedermayer	.05	.02	.01	
New Jersey Devils				
☐ 404 Bob Errey	.05	.02	.01	
San Jose Sharks				
☐ 405 Michal Pivonka	.05	.02	.01	
Washington Capitals				
☐ 406 Doug Lidster	.05	.02	.01	
New York Rangers				
☐ 407 Garry Valk	.05	.02	.01	
Anaheim Mighty Ducks				
☐ 408 Geoff Sanderson	.25	.11	.03	
Hartford Whalers				
☐ 409 Stewart Malgunas	.15	.07	.02	
Philadelphia Flyers				
☐ 410 Craig MacTavish	.05	.02	.01	
Edmonton Oilers				
☐ 411 Jaroslav Modry	.15	.07	.02	
New Jersey Devils				
☐ 412 Shawn Chambers	.05	.02	.01	
Tampa Bay Lightning				
☐ 413 Geoff Courtnall	.05	.02	.01	
Vancouver Canucks				
☐ 414 Mark Hardy	.05	.02	.01	
Los Angeles Kings				
☐ 415 Martin Straka	.40	.18	.05	
Pittsburgh Penguins				
☐ 416 Randy Burridge	.05	.02	.01	
Washington Capitals				
☐ 417 Kent Manderville	.05	.02	.01	
Toronto Maple Leafs				
☐ 418 Darren Rumble	.05	.02	.01	
Ottawa Senators				
☐ 419 Bill Houlder	.05	.02	.01	
Anaheim Mighty Ducks				
☐ 420 Chris Chelios	.08	.04	.01	
Chicago Blackhawks				
☐ 421 Jim Hrivnak	.05	.02	.01	
Winnipeg Jets				
☐ 422 Benoit Brunet	.05	.02	.01	
Montreal Canadiens				
☐ 423 Aaron Ward	.15	.07	.02	
Detroit Red Wings				
☐ 424 Alexei Gusarov	.05	.02	.01	
Quebec Nordiques				
☐ 425 Mats Sundin	.15	.07	.02	
Quebec Nordiques				
☐ 426 Kjell Samuelsson	.05	.02	.01	
Pittsburgh Penguins				
☐ 427 Mikael Andersson	.05	.02	.01	
Tampa Bay Lightning				
☐ 428 Ulf Dahlen	.05	.02	.01	

Dallas Stars
- [ ] 429 Nicklas Lidstrom .... .05 .02 .01
Detroit Red Wings
- [ ] 430 Tommy Soderstrom .... .15 .07 .02
Philadelphia Flyers
- [ ] 431 Darrin Madeley .... .20 .09 .03
Ottawa Senators
- [ ] 432 Kevin Dahl .... .05 .02 .01
Calgary Flames
- [ ] 433 Ron Hextall .... .08 .04 .01
New York Islanders
- [ ] 434 Patrick Carnback .... .15 .07 .02
Anaheim Mighty Ducks
- [ ] 435 Randy Moller .... .05 .02 .01
Buffalo Sabres
- [ ] 436 Dave Gagner .... .08 .04 .01
Dallas Stars
- [ ] 437 Corey Millen .... .05 .02 .01
New Jersey Devils
- [ ] 438 Olaf Kolzig .... .05 .02 .01
Washington Capitals
- [ ] 439 Gord Murphy .... .05 .02 .01
Florida Panthers
- [ ] 440 Cam Stewart .... .15 .07 .02
Boston Bruins
- [ ] 441 Darren McCarty .... .15 .07 .02
Detroit Red Wings
- [ ] 442 Frantisek Kucera .... .05 .02 .01
Chicago Blackhawks
- [ ] 443 Ted Drury .... .05 .02 .01
Calgary Flames
- [ ] 444 Troy Mallette .... .05 .02 .01
Anaheim Mighty Ducks
- [ ] 445 Robin Bawa .... .15 .07 .02
Anaheim Mighty Ducks
- [ ] 446 Steven Rice .... .05 .02 .01
Edmonton Oilers
- [ ] 447 Pat Elynuik .... .05 .02 .01
Tampa Bay Lightning
- [ ] 448 Jim Cummins .... .15 .07 .02
New York Rangers
- [ ] 449 Rob Niedermayer .... .60 .25 .08
Florida Panthers
- [ ] 450 Paul Coffey .... .15 .07 .02
Detroit Red Wings
- [ ] 451 Calle Johansson .... .05 .02 .01
Washington Capitals
- [ ] 452 Mike Needham .... .05 .02 .01
Pittsburgh Penguins
- [ ] 453 Glenn Healy .... .05 .02 .01
New York Islanders
- [ ] 454 Dixon Ward .... .05 .02 .01
Vancouver Canucks
- [ ] 455 Al Iafrate .... .05 .02 .01
Washington Capitals
- [ ] 456 Jon Casey .... .05 .02 .01
Boston Bruins
- [ ] 457 Kevin Stevens .... .15 .07 .02
Pittsburgh Penguins
- [ ] 458 Tony Amonte .... .08 .04 .01
New York Rangers
- [ ] 459 Chris Chelios .... .05 .02 .01
Chicago Blackhawks
- [ ] 460 Pat LaFontaine .... .15 .07 .02
Buffalo Sabres
- [ ] 461 Jamie Baker .... .05 .02 .01
San Jose Sharks
- [ ] 462 Andre Faust .... .05 .02 .01
Philadelphia Flyers
- [ ] 463 Bobby Dollas .... .05 .02 .01
Anaheim Mighty Ducks
- [ ] 464 Steven Finn .... .05 .02 .01
Quebec Nordiques
- [ ] 465 Scott Lachance .... .05 .02 .01
New York Islanders
- [ ] 466 Mike Hough .... .05 .02 .01
Florida Panthers
- [ ] 467 Bill Guerin .... .05 .02 .01
New Jersey Devils
- [ ] 468 Dimitri Filimonov .... .05 .02 .01
Ottawa Senators
- [ ] 469 Dave Ellett .... .05 .02 .01
Toronto Maple Leafs
- [ ] 470 Andy Moog .... .08 .04 .01
Dallas Stars
- [ ] 471 Scott Thomas .... .15 .07 .02
Buffalo Sabres
- [ ] 472 Trent Yawney .... .05 .02 .01
Calgary Flames
- [ ] 473 Tim Sweeney .... .05 .02 .01
Anaheim Mighty Ducks
- [ ] 474 Shjon Podein .... .15 .07 .02
Edmonton Oilers
- [ ] 475 J.J. Daigneault .... .05 .02 .01

Montreal Canadiens
- [ ] 476 Darren Turcotte .... .05 .02 .01
Hartford Whalers
- [ ] 477 Esa Tikkanen .... .08 .04 .01
New York Rangers
- [ ] 478 Vitali Karamnov .... .05 .02 .01
St. Louis Blues
- [ ] 479 Jocelyn Thibault .... .60 .25 .08
Quebec Nordiques
- [ ] 480 Pavel Bure .... 1.25 .55 .16
Vancouver Canucks
- [ ] 481 Steve Konowalchuk .... .05 .02 .01
Washington Capitals
- [ ] 482 Sylvain Turgeon .... .05 .02 .01
Ottawa Senators
- [ ] 483 Jeff Daniels .... .05 .02 .01
Pittsburgh Penguins
- [ ] 484 Dallas Drake .... .20 .09 .03
Detroit Red Wings
- [ ] 485 Iain Fraser .... .15 .07 .02
Quebec Nordiques
- [ ] 486 Joe Reekie .... .05 .02 .01
Tampa Bay Lightning
- [ ] 487 Evgeny Davydov .... .05 .02 .01
Florida Panthers
- [ ] 488 Jozef Stumpel .... .05 .02 .01
Boston Bruins
- [ ] 489 Brent Thompson .... .05 .02 .01
Los Angeles Kings
- [ ] 490 Terry Yake .... .05 .02 .01
Anaheim Mighty Ducks
- [ ] 491 Derek Plante .... .60 .25 .08
Buffalo Sabres
- [ ] 492 Dimitri Yushkevich .... .05 .02 .01
Philadelphia Flyers
- [ ] 493 Wayne McBean .... .05 .02 .01
New York Islanders
- [ ] 494 Derian Hatcher .... .05 .02 .01
Dallas Stars
- [ ] 495 Jeff Norton .... .05 .02 .01
San Jose Sharks
- [ ] 496 Adam Foote .... .05 .02 .01
Quebec Nordiques
- [ ] 497 Mike Peluso .... .05 .02 .01
New Jersey Devils
- [ ] 498 Rob Pearson .... .05 .02 .01
Toronto Maple Leafs
- [ ] 499 Checklist 251-375 .... .05 .02 .01
- [ ] 500 Checklist 376-500 .... .05 .02 .01

1993-94 Stadium Club
First Day Issue

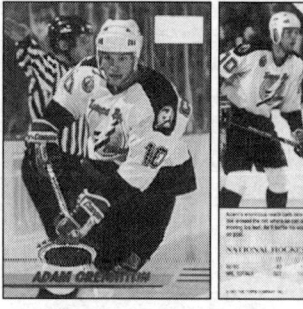

Randomly inserted into packs, this 500-card set measures the standard size (2 1/2" by 3 1/2") and is a parallel set to the regular issue set. The only difference is the holographic first day logo in the upper right. The cards are numbered on the back.

	MINT	EXC	G-VG
COMPLETE SET (500)	3000.00	1350.00	375.00
COMPLETE SERIES 1 (250)	1500.00	700.00	190.00
COMPLETE SERIES 2 (250)	1500.00	700.00	190.00
COMMON PLAYER (1-250)	5.00	2.30	.60

COMMON PLAYER (251-500).......... 5.00 2.30 .60
*UNLISTED STARS: 40X to 75X ......
*UNLISTED YOUNG STARS: 20X to 40X
*UNLISTED RCs: 10X to 25X...........

			MINT	EXC	G-VG
☐	10	Eric Lindros........................ Philadelphia Flyers	200.00	90.00	25.00
☐	20	Pat LaFontaine .... Buffalo Sabres	30.00	13.50	3.80
☐	45	Sergei Fedorov..................... Detroit Red Wings	70.00	32.00	8.75
☐	65	Brett Hull.............................. St. Louis Blues	50.00	23.00	6.25
☐	70	Steve Yzerman .... Detroit Red Wings	45.00	20.00	5.75
☐	91	Alexander Mogilny .... Buffalo Sabres	40.00	18.00	5.00
☐	98	Jaromir Jagr .... Pittsburgh Penguins	50.00	23.00	6.25
☐	99	Ed Belfour........................... Chicago Blackhawks	30.00	13.50	3.80
☐	130	Mike Modano .... Dallas Stars	25.00	11.50	3.10
☐	140	Doug Gilmour .... Toronto Maple Leafs	45.00	20.00	5.75
☐	141	Calder Trophy Winner .... Teemu Selanne Winnipeg Jets	35.00	16.00	4.40
☐	143	Hart Trophy Winner .... Mario Lemieux Pittsburgh Penguins	40.00	18.00	5.00
☐	146	Mario Lemieux.................... Pittsburgh Penguins Masterton Trophy Winner	40.00	18.00	5.00
☐	148	Mario Lemieux.................... Pittsburgh Penguins Art Ross Trophy Winner	40.00	18.00	5.00
☐	190	Jeremy Roenick .... Chicago Blackhawks	50.00	23.00	6.25
☐	200	Wayne Gretzky .... Los Angeles Kings	225.00	100.00	28.00
☐	202	Joe Juneau .... Boston Bruins	40.00	18.00	5.00
☐	210	Teemu Selanne .... Winnipeg Jets	70.00	32.00	8.75
☐	231	Patrick Roy .... Montreal Canadiens	100.00	45.00	12.50
☐	269	Mikael Renberg .... Philadelphia Flyers	50.00	23.00	6.25
☐	280	Felix Potvin .... Toronto Maple Leafs	80.00	36.00	10.00
☐	290	Chris Pronger..................... Hartford Whalers	40.00	18.00	5.00
☐	300	Alexandre Daigle .... Ottawa Senators	50.00	23.00	6.25
☐	310	Mario Lemieux .... Pittsburgh Penguins	140.00	65.00	17.50
☐	320	Chris Gratton .... Tampa Bay Lightning	40.00	18.00	5.00
☐	345	Jason Arnott .... Edmonton Oilers	80.00	36.00	10.00
☐	350	Chris Osgood .... Detroit Red Wings	30.00	13.50	3.80
☐	359	Alexei Yashin...................... Ottawa Senators	50.00	23.00	6.25
☐	380	Pierre Turgeon .... New York Islanders	30.00	13.50	3.80
☐	449	Rob Niedermayer .... Florida Panthers	40.00	18.00	5.00
☐	479	Jocelyn Thibault................. Quebec Nordiques	30.00	13.50	3.80
☐	480	Pavel Bure.......................... Vancouver Canucks	125.00	57.50	15.50
☐	491	Derek Plante....................... Buffalo Sabres	30.00	13.50	3.80

1993-94 Stadium Club All-Stars

Randomly inserted in first-series packs, each of these 23 standard-size (2 1/2" by 3 1/2") cards features two 1992-93 All-Stars, one from each conference. Both sides carry a posed color player photo superimposed over a stellar background. The player's name in gold foil appears on the bottom, while the words "NHL All-Star" are printed at the top. The cards are unnumbered and checklisted below in alphabetical order.

		MINT	EXC	G-VG
COMPLETE SET (23)......................		135.00	60.00	17.00
COMMON PAIR (1-23)...................		3.00	1.35	.40
☐ 1	Patrick Roy .... Montreal Canadiens Ed Belfour Chicago Blackhawks	20.00	9.00	2.50
☐ 2	Ray Bourque .... Boston Bruins Paul Coffey Detroit Red Wings	4.00	1.80	.50
☐ 3	Al Iafrate .... Washington Capitals Chris Chelios Chicago Blackhawks	3.00	1.35	.40
☐ 4	Jaromir Jagr .... Pittsburgh Penguins Brett Hull St. Louis Blues	12.00	5.50	1.50
☐ 5	Pat LaFontaine .... Buffalo Sabres Steve Yzerman Detroit Red Wings	10.00	4.50	1.25
☐ 6	Kevin Stevens .... Pittsburgh Penguins Pavel Bure Vancouver Canucks	15.00	6.75	1.90
☐ 7	Craig Billington .... Ottawa Senators Jon Casey Boston Bruins	3.00	1.35	.40
☐ 8	Steve Duchesne .... Quebec Nordiques Steve Chiasson Detroit Red Wings	3.00	1.35	.40
☐ 9	Scott Stevens...................... New Jersey Devils Phil Housley St. Louis Blues	3.00	1.35	.40
☐ 10	Peter Bondra....................... Washington Capitals Kelly Kisio Calgary Flames	3.00	1.35	.40
☐ 11	Adam Oates........................ Boston Bruins Brian Bradley Tampa Bay Lightning	4.00	1.80	.50
☐ 12	Alexander Mogilny .... Buffalo Sabres Jari Kurri Los Angeles Kings	7.00	3.10	.85
☐ 13	Peter Sidorkiewicz............... New Jersey Devils Mike Vernon Calgary Flames	3.00	1.35	.40
☐ 14	Zarley Zalapski .... Hartford Whalers Dave Manson Edmonton Oilers	3.00	1.35	.40
☐ 15	Brad Marsh .... Ottawa Senators Randy Carlyle Winnipeg Jets	3.00	1.35	.40
☐ 16	Kirk Muller .... Montreal Canadiens Gary Roberts Calgary Flames	3.00	1.35	.40
☐ 17	Joe Sakic .... Quebec Nordiques Doug Gilmour Toronto Maple Leafs	12.00	5.50	1.50

☐ 18	Mark Recchi	7.00	3.10	.85
	Philadelphia Flyers			
	Luc Robitaille			
	Los Angeles Kings			
☐ 19	Kevin Lowe	3.00	1.35	.40
	New York Rangers			
	Garth Butcher			
	St. Louis Blues			
☐ 20	Rick Tocchet	8.00	3.60	1.00
	Pittsburgh Penguins			
	Jeremy Roenick			
	Chicago Blackhawks			
☐ 21	Pierre Turgeon	10.00	4.50	1.25
	New York Islanders			
	Mike Modano			
	Dallas Stars			
☐ 22	Mike Gartner	10.00	4.50	1.25
	New York Rangers			
	Teemu Selanne			
	Winnipeg Jets			
☐ 23	Mario Lemieux	50.00	23.00	6.25
	Pittsburgh Penguins			
	Wayne Gretzky			
	Los Angeles Kings			

☐ NNO	Redemtion Single	1.00	.45	.13
☐ NNO	Redemption Set	4.00	1.80	.50

1993-94 Stadium Club Master Photos

Inserted one per U.S. box, and issued in two 12-card series, these 24 oversized cards measure 5" by 7". The fronts feature color player action shots framed by prismatic foil lines and set on a white card face. The player's name appears in prismatic-foil lettering atop a blue bar near the bottom of the photo. The white-bordered back carries the player's name in white lettering within the vertical red stripe in the middle. Career highlights are printed in the blue areas to the left and right. The cards are numbered on the back for both series as "X of 12," but are listed below as 1-24 to avoid confusion.

1993-94 Stadium Club Finest

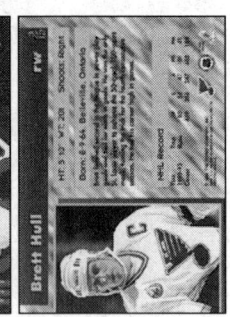

Randomly inserted in second-series packs, these 12 standard-size (2 1/2" by 3 1/2") cards feature color player action cutouts on their multicolored metallic fronts. The player's name in gold lettering appears on a silver bar at the lower left. The horizontal back carries a color player photo on the left. The player's name and position appear at the top, with biography, career highlights, and statistics following below on a background that resembles blue ruffled silk. The cards are numbered on the back as "X of 12."

	MINT	EXC	G-VG
COMPLETE SET (12)	70.00	32.00	8.75
COMMON PLAYER (1-12)	3.50	1.55	.45
☐ 1 Wayne Gretzky	18.00	8.00	2.30
Los Angeles Kings			
☐ 2 Jeff Brown	3.50	1.55	.45
St. Louis Blues			
☐ 3 Brett Hull	10.00	4.50	1.25
St. Louis Blues			
☐ 4 Paul Coffey	4.00	1.80	.50
Detroit Red Wings			
☐ 5 Felix Potvin	12.00	5.50	1.50
Toronto Maple Leafs			
☐ 6 Mike Gartner	4.00	1.80	.50
New York Rangers			
☐ 7 Luc Robitaille	5.00	2.30	.60
Los Angeles Kings			
☐ 8 Marty McSorley	3.50	1.55	.45
Pittsburgh Penguins			
☐ 9 Gary Roberts	4.00	1.80	.50
Calgary Flames			
☐ 10 Mario Lemieux	15.00	6.75	1.90
Pittsburgh Penguins			
☐ 11 Patrick Roy	12.00	5.50	1.50
Montreal Canadiens			
☐ 12 Ray Bourque	4.00	1.80	.50
Boston Bruins			

	MINT	EXC	G-VG
COMPLETE SET (24)	24.00	11.00	3.00
COMPLETE SERIES 1 (12)	15.00	6.75	1.90
COMPLETE SERIES 2 (12)	9.00	4.00	1.15
COMMON PLAYER (1-12)	1.00	.45	.13
COMMON PLAYER (13-24)	1.00	.45	.13
☐ 1 Pat LaFontaine	1.50	.65	.19
Buffalo Sabres			
☐ 2 Doug Gilmour	2.50	1.15	.30
Toronto Maple Leafs			
☐ 3 Ray Bourque	1.25	.55	.16
Boston Bruins			
☐ 4 Teemu Selanne	3.00	1.35	.40
Winnipeg Jets			
☐ 5 Eric Lindros	5.00	2.30	.60
Philadelphia Flyers			
☐ 6 Ray Ferraro	1.00	.45	.13
New York Rangers			
☐ 7 Patrick Roy	4.00	1.80	.50
Montreal Canadiens			
☐ 8 Wayne Gretzky	6.00	2.70	.75
Los Angeles Kings			
☐ 9 Brett Hull	3.00	1.35	.40
St. Louis Blues			
☐ 10 John Vanbiesbrouck	1.25	.55	.16
Florida Panthers			
☐ 11 Adam Oates	1.25	.55	.16
Boston Bruins			
☐ 12 Tom Barrasso	1.25	.55	.16
Pittsburgh Penguins			
☐ 13 Esa Tikkannen	1.25	.55	.16
New York Rangers			
☐ 14 Jari Kurri	1.25	.55	.16
Los Angeles Kings			
☐ 15 Grant Fuhr	1.25	.55	.16
Buffalo Sabres			
☐ 16 Scott Lachance	1.00	.45	.13
New York Islanders			
☐ 17 Theoren Fleury	1.25	.55	.16
Calgary Flames			
☐ 18 Adam Graves	1.50	.65	.19
New York Rangers			
☐ 19 Rick Tabaracci	1.00	.45	.13
Winnipeg Jets			
☐ 20 Pierre Turgeon	1.50	.65	.19
Buffalo Sabres			

		MINT	EXC	G-VG
☐ 21	Steven Finn .... Quebec Nordiques	1.00	.45	.13
☐ 22	Craig Janney .... St. Louis Blues	1.25	.55	.16
☐ 23	Mathieu Schneider .... Montreal Canadiens	1.00	.45	.13
☐ 24	Felix Potvin .... Toronto Maple Leafs	4.00	1.80	.50

1993-94 Stadium Club Team USA

Randomly inserted in second-series packs, these 23 standard-size (2 1/2" by 3 1/2") cards feature color player action shots on their borderless fronts. The player's name appears in gold-foil lettering over a blue stripe near the bottom. The gold foil USA Hockey logo appears in an upper corner. The horizontal back carries a color player photo on the left. The player's name, position, biography, career highlights, and statistics appear on a blue background on the right. The cards are numbered on the back as "X of 23."

		MINT	EXC	G-VG
COMPLETE SET (23)		35.00	16.00	4.40
COMMON PLAYER (1-23)		1.50	.65	.19
☐ 1	Mark Beaufait	1.50	.65	.19
☐ 2	Jim Campbell	2.00	.90	.25
☐ 3	Ted Crowley	1.50	.65	.19
☐ 4	Mike Dunham	2.00	.90	.25
☐ 5	Chris Ferraro	1.50	.65	.19
☐ 6	Peter Ferraro	2.50	1.15	.30
☐ 7	Brett Hauer	1.50	.65	.19
☐ 8	Darby Hendrickson	1.50	.65	.19
☐ 9	Jon Hillebrandt	1.50	.65	.19
☐ 10	Chris Imes	1.50	.65	.19
☐ 11	Craig Johnson	1.50	.65	.19
☐ 12	Peter Laviolette	1.50	.65	.19
☐ 13	John Lilley	2.00	.90	.25
☐ 14	Todd Marchant	1.50	.65	.19
☐ 15	Matt Martin	2.00	.90	.25
☐ 16	Ian Moran	1.50	.65	.19
☐ 17	Travis Richards	1.50	.65	.19
☐ 18	Barry Richter	2.00	.90	.25
☐ 19	David Roberts	2.00	.90	.25
☐ 20	Brian Rolston	2.00	.90	.25
☐ 21	David Sacco	3.00	1.35	.40
☐ 22	Jim Storm	2.00	.90	.25
☐ 23	Jeff Lazaro	2.00	.90	.25

1991 Star Pics Prospects

The premier edition of this 72-card set contains 57 of the top draft pick prospects, including 18 of the 22 first round picks. The standard-size (2 1/2" by 3 1/2") cards have glossy color action player photos, with a thin white border on a background picturing a hockey mask. The player's name appears in white lettering below the picture. The backs have

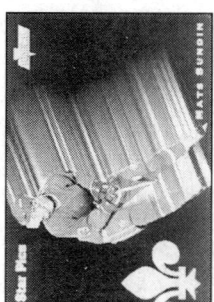
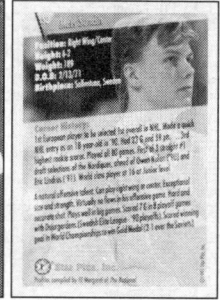

biography, personal background information, and a mini-scouting report by Al Morganti, superimposed on a partially washed out color player photo. The print run was supposedly limited to 225,000 individually numbered sets. Autographed cards were randomly inserted into the sets. The autographed cards are valued at 60 to 100 times the prices below for flashback cards and 20 to 40 times for the other cards. The set includes six flashback player cards (20, 30, 40, 50, 60, 70), and a Hall of Fame subset (4, 7, 10, 27, 52, 61) featuring sepia-toned photos and the recollections of former Detroit Red Wing Gary Bergman. The cards are numbered on the back.

		MINT	EXC	G-VG
COMPLETE SEALED SET (72)		9.00	3.75	.90
COMMON PLAYER (1-72)		.10	.04	.01
☐ 1	Draft Overview .... Al Morganti	.10	.04	.01
☐ 2	Pat Falloon	.75	.30	.07
☐ 3	Jamie Pushor	.10	.04	.01
☐ 4	Jean Beliveau FLB .... Hall of Fame	.25	.10	.02
☐ 5	Martin Lapointe	.20	.08	.02
☐ 6	Jamie Matthews	.10	.04	.01
☐ 7	Rod Gilbert FLB .... Hall of Fame	.25	.10	.02
☐ 8	Niklas Sundblad	.10	.04	.01
☐ 9	Steve Konowalchuk................	.15	.06	.01
☐ 10	Alex Delvecchio FLB.............. Hall of Fame	.15	.06	.01
☐ 11	Donevan Hextall	.10	.04	.01
☐ 12	Dody Wood	.10	.04	.01
☐ 13	Scott Niedermayer	.75	.30	.07
☐ 14	Trevor Halverson	.10	.04	.01
☐ 15	Terry Chitaroni	.10	.04	.01
☐ 16	Tyler Wright	.15	.06	.01
☐ 17	Andrei Lomakin UER	.20	.08	.02
☐ 18	Martin Hamrlik	.10	.04	.01
☐ 19	Dimitri Filimonov UER..........	.10	.04	.01
☐ 20	Ed Belfour FLB	.25	.10	.02
☐ 21	Andrew Verner	.15	.06	.01
☐ 22	Yanic Perreault	.20	.08	.02
☐ 23	Mikael Nylander	.25	.10	.02
☐ 24	Scott Lachance	.20	.08	.02
☐ 25	Pavel Bure	2.00	.80	.20
☐ 26	Mike Torchia	.10	.04	.01
☐ 27	Frank Mahovlich FLB............ Hall of Fame	.15	.06	.01
☐ 28	Philippe Boucher..................	.15	.06	.01
☐ 29	Jiri Slegr	.15	.06	.01
☐ 30	Sergei Fedorov FLB..............	.75	.30	.07
☐ 31	Rene Corbet	.15	.06	.01
☐ 32	Jamie McLennan	.20	.08	.02
☐ 33	Shane Peacock	.10	.04	.01
☐ 34	Mario Nobili	.10	.04	.01
☐ 35	Peter Forsberg	1.00	.40	.10
☐ 36	All-Rookie Team.................... Pat Falloon Tyler Wright Pat Poulin Philippe Boucher Andrew Verner Scott Lachance	.15	.06	.01
☐ 37	Arturs Irbe..........................	1.50	.60	.15
☐ 38	Alexei Zhitnik.....................	.25	.10	.02
☐ 39	Pat Peake	.40	.16	.04
☐ 40	Adam Oates FLB..................	.25	.10	.02
☐ 41	Markus Naslund...................	.20	.08	.02

☐ 42	Eric Lavigne	.10	.04	.01
☐ 43	Jeff Nelson	.15	.06	.01
☐ 44	Yanic Dupre UER	.10	.04	.01
☐ 45	Justin Morrison	.10	.04	.01
☐ 46	Alek Stojanov	.10	.04	.01
☐ 47	Marcel Cousineau	.10	.04	.01
☐ 48	Alexei Kovalev UER	1.00	.40	.10
☐ 49	Andrei Trefilov	.50	.20	.05
☐ 50	Mats Sundin FLB	.25	.10	.02
☐ 51	Steve Staios	.15	.06	.01
☐ 52	Glenn Hall FLB	.25	.10	.02
	Hall of Fame			
☐ 53	Brent Bilodeau	.10	.04	.01
☐ 54	Darcy Werenka	.10	.04	.01
☐ 55	Chris Osgood	.35	.14	.03
☐ 56	Nathan Lafayette	.25	.10	.02
☐ 57	Richard Matvichuk	.15	.06	.01
☐ 58	Dimitri Mironov UER	.15	.06	.01
☐ 59	Jason Dawe	.15	.06	.01
☐ 60	Mike Ricci FLB	.25	.10	.02
☐ 61	Gerry Cheevers FLB	.25	.10	.02
	Hall of Fame			
☐ 62	Jim Campbell	.15	.06	.01
☐ 63	Francois Groleau	.10	.04	.01
☐ 64	Glen Murray	.30	.12	.03
☐ 65	Jason Young	.10	.04	.01
☐ 66	Dean McAmmond	.15	.06	.01
☐ 67	Guy Leveque	.15	.06	.01
☐ 68	Patrick Poulin	.25	.10	.02
☐ 69	Bobby House	.10	.04	.01
☐ 70	Jaromir Jagr FLB	.75	.30	.07
☐ 71	Jassen Cullimore	.10	.04	.01
☐ 72	Checklist Card	.10	.04	.01

☐ 15	Russ Blinco MM	40.00	16.00	4.00
☐ 16	Herb Cain MM	50.00	20.00	5.00
☐ 17	Lionel Conacher MM	125.00	50.00	12.50
☐ 18	Alex Connell MM	100.00	40.00	10.00
☐ 19	Stewart Evans MM	40.00	16.00	4.00
☐ 20	Norman Gainor MM	40.00	16.00	4.00
☐ 21	Paul Haynes MM	40.00	16.00	4.00
☐ 22	Gus Marker MM	40.00	16.00	4.00
☐ 23	Baldy Northcott MM	40.00	16.00	4.00
☐ 24	Earl Robinson MM	40.00	16.00	4.00
☐ 25	Hooley Smith MM	80.00	32.00	8.00
☐ 26	Dave Trottier MM	40.00	16.00	4.00
☐ 27	Jimmy Ward MM	40.00	16.00	4.00
☐ 28	Marvin(Cy) Wentworth	40.00	16.00	4.00
	MM			
☐ 29	Eddie Shore BB	400.00	160.00	40.00
☐ 30	Babe Siebert BB	100.00	40.00	10.00
☐ 31	Nels Stewart BB	125.00	50.00	12.50
☐ 32	Cecil(Tiny) Thompson BB	100.00	40.00	10.00
☐ 33	Lorne Chabot CBH	50.00	20.00	5.00
☐ 34	Harold March CBH	40.00	16.00	4.00
☐ 35	Howie Morenz CBH	500.00	200.00	50.00
☐ 36	Larry Aurie DRW	40.00	16.00	4.00
☐ 37	Ebbie Goodfellow DRW	80.00	32.00	8.00
☐ 38	Herbie Lewis DRW	40.00	16.00	4.00
☐ 39	Ralph Weiland DRW	80.00	32.00	8.00
☐ 40	Bill Cook NYR	80.00	32.00	8.00
☐ 41	Fred Cook NYR	40.00	16.00	4.00
☐ 42	Ivan(Ching) Johnson NYR	100.00	40.00	10.00
☐ 43	Dave Kerr NYR	40.00	16.00	4.00
☐ 44	Frank(King) Clancy TML	400.00	160.00	40.00
☐ 45	Chuck Conacher TML	300.00	120.00	30.00
☐ 46	Red Horner TML	100.00	40.00	10.00
☐ 47	Harvey(Busher) Jackson	125.00	50.00	12.50
	TML			
☐ 48	Joe Primeau TML	100.00	40.00	10.00

1934-35 Sweet Caporal

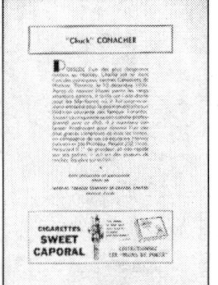

This colorful set of 48 large (approximately 6 3/4" by 10 1/2") pictures were actually inserts in Montreal Forum programs during Canadiens and Maroons home games during the 1934-35 season. Apparently a different photo was inserted each game. Players in the checklist below are identified as part of the following teams, Montreal Canadiens (MC), Montreal Maroons (MM), Boston Bruins (BB), Chicago Blackhawks (CBH), Detroit Red Wings (DRW), New York Rangers (NYR), and Toronto Maple Leafs (TML). The photos are blank backed and unnumbered.

	EX-MT	VG-E	GOOD
COMPLETE SET (48)	4000.00	1600.00	400.00
COMMON PLAYER (1-48)	40.00	16.00	4.00

☐ 1	Gerald Carson MC	40.00	16.00	4.00
☐ 2	Nels Crutchfield MC	40.00	16.00	4.00
☐ 3	Wilfrid Cude MC	40.00	16.00	4.00
☐ 4	Roger Jenkins MC	40.00	16.00	4.00
☐ 5	Aurel Joliat MC	250.00	100.00	25.00
☐ 6	Joe Lamb MC	40.00	16.00	4.00
☐ 7	Wildor Larochelle MC	40.00	16.00	4.00
☐ 8	Pete Lepine MC	40.00	16.00	4.00
☐ 9	Georges Mantha MC	40.00	16.00	4.00
☐ 10	Sylvio Mantha MC	80.00	32.00	8.00
☐ 11	Jack McGill MC	40.00	16.00	4.00
☐ 12	Armand Mondou MC	40.00	16.00	4.00
☐ 13	Paul Marcel Raymond MC	40.00	16.00	4.00
☐ 14	Jack Riley MC	40.00	16.00	4.00

1981-82 TCMA

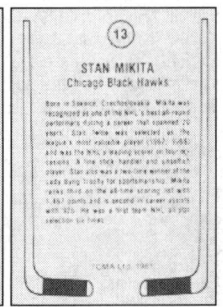

This 13-card set measures the standard size, 2 1/2" by 3 1/2". The front features a color posed photo, with a thin black border on white card stock. The cards are numbered on the back and have biographical information as well as career highlights between two hockey sticks drawn on the sides of the card backs. Supposedly there were only 3000 sets produced. The set features 11 Hockey Hall of Famers out the 13 players selected for the set.

	MINT	EXC	G-VG
COMPLETE SET (13)	50.00	20.00	5.00
COMMON PLAYER (1-13)	1.00	.40	.10

☐ 1	Norm Ullman	3.00	1.20	.30
	Detroit Red Wings			
☐ 2	Gump Worsley	5.00	2.00	.50
	New York Rangers			
☐ 3	J.C. Tremblay	1.25	.50	.12
	Montreal Canadiens			
☐ 4	Lou Fontinato	1.00	.40	.10
	New York Rangers			
☐ 5	Johnny Bucyk	3.00	1.20	.30
	Boston Bruins			
☐ 6	Harry Howell	2.00	.80	.20
	New York Rangers			
☐ 7	Henri Richard	4.00	1.60	.40
	Montreal Canadiens			

			MINT	EXC	G-VG
☐ 8	Andy Bathgate	3.00	1.20	.30
	New York Rangers			
☐ 9	Bobby Orr	25.00	10.00	2.50
	Boston Bruins			
☐ 10	Frank Mahovlich	6.00	2.40	.60
	Toronto Maple Leafs			
☐ 11	Jean Beliveau	8.00	3.25	.80
	Montreal Canadiens			
☐ 12	Jacques Plante	7.00	2.80	.70
	Montreal Canadiens			
☐ 13	Stan Mikita	7.00	2.80	.70
	Chicago Blackhawks			

1974 Team Canada L'Equipe WHA

This 24-photo set measures approximately 4 1/8" by 7 1/2" and features posed, glossy, black-and-white player photos on thin stock. The pictures are attached to red posterboard. The player's name and two Team Canada L'Equipe logos appear in the white margin at the bottom. The backs are blank. The cards are unnumbered and checklisted below in alphabetical order.

		NRMT	VG-E	GOOD
	COMPLETE SET (24)	40.00	16.00	4.00
	COMMON PLAYER (1-24)	1.25	.50	.12
☐ 1	Ralph Backstrom	1.50	.60	.15
☐ 2	Serge Bernier	1.25	.50	.12
☐ 3	Gerry Cheevers	6.00	2.40	.60
☐ 4	Al Hamilton	1.25	.50	.12
☐ 5	Billy Harris CO	1.25	.50	.12
☐ 6	Jim Harrison	1.25	.50	.12
☐ 7	Ben Hatzkin	1.25	.50	.12
☐ 8	Paul Henderson	2.00	.80	.20
☐ 9	Rejean Houle	1.25	.50	.12
☐ 10	Mark Howe	4.00	1.60	.40
☐ 11	Marty Howe	1.50	.60	.15
☐ 12	Bill Hunter	1.25	.50	.12
☐ 13	Gordon W. Jukes	1.25	.50	.12
☐ 14	Rick Ley	1.50	.60	.15
☐ 15	Frank Mahovlich	7.50	3.00	.75
☐ 16	John McKenzie	1.50	.60	.15
☐ 17	Don McLeod	1.25	.50	.12
☐ 18	Rick Noonan	1.25	.50	.12
☐ 19	Brad Selwood	1.25	.50	.12
☐ 20	Rick Smith	1.25	.50	.12
☐ 21	Pat Stapleton	1.50	.60	.15
☐ 22	Marc Tardif	1.50	.60	.15
☐ 23	Mike Walton	1.50	.60	.15
☐ 24	Tom Webster	2.00	.80	.20

1993 Titrex Guy Lafleur Insert

This standard-size (2 1/2" by 3 1/2") card was inserted in Canadian packages of Power Bar, made by Titrex International, a firm specializing in dietary products. Also included in the package was an order form in French for

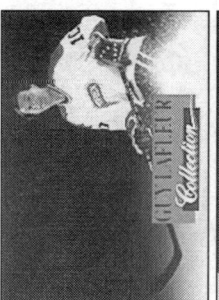

ordering the 24-card Guy Lafleur Collection set. The card features on its front and back a horizontal borderless shot of Guy Lafleur on ice wearing a Titrex jersey, with the Guy Lafleur Collection logo appearing at the bottom. The front has a glossy finish, and Lafleur's name is highlighted in gold foil. The unglossy back carries the Titrex logo at the upper left, and also has the years Lafleur played for each hockey team within a gray stripe down the left edge. The card is unnumbered.

		MINT	EXC	G-VG
	COMPLETE SET (1)	3.00	1.20	.30
	COMMON CARD	3.00	1.20	.30
☐ 1	Guy Lafleur	3.00	1.20	.30
	(Wearing Titrex jersey)			

1994 Titrex Guy Lafleur

This 24-card standard size (2 1/2" by 3 1/2") set presents the progression of Guy Lafleur's career from the beginning until the 1979 Stanley Cup win. The cards were printed on heavier card stock and came with a card storage album measuring approximately 6 1/4" by 8" and a certificate of authenticity. The borderless fronts feature both horizontal and vertical black-and-white photos. The Guy Lafleur Collection emblem appears inside a red rectangle at the bottom. On a white background with a fading red stripe to the left, the backs carry horizontal and vertical black-and-white photos with the date and a brief photo description (in French and English) below. The cards are unnumbered and checklisted below in chronological order. The set could be obtained by mailing in the order form (plus 24.95 Canadian) that accompanied the 1993 Titrex Guy Lafleur Power Bar Insert in packages of Titrex's Power Bar.

		MINT	EXC	G-VG
	COMPLETE SET (24)	25.00	10.00	2.50
	COMMON LAFLEUR (1-24)	1.50	.60	.15

☐ 1 Guy Lafleur 1956, Thurso	2.00	.80	.20
☐ 2 Guy Lafleur 1961-1962, Thurso	1.50	.60	.15
☐ 3 Guy Lafleur 1961-1962 (Mosquito's Team Trophy)	1.50	.60	.15
☐ 4 Guy Lafleur 1962 (Guy Wins The Red Story Trophy)	1.50	.60	.15
☐ 5 Guy Lafleur 1962, Hawkesbury	1.50	.60	.15
☐ 6 Guy Lafleur 1962 (First Participation In Quebec Pee-Wee International Hockey Tournament)	1.50	.60	.15
☐ 7 Guy Lafleur 1963-1964	1.50	.60	.15
☐ 8 Guy Lafleur 1964-1965	1.50	.60	.15
☐ 9 Guy Lafleur 1966-1967	1.50	.60	.15
☐ 10 Guy Lafleur 1967-1968	1.50	.60	.15
☐ 11 Guy Lafleur 1970 (His 75th Goal)	1.50	.60	.15
☐ 12 Guy Lafleur 1970 (After 76th Goal)	1.50	.60	.15
☐ 13 Guy Lafleur 1970-1971 (Holding Paul Lebel Trophy)	1.50	.60	.15
☐ 14 Guy Lafleur 1970-1971 (Last Season With Quebec Remparts)	1.50	.60	.15
☐ 15 Guy Lafleur 1970-1971, Quebec Winning The Memorial Cup)	1.50	.60	.15
☐ 16 Guy Lafleur Rejean Giroux Andre Savard 1970-1971	1.50	.60	.15
☐ 17 Guy Lafleur Rejean Lafleur, 1970-1971	1.50	.60	.15
☐ 18 Guy Lafleur Rejean Lafleur, 1971	1.50	.60	.15
☐ 19 Guy Lafleur 1971 (His Last Year With Quebec Remparts)	1.50	.60	.15
☐ 20 Guy Lafleur 1971 (Carrying The Memorial Cup)	1.50	.60	.15
☐ 21 Guy Lafleur Lieutenant Governor Roland Mitchener, 1971	1.50	.60	.15
☐ 22 Guy Lafleur 1971 (Leaving The Quebec Remparts)	1.50	.60	.15
☐ 23 Guy Lafleur 1971 (Holding The Memorial Cup)	1.50	.60	.15
☐ 24 Guy Lafleur 1979	2.00	.80	.20

1954-55 Topps

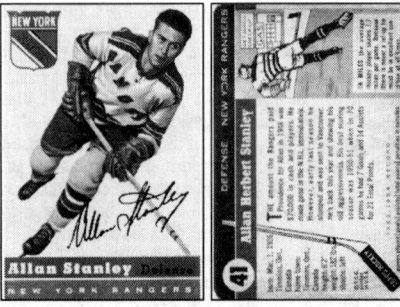

Topps introduced its first hockey set in 1954-55. The issue includes 60 cards of players on the four American (Boston,

Chicago, Detroit and New York) teams. Cards measure approximately 2 5/8" by 3 3/4". Color fronts feature the player on a white background with facsimile autograph and team logo. The player's name, team name and position appear in bottom borders that are in team colors. The backs, printed in red and blue, contain player biographies, 1953-54 statistics and a hockey fact section. The cards were printed in the USA. Rookie Cards include Camille Henry and Doug Mohns. An early and very popular card of Gordie Howe is the main attraction in this set.

	NRMT	VG-E	GOOD
COMPLETE SET (60)	4500.00	2000.00	575.00
COMMON PLAYER (1-60)	35.00	16.00	4.40
☐ 1 Dick Gamble	100.00	25.00	8.00
☐ 2 Bob Chrystal	35.00	16.00	4.40
☐ 3 Harry Howell	100.00	45.00	12.50
☐ 4 Johnny Wilson	35.00	16.00	4.40
☐ 5 Red Kelly	125.00	57.50	15.50
☐ 6 Real Chevrefils	35.00	16.00	4.40
☐ 7 Bob Armstrong	35.00	16.00	4.40
☐ 8 Gordie Howe	2200.00	1000.00	275.00
☐ 9 Benny Woit	35.00	16.00	4.40
☐ 10 Gump Worsley	200.00	90.00	25.00
☐ 11 Andy Bathgate	100.00	45.00	12.50
☐ 12 Bucky Hollingworth	35.00	16.00	4.40
☐ 13 Ray Timgren	35.00	16.00	4.40
☐ 14 Jack Evans	35.00	16.00	4.40
☐ 15 Paul Ronty	35.00	16.00	4.40
☐ 16 Glen Skov	35.00	16.00	4.40
☐ 17 Gus Mortson	35.00	16.00	4.40
☐ 18 Doug Mohns	60.00	27.00	7.50
☐ 19 Leo Labine	38.00	17.00	4.70
☐ 20 Bill Gadsby	60.00	27.00	7.50
☐ 21 Jerry Toppazzini	38.00	17.00	4.70
☐ 22 Wally Hergesheimer	35.00	16.00	4.40
☐ 23 Danny Lewicki	35.00	16.00	4.40
☐ 24 Metro Prystai	35.00	16.00	4.40
☐ 25 Fern Flaman	50.00	23.00	6.25
☐ 26 Al Rollins	55.00	25.00	7.00
☐ 27 Marcel Pronovost	55.00	25.00	7.00
☐ 28 Lou Jankowski	35.00	16.00	4.40
☐ 29 Nick Mickoski	35.00	16.00	4.40
☐ 30 Frank Martin	35.00	16.00	4.40
☐ 31 Lorne Ferguson	35.00	16.00	4.40
☐ 32 Camille Henry	50.00	23.00	6.25
☐ 33 Pete Conacher	38.00	17.00	4.70
☐ 34 Marty Pavelich	35.00	16.00	4.40
☐ 35 Don McKenney	40.00	18.00	5.00
☐ 36 Fleming Mackell	35.00	16.00	4.40
☐ 37 Jim Henry	55.00	25.00	7.00
☐ 38 Hal Laycoe	35.00	16.00	4.40
☐ 39 Alex Delvecchio	125.00	57.50	15.50
☐ 40 Larry Wilson	35.00	16.00	4.40
☐ 41 Allan Stanley	75.00	34.00	9.50
☐ 42 George Sullivan	35.00	16.00	4.40
☐ 43 Jack McIntyre	35.00	16.00	4.40
☐ 44 Ivan Irwin	35.00	16.00	4.40
☐ 45 Tony Leswick	35.00	16.00	4.40
☐ 46 Bob Goldham	35.00	16.00	4.40
☐ 47 Cal Gardner	38.00	17.00	4.70
☐ 48 Ed Sandford	35.00	16.00	4.40
☐ 49 Bill Quackenbush	55.00	25.00	7.00
☐ 50 Warren Godfrey	35.00	16.00	4.40
☐ 51 Ted Lindsay	130.00	57.50	16.50
☐ 52 Earl Reibel	38.00	17.00	4.70
☐ 53 Don Raleigh	35.00	16.00	4.40
☐ 54 Bill Mosienko	60.00	27.00	7.50
☐ 55 Larry Popein	35.00	16.00	4.40
☐ 56 Edgar Laprade	40.00	18.00	5.00
☐ 57 Bill Dineen	30.00	17.00	4.70
☐ 58 Terry Sawchuk	600.00	275.00	75.00
☐ 59 Marcel Bonin	35.00	16.00	4.40
☐ 60 Milt Schmidt	175.00	52.50	17.50

1957-58 Topps

After a two year hiatus, Topps returned to producing hockey cards for 1957-58. Reportedly, Topps spent the interim evaluating the hockey card market. This set is comprised of 66 color cards of players from the four U.S. based teams. Cards in the set were reduced to measure the standard

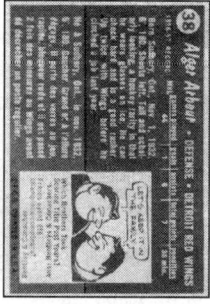

AL ARBOUR-defense
DETROIT RED WINGS

2 1/2" by 3 1/2". Bilingual backs feature 1956-57 statistics, a short player biography and a cartoon question and answer section. Rookie Cards in this include Johnny Bucyk, Glenn Hall, Pierre Pilote, and Norm Ullman.

	NRMT	VG-E	GOOD
COMPLETE SET (66)	2000.00	900.00	250.00
COMMON PLAYER (1-66)	16.00	7.25	2.00

☐ 1 Real Chevrefils	30.00	7.25	2.00
☐ 2 Jack Bionda	16.00	7.25	2.00
☐ 3 Bob Armstrong	16.00	7.25	2.00
☐ 4 Fern Flaman	20.00	9.00	2.50
☐ 5 Jerry Toppazzini	16.00	7.25	2.00
☐ 6 Larry Regan	16.00	7.25	2.00
☐ 7 Bronco Horvath	20.00	9.00	2.50
☐ 8 Jack Caffery	16.00	7.25	2.00
☐ 9 Leo Labine	16.00	7.25	2.00
☐ 10 Johnny Bucyk	175.00	80.00	22.00
☐ 11 Vic Stasiuk	16.00	7.25	2.00
☐ 12 Doug Mohns	20.00	9.00	2.50
☐ 13 Don McKenney	16.00	7.25	2.00
☐ 14 Don Simmons	20.00	9.00	2.50
☐ 15 Allan Stanley	30.00	13.50	3.80
☐ 16 Fleming Mackell	16.00	7.25	2.00
☐ 17 Larry Hillman	18.00	8.00	2.30
☐ 18 Leo Boivin	18.00	8.00	2.30
☐ 19 Bob Bailey	16.00	7.25	2.00
☐ 20 Glenn Hall	275.00	125.00	34.00
☐ 21 Ted Lindsay	45.00	20.00	5.75
☐ 22 Pierre Pilote	125.00	57.50	15.50
☐ 23 Jim Thomson	16.00	7.25	2.00
☐ 24 Eric Nesterenko	18.00	8.00	2.30
☐ 25 Gus Mortson	16.00	7.25	2.00
☐ 26 Ed Litzenberger	20.00	9.00	2.50
☐ 27 Elmer Vasko	25.00	11.50	3.10
☐ 28 Jack McIntyre	16.00	7.25	2.00
☐ 29 Ron Murphy	16.00	7.25	2.00
☐ 30 Glen Skov	16.00	7.25	2.00
☐ 31 Hec Lalonde	16.00	7.25	2.00
☐ 32 Nick Mickoski	16.00	7.25	2.00
☐ 33 Wally Hergesheimer	16.00	7.25	2.00
☐ 34 Alex Delvecchio	40.00	18.00	5.00
☐ 35 Terry Sawchuk UER	175.00	80.00	22.00
(Misspelled Sawchuck			
on card front)			
☐ 36 Guyle Fielder	18.00	8.00	2.30
☐ 37 Tom McCarthy	16.00	7.25	2.00
☐ 38 Al Arbour	35.00	16.00	4.40
☐ 39 Billy Dea	16.00	7.25	2.00
☐ 40 Lorne Ferguson	16.00	7.25	2.00
☐ 41 Warren Godfrey	16.00	7.25	2.00
☐ 42 Gordie Howe	600.00	275.00	75.00
☐ 43 Marcel Pronovost	20.00	9.00	2.50
☐ 44 Bill McNeil	16.00	7.25	2.00
☐ 45 Earl Reibel	18.00	8.00	2.30
☐ 46 Norm Ullman	175.00	80.00	22.00
☐ 47 Johnny Wilson	16.00	7.25	2.00
☐ 48 Red Kelly	40.00	18.00	5.00
☐ 49 Bill Dineen	18.00	8.00	2.30
☐ 50 Forbes Kennedy	25.00	11.50	3.10
☐ 51 Harry Howell	35.00	16.00	4.40
☐ 52 Jean-Guy Gendron	18.00	8.00	2.30
☐ 53 Gump Worsley	100.00	45.00	12.50
☐ 54 Larry Popein	16.00	7.25	2.00
☐ 55 Jack Evans	16.00	7.25	2.00
☐ 56 George Sullivan	16.00	7.25	2.00
☐ 57 Gerry Foley	16.00	7.25	2.00
☐ 58 Andy Hebenton	20.00	9.00	2.50
☐ 59 Larry Cahan	16.00	7.25	2.00
☐ 60 Andy Bathgate	35.00	16.00	4.40
☐ 61 Danny Lewicki	16.00	7.25	2.00
☐ 62 Dean Prentice	18.00	8.00	2.30
☐ 63 Camille Henry	20.00	9.00	2.50
☐ 64 Lou Fontinato	25.00	11.50	3.10
☐ 65 Bill Gadsby	25.00	11.50	3.10
☐ 66 Dave Creighton	30.00	7.25	2.00

1958-59 Topps

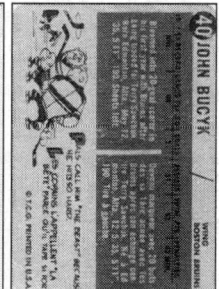

The 1958-59 Topps set contains 66 color cards of players from the four U.S. based teams. Cards measure 2 1/2" by 3 1/2". Bilingual backs feature 1957-58 statistics, player biographies and a cartoon information section on the player. The set features the Rookie Card of Bobby Hull. Due to being the last card and subject to wear as well as being chronically off-center, the Hull card is quite scarce in top grades. Other Rookie Cards include Eddie Shack and Ken Wharram.

	NRMT	VG-E	GOOD
COMPLETE SET (66)	4200.00	1900.00	525.00
COMMON PLAYER (1-66)	15.00	6.75	1.90

☐ 1 Bob Armstrong	30.00	9.00	3.00
☐ 2 Terry Sawchuk	150.00	70.00	19.00
☐ 3 Glen Skov	15.00	6.75	1.90
☐ 4 Leo Labine	15.00	6.75	1.90
☐ 5 Dollard St.Laurent	15.00	6.75	1.90
☐ 6 Danny Lewicki	15.00	6.75	1.90
☐ 7 John Hanna	15.00	6.75	1.90
☐ 8 Gordie Howe UER	500.00	230.00	65.00
(Misspelled Gordy			
on card front)			
☐ 9 Vic Stasiuk	15.00	6.75	1.90
☐ 10 Larry Regan	15.00	6.75	1.90
☐ 11 Forbes Kennedy	15.00	6.75	1.90
☐ 12 Elmer Vasko	16.00	7.25	2.00
☐ 13 Glenn Hall	135.00	60.00	17.00
☐ 14 Ken Wharram	20.00	9.00	2.50
☐ 15 Len Lunde	15.00	6.75	1.90
☐ 16 Ed Litzenberger	16.00	7.25	2.00
☐ 17 Norm Johnson	15.00	6.75	1.90
☐ 18 Earl Ingarfield	15.00	6.75	1.90
☐ 19 Les Colwill	15.00	6.75	1.90
☐ 20 Leo Boivin	16.00	7.25	2.00
☐ 21 Andy Bathgate	30.00	13.50	3.80
☐ 22 Johnny Wilson	15.00	6.75	1.90
☐ 23 Larry Cahan	15.00	6.75	1.90
☐ 24 Marcel Pronovost	18.00	8.00	2.30
☐ 25 Larry Hillman	16.00	7.25	2.00
☐ 26 Jim Bartlett	15.00	6.75	1.90
☐ 27 Nick Mickoski	15.00	6.75	1.90
☐ 28 Larry Popein	15.00	6.75	1.90
☐ 29 Fleming Mackell	15.00	6.75	1.90
☐ 30 Eddie Shack	120.00	55.00	15.00
☐ 31 Jack Evans	15.00	6.75	1.90
☐ 32 Dean Prentice	16.00	7.25	2.00
☐ 33 Claude LaForge	15.00	6.75	1.90
☐ 34 Bill Gadsby	20.00	9.00	2.50
☐ 35 Bronco Horvath	16.00	7.25	2.00
☐ 36 Pierre Pilote	55.00	25.00	7.00
☐ 37 Earl Balfour	15.00	6.75	1.90
☐ 38 Gus Mortson	15.00	6.75	1.90
☐ 39 Gump Worsley	60.00	27.00	7.50
☐ 40 Johnny Bucyk	90.00	40.00	11.50
☐ 41 Lou Fontinato	16.00	7.25	2.00

☐ 42	Tod Sloan	15.00	6.75	1.90
☐ 43	Charlie Burns	15.00	6.75	1.90
☐ 44	Don Simmons	16.00	7.25	2.00
☐ 45	Jerry Toppazzini	15.00	6.75	1.90
☐ 46	Andy Hebenton	16.00	7.25	2.00
☐ 47	Pete Goegan UER	15.00	6.75	1.90
	(Misspelled Geogan on card front)			
☐ 48	George Sullivan	15.00	6.75	1.90
☐ 49	Hank Ciesla	15.00	6.75	1.90
☐ 50	Doug Mohns	16.00	7.25	2.00
☐ 51	Jean-Guy Gendron	15.00	6.75	1.90
☐ 52	Alex Delvecchio	30.00	13.50	3.80
☐ 53	Eric Nesterenko	16.00	7.25	2.00
☐ 54	Camille Henry	15.00	6.75	1.90
☐ 55	Lorne Ferguson	15.00	6.75	1.90
☐ 56	Fern Flaman	18.00	8.00	2.30
☐ 57	Earl Reibel	16.00	7.25	2.00
☐ 58	Warren Godfrey	15.00	6.75	1.90
☐ 59	Ron Murphy	15.00	6.75	1.90
☐ 60	Harry Howell	30.00	13.50	3.80
☐ 61	Red Kelly	30.00	13.50	3.80
☐ 62	Don McKenney	15.00	6.75	1.90
☐ 63	Ted Lindsay	35.00	16.00	4.40
☐ 64	Al Arbour	25.00	11.50	3.10
☐ 65	Norm Ullman	90.00	40.00	11.50
☐ 66	Bobby Hull	3000.00	750.00	240.00

1959-60 Topps

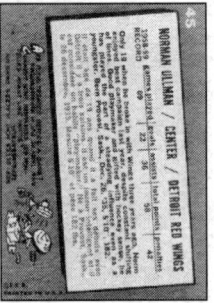

Norm Ullman center

The 1959-60 Topps set contains 66 color cards of players from the four U.S. based teams. Cards measure 2 1/2" by 3 1/2". The fronts have the player's name and position at the bottom with team name and logo at the top. Bilingual backs feature 1958-59 statistics, a short biography and a cartoon question section.

		NRMT	VG-E	GOOD
COMPLETE SET (66)		2000.00	900.00	250.00
COMMON PLAYER (1-66)		14.00	6.25	1.75
☐ 1	Eric Nesterenko	25.00	7.50	2.50
☐ 2	Pierre Pilote	40.00	18.00	5.00
☐ 3	Elmer Vasko	15.00	6.75	1.90
☐ 4	Peter Goegan	14.00	6.25	1.75
☐ 5	Lou Fontinato	14.00	6.25	1.75
☐ 6	Ted Lindsay	28.00	12.50	3.50
☐ 7	Leo Labine	14.00	6.25	1.75
☐ 8	Alex Delvecchio	28.00	12.50	3.50
☐ 9	Don McKenney UER	14.00	6.25	1.75
	(Misspelled McKenny on card front)			
☐ 10	Earl Ingarfield	14.00	6.25	1.75
☐ 11	Don Simmons	15.00	6.75	1.90
☐ 12	Glen Skov	14.00	6.25	1.75
☐ 13	Tod Sloan	14.00	6.25	1.75
☐ 14	Vic Stasiuk	14.00	6.25	1.75
☐ 15	Gump Worsley	45.00	20.00	5.75
☐ 16	Andy Hebenton	15.00	6.75	1.90
☐ 17	Dean Prentice	15.00	6.75	1.90
☐ 18	Action picture	15.00	6.75	1.90
☐ 19	Fleming Mackell	14.00	6.25	1.75
☐ 20	Harry Howell	25.00	11.50	3.10
☐ 21	Larry Popein	14.00	6.25	1.75
☐ 22	Len Lunde	14.00	6.25	1.75
☐ 23	Johnny Bucyk	50.00	23.00	6.25

☐ 24	Jean-Guy Gendron	14.00	6.25	1.75
☐ 25	Barry Cullen	14.00	6.25	1.75
☐ 26	Leo Boivin	15.00	6.75	1.90
☐ 27	Warren Godfrey	14.00	6.25	1.75
☐ 28	Action Picture	30.00	13.50	3.80
	(Glenn Hall and Camille Henry)			
☐ 29	Fern Flaman	16.00	7.25	2.00
☐ 30	Jack Evans	14.00	6.25	1.75
☐ 31	John Hanna	14.00	6.25	1.75
☐ 32	Glenn Hall	80.00	36.00	10.00
☐ 33	Murray Balfour	15.00	6.75	1.90
☐ 34	Andy Bathgate	25.00	11.50	3.10
☐ 35	Al Arbour	20.00	9.00	2.50
☐ 36	Jim Morrison	14.00	6.25	1.75
☐ 37	Nick Mickoski	14.00	6.25	1.75
☐ 38	Jerry Toppazzini	14.00	6.25	1.75
☐ 39	Bob Armstrong	14.00	6.25	1.75
☐ 40	Charlie Burns UER	14.00	6.25	1.75
	(Misspelled Charley on card front)			
☐ 41	Bill McNeil	14.00	6.25	1.75
☐ 42	Terry Sawchuk	125.00	57.50	15.50
☐ 43	Dollard St.Laurent	14.00	6.25	1.75
☐ 44	Marcel Pronovost	16.00	7.25	2.00
☐ 45	Norm Ullman	50.00	23.00	6.25
☐ 46	Camille Henry	15.00	6.75	1.90
☐ 47	Bobby Hull	600.00	275.00	75.00
☐ 48	Action Picture	90.00	40.00	11.50
	(Gordie Howe and Jack Evans)			
☐ 49	Lou Marcon	14.00	6.25	1.75
☐ 50	Earl Balfour	14.00	6.25	1.75
☐ 51	Jim Bartlett	14.00	6.25	1.75
☐ 52	Forbes Kennedy	14.00	6.25	1.75
☐ 53	Action Picture	15.00	6.75	1.90
	(Nick Mickoski and Johnny Hanna)			
☐ 54	Action Picture	25.00	11.50	3.10
	(Norm Johnson, Gump Worsley, and Harry Howell)			
☐ 55	Brian Cullen	14.00	6.25	1.75
☐ 56	Bronco Horvath	15.00	6.75	1.90
☐ 57	Eddie Shack	60.00	27.00	7.50
☐ 58	Doug Mohns	15.00	6.75	1.90
☐ 59	George Sullivan	14.00	6.25	1.75
☐ 60	Action Picture	15.00	6.75	1.90
	(Pierre Pilote and Flem Mackell)			
☐ 61	Ed Litzenberger	14.00	6.25	1.75
☐ 62	Bill Gadsby	18.00	8.00	2.30
☐ 63	Gordie Howe	450.00	200.00	57.50
☐ 64	Claude LaForge	14.00	6.25	1.75
☐ 65	Red Kelly	28.00	12.50	3.50
☐ 66	Ron Murphy	25.00	7.50	2.50

1960-61 Topps

Charlie Burns

The 1960-61 Topps set contains 66 color cards featuring players from Boston, Chicago and New York. Cards measure the standard 2 1/2" by 3 1/2". In addition to player and team names, the typical card front features color patterns according to the player's team. The backs are bilingual and have 1959-60 statistics and a cartoon trivia quiz. Cards titled "All-Time Greats" are an attractive feature to this set and include the likes of Georges Vezina and Eddie Shore. The All-Time Great players are indicated by ATG in the checklist below. Stan Mikita's Rookie Card is part of this set.

	NRMT	VG-E	GOOD
COMPLETE SET (66)	2000.00	900.00	250.00
COMMON PLAYER (1-66)	13.00	5.75	1.65
☐ 1 Lester Patrick ATG	50.00	12.50	4.00
☐ 2 Paddy Moran ATG	20.00	9.00	2.50
☐ 3 Joe Malone ATG	28.00	12.50	3.50
☐ 4 Ernest(Moose) Johnson ATG	15.00	6.75	1.90
☐ 5 Nels Stewart ATG	20.00	9.00	2.50
☐ 6 Bill(Red) Hay	15.00	6.75	1.90
☐ 7 Eddie Shack	40.00	18.00	5.00
☐ 8 Cy Denneny ATG	15.00	6.75	1.90
☐ 9 Jim Morrison	13.00	5.75	1.65
☐ 10 Bill Cook ATG	16.00	7.25	2.00
☐ 11 Johnny Bucyk	40.00	18.00	5.00
☐ 12 Murray Balfour	13.00	5.75	1.65
☐ 13 Leo Labine	13.00	5.75	1.65
☐ 14 Stan Mikita	450.00	200.00	57.50
☐ 15 George Hay ATG	15.00	6.75	1.90
☐ 16 Mervyn(Red) Dutton ATG	15.00	6.75	1.90
☐ 17 Dickie Boon ATG UER	15.00	6.75	1.90
(Misspelled Boone on card front)			
☐ 18 George Sullivan	13.00	5.75	1.65
☐ 19 Georges Vezina ATG	50.00	23.00	6.25
☐ 20 Eddie Shore ATG	50.00	23.00	6.25
☐ 21 Ed Litzenberger	13.00	5.75	1.65
☐ 22 Bill Gadsby	15.00	6.75	1.90
☐ 23 Elmer Vasko	13.00	5.75	1.65
☐ 24 Charlie Burns	13.00	5.75	1.65
☐ 25 Glenn Hall	65.00	29.00	8.25
☐ 26 Dit Clapper ATG	20.00	9.00	2.50
☐ 27 Art Ross ATG	35.00	16.00	4.40
☐ 28 Jerry Toppazzini	13.00	5.75	1.65
☐ 29 Frank Boucher ATG	16.00	7.25	2.00
☐ 30 Jack Evans	13.00	5.75	1.65
☐ 31 Jean-Guy Gendron	13.00	5.75	1.65
☐ 32 Chuck Gardiner ATG	20.00	9.00	2.50
☐ 33 Ab McDonald	13.00	5.75	1.65
☐ 34 Frank Frederickson ATG UER	16.00	7.25	2.00
(Misspelled Fredrickson on front)			
☐ 35 Frank Nighbor ATG	20.00	9.00	2.50
☐ 36 Gump Worsley	40.00	18.00	5.00
☐ 37 Dean Prentice	14.00	6.25	1.75
☐ 38 Hugh Lehman ATG	16.00	7.25	2.00
☐ 39 Jack McCartan	14.00	6.25	1.75
☐ 40 Don McKenney UER	13.00	5.75	1.65
(Misspelled McKenny on card front)			
☐ 41 Ron Murphy	13.00	5.75	1.65
☐ 42 Andy Hebenton	13.00	5.75	1.65
☐ 43 Don Simmons	14.00	6.25	1.75
☐ 44 Herb Gardiner ATG	15.00	6.75	1.90
☐ 45 Andy Bathgate	20.00	9.00	2.50
☐ 46 Cyclone Taylor ATG	25.00	11.50	3.10
☐ 47 King Clancy ATG	40.00	18.00	5.00
☐ 48 Newsy Lalonde ATG	25.00	11.50	3.10
☐ 49 Harry Howell	20.00	9.00	2.50
☐ 50 Ken Schinkel	13.00	5.75	1.65
☐ 51 Tod Sloan	13.00	5.75	1.65
☐ 52 Doug Mohns	14.00	6.25	1.75
☐ 53 Camille Henry	14.00	6.25	1.75
☐ 54 Bronco Horvath	13.00	5.75	1.65
☐ 55 Tiny Thompson ATG	25.00	11.50	3.10
☐ 56 Bob Armstrong	13.00	5.75	1.65
☐ 57 Bob Flaman	13.00	5.75	1.65
☐ 58 Bobby Hull	400.00	180.00	50.00
☐ 59 Howie Morenz ATG	50.00	23.00	6.25
☐ 60 Dick Irvin ATG	25.00	11.50	3.10
☐ 61 Lou Fontinato	13.00	5.75	1.65
☐ 62 Leo Boivin	14.00	6.25	1.75
☐ 63 Moose Goheen ATG	15.00	6.75	1.90
☐ 64 Al Arbour	18.00	8.00	2.30
☐ 65 Pierre Pilote	27.00	12.00	3.40
☐ 66 Vic Stasiuk	25.00	7.50	2.50

1960-61 Topps Stamps

There are 52 stamps in this scarce set. They were issued as pairs as an insert in with the 1960-61 Topps Hockey regular issue cards. The players in the set are either members of the Boston Bruins (BB), Chicago Blackhawks (CBH), New York

Rangers (NYR), or All-Time Greats (ATG). The stamps are unnumbered, so they are listed below alphabetically. Stan Mikita's stamp is notable in that it appears in Stan's Rookie Card year. Intact pairs of stamps with tabs are more difficult to find and would be valued 50 percent higher than the sum of the two players.

	NRMT	VG-E	GOOD
COMPLETE SET (52)	1350.00	550.00	135.00
COMMON PLAYER (1-52)	15.00	6.00	1.50
☐ 1 Murray Balfour CBH	15.00	6.00	1.50
☐ 2 Andy Bathgate NYR	30.00	12.00	3.00
☐ 3 Leo Boivin BB	25.00	10.00	2.50
☐ 4 Dickie Boon ATG	18.00	7.25	1.80
☐ 5 Frank Boucher ATG	18.00	7.25	1.80
☐ 6 Johnny Bucyk BB	35.00	14.00	3.50
☐ 7 Charlie Burns BB	15.00	6.00	1.50
☐ 8 King Clancy ATG	50.00	20.00	5.00
☐ 9 Dit Clapper ATG	25.00	10.00	2.50
☐ 10 Sprague Cleghorn ATG	18.00	7.25	1.80
☐ 11 Alex Connell ATG	18.00	7.25	1.80
☐ 12 Bill Cook ATG	18.00	7.25	1.80
☐ 13 Cy Denneny ATG	18.00	7.25	1.80
☐ 14 Jack Evans CBH	15.00	6.00	1.50
☐ 15 Frank Frederickson ATG	15.00	6.00	1.50
☐ 16 Chuck Gardiner ATG	18.00	7.25	1.80
☐ 17 Herb Gardiner ATG	15.00	6.00	1.50
☐ 18 Eddie Gerard ATG	15.00	6.00	1.50
☐ 19 Moose Goheen ATG	15.00	6.00	1.50
☐ 20 Glenn Hall CBH	50.00	20.00	5.00
☐ 21 Doug Harvey NYR	35.00	14.00	3.50
☐ 22 Bill(Red) Hay CBH	15.00	6.00	1.50
☐ 23 George Hay ATG	18.00	7.25	1.80
☐ 24 Andy Hebenton NYR	15.00	6.00	1.50
☐ 25 Camille Henry NYR	15.00	6.00	1.50
☐ 26 Bronco Horvath CBH	15.00	6.00	1.50
☐ 27 Harry Howell NYR	25.00	10.00	2.50
☐ 28 Bobby Hull CBH	125.00	50.00	12.50
☐ 29 Dick Irvin ATG	15.00	6.00	1.50
☐ 30 Ernest(Moose) Johnson ATG	18.00	7.25	1.80
☐ 31 Newsy Lalonde ATG	30.00	12.00	3.00
☐ 32 Albert Langlois NYR	15.00	6.00	1.50
☐ 33 Hugh Lehman ATG	15.00	6.00	1.50
☐ 34 Joe Malone ATG	25.00	10.00	2.50
☐ 35 Don McKenney BB	15.00	6.00	1.50
☐ 36 Stan Mikita CBH	100.00	40.00	10.00
☐ 37 Doug Mohns BB	18.00	7.25	1.80
☐ 38 Paddy Moran ATG	25.00	10.00	2.50
☐ 39 Howie Morenz ATG	75.00	30.00	7.50
☐ 40 Ron Murphy CBH	15.00	6.00	1.50
☐ 41 Frank Nighbor ATG	18.00	7.25	1.80
☐ 42 Murray Oliver BB	15.00	6.00	1.50
☐ 43 Pierre Pilote CBH	30.00	12.00	3.00
☐ 44 Dean Prentice NYR	18.00	7.25	1.80
☐ 45 Andre Pronovost BB	15.00	6.00	1.50
☐ 46 Art Ross ATG	30.00	12.00	3.00
☐ 47 Dallas Smith BB	18.00	7.25	1.80
☐ 48 Nels Stewart ATG	35.00	14.00	3.50
☐ 49 Cyclone Taylor ATG	30.00	12.00	3.00
☐ 50 Elmer Vasko CBH	15.00	6.00	1.50
☐ 51 Georges Vezina ATG	75.00	30.00	7.50
☐ 52 Gump Worsley NYR	40.00	16.00	4.00

1961-62 Topps

The 1961-62 Topps set contains 66 color cards featuring players from Boston, Chicago and New York. The card numbering in this set is basically by team order, e.g., Boston Bruins (1-22), Chicago Blackhawks (23-44), and

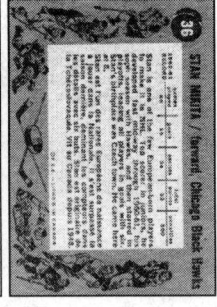

New York Rangers (45-65). Cards in the set measure 2 1/2" by 3 1/2". Bilingual backs contain 1960-61 statistics and a brief career highlights. For the first time, Topps cards were printed in Canada. Rookie Cards include Rod Gilbert and Jean Ratelle. The set marks the debut of team and checklist cards within Topps hockey card sets.

	NRMT	VG-E	GOOD
COMPLETE SET (66)	1600.00	700.00	200.00
COMMON PLAYER (1-66)	12.00	5.50	1.50
☐ 1 Phil Watson CO	25.00	7.50	2.50
☐ 2 Ted Green	35.00	16.00	4.40
☐ 3 Earl Balfour	12.00	5.50	1.50
☐ 4 Dallas Smith	25.00	11.50	3.10
☐ 5 Andre Pronovost UER	12.00	5.50	1.50
(Misspelled Provonost on card back)			
☐ 6 Dick Meissner	12.00	5.50	1.50
☐ 7 Leo Boivin	13.00	5.75	1.65
☐ 8 Johnny Bucyk	35.00	16.00	4.40
☐ 9 Jerry Toppazzini	12.00	5.50	1.50
☐ 10 Doug Mohns	13.00	5.75	1.65
☐ 11 Charlie Burns	12.00	5.50	1.50
☐ 12 Don McKenney	12.00	5.50	1.50
☐ 13 Bob Armstrong	12.00	5.50	1.50
☐ 14 Murray Oliver	12.00	5.50	1.50
☐ 15 Orland Kurtenbach	18.00	8.00	2.30
☐ 16 Terry Gray	12.00	5.50	1.50
☐ 17 Don Head	14.00	6.25	1.75
☐ 18 Pat Stapleton	25.00	11.50	3.10
☐ 19 Cliff Pennington	12.00	5.50	1.50
☐ 20 Team Picture	30.00	13.50	3.80
Boston Bruins			
☐ 21 Action Picture	13.00	5.75	1.65
(Earl Balfour and Fern Flaman)			
☐ 22 Action Picture	25.00	11.50	3.10
(Andy Bathgate and Glenn Hall)			
☐ 23 Rudy Pilous CO	15.00	6.75	1.90
☐ 24 Pierre Pilote	20.00	9.00	2.50
☐ 25 Elmer Vasko	12.00	5.50	1.50
☐ 26 Reg Fleming	15.00	6.75	1.90
☐ 27 Ab McDonald	12.00	5.50	1.50
☐ 28 Eric Nesterenko	13.00	5.75	1.65
☐ 29 Bobby Hull	350.00	160.00	45.00
☐ 30 Ken Wharram	13.00	5.75	1.65
☐ 31 Dollard St.Laurent	12.00	5.50	1.50
☐ 32 Glenn Hall	50.00	23.00	6.25
☐ 33 Murray Balfour	12.00	5.50	1.50
☐ 34 Ron Murphy	12.00	5.50	1.50
☐ 35 Bill(Red) Hay	12.00	5.50	1.50
☐ 36 Stan Mikita	175.00	80.00	22.00
☐ 37 Denis DeJordy	25.00	11.50	3.10
☐ 38 Wayne Hillman	13.00	5.75	1.65
☐ 39 Rino Robazzo	12.00	5.50	1.50
☐ 40 Bronco Horvath	12.00	5.50	1.50
☐ 41 Bob Turner	12.00	5.50	1.50
☐ 42 Blackhawks Team	30.00	13.50	3.80
☐ 43 Action Picture	13.00	5.75	1.65
(Ken Wharram)			
☐ 44 Action Picture	20.00	9.00	2.50
(Dollard St.Laurent helps Glenn Hall)			
☐ 45 Doug Harvey CO	25.00	11.50	3.10
☐ 46 Junior Langlois	12.00	5.50	1.50
☐ 47 Irv Spencer	12.00	5.50	1.50
☐ 48 George Sullivan	12.00	5.50	1.50
☐ 49 Earl Ingarfield	12.00	5.50	1.50
☐ 50 Gump Worsley	35.00	16.00	4.40

☐ 51 Harry Howell	18.00	8.00	2.30
☐ 52 Larry Cahan	12.00	5.50	1.50
☐ 53 Andy Bathgate	18.00	8.00	2.30
☐ 54 Dean Prentice	13.00	5.75	1.65
☐ 55 Andy Hebenton	12.00	5.50	1.50
☐ 56 Camille Henry	13.00	5.75	1.65
☐ 57 Jean-Guy Gendron	12.00	5.50	1.50
☐ 58 Pat Hannigan	12.00	5.50	1.50
☐ 59 Ted Hampson	12.00	5.50	1.50
☐ 60 Jean Ratelle	135.00	60.00	17.00
☐ 61 Al Lebrun	12.00	5.50	1.50
☐ 62 Rod Gilbert	135.00	60.00	17.00
☐ 63 Team Picture	30.00	13.50	3.80
New York Rangers			
☐ 64 Action Picture	20.00	9.00	2.50
(Dick Meissner and Gump Worsley)			
☐ 65 Action Picture	20.00	9.00	2.50
(Gump Worsley)			
☐ 66 Checklist Card	250.00	50.00	15.00

1962-63 Topps

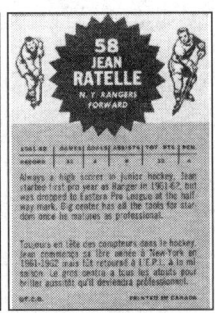

The 1962-63 Topps set contains 66 color cards featuring players from Boston, Chicago, and New York. The card numbering in this set is by team order, e.g., Boston Bruins (1-22), Chicago Blackhawks (23-44), and New York Rangers (45-65). Included within the numbering sequence are team cards. Cards measure 2 1/2" by 3 1/2". Bilingual backs feature 1961-62 statistics and career highlights. The cards were printed in Canada. Rookie Cards include Vic Hadfield and Chico Maki.

	NRMT	VG-E	GOOD
COMPLETE SET (66)	1300.00	575.00	160.00
COMMON PLAYER (1-66)	12.00	5.50	1.50
☐ 1 Phil Watson CO	20.00	6.00	2.00
☐ 2 Bob Perreault	13.00	5.75	1.65
☐ 3 Bruce Gamble	13.00	5.75	1.65
☐ 4 Warren Godfrey	12.00	5.50	1.50
☐ 5 Leo Boivin	13.00	5.75	1.65
☐ 6 Doug Mohns	13.00	5.75	1.65
☐ 7 Ted Green	15.00	6.75	1.90
☐ 8 Pat Stapleton	14.00	6.25	1.75
☐ 9 Dallas Smith	14.00	6.25	1.75
☐ 10 Don McKenney	12.00	5.50	1.50
☐ 11 Johnny Bucyk	30.00	13.50	3.80
☐ 12 Murray Oliver	12.00	5.50	1.50
☐ 13 Jerry Toppazzini	12.00	5.50	1.50
☐ 14 Cliff Pennington	12.00	5.50	1.50
☐ 15 Charlie Burns	12.00	5.50	1.50
☐ 16 Jean-Guy Gendron	12.00	5.50	1.50
☐ 17 Irv Spencer	12.00	5.50	1.50
☐ 18 Wayne Connelly	12.00	5.50	1.50
☐ 19 Andre Pronovost	12.00	5.50	1.50
☐ 20 Terry Gray	12.00	5.50	1.50
☐ 21 Tom Williams	15.00	6.75	1.90
☐ 22 Bruins Team	30.00	13.50	3.80
☐ 23 Rudy Pilous CO	13.00	5.75	1.65
☐ 24 Glenn Hall	45.00	20.00	5.75
☐ 25 Denis DeJordy	14.00	6.25	1.75
☐ 26 Jack Evans	12.00	5.50	1.50
☐ 27 Elmer Vasko	12.00	5.50	1.50
☐ 28 Pierre Pilote	18.00	8.00	2.30

☐	29 Bob Turner	12.00	5.50	1.50
☐	30 Dollard St.Laurent	12.00	5.50	1.50
☐	31 Wayne Hillman	13.00	5.75	1.65
☐	32 Al McNeil	12.00	5.50	1.50
☐	33 Bobby Hull	300.00	135.00	38.00
☐	34 Stan Mikita	125.00	57.50	15.50
☐	35 Bill(Red) Hay	12.00	5.50	1.50
☐	36 Murray Balfour	12.00	5.50	1.50
☐	37 Chico Maki	20.00	9.00	2.50
☐	38 Ab McDonald	12.00	5.50	1.50
☐	39 Ken Wharram	13.00	5.75	1.65
☐	40 Ron Murphy	12.00	5.50	1.50
☐	41 Eric Nesterenko	13.00	5.75	1.65
☐	42 Reg Fleming	13.00	5.75	1.65
☐	43 Murray Hall	12.00	5.50	1.50
☐	44 Blackhawks Team	30.00	13.50	3.80
☐	45 Gump Worsley	30.00	13.50	3.80
☐	46 Harry Howell	15.00	6.75	1.90
☐	47 Albert Langlois	12.00	5.50	1.50
☐	48 Larry Cahan	12.00	5.50	1.50
☐	49 Jim Neilson	15.00	6.75	1.90
☐	50 Al Lebrun	12.00	5.50	1.50
☐	51 Earl Ingarfield	12.00	5.50	1.50
☐	52 Andy Bathgate	15.00	6.75	1.90
☐	53 Dean Prentice	13.00	5.75	1.65
☐	54 Andy Hebenton	12.00	5.50	1.50
☐	55 Ted Hampson	12.00	5.50	1.50
☐	56 Dave Balon	12.00	5.50	1.50
☐	57 Bert Olmstead	13.00	5.75	1.65
☐	58 Jean Ratelle	45.00	20.00	5.75
☐	59 Rod Gilbert	45.00	20.00	5.75
☐	60 Vic Hadfield	35.00	16.00	4.40
☐	61 Frank Paice	12.00	5.50	1.50
☐	62 Camille Henry	13.00	5.75	1.65
☐	63 Bronco Horvath	12.00	5.50	1.50
☐	64 Pat Hannigan	12.00	5.50	1.50
☐	65 Rangers Team	30.00	13.50	3.80
☐	66 Checklist Card	250.00	50.00	15.00

1962-63 Topps Hockey Bucks

There are 12 double printed bucks in this 24-card set marked DP in the checklist below. The "bucks" are actually printed on thin paper stock. They were distributed as an inserted folded in one buck per wax pack. Since these bucks are unnumbered, they are ordered below in alphabetical order by player's name. The bucks are approximately 4 1/16" by 1 11/16"; there is no information on the backs, just a green-patterned design.

		NRMT	VG-E	GOOD
	COMPLETE SET (24)	750.00	300.00	75.00
	COMMON PLAYER (1-24)	20.00	8.00	2.00
	COMMON PLAYER DP	16.00	6.50	1.60
☐	1 Dave Balon DP	16.00	6.50	1.60
☐	2 Andy Bathgate	50.00	20.00	5.00
☐	3 Leo Boivin	40.00	16.00	4.00
☐	4 Johnny Bucyk DP	40.00	16.00	4.00
☐	5 Reg Fleming DP	16.00	6.50	1.60
☐	6 Warren Godfrey DP	16.00	6.50	1.60
☐	7 Ted Green	25.00	10.00	2.50
☐	8 Glenn Hall DP	50.00	20.00	5.00
☐	9 Bill(Red) Hay	20.00	8.00	2.00
☐	10 Andy Hebenton DP	16.00	6.50	1.60
☐	11 Harry Howell DP	25.00	10.00	2.50
☐	12 Bobby Hull	150.00	60.00	15.00
☐	13 Earl Ingarfield	20.00	8.00	2.00
☐	14 Albert Langlois	20.00	8.00	2.00
☐	15 Ab MacDonald DP	16.00	6.50	1.60
☐	16 Don McKenney	20.00	8.00	2.00
☐	17 Stan Mikita	75.00	30.00	7.50
☐	18 Doug Mohns	25.00	10.00	2.50
☐	19 Murray Oliver DP	16.00	6.50	1.60
☐	20 Pierre Pilote	40.00	16.00	4.00

☐	21 Dean Prentice	25.00	10.00	2.50
☐	22 Jerry Toppazzini DP	16.00	6.50	1.60
☐	23 Elmer Vasko DP	16.00	6.50	1.60
☐	24 Gump Worsley DP	50.00	20.00	5.00

1963-64 Topps

 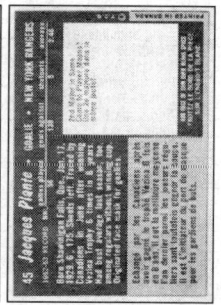

The 1963-64 Topps set contains 66 color cards featuring players and team cards from Boston, Chicago, and New York. Cards in the set measure 2 1/2" by 3 1/2". Bilingual backs contain 1962-63 statistics and a short player biography. A question section, the answer for which could be obtained by rubbing the edge of a coin over a blank space under the question, also appears on the card backs. The cards were printed in Canada. The notable Rookie Cards in this set are Ed Johnston, Gilles Villemure, and Ed Westfall. Jacques Plante makes his first appearance in a Topps set.

		NRMT	VG-E	GOOD
	COMPLETE SET (66)	1000.00	450.00	125.00
	COMMON PLAYER (1-66)	9.00	4.00	1.15
☐	1 Milt Schmidt CO	20.00	5.00	1.60
☐	2 Ed Johnston	30.00	13.50	3.80
☐	3 Doug Mohns	10.00	4.50	1.25
☐	4 Tom Johnson	10.00	4.50	1.25
☐	5 Leo Boivin	9.00	4.00	1.15
☐	6 Bob McCord	9.00	4.00	1.15
☐	7 Ted Green	10.00	4.50	1.25
☐	8 Ed Westfall	25.00	11.50	3.10
☐	9 Charlie Burns	9.00	4.00	1.15
☐	10 Murray Oliver	10.00	4.50	1.25
☐	11 Johnny Bucyk	25.00	11.50	3.10
☐	12 Tom Williams	10.00	4.50	1.25
☐	13 Dean Prentice	10.00	4.50	1.25
☐	14 Bob Leiter	9.00	4.00	1.15
☐	15 Andy Hebenton	9.00	4.00	1.15
☐	16 Jean-Guy Gendron	9.00	4.00	1.15
☐	17 Wayne Rivers	9.00	4.00	1.15
☐	18 Jerry Toppazzini	9.00	4.00	1.15
☐	19 Forbes Kennedy	9.00	4.00	1.15
☐	20 Orland Kurtenbach	10.00	4.50	1.25
☐	21 Bruins Team	30.00	13.50	3.80
☐	22 Billy Reay CO	10.00	4.50	1.25
☐	23 Glenn Hall	35.00	16.00	4.40
☐	24 Denis DeJordy	10.00	4.50	1.25
☐	25 Pierre Pilote	15.00	6.75	1.90
☐	26 Elmer Vasko	9.00	4.00	1.15
☐	27 Wayne Hillman	10.00	4.50	1.25
☐	28 Al McNeil	9.00	4.00	1.15
☐	29 Howie Young	9.00	4.00	1.15
☐	30 Ed Van Impe	10.00	4.50	1.25
☐	31 Reg Fleming	11.00	4.90	1.40
	(Gordie Howe			
	also shown)			
☐	32 Bob Turner	9.00	4.00	1.15
☐	33 Bobby Hull	225.00	100.00	28.00
☐	34 Bill(Red) Hay	9.00	4.00	1.15
☐	35 Murray Balfour	9.00	4.00	1.15
☐	36 Stan Mikita	90.00	40.00	11.50
☐	37 Ab McDonald	9.00	4.00	1.15
☐	38 Ken Wharram	10.00	4.50	1.25
☐	39 Eric Nesterenko	10.00	4.50	1.25

		NRMT	VG-E	GOOD
☐ 40	Ron Murphy	9.00	4.00	1.15
☐ 41	Chico Maki	9.00	4.00	1.15
☐ 42	John McKenzie	11.00	4.90	1.40
☐ 43	Blackhawks Team	30.00	13.50	3.80
☐ 44	George Sullivan	9.00	4.00	1.15
☐ 45	Jacques Plante	100.00	45.00	12.50
☐ 46	Gilles Villemure	25.00	11.50	3.10
☐ 47	Doug Harvey	20.00	9.00	2.50
☐ 48	Harry Howell	12.00	5.50	1.50
☐ 49	Albert Langlois	9.00	4.00	1.15
☐ 50	Jim Neilson	10.00	4.50	1.25
☐ 51	Larry Cahan	9.00	4.00	1.15
☐ 52	Andy Bathgate	12.00	5.50	1.50
☐ 53	Don McKenney	9.00	4.00	1.15
☐ 54	Vic Hadfield	12.00	5.50	1.50
☐ 55	Earl Ingarfield	9.00	4.00	1.15
☐ 56	Camille Henry	9.00	4.00	1.15
☐ 57	Rod Gilbert	30.00	13.50	3.80
☐ 58	Phil Goyette	11.00	4.90	1.40
	(Gordie Howe also shown in background)			
☐ 59	Don Marshall	9.00	4.00	1.15
☐ 60	Dick Meissner	9.00	4.00	1.15
☐ 61	Val Fonteyne	9.00	4.00	1.15
☐ 62	Ken Schinkel	9.00	4.00	1.15
☐ 63	Jean Ratelle	30.00	13.50	3.80
☐ 64	Don Johns	9.00	4.00	1.15
☐ 65	Rangers Team	30.00	13.50	3.80
☐ 66	Checklist Card	200.00	40.00	10.00

1964-65 Topps

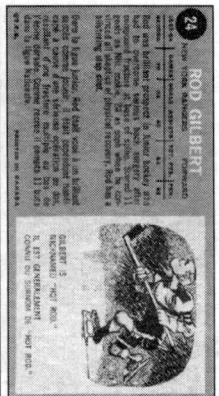

ROD GILBERT forward

The 1964-65 Topps hockey set features 110 color cards of players from all six NHL teams. The size of the card is larger than in previous years at 2 1/2" by 4 11/16". Colorful fronts contain a solid player background with team name at the top and player name and position at the bottom. Bilingual backs have 1963-64 statistics, a brief player bio and a cartoon section featuring a fact about the player. The cards were printed in Canada. Eleven of the numbers in the last series (56-110) appear to have been short printed. They are designated SP below. Rookie Cards include single prints of Gary Dornhoefer and Marcel Paille found in the last series. Other Rookie cards include Roger Crozier, Jim Pappin, Pit Martin, Rod Seiling and Lou Angotti.

	NRMT	VG-E	GOOD
COMPLETE SET (110)	6500.00	2900.00	800.00
COMMON PLAYER (1-55)	18.00	8.00	2.30
COMMON PLAYER (56-110)	45.00	20.00	5.75

☐ 1	Pit Martin	60.00	18.00	6.00
☐ 2	Gilles Tremblay	20.00	9.00	2.50
☐ 3	Terry Harper	20.00	9.00	2.50
☐ 4	John Ferguson	35.00	16.00	4.40
☐ 5	Elmer Vasko	18.00	8.00	2.30
☐ 6	Terry Sawchuk UER	100.00	45.00	12.50

	(Misspelled Sawchuck on card back)			
☐ 7	Bill(Red) Hay	18.00	8.00	2.30
☐ 8	Gary Bergman	25.00	11.50	3.10
☐ 9	Doug Barkley	18.00	8.00	2.30
☐ 10	Bob McCord	18.00	8.00	2.30
☐ 11	Parker MacDonald	18.00	8.00	2.30
☐ 12	Glenn Hall	50.00	23.00	6.25
☐ 13	Albert Langlois	18.00	8.00	2.30
☐ 14	Camille Henry	18.00	8.00	2.30
☐ 15	Norm Ullman	25.00	11.50	3.10
☐ 16	Ab McDonald	18.00	8.00	2.30
☐ 17	Charlie Hodge	20.00	9.00	2.50
☐ 18	Orland Kurtenbach	18.00	8.00	2.30
☐ 19	Dean Prentice	20.00	9.00	2.50
☐ 20	Bobby Hull	300.00	135.00	38.00
☐ 21	Ed Johnston	22.00	10.00	2.80
☐ 22	Denis DeJordy	20.00	9.00	2.50
☐ 23	Claude Provost	18.00	8.00	2.30
☐ 24	Rod Gilbert	40.00	18.00	5.00
☐ 25	Doug Mohns	20.00	9.00	2.50
☐ 26	Al McNeil	18.00	8.00	2.30
☐ 27	Billy Harris	18.00	8.00	2.30
☐ 28	Ken Wharram	20.00	9.00	2.50
☐ 29	George Sullivan	18.00	8.00	2.30
☐ 30	John McKenzie	21.00	9.50	2.60
☐ 31	Stan Mikita	100.00	45.00	12.50
☐ 32	Ted Green	20.00	9.00	2.50
☐ 33	Jean Beliveau	125.00	57.50	15.50
☐ 34	Arnie Brown	18.00	8.00	2.30
☐ 35	Reg Fleming	18.00	8.00	2.30
☐ 36	Jim Mikol	18.00	8.00	2.30
☐ 37	Dave Balon	18.00	8.00	2.30
☐ 38	Billy Reay CO	20.00	9.00	2.50
☐ 39	Marcel Pronovost	20.00	9.00	2.50
☐ 40	Johnny Bower	35.00	16.00	4.40
☐ 41	Wayne Hillman	18.00	8.00	2.30
☐ 42	Floyd Smith	18.00	8.00	2.30
☐ 43	Toe Blake CO	20.00	9.00	2.50
☐ 44	Red Kelly	25.00	11.50	3.10
☐ 45	Punch Imlach CO	20.00	9.00	2.50
☐ 46	Dick Duff	20.00	9.00	2.50
☐ 47	Roger Crozier	45.00	20.00	5.75
☐ 48	Henri Richard	70.00	32.00	8.75
☐ 49	Larry Jeffrey	18.00	8.00	2.30
☐ 50	Leo Boivin	18.00	8.00	2.30
☐ 51	Ed Westfall	20.00	9.00	2.50
☐ 52	Jean-Guy Talbot	18.00	8.00	2.30
☐ 53	Jacques Laperriere	25.00	11.50	3.10
☐ 54	1st Checklist	275.00	55.00	16.50
☐ 55	2nd Checklist	300.00	60.00	18.00
☐ 56	Ron Murphy	45.00	20.00	5.75
☐ 57	Bob Baun	48.00	22.00	6.00
☐ 58	Tom Williams SP	200.00	90.00	25.00
☐ 59	Pierre Pilote SP	250.00	115.00	31.00
☐ 60	Bob Pulford	50.00	23.00	6.25
☐ 61	Red Berenson	50.00	23.00	6.25
☐ 62	Vic Hadfield	50.00	23.00	6.25
☐ 63	Bob Leiter	45.00	20.00	5.75
☐ 64	Jim Pappin	60.00	27.00	7.50
☐ 65	Earl Ingarfield	45.00	20.00	5.75
☐ 66	Lou Angotti	50.00	23.00	6.25
☐ 67	Rod Seiling	50.00	23.00	6.25
☐ 68	Jacques Plante	150.00	70.00	19.00
☐ 69	George Armstrong	60.00	27.00	7.50
☐ 70	Milt Schmidt CO	50.00	23.00	6.25
☐ 71	Eddie Shack	60.00	27.00	7.50
☐ 72	Gary Dornhoefer SP	225.00	100.00	28.00
☐ 73	Chico Maki SP	200.00	90.00	25.00
☐ 74	Gilles Villemure SP	225.00	100.00	28.00
☐ 75	Carl Brewer	48.00	22.00	6.00
☐ 76	Bruce MacGregor	45.00	20.00	5.75
☐ 77	Bob Nevin	48.00	22.00	6.00
☐ 78	Ralph Backstrom	48.00	22.00	6.00
☐ 79	Murray Oliver	45.00	20.00	5.75
☐ 80	Bobby Rousseau SP	200.00	90.00	25.00
☐ 81	Don McKenney	45.00	20.00	5.75
☐ 82	Ted Lindsay	75.00	34.00	9.50
☐ 83	Harry Howell	50.00	23.00	6.25
☐ 84	Doug Robinson	45.00	20.00	5.75
☐ 85	Frank Mahovlich	125.00	57.50	15.50
☐ 86	Andy Bathgate	50.00	23.00	6.25
☐ 87	Phil Goyette	45.00	20.00	5.75
☐ 88	J.C. Tremblay	48.00	22.00	6.00
☐ 89	Gordie Howe	500.00	230.00	65.00
☐ 90	Murray Balfour	45.00	20.00	5.75
☐ 91	Eric Nesterenko SP	200.00	90.00	25.00
☐ 92	Marcel Paille SP	300.00	135.00	38.00
☐ 93	Sid Abel CO	50.00	23.00	6.25
☐ 94	Dave Keon	80.00	36.00	10.00
☐ 95	Alex Delvecchio	70.00	32.00	8.75
☐ 96	Bill Gadsby	50.00	23.00	6.25
☐ 97	Don Marshall	45.00	20.00	5.75
☐ 98	Bill Hicke SP	200.00	90.00	25.00

☐	99 Ron Stewart	45.00	20.00	5.75
☐	100 Johnny Bucyk	75.00	34.00	9.50
☐	101 Tom Johnson	48.00	22.00	6.00
☐	102 Tim Horton	125.00	57.50	15.50
☐	103 Jim Neilson	48.00	22.00	6.00
☐	104 Allan Stanley	50.00	23.00	6.25
☐	105 Tim Horton AS SP	275.00	125.00	34.00
☐	106 Stan Mikita AS SP	275.00	125.00	34.00
☐	107 Bobby Hull AS	200.00	90.00	25.00
☐	108 Ken Wharram AS	50.00	23.00	6.25
☐	109 Pierre Pilote AS	60.00	27.00	7.50
☐	110 Glenn Hall AS	125.00	38.00	12.50

1965-66 Topps

The 1965-66 Topps set contains 128 cards. Cards measure the standard 2 1/2" by 3 1/2". Bilingual backs contain 1964-65 statistics, a short biography and a scratch-off question section. The cards were printed in Canada. Cards 122-128 are quite scarce and considered Single Prints. The seven cards were not included checklist card 121. Rookie Cards include Gerry Cheevers, Yvan Cournoyer, Phil Esposito, Ed Giacomin, Ken Hodge, and Dennis Hull. Eleven cards in the set were double printed including Cournoyer's Rookie Card.

		NRMT	VG-E	GOOD
	COMPLETE SET (128)	2700.00	1200.00	350.00
	COMMON PLAYER (1-128)	8.00	3.60	1.00
☐	1 Toe Blake CO	20.00	5.00	1.60
☐	2 Gump Worsley	22.00	10.00	2.80
☐	3 Jacques Laperriere	15.00	6.75	1.90
☐	4 Jean-Guy Talbot	8.00	3.60	1.00
☐	5 Ted Harris	8.00	3.60	1.00
☐	6 Jean Beliveau	50.00	23.00	6.25
☐	7 Dick Duff	9.00	4.00	1.15
☐	8 Claude Provost DP	6.00	2.70	.75
☐	9 Red Berenson	9.00	4.00	1.15
☐	10 John Ferguson	9.00	4.00	1.15
☐	11 Punch Imlach CO	10.00	4.50	1.25
☐	12 Terry Sawchuk	60.00	27.00	7.50
☐	13 Bob Baun	9.00	4.00	1.15
☐	14 Kent Douglas	8.00	3.60	1.00
☐	15 Red Kelly	16.00	7.25	2.00
☐	16 Jim Pappin	8.50	3.80	1.05
☐	17 Dave Keon	27.00	12.00	3.40
☐	18 Bob Pulford	8.00	3.60	1.00
☐	19 George Armstrong	10.00	4.50	1.25
☐	20 Orland Kurtenbach	8.00	3.60	1.00
☐	21 Ed Giacomin	125.00	57.50	15.50
☐	22 Harry Howell	10.00	4.50	1.25
☐	23 Rod Seiling	8.00	3.60	1.00
☐	24 Mike McMahon	8.00	3.60	1.00
☐	25 Jean Ratelle	25.00	11.50	3.10
☐	26 Doug Robinson	8.00	3.60	1.00
☐	27 Vic Hadfield	8.50	3.80	1.05
☐	28 Garry Peters UER	8.00	3.60	1.00
	(Misspelled Gary on card front)			
☐	29 Don Marshall	8.00	3.60	1.00
☐	30 Bill Hicke	8.00	3.60	1.00
☐	31 Gerry Cheevers	125.00	57.50	15.50
☐	32 Leo Boivin	8.00	3.60	1.00
☐	33 Albert Langlois	8.00	3.60	1.00
☐	34 Murray Oliver DP	6.00	2.70	.75

☐	35 Tom Williams	8.00	3.60	1.00
☐	36 Ron Schock	8.00	3.60	1.00
☐	37 Ed Westfall	9.00	4.00	1.15
☐	38 Gary Dornhoefer	9.00	4.00	1.15
☐	39 Bob Dillabough	8.00	3.60	1.00
☐	40 Poul Popiel	8.00	3.60	1.00
☐	41 Sid Abel CO	10.00	4.50	1.25
☐	42 Roger Crozier	10.00	4.50	1.25
☐	43 Doug Barkley	8.00	3.60	1.00
☐	44 Bill Gadsby	8.00	3.60	1.00
☐	45 Bryan Watson	15.00	6.75	1.90
☐	46 Bob McCord	8.00	3.60	1.00
☐	47 Alex Delvecchio	16.00	7.25	2.00
☐	48 Andy Bathgate	10.00	4.50	1.25
☐	49 Norm Ullman	16.00	7.25	2.00
☐	50 Ab McDonald	8.00	3.60	1.00
☐	51 Paul Henderson	30.00	13.50	3.80
☐	52 Pit Martin	9.00	4.00	1.15
☐	53 Billy Harris DP	6.00	2.70	.75
☐	54 Billy Reay CO	9.00	4.00	1.15
☐	55 Glenn Hall	25.00	11.50	3.10
☐	56 Pierre Pilote	10.00	4.50	1.25
☐	57 Al McNeil	8.00	3.60	1.00
☐	58 Camille Henry	8.00	3.60	1.00
☐	59 Bobby Hull	175.00	80.00	22.00
☐	60 Stan Mikita	60.00	27.00	7.50
☐	61 Ken Wharram	9.00	4.00	1.15
☐	62 Bill(Red) Hay	8.00	3.60	1.00
☐	63 Fred Stanfield	10.00	4.50	1.25
☐	64 Dennis Hull DP	25.00	11.50	3.10
☐	65 Ken Hodge	25.00	11.50	3.10
☐	66 Checklist Card	175.00	26.00	8.75
☐	67 Charlie Hodge	9.00	4.00	1.15
☐	68 Terry Harper	8.00	3.60	1.00
☐	69 J.C. Tremblay	8.00	3.60	1.00
☐	70 Bobby Rousseau DP	6.00	2.70	.75
☐	71 Henri Richard	25.00	11.50	3.10
☐	72 Dave Balon	8.00	3.60	1.00
☐	73 Ralph Backstrom	9.00	4.00	1.15
☐	74 Jim Roberts	10.00	4.50	1.25
☐	75 Claude Larose	8.50	3.80	1.05
☐	76 Yvan Cournoyer UER DP	100.00	45.00	12.50
☐	77 Johnny Bower DP	12.00	5.50	1.50
☐	78 Carl Brewer	9.00	4.00	1.15
☐	79 Tim Horton	30.00	13.50	3.80
☐	80 Marcel Pronovost	8.00	3.60	1.00
☐	81 Frank Mahovlich	35.00	16.00	4.40
☐	82 Ron Ellis	25.00	11.50	3.10
☐	83 Larry Jeffrey	8.00	3.60	1.00
☐	84 Pete Stemkowski	12.00	5.50	1.50
☐	85 Eddie Joyal	8.00	3.60	1.00
☐	86 Mike Walton	10.00	4.50	1.25
☐	87 George Sullivan	8.00	3.60	1.00
☐	88 Don Simmons	9.00	4.00	1.15
☐	89 Jim Neilson	8.50	3.80	1.05
☐	90 Arnie Brown	8.00	3.60	1.00
☐	91 Rod Gilbert	25.00	11.50	3.10
☐	92 Phil Goyette	8.00	3.60	1.00
☐	93 Bob Nevin	8.50	3.80	1.05
☐	94 John McKenzie	9.00	4.00	1.15
☐	95 Ted Taylor	8.00	3.60	1.00
☐	96 Milt Schmidt CO DP	10.00	4.50	1.25
☐	97 Ed Johnston	9.00	4.00	1.15
☐	98 Ted Green	9.00	4.00	1.15
☐	99 Don Awrey	10.00	4.50	1.25
☐	100 Bob Woytowich DP	6.00	2.70	.75
☐	101 Johnny Bucyk	18.00	8.00	2.30
☐	102 Dean Prentice	9.00	4.00	1.15
☐	103 Ron Stewart	8.00	3.60	1.00
☐	104 Reg Fleming	8.00	3.60	1.00
☐	105 Parker MacDonald	8.00	3.60	1.00
☐	106 Hank Bassen	9.00	4.00	1.15
☐	107 Gary Bergman	8.00	3.60	1.00
☐	108 Gordie Howe DP	150.00	70.00	19.00
☐	109 Floyd Smith	8.00	3.60	1.00
☐	110 Bruce MacGregor	8.00	3.60	1.00
☐	111 Ron Murphy	8.00	3.60	1.00
☐	112 Don McKenney	8.00	3.60	1.00
☐	113 Denis DeJordy DP	6.50	2.90	.80
☐	114 Elmer Vasko	8.00	3.60	1.00
☐	115 Matt Ravlich	8.00	3.60	1.00
☐	116 Phil Esposito	400.00	180.00	50.00
☐	117 Chico Maki	8.00	3.60	1.00
☐	118 Doug Mohns	9.00	4.00	1.15
☐	119 Eric Nesterenko	9.00	4.00	1.15
☐	120 Pat Stapleton	9.00	4.00	1.15
☐	121 Checklist Card	175.00	26.00	8.75
	(600 Goals)			
☐	122 Gordie Howe SP	350.00	160.00	45.00
☐	123 Toronto Maple Leafs Team Card SP	65.00	29.00	8.25
☐	124 Chicago Blackhawks Team Card SP	65.00	29.00	8.25

	NRMT	VG-E	GOOD
☐ 125 Detroit Red Wings Team Card SP	65.00	29.00	8.25
☐ 126 Montreal Canadiens Team Card SP	70.00	32.00	8.75
☐ 127 New York Rangers Team Card SP	65.00	29.00	8.25
☐ 128 Boston Bruins Team Card SP	175.00	45.00	14.00

1966-67 Topps

 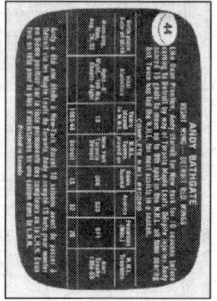

At 132 cards, the 1966-67 issue was the largest Topps set to date. The cards in the set measure 2 1/2" by 3 1/2". The front features a distinctive wood grain border with a television screen look. Bilingual backs feature a short biography, 1965-66 and career statistics. The cards were printed in Canada. The key card in the set is Bobby Orr's Rookie Card. Other Rookie Cards include Emile Francis, Harry Sinden and Peter Mahovlich. The backs of card numbers 127-132 form a puzzle of Bobby Orr.

	NRMT	VG-E	GOOD
COMPLETE SET (132)	4000.00	1800.00	500.00
COMMON PLAYER (1-132)	7.00	3.10	.85
☐ 1 Toe Blake CO	20.00	5.00	1.60
☐ 2 Gump Worsley	20.00	9.00	2.50
☐ 3 Jean-Guy Talbot	7.00	3.10	.85
☐ 4 Gilles Tremblay	7.00	3.10	.85
☐ 5 J.C. Tremblay	7.00	3.10	.85
☐ 6 Jim Roberts	7.50	3.40	.95
☐ 7 Bobby Rousseau	7.00	3.10	.85
☐ 8 Henri Richard	20.00	9.00	2.50
☐ 9 Claude Provost	7.00	3.10	.85
☐ 10 Claude Larose	7.50	3.40	.95
☐ 11 Punch Imlach CO	9.00	4.00	1.15
☐ 12 Johnny Bower	15.00	6.75	1.90
☐ 13 Terry Sawchuk	50.00	23.00	6.25
☐ 14 Mike Walton	7.50	3.40	.95
☐ 15 Pete Stemkowski	7.00	3.10	.85
☐ 16 Allan Stanley	10.00	4.50	1.25
☐ 17 Eddie Shack	15.00	6.75	1.90
☐ 18 Brit Selby	10.00	4.50	1.25
☐ 19 Bob Pulford	7.00	3.10	.85
☐ 20 Marcel Pronovost	7.00	3.10	.85
☐ 21 Emile Francis	20.00	9.00	2.50
☐ 22 Rod Seiling	7.00	3.10	.85
☐ 23 Ed Giacomin	40.00	18.00	5.00
☐ 24 Don Marshall	7.00	3.10	.85
☐ 25 Orland Kurtenbach	7.00	3.10	.85
☐ 26 Rod Gilbert	20.00	9.00	2.50
☐ 27 Bob Nevin	7.50	3.40	.95
☐ 28 Phil Goyette	7.00	3.10	.85
☐ 29 Jean Ratelle	20.00	9.00	2.50
☐ 30 Earl Ingarfield	7.00	3.10	.85
☐ 31 Harry Sinden	25.00	11.50	3.10
☐ 32 Ed Westfall	7.50	3.40	.95
☐ 33 Joe Watson	10.00	4.50	1.25
☐ 34 Bob Woytowich	7.00	3.10	.85
☐ 35 Bobby Orr	2500.00	1150.00	325.00
☐ 36 Gilles Marotte	10.00	4.50	1.25
☐ 37 Ted Green	7.50	3.40	.95
☐ 38 Tom Williams	7.00	3.10	.85
☐ 39 Johnny Bucyk	18.00	8.00	2.30
☐ 40 Wayne Connelly	7.00	3.10	.85
☐ 41 Pit Martin	7.50	3.40	.95
☐ 42 Sid Abel CO	7.00	3.10	.85
☐ 43 Roger Crozier	8.00	3.60	1.00
☐ 44 Andy Bathgate	9.00	4.00	1.15
☐ 45 Dean Prentice	7.00	3.10	.85
☐ 46 Paul Henderson	10.00	4.50	1.25
☐ 47 Gary Bergman	7.00	3.10	.85
☐ 48 Bryan Watson	7.50	3.40	.95
☐ 49 Bob Wall	7.00	3.10	.85
☐ 50 Leo Boivin	7.00	3.10	.85
☐ 51 Bert Marshall	7.00	3.10	.85
☐ 52 Norm Ullman	15.00	6.75	1.90
☐ 53 Billy Reay CO	7.50	3.40	.95
☐ 54 Glenn Hall	22.00	10.00	2.80
☐ 55 Wally Boyer	7.00	3.10	.85
☐ 56 Fred Stanfield	7.00	3.10	.85
☐ 57 Pat Stapleton	7.50	3.40	.95
☐ 58 Matt Ravlich	7.00	3.10	.85
☐ 59 Pierre Pilote	7.50	3.40	.95
☐ 60 Eric Nesterenko	7.50	3.40	.95
☐ 61 Doug Mohns	7.50	3.40	.95
☐ 62 Stan Mikita	50.00	23.00	6.25
☐ 63 Phil Esposito	125.00	57.50	15.50
☐ 64 Leading Scorer (Bobby Hull)	75.00	34.00	9.50
☐ 65 Vezina Trophy (Charlie Hodge/ Gump Worsley)	15.00	6.75	1.90
☐ 66 Checklist Card	200.00	33.00	10.00
☐ 67 Jacques Laperriere	10.00	4.50	1.25
☐ 68 Terry Harper	7.00	3.10	.85
☐ 69 Ted Harris	7.00	3.10	.85
☐ 70 John Ferguson	7.50	3.40	.95
☐ 71 Dick Duff	8.00	3.60	1.00
☐ 72 Yvan Cournoyer	45.00	20.00	5.75
☐ 73 Jean Beliveau	45.00	20.00	5.75
☐ 74 Dave Balon	7.00	3.10	.85
☐ 75 Ralph Backstrom	7.50	3.40	.95
☐ 76 Jim Pappin	7.50	3.40	.95
☐ 77 Frank Mahovlich	30.00	13.50	3.80
☐ 78 Dave Keon	20.00	9.00	2.50
☐ 79 Red Kelly	14.00	6.25	1.75
☐ 80 Tim Horton	25.00	11.50	3.10
☐ 81 Ron Ellis	7.50	3.40	.95
☐ 82 Kent Douglas	7.00	3.10	.85
☐ 83 Bob Baun	8.00	3.60	1.00
☐ 84 George Armstrong	10.00	4.50	1.25
☐ 85 Boom Boom Geoffrion	25.00	11.50	3.10
☐ 86 Vic Hadfield	7.50	3.40	.95
☐ 87 Wayne Hillman	7.00	3.10	.85
☐ 88 Jim Neilson	7.00	3.10	.85
☐ 89 Al McNeil	7.00	3.10	.85
☐ 90 Arnie Brown	7.00	3.10	.85
☐ 91 Harry Howell	10.00	4.50	1.25
☐ 92 Red Berenson	7.50	3.40	.95
☐ 93 Reg Fleming	7.00	3.10	.85
☐ 94 Ron Stewart	7.00	3.10	.85
☐ 95 Murray Oliver	7.00	3.10	.85
☐ 96 Ron Murphy	7.00	3.10	.85
☐ 97 John McKenzie	8.00	3.60	1.00
☐ 98 Bob Dillabough	7.00	3.10	.85
☐ 99 Ed Johnston	8.00	3.60	1.00
☐ 100 Ron Schock	7.00	3.10	.85
☐ 101 Dallas Smith	7.00	3.10	.85
☐ 102 Alex Delvecchio	14.00	6.25	1.75
☐ 103 Peter Mahovlich	25.00	11.50	3.10
☐ 104 Bruce MacGregor	7.00	3.10	.85
☐ 105 Murray Hall	7.00	3.10	.85
☐ 106 Floyd Smith	7.00	3.10	.85
☐ 107 Hank Bassen	7.50	3.40	.95
☐ 108 Val Fonteyne	7.00	3.10	.85
☐ 109 Gordie Howe	200.00	90.00	25.00
☐ 110 Chico Maki	7.00	3.10	.85
☐ 111 Doug Jarrett	7.00	3.10	.85
☐ 112 Bobby Hull	150.00	70.00	19.00
☐ 113 Dennis Hull	12.00	5.50	1.50
☐ 114 Ken Hodge	10.00	4.50	1.25
☐ 115 Denis DeJordy	8.00	3.60	1.00
☐ 116 Lou Angotti	7.00	3.10	.85
☐ 117 Ken Wharram	7.00	3.10	.85
☐ 118 Montreal Canadiens Team Card	18.00	8.00	2.30
☐ 119 Detroit Red Wings Team Card	18.00	8.00	2.30
☐ 120 Checklist Card	200.00	33.00	10.00
☐ 121 Gordie Howe AS	100.00	45.00	12.50
☐ 122 Jacques Laperriere AS	7.50	3.40	.95
☐ 123 Pierre Pilote AS	7.50	3.40	.95
☐ 124 Stan Mikita AS	30.00	13.50	3.80
☐ 125 Bobby Hull AS	75.00	34.00	9.50
☐ 126 Glenn Hall AS	15.00	6.75	1.90
☐ 127 Jean Beliveau AS	20.00	9.00	2.50
☐ 128 Allan Stanley AS	9.00	4.00	1.15

		NRMT	VG-E	GOOD
☐ 129	Pat Stapleton AS	9.00	4.00	1.15
☐ 130	Gump Worsley AS	18.00	8.00	2.30
☐ 131	Frank Mahovlich AS	18.00	8.00	2.30
☐ 132	Bobby Rousseau AS	20.00	5.00	1.45

1966-67 Topps USA Test

 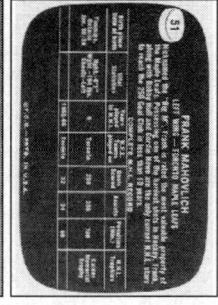

This 66-card set was apparently a test issue with limited distribution as it is quite scarce. The cards feature the same format as the 1966-67 Topps regular hockey cards. The cards are standard size, 2 1/2" by 3 1/2". The primary difference is that the card backs in this scarce issue are only printed in English, i.e., no French. The card numbering has some similarities to the regular issue, e.g., Bobby Orr is number 35 in both sets, however there are also many differences from the regular Topps Canadian version which was more mass produced. The wood grain border on the front of the cards is slightly lighter than that of the regular issue.

		NRMT	VG-E	GOOD
COMPLETE SET (66)		12000.	5000.	1200.
COMMON PLAYER (1-66)		35.00	14.00	3.50
☐ 1	Dennis Hull	50.00	20.00	5.00
☐ 2	Gump Worsley	125.00	50.00	12.50
☐ 3	Dallas Smith	40.00	16.00	4.00
☐ 4	Gilles Tremblay	35.00	14.00	3.50
☐ 5	J.C. Tremblay	40.00	16.00	4.00
☐ 6	Ralph Backstrom	40.00	16.00	4.00
☐ 7	Bobby Rousseau	40.00	16.00	4.00
☐ 8	Henri Richard	100.00	40.00	10.00
☐ 9	Claude Provost	40.00	16.00	4.00
☐ 10	Red Berenson	40.00	16.00	4.00
☐ 11	Punch Imlach CO	40.00	16.00	4.00
☐ 12	Johnny Bower	100.00	40.00	10.00
☐ 13	Yvan Cournoyer	125.00	50.00	12.50
☐ 14	Mike Walton	40.00	16.00	4.00
☐ 15	Pete Stemkowski	40.00	16.00	4.00
☐ 16	Allan Stanley	75.00	30.00	7.50
☐ 17	George Armstrong	100.00	40.00	10.00
☐ 18	Harry Howell	75.00	30.00	7.50
☐ 19	Vic Hadfield	40.00	16.00	4.00
☐ 20	Marcel Pronovost	75.00	30.00	7.50
☐ 21	Pete Mahovlich	50.00	20.00	5.00
☐ 22	Rod Seiling	35.00	14.00	3.50
☐ 23	Gordie Howe	900.00	360.00	90.00
☐ 24	Don Marshall	35.00	14.00	3.50
☐ 25	Orland Kurtenbach	40.00	16.00	4.00
☐ 26	Rod Gilbert	100.00	40.00	10.00
☐ 27	Bob Nevin	35.00	14.00	3.50
☐ 28	Phil Goyette	35.00	14.00	3.50
☐ 29	Jean Ratelle	100.00	40.00	10.00
☐ 30	Dave Keon	100.00	40.00	10.00
☐ 31	Jean Beliveau	250.00	100.00	25.00
☐ 32	Ed Westfall	40.00	16.00	4.00
☐ 33	Ron Murphy	35.00	14.00	3.50
☐ 34	Wayne Hillman	35.00	14.00	3.50
☐ 35	Bobby Orr	7500.00	3000.00	750.00
☐ 36	Boom Boom Geoffrion	175.00	70.00	18.00
☐ 37	Ted Green	45.00	18.00	4.50
☐ 38	Tom Williams	35.00	14.00	3.50
☐ 39	Johnny Bucyk	100.00	40.00	10.00
☐ 40	Bobby Hull	600.00	240.00	60.00
☐ 41	Ted Harris	35.00	14.00	3.50
☐ 42	Red Kelly	100.00	40.00	10.00
☐ 43	Roger Crozier	40.00	16.00	4.00
☐ 44	Ken Wharram	35.00	14.00	3.50
☐ 45	Dean Prentice	40.00	16.00	4.00
☐ 46	Paul Henderson	50.00	20.00	5.00
☐ 47	Gary Bergman	40.00	16.00	4.00
☐ 48	Arnie Brown	35.00	14.00	3.50
☐ 49	Jim Pappin	35.00	14.00	3.50
☐ 50	Denis DeJordy	40.00	16.00	4.00
☐ 51	Frank Mahovlich	150.00	60.00	15.00
☐ 52	Norm Ullman	100.00	40.00	10.00
☐ 53	Chico Maki	40.00	16.00	4.00
☐ 54	Reg Fleming	35.00	14.00	3.50
☐ 55	Jim Neilson	35.00	14.00	3.50
☐ 56	Bruce MacGregor	35.00	14.00	3.50
☐ 57	Pat Stapleton	40.00	16.00	4.00
☐ 58	Matt Ravlich	35.00	14.00	3.50
☐ 59	Pierre Pilote	75.00	30.00	7.50
☐ 60	Eric Nesterenko	40.00	16.00	4.00
☐ 61	Doug Mohns	40.00	16.00	4.00
☐ 62	Stan Mikita	200.00	80.00	20.00
☐ 63	Alex Delvecchio	100.00	40.00	10.00
☐ 64	Ed Johnston	50.00	20.00	5.00
☐ 65	John Ferguson	40.00	16.00	4.00
☐ 66	John McKenzie	40.00	16.00	4.00

1967-68 Topps

 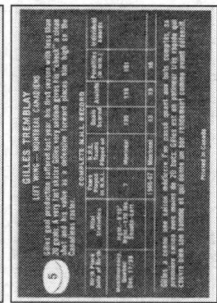

The 1967-68 Topps set features 132 cards. Players on the six expansion teams (Los Angeles, Minnesota, Oakland, Philadelphia, Pittsburgh, and St. Louis) were not included until 1968-69. Cards measure 2 1/2" by 3 1/2". Bilingual backs feature a short biography, 1966-67 and career records. The backs are identical in format to the 1966-67 cards. The cards were printed in Canada. Rookie Cards include Jacques Lemaire, Derek Sanderson, Glen Sather, and Rogatien Vachon.

		NRMT	VG-E	GOOD
COMPLETE SET (132)		2700.00	1200.00	350.00
COMMON PLAYER (1-132)		7.00	3.10	.85
☐ 1	Gump Worsley	35.00	10.50	3.50
☐ 2	Dick Duff	8.00	3.60	1.00
☐ 3	Jacques Lemaire	55.00	25.00	7.00
☐ 4	Claude Larose	7.50	3.40	.95
☐ 5	Gilles Tremblay	7.00	3.10	.85
☐ 6	Terry Harper	7.00	3.10	.85
☐ 7	Jacques Laperriere	9.00	4.00	1.15
☐ 8	Garry Monahan	7.00	3.10	.85
☐ 9	Carol Vadnais	10.00	4.50	1.25
☐ 10	Ted Harris	7.00	3.10	.85
☐ 11	Dave Keon	15.00	6.75	1.90
☐ 12	Pete Stemkowski	7.00	3.10	.85
☐ 13	Allan Stanley	9.00	4.00	1.15
☐ 14	Ron Ellis	7.50	3.40	.95
☐ 15	Mike Walton	7.50	3.40	.95
☐ 16	Tim Horton	22.00	10.00	2.80
☐ 17	Brian Conacher	7.00	3.10	.85
☐ 18	Bruce Gamble	8.00	3.60	1.00
☐ 19	Bob Pulford	7.00	3.10	.85
☐ 20	Duane Rupp	7.00	3.10	.85
☐ 21	Larry Jeffrey	7.00	3.10	.85
☐ 22	Wayne Hillman	7.00	3.10	.85

☐	23	Don Marshall	7.00	3.10	.85
☐	24	Red Berenson	7.50	3.40	.95
☐	25	Phil Goyette	7.00	3.10	.85
☐	26	Camille Henry	7.00	3.10	.85
☐	27	Rod Seiling	7.00	3.10	.85
☐	28	Bob Nevin	7.50	3.40	.95
☐	29	Boom Boom Geoffrion	20.00	9.00	2.50
☐	30	Reg Fleming	7.00	3.10	.85
☐	31	Jean Ratelle	18.00	8.00	2.30
☐	32	Phil Esposito	75.00	34.00	9.50
☐	33	Derek Sanderson	55.00	25.00	7.00
☐	34	Eddie Shack	12.00	5.50	1.50
☐	35	Ross Lonsberry	9.00	4.00	1.15
☐	36	Fred Stanfield	7.00	3.10	.85
☐	37	Don Awrey UER	7.00	3.10	.85

(Photo actually Skip Krake)

☐	38	Glen Sather	30.00	13.50	3.80
☐	39	John McKenzie	7.50	3.40	.95
☐	40	Tom Williams	7.00	3.10	.85
☐	41	Dallas Smith	7.00	3.10	.85
☐	42	Johnny Bucyk	15.00	6.75	1.90
☐	43	Gordie Howe	150.00	70.00	19.00
☐	44	Gary Jarrett	7.00	3.10	.85
☐	45	Dean Prentice	7.00	3.10	.85
☐	46	Bert Marshall	7.00	3.10	.85
☐	47	Gary Bergman	7.00	3.10	.85
☐	48	Roger Crozier	8.00	3.60	1.00
☐	49	Howie Young	7.00	3.10	.85
☐	50	Doug Roberts	7.00	3.10	.85
☐	51	Alex Delvecchio	12.00	5.50	1.50
☐	52	Floyd Smith	7.00	3.10	.85
☐	53	Doug Shelton	7.00	3.10	.85
☐	54	Gerry Goyer	7.00	3.10	.85
☐	55	Wayne Maki	7.00	3.10	.85
☐	56	Dennis Hull	9.00	4.00	1.15
☐	57	Dave Dryden	14.00	6.25	1.75
☐	58	Paul Terbenche	7.00	3.10	.85
☐	59	Gilles Marotte	7.00	3.10	.85
☐	60	Eric Nesterenko	7.50	3.40	.95
☐	61	Pat Stapleton	7.50	3.40	.95
☐	62	Pierre Pilote	7.00	3.10	.85
☐	63	Doug Mohns	7.00	3.10	.85
☐	64	Triple Winner	25.00	11.50	3.10

(Stan Mikita)

☐	65	Vezina Trophy	15.00	6.75	1.90

(Glenn Hall/ Denis DeJordy)

☐	66	Checklist Card	150.00	25.00	7.50
☐	67	Ralph Backstrom	7.50	3.40	.95
☐	68	Bobby Rousseau	7.00	3.10	.85
☐	69	John Ferguson	7.50	3.40	.95
☐	70	Yvan Cournoyer	25.00	11.50	3.10
☐	71	Claude Provost	7.00	3.10	.85
☐	72	Henri Richard	18.00	8.00	2.30
☐	73	J.C. Tremblay	7.00	3.10	.85
☐	74	Jean Beliveau	35.00	16.00	4.40
☐	75	Rogatien Vachon	75.00	34.00	9.50
☐	76	Johnny Bower	12.00	5.50	1.50
☐	77	Wayne Carleton	7.00	3.10	.85
☐	78	Jim Pappin	7.00	3.10	.85
☐	79	Frank Mahovlich	25.00	11.50	3.10
☐	80	Larry Hillman	7.00	3.10	.85
☐	81	Marcel Pronovost	7.00	3.10	.85
☐	82	Murray Oliver	7.00	3.10	.85
☐	83	George Armstrong	9.00	4.00	1.15
☐	84	Harry Howell	9.00	4.00	1.15
☐	85	Ed Giacomin	30.00	13.50	3.80
☐	86	Gilles Villemure	8.00	3.60	1.00
☐	87	Orland Kurtenbach	7.00	3.10	.85
☐	88	Vic Hadfield	7.50	3.40	.95
☐	89	Arnie Brown	7.00	3.10	.85
☐	90	Rod Gilbert	18.00	8.00	2.30
☐	91	Jim Neilson	7.00	3.10	.85
☐	92	Bobby Orr	750.00	350.00	95.00
☐	93	Skip Krake UER	7.00	3.10	.85

(Photo actually Don Awrey)

☐	94	Ted Green	7.50	3.40	.95
☐	95	Ed Westfall	7.50	3.40	.95
☐	96	Ed Johnston	8.00	3.60	1.00
☐	97	Gary Doak	9.00	4.00	1.15
☐	98	Ken Hodge	9.00	4.00	1.15
☐	99	Gerry Cheevers	40.00	18.00	5.00
☐	100	Ron Murphy	7.00	3.10	.85
☐	101	Norm Ullman	12.00	5.50	1.50
☐	102	Bruce MacGregor	7.00	3.10	.85
☐	103	Paul Henderson	7.50	3.40	.95
☐	104	Jean-Guy Talbot	7.00	3.10	.85
☐	105	Bart Crashley	7.00	3.10	.85
☐	106	Roy Edwards	8.00	3.60	1.00
☐	107	Jim Watson	7.00	3.10	.85
☐	108	Ted Hampson	7.00	3.10	.85
☐	109	Bill Orban	7.00	3.10	.85
☐	110	Geoffrey Powis	7.00	3.10	.85
☐	111	Chico Maki	7.00	3.10	.85
☐	112	Doug Jarrett	7.00	3.10	.85
☐	113	Bobby Hull	125.00	57.50	15.50
☐	114	Stan Mikita	45.00	20.00	5.75
☐	115	Denis DeJordy	8.00	3.60	1.00
☐	116	Pit Martin	7.50	3.40	.95
☐	117	Ken Wharram	7.00	3.10	.85
☐	118	Calder Trophy	250.00	115.00	31.00

(Bobby Orr)

☐	119	Norris Trophy	7.00	3.10	.85

(Harry Howell)

☐	120	Checklist Card	150.00	25.00	7.50
☐	121	Harry Howell AS	8.00	3.60	1.00
☐	122	Pierre Pilote AS	8.00	3.60	1.00
☐	123	Ed Giacomin AS	15.00	6.75	1.90
☐	124	Bobby Hull AS	65.00	29.00	8.25
☐	125	Ken Wharram AS	8.00	3.60	1.00
☐	126	Stan Mikita AS	25.00	11.50	3.10
☐	127	Tim Horton AS	12.00	5.50	1.50
☐	128	Bobby Orr AS	250.00	115.00	31.00
☐	129	Glenn Hall AS	15.00	6.75	1.90
☐	130	Don Marshall AS	8.00	3.60	1.00
☐	131	Gordie Howe AS	90.00	40.00	11.50
☐	132	Norm Ullman AS	18.00	5.50	1.80

1968-69 Topps

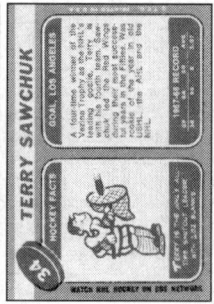

The 1968-69 Topps set consists of 132 cards featuring all 12 teams including the six expansion teams. Cards measure 2 1/2" by 3 1/2". The fronts feature a horizontal format with the player in the foreground and an artistically rendered hockey scene in the background. The backs include a short biography, 1967-68 and career statistics as well as a cartoon-illustrated fact about the player. With O-Pee-Chee printing cards for the Canadian market, text on back is English only. For the first time since 1960-61, Topps cards were printed in the U.S. The only Rookie Card of consequence is Bernie Parent.

	NRMT	VG-E	GOOD
COMPLETE SET (132)	650.00	300.00	80.00
COMMON PLAYER (1-132)	3.00	1.35	.40

☐	1	Gerry Cheevers	20.00	5.00	1.60
☐	2	Bobby Orr	200.00	90.00	25.00
☐	3	Don Awrey UER	3.00	1.35	.40

(Photo actually Skip Krake)

☐	4	Ted Green	3.50	1.55	.45
☐	5	Johnny Bucyk	6.00	2.70	.75
☐	6	Derek Sanderson	12.00	5.50	1.50
☐	7	Phil Esposito	30.00	13.50	3.80
☐	8	Ken Hodge	3.50	1.55	.45
☐	9	John McKenzie	3.50	1.55	.45
☐	10	Fred Stanfield	3.00	1.35	.40
☐	11	Tom Williams	3.00	1.35	.40
☐	12	Denis DeJordy	3.50	1.55	.45
☐	13	Doug Jarrett	3.00	1.35	.40
☐	14	Gilles Marotte	3.00	1.35	.40
☐	15	Pat Stapleton	3.50	1.55	.45
☐	16	Bobby Hull	60.00	27.00	7.50
☐	17	Chico Maki	3.00	1.35	.40

□	#	Player	NRMT	VG-E	GOOD
□	18	Pit Martin	3.50	1.55	.45
□	19	Doug Mohns	3.00	1.35	.40
□	20	Stan Mikita	20.00	9.00	2.50
□	21	Jim Pappin	3.00	1.35	.40
□	22	Ken Wharram	3.00	1.35	.40
□	23	Roger Crozier	3.50	1.55	.45
□	24	Bob Baun	3.50	1.55	.45
□	25	Gary Bergman	3.00	1.35	.40
□	26	Kent Douglas	3.00	1.35	.40
□	27	Ron Harris	3.00	1.35	.40
□	28	Alex Delvecchio	6.00	2.70	.75
□	29	Gordie Howe	75.00	34.00	9.50
□	30	Bruce MacGregor	3.00	1.35	.40
□	31	Frank Mahovlich	10.00	4.50	1.25
□	32	Dean Prentice	3.00	1.35	.40
□	33	Pete Stemkowski	3.00	1.35	.40
□	34	Terry Sawchuk	30.00	13.50	3.80
□	35	Larry Cahan	3.00	1.35	.40
□	36	Real Lemieux	3.00	1.35	.40
□	37	Bill White	4.00	1.80	.50
□	38	Gord Labossiere	3.00	1.35	.40
□	39	Ted Irvine	3.00	1.35	.40
□	40	Eddie Joyal	3.00	1.35	.40
□	41	Dale Rolfe	3.00	1.35	.40
□	42	Lowell MacDonald	4.00	1.80	.50
□	43	Skip Krake UER	3.00	1.35	.40
		(Photo actually Don Awrey)			
□	44	Terry Gray	3.00	1.35	.40
□	45	Cesare Maniago	3.50	1.55	.45
□	46	Mike McMahon	3.00	1.35	.40
□	47	Wayne Hillman	3.00	1.35	.40
□	48	Larry Hillman	3.00	1.35	.40
□	49	Bob Woytowich	3.00	1.35	.40
□	50	Wayne Connelly	3.00	1.35	.40
□	51	Claude Larose	3.00	1.35	.40
□	52	Danny Grant	5.00	2.30	.60
□	53	Andre Boudrias	3.00	1.35	.40
□	54	Ray Cullen	4.00	1.80	.50
□	55	Parker MacDonald	3.00	1.35	.40
□	56	Gump Worsley	7.00	3.10	.85
□	57	Terry Harper	3.00	1.35	.40
□	58	Jacques Laperriere	3.50	1.55	.45
□	59	J.C. Tremblay	3.00	1.35	.40
□	60	Ralph Backstrom	3.50	1.55	.45
□	61	Jean Beliveau	15.00	6.75	1.90
□	62	Yvan Cournoyer	10.00	4.50	1.25
□	63	Jacques Lemaire	12.00	5.50	1.50
□	64	Henri Richard	8.00	3.60	1.00
□	65	Bobby Rousseau	3.00	1.35	.40
□	66	Gilles Tremblay	3.00	1.35	.40
□	67	Ed Giacomin	12.00	5.50	1.50
□	68	Arnie Brown	3.00	1.35	.40
□	69	Harry Howell	3.50	1.55	.45
□	70	Jim Neilson	3.00	1.35	.40
□	71	Rod Seiling	3.00	1.35	.40
□	72	Rod Gilbert	7.00	3.10	.85
□	73	Phil Goyette	3.00	1.35	.40
□	74	Vic Hadfield	3.50	1.55	.45
□	75	Don Marshall	3.00	1.35	.40
□	76	Bob Nevin	3.50	1.55	.45
□	77	Jean Ratelle	7.00	3.10	.85
□	78	Charlie Hodge	3.50	1.55	.45
□	79	Bert Marshall	3.00	1.35	.40
□	80	Billy Harris	3.00	1.35	.40
□	81	Carol Vadnais	3.50	1.55	.45
□	82	Howie Young	3.00	1.35	.40
□	83	John Brenneman	3.00	1.35	.40
□	84	Gerry Ehman	3.00	1.35	.40
□	85	Ted Hampson	3.00	1.35	.40
□	86	Bill Hicke	3.00	1.35	.40
□	87	Gary Jarrett	3.00	1.35	.40
□	88	Doug Roberts	3.00	1.35	.40
□	89	Bernie Parent	75.00	34.00	9.50
□	90	Joe Watson	3.00	1.35	.40
□	91	Ed Van Impe	3.00	1.35	.40
□	92	Larry Zeidel	3.00	1.35	.40
□	93	John Miszuk	3.00	1.35	.40
□	94	Gary Dornhoefer	3.50	1.55	.45
□	95	Leon Rochefort	3.00	1.35	.40
□	96	Brit Selby	3.00	1.35	.40
□	97	Forbes Kennedy	3.00	1.35	.40
□	98	Ed Hoekstra	3.00	1.35	.40
□	99	Garry Peters	3.00	1.35	.40
□	100	Les Binkley	5.00	2.30	.60
□	101	Leo Boivin	3.00	1.35	.40
□	102	Earl Ingarfield	3.00	1.35	.40
□	103	Lou Angotti	3.00	1.35	.40
□	104	Andy Bathgate	3.50	1.55	.45
□	105	Wally Boyer	3.00	1.35	.40
□	106	Ken Schinkel	3.00	1.35	.40
□	107	Ab McDonald	3.00	1.35	.40
□	108	Charlie Burns	3.00	1.35	.40
□	109	Val Fonteyne	3.00	1.35	.40
□	110	Noel Price	3.00	1.35	.40
□	111	Glenn Hall	9.00	4.00	1.15
□	112	Bob Plager	7.00	3.10	.85
□	113	Jim Roberts	3.50	1.55	.45
□	114	Red Berenson	3.50	1.55	.45
□	115	Larry Keenan	3.00	1.35	.40
□	116	Camille Henry	3.00	1.35	.40
□	117	Gary Sabourin	3.00	1.35	.40
□	118	Ron Schock	3.00	1.35	.40
□	119	Gary Veneruzzo	3.00	1.35	.40
□	120	Gerry Melnyk	3.00	1.35	.40
□	121	Checklist Card	75.00	7.50	1.50
□	122	Johnny Bower	5.00	2.30	.60
□	123	Tim Horton	10.00	4.50	1.25
□	124	Pierre Pilote	3.50	1.55	.45
□	125	Marcel Pronovost	3.00	1.35	.40
□	126	Ron Ellis	3.50	1.55	.45
□	127	Paul Henderson	3.50	1.55	.45
□	128	Dave Keon	6.00	2.70	.75
□	129	Bob Pulford	3.50	1.55	.45
□	130	Floyd Smith	3.00	1.35	.40
□	131	Norm Ullman	5.00	2.30	.60
□	132	Mike Walton	5.00	1.50	.40

1969-70 Topps

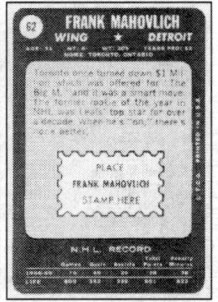

The 1969-70 Topps set consists of 132 cards. Cards measure 2 1/2" by 3 1/2". The backs contain 1968-69 and career statistics, a short biography and a cartoon-illustrated fact about the player. Those players in this set who were also included in the insert of stamps have a place on the card back for placing that player's stamp; this is not recommended. The only notable Rookie Card in the set is Serge Savard.

		NRMT	VG-E	GOOD
COMPLETE SET (132)		450.00	200.00	57.50
COMMON PLAYER (1-132)		2.00	.90	.25

□	#	Player	NRMT	VG-E	GOOD
□	1	Gump Worsley	15.00	3.80	1.20
□	2	Ted Harris	2.00	.90	.25
□	3	Jacques Laperriere	2.50	1.15	.30
□	4	Serge Savard	20.00	9.00	2.50
□	5	J.C. Tremblay	2.00	.90	.25
□	6	Yvan Cournoyer	7.00	3.10	.85
□	7	John Ferguson	2.50	1.15	.30
□	8	Jacques Lemaire	6.00	2.70	.75
□	9	Bobby Rousseau	2.00	.90	.25
□	10	Jean Beliveau	12.00	5.50	1.50
□	11	Henri Richard	7.00	3.10	.85
□	12	Glenn Hall	7.00	3.10	.85
□	13	Bob Plager	2.50	1.15	.30
□	14	Jim Roberts	2.50	1.15	.30
□	15	Jean-Guy Talbot	2.00	.90	.25
□	16	Andre Boudrias	2.00	.90	.25
□	17	Camille Henry	2.00	.90	.25
□	18	Ab McDonald	2.00	.90	.25
□	19	Gary Sabourin	2.00	.90	.25
□	20	Red Berenson	2.50	1.15	.30
□	21	Phil Goyette	2.00	.90	.25
□	22	Gerry Cheevers	10.00	4.50	1.25
□	23	Ted Green	2.50	1.15	.30
□	24	Bobby Orr	125.00	57.50	15.50
□	25	Dallas Smith	2.00	.90	.25
□	26	Johnny Bucyk	5.00	2.30	.60

		NRMT	VG-E	GOOD
☐ 27	Ken Hodge	2.50	1.15	.30
☐ 28	John McKenzie	2.50	1.15	.30
☐ 29	Ed Westfall	2.50	1.15	.30
☐ 30	Phil Esposito	20.00	9.00	2.50
☐ 31	Derek Sanderson	6.00	2.70	.75
☐ 32	Fred Stanfield	2.00	.90	.25
☐ 33	Ed Giacomin	10.00	4.50	1.25
☐ 34	Arnie Brown	2.00	.90	.25
☐ 35	Jim Neilson	2.00	.90	.25
☐ 36	Rod Seiling	2.00	.90	.25
☐ 37	Rod Gilbert	5.00	2.30	.60
☐ 38	Vic Hadfield	2.50	1.15	.30
☐ 39	Don Marshall	2.00	.90	.25
☐ 40	Bob Nevin	2.50	1.15	.30
☐ 41	Ron Stewart	2.00	.90	.25
☐ 42	Jean Ratelle	5.00	2.30	.60
☐ 43	Walt Tkaczuk	5.00	2.30	.60
☐ 44	Bruce Gamble	2.50	1.15	.30
☐ 45	Tim Horton	7.00	3.10	.85
☐ 46	Ron Ellis	2.50	1.15	.30
☐ 47	Paul Henderson	2.50	1.15	.30
☐ 48	Brit Selby	2.00	.90	.25
☐ 49	Floyd Smith	2.00	.90	.25
☐ 50	Mike Walton	2.50	1.15	.30
☐ 51	Dave Keon	5.00	2.30	.60
☐ 52	Murray Oliver	2.00	.90	.25
☐ 53	Bob Pulford	2.50	1.15	.30
☐ 54	Norm Ullman	4.00	1.80	.50
☐ 55	Roger Crozier	2.50	1.15	.30
☐ 56	Roy Edwards	2.50	1.15	.30
☐ 57	Bob Baun	2.50	1.15	.30
☐ 58	Gary Bergman	2.00	.90	.25
☐ 59	Carl Brewer	2.50	1.15	.30
☐ 60	Wayne Connelly	2.00	.90	.25
☐ 61	Gordie Howe	60.00	27.00	7.50
☐ 62	Frank Mahovlich	8.00	3.60	1.00
☐ 63	Bruce MacGregor	2.00	.90	.25
☐ 64	Alex Delvecchio	5.00	2.30	.60
☐ 65	Pete Stemkowski	2.00	.90	.25
☐ 66	Denis DeJordy	2.50	1.15	.30
☐ 67	Doug Jarrett	2.00	.90	.25
☐ 68	Gilles Marotte	2.00	.90	.25
☐ 69	Pat Stapleton	2.50	1.15	.30
☐ 70	Bobby Hull	50.00	23.00	6.25
☐ 71	Dennis Hull	2.50	1.15	.30
☐ 72	Doug Mohns	2.00	.90	.25
☐ 73	Jim Pappin	2.00	.90	.25
☐ 74	Ken Wharram	2.00	.90	.25
☐ 75	Pit Martin	2.50	1.15	.30
☐ 76	Stan Mikita	15.00	6.75	1.90
☐ 77	Charlie Hodge	2.50	1.15	.30
☐ 78	Gary Smith	2.50	1.15	.30
☐ 79	Harry Howell	2.50	1.15	.30
☐ 80	Bert Marshall	2.00	.90	.25
☐ 81	Doug Roberts	2.00	.90	.25
☐ 82	Carol Vadnais	2.50	1.15	.30
☐ 83	Gerry Ehman	2.00	.90	.25
☐ 84	Bill Hicke	2.00	.90	.25
☐ 85	Gary Jarrett	2.00	.90	.25
☐ 86	Ted Hampson	2.00	.90	.25
☐ 87	Earl Ingarfield	2.00	.90	.25
☐ 88	Doug Favell	5.00	2.30	.60
☐ 89	Bernie Parent	25.00	11.50	3.10
☐ 90	Larry Hillman	2.00	.90	.25
☐ 91	Wayne Hillman	2.00	.90	.25
☐ 92	Ed Van Impe	2.00	.90	.25
☐ 93	Joe Watson	2.00	.90	.25
☐ 94	Gary Dornhoefer	2.50	1.15	.30
☐ 95	Reg Fleming	2.00	.90	.25
☐ 96	Jean-Guy Gendron	2.00	.90	.25
☐ 97	Jim Johnson	2.00	.90	.25
☐ 98	Andre Lacroix	3.00	1.35	.40
☐ 99	Gerry Desjardins	4.00	1.80	.50
☐ 100	Dale Rolfe	2.00	.90	.25
☐ 101	Bill White	2.00	.90	.25
☐ 102	Bill Flett	2.00	.90	.25
☐ 103	Ted Irvine	2.00	.90	.25
☐ 104	Ross Lonsberry	2.50	1.15	.30
☐ 105	Leon Rochefort	2.00	.90	.25
☐ 106	Eddie Shack	4.00	1.80	.50
☐ 107	Dennis Hextall	3.50	1.55	.45
☐ 108	Eddie Joyal	2.00	.90	.25
☐ 109	Gord Labossiere	2.00	.90	.25
☐ 110	Les Binkley	2.50	1.15	.30
☐ 111	Tracy Pratt	2.00	.90	.25
☐ 112	Bryan Watson	2.00	.90	.25
☐ 113	Bob Woytowich	2.00	.90	.25
☐ 114	Keith McCreary	2.00	.90	.25
☐ 115	Dean Prentice	2.00	.90	.25
☐ 116	Glen Sather	4.00	1.80	.50
☐ 117	Ken Schinkel	2.00	.90	.25
☐ 118	Wally Boyer	2.00	.90	.25
☐ 119	Val Fonteyne	2.00	.90	.25
☐ 120	Ron Schock	2.00	.90	.25
☐ 121	Cesare Maniago	2.50	1.15	.30
☐ 122	Leo Boivin	2.00	.90	.25
☐ 123	Bob McCord	2.00	.90	.25
☐ 124	John Miszuk	2.00	.90	.25
☐ 125	Danny Grant	2.50	1.15	.30
☐ 126	Claude Larose	2.00	.90	.25
☐ 127	Jean-Paul Parise	2.50	1.15	.30
☐ 128	Tom Williams	2.00	.90	.25
☐ 129	Charlie Burns	2.00	.90	.25
☐ 130	Ray Cullen	2.00	.90	.25
☐ 131	Danny O'Shea	2.00	.90	.25
☐ 132	Checklist Card	60.00	6.00	1.20

1970-71 Topps

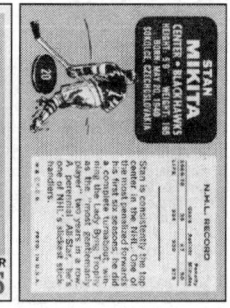

The 1970-71 Topps set consists of 132 cards. Cards measure 2 1/2" by 3 1/2". Card fronts have solid player backgrounds that differ in color according to team. The player's name, team and position are at the bottom. The backs feature the player's 1968-69 and career statistics as well as a short biography. Players from the expansion Buffalo Sabres and Vancouver Canucks are included. Rookie Cards include Wayne Cashman, Brad Park and Gilbert Perreault.

		NRMT	VG-E	GOOD
	COMPLETE SET (132)	400.00	180.00	50.00
	COMMON PLAYER (1-132)	1.50	.65	.19
☐ 1	Gerry Cheevers	15.00	4.50	1.50
☐ 2	Johnny Bucyk	4.00	1.80	.50
☐ 3	Bobby Orr	75.00	34.00	9.50
☐ 4	Don Awrey	1.50	.65	.19
☐ 5	Fred Stanfield	1.50	.65	.19
☐ 6	John McKenzie	2.00	.90	.25
☐ 7	Wayne Cashman	8.00	3.60	1.00
☐ 8	Ken Hodge	2.00	.90	.25
☐ 9	Wayne Carleton	1.50	.65	.19
☐ 10	Garnet Bailey	1.50	.65	.19
☐ 11	Phil Esposito	18.00	8.00	2.30
☐ 12	Lou Angotti	1.50	.65	.19
☐ 13	Jim Pappin	1.50	.65	.19
☐ 14	Dennis Hull	2.00	.90	.25
☐ 15	Bobby Hull	35.00	16.00	4.40
☐ 16	Doug Mohns	1.50	.65	.19
☐ 17	Pat Stapleton	2.00	.90	.25
☐ 18	Pit Martin	2.00	.90	.25
☐ 19	Eric Nesterenko	2.00	.90	.25
☐ 20	Stan Mikita	12.00	5.50	1.50
☐ 21	Roy Edwards	2.00	.90	.25
☐ 22	Frank Mahovlich	7.00	3.10	.85
☐ 23	Ron Harris	1.50	.65	.19
☐ 24	Bob Baun	2.00	.90	.25
☐ 25	Pete Stemkowski	1.50	.65	.19
☐ 26	Garry Unger	3.00	1.35	.40
☐ 27	Bruce MacGregor	1.50	.65	.19
☐ 28	Larry Jeffrey	1.50	.65	.19
☐ 29	Gordie Howe	50.00	23.00	6.25
☐ 30	Billy Dea	1.50	.65	.19
☐ 31	Denis DeJordy	2.00	.90	.25
☐ 32	Matt Ravlich	1.50	.65	.19
☐ 33	Dave Amadio	1.50	.65	.19
☐ 34	Gilles Marotte	1.50	.65	.19
☐ 35	Eddie Shack	3.00	1.35	.40

☐	36	Bob Pulford	2.00	.90	.25
☐	37	Ross Lonsberry	2.00	.90	.25
☐	38	Gord Labossiere	1.50	.65	.19
☐	39	Eddie Joyal	1.50	.65	.19
☐	40	Gump Worsley	5.00	2.30	.60
☐	41	Bob McCord	1.50	.65	.19
☐	42	Leo Boivin	1.50	.65	.19
☐	43	Tom Reid	1.50	.65	.19
☐	44	Charlie Burns	1.50	.65	.19
☐	45	Bob Barlow	1.50	.65	.19
☐	46	Bill Goldsworthy	2.00	.90	.25
☐	47	Danny Grant	2.00	.90	.25
☐	48	Norm Beaudin	1.50	.65	.19
☐	49	Rogatien Vachon	5.00	2.30	.60
☐	50	Yvan Cournoyer	5.00	2.30	.60
☐	51	Serge Savard	7.00	3.10	.85
☐	52	Jacques Laperriere	2.00	.90	.25
☐	53	Terry Harper	1.50	.65	.19
☐	54	Ralph Backstrom	2.00	.90	.25
☐	55	Jean Beliveau	10.00	4.50	1.25
☐	56	Claude Larose UER	1.50	.65	.19
		(Misspelled LaRose			
		on both sides)			
☐	57	Jacques Lemaire	5.00	2.30	.60
☐	58	Peter Mahovlich	2.00	.90	.25
☐	59	Tim Horton	5.00	2.30	.60
☐	60	Bob Nevin	1.50	.65	.19
☐	61	Dave Balon	1.50	.65	.19
☐	62	Vic Hadfield	2.00	.90	.25
☐	63	Rod Gilbert	4.00	1.80	.50
☐	64	Ron Stewart	1.50	.65	.19
☐	65	Ted Irvine	1.50	.65	.19
☐	66	Arnie Brown	1.50	.65	.19
☐	67	Brad Park	30.00	13.50	3.80
☐	68	Ed Giacomin	7.00	3.10	.85
☐	69	Gary Smith	2.00	.90	.25
☐	70	Carol Vadnais	2.00	.90	.25
☐	71	Doug Roberts	1.50	.65	.19
☐	72	Harry Howell	2.00	.90	.25
☐	73	Joe Szura	1.50	.65	.19
☐	74	Mike Laughton	1.50	.65	.19
☐	75	Gary Jarrett	1.50	.65	.19
☐	76	Bill Hicke	1.50	.65	.19
☐	77	Paul Andrea	1.50	.65	.19
☐	78	Bernie Parent	14.00	6.25	1.75
☐	79	Joe Watson	1.50	.65	.19
☐	80	Ed Van Impe	1.50	.65	.19
☐	81	Larry Hillman	1.50	.65	.19
☐	82	George Swarbrick	1.50	.65	.19
☐	83	Bill Sutherland	1.50	.65	.19
☐	84	Andre Lacroix	2.00	.90	.25
☐	85	Gary Dornhoefer	1.50	.65	.19
☐	86	Jean-Guy Gendron	1.50	.65	.19
☐	87	Al Smith	2.00	.90	.25
☐	88	Bob Woytowich	1.50	.65	.19
☐	89	Duane Rupp	1.50	.65	.19
☐	90	Jim Morrison	1.50	.65	.19
☐	91	Ron Schock	1.50	.65	.19
☐	92	Ken Schinkel	1.50	.65	.19
☐	93	Keith McCreary	1.50	.65	.19
☐	94	Bryan Hextall	2.00	.90	.25
☐	95	Wayne Hicks	1.50	.65	.19
☐	96	Gary Sabourin	1.50	.65	.19
☐	97	Ernie Wakely	1.50	.65	.19
☐	98	Bob Wall	1.50	.65	.19
☐	99	Barclay Plager	2.00	.90	.25
☐	100	Jean-Guy Talbot	1.50	.65	.19
☐	101	Gary Veneruzzo	1.50	.65	.19
☐	102	Tim Ecclestone	1.50	.65	.19
☐	103	Red Berenson	2.00	.90	.25
☐	104	Larry Keenan	1.50	.65	.19
☐	105	Bruce Gamble	2.00	.90	.25
☐	106	Jim Dorey	1.50	.65	.19
☐	107	Mike Pelyk	1.50	.65	.19
☐	108	Rick Ley	1.50	.65	.19
☐	109	Mike Walton	1.50	.65	.19
☐	110	Norm Ullman	3.00	1.35	.40
☐	111	Brit Selby	1.50	.65	.19
☐	112	Garry Monahan	1.50	.65	.19
☐	113	George Armstrong	2.00	.90	.25
☐	114	Gary Doak	1.50	.65	.19
☐	115	Darryl Sly	1.50	.65	.19
☐	116	Wayne Maki	1.50	.65	.19
☐	117	Orland Kurtenbach	1.50	.65	.19
☐	118	Murray Hall	1.50	.65	.19
☐	119	Marc Reaume	1.50	.65	.19
☐	120	Pat Quinn	3.00	1.35	.40
☐	121	Andre Boudrias	1.50	.65	.19
☐	122	Poul Popiel	1.50	.65	.19
☐	123	Paul Terbenche	1.50	.65	.19
☐	124	Howie Menard	1.50	.65	.19
☐	125	Gerry Meehan	2.50	1.15	.30
☐	126	Skip Krake	1.50	.65	.19

☐	127	Phil Goyette	1.50	.65	.19
☐	128	Reg Fleming	1.50	.65	.19
☐	129	Don Marshall	1.50	.65	.19
☐	130	Bill Inglis	1.50	.65	.19
☐	131	Gilbert Perreault	50.00	23.00	6.25
☐	132	Checklist Card	50.00	5.00	1.00

1970-71 Topps/OPC Sticker Stamps

This set consists of 33 unnumbered, full-color sticker stamps measuring 2 1/2" by 3 1/2". The backs are blank. The checklist below is ordered alphabetically for convenience. The sticker cards were issued as an insert in the regular issue wax packs of the 1970-71 Topps hockey as well as in first series wax packs of 1970-71 O-Pee-Chee.

		NRMT	VG-E	GOOD
COMPLETE SET (33)		175.00	70.00	18.00
COMMON PLAYER (1-33)		2.00	.80	.20
☐ 1	Jean Beliveau	18.00	7.25	1.80
☐ 2	Red Berenson	3.00	1.20	.30
☐ 3	Wayne Carleton	2.00	.80	.20
☐ 4	Tim Ecclestone	2.00	.80	.20
☐ 5	Ron Ellis	3.00	1.20	.30
☐ 6	Phil Esposito	20.00	8.00	2.00
☐ 7	Tony Esposito	15.00	6.00	1.50
☐ 8	Bill Flett	2.00	.80	.20
☐ 9	Ed Giacomin	6.00	2.40	.60
☐ 10	Rod Gilbert	6.00	2.40	.60
☐ 11	Danny Grant	3.00	1.20	.30
☐ 12	Bill Hicke	2.00	.80	.20
☐ 13	Gordie Howe	40.00	16.00	4.00
☐ 14	Bobby Hull	25.00	10.00	2.50
☐ 15	Earl Ingarfield	2.00	.80	.20
☐ 16	Eddie Joyal	2.00	.80	.20
☐ 17	Dave Keon	6.00	2.40	.60
☐ 18	Andre Lacroix	3.00	1.20	.30
☐ 19	Jacques Laperriere	4.00	1.60	.40
☐ 20	Jacques Lemaire	6.00	2.40	.60
☐ 21	Frank Mahovlich	12.00	5.00	1.20
☐ 22	Keith McCreary	2.00	.80	.20
☐ 23	Stan Mikita	15.00	6.00	1.50
☐ 24	Bobby Orr	50.00	20.00	5.00
☐ 25	Jean-Paul Parise	2.00	.80	.20
☐ 26	Jean Ratelle	6.00	2.40	.60
☐ 27	Derek Sanderson	4.00	1.60	.40
☐ 28	Frank St.Marseille	2.00	.80	.20
☐ 29	Ron Schock	2.00	.80	.20
☐ 30	Garry Unger	3.00	1.20	.30
☐ 31	Carol Vadnais	2.00	.80	.20
☐ 32	Ed Van Impe	2.00	.80	.20
☐ 33	Bob Woytowich	2.00	.80	.20

1971-72 Topps

The 1971-72 Topps set consists of 132 cards that measure 2 1/2" by 3 1/2". For the first time, Topps included the player's NHL year-by-year career record on back. A short player biography and a cartoon-illustrated fact about the

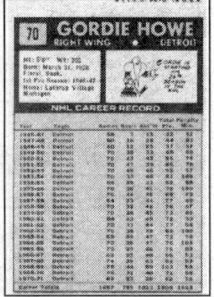

player also appear on back. A League Leaders (1-6) subset is exclusive to the Topps set of this year. Rookie Cards include Ken Dryden. An additional key card in the set is Gordie Howe (70). Howe does not have a regular card in the 1971-72 O-Pee-Chee set.

	NRMT	VG-E	GOOD
COMPLETE SET (132)	350.00	160.00	45.00
COMMON PLAYER (1-132)	1.00	.45	.13

		NRMT	VG-E	GOOD
☐ 1	Goal Leaders	15.00	4.50	1.50
	Phil Esposito			
	Johnny Bucyk			
	Bobby Hull			
☐ 2	Assists Leaders	15.00	6.75	1.90
	Bobby Orr			
	Phil Esposito			
	Johnny Bucyk			
☐ 3	Scoring Leaders	15.00	6.75	1.90
	Phil Esposito			
	Bobby Orr			
	Johnny Bucyk			
☐ 4	Goalies Win Leaders	8.00	3.60	1.00
	Tony Esposito			
	Ed Johnston			
	Gerry Cheevers			
	Ed Giacomin			
☐ 5	Shutouts Leaders	6.00	2.70	.75
	Ed Giacomin			
	Tony Esposito			
	Cesare Maniago			
☐ 6	Goals Against	10.00	4.50	1.25
	Average Leaders			
	Jacques Plante			
	Ed Giacomin			
	Tony Esposito			
☐ 7	Fred Stanfield	1.00	.45	.13
☐ 8	Mike Robitaille	1.00	.45	.13
☐ 9	Vic Hadfield	1.50	.65	.19
☐ 10	Jacques Plante	14.00	6.25	1.75
☐ 11	Bill White	1.00	.45	.13
☐ 12	Andre Boudrias	1.00	.45	.13
☐ 13	Jim Lorentz	1.00	.45	.13
☐ 14	Arnie Brown	1.00	.45	.13
☐ 15	Yvan Cournoyer	4.00	1.80	.50
☐ 16	Bryan Hextall	1.50	.65	.19
☐ 17	Gary Croteau	1.00	.45	.13
☐ 18	Gilles Villemure	1.50	.65	.19
☐ 19	Serge Bernier	1.50	.65	.19
☐ 20	Phil Esposito	14.00	6.25	1.75
☐ 21	Charlie Burns	1.00	.45	.13
☐ 22	Doug Barrie	1.00	.45	.13
☐ 23	Eddie Joyal	1.00	.45	.13
☐ 24	Rosaire Paiement	1.00	.45	.13
☐ 25	Pat Stapleton	1.50	.65	.19
☐ 26	Garry Unger	1.50	.65	.19
☐ 27	Al Smith	1.50	.65	.19
☐ 28	Bob Woytowich	1.00	.45	.13
☐ 29	Marc Tardif	1.50	.65	.19
☐ 30	Norm Ullman	2.50	1.15	.30
☐ 31	Tom Williams	1.00	.45	.13
☐ 32	Ted Harris	1.00	.45	.13
☐ 33	Andre Lacroix	1.50	.65	.19
☐ 34	Mike Byers	1.00	.45	.13
☐ 35	Johnny Bucyk	2.50	1.15	.30
☐ 36	Roger Crozier	1.50	.65	.19
☐ 37	Alex Delvecchio	3.50	1.55	.45
☐ 38	Frank St.Marseille	1.00	.45	.13
☐ 39	Pit Martin	1.50	.65	.19
☐ 40	Brad Park	12.00	5.50	1.50
☐ 41	Greg Polis	1.00	.45	.13
☐ 42	Orland Kurtenbach	1.00	.45	.13
☐ 43	Jim McKenny	1.00	.45	.13
☐ 44	Bob Nevin	1.00	.45	.13
☐ 45	Ken Dryden	100.00	45.00	12.50
☐ 46	Carol Vadnais	1.50	.65	.19
☐ 47	Bill Flett	1.00	.45	.13
☐ 48	Jim Johnson	1.00	.45	.13
☐ 49	Al Hamilton	1.00	.45	.13
☐ 50	Bobby Hull	25.00	11.50	3.10
☐ 51	Chris Bordeleau	1.00	.45	.13
☐ 52	Tim Ecclestone	1.00	.45	.13
☐ 53	Rod Seiling	1.00	.45	.13
☐ 54	Gerry Cheevers	5.00	2.30	.60
☐ 55	Bill Goldsworthy	1.50	.65	.19
☐ 56	Ron Schock	1.00	.45	.13
☐ 57	Jim Dorey	1.00	.45	.13
☐ 58	Wayne Maki	1.00	.45	.13
☐ 59	Terry Harper	1.00	.45	.13
☐ 60	Gilbert Perreault	18.00	8.00	2.30
☐ 61	Ernie Hicke	1.00	.45	.13
☐ 62	Wayne Hillman	1.00	.45	.13
☐ 63	Denis DeJordy	1.50	.65	.19
☐ 64	Ken Schinkel	1.00	.45	.13
☐ 65	Derek Sanderson	3.50	1.55	.45
☐ 66	Barclay Plager	1.50	.65	.19
☐ 67	Paul Henderson	1.50	.65	.19
☐ 68	Jude Drouin	1.00	.45	.13
☐ 69	Keith Magnuson	1.50	.65	.19
☐ 70	Gordie Howe	55.00	25.00	7.00
☐ 71	Jacques Lemaire	3.50	1.55	.45
☐ 72	Doug Favell	1.50	.65	.19
☐ 73	Bert Marshall	1.00	.45	.13
☐ 74	Gerry Meehan	1.50	.65	.19
☐ 75	Walt Tkaczuk	1.50	.65	.19
☐ 76	Bob Berry	2.50	1.15	.30
☐ 77	Syl Apps	2.50	1.15	.30
☐ 78	Tom Webster	1.50	.65	.19
☐ 79	Danny Grant	1.50	.65	.19
☐ 80	Dave Keon	2.50	1.15	.30
☐ 81	Ernie Wakely	1.00	.45	.13
☐ 82	John McKenzie	1.50	.65	.19
☐ 83	Doug Roberts	1.00	.45	.13
☐ 84	Peter Mahovlich	1.50	.65	.19
☐ 85	Dennis Hull	1.50	.65	.19
☐ 86	Juha Widing	1.00	.45	.13
☐ 87	Gary Doak	1.00	.45	.13
☐ 88	Phil Goyette	1.00	.45	.13
☐ 89	Gary Dornhoefer	1.00	.45	.13
☐ 90	Ed Giacomin	5.00	2.30	.60
☐ 91	Red Berenson	1.50	.65	.19
☐ 92	Mike Pelyk	1.00	.45	.13
☐ 93	Gary Jarrett	1.00	.45	.13
☐ 94	Bob Pulford	1.50	.65	.19
☐ 95	Dale Tallon	1.50	.65	.19
☐ 96	Eddie Shack	1.50	.65	.19
☐ 97	Jean Ratelle	3.50	1.55	.45
☐ 98	Jim Pappin	1.00	.45	.13
☐ 99	Roy Edwards	1.50	.65	.19
☐ 100	Bobby Orr	50.00	23.00	6.25
☐ 101	Ted Hampson	1.00	.45	.13
☐ 102	Mickey Redmond	3.00	1.35	.40
☐ 103	Bob Plager	1.50	.65	.19
☐ 104	Bruce Gamble	1.50	.65	.19
☐ 105	Frank Mahovlich	6.00	2.70	.75
☐ 106	Tony Featherstone	1.00	.45	.13
☐ 107	Tracy Pratt	1.00	.45	.13
☐ 108	Ralph Backstrom	1.50	.65	.19
☐ 109	Murray Hall	1.00	.45	.13
☐ 110	Tony Esposito	20.00	9.00	2.50
☐ 111	Checklist Card	40.00	4.00	.80
☐ 112	Jim Neilson	1.00	.45	.13
☐ 113	Ron Ellis	1.50	.65	.19
☐ 114	Bobby Clarke	30.00	13.50	3.80
☐ 115	Ken Hodge	1.50	.65	.19
☐ 116	Jim Roberts	1.50	.65	.19
☐ 117	Cesare Maniago	1.50	.65	.19
☐ 118	Jean Pronovost	1.50	.65	.19
☐ 119	Gary Bergman	1.00	.45	.13
☐ 120	Henri Richard	4.00	1.80	.50
☐ 121	Ross Lonsberry	1.00	.45	.13
☐ 122	Pat Quinn	1.50	.65	.19
☐ 123	Rod Gilbert	3.50	1.55	.45
☐ 124	Gary Smith	1.50	.65	.19
☐ 125	Stan Mikita	10.00	4.50	1.25
☐ 126	Ed Van Impe	1.00	.45	.13
☐ 127	Wayne Connelly	1.00	.45	.13
☐ 128	Dennis Hextall	1.50	.65	.19
☐ 129	Wayne Cashman	2.50	1.15	.30
☐ 130	J.C. Tremblay	1.00	.45	.13
☐ 131	Bernie Parent	9.00	4.00	1.15
☐ 132	Dunc McCallum	4.00	1.20	.40

1972-73 Topps

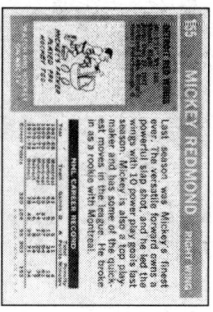

The 1972-73 production marked Topps' largest set to date at 176 cards. Expansion plays a part in the increase as the Atlanta Flames and New York Islanders join the league. Tan borders include team name down the left side. A tan colored bar that crosses the bottom portion of the player photo includes the player's name and team logo. Cards measure 2 1/2" by 3 1/2". The back contains the year by year NHL career record of the player, a short biography and a cartoon illustrated fact about the player. The key cards in the set are not Rookie Cards, but are the first Topps cards of Marcel Dionne and Guy Lafleur. The set was printed on two sheets of 132 cards each creating 88 double-printed cards. The double prints are noted in the checklist below by DP. Topps gives collectors a look at the various NHL hardware in the Trophy subset (170-176).

	NRMT	VG-E	GOOD
COMPLETE SET (176)	300.00	135.00	38.00
COMMON PLAYER (1-176)	.75	.35	.09

		NRMT	VG-E	GOOD
☐ 1	World Champions DP	4.00	1.00	.30
	Boston Bruins Team			
☐ 2	Playoff Game 1	1.00	.45	.13
	Bruins 6			
	Rangers 5			
☐ 3	Playoff Game 2	1.00	.45	.13
	Bruins 2			
	Rangers 1			
☐ 4	Playoff Game 3	1.00	.45	.13
	Rangers 5			
	Bruins 2			
☐ 5	Playoff Game 4 DP	1.00	.45	.13
	Bruins 3			
	Rangers 2			
☐ 6	Playoff Game 5 DP	1.00	.45	.13
	Rangers 3			
	Bruins 2			
☐ 7	Playoff Game 6 DP	1.00	.45	.13
	Bruins 3			
	Rangers 0			
☐ 8	Stanley Cup Trophy	3.50	1.55	.45
☐ 9	Ed Van Impe DP	.60	.25	.08
☐ 10	Yvan Cournoyer DP	2.50	1.15	.30
☐ 11	Syl Apps DP	.75	.35	.09
☐ 12	Bill Plager	1.50	.65	.19
☐ 13	Ed Johnston DP	.75	.35	.09
☐ 14	Walt Tkaczuk	1.00	.45	.13
☐ 15	Dale Tallon DP	.60	.25	.08
☐ 16	Gerry Meehan	1.00	.45	.13
☐ 17	Reggie Leach	3.00	1.35	.40
☐ 18	Marcel Dionne DP	18.00	8.00	2.30
☐ 19	Andre Dupont	2.00	.90	.25
☐ 20	Tony Esposito	12.00	5.50	1.50
☐ 21	Bob Berry DP	.75	.35	.09
☐ 22	Craig Cameron	.75	.35	.09
☐ 23	Ted Harris	.75	.35	.09
☐ 24	Jacques Plante	10.00	4.50	1.25
☐ 25	Jacques Lemaire DP	2.00	.90	.25
☐ 26	Simon Nolet DP	.75	.35	.09
☐ 27	Keith McCreary DP	.60	.25	.08
☐ 28	Duane Rupp	.75	.35	.09
☐ 29	Wayne Cashman	1.50	.65	.19
☐ 30	Brad Park	6.00	2.70	.75
☐ 31	Roger Crozier	1.00	.45	.13

☐ 32	Wayne Maki	.75	.35	.09
☐ 33	Tim Ecclestone	.75	.35	.09
☐ 34	Rick Smith	.75	.35	.09
☐ 35	Garry Unger DP	.75	.35	.09
☐ 36	Serge Bernier DP	.75	.35	.09
☐ 37	Brian Glennie	.75	.35	.09
☐ 38	Gerry Desjardins DP	.75	.35	.09
☐ 39	Danny Grant	1.00	.45	.13
☐ 40	Bill White DP	.60	.25	.08
☐ 41	Gary Dornhoefer DP	.60	.25	.08
☐ 42	Peter Mahovlich	1.00	.45	.13
☐ 43	Greg Polis DP	.60	.25	.08
☐ 44	Larry Hale DP	.60	.25	.08
☐ 45	Dallas Smith	.75	.35	.09
☐ 46	Orland Kurtenbach DP	.60	.25	.08
☐ 47	Steve Atkinson	.75	.35	.09
☐ 48	Joey Johnston DP	.60	.25	.08
☐ 49	Gary Bergman	.75	.35	.09
☐ 50	Jean Ratelle	3.00	1.35	.40
☐ 51	Rogatien Vachon DP	2.50	1.15	.30
☐ 52	Phil Roberto DP	.60	.25	.08
☐ 53	Brian Spencer DP	.75	.35	.09
☐ 54	Jim McKenny DP	.60	.25	.08
☐ 55	Gump Worsley	3.50	1.55	.45
☐ 56	Stan Mikita DP	5.00	2.30	.60
☐ 57	Guy Lapointe	2.00	.90	.25
☐ 58	Lew Morrison DP	.60	.25	.08
☐ 59	Ron Schock DP	.60	.25	.08
☐ 60	Johnny Bucyk	2.50	1.15	.30
☐ 61	Goals Leaders	9.00	4.00	1.15
	Phil Esposito			
	Vic Hadfield			
	Bobby Hull			
☐ 62	Assists Leaders DP	12.00	5.50	1.50
	Bobby Orr			
	Phil Esposito			
	Jean Ratelle			
☐ 63	Scoring Leaders DP	12.00	5.50	1.50
	Phil Esposito			
	Bobby Orr			
	Jean Ratelle			
☐ 64	Goals Against	5.00	2.30	.60
	Average Leaders			
	Tony Esposito			
	Gilles Villemure			
	Gump Worsley			
☐ 65	Penalty Minutes	.75	.35	.09
	Leaders DP			
	Bryan Watson			
	Keith Magnuson			
	Gary Dornhoefer			
☐ 66	Jim Neilson	.75	.35	.09
☐ 67	Nick Libett DP	.60	.25	.08
☐ 68	Jim Lorentz	.75	.35	.09
☐ 69	Gilles Meloche	4.00	1.80	.50
☐ 70	Pat Stapleton	1.00	.45	.13
☐ 71	Frank St.Marseille DP	.60	.25	.08
☐ 72	Butch Goring	2.00	.90	.25
☐ 73	Paul Henderson DP	.75	.35	.09
☐ 74	Doug Favell	1.00	.45	.13
☐ 75	Jocelyn Guevremont DP	.60	.25	.08
☐ 76	Tom Miller	.75	.35	.09
☐ 77	Bill MacMillan	.75	.35	.09
☐ 78	Doug Mohns	.75	.35	.09
☐ 79	Guy Lafleur DP	20.00	9.00	2.50
☐ 80	Rod Gilbert DP	2.00	.90	.25
☐ 81	Gary Doak	.75	.35	.09
☐ 82	Dave Burrows DP	.60	.25	.08
☐ 83	Gary Croteau	.75	.35	.09
☐ 84	Tracy Pratt DP	.60	.25	.08
☐ 85	Carol Vadnais DP	.60	.25	.08
☐ 86	Jacques Caron DP	.60	.25	.08
☐ 87	Keith Magnuson	1.50	.65	.19
☐ 88	Dave Keon	2.00	.90	.25
☐ 89	Mike Corrigan	.75	.35	.09
☐ 90	Bobby Clarke	15.00	6.75	1.90
☐ 91	Dunc Wilson DP	.75	.35	.09
☐ 92	Gerry Hart	.75	.35	.09
☐ 93	Lou Nanne	1.00	.45	.13
☐ 94	Checklist 1-176 DP	20.00	2.00	.40
☐ 95	Red Berenson DP	.75	.35	.09
☐ 96	Bob Plager	1.00	.45	.13
☐ 97	Jim Rutherford	3.50	1.55	.45
☐ 98	Rick Foley DP	.60	.25	.08
☐ 99	Pit Martin DP	.75	.35	.09
☐ 100	Bobby Orr DP	30.00	13.50	3.80
☐ 101	Stan Gilbertson	.75	.35	.09
☐ 102	Barry Wilkins	.75	.35	.09
☐ 103	Terry Crisp DP	.75	.35	.09
☐ 104	Cesare Maniago DP	.75	.35	.09
☐ 105	Marc Tardif	.75	.35	.09
☐ 106	Don Luce DP	.75	.35	.09
☐ 107	Mike Pelyk	.75	.35	.09

☐ 108	Juha Widing DP	.60	.25	.08
☐ 109	Phil Myre DP	2.00	.90	.25
☐ 110	Vic Hadfield	1.00	.45	.13
☐ 111	Arnie Brown DP	.60	.25	.08
☐ 112	Ross Lonsberry DP	.60	.25	.08
☐ 113	Dick Redmond	.75	.35	.09
☐ 114	Gary Smith	1.00	.45	.13
☐ 115	Bill Goldsworthy	1.00	.45	.13
☐ 116	Bryan Watson	.75	.35	.09
☐ 117	Dave Balon DP	.60	.25	.08
☐ 118	Bill Mikkelson DP	.60	.25	.08
☐ 119	Terry Harper DP	.60	.25	.08
☐ 120	Gilbert Perreault DP	6.00	2.70	.75
☐ 121	Tony Esposito AS1	5.00	2.30	.60
☐ 122	Bobby Orr AS1	18.00	8.00	2.30
☐ 123	Brad Park AS1	3.00	1.35	.40
☐ 124	Phil Esposito AS1	5.00	2.30	.60
	(Brother Tony pictured in background)			
☐ 125	Rod Gilbert AS1	2.50	1.15	.30
☐ 126	Bobby Hull AS1	15.00	6.75	1.90
☐ 127	Ken Dryden AS2 DP	10.00	4.50	1.25
☐ 128	Bill White AS2 DP	1.00	.45	.13
☐ 129	Pat Stapleton AS2 DP	1.00	.45	.13
☐ 130	Jean Ratelle AS2 DP	1.75	.80	.22
☐ 131	Yvan Cournoyer AS2 DP	1.75	.80	.22
☐ 132	Vic Hadfield AS2 DP	1.00	.45	.13
☐ 133	Ralph Backstrom DP	.75	.35	.09
☐ 134	Bob Baun DP	.75	.35	.09
☐ 135	Fred Stanfield DP	.60	.25	.08
☐ 136	Barclay Plager DP	.75	.35	.09
☐ 137	Gilles Villemure	1.00	.45	.13
☐ 138	Ron Harris DP	.60	.25	.08
☐ 139	Bill Flett DP	.60	.25	.08
☐ 140	Frank Mahovlich	4.00	1.80	.50
☐ 141	Alex Delvecchio DP	2.00	.90	.25
☐ 142	Poul Popiel	.75	.35	.09
☐ 143	Jean Pronovost DP	.75	.35	.09
☐ 144	Denis DeJordy DP	.75	.35	.09
☐ 145	Richard Martin DP	3.00	1.35	.40
☐ 146	Ivan Boldirev	2.00	.90	.25
☐ 147	Jack Egers	.75	.35	.09
☐ 148	Jim Pappin	.75	.35	.09
☐ 149	Rod Seiling	.75	.35	.09
☐ 150	Phil Esposito	9.00	4.00	1.15
☐ 151	Gary Edwards	1.00	.45	.13
☐ 152	Ron Ellis DP	.75	.35	.09
☐ 153	Jude Drouin	.75	.35	.09
☐ 154	Ernie Hicke DP	.60	.25	.08
☐ 155	Mickey Redmond	1.50	.65	.19
☐ 156	Joe Watson DP	.60	.25	.08
☐ 157	Bryan Hextall	.75	.35	.09
☐ 158	Andre Boudrias	.75	.35	.09
☐ 159	Ed Westfall	1.00	.45	.13
☐ 160	Ken Dryden	30.00	13.50	3.80
☐ 161	Rene Robert DP	2.50	1.15	.30
☐ 162	Bert Marshall DP	.60	.25	.08
☐ 163	Gary Sabourin	.75	.35	.09
☐ 164	Dennis Hull	1.00	.45	.13
☐ 165	Ed Giacomin DP	2.50	1.15	.30
☐ 166	Ken Hodge	1.00	.45	.13
☐ 167	Gilles Marotte DP	.60	.25	.08
☐ 168	Norm Ullman DP	1.50	.65	.19
☐ 169	Barry Gibbs	.75	.35	.09
☐ 170	Art Ross Trophy	1.50	.65	.19
☐ 171	Hart Memorial Trophy	1.50	.65	.19
☐ 172	James Norris Trophy	1.50	.65	.19
☐ 173	Vezina Trophy DP	1.00	.45	.13
☐ 174	Calder Trophy DP	1.00	.45	.13
☐ 175	Lady Byng Trophy DP	1.00	.45	.13
☐ 176	Conn Smythe Trophy DP	3.00	.75	.24

1973-74 Topps

Once again increasing in size, the 1973-74 Topps set consists of 198 cards. Cards measure 2 1/2" by 3 1/2". The fronts of the cards have distinct colored borders including blue and green which differs from O-Pee-Chee. The backs contain the player's 1972-73 season record, career numbers, a short biography and a cartoon-illustrated fact about the player. Team cards (92-107) give team and player records on the back. Since the set was printed on two 132-card sheets, there are 66 double-printed cards. These double prints are denoted in the checklist below by DP. Rookie Cards include Bill Barber, Billy Smith and Dave Schultz. Ken Dryden (10) is only in the Topps set.

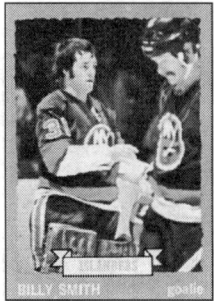
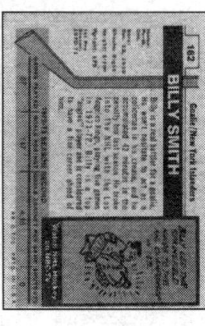

		NRMT	VG-E	GOOD
COMPLETE SET (198)		200.00	90.00	25.00
COMMON PLAYER (1-198)		.50	.23	.06
☐ 1	Goal Leaders	5.00	1.50	.50
	Phil Esposito			
	Rick MacLeish			
☐ 2	Assists Leaders	5.00	2.30	.60
	Phil Esposito			
	Bobby Clarke			
☐ 3	Scoring Leaders	5.00	2.30	.60
	Phil Esposito			
	Bobby Clarke			
☐ 4	Goals Against	6.00	2.70	.75
	Average Leaders			
	Ken Dryden			
	Tony Esposito			
☐ 5	Penalty Min. Leaders	1.50	.65	.19
	Jim Schoenfeld			
	Dave Schultz			
☐ 6	Power Play Goals	3.00	1.35	.40
	Leaders			
	Phil Esposito			
	Rick MacLeish			
☐ 7	Paul Henderson DP	.50	.23	.06
☐ 8	Gregg Sheppard DP UER	.40	.18	.05
	(Misspelled Greg on card front)			
☐ 9	Rod Seiling DP	.40	.18	.05
☐ 10	Ken Dryden	35.00	16.00	4.40
☐ 11	Jean Pronovost DP	.50	.23	.06
☐ 12	Dick Redmond	.50	.23	.06
☐ 13	Keith McCreary DP	.40	.18	.05
☐ 14	Ted Harris DP	.40	.18	.05
☐ 15	Garry Unger	.60	.25	.08
☐ 16	Neil Komadoski	.50	.23	.06
☐ 17	Marcel Dionne	12.00	5.50	1.50
☐ 18	Ernie Hicke DP	.40	.18	.05
☐ 19	Andre Boudrias	.50	.23	.06
☐ 20	Bill Flett	.50	.23	.06
☐ 21	Marshall Johnston	.50	.23	.06
☐ 22	Gerry Meehan	.60	.25	.08
☐ 23	Ed Johnston DP	.50	.23	.06
☐ 24	Serge Savard	1.25	.55	.16
☐ 25	Walt Tkaczuk	.60	.25	.08
☐ 26	Johnny Bucyk	2.00	.90	.25
☐ 27	Dave Burrows	.50	.23	.06
☐ 28	Cliff Koroll	.50	.23	.06
☐ 29	Rey Comeau DP	.40	.18	.05
☐ 30	Barry Gibbs	.50	.23	.06
☐ 31	Wayne Stephenson	.60	.25	.08
☐ 32	Dan Maloney DP	.50	.23	.06
☐ 33	Henry Boucha DP	.40	.18	.05
☐ 34	Gerry Hart	.50	.23	.06
☐ 35	Bobby Schmautz	.50	.23	.06
☐ 36	Ross Lonsberry DP	.40	.18	.05
☐ 37	Ted McAneeley	.50	.23	.06
☐ 38	Don Luce DP	.40	.18	.05
☐ 39	Jim McKenny DP	.40	.18	.05
☐ 40	Frank Mahovlich	3.50	1.55	.45
☐ 41	Bill Fairbairn	.50	.23	.06
☐ 42	Dallas Smith	.50	.23	.06
☐ 43	Bryan Hextall	.50	.23	.06
☐ 44	Keith Magnuson	.60	.25	.08
☐ 45	Dan Bouchard	.60	.25	.08
☐ 46	Jean-Paul Parise DP	.40	.18	.05
☐ 47	Barclay Plager	.60	.25	.08
☐ 48	Mike Corrigan	.50	.23	.06
☐ 49	Nick Libett DP	.40	.18	.05
☐ 50	Bobby Clarke	10.00	4.50	1.25
☐ 51	Bert Marshall DP	.40	.18	.05
☐ 52	Craig Patrick	1.50	.65	.19

☐ 53	Richard Lemieux	.50	.23	.06
☐ 54	Tracy Pratt DP	.40	.18	.05
☐ 55	Ron Ellis DP	.50	.23	.06
☐ 56	Jacques Lemaire	2.50	1.15	.30
☐ 57	Steve Vickers DP	.50	.23	.06
☐ 58	Carol Vadnais	.50	.23	.06
☐ 59	Jim Rutherford DP	.50	.23	.06
☐ 60	Dennis Hull	.60	.25	.08
☐ 61	Pat Quinn DP	.50	.23	.06
☐ 62	Bill Goldsworthy DP	.50	.23	.06
☐ 63	Fran Huck	.50	.23	.06
☐ 64	Rogatien Vachon DP	1.50	.65	.19
☐ 65	Gary Bergman DP	.40	.18	.05
☐ 66	Bernie Parent	4.50	2.00	.55
☐ 67	Ed Westfall	.60	.25	.08
☐ 68	Ivan Boldirev	.60	.25	.08
☐ 69	Don Tannahill DP	.40	.18	.05
☐ 70	Gilbert Perreault DP	6.00	2.70	.75
☐ 71	Mike Pelyk DP	.40	.18	.05
☐ 72	Guy Lafleur DP	15.00	6.75	1.90
☐ 73	Jean Ratelle	2.50	1.15	.30
☐ 74	Gilles Gilbert DP	2.50	1.15	.30
☐ 75	Greg Polis	.50	.23	.06
☐ 76	Doug Jarrett DP	.40	.18	.05
☐ 77	Phil Myre DP	.50	.23	.06
☐ 78	Fred Harvey DP	.40	.18	.05
☐ 79	Jack Egers	.50	.23	.06
☐ 80	Terry Harper	.50	.23	.06
☐ 81	Bill Barber	15.00	6.75	1.90
☐ 82	Roy Edwards DP	.50	.23	.06
☐ 83	Brian Spencer	.60	.25	.08
☐ 84	Reggie Leach DP	1.00	.45	.13
☐ 85	Dave Keon	1.50	.65	.19
☐ 86	Jim Schoenfeld	2.00	.90	.25
☐ 87	Henri Richard DP	1.50	.65	.19
☐ 88	Rod Gilbert DP	1.50	.65	.19
☐ 89	Don Marcotte DP	.40	.18	.05
☐ 90	Tony Esposito	7.00	3.10	.85
☐ 91	Joe Watson	.50	.23	.06
☐ 92	Flames Team	1.50	.65	.19
☐ 93	Bruins Team	2.00	.90	.25
☐ 94	Sabres Team DP	1.50	.65	.19
☐ 95	Golden Seals Team DP	1.50	.65	.19
☐ 96	Blackhawks Team	1.50	.65	.19
☐ 97	Red Wings Team DP	1.50	.65	.19
☐ 98	Kings Team DP	1.50	.65	.19
☐ 99	North Stars Team	1.50	.65	.19
☐ 100	Canadiens Team	2.00	.90	.25
☐ 101	Islanders Teams	1.50	.65	.19
☐ 102	Rangers Team DP	1.50	.65	.19
☐ 103	Flyers Team DP	2.00	.90	.25
☐ 104	Penguins Team	1.50	.65	.19
☐ 105	Blues Team	1.50	.65	.19
☐ 106	Maple Leafs Team	2.00	.90	.25
☐ 107	Canucks Team	1.50	.65	.19
☐ 108	Roger Crozier DP	.50	.23	.06
☐ 109	Tom Reid	.50	.23	.06
☐ 110	Hilliard Graves	.50	.23	.06
☐ 111	Don Lever	.60	.25	.08
☐ 112	Jim Pappin	.50	.23	.06
☐ 113	Ron Schock DP	.40	.18	.05
☐ 114	Gerry Desjardins	.60	.25	.08
☐ 115	Yvan Cournoyer DP	2.00	.90	.25
☐ 116	Checklist Card	18.00	1.80	.35
☐ 117	Bob Leiter	.50	.23	.06
☐ 118	Ab DeMarco	.50	.23	.06
☐ 119	Doug Favell	.60	.25	.08
☐ 120	Phil Esposito	6.00	2.70	.75
☐ 121	Mike Robitaille	.50	.23	.06
☐ 122	Real Lemieux	.50	.23	.06
☐ 123	Jim Neilson	.50	.23	.06
☐ 124	Tim Ecclestone DP	.40	.18	.05
☐ 125	Jude Drouin	.50	.23	.06
☐ 126	Gary Smith DP	.50	.23	.06
☐ 127	Walt McKechnie	.50	.23	.06
☐ 128	Lowell MacDonald	.50	.23	.06
☐ 129	Dale Tallon DP	.40	.18	.05
☐ 130	Billy Harris	.60	.25	.08
☐ 131	Randy Manery DP	.40	.18	.05
☐ 132	Darryl Sittler DP	7.00	3.10	.85
☐ 133	Ken Hodge	.60	.25	.08
☐ 134	Bob Plager	.60	.25	.08
☐ 135	Rick MacLeish	2.50	1.15	.30
☐ 136	Dennis Hextall	.50	.23	.06
☐ 137	Jacques Laperriere DP	.50	.23	.06
☐ 138	Butch Goring	1.00	.45	.13
☐ 139	Rene Robert	.60	.25	.08
☐ 140	Ed Giacomin	2.50	1.15	.30
☐ 141	Alex Delvecchio DP	1.50	.65	.19
☐ 142	Jocelyn Guevremont	.50	.23	.06
☐ 143	Joey Johnston	.50	.23	.06
☐ 144	Bryan Watson DP	.40	.18	.05
☐ 145	Stan Mikita	5.00	2.30	.60

☐ 146	Cesare Maniago	.60	.25	.08
☐ 147	Craig Cameron	.50	.23	.06
☐ 148	Norm Ullman DP	1.00	.45	.13
☐ 149	Dave Schultz	7.00	3.10	.85
☐ 150	Bobby Orr	28.00	12.50	3.50
☐ 151	Phil Roberto	.50	.23	.06
☐ 152	Curt Bennett	.50	.23	.06
☐ 153	Gilles Villemure DP	.50	.23	.06
☐ 154	Chuck Lefley	.50	.23	.06
☐ 155	Richard Martin	2.50	1.15	.30
☐ 156	Juha Widing	.50	.23	.06
☐ 157	Orland Kurtenbach	.50	.23	.06
☐ 158	Bill Collins DP	.40	.18	.05
☐ 159	Bob Stewart	.50	.23	.06
☐ 160	Syl Apps	.60	.25	.08
☐ 161	Danny Grant	.60	.25	.08
☐ 162	Billy Smith	25.00	11.50	3.10
☐ 163	Brian Glennie	.50	.23	.06
☐ 164	Pit Martin DP	.50	.23	.06
☐ 165	Brad Park	4.00	1.80	.50
☐ 166	Wayne Cashman DP	.50	.23	.06
☐ 167	Gary Dornhoefer	.50	.23	.06
☐ 168	Steve Durbano	.50	.23	.06
☐ 169	Jacques Richard	.50	.23	.06
☐ 170	Guy Lapointe	1.00	.45	.13
☐ 171	Jim Lorentz	.50	.23	.06
☐ 172	Bob Berry DP	.40	.18	.05
☐ 173	Dennis Kearns	.50	.23	.06
☐ 174	Red Berenson	.60	.25	.08
☐ 175	Gilles Meloche DP	.50	.23	.06
☐ 176	Al McDonough	.50	.23	.06
☐ 177	Dennis O'Brien	.50	.23	.06
☐ 178	Germaine Gagnon UER DP	.40	.18	.05
☐ 179	Rick Kehoe DP	.50	.23	.06
☐ 180	Bill White	.50	.23	.06
☐ 181	Vic Hadfield DP	.50	.23	.06
☐ 182	Derek Sanderson	2.00	.90	.25
☐ 183	Andre Dupont DP	.40	.18	.05
☐ 184	Gary Sabourin	.50	.23	.06
☐ 185	Larry Romanchych	.50	.23	.06
☐ 186	Peter Mahovlich	.60	.25	.08
☐ 187	Dave Dryden	.60	.25	.08
☐ 188	Gilles Marotte	.50	.23	.06
☐ 189	Bobby Lalonde	.50	.23	.06
☐ 190	Mickey Redmond	.60	.25	.08
☐ 191	Series A	.75	.35	.09
	Canadiens 4			
	Sabres 2			
☐ 192	Series B	.75	.35	.09
	Flyers 4			
	North Stars 2			
☐ 193	Series C	.75	.35	.09
	Blackhawks 4			
	Blues 2			
☐ 194	Series D	.75	.35	.09
	Rangers 4			
	Bruins			
☐ 195	Series E	.75	.35	.09
	Canadiens 4			
	Flyers 1			
☐ 196	Series F	.75	.35	.09
	Blackhawks 4			
	Rangers 1			
☐ 197	Series G	.75	.35	.09
	Canadiens 4			
	Blackhawks 2			
☐ 198	Stanley Cup Champs	2.50	.75	.25
	Montreal Canadiens			

1974-75 Topps

Topps produced its largest set of cards at 264 for 1974-75. Cards measure 2 1/2" by 3 1/2". Design of card fronts offers a hockey stick down the left side. The team name, player name and team logo appear at the bottom in a border that features one of the team colors. The backs feature the player's 1973-74 and career statistics, a short biography and a cartoon-illustrated fact about the player. Players from the 1974-75 expansion Washington Capitals and the now defunct Kansas City Scouts appear in this set. The set marks the return of coach cards including Rookie Cards of Don Cherry and Scotty Bowman. Other Rookie Cards include Lanny McDonald, Denis Potvin, Borje Salming and John Davidson.

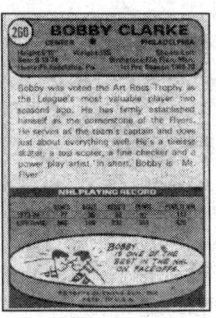

BOBBY CLARKE

FLYERS

BOBBY CLARKE

	NRMT	VG-E	GOOD
COMPLETE SET (264)	200.00	90.00	25.00
COMMON PLAYER (1-264)	.40	.18	.05

			NRMT	VG-E	GOOD
☐ 1	Goal Leaders		3.00	.90	.30
	Phil Esposito				
	Bill Goldsworthy				
☐ 2	Assists Leaders		5.00	2.30	.60
	Bobby Orr				
	Dennis Hextall				
☐ 3	Scoring Leaders		4.00	1.80	.50
	Phil Esposito				
	Bobby Clarke				
☐ 4	Goals Against Average		1.50	.65	.19
	Leaders				
	Doug Favell				
	Bernie Parent				
☐ 5	Penalty Min. Leaders		.60	.25	.08
	Bryan Watson				
	Dave Schultz				
☐ 6	Power Play Goal		.60	.25	.08
	Leaders				
	Mickey Redmond				
	Rick MacLeish				
☐ 7	Gary Bromley		.50	.23	.06
☐ 8	Bill Barber		5.00	2.30	.60
☐ 9	Emile Francis CO		.75	.35	.09
☐ 10	Gilles Gilbert		.50	.23	.06
☐ 11	John Davidson		5.00	2.30	.60
☐ 12	Ron Ellis		.50	.23	.06
☐ 13	Syl Apps		.40	.18	.05
☐ 14	Flames Leaders		.75	.35	.09
	Jacques Richard				
	Tom Lysiak				
	Tom Lysiak				
	Keith McCreary				
☐ 15	Dan Bouchard		.50	.23	.06
☐ 16	Ivan Boldirev		.50	.23	.06
☐ 17	Gary Coalter		.40	.18	.05
☐ 18	Bob Berry		.40	.18	.05
☐ 19	Red Berenson		.50	.23	.06
☐ 20	Stan Mikita		4.00	1.80	.50
☐ 21	Fred Shero CO		2.50	1.15	.30
☐ 22	Gary Smith		.50	.23	.06
☐ 23	Bill Mikkelson		.40	.18	.05
☐ 24	Jacques Lemaire UER		1.75	.80	.22
	(Shown in Sabres				
	sweater)				
☐ 25	Gilbert Perreault		4.00	1.80	.50
☐ 26	Cesare Maniago		.50	.23	.06
☐ 27	Bobby Schmautz		.40	.18	.05
☐ 28	Bruins Leaders		7.00	3.10	.85
	Phil Esposito				
	Bobby Orr				
	Phil Esposito				
	Johnny Bucyk				
☐ 29	Steve Vickers		.50	.23	.06
☐ 30	Lowell MacDonald		.40	.18	.05
☐ 31	Fred Stanfield		.40	.18	.05
☐ 32	Ed Westfall		.50	.23	.06
☐ 33	Curt Bennett		.40	.18	.05
☐ 34	Bep Guidolin CO		.40	.18	.05
☐ 35	Cliff Koroll		.40	.18	.05
☐ 36	Gary Croteau		.40	.18	.05
☐ 37	Mike Corrigan		.40	.18	.05
☐ 38	Henry Boucha		.40	.18	.05
☐ 39	Ron Low		.50	.23	.06
☐ 40	Darryl Sittler		5.00	2.30	.60
☐ 41	Tracy Pratt		.40	.18	.05
☐ 42	Sabres Leaders		.75	.35	.09
	Richard Martin				
	Rene Robert				
	Richard Martin				

			NRMT	VG-E	GOOD
	Richard Martin				
☐ 43	Larry Carriere		.40	.18	.05
☐ 44	Gary Dornhoefer		.40	.18	.05
☐ 45	Denis Herron		2.50	1.15	.30
☐ 46	Doug Favell		.50	.23	.06
☐ 47	Dave Gardner		.40	.18	.05
☐ 48	Morris Mott		.40	.18	.05
☐ 49	Marc Boileau CO		.40	.18	.05
☐ 50	Brad Park		3.00	1.35	.40
☐ 51	Bob Leiter		.40	.18	.05
☐ 52	Tom Reid		.40	.18	.05
☐ 53	Serge Savard		1.00	.45	.13
☐ 54	Checklist 1-132		12.00	1.20	.24
☐ 55	Terry Harper		.40	.18	.05
☐ 56	Golden Seals		.60	.25	.08
	Leaders				
	Joey Johnston				
	Joey Johnston				
	Joey Johnston				
	Walt McKechnie				
☐ 57	Guy Charron		.50	.23	.06
☐ 58	Pit Martin		.40	.18	.05
☐ 59	Chris Evans		.40	.18	.05
☐ 60	Bernie Parent		3.00	1.35	.40
☐ 61	Jim Lorentz		.40	.18	.05
☐ 62	Dave Kryskow		.40	.18	.05
☐ 63	Lou Angotti CO		.40	.18	.05
☐ 64	Bill Flett		.40	.18	.05
☐ 65	Vic Hadfield		.50	.23	.06
☐ 66	Wayne Merrick		.40	.18	.05
☐ 67	Andre Dupont		.40	.18	.05
☐ 68	Tom Lysiak		1.25	.55	.16
☐ 69	Blackhawks Leaders		.75	.35	.09
	Jim Pappin				
	Stan Mikita				
	J.P. Bordeleau				
	Stan Mikita				
☐ 70	Guy Lapointe		.75	.35	.09
☐ 71	Gerry O'Flaherty		.40	.18	.05
☐ 72	Marcel Dionne		8.00	3.60	1.00
☐ 73	Brent Hughes		.40	.18	.05
☐ 74	Butch Goring		.50	.23	.06
☐ 75	Keith Magnuson		.40	.18	.05
☐ 76	Red Kelly CO		1.00	.45	.13
☐ 77	Pete Stemkowski		.40	.18	.05
☐ 78	Jim Roberts		.40	.18	.05
	Montreal Canadiens				
☐ 79	Don Luce		.40	.18	.05
☐ 80	Don Awrey		.40	.18	.05
☐ 81	Rick Kehoe		.50	.23	.06
☐ 82	Billy Smith		7.00	3.10	.85
☐ 83	Jean-Paul Parise		.40	.18	.05
☐ 84	Red Wings Leaders		1.50	.65	.19
	Mickey Redmond				
	Marcel Dionne				
	Marcel Dionne				
	Bill Hogaboam				
☐ 85	Ed Van Impe		.40	.18	.05
☐ 86	Randy Manery		.40	.18	.05
☐ 87	Barclay Plager		.50	.23	.06
☐ 88	Inge Hammarstrom		.40	.18	.05
☐ 89	Ab Demarco		.40	.18	.05
☐ 90	Bill White		.40	.18	.05
☐ 91	Al Arbour CO		1.50	.65	.19
☐ 92	Bob Stewart		.40	.18	.05
☐ 93	Jack Egers		.40	.18	.05
☐ 94	Don Lever		.50	.23	.06
☐ 95	Reggie Leach		.75	.35	.09
☐ 96	Dennis O'Brien		.40	.18	.05
☐ 97	Peter Mahovlich		.50	.23	.06
☐ 98	Kings Leaders		.60	.25	.08
	Butch Goring				
	Frank St.Marseille				
	Butch Goring				
	Don Kozak				
☐ 99	Gerry Meehan		.50	.23	.06
☐ 100	Bobby Orr		25.00	11.50	3.10
☐ 101	Jean Potvin		.75	.35	.09
☐ 102	Rod Seiling		.40	.18	.05
☐ 103	Keith McCreary		.40	.18	.05
☐ 104	Phil Maloney CO		.40	.18	.05
☐ 105	Denis Dupere		.40	.18	.05
☐ 106	Steve Durbano		.40	.18	.05
☐ 107	Bob Plager UER		.50	.23	.06
	(Photo actually				
	Barclay Plager)				
☐ 108	Chris Oddleifson		.40	.18	.05
☐ 109	Jim Neilson		.40	.18	.05
☐ 110	Jean Pronovost		.50	.23	.06
☐ 111	Don Kozak		.40	.18	.05
☐ 112	North Stars		.60	.25	.08
	Leaders				
	Bill Goldsworthy				
	Dennis Hextall				

	Dennis Hextall			
	Danny Grant			
☐ 113	Jim Pappin	.40	.18	.05
☐ 114	Richard Lemieux	.40	.18	.05
☐ 115	Dennis Hextall	.40	.18	.05
☐ 116	Bill Hogaboam	.40	.18	.05
☐ 117	Canucks Leaders	.60	.25	.08
	Dennis Ververgaert			
	Bob Schmautz			
	Andre Boudrias			
	Andre Boudrias			
	Don Tannahill			
☐ 118	Jimmy Anderson CO	.40	.18	.05
☐ 119	Walt Tkaczuk	.50	.23	.06
☐ 120	Mickey Redmond	.50	.23	.06
☐ 121	Jim Schoenfeld	.75	.35	.09
☐ 122	Jocelyn Guevremont	.40	.18	.05
☐ 123	Bob Nystrom	1.50	.65	.19
☐ 124	Canadiens Leaders	2.00	.90	.25
	Yvan Cournoyer			
	Frank Mahovlich			
	Frank Mahovlich			
	Claude Larose			
☐ 125	Lew Morrison	.40	.18	.05
☐ 126	Terry Murray	.50	.23	.06
☐ 127	Richard Martin AS	.50	.23	.06
☐ 128	Ken Hodge AS	.50	.23	.06
☐ 129	Phil Esposito AS	2.50	1.15	.30
☐ 130	Bobby Orr AS	12.00	5.50	1.50
☐ 131	Brad Park AS	1.50	.65	.19
☐ 132	Gilles Gilbert AS	.50	.23	.06
☐ 133	Lowell MacDonald AS	.50	.23	.06
☐ 134	Bill Goldsworthy AS	.50	.23	.06
☐ 135	Bobby Clarke AS	4.00	1.80	.50
☐ 136	Bill White AS	.50	.23	.06
☐ 137	Dave Burrows AS	.50	.23	.06
☐ 138	Bernie Parent AS	1.50	.65	.19
☐ 139	Jacques Richard	.40	.18	.05
☐ 140	Yvan Cournoyer	2.50	1.15	.30
☐ 141	Rangers Leaders	1.50	.65	.19
	Rod Gilbert			
	Brad Park			
	Brad Park			
	Rod Gilbert			
☐ 142	Rene Robert	.50	.23	.06
☐ 143	J. Bob Kelly	.40	.18	.05
☐ 144	Ross Lonsberry	.40	.18	.05
☐ 145	Jean Ratelle	1.50	.65	.19
☐ 146	Dallas Smith	.40	.18	.05
☐ 147	BoomBoom Geoffrion CO	2.50	1.15	.30
☐ 148	Ted McAneeley	.40	.18	.05
☐ 149	Pierre Plante	.40	.18	.05
☐ 150	Dennis Hull	.50	.23	.06
☐ 151	Dave Keon	1.00	.45	.13
☐ 152	Dave Dunn	.40	.18	.05
☐ 153	Michel Belhumeur	.50	.23	.06
☐ 154	Flyers Leaders	2.00	.90	.25
	Bobby Clarke			
	Bobby Clarke			
	Bobby Clarke			
	Dave Schultz			
☐ 155	Ken Dryden	15.00	6.75	1.90
☐ 156	John Wright	.40	.18	.05
☐ 157	Larry Romanchych	.40	.18	.05
☐ 158	Ralph Stewart	.40	.18	.05
☐ 159	Mike Robitaille	.40	.18	.05
☐ 160	Ed Giacomin	2.00	.90	.25
☐ 161	Don Cherry CO	15.00	6.75	1.90
☐ 162	Checklist 133-264	12.00	1.20	.24
☐ 163	Rick MacLeish	1.00	.45	.13
☐ 164	Greg Polis	.40	.18	.05
☐ 165	Carol Vadnais	.40	.18	.05
☐ 166	Pete Laframboise	.40	.18	.05
☐ 167	Ron Schock	.40	.18	.05
☐ 168	Lanny McDonald	20.00	9.00	2.50
☐ 169	Scouts Emblem	1.00	.45	.13
	Draft Selections			
	on back			
☐ 170	Tony Esposito	5.00	2.30	.60
☐ 171	Pierre Jarry	.40	.18	.05
☐ 172	Dan Maloney	.50	.23	.06
☐ 173	Peter McDuffe	.50	.23	.06
☐ 174	Danny Grant	.50	.23	.06
☐ 175	John Stewart	.40	.18	.05
☐ 176	Floyd Smith CO	.40	.18	.05
☐ 177	Bert Marshall	.40	.18	.05
☐ 178	Chuck Lefley UER	.40	.18	.05
	(Photo actually			
	Pierre Bouchard)			
☐ 179	Gilles Villemure	.50	.23	.06
☐ 180	Borje Salming	9.00	4.00	1.15
☐ 181	Doug Mohns	.40	.18	.05
☐ 182	Barry Wilkins	.40	.18	.05
☐ 183	Penguins Leaders	.60	.25	.08

	Lowell MacDonald			
	Syl Apps			
	Syl Apps			
	Lowell MacDonald			
☐ 184	Gregg Sheppard	.40	.18	.05
☐ 185	Joey Johnston	.40	.18	.05
☐ 186	Dick Redmond	.40	.18	.05
☐ 187	Simon Nolet	.40	.18	.05
☐ 188	Ron Stackhouse	.40	.18	.05
☐ 189	Marshall Johnston	.40	.18	.05
☐ 190	Richard Martin	1.00	.45	.13
☐ 191	Andre Boudrias	.40	.18	.05
☐ 192	Steve Atkinson	.40	.18	.05
☐ 193	Nick Libett	.40	.18	.05
☐ 194	Bob Murdoch	.40	.18	.05
	Los Angeles Kings			
☐ 195	Denis Potvin	28.00	12.50	3.50
☐ 196	Dave Schultz	2.00	.90	.25
☐ 197	Blues Leaders	.75	.35	.09
	Garry Unger			
	Garry Unger			
	Garry Unger			
	Pierre Plante			
☐ 198	Jim McKenny	.40	.18	.05
☐ 199	Gerry Hart	.40	.18	.05
☐ 200	Phil Esposito	4.00	1.80	.50
☐ 201	Rod Gilbert	1.50	.65	.19
☐ 202	Jacques Laperriere	.50	.23	.06
☐ 203	Barry Gibbs	.40	.18	.05
☐ 204	Billy Reay CO	.50	.23	.06
☐ 205	Gilles Meloche	.50	.23	.06
☐ 206	Wayne Cashman	.50	.23	.06
☐ 207	Dennis Ververgaert	.40	.18	.05
☐ 208	Phil Roberto	.40	.18	.05
☐ 209	Quarter Finals	.75	.35	.09
	Flyers sweep			
	Flames			
☐ 210	Quarter Finals	.75	.35	.09
	Rangers over			
	Canadiens			
☐ 211	Quarter Finals	.75	.35	.09
	Bruins sweep			
	Maple Leafs			
☐ 212	Quarter Finals	.75	.35	.09
	Blackhawks over			
	L.A. Kings			
☐ 213	Stanley Cup Semifinals	.75	.35	.09
	Flyers over Rangers			
☐ 214	Stanley Cup Semifinals	.75	.35	.09
	Bruins over			
	Blackhawks			
☐ 215	Stanley Cup Finals	.75	.35	.09
	Flyers over Bruins			
☐ 216	Stanley Cup Champions	1.00	.45	.13
	Philadelphia Flyers			
☐ 217	Joe Watson	.40	.18	.05
☐ 218	Wayne Stephenson	.50	.23	.06
☐ 219	Maple Leaf Leaders	1.50	.65	.19
	Darryl Sittler			
	Norm Ullman			
	Darryl Sittler			
	Paul Henderson			
	Denis Dupere			
☐ 220	Bill Goldsworthy	.50	.23	.06
☐ 221	Don Marcotte	.40	.18	.05
☐ 222	Alex Delvecchio CO	1.00	.45	.13
☐ 223	Stan Gilbertson	.40	.18	.05
☐ 224	Mike Murphy	.40	.18	.05
☐ 225	Jim Rutherford	.50	.23	.06
☐ 226	Phil Russell	.40	.18	.05
☐ 227	Lynn Powis	.40	.18	.05
☐ 228	Billy Harris	.40	.18	.05
☐ 229	Bob Pulford CO	.50	.23	.06
☐ 230	Ken Hodge	.50	.23	.06
☐ 231	Bill Fairbairn	.40	.18	.05
☐ 232	Guy Lafleur	12.00	5.50	1.50
☐ 233	Islanders Leaders	2.50	1.15	.30
	Billy Harris			
	Ralph Stewart			
	Denis Potvin			
	Denis Potvin			
	Ralph Stewart			
☐ 234	Fred Barrett	.40	.18	.05
☐ 235	Rogatien Vachon	1.50	.65	.19
☐ 236	Norm Ullman	1.50	.65	.19
☐ 237	Garry Unger	.50	.23	.06
☐ 238	Jack Gordon CO	.40	.18	.05
☐ 239	Johnny Bucyk	1.50	.65	.19
☐ 240	Bob Dailey	.40	.18	.05
☐ 241	Dave Burrows	.40	.18	.05
☐ 242	Len Frig	.40	.18	.05
☐ 243	Masterton Trophy	1.00	.45	.13
	Henri Richard			
☐ 244	Hart Trophy	2.50	1.15	.30

		NRMT	VG-F	GOOD
	Phil Esposito			
☐ 245	Byng Trophy	1.00	.45	.13
	Johnny Bucyk			
☐ 246	Ross Trophy	2.50	1.15	.30
	Phil Esposito			
☐ 247	Prince of Wales Trophy	.75	.35	.09
	Boston Bruins			
☐ 248	Norris Trophy	12.00	5.50	1.50
	Bobby Orr			
☐ 249	Vezina Trophy	1.50	.65	.19
	Bernie Parent			
☐ 250	Stanley Cup	.75	.35	.09
	Philadelphia Flyers			
☐ 251	Smythe Trophy	1.50	.65	.19
	Bernie Parent			
☐ 252	Calder Trophy	7.00	3.10	.85
	Denis Potvin			
☐ 253	Campbell Trophy	.75	.35	.09
	Philadelphia Flyers			
☐ 254	Pierre Bouchard	.40	.18	.05
☐ 255	Jude Drouin	.40	.18	.05
☐ 256	Capitals Emblem	1.00	.45	.13
	(Draft Selections on back)			
☐ 257	Michel Plasse	.50	.23	.06
☐ 258	Juha Widing	.40	.18	.05
☐ 259	Bryan Watson	.40	.18	.05
☐ 260	Bobby Clarke	8.00	3.60	1.00
☐ 261	Scotty Bowman CO	9.00	4.00	1.15
☐ 262	Craig Patrick	.50	.23	.06
☐ 263	Craig Cameron	.40	.18	.05
☐ 264	Ted Irvine	1.00	.25	.05

1975-76 Topps

 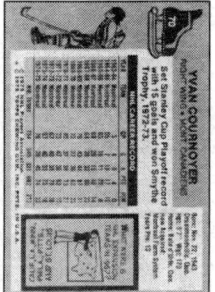

YVON COURNOYER

At 330 cards, the 1975-76 Topps set is the largest to date and the largest until 1990-91. Cards are the standard 2 1/2" by 3 1/2". Fronts feature team name at top and player name at the bottom. The players' position appears in a puck at the bottom. The backs contain year-by-year and NHL career records, a short biography and a cartoon-illustrated hockey fact or referee's signal with interpretaion. For the first time, team cards (81-98) with team checklist on back appear in a Topps set. Rookie Cards include Clark Gillies, Peter McNab, Ron Greschner and Pierre Larouche.

		NRMT	VG-F	GOOD
	COMPLETE SET (330)	150.00	70.00	19.00
	COMMON PLAYER (1-330)	.30	.14	.04
☐ 1	Stanley Cup Finals	1.50	.40	.08
	Philadelphia 4			
	Buffalo 2			
☐ 2	Semi-Finals	.50	.23	.06
	Philadelphia 4			
	N.Y. Islanders 3			
☐ 3	Semi-Finals	.50	.23	.06
	Buffalo 4			
	Montreal 2			
☐ 4	Quarter Finals	.50	.23	.06
	N.Y. Islanders 4			
	Pittsburgh 2			
☐ 5	Quarter Finals	.50	.23	.06
	Montreal 4			
	Vancouver 1			
☐ 6	Quarter Finals	.50	.23	.06
	Buffalo 4			
	Chicago 1			
☐ 7	Quarter Finals	.50	.23	.06
	Philadelphia 4			
	Toronto 0			
☐ 8	Curt Bennett	.30	.14	.04
☐ 9	Johnny Bucyk	1.25	.55	.16
☐ 10	Gilbert Perreault	3.00	1.35	.40
☐ 11	Darryl Edestrand	.30	.14	.04
☐ 12	Ivan Boldirev	.30	.14	.04
☐ 13	Nick Libett	.30	.14	.04
☐ 14	Jim McElmury	.30	.14	.04
☐ 15	Frank St.Marseille	.30	.14	.04
☐ 16	Blake Dunlop	.30	.14	.04
☐ 17	Yvon Lambert	.40	.18	.05
☐ 18	Gerry Hart	.30	.14	.04
☐ 19	Steve Vickers	.30	.14	.04
☐ 20	Rick MacLeish	.40	.18	.05
☐ 21	Bob Paradise	.30	.14	.04
☐ 22	Red Berenson	.40	.18	.05
☐ 23	Lanny McDonald	6.00	2.70	.75
☐ 24	Mike Robitaille	.30	.14	.04
☐ 25	Ron Low	.40	.18	.05
☐ 26	Bryan Hextall	.30	.14	.04
☐ 27	Carol Vadnais	.30	.14	.04
☐ 28	Jim Lorentz	.30	.14	.04
☐ 29	Gary Simmons	.40	.18	.05
☐ 30	Stan Mikita	3.00	1.35	.40
☐ 31	Bryan Watson	.30	.14	.04
☐ 32	Guy Charron	.30	.14	.04
☐ 33	Bob Murdoch	.30	.14	.04
	Los Angeles Kings			
☐ 34	Norm Gratton	.30	.14	.04
☐ 35	Ken Dryden	12.00	5.50	1.50
☐ 36	Jean Potvin	.30	.14	.04
☐ 37	Rick Middleton	3.00	1.35	.40
☐ 38	Ed Van Impe	.30	.14	.04
☐ 39	Rick Kehoe	.40	.18	.05
☐ 40	Garry Unger	.40	.18	.05
☐ 41	Ian Turnbull	.40	.18	.05
☐ 42	Dennis Ververgaert	.30	.14	.04
☐ 43	Mike Marson	.30	.14	.04
☐ 44	Randy Manery	.30	.14	.04
☐ 45	Gilles Gilbert	.40	.18	.05
☐ 46	Rene Robert	.40	.18	.05
☐ 47	Bob Stewart	.30	.14	.04
☐ 48	Pit Martin	.30	.14	.04
☐ 49	Danny Grant	.40	.18	.05
☐ 50	Peter Mahovlich	.40	.18	.05
☐ 51	Dennis Patterson	.30	.14	.04
☐ 52	Mike Murphy	.30	.14	.04
☐ 53	Dennis O'Brien	.30	.14	.04
☐ 54	Garry Howatt	.30	.14	.04
☐ 55	Ed Giacomin	1.50	.65	.19
☐ 56	Andre Dupont	.30	.14	.04
☐ 57	Chuck Arnason	.30	.14	.04
☐ 58	Bob Gassoff	.30	.14	.04
☐ 59	Ron Ellis	.40	.18	.05
☐ 60	Andre Boudrias	.30	.14	.04
☐ 61	Yvon Labre	.30	.14	.04
☐ 62	Hilliard Graves	.30	.14	.04
☐ 63	Wayne Cashman	.40	.18	.05
☐ 64	Danny Gare	2.00	.90	.25
☐ 65	Rick Hampton	.30	.14	.04
☐ 66	Darcy Rota	.30	.14	.04
☐ 67	Bill Hogaboam	.30	.14	.04
☐ 68	Denis Herron	.40	.18	.05
☐ 69	Sheldon Kannegiesser	.30	.14	.04
☐ 70	Yvan Cournoyer UER	1.50	.65	.19
	(Misspelled Yvon on card front)			
☐ 71	Ernie Hicke	.30	.14	.04
☐ 72	Bert Marshall	.30	.14	.04
☐ 73	Derek Sanderson	1.00	.45	.13
☐ 74	Tom Bladon	.40	.18	.05
☐ 75	Ron Schock	.30	.14	.04
☐ 76	Larry Sacharuk	.30	.14	.04
☐ 77	George Ferguson	.30	.14	.04
☐ 78	Ab DeMarco	.30	.14	.04
☐ 79	Tom Williams	.30	.14	.04
☐ 80	Phil Roberto	.30	.14	.04
☐ 81	Bruins Team	1.50	.65	.19
	(Checklist back)			
☐ 82	Seals Team	1.00	.45	.13
	(Checklist back)			
☐ 83	Sabres Team UER	1.00	.45	.13
	(Gary Desjardins, sic; checklist back)			
☐ 84	Blackhawks Team UER	1.00	.45	.13
	(Germain Gagnon, sic; checklist back)			
☐ 85	Flames Team	1.00	.45	.13

	(Checklist back)			
☐ 86	Kings Team	1.00	.45	.13
	(Checklist back)			
☐ 87	Red Wings Team	1.00	.45	.13
	(Checklist back)			
☐ 88	Scouts Team UER	1.00	.45	.13
	(Dennis Dupere, sic; checklist back)			
☐ 89	North Stars Team	1.00	.45	.13
	(Checklist back)			
☐ 90	Canadiens Team	1.50	.65	.19
	(Checklist back)			
☐ 91	Maple Leafs Team	1.50	.65	.19
	(Checklist back)			
☐ 92	Islanders Team	1.00	.45	.13
	(Checklist back)			
☐ 93	Penguins Team	1.00	.45	.13
	(Checklist back)			
☐ 94	Rangers Team	1.00	.45	.13
	(Checklist back)			
☐ 95	Flyers Team UER	1.00	.45	.13
	(Philadelphia misspelled on card back; checklist back)			
☐ 96	Blues Team	1.00	.45	.13
	(Checklist back)			
☐ 97	Canucks Team UER	1.00	.45	.13
	(242 Robitaille should be 24 and 42 Ververgaert not shown; checklist back)			
☐ 98	Capitals Team	1.00	.45	.13
	(Checklist back)			
☐ 99	Checklist 1-110	9.00	.90	.18
☐ 100	Bobby Orr	20.00	9.00	2.50
☐ 101	Germaine Gagnon UER	.30	.14	.04
	(Misspelled Germain on both sides)			
☐ 102	Phil Russell	.30	.14	.04
☐ 103	Billy Lochead	.30	.14	.04
☐ 104	Robin Burns	.30	.14	.04
☐ 105	Gary Edwards	.40	.18	.05
☐ 106	Dwight Bialowas	.30	.14	.04
☐ 107	Doug Risebrough UER	2.00	.90	.25
	(Photo actually Bob Gainey)			
☐ 108	Dave Lewis	.30	.14	.04
☐ 109	Bill Fairbairn	.30	.14	.04
☐ 110	Ross Lonsberry	.30	.14	.04
☐ 111	Ron Stackhouse	.30	.14	.04
☐ 112	Claude Larose	.30	.14	.04
☐ 113	Don Luce	.30	.14	.04
☐ 114	Errol Thompson	.30	.14	.04
☐ 115	Gary Smith	.40	.18	.05
☐ 116	Jack Lynch	.30	.14	.04
☐ 117	Jacques Richard	.30	.14	.04
☐ 118	Dallas Smith	.30	.14	.04
☐ 119	Dave Gardner	.30	.14	.04
☐ 120	Mickey Redmond	.40	.18	.05
☐ 121	John Marks	.30	.14	.04
☐ 122	Dave Hudson	.30	.14	.04
☐ 123	Bob Nevin	.30	.14	.04
☐ 124	Fred Barrett	.30	.14	.04
☐ 125	Gerry Desjardins	.40	.18	.05
☐ 126	Guy Lafleur UER	10.00	4.50	1.25
	(Listed as Defense on card front)			
☐ 127	Jean-Paul Parise	.30	.14	.04
☐ 128	Walt Tkaczuk	.40	.18	.05
☐ 129	Gary Dornhoefer	.30	.14	.04
☐ 130	Syl Apps	.30	.14	.04
☐ 131	Bob Plager	.40	.18	.05
☐ 132	Stan Weir	.30	.14	.04
☐ 133	Tracy Pratt	.30	.14	.04
☐ 134	Jack Egers	.30	.14	.04
☐ 135	Eric Vail	.30	.14	.04
☐ 136	Al Sims	.30	.14	.04
☐ 137	Larry Patey	.30	.14	.04
☐ 138	Jim Schoenfeld	.40	.18	.05
☐ 139	Cliff Koroll	.30	.14	.04
☐ 140	Marcel Dionne	6.00	2.70	.75
☐ 141	Jean-Guy Lagace	.30	.14	.04
☐ 142	Juha Widing	.30	.14	.04
☐ 143	Lou Nanne	.40	.18	.05
☐ 144	Serge Savard	.75	.35	.09
☐ 145	Glenn Resch	3.00	1.35	.40
☐ 146	Ron Greschner	2.50	1.15	.30
☐ 147	Dave Schultz	1.00	.45	.13
☐ 148	Barry Wilkins	.30	.14	.04
☐ 149	Floyd Thomson	.30	.14	.04
☐ 150	Darryl Sittler	4.00	1.80	.50
☐ 151	Paulin Bordeleau	.30	.14	.04
☐ 152	Ron Lalonde	.30	.14	.04
☐ 153	Larry Romanchych	.30	.14	.04
☐ 154	Larry Carriere	.30	.14	.04
☐ 155	Andre Savard	.30	.14	.04
☐ 156	Dave Hrechkosy	.30	.14	.04
☐ 157	Bill White	.30	.14	.04
☐ 158	Dave Kryskow	.30	.14	.04
☐ 159	Denis Dupere	.30	.14	.04
☐ 160	Rogatien Vachon	1.25	.55	.16
☐ 161	Doug Rombough	.30	.14	.04
☐ 162	Murray Wilson	.30	.14	.04
☐ 163	Bob Bourne	1.50	.65	.19
☐ 164	Gilles Marotte	.30	.14	.04
☐ 165	Vic Hadfield	.40	.18	.05
☐ 166	Reggie Leach	.40	.18	.05
☐ 167	Jerry Butler	.30	.14	.04
☐ 168	Inge Hammarstrom	.30	.14	.04
☐ 169	Chris Oddleifson	.30	.14	.04
☐ 170	Greg Joly	.30	.14	.04
☐ 171	Checklist 111-220	9.00	.90	.18
☐ 172	Pat Quinn	.40	.18	.05
☐ 173	Dave Forbes	.30	.14	.04
☐ 174	Len Frig	.30	.14	.04
☐ 175	Richard Martin	.40	.18	.05
☐ 176	Keith Magnuson	.30	.14	.04
☐ 177	Dan Maloney	.30	.14	.04
☐ 178	Craig Patrick	.40	.18	.05
☐ 179	Tom Williams	.30	.14	.04
☐ 180	Bill Goldsworthy	.40	.18	.05
☐ 181	Steve Shutt	3.00	1.35	.40
☐ 182	Ralph Stewart	.30	.14	.04
☐ 183	John Davidson	1.50	.65	.19
☐ 184	Bob Kelly	.30	.14	.04
☐ 185	Ed Johnston	.40	.18	.05
☐ 186	Dave Burrows	.30	.14	.04
☐ 187	Dave Dunn	.30	.14	.04
☐ 188	Dennis Kearns	.30	.14	.04
☐ 189	Bill Clement	1.00	.45	.13
☐ 190	Gilles Meloche	.40	.18	.05
☐ 191	Bob Leiter	.30	.14	.04
☐ 192	Jerry Korab	.30	.14	.04
☐ 193	Joey Johnston	.30	.14	.04
☐ 194	Walt McKechnie	.30	.14	.04
☐ 195	Wilf Paiement	.30	.14	.04
☐ 196	Bob Berry	.30	.14	.04
☐ 197	Dean Talafous	.30	.14	.04
☐ 198	Guy Lapointe	.40	.18	.05
☐ 199	Clark Gillies	5.00	2.30	.60
☐ 200	Phil Esposito	3.00	1.35	.40
☐ 201	Greg Polis	.30	.14	.04
☐ 202	Jim Watson	.40	.18	.05
☐ 203	Gord McRae	.40	.18	.05
☐ 204	Lowell MacDonald	.30	.14	.04
☐ 205	Barclay Plager	.40	.18	.05
☐ 206	Don Lever	.30	.14	.04
☐ 207	Bill Mikkelson	.30	.14	.04
☐ 208	Goals Leaders	3.50	1.55	.45
	Phil Esposito Guy Lafleur Richard Martin			
☐ 209	Assists Leaders	5.00	2.30	.60
	Bobby Clarke Bobby Orr Pete Mahovlich			
☐ 210	Scoring Leaders	5.00	2.30	.60
	Bobby Orr Phil Esposito Marcel Dionne			
☐ 211	Penalty Min. Leaders	.50	.23	.06
	Dave Schultz Andre Dupont Phil Russell			
☐ 212	Power Play	1.50	.65	.19
	Goal Leaders Phil Esposito Richard Martin Danny Grant			
☐ 213	Goals Against	5.00	2.30	.60
	Average Leaders Bernie Parent Rogatien Vachon Ken Dryden			
☐ 214	Barry Gibbs	.30	.14	.04
☐ 215	Ken Hodge	.40	.18	.05
☐ 216	Jocelyn Guevremont	.30	.14	.04
☐ 217	Warren Williams	.30	.14	.04
☐ 218	Dick Redmond	.30	.14	.04
☐ 219	Jim Rutherford	.40	.18	.05
☐ 220	Simon Nolet	.30	.14	.04
☐ 221	Butch Goring	.40	.18	.05
☐ 222	Glen Sather	.50	.23	.06
☐ 223	Mario Tremblay	1.50	.65	.19
☐ 224	Jude Drouin	.30	.14	.04
☐ 225	Rod Gilbert	1.25	.55	.16
☐ 226	Bill Barber	3.00	1.35	.40

☐	227 Gary Inness	.40	.18	.05
☐	228 Wayne Merrick	.30	.14	.04
☐	229 Rod Seiling	.30	.14	.04
☐	230 Tom Lysiak	.40	.18	.05
☐	231 Bob Dailey	.30	.14	.04
☐	232 Michel Belhumeur	.40	.18	.05
☐	233 Bill Hajt	.30	.14	.04
☐	234 Jim Pappin	.30	.14	.04
☐	235 Gregg Sheppard	.30	.14	.04
☐	236 Gary Bergman	.30	.14	.04
☐	237 Randy Rota	.30	.14	.04
☐	238 Neil Komadoski	.30	.14	.04
☐	239 Craig Cameron	.30	.14	.04
☐	240 Tony Esposito	3.00	1.35	.40
☐	241 Larry Robinson	7.00	3.10	.85
☐	242 Billy Harris	.30	.14	.04
☐	243 Jean Ratelle	1.25	.55	.16
☐	244 Ted Irvine UER (Photo actually Ted Harris)	.30	.14	.04
☐	245 Bob Kelly	.30	.14	.04
☐	246 Bobby Lalonde	.30	.14	.04
☐	247 Ron Jones	.30	.14	.04
☐	248 Rey Comeau	.30	.14	.04
☐	249 Michel Plasse	.40	.18	.05
☐	250 Bobby Clarke	6.00	2.70	.75
☐	251 Bobby Schmautz	.30	.14	.04
☐	252 Peter McNab	2.50	1.15	.30
☐	253 Al MacAdam	.30	.14	.04
☐	254 Dennis Hull	.40	.18	.05
☐	255 Terry Harper	.30	.14	.04
☐	256 Peter McDuffe	.40	.18	.05
☐	257 Jean Hamel	.30	.14	.04
☐	258 Jacques Lemaire	1.25	.55	.16
☐	259 Bob Nystrom	.40	.18	.05
☐	260 Brad Park	2.00	.90	.25
☐	261 Cesare Maniago	.40	.18	.05
☐	262 Don Saleski	.30	.14	.04
☐	263 J. Bob Kelly	.30	.14	.04
☐	264 Bob Hess	.30	.14	.04
☐	265 Blaine Stoughton	.75	.35	.09
☐	266 John Gould	.30	.14	.04
☐	267 Checklist 221-330	9.00	.90	.18
☐	268 Dan Bouchard	.40	.18	.05
☐	269 Don Marcotte	.30	.14	.04
☐	270 Jim Neilson	.30	.14	.04
☐	271 Craig Ramsay	.30	.14	.04
☐	272 Grant Mulvey	1.00	.45	.13
☐	273 Larry Giroux	.30	.14	.04
☐	274 Real Lemieux	.30	.14	.04
☐	275 Denis Potvin	9.00	4.00	1.15
☐	276 Don Kozak	.30	.14	.04
☐	277 Tom Reid	.30	.14	.04
☐	278 Bob Gainey	4.00	1.80	.50
☐	279 Nick Beverley	.30	.14	.04
☐	280 Jean Pronovost	.40	.18	.05
☐	281 Joe Watson	.30	.14	.04
☐	282 Chuck Lefley	.30	.14	.04
☐	283 Borje Salming	3.00	1.35	.40
☐	284 Garnet Bailey	.30	.14	.04
☐	285 Gregg Boddy	.30	.14	.04
☐	286 Bobby Clarke AS1	2.50	1.15	.30
☐	287 Denis Potvin AS1	3.00	1.35	.40
☐	288 Bobby Orr AS1	10.00	4.50	1.25
☐	289 Richard Martin AS1	.40	.18	.05
☐	290 Guy Lafleur AS1	3.00	1.35	.40
☐	291 Bernie Parent AS1	1.25	.55	.16
☐	292 Phil Esposito AS2	2.00	.90	.25
☐	293 Guy Lapointe AS2	.40	.18	.05
☐	294 Borje Salming AS2	1.00	.45	.13
☐	295 Steve Vickers AS2	.40	.18	.05
☐	296 Rene Robert AS2	.40	.18	.05
☐	297 Rogatien Vachon AS2	.75	.35	.09
☐	298 Buster Harvey	.30	.14	.04
☐	299 Gary Sabourin	.30	.14	.04
☐	300 Bernie Parent	2.50	1.16	.30
☐	301 Terry O'Reilly	1.00	.45	.13
☐	302 Ed Westfall	.40	.18	.05
☐	303 Pete Stemkowski	.30	.14	.04
☐	304 Pierre Bouchard	.30	.14	.04
☐	305 Pierre Larouche	4.00	1.80	.50
☐	306 Lee Fogolin	.30	.14	.04
☐	307 Gerry O'Flaherty	.30	.14	.04
☐	308 Phil Myre	.40	.18	.05
☐	309 Pierre Plante	.30	.14	.04
☐	310 Dennis Hextall	.30	.14	.04
☐	311 Jim McKenny	.30	.14	.04
☐	312 Vic Venasky	.30	.14	.04
☐	313 Flames Leaders Eric Vail Tom Lysiak Tom Lysiak Tom Lysiak	.40	.18	.05
☐	314 Bruins Leaders	5.00	2.30	.60

	Phil Esposito Bobby Orr Phil Esposito Johnny Bucyk			
☐	315 Sabres Leaders Richard Martin Rene Robert Rene Robert Richard Martin	.40	.18	.05
☐	316 Seals Leaders Dave Hrechkosy Larry Patey Stan Weir Stan Weir Larry Patey Dave Hrechkosy	.40	.18	.05
☐	317 Blackhawks Leaders Stan Mikita Jim Pappin Stan Mikita Stan Mikita Stan Mikita	1.00	.45	.13
☐	318 Red Wings Leaders Danny Grant Marcel Dionne Marcel Dionne Danny Grant	1.00	.45	.13
☐	319 Scouts Leaders Simon Nolet Wilf Paiement Simon Nolet Guy Charron Simon Nolet	.40	.18	.05
☐	320 Kings Leaders Bob Nevin Bob Nevin Bob Nevin Bob Nevin Juha Widing Bob Berry	.40	.18	.05
☐	321 North Stars Leaders Bill Goldsworthy Dennis Hextall Dennis Hextall Bill Goldsworthy	.40	.18	.05
☐	322 Canadiens Leaders Guy Lafleur Pete Mahovlich Guy Lafleur Guy Lafleur	1.50	.65	.19
☐	323 Islanders Leaders Bob Nystrom Denis Potvin Denis Potvin Clark Gillies	1.50	.65	.19
☐	324 Rangers Leaders Steve Vickers Steve Vickers Rod Gilbert Rod Gilbert Jean Ratelle	1.00	.45	.13
☐	325 Flyers Leaders Reggie Leach Bobby Clarke Bobby Clarke Reggie Leach	1.25	.55	.16
☐	326 Penguins Leaders Jean Pronovost Ron Schock Ron Schock Jean Pronovost	.40	.18	.05
☐	327 Blues Leaders Garry Unger Garry Unger Garry Unger Garry Unger Larry Sacharuk	.40	.18	.05
☐	328 Maple Leafs Leaders Darryl Sittler Darryl Sittler Darryl Sittler Darryl Sittler	1.50	.65	.19
☐	329 Canucks Leaders Don Lever Don Lever Andre Boudrias Andre Boudrias	.40	.18	.05
☐	330 Capitals Leaders Tommy Williams Garnet Bailey Tommy Williams Garnet Bailey Tommy Williams	.75	.18	.05

1976-77 Topps

GERRY CHEEVERS • GOALIE

The 1976-77 Topps set contains 264 color cards. Cards measure 2 1/2" by 3 1/2". The fronts contain team name and logo at the top with player name and position at the bottom. The backs feature 1975-76 and career statistics, career highlights and a cartoon-illustrated fact. The first cards of Colorado Rockies (formerly Kansas City) players appear this year. Rookie Cards in this set include Bryan Trottier and Dennis Maruk.

	NRMT	VG-E	GOOD
COMPLETE SET (264)	125.00	57.50	15.50
COMMON PLAYER (1-264)	.25	.11	.03

		NRMT	VG-E	GOOD
☐ 1	Goals Leaders Reggie Leach Guy Lafleur Pierre Larouche	2.00	.50	.10
☐ 2	Assists Leaders Bobby Clarke Peter Mahovlich Guy Lafleur Gilbert Perrault Jean Ratelle	2.00	.90	.25
☐ 3	Scoring Leaders Guy Lafleur Bobby Clarke Gilbert Perreault	2.00	.90	.25
☐ 4	Penalty Min. Leaders Steve Durbano Bryan Watson Dave Schultz	.35	.16	.04
☐ 5	Power Play Goals Leaders Phil Esposito Guy Lafleur Richard Martin Pierre Larouche Denis Potvin	2.00	.90	.25
☐ 6	Goals Against Average Leaders Ken Dryden Glenn Resch Michel Larocque	2.00	.90	.25
☐ 7	Gary Doak	.25	.11	.03
☐ 8	Jacques Richard	.25	.11	.03
☐ 9	Wayne Dillon	.25	.11	.03
☐ 10	Bernie Parent	2.00	.90	.25
☐ 11	Ed Westfall	.35	.16	.04
☐ 12	Dick Redmond	.25	.11	.03
☐ 13	Bryan Hextall	.25	.11	.03
☐ 14	Jean Pronovost	.35	.16	.04
☐ 15	Peter Mahovlich	.35	.16	.04
☐ 16	Danny Grant	.35	.16	.04
☐ 17	Phil Myre	.35	.16	.04
☐ 18	Wayne Merrick	.25	.11	.03
☐ 19	Steve Durbano	.25	.11	.03
☐ 20	Derek Sanderson	.75	.35	.09
☐ 21	Mike Murphy	.25	.11	.03
☐ 22	Borje Salming	1.25	.55	.16
☐ 23	Mike Walton	.25	.11	.03
☐ 24	Randy Manery	.25	.11	.03
☐ 25	Ken Hodge	.35	.16	.04
☐ 26	Mel Bridgman	1.25	.55	.16
☐ 27	Jerry Korab	.25	.11	.03
☐ 28	Gilles Gratton	.35	.16	.04
☐ 29	Andre St.Laurent	.25	.11	.03

		NRMT	VG-E	GOOD
☐ 30	Yvan Cournoyer	1.25	.55	.16
☐ 31	Phil Russell	.25	.11	.03
☐ 32	Dennis Hextall	.25	.11	.03
☐ 33	Lowell MacDonald	.25	.11	.03
☐ 34	Dennis O'Brien	.25	.11	.03
☐ 35	Gerry Meehan	.35	.16	.04
☐ 36	Gilles Meloche	.35	.16	.04
☐ 37	Wilf Paiement	.35	.16	.04
☐ 38	Bob MacMillan	.50	.23	.06
☐ 39	Ian Turnbull	.35	.16	.04
☐ 40	Rogatien Vachon	1.00	.45	.13
☐ 41	Nick Beverley	.25	.11	.03
☐ 42	Rene Robert	.35	.16	.04
☐ 43	Andre Savard	.25	.11	.03
☐ 44	Bob Gainey	2.50	1.15	.30
☐ 45	Joe Watson	.25	.11	.03
☐ 46	Billy Smith	2.00	.90	.25
☐ 47	Darcy Rota	.25	.11	.03
☐ 48	Rick Lapointe	.25	.11	.03
☐ 49	Pierre Jarry	.25	.11	.03
☐ 50	Syl Apps	.25	.11	.03
☐ 51	Eric Vail	.25	.11	.03
☐ 52	Greg Joly	.25	.11	.03
☐ 53	Don Lever	.25	.11	.03
☐ 54	Bob Murdoch Seals Right Wing	.25	.11	.03
☐ 55	Denis Herron	.35	.16	.04
☐ 56	Mike Bloom	.25	.11	.03
☐ 57	Bill Fairbairn	.25	.11	.03
☐ 58	Fred Stanfield	.25	.11	.03
☐ 59	Steve Shutt	2.00	.90	.25
☐ 60	Brad Park	1.50	.65	.19
☐ 61	Gilles Villemure	.35	.16	.04
☐ 62	Bert Marshall	.25	.11	.03
☐ 63	Chuck Lefley	.25	.11	.03
☐ 64	Simon Nolet	.25	.11	.03
☐ 65	Reggie Leach RB Most Goals, Playoffs	.35	.16	.04
☐ 66	Darryl Sittler RB Most Points, Game	1.00	.45	.13
☐ 67	Bryan Trottier RB Most Points, Season, Rookie	5.00	2.30	.60
☐ 68	Garry Unger RB Most Consecutive Games, Lifetime	.35	.16	.04
☐ 69	Ron Low	.35	.16	.04
☐ 70	Bobby Clarke	4.00	1.80	.50
☐ 71	Michel Bergeron	.25	.11	.03
☐ 72	Ron Stackhouse	.25	.11	.03
☐ 73	Bill Hogaboam	.25	.11	.03
☐ 74	Bob Murdoch Kings Defenseman	.25	.11	.03
☐ 75	Steve Vickers	.25	.11	.03
☐ 76	Pit Martin	.25	.11	.03
☐ 77	Gerry Hart	.25	.11	.03
☐ 78	Craig Ramsay	.25	.11	.03
☐ 79	Michel Larocque	.35	.16	.04
☐ 80	Jean Ratelle	1.00	.45	.13
☐ 81	Don Saleski	.25	.11	.03
☐ 82	Bill Clement	.60	.25	.08
☐ 83	Dave Burrows	.25	.11	.03
☐ 84	Wayne Thomas	.35	.16	.04
☐ 85	John Gould	.25	.11	.03
☐ 86	Dennis Maruk	2.50	1.15	.30
☐ 87	Ernie Hicke	.25	.11	.03
☐ 88	Jim Rutherford	.35	.16	.04
☐ 89	Dale Tallon	.25	.11	.03
☐ 90	Rod Gilbert	1.00	.45	.13
☐ 91	Marcel Dionne	4.00	1.80	.50
☐ 92	Chuck Arnason	.25	.11	.03
☐ 93	Jean Potvin	.25	.11	.03
☐ 94	Don Luce	.25	.11	.03
☐ 95	Johnny Bucyk	1.00	.45	.13
☐ 96	Larry Goodenough	.25	.11	.03
☐ 97	Mario Tremblay	.35	.16	.04
☐ 98	Nelson Pyatt	.25	.11	.03
☐ 99	Brian Glennie	.25	.11	.03
☐ 100	Tony Esposito	2.50	1.15	.30
☐ 101	Dan Maloney	.25	.11	.03
☐ 102	Barry Wilkins	.25	.11	.03
☐ 103	Dean Talafous	.25	.11	.03
☐ 104	Ed Staniowski	.35	.16	.04
☐ 105	Dallas Smith	.25	.11	.03
☐ 106	Jude Drouin	.25	.11	.03
☐ 107	Pat Hickey	.25	.11	.03
☐ 108	Jocelyn Guevremont	.25	.11	.03
☐ 109	Doug Risebrough	.50	.23	.06
☐ 110	Reggie Leach	.35	.16	.04
☐ 111	Dan Bouchard	.35	.16	.04
☐ 112	Chris Oddleifson	.25	.11	.03
☐ 113	Rick Hampton	.25	.11	.03
☐ 114	John Marks	.25	.11	.03

☐ 115	Bryan Trottier	30.00	13.50	3.80
☐ 116	Checklist 1-132	6.00	.60	.12
☐ 117	Greg Polis	.25	.11	.03
☐ 118	Peter McNab	.60	.25	.08
☐ 119	Jim Roberts	.25	.11	.03
	Montreal Canadiens			
☐ 120	Gerry Cheevers	2.00	.90	.25
☐ 121	Rick MacLeish	.35	.16	.04
☐ 122	Billy Lochead	.25	.11	.03
☐ 123	Tom Reid	.25	.11	.03
☐ 124	Rick Kehoe	.35	.16	.04
☐ 125	Keith Magnuson	.25	.11	.03
☐ 126	Clark Gillies	1.25	.55	.16
☐ 127	Rick Middleton	2.00	.90	.25
☐ 128	Bill Hajt	.25	.11	.03
☐ 129	Jacques Lemaire	.75	.35	.09
☐ 130	Terry O'Reilly	.50	.23	.06
☐ 131	Andre Dupont	.25	.11	.03
☐ 132	Flames Team	.75	.35	.09
	(Checklist back)			
☐ 133	Bruins Team	1.00	.45	.13
	(Checklist back)			
☐ 134	Sabres Team	.75	.35	.09
	(Checklist back)			
☐ 135	Seals Team	.75	.35	.09
	(Checklist back)			
☐ 136	Blackhawks Team	.75	.35	.09
	(Checklist back)			
☐ 137	Red Wings Team	.75	.35	.09
	(Checklist back)			
☐ 138	Scouts Team	.75	.35	.09
	(Checklist back)			
☐ 139	Kings Team	.75	.35	.09
	(Checklist back)			
☐ 140	North Stars Team	.75	.35	.09
	(Checklist back)			
☐ 141	Canadiens Team	1.00	.45	.13
	(Checklist back)			
☐ 142	Islanders Team	.75	.35	.09
	(Checklist back)			
☐ 143	Rangers Team	.75	.35	.09
	(Checklist back)			
☐ 144	Flyers Team	.75	.35	.09
	(Checklist back)			
☐ 145	Penguins Team	.75	.35	.09
	(Checklist back)			
☐ 146	Blues Team	.75	.35	.09
	(Checklist back)			
☐ 147	Maple Leafs Team	1.00	.45	.13
	(Checklist back)			
☐ 148	Canucks Team	.75	.35	.09
	(Checklist back)			
☐ 149	Capitals Team	.75	.35	.09
	(Checklist back)			
☐ 150	Dave Schultz	.50	.23	.06
☐ 151	Larry Robinson	4.00	1.80	.50
☐ 152	Al Smith	.35	.16	.04
☐ 153	Bob Nystrom	.35	.16	.04
☐ 154	Ron Greschner UER	.60	.25	.08
	(Shown as Penguin on front, should be Ranger)			
☐ 155	Gregg Sheppard	.25	.11	.03
☐ 156	Alain Daigle	.25	.11	.03
☐ 157	Ed Van Impe	.25	.11	.03
☐ 158	Tim Young	.50	.23	.06
☐ 159	Gary Bergman	.25	.11	.03
☐ 160	Ed Giacomin	1.25	.55	.16
☐ 161	Yvon Labre	.25	.11	.03
☐ 162	Jim Lorentz	.25	.11	.03
☐ 163	Guy Lafleur	8.00	3.60	1.00
☐ 164	Tom Bladon	.35	.16	.04
☐ 165	Wayne Cashman	.35	.16	.04
☐ 166	Pete Stemkowski	.25	.11	.03
☐ 167	Grant Mulvey	.25	.11	.03
☐ 168	Yves Belanger	.35	.16	.04
☐ 169	Bill Goldsworthy	.35	.16	.04
☐ 170	Denis Potvin	5.00	2.30	.60
☐ 171	Nick Libett	.25	.11	.03
☐ 172	Michel Plasse	.35	.16	.04
☐ 173	Lou Nanne	.25	.11	.03
☐ 174	Tom Lysiak	.35	.16	.04
☐ 175	Dennis Ververgaert	.25	.11	.03
☐ 176	Gary Simmons	.35	.16	.04
☐ 177	Pierre Bouchard	.25	.11	.03
☐ 178	Bill Barber	1.50	.65	.19
☐ 179	Darryl Edestrand	.25	.11	.03
☐ 180	Gilbert Perreault	2.00	.90	.25
☐ 181	Dave Maloney	.50	.23	.06
☐ 182	Jean-Paul Parise	.25	.11	.03
☐ 183	Bobby Sheehan	.25	.11	.03
☐ 184	Pete Lopresti	.35	.16	.04
☐ 185	Don Kozak	.25	.11	.03
☐ 186	Guy Charron	.25	.11	.03
☐ 187	Stan Gilbertson	.25	.11	.03

☐ 188	Bill Nyrop	.25	.11	.03
☐ 189	Bobby Schmautz	.25	.11	.03
☐ 190	Wayne Stephenson	.35	.16	.04
☐ 191	Brian Spencer	.25	.11	.03
☐ 192	Gilles Marotte	.25	.11	.03
☐ 193	Lorne Henning	.25	.11	.03
☐ 194	Bob Neely	.25	.11	.03
☐ 195	Dennis Hull	.35	.16	.04
☐ 196	Walt McKechnie	.25	.11	.03
☐ 197	Curt Ridley	.35	.16	.04
☐ 198	Dwight Bialowas	.25	.11	.03
☐ 199	Pierre Larouche	1.25	.55	.16
☐ 200	Ken Dryden	10.00	4.50	1.25
☐ 201	Ross Lonsberry	.25	.11	.03
☐ 202	Curt Bennett	.25	.11	.03
☐ 203	Hartland Monahan	.25	.11	.03
☐ 204	John Davidson	.50	.23	.06
☐ 205	Serge Savard	.25	.11	.03
☐ 206	Garry Howatt	.25	.11	.03
☐ 207	Darryl Sittler	3.00	1.35	.40
☐ 208	J.P. Bordeleau	.25	.11	.03
☐ 209	Henry Boucha	.25	.11	.03
☐ 210	Richard Martin	.35	.16	.04
☐ 211	Vic Venasky	.25	.11	.03
☐ 212	Buster Harvey	.25	.11	.03
☐ 213	Bobby Orr	18.00	8.00	2.30
☐ 214	French Connection	2.00	.90	.25
	Richard Martin			
	Gilbert Perreault			
	Rene Robert			
☐ 215	LCB Line	2.50	1.15	.30
	Reggie Leach			
	Bobby Clarke			
	Bill Barber			
☐ 216	Long Island Lightning	3.00	1.35	.40
	Clark Gillies			
	Bryan Trottier			
	Billy Harris			
☐ 217	Checking Line	.60	.25	.08
	Bob Gainey			
	Doug Jarvis			
	Jim Roberts			
☐ 218	Bicentennial Line	.35	.16	.04
	Lowell MacDonald			
	Syl Apps			
	Jean Pronovost			
☐ 219	Bob Kelly	.25	.11	.03
☐ 220	Walt Tkaczuk	.35	.16	.04
☐ 221	Dave Lewis	.25	.11	.03
☐ 222	Danny Gare	.60	.25	.08
☐ 223	Guy Lapointe	.35	.16	.04
☐ 224	Hank Nowak	.25	.11	.03
☐ 225	Stan Mikita	2.50	1.15	.30
☐ 226	Vic Hadfield	.35	.16	.04
☐ 227	Bernie Wolfe	.35	.16	.04
☐ 228	Bryan Watson	.25	.11	.03
☐ 229	Ralph Stewart	.25	.11	.03
☐ 230	Gerry Desjardins	.35	.16	.04
☐ 231	John Bednarski	.25	.11	.03
☐ 232	Yvon Lambert	.25	.11	.03
☐ 233	Orest Kindrachuk	.25	.11	.03
☐ 234	Don Marcotte	.25	.11	.03
☐ 235	Bill White	.25	.11	.03
☐ 236	Red Berenson	.35	.16	.04
☐ 237	Al MacAdam	.25	.11	.03
☐ 238	Rick Blight	.25	.11	.03
☐ 239	Butch Goring	.35	.16	.04
☐ 240	Cesare Maniago	.35	.16	.04
☐ 241	Jim Schoenfeld	.35	.16	.04
☐ 242	Cliff Koroll	.25	.11	.03
☐ 243	Mickey Redmond	.35	.16	.04
☐ 244	Rick Chartraw	.25	.11	.03
☐ 245	Phil Esposito	2.50	1.15	.30
☐ 246	Dave Forbes	.25	.11	.03
☐ 247	Joe Watson	.25	.11	.03
☐ 248	Ron Schock	.25	.11	.03
☐ 249	Fred Barrett	.25	.11	.03
☐ 250	Glenn Resch	1.25	.55	.16
☐ 251	Ivan Boldirev	.25	.11	.03
☐ 252	Billy Harris	.25	.11	.03
☐ 253	Lee Fogolin	.25	.11	.03
☐ 254	Murray Wilson	.25	.11	.03
☐ 255	Gilles Gilbert	.35	.16	.04
☐ 256	Gary Dornhoefer	.25	.11	.03
☐ 257	Carol Vadnais	.25	.11	.03
☐ 258	Checklist 133-264	6.00	.60	.12
☐ 259	Errol Thompson	.25	.11	.03
☐ 260	Garry Unger	.35	.16	.04
☐ 261	J. Bob Kelly	.25	.11	.03
☐ 262	Terry Harper	.25	.11	.03
☐ 263	Blake Dunlop	.25	.11	.03
☐ 264	Stanley Cup Champs	1.50	.45	.15
	Montreal Canadiens			

1976-77 Topps Glossy Inserts

This 22-card insert set was issued with the 1976-77 Topps hockey card set but not with the O-Pee-Chee hockey cards unlike the glossy insert produced "jointly" by Topps and O-Pee-Chee the next year. This set is very similar to (but much more difficult to find than) the glossy insert set of the following year. The cards were printed in the United States. These rounded-corner cards are approximately 2 1/4" by 3 1/4".

		NRMT	VG-E	GOOD
	COMPLETE SET (22)	60.00	24.00	6.00
	COMMON PLAYER (1-22)	1.00	.40	.10
☐ 1	Bobby Clarke	4.00	1.60	.40
☐ 2	Brad Park	2.50	1.00	.25
☐ 3	Tony Esposito	3.00	1.20	.30
☐ 4	Marcel Dionne	3.50	1.40	.35
☐ 5	Ken Dryden	6.00	2.40	.60
☐ 6	Glenn Resch	2.00	.80	.20
☐ 7	Phil Esposito	4.00	1.60	.40
☐ 8	Darryl Sittler	2.50	1.00	.25
☐ 9	Gilbert Perreault	2.00	.80	.20
☐ 10	Denis Potvin	3.00	1.20	.30
☐ 11	Guy Lafleur	6.00	2.40	.60
☐ 12	Bill Barber	2.50	1.00	.25
☐ 13	Syl Apps	1.00	.40	.10
☐ 14	Johnny Bucyk	2.50	1.00	.25
☐ 15	Bryan Trottier	10.00	4.00	1.00
☐ 16	Dennis Hull	1.50	.60	.15
☐ 17	Guy Lapointe	2.00	.80	.20
☐ 18	Rod Gilbert	2.00	.80	.20
☐ 19	Richard Martin	1.50	.60	.15
☐ 20	Bobby Orr	20.00	8.00	2.00
☐ 21	Reggie Leach	1.50	.60	.15
☐ 22	Jean Ratelle	2.00	.80	.20

1977-78 Topps

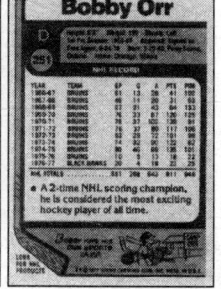

The 1977-78 Topps set consists of 264 cards. Cards 203 (Stan Gilbertson) and 255 (Bill Fairbairn) differ from those of O-Pee-Chee. Cards are the standard 2 1/2" by 3 1/2". Card fronts have team name and logo, player name and position at the bottom. Yearly statistics including minor league numbers are featured on the back along with a short biography and a cartoon-illustrated fact about the player. After the initial print run, Topps changed the photos on card numbers 131, 138, 149 and 152. Two of the changes (138 and 149) were necessary corrections. Rookie Cards include Mike Milbury and Mike Palmateer. This set marks Bobby Orr's last Topps appearance.

		NRMT	VG-E	GOOD
	COMPLETE SET (264)	100.00	45.00	12.50
	COMMON PLAYER (1-264)	.20	.09	.03
☐ 1	Goals Leaders	2.50	.75	.25
	Steve Shutt			
	Guy Lafleur			
	Marcel Dionne			
☐ 2	Assists Leaders	1.50	.65	.19
	Guy Lafleur			
	Marcel Dionne			
	Larry Robinson			
	Borje Salming			
	Tim Young			
☐ 3	Scoring Leaders	2.00	.90	.25
	Guy Lafleur			
	Marcel Dionne			
	Steve Shutt			
☐ 4	Penalty Min. Leaders	.35	.16	.04
	Dave(Tiger) Williams			
	Dennis Polonich			
	Bob Gassoff			
☐ 5	Power Play Goals Leaders	.75	.35	.09
	Lanny McDonald			
	Phil Esposito			
	Tom Williams			
☐ 6	Goals Against Average Leaders	1.00	.45	.13
	Michel Larocque			
	Ken Dryden			
	Glenn Resch			
☐ 7	Game Winning Goals Leaders	1.50	.65	.19
	Gilbert Perreault			
	Steve Shutt			
	Guy Lafleur			
	Rick MacLeish			
	Peter McNab			
☐ 8	Shutouts Leaders	2.00	.90	.25
	Ken Dryden			
	Rogatien Vachon			
	Bernie Parent			
	Dunc Wilson			
☐ 9	Brian Spencer	.20	.09	.03
☐ 10	Denis Potvin AS2	3.00	1.35	.40
☐ 11	Nick Fotiu	.50	.23	.06
☐ 12	Bob Murray	.20	.09	.03
☐ 13	Pete Lopresti	.25	.11	.03
☐ 14	J. Bob Kelly	.20	.09	.03
☐ 15	Rick MacLeish	.25	.11	.03
☐ 16	Terry Harper	.20	.09	.03
☐ 17	Willi Plett	1.50	.65	.19
☐ 18	Peter McNab	.25	.11	.03
☐ 19	Wayne Thomas	.25	.11	.03
☐ 20	Pierre Bouchard	.20	.09	.03
☐ 21	Dennis Maruk	.60	.25	.08
☐ 22	Mike Murphy	.20	.09	.03
☐ 23	Cesare Maniago	.25	.11	.03
☐ 24	Paul Gardner	.35	.16	.04
☐ 25	Rod Gilbert	.75	.35	.09
☐ 26	Orest Kindrachuk	.20	.09	.03
☐ 27	Bill Hajt	.20	.09	.03
☐ 28	John Davidson	.25	.11	.03
☐ 29	Jean-Paul Parise	.20	.09	.03
☐ 30	Larry Robinson AS1	3.00	1.35	.40
☐ 31	Yvon Labre	.20	.09	.03
☐ 32	Walt McKechnie	.20	.09	.03
☐ 33	Rick Kehoe	.25	.11	.03
☐ 34	Randy Holt	.20	.09	.03
☐ 35	Garry Unger	.25	.11	.03
☐ 36	Lou Nanne	.20	.09	.03
☐ 37	Dan Bouchard	.25	.11	.03
☐ 38	Darryl Sittler	2.00	.90	.25
☐ 39	Bob Murdoch	.20	.09	.03
☐ 40	Jean Ratelle	.75	.35	.09
☐ 41	Dave Maloney	.20	.09	.03
☐ 42	Danny Gare	.25	.11	.03
☐ 43	Jim Watson	.20	.09	.03
☐ 44	Tom Williams	.20	.09	.03

☐ 45	Serge Savard	.20	.09	.03
☐ 46	Derek Sanderson	.25	.11	.03
☐ 47	John Marks	.20	.09	.03
☐ 48	Al Cameron	.20	.09	.03
☐ 49	Dean Talafous	.20	.09	.03
☐ 50	Glenn Resch	.75	.35	.09
☐ 51	Ron Schock	.20	.09	.03
☐ 52	Gary Croteau	.20	.09	.03
☐ 53	Gerry Meehan	.25	.11	.03
☐ 54	Ed Staniowski	.25	.11	.03
☐ 55	Phil Esposito	2.50	1.15	.30
☐ 56	Dennis Ververgaert	.20	.09	.03
☐ 57	Rick Wilson	.20	.09	.03
☐ 58	Jim Lorentz	.20	.09	.03
☐ 59	Bobby Schmautz	.20	.09	.03
☐ 60	Guy Lapointe AS2	.25	.11	.03
☐ 61	Ivan Boldirev	.20	.09	.03
☐ 62	Bob Nystrom	.25	.11	.03
☐ 63	Rick Hampton	.20	.09	.03
☐ 64	Jack Valiquette	.20	.09	.03
☐ 65	Bernie Parent	1.25	.55	.16
☐ 66	Dave Burrows	.20	.09	.03
☐ 67	Butch Goring	.25	.11	.03
☐ 68	Checklist 1-132	3.50	.35	.07
☐ 69	Murray Wilson	.20	.09	.03
☐ 70	Ed Giacomin	1.00	.45	.13
☐ 71	Flames Team	.50	.23	.06
☐ 72	Bruins Team	.75	.35	.09
☐ 73	Sabres Team	.50	.23	.06
☐ 74	Blackhawks Team	.50	.23	.06
☐ 75	Barons Team	.50	.23	.06
☐ 76	Rockies Team	.50	.23	.06
☐ 77	Red Wings Team	.50	.23	.06
☐ 78	Kings Team	.50	.23	.06
☐ 79	North Stars Team	.50	.23	.06
☐ 80	Canadiens Team	.75	.35	.09
☐ 81	Islanders Team	.50	.23	.06
☐ 82	Rangers Team	.50	.23	.06
☐ 83	Flyers Team	.50	.23	.06
☐ 84	Penguins Team	.50	.23	.06
☐ 85	Blues Team	.50	.23	.06
☐ 86	Maple Leafs Team	.75	.35	.09
☐ 87	Canucks Team	.50	.23	.06
☐ 88	Capitals Team	.50	.23	.06
☐ 89	Keith Magnuson	.20	.09	.03
☐ 90	Walt Tkaczuk	.25	.11	.03
☐ 91	Bill Nyrop	.20	.09	.03
☐ 92	Michel Plasse	.25	.11	.03
☐ 93	Bob Bourne	.25	.11	.03
☐ 94	Lee Fogolin	.20	.09	.03
☐ 95	Gregg Sheppard	.20	.09	.03
☐ 96	Hartland Monahan	.20	.09	.03
☐ 97	Curt Bennett	.20	.09	.03
☐ 98	Bob Dailey	.20	.09	.03
☐ 99	Bill Goldsworthy	.25	.11	.03
☐ 100	Ken Dryden AS1	7.00	3.10	.85
☐ 101	Grant Mulvey	.20	.09	.03
☐ 102	Pierre Larouche	.50	.23	.06
☐ 103	Nick Libett	.20	.09	.03
☐ 104	Rick Smith	.20	.09	.03
☐ 105	Bryan Trottier	12.00	5.50	1.50
☐ 106	Pierre Jarry	.20	.09	.03
☐ 107	Red Berenson	.25	.11	.03
☐ 108	Jim Schoenfeld	.25	.11	.03
☐ 109	Gilles Meloche	.25	.11	.03
☐ 110	Lanny McDonald AS2	2.00	.90	.25
☐ 111	Don Lever	.20	.09	.03
☐ 112	Greg Polis	.20	.09	.03
☐ 113	Gary Sargent	.30	.14	.04
☐ 114	Earl Anderson	.20	.09	.03
☐ 115	Bobby Clarke	3.00	1.35	.40
☐ 116	Dave Lewis	.20	.09	.03
☐ 117	Darcy Rota	.20	.09	.03
☐ 118	Andre Savard	.20	.09	.03
☐ 119	Denis Herron	.25	.11	.03
☐ 120	Steve Shutt AS1	1.25	.55	.16
☐ 121	Mel Bridgman	.50	.23	.06
☐ 122	Buster Harvey	.20	.09	.03
☐ 123	Roland Eriksson	.20	.09	.03
☐ 124	Dale Tallon	.20	.09	.03
☐ 125	Gilles Gilbert	.25	.11	.03
☐ 126	Billy Harris	.20	.09	.03
☐ 127	Tom Lysiak	.25	.11	.03
☐ 128	Jerry Korab	.20	.09	.03
☐ 129	Bob Gainey	1.25	.55	.16
☐ 130	Wilf Paiement	.25	.11	.03
☐ 131A	Tom Bladon (Standing)	2.00	.90	.25
☐ 131B	Tom Bladon (Crouched for face off)	.20	.09	.03
☐ 132	Ernie Hicke	.20	.09	.03
☐ 133	J.P. LeBlanc	.20	.09	.03
☐ 134	Mike Milbury	1.50	.65	.19
☐ 135	Pit Martin	.20	.09	.03
☐ 136	Steve Vickers	.20	.09	.03
☐ 137	Don Awrey	.20	.09	.03
☐ 138A	Bernie Wolfe ERR (Photo actually Al MacAdam looking straight ahead)	2.00	.90	.25
☐ 138B	Bernie Wolfe COR	.20	.09	.03
☐ 139	Doug Jarvis	.40	.18	.05
☐ 140	Borje Salming AS1	1.00	.45	.13
☐ 141	Bob MacMillan	.20	.09	.03
☐ 142	Wayne Stephenson	.25	.11	.03
☐ 143	Dave Forbes	.20	.09	.03
☐ 144	Jean Potvin	.20	.09	.03
☐ 145	Guy Charron	.20	.09	.03
☐ 146	Cliff Koroll	.20	.09	.03
☐ 147	Danny Grant	.25	.11	.03
☐ 148	Bill Hogaboam UER (Photo actually Michel Bergeron)	.20	.09	.03
☐ 149A	Al MacAdam ERR (Photo actually Bernie Wolfe, looking left)	2.00	.90	.25
☐ 149B	Al MacAdam COR	.20	.09	.03
☐ 150	Gerry Desjardins	.25	.11	.03
☐ 151	Yvon Lambert	.20	.09	.03
☐ 152A	Rick Lapointe (Shooting, facing right, without mustache)	2.00	.90	.25
☐ 152B	Rick Lapointe (With mustache)	.20	.09	.03
☐ 153	Ed Westfall	.25	.11	.03
☐ 154	Carol Vadnais	.20	.09	.03
☐ 155	Johnny Bucyk	.60	.25	.08
☐ 156	J.P. Bordeleau	.20	.09	.03
☐ 157	Ron Stackhouse	.20	.09	.03
☐ 158	Glen Sharpley	.20	.09	.03
☐ 159	Michel Bergeron	.20	.09	.03
☐ 160	Rogatien Vachon AS2	.60	.25	.08
☐ 161	Fred Stanfield	.20	.09	.03
☐ 162	Gerry Hart	.20	.09	.03
☐ 163	Mario Tremblay	.25	.11	.03
☐ 164	Andre Dupont	.20	.09	.03
☐ 165	Don Marcotte	.20	.09	.03
☐ 166	Wayne Dillon	.20	.09	.03
☐ 167	Claude Larose	.20	.09	.03
☐ 168	Eric Vail	.20	.09	.03
☐ 169	Tom Edur	.20	.09	.03
☐ 170	Tony Esposito	1.50	.65	.19
☐ 171	Andre St.Laurent	.20	.09	.03
☐ 172	Dan Maloney	.20	.09	.03
☐ 173	Dennis O'Brien	.20	.09	.03
☐ 174	Blair Chapman	.20	.09	.03
☐ 175	Dennis Kearns	.20	.09	.03
☐ 176	Wayne Merrick	.20	.09	.03
☐ 177	Michel Larocque	.25	.11	.03
☐ 178	Bob Kelly	.20	.09	.03
☐ 179	Dave Farrish	.20	.09	.03
☐ 180	Richard Martin AS2	.25	.11	.03
☐ 181	Gary Doak	.20	.09	.03
☐ 182	Jude Drouin	.20	.09	.03
☐ 183	Barry Dean	.20	.09	.03
☐ 184	Gary Smith	.25	.11	.03
☐ 185	Reggie Leach	.25	.11	.03
☐ 186	Ian Turnbull	.25	.11	.03
☐ 187	Vic Venasky	.20	.09	.03
☐ 188	Wayne Bianchin	.20	.09	.03
☐ 189	Doug Risebrough	.25	.11	.03
☐ 190	Brad Park	1.25	.55	.16
☐ 191	Craig Ramsay	.20	.09	.03
☐ 192	Ken Hodge	.25	.11	.03
☐ 193	Phil Myre	.25	.11	.03
☐ 194	Garry Howatt	.20	.09	.03
☐ 195	Stan Mikita	2.50	1.15	.30
☐ 196	Garnet Bailey	.20	.09	.03
☐ 197	Dennis Hextall	.20	.09	.03
☐ 198	Nick Beverley	.20	.09	.03
☐ 199	Larry Patey	.20	.09	.03
☐ 200	Guy Lafleur AS1	5.00	2.30	.60
☐ 201	Don Edwards	1.50	.65	.19
☐ 202	Gary Dornhoefer	.20	.09	.03
☐ 203	Stan Gilbertson	.20	.09	.03
☐ 204	Alex Pirus	.20	.09	.03
☐ 205	Peter Mahovlich	.25	.11	.03
☐ 206	Bert Marshall	.20	.09	.03
☐ 207	Gilles Gratton	.25	.11	.03
☐ 208	Alain Daigle	.20	.09	.03
☐ 209	Chris Oddleifson	.20	.09	.03
☐ 210	Gilbert Perreault AS2	1.50	.65	.19
☐ 211	Mike Palmateer	2.00	.90	.25
☐ 212	Billy Lochead	.20	.09	.03
☐ 213	Dick Redmond	.20	.09	.03

		NRMT	VG-E	GOOD
☐ 214	Guy Lafleur RB.................. Most Points, RW, Season	1.50	.65	.19
☐ 215	Ian Turnbull RB.................. Most Goals, Defenseman, Game	.20	.09	.03
☐ 216	Guy Lafleur RB.................. Longest Point Scoring Streak	1.50	.65	.19
☐ 217	Steve Shutt RB.................. Most Goals, LW, Season	.40	.18	.05
☐ 218	Guy Lafleur RB.................. Most Assists, RW, Season	1.50	.65	.19
☐ 219	Lorne Henning	.20	.09	.03
☐ 220	Terry O'Reilly	.35	.16	.04
☐ 221	Pat Hickey	.20	.09	.03
☐ 222	Rene Robert......................	.25	.11	.03
☐ 223	Tim Young	.20	.09	.03
☐ 224	Dunc Wilson	.25	.11	.03
☐ 225	Dennis Hull	.25	.11	.03
☐ 226	Rod Seiling	.20	.09	.03
☐ 227	Bill Barber	.75	.35	.09
☐ 228	Dennis Polonich................	.20	.09	.03
☐ 229	Billy Smith........................	1.25	.55	.16
☐ 230	Yvan Cournoyer	1.00	.45	.13
☐ 231	Don Luce..........................	.20	.09	.03
☐ 232	Mike McEwen	.35	.16	.04
☐ 233	Don Saleski......................	.20	.09	.03
☐ 234	Wayne Cashman	.25	.11	.03
☐ 235	Phil Russell......................	.20	.09	.03
☐ 236	Mike Corrigan...................	.20	.09	.03
☐ 237	Guy Chouinard	.25	.11	.03
☐ 238	Steve Jensen....................	.20	.09	.03
☐ 239	Jim Rutherford..................	.25	.11	.03
☐ 240	Marcel Dionne AS1	3.50	1.55	.45
☐ 241	Rejean Houle....................	.20	.09	.03
☐ 242	Jocelyn Guevremont	.20	.09	.03
☐ 243	Jim Harrison.....................	.20	.09	.03
☐ 244	Don Murdoch.....................	.20	.09	.03
☐ 245	Rick Green	.60	.25	.08
☐ 246	Rick Middleton..................	1.25	.55	.16
☐ 247	Joe Watson	.20	.09	.03
☐ 248	Syl Apps...........................	.20	.09	.03
☐ 249	Checklist 133-264	3.50	.35	.07
☐ 250	Clark Gillies......................	.50	.23	.06
☐ 251	Bobby Orr	15.00	6.75	1.90
☐ 252	Nelson Pyatt.....................	.20	.09	.03
☐ 253	Gary McAdam	.20	.09	.03
☐ 254	Jacques Lemaire	.60	.25	.08
☐ 255	Bill Fairbairn.....................	.20	.09	.03
☐ 256	Ron Greschner..................	.25	.11	.03
☐ 257	Ross Lonsberry.................	.20	.09	.03
☐ 258	Dave Gardner	.20	.09	.03
☐ 259	Rick Blight........................	.20	.09	.03
☐ 260	Gerry Cheevers	1.25	.55	.16
☐ 261	Jean Pronovost	.25	.11	.03
☐ 262	Semi-Finals .... Canadiens Skate Past Islanders	.35	.16	.04
☐ 263	Semi-Finals .... Bruins Advance to Finals	.35	.16	.04
☐ 264	Finals .... Canadiens Win 20th Stanley Cup	1.00	.25	.08

☐ 1	Wayne Cashman	.35	.14	.03
☐ 2	Gerry Cheevers	1.25	.50	.12
☐ 3	Bobby Clarke....................	1.50	.60	.15
☐ 4	Marcel Dionne	1.50	.60	.15
☐ 5	Ken Dryden	2.50	1.00	.25
☐ 6	Clark Gillies......................	.35	.14	.03
☐ 7	Guy Lafleur	2.50	1.00	.25
☐ 8	Reggie Leach	.25	.10	.02
☐ 9	Rick MacLeish...................	.50	.20	.05
☐ 10	Dave Maloney	.25	.10	.02
☐ 11	Richard Martin..................	.35	.14	.03
☐ 12	Don Murdoch.....................	.25	.10	.02
☐ 13	Brad Park.........................	.75	.30	.07
☐ 14	Gilbert Perreault...............	1.00	.40	.10
☐ 15	Denis Potvin.....................	1.00	.40	.10
☐ 16	Jean Ratelle.....................	.75	.30	.07
☐ 17	Glenn Resch.....................	.60	.24	.06
☐ 18	Larry Robinson	1.25	.50	.12
☐ 19	Steve Shutt	.75	.30	.07
☐ 20	Darryl Sittler....................	1.00	.40	.10
☐ 21	Rogatien Vachon	.60	.24	.06
☐ 22	Tim Young	.25	.10	.02

1978-79 Topps

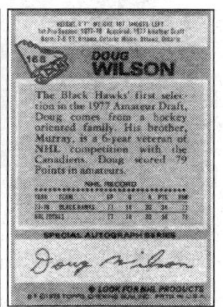

1977-78 Topps/O-Pee-Chee Glossy

This set of 22 numbered cards was issued with either square or round corners as an insert with both the Topps and O-Pee-Chee hockey cards of 1977-78. Cards were numbered on the back and measure 2 1/4" by 3 1/4". They are essentially the same as the O-Pee-Chee insert issue of the same year. The O-Pee-Chee inserts have the same card numbers and pictures, same prices, but different copyright lines on the reverses. The cards are priced below for the round cornered version; the square cornered cards are worth approximately 10 percent more than the the prices below.

	NRMT	VG-E	GOOD
COMPLETE SET (22).......................	12.00	5.00	1.20
COMMON PLAYER (1-22)................	.25	.10	.02

The 1978-79 Topps set consists of 264 cards. Cards measure 2 1/2" by 3 1/2". Card fronts have team name, logo and player position in the top left corner. The player's name is within the top border. A short biography, yearly statistics including minor leagues and a facsimile autograph are included on the back. The key Rookie Cards in this set are Mike Bossy, Bernie Federko, and Doug Wilson.

	NRMT	VG-E	GOOD
COMPLETE SET (264).......................	75.00	34.00	9.50
COMMON PLAYER (1-264)...............	.15	.07	.02
☐ 1 Mike Bossy HL....................... Goals by Rookie	5.00	1.25	.25
☐ 2 Phil Esposito HL..................... 29th Hat Trick	.75	.35	.09
☐ 3 Guy Lafleur HL........................ Scores Against Every Team	1.00	.45	.13
☐ 4 Darryl Sittler HL.......................	.50	.23	.06

	Goals In Nine Straight Games			
☐ 5	Garry Unger HL	.20	.09	.03
	803 Consecutive Games			
☐ 6	Gary Edwards	.20	.09	.03
☐ 7	Rick Blight	.15	.07	.02
☐ 8	Larry Patey	.15	.07	.02
☐ 9	Craig Ramsay	.15	.07	.02
☐ 10	Bryan Trottier AS1	5.00	2.30	.60
☐ 11	Don Murdoch	.15	.07	.02
☐ 12	Phil Russell	.15	.07	.02
☐ 13	Doug Jarvis	.20	.09	.03
☐ 14	Gene Carr	.15	.07	.02
☐ 15	Bernie Parent	1.00	.45	.13
☐ 16	Perry Miller	.15	.07	.02
☐ 17	Kent-Erik Andersson	.15	.07	.02
☐ 18	Gregg Sheppard	.15	.07	.02
☐ 19	Dennis Owchar	.15	.07	.02
☐ 20	Rogatien Vachon	.50	.23	.06
☐ 21	Dan Maloney	.15	.07	.02
☐ 22	Guy Charron	.15	.07	.02
☐ 23	Dick Redmond	.15	.07	.02
☐ 24	Checklist 1-132	2.50	.30	.05
☐ 25	Anders Hedberg	.20	.09	.03
☐ 26	Mel Bridgman	.20	.09	.03
☐ 27	Lee Fogolin	.15	.07	.02
☐ 28	Gilles Meloche	.20	.09	.03
☐ 29	Garry Howatt	.15	.07	.02
☐ 30	Darryl Sittler AS2	1.25	.55	.16
☐ 31	Curt Bennett	.15	.07	.02
☐ 32	Andre St.Laurent	.15	.07	.02
☐ 33	Blair Chapman	.15	.07	.02
☐ 34	Keith Magnuson	.15	.07	.02
☐ 35	Pierre Larouche	.20	.09	.03
☐ 36	Michel Plasse	.20	.09	.03
☐ 37	Gary Sargent	.15	.07	.02
☐ 38	Mike Walton	.15	.07	.02
☐ 39	Robert Picard	.25	.11	.03
☐ 40	Terry O'Reilly AS2	.25	.11	.03
☐ 41	Dave Farrish	.15	.07	.02
☐ 42	Gary McAdam	.15	.07	.02
☐ 43	Joe Watson	.15	.07	.02
☐ 44	Yves Belanger	.20	.09	.03
☐ 45	Steve Jensen	.15	.07	.02
☐ 46	Bob Stewart	.15	.07	.02
☐ 47	Darcy Rota	.15	.07	.02
☐ 48	Dennis Hextall	.15	.07	.02
☐ 49	Bert Marshall	.15	.07	.02
☐ 50	Ken Dryden AS1	5.00	2.30	.60
☐ 51	Peter Mahovlich	.20	.09	.03
☐ 52	Dennis Ververgaert	.15	.07	.02
☐ 53	Inge Hammarstrom	.15	.07	.02
☐ 54	Doug Favell	.20	.09	.03
☐ 55	Steve Vickers	.15	.07	.02
☐ 56	Syl Apps	.15	.07	.02
☐ 57	Errol Thompson	.15	.07	.02
☐ 58	Don Luce	.15	.07	.02
☐ 59	Mike Milbury	.35	.16	.04
☐ 60	Yvan Cournoyer	.75	.35	.09
☐ 61	Kirk Bowman	.15	.07	.02
☐ 62	Billy Smith	.75	.35	.09
☐ 63	Goal Leaders	2.50	1.15	.30
	Guy Lafleur			
	Mike Bossy			
	Steve Shutt			
☐ 64	Assist Leaders	1.50	.65	.19
	Bryan Trottier			
	Guy Lafleur			
	Darryl Sittler			
☐ 65	Scoring Leaders	1.50	.65	.19
	Guy Lafleur			
	Bryan Trottier			
	Darryl Sittler			
☐ 66	Penalty Minutes	.30	.14	.04
	Leaders			
	Dave Schultz			
	Dave(Tiger) Williams			
	Dennis Polonich			
☐ 67	Power Play Goal	2.00	.90	.25
	Leaders			
	Mike Bossy			
	Phil Esposito			
	Steve Shutt			
☐ 68	Goals Against	1.50	.65	.19
	Average Leaders			
	Ken Dryden			
	Bernie Parent			
	Gilles Gilbert			
☐ 69	Game Winning	1.50	.65	.19
	Goal Leaders			
	Guy Lafleur			
	Bill Barber			
	Darryl Sittler			
	Bob Bourne			
☐ 70	Shutout Leaders	2.50	1.15	.30
	Bernie Parent			
	Ken Dryden			
	Don Edwards			
	Tony Esposito			
	Mike Palmateer			
☐ 71	Bob Kelly	.15	.07	.02
☐ 72	Ron Stackhouse	.15	.07	.02
☐ 73	Wayne Dillon	.15	.07	.02
☐ 74	Jim Rutherford	.20	.09	.03
☐ 75	Stan Mikita	1.75	.80	.22
☐ 76	Bob Gainey	1.00	.45	.13
☐ 77	Gerry Hart	.15	.07	.02
☐ 78	Lanny McDonald	1.00	.45	.13
☐ 79	Brad Park	1.00	.45	.13
☐ 80	Richard Martin	.20	.09	.03
☐ 81	Bernie Wolfe	.20	.09	.03
☐ 82	Bob MacMillan	.15	.07	.02
☐ 83	Brad Maxwell	.15	.07	.02
☐ 84	Mike Fidler	.15	.07	.02
☐ 85	Carol Vadnais	.15	.07	.02
☐ 86	Don Lever	.15	.07	.02
☐ 87	Phil Myre	.20	.09	.03
☐ 88	Paul Gardner	.15	.07	.02
☐ 89	Bob Murray	.15	.07	.02
☐ 90	Guy Lafleur AS1	3.50	1.55	.45
☐ 91	Bob Murdoch	.15	.07	.02
☐ 92	Ron Ellis	.20	.09	.03
☐ 93	Jude Drouin	.15	.07	.02
☐ 94	Jocelyn Guevremont	.15	.07	.02
☐ 95	Gilles Gilbert	.20	.09	.03
☐ 96	Bob Sirois	.15	.07	.02
☐ 97	Tom Lysiak	.20	.09	.03
☐ 98	Andre Dupont	.15	.07	.02
☐ 99	Per-Olov Brasar	.15	.07	.02
☐ 100	Phil Esposito	2.00	.90	.25
☐ 101	J.P. Bordeleau	.15	.07	.02
☐ 102	Pierre Mondou	.50	.23	.06
☐ 103	Wayne Bianchin	.15	.07	.02
☐ 104	Dennis O'Brien	.15	.07	.02
☐ 105	Glenn Resch	.40	.18	.05
☐ 106	Dennis Polonich	.15	.07	.02
☐ 107	Kris Manery	.15	.07	.02
☐ 108	Bill Hajt	.15	.07	.02
☐ 109	Jere Gillis	.15	.07	.02
☐ 110	Garry Unger	.20	.09	.03
☐ 111	Nick Beverly	.15	.07	.02
☐ 112	Pat Hickey	.15	.07	.02
☐ 113	Rick Middleton	.75	.35	.09
☐ 114	Orest Kindrachuk	.15	.07	.02
☐ 115	Mike Bossy	25.00	11.50	3.10
☐ 116	Pierre Bouchard	.15	.07	.02
☐ 117	Alain Daigle	.15	.07	.02
☐ 118	Terry Martin	.15	.07	.02
☐ 119	Tom Edur	.15	.07	.02
☐ 120	Marcel Dionne	2.50	1.15	.30
☐ 121	Barry Beck	1.00	.45	.13
☐ 122	Billy Lochead	.15	.07	.02
☐ 123	Paul Harrison	.20	.09	.03
☐ 124	Wayne Cashman	.20	.09	.03
☐ 125	Rick MacLeish	.20	.09	.03
☐ 126	Bob Bourne	.20	.09	.03
☐ 127	Ian Turnbull	.15	.07	.02
☐ 128	Gerry Meehan	.20	.09	.03
☐ 129	Eric Vail	.15	.07	.02
☐ 130	Gilbert Perreault	1.00	.45	.13
☐ 131	Bob Dailey	.15	.07	.02
☐ 132	Dale McCourt	.35	.16	.04
☐ 133	John Wensink	.50	.23	.06
☐ 134	Bill Nyrop	.15	.07	.02
☐ 135	Ivan Boldirev	.15	.07	.02
☐ 136	Lucien DeBlois	.30	.14	.04
☐ 137	Brian Spencer	.15	.07	.02
☐ 138	Tim Young	.15	.07	.02
☐ 139	Ron Sedlbauer	.15	.07	.02
☐ 140	Gerry Cheevers	1.00	.45	.13
☐ 141	Dennis Maruk	.20	.09	.03
☐ 142	Barry Dean	.15	.07	.02
☐ 143	Bernie Federko	8.00	3.60	1.00
☐ 144	Stefan Persson	.35	.16	.04
☐ 145	Wilf Paiement	.20	.09	.03
☐ 146	Dale Tallon	.15	.07	.02
☐ 147	Yvon Lambert	.15	.07	.02
☐ 148	Greg Joly	.15	.07	.02
☐ 149	Dean Talafous	.15	.07	.02
☐ 150	Don Edwards AS2	.20	.09	.03
☐ 151	Butch Goring	.20	.09	.03
☐ 152	Tom Bladon	.15	.07	.02
☐ 153	Bob Nystrom	.20	.09	.03
☐ 154	Ron Greschner	.20	.09	.03
☐ 155	Jean Ratelle	.60	.25	.08
☐ 156	Russ Anderson	.15	.07	.02
☐ 157	John Marks	.15	.07	.02

☐ 158	Michel Larocque	.20	.09	.03
☐ 159	Paul Woods	.15	.07	.02
☐ 160	Mike Palmateer	.20	.09	.03
☐ 161	Jim Lorentz	.15	.07	.02
☐ 162	Dave Lewis	.15	.07	.02
☐ 163	Harvey Bennett	.15	.07	.02
☐ 164	Rick Smith	.15	.07	.02
☐ 165	Reggie Leach	.20	.09	.03
☐ 166	Wayne Thomas	.20	.09	.03
☐ 167	Dave Forbes	.15	.07	.02
☐ 168	Doug Wilson	8.00	3.60	1.00
☐ 169	Dan Bouchard	.20	.09	.03
☐ 170	Steve Shutt AS2	.75	.35	.09
☐ 171	Mike Kaszycki	.15	.07	.02
☐ 172	Denis Herron	.20	.09	.03
☐ 173	Rick Bowness	.20	.09	.03
☐ 174	Rick Hampton	.15	.07	.02
☐ 175	Glen Sharpley	.15	.07	.02
☐ 176	Bill Barber	.60	.25	.08
☐ 177	Ron Duguay	2.00	.90	.25
☐ 178	Jim Schoenfeld	.20	.09	.03
☐ 179	Pierre Plante	.15	.07	.02
☐ 180	Jacques Lemaire	.40	.18	.05
☐ 181	Stan Jonathan	.15	.07	.02
☐ 182	Billy Harris	.15	.07	.02
☐ 183	Chris Oddleifson	.15	.07	.02
☐ 184	Jean Pronovost	.20	.09	.03
☐ 185	Fred Barrett	.15	.07	.02
☐ 186	Ross Lonsberry	.15	.07	.02
☐ 187	Mike McEwen	.15	.07	.02
☐ 188	Rene Robert	.20	.09	.03
☐ 189	J. Bob Kelly	.15	.07	.02
☐ 190	Serge Savard AS2	.20	.09	.03
☐ 191	Dennis Kearns	.15	.07	.02
☐ 192	Flames Team	.35	.16	.04
☐ 193	Bruins Team	.45	.20	.06
☐ 194	Sabres Team	.35	.16	.04
☐ 195	Blackhawks Team	.35	.16	.04
☐ 196	Rockies Team	.35	.16	.04
☐ 197	Red Wings Team	.35	.16	.04
☐ 198	Kings Team	.35	.16	.04
☐ 199	North Stars Team	.35	.16	.04
☐ 200	Canadiens Team	.45	.20	.06
☐ 201	Islanders Team	.35	.16	.04
☐ 202	Rangers Team	.35	.16	.04
☐ 203	Flyers Team	.35	.16	.04
☐ 204	Penguins Team	.35	.16	.04
☐ 205	Blues Team	.35	.16	.04
☐ 206	Maple Leafs Team	.45	.20	.06
☐ 207	Canucks Team	.35	.16	.04
☐ 208	Capitals Team	.35	.16	.04
☐ 209	Danny Gare	.20	.09	.03
☐ 210	Larry Robinson AS1	1.25	.55	.16
☐ 211	John Davidson	.20	.09	.03
☐ 212	Peter McNab	.20	.09	.03
☐ 213	Rick Kehoe	.20	.09	.03
☐ 214	Terry Harper	.15	.07	.02
☐ 215	Bobby Clarke	2.00	.90	.25
☐ 216	Bryan Maxwell UER	.15	.07	.02
	(Photo actually			
	Brad Maxwell)			
☐ 217	Ted Bulley	.15	.07	.02
☐ 218	Red Berenson	.20	.09	.03
☐ 219	Ron Grahame	.20	.09	.03
☐ 220	Clark Gillies AS1	.20	.09	.03
☐ 221	Dave Maloney	.15	.07	.02
☐ 222	Derek Smith	.15	.07	.02
☐ 223	Wayne Stephenson	.20	.09	.03
☐ 224	John Van Boxmeer	.15	.07	.02
☐ 225	Dave Schultz	.25	.11	.03
☐ 226	Reed Larson	.50	.23	.06
☐ 227	Rejean Houle	.15	.07	.02
☐ 228	Doug Hicks	.15	.07	.02
☐ 229	Mike Murphy	.15	.07	.02
☐ 230	Pete Lopresti	.20	.09	.03
☐ 231	Jerry Korab	.15	.07	.02
☐ 232	Ed Westfall	.20	.09	.03
☐ 233	Greg Malone	.15	.07	.02
☐ 234	Paul Holmgren	.35	.16	.04
☐ 235	Walt Tkaczuk	.20	.09	.03
☐ 236	Don Marcotte	.15	.07	.02
☐ 237	Ron Low	.20	.09	.03
☐ 238	Rick Chartraw	.15	.07	.02
☐ 239	Cliff Koroll	.15	.07	.02
☐ 240	Borje Salming AS1	.60	.25	.08
☐ 241	Roland Eriksson	.15	.07	.02
☐ 242	Ric Seiling	.15	.07	.02
☐ 243	Jim Bedard	.20	.09	.03
☐ 244	Peter Lee	.20	.09	.03
☐ 245	Denis Potvin AS2	2.00	.90	.25
☐ 246	Greg Polis	.15	.07	.02
☐ 247	Jim Watson	.15	.07	.02
☐ 248	Bobby Schmautz	.15	.07	.02

☐ 249	Doug Risebrough	.20	.09	.03
☐ 250	Tony Esposito	1.25	.55	.16
☐ 251	Nick Libett	.15	.07	.02
☐ 252	Ron Zanussi	.15	.07	.02
☐ 253	Andre Savard	.15	.07	.02
☐ 254	Dave Burrows	.15	.07	.02
☐ 255	Ulf Nilsson	.25	.11	.03
☐ 256	Richard Mulhern	.15	.07	.02
☐ 257	Don Saleski	.15	.07	.02
☐ 258	Wayne Merrick	.15	.07	.02
☐ 259	Checklist 133-264	2.50	.30	.05
☐ 260	Guy Lapointe	.20	.09	.03
☐ 261	Grant Mulvey	.15	.07	.02
☐ 262	Stanley Cup: Semis	.30	.14	.04
	Canadiens sweep			
	Maple Leafs			
☐ 263	Stanley Cup: Semis	.30	.14	.04
	Bruins skate			
	past Flyers			
☐ 264	Stanley Cup: Finals	.75	.19	.08
	Canadiens win 3rd			
	Straight Cup			

1979-80 Topps

 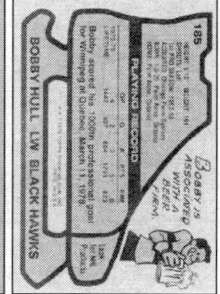

The 1979-80 Topps set consists of 264 cards. Card numbers 81 and 82 (Stanley Cup Playoffs), 163 (Ulf Nilsson RB) and 261 (NHL Entries) differ from those of O-Pee-Chee. The cards measure 2 1/2" by 3 1/2". The fronts contain a blue border that is prone to chipping. The player's name, team and position are at the top with team logo at the bottom. Career and 1978-79 statistics, short biography and a cartoon-illustrated fact about the player appear on the back. Included in this set are players from the four remaining WHA franchises that were absorbed by the NHL. The franchises are the Edmonton Oilers, Hartford Whalers, Quebec Nordiques and Winnipeg Jets. The set features the Rookie Card of Wayne Gretzky and the last cards of a Hall of Fame crop including Gordie Howe, Bobby Hull, Ken Dryden and Stan Mikita. In additon to Gretzky, Rookie Cards include Charlie Simmer, Bobby Smith, and John Tonelli.

	MINT	EXC	G-VG
COMPLETE SET (264)	500.00	230.00	65.00
COMMON PLAYER (1-264)	.25	.11	.03

☐ 1	Goal Leaders	2.00	.90	.25
	Mike Bossy			
	Marcel Dionne			
	Guy Lafleur			
☐ 2	Assist Leaders	1.75	.80	.22
	Bryan Trottier			
	Guy Lafleur			
	Marcel Dionne			
	Bob MacMillan			
☐ 3	Scoring Leaders	1.75	.80	.22
	Bryan Trottier			
	Marcel Dionne			
	Guy Lafleur			
☐ 4	Penalty Minutes	.40	.18	.05
	Leaders			
	Dave(Tiger) Williams			
	Randy Holt			

	Dave Schultz			
☐ 5	Power Play	1.50	.65	.19
	Goal Leaders			
	Mike Bossy			
	Marcel Dionne			
	Paul Gardner			
	Lanny McDonald			
☐ 6	Goals Against	1.50	.65	.19
	Average Leaders			
	Ken Dryden			
	Glenn Resch			
	Bernie Parent			
☐ 7	Game Winning	2.00	.90	.25
	Goals Leaders			
	Guy Lafleur			
	Mike Bossy			
	Bryan Trottier			
	Jean Pronovost			
	Ted Bulley			
☐ 8A	Shutout Leaders ERR	8.00	3.60	1.00
	Ken Dryden			
	Tony Esposito			
	Mario Lessard			
	Mike Palmateer			
	Bernie Parent			
	(Palmateer and Lessard photos switched)			
☐ 8B	Shutout Leaders COR	2.00	.90	.25
	Ken Dryden			
	Tony Esposito			
	Mario Lessard			
	Mike Palmateer			
	Bernie Parent			
☐ 9	Greg Malone	.25	.11	.03
☐ 10	Rick Middleton	.60	.25	.08
☐ 11	Greg Smith	.25	.11	.03
☐ 12	Rene Robert	.30	.14	.04
☐ 13	Doug Risebrough	.30	.14	.04
☐ 14	Bob Kelly	.25	.11	.03
☐ 15	Walt Tkaczuk	.30	.14	.04
☐ 16	John Marks	.25	.11	.03
☐ 17	Willie Huber	.25	.11	.03
☐ 18	Wayne Gretzky UER	400.00	180.00	50.00
	(Games played should be 80, not 60)			
☐ 19	Ron Sedlbauer	.25	.11	.03
☐ 20	Glenn Resch AS2	.40	.18	.05
☐ 21	Blair Chapman	.25	.11	.03
☐ 22	Ron Zanussi	.25	.11	.03
☐ 23	Brad Park	.60	.25	.08
☐ 24	Yvon Lambert	.25	.11	.03
☐ 25	Andre Savard	.25	.11	.03
☐ 26	Jim Watson	.25	.11	.03
☐ 27	Hal Philipoff	.25	.11	.03
☐ 28	Dan Bouchard	.30	.14	.04
☐ 29	Bob Sirois	.25	.11	.03
☐ 30	Ulf Nilsson	.30	.14	.04
☐ 31	Mike Murphy	.25	.11	.03
☐ 32	Stefan Persson	.25	.11	.03
☐ 33	Garry Unger	.30	.14	.04
☐ 34	Rejean Houle	.25	.11	.03
☐ 35	Barry Beck	.30	.14	.04
☐ 36	Tim Young	.25	.11	.03
☐ 37	Rick Dudley	.25	.11	.03
☐ 38	Wayne Stephenson	.30	.14	.04
☐ 39	Peter McNab	.30	.14	.04
☐ 40	Borje Salming AS2	.50	.23	.06
☐ 41	Tom Lysiak	.25	.11	.03
☐ 42	Don Maloney	.75	.35	.09
☐ 43	Mike Rogers	.35	.16	.04
☐ 44	Dave Lewis	.25	.11	.03
☐ 45	Peter Lee	.25	.11	.03
☐ 46	Marty Howe	.30	.14	.04
☐ 47	Serge Bernier	.25	.11	.03
☐ 48	Paul Woods	.25	.11	.03
☐ 49	Bob Sauve	.30	.14	.04
☐ 50	Larry Robinson AS1	1.25	.55	.16
☐ 51	Tom Gorence	.25	.11	.03
☐ 52	Gary Sargent	.25	.11	.03
☐ 53	Thomas Gradin	1.25	.55	.16
☐ 54	Dean Talafous	.25	.11	.03
☐ 55	Bob Murray	.25	.11	.03
☐ 56	Bob Bourne	.30	.14	.04
☐ 57	Larry Patey	.25	.11	.03
☐ 58	Ross Lonsberry	.25	.11	.03
☐ 59	Rick Smith	.25	.11	.03
☐ 60	Guy Chouinard	.30	.14	.04
☐ 61	Danny Gare	.30	.14	.04
☐ 62	Jim Bedard	.30	.14	.04
☐ 63	Dale McCourt	.25	.11	.03
☐ 64	Steve Payne	.35	.16	.04
☐ 65	Pat Hughes	.25	.11	.03
☐ 66	Mike McEwen	.25	.11	.03
☐ 67	Reg Kerr	.25	.11	.03
☐ 68	Walt McKechnie	.25	.11	.03
☐ 69	Michel Plasse	.30	.14	.04
☐ 70	Denis Potvin AS1	1.25	.55	.16
☐ 71	Dave Dryden	.30	.14	.04
☐ 72	Gary McAdam	.25	.11	.03
☐ 73	Andre St.Laurent	.25	.11	.03
☐ 74	Jerry Korab	.25	.11	.03
☐ 75	Rick MacLeish	.30	.14	.04
☐ 76	Dennis Kearns	.25	.11	.03
☐ 77	Jean Pronovost	.30	.14	.04
☐ 78	Ron Greschner	.30	.14	.04
☐ 79	Wayne Cashman	.30	.14	.04
☐ 80	Tony Esposito	1.25	.55	.16
☐ 81	Cup Semi-Finals	.40	.18	.05
	Canadiens squeak past Bruins			
☐ 82	Cup Semi-Finals	.40	.18	.05
	Rangers upset Islanders in Six			
☐ 83	Stanley Cup Finals	.50	.23	.06
	Canadiens Make It Four Straight Cups			
☐ 84	Brian Sutter	2.50	1.15	.30
☐ 85	Gerry Cheevers	.75	.35	.09
☐ 86	Pat Hickey	.25	.11	.03
☐ 87	Mike Kaszycki	.25	.11	.03
☐ 88	Grant Mulvey	.25	.11	.03
☐ 89	Derek Smith	.25	.11	.03
☐ 90	Steve Shutt	.60	.25	.08
☐ 91	Robert Picard	.25	.11	.03
☐ 92	Dan Labraaten	.25	.11	.03
☐ 93	Glen Sharpley	.25	.11	.03
☐ 94	Denis Herron	.30	.14	.04
☐ 95	Reggie Leach	.30	.14	.04
☐ 96	John Van Boxmeer	.25	.11	.03
☐ 97	Dave(Tiger) Williams	.40	.18	.05
☐ 98	Butch Goring	.30	.14	.04
☐ 99	Don Marcotte	.25	.11	.03
☐ 100	Bryan Trottier AS1	2.50	1.15	.30
☐ 101	Serge Savard AS2	.30	.14	.04
☐ 102	Cliff Koroll	.25	.11	.03
☐ 103	Gary Smith	.30	.14	.04
☐ 104	Al MacAdam	.25	.11	.03
☐ 105	Don Edwards	.30	.14	.04
☐ 106	Errol Thompson	.25	.11	.03
☐ 107	Andre Lacroix	.30	.14	.04
☐ 108	Marc Tardif	.25	.11	.03
☐ 109	Rick Kehoe	.30	.14	.04
☐ 110	John Davidson	.30	.14	.04
☐ 111	Behn Wilson	.35	.16	.04
☐ 112	Doug Jarvis	.30	.14	.04
☐ 113	Tom Rowe	.25	.11	.03
☐ 114	Mike Milbury	.30	.14	.04
☐ 115	Billy Harris	.25	.11	.03
☐ 116	Greg Fox	.25	.11	.03
☐ 117	Curt Fraser	.35	.16	.04
☐ 118	Jean-Paul Parise	.25	.11	.03
☐ 119	Ric Seiling	.25	.11	.03
☐ 120	Darryl Sittler	1.00	.45	.13
☐ 121	Rick Lapointe	.25	.11	.03
☐ 122	Jim Rutherford	.30	.14	.04
☐ 123	Mario Tremblay	.30	.14	.04
☐ 124	Randy Carlyle	1.00	.45	.13
☐ 125	Bobby Clarke	1.25	.55	.16
☐ 126	Wayne Thomas	.30	.14	.04
☐ 127	Ivan Boldirev	.25	.11	.03
☐ 128	Ted Bulley	.25	.11	.03
☐ 129	Dick Redmond	.25	.11	.03
☐ 130	Clark Gillies AS1	.30	.14	.04
☐ 131	Checklist 1-132	4.00	.40	.08
☐ 132	Vaclav Nedomansky	.25	.11	.03
☐ 133	Richard Mulhern	.25	.11	.03
☐ 134	Dave Schultz	.30	.14	.04
☐ 135	Guy Lapointe	.30	.14	.04
☐ 136	Gilles Meloche	.30	.14	.04
☐ 137	Randy Pierce UER	.25	.11	.03
	(Photo actually Ron Delorme)			
☐ 138	Cam Connor	.25	.11	.03
☐ 139	George Ferguson	.25	.11	.03
☐ 140	Bill Barber	.50	.23	.06
☐ 141	Mike Walton	.25	.11	.03
☐ 142	Wayne Babych	.50	.23	.06
☐ 143	Phil Russell	.25	.11	.03
☐ 144	Bobby Schmautz	.25	.11	.03
☐ 145	Carol Vadnais	.25	.11	.03
☐ 146	John Tonelli	5.00	2.30	.60
☐ 147	Peter Marsh	.25	.11	.03
☐ 148	Thommie Bergman	.25	.11	.03
☐ 149	Richard Martin	.30	.14	.04
☐ 150	Ken Dryden AS1	4.00	1.80	.50
☐ 151	Kris Manery	.25	.11	.03
☐ 152	Guy Charron	.25	.11	.03

☐ 153	Lanny McDonald	1.00	.45	.13
☐ 154	Ron Stackhouse	.25	.11	.03
☐ 155	Stan Mikita	1.50	.65	.19
☐ 156	Paul Holmgren	.30	.14	.04
☐ 157	Perry Miller	.25	.11	.03
☐ 158	Gary Croteau	.25	.11	.03
☐ 159	Dave Maloney	.25	.11	.03
☐ 160	Marcel Dionne AS2	2.00	.90	.25
☐ 161	Mike Bossy RB	2.00	.90	.25
	Most Goals,			
	RW Season			
☐ 162	Don Maloney RB	.40	.18	.05
	Rookie Most Points,			
	Playoff Series			
☐ 163	Ulf Nilsson RB	.40	.18	.05
	Highest Scoring			
	Percentage, Season			
☐ 164	Brad Park RB	.40	.18	.05
	Most Career Playoff			
	Goals, Defenseman			
☐ 165	Bryan Trottier RB	.75	.35	.09
	Most Points, Period			
☐ 166	Al Hill	.25	.11	.03
☐ 167	Gary Bromley	.30	.14	.04
☐ 168	Don Murdoch	.25	.11	.03
☐ 169	Wayne Merrick	.25	.11	.03
☐ 170	Bob Gainey	.60	.25	.08
☐ 171	Jim Schoenfeld	.25	.11	.03
☐ 172	Gregg Sheppard	.25	.11	.03
☐ 173	Dan Bolduc	.25	.11	.03
☐ 174	Blake Dunlop	.25	.11	.03
☐ 175	Gordie Howe	20.00	9.00	2.50
☐ 176	Richard Brodeur	.75	.35	.09
☐ 177	Tom Younghans	.25	.11	.03
☐ 178	Andre Dupont	.25	.11	.03
☐ 179	Ed Johnstone	.25	.11	.03
☐ 180	Gilbert Perreault	1.00	.45	.13
☐ 181	Bob Lorimer	.25	.11	.03
☐ 182	John Wensink	.25	.11	.03
☐ 183	Lee Fogolin	.25	.11	.03
☐ 184	Greg Carroll	.25	.11	.03
☐ 185	Bobby Hull	15.00	6.75	1.90
☐ 186	Harold Snepsts	.40	.18	.05
☐ 187	Peter Mahovlich	.30	.14	.04
☐ 188	Eric Vail	.25	.11	.03
☐ 189	Phil Myre	.30	.14	.04
☐ 190	Wilf Paiement	.30	.14	.04
☐ 191	Charlie Simmer	4.00	1.80	.50
☐ 192	Per-Olov Brasar	.25	.11	.03
☐ 193	Lorne Henning	.25	.11	.03
☐ 194	Don Luce	.25	.11	.03
☐ 195	Steve Vickers	.25	.11	.03
☐ 196	Bob Miller	.25	.11	.03
☐ 197	Mike Palmateer	.30	.14	.04
☐ 198	Nick Libett	.25	.11	.03
☐ 199	Pat Ribble	.25	.11	.03
☐ 200	Guy Lafleur AS1	3.50	1.55	.45
☐ 201	Mel Bridgman	.30	.14	.04
☐ 202	Morris Lukowich	.35	.16	.04
☐ 203	Don Lever	.25	.11	.03
☐ 204	Tom Bladon	.25	.11	.03
☐ 205	Garry Howatt	.25	.11	.03
☐ 206	Bobby Smith	5.00	2.30	.60
☐ 207	Craig Ramsay	.25	.11	.03
☐ 208	Ron Duguay	.35	.16	.04
☐ 209	Gilles Gilbert	.30	.14	.04
☐ 210	Bob MacMillan	.25	.11	.03
☐ 211	Pierre Mondou	.25	.11	.03
☐ 212	J.P. Bordeleau	.25	.11	.03
☐ 213	Reed Larson	.30	.14	.04
☐ 214	Dennis Ververgaert	.25	.11	.03
☐ 215	Bernie Federko	2.50	1.15	.30
☐ 216	Mark Howe	1.50	.65	.19
☐ 217	Bob Nystrom	.30	.14	.04
☐ 218	Orest Kindrachuk	.25	.11	.03
☐ 219	Mike Fidler	.25	.11	.03
☐ 220	Phil Esposito	2.00	.90	.25
☐ 221	Bill Hajt	.25	.11	.03
☐ 222	Mark Napier	.30	.14	.04
☐ 223	Dennis Maruk	.30	.14	.04
☐ 224	Dennis Polonich	.25	.11	.03
☐ 225	Jean Ratelle	.75	.35	.09
☐ 226	Bob Dailey	.25	.11	.03
☐ 227	Alain Daigle	.25	.11	.03
☐ 228	Ian Turnbull	.25	.11	.03
☐ 229	Jack Valiquette	.25	.11	.03
☐ 230	Mike Bossy AS2	10.00	4.50	1.25
☐ 231	Brad Maxwell	.25	.11	.03
☐ 232	Dave Taylor	5.00	2.30	.60
☐ 233	Pierre Larouche	.30	.14	.04
☐ 234	Rod Schutt	.25	.11	.03
☐ 235	Rogatien Vachon	.50	.23	.06
☐ 236	Ryan Walter	1.00	.45	.13

☐ 237	Checklist 133-264	4.00	.40	.08
☐ 238	Terry O'Reilly	.30	.14	.04
☐ 239	Real Cloutier	.30	.14	.04
☐ 240	Anders Hedberg	.30	.14	.04
☐ 241	Ken Linseman	2.50	1.15	.30
☐ 242	Billy Smith	.75	.35	.09
☐ 243	Rick Chartraw	.25	.11	.03
☐ 244	Flames Team	1.00	.45	.13
☐ 245	Bruins Team	1.25	.55	.16
☐ 246	Sabres Team	1.00	.45	.13
☐ 247	Blackhawks Team	1.00	.45	.13
☐ 248	Rockies Team	1.00	.45	.13
☐ 249	Red Wings Team	1.00	.45	.13
☐ 250	Kings Team	1.00	.45	.13
☐ 251	North Stars Team	1.00	.45	.13
☐ 252	Canadiens Team	1.25	.55	.16
☐ 253	Islanders Team	1.25	.55	.16
☐ 254	Rangers Team	1.00	.45	.13
☐ 255	Flyers Team	1.00	.45	.13
☐ 256	Penguins Team	1.00	.45	.13
☐ 257	Blues Team	1.00	.45	.13
☐ 258	Maple Leafs Team	1.25	.55	.16
☐ 259	Canucks Team	1.00	.45	.13
☐ 260	Capitals Team	1.00	.45	.13
☐ 261	New NHL Entries	7.00	3.10	.85
	Edmonton Oilers			
	Hartford Whalers			
	Quebec Nordiques			
	Winnipeg Jets			
☐ 262	Jean Hamel	.25	.11	.03
☐ 263	Stan Jonathan	.25	.11	.03
☐ 264	Russ Anderson	.50	.11	.03

1979-80 Topps Team Inserts

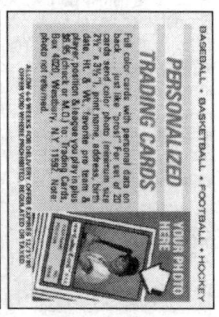

This set of 21 team inserts measures the standard size, 2 1/2" by 3 1/2". They were issued one per wax pack. Each team insert consists of two decals: a team logo decal, and a second decal that is subdivided into three mini-decals. The three mini-decals picture a pair of hockey sticks, a hockey word (goal, wing, score, defense), and a one-digit number. The horizontally oriented back has an offer for personalized trading cards which expires as of 12/31/80.

		NRMT	VG-E	GOOD
COMPLETE SET (21)		12.00	5.00	1.20
COMMON CARD (1-21)		1.00	.40	.10
☐ 1	Atlanta Flames	1.00	.40	.10
☐ 2	Boston Bruins	1.50	.60	.15
☐ 3	Buffalo Sabres	1.00	.40	.10
☐ 4	Chicago Blackhawks	1.50	.60	.15
☐ 5	Colorado Rockies	1.50	.60	.15
☐ 6	Detroit Red Wings	1.50	.60	.15
☐ 7	Edmonton Oilers	1.50	.60	.15
☐ 8	Hartford Whalers	1.00	.40	.10
☐ 9	Los Angeles Kings	1.00	.40	.10
☐ 10	Minnesota North Stars	1.00	.40	.10
☐ 11	Montreal Canadiens	1.50	.60	.15
☐ 12	New York Islanders	1.50	.60	.15
☐ 13	New York Rangers	1.50	.60	.15
☐ 14	Philadelphia Flyers	1.50	.60	.15
☐ 15	Pittsburgh Penguins UER	1.50	.60	.15
	(Triangle in Penguins			
	logo is upside down)			
☐ 16	Quebec Nordiques	1.50	.60	.15

☐ 17	St. Louis Blues	1.00	.40	.10
☐ 18	Toronto Maple Leafs	1.50	.60	.15
☐ 19	Vancouver Canucks	1.50	.60	.15
☐ 20	Washington Capitals	1.00	.40	.10
☐ 21	Winnipeg Jets	1.00	.40	.10

1980-81 Topps

 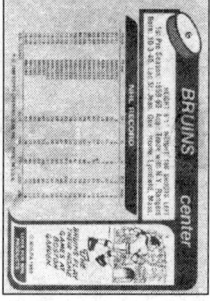

The 1980-81 Topps set features 264 cards that measure the standard 2 1/2" by 3 1/2". The fronts contain a puck (black ink) at the bottom right which can be scratched-off to reveal the player's name. Cards that have been scratched off are considered to be, at best, one quarter to one half the value of the Mint price below. Yearly statistics including minor leagues, a short biography and a cartoon-illustrated hockey fact are included on the back. Members of the U.S. Olympic team are designated by USA. Rookie Cards in this set include Ray Bourque, Dave Christian, Mike Foligno, Mike Gartner, Michel Goulet, Mike Liut, Kent Nilsson, Brian Propp, Rob Ramage and Rick Vaive.

		MINT	EXC	G-VG
	COMPLETE SET (264)	300.00	135.00	38.00
	COMMON PLAYER (1-264)	.20	.09	.03
	*SCRATCHED: .25X to .50X VALUE..			
☐ 1	Phila. Flyers RB	.50	.23	.06
	35 Game Streak, Long-			
	est in Sports History			
☐ 2	Ray Bourque RB	6.00	2.70	.75
	65 Pts.; Record for			
	Rookie Defenseman			
☐ 3	Wayne Gretzky RB	20.00	9.00	2.50
	Youngest Ever,			
	50-goal Scorer			
☐ 4	Charlie Simmer RB	.30	.14	.04
	Scores in 13th Straight			
	Game, NHL Record			
☐ 5	Billy Smith RB	.30	.14	.04
	First Goalie to			
	Score a Goal			
☐ 6	Jean Ratelle	.50	.23	.06
☐ 7	Dave Maloney	.20	.09	.03
☐ 8	Phil Myre	.20	.09	.03
☐ 9	Ken Morrow USA	1.00	.45	.13
☐ 10	Guy Lafleur	2.50	1.15	.30
☐ 11	Bill Derlago	.25	.11	.03
☐ 12	Doug Wilson	2.00	.90	.25
☐ 13	Craig Ramsay	.20	.09	.03
☐ 14	Pat Boutette	.20	.09	.03
☐ 15	Eric Vail	.20	.09	.03
☐ 16	Red Wings Leaders	.35	.16	.04
	Mike Foligno			
☐ 17	Bobby Smith	1.25	.55	.16
☐ 18	Rick Kehoe	.25	.11	.03
☐ 19	Joel Quenneville	.20	.09	.03
☐ 20	Marcel Dionne	1.25	.55	.16
☐ 21	Kevin McCarthy	.20	.09	.03
☐ 22	Jim Craig USA	.75	.35	.09
☐ 23	Steve Vickers	.20	.09	.03
☐ 24	Ken Linseman	.75	.35	.09
☐ 25	Mike Bossy	5.00	2.30	.60
☐ 26	Serge Savard	.25	.11	.03
☐ 27	Blackhawks Leaders	.30	.14	.04

	Grant Mulvey			
☐ 28	Pat Hickey	.20	.09	.03
☐ 29	Peter Sullivan	.20	.09	.03
☐ 30	Blaine Stoughton	.25	.11	.03
☐ 31	Mike Liut	5.00	2.30	.60
☐ 32	Blair MacDonald	.20	.09	.03
☐ 33	Rick Green	.20	.09	.03
☐ 34	Al MacAdam	.20	.09	.03
☐ 35	Robbie Ftorek	.25	.11	.03
☐ 36	Dick Redmond	.20	.09	.03
☐ 37	Ron Duguay	.25	.11	.03
☐ 38	Sabres Leaders	.30	.14	.04
	Danny Gare			
☐ 39	Brian Propp	5.00	2.30	.60
☐ 40	Bryan Trottier	1.50	.65	.19
☐ 41	Rich Preston	.20	.09	.03
☐ 42	Pierre Mondou	.20	.09	.03
☐ 43	Reed Larson	.25	.11	.03
☐ 44	George Ferguson	.20	.09	.03
☐ 45	Guy Chouinard	.25	.11	.03
☐ 46	Billy Harris	.20	.09	.03
☐ 47	Gilles Meloche	.25	.11	.03
☐ 48	Blair Chapman	.20	.09	.03
☐ 49	Capitals Leaders	4.00	1.80	.50
	Mike Gartner			
☐ 50	Darryl Sittler	.75	.35	.09
☐ 51	Richard Martin	.25	.11	.03
☐ 52	Ivan Boldirev	.20	.09	.03
☐ 53	Craig Norwich	.20	.09	.03
☐ 54	Dennis Polonich	.20	.09	.03
☐ 55	Bobby Clarke	1.00	.45	.13
☐ 56	Terry O'Reilly	.25	.11	.03
☐ 57	Carol Vadnais	.20	.09	.03
☐ 58	Bob Gainey	.50	.23	.06
☐ 59	Whalers Leaders	.30	.14	.04
	Blaine Stoughton			
☐ 60	Billy Smith	.50	.23	.06
☐ 61	Mike O'Connell	.40	.18	.05
☐ 62	Lanny McDonald	.75	.35	.09
☐ 63	Lee Fogolin	.20	.09	.03
☐ 64	Rocky Saganiuk	.20	.09	.03
☐ 65	Rolf Edberg	.20	.09	.03
☐ 66	Paul Shmyr	.20	.09	.03
☐ 67	Michel Goulet	15.00	6.75	1.90
☐ 68	Dan Bouchard	.25	.11	.03
☐ 69	Mark Johnson USA	.50	.23	.06
☐ 70	Reggie Leach	.25	.11	.03
☐ 71	Blues Leaders	.40	.18	.05
	Bernie Federko			
☐ 72	Peter Mahovlich	.25	.11	.03
☐ 73	Anders Hedberg	.25	.11	.03
☐ 74	Brad Park	.50	.23	.06
☐ 75	Clark Gillies	.25	.11	.03
☐ 76	Doug Jarvis	.25	.11	.03
☐ 77	John Garrett	.20	.09	.03
☐ 78	Dave Hutchinson	.20	.09	.03
☐ 79	John Anderson	.30	.14	.04
☐ 80	Gilbert Perreault	.75	.35	.09
☐ 81	Marcel Dionne AS1	.60	.25	.08
☐ 82	Guy Lafleur AS1	1.00	.45	.13
☐ 83	Charlie Simmer AS1	.30	.14	.04
☐ 84	Larry Robinson AS1	.30	.14	.04
☐ 85	Borje Salming AS1	.35	.16	.04
☐ 86	Tony Esposito AS1	.50	.23	.06
☐ 87	Wayne Gretzky AS2	25.00	11.50	3.10
☐ 88	Danny Gare AS2	.30	.14	.04
☐ 89	Steve Shutt AS2	.35	.16	.04
☐ 90	Barry Beck AS2	.30	.14	.04
☐ 91	Mark Howe AS2	.35	.16	.04
☐ 92	Don Edwards AS2	.30	.14	.04
☐ 93	Tom McCarthy	.35	.16	.04
☐ 94	Bruins Leaders	.30	.14	.04
	Peter McNab			
	Rick Middleton			
☐ 95	Mike Palmateer	.20	.09	.03
☐ 96	Jim Schoenfeld	.20	.09	.03
☐ 97	Jordy Douglas	.20	.09	.03
☐ 98	Keith Brown	.40	.18	.05
☐ 99	Dennis Ververgaert	.20	.09	.03
☐ 100	Phil Esposito	1.25	.55	.16
☐ 101	Jack Brownschidle	.20	.09	.03
☐ 102	Bob Nystrom	.20	.09	.03
☐ 103	Steve Christoff USA	.30	.14	.04
☐ 104	Rob Palmer	.20	.09	.03
☐ 105	Dave(Tiger) Williams	.25	.11	.03
☐ 106	Flames Leaders	.40	.18	.05
	Kent Nilsson			
☐ 107	Morris Lukowich	.25	.11	.03
☐ 108	Jack Valiquette	.20	.09	.03
☐ 109	Richie Dunn	.20	.09	.03
☐ 110	Rogatien Vachon	.35	.16	.04
☐ 111	Mark Napier	.20	.09	.03
☐ 112	Gordie Roberts	.25	.11	.03
☐ 113	Stan Jonathan	.20	.09	.03

☐ 114	Brett Callighen	.20	.09	.03
☐ 115	Rick MacLeish	.25	.11	.03
☐ 116	Ulf Nilsson	.25	.11	.03
☐ 117	Penguins Leaders	.30	.14	.04
	Rick Kehoe			
☐ 118	Dan Maloney	.20	.09	.03
☐ 119	Terry Ruskowski	.20	.09	.03
☐ 120	Denis Potvin	1.00	.45	.13
☐ 121	Wayne Stephenson	.20	.09	.03
☐ 122	Rich Leduc	.20	.09	.03
☐ 123	Checklist 1-132	2.50	.25	.05
☐ 124	Don Lever	.20	.09	.03
☐ 125	Jim Rutherford	.20	.09	.03
☐ 126	Ray Allison	.20	.09	.03
☐ 127	Mike Ramsey USA	2.00	.90	.25
☐ 128	Canucks Leaders	.30	.14	.04
	Stan Smyl			
☐ 129	Al Secord	2.00	.90	.25
☐ 130	Denis Herron	.20	.09	.03
☐ 131	Bob Dailey	.20	.09	.03
☐ 132	Dean Talafous	.20	.09	.03
☐ 133	Ian Turnbull	.20	.09	.03
☐ 134	Ron Sedlbauer	.20	.09	.03
☐ 135	Tom Bladon	.20	.09	.03
☐ 136	Bernie Federko	1.50	.65	.19
☐ 137	Dave Taylor	2.50	1.15	.30
☐ 138	Bob Lorimer	.20	.09	.03
☐ 139	North Stars Leaders	.30	.14	.04
	Al MacAdam			
	Steve Payne			
☐ 140	Ray Bourque	75.00	34.00	9.50
☐ 141	Glen Hanlon	.35	.16	.04
☐ 142	Willy Lindstrom	.20	.09	.03
☐ 143	Mike Rogers	.25	.11	.03
☐ 144	Tony McKegney	.40	.18	.05
☐ 145	Behn Wilson	.20	.09	.03
☐ 146	Lucien DeBlois	.20	.09	.03
☐ 147	Dave Burrows	.20	.09	.03
☐ 148	Paul Woods	.20	.09	.03
☐ 149	Rangers Leaders	.40	.18	.05
	Phil Esposito			
☐ 150	Tony Esposito	1.00	.45	.13
☐ 151	Pierre Larouche	.25	.11	.03
☐ 152	Brad Maxwell	.20	.09	.03
☐ 153	Stan Weir	.20	.09	.03
☐ 154	Ryan Walter	.25	.11	.03
☐ 155	Dale Hoganson	.20	.09	.03
☐ 156	Anders Kallur	.20	.09	.03
☐ 157	Paul Reinhart	1.00	.45	.13
☐ 158	Greg Millen	.75	.35	.09
☐ 159	Ric Seiling	.20	.09	.03
☐ 160	Mark Howe	.75	.35	.09
☐ 161	Goals Leaders	.30	.14	.04
	Danny Gare (1)			
	Charlie Simmer (1)			
	Blaine Stoughton (1)			
☐ 162	Assists Leaders	10.00	4.50	1.25
	Wayne Gretzky (1)			
	Marcel Dionne (2)			
	Guy Lafleur (3)			
☐ 163	Scoring Leaders	10.00	4.50	1.25
	Marcel Dionne (1)			
	Wayne Gretzky (1)			
	Guy Lafleur (3)			
☐ 164	Penalty Minutes	.30	.14	.04
	Leaders			
	Jimmy Mann (1)			
	Dave(Tiger) Williams (2)			
	Paul Holmgren (3)			
☐ 165	Power Play Goals	.50	.23	.06
	Leaders			
	Charlie Simmer (1)			
	Marcel Dionne (2)			
	Danny Gare (2)			
	Steve Shutt (2)			
	Darryl Sittler (2)			
☐ 166	Goals Against Average	.30	.14	.04
	Leaders			
	Bob Sauve (1)			
	Denis Herron (2)			
	Don Edwards (3)			
☐ 167	Game-Winning Goals	.30	.14	.04
	Leaders			
	Danny Gare (1)			
	Peter McNab (2)			
	Blaine Stoughton (2)			
☐ 168	Shutout Leaders	1.00	.45	.13
	Tony Esposito (1)			
	Gerry Cheevers (2)			
	Bob Sauve (2)			
	Rogatien Vachon (2)			
☐ 169	Perry Turnbull	.35	.16	.04
☐ 170	Barry Beck	.25	.11	.03
☐ 171	Kings Leaders	.40	.18	.05
	Charlie Simmer			
☐ 172	Paul Holmgren	.25	.11	.03
☐ 173	Willie Huber	.20	.09	.03
☐ 174	Tim Young	.20	.09	.03
☐ 175	Gilles Gilbert	.20	.09	.03
☐ 176	Dave Christian USA	2.00	.90	.25
☐ 177	Lars Lindgren	.20	.09	.03
☐ 178	Real Cloutier	.20	.09	.03
☐ 179	Laurie Boschman	.50	.23	.06
☐ 180	Steve Shutt	.40	.18	.05
☐ 181	Bob Murray	.20	.09	.03
☐ 182	Oilers Leaders	14.00	6.25	1.75
	Wayne Gretzky			
☐ 183	John Van Boxmeer	.20	.09	.03
☐ 184	Nick Fotiu	.25	.11	.03
☐ 185	Mike McEwen	.20	.09	.03
☐ 186	Greg Malone	.20	.09	.03
☐ 187	Mike Foligno	3.50	1.55	.45
☐ 188	Dave Langevin	.30	.14	.04
☐ 189	Mel Bridgman	.20	.09	.03
☐ 190	John Davidson	.25	.11	.03
☐ 191	Mike Milbury	.25	.11	.03
☐ 192	Ron Zanussi	.20	.09	.03
☐ 193	Maple Leafs Leaders	.35	.16	.04
	Darryl Sittler			
☐ 194	John Marks	.20	.09	.03
☐ 195	Mike Gartner	40.00	18.00	5.00
☐ 196	Dave Lewis	.20	.09	.03
☐ 197	Kent Nilsson	2.00	.90	.25
☐ 198	Rick Ley	.20	.09	.03
☐ 199	Derek Smith	.20	.09	.03
☐ 200	Bill Barber	.35	.16	.04
☐ 201	Guy Lapointe	.25	.11	.03
☐ 202	Vaclav Nedomansky	.20	.09	.03
☐ 203	Don Murdoch	.20	.09	.03
☐ 204	Islanders Leaders	1.00	.45	.13
	Mike Bossy			
☐ 205	Pierre Hamel	.20	.09	.03
☐ 206	Mike Eaves	.20	.09	.03
☐ 207	Doug Halward	.20	.09	.03
☐ 208	Stan Smyl	.75	.35	.09
☐ 209	Mike Zuke	.20	.09	.03
☐ 210	Borje Salming	.20	.09	.03
☐ 211	Walt Tkaczuk	.25	.11	.03
☐ 212	Grant Mulvey	.20	.09	.03
☐ 213	Rob Ramage	2.00	.90	.25
☐ 214	Tom Rowe	.20	.09	.03
☐ 215	Don Edwards	.20	.09	.03
☐ 216	Canadiens Leaders	.75	.35	.09
	Guy Lafleur			
	Pierre Larouche			
☐ 217	Dan Labraaten	.20	.09	.03
☐ 218	Glen Sharpley	.20	.09	.03
☐ 219	Stefan Persson	.20	.09	.03
☐ 220	Peter McNab	.25	.11	.03
☐ 221	Doug Hicks	.20	.09	.03
☐ 222	Bengt Gustafsson	.35	.16	.04
☐ 223	Michel Dion	.20	.09	.03
☐ 224	Jim Watson	.20	.09	.03
☐ 225	Wilf Paiement	.25	.11	.03
☐ 226	Phil Russell	.20	.09	.03
☐ 227	Jets Leaders	.30	.14	.04
	Morris Lukowich			
☐ 228	Ron Stackhouse	.20	.09	.03
☐ 229	Ted Bulley	.20	.09	.03
☐ 230	Larry Robinson	.75	.35	.09
☐ 231	Don Maloney	.25	.11	.03
☐ 232	Rob McClanahan USA	.30	.14	.04
☐ 233	Al Sims	.20	.09	.03
☐ 234	Errol Thompson	.20	.09	.03
☐ 235	Glenn Resch	.25	.11	.03
☐ 236	Bob Miller	.20	.09	.03
☐ 237	Gary Sargent	.20	.09	.03
☐ 238	Nordiques Leaders	.30	.14	.04
	Real Cloutier			
☐ 239	Rene Robert	.25	.11	.03
☐ 240	Charlie Simmer	1.25	.55	.16
☐ 241	Thomas Gradin	.35	.16	.04
☐ 242	Rick Vaive	2.00	.90	.25
☐ 243	Ron Wilson	.50	.23	.06
☐ 244	Brian Sutter	1.25	.55	.16
☐ 245	Dale McCourt	.20	.09	.03
☐ 246	Yvon Lambert	.20	.09	.03
☐ 247	Tom Lysiak	.20	.09	.03
☐ 248	Ron Greschner	.20	.09	.03
☐ 249	Flyers Leaders	.30	.14	.04
	Reggie Leach			
☐ 250	Wayne Gretzky UER	100.00	45.00	12.50
	(1978-79 GP should			
	be 80, not 60)			
☐ 251	Rick Middleton	.40	.18	.05
☐ 252	Al Smith	.20	.09	.03

		MINT	EXC	G-VG
☐ 253	Fred Barrett	.20	.09	.03
☐ 254	Butch Goring	.25	.11	.03
☐ 255	Robert Picard	.20	.09	.03
☐ 256	Marc Tardif	.20	.09	.03
☐ 257	Checklist 133-264	2.50	.25	.05
☐ 258	Barry Long	.20	.09	.03
☐ 259	Rockies Leaders	.30	.14	.04
	Rene Robert			
☐ 260	Danny Gare	.25	.11	.03
☐ 261	Rejean Houle	.20	.09	.03
☐ 262	Stanley Cup Semifinals	.30	.14	.04
	Islanders-Sabres			
☐ 263	Stanley Cup Semifinals	.30	.14	.04
	Flyers-North Stars			
☐ 264	Stanley Cup Finals	.60	.25	.08
	Islanders win 1st			

1980-81 Topps Team Posters

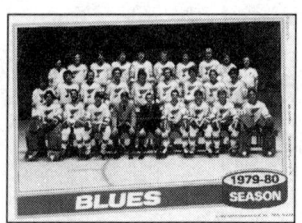

The 1980-81 Topps pin-up posters were issued as folded inserts (approximately 5" by 7" horizontal) to the 1980-81 Topps regular hockey issue. These 16 numbered posters are in full color with a white border on very thin stock. The posters feature posed shots (on ice) of the entire 1979-80 hockey team. The name of the team is indicated in large letters to the left of the hockey puck, which contains the designation 1979-80 Season. Fold lines or creases are natural and do not detract from the condition of the poster. For some reason the Edmonton Oilers, Quebec Nordiques, and Winnipeg Jets were not included in this set.

		MINT	EXC	G-VG
COMPLETE SET (16)		18.00	7.25	1.80
COMMON TEAM (1-16)		1.25	.50	.12
☐ 1	New York Islanders	2.00	.80	.20
☐ 2	New York Rangers	1.50	.60	.15
☐ 3	Philadelphia Flyers	1.50	.60	.15
☐ 4	Boston Bruins	2.00	.80	.20
☐ 5	Hartford Whalers	3.00	1.20	.30
	(Gordie Howe included)			
☐ 6	Buffalo Sabres	1.25	.50	.12
☐ 7	Chicago Blackhawks	1.50	.60	.15
☐ 8	Detroit Red Wings	1.50	.60	.15
☐ 9	Minn. North Stars	1.25	.50	.12
☐ 10	Toronto Maple Leafs	2.00	.80	.20
☐ 11	Montreal Canadiens	2.00	.80	.20
☐ 12	Colorado Rockies	2.00	.80	.20
☐ 13	Los Angeles Kings	1.25	.50	.12
☐ 14	Vancouver Canucks	1.50	.60	.15
☐ 15	St. Louis Blues	1.25	.50	.12
☐ 16	Washington Capitals	1.25	.50	.12

1981-82 Topps

Topps regionalized its set for 1981-82. While the first 66 cards of the set were distributed nationwide, cards numbered 67 East through 132 East and 67 West through 132 West were distributed regionally. Cards measure the standard 2 1/2" by 3 1/2". The card fronts contain the Topps logo at the top, with team logo, player name and position at the bottom. The team name appears in large letters placed

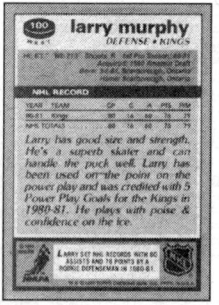

over the bottom portion of the photo. The backs feature player biographies and yearly statistics including minor leagues. The card numbering is according to teams, for example, Boston Bruins (E67-E74), Buffalo Sabres (E75-E80), Pittsburgh Penguins (E81, E112-E114, E116), Hartford Whalers (E82-E86, E108, E115), New York Islanders (E87-E93), New York Rangers (E94-E102), Philadelphia Flyers (E103-E110, E109-E110), Washington Capitals (E117-E122), Chicago Blackhawks (W67-W72), Winnipeg Jets (W79), Colorado Rockies (W80-W85), Detroit Red Wings (W87-W95), Los Angeles Kings (W96-W98, W100-W101), Toronto Maple Leafs (W99), Minnesota North Stars (W102-113), and St. Louis Blues (W114-W119, W121-W124). The key Rookie Cards in this set are Don Beaupre, Dino Ciccarelli, Jari Kurri, Larry Murphy, Denis Savard, and Peter Stastny.

		MINT	EXC	G-VG
COMPLETE SET (198)		85.00	38.00	10.50
COMMON CARD (1-66)		.06	.03	.01
COMMON CARD (E67-E132)		.10	.05	.01
COMMON CARD (W67-W132)		.25	.11	.03
☐ 1	Dave Babych	.50	.13	.05
☐ 2	Bill Barber	.20	.09	.03
☐ 3	Barry Beck	.08	.04	.01
☐ 4	Mike Bossy	1.50	.65	.19
☐ 5	Ray Bourque	4.00	1.80	.50
☐ 6	Guy Chouinard	.06	.03	.01
☐ 7	Dave Christian	.11	.05	.01
☐ 8	Bill Derlago	.06	.03	.01
☐ 9	Marcel Dionne	.75	.35	.09
☐ 10	Brian Engblom	.06	.03	.01
☐ 11	Tony Esposito	.50	.23	.06
☐ 12	Bernie Federko	.35	.16	.04
☐ 13	Bob Gainey	.25	.11	.03
☐ 14	Danny Gare	.06	.03	.01
☐ 15	Thomas Gradin	.08	.04	.01
☐ 16	Wayne Gretzky UER	12.00	5.50	1.50
	(1978-79 GP should			
	be 80, not 60)			
☐ 17	Rick Kehoe	.06	.03	.01
☐ 18	Jari Kurri	6.00	2.70	.75
☐ 19	Guy Lafleur	1.00	.45	.13
☐ 20	Mike Liut	.40	.18	.05
☐ 21	Dale McCourt	.06	.03	.01
☐ 22	Rick Middleton	.25	.11	.03
☐ 23	Mark Napier	.06	.03	.01
☐ 24	Kent Nilsson	.08	.04	.01
☐ 25	Wilf Paiement	.08	.04	.01
☐ 26	Willi Plett	.06	.03	.01
☐ 27	Denis Potvin	.50	.23	.06
☐ 28	Paul Reinhart	.00	.04	.01
☐ 29	Jacques Richard	.06	.03	.01
☐ 30	Pat Riggin	.25	.11	.03
☐ 31	Larry Robinson	.30	.14	.04
☐ 32	Mike Rogers	.08	.04	.01
☐ 33	Borje Salming	.08	.04	.01
☐ 34	Steve Shutt	.25	.11	.03
☐ 35	Charlie Simmer	.25	.11	.03
☐ 36	Darryl Sittler	.35	.16	.04
☐ 37	Bobby Smith	.25	.11	.03
☐ 38	Stan Smyl	.08	.04	.01
☐ 39	Peter Stastny	4.00	1.80	.50
☐ 40	Dave Taylor	.50	.23	.06
☐ 41	Bryan Trottier	.75	.35	.09
☐ 42	Ian Turnbull	.06	.03	.01

☐ 43	Eric Vail	.06	.03	.01
☐ 44	Rick Vaive	.25	.11	.03
☐ 45	Behn Wilson	.06	.03	.01
☐ 46	Boston Scoring: Rick Middleton	.15	.07	.02
☐ 47	Buffalo Scoring: Danny Gare	.10	.05	.01
☐ 48	Calgary Flames Scoring Leaders Kent Nilsson	.15	.07	.02
☐ 49	Chicago Blackhawks Scoring Leaders Tom Lysiak	.10	.05	.01
☐ 50	Colorado Rockies Scoring Leaders Lanny McDonald	.15	.07	.02
☐ 51	Red Wings Scoring: Dale McCourt	.10	.05	.01
☐ 52	Edmonton Scoring: Wayne Gretzky	3.00	1.35	.40
☐ 53	Hartford Whalers Scoring Leaders Mike Rogers	.10	.05	.01
☐ 54	L.A.Kings Scoring: Marcel Dionne	.25	.11	.03
☐ 55	Minnesota North Stars Scoring Leaders Bobby Smith	.15	.07	.02
☐ 56	Montreal Scoring: Steve Shutt	.15	.07	.02
☐ 57	Islanders Scoring: Mike Bossy	.30	.14	.04
☐ 58	Rangers Scoring: Anders Hedberg	.10	.05	.01
☐ 59	Flyers Scoring: Bill Barber	.10	.05	.01
☐ 60	Penguins Scoring: Rick Kehoe	.10	.05	.01
☐ 61	Quebec Nordiques Scoring Leaders Peter Stastny	.30	.14	.04
☐ 62	Blues Scoring: Bernie Federko	.15	.07	.02
☐ 63	Toronto Scoring: Wilf Paiement	.10	.05	.01
☐ 64	Vancouver Canucks Scoring Leaders Thomas Gradin	.10	.05	.01
☐ 65	Washington Capitals Scoring Leaders Dennis Maruk	.10	.05	.01
☐ 66	Winnepeg Jets Scoring Leaders Dave Christian	.15	.07	.02
☐ E67	Dwight Foster	.10	.05	.01
☐ E68	Steve Kasper	1.00	.45	.13
☐ E69	Peter McNab	.15	.07	.02
☐ E70	Mike O'Connell	.15	.07	.02
☐ E71	Terry O'Reilly	.15	.07	.02
☐ E72	Brad Park	.35	.16	.04
☐ E73	Dick Redmond	.10	.05	.01
☐ E74	Rogatien Vachon	.30	.14	.04
☐ E75	Don Edwards	.10	.05	.01
☐ E76	Tony McKegney	.15	.07	.02
☐ E77	Bob Sauve	.10	.05	.01
☐ E78	Andre Savard	.10	.05	.01
☐ E79	Derek Smith	.10	.05	.01
☐ E80	John Van Boxmeer	.10	.05	.01
☐ E81	Pat Boutette	.10	.05	.01
☐ E82	Mark Howe	.35	.16	.04
☐ E83	Dave Keon	.25	.11	.03
☐ E84	Warren Miller	.10	.05	.01
☐ E85	Al Sims	.10	.05	.01
☐ E86	Blaine Stoughton	.15	.07	.02
☐ E87	Bob Bourne	.10	.05	.01
☐ E88	Clark Gillies	.15	.07	.02
☐ E89	Butch Goring	.15	.07	.02
☐ E90	Anders Kallur	.10	.05	.01
☐ E91	Ken Morrow	.15	.07	.02
☐ E92	Stefan Persson	.10	.05	.01
☐ E93	Billy Smith	.25	.11	.03
☐ E94	Mike Allison	.10	.05	.01
☐ E95	John Davidson	.15	.07	.02
☐ E96	Ron Duguay	.15	.07	.02
☐ E97	Ron Greschner	.10	.05	.01
☐ E98	Anders Hedberg	.15	.07	.02
☐ E99	Ed Johnstone	.10	.05	.01
☐ E100	Dave Maloney	.10	.05	.01
☐ E101	Don Maloney	.15	.07	.02
☐ E102	Ulf Nilsson	.15	.07	.02
☐ E103	Bobby Clarke	.60	.25	.08
☐ E104	Bob Dailey	.10	.05	.01
☐ E105	Paul Holmgren	.10	.05	.01
☐ E106	Reggie Leach	.15	.07	.02
☐ E107	Ken Linseman	.15	.07	.02
☐ E108	Rick MacLeish	.15	.07	.02
☐ E109	Pete Peeters	.50	.23	.06
☐ E110	Brian Propp	.75	.35	.09
☐ E111	Checklist 1-132	.75	.08	.02
☐ E112	Randy Carlyle	.15	.07	.02
☐ E113	Paul Gardner	.10	.05	.01
☐ E114	Peter Lee	.10	.05	.01
☐ E115	Greg Millen	.15	.07	.02
☐ E116	Rod Schutt	.10	.05	.01
☐ E117	Mike Gartner	5.00	2.30	.60
☐ E118	Rick Green	.10	.05	.01
☐ E119	Bob Kelly	.10	.05	.01
☐ E120	Dennis Maruk	.15	.07	.02
☐ E121	Mike Palmateer	.10	.05	.01
☐ E122	Ryan Walter	.15	.07	.02
☐ E123	Bill Barber SA	.15	.07	.02
☐ E124	Barry Beck SA	.10	.05	.01
☐ E125	Mike Bossy SA	1.00	.45	.13
☐ E126	Ray Bourque SA	2.00	.90	.25
☐ E127	Danny Gare SA	.10	.05	.01
☐ E128	Rick Kehoe SA	.10	.05	.01
☐ E129	Rick Middleton SA	.12	.05	.02
☐ E130	Denis Potvin SA	.40	.18	.05
☐ E131	Mike Rogers SA	.10	.05	.01
☐ E132	Bryan Trottier SA	.50	.23	.06
☐ W67	Keith Brown	.25	.11	.03
☐ W68	Ted Bulley	.25	.11	.03
☐ W69	Tim Higgins	.25	.11	.03
☐ W70	Reg Kerr	.25	.11	.03
☐ W71	Tom Lysiak	.25	.11	.03
☐ W72	Grant Mulvey	.25	.11	.03
☐ W73	Bob Murray	.25	.11	.03
☐ W74	Terry Ruskowski	.25	.11	.03
☐ W75	Denis Savard	12.00	5.50	1.50
☐ W76	Glen Sharpley	.25	.11	.03
☐ W77	Darryl Sutter	1.00	.45	.13
☐ W78	Doug Wilson	1.00	.45	.13
☐ W79	Lucien DeBlois	.25	.11	.03
☐ W80	Paul Gagne	.25	.11	.03
☐ W81	Merlin Malinowski	.25	.11	.03
☐ W82	Lanny McDonald	.40	.18	.05
☐ W83	Joel Quenneville	.25	.11	.03
☐ W84	Rob Ramage	.30	.14	.04
☐ W85	Glenn Resch	.30	.14	.04
☐ W86	Steve Tambellini	.25	.11	.03
☐ W87	Mike Foligno	.50	.23	.06
☐ W88	Gilles Gilbert	.25	.11	.03
☐ W89	Willie Huber	.25	.11	.03
☐ W90	Mark Kirton	.25	.11	.03
☐ W91	Jim Korn	.25	.11	.03
☐ W92	Reed Larson	.30	.14	.04
☐ W93	Gary McAdam	.25	.11	.03
☐ W94	Vaclav Nedomansky	.25	.11	.03
☐ W95	John Ogrodnick	.50	.23	.06
☐ W96	Billy Harris	.25	.11	.03
☐ W97	Jerry Korab	.25	.11	.03
☐ W98	Mario Lessard	.25	.11	.03
☐ W99	Don Luce	.25	.11	.03
☐ W100	Larry Murphy	8.00	3.60	1.00
☐ W101	Mike Murphy	.25	.11	.03
☐ W102	Kent-Erik Andersson	.25	.11	.03
☐ W103	Don Beaupre	3.50	1.55	.45
☐ W104	Steve Christoff	.25	.11	.03
☐ W105	Dino Ciccarelli	12.00	5.50	1.50
☐ W106	Craig Hartsburg	.30	.14	.04
☐ W107	Al MacAdam	.25	.11	.03
☐ W108	Tom McCarthy	.30	.14	.04
☐ W109	Gilles Meloche	.30	.14	.04
☐ W110	Steve Payne	.25	.11	.03
☐ W111	Gordie Roberts	.30	.14	.04
☐ W112	Greg Smith	.25	.11	.03
☐ W113	Tim Young	.25	.11	.03
☐ W114	Wayne Babych	.25	.11	.03
☐ W115	Blair Chapman	.25	.11	.03
☐ W116	Tony Currie	.25	.11	.03
☐ W117	Blake Dunlop	.25	.11	.03
☐ W118	Ed Kea	.25	.11	.03
☐ W119	Rick Lapointe	.25	.11	.03
☐ W120	Checklist 1-132	1.50	.15	.03
☐ W121	Jorgen Pettersson	.25	.11	.03
☐ W122	Brian Sutter	.50	.23	.06
☐ W123	Perry Turnbull	.25	.11	.03
☐ W124	Mike Zuke	.25	.11	.03
☐ W125	Marcel Dionne SA	.50	.23	.06
☐ W126	Tony Esposito SA	.50	.23	.06
☐ W127	Bernie Federko SA	.40	.18	.05
☐ W128	Mike Liut SA	.35	.16	.04
☐ W129	Dale McCourt SA	.25	.11	.03
☐ W130	Charlie Simmer SA	.30	.14	.04
☐ W131	Bobby Smith SA	.35	.16	.04
☐ W132	Dave Taylor SA	.75	.25	.11

1984-85 Topps

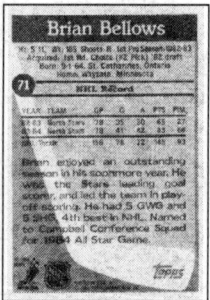

After a two year hiatus, Topps returned to hockey with a set of 165 standard size (2 1/2" by 3 1/2") cards. The set contains 66 single print cards which are noted in the checklist by SP. Teams from the United States have a greater player representation than the Canadian teams. Card fronts (much like 1983 Topps baseball) are color coordinated by team and feature two photos. A small photo at bottom right has player name, position and team name to the left. Card backs contain complete career statistics. Rookie Cards include Dave Andreychuk, Tom Barrasso, Pat LaFontaine, Pat Verbeek and Steve Yzerman.

	MINT	EXC	G-VG
COMPLETE SET (165)	35.00	16.00	4.40
COMMON PLAYER (1-165)	.05	.02	.01

	MINT	EXC	G-VG
☐ 1 Ray Bourque	1.50	.65	.19
☐ 2 Keith Crowder SP	.15	.07	.02
☐ 3 Tom Fergus	.10	.05	.01
☐ 4 Doug Keans	.05	.02	.01
☐ 5 Gord Kluzak SP	.15	.07	.02
☐ 6 Mike Krushelnyski SP	.30	.14	.04
☐ 7 Nevin Markwart	.05	.02	.01
☐ 8 Rick Middleton	.15	.07	.02
☐ 9 Mike O'Connell	.05	.02	.01
☐ 10 Terry O'Reilly SP	.20	.09	.03
☐ 11 Barry Pederson	.10	.05	.01
☐ 12 Pete Peeters	.10	.05	.01
☐ 13 Dave Andreychuk SP	7.00	3.10	.85
☐ 14 Tom Barrasso	3.50	1.55	.45
☐ 15 Real Cloutier SP	.15	.07	.02
☐ 16 Mike Foligno	.10	.05	.01
☐ 17 Bill Hajt SP	.15	.07	.02
☐ 18 Phil Housley SP	2.00	.90	.25
☐ 19 Gilbert Perreault	.25	.11	.03
☐ 20 Larry Playfair SP	.15	.07	.02
☐ 21 Craig Ramsay SP	.15	.07	.02
☐ 22 Mike Ramsey	.10	.05	.01
☐ 23 Lindy Ruff SP	.15	.07	.02
☐ 24 Ed Beers	.05	.02	.01
☐ 25 Rejean Lemelin SP	.25	.11	.03
☐ 26 Lanny McDonald	.15	.07	.02
☐ 27 Murray Bannerman	.05	.02	.01
☐ 28 Keith Brown SP	.15	.07	.02
☐ 29 Curt Fraser	.05	.02	.01
☐ 30 Steve Larmer	1.50	.65	.19
☐ 31 Tom Lysiak	.05	.02	.01
☐ 32 Bob Murray	.05	.02	.01
☐ 33 Jack O'Callahan SP	.15	.07	.02
☐ 34 Rich Preston	.05	.02	.01
☐ 35 Denis Savard	.50	.23	.06
☐ 36 Darryl Sutter	.05	.02	.01
☐ 37 Doug Wilson	.10	.05	.01
☐ 38 Ivan Boldirev	.05	.02	.01
☐ 39 Colin Campbell SP	.15	.07	.02
☐ 40 Ron Duguay SP	.20	.09	.03
☐ 41 Dwight Foster SP	.15	.07	.02
☐ 42 Danny Gare SP	.15	.07	.02
☐ 43 Ed Johnstone	.05	.02	.01
☐ 44 Reed Larson SP	.20	.09	.03
☐ 45 Eddie Mio SP	.15	.07	.02
☐ 46 John Ogrodnick	.10	.05	.01
☐ 47 Brad Park	.05	.02	.01
☐ 48 Greg Stefan SP	.25	.11	.03
☐ 49 Steve Yzerman	12.00	5.50	1.50
☐ 50 Paul Coffey	2.00	.90	.25
☐ 51 Wayne Gretzky	10.00	4.50	1.25
☐ 52 Jari Kurri	1.00	.45	.13
☐ 53 Bob Crawford	.05	.02	.01
☐ 54 Ron Francis	1.00	.45	.13
☐ 55 Marty Howe	.10	.05	.01
☐ 56 Mark Johnson SP	.15	.07	.02
☐ 57 Greg Malone SP	.15	.07	.02
☐ 58 Greg Millen SP	.20	.09	.03
☐ 59 Ray Neufeld	.05	.02	.01
☐ 60 Joel Quenneville SP	.15	.07	.02
☐ 61 Risto Siltanen	.05	.02	.01
☐ 62 Sylvain Turgeon	.50	.23	.06
☐ 63 Mike Zuke SP	.15	.07	.02
☐ 64 Marcel Dionne	.25	.11	.03
☐ 65 Brian Engblom SP	.15	.07	.02
☐ 66 Jim Fox SP	.15	.07	.02
☐ 67 Bernie Nicholls	1.00	.45	.13
☐ 68 Terry Ruskowski SP	.15	.07	.02
☐ 69 Charlie Simmer	.10	.05	.01
☐ 70 Don Beaupre	.10	.05	.01
☐ 71 Brian Bellows	1.00	.45	.13
☐ 72 Neal Broten SP	.40	.18	.05
☐ 73 Dino Ciccarelli	.40	.18	.05
☐ 74 Paul Holmgren SP	.15	.07	.02
☐ 75 Al MacAdam SP	.15	.07	.02
☐ 76 Dennis Maruk	.10	.05	.01
☐ 77 Brad Maxwell SP	.15	.07	.02
☐ 78 Tom McCarthy SP	.15	.07	.02
☐ 79 Gilles Meloche SP	.15	.07	.02
☐ 80 Steve Payne	.05	.02	.01
☐ 81 Guy Lafleur	.50	.23	.06
☐ 82 Larry Robinson	.20	.09	.03
☐ 83 Bobby Smith	.15	.07	.02
☐ 84 Mel Bridgman	.05	.02	.01
☐ 85 Joe Cirella	.05	.02	.01
☐ 86 Don Lever	.05	.02	.01
☐ 87 Dave Lewis	.05	.02	.01
☐ 88 Jan Ludvig	.05	.02	.01
☐ 89 Glenn Resch	.15	.07	.02
☐ 90 Pat Verbeek	2.00	.90	.25
☐ 91 Mike Bossy	.50	.23	.06
☐ 92 Bob Bourne	.05	.02	.01
☐ 93 Greg Gilbert	.20	.09	.03
☐ 94 Clark Gillies SP	.20	.09	.03
☐ 95 Butch Goring SP	.20	.09	.03
☐ 96 Pat LaFontaine SP	10.00	4.50	1.25
☐ 97 Ken Morrow	.05	.02	.01
☐ 98 Bob Nystrom SP	.15	.07	.02
☐ 99 Stefan Persson SP	.15	.07	.02
☐ 100 Denis Potvin	.20	.09	.03
☐ 101 Billy Smith SP	.25	.11	.03
☐ 102 Brent Sutter SP	.50	.23	.06
☐ 103 John Tonelli	.10	.05	.01
☐ 104 Bryan Trottier	.25	.11	.03
☐ 105 Barry Beck	.10	.05	.01
☐ 106 Glen Hanlon SP	.20	.09	.03
☐ 107 Anders Hedberg SP	.20	.09	.03
☐ 108 Pierre Larouche SP	.20	.09	.03
☐ 109 Don Maloney SP	.15	.07	.02
☐ 110 Mark Osborne SP	.15	.07	.02
☐ 111 Larry Patey	.05	.02	.01
☐ 112 James Patrick	1.00	.45	.13
☐ 113 Mark Pavelich SP	.15	.07	.02
☐ 114 Mike Rogers SP	.20	.09	.03
☐ 115 Reijo Ruotsalainen SP	.15	.07	.02
☐ 116 Peter Sundstrom SP	.25	.11	.03
☐ 117 Bob Froese	.10	.05	.01
☐ 118 Mark Howe	.10	.05	.01
☐ 119 Tim Kerr SP	.25	.11	.03
☐ 120 Dave Poulin	1.00	.45	.13
☐ 121 Darryl Sittler SP	.25	.11	.03
☐ 122 Ron Sutter	.40	.18	.05
☐ 123 Mike Bullard SP	.20	.09	.03
☐ 124 Ron Flockhart SP	.15	.07	.02
☐ 125 Rick Kehoe	.05	.02	.01
☐ 126 Kevin McCarthy SP	.15	.07	.02
☐ 127 Mark Taylor	.05	.02	.01
☐ 128 Dan Bouchard SP	.20	.09	.03
☐ 129 Michel Goulet	.40	.18	.05
☐ 130 Peter Stastny SP	1.50	.65	.19
☐ 131 Bernie Federko	.15	.07	.02
☐ 132 Mike Liut	.15	.07	.02
☐ 133 Joe Mullen SP	1.50	.65	.19
☐ 134 Rob Ramage	.05	.02	.01
☐ 135 Brian Sutter	.15	.07	.02
☐ 136 John Anderson SP	.15	.07	.02
☐ 137 Dan Daoust	.05	.02	.01
☐ 138 Rick Vaive	.10	.05	.01
☐ 139 Darcy Rota SP	.15	.07	.02
☐ 140 Stan Smyl SP	.20	.09	.03
☐ 141 Tony Tanti	.10	.05	.01
☐ 142 Dave Christian SP	.20	.09	.03

			MINT	EXC	G-VG
☐	143	Mike Gartner SP	1.50	.65	.19
☐	144	Bengt Gustafsson SP	.15	.07	.02
☐	145	Doug Jarvis	.05	.02	.01
☐	146	Al Jensen	.05	.02	.01
☐	147	Rod Langway	.25	.11	.03
☐	148	Pat Riggin	.05	.02	.01
☐	149	Scott Stevens SP	2.50	1.15	.30
☐	150	Dave Babych	.10	.05	.01
☐	151	Laurie Boschman	.05	.02	.01
☐	152	Dale Hawerchuk	1.00	.45	.13
☐	153	Michel Goulet AS	.15	.07	.02
☐	154	Wayne Gretzky AS	2.50	1.15	.30
☐	155	Mike Bossy AS	.20	.09	.03
☐	156	Rod Langway AS	.10	.05	.01
☐	157	Ray Bourque AS	.50	.23	.06
☐	158	Tom Barrasso AS	.50	.23	.06
☐	159	Mark Messier AS	1.50	.65	.19
☐	160	Bryan Trottier AS	.20	.09	.03
☐	161	Jari Kurri AS	.35	.16	.04
☐	162	Denis Potvin AS	.15	.07	.02
☐	163	Paul Coffey AS	.50	.23	.06
☐	164	Pat Riggin AS	.10	.05	.01
☐	165	Checklist 1-165 SP	1.50	.15	.03

1985-86 Topps

 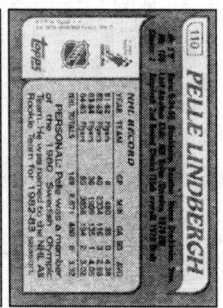

This set of 165 cards measuring 2 1/2" by 3 1/2" is very similar to Topps' hockey set of the previous season in that there are 66 single prints. The single prints are noted in the checklist by SP. The fronts have player name and position at the bottom with team log at the top right or left. Backs contain complete career statistics and personal notes. Wax boxes from this year had cards printed on the bottom with four players per box; these wax box cards are "lettered" A-P rather than numbered. The set is considered complete without the wax box cards. The key Rookie Card in this set is Mario Lemieux. Other Rookie Cards include Kevin Dineen, Kelly Hrudey, Kirk Muller, Tomas Sandstrom, and Peter Zezel.

		MINT	EXC	G-VG
COMPLETE SET (165)		250.00	115.00	31.00
COMMON PLAYER (1-165)		.20	.09	.03

			MINT	EXC	G-VG
☐	1	Lanny McDonald	.40	.18	.05
☐	2	Mike O'Connell SP	.35	.16	.04
☐	3	Curt Fraser SP	.35	.16	.04
☐	4	Steve Penney	.20	.09	.03
☐	5	Brian Engblom	.20	.09	.03
☐	6	Ron Sutter	.25	.11	.03
☐	7	Joe Mullen	1.00	.45	.13
☐	8	Rod Langway	.25	.11	.03
☐	9	Mario Lemieux	175.00	80.00	22.00
☐	10	Dave Babych	.20	.09	.03
☐	11	Bob Nystrom	.20	.09	.03
☐	12	Andy Moog SP	2.50	1.15	.30
☐	13	Dino Ciccarelli	.75	.35	.09
☐	14	Dwight Foster SP	.35	.16	.04
☐	15	James Patrick SP	.40	.18	.05
☐	16	Thomas Gradin SP	.35	.16	.04
☐	17	Mike Foligno	.25	.11	.03
☐	18	Mario Gosselin	.25	.11	.03
☐	19	Mike Zuke SP	.35	.16	.04
☐	20	John Anderson SP	.35	.16	.04
☐	21	Dave Pichette	.20	.09	.03
☐	22	Nick Fotiu SP	.40	.18	.05
☐	23	Tom Lysiak	.20	.09	.03
☐	24	Peter Zezel	2.00	.90	.25
☐	25	Denis Potvin	.35	.16	.04
☐	26	Bob Carpenter	.25	.11	.03
☐	27	Murray Bannerman SP	.35	.16	.04
☐	28	Gordie Roberts SP	.35	.16	.04
☐	29	Steve Yzerman	15.00	6.75	1.90
☐	30	Phil Russell	.20	.09	.03
☐	31	Peter Stastny	1.00	.45	.13
☐	32	Craig Ramsay SP	.40	.18	.05
☐	33	Terry Ruskowski SP	.35	.16	.04
☐	34	Kevin Dineen SP	5.00	2.30	.60
☐	35	Mark Howe	.25	.11	.03
☐	36	Glenn Resch	.25	.11	.03
☐	37	Danny Gare SP	.35	.16	.04
☐	38	Doug Bodger	.75	.35	.09
☐	39	Mike Rogers	.25	.11	.03
☐	40	Ray Bourque	2.50	1.15	.30
☐	41	John Tonelli	.25	.11	.03
☐	42	Mel Bridgman	.20	.09	.03
☐	43	Sylvain Turgeon SP	.40	.18	.05
☐	44	Mark Johnson	.20	.09	.03
☐	45	Doug Wilson	.25	.11	.03
☐	46	Mike Gartner	1.75	.80	.22
☐	47	Brent Peterson	.20	.09	.03
☐	48	Paul Reinhart SP	.35	.16	.04
☐	49	Mike Krushelnyski	.25	.11	.03
☐	50	Brian Bellows	1.25	.55	.16
☐	51	Chris Chelios	3.50	1.55	.45
☐	52	Barry Pederson SP	.35	.16	.04
☐	53	Murray Craven SP	.75	.35	.09
☐	54	Pierre Larouche SP	.40	.18	.05
☐	55	Reed Larson	.25	.11	.03
☐	56	Pat Verbeek SP	1.00	.45	.13
☐	57	Randy Carlyle	.25	.11	.03
☐	58	Ray Neufeld SP	.35	.16	.04
☐	59	Keith Brown SP	.35	.16	.04
☐	60	Bryan Trottier	.35	.16	.04
☐	61	Jim Fox SP	.35	.16	.04
☐	62	Scott Stevens	2.50	1.15	.30
☐	63	Phil Housley	1.25	.55	.16
☐	64	Rick Middleton	.25	.11	.03
☐	65	Steve Payne	.20	.09	.03
☐	66	Dave Lewis	.20	.09	.03
☐	67	Mike Bullard	.25	.11	.03
☐	68	Stan Smyl SP	.40	.18	.05
☐	69	Mark Pavelich SP	.35	.16	.04
☐	70	John Ogrodnick	.25	.11	.03
☐	71	Bill Derlago SP	.35	.16	.04
☐	72	Brad Marsh SP	.40	.18	.05
☐	73	Denis Savard	.75	.35	.09
☐	74	Mark Fusco	.20	.09	.03
☐	75	Pete Peeters	.25	.11	.03
☐	76	Doug Gilmour	15.00	6.75	1.90
☐	77	Mike Ramsey	.20	.09	.03
☐	78	Anton Stastny SP	.35	.16	.04
☐	79	Steve Kasper SP	.35	.16	.04
☐	80	Bryan Erickson SP	.35	.16	.04
☐	81	Clark Gillies	.20	.09	.03
☐	82	Keith Acton	.20	.09	.03
☐	83	Pat Flatley	.25	.11	.03
☐	84	Kirk Muller	9.00	4.00	1.15
☐	85	Paul Coffey	2.50	1.15	.30
☐	86	Ed Olczyk	1.00	.45	.13
☐	87	Charlie Simmer SP	.40	.18	.05
☐	88	Mike Liut	.25	.11	.03
☐	89	Dave Maloney	.20	.09	.03
☐	90	Marcel Dionne	.35	.16	.04
☐	91	Tim Kerr	.25	.11	.03
☐	92	Ivan Boldirev SP	.35	.16	.04
☐	93	Ken Morrow SP	.35	.16	.04
☐	94	Don Maloney SP	.35	.16	.04
☐	95	Rejean Lemelin	.25	.11	.03
☐	96	Curt Giles	.20	.09	.03
☐	97	Bob Bourne	.20	.09	.03
☐	98	Joe Cirella	.20	.09	.03
☐	99	Dave Christian SP	.40	.18	.05
☐	100	Darryl Sutter	.20	.09	.03
☐	101	Kelly Kisio	.35	.16	.04
☐	102	Mats Naslund	.25	.11	.03
☐	103	Joel Quenneville SP	.35	.16	.04
☐	104	Bernie Federko	.30	.14	.04
☐	105	Tom Barrasso	2.50	1.15	.30
☐	106	Rick Vaive	.25	.11	.03
☐	107	Brent Sutter	.35	.16	.04
☐	108	Wayne Babych	.20	.09	.03
☐	109	Dale Hawerchuk	1.50	.65	.19
☐	110	Pelle Lindbergh SP	12.00	5.50	1.50
☐	111	Dennis Maruk SP	.40	.18	.05
☐	112	Reijo Ruotsalainen SP	.35	.16	.04
☐	113	Tom Fergus SP	.40	.18	.05

		MINT	EXC	G-VG
☐ 114 Bob Murray SP	.35	.16	.04
☐ 115 Patrik Sundstrom	.20	.09	.03
☐ 116 Ron Duguay SP	.40	.18	.05
☐ 117 Alan Haworth SP	.35	.16	.04
☐ 118 Greg Malone	.20	.09	.03
☐ 119 Bill Hajt	.20	.09	.03
☐ 120 Wayne Gretzky	18.00	8.00	2.30
☐ 121 Craig Redmond	.20	.09	.03
☐ 122 Kelly Hrudey	5.00	2.30	.60
☐ 123 Tomas Sandstrom	6.00	2.70	.75
☐ 124 Neal Broten	.25	.11	.03
☐ 125 Moe Mantha SP	.35	.16	.04
☐ 126 Greg Gilbert SP	.35	.16	.04
☐ 127 Bruce Driver SP	1.00	.45	.13
☐ 128 Dave Poulin	.25	.11	.03
☐ 129 Morris Lukowich SP	.35	.16	.04
☐ 130 Mike Bossy	.75	.35	.09
☐ 131 Larry Playfair SP	.35	.16	.04
☐ 132 Steve Larmer	2.00	.90	.25
☐ 133 Doug Keans SP	.35	.16	.04
☐ 134 Bob Manno	.20	.09	.03
☐ 135 Brian Sutter	.30	.14	.04
☐ 136 Pat Riggin	.20	.09	.03
☐ 137 Pat LaFontaine	12.00	5.50	1.50
☐ 138 Barry Beck SP	.40	.18	.05
☐ 139 Rich Preston SP	.35	.16	.04
☐ 140 Ron Francis	1.25	.55	.16
☐ 141 Brian Propp SP	.40	.18	.05
☐ 142 Don Beaupre	.25	.11	.03
☐ 143 Dave Andreychuk SP	6.00	2.70	.75
☐ 144 Ed Beers	.20	.09	.03
☐ 145 Paul MacLean	.25	.11	.03
☐ 146 Troy Murray SP	.60	.25	.08
☐ 147 Larry Robinson	.30	.14	.04
☐ 148 Bernie Nicholls	1.00	.45	.13
☐ 149 Glen Hanlon SP	.40	.18	.05
☐ 150 Michel Goulet	.60	.25	.08
☐ 151 Doug Jarvis SP	.35	.16	.04
☐ 152 Warren Young	.20	.09	.03
☐ 153 Tony Tanti	.25	.11	.03
☐ 154 Tomas Jonsson SP	.35	.16	.04
☐ 155 Jari Kurri	1.50	.65	.19
☐ 156 Tony McKegney	.20	.09	.03
☐ 157 Greg Stefan SP	.35	.16	.04
☐ 158 Brad McCrimmon SP	.35	.16	.04
☐ 159 Keith Crowder SP	.35	.16	.04
☐ 160 Gilbert Perreault	.30	.14	.04
☐ 161 Tim Bothwell SP	.35	.16	.04
☐ 162 Bob Crawford SP	.35	.16	.04
☐ 163 Paul Gagne SP	.35	.16	.04
☐ 164 Dan Daoust SP	.35	.16	.04
☐ 165 Checklist 1-165 SP	2.50	.25	.05

	MINT	EXC	G-VG
COMPLETE SET (33)	20.00	8.00	2.00
COMMON PLAYER (1-12)	.25	.10	.02
COMMON TEAM (13-33)	.15	.06	.01
☐ 1 John Ogrodnick	.25	.10	.02
☐ 2 Wayne Gretzky	10.00	4.00	1.00
☐ 3 Jari Kurri	.75	.30	.07
☐ 4 Paul Coffey	1.25	.50	.12
☐ 5 Ray Bourque	1.50	.60	.15
☐ 6 Pelle Lindbergh	5.00	2.00	.50
☐ 7 John Tonelli	.25	.10	.02
☐ 8 Dale Hawerchuk	.75	.30	.07
☐ 9 Mike Bossy	1.25	.50	.12
☐ 10 Rod Langway	.35	.14	.03
☐ 11 Doug Wilson	.35	.14	.03
☐ 12 Tom Barrasso	.75	.30	.07
☐ 13 Toronto Maple Leafs	.15	.06	.01
☐ 14 Buffalo Sabres	.15	.06	.01
☐ 15 Detroit Red Wings	.15	.06	.01
☐ 16 Pittsburgh Penguins	.15	.06	.01
☐ 17 New York Rangers	.15	.06	.01
☐ 18 Calgary Flames	.15	.06	.01
☐ 19 Winnipeg Jets	.15	.06	.01
☐ 20 Quebec Nordiques	.15	.06	.01
☐ 21 Chicago Blackhawks	.15	.06	.01
☐ 22 Los Angeles Kings	.15	.06	.01
☐ 23 Montreal Canadiens	.15	.06	.01
☐ 24 Vancouver Canucks	.15	.06	.01
☐ 25 Hartford Whalers	.15	.06	.01
☐ 26 Philadelphia Flyers	.15	.06	.01
☐ 27 New Jersey Devils	.15	.06	.01
☐ 28 St. Louis Blues	.15	.06	.01
☐ 29 Minnesota North Stars	.15	.06	.01
☐ 30 Washington Capitals	.15	.06	.01
☐ 31 Boston Bruins	.15	.06	.01
☐ 32 New York Islanders	.15	.06	.01
☐ 33 Edmonton Oilers	.15	.06	.01

1986-87 Topps

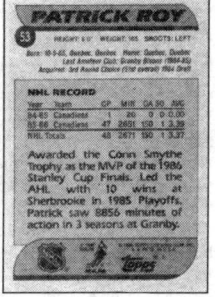

1985-86 Topps Sticker Inserts

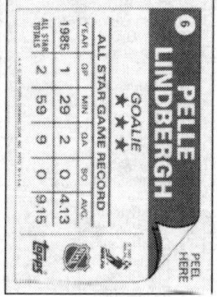

This set of 33 "Hockey Helmet Stickers" features stickers of 12 All-Star players (1-12) and 21 stickers of team logos, pucks, and numbers. The stickers were inserted in with the 1985-86 Topps hockey regular issue wax packs and as such are also 2 1/2" by 3 1/2". The card backs are printed in blue and red on white card stock. These inserts were also included in some O-Pee-Chee packs that year, which may explain why this particular year of stickers is relatively plentiful. The last seven team stickers can be found with the team logos on the top or bottom.

This set of 198 cards measures the standard 2 1/2" by 3 1/2". There are 66 double prints that are noted in the checklist by DP. Card fronts feature player name, team, team logo and position at the bottom. Card backs contain complete career statistics and career highlights. There were also 16 cards printed on the bottom of the wax pack boxes, four to a box. These cards are "lettered" rather than numbered and are not considered part of the complete set. The key Rookie Card in this set is Patrick Roy. Other Rookie Cards include Greg Adams, Randy Durridge, Wendel Clark, Russ Courtnall, Ray Ferraro, Dirk Graham, Petr Klima, John MacLean, Craig MacTavish, Mike Ridley, Gary Suter, and John Vanbiesbrouck.

	MINT	EXC	G-VG
COMPLETE SET (198)	140.00	65.00	17.50
COMMON PLAYER (1-198)	.12	.05	.02
☐ 1 Ray Bourque	2.00	.65	.20
☐ 2 Pat LaFontaine DP	4.00	1.80	.50
☐ 3 Wayne Gretzky	16.00	7.25	2.00
☐ 4 Lindy Ruff	.12	.05	.02
☐ 5 Brad McCrimmon	.12	.05	.02

☐ 6	Dave(Tiger) Williams	.15	.07	.02
☐ 7	Denis Savard DP	.40	.18	.05
☐ 8	Lanny McDonald	.20	.09	.03
☐ 9	John Vanbiesbrouck DP	6.50	2.90	.80
☐ 10	Greg Adams	1.50	.65	.19
	New Jersey Devils			
☐ 11	Steve Yzerman	7.00	3.10	.85
☐ 12	Craig Hartsburg	.12	.05	.02
☐ 13	John Anderson DP	.08	.04	.01
☐ 14	Bob Bourne DP	.08	.04	.01
☐ 15	Kjell Dahlin	.12	.05	.02
☐ 16	Dave Andreychuk	3.50	1.55	.45
☐ 17	Rob Ramage DP	.08	.04	.01
☐ 18	Ron Greschner DP	.08	.04	.01
☐ 19	Bruce Driver	.15	.07	.02
☐ 20	Peter Stastny	.75	.35	.09
☐ 21	Dave Christian	.15	.07	.02
☐ 22	Doug Keans	.12	.05	.02
☐ 23	Scott Bjugstad	.12	.05	.02
☐ 24	Doug Bodger DP	.10	.05	.01
☐ 25	Troy Murray DP	.10	.05	.01
☐ 26	Al Iafrate	3.50	1.55	.45
☐ 27	Kelly Hrudey	1.25	.55	.16
☐ 28	Doug Jarvis	.12	.05	.02
☐ 29	Rich Sutter	.12	.05	.02
☐ 30	Marcel Dionne	.30	.14	.04
☐ 31	Curt Fraser	.12	.05	.02
☐ 32	Doug Lidster	.15	.07	.02
☐ 33	Brian MacLellan	.12	.05	.02
☐ 34	Barry Pederson	.12	.05	.02
☐ 35	Craig Laughlin	.12	.05	.02
☐ 36	Ilkka Sinisalo DP	.08	.04	.01
☐ 37	John MacLean	4.00	1.80	.50
☐ 38	Brian Mullen	.15	.07	.02
☐ 39	Duane Sutter DP	.08	.04	.01
☐ 40	Brian Engblom	.12	.05	.02
☐ 41	Chris Cichocki	.12	.05	.02
☐ 42	Gordie Roberts	.12	.05	.02
☐ 43	Ron Francis	.60	.25	.08
☐ 44	Joe Mullen	.50	.23	.06
☐ 45	Moe Mantha DP	.08	.04	.01
☐ 46	Pat Verbeek	.35	.16	.04
☐ 47	Clint Malarchuk	.75	.35	.09
☐ 48	Bob Brooke DP	.08	.04	.01
☐ 49	Darryl Sutter DP	.08	.04	.01
☐ 50	Stan Smyl DP	.10	.05	.01
☐ 51	Greg Stefan	.12	.05	.02
☐ 52	Bill Hajt DP	.08	.04	.01
☐ 53	Patrick Roy	70.00	32.00	8.75
☐ 54	Gord Kluzak	.12	.05	.02
☐ 55	Bob Froese DP	.08	.04	.01
☐ 56	Grant Fuhr	1.00	.45	.13
☐ 57	Mark Hunter DP	.08	.04	.01
☐ 58	Dana Murzyn	.20	.09	.03
☐ 59	Mike Gartner	.75	.35	.09
☐ 60	Dennis Maruk	.15	.07	.02
☐ 61	Rich Preston	.12	.05	.02
☐ 62	Larry Robinson DP	.12	.05	.02
☐ 63	Dave Taylor DP	.12	.05	.02
☐ 64	Bob Murray DP	.08	.04	.01
☐ 65	Ken Morrow	.12	.05	.02
☐ 66	Mike Ridley	2.50	1.15	.30
☐ 67	John Tucker	.30	.14	.04
☐ 68	Miroslav Frycer	.12	.05	.02
☐ 69	Danny Gare	.12	.05	.02
☐ 70	Randy Burridge	1.00	.45	.13
☐ 71	Dave Poulin	.15	.07	.02
☐ 72	Brian Sutter	.20	.09	.03
☐ 73	Dave Babych	.12	.05	.02
☐ 74	Dale Hawerchuk DP	.75	.35	.09
☐ 75	Brian Bellows	.60	.25	.08
☐ 76	Dave Pasin DP	.08	.04	.01
☐ 77	Pete Peeters DP	.10	.05	.01
☐ 78	Tomas Jonsson DP	.08	.04	.01
☐ 79	Gilbert Perreault DP	.12	.05	.02
☐ 80	Glenn Anderson DP	.50	.23	.06
☐ 81	Don Maloney	.12	.05	.02
☐ 82	Ed Olczyk DP	.20	.09	.03
☐ 83	Mike Bullard DP	.10	.05	.01
☐ 84	Tim Fergus	.12	.05	.02
☐ 85	Dave Lewis	.12	.05	.02
☐ 86	Brian Propp	.20	.09	.03
☐ 87	John Ogrodnick	.15	.07	.02
☐ 88	Kevin Dineen DP	.75	.35	.09
☐ 89	Don Beaupre	.15	.07	.02
☐ 90	Mike Bossy DP	.50	.23	.06
☐ 91	Tom Barrasso DP	.75	.35	.09
☐ 92	Michel Goulet DP	.25	.11	.03
☐ 93	Doug Gilmour	7.00	3.10	.85
☐ 94	Kirk Muller	2.00	.90	.25
☐ 95	Larry Melnyk DP	.08	.04	.01
☐ 96	Bob Gainey DP	.10	.05	.01
☐ 97	Steve Kasper	.12	.05	.02
☐ 98	Petr Klima	1.25	.55	.16
☐ 99	Neal Broten DP	.10	.05	.01
☐ 100	Al Secord DP	.10	.05	.01
☐ 101	Bryan Erickson DP	.08	.04	.01
☐ 102	Rejean Lemelin	.15	.07	.02
☐ 103	Sylvain Turgeon	.12	.05	.02
☐ 104	Bob Nystrom	.12	.05	.02
☐ 105	Bernie Federko	.20	.09	.03
☐ 106	Doug Wilson DP	.10	.05	.01
☐ 107	Alan Haworth	.12	.05	.02
☐ 108	Jari Kurri	1.00	.45	.13
☐ 109	Ron Sutter	.15	.07	.02
☐ 110	Reed Larson DP	.08	.04	.01
☐ 111	Terry Ruskowski DP	.08	.04	.01
☐ 112	Mark Johnson DP	.08	.04	.01
☐ 113	James Patrick	.15	.07	.02
☐ 114	Paul MacLean	.15	.07	.02
☐ 115	Mike Ramsey DP	.08	.04	.01
☐ 116	Kelly Kisio DP	.10	.05	.01
☐ 117	Brent Sutter	.15	.07	.02
☐ 118	Joel Quenneville	.12	.05	.02
☐ 119	Curt Giles DP	.08	.04	.01
☐ 120	Tony Tanti DP	.08	.04	.01
☐ 121	Doug Sulliman DP	.08	.04	.01
☐ 122	Mario Lemieux	40.00	18.00	5.00
☐ 123	Mark Howe DP	.10	.05	.01
☐ 124	Bob Sauve	.12	.05	.02
☐ 125	Anton Stastny	.12	.05	.02
☐ 126	Scott Stevens DP	.60	.25	.08
☐ 127	Mike Foligno	.15	.07	.02
☐ 128	Reijo Ruotsalainen DP	.08	.04	.01
☐ 129	Denis Potvin	.25	.11	.03
☐ 130	Keith Crowder	.12	.05	.02
☐ 131	Bob Janecyk DP	.08	.04	.01
☐ 132	John Tonelli	.15	.07	.02
☐ 133	Mike Liut DP	.10	.05	.01
☐ 134	Tim Kerr DP	.10	.05	.01
☐ 135	Al Jensen	.12	.05	.02
☐ 136	Mel Bridgman	.12	.05	.02
☐ 137	Paul Coffey DP	1.00	.45	.13
☐ 138	Dino Ciccarelli DP	.30	.14	.04
☐ 139	Steve Larmer	1.00	.45	.13
☐ 140	Mike O'Connell	.12	.05	.02
☐ 141	Clark Gillies	.12	.05	.02
☐ 142	Phil Russell DP	.08	.04	.01
☐ 143	Dirk Graham DP	1.50	.65	.19
☐ 144	Randy Carlyle	.15	.07	.02
☐ 145	Charlie Simmer	.15	.07	.02
☐ 146	Ron Flockhart DP	.08	.04	.01
☐ 147	Tom Laidlaw	.12	.05	.02
☐ 148	Dave Tippett	.35	.16	.04
☐ 149	Wendel Clark DP	12.00	5.50	1.50
☐ 150	Bob Carpenter DP	.10	.05	.01
☐ 151	Bill Watson	.12	.05	.02
☐ 152	Roberto Romano DP	.25	.11	.03
☐ 153	Doug Shedden	.12	.05	.02
☐ 154	Phil Housley	.50	.23	.06
☐ 155	Bryan Trottier	.25	.11	.03
☐ 156	Patrik Sundstrom DP	.08	.04	.01
☐ 157	Rick Middleton DP	.10	.05	.01
☐ 158	Glenn Resch	.15	.07	.02
☐ 159	Bernie Nicholls DP	.30	.14	.04
☐ 160	Ray Ferraro	2.00	.90	.25
☐ 161	Mats Naslund DP	.10	.05	.01
☐ 162	Pat Flatley DP	.08	.04	.01
☐ 163	Joe Cirella	.12	.05	.02
☐ 164	Rod Langway DP	.10	.05	.01
☐ 165	Checklist 1-99	1.00	.10	.02
☐ 166	Carey Wilson	.12	.05	.02
☐ 167	Murray Craven	.12	.05	.02
☐ 168	Paul Gillis	.12	.05	.02
☐ 169	Borje Salming	.15	.07	.02
☐ 170	Perry Turnbull	.12	.05	.02
☐ 171	Chris Chelios	1.50	.65	.19
☐ 172	Keith Acton	.12	.05	.02
☐ 173	Al MacInnis	6.00	2.70	.75
☐ 174	Russ Courtnall	4.00	1.80	.50
☐ 175	Brad Marsh	.15	.07	.02
☐ 176	Guy Carbonneau	.35	.16	.04
☐ 177	Ray Neufeld	.12	.05	.02
☐ 178	Craig MacTavish	1.25	.55	.16
☐ 179	Rick Lanz	.12	.05	.02
☐ 180	Murray Bannerman	.12	.05	.02
☐ 181	Brent Ashton	.12	.05	.02
☐ 182	Jim Peplinski	.12	.05	.02
☐ 183	Mark Napier	.12	.05	.02
☐ 184	Laurie Boschman	.12	.05	.02
☐ 185	Larry Murphy	.40	.18	.05
☐ 186	Mark Messier	3.00	1.35	.40
☐ 187	Risto Siltanen	.12	.05	.02
☐ 188	Bobby Smith	.15	.07	.02
☐ 189	Gary Suter	2.00	.90	.25
☐ 190	Peter Zezel	.40	.18	.05

☐ 191	Rick Vaive	.15	.07	.02
☐ 192	Dale Hunter	.15	.07	.02
☐ 193	Mike Krushelnyski	.15	.07	.02
☐ 194	Scott Arniel	.12	.05	.02
☐ 195	Larry Playfair	.12	.05	.02
☐ 196	Doug Risebrough	.12	.05	.02
☐ 197	Kevin Lowe	.30	.14	.04
☐ 198	Checklist 100-198	1.00	.10	.02

1986-87 Topps Sticker Inserts

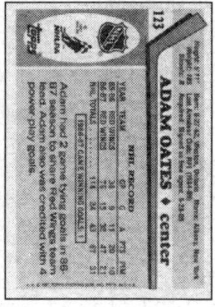

This set of 33 "Hockey Helmet Stickers" features stickers of 12 All-Star players (1-12) and 21 stickers of team logos, pucks, and numbers. The stickers were inserted in with the 1986-87 Topps hockey regular issue wax packs and as such are also 2 1/2" by 3 1/2". The card backs are printed in blue and red on white card stock. The last seven team stickers can be found with the team logos on the top or bottom.

	MINT	EXC	G-VG
COMPLETE SET (33)	20.00	8.00	2.00
COMMON PLAYER (1-12)	.25	.10	.02
COMMON TEAM (13-33)	.15	.06	.01

☐ 1	John Vanbiesbrouck	2.00	.80	.20
☐ 2	Michel Goulet	.50	.20	.05
☐ 3	Wayne Gretzky	8.00	3.25	.80
☐ 4	Mike Bossy	1.00	.40	.10
☐ 5	Paul Coffey	1.00	.40	.10
☐ 6	Mark Howe	.35	.14	.03
☐ 7	Bob Froese	.25	.10	.02
☐ 8	Mats Naslund	.35	.14	.03
☐ 9	Mario Lemieux	8.00	3.25	.80
☐ 10	Jari Kurri	.75	.30	.07
☐ 11	Ray Bourque	1.25	.50	.12
☐ 12	Larry Robinson	.50	.20	.05
☐ 13	Toronto Maple Leafs	.15	.06	.01
☐ 14	Buffalo Sabres	.15	.06	.01
☐ 15	Detroit Red Wings	.15	.06	.01
☐ 16	Pittsburgh Penguins	.15	.06	.01
☐ 17	New York Rangers	.15	.06	.01
☐ 18	Calgary Flames	.15	.06	.01
☐ 19	Winnipeg Jets	.15	.06	.01
☐ 20	Quebec Nordiques	.15	.06	.01
☐ 21	Chicago Blackhawks	.15	.06	.01
☐ 22	Los Angeles Kings	.15	.06	.01
☐ 23	Montreal Canadiens	.15	.06	.01
☐ 24	Vancouver Canucks	.15	.06	.01
☐ 25	Hartford Whalers	.15	.06	.01
☐ 26	Philadelphia Flyers	.15	.06	.01
☐ 27	New Jersey Devils	.15	.06	.01
☐ 28	St. Louis Blues	.15	.06	.01
☐ 29	Minnesota North Stars	.15	.06	.01
☐ 30	Washington Capitals	.15	.06	.01
☐ 31	Boston Bruins	.15	.06	.01
☐ 32	New York Islanders	.15	.06	.01
☐ 33	Edmonton Oilers	.15	.06	.01

1987-88 Topps

The 1987-88 Topps hockey set contains 198 standard size (2 1/2" by 3 1/2") cards. There are 66 double printed cards whcih are indicated by DP below. The fronts feature a design that includes a hockey stick at the bottom with which the player's name is located. At bottom right, the team name appears in a large puck. The card backs contain career statistics, game winning goals from 1986-87 and highlights. There were cards printed on the bottoms of the wax boxes; these cards are similar to the regular issue cards but are "lettered" A-P rather than numbered. These wax box cards are not considered part of the complete set price below. Rookie Cards in this set include Jimmy Carson, Kevin Hatcher, Ron Hextall, Adam Oates, Bill Ranford, Luc Robitaille, Craig Simpson, Ulf Samuelsson, Esa Tikkanen, and Rick Tocchet.

	MINT	EXC	G-VG
COMPLETE SET (198)	120.00	55.00	15.00
COMMON PLAYER (1-198)	.10	.05	.01

☐ 1	Denis Potvin DP	.25	.11	.03
☐ 2	Rick Tocchet	9.00	4.00	1.15
☐ 3	Dave Andreychuk	1.50	.65	.19
☐ 4	Stan Smyl	.15	.07	.02
☐ 5	Dave Babych DP	.05	.02	.01
☐ 6	Pat Verbeek	.25	.11	.03
☐ 7	Esa Tikkanen	6.00	2.70	.75
☐ 8	Mike Ridley	.40	.18	.05
☐ 9	Randy Carlyle	.15	.07	.02
☐ 10	Greg Paslawski	.25	.11	.03
☐ 11	Neal Broten	.15	.07	.02
☐ 12	Wendel Clark DP	2.50	1.15	.30
☐ 13	Bill Ranford DP	5.00	2.30	.60
☐ 14	Doug Wilson	.15	.07	.02
☐ 15	Mario Lemieux	25.00	11.50	3.10
☐ 16	Mats Naslund	.15	.07	.02
☐ 17	Mel Bridgman	.10	.05	.01
☐ 18	James Patrick DP	.05	.02	.01
☐ 19	Rollie Melanson	.10	.05	.01
☐ 20	Lanny McDonald	.20	.09	.03
☐ 21	Peter Stastny	.50	.23	.06
☐ 22	Murray Craven	.10	.05	.01
☐ 23	Ulf Samuelsson DP	3.00	1.35	.40
☐ 24	Michael Thelven DP UER	.05	.02	.01
	(Misspelled Thelvin on card front)			
☐ 25	Scott Stevens	.60	.25	.08
☐ 26	Petr Klima	.35	.16	.04
☐ 27	Brent Sutter DP	.10	.05	.01
☐ 28	Tomas Sandstrom	.75	.35	.09
☐ 29	Tim Bothwell	.10	.05	.01
☐ 30	Bob Carpenter DP	.10	.05	.01
☐ 31	Brian MacLellan DP	.05	.02	.01
☐ 32	John Chabot	.10	.05	.01
☐ 33	Phil Housley DP	.25	.11	.03
☐ 34	Patrik Sundstrom DP	.05	.02	.01
☐ 35	Dave Ellett	.50	.23	.06
☐ 36	John Vanbiesbrouck	2.50	1.15	.30
☐ 37	Dave Lewis	.10	.05	.01
☐ 38	Tom McCarthy DP	.05	.02	.01
☐ 39	Dave Poulin	.15	.07	.02
☐ 40	Mike Foligno	.15	.07	.02
☐ 41	Gordie Roberts	.10	.05	.01
☐ 42	Luc Robitaille	35.00	16.00	4.40
☐ 43	Duane Sutter	.10	.05	.01
☐ 44	Pete Peeters	.15	.07	.02
☐ 45	John Anderson	.10	.05	.01
☐ 46	Aaron Broten	.10	.05	.01
☐ 47	Keith Brown	.10	.05	.01
☐ 48	Bobby Smith	.15	.07	.02

☐ 49	Don Maloney	.10	.05	.01
☐ 50	Mark Hunter	.10	.05	.01
☐ 51	Moe Mantha	.10	.05	.01
☐ 52	Charlie Simmer	.15	.07	.02
☐ 53	Wayne Gretzky	14.00	6.25	1.75
☐ 54	Mark Howe	.15	.07	.02
☐ 55	Bob Gould	.10	.05	.01
☐ 56	Steve Yzerman DP	3.00	1.35	.40
☐ 57	Larry Playfair	.10	.05	.01
☐ 58	Alain Chevrier	.10	.05	.01
☐ 59	Steve Larmer	.50	.23	.06
☐ 60	Bryan Trottier	.20	.09	.03
☐ 61	Stewart Gavin DP	.05	.02	.01
☐ 62	Russ Courtnall DP	.60	.25	.08
☐ 63	Mike Ramsey DP	.05	.02	.01
☐ 64	Bob Brooke	.10	.05	.01
☐ 65	Rick Wamsley DP	.05	.02	.01
☐ 66	Ken Morrow DP	.05	.02	.01
☐ 67	Gerard Gallant UER	.35	.16	.04
	(Misspelled Gerald on card front)			
☐ 68	Kevin Hatcher	5.00	2.30	.60
☐ 69	Cam Neely	3.50	1.55	.45
☐ 70	Sylvain Turgeon DP	.05	.02	.01
☐ 71	Peter Zezel	.15	.07	.02
☐ 72	Al MacInnis	2.50	1.15	.30
☐ 73	Terry Ruskowski DP	.05	.02	.01
☐ 74	Troy Murray	.10	.05	.01
☐ 75	Jim Fox DP	.05	.02	.01
☐ 76	Kelly Kisio	.15	.07	.02
☐ 77	Michel Goulet DP	.15	.07	.02
☐ 78	Tom Barrasso DP	.35	.16	.04
☐ 79	Bruce Driver DP	.10	.05	.01
☐ 80	Craig Simpson DP	1.00	.45	.13
☐ 81	Dino Ciccarelli	.35	.16	.04
☐ 82	Gary Nylund DP	.05	.02	.01
☐ 83	Bernie Federko	.20	.09	.03
☐ 84	John Tonelli DP	.10	.05	.01
☐ 85	Brad McCrimmon DP	.05	.02	.01
☐ 86	Dave Tippett DP	.05	.02	.01
☐ 87	Ray Bourque DP	1.00	.45	.13
☐ 88	Dave Christian	.15	.07	.02
☐ 89	Glen Hanlon	.15	.07	.02
☐ 90	Brian Curran	.10	.05	.01
☐ 91	Paul MacLean	.15	.07	.02
☐ 92	Jimmy Carson	1.00	.45	.13
☐ 93	Willie Huber	.10	.05	.01
☐ 94	Brian Bellows	.35	.16	.04
☐ 95	Doug Jarvis DP	.05	.02	.01
☐ 96	Clark Gillies	.10	.05	.01
☐ 97	Tony Tanti	.10	.05	.01
☐ 98	Pelle Eklund DP	.40	.18	.05
☐ 99	Paul Coffey	1.00	.45	.13
☐ 100	Brent Ashton DP	.05	.02	.01
☐ 101	Mark Johnson	.10	.05	.01
☐ 102	Greg Johnston	.10	.05	.01
☐ 103	Ron Flockhart	.10	.05	.01
☐ 104	Ed Olczyk	.10	.05	.01
☐ 105	Mike Bossy	.40	.18	.05
☐ 106	Chris Chelios	.75	.35	.09
☐ 107	Gilles Meloche	.10	.05	.01
☐ 108	Rod Langway	.15	.07	.02
☐ 109	Ray Ferraro DP	.50	.23	.06
☐ 110	Ron Duguay DP	.10	.05	.01
☐ 111	Al Secord DP	.05	.02	.01
☐ 112	Mark Messier	1.75	.80	.22
☐ 113	Ron Sutter	.10	.05	.01
☐ 114	Darren Veitch	.10	.05	.01
☐ 115	Rick Middleton DP	.10	.05	.01
☐ 116	Doug Sulliman	.10	.05	.01
☐ 117	Dennis Maruk DP	.10	.05	.01
☐ 118	Dave Taylor	.20	.09	.03
☐ 119	Kelly Hrudey	.50	.23	.06
☐ 120	Tom Fergus	.10	.05	.01
☐ 121	Christian Ruuttu	.50	.23	.06
☐ 122	Brian Benning	.25	.11	.03
☐ 123	Adam Oates	25.00	11.50	3.10
☐ 124	Kevin Dineen	.40	.18	.05
☐ 125	Doug Bodger DP	.05	.02	.01
☐ 126	Joe Mullen	.35	.16	.04
☐ 127	Denis Savard	.35	.16	.04
☐ 128	Brad Marsh	.15	.07	.02
☐ 129	Marcel Dionne DP	.20	.09	.03
☐ 130	Bryan Erickson	.10	.05	.01
☐ 131	Reed Larson DP	.05	.02	.01
☐ 132	Don Beaupre	.15	.07	.02
☐ 133	Larry Murphy DP	.25	.11	.03
☐ 134	John Ogrodnick DP	.10	.05	.01
☐ 135	Greg Adams DP	.10	.05	.01
	New Jersey Devils			
☐ 136	Pat Flatley	.10	.05	.01
☐ 137	Scott Arniel DP	.05	.02	.01
☐ 138	Dana Murzyn	.10	.05	.01

☐ 139	Greg C. Adams	.10	.05	.01
	Washington Capitals			
☐ 140	Bob Sauve	.10	.05	.01
☐ 141	Mike O'Connell	.10	.05	.01
☐ 142	Walt Poddubny DP	.10	.05	.01
☐ 143	Paul Reinhart	.10	.05	.01
☐ 144	Tim Kerr DP	.10	.05	.01
☐ 145	Brian Lawton	.10	.05	.01
☐ 146	Gino Cavallini	.25	.11	.03
☐ 147	Doug Keans DP	.05	.02	.01
☐ 148	Jari Kurri	.50	.23	.06
☐ 149	Dale Hawerchuk	.60	.25	.08
☐ 150	Randy Cunneyworth	.20	.09	.03
☐ 151	Jay Wells	.10	.05	.01
☐ 152	Mike Liut DP	.10	.05	.01
☐ 153	Steve Konroyd	.10	.05	.01
☐ 154	John Tucker	.10	.05	.01
☐ 155	Rick Vaive DP	.10	.05	.01
☐ 156	Bob Murray	.10	.05	.01
☐ 157	Kirk Muller DP	.75	.35	.09
☐ 158	Brian Propp	.20	.09	.03
☐ 159	Ron Greschner	.10	.05	.01
☐ 160	Rob Ramage	.10	.05	.01
☐ 161	Craig Laughlin	.10	.05	.01
☐ 162	Steve Kasper DP	.05	.02	.01
☐ 163	Patrick Roy	22.00	10.00	2.80
☐ 164	Shawn Burr DP	.25	.11	.03
☐ 165	Craig Hartsburg DP	.05	.02	.01
☐ 166	Dean Evason	.25	.11	.03
☐ 167	Bob Bourne	.10	.05	.01
☐ 168	Mike Gartner	.50	.23	.06
☐ 169	Ron Hextall	4.00	1.80	.50
☐ 170	Joe Cirella	.10	.05	.01
☐ 171	Dan Quinn DP	.05	.02	.01
☐ 172	Tony McKegney	.10	.05	.01
☐ 173	Pat LaFontaine DP	2.50	1.15	.30
☐ 174	Allen Pedersen DP	.05	.02	.01
☐ 175	Doug Gilmour	4.00	1.80	.50
☐ 176	Gary Suter DP	.25	.11	.03
☐ 177	Barry Pederson DP	.05	.02	.01
☐ 178	Grant Fuhr	.50	.23	.06
☐ 179	Wayne Presley	.40	.18	.05
☐ 180	Wilf Paiement	.15	.07	.02
☐ 181	Doug Smail	.10	.05	.01
☐ 182	Doug Crossman DP	.05	.02	.01
☐ 183	Bernie Nicholls UER	.35	.16	.04
	(Misspelled Nichols on card front)			
☐ 184	Dirk Graham UER	.25	.11	.03
	(Misspelled Dick on card front)			
☐ 185	Anton Stastny	.10	.05	.01
☐ 186	Greg Stefan	.10	.05	.01
☐ 187	Ron Francis	.40	.18	.05
☐ 188	Steve Thomas DP	.60	.25	.08
☐ 189	Kelly Miller	.75	.35	.09
☐ 190	Tomas Jonsson	.10	.05	.01
☐ 191	John MacLean	.75	.35	.09
☐ 192	Larry Robinson DP	.10	.05	.01
☐ 193	Doug Wickenheiser DP	.05	.02	.01
☐ 194	Keith Crowder DP	.05	.02	.01
☐ 195	Bob Froese	.10	.05	.01
☐ 196	Jim Johnson	.10	.05	.01
☐ 197	Checklist 1-99	.75	.08	.02
☐ 198	Checklist 100-198	.75	.08	.02

1987-88 Topps Sticker Inserts

This set of 33 "Hockey Helmet Stickers" features stickers of 12 All-Star players (1-12) and 21 stickers of team logos, pucks, and numbers. The stickers were inserted in with the 1987-88 Topps hockey regular issue wax packs and as such are also 2 1/2" by 3 1/2". The card backs are printed in blue and red on white card stock. The last seven team stickers can be found with the team logos on the top or bottom.

	MINT	EXC	G-VG
COMPLETE SET (33)	18.00	7.25	1.80
COMMON PLAYER (1-12)	.25	.10	.02
COMMON TEAM (13-33)	.15	.06	.01
☐ 1 Ray Bourque	1.25	.50	.12
☐ 2 Ron Hextall	.50	.20	.05
☐ 3 Mark Howe	.35	.14	.03
☐ 4 Jari Kurri	.75	.30	.07
☐ 5 Wayne Gretzky	6.00	2.40	.60
☐ 6 Michel Goulet	.50	.20	.05
☐ 7 Larry Murphy	.50	.20	.05
☐ 8 Mike Liut	.35	.14	.03
☐ 9 Al MacInnis	.75	.30	.07
☐ 10 Tim Kerr	.25	.10	.02
☐ 11 Mario Lemieux	6.00	2.40	.60
☐ 12 Luc Robitaille	6.00	2.40	.60
☐ 13 Toronto Maple Leafs	.15	.06	.01
☐ 14 Buffalo Sabres	.15	.06	.01
☐ 15 Detroit Red Wings	.15	.06	.01
☐ 16 Pittsburgh Penguins	.15	.06	.01
☐ 17 New York Rangers	.15	.06	.01
☐ 18 Calgary Flames	.15	.06	.01
☐ 19 Winnipeg Jets	.15	.06	.01
☐ 20 Quebec Nordiques	.15	.06	.01
☐ 21 Chicago Blackhawks	.15	.06	.01
☐ 22 Los Angeles Kings	.15	.06	.01
☐ 23 Montreal Canadiens	.15	.06	.01
☐ 24 Vancouver Canucks	.15	.06	.01
☐ 25 Hartford Whalers	.15	.06	.01
☐ 26 Philadelphia Flyers	.15	.06	.01
☐ 27 New Jersey Devils	.15	.06	.01
☐ 28 St. Louis Blues	.15	.06	.01
☐ 29 Minnesota North Stars	.15	.06	.01
☐ 30 Washington Capitals	.15	.06	.01
☐ 31 Boston Bruins	.15	.06	.01
☐ 32 New York Islanders	.15	.06	.01
☐ 33 Edmonton Oilers	.15	.06	.01

1988-89 Topps

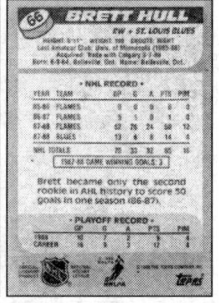

The 1988-89 Topps hockey set contains 198 standard size (2 1/2" by 3 1/2") cards. There are 66 double printed cards that are indicated by DP in the checklist below. The fronts feature colored borders and each player's team logo. The backs contain yearly statistics, playoff statistics, game winning goals from 1987-88 and highlights. There were cards printed on the bottoms of the wax boxes; these cards are similar to the regular issue cards but are "lettered" A-P rather than numbered. These wax box cards are not considered part of the complete set price below. Wayne Gretzky (120) appears as a King for the first time. The photo is of the press conference with Gretzky holding his new Kings jersey. Rookie Cards in this set include Sean Burke, Ulf Dahlen, Steve Duchesne, Brett Hull, Joe Nieuwendyk,

Bob Probert, Brendan Shanahan, Ray Sheppard, Pierre Turgeon and Glen Wesley.

	MINT	EXC	G-VG
COMPLETE SET (198)	110.00	50.00	14.00
COMMON PLAYER (1-198)	.08	.04	.01
☐ 1 Mario Lemieux DP	6.00	2.70	.75
☐ 2 Bob Joyce DP	.05	.02	.01
☐ 3 Joel Quenneville DP	.05	.02	.01
☐ 4 Tony McKegney	.08	.04	.01
☐ 5 Stephane Richer DP	1.00	.45	.13
☐ 6 Mark Howe DP	.08	.04	.01
☐ 7 Brent Sutter DP	.08	.04	.01
☐ 8 Gilles Meloche DP	.05	.02	.01
☐ 9 Jimmy Carson DP	.30	.14	.04
☐ 10 John MacLean	.35	.16	.04
☐ 11 Gary Leeman	.08	.04	.01
☐ 12 Gerard Gallant DP	.08	.04	.01
☐ 13 Marcel Dionne	.20	.09	.03
☐ 14 Dave Christian DP	.08	.04	.01
☐ 15 Gary Nylund	.08	.04	.01
☐ 16 Joe Nieuwendyk	7.00	3.10	.85
☐ 17 Billy Smith DP	.10	.05	.01
☐ 18 Christian Ruuttu	.08	.04	.01
☐ 19 Randy Cunneyworth	.08	.04	.01
☐ 20 Brian Lawton	.08	.04	.01
☐ 21 Scott Mellanby DP	.30	.14	.04
☐ 22 Peter Stastny DP	.25	.11	.03
☐ 23 Gord Kluzak	.08	.04	.01
☐ 24 Sylvain Turgeon	.08	.04	.01
☐ 25 Clint Malarchuk	.12	.05	.02
☐ 26 Denis Savard	.25	.11	.03
☐ 27 Craig Simpson	.25	.11	.03
☐ 28 Petr Klima	.12	.05	.02
☐ 29 Pat Verbeek	.20	.09	.03
☐ 30 Moe Mantha	.08	.04	.01
☐ 31 Chris Nilan	.12	.05	.02
☐ 32 Barry Pederson	.08	.04	.01
☐ 33 Randy Burridge	.15	.07	.02
☐ 34 Ron Hextall	1.00	.45	.13
☐ 35 Gaston Gingras	.08	.04	.01
☐ 36 Kevin Dineen DP	.20	.09	.03
☐ 37 Tom Laidlaw	.08	.04	.01
☐ 38 Paul MacLean DP	.05	.02	.01
☐ 39 John Chabot DP	.05	.02	.01
☐ 40 Lindy Ruff	.08	.04	.01
☐ 41 Dan Quinn DP	.05	.02	.01
☐ 42 Don Beaupre	.12	.05	.02
☐ 43 Gary Suter	.15	.07	.02
☐ 44 Mikko Makela DP	.05	.02	.01
☐ 45 Mark Johnson DP	.05	.02	.01
☐ 46 Dave Taylor	.15	.07	.02
☐ 47 Ulf Dahlen DP	.75	.35	.09
☐ 48 Jeff Sharples	.08	.04	.01
☐ 49 Chris Chelios	.35	.16	.04
☐ 50 Mike Gartner DP	.20	.09	.03
☐ 51 Darren Pang DP	.20	.09	.03
☐ 52 Ron Francis	.25	.11	.03
☐ 53 Ken Morrow	.08	.04	.01
☐ 54 Michel Goulet	.12	.05	.02
☐ 55 Ray Sheppard	4.00	1.80	.50
☐ 56 Doug Gilmour	2.50	1.15	.30
☐ 57 David Shaw DP	.05	.02	.01
☐ 58 Cam Neely DP	1.00	.45	.13
☐ 59 Grant Fuhr DP	.35	.16	.04
☐ 60 Scott Stevens	.30	.14	.04
☐ 61 Bob Brooke	.08	.04	.01
☐ 62 Dave Hunter	.08	.04	.01
☐ 63 Alan Kerr	.08	.04	.01
☐ 64 Brad Marsh	.12	.05	.02
☐ 65 Dale Hawerchuk DP	.35	.16	.04
☐ 66 Brett Hull DP	35.00	16.00	4.40
☐ 67 Patrik Sundstrom DP	.05	.02	.01
☐ 68 Greg Stefan	.08	.04	.01
☐ 69 James Patrick	.08	.04	.01
☐ 70 Dale Hunter DP	.08	.04	.01
☐ 71 Al Iafrate	.35	.16	.04
☐ 72 Bob Carpenter	.12	.05	.02
☐ 73 Ray Bourque DP	.50	.23	.06
☐ 74 John Tucker DP	.05	.02	.01
☐ 75 Carey Wilson	.08	.04	.01
☐ 76 Joe Mullen	.25	.11	.03
☐ 77 Rick Vaive	.08	.04	.01
☐ 78 Shawn Burr DP	.05	.02	.01
☐ 79 Murray Craven DP	.05	.02	.01
☐ 80 Clark Gillies	.08	.04	.01
☐ 81 Bernie Federko	.10	.05	.01
☐ 82 Tony Tanti	.08	.04	.01
☐ 83 Greg Gilbert	.08	.04	.01
☐ 84 Kirk Muller	.50	.23	.06
☐ 85 Dave Tippett	.08	.04	.01
☐ 86 Kevin Hatcher DP	1.00	.45	.13

☐ 87	Rick Middleton DP	.08	.04	.01
☐ 88	Bobby Smith	.12	.05	.02
☐ 89	Doug Wilson DP	.08	.04	.01
☐ 90	Scott Arniel	.08	.04	.01
☐ 91	Brian Mullen	.12	.05	.02
☐ 92	Mike O'Connell DP	.05	.02	.01
☐ 93	Mark Messier DP	.75	.35	.09
☐ 94	Sean Burke	1.00	.45	.13
☐ 95	Brian Bellows DP	.20	.09	.03
☐ 96	Doug Bodger	.08	.04	.01
☐ 97	Bryan Trottier	.15	.07	.02
☐ 98	Anton Stastny	.08	.04	.01
☐ 99	Checklist 1-99	.35	.07	.02
☐ 100	Dave Poulin DP	.08	.04	.01
☐ 101	Bob Bourne DP	.05	.02	.01
☐ 102	John Vanbiesbrouck	.75	.35	.09
☐ 103	Allen Pedersen	.08	.04	.01
☐ 104	Mike Ridley	.12	.05	.02
☐ 105	Andrew McBain	.08	.04	.01
☐ 106	Troy Murray DP	.05	.02	.01
☐ 107	Tom Barrasso	.25	.11	.03
☐ 108	Tomas Jonsson	.08	.04	.01
☐ 109	Rob Brown	.40	.18	.05
☐ 110	Hakan Loob DP	.05	.02	.01
☐ 111	Ilkka Sinisalo DP	.05	.02	.01
☐ 112	Dave Archibald	.08	.04	.01
☐ 113	Doug Halward	.08	.04	.01
☐ 114	Ray Ferraro	.12	.05	.02
☐ 115	Doug Brown	.35	.16	.04
☐ 116	Patrick Roy DP	4.00	1.80	.50
☐ 117	Greg Millen	.08	.04	.01
☐ 118	Ken Linseman	.08	.04	.01
☐ 119	Phil Housley DP	.20	.09	.03
☐ 120	Wayne Gretzky	35.00	16.00	4.40
	(Holding up Kings sweater)			
☐ 121	Tomas Sandstrom	.40	.18	.05
☐ 122	Brendan Shanahan	10.00	4.50	1.25
☐ 123	Pat LaFontaine	1.25	.55	.16
☐ 124	Luc Robitaille DP	4.00	1.80	.50
☐ 125	Ed Olczyk DP	.08	.04	.01
☐ 126	Ron Sutter	.08	.04	.01
☐ 127	Mike Liut	.12	.05	.02
☐ 128	Brent Ashton DP	.05	.02	.01
☐ 129	Tony Hrkac	.20	.09	.03
☐ 130	Kelly Miller	.12	.05	.02
☐ 131	Alan Haworth	.08	.04	.01
☐ 132	Dave McIlwain	.15	.07	.02
☐ 133	Mike Ramsey	.08	.04	.01
☐ 134	Bob Sweeney	.25	.11	.03
☐ 135	Dirk Graham DP	.08	.04	.01
☐ 136	Ulf Samuelsson	.50	.23	.06
☐ 137	Petri Skriko	.08	.04	.01
☐ 138	Aaron Broten DP	.05	.02	.01
☐ 139	Jim Fox	.08	.04	.01
☐ 140	Randy Wood DP	.25	.11	.03
☐ 141	Larry Murphy	.15	.07	.02
☐ 142	Daniel Berthiaume DP	.05	.02	.01
☐ 143	Kelly Kisio	.08	.04	.01
☐ 144	Neal Broten	.12	.05	.02
☐ 145	Reed Larson	.08	.04	.01
☐ 146	Peter Zezel DP	.08	.04	.01
☐ 147	Jari Kurri	.35	.16	.04
☐ 148	Jim Johnson	.08	.04	.01
☐ 149	Gino Cavallini DP	.05	.02	.01
☐ 150	Glen Hanlon DP	.05	.02	.01
☐ 151	Bengt Gustafsson	.08	.04	.01
☐ 152	Mike Bullard DP	.05	.02	.01
☐ 153	John Ogrodnick	.12	.05	.02
☐ 154	Steve Larmer	.35	.16	.04
☐ 155	Kelly Hrudey	.25	.11	.03
☐ 156	Mats Naslund	.12	.05	.02
☐ 157	Bruce Driver	.08	.04	.01
☐ 158	Randy Hillier	.08	.04	.01
☐ 159	Craig Hartsburg	.08	.04	.01
☐ 160	Rollie Melanson	.08	.04	.01
☐ 161	Adam Oates DP	3.00	1.35	.40
☐ 162	Greg Adams DP	.08	.04	.01
	Vancouver Canucks			
☐ 163	Dave Andreychuk DP	.50	.23	.06
☐ 164	Dave Babych	.08	.04	.01
☐ 165	Brian Noonan	.50	.23	.06
☐ 166	Glen Wesley	1.00	.45	.13
☐ 167	Dave Ellett	.12	.05	.02
☐ 168	Brian Propp	.12	.05	.02
☐ 169	Bernie Nicholls	.25	.11	.03
☐ 170	Walt Poddubny	.08	.04	.01
☐ 171	Steve Konroyd	.08	.04	.01
☐ 172	Doug Sulliman DP	.05	.02	.01
☐ 173	Mario Gosselin	.08	.04	.01
☐ 174	Brian Benning	.08	.04	.01
☐ 175	Dino Ciccarelli	.15	.07	.02
☐ 176	Steve Kasper	.08	.04	.01

☐ 177	Rick Tocchet	2.00	.90	.25
☐ 178	Brad McCrimmon	.08	.04	.01
☐ 179	Paul Coffey	.60	.25	.08
☐ 180	Pete Peeters	.12	.05	.02
☐ 181	Bob Probert DP	2.50	1.15	.30
☐ 182	Steve Duchesne DP	2.00	.90	.25
☐ 183	Russ Courtnall	.35	.16	.04
☐ 184	Mike Foligno DP	.08	.04	.01
☐ 185	Wayne Presley DP	.05	.02	.01
☐ 186	Rejean Lemelin	.12	.05	.02
☐ 187	Mark Hunter	.08	.04	.01
☐ 188	Joe Cirella	.08	.04	.01
☐ 189	Glenn Anderson DP	.25	.11	.03
☐ 190	John Anderson	.08	.04	.01
☐ 191	Pat Flatley	.08	.04	.01
☐ 192	Rod Langway	.12	.05	.02
☐ 193	Brian MacLellan	.08	.04	.01
☐ 194	Pierre Turgeon	15.00	6.75	1.90
☐ 195	Brian Hayward	.08	.04	.01
☐ 196	Steve Yzerman DP	1.50	.65	.19
☐ 197	Doug Crossman	.08	.04	.01
☐ 198	Checklist 100-198	.35	.07	.02

1988-89 Topps Sticker Inserts

This set of 33 "Hockey Helmet Stickers" features stickers of 12 All-Star players (1-12) and 21 stickers of team logos, pucks, and numbers. The stickers were inserted in with the 1988-89 Topps hockey regular issue wax packs and as such are also 2 1/2" by 3 1/2". The card backs are printed in blue and red on white card stock. The last seven team stickers can be found with the team logos on the top or bottom.

	MINT	EXC	G-VG
COMPLETE SET (33)	14.00	5.75	1.40
COMMON PLAYER (1-12)	.25	.10	.02
COMMON TEAM (13-33)	.15	.06	.01

☐ 1	Luc Robitaille	1.50	.60	.15
☐ 2	Mario Lemieux	5.00	2.00	.50
☐ 3	Hakan Loob	.25	.10	.02
☐ 4	Scott Stevens	.50	.20	.05
☐ 5	Ray Bourque	.75	.30	.07
☐ 6	Grant Fuhr	.50	.20	.05
☐ 7	Michel Goulet	.50	.20	.05
☐ 8	Wayne Gretzky	5.00	2.00	.50
☐ 9	Cam Neely	.75	.30	.07
☐ 10	Brad McCrimmon	.25	.10	.02
☐ 11	Gary Suter	.35	.14	.03
☐ 12	Patrick Roy	2.50	1.00	.25
☐ 13	Toronto Maple Leafs	.15	.06	.01
☐ 14	Buffalo Sabres	.15	.06	.01
☐ 15	Detroit Red Wings	.15	.06	.01
☐ 16	Pittsburgh Penguins	.15	.06	.01
☐ 17	New York Rangers	.15	.06	.01
☐ 18	Calgary Flames	.15	.06	.01
☐ 19	Winnipeg Jets	.15	.06	.01
☐ 20	Quebec Nordiques	.15	.06	.01
☐ 21	Chicago Blackhawks	.15	.06	.01
☐ 22	Los Angeles Kings	.15	.06	.01
☐ 23	Montreal Canadiens	.15	.06	.01
☐ 24	Vancouver Canucks	.15	.06	.01
☐ 25	Hartford Whalers	.15	.06	.01
☐ 26	Philadelphia Flyers	.15	.06	.01
☐ 27	New Jersey Devils	.15	.06	.01
☐ 28	St. Louis Blues	.15	.06	.01

☐ 29 Minnesota North Stars	.15	.06	.01
☐ 30 Washington Capitals	.15	.06	.01
☐ 31 Boston Bruins	.15	.06	.01
☐ 32 New York Islanders	.15	.06	.01
☐ 33 Edmonton Oilers	.15	.06	.01

1989-90 Topps

The 1989-90 Topps set contains 198 cards measuring the standard size (2 1/2" by 3 1/2"). There are 66 double-printed cards which are marked as DP in the checklist below. The fronts feature blue borders on top and bottom that are prone to chipping. An ice blue border is on either side. A team logo and the player's name are at the bottom. The backs contain yearly statistics, playoff statistics, game-winning goals from 1988-89 and highlights. Rookie Cards in this set include Jon Casey, Geoff Courtnall, Tony Granato, Craig Janney, Derek King, Trevor Linden, Brian Leetch, Dave Manson, Kirk McLean, Cliff Ronning and Joe Sakic.

	MINT	EXC	G-VG
COMPLETE SET (198)	40.00	18.00	5.00
COMMON PLAYER (1-198)	.05	.02	.01

☐ 1 Mario Lemieux	2.50	1.15	.30
☐ 2 Ulf Dahlen DP	.08	.04	.01
☐ 3 Terry Carkner	.15	.07	.02
☐ 4 Tony McKegney	.05	.02	.01
☐ 5 Denis Savard	.10	.05	.01
☐ 6 Derek King DP	.60	.25	.08
☐ 7 Lanny McDonald	.08	.04	.01
☐ 8 John Tonelli	.08	.04	.01
☐ 9 Tom Kurvers DP	.05	.02	.01
☐ 10 Dave Archibald	.05	.02	.01
☐ 11 Peter Sidorkiewicz	.25	.11	.03
☐ 12 Esa Tikkanen	.25	.11	.03
☐ 13 Dave Barr	.05	.02	.01
☐ 14 Brent Sutter	.08	.04	.01
☐ 15 Cam Neely	.50	.23	.06
☐ 16 Calle Johansson	.25	.11	.03
☐ 17 Patrick Roy DP	1.25	.55	.16
☐ 18 Dale DeGray DP	.05	.02	.01
☐ 19 Phil Bourque	.25	.11	.03
☐ 20 Kevin Dineen	.08	.04	.01
☐ 21 Mike Bullard DP	.05	.02	.01
☐ 22 Gary Leeman	.05	.02	.01
☐ 23 Greg Stefan DP	.05	.02	.01
☐ 24 Brian Mullen	.08	.04	.01
☐ 25 Pierre Turgeon DP	1.00	.45	.13
☐ 26 Bob Rouse DP	.05	.02	.01
☐ 27 Peter Zezel	.08	.04	.01
☐ 28 Jeff Brown DP	.30	.14	.04
☐ 29 Andy Brickley DP	.10	.05	.01
☐ 30 Mike Gartner	.25	.11	.03
☐ 31 Darren Pang	.05	.02	.01
☐ 32 Pat Verbeek	.10	.05	.01
☐ 33 Petri Skriko DP	.05	.02	.01
☐ 34 Tom Laidlaw	.05	.02	.01
☐ 35 Randy Wood	.05	.02	.01
☐ 36 Tom Barrasso DP	.10	.05	.01
☐ 37 John Tucker DP	.05	.02	.01
☐ 38 Andrew McBain	.05	.02	.01
☐ 39 David Shaw DP	.05	.02	.01

☐ 40 Rejean Lemelin	.08	.04	.01
☐ 41 Dino Ciccarelli DP	.08	.04	.01
☐ 42 Jeff Sharples	.05	.02	.01
☐ 43 Jari Kurri	.25	.11	.03
☐ 44 Murray Craven DP	.05	.02	.01
☐ 45 Cliff Ronning DP	1.00	.45	.13
☐ 46 Dave Babych	.05	.02	.01
☐ 47 Bernie Nicholls DP	.10	.05	.01
☐ 48 Jon Casey	.60	.25	.08
☐ 49 Al MacInnis	.25	.11	.03
☐ 50 Bob Errey DP	.20	.09	.03
☐ 51 Glen Wesley	.08	.04	.01
☐ 52 Dirk Graham	.08	.04	.01
☐ 53 Guy Carbonneau DP	.08	.04	.01
☐ 54 Tomas Sandstrom	.08	.04	.01
☐ 55 Rod Langway DP	.05	.02	.01
☐ 56 Patrik Sundstrom	.05	.02	.01
☐ 57 Michel Goulet	.08	.04	.01
☐ 58 Dave Taylor	.08	.04	.01
☐ 59 Phil Housley	.08	.04	.01
☐ 60 Pat LaFontaine DP	.35	.16	.04
☐ 61 Kirk McLean DP	2.50	1.15	.30
☐ 62 Ken Linseman	.05	.02	.01
☐ 63A Randy Cunneyworth ERR.... (Pittsburgh Penguins)	10.00	4.50	1.25
☐ 63B Randy Cunneyworth COR ... (Winnipeg Jets)	.05	.02	.01
☐ 64 Tony Hrkac DP	.05	.02	.01
☐ 65 Mark Messier DP	.50	.23	.06
☐ 66 Carey Wilson DP	.05	.02	.01
☐ 67 Stephen Leach	.35	.16	.04
☐ 68 Christian Ruuttu	.05	.02	.01
☐ 69 Dave Ellett	.08	.04	.01
☐ 70 Ray Ferraro	.08	.04	.01
☐ 71 Colin Patterson	.05	.02	.01
☐ 72 Tim Kerr	.08	.04	.01
☐ 73 Bob Joyce	.05	.02	.01
☐ 74 Doug Gilmour DP	.75	.35	.09
☐ 75 Lee Norwood DP	.05	.02	.01
☐ 76 Dale Hunter	.08	.04	.01
☐ 77 Jim Johnson DP	.05	.02	.01
☐ 78 Mike Foligno DP	.08	.04	.01
☐ 79 Al Iafrate DP	.25	.11	.03
☐ 80 Rick Tocchet DP	.20	.09	.03
☐ 81 Greg Hawgood DP	.25	.11	.03
☐ 82 Steve Thomas	.08	.04	.01
☐ 83 Steve Yzerman DP	.50	.23	.06
☐ 84 Mike McPhee	.08	.04	.01
☐ 85 David Volek DP	.20	.09	.03
☐ 86 Brian Benning	.05	.02	.01
☐ 87 Neal Broten	.08	.04	.01
☐ 88 Luc Robitaille	1.00	.45	.13
☐ 89 Trevor Linden	3.50	1.55	.45
☐ 90 James Patrick DP	.05	.02	.01
☐ 91 Brian Lawton	.05	.02	.01
☐ 92 Sean Burke DP	.08	.04	.01
☐ 93 Scott Stevens	.10	.05	.01
☐ 94 Pat Elynuik DP	.20	.09	.03
☐ 95 Paul Coffey	.35	.16	.04
☐ 96 Jan Erixon DP	.05	.02	.01
☐ 97 Mike Liut	.08	.04	.01
☐ 98 Wayne Presley	.05	.02	.01
☐ 99 Craig Simpson	.08	.04	.01
☐ 100 Kjell Samuelsson	.30	.14	.04
☐ 101 Shawn Burr DP	.05	.02	.01
☐ 102 John MacLean	.08	.04	.01
☐ 103 Tom Fergus	.05	.02	.01
☐ 104 Mike Krushelnyski	.05	.02	.01
☐ 105 Gary Nylund	.05	.02	.01
☐ 106 Dave Andreychuk	.35	.16	.04
☐ 107 Bernie Federko	.08	.04	.01
☐ 108 Gary Suter	.08	.04	.01
☐ 109 Dave Gagner DP	.25	.11	.03
☐ 110 Ray Bourque	.40	.18	.05
☐ 111 Geoff Courtnall	1.25	.55	.16
☐ 112 Doug Wilson	.08	.04	.01
☐ 113 Joe Sakic	7.00	3.10	.85
☐ 114 John Vanbiesbrouck	.35	.16	.04
☐ 115 Dave Poulin	.08	.04	.01
☐ 116 Rick Meagher	.05	.02	.01
☐ 117 Kirk Muller DP	.15	.07	.02
☐ 118 Mats Naslund	.08	.04	.01
☐ 119 Ray Sheppard	.50	.23	.06
☐ 120 Jeff Norton	.30	.14	.04
☐ 121 Randy Burridge DP	.08	.04	.01
☐ 122 Dale Hawerchuk DP	.15	.07	.02
☐ 123 Steve Duchesne	.25	.11	.03
☐ 124 John Anderson	.05	.02	.01
☐ 125 Rick Vaive DP	.05	.02	.01
☐ 126 Randy Hillier	.05	.02	.01
☐ 127 Jimmy Carson	.08	.04	.01
☐ 128 Larry Murphy	.08	.04	.01
☐ 129 Paul MacLean DP	.05	.02	.01

□	130	Joe Cirella	.05	.02	.01
□	131	Kelly Miller DP	.08	.04	.01
□	132	Alain Chevrier DP	.05	.02	.01
□	133	Ed Olczyk	.05	.02	.01
□	134	Dave Tippett	.05	.02	.01
□	135	Bob Sweeney	.05	.02	.01
□	136	Brian Leetch	10.00	4.50	1.25
□	137	Greg Millen	.05	.02	.01
□	138	Joe Nieuwendyk	.50	.23	.06
□	139	Brian Propp	.08	.04	.01
□	140	Mike Ramsey	.05	.02	.01
□	141	Mike Allison	.05	.02	.01
□	142	Shawn Chambers	.15	.07	.02
□	143	Peter Stastny DP	.08	.04	.01
□	144	Glen Hanlon	.05	.02	.01
□	145	John Cullen	.50	.23	.06
□	146	Kevin Hatcher	.25	.11	.03
□	147	Brendan Shanahan	1.50	.65	.19
□	148	Paul Reinhart	.05	.02	.01
□	149	Bryan Trottier	.08	.04	.01
□	150	Dave Manson	.50	.23	.06
□	151	Marc Habscheid DP	.05	.02	.01
□	152	Dan Quinn	.05	.02	.01
□	153	Stephane Richer DP	.25	.11	.03
□	154	Doug Bodger DP	.05	.02	.01
□	155	Ron Hextall	.25	.11	.03
□	156	Wayne Gretzky	3.00	1.35	.40
□	157	Steve Tuttle DP	.05	.02	.01
□	158	Charlie Huddy DP	.05	.02	.01
□	159	Dave Christian DP	.08	.04	.01
□	160	Andy Moog	.25	.11	.03
□	161	Tony Granato	.60	.25	.08
□	162	Sylvain Cote	.08	.04	.01
□	163	Mike Vernon	.30	.14	.04
□	164	Steve Chiasson	.35	.16	.04
□	165	Mike Ridley	.08	.04	.01
□	166	Kelly Hrudey	.08	.04	.01
□	167	Bob Carpenter DP	.05	.02	.01
□	168	Zarley Zalapski	.35	.16	.04
□	169	Derek Laxdal	.05	.02	.01
□	170	Clint Malarchuk DP	.08	.04	.01
□	171	Kelly Kisio	.05	.02	.01
□	172	Gerard Gallant	.05	.02	.01
□	173	Ron Sutter	.05	.02	.01
□	174	Chris Chelios	.10	.05	.01
□	175	Ron Francis	.25	.11	.03
□	176	Gino Cavallini	.05	.02	.01
□	177	Brian Bellows DP	.08	.04	.01
□	178	Greg C. Adams DP	.05	.02	.01
		Vancouver Canucks			
□	179	Steve Larmer	.25	.11	.03
□	180	Aaron Broten	.05	.02	.01
□	181	Brent Ashton DP	.05	.02	.01
□	182	Gerald Diduck DP	.05	.02	.01
□	183	Paul MacDermid	.05	.02	.01
□	184	Walt Poddubny DP	.05	.02	.01
□	185	Adam Oates	.75	.35	.09
□	186	Brett Hull	5.00	2.30	.60
□	187	Scott Arniel	.05	.02	.01
□	188	Bobby Smith	.08	.04	.01
□	189	Guy Lafleur	.25	.11	.03
□	190	Craig Janney	3.00	1.35	.40
□	191	Mark Howe	.08	.04	.01
□	192	Grant Fuhr DP	.15	.07	.02
□	193	Rob Brown	.05	.02	.01
□	194	Steve Kasper DP	.05	.02	.01
□	195	Pete Peeters	.08	.04	.01
□	196	Joe Mullen	.20	.09	.03
□	197	Checklist 1-99	.15	.03	.01
□	198	Checklist 100-198 DP	.15	.03	.01

1989-90 Topps Sticker Inserts

This 33-card set which measures the standard 2 1/2" by 3 1/2" was issued as a one per pack insert in the 1989-90 Topps Hockey packs. This set is divided into the first 12 cards being the 1989-90 NHL all-stars and the next 21 cards being the various team logos along with some number stickers and stickers of hockey pucks. For some reason Topps apparently printed these sticker cards on sheets in such a way that there were three complete sets of 33 and then three more rows of 11 double-printed cards instead of merely printing four complete sets on the printing sheet. The last seven team stickers can be found with the team logos on the top or bottom.

		MINT	EXC	G-VG
COMPLETE SET (33)		10.00	4.00	1.00
COMMON PLAYER (1-12)		.25	.10	.02
COMMON DP (2/5/9/10)		.15	.06	.01
COMMON TEAM (13-26)		.15	.06	.01
COMMON TEAM DP (27-33)		.10	.04	.01

□	1	Chris Chelios	.50	.20	.05
□	2	Gerard Gallant DP	.15	.06	.01
□	3	Mario Lemieux	4.00	1.60	.40
□	4	Al MacInnis	.60	.24	.06
□	5	Joe Mullen DP	.25	.10	.02
□	6	Patrick Roy	1.50	.60	.15
□	7	Ray Bourque	.75	.30	.07
□	8	Rob Brown	.25	.10	.02
□	9	Geoff Courtnall DP	.25	.10	.02
□	10	Steve Duchesne DP	.15	.06	.01
□	11	Wayne Gretzky	4.00	1.60	.40
□	12	Mike Vernon	.35	.14	.03
□	13	Toronto Maple Leafs	.15	.06	.01
□	14	Buffalo Sabres	.15	.06	.01
□	15	Detroit Red Wings	.15	.06	.01
□	16	Pittsburgh Penguins	.15	.06	.01
□	17	New York Rangers	.15	.06	.01
□	18	Calgary Flames	.15	.06	.01
□	19	Winnipeg Jets	.15	.06	.01
□	20	Quebec Nordiques	.15	.06	.01
□	21	Chicago Blackhawks	.15	.06	.01
□	22	Los Angeles Kings	.15	.06	.01
□	23	Montreal Canadiens	.15	.06	.01
□	24	Vancouver Canucks	.15	.06	.01
□	25	Hartford Whalers	.15	.06	.01
□	26	Philadelphia Flyers	.15	.06	.01
□	27	New Jersey Devils DP	.10	.04	.01
□	28	St. Louis Blues DP	.10	.04	.01
□	29	Minn. North Stars DP	.10	.04	.01
□	30	Washington Capitals DP	.10	.04	.01
□	31	Boston Bruins DP	.10	.04	.01
□	32	New York Islanders DP	.10	.04	.01
□	33	Edmonton Oilers DP	.10	.04	.01

1990-91 Topps

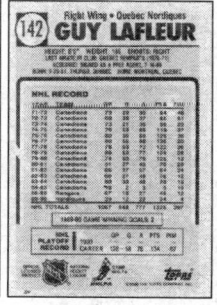

The 1990-91 Topps hockey set contains 396 cards measuring the standard size, 2 1/2" by 3 1/2". The fronts feature color action photos with color borders (according to team) on all four sides. A hockey stick is superimposed over the picture at the top border. The backs have yearly statistics, playoff statistics, and game winning goals from 1989-90. Included in the set is a three-card Tribute to Wayne Gretzky (1-3). Team cards have action scenes with the team's previous season standings and power play stats on back. The set was also produced in a high-gloss Tiffany version with supposedly just 3000 sets produced; the values for the Tiffany version are approximately five times the values listed below. Rookie Cards in this set include Rod Brind'Amour, Curtis Joseph, Bob Kudelski, Mike Modano, Alexander Mogilny, Mark Recchi, Mike Richter, Jeremy Roenick, Kevin Stevens and Chris Terreri.

	MINT	EXC	G-VG
COMPLETE SET (396)	15.00	6.75	1.90
COMPLETE FACT.SET (396)	15.00	6.75	1.90
COMMON PLAYER (1-396)	.05	.02	.01

☐ 1	Gretzky Tribute	.35	.16	.04
	Indianapolis Racers			
☐ 2	Gretzky Tribute	.30	.14	.04
	Edmonton Oilers			
☐ 3	Gretzky Tribute	.30	.14	.04
	Los Angeles Kings			
☐ 4	Brett Hull HL	.20	.09	.03
☐ 5	Jari Kurri HL UER	.08	.04	.01
	(Jari, not Jarri)			
☐ 6	Bryan Trottier HL	.05	.02	.01
☐ 7	Jeremy Roenick	1.25	.55	.16
☐ 8	Brian Propp	.08	.04	.01
☐ 9	Jim Hrivnak	.15	.07	.02
☐ 10	Mick Vukota	.05	.02	.01
☐ 11	Tom Kurvers	.05	.02	.01
☐ 12	Ulf Dahlen	.08	.04	.01
☐ 13	Bernie Nicholls	.10	.05	.01
☐ 14	Peter Sidorkiewicz	.05	.02	.01
☐ 15	Peter Zezel	.05	.02	.01
☐ 16	Mike Hartman	.05	.02	.01
☐ 17	Kings Team	.05	.02	.01
☐ 18	Jim Sandlak	.05	.02	.01
☐ 19	Rob Brown	.05	.02	.01
☐ 20	Paul Ranheim	.10	.05	.01
☐ 21	Rick Zombo	.05	.02	.01
☐ 22	Paul Gillis	.05	.02	.01
☐ 23	Brian Hayward	.05	.02	.01
☐ 24	Brent Ashton	.05	.02	.01
☐ 25	Mark Lamb	.05	.02	.01
☐ 26	Rick Tocchet	.08	.04	.01
☐ 27	Viacheslav Fetisov	.15	.07	.02
☐ 28	Denis Savard	.08	.04	.01
☐ 29	Chris Chelios	.08	.04	.01
☐ 30	Janne Ojanen	.05	.02	.01
☐ 31	Don Maloney	.05	.02	.01
☐ 32	Allan Bester	.05	.02	.01
☐ 33	Geoff Smith	.05	.02	.01
☐ 34	Daniel Shank	.05	.02	.01
☐ 35	Mikael Andersson	.10	.05	.01
☐ 36	Gino Cavallini	.05	.02	.01
☐ 37	Rob Murphy	.05	.02	.01
☐ 38	Flames Team	.05	.02	.01
☐ 39	Laurie Boschman	.05	.02	.01
☐ 40	Craig Wolanin	.05	.02	.01
☐ 41	Phil Bourque	.05	.02	.01
☐ 42	Alexander Mogilny	.75	.35	.09
☐ 43	Ray Bourque	.20	.09	.03
☐ 44	Mike Liut	.08	.04	.01
☐ 45	Ron Sutter	.05	.02	.01
☐ 46	Bob Kudelski	.35	.16	.04
☐ 47	Larry Murphy	.08	.04	.01
☐ 48	Darren Turcotte	.20	.09	.03
☐ 49	Paul Ysebaert	.15	.07	.02
☐ 50	Alan Kerr	.05	.02	.01
☐ 51	Randy Carlyle	.05	.02	.01
☐ 52	Iiro Jarvi	.05	.02	.01
☐ 53	Don Barber	.05	.02	.01
☐ 54	Carey Wilson UER	.05	.02	.01
	(Misspelled Cary			
	on both sides)			
☐ 55	Joey Kocur	.05	.02	.01
☐ 56	Steve Larmer	.08	.04	.01
☐ 57	Paul Cavallini	.05	.02	.01
☐ 58	Shayne Corson	.08	.04	.01
☐ 59	Canucks Team	.05	.02	.01
☐ 60	Sergei Makarov	.35	.16	.04
☐ 61	Kjell Samuelsson	.05	.02	.01
☐ 62	Tony Granato	.08	.04	.01
☐ 63	Tom Fergus	.05	.02	.01
☐ 64	Martin Gelinas	.15	.07	.02
☐ 65	Tom Barrasso	.10	.05	.01

☐ 66	Pierre Turgeon	.25	.11	.03
☐ 67	Randy Cunneyworth	.05	.02	.01
☐ 68	Michal Pivonka	.20	.09	.03
☐ 69	Cam Neely	.20	.09	.03
☐ 70	Brian Bellows	.08	.04	.01
☐ 71	Pat Elynuik	.05	.02	.01
☐ 72	Doug Crossman	.05	.02	.01
☐ 73	Sylvain Turgeon	.05	.02	.01
☐ 74	Shawn Burr	.05	.02	.01
☐ 75	John Vanbiesbrouck	.15	.07	.02
☐ 76	Steve Bozek	.05	.02	.01
☐ 77	Brett Hull	.75	.35	.09
☐ 78	Zarley Zalapski	.08	.04	.01
☐ 79	Wendel Clark	.15	.07	.02
☐ 80	Flyers Team	.05	.02	.01
☐ 81	Kelly Miller	.05	.02	.01
☐ 82	Mark Pederson	.05	.02	.01
☐ 83	Adam Creighton	.05	.02	.01
☐ 84	Scott Young	.05	.02	.01
☐ 85	Petr Klima	.08	.04	.01
☐ 86	Steve Duchesne	.08	.04	.01
☐ 87	Joe Nieuwendyk	.15	.07	.02
☐ 88	Andy Brickley	.05	.02	.01
☐ 89	Phil Housley	.08	.04	.01
☐ 90	Neal Broten	.08	.04	.01
☐ 91	Al Iafrate	.08	.04	.01
☐ 92	Steve Thomas	.08	.04	.01
☐ 93	Guy Carbonneau	.08	.04	.01
☐ 94	Steve Chiasson	.05	.02	.01
☐ 95	Mike Tomlak	.05	.02	.01
☐ 96	Roger Johansson	.05	.02	.01
☐ 97	Randy Wood	.05	.02	.01
☐ 98	Jim Johnson	.05	.02	.01
☐ 99	Bob Sweeney	.05	.02	.01
☐ 100	Dino Ciccarelli	.08	.04	.01
☐ 101	Rangers Team	.05	.02	.01
☐ 102	Mike Ramsey	.05	.02	.01
☐ 103	Kelly Hrudey	.08	.04	.01
☐ 104	Dave Ellett	.05	.02	.01
☐ 105	Bob Brooke	.05	.02	.01
☐ 106	Greg Adams	.05	.02	.01
	Vancouver Canucks			
☐ 107	Joe Cirella	.05	.02	.01
☐ 108	Jari Kurri	.10	.05	.01
☐ 109	Pete Peeters	.08	.04	.01
☐ 110	Paul MacLean	.05	.02	.01
☐ 111	Doug Wilson	.08	.04	.01
☐ 112	Pat Verbeek	.08	.04	.01
☐ 113	Bob Beers	.10	.05	.01
☐ 114	Mike O'Connell	.05	.02	.01
☐ 115	Brian Bradley	.08	.04	.01
☐ 116	Paul Coffey	.15	.07	.02
☐ 117	Doug Brown	.05	.02	.01
☐ 118	Aaron Broten	.05	.02	.01
☐ 119	Bob Essensa	.20	.09	.03
☐ 120	Wayne Gretzky UER	1.00	.45	.13
	(1302 career assists,			
	not 13102)			
☐ 121	Vincent Damphousse	.08	.04	.01
☐ 122	Nordiques Team	.05	.02	.01
☐ 123	Mike Foligno	.08	.04	.01
☐ 124	Russ Courtnall	.08	.04	.01
☐ 125	Rick Meagher	.05	.02	.01
☐ 126	Craig Fisher	.05	.02	.01
☐ 127	Al MacInnis	.10	.05	.01
☐ 128	Derek King	.08	.04	.01
☐ 129	Dale Hunter	.08	.04	.01
☐ 130	Mark Messier UER	.25	.11	.03
	(Shown as LW,			
	should be C)			
☐ 131	James Patrick UER	.05	.02	.01
	(Orange border,			
	should be blue)			
☐ 132	Checklist 1-132 UER	.06	.02	.01
	(54 Cary Wilson,			
	should be Carey)			
☐ 133	Red Wings Team	.05	.02	.01
☐ 134	Barry Pederson	.05	.02	.01
☐ 135	Gary Leeman	.05	.02	.01
☐ 136	Doug Gilmour	.35	.16	.04
☐ 137	Mike McPhee	.05	.02	.01
☐ 138	Bob Murray	.05	.02	.01
☐ 139	Bob Carpenter	.05	.02	.01
☐ 140	Sean Burke	.08	.04	.01
☐ 141	Dale Hawerchuk	.08	.04	.01
☐ 142	Guy Lafleur	.05	.02	.01
☐ 143	Lindy Ruff	.05	.02	.01
☐ 144	Whalers Team	.05	.02	.01
☐ 145	Glenn Anderson	.10	.05	.01
☐ 146	Dave Chyzowski	.05	.02	.01
☐ 147	Kevin Hatcher	.05	.02	.01
☐ 148	Rick Vaive	.05	.02	.01
☐ 149	Adam Oates	.15	.07	.02

□	#	Name			
□	150	Garth Butcher	.08	.04	.01
□	151	Basil McRae	.08	.04	.01
□	152	Ilkka Sinisalo	.05	.02	.01
□	153	Steve Kasper	.05	.02	.01
□	154	Greg Paslawski	.05	.02	.01
□	155	Brad Marsh	.08	.04	.01
□	156	Esa Tikkanen	.08	.04	.01
□	157	Tony Tanti	.05	.02	.01
□	158	Mario Marois	.05	.02	.01
		(oi in last name line below rest of name)			
□	159	Sylvain Lefebvre	.05	.02	.01
□	160	Troy Murray	.05	.02	.01
□	161	Gary Roberts	.20	.09	.03
□	162	Randy Ladouceur	.05	.02	.01
□	163	John Chabot	.05	.02	.01
□	164	Calle Johansson	.05	.02	.01
□	165	Bruins Team	.05	.02	.01
□	166	Jeff Norton	.05	.02	.01
□	167	Mike Krushelnyski	.05	.02	.01
□	168	Dave Gagner	.08	.04	.01
□	169	Dave Andreychuk	.20	.09	.03
□	170	Dave Capuano	.05	.02	.01
□	171	Curtis Joseph	.75	.35	.09
□	172	Bruce Driver	.05	.02	.01
□	173	Scott Mellanby	.08	.04	.01
□	174	John Ogrodnick	.05	.02	.01
□	175	Mario Lemieux	1.00	.45	.13
□	176	Marc Fortier	.05	.02	.01
□	177	Vincent Riendeau	.15	.07	.02
□	178	Mark Johnson	.05	.02	.01
□	179	Dirk Graham	.08	.04	.01
□	180	Jets Team	.05	.02	.01
□	181	Robb Stauber	.20	.09	.03
□	182	Christian Ruuttu	.05	.02	.01
□	183	Dave Tippett	.05	.02	.01
□	184	Pat LaFontaine	.25	.11	.03
□	185	Mark Howe	.08	.04	.01
□	186	Stephane Richer	.08	.04	.01
□	187	Jan Erixon	.05	.02	.01
□	188	Neil Sheehy	.05	.02	.01
□	189	Craig MacTavish	.08	.04	.01
□	190	Randy Burridge	.05	.02	.01
□	191	Bernie Federko	.08	.04	.01
□	192	Shawn Chambers	.05	.02	.01
□	193	Mark Messier AS1	.08	.04	.01
□	194	Luc Robitaille AS1	.08	.04	.01
□	195	Brett Hull AS1	.25	.11	.03
□	196	Ray Bourque AS1	.08	.04	.01
□	197	Al Macinnis AS1	.08	.04	.01
□	198	Patrick Roy AS1	.35	.16	.04
□	199	Wayne Gretzky AS2	.35	.16	.04
□	200	Brian Bellows AS2	.05	.02	.01
□	201	Cam Neely AS2	.08	.04	.01
□	202	Paul Coffey AS2	.08	.04	.01
□	203	Doug Wilson AS2	.05	.02	.01
□	204	Daren Puppa AS2 UER	.05	.02	.01
		(Misspelled Darren on front and back)			
□	205	Gary Suter	.08	.04	.01
□	206	Ed Olczyk	.05	.02	.01
□	207	Doug Lidster	.05	.02	.01
□	208	John Cullen	.08	.04	.01
□	209	Luc Robitaille	.25	.11	.03
□	210	Tim Kerr	.08	.04	.01
□	211	Scott Stevens	.10	.05	.01
□	212	Craig Janney	.20	.09	.03
□	213	Kevin Dineen	.08	.04	.01
□	214	Jimmy Waite	.20	.09	.03
□	215	Benoit Hogue	.08	.04	.01
□	216	Curtis Leschyshyn	.05	.02	.01
□	217	Brad Lauer	.05	.02	.01
□	218	Joe Mullen	.10	.05	.01
□	219	Patrick Roy	.75	.35	.09
□	220	Blues Team	.05	.02	.01
□	221	Brian Leetch	.50	.23	.06
□	222	Steve Yzerman	.35	.16	.04
□	223	Stephane Beauregard	.10	.05	.01
□	224	John MacLean	.08	.04	.01
□	225	Trevor Linden	.25	.11	.03
□	226	Bill Ranford	.10	.05	.01
□	227	Mark Osborne	.05	.02	.01
□	228	Curt Giles	.05	.02	.01
□	229	Mikko Makela	.05	.02	.01
□	230	Bob Errey	.05	.02	.01
□	231	Jimmy Carson	.08	.04	.01
□	232	Kay Whitmore	.15	.07	.02
□	233	Gary Nylund	.05	.02	.01
□	234	Jiri Hrdina	.05	.02	.01
□	235	Stephen Leach	.05	.02	.01
□	236	Greg Hawgood UER	.05	.02	.01
		(Photo actually Don Sweeney)			
□	237	Jocelyn Lemieux	.05	.02	.01
□	238	Daren Puppa	.08	.04	.01
□	239	Kelly Kisio	.05	.02	.01
□	240	Craig Simpson	.08	.04	.01
□	241	Maple Leafs Team	.05	.02	.01
□	242	Fredrik Olausson	.08	.04	.01
□	243	Ron Hextall	.08	.04	.01
□	244	Sergio Momesso	.15	.07	.02
□	245	Kirk Muller	.08	.04	.01
□	246	Petr Svoboda	.05	.02	.01
□	247	Daniel Berthiaume	.05	.02	.01
□	248	Andrew McBain	.05	.02	.01
□	249	Jeff Jackson UER	.05	.02	.01
		(Game total for '89-90 is 65, not 0)			
□	250	Randy Gilhen	.05	.02	.01
□	251	Oilers Team	.05	.02	.01
□	252	Rick Bennett	.05	.02	.01
□	253	Don Beaupre	.08	.04	.01
□	254	Pelle Eklund	.05	.02	.01
□	255	Greg Gilbert	.05	.02	.01
□	256	Gordie Roberts	.05	.02	.01
□	257	Kirk McLean	.20	.09	.03
□	258	Brent Sutter	.08	.04	.01
□	259	Brendan Shanahan	.25	.11	.03
□	260	Todd Krygier	.05	.02	.01
□	261	Larry Robinson UER	.08	.04	.01
		(No '80-81 stats on card, totals wrong)			
□	262	Sabres Team	.05	.02	.01
□	263	Dave Christian	.05	.02	.01
□	264	Checklist 133-264	.06	.02	.01
□	265	Jamie Macoun	.05	.02	.01
□	266	Glen Hanlon	.05	.02	.01
□	267	Daniel Marois	.05	.02	.01
□	268	Doug Smail	.05	.02	.01
□	269	Jon Casey	.08	.04	.01
□	270	Brian Skrudland	.05	.02	.01
□	271	Michel Petit	.05	.02	.01
□	272	Dan Quinn	.05	.02	.01
□	273	Geoff Courtnall	.08	.04	.01
□	274	Mike Bullard	.05	.02	.01
□	275	Randy Gregg	.05	.02	.01
□	276	Keith Brown	.05	.02	.01
□	277	Troy Mallette	.05	.02	.01
□	278	Steve Tuttle	.05	.02	.01
□	279	Brad Shaw	.05	.02	.01
□	280	Mark Recchi	.75	.35	.09
□	281	John Tonelli	.08	.04	.01
□	282	Doug Bodger	.05	.02	.01
□	283	Thomas Steen	.08	.04	.01
□	284	Devils Team	.05	.02	.01
□	285	Lee Norwood	.05	.02	.01
□	286	Dave MacLellan	.05	.02	.01
□	287	Bobby Smith	.08	.04	.01
□	288	Rob Cimetta	.05	.02	.01
□	289	Rob Zettler	.05	.02	.01
□	290	David Reid	.05	.02	.01
□	291	Bryan Trottier	.08	.04	.01
□	292	Brian Mullen	.08	.04	.01
□	293	Paul Reinhart	.05	.02	.01
□	294	Andy Moog	.10	.05	.01
□	295	Jeff Brown	.08	.04	.01
□	296	Ryan Walter	.05	.02	.01
□	297	Trent Yawney	.05	.02	.01
□	298	John Druce	.05	.02	.01
□	299	Dave McLlwain UER	.05	.02	.01
		(Card says shoots right, should be left)			
□	300	David Volek	.05	.02	.01
□	301	Tomas Sandstrom	.08	.04	.01
□	302	Gord Murphy	.05	.02	.01
□	303	Lou Franceschetti	.05	.02	.01
□	304	Dana Murzyn	.05	.02	.01
□	305	North Stars Team	.05	.02	.01
□	306	Patrik Sundstrom	.05	.02	.01
□	307	Kevin Lowe	.08	.04	.01
□	308	Dave Barr	.05	.02	.01
□	309	Wendell Young	.05	.02	.01
□	310	Darrin Shannon	.15	.07	.02
□	311	Ron Francis	.10	.05	.01
□	312	Stephane Fiset	.25	.11	.03
□	313	Paul Fenton	.05	.02	.01
□	314	Dave Taylor	.08	.04	.01
□	315	Islanders Team	.05	.02	.01
□	316	Petri Skriko	.05	.02	.01
□	317	Rob Ramage	.05	.02	.01
□	318	Murray Craven	.05	.02	.01
□	319	Gaetan Duchesne	.05	.02	.01
□	320	Brad McCrimmon	.05	.02	.01
□	321	Grant Fuhr	.10	.05	.01
□	322	Gerard Gallant	.05	.02	.01
□	323	Tommy Albelin	.05	.02	.01

			MINT	EXC	G-VG
☐	324	Scott Arniel	.05	.02	.01
☐	325	Mike Keane	.20	.09	.03
☐	326	Penguins Team	.05	.02	.01
☐	327	Mike Ridley	.08	.04	.01
☐	328	Dave Babych	.05	.02	.01
☐	329	Michel Goulet	.08	.04	.01
☐	330	Mike Richter	1.00	.45	.13
☐	331	Garry Galley	.15	.07	.02
☐	332	Rod Brind'Amour	.50	.23	.06
☐	333	Tony McKegney	.05	.02	.01
☐	334	Peter Stastny	.08	.04	.01
☐	335	Greg Millen	.05	.02	.01
☐	336	Ray Ferraro	.08	.04	.01
☐	337	Miloslav Horava	.05	.02	.01
☐	338	Paul MacDermid	.05	.02	.01
☐	339	Craig Coxe	.05	.02	.01
☐	340	Dave Snuggerud	.05	.02	.01
☐	341	Mike Lalor	.05	.02	.01
☐	342	Marc Habscheid	.05	.02	.01
☐	343	Rejean Lemelin	.08	.04	.01
☐	344	Charlie Huddy	.05	.02	.01
☐	345	Ken Linseman	.05	.02	.01
☐	346	Canadiens Team	.05	.02	.01
☐	347	Troy Loney	.05	.02	.01
☐	348	Mike Modano	.75	.35	.09
☐	349	Jeff Reese	.10	.05	.01
☐	350	Pat Flatley	.05	.02	.01
☐	351	Mike Vernon	.08	.04	.01
☐	352	Todd Elik	.20	.09	.03
☐	353	Rod Langway	.05	.02	.01
☐	354	Moe Mantha	.05	.02	.01
☐	355	Keith Acton	.05	.02	.01
☐	356	Scott Pearson	.05	.02	.01
☐	357	Perry Berezan	.05	.02	.01
☐	358	Alexei Kasatonov	.15	.07	.02
☐	359	Igor Larionov	.30	.14	.04
☐	360	Kevin Stevens	.60	.25	.08
☐	361	Yves Racine	.15	.07	.02
☐	362	Dave Poulin	.08	.04	.01
☐	363	Blackhawks Team	.05	.02	.01
☐	364	Yvon Corriveau	.05	.02	.01
☐	365	Brian Benning	.05	.02	.01
☐	366	Hubie McDonough	.05	.02	.01
☐	367	Ron Tugnutt	.08	.04	.01
☐	368	Steve Smith	.08	.04	.01
☐	369	Joel Otto	.05	.02	.01
☐	370	Dave Lowry	.05	.02	.01
☐	371	Clint Malarchuk	.08	.04	.01
☐	372	Mathieu Schneider	.20	.09	.03
☐	373	Mike Gartner	.10	.05	.01
☐	374	John Tucker	.05	.02	.01
☐	375	Chris Terreri	.25	.11	.03
☐	376	Dean Evason	.05	.02	.01
☐	377	Jamie Leach	.05	.02	.01
☐	378	Jacques Cloutier	.05	.02	.01
☐	379	Glen Wesley	.08	.04	.01
☐	380	Vladimir Krutov	.05	.02	.01
☐	381	Terry Carkner	.05	.02	.01
☐	382	John McIntyre	.05	.02	.01
☐	383	Ville Siren	.05	.02	.01
☐	384	Joe Sakic	.40	.18	.05
☐	385	Teppo Numminen	.15	.07	.02
☐	386	Theoren Fleury	.25	.11	.03
☐	387	Glen Featherstone	.05	.02	.01
☐	388	Stephan Lebeau	.30	.14	.04
☐	389	Kevin McClelland	.05	.02	.01
☐	390	Uwe Krupp	.08	.04	.01
☐	391	Mark Janssens	.05	.02	.01
☐	392	Marty McSorley	.08	.04	.01
☐	393	Vladimir Ruzicka	.15	.07	.02
☐	394	Capitals Team	.05	.02	.01
☐	395	Mark Fitzpatrick	.15	.07	.02
☐	396	Checklist 265-396	.06	.02	.01

1990-91 Topps
Team Scoring Leaders

This 21-card standard size (2 1/2" by 3 1/2") set was included as an insert in the 1990-91 Topps hockey packs. This set has a glossy front with a full color action shot of the team's leading scorer while the back of the card has a list of the ten leading scorers for each team.

	MINT	EXC	G-VG
COMPLETE SET (21)	6.00	2.40	.60
COMMON PLAYER (1-21)	.10	.04	.01

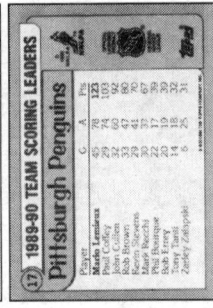

			MINT	EXC	G-VG
☐	1	Steve Larmer	.20	.08	.02
☐	2	Brett Hull	1.00	.40	.10
☐	3	Cam Neely	.50	.20	.05
☐	4	Stephane Richer	.20	.08	.02
☐	5	Paul Reinhart	.10	.04	.01
☐	6	Dino Ciccarelli	.20	.08	.02
☐	7	Kirk Muller	.30	.12	.03
☐	8	Joe Nieuwendyk	.40	.16	.04
☐	9	Rick Tocchet	.30	.12	.03
☐	10	Pat LaFontaine	.75	.30	.07
☐	11	Dale Hawerchuk	.20	.08	.02
☐	12	Wayne Gretzky	2.00	.80	.20
☐	13	Gary Leeman	.10	.04	.01
☐	14	Joe Sakic	.75	.30	.07
☐	15	Brian Bellows	.20	.08	.02
☐	16	Mark Messier	.75	.30	.07
☐	17	Mario Lemieux	1.50	.60	.15
☐	18	John Ogrodnick	.10	.04	.01
☐	19	Steve Yzerman	.75	.30	.07
☐	20	Pierre Turgeon	.60	.24	.06
☐	21	Ron Francis	.20	.08	.02

1991-92 Topps/Bowman
Preview Sheet

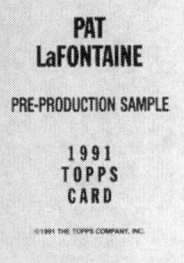

This nine-card unperforated sheet of Topps and Bowman hockey cards was sent to dealers to show them the graphic design of the coming year's hockey cards. The fronts of these preview cards are identical to the regular issue. In blue lettering, the backs have the player's name, the words "Pre-Production Sample", "1991 Topps (or as the case may be, Bowman) Card", and a tagline. The cards are unnumbered on the back and hence are listed below beginning with the upper left corner, counting across, and ending with the lower right corner. The cards are arranged so that Topps and Bowman cards alternate with one another.

	MINT	EXC	G-VG
COMPLETE SET (9)	10.00	4.00	1.00
COMMON PLAYER (1-9)	1.00	.40	.10
☐ 1 Mario Lemieux (Topps)	2.50	1.00	.25

			MINT	EXC	G-VG
☐	2	Wayne Gretzky (Bowman)	3.00	1.20	.30
☐	3	Joe Sakic (Topps)	1.00	.40	.10
☐	4	Ray Bourque (Bowman)	1.00	.40	.10
☐	5	Ed Belfour (Topps)	1.00	.40	.10
☐	6	Mark Messier (Bowman)	1.50	.60	.15
☐	7	Pat LaFontaine (Topps)	1.50	.60	.15
☐	8	Steve Yzerman (Bowman)	1.50	.60	.15
☐	9	Brett Hull (Topps)	2.00	.80	.20

☐	13	New York Islanders Rick Tocchet	.20	.08	.02
☐	14	Philadelphia Flyers Theoren Fleury UER (Misspelled Fluery on card back)	.20	.08	.02
☐	15	Calgary Flames John MacLean	.15	.06	.01
☐	16	New Jersey Devils Kevin Hatcher	.15	.06	.01
☐	17	Washington Capitals Trevor Linden	.50	.20	.05
☐	18	Vancouver Canucks Russ Courtnall	.15	.06	.01
☐	19	Montreal Canadiens Ray Bourque	.50	.20	.05
☐	20	Boston Bruins Brett Hull	1.00	.40	.10
☐	21	St. Louis Blues Steve Larmer	.15	.06	.01
		Chicago Blackhawks			

1991-92 Topps
Team Scoring Leaders

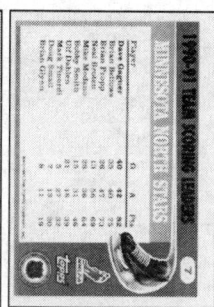

This 21-card set, with each card measuring the standard 2 1/2" by 3 1/2", features fronts with color action shots enclosed by white borders. A yellow, black, and orange hockey stick flanks the right of the photo and carries the team name in the blade. The player's name is at the bottom left in a screened aqua border while '90-'91 Team Scoring Leader appears in the narrow yellow border at the bottom. The horizontally oriented backs are accented in red and aqua and present the players' scoring (goals and assists) statistics. These 21 Team Scoring Leader cards were inserted, one per pack, in 1991-92 Topps cello packs. The backs are numbered in the upper right corner, while a hockey skate and various logos appear down the right side.

			MINT	EXC	G-VG
	COMPLETE SET (21)		6.00	2.40	.60
	COMMON PLAYER (1-21)		.10	.04	.01
☐	1	Pat Verbeek Hartford Whalers	.15	.06	.01
☐	2	Dale Hawerchuk Buffalo Sabres	.20	.08	.02
☐	3	Steve Yzerman Detroit Red Wings	.75	.30	.07
☐	4	Brian Leetch New York Rangers	.60	.24	.06
☐	5	Mark Recchi Pittsburgh Penguins	.60	.24	.06
☐	6	Esa Tikkanen Edmonton Oilers	.15	.06	.01
☐	7	Dave Gagner Minnesota North Stars	.10	.04	.01
☐	8	Joe Sakic Quebec Nordiques	.50	.20	.05
☐	9	Vincent Damphousse Toronto Maple Leafs	.20	.08	.02
☐	10	Wayne Gretzky Los Angeles Kings	1.50	.60	.15
☐	11	Phil Housley Winnipeg Jets	.25	.10	.02
☐	12	Pat LaFontaine	.75	.30	.07

1992-93 Topps

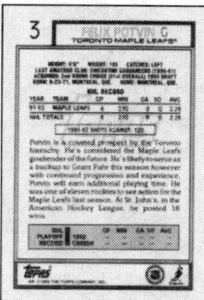

The 1992-93 Topps set contains 529 cards measuring the standard size, 2 1/2" by 3 1/2". Gold foil versions of all the cards were produced. One Gold card was inserted in each foil pack and three per jumbo pack. There were 20 such cards included in factory sets as a bonus. Topps switched to white card stock this year allowing for a better looking product. Card fronts have team and player name at the bottom. Colorful backs include yearly statistics, playoff statistics and game-winning goals from 1991-92. The early print-run cards of Randy Moller (407) suffer from a print flaw which appears to be large finger impression on the card face. Rookie Cards include Guy Hebert and Bill Guerin.

			MINT	EXC	G-VG
	COMPLETE SET (529)		20.00	9.00	2.50
	COMPLETE FACT.SET (549)		28.00	12.50	3.50
	COMMON PLAYER (1-529)		.05	.02	.01
☐	1	Wayne Gretzky Los Angeles Kings	1.00	.45	.13
☐	2	Brett Hull St. Louis Blues	.50	.23	.06
☐	3	Felix Potvin Toronto Maple Leafs	1.00	.45	.13
☐	4	Mark Tinordi Minnesota North Stars	.08	.04	.01
☐	5	Paul Coffey HL Los Angeles Kings	.06	.03	.01
☐	6	Tony Amonte New York Rangers	.15	.07	.02
☐	7	Pat Falloon San Jose Sharks	.15	.07	.02
☐	8	Pavel Bure Vancouver Canucks	.50	.23	.06
☐	9	Nicklas Lidstrom Detroit Red Wings	.08	.04	.01
☐	10	Dominic Roussel Philadelphia Flyers	.10	.05	.01
☐	11	Nelson Emerson	.08	.04	.01

St. Louis Blues
☐ 12 Donald Audette .06 .03 .01
Buffalo Sabres
☐ 13 Gilbert Dionne .06 .03 .01
Montreal Canadiens
☐ 14 Vladimir Konstantinov .06 .03 .01
Detroit Red Wings
☐ 15 Kevin Todd .06 .03 .01
New Jersey Devils
☐ 16 Steve Leach .05 .02 .01
Boston Bruins
☐ 17 Ed Olczyk .05 .02 .01
Winnipeg Jets
☐ 18 Jim Hrivnak .05 .02 .01
Washington Capitals
☐ 19 Gilbert Dionne .05 .02 .01
Montreal Canadiens
☐ 20 Mike Vernon .08 .04 .01
Calgary Flames
☐ 21 Dave Christian .05 .02 .01
St. Louis Blues
☐ 22 Ed Belfour .25 .11 .03
Chicago Blackhawks
☐ 23 Andrew Cassels .05 .02 .01
Hartford Whalers
☐ 24 Jaromir Jagr .50 .23 .06
Pittsburgh Penguins
☐ 25 Arturs Irbe .40 .18 .05
San Jose Sharks
☐ 26 Petr Klima .05 .02 .01
Edmonton Oilers
☐ 27 Randy Gilhen .05 .02 .01
New York Rangers
☐ 28 Ulf Dahlen .05 .02 .01
Minnesota North Stars
☐ 29 Kelly Hrudey .08 .04 .01
Los Angeles Kings
☐ 30 Dave Ellett .05 .02 .01
Toronto Maple Leafs
☐ 31 Tom Fitzgerald .05 .02 .01
New York Rangers
☐ 32 Cam Neely .08 .04 .01
Boston Bruins
☐ 33 Greg Paslawski .05 .02 .01
Quebec Nordiques
☐ 34 Brad May .05 .02 .01
Buffalo Sabres
☐ 35 Vyacheslav Kozlov .60 .25 .08
Detroit Red Wings
☐ 36 Mark Hunter .05 .02 .01
Washington Capitals
☐ 37 Steve Chiasson .05 .02 .01
Detroit Red Wings
☐ 38 Joe Murphy .05 .02 .01
Edmonton Oilers
☐ 39 Darryl Sydor .08 .04 .01
Los Angeles Kings
☐ 40 Ron Hextall .08 .04 .01
Quebec Nordiques
☐ 41 Jim Sandlak .05 .02 .01
Vancouver Canucks
☐ 42 Dave Lowry .05 .02 .01
St. Louis Blues
☐ 43 Claude Lemieux .08 .04 .01
New Jersey Devils
☐ 44 Gerald Diduck .05 .02 .01
Vancouver Canucks
☐ 45 Mike McPhee .05 .02 .01
Montreal Canadiens
☐ 46 Rod Langway .05 .02 .01
Washington Capitals
☐ 47 Guy Larose .05 .02 .01
Toronto Maple Leafs
☐ 48 Craig Billington .05 .02 .01
New Jersey Devils
☐ 49 Daniel Marois .05 .02 .01
New York Islanders
☐ 50 Todd Nelson .05 .02 .01
Pittsburgh Penguins
☐ 51 Jari Kurri .10 .05 .01
Los Angeles Kings
☐ 52 Keith Brown .05 .02 .01
Chicago Blackhawks
☐ 53 Valeri Kamensky .15 .07 .02
Quebec Nordiques
☐ 54 Jim Johnson .05 .02 .01
Minnesota North Stars
☐ 55 Vincent Damphousse .08 .04 .01
Edmonton Oilers
☐ 56 Pat Elynuik .05 .02 .01
Winnipeg Jets
☐ 57 Jeff Beukeboom .05 .02 .01
New York Rangers
☐ 58 Paul Ysebaert .05 .02 .01

Detroit Red Wings
☐ 59 Ken Sutton .05 .02 .01
Buffalo Sabres
☐ 60 Dale Craigwell .05 .02 .01
San Jose Sharks
☐ 61 Marc Bergevin .05 .02 .01
Hartford Whalers
☐ 62 Stephane Beauregard .05 .02 .01
Winnipeg Jets
☐ 63 Bob Probert .05 .02 .01
Detroit Red Wings
☐ 64 Jergus Baca .05 .02 .01
Hartford Whalers
☐ 65 Brian Propp .08 .04 .01
Minnesota North Stars
☐ 66 Jacques Cloutier .05 .02 .01
Quebec Nordiques
☐ 67 Jim Thomson .05 .02 .01
Ottawa Senators
☐ 68 Anatoli Semenov .05 .02 .01
Tampa Bay Lightning
☐ 69 Stephan Lebeau .05 .02 .01
Montreal Canadiens
☐ 70 Rick Tocchet .08 .04 .01
Pittsburgh Penguins
☐ 71 James Patrick .05 .02 .01
New York Rangers
☐ 72 Rob Brown .05 .02 .01
Chicago Blackhawks
☐ 73 Peter Ahola .05 .02 .01
Los Angeles Kings
☐ 74 Bob Corkum .05 .02 .01
Buffalo Sabres
☐ 75 Brent Sutter .08 .04 .01
Chicago Blackhawks
☐ 76 Neil Wilkinson .05 .02 .01
San Jose Sharks
☐ 77 Mark Osborne .05 .02 .01
Toronto Maple Leafs
☐ 78 Ron Wilson .05 .02 .01
St. Louis Blues
☐ 79 Todd Richards .05 .02 .01
Hartford Whalers
☐ 80 Robert Kron .05 .02 .01
Vancouver Canucks
☐ 81 Cliff Ronning .05 .02 .01
Vancouver Canucks
☐ 82 Zarley Zalapski .05 .02 .01
Hartford Whalers
☐ 83 Randy Burridge .05 .02 .01
Washington Capitals
☐ 84 Jarrod Skalde .05 .02 .01
New Jersey Devils
☐ 85 Gary Leeman .05 .02 .01
Calgary Flames
☐ 86 Mike Ricci .08 .04 .01
Quebec Nordiques
☐ 87 Dennis Vaske .05 .02 .01
New York Islanders
☐ 88 John LeBlanc .05 .02 .01
Winnipeg Jets
☐ 89 Brad Shaw .05 .02 .01
Ottawa Senators
☐ 90 Rod Brind'Amour .15 .07 .02
Philadelphia Flyers
☐ 91 Colin Patterson .05 .02 .01
Buffalo Sabres
☐ 92 Gerard Gallant .05 .02 .01
Detroit Red Wings
☐ 93 Per Djoos .05 .02 .01
New York Rangers
☐ 94 Claude Lapointe .05 .02 .01
Quebec Nordiques
☐ 95 Bob Errey .05 .02 .01
Pittsburgh Penguins
☐ 96 Norm Maciver .05 .02 .01
Edmonton Oilers
☐ 97 Todd Elik .05 .02 .01
Minnesota North Stars
☐ 98 Chris Chelios .08 .04 .01
Chicago Blackhawks
☐ 99 Keith Primeau .08 .04 .01
Detroit Red Wings
☐ 100 Jim Waite .05 .02 .01
Chicago Blackhawks
☐ 101 Luc Robitaille .15 .07 .02
Los Angeles Kings
☐ 102 Keith Tkachuk .30 .14 .04
Winnipeg Jets
☐ 103 Benoit Hogue .05 .02 .01
New York Islanders
☐ 104 Brian Mullen .08 .04 .01
San Jose Sharks
☐ 105 Joe Nieuwendyk .08 .04 .01

☐ 106	Randy McKay	.05	.02	.01
	Calgary Flames			
	New Jersey Devils			
☐ 107	Michal Pivonka	.08	.04	.01
	Washington Capitals			
☐ 108	Darcy Wakaluk	.08	.04	.01
	Minnesota North Stars			
☐ 109	Andy Brickley	.05	.02	.01
	Boston Bruins			
☐ 110	Goals Against	.25	.11	.03
	Average Leader			
	Patrick Roy			
	Montreal Canadiens			
☐ 111	Bob Sweeney	.05	.02	.01
	Boston Bruins			
☐ 112	Guy Hebert	.40	.18	.05
	St. Louis Blues			
☐ 113	Joe Mullen	.08	.04	.01
	Pittsburgh Penguins			
☐ 114	Gord Murphy	.05	.02	.01
	Boston Bruins			
☐ 115	Evgeny Davydov	.05	.02	.01
	Winnipeg Jets			
☐ 116	Gary Roberts	.08	.04	.01
	Calgary Flames			
☐ 117	Pelle Eklund	.05	.02	.01
	Philadelphia Flyers			
☐ 118	Tom Kurvers	.05	.02	.01
	New York Islanders			
☐ 119	John Tonelli	.08	.04	.01
	Quebec Nordiques			
☐ 120	Fredrik Olausson	.05	.02	.01
	Winnipeg Jets			
☐ 121	Mike Donnelly	.05	.02	.01
	Los Angeles Kings			
✗ 122	Doug Gilmour	.25	.11	.03
	Toronto Maple Leafs			
☐ 123	Wayne Gretzky	.40	.18	.05
	Assists Leader			
	Los Angeles Kings			
☐ 124	Curtis Leschyshyn	.05	.02	.01
	Quebec Nordiques			
☐ 125	Guy Carbonneau	.08	.04	.01
	Montreal Canadiens			
☐ 126	Bill Ranford	.08	.04	.01
	Edmonton Oilers			
☐ 127	Ulf Samuelsson	.08	.04	.01
	Pittsburgh Penguins			
☐ 128	Joey Kocur	.05	.02	.01
	New York Rangers			
☐ 129	Kevin Miller	.08	.04	.01
	Detroit Red Wings			
☐ 130	Kirk McLean	.20	.09	.03
	Vancouver Canucks			
☐ 131	Kevin Dineen	.08	.04	.01
	Philadelphia Flyers			
☐ 132	John Cullen	.05	.02	.01
	Hartford Whalers			
☐ 133	Al Iafrate	.08	.04	.01
	Washington Capitals			
☐ 134	Craig Janney	.10	.05	.01
	St. Louis Blues			
☐ 135	Patrick Flatley	.05	.02	.01
	New York Islanders			
☐ 136	Dominik Hasek	.40	.18	.05
	Chicago Blackhawks			
☐ 137	Benoit Brunet	.05	.02	.01
	Montreal Canadiens			
☐ 138	Dave Babych	.05	.02	.01
	Vancouver Canucks			
☐ 139	Doug Brown	.05	.02	.01
	New Jersey Devils			
☐ 140	Mike Lalor	.05	.02	.01
	Winnipeg Jets			
☐ 141	Thomas Steen	.05	.02	.01
	Winnipeg Jets			
☐ 142	Frantisek Musil	.05	.02	.01
	Calgary Flames			
☐ 143	Dan Quinn	.05	.02	.01
	Philadelphia Flyers			
☐ 144	Dmitri Mironov	.08	.04	.01
	Toronto Maple Leafs			
☐ 145	Bob Kudelski	.08	.04	.01
	Los Angeles Kings			
☐ 146	Mike Bullard	.05	.02	.01
	Toronto Maple Leafs			
☐ 147	Randy Carlyle	.05	.02	.01
	Winnipeg Jets			
☐ 148	Kent Manderville	.05	.02	.01
	Toronto Maple Leafs			
☐ 149	Kevin Hatcher	.08	.04	.01
	Washington Capitals			
☐ 150	Steve Kasper	.05	.02	.01
	Philadelphia Flyers			
☐ 151	Mikael Andersson	.05	.02	.01
	Hartford Whalers			
☐ 152	Alexei Kasatonov	.05	.02	.01
	New Jersey Devils			
☐ 153	Jan Erixon	.05	.02	.01
	New York Rangers			
☐ 154	Craig Ludwig	.05	.02	.01
	Minnesota North Stars			
☐ 155	Dave Poulin	.05	.02	.01
	Boston Bruins			
☐ 156	Scott Stevens	.10	.05	.01
	New Jersey Devils			
☐ 157	Robert Reichel	.08	.04	.01
	Calgary Flames			
☐ 158	Uwe Krupp	.05	.02	.01
	New York Islanders			
☐ 159	Brian Noonan	.05	.02	.01
	Chicago Blackhawks			
☐ 160	Stephane Richer	.08	.04	.01
	New Jersey Devils			
☐ 161	Brent Thompson	.05	.02	.01
	Los Angeles Kings			
☐ 162	Glenn Anderson	.08	.04	.01
	Toronto Maple Leafs			
☐ 163	Joe Cirella	.05	.02	.01
	New York Rangers			
☐ 164	Dave Andreychuk	.15	.07	.02
	Buffalo Sabres			
☐ 165	Vladimir Konstantinov	.05	.02	.01
	Detroit Red Wings			
☐ 166	Mike McNeill	.05	.02	.01
	Quebec Nordiques			
☐ 167	Darrin Shannon	.05	.02	.01
	Winnipeg Jets			
☐ 168	Rob Pearson	.05	.02	.01
	Toronto Maple Leafs			
☐ 169	John Vanbiesbrouck	.10	.05	.01
	New York Rangers			
☐ 170	Randy Wood	.05	.02	.01
	Buffalo Sabres			
☐ 171	Marty McSorley	.08	.04	.01
	Los Angeles Kings			
☐ 172	Mike Hudson	.05	.02	.01
	Chicago Blackhawks			
☐ 173	Paul Fenton	.05	.02	.01
	San Jose Sharks			
☐ 174	Jeff Brown	.08	.04	.01
	St. Louis Blues			
☐ 175	Mark Greig	.05	.02	.01
	Hartford Whalers			
☐ 176	Gordie Roberts	.05	.02	.01
	Pittsburgh Penguins			
☐ 177	Josef Beranek	.15	.07	.02
	Edmonton Oilers			
☐ 178	Shawn Burr	.05	.02	.01
	Detroit Red Wings			
☐ 179	Marc Bureau	.05	.02	.01
	Minnesota North Stars			
☐ 180	Mikhail Tatarinov	.05	.02	.01
	Quebec Nordiques			
☐ 181	Robert Cimetta	.05	.02	.01
	Toronto Maple Leafs			
☐ 182	Paul Coffey UER	.15	.07	.02
	(Still pictured			
	as a Penguin)			
	Los Angeles Kings			
☐ 183	Bob Essensa	.08	.04	.01
	Winnipeg Jets			
☐ 184	Joe Reekie	.05	.02	.01
	Tampa Bay Lightning			
☐ 185	Jeff Hackett	.05	.02	.01
	San Jose Sharks			
☐ 186	Tomas Forslund	.05	.02	.01
	Calgary Flames			
☐ 187	Claude Vilgrain	.05	.02	.01
	New Jersey Devils			
☐ 188	John Druce	.05	.02	.01
	Washington Capitals			
☐ 189	Patrice Brisebois	.05	.02	.01
	Montreal Canadiens			
☐ 190	Peter Douris	.05	.02	.01
	Boston Bruins			
☐ 191	Brent Ashton	.05	.02	.01
	Boston Bruins			
☐ 192	Eric Desjardins	.05	.02	.01
	Montreal Canadiens			
☐ 193	Nick Kypreos	.05	.02	.01
	Washington Capitals			
☐ 194	Dana Murzyn	.05	.02	.01
	Vancouver Canucks			
☐ 195	Don Beaupre	.08	.04	.01
	Washington Capitals			
☐ 196	Jeff Chychrun	.05	.02	.01

Pittsburgh Penguins			
☐ 197 Dave Barr	.05	.02	.01
New Jersey Devils			
☐ 198 Brian Glynn	.05	.02	.01
Edmonton Oilers			
☐ 199 Keith Acton	.05	.02	.01
Philadelphia Flyers			
☐ 200 Igor Kravchuk	.05	.02	.01
Chicago Blackhawks			
☐ 201 Shayne Corson	.08	.04	.01
Montreal Canadiens			
☐ 202 Curt Giles	.05	.02	.01
St. Louis Blues			
☐ 203 Darren Turcotte	.05	.02	.01
New York Rangers			
☐ 204 David Volek	.05	.02	.01
New York Islanders			
☐ 205 Ray Whitney	.20	.09	.03
San Jose Sharks			
☐ 206 Donald Audette	.05	.02	.01
Buffalo Sabres			
☐ 207 Steve Yzerman	.25	.11	.03
Detroit Red Wings			
☐ 208 Craig Berube	.05	.02	.01
Calgary Flames			
☐ 209 Bob McGill	.05	.02	.01
Detroit Red Wings			
☐ 210 Stu Barnes	.05	.02	.01
Winnipeg Jets			
☐ 211 Rob Blake	.10	.05	.01
Los Angeles Kings			
☐ 212 Mario Lemieux	.75	.35	.09
Pittsburgh Penguins			
☐ 213 Dominic Roussel	.15	.07	.02
Philadelphia Flyers			
☐ 214 Sergio Momesso	.05	.02	.01
Vancouver Canucks			
☐ 215 Brad Marsh	.08	.04	.01
Detroit Red Wings			
☐ 216 Mark Fitzpatrick	.08	.04	.01
New York Islanders			
☐ 217 Ken Baumgartner	.05	.02	.01
Toronto Maple Leafs			
☐ 218 Greg Gilbert	.05	.02	.01
Chicago Blackhawks			
☐ 219 Ric Nattress	.05	.02	.01
Toronto Maple Leafs			
☐ 220 Theoren Fleury	.10	.05	.01
Calgary Flames			
☐ 221 Ray Bourque	.15	.07	.02
Boston Bruins			
☐ 222 Steve Thomas	.08	.04	.01
New York Islanders			
☐ 223 Scott Niedermayer	.25	.11	.03
New Jersey Devils			
☐ 224 Jeff Lazaro	.05	.02	.01
Ottawa Senators			
☐ 225 Wins Leaders	.08	.04	.01
Tim Cheveldae			
Detroit Red Wings			
Kirk McLean			
Vancouver Canucks			
☐ 226 Marc Fortier	.05	.02	.01
Quebec Nordiques			
☐ 227 Rob Zettler	.05	.02	.01
San Jose Sharks			
☐ 228 Kevin Todd	.05	.02	.01
New Jersey Devils			
☐ 229 Tony Amonte	.20	.09	.03
New York Rangers			
☐ 230 Mark Lamb	.05	.02	.01
Ottawa Senators			
☐ 231 Chris Dahlquist	.05	.02	.01
Minnesota North Stars			
☐ 232 James Black	.05	.02	.01
Hartford Whalers			
☐ 233 Paul Cavallini	.05	.02	.01
St. Louis Blues			
☐ 234 Gino Cavallini	.05	.02	.01
Quebec Nordiques			
☐ 235 Tony Tanti	.05	.02	.01
Buffalo Sabres			
☐ 236 Mike Ridley	.08	.04	.01
Washington Capitals			
☐ 237 Curtis Joseph	.25	.11	.03
St. Louis Blues			
☐ 238 Mike Craig	.05	.02	.01
Minnesota North Stars			
☐ 239 Luciano Borsato	.05	.02	.01
Winnipeg Jets			
☐ 240 Brian Bellows	.08	.04	.01
Minnesota North Stars			
☐ 241 Barry Pederson	.05	.02	.01
Boston Bruins			
☐ 242 Tony Granato	.05	.02	.01
Los Angeles Kings			
☐ 243 Jim Paek	.05	.02	.01
Pittsburgh Penguins			
☐ 244 Tim Bergland	.05	.02	.01
Tampa Bay Lightning			
☐ 245 Jayson More	.05	.02	.01
San Jose Sharks			
☐ 246 Laurie Boschman	.05	.02	.01
New Jersey Devils			
☐ 247 Doug Bodger	.05	.02	.01
Buffalo Sabres			
☐ 248 Murray Craven	.05	.02	.01
Hartford Whalers			
☐ 249 Kris Draper	.05	.02	.01
Winnipeg Jets			
☐ 250 Brian Benning	.05	.02	.01
Philadelphia Flyers			
☐ 251 Jarmo Myllys	.05	.02	.01
San Jose Sharks			
☐ 252 Sergei Fedorov	.60	.25	.08
Detroit Red Wings			
☐ 253 Mathieu Schneider	.08	.04	.01
Montreal Canadiens			
☐ 254 Dave Gagner	.08	.04	.01
Minnesota North Stars			
☐ 255 Michel Goulet	.08	.04	.01
Chicago Blackhawks			
☐ 256 Alexander Godynyuk	.05	.02	.01
Calgary Flames			
☐ 257 Ray Sheppard	.08	.04	.01
Detroit Red Wings			
☐ 258 Mark Messier AS	.10	.05	.01
New York Rangers			
☐ 259 Kevin Stevens AS	.10	.05	.01
Pittsburgh Penguins			
☐ 260 Brett Hull AS	.20	.09	.03
St. Louis Blues			
☐ 261 Brian Leetch AS	.15	.07	.02
New York Rangers			
☐ 262 Ray Bourque AS	.08	.04	.01
Boston Bruins			
☐ 263 Patrick Roy AS	.25	.11	.03
Montreal Canadiens			
☐ 264 Mike Gartner HL	.06	.03	.01
New York Rangers			
☐ 265 Mario Lemieux AS	.25	.11	.03
Pittsburgh Penguins			
☐ 266 Luc Robitaille AS	.08	.04	.01
Los Angeles Kings			
☐ 267 Mark Recchi AS	.08	.04	.01
Philadelphia Flyers			
☐ 268 Phil Housley AS	.08	.04	.01
Winnipeg Jets			
☐ 269 Scott Stevens AS	.08	.04	.01
New Jersey Devils			
☐ 270 Kirk McLean AS	.08	.04	.01
Vancouver Canucks			
☐ 271 Steve Duchesne	.08	.04	.01
Quebec Nordiques			
☐ 272 Jiri Hrdina	.05	.02	.01
Pittsburgh Penguins			
☐ 273 John MacLean	.08	.04	.01
New Jersey Devils			
☐ 274 Mark Messier	.20	.09	.03
New York Rangers			
☐ 275 Geoff Smith	.05	.02	.01
Edmonton Oilers			
☐ 276 Russ Courtnall	.08	.04	.01
Montreal Canadiens			
☐ 277 Yves Racine	.05	.02	.01
Detroit Red Wings			
☐ 278 Tom Draper	.05	.02	.01
Buffalo Sabres			
☐ 279 Charlie Huddy	.05	.02	.01
Los Angeles Kings			
☐ 280 Trevor Kidd	.08	.04	.01
Calgary Flames			
☐ 281 Garth Butcher	.05	.02	.01
St. Louis Blues			
☐ 282 Mike Sullivan	.05	.02	.01
San Jose Sharks			
☐ 283 Adam Burt	.05	.02	.01
Hartford Whalers			
☐ 284 Troy Murray	.05	.02	.01
Winnipeg Jets			
☐ 285 Stephane Fiset	.08	.04	.01
Quebec Nordiques			
☐ 286 Perry Anderson	.05	.02	.01
San Jose Sharks			
☐ 287 Sergei Nemchinov	.08	.04	.01
New York Rangers			
☐ 288 Rick Zombo	.05	.02	.01

St. Louis Blues
☐ 289 Pierre Turgeon	.20	.09	.03

New York Islanders
☐ 290 Kevin Lowe .05 .02 .01
Edmonton Oilers
☐ 291 Brian Bradley .05 .02 .01
Tampa Bay Lightning
☐ 292 Martin Gelinas UER .05 .02 .01
(Transaction date should
be 8-9-88, not 8-9-89)
Edmonton Oilers
☐ 293 Brian Leetch .30 .14 .04
New York Rangers
☐ 294 Peter Bondra .08 .04 .01
Washington Capitals
☐ 295 Brendan Shanahan .20 .09 .03
St. Louis Blues
☐ 296 Dale Hawerchuk .08 .04 .01
Buffalo Sabres
☐ 297 Mike Hough .05 .02 .01
Quebec Nordiques
☐ 298 Rollie Melanson .05 .02 .01
Montreal Canadiens
☐ 299 Brad Jones .05 .02 .01
Philadelphia Flyers
☐ 300 Jocelyn Lemieux .05 .02 .01
Chicago Blackhawks
☐ 301 Brad McCrimmon .05 .02 .01
Detroit Red Wings
☐ 302 Marty McInnis .05 .02 .01
New York Islanders
☐ 303 Chris Terreri .08 .04 .01
New Jersey Devils
☐ 304 Dean Evason .05 .02 .01
San Jose Sharks
☐ 305 Glenn Healy .08 .04 .01
New York Islanders
☐ 306 Ken Hodge Jr. .05 .02 .01
Boston Bruins
☐ 307 Mike Liut .08 .04 .01
Washington Capitals
☐ 308 Gary Suter .08 .04 .01
Calgary Flames
☐ 309 Neal Broten .08 .04 .01
Minnesota North Stars
☐ 310 Tim Cheveldae .08 .04 .01
Detroit Red Wings
☐ 311 Tom Fergus .05 .02 .01
Vancouver Canucks
☐ 312 Petr Svoboda .05 .02 .01
Buffalo Sabres
☐ 313 Tom Chorske .05 .02 .01
New Jersey Devils
☐ 314 Paul Ysebaert .08 .04 .01
Plus/Minus Leader
Detroit Red Wings
☐ 315 Steve Smith .08 .04 .01
Chicago Blackhawks
☐ 316 Stephane Morin .05 .02 .01
Quebec Nordiques
☐ 317 Pat MacLeod .05 .02 .01
San Jose Sharks
☐ 318 Dino Ciccarelli .08 .04 .01
Washington Capitals
☐ 319 Peter Zezel .05 .02 .01
Toronto Maple Leafs
☐ 320 Chris Lindberg .05 .02 .01
Calgary Flames
☐ 321 Grant Ledyard .05 .02 .01
Buffalo Sabres
☐ 322 Ron Francis .08 .04 .01
Pittsburgh Penguins
☐ 323 Adrien Plavsic .05 .02 .01
Vancouver Canucks
☐ 324 Ray Ferraro .05 .02 .01
New York Islanders
☐ 325 Wendel Clark .10 .05 .01
Toronto Maple Leafs
☐ 326 Corey Millen .08 .04 .01
Los Angeles Kings
☐ 327 Mark Pederson .05 .02 .01
Philadelphia Flyers
☐ 328 Patrick Poulin .05 .02 .01
Hartford Whalers
☐ 329 Adam Graves .25 .11 .03
New York Rangers
☐ 330 Bobby Holik .05 .02 .01
Hartford Whalers
☐ 331 Kelly Kisio .05 .02 .01
San Jose Sharks
☐ 332 Peter Sidorkiewicz .05 .02 .01
Ottawa Senators
☐ 333 Vladimir Ruzicka .05 .02 .01
Boston Bruins

☐ 334 J.J. Daigneault .05 .02 .01
Montreal Canadiens
☐ 335 Troy Mallette .05 .02 .01
New Jersey Devils
☐ 336 Craig MacTavish .05 .02 .01
Edmonton Oilers
☐ 337 Michel Petit .05 .02 .01
Calgary Flames
☐ 338 Claude Loiselle .05 .02 .01
New York Islanders
☐ 339 Teppo Numminen .05 .02 .01
Winnipeg Jets
☐ 340 Brett Hull .20 .09 .03
Goal Scoring Leader
St. Louis Blues
☐ 341 Sylvain Lefebvre .05 .02 .01
Montreal Canadiens
☐ 342 Perry Berezan .05 .02 .01
San Jose Sharks
☐ 343 Kevin Stevens .20 .09 .03
Pittsburgh Penguins
☐ 344 Randy Ladouceur .05 .02 .01
Hartford Whalers
☐ 345 Pat LaFontaine .20 .09 .03
Buffalo Sabres
☐ 346 Glen Wesley .05 .02 .01
Boston Bruins
☐ 347 Michel Goulet HL .06 .03 .01
Chicago Blackhawks
☐ 348 Jamie Macoun .05 .02 .01
Toronto Maple Leafs
☐ 349 Owen Nolan .05 .02 .01
Quebec Nordiques
☐ 350 Grant Fuhr .08 .04 .01
Toronto Maple Leafs
☐ 351 Tim Kerr .08 .04 .01
New York Rangers
☐ 352 Kjell Samuelsson .05 .02 .01
Pittsburgh Penguins
☐ 353 Pavel Bure 1.00 .45 .13
Vancouver Canucks
☐ 354 Murray Baron .05 .02 .01
St. Louis Blues
☐ 355 Paul Broten .05 .02 .01
New York Rangers
☐ 356 Craig Simpson .05 .02 .01
Edmonton Oilers
☐ 357 Ken Daneyko .05 .02 .01
New Jersey Devils
☐ 358 Greg Hawgood .05 .02 .01
Edmonton Oilers
☐ 359 Johan Garpenlov .05 .02 .01
San Jose Sharks
☐ 360 Garry Galley .05 .02 .01
Philadelphia Flyers
☐ 361 Paul DiPietro .05 .02 .01
Montreal Canadiens
☐ 362 Jamie Leach .05 .02 .01
Pittsburgh Penguins
☐ 363 Clint Malarchuk .08 .04 .01
Buffalo Sabres
☐ 364 Dan Lambert .05 .02 .01
Quebec Nordiques
☐ 365 Joe Juneau UER .75 .35 .09
(Shoots left, not right)
Boston Bruins
☐ 366 Scott Lachance .05 .02 .01
New York Islanders
☐ 367 Mike Richter .25 .11 .03
New York Rangers
☐ 368 Sheldon Kennedy .05 .02 .01
Detroit Red Wings
☐ 369 John McIntyre .05 .02 .01
Los Angeles Kings
☐ 370 Glen Murray UER .05 .02 .01
(Misspelled Glenn
on both sides)
Boston Bruins
☐ 371 Ron Sutter .05 .02 .01
St. Louis Blues
☐ 372 David Williams .10 .05 .01
San Jose Sharks
☐ 373 Bill Lindsay .10 .05 .01
Quebec Nordiques
☐ 374 Todd Gill .05 .02 .01
Toronto Maple Leafs
☐ 375 Sylvain Turgeon .05 .02 .01
Ottawa Senators
☐ 376 Dirk Graham .05 .02 .01
Chicago Blackhawks
☐ 377 Brad Schlegel .05 .02 .01
Washington Capitals
☐ 378 Bob Carpenter .05 .02 .01

Boston Bruins				
☐ 379 Jon Casey	.08	.04	.01
Minnesota North Stars				
☐ 380 Andrei Lomakin	.05	.02	.01
Philadelphia Flyers				
☐ 381 Kay Whitmore	.05	.02	.01
Hartford Whalers				
☐ 382 Alexander Mogilny	.40	.18	.05
Buffalo Sabres				
☐ 383 Garry Valk	.05	.02	.01
Vancouver Canucks				
☐ 384 Bruce Driver	.05	.02	.01
New Jersey Devils				
☐ 385 Jeff Reese	.05	.02	.01
Calgary Flames				
☐ 386 Brent Gilchrist	.05	.02	.01
Montreal Canadiens				
☐ 387 Kerry Huffman	.05	.02	.01
Quebec Nordiques				
☐ 388 Bobby Smith	.08	.04	.01
Minnesota North Stars				
☐ 389 Dave Manson	.05	.02	.01
Edmonton Oilers				
☐ 390 Russ Romaniuk	.05	.02	.01
Winnipeg Jets				
☐ 391 Paul MacDermid	.05	.02	.01
Washington Capitals				
☐ 392 Louie DeBrusk	.05	.02	.01
Edmonton Oilers				
☐ 393 Dave McIlwain	.05	.02	.01
Toronto Maple Leafs				
☐ 394 Andy Moog	.08	.04	.01
Boston Bruins				
☐ 395 Tie Domi	.05	.02	.01
New York Rangers				
☐ 396 Pat Jablonski	.05	.02	.01
Tampa Bay Lightning				
☐ 397 Troy Loney	.05	.02	.01
Pittsburgh Penguins				
☐ 398 Jimmy Carson	.05	.02	.01
Detroit Red Wings				
☐ 399 Eric Weinrich	.05	.02	.01
New Jersey Devils				
☐ 400 Jeremy Roenick	.50	.23	.06
Chicago Blackhawks				
☐ 401 Brent Fedyk	.05	.02	.01
Detroit Red Wings				
☐ 402 Geoff Sanderson	.30	.14	.04
Hartford Whalers				
☐ 403 Doug Lidster	.05	.02	.01
Vancouver Canucks				
☐ 404 Mike Gartner	.10	.05	.01
New York Rangers				
☐ 405 Derian Hatcher	.05	.02	.01
Minnesota North Stars				
☐ 406 Gaetan Duchesne	.05	.02	.01
Minnesota North Stars				
☐ 407 Randy Moller	.05	.02	.01
Buffalo Sabres				
☐ 408 Brian Skrudland	.05	.02	.01
Montreal Canadiens				
☐ 409 Luke Richardson	.05	.02	.01
Edmonton Oilers				
☐ 410 Mark Recchi	.25	.11	.03
Philadelphia Flyers				
☐ 411 Steve Konroyd	.05	.02	.01
Hartford Whalers				
☐ 412 Troy Gamble	.05	.02	.01
Vancouver Canucks				
☐ 413 Greg Johnston	.05	.02	.01
Toronto Maple Leafs				
☐ 414 Denis Savard	.08	.04	.01
Montreal Canadiens				
☐ 415 Mats Sundin	.20	.09	.03
Quebec Nordiques				
☐ 416 Bryan Trottier	.08	.04	.01
Pittsburgh Penguins				
☐ 417 Don Sweeney	.05	.02	.01
Boston Bruins				
☐ 418 Pat Falloon	.15	.07	.02
San Jose Sharks				
☐ 419 Alexander Semak	.05	.02	.01
New Jersey Devils				
☐ 420 David Shaw	.05	.02	.01
Minnesota North Stars				
☐ 421 Tomas Sandstrom	.05	.02	.01
Los Angeles Kings				
☐ 422 Petr Nedved	.10	.05	.01
Vancouver Canucks				
☐ 423 Peter Ing	.05	.02	.01
Edmonton Oilers				
☐ 424 Wayne Presley	.05	.02	.01
Buffalo Sabres				
☐ 425 Rick Wamsley	.05	.02	.01

Toronto Maple Leafs				
☐ 426 Rob Zamuner	.10	.05	.01
New York Rangers				
☐ 427 Claude Boivin	.05	.02	.01
Philadelphia Flyers				
☐ 428 Sylvain Cote	.05	.02	.01
Washington Capitals				
☐ 429 Kevin Stevens HL	.06	.03	.01
Pittsburgh Penguins				
☐ 430 Randy Velischek	.05	.02	.01
Quebec Nordiques				
☐ 431 Derek King	.05	.02	.01
New York Islanders				
☐ 432 Terry Yake	.05	.02	.01
Hartford Whalers				
☐ 433 Philippe Bozon	.05	.02	.01
St. Louis Blues				
☐ 434 Rich Sutter	.05	.02	.01
St. Louis Blues				
☐ 435 Brian Lawton	.05	.02	.01
San Jose Sharks				
☐ 436 Brian Hayward	.05	.02	.01
San Jose Sharks				
☐ 437 Robert Dirk	.05	.02	.01
Vancouver Canucks				
☐ 438 Bernie Nicholls	.08	.04	.01
Edmonton Oilers				
☐ 439 Michel Picard	.05	.02	.01
Hartford Whalers				
☐ 440 Nicklas Lidstrom	.15	.07	.02
Detroit Red Wings				
☐ 441 Mike Modano	.25	.11	.03
Minnesota North Stars				
☐ 442 Phil Bourque	.05	.02	.01
Pittsburgh Penguins				
☐ 443 Wayne McBean	.05	.02	.01
New York Islanders				
☐ 444 Scott Mellanby	.05	.02	.01
Edmonton Oilers				
☐ 445 Kevin Haller	.05	.02	.01
Montreal Canadiens				
☐ 446 Dave Taylor UER	.08	.04	.01
(Games played total				
***, should be 1,030)				
Los Angeles Kings				
☐ 447 Larry Murphy	.08	.04	.01
Pittsburgh Penguins				
☐ 448 David Bruce	.05	.02	.01
San Jose Sharks				
☐ 449 Steven Finn	.05	.02	.01
Quebec Nordiques				
☐ 450 Mike Krushelnyski	.05	.02	.01
Toronto Maple Leafs				
☐ 451 Adam Creighton	.05	.02	.01
New York Islanders				
☐ 452 Al MacInnis	.10	.05	.01
Calgary Flames				
☐ 453 Rick Tabaracci	.05	.02	.01
Winnipeg Jets				
☐ 454 Bob Bassen	.05	.02	.01
St. Louis Blues				
☐ 455 Kelly Buchberger	.05	.02	.01
Edmonton Oilers				
☐ 456 Phil Housley	.08	.04	.01
Winnipeg Jets				
☐ 457 Daren Puppa	.08	.04	.01
Buffalo Sabres				
☐ 458 Viacheslav Fetisov	.05	.02	.01
New Jersey Devils				
☐ 459 Doug Smail	.05	.02	.01
Quebec Nordiques				
☐ 460 Paul Stanton	.05	.02	.01
Pittsburgh Penguins				
☐ 461 Steve Weeks	.05	.02	.01
Los Angeles Kings				
☐ 462 Valeri Zelepukin	.15	.07	.02
New Jersey Devils				
☐ 463 Stephane Matteau	.05	.02	.01
Chicago Blackhawks				
☐ 464 Dale Hunter	.08	.04	.01
Washington Capitals				
☐ 465 Terry Carkner	.05	.02	.01
Philadelphia Flyers				
☐ 466 Vincent Riendeau	.05	.02	.01
Detroit Red Wings				
☐ 467 Sergei Makarov	.08	.04	.01
Calgary Flames				
☐ 468 Igor Ulanov	.05	.02	.01
Winnipeg Jets				
☐ 469 Peter Stastny	.08	.04	.01
New Jersey Devils				
☐ 470 Dimitri Khristich	.08	.04	.01
Washington Capitals				
☐ 471 Joel Otto	.05	.02	.01

Calgary Flames
☐ 472 Geoff Courtnall .... .05 .02 .01
Vancouver Canucks
☐ 473 Mike Ramsey .... .05 .02 .01
Buffalo Sabres
☐ 474 Yvon Corriveau .... .05 .02 .01
Hartford Whalers
☐ 475 Adam Oates....................... .15 .07 .02
Boston Bruins
☐ 476 Esa Tikkanen .... .08 .04 .01
Edmonton Oilers
☐ 477 Doug Weight .... .08 .04 .01
New York Rangers
☐ 478 Mike Keane .... .05 .02 .01
Montreal Canadiens
☐ 479 Kelly Miller .... .05 .02 .01
Detroit Red Wings
☐ 480 Nelson Emerson.................. .15 .07 .02
St. Louis Blues
☐ 481 Shawn McEachern .... .15 .07 .02
Pittsburgh Penguins
☐ 482 Doug Wilson .... .08 .04 .01
San Jose Sharks
☐ 483 Jeff Odgers .... .05 .02 .01
San Jose Sharks
☐ 484 Stephane Quintal................ .05 .02 .01
St. Louis Blues
☐ 485 Christian Ruuttu .... .05 .02 .01
Buffalo Sabres
☐ 486 Paul Ranheim .... .05 .02 .01
Calgary Flames
☐ 487 Craig Wolanin .... .05 .02 .01
Quebec Nordiques
☐ 488 Rob DiMaio .... .05 .02 .01
New York Islanders
☐ 489 Shawn Cronin .... .05 .02 .01
Winnipeg Jets
☐ 490 Kirk Muller .... .08 .04 .01
Montreal Canadiens
☐ 491 Patrick Roy .... .25 .11 .03
Leader
Save Percentage
Montreal Canadiens
☐ 492 Rich Pilon .... .05 .02 .01
New York Islanders
☐ 493 Pat Verbeek .... .08 .04 .01
Hartford Whalers
☐ 494 Ken Wregget .... .05 .02 .01
Pittsburgh Penguins
☐ 495 Joe Sakic .... .20 .09 .03
Quebec Nordiques
☐ 496 Zdeno Ciger .... .05 .02 .01
New Jersey Devils
☐ 497 Steve Larmer...................... .08 .04 .01
Chicago Blackhawks
☐ 498 Calle Johansson .... .05 .02 .01
Washington Capitals
☐ 499 Trevor Linden...................... .20 .09 .03
Vancouver Canucks
☐ 500 John LeClair....................... .05 .02 .01
Montreal Canadiens
☐ 501 Bryan Marchment .... .05 .02 .01
Chicago Blackhawks
☐ 502 Todd Krygier .... .05 .02 .01
Washington Capitals
☐ 503 Tom Barrasso .... .08 .04 .01
Pittsburgh Penguins
☐ 504 Mario Lemieux .... .25 .11 .03
Points Leader
Pittsburgh Penguins
☐ 505 Daniel Berthiaume UER .... .05 .02 .01
(Headings on back
are for skaters)
Boston Bruins
☐ 506 Jamie Baker .... .05 .02 .01
Quebec Nordiques
☐ 507 Greg Adams .... .05 .02 .01
Vancouver Canucks
☐ 508 Patrick Roy .... .50 .23 .06
Montreal Canadiens
☐ 509 Kris King .... .05 .02 .01
New York Rangers
☐ 510 Jyrki Lumme .... .05 .02 .01
Vancouver Canucks
☐ 511 Darin Kimble .... .05 .02 .01
Tampa Bay Lightning
☐ 512 Igor Larionov .... .08 .04 .01
Vancouver Canucks
☐ 513 Martin Brodeur.................... .40 .18 .05
New Jersey Devils
☐ 514 Denny Felsner .... .15 .07 .02
St. Louis Blues
☐ 515 Yanic Dupre .... .05 .02 .01
Philadelphia Flyers

☐ 516 Bill Guerin .... .20 .09 .03
New Jersey Devils
☐ 517 Bret Hedican UER............... .15 .07 .02
(Misspelled Brett
on both sides)
St. Louis Blues
☐ 518 Mike Hartman .... .05 .02 .01
Winnipeg Jets
☐ 519 Steve Heinze UER............... .05 .02 .01
(Photo actually
Gord Hynes)
Boston Bruins
☐ 520 Frantisek Kucera .... .05 .02 .01
Chicago Blackhawks
☐ 521 Dave Reid .... .05 .02 .01
Boston Bruins
☐ 522 Frank Pietrangelo .... .05 .02 .01
Hartford Whalers
☐ 523 Martin Rucinsky.................. .15 .07 .02
Quebec Nordiques
☐ 524 Tony Hrkac......................... .05 .02 .01
Chicago Blackhawks
☐ 525 Checklist 1-132 .... .05 .02 .01
☐ 526 Checklist 133-264 .... .05 .02 .01
☐ 527 Checklist 265-396 .... .05 .02 .01
☐ 528 Checklist 397-528 UER ...... .05 .02 .01
(529 not listed)
☐ 529 Eric Lindros UER................ 4.00 1.80 .50
(Acquired 6-30-92,
not 6-20-92)
Philadelphia Flyers

1992-93 Topps Gold

 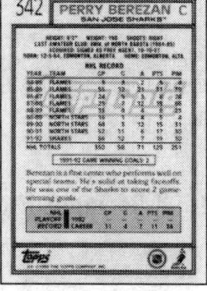

The 1992-93 Topps Gold hockey set consists of 529 standard-size (2 1/2" by 3 1/2") cards. The cards are identical in design to the regular series, except that the name plaque on the front is in gold foil. One Topps Gold card was inserted in each wax pack, while three gold cards were included in each jumbo pack and 20 per factory set. Player cards that replaced the regular series checklist cards are listed below. Cards 525-528 are player cards as opposed to checklists in the basic Topps issue.

	MINT	EXC	G-VG
COMPLETE SET (529)......................	400.00	180.00	50.00
COMMON PLAYER (1G-529G)...........	.30	.14	.04

*UNLISTED VETERAN STARS: 5X to 10X VALUE
*UNLISTED YOUNG STARS: 3X to 6X VALUE
*UNLISTED RCs: 2X to 4X VALUE....

☐ 1G Wayne Gretzky..................... 40.00 18.00 5.00
Los Angeles Kings
☐ 2G Brett Hull.......................... 18.00 8.00 2.30
St. Louis Blues
☐ 3G Felix Potvin 18.00 8.00 2.30
Toronto Maple Leafs
☐ 90G Rod Brind'Amour HOR 8.00 3.60 1.00
Philadelphia Flyers
☐ 110G Goals Against 9.00 4.00 1.15
Average Leader
Patrick Roy
Montreal Canadiens
☐ 122G Doug Gilmour 8.00 3.60 1.00
Toronto Maple Leafs

☐ 123G Wayne Gretzky..................	9.00	4.00	1.15
Assists Leader			
Los Angeles Kings			
☐ 144G Dmitri Mironov...............	4.00	1.80	.50
Toronto Maple Leafs			
☐ 164G Dave Andreychuk HOR	12.00	5.50	1.50
Buffalo Sabres			
☐ 195G Don Beaupre HOR	8.00	3.60	1.00
Washington Capitals			
☐ 207G Steve Yzerman..................	6.00	2.70	.75
Detroit Red Wings			
☐ 212G Mario Lemieux..................	25.00	11.50	3.10
Pittsburgh Penguins			
☐ 222G Steve Thomas..................	4.00	1.80	.50
New York Islanders			
☐ 229G Tony Amonte....................	4.00	1.80	.50
New York Rangers			
☐ 263G Patrick Roy AS................	9.00	4.00	1.15
Montreal Canadiens			
☐ 265G Mario Lemieux AS	6.00	2.70	.75
Pittsburgh Penguins			
☐ 274G Mark Messier....................	8.00	3.60	1.00
New York Rangers			
☐ 345G Pat LaFontaine.................	5.00	2.30	.60
Buffalo Sabres			
☐ 353G Pavel Bure	20.00	9.00	2.50
Vancouver Canucks			
☐ 365G Joe Juneau UER	15.00	6.75	1.90
(Shoots left, not right)			
Boston Bruins			
☐ 366G Scott Lachance HOR........	8.00	3.60	1.00
New York Islanders			
☐ 491G Patrick Roy	9.00	4.00	1.15
Leader			
Save Percentage			
Montreal Canadiens			
☐ 497G Steve Larmer...................	4.00	1.80	.50
Chicago Blackhawks			
☐ 504G Mario Lemieux.................	6.00	2.70	.75
Points Leader			
Pittsburgh Penguins			
☐ 508G Patrick Roy HOR..............	25.00	11.50	3.10
Montreal Canadiens			
☐ 513G Martin Brodeur	7.00	3.10	.85
New Jersey Devils			
☐ 529G Eric Lindros.....................	40.00	18.00	5.00
Philadelphia Flyers			

1993-94 Topps Premier Promo Sheet

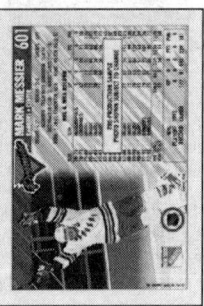

This nine-card promo sheet measures approximately 7 3/4" by 10 3/4" and features white-bordered color player photos on the front. The player's name and position appear at the bottom of each card within a team color-coded stripe, and the Premier logo is displayed in the lower left. The horizontal backs carry color player action shots on their left sides. At the top, the player's name, uniform number, team, and position appear within a team color-coded stripe. Below this, and to the right of the player photo, appear the player's biography and stats on a background that resembles white ruffled silk. The team, NHL, and NHLPA logos in the lower left round out the back. The cards are numbered on the back.

	MINT	EXC	G-VG
COMPLETE SET (9)...........................	4.00	1.60	.40
COMMON PLAYER..........................	.25	.10	.02
☐ 1 Patrick Roy	1.50	.60	.15
Montreal Canadiens			
☐ 15 Mike Vernon......................	.35	.14	.03
Calgary Flames			
☐ 22 Jamie Baker	.25	.10	.02
Ottawa Senators			
☐ 100 Theoren Fleury....................	.35	.14	.03
Calgary Flames			
☐ 156 Geoff Sanderson	.50	.20	.05
Hartford Whalers			
☐ 244 Dave Lowry........................	.25	.10	.02
Florida Panthers			
☐ 257 Scott Lachance	.35	.14	.03
New York Islanders			
☐ 601 Mark Messier.....................	.75	.30	.07
New York Rangers			
☐ 602 Ray Bourque	.50	.20	.05
Boston Bruins			

1993-94 Topps/OPC Premier

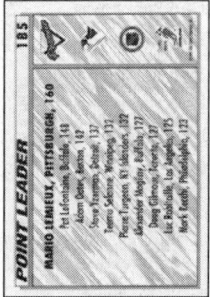

Both series of the 1993-94 Topps (and O-Pee-Chee) Premier hockey set consisted of 264 standard-size (2 1/2" by 3 1/2") cards. The fronts feature white-bordered color player photos. The player's name and position appear at the bottom of each card within a team color-coded stripe, and the Premier logo is displayed in the lower left. The horizontal backs carry color player action shots on their left sides. At the top, the player's name, uniform number, team, and position appear within a team color-coded stripe. Below this, and to the right of the player photo, appear the player's biography and stats on a background that resembles white ruffled silk. The team, NHL, and NHLPA logos in the lower left round out the back. The cards are numbered on the back. Topical subsets featured are Super Rookies (121-130), and 1st Team All-Stars, 2nd Team All-Stars, and League Leaders scattered throughout the set. Except for some information in French on the backs, the 1993-94 O-Pee-Chee Premier set is identical to the 1993-94 Topps Premier set but carry a premium of up to 1.25 times the prices below. Every 12-card pack included 11 regular cards plus one Premier Gold card. One in four packs featured ten regular cards plus two Premier Gold cards. Four gold cards were inserted in every Topps jumbo pack. Moreover, Black Gold cards were randomly inserted at a rate of one per 36 Topps and O-Pee-Chee packs.

	MINT	EXC	G-VG
COMPLETE SET (528)......................	30.00	13.50	3.80
COMPLETE SERIES 1 (264)..............	15.00	6.75	1.90
COMPLETE SERIES 2 (264)..............	15.00	6.75	1.90
COMMON PLAYER (1-264)................	.05	.02	.01
COMMON PLAYER (265-528)............	.05	.02	.01
*OPC VALUED: 1X to 1.25X.............			

□	#	Player			
□	1	Patrick Roy	.50	.23	.06
		Montreal Canadiens			
□	2	Alexei Zhitnik	.05	.02	.01
		Los Angeles Kings			
□	3	Uwe Krupp	.05	.02	.01
		New York Islanders			
□	4	Todd Gill	.05	.02	.01
		Toronto Maple Leafs			
□	5	Paul Stanton	.05	.02	.01
		Pittsburgh Penguins			
□	6	Sergio Momesso	.05	.02	.01
		Vancouver Canucks			
□	7	Dale Hawerchuk	.08	.04	.01
		Buffalo Sabres			
□	8	Kevin Miller	.05	.02	.01
		St. Louis Blues			
□	9	Nicklas Lidstrom	.08	.04	.01
		Detroit Red Wings			
□	10	Joe Sakic	.15	.07	.02
		Quebec Nordiques			
□	11	Thomas Steen	.05	.02	.01
		Winnipeg Jets			
□	12	Peter Bondra	.08	.04	.01
		Washington Capitals			
□	13	Brian Noonan	.05	.02	.01
		Chicago Blackhawks			
□	14	Glen Featherstone	.05	.02	.01
		Boston Bruins			
□	15	Mike Vernon	.08	.04	.01
		Calgary Flames			
□	16	Janne Ojanen	.05	.02	.01
		New Jersey Devils			
□	17	Neil Brady	.05	.02	.01
		Ottawa Senators			
□	18	Dimitri Yushkevich	.05	.02	.01
		Philadelphia Flyers			
□	19	Rob Zamuner	.05	.02	.01
		Tampa Bay Lightning			
□	20	Zarley Zalapski	.05	.02	.01
		Hartford Whalers			
□	21	Mike Sullivan	.05	.02	.01
		San Jose Sharks			
□	22	Jamie Baker	.05	.02	.01
		Ottawa Senators			
□	23	Craig MacTavish	.05	.02	.01
		Edmonton Oilers			
□	24	Mark Tinordi	.05	.02	.01
		Minnesota North Stars			
□	25	Brian Leetch	.20	.09	.03
		New York Rangers			
□	26	Brian Skrudland	.05	.02	.01
		Calgary Flames			
□	27	Keith Tkachuk	.15	.07	.02
		Winnipeg Jets			
□	28	Patrick Flatley	.05	.02	.01
		New York Islanders			
□	29	Doug Bodger	.05	.02	.01
		Buffalo Sabres			
□	30	Felix Potvin	.60	.25	.08
		Toronto Maple Leafs			
□	31	Shawn Antoski	.05	.02	.01
		Vancouver Canucks			
□	32	Eric Desjardins	.05	.02	.01
		Montreal Canadiens			
□	33	Mike Donnelly	.05	.02	.01
		Los Angeles Kings			
□	34	Kjell Samuelsson	.05	.02	.01
		Pittsburgh Penguins			
□	35	Nelson Emerson	.08	.04	.01
		St. Louis Blues			
□	36	Phil Housley	.08	.04	.01
		Winnipeg Jets			
□	37	Mario Lemieux	.25	.11	.03
		Pittsburgh Penguins			
□	38	Shayne Corson	.05	.02	.01
		Edmonton Oilers			
□	39	Steve Smith	.05	.02	.01
		Chicago Blackhawks			
□	40	Bob Kudelski	.08	.04	.01
		Ottawa Senators			
□	41	Joe Cirella	.05	.02	.01
		New York Rangers			
□	42	Sergei Nemchinov	.05	.02	.01
		New York Rangers			
□	43	Kerry Huffman	.05	.02	.01
		Quebec Nordiques			
□	44	Bob Beers	.05	.02	.01
		Tampa Bay Lightning			
□	45	Al Iafrate	.08	.04	.01
		Washington Capitals			
□	46	Mike Modano	.20	.09	.03
		Minnesota North Stars			
□	47	Pat Verbeek	.08	.04	.01
		Hartford Whalers			
□	48	Joel Otto	.05	.02	.01
		Calgary Flames			
□	49	Dino Ciccarelli	.08	.04	.01
		Detroit Red Wings			
□	50	Adam Oates	.15	.07	.02
		Boston Bruins			
□	51	Pat Elynuik	.05	.02	.01
		Washington Capitals			
□	52	Bobby Holik	.05	.02	.01
		New Jersey Devils			
□	53	Johan Garpenlov	.05	.02	.01
		San Jose Sharks			
□	54	Jeff Beukeboom	.05	.02	.01
		New York Rangers			
□	55	Tommy Soderstrom	.15	.07	.02
		Philadelphia Flyers			
□	56	Rob Blake	.08	.04	.01
		Los Angeles Kings			
□	57	Marty McInnis	.05	.02	.01
		New York Islanders			
□	58	Dixon Ward	.05	.02	.01
		Vancouver Canucks			
□	59	Patrice Brisebois	.05	.02	.01
		Montreal Canadiens			
□	60	Ed Belfour	.15	.07	.02
		Chicago Blackhawks			
□	61	Donald Audette	.05	.02	.01
		Buffalo Sabres			
□	62	Mike Ricci	.08	.04	.01
		Quebec Nordiques			
□	63	Fredrik Olausson	.05	.02	.01
		Winnipeg Jets			
□	64	Norm Maciver	.05	.02	.01
		Ottawa Senators			
□	65	Andrew Cassels	.05	.02	.01
		Hartford Whalers			
□	66	Tim Cheveldae	.08	.04	.01
		Detroit Red Wings			
□	67	Dave Reid	.05	.02	.01
		Boston Bruins			
□	68	Philippe Bozon	.05	.02	.01
		St. Louis Blues			
□	69	Drake Berehowsky	.05	.02	.01
		Toronto Maple Leafs			
□	70	Tony Amonte	.05	.02	.01
		New York Rangers			
□	71	Dave Manson	.05	.02	.01
		Edmonton Oilers			
□	72	Rick Tocchet	.08	.04	.01
		Pittsburgh Penguins			
□	73	Steve Kasper	.05	.02	.01
		Philadelphia Flyers			
□	74	Adam Oates	.05	.02	.01
		Assist Leader			
		Boston Bruins			
□	75	Ulf Dahlen	.05	.02	.01
		Minnesota North Stars			
□	76	Chris Lindberg	.05	.02	.01
		Calgary Flames			
□	77	Doug Wilson	.08	.04	.01
		San Jose Sharks			
□	78	Mike Ridley	.08	.04	.01
		Washington Capitals			
□	79	Viacheslav Butsayev	.05	.02	.01
		Philadelphia Flyers			
□	80	Scott Stevens	.08	.04	.01
		New Jersey Devils			
□	81	Cliff Ronning	.05	.02	.01
		Vancouver Canucks			
□	82	Andrei Lomakin	.05	.02	.01
		Philadelphia Flyers			
□	83	Shawn Burr	.05	.02	.01
		Detroit Red Wings			
□	84	Benoit Brunet	.05	.02	.01
		Montreal Canadiens			
□	85	Valeri Kamensky	.15	.07	.02
		Quebec Nordiques			
□	86	Randy Carlyle	.05	.02	.01
		Winnipeg Jets			
□	87	Chris Joseph	.05	.02	.01
		Edmonton Oilers			
□	88	Dirk Graham	.05	.02	.01
		Chicago Blackhawks			
□	89	Ken Sutton	.05	.02	.01
		Buffalo Sabres			
□	90	Luc Robitaille	.05	.02	.01
		Los Angeles Kings			
□	91	Mario Lemieux	.25	.11	.03
		Pittsburgh Penguins			
□	92	Teemu Selanne	.30	.14	.04
		Winnipeg Jets			
□	93	Ray Bourque	.05	.02	.01
		Boston Bruins			

☐ 94	Chris Chelios	.08	.04	.01
	Chicago Blackhawks			
☐ 95	Ed Belfour	.05	.02	.01
	Chicago Blackhawks			
☐ 96	Keith Jones	.05	.02	.01
	Washington Capitals			
☐ 97	Sylvain Turgeon	.05	.02	.01
	Ottawa Senators			
☐ 98	Jim Johnson	.05	.02	.01
	Minnesota North Stars			
☐ 99	Mikael Nylander	.15	.07	.02
	Hartford Whalers			
☐ 100	Theoren Fleury	.10	.05	.01
	Calgary Flames			
☐ 101	Shawn Chambers	.05	.02	.01
	Tampa Bay Lightning			
☐ 102	Alexander Semak	.05	.02	.01
	New Jersey Devils			
☐ 103	Ron Sutter	.05	.02	.01
	St. Louis Blues			
☐ 104	Glenn Anderson	.08	.04	.01
	Toronto Maple Leafs			
☐ 105	Jaromir Jagr	.35	.16	.04
	Pittsburgh Penguins			
☐ 106	Adam Graves	.20	.09	.03
	New York Rangers			
☐ 107	Nikolai Borschevsky	.15	.07	.02
	Toronto Maple Leafs			
☐ 108	Vladimir Konstantinov	.05	.02	.01
	Detroit Red Wings			
☐ 109	Robb Stauber	.05	.02	.01
	Los Angeles Kings			
☐ 110	Arturs Irbe	.10	.05	.01
	San Jose Sharks			
☐ 111	G.A.A.Leader	.30	.14	.04
	Felix Potvin			
	Toronto Maple Leafs			
☐ 112	Darius Kasparaitis	.05	.02	.01
	New York Islanders			
☐ 113	Kirk McLean	.10	.05	.01
	Vancouver Canucks			
☐ 114	Glen Wesley	.05	.02	.01
	Boston Bruins			
☐ 115	Rod Brind'Amour	.10	.05	.01
	Philadelphia Flyers			
☐ 116	Mike Eagles	.05	.02	.01
	Winnipeg Jets			
☐ 117	Brian Bradley	.05	.02	.01
	Tampa Bay Lightning			
☐ 118	Dave Christian	.05	.02	.01
	Chicago Blackhawks			
☐ 119	Randy Wood	.05	.02	.01
	Buffalo Sabres			
☐ 120	Craig Janney	.10	.05	.01
	Boston Bruins			
☐ 121	Eric Lindros	.75	.35	.09
	Philadelphia Flyers			
☐ 122	Tommy Soderstrom	.08	.04	.01
	Philadelphia Flyers			
☐ 123	Shawn McEachern	.08	.04	.01
	Pittsburgh Penguins			
☐ 124	Andrei Kovalenko	.08	.04	.01
	Quebec Nordiques			
☐ 125	Joe Juneau	.25	.11	.03
	Boston Bruins			
☐ 126	Felix Potvin	.30	.14	.04
	Toronto Maple Leafs			
☐ 127	Dixon Ward	.08	.04	.01
	Vancouver Canucks			
☐ 128	Alexei Zhamnov	.15	.07	.02
	Winnipeg Jets			
☐ 129	Vladimir Malakhov	.11	.05	.01
	New York Islanders			
☐ 130	Teemu Selanne	.50	.23	.06
	Winnipeg Jets			
☐ 131	Neal Broten	.08	.04	.01
	Minnesota North Stars			
☐ 132	Ulf Samuelsson	.08	.04	.01
	Pittsburgh Penguins			
☐ 133	Mark Janssens	.05	.02	.01
	Hartford Whalers			
☐ 134	Claude Lemieux	.08	.04	.01
	New Jersey Devils			
☐ 135	Mike Richter	.15	.07	.02
	New York Rangers			
☐ 136	Doug Weight	.08	.04	.01
	Edmonton Oilers			
☐ 137	Rob Pearson	.05	.02	.01
	Toronto Maple Leafs			
☐ 138	Sylvain Cote	.05	.02	.01
	Washington Capitals			
☐ 139	Mike Keane	.05	.02	.01
	Montreal Canadiens			
☐ 140	Benoit Hogue	.05	.02	.01
	New York Islanders			
☐ 141	Michel Petit	.05	.02	.01
	Calgary Flames			
☐ 142	Mark Freer	.05	.02	.01
	Ottawa Senators			
☐ 143	Doug Zmolek	.05	.02	.01
	San Jose Sharks			
☐ 144	Tony Granato	.05	.02	.01
	Los Angeles Kings			
☐ 145	Paul Coffey	.15	.07	.02
	Detroit Red Wings			
☐ 146	Ted Donato	.05	.02	.01
	Boston Bruins			
☐ 147	Brent Sutter	.08	.04	.01
	Chicago Blackhawks			
☐ 148	Goal Scoring Leader	.20	.09	.03
	Alexander Mogilny			
	Buffalo Sabres			
	Teemu Selanne			
	Winnipeg Jets			
☐ 149	James Patrick	.05	.02	.01
	New York Rangers			
☐ 150	Mikael Andersson	.05	.02	.01
	Tampa Bay Lightning			
☐ 151	Steve Duchesne	.08	.04	.01
	Quebec Nordiques			
☐ 152	Terry Carkner	.05	.02	.01
	Philadelphia Flyers			
☐ 153	Russ Courtnall	.08	.04	.01
	Minnesota North Stars			
☐ 154	Brian Mullen	.08	.04	.01
	New York Islanders			
☐ 155	Martin Straka	.25	.11	.03
	Pittsburgh Penguins			
☐ 156	Geoff Sanderson	.15	.07	.02
	Hartford Whalers			
☐ 157	Mark Howe	.08	.04	.01
	Detroit Red Wings			
☐ 158	Stephane Richer	.08	.04	.01
	New Jersey Devils			
☐ 159	Doug Crossman	.05	.02	.01
	St. Louis Blues			
☐ 160	John Vanbiesbrouck	.10	.05	.01
	New York Rangers			
☐ 161	Bob Essensa	.08	.04	.01
	Winnipeg Jets			
☐ 162	Wayne Presley	.05	.02	.01
	Buffalo Sabres			
☐ 163	Mathieu Schneider	.08	.04	.01
	Montreal Canadiens			
☐ 164	Jiri Slegr	.05	.02	.01
	Vancouver Canucks			
☐ 165	Stephane Fiset	.05	.02	.01
	Quebec Nordiques			
☐ 166	Wendell Young	.05	.02	.01
	Tampa Bay Lightning			
☐ 167	Kevin Dineen	.08	.04	.01
	Philadelphia Flyers			
☐ 168	Sandis Ozolinsh	.15	.07	.02
	San Jose Sharks			
☐ 169	Mike Krushelnyski	.05	.02	.01
	Toronto Maple Leafs			
☐ 170	Kevin Stevens	.05	.02	.01
	Pittsburgh Penguins			
☐ 171	Pat LaFontaine	.05	.02	.01
	Buffalo Sabres			
☐ 172	Alexander Mogilny	.15	.07	.02
	Buffalo Sabres			
☐ 173	Larry Murphy	.08	.04	.01
	Pittsburgh Penguins			
☐ 174	Al Iafrate	.08	.04	.01
	Washington Capitals			
☐ 175	Tom Barrasso	.08	.04	.01
	Pittsburgh Penguins			
☐ 176	Derek King	.05	.02	.01
	New York Islanders			
☐ 177	Bob Probert	.05	.02	.01
	Detroit Red Wings			
☐ 178	Gary Suter	.08	.04	.01
	Calgary Flames			
☐ 179	David Shaw	.05	.02	.01
	Boston Bruins			
☐ 180	Luc Robitaille	.15	.07	.02
	Los Angeles Kings			
☐ 181	John LeClair	.05	.02	.01
	Montreal Canadiens			
☐ 182	Troy Murray	.05	.02	.01
	Chicago Blackhawks			
☐ 183	Dave Gagner	.08	.04	.01
	Minnesota North Stars			
☐ 184	Darcy Loewen	.05	.02	.01
	Ottawa Senators			

☐ 185 Point Leader	.25	.11	.03
Mario Lemieux			
Pittsburgh Penguins			
☐ 186 Pat Jablonski	.05	.02	.01
Tampa Bay Lightning			
☐ 187 Alexei Kovalev	.30	.14	.04
New York Rangers			
☐ 188 Todd Krygier	.05	.02	.01
Washington Capitals			
☐ 189 Larry Murphy	.08	.04	.01
Pittsburgh Penguins			
☐ 190 Pierre Turgeon	.15	.07	.02
New York Islanders			
☐ 191 Craig Ludwig	.05	.02	.01
Minnesota North Stars			
☐ 192 Brad May	.05	.02	.01
Buffalo Sabres			
☐ 193 John MacLean	.08	.04	.01
New Jersey Devils			
☐ 194 Ron Wilson	.05	.02	.01
St. Louis Blues			
☐ 195 Eric Weinrich	.05	.02	.01
Hartford Whalers			
☐ 196 Steve Chiasson	.05	.02	.01
Detroit Red Wings			
☐ 197 Dmitri Kvartalnov	.05	.02	.01
Boston Bruins			
☐ 198 Andrei Kovalenko	.05	.02	.01
Quebec Nordiques			
☐ 199 Rob Gaudreau	.15	.07	.02
San Jose Sharks			
☐ 200 Evgeny Davydov	.05	.02	.01
Winnipeg Jets			
☐ 201 Adrien Plavsic	.05	.02	.01
Vancouver Canucks			
☐ 202 Brian Bellows	.08	.04	.01
Montreal Canadiens			
☐ 203 Doug Evans	.05	.02	.01
Philadelphia Flyers			
☐ 204 Win Leader	.05	.02	.01
Tom Barrasso			
Pittsburgh Penguins			
☐ 205 Joe Nieuwendyk	.08	.04	.01
Calgary Flames			
☐ 206 Jari Kurri	.10	.05	.01
Los Angeles Kings			
☐ 207 Bob Rouse	.05	.02	.01
Toronto Maple Leafs			
☐ 208 Yvon Corriveau	.05	.02	.01
Hartford Whalers			
☐ 209 John Blue	.05	.02	.01
Boston Bruins			
☐ 210 Dimitri Khristich	.08	.04	.01
Washington Capitals			
☐ 211 Brent Fedyk	.05	.02	.01
Philadelphia Flyers			
☐ 212 Jody Hull	.05	.02	.01
Ottawa Senators			
☐ 213 Chris Terreri	.08	.04	.01
New Jersey Devils			
☐ 214 Mike McPhee	.05	.02	.01
Minnesota North Stars			
☐ 215 Chris Kontos	.05	.02	.01
Tampa Bay Lightning			
☐ 216 Greg Gilbert	.05	.02	.01
Chicago Blackhawks			
☐ 217 Sergei Zubov	.35	.16	.04
New York Rangers			
☐ 218 Grant Fuhr	.08	.04	.01
Buffalo Sabres			
☐ 219 Charlie Huddy	.05	.02	.01
Los Angeles Kings			
☐ 220 Mario Lemieux	.75	.35	.09
Pittsburgh Penguins			
☐ 221 Sheldon Kennedy	.05	.02	.01
Detroit Red Wings			
☐ 222 Save PCT.Leader	.05	.02	.01
Curtis Joseph			
St. Louis Blues			
☐ 223 Brad Dalgarno	.05	.02	.01
New York Islanders			
☐ 224 Bret Hedican	.05	.02	.01
St. Louis Blues			
☐ 225 Trevor Linden	.10	.05	.01
Vancouver Canucks			
☐ 226 Darryl Sydor	.08	.04	.01
Los Angeles Kings			
☐ 227 Jayson More	.05	.02	.01
San Jose Sharks			
☐ 228 Dave Poulin	.05	.02	.01
Boston Bruins			
☐ 229 Frantisek Musil	.05	.02	.01
Calgary Flames			
☐ 230 Mark Recchi	.15	.07	.02
Philadelphia Flyers			
☐ 231 Craig Simpson	.05	.02	.01
Edmonton Oilers			
☐ 232 Gino Cavallini	.05	.02	.01
Quebec Nordiques			
☐ 233 Vincent Damphousse	.08	.04	.01
Montreal Canadiens			
☐ 234 Luciano Borsato	.05	.02	.01
Winnipeg Jets			
☐ 235 Dave Andreychuk	.10	.05	.01
Toronto Maple Leafs			
☐ 236 Ken Daneyko	.05	.02	.01
New Jersey Devils			
☐ 237 Chris Chelios	.08	.04	.01
Chicago Blackhawks			
☐ 238 Andrew McBain	.05	.02	.01
Ottawa Senators			
☐ 239 Rick Tabaracci	.05	.02	.01
Winnipeg Jets			
☐ 240 Steve Larmer	.08	.04	.01
Chicago Blackhawks			
☐ 241 Sean Burke	.08	.04	.01
Hartford Whalers			
☐ 242 Rob DiMaio	.05	.02	.01
Tampa Bay Lightning			
☐ 243 Jim Paek	.05	.02	.01
Pittsburgh Penguins			
☐ 244 Dave Lowry	.05	.02	.01
St. Louis Blues			
☐ 245 Alexander Mogilny	.30	.14	.04
Buffalo Sabres			
☐ 246 Darren Turcotte	.05	.02	.01
New York Rangers			
☐ 247 Brendan Shanahan	.15	.07	.02
St. Louis Blues			
☐ 248 Peter Taglianetti	.05	.02	.01
Pittsburgh Penguins			
☐ 249 Scott Mellanby	.05	.02	.01
Edmonton Oilers			
☐ 250 Guy Carbonneau	.08	.04	.01
Montreal Canadiens			
☐ 251 Claude LaPointe	.05	.02	.01
Quebec Nordiques			
☐ 252 Pat Conacher	.05	.02	.01
Los Angeles Kings			
☐ 253 Roger Johansson	.05	.02	.01
Calgary Flames			
☐ 254 Cam Neely	.08	.04	.01
Boston Bruins			
☐ 255 Garry Galley	.05	.02	.01
Philadelphia Flyers			
☐ 256 Keith Primeau	.08	.04	.01
Detroit Red Wings			
☐ 257 Scott Lachance	.05	.02	.01
New York Islanders			
☐ 258 Bill Ranford	.08	.04	.01
Edmonton Oilers			
☐ 259 Pat Fallon	.05	.02	.01
San Jose Sharks			
☐ 260 Pavel Bure	1.00	.45	.13
Vancouver Canucks			
☐ 261 Darrin Shannon	.05	.02	.01
Winnipeg Jets			
☐ 262 Mike Foligno	.05	.02	.01
Toronto Maple Leafs			
☐ 263 Checklist 1-132	.05	.02	.01
☐ 264 Checklist 133-264	.05	.02	.01
☐ 265 Peter Douris	.05	.02	.01
Anaheim Mighty Ducks			
☐ 266 Warren Rychel	.05	.02	.01
Los Angeles Kings			
☐ 267 Owen Nolan	.08	.04	.01
Quebec Nordiques			
☐ 268 Mark Osborne	.05	.02	.01
Toronto Maple Leafs			
☐ 269 Teppo Numminen	.05	.02	.01
Winnipeg Jets			
☐ 270 Rob Niedermayer	.35	.16	.04
Florida Panthers			
☐ 271 Mark Lamb	.05	.02	.01
Edmonton Oilers			
☐ 272 Curtis Joseph	.15	.07	.02
St. Louis Blues			
☐ 273 Joe Murphy	.05	.02	.01
Chicago Blackhawks			
☐ 274 Bernie Nicholls	.08	.04	.01
New Jersey Devils			
☐ 275 Gord Roberts	.05	.02	.01
Florida Panthers			
☐ 276 Al MacInnis	.10	.05	.01
Calgary Flames			
☐ 277 Ken Wregget	.05	.02	.01

Pittsburgh Penguins
☐ 278 Calle Johansson	.05	.02	.01

Washington Capitals
☐ 279 Tom Kurvers	.05	.02	.01

New York Islanders
☐ 280 Steve Yzerman	.25	.11	.03

Detroit Red Wings
☐ 281 Roman Hamrlik	.15	.07	.02

Tampa Bay Lightning
☐ 282 Esa Tikkanen	.08	.04	.01

New York Rangers
☐ 283 Darrin Madeley	.10	.05	.01

Ottawa Senators
☐ 284 Robert Dirk	.05	.02	.01

Vancouver Canucks
☐ 285 Derek Plante	.40	.18	.05

Buffalo Sabres
☐ 286 Ron Tugnutt	.05	.02	.01

Anaheim Mighty Ducks
☐ 287 Frank Pietrangelo	.05	.02	.01

Hartford Whalers
☐ 288 Paul DiPietro	.05	.02	.01

Montreal Canadiens
☐ 289 Alexander Godynyuk	.05	.02	.01

Hartford Whalers
☐ 290 Kirk Maltby	.10	.05	.01

Edmonton Oilers
☐ 291 Olaf Kolzig	.05	.02	.01

Washington Capitals
☐ 292 Vitali Karamnov	.05	.02	.01

St. Louis Blues
☐ 293 Alexei Gusarov	.05	.02	.01

Quebec Nordiques
☐ 294 Bryan Erickson	.05	.02	.01

Winnipeg Jets
☐ 295 Jocelyn Lemieux	.05	.02	.01

Chicago Blackhawks
☐ 296 Bryan Trottier	.08	.04	.01

Pittsburgh Penguins
☐ 297 Dave Ellett	.05	.02	.01

Toronto Maple Leafs
☐ 298 Tim Watters	.05	.02	.01

Los Angeles Kings
☐ 299 Joe Juneau	.40	.18	.05

Boston Bruins
☐ 300 Steve Thomas	.08	.04	.01

New York Islanders
☐ 301 Mark Greig	.05	.02	.01

Hartford Whalers
☐ 302 Jeff Reese	.05	.02	.01

Calgary Flames
☐ 303 Steven King	.05	.02	.01

Anaheim Mighty Ducks
☐ 304 Don Beaupre	.08	.04	.01

Washington Capitals
☐ 305 Denis Savard	.10	.05	.01

Tampa Bay Lightning
☐ 306 Greg Smyth	.05	.02	.01

Calgary Flames
☐ 307 Jaroslav Modry	.10	.05	.01

New Jersey Devils
☐ 308 Petr Svoboda	.05	.02	.01

Buffalo Sabres
☐ 309 Mike Craig	.05	.02	.01

Dallas Stars
☐ 310 Eric Lindros	1.50	.65	.19

Philadelphia Flyers
☐ 311 Dana Murzyn	.05	.02	.01

Vancouver Canucks
☐ 312 Sean Hill	.05	.02	.01

Anaheim Mighty Ducks
☐ 313 Andre Racicot	.05	.02	.01

Montreal Canadiens
☐ 314 John Vanbiesbrouck	.15	.07	.02

Florida Panthers
☐ 315 Doug Lidster	.05	.02	.01

New York Rangers
☐ 316 Garth Butcher	.05	.02	.01

St. Louis Blues
☐ 317 Alexei Yashin	.50	.23	.06

Ottawa Senators
☐ 318 Sergei Fedorov	.50	.23	.06

Detroit Red Wings
☐ 319 Louie DeBrusk	.05	.02	.01

Edmonton Oilers
☐ 320 Dominik Hasek	.10	.05	.01

Buffalo Sabres
☐ 321 Michal Pivonka	.05	.02	.01

Washington Capitals
☐ 322 Bobby Holik	.05	.02	.01

Hartford Whalers
☐ 323 Roman Hamrlik	.15	.07	.02

Tampa Bay Lightning
☐ 324 Petr Svoboda	.05	.02	.01

Buffalo Sabres
☐ 325 Jaromir Jagr	.35	.16	.04

Pittsburgh Penguins
☐ 326 Steven Finn	.05	.02	.01

Quebec Nordiques
☐ 327 Stephane Richer	.08	.04	.01

New Jersey Devils
☐ 328 Claude Loiselle	.05	.02	.01

New York Islanders
☐ 329 Joe Sacco	.05	.02	.01

Anaheim Mighty Ducks
☐ 330 Wayne Gretzky	1.00	.45	.13

Los Angeles Kings
☐ 331 Sylvain Lefebvre	.05	.02	.01

Toronto Maple Leafs
☐ 332 Sergei Bautin	.05	.02	.01

Winnipeg Jets
☐ 333 Craig Simpson	.05	.02	.01

Buffalo Sabres
☐ 334 Don Sweeney	.05	.02	.01

Boston Bruins
☐ 335 Dominic Roussel	.15	.07	.02

Philadelphia Flyers
☐ 336 Scott Thomas	.10	.05	.01

Buffalo Sabres
☐ 337 Geoff Courtnall	.05	.02	.01

Vancouver Canucks
☐ 338 Tom Fitzgerald	.05	.02	.01

Florida Panthers
☐ 339 Kevin Haller	.05	.02	.01

Buffalo Sabres
☐ 340 Troy Loney	.05	.02	.01

Anaheim Mighty Ducks
☐ 341 Ronnie Stern	.05	.02	.01

Calgary Flames
☐ 342 Mark Astley	.10	.05	.01

Calgary Flames
☐ 343 Jeff Daniels	.05	.02	.01

Pittsburgh Penguins
☐ 344 Marc Bureau	.05	.02	.01

Tampa Bay Lightning
☐ 345 Micah Aivazoff	.10	.05	.01

Detroit Red Wings
☐ 346 Matthew Barnaby	.15	.07	.02

Buffalo Sabres
☐ 347 C.J. Young	.05	.02	.01

Florida Panthers
☐ 348 Dale Craigwell	.05	.02	.01

San Jose Sharks
☐ 349 Ray Ferraro	.05	.02	.01

New York Islanders
☐ 350 Ray Bourque	.15	.07	.02

Boston Bruins
☐ 351 Stu Barnes	.05	.02	.01

Florida Panthers
☐ 352 Allan Conroy	.10	.05	.01

Philadelphia Flyers
☐ 353 Shawn McEachern	.05	.02	.01

Los Angeles Kings
☐ 354 Garry Valk	.05	.02	.01

Anaheim Mighty Ducks
☐ 355 Christian Ruuttu	.05	.02	.01

Chicago Blackhawks
☐ 356 Darren Rumble	.05	.02	.01

Ottawa Senators
☐ 357 Stu Grimson	.05	.02	.01

Anaheim Mighty Ducks
☐ 358 Alexander Karpovtsev	.08	.04	.01

New York Rangers
☐ 359 Wendel Clark	.10	.05	.01

Toronto Maple Leafs
☐ 360 Michal Pivonka	.05	.02	.01

Washington Capitals
☐ 361 Peter Popovic	.10	.05	.01

Montreal Canadiens
☐ 362 Kevin Dahl	.05	.02	.01

Calgary Flames
☐ 363 Jeff Brown	.08	.04	.01

St. Louis Blues
☐ 364 Daren Puppa	.08	.04	.01

Tampa Bay Lightning
☐ 365 Dallas Drake	.15	.07	.02

Detroit Red Wings
☐ 366 Dean McAmmond	.05	.02	.01

Chicago Blackhawks
☐ 367 Martin Rucinsky	.05	.02	.01

Quebec Nordiques
☐ 368 Shane Churla	.05	.02	.01

Dallas Stars
☐ 369 Todd Ewen	.05	.02	.01

Anaheim Mighty Ducks
☐ 370 Kevin Stevens	.20	.09	.03

Pittsburgh Penguins
☐ 371 David Volek	.05	.02	.01

New York Islanders			
☐ 372 J.J. Daigneault	.05	.02	.01
Montreal Canadiens			
☐ 373 Marc Bergevin	.05	.02	.01
Tampa Bay Lightning			
☐ 374 Craig Billington	.05	.02	.01
Ottawa Senators			
☐ 375 Mike Gartner	.10	.05	.01
New York Rangers			
☐ 376 Jimmy Carson	.05	.02	.01
Los Angeles Kings			
☐ 377 Bruce Driver	.05	.02	.01
New Jersey Devils			
☐ 378 Steve Heinze	.05	.02	.01
Boston Bruins			
☐ 379 Patrick Carnback	.10	.05	.01
Anaheim Mighty Ducks			
☐ 380 Wayne Gretzky	.50	.23	.06
Los Angeles Kings			
☐ 381 Jeff Brown	.08	.04	.01
St. Louis Blues			
☐ 382 Gary Roberts	.11	.05	.01
Calgary Flames			
☐ 383 Ray Bourque	.08	.04	.01
Boston Bruins			
☐ 384 Mike Gartner	.08	.04	.01
New York Rangers			
☐ 385 Felix Potvin	.40	.18	.05
Toronto Maple Leafs			
☐ 386 Michel Goulet	.08	.04	.01
Chicago Blackhawks			
☐ 387 Dave Tippett	.05	.02	.01
Pittsburgh Penguins			
☐ 388 Jim Waite	.05	.02	.01
San Jose Sharks			
☐ 389 Yuri Khmylev	.08	.04	.01
Buffalo Sabres			
☐ 390 Doug Gilmour	.25	.11	.03
Toronto Maple Leafs			
☐ 391 Brad McCrimmon	.05	.02	.01
Detroit Red Wings			
☐ 392 Brent Severyn	.10	.05	.01
Florida Panthers			
☐ 393 Jocelyn Thibault	.50	.23	.06
Quebec Nordiques			
☐ 394 Boris Mironov	.05	.02	.01
Winnipeg Jets			
☐ 395 Marty McSorley	.08	.04	.01
Pittsburgh Penguins			
☐ 396 Shaun Van Allen	.05	.02	.01
Edmonton Oilers			
☐ 397 Gary Leeman	.05	.02	.01
Montreal Canadiens			
☐ 398 Ed Olczyk	.05	.02	.01
New York Rangers			
☐ 399 Darcy Wakaluk	.05	.02	.01
Dallas Stars			
☐ 400 Murray Craven	.05	.02	.01
Vancouver Canucks			
☐ 401 Martin Brodeur	.30	.14	.04
New Jersey Devils			
☐ 402 Paul Laus	.10	.05	.01
Florida Panthers			
☐ 403 Bill Houlder	.05	.02	.01
Anaheim Mighty Ducks			
☐ 404 Robert Reichel	.08	.04	.01
Calgary Flames			
☐ 405 Alexandre Daigle	.40	.18	.05
Ottawa Senators			
☐ 406 Brent Thompson	.05	.02	.01
Los Angeles Kings			
☐ 407 Keith Acton	.05	.02	.01
Philadelphia Flyers			
☐ 408 Dave Karpa	.05	.02	.01
Quebec Nordiques			
☐ 409 Igor Korolev	.05	.02	.01
St. Louis Blues			
☐ 410 Chris Gratton	.35	.16	.04
Tampa Bay Lightning			
☐ 411 Vincent Riendeau	.05	.02	.01
Detroit Red Wings			
☐ 412 Darren McCarty	.10	.05	.01
Detroit Red Wings			
☐ 413 Bob Carpenter	.05	.02	.01
Washington Capitals			
☐ 414 Joe Cirella	.05	.02	.01
Florida Panthers			
☐ 415 Stephane Matteau	.05	.02	.01
Chicago Blackhawks			
☐ 416 Jozef Stumpel	.05	.02	.01
Boston Bruins			
☐ 417 Rich Pilon	.05	.02	.01
New York Islanders			
☐ 418 Mattias Norstrom	.10	.05	.01
New York Rangers			
☐ 419 Dmitri Moronov	.05	.02	.01
Toronto Maple Leafs			
☐ 420 Alexei Zhamnov	.25	.11	.03
Winnipeg Jets			
☐ 421 Bill Guerin	.05	.02	.01
New Jersey Devils			
☐ 422 Greg Hawgood	.05	.02	.01
Florida Panthers			
☐ 423 Randy Cunneyworth	.05	.02	.01
Hartford Whalers			
☐ 424 Ron Francis	.08	.04	.01
Pittsburgh Penguins			
☐ 425 Brett Hull	.40	.18	.05
St. Louis Blues			
☐ 426 Tim Sweeney	.05	.02	.01
Anaheim Mighty Ducks			
☐ 427 Mike Rathje	.05	.02	.01
San Jose Sharks			
☐ 428 Dave Babych	.05	.02	.01
Vancouver Canucks			
☐ 429 Chris Tancill	.05	.02	.01
Dallas Stars			
☐ 430 Mark Messier	.15	.07	.02
New York Rangers			
☐ 431 Bob Sweeney	.05	.02	.01
Buffalo Sabres			
☐ 432 Terry Yake	.05	.02	.01
Anaheim Mighty Ducks			
☐ 433 Joe Reekie	.05	.02	.01
Tampa Bay Lightning			
☐ 434 Tomas Sandstrom	.05	.02	.01
Los Angeles Kings			
☐ 435 Kevin Hatcher	.08	.04	.01
Washington Capitals			
☐ 436 Bill Lindsay	.05	.02	.01
Florida Panthers			
☐ 437 Jon Casey	.08	.04	.01
Boston Bruins			
☐ 438 Dennis Vaske	.05	.02	.01
New York Islanders			
☐ 439 Allen Pedersen	.05	.02	.01
Hartford Whalers			
☐ 440 Pavel Bure	.60	.25	.08
Vancouver Canucks			
☐ 441 Sergei Fedorov	.30	.14	.04
Detroit Red Wings			
☐ 442 Arturs Irbe	.20	.09	.03
San Jose Sharks			
☐ 443 Darius Kasparaitis	.05	.02	.01
New York Islanders			
☐ 444 Evgeny Davydov	.05	.02	.01
Florida Panthers			
☐ 445 Vladimir Malakhov	.15	.07	.02
New York Islanders			
☐ 446 Tom Barrasso	.08	.04	.01
Pittsburgh Penguins			
☐ 447 Jeff Norton	.05	.02	.01
San Jose Sharks			
☐ 448 David Emma	.05	.02	.01
New Jersey Devils			
☐ 449 Pelle Eklund	.05	.02	.01
Philadelphia Flyers			
☐ 450 Jeremy Roenick	.35	.16	.04
Chicago Blackhawks			
☐ 451 Jesse Belanger	.15	.07	.02
Florida Panthers			
☐ 452 Vitali Prokhorov	.05	.02	.01
St. Louis Blues			
☐ 453 Arto Blomsten	.05	.02	.01
Winnipeg Jets			
☐ 454 Peter Zezel	.05	.02	.01
Toronto Maple Leafs			
☐ 455 Kelly Kisio	.05	.02	.01
Calgary Flames			
☐ 456 Zdeno Ciger	.05	.02	.01
Edmonton Oilers			
☐ 457 Greg Johnson	.05	.02	.01
Detroit Red Wings			
☐ 458 Dave Archibald	.05	.02	.01
Ottawa Senators			
☐ 459 Vladimir Vujtek	.05	.02	.01
Edmonton Oilers			
☐ 460 Mats Sundin	.20	.09	.03
Quebec Nordiques			
☐ 461 Dan Keczmer	.05	.02	.01
San Jose Sharks			
☐ 462 Stephan Lebeau	.05	.02	.01
Montreal Canadiens			
☐ 463 Dominik Hasek	.10	.05	.01
Buffalo Sabres			
☐ 464 Kevin Lowe	.05	.02	.01
New York Rangers			
☐ 465 Gord Murphy	.05	.02	.01

	Florida Panthers			
☐ 466	Bryan Smolinski................	.30	.14	.04
	Boston Bruins			
☐ 467	Josef Beranek	.08	.04	.01
	Philadelphia Flyers			
☐ 468	Ron Hextall	.08	.04	.01
	New York Islanders			
☐ 469	Randy Ladouceur..............	.05	.02	.01
	Anaheim Mighty Ducks			
☐ 470	Scott Niedermayer	.15	.07	.02
	New Jersey Devils			
☐ 471	Kelly Hrudey....................	.08	.04	.01
	Los Angeles Kings			
☐ 472	Mike Needham	.05	.02	.01
	Pittsburgh Penguins			
☐ 473	John Tucker	.05	.02	.01
	Tampa Bay Lightning			
☐ 474	Kelly Miller	.05	.02	.01
	Washington Capitals			
☐ 475	Jyrki Lumme	.05	.02	.01
	Vancouver Canucks			
☐ 476	Andy Moog	.08	.04	.01
	Dallas Stars			
☐ 477	Glen Murray	.05	.02	.01
	Boston Bruins			
☐ 478	Mark Ferner......................	.10	.05	.01
	Anaheim Mighty Ducks			
☐ 479	John Cullen	.05	.02	.01
	Toronto Maple Leafs			
☐ 480	Gilbert Dionne	.05	.02	.01
	Montreal Canadiens			
☐ 481	Paul Ranheim....................	.05	.02	.01
	Calgary Flames			
☐ 482	Mike Hough.......................	.05	.02	.01
	Florida Panthers			
☐ 483	Teemu Selanne.................	.60	.25	.08
	Winnipeg Jets			
☐ 484	Aaron Ward.......................	.10	.05	.01
	Detroit Red Wings			
☐ 485	Chris Pronger....................	.35	.16	.04
	Hartford Whalers			
☐ 486	Glenn Healy	.05	.02	.01
	New York Rangers			
☐ 487	Curtis Leschyshyn..............	.05	.02	.01
	Quebec Nordiques			
☐ 488	Jim Montgomery................	.10	.05	.01
	St. Louis Blues			
☐ 489	Travis Green.....................	.05	.02	.01
	New York Islanders			
☐ 490	Pat LaFontaine	.20	.09	.03
	Buffalo Sabres			
☐ 491	Bobby Dollas.....................	.10	.05	.01
	Anaheim Mighty Ducks			
☐ 492	Alexei Kasatonov..............	.05	.02	.01
	Anaheim Mighty Ducks			
☐ 493	Corey Millen......................	.05	.02	.01
	New Jersey Devils			
☐ 494	Vyacheslav Kozlov.............	.30	.14	.04
	Detroit Red Wings			
☐ 495	Igor Kravchuk	.05	.02	.01
	Edmonton Oilers			
☐ 496	Dimitri Filimonov...............	.05	.02	.01
	Ottawa Senators			
☐ 497	Jeff Odgers	.05	.02	.01
	San Jose Sharks			
☐ 498	Joe Mullen	.08	.04	.01
	Pittsburgh Penguins			
☐ 499	Gary Shuchuk	.05	.02	.01
	Los Angeles Kings			
☐ 500	Jeremy Roenick	.30	.14	.04
	Chicago Blackhawks			
☐ 501	Tom Barrasso	.05	.02	.01
	Pittsburgh Penguins			
☐ 502	Keith Tkachuk	.12	.05	.02
	Winnipeg Jets			
☐ 503	Phil Housley	.08	.04	.01
	St. Louis Blues			
☐ 504	Tony Granato	.08	.04	.01
	Los Angeles Kings			
☐ 505	Brian Leetch	.15	.07	.02
	New York Rangers			
☐ 506	Anatoli Semenov	.05	.02	.01
	Anaheim Mighty Ducks			
☐ 507	Steve Leach......................	.05	.02	.01
	Boston Bruins			
☐ 508	Brian Skrudland	.05	.02	.01
	Florida Panthers			
☐ 509	Kirk Muller	.08	.04	.01
	Montreal Canadiens			
☐ 510	Gary Roberts	.08	.04	.01
	Calgary Flames			
☐ 511	Gerard Gallant	.05	.02	.01
	Tampa Bay Lightning			
☐ 512	Joey Kocur........................	.05	.02	.01

	New York Rangers			
☐ 513	Tie Domi	.05	.02	.01
	Winnipeg Jets			
☐ 514	Kay Whitmore....................	.05	.02	.01
	Dallas Stars			
☐ 515	Vladimir Malakhov..............	.15	.07	.02
	New York Islanders			
☐ 516	Stewart Malgunas	.10	.05	.01
	Philadelphia Flyers			
☐ 517	Jamie Macoun....................	.05	.02	.01
	Toronto Maple Leafs			
☐ 518	Alan May	.05	.02	.01
	Washington Capitals			
☐ 519	Guy Hebert.......................	.15	.07	.02
	Anaheim Mighty Ducks			
☐ 520	Derian Hatcher	.05	.02	.01
	Dallas Stars			
☐ 521	Richard Smehlik.................	.08	.04	.01
	Buffalo Sabres			
☐ 522	Joby Messier.....................	.10	.05	.01
	New York Rangers			
☐ 523	Trent Klatt	.05	.02	.01
	Dallas Stars			
☐ 524	Tom Chorske......................	.05	.02	.01
	New Jersey Devils			
☐ 525	Iain Fraser.......................	.10	.05	.01
	Quebec Nordiques			
☐ 526	Daniel Laperriere................	.05	.02	.01
	St. Louis Blues			
☐ 527	Checklist	.05	.02	.01
☐ 528	Checklist	.05	.02	.01

1993-94 Topps/OPC Premier Gold

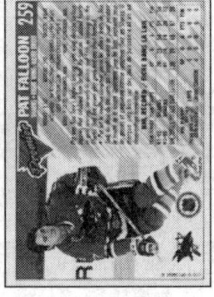

This parallel insert set to the regular issue '93-94 Topps/OPC Premier set comprises 528 standard-size (2 1/2" by 3 1/2") cards. Every regular Premier 12-card pack included 11 regular cards plus one Premier Gold card. Also, one in four packs contained 10 regular cards plus two Premier Gold cards; and four Gold cards were inserted in every Topps jumbo pack. Aside from the gold-foil, the Premier Gold cards are identical to their regular issue counterparts. The four regular issue Premier checklists were replaced by Gold cards of the players listed below. The cards are numbered on the back. Except for some information in French on the backs, the 1993-94 O-Pee-Chee Premier Gold set is identical to the 1993-94 Topps Premier Gold set. Cards 263, 264, 527 and 528 are checklist replacement cards.

	MINT	EXC	G-VG
COMPLETE TOPPS SET (528)	150.00	70.00	19.00
COMPLETE OPC SET (528)...............	240.00	110.00	30.00
COMP.TOPPS SERIES 1 (264)..........	75.00	34.00	9.50
COMP.OPC SERIES 1 (264).............	120.00	55.00	15.00
COMP.TOPPS SERIES 2 (264)..........	75.00	34.00	9.50
COMP.OPC SERIES 2 (264).............	120.00	55.00	15.00
COMMON GOLD (1G-264G).............	.25	.11	.03
COMMON GOLD (265G-528G)...........	.25	.11	.03
*TOPPS VETERAN STARS: 2X to 5X VALUE			
*TOPPS YOUNG STARS: 2X to 4X VALUE			
*TOPPS RCs: 1.5X to 3X VALUE			
*OPC VETERAN STARS: 4X to 7X VALUE			

*OPC YOUNG STARS: 3X to 5X VALUE
*OPC RCs: 2X to 4X VALUE.............

		MINT	EXC	G-VG
☐	263G Martin Lapointe	1.00	.45	.13
	Detroit Red Wings			
☐	264G Kevin Miehm...................	1.00	.45	.13
	St. Louis Blues			
☐	527G Myles O'Connor..............	1.00	.45	.13
	New Jersey Devils			
☐	528G Jamie Leach	1.00	.45	.13
	Pittsburgh Penguins			

1993-94 Topps Premier Black Gold

PAUL COFFEY

Randomly inserted in Topps packs, these 24 standard-size (2 1/2" by 3 1/2") cards feature on their white-bordered fronts color player action shots set on ghosted and darkened backgrounds. Gold foil inner borders at the top and bottom carry multiple Premier Black Gold logos. The player's name appears in white lettering within a black stripe across the lower gold-foil inner margin. The horizontal back carries a color action cutout set on a bluish background on the left. Career highlights appear within a purple area on the right. The player's name and team name appear within a black bar across the top. The cards are numbered on the back. Collectors could also find in packs a Winner Card A, redeemable for the entire 12-card first-series set; a Winner Card B, redeemable for the 12-card second series; and a Winner Card AB, redeemable for the entire 24 card set. The Winner cards expired May 31, 1994.

		MINT	EXC	G-VG
	COMPLETE SET (24)......................	50.00	23.00	6.25
	COMPLETE SERIES 1 (12)...............	25.00	11.50	3.10
	COMPLETE SERIES 2 (12)...............	25.00	11.50	3.10
	COMMON PLAYER (1-12)................	2.00	.90	.25
	COMMON PLAYER (13-24).............	2.00	.90	.25
☐ 1	Teemu Selanne	5.00	2.30	.60
	Winnipeg Jets			
☐ 2	Steve Duchesne	2.00	.90	.25
	Quebec Nordiques			
☐ 3	Felix Potvin	6.00	2.70	.75
	Toronto Maple Leafs			
☐ 4	Shawn McEachern	2.00	.90	.25
	Pittsburgh Penguins			
☐ 5	Adam Oates..........................	2.50	1.15	.30
	Boston Bruins			
☐ 6	Paul Coffey...........................	2.50	1.15	.30
	Detroit Red Wings			
☐ 7	Wayne Gretzky	9.00	4.00	1.15
	Los Angeles Kings			
☐ 8	Alexei Zhamnov.....................	2.50	1.15	.30
	Winnipeg Jets			
☐ 9	Mario Lemieux	7.00	3.10	.85
	Pittsburgh Penguins			
☐ 10	Gary Suter............................	2.50	1.15	.30
	Calgary Flames			
☐ 11	Tom Barrasso	2.50	1.15	.30
	Pittsburgh Penguins			
☐ 12	Joe Juneau...........................	4.00	1.80	.50
	Boston Bruins			
☐ 13	Eric Lindros...........................	9.00	4.00	1.15

		MINT	EXC	G-VG
	Philadelphia Flyers			
☐ 14	Ed Belfour	4.00	1.80	.50
	Chicago Blackhawks			
☐ 15	Ray Bourque	2.50	1.15	.30
	Boston Bruins			
☐ 16	Steve Yzerman	4.00	1.80	.50
	Detroit Red Wings			
☐ 17	Andrei Kovalenko	2.00	.90	.25
	Quebec Nordiques			
☐ 18	Curtis Joseph	3.00	1.35	.40
	St. Louis Blues			
☐ 19	Phil Housley..........................	2.00	.90	.25
	St. Louis Blues			
☐ 20	Pierre Turgeon	3.00	1.35	.40
	New York Islanders			
☐ 21	Brett Hull..............................	5.00	2.30	.60
	St. Louis Blues			
☐ 22	Patrick Roy	6.00	2.70	.75
	Montreal Canadiens			
☐ 23	Larry Murphy	2.50	1.15	.30
	Pittsburgh Penguins			
☐ 24	Pat LaFontaine	3.00	1.35	.40
	Buffalo Sabres			
☐ A	Winner 1-12 Expired...............	3.00	1.35	.40
☐ B	Winner 13-24 Expired.............	3.00	1.35	.40
☐ AB	Winner 1-24 Expired.............	6.00	2.70	.75

1993-94 Topps Premier Finest

Randomly inserted in both Topps and OPC second-series packs, these 12 standard-size (2 1/2" by 3 1/2") cards feature on their metallic fronts color player action shots framed by a gold line and bordered in blue. The player's name and position appear in gold lettering in the lower blue margin. The horizontal blue and gray back carries a color player action shot on the right, which carries the date of the player's NHL debut in its lower left corner. On the left are displayed the team name, player name, position, biography, and statistics. The cards are numbered on the back as "X of 12."

		MINT	EXC	G-VG
	COMPLETE SET (12)......................	50.00	23.00	6.25
	COMPLETE SET (12)......................	50.00	23.00	6.25
	COMMON PLAYER (1-12)................	2.50	1.15	.30
☐ 1	Alexandre Daigle	7.00	3.10	.85
	Ottawa Senators			
☐ 2	Roman Hamrlik......................	2.50	1.15	.30
	Tampa Bay Lightning			
☐ 3	Eric Lindros..........................	18.00	8.00	2.30
	Philadelphia Flyers			
☐ 4	Owen Nolan..........................	2.50	1.15	.30
	Quebec Nordiques			
☐ 5	Mats Sundin..........................	5.00	2.30	.60
	Quebec Nordiques			
☐ 6	Mike Modano	5.00	2.30	.60
	Dallas Stars			
☐ 7	Pierre Turgeon	5.00	2.30	.60
	New York Islanders			
☐ 8	Joe Murphy...........................	2.50	1.15	.30
	Chicago Blackhawks			
☐ 9	Wendel Clark	5.00	2.30	.60
	Toronto Maple Leafs			
☐ 10	Mario Lemieux	12.00	5.50	1.50

Pittsburgh Penguins
☐	11	Dale Hawerchuk	3.00	1.35	.40

Buffalo Sabres
☐	12	Rob Ramage	2.50	1.15	.30

Philadelphia Flyers
☐	NNO	OPC Redemption Single	2.00	.90	.25
☐	NNO	OPC Redemption Set	5.00	2.30	.60
☐	NNO	Topps Redemption Single	1.00	.45	.13
☐	NNO	Topps Redemption Set	4.00	1.80	.50

1993-94 Topps Premier Team USA

Randomly inserted in second-series Topps Premier packs, these 23 standard-size (2 1/2" by 3 1/2") cards feature borderless color player photos on their fronts. The player's name and the USA Hockey logo appear at the bottom in gold foil. The red, white, and blue back carries the player's name and position at the top, followed below by biography, player photo, career highlights, and statistics. The cards are numbered on the back as "X of 23."

		MINT	EXC	G-VG
COMPLETE SET (23)		35.00	16.00	4.40
COMMON PLAYER (1-23)		1.50	.65	.19

			MINT	EXC	G-VG
☐	1	Mike Dunham	2.00	.90	.25
☐	2	Ian Moran	1.50	.65	.19
☐	3	Peter Laviolette	1.50	.65	.19
☐	4	Darby Hendrickson	1.50	.65	.19
☐	5	Brian Rolston	3.00	1.35	.40
☐	6	Mark Beaufait	1.50	.65	.19
☐	7	Travis Richards	2.00	.90	.25
☐	8	John Lilley	2.00	.90	.25
☐	9	Chris Ferraro	2.00	.90	.25
☐	10	Jon Hillebrandt	1.50	.65	.19
☐	11	Chris Imes	1.50	.65	.19
☐	12	Ted Crowley	1.50	.65	.19
☐	13	David Sacco	2.00	.90	.25
☐	14	Todd Marchant	2.00	.90	.25
☐	15	Peter Ferraro	3.00	1.35	.40
☐	16	David Roberts	2.00	.90	.25
☐	17	Jim Campbell	2.00	.90	.25
☐	18	Barry Richter	2.00	.90	.25
☐	19	Craig Johnson	1.50	.65	.19
☐	20	Brett Hauer	1.50	.65	.19
☐	21	Jeff Lazaro	1.50	.65	.19
☐	22	Jim Storm	2.00	.90	.25
☐	23	Matt Marllli	1.50	.65	.19

1963-64 Toronto Star

This set of 42 photos was distributed one per week with the Toronto Star and was also available as a complete set directly. The photos measure approximately 4 3/4" by 6 3/4" and are entitled, "Hockey Stars in Action." There is a short write-up on the back of each photo. The player's team is identified in the checklist below, Boston Bruins (BB), Chicago Blackhawks (CBH), Detroit Red Wings (DRW), Montreal Canadiens (MC), New York Rangers (NYR), and

 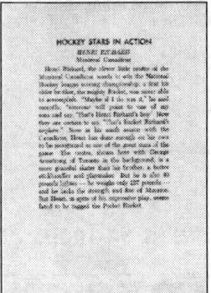

Toronto Maple Leafs (TML). Since the photos are unnumbered, they are listed below in alphabetical order.

		NRMT	VG-E	GOOD
COMPLETE SET (42)		300.00	120.00	30.00
COMMON PLAYER (1-42)		4.00	1.60	.40

			NRMT	VG-E	GOOD
☐	1	George Armstrong TML	8.00	3.25	.80
☐	2	Andy Bathgate NYR	8.00	3.25	.80
☐	3	Bob Baun TML	5.00	2.00	.50
☐	4	Jean Beliveau MC	15.00	6.00	1.50
☐	5	Leo Boivin BB	6.00	2.40	.60
☐	6	Johnny Bower TML	8.00	3.25	.80
☐	7	Carl Brewer TML	5.00	2.00	.50
☐	8	Johnny Bucyk BB	9.00	3.75	.90
☐	9	Alec Delvecchio DRW	9.00	3.75	.90
☐	10	Kent Douglas TML	4.00	1.60	.40
☐	11	Dick Duff TML	5.00	2.00	.50
☐	12	Bill Gadsby DRW	6.00	2.40	.60
☐	13	Jean-Guy Gendron BB	4.00	1.60	.40
☐	14	BoomBoom Geoffrion MC	12.00	5.00	1.20
☐	15	Glenn Hall CBH	10.00	4.00	1.00
☐	16	Doug Harvey NYR	9.00	3.75	.90
☐	17	Bill(Red) Hay CBH	4.00	1.60	.40
☐	18	Camille Henry NYR	5.00	2.00	.50
☐	19	Tim Horton TML	10.00	4.00	1.00
☐	20	Gordie Howe DRW	40.00	16.00	4.00
☐	21	Bobby Hull CBH	25.00	10.00	2.50
☐	22	Red Kelly TML	9.00	3.75	.90
☐	23	Dave Keon TML	8.00	3.25	.80
☐	24	Parker MacDonald DRW	4.00	1.60	.40
☐	25	Frank Mahovlich TML	12.00	5.00	1.20
☐	26	Stan Mikita CBH	12.00	5.00	1.20
☐	27	Dickie Moore MC	9.00	3.75	.90
☐	28	Eric Nesterenko CBH	5.00	2.00	.50
☐	29	Marcel Pronovost DRW	6.00	2.40	.60
☐	30	Claude Provost MC	5.00	2.00	.50
☐	31	Bob Pulford TML	6.00	2.40	.60
☐	32	Henri Richard MC	10.00	4.00	1.00
☐	33	Terry Sawchuk DRW	15.00	6.00	1.50
☐	34	Eddie Shack TML	7.00	2.80	.70
☐	35	Allan Stanley TML	7.00	2.80	.70
☐	36	Ron Stewart TML	4.00	1.60	.40
☐	37	Jean-Guy Talbot MC	5.00	2.00	.50
☐	38	Gilles Tremblay MC	4.00	1.60	.40
☐	39	J.C. Tremblay MC	5.00	2.00	.50
☐	40	Norm Ullman DRW	8.00	3.25	.80
☐	41	Elmer(Moose) Vasko CBH	4.00	1.60	.40
☐	42	Ken Wharram CBH	4.00	1.60	.40

1964-65 Toronto Star

This set of 48 photos was distributed one per week with the Toronto Star and was also available as a complete set directly. The direct complete sets also included a booklet and glossy photo of Dave Keon in the mail-away package. These blank-backed photos measure approximately 4 1/8" by 5 1/8". The player's team is identified in the checklist below, Boston Bruins (BB), Chicago Blackhawks (CBH), Detroit Red Wings (DRW), Montreal Canadiens (MC), New York Rangers (NYR), and Toronto Maple Leafs (TML). Since the photos are unnumbered, they are listed below in alphabetical order. There was an album (actually a folder) available for each team to slot in cards. However when the

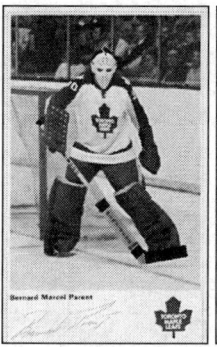

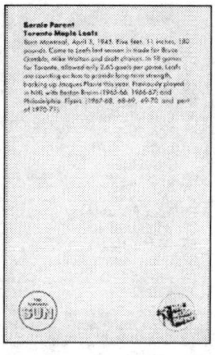

cards were placed in the album it rendered the card's caption unreadable as only the action photo was visible.

	NRMT	VG-E	GOOD
COMPLETE SET (48)	250.00	100.00	25.00
COMMON PLAYER (1-48)	4.00	1.60	.40
☐ 1 Dave Balon MC	4.00	1.60	.40
☐ 2 Andy Bathgate TML	8.00	3.25	.80
☐ 3 Bob Baun TML	5.00	2.00	.50
☐ 4 Jean Beliveau MC	15.00	6.00	1.50
☐ 5 Red Berenson MC	5.00	2.00	.50
☐ 6 Leo Boivin BB	6.00	2.40	.60
☐ 7 Carl Brewer TML	5.00	2.00	.50
☐ 8 Alex Delvecchio DRW	9.00	3.75	.90
☐ 9 Rod Gilbert NYR	8.00	3.25	.80
☐ 10 Ted Green BB	5.00	2.00	.50
☐ 11 Glenn Hall CBH	10.00	4.00	1.00
☐ 12 Billy Harris TML	4.00	1.60	.40
☐ 13 Bill(Red) Hay CBH	4.00	1.60	.40
☐ 14 Paul Henderson DRW	5.00	2.00	.50
☐ 15 Wayne Hillman CBH	4.00	1.60	.40
☐ 16 Charlie Hodge MC	5.00	2.00	.50
☐ 17 Tim Horton TML	10.00	4.00	1.00
☐ 18 Gordie Howe DRW	40.00	16.00	4.00
☐ 19 Harry Howell NYR	6.00	2.40	.60
☐ 20 Bobby Hull BB	25.00	10.00	2.50
☐ 21 Larry Jeffrey DRW	4.00	1.60	.40
☐ 22 Tom Johnson BB	6.00	2.40	.60
☐ 23 Forbes Kennedy BB	4.00	1.60	.40
☐ 24 Dave Keon TML	8.00	3.25	.80
☐ 25 Orland Kurtenbach BB	5.00	2.00	.50
☐ 26 Jacques Laperriere MC	6.00	2.40	.60
☐ 27 Parker MacDonald DRW	4.00	1.60	.40
☐ 28 Al MacNeil CBH	4.00	1.60	.40
☐ 29 Frank Mahovlich TML	12.00	5.00	1.20
☐ 30 Chico Maki CBH	4.00	1.60	.40
☐ 31 Don McKenney TML	4.00	1.60	.40
☐ 32 John McKenzie CBH	4.00	1.60	.40
☐ 33 Stan Mikita CBH	12.00	5.00	1.20
☐ 34 Jim Nielson NYR	4.00	1.60	.40
☐ 35 Jim Pappin TML	4.00	1.60	.40
☐ 36 Pierre Pilote CBH	6.00	2.40	.60
☐ 37 Jacques Plante NYR	12.00	5.00	1.20
☐ 38 Marcel Pronovost DRW	6.00	2.40	.60
☐ 39 Claude Provost MC	5.00	2.00	.50
☐ 40 Bob Pulford TML	6.00	2.40	.60
☐ 41 Henri Richard MC	10.00	4.00	1.00
☐ 42 Wayne Rivers BB	4.00	1.60	.40
☐ 43 Floyd Smith DRW	4.00	1.60	.40
☐ 44 Allan Stanley TML	7.00	2.80	.70
☐ 45 Ron Stewart TML	4.00	1.60	.40
☐ 46 J.C. Tremblay MC	5.00	2.00	.50
☐ 47 Norm Ullman DRW	8.00	3.25	.80
☐ 48 Elmer Vasko CBH	4.00	1.60	.40
☐ xx Album/Folder	20.00	8.00	2.00

1971-72 Toronto Sun

This set of 294 photo cards with two punch holes has never been very popular with collectors. The photos are quite fragile, printed on thin paper, and measure approximately 5" by 7". The checklist below is in team order as follows: Boston Bruins (1-21), Buffalo Sabres (22-41), California Golden Seals (42-61), Chicago Blackhawks (62-82), Detroit Red Wings (83-103), Los Angeles Kings (104-124), Minnesota North Stars (125-145), Montreal Canadiens (146-

166), New York Rangers (167-186), Philadelphia Flyers (187-208), Pittsburgh Penguins (209-230), St. Louis Blues (231-252), Toronto Maple Leafs (253-274), and Vancouver Canucks (275-294). The cards were intended to fit in a two-ring binder specially made to hold the cards. There was an Introduction "photo" written by Scott Young which obviously was an introduction to the collection.

	NRMT	VG-E	GOOD
COMPLETE SET (294)	400.00	160.00	40.00
COMMON PLAYER (1-294)	.75	.30	.07
☐ 1 Boston Bruins	.75	.30	.07
Team Crest			
☐ 2 Don Awrey	.75	.30	.07
☐ 3 Garnet Bailey	.75	.30	.07
☐ 4 Ivan Boldirev	.75	.30	.07
☐ 5 Johnny Bucyk	5.00	2.00	.50
☐ 6 Wayne Cashman	1.25	.50	.12
☐ 7 Gerry Cheevers	5.00	2.00	.50
☐ 8 Phil Esposito	10.00	4.00	1.00
☐ 9 Ted Green	1.00	.40	.10
☐ 10 Ken Hodge	1.25	.50	.12
☐ 11 Ed Johnston	1.25	.50	.12
☐ 12 Reggie Leach	1.00	.40	.10
☐ 13 Don Marcotte	.75	.30	.07
☐ 14 John McKenzie	.75	.30	.07
☐ 15 Bobby Orr	50.00	20.00	5.00
☐ 16 Derek Sanderson	2.00	.80	.20
☐ 17 Dallas Smith	1.00	.40	.10
☐ 18 Richard Allan Smith	.75	.30	.07
☐ 19 Fred Stanfield	.75	.30	.07
☐ 20 Mike Walton	1.00	.40	.10
☐ 21 Ed Westfall	1.00	.40	.10
☐ 22 Buffalo Sabres	.75	.30	.07
Team Crest			
☐ 23 Doug Barrie	.75	.30	.07
☐ 24 Roger Crozier	1.00	.40	.10
☐ 25 Dave Dryden	1.00	.40	.10
☐ 26 Dick Duff	1.00	.40	.10
☐ 27 Phil Goyette	.75	.30	.07
☐ 28 Al Hamilton	.75	.30	.07
☐ 29 Larry Keenan	.75	.30	.07
☐ 30 Danny Lawson	.75	.30	.07
☐ 31 Don Luce	.75	.30	.07
☐ 32 Richard Martin	1.50	.60	.15
☐ 33 Ray McKay	.75	.30	.07
☐ 34 Gerry Meehan	1.25	.50	.12
☐ 35 Kevin O'Shea	.75	.30	.07
☐ 36 Gilbert Perreault	6.00	2.40	.60
☐ 37 Tracy Pratt	.75	.30	.07
☐ 38 Mike Robitaille	.75	.30	.07
☐ 39 Eddie Shack	2.00	.80	.20
☐ 40 Jim Watson	.75	.30	.07
☐ 41 Rod Zaine	.75	.30	.07
☐ 42 California Seals	1.00	.40	.10
Team Crest			
☐ 43 Wayne Carleton	.75	.30	.07
☐ 44 Lyle Carter	.75	.30	.07
☐ 45 Gary Croteau	.75	.30	.07
☐ 46 Norm Ferguson	.75	.30	.07
☐ 47 Stan Gilbertson	.75	.30	.07
☐ 48 Ernie Hicke	.75	.30	.07
☐ 49 Gary Jarrett	.75	.30	.07
☐ 50 Joey Johnston	.75	.30	.07
☐ 51 Marshall Johnston	.75	.30	.07
☐ 52 Bert Marshall	.75	.30	.07
☐ 53 Walt McKechnie	.75	.30	.07

☐	54	Don O'Donoghue	.75	.30	.07
☐	55	Gerry Pinder	1.00	.40	.10
☐	56	Dick Redmond	.75	.30	.07
☐	57	Robert Sheehan	.75	.30	.07
☐	58	Paul Shmyr	.75	.30	.07
☐	59	Ron Stackhouse SP	10.00	4.00	1.00
☐	60	Carol Vadnais	.75	.30	.07
☐	61	Tom Williams	.75	.30	.07
☐	62	Chicago Blackhawks Team Crest	.75	.30	.07
☐	63	Lou Angotti	.75	.30	.07
☐	64	Bryan Campbell	.75	.30	.07
☐	65	Tony Esposito	6.00	2.40	.60
☐	66	Bobby Hull	25.00	10.00	2.50
☐	67	Dennis Hull	1.50	.60	.15
☐	68	Doug Jarrett	.75	.30	.07
☐	69	Jerry Korab	.75	.30	.07
☐	70	Cliff Koroll	.75	.30	.07
☐	71	Darryl Maggs	.75	.30	.07
☐	72	Keith Magnuson	1.00	.40	.10
☐	73	Chico Maki	1.00	.40	.10
☐	74	Dan Maloney	1.00	.40	.10
☐	75	Pit Martin	1.00	.40	.10
☐	76	Stan Mikita	10.00	4.00	1.00
☐	77	Eric Nesterenko	1.00	.40	.10
☐	78	Danny O'Shea	.75	.30	.07
☐	79	Jim Pappin	1.00	.40	.10
☐	80	Gary Smith	1.00	.40	.10
☐	81	Pat Stapleton	1.00	.40	.10
☐	82	Bill White	1.00	.40	.10
☐	83	Detroit Red Wings Team Crest	.75	.30	.07
☐	84	Red Berenson	1.25	.50	.12
☐	85	Gary Bergman	1.00	.40	.10
☐	86	Arnie Brown	.75	.30	.07
☐	87	Guy Charron	.75	.30	.07
☐	88	Bill Collins	.75	.30	.07
☐	89	Brian Conacher	.75	.30	.07
☐	90	Joe Daley	1.00	.40	.10
☐	91	Alex Delvecchio	5.00	2.00	.50
☐	92	Marcel Dionne	20.00	8.00	2.00
☐	93	Tim Ecclestone	.75	.30	.07
☐	94	Ron Harris	.75	.30	.07
☐	95	Gerry Hart	.75	.30	.07
☐	96	Gordie Howe	50.00	20.00	5.00
☐	97	Al Karlander	.75	.30	.07
☐	98	Nick Libett	1.00	.40	.10
☐	99	Ab McDonald	.75	.30	.07
☐	100	James Niekamp	.75	.30	.07
☐	101	Mickey Redmond	1.50	.60	.15
☐	102	Leon Rochefort	.75	.30	.07
☐	103	Al Smith	1.00	.40	.10
☐	104	Los Angeles Kings Team Crest	.75	.30	.07
☐	105	Ralph Backstrom	1.00	.40	.10
☐	106	Bob Berry	1.00	.40	.10
☐	107	Mike Byers	.75	.30	.07
☐	108	Larry Cahan	.75	.30	.07
☐	109	Paul Curtis	.75	.30	.07
☐	110	Denis DeJordy	1.25	.50	.12
☐	111	Gary Edwards	1.00	.40	.10
☐	112	Bill Flett	.75	.30	.07
☐	113	Butch Goring	1.25	.50	.12
☐	114	Lucien Grenier	.75	.30	.07
☐	115	Larry Hillman	.75	.30	.07
☐	116	Dale Hoganson	.75	.30	.07
☐	117	Harry Howell	2.00	.80	.20
☐	118	Eddie Joyal	.75	.30	.07
☐	119	Real Lemieux	.75	.30	.07
☐	120	Ross Lonsberry	.75	.30	.07
☐	121	Al McDonough	.75	.30	.07
☐	122	Jean Potvin	1.00	.40	.10
☐	123	Bob Pulford	2.00	.80	.20
☐	124	Juha Widing	.75	.30	.07
⊓	125	Minnesota North Stars Team Crest	.75	.30	.07
☐	126	Fred Barrett	.75	.30	.07
☐	127	Charlie Burns	.75	.30	.07
☐	128	Jude Drouin	.75	.30	.07
☐	129	Barry Gibbs	.75	.30	.07
☐	130	Gilles Gilbert	1.00	.40	.10
☐	131	Bill Goldsworthy	1.50	.60	.15
☐	132	Danny Grant	1.00	.40	.10
☐	133	Ted Hampson	.75	.30	.07
☐	134	Ted Harris	.75	.30	.07
☐	135	Fred Harvey	.75	.30	.07
☐	136	Cesare Maniago	1.25	.50	.12
☐	137	Doug Mohns	1.00	.40	.10
☐	138	Lou Nanne	1.00	.40	.10
☐	139	Bob Nevin	1.00	.40	.10
☐	140	Dennis O'Brien	.75	.30	.07
☐	141	Murray Oliver	.75	.30	.07
☐	142	Jean-Paul Parise	1.00	.40	.10
☐	143	Dean Prentice	1.00	.40	.10
☐	144	Tom Reid	.75	.30	.07
☐	145	Gump Worsley	5.00	2.00	.50
☐	146	Montreal Canadiens Team Crest	1.00	.40	.10
☐	147	Pierre Bouchard	1.00	.40	.10
☐	148	Yvan Cournoyer	5.00	2.00	.50
☐	149	Ken Dryden	25.00	10.00	2.50
☐	150	Terry Harper	1.00	.40	.10
☐	151	Rejean Houle	.75	.30	.07
☐	152	Guy Lafleur	25.00	10.00	2.50
☐	153	Jacques Laperriere	2.00	.80	.20
☐	154	Guy Lapointe	3.00	1.20	.30
☐	155	Claude Larose	.75	.30	.07
☐	156	Jacques Lemaire	4.00	1.60	.40
☐	157	Frank Mahovlich	10.00	4.00	1.00
☐	158	Pete Mahovlich	1.25	.50	.12
☐	159	Phil Myre	1.00	.40	.10
☐	160	Larry Pleau	1.00	.40	.10
☐	161	Henri Richard	6.00	2.40	.60
☐	162	Phil Roberto	.75	.30	.07
☐	163	Serge Savard	3.00	1.20	.30
☐	164	Marc Tardif	1.00	.40	.10
☐	165	J.C. Tremblay	1.00	.40	.10
☐	166	Rogatien Vachon	4.00	1.60	.40
☐	167	New York Rangers Team Crest	.75	.30	.07
☐	168	Dave Balon	.75	.30	.07
☐	169	Ab DeMarco	.75	.30	.07
☐	170	Jack Egers	.75	.30	.07
☐	171	Bill Fairbairn	.75	.30	.07
☐	172	Ed Giacomin	4.00	1.60	.40
☐	173	Rod Gilbert	3.00	1.20	.30
☐	174	Vic Hadfield	1.25	.50	.12
☐	175	Ted Irvine	.75	.30	.07
☐	176	Bruce MacGregor	.75	.30	.07
☐	177	Jim Neilson	.75	.30	.07
☐	178	Brad Park	5.00	2.00	.50
☐	179	Jean Ratelle	3.00	1.20	.30
☐	180	Dale Rolfe	.75	.30	.07
☐	181	Bobby Rousseau	1.00	.40	.10
☐	182	Glen Sather	2.00	.80	.20
☐	183	Rod Seiling	.75	.30	.07
☐	184	Pete Stemkowski	1.00	.40	.10
☐	185	Walt Tkaczuk	1.00	.40	.10
☐	186	Gilles Villemure	1.50	.60	.15
☐	187	Philadelphia Flyers Team Crest	.75	.30	.07
☐	188	Barry Ashbee	1.50	.60	.15
☐	189	Serge Bernier	.75	.30	.07
☐	190	Larry Brown	.75	.30	.07
☐	191	Bobby Clarke	10.00	4.00	1.00
☐	192	Gary Dornhoefer	1.00	.40	.10
☐	193	Doug Favell	1.00	.40	.10
☐	194	Bruce Gamble	.75	.30	.07
☐	195	Jean-Guy Gendron	.75	.30	.07
☐	196	Larry Hale	.75	.30	.07
☐	197	Wayne Hillman	.75	.30	.07
☐	198	Brent Hughes	.75	.30	.07
☐	199	Jim Johnson	.75	.30	.07
☐	200	Bob Kelly	1.00	.40	.10
☐	201	Andre Lacroix	1.00	.40	.10
☐	202	Bill Lesuk	.75	.30	.07
☐	203	Rick MacLeish	2.00	.80	.20
☐	204	Larry Mickey	.75	.30	.07
☐	205	Simon Nolet	.75	.30	.07
☐	206	Pierre Plante	.75	.30	.07
☐	207	Ed Van Impe	.75	.30	.07
☐	208	Joe Watson	.75	.30	.07
☐	209	Pittsburgh Penguins Team Crest	.75	.30	.07
☐	210	Syl Apps	1.00	.40	.10
☐	211	Les Binkley	1.00	.40	.10
☐	212	Wally Boyer	.75	.30	.07
☐	213	Darryl Edestrand	.75	.30	.07
☐	214	Roy Edwards	1.00	.40	.10
☐	215	Nick Harbaruk	.75	.30	.07
☐	216	Bryan Hextall	1.00	.40	.10
☐	217	Bill Hicke	.75	.30	.07
☐	218	Tim Horton	6.00	2.40	.60
☐	219	Sheldon Kannegeisser	.75	.30	.07
☐	220	Bob Leiter	.75	.30	.07
☐	221	Keith McCreary	.75	.30	.07
☐	222	Joe Noris	.75	.30	.07
☐	223	Greg Polis	.75	.30	.07
☐	224	Jean Pronovost	1.00	.40	.10
☐	225	Rene Robert	1.25	.50	.12
☐	226	Duane Rupp	.75	.30	.07
☐	227	Ken Schinkel	.75	.30	.07
☐	228	Ron Schock	.75	.30	.07
☐	229	Bryan Watson	1.00	.40	.10
☐	230	Bob Woytowich	.75	.30	.07
☐	231	St. Louis Blues	.75	.30	.07

Team Crest

☐	232	Al Arbour	2.00	.80	.20
☐	233	John Arbour	.75	.30	.07
☐	234	Chris Bordeleau	.75	.30	.07
☐	235	Carl Brewer	1.00	.40	.10
☐	236	Gene Carr	.75	.30	.07
☐	237	Wayne Connelly	.75	.30	.07
☐	238	Terry Crisp	1.25	.50	.12
☐	239	Jim Lorentz	.75	.30	.07
☐	240	Peter McDuffe	.75	.30	.07
☐	241	George Morrison	.75	.30	.07
☐	242	Michel Parizeau	.75	.30	.07
☐	243	Noel Picard	.75	.30	.07
☐	244	Barclay Plager	1.25	.50	.12
☐	245	Bob Plager	1.25	.50	.12
☐	246	Jim Roberts	1.00	.40	.10
☐	247	Gary Sabourin	.75	.30	.07
☐	248	Jim Shires	.75	.30	.07
☐	249	Frank St.Marseille	.75	.30	.07
☐	250	Bill Sutherland	.75	.30	.07
☐	251	Garry Unger	1.50	.60	.15
☐	252	Ernie Wakely	.75	.30	.07
☐	253	Toronto Maple Leafs	.75	.30	.07

Team Crest

☐	254	Bob Baun	1.00	.40	.10
☐	255	Jim Dorey	.75	.30	.07
☐	256	Denis Dupere	.75	.30	.07
☐	257	Ron Ellis	1.00	.40	.10
☐	258	Brian Glennie	.75	.30	.07
☐	259	Jim Harrison	.75	.30	.07
☐	260	Paul Henderson	1.25	.50	.12
☐	261	Dave Keon	5.00	2.00	.50
☐	262	Rick Ley	1.00	.40	.10
☐	263	Billy MacMillan	.75	.30	.07
☐	264	Don Marshall	.75	.30	.07
☐	265	Jim McKenny	.75	.30	.07
☐	266	Garry Monahan	.75	.30	.07
☐	267	Bernie Parent	6.00	2.40	.60
☐	268	Mike Pelyk	.75	.30	.07
☐	269	Jacques Plante	10.00	4.00	1.00
☐	270	Brad Selwood	.75	.30	.07
☐	271	Darryl Sittler	6.00	2.40	.60
☐	272	Brian Spencer	1.25	.50	.12
☐	273	Guy Trottier	.75	.30	.07
☐	274	Norm Ullman	4.00	1.60	.40
☐	275	Vancouver Canucks	.75	.30	.07

Team Crest

☐	276	Andre Boudrias	.75	.30	.07
☐	277	George Gardiner	.75	.30	.07
☐	278	Jocelyn Guevremont	1.00	.40	.10
☐	279	Murray Hall	.75	.30	.07
☐	280	Danny Johnson	.75	.30	.07
☐	281	Dennis Kearns	.75	.30	.07
☐	282	Orland Kurtenbach	1.00	.40	.10
☐	283	Bobby Lalonde	.75	.30	.07
☐	284	Wayne Maki	.75	.30	.07
☐	285	Rosaire Paiement	1.00	.40	.10
☐	286	Paul Popiel	1.00	.40	.10
☐	287	Pat Quinn	1.50	.60	.15
☐	288	John Schella	.75	.30	.07
☐	289	Bobby Schmautz	1.00	.40	.10
☐	290	Fred Speck	.75	.30	.07
☐	291	Dale Tallon	1.00	.40	.10
☐	292	Ron Ward	.75	.30	.07
☐	293	Barry Wilkins	.75	.30	.07
☐	294	Dunc Wilson	1.00	.40	.10
☐	NNO	Introduction Card	2.50	1.00	.25
		(Written by Scott Young)			
☐	xx	Binder	20.00	8.00	2.00

1991 Tri-Globe Fedorov

This five-card set honoring Sergei Fedorov is the product of a joint venture between Tri-Globe International, Inc. and Ivan Fiodorov Press. The cards measure approximately 2 1/2" by 3 3/4" and are printed on a grainy cardboard stock. The fronts feature color action game shots. The first card has the player's name printed in a green stripe to the right of the picture. In a yellow stripe below the picture, card numbers 2-5 have a caption and a drawing of a leopard, elk, bears, and lion respectively. The backs of all the cards have smaller color action shots and career summary in English and Russian. The cards are numbered on the back. Dealers who purchased 50 or more sets received a promotion poster,

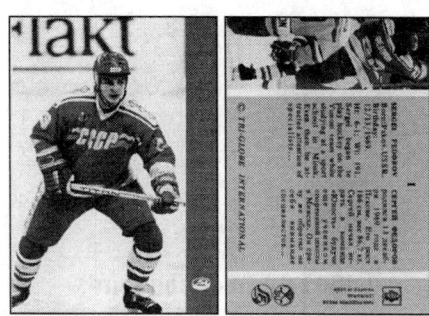

which uses the same player photo as on card number 1. According to Tri-Globe, 600 uncut, numbered sheets were printed, producing the equivalent of 3,000 sets, as well as 1,000 uncut, numbered five-card strips. Moreover, 100,000 five-card sets were reportedly produced.

		MINT	EXC	G-VG
COMPLETE SET (5)		5.00	2.00	.50
COMMON PLAYER (1-5)		1.25	.50	.12
☐ 1	Sergei Fedorov	1.25	.50	.12
☐ 2	Sergei Fedorov	1.25	.50	.12
	Some men are faster			
☐ 3	Sergei Fedorov	1.25	.50	.12
	Some men are tougher			
☐ 4	Sergei Fedorov	1.25	.50	.12
	Some men are stronger			
☐ 5	Sergei Fedorov	1.25	.50	.12
	Some men are better			

1991-92 Tri-Globe Kamensky

This standard-size (2-1/2" by 3-1/2") five-card set was produced by Tri-Globe as part of the "The Magnificent Five" series. These sets spotlight five Russian hockey stars currently playing in the NHL, with set 1 featuring Valeri Kamensky. It is claimed that 5,000 numbered display boxes were produced, each containing 40 sets (ten for each player). Printed in Russia on heavy laminated textured stock, card fronts feature full-color action shots in various formats and accented predominantly in purple. In a horizontal format, the lavender backs carry another full-color photo and career statistics printed in English and French. The card number appears in a circle at the top right along with the sponsor's logo. Each set includes a checklist on the back of a Sergei Fedorov promo card.

	MINT	EXC	G-VG
COMPLETE SET (6)	3.00	1.20	.30
COMMON PLAYER (1-5)	.75	.30	.07

☐ 1	Valeri Kamensky	.75	.30	.07
	One of the World's Best			
☐ 2	Valeri Kamensky	.75	.30	.07
	A World Champion			
☐ 3	Valeri Kamensky	.75	.30	.07
	A World Class Forward			
☐ 4	Valeri Kamensky	.75	.30	.07
	Champion of the USSR			
☐ 5	Valeri Kamensky	.75	.30	.07
	There are only few			
	of them			
☐ NNO	Sergei Fedorov..................	1.00	.40	.10
	Checklist			

1991-92 Tri-Globe Bure

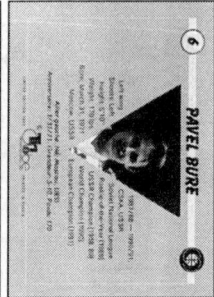

player). Printed in Russia on heavy laminated textured stock, card fronts feature full-color action shots in various formats and accented predominantly in aqua. In a horizontal format, the aqua backs carry another full-color photo and career statistics printed in English and French. The card number appears in a circle at the top right along with the sponsor's logo. Each set includes a checklist on the back of a Sergei Fedorov promo card.

	MINT	EXC	G-VG
COMPLETE SET (6)..........................	3.00	1.20	.30
COMMON PLAYER (11-15)..............	.75	.30	.07

☐ 11	Anatoli Semenov	.75	.30	.07
	One of the World's Best			
☐ 12	Anatoli Semenov	.75	.30	.07
	An Olympic Champion			
☐ 13	Anatoli Semenov	.75	.30	.07
	A World Class Forward			
☐ 14	Anatoli Semenov...................	.75	.30	.07
	Champion of the USSR			
☐ 15	Anatoli Semenov...................	.75	.30	.07
	There are only few			
	of them			
☐ NNO	Sergei Fedorov..................	1.00	.40	.10
	Checklist			

This standard-size (2-1/2" by 3-1/2") five-card set was produced by Tri-Globe as part of the "The Magnificent Five" series. These sets spotlight five Russian hockey stars currently playing in the NHL, with set 2 featuring Pavel Bure. It is claimed that 5,000 numbered display boxes were produced, each containing 40 sets (ten for each player). Printed in Russia on heavy laminated textured stock, card fronts feature full-color action shots in various formats and accented predominantly in green. In a horizontal format, the green backs carry another full-color photo and career statistics printed in English and French. The card number appears in a circle at the top right along with the sponsor's logo. Each set includes a checklist on the back of a Sergei Fedorov promo card.

1991-92 Tri-Globe Irbe

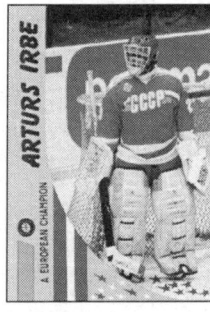

	MINT	EXC	G-VG
COMPLETE SET (6)........................	7.00	2.80	.70
COMMON PLAYER (6-10)...............	1.50	.60	.15

☐ 6	Pavel Bure..............................	1.50	.60	.15
	One of the World's Best			
☐ 7	Pavel Bure.............................	1.50	.60	.15
	A World Champion			
☐ 8	Pavel Bure.............................	1.50	.60	.15
	A World Class Forward			
☐ 9	Pavel Bure.............................	1.50	.60	.15
	Champion of the USSR			
☐ 10	Pavel Bure............................	1.50	.60	.15
	A European Champion			
☐ NNO	Sergei Fedorov..................	1.00	.40	.10
	Checklist			

1991-92 Tri-Globe Semenov

This standard-size (2-1/2" by 3-1/2") five-card set was produced by Tri-Globe as part of the "The Magnificent Five" series. These sets spotlight five Russian hockey stars currently playing in the NHL, with set three featuring Anatoli Semenov. It is claimed that 5,000 numbered display boxes were produced, each containing 40 sets (ten for each

This standard-size (2-1/2" by 3-1/2") five-card set was produced by Tri-Globe as part of the "The Magnificent Five" series. These sets spotlight five Russian hockey stars currently playing in the NHL, with set four featuring Arturs Irbe. It is claimed that 5,000 numbered display boxes were produced, each containing 40 sets (ten for each player). Printed in Russia on heavy laminated textured stock, card fronts feature full-color action shots in various formats and accented predominantly in yellowish orange. In a horizontal format, the yellowish orange backs carry another full-color photo and career statistics printed in English and French. The card number appears in a circle at the top right along with the sponsor's logo. Each set includes a checklist on the back of a Sergei Fedorov promo card.

	MINT	EXC	G-VG
COMPLETE SET (6)	5.00	2.00	.50
COMMON PLAYER (16-20)	1.25	.50	.12
☐ 16 Arturs Irbe	1.25	.50	.12
One of the World's Best			
☐ 17 Arturs Irbe	1.25	.50	.12
A European Champion			
☐ 18 Arturs Irbe	1.25	.50	.12
A World Class Goaltender			
☐ 19 Arturs Irbe	1.25	.50	.12
A World Champion			
☐ 20 Arturs Irbe	1.25	.50	.12
There are only few of them			
☐ NNO Sergei Fedorov	1.00	.40	.10
Checklist			

1992 Tri-Globe From Russia With Puck

 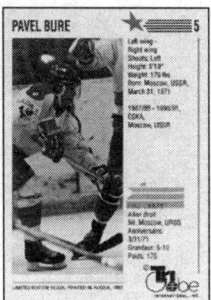

Twelve Russian hockey stars who are currently playing in the NHL are featured in this 24-card boxed set, with two cards devoted to each player. The production run was reportedly 50,000 sets. The cards measure the standard size (2 1/2" by 3 1/2"). The fronts of all cards display color action player photos. The fronts of all cards display color action player photos. On the player's first card (i.e., an odd-numbered card), his name appears at the top in a silver stripe, and red, white, and blue stripes accent the picture on three sides. On his second card (i.e., an even-numbered card), black-and-white speckled stripes edge the picture above and below. The back of the player's first card carries a second color action photo and biographical information, while the back of his second card has a close-up color photo and career statistics. All text is in French and English. The cards are numbered on the back.

	MINT	EXC	G-VG
COMPLETE SET (24)	10.00	4.00	1.00
COMMON PLAYER (1-24)	.50	.20	.05
☐ 1 Igor Larionov	.75	.30	.07
☐ 2 Igor Larionov	.75	.30	.07
☐ 3 Andrei Lomakin	.60	.24	.06
☐ 4 Andrei Lomakin	.60	.24	.06
☐ 5 Pavel Bure	3.00	1.20	.30
☐ 6 Pavel Bure	3.00	1.20	.30
☐ 7 Alexei Zhamnov	1.25	.50	.12
☐ 8 Alexei Zhamnov	1.25	.50	.12
☐ 9 Sergei Krivokrasov	.60	.24	.06
☐ 10 Sergei Krivokrasov	.60	.24	.06
☐ 11 Valeri Kamensky	.75	.30	.07
☐ 12 Valeri Kamensky	.75	.30	.07
☐ 13 Viacheslav Kozlov	1.50	.60	.15
☐ 14 Viacheslav Kozlov	1.50	.60	.15
☐ 15 Valeri Zelepukhin	.60	.24	.06
☐ 16 Valeri Zelepukhin	.60	.24	.06
☐ 17 Igor Kravchuk	.50	.20	.05
☐ 18 Igor Kravchuk	.50	.20	.05
☐ 19 Vladimir Malakhov	.75	.30	.07
☐ 20 Vladimir Malakhov	.75	.30	.07
☐ 21 Boris Mironov	.50	.20	.05
☐ 22 Boris Mironov	.50	.20	.05
☐ 23 Arturs Irbe	1.50	.60	.15
☐ 24 Arturs Irbe	1.50	.60	.15

1936 Triumph Postcards

 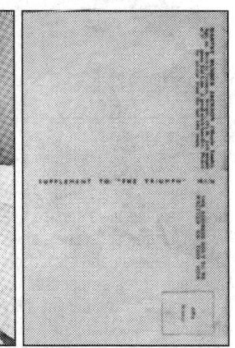

Harvey Busher Jackson
MAPLE LEAFS

This ten-card set was issued as a supplement to The Triumph (a newspaper). The cards measure approximately 3 1/2" by 5 1/2" and are in the postcard format. The borderless fronts feature full-length black and white posed action shots. The player's name and team name appear in the lower left corner. The back carries the typical postcard design with each player's name and biographical information in the upper corner. Different dates appear on the back of the cards, which represent the date each card was distributed. The cards were issued three the first week with The Triumph, then one per week thereafter. The cards are unnumbered and checklisted below in alphabetical order. The date mentioned below is the issue date as noted on the card back in Canadian style, day/month/year.

	EX-MT	VG-E	GOOD
COMPLETE SET (10)	1000.00	400.00	100.00
COMMON PLAYER (1-10)	60.00	24.00	6.00
☐ 1 Lionel Conacher	200.00	80.00	20.00
22/2/36			
☐ 2 Harvey(Busher) Jackson	125.00	50.00	12.50
Toronto Maple Leafs			
18/1/36			
☐ 3 Ivan(Ching) Johnson	100.00	40.00	10.00
New York Rangers			
8/2/36			
☐ 4 Herbie Lewis	60.00	24.00	6.00
7/3/36			
☐ 5 Sylvio Mantha	100.00	40.00	10.00
Montreal Canadiens			
18/1/36			
☐ 6 Nick Metz	60.00	24.00	6.00
Toronto Maple Leafs			
15/2/36			
☐ 7 Baldy Northcott	75.00	30.00	7.50
Montreal Maroons			
1/2/36			
☐ 8 Eddie Shore	250.00	100.00	25.00
Boston Bruins			
25/1/36			
☐ 9 Paul Thompson	60.00	24.00	6.00
Chicago Blackhawks			
29/2/36			
☐ 10 Roy Worters	100.00	40.00	10.00
New York Americans			
18/1/36			

1991 Ultimate Draft Promos

This three-card set was given out to dealers and collectors to promote the new Ultimate hockey draft picks cards. The cards measure the standard size (2 1/2" by 3 1/2"). The front design is basically the same as the regular issue. The Torchia card displays a different player photo, while the Stojanov card is cropped differently. Also the promos have the team name below the player's name rather than city name as with their regular issue. The backs of the promos differ from those of the regular issue in that the photos on the back are more ghosted and the word "Sample" is stenciled over them. Also the player information on the Stojanov card back is arranged differently on the promo. The cards are unnumbered and checklisted below in alphabetical order.

	MINT	EXC	G-VG
COMPLETE SET (3)	2.50	1.00	.25
COMMON PLAYER (1-3)	.75	.30	.07
☐ 1 Pat Falloon	2.00	.80	.20
San Jose Sharks			
☐ 2 Alex Stojanov	.50	.20	.05
Vancouver Canucks			
☐ 3 Mike Torchia	.50	.20	.05
Minnesota North Stars			

1991 Ultimate Draft

The 1991 Ultimate/Smokey's Draft Picks hockey set contains 90 cards measuring the standard-size (2 1/2" by 3 1/2"). The front design has glossy, color action player photos, bordered in white. The upper left corner of the picture is cut off to allow space for a logo with the words "Sportscards Ultimate Hockey". The player's name, position, and team appear in white lettering in a blue-gray rectangle near the card bottom. The backs have biography, statistics,

and player profile overlaying a player photo that is ghosted except for the head. The cards are numbered on the back. Cards 58-74 are a special subset of First Draft Picks (FDP) and cards 78-87 are a special subset of black-and-white photos (BW). Reportedly production quantities were as follows: 6,000 American set cases equalling 120,000 sets, 750 French set cases equalling 15,000 sets, 5,000 American ten-box wax cases, 1,500 French ten-box wax cases, and 500 autographed sets. Currently the French and English cards are valued equally.

	MINT	EXC	G-VG
COMPLETE SET (90)	6.00	2.40	.60
COMMON PLAYER (1-90)	.04	.02	.00
☐ 1 Ultimate/Preview	.04	.02	.00
☐ 2 Pat Falloon	.40	.16	.04
☐ 3 Scott Niedermayer	.40	.16	.04
☐ 4 Scott Lachance	.15	.06	.01
☐ 5 Peter Forsberg	.50	.20	.05
☐ 6 Alek Stojanov	.07	.03	.01
☐ 7 Richard Matvichuk	.10	.04	.01
☐ 8 Patrick Poulin	.15	.06	.01
☐ 9 Martin Lapointe	.15	.06	.01
☐ 10 Tyler Wright	.10	.04	.01
☐ 11 Philippe Boucher	.10	.04	.01
☐ 12 Pat Peake	.25	.10	.02
☐ 13 Markus Naslund	.15	.06	.01
☐ 14 Brent Bilodeau	.10	.04	.01
☐ 15 Glen Murray	.20	.08	.02
☐ 16 Niklas Sundblad	.07	.03	.01
☐ 17 Trevor Halverson	.10	.04	.01
☐ 18 Dean McAmmond UER	.10	.04	.01
☐ 19 Jim Campbell	.10	.04	.01
☐ 20 Rene Corbet	.10	.04	.01
☐ 21 Eric Lavigne	.07	.03	.01
☐ 22 Steve Staios	.10	.04	.01
☐ 23 Jassen Cullimore	.07	.03	.01
☐ 24 Jamie Pushor	.07	.03	.01
☐ 25 Donevan Hextall	.07	.03	.01
☐ 26 Andrew Verner	.10	.04	.01
☐ 27 Jason Dawe	.10	.04	.01
☐ 28 Jeff Nelson	.10	.04	.01
☐ 29 Darcy Werenka	.04	.02	.00
☐ 30 Francois Groleau	.07	.03	.01
☐ 31 Guy Leveque	.10	.04	.01
☐ 32 Jamie Matthews	.07	.03	.01
☐ 33 Dody Wood	.07	.03	.01
☐ 34 Yanick Perreault	.12	.05	.01
☐ 35 Jamie McLennan UER	.15	.06	.01
☐ 36 Yanic Dupre	.07	.03	.01
☐ 37 1st Round Checklist	.04	.02	.00
☐ 38 Chris Osgood	.25	.10	.02
☐ 39 Fredrik Lindquist	.07	.03	.01
☐ 40 Jason Young	.07	.03	.01
☐ 41 Steve Konowalchuk	.10	.04	.01
☐ 42 Mikael Nylander	.15	.06	.01
☐ 43 Shane Peacock	.07	.03	.01
☐ 44 Yves Sarault	.07	.03	.01
☐ 45 Marcel Cousineau	.07	.03	.01
☐ 46 Nathan Lafayette	.15	.06	.01
☐ 47 Bobby House	.04	.02	.00
☐ 48 Kerry Toporowski	.07	.03	.01
☐ 49 Terry Chitaroni	.07	.03	.01
☐ 50 Mike Torchia	.07	.03	.01
☐ 51 Mario Nobili	.07	.03	.01
☐ 52 Justin Morrison	.04	.02	.00
☐ 53 Grayden Reid	.07	.03	.01
☐ 54 Yanick Perreault	.07	.03	.01
Underdog			
☐ 55 2nd Round Checklist	.04	.02	.00
☐ 56 Niedermayer, Falloon,	.25	.10	.02
and Lachance			
☐ 57 The Goalies	.20	.08	.02
☐ 58 Pat Falloon FDP	.25	.10	.02
☐ 59 Scott Niedermayer FDP	.20	.08	.02
☐ 60 Scott Lachance FDP	.10	.04	.01
☐ 61 Peter Forsberg FDP	.25	.10	.02
☐ 62 Alek Stojanov FDP	.04	.02	.00
☐ 63 Richard Matvichuk FDP	.07	.03	.01
☐ 64 Patrick Poulin FDP	.10	.04	.01
☐ 65 Martin Lapointe FDP	.07	.03	.01
☐ 66 Tyler Wright FDP	.07	.03	.01
☐ 67 Philippe Boucher FDP	.07	.03	.01
☐ 68 Pat Peake FDP	.10	.04	.01
☐ 69 Markus Naslund FDP	.10	.04	.01
☐ 70 Brent Bilodeau FDP	.07	.03	.01
☐ 71 Glen Murray FDP	.07	.03	.01
☐ 72 Niklas Sundblad FDP	.04	.02	.00
☐ 73 Trevor Halverson FDP	.07	.03	.01

☐ 74	Dean McCammond FDP	.07	.03	.01
☐ 75	Award Winners	.10	.04	.01
	Philippe Boucher			
	Jeff Nelson			
	Scott Niedermayer			
☐ 76	The Swedes	.25	.10	.02
	Markus Naslund			
	Peter Forsberg			
☐ 77	3rd and 4th Round	.04	.02	.00
	Checklist			
☐ 78	Pat Falloon BW	.25	.10	.02
☐ 79	Scott Niedermayer BW	.20	.08	.02
☐ 80	Falloon/Niedermayer BW	.15	.06	.01
☐ 81	Scott Lachance BW	.10	.04	.01
☐ 82	Philippe Boucher BW	.07	.03	.01
☐ 83	Markus Naslund BW	.10	.04	.01
☐ 84	Glen Murray BW	.07	.03	.01
☐ 85	Niklas Sundblad BW	.04	.02	.00
☐ 86	Jason Dawe BW	.07	.03	.01
☐ 87	Yanick Perreault BW	.07	.03	.01
☐ 88	Offensive Threats	.10	.04	.01
	Yanic Dupre			
	Mikael Nylander			
☐ 89	Group Shot/Overview	.07	.03	.01
☐ 90	Face the Future/	.07	.03	.01
	Ultimate			

1991-92 Ultimate Original Six

 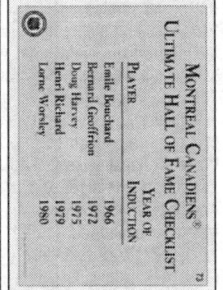

Produced by the Ultimate Trading Card Company, this 100-card set celebrates the 75th anniversary of the NHL by featuring players from the original six teams in the NHL. The standard-size (2 1/2" by 3 1/2") cards were available only in foil, with a production run reportedly of 25,000 foil cases. Each foil pack included a sweepstake card; prizes offered included 250 autographed Bobby Hull holograms and 500 sets autographed by those players living at the time. The fronts feature color action photos with white borders, with the player's name in a silver bar at the top and the left lower corner of the picture rolled back to allow space for the producer's logo. The backs have a career summary presented in the format of a newspaper article (with different headlines), with biography and career statistics appearing in a silver box toward the bottom of the card. The cards are numbered on the back and checklisted below as follows: Team Checklists (1-6), Montreal Canadiens (7-17), New York Rangers (18-29), Toronto Maple Leafs (30-46), Boston Bruins (47-56), Chicago Blackhawks (57-65), Detroit Red Wings (66-72), Ultimate Hall of Fame (73-78), All Ultimate Team (79-84), Referees (85-87), Bobby Hull (88-92), and Great Moments (93-97). The cards were produced in both English and French versions.

	MINT	EXC	G-VG
COMPLETE SET (100)	9.00	3.75	.90
COMMON PLAYER (1-100)	.10	.04	.01
*FRENCH: SAME VALUE:			

☐ 1	Montreal Canadiens	.15	.06	.01
	Checklist			

☐ 2	New York Rangers	.10	.04	.01
	Checklist			
☐ 3	Toronto Maple Leafs	.10	.04	.01
	Checklist			
☐ 4	Boston Bruins	.10	.04	.01
	Checklist			
☐ 5	Chicago Blackhawks	.10	.04	.01
	Checklist			
☐ 6	Detroit Red Wings	.10	.04	.01
	Checklist			
☐ 7	Ralph Backstrom	.10	.04	.01
☐ 8	Emile(Butch) Bouchard	.20	.08	.02
☐ 9	John Ferguson	.10	.04	.01
☐ 10	BoomBoom Geoffrion	.75	.30	.07
☐ 11	Phil Goyette	.10	.04	.01
☐ 12	Doug Harvey	.50	.20	.05
☐ 13	Don Marshall	.10	.04	.01
☐ 14	Henri Richard	.50	.20	.05
☐ 15	Dollard St.Laurent	.10	.04	.01
☐ 16	Jean-Guy Talbot	.15	.06	.01
☐ 17	Gump Worsley	.50	.20	.05
☐ 18	Andy Bathgate	.30	.12	.03
☐ 19	Lou Fontinato	.10	.04	.01
☐ 20	Ed Giacomin	.30	.12	.03
☐ 21	Vic Hadfield	.15	.06	.01
☐ 22	Camille Henry	.10	.04	.01
☐ 23	Harry Howell	.20	.08	.02
☐ 24	Orland Kurtenbach	.15	.06	.01
☐ 25	Jim Neilson	.10	.04	.01
☐ 26	Bob Nevin	.10	.04	.01
☐ 27	Dean Prentice	.15	.06	.01
☐ 28	Leo Reise Jr.	.10	.04	.01
☐ 29	George Sullivan	.10	.04	.01
☐ 30	Bob Baun	.15	.06	.01
☐ 31	Gus Bodnar	.10	.04	.01
☐ 32	Johnny Bower	.30	.12	.03
☐ 33	Bob Davidson	.10	.04	.01
☐ 34	Ron Ellis	.15	.06	.01
☐ 35	Billy Harris	.10	.04	.01
☐ 36	Larry Hillman	.10	.04	.01
☐ 37	Tim Horton	.50	.20	.05
☐ 38	Red Kelly	.40	.16	.04
☐ 39	Dave Keon	.30	.12	.03
☐ 40	Frank Mahovlich	.60	.24	.06
☐ 41	Eddie Shack	.25	.10	.02
☐ 42	Tod Sloan	.10	.04	.01
☐ 43	Sid Smith	.15	.06	.01
☐ 44	Allan Stanley	.25	.10	.02
☐ 45	Gaye Stewart	.10	.04	.01
☐ 46	Harry Watson	.20	.08	.02
☐ 47	Wayne Carleton	.10	.04	.01
☐ 48	Fern Flaman	.20	.08	.02
☐ 49	Ken Hodge UER	.15	.06	.01
	(Photo actually			
	Ed Westfall)			
☐ 50	Leo Labine	.10	.04	.01
☐ 51	Harry Lumley	.30	.12	.03
☐ 52	John McKenzie	.15	.06	.01
☐ 53	Doug Mohns	.15	.06	.01
☐ 54	Fred Stanfield	.10	.04	.01
☐ 55	Jerry Toppazzini	.10	.04	.01
☐ 56	Ed Westfall	.15	.06	.01
☐ 57	Bobby Hull	1.25	.50	.12
☐ 58	Ed Litzenberger	.10	.04	.01
☐ 59	Gilles Marotte	.10	.04	.01
☐ 60	Ab McDonald	.10	.04	.01
☐ 61	Bill Mosienko	.20	.08	.02
☐ 62	Jim Pappin	.10	.04	.01
☐ 63	Pierre Pilote	.20	.08	.02
☐ 64	Elmer Vasko	.10	.04	.01
☐ 65	Johnny Wilson	.10	.04	.01
☐ 66	Sid Abel	.25	.10	.02
☐ 67	Gary Bergman	.10	.04	.01
☐ 68	Alex Delvecchio	.40	.16	.04
☐ 69	Bill Gadsby	.30	.12	.03
☐ 70	Ted Lindsay	.50	.20	.05
☐ 71	Marcel Pronovost	.20	.08	.02
☐ 72	Norm Ullman	.30	.12	.03
☐ 73	BoomBoom Geoffrion	.75	.30	.07
☐ 74	Andy Bathgate	.30	.12	.03
☐ 75	Allan Stanley	.25	.10	.02
☐ 76	Fern Flaman	.20	.08	.02
☐ 77	Bobby Hull	1.25	.50	.12
☐ 78	Norm Ullman	.30	.12	.03
☐ 79	Red Kelly	.40	.16	.04
☐ 80	Johnny Bower	.40	.16	.04
☐ 81	Henri Richard	.50	.20	.05
☐ 82	Bobby Hull	1.25	.50	.12
☐ 83	BoomBoom Geoffrion	.75	.30	.07
☐ 84	Tim Horton	.50	.20	.05
☐ 85	Bill Friday REF	.10	.04	.01
☐ 86	Bruce Hood REF	.10	.04	.01
☐ 87	Ron Wicks REF	.10	.04	.01

☐	88	Bobby Hull	.60	.24	.06
		Electric Slap Shot			
☐	89	Bobby Hull	.60	.24	.06
		The Point Race			
☐	90	Bobby Hull	.60	.24	.06
		1960-61 Stanley Cup			
☐	91	Bobby Hull	.60	.24	.06
		The Curse of Muldoon is lifted			
☐	92	Bobby Hull	.60	.24	.06
		Million Dollar Man			
☐	93	Bobby Baun	.10	.04	.01
		Baun's Heroics			
☐	94	Ted Lindsay	.20	.08	.02
		Lindsay's comeback			
☐	95	Henri Richard	.20	.08	.02
		Richard's 99-year record			
☐	96	Bobby Hull	.60	.24	.06
		Hull breaks 50 goal barrier			
☐	97	Tim Horton	.30	.12	.03
		A Tribute to Horton			
☐	98	Keith McCreary	.10	.04	.01
☐	99	Checklist 1	.10	.04	.01
☐	100	Checklist 2	.10	.04	.01
☐	NNO	Bobby Hull Hologram	50.00	20.00	5.00

1991-92 Ultimate Original Six Box Bottoms

This four-card set was issued on the bottom of foil boxes. The cards measure the standard 2 1/2" by 3 1/2" and feature on the fronts four-color or black and white action photos, with the lower left corner turned upward to allow space for the Ultimate logo. The player's name appears in black in a silver border at the top and the NHL logo is placed toward the end of the silver bar. Bobby Hull's card features red to black screened bars on two sides enclosing an artwork collage. The cards are unnumbered and checklisted below in alphabetical order.

		MINT	EXC	G-VG
COMPLETE SET (4)		1.50	.60	.15
COMMON PLAYER (1-4)		.25	.10	.02
☐	1 Ed Giacomin	.50	.20	.05
☐	2 Bobby Hull	1.00	.40	.10
	The Golden Jet			
☐	3 Marcel Pronovost	.25	.10	.02
☐	4 Eddie Shack	.25	.10	.02

1992-93 Ultra

The 1992-93 Fleer Ultra hockey set consists of 450 standard-size (2 1/2" by 3 1/2") cards. Twelve Ultra All-Stars, ten Ultra Award Winners, ten Jeremy Roenick Performance Highlights and eight Ultra Rookies were randomly inserted

in first series foil packs. Roenick autographed more than 2,000 of his cards. The basic Ultra card has glossy color action player photos on the fronts that are full-bleed except at the bottom where a diagonal gold-foil stripe edges a "blue ice" border. The player's name and team appear on two team color-coded bars that overlay the bottom border. The horizontally oriented backs display action and close-up cut-out player photos against a hockey rink background. The team logo and biographical information appear in a blue ice bar edging the right side, while the player's name and statistics are given in bars running across the card bottom. The cards are numbered on the back and checklisted below alphabetically according to team as follows: Boston Bruins (1-11), Buffalo Sabres (12-20), Calgary Flames (21-31), Chicago Blackhawks (32-43), Detroit Red Wings (44-55), Edmonton Oilers (56-67), Hartford Whalers (68-77), Los Angeles Kings (78-88), Minnesota North Stars (89-99), Montreal Canadiens (100-111), New Jersey Devils (112-122), New York Islanders (123-132), New York Rangers (133-144), Ottawa Senators (145-150), Philadelphia Flyers (151-161), Pittsburgh Penguins (162-172), Quebec Nordiques (173-181), St. Louis Blues (182-190), San Jose Sharks (191-199), Tampa Bay Lightning (200-206), Toronto Maple Leafs (207-216), Vancouver Canucks (217-228), Washington Capitals (229-238), and Winnipeg Jets (239-247). The first series closes with checklist cards (248-250). The second series consists of 200 cards, including more than 50 rookies, traded players, and veterans who were omitted from series I. First year player cards carry an Ultra Rookie gold foil logo. A 25-card Ultra Imports set featuring NHL players from Europe, Russia, and Scandinavia was randomly inserted in all series II packs. The cards are numbered on the back, grouped alphabetically within teams, and checklisted below alphabetically according to teams as follows: Boston Bruins (251-257), Buffalo Sabres (258-265), Calgary Flames (266-272), Chicago Blackhawks (273-281), Detroit Red Wings (282-290), Edmonton Oilers (291-299), Hartford Whalers (300-306), Los Angeles Kings (307-314), Minnesota North Stars (315-323), Montreal Canadiens (324-333), New Jersey Devils (334-341), New York Islanders (342-350), New York Rangers (351-359), Ottawa Senators (360-367), Philadelphia Flyers (368-375), Pittsburgh Penguins (376-383), Quebec Nordiques (384-391), St. Louis Blues (392-398), San Jose Sharks (399-405), Tampa Bay Lightning (406-415), Toronto Maple Leafs (416-423), Vancouver Canucks (424-431), Washington Capitals (432-439), and Winnipeg Jets (440-447). The second series also closes with checklists (448-450). The key Rookie Cards in the set are Nikolai Borschevsky, Roman Hamrlik, Andrei Kovalenko, Dmitri Kvartalnov, Tommy Soderstrom, and Martin Straka.

		MINT	EXC	G-VG
	COMPLETE SET (450)	35.00	16.00	4.40
	COMPLETE SERIES 1 (250)	18.00	8.00	2.30
	COMPLETE SERIES 2 (200)	17.00	7.75	2.10
	COMMON PLAYER (1-250)	.07	.03	.01
	COMMON PLAYER (251-450)	.07	.03	.01
☐ 1	Brent Ashton	.07	.03	.01
☐ 2	Ray Bourque	.25	.11	.03
☐ 3	Steve Heinze	.07	.03	.01
☐ 4	Joe Juneau UER	1.75	.80	.22
	(Shoots left, not right)			
☐ 5	Stephen Leach	.07	.03	.01
☐ 6	Andy Moog	.07	.03	.01
☐ 7	Cam Neely	.25	.11	.03
☐ 8	Adam Oates	.20	.09	.03
☐ 9	Dave Poulin	.07	.03	.01
☐ 10	Vladimir Ruzicka	.07	.03	.01
☐ 11	Glen Wesley	.07	.03	.01
☐ 12	Dave Andreychuk	.25	.11	.03
☐ 13	Keith Carney	.07	.03	.01
☐ 14	Tom Draper	.07	.03	.01
☐ 15	Dale Hawerchuk	.10	.05	.01
☐ 16	Pat LaFontaine	.35	.16	.04
☐ 17	Brad May	.07	.03	.01
☐ 18	Alexander Mogilny	.75	.35	.09
☐ 19	Mike Ramsey	.07	.03	.01
☐ 20	Ken Sutton	.07	.03	.01
☐ 21	Theoren Fleury	.15	.07	.02
☐ 22	Gary Leeman	.07	.03	.01
☐ 23	Al MacInnis	.15	.07	.02
☐ 24	Sergei Makarov	.10	.05	.01
☐ 25	Joe Nieuwendyk	.10	.05	.01
☐ 26	Joel Otto	.07	.03	.01
☐ 27	Paul Ranheim	.07	.03	.01
☐ 28	Robert Reichel	.10	.05	.01
☐ 29	Gary Roberts	.10	.05	.01
☐ 30	Gary Suter	.10	.05	.01
☐ 31	Mike Vernon	.10	.05	.01
☐ 32	Ed Belfour	.40	.18	.05
☐ 33	Rob Brown	.07	.03	.01
☐ 34	Chris Chelios	.10	.05	.01
☐ 35	Michel Goulet	.10	.05	.01
☐ 36	Dirk Graham	.07	.03	.01
☐ 37	Mike Hudson	.07	.03	.01
☐ 38	Igor Kravchuk	.07	.03	.01
☐ 39	Steve Larmer	.10	.05	.01
☐ 40	Dean McAmmond	.25	.11	.03
☐ 41	Jeremy Roenick	1.00	.45	.13
☐ 42	Steve Smith	.10	.05	.01
☐ 43	Brent Sutter	.10	.05	.01
☐ 44	Shawn Burr	.07	.03	.01
☐ 45	Jimmy Carson	.07	.03	.01
☐ 46	Tim Cheveldae	.10	.05	.01
☐ 47	Dino Ciccarelli	.10	.05	.01
☐ 48	Sergei Fedorov	1.25	.55	.16
☐ 49	Vladimir Konstantinov	.07	.03	.01
☐ 50	Vyacheslav Kozlov	1.25	.55	.16
☐ 51	Nicklas Lidstrom	.25	.11	.03
☐ 52	Brad McCrimmon	.07	.03	.01
☐ 53	Bob Probert	.07	.03	.01
☐ 54	Paul Ysebaert	.07	.03	.01
☐ 55	Steve Yzerman	.40	.18	.05
☐ 56	Josef Beranek	.25	.11	.03
☐ 57	Shayne Corson	.10	.05	.01
☐ 58	Brian Glynn	.07	.03	.01
☐ 59	Petr Klima	.07	.03	.01
☐ 60	Kevin Lowe	.07	.03	.01
☐ 61	Norm Maciver	.07	.03	.01
☐ 62	Dave Manson	.07	.03	.01
☐ 63	Joe Murphy	.07	.03	.01
☐ 64	Bernie Nicholls	.10	.05	.01
☐ 65	Bill Ranford	.10	.05	.01
☐ 66	Craig Simpson	.07	.03	.01
☐ 67	Esa Tikkanen	.10	.05	.01
☐ 68	Sean Burke	.10	.05	.01
☐ 69	Adam Burt	.07	.03	.01
☐ 70	Andrew Cassels	.07	.03	.01
☐ 71	Murray Craven	.07	.03	.01
☐ 72	John Cullen	.07	.03	.01
☐ 73	Randy Cunneyworth	.07	.03	.01
☐ 74	Tim Kerr	.10	.05	.01
☐ 75	Geoff Sanderson	.50	.23	.06
☐ 76	Eric Weinrich	.07	.03	.01
☐ 77	Zarley Zalapski	.07	.03	.01
☐ 78	Peter Ahola	.07	.03	.01
☐ 79	Rob Blake	.15	.07	.02
☐ 80	Paul Coffey	.25	.11	.03
☐ 81	Mike Donnelly	.07	.03	.01
☐ 82	Tony Granato	.07	.03	.01
☐ 83	Wayne Gretzky	1.50	.65	.19
☐ 84	Kelly Hrudey	.10	.05	.01
☐ 85	Jari Kurri	.15	.07	.02
☐ 86	Corey Millen	.10	.05	.01
☐ 87	Luc Robitaille	.30	.14	.04
☐ 88	Tomas Sandstrom	.07	.03	.01
☐ 89	Neal Broten	.10	.05	.01
☐ 90	Jon Casey	.10	.05	.01
☐ 91	Russ Courtnall	.10	.05	.01
☐ 92	Ulf Dahlen	.07	.03	.01
☐ 93	Todd Elik	.07	.03	.01
☐ 94	Dave Gagner	.10	.05	.01
☐ 95	Jim Johnson	.07	.03	.01
☐ 96	Mike Modano UER	.40	.18	.05
	(Born in Livonia, Michigan, not Minnesota)			
☐ 97	Bobby Smith	.10	.05	.01
☐ 98	Mark Tinordi	.10	.05	.01
☐ 99	Darcy Wakaluk	.10	.05	.01
☐ 100	Brian Bellows	.10	.05	.01
☐ 101	Benoit Brunet	.07	.03	.01
☐ 102	Guy Carbonneau	.10	.05	.01
☐ 103	Vincent Damphousse	.10	.05	.01
☐ 104	Eric Desjardins	.07	.03	.01
☐ 105	Gilbert Dionne	.07	.03	.01
☐ 106	Mike Keane	.07	.03	.01
☐ 107	Kirk Muller	.10	.05	.01
☐ 108	Patrick Roy	1.00	.45	.13
☐ 109	Denis Savard	.10	.05	.01
☐ 110	Mathieu Schneider	.10	.05	.01
☐ 111	Brian Skrudland	.07	.03	.01
☐ 112	Tom Chorske	.07	.03	.01
☐ 113	Zdeno Ciger	.07	.03	.01
☐ 114	Claude Lemieux	.10	.05	.01
☐ 115	John MacLean	.10	.05	.01
☐ 116	Scott Niedermayer	.50	.23	.06
☐ 117	Stephane Richer	.10	.05	.01
☐ 118	Peter Stastny	.10	.05	.01
☐ 119	Scott Stevens	.15	.07	.02
☐ 120	Chris Terreri	.10	.05	.01
☐ 121	Kevin Todd	.07	.03	.01
☐ 122	Valeri Zelepukin	.25	.11	.03
☐ 123	Ray Ferraro	.07	.03	.01
☐ 124	Mark Fitzpatrick	.10	.05	.01
☐ 125	Patrick Flatley	.07	.03	.01
☐ 126	Glenn Healy	.10	.05	.01
☐ 127	Benoit Hogue	.07	.03	.01
☐ 128	Derek King	.07	.03	.01
☐ 129	Uwe Krupp	.07	.03	.01
☐ 130	Scott Lachance	.07	.03	.01
☐ 131	Steve Thomas	.10	.05	.01
☐ 132	Pierre Turgeon	.30	.14	.04
☐ 133	Tony Amonte	.25	.11	.03
☐ 134	Paul Broten	.07	.03	.01
☐ 135	Mike Gartner	.15	.07	.02
☐ 136	Adam Graves	.40	.18	.05
☐ 137	Alexei Kovalev	1.25	.55	.16
☐ 138	Brian Leetch	.40	.18	.05
☐ 139	Mark Messier	.30	.14	.04
☐ 140	Sergei Nemchinov	.10	.05	.01
☐ 141	James Patrick	.07	.03	.01
☐ 142	Mike Richter	.35	.16	.04
☐ 143	Darren Turcotte	.07	.03	.01
☐ 144	John Vanbiesbrouck	.15	.07	.02
☐ 145	Dominic Lavoie	.07	.03	.01
☐ 146	Lonnie Loach	.07	.03	.01
☐ 147	Andrew McBain	.07	.03	.01
☐ 148	Darren Rumble	.07	.03	.01
☐ 149	Sylvain Turgeon	.07	.03	.01
☐ 150	Peter Sidorkiewicz	.07	.03	.01
☐ 151	Brian Benning	.07	.03	.01
☐ 152	Rod Brind'Amour	.25	.11	.03
☐ 153	Viacheslav Butsayev	.20	.09	.03
☐ 154	Kevin Dineen	.10	.05	.01
☐ 155	Pelle Eklund	.07	.03	.01
☐ 156	Garry Galley	.07	.03	.01
☐ 157	Eric Lindros	5.00	2.30	.60
☐ 158	Mark Recchi	.35	.16	.04
☐ 159	Dominic Roussel	.25	.11	.03
☐ 160	Tommy Soderstrom	.50	.23	.06
☐ 161	Dimitri Yushkevich	.25	.11	.03
☐ 162	Tom Barrasso	.10	.05	.01
☐ 163	Ron Francis	.10	.05	.01
☐ 164	Jaromir Jagr	1.00	.45	.13
☐ 165	Mario Lemieux	1.25	.55	.16
☐ 166	Joe Mullen	.10	.05	.01
☐ 167	Larry Murphy	.10	.05	.01
☐ 168	Jim Paek	.07	.03	.01
☐ 169	Kjell Samuelsson	.07	.03	.01
☐ 170	Ulf Samuelsson	.07	.03	.01
☐ 171	Kevin Stevens	.35	.16	.04
☐ 172	Rick Tocchet	.10	.05	.01
☐ 173	Alexei Gusarov	.07	.03	.01
☐ 174	Ron Hextall	.10	.05	.01
☐ 175	Mike Hough	.07	.03	.01
☐ 176	Claude Lapointe	.07	.03	.01
☐ 177	Owen Nolan	.20	.09	.03

178	Mike Ricci	.20	.09	.03
179	Joe Sakic	.30	.14	.04
180	Mats Sundin	.35	.16	.04
181	Mikhail Tatarinov	.07	.03	.01
182	Bob Bassen	.07	.03	.01
183	Jeff Brown	.10	.05	.01
184	Garth Butcher	.07	.03	.01
185	Paul Cavallini	.07	.03	.01
186	Brett Hull	1.00	.45	.13
187	Craig Janney	.20	.09	.03
188	Curtis Joseph	.40	.18	.05
189	Brendan Shanahan	.35	.16	.04
190	Ron Sutter	.07	.03	.01
191	David Bruce	.07	.03	.01
192	Dale Craigwell	.07	.03	.01
193	Dean Evason	.07	.03	.01
194	Pat Falloon	.25	.11	.03
195	Jeff Hackett	.07	.03	.01
196	Kelly Kisio	.07	.03	.01
197	Brian Lawton	.07	.03	.01
198	Neil Wilkinson	.07	.03	.01
199	Doug Wilson	.10	.05	.01
200	Marc Bergevin	.07	.03	.01
201	Roman Hamrlik	.60	.25	.08
202	Pat Jablonski	.07	.03	.01
203	Michel Mongeau	.07	.03	.01
204	Peter Taglianetti	.07	.03	.01
205	Steve Tuttle	.07	.03	.01
206	Wendell Young	.07	.03	.01
207	Glenn Anderson	.10	.05	.01
208	Wendel Clark	.15	.07	.02
209	Dave Ellett	.07	.03	.01
210	Grant Fuhr	.10	.05	.01
211	Doug Gilmour	.40	.18	.05
212	Jamie Macoun	.07	.03	.01
213	Felix Potvin	2.00	.90	.25
214	Bob Rouse	.07	.03	.01
215	Joe Sacco	.07	.03	.01
216	Peter Zezel	.07	.03	.01
217	Greg Adams	.07	.03	.01
218	Dave Babych	.07	.03	.01
219	Pavel Bure	2.50	1.15	.30
220	Geoff Courtnall	.07	.03	.01
221	Doug Lidster	.07	.03	.01
222	Trevor Linden	.30	.14	.04
223	Jyrki Lumme	.07	.03	.01
224	Kirk McLean	.30	.14	.04
225	Sergio Momesso	.07	.03	.01
226	Petr Nedved	.30	.14	.04
227	Cliff Ronning	.07	.03	.01
228	Jim Sandlak	.07	.03	.01
229	Don Beaupre	.10	.05	.01
230	Peter Bondra	.10	.05	.01
231	Kevin Hatcher	.10	.05	.01
232	Dale Hunter	.10	.05	.01
233	Al Iafrate	.10	.05	.01
234	Calle Johansson	.07	.03	.01
235	Dimitri Khristich	.10	.05	.01
236	Kelly Miller	.07	.03	.01
237	Michal Pivonka	.10	.05	.01
238	Mike Ridley	.10	.05	.01
239	Luciano Borsato	.07	.03	.01
240	Bob Essensa	.10	.05	.01
241	Phil Housley	.10	.05	.01
242	Troy Murray	.07	.03	.01
243	Teppo Numminen	.07	.03	.01
244	Fredrik Olausson	.07	.03	.01
245	Ed Olczyk	.07	.03	.01
246	Darrin Shannon	.07	.03	.01
247	Thomas Steen	.07	.03	.01
248	Checklist 1	.10	.03	.01
249	Checklist 2	.10	.03	.01
250	Checklist 3	.10	.03	.01
251	Ted Donato	.07	.03	.01
252	Dmitri Kvartalnov	.30	.14	.04
253	Gord Murphy	.07	.03	.01
254	Gregori Panteleyev	.15	.07	.02
255	Gordie Roberts	.07	.03	.01
256	David Shaw	.07	.03	.01
257	Don Sweeney	.07	.03	.01
258	Doug Bodger	.07	.03	.01
259	Gord Donnelly	.07	.03	.01
260	Yuri Khmylev	.40	.18	.05
261	Daren Puppa	.10	.05	.01
262	Richard Smehlik	.30	.14	.04
263	Petr Svoboda	.07	.03	.01
264	Bob Sweeney	.07	.03	.01
265	Randy Wood	.07	.03	.01
266	Kevin Dahl	.07	.03	.01
267	Chris Dahlquist	.07	.03	.01
268	Roger Johansson	.07	.03	.01
269	Chris Lindberg	.07	.03	.01
270	Frank Musil	.07	.03	.01
271	Ronnie Stern	.07	.03	.01
272	Carey Wilson	.07	.03	.01
273	Dave Christian	.07	.03	.01
274	Karl Dykhuis	.07	.03	.01
275	Greg Gilbert	.07	.03	.01
276	Sergei Krivokrasov	.25	.11	.03
277	Frantisek Kucera	.07	.03	.01
278	Bryan Marchment	.07	.03	.01
279	Stephane Matteau	.07	.03	.01
280	Brian Noonan	.07	.03	.01
281	Christian Ruuttu	.07	.03	.01
282	Steve Chiasson	.07	.03	.01
283	Dino Ciccarelli	.10	.05	.01
284	Gerard Gallant	.07	.03	.01
285	Mark Howe	.10	.05	.01
286	Keith Primeau	.10	.05	.01
287	Yves Racine	.07	.03	.01
288	Vincent Riendeau	.07	.03	.01
289	Ray Sheppard	.10	.05	.01
290	Mike Sillinger	.07	.03	.01
291	Kelly Buchberger	.07	.03	.01
292	Shayne Corson	.10	.05	.01
293	Brent Gilchrist	.07	.03	.01
294	Craig MacTavish	.07	.03	.01
295	Scott Mellanby	.07	.03	.01
296	Craig Muni	.07	.03	.01
297	Luke Richardson	.07	.03	.01
298	Ron Tugnutt	.07	.03	.01
299	Shaun Van Allen	.07	.03	.01
300	Steve Konroyd	.07	.03	.01
301	Nick Kypreos	.07	.03	.01
302	Robert Petrovicky	.25	.11	.03
303	Frank Pietrangelo	.07	.03	.01
304	Patrick Poulin	.07	.03	.01
305	Pat Verbeek	.10	.05	.01
306	Eric Weinrich	.07	.03	.01
307	Jim Hiller	.15	.07	.02
308	Charlie Huddy	.07	.03	.01
309	Lonnie Loach	.07	.03	.01
310	Marty McSorley	.10	.05	.01
311	Robb Stauber	.07	.03	.01
312	Darryl Sydor	.10	.05	.01
313	Dave Taylor	.10	.05	.01
314	Alexei Zhitnik	.30	.14	.04
315	Shane Churla	.07	.03	.01
316	Russ Courtnall	.10	.05	.01
317	Mike Craig	.07	.03	.01
318	Gaetan Duchesne	.07	.03	.01
319	Derian Hatcher	.07	.03	.01
320	Craig Ludwig	.07	.03	.01
321	Richard Matvichuk	.20	.09	.03
322	Mike McPhee	.07	.03	.01
323	Tommy Sjodin	.15	.07	.02
324	Brian Bellows	.10	.05	.01
325	Patrice Brisebois	.07	.03	.01
326	J.J.Daigneault	.07	.03	.01
327	Kevin Haller	.07	.03	.01
328	Sean Hill	.20	.09	.03
329	Stephan Lebeau	.07	.03	.01
330	John LeClair	.07	.03	.01
331	Lyle Odelein	.07	.03	.01
332	Andre Racicot	.07	.03	.01
333	Ed Ronan	.15	.07	.02
334	Craig Billington	.07	.03	.01
335	Ken Daneyko	.07	.03	.01
336	Bruce Driver	.07	.03	.01
337	Viacheslav Fetisov	.07	.03	.01
338	Bill Guerin	.35	.16	.04
339	Bobby Holik	.07	.03	.01
340	Alexei Kasatonov	.07	.03	.01
341	Alexander Semak	.07	.03	.01
342	Tom Fitzgerald	.07	.03	.01
343	Travis Green	.20	.09	.03
344	Darius Kasparaitis	.20	.09	.03
345	Danny Lorenz	.07	.03	.01
346	Vladimir Malakhov	.30	.14	.04
347	Marty McInnis	.07	.03	.01
348	Brian Mullen	.10	.05	.01
349	Jeff Norton	.07	.03	.01
350	David Volek	.07	.03	.01
351	Jeff Beukeboom	.07	.03	.01
352	Phil Bourque	.07	.03	.01
353	Paul Broten	.07	.03	.01
354	Mark Hardy	.07	.03	.01
355	Steven King	.20	.09	.03
356	Kevin Lowe	.07	.03	.01
357	Ed Olczyk	.07	.03	.01
358	Doug Weight	.10	.05	.01
359	Sergei Zubov	3.00	1.35	.40
360	Jamie Baker	.07	.03	.01
361	Daniel Berthiaume	.07	.03	.01
362	Chris Luongo	.07	.03	.01
363	Norm Maciver	.07	.03	.01

☐	364 Brad Marsh	.10	.05	.01
☐	365 Mike Peluso	.07	.03	.01
☐	366 Brad Shaw	.07	.03	.01
☐	367 Peter Sidorkiewicz	.07	.03	.01
☐	368 Keith Acton	.07	.03	.01
☐	369 Stephane Beauregard	.07	.03	.01
☐	370 Terry Carkner	.07	.03	.01
☐	371 Brent Fedyk	.07	.03	.01
☐	372 Andrei Lomakin	.07	.03	.01
☐	373 Ryan McGill	.15	.07	.02
☐	374 Ric Nattress	.07	.03	.01
☐	375 Greg Paslawski	.07	.03	.01
☐	376 Peter Ahola	.07	.03	.01
☐	377 Jeff Daniels	.07	.03	.01
☐	378 Troy Loney	.07	.03	.01
☐	379 Shawn McEachern	.25	.11	.03
☐	380 Mike Needham	.15	.07	.02
☐	381 Paul Stanton	.07	.03	.01
☐	382 Martin Straka	1.50	.65	.19
☐	383 Ken Wregget	.07	.03	.01
☐	384 Steve Duchesne	.10	.05	.01
☐	385 Ron Hextall	.10	.05	.01
☐	386 Kerry Huffman	.07	.03	.01
☐	387 Andrei Kovalenko	.40	.18	.05
☐	388 Bill Lindsay	.15	.07	.02
☐	389 Mike Ricci	.10	.05	.01
☐	390 Martin Rucinsky	.15	.07	.02
☐	391 Scott Young	.07	.03	.01
☐	392 Philippe Bozon	.07	.03	.01
☐	393 Nelson Emerson	.25	.11	.03
☐	394 Guy Hebert	.60	.25	.08
☐	395 Igor Korolev	.20	.09	.03
☐	396 Kevin Miller	.10	.05	.01
☐	397 Vitali Prokhorov	.20	.09	.03
☐	398 Rich Sutter	.07	.03	.01
☐	399 John Carter	.07	.03	.01
☐	400 Johan Garpenlov	.07	.03	.01
☐	401 Arturs Irbe	.60	.25	.08
☐	402 Sandis Ozolinsh	.60	.25	.08
☐	403 Tom Pederson	.20	.09	.03
☐	404 Michel Picard	.07	.03	.01
☐	405 Doug Zmolek	.20	.09	.03
☐	406 Mikael Andersson	.07	.03	.01
☐	407 Bob Beers	.07	.03	.01
☐	408 Brian Bradley	.07	.03	.01
☐	409 Adam Creighton	.07	.03	.01
☐	410 Doug Crossman	.07	.03	.01
☐	411 Ken Hodge	.07	.03	.01
☐	412 Chris Kontos	.20	.09	.03
☐	413 Rob Ramage	.07	.03	.01
☐	414 John Tucker	.07	.03	.01
☐	415 Rob Zamuner	.15	.07	.02
☐	416 Ken Baumgartner	.07	.03	.01
☐	417 Drake Berehowsky	.07	.03	.01
☐	418 Nikolai Borschevsky	.50	.23	.06
☐	419 John Cullen	.07	.03	.01
☐	420 Mike Foligno	.07	.03	.01
☐	421 Mike Krushelnyski	.07	.03	.01
☐	422 Dmitri Mironov	.10	.05	.01
☐	423 Rob Pearson	.07	.03	.01
☐	424 Gerald Diduck	.07	.03	.01
☐	425 Robert Dirk	.07	.03	.01
☐	426 Tom Fergus	.07	.03	.01
☐	427 Gino Odjick	.07	.03	.01
☐	428 Adrien Plavsic	.07	.03	.01
☐	429 Anatoli Semenov	.07	.03	.01
☐	430 Jiri Slegr	.07	.03	.01
☐	431 Dixon Ward	.20	.09	.03
☐	432 Paul Cavallini	.07	.03	.01
☐	433 Sylvain Cote	.07	.03	.01
☐	434 Pat Elynuik	.07	.03	.01
☐	435 Jim Hrivnak	.07	.03	.01
☐	436 Keith Jones	.20	.09	.03
☐	437 Steve Konowalchuk	.20	.09	.03
☐	438 Todd Krygier	.07	.03	.01
☐	439 Paul MacDermid	.07	.03	.01
☐	440 Sergei Bautin	.15	.07	.02
☐	441 Evgeny Davydov	.07	.03	.01
☐	442 John Druce	.07	.03	.01
☐	443 Troy Murray	.07	.03	.01
☐	444 Teemu Selanne	2.00	.90	.25
☐	445 Rick Tabaracci	.07	.03	.01
☐	446 Keith Tkachuk	.40	.18	.05
☐	447 Alexei Zhamnov	.60	.25	.08
☐	448 Checklist 4	.10	.03	.01
☐	449 Checklist 5	.10	.03	.01
☐	450 Checklist 6	.10	.03	.01

1992-93 Ultra All-Stars

This 12-card standard-size (2 1/2" by 3 1/2") set was randomly inserted in 1992-93 Fleer Ultra first series foil packs. The cards depict First Team All-Stars by conference. The glossy color action player photos on the fronts are full-bleed except at the bottom where a diagonal gold-foil stripe edges a beige marbleized border. A gold-foil insignia with a star is superimposed on the beige border. The fronts feature color, action player photos from the 1992 All-Star Game. A brown marbleized border runs diagonally across the bottom. This border is separated from the photo by a thin gold foil stripe. The player's name and the words "NHL All-Star" are printed in gold foil on the marbleized border. On a gray marbleized background, the horizontal backs feature a cut-out color close-up player photo and a season summary. The cards are numbered on the back.

	MINT	EXC	G-VG
COMPLETE SET (12)	35.00	16.00	4.40
COMMON PLAYER (1-12)	2.00	.90	.25
☐ 1 Paul Coffey UER	2.00	.90	.25
(Photo on back actually Kevin Stevens) Pittsburgh Penguins			
☐ 2 Ray Bourque	2.00	.90	.25
Boston Bruins			
☐ 3 Patrick Roy	6.00	2.70	.75
Montreal Canadiens			
☐ 4 Mario Lemieux	7.00	3.10	.85
Pittsburgh Penguins			
☐ 5 Kevin Stevens UER	3.00	1.35	.40
(Photo on back actually Paul Coffey) Pittsburgh Penguins			
☐ 6 Jaromir Jagr	4.00	1.80	.50
Pittsburgh Penguins			
☐ 7 Chris Chelios	2.00	.90	.25
Chicago Blackhawks			
☐ 8 Al MacInnis	2.00	.90	.25
Calgary Flames			
☐ 9 Ed Belfour	3.00	1.35	.40
Chicago Blackhawks			
☐ 10 Wayne Gretzky	8.00	3.60	1.00
Los Angeles Kings			
☐ 11 Luc Robitaille	3.00	1.35	.40
Los Angeles Kings			
☐ 12 Brett Hull	4.00	1.80	.50
St. Louis Blues			

1992-93 Ultra Award Winners

This ten-card standard-size (2 1/2" by 3 1/2") set was randomly inserted in 1992-93 Fleer Ultra first series foil packs. The cards feature 1991-92 award winners. The glossy color action player photos on the fronts are full-bleed except at the bottom where a gold-foil stripe edges into a marbleized border.

	MINT	EXC	G-VG
COMPLETE SET (10)........................	30.00	13.50	3.80
COMMON PLAYER (1-10)................	2.00	.90	.25
☐ 1 Mark Messier.........................	3.00	1.35	.40
New York Rangers			
☐ 2 Brian Leetch.........................	3.50	1.55	.45
New York Rangers			
☐ 3 Guy Carbonneau....................	2.00	.90	.25
Montreal Canadiens			
☐ 4 Patrick Roy..........................	6.00	2.70	.75
Montreal Canadiens			
☐ 5 Mario Lemieux........................	7.00	3.10	.85
Pittsburgh Penguins			
☐ 6 Wayne Gretzky.......................	8.00	3.60	1.00
Los Angeles Kings			
☐ 7 Mark Fitzpatrick.....................	2.00	.90	.25
New York Islanders			
☐ 8 Ray Bourque.........................	2.00	.90	.25
Boston Bruins			
☐ 9 Pavel Bure...........................	8.00	3.60	1.00
Vancouver Canucks			
☐ 10 Mark Messier.......................	3.00	1.35	.40
New York Rangers			

		MINT	EXC	G-VG
	Boston Bruins			
☐ 13	Nicklas Lidstrom...................	2.50	1.15	.30
	Detroit Red Wings			
☐ 14	Vladimir Malakhov...............	3.00	1.35	.40
	New York Islanders			
☐ 15	Dmitri Mironov....................	2.50	1.15	.30
	Toronto Maple Leafs			
☐ 16	Alexander Mogilny...............	6.00	2.70	.75
	Buffalo Sabres			
☐ 17	Petr Nedved......................	5.00	2.30	.60
	Vancouver Canucks			
☐ 18	Fredrik Olausson.................	2.50	1.15	.30
	Winnipeg Jets			
☐ 19	Sandis Ozolinsh..................	5.00	2.30	.60
	San Jose Sharks			
☐ 20	Ulf Samuelsson...................	2.50	1.15	.30
	Pittsburgh Penguins			
☐ 21	Teemu Selanne...................	8.00	3.60	1.00
	Winnipeg Jets			
☐ 22	Richard Smehlik..................	2.50	1.15	.30
	Buffalo Sabres			
☐ 23	Tommy Soderstrom..............	3.00	1.35	.40
	Philadelphia Flyers			
☐ 24	Peter Stastny.....................	3.00	1.35	.40
	New Jersey Devils			
☐ 25	Mats Sundin......................	5.00	2.30	.60
	Quebec Nordiques			

1992-93 Ultra Imports

1992-93 Ultra Jeremy Roenick

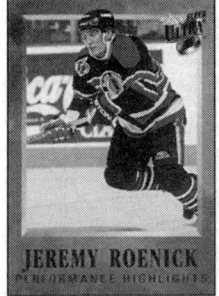
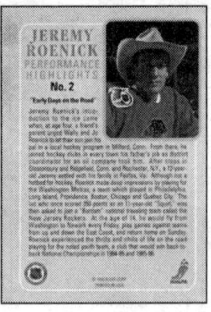

Randomly inserted in second series 1992-93 Fleer Ultra foil packs, this 25-card set measures the standard size (2 1/2" by 3 1/2"). The cards depict foreign players in the National Hockey League. Fronts feature color action cut-out player photos against a purple surreal background showing the player on ice with a globe design in the distance. The player's name is silver foil stamped at the bottom. The horizontal backs carry a close-up of the player, the player's name, and player information. The background is similar to the front. The cards are numbered on the back.

	MINT	EXC	G-VG
COMPLETE SET (25).......................	70.00	32.00	8.75
COMMON PLAYER (1-25)................	2.50	1.15	.30
☐ 1 Nikolai Borschevsky...............	3.00	1.35	.40
Toronto Maple Leafs			
☐ 2 Pavel Bure...........................	15.00	6.75	1.90
Vancouver Canucks			
☐ 3 Sergei Fedorov....................	8.00	3.60	1.00
Detroit Red Wings			
☐ 4 Roman Hamrlik.....................	3.00	1.35	.40
Tampa Bay Lightning			
☐ 5 Arturs Irbe..........................	7.00	3.10	.85
San Jose Sharks			
☐ 6 Jaromir Jagr.........................	6.00	2.70	.75
Pittsburgh Penguins			
☐ 7 Dimitri Khristich....................	2.50	1.15	.30
Washington Capitals			
☐ 8 Petr Klima...........................	2.50	1.15	.30
Edmonton Oilers			
☐ 9 Andrei Kovalenko..................	2.50	1.15	.30
Quebec Nordiques			
☐ 10 Alexei Kovalev.....................	6.00	2.70	.75
New York Rangers			
☐ 11 Jari Kurri...........................	3.00	1.35	.40
Los Angeles Kings			
☐ 12 Dmitri Kvartalnov.................	2.50	1.15	.30

Randomly inserted in first series 1992-93 Fleer Ultra foil packs, this 12-card set measures the standard size (2 1/2" by 3 1/2"). Two of the cards (11, 12) were available through a mail-in offer which was not availbale in Canada. The set, which features color action photos on front and career highlights on back, spotlights the career of Chicago Blackhawks' Jeremy Roenick. Roenick personally autographed more than 2,000 of his cards. The cards are numbered on back.

	MINT	EXC	G-VG
COMPLETE SET (10).......................	40.00	18.00	5.00
COMMON ROENICK (1-10).............	4.00	1.80	.50
COMMON MAIL-IN (11-12).............	6.00	2.70	.75
☐ 1 Jeremy Roenick....................	4.00	1.80	.50
Blast From The Past			
☐ 2 Jeremy Roenick....................	4.00	1.80	.50
Early Days on the Road			
☐ 3 Jeremy Roenick....................	4.00	1.80	.50
Prep School Phenom			
☐ 4 Jeremy Roenick....................	4.00	1.80	.50
Blackhawk-Bound			
☐ 5 Jeremy Roenick....................	4.00	1.80	.50
Breakfast With A			
Champion			
☐ 6 Jeremy Roenick....................	4.00	1.80	.50
The Fast Track			
☐ 7 Jeremy Roenick....................	4.00	1.80	.50
Boy To Man			
☐ 8 Jeremy Roenick....................	4.00	1.80	.50
Great Expectations			
☐ 9 Jeremy Roenick....................	4.00	1.80	.50
Changing of the Guard			
☐ 10 Jeremy Roenick....................	4.00	1.80	.50
Superstar			

		MINT	EXC	G-VG
☐ 11	Jeremy Roenick	6.00	2.70	.75
	Impressive Impressions (Skating, front shot)			
☐ 12	Jeremy Roenick	6.00	2.70	.75
	Roenick on Roenick (Skating, side view)			
☐ AU	Jeremy Roenick AU	200.00	90.00	25.00
	(Certified autograph)			

1992-93 Ultra Rookies

This eight-card standard-size (2 1/2" by 3 1/2") set was randomly inserted in 1992-93 Fleer Ultra series one foil packs. The card fronts feature color, action player photos. A brown marbleized border runs diagonally across the bottom. This border is separated from the photo by a thin gold foil stripe. The player's name and the words "Ultra Rookie" are printed in gold foil on the marbleized border. The backs show a close-up picture with a player profile against a gray marbleized background. The cards are numbered on the back.

		MINT	EXC	G-VG
COMPLETE SET (8)		25.00	11.50	3.10
COMMON PLAYER (1-8)		2.00	.90	.25
☐ 1	Tony Amonte	3.00	1.35	.40
	New York Rangers			
☐ 2	Donald Audette	2.00	.90	.25
	Buffalo Sabres			
☐ 3	Pavel Bure	8.00	3.60	1.00
	Vancouver Canucks			
☐ 4	Gilbert Dionne	2.00	.90	.25
	Montreal Canadiens			
☐ 5	Nelson Emerson	3.00	1.35	.40
	St. Louis Blues			
☐ 6	Pat Falloon	4.00	1.80	.50
	San Jose Sharks			
☐ 7	Nicklas Lidstrom	2.00	.90	.25
	Detroit Red Wings			
☐ 8	Kevin Todd	2.00	.90	.25
	New Jersey Devils			

1993-94 Ultra

The 1993-94 Ultra hockey set consists of 500 standard-size (2 1/2" by 3 1/2") cards. Both the first and second series contained 250 cards. The color action player photos on the fronts are full-bleed except at the bottom where a diagonal gold foil stripe separates the picture from a gray ice border. The player's name, team name, and position are gold foil-stamped on team color-coded bars. The horizontal backs display two color player cut-outs superimposed on a hockey stadium background, with biography, statistics, and team logo overprinted. The cards are numbered on the back. Randomly inserted in various first and second series packs

were ten different insert sets. The checkists for both series are alphabetical by team.

		MINT	EXC	G-VG
COMPLETE SET (500)		45.00	20.00	5.75
COMPLETE SERIES 1 (250)		20.00	9.00	2.50
COMPLETE SERIES 2 (250)		25.00	11.50	3.10
COMMON PLAYER (1-250)		.08	.04	.01
COMMON PLAYER (251-500)		.08	.04	.01
☐ 1	Ray Bourque	.20	.09	.03
	Boston Bruins			
☐ 2	Andy Moog	.10	.05	.01
	Dallas Stars			
☐ 3	Brian Benning	.08	.04	.01
	Edmonton Oilers			
☐ 4	Brian Bellows	.10	.05	.01
	Montreal Canadiens			
☐ 5	Claude Lemieux	.10	.05	.01
	New Jersey Devils			
☐ 6	Jamie Baker	.08	.04	.01
	Ottawa Senators			
☐ 7	Steve Duchesne	.10	.05	.01
	Quebec Nordiques			
☐ 8	Ed Courtenay	.08	.04	.01
	San Jose Sharks			
☐ 9	Glenn Anderson	.10	.05	.01
	Toronto Maple Leafs			
☐ 10	Sergei Bautin	.08	.04	.01
	Winnipeg Jets			
☐ 11	Al Iafrate	.10	.05	.01
	Washington Capitals			
☐ 12	Gary Shuchuk	.08	.04	.01
	Los Angeles Kings			
☐ 13	Matthew Barnaby	.20	.09	.03
	Buffalo Sabres			
☐ 14	Tim Cheveldae	.10	.05	.01
	Detroit Red Wings			
☐ 15	Sean Burke	.10	.05	.01
	Hartford Whalers			
☐ 16	Ray Ferraro	.08	.04	.01
	New York Islanders			
☐ 17	Josef Beranek	.10	.05	.01
	Philadelphia Flyers			
☐ 18	Bob Beers	.08	.04	.01
	Tampa Bay Lightning			
☐ 19	Greg Adams	.08	.04	.01
	Vancouver Canucks			
☐ 20	John Cullen	.08	.04	.01
	Toronto Maple Leafs			
☐ 21	Kirk Muller	.10	.05	.01
	Montreal Canadiens			
☐ 22	Ed Belfour	.25	.11	.03
	Chicago Blackhawks			
☐ 23	Kevin Dahl	.08	.04	.01
	Calgary Flames			
☐ 24	Rob Blake	.10	.05	.01
	Los Angeles Kings			
☐ 25	Mike Gartner	.15	.07	.02
	New York Rangers			
☐ 26	Tom Barrasso	.10	.05	.01
	Pittsburgh Penguins			
☐ 27	Garth Butcher	.08	.04	.01
	St. Louis Blues			
☐ 28	Don Beaupre	.10	.05	.01
	Washington Capitals			
☐ 29	Kirk McLean	.15	.07	.02
	Vancouver Canucks			
☐ 30	Felix Potvin	1.00	.45	.13
	Toronto Maple Leafs			
☐ 31	Doug Bodger	.08	.04	.01
	Buffalo Sabres			
☐ 32	Dino Ciccarelli	.10	.05	.01

#	Team / Player			
	Detroit Red Wings			
☐ 33	Andrew Cassels	.08	.04	.01
	Hartford Whalers			
☐ 34	Patrick Flatley	.08	.04	.01
	New York Islanders			
☐ 35	Jason Bowen	.15	.07	.02
	Philadelphia Flyers			
☐ 36	Brian Bradley	.08	.04	.01
	Tampa Bay Lightning			
☐ 37	Pavel Bure	1.25	.55	.16
	Vancouver Canucks			
☐ 38	Dave Ellett	.08	.04	.01
	Toronto Maple Leafs			
☐ 39	Patrick Roy	.75	.35	.09
	Montreal Canadiens			
☐ 40	Chris Chelios	.10	.05	.01
	Chicago Blackhawks			
☐ 41	Theoren Fleury	.15	.07	.02
	Calgary Flames			
☐ 42	Jimmy Carson	.08	.04	.01
	Los Angeles Kings			
☐ 43	Adam Graves	.30	.14	.04
	New York Rangers			
☐ 44	Ron Francis	.10	.05	.01
	Pittsburgh Penguins			
☐ 45	Nelson Emerson	.10	.05	.01
	St. Louis Blues			
☐ 46	Peter Bondra	.10	.05	.01
	Washington Capitals			
☐ 47	Sergio Momesso	.08	.04	.01
	Vancouver Canucks			
☐ 48	Teemu Selanne	1.00	.45	.13
	Winnipeg Jets			
☐ 49	Joe Juneau	.75	.35	.09
	Boston Bruins			
☐ 50	Russ Courtnall	.10	.05	.01
	Dallas Stars			
☐ 51	Shayne Corson	.08	.04	.01
	Edmonton Oilers			
☐ 52	Patrice Brisebois	.08	.04	.01
	Montreal Canadiens			
☐ 53	John MacLean	.10	.05	.01
	New Jersey Devils			
☐ 54	Daniel Berthiaume	.08	.04	.01
	Ottawa Senators			
☐ 55	Stephane Fiset	.08	.04	.01
	Quebec Nordiques			
☐ 56	Pat Falloon	.10	.05	.01
	San Jose Sharks			
☐ 57	Dave Andreychuk	.15	.07	.02
	Toronto Maple Leafs			
☐ 58	Evgeny Davydov	.08	.04	.01
	Winnipeg Jets			
☐ 59	Dimitri Khristich	.10	.05	.01
	Washington Capitals			
☐ 60	Darryl Sydor	.10	.05	.01
	Los Angeles Kings			
☐ 61	Dirk Graham	.08	.04	.01
	Chicago Blackhawks			
☐ 62	Chris Lindberg	.08	.04	.01
	Calgary Flames			
☐ 63	Tony Granato	.08	.04	.01
	Los Angeles Kings			
☐ 64	Corey Hirsch	.25	.11	.03
	New York Rangers			
☐ 65	Jaromir Jagr	.60	.25	.08
	Pittsburgh Penguins			
☐ 66	Bret Hedican	.08	.04	.01
	St. Louis Blues			
☐ 67	Pat Elynuik	.08	.04	.01
	Washington Capitals			
☐ 68	Petr Nedved	.10	.05	.01
	Vancouver Canucks			
☐ 69	Thomas Steen	.08	.04	.01
	Winnipeg Jets			
☐ 70	Philippe Boucher	.08	.04	.01
	Buffalo Sabres			
☐ 71	Paul Coffey	.20	.09	.03
	Detroit Red Wings			
☐ 72	Mike Lenarduzzi	.15	.07	.02
	Hartford Whalers			
☐ 73	Iain Fraser	.20	.09	.03
	New York Islanders			
☐ 74	Rod Brind'Amour	.20	.09	.03
	Philadelphia Flyers			
☐ 75	Shawn Chambers	.08	.04	.01
	Tampa Bay Lightning			
☐ 76	Geoff Courtnall	.08	.04	.01
	Vancouver Canucks			
☐ 77	Todd Gill	.08	.04	.01
	Toronto Maple Leafs			
☐ 78	Mathieu Schneider	.10	.05	.01
	Montreal Canadiens			
☐ 79	Vincent Damphousse	.10	.05	.01
	Montreal Canadiens			
☐ 80	Igor Kravchuk	.08	.04	.01
	Edmonton Oilers			
☐ 81	Ulf Dahlen	.08	.04	.01
	Dallas Stars			
☐ 82	Dmitri Kvartalnov	.08	.04	.01
	Boston Bruins			
☐ 83	Johan Garpenlov	.08	.04	.01
	San Jose Sharks			
☐ 84	Valeri Kamensky	.20	.09	.03
	Quebec Nordiques			
☐ 85	Bob Kudelski	.10	.05	.01
	Ottawa Senators			
☐ 86	Bernie Nicholls	.10	.05	.01
	New Jersey Devils			
☐ 87	Alexei Zhitnik	.20	.09	.03
	Los Angeles Kings			
☐ 88	Kelly Miller	.08	.04	.01
	Washington Capitals			
☐ 89	Bob Essensa	.10	.05	.01
	Winnipeg Jets			
☐ 90	Drake Berehowsky	.08	.04	.01
	Toronto Maple Leafs			
☐ 91	Jon Casey	.10	.05	.01
	Boston Bruins			
☐ 92	Dave Gagner	.10	.05	.01
	Dallas Stars			
☐ 93	Dave Manson	.08	.04	.01
	Edmonton Oilers			
☐ 94	Eric Desjardins	.08	.04	.01
	Montreal Canadiens			
☐ 95	Scott Niedermayer	.20	.09	.03
	New Jersey Devils			
☐ 96	Chris Luongo	.08	.04	.01
	New York Islanders			
☐ 97	Dave Karpa	.08	.04	.01
	Quebec Nordiques			
☐ 98	Rob Gaudreau	.25	.11	.03
	San Jose Sharks			
☐ 99	Nikolai Borschevsky	.20	.09	.03
	Toronto Maple Leafs			
☐ 100	Phil Housley	.10	.05	.01
	Winnipeg Jets			
☐ 101	Michal Pivonka	.10	.05	.01
	Washington Capitals			
☐ 102	Dixon Ward	.08	.04	.01
	Vancouver Canucks			
☐ 103	Grant Fuhr	.10	.05	.01
	Buffalo Sabres			
☐ 104	Dallas Drake	.20	.09	.03
	Detroit Red Wings			
☐ 105	Michael Nylander	.20	.09	.03
	Hartford Whalers			
☐ 106	Glenn Healy	.08	.04	.01
	New York Rangers			
☐ 107	Kevin Dineen	.10	.05	.01
	Philadelphia Flyers			
☐ 108	Roman Hamrlik	.15	.07	.02
	Tampa Bay Lightning			
☐ 109	Trevor Linden	.15	.07	.02
	Vancouver Canucks			
☐ 110	Doug Gilmour	.40	.18	.05
	Toronto Maple Leafs			
☐ 111	Keith Tkachuk	.25	.11	.03
	Winnipeg Jets			
☐ 112	Sergei Krivokrasov	.08	.04	.01
	Chicago Blackhawks			
☐ 113	Al MacInnis	.15	.07	.02
	Calgary Flames			
☐ 114	Wayne Gretzky	2.00	.90	.25
	Los Angeles Kings			
☐ 115	Alexei Kovalev	.60	.25	.08
	New York Rangers			
☐ 116	Mario Lemieux	1.25	.55	.16
	Pittsburgh Penguins			
☐ 117	Brett Hull	.75	.35	.09
	St. Louis Blues			
☐ 118	Kevin Hatcher	.10	.05	.01
	Washington Capitals			
☐ 119	Cliff Ronning	.08	.04	.01
	Vancouver Canucks			
☐ 120	Viktor Gordijuk	.08	.04	.01
	Buffalo Sabres			
☐ 121	Sergei Fedorov	1.00	.45	.13
	Detroit Red Wings			
☐ 122	Patrick Poulin	.08	.04	.01
	Hartford Whalers			
☐ 123	Benoit Hogue	.08	.04	.01
	New York Islanders			
☐ 124	Garry Galley	.08	.04	.01
	Philadelphia Flyers			
☐ 125	Pat Jablonski	.08	.04	.01
	Tampa Bay Lightning			
☐ 126	Jyrki Lumme	.08	.04	.01

Vancouver Canucks			
☐ 127 Dimitri Mironov	.08	.04	.01
Toronto Maple Leafs			
☐ 128 Alexei Zhamnov	.40	.18	.05
Winnipeg Jets			
☐ 129 Steve Larmer	.10	.05	.01
Chicago Blackhawks			
☐ 130 Joe Nieuwendyk	.10	.05	.01
Calgary Flames			
☐ 131 Kelly Hrudey	.10	.05	.01
Los Angeles Kings			
☐ 132 Brian Leetch	.30	.14	.04
New York Rangers			
☐ 133 Shawn McEachern	.15	.07	.02
Pittsburgh Penguins			
☐ 134 Craig Janney	.15	.07	.02
St. Louis Blues			
☐ 135 Dale Hunter	.10	.05	.01
Washington Capitals			
☐ 136 Jiri Slegr	.08	.04	.01
Vancouver Canucks			
☐ 137 Mats Sundin	.25	.11	.03
Quebec Nordiques			
☐ 138 Cam Neely	.10	.05	.01
Boston Bruins			
☐ 139 Derian Hatcher	.08	.04	.01
Dallas Stars			
☐ 140 Shjon Podein	.20	.09	.03
Edmonton Oilers			
☐ 141 Gilbert Dionne	.08	.04	.01
Montreal Canadiens			
☐ 142 Scott Pellerin	.20	.09	.03
New Jersey Devils			
☐ 143 Norm Maciver	.08	.04	.01
Ottawa Senators			
☐ 144 Andrei Kovalenko	.20	.09	.03
Quebec Nordiques			
☐ 145 Arturs Irbe	.40	.18	.05
San Jose Sharks			
☐ 146 Wendel Clark	.15	.07	.02
Toronto Maple Leafs			
☐ 147 Fredrik Olausson	.08	.04	.01
Winnipeg Jets			
☐ 148 Mike Ridley	.10	.05	.01
Washington Capitals			
☐ 149 Dale Hawerchuk	.10	.05	.01
Buffalo Sabres			
☐ 150 Vladimir Konstantinov	.08	.04	.01
Detroit Red Wings			
☐ 151 Geoff Sanderson	.25	.11	.03
Hartford Whalers			
☐ 152 Stephane Richer	.10	.05	.01
New Jersey Devils			
☐ 153 Darren Rumble	.08	.04	.01
Ottawa Senators			
☐ 154 Owen Nolan	.10	.05	.01
Quebec Nordiques			
☐ 155 Kelly Kisio	.08	.04	.01
San Jose Sharks			
☐ 156 Adam Oates	.20	.09	.03
Boston Bruins			
☐ 157 Trent Klatt	.08	.04	.01
Dallas Stars			
☐ 158 Bill Ranford	.10	.05	.01
Edmonton Oilers			
☐ 159 Paul DiPietro	.08	.04	.01
Montreal Canadiens			
☐ 160 Darius Kasparaitis	.08	.04	.01
New York Islanders			
☐ 161 Eric Lindros	3.00	1.35	.40
Philadelphia Flyers			
☐ 162 Chris Kontos	.08	.04	.01
Tampa Bay Lightning			
☐ 163 Joe Murphy	.08	.04	.01
Chicago Blackhawks			
☐ 164 Robert Reichel	.10	.05	.01
Calgary Flames			
☐ 165 Jari Kurri	.15	.07	.02
Los Angeles Kings			
☐ 166 Alexander Semak	.08	.04	.01
New Jersey Devils			
☐ 167 Brad Shaw	.08	.04	.01
Ottawa Senators			
☐ 168 Mike Ricci	.10	.05	.01
Quebec Nordiques			
☐ 169 Sandis Ozolinsh	.25	.11	.03
San Jose Sharks			
☐ 170 Joby Messier	.15	.07	.02
New York Rangers			
☐ 171 Joe Mullen	.10	.05	.01
Pittsburgh Penguins			
☐ 172 Curtis Joseph	.25	.11	.03
St. Louis Blues			
☐ 173 Yuri Khmylev	.10	.05	.01

Buffalo Sabres			
☐ 174 Vyacheslav Kozlov	.75	.35	.09
Detroit Red Wings			
☐ 175 Pat Verbeek	.10	.05	.01
Hartford Whalers			
☐ 176 Derek King	.08	.04	.01
New York Islanders			
☐ 177 Ryan McGill	.08	.04	.01
Philadelphia Flyers			
☐ 178 Chris LiPuma	.15	.07	.02
Tampa Bay Lightning			
☐ 179 Gregori Pantaleyev	.08	.04	.01
Boston Bruins			
☐ 180 Richard Matvichuk	.08	.04	.01
Dallas Stars			
☐ 181 Steven Rice	.08	.04	.01
Edmonton Oilers			
☐ 182 Sean Hill	.08	.04	.01
Anaheim Mighty Ducks			
☐ 183 Mark Messier	.20	.09	.03
New York Rangers			
☐ 184 Larry Murphy	.10	.05	.01
Pittsburgh Penguins			
☐ 185 Igor Korolev	.08	.04	.01
St. Louis Blues			
☐ 186 Jeremy Roenick	.75	.35	.09
Chicago Blackhawks			
☐ 187 Gary Roberts	.10	.05	.01
Calgary Flames			
☐ 188 Robert Lang	.08	.04	.01
Los Angeles Kings			
☐ 189 Scott Stevens	.10	.05	.01
New Jersey Devils			
☐ 190 Sylvain Turgeon	.08	.04	.01
Ottawa Senators			
☐ 191 Martin Rucinsky	.08	.04	.01
Quebec Nordiques			
☐ 192 J.F. Quintin	.08	.04	.01
San Jose Sharks			
☐ 193 Dave Poulin	.08	.04	.01
Boston Bruins			
☐ 194 Mike Modano	.30	.14	.04
Dallas Stars			
☐ 195 Doug Weight	.10	.05	.01
Edmonton Oilers			
☐ 196 Mike Keane	.08	.04	.01
Montreal Canadiens			
☐ 197 Pierre Turgeon	.30	.14	.04
New York Islanders			
☐ 198 Dimitri Yushkevich	.08	.04	.01
Philadelphia Flyers			
☐ 199 Rob Zamuner	.08	.04	.01
Tampa Bay Lightning			
☐ 200 Richard Smehlik	.10	.05	.01
Buffalo Sabres			
☐ 201 Steve Yzerman	.40	.18	.05
Detroit Red Wings			
☐ 202 Tony Amonte	.10	.05	.01
New York Rangers			
☐ 203 Sergei Nemchinov	.08	.04	.01
New York Rangers			
☐ 204 Ulf Samuelsson	.10	.05	.01
Pittsburgh Penguins			
☐ 205 Kevin Miehm	.08	.04	.01
St. Louis Blues			
☐ 206 Brent Sutter	.10	.05	.01
Chicago Blackhawks			
☐ 207 Mike Vernon	.10	.05	.01
Calgary Flames			
☐ 208 Luc Robitaille	.20	.09	.03
Los Angeles Kings			
☐ 209 Chris Terreri	.10	.05	.01
New Jersey Devils			
☐ 210 Philippe Bozon	.08	.04	.01
St. Louis Blues			
☐ 211 John Tucker	.08	.04	.01
Tampa Bay Lightning			
☐ 212 Jozef Stumpel	.08	.04	.01
Boston Bruins			
☐ 213 Mark Tinordi	.08	.04	.01
Dallas Stars			
☐ 214 Bruce Driver	.08	.04	.01
New Jersey Devils			
☐ 215 John LeClair	.08	.04	.01
Montreal Canadiens			
☐ 216 Steve Thomas	.10	.05	.01
New York Islanders			
☐ 217 Tommy Soderstrom	.20	.09	.03
Philadelphia Flyers			
☐ 218 Kevin Miller	.08	.04	.01
St. Louis Blues			
☐ 219 Pat LaFontaine	.30	.14	.04
Buffalo Sabres			
☐ 220 Nicklas Lidstrom	.10	.05	.01

Detroit Red Wings
☐ 221	Terry Yake	.08	.04	.01

Anaheim Mighty Ducks
☐ 222	Valeri Zelepukin	.10	.05	.01

New Jersey Devils
☐ 223	Jeff Brown	.10	.05	.01

St. Louis Blues
☐ 224	Chris Simon	.20	.09	.03

Quebec Nordiques
☐ 225	Rick Tocchet	.10	.05	.01

Pittsburgh Penguins
☐ 226	Gary Suter	.10	.05	.01

Calgary Flames
☐ 227	Marty McSorley	.10	.05	.01

Los Angeles Kings
☐ 228	Mike Richter	.25	.11	.03

New York Rangers
☐ 229	Kevin Stevens	.30	.14	.04

Pittsburgh Penguins
☐ 230	Doug Wilson	.10	.05	.01

San Jose Sharks
☐ 231	Steve Smith	.08	.04	.01

Chicago Blackhawks
☐ 232	Bryan Smolinski	.60	.25	.08

Boston Bruins
☐ 233	Tommy Sjodin	.08	.04	.01

Dallas Stars
☐ 234	Zarley Zalapski	.08	.04	.01

Hartford Whalers
☐ 235	Vladimir Malakhov	.20	.09	.03

New York Islanders
☐ 236	Mark Recchi	.30	.14	.04

Philadelphia Flyers
☐ 237	David Littman	.15	.07	.02

Tampa Bay Lightning
☐ 238	Alexander Mogilny	.50	.23	.06

Buffalo Sabres
☐ 239	Keith Primeau	.10	.05	.01

Detroit Red Wings
☐ 240	Tyler Wright	.08	.04	.01

Edmonton Oilers
☐ 241	Stephan Lebeau	.08	.04	.01

Montreal Canadiens
☐ 242	Joe Sakic	.25	.11	.03

Quebec Nordiques
☐ 243	Sergei Zubov	.60	.25	.08

New York Rangers
☐ 244	Martin Straka	.50	.23	.06

Pittsburgh Penguins
☐ 245	Brendan Shanahan	.25	.11	.03

St. Louis Blues
☐ 246	Tomas Sandstrom	.08	.04	.01

Los Angeles Kings
☐ 247	Milan Tichy	.20	.09	.03

Florida Panthers
☐ 248	C.J. Young	.08	.04	.01

Boston Bruins
☐ 249	Checklist	.25	.06	.02

Eric Lindros
☐ 250	Checklist	.20	.05	.01

Teemu Selanne
☐ 251	Patrick Carnback	.15	.07	.02
☐ 252	Todd Ewen	.08	.04	.01
☐ 253	Stu Grimson	.08	.04	.01
☐ 254	Guy Hebert	.20	.09	.03
☐ 255	Sean Hill	.08	.04	.01
☐ 256	Bill Houlder	.08	.04	.01
☐ 257	Alexei Kasatonov	.08	.04	.01
☐ 258	Steven King	.08	.04	.01
☐ 259	Troy Loney	.08	.04	.01
☐ 260	Joe Sacco	.08	.04	.01
☐ 261	Anatoli Semenov	.08	.04	.01
☐ 262	Tim Sweeney	.08	.04	.01
☐ 263	Ron Tugnutt	.08	.04	.01
☐ 264	Shaun Van Allen	.08	.04	.01
☐ 265	Terry Yake	.08	.04	.01
☐ 266	Jon Casey	.10	.05	.01
☐ 267	Ted Donato	.08	.04	.01
☐ 268	Steve Leach	.08	.04	.01
☐ 269	Dave Reid	.08	.04	.01
☐ 270	Cam Stewart	.20	.09	.03
☐ 271	Don Sweeney	.08	.04	.01
☐ 272	Glen Wesley	.08	.04	.01
☐ 273	Donald Audette	.08	.04	.01
☐ 274	Dominik Hasek	.15	.07	.02
☐ 275	Sergei Petrenko	.08	.04	.01
☐ 276	Derek Plante	.75	.35	.09
☐ 277	Craig Simpson	.08	.04	.01
☐ 278	Bob Sweeney	.08	.04	.01
☐ 279	Randy Wood	.08	.04	.01
☐ 280	Ted Drury	.08	.04	.01
☐ 281	Trevor Kidd	.10	.05	.01
☐ 282	Kelly Kisio	.08	.04	.01
☐ 283	Frank Musil	.08	.04	.01

☐ 284	Jason Muzzatti	.15	.07	.02
☐ 285	Joel Otto	.08	.04	.01
☐ 286	Paul Ranheim	.08	.04	.01
☐ 287	Wes Walz	.08	.04	.01
☐ 288	Ivan Droppa	.15	.07	.02
☐ 289	Michel Goulet	.10	.05	.01
☐ 290	Stephane Matteau	.08	.04	.01
☐ 291	Brian Noonan	.08	.04	.01
☐ 292	Patrick Poulin	.08	.04	.01
☐ 293	Rich Sutter	.08	.04	.01
☐ 294	Kevin Todd	.08	.04	.01
☐ 295	Eric Weinrich	.08	.04	.01
☐ 296	Neal Broten	.08	.04	.01
☐ 297	Mike Craig	.08	.04	.01
☐ 298	Dean Evason	.08	.04	.01
☐ 299	Grant Ledyard	.08	.04	.01
☐ 300	Mike McPhee	.08	.04	.01
☐ 301	Andy Moog	.10	.05	.01
☐ 302	Jarkko Varvio	.20	.09	.03
☐ 303	Micah Aivazoff	.20	.09	.03
☐ 304	Terry Carkner	.08	.04	.01
☐ 305	Steve Chiasson	.08	.04	.01
☐ 306	Greg Johnson	.08	.04	.01
☐ 307	Darren McCarty	.25	.11	.03
☐ 308	Chris Osgood	.75	.35	.09
☐ 309	Bob Probert	.08	.04	.01
☐ 310	Ray Sheppard	.08	.04	.01
☐ 311	Mike Sillinger	.08	.04	.01
☐ 312	Jason Arnott	2.00	.90	.25
☐ 313	Fred Brathwaite	.15	.07	.02
☐ 314	Kelly Buchberger	.08	.04	.01
☐ 315	Zdeno Ciger	.08	.04	.01
☐ 316	Craig MacTavish	.08	.04	.01
☐ 317	Dean McAmmond	.08	.04	.01
☐ 318	Luke Richardson	.08	.04	.01
☐ 319	Vladimir Vujtek	.08	.04	.01
☐ 320	Jesse Belanger	.20	.09	.03
☐ 321	Brian Benning	.08	.04	.01
☐ 322	Keith Brown	.08	.04	.01
☐ 323	Evgeny Davydov	.08	.04	.01
☐ 324	Tom Fitzgerald	.08	.04	.01
☐ 325	Alexander Godynyuk	.08	.04	.01
☐ 326	Scott Levins	.20	.09	.03
☐ 327	Andrei Lomakin	.08	.04	.01
☐ 328	Scott Mellanby	.08	.04	.01
☐ 329	Gord Murphy	.08	.04	.01
☐ 330	Rob Niedermayer	.75	.35	.09
☐ 331	Brent Severyn	.15	.07	.02
☐ 332	Brian Skrudland	.08	.04	.01
☐ 333	John Vanbiesbrouck	.20	.09	.03
☐ 334	Mark Greig	.08	.04	.01
☐ 335	Bryan Marchment	.08	.04	.01
☐ 336	James Patrick	.08	.04	.01
☐ 337	Robert Petrovicky	.08	.04	.01
☐ 338	Frank Pietrangelo	.08	.04	.01
☐ 339	Chris Pronger	.75	.35	.09
☐ 340	Brian Propp	.10	.05	.01
☐ 341	Darren Turcotte	.08	.04	.01
☐ 342	Pat Conacher	.08	.04	.01
☐ 343	Mark Hardy	.08	.04	.01
☐ 344	Charlie Huddy	.08	.04	.01
☐ 345	Shawn McEachern	.15	.07	.02
☐ 346	Warren Rychel	.08	.04	.01
☐ 347	Robb Stauber	.08	.04	.01
☐ 348	Dave Taylor	.10	.05	.01
☐ 349	Benoit Brunet	.08	.04	.01
☐ 350	Guy Carbonneau	.10	.05	.01
☐ 351	J.J. Daigneault	.08	.04	.01
☐ 352	Kevin Haller	.08	.04	.01
☐ 353	Gary Leeman	.08	.04	.01
☐ 354	Lyle Odelein	.08	.04	.01
☐ 355	Andre Racicot	.08	.04	.01
☐ 356	Ron Wilson	.08	.04	.01
☐ 357	Martin Brodeur	.50	.23	.06
☐ 358	Ken Daneyko	.08	.04	.01
☐ 359	Bill Guerin	.08	.04	.01
☐ 360	Bobby Holik	.08	.04	.01
☐ 361	Corey Millen	.08	.04	.01
☐ 362	Jaroslav Modry	.20	.09	.03
☐ 363	Jason Smith	.15	.07	.02
☐ 364	Brad Dalgarno	.08	.04	.01
☐ 365	Travis Green	.08	.04	.01
☐ 366	Ron Hextall	.10	.05	.01
☐ 367	Steve Junker	.08	.04	.01
☐ 368	Tom Kurvers	.08	.04	.01
☐ 369	Scott Lachance	.08	.04	.01
☐ 370	Marty McInnis	.08	.04	.01
☐ 371	Glenn Healy	.08	.04	.01
☐ 372	Alexander Karpovtsev	.08	.04	.01
☐ 373	Steve Larmer	.10	.05	.01
☐ 374	Doug Lidster	.08	.04	.01
☐ 375	Kevin Lowe	.08	.04	.01
☐ 376	Mattias Norstrom	.15	.07	.02

		MINT	EXC	G-VG

☐ 377 Esa Tikkanen .... .10 .05 .01
☐ 378 Craig Billington .... .08 .04 .01
☐ 379 Robert Burakovsky .... .08 .04 .01
☐ 380 Alexandre Daigle .... .75 .35 .09
☐ 381 Dmitri Filimonov .... .08 .04 .01
☐ 382 Darrin Madeley .... .20 .09 .03
☐ 383 Vladimir Ruzicka .... .08 .04 .01
☐ 384 Alexei Yashin .... .75 .35 .09
☐ 385 Viacheslav Butsayev .... .08 .04 .01
☐ 386 Pelle Eklund .... .08 .04 .01
☐ 387 Brent Fedyk .... .08 .04 .01
☐ 388 Greg Hawgood .... .08 .04 .01
☐ 389 Milos Holan .... .15 .07 .02
☐ 390 Stewart Malgunas .... .15 .07 .02
☐ 391 Mikael Renberg .... .75 .35 .09
☐ 392 Dominic Roussel .... .15 .07 .02
☐ 393 Doug Brown .... .08 .04 .01
☐ 394 Marty McSorley .... .08 .04 .01
☐ 395 Markus Naslund .... .20 .09 .03
☐ 396 Mike Ramsey .... .08 .04 .01
☐ 397 Peter Taglianetti .... .08 .04 .01
☐ 398 Bryan Trottier .... .10 .05 .01
☐ 399 Ken Wregget .... .08 .04 .01
☐ 400 Iain Fraser .... .15 .07 .02
☐ 401 Martin Gelinas .... .08 .04 .01
☐ 402 Kerry Huffman .... .08 .04 .01
☐ 403 Claude Lapointe .... .08 .04 .01
☐ 404 Curtis Leschyshyn .... .08 .04 .01
☐ 405 Chris Lindberg .... .08 .04 .01
☐ 406 Jocelyn Thibault .... .75 .35 .09
☐ 407 Murray Baron .... .08 .04 .01
☐ 408 Bob Bassen .... .08 .04 .01
☐ 409 Phil Housley .... .10 .05 .01
☐ 410 Jim Hrivnak .... .08 .04 .01
☐ 411 Tony Hrkac .... .08 .04 .01
☐ 412 Vitali Karamnov .... .08 .04 .01
☐ 413 Jim Montgomery .... .20 .09 .03
☐ 414 Vlastimil Kroupa .... .25 .11 .03
☐ 415 Igor Larionov .... .08 .04 .01
☐ 416 Sergei Makarov .... .10 .05 .01
☐ 417 Jeff Norton .... .08 .04 .01
☐ 418 Mike Rathje .... .08 .04 .01
☐ 419 Jim Waite .... .08 .04 .01
☐ 420 Ray Whitney .... .08 .04 .01
☐ 421 Mikael Andersson .... .08 .04 .01
☐ 422 Donald Dufresne .... .08 .04 .01
☐ 423 Chris Gratton .... .75 .35 .09
☐ 424 Brent Gretzky .... .30 .14 .04
☐ 425 Petr Klima .... .08 .04 .01
☐ 426 Bill McDougall .... .08 .04 .01
☐ 427 Daren Puppa .... .10 .05 .01
☐ 428 Denis Savard .... .10 .05 .01
☐ 429 Ken Baumgartner .... .08 .04 .01
☐ 430 Sylvain Lefebvre .... .08 .04 .01
☐ 431 Jamie Macoun .... .08 .04 .01
☐ 432 Matt Martin .... .20 .09 .03
☐ 433 Mark Osborne .... .08 .04 .01
☐ 434 Rob Pearson .... .08 .04 .01
☐ 435 Damian Rhodes .... .30 .14 .04
☐ 436 Peter Zezel .... .08 .04 .01
☐ 437 Shawn Antoski .... .08 .04 .01
☐ 438 Jose Charbonneau .... .08 .04 .01
☐ 439 Murray Craven .... .08 .04 .01
☐ 440 Gerald Diduck .... .08 .04 .01
☐ 441 Dana Murzyn .... .08 .04 .01
☐ 442 Gino Odjick .... .08 .04 .01
☐ 443 Kay Whitmore .... .08 .04 .01
☐ 444 Randy Burridge .... .08 .04 .01
☐ 445 Sylvain Cote .... .08 .04 .01
☐ 446 Keith Jones .... .08 .04 .01
☐ 447 Olaf Kolzig .... .08 .04 .01
☐ 448 Todd Krygier .... .08 .04 .01
☐ 449 Pat Peake .... .10 .05 .01
☐ 450 Dave Poulin .... .08 .04 .01
☐ 451 Stephane Beauregard .... .08 .04 .01
☐ 452 Luciano Borsato .... .08 .04 .01
☐ 453 Nelson Emerson .... .10 .05 .01
☐ 454 Boris Mironov .... .08 .04 .01
☐ 455 Teppo Numminen .... .08 .04 .01
☐ 456 Stephane Quintal .... .08 .04 .01
☐ 457 Paul Ysebaert .... .08 .04 .01
☐ 458 Adrian Aucoin .... .25 .11 .03
☐ 459 Todd Brost .... .15 .07 .02
☐ 460 Martin Gendron .... .35 .16 .04
☐ 461 David Harlock .... .15 .07 .02
☐ 462 Corey Hirsch .... .25 .11 .03
☐ 463 Todd Hlushko .... .20 .09 .03
☐ 464 Fabian Joseph .... .20 .09 .03
☐ 465 Paul Kariya .... 4.00 1.80 .50
☐ 466 Brett Lindros .... 6.00 2.70 .75
☐ 467 Ken Lovsin .... .15 .07 .02
☐ 468 Jason Marshall .... .15 .07 .02
☐ 469 Derek Mayer .... .15 .07 .02

☐ 470 Dwayne Norris .... .20 .09 .03
☐ 471 Russ Romaniuk .... .15 .07 .02
☐ 472 Brian Savage .... .30 .14 .04
☐ 473 Trevor Sim .... .15 .07 .02
☐ 474 Chris Therien .... .15 .07 .02
☐ 475 Brad Turner .... .20 .09 .03
☐ 476 Todd Warriner .... .60 .25 .08
☐ 477 Craig Woodcroft .... .15 .07 .02
☐ 478 Mark Beaufait .... .15 .07 .02
☐ 479 Jim Campbell .... .20 .09 .03
☐ 480 Ted Crowley .... .20 .09 .03
☐ 481 Mike Dunham .... .25 .11 .03
☐ 482 Chris Ferraro .... .20 .09 .03
☐ 483 Peter Ferraro .... .20 .09 .03
☐ 484 Brett Hauer .... .15 .07 .02
☐ 485 Darby Hendrickson .... .20 .09 .03
☐ 486 Chris Imes .... .15 .07 .02
☐ 487 Craig Johnson .... .20 .09 .03
☐ 488 Peter Laviolette .... .15 .07 .02
☐ 489 Jeff Lazaro .... .15 .07 .02
☐ 490 John Lilley .... .25 .11 .03
☐ 491 Todd Marchant .... .20 .09 .03
☐ 492 Ian Moran .... .15 .07 .02
☐ 493 Travis Richards .... .20 .09 .03
☐ 494 Barry Richter .... .25 .11 .03
☐ 495 David Roberts .... .25 .11 .03
☐ 496 Brian Rolston .... .50 .23 .06
☐ 497 David Sacco .... .25 .11 .03
☐ 498 Checklist Card .... .08 .04 .01
☐ 499 Checklist Card .... .08 .04 .01
☐ 500 Checklist Card .... .08 .04 .01

1993-94 Ultra All-Rookies

 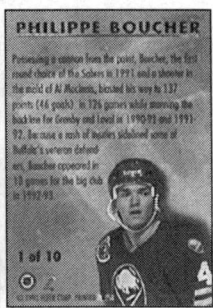

Randomly inserted in 19-card first-series jumbo packs, this 10-card standard-size (2 1/2" by 3 1/2") set features on its borderless fronts color player action cutouts "breaking out" of their simulated ice backgrounds. The player's name appears in gold-foil lettering at a lower corner. The blue back carries the player's name at the top in gold-foil lettering, followed below by career highlights and a color player action cutout. The cards are numbered on the back as "X of 10."

	MINT	EXC	G-VG
COMPLETE SET (10)	50.00	23.00	6.25
COMMON PLAYER (1-10)	5.00	2.30	.60

☐ 1 Philippe Boucher .... 5.00 2.30 .60
    Buffalo Sabres
☐ 2 Viktor Gordiouk .... 5.00 2.30 .60
    Buffalo Sabres
☐ 3 Corey Hirsch .... 6.00 2.70 .75
    New York Rangers
☐ 4 Chris LiPuma .... 5.00 2.30 .60
    Tampa Bay Lightning
☐ 5 David Littman .... 5.00 2.30 .60
    Tampa Bay Lightning
☐ 6 Joby Messier .... 5.00 2.30 .60
    New York Rangers
☐ 7 Chris Simon .... 5.00 2.30 .60
    Quebec Nordiques
☐ 8 Bryan Smolinski 9.00 4.00 1.15
    Boston Bruins
☐ 9 Jozef Stumpel .... 5.00 2.30 .60

		MINT	EXC	G-VG
Boston Bruins				
☐ 10	Milan Tichy	5.00	2.30	.60
Florida Panthers				

1993-94 Ultra All-Stars

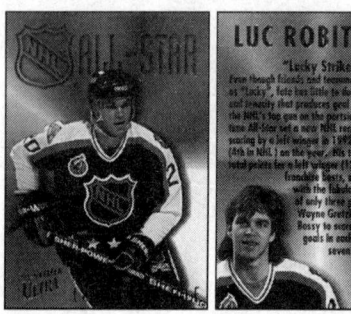

Randomly inserted into all first series packs, this 18-card standard-size (2 1/2" by 3 1/2") focuses on 18 of the NHL's best players. The set numbering is by conference All-Stars, Wales (1-9) and Campbell (10-18).

		MINT	EXC	G-VG
COMPLETE SET (18)		75.00	34.00	9.50
COMMON PLAYER (1-18)		2.50	1.15	.30
☐ 1	Patrick Roy	8.00	3.60	1.00
	Montreal Canadiens			
☐ 2	Ray Bourque	3.00	1.35	.40
	Boston Bruins			
☐ 3	Pierre Turgeon	4.00	1.80	.50
	New York Islanders			
☐ 4	Pat LaFontaine	3.50	1.55	.45
	Buffalo Sabres			
☐ 5	Alexander Mogilny	4.00	1.80	.50
	Buffalo Sabres			
☐ 6	Kevin Stevens	3.00	1.35	.40
	Pittsburgh Penguins			
☐ 7	Adam Oates	3.00	1.35	.40
	Boston Bruins			
☐ 8	Al Iafrate	2.50	1.15	.30
	Washington Capitals			
☐ 9	Kirk Muller	2.50	1.15	.30
	Montreal Canadiens			
☐ 10	Ed Belfour	4.00	1.80	.50
	Chicago Blackhawks			
☐ 11	Teemu Selanne	6.00	2.70	.75
	Winnipeg Jets			
☐ 12	Steve Yzerman	6.00	2.70	.75
	Detroit Red Wings			
☐ 13	Luc Robitaille	3.00	1.35	.40
	Los Angeles Kings			
☐ 14	Chris Chelios	2.50	1.15	.30
	Chicago Blackhawks			
☐ 15	Wayne Gretzky	12.00	5.50	1.50
	Los Angeles Kings			
☐ 16	Doug Gilmour	6.00	2.70	.75
	Toronto Maple Leafs			
☐ 17	Pavel Bure	10.00	4.50	1.25
	Vancouver Canucks			
☐ 18	Phil Housley	2.50	1.15	.30
	Winnipeg Jets			

1993-94 Ultra Award Winners

Randomly inserted into all first series packs, this six-card standard-size (2 1/2" by 3 1/2") set honors NHL award winners of the previous season. Each borderless front features the player with his award. The back has an action photo and career highlights. The cards are numbered "X of 6".

		MINT	EXC	G-VG
COMPLETE SET (6)		30.00	13.50	3.80
COMMON PLAYER (1-6)		3.00	1.35	.40
☐ 1	Ed Belfour	4.00	1.80	.50
	Chicago Blackhawks			
	Jennings/Vezina			
	Trophies			
☐ 2	Chris Chelios	3.00	1.35	.40
	Chicago Blackhawks			
	Norris Trophy			
☐ 3	Doug Gilmour	5.00	2.30	.60
	Toronto Maple Leafs			
	Selke Trophy			
☐ 4	Mario Lemieux	8.00	3.60	1.00
	Pittsburgh Penguins			
	Masterton Memorial/			
	Ross/Hart Memorial			
	Trophies			
☐ 5	Dave Poulin	3.00	1.35	.40
	Boston Bruins			
	King Clancy Trophy			
☐ 6	Teemu Selanne	6.00	2.70	.75
	Winnipeg Jets			
	Calder Trophy			

1993-94 Ultra Adam Oates

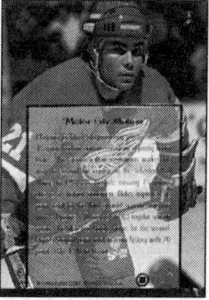

As part of Ultra's Signature series, this 12-card standard-size (2 1/2" by 3 1/2") set presents career highlights of Adam Oates. These cards were randomly inserted throughout all packs, and Oates autographed more than 2,000 of his cards. Two additional cards (11, 12) were available only by mail for ten Ultra wrappers plus 1.00. The cards are numbered on the back.

		MINT	EXC	G-VG
COMPLETE SET (10)		10.00	4.50	1.25
COMMON OATES (1-10)		1.00	.45	.13
COMMON MAIL-IN (11-12)		2.00	.90	.25
☐ 1	Adam Oates	1.00	.45	.13
	A Challenge Met			
☐ 2	Adam Oates	1.00	.45	.13
	Sowing His Oates			

			MINT	EXC	G-VG
☐	3	Adam Oates............................	1.00	.45	.13
		Wanted Man			
☐	4	Adam Oates............................	1.00	.45	.13
		Making the Grade			
☐	5	Adam Oates............................	1.00	.45	.13
		Motor City Motion			
☐	6	Adam Oates............................	1.00	.45	.13
		Hello and Goodbye			
☐	7	Adam Oates............................	1.00	.45	.13
		Blues Brother			
☐	8	Adam Oates............................	1.00	.45	.13
		Hit the Ignition			
☐	9	Adam Oates............................	1.00	.45	.13
		The Breakup			
☐	10	Adam Oates............................	1.00	.45	.13
		The Spotlight Shines			
☐	11	Adam Oates............................	2.00	.90	.25
		North American Dream			
☐	12	Adam Oates............................	2.00	.90	.25
		Giving 'till it Hurts			
☐	AU	Adam Oates AU	100.00	45.00	12.50
		(Certified autograph)			

1993-94 Ultra Premier Pivots

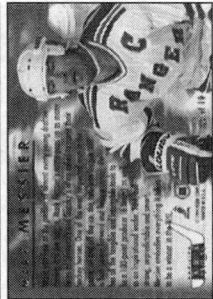

Randomly inserted in all series II packs, these ten standard-size (2 1/2" by 3 1/2") cards feature some of the NHL's greatest centers. The borderless fronts have color player action shots on motion-streaked backgrounds. The player's name appears in silver foil at the upper right. The horizontal back carries another borderless color player action shot offset to the right. The on-ice background is ghosted and again motion-streaked. The player's name appears in silver foil at the upper left, followed below by career highlights. The cards are numbered on the back as "X of 10."

			MINT	EXC	G-VG
		COMPLETE SET (10)........................	30.00	13.50	3.80
		COMMON PLAYER (1-10)................	1.50	.65	.19
☐	1	Doug Gilmour	4.00	1.80	.50
		Toronto Maple Leafs			
☐	2	Wayne Gretzky	8.00	3.60	1.00
		Los Angeles Kings			
☐	3	Pat LaFontaine	2.00	.90	.25
		Buffalo Sabres			
☐	4	Mario Lemieux	6.00	2.70	.75
		Pittsburgh Penguins			
☐	5	Eric Lindros..........................	8.00	3.60	1.00
		Philadelphia Flyers			
☐	6	Mark Messier	2.00	.90	.25
		New York Rangers			
☐	7	Adam Oates	1.50	.65	.19
		Boston Bruins			
☐	8	Jeremy Roenick	3.50	1.55	.45
		Chicago Blackhawks			
☐	9	Pierre Turgeon	2.00	.90	.25
		New York Islanders			
☐	10	Steve Yzerman	3.50	1.55	.45
		Detroit Red Wings			

1993-94 Ultra Prospects

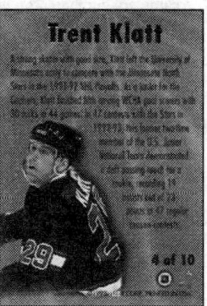

Randomly inserted into first series foil packs, the Ultra Prospects consists of ten standard-size (2 1/2" by 3 1/2") cards. Borderless fronts feature the player emerging from a solid background. The backs contain a photo and career highlights. The cards are numbered as "X of 10".

			MINT	EXC	G-VG
		COMPLETE SET (10)........................	12.00	5.50	1.50
		COMMON PLAYER (1-10)................	1.50	.65	.19
☐	1	Iain Fraser	1.50	.65	.19
		New York Islanders			
☐	2	Rob Gaudreau	2.00	.90	.25
		San Jose Sharks			
☐	3	Dave Karpa............................	1.50	.65	.19
		Quebec Nordiques			
☐	4	Trent Klatt	1.50	.65	.19
		Dallas Stars			
☐	5	Mike Lenarduzzi	1.50	.65	.19
		Hartford Whalers			
☐	6	Kevin Miehm	1.50	.65	.19
		St. Louis Blues			
☐	7	Michael Nylander	2.00	.90	.25
		Hartford Whalers			
☐	8	J.F. Quintin............................	1.50	.65	.19
		San Jose Sharks			
☐	9	Gary Shuchuk	1.50	.65	.19
		Los Angeles Kings			
☐	10	Tyler Wright	1.50	.65	.19
		Edmonton Oilers			

1993-94 Ultra Red Light Specials

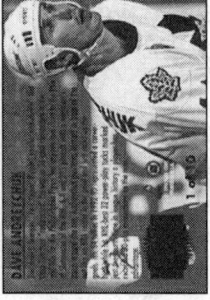

Randomly inserted in series 2 packs, this ten-card standard-size (2 1/2" by 3 1/2") set highlights some of the NHL's best goal scorers. The borderless fronts feature two color player action shots, one superposed upon the other. The player's name appears in red foil at the bottom. The horizontal back carries an on-ice closeup of the player set off to the right. The player's name appears in red foil at the upper left, followed below by the player's goal-scoring highlights, all on the red-screened background from the player closeup. The cards are numbered on the back as "X of 10."

	MINT	EXC	G-VG
COMPLETE SET (10)........................	28.00	12.50	3.50
COMMON PLAYER (1-10)................	.75	.35	.09
☐ 1 Dave Andreychuk.................. Toronto Maple Leafs	1.00	.45	.13
☐ 2 Pavel Bure............................. Vancouver Canucks	7.00	3.10	.85
☐ 3 Mike Gartner.......................... New York Rangers	.75	.35	.09
☐ 4 Brett Hull............................... St. Louis Blues	4.00	1.80	.50
☐ 5 Jaromir Jagr........................... Pittsburgh Penguins	3.00	1.35	.40
☐ 6 Mario Lemieux........................ Pittsburgh Penguins	5.00	2.30	.60
☐ 7 Alexander Mogilny................. Buffalo Sabres	2.50	1.15	.30
☐ 8 Mark Recchi........................... Philadelphia Flyers	1.00	.45	.13
☐ 9 Luc Robitaille.......................... Los Angeles Kings	1.00	.45	.13
☐ 10 Teemu Selanne.................... Winnipeg Jets	4.00	1.80	.50

1993-94 Ultra Scoring Kings

Randomly inserted into all first series packs, this six-card standard-size (2 1/2" by 3 1/2") set showcases six of the NHL's top scorers. Borderless fronts have action player photos. Backs feature a player photo and career highlights. the player's name appears in gold at the top. The card are numbered "X of 6".

	MINT	EXC	G-VG
COMPLETE SET (6)........................	40.00	18.00	5.00
COMMON PLAYER (1-6)................	5.00	2.30	.60
☐ 1 Pat LaFontaine....................... Buffalo Sabres	5.00	2.30	.60
☐ 2 Wayne Gretzky...................... Los Angeles Kings	12.00	5.50	1.50
☐ 3 Brett Hull.............................. St. Louis Blues	7.00	3.10	.85
☐ 4 Mario Lemieux........................ Pittsburgh Penguins	10.00	4.50	1.25
☐ 5 Pierre Turgeon....................... New York Islanders	5.00	2.30	.60
☐ 6 Steve Yzerman....................... Detroit Red Wings	6.00	2.70	.75

1993-94 Ultra Speed Merchants

Randomly inserted in second series jumbo packs, this 10-card standard-size (2 1/2" by 3 1/2") set sports fronts of motion-streaked color player action cutouts set on

borderless indigo backgrounds highlighted by ice spray. The horizontal borderless back carries a motion-streaked color player action cutout on one side, with the player's name in silver foil and career highlights on the other, all on a grayish background. The cards are numbered on the back as "X of 10."

	MINT	EXC	G-VG
COMPLETE SET (10)........................	125.00	57.50	15.50
COMMON PLAYER (1-10)................	6.00	2.70	.75
☐ 1 Pavel Bure............................. Vancouver Canucks	30.00	13.50	3.80
☐ 2 Russ Courtnall....................... Dallas Stars	6.00	2.70	.75
☐ 3 Sergei Fedorov...................... Detroit Red Wings	24.00	11.00	3.00
☐ 4 Mike Gartner.......................... New York Rangers	6.00	2.70	.75
☐ 5 Al Iafrate............................... Washington Capitals	6.00	2.70	.75
☐ 6 Pat LaFontaine....................... Buffalo Sabres	9.00	4.00	1.15
☐ 7 Alexander Mogilny................. Buffalo Sabres	10.00	4.50	1.25
☐ 8 Rob Niedermayer.................... Florida Panthers	10.00	4.50	1.25
☐ 9 Geoff Sanderson................... Hartford Whalers	9.00	4.00	1.15
☐ 10 Teemu Selanne.................... Winnipeg Jets	15.00	6.75	1.90

1993-94 Ultra Wave of the Future

Randomly inserted in series II packs, these 20 standard-size (2 1/2" by 3 1/2") cards highlight players in their first or second NHL season. The borderless fronts feature color player action shots with "rippled" on-ice backgrounds. The player's name appears in gold foil at a lower corner. The borderless horizontal back carries a player color closeup on the right. The player's name, and the card's descriptive title, appear in gold foil at the upper left; below are career highlights. The "rippled" background is a solid team color. The cards are numbered on the back as "X of 20."

	MINT	EXC	G-VG
COMPLETE SET (20)	35.00	16.00	4.40
COMMON PLAYER (1-20)	.75	.35	.09
☐ 1 Jason Arnott	7.00	3.10	.85
Edmonton Oilers			
☐ 2 Martin Brodeur	6.00	2.70	.75
New Jersey Devils			
☐ 3 Alexandre Daigle	4.00	1.80	.50
Ottawa Senators			
☐ 4 Ted Drury	.75	.35	.09
Calgary Flames			
☐ 5 Chris Gratton	3.00	1.35	.40
Tampa Bay Lightning			
☐ 6 Milos Holan	.75	.35	.09
Philadelphia Flyers			
☐ 7 Greg Johnson	.75	.35	.09
Detroit Red Wings			
☐ 8 Boris Mironov	.75	.35	.09
Winnipeg Jets			
☐ 9 Jaroslav Modry	.75	.35	.09
New Jersey Devils			
☐ 10 Markus Naslund	.75	.35	.09
Pittsburgh Penguins			
☐ 11 Rob Niedermayer	3.00	1.35	.40
Florida Panthers			
☐ 12 Chris Osgood	2.50	1.15	.30
Detroit Red Wings			
☐ 13 Derek Plante	2.50	1.15	.30
Buffalo Sabres			
☐ 14 Chris Pronger	3.00	1.35	.40
Hartford Whalers			
☐ 15 Mike Rathje	.75	.35	.09
San Jose Sharks			
☐ 16 Mikael Renberg	4.00	1.80	.50
Philadelphia Flyers			
☐ 17 Jason Smith	.75	.35	.09
New Jersey Devils			
☐ 18 Jocelyn Thibault	2.50	1.15	.30
Quebec Nordiques			
☐ 19 Jarkko Varvio	.75	.35	.09
Dallas Stars			
☐ 20 Alexei Yashin	4.00	1.80	.50
Ottawa Senators			

1990-91 Upper Deck Promos

The 1990-91 Upper Deck Promo set is a two-card set featuring Wayne Gretzky and Patrick Roy both numbered as card number 241. The cards were first handed out as samples at the 1990 National Sports Collectors Convention in Arlington. The Arlington National promos were issued as a set in a special screw-down holder commemorating the National; these sets are much more limited and are rarely offered for sale. The photos on the front and back of both of the cards were changed in the regular set, as were the card numbers.

	MINT	EXC	G-VG
COMPLETE SET (2)	40.00	16.00	4.00
COMMON PLAYER	15.00	6.00	1.50
☐ 241A Wayne Gretzky UER	30.00	12.00	3.00
(Wrong height, feet			
and inches reversed)			

	MINT	EXC	G-VG
☐ 241B Patrick Roy UER	15.00	6.00	1.50
(Wrong height, feet			
and inches reversed)			

1990-91 Upper Deck

 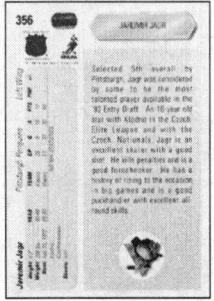

The 1990-91 Upper Deck Hockey set contains 550 cards, each measuring the standard size, 2 1/2" by 3 1/2". The set was released in two series of 400 and 150 cards, respectively. The card fronts feature color action photos, bordered on the right and bottom in the team's colors with the team logo in the lower right hand corner. The player's name and position in black lettering appear in a pale blue bar at the top of the card front. Two-thirds of back shows another color action photo, while the remaining third presents biographical information and career statistics in pale blue box running the length of the card. The second (or extended) series contains 150 cards and includes newest rookies, traded players, All Stars, Heroes of the NHL, and members of the Canadian National Junior Team. It should also be noted that the Canada's Captains card (473) shows Eric Lindros along with Kris Draper and Steven Rice. The French version of 1990-91 Upper Deck was produced in smaller quantities compared to the English version and commands up to 1.5 times the values below. Rookie Cards in the set include Ed Belfour, Pavel Bure, Pat Falloon, Sergei Fedorov, Jaromir Jagr, Alexander Mogilny, Petr Nedved, Scott Niedermayer, Owen Nolan, Felix Potvin, Mark Recchi, Mike Ricci, Jeremy Roenick, Kevin Stevens, and Mats Sundin.

	MINT	EXC	G-VG
COMPLETE SET (550)	70.00	32.00	8.75
COMPLETE LO SERIES (400)	35.00	16.00	4.40
COMPLETE HI SERIES (150)	35.00	16.00	4.40
COMPLETE HI FACT.SER.(150)	35.00	16.00	4.40
COMMON PLAYER (1-400)	.08	.04	.01
COMMON PLAYER (401-550)	.08	.04	.01
*FRENCH VERSION: 1X TO 2X			
☐ 1 David Volek	.08	.04	.01
☐ 2 Brian Propp	.12	.05	.02
☐ 3 Wendel Clark	.40	.18	.05
☐ 4 Adam Creighton	.08	.04	.01
☐ 5 Mark Osborne	.08	.04	.01
☐ 6 Murray Craven	.08	.04	.01
☐ 7 Doug Crossman	.08	.04	.01
☐ 8 Mario Marois	.08	.04	.01
☐ 9 Curt Giles	.08	.04	.01
☐ 10 Rick Wamsley	.08	.04	.01
☐ 11 Troy Mallette	.08	.04	.01
☐ 12 John Cullen	.12	.05	.02
☐ 13 Miloslav Horava	.08	.04	.01
☐ 14 Kevin Stevens	2.00	.90	.25
☐ 15 David Shaw	.08	.04	.01
☐ 16 Randy Wood	.08	.04	.01
☐ 17 Peter Zezel	.12	.05	.02
☐ 18 Glenn Healy	.50	.23	.06
☐ 19 Sergio Momesso	.35	.16	.04

20	Don Maloney	.08	.04	.01
21	Craig Muni	.08	.04	.01
22	Phil Housley	.12	.05	.02
23	Martin Gelinas	.25	.11	.03
24	Alexander Mogilny	3.00	1.35	.40
25	John Byce	.08	.04	.01
26	Joe Nieuwendyk	.25	.11	.03
27	Ron Tugnutt	.12	.05	.02
28	Don Barber	.08	.04	.01
29	Gary Roberts	.35	.16	.04
30	Basil McRae	.12	.05	.02
31	Phil Bourque	.08	.04	.01
32	Mike Richter	2.00	.90	.25
33	Zarley Zalapski	.12	.05	.02
34	Bernie Nicholls	.15	.07	.02
35	Bob Corkum	.25	.11	.03
36	Rod Brind'Amour	1.50	.65	.19
37	Mark Fitzpatrick UER (Back says catches right, not left)	.25	.11	.03
38	Gino Cavallini	.08	.04	.01
39	Mick Vukota	.08	.04	.01
40	Mike Lalor	.08	.04	.01
41	Dave Andreychuk	.30	.14	.04
42	Bill Ranford	.25	.11	.03
43	Pierre Turgeon	.60	.25	.08
44	Mark Messier	.50	.23	.06
45	Rob Blake	1.00	.45	.13
46	Mike Modano (With Norm Green)	2.50	1.15	.30
47	Theoren Fleury	.40	.18	.05
48	Neal Broten	.12	.05	.02
49	Paul Gillis	.08	.04	.01
50	Doug Bodger UER (Birthplace should be Chemainus)	.08	.04	.01
51	Stephan Lebeau	.60	.25	.08
52	Larry Robinson	.12	.05	.02
53	Dale Hawerchuk	.15	.07	.02
54	Wayne Gretzky	2.00	.90	.25
55	Ed Belfour UER (Turned pro with Gears, should be Generals)	3.00	1.35	.40
56	Steve Yzerman	.75	.35	.09
57	Rod Langway	.08	.04	.01
58	Bernie Federko	.12	.05	.02
59	Lemieux's Scoring Streak	.50	.23	.06
60	Doug Lidster	.08	.04	.01
61	Dave Christian	.08	.04	.01
62	Rob Ramage	.08	.04	.01
63	Jeremy Roenick	4.00	1.80	.50
64	Ray Bourque	.40	.18	.05
65	Jon Morris	.08	.04	.01
66	Sean Burke	.12	.05	.02
67	Ron Francis	.15	.07	.02
68	Ron Sutter	.08	.04	.01
69	Peter Sidorkiewicz	.08	.04	.01
70	Sylvain Turgeon	.08	.04	.01
71	Dave Ellett	.08	.04	.01
72	Bobby Smith	.12	.05	.02
73	Luc Robitaille	.50	.23	.06
74	Pat Elynuik	.08	.04	.01
75	Jason Soules	.08	.04	.01
76	Dino Ciccarelli	.12	.05	.02
77	Vladimir Krutov	.08	.04	.01
78	Lee Norwood	.08	.04	.01
79	Brian Bradley	.20	.09	.03
80	Michal Pivonka	.40	.18	.05
81	Mark LaForest	.08	.04	.01
82	Trent Yawney	.08	.04	.01
83	Tom Fergus	.08	.04	.01
84	Andy Brickley	.08	.04	.01
85	Dave Manson	.12	.05	.02
86	Gord Murphy	.20	.09	.03
87	Scott Young	.08	.04	.01
88	Tommy Albelin	.08	.04	.01
89	Ken Wregget	.12	.05	.02
90	Brad Shaw	.08	.04	.01
91	Mario Gosselin	.08	.04	.01
92	Paul Fenton	.08	.04	.01
93	Brian Skrudland	.08	.04	.01
94	Thomas Steen	.12	.05	.02
95	John Tonelli	.12	.05	.02
96	Steve Chiasson UER (Back photo actually Yves Racine)	.12	.05	.02
97	Mike Ridley	.12	.05	.02
98	Garth Butcher	.12	.05	.02
99	Daniel Shank	.08	.04	.01
100	Checklist 1-100	.08	.03	.01
101	Jamie Macoun	.08	.04	.01
102	Wendell Young	.08	.04	.01
103	Laurie Boschman	.08	.04	.01
104	Paul Ranheim	.20	.09	.03
105	Doug Smail	.08	.04	.01
106	Shawn Chambers	.08	.04	.01
107	Steve Weeks	.08	.04	.01
108	Gaetan Duchesne	.08	.04	.01
109	Kevin Hatcher	.12	.05	.02
110	Paul Reinhart	.08	.04	.01
111	Shawn Burr	.08	.04	.01
112	Troy Murray	.08	.04	.01
113	John Chabot	.08	.04	.01
114	Jacques Cloutier	.08	.04	.01
115	Rick Zombo	.08	.04	.01
116	Kjell Samuelsson	.08	.04	.01
117	Tim Watters	.08	.04	.01
118	Pat Flatley	.08	.04	.01
119	Tom Laidlaw	.08	.04	.01
120	Ilkka Sinisalo	.08	.04	.01
121	Tom Barrasso	.15	.07	.02
122	Bob Essensa	.40	.18	.05
123	Sergei Makarov	.75	.35	.09
124	Paul Coffey	.30	.14	.04
125	Bob Beers	.20	.09	.03
126	Brian Bellows	.12	.05	.02
127	Mike Liut	.12	.05	.02
128	Igor Larionov	.75	.35	.09
129	Craig Simpson	.12	.05	.02
130	Kelly Miller	.08	.04	.01
131	Dirk Graham	.12	.05	.02
132	Jimmy Carson	.12	.05	.02
133	Michel Goulet	.12	.05	.02
134	Gerard Gallant	.08	.04	.01
135	Bruce Hoffort	.08	.04	.01
136	Steve Duchesne	.12	.05	.02
137	Bryan Trottier	.15	.07	.02
138	Pelle Eklund	.08	.04	.01
139	Gary Nylund	.08	.04	.01
140	Steve Kasper	.08	.04	.01
141	Joel Otto	.08	.04	.01
142	Rob Brown	.08	.04	.01
143	Al MacInnis	.15	.07	.02
144	Mario Lemieux	1.75	.80	.22
145	Peter Eriksson UER (Photo actually Tommy Lehmann)	.08	.04	.01
146	Jari Kurri	.15	.07	.02
147	Petri Skriko	.08	.04	.01
148	Steve Smith	.12	.05	.02
149	Calle Johansson	.08	.04	.01
150	Stewart Gavin	.08	.04	.01
151	Randy Ladouceur	.08	.04	.01
152	Vincent Riendeau	.25	.11	.03
153	Patrick Roy UER (Feet and inches reversed in stat table)	1.50	.65	.19
154	Brett Hull	1.50	.65	.19
155	Craig Fisher UER (Photo actually Jay Wells)	.08	.04	.01
156	Cam Neely	.40	.18	.05
157	Al Iafrate	.15	.07	.02
158	Bob Carpenter	.08	.04	.01
159	Doug Brown	.08	.04	.01
160	Tom Kurvers	.08	.04	.01
161	John MacLean	.12	.05	.02
162	Guy Lafleur	.08	.04	.01
163	Peter Stastny	.12	.05	.02
164	Joe Sakic	1.00	.45	.13
165	Robb Stauber	.35	.16	.04
166	Daren Puppa	.12	.05	.02
167	Esa Tikkanen	.12	.05	.02
168	Mike Ramsey	.08	.04	.01
169	Craig MacTavish	.12	.05	.02
170	Christian Ruuttu	.08	.04	.01
171	Brian Hayward	.08	.04	.01
172	Pat Verbeek	.15	.07	.02
173	Adam Oates	.40	.18	.05
174	Chris Chelios	.15	.07	.02
175	Curtis Joseph	2.00	.90	.25
176	Viacheslav Fetisov	.30	.14	.04
177	Dave Poulin	.12	.05	.02
178	Mark Recchi	3.00	1.35	.40
179	Daniel Marois	.08	.04	.01
180	Mark Johnson	.08	.04	.01
181	Michel Petit	.08	.04	.01
182	Brian Mullen	.12	.05	.02
183	Chris Terreri	.60	.25	.08
184	Tony Hrkac	.08	.04	.01
185	James Patrick	.08	.04	.01
186	Craig Ludwig	.08	.04	.01
187	Uwe Krupp	.12	.05	.02
188	Guy Carbonneau	.12	.05	.02
189	Dave Snuggerud	.08	.04	.01

□	#	Card				□	#	Card			
□	190	Joe Murphy	.75	.35	.09	☒	271	Doug Gilmour	.75	.35	.09
□	191	Jeff Brown	.12	.05	.02	□	272	Tony Granato	.12	.05	.02
□	192	Dean Evason	.08	.04	.01	□	273	Gary Suter	.12	.05	.02
□	193	Petr Svoboda	.08	.04	.01	□	274	Darren Turcotte	.35	.16	.04
□	194	Dave Babych	.08	.04	.01	□	275	Murray Baron	.08	.04	.01
□	195	Steve Tuttle	.08	.04	.01	□	276	Stephane Richer	.15	.07	.02
□	196	Randy Burridge	.08	.04	.01	□	277	Mike Gartner	.20	.09	.03
□	197	Tony Tanti	.08	.04	.01	□	278	Kirk McLean	.75	.35	.09
□	198	Bob Sweeney	.08	.04	.01	□	279	John Vanbiesbrouck	.30	.14	.04
□	199	Brad Marsh	.12	.05	.02	□	280	Shayne Corson	.12	.05	.02
□	200	Checklist 101-200	.08	.03	.01	□	281	Paul Cavallini	.08	.04	.01
□	201	Conn Smythe Trophy Bill Ranford	.08	.04	.01	□	282	Petr Klima	.12	.05	.02
□	202	Calder Trophy Sergei Makarov	.25	.11	.03	□	283	Ulf Dahlen	.12	.05	.02
□	203	Lady Byng Trophy Brett Hull	.25	.11	.03	□	284	Glenn Anderson	.15	.07	.02
□	204	Norris Trophy Ray Bourque	.08	.04	.01	□	285	Rick Meagher	.08	.04	.01
□	205	Art Ross Trophy Wayne Gretzky	.50	.23	.06	□	286	Alexei Kasatonov	.25	.11	.03
□	206	Hart Trophy Mark Messier	.15	.07	.02	□	287	Ulf Samuelsson	.12	.05	.02
□	207	Vezina Trophy Patrick Roy	.50	.23	.06	□	288	Patrik Sundstrom	.08	.04	.01
□	208	Frank Selke Trophy Rick Meagher	.08	.04	.01	□	289	Ray Ferraro	.12	.05	.02
□	209	William Jennings Trophy Andy Moog and Reggie Lemelin	.08	.04	.01	□	290	Janne Ojanen	.08	.04	.01
□	210	Aaron Broten	.08	.04	.01	□	291	Jeff Jackson	.08	.04	.01
□	211	John Carter	.08	.04	.01	□	292	Jiri Hrdina	.08	.04	.01
□	212	Marty McSorley	.20	.09	.03	□	293	Joe Cirella	.08	.04	.01
□	213	Greg Millen	.08	.04	.01	□	294	Brad McCrimmon	.08	.04	.01
□	214	Dave Taylor	.12	.05	.02	□	295	Curtis Leschyshyn	.08	.04	.01
□	215	Rejean Lemelin	.12	.05	.02	□	296	Kelly Kisio	.08	.04	.01
□	216	Dave McLlwain UER (Shoots left, not right)	.08	.04	.01	□	297	Jyrki Lumme	.25	.11	.03
□	217	Don Beaupre	.12	.05	.02	□	298	Mark Janssens	.08	.04	.01
□	218	Paul MacDermid	.08	.04	.01	□	299	Stan Smyl	.08	.04	.01
□	219	Dale Hunter	.12	.05	.02	□	300	Checklist 201-300	.08	.03	.01
□	220	Brent Ashton	.08	.04	.01	□	301	Quebec Nordiques TC Joe Sakic	.25	.11	.03
□	221	Steve Thomas	.12	.05	.02	□	302	Vancouver Canucks TC Petri Skriko	.08	.04	.01
□	222	Ed Olczyk	.08	.04	.01	□	303	Detroit Red Wings TC Steve Yzerman	.20	.09	.03
□	223	Doug Wilson	.12	.05	.02	□	304	Phila. Flyers TC Tim Kerr	.12	.05	.02
□	224	Vincent Damphousse	.25	.11	.03	□	305	Pitts. Penguins TC Mario Lemieux	.40	.18	.05
□	225	Rob DiMaio	.08	.04	.01	□	306	N.Y. Islanders TC Pat LaFontaine	.15	.07	.02
□	226	Hubie McDonough	.08	.04	.01	□	307	L.A. Kings TC Wayne Gretzky	.50	.23	.06
□	227	Ron Hextall	.12	.05	.02	□	308	Minn. North Stars TC Brian Bellows	.12	.05	.02
□	228	Dave Chyzowski	.08	.04	.01	□	309	Wash. Capitals TC Rod Langway	.08	.04	.01
□	229	Larry Murphy	.12	.05	.02	□	310	Tor. Maple Leafs TC Gary Leeman	.08	.04	.01
□	230	Mike Bullard	.08	.04	.01	□	311	N.J. Devils TC Kirk Muller	.12	.05	.02
□	231	Kelly Hrudey	.12	.05	.02	□	312	St. Louis Blues TC Brett Hull	.25	.11	.03
□	232	Andy Moog	.20	.09	.03	□	313	Winnipeg Jets TC Thomas Steen	.08	.04	.01
□	233	Todd Elik	.35	.16	.04	□	314	Hartford Whalers TC Ron Francis	.12	.05	.02
□	234	Craig Janney	.40	.18	.05	□	315	N.Y. Rangers TC Brian Leetch	.12	.05	.02
□	235	Peter Lappin	.08	.04	.01	□	316	Chic. Blackhawks TC Jeremy Roenick	.40	.18	.05
□	236	Scott Stevens	.15	.07	.02	□	317	Mont. Canadiens TC Patrick Roy	.50	.23	.06
□	237	Fredrik Olausson	.12	.05	.02	□	318	Buffalo Sabres TC Pierre Turgeon	.20	.09	.03
□	238	Geoff Courtnall	.12	.05	.02	□	319	Calgary Flames TC Al MacInnis	.12	.05	.02
□	239	Greg Paslawski	.08	.04	.01	□	320	Boston Bruins TC Ray Bourque	.12	.05	.02
□	240	Alan May	.08	.04	.01	□	321	Edmonton Oilers TC Mark Messier	.12	.05	.02
□	241	Allan Bester	.08	.04	.01	□	322	Jody Hull	.08	.04	.01
□	242	Steve Larmer	.12	.05	.02	□	323	Chris Joseph	.08	.04	.01
□	243	Gary Leeman	.08	.04	.01	□	324	Adam Burt	.08	.04	.01
□	244	Denis Savard	.15	.07	.02	□	325	Jason Herter	.08	.04	.01
□	245	Eric Weinrich	.20	.09	.03	□	326	Geoff Smith ART	.08	.04	.01
□	246	Pat LaFontaine	.50	.23	.06	□	327	Brad Shaw ART	.08	.04	.01
□	247	Tim Kerr	.12	.05	.02	□	328	Rich Sutter	.08	.04	.01
□	248	Dave Gagner	.12	.05	.02	□	329	Barry Pederson	.08	.04	.01
□	249	Brent Sutter	.12	.05	.02	□	330	Paul MacLean	.08	.04	.01
□	250	Claude Vilgrain	.08	.04	.01	□	331	Randy Carlyle	.08	.04	.01
□	251	Tomas Sandstrom	.12	.05	.02	□	332	Donald Dufresne UER (Says shoots right, should say left)	.08	.04	.01
□	252	Joe Mullen	.15	.07	.02	□	333	Brent Hughes	.15	.07	.02
□	253	Brian Leetch	1.00	.45	.13	□	334	Mathieu Schneider	.75	.35	.09
□	254	Mike Vernon	.12	.05	.02	□	335	Jason Miller	.08	.04	.01
□	255	Daniel Dore	.08	.04	.01	□	336	Sergei Makarov ART	.25	.11	.03
□	256	Trevor Linden	.75	.35	.09	□	337	Bob Essensa ART	.12	.05	.02
□	257	Dave Barr	.08	.04	.01	□	338	Claude Loiselle	.08	.04	.01
□	258	John Ogrodnick	.08	.04	.01	□	339	Wayne Presley	.08	.04	.01
□	259	Russ Courtnall	.12	.05	.02	□	340	Tony McKegney	.08	.04	.01
□	260	Dan Quinn	.08	.04	.01						
□	261	Mark Howe	.12	.05	.02						
□	262	Kevin Lowe	.12	.05	.02						
□	263	Rick Tocchet	.15	.07	.02						
□	264	Grant Fuhr	.15	.07	.02						
□	265	Andrew Cassels	.40	.18	.05						
□	266	Kevin Dineen	.12	.05	.02						
□	267	Kirk Muller	.12	.05	.02						
□	268	Randy Cunneyworth	.08	.04	.01						
□	269	Brendan Shanahan	.50	.23	.06						
□	270	Dave Tippett	.08	.04	.01						

341	Charlie Huddy	.08	.04	.01
342	Greg Adams UER (Front photo actually Igor Larionov)	.12	.05	.02
343	Mike Tomlak	.08	.04	.01
344	Adam Graves	3.00	1.35	.40
345	Michel Mongeau	.08	.04	.01
346	Mike Modano UER ART ('89 Entry Draft, should say '88)	.50	.23	.06
347	Rod Brind'Amour ART	.25	.11	.03
348	Dana Murzyn	.08	.04	.01
349	Dave Lowry	.08	.04	.01
350	Star Rookie CL	.08	.04	.01
351	First Four Picks Owen Nolan Keith Primeau Petr Nedved Mike Ricci Top Ten Draft Pick CL	.75	.35	.09
352	Owen Nolan FDP	1.25	.55	.16
353	Petr Nedved	1.50	.65	.19
354	Keith Primeau	.75	.35	.09
355	Mike Ricci UER (Born October, not November 27)	1.00	.45	.13
356	Jaromir Jagr (With Craig Patrick)	3.50	1.55	.45
357	Scott Scissons	.08	.04	.01
358	Daryl Sydor	.50	.23	.06
359	Derian Hatcher (With Norm Green)	.50	.23	.06
360	John Slaney	.25	.11	.03
361	Drake Berehowsky	.40	.18	.05
362	Luke Richardson	.08	.04	.01
363	Lucien DeBlois	.08	.04	.01
364	David Reid	.10	.05	.01
365	Mats Sundin	2.00	.90	.25
366	Jan Erixon UER (Wrong position Wing, should be Right Wing)	.08	.04	.01
367	Troy Loney	.08	.04	.01
368	Chris Nilan	.12	.05	.02
369	Gord Dineen	.08	.04	.01
370	Jeff Bloemberg	.08	.04	.01
371	John Druce	.08	.04	.01
372	Brian MacLellan	.08	.04	.01
373	Bruce Driver	.08	.04	.01
374	Marc Habscheid	.08	.04	.01
375	Paul Ysebaert	.25	.11	.03
376	Rick Vaive	.08	.04	.01
377	Glen Wesley	.12	.05	.02
378	Mike Foligno	.12	.05	.02
379	Garry Galley	.40	.18	.05
380	Dean Kennedy	.08	.04	.01
381	Daniel Berthiaume	.08	.04	.01
382	Mike Keane	.35	.16	.04
383	Frantisek Musil	.08	.04	.01
384	Mike McPhee	.08	.04	.01
385	Jon Casey	.12	.05	.02
386	Jeff Norton	.08	.04	.01
387	John Tucker	.08	.04	.01
388	Alan Kerr	.08	.04	.01
389	Bob Rouse	.08	.04	.01
390	Gerald Diduck	.08	.04	.01
391	Greg Hawgood	.08	.04	.01
392	Randy Velischek	.08	.04	.01
393	Tim Cheveldae	.50	.23	.06
394	Mike Krushelnyski	.08	.04	.01
395	Glen Hanlon	.08	.04	.01
396	Lou Franceschetti	.08	.04	.01
397	Scott Arniel	.08	.04	.01
398	Terry Carkner	.08	.04	.01
399	Clint Malarchuk	.12	.05	.02
400	Checklist 301-400	.08	.03	.01
401	Mikhail Tatarinov	.15	.07	.02
402	Benoit Hogue	.12	.05	.02
403	Frank Pietrangelo	.08	.04	.01
404	Paul Stanton	.08	.04	.01
405	Anatoli Semenov	.30	.14	.04
406	Bobby Smith	.12	.05	.02
407	Derek King	.12	.05	.02
408	J.C. Bergeron	.08	.04	.01
409	Brian Propp	.12	.05	.02
410	Jiri Latal	.08	.04	.01
411	Joey Kocur	.08	.04	.01
412	Daniel Berthiaume	.08	.04	.01
413	Dave Ellett	.08	.04	.01
414	Jay Miller	.10	.05	.01
415	Stephane Beauregard	.15	.07	.02
416	Mark Hardy	.08	.04	.01
417	Todd Krygier	.08	.04	.01
418	Randy Moller	.08	.04	.01
419	Doug Crossman	.08	.04	.01
420	Ray Sheppard	.25	.11	.03
421	Sylvain Lefebvre	.08	.04	.01
422	Chris Chelios	.15	.07	.02
423	Joe Mullen	.15	.07	.02
424	Pete Peeters	.12	.05	.02
425	Bryan Trottier	.15	.07	.02
426	Denis Savard	.15	.07	.02
427	Ken Daneyko	.08	.04	.01
428	Eric Desjardins	.50	.23	.06
429	Zdeno Ciger	.30	.14	.04
430	Brad McCrimmon	.08	.04	.01
431	Ed Olczyk	.08	.04	.01
432	Peter Ing	.08	.04	.01
433	Bob Kudelski	1.00	.45	.13
434	Troy Gamble	.08	.04	.01
435	Phil Housley	.12	.05	.02
436	Scott Stevens	.15	.07	.02
437	Normand Rochefort	.08	.04	.01
438	Geoff Courtnall	.12	.05	.02
439	Ken Baumgartner	.08	.04	.01
440	Kris King	.20	.09	.03
441	Troy Crowder	.08	.04	.01
442	Chris Nilan	.12	.05	.02
443	Dale Hawerchuk	.15	.07	.02
444	Kevin Miller	.40	.18	.05
445	Keith Acton	.08	.04	.01
446	Jeff Chychrun	.08	.04	.01
447	Claude Lemieux	.12	.05	.02
448	Bob Probert	.40	.18	.05
449	Brian Hayward	.08	.04	.01
450	Craig Berube	.08	.04	.01
451	Team Canada Canadian National Junior Team Photo	.50	.23	.06
452	Mike Sillinger	.25	.11	.03
453	Jason Marshall	.20	.09	.03
454	Patrice Brisebois	.50	.23	.06
455	Brad May	.50	.23	.06
456	Pierre Sevigny	.30	.14	.04
457	John Slaney	.25	.11	.03
458	Felix Potvin	12.00	5.50	1.50
459	Scott Thornton	.15	.07	.02
460	Greg Johnson	.75	.35	.09
461	Scott Niedermayer	2.00	.90	.25
462	Steven Rice	.20	.09	.03
463	Trevor Kidd	.75	.35	.09
464	Dale Craigwell	.25	.11	.03
465	Kent Manderville	.25	.11	.03
466	Kris Draper	.30	.14	.04
467	Martin Lapointe	.50	.23	.06
468	Chris Snell	.20	.09	.03
469	Pat Falloon	1.50	.65	.19
470	David Harlock	.25	.11	.03
471	Karl Dykhuis	.15	.07	.02
472	Mike Craig	.30	.14	.04
473	Canada's Captains Kris Draper Steven Rice Eric Lindros	5.00	2.30	.60
474	Brett Hull AS	.40	.18	.05
475	Darren Turcotte AS	.12	.05	.02
476	Wayne Gretzky AS	.75	.35	.09
477	Steve Yzerman AS	.25	.11	.03
478	Theoren Fleury AS	.12	.05	.02
479	Pat LaFontaine AS	.25	.11	.03
480	Trevor Linden AS	.25	.11	.03
481	Jeremy Roenick AS	.50	.23	.06
482	Scott Stevens AS	.12	.05	.02
483	Adam Oates AS	.08	.04	.01
484	Vincent Damphousse AS	.12	.05	.02
485	Brian Leetch AS	.35	.16	.04
486	Kevin Hatcher AS	.08	.04	.01
487	Mark Recchi AS	.35	.16	.04
488	Rick Tocchet AS	.08	.04	.01
489	Ray Bourque AS	.08	.04	.01
490	Joe Sakic AS	.25	.11	.03
491	Chris Chelios AS	.08	.04	.01
492	John Cullen AS	.08	.04	.01
493	Cam Neely AS	.12	.05	.02
494	Mark Messier AS	.08	.04	.01
495	Mike Vernon AS	.08	.04	.01
496	Patrick Roy AS	.60	.25	.08
497	Al MacInnis AS	.12	.05	.02
498	Paul Coffey AS	.12	.05	.02
499	Steve Larmer AS	.08	.04	.01
500	Checklist 401-500	.08	.03	.01
501	Heroes Checklist	.08	.03	.01
502	Red Kelly HERO	.08	.04	.01
503	Eric Nesterenko HERO	.08	.04	.01
504	Darryl Sittler HERO	.08	.04	.01
505	Jim Schoenfeld HERO	.08	.04	.01
506	Serge Savard HERO	.08	.04	.01

☐ 507 Glenn Resch HERO	.08	.04	.01
☐ 508 Lanny McDonald HERO	.08	.04	.01
☐ 509 Bobby Clarke HERO	.08	.04	.01
☐ 510 Phil Esposito HERO	.08	.04	.01
☐ 511 Harry Howell HERO	.08	.04	.01
☐ 512 Rod Gilbert HERO	.08	.04	.01
☐ 513 Pit Martin HERO	.08	.04	.01
☐ 514 Jimmy Watson HERO	.08	.04	.01
☐ 515 Denis Potvin HERO	.08	.04	.01
☐ 516 Robert Ray	.08	.04	.01
☐ 517 Danton Cole	.15	.07	.02
☐ 518 Gino Odjick	.50	.23	.06
☐ 519 Donald Audette	.50	.23	.06
☐ 520 Rick Tabaracci	.35	.16	.04
☐ 521 Young Guns Checklist	.50	.23	.06
Sergei Fedorov			
Johan Garpenlov			
☐ 522 Kip Miller YG	.10	.05	.01
☐ 523 Johan Garpenlov YG	.35	.16	.04
☐ 524 Stephane Morin YG	.10	.05	.01
☐ 525 Sergei Fedorov YG UER	10.00	4.50	1.25
(Birthplace listed			
as Pskow, should be			
Appatity)			
☐ 526 Pavel Bure YG	18.00	8.00	2.30
☐ 527 Wes Walz YG	.20	.09	.03
☐ 528 Robert Kron YG	.35	.16	.04
☐ 529 Ken Hodge Jr. YG	.10	.05	.01
☐ 530 Garry Valk YG	.15	.07	.02
☐ 531 Tim Sweeney YG	.15	.07	.02
☐ 532 Mark Pederson YG	.10	.05	.01
☐ 533 Robert Reichel YG	1.00	.45	.13
☐ 534 Bobby Holik YG	.75	.35	.09
☐ 535 Stephane Matteau YG	.50	.23	.06
☐ 536 Peter Bondra YG	.75	.35	.09
☐ 537 Dimitri Khristich	.75	.35	.09
☐ 538 Vladimir Ruzicka	.25	.11	.03
☐ 539 Al Iafrate	.15	.07	.02
☐ 540 Rick Bennett	.08	.04	.01
☐ 541 Daryl Reaugh	.08	.04	.01
☐ 542 Martin Hostak	.08	.04	.01
☐ 543 Kari Takko	.08	.04	.01
☐ 544 Jocelyn Lemieux	.08	.04	.01
☐ 545 Gretzky's 2000th	1.00	.45	.13
Point			
☐ 546 Hull's 50 Goals	.50	.23	.06
☐ 547 Neil Wilkinson	.25	.11	.03
☐ 548 Bryan Fogarty	.08	.04	.01
☐ 549 Zamboni Machine	.08	.04	.01
☐ 550 Checklist Card	.08	.04	.01

1990-91 Upper Deck Holograms

The nine cards in this set were randomly inserted in 1990-91 Upper Deck foil packs (low and high series). The cards measure the standard size (2 1/2" by 3 1/2") and are best described as stereograms because the players show movement when the cards are slowly rotated. On the fronts, the stereograms are enclosed by a frame with rounded corners. The Upper Deck logo and title line "Hockey Superstars" appear in a bar at the top. The backs are blank and can be peeled off to stick the stereogram on a surface. The cards are unnumbered and checklisted below in alphabetical order.

	MINT	EXC	G-VG
COMPLETE SET (9)	10.00	4.00	1.00
COMMON PLAYER (1-9)	1.25	.50	.12
☐ 1 Wayne Gretzky	2.00	.80	.20
Stopping			
☐ 2 Wayne Gretzky	2.00	.80	.20
Shooting			
☐ 3 Wayne Gretzky	2.00	.80	.20
Standing			
☐ 4 Brett Hull	1.25	.50	.12
☐ 5 Mark Messier	1.25	.50	.12
☐ 6 Mark Messier and	1.25	.50	.12
Brett Hull			
☐ 7 Mark Messier and	1.25	.50	.12
Steve Yzerman			
☐ 8 Steve Yzerman	1.25	.50	.12
☐ 9 Steve Yzerman	1.25	.50	.12

1990-91 Upper Deck Sheets

As an advertising promotion, Upper Deck produced hockey commemorative sheets that were given away during the 1990-91 season at selected games in large arenas. Each sheet measures 8 1/2" by 11" and is printed on card stock. The fronts of the team commemorative sheets feature the team logo and a series of Upper Deck cards of star players on that team. Some of these sheets have a brief history of the team, which is tied in with an Upper Deck advertisement. The All-Star game sheet is distinguished by a hockey stick facsimile autographed by those All-Star players whose cards are displayed. All the sheets have an Upper Deck stamp indicating the production quota; in addition, some of the sheets have the serial number. The backs are blank. The sheets are listed below in chronological order.

	MINT	EXC	G-VG
COMPLETE SET (11)	175.00	70.00	18.00
COMMON PLAYER (1-11)	10.00	4.00	1.00
☐ 1 Toronto Maple Leafs	25.00	10.00	2.50
vs. Detroit Red Wings			
Nov. 17, 1990 (20,000)			
Al Iafrate			
Ed Olcyzk			
Vincent Damphousse			
Wendel Clark			
Gary Leeman			
Drake Berehowsky			
☐ 2 Detroit Red Wings I	15.00	6.00	1.50
vs. Boston Bruins			
Dec. 4, 1990 (22,000)			
Keith Primeau			
Shawn Burr			
Steve Yzerman			
Jimmy Carson			
Tim Cheveldae			
Steve Chiasson			
☐ 3 Los Angeles Kings	15.00	6.00	1.50

vs. Calgary Flames
Dec. 13, 1990 (19,500)
Steve Duchesne
Luc Robitaille
Rob Blake
Wayne Gretzky
Tony Granato
Tomas Sandstrom

☐ 4	New York Rangers I	10.00	4.00	1.00

vs. Hartford Whalers
Jan. 13, 1991 (25,700)
Mike Richter
Ray Sheppard
Troy Mallette
Normand Rochefort
Mark Janssens
Dennis Vial
John Ogrodnick
Lindy Ruff
Brian Leetch

☐ 5	New York Rangers II	10.00	4.00	1.00

vs. Chicago Blackhawks
Jan. 17, 1991 (25,700)
David Shaw
Miloslav Horava
Darren Turcotte
Jan Erixon
Kelly Kisio
Brian Mullen
Bernie Nicholls
John Vanbiesbrouck
James Patrick

☐ 6	Campbell All-Stars	30.00	12.00	3.00

Chicago Stadium
Jan. 19, 1991 (15,100)
Wayne Gretzky
Chris Chelios
Luc Robitaille
Brett Hull
Al MacInnis
Mike Vernon

☐ 7	Wales All-Stars	25.00	10.00	2.50

Chicago Stadium
Jan. 19, 1991 (15,100)
Ray Bourque
Rick Tocchet
Joe Sakic
Paul Coffey
Cam Neely
Patrick Roy

☐ 8	St. Louis Blues	15.00	6.00	1.50

vs. Buffalo Sabres
Jan. 29, 1991 (21,000)
Jeff Brown
Vincent Riendeau
Brent Hull
Paul Cavallini
Curtis Joseph
Gino Cavallini
Adam Oates
Scott Stevens
Rod Brind'Amour

☐ 9	Detroit Red Wings II	12.00	5.00	1.20

vs. Minnesota North Stars
Feb. 16, 1991 (23,000)
Joey Kocur
Rick Zombo
Sergei Fedorov
Gerard Gallant
Johan Garpenlov
Glen Hanlon
Dave Barr
John Chabot
Bob Probert

☐ 10	New York Rangers III	10.00	4.00	1.00

vs. New York Islanders
Feb. 18, 1991 (25,700)
Tie Domi
Randy Moller
Mike Gartner
Kevin Miller
Mark Hardy
Jody Hull
Kris King
Bob Froese
Paul Broten

☐ 11	All-Rookie Team	25.00	10.00	2.50

June 21, 1991 (16,000)
Eric Weinrich
Jaromir Jagr
Ed Belfour
Sergei Fedorov
Rob Blake
Ken Hodge

1991-92 Upper Deck

The 1991-92 Upper Deck hockey set contains 700 cards, each measuring the standard-size (2 1/2" by 3 1/2"). The set was released in two series of 500 and 200 cards, respectively. The front design features glossy color action player photos with white borders. The player's name and position appear in the top white border, while the team name is given in the bottom white border. Biographical information, statistics, or player profile are displayed on the back alongside a second color photo. The set includes several distinctive subsets. The teams that played in the Canada Cup are represented as follows: Soviet Union (1-6), Canada (8-15), Czechoslovakia (16-20), Finland (21-25), Sweden (26-31), and United States (32-37). Cards 1-6 even have the phrase "Soviet Stars" translated into Russian on both sides. Other subsets include All-Rookie Team (39-44), first round draft picks (64-77), team checklists illustrated by artist Steve Cusano (78-99), and Star Rookies (441-462). The All-Rookie Team and the Star Rookies are marked by the abbreviations ART and SR respectively in the list below. Nine hologram cards were randomly inserted in packs (low and high series) and represent trophy winners from the previous season. The first three holograms released were Wayne Gretzky, Ed Belfour, and Brett Hull. Finally a Heroes Bonus Set of ten cards highlights the career of Brett Hull. Hull autographed 2,500 of card number 9, and these were randomly inserted in low series packs. Also included in the foil packs was a randomly inserted Glasnost card (SP1) featuring Wayne Gretzky and Valeri Kamensky and ballots by which fans could vote for their favorite NHL All-Stars. The cards are numbered on the back and checklisted below accordingly. Three Award Winner hologram cards were randomly inserted in High Series foil packs. Special subsets featured in the second series include Canada Cup players (Canada 502-507 and USA 508-513), Young Guns (584-599), All-Stars (611-634), Heroes (635-643), Bloodlines (644-648), and members of the teams that participated in the IIHF World Junior Championships. The World Junior Championship teams included Commonwealth of Independent States (650-662), Switzerland (663-670), Finland (671-677), Germany (678-683), Canada (684-691), and USA (692-699). Rookie Cards in this set include Tony Amonte, Josef Beranek, Gilbert Dionne, Peter Forsberg, Dominik Hasek, Valeri Kamensky, Darius Kasparaitis, Alexei Kovalev, Viacheslav Kozlov, Sergei Krivokrasov, Nicklas Lidstrom, Sandis Ozolinsh, Pat Peake, Rob Pearson, Geoff Sanderson, Teemu Selanne, Keith Tkachuk, Alexei Yashin, Valeri Zelepukin, Alexei Zhamnov, and Alexei Zhitnik.

		MINT	EXC	G-VG
	COMPLETE SET (700)	45.00	20.00	5.75
	COMPLETE LO SET (500)	30.00	13.50	3.80
	COMPLETE HI SET (200)	15.00	6.75	1.90
	COMPLETE HI FACT.SET (200)	15.00	6.75	1.90
	COMMON PLAYER (1-500)	.05	.02	.01
	COMMON PLAYER (501-700)	.05	.02	.01
	*FRENCH VERSION: 1X to 1.2X			
1	Vladimir Malakhov SS	.75	.35	.09
2	Alexei Zhamnov SS	2.00	.90	.25
3	Dimitri Filiminov SS	.25	.11	.03
4	Alexander Semak SS	.35	.16	.04
5	Viacheslav Kozlov SS	2.00	.90	.25
6	Sergei Fedorov SS	.60	.25	.08
7	Canada Cup Checklist (Eric Lindros and Brett Hull)	1.00	.45	.13
8	Al MacInnis CC	.10	.05	.01
9	Eric Lindros CC	6.00	2.70	.75
10	Bill Ranford CC	.10	.05	.01
11	Paul Coffey CC	.10	.05	.01
12	Dale Hawerchuk CC	.10	.05	.01
13	Wayne Gretzky CC	.75	.35	.09
14	Mark Messier CC	.20	.09	.03
15	Steve Larmer CC	.10	.05	.01
16	Zigmund Palffy CC	.40	.18	.05
17	Josef Beranek CC	.50	.23	.06
18	Jiri Slegr CC	.40	.18	.05
19	Martin Rucinsky CC	.25	.11	.03
20	Jaromir Jagr CC	.50	.23	.06
21	Teemu Selanne CC	7.00	3.10	.85
22	Janne Laukkanen CC	.15	.07	.02
23	Markus Ketterer CC	.25	.11	.03
24	Jari Kurri CC	.10	.05	.01
25	Janne Ojanen CC	.07	.03	.01
26	Nicklas Lidstrom CC	.75	.35	.09
27	Thomas Forslund CC	.07	.03	.01
28	Johan Garpenlov CC	.07	.03	.01
29	Niclas Andersson CC	.15	.07	.02
30	Tomas Sandstrom CC	.07	.03	.01
31	Mats Sundin CC	.15	.07	.02
32	Mike Modano CC	.25	.11	.03
33	Brett Hull CC	.35	.16	.04
34	Mike Richter CC	.20	.09	.03
35	Brian Leetch CC	.25	.11	.03
36	Jeremy Roenick CC	.50	.23	.06
37	Chris Chelios CC	.10	.05	.01
38	Wayne Gretzky 99	.75	.35	.09
39	Ed Belfour ART	.15	.07	.02
40	Sergei Fedorov ART	.40	.18	.05
41	Ken Hodge Jr. ART	.07	.03	.01
42	Jaromir Jagr ART	.25	.11	.03
43	Rob Blake ART	.10	.05	.01
44	Eric Weinrich ART	.07	.03	.01
45	The 50/50 Club (Mario Lemieux, Wayne Gretzky, Brett Hull)	.35	.16	.04
46	Russ Romaniuk	.10	.05	.01
47	White House Welcome (George Bush and Mario Lemieux)	.25	.11	.03
48	Michel Picard	.05	.02	.01
49	Dennis Vaske	.05	.02	.01
50	Eric Murano	.05	.02	.01
51	Enrico Ciccone	.05	.02	.01
52	Shaun Van Allen	.15	.07	.02
53	Stu Barnes	.08	.04	.01
54	Pavel Bure	2.50	1.15	.30
55	Neil Wilkinson	.05	.02	.01
56	Tony Hrkac	.05	.02	.01
57	Brian Mullen	.08	.04	.01
58	Jeff Hackett	.05	.02	.01
59	Brian Hayward	.05	.02	.01
60	Craig Coxe	.05	.02	.01
61	Rob Zettler	.05	.02	.01
62	Bob McGill	.05	.02	.01
63	Draft Picks Checklist (Martin Lapointe and Jamie Pushor)	.05	.02	.01
64	Peter Forsberg	3.50	1.55	.45
65	Patrick Poulin	.40	.18	.05
66	Martin Lapointe	.15	.07	.02
67	Tyler Wright	.20	.09	.03
68	Philippe Boucher	.25	.11	.03
69	Glen Murray	.30	.14	.04
70	Martin Rucinsky	.25	.11	.03
71	Zigmund Palffy	.40	.18	.05
72	Jassen Cullimore	.10	.05	.01
73	Jamie Pushor	.10	.05	.01
74	Andrew Verner	.10	.05	.01
75	Jason Dawe	.25	.11	.03
76	Jamie Matthews	.15	.07	.02
77	Sandy McCarthy	.25	.11	.03
78	Cam Neely TC	.10	.05	.01
79	Dale Hawerchuk TC	.10	.05	.01
80	Theoren Fleury TC	.10	.05	.01
81	Ed Belfour TC	.15	.07	.02
82	Sergei Fedorov TC	.25	.11	.03
83	Esa Tikkanen TC	.07	.03	.01
84	John Cullen TC	.07	.03	.01
85	Tomas Sandstrom TC	.07	.03	.01
86	Dave Gagner TC	.07	.03	.01
87	Russ Courtnall TC	.07	.03	.01
88	John MacLean TC	.07	.03	.01
89	David Volek TC	.07	.03	.01
90	Darren Turcotte TC	.07	.03	.01
91	Rick Tocchet TC	.10	.05	.01
92	Mark Recchi TC	.15	.07	.02
93	Mats Sundin TC	.15	.07	.02
94	Neil Wilkinson TC	.07	.03	.01
95	Adam Oates TC	.10	.05	.01
96	Dave Ellett TC	.07	.03	.01
97	Trevor Linden TC	.10	.05	.01
98	Kevin Hatcher TC	.07	.03	.01
99	Ed Olczyk TC	.07	.03	.01
100	Checklist 1-100	.07	.03	.01
101	Bob Essensa	.08	.04	.01
102	Uwe Krupp	.05	.02	.01
103	Pelle Eklund	.05	.02	.01
104	Christian Ruuttu	.05	.02	.01
105	Kevin Dineen	.08	.04	.01
106	Phil Housley	.08	.04	.01
107	Pat Jablonski	.15	.07	.02
108	Jarmo Kekalainen	.05	.02	.01
109	Pat Elynuik	.05	.02	.01
110	Corey Millen	.35	.16	.04
111	Petr Klima	.05	.02	.01
112	Mike Ridley	.08	.04	.01
113	Peter Stastny	.08	.04	.01
114	Jyrki Lumme	.05	.02	.01
115	Chris Terreri	.08	.04	.01
116	Tom Barrasso	.08	.04	.01
117	Bill Ranford	.08	.04	.01
118	Peter Ing	.05	.02	.01
119	John Tanner	.05	.02	.01
120	Troy Gamble	.05	.02	.01
121	Stephane Matteau	.05	.02	.01
122	Rick Tocchet	.08	.04	.01
123	Wes Walz	.05	.02	.01
124	Dave Andreychuk	.20	.09	.03
125	Mike Craig	.05	.02	.01
126	Dale Hawerchuk	.08	.04	.01
127	Dean Evason	.05	.02	.01
128	Craig Janney	.20	.09	.03
129	Tim Cheveldae	.08	.04	.01
130	Rick Wamsley	.05	.02	.01
131	Peter Bondra	.20	.09	.03
132	Scott Stevens	.10	.05	.01
133	Kelly Miller	.05	.02	.01
134	Mats Sundin	.60	.25	.08
135	Mick Vukota	.05	.02	.01
136	Vincent Damphousse	.08	.04	.01
137	Patrick Roy	1.00	.45	.13
138	Hubie McDonough	.05	.02	.01
139	Curtis Joseph	.40	.18	.05
140	Brent Sutter	.08	.04	.01
141	Tomas Sandstrom	.08	.04	.01
142	Kevin Miller	.08	.04	.01
143	Mike Ricci	.25	.11	.03
144	Sergei Fedorov	1.25	.55	.16
145	Luc Robitaille	.25	.11	.03
146	Steve Yzerman	.40	.18	.05
147	Andy Moog	.10	.05	.01
148	Rob Blake	.25	.11	.03
149	Kirk Muller	.08	.04	.01
150	Daniel Berthiaume	.05	.02	.01
151	John Druce	.05	.02	.01
152	Garry Valk	.05	.02	.01
153	Brian Leetch	.60	.25	.08
154	Kevin Stevens	.50	.23	.06
155	Darren Turcotte	.05	.02	.01
156	Mario Lemieux	1.00	.45	.13
157	Dimitri Khristich	.08	.04	.01
158	Brian Glynn	.05	.02	.01
159	Benoit Hogue UER (Back photo actually Dean Kennedy)	.05	.02	.01
160	Mike Modano	.60	.25	.08
161	Jimmy Carson	.08	.04	.01
162	Steve Thomas	.08	.04	.01
163	Mike Vernon	.08	.04	.01
164	Ed Belfour	.60	.25	.08
165	Joel Otto	.05	.02	.01
166	Jeremy Roenick	1.00	.45	.13
167	Johan Garpenlov	.05	.02	.01
168	Russ Courtnall	.08	.04	.01
169	John MacLean	.08	.04	.01
170	J.J. Daigneault	.05	.02	.01

☐	171	Sylvain Lefebvre	.05	.02	.01	☐	264	Grant Fuhr	.08	.04	.01
☐	172	Tony Granato	.08	.04	.01	☐	265	Guy Carbonneau	.08	.04	.01
☐	173	David Volek	.05	.02	.01	☐	266	Martin Gelinas	.05	.02	.01
☐	174	Trevor Linden	.30	.14	.04	☐	267	Alexander Mogilny	.75	.35	.09
☐	175	Mike Richter	.50	.23	.06	☐	268	Adam Graves	.40	.18	.05
☐	176	Pierre Turgeon	.30	.14	.04	☐	269	Anatoli Semenov	.05	.02	.01
☐	177	Paul Coffey	.20	.09	.03	☐	270	Dave Taylor	.08	.04	.01
☐	178	Jan Erixon	.05	.02	.01	☐	271	Dirk Graham	.05	.02	.01
☐	179	Rick Vaive	.05	.02	.01	☐	272	Gary Leeman	.05	.02	.01
☐	180	Dave Gagner	.08	.04	.01	☐	273	Valeri Kamensky	.50	.23	.06
☐	181	Thomas Steen	.05	.02	.01	☐	274	Marc Bureau	.05	.02	.01
☐	182	Esa Tikkanen	.08	.04	.01	☐	275	James Patrick	.05	.02	.01
☐	183	Sean Burke	.08	.04	.01	☐	276	Dino Ciccarelli	.08	.04	.01
☐	184	Paul Cavallini	.05	.02	.01	☐	277	Ron Tugnutt	.05	.02	.01
☐	185	Alexei Kasatonov	.08	.04	.01	☐	278	Paul Ysebaert	.05	.02	.01
☐	186	Kevin Lowe	.08	.04	.01	☐	279	Laurie Boschman	.05	.02	.01
☐	187	Gino Cavallini	.05	.02	.01	☐	280	Dave Manson	.08	.04	.01
☒	188	Doug Gilmour	.40	.18	.05	☐	281	Dave Chyzowski	.05	.02	.01
☐	189	Rod Brind'Amour	.25	.11	.03	☐	282	Shayne Corson	.08	.04	.01
☐	190	Gary Roberts	.08	.04	.01	☐	283	Steve Chiasson	.05	.02	.01
☐	191	Kirk McLean	.30	.14	.04	☐	284	Craig MacTavish	.05	.02	.01
☐	192	Kevin Haller	.15	.07	.02	☐	285	Petr Svoboda	.05	.02	.01
☐	193	Pat Verbeek	.08	.04	.01	☐	286	Craig Simpson	.08	.04	.01
☐	194	Dave Snuggerud	.05	.02	.01	☐	287	Ron Hoover	.05	.02	.01
☐	195	Gino Odjick	.08	.04	.01	☐	288	Vladimir Ruzicka	.05	.02	.01
☐	196	Dave Ellett	.05	.02	.01	☐	289	Randy Wood	.05	.02	.01
☐	197	Don Beaupre	.08	.04	.01	☐	290	Doug Lidster	.05	.02	.01
☐	198	Rob Brown	.05	.02	.01	☐	291	Kay Whitmore	.05	.02	.01
☐	199	Marty McSorley	.08	.04	.01	☐	292	Bruce Driver	.05	.02	.01
☐	200	Checklist 101-200	.07	.03	.01	☐	293	Bobby Smith	.08	.04	.01
☐	201	Joe Mullen	.10	.05	.01	☐	294	Claude Lemieux	.08	.04	.01
☐	202	Dave Capuano	.05	.02	.01	☐	295	Mark Tinordi	.08	.04	.01
☐	203	Paul Stanton	.05	.02	.01	☐	296	Mark Osborne	.05	.02	.01
☐	204	Terry Carkner	.05	.02	.01	☐	297	Brad Shaw	.05	.02	.01
☐	205	Jon Casey	.08	.04	.01	☐	298	Igor Larionov	.08	.04	.01
☐	206	Ken Wregget	.05	.02	.01	☐	299	Ron Francis	.08	.04	.01
☐	207	Gaetan Duchesne	.05	.02	.01	☐	300	Checklist 201-300	.07	.03	.01
☐	208	Cliff Ronning	.08	.04	.01	☐	301	Bob Kudelski	.08	.04	.01
☐	209	Dale Hunter	.08	.04	.01	☐	302	Larry Murphy	.08	.04	.01
☐	210	Danton Cole	.05	.02	.01	☐	303	Brent Ashton	.05	.02	.01
☐	211	Jeff Brown	.08	.04	.01	☐	304	Brad Jones	.05	.02	.01
☐	212	Mike Foligno	.05	.02	.01	☐	305	Gord Donnelly	.05	.02	.01
☐	213	Michel Mongeau	.05	.02	.01	☐	306	Murray Craven	.05	.02	.01
☐	214	Doug Brown	.05	.02	.01	☐	307	Chris Dahlquist	.05	.02	.01
☐	215	Todd Krygier	.05	.02	.01	☐	308	Jim Paek	.15	.07	.02
☐	216	Jon Morris	.05	.02	.01	☐	309	Ron Sutter	.05	.02	.01
☐	217	David Reid	.05	.02	.01	☐	310	Mike Tomlak	.05	.02	.01
☐	218	John McIntyre	.05	.02	.01	☐	311	Ray Ferraro	.08	.04	.01
☐	219	Guy Lafleur's Farewell	.08	.04	.01	☐	312	Dave Hannan	.05	.02	.01
☐	220	Vincent Riendeau	.05	.02	.01	☐	313	Randy McKay	.05	.02	.01
☐	221	Tim Hunter	.05	.02	.01	☐	314	Rod Langway	.05	.02	.01
☐	222	Dave McLlwain	.05	.02	.01	☐	315	Shawn Burr	.05	.02	.01
☐	223	Robert Reichel	.25	.11	.03	☐	316	Calle Johansson	.05	.02	.01
☐	224	Glenn Healy	.08	.04	.01	☐	317	Rich Sutter	.05	.02	.01
☐	225	Robert Kron	.05	.02	.01	☐	318	Al Iafrate	.08	.04	.01
☐	226	Pat Flatley	.05	.02	.01	☐	319	Bob Bassen	.05	.02	.01
☐	227	Petr Nedved	.30	.14	.04	☐	320	Mike Krushelnyski	.05	.02	.01
☐	228	Mark Janssens	.05	.02	.01	☐	321	Sergei Makarov	.25	.11	.03
☐	229	Michal Pivonka	.08	.04	.01	☐	322	Darrin Shannon	.05	.02	.01
☐	230	Ulf Samuelsson	.08	.04	.01	☐	323	Terry Yake	.08	.04	.01
☐	231	Zarley Zalapski	.05	.02	.01	☐	324	John Vanbiesbrouck	.25	.11	.03
☐	232	Neal Broten	.08	.04	.01	☐	325	Peter Sidorkiewicz	.05	.02	.01
☐	233	Bobby Holik	.08	.04	.01	☐	326	Troy Mallette	.05	.02	.01
☐	234	Cam Neely	.20	.09	.03	☐	327	Ron Hextall	.08	.04	.01
☐	235	John Cullen	.05	.02	.01	☐	328	Mathieu Schneider	.08	.04	.01
☐	236	Brian Bellows	.08	.04	.01	☐	329	Bryan Trottier	.08	.04	.01
☐	237	Chris Nilan	.08	.04	.01	☐	330	Kris King	.05	.02	.01
☐	238	Mikael Andersson	.05	.02	.01	☐	331	Daniel Marois	.05	.02	.01
☐	239	Bob Probert	.08	.04	.01	☐	332	Shayne Stevenson	.05	.02	.01
☐	240	Teppo Numminen	.05	.02	.01	☐	333	Joe Sakic	.50	.23	.06
☐	241	Peter Zezel	.05	.02	.01	☐	334	Petri Skriko	.05	.02	.01
☐	242	Denis Savard	.08	.04	.01	☐	335	Dominik Hasek	2.50	1.15	.30
☐	243	Al MacInnis	.10	.05	.01	☐	336	Scott Pearson	.05	.02	.01
☐	244	Stephane Richer	.08	.04	.01	☐	337	Bryan Fogarty	.05	.02	.01
☐	245	Theoren Fleury	.20	.09	.03	☐	338	Don Sweeney	.05	.02	.01
☐	246	Mark Messier	.35	.16	.04	☐	339	Rick Tabaracci	.05	.02	.01
☐	247	Mike Gartner	.10	.05	.01	☐	340	Steven Finn	.05	.02	.01
☐	248	Daren Puppa	.08	.04	.01	☐	341	Gary Suter	.08	.04	.01
☐	249	Louie DeBrusk	.05	.02	.01	☐	342	Troy Crowder	.05	.02	.01
☐	250	Glenn Anderson	.08	.04	.01	☐	343	Jim Hrivnak	.05	.02	.01
☐	251	Ken Hodge Jr.	.05	.02	.01	☐	344	Eric Weinrich	.05	.02	.01
☐	252	Adam Oates	.25	.11	.03	☐	345	John LeClair	.25	.11	.03
☐	253	Pat LaFontaine	.30	.14	.04	☐	346	Mark Recchi	.75	.35	.09
☐	254	Adam Creighton	.05	.02	.01	☐	347	Dan Currie	.05	.02	.01
☐	255	Ray Bourque	.25	.11	.03	☐	348	Ulf Dahlen	.08	.04	.01
☐	256	Jaromir Jagr	1.00	.45	.13	☐	349	Robert Ray	.05	.02	.01
☐	257	Steve Larmer	.08	.04	.01	☐	350	Steve Smith	.05	.02	.01
☐	258	Keith Primeau	.25	.11	.03	☐	351	Shawn Antoski	.05	.02	.01
☐	259	Mike Liut	.08	.04	.01	☐	352	Cam Russell	.05	.02	.01
☐	260	Brian Propp	.08	.04	.01	☐	353	Scott Thornton	.05	.02	.01
☐	261	Stephan Lebeau	.15	.07	.02	☐	354	Chris Chelios	.08	.04	.01
☐	262	Kelly Hrudey	.08	.04	.01	☐	355	Sergei Nemchinov	.20	.09	.03
☐	263	Joe Nieuwendyk	.10	.05	.01	☐	356	Bernie Nicholls	.08	.04	.01

☐ 357	Jeff Norton	.05	.02	.01
☐ 358	Dan Quinn	.05	.02	.01
☐ 359	Michel Petit	.05	.02	.01
☐ 360	Eric Desjardins	.08	.04	.01
☐ 361	Kevin Hatcher	.08	.04	.01
☐ 362	Jiri Sejba	.05	.02	.01
☐ 363	Mark Pederson	.05	.02	.01
☐ 364	Jeff Lazaro	.05	.02	.01
☐ 365	Alexei Gusarov	.10	.05	.01
☐ 366	Jari Kurri	.10	.05	.01
☐ 367	Owen Nolan	.20	.09	.03
☐ 368	Clint Malarchuk	.08	.04	.01
☐ 369	Patrik Sundstrom	.05	.02	.01
☐ 370	Glen Wesley	.05	.02	.01
☐ 371	Wayne Presley	.05	.02	.01
☐ 372	Craig Muni	.05	.02	.01
☐ 373	Brent Fedyk	.05	.02	.01
☐ 374	Michel Goulet	.08	.04	.01
☐ 375	Tim Sweeney	.05	.02	.01
☐ 376	Gary Shuchuk	.05	.02	.01
☐ 377	Andre Racicot	.15	.07	.02
☐ 378	Jay Mazur	.05	.02	.01
☐ 379	Andrew Cassels	.08	.04	.01
☐ 380	Brian Noonan	.05	.02	.01
☐ 381	Sergei Kharin	.05	.02	.01
☐ 382	Derek King	.08	.04	.01
☐ 383	Fredrik Olausson	.08	.04	.01
☐ 384	Tom Fergus	.05	.02	.01
☐ 385	Zdeno Ciger	.05	.02	.01
☐ 386	Wendel Clark	.25	.11	.03
☐ 387	Ed Olczyk	.05	.02	.01
☐ 388	Basil McRae	.05	.02	.01
☐ 389	Tom Fitzgerald	.05	.02	.01
☐ 390	Ray Sheppard	.08	.04	.01
☐ 391	Bob Sweeney	.05	.02	.01
☐ 392	Gord Murphy	.05	.02	.01
☐ 393	John Chabot	.05	.02	.01
☐ 394	Jeff Beukeboom	.05	.02	.01
☐ 395	Rick Zombo	.05	.02	.01
☐ 396	Kjell Samuelsson	.05	.02	.01
☐ 397	Garth Butcher	.05	.02	.01
☐ 398	Phil Bourque	.05	.02	.01
☐ 399	Lou Franceschetti	.05	.02	.01
☐ 400	Checklist 301-400	.07	.03	.01
☐ 401	Kevin Todd	.20	.09	.03
☐ 402	Ken Baumgartner	.05	.02	.01
☐ 403	Peter Douris	.05	.02	.01
☐ 404	Jiri Latal	.05	.02	.01
☐ 405	Marc Potvin	.10	.05	.01
☐ 406	Gary Nylund	.05	.02	.01
☐ 407	Yvon Corriveau	.05	.02	.01
☐ 408	Sheldon Kennedy	.05	.02	.01
☐ 409	David Shaw	.05	.02	.01
☐ 410	Viacheslav Fetisov	.08	.04	.01
☐ 411	Mario Doyon	.05	.02	.01
☐ 412	Jamie Macoun	.05	.02	.01
☐ 413	Curtis Leschyshyn	.05	.02	.01
☐ 414	Mike Peluso	.05	.02	.01
☐ 415	Brian Benning	.05	.02	.01
☐ 416	Stu Grimson	.25	.11	.03
☐ 417	Ken Sabourin	.05	.02	.01
☐ 418	Luke Richardson	.05	.02	.01
☐ 419	Ken Quinney	.05	.02	.01
☐ 420	Mike Donnelly	.20	.09	.03
☐ 421	Darcy Loewen	.05	.02	.01
☐ 422	Brian Skrudland	.05	.02	.01
☐ 423	Joel Savage	.05	.02	.01
☐ 424	Adrien Plavsic	.05	.02	.01
☐ 425	Jergus Baca	.05	.02	.01
☐ 426	Greg Adams	.05	.02	.01
☐ 427	Tom Chorske	.05	.02	.01
☐ 428	Scott Scissons	.05	.02	.01
☐ 429	Dale Kushner	.05	.02	.01
☐ 430	Todd Richards	.05	.02	.01
☐ 431	Kip Miller	.05	.02	.01
☐ 432	Jason Prosofsky	.05	.02	.01
☐ 433	Stephane Morin	.05	.02	.01
☐ 434	Brian McReynolds	.05	.02	.01
☐ 435	Ken Daneyko	.05	.02	.01
☐ 436	Chris Joseph	.05	.02	.01
☐ 437	Wayne Gretzky	1.25	.55	.16
☐ 438	Jocelyn Lemieux	.05	.02	.01
☐ 439	Garry Galley	.08	.04	.01
☐ 440	Super Rookie Checklist	.25	.11	.03
	(Tony Amonte,			
	Doug Weight,			
	and Steven Rice)			
☐ 441	Steven Rice SR	.07	.03	.01
☐ 442	Patrice Brisebois SR	.20	.09	.03
☐ 443	Jimmy Waite SR	.10	.05	.01
☐ 444	Doug Weight SR	.50	.23	.06
☐ 445	Nelson Emerson SR	.40	.18	.05
☐ 446	Jarrod Skalde SR	.20	.09	.03

☐ 447	Jamie Leach SR	.07	.03	.01
☐ 448	Gilbert Dionne SR	.35	.16	.04
☐ 449	Trevor Kidd SR	.10	.05	.01
☐ 450	Tony Amonte SR	.50	.23	.06
☐ 451	Pat Murray SR	.07	.03	.01
☐ 452	Stephane Fiset SR	.25	.11	.03
☐ 453	Patrick Lebeau SR	.15	.07	.02
☐ 454	Chris Taylor SR	.07	.03	.01
☐ 455	Chris Tancill SR	.07	.03	.01
☐ 456	Mark Greig SR	.07	.03	.01
☐ 457	Mike Sillinger SR	.07	.03	.01
☐ 458	Ken Sutton SR	.10	.05	.01
☐ 459	Len Barrie SR	.07	.03	.01
☐ 460	Felix Potvin SR	2.00	.90	.25
☐ 461	Brian Sakic SR	.07	.03	.01
☐ 462	Viacheslav Kozlov SR	2.00	.90	.25
☐ 463	Matt DelGuidice	.05	.02	.01
☐ 464	Brett Hull	1.00	.45	.13
☐ 465	Norm Foster	.05	.02	.01
☐ 466	Alexander Godynyuk	.05	.02	.01
☐ 467	Geoff Courtnall	.08	.04	.01
☐ 468	Frantisek Kucera	.05	.02	.01
☐ 469	Benoit Brunet	.15	.07	.02
☐ 470	Mark Vermette	.05	.02	.01
☐ 471	Tim Watters	.05	.02	.01
☐ 472	Paul Ranheim	.05	.02	.01
☐ 473	Martin Hostak	.05	.02	.01
☐ 474	Joe Murphy	.08	.04	.01
☐ 475	Claude Boivin	.10	.05	.01
☐ 476	John Ogrodnick	.05	.02	.01
☐ 477	Doug Bodger	.05	.02	.01
☐ 478	Shawn Cronin	.05	.02	.01
☐ 479	Mark Hunter	.05	.02	.01
☐ 480	Dave Tippett	.05	.02	.01
☐ 481	Rob DiMaio	.05	.02	.01
☐ 482	Lyle Odelein	.05	.02	.01
☐ 483	Joe Reekie	.05	.02	.01
☐ 484	Randy Velischek	.05	.02	.01
☐ 485	Myles O'Connor	.05	.02	.01
☐ 486	Craig Wolanin	.05	.02	.01
☐ 487	Mike McPhee	.05	.02	.01
☐ 488	Claude Lapointe	.10	.05	.01
☐ 489	Troy Loney	.05	.02	.01
☐ 490	Bob Beers	.05	.02	.01
☐ 491	Sylvain Couturier	.05	.02	.01
☐ 492	Kimbi Daniels	.05	.02	.01
☐ 493	Darryl Shannon	.05	.02	.01
☐ 494	Jim McKenzie	.05	.02	.01
☐ 495	Don Gibson	.05	.02	.01
☐ 496	Ralph Barahona	.05	.02	.01
☐ 497	Murray Baron	.05	.02	.01
☐ 498	Yves Racine	.05	.02	.01
☐ 499	Larry Robinson	.08	.04	.01
☐ 500	Checklist 401-500	.07	.03	.01
☐ 501	Canada Cup Checklist	.25	.11	.03
	(Paul Coffey and			
	Wayne Gretzky)			
☐ 502	Dirk Graham CC	.07	.03	.01
☐ 503	Rick Tocchet CC	.10	.05	.01
☐ 504	Eric Desjardins CC	.07	.03	.01
☐ 505	Shayne Corson CC	.07	.03	.01
☐ 506	Theoren Fleury CC	.10	.05	.01
☐ 507	Luc Robitaille CC	.10	.05	.01
☐ 508	Tony Granato CC	.07	.03	.01
☐ 509	Eric Weinrich CC	.07	.03	.01
☐ 510	Gary Suter CC	.07	.03	.01
☐ 511	Kevin Hatcher CC	.07	.03	.01
☐ 512	Craig Janney CC	.10	.05	.01
☐ 513	Darren Turcotte CC	.07	.03	.01
☐ 514	Chris Winnes	.05	.02	.01
	Boston Bruins			
☐ 515	Kelly Kisio	.05	.02	.01
	San Jose Sharks			
☐ 516	Joe Day	.05	.02	.01
	Hartford Whalers			
☐ 517	Ed Courtenay	.05	.02	.01
	San Jose Sharks			
☐ 518	Andrei Lomakin	.05	.02	.01
	Philadelphia Flyers			
☐ 519	Kirk Muller	.08	.04	.01
	Montreal Canadiens			
☐ 520	Rick Lessard	.05	.02	.01
	San Jose Sharks			
☐ 521	Scott Thornton	.05	.02	.01
	Edmonton Oilers			
☐ 522	Luke Richardson	.05	.02	.01
	Edmonton Oilers			
☐ 523	Mike Eagles	.05	.02	.01
	Winnipeg Jets			
☐ 524	Mike McNeill	.05	.02	.01
	Quebec Nordiques			
☐ 525	Ken Priestlay	.05	.02	.01
	Pittsburgh Penguins			

☐ 526 Louie DeBrusk	.05	.02	.01
Edmonton Oilers			
☐ 527 Dave McLlwain	.05	.02	.01
New York Islanders			
☐ 528 Gary Leeman	.05	.02	.01
Calgary Flames			
☐ 529 Adam Foote	.05	.02	.01
Quebec Nordiques			
☐ 530 Kevin Dineen	.08	.04	.01
Philadelphia Flyers			
☐ 531 David Reid	.05	.02	.01
Boston Bruins			
☐ 532 Arturs Irbe	1.00	.45	.13
San Jose Sharks			
☐ 533 Mark Osiecki	.05	.02	.01
Calgary Flames			
☐ 534 Steve Thomas	.08	.04	.01
New York Islanders			
☐ 535 Vincent Damphousse	.08	.04	.01
Edmonton Oilers			
☐ 536 Stephane Richer	.08	.04	.01
New Jersey Devils			
☐ 537 Jarmo Myllys	.05	.02	.01
San Jose Sharks			
☐ 538 Carey Wilson	.05	.02	.01
Calgary Flames			
☐ 539 Scott Stevens	.10	.05	.01
New Jersey Devils			
☐ 540 Uwe Krupp	.05	.02	.01
New York Islanders			
☐ 541 Dave Christian	.05	.02	.01
St. Louis Blues			
☐ 542 Scott Mellanby	.05	.02	.01
Edmonton Oilers			
☐ 543 Peter Ahola	.05	.02	.01
Los Angeles Kings			
☐ 544 Todd Elik	.05	.02	.01
Minnesota North Stars			
☐ 545 Mark Messier	.40	.18	.05
New York Rangers			
☐ 546 Derian Hatcher	.08	.04	.01
Minnesota North Stars			
☐ 547 Rod Brind'Amour	.25	.11	.03
Philadelphia Flyers			
☐ 548 Dave Manson	.08	.04	.01
Edmonton Oilers			
☐ 549 Daryl Sydor	.08	.04	.01
Los Angeles Kings			
☐ 550 Paul Broten	.05	.02	.01
New York Rangers			
☐ 551 Andrew Cassels	.08	.04	.01
Hartford Whalers			
☐ 552 Tom Draper	.10	.05	.01
Buffalo Sabres			
☐ 553 Grant Fuhr	.08	.04	.01
Toronto Maple Leafs			
☐ 554 Pierre Turgeon	.35	.16	.04
New York Islanders			
☐ 555 Pavel Bure	2.00	.90	.25
Vancouver Canucks			
☐ 556 Pat LaFontaine	.30	.14	.04
Buffalo Sabres			
☐ 557 Dave Thomlinson	.05	.02	.01
Boston Bruins			
☒ 558 Doug Gilmour	.50	.23	.06
Toronto Maple Leafs			
☐ 559 Craig Billington	.25	.11	.03
New Jersey Devils			
☐ 560 Dean Evason	.05	.02	.01
San Jose Sharks			
☐ 561 Brendan Shanahan	.35	.16	.04
St. Louis Blues			
☐ 562 Mike Hough	.05	.02	.01
Quebec Nordiques			
☐ 563 Dan Quinn	.05	.02	.01
Philadelphia Flyers			
☐ 564 Jeff Daniels	.05	.02	.01
Pittsburgh Penguins			
☐ 565 Troy Murray	.05	.02	.01
Winnipeg Jets			
☐ 566 Bernie Nicholls	.08	.04	.01
Edmonton Oilers			
☐ 567 Randy Burridge	.05	.02	.01
Washington Capitals			
☐ 568 Todd Hartje	.05	.02	.01
Winnipeg Jets			
☐ 569 Charlie Huddy	.05	.02	.01
Los Angeles Kings			
☐ 570 Steve Duchesne	.08	.04	.01
Philadelphia Flyers			
☐ 571 Sergio Momesso	.05	.02	.01
Vancouver Canucks			
☐ 572 Brian Lawton	.05	.02	.01
San Jose Sharks			
☐ 573 Ray Sheppard	.08	.04	.01
Detroit Red Wings			
☐ 574 Adam Graves	.50	.23	.06
New York Rangers			
☐ 575 Rollie Melanson	.05	.02	.01
Montreal Canadiens			
☐ 576 Steve Kasper	.05	.02	.01
Philadelphia Flyers			
☐ 577 Jim Sandlak	.05	.02	.01
Vancouver Canucks			
☐ 578 Pat MacLeod	.05	.02	.01
San Jose Sharks			
☐ 579 Sylvain Turgeon	.05	.02	.01
Montreal Canadiens			
☐ 580 James Black	.05	.02	.01
Hartford Whalers			
☐ 581 Darrin Shannon	.05	.02	.01
Winnipeg Jets			
☐ 582 Todd Krygier	.05	.02	.01
Washington Capitals			
☐ 583 Dominic Roussel	.50	.23	.06
Philadelphia Flyers			
☐ 584 Young Guns Checklist	.15	.07	.02
(Nicklas Lidstrom)			
☐ 585 Donald Audette YG	.07	.03	.01
Buffalo Sabres			
☐ 586 Tomas Forslund YG	.07	.03	.01
Calgary Flames			
☐ 587 Nicklas Lidstrom YG	.40	.18	.05
Detroit Red Wings			
☐ 588 Geoff Sanderson YG	2.00	.90	.25
Hartford Whalers			
☐ 589 Valeri Zelepukin YG	.60	.25	.08
New Jersey Devils			
☐ 590 Igor Ulanov YG	.15	.07	.02
Winnipeg Jets			
☐ 591 Corey Foster YG	.07	.03	.01
Philadelphia Flyers			
☐ 592 Dan Lambert YG	.07	.03	.01
Quebec Nordiques			
☐ 593 Pat Falloon YG	.40	.18	.05
San Jose Sharks			
☐ 594 Vladimir Konstantinov YG	.25	.11	.03
Detroit Red Wings			
☐ 595 Josef Beranek YG	.30	.14	.04
Edmonton Oilers			
☐ 596 Brad May YG	.10	.05	.01
Buffalo Sabres			
☐ 597 Jeff Odgers YG	.15	.07	.02
San Jose Sharks			
☐ 598 Rob Pearson YG	.25	.11	.03
Toronto Maple Leafs			
☐ 599 Luciano Borsato YG	.15	.07	.02
Winnipeg Jets			
☐ 600 Checklist 501-600	.07	.03	.01
☐ 601 Peter Douris	.05	.02	.01
Boston Bruins			
☐ 602 Mark Fitzpatrick	.08	.04	.01
New York Islanders			
☐ 603 Randy Gilhen	.05	.02	.01
New York Rangers			
☐ 604 Corey Millen	.20	.09	.03
Los Angeles Kings			
☐ 605 Jason Cirone	.05	.02	.01
Winnipeg Jets			
☐ 606 Kyosti Karjalainen	.05	.02	.01
Los Angeles Kings			
☐ 607 Garry Galley	.08	.04	.01
Philadelphia Flyers			
☐ 608 Brent Thompson	.10	.05	.01
Los Angeles Kings			
☐ 609 Alexander Godynyuk	.05	.02	.01
Calgary Flames			
☐ 610 All-Star Checklist	.35	.16	.04
Mark Messier			
Mike Richter			
Brian Leetch			
☐ 611 Mario Lemieux AS	.40	.18	.05
Pittsburgh Penguins			
☐ 612 Brian Leetch AS	.20	.09	.03
New York Rangers			
☐ 613 Kevin Stevens AS	.15	.07	.02
Pittsburgh Penguins			
☐ 614 Patrick Roy AS	.40	.18	.05
Montreal Canadiens			
☐ 615 Paul Coffey AS	.10	.05	.01
Pittsburgh Penguins			
☐ 616 Joe Sakic AS	.15	.07	.02
Quebec Nordiques			
☐ 617 Jaromir Jagr AS	.20	.09	.03
Pittsburgh Penguins			
☐ 618 Alexander Mogilny AS	.20	.09	.03
Buffalo Sabres			

☐ 619	Owen Nolan AS	.10	.05	.01
	Quebec Nordiques			
☐ 620	Mark Messier AS	.20	.09	.03
	New York Rangers			
☐ 621	Wayne Gretzky AS	.75	.35	.09
	Los Angeles Kings			
☐ 622	Brett Hull AS	.25	.11	.03
	St. Louis Blues			
☐ 623	Luc Robitaille AS	.15	.07	.02
	Los Angeles Kings			
☐ 624	Phil Housley AS	.07	.03	.01
	Winnipeg Jets			
☐ 625	Ed Belfour AS	.15	.07	.02
	Chicago Blackhawks			
☐ 626	Steve Yzerman AS	.20	.09	.03
	Detroit Red Wings			
☐ 627	Adam Oates AS	.07	.03	.01
	St. Louis Blues			
☐ 628	Trevor Linden AS	.15	.07	.02
	Vancouver Canucks			
☐ 629	Jeremy Roenick AS	.25	.11	.03
	Chicago Blackhawks			
☐ 630	Theoren Fleury AS	.10	.05	.01
	Calgary Flames			
☐ 631	Sergei Fedorov AS	.30	.14	.04
	Detroit Red Wings			
☐ 632	Al MacInnis AS	.10	.05	.01
	Calgary Flames			
☐ 633	Ray Bourque AS	.10	.05	.01
	Boston Bruins			
☐ 634	Mike Richter AS	.10	.05	.01
	New York Rangers			
☐ 635	Al Secord HERO	.07	.03	.01
☐ 636	Marcel Dionne HERO	.10	.05	.01
☐ 637	Ken Morrow HERO	.07	.03	.01
☐ 638	Guy Lafleur HERO	.10	.05	.01
☐ 639	Ed Mio HERO	.07	.03	.01
☐ 640	Clark Gillies HERO	.07	.03	.01
☐ 641	Bob Nystrom HERO	.07	.03	.01
☐ 642	Pete Peeters HERO	.07	.03	.01
☐ 643	Ulf Nilsson HERO	.07	.03	.01
☐ 644	Stephan Lebeau and	.10	.05	.01
	Patrick Lebeau			
☐ 645	The Sutter Brothers	.07	.03	.01
	Brian Sutter			
	Duane Sutter			
	Darryl Sutter			
	Brent Sutter			
	Rich Sutter			
	Ron Sutter			
☐ 646	Gino Cavallini and	.07	.03	.01
	Paul Cavallini			
☐ 647	Valeri Bure UER	1.00	.45	.13
	and Pavel Bure			
	(Name misspelled			
	Valery on both sides)			
☐ 648	Chris Ferraro and	.40	.18	.05
	Peter Ferraro			
☐ 649	World Jr. Checklist	.25	.11	.03
	CCCP Team Photo			
☐ 650	Darius Kasparaitis	.50	.23	.06
☐ 651	Alexei Yashin	4.00	1.80	.50
☐ 652	Nikolai Khabibulin	.25	.11	.03
☐ 653	Denis Metlyuk	.10	.05	.01
☐ 654	Konstantin Korotkov	.10	.05	.01
☐ 655	Alexei Kovalev	4.00	1.80	.50
☐ 656	Alexander Kuzminsky	.10	.05	.01
☐ 657	Alexander Cherbayev	.50	.23	.06
☐ 658	Sergei Krivokrasov	.60	.25	.08
☐ 659	Sergei Zholtok	.25	.11	.03
☐ 660	Alexei Zhitnik	1.00	.45	.13
☐ 661	Sandis Ozolinch	1.75	.80	.22
☐ 662	Boris Mironov	.50	.23	.06
☐ 663	Pauli Jaks	.25	.11	.03
☐ 664	Gaetan Voisard	.10	.05	.01
☐ 665	Nicola Celio	.10	.05	.01
☐ 666	Marc Weber	.10	.05	.01
☐ 667	Bernhard Schumperli	.10	.05	.01
☐ 668	Laurent Bucher	.10	.05	.01
☐ 669	Michael Blaha	.10	.05	.01
☐ 670	Tiziano Gianini	.10	.05	.01
☐ 671	Marko Kiprusoff	.10	.05	.01
☐ 672	Janne Gronvall	.20	.09	.03
☐ 673	Juha Ylonen	.20	.09	.03
☐ 674	Sami Kapanen	.10	.05	.01
☐ 675	Marko Tuomainen	.20	.09	.03
☐ 676	Jarkko Varvio	.40	.18	.05
☐ 677	Tuomas Gronman	.20	.09	.03
☐ 678	Andreas Naumann	.10	.05	.01
☐ 679	Steffen Ziesche	.10	.05	.01
☐ 680	Jens Schwabe	.10	.05	.01
☐ 681	Thomas Schubert	.10	.05	.01
☐ 682	Hans-Jorg Mayer	.10	.05	.01

☐ 683	Marc Seliger	.10	.05	.01
☐ 684	Trevor Kidd	.15	.07	.02
☐ 685	Martin Lapointe	.10	.05	.01
☐ 686	Tyler Wright	.10	.05	.01
☐ 687	Kimbi Daniels	.10	.05	.01
☐ 688	Karl Dykhuis	.10	.05	.01
☐ 689	Jeff Nelson	.20	.09	.03
☐ 690	Jassen Cullimore	.10	.05	.01
☐ 691	Turner Stevenson	.15	.07	.02
☐ 692	Scott Lachance	.30	.14	.04
☐ 693	Mike Dunham	.75	.35	.09
☐ 694	Brent Bilodeau	.20	.09	.03
☐ 695	Ryan Sittler	.75	.35	.09
☐ 696	Peter Ferraro	.75	.35	.09
☐ 697	Pat Peake	1.50	.65	.19
☐ 698	Keith Tkachuk	2.00	.90	.25
☐ 699	Brian Rolston	1.00	.45	.13
☐ 700	Checklist 601-700	.07	.03	.01
☐ SP1	Glasnost On Ice	5.00	2.30	.60
	Wayne Gretzky and Valeri Kamensky			

1991-92 Upper Deck
Award Winner Holograms

This nine-card standard-size (2 1/2" by 3 1/2") hologram set features award-winning hockey players with their respective trophies for most outstanding performance. The name of the award appears in the left border stripe, while the player's name and position are printed in the bottom border stripe. The backs have a color photo of the player with the trophy as well as biographical information. The holograms were randomly inserted into foil packs and subdivided into three groups: AW1-AW3 (low series); AW5-AW7 (late winter, low series); and AW4, AW8, and AW9 (high series). The holograms are numbered on the back with an "AW" prefix.

		MINT	EXC	G-VG
COMPLETE SET (9)		8.00	3.25	.80
COMMON PLAYER (1-9)		.60	.24	.06
☐ 1	Wayne Gretzky	2.00	.80	.20
	Art Ross Trophy			
☐ 2	Ed Belfour	1.00	.40	.10
	William M. Jennings			
	Trophy			
☐ 3	Brett Hull	1.25	.50	.12
	Hart Trophy			
☐ 4	Ed Belfour	1.00	.40	.10
	Calder Trophy			
☐ 5A	Ray Bourque ERR	1.00	.40	.10
	Norris Trophy			
	(No best defenseman			
	notation on back)			
☐ 5B	Ray Bourque COR	1.00	.40	.10
	Norris Trophy			
	(Best defenseman			
	notation on back)			
☐ 6	Wayne Gretzky	2.00	.80	.20
	Lady Byng Trophy			
☐ 7	Ed Belfour	1.00	.40	.10
	Vezina Trophy			
☐ 8	Dirk Graham	.60	.24	.06
	Frank J. Selke Trophy			
☐ 9	Mario Lemieux	1.50	.60	.15
	Conn Smythe Trophy			

1991-92 Upper Deck Box Bottoms

These five box bottoms are printed on glossy cover stock and measure approximately 5 1/2" by 9". Though they were issued with both French and English hockey sets, the New York Rangers' Mark Messier box bottom was available only with the high series. Each bottom features a four-color action photo enclosed by white borders. The Upper Deck logo, player's name, and position appear above the photo while the team name and the 75th NHL Anniversary logo appear beneath the picture superimposed on small black lines. The box bottoms are unnumbered and checklisted below alphabetically.

	MINT	EXC	G-VG
COMPLETE SET (5)	6.00	2.40	.60
COMMON PLAYER (1-5)	1.00	.40	.10
☐ 1 Wayne Gretzky	2.00	.80	.20
Los Angeles Kings			
☐ 2 Brett Hull	1.25	.50	.12
St. Louis Blues			
☐ 3 Mark Messier	1.00	.40	.10
Edmonton Oilers			
☐ 4 Mark Messier	2.00	.80	.20
New York Rangers			
☐ 5 Steve Yzerman	1.00	.40	.10
Detroit Red Wings			

1991-92 Upper Deck Euro-Stars

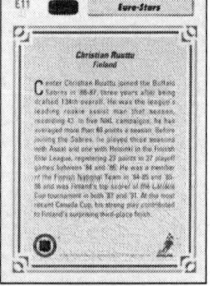

This 18-card set spotlights NHL players from Finland, the former Soviet Union, Czechoslovakia, and Sweden. One Euro-Star card was inserted in each 1991-92 Upper Deck hockey jumbo pack in both English and French editions. The front design of the standard-size (2 1/2" by 3 1/2") cards is the same as the regular issue except that a Euro-Stars

emblem featuring a segment of the player's homeland flag, appears in the lower right corner. On a textured background, the backs present career summary. The cards are numbered on the back and checklisted below accordingly.

	MINT	EXC	G-VG
COMPLETE SET (18)	12.00	5.50	1.50
COMMON PLAYER (1-18)	.50	.23	.06
*FRENCH VERSION: 1X to 1.25X			
☐ 1 Jarmo Kekalainen	.50	.23	.06
Boston Bruins			
☐ 2 Alexander Mogilny	2.00	.90	.25
Buffalo Sabres			
☐ 3 Bobby Holik	.50	.23	.06
Hartford Whalers			
☐ 4 Anatoli Semenov	.50	.23	.06
Edmonton Oilers			
☐ 5 Petr Nedved	1.50	.65	.19
Vancouver Canucks			
☐ 6 Jaromir Jagr	2.50	1.15	.30
Pittsburgh Penguins			
☐ 7 Tomas Sandstrom	.75	.35	.09
Los Angeles Kings			
☐ 8 Robert Kron	.50	.23	.06
Vancouver Canucks			
☐ 9 Sergei Fedorov	3.50	1.55	.45
Detroit Red Wings			
☐ 10 Esa Tikkanen	.75	.35	.09
Edmonton Oilers			
☐ 11 Christian Ruuttu	.50	.23	.06
Buffalo Sabres			
☐ 12 Peter Bondra	.75	.35	.09
Washington Capitals			
☐ 13 Mats Sundin	2.00	.90	.25
Quebec Nordiques			
☐ 14 Dominik Hasek	3.00	1.35	.40
Chicago Blackhawks			
☐ 15 Johan Garpenlov	1.00	.45	.13
Detroit Red Wings			
☐ 16 Alexander Godynyuk	.50	.23	.06
Toronto Maple Leafs			
☐ 17 Ulf Samuelsson	.50	.23	.06
Pittsburgh Penguins			
☐ 18 Igor Larionov	1.00	.45	.13
Vancouver Canucks			

1991-92 Upper Deck Brett Hull Heroes

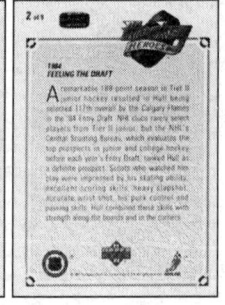

This ten-card standard-size (2 1/2" by 3 1/2") set was inserted in 1991-92 Upper Deck low series foil packs (French as well as English editions). On a light gray textured background, the fronts have color player photos cut out and superimposed on an emblem. The textured background is enclosed by thin tan border stripes. On the same textured background, the backs summarize various moments in Hull's career. Brett Hull personally signed and numbered 2,500 of the checklist card number 9; these autographed cards were randomly inserted in packs and are very difficult to find. The signed cards are numbered by hand on the front.

	MINT	EXC	G-VG
COMPLETE SET (10)........................	15.00	6.75	1.90
COMMON HULL HEROES (1-9)	1.00	.45	.13
☐ 1 Brett Hull.............................. Penticton's 105-Goal Man	1.00	.45	.13
☐ 2 Brett Hull.............................. Feeling the Draft	1.00	.45	.13
☐ 3 Brett Hull.............................. NCAA's Goal-Scoring Leader	1.00	.45	.13
☐ 4 Brett Hull.............................. AHL's Rookie-of- the-Year	1.00	.45	.13
☐ 5 Brett Hull.............................. A Full-Time Flame	1.00	.45	.13
☐ 6 Brett Hull.............................. 40-Goal Plateau	1.00	.45	.13
☐ 7 Brett Hull.............................. NHL's New 70-Goal Scorer	1.00	.45	.13
☐ 8 Brett Hull.............................. A Season With Hart	1.00	.45	.13
☐ 9 Brett Hull.............................. (Vernon Wells Artwork)	1.00	.45	.13
☐ AU1 Brett Hull .... (Certified autograph)	350.00	160.00	45.00
☐ NNO Hull Header SP	9.00	4.00	1.15

1991-92 Upper Deck Sheets

For the second straight year, Upper Deck produced hockey commemorative sheets that were given away during the 1991-92 season at selected games in large arenas. Each sheet measures approximately 8 1/2" by 11" and is printed on card stock. The fronts of the team commemorative sheets feature the team logo and a series of Upper Deck cards of star players on that team. The Alumni sheet features player portraits by sports artist Alan Studt. All the sheets have an Upper Deck stamp indicating the production quota and the serial number. The backs are blank. The sheets are listed below in chronological order.

	MINT	EXC	G-VG
COMPLETE SET (19)........................	225.00	90.00	22.00
COMMON PLAYER (1-19).................	10.00	4.00	1.00
☐ 1 Los Angeles Kings 25th .... vs. Edmonton Oilers Oct. 8, 1991 (20,000) Rob Blake Jari Kurri Tomas Sandstrom Wayne Gretzky Marty McSorley Kelly Hrudey	12.00	5.00	1.20
☐ 2 New York Rangers I .... vs. Calgary Flames	10.00	4.00	1.00

	MINT	EXC	G-VG
Nov. 4, 1991 (21,500) Randy Moller Paul Broten Jody Hull Jan Erixon Mark Janssens Brian Leetch Mike Gartner Joey Kocur Mark Hardy			
☐ 3 St. Louis Blues...................... vs. Philadelpha Flyers Nov. 5, 1991 (21,500) Adam Oates Nelson Emerson Paul Cavallini Curtis Joseph Brett Hull Jeff Brown	12.00	5.00	1.20
☐ 4 New Jersey Devils 10th.......... vs. Chicago Blackhawks Dec. 21, 1991 (24,000) (New Jersey Devils Tenth Anniversary) Walt Poddubny John MacLean Scott Stevens Peter Stastny Claude Lemieux Stephane Richer	10.00	4.00	1.00
☐ 5 Calgary Flames I...................... Tenth Annual Clinic Dec. 27, 1991 (26,000) Robert Reichel Doug Gilmour Theoren Fleury Al MacInnis Joel Otto Gary Roberts	15.00	6.00	1.50
☐ 6 New York Rangers II .... vs. St. Louis Blues Jan. 8, 1992 (23,000) Mike Richter Kris King Tie Domi Tony Amonte Mark Messier Joe Cirella James Patrick Sergei Nemchinov	10.00	4.00	1.00
☐ 7 Philadelphia Flyers I .... Alumni vs. NHL Heroes Jan. 17, 1992 (21,000) Bill Barber Bill Clement Keith Allen Joe Watson Bobby Clarke Bernie Parent	10.00	4.00	1.00
☐ 8 Campbell All-Stars .... Philadelphia Spectrum Jan. 18, 1992 (13,500) Brett Hull Al MacInnis Luc Robitaille Chris Chelios Wayne Gretzky Ed Belfour	25.00	10.00	2.50
☐ 9 Wales All-Stars .... Philadelphia Spectrum Jan. 18, 1992 (13,500) Mario Lemieux Patrick Roy Kevin Stevens Paul Coffey Jaromir Jagr Ray Bourque	25.00	10.00	2.50
☐ 10 Detroit Red Wings I.............. vs. Toronto Maple Leafs Feb. 7, 1992 (25,000) Niklas Lidstrom Steve Yzerman Tim Cheveldae Bob Probert Steve Chiasson Sergei Fedorov	10.00	4.00	1.00
☐ 11 Washington Capitals .... vs. New York Rangers Feb. 7, 1992 (20,500) Kevin Hatcher Dimitri Khristich Calle Johansson Michal Pivonka Al Iafrate	10.00	4.00	1.00

☐ 12	Dino Ciccarelli Minnesota North Stars	15.00	6.00	1.50

Dream Team
Feb.15, 1992 (19,000)
Brian Bellows
Neal Broten
Bill Goldsworthy
Curt Giles
Jon Casey
Craig Hartsburg

☐ 13	Pittsburgh Penguins	15.00	6.00	1.50

vs. Toronto Maple Leafs
Feb. 18, 1992 (21,000)
Kevin Stevens
Jaromir Jagr
Ulf Samuelsson
Tom Barrasso
Mark Recchi
Joe Mullen

☐ 14	New York Rangers III	12.00	5.00	1.20

vs. Philadelphia Flyers
Feb. 23, 1992 (23,000)
John Vanbiesbrouck
Kris King
Normand Rochefort
John Ogrodnick
Mark Messier
Jeff Beukeboom
Adam Graves
Darren Turcotte

☐ 15	Edmonton Oilers	12.00	5.00	1.20

vs. Philadelphia Flyers
Feb. 28, 1992 (22,000)
Kevin Lowe
Craig MacTavish
Esa Tikkanen
Bill Ranford
Craig Simpson
Vincent Damphousse

☐ 16	Minnesota North Stars	10.00	4.00	1.00

vs. Detroit Red Wings
March 14, 1992 (19,000)
Bobby Smith
Dave Gagner
Mike Modano
Ulf Dahlen
Mark Tinordi
Basil McRae

☐ 17	Calgary Flames II	12.00	5.00	1.20

vs. Minnesota North Stars
Eighth Fan
Appreciation Night
March 28, 1992 (24,000)
Mike Vernon
Joe Nieuwendyk
Gary Suter
Paul Ranheim
Sergei Makarov
Carey Wilson

☐ 18	Detroit Red Wings II	10.00	4.00	1.00

vs. Chicago Blackhawks
March 31, 1992 (25,000)
Paul Ysebaert
Yves Racine
Vladimir Konstantinov
Ray Sheppard
Kevin Miller
Jimmy Carson

☐ 19	Philadelphia Flyers II	10.00	4.00	1.00

Toronto Maple Leafs
April 5, 1992 (21,000)
Mike Ricci
Kevin Dineen
Garry Galley
Steve Duchesne
Rod Brind'Amour
Claude Boivin

1991-92 Upper Deck Kings
Season Ticket

This approximately 5" by 3 1/2" horizontally oriented card was sent out to 7,000 Los Angeles Kings season ticket holders along with a Christmas card from Upper Deck in December 1991 celebrating the Kings' 25th anniversary. The front features a borderless color action shot of several Kings players and opponent(s) in a pileup in front of the Kings' net with Kings' goalie Kelly Hrudey. The limited edition seal with production number is placed in the upper left. The Upper Deck Hockey logo is in the upper right. The horizontal back carries a drawing of Wayne Gretzky, Rogie Vachon, Bruce McNall, Marcel Dionne, and Luc Robitaille.

	MINT	EXC	G-VG
COMPLETE SET (1)	125.00	50.00	12.50
COMMON CARD	125.00	50.00	12.50
☐ 1 Los Angeles Kings	125.00	50.00	12.50

Season Ticket Holders
25th Anniversary
Kelly Hrudey

1991-92 Upper Deck McDonald's

This 31-card set, which features 25 regular cards and six hologram cards and was produced by Upper Deck for McDonald's Restaurants across Canada to honor NHL All-Stars. For 29 cents plus tax, with the purchase of any soft drink, customers could receive a pack with three regular cards and one hologram sticker card. The fronts of these standard-size (2 1/2" by 3 1/2") cards feature a mix of posed and action pictures enclosed in red and white borders. The Upper Deck logo appears in the upper right corner while the McDonald's All-Stars logo appears in a red circle in the lower right corner. The player's name and position appear in the bottom white border. The backs carry a second color photo and career summary is presented in English and French. Upper Deck's unique anti-counterfeiting device appears in the upper right corner in the shape of McDonald's golden arches. The cards are numbered on the back. Six players wearing their 1991 All-Star uniforms on the regular cards appear on the hologram cards in their regular team uniforms. The holograms have blank backs and are numbered on the front. The card numbers show a "Mc" prefix.

		MINT	EXC	G-VG
COMPLETE SET (31)		20.00	8.00	2.00
COMMON PLAYER (1-25)		.35	.14	.03
COMMON HOLOGRAM (H1-H6)		.75	.30	.07
☐ 1	Cam Neely	1.00	.40	.10
☐ 2	Rick Tocchet	.50	.20	.05
☐ 3	Kevin Stevens	.75	.30	.07
☐ 4	Mark Recchi	.75	.30	.07
☐ 5	Joe Sakic	1.00	.40	.10
☐ 6	Pat LaFontaine	1.00	.40	.10
☐ 7	Darren Turcotte	.35	.14	.03
☐ 8	Patrick Roy	2.00	.80	.20
☐ 9	Andy Moog	.50	.20	.05
☐ 10	Ray Bourque	.75	.30	.07
☐ 11	Paul Coffey	1.00	.40	.10

		MINT	EXC	G-VG
☐ 12	Brian Leetch	1.25	.50	.12
☐ 13	Brett Hull	1.50	.60	.15
☐ 14	Luc Robitaille	1.00	.40	.10
☐ 15	Steve Larmer	.50	.20	.05
☐ 16	Vincent Damphousse	.50	.20	.05
☐ 17	Wayne Gretzky	3.00	1.20	.30
☐ 18	Theoren Fleury	.75	.30	.07
☐ 19	Steve Yzerman	1.25	.50	.12
☐ 20	Mike Vernon	.35	.14	.03
☐ 21	Bill Ranford	.50	.20	.05
☐ 22	Chris Chelios	.50	.20	.05
☐ 23	Al MacInnis	.50	.20	.05
☐ 24	Scott Stevens	.35	.14	.03
☐ 25	Checklist	.35	.14	.03
☐ H1	Wayne Gretzky	4.00	1.60	.40
☐ H2	Chris Chelios	.75	.30	.07
☐ H3	Ray Bourque	1.00	.40	.10
☐ H4	Brett Hull	2.00	.80	.20
☐ H5	Cam Neely	1.25	.50	.12
☐ H6	Patrick Roy	2.00	.80	.20

1991-92 Upper Deck World Junior Tournament

This 100-card set features outstanding players from the 1991 World Junior Championships including Czechoslovakian, U.S.A., Canadian, German, Russian, Swiss, and Finnish teams. Two Wayne Gretzky holograms were randomly inserted in the foil packs. The cards measure the standard size (2 1/2" by 3 1/2"). Inside white borders, the fronts display glossy color action photos of the players in their national team uniforms. The player's name and position appear in the top border, while the World Junior Tournament logo and an emblem of their national flag overlay the bottom of the picture. The backs carry a second color player photo; alongside in a gray box, the player's position and a brief profile are printed in English and Czech. The cards are numbered on the back and checklisted below according to teams as follows: C.I.S. (1-23), Switzerland (24-31), Finland (32-40), Germany (41-46), Canada (47-65), U.S.A. (66-86), and Czechoslovakia (87-99). These cards were made by Upper Deck for distribution in Eastern Europe. An album was also made to house the set.

		MINT	EXC	G-VG
COMPLETE SET (100)		40.00	16.00	4.00
COMMON PLAYER (1-100)		.25	.10	.02
☐ 1	Description Card	.50	.20	.05
☐ 2	Vladislav Buljin	.35	.14	.03
☐ 3	Ravil Gusmanov	.25	.10	.02
☐ 4	Denis Vinokurov	.25	.10	.02
☐ 5	Mikhail Volkov	.25	.10	.02
☐ 6	Alexei Troschinsky	.25	.10	.02
☐ 7	Andrei Nikolishin	.50	.20	.05
☐ 8	Alexander Sverztov	.25	.10	.02
☐ 9	Artem Kopot	.25	.10	.02

☐ 10	Ildar Mukhometov	.25	.10	.02
☐ 11	Darius Kasparaitis	2.00	.80	.20
☐ 12	Alexei Yashin	5.00	2.00	.50
☐ 13	Nicolai Khabibulin	.75	.30	.07
☐ 14	Denis Metlyuk	.75	.30	.07
☐ 15	Konstantin Korotkov	.25	.10	.02
☐ 16	Alexei Kovalev	6.00	2.40	.60
☐ 17	Alexander Kuzminsky	.25	.10	.02
☐ 18	Alexander Cherbayev	1.00	.40	.10
☐ 19	Sergei Krivokrasov	1.50	.60	.15
☐ 20	Sergei Zholtok	1.00	.40	.10
☐ 21	Alexei Zhitnik	2.00	.80	.20
☐ 22	Sandis Ozolinsh	2.50	1.00	.25
☐ 23	Boris Mironov	1.00	.40	.10
☐ 24	Pauli Jaks	.75	.30	.07
☐ 25	Gaetan Voisard	.25	.10	.02
☐ 26	Nicola Celio	.25	.10	.02
☐ 27	Marc Weber	.25	.10	.02
☐ 28	Bernhard Schumperli	.25	.10	.02
☐ 29	Laurent Bucher	.25	.10	.02
☐ 30	Michael Blaha	.25	.10	.02
☐ 31	Tiziano Gianini	.25	.10	.02
☐ 32	Tero Lehtera	.25	.10	.02
☐ 33	Mikko Luovi	.25	.10	.02
☐ 34	Marko Kiprusoff	.25	.10	.02
☐ 35	Janne Gronvall	.75	.30	.07
☐ 36	Juha Ylonen	.50	.20	.05
☐ 37	Sami Kapanen	.25	.10	.02
☐ 38	Marko Tuomainen	.75	.30	.07
☐ 39	Jarkko Varvio	1.00	.40	.10
☐ 40	Tuomas Gronman	.75	.30	.07
☐ 41	Andreas Naumann	.25	.10	.02
☐ 42	Steffen Ziesche	.25	.10	.02
☐ 43	Jens Schwabe	.35	.14	.03
☐ 44	Thomas Schubert	.25	.10	.02
☐ 45	Hans-Jorg Mayer	.25	.10	.02
☐ 46	Marc Seliger	.25	.10	.02
☐ 47	Ryan Hughes	.35	.14	.03
☐ 48	Richard Matvichuk	.50	.20	.05
☐ 49	David St.Pierre	.35	.14	.03
☐ 50	Paul Kariya	10.00	4.00	1.00
☐ 51	Patrick Poulin	1.00	.40	.10
☐ 52	Mike Fountain	.50	.20	.05
☐ 53	Scott Niedermayer	2.50	1.00	.25
☐ 54	John Slaney	.75	.30	.07
☐ 55	Brad Bombardir	.75	.30	.07
☐ 56	Andy Schneider	.35	.14	.03
☐ 57	Steve Junker	.75	.30	.07
☐ 58	Trevor Kidd	1.50	.60	.15
☐ 59	Martin Lapointe	1.00	.40	.10
☐ 60	Tyler Wright	.75	.30	.07
☐ 61	Kimbi Daniels	.75	.30	.07
☐ 62	Karl Dykhuis	.50	.20	.05
☐ 63	Jeff Nelson	.50	.20	.05
☐ 64	Jassen Cullimore	.50	.20	.05
☐ 65	Turner Stevenson	.75	.30	.07
☐ 66	Brian Mueller	.35	.14	.03
☐ 67	Chris Tucker	.35	.14	.03
☐ 68	Marty Schriner	.35	.14	.03
☐ 69	Mike Pendergast	.35	.14	.03
☐ 70	John Lilley	.75	.30	.07
☐ 71	Jim Campbell	.75	.30	.07
☐ 72	Brian Holzinger	.35	.14	.03
☐ 73	Steve Konowalchuk	.75	.30	.07
☐ 74	Chris Ferraro	1.00	.40	.10
☐ 75	Chris Imes	.50	.20	.05
☐ 76	Rich Brennan	.35	.14	.03
☐ 77	Todd Hall	.35	.14	.03
☐ 78	Brian Rafalski	.50	.20	.05
☐ 79	Scott Lachance	1.50	.60	.15
☐ 80	Mike Dunham	2.00	.80	.20
☐ 81	Brent Bilodeau	.75	.30	.07
☐ 82	Ryan Sittler	2.00	.80	.20
☐ 83	Peter Ferraro	2.00	.80	.20
☐ 84	Pat Peake	2.00	.80	.20
☐ 85	Keith Tkachuk	4.00	1.60	.40
☐ 86	Brian Rolston	1.50	.60	.15
☐ 87	Milan Hnilicka	.50	.20	.05
☐ 88	Roman Hamrlik	2.50	1.00	.25
☐ 89	Milan Nedoma	.35	.14	.03
☐ 90	Patrik Luza	.50	.20	.05
☐ 91	Jan Caloun	.50	.20	.05
☐ 92	Viktor Ujcik	.35	.14	.03
☐ 93	Robert Petrovicky	.75	.30	.07
☐ 94	Roman Meluzin	.25	.10	.02
☐ 95	Jan Vopat	.50	.20	.05
☐ 96	Martin Prochazka	.25	.10	.02
☐ 97	Zigmund Palffy	1.00	.40	.10
☐ 98	Ivan Droppa	.75	.30	.07
☐ 99	Martin Straka	2.50	1.00	.25
☐ 100	Checklist 1-100	.35	.14	.03
☐ NNO	Gretzky Hologram 1	4.00	1.60	.40
☐ NNO	Gretzky Hologram 2	4.00	1.60	.40

1992-93 Upper Deck

The 1992-93 Upper Deck hockey set contains 660 cards, measuring the standard size (2 1/2" by 3 1/2"). The set was released in two series of 440 and 220 cards, respectively. First series foil packs also included the following inserts: a Pavel Bure SP card, Wayne Gretzky "Hockey Heroes," All-Rookie Team, and Euro-Rookie Team Holograms. Second series insert sets include: Calder Candidates, Euro-Rookies, Gordie Howe Heroes, Gordie Howe Selects, and World Junior Grads. The cards, which are printed on a whiter, heavier card stock, display glossy color action photos on the fronts. Special subsets featured include Team Checklists (1-24), Bloodlines (35-39), '92 World Juniors (222-236), Russian Stars from Moscow Dynamo (333-353), Rookie Report (354-368), '92 World Championships (369-386), Team USA (392-397), Star Rookies (398-422), and Award Winners (431-440). Pavel Bure is showcased on a special card (SP2) that was randomly inserted in first series foil and jumbo packs. A special card (SP3), titled "World Champions," honors the Canada's 1993 IIHF World Junior Champions team. High series subsets featured are Lethal Lines (453-456), Young Guns (554-583), and World Junior Champions (584-619). The World Junior Champions subset is grouped according to national teams as follows: Canada (585-594), Sweden (595-599), Czechoslovakia (600-604), USA (605-609), Russia (610-614), and Finland (615-619). An Upper Deck Profiles (620-640) subset closes out the set. The cards are numbered on the back. Rookie Cards include Nikolai Borschevsky, Alexandre Daigle, Chris Gratton, Roman Hamrlik, Yan Kaminsky, Paul Kariya, Viktor Kozlov, Martin Straka, Markus Naslund, Rob Niedermayer, Chris Pronger, Mikael Renberg, Tommy Soderstrom, Niklas Sundstrom and Sergei Zubov. Card No. 88, Eric Lindros, was short-printed (SP) as it was not included in second series packaging. This was brought about because of a controversy over Lindros' head being superimposed on a teammate's body.

	MINT	EXC	G-VG
COMPLETE SET (640)	60.00	27.00	7.50
COMPLETE LO SET (440)	25.00	11.50	3.10
COMPLETE HI SET (200)	35.00	16.00	4.40
COMMON PLAYER (1-440)	.05	.02	.01
COMMON PLAYER (441-640)	.05	.02	.01
☐ 1 Andy Moog TC	.08	.04	.01
Boston Bruins			
☐ 2 Donald Audette TC	.05	.02	.01
Buffalo Sabres			
☐ 3 Tomas Forslund TC	.05	.02	.01
Calgary Flames			
☐ 4 Steve Larmer TC	.08	.04	.01
Chicago Blackhawks			
☐ 5 Tim Cheveldae TC	.08	.04	.01
Detroit Red Wings			
☐ 6 Vincent Damphousse TC	.08	.04	.01

Edmonton Oilers			
☐ 7 Pat Verbeek TC	.05	.02	.01
Hartford Whalers			
☐ 8 Luc Robitaille TC	.08	.04	.01
Los Angeles Kings			
☐ 9 Mike Modano TC	.08	.04	.01
Minnesota North Stars			
☐ 10 Denis Savard TC	.08	.04	.01
Montreal Canadiens			
☐ 11 Kevin Todd TC	.05	.02	.01
New Jersey Devils			
☐ 12 Ray Ferraro TC	.05	.02	.01
New York Islanders			
☐ 13 Tony Amonte TC	.08	.04	.01
New York Rangers			
☐ 14 Peter Sidorkiewicz TC	.05	.02	.01
Ottawa Senators			
☐ 15 Rod Brind'Amour TC	.08	.04	.01
Philadelphia Flyers			
☐ 16 Jaromir Jagr TC	.20	.09	.03
Pittsburgh Penguins			
☐ 17 Owen Nolan TC	.05	.02	.01
Quebec Nordiques			
☐ 18 Nelson Emerson TC	.08	.04	.01
St. Louis Blues			
☐ 19 Pat Falloon TC	.05	.02	.01
San Jose Sharks			
☐ 20 Anatoli Semenov TC	.05	.02	.01
Tampa Bay Lightning			
☒ 21 Doug Gilmour TC	.15	.07	.02
Toronto Maple Leafs			
☐ 22 Kirk McLean TC	.08	.04	.01
Vancouver Canucks			
☐ 23 Don Beaupre TC	.05	.02	.01
Washington Capitals			
☐ 24 Phil Housley TC	.08	.04	.01
Winnipeg Jets			
☐ 25 Wayne Gretzky	1.25	.55	.16
Los Angeles Kings			
☐ 26 Mario Lemieux	1.00	.45	.13
Pittsburgh Penguins			
☐ 27 Valeri Kamensky	.20	.09	.03
Quebec Nordiques			
☐ 28 Jaromir Jagr	.60	.25	.08
Pittsburgh Penguins			
☐ 29 Brett Hull	.75	.35	.09
St. Louis Blues			
☐ 30 Neil Wilkinson	.05	.02	.01
San Jose Sharks			
☐ 31 Dominic Roussel	.20	.09	.03
Philadelphia Flyers			
☐ 32 Kent Manderville	.05	.02	.01
Toronto Maple Leafs			
☐ 33 Gretzky 1500	.50	.23	.06
Los Angeles Kings			
☐ 34 Presidents' Cup	.25	.11	.03
New York Rangers			
☐ 35 Kip Miller BL	.05	.02	.01
Minnesota North Stars			
Kevin Miller			
Washington Capitals			
Kelly Miller			
Washington Capitals			
☐ 36 Brian Sakic BL	.15	.07	.02
New York Rangers			
Joe Sakic			
Quebec Nordiques			
☐ 37 Wayne Gretzky BL	.50	.23	.06
Los Angeles Kings			
Keith Gretzky			
San Diego Gulls			
Brent Gretzky			
Tampa Bay Lightning			
☐ 38 Jamie Linden BL	.15	.07	.02
Spokane Chiefs			
Trevor Linden			
Vancouver Canucks			
☐ 39 Geoff Courtnall BL	.05	.02	.01
Vancouver Canucks			
Russ Courtnall			
Montreal Canadiens			
☐ 40 Dale Craigwell	.05	.02	.01
San Jose Sharks			
☐ 41 Peter Ahola	.05	.02	.01
Los Angeles Kings			
☐ 42 Robert Reichel	.08	.04	.01
Calgary Flames			
☐ 43 Chris Terreri	.08	.04	.01
New Jersey Devils			
☐ 44 John Vanbiesbrouck	.12	.05	.02
New York Rangers			
☐ 45 Alexander Semak	.05	.02	.01
New Jersey Devils			
☐ 46 Mike Sullivan	.05	.02	.01

	San Jose Sharks			
☐ 47	Bob Sweeney	.05	.02	.01
	Boston Bruins			
☐ 48	Corey Millen	.08	.04	.01
	Los Angeles Kings			
☐ 49	Murray Craven	.05	.02	.01
	Hartford Whalers			
☐ 50	Dennis Vaske	.05	.02	.01
	New York Islanders			
☐ 51	David Williams	.10	.05	.01
	San Jose Sharks			
☐ 52	Tom Fitzgerald	.05	.02	.01
	New York Islanders			
☐ 53	Corey Foster	.05	.02	.01
	Philadelphia Flyers			
☐ 54	Al Iafrate	.08	.04	.01
	Washington Capitals			
☐ 55	John LeClair	.05	.02	.01
	Montreal Canadiens			
☐ 56	Stephane Richer	.08	.04	.01
	New Jersey Devils			
☐ 57	Claude Boivin	.05	.02	.01
	Philadelphia Flyers			
☐ 58	Rick Tabaracci	.05	.02	.01
	Winnipeg Jets			
☐ 59	Johan Garpenlov	.05	.02	.01
	San Jose Sharks			
☐ 60	Checklist 1-110	.05	.02	.01
☐ 61	Steve Leach	.05	.02	.01
	Boston Bruins			
☐ 62	Trent Klatt	.25	.11	.03
	Minnesota North Stars			
☐ 63	Darryl Sydor	.08	.04	.01
	Los Angeles Kings			
☐ 64	Brian Glynn	.05	.02	.01
	Edmonton Oilers			
☐ 65	Mike Craig	.05	.02	.01
	Minnesota North Stars			
☐ 66	Gary Leeman	.05	.02	.01
	Calgary Flames			
☐ 67	Jim Waite	.05	.02	.01
	Chicago Blackhawks			
☐ 68	Jason Marshall	.05	.02	.01
	St. Louis Blues			
☐ 69	Robert Kron	.05	.02	.01
	Vancouver Canucks			
☐ 70	Yanic Perreault	.25	.11	.03
	Toronto Maple Leafs			
☐ 71	Daniel Marois	.05	.02	.01
	New York Islanders			
☐ 72	Mark Osborne	.05	.02	.01
	Toronto Maple Leafs			
☐ 73	Mark Tinordi	.08	.04	.01
	Minnesota North Stars			
☐ 74	Brad May	.05	.02	.01
	Buffalo Sabres			
☐ 75	Kimbi Daniels	.05	.02	.01
	Philadelphia Flyers			
☐ 76	Kay Whitmore	.05	.02	.01
	Hartford Whalers			
☐ 77	Luciano Borsato	.05	.02	.01
	Winnipeg Jets			
☐ 78	Kris King	.05	.02	.01
	New York Rangers			
☐ 79	Felix Potvin	1.25	.55	.16
	Toronto Maple Leafs			
☐ 80	Benoit Brunet	.05	.02	.01
	Montreal Canadiens			
☐ 81	Shawn Antoski	.05	.02	.01
	Vancouver Canucks			
☐ 82	Randy Gilhen	.05	.02	.01
	New York Rangers			
☐ 83	Dimitri Mironov	.08	.04	.01
	Toronto Maple Leafs			
☐ 84	Dave Manson	.05	.02	.01
	Edmonton Oilers			
☐ 85	Sergio Momesso	.05	.02	.01
	Vancouver Canucks			
☐ 86	Cam Neely	.20	.09	.03
	Boston Bruins			
☐ 87	Mike Krushelnyski	.05	.02	.01
	Toronto Maple Leafs			
☐ 88	Eric Lindros UER SP	6.00	2.70	.75
	(8 games with Canadian Olympic Team, not 7)			
	Philadelphia Flyers			
☐ 89	Wendel Clark	.12	.05	.02
	Toronto Maple Leafs			
☐ 90	Enrico Ciccone	.05	.02	.01
	Minnesota North Stars			
☐ 91	Jarrod Skalde	.05	.02	.01
	New Jersey Devils			
☐ 92	Dominik Hasek	.50	.23	.06
	Chicago Blackhawks			
☐ 93	Dave McLlwain	.05	.02	.01
	Toronto Maple Leafs			
☐ 94	Russ Courtnall	.08	.04	.01
	Montreal Canadiens			
☐ 95	Tim Sweeney	.05	.02	.01
	Calgary Flames			
☐ 96	Alexei Kasatonov	.05	.02	.01
	New Jersey Devils			
☐ 97	Chris Lindberg	.05	.02	.01
	Calgary Flames			
☐ 98	Steven Rice	.05	.02	.01
	Edmonton Oilers			
☐ 99	Tie Domi	.05	.02	.01
	New York Rangers			
☐ 100	Paul Stanton	.05	.02	.01
	Pittsburgh Penguins			
☐ 101	Brad Schlegel	.05	.02	.01
	Washington Capitals			
☐ 102	David Bruce	.05	.02	.01
	San Jose Sharks			
☐ 103	Mikael Andersson	.05	.02	.01
	Tampa Bay Lightning			
☐ 104	Shawn Chambers	.05	.02	.01
	Tampa Bay Lightning			
☐ 105	Rob Ramage	.05	.02	.01
	Tampa Bay Lightning			
☐ 106	Joe Reekie	.05	.02	.01
	Tampa Bay Lightning			
☐ 107	Sylvain Turgeon	.05	.02	.01
	Ottawa Senators			
☐ 108	Rob Murphy	.05	.02	.01
	Ottawa Senators			
☐ 109	Brad Shaw	.05	.02	.01
	Ottawa Senators			
☐ 110	Darren Rumble	.10	.05	.01
	Ottawa Senators			
☐ 111	Kyosti Karjalainen	.05	.02	.01
	Los Angeles Kings			
☐ 112	Mike Vernon	.08	.04	.01
	Calgary Flames			
☐ 113	Michel Goulet	.08	.04	.01
	Chicago Blackhawks			
☐ 114	Garry Valk	.05	.02	.01
	Vancouver Canucks			
☐ 115	Peter Bondra	.08	.04	.01
	Washington Capitals			
☐ 116	Paul Coffey	.15	.07	.02
	Los Angeles Kings			
☐ 117	Brian Noonan	.05	.02	.01
	Chicago Blackhawks			
☐ 118	John McIntyre	.05	.02	.01
	Los Angeles Kings			
☐ 119	Scott Mellanby	.05	.02	.01
	Edmonton Oilers			
☐ 120	Jim Sandlak	.05	.02	.01
	Vancouver Canucks			
☐ 121	Mats Sundin	.25	.11	.03
	Quebec Nordiques			
☐ 122	Brendan Shanahan	.30	.14	.04
	St. Louis Blues			
☐ 123	Kelly Buchberger	.05	.02	.01
	Edmonton Oilers			
☐ 124	Doug Smail	.05	.02	.01
	Quebec Nordiques			
☐ 125	Craig Janney	.15	.07	.02
	St. Louis Blues			
☐ 126	Mike Gartner	.12	.05	.02
	New York Rangers			
☐ 127	Alexei Gusarov	.05	.02	.01
	Quebec Nordiques			
☐ 128	Joe Nieuwendyk	.08	.04	.01
	Calgary Flames			
☐ 129	Troy Murray	.05	.02	.01
	Winnipeg Jets			
☐ 130	Jamie Baker	.05	.02	.01
	Quebec Nordiques			
☐ 131	Dale Hunter	.08	.04	.01
	Washington Capitals			
☐ 132	Darrin Shannon	.05	.02	.01
	Winnipeg Jets			
☐ 133	Adam Oates	.20	.09	.03
	Boston Bruins			
☐ 134	Trevor Kidd	.08	.04	.01
	Calgary Flames			
☐ 135	Steve Larmer	.08	.04	.01
	Chicago Blackhawks			
☐ 136	Fredrik Olausson	.05	.02	.01
	Winnipeg Jets			
☐ 137	Jyrki Lumme	.05	.02	.01
	Vancouver Canucks			
☐ 138	Tony Amonte	.20	.09	.03
	New York Rangers			
☐ 139	Calle Johansson	.05	.02	.01

Washington Capitals			
☐ 140 Rob Blake	.12	.05	.02
Los Angeles Kings			
☐ 141 Phil Bourque	.05	.02	.01
Pittsburgh Penguins			
☐ 142 Yves Racine	.05	.02	.01
Detroit Red Wings			
☐ 143 Rich Sutter	.05	.02	.01
St. Louis Blues			
☐ 144 Joe Mullen	.08	.04	.01
Pittsburgh Penguins			
☐ 145 Mike Richter	.30	.14	.04
New York Rangers			
☐ 146 Pat MacLeod	.05	.02	.01
San Jose Sharks			
☐ 147 Claude Lapointe	.05	.02	.01
Quebec Nordiques			
☐ 148 Paul Broten	.05	.02	.01
New York Rangers			
☐ 149 Patrick Roy	.60	.25	.08
Montreal Canadiens			
☐ 150 Doug Wilson	.08	.04	.01
San Jose Sharks			
☐ 151 Jim Hrivnak	.05	.02	.01
Washington Capitals			
☐ 152 Joe Murphy	.05	.02	.01
Edmonton Oilers			
☐ 153 Randy Burridge	.05	.02	.01
Washington Capitals			
☐ 154 Thomas Steen	.05	.02	.01
Winnipeg Jets			
☐ 155 Steve Yzerman	.30	.14	.04
Detroit Red Wings			
☐ 156 Pavel Bure	1.25	.55	.16
Vancouver Canucks			
☐ 157 Sergei Fedorov	.75	.35	.09
Detroit Red Wings			
☐ 158 Trevor Linden	.20	.09	.03
Vancouver Canucks			
☐ 159 Chris Chelios	.08	.04	.01
Chicago Blackhawks			
☐ 160 Cliff Ronning	.05	.02	.01
Vancouver Canucks			
☐ 161 Jeff Beukeboom	.05	.02	.01
New York Rangers			
☐ 162 Denis Savard	.08	.04	.01
Montreal Canadiens			
☐ 163 Claude Lemieux	.08	.04	.01
New Jersey Devils			
☐ 164 Mike Keane	.05	.02	.01
Montreal Canadiens			
☐ 165 Pat LaFontaine	.25	.11	.03
Buffalo Sabres			
☐ 166 Nelson Emerson	.20	.09	.03
St. Louis Blues			
☐ 167 Alexander Mogilny	.50	.23	.06
Buffalo Sabres			
☐ 168 Jamie Leach	.05	.02	.01
Pittsburgh Penguins			
☐ 169 Darren Turcotte	.05	.02	.01
New York Rangers			
☐ 170 Checklist 111-220	.05	.02	.01
☐ 171 Steve Thomas	.08	.04	.01
New York Islanders			
☐ 172 Brian Bellows	.08	.04	.01
Minnesota North Stars			
☐ 173 Mike Ridley	.08	.04	.01
Washington Capitals			
☐ 174 Dave Gagner	.08	.04	.01
Minnesota North Stars			
☐ 175 Pierre Turgeon	.25	.11	.03
New York Islanders			
☐ 176 Paul Ysebaert	.05	.02	.01
Detroit Red Wings			
☐ 177 Brian Propp	.08	.04	.01
Minnesota North Stars			
☐ 178 Nicklas Lidstrom	.20	.09	.03
Detroit Red Wings			
☐ 179 Kelly Miller	.05	.02	.01
Washington Capitals			
☐ 180 Kirk Muller	.08	.04	.01
Montreal Canadiens			
☐ 181 Bob Bassen	.05	.02	.01
St. Louis Blues			
☐ 182 Tony Tanti	.05	.02	.01
Buffalo Sabres			
☐ 183 Mikhail Tatarinov	.05	.02	.01
Quebec Nordiques			
☐ 184 Ron Sutter	.05	.02	.01
St. Louis Blues			
☐ 185 Tony Granato	.05	.02	.01
Los Angeles Kings			
☐ 186 Curtis Joseph	.30	.14	.04
St. Louis Blues			

☐ 187 Uwe Krupp	.05	.02	.01
New York Islanders			
☐ 188 Esa Tikkanen	.08	.04	.01
Edmonton Oilers			
☐ 189 Ulf Samuelsson	.08	.04	.01
Pittsburgh Penguins			
☐ 190 Jon Casey	.08	.04	.01
Minnesota North Stars			
☐ 191 Derek King	.05	.02	.01
New York Islanders			
☐ 192 Greg Adams	.05	.02	.01
Vancouver Canucks			
☐ 193 Ray Ferraro	.05	.02	.01
New York Islanders			
☐ 194 Dave Christian	.05	.02	.01
St. Louis Blues			
☐ 195 Eric Weinrich	.05	.02	.01
New Jersey Devils			
☐ 196 Josef Beranek	.15	.07	.02
Edmonton Oilers			
☐ 197 Tim Cheveldae	.08	.04	.01
Detroit Red Wings			
☐ 198 Kevin Hatcher	.08	.04	.01
Washington Capitals			
☐ 199 Brent Sutter	.08	.04	.01
Chicago Blackhawks			
☐ 200 Bruce Driver	.05	.02	.01
New Jersey Devils			
☐ 201 Tom Draper	.05	.02	.01
Buffalo Sabres			
☐ 202 Ted Donato	.05	.02	.01
Boston Bruins			
☐ 203 Ed Belfour	.30	.14	.04
Chicago Blackhawks			
☐ 204 Pat Verbeek	.08	.04	.01
Hartford Whalers			
☐ 205 John Druce	.05	.02	.01
Washington Capitals			
☐ 206 Neal Broten	.08	.04	.01
Minnesota North Stars			
☐ 207 Doug Bodger	.05	.02	.01
Buffalo Sabres			
☐ 208 Troy Loney	.05	.02	.01
Pittsburgh Penguins			
☐ 209 Mark Pederson	.05	.02	.01
Philadelphia Flyers			
☐ 210 Todd Elik	.05	.02	.01
Minnesota North Stars			
☐ 211 Ed Olczyk	.05	.02	.01
Winnipeg Jets			
☐ 212 Paul Cavallini	.05	.02	.01
St. Louis Blues			
☐ 213 Stephan Lebeau	.05	.02	.01
Montreal Canadiens			
☐ 214 Dave Ellett	.05	.02	.01
Toronto Maple Leafs			
☒ 215 Doug Gilmour	.30	.14	.04
Toronto Maple Leafs			
☐ 216 Luc Robitaille	.20	.09	.03
Los Angeles Kings			
☐ 217 Bob Essensa	.08	.04	.01
Winnipeg Jets			
☐ 218 Jari Kurri	.12	.05	.02
Los Angeles Kings			
☐ 219 Dimitri Khristich	.08	.04	.01
Washington Capitals			
☐ 220 Joel Otto	.05	.02	.01
Calgary Flames			
☐ 221 Checklist 221-280	.05	.02	.01
☐ 222 Jonas Hoglund	.15	.07	.02
Team Sweden			
☐ 223 Rolf Wanhainen	.15	.07	.02
Team Sweden			
☐ 224 Stefan Klockare	.15	.07	.02
Team Sweden			
☐ 225 Johan Norgren	.15	.07	.02
Team Sweden			
☐ 226 Roger Kyro	.15	.07	.02
Team Sweden			
☐ 227 Niklas Sunblad	.30	.14	.04
Team Sweden			
☐ 228 Calle Carlsson	.15	.07	.02
Team Sweden			
☐ 229 Jakob Karlsson	.15	.07	.02
Team Sweden			
☐ 230 Fredrik Jax	.20	.09	.03
Team Sweden			
☐ 231 Bjorn Nord	.15	.07	.02
Team Sweden			
☐ 232 Kristian Gahn	.15	.07	.02
Team Sweden			
☐ 233 Mikael Renberg	3.00	1.35	.40
Team Sweden			

234	Markus Naslund	.50	.23	.06
	Team Sweden			
235	Peter Forsberg	.50	.23	.06
	Team Sweden			
236	Mikael Nylander	.40	.18	.05
	Team Sweden			
237	Stanley Cup Centennial	.05	.02	.01
238	Rick Tocchet	.08	.04	.01
	Pittsburgh Penguins			
239	Igor Kravchuk	.05	.02	.01
	Chicago Blackhawks			
240	Geoff Courtnall	.05	.02	.01
	Vancouver Canucks			
241	Larry Murphy	.08	.04	.01
	Pittsburgh Penguins			
242	Mark Messier	.25	.11	.03
	New York Rangers			
243	Tom Barrasso	.08	.04	.01
	Pittsburgh Penguins			
244	Glen Wesley	.05	.02	.01
	Boston Bruins			
245	Randy Wood	.05	.02	.01
	Buffalo Sabres			
246	Gerard Gallant	.05	.02	.01
	Detroit Red Wings			
247	Kip Miller	.05	.02	.01
	Minnesota North Stars			
248	Bob Probert	.05	.02	.01
	Detroit Red Wings			
249	Gary Suter	.08	.04	.01
	Calgary Flames			
250	Ulf Dahlen	.05	.02	.01
	Minnesota North Stars			
251	Dan Lambert	.05	.02	.01
	Quebec Nordiques			
252	Bobby Holik	.05	.02	.01
	Hartford Whalers			
253	Jimmy Carson	.05	.02	.01
	Detroit Red Wings			
254	Ken Hodge Jr.	.05	.02	.01
	Boston Bruins			
255	Joe Sakic	.25	.11	.03
	Quebec Nordiques			
256	Kevin Dineen	.08	.04	.01
	Philadelphia Flyers			
257	Al MacInnis	.12	.05	.02
	Calgary Flames			
258	Vladimir Ruzicka	.05	.02	.01
	Boston Bruins			
259	Ken Daneyko	.05	.02	.01
	New Jersey Devils			
260	Guy Carbonneau	.08	.04	.01
	Montreal Canadiens			
261	Michal Pivonka	.08	.04	.01
	Washington Capitals			
262	Bill Ranford	.08	.04	.01
	Edmonton Oilers			
263	Petr Nedved	.25	.11	.03
	Vancouver Canucks			
264	Rod Brind'Amour	.20	.09	.03
	Philadelphia Flyers			
265	Ray Bourque	.20	.09	.03
	Boston Bruins			
266	Joe Sacco	.05	.02	.01
	Toronto Maple Leafs			
267	Vladimir Konstantinov	.05	.02	.01
	Detroit Red Wings			
268	Eric Desjardins	.05	.02	.01
	Montreal Canadiens			
269	Dave Andreychuk	.20	.09	.03
	Buffalo Sabres			
270	Kelly Hrudey	.08	.04	.01
	Los Angeles Kings			
271	Grant Fuhr	.08	.04	.01
	Toronto Maple Leafs			
272	Dirk Graham	.05	.02	.01
	Chicago Blackhawks			
273	Frank Pietrangelo	.05	.02	.01
	Hartford Whalers			
274	Jeremy Roenick	.60	.25	.08
	Chicago Blackhawks			
275	Kevin Stevens	.30	.14	.04
	Pittsburgh Penguins			
276	Phil Housley	.08	.04	.01
	Winnipeg Jets			
277	Patrice Brisebois	.05	.02	.01
	Montreal Canadiens			
278	Viacheslav Fetisov	.05	.02	.01
	New Jersey Devils			
279	Doug Weight	.08	.04	.01
	New York Rangers			
280	Checklist 281-330	.05	.02	.01
281	Dean Evason	.05	.02	.01
	San Jose Sharks			
282	Martin Gelinas	.05	.02	.01
	Edmonton Oilers			
283	Philippe Bozon	.05	.02	.01
	St. Louis Blues			
284	Brian Leetch	.35	.16	.04
	New York Rangers			
285	Theoren Fleury	.12	.05	.02
	Calgary Flames			
286	Pat Falloon	.20	.09	.03
	San Jose Sharks			
287	Derian Hatcher	.05	.02	.01
	Minnesota North Stars			
288	Andrew Cassels	.05	.02	.01
	Hartford Whalers			
289	Gary Roberts	.08	.04	.01
	Calgary Flames			
290	Bernie Nicholls	.08	.04	.01
	Edmonton Oilers			
291	Ron Francis	.08	.04	.01
	Pittsburgh Penguins			
292	Tom Kurvers	.05	.02	.01
	New York Islanders			
293	Geoff Sanderson	.35	.16	.04
	Hartford Whalers			
294	Vyacheslav Kozlov	.75	.35	.09
	Detroit Red Wings			
295	Valeri Zelepukin	.20	.09	.03
	New Jersey Devils			
296	Ray Sheppard	.08	.04	.01
	Detroit Red Wings			
297	Scott Stevens	.12	.05	.02
	New Jersey Devils			
298	Sergei Nemchinov	.08	.04	.01
	New York Rangers			
299	Kirk McLean	.15	.07	.02
	Vancouver Canucks			
300	Igor Ulanov	.05	.02	.01
	Winnipeg Jets			
301	Brian Benning	.05	.02	.01
	Philadelphia Flyers			
302	Dale Hawerchuk	.08	.04	.01
	Buffalo Sabres			
303	Kevin Todd	.05	.02	.01
	New Jersey Devils			
304	John Cullen	.05	.02	.01
	Hartford Whalers			
305	Mike Modano	.30	.14	.04
	Minnesota North Stars			
306	Donald Audette	.05	.02	.01
	Buffalo Sabres			
307	Vincent Damphousse	.08	.04	.01
	Edmonton Oilers			
308	Jeff Hackett	.05	.02	.01
	San Jose Sharks			
309	Craig Simpson	.05	.02	.01
	Edmonton Oilers			
310	Don Beaupre	.08	.04	.01
	Washington Capitals			
311	Adam Creighton	.05	.02	.01
	New York Islanders			
312	Pat Elynuik	.05	.02	.01
	Winnipeg Jets			
313	David Volek	.05	.02	.01
	New York Islanders			
314	Sergei Makarov	.08	.04	.01
	Calgary Flames			
315	Craig Billington	.05	.02	.01
	New Jersey Devils			
316	Zarley Zalapski	.05	.02	.01
	Hartford Whalers			
317	Brian Mullen	.08	.04	.01
	San Jose Sharks			
318	Rob Pearson	.05	.02	.01
	Toronto Maple Leafs			
319	Garry Galley	.05	.02	.01
	Philadelphia Flyers			
320	James Patrick	.05	.02	.01
	New York Rangers			
321	Owen Nolan	.08	.04	.01
	Quebec Nordiques			
322	Marty McSorley	.08	.04	.01
	Los Angeles Kings			
323	James Black	.05	.02	.01
	Hartford Whalers			
324	Jacques Cloutier	.05	.02	.01
	Quebec Nordiques			
325	Benoit Hogue	.05	.02	.01
	New York Islanders			
326	Teppo Numminen	.05	.02	.01
	Winnipeg Jets			
327	Mark Recchi	.30	.14	.04
	Philadelphia Flyers			
328	Paul Ranheim	.05	.02	.01

Calgary Flames
☐ 329 Andy Moog	.08	.04	.01

Boston Bruins
☐ 330 Shayne Corson	.08	.04	.01

Montreal Canadiens
☐ 331 J.J. Daigneault	.05	.02	.01

Montreal Canadiens
☐ 332 Mark Fitzpatrick	.08	.04	.01

New York Islanders
☐ 333 Russian Stars CL	.20	.09	.03

Alexander Yudin
Dmitri Yushkevich
Yan Kaminsky
Alexander Andriyevski
☐ 334 Alexei Yashin RS	1.00	.45	.13
☐ 335 Darius Kasparaitis RS	.15	.07	.02
☐ 336 Alexander Yudin RS	.20	.09	.03
☐ 337 Sergei Bautin RS	.15	.07	.02
☐ 338 Igor Korolev RS	.15	.07	.02
☐ 339 Sergei Klimovich RS	.20	.09	.03
☐ 340 Andrei Nikolishin RS	.25	.11	.03
☐ 341 Vitali Karamnov RS	.15	.07	.02
☐ 342 Alexander Andriyevski RS	.15	.07	.02
☐ 343 Sergei Sorokin RS	.20	.09	.03
☐ 344 Yan Kaminsky RS	.40	.18	.05
☐ 345 Andrei Trefilov RS	.50	.23	.06
☐ 346 Sergei Petrenko RS	.25	.11	.03
☐ 347 Ravil Khaidarov RS	.15	.07	.02
☐ 348 Dmitri Frolov RS	.15	.07	.02
☐ 349 Ravil Yakubov RS	.20	.09	.03
☐ 350 Dmitri Yushkevich RS	.20	.09	.03
☐ 351 Alexander Karpovtsev RS	.40	.18	.05
☐ 352 Igor Dorofeyev RS	.15	.07	.02
☐ 353 Alexander Galchenyuk RS	.15	.07	.02
☐ 354 Joe Juneau RR	.75	.35	.09

Boston Bruins
☐ 355 Pat Falloon RR	.15	.07	.02

San Jose Sharks
☐ 356 Gilbert Dionne RR	.08	.04	.01

Montreal Canadiens
☐ 357 Vladimir Konstantinov RR	.08	.04	.01

Detroit Red Wings
☐ 358 Rick Tabaracci RR	.08	.04	.01

Winnipeg Jets
☐ 359 Tony Amonte RR	.15	.07	.02

New York Rangers
☐ 360 Scott Lachance RR	.08	.04	.01

New York Islanders
☐ 361 Tom Draper RR	.08	.04	.01

Buffalo Sabres
☐ 362 Pavel Bure RR	.75	.35	.09

Vancouver Canucks
☐ 363 Nicklas Lidstrom RR	.15	.07	.02

Detroit Red Wings
☐ 364 Keith Tkachuk RR	.30	.14	.04

Winnipeg Jets
☐ 365 Kevin Todd RR	.08	.04	.01

New Jersey Devils
☐ 366 Dominik Hasek RR	.30	.14	.04

Chicago Blackhawks
☐ 367 Igor Kravchuk RR	.08	.04	.01

Chicago Blackhawks
☐ 368 Shawn McEachern RR	.15	.07	.02

Pittsburgh Penguins
☐ 369 '92 World Championships Checklist	.25	.11	.03

Arto Blomsten
Peter Forsberg
☐ 370 Dieter Hegen	.08	.04	.01

Team Germany
☐ 371 Stefan Ustorf	.15	.07	.02

Team Germany
☐ 372 Ernst Kopf	.08	.04	.01

Team Germany
☐ 373 Raimond Hilger	.08	.04	.01

Team Germany
☐ 374 Mats Sundin	.20	.09	.03

Team Sweden
☐ 375 Peter Forsberg	.50	.23	.06

Team Sweden
☐ 376 Arto Blomsten	.15	.07	.02

Team Sweden
☐ 377 Tommy Soderstrom	.40	.18	.05

Team Sweden
☐ 378 Mikael Nylander	.40	.18	.05

Team Sweden
☐ 379 David Jensen	.08	.04	.01

Team USA
☐ 380 Chris Winnes	.08	.04	.01

Team USA
☐ 381 Ray LeBlanc	.08	.04	.01

Team USA
☐ 382 Joe Sacco	.08	.04	.01

Team USA
☐ 383 Dennis Vaske	.08	.04	.01

Team USA
☐ 384 Jorg Eberle	.08	.04	.01

Team Sweden
☐ 385 Trevor Kidd	.12	.05	.02

Calgary Flames
☐ 386 Pat Falloon	.20	.09	.03

San Jose Sharks
☐ 387 Rob Brown	.05	.02	.01

Chicago Blackhawks
☐ 388 Adam Graves	.30	.14	.04

New York Rangers
☐ 389 Peter Zezel	.05	.02	.01

Toronto Maple Leafs
☐ 390 Checklist 391-440	.05	.02	.01
☐ 391 Don Sweeney	.05	.02	.01

Boston Bruins
☐ 392 Sean Hill	.20	.09	.03

Team USA
☐ 393 Ted Donato	.08	.04	.01

Team USA
☐ 394 Marty McInnis	.08	.04	.01

Team USA
☐ 395 C.J. Young	.10	.05	.01

Team USA
☐ 396 Ted Drury	.25	.11	.03

Team USA
☐ 397 Scott Young	.08	.04	.01

Team USA
☐ 398 Star Rookie CL	.25	.11	.03

Scott Lachance
New York Islanders
Keith Tkachuk
Winnipeg Jets
☐ 399 Joe Juneau SR UER	1.00	.45	.13

(Olympic stats should
read 8 games, 9 assists,
15 points, and 4 PIM)
Boston Bruins
☐ 400 Steve Heinze SR	.08	.04	.01

Boston Bruins
☐ 401 Glen Murray SR	.08	.04	.01

Boston Bruins
☐ 402 Keith Carney SR	.15	.07	.02

Buffalo Sabres
☐ 403 Dean McAmmond SR	.20	.09	.03

Chicago Blackhawks
☐ 404 Karl Dykhuis SR	.08	.04	.01

Chicago Blackhawks
☐ 405 Martin Lapointe SR	.08	.04	.01

Detroit Red Wings
☐ 406 Scott Niedermayer SR	.30	.14	.04

New Jersey Devils
☐ 407 Ray Whitney SR	.25	.11	.03

San Jose Sharks
☐ 408 Martin Brodeur SR	.75	.35	.09

New Jersey Devils
☐ 409 Scott Lachance SR	.08	.04	.01

New York Islanders
☐ 410 Marty McInnis SR	.08	.04	.01

New York Islanders
☐ 411 Bill Guerin SR	.25	.11	.03

New Jersey Devils
☐ 412 Shawn McEachern SR	.20	.09	.03

Pittsburgh Penguins
☐ 413 Denny Felsner SR	.20	.09	.03

St. Louis Blues
☐ 414 Bret Hedican SR	.20	.09	.03

St. Louis Blues
☐ 415 Drake Berehowsky SR	.08	.04	.01

Toronto Maple Leafs
☐ 416 Patrick Poulin SR	.08	.04	.01

Hartford Whalers
☐ 417 Vladimir Vujtek SR	.15	.07	.02

Montreal Canadiens
☐ 418 Steve Konowalchuk SR	.15	.07	.02

Washington Capitals
☐ 419 Keith Tkachuk SR	.35	.16	.04

Winnipeg Jets
☐ 420 Evgeny Davydov SR	.08	.04	.01

Winnipeg Jets
☐ 421 Yanick Dupre SR	.08	.04	.01

Philadelphia Flyers
☐ 422 Jason Woolley SR	.10	.05	.01

Washington Capitals
☐ 423 Back-to-Back	.50	.23	.06

Brett Hull
St. Louis Blues
Wayne Gretzky

	Los Angeles Kings			
☐ 424	Tomas Sandstrom..............	.05	.02	.01
	Los Angeles Kings			
☐ 425	Craig MacTavish	.05	.02	.01
	Edmonton Oilers			
☐ 426	Stu Barnes	.05	.02	.01
	Winnipeg Jets			
☐ 427	Gilbert Dionne	.05	.02	.01
	Montreal Canadiens			
☐ 428	Andrei Lomakin	.05	.02	.01
	Philadelphia Flyers			
☐ 429	Tomas Forslund	.05	.02	.01
	Calgary Flames			
☐ 430	Andre Racicot	.05	.02	.01
	Montreal Canadiens			
☐ 431	Pavel Bure AW	.75	.35	.09
	Vancouver Canucks			
	Calder Memorial			
☐ 432	Mark Messier AW	.15	.07	.02
	New York Rangers			
	Lester B. Pearson			
☐ 433	Mario Lemieux AW.............	.25	.11	.03
	Pittsburgh Penguins			
	Art Ross			
☐ 434	Brian Leetch AW	.15	.07	.02
	New York Rangers			
	Norris			
☐ 435	Wayne Gretzky AW.............	.50	.23	.06
	Los Angeles Kings			
	Lady Byng			
☐ 436	Mario Lemieux AW.............	.25	.11	.03
	Pittsburgh Penguins			
	Conn Smythe			
☐ 437	Mark Messier AW	.15	.07	.02
	New York Rangers			
	Hart			
☐ 438	Patrick Roy AW	.40	.18	.05
	Montreal Canadiens			
	Vezina			
☐ 439	Guy Carbonneau AW	.05	.02	.01
	Montreal Canadiens			
	Frank J. Selke			
☐ 440	Patrick Roy AW	.40	.18	.05
	Montreal Canadiens			
	William M. Jennings			
☐ 441	Russ Courtnall	.08	.04	.01
	Minnesota North Stars			
☐ 442	Jeff Reese	.05	.02	.01
	Calgary Flames			
☐ 443	Brent Fedyk	.05	.02	.01
	Philadelphia Flyers			
☐ 444	Kerry Huffman	.05	.02	.01
	Quebec Nordiques			
☐ 445	Mark Freer	.05	.02	.01
	Ottawa Senators			
☐ 446	Christian Ruuttu	.05	.02	.01
	Chicago Blackhawks			
☐ 447	Nick Kypreos.....................	.05	.02	.01
	Hartford Whalers			
☐ 448	Mike Hurlbut	.05	.02	.01
	New York Rangers			
☐ 449	Bob Sweeney	.05	.02	.01
	Buffalo Sabres			
☐ 450	Checklist 491-540	.05	.02	.01
☐ 451	Perry Berezan....................	.05	.02	.01
	San Jose Sharks			
☐ 452	Phil Bourque	.05	.02	.01
	New York Rangers			
☐ 453	New York Rangers LL	.40	.18	.05
	Mark Messier			
	Tony Amonte			
	Adam Graves			
☐ 454	Pittsburgh Penguins LL	.30	.14	.04
	Mario Lemieux			
	Kevin Stevens			
	Rick Tocchet			
☐ 455	Boston Bruins LL	.25	.11	.03
	Adam Oates			
	Joe Juneau			
	Dmitri Kvartalnov			
☐ 456	Buffalo Sabres LL..............	.25	.11	.03
	Pat LaFontaine			
	Dave Andreychuk			
	Alexander Mogilny			
☐ 457	Zdeno Ciger......................	.05	.02	.01
	New Jersey Devils			
☐ 458	Pat Jablonski....................	.05	.02	.01
	Tampa Bay Lightning			
☐ 459	Brent Gilchrist	.05	.02	.01
	Edmonton Oilers			
☐ 460	Yvon Corriveau	.05	.02	.01
	San Jose Sharks			
☐ 461	Dino Ciccarelli	.08	.04	.01
	Detroit Red Wings			

☐ 462	David Emma.......................	.05	.02	.01
	New Jersey Devils			
☐ 463	Corey Hirsch	.50	.23	.06
	New York Rangers			
☐ 464	Jamie Baker	.05	.02	.01
	Ottawa Senators			
☐ 465	John Cullen	.05	.02	.01
	Toronto Maple Leafs			
☐ 466	Lonnie Loach	.05	.02	.01
	Los Angeles Kings			
☐ 467	Louie DeBrusk...................	.05	.02	.01
	Edmonton Oilers			
☐ 468	Brian Mullen.....................	.08	.04	.01
	New York Islanders			
☐ 469	Gaeten Duchesne	.05	.02	.01
	Minnesota North Stars			
☐ 470	Eric Lindros.....................	4.00	1.80	.50
	Philadelphia Flyers			
☐ 471	Brian Bellows	.08	.04	.01
	Montreal Canadiens			
☐ 472	Bill Lindsay	.15	.07	.02
	Quebec Nordiques			
☐ 473	Dave Archibald	.05	.02	.01
	Ottawa Senators			
☐ 474	Reggie Savage	.05	.02	.01
	Washington Capitals			
☐ 475	Tommy Soderstrom............	.25	.11	.03
	Philadelphia Flyers			
☐ 476	Vin Damphousse	.08	.04	.01
	Montreal Canadiens			
☐ 477	Mike Ricci	.08	.04	.01
	Quebec Nordiques			
☐ 478	Bob Carpenter	.05	.02	.01
	Washington Capitals			
☐ 479	Kevin Haller	.05	.02	.01
	Montreal Canadiens			
☐ 480	Peter Sidorkiewicz.............	.05	.02	.01
	Ottawa Senators			
☐ 481	Peter Andersson	.10	.05	.01
	New York Rangers			
☐ 482	Kevin Miller......................	.08	.04	.01
	St. Louis Blues			
☐ 483	Jean-Francois Quintin	.05	.02	.01
	San Jose Sharks			
☐ 484	Philippe Boucher...............	.05	.02	.01
	Buffalo Sabres			
☐ 485	Jozef Stumpel	.05	.02	.01
	Boston Bruins			
☐ 486	Vitali Prokhorov	.15	.07	.02
	St. Louis Blues			
☐ 487	Stan Drulia	.05	.02	.01
	Tampa Bay Lightning			
☐ 488	Jayson More	.05	.02	.01
	San Jose Sharks			
☐ 489	Mike Needham	.15	.07	.02
	Pittsburgh Penguins			
☐ 490	Glenn Mulvenna	.05	.02	.01
	Philadelphia Flyers			
☐ 491	Ed Ronan	.15	.07	.02
	Montreal Canadiens			
☐ 492	Grigori Panteleyev..............	.10	.05	.01
	Boston Bruins			
☐ 493	Kevin Dahl........................	.05	.02	.01
	Calgary Flames			
☐ 494	Ryan McGill.......................	.10	.05	.01
	Philadelphia Flyers			
☐ 495	Robb Stauber.....................	.05	.02	.01
	Los Angeles Kings			
☐ 496	Vladimir Vujtek..................	.15	.07	.02
	Edmonton Oilers			
☐ 497	Tomas Jelinek	.05	.02	.01
	Ottawa Senators			
☐ 498	Patrik Kjellberg.................	.05	.02	.01
	Montreal Canadiens			
☐ 499	Sergei Bautin.....................	.05	.02	.01
	Winnipeg Jets			
☐ 500	Bobby Holik.......................	.05	.02	.01
	New Jersey Devils			
☐ 501	Guy Hebert........................	.50	.23	.06
	St. Louis Blues			
☐ 502	Chris Kontos	.15	.07	.02
	Tampa Bay Lightning			
☐ 503	Vyatcheslav Butsayev..........	.20	.09	.03
	Philadelphia Flyers			
☐ 504	Yuri Khymlev.....................	.35	.16	.04
	Buffalo Sabres			
☐ 505	Richard Matvichuk.............	.15	.07	.02
	Minnesota North Stars			
☐ 506	Dominik Hasek...................	.50	.23	.06
	Buffalo Sabres			
☐ 507	Ed Courtenay.....................	.05	.02	.01
	San Jose Sharks			
☐ 508	Jeff Daniels	.05	.02	.01

Pittsburgh Penguins
☐ 509 Doug Zmolek	.15	.07	.02

San Jose Sharks
☐ 510 Vitali Karamnov	.05	.02	.01

St. Louis Blues
☐ 511 Norm MacIver	.05	.02	.01

Ottawa Senators
☐ 512 Terry Yake	.05	.02	.01

Hartford Whalers
☐ 513 Steve Duchesne	.08	.04	.01

Quebec Nordiques
☐ 514 Andrei Trefilov	.25	.11	.03

Calgary Flames
☐ 515 Jiri Slegr	.05	.02	.01

Vancouver Canucks
☐ 516 Sergei Zubov	2.50	1.15	.30

New York Rangers
☐ 517 Dave Karpa	.10	.05	.01

Quebec Nordiques
☐ 518 Sean Burke	.08	.04	.01

Hartford Whalers
☐ 519 Adrien Plavsic	.05	.02	.01

Vancouver Canucks
☐ 520 Mikael Nylander	.20	.09	.03

Hartford Whalers
☐ 521 John MacLean	.08	.04	.01

New Jersey Devils
☐ 522 Jason Ruff	.10	.05	.01

St. Louis Blues
☐ 523 Sean Hill	.05	.02	.01

Montreal Canadiens
☐ 524 Mike Sillinger	.05	.02	.01

Detroit Red Wings
☐ 525 Daniel Laperriere	.15	.07	.02

St. Louis Blues
☐ 526 Peter Ahola	.05	.02	.01

Pittsburgh Penguins
☐ 527 Guy Larose	.05	.02	.01

Toronto Maple Leafs
☐ 528 Tommy Sjodin	.10	.05	.01

Minnesota North Stars
☐ 529 Rob Dimaio	.05	.02	.01

Tampa Bay Lightning
☐ 530 Mark Howe	.08	.04	.01

Detroit Red Wings
☐ 531 Greg Paslawski	.05	.02	.01

Philadelphia Flyers
☐ 532 Ron Hextall	.08	.04	.01

Quebec Nordiques
☐ 533 Keith Jones	.15	.07	.02

Washington Capitals
☐ 534 Chris Luongo	.05	.02	.01

Ottawa Senators
☐ 535 Anatoli Semenov	.05	.02	.01

Vancouver Canucks
☐ 536 Stephane Beauregard	.05	.02	.01

Philadelphia Flyers
☐ 537 Pat Elynuik	.05	.02	.01

Washington Capitals
☐ 538 Mike McPhee	.05	.02	.01

Minnesota North Stars
☐ 539 Jody Hull	.05	.02	.01

Ottawa Senators
☐ 540 Stephane Matteau	.05	.02	.01

Chicago Blackhawks
☐ 541 Shayne Corson	.08	.04	.01

Edmonton Oilers
☐ 542 Mikhail Kravets	.15	.07	.02

San Jose Sharks
☐ 543 Kevin Miehm	.05	.02	.01

St. Louis Blues
☐ 544 Brian Bradley	.05	.02	.01

Tampa Bay Lightning
☐ 545 Mathieu Schneider	.08	.04	.01

Montreal Canadiens
☐ 546 Steve Chiasson	.05	.02	.01

Detroit Red Wings
☐ 547 Warren Rychel	.15	.07	.02

Los Angeles Kings
☐ 548 John Tucker	.05	.02	.01

Tampa Bay Lightning
☐ 549 Todd Ewen	.05	.02	.01

Montreal Canadiens
☐ 550 Checklist 591-640	.05	.02	.01
☐ 551 Petr Klima	.05	.02	.01

Edmonton Oilers
☐ 552 Robert Lang	.25	.11	.03

Los Angeles Kings
☐ 553 Eric Weinrich	.05	.02	.01

Hartford Whalers
☐ 554 Young Guns Checklist	.20	.09	.03
☐ 555 Roman Hamrlik YG	.50	.23	.06

Tampa Bay Lightning
☐ 556 Martin Rucinsky YG	.15	.07	.02

Quebec Nordiques
☐ 557 Patrick Poulin YG	.08	.04	.01

Hartford Whalers
☐ 558 Tyler Wright YG	.08	.04	.01

Edmonton Oilers
☐ 559 Martin Straka YG	1.00	.45	.13

Pittsburgh Penguins
☐ 560 Jim Hiller YG	.10	.05	.01

Los Angeles Kings
☐ 561 Dmitri Kvartalnov YG	.25	.11	.03

Boston Bruins
☐ 562 Scott Niedermayer YG	.30	.14	.04

New Jersey Devils
☐ 563 Darius Kasparaitis YG	.15	.07	.02

New York Islanders
☐ 564 Richard Smehlik YG	.25	.11	.03

Buffalo Sabres
☐ 565 Shawn McEachern YG	.20	.09	.03

Pittsburgh Penguins
☐ 566 Alexei Zhitnik YG	.20	.09	.03

Los Angeles Kings
☐ 567 Andrei Kovalenko YG	.30	.14	.04

Quebec Nordiques
☐ 568 Sandis Ozolinsh YG	.50	.23	.06

San Jose Sharks
☐ 569 Robert Petrovicky YG	.20	.09	.03

Hartford Whalers
☐ 570 Dimitri Yushkevich YG	.15	.07	.02

Philadelphia Flyers
☐ 571 Scott Lachance YG	.08	.04	.01

New York Islanders
☐ 572 Nikolai Borschevsky YG	.50	.23	.06

Toronto Maple Leafs
☐ 573 Alexei Kovalev YG	.75	.35	.09

New York Rangers
☐ 574 Teemu Selanne YG	1.50	.65	.19

Winnipeg Jets
☐ 575 Steven King YG	.20	.09	.03

New York Rangers
☐ 576 Guy Leveque YG	.15	.07	.02

Los Angeles Kings
☐ 577 Vladimir Malakhov YG	.25	.11	.03

New York Islanders
☐ 578 Alexei Zhamnov YG	.50	.23	.06

Winnipeg Jets
☐ 579 Viktor Gordijuk YG	.20	.09	.03

Buffalo Sabres
☐ 580 Dixon Ward YG	.20	.09	.03

Vancouver Canucks
☐ 581 Igor Korolev YG	.08	.04	.01

St. Louis Blues
☐ 582 Sergei Krivokrasov YG	.20	.09	.03

Chicago Blackhawks
☐ 583 Rob Zamuner YG	.15	.07	.02

Tampa Bay Lightning
☐ 584 World Jr.	.15	.07	.02

Championship Checklist
☐ 585 Martin Legace	.60	.25	.08
☐ 586 Paul Kariya	5.00	2.30	.60
☐ 587 Alexandre Daigle	4.00	1.80	.50
☐ 588 Nathan Lafeyette	.60	.25	.08
☐ 589 Mike Rathje	.75	.35	.09
☐ 590 Chris Gratton	2.00	.90	.25
☐ 591 Chris Pronger	2.00	.90	.25
☐ 592 Brent Tully	.35	.16	.04
☐ 593 Rob Niedermayer UER	2.00	.90	.25
(Hometown is Cassiar, not Kassier)			
☐ 594 Darcy Werenka	.25	.11	.03
☐ 595 Peter Forsberg	.50	.23	.06
☐ 596 Kenny Jonsson	1.00	.45	.13
☐ 597 Niklas Sundstrom	1.00	.45	.13
☐ 598 Reine Rauhala	.15	.07	.02
☐ 599 Daniel Johansson	.20	.09	.03
☐ 600 David Vyborny	.50	.23	.06
☐ 601 Jan Vopat	.40	.18	.05
☐ 602 Pavol Demitra	.40	.18	.05
☐ 603 Michal Cerny	.20	.09	.03
☐ 604 Ondrej Steiner	.20	.09	.03
☐ 605 Jim Campbell	.50	.23	.06
☐ 606 Todd Marchant	.50	.23	.06
☐ 607 Mike Pomichter	.40	.18	.05
☐ 608 John Emmons	.20	.09	.03
☐ 609 Adam Deadmarsh	.50	.23	.06
☐ 610 Nikolai Semin	.20	.09	.03
☐ 611 Igor Alexandrov	.20	.09	.03
☐ 612 Vadim Sharifjanov	.75	.35	.09
☐ 613 Viktor Kozlov	2.00	.90	.25
☐ 614 Nikolai Tsulygin	.40	.18	.05
☐ 615 Jere Lehtinen	.25	.11	.03
☐ 616 Ville Peltonen	.40	.18	.05
☐ 617 Saku Koivu	1.00	.45	.13
☐ 618 Kimmo Rintanen	.10	.05	.01
☐ 619 Jonni Vauhkonen	.25	.11	.03

☐ 620 Brett Hull	.25	.11	.03
St. Louis Blues			
☐ 621 Wayne Gretzky	.50	.23	.06
Los Angeles Kings			
☐ 622 Jaromir Jagr	.25	.11	.03
Pittsburgh Penguins			
☐ 623 Darius Kasparaitis	.10	.05	.01
New York Islanders			
☐ 624 Bernie Nicholls	.10	.05	.01
Edmonton Oilers			
☐ 625 Gilbert Dionne	.10	.05	.01
Montreal Canadiens			
☐ 626 Ray Bourque	.12	.05	.02
Boston Bruins			
☐ 627 Mike Ricci	.10	.05	.01
Quebec Nordiques			
☐ 628 Phil Housley	.10	.05	.01
Winnipeg Jets			
☐ 629 Chris Chelios	.10	.05	.01
Chicago Blackhawks			
☐ 630 Kevin Stevens	.20	.09	.03
Pittsburgh Penguins			
☐ 631 Roman Hamrlik	.15	.07	.02
Tampa Bay Lightning			
☐ 632 Sergei Fedorov	.35	.16	.04
Detroit Red Wings			
☐ 633 Alexei Kovalev	.25	.11	.03
New York Rangers			
☐ 634 Shawn McEachern	.15	.07	.02
Pittsburgh Penguins			
☐ 635 Tony Amonte	.10	.05	.01
New York Rangers			
☐ 636 Brian Bellows	.10	.05	.01
Minnesota North Stars			
☐ 637 Adam Oates	.12	.05	.02
Boston Bruins			
☐ 638 Denis Savard	.12	.05	.02
Montreal Canadiens			
☑ 639 Doug Gilmour	.25	.11	.03
Toronto Maple Leafs			
☐ 640 Brian Leetch	.12	.05	.02
New York Rangers			
☐ SP2 Pavel Bure	8.00	3.60	1.00
All-Rookie Team			
Vancouver Canucks			
☐ SP3 World Jr. Champs	5.00	2.30	.60
Gold medal winner			
Canada			

1992-93 Upper Deck All-Rookie Team

This seven-card set was inserted only in low series U.S. foil packs and features six of the NHL's brightest rookies from the 1991-92 season. The fronts show a triple-pose player photo and have a diagonal silver foil stripe in the lower right corner with the words "All-Rookie Team". The backs provide biographical information and a color photo of the player in civilian dress. The checklist card has a group photo of all six players. The cards are numbered on the back with an "AR" prefix.

	MINT	EXC	G-VG
COMPLETE SET (7)	30.00	13.50	3.80
COMMON PLAYER (AR1-AR7)	4.00	1.80	.50

☐ AR1 Tony Amonte	5.00	2.30	.60
New York Rangers			
☐ AR2 Gilbert Dionne	4.00	1.80	.50
Montreal Canadiens			
☐ AR3 Kevin Todd	4.00	1.80	.50
New Jersey Devils			
☐ AR4 Nicklas Lidstrom	4.00	1.80	.50
Detroit Red Wings			
☐ AR5 Vladimir Konstantinov	4.00	1.80	.50
Detroit Red Wings			
☐ AR6 Dominik Hasek	8.00	3.60	1.00
Chicago Blackhawks			
☐ AR7 Checklist Card	18.00	8.00	2.30
Tony Amonte			
Gilbert Dionne			
Kevin Todd			
Nicklas Lidstrom			
Vladimir Konstantinov			
Dominik Hasek			

1992-93 Upper Deck All-World Team

This six-card set was randomly inserted only in Canadian low series foil packs. These standard size (2 1/2" by 3 1/2") cards are full bleed with a gold "All-World Team" logo at the bottom of the card. The cards are numbered on the back with a "W" prefix.

	MINT	EXC	G-VG
COMPLETE SET (6)	30.00	13.50	3.80
COMMON PLAYER (W1-W6)	3.00	1.35	.40

☐ W1 Wayne Gretzky	9.00	4.00	1.15
Los Angeles Kings			
☐ W2 Brett Hull	6.00	2.70	.75
St. Louis Blues			
☐ W3 Jaromir Jagr	6.00	2.70	.75
Pittsburgh Penguins			
☐ W4 Nicklas Lidstrom	3.00	1.35	.40
Detroit Red Wings			
☐ W5 Vladimir Konstantinov	3.00	1.35	.40
Detroit Red Wings			
☐ W6 Patrick Roy	9.00	4.00	1.15
Montreal Canadiens			

1992-93 Upper Deck Ameri/Can Holograms

Randomly inserted in high series foil packs, this six-card hologram set spotlights the top rookies of either U.S. or Canadian heritage at each position. The cards have the photo superimposed over the hologram. These standard size (2 1/2" by 3 1/2") cards are numbered on the back.

	MINT	EXC	G-VG
COMPLETE SET (6)	15.00	6.75	1.90
COMMON PLAYER (1-6)	2.50	1.15	.30

☐ 1 Joe Juneau	4.00	1.80	.50
Boston Bruins			

		MINT	EXC	G-VG
☐ 2	Keith Tkachuk .... Winnipeg Jets	3.50	1.55	.45
☐ 3	Steve Heinze .... Boston Bruins	2.50	1.15	.30
☐ 4	Scott Lachance .... New York Islanders	2.50	1.15	.30
☐ 5	Scott Niedermayer .... New Jersey Devils	3.00	1.35	.40
☐ 6	Dominic Roussel.................... Philadelphia Flyers	2.50	1.15	.30

1992-93 Upper Deck Calder Candidates

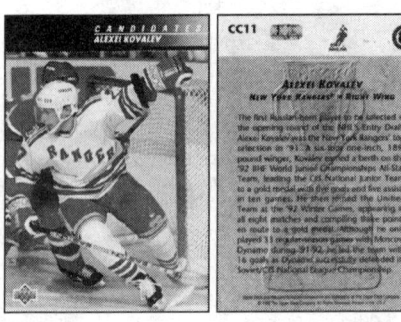

Randomly inserted into 1992-93 Upper Deck U.S. High Series retail foil packs only, this 20-card set spotlights top rookies eligible to win the Calder Memorial Trophy for the 1992-93 season. The full-bleed photos on the front are bordered on the top by a gold foil stripe. The team name and player's name appears in bar that shades from black to white. On a background consisting of a stone slab carved with an image of the Calder trophy, the backs present a career summary. The card number appears in a white stripe that cuts across the top of the card. These standard size (2 1/2" by 3 1/2") cards are numbered with a "CC" prefix

		MINT	EXC	G-VG
COMPLETE SET (20)....................		90.00	40.00	11.50
COMMON PLAYER (CC1-CC20)........		3.00	1.35	.40
☐ CC1	Dixon Ward........................ Vancouver Canucks	3.00	1.35	.40
☐ CC2	Igor Korolev...................... St. Louis Blues	3.00	1.35	.40
☐ CC3	Felix Potvin....................... Toronto Maple Leafs	12.00	5.50	1.50
☐ CC4	Rob Zamuner...................... Tampa Bay Lightning	3.00	1.35	.40
☐ CC5	Scott Niedermayer .... New Jersey Devils	5.00	2.30	.60
☐ CC6	Eric Lindros....................... Philadelphia Flyers	20.00	9.00	2.50

☐ CC7	Alexei Zhitnik..................... Los Angeles Kings	5.00	2.30	.60
☐ CC8	Roman Hamrlik................... Tampa Bay Lightning	4.00	1.80	.50
☐ CC9	Joe Juneau .... Boston Bruins	8.00	3.60	1.00
☐ CC10	Teemu Selanne................. Winnipeg Jets	10.00	4.50	1.25
☐ CC11	Alexei Kovalev.................. New York Rangers	8.00	3.60	1.00
☐ CC12	Vladimir Malakhov........... New York Islanders	4.00	1.80	.50
☐ CC13	Darius Kasparaitis............ New York Islanders	3.00	1.35	.40
☐ CC14	Shawn McEachern........... Pittsburgh Penguins	3.00	1.35	.40
☐ CC15	Keith Tkachuk.................. Winnipeg Jets	6.00	2.70	.75
☐ CC16	Scott Lachance................ New York Islanders	3.00	1.35	.40
☐ CC17	Andrei Kovalenko............. Quebec Nordiques	3.00	1.35	.40
☐ CC18	Patrick Poulin .... Hartford Whalers	3.00	1.35	.40
☐ CC19	Evgeny Davydov .... Winnipeg Jets	3.00	1.35	.40
☐ CC20	Dimitri Yushkevich .... Philadelphia Flyers	3.00	1.35	.40

1992-93 Upper Deck Euro-Rookie Team

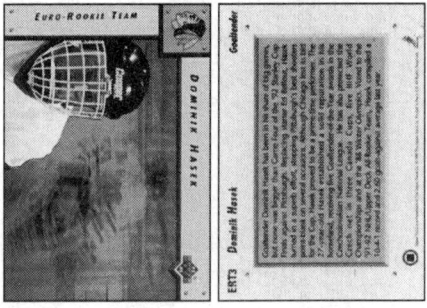

This six-card set was randomly inserted in 1992-93 Upper Deck low series packs. The cards measure the standard size (2 1/2" by 3 1/2") and feature cut-out color player photos superimposed on a hologram that shows the player in action. The horizontal fronts are bordered on the left and top by gray wood-textured panels. The team logo appears at the top left on a tan wood-textured panel. The horizontal backs feature a player profile on a tan background bordered by gray wood-textured panels. The cards are numbered on the back with an "ERT" prefix.

		MINT	EXC	G-VG
COMPLETE SET (6)........................		18.00	8.00	2.30
COMMON PLAYER (1-6).................		2.00	.90	.25
☐ 1	Pavel Bure............................ Vancouver Canucks	0.00	4.00	1.15
☐ 2	Nicklas Lidstrom .... Detroit Red Wings	2.00	.90	.25
☐ 3	Dominik Hasek...................... Chicago Blackhawks	6.00	2.70	.75
☐ 4	Peter Ahola.......................... Los Angeles Kings	2.00	.90	.25
☐ 5	Alexander Semak .... New Jersey Devils	2.00	.90	.25
☐ 6	Tomas Forslund .... Calgary Flames	2.00	.90	.25

1992-93 Upper Deck Euro-Rookies

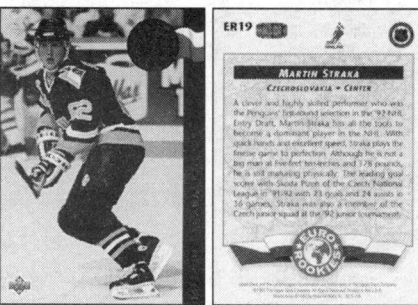

One per high series jumbo pack, this 20-card standard-size (2 1/2" by 3 1/2") set spotlights European born rookies. The color action player photos on the fronts are full-bleed except on the right side, where a black stripe carries the player's name in bronze foil lettering. At the upper right corner appears a bronze foil "Euro-Rookies" seal, with the flag of the player's country immediately to the right. The cards are numbered on the back with an "ER" prefix.

	MINT	EXC	G-VG
COMPLETE SET (20)	25.00	11.50	3.10
COMMON PLAYER (ER1-ER20)	1.00	.45	.13
☐ ER1 Richard Smehlik Buffalo Sabres	1.00	.45	.13
☐ ER2 Mikael Nylander Hartford Whalers	1.50	.65	.19
☐ ER3 Igor Korolev St. Louis Blues	1.00	.45	.13
☐ ER4 Robert Lang Los Angeles Kings	1.00	.45	.13
☐ ER5 Sergei Krivokrasov Chicago Blackhawks	1.50	.65	.19
☐ ER6 Teemu Selanne Winnipeg Jets	7.00	3.10	.85
☐ ER7 Darius Kasparaitis New York Islanders	1.50	.65	.19
☐ ER8 Alexei Zhamnov Winnipeg Jets	4.00	1.80	.50
☐ ER9 Jiri Slegr Vancouver Canucks	1.00	.45	.13
☐ ER10 Alexei Kovalev New York Rangers	5.00	2.30	.60
☐ ER11 Roman Hamrlik Tampa Bay Lightning	1.50	.65	.19
☐ ER12 Dimitri Yushkevich Philadelphia Flyers	1.50	.65	.19
☐ ER13 Alexei Zhitnik Los Angeles Kings	1.50	.65	.19
☐ ER14 Andrei Kovalenko Quebec Nordiques	1.50	.65	.19
☐ ER15 Vladimir Malakhov New York Islanders	1.50	.65	.19
☐ ER16 Sandis Ozolinsh San Jose Sharks	3.00	1.35	.40
☐ ER17 Evgeny Davydov Winnipeg Jets	1.00	.45	.13
☐ ER18 Viktor Gordijuk Buffalo Sabres	1.00	.45	.13
☐ ER19 Martin Straka Pittsburgh Penguins	3.00	1.35	.40
☐ ER20 Robert Petrovicky Hartford Whalers	1.00	.45	.13

1992-93 Upper Deck Euro-Stars

This 20-card set, issued one per low series jumbo pack, measures the standard size (2 1/2" by 3 1/2") and features action color player photos with a silver foil border. The borders are prone to chipping. The pictures are silver-foil

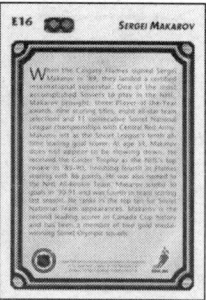

stamped with the player's name and with the "Euro Stars" emblem which hangs down from a white, red, and blue ribbon at the upper right corner. The backs display player profile information against a light gray panel with a black, silver, and gold frame design. The cards are numbered on the back with an "E" prefix.

	MINT	EXC	G-VG
COMPLETE SET (20)	40.00	18.00	5.00
COMMON PLAYER (E1-E20)	1.50	.65	.19
☐ E1 Sergei Fedorov Detroit Red Wings	6.00	2.70	.75
☐ E2 Pavel Bure Vancouver Canucks	10.00	4.50	1.25
☐ E3 Dominik Hasek Chicago Blackhawks	5.00	2.30	.60
☐ E4 Vladimir Ruzicka Boston Bruins	1.50	.65	.19
☐ E5 Peter Ahola Los Angeles Kings	1.50	.65	.19
☐ E6 Kyosti Karjalainen Los Angeles Kings	1.50	.65	.19
☐ E7 Igor Kravchuk Chicago Blackhawks	1.50	.65	.19
☐ E8 Evgeny Davydov Winnipeg Jets	1.50	.65	.19
☐ E9 Nicklas Lidstrom Detroit Red Wings	2.00	.90	.25
☐ E10 Vlad. Konstantinov Detroit Red Wings	1.50	.65	.19
☐ E11 Josef Beranek Edmonton Oilers	2.00	.90	.25
☐ E12 Valeri Zelepukin New Jersey Devils	1.75	.80	.22
☐ E13 Sergei Nemchinov New York Rangers	1.75	.80	.22
☐ E14 Jaromir Jagr Pittsburgh Penguins	5.00	2.30	.60
☐ E15 Igor Ulanov Winnipeg Jets	1.50	.65	.19
☐ E16 Sergei Makarov Calgary Flames	1.75	.80	.22
☐ E17 Andrei Lomakin Philadelphia Flyers	1.50	.65	.19
☐ E18 Mats Sundin Quebec Nordiques	4.00	1.80	.50
☐ E19 Jarmo Myllys San Jose Sharks	1.50	.65	.19
☐ E20 Valeri Kamensky Quebec Nordiques	2.00	.90	.25

1992-93 Upper Deck Wayne Gretzky Heroes

Randomly inserted in low series foil packs, this ten-card "Hockey Heroes" set pays tribute to Wayne Gretzky by chronicling his career. The cards are numbered on the back and measure the standard size (2 1/2" by 3 1/2"). Inside white borders on a gray ice background, the fronts display color photos that are cut out to fit a emblem design. On a gray ice background accented by black, the backs capture

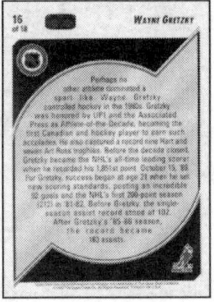

'..ghlights in Gretzky's career. The cards are numbered on the back.

	MINT	EXC	G-VG
COMPLETE SET (10)	50.00	23.00	6.25
COMMON GRETZKY (10-18)	5.00	2.30	.60
☐ 10 The Untouchable Greyhound	5.00	2.30	.60
☐ 11 17-Year-Old Pro	5.00	2.30	.60
☐ 12 Hart Trophy in NHL Debut	5.00	2.30	.60
☐ 13 Four Cups in Five Seasons	5.00	2.30	.60
☐ 14 Wrapped In The Maple Leaf	5.00	2.30	.60
☐ 15 The Trade That Rocked Sports	5.00	2.30	.60
☐ 16 Athlete-Of-The-Decade	5.00	2.30	.60
☐ 17 New Goals	5.00	2.30	.60
☐ 18 Checklist	5.00	2.30	.60
☐ NNO Title/Header Card SP	12.00	5.50	1.50

1992-93 Upper Deck Gordie Howe Heroes

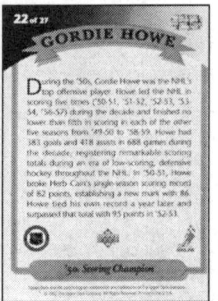

Randomly inserted in high series foil packs, this ten-card "Hockey Heroes" set showcases Gordie Howe, the NHL's former all-time leader in goals, assists, and points. The cards measure the standard size (2 1/2" by 3 1/2"). The backs capture highlights in Howe's career. The cards are numbered on the back and continue from where the Gretzky Heroes left off.

	MINT	EXC	G-VG
COMPLETE SET (10)	20.00	9.00	2.50
COMMON HOWE (19-27)	2.00	.90	.25
☐ 19 Gordie Howe The Early Years	2.00	.90	.25
☐ 20 Gordie Howe Dynasty in Detroit	2.00	.90	.25
☐ 21 Gordie Howe The First Production Line	2.00	.90	.25

	MINT	EXC	G-VG
☐ 22 Gordie Howe '50s Scoring Champion	2.00	.90	.25
☐ 23 Gordie Howe Six-time Hart Trophy Winner	2.00	.90	.25
☐ 24 Gordie Howe Hall of Fame	2.00	.90	.25
☐ 25 Gordie Howe The Comeback	2.00	.90	.25
☐ 26 Gordie Howe Wayne Gretzky "Mr. Hockey" and "The Great One"	2.00	.90	.25
☐ 27 Checklist Card (Artwork by Steve Cusano)	2.00	.90	.25
☐ NNO Cover/Header Card SP	6.00	2.70	.75

1992-93 Upper Deck Gordie Howe Selects

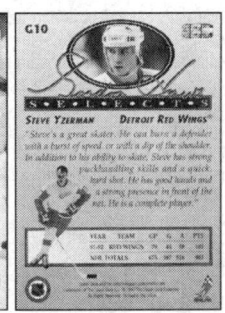

Randomly inserted throughout U.S. high series hobby packs only, this 20-card set features Gordie Howe's selections of ten current NHL superstars and ten rookies he believes are the NHL's best. The cards measure the standard size (2 1/2" by 3 1/2"). The fronts carry full-bleed color player photos. Howe's signature in gold foil sits on top of a black bar (carrying the word "Selects") toward the bottom of the picture, with the player's name and position immediately below. The backs have a color head shot in an oval and a quote of Howe's evaluation of the player's strengths. A small color player cut-out of Howe and the player's statistics complete the back. The cards are numbered on the back with a "G" prefix.

	MINT	EXC	G-VG
COMPLETE SET (20)	100.00	45.00	12.50
COMMON PLAYER (1-20)	3.50	1.55	.45
☐ 1 Brian Bellows Montreal Canadiens	4.00	1.80	.50
☐ 2 Luc Robitaille Los Angeles Kings	5.00	2.30	.60
☐ 3 Pat LaFontaine Buffalo Sabres	6.00	2.70	.75
☐ 4 Kevin Stevens Pittsburgh Penguins	5.00	2.30	.60
☐ 5 Wayne Gretzky Los Angeles Kings	20.00	9.00	2.50
☐ 6 Steve Larmer Chicago Blackhawks	4.00	1.80	.50
☐ 7 Brett Hull St. Louis Blues	8.00	3.60	1.00
☐ 8 Jeremy Roenick Chicago Blackhawks	9.00	4.00	1.15
☐ 9 Mario Lemieux Pittsburgh Penguins	15.00	6.75	1.90
☐ 10 Steve Yzerman Detroit Red Wings	8.00	3.60	1.00
☐ 11 Joe Juneau Boston Bruins	9.00	4.00	1.15
☐ 12 Vladimir Malakhov New York Islanders	4.00	1.80	.50

		MINT	EXC	G-VG
☐ 13	Alexei Kovalev	8.00	3.60	1.00
	New York Rangers			
☐ 14	Eric Lindros	20.00	9.00	2.50
	Philadelphia Flyers			
☐ 15	Teemu Selanne	10.00	4.50	1.25
	Winnipeg Jets			
☐ 16	Patrick Poulin	3.50	1.55	.45
	Hartford Whalers			
☐ 17	Shawn McEachern	3.50	1.55	.45
	Pittsburgh Penguins			
☐ 18	Keith Tkachuk	6.00	2.70	.75
	New York Islanders			
☐ 19	Andrei Kovalenko	3.50	1.55	.45
	Quebec Nordiques			
☐ 20	Ted Donato	3.50	1.55	.45
	Boston Bruins			

		MINT	EXC	G-VG
☐ WG14	Trevor Linden	7.00	3.10	.85
	Vancouver Canucks			
☐ WG15	Brian Leetch	8.00	3.60	1.00
	New York Rangers			
☐ WG16	Sergei Fedorov	12.00	5.50	1.50
	Detroit Red Wings			
☐ WG17	Mats Sundin	6.00	2.70	.75
	Quebec Nordiques			
☐ WG18	Alexander Mogilny	8.00	3.60	1.00
	Buffalo Sabres			
☐ WG19	Jeremy Roenick	9.00	4.00	1.15
	Chicago Blackhawks			
☐ WG20	Luc Robitaille	5.00	2.30	.60
	Los Angeles Kings			

1992-93 Upper Deck World Junior Grads

1992-93 Upper Deck Sheets

Randomly inserted in Canadian high series foil packs, this 20-card standard-size (2 1/2" by 3 1/2") set features top players in the world who have participated in the IIHF Junior Championships. Beneath a black stripe carrying the player's name, the fronts display full-bleed color action player photos. The top portion of a globe and the words "World Junior Grads" are silver foil-stamped at the bottom of the picture. On the backs, a full-size globe serves as a panel for displaying a career summary and a color action player cut-out. The back also includes the year the player participated in the IIHF World Junior Championships. The cards are numbered on the back with a "WG" prefix.

	MINT	EXC	G-VG
COMPLETE SET (20)	100.00	45.00	12.50
COMMON PLAYER (WG1-WG20)	3.50	1.55	.45

		MINT	EXC	G-VG
☐ WG1	Scott Niedermayer	5.00	2.30	.60
	New Jersey Devils			
☐ WG2	Vyacheslav Kozlov	9.00	4.00	1.15
	Detroit Red Wings			
☐ WG3	Chris Chelios	3.50	1.55	.45
	Chicago Blackhawks			
☐ WG4	Jari Kurri	3.50	1.55	.45
	Los Angeles Kings			
☐ WG5	Pavel Bure	15.00	6.75	1.90
	Vancouver Canucks			
☐ WG6	Jaromir Jagr	9.00	4.00	1.15
	Pittsburgh Penguins			
☐ WG7	Steve Yzerman	8.00	3.60	1.00
	Detroit Red Wings			
☐ WG8	Joe Sakic	6.00	2.70	.75
	Quebec Nordiques			
☐ WG9	Alexei Kovalev	8.00	3.60	1.00
	New York Rangers			
☐ WG10	Wayne Gretzky	20.00	9.00	2.50
	Los Angeles Kings			
☐ WG11	Mario Lemieux	15.00	6.75	1.90
	Pittsburgh Penguins			
☐ WG12	Eric Lindros	20.00	9.00	2.50
	Philadelphia Flyers			
☐ WG13	Pat Falloon	5.00	2.30	.60
	San Jose Sharks			

For the third straight year, Upper Deck produced hockey commemorative sheets that were given away during the 1992-93 season at selected games in large arenas. Each sheet measures 8 1/2" by 11" and is printed on card stock. The fronts of the team commemorative sheets feature a series of Upper Deck cards of star players on a particular team and the team logo. The 1993 All-Star Game sheets feature a series of Upper Deck cards of players that participated in the All-Star Game. All the sheets have an Upper Deck stamp indicating the production quota and the serial number. The backs of the sheets are blank. The players are listed as they appear from left to right.

	MINT	EXC	G-VG
COMPLETE SET (17)	175.00	70.00	18.00
COMMON SHEET (1-17)	10.00	4.00	1.00

		MINT	EXC	G-VG
☐ 1	'91-92 All-Rookie Team	15.00	6.00	1.50
	June 1992 (17,000)			
	Gilbert Dionne			
	Kevin Todd			
	Vladimir Konstantinov			
	Tony Amonte			
	Nicklas Lidstrom			
	Dominik Hasek			
☐ 2	New York Rangers	10.00	4.00	1.00
	Defending Season Champs			
	Undated (18,000)			
	Peter Andersson			
	Phil Bourque			
	Joe Kocur			
	Doug Weight			
	Randy Gilhen			
	John Vanbiesbrouck			
	Adam Graves			
	Mark Messier			
☐ 3	Gordie Howe Birthday	10.00	4.00	1.00
	Undated (NNO)			

65th Birthday
Celebration Tour
(Nine Howe Hockey Heroes
Cards Pictured)

☐ 4 Gordie Howe Birthday 10.00 4.00 1.00
Undated (NNO)
Hamilton McDonald's

☐ 5 Wayne Gretzky Heroes 15.00 6.00 1.50
Mail-In (NNO)

☐ 6 New York Rangers 10.00 4.00 1.00
vs. Quebec Nordiques
Oct. 29, 1992 (18,000)
Paul Broten
Mike Richter
Sergei Nemchinov
Tie Domi
Kris King
Jeff Beukeboom
Brian Leetch Norris
Tony Amonte

☐ 7 Los Angeles Kings 12.00 5.00 1.20
vs. Vancouver Canucks
Nov. 12, 1992 (18,000)
Luc Robitaille
Paul Coffey
Tony Granato
Rob Blake
Tomas Sandstrom
Kelly Hrudey

☐ 8 Minnesota North Stars 15.00 6.00 1.50
vs. San Jose Sharks
Nov. 28, 1992 (16,500)

☐ 9 Edmonton Oilers 10.00 4.00 1.00
vs. Calgary Flames
Dec. 8, 1992 (18,500)
Brian Glynn
Scott Mellanby
Dave Manson
Craig MacTavish
Bernie Nicholls
Bill Ranford

☐ 10 Philadelphia Flyers 10.00 4.00 1.00
vs. Pittsburgh Penguins
Dec. 17, 1992 (19,000)
Kevin Dineen
Mark Recchi
Garry Galley
Dominic Roussel
Brian Benning
Rod Brind'Amour

☐ 11 Minnesota North Stars 12.00 5.00 1.20
vs. Tampa Bay Lightning
Jan. 30, 1993 (16,500)
Dave Gagner
Neal Broten
Ulf Dahlen
Todd Elik
Tommy Sjodin
Gaetan Duchesne

☐ 12 Campbell All-Stars 10.00 4.00 1.00
Montreal Forum
Feb. 6, 1993 (NNO)
Ed Belfour
Paul Coffey
Chris Chelios
Steve Yzerman
Brett Hull
Pavel Bure

☐ 13 Wales All-Stars 10.00 4.00 1.00
Montreal Forum
Feb. 6, 1993 (NNO)
Patrick Roy
Brian Leetch
Ray Bourque
Kevin Stevens
Mario Lemieux
Jaromir Jagr

☐ 14 Washington Capitals 10.00 4.00 1.00
vs. St. Louis Blues
Feb. 21, 1993 (17,000)
Jim Hrivnak
Mike Ridley
Peter Bondra
Dale Hunter
Kelly Miller
Don Beaupre

☐ 15 Los Angeles Kings 12.00 5.00 1.20
vs. Ottawa Senators
Mar. 4, 1993 (18,000)
Jari Kurri
Corey Millen
Marty McSorley
Darryl Sydor
Wayne Gretzky

Robb Stauber

☐ 16 Quebec Nordiques 15.00 6.00 1.50
vs. Hartford Whalers
Mar. 8, 1993 (15,000)

☐ 17 St.Louis Blues 10.00 4.00 1.00
vs. Vancouver Canucks
Mar. 30, 1993 (17,500)

1992-93 Upper Deck Flyers Sheets

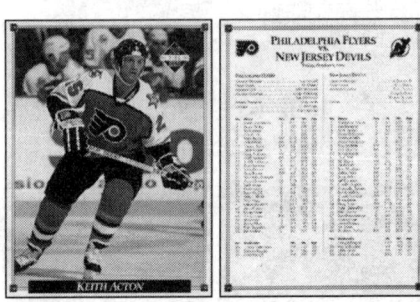

The 44 commemorative sheets in this set were distributed individually at Philadelphia Flyers games during the 1992-93 season in Flyer magazine. The sheets measure approximately 8 1/2" by 11" and feature color, posed and action, player photos with orange and white borders. A black bar with an orange accent stripe above it carries either the player's name or a picture title. On sheets with a title, the player's name is printed on the photo in either orange or white lettering. A black diamond design is printed with the individual sheet number and the production run. The backs display the game date and teams playing. All sheets are the Flyers versus another NHL team. The roster and management of each team is also given. The sheets are unnumbered and checklisted below in chronological order.

	MINT	EXC	G-VG
COMPLETE SET (44)	250.00	100.00	25.00
COMMON SHEET (1-44)	4.00	1.60	.40

☐ 1 Quebec Nordiques .... 5.00 2.00 .50
Sept. 19, 1992 (4,500)
Kevin Dineen

☐ 2 New Jersey Devils .... 4.00 1.60 .40
Sept. 24, 1992 (4,500)
Brian Benning

☐ 3 Washington Capitals 10.00 4.00 1.00
Oct. 3, 1992 (4,500)
Mark Recchi

☐ 4 New Jersey Devils .... 4.00 1.60 .40
Oct. 9, 1992 (7,500)
Keith Acton

☐ 5 New York Islanders .... 7.50 3.00 .75
Oct. 15, 1992 (4,500)
Rod Brind'Amour

☐ 6 Winnipeg Jets .... 5.00 2.00 .50
Oct. 18, 1992 (4,500)
Dave Brown

☐ 7 Vancouver Canucks .... 7.50 3.00 .75
Oct. 22, 1992 (4,500)
Dominic Roussel

☐ 8 Montreal Canadiens .... 4.00 1.60 .40
Oct. 24, 1992 (4,500)
Gord Hynes

☐ 9 St. Louis Blues .... 4.00 1.60 .40
Nov. 7, 1992 (4,500)
Claude Boivin

☐ 10 New York Islanders .... 6.00 2.40 .60
Nov. 12, 1992 (4,500)
Dimitri Yushkevich

☐ 11 Ottawa Senators 40.00 16.00 4.00
Nov. 15, 1992 (5,500)
Eric Lindros

☐ 12 New York Rangers .... 4.00 1.60 .40
Nov. 19, 1992 (4,500)

Steve Kasper
- [ ] 13 Buffalo Sabres.................. 12.00 5.00 1.20
  Nov. 22, 1992 (4,500)
  1992-93 Team Picture
- [ ] 14 New York Islanders.............. 4.00 1.60 .40
  Nov. 27, 1992 (5,500)
  Greg Paslawski
- [ ] 15 Quebec Nordiques.............. 4.00 1.60 .40
  Dec. 3, 1992 (4,500)
  Terry Carkner
- [ ] 16 Boston Bruins...................... 4.00 1.60 .40
  Dec. 6, 1992 (4,500)
  Shawn Cronin
- [ ] 17 Washington Capitals .... 5.00 2.00 .50
  Dec. 12, 1992 (4,500)
  Brent Fedyk
- [ ] 18 Pittsburgh Penguins .... 5.00 2.00 .50
  Dec. 17, 1992 (4,500)
  Garry Galley
- [ ] 19 Chicago Blackhawks .... 5.00 2.00 .50
  Dec. 19, 1992 (5,000)
  Andrei Lomakin
- [ ] 20 Pittsburgh Penguins .... 5.00 2.00 .50
  Dec. 23, 1992 (5,500)
  Bill and Kevin Dineen
- [ ] 21 Washington Capitals .... 4.00 1.60 .40
  Jan. 7, 1993 (4,500)
  Stephane Beauregard
- [ ] 22 New York Rangers 10.00 4.00 1.00
  Jan. 9, 1993 (6,000)
  Mark Recchi
- [ ] 23 Edmonton Oilers .... 4.00 1.60 .40
  Jan. 10, 1993 (5,000)
  Ryan McGill
- [ ] 24 Calgary Flames.................... 4.00 1.60 .40
  Jan. 14, 1993 (6,500)
  Doug Evans
- [ ] 25 Detroit Red Wings............... 6.00 2.40 .60
  Jan. 17, 1993 (5,000)
  The Captains
  Kevin Dineen
  Keith Acton
  Terry Carkner
- [ ] 26 Boston Bruins .... 4.00 1.60 .40
  Jan. 21, 1993 (5,000)
  Ric Nattress
- [ ] 27 Hartford Whalers.................. 7.50 3.00 .75
  Jan. 24, 1993 (5,000)
  Rod Brind'Amour
- [ ] 28 Buffalo Sabres.................... 6.00 2.40 .60
  Jan. 26, 1993 (5,000)
  Tommy Soderstrom
- [ ] 29 Quebec Nordiques............... 4.00 1.60 .40
  Jan. 28, 1993 (5,000)
  Pelle Eklund
- [ ] 30 Ottawa Senators.................. 5.00 2.00 .50
  Feb. 9, 1993 (5,000)
  Dave Brown
- [ ] 31 Montreal Canadiens 20.00 8.00 2.00
  Feb. 11, 1993 (5,500)
  The Rookies
  Tommy Soderstrom
  Dimitri Yushkevich
  Dominic Roussel
  Ryan McGill
  Eric Lindros
- [ ] 32 New Jersey Devils............... 6.00 2.40 .60
  Feb. 14, 1993 (5,000)
  Josef Beranek
- [ ] 33 New Jersey Devils............... 4.00 1.60 .40
  Feb. 25, 1993 (6,000)
  Greg Paslawski
- [ ] 34 New York Islanders.............. 4.00 1.60 .40
  Feb. 27, 1993 (5,000)
  The Coaches
  Craig Hartsburg
  Bill Dineen
  Ken Hitchcock
- [ ] 35 Pittsburgh Penguins .... 4.00 1.60 .40
  Mar. 2, 1993 (5,000)
  Keith Acton
- [ ] 36 Washington Capitals 10.00 4.00 1.00
  Mar. 11, 1993 (5,500)
  NHL All-Star
  Mark Recchi
- [ ] 37 Los Angeles Kings .... 5.00 2.00 .50
  Mar. 13, 1993 (5,500)
  Garry Galley
- [ ] 38 Minnesota North Stars .... 4.00 1.60 .40
  Mar. 16, 1993 (5,000)
  Terry Carkner
- [ ] 39 New Jersey Devils................ 7.50 3.00 .75
  Mar. 21, 1993 (5,000)
  Dominic Roussel

- [ ] 40 San Jose Sharks .... 4.00 1.60 .40
  Mar. 25, 1993 (5,000)
  Greg Hawgood
- [ ] 41 Tampa Bay Lightning .... 6.00 2.40 .60
  Apr. 3, 1993 (5,500)
  Viacheslav Butsayev
- [ ] 42 Toronto Maple Leafs 20.00 8.00 2.00
  Apr. 4, 1993 (6,000)
  Crazy 8's
  Mark Recchi
  Eric Lindros
  Brent Fedyk
- [ ] 43 Washington Capitals .... 7.50 3.00 .75
  Apr. 8, 1993 (5,500)
  European Style
  Andrei Lomakin
  Dimitri Yushkevich
  Viacheslav Butsayev
- [ ] 44 New York Rangers 10.00 4.00 1.00
  Apr. 12, 1993 (5,500)
  Hockey Hall of Famers
  Bob Clarke
  Ed Snider
  Bill Barber
  Bernie Parent
  Keith Allen

1992-93 Upper Deck McDonald's

Produced by Upper Deck for McDonald's of Canada, this set consists of 27 regular cards and six hologram cards in honor of 33 of hockey's most exciting players. Four-card packs were available for 39 cents plus tax with a purchase at participating McDonald's restaurants. All cards measure the standard size (2 1/2" by 3 1/2"). The regular cards feature color action photos of the players in their 1992 All-Star uniforms. A black border, which edges the photo on three sides, contains the player's name and position. Featuring six NHL post-season First Team All-Stars, the six hologram cards were randomly inserted in a limited number of card packs. The full-bleed cards feature a small, cut-out action player photos against a facial shot. The player's name appears in a stripe across the bottom. The backs of the regular cards and holograms are identical, each showing a narrow, vertical player photo against a white background with a bilingual (English and French) player profile to the right. The regular cards are arranged according to conference: Campbell (1-14) and Wales (15-27). The cards are numbered on the back with an "McD" prefix.

	MINT	EXC	G-VG
COMPLETE SET (34)......................	25.00	10.00	2.50
COMMON PLAYER (1-27)............	.35	.14	.03
COMMON HOLOGRAM (H1-H6)	1.00	.40	.10

- [ ] 1 Ed Belfour .... 1.00 .40 .10
- [ ] 2 Brian Bellows .... .35 .14 .03
- [ ] 3 Chris Chelios........................... .50 .20 .05
- [ ] 4 Vincent Damphousse .... .50 .20 .05
- [ ] 5 Dave Ellett............................. .35 .14 .03
- [ ] 6 Sergei Fedorov .... 2.00 .80 .20

☐	7	Theoren Fleury	.50	.20	.05
☐	8	Phil Housley	.50	.20	.05
☐	9	Trevor Linden	.75	.30	.07
☐	10	Al MacInnis	.75	.30	.07
☐	11	Adam Oates	1.00	.40	.10
☐	12	Luc Robitaille	1.25	.50	.12
☐	13	Jeremy Roenick	1.50	.60	.15
☐	14	Steve Yzerman	1.25	.50	.12
☐	15	Don Beaupre	.35	.14	.03
☐	16	Rod Brind'Amour	.50	.20	.05
☐	17	Paul Coffey	.75	.30	.07
☐	18	John Cullen	.35	.14	.03
☐	19	Kevin Hatcher	.50	.20	.05
☐	20	Jaromir Jagr	1.50	.60	.15
☐	21	Mario Lemieux	3.00	1.20	.30
☐	22	Alexander Mogilny	1.25	.50	.12
☐	23	Kirk Muller	.50	.20	.05
☐	24	Owen Nolan	.50	.20	.05
☐	25	Mike Richter	.75	.30	.07
☐	26	Joe Sakic	1.00	.40	.10
☐	27	Scott Stevens	.50	.20	.05
☐	H1	Mark Messier HOLO	2.00	.80	.20
☐	H2	Brett Hull HOLO	2.50	1.00	.25
☐	H3	Kevin Stevens HOLO	1.00	.40	.10
☐	H4	Brian Leetch HOLO	1.50	.60	.15
☐	H5	Ray Bourque HOLO	1.00	.40	.10
☐	H6	Patrick Roy HOLO	2.50	1.00	.25
☐	NNO	Checklist UER SP	1.00	.40	.10

(Bourque listed as 4
and Leetch as 5)

1992-93 Upper Deck
Best of the Blues

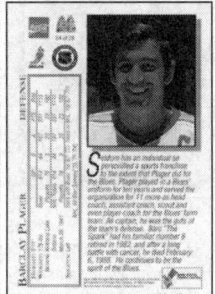

This 28-card set, subtitled "Best of the Blues" was distributed at McDonald's restaurants of St. Louis and Metro East and showcases St. Louis Blues' players from the past 25 years. Proceeds from the cards benefitted Ronald McDonald Children's Charities of St. Louis and Metro East. The cards were available in six-card packs for 99 cents with the purchase of any large sandwich, or any breakfast sandwich. The offer was valid through March 4. Also, 100 autographed Brett Hull cards were randomly inserted in the packs. The cards are standard size (2 1/2" by 3 1/2"). The fronts feature color action player photos. Black-and-white photos appear on the reverse of some cards. On Monday nights beginning on February 15 and running through March 30, "Best of the Blues" trading card nights were held at participating restaurants to enable collectors to assemble complete sets. In conjunction with these events, a giant Brett Hull card was raffled off at each restaurant on the last trading card night (March 30, 1993). Finally, a holder to display the set was available through a mail-in offer for 8.50. The fronts features color action player photos with silver borders that give a shadow effect against the white card face. The player's name is printed in a black stripe across the bottom. The Best of the Blues logo is superimposed over the picture at the upper left. The backs carry a small,

shadow-bordered, close-up photo. A player profile appears below the picture. Statistics are printed in a horizontally oriented box. The cards are numbered on the back.

		MINT	EXC	G-VG
COMPLETE SET (28)		35.00	14.00	3.50
COMMON PLAYER (1-28)		.75	.30	.07

☐	1	Glenn Hall	2.00	.80	.20
☐	2	Doug Gilmour	5.00	2.00	.50
☐	3	Al Arbour	1.00	.40	.10
☐	4	Mike Liut	1.00	.40	.10
☐	5	Blake Dunlop	.75	.30	.07
☐	6	Noel Picard	.75	.30	.07
☐	7	Bob Plager	1.25	.50	.12
☐	8	Ab McDonald	.75	.30	.07
☐	9	Curtis Joseph	2.50	1.00	.25
☐	10	Wayne Babych	.75	.30	.07
☐	11	Red Berenson	1.00	.40	.10
☐	12	Brett Hull	5.00	2.00	.50
☐	13	Bob Gassoff	1.00	.40	.10
☐	14	Bernie Federko	1.50	.60	.15
☐	15	Gary Sabourin	.75	.30	.07
☐	16	Joe Mullen	1.25	.50	.12
☐	17	Adam Oates	3.00	1.20	.30
☐	18	Jorgen Pettersson	.75	.30	.07
☐	19	Frank St. Marseille	.75	.30	.07
☐	20	Scott Stevens	1.50	.60	.15
☐	21	Rob Ramage	1.00	.40	.10
☐	22	Jacques Plante	2.50	1.00	.25
☐	23	Rick Meagher	.75	.30	.07
☐	24	Barclay Plager	1.25	.50	.12
☐	25	Brian Sutter	1.25	.50	.12
☐	26	Perry Turnbull	.75	.30	.07
☐	27	Garry Unger	1.00	.40	.10
☐	28	Checklist SP	6.00	2.40	.60

1993 Upper Deck Locker All-Stars

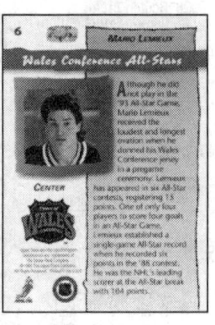

This 60-card set measures the standard size (2 1/2" by 3 1/2") and was issued as the 1992-93 Upper Deck NHL All-Star Locker Series. The set came in a plastic locker box. Personally signed Gordie Howe "Hockey Heroes" cards were randomly inserted throughout the locker boxes; the odds of finding one are one in 120 boxes. The fronts feature full-bleed, color, action player photos. The player's name is printed in gold foil above a blue and gold-foil curving stripe at the bottom. The 44th NHL All-Star game logo overlaps the stripe and is printed in the lower right corner. The backs carry a small, close-up picture within a bright blue rough-edged border that gives the effect of torn paper. This photo overlaps a gray panel with the same rough-edge look. This panel carries player profile information. After presenting the NHL All-Stars by conference, Campbell Conference All-Stars (1-18) and Wales Conference All-Stars (19-36), the set features the following special subsets, All-Star Skills Winners (37-40), All-Star Heroes (41-50), and Future All-Stars (51-60). The cards are numbered on the back. The card pictures for this set were taken during the 1993 NHL All-Star Weekend in Montreal.

	MINT	EXC	G-VG
COMPLETE SET (60).........................	10.00	4.00	1.00
COMMON PLAYER (1-60)................	.10	.04	.01

		MINT	EXC	G-VG
☐ 1	Peter Bondra.......................... Washington Capitals	.10	.04	.01
☐ 2	Steve Duchesne....................... Quebec Nordiques	.10	.04	.01
☐ 3	Jaromir Jagr .... Pittsburgh Penguins	.50	.20	.05
☐ 4	Pat LaFontaine .... Buffalo Sabres	.40	.16	.04
☐ 5	Brian Leetch........................... New York Rangers	.30	.12	.03
☐ 6	Mario Lemieux .... Pittsburgh Penguins	1.00	.40	.10
☐ 7	Mark Messier .... New York Rangers	.40	.16	.04
☐ 8	Alexander Mogilny .... Buffalo Sabres	.40	.16	.04
☐ 9	Kirk Muller............................ New Jersey Devils	.20	.08	.02
☐ 10	Adam Oates............................ St. Louis Blues	.30	.12	.03
☐ 11	Mark Recchi .... Philadelphia Flyers	.30	.12	.03
☐ 12	Patrick Roy .... Montreal Canadiens	1.00	.40	.10
☐ 13	Joe Sakic.............................. Quebec Nordiques	.30	.12	.03
☐ 14	Kevin Stevens .... Pittsburgh Penguins	.30	.12	.03
☐ 15	Scott Stevens .... New Jersey Devils	.15	.06	.01
☐ 16	Rick Tocchet .... Pittsburgh Penguins	.15	.06	.01
☐ 17	Pierre Turgeon .... New York Islanders	.40	.16	.04
☐ 18	Zarley Zalapski .... Hartford Whalers	.10	.04	.01
☐ 19	Ed Belfour............................. Chicago Blackhawks	.40	.16	.04
☐ 20	Brian Bradley.......................... Tampa Bay Lightning	.10	.04	.01
☐ 21	Pavel Bure............................ Vancouver Canucks	1.25	.50	.12
☐ 22	Chris Chelios .... Chicago Blackhawks	.15	.06	.01
☐ 23	Paul Coffey .... Detroit Red Wings	.25	.10	.02
☐ 24	Doug Gilmour .... Toronto Maple Leafs	.50	.20	.05
☐ 25	Wayne Gretzky .... Los Angeles Kings	1.25	.50	.12
☐ 26	Phil Housley.......................... Winnipeg Jets	.15	.06	.01
☐ 27	Brett Hull............................. St. Louis Blues	.75	.30	.07
☐ 28	Kelly Kisio............................ San Jose Sharks	.10	.04	.01
☐ 29	Jari Kurri .... Los Angeles Kings	.15	.06	.01
☐ 30	Dave Manson .... Edmonton Oilers	.10	.04	.01
☐ 31	Mike Modano.......................... Minnesota North Stars	.30	.12	.03
☐ 32	Gary Roberts........................... Calgary Flames	.15	.06	.01
☐ 33	Luc Robitaille .... Los Angeles Kings	.30	.12	.03
☐ 34	Jeremy Roenick .... Chicago Blackhawks	.75	.30	.07
☐ 35	Teemu Selanne .... Winnipeg Jets	.75	.30	.07
☐ 36	Steve Yzerman .... Detroit Red Wings	.50	.20	.05
☐ 37	Al Iafrate .... Washington Capitals	.20	.08	.02
☐ 38	Mike Gartner .... New York Rangers	.25	.10	.02
☐ 39	Ray Bourque .... Boston Bruins	.30	.12	.03
☐ 40	Jon Casey .... Minnesota North Stars	.15	.06	.01
☐ 41	Bob Gainey............................	.15	.06	.01
☐ 42	Gordie Howe..........................	.60	.24	.06
☐ 43	Bobby Hull............................	.50	.20	.05
☐ 44	Frank Mahovlich.....................	.30	.12	.03
☐ 45	Lanny McDonald	.20	.08	.02
☐ 46	Stan Mikita............................	.25	.10	.02
☐ 47	Henri Richard	.25	.10	.02
☐ 48	Larry Robinson	.15	.06	.01
☐ 49	Glen Sather	.10	.04	.01
☐ 50	Bryan Trottier.......................	.20	.08	.02

		MINT	EXC	G-VG
☐ 51	Tony Amonte......................... New York Rangers	.20	.08	.02
☐ 52	Pat Falloon .... San Jose Sharks	.20	.08	.02
☐ 53	Joe Juneau............................ Boston Bruins	.60	.24	.06
☐ 54	Alexei Kovalev .... New York Rangers	.60	.24	.06
☐ 55	Dmitri Kvartalnov .... Boston Bruins	.20	.08	.02
☐ 56	Eric Lindros.......................... Philadelphia Flyers	1.50	.60	.15
☐ 57	Vladimir Malakhov .... New York Islanders	.30	.12	.03
☐ 58	Felix Potvin .... Toronto Maple Leafs	.75	.30	.07
☐ 59	Mats Sundin.......................... Quebec Nordiques	.50	.20	.05
☐ 60	Alexei Zhamnov...................... Winnipeg Jets	.40	.16	.04
☐ AU	Gordie Howe AU.................. (Certified autograph)	200.00	80.00	20.00

1993-94 Upper Deck

The 1993-94 Upper Deck hockey set contains 575 cards, measuring the standard size (2 1/2" by 3 1/2"). The set was released in two series of 310 and 265 cards respectively. The white-bordered fronts feature color action player photos with team color-coded inner borders. The player's name, position and team name are printed in the lower margins. The same border design continues on the backs, which carry color player photos in their upper portions. The player's biography, name, statistics, career highlights, and team logo follow below. Following subsets are included in this set: 100-Point Club (220-235), NHL Star Rookies (236-249), World Jr. Championships (Canada [250-260], Czechoslovakia [261-267], Finland [268-271], and Russia [272-279]), All-Rookie Team (280-285), and Team Point Leaders (286-309). After a World Junior Championships (530-568) subset, which is organized according to countries (Canada [531-550]; USA [551-568]; Sweden [570, 572]; Czechoslovakia [573]; Russia [571, 574]), the set closes with an All-World Junior Team subset (569-574). The cards are numbered on the back.

	MINT	EXC	G-VG
COMPLETE SET (575)..................	40.00	18.00	5.00
COMPLETE SERIES 1 (310).............	22.00	10.00	2.80
COMPLETE SERIES 2 (265).............	18.00	8.00	2.30
COMMON PLAYER (1-310)...........	.05	.02	.01
COMMON PLAYER (311-575).........	.05	.02	.01

		MINT	EXC	G-VG
☐ 1	Guy Hebert........................... Anaheim Mighty Ducks	.15	.07	.02
☐ 2	Bob Bassen .... St. Louis Blues	.05	.02	.01
☐ 3	Theoren Fleury .... Calgary Flames	.10	.05	.01
☐ 4	Ray Whitney.......................... San Jose Sharks	.08	.04	.01

☐ 5	Donald Audette	.05	.02	.01
	Buffalo Sabres			
☐ 6	Martin Rucinsky	.05	.02	.01
	Quebec Nordiques			
☐ 7	Lyle Odelein	.05	.02	.01
	Montreal Canadiens			
☐ 8	John Vanbiesbrouck	.15	.07	.02
	Florida Panthers			
☐ 9	Tim Cheveldae........................	.08	.04	.01
	Detroit Red Wings			
☐ 10	Jock Callander........................	.05	.02	.01
	Tampa Bay Lightning			
☐ 11	Nick Kypreos..........................	.05	.02	.01
	Hartford Whalers			
☐ 12	Jarrod Shalde..........................	.05	.02	.01
	Anaheim Mighty Ducks			
☐ 13	Gary Shuchuk	.05	.02	.01
	Los Angeles Kings			
☐ 14	Kris King	.05	.02	.01
	Winnipeg Jets			
☐ 15	Josef Beranek	.08	.04	.01
	Philadelphia Flyers			
☐ 16	Sean Hill	.05	.02	.01
	Anaheim Mighty Ducks			
☐ 17	Bob Kudelski..........................	.08	.04	.01
	Ottawa Senators			
☐ 18	Jiri Slegr	.05	.02	.01
	Vancouver Canucks			
☐ 19	Dmitri Kvartalnov	.05	.02	.01
	Boston Bruins			
☐ 20	Drake Berehowsky	.05	.02	.01
	Toronto Maple Leafs			
☐ 21	Jean Francois Quintin............	.05	.02	.01
	San Jose Sharks			
☐ 22	Randy Wood	.05	.02	.01
	Buffalo Sabres			
☐ 23	Jim McKenzie..........................	.05	.02	.01
	Hartford Whalers			
☐ 24	Steven King	.05	.02	.01
	Anaheim Mighty Ducks			
☐ 25	Scott Niedermayer	.15	.07	.02
	New Jersey Devils			
☐ 26	Alexander Andrijevski............	.05	.02	.01
	Chicago Blackhawks			
☐ 27	Alexei Kovalev	.40	.18	.05
	New York Rangers			
☐ 28	Steve Konowalchuk................	.05	.02	.01
	Washington Capitals			
☐ 29	Vladimir Malakhov	.15	.07	.02
	New York Islanders			
☐ 30	Eric Lindros............................	2.00	.90	.25
	Philadelphia Flyers			
☐ 31	Mathieu Schneider	.08	.04	.01
	Montreal Canadiens			
☐ 32	Russ Courtnall	.08	.04	.01
	Dallas Stars			
☐ 33	Ron Sutter..............................	.05	.02	.01
	St. Louis Blues			
☐ 34	Radek Hamr	.15	.07	.02
	Ottawa Senators			
☐ 35	Pavel Bure..............................	1.00	.45	.13
	Vancouver Canucks			
☐ 36	Joe Sacco	.05	.02	.01
	Anaheim Mighty Ducks			
☐ 37	Robert Petrovicky	.05	.02	.01
	Hartford Whalers			
☐ 38	Anatoli Fedotov	.15	.07	.02
	Anaheim Mighty Ducks			
☐ 39	Pat Falloon	.08	.04	.01
	San Jose Sharks			
☐ 40	Martin Straka	.40	.18	.05
	Pittsburgh Penguins			
☐ 41	Brad Werenka	.05	.02	.01
	Edmonton Oilers			
☐ 42	Mike Richter............................	.20	.09	.03
	New York Rangers			
☐ 43	Mike McPhee	.05	.02	.01
	Dallas Stars			
☐ 44	Sylvain Turgeon	.05	.02	.01
	Ottawa Senators			
☐ 45	Tom Barrasso	.08	.04	.01
	Pittsburgh Penguins			
☐ 46	Anatoli Semenov	.05	.02	.01
	Anaheim Mighty Ducks			
☐ 47	Joe Murphy.............................	.05	.02	.01
	Chicago Blackhawks			
☐ 48	Rob Pearson	.05	.02	.01
	Toronto Maple Leafs			
☐ 49	Patrick Roy	.60	.25	.08
	Montreal Canadiens			
☐ 50	Dallas Drake...........................	.20	.09	.03
	Detroit Red Wings			
☐ 51	Mark Messier	.15	.07	.02

	New York Rangers			
☐ 52	Scott Pellerin.........................	.15	.07	.02
	New Jersey Devils			
☐ 53	Teppo Numminen	.05	.02	.01
	Winnipeg Jets			
☐ 54	Chris Kontos	.05	.02	.01
	Tampa Bay Lightning			
☐ 55	Richard Matvichuk	.05	.02	.01
	Dallas Stars			
☐ 56	Dale Craigwell	.05	.02	.01
	San Jose Sharks			
☐ 57	Mike Eastwood.......................	.05	.02	.01
	Toronto Maple Leafs			
☐ 58	Bernie Nicholls.......................	.08	.04	.01
	New Jersey Devils			
☐ 59	Travis Green...........................	.05	.02	.01
	New York Islanders			
☐ 60	Shjon Podein..........................	.15	.07	.02
	Edmonton Oilers			
☐ 61	Darrin Madeley.......................	.20	.09	.03
	Ottawa Senators			
☐ 62	Dixon Ward	.05	.02	.01
	Vancouver Canucks			
☐ 63	Andre Faust............................	.05	.02	.01
	Philadelphia Flyers			
☐ 64	Tony Amonte..........................	.08	.04	.01
	New York Rangers			
☐ 65	Joe Cirella	.05	.02	.01
	Florida Panthers			
☐ 66	Michel Petit............................	.05	.02	.01
	Calgary Flames			
☐ 67	David Lowry............................	.05	.02	.01
	Florida Panthers			
☐ 68	Shawn Chambers....................	.05	.02	.01
	Tampa Bay Lightning			
☐ 69	Joe Sakic...............................	.20	.09	.03
	Quebec Nordiques			
☐ 70	Michael Nylander	.15	.07	.02
	Hartford Whalers			
☐ 71	Peter Andersson	.05	.02	.01
	New York Rangers			
☐ 72	Sandis Ozolinsh	.20	.09	.03
	San Jose Sharks			
☐ 73	Joby Messier..........................	.15	.07	.02
	New York Rangers			
☐ 74	John Blue...............................	.05	.02	.01
	Boston Bruins			
☐ 75	Pat Elynuik	.05	.02	.01
	Washington Capitals			
☐ 76	Keith Osborne	.10	.05	.01
	Tampa Bay Lightning			
☐ 77	Greg Adamas	.05	.02	.01
	Vancouver Canucks			
☐ 78	Chris Gratton.........................	.50	.23	.06
	Tampa Bay Lightning			
☐ 79	Louie DeBrusk........................	.05	.02	.01
	Edmonton Oilers			
☐ 80	Todd Harkins..........................	.10	.05	.01
	Calgary Flames			
☐ 81	Neil Brady	.05	.02	.01
	Ottawa Senators			
☐ 82	Philippe Boucher....................	.05	.02	.01
	Buffalo Sabres			
☐ 83	Darryl Sydor...........................	.08	.04	.01
	Los Angeles Kings			
☐ 84	Oleg Petrov............................	.20	.09	.03
	Montreal Canadiens			
☐ 85	Andrei Kovalenko	.15	.07	.02
	Quebec Nordiques			
☐ 86	Dave Andreychuk	.10	.05	.01
	Toronto Maple Leafs			
☐ 87	Jeff Daniels	.05	.02	.01
	Pittsburgh Penguins			
☐ 88	Kevin Todd	.05	.02	.01
	Edmonton Oilers			
☐ 89	Mark Tinordi	.05	.02	.01
	Dallas Stars			
☐ 90	Garry Galley	.05	.02	.01
	Philadelphia Flyers			
☐ 91	Shawn Burr............................	.05	.02	.01
	Detroit Red Wings			
☐ 92	Tom Pederson........................	.05	.02	.01
	San Jose Sharks			
☐ 93	Warren Rychel	.05	.02	.01
	Los Angeles Kings			
☐ 94	Stu Barnes	.05	.02	.01
	Winnipeg Jets			
☐ 95	Peter Bondra..........................	.08	.04	.01
	Washington Capitals			
☐ 96	Brian Skrudland	.05	.02	.01
	Florida Panthers			
☐ 97	Doug MacDonald	.15	.07	.02
	Buffalo Sabres			
☐ 98	Rob Niedermayer....................	.50	.23	.06

☐	Florida Panthers 99 Wayne Gretzky	1.00	.45	.13
☐	Los Angeles Kings 100 Peter Taglianetti	.05	.02	.01
☐	Pittsburgh Penguins 101 Don Sweeney	.05	.02	.01
☐	Boston Bruins 102 Andrei Lomakin	.05	.02	.01
☐	Florida Panthers 103 Checklist 1-103	.05	.02	.01
☐	104 Sergio Momesso	.05	.02	.01
☐	Vancouver Canucks 105 Dave Archibald	.05	.02	.01
☐	Ottawa Senators 106 Karl Dykhuis	.05	.02	.01
☐	Chicago Blackhawks 107 Scott Mellanby	.05	.02	.01
☐	Florida Panthers 108 Paul DiPietro	.05	.02	.01
☐	Montreal Canadiens 109 Neal Broten	.08	.04	.01
☐	Dallas Stars 110 Chris Terreri	.08	.04	.01
☐	New Jersey Devils 111 Craig MacTavish	.05	.02	.01
☐	Edmonton Oilers 112 Jody Hull	.05	.02	.01
☐	Ottawa Senators 113 Philippe Bozon	.05	.02	.01
☐	St. Louis Blues 114 Geoff Courtnall	.05	.02	.01
☐	Vancouver Canucks 115 Ed Olcyzk	.05	.02	.01
☐	New York Rangers 116 Ray Bourque	.15	.07	.02
☐	Boston Bruins 117 Gilbert Dionne	.05	.02	.01
☐	Montreal Canadiens 118 Valeri Kamensky	.15	.07	.02
☐	Quebec Nordiques 119 Scott Stevens	.08	.04	.01
☐	New Jersey Devils 120 Pelle Eklund	.05	.02	.01
☐	Philadelphia Flyers 121 Brian Bradley	.05	.02	.01
☐	Tampa Bay Lightning 122 Steve Thomas	.08	.04	.01
☐	New York Islanders 123 Don Beaupre	.08	.04	.01
☐	Washington Capitals 124 Joel Otto	.05	.02	.01
☐	Calgary Flames 125 Arturs Irbe	.35	.16	.04
☐	San Jose Sharks 126 Kevin Stevens	.20	.09	.03
☐	Pittsburgh Penguins 127 Dimitri Yushkevich	.05	.02	.01
☐	Philadelphia Flyers 128 Adam Graves	.25	.11	.03
☐	New York Rangers 129 Chris Chelios	.08	.04	.01
☐	Chicago Blackhawks 130 Jeff Brown	.08	.04	.01
☐	St. Louis Blues 131 Paul Ranheim	.05	.02	.01
☐	Calgary Flames 132 Shayne Corson	.05	.02	.01
☐	Edmonton Oilers 133 Curtis Leschyshyn	.05	.02	.01
☐	Quebec Nordiques 134 John MacLean	.08	.04	.01
☐	New Jersey Devils 135 Dimitri Khristich	.08	.04	.01
☐	Washington Capitals 136 Dino Ciccarelli	.08	.04	.01
☐	Detroit Red Wings 137 Pat LaFontaine	.20	.09	.03
☐	Buffalo Sabres 138 Patrick Poulin	.05	.02	.01
☐	Hartford Whalers 139 Jaromir Jagr	.40	.18	.05
☐	Pittsburgh Penguins 140 Kevin Hatcher	.08	.04	.01
☐	Washington Capitals 141 Christian Ruuttu	.05	.02	.01
☐	Chicago Blackhawks 142 Ulf Samuelsson	.08	.04	.01
☐	Pittsburgh Penguins 143 Ted Donato	.05	.02	.01
☐	Boston Bruins 144 Bob Essensa	.08	.04	.01
☐	Winnipeg Jets 145 Dave Gagner	.08	.04	.01
	Dallas Stars			

☐	146 Tony Granato	.05	.02	.01
☐	Los Angeles Kings 147 Ed Belfour	.20	.09	.03
☐	Chicago Blackhawks 148 Kirk Muller	.08	.04	.01
☐	Montreal Canadiens 149 Rob Gaudreau	.20	.09	.03
☐	San Jose Sharks 150 Nicklas Lidstrom	.08	.04	.01
☐	Detroit Red Wings 151 Gary Roberts	.08	.04	.01
☐	Calgary Flames 152 Trent Klatt	.05	.02	.01
☐	Dallas Stars 153 Ray Ferraro	.05	.02	.01
☐	New York Islanders 154 Michal Pivonka	.05	.02	.01
☐	Washington Capitals 155 Mike Foligno	.05	.02	.01
☐	Toronto Maple Leafs 156 Kirk McLean	.10	.05	.01
☐	Vancouver Canucks 157 Curtis Joseph	.20	.09	.03
☐	St. Louis Blues 158 Roman Hamrlik	.15	.07	.02
☐	Tampa Bay Lightning 159 Felix Potvin	1.00	.45	.13
☐	Toronto Maple Leafs 160 Brett Hull	.50	.23	.06
☐	St. Louis Blues 161 Alexei Zhitnik	.15	.07	.02
☐	Los Angeles Kings 162 Alexei Zhamnov	.30	.14	.04
☐	Winnipeg Jets 163 Grant Fuhr	.08	.04	.01
☐	Buffalo Sabres 164 Nikolai Borschevsky	.15	.07	.02
☐	Toronto Maple Leafs 165 Tomas Jelinek	.05	.02	.01
☐	Ottawa Senators 166 Thomas Steen	.05	.02	.01
☐	Winnipeg Jets 167 John LeClair	.05	.02	.01
☐	Montreal Canadiens 168 Vladimir Vujtek	.05	.02	.01
☐	Edmonton Oilers 169 Richard Smehlik	.08	.04	.01
☐	Buffalo Sabres 170 Alexandre Daigle	.60	.25	.08
☐	Ottawa Senators 171 Sergei Fedorov	.75	.35	.09
☐	Detroit Red Wings 172 Steve Larmer	.08	.04	.01
☐	Chicago Blackhawks 173 Darius Kasparaitis	.05	.02	.01
☐	New York Islanders 174 Igor Kravchuk	.05	.02	.01
☐	Edmonton Oilers 175 Owen Nolan	.08	.04	.01
☐	Quebec Nordiques 176 Rob Dimaio	.05	.02	.01
☐	Tampa Bay Lightning 177 Mike Vernon	.08	.04	.01
☐	Calgary Flames 178 Alexander Semak	.05	.02	.01
☐	New Jersey Devils 179 Rick Tocchet	.08	.04	.01
☐	Pittsburgh Penguins 180 Bill Ranford	.08	.04	.01
☐	Edmonton Oilers 181 Sergei Zubov	.40	.18	.05
☐	New York Rangers 182 Tommy Soderstrom	.15	.07	.02
☐	Philadelphia Flyers 183 Al Iafrate	.08	.04	.01
☐	Washington Capitals 184 Eric Desjardins	.05	.02	.01
☐	Montreal Canadiens 185 Bret Hedican	.05	.02	.01
☐	St. Louis Blues 186 Joe Mullen	.08	.04	.01
☐	Pittsburgh Penguins 187 Doug Bodger	.05	.02	.01
☐	Buffalo Sabres 188 Tomas Sandstrom	.05	.02	.01
☐	Los Angeles Kings 189 Glen Murray	.05	.02	.01
☐	Boston Bruins 190 Chris Pronger	.50	.23	.06
☐	Hartford Whalers 191 Mike Craig	.05	.02	.01
☐	Dallas Stars 192 Jim Paek	.05	.02	.01

Pittsburgh Penguins				
☐ 193 Doug Zmolek	.05	.02	.01
San Jose Sharks				
☐ 194 Yves Racine	.05	.02	.01
Detroit Red Wings				
☐ 195 Keith Thachuk	.20	.09	.03
Winnipeg Jets				
☐ 196 Chris Lindberg	.05	.02	.01
Calgary Flames				
☐ 197 Kelly Buchberger	.05	.02	.01
Edmonton Oilers				
☐ 198 Mark Janssens	.05	.02	.01
Hartford Whalers				
☐ 199 Peter Zezel	.05	.02	.01
Toronto Maple Leafs				
☐ 200 Bob Probert	.05	.02	.01
Detroit Red Wings				
☐ 201 Brad May	.05	.02	.01
Buffalo Sabres				
☐ 202 Rob Zamuner	.05	.02	.01
Tampa Bay Lightning				
☐ 203 Stephane Fiset	.05	.02	.01
Quebec Nordiques				
☐ 204 Derian Hatcher	.05	.02	.01
Dallas Stars				
☐ 205 Mike Gartner	.10	.05	.01
New York Rangers				
☐ 206 Checklist 104-206	.05	.02	.01
☐ 207 Todd Krygier	.05	.02	.01
Washington Capitals				
☐ 208 Glen Wesley	.05	.02	.01
Boston Bruins				
☐ 209 Fredrik Olausson	.05	.02	.01
Winnipeg Jets				
☐ 210 Patrick Flatley	.05	.02	.01
New York Islanders				
☐ 211 Cliff Ronning	.05	.02	.01
Vancouver Canucks				
☐ 212 Kevin Dineen	.08	.04	.01
Philadelphia Flyers				
☐ 213 Zarley Zalapski	.05	.02	.01
Hartford Whalers				
☐ 214 Stephane Matteau	.05	.02	.01
Chicago Blackhawks				
☐ 215 Dave Ellett	.05	.02	.01
Toronto Maple Leafs				
☐ 216 Kelly Hrudey	.08	.04	.01
Los Angeles Kings				
☐ 217 Steve Duchesne	.08	.04	.01
Quebec Nordiques				
☐ 218 Bobby Holik	.05	.02	.01
New Jersey Devils				
☐ 219 Brad Dalgarno	.05	.02	.01
New York Islanders				
☐ 220 Mats Sundin 100 CL	.10	.05	.01
Quebec Nordiques				
☐ 221 Pat LaFontaine 100	.15	.07	.02
Buffalo Sabres				
☐ 222 Mark Recchi 100	.10	.05	.01
Philadelphia Flyers				
☐ 223 Joe Sakic 100	.10	.05	.01
Quebec Nordiques				
☐ 224 Pierre Turgeon 100	.10	.05	.01
New York Islanders				
☐ 225 Craig Janney 100	.08	.04	.01
St. Louis Blues				
☐ 226 Adam Oates 100	.10	.05	.01
Boston Bruins				
☐ 227 Steve Yzerman 100	.15	.07	.02
Detroit Red Wings				
☐ 228 Mats Sundin 100	.10	.05	.01
Quebec Nordiques				
☐ 229 Theoren Fleury 100	.08	.04	.01
Calgary Flames				
☐ 230 Kevin Stevens 100	.10	.05	.01
Pittsburgh Penguins				
☐ 231 Luc Robitaille 100	.10	.05	.01
Los Angeles Kings				
☐ 232 Brett Hull 100	.25	.11	.03
St. Louis Blues				
☐ 233 Rick Tocchet 100	.05	.02	.01
Pittsburgh Penguins				
☐ 234 Alexander Mogilny 100	.20	.09	.03
Buffalo Sabres				
☐ 235 Jeremy Roenick 100	.25	.11	.03
Chicago Blackhawks				
☐ 236 Guy Leveque SR CL	.05	.02	.01
Los Angeles Kings				
Turner Stevenson				
Montreal Canadiens				
Checklist				
☐ 237 Adam Bennett SR	.10	.05	.01
Chicago Blackhawks				
☐ 238 Dody Wood SR	.10	.05	.01

San Jose Sharks				
☐ 239 Niclas Andersson SR	.05	.02	.01
Quebec Nordiques				
☐ 240 Jason Bowen SR	.15	.07	.02
Philadelphia Flyers				
☐ 241 Steve Junker SR	.10	.05	.01
New York Islanders				
☐ 242 Bryan Smolinski SR	.50	.23	.06
Boston Bruins				
☐ 243 Chris Simon SR	.15	.07	.02
Quebec Nordiques				
☐ 244 Sergei Zholtok SR	.05	.02	.01
Boston Bruins				
☐ 245 Dan Ratushny SR	.10	.05	.01
Vancouver Canucks				
☐ 246 Guy Leveque SR	.05	.02	.01
Los Angeles Kings				
☐ 247 Scott Thomas SR	.15	.07	.02
Buffalo Sabres				
☐ 248 Turner Stevenson SR	.05	.02	.01
Montreal Canadiens				
☐ 249 Dan Keczmer SR	.05	.02	.01
Hartford Whalers				
☐ 250 Alexandre Daigle WJC	.40	.18	.05
Checklist				
☐ 251 Adrian Aucoin WJC	.20	.09	.03
☐ 252 Jason Smith WJC	.15	.07	.02
☐ 253 Ralph Intranouvo WJC	.25	.11	.03
☐ 254 Jason Dawe WJC	.20	.09	.03
☐ 255 Jeff Bes WJC	.40	.18	.05
☐ 256 Tyler Wright WJC	.15	.07	.02
☐ 257 Martin Lapointe WJC	.15	.07	.02
☐ 258 Jeff Shantz WJC	.20	.09	.03
☐ 259 Martin Gendron WJC	.35	.16	.04
☐ 260 Philippe DeRouville	.40	.18	.05
WJC				
☐ 261 Frantisek Kaberle WJC	.15	.07	.02
☐ 262 Radim Bicanek WJC	.20	.09	.03
☐ 263 Tomas Klimt WJC	.15	.07	.02
☐ 264 Tomas Nemcicky WJC	.15	.07	.02
☐ 265 Richard Kapus WJC	.20	.09	.03
☐ 266 Patrik Krisak WJC	.20	.09	.03
☐ 267 Roman Kadera WJC	.20	.09	.03
☐ 268 Kimmo Timonen WJC	.20	.09	.03
☐ 269 Jukka Ollila WJC	.15	.07	.02
☐ 270 Tuomas Gronman WJC	.15	.07	.02
☐ 271 Mikko Luovi WJC	.15	.07	.02
☐ 272 Sergei Gonchar WJC	.40	.18	.05
☐ 273 Maxim Golanov WJC	.25	.11	.03
☐ 274 Oleg Belov WJC	.25	.11	.03
☐ 275 Sergei Klimovich WJC	.25	.11	.03
☐ 276 Sergei Brylin WJC	.25	.11	.03
☐ 277 Alexei Yashin WJC	.60	.25	.08
☐ 278 Vitali Tomilin WJC	.20	.09	.03
☐ 279 Alexander Cherbaev	.20	.09	.03
WJC				
☐ 280 Eric Lindros ART	1.00	.45	.13
Philadelphia Flyers				
☐ 281 Teemu Selanne ART	.50	.23	.06
Winnipeg Jets				
☐ 282 Joe Juneau ART	.30	.14	.04
Boston Bruins				
☐ 283 Vladimir Malakhov ART	.15	.07	.02
New York Islanders				
☐ 284 Scott Niedermayer ART	.15	.07	.02
New Jersey Devils				
☐ 285 Felix Potvin ART	.50	.23	.06
Toronto Maple Leafs				
☐ 286 Adam Oates TL	.10	.05	.01
Boston Bruins				
☐ 287 Pat LaFontaine TL	.10	.05	.01
Buffalo Sabres				
☐ 288 Theoren Fleury TL	.08	.04	.01
Calgary Flames				
☐ 289 Jeremy Roenick TL	.20	.09	.03
Chicago Blackhawks				
☐ 290 Steve Yzerman TL	.15	.07	.02
Detroit Red Wings				
☐ 291 Petr Klima TL	.05	.02	.01
Doug Weight TL				
Edmonton Oilers				
☐ 292 Geoff Sanderson TL	.15	.07	.02
Hartford Whalers				
☐ 293 Luc Robitaille TL	.10	.05	.01
Los Angeles Kings				
☐ 294 Mike Modano TL	.10	.05	.01
Dallas Stars				
☐ 295 Vincent Damphousse TL	.05	.02	.01
Montreal Canadiens				
☐ 296 Claude Lemieux TL	.05	.02	.01
New Jersey Devils				
☐ 297 Pierre Turgeon TL	.10	.05	.01
New York Islanders				
☐ 298 Mark Messier TL	.10	.05	.01

New York Rangers			
☐ 299 Norm Maciver TL	.05	.02	.01
Ottawa Senators			
☐ 300 Mark Recchi TL	.10	.05	.01
Philadelphia Flyers			
☐ 301 Mario Lemieux TL	.30	.14	.04
Pittsburgh Penguins			
☐ 302 Mats Sundin TL	.10	.05	.01
Quebec Nordiques			
☐ 303 Craig Janney TL	.08	.04	.01
St. Louis Blues			
☐ 304 Kelly Kisio TL	.05	.02	.01
San Jose Sharks			
☐ 305 Brian Bradley TL	.05	.02	.01
Tampa Bay Lightning			
☐ 306 Doug Gilmour TL	.15	.07	.02
Toronto Maple Leafs			
☐ 307 Pavel Bure TL	.50	.23	.06
Vancouver Canucks			
☐ 308 Peter Bondra TL	.05	.02	.01
Washington Capitals			
☐ 309 Teemu Selanne TL	.50	.23	.06
Winnipeg Jets			
☐ 310 Checklist 207-310	.05	.02	.01
☐ 311 Terry Yake	.05	.02	.01
Anaheim Mighty Ducks			
☐ 312 Bob Sweeney	.05	.02	.01
Buffalo Sabres			
☐ 313 Robert Reichel	.08	.04	.01
Calgary Flames			
☐ 314 Jeremy Roenick	.40	.18	.05
Chicago Blackhawks			
☐ 315 Paul Coffey	.15	.07	.02
Detroit Red Wings			
☐ 316 Geoff Sanderson	.25	.11	.03
Hartford Whalers			
☐ 317 Rob Blake	.08	.04	.01
Los Angeles Kings			
☐ 318 Patrice Brisebois	.05	.02	.01
Montreal Canadiens			
☐ 319 Jaroslav Modry	.15	.07	.02
New Jersey Devils			
☐ 320 Scott Lachance	.05	.02	.01
New York Islanders			
☐ 321 Glenn Healy	.05	.02	.01
New York Rangers			
☐ 322 Martin Gelinas	.05	.02	.01
Quebec Nordiques			
☐ 323 Craig Janney	.10	.05	.01
St. Louis Blues			
☐ 324 Bill McDougall	.05	.02	.01
Tampa Bay Lightning			
☐ 325 Shawn Antoski	.05	.02	.01
Vancouver Canucks			
☐ 326 Olaf Kolzig	.05	.02	.01
Washington Capitals			
☐ 327 Adam Oates	.15	.07	.02
Boston Bruins			
☐ 328 Dirk Graham	.05	.02	.01
Chicago Blackhawks			
☐ 329 Brent Gilchrist	.05	.02	.01
Dallas Stars			
☐ 330 Zdeno Ciger	.05	.02	.01
Edmonton Oilers			
☐ 331 Pat Verbeek	.08	.04	.01
Hartford Whalers			
☐ 332 Jari Kurri	.10	.05	.01
Los Angeles Kings			
☐ 333 Kevin Haller	.05	.02	.01
Montreal Canadiens			
☐ 334 Martin Brodeur	.40	.18	.05
New Jersey Devils			
☐ 335 Norm Maciver	.05	.02	.01
Ottawa Senators			
☐ 336 Dominic Roussel	.15	.07	.02
Philadelphia Flyers			
☐ 337 Iain Fraser	.15	.07	.02
Quebec Nordiques			
☐ 338 Vitali Karamnov	.05	.02	.01
St. Louis Blues			
☐ 339 Rene Corbet	.25	.11	.03
Quebec Nordiques			
☐ 340 Wendel Clark	.10	.05	.01
Toronto Maple Leafs			
☐ 341 Mike Ridley	.08	.04	.01
Washington Capitals			
☐ 342 Nelson Emerson	.08	.04	.01
Winnipeg Jets			
☐ 343 Joe Juneau	.50	.23	.06
Boston Bruins			
☐ 344 Vesa Viitakoski	.15	.07	.02
Calgary Flames			
☐ 345 Steve Chiasson	.05	.02	.01
Detroit Red Wings			
☐ 346 Andrew Cassels	.05	.02	.01
Hartford Whalers			
☐ 347 Pierre Turgeon	.25	.11	.03
New York Islanders			
☐ 348 Brian Leetch	.05	.02	.01
New York Rangers			
☐ 349 Alexei Yashin	.60	.25	.08
Ottawa Senators			
☐ 350 Mark Recchi	.20	.09	.03
Philadelphia Flyers			
☐ 351 Ron Francis	.08	.04	.01
Pittsburgh Penguins			
☐ 352 Mike Ricci	.08	.04	.01
Quebec Nordiques			
☐ 353 Igor Korolev	.05	.02	.01
St. Louis Blues			
☐ 354 Brent Gretzky	.25	.11	.03
Tampa Bay Lightning			
☐ 355 Dave Poulin	.05	.02	.01
Washington Capitals			
☐ 356 Cam Neely	.08	.04	.01
Boston Bruins			
☐ 357 Gary Suter	.08	.04	.01
Calgary Flames			
☐ 358 Dave Manson	.05	.02	.01
Edmonton Oilers			
☐ 359 Robert Kron	.05	.02	.01
Hartford Whalers			
☐ 360 Ulf Dahlen	.05	.02	.01
Dallas Stars			
☐ 361 Rod Brind'Amour	.15	.07	.02
Philadelphia Flyers			
☐ 362 Alexei Gusarov	.05	.02	.01
Quebec Nordiques			
☐ 363 Vitali Prokhorov	.05	.02	.01
St. Louis Blues			
☐ 364 Damian Rhodes	.25	.11	.03
Toronto Maple Leafs			
☐ 365 Paul Ysebaert	.05	.02	.01
Winnipeg Jets			
☐ 366 Vladimir Konstantinov	.05	.02	.01
Detroit Red Wings			
☐ 367 Steven Rice	.05	.02	.01
Edmonton Oilers			
☐ 368 Brian Propp	.08	.04	.01
Hartford Whalers			
☐ 369 Valeri Zelepukin	.08	.04	.01
New Jersey Devils			
☐ 370 David Volek	.05	.02	.01
New York Islanders			
☐ 371 Sergei Nemchinov	.05	.02	.01
New York Rangers			
☐ 372 Pavol Demitra	.10	.05	.01
Ottawa Senators			
☐ 373 Brent Fedyk	.05	.02	.01
Philadelphia Flyers			
☐ 374 Larry Murphy	.08	.04	.01
Pittsburgh Penguins			
☐ 375 Dave Karpa	.05	.02	.01
Quebec Nordiques			
☐ 376 Dave Babych	.05	.02	.01
Vancouver Canucks			
☐ 377 Keith Jones	.05	.02	.01
Washington Capitals			
☐ 378 Neil Wilkinson	.05	.02	.01
Chicago Blackhawks			
☐ 379 Jozef Stumpel	.05	.02	.01
Boston Bruins			
☐ 380 Vincent Damphousse	.08	.04	.01
Montreal Canadiens			
☐ 381 Tom Kurvers	.05	.02	.01
New York Islanders			
☐ 382 Doug Gilmour	.30	.14	.04
Toronto Maple Leafs			
☐ 383 Trevor Linden	.10	.05	.01
Vancouver Canucks			
☐ 384 Kelly Miller	.05	.02	.01
Washington Capitals			
☐ 385 Tim Sweeney	.05	.02	.01
Anaheim Mighty Ducks			
☐ 386 Mikhail Tatarinov	.05	.02	.01
Boston Bruins			
☐ 387 Dominic Hasek	.10	.05	.01
Buffalo Sabres			
☐ 388 Steve Yzerman	.30	.14	.04
Detroit Red Wings			
☐ 389 Scott Pearson	.05	.02	.01
Edmonton Oilers			
☐ 390 Brian Bellows	.08	.04	.01
Montreal Canadiens			
☐ 391 Claude Lemieux	.08	.04	.01
New Jersey Devils			
☐ 392 Marty McInnis	.05	.02	.01

New York Islanders
☐ 393 Jim Sandlak	.05	.02	.01

Hartford Whalers
☐ 394 Jocelyn Thibault	.60	.25	.08

Quebec Nordiques
☐ 395 John Cullen	.05	.02	.01

Toronto Maple Leafs
☐ 396 Joe Nieuwendyk	.08	.04	.01

Calgary Flames
☐ 397 Mike Modano	.25	.11	.03

Dallas Stars
☐ 398 Ray Sheppard	.05	.02	.01

Detroit Red Wings
☐ 399 Trevor Kidd	.08	.04	.01

Calgary Flames
☐ 400 Checklist	.05	.02	.01
☐ 401 Frank Pietrangelo	.05	.02	.01

Hartford Whalers
☐ 402 Stephan Lebeau	.05	.02	.01

Montreal Canadiens
☐ 403 Stephane Richer.................	.08	.04	.01

New Jersey Devils
☐ 404 Greg Gilbert......................	.05	.02	.01

New York Rangers
☐ 405 Dmitri Filimonov	.05	.02	.01

Ottawa Senators
☐ 406 Vyacheslav Butsayev..........	.05	.02	.01

Philadelphia Flyers
☐ 407 Mario Lemieux	.75	.35	.09

Pittsburgh Penguins
☐ 408 Kevin Miller	.05	.02	.01

St. Louis Blues
☐ 409 John Tucker	.05	.02	.01

Tampa Bay Lightning
☐ 410 Murray Craven	.05	.02	.01

Vancouver Canucks
☐ 411 Dale Hawerchuk	.08	.04	.01

Buffalo Sabres
☐ 412 Al MacInnis........................	.10	.05	.01

Calgary Flames
☐ 413 Keith Primeau	.08	.04	.01

Detroit Red Wings
☐ 414 Luc Robitaille.....................	.15	.07	.02

Los Angeles Kings
☐ 415 Benoit Brunet.....................	.05	.02	.01

Montreal Canadiens
☐ 416 Tom Chorske......................	.05	.02	.01

New Jersey Devils
☐ 417 Derek King	.05	.02	.01

New York Islanders
☐ 418 Troy Mallette......................	.05	.02	.01

Ottawa Senators
☐ 419 Mats Sundin.......................	.20	.09	.03

Quebec Nordiques
☐ 420 Kent Manderville	.05	.02	.01

Toronto Maple Leafs
☐ 421 Kip Miller	.05	.02	.01

San Jose Sharks
☐ 422 Jarkko Varvio	.15	.07	.02

Dallas Stars
☐ 423 Jason Arnott	2.00	.90	.25

Edmonton Oilers
☐ 424 Craig Billington	.05	.02	.01

Ottawa Senators
☐ 425 Stewart Malgunas	.10	.05	.01

Philadelphia Flyers
☐ 426 Ron Tugnutt.......................	.05	.02	.01

Anaheim Mighty Ducks
☐ 427 Alexei Kudashov.................	.15	.07	.02

Toronto Maple Leafs
☐ 428 Harijs Vitolinsh..................	.05	.02	.01

Winnipeg Jets
☐ 429 Bill Houlder	.05	.02	.01

Anaheim Mighty Ducks
☐ 430 Craig Simpson	.05	.02	.01

Buffalo Sabres
☐ 431 Wes Walz	.05	.02	.01

Calgary Flames
☐ 432 Micah Aivazoff....................	.15	.07	.02

Detroit Red Wings
☐ 433 Scott Levins	.15	.07	.02

Florida Panthers
☐ 434 Ron Hextall	.08	.04	.01

New York Islanders
☐ 435 Frank Brathwaite	.15	.07	.02

Edmonton Oilers
☐ 436 Chad Penney	.25	.11	.03

Ottawa Senators
☐ 437 Vlastimil Kroupa.................	.20	.09	.03

San Jose Sharks
☐ 438 Troy Loney	.05	.02	.01

Anaheim Mighty Ducks
☐ 439 Matthew Barnaby	.15	.07	.02

Buffalo Sabres

☐ 440 Kevin Todd........................	.05	.02	.01

Chicago Blackhawks
☐ 441 Paul Cavallini.....................	.05	.02	.01

Dallas Stars
☐ 442 Doug Weight......................	.08	.04	.01

Edmonton Oilers
☐ 443 Evgeny Davydov.................	.05	.02	.01

Florida Panthers
☐ 444 Dominic Lavoie	.05	.02	.01

Los Angeles Kings
☐ 445 Peter Popovic.....................	.15	.07	.02

Montreal Canadiens
☐ 446 Sergei Makarov	.08	.04	.01

San Jose Sharks
☐ 447 Matt Martin	.15	.07	.02

Toronto Maple Leafs
☐ 448 Teemu Selanne	.75	.35	.09

Winnipeg Jets
☐ 449 Todd Ewen	.05	.02	.01

Anaheim Mighty Ducks
☐ 450 Sergei Petrenko..................	.05	.02	.01

Buffalo Sabres
☐ 451 Jeff Shantz	.15	.07	.02

Chicago Blackhawks
☐ 452 Greg Johnson	.05	.02	.01

Detroit Red Wings
☐ 453 Brent Severyn	.15	.07	.02

Florida Panthers
☐ 454 Shawn McEachern..............	.15	.07	.02

Los Angeles Kings
☐ 455 Pierre Sevigny....................	.05	.02	.01

Montreal Canadiens
☐ 456 Benoit Hogue	.05	.02	.01

New York Islanders
☐ 457 Esa Tikkanen	.08	.04	.01

New York Rangers
☐ 458 Brian Glynn	.05	.02	.01

Ottawa Senators
☐ 459 Doug Brown	.05	.02	.01

Pittsburgh Penguins
☐ 460 Mike Rathje	.05	.02	.01

San Jose Sharks
☐ 461 Rudy Poeschek	.05	.02	.01

Tampa Bay Lightning
☐ 462 Jason Woolley.....................	.05	.02	.01

Washington Capitals
☐ 463 Patrick Carnback	.10	.05	.01

Anaheim Mighty Ducks
☐ 464 Cam Stewart	.15	.07	.02

Boston Bruins
☐ 465 Petr Svoboda	.05	.02	.01

Buffalo Sabres
☐ 466 Ted Drury	.05	.02	.01

Calgary Flames
☐ 467 Ladislav Karabin.................	.10	.05	.01

Pittsburgh Penguins
☐ 468 Paul Broten	.05	.02	.01

Dallas Stars
☐ 469 Alexander Godynyuk	.05	.02	.01

Florida Panthers
☐ 470 Bob Jay	.10	.05	.01

Los Angeles Kings
☐ 471 Steve Larmer......................	.08	.04	.01

New York Rangers
☐ 472 Jim Montgomery.................	.15	.07	.02

St. Louis Blues
☐ 473 Darren Puppa.....................	.08	.04	.01

Tampa Bay Lightning
☐ 474 Alexei Kasatonov................	.05	.02	.01

Anaheim Mighty Ducks
☐ 475 Derek Plante.......................	.60	.25	.08

Buffalo Sabres
☐ 476 German Titov	.40	.18	.05

Calgary Flames
☐ 477 Steve Dubinsky	.20	.09	.03

Chicago Blackhawks
☐ 478 Andy Moog	.08	.04	.01

Dallas Stars
☐ 479 Aaron Ward	.15	.07	.02

Detroit Red Wings
☐ 480 Dean McAmmond	.05	.02	.01

Edmonton Oilers
☐ 481 Randy Gilhen	.05	.02	.01

Florida Panthers
☐ 482 Jason Muzzatti	.10	.05	.01

Calgary Flames
☐ 483 Corey Millen.......................	.05	.02	.01

New Jersey Devils
☐ 484 Alexander Karpovtsev	.08	.04	.01

New York Rangers
☐ 485 Bill Huard	.10	.05	.01

Ottawa Senators
☐ 486 Mikael Renberg...................	.60	.25	.08

Philadelphia Flyers			
☐ 487 Marty McSorley	.08	.04	.01
Pittsburgh Penguins			
☐ 488 Alexander Mogilny	.35	.16	.04
Buffalo Sabres			
☐ 489 Michal Sykora	.25	.11	.03
San Jose Sharks			
☐ 490 Checklist	.05	.02	.01
☐ 491 Tom Tilley	.05	.02	.01
St. Louis Blues			
☐ 492 Boris Mironov	.05	.02	.01
Winnipeg Jets			
☐ 493 Sandy McCarthy	.05	.02	.01
Calgary Flames			
☐ 494 Mark Astley	.15	.07	.02
Buffalo Sabres			
☐ 495 Vyacheslav Kozlov	.40	.18	.05
Detroit Red Wings			
☐ 496 Brian Benning	.05	.02	.01
Florida Panthers			
☐ 497 Eric Weinrich	.05	.02	.01
Chicago Blackhawks			
☐ 498 Robert Burakovsky	.05	.02	.01
Ottawa Senators			
☐ 499 Patrick Lebeau	.05	.02	.01
Florida Panthers			
☐ 500 Markus Naslund	.15	.07	.02
Pittsburgh Penguins			
☐ 501 Jimmy Waite	.05	.02	.01
San Jose Sharks			
☐ 502 Denis Savard	.10	.05	.01
Tampa Bay Lightning			
☐ 503 Jose Charbonneau	.05	.02	.01
Vancouver Canucks			
☐ 504 Randy Burridge	.05	.02	.01
Washington Capitals			
☐ 505 Arto Blomsten	.05	.02	.01
Winnipeg Jets			
☐ 506 Shaun Van Allen	.05	.02	.01
Anaheim Mighty Ducks			
☐ 507 Jon Casey	.08	.04	.01
Boston Bruins			
☐ 508 Darren McCarty	.15	.07	.02
Detroit Red Wings			
☐ 509 Roman Oksyuta	.10	.05	.01
Edmonton Oilers			
☐ 510 Jody Hull	.05	.02	.01
Florida Panthers			
☐ 511 Scott Scissons	.05	.02	.01
New York Islanders			
☐ 512 Jeff Norton	.05	.02	.01
San Jose Sharks			
☐ 513 Dmitri Mironov	.05	.02	.01
Toronto Maple Leafs			
☐ 514 Sergei Bautin	.05	.02	.01
Winnipeg Jets			
☐ 515 Garry Valk	.05	.02	.01
Anaheim Mighty Ducks			
☐ 516 Keith Carney	.05	.02	.01
Buffalo Sabres			
☐ 517 James Black	.05	.02	.01
Dallas Stars			
☐ 518 Pat Peake	.15	.07	.02
Washington Capitals			
☐ 519 Chris Osgood	.50	.23	.06
Detroit Red Wings			
☐ 520 Kirk Maltby	.15	.07	.02
Edmonton Oilers			
☐ 521 Gord Murphy	.05	.02	.01
Florida Panthers			
☐ 522 Mattias Norstrom	.10	.05	.01
New York Rangers			
☐ 523 Milos Holan	.10	.05	.01
Philadelphia Flyers			
☐ 524 Dave McLlwain	.05	.02	.01
Ottawa Senators			
☐ 525 Phil Housley	.08	.04	.01
St. Louis Blues			
☐ 526 Petr Klima	.05	.02	.01
Tampa Bay Lightning			
☐ 527 John McIntyre	.05	.02	.01
Vancouver Canucks			
☐ 528 Enrico Ciccone	.05	.02	.01
Washington Capitals			
☐ 529 Stephane Quintal	.05	.02	.01
Winnipeg Jets			
☐ 530 World Junior	.15	.07	.02
Checklist			
☐ 531 Anson Carter	.30	.14	.04
☐ 532 Jeff Friesen	1.25	.55	.16
☐ 533 Yanick Dube	.60	.25	.08
☐ 534 Jason Botterill	.60	.25	.08
☐ 535 Todd Harvey	.75	.35	.09
☐ 536 Manny Fernandez	.50	.23	.06

☐ 537 Jason Allison	1.00	.45	.13
☐ 538 Jamie Storr	2.00	.90	.25
☐ 539 Rick Girrard	.40	.18	.05
☐ 540 Martin Gendron	.25	.11	.03
☐ 541 Joel Bouchard	.15	.07	.02
☐ 542 Mike Peca	.50	.23	.06
☐ 543 Nick Stajduhar	.40	.18	.05
☐ 544 Brendan Witt	.50	.23	.06
☐ 545 Aaron Gavey	.75	.35	.09
☐ 546 Chris Armstrong	.15	.07	.02
☐ 547 Curtis Bowen	.30	.14	.04
☐ 548 Brandon Convery	.40	.18	.05
☐ 549 Bryan McCabe	.25	.11	.03
☐ 550 Marty Murray	.40	.18	.05
☐ 551 Ryan Sittler	.20	.09	.03
☐ 552 Jason McBain	.15	.07	.02
☐ 553 Richard Park	.50	.23	.06
☐ 554 Aaron Ellis	.15	.07	.02
☐ 555 Tobi Kvalevog	.15	.07	.02
☐ 556 Jay Pandolfo	.20	.09	.03
☐ 557 John Emmons	.15	.07	.02
☐ 558 David Wilkie	.25	.11	.03
☐ 559 John Varga	.25	.11	.03
☐ 560 Jason Bonsignore	1.00	.45	.13
☐ 561 Blake Sloan	.30	.14	.04
☐ 562 Adam Deadmarsh	.20	.09	.03
☐ 563 Jon Coleman	.20	.09	.03
☐ 564 Bob Lachance	.15	.07	.02
☐ 565 Chris O'Sullivan	.20	.09	.03
☐ 566 Jamie Langenbrunner	.35	.16	.04
☐ 567 Kevin Hilton	.20	.09	.03
☐ 568 Kevyn Adams	.50	.23	.06
☐ 569 Saku Koivu	.50	.23	.06
☐ 570 Mats Lindgren	.35	.16	.04
☐ 571 Nikolai Tsulygin	1.00	.45	.13
☐ 572 Edvin Frylen	.20	.09	.03
☐ 573 Jaroslav Miklenda	.25	.11	.03
☐ 574 Vadim Sharifjanov	.30	.14	.04
☐ 575 Checklist Card	.05	.02	.01
☐ SP4 Teemu Selanne Holo	5.00	2.30	.60
Winnipeg Jets			

1993-94 Upper Deck Award Winners

Randomly inserted in Canadian first-series foil packs, this eight-card set measures the standard size (2 1/2" by 3 1/2"). The fronts feature a black-and-white photo of the player and his trophy. The player's name appears in a colored bar at the bottom and also in vertical silver-foil letters on the left side. The backs carry a color action player photo, along with the player's name, position, and profile, the team logo, and the name of the trophy. The cards are numbered on the back with an "AW" prefix.

	MINT	EXC	G-VG
COMPLETE SET (8)	30.00	13.50	3.80
COMMON PLAYER (AW1-AW8)	2.00	.90	.25
☐ AW1 Mario Lemieux	8.00	3.60	1.00
Hart Trophy			
Art Ross Trophy			
Lester B. Pearson Award			
Bill Master Trophy			
☐ AW2 Teemu Selanne	5.00	2.30	.60
Calder Trophy			

☐ AW3 Ed Belfour..........................		3.00	1.35	.40
Jennings Trophy				
Vezina Trophy				
☐ AW4 Patrick Roy........................		7.00	3.10	.85
Conn Smythe Trophy				
☐ AW5 Chris Chelios....................		2.00	.90	.25
Jack Norris Trophy				
☐ AW6 Doug Gilmour....................		4.00	1.80	.50
Frank J. Selke Trophy				
☐ AW7 Pierre Turgeon..................		3.00	1.35	.40
Lady Byng Trophy				
☐ AW8 Dave Poulin......................		2.00	.90	.25
King Clancy				

1993-94 Upper Deck Wayne Gretzky Box Bottom

Issued on the bottom of Upper Deck boxes, this card measures approximately 5" by 7" and features Wayne Gretzky on the front. The design is the same as his regular issue card. The back is blank. The card is unnumbered.

	MINT	EXC	G-VG
COMPLETE SET (1)..........................	1.00	.40	.10
COMMON PLAYER..........................	1.00	.40	.10
☐ 1 Wayne Gretzky.......................	1.00	.40	.10
Los Angeles Kings			

1993-94 Upper Deck Future Heroes

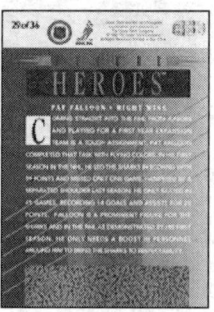

Randomly inserted in first-series U.S. hobby packs, this 10-card set measures the standard size (2 1/2" by 3 1/2"). The tan-bordered fronts feature sepia-toned action player photos with the player's name in white lettering within a black bar above the photo. The set's title appears below the photo, with the word "Heroes" printed in copper foil. On a gray background, the back carries a player profile. The cards are numbered on the back as a continuation of Upper Deck's 1991 and 1992 Heroes series ("X of 36.")

	MINT	EXC	G-VG
COMPLETE SET (10).......................	125.00	57.50	15.50
COMMON PLAYER (28-36)..............	5.00	2.30	.60
☐ 28 Felix Potvin	20.00	9.00	2.50
Toronto Maple Leafs			
☐ 29 Pat Falloon	5.00	2.30	.60
San Jose Sharks			
☐ 30 Pavel Bure...........................	25.00	11.50	3.10
Vancouver Canucks			
☐ 31 Eric Lindros.........................	35.00	16.00	4.40
Philadelphia Flyers			
☐ 32 Teemu Selanne	12.00	5.50	1.50
Winnipeg Jets			
☐ 33 Jaromir Jagr	10.00	4.50	1.25
Pittsburgh Penguins			
☐ 34 Alexander Mogilny	9.00	4.00	1.15
Buffalo Sabres			
☐ 35 Joe Juneau..........................	10.00	4.50	1.25
Boston Bruins			
☐ 36 Checklist	25.00	11.50	3.10
☐ NNO Header Card......................	22.00	10.00	2.80

1993-94 Upper Deck Gretzky's Great Ones

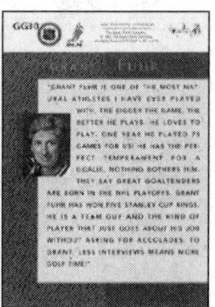

Randomly inserted in series one packs and one per series one jumbo, this 10-card set measures the standard size (2 1/2" by 3 1/2"). The fronts feature color player photos with blue and gray bars above, below, and to the left. The player's name and the words "Gretzky's Great Ones" in copper-foil letters appear below and above the photo, respectively. The backs carry a small head shot of Wayne Gretzky along with his comments on the featured player. The cards are numbered on the back with a "GG" prefix.

	MINT	EXC	G-VG
COMPLETE SET (10).......................	18.00	8.00	2.30
COMMON PLAYER (GG1-GG10).......	1.50	.65	.19
☐ GG1 Denis Savard.....................	1.50	.65	.19
Montreal Canadiens			
☐ GG2 Chris Chelios.....................	1.50	.65	.19
Chicago Blackhawks			
☐ GG3 Brett Hull..........................	2.50	1.15	.30
St. Louis Blues			
☐ GG4 Mario Lemieux	5.00	2.30	.60
Pittsburgh Penguins			
☐ GG5 Mark Messier	2.00	.90	.25
New York Rangers			
☐ GG6 Paul Coffey........................	1.50	.65	.19
Detroit Red Wings			
☐ GG7 Theoren Fleury	1.50	.65	.19
Calgary Flames			
☐ GG8 Luc Robitaille	2.00	.90	.25
Los Angeles Kings			
☐ GG9 Marty McSorley..................	1.50	.65	.19
Los Angeles Kings			
☐ GG10 Grant Fuhr.......................	1.50	.65	.19
Buffalo Sabres			

1993-94 Upper Deck Hat Tricks

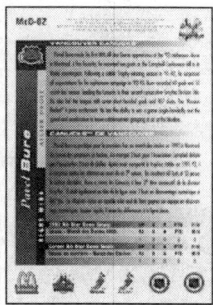

Inserted one per series one jumbo pack, this 20-card set measures the standard size (2 1/2" by 3 1/2"). The fronts feature color player photos that are borderless, except on the right, where a strip that fades from brown to black carries the player's name. The backs carry the player's name, team name, and description of his hat trick performances. The cards are numbered on the back with an "HT" prefix.

	MINT	EXC	G-VG
COMPLETE SET (20)	15.00	6.75	1.90
COMMON PLAYER (HT1-HT20)	.50	.23	.06
☐ HT1 Adam Graves	1.00	.45	.13
New York Rangers			
☐ HT2 Geoff Sanderson	.75	.35	.09
Hartford Whalers			
☐ HT3 Gary Roberts	.60	.25	.08
Calgary Flames			
☐ HT4 Robert Reichel	.60	.25	.08
Calgary Flames			
☐ HT5 Adam Oates	.75	.35	.09
Boston Bruins			
☐ HT6 Steve Yzerman	1.50	.65	.19
Detroit Red Wings			
☐ HT7 Alexei Kovalev	1.50	.65	.19
New York Rangers			
☐ HT8 Vincent Damphousse	.60	.25	.08
Montreal Canadiens			
☐ HT9 Rob Gaudreau	.50	.23	.06
San Jose Sharks			
☐ HT10 Pat LaFontaine	1.00	.45	.13
Buffalo Sabres			
☐ HT11 Pierre Turgeon	1.00	.45	.13
New York Islanders			
☐ HT12 Rick Tocchet	.60	.25	.08
Pittsburgh Penguins			
☐ HT13 Michael Nylander	.50	.23	.06
Hartford Whalers			
☐ HT14 Steve Larmer	.60	.25	.08
Chicago Blackhawks			
☐ HT15 Alexander Mogilny	1.25	.55	.16
Buffalo Sabres			
☐ HT16 Owen Nolan	.50	.23	.06
Quebec Nordiques			
☐ HT17 Luc Robitaille	.75	.35	.09
Los Angeles Kings			
☐ HT18 Jeremy Roenick	2.00	.90	.25
Chicago Blackhawks			
☐ HT19 Kevin Stevens	1.00	.45	.13
Pittsburgh Penguins			
☐ HT20 Mats Sundin	1.00	.45	.13
Quebec Nordiques			

1993-94 Upper Deck McDonald's

Produced by Upper Deck for McDonald's of Canada, this set is similar in concept to the previous year's Upper Deck McDonald's set. The 27 regular cards and six hologram-type cards honor 33 of the NHL's most exciting players. The holograms were random inserts in the four-card packs. An oversized (4" by 5 1/2") Patrick Roy card (23) was also available via a redemption card randomly inserted in packs. The redemption card could be redeemed at McDonald's or throught the mail. Also, Upper Deck has confirmed that the unnumbered checklist card was short-printed. All cards measure the standard size (2 1/2" by 3 1/2"). The regular cards feature on their fronts white-bordered color action shots of players in their 1993 All-Star uniforms. The player's name and position appear at the bottom. A small black-and-white head shot, along with the Upper Deck and McDonald's logos, appear within a blue and black stripe to the right of the main photo. The back carries the player's name and position vertically on the left. Highlights and statistics from the 1993 All-Star Game appear in both English and French. The hologram cards are horizontal on their fronts and backs. The front of each card features a hologram-type action photo of a first team All-Star on the right and a posed closeup on the left. The player's name and position appear within blue, black, and gray stripes near the bottom. The back carries the player's All-Star highlights in both English and French. The regular cards are arranged according to conference: Campbell (1-13) and Wales (14-27). The regular cards are numbered on the back with an "McD" prefix; the hologram-types are numbered with an "McH" prefix.

	MINT	EXC	G-VG
COMPLETE SET (34)	15.00	6.00	1.50
COMMON PLAYER (1-27)	.25	.10	.02
COMMON HOLOGRAM (H1-H6)	1.00	.40	.10
☐ 1 Brian Bradley	.25	.10	.02
☐ 2 Pavel Bure	2.00	.80	.20
☐ 3 Jon Casey	.25	.10	.02
☐ 4 Paul Coffey	.50	.20	.05
☐ 5 Doug Gilmour	1.00	.40	.10
☐ 6 Phil Housley	.25	.10	.02
☐ 7 Brett Hull	1.00	.40	.10
☐ 8 Jari Kurri	.35	.14	.03
☐ 9 Dave Manson	.25	.10	.02
☐ 10 Mike Modano	.75	.30	.07
☐ 11 Gary Roberts	.25	.10	.02
☐ 12 Jeremy Roenick	1.25	.50	.12
☐ 13 Steve Yzerman	1.00	.40	.10
☐ 14 Steve Duchesne	.25	.10	.02
☐ 15 Mike Gartner	.50	.20	.05
☐ 16 Al Iafrate	.35	.14	.03
☐ 17 Jaromir Jagr	1.00	.40	.10
☐ 18 Pat LaFontaine	.75	.30	.07
☐ 19 Alexander Mogilny	.75	.30	.07
☐ 20 Kirk Muller	.35	.14	.03
☐ 21 Adam Oates	.75	.30	.07
☐ 22 Mark Recchi	.50	.20	.05
☐ 23 Patrick Roy	1.50	.60	.15
☐ 23L Patrick Roy Large	12.00	5.00	1.20
(4" by 5 1/2"; only			
available from			
redemption card)			
☐ 24 Joe Sakic	.75	.30	.07
☐ 25 Kevin Stevens	.50	.20	.05
☐ 26 Scott Stevens	.35	.14	.03
☐ 27 Pierre Turgeon	.75	.30	.07
☐ H1 Mario Lemieux	3.00	1.20	.30

☐	H2 Teemu Selanne	2.00	.80	.20
☐	H3 Luc Robitaille	1.25	.50	.12
☐	H4 Ray Bourque	1.00	.40	.10
☐	H5 Chris Chelios	1.00	.40	.10
☐	H6 Ed Belfour	1.00	.40	.10
☐	NNO Checklist SP	2.00	.80	.20

1993-94 Upper Deck Next In Line

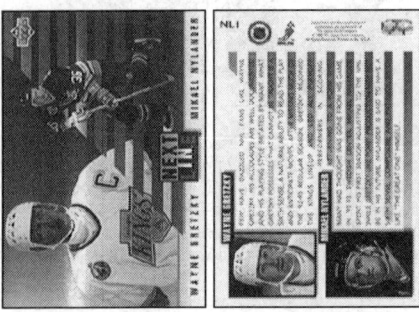

name and an advertisement for the NHLPA apparel. The cards are numbered on the back. The entire set could also be purchased by mail. The first series came out in 1993, while the second series came out in 1994.

Randomly inserted in all first-series packs, this six-card set measures the standard-size (2 1/2" by 3 1/2"). The horizontal metallic and prismatic fronts feature photos of two NHL players, diagonally divided in the middle. The players' names appear under the photos. The horizontal backs carry small head shots of both players, along with player profiles. The cards are numbered on the back with an "NL" prefix.

	MINT	EXC	G-VG
COMPLETE SET (6)	30.00	13.50	3.80
COMMON PAIR (NL1-NL6)	3.00	1.35	.40

		MINT	EXC	G-VG
☐	NL1 Wayne Gretzky Los Angeles Kings Michael Nylander Hartford Whalers	10.00	4.50	1.25
☐	NL2 Brett Hull St. Louis Blues Patrick Poulin Hartford Whalers	5.00	2.30	.60
☐	NL3 Steve Yzerman Detroit Red Wings Joe Sakic Quebec Nordiques	5.00	2.30	.60
☐	NL4 Ray Bourque Boston Bruins Brian Leetch New York Rangers	3.00	1.35	.40
☐	NL5 Doug Gilmour Toronto Maple Leafs Keith Tkachuk Winnipeg Jets	7.00	3.10	.85
☐	NL6 Patrick Roy Montreal Canadiens Felix Potvin Toronto Maple Leafs	10.00	4.50	1.25

1993-94 Upper Deck NHLPA/Roots

Teamed with the NHL Players Association, Upper Deck issued these clothing tags as a promotion for a new line of clothing produced by the clothing manufacturer, Roots Canada. Called "Hang Out," each article of clothing came with one of ten "hang tag" cards featuring on their fronts a full-bleed photo of the NHL player wearing the clothing. The clothing tags measure the standard size (2 1/2" by 3 1/2") and are punchholed in the upper left corner. Versions of these cards without the punchhole also exist. With a faded and enlarged Upper Deck logo, the backs carry the player's

	MINT	EXC	G-VG
COMPLETE SET (20)	20.00	8.00	2.00
COMPLETE SERIES 1 (10)	10.00	4.00	1.00
COMPLETE SERIES 2 (10)	10.00	4.00	1.00
COMMON PLAYER (1-10)	.50	.20	.05
COMMON PLAYER (11-20)	.50	.20	.05

		MINT	EXC	G-VG
☐	1 Trevor Linden Vancouver Canucks	1.00	.40	.10
☐	2 Patrick Roy Montreal Canadiens	3.00	1.20	.30
☐	3 Felix Potvin Toronto Maple Leafs	2.50	1.00	.25
☐	4 Steve Yzerman Detroit Red Wings	1.50	.60	.15
☐	5 Doug Gilmour Toronto Maple Leafs	2.00	.80	.20
☐	6 Wendel Clark Toronto Maple Leafs	1.00	.40	.10
☐	7 Kirk McLean Vancouver Canucks	.75	.30	.07
☐	8 Larry Murphy Pittsburgh Penguins	.50	.20	.05
☐	9 Guy Carbonneau Montreal Canadiens	.50	.20	.05
☐	10 Mike Ricci Quebec Nordiques	.75	.30	.07
☐	11 Doug Gilmour Toronto Maple Leafs	2.00	.80	.20
☐	12 Sergei Fedorov Detroit Red Wings	2.50	1.00	.25
☐	13 Shayne Corson Edmonton Oilers	.50	.20	.05
☐	14 Alexei Yashin Ottawa Senators	1.50	.60	.15
☐	15 Pavel Bure Vancouver Canucks	4.00	1.60	.40
☐	16 Joe Sakic Quebec Nordiques	1.25	.50	.12
☐	17 Teemu Selanne Winnipeg Jets	2.00	.80	.20
☐	18 Dave Andreychuk Toronto Maple Leafs	.75	.30	.07
☐	19 Al MacInnis Calgary Flames	.75	.30	.07
☐	20 Rob Blake Los Angeles Kings	.75	.30	.07

1993-94 Upper Deck NHL's Best

Randomly inserted in first-series U.S. retail packs, this 10-card set measures the standard size (2 1/2" by 3 1/2"). The fronts feature color action player photos that are borderless, except at the bottom, where a black bar carries the player's name. On a white background, the backs carry a small color action player photo, along with career highlights. The player's name appears vertically in the black bar to the left. The cards are numbered on the back with an "HB" prefix.

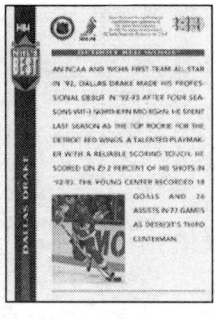

6), Boston Bruins (7-12), Buffalo Sabres (13-19), Calgary Flames (20-26), Chicago Blackhawks (27-33), Dallas Stars (34-40), Detroit Red Wings (41-47), Edmonton Oilers (48-54), Florida Panthers (55-60), Hartford Whalers (61-67), Los Angeles Kings (68-75), Montreal Canadiens (76-82), New Jersey Devils (83-89), New York Islanders (90-96), New York Rangers (97-104), Ottawa Senators (105-112), Philadelphia Flyers (113-119), Pittsburgh Penguins (120-126), Quebec Nordiques (127-133), St. Louis Blues (134-140), San Jose Sharks (141-147), Tampa Bay Lightning (148-154), Toronto Maple Leafs (155-160), Vancouver Canucks (161-167), Washington Capitals (168-173), and Winnipeg Jets (174-180).

	MINT	EXC	G-VG
COMPLETE SET (180)	125.00	57.50	15.50
COMMON PLAYER (1-180)	.30	.14	.04

		MINT	EXC	G-VG
☐ 1	Sean Hill	.30	.14	.04
☐ 2	Troy Loney	.30	.14	.04
☐ 3	Joe Sacco	.30	.14	.04
☐ 4	Anatoli Semenov	.30	.14	.04
☐ 5	Ron Tugnutt	.30	.14	.04
☐ 6	Terry Yake	.30	.14	.04
☐ 7	Ray Bourque	.60	.25	.08
☐ 8	Jon Casey	.35	.16	.04
☐ 9	Joe Juneau	2.00	.90	.25
☐ 10	Cam Neely	.50	.23	.06
☐ 11	Adam Oates	.60	.25	.08
☐ 12	Bryan Smolinski	1.50	.65	.19
☐ 13	Matthew Barnaby	.30	.14	.04
☐ 14	Philippe Boucher	.30	.14	.04
☐ 15	Grant Fuhr	.35	.16	.04
☐ 16	Dale Hawerchuk	.35	.16	.04
☐ 17	Pat LaFontaine	.75	.35	.09
☐ 18	Alexander Mogilny	1.25	.55	.16
☐ 19	Craig Simpson	.30	.14	.04
☐ 20	Ted Drury	.30	.14	.04
☐ 21	Theoren Fleury	.40	.18	.05
☐ 22	Al MacInnis	.40	.18	.05
☐ 23	Joe Nieuwendyk	.35	.16	.04
☐ 24	Joel Otto	.30	.14	.04
☐ 25	Gary Roberts	.35	.16	.04
☐ 26	Vesa Viitakoski	.30	.14	.04
☐ 27	Ed Belfour	.75	.35	.09
☐ 28	Chris Chelios	.35	.16	.04
☐ 29	Joe Murphy	.30	.14	.04
☐ 30	Patrick Poulin	.30	.14	.04
☐ 31	Jeremy Roenick	2.00	.90	.25
☐ 32	Jeff Shantz	.30	.14	.04
☐ 33	Kevin Todd	.30	.14	.04
☐ 34	Neal Broten	.35	.16	.04
☐ 35	Paul Cavallini	.30	.14	.04
☐ 36	Russ Courtnall	.35	.16	.04
☐ 37	Derian Hatcher	.30	.14	.04
☐ 38	Mike Modano	1.00	.45	.13
☐ 39	Andy Moog	.35	.16	.04
☐ 40	Jarkko Varvio	.30	.14	.04
☐ 41	Dino Ciccarelli	.35	.16	.04
☐ 42	Paul Coffey	.50	.23	.06
☐ 43	Dallas Drake	.50	.23	.06
☐ 44	Sergei Fedorov	3.00	1.35	.40
☐ 45	Keith Primeau	.50	.23	.06
☐ 46	Bob Probert	.30	.14	.04
☐ 47	Steve Yzerman	1.25	.55	.16
☐ 48	Jason Arnott	6.00	2.70	.75
☐ 49	Shayne Corson	.30	.14	.04
☐ 50	Dave Manson	.30	.14	.04
☐ 51	Dean McAmmond	.30	.14	.04
☐ 52	Bill Ranford	.35	.16	.04
☐ 53	Doug Weight	.35	.16	.04
☐ 54	Brad Werenka	.30	.14	.04
☐ 55	Egeny Davydov	.30	.14	.04
☐ 56	Scott Levins	.30	.14	.04
☐ 57	Scott Mellanby	.30	.14	.04
☐ 58	Rob Niedermayer	1.25	.55	.16
☐ 59	Brian Skrudland	.30	.14	.04
☐ 60	John Vanbiesbrouck	.50	.23	.06
☐ 61	Robert Kron	.30	.14	.04
☐ 62	Michael Nylander	.50	.23	.06
☐ 63	Robert Petrovicky	.30	.14	.04
☐ 64	Chris Pronger	1.25	.55	.16
☐ 65	Geoff Sanderson	.75	.35	.09
☐ 66	Darren Turcotte	.30	.14	.04
☐ 67	Pat Verbeek	.35	.16	.04
☐ 68	Rob Blake	.35	.16	.04
☐ 69	Tony Granato	.30	.14	.04
☐ 70	Wayne Gretzky	10.00	4.50	1.25
☐ 71	Kelly Hrudey	.35	.16	.04

	MINT	EXC	G-VG
COMPLETE SET (10)	140.00	65.00	17.50
COMMON PLAYER (HB1-HB10)	4.00	1.80	.50

		MINT	EXC	G-VG
☐ HB1	Alexander Mogilny Best Goalscorer	10.00	4.50	1.25
☐ HB2	Rob Gaudreau Future Best Goalscorer	4.00	1.80	.50
☐ HB3	Brett Hull Best Shot	12.00	5.50	1.50
☐ HB4	Dallas Drake Future Best Shot	4.00	1.80	.50
☐ HB5	Pavel Bure Most Exciting Player	25.00	11.50	3.10
☐ HB6	Alexei Kovalev Future Most Exciting Player	12.00	5.50	1.50
☐ HB7	Mario Lemieux Best All-Around Player	25.00	11.50	3.10
☐ HB8	Eric Lindros Future Best All-Around Player	40.00	18.00	5.00
☐ HB9	Wayne Gretzky Best Passer	40.00	18.00	5.00
☐ HB10	Joe Juneau Future Best Passer	10.00	4.50	1.25

1993-94 Upper Deck SP

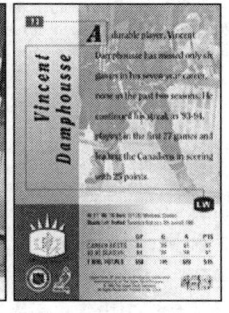

Inserted one per second-series pack and two per second-series jumbo, these 180 standard-size (2 1/2" by 3 1/2") cards feature color player action shots on their fronts. The photos are borderless, except at the bottom, where a team color-coded margin carries the player's name and position in white lettering. The player's team name appears in a silver-foil arc above him. The silver-foil set logo rests at the lower right. The back carries a ghosted and team color-screened action shot at the upper right, overprinted with player profile. Biography and statistics appear below. The cards are numbered on the back, grouped alphabetically within teams, and checklisted below alphabetically according to teams as follows: Anaheim Mighty Ducks (1-

☐	72 Shawn McEachern	.30	.14	.04
☐	73 Luc Robitaille	.75	.35	.09
☐	74 Darryl Sydor	.35	.16	.04
☐	75 Alexei Zhitnik	.50	.23	.06
☐	76 Brian Bellows	.35	.16	.04
☐	77 Vincent Damphousse	.35	.16	.04
☐	78 Stephan Lebeau	.30	.14	.04
☐	79 John LeClair	.30	.14	.04
☐	80 Kirk Muller	.35	.16	.04
☐	81 Patrick Roy	7.00	3.10	.85
☐	82 Pierre Sevigny	.30	.14	.04
☐	83 Claude Lemieux	.35	.16	.04
☐	84 Corey Millen	.30	.14	.04
☐	85 Bernie Nicholls	.35	.16	.04
☐	86 Scott Niedermayer	.60	.25	.08
☐	87 Stephane Richer	.35	.16	.04
☐	88 Alexander Semak	.30	.14	.04
☐	89 Scott Stevens	.35	.16	.04
☐	90 Ray Ferraro	.30	.14	.04
☐	91 Darius Kasparaitis	.30	.14	.04
☐	92 Scott Lachance	.30	.14	.04
☐	93 Vladimir Malakhov	.50	.23	.06
☐	94 Scott Scissons	.30	.14	.04
☐	95 Steve Thomas	.35	.16	.04
☐	96 Pierre Turgeon	.75	.35	.09
☐	97 Tony Amonte	.35	.16	.04
☐	98 Mike Gartner	.40	.18	.05
☐	99 Adam Graves	.75	.35	.09
☐	100 Alexander Karpovtsev	.35	.16	.04
☐	101 Alexei Kovalev	1.25	.55	.16
☐	102 Brian Leetch	1.00	.45	.13
☐	103 Mark Messier	.75	.35	.09
☐	104 Esa Tikkanen	.35	.16	.04
☐	105 Craig Billington	.30	.14	.04
☐	106 Robert Burakovsky	.30	.14	.04
☐	107 Alexandre Daigle	2.00	.90	.25
☐	108 Pavol Demitra	.30	.14	.04
☐	109 Dmitri Filimonov	.30	.14	.04
☐	110 Bob Kudelski	.35	.16	.04
☐	111 Norm Maciver	.30	.14	.04
☐	112 Alexei Yashin	2.50	1.15	.30
☐	113 Josef Beranek	.35	.16	.04
☐	114 Rod Brind'Amour	.50	.23	.06
☐	115 Milos Holan	.30	.14	.04
☐	116 Eric Lindros	10.00	4.50	1.25
☐	117 Mark Recchi	.75	.35	.09
☐	118 Mikael Renberg	2.50	1.15	.30
☐	119 Dimitri Yushkevich	.30	.14	.04
☐	120 Tom Barrasso	.35	.16	.04
☐	121 Jaromir Jagr	1.75	.80	.22
☐	122 Mario Lemieux	7.00	3.10	.85
☐	123 Markus Naslund	.50	.23	.06
☐	124 Kevin Stevens	.60	.25	.08
☐	125 Martin Straka	.60	.25	.08
☐	126 Rick Tocchet	.35	.16	.04
☐	127 Martin Gelinas	.30	.14	.04
☐	128 Owen Nolan	.35	.16	.04
☐	129 Mike Ricci	.35	.16	.04
☐	130 Joe Sakic	.75	.35	.09
☐	131 Chris Simon	.30	.14	.04
☐	132 Mats Sundin	1.00	.45	.13
☐	133 Jocelyn Thibault	2.00	.90	.25
☐	134 Philippe Bozon	.30	.14	.04
☐	135 Jeff Brown	.35	.16	.04
☐	136 Phil Housley	.35	.16	.04
☐	137 Brett Hull	3.00	1.35	.40
☐	138 Craig Janney	.40	.18	.05
☐	139 Curtis Joseph	.75	.35	.09
☐	140 Brendan Shanahan	.75	.35	.09
☐	141 Pat Falloon	.35	.16	.04
☐	142 Johan Garpenlov	.30	.14	.04
☐	143 Rob Gaudreau	.30	.14	.04
☐	144 Vlastimil Kroupa	.30	.14	.04
☐	145 Sergei Makarov	.35	.16	.04
☐	146 Sandis Ozolinsh	.60	.25	.08
☐	147 Mike Rathje	.30	.14	.04
☐	148 Brian Bradley	.30	.14	.04
☐	149 Chris Gratton	1.25	.55	.16
☐	150 Brent Gretzky	.75	.35	.09
☐	151 Roman Hamrlik	.50	.23	.06
☐	152 Petr Klima	.30	.14	.04
☐	153 Denis Savard	.40	.18	.05
☐	154 Rob Zamuner	.30	.14	.04
☐	155 Dave Andreychuk	.50	.23	.06
☐	156 Nikolai Borschevsky	.50	.23	.06
☐	157 Dave Ellett	.30	.14	.04
☐	158 Doug Gilmour	1.50	.65	.19
☐	159 Alexei Kudashov	.30	.14	.04
☐	160 Felix Potvin	5.00	2.30	.60
☐	161 Greg Adams	.30	.14	.04
☐	162 Pavel Bure	7.50	3.40	.95
☐	163 Geoff Courtnall	.30	.14	.04
☐	164 Trevor Linden	.75	.35	.09

☐	165 Kirk McLean	.75	.35	.09
☐	166 Jiri Slegr	.30	.14	.04
☐	167 Dixon Ward	.30	.14	.04
☐	168 Peter Bondra	.35	.16	.04
☐	169 Kevin Hatcher	.35	.16	.04
☐	170 Al Lafrate	.30	.14	.04
☐	171 Dimitri Khristich	.35	.16	.04
☐	172 Pat Peake	.50	.23	.06
☐	173 Mike Ridley	.35	.16	.04
☐	174 Arto Blomsten	.30	.14	.04
☐	175 Nelson Emerson	.35	.16	.04
☐	176 Boris Mironov	.30	.14	.04
☐	177 Teemu Selanne	3.00	1.35	.40
☐	178 Keith Tkachuk	.75	.35	.09
☐	179 Paul Ysebaert	.30	.14	.04
☐	180 Alexei Zhamnov	1.00	.45	.13

1993-94 Upper Deck Program of Excellence

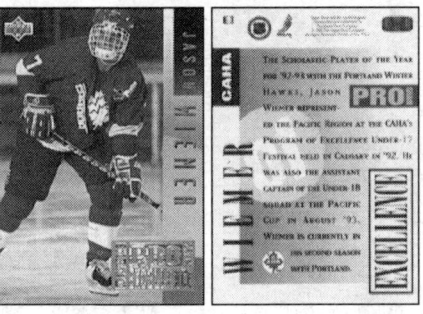

Randomly inserted in Canadian second series packs, this 15-card set measures the standard size (2 1/2" by 3 1/2"). The fronts feature color action player photos that are borderless, except at the right, where the margin carries the player's name in silver-foil letters. The silver-foil "Program of Excellence" logo rests at the lower right. The backs carry the player's name and career highlights. The cards are numbered on the back with an "E" prefix.

	MINT	EXC	G-VG
COMPLETE SET (15)	175.00	80.00	22.00
COMMON PLAYER (E1-E15)	8.00	3.60	1.00
☐ E1 Adam Smith Canada	8.00	3.60	1.00
☐ E2 Jason Podollan Canada	10.00	4.50	1.25
☐ E3 Jason Wiemer Canada	12.00	5.50	1.50
☐ E4 Jeff O'Neill Canada	15.00	6.75	1.90
☐ E5 Daniel Goneau Canada	8.00	3.60	1.00
☐ E6 Christian Laflamme Canada	8.00	3.60	1.00
☐ E7 Daymond Langkow Canada	12.00	5.50	1.50
☐ E8 Jeff Friesen Canada	18.00	8.00	2.30
☐ E9 Wayne Primeau Canada	12.00	5.50	1.50
☐ E10 Paul Kariya Canada	25.00	11.50	3.10
☐ E11 Rob Niedermayer Florida Panthers	10.00	4.50	1.25
☐ E12 Eric Lindros Philadelphia Flyers	40.00	18.00	5.00
☐ E13 Mario Lemieux Pittsburgh Penguins	28.00	12.50	3.50
☐ E14 Steve Yzerman Detroit Red Wings	14.00	6.25	1.75
☐ E15 Alexandre Daigle Ottawa Senators	12.00	5.50	1.50

1993-94 Upper Deck Silver Skates Hobby

Randomly inserted in second-series hobby packs, these 10 die-cut cards measure the standard size (2 1/2" by 3 1/2"). The fronts feature color player action cutouts set on red and black backgrounds. The player's name appears in black lettering within the die-cut silver-foil top edge. The back carries a color player action shot and career highlights. The cards are numbered on the back with an "H" prefix.

	MINT	EXC	G-VG
COMPLETE SET (10)	125.00	57.50	15.50
COMMON PLAYER (H1-H10)	7.00	3.10	.85
☐ H1 Mario Lemieux	28.00	12.50	3.50
Pittsburgh Penguins			
☐ H2 Pavel Bure	25.00	11.50	3.10
Vancouver Canucks			
☐ H3 Eric Lindros	35.00	16.00	4.40
Philadelphia Flyers			
☐ H4 Rob Niedermayer	10.00	4.50	1.25
Florida Panthers			
☐ H5 Chris Pronger	10.00	4.50	1.25
Hartford Whalers			
☐ H6 Adam Oates	7.00	3.10	.85
Boston Bruins			
☐ H7 Pierre Turgeon	7.00	3.10	.85
New York Islanders			
☐ H8 Alexei Yashin	14.00	6.25	1.75
Ottawa Senators			
☐ H9 Joe Sakic	8.00	3.60	1.00
Quebec Nordiques			
☐ H10 Alexander Mogilny	8.00	3.60	1.00
Buffalo Sabres			
☐ NNO Gold Trade Card	15.00	6.75	1.90
Wayne Gretzky			
☐ NNO Silver Trade Card	8.00	3.60	1.00
Wayne Gretzky			

1993-94 Upper Deck Silver Skates Retail

Randomly inserted in second-series retail packs, this 10-card set measures the standard size (2 1/2" by 3 1/2"). The fronts feature color player action cutouts set on red and black backgrounds. The player's name appears in black lettering within the die-cut silver-foil top edge. The back carries a color player action shot and career highlights. The cards are numbered on the back with an "R" prefix.

	MINT	EXC	G-VG
COMPLETE SET (10)	125.00	57.50	15.50
COMMON DIE-CUT (R1-R10)	10.00	4.50	1.25
*GOLD REDEEMED CARDS: 1X to 1.5X HI COLUMN VALUE			
☐ R1 Wayne Gretzky	35.00	16.00	4.40
Los Angeles Kings			
☐ R2 Teemu Selanne	15.00	6.75	1.90
Winnipeg Jets			
☐ R3 Alexandre Daigle	15.00	6.75	1.90
Ottawa Senators			
☐ R4 Chris Gratton	10.00	4.50	1.25
Tampa Bay Lightning			
☐ R5 Brett Hull	12.00	5.50	1.50
St. Louis Blues			
☐ R6 Steve Yzerman	12.00	5.50	1.50
Detroit Red Wings			
☐ R7 Doug Gilmour	12.00	5.50	1.50
Toronto Maple Leafs			
☐ R8 Jaromir Jagr	12.00	5.50	1.50
Pittsburgh Penguins			
☐ R9 Jason Arnott	20.00	9.00	2.50
Edmonton Oilers			
☐ R10 Jeremy Roenick	12.00	5.50	1.50
Chicago Blackhawks			

1994 Upper Deck NHLPA/Be A Player

This special 45-card set features the NHL's top players in unique settings. Upper Deck sent three top photographers, including Walter Iooss, to capture on film players in off-ice situations. Production was limited to 25,000 numbered cases. The first 18 cards bear Iooss' photos (Walter Iooss Collection) and are arranged alphabetically. Cards 19-40 are also arranged alphabetically and carry photos of the other photographers. The final five cards feature Doug Gilmour: A Canadian Hero (41-45). The cards promote the NHLPA line of clothing. All NHLPA clothing proceeds benefit a Special Assistance Fund for Former NHL Players. The front of each card features a borderless posed shot of the player relaxing in NHLPA clothing. The gold-foil Upper Deck logo appears in an upper corner. A gold-foil and motion-streaked hockey puck icon rests in a lower corner. The words "Be a Player" appear vertically in white lettering near the left edge. The back carries the player's name, position and team, along with information about the NHLPA clothes and Special Assistance Fund. The left side of the card back has either a quote from Iooss or personal information about the player. The cards are numbered on the back. The set was issued in a box with a checklist on its back.

		MINT	EXC	G-VG
COMPLETE SET (40)		20.00	8.00	2.00
COMMON PLAYER (1-40)		.25	.10	.02
☐ 1	Tony Amonte	.35	.14	.03
	New York Rangers			
☐ 2	Chris Chelios	.35	.14	.03
	Chicago Blackhawks			
☐ 3	Alexandre Daigle	1.00	.40	.10
	Ottawa Senators			
☐ 4	Dave Ellett	.25	.10	.02
	Toronto Maple Leafs			
☐ 5	Sergei Fedorov	1.50	.60	.15
	Detroit Red Wings			
☐ 6	Chris Gratton	.75	.30	.07
	Tampa Bay Lightning			
☐ 7	Wayne Gretzky	3.00	1.20	.30
	Los Angeles Kings			
☐ 8	Brett Hull	1.25	.50	.12
	St. Louis Blues			
☐ 9	Brian Leetch	.75	.30	.07
	New York Rangers			
☐ 10	Rob Niedermayer	.75	.30	.07
	Florida Panthers			
☐ 11	Felix Potvin	1.50	.60	.15
	Toronto Maple Leafs			
☐ 12	Luc Robitaille	.75	.30	.07
	Los Angeles Kings			
☐ 13	Jeremy Roenick	1.25	.50	.12
	Chicago Blackhawks			
☐ 14	Joe Sakic	.50	.20	.05
	Quebec Nordiques			
☐ 15	Teemu Selanne	1.25	.50	.12
	Winnipeg Jets			
☐ 16	Brendan Shanahan	.75	.30	.07
	St. Louis Blues			
☐ 17	Alexei Yashin	1.00	.40	.10
	Ottawa Senators			
☐ 18	Steve Yzerman	1.00	.40	.10
	Detroit Red Wings			
☐ 19	Jason Arnott	1.00	.40	.10
	Edmonton Oilers			
☐ 20	Pavel Bure	2.00	.80	.20
	Vancouver Canucks			
☐ 21	Theoren Fleury	.35	.14	.03
	Calgary Flames			
☐ 22	Mike Gartner	.35	.14	.03
	New York Rangers			
☐ 23	Kevin Haller	.25	.10	.02
	Montreal Canadiens			
☐ 24	Derian Hatcher	.25	.10	.02
	Dallas Stars			
☐ 25	Mark Howe	.75	.30	.07
	Gordie Howe			
	Detroit Red Wings			
☐ 26	Al Iafrate	.35	.14	.03
	Washington Capitals			
☐ 27	Joe Juneau	.75	.30	.07
	Boston Bruins			
☐ 28	Pat LaFontaine	.75	.30	.07
	Buffalo Sabres			
☐ 29	Eric Lindros	3.00	1.20	.30
	Philadelphia Flyers			
☐ 30	Dave Manson	.25	.10	.02
	Winnipeg Jets			
☐ 31	Mike Modano	.75	.30	.07
	Dallas Stars			
☐ 32	Scott Niedermayer	.35	.14	.03
	New Jersey Devils			
☐ 33	Owen Nolan	.35	.14	.03
	Quebec Nordiques			
☐ 34	Joel Otto	.25	.10	.02
	Calgary Flames			
☐ 35	Chris Pronger	.75	.30	.07
	Hartford Whalers			
☐ 36	Scott Stevens	.35	.14	.03
	New Jersey Devils			
☐ 37	Pierre Turgeon	.75	.30	.07
	New York Islanders			
☐ 38	Pat Verbeek	.25	.10	.02
	Hartford Whalers			
☐ 39	Doug Weight	.25	.10	.02
	Edmonton Oilers			
☐ 40	Terry Yake	.25	.10	.02
	Anaheim Mighty Ducks			
☐ 41	Doug Gilmour	.50	.20	.05
	(Two-Year Old Doug With A Hockey Stick)			
☐ 42	Doug Gilmour	.50	.20	.05
	(Nine-Year Old Doug On The Ice)			
☐ 43	Doug Gilmour	.50	.20	.05
	(Standing Next To A Little Girl)			
☐ 44	Doug Gilmour	.50	.20	.05
	(Sitting On Motorcycle)			
☐ 45	Doug Gilmour	.50	.20	.05
	(With Fishing Rod)			

1983-84 Vachon

 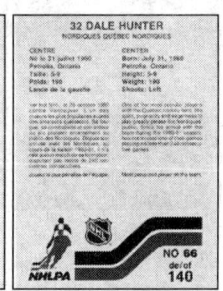

This set of 140 cards was issued by Vachon Foods as panels of two cards cards. The individual cards measure the standard 2 1/2" by 3 1/2". The set includes players from the seven Canadian NHL teams. The cards were also available as a set directly from Vachon. The first printing contained an error in that number 96 pictures Peter Ihnacek instead of Walt Poddubny. The error was corrected for the second printing. The card backs are written in French and English. The Vachon logo is on the front of every card in the lower right corner. The set is difficult to collect in uncut panels of two; the prices below are for individual cards, the panel prices are 50 percent greater than the prices listed below.

		MINT	EXC	G-VG
COMPLETE SET (140)		175.00	70.00	18.00
COMMON PLAYER (1-140)		.75	.30	.07
☐ 1	Paul Baxter	.75	.30	.07
☐ 2	Ed Beers	.75	.30	.07
☐ 3	Steve Bozek	.75	.30	.07
☐ 4	Mike Eaves	.75	.30	.07
☐ 5	Don Edwards	1.00	.40	.10
☐ 6	Kari Eloranta	.75	.30	.07
☐ 7	Dave Hindmarch	.75	.30	.07
☐ 8	Jamie Hislop	.75	.30	.07
☐ 9	Steve Konroyd	.75	.30	.07
☐ 10	Reggie Lemelin	1.00	.40	.10
☐ 11	Hakan Loob	1.25	.50	.12
☐ 12	Jamie Macoun	.75	.30	.07
☐ 13	Lanny McDonald	3.00	1.20	.30
☐ 14	Kent Nilsson	1.00	.40	.10
☐ 15	Colin Patterson	.75	.30	.07
☐ 16	Jim Peplinski	1.00	.40	.10
☐ 17	Paul Reinhart	1.00	.40	.10
☐ 18	Doug Risebrough	1.00	.40	.10
☐ 19	Steve Tambellini	.75	.30	.07
☐ 20	Mickey Volcan	.75	.30	.07
☐ 21	Glenn Anderson	3.00	1.20	.30
☐ 22	Paul Coffey	12.00	5.00	1.20
☐ 23	Lee Fogolin	.75	.30	.07
☐ 24	Grant Fuhr	5.00	2.00	.50
☐ 25	Randy Gregg	.75	.30	.07
☐ 26	Wayne Gretzky	50.00	20.00	5.00
☐ 27	Charlie Huddy	.75	.30	.07
☐ 28	Pat Hughes	.75	.30	.07
☐ 29	Dave Hunter	.75	.30	.07
☐ 30	Don Jackson	.75	.30	.07
☐ 31	Jari Kurri	5.00	2.00	.50
☐ 32	Willy Lindstrom	.75	.30	.07
☐ 33	Ken Linseman	1.00	.40	.10
☐ 34	Kevin Lowe	1.50	.60	.15
☐ 35	Dave Lumley	.75	.30	.07
☐ 36	Mark Messier	15.00	6.00	1.50
☐ 37	Andy Moog	5.00	2.00	.50
☐ 38	Jaroslav Pouzar	.75	.30	.07
☐ 39	Tom Roulston	.75	.30	.07
☐ 40	Dave Semenko	.75	.30	.07

☐ 41	Guy Carbonneau	3.00	1.20	.30
☐ 42	Kent Carlson	1.00	.40	.10
☐ 43	Gilbert Delorme	.75	.30	.07
☐ 44	Bob Gainey	2.00	.80	.20
☐ 45	Jean Hamel	.75	.30	.07
☐ 46	Mark Hunter	.75	.30	.07
☐ 47	Guy Lafleur	6.00	2.40	.60
☐ 48	Craig Ludwig	.75	.30	.07
☐ 49	Pierre Mondou	.75	.30	.07
☐ 50	Mats Naslund	1.25	.50	.12
☐ 51	Chris Nilan	1.00	.40	.10
☐ 52	Greg Paslawski	.75	.30	.07
☐ 53	Larry Robinson	2.00	.80	.20
☐ 54	Richard Sevigny	1.00	.40	.10
☐ 55	Steve Shutt	2.00	.80	.20
☐ 56	Bobby Smith	1.50	.60	.15
☐ 57	Mario Tremblay	.75	.30	.07
☐ 58	Ryan Walter	1.00	.40	.10
☐ 59	Rick Wamsley	1.00	.40	.10
☐ 60	Doug Wickenheiser	.75	.30	.07
☐ 61	Bo Berglund	.75	.30	.07
☐ 62	Dan Bouchard	.75	.30	.07
☐ 63	Alain Cote	.75	.30	.07
☐ 64	Brian Ford	.75	.30	.07
☐ 65	Michel Goulet	2.50	1.00	.25
☐ 66	Dale Hunter	2.00	.80	.20
☐ 67	Mario Marois	1.00	.40	.10
☐ 68	Tony McKegney	1.00	.40	.10
☐ 69	Randy Moller	.75	.30	.07
☐ 70	Wilf Paiement	1.00	.40	.10
☐ 71	Pat Price	.75	.30	.07
☐ 72	Normand Rochefort	.75	.30	.07
☐ 73	Andre Savard	.75	.30	.07
☐ 74	Louis Sleigher	.75	.30	.07
☐ 75	Anton Stastny	1.00	.40	.10
☐ 76	Marian Stastny	1.00	.40	.10
☐ 77	Peter Stastny	6.00	2.40	.60
☐ 78	John Van Boxmeer	.75	.30	.07
☐ 79	Wally Weir	.75	.30	.07
☐ 80	Blake Wesley	.75	.30	.07
☐ 81	John Anderson	1.00	.40	.10
☐ 82	Jim Benning	.75	.30	.07
☐ 83	Dan Daoust	.75	.30	.07
☐ 84	Bill Derlago	.75	.30	.07
☐ 85	Dave Farrish	.75	.30	.07
☐ 86	Miroslav Frycer	.75	.30	.07
☐ 87	Stewart Gavin	1.00	.40	.10
☐ 88	Gaston Gingras	.75	.30	.07
☐ 89	Billy Harris	.75	.30	.07
☐ 90	Peter Inhacak	1.00	.40	.10
☐ 91	Jim Korn	.75	.30	.07
☐ 92	Terry Martin	.75	.30	.07
☐ 93	Dale McCourt	1.00	.40	.10
☐ 94	Gary Nylund	1.00	.40	.10
☐ 95	Mike Palmateer	1.00	.40	.10
☐ 96A	Walt Poddubny ERR	10.00	4.00	1.00
	(Photo actually			
	Peter Inhacek,			
	no mustache)			
☐ 96B	Walt Poddubny COR	2.50	1.00	.25
	(With mustache)			
☐ 97	Borje Salming	2.00	.80	.20
☐ 98	Rick St.Croix	.75	.30	.07
☐ 99	Greg P. Terrion	.75	.30	.07
☐ 100	Rick Vaive	1.00	.40	.10
☐ 101	Richard Brodeur	1.00	.40	.10
☐ 102	Jiri Bubla	.75	.30	.07
☐ 103	Garth Butcher	1.50	.60	.15
☐ 104	Ron Delorme	.75	.30	.07
☐ 105	John Garrett	1.00	.40	.10
☐ 106	Jere Gillis	.75	.30	.07
☐ 107	Thomas Gradin	1.00	.40	.10
☐ 108	Doug Halward	.75	.30	.07
☐ 109	Mark Kirton	.75	.30	.07
☐ 110	Rick Lanz	.75	.30	.07
☐ 111	Gary Lupul	.75	.30	.07
☐ 112	Kevin McCarthy	.75	.30	.07
☐ 113	Lars Molin	.75	.30	.07
☐ 114	Jim Nill	.75	.30	.07
☐ 115	Darcy Rota	.75	.30	.07
☐ 116	Stan Smyl	1.00	.40	.10
☐ 117	Harold Snepsts	1.25	.50	.12
☐ 118	Patrik Sundstrom	1.00	.40	.10
☐ 119	Tony Tanti	1.00	.40	.10
☐ 120	Dave(Tiger) Williams	1.25	.50	.12
☐ 121	Scott Arniel	.75	.30	.07
☐ 122	Dave Babych	1.00	.40	.10
☐ 123	Laurie Boschmann	.75	.30	.07
☐ 124	Wade Campbell	.75	.30	.07
☐ 125	Lucien DeBlois	.75	.30	.07
☐ 126	Dale Hawerchuk	6.00	2.40	.60
☐ 127	Brian Hayward	1.25	.50	.12
☐ 128	Jim Kyte	.75	.30	.07

☐ 129	Morris Lukowich	.75	.30	.07
☐ 130	Bengt Lundholm	.75	.30	.07
☐ 131	Paul MacLean	1.00	.40	.10
☐ 132	Moe Mantha	.75	.30	.07
☐ 133	Andrew McBain	.75	.30	.07
☐ 134	Brian Mullen	1.50	.60	.15
☐ 135	Robert Picard	.75	.30	.07
☐ 136	Doug Smail	1.00	.40	.10
☐ 137	Doug Soetaert	.75	.30	.07
☐ 138	Thomas Steen	1.25	.50	.12
☐ 139	Tim Watters	.75	.30	.07
☐ 140	Tim Young	.75	.30	.07

1923-24 V128-1 Paulins Candy

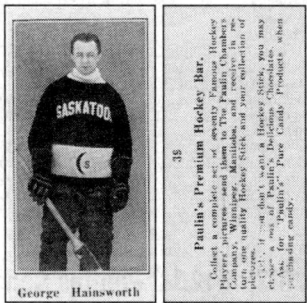

This 70-card set was issued during the 1923-24 season and featured players from the WCHL. The horizontal back explains how to obtain either a hockey stick or a box of Paulin's chocolates by collecting and sending in the complete Famous Hockey Players set. The cards were to be returned to the collector with the hockey stick or chocolates. The cards are in black and white and measure approximately 1 3/8" by 2 3/4". The cards are numbered on the back.

		EX-MT	VG-E	GOOD
COMPLETE SET (70)		8500.00	3750.00	850.00
COMMON PLAYER (1-70)		100.00	40.00	10.00
☐ 1	Bill Borland	150.00	60.00	15.00
☐ 2	Pete Speirs	100.00	40.00	10.00
☐ 3	Jack Hughes	100.00	40.00	10.00
☐ 4	Errol Gillis	100.00	40.00	10.00
☐ 5	Cecil Browne	100.00	40.00	10.00
☐ 6	W. Roberts	100.00	40.00	10.00
☐ 7	Howard Brandon	100.00	40.00	10.00
☐ 8	Fred Comfort	100.00	40.00	10.00
☐ 9	Cliff O'Meara	100.00	40.00	10.00
☐ 10	Leo Benard	100.00	40.00	10.00
☐ 11	Lloyd Harvey	100.00	40.00	10.00
☐ 12	Bobby Connors	100.00	40.00	10.00
☐ 13	Daddy Dalman	100.00	40.00	10.00
☐ 14	Dub Mackie	100.00	40.00	10.00
☐ 15	Lorne Chabot	150.00	60.00	15.00
☐ 16	Phat Wilson	100.00	40.00	10.00
☐ 17	Wilf L'Heureux	100.00	40.00	10.00
☐ 18	Danny Cox	100.00	40.00	10.00
☐ 19	Bill Brydge	100.00	40.00	10.00
☐ 20	Alex Gray	100.00	40.00	10.00
☐ 21	Albert Pudas	100.00	40.00	10.00
☐ 22	Jack Irwin	100.00	40.00	10.00
☐ 23	Puss Traub	100.00	40.00	10.00
☐ 24	Red McCusker	100.00	40.00	10.00
☐ 25	Jack Asseltine	100.00	40.00	10.00
☐ 26	Duke Dutkowski	100.00	40.00	10.00
☐ 27	Charley McVeigh	100.00	40.00	10.00
☐ 28	George Hay	200.00	80.00	20.00
☐ 29	Amby Moran	100.00	40.00	10.00
☐ 30	Barney Stanley	200.00	80.00	20.00
☐ 31	Art Gagne	100.00	40.00	10.00
☐ 32	Louis Berlinquette	100.00	40.00	10.00
☐ 33	P.C. Stevens	100.00	40.00	10.00
☐ 34	W.D. Elmer	100.00	40.00	10.00
☐ 35	Bill Cook	300.00	120.00	30.00
☐ 36	Leo Reise	100.00	40.00	10.00
☐ 37	Curly Headley	200.00	80.00	20.00
☐ 38	Newsy Lalonde	500.00	200.00	50.00

☐ 39	George Hainsworth	400.00	160.00	40.00
☐ 40	Laurie Scott	100.00	40.00	10.00
☐ 41	Joe Simpson	300.00	120.00	30.00
☐ 42	Bob Trapp	100.00	40.00	10.00
☐ 43	Joe McCormick	100.00	40.00	10.00
☐ 44	Ty Arbour	100.00	40.00	10.00
☐ 45	Duke Keats	100.00	40.00	10.00
☐ 46	Hal Winkler	100.00	40.00	10.00
☐ 47	Johnny Sheppard	100.00	40.00	10.00
☐ 48	Crutchy Morrison	100.00	40.00	10.00
☐ 49	Spunk Sparrow	100.00	40.00	10.00
☐ 50	Percy McGregor	100.00	40.00	10.00
☐ 51	Harry Tuckwell	100.00	40.00	10.00
☐ 52	Chubby Scott	100.00	40.00	10.00
☐ 53	Scotty Fraser	100.00	40.00	10.00
☐ 54	Bob Davis	100.00	40.00	10.00
☐ 55	Clucker White	100.00	40.00	10.00
☐ 56	Bob Armstrong	100.00	40.00	10.00
☐ 57	Doc Longtry	100.00	40.00	10.00
☐ 58	Darb Sommers	100.00	40.00	10.00
☐ 59	Frank Hacquoil	100.00	40.00	10.00
☐ 60	Stan Evans	100.00	40.00	10.00
☐ 61	Ed Oatman	100.00	40.00	10.00
☐ 62	Mervyn(Red) Dutton	300.00	120.00	30.00
☐ 63	Herb Gardiner	200.00	80.00	20.00
☐ 64	Bernie Morris	100.00	40.00	10.00
☐ 65	Bobbie Benson	100.00	40.00	10.00
☐ 66	Ernie Anderson	100.00	40.00	10.00
☐ 67	Cully Wilson	100.00	40.00	10.00
☐ 68	Charlie Reid	100.00	40.00	10.00
☐ 69	Harry Oliver	200.00	80.00	20.00
☐ 70	Rusty Crawford	200.00	80.00	20.00

1928-29 V128-2 Paulins Candy

This scarce set of 90 black and white cards was produced and distributed in Western Canada and features Western Canadian teams and players. The cards are numbered on the back and measure approximately 1 3/8" by 2 5/8". The card back details an offer (expiring June 1st, 1929) of a hockey stick prize (or box of chocolates for girls) if someone could bring in a complete set of 90 cards; perhaps that is why, after all these years, there are still two cards unknown. Players on the Calgary Jimmies are not explicitly identified on the card so they are listed below without a specific player name. The complete set price below does not include either of the unknown cards, numbers 9 and 20.

	EX-MT	VG-E	GOOD
COMPLETE SET (88)	6000.00	2500.00	600.00
COMMON TEAM (1-40)	75.00	30.00	7.50
COMMON PLAYER (41-90)	75.00	30.00	7.50

☐ 1	Univ. of Man. Girls Hockey Team	100.00	40.00	10.00
☐ 2	Elgin Hockey Team	75.00	30.00	7.50
☐ 3	Brandon Schools Boy Champions	75.00	30.00	7.50
☐ 4	Port Arthur Hockey Team	75.00	30.00	7.50
☐ 5	Enderby Hockey Team	75.00	30.00	7.50
☐ 6	Humboldt High School Team	75.00	30.00	7.50
☐ 7	Regina Collegiate Hockey Team	75.00	30.00	7.50
☐ 8	Weyburn Reavers	75.00	30.00	7.50
☐ 10	M.A.C. Junior Hockey	75.00	30.00	7.60
☐ 11	Vermillion Agri-cultural School	75.00	30.00	7.50
☐ 12	Rovers, Cranbrook, B.C.	75.00	30.00	7.50
☐ 13	Empire School, Moose Jaw	75.00	30.00	7.50
☐ 14	Arts Senior Hockey	75.00	30.00	7.50
☐ 15	Juvenile Varsity Hockey	75.00	30.00	7.50
☐ 16	St. Peter's College Hockey	75.00	30.00	7.50
☐ 17	Arts Girls Hockey	100.00	40.00	10.00
☐ 18	Swan River Hockey Team	75.00	30.00	7.50
☐ 19	U.M.S.U. Junior Hockey Team	75.00	30.00	7.50
☐ 21	Drinkwater Hockey Team	75.00	30.00	7.50
☐ 22	Elks Hockey Team,	75.00	30.00	7.50

☐ 23	Biggar, Saskatchewan South Calgary High School	75.00	30.00	7.50
☐ 24	Meota Hockey	75.00	30.00	7.50
☐ 25	Chartered Accountants	100.00	40.00	10.00
☐ 26	Nutana Collegiate Hockey Team	75.00	30.00	7.50
☐ 27	MacLeod Hockey Team	75.00	30.00	7.50
☐ 28	Arts Junior Hockey	75.00	30.00	7.50
☐ 29	Fort William Juniors	75.00	30.00	7.50
☐ 30	Swan Lake Hockey Team	75.00	30.00	7.50
☐ 31	Dauphin Hockey Team	75.00	30.00	7.50
☐ 32	Mount Royal Hockey Team	75.00	30.00	7.50
☐ 33	Port Arthur W. End Junior Hockey	75.00	30.00	7.50
☐ 34	Hanna Hockey Club	75.00	30.00	7.50
☐ 35	Vermillion Junior Hockey	75.00	30.00	7.50
☐ 36	Smithers Hockey Team	75.00	30.00	7.50
☐ 37	Lloydminster High School	75.00	30.00	7.50
☐ 38	Winnipeg Rangers	100.00	40.00	10.00
☐ 39	Delisle Intermediate Hockey	75.00	30.00	7.50
☐ 40	Moose Jaw College Senior Hockey	75.00	30.00	7.50
☐ 41	Art Bonneyman	75.00	30.00	7.50
☐ 42	Jimmy Graham	75.00	30.00	7.50
☐ 43	Pat O'Hunter	75.00	30.00	7.50
☐ 44	Leo Moret	75.00	30.00	7.50
☐ 45	Blondie McLennan	75.00	30.00	7.50
☐ 46	Red Beattie	75.00	30.00	7.50
☐ 47	Frank Peters	75.00	30.00	7.50
☐ 48	Lloyd McIntyre	75.00	30.00	7.50
☐ 49	Art Somers	75.00	30.00	7.50
☐ 50	Ikey Morrison	75.00	30.00	7.50
☐ 51	Jimmies, Calgary	75.00	30.00	7.50
☐ 52	Don Cummings	75.00	30.00	7.50
☐ 53	Jimmies, Calgary	75.00	30.00	7.50
☐ 54	P. Gerlitz	75.00	30.00	7.50
☐ 55	A. Kay	75.00	30.00	7.50
☐ 56	Paul Runge	75.00	30.00	7.50
☐ 57	J. Gerlitz	75.00	30.00	7.50
☐ 58	H. Gerlitz	75.00	30.00	7.50
☐ 59	C. Biles	75.00	30.00	7.50
☐ 60	Jimmy Evans	75.00	30.00	7.50
☐ 61	Ira Stuart	75.00	30.00	7.50
☐ 62	Berg Irving	75.00	30.00	7.50
☐ 63	Cecil Browne	75.00	30.00	7.50
☐ 64	Nick Wasnie	75.00	30.00	7.50
☐ 65	Gordon Teal	75.00	30.00	7.50
☐ 66	Jack Hughes	75.00	30.00	7.50
☐ 67	D. Yeatman	75.00	30.00	7.50
☐ 68	Connie Johanneson	75.00	30.00	7.50
☐ 69	S. Walters	75.00	30.00	7.50
☐ 70	Harold McMunn	75.00	30.00	7.50
☐ 71	Smokey Harris	75.00	30.00	7.50
☐ 72	Jimmies, Calgary	75.00	30.00	7.50
☐ 73	Bernie Morris	75.00	30.00	7.50
☐ 74	J. Fowler	75.00	30.00	7.50
☐ 75	Jimmies, Calgary	75.00	30.00	7.50
☐ 76	Pete Spiers	75.00	30.00	7.50
☐ 77	Bill Borland	75.00	30.00	7.50
☐ 78	Cliff O'Meara	75.00	30.00	7.50
☐ 79	F. Porteous	75.00	30.00	7.50
☐ 80	W. Brooks	75.00	30.00	7.50
☐ 81	Everett McGowan	75.00	30.00	7.50
☐ 82	Jimmies, Calgary	75.00	30.00	7.50
☐ 83	George Dame	75.00	30.00	7.50
☐ 84	Jimmies, Calgary	75.00	30.00	7.50
☐ 85	Jimmies, Calgary	75.00	30.00	7.50
☐ 86	Jimmies, Calgary	75.00	30.00	7.50
☐ 87	Heck Fowler	75.00	30.00	7.50
☐ 88	Jimmy Hoyle	75.00	30.00	7.50
☐ 89	Charlie Gardiner	125.00	50.00	12.50
☐ 90	Jimmies, Calgary	75.00	30.00	7.50

1933-34 V129

This 50-card set was issued anonymously during the 1933-34 season. The cards are sepia tone and measure approximately 1 5/8" by 2 7/8". The cards are numbered on the back with the capsule biography both in French and in English. Card number 39 is now known to exist but is quite scarce as it was the card that the company (allegedly) purposely withheld in order to make it difficult to complete

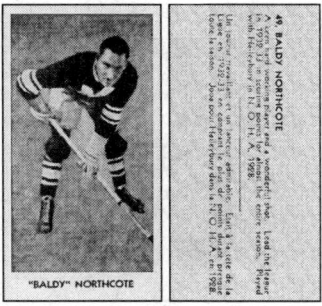

"BALDY" NORTHCOTE

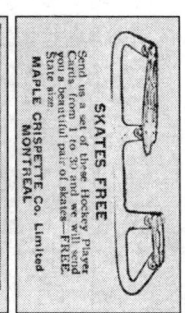

Aurel Joliat   14

the set. The short-printed Oliver card is not included in the complete set price below.

	EX-MT	VG-E	GOOD
COMPLETE SET (49)	13500.	5500.	1350.
COMMON PLAYER (1-50)	150.00	60.00	15.00
□ 1 Red Horner	400.00	160.00	40.00
□ 2 Clarence(Hap) Day	300.00	120.00	30.00
□ 3 Ace Bailey	500.00	200.00	50.00
□ 4 Buzz Boll	150.00	60.00	15.00
□ 5 Charlie Conacher	750.00	300.00	75.00
□ 6 Harvey(Busher) Jackson	400.00	160.00	40.00
□ 7 Joe Primeau	350.00	140.00	35.00
□ 8 King Clancy	750.00	300.00	75.00
□ 9 Alex Levinsky	175.00	70.00	18.00
□ 10 Bill Thoms	150.00	60.00	15.00
□ 11 Andy Blair	150.00	60.00	15.00
□ 12 Harold Cotton	150.00	60.00	15.00
□ 13 George Hainsworth	400.00	160.00	40.00
□ 14 Ken Doraty	150.00	60.00	15.00
□ 15 Fred Robertson	150.00	60.00	15.00
□ 16 Charlie Sands	150.00	60.00	15.00
□ 17 Hec Kilrea	150.00	60.00	15.00
□ 18 John Ross Roach	150.00	60.00	15.00
□ 19 Larry Aurie	150.00	60.00	15.00
□ 20 Ebbie Goodfellow	300.00	120.00	30.00
□ 21 Normie Himes	150.00	60.00	15.00
□ 22 Bill Brydge	150.00	60.00	15.00
□ 23 Mervyn(Red) Dutton	300.00	120.00	30.00
□ 24 Cooney Weiland	300.00	120.00	30.00
□ 25 Bill Beveridge	150.00	60.00	15.00
□ 26 Frank Finnigan	150.00	60.00	15.00
□ 27 Albert Leduc	175.00	70.00	18.00
(Battleship)			
□ 28 Babe Siebert	400.00	160.00	40.00
□ 29 Murray Murdock	150.00	60.00	15.00
□ 30 Butch Keeling	150.00	60.00	15.00
□ 31 Bill Cook	300.00	120.00	30.00
□ 32 Cecil Dillon	150.00	60.00	15.00
□ 33 Ivan(Ching) Johnson	400.00	160.00	40.00
□ 34 Ott Heller	150.00	60.00	15.00
□ 35 Red Beattie	150.00	60.00	15.00
□ 36 Dit Clapper	400.00	160.00	40.00
□ 37 Eddie Shore	1800.00	725.00	180.00
□ 38 Marty Barry	350.00	140.00	35.00
□ 39 Harry Oliver SP	6000.00	2500.00	600.00
□ 40 Bob Gracie	150.00	60.00	15.00
□ 41 Howie Morenz	2000.00	800.00	200.00
□ 42 Pit Lepine	150.00	60.00	15.00
□ 43 Johnny Gagnon	150.00	60.00	15.00
□ 44 Armand Mondou	150.00	60.00	15.00
□ 45 Lorne Chabot	175.00	70.00	18.00
□ 46 Bun Cook	175.00	70.00	18.00
□ 47 Alex Smith	150.00	60.00	15.00
□ 48 Danny Cox	150.00	60.00	15.00
□ 49 Baldy Northcott	175.00	70.00	18.00
□ 50 Paul Thompson	175.00	70.00	18.00

1924-25 V130 Maple Crispette

This 30-card set was issued during the 1924-25 season in the Montreal area. The cards are in black and white and measure approximately 1 3/8" by 2 3/8". There was a prize offer detailed on the reverse of every card offering a pair of hockey skates for a complete set of the cards. Card number

15 apparently was the "impossible" card that prevented most collectors of that day from ever getting the skates. The cards are numbered on the front in the lower right hand corner. The set is considered complete without the short-printed Cleghorn.

	EX-MT	VG-E	GOOD
COMPLETE SET (29)	7000.00	2750.00	700.00
COMMON PLAYER (1-30)	125.00	50.00	12.50
□ 1 Capt. Dunc Munro	175.00	70.00	18.00
□ 2 Clint Benedict	250.00	100.00	25.00
□ 3 Norman Fowler	125.00	50.00	12.50
Boston			
□ 4 Curly Headley	125.00	50.00	12.50
Boston			
□ 5 Alf Skinner	125.00	50.00	12.50
Boston			
□ 6 Bill Cook	250.00	100.00	25.00
Boston			
□ 7 Smokey Harris	125.00	50.00	12.50
Boston			
□ 8 Jim Herberts	125.00	50.00	12.50
Boston			
□ 9 Carson Cooper	125.00	50.00	12.50
Boston			
□ 10 Red Greenilton	125.00	50.00	12.50
Hamilton			
□ 11 Billy Boucher	125.00	50.00	12.50
□ 12 Howie Morenz	1500.00	200.00	50.00
□ 13 Georges Vezina	1000.00	400.00	100.00
□ 14 Aurel Joliat	600.00	240.00	60.00
□ 15 Sprague Cleghorn SP	6000.00	2500.00	600.00
□ 16 Dutch Cain	125.00	50.00	12.50
□ 17 Charlie Dinsmore	125.00	50.00	12.50
□ 18 Punch Broadbent	250.00	100.00	25.00
□ 19 Sam Rothschild	125.00	50.00	12.50
□ 20 George Carroll	125.00	50.00	12.50
□ 21 Billy Burch	250.00	100.00	25.00
Hamilton			
□ 22 Shorty Green	250.00	100.00	25.00
Hamilton			
□ 23 Mickey Roach	125.00	50.00	12.50
Hamilton			
□ 24 Ken Randall	125.00	50.00	12.50
Hamilton			
□ 25 Vernon Forbes	125.00	50.00	12.50
Hamilton			
□ 26 Charlie Langlois	125.00	50.00	12.50
□ 27 Newsy Lalonde	500.00	200.00	50.00
□ 28 Fred(Frock) Lowrey	125.00	50.00	12.50
□ 29 Ganton Scott	125.00	50.00	12.50
□ 30 Louis Berlinguette	150.00	60.00	15.00

1923-24 V145-1

This relatively unattractive 40-card set is printed in sepia tone. The cards measure approximately 2" by 3 1/4". The cards have blank backs. The cards are numbered on the front in the lower left corner. The player's name, team, and National Hockey League are at the bottom of each card. The issuer of the set is not indicated in any way on the card. This set is easily confused with the other V145 set. Except for the

tint and size differences and the different card name/number correspondence, these sets are essentially the same. Thankfully the only player with the same number in both sets is number 3 King Clancy. Supposedly card 25 Bert Corbeau is hard to find and may have been short printed, but is nevertheless included in the complete set price below.

	EX-MT	VG-E	GOOD
COMPLETE SET (40)	12000.	5000.	1250.
COMMON PLAYER (1-40)	100.00	40.00	10.00

		EX-MT	VG-E	GOOD
☐ 1	Eddie Gerard	250.00	100.00	25.00
☐ 2	Frank Nighbor	300.00	120.00	30.00
☐ 3	King Clancy	1500.00	600.00	150.00
☐ 4	Jack Darragh	200.00	80.00	20.00
☐ 5	Harry Helman	100.00	40.00	10.00
☐ 6	George(Buck) Boucher	200.00	80.00	20.00
☐ 7	Clint Benedict	200.00	80.00	20.00
☐ 8	Lionel Hitchman	100.00	40.00	10.00
☐ 9	Punch Broadbent	250.00	100.00	25.00
☐ 10	Cy Denneny	350.00	140.00	35.00
☐ 11	Sprague Cleghorn	250.00	100.00	25.00
☐ 12	Sylvio Mantha	200.00	80.00	20.00
☐ 13	Joe Malone	300.00	120.00	30.00
☐ 14	Aurel Joliat	1200.00	500.00	125.00
☐ 15	Howie Morenz	2500.00	1000.00	250.00
☐ 16	Billy Boucher	100.00	40.00	10.00
☐ 17	Billy Coutu	100.00	40.00	10.00
☐ 18	Odie Cleghorn	125.00	50.00	12.50
☐ 19	Georges Vezina	1200.00	500.00	125.00
☐ 20	Amos Arbour	100.00	40.00	10.00
☐ 21	Lloyd Andrews	100.00	40.00	10.00
☐ 22	Red Stuart	100.00	40.00	10.00
☐ 23	Cecil(Babe) Dye	300.00	120.00	30.00
☐ 24	Jack Adams	300.00	120.00	30.00
☐ 25	Bert Corbeau SP	1500.00	600.00	150.00
☐ 26	Reg Noble	200.00	80.00	20.00
☐ 27	Stan Jackson	100.00	40.00	10.00
☐ 28	John Ross Roach	100.00	40.00	10.00
☐ 29	Vernon Forbes	100.00	40.00	10.00
☐ 30	Shorty Green	200.00	80.00	20.00
☐ 31	Red Green	100.00	40.00	10.00
☐ 32	Goldie Prodgers	100.00	40.00	10.00
☐ 33	Leo Reise	100.00	40.00	10.00
☐ 34	Ken Randall	100.00	40.00	10.00
☐ 35	Billy Burch	200.00	80.00	20.00
☐ 36	Jesse Spring	100.00	40.00	10.00
☐ 37	Eddie Bouchard	100.00	40.00	10.00
☐ 38	Mickey Roach	100.00	40.00	10.00
☐ 39	Chas. Fraser	100.00	40.00	10.00
☐ 40	Corbett Denneny	150.00	60.00	15.00

1924-25 V145-2

This 60-card set was issued anonymously during the 1924-25 season. The cards have a green-black tint and measure approximately 1 3/4" by 3 1/4". Cards are numbered in the lower left corner and have a blank back. The player's name, team, and National Hockey League are at the bottom of each card. The issuer of the set is not indicated in any way on the card. This set is easily confused with the other V145 set. Except for the tint and size differences and the different card name/number correspondence, these sets are essentially the

same. Thankfully the only player with the same number in both sets is number 3 King Clancy.

	EX-MT	VG-E	GOOD
COMPLETE SET (60)	11000.	4500.	1100.
COMMON PLAYER (1-60)	100.00	40.00	10.00

		EX-MT	VG-E	GOOD
☐ 1	Joe Ironstone	150.00	60.00	15.00
☐ 2	George(Buck) Boucher	200.00	80.00	20.00
☐ 3	King Clancy	1500.00	600.00	150.00
☐ 4	Lionel Hitchman	100.00	40.00	10.00
☐ 5	Hooley Smith	250.00	100.00	25.00
☐ 6	Frank Nighbor	200.00	80.00	20.00
☐ 7	Cy Denneny	250.00	100.00	25.00
☐ 8	Spiff Campbell	100.00	40.00	10.00
☐ 9	Frank Finnigan	150.00	60.00	15.00
☐ 10	Alex Connell	250.00	100.00	25.00
☐ 11	Vernon Forbes	100.00	40.00	10.00
☐ 12	Ken Randall	100.00	40.00	10.00
☐ 13	Billy Burch	200.00	80.00	20.00
☐ 14	Shorty Green	200.00	80.00	20.00
☐ 15	Red Green	100.00	40.00	10.00
☐ 16	Alex McKinnon	100.00	40.00	10.00
☐ 17	Charlie Langlois	100.00	40.00	10.00
☐ 18	Mickey Roach	100.00	40.00	10.00
☐ 19	Eddie Bouchard	100.00	40.00	10.00
☐ 20	Jesse Spring	100.00	40.00	10.00
☐ 21	Carson Cooper	100.00	40.00	10.00
☐ 22	Smokey Harris	100.00	40.00	10.00
☐ 23	Gopher Headley	100.00	40.00	10.00
☐ 24	Bill Cook	200.00	80.00	20.00
☐ 25	Jim Herberts	100.00	40.00	10.00
☐ 26	Werner Schnarr	100.00	40.00	10.00
☐ 27	Alf Skinner	100.00	40.00	10.00
☐ 28	George Redding	100.00	40.00	10.00
☐ 29	Herbie Mitchell	100.00	40.00	10.00
☐ 30	Hek Fowler	100.00	40.00	10.00
☐ 31	Red Stuart	100.00	40.00	10.00
☐ 32	Clint Benedict	200.00	80.00	20.00
☐ 33	Gerald Munro	100.00	40.00	10.00
☐ 34	Dunc Munro	100.00	40.00	10.00
☐ 35	Dutch Cain	100.00	40.00	10.00
☐ 36	Fred(Frock) Lowrey	100.00	40.00	10.00
☐ 37	Sam Rothschild	100.00	40.00	10.00
☐ 38	Ganton Scott	100.00	40.00	10.00
☐ 39	Punch Broadbent	250.00	100.00	25.00
☐ 40	Charlie Dinsmore	100.00	40.00	10.00
☐ 41	Louis Berlinquette	100.00	40.00	10.00
☐ 42	George Carroll	100.00	40.00	10.00
☐ 43	Georges Vezina	800.00	320.00	80.00
☐ 44	Billy Coutu	100.00	40.00	10.00
☐ 45	Odie Cleghorn	125.00	50.00	12.50
☐ 46	Billy Boucher	100.00	40.00	10.00
☐ 47	Howie Morenz	2000.00	800.00	200.00
☐ 48	Aurel Joliat	800.00	320.00	80.00
☐ 49	Sprague Cleghorn	200.00	80.00	20.00
☐ 50	Billy Mantha	100.00	40.00	10.00
☐ 51	Reg Noble	200.00	80.00	20.00
☐ 52	John Ross Roach	100.00	40.00	10.00
☐ 53	Jack Adams	200.00	80.00	20.00
☐ 54	Cecil(Babe) Dye	200.00	80.00	20.00
☐ 55	Reg Reid	100.00	40.00	10.00
☐ 56	Albert Holway	100.00	40.00	10.00
☐ 57	Bert McCaffery	100.00	40.00	10.00
☐ 58	Bert Corbeau	125.00	50.00	12.50
☐ 59	Lloyd Andrews	100.00	40.00	10.00
☐ 60	Stan Jackson	125.00	50.00	12.50

1933-34 V252 Canadian Gum

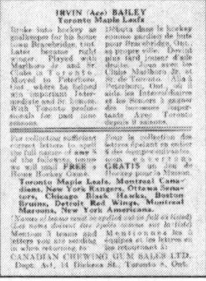

This unnumbered set of 50 cards was designated V252 by the American Card Catalog. Cards are black and white pictures with a red border. Backs are written in both French and English. Cards measure approximately 2 1/2" by 3 1/4" including a 3/4" tab at the bottom describing a premium (contest) offer and containing one large letter. When enough of these letters were saved so that the collector could spell out the names of five NHL teams, they could be redeemed for a free home hockey game according to the details given on the card backs. The cards are checklisted in alphabetical order.

	EX-MT	VG-E	GOOD
COMPLETE SET (50)	8000.00	3250.00	800.00
COMMON PLAYER (1-50)	90.00	36.00	9.00

		EX-MT	VG-E	GOOD
☐ 1	Clarence(Taffy) Abel	125.00	50.00	12.50
☐ 2	Larry Aurie	90.00	36.00	9.00
☐ 3	Ace Bailey	300.00	120.00	30.00
☐ 4	Helge Bostrom	90.00	36.00	9.00
☐ 5	Bill Brydge	90.00	36.00	9.00
☐ 6	Glyn Brydson	90.00	36.00	9.00
☐ 7	Marty Burke	90.00	36.00	9.00
☐ 8	Gerald Carson	90.00	36.00	9.00
☐ 9	Lorne Chabot	125.00	50.00	12.50
☐ 10	King Clancy	600.00	240.00	60.00
☐ 11	Dit Clapper	250.00	100.00	25.00
☐ 12	Charlie Conacher	500.00	200.00	50.00
☐ 13	Lionel Conacher	300.00	120.00	30.00
☐ 14	Alex Connell	175.00	70.00	18.00
☐ 15	Bun Cook	125.00	50.00	12.50
☐ 16	Danny Cox	90.00	36.00	9.00
☐ 17	Clarence(Hap) Day	200.00	80.00	20.00
☐ 18	Cecil Dillon	90.00	36.00	9.00
☐ 19	Lorne Duguid	125.00	50.00	12.50
☐ 20	Duke Dutkowski	90.00	36.00	9.00
☐ 21	Mervyn(Red) Dutton	175.00	70.00	18.00
☐ 22	Happy Emms	90.00	36.00	9.00
☐ 23	Frank Finnigan	125.00	50.00	12.50
☐ 24	Chuck Gardiner	175.00	70.00	18.00
☐ 25	Ebbie Goodfellow	175.00	70.00	18.00
☐ 26	Johnny Gottselig	125.00	50.00	12.50
☐ 27	Bob Gracie	90.00	36.00	9.00
☐ 28	George Hainsworth	175.00	70.00	18.00
☐ 29	Ott Heller	90.00	36.00	9.00
☐ 30	Normie Himes	90.00	36.00	9.00
☐ 31	Red Horner	200.00	80.00	20.00
☐ 32	Harvey(Busher) Jackson	300.00	120.00	30.00
☐ 33	Walter(Red) Jackson	90.00	36.00	9.00
☐ 34	Aurel Joliat	500.00	200.00	50.00
☐ 35	Dave Kerr	90.00	36.00	9.00
☐ 36	Pit Lepine	90.00	36.00	9.00
☐ 37	Georges Mantha	90.00	36.00	9.00
☐ 38	Howie Morenz	1000.00	400.00	100.00
☐ 39	Murray Murdoch	90.00	36.00	9.00
☐ 40	Baldy Northcott	125.00	50.00	12.50
☐ 41	John Ross Roach	90.00	36.00	9.00
☐ 42	Johnny Sheppard	90.00	36.00	9.00
☐ 43	Babe Siebert	200.00	80.00	20.00
☐ 44	Alex Smith	90.00	36.00	9.00
☐ 45	John Sorrell	90.00	36.00	9.00
☐ 46	Nelson Stewart	400.00	160.00	40.00
☐ 47	Dave Trottier	90.00	36.00	9.00
☐ 48	Bill Touhey	90.00	36.00	9.00
☐ 49	Jimmy Ward	90.00	36.00	9.00
☐ 50	Nick Wasnie	90.00	36.00	9.00

1933-34 V288 Hamilton Gum

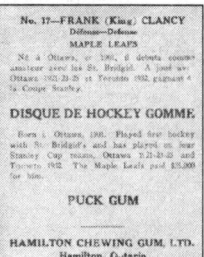

This skip-numbered set of 21 cards was designated V288 by the American Card Catalog. Cards are black and white pictures with a beige, blue, green, or orange background. Backs are written in both French and English. Cards measure approximately 2 3/8" by 2 3/4".

	EX-MT	VG-E	GOOD
COMPLETE SET (21)	5000.00	2000.00	500.00
COMMON PLAYER (1-49)	90.00	36.00	9.00

		EX-MT	VG-E	GOOD
☐ 1	Nick Wasnie	125.00	50.00	12.50
☐ 2	Joe Primeau	300.00	120.00	30.00
☐ 3	Marty Burke	90.00	36.00	9.00
☐ 7	Bill Thoms	90.00	36.00	9.00
☐ 8	Howie Morenz	1000.00	400.00	100.00
☐ 9	Andy Blair	90.00	36.00	9.00
☐ 11	Ace Bailey	300.00	120.00	30.00
☐ 14	Wildor Larochelle	90.00	36.00	9.00
☐ 17	King Clancy	600.00	240.00	60.00
☐ 18	Sylvio Mantha	175.00	70.00	18.00
☐ 21	Red Horner	200.00	80.00	20.00
☐ 23	Pit Lepine	90.00	36.00	9.00
☐ 27	Aurel Joliat	500.00	200.00	50.00
☐ 29	Harvey(Busher) Jackson	300.00	120.00	30.00
☐ 30	Lorne Chabot	125.00	50.00	12.50
☐ 33	Clarence(Hap) Day	200.00	80.00	20.00
☐ 36	Alex Levinsky	125.00	50.00	12.50
☐ 39	Harold Cotton	90.00	36.00	9.00
☐ 42	Ebbie Goodfellow	175.00	70.00	18.00
☐ 44	Larry Aurie	90.00	36.00	9.00
☐ 49	Charlie Conacher	600.00	240.00	60.00

1936-37 V356 Worldwide Gum

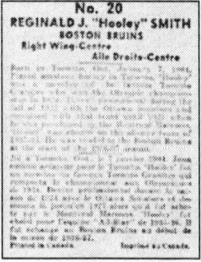

These rather crude greenish-gray cards feature the player's name and card number on the front and the card number, the player's name, his position and biographical data (in both English and French) on the back. Cards are approximately 2 3/8" by 2 7/8". Although the backs of the cards state that the cards were printed in Canada, no mention of the issuer, World Wide Gum, is apparent anywhere on the card.

	EX-MT	VG-E	GOOD
COMPLETE SET (135)	18000.	7500.	1800.
COMMON PLAYER (1-135)	90.00	36.00	9.00
☐ 1 Charlie Conacher	750.00	250.00	50.00
☐ 2 Jimmy Ward	90.00	36.00	9.00
☐ 3 Babe Siebert	200.00	80.00	20.00
☐ 4 Marty Barry	175.00	70.00	18.00
☐ 5 Eddie Shore	900.00	360.00	90.00
☐ 6 Paul Thompson	90.00	36.00	9.00
☐ 7 Roy Worters	200.00	80.00	20.00
☐ 8 Red Horner	200.00	80.00	20.00
☐ 9 Wilfred Cude	125.00	50.00	12.50
☐ 10 Lionel Conacher	300.00	120.00	30.00
☐ 11 Ebbie Goodfellow	200.00	80.00	20.00
☐ 12 Tiny Thompson	250.00	100.00	25.00
☐ 13 Harold(Mush) March	90.00	36.00	9.00
☐ 14 Mervyn(Red) Dutton	200.00	80.00	20.00
☐ 15 Butch Keeling	90.00	36.00	9.00
☐ 16 Frank Boucher	200.00	80.00	20.00
☐ 17 Tommy Gorman	90.00	36.00	9.00
☐ 18 Howie Morenz	1500.00	600.00	150.00
☐ 19 Marvin Wentworth	90.00	36.00	9.00
☐ 20 Hooley Smith	200.00	80.00	20.00
☐ 21 Ivan(Ching) Johnson	250.00	100.00	25.00
☐ 22 Baldy Northcott	125.00	50.00	12.50
☐ 23 Syl Apps	300.00	120.00	30.00
☐ 24 Hec Kilrea	90.00	36.00	9.00
☐ 25 John Sorrell	90.00	36.00	9.00
☐ 26 Lorne Carr	90.00	36.00	9.00
☐ 27 Charlie Sands	90.00	36.00	9.00
☐ 28 Nick Metz	90.00	36.00	9.00
☐ 29 King Clancy	750.00	300.00	75.00
☐ 30 Russ Blinco	90.00	36.00	9.00
☐ 31 Pete Kelly	90.00	36.00	9.00
☐ 32 Walter Buswell	90.00	36.00	9.00
☐ 33 Paul Haynes	90.00	36.00	9.00
☐ 34 Wildor Larochelle	90.00	36.00	9.00
☐ 35 Harold Cotton	90.00	36.00	9.00
☐ 36 Dit Clapper	300.00	120.00	30.00
☐ 37 Joe Lamb	90.00	36.00	9.00
☐ 38 Bob Gracie	90.00	36.00	9.00
☐ 39 Jack Shill	90.00	36.00	9.00
☐ 40 Buzz Boll	90.00	36.00	9.00
☐ 41 John Gallagher	90.00	36.00	9.00
☐ 42 Art Chapman	90.00	36.00	9.00
☐ 43 Tom Cook	90.00	36.00	9.00
☐ 44 Bill MacKenzie	90.00	36.00	9.00
☐ 45 Georges Mantha	90.00	36.00	9.00
☐ 46 Herb Cain	100.00	40.00	10.00
☐ 47 Mud Bruneteau	100.00	40.00	10.00
☐ 48 Bob Davidson	90.00	36.00	9.00
☐ 49 Doug Young	90.00	36.00	9.00
☐ 50 Paul Drouin	90.00	36.00	9.00
☐ 51 Harvey(Busher) Jackson	300.00	120.00	30.00
☐ 52 Clarence(Hap) Day	250.00	100.00	25.00
☐ 53 Dave Kerr	90.00	36.00	9.00
☐ 54 Al Murray	90.00	36.00	9.00
☐ 55 Johnny Gottselig	90.00	36.00	9.00
☐ 56 Andy Blair	90.00	36.00	9.00
☐ 57 Lynn Patrick	250.00	100.00	25.00
☐ 58 Sweeney Schriner	250.00	100.00	25.00
☐ 59 Happy Emms	90.00	36.00	9.00
☐ 60 Allan Shields	90.00	36.00	9.00
☐ 61 Alex Levinsky	125.00	50.00	12.50
☐ 62 Flash Hollett	90.00	36.00	9.00
☐ 63 Peggy O'Neil	90.00	36.00	9.00
☐ 64 Herbie Lewis	200.00	80.00	20.00
☐ 65 Aurel Joliat	600.00	240.00	60.00
☐ 66 Carl Voss	200.00	80.00	20.00
☐ 67 Stewart Evans	90.00	36.00	9.00
☐ 68 Bun Cook	125.00	50.00	12.50
☐ 69 Cooney Weiland	200.00	80.00	20.00
☐ 70 Dave Trottier	90.00	36.00	9.00
☐ 71 Louis Trudel	90.00	36.00	9.00
☐ 72 Marty Burke	90.00	36.00	9.00
☐ 73 Leroy Goldsworthy	90.00	36.00	9.00
☐ 74 Normie Smith	90.00	36.00	9.00
☐ 75 Syd Howe	250.00	100.00	25.00
☐ 76 Gordon Pettinger	90.00	36.00	9.00
☐ 77 Jack McGill	90.00	36.00	9.00
☐ 78 Pit Lepine	90.00	36.00	9.00
☐ 79 Sammy McManus	90.00	36.00	9.00
☐ 80 Phil Watson	125.00	50.00	12.50
☐ 81 Paul Runge	90.00	36.00	9.00
☐ 82 Bill Beveridge	90.00	36.00	9.00
☐ 83 Johnny Gagnon	90.00	36.00	9.00
☐ 84 Bucko MacDonald	90.00	36.00	9.00
☐ 85 Earl Robinson	90.00	36.00	9.00
☐ 86 Pep Kelly	90.00	36.00	9.00
☐ 87 Ott Heller	90.00	36.00	9.00
☐ 88 Murray Murdock	90.00	36.00	9.00
☐ 89 Mac Colville	90.00	36.00	9.00
☐ 90 Alex Shibicky	125.00	50.00	12.50

	EX-MT	VG-E	GOOD
☐ 91 Neil Colville	200.00	80.00	20.00
☐ 92 Normie Himes	90.00	36.00	9.00
☐ 93 Charley McVeigh	90.00	36.00	9.00
☐ 94 Lester Patrick	250.00	100.00	25.00
☐ 95 Connie Smythe	350.00	140.00	35.00
☐ 96 Art Ross	250.00	100.00	25.00
☐ 97 Cecil M.Hart	200.00	80.00	20.00
☐ 98 Dutch Gainor	90.00	36.00	9.00
☐ 99 Jack Adams	200.00	80.00	20.00
☐ 100 Howie Morenz Jr.	200.00	80.00	20.00
☐ 101 Buster Mundy	90.00	36.00	9.00
☐ 102 Johnny Wing	90.00	36.00	9.00
☐ 103 Morris Croghan	90.00	36.00	9.00
☐ 104 Pete Jotkus	90.00	36.00	9.00
☐ 105 Doug MacQuisten	90.00	36.00	9.00
☐ 106 Lester Brennan	90.00	36.00	9.00
☐ 107 Jack O'Connell	90.00	36.00	9.00
☐ 108 Ray Malenfant	90.00	36.00	9.00
☐ 109 Ken Murray	90.00	36.00	9.00
☐ 110 Frank Stangle	90.00	36.00	9.00
☐ 111 Dave Neville	90.00	36.00	9.00
☐ 112 Claude Burke	90.00	36.00	9.00
☐ 113 Herman Murray	90.00	36.00	9.00
☐ 114 Buddy O'Connor	250.00	100.00	25.00
☐ 115 Albert Perreault	90.00	36.00	9.00
☐ 116 Johnny Taugher	90.00	36.00	9.00
☐ 117 Rene Boudreau	90.00	36.00	9.00
☐ 118 Kenny McKinnon	90.00	36.00	9.00
☐ 119 Alex Bolduc	90.00	36.00	9.00
☐ 120 Jimmy Keiller	90.00	36.00	9.00
☐ 121 Lloyd McIntyre	90.00	36.00	9.00
☐ 122 Emile Fortin	90.00	36.00	9.00
☐ 123 Mike Karakas	90.00	36.00	9.00
☐ 124 Art Wiebe	90.00	36.00	9.00
☐ 125 Louis Denis	90.00	36.00	9.00
☐ 126 Stan Pratt	90.00	36.00	9.00
☐ 127 Jules Cholette	90.00	36.00	9.00
☐ 128 Jimmy Muir	90.00	36.00	9.00
☐ 129 Pete Morin	90.00	36.00	9.00
☐ 130 Jimmy Heffernan	90.00	36.00	9.00
☐ 131 Morris Bastien	90.00	36.00	9.00
☐ 132 Tuffy Griffiths	90.00	36.00	9.00
☐ 133 Johnny Mahaffey	90.00	36.00	9.00
☐ 134 Trueman Donnelly	90.00	36.00	9.00
☐ 135 Bill Stewart	150.00	60.00	15.00

1933-34 V357 Ice Kings

This interesting and attractive set of 72 cards features black and white photos on the front, upon which the head of the player portrayed has been tinted in flesh tones. The cards measure approximately 2 3/8" by 2 7/8". The player's name appears on the front of the card. The card number, position, team and player's name is listed on the back as are brief biographies in both French and English. Some cards appear with the resumes in English only. Printed in Canada and issued by World Wide Gum, the ACC designation for this set is V357.

	EX-MT	VG-E	GOOD
COMPLETE SET (72)	9500.00	4000.00	900.00
COMMON PLAYER (1-48)	75.00	30.00	7.50
COMMON PLAYER (49-72)	100.00	40.00	10.00
☐ 1 Dit Clapper	250.00	100.00	25.00
☐ 2 Bill Brydge	75.00	30.00	7.50

☐ 3	Aurel Joliat	500.00	200.00	50.00
☐ 4	Andy Blair	75.00	30.00	7.50
☐ 5	Earl Robinson	75.00	30.00	7.50
☐ 6	Paul Haynes	75.00	30.00	7.50
☐ 7	Ronnie Martin	75.00	30.00	7.50
☐ 8	Babe Siebert	200.00	80.00	20.00
☐ 9	Archie Wilcox	75.00	30.00	7.50
☐ 10	Clarence(Hap) Day	200.00	80.00	20.00
☐ 11	Roy Worters	200.00	80.00	20.00
☐ 12	Nelson Stewart	350.00	140.00	35.00
☐ 13	King Clancy	600.00	240.00	60.00
☐ 14	Marty Burke	150.00	60.00	15.00
☐ 15	Cecil Dillon	75.00	30.00	7.50
☐ 16	Red Horner	175.00	70.00	18.00
☐ 17	Armand Mondou	75.00	30.00	7.50
☐ 18	Paul Raymond	75.00	30.00	7.50
☐ 19	Dave Kerr	75.00	30.00	7.50
☐ 20	Butch Keeling	75.00	30.00	7.50
☐ 21	Johnny Gagnon	75.00	30.00	7.50
☐ 22	Ace Bailey	300.00	120.00	30.00
☐ 23	Harry Oliver	150.00	60.00	15.00
☐ 24	Gerald Carson	75.00	30.00	7.50
☐ 25	Mervyn(Red) Dutton	150.00	60.00	15.00
☐ 26	Georges Mantha	75.00	30.00	7.50
☐ 27	Marty Barry	175.00	70.00	18.00
☐ 28	Wildor Larochelle	75.00	30.00	7.50
☐ 29	Red Beattie	75.00	30.00	7.50
☐ 30	Bill Cook	150.00	60.00	15.00
☐ 31	Hooley Smith	150.00	60.00	15.00
☐ 32	Art Chapman	75.00	30.00	7.50
☐ 33	Harold Cotton	75.00	30.00	7.50
☐ 34	Lionel Hitchman	75.00	30.00	7.50
☐ 35	George Patterson	75.00	30.00	7.50
☐ 36	Howie Morenz	1000.00	400.00	100.00
☐ 37	Jimmy Ward	75.00	30.00	7.50
☐ 38	Charley McVeigh	75.00	30.00	7.50
☐ 39	Glen Brydson	75.00	30.00	7.50
☐ 40	Joe Primeau	250.00	100.00	25.00
☐ 41	Joe Lamb	75.00	30.00	7.50
☐ 42	Sylvio Mantha	150.00	60.00	15.00
☐ 43	Cy Wentworth	75.00	30.00	7.50
☐ 44	Normie Himes	75.00	30.00	7.50
☐ 45	Doug Brennan	75.00	30.00	7.50
☐ 46	Pit Lepine	75.00	30.00	7.50
☐ 47	Alex Levinsky	100.00	40.00	10.00
☐ 48	Baldy Northcott	100.00	40.00	10.00
☐ 49	Ken Doraty	100.00	40.00	10.00
☐ 50	Bill Thoms	100.00	40.00	10.00
☐ 51	Vernon Ayers	100.00	40.00	10.00
☐ 52	Lorne Duguid	100.00	40.00	10.00
☐ 53	Wally Kilrea	100.00	40.00	10.00
☐ 54	Vic Ripley	100.00	40.00	10.00
☐ 55	Happy Emms	100.00	40.00	10.00
☐ 56	Duke Dutkowski	100.00	40.00	10.00
☐ 57	Tiny Thompson	200.00	80.00	20.00
☐ 58	Charlie Sands	100.00	40.00	10.00
☐ 59	Larry Aurie	100.00	40.00	10.00
☐ 60	Bill Beveridge	100.00	40.00	10.00
☐ 61	Bill McKenzie	100.00	40.00	10.00
☐ 62	Earl Roche	100.00	40.00	10.00
☐ 63	Bob Gracie	100.00	40.00	10.00
☐ 64	Hec Kilrea	100.00	40.00	10.00
☐ 65	Cooney Weiland	250.00	100.00	25.00
☐ 66	Bun Cook	125.00	50.00	12.50
☐ 67	John Roach	100.00	40.00	10.00
☐ 68	Murray Murdock	100.00	40.00	10.00
☐ 69	Danny Cox	100.00	40.00	10.00
☐ 70	Desse Roche	100.00	40.00	10.00
☐ 71	Lorne Chabot	125.00	50.00	12.50
☐ 72	Syd Howe	250.00	100.00	25.00

1933-34 V357-2 Ice Kings Premiums

These six black-and-white large cards are actually premiums. The cards measure approximately 7" by 9". The cards are unnumbered and rather difficult to find now.

	EX-MT	VG-E	GOOD
COMPLETE SET (6)	3500.00	1500.00	350.00
COMMON PLAYER (1-6)	150.00	60.00	15.00
☐ 1 King Clancy	900.00	360.00	90.00
☐ 2 Clarence(Hap) Day	300.00	120.00	30.00
☐ 3 Aurelel Joliat	750.00	300.00	75.00
☐ 4 Howie Morenz	1500.00	600.00	150.00
☐ 5 Allan Shields	150.00	60.00	15.00
☐ 6 Reginald(Hooley) Smith	250.00	100.00	25.00

1984-85 Whalers Junior Wendy's

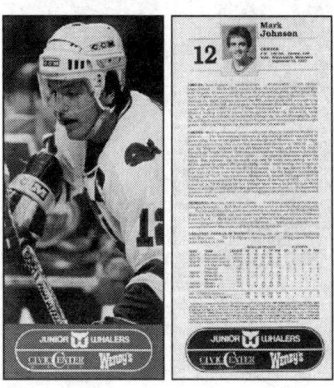

This 22-card set was sponsored by Wendy's and The Civic Center Mall. The cards measure approximately 3 3/4" by 8 1/4" and feature color action player photos. The pictures are full-bleed except for a bright blue bottom border that contains an oval that is divided in half horizontally with the top half being green and the bottom red. The design contains the team name and sponsors in white print. The backs have a black and white head shot, biography, 1983-84 season summary, career summary, miscellaneous player information, and statistics. The oval design is repeated on the back in black. The cards are unnumbered and checklisted below in alphabetical order.

	MINT	EXC	G-VG
COMPLETE SET (22)	25.00	10.00	2.50
COMMON PLAYER (1-22)	1.00	.40	.10
☐ 1 Jack Brownschidle	1.00	.40	.10
☐ 2 Sylvain Cote	1.00	.40	.10
☐ 3 Bob Crawford	1.00	.40	.10
☐ 4 Mike Crombeen	1.00	.40	.10
☐ 5 Tony Currie	1.00	.40	.10
☐ 6 Ron Francis	5.00	2.00	.50
☐ 7 Mark Fusco	1.00	.40	.10
☐ 8 Dave Jensen	1.00	.40	.10
☐ 9 Mark Johnson	1.50	.60	.15
☐ 10 Chris Kotsopoulos	1.00	.40	.10
☐ 11 Greg Malone	1.00	.40	.10
☐ 12 Greg Millen	2.00	.80	.20
☐ 13 Ray Neufeld	1.00	.40	.10
☐ 14 Randy Pierce	1.00	.40	.10
☐ 15 Joel Quenneville	1.00	.40	.10
☐ 16 Torrie Robertson	1.00	.40	.10
☐ 17 Ulf Samuelsson	4.00	1.60	.40
☐ 18 Risto Siltanen	1.00	.40	.10
☐ 19 Dave Tippett	1.00	.40	.10
☐ 20 Sylvain Turgeon	2.00	.80	.20
☐ 21 Steve Weeks	1.50	.60	.15
☐ 22 Mike Zuke	1.00	.40	.10

1985-86 Whalers Junior Wendy's

Sponsored by Wendy's, this 23-card set measures approximately 3 3/4" by 8 1/4". The fronts feature full-bleed color action player photos, except at the bottom where a bright blue stripe contains an oval that is divided in half horizontally with the top half being green and the bottom red. The design contains the sponsor's name in the top portion, while the team name appears in the bottom portion, both in white letters. The white backs carry a black-and-white headshot, biography, 1984-85 season summary,

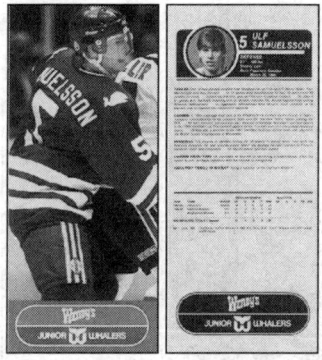

career summary, personal information, and statistics. The oval design is repeated on the back in black-and-white. The cards are unnumbered and checklisted below in alphabetical order.

	MINT	EXC	G-VG
COMPLETE SET (23)	25.00	10.00	2.50
COMMON PLAYER (1-23)	1.00	.40	.10
☐ 1 Jack Brownschidle	1.00	.40	.10
☐ 2 Sylvain Cote	1.00	.40	.10
☐ 3 Bob Crawford	1.00	.40	.10
☐ 4 Kevin Dineen	4.00	1.60	.40
☐ 5 Paul Fenton	1.00	.40	.10
☐ 6 Ray Ferraro	3.00	1.20	.30
☐ 7 Ron Francis	4.00	1.60	.40
☐ 8 Scott Kleinendorst	1.00	.40	.10
☐ 9 Paul Lawless	1.00	.40	.10
☐ 10 Mike Liut	3.00	1.20	.30
☐ 11 Paul MacDermid	1.00	.40	.10
☐ 12 Greg Malone	1.00	.40	.10
☐ 13 Dana Murzyn	1.00	.40	.10
☐ 14 Ray Neufeld	1.00	.40	.10
☐ 15 Jorgen Pettersson	1.00	.40	.10
☐ 16 Joel Quenneville	1.00	.40	.10
☐ 17 Torrie Robertson	1.00	.40	.10
☐ 18 Ulf Samuelsson	3.00	1.20	.30
☐ 19 Risto Siltanen	1.00	.40	.10
☐ 20 Dave Tippett	1.00	.40	.10
☐ 21 Sylvain Turgeon	2.00	.80	.20
☐ 22 Steve Weeks	1.50	.60	.15
☐ 23 Mike Zuke	1.00	.40	.10

1988-89 Whalers Junior Ground Round

This 18-card set of Hartford Whalers was sponsored by Ground Round restaurants. The cards measure

approximately 3 11/16" by 8 1/4". The front features a borderless full color photo of the player. The team logo and a Ground Round advertisement appear in the blue and green stripes that cut across the bottom of the card face. The back has a black and white head shot of the player at the upper left hand corner as well as extensive player information and career statistics. Another Ground Round advertisement and a Ground Round Drug Tip (an anti-drug and alcohol message) appear at the bottom of the card. The cards are unnumbered and hence are checklisted below in alphabetical order.

	MINT	EXC	G-VG
COMPLETE SET (18)	20.00	8.00	2.00
COMMON PLAYER (1-18)	1.00	.40	.10
☐ 1 John Anderson	1.25	.50	.12
☐ 2 Dave Babych	1.50	.60	.15
☐ 3 Sylvain Cote	1.00	.40	.10
☐ 4 Kevin Dineen	2.00	.80	.20
☐ 5 Dean Evason	1.25	.50	.12
☐ 6 Ray Ferraro	2.00	.80	.20
☐ 7 Ron Francis	3.00	1.20	.30
☐ 8 Scot Kleinendorst	1.00	.40	.10
☐ 9 Randy Ladouceur	1.00	.40	.10
☐ 10 Mike Liut	2.00	.80	.20
☐ 11 Paul MacDermid	1.00	.40	.10
☐ 12 Brent Peterson	1.00	.40	.10
☐ 13 Joel Quenneville	1.00	.40	.10
☐ 14 Torrie Robertson	1.00	.40	.10
☐ 15 Ulf Samuelsson	2.00	.80	.20
☐ 16 Dave Tippett	1.00	.40	.10
☐ 17 Sylvain Turgeon	1.50	.60	.15
☐ 18 Carey Wilson	1.00	.40	.10

1989-90 Whalers Junior Milk

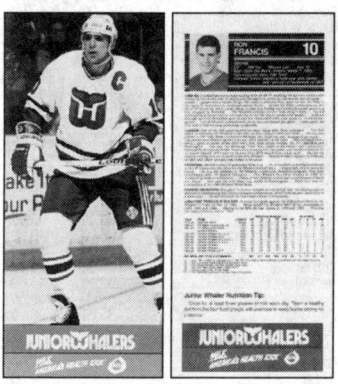

This 23-card set of Hartford Whalers was sponsored by Milk, America's Health Kick. The cards measure approximately 3 11/16" by 8 1/4". The front features a borderless full color photo of the player. The team logo and a Milk advertisement appear in the blue and green stripes that cut across the bottom of the card face. The back has a black and white head shot of the player at the upper left hand corner as well as extensive player information and career statistics. A Junior Whaler Nutrition Tip and another Milk advertisement appear at the bottom of the card's reverse. The cards are unnumbered and hence are checklisted below in alphabetical order. Three cards (11, 12, 21) were added to the set at the end of the season and are marked as SP in the checklist below.

	MINT	EXC	G-VG
COMPLETE SET (23)	20.00	8.00	2.00
COMMON PLAYER (1-23)	.75	.30	.07

		MINT	EXC	G-VG
☐ 1	Mikael Andersson	1.00	.40	.10
☐ 2	Dave Babych	1.00	.40	.10
☐ 3	Sylvain Cote	.75	.30	.07
☐ 4	Randy Cunneyworth	.75	.30	.07
☐ 5	Kevin Dineen	1.50	.60	.15
☐ 6	Dean Evason	1.00	.40	.10
☐ 7	Ray Ferraro	1.25	.50	.12
☐ 8	Ron Francis	2.50	1.00	.25
☐ 9	Jody Hull	.75	.30	.07
☐ 10	Grant Jennings	.75	.30	.07
☐ 11	Ed Kastelic SP	2.50	1.00	.25
☐ 12	Todd Krygier SP	2.50	1.00	.25
☐ 13	Randy Ladouceur	.75	.30	.07
☐ 14	Mike Liut	1.50	.60	.15
☐ 15	Paul MacDermid	.75	.30	.07
☐ 16	Joel Quenneville	.75	.30	.07
☐ 17	Ulf Samuelsson	2.00	.80	.20
☐ 18	Brad Shaw	1.00	.40	.10
☐ 19	Peter Sidorkiewicz	1.00	.40	.10
☐ 20	Dave Tippett	.75	.30	.07
☐ 21	Mike Tomlak SP	2.50	1.00	.25
☐ 22	Pat Verbeek	2.00	.80	.20
☐ 23	Scott Young	1.25	.50	.12

1990-91 Whalers Jr. 7-Eleven

This 27-card set of Hartford Whalers was issued by 7-Eleven and sent out as a premium to all members of the Hartford Junior Whalers. This set features full-color photographs on the front while the backs contain the same information about the players that is available in the media guides. The set has been checklisted alphabetically for convenient reference. The set measures approximately 3 3/4" by 8 1/4" and has the players of the Hartford Whalers along with a special Gordie Howe card. Four cards (3, 12, 19, 20) were added to the set at the end of the season and their backs are blank.

		MINT	EXC	G-VG
	COMPLETE SET (27)	20.00	8.00	2.00
	COMMON PLAYER (1-27)	.60	.24	.06
	COMMON PLAYER SP	2.00	.80	.20
☐ 1	Mikael Andersson	.75	.30	.07
☐ 2	Dave Babych	.75	.30	.07
☐ 3	Rob Brown SP	2.00	.80	.20
☐ 4	Yvon Corriveau	.60	.24	.06
☐ 5	Sylvain Cote	.60	.24	.06
☐ 6	Doug Crossman	.75	.30	.07
☐ 7	Randy Cunneyworth	.60	.24	.06
☐ 8	Paul Cyr	.60	.24	.06
☐ 9	Kevin Dineen	1.25	.50	.12
☐ 10	Dean Evason	.75	.30	.07
☐ 11	Ron Francis	2.00	.80	.20
☐ 12	Chris Govedaris SP	2.00	.80	.20
☐ 13	Bobby Holik	2.00	.80	.20
☐ 14	Gordie Howe	6.00	2.40	.60
☐ 15	Grant Jennings	.60	.24	.06
☐ 16	Ed Kastelic	.60	.24	.06
☐ 17	Todd Krygier	.75	.30	.07

		MINT	EXC	G-VG
☐ 18	Randy Ladouceur	.60	.24	.06
☐ 19	Jim McKenzie SP	2.00	.80	.20
☐ 20	Daryl Reaugh SP	2.00	.80	.20
☐ 21	Ulf Samuelsson	1.50	.60	.15
☐ 22	Brad Shaw	.75	.30	.07
☐ 23	Peter Sidorkiewicz	1.00	.40	.10
☐ 24	Mike Tomlak	.60	.24	.06
☐ 25	Pat Verbeek	1.25	.50	.12
☐ 26	Carey Wilson	.60	.24	.06
☐ 27	Scott Young	1.00	.40	.10

1991-92 Whalers Jr. 7-Eleven

This 28-card set of Hartford Whalers was issued by 7-Eleven and sent out as a premium to all members of the Hartford Junior Whalers. This set features full-color photographs on the front while the backs contain the same information about the players that is available in the media guides. The set has been checklisted alphabetically for convenient reference. The set measures approximately 3 3/4" by 8 1/4" and contains the players of the Hartford Whalers. Six cards (3, 6, 10, 12, 18, 19) were issued late in the season and their backs are blank.

		MINT	EXC	G-VG
	COMPLETE SET (28)	20.00	8.00	2.00
	COMMON PLAYER (1-28)	.50	.20	.05
	COMMON PLAYER SP	1.50	.60	.15
☐ 1	Mikael Andersson	.60	.24	.06
☐ 2	Marc Bergevin	.50	.20	.05
☐ 3	James Black SP	1.50	.60	.15
☐ 4	Rob Brown	.60	.24	.06
☐ 5	Adam Burt	.50	.20	.05
☐ 6	Andrew Cassels SP	3.00	1.20	.30
☐ 7	Murray Craven	.75	.30	.07
☐ 8	John Cullen	1.00	.40	.10
☐ 9	Randy Cunneyworth	.50	.20	.05
☐ 10	Paul Cyr SP	1.50	.60	.15
☐ 11	Joe Day	.50	.20	.05
☐ 12	Paul Gillis SP	1.50	.60	.15
☐ 13	Mark Greig	.60	.24	.06
☐ 14	Bobby Holik	1.25	.50	.12
☐ 15	Doug Houda	.50	.20	.05
☐ 16	Mark Hunter	.50	.20	.05
☐ 17	Ed Kastelic	.50	.20	.05
☐ 18	Dan Keczmer SP	1.50	.60	.15
☐ 19	Steve Konroyd SP	1.50	.60	.15
☐ 20	Randy Ladouceur	.50	.20	.05
☐ 21	Jim McKenzie	.50	.20	.05
☐ 22	Michel Picard	.50	.20	.05
☐ 23	Geoff Sanderson	5.00	2.00	.50
☐ 24	Brad Shaw	.60	.24	.06
☐ 25	Peter Sidorkiewicz	.75	.30	.07
☐ 26	Pat Verbeek	1.25	.50	.12
☐ 27	Kay Whitmore	1.00	.40	.10
☐ 28	Zarley Zalapski	.75	.30	.07

1992-93 Whalers Dairymart

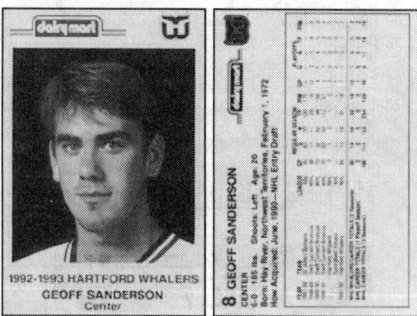

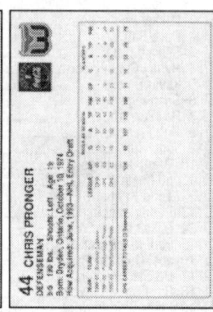

	MINT	EXC	G-VG
COMPLETE SET (24)	15.00	6.00	1.50
COMMON PLAYER (1-24)	.50	.20	.05
☐ 1 Sean Burke	1.00	.40	.10
☐ 2 Adam Burt	.60	.24	.06
☐ 3 Andrew Cassels	1.00	.40	.10
☐ 4 Randy Cunneyworth	.50	.20	.05
☐ 5 Alexander Godynyuk	.50	.20	.05
☐ 6 Mark Greig	.50	.20	.05
☐ 7 Mark Janssens	.50	.20	.05
☐ 8 Robert Kron	.60	.24	.06
☐ 9 Bryan Marchment	.60	.24	.06
☐ 10 Brad McCrimmon	.60	.24	.06
☐ 11 Pierre McGuire CO	.60	.24	.06
☐ 12 Michael Nylander	.75	.30	.07
☐ 13 James Patrick	.60	.24	.06
☐ 14 Frank Pietrangelo	.75	.30	.07
☐ 15 Marc Potvin	.50	.20	.05
☐ 16 Chris Pronger	4.00	1.60	.40
☐ 17 Brian Propp	.60	.24	.06
☐ 18 Jeff Reese	.60	.24	.06
☐ 19 Geoff Sanderson	2.00	.80	.20
☐ 20 Jim Sandlak	.60	.24	.06
☐ 21 Jim Storm	.50	.20	.05
☐ 22 Darren Turcotte	.75	.30	.07
☐ 23 Pat Verbeek	1.00	.40	.10
☐ 24 Zarley Zalapski	.75	.30	.07

Sponsored by Dairymart, this 26-card set features white-bordered glossy color studio head shots on cards that measure approximately 2 3/8" by 3 1/2". The Dairymart and Whalers logos are displayed above the player photo, and the player's name and position, along with "1992-93 Hartford Whalers," appear beneath his image. The white horizontal back carries the player's name, uniform number, position, and biography above a stat table. The Dairymart and Whalers logos in the upper right complete the card. The cards are unnumbered and checklisted below in alphabetical order.

	MINT	EXC	G-VG
COMPLETE SET (26)	15.00	6.00	1.50
COMMON PLAYER (1-26)	.50	.20	.05
☐ 1 Jim Agnew	.50	.20	.05
☐ 2 Sean Burke	1.00	.40	.10
☐ 3 Adam Burt	.50	.20	.05
☐ 4 Andrew Cassels	1.00	.40	.10
☐ 5 Murray Craven	.75	.30	.07
☐ 6 Randy Cunneyworth	.50	.20	.05
☐ 7 Paul Gillis	.50	.20	.05
☐ 8 Paul Holmgren CO	.60	.24	.06
☐ 9 Doug Houda	.50	.20	.05
☐ 10 Mark Janssens	.50	.20	.05
☐ 11 Tim Kerr	.75	.30	.07
☐ 12 Steve Konroyd	.50	.20	.05
☐ 13 Nick Kypreos	.50	.20	.05
☐ 14 Randy Ladouceur	.50	.20	.05
☐ 15 Jim McKenzie	.50	.20	.05
☐ 16 Michael Nylander	1.25	.50	.12
☐ 17 Allen Pedersen	.50	.20	.05
☐ 18 Robert Petrovicky	.75	.30	.07
☐ 19 Frank Pietrangelo	.75	.30	.07
☐ 20 Patrick Poulin	1.25	.50	.12
☐ 21 Geoff Sanderson	4.00	1.60	.40
☐ 22 Pat Verbeek	1.00	.40	.10
☐ 23 Eric Weinrich	.75	.30	.07
☐ 24 Terry Yake	.60	.24	.06
☐ 25 Zarley Zalapski	.75	.30	.07
☐ 26 Junior Whalers	.50	.20	.05
Member Card			

1993-94 Whalers Coke

Sponsored by Coca-Cola, this 24-card set features white-bordered color studio head shots on cards that measure approximately 2 3/8" by 3 1/2". The Coca-Cola and Whalers logos are displayed above the player photo, while the player's name and position appear beneath his image. The white horizontal backs carry the player's name, uniform number, position, and biography above a stat table. The Coca-Cola and Whalers logos in the upper right corner complete the backs. The cards are unnumbered and checklisted below in alphabetical order.

1960-61 Wonder Bread Premium Photos

Produced and issued in Canada, the 1960-61 Wonder Bread set features four hockey stars. This set of premium photos measure approximately 5" by 7" and are unnumbered. There were actually two sets produced: Bread Labels and Premium Photos. The bread labels are valued at 25 percent of the values listed below. Reportedly the premium photo was inside the bread package and there was also a small picture of the player on the end of the bread wrapper.

	NRMT	VG-E	GOOD
COMPLETE SET (4)	400.00	160.00	40.00
COMMON PLAYER (1-4)	40.00	16.00	4.00
☐ 1 Gordie Howe	200.00	80.00	20.00
☐ 2 Bobby Hull	100.00	40.00	10.00
☐ 3 Dave Keon	40.00	16.00	4.00
☐ 4 Maurice Richard	150.00	60.00	15.00

1960-61 York Premium Photos

This set of 37 photos is very difficult to put together. These unnumbered photos measure approximately 5" by 7" and feature members of the Montreal Canadiens (MC) and Toronto Maple Leafs (TML). The checklist below is ordered alphabetically. These large black and white cards were

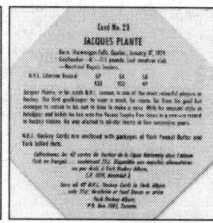

supposedly available from York Peanut Butter as a mail-in premium in return for two proofs of purchase; unfortunately there are no identifying marking on the photo that indicate the producer or the year of issue. The photos are action shots with a facsimile autograph of the player on the photo. The cards were apparently issued very late in the 1960-61 season since the set includes Eddie Shack as a Maple Leaf (he was acquired by Toronto from the Rangers during the 1960-61 season), Gilles Tremblay (his first NHL season was 1960-61 with the Canadiens), and several players (Jean-Guy Gendron, Larry Regan, Bob Turner) who were with other teams for the 1961-62 season.

	NRMT	VG-E	GOOD
COMPLETE SET (37)	2000.00	800.00	200.00
COMMON PLAYER (1-37)	40.00	16.00	4.00
☐ 1 George Armstrong TML	70.00	28.00	7.00
☐ 2 Ralph Backstrom MC	45.00	18.00	4.50
☐ 3 Bob Baun TML	45.00	18.00	4.50
☐ 4 Jean Beliveau MC	125.00	50.00	12.50
☐ 5 Marcel Bonin MC	40.00	16.00	4.00
☐ 6 Johnny Bower TML	70.00	28.00	7.00
☐ 7 Carl Brewer TML	40.00	16.00	4.00
☐ 8 Dick Duff TML	45.00	18.00	4.50
☐ 9 Jean-Guy Gendron MC	40.00	16.00	4.00
☐ 10 Boom Boom Geoffrion MC	100.00	40.00	10.00
☐ 11 Phil Goyette MC	40.00	16.00	4.00
☐ 12 Billy Harris TML	40.00	16.00	4.00
☐ 13 Doug Harvey MC	80.00	32.00	8.00
☐ 14 Bill Hicke MC	40.00	16.00	4.00
☐ 15 Larry Hillman TML	40.00	16.00	4.00
☐ 16 Charlie Hodge MC	50.00	20.00	5.00
☐ 17 Tim Horton TML	80.00	32.00	8.00
☐ 18 Tom Johnson MC	50.00	20.00	5.00
☐ 19 Red Kelly TML	70.00	28.00	7.00
☐ 20 Dave Keon TML	60.00	24.00	6.00
☐ 21 Albert Langlois MC	40.00	16.00	4.00
☐ 22 Frank Mahovlich TML	90.00	36.00	9.00
☐ 23 Don Marshall MC	40.00	16.00	4.00
☐ 24 Dickie Moore MC	70.00	28.00	7.00
☐ 25 Bob Nevin TML	40.00	16.00	4.00
☐ 26 Bert Olmstead TML	50.00	20.00	5.00
☐ 27 Jacques Plante MC	125.00	50.00	12.50
☐ 28 Claude Provost MC	45.00	18.00	4.50
☐ 29 Bob Pulford TML	50.00	20.00	5.00
☐ 30 Larry Regan TML	40.00	16.00	4.00
☐ 31 Henri Richard MC	80.00	32.00	8.00
☐ 32 Eddie Shack TML	70.00	28.00	7.00
☐ 33 Allan Stanley TML	60.00	24.00	6.00
☐ 34 Ron Stewart TML	40.00	16.00	4.00
☐ 35 Jean-Guy Talbot MC	45.00	18.00	4.50
☐ 36 Gilles Tremblay MC	40.00	16.00	4.00
☐ 37 Bob Turner MC	40.00	16.00	4.00

1961-62 York Yellow Backs

This set of 42 octagonal cards was issued by York Peanut Butter. The cards are numbered on the backs at the top. An album was originally available as a send-in offer or at certain food stores for 25 cents. The cards measure approximately 2 1/2" in diameter. The set can be dated as a 1961-62 set by referring to the career totals given on the back of each player's cards. The card backs were written in both French and English. The set is considered complete without the album.

	NRMT	VG-E	GOOD
COMPLETE SET (42)	600.00	240.00	60.00
COMMON PLAYER (1-42)	10.00	4.00	1.00
☐ 1 Bob Baun	12.00	5.00	1.20
☐ 2 Dick Duff	12.00	5.00	1.20
☐ 3 Frank Mahovlich	25.00	10.00	2.50
☐ 4 Gilles Tremblay	10.00	4.00	1.00
☐ 5 Dickie Moore	16.00	6.50	1.60
☐ 6 Don Marshall	10.00	4.00	1.00
☐ 7 Tim Horton	20.00	8.00	2.00
☐ 8 Johnny Bower	18.00	7.25	1.80
☐ 9 Allan Stanley	15.00	6.00	1.50
☐ 10 Jean Beliveau	35.00	14.00	3.50
☐ 11 Tom Johnson	15.00	6.00	1.50
☐ 12 Jean-Guy Talbot	12.00	5.00	1.20
☐ 13 Carl Brewer	10.00	4.00	1.00
☐ 14 Bob Pulford	15.00	6.00	1.50
☐ 15 Billy Harris	10.00	4.00	1.00
☐ 16 Bill Hicke	10.00	4.00	1.00
☐ 17 Claude Provost	12.00	5.00	1.20
☐ 18 Henri Richard	20.00	8.00	2.00
☐ 19 Bert Olmstead	15.00	6.00	1.50
☐ 20 Ron Stewart	10.00	4.00	1.00
☐ 21 Red Kelly	18.00	7.25	1.80
☐ 22 Hector(Toe) Blake CO	15.00	6.00	1.50
☐ 23 Jacques Plante	30.00	12.00	3.00
☐ 24 Ralph Backstrom	12.00	5.00	1.20
☐ 25 Eddie Shack	18.00	7.25	1.80
☐ 26 Bob Nevin	10.00	4.00	1.00
☐ 27 Dave Keon	18.00	7.25	1.80
☐ 28 Boom Boom Geoffrion	25.00	10.00	2.50
☐ 29 Marcel Bonin	10.00	4.00	1.00
☐ 30 Phil Goyette	10.00	4.00	1.00
☐ 31 Larry Hillman	10.00	4.00	1.00
☐ 32 Larry Keenan	10.00	4.00	1.00
☐ 33 Al Arbour	15.00	6.00	1.50
☐ 34 J.C. Tremblay	12.00	5.00	1.20
☐ 35 Bobby Rousseau	10.00	4.00	1.00
☐ 36 Al McNeil	10.00	4.00	1.00
☐ 37 George Armstrong	16.00	6.50	1.60
☐ 38 Punch Imlach CO	12.00	5.00	1.20
☐ 39 King Clancy	20.00	8.00	2.00
☐ 40 Lou Fontinato	10.00	4.00	1.00
☐ 41 Cesare Maniago	12.00	5.00	1.20
☐ 42 Jean Gauthier	10.00	4.00	1.00
☐ xx Album	30.00	12.00	3.00

1962-63 York Iron-On Transfers

These iron-on transfers are very difficult to find. They measure approximately 2 1/4" by 4 1/4". There is some dispute with regard to the year of issue but the 1962-63

season seems to be a likely date based on the careers of the players selected for and included in the set. These transfers are numbered at the bottom.

	NRMT	VG-E	GOOD
COMPLETE SET (36)	1500.00	600.00	150.00
COMMON PLAYER (1-36)	25.00	10.00	2.50

		NRMT	VG-E	GOOD
☐ 1	Johnny Bower	50.00	20.00	5.00
☐ 2	Jacques Plante	75.00	30.00	7.50
☐ 3	Tim Horton	60.00	24.00	6.00
☐ 4	Jean-Guy Talbot	30.00	12.00	3.00
☐ 5	Carl Brewer	25.00	10.00	2.50
☐ 6	J.C. Tremblay	30.00	12.00	3.00
☐ 7	Dick Duff	30.00	12.00	3.00
☐ 8	Jean Beliveau	90.00	36.00	9.00
☐ 9	Dave Keon	45.00	18.00	4.50
☐ 10	Henri Richard	50.00	20.00	5.00
☐ 11	Frank Mahovlich	60.00	24.00	6.00
☐ 12	BoomBoom Geoffrion	60.00	24.00	6.00
☐ 13	Kent Douglas	25.00	10.00	2.50
☐ 14	Claude Provost	30.00	12.00	3.00
☐ 15	Bob Pulford	35.00	14.00	3.50
☐ 16	Ralph Backstrom	30.00	12.00	3.00
☐ 17	George Armstrong	45.00	18.00	4.50
☐ 18	Bobby Rousseau	25.00	10.00	2.50
☐ 19	Gordie Howe	250.00	100.00	25.00
☐ 20	Red Kelly	50.00	20.00	5.00
☐ 21	Alex Delvecchio	50.00	20.00	5.00
☐ 22	Dickie Moore	50.00	20.00	5.00
☐ 23	Marcel Pronovost	35.00	14.00	3.50
☐ 24	Doug Barkley	25.00	10.00	2.50
☐ 25	Terry Sawchuk	75.00	30.00	7.50
☐ 26	Billy Harris	25.00	10.00	2.50
☐ 27	Parker MacDonald	25.00	10.00	2.50
☐ 28	Don Marshall	25.00	10.00	2.50
☐ 29	Norm Ullman	45.00	18.00	4.50
☐ 30A	Andre Pronovost	25.00	10.00	2.50
☐ 30B	Vic Stasiuk	25.00	10.00	2.50
☐ 31	Bill Gadsby	35.00	14.00	3.50
☐ 32	Eddie Shack	40.00	16.00	4.00
☐ 33	Larry Jeffrey	25.00	10.00	2.50
☐ 34	Gilles Tremblay	25.00	10.00	2.50
☐ 35	Howie Young	25.00	10.00	2.50
☐ 36	Bruce MacGregor	25.00	10.00	2.50

☐ 9	Dick Duff	12.00	5.00	1.20
☐ 10	Billy Harris	10.00	4.00	1.00
☐ 11	Larry Hillman	10.00	4.00	1.00
☐ 12	Red Kelly	16.00	6.50	1.60
☐ 13	Kent Douglas	10.00	4.00	1.00
☐ 14	Allan Stanley	15.00	6.00	1.50
☐ 15	Don Simmons	10.00	4.00	1.00
☐ 16	George Armstrong	16.00	6.50	1.60
☐ 17	Carl Brewer	10.00	4.00	1.00
☐ 18	Bob Pulford	15.00	6.00	1.50
☐ 19	Henri Richard	20.00	8.00	2.00
☐ 20	BoomBoom Geoffrion	25.00	10.00	2.50
☐ 21	Gilles Tremblay	10.00	4.00	1.00
☐ 22	Gump Worsley	20.00	8.00	2.00
☐ 23	Jean-Guy Talbot	12.00	5.00	1.20
☐ 24	J.C. Tremblay	12.00	5.00	1.20
☐ 25	Bobby Rousseau	10.00	4.00	1.00
☐ 26	Jean Beliveau	35.00	14.00	3.50
☐ 27	Ralph Backstrom	12.00	5.00	1.20
☐ 28	Claude Provost	12.00	5.00	1.20
☐ 29	Jean Gauthier	10.00	4.00	1.00
☐ 30	Bill Hicke	10.00	4.00	1.00
☐ 31	Terry Harper	12.00	5.00	1.20
☐ 32	Marc Reaume	10.00	4.00	1.00
☐ 33	Dave Balon	10.00	4.00	1.00
☐ 34	Jacques Laperriere	15.00	6.00	1.50
☐ 35	John Ferguson	12.00	5.00	1.20
☐ 36	Red Berenson	12.00	5.00	1.20
☐ 37	Terry Sawchuk	35.00	14.00	3.50
☐ 38	Marcel Pronovost	15.00	6.00	1.50
☐ 39	Bill Gadsby	15.00	6.00	1.50
☐ 40	Parker MacDonald	10.00	4.00	1.00
☐ 41	Larry Jeffrey	10.00	4.00	1.00
☐ 42	Floyd Smith	10.00	4.00	1.00
☐ 43	Andre Pronovost	10.00	4.00	1.00
☐ 44	Art Stratton	10.00	4.00	1.00
☐ 45	Gordie Howe	100.00	40.00	10.00
☐ 46	Doug Barkley	10.00	4.00	1.00
☐ 47	Norm Ullman	16.00	6.50	1.60
☐ 48	Eddie Joyal	10.00	4.00	1.00
☐ 49	Alex Faulkner	10.00	4.00	1.00
☐ 50	Alex Delvecchio	16.00	6.50	1.60
☐ 51	Bruce MacGregor	10.00	4.00	1.00
☐ 52	Ted Hampson	10.00	4.00	1.00
☐ 53	Pete Goegan	10.00	4.00	1.00
☐ 54	Ron Ingram	10.00	4.00	1.00
☐ xx	Album	25.00	10.00	2.50

1963-64 York White Backs

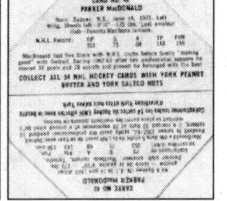

This set of 54 octagonal cards was issued by York Peanut Butter and York Salted Nuts. The cards are numbered on the backs at the top. The cards measure approximately 2 1/2" in diameter. The set can be dated as a 1963-64 set by referring to the career totals given on the back of each player's cards. The card backs were written in both French and English. An album was originally available for holding the set; the set is considered complete without the album.

	NRMT	VG-E	GOOD
COMPLETE SET (54)	750.00	300.00	75.00
COMMON PLAYER (1-54)	10.00	4.00	1.00

		NRMT	VG-E	GOOD
☐ 1	Tim Horton	20.00	8.00	2.00
☐ 2	Johnny Bower	16.00	6.50	1.60
☐ 3	Ron Stewart	10.00	4.00	1.00
☐ 4	Eddie Shack	16.00	6.50	1.60
☐ 5	Frank Mahovlich	20.00	8.00	2.00
☐ 6	Dave Keon	16.00	6.50	1.60
☐ 7	Bob Baun	12.00	5.00	1.20
☐ 8	Bob Nevin	10.00	4.00	1.00

1967-68 York Action Octagons

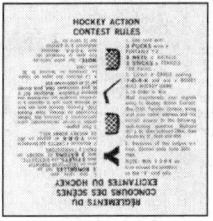

This 36-card set was issued by York Peanut Butter. Only cards 13-36 are numbered. The twelve unnumbered cards have been assigned the numbers 1-12 based on alphabetizing the names of the first player listed on each card. Each card shows an action scene involving two or three players. Uniform (sweater) numbers are also given on the cards. The card backs give the details of a send-in contest ending June 30, 1968. Collecting four cards spelling "YORK" entitled one to receive a Bobby Hull Hockey Game. These octagonal cards measure approximately 2 7/8" in diameter. The card backs were written in both French and English.

	NRMT	VG-E	GOOD
COMPLETE SET (36)	450.00	180.00	45.00
COMMON CARD (1-36)	10.00	4.00	1.00

		NRMT	VG-E	GOOD
☐ 1	Brian Conacher 22 Allan Stanley 26	10.00	4.00	1.00

	Leon Rochefort 25			
☐ 2	Terry Harper 19.....................	12.00	5.00	1.20
	Gump Worsley 30			
	Mike Walton 16			
☐ 3	Tim Horton 7..........................	25.00	10.00	2.50
	George Armstrong 10			
	Jean Beliveau 4			
☐ 4	Dave Keon 14.........................	12.00	5.00	1.20
	George Armstrong 10			
	Claude Provost 14			
☐ 5	Jacques Laperriere 2..............	12.00	5.00	1.20
	Rogatien Vachon 29			
	Bob Pulford 20			
☐ 6	Bob Pulford 20.......................	10.00	4.00	1.00
	Brian Conacher 22			
	Claude Provost 14			
☐ 7	Bob Pulford 20.......................	10.00	4.00	1.00
	Jim Pappin 18			
	Terry Harper 19			
☐ 8	Pete Stemkowski 12................	10.00	4.00	1.00
	Jim Pappin 18			
	Harris 10			
☐ 9	J.C. Tremblay 3......................	10.00	4.00	1.00
	Rogatien Vachon 29			
	Pete Stemkowski 12			
☐ 10	Rogatien Vachon 29..............	12.00	5.00	1.20
	Ralph Backstrom 6			
	Bob Pulford 20			
☐ 11	Rogatien Vachon 29..............	12.00	5.00	1.20
	Jacques Laperriere 2			
	Mike Walton 16			
☐ 12	Mike Walton 16......................	10.00	4.00	1.00
	Pete Stemkowski 12			
	J.C. Tremblay 3			
☐ 13	Dave Keon 14.........................	10.00	4.00	1.00
	Mike Walton 16			
	J.C. Tremblay 3			
☐ 14	Pete Stemkowski 12................	10.00	4.00	1.00
	Ralph Backstrom 6			
☐ 15	Rogatien Vachon 29..............	12.00	5.00	1.20
	Bob Pulford 20			
☐ 16	Johnny Bower 1......................	12.00	5.00	1.20
	Ron Ellis 8			
	John Ferguson 22			
☐ 17	Ron Ellis 8.............................	12.00	5.00	1.20
	Gump Worsley 30			
☐ 18	Gump Worsley 30	20.00	8.00	2.00
	Jacques Laperriere 2			
	Frank Mahovlich 27			
☐ 19	J.C. Tremblay 3......................	12.00	5.00	1.20
	Dave Keon 14			
☐ 20	Claude Provost 14..................	15.00	6.00	1.50
	Frank Mahovlich 27			
☐ 21	John Ferguson 22	15.00	6.00	1.50
	Tim Horton 7			
☐ 22	Gump Worsley 30	12.00	5.00	1.20
	Ron Ellis 8			
☐ 23	Johnny Bower 1	15.00	6.00	1.50
	Mike Walton 16			
	Jean Beliveau 4			
☐ 24	J.C. Tremblay 3......................	15.00	6.00	1.50
	Gump Worsley 30			
	Bob Pulford 20			
☐ 25	Tim Horton 7..........................	25.00	10.00	2.50
	Johnny Bower 1			
	Jean Beliveau 4			
☐ 26	Allan Stanley 26	15.00	6.00	1.50
	Johnny Bower 1			
	Dick Duff 8			
☐ 27	Ralph Backstrom 6.................	12.00	5.00	1.20
	Johnny Bower 1			
☐ 28	Yvan Cournoyer 12	30.00	12.00	3.00
	Jean Beliveau 4			
	Frank Mahovlich 27			
☐ 29	Johnny Bower 1	15.00	6.00	1.50
	Larry Hillman 2			
	Yvan Cournoyer 12			
☐ 30	Johnny Bower 1	15.00	6.00	1.50
	Yvan Cournoyer 12			
☐ 31	Tim Horton 7..........................	15.00	6.00	1.50
	Rogatien Vachon 29			
☐ 32	Jim Pappin 18........................	12.00	5.00	1.20
	Bob Pulford 20			
	Rogatien Vachon 29			
☐ 33	Terry Harper 19.....................	10.00	4.00	1.00
	Bobby Rousseau 15			
	Pronovost 3			
☐ 34	Johnny Bower 1	10.00	4.00	1.00
	Pronovost 3			
	Ralph Backstrom 6			
☐ 35	Frank Mahovlich 27...............	20.00	8.00	2.00
	Gump Worsley 30			
☐ 36	Claude Provost 14..................	10.00	4.00	1.00
	Johnny Bower 1			

1992-93 Zellers Masters of Hockey

 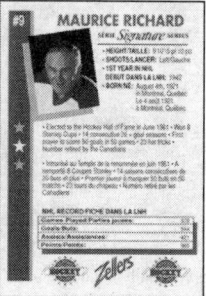

This seven-card "Signature Series" set, featuring former NHL greats, was a promotion by Zellers, a discount retailer with over 275 stores across Canada. This promotion provided additional revenue and benefited children's hospitals in Canada that received 10,000 dollar donations on behalf of each of the players involved. "Club Z" members receive points for purchasing merchandise at Zellers (100 points per dollar spent). They may redeem these points for any gifts in the Club Z rewards catalog. For example, the consumer received a seven-card unsigned set for 50,000 points, and a seven-card signed set for 250,000 points. Jerseys, pucks, photos, and posters were also offered; the Club Z catalog offering all these items was valid from September 9, 1992 until January 1, 1994. Also one personally autographed hockey stick was given away each month in each Zellers store. According to the certificate of authenticity, the production run was 1,000 sets. The cards measure the standard size (2 1/2" by 3 1/2") and have posed color player photos inside white borders. A blue stripe above the picture carries the player's name and is accented by a thin mustard stripe. A silver foil facsimile signature is inscribed across the picture. The backs have the blue and mustard stripes running down the left side and carrying the player's jersey number. In English and French, biography, career highlights, and statistics are included on a white background. A close-up color player photo with a shadow border partially overlaps the stripe near the top. The cards are unnumbered and checklisted below in alphabetical order. There was also a large Marcel Dionne card reportedly given out at various store signings.

	MINT	EXC	G-VG
COMPLETE SET (7).........................	20.00	8.00	2.00
COMMON CARD (1-7)	2.00	.80	.20
☐ 1 Johnny Bower.......................	3.00	1.20	.30
☐ 2 Rod Gilbert..........................	3.00	1.20	.30
☐ 3 Ted Lindsay..........................	3.00	1.20	.30
☐ 4 Frank Mahovlich....................	4.00	1.60	.40
☐ 5 Stan Mikita	4.00	1.60	.40
☐ 6 Maurice Richard....................	6.00	2.40	.60
☐ 7 Certificate of........................	2.00	.80	.20
Authenticity			
☐ NNO Marcel Dionne Large.........	20.00	8.00	2.00

1981-82 O-Pee-Chee Stickers

Similar in size and format to the baseball and football stickers of recent years, this 269-sticker set features foil cards of significant events and star players. Stickers measure approximately 1 15/16" by 2 9/16". The backs

 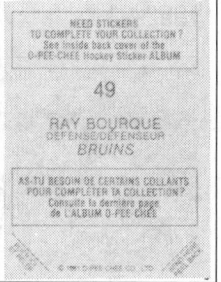

printed in both English and French contain the card number, the player's name and team, an advertisement for an O-Pee-Chee hockey sticker album, and a 1981 O-Pee-Chee copyright date. The sticker number also appears within the border at the lower left corner on the front. On the inside back cover of the sticker album the company offered (via direct mail-order) any ten different stickers (but no more than two foil) of your choice for one dollar; this is one reason why the values of the most popular players in these sticker sets are somewhat depressed compared to traditional card set prices.

	MINT	EXC	G-VG
COMPLETE SET (269)	35.00	14.00	3.50
COMMON PLAYER (1-269)	.05	.02	.00
COMMON FOIL	.15	.06	.01

		MINT	EXC	G-VG
☐ 1	The Stanley Cup FOIL	.25	.10	.02
☐ 2	The Stanley Cup FOIL	.15	.06	.01
☐ 3	The Stanley Cup FOIL	.15	.06	.01
☐ 4	The Stanley Cup FOIL	.15	.06	.01
☐ 5	The Stanley Cup FOIL	.15	.06	.01
☐ 6	The Stanley Cup FOIL	.15	.06	.01
☐ 7	Oilers vs. Islanders	.05	.02	.00
☐ 8	Oilers vs. Islanders	.05	.02	.00
☐ 9	Oilers vs. Islanders	.05	.02	.00
☐ 10	Oilers vs. Islanders	.05	.02	.00
☐ 11	Jari Kurri	1.25	.50	.12
☐ 12	Pat Riggin	.05	.02	.00
☐ 13	Flames vs. Flyers	.05	.02	.00
☐ 14	Flames vs. Flyers	.05	.02	.00
☐ 15	Flames vs. Flyers	.05	.02	.00
☐ 16	Flames vs. Flyers	.05	.02	.00
☐ 17	Stanley Cup Winner 1980-81	.05	.02	.00
☐ 18	Stanley Cup Winner 1980-81	.05	.02	.00
☐ 19	Conn Smythe Trophy FOIL	.20	.08	.02
☐ 20	Butch Goring	.05	.02	.00
☐ 21	North Stars vs. Islanders	.05	.02	.00
☐ 22	Steve Payne	.05	.02	.00
☐ 23	North Stars vs. Islanders	.05	.02	.00
☐ 24	North Stars vs. Islanders	.05	.02	.00
☐ 25	North Stars vs. Islanders	.05	.02	.00
☐ 26	North Stars vs. Islanders	.05	.02	.00
☐ 27	Prince of Wales Trophy FOIL	.15	.06	.01
☐ 28	Prince of Wales Trophy FOIL	.15	.06	.01
☐ 29	Guy Lafleur	.35	.14	.03
☐ 30	Bob Gainey	.20	.08	.02
☐ 31	Larry Robinson	.20	.08	.02
☐ 32	Steve Shutt	.15	.06	.01
☐ 33	Brian Engblom	.05	.02	.00
☐ 34	Doug Jarvis	.05	.02	.00
☐ 35	Yvon Lambert	.05	.02	.00
☐ 36	Mark Napier	.05	.02	.00

		MINT	EXC	G-VG
☐ 37	Rejean Houle	.05	.02	.00
☐ 38	Pierre Larouche	.08	.03	.01
☐ 39	Rod Langway	.15	.06	.01
☐ 40	Richard Sevigny	.05	.02	.00
☐ 41	Guy Lafleur	.35	.14	.03
☐ 42	Larry Robinson	.20	.08	.02
☐ 43	Bob Gainey	.20	.08	.02
☐ 44	Steve Shutt	.15	.06	.01
☐ 45	Rick Middleton	.10	.04	.01
☐ 46	Peter McNab	.05	.02	.00
☐ 47	Rogatien Vachon	.15	.06	.01
☐ 48	Brad Park	.20	.08	.02
☐ 49	Ray Bourque	.75	.30	.07
☐ 50	Terry O'Reilly	.08	.03	.01
☐ 51	Steve Kasper	.08	.03	.01
☐ 52	Dwight Foster	.05	.02	.00
☐ 53	Danny Gare	.05	.02	.00
☐ 54	Andre Savard	.05	.02	.00
☐ 55	Don Edwards	.08	.03	.01
☐ 56	Bob Sauve	.08	.03	.01
☐ 57	Tony McKegney	.05	.02	.00
☐ 58	John Van Boxmeer	.05	.02	.00
☐ 59	Derek Smith	.05	.02	.00
☐ 60	Gilbert Perreault	.20	.08	.02
☐ 61	Mike Rogers	.05	.02	.00
☐ 62	Mark Howe	.12	.05	.01
☐ 63	Blaine Stoughton	.05	.02	.00
☐ 64	Rick Ley	.05	.02	.00
☐ 65	Jordy Douglas	.05	.02	.00
☐ 66	Al Sims	.05	.02	.00
☐ 67	Norm Barnes	.05	.02	.00
☐ 68	John Garrett	.05	.02	.00
☐ 69	Peter Stastny	1.25	.50	.12
☐ 70	Anton Stastny	.08	.03	.01
☐ 71	Jacques Richard	.05	.02	.00
☐ 72	Robbie Ftorek	.08	.03	.01
☐ 73	Dan Bouchard	.05	.02	.00
☐ 74	Real Cloutier	.05	.02	.00
☐ 75	Michel Goulet	.75	.30	.07
☐ 76	Marc Tardif	.08	.03	.01
☐ 77	Capitals vs. Maple Leafs	.05	.02	.00
☐ 78	Capitals vs. Maple Leafs	.05	.02	.00
☐ 79	Capitals vs. Maple Leafs	.05	.02	.00
☐ 80	Capitals vs. Maple Leafs	.05	.02	.00
☐ 81	Whalers vs. Capitals	.05	.02	.00
☐ 82	Whalers vs. Capitals	.05	.02	.00
☐ 83	Canadiens vs. Capitals	.05	.02	.00
☐ 84	Dan Bouchard	.05	.02	.00
☐ 85	North Stars vs. Capitals	.05	.02	.00
☐ 86	North Stars vs. Capitals	.05	.02	.00
☐ 87	Bruins vs. Capitals	.05	.02	.00
☐ 88	Bobby Smith	.25	.10	.02
☐ 89	Don Beaupre	.15	.06	.01
☐ 90	Al MacAdam	.05	.02	.00
☐ 91	Craig Hartsburg	.05	.02	.00
☐ 92	Steve Payne	.05	.02	.00
☐ 93	Gilles Meloche	.08	.03	.01
☐ 94	Tim Young	.05	.02	.00
☐ 95	Tom McCarthy	.05	.02	.00
☐ 96	Wilf Paiement	.05	.02	.00
☐ 97	Darryl Sittler	.20	.08	.02
☐ 98	Borje Salming	.15	.06	.01
☐ 99	Bill Derlago	.05	.02	.00
☐ 100	Ian Turnbull	.05	.02	.00
☐ 101	Rick Vaive	.10	.04	.01
☐ 102	Dan Maloney	.05	.02	.00
☐ 103	Laurie Boschman	.05	.02	.00
☐ 104	Pat Hickey	.05	.02	.00
☐ 105	Michel Larocque	.08	.03	.01
☐ 106	Jiri Crha	.05	.02	.00
☐ 107	John Anderson	.08	.03	.01
☐ 108	Bill Derlago	.05	.02	.00
☐ 109	Darryl Sittler	.20	.08	.02
☐ 110	Wilf Paiement	.05	.02	.00
☐ 111	Borje Salming	.15	.06	.01
☐ 112	Denis Savard	1.25	.50	.12
☐ 113	Tony Esposito	.25	.10	.02
☐ 114	Tom Lysiak	.05	.02	.00
☐ 115	Keith Brown	.10	.04	.01
☐ 116	Glen Sharpley	.05	.02	.00
☐ 117	Terry Ruskowski	.08	.03	.01
☐ 118	Reg Kerr	.05	.02	.00
☐ 119	Bob Murray	.05	.02	.00
☐ 120	Dale McCourt	.05	.02	.00
☐ 121	John Ogrodnick	.10	.04	.01
☐ 122	Mike Foligno	.08	.03	.01
☐ 123	Gilles Gilbert	.08	.03	.01

☐ 124	Reed Larson	.05	.02	.00
☐ 125	Vaclav Nedomansky	.05	.02	.00
☐ 126	Willie Huber	.05	.02	.00
☐ 127	Jim Korn	.05	.02	.00
☐ 128	Bernie Federko	.15	.06	.01
☐ 129	Mike Liut	.15	.06	.01
☐ 130	Wayne Babych	.05	.02	.00
☐ 131	Blake Dunlop	.05	.02	.00
☐ 132	Mike Zuke	.05	.02	.00
☐ 133	Brian Sutter	.15	.06	.01
☐ 134	Rick Lapointe	.05	.02	.00
☐ 135	Jorgen Pettersson	.05	.02	.00
☐ 136	Dave Christian	.15	.06	.01
☐ 137	Dave Babych	.08	.03	.01
☐ 138	Morris Lukowich	.05	.02	.00
☐ 139	Norm Dupont	.05	.02	.00
☐ 140	Ron Wilson	.05	.02	.00
☐ 141	Dan Geoffrion	.05	.02	.00
☐ 142	Barry Long	.05	.02	.00
☐ 143	Pierre Hamel	.05	.02	.00
☐ 144	Charlie Simmer AS FOIL	.25	.10	.02
☐ 145	Mark Howe AS FOIL	.30	.12	.03
☐ 146	Don Beaupre AS FOIL	.40	.16	.04
☐ 147	Marcel Dionne AS FOIL	.50	.20	.05
☐ 148	Larry Robinson AS FOIL	.45	.18	.04
☐ 149	Dave Taylor AS FOIL	.25	.10	.02
☐ 150	Mike Bossy AS FOIL	.75	.30	.07
☐ 151	Denis Potvin AS FOIL	.50	.20	.05
☐ 152	Bryan Trottier AS FOIL	.50	.20	.05
☐ 153	Mike Liut AS FOIL	.25	.10	.02
☐ 154	Rob Ramage AS FOIL	.20	.08	.02
☐ 155	Bill Barber AS FOIL	.30	.12	.03
☐ 156	Campbell Bowl FOIL	.15	.06	.01
☐ 157	Campbell Bowl FOIL	.15	.06	.01
☐ 158	Mike Bossy	.40	.16	.04
☐ 159	Denis Potvin	.25	.10	.02
☐ 160	Bryan Trottier	.25	.10	.02
☐ 161	Billy Smith	.15	.06	.01
☐ 162	Anders Kallur	.05	.02	.00
☐ 163	Bob Bourne	.05	.02	.00
☐ 164	Clark Gillies	.08	.03	.01
☐ 165	Ken Morrow	.08	.03	.01
☐ 166	Anders Hedberg	.08	.03	.01
☐ 167	Ron Greschner	.08	.03	.01
☐ 168	Barry Beck	.08	.03	.01
☐ 169	Ed Johnstone	.05	.02	.00
☐ 170	Don Maloney	.05	.02	.00
☐ 171	Ron Duguay	.08	.03	.01
☐ 172	Ulf Nilsson	.08	.03	.01
☐ 173	Dave Maloney	.08	.03	.01
☐ 174	Bill Barber	.15	.06	.01
☐ 175	Behn Wilson	.05	.02	.00
☐ 176	Ken Linseman	.08	.03	.01
☐ 177	Pete Peeters	.15	.06	.01
☐ 178	Bobby Clarke	.25	.10	.02
☐ 179	Paul Holmgren	.08	.03	.01
☐ 180	Brian Propp	.15	.06	.01
☐ 181	Reggie Leach	.08	.03	.01
☐ 182	Rick Kehoe	.08	.03	.01
☐ 183	Randy Carlyle	.08	.03	.01
☐ 184	George Ferguson	.05	.02	.00
☐ 185	Peter Lee	.05	.02	.00
☐ 186	Rod Schutt	.05	.02	.00
☐ 187	Paul Gardner	.05	.02	.00
☐ 188	Ron Stackhouse	.05	.02	.00
☐ 189	Mario Faubert	.05	.02	.00
☐ 190	Mike Gartner	1.00	.40	.10
☐ 191	Dennis Maruk	.08	.03	.01
☐ 192	Ryan Walter	.08	.03	.01
☐ 193	Rick Green	.05	.02	.00
☐ 194	Mike Palmateer	.08	.03	.01
☐ 195	Bob Kelly	.08	.03	.01
☐ 196	Jean Pronovost	.08	.03	.01
☐ 197	Al Hangsleben	.05	.02	.00
☐ 198	Flames vs. Capitals	.05	.02	.00
☐ 199	Oilers vs. Islanders	.05	.02	.00
☐ 200	Oilers vs. Islanders	.05	.02	.00
☐ 201	Oilers vs. Islanders	.05	.02	.00
☐ 202	Oilers vs. Islanders	.05	.02	.00
☐ 203	Rangers vs. Islanders	.05	.02	.00
☐ 204	Rangers vs. Islanders	.05	.02	.00
☐ 205	Flyers vs. Capitals	.05	.02	.00
☐ 206	Flyers vs. Capitals	.05	.02	.00
☐ 207	Rangers vs. Capitals	.05	.02	.00
☐ 208	Canadiens vs. Capitals	.05	.02	.00
☐ 209	Wayne Gretzky	6.00	2.40	.60
☐ 210	Mark Messier	2.50	1.00	.25
☐ 211	Jari Kurri	1.25	.50	.12
☐ 212	Brett Callighen	.05	.02	.00

☐ 213	Matti Hagman	.05	.02	.00
☐ 214	Risto Siltanen	.05	.02	.00
☐ 215	Lee Fogolin	.05	.02	.00
☐ 216	Eddie Mio	.08	.03	.01
☐ 217	Glenn Anderson	.60	.24	.06
☐ 218	Kent Nilsson	.08	.03	.01
☐ 219	Guy Chouinard	.08	.03	.01
☐ 220	Eric Vail	.08	.03	.01
☐ 221	Pat Riggin	.10	.04	.01
☐ 222	Willi Plett	.05	.02	.00
☐ 223	Pekka Rautakallio	.05	.02	.00
☐ 224	Paul Reinhart	.08	.03	.01
☐ 225	Brad Marsh	.08	.03	.01
☐ 226	Phil Russell	.05	.02	.00
☐ 227	Lanny McDonald	.20	.08	.02
☐ 228	Merlin Malinowski	.05	.02	.00
☐ 229	Rob Ramage	.15	.06	.01
☐ 230	Glenn Resch	.12	.05	.01
☐ 231	Ron Delorme	.05	.02	.00
☐ 232	Lucien DeBlois	.05	.02	.00
☐ 233	Paul Gagne	.05	.02	.00
☐ 234	Joel Quenneville	.05	.02	.00
☐ 235	Marcel Dionne	.25	.10	.02
☐ 236	Charlie Simmer	.12	.05	.01
☐ 237	Dave Taylor	.12	.05	.01
☐ 238	Mario Lessard	.08	.03	.01
☐ 239	Larry Murphy	.60	.24	.06
☐ 240	Jerry Korab	.05	.02	.00
☐ 241	Mike Murphy	.05	.02	.00
☐ 242	Billy Harris	.05	.02	.00
☐ 243	Thomas Gradin	.08	.03	.01
☐ 244	Per-Olov Brasar	.05	.02	.00
☐ 245	Glen Hanlon	.08	.03	.01
☐ 246	Chris Oddleifson	.05	.02	.00
☐ 247	Dave(Tiger) Williams	.08	.03	.01
☐ 248	Kevin McCarthy	.05	.02	.00
☐ 249	Dennis Kearns	.05	.02	.00
☐ 250	Harold Snepsts	.08	.03	.01
☐ 251	Art Ross Trophy FOIL	.20	.08	.02
☐ 252	Wayne Gretzky	6.00	2.40	.60
☐ 253	Mike Bossy	.50	.20	.05
☐ 254	Norris Trophy FOIL	.20	.08	.02
☐ 255	Randy Carlyle	.08	.03	.01
☐ 256	Richard Sevigny	.08	.03	.01
☐ 257	Vezina Trophy FOIL	.20	.08	.02
☐ 258	Denis Herron	.08	.03	.01
☐ 259	Michel Larocque	.08	.03	.01
☐ 260	Lady Byng Trophy FOIL	.20	.08	.02
☐ 261	Rick Kehoe	.08	.03	.01
☐ 262	Calder Trophy FOIL	.20	.08	.02
☐ 263	Peter Stastny	1.25	.50	.12
☐ 264	Wayne Gretzky	6.00	2.40	.60
☐ 265	Hart Trophy FOIL	.20	.08	.02
☐ 266	Charlie Simmer	.15	.06	.01
☐ 267	Marcel Dionne	.25	.10	.02
☐ 268	Dave Taylor	.12	.05	.01
☐ 269	Bob Gainey	.20	.08	.02
☐ xx	Sticker Album	2.00	.80	.20

1982-83 O-Pee-Chee Stickers

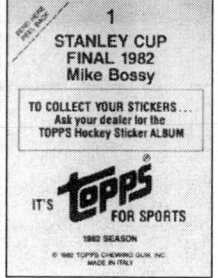

This set of 263 stickers is exactly the same as the Topps stickers issued this year except for minor back differences. Foil cards of players and trophies are contained within this set. The stickers in the set are 1 15/16" by 2 9/16". The card numbers appear at the lower right within the border on the fronts of the cards as well as appearing on the back. The backs of the stickers contain an ad for an O-Pee-Chee hockey sticker album (in both English and French), the player's name and team, a 1982 Topps copyright date, and a statement to the fact that these cards were made in Italy. The checklist and prices below apply to both O-Pee-Chee and Topps stickers for this year. On the inside back cover of the sticker album the company offered (via direct mail-order) any ten different stickers (but no more than two foil) of your choice for one dollar; this is one reason why the values of the most popular players in these sticker sets are somewhat depressed compared to traditional card set prices.

	MINT	EXC	G-VG
COMPLETE SET (263)	35.00	14.00	3.50
COMMON PLAYER (1-263)	.05	.02	.00
COMMON FOIL	.15	.06	.01

		MINT	EXC	G-VG
☐	1 Mike Bossy	.40	.16	.04
☐	2 Conn Smythe Trophy FOIL	.20	.08	.02
☐	3 1981-82 Stanley Cup Winners	.05	.02	.00
☐	4 1981-82 Stanley Cup Winners	.05	.02	.00
☐	5 Stanley Cup Finals	.05	.02	.00
☐	6 Stanley Cup Finals	.05	.02	.00
☐	7 Richard Brodeur	.08	.03	.01
☐	8 Victory/Victoire	.05	.02	.00
☐	9 Stanley Cup Finals	.05	.02	.00
☐	10 Stanley Cup Finals	.05	.02	.00
☐	11 Canucks vs. Chicago	.05	.02	.00
☐	12 Canucks vs. Chicago	.05	.02	.00
☐	13 Canucks vs. Chicago	.05	.02	.00
☐	14 Tom Lysiak	.05	.02	.00
☐	15 Peter Stastny	.40	.16	.04
☐	16 Islanders vs. Quebec	.05	.02	.00
☐	17 Islanders vs. Quebec	.05	.02	.00
☐	18 Islanders vs. Quebec	.05	.02	.00
☐	19 Peter Stastny	.40	.16	.04
☐	20 Marian Stastny	.05	.02	.00
☐	21 Marc Tardif	.05	.02	.00
☐	22 Wilf Paiement	.05	.02	.00
☐	23 Real Cloutier	.05	.02	.00
☐	24 Anton Stastny	.08	.03	.01
☐	25 Michel Goulet	.25	.10	.02
☐	26 Dale Hunter	.20	.08	.02
☐	27 Dan Bouchard	.05	.02	.00
☐	28 Guy Lafleur	.30	.12	.03
☐	29 Guy Lafleur	.30	.12	.03
☐	30 Mario Tremblay	.05	.02	.00
☐	31 Larry Robinson	.20	.08	.02
☐	32 Steve Shutt	.15	.06	.01
☐	33 Steve Shutt	.15	.06	.01
☐	34 Rod Langway	.10	.04	.01
☐	35 Pierre Mondou	.05	.02	.00
☐	36 Bob Gainey	.15	.06	.01
☐	37 Rick Wamsley	.08	.03	.01
☐	38 Mark Napier	.05	.02	.00
☐	39 Mark Napier	.05	.02	.00
☐	40 Doug Jarvis	.08	.03	.01
☐	41 Denis Herron	.08	.03	.01
☐	42 Keith Acton	.05	.02	.00
☐	43 Keith Acton	.05	.02	.00
☐	44 Prince of Wales Trophy FOIL	.15	.06	.01
☐	45 Prince of Wales Trophy FOIL	.15	.06	.01
☐	46 Denis Potvin	.25	.10	.02
☐	47 Bryan Trottier	.25	.10	.02
☐	48 Bryan Trottier	.25	.10	.02
☐	49 John Tonelli	.08	.03	.01
☐	50 Mike Bossy	.40	.16	.04
☐	51 Mike Bossy	.40	.16	.04
☐	52 Duane Sutter	.10	.04	.01
☐	53 Bob Bourne	.05	.02	.00
☐	54 Clark Gillies	.08	.03	.01
☐	55 Clark Gillies	.08	.03	.01
☐	56 Brent Sutter	.25	.10	.02
☐	57 Anders Kallur	.05	.02	.00
☐	58 Ken Morrow	.08	.03	.01
☐	59 Bob Nystrom	.05	.02	.00
☐	60 Billy Smith	.20	.08	.02
☐	61 Billy Smith	.20	.08	.02
☐	62 Rick Vaive	.08	.03	.01
☐	63 Rick Vaive	.08	.03	.01
☐	64 Jim Benning	.05	.02	.00
☐	65 Miroslav Frycer	.05	.02	.00

		MINT	EXC	G-VG
☐	66 Terry Martin	.05	.02	.00
☐	67 Bill Derlago	.05	.02	.00
☐	68 Bill Derlago	.05	.02	.00
☐	69 Rocky Saganiuk	.05	.02	.00
☐	70 Vincent Tremblay	.05	.02	.00
☐	71 Bob Manno	.05	.02	.00
☐	72 Dan Maloney	.08	.03	.01
☐	73 John Anderson	.05	.02	.00
☐	74 John Anderson	.05	.02	.00
☐	75 Borje Salming	.10	.04	.01
☐	76 Borje Salming	.10	.04	.01
☐	77 Michel Larocque	.08	.03	.01
☐	78 Rick Middleton	.10	.04	.01
☐	79 Rick Middleton	.10	.04	.01
☐	80 Keith Crowder	.05	.02	.00
☐	81 Steve Kasper	.08	.03	.01
☐	82 Brad Park	.15	.06	.01
☐	83 Peter McNab	.05	.02	.00
☐	84 Peter McNab	.05	.02	.00
☐	85 Terry O'Reilly	.08	.03	.01
☐	86 Ray Bourque	.50	.20	.05
☐	87 Ray Bourque	.50	.20	.05
☐	88 Tom Fergus	.05	.02	.00
☐	89 Mike O'Connell	.05	.02	.00
☐	90 Brad McCrimmon	.08	.03	.01
☐	91 Don Marcotte	.05	.02	.00
☐	92 Barry Pederson	.08	.03	.01
☐	93 Barry Pederson	.08	.03	.01
☐	94 Mark Messier	1.25	.50	.12
☐	95 Grant Fuhr	1.25	.50	.12
☐	96 Kevin Lowe	.35	.14	.03
☐	97 Wayne Gretzky	5.00	2.00	.50
☐	98 Wayne Gretzky	5.00	2.00	.50
☐	99 Glenn Anderson	.20	.08	.02
☐	100 Glenn Anderson	.20	.08	.02
☐	101 Dave Lumley	.05	.02	.00
☐	102 Dave Hunter	.05	.02	.00
☐	103 Matti Hagman	.05	.02	.00
☐	104 Paul Coffey	1.25	.50	.12
☐	105 Paul Coffey	1.25	.50	.12
☐	106 Lee Fogolin	.05	.02	.00
☐	107 Ron Low	.08	.03	.01
☐	108 Jari Kurri	.50	.20	.05
☐	109 Jari Kurri	.50	.20	.05
☐	110 Bill Barber	.15	.06	.01
☐	111 Brian Propp	.10	.04	.01
☐	112 Ken Linseman	.08	.03	.01
☐	113 Ron Flockhart	.08	.03	.01
☐	114 Darryl Sittler	.15	.06	.01
☐	115 Bobby Clarke	.30	.12	.03
☐	116 Paul Holmgren	.08	.03	.01
☐	117 Pete Peeters	.10	.04	.01
☐	118 Gilbert Perreault	.20	.08	.02
☐	119 Dale McCourt	.05	.02	.00
☐	120 Mike Foligno	.05	.02	.00
☐	121 John Van Boxmeer	.05	.02	.00
☐	122 Tony McKegney	.08	.03	.01
☐	123 Ric Seiling	.05	.02	.00
☐	124 Don Edwards	.08	.03	.01
☐	125 Yvon Lambert	.05	.02	.00
☐	126 Blaine Stoughton	.08	.03	.01
☐	127 Pierre Larouche	.08	.03	.01
☐	128 Doug Sulliman	.05	.02	.00
☐	129 Ron Francis	1.25	.50	.12
☐	130 Greg Millen	.08	.03	.01
☐	131 Mark Howe	.10	.04	.01
☐	132 Chris Kotsopoulos	.05	.02	.00
☐	133 Garry Howatt	.05	.02	.00
☐	134 Ron Duguay	.08	.03	.01
☐	135 Barry Beck	.08	.03	.01
☐	136 Mike Rogers	.05	.02	.00
☐	137 Don Maloney	.05	.02	.00
☐	138 Mark Pavelich	.08	.03	.01
☐	139 Ed Johnstone	.05	.02	.00
☐	140 Dave Maloney	.05	.02	.00
☐	141 Steve Weeks	.08	.03	.01
☐	142 Eddie Mio	.08	.03	.01
☐	143 Rick Kehoe	.08	.03	.01
☐	144 Randy Carlyle	.08	.03	.01
☐	145 Paul Gardner	.05	.02	.00
☐	146 Michel Dion	.08	.03	.01
☐	147 Rick MacLeish	.10	.04	.01
☐	148 Pat Boutette	.05	.02	.00
☐	149 Mike Bullard	.08	.03	.01
☐	150 George Ferguson	.05	.02	.00
☐	151 Dennis Maruk	.08	.03	.01
☐	152 Ryan Walter	.08	.03	.01
☐	153 Mike Gartner	.50	.20	.05
☐	154 Bob Carpenter	.30	.12	.03
☐	155 Chris Valentine	.05	.02	.00
☐	156 Rick Green	.08	.03	.01
☐	157 Bengt Gustafsson	.05	.02	.00
☐	158 Dave Parro	.05	.02	.00

☐ 159 Mark Messier AS FOIL	1.50	.60	.15
☐ 160 Paul Coffey AS FOIL	1.50	.60	.15
☐ 161 Grant Fuhr AS FOIL	1.50	.60	.15
☐ 162 Wayne Gretzky AS FOIL	6.00	2.40	.60
☐ 163 Doug Wilson AS FOIL	.35	.14	.03
☐ 164 Dave Taylor AS FOIL	.25	.10	.02
☐ 165 Mike Bossy AS FOIL	.75	.30	.07
☐ 166 Ray Bourque AS FOIL	.75	.30	.07
☐ 167 Peter Stastny AS FOIL	.75	.30	.07
☐ 168 Michel Dion AS FOIL	.20	.08	.02
☐ 169 Larry Robinson AS FOIL	.35	.14	.03
☐ 170 Bill Barber AS FOIL	.30	.12	.03
☐ 171 Denis Savard	.40	.16	.04
☐ 172 Doug Wilson	.15	.06	.01
☐ 173 Grant Mulvey	.08	.03	.01
☐ 174 Tom Lysiak	.08	.03	.01
☐ 175 Al Secord	.08	.03	.01
☐ 176 Reg Kerr	.05	.02	.00
☐ 177 Tim Higgins	.05	.02	.00
☐ 178 Terry Ruskowski	.08	.03	.01
☐ 179 John Ogrodnick	.08	.03	.01
☐ 180 Reed Larson	.05	.02	.00
☐ 181 Bob Sauve	.08	.03	.01
☐ 182 Mark Osborne	.05	.02	.00
☐ 183 Jim Schoenfeld	.08	.03	.01
☐ 184 Danny Gare	.08	.03	.01
☐ 185 Willie Huber	.05	.02	.00
☐ 186 Walt McKechnie	.05	.02	.00
☐ 187 Paul Woods	.05	.02	.00
☐ 188 Bobby Smith	.12	.05	.01
☐ 189 Dino Ciccarelli	.50	.20	.05
☐ 190 Neal Broten	.25	.10	.02
☐ 191 Steve Payne	.08	.03	.01
☐ 192 Craig Hartsburg	.05	.02	.00
☐ 193 Don Beaupre	.12	.05	.01
☐ 194 Steve Christoff	.08	.03	.01
☐ 195 Gilles Meloche	.08	.03	.01
☐ 196 Mike Liut	.10	.04	.01
☐ 197 Bernie Federko	.12	.05	.01
☐ 198 Brian Sutter	.12	.05	.01
☐ 199 Blake Dunlop	.05	.02	.00
☐ 200 Joe Mullen	1.50	.60	.15
☐ 201 Wayne Babych	.05	.02	.00
☐ 202 Jorgen Pettersson	.05	.02	.00
☐ 203 Perry Turnbull	.05	.02	.00
☐ 204 Dale Hawerchuk	2.00	.80	.20
☐ 205 Morris Lukowich	.05	.02	.00
☐ 206 Dave Christian	.08	.03	.01
☐ 207 Dave Babych	.08	.03	.01
☐ 208 Paul MacLean	.10	.04	.01
☐ 209 Willy Lindstrom	.05	.02	.00
☐ 210 Ed Staniowski	.05	.02	.00
☐ 211 Doug Soetaert	.05	.02	.00
☐ 212 Lucien DeBlois	.05	.02	.00
☐ 213 Mel Bridgman	.05	.02	.00
☐ 214 Lanny McDonald	.20	.08	.02
☐ 215 Guy Chouinard	.05	.02	.00
☐ 216 Jim Peplinski	.08	.03	.01
☐ 217 Kent Nilsson	.08	.03	.01
☐ 218 Rekka Rautakallio	.08	.03	.01
☐ 219 Paul Reinhart	.08	.03	.01
☐ 220 Kevin Lavalee	.05	.02	.00
☐ 221 Ken Houston	.05	.02	.00
☐ 222 Glenn Resch	.12	.05	.01
☐ 223 Rob Ramage	.08	.03	.01
☐ 224 Don Lever	.05	.02	.00
☐ 225 Bob MacMillan	.05	.02	.00
☐ 226 Steve Tambellini	.05	.02	.00
☐ 227 Brent Ashton	.05	.02	.00
☐ 228 Bob Lorimer	.05	.02	.00
☐ 229 Merlin Malinowski	.05	.02	.00
☐ 230 Marcel Dionne	.25	.10	.02
☐ 231 Dave Taylor	.10	.04	.01
☐ 232 Larry Murphy	.25	.10	.02
☐ 233 Steve Bozek	.05	.02	.00
☐ 234 Greg Terrion	.05	.02	.00
☐ 235 Jim Fox	.05	.02	.00
☐ 236 Mario Lessard	.08	.03	.01
☐ 237 Charlie Simmer	.12	.05	.01
☐ 238 Campbell Bowl FOIL	.15	.06	.01
☐ 239 Campbell Bowl FOIL	.15	.06	.01
☐ 240 Thomas Gradin	.08	.03	.01
☐ 241 Ivan Boldirev	.05	.02	.00
☐ 242 Stan Smyl	.08	.03	.01
☐ 243 Harold Snepsts	.08	.03	.01
☐ 244 Curt Fraser	.05	.02	.00
☐ 245 Lars Molin	.05	.02	.00
☐ 246 Kevin McCarthy	.05	.02	.00
☐ 247 Richard Brodeur	.08	.03	.01
☐ 248 Calder Trophy FOIL	.15	.06	.01

☐ 249 Dale Hawerchuk	1.25	.50	.12
☐ 250 Vezina Trophy FOIL	.15	.06	.01
☐ 251 Billy Smith	.12	.05	.01
☐ 252 Denis Herron and Rick Wamsley	.06	.02	.00
☐ 253 Steve Kasper	.06	.02	.00
☐ 254 Doug Wilson	.15	.06	.01
☐ 255 Norris Trophy FOIL	.20	.08	.02
☐ 256 Wayne Gretzky	3.00	1.20	.30
☐ 257 Wayne Gretzky	3.00	1.20	.30
☐ 258 Wayne Gretzky	3.00	1.20	.30
☐ 259 Wayne Gretzky	3.00	1.20	.30
☐ 260 Hart Trophy FOIL	.15	.06	.01
☐ 261 Art Ross Trophy FOIL	.15	.06	.01
☐ 262 Rick Middleton	.10	.04	.01
☐ 263 Lady Byng Trophy FOIL	.20	.08	.02
☐ xx Sticker Album	2.00	.80	.20

1983-84 O-Pee-Chee Stickers

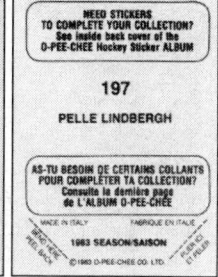

This sticker set consists of 330 stickers in full color and was put out by both O-Pee-Chee and Topps. The foil stickers are numbers 1-4, 15, 22-24, 299-300, 304-305, 308-311, 314-315, 319-330. Stickers measure 1 15/16" by 2 9/16". An album is available for these stickers. The Topps set is distinguishable only by minor back differences. The checklist and prices below apply to both O-Pee-Chee and Topps stickers for this year. On the inside back cover of the sticker album the company offered (via direct mail-order) any ten different stickers of your choice for one dollar; this is one reason why the values of the most popular players in these sticker sets are somewhat depressed compared to traditional card set prices.

	MINT	EXC	G-VG
COMPLETE SET (330)	35.00	14.00	3.50
COMMON PLAYER (1-330)	.05	.02	.00
COMMON FOIL	.15	.06	.01
☐ 1 Marcel Dionne FOIL	.50	.20	.05
☐ 2 Guy Lafleur FOIL	.60	.24	.06
☐ 3 Darryl Sittler FOIL	.35	.14	.03
☐ 4 Gilbert Perreault FOIL	.35	.14	.03
☐ 5 Bill Barber	.15	.06	.01
☐ 6 Steve Shutt	.15	.06	.01
☐ 7 Wayne Gretzky	4.00	1.60	.40
☐ 8 Lanny McDonald	.20	.08	.02
☐ 9 Reggie Leach	.08	.03	.01
☐ 10 Mike Bossy	.40	.16	.04
☐ 11 Rick Kehoe	.08	.03	.01
☐ 12 Bobby Clarke	.30	.12	.03
☐ 13 Butch Goring	.08	.03	.01
☐ 14 Rick Middleton	.10	.04	.01
☐ 15 Conn Smythe Trophy FOIL	.20	.08	.02
☐ 16 Billy Smith	.15	.06	.01
☐ 17 Lee Fogolin	.05	.02	.00
☐ 18 Stanley Cup Finals	.05	.02	.00
☐ 19 Stanley Cup Finals	.05	.02	.00
☐ 20 Stanley Cup Finals	.05	.02	.00
☐ 21 Stanley Cup Finals	.05	.02	.00
☐ 22 Stanley Cup FOIL	.15	.06	.01
☐ 23 Stanley Cup FOIL	.15	.06	.01
☐ 24 Stanley Cup FOIL	.15	.06	.01

☐ 25	Rick Vaive	.08	.03	.01
☐ 26	Rick Vaive	.08	.03	.01
☐ 27	Billy Harris	.05	.02	.00
☐ 28	Dan Daoust	.05	.02	.00
☐ 29	Dan Daoust	.05	.02	.00
☐ 30	John Anderson	.05	.02	.00
☐ 31	John Anderson	.05	.02	.00
☐ 32	Peter Ihnacak	.05	.02	.00
☐ 33	Borje Salming	.10	.04	.01
☐ 34	Borje Salming	.10	.04	.01
☐ 35	Bill Derlago	.05	.02	.00
☐ 36	Rick St.Croix	.05	.02	.00
☐ 37	Greg Terrion	.05	.02	.00
☐ 38	Miroslav Frycer	.05	.02	.00
☐ 39	Mike Palmateer	.08	.03	.01
☐ 40	Gaston Gingras	.05	.02	.00
☐ 41	Pete Peeters	.08	.03	.01
☐ 42	Pete Peeters	.08	.03	.01
☐ 43	Mike Krushelnyski	.08	.03	.01
☐ 44	Rick Middleton	.10	.04	.01
☐ 45	Rick Middleton	.10	.04	.01
☐ 46	Ray Bourque	.50	.20	.05
☐ 47	Ray Bourque	.50	.20	.05
☐ 48	Brad Park	.20	.08	.02
☐ 49	Barry Pederson	.08	.03	.01
☐ 50	Barry Pederson	.08	.03	.01
☐ 51	Peter McNab	.05	.02	.00
☐ 52	Mike O'Connell	.05	.02	.00
☐ 53	Steve Kasper	.08	.03	.01
☐ 54	Marty Howe	.05	.02	.00
☐ 55	Tom Fergus	.05	.02	.00
☐ 56	Keith Crowder	.05	.02	.00
☐ 57	Steve Shutt	.15	.06	.01
☐ 58	Guy Lafleur	.30	.12	.03
☐ 59	Guy Lafleur	.30	.12	.03
☐ 60	Larry Robinson	.20	.08	.02
☐ 61	Larry Robinson	.20	.08	.02
☐ 62	Ryan Walter	.08	.03	.01
☐ 63	Ryan Walter	.08	.03	.01
☐ 64	Mark Napier	.08	.03	.01
☐ 65	Mark Napier	.08	.03	.01
☐ 66	Bob Gainey	.15	.06	.01
☐ 67	Doug Wickenheiser	.05	.02	.00
☐ 68	Pierre Mondou	.05	.02	.00
☐ 69	Mario Tremblay	.05	.02	.00
☐ 70	Gilbert Delorme	.05	.02	.00
☐ 71	Mats Naslund	.25	.10	.02
☐ 72	Rick Wamsley	.08	.03	.01
☐ 73	Ken Morrow	.08	.03	.01
☐ 74	John Tonelli	.08	.03	.01
☐ 75	John Tonelli	.08	.03	.01
☐ 76	Bryan Trottier	.25	.10	.02
☐ 77	Bryan Trottier	.25	.10	.02
☐ 78	Mike Bossy	.40	.16	.04
☐ 79	Mike Bossy	.40	.16	.04
☐ 80	Bob Bourne	.05	.02	.00
☐ 81	Denis Potvin	.20	.08	.02
☐ 82	Denis Potvin	.20	.08	.02
☐ 83	Dave Langevin	.05	.02	.00
☐ 84	Clark Gillies	.08	.03	.01
☐ 85	Bob Nystrom	.08	.03	.01
☐ 86	Billy Smith	.15	.06	.01
☐ 87	Tomas Jonsson	.05	.02	.00
☐ 88	Rollie Melanson	.08	.03	.01
☐ 89	Wayne Gretzky	4.00	1.60	.40
☐ 90	Wayne Gretzky	4.00	1.60	.40
☐ 91	Willy Lindstrom	.05	.02	.00
☐ 92	Glenn Anderson	.15	.06	.01
☐ 93	Glenn Anderson	.15	.06	.01
☐ 94	Paul Coffey	.60	.24	.06
☐ 95	Paul Coffey	.60	.24	.06
☐ 96	Charlie Huddy	.05	.02	.00
☐ 97	Mark Messier	1.00	.40	.10
☐ 98	Mark Messier	1.00	.40	.10
☐ 99	Andy Moog	.60	.24	.06
☐ 100	Lee Fogolin	.06	.02	.00
☐ 101	Kevin Lowe	.15	.06	.01
☐ 102	Ken Linseman	.05	.02	.00
☐ 103	Tom Roulston	.05	.02	.00
☐ 104	Jari Kurri	.35	.14	.03
☐ 105	Darryl Sutter	.08	.03	.01
☐ 106	Denis Savard	.20	.08	.02
☐ 107	Denis Savard	.20	.08	.02
☐ 108	Steve Larmer	1.00	.40	.10
☐ 109	Bob Murray	.05	.02	.00
☐ 110	Tom Lysiak	.08	.03	.01
☐ 111	Al Secord	.08	.03	.01
☐ 112	Doug Wilson	.15	.06	.01
☐ 113	Murray Bannerman	.08	.03	.01
☐ 114	Gordie Roberts	.05	.02	.00
☐ 115	Tom McCarthy	.05	.02	.00
☐ 116	Bobby Smith	.15	.06	.01
☐ 117	Craig Hartsburg	.05	.02	.00
☐ 118	Dino Ciccarelli	.35	.14	.03
☐ 119	Dino Ciccarelli	.35	.14	.03
☐ 120	Neal Broten	.15	.06	.01
☐ 121	Steve Payne	.05	.02	.00
☐ 122	Don Beaupre	.10	.04	.01
☐ 123	Jorgen Pettersson	.05	.02	.00
☐ 124	Perry Turnbull	.05	.02	.00
☐ 125	Bernie Federko	.15	.06	.01
☐ 126	Mike Crombeen	.05	.02	.00
☐ 127	Brian Sutter	.10	.04	.01
☐ 128	Brian Sutter	.10	.04	.01
☐ 129	Mike Liut	.08	.03	.01
☐ 130	Rob Ramage	.08	.03	.01
☐ 131	Blake Dunlop	.05	.02	.00
☐ 132	Ivan Boldirev	.05	.02	.00
☐ 133	Dwight Foster	.05	.02	.00
☐ 134	Reed Larson	.05	.02	.00
☐ 135	Danny Gare	.08	.03	.01
☐ 136	Jim Schoenfeld	.08	.03	.01
☐ 137	John Ogrodnick	.08	.03	.01
☐ 138	John Ogrodnick	.08	.03	.01
☐ 139	Willie Huber	.05	.02	.00
☐ 140	Greg Smith	.05	.02	.00
☐ 141	Ed Beers	.05	.02	.00
☐ 142	Brian Bellows	1.00	.40	.10
☐ 143	Jiri Bubla	.05	.02	.00
☐ 144	Daryl Evans	.05	.02	.00
☐ 145	Randy Gregg	.08	.03	.01
☐ 146	Jim Jackson	.05	.02	.00
☐ 147	Corrado Micalef	.05	.02	.00
☐ 148	Brian Mullen	.25	.10	.02
☐ 149	Frank Nigro	.05	.02	.00
☐ 150	Walt Poddubny	.08	.03	.01
☐ 151	Jaroslav Pouzar	.05	.02	.00
☐ 152	Patrik Sundstrom	.15	.06	.01
☐ 153	Denis Savard	.20	.08	.02
☐ 154	Dave Hunter	.05	.02	.00
☐ 155	Andy Moog	.60	.24	.06
☐ 156	Al Secord	.08	.03	.01
☐ 157	Mark Messier	1.00	.40	.10
☐ 158	Glenn Anderson	.15	.06	.01
☐ 159	Jaroslav Pouzar	.05	.02	.00
☐ 160	Al Secord AS	.05	.02	.00
☐ 161	Wayne Gretzky AS	2.50	1.00	.25
☐ 162	Lanny McDonald AS	.15	.06	.01
☐ 163	Dave Babych AS	.08	.03	.01
☐ 164	Murray Bannerman AS	.08	.03	.01
☐ 165	Doug Wilson AS	.10	.04	.01
☐ 166	Michel Goulet AS	.15	.06	.01
☐ 167	Peter Stastny AS	.20	.08	.02
☐ 168	Marian Stastny AS	.05	.02	.00
☐ 169	Denis Potvin AS	.15	.06	.01
☐ 170	Pete Peeters AS	.08	.03	.01
☐ 171	Mark Howe AS	.08	.03	.01
☐ 172	Luc Dufour	.05	.02	.00
☐ 173	Ray Bourque	.50	.20	.05
☐ 174	Bob Bourne	.05	.02	.00
☐ 175	Denis Potvin	.15	.06	.01
☐ 176	Mike Bossy	.35	.14	.03
☐ 177	Butch Goring	.07	.03	.01
☐ 178	Brad Park	.20	.08	.02
☐ 179	Murray Brumwell	.05	.02	.00
☐ 180	Guy Carbonneau	.75	.30	.07
☐ 181	Lindsay Carson	.05	.02	.00
☐ 182	Luc Dufour	.05	.02	.00
☐ 183	Bob Froese	.15	.06	.01
☐ 184	Mats Hallin	.05	.02	.00
☐ 185	Gord Kluzak	.08	.03	.01
☐ 186	Jeff Larmer	.05	.02	.00
☐ 187	Milan Novy	.05	.02	.00
☐ 188	Scott Stevens	2.00	.80	.20
☐ 189	Bob Sullivan	.05	.02	.00
☐ 190	Mark Taylor	.05	.02	.00
☐ 191	Darryl Sittler	.20	.08	.02
☐ 192	Ron Flockhart	.05	.02	.00
☐ 193	Brad McCrimmon	.08	.03	.01
☐ 194	Bill Barber	.15	.06	.01
☐ 195	Mark Howe	.10	.04	.01
☐ 196	Mark Howe	.10	.04	.01
☐ 197	Pelle Lindbergh	5.00	2.00	.50
☐ 198	Bobby Clarke	.30	.12	.03
☐ 199	Brian Propp	.10	.04	.01
☐ 200	Ken Houston	.05	.02	.00
☐ 201	Rod Langway	.10	.04	.01
☐ 202	Al Jensen	.08	.03	.01
☐ 203	Brian Engblom	.05	.02	.00
☐ 204	Dennis Maruk	.08	.03	.01
☐ 205	Dennis Maruk	.08	.03	.01
☐ 206	Bob Carpenter	.10	.04	.01
☐ 207	Mike Gartner	.30	.12	.03
☐ 208	Doug Jarvis	.08	.03	.01
☐ 209	Eddie Mio	.08	.03	.01
☐ 210	Barry Beck	.08	.03	.01

☐ 211	Dave Maloney	.08	.03	.01
☐ 212	Don Maloney	.05	.02	.00
☐ 213	Mark Pavelich	.08	.03	.01
☐ 214	Mark Pavelich	.08	.03	.01
☐ 215	Anders Hedberg	.08	.03	.01
☐ 216	Reijo Ruotsalainen	.05	.02	.00
☐ 217	Mike Rogers	.08	.03	.01
☐ 218	Don Lever	.05	.02	.00
☐ 219	Steve Tambellini	.05	.02	.00
☐ 220	Bob MacMillan	.05	.02	.00
☐ 221	Hector Marini	.05	.02	.00
☐ 222	Glenn Resch	.12	.05	.01
☐ 223	Glenn Resch	.12	.05	.01
☐ 224	Carol Vadnais	.05	.02	.00
☐ 225	Joel Quenneville	.05	.02	.00
☐ 226	Aaron Broten	.05	.02	.00
☐ 227	Randy Carlyle	.08	.03	.01
☐ 228	Doug Shedden	.05	.02	.00
☐ 229	Greg Malone	.05	.02	.00
☐ 230	Paul Gardner	.05	.02	.00
☐ 231	Rick Kehoe	.08	.03	.01
☐ 232	Rick Kehoe	.08	.03	.01
☐ 233	Pat Boutette	.05	.02	.00
☐ 234	Michel Dion	.08	.03	.01
☐ 235	Mike Bullard	.08	.03	.01
☐ 236	Dale McCourt	.05	.02	.00
☐ 237	Mike Foligno	.08	.03	.01
☐ 238	Phil Housley	1.50	.60	.15
☐ 239	Tony McKegney	.05	.02	.00
☐ 240	Gilbert Perreault	.15	.06	.01
☐ 241	Gilbert Perreault	.15	.06	.01
☐ 242	Bob Sauve	.08	.03	.01
☐ 243	Mike Ramsey	.08	.03	.01
☐ 244	John Van Boxmeer	.05	.02	.00
☐ 245	Dan Bouchard	.08	.03	.01
☐ 246	Real Cloutier	.05	.02	.00
☐ 247	Marc Tardif	.08	.03	.01
☐ 248	Randy Moller	.05	.02	.00
☐ 249	Michel Goulet	.20	.08	.02
☐ 250	Michel Goulet	.20	.08	.02
☐ 251	Marian Stastny	.08	.03	.01
☐ 252	Anton Stastny	.08	.03	.01
☐ 253	Peter Stastny	.30	.12	.03
☐ 254	Mark Johnson	.08	.03	.01
☐ 255	Ron Francis	.30	.12	.03
☐ 256	Doug Sulliman	.05	.02	.00
☐ 257	Risto Siltanen	.05	.02	.00
☐ 258	Blaine Stoughton	.08	.03	.01
☐ 259	Blaine Stoughton	.08	.03	.01
☐ 260	Ray Neufeld	.05	.02	.00
☐ 261	Pierre Lacroix	.05	.02	.00
☐ 262	Greg Millen	.08	.03	.01
☐ 263	Lanny McDonald	.20	.08	.02
☐ 264	Paul Reinhart	.08	.03	.01
☐ 265	Mel Bridgman	.08	.03	.01
☐ 266	Rejean Lemelin	.10	.04	.01
☐ 267	Kent Nilsson	.08	.03	.01
☐ 268	Kent Nilsson	.08	.03	.01
☐ 269	Doug Risebrough	.08	.03	.01
☐ 270	Kari Eloranta	.05	.02	.00
☐ 271	Phil Russell	.05	.02	.00
☐ 272	Darcy Rota	.05	.02	.00
☐ 273	Thomas Gradin	.08	.03	.01
☐ 274	Stan Smyl	.08	.03	.01
☐ 275	John Garrett	.08	.03	.01
☐ 276	Richard Brodeur	.08	.03	.01
☐ 277	Richard Brodeur	.08	.03	.01
☐ 278	Doug Halward	.05	.02	.00
☐ 279	Kevin McCarthy	.05	.02	.00
☐ 280	Rick Lanz	.05	.02	.00
☐ 281	Morris Lukowich	.05	.02	.00
☐ 282	Dale Hawerchuk	.50	.20	.05
☐ 283	Paul MacLean	.08	.03	.01
☐ 284	Lucien DeBlois	.05	.02	.00
☐ 285	Dave Babych	.08	.03	.01
☐ 286	Dave Babych	.08	.03	.01
☐ 287	Doug Smail	.08	.03	.01
☐ 288	Doug Soetart	.05	.02	.00
☐ 289	Thomas Steen	.10	.04	.01
☐ 290	Charlie Simmer	.10	.04	.01
☐ 291	Terry Ruskowski	.08	.03	.01
☐ 292	Bernie Nicholls	1.00	.40	.10
☐ 293	Jim Fox	.05	.02	.00
☐ 294	Marcel Dionne	.25	.10	.02
☐ 295	Marcel Dionne	.25	.10	.02
☐ 296	Gary Laskoski	.05	.02	.00
☐ 297	Jerry Korab	.05	.02	.00
☐ 298	Larry Murphy	.25	.10	.02
☐ 299	Hart Trophy FOIL	.20	.08	.02
☐ 300	Hart Trophy FOIL	.20	.08	.02
☐ 301	Wayne Gretzky	3.00	1.20	.30
☐ 302	Bobby Clarke	.30	.12	.03
☐ 303	Lanny McDonald	.20	.08	.02

☐ 304	Lady Byng Trophy FOIL	.15	.06	.01
☐ 305	Lady Byng Trophy FOIL	.15	.06	.01
☐ 306	Mike Bossy	.35	.14	.03
☐ 307	Wayne Gretzky	3.00	1.20	.30
☐ 308	Art Ross Trophy FOIL	.20	.08	.02
☐ 309	Art Ross Trophy FOIL	.20	.08	.02
☐ 310	Calder Trophy FOIL	.15	.06	.01
☐ 311	Calder Trophy FOIL	.15	.06	.01
☐ 312	Steve Larmer	.75	.30	.07
☐ 313	Rod Langway	.08	.03	.01
☐ 314	Norris Trophy FOIL	.15	.06	.01
☐ 315	Norris Trophy FOIL	.15	.06	.01
☐ 316	Billy Smith	.15	.06	.01
☐ 317	Roland Melanson	.08	.03	.01
☐ 318	Pete Peeters	.08	.03	.01
☐ 319	Vezina Trophy FOIL	.15	.06	.01
☐ 320	Vezina Trophy FOIL	.15	.06	.01
☐ 321	Mike Bossy FOIL	.50	.20	.05
☐ 322	Mike Bossy FOIL	.50	.20	.05
☐ 323	Marcel Dionne FOIL	.40	.16	.04
☐ 324	Marcel Dionne FOIL	.40	.16	.04
☐ 325	Wayne Gretzky FOIL	3.00	1.20	.30
☐ 326	Wayne Gretzky FOIL	3.00	1.20	.30
☐ 327	Pat Hughes FOIL	.15	.06	.01
☐ 328	Pat Hughes FOIL	.15	.06	.01
☐ 329	Rick Middleton FOIL	.25	.10	.02
☐ 330	Rick Middleton FOIL	.25	.10	.02
☐ xx	Sticker Album	2.00	.80	.20

1984-85 O-Pee-Chee Stickers

This sticker set consists of 292 stickers in full color and was put out by O-Pee-Chee. The foil stickers are listed in the checklist below explicitly. The stickers measure approximately 1 15/16" by 2 9/16". An album is available for these stickers. Those stickers which are pairs are indicated in the checklist by noting parenthetically the other member of the pair. On the inside back cover of the sticker album the company offered (via direct mail-order) any ten different stickers of your choice for one dollar; this is one reason why the values of the most popular players in these sticker sets are somewhat depressed compared to traditional card set prices.

	MINT	EXC	G-VG
COMPLETE SET (292)	30.00	12.00	3.00
COMMON PLAYER (1-292)	.05	.02	.00
COMMON FOILS	.15	.06	.01
COMMON HALF FOILS	.10	.04	.01

☐ 1	Stanley Cup	.08	.03	.01
☐ 2	Stanley Cup	.05	.02	.00
☐ 3	Stanley Cup	.05	.02	.00
☐ 4	Stanley Cup	.05	.02	.00
☐ 5	Mark Messier	.50	.20	.05
☐ 6	Maple Leafs Logo (23) FOIL	.10	.04	.01
☐ 7	Borje Salming	.08	.03	.01
☐ 8	Borje Salming	.08	.03	.01
☐ 9	Dan Daoust	.05	.02	.00

☐	10	Dan Daoust	.05	.02	.00
☐	11	Rick Vaive	.08	.03	.01
☐	12	Rick Vaive	.08	.03	.01
☐	13	Dale McCourt	.05	.02	.00
☐	14	Bill Derlago	.05	.02	.00
☐	15	Gary Nylund	.08	.03	.01
☐	16	Gary Nylund	.08	.03	.01
☐	17	Jim Korn	.05	.02	.00
☐	18	John Anderson	.05	.02	.00
☐	19	Greg Terrion	.05	.02	.00
☐	20	Allan Bester	.05	.02	.00
☐	21	Jim Benning	.05	.02	.00
☐	22	Mike Palmateer	.08	.03	.01
☐	23	Blackhawks Logo (6)	.10	.04	.01
		FOIL			
☐	24	Denis Savard	.20	.08	.02
☐	25	Denis Savard	.20	.08	.02
☐	26	Bob Murray	.05	.02	.00
☐	27	Doug Wilson	.12	.05	.01
☐	28	Keith Brown	.08	.03	.01
☐	29	Steve Larmer	.40	.16	.04
☐	30	Darryl Sutter	.08	.03	.01
☐	31	Tom Lysiak	.08	.03	.01
☐	32	Murray Bannerman	.08	.03	.01
☐	33	Red Wings Logo (43)	.10	.04	.01
		FOIL			
☐	34	John Ogrodnick	.08	.03	.01
☐	35	John Ogrodnick	.08	.03	.01
☐	36	Reed Larson	.05	.02	.00
☐	37	Steve Yzerman	5.00	2.00	.50
☐	38	Brad Park	.15	.06	.01
☐	39	Ivan Boldirev	.05	.02	.00
☐	40	Kelly Kisio	.08	.03	.01
☐	41	Greg Stefan	.08	.03	.01
☐	42	Ron Duguay	.08	.03	.01
☐	43	North Stars Logo (33)	.10	.04	.01
		FOIL			
☐	44	Brian Bellows	.35	.14	.03
☐	45	Brian Bellows	.35	.14	.03
☐	46	Neal Broten	.12	.05	.01
☐	47	Dino Ciccarelli	.20	.08	.02
☐	48	Dennis Maruk	.08	.03	.01
☐	49	Steve Payne	.05	.02	.00
☐	50	Brad Maxwell	.05	.02	.00
☐	51	Gilles Meloche	.08	.03	.01
☐	52	Tom McCarthy	.05	.02	.00
☐	53	Blues Logo (67)	.10	.04	.01
		FOIL			
☐	54	Bernie Federko	.12	.05	.01
☐	55	Bernie Federko	.12	.05	.01
☐	56	Brian Sutter	.10	.04	.01
☐	57	Mike Liut	.08	.03	.01
☐	58	Doug Wickenheiser	.05	.02	.00
☐	59	Jorgen Pettersson	.05	.02	.00
☐	60	Doug Gilmour	5.00	2.00	.50
☐	61	Joe Mullen	.25	.10	.02
☐	62	Rob Ramage	.08	.03	.01
☐	63	Wayne Gretzky (64)	1.25	.50	.12
		FOIL			
☐	64	Michel Goulet (63)	.15	.06	.01
		FOIL			
☐	65	Pat Riggin (66)	.10	.04	.01
		FOIL			
☐	66	Denis Potvin (65)	.20	.08	.02
		FOIL			
☐	67	Devils Logo (53)	.10	.04	.01
		FOIL			
☐	68	Glenn Resch	.10	.04	.01
☐	69	Glenn Resch	.10	.04	.01
☐	70	Don Lever	.05	.02	.00
☐	71	Mel Bridgman	.08	.03	.01
☐	72	Bob MacMillan	.05	.02	.00
☐	73	Pat Verbeek	.60	.24	.06
☐	74	Joe Cirella	.08	.03	.01
☐	75	Phil Russell	.05	.02	.00
☐	76	Jan Ludvig	.05	.02	.00
☐	77	Islanders Logo (94)	.10	.04	.01
		FOIL			
☐	78	Denis Potvin	.20	.08	.02
☐	79	Denis Potvin	.20	.08	.02
☐	80	John Tonelli	.08	.03	.01
☐	81	John Tonelli	.08	.03	.01
☐	82	Mike Bossy	.40	.16	.04
☐	83	Mike Bossy	.40	.16	.04
☐	84	Butch Goring	.08	.03	.01
☐	85	Bob Nystrom	.05	.02	.00
☐	86	Bryan Trottier	.25	.10	.02
☐	87	Bryan Trottier	.25	.10	.02
☐	88	Brent Sutter	.08	.03	.01
☐	89	Bob Bourne	.05	.02	.00
☐	90	Greg Gilbert	.08	.03	.01
☐	91	Billy Smith	.15	.06	.01
☐	92	Rollie Melanson	.08	.03	.01
☐	93	Ken Morrow	.08	.03	.01
☐	94	Rangers Logo (77)	.10	.04	.01
		FOIL			
☐	95	Don Maloney	.05	.02	.00
☐	96	Don Maloney	.05	.02	.00
☐	97	Mark Pavelich	.05	.02	.00
☐	98	Glen Hanlon	.08	.03	.01
☐	99	Mike Rogers	.08	.03	.01
☐	100	Barry Beck	.08	.03	.01
☐	101	Reijo Ruotsalainen	.05	.02	.00
☐	102	Anders Hedberg	.08	.03	.01
☐	103	Pierre Larouche	.08	.03	.01
☐	104	Flyers Logo (114)	.10	.04	.01
		FOIL			
☐	105	Tim Kerr	.12	.05	.01
☐	106	Tim Kerr	.12	.05	.01
☐	107	Ron Sutter	.10	.04	.01
☐	108	Darryl Sittler	.15	.06	.01
☐	109	Mark Howe	.10	.04	.01
☐	110	Dave Poulin	.12	.05	.01
☐	111	Rich Sutter	.10	.04	.01
☐	112	Brian Propp	.10	.04	.01
☐	113	Bob Froese	.08	.03	.01
☐	114	Penguins Logo (104)	.10	.04	.01
		FOIL			
☐	115	Ron Flockhart	.05	.02	.00
☐	116	Ron Flockhart	.05	.02	.00
☐	117	Rick Kehoe	.08	.03	.01
☐	118	Mike Bullard	.08	.03	.01
☐	119	Kevin McCarthy	.05	.02	.00
☐	120	Doug Shedden	.05	.02	.00
☐	121	Mark Taylor	.05	.02	.00
☐	122	Denis Herron	.08	.03	.01
☐	123	Tom Roulston	.05	.02	.00
☐	124	Capitals Logo (146)	.10	.04	.01
		FOIL			
☐	125	Rod Langway	.08	.03	.01
☐	126	Rod Langway	.08	.03	.01
☐	127	Larry Murphy	.15	.06	.01
☐	128	Al Jensen	.08	.03	.01
☐	129	Doug Jarvis	.08	.03	.01
☐	130	Bengt Gustafsson	.05	.02	.00
☐	131	Mike Gartner	.25	.10	.02
☐	132	Bob Carpenter	.10	.04	.01
☐	133	Dave Christian	.08	.03	.01
☐	134	Paul Coffey FOIL	.75	.30	.07
☐	135	Murray Bannerman	.15	.06	.01
		FOIL			
☐	136	Rob Ramage FOIL	.15	.06	.01
☐	137	John Ogrodnick	.15	.06	.01
		FOIL			
☐	138	Wayne Gretzky	2.50	1.00	.25
		FOIL			
☐	139	Rick Vaive FOIL	.15	.06	.01
☐	140	Michel Goulet	.35	.14	.03
		FOIL			
☐	141	Peter Stastny FOIL	.50	.20	.05
☐	142	Rick Middleton	.25	.10	.02
		FOIL			
☐	143	Ray Bourque FOIL	.75	.30	.07
☐	144	Pete Peeters FOIL	.20	.08	.02
☐	145	Denis Potvin FOIL	.40	.16	.04
☐	146	Canadiens Logo (124)	.10	.04	.01
		FOIL			
☐	147	Larry Robinson	.15	.06	.01
☐	148	Larry Robinson	.15	.06	.01
☐	149	Guy Lafleur	.25	.10	.02
☐	150	Guy Lafleur	.25	.10	.02
☐	151	Bobby Smith	.10	.04	.01
☐	152	Bobby Smith	.10	.04	.01
☐	153	Bob Gainey	.15	.06	.01
☐	154	Craig Ludwig	.05	.02	.00
☐	155	Mats Naslund	.08	.03	.01
☐	156	Mats Naslund	.08	.03	.01
☐	157	Rick Wamsley	.08	.03	.01
☐	158	Jean Hamel	.05	.02	.00
☐	159	Ryan Walter	.08	.03	.01
☐	160	Guy Carbonneau	.20	.08	.02
☐	161	Mario Tremblay	.05	.02	.00
☐	162	Pierre Mondou	.05	.02	.00
☐	163	Nordiques Logo (180)	.10	.04	.01
		FOIL			
☐	164	Peter Stastny	.20	.08	.02
☐	165	Peter Stastny	.20	.08	.02
☐	166	Mario Marois	.05	.02	.00
☐	167	Mario Marois	.05	.02	.00
☐	168	Michel Goulet	.15	.06	.01
☐	169	Michel Goulet	.15	.06	.01
☐	170	Andre Savard	.05	.02	.00
☐	171	Tony McKegney	.05	.02	.00
☐	172	Dan Bouchard	.05	.02	.00
☐	173	Dan Bouchard	.05	.02	.00
☐	174	Randy Moller	.05	.02	.00

☐ 175 Wilf Paiement	.08	.03	.01
☐ 176 Normand Rochefort	.05	.02	.00
☐ 177 Marian Stastny	.08	.03	.01
☐ 178 Anton Stastny	.08	.03	.01
☐ 179 Dale Hunter	.15	.06	.01
☐ 180 Bruins Logo (163) FOIL	.10	.04	.01
☐ 181 Rick Middleton	.10	.04	.01
☐ 182 Rick Middleton	.10	.04	.01
☐ 183 Ray Bourque	.40	.16	.04
☐ 184 Pete Peeters	.08	.03	.01
☐ 185 Mike O'Connell	.05	.02	.00
☐ 186 Gord Kluzak	.08	.03	.01
☐ 187 Barry Pederson	.08	.03	.01
☐ 188 Mike Krushelnyski	.08	.03	.01
☐ 189 Tom Fergus	.08	.03	.01
☐ 190 Whalers Logo (200) FOIL	.10	.04	.01
☐ 191 Sylvain Turgeon	.08	.03	.01
☐ 192 Sylvain Turgeon	.08	.03	.01
☐ 193 Mark Johnson	.08	.03	.01
☐ 194 Greg Malone	.05	.02	.00
☐ 195 Mike Zuke	.05	.02	.00
☐ 196 Ron Francis	.25	.10	.02
☐ 197 Bob Crawford	.05	.02	.00
☐ 198 Greg Millen	.08	.03	.01
☐ 199 Ray Neufeld	.05	.02	.00
☐ 200 Sabres Logo (190) FOIL	.10	.04	.01
☐ 201 Gilbert Perreault	.15	.06	.01
☐ 202 Gilbert Perreault	.15	.06	.01
☐ 203 Phil Housley	.35	.14	.03
☐ 204 Phil Housley	.35	.14	.03
☐ 205 Tom Barrasso	1.25	.50	.12
☐ 206 Tom Barrasso	1.25	.50	.12
☐ 207 Larry Playfair	.05	.02	.00
☐ 208 Bob Sauve	.08	.03	.01
☐ 209 Dave Andreychuk	1.50	.60	.15
☐ 210 Dave Andreychuk	1.50	.60	.15
☐ 211 Mike Ramsey	.05	.02	.00
☐ 212 Mike Foligno	.08	.03	.01
☐ 213 Lindy Ruff	.05	.02	.00
☐ 214 Bill Hajt	.05	.02	.00
☐ 215 Craig Ramsay	.05	.02	.00
☐ 216 Ric Seiling	.05	.02	.00
☐ 217 Hart Trophy (224) FOIL	.10	.04	.01
☐ 218 Vezina Trophy (223) FOIL	.10	.04	.01
☐ 219 Jennings Trophy (221) FOIL	.10	.04	.01
☐ 220 Calder Trophy (225) FOIL	.10	.04	.01
☐ 221 Art Ross Trophy (219) FOIL	.10	.04	.01
☐ 222 Norris Trophy (283) FOIL	.10	.04	.01
☐ 223 Masterton Trophy (218) FOIL	.10	.04	.01
☐ 224 Selke Trophy (217) FOIL	.10	.04	.01
☐ 225 Lady Byng Trophy(220) FOIL	.10	.04	.01
☐ 226 Wayne Gretzky (227)	1.00	.40	.10
☐ 227 Tom Barrasso (226)	.50	.20	.05
☐ 228 Tom Barrasso (229)	.50	.20	.05
☐ 229 Wayne Gretzky (228)	1.00	.40	.10
☐ 230 Rod Langway (230)	.05	.02	.00
☐ 231 Brad Park (230)	.10	.04	.01
☐ 232 Al Jensen (233)	.05	.02	.00
☐ 233 Pat Riggin (232)	.05	.02	.00
☐ 234 Doug Jarvis (235)	.05	.02	.00
☐ 235 Mike Bossy (234)	.15	.06	.01
☐ 236 Flames Logo (246) FOIL	.10	.04	.01
☐ 237 Lanny McDonald	.20	.08	.02
☐ 238 Lanny McDonald	.20	.08	.02
☐ 239 Steve Tambellini	.08	.03	.01
☐ 240 Rejean Lemelin	.08	.03	.01
☐ 241 Doug Risebrough	.08	.03	.01
☐ 242 Hakan Loob	.08	.03	.01
☐ 243 Ed Beers	.05	.02	.00
☐ 244 Mike Eaves	.05	.02	.00
☐ 245 Kent Nilsson	.08	.03	.01
☐ 246 Oilers Logo (236) FOIL	.10	.04	.01
☐ 247 Glenn Anderson	.15	.06	.01
☐ 248 Glenn Anderson	.15	.06	.01
☐ 249 Jari Kurri	.30	.12	.03
☐ 250 Jari Kurri	.30	.12	.03
☐ 251 Paul Coffey	.50	.20	.05
☐ 252 Paul Coffey	.50	.20	.05
☐ 253 Kevin Lowe	.15	.06	.01

☐ 254 Lee Fogolin	.05	.02	.00
☐ 255 Wayne Gretzky	2.00	.80	.20
☐ 256 Wayne Gretzky	2.00	.80	.20
☐ 257 Randy Gregg	.08	.03	.01
☐ 258 Charlie Huddy	.08	.03	.01
☐ 259 Grant Fuhr	.35	.14	.03
☐ 260 Willy Lindstrom	.05	.02	.00
☐ 261 Mark Messier	.75	.30	.07
☐ 262 Andy Moog	.35	.14	.03
☐ 263 Kings Logo (273) FOIL	.10	.04	.01
☐ 264 Marcel Dionne	.25	.10	.02
☐ 265 Marcel Dionne	.25	.10	.02
☐ 266 Charlie Simmer	.10	.04	.01
☐ 267 Dave Taylor	.10	.04	.01
☐ 268 Jim Fox	.05	.02	.00
☐ 269 Bernie Nicholls	.40	.16	.04
☐ 270 Terry Ruskowski	.08	.03	.01
☐ 271 Brian Engblom	.05	.02	.00
☐ 272 Mark Hardy	.05	.02	.00
☐ 273 Canucks Logo (263) FOIL	.10	.04	.01
☐ 274 Tony Tanti	.08	.03	.01
☐ 275 Tony Tanti	.08	.03	.01
☐ 276 Rick Lanz	.05	.02	.00
☐ 277 Richard Brodeur	.08	.03	.01
☐ 278 Doug Halward	.05	.02	.00
☐ 279 Patrik Sundstrom	.08	.03	.01
☐ 280 Darcy Rota	.05	.02	.00
☐ 281 Stan Smyl	.08	.03	.01
☐ 282 Thomas Gradin	.08	.03	.01
☐ 283 Jets Logo (222) FOIL	.10	.04	.01
☐ 284 Dale Hawerchuk	.35	.14	.03
☐ 285 Dale Hawerchuk	.35	.14	.03
☐ 286 Scott Arniel	.05	.02	.00
☐ 287 Dave Babych	.08	.03	.01
☐ 288 Laurie Boschman	.08	.03	.01
☐ 289 Paul MacLean	.08	.03	.01
☐ 290 Lucien DeBlois	.05	.02	.00
☐ 291 Randy Carlyle	.08	.03	.01
☐ 292 Thomas Steen	.10	.04	.01
☐ xx Sticker Album	2.00	.80	.20

1985-86 O-Pee-Chee Stickers

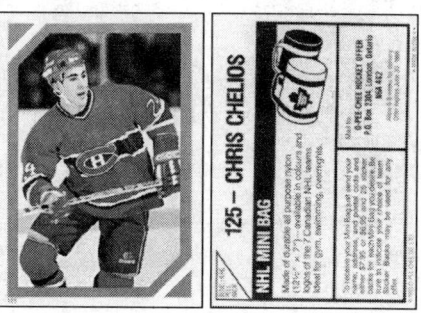

This sticker set consists of 255 stickers in full color and was put out by O-Pee-Chee. The foil stickers are listed in the checklist below explicitly. The stickers measure approximately 2 1/8" by 3". An album is available for these stickers. Those stickers which are pairs are indicated in the checklist below by noting parenthetically the other member of the pair. On the inside back cover of the sticker album the company offered (via direct mail-order) any ten different stickers of your choice for one dollar; this is one reason why the values of the most popular players in these sticker sets are somewhat depressed compared to traditional card set prices. For example, anyone wanting Mario Lemieux, Wayne Gretzky, and eight others could get them for one dollar directly through this offer.

		MINT	EXC	G-VG
COMPLETE SET (255)		30.00	12.00	3.00
COMMON PLAYER (1-255)		.05	.02	.00
COMMON HALF PLAYER		.03	.01	.00
COMMON FOILS		.15	.06	.01
COMMON HALF FOILS		.10	.04	.01
☐ 1	Stanley Cup Finals	.08	.03	.01
☐ 2	Stanley Cup Finals	.05	.02	.00
☐ 3	Stanley Cup Finals	.05	.02	.00
☐ 4	Stanley Cup Finals	.05	.02	.00
☐ 5	Wayne Gretzky	2.50	1.00	.25
☐ 6	Rick Vaive	.08	.03	.01
☐ 7	Bill Derlago	.05	.02	.00
☐ 8	Rick St. Croix (136)	.03	.01	.00
☐ 9	Tim Bernhardt (137)	.03	.01	.00
☐ 10	John Anderson (138)	.03	.01	.00
☐ 11	Dan Daoust (139)	.03	.01	.00
☐ 12	Borje Salming	.08	.03	.01
☐ 13	Al Iafrate (143)	.60	.24	.06
☐ 14	Gary Nylund (144)	.03	.01	.00
☐ 15	Bob McGill (145)	.03	.01	.00
☐ 16	Jim Benning (146)	.03	.01	.00
☐ 17	Stewart Gavin (148)	.03	.01	.00
☐ 18	Greg Terrion (149)	.03	.01	.00
☐ 19	Peter Ihnacak (150)	.03	.01	.00
☐ 20	Russ Courtnall (151)	.60	.24	.06
☐ 21	Miroslav Frycer	.05	.02	.00
☐ 22	Denis Savard	.15	.06	.01
☐ 23	Steve Yzerman (152)	1.00	.40	.10
☐ 24	Curt Fraser (153)	.03	.01	.00
☐ 25	Doug Wilson	.10	.04	.01
☐ 26	Ed Olczyk (154)	.30	.12	.03
☐ 27	Murray Bannerman (155)	.03	.01	.00
☐ 28	Steve Larmer (158)	.12	.05	.01
☐ 29	Troy Murray (159)	.08	.03	.01
☐ 30	Steve Yzerman	2.00	.80	.20
☐ 31	Greg Stefan (161)	.05	.02	.00
☐ 32	Ron Duguay (162)	.05	.02	.00
☐ 33	Reed Larson (163)	.03	.01	.00
☐ 34	Ivan Boldirev (164)	.03	.01	.00
☐ 35	Danny Gare (166)	.05	.02	.00
☐ 36	Darryl Sittler (167)	.10	.04	.01
☐ 37	John Ogrodnick	.08	.03	.01
☐ 38	Keith Acton	.05	.02	.00
☐ 39	Dino Ciccarelli (168)	.10	.04	.01
☐ 40	Neal Broten (169)	.05	.02	.00
☐ 41	Brian Bellows	.25	.10	.02
☐ 42	Steve Payne (170)	.03	.01	.00
☐ 43	Gordie Roberts (171)	.03	.01	.00
☐ 44	Harold Snepsts (175)	.05	.02	.00
☐ 45	Tony McKegney (176)	.03	.01	.00
☐ 46	Brian Sutter	.10	.04	.01
☐ 47	Joe Mullen (177)	.10	.04	.01
☐ 48	Doug Gilmour (178)	1.00	.40	.10
☐ 49	Tim Bothwell (180)	.03	.01	.00
☐ 50	Mark Johnson (181)	.03	.01	.00
☐ 51	Greg Millen (182)	.05	.02	.00
☐ 52	Doug Wickenheiser (183)	.03	.01	.00
☐ 53	Bernie Federko	.10	.04	.01
☐ 54	Wayne Gretzky (197) FOIL	1.00	.40	.10
☐ 55	Tom Barrasso (203) FOIL	.25	.10	.02
☐ 56	Paul Coffey (204) FOIL	.40	.16	.04
☐ 57	Mel Bridgman	.05	.02	.00
☐ 58	Phil Russell (184)	.03	.01	.00
☐ 59	Dave Lewis (185)	.03	.01	.00
☐ 60	Paul Gagne (186)	.03	.01	.00
☐ 61	Glenn Resch (187)	.08	.03	.01
☐ 62	Aaron Broten (189)	.03	.01	.00
☐ 63	Dave Pichette (190)	.03	.01	.00
☐ 64	Kirk Muller	1.25	.50	.12
☐ 65	Bryan Trottier	.20	.08	.02
☐ 66	Mike Bossy	.30	.12	.03
☐ 67	Bob Bourne (191)	.03	.01	.00
☐ 68	Clark Gillies (192)	.05	.02	.00
☐ 69	Bob Nystrom (193)	.03	.01	.00
☐ 70	Denis Potvin (198)	.10	.04	.01
☐ 71	Brent Sutter	.08	.03	.01
☐ 72	Duane Sutter (199)	.05	.02	.00
☐ 73	Pat Flatley (200)	.05	.02	.00
☐ 74	Pat LaFontaine (201)	1.00	.40	.10
☐ 75	Greg Gilbert (202)	.03	.01	.00
☐ 76	Billy Smith (209)	.08	.03	.01
☐ 77	Gordie Lane (210)	.03	.01	.00
☐ 78	Tomas Jonsson (211)	.03	.01	.00
☐ 79	Kelly Hrudey (212)	.50	.20	.05
☐ 80	John Tonelli	.08	.03	.01
☐ 81	Reijo Ruotsalainen	.05	.02	.00
☐ 82	Barry Beck (213)	.05	.02	.00
☐ 83	James Patrick (214)	.15	.06	.01
☐ 84	Mark Pavelich	.05	.02	.00
☐ 85	Pierre Larouche	.08	.03	.01
☐ 86	Mike Rogers (219)	.03	.01	.00
☐ 87	Glen Hanlon (220)	.05	.02	.00
☐ 88	John Vanbiesbrouck (221)	.75	.30	.07
☐ 89	Dave Poulin	.08	.03	.01
☐ 90	Brian Propp (223)	.08	.03	.01
☐ 91	Pelle Lindbergh (224)	1.50	.60	.15
☐ 92	Brad McCrimmon (225)	.05	.02	.00
☐ 93	Mark Howe (226)	.08	.03	.01
☐ 94	Peter Zezel (227)	.25	.10	.02
☐ 95	Murray Craven (228)	.05	.02	.00
☐ 96	Tim Kerr	.08	.03	.01
☐ 97	Mario Lemieux	7.50	3.00	.75
☐ 98	Moe Mantha (229)	.03	.01	.00
☐ 99	Doug Bodger (230)	.05	.02	.00
☐ 100	Warren Young	.08	.03	.01
☐ 101	John Chabot (233)	.03	.01	.00
☐ 102	Doug Shedden (234)	.03	.01	.00
☐ 103	Wayne Babych (236)	.03	.01	.00
☐ 104	Mike Bullard (237)	.03	.01	.00
☐ 105	Rod Langway	.08	.03	.01
☐ 106	Pat Riggin (238)	.05	.02	.00
☐ 107	Scott Stevens (239)	.20	.08	.02
☐ 108	Alan Haworth (241)	.03	.01	.00
☐ 109	Doug Jarvis (242)	.03	.01	.00
☐ 110	Dave Christian (243)	.05	.02	.00
☐ 111	Mike Gartner (244)	.12	.05	.01
☐ 112	Bob Carpenter	.08	.03	.01
☐ 113	Rod Langway FOIL	.15	.06	.01
☐ 114	Tom Barrasso FOIL	.25	.10	.02
☐ 115	Ray Bourque FOIL	.50	.20	.05
☐ 116	John Tonelli FOIL	.15	.06	.01
☐ 117	Brent Sutter FOIL	.15	.06	.01
☐ 118	Mike Bossy FOIL	.45	.18	.04
☐ 119	John Ogrodnick FOIL	.15	.06	.01
☐ 120	Wayne Gretzky FOIL	2.00	.80	.20
☐ 121	Jari Kurri FOIL	.45	.18	.04
☐ 122	Doug Wilson FOIL	.25	.10	.02
☐ 123	Andy Moog FOIL	.40	.16	.04
☐ 124	Paul Coffey FOIL	.50	.20	.05
☐ 125	Chris Chelios	.60	.24	.06
☐ 126	Steve Penney	.08	.03	.01
☐ 127	Chris Nilan (245)	.05	.02	.00
☐ 128	Ron Flockhart (246)	.03	.01	.00
☐ 129	Tom Kurvers (249)	.03	.01	.00
☐ 130	Craig Ludwig (250)	.03	.01	.00
☐ 131	Mats Naslund	.10	.04	.01
☐ 132	Bobby Smith (252)	.08	.03	.01
☐ 133	Pierre Mondou (253)	.03	.01	.00
☐ 134	Mario Tremblay (254)	.03	.01	.00
☐ 135	Guy Carbonneau (255)	.08	.03	.01
☐ 136	Doug Soetaert (8)	.03	.01	.00
☐ 137	Mark Hunter (9)	.03	.01	.00
☐ 138	Bob Gainey (10)	.08	.03	.01
☐ 139	Petr Svoboda (11)	.10	.04	.01
☐ 140	Larry Robinson	.12	.05	.01
☐ 141	Michel Goulet	.15	.06	.01
☐ 142	Bruce Bell	.05	.02	.00
☐ 143	Dan Bouchard (13)	.03	.01	.00
☐ 144	Mario Marois (14)	.03	.01	.00
☐ 145	Randy Moller (15)	.03	.01	.00
☐ 146	Mario Gosselin (16)	.03	.01	.00
☐ 147	Anton Stastny	.05	.02	.00
☐ 148	Normand Rochefort (17)	.03	.01	.00
☐ 149	Alain Cote (18)	.03	.01	.00
☐ 150	Paul Gillis (19)	.03	.01	.00
☐ 151	Dale Hunter (20)	.08	.03	.01
☐ 152	Wilf Paiement (23)	.03	.01	.00
☐ 153	Brent Ashton (24)	.03	.01	.00
☐ 154	Brad Maxwell (26)	.03	.01	.00
☐ 155	J.F. Sauve (27)	.03	.01	.00
☐ 156	Peter Stastny	.20	.08	.02
☐ 157	Ray Bourque	.35	.14	.03
☐ 158	Charlie Simmer (28)	.08	.03	.01
☐ 159	Rick Middleton (29)	.08	.03	.01
☐ 160	Pete Peeters	.08	.03	.01
☐ 161	Mike O'Connell (31)	.03	.01	.00
☐ 162	Terry O'Reilly (32)	.05	.02	.00
☐ 163	Keith Crowder (33)	.03	.01	.00
☐ 164	Tom Fergus (34)	.03	.01	.00
☐ 165	Sylvain Turgeon	.05	.02	.00
☐ 166	Greg Malone (35)	.03	.01	.00
☐ 167	Bob Crawford (36)	.03	.01	.00
☐ 168	Kevin Dineen (39)	.30	.12	.03
☐ 169	Mike Liut (40)	.08	.03	.01
☐ 170	Joel Quenneville (42)	.03	.01	.00
☐ 171	Ray Neufeld (43)	.03	.01	.00
☐ 172	Ron Francis	.20	.08	.02
☐ 173	Phil Housley	.25	.10	.02
☐ 174	Mike Foligno	.05	.02	.00

☐ 175 Craig Ramsay (44)	.03	.01	.00
☐ 176 Bill Hajt (45)	.03	.01	.00
☐ 177 Dave Maloney (47)	.03	.01	.00
☐ 178 Brent Peterson (48)	.03	.01	.00
☐ 179 Tom Barrasso	.25	.10	.02
☐ 180 Mike Ramsey (49)	.03	.01	.00
☐ 181 Bob Sauve (50)	.05	.02	.00
☐ 182 Ric Seiling (51)	.03	.01	.00
☐ 183 Paul Cyr (52)	.03	.01	.00
☐ 184 John Tucker (58)	.03	.01	.00
☐ 185 Gilles Hamel (59)	.03	.01	.00
☐ 186 Malcolm Davis (60)	.03	.01	.00
☐ 187 Dave Andreychuk (61)	.35	.14	.03
☐ 188 Gilbert Perreault	.15	.06	.01
☐ 189 Tom Barrasso (62)	.25	.10	.02
☐ 190 Bob Sauve (63)	.05	.02	.00
☐ 191 Paul Coffey (67)	.25	.10	.02
☐ 192 Craig Ramsay (68)	.03	.01	.00
☐ 193 Pelle Lindbergh (69)	1.50	.60	.15
☐ 194 Jennings Trophy (205) FOIL	.10	.04	.01
☐ 195 Norris Trophy (206) FOIL	.10	.04	.01
☐ 196 Selke Trophy (207) FOIL	.10	.04	.01
☐ 197 Vezina Trophy (54) FOIL	.10	.04	.01
☐ 198 Wayne Gretzky (70)	1.00	.40	.10
☐ 199 Mario Lemieux (72)	3.00	1.20	.30
☐ 200 Anders Hedberg (73)	.05	.02	.00
☐ 201 Jari Kurri (74)	.15	.06	.01
☐ 202 Wayne Gretzky (75)	1.00	.40	.10
☐ 203 Hart Trophy (55) FOIL	.10	.04	.01
☐ 204 Calder Trophy (56) FOIL	.10	.04	.01
☐ 205 Masterton Trophy(194) FOIL	.10	.04	.01
☐ 206 Lady Byng Trophy(195) FOIL	.10	.04	.01
☐ 207 Art Ross Trophy (207) FOIL	.10	.04	.01
☐ 208 Kent Nilsson	.08	.03	.01
☐ 209 Paul Reinhart (76)	.05	.02	.00
☐ 210 Rejean Lemelin (77)	.05	.02	.00
☐ 211 Al MacInnis (78)	2.00	.80	.20
☐ 212 Jamie Macoun (79)	.05	.02	.00
☐ 213 Carey Wilson (82)	.03	.01	.00
☐ 214 Ed Beers (83)	.03	.01	.00
☐ 215 Lanny McDonald	.15	.06	.01
☐ 216 Charlie Huddy	.05	.02	.00
☐ 217 Paul Coffey	.40	.16	.04
☐ 218 Lee Fogolin (85)	.03	.01	.00
☐ 219 Kevin Lowe (86)	.08	.03	.01
☐ 220 Andy Moog (87)	.20	.08	.02
☐ 221 Grant Fuhr (88)	.20	.08	.02
☐ 222 Wayne Gretzky	2.00	.80	.20
☐ 223 Mike Krushelnyski(90)	.05	.02	.00
☐ 224 Billy Carroll (91)	.03	.01	.00
☐ 225 Randy Gregg (92)	.05	.02	.00
☐ 226 Willy Lindstrom (93)	.03	.01	.00
☐ 227 Glenn Anderson (94)	.08	.03	.01
☐ 228 Mark Messier (95)	.30	.12	.03
☐ 229 Pat Hughes (98)	.03	.01	.00
☐ 230 Kevin McClelland (99)	.03	.01	.00
☐ 231 Jari Kurri	.25	.10	.02
☐ 232 Bernie Nicholls	.25	.10	.02
☐ 233 Brian Engblom (101)	.03	.01	.00
☐ 234 Mark Hardy (102)	.03	.01	.00
☐ 235 Marcel Dionne	.25	.10	.02
☐ 236 Jim Fox (103)	.03	.01	.00
☐ 237 Terry Ruskowski (104)	.05	.02	.00
☐ 238 Dave Taylor (106)	.05	.02	.00
☐ 239 Bob Janecyk (107)	.05	.02	.00
☐ 240 Thomas Gradin	.08	.03	.01
☐ 241 Patrik Sundstrom(108)	.05	.02	.00
☐ 242 Al MacAdam (109)	.03	.01	.00
☐ 243 Doug Halward (110)	.03	.01	.00
☐ 244 Peter McNab (111)	.03	.01	.00
☐ 245 Tony Tanti (127)	.05	.02	.00
☐ 246 Moe Lemay (128)	.03	.01	.00
☐ 247 Stan Smyl	.05	.02	.00
☐ 248 Dale Hawerchuk	.30	.12	.03
☐ 249 Dave Babych (129)	.06	.02	.00
☐ 250 Paul MacLean (130)	.06	.02	.00
☐ 251 Randy Carlyle	.05	.02	.00
☐ 252 Robert Picard (132)	.03	.01	.00
☐ 253 Thomas Steen (133)	.05	.02	.00
☐ 254 Laurie Boschman (134)	.03	.01	.00
☐ 255 Doug Smail (135)	.05	.02	.00
☐ xx Sticker Album	2.00	.80	.20

1986-87 O-Pee-Chee Stickers

This sticker set consists of 255 stickers in full color and was put out by O-Pee-Chee. The foil stickers are listed in the checklist below explicitly. The stickers measure approximately 2 1/8" by 3". An album is available for these stickers. Those stickers which are pairs are indicated in the checklist below by noting parenthetically the other member of the pair. On the inside back cover of the sticker album the company offered (via direct mail-order) any ten different stickers of your choice for one dollar; this is one reason why the values of the most popular players in these sticker sets are somewhat depressed compared to traditional card set prices.

	MINT	EXC	G-VG
COMPLETE SET (255)	30.00	12.00	3.00
COMMON PLAYER (1-255)	.05	.02	.00
COMMON HALF STICKER	.03	.01	.00
COMMON FOILS	.15	.06	.01
COMMON HALF FOILS	.10	.04	.01
☐ 1 Stanley Cup Action	.25	.10	.02
☐ 2 Stanley Cup Action	.15	.06	.01
☐ 3 Stanley Cup Action	.15	.06	.01
☐ 4 Stanley Cup Action	.15	.06	.01
☐ 5 Patrick Roy FOIL	9.00	3.75	.90
☐ 6 Chris Chelios (151)	.20	.08	.02
☐ 7 Guy Carbonneau (152)	.10	.04	.01
☐ 8 Larry Robinson	.15	.06	.01
☐ 9 Mario Tremblay (154)	.03	.01	.00
☐ 10 Tom Kurvers (155)	.03	.01	.00
☐ 11 Mats Naslund	.08	.03	.01
☐ 12 Bob Gainey	.12	.05	.01
☐ 13 Bobby Smith	.08	.03	.01
☐ 14 Craig Ludwig (156)	.03	.01	.00
☐ 15 Mike McPhee (157)	.05	.02	.00
☐ 16 Doug Soetaert (159)	.03	.01	.00
☐ 17 Petr Svoboda (160)	.05	.02	.00
☐ 18 Kjell Dahlin	.10	.04	.01
☐ 19 Patrick Roy	6.00	2.40	.60
☐ 20 Alain Cote (161)	.03	.01	.00
☐ 21 Mario Gosselin (162)	.03	.01	.00
☐ 22 Michel Goulet	.15	.06	.01
☐ 23 J.F. Sauve (163)	.03	.01	.00
☐ 24 Paul Gillis (164)	.03	.01	.00
☐ 25 Brent Ashton	.05	.02	.00
☐ 26 Peter Stastny	.20	.08	.02
☐ 27 Anton Stastny	.05	.02	.00
☐ 28 Gilbert Delorme (167)	.03	.01	.00
☐ 29 Risto Siltanen (168)	.03	.01	.00
☐ 30 Robert Picard (170)	.03	.01	.00
☐ 31 David Shaw (171)	.05	.02	.00
☐ 32 Dale Hunter	.08	.03	.01
☐ 33 Clint Malarchuk	.08	.03	.01
☐ 34 Ray Bourque	.35	.14	.03
☐ 35 Rick Middleton (172)	.08	.03	.01
☐ 36 Charlie Simmer (173)	.05	.02	.00
☐ 37 Keith Crowder	.05	.02	.00
☐ 38 Barry Pederson (175)	.05	.02	.00
☐ 39 Reed Larson (176)	.03	.01	.00
☐ 40 Steve Kasper (177)	.05	.02	.00
☐ 41 Pat Riggin (178)	.05	.02	.00
☐ 42 Mike Foligno	.05	.02	.00
☐ 43 Gilbert Perreault (179)	.10	.04	.01

☐ 44 Mike Ramsey (180)	.05	.02	.00
☐ 45 Tom Barrasso (186)	.15	.06	.01
☐ 46 Brian Engblom (187)	.03	.01	.00
☐ 47 Phil Housley (188)	.15	.06	.01
☐ 48 John Tucker (189)	.05	.02	.00
☐ 49 Dave Andreychuk	.25	.10	.02
☐ 50 Dave Babych	.08	.03	.01
☐ 51 Ron Francis (190)	.08	.03	.01
☐ 52 Mike Liut (191)	.08	.03	.01
☐ 53 Sylvain Turgeon	.08	.03	.01
☐ 54 John Anderson (192)	.03	.01	.00
☐ 55 Joel Quenneville (193)	.03	.01	.00
☐ 56 Kevin Dineen (194)	.08	.03	.01
☐ 57 Ray Ferraro (195)	.15	.06	.01
☐ 58 Action Sticker	.05	.02	.00
☐ 59 Action Sticker	.05	.02	.00
☐ 60 Action Sticker	.05	.02	.00
☐ 61 Action Sticker	.05	.02	.00
☐ 62 Action Sticker	.05	.02	.00
☐ 63 Action Sticker	.05	.02	.00
☐ 64 Action Sticker	.05	.02	.00
☐ 65 Action Sticker	.05	.02	.00
☐ 66 Andy Moog (197)	.15	.06	.01
☐ 67 Grant Fuhr (198)	.15	.06	.01
☐ 68 Paul Coffey	.35	.14	.03
☐ 69 Charlie Huddy (199)	.05	.02	.00
☐ 70 Kevin Lowe (200)	.08	.03	.01
☐ 71 Lee Fogolin	.05	.02	.00
☐ 72 Wayne Gretzky	1.50	.60	.15
☐ 73 Jari Kurri	.25	.10	.02
☐ 74 Mike Krushelnyski (201)	.05	.02	.00
☐ 75 Mark Napier (202)	.05	.02	.00
☐ 76 Craig MacTavish (204)	.15	.06	.01
☐ 77 Kevin McClelland (205)	.03	.01	.00
☐ 78 Glenn Anderson	.15	.06	.01
☐ 79 Mark Messier	.50	.20	.05
☐ 80 Lanny McDonald	.15	.06	.01
☐ 81 John Tonelli (207)	.05	.02	.00
☐ 82 Joe Mullen (208)	.12	.05	.01
☐ 83 Reggie Lemelin	.08	.03	.01
☐ 84 Jim Peplinski (212)	.03	.01	.00
☐ 85 Jamie Macoun (213)	.03	.01	.00
☐ 86 Al MacInnis (214)	.50	.20	.05
☐ 87 Dan Quinn (215)	.05	.02	.00
☐ 88 Marcel Dionne	.20	.08	.02
☐ 89 Jim Fox (219)	.03	.01	.00
☐ 90 Dave Taylor (220)	.05	.02	.00
☐ 91 Bob Janecyk (222)	.05	.02	.00
☐ 92 Jay Wells (223)	.03	.01	.00
☐ 93 Bryan Erickson (224)	.03	.01	.00
☐ 94 Dave(Tiger) Williams (225)	.05	.02	.00
☐ 95 Bernie Nicholls	.25	.10	.02
☐ 96 Stan Smyl	.05	.02	.00
☐ 97 Doug Halward (227)	.03	.01	.00
☐ 98 Richard Brodeur (228)	.05	.02	.00
☐ 99 Tony Tanti	.08	.03	.01
☐ 100 Brent Peterson (229)	.03	.01	.00
☐ 101 Patrik Sundstrom (230)	.05	.02	.00
☐ 102 Doug Lidster (231)	.05	.02	.00
☐ 103 Petri Skriko (232)	.05	.02	.00
☐ 104 Dale Hawerchuk	.25	.10	.02
☐ 105 Bill Derlago (234)	.03	.01	.00
☐ 106 Ray Neufeld (235)	.03	.01	.00
☐ 107 Randy Carlyle (237)	.05	.02	.00
☐ 108 Paul MacLean (238)	.05	.02	.00
☐ 109 Brian Mullen (242)	.05	.02	.00
☐ 110 Thomas Steen (243)	.05	.02	.00
☐ 111 Laurie Boschman	.05	.02	.00
☐ 112 Paul Coffey (126) FOIL	.30	.12	.03
☐ 113 Michel Goulet (127) FOIL	.20	.08	.02
☐ 114 John Vanbiesbrouck (128) FOIL	.25	.10	.02
☐ 115 Wayne Gretzky (129) FOIL	1.00	.40	.10
☐ 116 Mark Howe (130) FOIL	.12	.05	.01
☐ 117 Mike Bossy (131) FOIL	.20	.08	.02
☐ 118 Jari Kurri (132) FOIL	.15	.06	.01
☐ 119 Ray Bourque (133) FOIL	.25	.10	.02
☐ 120 Mario Lemieux (134) FOIL	1.50	.60	.15
☐ 121 Grant Fuhr (135) FOIL	.20	.08	.02
☐ 122 Mats Naslund (182)	.10	.04	.01

FOIL			
☐ 123 Larry Robinson (183)	.15	.06	.01
FOIL			
☐ 124 Chris Cichocki (184)	.10	.04	.01
FOIL			
☐ 125 Wendel Clark (185)	1.00	.40	.10
FOIL			
☐ 126 Kjell Dahlin (112)	.12	.05	.01
FOIL			
☐ 127 Pelle Eklund (113)	.12	.05	.01
FOIL			
☐ 128 Jim Johnson (114)	.10	.04	.01
FOIL			
☐ 129 Petr Klima (115)	.25	.10	.02
FOIL			
☐ 130 Joel Otto (116)	.15	.06	.01
FOIL			
☐ 131 Mike Ridley (117)	.30	.12	.03
FOIL			
☐ 132 Patrick Roy (118)	4.00	1.60	.40
FOIL			
☐ 133 David Shaw (119)	.12	.05	.01
FOIL			
☐ 134 Gary Suter (120)	.35	.14	.03
FOIL			
☐ 135 Steve Thomas (121)	.20	.08	.02
FOIL			
☐ 136 Borje Salming (244)	.08	.03	.01
☐ 137 Gary Nylund (245)	.05	.02	.00
☐ 138 Rick Vaive	.08	.03	.01
☐ 139 Don Edwards (249)	.05	.02	.00
☐ 140 Steve Thomas (250)	.05	.02	.00
☐ 141 Wendel Clark	1.00	.40	.10
☐ 142 Miroslav Frycer	.05	.02	.00
☐ 143 Tom Fergus	.05	.02	.00
☐ 144 Marian Stastny (252)	.03	.01	.00
☐ 145 Brad Maxwell (253)	.03	.01	.00
☐ 146 Dan Daoust (254)	.03	.01	.00
☐ 147 Greg Terrion (255)	.03	.01	.00
☐ 148 Al Iafrate	.40	.16	.04
☐ 149 Russ Courtnall	.30	.12	.03
☐ 150 Denis Savard	.15	.06	.01
☐ 151 Darryl Sutter (6)	.05	.02	.00
☐ 152 Bob Sauve (7)	.05	.02	.00
☐ 153 Doug Wilson	.12	.05	.01
☐ 154 Troy Murray (9)	.05	.02	.00
☐ 155 Al Secord (10)	.05	.02	.00
☐ 156 Ed Olczyk (14)	.12	.05	.01
☐ 157 Steve Larmer (15)	.12	.05	.01
☐ 158 John Ogrodnick	.08	.03	.01
☐ 159 Danny Gare (16)	.05	.02	.00
☐ 160 Petr Svoboda (160)	.05	.02	.00
☐ 161 Steve Yzerman (20)	.75	.30	.07
☐ 162 Petr Klima (21)	.15	.06	.01
☐ 163 Kelly Kisio (23)	.05	.02	.00
☐ 164 Doug Shedden (24)	.03	.01	.00
☐ 165 Greg Stefan	.08	.03	.01
☐ 166 Neal Broten	.08	.03	.01
☐ 167 Brian Bellows (28)	.10	.04	.01
☐ 168 Scott Bjugstad (29)	.03	.01	.00
☐ 169 Dino Ciccarelli	.12	.05	.01
☐ 170 Dennis Maruk (30)	.05	.02	.00
☐ 171 Dirk Graham (31)	.25	.10	.02
☐ 172 Curt Giles (35)	.03	.01	.00
☐ 173 Craig Hartsburg (36)	.03	.01	.00
☐ 174 Bernie Federko	.10	.04	.01
☐ 175 Brian Sutter (38)	.05	.02	.00
☐ 176 Ron Flockhart (39)	.03	.01	.00
☐ 177 Doug Gilmour (40)	.75	.30	.07
☐ 178 Charlie Bourgeois (41)	.03	.01	.00
☐ 179 Rick Wamsley (43)	.05	.02	.00
☐ 180 Rob Ramage (44)	.05	.02	.00
☐ 181 Mark Hunter	.05	.02	.00
☐ 182 Bob Froese (122) FOIL	.10	.04	.01
☐ 183 Wayne Gretzky (123) FOIL	1.00	.40	.10
☐ 184 Mark Howe (124) FOIL	.12	.05	.01
☐ 185 Jari Kurri (125) FOIL	.20	.08	.02
☐ 186 Bob Froese (45)	.05	.02	.00
☐ 187 Darren Jensen (46)	.05	.02	.00
☐ 188 Paul Coffey (47)	.20	.08	.02
☐ 189 Troy Murray (48)	.08	.03	.01
☐ 190 John Vanbiesbrouck (51)	.30	.12	.03
☐ 191 Wayne Gretzky (52)	1.00	.40	.10
☐ 192 Gary Suter (54)	.10	.04	.01
☐ 193 Bob Froese (55)	.08	.03	.01
☐ 194 Mike Bossy (56)	.15	.06	.01
☐ 195 Wayne Gretzky (57)	1.00	.40	.10
☐ 196 Greg Adams	.05	.02	.00

		MINT	EXC	G-VG
☐ 197	Dave Lewis (66)	.03	.01	.00
☐ 198	Joe Cirella (67)	.05	.02	.00
☐ 199	Rich Preston (69)	.03	.01	.00
☐ 200	Mark Johnson (70)	.05	.02	.00
☐ 201	Kirk Muller (74)	.25	.10	.02
☐ 202	Pat Verbeek (75)	.12	.05	.01
☐ 203	Mel Bridgman	.05	.02	.00
☐ 204	Bob Nystrom (76)	.03	.01	.00
☐ 205	Clark Gillies (77)	.05	.02	.00
☐ 206	Pat LaFontaine	.75	.30	.07
☐ 207	Pat Flatley (81)	.03	.01	.00
☐ 208	Bob Bourne (82)	.03	.01	.00
☐ 209	Denis Potvin	.15	.06	.01
☐ 210	Duane Sutter	.08	.03	.01
☐ 211	Brent Sutter	.08	.03	.01
☐ 212	Kelly Hrudey (84)	.15	.06	.01
☐ 213	Billy Smith (85)	.08	.03	.01
☐ 214	Tomas Jonsson (86)	.05	.02	.00
☐ 215	Ken Morrow (87)	.03	.01	.00
☐ 216	Bryan Trottier	.20	.08	.02
☐ 217	Mike Bossy	.30	.12	.03
☐ 218	John Vanbiesbrouck	.40	.16	.04
☐ 219	Bob Brooke (89)	.03	.01	.00
☐ 220	James Patrick (90)	.05	.02	.00
☐ 221	Mike Ridley	.35	.14	.03
☐ 222	Ron Greschner (91)	.05	.02	.00
☐ 223	Tom Laidlaw (92)	.03	.01	.00
☐ 224	Larry Melnyk (93)	.03	.01	.00
☐ 225	Reijo Ruotsalainen (94)	.03	.01	.00
☐ 226	Terry Ruskowski	.08	.03	.01
☐ 227	Willy Lindstrom (97)	.03	.01	.00
☐ 228	Mike Bullard (98)	.03	.01	.00
☐ 229	Roberto Romano (100)	.03	.01	.00
☐ 230	John Chabot (101)	.03	.01	.00
☐ 231	Moe Mantha (102)	.03	.01	.00
☐ 232	Doug Bodger (103)	.05	.02	.00
☐ 233	Mario Lemieux	4.00	1.60	.40
☐ 234	Glenn Resch (105)	.08	.03	.01
☐ 235	Brad Marsh (106)	.05	.02	.00
☐ 236	Bob Froese	.08	.03	.01
☐ 237	Doug Crossman (107)	.03	.01	.00
☐ 238	Ilkka Sinisalo (108)	.03	.01	.00
☐ 239	Brian Propp	.08	.03	.01
☐ 240	Tim Kerr	.08	.03	.01
☐ 241	Dave Poulin	.08	.03	.01
☐ 242	Rich Sutter (109)	.05	.02	.00
☐ 243	Ron Sutter (110)	.05	.02	.00
☐ 244	Murray Craven (136)	.05	.02	.00
☐ 245	Peter Zezel (137)	.10	.04	.01
☐ 246	Mark Howe	.08	.03	.01
☐ 247	Brad McCrimmon	.08	.03	.01
☐ 248	Dave Christian	.08	.03	.01
☐ 249	Rod Langway (139)	.08	.03	.01
☐ 250	Bob Carpenter (140)	.08	.03	.01
☐ 251	Mike Gartner	.15	.06	.01
☐ 252	Al Jensen (144)	.05	.02	.00
☐ 253	Craig Laughlin (145)	.03	.01	.00
☐ 254	Scott Stevens (146)	.12	.05	.01
☐ 255	Alan Haworth (147)	.03	.01	.00
☐ xx	Sticker Album	1.50	.60	.15

1987-88 O-Pee-Chee Stickers

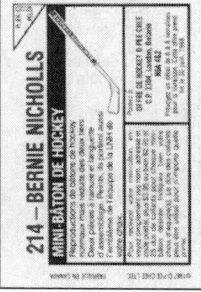

This sticker set consists of 255 stickers in full color and was put out by O-Pee-Chee. There are no foil stickers in this set. The stickers measure approximately 2 1/8" by 3". An album is available for these stickers. Those stickers which are pairs are indicated in the checklist below by noting parenthetically the other member of the pair. On the inside back cover of the sticker album the company offered (via direct mail-order) up to 25 different stickers of your choice for ten cents each; this is one reason why the values of the most popular players in these sticker sets are somewhat depressed compared to traditional card set prices.

		MINT	EXC	G-VG
COMPLETE SET (255)		20.00	8.00	2.00
COMMON PLAYER (1-255)		.05	.02	.00
COMMON HALF STICKER		.03	.01	.00
☐ 1	Ron Hextall MVP	.20	.08	.02
☐ 2	Stanley Cup Action	.05	.02	.00
☐ 3	Stanley Cup Action	.05	.02	.00
☐ 4	Stanley Cup Action	.05	.02	.00
☐ 5	Stanley Cup Action	.05	.02	.00
☐ 6	Mats Naslund	.08	.03	.01
☐ 7	Guy Carbonneau (146)	.08	.03	.01
☐ 8	Gaston Gingras (147)	.03	.01	.00
☐ 9	Chris Chelios	.20	.08	.02
☐ 10	Bobby Smith	.08	.03	.01
☐ 11	Rick Green (149)	.03	.01	.00
☐ 12	Bob Gainey (150)	.08	.03	.01
☐ 13	Patrick Roy	2.00	.80	.20
☐ 14	Kjell Dahlin (153)	.05	.02	.00
☐ 15	Chris Nilan (154)	.05	.02	.00
☐ 16	Larry Robinson	.12	.05	.01
☐ 17	Ryan Walter (157)	.05	.02	.00
☐ 18	Petr Svoboda (158)	.05	.02	.00
☐ 19	Claude Lemieux	.75	.30	.07
☐ 20	Rob Ramage (160)	.05	.02	.00
☐ 21	Mark Hunter (161)	.03	.01	.00
☐ 22	Rick Wamsley (163)	.05	.02	.00
☐ 23	Greg Paslawski (164)	.03	.01	.00
☐ 24	Bernie Federko	.08	.03	.01
☐ 25	Ron Flockhart (166)	.03	.01	.00
☐ 26	Tim Bothwell (167)	.03	.01	.00
☐ 27	Doug Gilmour	.60	.24	.06
☐ 28	Kelly Kisio (168)	.05	.02	.00
☐ 29	Don Maloney (169)	.03	.01	.00
☐ 30	James Patrick (171)	.05	.02	.00
☐ 31	Willie Huber (172)	.03	.01	.00
☐ 32	Walt Poddubny	.05	.02	.00
☐ 33	John Vanbiesbrouck (178)	.15	.06	.01
☐ 34	Marcel Dionne (179)	.12	.05	.01
☐ 35	Tomas Sandstrom	.15	.06	.01
☐ 36	Joe Mullen	.15	.06	.01
☐ 37	Mike Bullard (180)	.03	.01	.00
☐ 38	Neil Sheehy (181)	.03	.01	.00
☐ 39	Paul Reinhart	.05	.02	.00
☐ 40	Al MacInnis	.40	.16	.04
☐ 41	Mike Vernon (182)	.20	.08	.02
☐ 42	Joel Otto (183)	.05	.02	.00
☐ 43	Lanny McDonald	.15	.06	.01
☐ 44	Hakan Loob (184)	.05	.02	.00
☐ 45	Carey Wilson (185)	.03	.01	.00
☐ 46	Jim Peplinski	.05	.02	.00
☐ 47	John Tonelli (186)	.05	.02	.00
☐ 48	Jamie Macoun (187)	.03	.01	.00
☐ 49	Gary Suter	.15	.06	.01
☐ 50	Dennis Maruk (189)	.05	.02	.00
☐ 51	Don Beaupre (190)	.05	.02	.00
☐ 52	Neal Broten (193)	.05	.02	.00
☐ 53	Brian Bellows (194)	.10	.04	.01
☐ 54	Craig Hartsburg	.05	.02	.00
☐ 55	Gordie Roberts (196)	.03	.01	.00
☐ 56	Steve Payne (197)	.03	.01	.00
☐ 57	Dino Ciccarelli	.12	.05	.01
☐ 58	Pat Verbeek (199)	.08	.03	.01
☐ 59	Doug Sulliman (200)	.03	.01	.00
☐ 60	Bruce Driver (202)	.03	.01	.00
☐ 61	Joe Cirella (203)	.05	.02	.00
☐ 62	Aaron Broten	.05	.02	.00
☐ 63	Alain Chevrier (204)	.05	.02	.00
☐ 64	Mark Johnson (205)	.05	.02	.00
☐ 65	Kirk Muller	.25	.10	.02
☐ 66A	Face-Off Action (Sandlak)	.05	.02	.00
☐ 66B	Face-Off Action (Kasper)	.05	.02	.00
☐ 67	Action Sticker	.05	.02	.00
☐ 68	Action Sticker	.05	.02	.00
☐ 69	Murray Craven IA	.05	.02	.00
☐ 70	Bruins Action	.05	.02	.00
☐ 71	Islanders Action	.05	.02	.00
☐ 72	Action Sticker	.05	.02	.00
☐ 73	Action Sticker	.05	.02	.00

☐ 74	Al Secord (207)	.05	.02	.00
☐ 75	Bob Sauve (208)	.05	.02	.00
☐ 76	Ed Olczyk (210)	.08	.03	.01
☐ 77	Doug Wilson (211)	.08	.03	.01
☐ 78	Denis Savard	.15	.06	.01
☐ 79	Troy Murray (212)	.05	.02	.00
☐ 80	Gary Nylund (213)	.05	.02	.00
☐ 81	Steve Larmer	.15	.06	.01
☐ 82	Jari Kurri	.20	.08	.02
☐ 83	Esa Tikkanen (215)	.50	.20	.05
☐ 84	Kevin Lowe (216)	.08	.03	.01
☐ 85	Grant Fuhr	.20	.08	.02
☐ 86	Wayne Gretzky	1.25	.50	.12
☐ 87	Charlie Huddy (219)	.05	.02	.00
☐ 88	Kent Nilsson (220)	.05	.02	.00
☐ 89	Paul Coffey	.25	.10	.02
☐ 90	Mike Krushelnyski (223)	.05	.02	.00
☐ 91	Craig MacTavish (224)	.08	.03	.01
☐ 92	Mark Messier	.30	.12	.03
☐ 93	Andy Moog (226)	.12	.05	.01
☐ 94	Randy Gregg (227)	.05	.02	.00
☐ 95	Glenn Anderson	.12	.05	.01
☐ 96	Peter Zezel (229)	.05	.02	.00
☐ 97	Brian Propp (230)	.08	.03	.01
☐ 98	Dave Poulin (232)	.05	.02	.00
☐ 99	Brad McCrimmon (233)	.05	.02	.00
☐ 100	Mark Howe	.08	.03	.01
☐ 101	Ron Hextall (234)	.15	.06	.01
☐ 102	Ron Sutter (235)	.05	.02	.00
☐ 103	Tim Kerr	.08	.03	.01
☐ 104	Petr Klima (237)	.10	.04	.01
☐ 105	Adam Oates (238)	1.25	.50	.12
☐ 106	Gerard Gallant (240)	.07	.03	.01
☐ 107	Mike O'Connell (241)	.03	.01	.00
☐ 108	Brent Ashton	.05	.02	.00
☐ 109	Glen Hanlon (242)	.05	.02	.00
☐ 110	Harold Snepsts (243)	.03	.01	.00
☐ 111	Steve Yzerman	.60	.24	.06
☐ 112	Mark Howe (124)	.08	.03	.01
☐ 113	Michel Goulet (125)	.08	.03	.01
☐ 114	Ron Hextall (126)	.15	.06	.01
☐ 115	Wayne Gretzky (127)	.75	.30	.07
☐ 116	Ray Bourque (128)	.15	.06	.01
☐ 117	Jari Kurri (129)	.12	.05	.01
☐ 118	Dino Ciccarelli (130)	.08	.03	.01
☐ 119	Larry Murphy (131)	.10	.04	.01
☐ 120	Mario Lemieux (132)	.75	.30	.07
☐ 121	Mike Liut (133)	.05	.02	.00
☐ 122	Luc Robitaille (134)	1.50	.60	.15
☐ 123	Al MacInnis (135)	.20	.08	.02
☐ 124	Brian Benning (112)	.03	.01	.00
☐ 125	Shawn Burr (113)	.03	.01	.00
☐ 126	Jimmy Carson (114)	.25	.10	.02
☐ 127	Shayne Corson (115)	.20	.08	.02
☐ 128	Vincent Damphousse (116)	.35	.14	.03
☐ 129	Ron Hextall (117)	.15	.06	.01
☐ 130	Jason Lafreniere (118)	.03	.01	.00
☐ 131	Ken Leiter (119)	.03	.01	.00
☐ 132	Allen Pedersen (120)	.03	.01	.00
☐ 133	Luc Robitaille (121)	1.50	.60	.15
☐ 134	Christian Ruuttu (122)	.08	.03	.01
☐ 135	Jim Sandlak (123)	.03	.01	.00
☐ 136	Keith Crowder (245)	.03	.01	.00
☐ 137	Charlie Simmer (246)	.05	.02	.00
☐ 138	Rick Middleton (248)	.05	.02	.00
☐ 139	Doug Keans (249)	.05	.02	.00
☐ 140	Ray Bourque	.25	.10	.02
☐ 141	Tom McCarthy (250)	.03	.01	.00
☐ 142	Reed Larson (251)	.03	.01	.00
☐ 143	Cam Neely	.75	.30	.07
☐ 144	Christian Ruuttu (253)	.05	.02	.00
☐ 145	John Tucker (254)	.05	.02	.00
☐ 146	Steve Dykstra (7)	.03	.01	.00
☐ 147	Dave Andreychuk (8)	.15	.06	.01
☐ 148	Tom Barrasso	.15	.06	.01
☐ 149	Mike Ramsey (11)	.03	.01	.00
☐ 150	Mike Foligno (12)	.03	.01	.00
☐ 151	Phil Housley	.15	.06	.01
☐ 152	Wendel Clark	.25	.10	.02
☐ 153	Greg Terrion (14)	.03	.01	.00
☐ 154	Steve Thomas (15)	.05	.02	.00
☐ 155	Rick Vaive	.05	.02	.00
☐ 156	Russ Courtnall	.30	.12	.03
☐ 157	Rick Lanz (17)	.03	.01	.00
☐ 158	Miroslav Frycer (18)	.03	.01	.00
☐ 159	Tom Fergus	.05	.02	.00
☐ 160	Al Iafrate (20)	.20	.08	.02
☐ 161	Gary Leeman (21)	.05	.02	.00
☐ 162	Allan Bester	.05	.02	.00
☐ 163	Todd Gill (22)	.03	.01	.00
☐ 164	Ken Wregget (23)	.10	.04	.01
☐ 165	Borje Salming	.08	.03	.01
☐ 166	Craig Simpson (25)	.20	.08	.02
☐ 167	Terry Ruskowski (26)	.05	.02	.00
☐ 168	Gilles Meloche (28)	.05	.02	.00
☐ 169	John Chabot (29)	.03	.01	.00
☐ 170	Mario Lemieux	2.00	.80	.20
☐ 171	Moe Mantha (30)	.03	.01	.00
☐ 172	Jim Johnson (31)	.03	.01	.00
☐ 173	Dan Quinn	.05	.02	.00
☐ 174	Wayne Gretzky (176)	.75	.30	.07
☐ 175	Brian Hayward (177)	.08	.03	.01
☐ 176	Mark Howe (174)	.08	.03	.01
☐ 177	Luc Robitaille (175)	1.50	.60	.15
☐ 178	Ray Bourque (33)	.15	.06	.01
☐ 179	Dave Poulin (34)	.05	.02	.00
☐ 180	Wayne Gretzky (37) Hart Trophy Winner	.75	.30	.07
☐ 181	Wayne Gretzky (38) Ross Trophy Winner	.75	.30	.07
☐ 182	Ron Hextall (41)	.15	.06	.01
☐ 183	Doug Jarvis (42)	.03	.01	.00
☐ 184	Brian Hayward (44)	.08	.03	.01
☐ 185	Patrick Roy (45)	1.00	.40	.10
☐ 186	Joe Mullen (47)	.15	.06	.01
☐ 187	Luc Robitaille (48)	1.50	.60	.15
☐ 188	Barry Pederson (50)	.08	.03	.01
☐ 189	Richard Brodeur (50)	.05	.02	.00
☐ 190	Dave Richter (51)	.03	.01	.00
☐ 191	Doug Lidster	.05	.02	.00
☐ 192	Petri Skriko	.08	.03	.01
☐ 193	Rich Sutter (52)	.05	.02	.00
☐ 194	Jim Sandlak (53)	.08	.03	.01
☐ 195	Tony Tanti	.08	.03	.01
☐ 196	Michel Petit (55)	.05	.02	.00
☐ 197	Jim Benning (56)	.03	.01	.00
☐ 198	Stan Smyl	.05	.02	.00
☐ 199	Brent Peterson (58)	.03	.01	.00
☐ 200	Garth Butcher (59)	.20	.08	.02
☐ 201	Patrik Sundstrom	.08	.03	.01
☐ 202	Kevin Dineen (60)	.08	.03	.01
☐ 203	Sylvain Turgeon (61)	.05	.02	.00
☐ 204	John Anderson (63)	.03	.01	.00
☐ 205	Ulf Samuelsson (64)	.25	.10	.02
☐ 206	Ron Francis	.15	.06	.01
☐ 207	Doug Jarvis (74)	.03	.01	.00
☐ 208	Dave Babych (75)	.03	.01	.00
☐ 209	Mike Liut	.08	.03	.01
☐ 210	Jimmy Carson (76)	.25	.10	.02
☐ 211	Larry Playfair (77)	.03	.01	.00
☐ 212	Jay Wells (79)	.03	.01	.00
☐ 213	Rollie Melanson (80)	.05	.02	.00
☐ 214	Bernie Nicholls	.20	.08	.02
☐ 215	Dave Taylor (83)	.05	.02	.00
☐ 216	Jim Fox (84)	.03	.01	.00
☐ 217	Luc Robitaille	2.50	1.00	.25
☐ 218	John Ogrodnick (86)	.08	.03	.01
☐ 219	Jason Lafreniere (87)	.03	.01	.00
☐ 220	Mike Hough (88)	.03	.01	.00
☐ 221	Paul Gillis	.05	.02	.00
☐ 222	Peter Stastny	.20	.08	.02
☐ 223	David Shaw (90)	.03	.01	.00
☐ 224	Bill Derlago (91)	.03	.01	.00
☐ 225	Michel Goulet	.15	.06	.01
☐ 226	Doug Shedden (93)	.03	.01	.00
☐ 227	Basil McRae (94)	.03	.01	.00
☐ 228	Anton Stastny	.05	.02	.00
☐ 229	Randy Moller (96)	.03	.01	.00
☐ 230	Robert Picard (97)	.03	.01	.00
☐ 231	Mario Gosselin	.08	.03	.01
☐ 232	Larry Murphy (98)	.08	.03	.01
☐ 233	Scott Stevens (99)	.10	.04	.01
☐ 234	Mike Ridley (101)	.08	.03	.01
☐ 235	Dave Christian (102)	.05	.02	.00
☐ 236	Rod Langway	.08	.03	.01
☐ 237	Bob Gould (104)	.03	.01	.00
☐ 238	Bob Mason (105)	.03	.01	.00
☐ 239	Mike Gartner	.20	.08	.02
☐ 240	Bryan Trottier (106)	.12	.05	.01
☐ 241	Brent Sutter (107)	.08	.03	.01
☐ 242	Kelly Hrudey (109)	.10	.04	.01
☐ 243	Pat LaFontaine (110)	.40	.16	.04
☐ 244	Mike Bossy	.35	.14	.03
☐ 245	Pat Flatley (136)	.05	.02	.00
☐ 246	Ken Morrow (137)	.03	.01	.00
☐ 247	Denis Potvin	.15	.06	.01
☐ 248	Randy Carlyle (138)	.05	.02	.00
☐ 249	Daniel Berthiaume (139)	.08	.03	.01
☐ 250	Mario Marois (141)	.03	.01	.00
☐ 251	Dave Ellett (142)	.08	.03	.01

		MINT	EXC	G-VG
☐ 252	Paul MacLean	.06	.02	.00
☐ 253	Gilles Hamel (144)	.03	.01	.00
☐ 254	Doug Smail (145)	.04	.02	.00
☐ 255	Dale Hawerchuk	.25	.10	.02
☐ xx	Sticker Album	1.50	.60	.15

1988-89 O-Pee-Chee Stickers

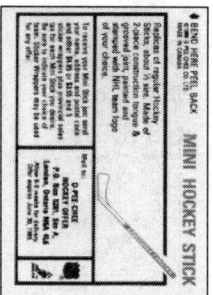

This sticker set consists of 270 stickers in full color and was put out by O-Pee-Chee. There are no foil stickers in this set. The stickers measure approximately 2 1/8" by 3". An album is available for these stickers. Those stickers which are pairs are indicated in the checklist below by noting parenthetically the other member of the pair. The backs of the stickers are three types: trivia questions and answers (42 different red Level I and blue Level II), various souvenir offers, and the colorful Future Stars (which are considered a separate set in their own right). On the inside back cover of the sticker album the company offered (via direct mail-order) up to 20 different stickers of your choice for ten cents each; this is one reason why the values of the most popular players in these sticker sets are somewhat depressed compared to traditional card set prices.

		MINT	EXC	G-VG
COMPLETE SET (270)		20.00	8.00	2.00
COMMON PLAYER (1-270)		.05	.02	.00
COMMON HALF STICKER		.03	.01	.00
☐ 1	Wayne Gretzky MVP	1.25	.50	.12
☐ 2	Oilers/Bruins Action	.05	.02	.00
☐ 3	Oilers/Bruins Action	.05	.02	.00
☐ 4	Oilers/Bruins Action	.05	.02	.00
☐ 5	Oilers/Bruins Action	.05	.02	.00
☐ 6	Doug Wilson (135)	.08	.03	.01
☐ 7	Dirk Graham (136)	.05	.02	.00
☐ 8	Darren Pang (137)	.05	.02	.00
☐ 9	Rick Vaive (138)	.05	.02	.00
☐ 10	Troy Murray (139)	.05	.02	.00
☐ 11	Brian Noonan (140)	.05	.02	.00
☐ 12	Steve Larmer	.12	.05	.01
☐ 13	Denis Savard	.12	.05	.01
☐ 14	Mark Hunter (141)	.03	.01	.00
☐ 15	Brian Sutter (142)	.05	.02	.00
☐ 16	Brett Hull (145)	2.00	.80	.20
☐ 17	Tony McKegney (146)	.03	.01	.00
☐ 18	Brian Benning (151)	.03	.01	.00
☐ 19	Tony Hrkac (152)	.05	.02	.00
☐ 20	Doug Gilmour	.50	.20	.05
☐ 21	Bernie Federko	.08	.03	.01
☐ 22	Cam Neely	.35	.14	.03
☐ 23	Ray Bourque	.30	.12	.03
☐ 24	Rejean Lemelin (153)	.05	.02	.00
☐ 25	Gord Kluzak (154)	.03	.01	.00
☐ 26	Rick Middleton (155)	.08	.03	.01
☐ 27	Steve Kasper (156)	.05	.02	.00
☐ 28	Bob Sweeney (168)	.03	.01	.00
☐ 29	Randy Burridge (169)	.05	.02	.00
☐ 30	Bruins/Whalers Action	.05	.02	.00
☐ 31	Canadiens/Bruins	.05	.02	.00
☐ 32	Canadiens/Bruins Action	.05	.02	.00
☐ 33	Blues/Red Wings Action	.05	.02	.00
☐ 34	Canadiens/Bruins Action	.05	.02	.00
☐ 35	Canadiens/Bruins Action	.05	.02	.00
☐ 36	Canadiens/Bruins Action	.05	.02	.00
☐ 37	Canadiens/Bruins Action	.05	.02	.00
☐ 38	Canadiens/Bruins Action	.05	.02	.00
☐ 39	Larry Robinson (170)	.08	.03	.01
☐ 40	Ryan Walter (171)	.03	.01	.00
☐ 41	Guy Carbonneau (172)	.08	.03	.01
☐ 42	Bob Gainey (173)	.08	.03	.01
☐ 43	Claude Lemieux (176)	.15	.06	.01
☐ 44	Petr Svoboda (177)	.05	.02	.00
☐ 45	Patrick Roy	1.00	.40	.10
☐ 46	Bobby Smith	.08	.03	.01
☐ 47	Mike McPhee (182)	.05	.02	.00
☐ 48	Craig Ludwig (183)	.03	.01	.00
☐ 49	Stephane Richer	.30	.12	.03
☐ 50	Mats Naslund	.08	.03	.01
☐ 51	Chris Chelios	.15	.06	.01
☐ 52	Brian Hayward	.08	.03	.01
☐ 53	Larry Melnyk (184)	.03	.01	.00
☐ 54	Garth Butcher (185)	.08	.03	.01
☐ 55	Kirk McLean (186)	.50	.20	.05
☐ 56	Doug Wickenheiser (187)	.03	.01	.00
☐ 57	Rich Sutter (190)	.05	.02	.00
☐ 58	Jim Benning (191)	.03	.01	.00
☐ 59	Tony Tanti	.05	.02	.00
☐ 60	Stan Smyl	.05	.02	.00
☐ 61	David Saunders (196)	.03	.01	.00
☐ 62	Steve Tambellini (197)	.03	.01	.00
☐ 63	Doug Lidster	.05	.02	.00
☐ 64	Petri Skriko	.05	.02	.00
☐ 65	Barry Pederson	.05	.02	.00
☐ 66	Greg Adams	.08	.03	.01
☐ 67	Mike Gartner	.20	.08	.02
☐ 68	Scott Stevens	.15	.06	.01
☐ 69	Rod Langway (198)	.05	.02	.00
☐ 70	Dave Christian (199)	.05	.02	.00
☐ 71	Larry Murphy (200)	.10	.04	.01
☐ 72	Clint Malarchuk (201)	.05	.02	.00
☐ 73	Dale Hunter (204)	.08	.03	.01
☐ 74	Mike Ridley (205)	.05	.02	.00
☐ 75	Kirk Muller	.25	.10	.02
☐ 76	Aaron Broten	.05	.02	.00
☐ 77	Bruce Driver (206)	.03	.01	.00
☐ 78	John MacLean (207)	.15	.06	.01
☐ 79	Joe Cirella (208)	.05	.02	.00
☐ 80	Doug Brown (209)	.05	.02	.00
☐ 81	Pat Verbeek (210)	.08	.03	.01
☐ 82	Sean Burke (211)	.25	.10	.02
☐ 83	Joel Otto (212)	.05	.02	.00
☐ 84	Rob Ramage (213)	.05	.02	.00
☐ 85	Lanny McDonald (215)	.10	.04	.01
☐ 86	Mike Vernon (216)	.15	.06	.01
☐ 87	John Tonelli (217)	.05	.02	.00
☐ 88	Jim Peplinski (218)	.03	.01	.00
☐ 89	Gary Suter	.10	.04	.01
☐ 90	Joe Nieuwendyk	1.25	.50	.12
☐ 91	Ric Nattress (219)	.03	.01	.00
☐ 92	Al MacInnis (220)	.20	.08	.02
☐ 93	Mike Bullard	.05	.02	.00
☐ 94	Hakan Loob	.08	.03	.01
☐ 95	Joe Mullen	.12	.05	.01
☐ 96	Brad McCrimmon	.08	.03	.01
☐ 97	Brian Propp (221)	.05	.02	.00
☐ 98	Murray Craven (222)	.05	.02	.00
☐ 99	Rick Tocchet (225)	.40	.16	.04
☐ 100	Doug Crossman (226)	.03	.01	.00
☐ 101	Brad Marsh (233)	.05	.02	.00
☐ 102	Peter Zezel (234)	.05	.02	.00
☐ 103	Ron Hextall	.15	.06	.01
☐ 104	Mark Howe	.10	.04	.01
☐ 105	Brent Sutter (235)	.05	.02	.00
☐ 106	Alan Kerr (236)	.03	.01	.00
☐ 107	Randy Wood (237)	.03	.01	.00
☐ 108	Mikko Makela (238)	.03	.01	.00
☐ 109	Kelly Hrudey (241)	.08	.03	.01
☐ 110	Steve Konroyd (242)	.03	.01	.00
☐ 111	Pat LaFontaine	.40	.16	.04
☐ 112	Bryan Trottier	.20	.08	.02
☐ 113	Gary Suter (243)	.05	.02	.00
☐ 114	Luc Robitaille (244)	.50	.20	.05
☐ 115	Patrick Roy (245)	.50	.20	.05

☐ 116	Mario Lemieux (246)	.75	.30	.07
☐ 117	Ray Bourque (247)	.15	.06	.01
☐ 118	Hakan Loob (248)	.05	.02	.00
☐ 119	Mike Bullard (249)	.03	.01	.00
☐ 120	Brad McCrimmon (250)	.05	.02	.00
☐ 121	Wayne Gretzky (251)	1.00	.40	.10
☐ 122	Grant Fuhr (252)	.15	.06	.01
☐ 123	Craig Simpson (255)	.10	.04	.01
☐ 124	Mark Howe (256)	.06	.02	.00
☐ 125	Joe Nieuwendyk (257)	.50	.20	.05
☐ 126	Ray Sheppard (258)	.25	.10	.02
☐ 127	Brett Hull (259)	2.00	.80	.20
☐ 128	Ulf Dahlen (260)	.10	.04	.01
☐ 129	Tony Hrkac (265)	.05	.02	.00
☐ 130	Bob Sweeney (266)	.05	.02	.00
☐ 131	Rob Brown (267)	.10	.04	.01
☐ 132	Iain Duncan (268)	.03	.01	.00
☐ 133	Pierre Turgeon (269)	.75	.30	.07
☐ 134	Calle Johansson (270)	.05	.02	.00
☐ 135	Darren Pang (6)	.05	.02	.00
☐ 136	Kirk McLean (7)	.50	.20	.05
☐ 137	Doug Smail (8)	.05	.02	.00
☐ 138	Thomas Steen (9)	.05	.02	.00
☐ 139	Laurie Boschman (10)	.03	.01	.00
☐ 140	Iain Duncan (11)	.03	.01	.00
☐ 141	Ray Neufeld (14)	.03	.01	.00
☐ 142	Mario Marois (15)	.03	.01	.00
☐ 143	Dale Hawerchuk	.15	.06	.01
☐ 144	Paul MacLean	.05	.02	.00
☐ 145	Jim Kyte (16)	.03	.01	.00
☐ 146	Pokey Reddick (17)	.05	.02	.00
☐ 147	Andrew McBain	.05	.02	.00
☐ 148	Randy Carlyle	.08	.03	.01
☐ 149	Daniel Berthiaume	.08	.03	.01
☐ 150	Dave Ellett	.08	.03	.01
☐ 151	Roland Melanson (18)	.04	.02	.00
☐ 152	Steve Duchesne (19)	.15	.06	.01
☐ 153	Bob Carpenter (24)	.05	.02	.00
☐ 154	Jim Fox (25)	.03	.01	.00
☐ 155	Dave Taylor (26)	.05	.02	.00
☐ 156	Bernie Nicholls (27)	.15	.06	.01
☐ 157	Luc Robitaille	.75	.30	.07
☐ 158	Jimmy Carson	.15	.06	.01
☐ 159	Canadiens/Bruins Action	.05	.02	.00
☐ 160	Devils/Nordiques Action	.05	.02	.00
☐ 161	Devils/Nordiques Action	.05	.02	.00
☐ 162	Devils/North Stars Action	.05	.02	.00
☐ 163	Oilers/Flames Action	.05	.02	.00
☐ 164	Oilers/Flames Action	.05	.02	.00
☐ 165	Oilers/Flames Action	.05	.02	.00
☐ 166	Oilers/Flames Action	.05	.02	.00
☐ 167	Canadiens/Bruins Action	.05	.02	.00
☐ 168	Mark Osborne (28)	.03	.01	.00
☐ 169	Dan Daoust (29)	.03	.01	.00
☐ 170	Tom Fergus (39)	.03	.01	.00
☐ 171	Vincent Damphousse (40)	.20	.08	.02
☐ 172	Wendel Clark (41)	.25	.10	.02
☐ 173	Luke Richardson (42)	.05	.02	.00
☐ 174	Borje Salming	.08	.03	.01
☐ 175	Russ Courtnall	.12	.05	.01
☐ 176	Rick Lanz (43)	.03	.01	.00
☐ 177	Ken Wregget (44)	.08	.03	.01
☐ 178	Gary Leeman	.08	.03	.01
☐ 179	Al Secord	.08	.03	.01
☐ 180	Al Iafrate	.15	.06	.01
☐ 181	Ed Olczyk	.10	.04	.01
☐ 182	Normand Rochefort (47)	.03	.01	.00
☐ 183	Lane Lambert (48)	.03	.01	.00
☐ 184	Tommy Albelin (53)	.03	.01	.00
☐ 185	Jason Lafreniere (54)	.03	.01	.00
☐ 186	Alain Cote (55)	.03	.01	.00
☐ 187	Gaetan Duchesne (56)	.03	.01	.00
☐ 188	Michel Goulet	.15	.06	.01
☐ 189	Peter Stastny	.20	.08	.02
☐ 190	Jeff Jackson (57)	.03	.01	.00
☐ 191	Mike Eagles (58)	.03	.01	.00
☐ 192	Jeff Brown	.40	.16	.04
☐ 193	Mario Gosselin	.08	.03	.01
☐ 194	Anton Stastny	.05	.02	.00
☐ 195	Alan Haworth	.05	.02	.00
☐ 196	Don Beaupre (61)	.08	.03	.01
☐ 197	Brian MacLellan (62)	.03	.01	.00
☐ 198	Brian Lawton (69)	.03	.01	.00
☐ 199	Craig Hartsburg (70)	.03	.01	.00
☐ 200	Moe Mantha (71)	.03	.01	.00
☐ 201	Neal Broten (72)	.05	.02	.00
☐ 202	Dino Ciccarelli	.15	.06	.01
☐ 203	Brian Bellows	.15	.06	.01
☐ 204	Mario Lemieux (73)	.75	.30	.07
☐ 205	Joe Nieuwendyk (74)	.50	.20	.05
☐ 206	Brad McCrimmon (77)	.05	.02	.00
☐ 207	Pete Peeters (78)	.05	.02	.00
☐ 208	Norris Trophy Winner Ray Bourque (79)	.12	.05	.01
☐ 209	Frank J. Selke Trophy Winner Guy Carbonneau (80)	.05	.02	.00
☐ 210	Hart Trophy Winner Mario Lemieux (81)	.75	.30	.07
☐ 211	Art Ross Trophy Winner Mario Lemieux (82)	.75	.30	.07
☐ 212	Vezina Trophy Winner Grant Fuhr (83)	.10	.04	.01
☐ 213	Bill Masterton Trophy Winner Bob Bourne (84)	.03	.01	.00
☐ 214	William Jennings Trophy Winners Brian Hayward and Patrick Roy	.35	.14	.03
☐ 215	Lady Byng Trophy Winner Mats Naslund (85)	.05	.02	.00
☐ 216	Calder Trophy Winner Joe Nieuwendyk (86)	.50	.20	.05
☐ 217	Craig MacTavish (87)	.03	.01	.00
☐ 218	Chris Joseph (88)	.03	.01	.00
☐ 219	Kevin Lowe (91)	.05	.02	.00
☐ 220	Esa Tikkanen (92)	.25	.10	.02
☐ 221	Charlie Huddy (97)	.04	.02	.00
☐ 222	Geoff Courtnall (98)	.50	.20	.05
☐ 223	Grant Fuhr	.15	.06	.01
☐ 224	Wayne Gretzky	1.50	.60	.15
☐ 225	Steve Smith (99)	.25	.10	.02
☐ 226	Mike Krushelnyski (100)	.05	.02	.00
☐ 227	Jari Kurri	.15	.06	.01
☐ 228	Craig Simpson	.12	.05	.01
☐ 229	Glenn Anderson	.12	.05	.01
☐ 230	Mark Messier	.40	.16	.04
☐ 231	Randy Cunneyworth	.05	.02	.00
☐ 232	Mario Lemieux	1.50	.60	.15
☐ 233	Paul Coffey (101)	.15	.06	.01
☐ 234	Doug Bodger (102)	.05	.02	.00
☐ 235	Dave Hunter (105)	.03	.01	.00
☐ 236	Dan Quinn (106)	.03	.01	.00
☐ 237	Rob Brown (107)	.10	.04	.01
☐ 238	Gilles Meloche (108)	.05	.02	.00
☐ 239	Kelly Kisio	.05	.02	.00
☐ 240	Walt Poddubny	.05	.02	.00
☐ 241	John Vanbiesbrouck (109)	.15	.06	.01
☐ 242	Tomas Sandstrom (110)	.10	.04	.01
☐ 243	David Shaw (113)	.05	.02	.00
☐ 244	Marcel Dionne (114)	.12	.05	.01
☐ 245	Chris Nilan (115)	.05	.02	.00
☐ 246	James Patrick (116)	.05	.02	.00
☐ 247	Bob Probert (117)	.50	.20	.05
☐ 248	Mike O'Connell (118)	.03	.01	.00
☐ 249	Jeff Sharples (119)	.03	.01	.00
☐ 250	Brent Ashton (120)	.03	.01	.00
☐ 251	Petr Klima (121)	.05	.02	.00
☐ 252	Greg Stefan (122)	.05	.02	.00
☐ 253	Steve Yzerman	.50	.20	.05
☐ 254	Gerard Gallant	.10	.04	.01
☐ 255	Phil Housley (123)	.10	.04	.01
☐ 256	Christian Ruuttu (124)	.03	.01	.00
☐ 257	Mike Foligno (125)	.03	.01	.00
☐ 258	Scott Arniel (126)	.03	.01	.00
☐ 259	Tom Barrasso (127)	.10	.04	.01
☐ 260	Mike Ramsey (128)	.03	.01	.00
☐ 261	Dave Andreychuk	.20	.08	.02
☐ 262	Ray Sheppard	.35	.14	.03
☐ 263	Mike Liut	.08	.03	.01
☐ 264	Ron Francis	.12	.05	.01
☐ 265	Ulf Samuelsson (129)	.10	.04	.01
☐ 266	Carey Wilson (130)	.03	.01	.00
☐ 267	Dave Babych (131)	.05	.02	.00
☐ 268	Ray Ferraro (132)	.05	.02	.00
☐ 269	Kevin Dineen (133)	.05	.02	.00
☐ 270	John Anderson (134)	.03	.01	.00
☐ xx	Sticker Album	1.50	.60	.15

1989-90 O-Pee-Chee Stickers

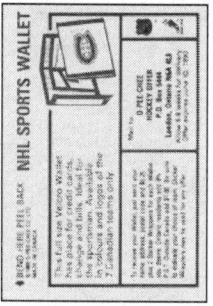

The 1989-90 O-Pee-Chee set contains 270 stickers. The standard size stickers measure 2 1/8" by 3"; some stickers consist of two half-size stickers. The fronts feature color action photos of players, teams, and trophies. The sticker backs are of four types: trivia questions and answers (green Level III), souvenir offers, Future Stars, and All-Stars. A full-color glossy album was issued with the set for holding the stickers. Some team action shots are a composite of two or four stickers; in the checklist below these stickers are denoted by L (left half) and R (right half), with the additional prefixes U (upper) and L (lower) for the four sticker pictures. The stickers are numbered on the front and are checklisted below accordingly. For those stickers that consist of two half-size stickers, we have noted the other number of the pair parenthetically after the player's name.

	MINT	EXC	G-VG
COMPLETE SET (270)	20.00	8.00	2.00
COMMON PLAYER (1-270)	.05	.02	.00
COMMON HALF STICKER	.03	.01	.00
☐ 1 Flames/Canadiens action UL	.08	.03	.01
☐ 2 Flames/Canadiens action UR	.05	.02	.00
☐ 3 Flames/Canadiens action LL	.05	.02	.00
☐ 4 Flames/Canadiens action LR	.05	.02	.00
☐ 5 Al MacInnis Conn Smythe Trophy Winner	.20	.08	.02
☐ 6 Flames/Canadiens action UL	.05	.02	.00
☐ 7 Flames/Canadiens action UR	.05	.02	.00
☐ 8 Flames/Canadiens action LL	.05	.02	.00
☐ 9 Flames/Canadiens action LR	.05	.02	.00
☐ 10 Darren Pang (150)	.03	.01	.00
☐ 11 Troy Murray (151)	.05	.02	.00
☐ 12 Dirk Graham (152)	.05	.02	.00
☐ 13 Dave Manson (153)	.10	.04	.01
☐ 14 Doug Wilson (156)	.08	.03	.01
☐ 15 Steve Thomas (157)	.05	.02	.00
☐ 16 Denis Savard	.12	.05	.01
☐ 17 Steve Larmer	.12	.05	.01
☐ 18 Paul MacLean (158)	.05	.02	.00
☐ 19 Paul Cavallini (159)	.05	.02	.00
☐ 20 Cliff Ronning (160)	.20	.08	.02
☐ 21 Gaston Gingras (161)	.03	.01	.00
☐ 22 Brett Hull	.75	.30	.07
☐ 23 Peter Zezel	.08	.03	.01
☐ 24 Brian Benning (162)	.05	.02	.00
☐ 25 Tony Hrkac (163)	.03	.01	.00
☐ 26 Ken Linseman (164)	.03	.01	.00
☐ 27 Glen Wesley (165)	.08	.03	.01
☐ 28 Randy Burridge (166)	.05	.02	.00
☐ 29 Craig Janney (167)	.40	.16	.04
☐ 30 Andy Moog (170)	.12	.05	.01
☐ 31 Bob Joyce (171)	.05	.02	.00
☐ 32 Ray Bourque	.25	.10	.02
☐ 33 Cam Neely	.30	.12	.03
☐ 34 Sean Burke (174)	.12	.05	.01
☐ 35 Pat Elynuik (175)	.10	.04	.01
☐ 36 Tony Granato (176)	.10	.04	.01
☐ 37 Benoit Hogue (177)	.15	.06	.01
☐ 38 Craig Janney (180)	.40	.16	.04
☐ 39 Brian Leetch (181)	.75	.30	.07
☐ 40 Trevor Linden (184)	.60	.24	.06
☐ 41 Joe Sakic (185)	.75	.30	.07
☐ 42 Peter Sidorkiewicz (188)	.05	.02	.00
☐ 43 Dave Volek (189)	.08	.03	.01
☐ 44 Scott Young (190)	.05	.02	.00
☐ 45 Zarley Zalapski (191)	.10	.04	.01
☐ 46 Mats Naslund	.05	.02	.00
☐ 47 Bobby Smith	.08	.03	.01
☐ 48 Guy Carbonneau (194)	.05	.02	.00
☐ 49 Shayne Corson (195)	.08	.03	.01
☐ 50 Brian Hayward	.08	.03	.01
☐ 51 Stephane Richer	.15	.06	.01
☐ 52 Claude Lemieux (196)	.10	.04	.01
☐ 53 Russ Courtnall (197)	.08	.03	.01
☐ 54 Petr Svoboda (198)	.05	.02	.00
☐ 55 Larry Robinson (199)	.08	.03	.01
☐ 56 Chris Chelios	.15	.06	.01
☐ 57 Patrick Roy	.75	.30	.07
☐ 58 Bob Gainey (200)	.08	.03	.01
☐ 59 Mike McPhee (201)	.05	.02	.00
☐ 60 Barry Pederson	.05	.02	.00
☐ 61 Trevor Linden	1.00	.40	.10
☐ 62 Rich Sutter (204)	.05	.02	.00
☐ 63 Brian Bradley (205)	.12	.05	.01
☐ 64 Kirk McLean	.35	.14	.03
☐ 65 Paul Reinhart	.05	.02	.00
☐ 66 Robert Nordmark (206)	.03	.01	.00
☐ 67 Steve Bozek (207)	.03	.01	.00
☐ 68 Stan Smyl (208)	.05	.02	.00
☐ 69 Doug Lidster (209)	.03	.01	.00
☐ 70 Petri Skriko	.05	.02	.00
☐ 71 Tony Tanti	.05	.02	.00
☐ 72 Garth Butcher (210)	.08	.03	.01
☐ 73 Larry Melnyk (212)	.03	.01	.00
☐ 74 Kelly Miller (213)	.08	.03	.01
☐ 75 Dino Ciccarelli (214)	.08	.03	.01
☐ 76 Scott Stevens (215)	.10	.04	.01
☐ 77 Rod Langway (216)	.05	.02	.00
☐ 78 Dave Christian (219)	.05	.02	.00
☐ 79 Stephen Leach (220)	.08	.03	.01
☐ 80 Geoff Courtnall	.30	.12	.03
☐ 81 Mike Ridley	.08	.03	.01
☐ 82 Patrik Sundstrom (223)	.05	.02	.00
☐ 83 Kirk Muller (224)	.10	.04	.01
☐ 84 Tom Kurvers (225)	.03	.01	.00
☐ 85 Walt Poddubny (226)	.03	.01	.00
☐ 86 Sean Burke	.15	.06	.01
☐ 87 John MacLean	.15	.06	.01
☐ 88 Aaron Broten (229)	.03	.01	.00
☐ 89 Brendan Shanahan (230)	.35	.14	.03
☐ 90 Joe Mullen	.12	.05	.01
☐ 91 Brad McCrimmon	.08	.03	.01
☐ 92 Lanny McDonald (231)	.10	.04	.01
☐ 93 Rick Wamsley (232)	.05	.02	.00
☐ 94 Mike Vernon	.15	.06	.01
☐ 95 Al MacInnis	.20	.08	.02
☐ 96 Joel Otto (233)	.03	.01	.00
☐ 97 Jiri Hrdina (234)	.03	.01	.00
☐ 98 Gary Roberts (235)	.30	.12	.03
☐ 99 Jim Peplinski (236)	.03	.01	.00
☐ 100 Gary Suter	.10	.04	.01
☐ 101 Joe Nieuwendyk	.25	.10	.02
☐ 102 Colin Patterson (239)	.03	.01	.00
☐ 103 Doug Gilmour (240)	.30	.12	.03
☐ 104 Mike Bullard (241)	.03	.01	.00
☐ 105 Pelle Eklund (242)	.05	.02	.00
☐ 106 Brian Propp (245)	.05	.02	.00
☐ 107 Ron Sutter (246)	.05	.02	.00
☐ 108 Rick Tocchet (247)	.12	.05	.01
☐ 109 Mark Howe (248)	.08	.03	.01
☐ 110 Tim Kerr	.08	.03	.01
☐ 111 Ron Hextall	.12	.05	.01
☐ 112 Mikko Makela (249)	.03	.01	.00
☐ 113 Dave Volek (250)	.03	.01	.00
☐ 114 Gary Nylund (251)	.03	.01	.00
☐ 115 Brent Sutter (252)	.05	.02	.00
☐ 116 Derek King (255)	.20	.08	.02
☐ 117 Gerald Diduck (256)	.03	.01	.00
☐ 118 Bryan Trottier	.15	.06	.01
☐ 119 Pat LaFontaine	.35	.14	.03
☐ 120 Blues/Bruins action L	.05	.02	.00
☐ 121 Blues/Bruins action R	.05	.02	.00
☐ 122 Bruins/Rangers	.05	.02	.00

	action L			
☐	123 Bruins/Rangers	.05	.02	.00
	action R			
☐	124 Blackhawks action	.05	.02	.00
☐	125 Bruins/Canadiens	.12	.05	.01
	action (Ray Bourque)			
☐	126 Devils/Bruins action	.05	.02	.00
☐	127 Flames/Devils action	.05	.02	.00
☐	128 Canadiens/Flyers	.05	.02	.00
	action			
☐	129 Flyers/Oilers action	.05	.02	.00
☐	130 Canucks/Bruins	.05	.02	.00
	action L			
☐	131 Canucks/Bruins	.05	.02	.00
	action R			
☐	132 North Stars/Bruins	.05	.02	.00
	action L			
☐	133 North Stars/Bruins	.05	.02	.00
	action R			
☐	134 Dale Hawerchuk	.15	.06	.01
☐	135 Andrew McBain	.05	.02	.00
☐	136 Iain Duncan (257)	.03	.01	.00
☐	137 Eldon Reddick (258)	.08	.03	.01
☐	138 Brent Ashton	.05	.02	.00
☐	139 Dave Ellett	.05	.02	.00
☐	140 Jim Kyte (259)	.03	.01	.00
☐	141 Doug Smail (260)	.05	.02	.00
☐	142 Pat Elynuik (263)	.10	.04	.01
☐	143 Randy Carlyle (264)	.05	.02	.00
☐	144 Thomas Steen	.08	.03	.01
☐	145 Hannu Jarvenpaa	.05	.02	.00
☐	146 Peter Taglianetti	.03	.01	.00
	(265)			
☐	147 Laurie Boschman (266)	.03	.01	.00
☐	148 Luc Robitaille (267)	.25	.10	.02
☐	149 Kelly Hrudey (268)	.08	.03	.01
☐	150 Steve Duchesne (10)	.08	.03	.01
☐	151 Dave Taylor (11)	.05	.02	.00
☐	152 Steve Kasper (12)	.05	.02	.00
☐	153 Mike Krushelnyski	.05	.02	.00
	(13)			
☐	154 Wayne Gretzky	1.00	.40	.10
☐	155 Bernie Nicholls	.15	.06	.01
☐	156 Chris Chelios (14)	.10	.04	.01
☐	157 Gerard Gallant (15)	.05	.02	.00
☐	158 Mario Lemieux (18)	.50	.20	.05
☐	159 Al MacInnis (19)	.12	.05	.01
☐	160 Joe Mullen (20)	.08	.03	.01
☐	161 Patrick Roy (21)	.35	.14	.03
☐	162 Ray Bourque (24)	.15	.06	.01
☐	163 Rob Brown (25)	.05	.02	.00
☐	164 Geoff Courtnall (26)	.10	.04	.01
☐	165 Steve Duchesne (27)	.08	.03	.01
☐	166 Wayne Gretzky (28)	.50	.20	.05
☐	167 Mike Vernon (29)	.10	.04	.01
☐	168 Gary Leeman	.05	.02	.00
☐	169 Allan Bester	.05	.02	.00
☐	170 David Reid (30)	.05	.02	.00
☐	171 Craig Laughlin (31)	.03	.01	.00
☐	172 Ed Olczyk (31)	.08	.03	.01
☐	173 Tom Fergus	.05	.02	.00
☐	174 Mark Osborne (34)	.03	.01	.00
☐	175 Brad Marsh (35)	.05	.02	.00
☐	176 Daniel Marois (36)	.05	.02	.00
☐	177 Dan Daoust (37)	.03	.01	.00
☐	178 Al Iafrate	.15	.06	.01
☐	179 Vincent Damphousse	.20	.08	.02
☐	180 Chris Kotsopoulos	.03	.01	.00
	(38)			
☐	181 Derek Laxdal (39)	.03	.01	.00
☐	182 Peter Stastny	.15	.06	.01
☐	183 Paul Gillis	.05	.02	.00
☐	184 Jeff Jackson (40)	.03	.01	.00
☐	185 Mario Marois (41)	.03	.01	.00
☐	186 Michel Goulet	.12	.05	.01
☐	187 Joe Sakic	1.50	.60	.15
☐	188 Bob Mason (42)	.03	.01	.00
☐	189 Marc Fortier (43)	.03	.01	.00
☐	190 Robert Picard (44)	.03	.01	.00
☐	191 Steven Finn (45)	.03	.01	.00
☐	192 Iiro Jarvi	.05	.02	.00
☐	193 Jeff Brown	.12	.05	.01
☐	194 Gaetan Duchesne (48)	.03	.01	.00
☐	195 Randy Moller (49)	.03	.01	.00
☐	196 Mike Gartner (52)	.10	.04	.01
☐	197 Jon Casey (53)	.20	.08	.02
☐	198 Marc Habscheid (54)	.03	.01	.00
☐	199 Larry Murphy (55)	.08	.03	.01
☐	200 Brian Bellows (58)	.05	.02	.00
☐	201 Dave Archibald (59)	.03	.01	.00
☐	202 Neal Broten	.05	.02	.00
☐	203 Dave Gagner	.25	.10	.02
☐	204 Vezina Trophy (62)	.03	.01	.00
☐	205 Jennings Trophy (63)	.03	.01	.00

☐	206 Selke Trophy (66)	.03	.01	.00
☐	207 Masterton Trophy (67)	.03	.01	.00
☐	208 Mario Lemieux (68)	.50	.20	.05
	Ross Trophy Winner			
☐	209 Wayne Gretzky (69)	.60	.24	.06
	Hart Trophy Winner			
☐	210 Patrick Roy (72)	.35	.14	.03
	Vezina Trophy Winner			
☐	211 Patrick Roy and	.20	.08	.02
	Brian Hayward			
	Jennings Trophy Winners			
☐	212 Chris Chelios (73)	.10	.04	.01
	Norris Trophy Winner			
☐	213 Guy Carbonneau (74)	.05	.02	.00
	Selke Trophy Winner			
☐	214 Joe Mullen (75)	.05	.02	.00
	Lady Byng Trophy Winner			
☐	215 Brian Leetch (76)	.40	.16	.04
	Calder Trophy Winner			
☐	216 Tim Kerr (77)	.03	.01	.00
	Masterton Trophy Winner			
☐	217 Craig Simpson	.10	.04	.01
☐	218 Glenn Anderson	.10	.04	.01
☐	219 Esa Tikkanen (78)	.08	.03	.01
☐	220 Charlie Huddy (79)	.05	.02	.00
☐	221 Jari Kurri	.15	.06	.01
☐	222 Jimmy Carson	.08	.03	.01
☐	223 Steve Smith (82)	.08	.03	.01
☐	224 Kevin Lowe (83)	.08	.03	.01
☐	225 Chris Joseph (84)	.03	.01	.00
☐	226 Craig MacTavish (85)	.05	.02	.00
☐	227 Mark Messier	.40	.16	.04
☐	228 Grant Fuhr	.15	.06	.01
☐	229 Craig Muni (88)	.03	.01	.00
☐	230 Bill Ranford (89)	.35	.14	.03
☐	231 John Cullen (92)	.20	.08	.02
☐	232 Zarley Zalapski (93)	.08	.03	.01
☐	233 Bob Errey (96)	.03	.01	.00
☐	234 Dan Quinn (97)	.03	.01	.00
☐	235 Tom Barrasso (98)	.08	.03	.01
☐	236 Rob Brown (99)	.05	.02	.00
☐	237 Paul Coffey	.20	.08	.02
☐	238 Mario Lemieux	1.00	.40	.10
☐	239 Carey Wilson (102)	.03	.01	.00
☐	240 Brian Leetch (103)	.75	.30	.07
☐	241 Tony Granato (104)	.10	.04	.01
☐	242 James Patrick (105)	.05	.02	.00
☐	243 Brian Mullen	.08	.03	.01
☐	244 Tomas Sandstrom	.10	.04	.01
☐	245 Guy Lafleur (106)	.15	.06	.01
☐	246 John Vanbiesbrouck	.10	.04	.01
	(107)			
☐	247 Bernie Federko (108)	.05	.02	.00
☐	248 Greg Stefan (109)	.05	.02	.00
☐	249 Mike O'Connell (112)	.03	.01	.00
☐	250 Dave Barr (113)	.03	.01	.00
☐	251 Lee Norwood (114)	.03	.01	.00
☐	252 Shawn Burr (115)	.03	.01	.00
☐	253 Gerard Gallant	.05	.02	.00
☐	254 Steve Yzerman	.40	.16	.04
☐	255 Christian Ruuttu	.03	.01	.00
	(116)			
☐	256 Rick Vaive (117)	.03	.01	.00
☐	257 Doug Bodger (136)	.03	.01	.00
☐	258 Dave Andreychuk (137)	.10	.04	.01
☐	259 Ray Sheppard (140)	.08	.03	.01
☐	260 Mike Foligno (141)	.03	.01	.00
☐	261 Phil Housley	.12	.05	.01
☐	262 Pierre Turgeon	.50	.20	.05
☐	263 Ray Ferraro (142)	.08	.03	.01
☐	264 Scott Young (143)	.05	.02	.00
☐	265 Dave Babych (146)	.05	.02	.00
☐	266 Paul MacDermid (147)	.03	.01	.00
☐	267 Mike Liut (148)	.05	.02	.00
☐	268 Dave Tippett (149)	.03	.01	.00
☐	269 Ron Francis	.10	.04	.01
☐	270 Kevin Dineen	.08	.03	.01
☐	xx Sticker Album	1.50	.60	.15

1979 Panini Stickers

This "global" hockey set was produced by Figurine Panini and printed in Italy. Each sticker measures approximately 1 15/16" by 2 3/4". The set also has an album available. This set is complete with 400 numbered small cards featuring hockey players from all over the world. The numbering

within the cards in the set is organized by topical subgroups, i.e., Referee Signals (1-19), Action Pairs (20-39), National Team Logos (40-47), Four Part Photo (48-51), Canadien Players (52-69), Four Part Photo (70-73), Czech Players (74-91), Four Part Photo (92-95), FDR Players (96-113), Four Part Photo (114-117), Poland Players (118-135), Four Part Photo (136-139), USSR Players (140-157), Four Part Photo (158-161), Finland Players (162-179), Four Part Photo (180-183), Sweden Players (184-201), Four Part Photo (202-205), USA Players (206-223), Action Pairs (225-238), National Team Logos (239-246), DDR (247-255), Switzerland (256-264), Hungary (265-273), Netherlands (274-282), Japan (283-291), Norway (292-300), Austria (301-309), Romania (310-318), Action Pairs (320-328), National Team Logos (329-336), Belgium (337-344), Bulgaria (345-352), China (353-360), Denmark (361-368), Spain (369-376), France (377-384), Italy (385-392), and Yugoslavia (393-400).

	NRMT	VG-E	GOOD
COMPLETE SET (400)	100.00	40.00	10.00
COMMON CARD (1-400)	.35	.14	.03

		NRMT	VG-E	GOOD
☐ 1	Goal Disallowed	.50	.20	.05
☐ 2	Butt-Ending	.35	.14	.03
☐ 3	Slow Whistle	.35	.14	.03
☐ 4	Hooking	.35	.14	.03
☐ 5	Charging	.35	.14	.03
☐ 6	Misconduct Penalty	.35	.14	.03
☐ 7	Holding	.35	.14	.03
☐ 8	High-Sticking	.35	.14	.03
☐ 9	Tripping	.35	.14	.03
☐ 10	Cross-Checking	.35	.14	.03
☐ 11	Elbowing	.35	.14	.03
☐ 12	Icing (I)	.35	.14	.03
☐ 13	Icing (II)	.35	.14	.03
☐ 14	Boarding	.35	.14	.03
☐ 15	Kneeing	.35	.14	.03
☐ 16	Slashing	.35	.14	.03
☐ 17	Excessive Roughness	.35	.14	.03
☐ 18	Spearing	.35	.14	.03
☐ 19	Interference	.35	.14	.03
☐ 20	Poster	.35	.14	.03
☐ 21	Czech.-USSR 6-4	.50	.20	.05
☐ 22	Czech.-USSR 6-4	.50	.20	.05
☐ 23	USSR-Czech. 3-1	.50	.20	.05
☐ 24	USSR-Czech. 3-1	.50	.20	.05
☐ 25	USSR-Czech. 3-1	.50	.20	.05
☐ 26	USSR-Czech. 3-1	.50	.20	.05
☐ 27	Can-Sweden 3-2	.50	.20	.05
☐ 28	Can-Sweden 3-2	.50	.20	.05
☐ 29	USSR-Canada 5-1	.75	.30	.07
☐ 30	USSR-Canada 5-1	.75	.30	.07
☐ 31	Czech.-Canada 3-2	.50	.20	.05
☐ 32	Czech.-Canada 3-2	.50	.20	.05
☐ 33	USSR-Sweden 7-1	.50	.20	.05
☐ 34	USSR-Sweden 7-1	.50	.20	.05
☐ 35	USA-Finland 4-3	.50	.20	.05
☐ 36	USA-Finland 4-3	.50	.20	.05
☐ 37	Finland-DDR 7-2	.35	.14	.03
☐ 38	DDR-BRD 0-0	.35	.14	.03
☐ 39	DDR-BRD 0-0	.35	.14	.03
☐ 40	Czechoslovakia	.35	.14	.03
☐ 41	Poland	.35	.14	.03
☐ 42	USSR	1.25	.50	.12
☐ 43	USA	1.25	.50	.12
☐ 44	Canada	1.25	.50	.12
☐ 45	Deutschland-BRD	.35	.14	.03
☐ 46	Finland	.35	.14	.03
☐ 47	Sweden	.50	.20	.05
☐ 48	Canada Team Picture (upper left)	.75	.30	.07
☐ 49	Canada Team Picture (upper right)	.75	.30	.07
☐ 50	Canada Team Picture (lower left)	.75	.30	.07
☐ 51	Canada Team Picture (lower right)	.75	.30	.07
☐ 52	Denis Herron	.75	.30	.07
☐ 53	Dan Bouchard	.75	.30	.07
☐ 54	Rick Hampton	.50	.20	.05
☐ 55	Robert Picard	.50	.20	.05
☐ 56	Brad Maxwell	.50	.20	.05
☐ 57	David Shand	.50	.20	.05
☐ 58	Dennis Kearns	.50	.20	.05
☐ 59	Tom Lysiak	.75	.30	.07
☐ 60	Dennis Maruk	1.00	.40	.10
☐ 61	Marcel Dionne	6.00	2.40	.60
☐ 62	Guy Charron	.50	.20	.05
☐ 63	Glen Sharpley	.50	.20	.05
☐ 64	Jean Pronovost	.75	.30	.07
☐ 65	Don Lever	.50	.20	.05
☐ 66	Bob MacMillan	.75	.30	.07
☐ 67	Wilf Paiement	.75	.30	.07
☐ 68	Pat Hickey	.75	.30	.07
☐ 69	Mike Murphy	.50	.20	.05
☐ 70	Czechoslovakia Team Picture (upper left)	.50	.20	.05
☐ 71	Czechoslovakia Team Picture (upper right)	.50	.20	.05
☐ 72	Czechoslovakia Team Picture (lower left)	.50	.20	.05
☐ 73	Czechoslovakia Team Picture (lower right)	.50	.20	.05
☐ 74	Jiri Holecek	.75	.30	.07
☐ 75	Jiri Crha	.75	.30	.07
☐ 76	Jiri Bubla	.75	.30	.07
☐ 77	Milan Kajki	.35	.14	.03
☐ 78	Miroslav Dvorak	.50	.20	.05
☐ 79	Milan Chalupa	.50	.20	.05
☐ 80	Frantisek Kaberle	.35	.14	.03
☐ 81	Jan Zajicek	.35	.14	.03
☐ 82	Jiri Novak	.35	.14	.03
☐ 83	Ivan Hlinka	.50	.20	.05
☐ 84	Peter Stastny	7.50	3.00	.75
☐ 85	Milan Novy	.50	.20	.05
☐ 86	Vladimir Martinec	.35	.14	.03
☐ 87	Jaroslav Pouzar	.50	.20	.05
☐ 88	Pavel Richter	.35	.14	.03
☐ 89	Bohuslav Ebermann	.35	.14	.03
☐ 90	Marian Stastny	1.00	.40	.10
☐ 91	Frantisek Cernick	.35	.14	.03
☐ 92	FDR Team Picture (upper left)	.35	.14	.03
☐ 93	FDR Team Picture (upper right)	.35	.14	.03
☐ 94	FDR Team Picture (lower left)	.35	.14	.03
☐ 95	FDR Team Picture (lower right)	.35	.14	.03
☐ 96	Erich Weishaupt	.35	.14	.03
☐ 97	Bernh. Engelbrect	.35	.14	.03
☐ 98	Ignaz Berndaner	.35	.14	.03
☐ 99	Robert Murray	.35	.14	.03
☐ 100	Udo Kiessling	.50	.20	.05
☐ 101	Klaus Auhuber	.35	.14	.03
☐ 102	Horst Kretschmer	.35	.14	.03
☐ 103	Erich Kuhnhackl	.50	.20	.05
☐ 104	Martin Wild	.35	.14	.03
☐ 105	Lorenz Funk	.35	.14	.03
☐ 106	M. Hinterstocker	.35	.14	.03
☐ 107	Alois Schloder	.35	.14	.03
☐ 108	Rainer Philipp	.35	.14	.03
☐ 109	H. Hinterstocker	.35	.14	.03
☐ 110	Franz Reindl	.35	.14	.03
☐ 111	Walter Koberle	.50	.20	.05
☐ 112	Johann Zach	.35	.14	.03
☐ 113	Marcus Kuhl	.35	.14	.03
☐ 114	Poland Team Picture (upper left)	.35	.14	.03
☐ 115	Poland Team Picture (upper right)	.35	.14	.03
☐ 116	Poland Team Picture (lower left)	.35	.14	.03
☐ 117	Poland Team Picture	.35	.14	.03

(lower right)

☐ 118	Henryk Wojtynek	.35	.14	.03
☐ 119	T. Slowakiewicz	.35	.14	.03
☐ 120	Henryk Janiszewski	.50	.20	.05
☐ 121	Henryk Gruth	.35	.14	.03
☐ 122	Andr. Slowakiewicz	.35	.14	.03
☐ 123	Andrzej Eskrzycki	.35	.14	.03
☐ 124	Jerzy Potz	.50	.20	.05
☐ 125	Marek Marcinczak	.35	.14	.03
☐ 126	Jozef Batkiewicz	.35	.14	.03
☐ 127	Stefan Chowaniec	.35	.14	.03
☐ 128	Andrzej Malysiak	.35	.14	.03
☐ 129	Walenty Zietara	.35	.14	.03
☐ 130	Henryk Pytel	.35	.14	.03
☐ 131	Andrezei Zabawa	.35	.14	.03
☐ 133	Tadeusz Oboj	.35	.14	.03
☐ 134	Jan Piecko	.35	.14	.03
☐ 135	Leszek Tokarz	.35	.14	.03
☐ 136	USSR Team Picture	.75	.30	.07

(upper left)

| ☐ 137 | USSR Team Picture | .75 | .30 | .07 |

(upper right)

| ☐ 138 | USSR Team Picture | .75 | .30 | .07 |

(lower left)

| ☐ 139 | USSR Team Picture | .75 | .30 | .07 |

(lower right)

☐ 140	Vladislav Tretiak	7.50	3.00	.75
☐ 141	Viacheslav Fetisov	4.00	1.60	.40
☐ 142	Vladimir Lutchenko	1.00	.40	.10
☐ 143	Vasilij Pervukhin	.75	.30	.07
☐ 144	Valeri Vasiliev	2.00	.80	.20
☐ 145	Gennady Tsygankov	1.00	.40	.10
☐ 146	Juri Fedorov	.75	.30	.07
☐ 147	Vladimir Petrov	2.00	.80	.20
☐ 148	Vladimir Golkov	1.00	.40	.10
☐ 149	Victor Zhluktov	1.00	.40	.10
☐ 150	Boris Mikhailov	2.00	.80	.20
☐ 151	Valeri Kharlamov	5.00	2.00	.50
☐ 152	Helmut Balderis	1.25	.50	.12
☐ 153	Sergej Kapustin	1.00	.40	.10
☐ 154	Alexander Golikov	.75	.30	.07
☐ 155	Alexander Maltsev	3.00	1.20	.30
☐ 156	Yuri Lebedev	1.00	.40	.10
☐ 157	Sergei Makarov	6.00	2.40	.60
☐ 158	Finland	.35	.14	.03

Team Picture
(upper left)

| ☐ 159 | Finland | .35 | .14 | .03 |

Team Picture
(upper right)

| ☐ 160 | Finland | .35 | .14 | .03 |

Team Picture
(lower left)

| ☐ 161 | Finland | .35 | .14 | .03 |

Team Picture
(lower right)

☐ 162	Urpo Ylonen	.35	.14	.03
☐ 163	Antero Kivela	.35	.14	.03
☐ 164	Pekka Rautakallio	1.00	.40	.10
☐ 165	Timo Nummelin	.35	.14	.03
☐ 166	Risto Siltanen	1.00	.40	.10
☐ 167	Pekka Marjamaki	.35	.14	.03
☐ 168	Tapio Levo	.35	.14	.03
☐ 169	Lasse Litma	.35	.14	.03
☐ 170	Esa Peitonen	.35	.14	.03
☐ 171	Martti Jarkko	.35	.14	.03
☐ 172	Matti Hagman	.50	.20	.05
☐ 173	Seppo Repo	.35	.14	.03
☐ 174	Pertti Korvulahti	.35	.14	.03
☐ 175	Seppo Ahokainen	.35	.14	.03
☐ 176	Juhani Tamminen	.35	.14	.03
☐ 177	Jukko Provari	.35	.14	.03
☐ 178	Mikko Leinonen	.75	.30	.07
☐ 179	Matti Rautiainen	.35	.14	.03
☐ 180	Sweden Team Picture	.50	.20	.05

(upper left)

| ☐ 181 | Sweden Team Picture | .50 | .20 | .05 |

(upper right)

| ☐ 182 | Sweden Team Picture | .50 | .20 | .05 |

(lower left)

| ☐ 183 | Sweden Team Picture | .50 | .20 | .05 |

(lower right)

☐ 184	Goran Hogasta	.35	.14	.03
☐ 185	Hardy Astrom	.75	.30	.07
☐ 186	Stig Ostling	.35	.14	.03
☐ 187	Ulf Weinstock	.35	.14	.03
☐ 188	Mats Waltin	.35	.14	.03
☐ 189	Stig Salming	.50	.20	.05
☐ 190	Lars Zetterstrom	.35	.14	.03
☐ 191	Lars Lindgren	.50	.20	.05
☐ 192	Leif Holmgren	.35	.14	.03
☐ 193	Roland Ericksson	.35	.14	.03
☐ 194	Rolf Edberg	.35	.14	.03
☐ 195	Per-Olov Brasar	.50	.20	.05

☐ 196	Mats Ahlberg	.35	.14	.03
☐ 197	Bengt Lundholm	.50	.20	.05
☐ 198	Lars Gunnar Lundberg	.35	.14	.03
☐ 199	Nils-Olov Olsson	.35	.14	.03
☐ 200	Kent-Erik Anderson	.75	.30	.07
☐ 201	Thomas Gradin	1.25	.50	.12
☐ 202	USA Team Picture	.75	.30	.07

(upper left)

| ☐ 203 | USA Team Picture | .75 | .30 | .07 |

(upper right)

| ☐ 204 | USA Team Picture | .75 | .30 | .07 |

(lower left)

| ☐ 205 | USA Team Picture | .75 | .30 | .07 |

(lower right)

☐ 206	Peter Lopresti	.75	.30	.07
☐ 207	Jim Warden	.50	.20	.05
☐ 208	Dick Lamby	.50	.20	.05
☐ 209	Craig Norwich	.50	.20	.05
☐ 210	Glen Patrick	.50	.20	.05
☐ 211	Patrick Westrum	.50	.20	.05
☐ 212	Don Jackson	.50	.20	.05
☐ 213	Mark Johnson	1.00	.40	.10
☐ 214	Curt Bennett	.50	.20	.05
☐ 215	Dave Debol	.50	.20	.05
☐ 216	Bob Collyard	.50	.20	.05
☐ 217	Mike Fidler	.50	.20	.05
☐ 218	Tom Younghans	.50	.20	.05
☐ 219	Harvey Bennett	.50	.20	.05
☐ 220	Steve Jensen	.75	.30	.07
☐ 221	Jim Warner	.50	.20	.05
☐ 222	Mike Eaves	.50	.20	.05
☐ 223	William Gilligan	.50	.20	.05
☐ 224	Poster	.50	.20	.05
☐ 225	Poland-Rom. 8-6	.35	.14	.03
☐ 226	Poland-Rom. 8-6	.35	.14	.03
☐ 227	Poland-Rom. 8-6	.35	.14	.03
☐ 228	Poland-Rom. 8-6	.35	.14	.03
☐ 229	Poland-Hun. 7-2	.35	.14	.03
☐ 230	Poland-Hun. 7-2	.35	.14	.03
☐ 231	Japan-Yug. 6-1	.35	.14	.03
☐ 232	Japan-Yug. 6-1	.35	.14	.03
☐ 233	Italy-Yug. 6-1	.35	.14	.03
☐ 234	Italy-Yug. 6-1	.35	.14	.03
☐ 235	Rom.-Italy 5-5	.35	.14	.03
☐ 236	Rom.-Italy 5-5	.35	.14	.03
☐ 237	Poland	.35	.14	.03
☐ 238	Poland	.35	.14	.03
☐ 239	Deutschland-DDR	.35	.14	.03
☐ 240	Hungary	.35	.14	.03
☐ 241	Netherland	.35	.14	.03
☐ 242	Romania	.35	.14	.03
☐ 243	Switzerland	.35	.14	.03
☐ 244	Japan	.35	.14	.03
☐ 245	Norway	.35	.14	.03
☐ 246	Austria	.35	.14	.03
☐ 247	DDR	.35	.14	.03
☐ 248	DDR	.35	.14	.03
☐ 249	Herzig and Kraske	.35	.14	.03
☐ 250	Simon and Peters	.35	.14	.03
☐ 251	Frenzel and Lempio	.35	.14	.03
☐ 252	Fengler and Slapke	.35	.14	.03
☐ 253	Patschinski and	.35	.14	.03

Bielas 1

| ☐ 254 | Peters and Scholz | .35 | .14 | .03 |
| ☐ 255 | Bogelsack and | .35 | .14 | .03 |

Stasche

☐ 256	Switzerland	.35	.14	.03
☐ 257	Switzerland	.35	.14	.03
☐ 258	Grubauer and Anken	.35	.14	.03
☐ 259	Zenhausern and	.35	.14	.03

Meyer

| ☐ 260 | Kolliker and | .35 | .14 | .03 |

Locher

| ☐ 261 | Mattli and Conte | .35 | .14 | .03 |
| ☐ 262 | Holzer and | .35 | .14 | .03 |

Dellsberger

| ☐ 263 | Horisberger and | .35 | .14 | .03 |

Rossetti

☐ 264	Berger and Schmid	.35	.14	.03
☐ 265	Hungary	.35	.14	.03
☐ 266	Hungary	.35	.14	.03
☐ 267	Balagh and Farkas	.35	.14	.03
☐ 268	Kovacs and Hajzer	.35	.14	.03
☐ 269	Flora and Kereszty	.35	.14	.03
☐ 270	Palla and Meszoly	.35	.14	.03
☐ 271	Menyhart and	.35	.14	.03

Havran

☐ 272	Poth and Muhr	.35	.14	.03
☐ 273	Buzas and Pek	.35	.14	.03
☐ 274	Netherlands	.35	.14	.03
☐ 275	Netherlands	.35	.14	.03
☐ 276	Van Bilsen and	.35	.14	.03

Krikke

☐ 277 Van Soldt and...................... .35 .14 .03
    Peternousek
☐ 278 Kolijn and Van Den.............. .35 .14 .03
    Broek
☐ 279 Van Wieren and.................. .35 .14 .03
    Toren
☐ 280 Van Onlangs and................ .35 .14 .03
    Schaffer
☐ 281 Janssen and Van Der .... .35 .14 .03
    Griendt
☐ 282 De Heer and .... .35 .14 .03
    Koopmans
☐ 283 Japan.................................. .35 .14 .03
☐ 284 Japan.................................. .35 .14 .03
☐ 285 Iwamoto and Misaw............ .35 .14 .03
☐ 286 Ito and Tonozaki................. .35 .14 .03
☐ 287 Hori and Nakayama............ .35 .14 .03
☐ 288 Tanaka and Kyoya .... .35 .14 .03
☐ 289 Kawamura and .... .35 .14 .03
    Hoshino
☐ 290 Misawa and Sakurai........... .35 .14 .03
☐ 291 Honma and Hanzawa .... .35 .14 .03
☐ 292 Norway................................ .35 .14 .03
☐ 293 Norway................................ .35 .14 .03
☐ 294 Walberg and....................... .35 .14 .03
    Goldstein
☐ 295 Martinsen and .... .35 .14 .03
    Molberg
☐ 296 Nilsen and Erevik .... .35 .14 .03
☐ 297 Lien and Roymark............... .35 .14 .03
☐ 298 Eriksen and .... .35 .14 .03
    Ovstedal
☐ 299 Johansen and..................... .35 .14 .03
    Haraldsen
☐ 300 Stethereng and .... .35 .14 .03
    Throrkildsen
☐ 301 Austria .... .35 .14 .03
☐ 302 Austria .... .35 .14 .03
☐ 303 Schilcherl and .... .35 .14 .03
    Prohaska
☐ 304 Hyytaienen and .... .35 .14 .03
    Russ
☐ 305 Staribacher and.................. .35 .14 .03
    Schneider
☐ 306 Kotnauer and Pok............... .35 .14 .03
☐ 307 Sadjina and Konig .... .35 .14 .03
☐ 308 Mortl and Pepeunig............ .35 .14 .03
☐ 309 Schilchner and .... .35 .14 .03
    Haiszan
☐ 310 Romania.............................. .35 .14 .03
☐ 311 Romania.............................. .35 .14 .03
☐ 312 Hutan and Netedu .... .35 .14 .03
☐ 313 Antal and Gall..................... .35 .14 .03
☐ 314 Lustinian and .... .35 .14 .03
    Lonita
☐ 315 Hutanu and Halauca .... .35 .14 .03
☐ 316 Tureanu and Axinte .... .35 .14 .03
☐ 317 Nagy and Costea .... .35 .14 .03
☐ 318 Nistor and Olenici............... .35 .14 .03
☐ 319 Poster .... .35 .14 .03
☐ 320 Den.-Net 3-3........................ .35 .14 .03
☐ 321 Den.-Net 3-3........................ .35 .14 .03
☐ 322 Net.-Spain 19-0................... .35 .14 .03
☐ 323 Net.-Spain 19-0................... .35 .14 .03
☐ 324 Aus.-Den 7-4....................... .35 .14 .03
☐ 325 Aus.-Den 7-4....................... .35 .14 .03
☐ 326 Net.-Bul. 8-0........................ .35 .14 .03
☐ 327 China-Den. 3-2.................... .35 .14 .03
☐ 328 China-France 8-4................. .35 .14 .03
☐ 329 Bulgaria.............................. .35 .14 .03
☐ 330 France .... .35 .14 .03
☐ 331 Italy.................................... .35 .14 .03
☐ 332 Yugoslavia .... .35 .14 .03
☐ 333 Belgium............................... .35 .14 .03
☐ 334 China.................................. .35 .14 .03
☐ 335 Denmark.............................. .35 .14 .03
☐ 336 Spain.................................. .35 .14 .03
☐ 337 Belgium............................... .35 .14 .03
☐ 338 Belgium............................... .35 .14 .03
☐ 339 Smeets and Lauwers........... .35 .14 .03
☐ 340 Adriaensen and .... .35 .14 .03
    Zwikel
☐ 341 Cuvelier and .... .35 .14 .03
    Sarazin
☐ 342 Vermeulen and.................... .35 .14 .03
    Voskertian
☐ 343 Verschraegen and .... .35 .14 .03
    Arnould
☐ 344 Lejeune and Langh.............. .35 .14 .03
☐ 345 Bulgaria.............................. .35 .14 .03
☐ 346 Bulgaria.............................. .35 .14 .03
☐ 347 Iliev and Lazarov .... .35 .14 .03
☐ 348 Iliev and .... .35 .14 .03
    Krastinov
☐ 349 Hristov and Petrov .... .35 .14 .03
☐ 350 Atanasov and Nenov .... .35 .14 .03
☐ 351 Todorov and Stoilov........... .35 .14 .03
☐ 352 Guerasimov and.................. .35 .14 .03
    Batchvarov
☐ 353 China.................................. .35 .14 .03
☐ 354 China.................................. .35 .14 .03
☐ 355 Ting Wen and...................... .35 .14 .03
    Yung Ke
☐ 356 Ke and Shao Tang .... .35 .14 .03
☐ 357 Ta Chun and........................ .35 .14 .03
    Ung Sheng
☐ 358 Hsi Kiang and..................... .35 .14 .03
    Chang Shun
☐ 359 Cheng Hsin and .... .35 .14 .03
    Te Hsi
☐ 360 Shu Ching and .... .35 .14 .03
    Sheng Wen
☐ 361 Denmark.............................. .35 .14 .03
☐ 362 Denmark.............................. .35 .14 .03
☐ 363 Hansen and Holten.............. .35 .14 .03
    Moller
☐ 364 Andersen and .... .35 .14 .03
    Pedersen
☐ 365 Henriksen and .... .35 .14 .03
    Hviid
☐ 366 Nielsen and Thomsen......... .35 .14 .03
☐ 367 Nielsen and Kahl .... .35 .14 .03
☐ 368 Jensen and......................... .35 .14 .03
    Gjerding
☐ 369 Spain.................................. .35 .14 .03
☐ 370 Spain.................................. .35 .14 .03
☐ 371 Estrada and .... .35 .14 .03
    Lizarraga
☐ 372 Gonzalez and...................... .35 .14 .03
    Munitiz
☐ 373 Marin and Aguado............... .35 .14 .03
☐ 374 Raventos and .... .35 .14 .03
    Encinas
☐ 375 Capillas and....................... .35 .14 .03
    Sarazirar
☐ 376 Labayen and Plaza .... .35 .14 .03
☐ 377 France .... .35 .14 .03
☐ 378 France .... .35 .14 .03
☐ 379 Maric and .... .35 .14 .03
    Del Monaco
☐ 380 Oprandi and Combe .... .35 .14 .03
☐ 381 Allard and........................... .35 .14 .03
    Le Blond
☐ 382 Vassieux and Rey................ .35 .14 .03
☐ 383 Galiay and .... .35 .14 .03
    Le Blond
☐ 384 Vinard and.......................... .35 .14 .03
    Smaniotto
☐ 385 Italy.................................... .35 .14 .03
☐ 386 Italy.................................... .35 .14 .03
☐ 387 Tigliani and Gasser............. .35 .14 .03
☐ 388 Kostner and........................ .35 .14 .03
    Pasqualotto
☐ 389 Lacedelli and Polloni .... .35 .14 .03
☐ 390 Insam and De Toni.............. .35 .14 .03
☐ 391 Strohmaier and .... .35 .14 .03
    Kasslatter
☐ 392 De Marchi and .... .35 .14 .03
    Pugliese
☐ 393 Yugoslavia .... .35 .14 .03
☐ 394 Yugoslavia .... .35 .14 .03
☐ 395 Zbontar and Scap............... .35 .14 .03
☐ 396 Kumar and Kosir .... .35 .14 .03
☐ 397 Kavec and Smolej............... .35 .14 .03
☐ 398 Kafner and Lepsa .... .35 .14 .03
☐ 399 Poljansek and Kosir .... .35 .14 .03
☐ 400 Klemenc and Jan................ .50 .20 .05
☐ xx Sticker Album.................. 20.00 8.00 2.00

1987-88 Panini Stickers

This set of 396 hockey stickers was produced and distributed by Panini. The full-color stickers are very attractive. The sticker number is only on the backing of the sticker. The stickers measure approximately 2 1/8" by 2 11/16". The team logos are foil stickers. On the inside back cover of the sticker album the company offered (via direct mail-order) up to 30 different stickers of your choice for either ten cents each or in trade one-for-one for your

unwanted extra stickers plus 1.00 for postage and handling; this is one reason why the values of the most popular players in these sticker sets are somewhat depressed compared to traditional card set prices.

		MINT	EXC	G-VG
	COMPLETE SET (396)	35.00	14.00	3.50
	COMMON PLAYER (1-396)	.05	.02	.00
☐ 1	Stanley Cup	.10	.04	.01
☐ 2	Bruins Action	.05	.02	.00
☐ 3	Bruins Emblem	.05	.02	.00
☐ 4	Doug Keans	.05	.02	.00
☐ 5	Bill Ranford	1.00	.40	.10
☐ 6	Ray Bourque	.30	.12	.03
☐ 7	Reed Larson	.05	.02	.00
☐ 8	Mike Milbury	.08	.03	.01
☐ 9	Michael Thelven	.05	.02	.00
☐ 10	Cam Neely	.35	.14	.03
☐ 11	Charlie Simmer	.08	.03	.01
☐ 12	Rick Middleton	.08	.03	.01
☐ 13	Tom McCarthy	.05	.02	.00
☐ 14	Keith Crowder	.05	.02	.00
☐ 15	Steve Kasper	.05	.02	.00
☐ 16	Ken Linseman	.05	.02	.00
☐ 17	Dwight Foster	.05	.02	.00
☐ 18	Jay Miller	.05	.02	.00
☐ 19	Sabres Action	.05	.02	.00
☐ 20	Sabres Emblem	.05	.02	.00
☐ 21	Jacques Cloutier	.08	.03	.01
☐ 22	Tom Barrasso	.20	.08	.02
☐ 23	Daren Puppa	.25	.10	.02
☐ 24	Phil Housley	.25	.10	.02
☐ 25	Mike Ramsey	.05	.02	.00
☐ 26	Bill Hajt	.05	.02	.00
☐ 27	Dave Andreychuk	.35	.14	.03
☐ 28	Christian Ruuttu	.10	.04	.01
☐ 29	Mike Foligno	.05	.02	.00
☐ 30	John Tucker	.05	.02	.00
☐ 31	Adam Creighton	.15	.06	.01
☐ 32	Wilf Paiement	.05	.02	.00
☐ 33	Paul Cyr	.05	.02	.00
☐ 34	Clark Gillies	.08	.03	.01
☐ 35	Lindy Ruff	.05	.02	.00
☐ 36	Whalers Action	.05	.02	.00
☐ 37	Whalers Emblem	.05	.02	.00
☐ 38	Mike Liut	.08	.03	.01
☐ 39	Steve Weeks	.08	.03	.01
☐ 40	Dave Babych	.08	.03	.01
☐ 41	Ulf Samuelsson	.40	.16	.04
☐ 42	Dana Murzyn	.05	.02	.00
☐ 43	Ron Francis	.15	.06	.01
☐ 44	Kevin Dineen	.10	.04	.01
☐ 45	John Anderson	.05	.02	.00
☐ 46	Ray Ferraro	.30	.12	.03
☐ 47	Dean Evason	.05	.02	.00
☐ 48	Paul Lawless	.05	.02	.00
☐ 49	Stewart Gavin	.05	.02	.00
☐ 50	Sylvain Turgeon	.08	.03	.01
☐ 51	Dave Tippett	.05	.02	.00
☐ 52	Doug Jarvis	.08	.03	.01
☐ 53	Canadiens Action	.05	.02	.00
☐ 54	Canadiens Emblem	.05	.02	.00
☐ 55	Brian Hayward	.10	.04	.01
☐ 56	Patrick Roy	1.50	.60	.15
☐ 57	Larry Robinson	.15	.06	.01
☐ 58	Chris Chelios	.15	.06	.01
☐ 59	Craig Ludwig	.05	.02	.00
☐ 60	Rick Green	.05	.02	.00
☐ 61	Mats Naslund	.08	.03	.01
☐ 62	Bobby Smith	.08	.03	.01
☐ 63	Claude Lemieux	.75	.30	.07
☐ 64	Guy Carbonneau	.10	.04	.01
☐ 65	Stephane Richer	.75	.30	.07
☐ 66	Mike McPhee	.10	.04	.01
☐ 67	Brian Skrudland	.08	.03	.01
☐ 68	Chris Nilan	.08	.03	.01
☐ 69	Bob Gainey	.15	.06	.01
☐ 70	Devils Action	.05	.02	.00
☐ 71	Devils Emblem	.05	.02	.00
☐ 72	Craig Billington	.25	.10	.02
☐ 73	Alain Chevrier	.08	.03	.01
☐ 74	Bruce Driver	.10	.04	.01
☐ 75	Joe Cirella	.08	.03	.01
☐ 76	Ken Daneyko	.08	.03	.01
☐ 77	Craig Wolanin	.05	.02	.00
☐ 78	Aaron Broten	.05	.02	.00
☐ 79	Kirk Muller	.35	.14	.03
☐ 80	John MacLean	.25	.10	.02
☐ 81	Pat Verbeek	.15	.06	.01
☐ 82	Doug Sulliman	.05	.02	.00
☐ 83	Mark Johnson	.08	.03	.01
☐ 84	Greg Adams	.08	.03	.01
☐ 85	Claude Loiselle	.05	.02	.00
☐ 86	Andy Brickley	.08	.03	.01
☐ 87	Islanders Action	.05	.02	.00
☐ 88	Islanders Emblem	.05	.02	.00
☐ 89	Billy Smith	.15	.06	.01
☐ 90	Kelly Hrudey	.25	.10	.02
☐ 91	Denis Potvin	.15	.06	.01
☐ 92	Tomas Jonsson	.05	.02	.00
☐ 93	Ken Leiter	.05	.02	.00
☐ 94	Ken Morrow	.08	.03	.01
☐ 95	Brian Curran	.05	.02	.00
☐ 96	Bryan Trottier	.20	.08	.02
☐ 97	Mike Bossy	.30	.12	.03
☐ 98	Pat LaFontaine	.50	.20	.05
☐ 99	Brent Sutter	.10	.04	.01
☐ 100	Mikko Makela	.05	.02	.00
☐ 101	Pat Flatley	.05	.02	.00
☐ 102	Duane Sutter	.08	.03	.01
☐ 103	Rich Kromm	.05	.02	.00
☐ 104	Rangers Action	.05	.02	.00
☐ 105	Rangers Emblem	.05	.02	.00
☐ 106	John Vanbiesbrouck	.35	.14	.03
☐ 107	James Patrick	.08	.03	.01
☐ 108	Ron Greschner	.08	.03	.01
☐ 109	Willie Huber	.05	.02	.00
☐ 110	Curt Giles	.05	.02	.00
☐ 111	Larry Melnyk	.05	.02	.00
☐ 112	Walt Poddubny	.08	.03	.01
☐ 113	Marcel Dionne	.25	.10	.02
☐ 114	Tomas Sandstrom	.15	.06	.01
☐ 115	Kelly Kisio	.08	.03	.01
☐ 116	Pierre Larouche	.08	.03	.01
☐ 117	Don Maloney	.05	.02	.00
☐ 118	Tony McKegney	.05	.02	.00
☐ 119	Ron Duguay	.08	.03	.01
☐ 120	Jan Erixon	.08	.03	.01
☐ 121	Flyers Action	.05	.02	.00
☐ 122	Flyers Emblem	.05	.02	.00
☐ 123	Ron Hextall	.35	.14	.03
☐ 124	Mark Howe	.10	.04	.01
☐ 125	Doug Crossman	.08	.03	.01
☐ 126	Brad McCrimmon	.08	.03	.01
☐ 127	Brad Marsh	.08	.03	.01
☐ 128	Tim Kerr	.08	.03	.01
☐ 129	Peter Zezel	.08	.03	.01
☐ 130	Dave Poulin	.08	.03	.01
☐ 131	Brian Propp	.08	.03	.01
☐ 132	Pelle Eklund	.08	.03	.01
☐ 133	Murray Craven	.08	.03	.01
☐ 134	Rick Tocchet	1.25	.50	.12
☐ 135	Derrick Smith	.08	.03	.01
☐ 136	Ilkka Sinisalo	.08	.03	.01
☐ 137	Ron Sutter	.08	.03	.01
☐ 138	Penguins Action	.05	.02	.00
☐ 139	Penguins Emblem	.05	.02	.00
☐ 140	Gilles Meloche	.08	.03	.01
☐ 141	Doug Bodger	.08	.03	.01
☐ 142	Moe Mantha	.05	.02	.00
☐ 143	Jim Johnson	.05	.02	.00
☐ 144	Rod Buskas	.05	.02	.00
☐ 145	Randy Hillier	.05	.02	.00
☐ 146	Mario Lemieux	2.00	.80	.20
☐ 147	Dan Quinn	.08	.03	.01
☐ 148	Randy Cunneyworth	.05	.02	.00
☐ 149	Craig Simpson	.25	.10	.02
☐ 150	Terry Ruskowski	.08	.03	.01
☐ 151	John Chabot	.05	.02	.00
☐ 152	Bob Errey	.05	.02	.00
☐ 153	Dan Frawley	.05	.02	.00
☐ 154	Dave Hannan	.05	.02	.00
☐ 155	Nordiques Action	.05	.02	.00
☐ 156	Nordiques Emblem	.05	.02	.00
☐ 157	Mario Gosselin	.08	.03	.01
☐ 158	Clint Malarchuk	.10	.04	.01

159	Risto Siltanen	.05	.02	.00
160	Robert Picard	.05	.02	.00
161	Normand Rochefort	.05	.02	.00
162	Randy Moller	.05	.02	.00
163	Michel Goulet	.15	.06	.01
164	Peter Stastny	.20	.08	.02
165	John Ogrodnick	.08	.03	.01
166	Anton Stastny	.08	.03	.01
167	Paul Gillis	.05	.02	.00
168	Dale Hunter	.12	.05	.01
169	Alain Cote	.05	.02	.00
170	Mike Eagles	.05	.02	.00
171	Jason Lafreniere	.05	.02	.00
172	Capitals Action	.05	.02	.00
173	Capitals Emblem	.05	.02	.00
174	Pete Peeters	.08	.03	.01
175	Bob Mason	.08	.03	.01
176	Larry Murphy	.20	.08	.02
177	Scott Stevens	.20	.08	.02
178	Rod Langway	.10	.04	.01
179	Kevin Hatcher	.75	.30	.07
180	Mike Gartner	.20	.08	.02
181	Mike Ridley	.12	.05	.01
182	Craig Laughlin	.05	.02	.00
183	Gaetan Duchesne	.05	.02	.00
184	Dave Christian	.08	.03	.01
185	Greg Adams	.08	.03	.01
186	Kelly Miller	.08	.03	.01
187	Alan Haworth	.05	.02	.00
188	Lou Franceschetti	.05	.02	.00
189	Stanley Cup (top half)	.08	.03	.01
190	Stanley Cup (bottom half)	.08	.03	.01
191	Ron Hextall	.35	.14	.03
192	Wayne Gretzky	2.00	.80	.20
193	Brian Propp	.10	.04	.01
194	Mark Messier	.50	.20	.05
195	Flyers/Oilers Action	.10	.04	.01
196	Flyers/Oilers Action	.10	.04	.01
197	Gretzky Holding Cup (upper left)	.75	.30	.07
198	Gretzky Holding Cup (upper right)	.75	.30	.07
199	Gretzky Holding Cup (lower left)	.75	.30	.07
200	Gretzky Holding Cup (lower right)	.75	.30	.07
201	Flames Action	.05	.02	.00
202	Flames Emblem	.05	.02	.00
203	Mike Vernon	.40	.16	.04
204	Rejean Lemelin	.08	.03	.01
205	Al MacInnis	.40	.16	.04
206	Paul Reinhart	.08	.03	.01
207	Gary Suter	.12	.05	.01
208	Jamie Macoun	.05	.02	.00
209	Neil Sheehy	.05	.02	.00
210	Joe Mullen	.15	.06	.01
211	Carey Wilson	.05	.02	.00
212	Joel Otto	.05	.02	.00
213	Jim Peplinski	.08	.03	.01
214	Hakan Loob	.08	.03	.01
215	Lanny McDonald	.20	.08	.02
216	Tim Hunter	.05	.02	.00
217	Gary Roberts	.75	.30	.07
218	Blackhawks Action	.05	.02	.00
219	Blackhawks Emblem	.05	.02	.00
220	Bob Sauve	.08	.03	.01
221	Murray Bannerman	.05	.02	.00
222	Doug Wilson	.10	.04	.01
223	Bob Murray	.05	.02	.00
224	Gary Nylund	.05	.02	.00
225	Denis Savard	.15	.06	.01
226	Steve Larmer	.15	.06	.01
227	Troy Murray	.10	.04	.01
228	Wayne Presley	.05	.02	.00
229	Al Secord	.08	.03	.01
230	Ed Olczyk	.10	.04	.01
231	Curt Fraser	.05	.02	.00
232	Bill Watson	.05	.02	.00
233	Keith Brown	.08	.03	.01
234	Darryl Sutter	.08	.03	.01
235	Red Wings Action	.05	.02	.00
236	Red Wings Emblem	.05	.02	.00
237	Greg Stefan	.08	.03	.01
238	Glen Hanlon	.08	.03	.01
239	Darren Veitch	.08	.03	.01
240	Mike O'Connell	.05	.02	.00
241	Harold Snepsts	.08	.03	.01
242	Dave Lewis	.05	.02	.00
243	Steve Yzerman	.60	.24	.06
244	Brent Ashton	.05	.02	.00
245	Gerard Gallant	.12	.05	.01
246	Petr Klima	.10	.04	.01
247	Shawn Burr	.08	.03	.01
248	Adam Oates	2.50	1.00	.25
249	Mel Bridgman	.08	.03	.01
250	Tim Higgins	.05	.02	.00
251	Joey Kocur	.15	.06	.01
252	Oilers Action	.05	.02	.00
253	Oilers Emblem	.05	.02	.00
254	Grant Fuhr	.20	.08	.02
255	Andy Moog	.20	.08	.02
256	Paul Coffey	.30	.12	.03
257	Kevin Lowe	.08	.03	.01
258	Craig Muni	.05	.02	.00
259	Steve Smith	.30	.12	.03
260	Charlie Huddy	.08	.03	.01
261	Wayne Gretzky	2.00	.80	.20
262	Jari Kurri	.20	.08	.02
263	Mark Messier	.50	.20	.05
264	Esa Tikkanen	1.00	.40	.10
265	Glenn Anderson	.12	.05	.01
266	Mike Krushelnyski	.08	.03	.01
267	Craig MacTavish	.10	.04	.01
268	Dave Hunter	.05	.02	.00
269	Kings Action	.05	.02	.00
270	Kings Emblem	.05	.02	.00
271	Roland Melanson	.08	.03	.01
272	Darren Eliot	.05	.02	.00
273	Grant Ledyard	.05	.02	.00
274	Jay Wells	.05	.02	.00
275	Mark Hardy	.05	.02	.00
276	Dean Kennedy	.05	.02	.00
277	Luc Robitaille	3.00	1.20	.30
278	Bernie Nicholls	.20	.08	.02
279	Jimmy Carson	.30	.12	.03
280	Dave Taylor	.08	.03	.01
281	Jim Fox	.05	.02	.00
282	Bryan Erickson	.05	.02	.00
283	Dave(Tiger) Williams	.08	.03	.01
284	Sean McKenna	.05	.02	.00
285	Phil Sykes	.05	.02	.00
286	North Stars Action	.05	.02	.00
287	North Stars Emblem	.05	.02	.00
288	Kari Takko	.08	.03	.01
289	Don Beaupre	.08	.03	.01
290	Craig Hartsburg	.05	.02	.00
291	Ron Wilson	.05	.02	.00
292	Frantisek Musil	.10	.04	.01
293	Dino Ciccarelli	.15	.06	.01
294	Brian MacLellan	.05	.02	.00
295	Dirk Graham	.10	.04	.01
296	Brian Bellows	.10	.04	.01
297	Neal Broten	.08	.03	.01
298	Dennis Maruk	.08	.03	.01
299	Keith Acton	.05	.02	.00
300	Brian Lawton	.08	.03	.01
301	Bob Brooke	.05	.02	.00
302	Willi Plett	.05	.02	.00
303	Blues Action	.05	.02	.00
304	Blues Emblem	.05	.02	.00
305	Rick Wamsley	.08	.03	.01
306	Rob Ramage	.08	.03	.01
307	Ric Nattress	.05	.02	.00
308	Bruce Bell	.05	.02	.00
309	Charlie Bourgeois	.05	.02	.00
310	Jim Pavese	.05	.02	.00
311	Doug Gilmour	.60	.24	.06
312	Bernie Federko	.10	.04	.01
313	Mark Hunter	.05	.02	.00
314	Greg Paslawski	.05	.02	.00
315	Gino Cavallini	.08	.03	.01
316	Rick Meagher	.08	.03	.01
317	Ron Flockhart	.05	.02	.00
318	Doug Wickenheiser	.05	.02	.00
319	Jocelyn Lemieux	.06	.02	.00
320	Maple Leafs Action	.05	.02	.00
321	Maple Leafs Emblem	.05	.02	.00
322	Ken Wregget	.15	.06	.01
323	Allan Bester	.08	.03	.01
324	Todd Gill	.05	.02	.00
325	Al Iafrate	.25	.10	.02
326	Borje Salming	.10	.04	.01
327	Russ Courtnall	.35	.14	.03
328	Rick Vaive	.08	.03	.01
329	Steve Thomas	.10	.04	.01
330	Wendel Clark	.75	.30	.07
331	Gary Leeman	.08	.03	.01
332	Tom Fergus	.05	.02	.00
333	Vincent Damphousse	1.00	.40	.10
334	Peter Ihnacak	.05	.02	.00
335	Brad Smith	.05	.02	.00
336	Miroslav Ihnacak	.05	.02	.00
337	Canucks Action	.05	.02	.00
338	Canucks Emblem	.05	.02	.00

☐	339	Frank Caprice	.05	.02	.00
☐	340	Richard Brodeur	.08	.03	.01
☐	341	Doug Lidster	.05	.02	.00
☐	342	Michel Petit	.05	.02	.00
☐	343	Garth Butcher	.15	.06	.01
☐	344	Dave Richter	.05	.02	.00
☐	345	Tony Tanti	.08	.03	.01
☐	346	Barry Pederson	.08	.03	.01
☐	347	Petri Skriko	.08	.03	.01
☐	348	Patrik Sundstrom	.08	.03	.01
☐	349	Stan Smyl	.08	.03	.01
☐	350	Rich Sutter	.08	.03	.01
☐	351	Steve Tambellini	.05	.02	.00
☐	352	Jim Sandlak	.10	.04	.01
☐	353	Dave Lowry	.05	.02	.00
☐	354	Jets Action	.05	.02	.00
☐	355	Jets Emblem	.05	.02	.00
☐	356	Daniel Berthiaume	.10	.04	.01
☐	357	Pokey Reddick	.25	.10	.02
☐	358	Dave Ellett	.10	.04	.01
☐	359	Mario Marois	.05	.02	.00
☐	360	Randy Carlyle	.08	.03	.01
☐	361	Fredrick Olausson	.25	.10	.02
☐	362	Jim Kyte	.05	.02	.00
☐	363	Dale Hawerchuk	.20	.08	.02
☐	364	Paul MacLean	.08	.03	.01
☐	365	Thomas Steen	.10	.04	.01
☐	366	Gilles Hamel	.05	.02	.00
☐	367	Doug Smail	.05	.02	.00
☐	368	Laurie Boschman	.05	.02	.00
☐	369	Ray Neufeld	.05	.02	.00
☐	370	Andrew McBain	.05	.02	.00
☐	371	Wayne Gretzky	1.25	.50	.12
☐	372	Hart Trophy	.05	.02	.00
☐	373	Wayne Gretzky	1.25	.50	.12
☐	374	Art Ross Trophy	.05	.02	.00
☐	375	Jennings Trophy	.05	.02	.00
☐	376A	Brian Hayward	.08	.03	.01
☐	376B	Patrick Roy	.60	.24	.06
☐	377	Vezina Trophy	.05	.02	.00
☐	378	Ron Hextall	.20	.08	.02
☐	379	Luc Robitaille	2.50	1.00	.25
☐	380	Calder Trophy	.05	.02	.00
☐	381	Ray Bourque	.15	.06	.01
☐	382	Norris Trophy	.05	.02	.00
☐	383	Lady Byng Trophy	.05	.02	.00
☐	384	Joe Mullen	.12	.05	.01
☐	385	Frank Selke Trophy	.05	.02	.00
☐	386	Dave Poulin	.07	.03	.01
☐	387	Doug Jarvis	.05	.02	.00
☐	388	Masterton Trophy	.05	.02	.00
☐	389	Wayne Gretzky	1.25	.50	.12
☐	390	Emery Edge Award	.05	.02	.00
☐	391	Flyers Team Photo (left half)	.10	.04	.01
☐	392	Flyers Team Photo (right half)	.10	.04	.01
☐	393	Prince of Wales Trophy	.05	.02	.00
☐	394	Clarence S. Campbell Bowl	.05	.02	.00
☐	395	Oilers Team Photo (left half)	.15	.06	.01
☐	396	Oilers Team Photo (right half)	.15	.06	.01
☐	xx	Sticker Album	2.50	1.00	.25

1988-89 Panini Stickers

This set of 408 hockey stickers was produced and distributed by Panini. These full-color stickers are very attractive. The sticker number is only on the backing of the sticker. The stickers measure approximately 2 1/8" by 2 11/16". The team picture cards are double stickers with each sticker showing half of the photo; in the checklist below these halves are denoted by LH (left half) and RH (right half). There was an album issued with the set for holding the stickers. On the inside back cover of the sticker album the company offered (via direct mail-order) up to 30 different stickers of your choice for either ten cents each or in trade one-for-one for your unwanted extra stickers plus 1.00 for postage and handling; this is one reason why the values of the most popular players in these sticker sets are somewhat depressed compared to traditional card set prices.

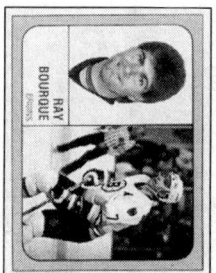
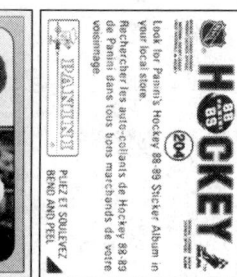

			MINT	EXC	G-VG
	COMPLETE SET (408)		30.00	12.00	3.00
	COMMON PLAYER (1-408)		.05	.02	.00
☐	1	Road to the Cup / Stanley Cup Draw	.10	.04	.01
☐	2	Flames Emblem	.05	.02	.00
☐	3	Flames Uniform	.05	.02	.00
☐	4	Mike Vernon	.15	.06	.01
☐	5	Al MacInnis	.20	.08	.02
☐	6	Brad McCrimmon	.08	.03	.01
☐	7	Gary Suter	.10	.04	.01
☐	8	Mike Bullard	.05	.02	.00
☐	9	Hakan Loob	.08	.03	.01
☐	10	Lanny McDonald	.15	.06	.01
☐	11	Joe Mullen	.15	.06	.01
☐	12	Joe Nieuwendyk	1.25	.50	.12
☐	13	Joel Otto	.08	.03	.01
☐	14	Jim Peplinski	.05	.02	.00
☐	15	Gary Roberts	.30	.12	.03
☐	16	Flames Team LH	.05	.02	.00
☐	17	Flames Team RH	.05	.02	.00
☐	18	Blackhawks Emblem	.05	.02	.00
☐	19	Blackhawks Uniform	.05	.02	.00
☐	20	Bob Mason	.05	.02	.00
☐	21	Darren Pang	.05	.02	.00
☐	22	Bob Murray	.05	.02	.00
☐	23	Gary Nylund	.05	.02	.00
☐	24	Doug Wilson	.10	.04	.01
☐	25	Dirk Graham	.08	.03	.01
☐	26	Steve Larmer	.12	.05	.01
☐	27	Troy Murray	.08	.03	.01
☐	28	Brian Ashton	.10	.04	.01
☐	29	Denis Savard	.12	.05	.01
☐	30	Steve Thomas	.08	.03	.01
☐	31	Rick Vaive	.08	.03	.01
☐	32	Blackhawks Team LH	.05	.02	.00
☐	33	Blackhawks Team RH	.05	.02	.00
☐	34	Red Wings Emblem	.05	.02	.00
☐	35	Red Wings Uniform	.05	.02	.00
☐	36	Glen Hanlon	.08	.03	.01
☐	37	Greg Stefan	.08	.03	.01
☐	38	Jeff Sharples	.05	.02	.00
☐	39	Darren Veitch	.05	.02	.00
☐	40	Brent Ashton	.05	.02	.00
☐	41	Shawn Burr	.05	.02	.00
☐	42	John Chabot	.05	.02	.00
☐	43	Gerard Gallant	.08	.03	.01
☐	44	Petr Klima	.08	.03	.01
☐	45	Adam Oates	.50	.20	.05
☐	46	Bob Probert	.75	.30	.07
☐	47	Steve Yzerman	.50	.20	.05
☐	48	Red Wings Team LH	.05	.02	.00
☐	49	Red Wings Team RH	.05	.02	.00
☐	50	Oilers Emblem	.05	.02	.00
☐	51	Oilers Uniform	.05	.02	.00
☐	52	Grant Fuhr	.15	.06	.01
☐	53	Charlie Huddy	.08	.03	.01
☐	54	Kevin Lowe	.08	.03	.01
☐	55	Steve Smith	.25	.10	.02
☐	56	Jeff Beukeboom	.05	.02	.00
☐	57	Glenn Anderson	.12	.05	.01
☐	58	Wayne Gretzky	1.25	.50	.12
☐	59	Jari Kurri	.15	.06	.01
☐	60	Craig MacTavish	.10	.04	.01
☐	61	Mark Messier	.50	.20	.05
☐	62	Craig Simpson	.12	.05	.01
☐	63	Esa Tikkanen	.20	.08	.02
☐	64	Oilers Team LH	.05	.02	.00
☐	65	Oilers Team RH	.05	.02	.00
☐	66	Kings Emblem	.05	.02	.00
☐	67	Kings Uniform	.05	.02	.00
☐	68	Glenn Healy	.08	.03	.01
☐	69	Roland Melanson	.08	.03	.01

☐ 70	Steve Duchesne	.30	.12	.03
☐ 71	Tom Laidlaw	.05	.02	.00
☐ 72	Jay Wells	.05	.02	.00
☐ 73	Mike Allison	.05	.02	.00
☐ 74	Bob Carpenter	.08	.03	.01
☐ 75	Jimmy Carson	.12	.05	.01
☐ 76	Jim Fox	.05	.02	.00
☐ 77	Bernie Nicholls	.15	.06	.01
☐ 78	Luc Robitaille	.75	.30	.07
☐ 79	Dave Taylor	.10	.04	.01
☐ 80	Kings Team LH	.05	.02	.00
☐ 81	Kings Team RH	.05	.02	.00
☐ 82	North Stars Emblem	.05	.02	.00
☐ 83	North Stars Uniform	.05	.02	.00
☐ 84	Don Beaupre	.10	.04	.01
☐ 85	Kari Takko	.08	.03	.01
☐ 86	Craig Hartsburg	.05	.02	.00
☐ 87	Frantisek Musil	.08	.03	.01
☐ 88	Dave Archibald	.05	.02	.00
☐ 89	Brian Bellows	.10	.04	.01
☐ 90	Scott Bjugstad	.05	.02	.00
☐ 91	Bob Brooke	.05	.02	.00
☐ 92	Neal Broten	.08	.03	.01
☐ 93	Dino Ciccarelli	.15	.06	.01
☐ 94	Brian Lawton	.05	.02	.00
☐ 95	Brian MacLellan	.05	.02	.00
☐ 96	North Stars Team LH	.05	.02	.00
☐ 97	North Stars Team RH	.05	.02	.00
☐ 98	Blues Emblem	.05	.02	.00
☐ 99	Blues Uniform	.05	.02	.00
☐ 100	Greg Millen	.08	.03	.01
☐ 101	Brian Benning	.05	.02	.00
☐ 102	Gordie Roberts	.05	.02	.00
☐ 103	Gino Cavallini	.08	.03	.01
☐ 104	Bernie Federko	.10	.04	.01
☐ 105	Doug Gilmour	.50	.20	.05
☐ 106	Tony Hrkac	.08	.03	.01
☐ 107	Brett Hull	3.00	1.20	.30
☐ 108	Mark Hunter	.05	.02	.00
☐ 109	Tony McKegney	.05	.02	.00
☐ 110	Rick Meagher	.05	.02	.00
☐ 111	Brian Sutter	.08	.03	.01
☐ 112	Blues Team LH	.05	.02	.00
☐ 113	Blues Team RH	.05	.02	.00
☐ 114	Maple Leafs Emblem	.05	.02	.00
☐ 115	Maple Leafs Uniform	.05	.02	.00
☐ 116	Allan Bester	.05	.02	.00
☐ 117	Ken Wregget	.08	.03	.01
☐ 118	Al Iafrate	.15	.06	.01
☐ 119	Luke Richardson	.05	.02	.00
☐ 120	Borje Salming	.10	.04	.01
☐ 121	Wendel Clark	.25	.10	.02
☐ 122	Russ Courtnall	.15	.06	.01
☐ 123	Vincent Damphousse	.35	.14	.03
☐ 124	Dan Daoust	.05	.02	.00
☐ 125	Gary Leeman	.08	.03	.01
☐ 126	Ed Olczyk	.08	.03	.01
☐ 127	Mark Osborne	.05	.02	.00
☐ 128	Maple Leafs Team LH	.05	.02	.00
☐ 129	Maple Leafs Team RH	.05	.02	.00
☐ 130	Canucks Emblem	.05	.02	.00
☐ 131	Canucks Uniform	.05	.02	.00
☐ 132	Kirk McLean	.75	.30	.07
☐ 133	Jim Benning	.05	.02	.00
☐ 134	Garth Butcher	.10	.04	.01
☐ 135	Doug Lidster	.05	.02	.00
☐ 136	Greg Adams	.08	.03	.01
☐ 137	David Bruce	.08	.03	.01
☐ 138	Barry Pederson	.05	.02	.00
☐ 139	Jim Sandlak	.08	.03	.01
☐ 140	Petri Skriko	.08	.03	.01
☐ 141	Stan Smyl	.05	.02	.00
☐ 142	Rich Sutter	.08	.03	.01
☐ 143	Tony Tanti	.08	.03	.01
☐ 144	Canucks Team LH	.05	.02	.00
☐ 145	Canucks Team RH	.05	.02	.00
☐ 146	Jets Emblem	.05	.02	.00
☐ 147	Jets Uniform	.05	.02	.00
☐ 148	Daniel Berthiaume	.10	.04	.01
☐ 149	Randy Carlyle	.08	.03	.01
☐ 150	Dave Ellett	.08	.03	.01
☐ 151	Mario Marois	.05	.02	.00
☐ 152	Peter Taglianetti	.05	.02	.00
☐ 153	Laurie Boschman	.05	.02	.00
☐ 154	Iain Duncan	.05	.02	.00
☐ 155	Dale Hawerchuk	.15	.06	.01
☐ 156	Paul MacLean	.08	.03	.01
☐ 157	Andrew McBain	.05	.02	.00
☐ 158	Doug Smail	.08	.03	.01
☐ 159	Thomas Steen	.08	.03	.01
☐ 160	Jets Team LH	.05	.02	.00
☐ 161	Jets Team RH	.05	.02	.00
☐ 162	Prince of Wales	.05	.02	.00
	Trophy			
☐ 163	Caps/Flyers Action	.05	.02	.00
☐ 164	Bruins/Canadiens	.05	.02	.00
	Action			
☐ 165	Caps/Devils Action	.05	.02	.00
☐ 166	Bruins/Devils	.05	.02	.00
	Action LH			
☐ 167	Bruins/Devils	.05	.02	.00
	Action RH			
☐ 168	Flames/Kings Action	.05	.02	.00
☐ 169	Clarence S. Campbell	.05	.02	.00
	Bowl			
☐ 170	Oilers/Flames Action	.05	.02	.00
☐ 171	Blues/Red Wings Action	.05	.02	.00
☐ 172	Oilers/Red Wings	.05	.02	.00
	Action LH			
☐ 173	Oilers/Red Wings	.05	.02	.00
	Action RH			
☐ 174	Oilers Celebrate	.05	.02	.00
☐ 175	Oilers/Bruins Action	.05	.02	.00
☐ 176	Stanley Cup	.08	.03	.01
	(top half)			
☐ 177	Stanley Cup	.08	.03	.01
	(bottom half)			
☐ 178	Oilers/Bruins	.08	.03	.01
	Action LH			
☐ 179	Oilers/Bruins	.08	.03	.01
	Action RH			
☐ 180	Oilers/Bruins Action	.08	.03	.01
☐ 181	Wayne Gretzky	1.25	.50	.12
☐ 182	Conn Smythe Trophy	.05	.02	.00
☐ 183	Oilers Celebrate UL	.08	.03	.01
☐ 184	Oilers Celebrate UR	.08	.03	.01
☐ 185	Oilers Celebrate LL	.08	.03	.01
☐ 186	Oilers Celebrate LR	.08	.03	.01
☐ 187	Flames Action	.05	.02	.00
☐ 188	Grant Fuhr	.15	.06	.01
☐ 189	Devils Action	.05	.02	.00
☐ 190	Marcel Dionne	.15	.06	.01
☐ 191	Bruins Action	.05	.02	.00
☐ 192	Capitals Action	.05	.02	.00
☐ 193	Wayne Gretzky	1.25	.50	.12
☐ 194	Oilers Action	.08	.03	.01
☐ 195	Bruins/Canadiens	.05	.02	.00
	Action			
☐ 196	Blues Action	.05	.02	.00
☐ 197	Caps/Flyers Action	.05	.02	.00
☐ 198	Islanders Action	.05	.02	.00
☐ 199	Flames Action	.05	.02	.00
☐ 200	Penguins Action	.05	.02	.00
☐ 201	Bruins Emblem	.05	.02	.00
☐ 202	Bruins Uniform	.05	.02	.00
☐ 203	Rejean Lemelin	.08	.03	.01
☐ 204	Ray Bourque	.25	.10	.02
☐ 205	Gord Kluzak	.05	.02	.00
☐ 206	Michael Thelven	.05	.02	.00
☐ 207	Glen Wesley	.12	.05	.01
☐ 208	Randy Burridge	.15	.06	.01
☐ 209	Keith Crowder	.05	.02	.00
☐ 210	Steve Kasper	.08	.03	.01
☐ 211	Ken Linseman	.05	.02	.00
☐ 212	Jay Miller	.05	.02	.00
☐ 213	Cam Neely	.30	.12	.03
☐ 214	Bob Sweeney	.05	.02	.00
☐ 215	Bruins Team LH	.05	.02	.00
☐ 216	Bruins Team RH	.05	.02	.00
☐ 217	Sabres Emblem	.05	.02	.00
☐ 218	Sabres Uniform	.05	.02	.00
☐ 219	Tom Barrasso	.20	.08	.02
☐ 220	Phil Housley	.20	.08	.02
☐ 221	Calle Johansson	.10	.04	.01
☐ 222	Mike Ramsey	.05	.02	.00
☐ 223	Dave Andreychuk	.25	.10	.02
☐ 224	Scott Arniel	.05	.02	.00
☐ 225	Adam Creighton	.10	.04	.01
☐ 226	Mike Foligno	.05	.02	.00
☐ 227	Christian Ruuttu	.05	.02	.00
☐ 228	Ray Sheppard	.20	.08	.02
☐ 229	John Tucker	.05	.02	.00
☐ 230	Pierre Turgeon	1.50	.60	.15
☐ 231	Sabres Team LH	.05	.02	.00
☐ 232	Sabres Team RH	.05	.02	.00
☐ 233	Whalers Emblem	.05	.02	.00
☐ 234	Whalers Uniform	.05	.02	.00
☐ 235	Mike Liut	.08	.03	.01
☐ 236	Dave Babych	.08	.03	.01
☐ 237	Sylvain Cote	.05	.02	.00
☐ 238	Ulf Samuelsson	.15	.06	.00
☐ 239	John Anderson	.05	.02	.00
☐ 240	Kevin Dineen	.10	.04	.01
☐ 241	Ray Ferraro	.08	.03	.01
☐ 242	Ron Francis	.12	.05	.01
☐ 243	Paul MacDermid	.05	.02	.00
☐ 244	Dave Tippett	.05	.02	.00

☐	245	Sylvain Turgeon	.08	.03	.01			
☐	246	Carey Wilson	.05	.02	.00			
☐	247	Whalers Team LH	.05	.02	.00			
☐	248	Whalers Team RH	.05	.02	.00			
☐	249	Canadiens Emblem	.05	.02	.00			
☐	250	Canadiens Uniform	.05	.02	.00			
☐	251	Brian Hayward	.08	.03	.01			
☐	252	Patrick Roy	.75	.30	.07			
☐	253	Chris Chelios	.15	.06	.01			
☐	254	Craig Ludwig	.05	.02	.00			
☐	255	Petr Svoboda	.08	.03	.01			
☐	256	Guy Carbonneau	.10	.04	.01			
☐	257	Claude Lemieux	.25	.10	.02			
☐	258	Mike McPhee	.08	.03	.01			
☐	259	Mats Naslund	.08	.03	.01			
☐	260	Stephane Richer	.20	.08	.02			
☐	261	Bobby Smith	.08	.03	.01			
☐	262	Ryan Walter	.08	.03	.01			
☐	263	Canadiens Team LH	.05	.02	.00			
☐	264	Canadiens Team RH	.05	.02	.00			
☐	265	Devils Emblem	.05	.02	.00			
☐	266	Devils Uniform	.05	.02	.00			
☐	267	Sean Burke	.20	.08	.02			
☐	268	Joe Cirella	.08	.03	.01			
☐	269	Bruce Driver	.08	.03	.01			
☐	270	Craig Wolanin	.05	.02	.00			
☐	271	Aaron Broten	.05	.02	.00			
☐	272	Doug Brown	.05	.02	.00			
☐	273	Claude Loiselle	.05	.02	.00			
☐	274	John MacLean	.15	.06	.01			
☐	275	Kirk Muller	.25	.10	.02			
☐	276	Brendan Shanahan	1.50	.60	.15			
☐	277	Patrik Sundstrom	.08	.03	.01			
☐	278	Pat Verbeek	.10	.04	.01			
☐	279	Devils Team LH	.05	.02	.00			
☐	280	Devils Team RH	.05	.02	.00			
☐	281	Islanders Emblem	.05	.02	.00			
☐	282	Islanders Uniform	.05	.02	.00			
☐	283	Kelly Hrudey	.12	.05	.01			
☐	284	Steve Konroyd	.05	.02	.00			
☐	285	Ken Morrow	.08	.03	.01			
☐	286	Pat Flatley	.08	.03	.01			
☐	287	Greg Gilbert	.05	.02	.00			
☐	288	Alan Kerr	.05	.02	.00			
☐	289	Derek King	.30	.12	.03			
☐	290	Pat LaFontaine	.40	.16	.04			
☐	291	Mikko Makela	.05	.02	.00			
☐	292	Brent Sutter	.08	.03	.01			
☐	293	Bryan Trottier	.20	.08	.02			
☐	294	Randy Wood	.08	.03	.01			
☐	295	Islanders Team	.05	.02	.00			
☐	296	Islanders Team	.05	.02	.00			
☐	297	Rangers Emblem	.05	.02	.00			
☐	298	Rangers Uniform	.05	.02	.00			
☐	299	Bob Froese	.08	.03	.01			
☐	300	John Vanbiesbrouck	.25	.10	.02			
☐	301	Brian Leetch	2.50	1.00	.25			
☐	302	Norm Maciver	.08	.03	.01			
☐	303	James Patrick	.08	.03	.01			
☐	304	Michel Petit	.08	.03	.01			
☐	305	Ulf Dahlen	.08	.03	.01			
☐	306	Jan Erixon	.08	.03	.01			
☐	307	Kelly Kisio	.08	.03	.01			
☐	308	Don Maloney	.05	.02	.00			
☐	309	Walt Poddubny	.05	.02	.00			
☐	310	Tomas Sandstrom	.10	.04	.01			
☐	311	Rangers Team LH	.05	.02	.00			
☐	312	Rangers Team RH	.05	.02	.00			
☐	313	Flyers Emblem	.05	.02	.00			
☐	314	Flyers Uniform	.05	.02	.00			
☐	315	Ron Hextall	.15	.06	.01			
☐	316	Mark Howe	.10	.04	.01			
☐	317	Kerry Huffman	.05	.02	.00			
☐	318	Kjell Samuelsson	.08	.03	.01			
☐	319	Dave Brown	.05	.02	.00			
☐	320	Murray Craven	.08	.03	.01			
☐	321	Tim Kerr	.08	.03	.01			
☐	322	Scott Mellanby	.08	.03	.01			
☐	323	Dave Poulin	.08	.03	.01			
☐	324	Brian Propp	.08	.03	.01			
☐	325	Ilkka Sinisalo	.05	.02	.00			
☐	326	Rick Tocchet	.25	.10	.02			
☐	327	Flyers Team LH	.05	.02	.00			
☐	328	Flyers Team RH	.05	.02	.00			
☐	329	Penguins Emblem	.05	.02	.00			
☐	330	Penguins Uniform	.05	.02	.00			
☐	331	Frank Pietrangelo	.20	.08	.02			
☐	332	Doug Bodger	.08	.03	.01			
☐	333	Paul Coffey	.30	.12	.03			
☐	334	Jim Johnson	.05	.02	.00			
☐	335	Ville Siren	.05	.02	.00			
☐	336	Rob Brown	.12	.05	.01			
☐	337	Randy Cunneyworth	.05	.02	.00			
☐	338	Dan Frawley	.05	.02	.00			
☐	339	Dave Hunter	.05	.02	.00			
☐	340	Mario Lemieux	1.50	.60	.15			
☐	341	Troy Loney	.05	.02	.00			
☐	342	Dan Quinn	.05	.02	.00			
☐	343	Penguins Team LH	.05	.02	.00			
☐	344	Penguins Team RH	.05	.02	.00			
☐	345	Nordiques Emblem	.05	.02	.00			
☐	346	Nordiques Uniform	.05	.02	.00			
☐	347	Mario Gosselin	.05	.02	.00			
☐	348	Tommy Albelin	.05	.02	.00			
☐	349	Jeff Brown	.30	.12	.03			
☐	350	Steven Finn	.05	.02	.00			
☐	351	Randy Moller	.05	.02	.00			
☐	352	Alain Cote	.05	.02	.00			
☐	353	Gaetan Duchesne	.05	.02	.00			
☐	354	Mike Eagles	.05	.02	.00			
☐	355	Michel Goulet	.12	.05	.01			
☐	356	Lane Lambert	.05	.02	.00			
☐	357	Anton Stastny	.05	.02	.00			
☐	358	Peter Stastny	.15	.06	.01			
☐	359	Nordiques Team LH	.05	.02	.00			
☐	360	Nordiques Team RH	.05	.02	.00			
☐	361	Capitals Emblem	.05	.02	.00			
☐	362	Capitals Uniform	.05	.02	.00			
☐	363	Clint Malarchuk	.08	.03	.01			
☐	364	Pete Peeters	.08	.03	.01			
☐	365	Kevin Hatcher	.25	.10	.02			
☐	366	Rod Langway	.08	.03	.01			
☐	367	Larry Murphy	.10	.04	.01			
☐	368	Scott Stevens	.12	.05	.01			
☐	369	Dave Christian	.08	.03	.01			
☐	370	Mike Gartner	.15	.06	.01			
☐	371	Bengt Gustafsson	.05	.02	.00			
☐	372	Dale Hunter	.10	.04	.01			
☐	373	Kelly Miller	.08	.03	.01			
☐	374	Mike Ridley	.10	.04	.01			
☐	375	Capitals Team LH	.05	.02	.00			
☐	376	Capitals Team RH	.05	.02	.00			
☐	377	Hockey Rink Schematic	.05	.02	.00			
☐	378	Hockey Rink Schematic	.05	.02	.00			
☐	379	Cross-checking	.05	.02	.00			
☐	380	Elbowing	.05	.02	.00			
☐	381	High-sticking	.05	.02	.00			
☐	382	Holding	.05	.02	.00			
☐	383	Hooking	.05	.02	.00			
☐	384	Interference	.05	.02	.00			
☐	385	Spearing	.05	.02	.00			
☐	386	Tripping	.05	.02	.00			
☐	387	Boarding	.05	.02	.00			
☐	388	Charging	.05	.02	.00			
☐	389	Delayed Calling of Penalty	.05	.02	.00			
☐	390	Kneeing	.05	.02	.00			
☐	391	Misconduct	.05	.02	.00			
☐	392	Roughing	.05	.02	.00			
☐	393	Slashing	.05	.02	.00			
☐	394	Unsportsmanlike Conduct	.05	.02	.00			
☐	395	Wash-out	.05	.02	.00			
☐	396	Icing	.05	.02	.00			
☐	397	Off-side	.05	.02	.00			
☐	398	Wash-out	.05	.02	.00			
☐	399	Bill Masterton Memorial Trophy Bob Bourne	.05	.02	.00			
☐	400	Hart Memorial Trophy Mario Lemieux	.75	.30	.07			
☐	401	Art Ross Trophy Mario Lemieux	.75	.30	.07			
☐	402	William M. Jennings Trophy Brian Hayward and Patrick Roy	.25	.10	.02			
☐	403	Vezina Trophy Grant Fuhr	.12	.05	.01			
☐	404	Calder Memorial Trophy Joe Nieuwendyk	.25	.10	.02			
☐	405	James Norris Memorial Trophy Ray Bourque	.15	.06	.01			
☐	406	Lady Byng Trophy Mats Naslund	.08	.03	.01			
☐	407	Frank J. Selke Trophy Guy Carbonneau	.05	.02	.00			
☐	408	Emery Edge Award Brad McCrimmon	.05	.02	.00			
☐	xx	Sticker Album	2.00	.80	.20			

1989-90 Panini Stickers

Trading double stickers is a fun way to meet new friends and complete your album faster.

L'échange d'autocollants en double est une façon amusante de rencontrer de nouveaux amis et de compléter votre album plus rapidement.

Printed in Modena Italy

This set of 384 hockey stickers was produced and distributed by Panini. The full color stickers are very attractive. The stickers are numbered on the back and measure 1 7/8" by 3". The stickers display color action shots of players, teams, arenas, and logos. Some team pictures consist of two stickers, each showing half of the photo; in the checklist below these halves are denoted by LH (left half) and RH (right half), and in the case of a four sticker picture, note the additional prefixes U (upper) and L (lower). A 52-page, full-color glossy album was issued with the set for holding the stickers. The album includes player information and statistics in English and French.

		MINT	EXC	G-VG
COMPLETE SET (384)		25.00	10.00	2.50
COMMON PLAYER (1-384)		.05	.02	.00
☐ 1	NHL Logo	.08	.03	.01
☐ 2	Playoff schedule	.05	.02	.00
☐ 3	Flames/Blackhawks action	.05	.02	.00
☐ 4	Flames/Canucks action	.05	.02	.00
☐ 5	Kings/Oilers action	.05	.02	.00
☐ 6	Vernon goal LH	.08	.03	.01
☐ 7	Vernon goal RH	.08	.03	.01
☐ 8	Bruins/Sabres action	.05	.02	.00
☐ 9	Canadiens/Bruins action	.05	.02	.00
☐ 10	Flyers score	.05	.02	.00
☐ 11	Canadiens/Flyers action LH	.05	.02	.00
☐ 12	Canadiens/Flyers action RH	.05	.02	.00
☐ 13	Canadiens/Flames action	.05	.02	.00
☐ 14	Canadiens celebration	.05	.02	.00
☐ 15	Canadiens/Flames action	.05	.02	.00
☐ 16	Canadiens/Flames action	.05	.02	.00
☐ 17	Flames celebration	.05	.02	.00
☐ 18	Flames/Canadiens action LH	.05	.02	.00
☐ 19	Flames/Canadiens action RH	.05	.02	.00
☐ 20	Al MacInnis Conn Smythe Trophy	.15	.06	.01
☐ 21	Stanley Cup/Flames UL	.05	.02	.00
☐ 22	Stanley Cup/Flames UR	.05	.02	.00
☐ 23	Stanley Cup/Flames LL	.05	.02	.00
☐ 24	Stanley Cup/Flames LR	.05	.02	.00
☐ 25	Stanley Cup	.08	.03	.01
☐ 26	Calgary Flames logo	.05	.02	.00
☐ 27	Joe Mullen	.10	.04	.01
☐ 28	Doug Gilmour	.40	.16	.04
☐ 29	Joe Nieuwendyk	.15	.06	.01

☐ 30	Gary Suter	.08	.03	.01
☐ 31	Flames team	.05	.02	.00
☐ 32	Al MacInnis	.15	.06	.01
☐ 33	Brad McCrimmon	.08	.03	.01
☐ 34	Mike Vernon	.10	.04	.01
☐ 35	Gary Roberts	.15	.06	.01
☐ 36	Colin Patterson	.05	.02	.00
☐ 37	Jim Peplinski	.08	.03	.01
☐ 38	Jamie Macoun	.05	.02	.00
☐ 39	Lanny McDonald	.15	.06	.01
☐ 40	Saddledome	.05	.02	.00
☐ 41	Chicago Blackhawks logo	.05	.02	.00
☐ 42	Darren Pang	.08	.03	.01
☐ 43	Steve Larmer	.12	.05	.01
☐ 44	Dirk Graham	.08	.03	.01
☐ 45	Doug Wilson	.10	.04	.01
☐ 46	Blackhawks/Oilers action (Ed Belfour shown)	.75	.30	.07
☐ 47	Dave Manson	.15	.06	.01
☐ 48	Troy Murray	.08	.03	.01
☐ 49	Denis Savard	.12	.05	.01
☐ 50	Steve Thomas	.08	.03	.01
☐ 51	Adam Creighton	.08	.03	.01
☐ 52	Wayne Presley	.05	.02	.00
☐ 53	Trent Yawney	.08	.03	.01
☐ 54	Alain Chevrier	.08	.03	.01
☐ 55	Chicago Stadium	.05	.02	.00
☐ 56	Detroit Red Wings logo	.05	.02	.00
☐ 57	Steve Yzerman	.40	.16	.04
☐ 58	Gerard Gallant	.08	.03	.01
☐ 59	Greg Stefan	.08	.03	.01
☐ 60	Dave Barr	.05	.02	.00
☐ 61	Red Wings team	.05	.02	.00
☐ 62	Steve Chiasson	.08	.03	.01
☐ 63	Shawn Burr	.08	.03	.01
☐ 64	Rick Zombo	.08	.03	.01
☐ 65	Glen Hanlon	.08	.03	.01
☐ 66	Jeff Sharples	.08	.03	.01
☐ 67	Joey Kocur	.05	.02	.00
☐ 68	Lee Norwood	.05	.02	.00
☐ 69	Mike O'Connell	.05	.02	.00
☐ 70	Joe Louis Arena	.05	.02	.00
☐ 71	Edmonton Oilers logo	.05	.02	.00
☐ 72	Jimmy Carson	.10	.04	.01
☐ 73	Jari Kurri	.15	.06	.01
☐ 74	Mark Messier	.40	.16	.04
☐ 75	Craig Simpson	.08	.03	.01
☐ 76	Oilers/Flyers action	.05	.02	.00
☐ 77	Glenn Anderson	.10	.04	.01
☐ 78	Craig MacTavish	.08	.03	.01
☐ 79	Kevin Lowe	.08	.03	.01
☐ 80	Craig Muni	.05	.02	.00
☐ 81	Bill Ranford	.30	.12	.03
☐ 82	Charlie Huddy	.08	.03	.01
☐ 83	Steve Smith	.12	.05	.01
☐ 84	Normand Lacombe	.05	.02	.00
☐ 85	Northlands Coliseum	.05	.02	.00
☐ 86	L.A. Kings logo	.05	.02	.00
☐ 87	Wayne Gretzky	1.00	.40	.10
☐ 88	Bernie Nicholls	.15	.06	.01
☐ 89	Kelly Hrudey	.12	.05	.01
☐ 90	John Tonelli	.08	.03	.01
☐ 91	Oilers/Kings action	.05	.02	.00
☐ 92	Steve Kasper	.05	.02	.00
☐ 93	Steve Duchesne	.08	.03	.01
☐ 94	Mike Krushelnyski	.08	.03	.01
☐ 95	Luc Robitaille	.50	.20	.05
☐ 96	Ron Duguay	.08	.03	.01
☐ 97	Glenn Healy	.08	.03	.01
☐ 98	Dave Taylor	.08	.03	.01
☐ 99	Marty McSorley	.35	.14	.03
☐ 100	The Great Western Forum	.05	.02	.00
☐ 101	Minnesota North Stars logo	.05	.02	.00
☐ 102	Kari Takko	.08	.03	.01
☐ 103	Dave Gagner	.20	.08	.02
☐ 104	Mike Gartner	.15	.06	.01
☐ 105	Brian Bellows	.10	.04	.01
☐ 106	North Stars team	.05	.02	.00
☐ 107	Neal Broten	.08	.03	.01
☐ 108	Larry Murphy	.10	.04	.01
☐ 109	Basil McRae	.05	.02	.00
☐ 110	Perry Berezan	.05	.02	.00
☐ 111	Shawn Chambers	.05	.02	.00
☐ 112	Curt Giles	.05	.02	.00
☐ 113	Stewart Gavin	.05	.02	.00
☐ 114	Jon Casey	.25	.10	.02
☐ 115	Metropolitan Sports Center	.05	.02	.00

☐ 116	St. Louis Blues logo	.05	.02	.00
☐ 117	Brett Hull	.75	.30	.07
☐ 118	Peter Zezel	.05	.02	.00
☐ 119	Tony Hrkac	.05	.02	.00
☐ 120	Vincent Riendeau	.25	.10	.02
☐ 121	Blues/Islanders action	.05	.02	.00
☐ 122	Cliff Ronning	.25	.10	.02
☐ 123	Gino Cavallini	.08	.03	.01
☐ 124	Brian Benning	.05	.02	.00
☐ 125	Rick Meagher	.05	.02	.00
☐ 126	Steve Tuttle	.05	.02	.00
☐ 127	Paul Cavallini	.05	.02	.00
☐ 128	Tom Tilley	.05	.02	.00
☐ 129	Greg Millen	.08	.03	.01
☐ 130	St. Louis Arena	.05	.02	.00
☐ 131	Toronto Maple Leafs logo	.05	.02	.00
☐ 132	Ed Olczyk	.10	.04	.01
☐ 133	Gary Leeman	.08	.03	.01
☐ 134	Vincent Damphousse	.20	.08	.02
☐ 135	Tom Fergus	.05	.02	.00
☐ 136	Maple Leafs action	.05	.02	.00
☐ 137	Daniel Marois	.08	.03	.01
☐ 138	Mark Osborne	.05	.02	.00
☐ 139	Allan Bester	.05	.02	.00
☐ 140	Al Iafrate	.15	.06	.01
☐ 141	Brad Marsh	.08	.03	.01
☐ 142	Luke Richardson	.05	.02	.00
☐ 143	Todd Gill	.08	.03	.01
☐ 144	Wendel Clark	.20	.08	.02
☐ 145	Maple Leafs Gardens	.05	.02	.00
☐ 146	Vancouver Canucks logo	.05	.02	.00
☐ 147	Petri Skriko	.05	.02	.00
☐ 148	Trevor Linden	.75	.30	.07
☐ 149	Tony Tanti	.08	.03	.01
☐ 150	Steve Weeks	.08	.03	.01
☐ 151	Canucks/Islanders action	.05	.02	.00
☐ 152	Brian Bradley	.20	.08	.02
☐ 153	Barry Pederson	.08	.03	.01
☐ 154	Greg Adams	.08	.03	.01
☐ 155	Kirk McLean	.25	.10	.02
☐ 156	Jim Sandlak	.08	.03	.01
☐ 157	Rich Sutter	.08	.03	.01
☐ 158	Garth Butcher	.08	.03	.01
☐ 159	Stan Smyl	.05	.02	.00
☐ 160	Pacific Coliseum	.05	.02	.00
☐ 161	Winnipeg Jets logo	.05	.02	.00
☐ 162	Dale Hawerchuk	.15	.06	.01
☐ 163	Thomas Steen	.08	.03	.01
☐ 164	Brent Ashton	.05	.02	.00
☐ 165	Pat Elynuik	.10	.04	.01
☐ 166	Jets/Islanders action	.05	.02	.00
☐ 167	Dave Ellett	.08	.03	.01
☐ 168	Randy Carlyle	.08	.03	.01
☐ 169	Laurie Boschman	.05	.02	.00
☐ 170	Iain Duncan	.05	.02	.00
☐ 171	Doug Smail	.08	.03	.01
☐ 172	Teppo Numminen	.10	.04	.01
☐ 173	Bob Essensa	.25	.10	.02
☐ 174	Peter Taglianetti	.05	.02	.00
☐ 175	Winnipeg Arena	.05	.02	.00
☐ 176	Steve Duchesne AS	.08	.03	.01
☐ 177	Luc Robitaille AS	.25	.10	.02
☐ 178	Mike Vernon AS	.10	.04	.01
☐ 179	Wayne Gretzky AS	.50	.20	.05
☐ 180	Kevin Lowe AS	.08	.03	.01
☐ 181	Jari Kurri AS	.15	.06	.01
☐ 182	Cam Neely AS	.20	.08	.02
☐ 183	Paul Coffey AS	.15	.06	.01
☐ 184	Mario Lemieux AS	.40	.16	.04
☐ 185	Sean Burke AS	.08	.03	.01
☐ 186	Rob Brown AS	.05	.02	.00
☐ 187	Ray Bourque AS	.15	.00	.01
☐ 188	Boston Bruins logo	.05	.02	.00
☐ 189	Greg Hawgood	.05	.02	.00
☐ 190	Ken Linseman	.05	.02	.00
☐ 191	Andy Moog	.12	.05	.01
☐ 192	Cam Neely	.30	.12	.03
☐ 193	Bruins/Flyers action	.05	.02	.00
☐ 194	Andy Brickley	.08	.03	.01
☐ 195	Rejean Lemelin	.08	.03	.01
☐ 196	Bob Carpenter	.08	.03	.01
☐ 197	Randy Burridge	.08	.03	.01
☐ 198	Craig Janney	.50	.20	.05
☐ 199	Bob Joyce	.05	.02	.00
☐ 200	Glen Wesley	.10	.04	.01
☐ 201	Ray Bourque	.15	.06	.01
☐ 202	Boston Garden	.05	.02	.00
☐ 203	Buffalo Sabres logo	.05	.02	.00
☐ 204	Pierre Turgeon	.35	.14	.03
☐ 205	Phil Housley	.12	.05	.01
☐ 206	Rick Vaive	.08	.03	.01
☐ 207	Christian Ruuttu	.08	.03	.01
☐ 208	Flyers/Sabres action	.05	.02	.00
☐ 209	Doug Bodger	.05	.02	.00
☐ 210	Mike Foligno	.05	.02	.00
☐ 211	Ray Sheppard	.20	.08	.02
☐ 212	John Tucker	.05	.02	.00
☐ 213	Scott Arniel	.05	.02	.00
☐ 214	Daren Puppa	.10	.04	.01
☐ 215	Dave Andreychuk	.20	.08	.02
☐ 216	Uwe Krupp	.05	.02	.00
☐ 217	Memorial Auditorium	.05	.02	.00
☐ 218	Hartford Whalers logo	.05	.02	.00
☐ 219	Kevin Dineen	.08	.03	.01
☐ 220	Peter Sidorkiewicz	.08	.03	.01
☐ 221	Ron Francis	.10	.04	.01
☐ 222	Ray Ferraro	.10	.04	.01
☐ 223	Islanders/Whalers action	.05	.02	.00
☐ 224	Scott Young	.08	.03	.01
☐ 225	Dave Babych	.08	.03	.01
☐ 226	Dave Tippett	.05	.02	.00
☐ 227	Paul MacDermid	.05	.02	.00
☐ 228	Ulf Samuelsson	.12	.05	.01
☐ 229	Sylvain Cote	.05	.02	.00
☐ 230	Jody Hull	.05	.02	.00
☐ 231	Don Maloney	.05	.02	.00
☐ 232	Hartford Civic Center	.05	.02	.00
☐ 233	Montreal Canadiens logo	.05	.02	.00
☐ 234	Mats Naslund	.08	.03	.01
☐ 235	Patrick Roy	.40	.16	.04
☐ 236	Bobby Smith	.08	.03	.01
☐ 237	Chris Chelios	.15	.06	.01
☐ 238	Flames/Canadiens action	.05	.02	.00
☐ 239	Stephane Richer	.15	.06	.01
☐ 240	Claude Lemieux	.15	.06	.01
☐ 241	Guy Carbonneau	.10	.04	.01
☐ 242	Shayne Corson	.15	.06	.01
☐ 243	Mike McPhee	.08	.03	.01
☐ 244	Petr Svoboda	.08	.03	.01
☐ 245	Larry Robinson	.15	.06	.01
☐ 246	Brian Hayward	.08	.03	.01
☐ 247	Montreal Forum	.08	.03	.01
☐ 248	New Jersey Devils logo	.05	.02	.00
☐ 249	John MacLean	.12	.05	.01
☐ 250	Patrik Sundstrom	.08	.03	.01
☐ 251	Kirk Muller	.15	.06	.01
☐ 252	Tom Kurvers	.05	.02	.00
☐ 253	Bruins/Devils action	.05	.02	.00
☐ 254	Aaron Broten	.05	.02	.00
☐ 255	Brendan Shanahan	.40	.16	.04
☐ 256	Sean Burke	.12	.05	.01
☐ 257	Tommy Albelin	.05	.02	.00
☐ 258	Ken Daneyko	.08	.03	.01
☐ 259	Randy Velischek	.05	.02	.00
☐ 260	Mark Johnson	.05	.02	.00
☐ 261	Jim Korn	.05	.02	.00
☐ 262	Brendan Byrne Arena	.05	.02	.00
☐ 263	New York Islanders logo	.05	.02	.00
☐ 264	Pat LaFontaine	.40	.16	.04
☐ 265	Mark Fitzpatrick	.25	.10	.02
☐ 266	Brent Sutter	.08	.03	.01
☐ 267	David Volek	.05	.02	.00
☐ 268	Islanders/Rangers action	.05	.02	.00
☐ 269	Bryan Trottier	.15	.06	.01
☐ 270	Mikko Makela	.05	.02	.00
☐ 271	Derek King	.15	.06	.01
☐ 272	Pat Flatley	.05	.02	.00
☐ 273	Jeff Norton	.08	.03	.01
☐ 274	Gerald Diduck	.05	.02	.00
☐ 275	Alan Kerr	.05	.02	.00
☐ 276	Jeff Hackett	.20	.00	.02
☐ 277	Nassau Veterans Memorial Coliseum	.05	.02	.00
☐ 278	New York Rangers logo	.05	.02	.00
☐ 279	Brian Leetch	.75	.30	.07
☐ 280	Carey Wilson	.05	.02	.00
☐ 281	Tomas Sandstrom	.10	.04	.01
☐ 282	John Vanbiesbrouck	.20	.08	.02
☐ 283	Oilers/Rangers action	.05	.02	.00
☐ 284	Bob Froese	.08	.03	.01
☐ 285	Tony Granato	.10	.04	.01
☐ 286	Brian Mullen	.08	.03	.01
☐ 287	Kelly Kisio	.08	.03	.01
☐ 288	Ulf Dahlen	.08	.03	.01

☐ 289	James Patrick	.08	.03	.01
☐ 290	John Ogrodnick	.08	.03	.01
☐ 291	Michel Petit	.08	.03	.01
☐ 292	Madison Square Garden	.05	.02	.00
☐ 293	Philadelphia Flyers logo	.05	.02	.00
☐ 294	Tim Kerr	.08	.03	.01
☐ 295	Rick Tocchet	.15	.06	.01
☐ 296	Pelle Eklund	.08	.03	.01
☐ 297	Terry Carkner	.08	.03	.01
☐ 298	Flyers/Canadiens action	.05	.02	.00
☐ 299	Ron Sutter	.08	.03	.01
☐ 300	Mark Howe	.08	.03	.01
☐ 301	Keith Acton	.05	.02	.00
☐ 302	Ron Hextall	.10	.04	.01
☐ 303	Gord Murphy	.05	.02	.00
☐ 304	Derrick Smith	.05	.02	.00
☐ 305	Dave Poulin	.05	.02	.00
☐ 306	Brian Propp	.08	.03	.01
☐ 307	The Spectrum	.05	.02	.00
☐ 308	Pittsburgh Penguins logo	.05	.02	.00
☐ 309	Mario Lemieux	.75	.30	.07
☐ 310	Rob Brown	.08	.03	.01
☐ 311	Paul Coffey	.20	.08	.02
☐ 312	Tom Barrasso	.15	.06	.01
☐ 313	Penguins/Flyers action	.05	.02	.00
☐ 314	Dan Quinn	.05	.02	.00
☐ 315	Bob Errey	.05	.02	.00
☐ 316	John Cullen	.20	.08	.02
☐ 317	Phil Bourque	.05	.02	.00
☐ 318	Zarley Zalapski	.08	.03	.01
☐ 319	Troy Loney	.08	.03	.01
☐ 320	Jim Johnson	.05	.02	.00
☐ 321	Kevin Stevens	1.50	.60	.15
☐ 322	Civic Arena	.05	.02	.00
☐ 323	Quebec Nordiques logo	.05	.02	.00
☐ 324	Peter Stastny	.15	.06	.01
☐ 325	Jeff Brown	.10	.04	.01
☐ 326	Michel Goulet	.10	.04	.01
☐ 327	Joe Sakic	1.50	.60	.15
☐ 328	Flyers/Nordiques action	.05	.02	.00
☐ 329	Iiro Jarvi	.05	.02	.00
☐ 330	Paul Gillis	.05	.02	.00
☐ 331	Randy Moller	.05	.02	.00
☐ 332	Ron Tugnutt	.20	.08	.02
☐ 333	Robert Picard	.05	.02	.00
☐ 334	Curtis Leschyshyn	.08	.03	.01
☐ 335	Marc Fortier	.05	.02	.00
☐ 336	Mario Marois	.05	.02	.00
☐ 337	Le Colisee	.05	.02	.00
☐ 338	Washington Capitals	.05	.02	.00
☐ 339	Mike Ridley	.08	.03	.01
☐ 340	Geoff Courtnall	.15	.06	.01
☐ 341	Scott Stevens	.10	.04	.01
☐ 342	Dino Ciccarelli	.10	.04	.01
☐ 343	Capitals/Flames action	.05	.02	.00
☐ 344	Bob Mason	.05	.02	.00
☐ 345	Dave Christian	.08	.03	.01
☐ 346	Dale Hunter	.08	.03	.01
☐ 347	Kevin Hatcher	.15	.06	.01
☐ 348	Kelly Miller	.08	.03	.01
☐ 349	Stephen Leach	.08	.03	.01
☐ 350	Rod Langway	.08	.03	.01
☐ 351	Bob Rouse	.05	.02	.00
☐ 352	Capital Centre	.05	.02	.00
☐ 353	Calgary Flames logo	.05	.02	.00
☐ 354	Edmonton Oilers logo	.05	.02	.00
☐ 355	Winnipeg Jets logo	.05	.02	.00
☐ 356	Toronto Maple Leafs logo	.05	.02	.00
☐ 357	Buffalo Sabres logo	.05	.02	.00
☐ 358	Montreal Canadiens logo	.05	.02	.00
☐ 359	Quebec Nordiques logo	.05	.02	.00
☐ 360	New Jersey Devils logo	.05	.02	.00
☐ 361	Boston Bruins logo	.05	.02	.00
☐ 362	Hartford Whalers logo	.05	.02	.00
☐ 363	Vancouver Canucks logo	.05	.02	.00
☐ 364	Minnesota North Stars logo	.05	.02	.00
☐ 365	Los Angeles Kings logo	.05	.02	.00
☐ 366	St. Louis Blues logo	.05	.02	.00
☐ 367	Chicago Blackhawks logo	.05	.02	.00
☐ 368	Detroit Red Wings logo	.05	.02	.00
☐ 369	Pittsburgh Penguins logo	.05	.02	.00
☐ 370	Washington Capitals logo	.05	.02	.00
☐ 371	Philadelphia Flyers logo	.05	.02	.00
☐ 372	New York Rangers logo	.05	.02	.00
☐ 373	New York Islanders logo	.05	.02	.00
☐ 374	Wayne Gretzky	.75	.30	.07
☐ 375	Mario Lemieux	.50	.20	.05
☐ 376	Patrick Roy and Brian Hayward	.25	.10	.02
☐ 377	Tim Kerr	.08	.03	.01
☐ 378	Brian Leetch	.40	.16	.04
☐ 379	Chris Chelios	.10	.04	.01
☐ 380	Joe Mullen	.08	.03	.01
☐ 381	Guy Carbonneau	.08	.03	.01
☐ 382	Bryan Trottier	.15	.06	.01
☐ 383	Patrick Roy	.35	.14	.03
☐ 384	Joe Mullen	.08	.03	.01
☐ xx	Sticker Album	1.50	.60	.15

1990-91 Panini Stickers

Theo Fleury

Collect these stickers in the Panini Hockey '90-'91 album.

Collectionnez les autocollants et conservez-les dans votre album Hockey 90-91 de Panini.

PLIEZ ET SOULEVEZ/BEND AND PEEL

This set of 351 hockey stickers was produced and distributed by Panini. The stickers are numbered on the back and measure approximately 2 1/16" by 2 15/16". The fronts feature full color action photos of the players. Different color triangles (in one of the team's colors) overlay the upper left corner of the pictures, with the team name in white lettering. A variegated stripe appears below the player photos, with the player's name below. The team logo and conference stickers are in foil. The stickers are arranged according to teams as follows: Boston Bruins (4-18, 322, 327), Buffalo Sabres (19-33, 338), Hartford Whalers (34-48, 344), Montreal Canadiens (49-63, 323), New Jersey Devils (64-78, 335, 339), New York Islanders (79-93), New York Rangers (94-108, 345), Philadelphia Flyers (109-123, 325), Pittsburgh Penguins (124-138, 324, 326, 341), Quebec Nordiques (139-153), Washington Capitals (154-168), Calgary Flames (172-186, 328-29, 334, 342), Chicago Blackhawks (187-201), Detroit Red Wings (202-216), Edmonton Oilers (217-231, 330), Los Angeles Kings (232-246), Minnesota North Stars (247-261), St. Louis Blues (262-276, 333, 343), Toronto Maple Leafs (277-291), Vancouver Canucks (292-306, 336-37), and Winnipeg Jets (307-321).

	MINT	EXC	G-VG
COMPLETE SET (351)	20.00	8.00	2.00
COMMON PLAYER (1-351)	.05	.02	.00
☐ 1 Prince of Wales Conference	.08	.03	.01
☐ 2 Clarence Campbell Conference	.05	.02	.00

3	Stanley Cup	.08	.03	.01
4	Dave Poulin	.05	.02	.00
5	Brian Propp	.08	.03	.01
6	Glen Wesley	.08	.03	.01
7	Bob Carpenter	.08	.03	.01
8	John Carter	.05	.02	.00
9	Cam Neely	.20	.08	.02
10	Greg Hawgood	.05	.02	.00
11	Andy Moog	.12	.05	.01
12	Boston Bruins logo	.05	.02	.00
13	Rejean Lemelin	.08	.03	.01
14	Craig Janney	.15	.06	.01
15	Bob Sweeney	.05	.02	.00
16	Andy Brickley	.05	.02	.00
17	Ray Bourque	.15	.06	.01
18	Dave Christian	.08	.03	.01
19	Dave Snuggerud	.05	.02	.00
20	Christian Ruuttu	.05	.02	.00
21	Phil Housley	.12	.05	.01
22	Uwe Krupp	.05	.02	.00
23	Rick Vaive	.08	.03	.01
24	Mike Ramsey	.05	.02	.00
25	Mike Foligno	.05	.02	.00
26	Clint Malarchuk	.08	.03	.01
27	Buffalo Sabres logo	.05	.02	.00
28	Pierre Turgeon	.30	.12	.03
29	Dave Andreychuk	.15	.06	.01
30	Scott Arniel	.05	.02	.00
31	Daren Puppa	.08	.03	.01
32	Mike Hartman	.05	.02	.00
33	Doug Bodger	.08	.03	.01
34	Scott Young	.08	.03	.01
35	Todd Krygier	.08	.03	.01
36	Pat Verbeek	.08	.03	.01
37	Dave Tippett	.05	.02	.00
38	Peter Sidorkiewicz	.08	.03	.01
39	Ron Francis	.10	.04	.01
40	Dave Babych	.08	.03	.01
41	Randy Ladouceur	.05	.02	.00
42	Hartford Whalers logo	.05	.02	.00
43	Kevin Dineen	.08	.03	.01
44	Dean Evason	.08	.03	.01
45	Ray Ferraro	.08	.03	.01
46	Mike Tomlak	.05	.02	.00
47	Mikael Andersson	.05	.02	.00
48	Brad Shaw	.05	.02	.00
49	Chris Chelios	.12	.05	.01
50	Petr Svoboda	.05	.02	.00
51	Patrick Roy	.35	.14	.03
52	Bobby Smith	.08	.03	.01
53	Stephane Richer	.10	.04	.01
54	Shayne Corson	.10	.04	.01
55	Brian Skrudland	.05	.02	.00
56	Russ Courtnall	.10	.04	.01
57	Montreal Canadiens logo	.05	.02	.00
58	Guy Carbonneau	.08	.03	.01
59	Sylvain Lefebvre	.08	.03	.01
60	Mathieu Schneider	.12	.05	.01
61	Brian Hayward	.08	.03	.01
62	Mats Naslund	.08	.03	.01
63	Mike McPhee	.08	.03	.01
64	Brendan Shanahan	.30	.12	.03
65	Patrik Sundstrom	.08	.03	.01
66	Mark Johnson	.05	.02	.00
67	Doug Brown	.05	.02	.00
68	Chris Terreri	.25	.10	.02
69	Bruce Driver	.05	.02	.00
70	Peter Stastny	.12	.05	.01
71	Sylvain Turgeon	.08	.03	.01
72	New Jersey Devils logo	.05	.02	.00
73	Kirk Muller	.15	.06	.01
74	John MacLean	.12	.05	.01
75	Viacheslav Fetisov	.20	.08	.02
76	Tommy Albelin	.05	.02	.00
77	Sean Durko	.10	.04	.01
78	Janne Ojanen	.05	.02	.00
79	Randy Wood	.05	.02	.00
80	Gary Nylund	.05	.02	.00
81	Pat LaFontaine	.30	.12	.03
82	Pat Flatley	.05	.02	.00
83	Bryan Trottier	.15	.06	.01
84	Don Maloney	.05	.02	.00
85	Gerald Diduck	.05	.02	.00
86	Mark Fitzpatrick	.10	.04	.01
87	New York Islanders logo	.05	.02	.00
88	Glenn Healy	.08	.03	.01
89	Alan Kerr	.05	.02	.00
90	Brent Sutter	.08	.03	.01
91	Doug Crossman	.05	.02	.00
92	Hubie McDonough	.05	.02	.00
93	Jeff Norton	.08	.03	.01
94	Kelly Kisio	.08	.03	.01
95	Brian Leetch	.35	.14	.03
96	Brian Mullen	.08	.03	.01
97	James Patrick	.08	.03	.01
98	Mike Richter	.50	.20	.05
99	John Ogrodnick	.08	.03	.01
100	Troy Mallette	.05	.02	.00
101	Mark Janssens	.05	.02	.00
102	New York Rangers logo	.05	.02	.00
103	Mike Gartner	.15	.06	.01
104	Jan Erixon	.05	.02	.00
105	Carey Wilson	.05	.02	.00
106	Bernie Nicholls	.10	.04	.01
107	Darren Turcotte	.10	.04	.01
108	John Vanbiesbrouck	.15	.06	.01
109	Ron Sutter	.08	.03	.01
110	Kjell Samuelsson	.05	.02	.00
111	Ken Linseman	.05	.02	.00
112	Ken Wregget	.08	.03	.01
113	Pelle Eklund	.08	.03	.01
114	Terry Carkner	.05	.02	.00
115	Gord Murphy	.05	.02	.00
116	Murray Craven	.05	.02	.00
117	Philadelphia Flyers logo	.05	.02	.00
118	Ron Hextall	.10	.04	.01
119	Mike Bullard	.05	.02	.00
120	Tim Kerr	.08	.03	.01
121	Rick Tocchet	.12	.05	.01
122	Mark Howe	.08	.03	.01
123	Ilkka Sinisalo	.05	.02	.00
124	Tony Tanti	.05	.02	.00
125	John Cullen	.08	.03	.01
126	Zarley Zalapski	.08	.03	.01
127	Wendell Young	.08	.03	.01
128	Rob Brown	.08	.03	.01
129	Phil Bourque	.05	.02	.00
130	Mark Recchi	.60	.24	.06
131	Kevin Stevens	.60	.24	.06
132	Pittsburgh Penguins logo	.05	.02	.00
133	Bob Errey	.05	.02	.00
134	Tom Barrasso	.12	.05	.00
135	Paul Coffey	.15	.06	.01
136	Mario Lemieux	.60	.24	.06
137	Randy Hillier	.05	.02	.00
138	Troy Loney	.05	.02	.00
139	Joe Sakic	.35	.14	.03
140	Lucien DeBlois	.05	.02	.00
141	Joe Cirella	.05	.02	.00
142	Ron Tugnutt	.12	.05	.01
143	Paul Gillis	.05	.02	.00
144	Bryan Fogarty	.08	.03	.01
145	Guy Lafleur	.15	.06	.01
146	Tony Hrkac	.05	.02	.00
147	Quebec Nordiques logo	.05	.02	.00
148	Michel Petit	.05	.02	.00
149	Tony McKegney	.05	.02	.00
150	Curtis Leschyshyn	.05	.02	.00
151	Claude Loiselle	.05	.02	.00
152	Mario Brunetta	.05	.02	.00
153	Marc Fortier	.05	.02	.00
154	Michal Pivonka	.10	.04	.01
155	Scott Stevens	.10	.04	.01
156	Kelly Miller	.08	.03	.01
157	John Tucker	.05	.02	.00
158	Don Beaupre	.08	.03	.01
159	Geoff Courtnall	.10	.04	.01
160	Alan May	.05	.02	.00
161	Dino Ciccarelli	.10	.04	.01
162	Washington Capitals logo	.05	.02	.00
163	Mike Ridley	.08	.03	.01
164	Bob Rouse	.05	.02	.00
165	Mike Liut	.08	.03	.01
166	Stephen Leach	.08	.03	.01
167	Kevin Hatcher	.12	.05	.01
168	Dale Hunter	.10	.04	.01
169	Prince of Wales Trophy	.05	.02	.00
170	Clarence Campbell Trophy	.05	.02	.00
171	Stanley Cup Championship	.08	.03	.01
172	Doug Gilmour	.40	.16	.04
173	Brad McCrimmon	.08	.03	.01
174	Joe Nieuwendyk	.15	.06	.01
175	Mike Vernon	.12	.05	.01
176	Theoren Fleury	.20	.08	.02
177	Gary Suter	.08	.03	.01
178	Jamie Macoun	.05	.02	.00
179	Gary Roberts	.12	.05	.01
180	Calgary Flames logo	.05	.02	.00

☐ 181	Paul Ranheim	.08	.03	.01
☐ 182	Jiri Hrdina	.05	.02	.00
☐ 183	Joe Mullen	.10	.04	.01
☐ 184	Sergei Makarov	.20	.08	.02
☐ 185	Al MacInnis	.15	.06	.01
☐ 186	Rick Wamsley	.08	.03	.01
☐ 187	Trent Yawney	.05	.02	.00
☐ 188	Greg Millen	.08	.03	.01
☐ 189	Doug Wilson	.08	.03	.01
☐ 190	Jocelyn Lemieux	.05	.02	.00
☐ 191	Dirk Graham	.08	.03	.01
☐ 192	Keith Brown	.05	.02	.00
☐ 193	Adam Creighton	.08	.03	.01
☐ 194	Steve Larmer	.10	.04	.01
☐ 195	Chicago Blackhawks logo	.05	.02	.00
☐ 196	Greg Gilbert	.05	.02	.00
☐ 197	Jacques Cloutier	.05	.02	.00
☐ 198	Denis Savard	.10	.04	.01
☐ 199	Dave Manson	.08	.03	.01
☐ 200	Troy Murray	.08	.03	.01
☐ 201	Jeremy Roenick	1.25	.50	.12
☐ 202	Lee Norwood	.05	.02	.00
☐ 203	Glen Hanlon	.08	.03	.01
☐ 204	Marc Habscheid	.05	.02	.00
☐ 205	Gerard Gallant	.08	.03	.01
☐ 206	Rick Zombo	.05	.02	.00
☐ 207	Steve Chiasson	.08	.03	.01
☐ 208	Steve Yzerman	.40	.16	.04
☐ 209	Bernie Federko	.10	.04	.01
☐ 210	Detroit Red Wings logo	.05	.02	.00
☐ 211	Joey Kocur	.08	.03	.01
☐ 212	Tim Cheveldae	.25	.10	.02
☐ 213	Shawn Burr	.05	.02	.00
☐ 214	Jimmy Carson	.08	.03	.01
☐ 215	Mike O'Connell	.05	.02	.00
☐ 216	John Chabot	.05	.02	.00
☐ 217	Craig Muni	.05	.02	.00
☐ 218	Bill Ranford	.15	.06	.01
☐ 219	Mark Messier	.35	.14	.03
☐ 220	Craig MacTavish	.08	.03	.01
☐ 221	Charlie Huddy	.05	.02	.00
☐ 222	Jari Kurri	.15	.06	.01
☐ 223	Esa Tikkanen	.10	.04	.01
☐ 224	Kevin Lowe	.08	.03	.01
☐ 225	Edmonton Oilers logo	.06	.02	.00
☐ 226	Steve Smith	.10	.04	.01
☐ 227	Glenn Anderson	.10	.04	.01
☐ 228	Petr Klima	.08	.03	.01
☐ 229	Craig Simpson	.08	.03	.01
☐ 230	Grant Fuhr	.12	.05	.01
☐ 231	Randy Gregg	.05	.02	.00
☐ 232	Bob Kudelski	.10	.04	.01
☐ 233	Luc Robitaille	.25	.10	.02
☐ 234	Marty McSorley	.20	.08	.02
☐ 235	John Tonelli	.08	.03	.01
☐ 236	Dave Taylor	.08	.03	.01
☐ 237	Mikko Makela	.05	.02	.00
☐ 238	Steve Kasper	.05	.02	.00
☐ 239	Tony Granato	.10	.04	.01
☐ 240	Los Angeles Kings logo	.05	.02	.00
☐ 241	Steve Duchesne	.08	.03	.01
☐ 242	Wayne Gretzky	.75	.30	.07
☐ 243	Tomas Sandstrom	.10	.04	.01
☐ 244	Larry Robinson	.10	.04	.01
☐ 245	Mike Krushelnyski	.08	.03	.01
☐ 246	Kelly Hrudey	.10	.04	.01
☐ 247	Aaron Broten	.05	.02	.00
☐ 248	Dave Gagner	.10	.04	.01
☐ 249	Basil McRae	.05	.02	.00
☐ 250	Curt Giles	.05	.02	.00
☐ 251	Larry Murphy	.10	.04	.01
☐ 252	Shawn Chambers	.05	.02	.00
☐ 253	Mike Modano	.50	.20	.05
☐ 254	Jon Casey	.10	.04	.01
☐ 255	Minnesota North Stars logo	.05	.02	.00
☐ 256	Gaetan Duchesne	.05	.02	.00
☐ 257	Brian Bellows	.10	.04	.01
☐ 258	Frantisek Musil	.05	.02	.00
☐ 259	Don Barber	.05	.02	.00
☐ 260	Stewart Gavin	.05	.02	.00
☐ 261	Neal Broten	.08	.03	.01
☐ 262	Brett Hull	.60	.24	.06
☐ 263	Sergio Momesso	.08	.03	.01
☐ 264	Peter Zezel	.05	.02	.00
☐ 265	Gino Cavallini	.05	.02	.00
☐ 266	Rod Brind'Amour	.30	.12	.03
☐ 267	Mike Lalor	.05	.02	.00
☐ 268	Vincent Riendeau	.12	.05	.01
☐ 269	Gordie Roberts	.05	.02	.00
☐ 270	St. Louis Blues logo	.05	.02	.00
☐ 271	Paul MacLean	.05	.02	.00
☐ 272	Curtis Joseph	.50	.20	.05
☐ 273	Rick Meagher	.05	.02	.00
☐ 274	Jeff Brown	.10	.04	.01
☐ 275	Adam Oates	.20	.08	.02
☐ 276	Paul Cavallini	.05	.02	.00
☐ 277	Brad Marsh	.08	.03	.01
☐ 278	Mark Osborne	.05	.02	.00
☐ 279	Gary Leeman	.08	.03	.01
☐ 280	Rob Ramage	.08	.03	.01
☐ 281	Jeff Reese	.08	.03	.01
☐ 282	Tom Fergus	.05	.02	.00
☐ 283	Ed Olczyk	.08	.03	.01
☐ 284	Daniel Marois	.05	.02	.00
☐ 285	Toronto Maple Leafs logo	.05	.02	.00
☐ 286	Wendel Clark	.20	.08	.02
☐ 287	Tom Kurvers	.05	.02	.00
☐ 288	Gilles Thibaudeau	.05	.02	.00
☐ 289	Lou Franceschetti	.05	.02	.00
☐ 290	Al Iafrate	.15	.06	.01
☐ 291	Vincent Damphousse	.12	.05	.01
☐ 292	Stan Smyl	.05	.02	.00
☐ 293	Paul Reinhart	.05	.02	.00
☐ 294	Igor Larionov	.15	.06	.01
☐ 295	Doug Lidster	.05	.02	.00
☐ 296	Kirk McLean	.20	.08	.02
☐ 297	Andrew McBain	.05	.02	.00
☐ 298	Petri Skriko	.05	.02	.00
☐ 299	Trevor Linden	.30	.12	.03
☐ 300	Vancouver Canucks logo	.05	.02	.00
☐ 301	Steve Bozek	.05	.02	.00
☐ 302	Brian Bradley	.12	.05	.01
☐ 303	Greg Adams	.08	.03	.01
☐ 304	Vladimir Krutov	.05	.02	.00
☐ 305	Dan Quinn	.05	.02	.00
☐ 306	Jim Sandlak	.08	.03	.01
☐ 307	Teppo Numminen	.05	.02	.00
☐ 308	Doug Smail	.05	.02	.00
☐ 309	Greg Paslawski	.05	.02	.00
☐ 310	Dave Ellett	.08	.03	.01
☐ 311	Bob Essensa	.12	.05	.01
☐ 312	Pat Elynuik	.08	.03	.01
☐ 313	Paul Fenton	.05	.02	.00
☐ 314	Randy Carlyle	.08	.03	.01
☐ 315	Winnipeg Jets logo	.05	.02	.00
☐ 316	Thomas Steen	.08	.03	.01
☐ 317	Dale Hawerchuk	.12	.05	.01
☐ 318	Fredrik Olausson	.08	.03	.01
☐ 319	Dave McLlwain	.05	.02	.00
☐ 320	Laurie Boschman	.05	.02	.00
☐ 321	Brent Ashton	.05	.02	.00
☐ 322	Ray Bourque	.15	.06	.01
☐ 323	Patrick Roy	.35	.14	.03
☐ 324	Paul Coffey	.15	.06	.01
☐ 325	Brian Propp	.08	.03	.01
☐ 326	Mario Lemieux	.60	.24	.06
☐ 327	Cam Neely	.20	.08	.02
☐ 328	Al MacInnis	.15	.06	.01
☐ 329	Mike Vernon	.10	.04	.01
☐ 330	Kevin Lowe	.08	.03	.01
☐ 331	Luc Robitaille	.25	.10	.02
☐ 332	Wayne Gretzky	.75	.30	.07
☐ 333	Brett Hull	.50	.20	.05
☐ 334	Sergei Makarov	.20	.08	.02
☐ 335	Alexei Kasatonov	.10	.04	.01
☐ 336	Igor Larionov	.15	.06	.01
☐ 337	Vladimir Krutov	.05	.02	.00
☐ 338	Alexander Mogilny	.75	.30	.07
☐ 339	Viacheslav Fetisov	.15	.06	.01
☐ 340	Mike Modano	.50	.20	.05
☐ 341	Mark Recchi	.50	.20	.05
☐ 342	Paul Ranheim	.08	.03	.01
☐ 343	Rod Brind'Amour	.30	.12	.03
☐ 344	Shaw Shaw	.05	.02	.00
☐ 345	Mike Richter	.40	.16	.04
☐ 346	Hart Trophy	.08	.03	.01
☐ 347	Art Ross Trophy	.08	.03	.01
☐ 348	Calder Memorial Trophy	.08	.03	.01
☐ 349	Lady Byng Trophy	.08	.03	.01
☐ 350	Norris Trophy	.08	.03	.01
☐ 351	Vezina Trophy	.08	.03	.01
☐ xx	Sticker Album	1.50	.60	.15

1991-92 Panini Stickers

This set of 344 stickers was produced by Panini. They measure approximately 1 7/8" by 2 7/8" and were to be

pasted in a 8 1/4" by 10 1/2" bilingual sticker album. The fronts feature color action shots of the players. Pages 2-5 of the album picture highlights of the 1991 Stanley Cup playoffs and finals. Team pages have team colors that highlight player stickers. The NHL 75th Anniversary logo (3-4) and the circular-shaped team logos (148-169) are foil. The stickers are numbered on the back and checklisted below alphabetically according to teams in the Clarence Campbell and Prince of Wales conferences as follows: Chicago Blackhawks (8-21), St. Louis Blues (22-35), Vancouver Canucks (36-49), Calgary Flames (50-63), Winnipeg Jets (64-77), Los Angeles Kings (78-91), Toronto Maple Leafs (92-105), Minnesota North Stars (106-119), Edmonton Oilers (120-133), Detroit Red Wings (134-147), Boston Bruins (170-183), Montreal Canadiens (184-197), Washington Capitals (198-211), New Jersey Devils (212-225), Philadelphia Flyers (226-239), New York Islanders (240-253), Quebec Nordiques (254-267), Pittsburgh Penguins (268-281), New York Rangers (282-295), Buffalo Sabres (296-309), and Hartford Whalers (310-323). The album closes with topical subsets focusing on the NHL All-Star game (324-336) and top NHL rookies (337-344).

	MINT	EXC	G-VG
COMPLETE SET (344)	15.00	6.00	1.50
COMMON PLAYER (1-344)	.05	.02	.00
☐ 1 NHL Logo	.08	.03	.01
☐ 2 NHLPA Logo	.05	.02	.00
☐ 3 NHL Logo 75th	.05	.02	.00
Anniversary (Left)			
☐ 4 NHL Logo 75th	.05	.02	.00
Anniversary (Right)			
☐ 5 Clarence Campbell	.05	.02	.00
Conference Logo			
☐ 6 Prince of Wales	.05	.02	.00
Conference Logo			
☐ 7 Stanley Cup	.05	.02	.00
Championship Logo			
☐ 8 Steve Larmer	.10	.04	.01
☐ 9 Ed Belfour	.35	.14	.03
☐ 10 Chris Chelios	.12	.05	.01
☐ 11 Michel Goulet	.10	.04	.01
☐ 12 Jeremy Roenick	.50	.20	.05
☐ 13 Adam Creighton	.08	.03	.01
☐ 14 Steve Thomas	.08	.03	.01
☐ 15 Dave Manson	.08	.03	.01
☐ 16 Dirk Graham	.08	.03	.01
☐ 17 Troy Murray	.08	.03	.01
☐ 18 Doug Wilson	.08	.03	.01
☐ 19 Wayne Presley	.05	.02	.00
☐ 20 Jocelyn Lemieux	.05	.02	.00
☐ 21 Keith Brown	.05	.02	.00
☐ 22 Curtis Joseph	.25	.10	.02
☐ 23 Jeff Brown	.10	.04	.01
☐ 24 Gino Cavallini	.05	.02	.00
☐ 25 Brett Hull	.40	.16	.04
☐ 26 Scott Stevens	.10	.04	.01
☐ 27 Dan Quinn	.05	.02	.00
☐ 28 Garth Butcher	.08	.03	.01
☐ 29 Bob Bassen	.05	.02	.00
☐ 30 Rod Brind'Amour	.15	.06	.01
☐ 31 Adam Oates	.15	.06	.01

☐ 32 Dave Lowry	.05	.02	.00
☐ 33 Rich Sutter	.08	.03	.01
☐ 34 Ron Wilson	.05	.02	.00
☐ 35 Paul Cavallini	.05	.02	.00
☐ 36 Trevor Linden	.20	.08	.02
☐ 37 Troy Gamble	.15	.06	.01
☐ 38 Geoff Courtnall	.08	.03	.01
☐ 39 Greg Adams	.08	.03	.01
☐ 40 Doug Lidster	.05	.02	.00
☐ 41 Dave Capuano	.05	.02	.00
☐ 42 Igor Larionov	.10	.04	.01
☐ 43 Tom Kurvers	.05	.02	.00
☐ 44 Sergio Momesso	.08	.03	.01
☐ 45 Kirk McLean	.15	.06	.01
☐ 46 Cliff Ronning	.10	.04	.01
☐ 47 Robert Kron	.08	.03	.01
☐ 48 Steve Bozek	.05	.02	.00
☐ 49 Petr Nedved	.60	.24	.06
☐ 50 Al MacInnis	.15	.06	.01
☐ 51 Theoren Fleury	.12	.05	.01
☐ 52 Gary Roberts	.10	.04	.01
☐ 53 Joe Nieuwendyk	.10	.04	.01
☐ 54 Paul Ranheim	.05	.02	.00
☐ 55 Mike Vernon	.10	.04	.01
☐ 56 Carey Wilson	.05	.02	.00
☐ 57 Gary Suter	.08	.03	.01
☐ 58 Sergei Makarov	.15	.06	.01
☐ 59 Doug Gilmour	.35	.14	.03
☐ 60 Joel Otto	.08	.03	.01
☐ 61 Jamie Macoun	.05	.02	.00
☐ 62 Stephane Matteau	.08	.03	.01
☐ 63 Robert Reichel	.30	.12	.03
☐ 64 Ed Olczyk	.08	.03	.01
☐ 65 Phil Housley	.10	.04	.01
☐ 66 Pat Elynuik	.08	.03	.01
☐ 67 Fredrik Olausson	.08	.03	.01
☐ 68 Thomas Steen	.08	.03	.01
☐ 69 Paul MacDermid	.05	.02	.00
☐ 70 Brent Ashton	.05	.02	.00
☐ 71 Teppo Numminen	.05	.02	.00
☐ 72 Danton Cole	.05	.02	.00
☐ 73 Dave McLlwain	.05	.02	.00
☐ 74 Scott Arniel	.05	.02	.00
☐ 75 Bob Essensa	.08	.03	.01
☐ 76 Randy Carlyle	.08	.03	.01
☐ 77 Mark Osborne	.05	.02	.00
☐ 78 Wayne Gretzky	.75	.30	.07
☐ 79 Tomas Sandstrom	.10	.04	.01
☐ 80 Steve Duchesne	.08	.03	.01
☐ 81 Kelly Hrudey	.10	.04	.01
☐ 82 Larry Robinson	.10	.04	.01
☐ 83 Tony Granato	.08	.03	.01
☐ 84 Marty McSorley	.15	.06	.01
☐ 85 Todd Elik	.08	.03	.01
☐ 86 Rob Blake	.20	.08	.02
☐ 87 Bob Kudelski	.08	.03	.01
☐ 88 Steve Kasper	.05	.02	.00
☐ 89 Dave Taylor	.08	.03	.01
☐ 90 John Tonelli	.08	.03	.01
☐ 91 Luc Robitaille	.20	.08	.02
☐ 92 Vincent Damphousse	.12	.05	.01
☐ 93 Brian Bradley	.10	.04	.01
☐ 94 Dave Ellett	.08	.03	.01
☐ 95 Daniel Marois	.05	.02	.00
☐ 96 Rob Ramage	.08	.03	.01
☐ 97 Mike Krushelnyski	.08	.03	.01
☐ 98 Michel Petit	.05	.02	.00
☐ 99 Peter Ing	.08	.03	.01
☐ 100 Lucien DeBlois	.05	.02	.00
☐ 101 Bob Rouse	.05	.02	.00
☐ 102 Wendel Clark	.15	.06	.01
☐ 103 Peter Zezel	.08	.03	.01
☐ 104 David Reid	.05	.02	.00
☐ 105 Aaron Broten	.05	.02	.00
☐ 106 Brian Hayward	.08	.03	.01
☐ 107 Neal Broten	.08	.03	.01
☐ 108 Brian Bellows	.08	.03	.01
☐ 109 Mark Tinordi	.10	.04	.01
☐ 110 Ulf Dahlen	.08	.03	.01
☐ 111 Doug Smail	.08	.03	.01
☐ 112 Dave Gagner	.08	.03	.01
☐ 113 Bobby Smith	.08	.03	.01
☐ 114 Brian Glynn	.05	.02	.00
☐ 115 Brian Propp	.08	.03	.01
☐ 116 Mike Modano	.25	.10	.02
☐ 117 Gaetan Duchesne	.05	.02	.00
☐ 118 Jon Casey	.10	.04	.01
☐ 119 Basil McRae	.05	.02	.00
☐ 120 Glenn Anderson	.10	.04	.01
☐ 121 Steve Smith	.10	.04	.01
☐ 122 Adam Graves	.35	.14	.03
☐ 123 Esa Tikkanen	.10	.04	.01
☐ 124 Mark Messier	.40	.16	.04

☐	125	Bill Ranford	.15	.06	.01	☐	196	Shayne Corson	.08	.03	.01
☐	126	Petr Klima	.08	.03	.01	☐	197	Guy Carbonneau	.08	.03	.01
☐	127	Anatoli Semenov	.10	.04	.01	☐	198	Kevin Hatcher	.10	.04	.01
☐	128	Martin Gelinas	.10	.04	.01	☐	199	Mike Ridley	.08	.03	.01
☐	129	Charlie Huddy	.05	.02	.00	☐	200	John Druce	.05	.02	.00
☐	130	Craig Simpson	.08	.03	.01	☐	201	Don Beaupre	.08	.03	.01
☐	131	Kevin Lowe	.08	.03	.01	☐	202	Kelly Miller	.08	.03	.01
☐	132	Craig MacTavish	.08	.03	.01	☐	203	Dale Hunter	.08	.03	.01
☐	133	Craig Muni	.05	.02	.00	☐	204	Nick Kypreos	.05	.02	.00
☐	134	Steve Yzerman	.35	.14	.03	☐	205	Calle Johansson	.05	.02	.00
☐	135	Shawn Burr	.05	.02	.00	☐	206	Michal Pivonka	.15	.06	.01
☐	136	Tim Cheveldae	.15	.06	.01	☐	207	Dino Ciccarelli	.10	.04	.01
☐	137	Rick Zombo	.05	.02	.00	☐	208	Al Iafrate	.12	.05	.01
☐	138	Marc Habscheid	.05	.02	.00	☐	209	Rod Langway	.08	.03	.01
☐	139	Jimmy Carson	.08	.03	.01	☐	210	Mikhail Tatarinov	.10	.04	.01
☐	140	Brent Fedyk	.08	.03	.01	☐	211	Stephen Leach	.08	.03	.01
☐	141	Yves Racine	.05	.02	.00	☐	212	Sean Burke	.10	.04	.01
☐	142	Gerard Gallant	.08	.03	.01	☐	213	John MacLean	.08	.03	.01
☐	143	Steve Chiasson	.08	.03	.01	☐	214	Lee Norwood	.05	.02	.00
☐	144	Johan Garpenlov	.12	.05	.01	☐	215	Laurie Boschman	.05	.02	.00
☐	145	Sergei Fedorov	.75	.30	.07	☐	216	Alexei Kasatonov	.08	.03	.01
☐	146	Bob Probert	.12	.05	.01	☐	217	Patrik Sundstrom	.08	.03	.01
☐	147	Rick Green	.05	.02	.00	☐	218	Ken Daneyko	.08	.03	.01
☐	148	Chicago Blackhawks Logo	.05	.02	.00	☐	219	Kirk Muller	.12	.05	.01
☐	149	Detroit Red Wings Logo	.05	.02	.00	☐	220	Peter Stastny	.12	.05	.01
						☐	221	Chris Terreri	.10	.04	.01
☐	150	Minnesota North Stars Logo	.05	.02	.00	☐	222	Brendan Shanahan	.20	.08	.02
☐	151	St. Louis Blues Logo	.05	.02	.00	☐	223	Eric Weinrich	.08	.03	.01
						☐	224	Claude Lemieux	.10	.04	.01
☐	152	Toronto Maple Leafs Logo	.05	.02	.00	☐	225	Bruce Driver	.08	.03	.01
						☐	226	Tim Kerr	.08	.03	.01
☐	153	Calgary Flames Logo	.05	.02	.00	☐	227	Ron Hextall	.10	.04	.01
						☐	228	Pelle Eklund	.08	.03	.01
☐	154	Edmonton Oilers Logo	.05	.02	.00	☐	229	Rick Tocchet	.10	.04	.01
						☐	230	Gord Murphy	.05	.02	.00
☐	155	Los Angeles Kings Logo	.05	.02	.00	☐	231	Mike Ricci	.30	.12	.03
						☐	232	Derrick Smith	.05	.02	.00
☐	156	San Jose Sharks Logo	.25	.10	.02	☐	233	Ron Sutter	.08	.03	.01
						☐	234	Murray Craven	.05	.02	.00
☐	157	Vancouver Canucks Logo	.05	.02	.00	☐	235	Terry Carkner	.05	.02	.00
						☐	236	Ken Wregget	.08	.03	.01
☐	158	Winnipeg Jets Logo	.05	.02	.00	☐	237	Keith Acton	.05	.02	.00
						☐	238	Scott Mellanby	.05	.02	.00
☐	159	Boston Bruins Logo	.05	.02	.00	☐	239	Kjell Samuelsson	.05	.02	.00
						☐	240	Jeff Hackett	.08	.03	.01
☐	160	Buffalo Sabres Logo	.05	.02	.00	☐	241	David Volek	.05	.02	.00
						☐	242	Craig Ludwig	.05	.02	.00
☐	161	Hartford Whalers Logo	.05	.02	.00	☐	243	Pat LaFontaine	.35	.14	.03
						☐	244	Randy Wood	.05	.02	.00
☐	162	Montreal Canadiens Logo	.08	.03	.01	☐	245	Pat Flatley	.05	.02	.00
						☐	246	Brent Sutter	.08	.03	.01
☐	163	Quebec Nordiques Logo	.05	.02	.00	☐	247	Derek King	.10	.04	.01
						☐	248	Jeff Norton	.08	.03	.01
☐	164	New Jersey Devils Logo	.05	.02	.00	☐	249	Glenn Healy	.08	.03	.01
						☐	250	Ray Ferraro	.08	.03	.01
☐	165	New York Islanders Logo	.05	.02	.00	☐	251	Gary Nylund	.05	.02	.00
						☐	252	Joe Reekie	.05	.02	.00
☐	166	New York Rangers Logo	.05	.02	.00	☐	253	Dave Chyzowski	.05	.02	.00
						☐	254	Mike Hough	.05	.02	.00
☐	167	Philadelphia Flyers Logo	.05	.02	.00	☐	255	Mats Sundin	.35	.14	.03
						☐	256	Curtis Leschyshyn	.08	.03	.01
☐	168	Pittsburgh Penguins Logo	.05	.02	.00	☐	257	Joe Sakic	.30	.12	.03
						☐	258	Stephane Fiset	.15	.06	.01
☐	169	Washington Capitals Logo	.05	.02	.00	☐	259	Bryan Fogarty	.08	.03	.01
						☐	260	Alexei Gusarov	.08	.03	.01
☐	170	Craig Janney	.12	.05	.01	☐	261	Steven Finn	.05	.02	.00
☐	171	Ray Bourque	.15	.06	.01	☐	262	Everett Sanipass	.05	.02	.00
☐	172	Rejean Lemelin	.08	.03	.01	☐	263	Stephane Morin	.08	.03	.01
☐	173	Dave Christian	.08	.03	.01	☐	264	Craig Wolanin	.05	.02	.00
☐	174	Randy Burridge	.08	.03	.01	☐	265	Randy Velischek	.05	.02	.00
☐	175	Garry Galley	.08	.03	.01	☐	266	Owen Nolan	.40	.16	.04
☐	176	Cam Neely	.20	.08	.02	☐	267	Ron Tugnutt	.10	.04	.01
☐	177	Bob Sweeney	.05	.02	.00	☐	268	Mario Lemieux	.50	.20	.05
☐	178	Ken Hodge Jr.	.08	.03	.01	☐	269	Kevin Stevens	.30	.12	.03
☐	179	Andy Moog	.12	.05	.01	☐	270	Larry Murphy	.10	.04	.01
☐	180	Don Sweeney	.05	.02	.00	☐	271	Tom Barrasso	.10	.04	.01
☐	181	Bob Carpenter	.08	.03	.01	☐	272	Phil Bourque	.05	.02	.00
☐	182	Glen Wesley	.08	.03	.01	☐	273	Scott Young	.08	.03	.01
☐	183	Chris Nilan	.08	.03	.01	☐	274	Paul Stanton	.05	.02	.00
☐	184	Patrick Roy	.35	.14	.03	☐	275	Jaromir Jagr	.60	.24	.06
☐	185	Petr Svoboda	.08	.03	.01	☐	276	Paul Coffey	.15	.06	.01
☐	186	Russ Courtnall	.08	.03	.01	☐	277	Ulf Samuelsson	.08	.03	.01
☐	187	Denis Savard	.10	.04	.01	☐	278	Joe Mullen	.08	.03	.01
☐	188	Mike McPhee	.08	.03	.01	☐	279	Bob Errey	.05	.02	.00
☐	189	Eric Desjardins	.08	.03	.01	☐	280	Mark Recchi	.30	.12	.03
☐	190	Mike Keane	.08	.03	.01	☐	281	Ron Francis	.10	.04	.01
☐	191	Stephan Lebeau	.15	.06	.01	☐	282	John Vanbiesbrouck	.15	.06	.01
☐	192	J.J. Daigneault	.08	.03	.01	☐	283	Jan Erixon	.05	.02	.00
☐	193	Stephane Richer	.10	.04	.01	☐	284	Brian Leetch	.30	.12	.03
☐	194	Brian Skrudland	.05	.02	.00	☐	285	Darren Turcotte	.08	.03	.01
☐	195	Mathieu Schneider	.10	.04	.01	☐	286	Ray Sheppard	.08	.03	.01
						☐	287	James Patrick	.08	.03	.01
						☐	288	Bernie Nicholls	.10	.04	.01

☐ 289 Brian Mullen	.08	.03	.01
☐ 290 Mike Richter	.25	.10	.02
☐ 291 Kelly Kisio	.08	.03	.01
☐ 292 Mike Gartner	.12	.05	.01
☐ 293 John Ogrodnick	.08	.03	.01
☐ 294 David Shaw	.08	.03	.01
☐ 295 Troy Mallette	.05	.02	.00
☐ 296 Dale Hawerchuk	.12	.05	.01
☐ 297 Rick Vaive	.08	.03	.01
☐ 298 Daren Puppa	.08	.03	.01
☐ 299 Mike Ramsey	.08	.03	.01
☐ 300 Benoit Hogue	.10	.04	.01
☐ 301 Clint Malarchuk	.08	.03	.01
☐ 302 Mikko Makela	.05	.02	.00
☐ 303 Pierre Turgeon	.25	.10	.02
☐ 304 Alexander Mogilny	.40	.16	.04
☐ 305 Uwe Krupp	.08	.03	.01
☐ 306 Christian Ruuttu	.05	.02	.00
☐ 307 Doug Bodger	.08	.03	.01
☐ 308 Dave Snuggerud	.05	.02	.00
☐ 309 Dave Andreychuk	.15	.06	.01
☐ 310 Peter Sidorkiewicz	.08	.03	.01
☐ 311 Brad Shaw	.08	.03	.01
☐ 312 Dean Evason	.05	.02	.00
☐ 313 Pat Verbeek	.08	.03	.01
☐ 314 John Cullen	.10	.04	.01
☐ 315 Rob Brown	.08	.03	.01
☐ 316 Bobby Holik	.20	.08	.02
☐ 317 Todd Krygier	.08	.03	.01
☐ 318 Adam Burt	.05	.02	.00
☐ 319 Mike Tomlak	.05	.02	.00
☐ 320 Randy Cunneyworth	.05	.02	.00
☐ 321 Paul Cyr	.05	.02	.00
☐ 322 Zarley Zalapski	.08	.03	.01
☐ 323 Kevin Dineen	.08	.03	.01
☐ 324 Luc Robitaille	.20	.08	.02
☐ 325 Brett Hull	.30	.12	.03
☐ 326 All-Star Game Logo	.08	.03	.01
☐ 327 Wayne Gretzky	.50	.20	.05
☐ 328 Mike Vernon	.10	.04	.01
☐ 329 Chris Chelios	.10	.04	.01
☐ 330 Al MacInnis	.10	.04	.01
☐ 331 Rick Tocchet	.10	.04	.01
☐ 332 Cam Neely	.15	.06	.01
☐ 333 Patrick Roy	.25	.10	.02
☐ 334 Joe Sakic	.25	.10	.02
☐ 335 Ray Bourque	.15	.06	.01
☐ 336 Paul Coffey	.15	.06	.01
☐ 337 Ed Belfour	.30	.12	.03
☐ 338 Mike Ricci	.25	.10	.02
☐ 339 Rob Blake	.12	.05	.01
☐ 340 Sergei Fedorov	.75	.30	.07
☐ 341 Ken Hodge Jr.	.08	.03	.01
☐ 342 Bobby Holik	.15	.06	.01
☐ 343 Robert Reichel	.15	.06	.01
☐ 344 Jaromir Jagr	.60	.24	.06
☐ xx Sticker Album	1.25	.50	.12

1992-93 Panini Stickers

This set of 330 stickers was produced by Panini. They measure approximately 2 3/8" by 3 3/8" and were to be pasted in a 9" by 11" album. The fronts have action color player photos with statistics running down the right side in a colored bar. The player's name appears at the top. The team logo is superimposed on the photo at the lower left corner.

The backs feature questions and answers that go with the Slap-shot game that is included in the album. The team logos scattered throughout the set are foil. The stickers are numbered on the front on a puck icon at the lower right corner. They are checklisted below alphabetically according to teams in the Campbell and Wales Conferences as follows: Chicago Blackhawks (2-13), St. Louis Blues (14-25), Vancouver Canucks (26-37), Calgary Flames (38-49), Winnipeg Jets (50-61), Los Angeles Kings (62-73), Toronto Maple Leafs (74-85), Minnesota North Stars (86-97), Edmonton Oilers (98-109), Detroit Red Wings (110-121), San Jose Sharks (122-133), Boston Bruins (134-145), Montreal Canadiens (146-157), Washington Capitals (158-169), New Jersey Devils (170-181), Philadelphia Flyers (182-193), New York Islanders (194-205), Quebec Nordiques (206-217), Pittsburgh Penguins (218-229), New York Rangers (230-241), Buffalo Sabres (242-253), Hartford Whalers (254-265), Tampa Bay Lightning (266-267), and Ottawa Senators (268-269). Also included are subsets of the 1992 NHL's Top Rookies (270-275), the 1992 All-Star Game (276-289), the European Invasion (290-302), and The Trophies (303-308). Randomly inserted throughout the packs were 22 lettered "Ice-Breaker" stickers, each featuring a star player from each of the 22 NHL teams (minus the new expansion teams, the Tampa Bay Lightning and the Ottawa Senators). On a silver metallic background, the fronts have action color player photos with biography and statistics running down the right side in a colored bar.

	MINT	EXC	G-VG
COMPLETE SET (330)	30.00	12.00	3.00
COMMON PLAYER (1-308)	.05	.02	.00
COMMON PLAYER (A-V)	.35	.14	.03

☐ 1 Stanley Cup	.08	.03	.01
☐ 2 Blackhawks logo	.05	.02	.00
☐ 3 Ed Belfour	.30	.12	.03
☐ 4 Jeremy Roenick	.40	.16	.04
☐ 5 Steve Larmer	.10	.04	.01
☐ 6 Michel Goulet	.10	.04	.01
☐ 7 Dirk Graham	.08	.03	.01
☐ 8 Jocelyn Lemieux	.05	.02	.00
☐ 9 Brian Noonan	.08	.03	.01
☐ 10 Rob Brown	.08	.03	.01
☐ 11 Chris Chelios	.10	.04	.01
☐ 12 Steve Smith	.08	.03	.01
☐ 13 Keith Brown	.05	.02	.00
☐ 14 St. Louis Blues	.05	.02	.00
☐ 15 Curtis Joseph	.20	.08	.02
☐ 16 Brett Hull	.35	.14	.03
☐ 17 Brendan Shanahan	.20	.08	.02
☐ 18 Ron Wilson	.05	.02	.00
☐ 19 Rich Sutter	.08	.03	.01
☐ 20 Ron Sutter	.08	.03	.01
☐ 21 Dave Lowry	.05	.02	.00
☐ 22 Craig Janney	.15	.06	.01
☐ 23 Paul Cavallini	.05	.02	.00
☐ 24 Garth Butcher	.08	.03	.01
☐ 25 Jeff Brown	.10	.04	.01
☐ 26 Canucks Logo	.05	.02	.00
☐ 27 Kirk McLean	.12	.05	.01
☐ 28 Trevor Linden	.15	.06	.01
☐ 29 Geoff Courtnall	.08	.03	.01
☐ 30 Cliff Ronning	.08	.03	.01
☐ 31 Petr Nedved	.25	.10	.02
☐ 32 Igor Larionov	.10	.04	.01
☐ 33 Robert Kron	.08	.03	.01
☐ 34 Jim Sandlak	.08	.03	.01
☐ 35 Dave Babych	.08	.03	.01
☐ 36 Jyrki Lumme	.08	.03	.01
☐ 37 Doug Lidster	.05	.02	.01
☐ 38 Flames Logo	.05	.02	.00
☐ 39 Mike Vernon	.10	.04	.01
☐ 40 Joe Nieuwendyk	.10	.04	.01
☐ 41 Gary Leeman	.05	.02	.00
☐ 42 Robert Reichel	.10	.04	.01
☐ 43 Joel Otto	.05	.02	.00
☐ 44 Paul Ranheim	.05	.02	.00
☐ 45 Gary Roberts	.10	.04	.01
☐ 46 Theo Fleury	.12	.05	.01
☐ 47 Sergei Makarov	.15	.06	.01
☐ 48 Gary Suter	.08	.03	.01
☐ 49 Al MacInnis	.12	.05	.01

☐ 50	Jets Logo	.05	.02	.00
☐ 51	Bob Essensa	.10	.04	.01
☐ 52	Teppo Numminen	.05	.02	.00
☐ 53	Thomas Steen	.08	.03	.01
☐ 54	Pat Elynuik	.08	.03	.01
☐ 55	Ed Olczyk	.08	.03	.01
☐ 56	Danton Cole	.05	.02	.00
☐ 57	Troy Murray	.08	.03	.01
☐ 58	Darrin Shannon	.08	.03	.01
☐ 59	Russ Romaniuk	.05	.02	.00
☐ 60	Fredrik Olausson	.08	.03	.01
☐ 61	Phil Housley	.10	.04	.01
☐ 62	Kings Logo	.05	.02	.00
☐ 63	Kelly Hrudey	.10	.04	.01
☐ 64	Wayne Gretzky	.60	.24	.06
☐ 65	Luc Robitaille	.20	.08	.02
☐ 66	Jari Kurri	.12	.05	.01
☐ 67	Tomas Sandstrom	.10	.04	.01
☐ 68	Tony Granato	.08	.03	.01
☐ 69	Bob Kudelski	.08	.03	.01
☐ 70	Corey Millen	.15	.06	.01
☐ 71	Rob Blake	.10	.04	.01
☐ 72	Paul Coffey	.15	.06	.01
☐ 73	Marty McSorley	.15	.06	.01
☐ 74	Maple Leafs Logo	.05	.02	.00
☐ 75	Grant Fuhr	.10	.04	.01
☐ 76	Glenn Anderson	.10	.04	.01
☐ 77	Doug Gilmour	.35	.14	.03
☐ 78	Mike Krushelnyski	.08	.03	.01
☐ 79	Wendel Clark	.15	.06	.01
☐ 80	Rob Pearson	.12	.05	.01
☐ 81	Peter Zezel	.08	.03	.01
☐ 82	Todd Gill	.05	.02	.00
☐ 83	Dave Ellett	.08	.03	.01
☐ 84	Mike Foligno	.05	.02	.00
☐ 85	Ken Baumgartner	.05	.02	.00
☐ 86	North Stars Logo	.05	.02	.00
☐ 87	Jon Casey	.10	.04	.00
☐ 88	Brian Bellows	.10	.04	.01
☐ 89	Neal Broten	.08	.03	.01
☐ 90	Dave Gagner	.08	.03	.01
☐ 91	Mike Modano	.25	.10	.02
☐ 92	Ulf Dahlen	.05	.02	.00
☐ 93	Brian Propp	.08	.03	.01
☐ 94	Jim Johnson	.05	.02	.00
☐ 95	Mike Craig	.08	.03	.01
☐ 96	Bobby Smith	.08	.03	.01
☐ 97	Mark Tinordi	.08	.03	.01
☐ 98	Oilers Logo	.05	.02	.00
☐ 99	Bill Ranford	.10	.04	.01
☐ 100	Joe Murphy	.08	.03	.01
☐ 101	Craig MacTavish	.08	.03	.01
☐ 102	Craig Simpson	.08	.03	.01
☐ 103	Esa Tikkanen	.10	.04	.01
☐ 104	Vincent Damphousse	.12	.05	.01
☐ 105	Petr Klima	.08	.03	.01
☐ 106	Martin Gelinas	.08	.03	.01
☐ 107	Kevin Lowe	.08	.03	.01
☐ 108	Dave Manson	.08	.03	.01
☐ 109	Bernie Nicholls	.10	.04	.01
☐ 110	Red Wings Logo	.05	.02	.00
☐ 111	Tim Cheveldae	.12	.05	.01
☐ 112	Steve Yzerman	.35	.14	.03
☐ 113	Sergei Fedorov	.50	.20	.05
☐ 114	Jimmy Carson	.10	.04	.01
☐ 115	Kevin Miller	.08	.03	.01
☐ 116	Gerard Gallant	.05	.02	.00
☐ 117	Keith Primeau	.15	.06	.01
☐ 118	Paul Ysebaert	.10	.04	.01
☐ 119	Yves Racine	.05	.02	.00
☐ 120	Steve Chiasson	.08	.03	.01
☐ 121	Ray Sheppard	.10	.04	.01
☐ 122	Sharks Logo	.15	.06	.01
☐ 123	Jeff Hackett	.10	.04	.01
☐ 124	Kelly Kisio	.08	.03	.01
☐ 125	Brian Mullen	.08	.03	.01
☐ 126	David Bruce	.08	.03	.01
☐ 127	Rob Zettler	.08	.03	.01
☐ 128	Neil Wilkinson	.08	.03	.01
☐ 129	Doug Wilson	.08	.03	.01
☐ 130	Jeff Odgers	.05	.02	.00
☐ 131	Dean Evason	.05	.02	.00
☐ 132	Brian Lawton	.05	.02	.00
☐ 133	Dale Craigwell	.08	.03	.01
☐ 134	Bruins Logo	.05	.02	.00
☐ 135	Andy Moog	.10	.04	.01
☐ 136	Adam Oates	.15	.06	.01
☐ 137	Dave Poulin	.05	.02	.00
☐ 138	Vladimir Ruzicka	.08	.03	.01
☐ 139	Jeff Lazaro	.05	.02	.00
☐ 140	Bob Carpenter	.08	.03	.01
☐ 141	Peter Douris	.05	.02	.00
☐ 142	Glen Murray	.10	.04	.01
☐ 143	Cam Neely	.15	.06	.01
☐ 144	Ray Bourque	.12	.05	.01
☐ 145	Glen Wesley	.08	.03	.01
☐ 146	Canadiens Logo	.05	.02	.00
☐ 147	Patrick Roy	.25	.10	.02
☐ 148	Kirk Muller	.12	.05	.01
☐ 149	Guy Carbonneau	.08	.03	.01
☐ 150	Shayne Corson	.08	.03	.01
☐ 151	Stephan Lebeau	.08	.03	.01
☐ 152	Denis Savard	.10	.04	.01
☐ 153	Brent Gilchrist	.05	.02	.00
☐ 154	Russ Courtnall	.08	.03	.01
☐ 155	Patrice Brisebois	.08	.03	.01
☐ 156	Eric Desjardins	.08	.03	.01
☐ 157	Matt Schneider	.10	.04	.01
☐ 158	Capitals Logo	.05	.02	.00
☐ 159	Don Beaupre	.08	.03	.01
☐ 160	Dino Ciccarelli	.10	.04	.01
☐ 161	Michal Pivonka	.10	.04	.01
☐ 162	Mike Ridley	.08	.03	.01
☐ 163	Randy Burridge	.08	.03	.01
☐ 164	Peter Bondra	.08	.03	.01
☐ 165	Dale Hunter	.08	.03	.01
☐ 166	Kelly Miller	.08	.03	.01
☐ 167	Kevin Hatcher	.10	.04	.01
☐ 168	Al Iafrate	.12	.05	.01
☐ 169	Rod Langway	.08	.03	.01
☐ 170	Devils Logo	.05	.02	.00
☐ 171	Chris Terreri	.08	.03	.01
☐ 172	Claude Lemieux	.10	.04	.01
☐ 173	Stephane Richer	.10	.04	.01
☐ 174	Peter Stastny	.10	.04	.01
☐ 175	Zdeno Ciger	.05	.02	.00
☐ 176	Alexander Semak	.15	.06	.01
☐ 177	Valeri Zelepukin	.10	.04	.01
☐ 178	Bruce Driver	.08	.03	.01
☐ 179	Scott Niedermayer	.25	.10	.02
☐ 180	Alexei Kasatonov	.12	.05	.01
☐ 181	Scott Stevens	.10	.04	.01
☐ 182	Flyers Logo	.05	.02	.00
☐ 183	Dominic Roussel	.15	.06	.01
☐ 184	Mike Ricci	.15	.06	.01
☐ 185	Mark Recchi	.25	.10	.02
☐ 186	Kevin Dineen	.08	.03	.01
☐ 187	Rod Brind'Amour	.12	.05	.01
☐ 188	Mark Pederson	.05	.02	.00
☐ 189	Pelle Eklund	.08	.03	.01
☐ 190	Terry Carkner	.05	.02	.00
☐ 191	Mark Howe	.08	.03	.01
☐ 192	Steve Duchesne	.08	.03	.01
☐ 193	Andrei Lomakin	.08	.03	.01
☐ 194	Islanders Logo	.05	.02	.00
☐ 195	Mark Fitzpatrick	.10	.04	.01
☐ 196	Pierre Turgeon	.25	.10	.02
☐ 197	Benoit Hogue	.10	.04	.01
☐ 198	Ray Ferraro	.10	.04	.01
☐ 199	Derek King	.10	.04	.01
☐ 200	David Volek	.05	.02	.00
☐ 201	Patrick Flatley	.05	.02	.00
☐ 202	Uwe Krupp	.05	.02	.00
☐ 203	Steve Thomas	.08	.03	.01
☐ 204	Adam Creighton	.05	.02	.00
☐ 205	Jeff Norton	.05	.02	.00
☐ 206	Nordiques Logo	.05	.02	.00
☐ 207	Stephane Fiset	.10	.04	.01
☐ 208	Mikhail Tatarinov	.08	.03	.01
☐ 209	Joe Sakic	.25	.10	.02
☐ 210	Owen Nolan	.20	.08	.02
☐ 211	Mike Hough	.05	.02	.00
☐ 212	Mats Sundin	.25	.10	.02
☐ 213	Claude Lapointe	.10	.04	.01
☐ 214	Stephane Morin	.08	.03	.01
☐ 215	Alexei Gusarov	.08	.03	.01
☐ 216	Steven Finn	.05	.02	.00
☐ 217	Curtis Leschyshyn	.08	.03	.01
☐ 218	Penguins Logo	.05	.02	.00
☐ 219	Tom Barrasso	.10	.04	.01
☐ 220	Mario Lemieux	.50	.20	.05
☐ 221	Kevin Stevens	.30	.12	.03
☐ 222	Shawn McEachern	.30	.12	.03
☐ 223	Joe Mullen	.10	.04	.01
☐ 224	Ron Francis	.10	.04	.01
☐ 225	Phil Bourque	.05	.02	.00
☐ 226	Rick Tocchet	.10	.04	.01
☐ 227	Bryan Trottier	.12	.05	.01
☐ 228	Larry Murphy	.10	.04	.01
☐ 229	Ulf Samuelsson	.08	.03	.01
☐ 230	Rangers Logo	.05	.02	.00
☐ 231	Mike Richter	.25	.10	.02
☐ 232	John Vanbiesbrouck	.15	.06	.01
☐ 233	Mark Messier	.35	.14	.03
☐ 234	Sergei Nemchinov	.10	.04	.01
☐ 235	Darren Turcotte	.10	.04	.01

☐	236	Doug Weight	.10	.04	.01
☐	237	Mike Gartner	.12	.05	.01
☐	238	Adam Graves	.25	.10	.02
☐	239	Brian Leetch	.20	.08	.02
☐	240	James Patrick	.05	.02	.00
☐	241	Jan Erixon	.05	.02	.00
☐	242	Sabres Logo	.05	.02	.00
☐	243	Tom Draper	.10	.04	.01
☐	244	Grant Ledyard	.05	.02	.00
☐	245	Doug Bodger	.05	.02	.00
☐	246	Pat LaFontaine	.35	.14	.03
☐	247	Dale Hawerchuk	.12	.05	.01
☐	248	Alexander Mogilny	.35	.14	.03
☐	249	Dave Andreychuk	.15	.06	.01
☐	250	Christian Ruuttu	.05	.02	.00
☐	251	Randy Wood	.05	.02	.00
☐	252	Brad May	.08	.03	.01
☐	253	Mike Ramsey	.05	.02	.00
☐	254	Whalers Logo	.05	.02	.00
☐	255	Kay Whitmore	.10	.04	.01
☐	256	Pat Verbeek	.08	.03	.01
☐	257	John Cullen	.08	.03	.01
☐	258	Mikael Andersson	.08	.03	.01
☐	259	Yvon Corriveau	.05	.02	.00
☐	260	Randy Cunneyworth	.08	.03	.01
☐	261	Robert Holik	.10	.04	.01
☐	262	Murray Craven	.05	.02	.00
☐	263	Zarley Zalapski	.08	.03	.01
☐	264	Adam Burt	.05	.02	.00
☐	265	Brad Shaw	.05	.02	.00
☐	266	Lightning Logo	.08	.03	.01
☐	267	Lightning Jersey	.08	.03	.01
☐	268	Senators Logo	.05	.02	.00
☐	269	Senators Jersey	.05	.02	.00
☐	270	Tony Amonte	.20	.08	.02
☐	271	Pavel Bure	1.00	.40	.10
☐	272	Gilbert Dionne	.25	.10	.02
☐	273	Pat Falloon	.25	.10	.02
☐	274	Nicklas Lidstrum	.20	.08	.02
☐	275	Kevin Todd	.10	.04	.01
☐	276	Prince of Wales Conference Logo	.05	.02	.00
☐	277	Patrick Roy AS	.25	.10	.02
☐	278	Paul Coffey AS	.12	.05	.01
☐	279	Ray Bourque AS	.12	.05	.01
☐	280	Mario Lemieux AS	.35	.14	.03
☐	281	Kevin Stevens AS	.20	.08	.02
☐	282	Jaromir Jagr AS	.30	.12	.03
☐	283	Clarence Campbell Conference Logo	.05	.02	.00
☐	284	Ed Belfour AS	.20	.08	.02
☐	285	Al MacInnis AS	.10	.04	.01
☐	286	Chris Chelios AS	.10	.04	.01
☐	287	Wayne Gretzky AS	.50	.20	.05
☐	288	Luc Robitaille AS	.15	.06	.01
☐	289	Brett Hull AS	.25	.10	.02
☐	290	Pavel Bure	.60	.24	.06
☐	291	Sergei Fedorov	.40	.16	.04
☐	292	Dominik Hasek	.15	.06	.01
☐	293	Robert Holik	.10	.04	.01
☐	294	Jaromir Jagr	.30	.12	.03
☐	295	Valeri Kamensky	.15	.06	.01
☐	296	Alexander Semak	.20	.08	.02
☐	297	Igor Kravchuk	.10	.04	.01
☐	298	Nicklas Lidstrom	.15	.06	.01
☐	299	Alexander Mogilny	.25	.10	.02
☐	300	Petr Nedved	.20	.08	.02
☐	301	Robert Reichel	.12	.05	.01
☐	302	Mats Sundin	.20	.08	.02
☐	303	Calder Trophy	.05	.02	.00
☐	304	Hart Trophy	.05	.02	.00
☐	305	Lady Byng Trophy	.05	.02	.00
☐	306	Norris Trophy	.05	.02	.00
☐	307	Selke Trophy	.05	.02	.00
☐	308	Vezina Trophy	.05	.02	.00
☐	A	Igor Kravchuk	.35	.14	.03
☐	B	Nelson Emerson	.50	.20	.05
☐	C	Pavel Bure	3.00	1.20	.30
☐	D	Tomas Forslund	.35	.14	.03
☐	E	Luciano Borsato	.35	.14	.03
☐	F	Darryl Sydor	.50	.20	.05
☐	G	Felix Potvin	1.50	.60	.15
☐	H	Derian Hatcher	.50	.20	.05
☐	I	Joseph Beranek	.50	.20	.05
☐	J	Nicklas Lidstrom	.75	.30	.07
☐	K	Pat Falloon	1.00	.40	.10
☐	L	Joe Juneau	1.50	.60	.15
☐	M	Gilbert Dionne	.75	.30	.07
☐	N	Dimitri Khristich	.75	.30	.07
☐	O	Kevin Todd	.50	.20	.05
☐	P	Eric Lindros	6.00	2.40	.60
☐	Q	Scott Lachance	.50	.20	.05
☐	R	Valeri Kamensky	.50	.20	.05
☐	S	Jaromir Jagr	1.50	.60	.15
☐	T	Tony Amonte	.75	.30	.07
☐	U	Donald Audette	.50	.20	.05
☐	V	Geoff Sanderson	1.25	.50	.12
☐	xx	Sticker Album	1.25	.50	.12

1993-94 Panini Stickers

This set of 300 stickers was produced by Panini. They measure approximately 2 3/8" by 3 3/8" and were to be pasted in a 9" by 11" sticker album. The fronts have action color player photos with the player's name and the team name printed to the left side of the photo. The backs promote collecting Panini stickers. They are checklisted below alphabetically according to teams in the Wales and Campbell Conference as follows: Boston Bruins (1-11), Montreal Canadiens (12-22), Washington Capitals (23-33), New Jersey Devils (34-44), Philadelphia Flyers (45-55), New York Islanders (56-66), Quebec Nordiques (67-77), Pittsburgh Penguins (78-88), New York Rangers (89-99), Buffalo Sabres (100-110), Ottawa Senators (111-121), Hartford Whalers (122-132), Chicago Blackhawks (145-155), St. Louis Blues (156-166), Vancouver Canucks (167-177), Calgary Flames (178-188), Winnipeg Jets (189-199), Los Angeles Kings (200-210), Tampa Bay Lightning (211-221), Toronto Maple Leafs (222-232), Edmonton Oilers (233-243), Detroit Red Wings (244-254), San Jose Sharks (255-265), and Dallas Stars (266-276). Also included are a subset Best of the Best (133-144), and a subset of 24 glitter stickers of Panini's superstars (A-X), one per team. The stickers are numbered on the back. The album also includes players' statistics and and a Stanley Cup final review.

	MINT	EXC	G-VG
COMPLETE SET (300)	25.00	10.00	2.50
COMMON PLAYER (1-276)	.05	.02	.00
COMMON GLITTER (A-X)	.35	.14	.03

☐	1	Bruins Logo	.08	.03	.01
☐	2	Adam Oates	.15	.06	.01
☐	3	Cam Neely	.15	.06	.01
☐	4	Dave Poulin	.08	.03	.01
☐	5	Steve Leach	.05	.02	.00
☐	6	Glen Wesley	.08	.03	.01
☐	7	Dmitri Kvartalnov	.10	.04	.01
☐	8	Ted Donato	.08	.03	.01
☐	9	Andy Moog	.10	.04	.01
☐	10	Ray Bourque	.15	.06	.01
☐	11	Don Sweeney	.08	.03	.01
☐	12	Canadiens Logo	.08	.03	.01
☐	13	Vincent Damphousse	.10	.04	.01
☐	14	Kirk Muller	.12	.05	.01
☐	15	Brian Bellows	.10	.04	.01
☐	16	Stephan Lebeau	.10	.04	.01
☐	17	Denis Savard	.08	.03	.01
☐	18	Gilbert Dionne	.08	.03	.01
☐	19	Guy Carbonneau	.08	.03	.01
☐	20	Benoit Brunet	.08	.03	.01
☐	21	Eric Desjardins	.08	.03	.01

☐ 22	Mathieu Schneider	.08	.03	.01
☐ 23	Capitals Logo	.05	.02	.00
☐ 24	Peter Bondra	.08	.03	.01
☐ 25	Mike Ridley	.08	.03	.01
☐ 26	Dale Hunter	.08	.03	.01
☐ 27	Michal Pivonka	.08	.03	.01
☐ 28	Dimitri Khristich	.08	.03	.01
☐ 29	Pat Elynuik	.05	.02	.00
☐ 30	Kelly Miller	.08	.03	.01
☐ 31	Calle Johansson	.05	.02	.00
☐ 32	Al Iafrate	.12	.05	.01
☐ 33	Don Beaupre	.08	.03	.01
☐ 34	Devils Logo	.05	.02	.00
☐ 35	Claude Lemieux	.10	.04	.01
☐ 36	Alexander Semak	.10	.04	.01
☐ 37	Stephane Richer	.10	.04	.01
☐ 38	Valeri Zelepukin	.08	.03	.01
☐ 39	Bernie Nicholls	.10	.04	.01
☐ 40	John MacLean	.10	.04	.01
☐ 41	Peter Stastny	.10	.04	.01
☐ 42	Scott Niedermayer	.10	.04	.01
☐ 43	Scott Stevens	.10	.04	.01
☐ 44	Bruce Driver	.08	.03	.01
☐ 45	Flyers Logo	.05	.02	.00
☐ 46	Mark Recchi	.25	.10	.02
☐ 47	Rod Brind'Amour	.10	.04	.01
☐ 48	Brent Fedyk	.08	.03	.01
☐ 49	Kevin Dineen	.08	.03	.01
☐ 50	Keith Acton	.05	.02	.00
☐ 51	Pelle Eklund	.08	.03	.01
☐ 52	Andrei Lomakin	.05	.02	.00
☐ 53	Garry Galley	.08	.03	.01
☐ 54	Terry Carkner	.05	.02	.00
☐ 55	Tommy Soderstrom	.10	.04	.01
☐ 56	Islanders Logo	.05	.02	.00
☐ 57	Steve Thomas	.08	.03	.01
☐ 58	Derek King	.08	.03	.01
☐ 59	Benoit Hogue	.08	.03	.01
☐ 60	Patrick Flatley	.05	.02	.00
☐ 61	Brian Mullen	.08	.03	.01
☐ 62	Marty McInnis	.05	.02	.00
☐ 63	Scott Lachance	.08	.03	.01
☐ 64	Jeff Norton	.08	.03	.01
☐ 65	Glenn Healy	.08	.03	.01
☐ 66	Mark Fitzpatrick	.08	.03	.01
☐ 67	Nordiques Logo	.05	.02	.00
☐ 68	Mats Sundin	.25	.10	.02
☐ 69	Mike Ricci	.15	.06	.01
☐ 70	Owen Nolan	.20	.08	.02
☐ 71	Andrei Kovalenko	.10	.04	.01
☐ 72	Valeri Kamensky	.10	.04	.01
☐ 73	Scott Young	.08	.03	.01
☐ 74	Martin Rucinsky	.08	.03	.01
☐ 75	Steven Finn	.05	.02	.00
☐ 76	Steve Duchesne	.08	.03	.01
☐ 77	Ron Hextall	.10	.04	.01
☐ 78	Penguins Logo	.05	.02	.00
☐ 79	Kevin Stevens	.25	.10	.02
☐ 80	Rick Tocchet	.12	.05	.01
☐ 81	Ron Francis	.10	.04	.01
☐ 82	Jaromir Jagr	.30	.12	.03
☐ 83	Joe Mullen	.08	.03	.01
☐ 84	Shawn McEachern	.12	.05	.01
☐ 85	Dave Tippett	.05	.02	.00
☐ 86	Larry Murphy	.08	.03	.01
☐ 87	Ulf Samuelsson	.08	.03	.01
☐ 88	Tom Barrasso	.10	.04	.01
☐ 89	Rangers Logo	.05	.02	.00
☐ 90	Tony Amonte	.10	.04	.01
☐ 91	Mike Gartner	.15	.06	.01
☐ 92	Adam Graves	.15	.06	.01
☐ 93	Sergei Nemchinov	.10	.04	.01
☐ 94	Darren Turcotte	.08	.03	.01
☐ 95	Esa Tikkanen	.10	.04	.01
☐ 96	Brian Leetch	.20	.08	.02
☐ 97	Kevin Lowe	.08	.03	.01
☐ 98	John Vanbiesbrouck	.15	.06	.01
☐ 99	Mike Richter	.20	.08	.02
☐ 100	Sabres Logo	.05	.02	.00
☐ 101	Pat LaFontaine	.30	.12	.03
☐ 102	Dale Hawerchuk	.12	.05	.01
☐ 103	Donald Audette	.05	.02	.00
☐ 104	Bob Sweeney	.05	.02	.00
☐ 105	Randy Wood	.05	.02	.00
☐ 106	Yuri Khmylev	.08	.03	.01
☐ 107	Wayne Presley	.05	.02	.00
☐ 108	Grant Fuhr	.10	.04	.01
☐ 109	Doug Bodger	.05	.02	.00
☐ 110	Richard Smehlik	.05	.02	.00
☐ 111	Senators Logo	.05	.02	.00
☐ 112	Norm Maciver	.05	.02	.00
☐ 113	Jamie Baker	.05	.02	.00
☐ 114	Bob Kudelski	.08	.03	.01
☐ 115	Jody Hull	.05	.02	.00
☐ 116	Mike Peluso	.05	.02	.00
☐ 117	Mark Lamb	.05	.02	.00
☐ 118	Mark Freer	.05	.02	.00
☐ 119	Neil Brady	.05	.02	.00
☐ 120	Brad Shaw	.05	.02	.00
☐ 121	Peter Sidorkiewicz	.08	.03	.01
☐ 122	Whalers Logo	.05	.02	.00
☐ 123	Andrew Cassels	.08	.03	.01
☐ 124	Pat Verbeek	.08	.03	.01
☐ 125	Terry Yake	.05	.02	.00
☐ 126	Patrick Poulin	.05	.02	.00
☐ 127	Mark Jansens	.05	.02	.00
☐ 128	Mikael Nylander	.08	.03	.01
☐ 129	Zarley Zalapski	.08	.03	.01
☐ 130	Eric Weinrich	.08	.03	.01
☐ 131	Sean Burke	.10	.04	.01
☐ 132	Frank Pietrangelo	.08	.03	.01
☐ 133	Phil Housley	.10	.04	.01
	Winnipeg Jets			
☐ 134	Paul Coffey	.12	.05	.01
	Detroit Red Wings			
☐ 135	Larry Murphy	.10	.04	.01
	Pittsburgh Penguins			
☐ 136	Mario Lemieux	.50	.20	.05
	Pittsburgh Penguins			
☐ 137	Pat LaFontaine	.30	.12	.03
	Buffalo Sabres			
☐ 138	Adam Oates	.20	.08	.02
	Boston Bruins			
☐ 139	Felix Potvin	.50	.20	.05
	Toronto Maple Leafs			
☐ 140	Ed Belfour	.30	.12	.03
	Chicago Blackhawks			
☐ 141	Tom Barrasso	.10	.04	.01
	Pittsburgh Penguins			
☐ 142	Teemu Selanne	.75	.30	.07
	Winnipeg Jets			
☐ 143	Joe Juneau	.35	.14	.03
	Boston Bruins			
☐ 144	Eric Lindros	2.00	.80	.20
	Philadelphia Flyers			
☐ 145	Blackhawks Logo	.05	.02	.00
☐ 146	Steve Larmer	.10	.04	.01
☐ 147	Dirk Graham	.08	.03	.01
☐ 148	Michel Goulet	.10	.04	.01
☐ 149	Brian Noonan	.08	.03	.01
☐ 150	Stephane Matteau	.08	.03	.01
☐ 151	Brent Sutter	.08	.03	.01
☐ 152	Jocelyn Lemieux	.05	.02	.00
☐ 153	Chris Chelios	.10	.04	.01
☐ 154	Steve Smith	.08	.03	.01
☐ 155	Ed Belfour	.30	.12	.03
☐ 156	Blues Logo	.05	.02	.00
☐ 157	Craig Janney	.10	.04	.01
☐ 158	Brendan Shanahan	.15	.06	.01
☐ 159	Nelson Emerson	.10	.04	.01
☐ 160	Rich Sutter	.08	.03	.01
☐ 161	Ron Sutter	.08	.03	.01
☐ 162	Ron Wilson	.05	.02	.00
☐ 163	Bob Bassen	.05	.02	.00
☐ 164	Garth Butcher	.08	.03	.01
☐ 165	Jeff Brown	.08	.03	.01
☐ 166	Curtis Joseph	.15	.06	.01
☐ 167	Canucks Logo	.05	.02	.00
☐ 168	Cliff Ronning	.08	.03	.01
☐ 169	Murray Craven	.05	.02	.00
☐ 170	Geoff Courtnall	.08	.03	.01
☐ 171	Petr Nedved	.20	.08	.02
☐ 172	Trevor Linden	.20	.08	.02
☐ 173	Greg Adams	.08	.03	.01
☐ 174	Anatoli Semenov	.05	.02	.00
☐ 175	Jyrki Lumme	.05	.02	.00
☐ 176	Doug Lidster	.05	.02	.00
☐ 177	Kirk McLean	.15	.06	.01
☐ 178	Flames Logo	.05	.02	.00
☐ 179	Theoren Fleury	.12	.05	.01
☐ 180	Robert Reichel	.08	.03	.01
☐ 181	Gary Roberts	.10	.04	.01
☐ 182	Joe Nieuwendyk	.10	.04	.01
☐ 183	Sergei Makarov	.12	.05	.01
☐ 184	Paul Ranheim	.05	.02	.00
☐ 185	Joel Otto	.05	.02	.00
☐ 186	Gary Suter	.08	.03	.01
☐ 187	Jeff Reese	.08	.03	.01
☐ 188	Mike Vernon	.10	.04	.01
☐ 189	Jets Logo	.05	.02	.00
☐ 190	Alexei Zhamnov	.25	.10	.02
☐ 191	Thomas Steen	.08	.03	.01
☐ 192	Darrin Shannon	.08	.03	.01
☐ 193	Keith Tkachuk	.15	.06	.01
☐ 194	Evgeny Davydov	.10	.04	.01
☐ 195	Luciano Borsato	.05	.02	.00

☐	196	Phil Housley	.10	.04	.01
☐	197	Teppo Numminen	.05	.02	.00
☐	198	Fredrik Olausson	.08	.03	.01
☐	199	Bob Essensa	.08	.03	.01
☐	200	Kings Logo	.05	.02	.00
☐	201	Luc Robitaille	.20	.08	.02
☐	202	Jari Kurri	.12	.05	.01
☐	203	Tony Granato	.08	.03	.01
☐	204	Jimmy Carson	.08	.03	.01
☐	205	Tomas Sandstrom	.10	.04	.01
☐	206	Dave Taylor	.08	.03	.01
☐	207	Corey Millen	.10	.04	.01
☐	208	Marty McSorley	.10	.04	.01
☐	209	Rob Blake	.10	.04	.01
☐	210	Kelly Hrudey	.10	.04	.01
☐	211	Lightning Logo	.08	.03	.01
☐	212	John Tucker	.05	.02	.00
☐	213	Chris Kontos	.08	.03	.01
☐	214	Rob Zamuner	.05	.02	.00
☐	215	Adam Creighton	.05	.02	.00
☐	216	Mikael Andersson	.08	.03	.01
☐	217	Bob Beers	.05	.02	.00
☐	218	Rob DiMaio	.05	.02	.00
☐	219	Shawn Chambers	.05	.02	.00
☐	220	J.C. Bergeron	.05	.02	.00
☐	221	Wendell Young	.08	.03	.01
☐	222	Maple Leafs Logo	.05	.02	.00
☐	223	Dave Andreychuk	.15	.06	.01
☐	224	Nikolai Borschevsky	.10	.04	.01
☐	225	Glenn Anderson	.10	.04	.01
☐	226	John Cullen	.10	.04	.01
☐	227	Wendel Clark	.15	.06	.01
☐	228	Mike Foligno	.05	.02	.00
☐	229	Mike Krushelnyski	.08	.03	.01
☐	230	James Macoun	.05	.02	.00
☐	231	Dave Ellett	.08	.03	.01
☐	232	Felix Potvin	.60	.24	.06
☐	233	Oilers Logo	.05	.02	.00
☐	234	Petr Klima	.08	.03	.01
☐	235	Doug Weight	.08	.03	.01
☐	236	Shayne Corson	.08	.03	.01
☐	237	Craig Simpson	.08	.03	.01
☐	238	Todd Elik	.08	.03	.01
☐	239	Zdeno Ciger	.05	.02	.00
☐	240	Craig MacTavish	.08	.03	.01
☐	241	Kelly Buchberger	.05	.02	.00
☐	242	Dave Manson	.08	.03	.01
☐	243	Scott Mellanby	.08	.03	.01
☐	244	Red Wings Logo	.05	.02	.00
☐	245	Dino Ciccarelli	.10	.04	.01
☐	246	Sergei Fedorov	.60	.24	.06
☐	247	Ray Sheppard	.10	.04	.01
☐	248	Paul Ysebaert	.08	.03	.01
☐	249	Bob Probert	.10	.04	.01
☐	250	Keith Primeau	.10	.04	.01
☐	251	Steve Chiasson	.05	.02	.00
☐	252	Paul Coffey	.12	.05	.01
☐	253	Nicklas Lidstrom	.08	.03	.01
☐	254	Tim Cheveldae	.10	.04	.01
☐	255	Sharks Logo	.15	.06	.01
☐	256	Kelly Kisio	.08	.03	.01
☐	257	Johan Garpenlov	.08	.03	.01
☐	258	Robert Gaudreau	.08	.03	.01
☐	259	Dean Evason	.05	.02	.00
☐	260	Jeff Odgers	.05	.02	.00
☐	261	Ed Courtenay	.05	.02	.00
☐	262	Mike Sullivan	.08	.03	.01
☐	263	Doug Zmolek	.08	.03	.01
☐	264	Doug Wilson	.08	.03	.01
☐	265	Brian Hayward	.08	.03	.01
☐	266	Stars Logo	.05	.02	.00
☐	267	Brian Propp	.08	.03	.01
☐	268	Russ Courtnall	.08	.03	.01
☐	269	Dave Gagner	.08	.03	.01
☐	270	Ulf Dahlen	.08	.03	.01
☐	271	Mike Craig	.08	.03	.01
☐	272	Neal Broten	.08	.03	.01
☐	273	Gaetan Duchesne	.05	.02	.00
☐	274	Derian Hatcher	.08	.03	.01
☐	275	Mark Tinordi	.08	.03	.01
☐	276	Jon Casey	.08	.03	.01
☐	A	Joe Juneau	1.00	.40	.10
		Boston Bruins			
☐	B	Patrick Roy	1.50	.60	.15
		Montreal Canadiens			
☐	C	Kevin Hatcher	.50	.20	.05
		Washington Capitals			
☐	D	Chris Terreri	.35	.14	.03
		New Jersey Devils			
☐	E	Eric Lindros	4.00	1.60	.40
		Philadelphia Flyers			
☐	F	Pierre Turgeon	.75	.30	.07
		New York Islanders			

☐	G	Joe Sakic	.75	.30	.07
		Quebec Nordiques			
☐	H	Mario Lemieux	1.50	.60	.15
		Pittsburgh Penguins			
☐	I	Mark Messier	1.00	.40	.10
		New York Rangers			
☐	J	Alexander Mogilny	.75	.30	.07
		Buffalo Sabres			
☐	K	Sylvain Turgeon	.35	.14	.03
		Ottawa Senators			
☐	L	Geoff Sanderson	.75	.30	.07
		Hartford Whalers			
☐	M	Jeremy Roenick	1.00	.40	.10
		Chicago Blackhawks			
☐	N	Brett Hull	1.00	.40	.10
		St. Louis Blues			
☐	O	Pavel Bure	2.50	1.00	.25
		Vancouver Canucks			
☐	P	Al MacInnis	.75	.30	.07
		Calgary Flames			
☐	Q	Teemu Selanne	1.50	.60	.15
		Winnipeg Jets			
☐	R	Wayne Gretzky	3.00	1.20	.30
		Los Angeles Kings			
☐	S	Brian Bradley	.50	.20	.05
		Tampa Bay Lightning			
☐	T	Doug Gilmour	1.00	.40	.10
		Toronto Maple Leafs			
☐	U	Bill Ranford	.75	.30	.07
		Edmonton Oilers			
☐	V	Steve Yzerman	1.00	.40	.10
		Detroit Red Wings			
☐	W	Pat Falloon	.75	.30	.07
		San Jose Sharks			
☐	X	Mike Modano	.75	.30	.07
		Dallas Stars			

1991-92 Air Canada SJHL

 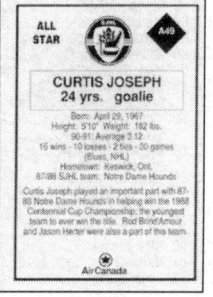

This 250-card set features players in the Saskatchewan Junior Hockey League. The set included an entry form for a contest sponsored by Air Canada and Old Dutch, which entitled the winner to a trip for two to anywhere in North America. The cards measure the standard size (2 1/2" by 3 1/2") and features posed color player photos with team color-coded shadow borders. The pictures are set on thin, white card stock with the team name in a yellow bar at the top. The player's name appears in the white margin at the bottom. The backs are white and carry biographical information and a player profile. The cards are numbered on the back and were issued in five series denoted by the letters A, B, C, D, and E as card number prefixes.

	MINT	EXC	G-VG
COMPLETE SET (250)	35.00	14.00	3.50
COMMON PLAYER (A1-A49)	.20	.08	.02
COMMON PLAYER (B1-B51)	.20	.08	.02
COMMON PLAYER (C1-A50)	.20	.08	.02
COMMON PLAYER (D1-D50)	.20	.08	.02
COMMON PLAYER (E1-E50)	.20	.08	.02

☐	A1	Dean Normand	.30	.12	.03
		Humboldt Broncos			
☐	A2	Dan Meyers	.20	.08	.02

Estevan Bruins			
A3 Tyson Balog	.20	.08	.02
Weyburn Red Wings			
A4 Tyler McMillan	.20	.08	.02
Weyburn Red Wings			
A5 Jason Selkirk	.20	.08	.02
Saskatoon Titans			
A6 Bryce Bohun	.20	.08	.02
North Battleford North Stars			
A7 Blaire Hornung	.20	.08	.02
Saskatoon Titans			
A8 Craig McKechnie	.20	.08	.02
Melville Millionaires			
A9 Rejean Stringer	.20	.08	.02
Nipawin Hawks			
A10 Corri Moffat	.20	.08	.02
Melville Millionaires			
A11 Dion Johnson	.20	.08	.02
Nipawin Hawks			
A12 Rod Krushel	.20	.08	.02
Melville Millionaires			
A13 Mike Langen	.20	.08	.02
Weyburn Red Wings			
A14 Jeff Hassman	.20	.08	.02
Melville Millionaires			
A15 Dean Moore	.20	.08	.02
Notre Dame Hounds			
A16 Trevor Wathen	.20	.08	.02
Minot Americans			
A17 Curtis Knight	.20	.08	.02
Humboldt Broncos			
A18 Chris Morgan	.20	.08	.02
Minot Americans			
A19 Trevor Thurstan	.20	.08	.02
Flin Flon Bombers			
A20 Wayne Filipenko	.20	.08	.02
Minot Americans			
A21 Jason Feiffer	.20	.08	.02
Weyburn Red Wings			
A22 Layne Douglas	.20	.08	.02
Minot Americans			
A23 Dave Gardner	.20	.08	.02
Nipawin Hawks			
A24 Ryan Sandholm	.20	.08	.02
Notre Dame Hounds			
A25 Corey McKee	.20	.08	.02
Melfort Mustangs			
A26 Trevor Schmiess	.20	.08	.02
Humboldt Broncos			
A27 Todd Hollinger	.50	.20	.05
Saskatoon Titans			
A28 Jay Dunn	.20	.08	.02
Nipawin Hawks			
A29 Jamie Ling	.50	.20	.05
Notre Dame Hounds			
A30 Todd Small	.20	.08	.02
Saskatoon Titans			
A31 Barret Kropf	.20	.08	.02
Melfort Mustangs			
A32 Dean Gerard	.20	.08	.02
Melfort Mustangs			
A33 Christian Dutil	.20	.08	.02
Yorkton Terriers			
A34 Tyler Scheidt	.20	.08	.02
Aaron Campbell Melfort Mustangs			
A35 Dean Sideroff	.20	.08	.02
Humboldt Broncos			
A36 Dan Dufresne	.20	.08	.02
Notre Dame Hounds			
A37 Cam Yager	.20	.08	.02
North Battleford North Stars			
A38 Richard Nagy	.20	.08	.02
Flin Flon Bombers			
A39 Aaron Cain	.50	.20	.05
Flin Flon Bombers			
A40 Rob Beck	.20	.08	.02
Flin Flon Bombers			
A41 Blair Wagar	.20	.08	.02
Yorkton Terriers			
A42 Kim Maier	.20	.08	.02
Estevan Bruins			
A43 Brent Hoiness	.20	.08	.02
North Battleford North Stars			
A44 Troy Edwards	.20	.08	.02
Estevan Bruins			
A45 Evan Anderson	.20	.08	.02
Estevan Bruins			
A46 Carlin Nordstrom	.20	.08	.02
North Battleford North Stars			
A47 Dean Seymour	.20	.08	.02
Yorkton Terriers			
A48 Scott Wotton	.20	.08	.02
Yorkton Terriers			
A49 Curtis Joseph	2.00	.80	.20
SJHL All Star			
B1 Richard Boscher	.20	.08	.02
Saskatoon Titans			
B2 James Schaeffler	.20	.08	.02
Saskatoon Titans			
B3 Wes Rommel	.20	.08	.02
Nipawin Hawks			
B4 Corey Thompson	.20	.08	.02
Nipawin Hawks			
B5 Rob Phillips	.20	.08	.02
Nipawin Hawks			
B6 Jim McLean	.20	.08	.02
Nipawin Hawks			
B7 Trevor Warrener	.50	.20	.05
Saskatoon Titans			
B8 Peter Boake	.20	.08	.02
Weyburn Red Wings			
B9 Kevin Riffel	.20	.08	.02
Estevan Bruins			
B10 Tom Perry	.20	.08	.02
Humboldt Broncos			
B11 Mark Baird	.20	.08	.02
Humboldt Broncos			
B12 Stacy Prevost	.20	.08	.02
Yorkton Terriers			
B13 Taras Lendzyk	.20	.08	.02
Humboldt Broncos			
B14 Shawn Reis	.20	.08	.02
Melfort Mustangs			
B15 Shawn Thompson	.20	.08	.02
Future Prospect			
B16 Curtis Kleisinger	.20	.08	.02
Notre Dame Hounds			
B17 Kent Rogers	.20	.08	.02
Saskatoon Titans			
B18 Scott Christion	.30	.12	.03
Notre Dame Hounds			
B19 Gerald Tallaire	.30	.12	.03
Estevan Bruins			
B20 Kelly Hollingshead	.20	.08	.02
Estevan Bruins			
B21 Mike Savard	.20	.08	.02
North Battleford North Stars			
B22 Darren Maloney	.20	.08	.02
Melville Millionaires			
B23 Jason Hynd	.20	.08	.02
North Battleford North Stars			
B24 Scott Stewart	.20	.08	.02
Flin Flon Bombers			
B25 Scott Beattie	.30	.12	.03
SJHL All Star			
B26 Dave McAmmond	.20	.08	.02
Flin Flon Bombers			
B27 Myles Gibb	.20	.08	.02
North Battleford North Stars			
B28 Ryan Bach	.50	.20	.05
Notre Dame Hounds			
B29 Martin Smith	.20	.08	.02
North Battleford North Stars			
B30 Leigh Brookbank	.20	.08	.02
Yorkton Terriers			
B31 Todd Markus	.20	.08	.02
Melfort Mustangs			
B32 The Boys From PA	.30	.12	.03
Dean Gerard Darryn Listwan Scott Rogers Brad Federenko Derek Simonson Jeff Greenwood Melfort Mustangs			
B33 Randy Muise	.20	.08	.02
Weyburn Red Wings			
B34 George Gervais	.20	.08	.02
Estevan Bruins			
B35 Keith Harris	.20	.08	.02
Weyburn Red Wings			
B36 Jamie Stelmak	.20	.08	.02
Melville Millionaires			
B37 Bart Vanstaalduinen	.20	.08	.02
Notre Dame Hounds			
B38 Scott Murray	.20	.08	.02
Minot Americans			
B39 Danny Galarneau	.20	.08	.02

Yorkton Terriers

☐ B40 Keith Murphy	.20	.08	.02

Melville Millionaires

☐ B41 Jeff Kungle	.30	.12	.03

Melfort Mustangs

☐ B42 Michel Cook	.20	.08	.02

Yorkton Terriers

☐ B43 Daryl Krauss	.20	.08	.02

Weyburn Red Wings

☐ B44 Derek Wynne	.20	.08	.02

Minot Americans

☐ B45 Derek Crimin	.20	.08	.02

Minot Americans

☐ B46 Jason Brown	.20	.08	.02

Flin Flon Bombers

☐ B47 Bruce Matatall	.20	.08	.02

Minot Americans

☐ B48 Chris Hatch	.20	.08	.02

Flin Flon Bombers

☐ B49 Kurtise Souchotte	.20	.08	.02

Melville Millionaires

☐ B50 Michael Brennan	.20	.08	.02

Humboldt Broncos

☐ B51 Orrin Hergott	.20	.08	.02

Future Prospect

☐ C1 Craig Matatall	.20	.08	.02

Notre Dame Hounds

☐ C2 Brad Prefontaine	.20	.08	.02

Melville Millionaires

☐ C3 Mike Evans	.20	.08	.02

Notre Dame Hounds

☐ C4 Jody Reiter	.20	.08	.02

North Battleford
North Stars

☐ C5 Jeremy Mylymok	.20	.08	.02

Notre Dame Hounds

☐ C6 Dave Doucet	.20	.08	.02

Melville Millionaires

☐ C7 Randy Kerr	.20	.08	.02

Melville Millionaires

☐ C8 Gordon McCann	.20	.08	.02

Melville Millionaires

☐ C9 Quinn Fair	.20	.08	.02

Notre Dame Hounds

☐ C10 Kyle Niemegeers	.20	.08	.02

Estevan Bruins

☐ C11 Ryan Smith	.75	.30	.07

North Battleford
North Stars

☐ C12 Mike Hillock	.20	.08	.02

Minot Americans

☐ C13 Vern Anderson	.20	.08	.02

North Battleford
North Stars

☐ C14 Trent Hamm	.20	.08	.02

Nipawin Hawks

☐ C15 Curtis Folkett ACO	.20	.08	.02

Estevan Bruins

☐ C16 Warren Pickford	.20	.08	.02

Nipawin Hawks

☐ C17 Craig Volstad	.20	.08	.02

Nipawin Hawks

☐ C18 Sean Tallaire	.30	.12	.03

Estevan Bruins

☐ C19 Jason Yaganiski	.20	.08	.02

Minot Americans

☐ C20 Jim McLarty	.20	.08	.02

Nipawin Hawks

☐ C21 Jamie Fyfuglien	.20	.08	.02

Minot Americans

☐ C22 Terry Metro	.20	.08	.02

Minot Americans

☐ C23 Todd Kozak	.20	.08	.02

North Battleford
North Stars

☐ C24 Jeff Huckle	.20	.08	.02

Saskatoon Titans

☐ C25 Darren McLean	.20	.08	.02

Estevan Bruins

☐ C26 Bret Mohninger	.20	.08	.02

Saskatoon Titans

☐ C27 Tim Slukynsky	.20	.08	.02

Yorkton Terriers

☐ C28 Roman Mrhalek	.20	.08	.02

Yorkton Terriers

☐ C29 Joel Martinson	.20	.08	.02

Humboldt Broncos

☐ C30 Ron Patterson	.20	.08	.02

Flin Flon Bombers

☐ C31 Mark Gorgi	.20	.08	.02

Melfort Mustangs

☐ C32 Tom Thomson	.20	.08	.02

Saskatoon Titans

☐ C33 Greg Wahl	.20	.08	.02

Saskatoon Titans

☐ C34 Craig Perrett	.20	.08	.02

Melfort Mustangs

☐ C35 Mike Harder	.20	.08	.02

Weyburn Red Wings

☐ C36 Jeff Cole	.20	.08	.02

Humboldt Broncos

☐ C37 Justin Christoffer	.20	.08	.02

Humboldt Broncos

☐ C38 Nolan Weir	.20	.08	.02

Flin Flon Bombers

☐ C39 Jeff Knight	.20	.08	.02

Melfort Mustangs

☐ C40 Lyle Vaughan	.20	.08	.02

Yorkton Terriers

☐ C41 Scott Bellefontaine	.20	.08	.02

Yorkton Terriers

☐ C42 Trevor Mathias	.20	.08	.02

Weyburn Red Wings

☐ C43 Chris Schinkel	.20	.08	.02

Humboldt Broncos

☐ C44 Scott Rogers	.20	.08	.02

Melfort Mustangs

☐ C45 Shane Holunga	.20	.08	.02

Weyburn Red Wings

☐ C46 Dwayne Rhinehart	.20	.08	.02

Flin Flon Bombers

☐ C47 Eddy Marchant	.20	.08	.02

Flin Flon Bombers

☐ C48 Travis Smith	.20	.08	.02

Weyburn Red Wings

☐ C49 Not Known	.20	.08	.02
☐ C50 Mike Hidlebaugh	.20	.08	.02

Future Prospect

☐ D1 Darcy Herlick	.20	.08	.02

Weyburn Red Wings

☐ D2 Joel Appleton	.20	.08	.02

Humboldt Broncos

☐ D3 Bobby Standish	.20	.08	.02

Melfort Mustangs

☐ D4 Kory Karlander	.30	.12	.03

Saskatoon Titans

☐ D5 Brett Kinaschuk	.20	.08	.02

Humboldt Broncos

☐ D6 Kevin Messer	.20	.08	.02

Nipawin Hawks

☐ D7 Jason Martin	.20	.08	.02

Weyburn Red Wings

☐ D8 Devin Zimmer	.20	.08	.02

Minot Americans

☐ D9 David Foster	.20	.08	.02

Humboldt Broncos

☐ D10 Bob Schwark	.20	.08	.02

Melfort Mustangs

☐ D11 Ted Grayling	.20	.08	.02

Melville Millionaires

☐ D12 Travis Vantighem	.20	.08	.02

Melville Millionaires

☐ D13 Darren Houghton	.20	.08	.02

Melville Millionaires

☐ D14 Wade Welte	.20	.08	.02

Melville Millionaires

☐ D15 1991 NB All Stars	.50	.20	.05

Martin Smith
Ron Gunville
Derek Knorr
Geoff McMaster
Trevor Converse
North Battleford
North Stars

☐ D16 Kevin Powell	.20	.08	.02

Minot Americans

☐ D17 Returning Hounds	.30	.12	.03

Dave Lovesin
Bernie Adlys
Bart Vanstaalduinen
Scott Christion
Bob MacIntosh
Rice Thompson
Adam Thompson
Notre Dame Hounds

☐ D18 Dennis Budeau	.20	.08	.02

Minot Americans

☐ D19 Darren Opp	.20	.08	.02

Nipawin Hawks

☐ D20 Jeff Greenwood	.20	.08	.02

Nipawin Hawks

☐ D21 Mark Daniels	.50	.20	.05

Saskatoon Titans

☐ D22 Todd Murphy	.20	.08	.02

Nipawin Hawks

☐ D23 Scott Weaver	.20	.08	.02

Minot Americans

☐ D24 Robby Bear	.20	.08	.02

Yorkton Terriers
□ D25 Nigel Werenka .... .30 .12 .03
Yorkton Terriers
□ D26 Sean Timmins .... .20 .08 .02
Notre Dame Hounds
□ D27 Ken Malenfant .... .20 .08 .02
Saskatoon Titans
□ D28 Greg Taylor .... .20 .08 .02
Melfort Mustangs
□ D29 Sheldon Bylsma .... .20 .08 .02
Yorkton Terriers
□ D30 Clint Hooge .... .20 .08 .02
Flin Flon Bombers
□ D31 Bob McIntosh .... .20 .08 .02
Notre Dame Hounds
□ D32 Dave Lovsin .... .20 .08 .02
Notre Dame Hounds
□ D33 Jeremy Mathies .... .20 .08 .02
North Battleford
North Stars
□ D34 Blaine Fomradas .... .20 .08 .02
Weyburn Red Wings
□ D35 Cory Borys .... .20 .08 .02
Yorkton Terriers
□ D36 Brad Purdie .... .20 .08 .02
Weyburn Red Wings
□ D37 J. Sotropa .... .20 .08 .02
Saskatoon Titans
□ D38 Duane Vardale .... .20 .08 .02
North Battleford
North Stars
□ D39 Jim Nellis .... .20 .08 .02
North Battleford
North Stars
□ D40 Brent Sheppard .... .20 .08 .02
Humboldt Broncos
□ D41 Cam Bristow .... .20 .08 .02
Melfort Mustangs
□ D42 Steven Brent .... .20 .08 .02
Estevan Bruins
□ D43 Mike Matteucci .... .20 .08 .02
Estevan Bruins
□ D44 Bryan Cossette .... .20 .08 .02
Estevan Bruins
□ D45 Tyler Kuhn .... .20 .08 .02
Flin Flon Bombers
□ D46 Dave Debusschere .... .50 .20 .05
Estevan Bruins
□ D47 Darryl Dickson .... .20 .08 .02
Flin Flon Bombers
□ D48 Derek Meikle .... .20 .08 .02
Flin Flon Bombers
□ D49 Parris Duffus .... .50 .20 .05
Ex SJHLer
□ D50 Lance Wakefield .... .30 .12 .03
Future Prospect
□ E1 Brooke Battersby .... .20 .08 .02
Estevan Bruins
□ E2 Jay Dobrescu .... .20 .08 .02
Estevan Bruins
□ E3 Blair Allison .... .20 .08 .02
Estevan Bruins
□ E4 Shane Johnson .... .20 .08 .02
Estevan Bruins
□ E5 Carson Cardinal .... .20 .08 .02
Estevan Bruins
□ E6 Dean Pooyak .... .20 .08 .02
Flin Flon Bombers
□ E7 Mark Loeppky .... .20 .08 .02
Flin Flon Bombers
□ E8 Travis Cheyne .... .20 .08 .02
Flin Flon Bombers
□ E9 Karl Johnson .... .20 .08 .02
Flin Flon Bombers
□ E10 Jason Ahenakew .... .20 .08 .02
Flin Flon Bombers
□ E11 Darren Schmidt .... .20 .08 .02
Humboldt Broncos
□ E12 Larry Empey .... .20 .08 .02
Humboldt Broncos
□ E13 Colin Froese .... .20 .08 .02
Humboldt Broncos
□ E14 Darryn Listwan .... .20 .08 .02
Melfort Mustangs
□ E15 Todd MacMillan .... .20 .08 .02
Melfort Mustangs
□ E16 Ken Ruddock .... .20 .08 .02
Melfort Mustangs
□ E17 Derek Simonson .... .20 .08 .02
Melfort Mustangs
□ E18 Lyle Ehrmantraut .... .20 .08 .02
Minot Americans
□ E19 Jody Weller .... .20 .08 .02
Nipawin Hawks

□ E20 Danny Dennis .... .20 .08 .02
Melville Millionaires
□ E21 Trent Harper .... .20 .08 .02
Melville Millionaires
□ E22 Jason Prokopetz .... .20 .08 .02
Melville Millionaires
□ E23 Tom Thomson .... .20 .08 .02
Saskatoon Titans
□ E24 Trent Dumaine .... .20 .08 .02
North Battleford
North Stars
□ E25 Mike Wevers .... .20 .08 .02
Saskatoon Titans
□ E26 Darren Duncalfe .... .20 .08 .02
Weyburn Red Wings
□ E27 Regan Simpson .... .20 .08 .02
North Battleford
North Stars
□ E28 Jeff Bloski .... .20 .08 .02
North Battleford
North Stars
□ E29 Blake Sutton .... .20 .08 .02
North Battleford
North Stars
□ E30 Darcy Blair .... .20 .08 .02
North Battleford
North Stars
□ E31 Marty Craigdallie .... .20 .08 .02
Notre Dame Hounds
□ E32 Jason Krug .... .20 .08 .02
Notre Dame Hounds
□ E33 Mark Hansen .... .20 .08 .02
Notre Dame Hounds
□ E34 Bernie Adlys .... .20 .08 .02
Notre Dame Hounds
□ E35 Brett Colborne .... .20 .08 .02
Notre Dame Hounds
□ E36 Tony Bergin .... .20 .08 .02
Notre Dame Hounds
□ E37 Ian Adamson .... .20 .08 .02
Nipawin Hawks
□ E38 Darren MacMillan .... .20 .08 .02
Nipawin Hawks
□ E39 Rob Neighbour .... .20 .08 .02
Nipawin Hawks
□ E40 Jeff Lawson .... .20 .08 .02
Nipawin Hawks
□ E41 Derrick Brucks .... .20 .08 .02
Saskatoon Titans
□ E42 Todd Schoenroth .... .20 .08 .02
Saskatoon Titans
□ E43 Jody Forseth .... .20 .08 .02
Weyburn Red Wings
□ E44 Derek Beuselinck .... .20 .08 .02
Weyburn Red Wings
□ E45 Clint Wensley .... .20 .08 .02
Weyburn Red Wings
□ E46 Darren Donald .... .20 .08 .02
Weyburn Red Wings
□ E47 Shane Stangby .... .20 .08 .02
Yorkton Terriers
□ E48 Jamie Dunn .... .20 .08 .02
Yorkton Terriers
□ E49 Steve Sabo .... .20 .08 .02
Yorkton Terriers
□ E50 Anthony Toth .... .20 .08 .02
Yorkton Terriers

1991-92 Air Canada SJHL All-Stars

This 50-card set features Saskatchewan Junior Hockey League All-Stars. The set included an entry form for a contest sponsored by Air Canada and Old Dutch, which entitled the winner to a trip for two to anywhere in North America. The cards measure the standard size (2 1/2" by 3 1/2") and feature posed color player photos with yellow shadow borders. The pictures are set against a white card face accented with an screened pale purple star pattern. The words "All Star" appear in red within a yellow and black striped bar at the top, while the player's name is printed below the photo. The backs carry the player's name, biographical information, and a player profile. The cards are numbered on the back.

	MINT	EXC	G-VG
COMPLETE SET (50)	12.00	5.00	1.20
COMMON PLAYER (1-50)	.25	.10	.02
☐ 1 Jeff Kungle	.35	.14	.03
Melfort Mustangs			
☐ 2 Jay Dunn	.25	.10	.02
Nipawin Hawks			
☐ 3 Kevin Dickie	.25	.10	.02
Melfort Mustangs			
☐ 4 Martin Smith	.25	.10	.02
North Battleford North Stars			
☐ 5 Jeff Cole	.25	.10	.02
Humboldt Broncos			
☐ 6 Trent Hamm	.25	.10	.02
Nipawin Hawks			
☐ 7 Kent Rogers	.25	.10	.02
Saskatoon Titans			
☐ 8 Dean Gerard	.25	.10	.02
Melfort Mustangs			
☐ 9 Jim McLarty	.25	.10	.02
Nipawin Hawks			
☐ 10 Malcolm Kostuchenko	.25	.10	.02
North Battleford North Stars			
☐ 11 Mark Scollan	.25	.10	.02
Melville Millionaires			
☐ 12 Brad Federenko	.50	.20	.05
Melfort Mustangs			
☐ 13 Rob Beck	.25	.10	.02
Flin Flon Bombers			
☐ 14 Bryce Bohun	.25	.10	.02
North Battleford North Stars			
☐ 15 Kory Karlander	.35	.14	.03
Saskatoon Titans			
☐ 16 Scott Christion	.35	.14	.03
Notre Dame Hounds			
☐ 17 Tyler Kuhn	.25	.10	.02
Flin Flon Bombers			
☐ 18 Corri Moffatt	.25	.10	.02
Melville Millionaires			
☐ 19 Layne Douglas	.25	.10	.02
Minot Americans			
☐ 20 Shane Holunga	.25	.10	.02
Weyburn Red Wings			
☐ 21 Mike Matteucci	.25	.10	.02
Estevan Bruins			
☐ 22 Bart Vanstaalduinen	.25	.10	.02
Notre Dame Hounds			
☐ 23 Brad McEwen	.25	.10	.02
Melville Millionaires			
☐ 24 Kim Maier	.25	.10	.02
Estevan Bruins			
☐ 25 Jamie Ling	.35	.14	.03
Notre Dame Hounds			
☐ 26 Dean Seymour	.25	.10	.02
Yorkton Terriers			
☐ 27 Derek Crimin	.25	.10	.02
Minot Americans			
☐ 28 Evan Anderson	.25	.10	.02
Estevan Bruins			
☐ 29 Craig Matatall	.25	.10	.02
Notre Dame Hounds			
☐ 30 Keith Murphy	.25	.10	.02
Melville Millionaires			
☐ 31 Jason Feiffer	.25	.10	.02
Weyburn Red Wings			
☐ 32 Michel Cook	.25	.10	.02
Yorkton Terriers			
☐ 33 Rod Krushel	.25	.10	.02
☐ 34 Tyler Rice	.35	.14	.03
Melville Millionaires			
☐ 35 Gerald Tallaire	.35	.14	.03
Notre Dame Hounds			
☐ 36 Richard Nagy	.25	.10	.02
Estevan Bruins			
☐ 37 Taras Lendzyk	.25	.10	.02
Flin Flon Bombers			
☐ 38 Jeff Knight	.25	.10	.02
Humboldt Broncos			
☐ 39 Darren Opp	.25	.10	.02
Melfort Mustangs			
☐ 40 Dwayne Rhinehart	.25	.10	.02
Nipawin Hawks			
☐ 41 Minot Americans	.25	.10	.02
Layne Douglas Derek Crimin			
☐ 42 Scott Bellefontaine	.25	.10	.02
Yorkton Terriers			
☐ 43 Darren Maloney	.25	.10	.02
Melville Millionaires			
☐ 44 North Division	.75	.30	.07
All-Star Team Team Photo			
☐ 45 Yorkton Terriers	.75	.30	.07
All Stars Michel Cook Dean Seymour Scott Bellefontaine			
☐ 46 Melville Millionaires	.75	.30	.07
All Stars Team Photo			
☐ 47 Best 1992 All-Stars	.75	.30	.07
Kevin Dickie CO Mike Matteucci Kory Karlander Kim Maier Darren Opp Richard Nagy Mark Scollan			
☐ 48 Estevan Bruins	.75	.30	.07
All Stars Gerald Tallaire Kim Maier Mike Matteucci Evan Anderson			
☐ 49 Notre Dame Hounds	.75	.30	.07
All Stars Tyler Rice Scott Christion Bart Van Staalduinen Jamie Ling Craig Matatall			
☐ 50 Bob Robson CO	.35	.14	.03
Estevan Bruins			

1991-92 British Columbia JHL

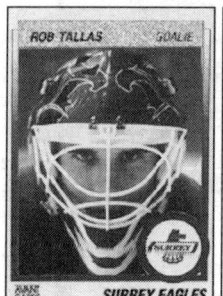
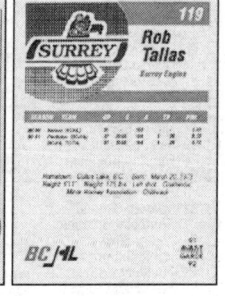

This 172-card set features players of the British Columbia Junior Hockey League and measures the standard size (2 1/2" by 3 1/2") and features action and posed color player photos. A border design that frames the picture is royal blue at the bottom and fades to pale blue and white at the top. Overlapping this frame at the top is a bar with a blue speckled pattern, which contains the player's name, team name, or card title. The team logo appears within a royal blue circle that is superimposed over the lower right corner of the picture. The backs carry a black-and-white close-up, statistics, and biographical information. Topical subsets featured are Stars of the Future (81, 91, 93, 106, 146-147, 164, 166, 168-169), Coastal All-Stars (151-154, 163), and Interior All-Stars (155-162). The cards are numbered on the back and checklisted below according to teams as follows: Vernon Lakers (1-17, 23-25), Kelowna Spartans (18-22, 26-41), Nanaimo Clippers (42-62, 79-80, 153), Merritt Centennials (63-78, 82, 107), Chilliwack Chiefs (81, 127-145), Surrey Eagles (83, 106, 108-117, 119-126), and Penticton Panthers (85-105, 118, 147).

	MINT	EXC	G-VG
COMPLETE SET (173)	30.00	12.00	3.00
COMMON PLAYER (1-170)	.15	.06	.01

		MINT	EXC	G-VG
☐ 1	Vernon Lakers Team Photo	.25	.10	.02
☐ 2	Scott Longstaff	.15	.06	.01
☐ 3	Rick Crowe	.15	.06	.01
☐ 4	Sheldon Wolitski	.15	.06	.01
☐ 5	Kevan Rilcof	.15	.06	.01
☐ 6	Greg Buchanan	.15	.06	.01
☐ 7	Vernon Lakers Executives	.15	.06	.01
☐ 8	Murray Caton	.15	.06	.01
☐ 9	Adrain Bubola	.15	.06	.01
☐ 10	Troy Becker	.15	.06	.01
☐ 11	Shawn Potyok	.15	.06	.01
☐ 12	John Morabito	.15	.06	.01
☐ 13	Peter Zurba	.15	.06	.01
☐ 14	Chad Schraeder	.15	.06	.01
☐ 15	Shawn Bourgeois	.15	.06	.01
☐ 16	Michal Sup	.15	.06	.01
☐ 17	Rick Eremenko	.15	.06	.01
☐ 18	David Lemanowicz	.15	.06	.01
☐ 19	Daniel Blasko	.15	.06	.01
☐ 20	Gary Audette	.25	.10	.02
☐ 21	Graham Harder	.15	.06	.01
☐ 22	Ryan Nessman	.15	.06	.01
☐ 23	Jason Switzer	.15	.06	.01
☐ 24	Roland Ramoser	.15	.06	.01
☐ 25	Dusty McLellan	.15	.06	.01
☐ 26	Dustin Green	.15	.06	.01
☐ 27	Steve Roberts	.15	.06	.01
☐ 28	Jason Lowe	.15	.06	.01
☐ 29	Brad Knight	.15	.06	.01
☐ 30	Pavel Suchanek	.15	.06	.01
☐ 31	Ken Crockett	.15	.06	.01
☐ 32	Adam Smith	.35	.14	.03
☐ 33	Glen Pullishy	.15	.06	.01
☐ 34	Mike Zambon	.15	.06	.01
☐ 35	Scott Chartier	.35	.14	.03
☐ 36	Donny Hearn	.15	.06	.01
☐ 37	Jeff Denham	.15	.06	.01
☐ 38	Jamie Marriott	.15	.06	.01
☐ 39	Silverio Mirao	.15	.06	.01
☐ 40	Darren Tymchyshyn	.15	.06	.01
☐ 41	Mark Basanta	.15	.06	.01
☐ 42	Trevor Prest	.15	.06	.01
☐ 43	Jim Lessard	.15	.06	.01
☐ 44	Jade Kersey	.15	.06	.01
☐ 45	Geordie Young	.15	.06	.01
☐ 46	Darren Holmes	.15	.06	.01
☐ 47	Wade Dayley	.15	.06	.01
☐ 48	Dan Murphy	.15	.06	.01
☐ 49	Paul Taylor	.15	.06	.01
☐ 50	Sjon Wynia	.15	.06	.01
☐ 51	Ryan Loxam	.15	.06	.01
☐ 52	Andy Faulkner	.15	.06	.01
☐ 53	Scott Kowalski	.15	.06	.01
☐ 54	Mickey McGuire	.15	.06	.01
☐ 55	Jason Disiewich	.15	.06	.01
☐ 56	Jim Ingram	.15	.06	.01
☐ 57	Ryan Keller	.15	.06	.01
☐ 58	Brian Schiebel	.15	.06	.01
☐ 59	Shawn York	.15	.06	.01
☐ 60	Sean Krause	.15	.06	.01
☐ 61	Casey Hungle	.15	.06	.01
☐ 62	Chris Jones	.15	.06	.01
☐ 63	Doug Stewart	.15	.06	.01
☐ 64	Jason Sirota	.25	.10	.02
☐ 65	Dave Dunnigan	.15	.06	.01
☐ 66	Aaron Hoffman	.15	.06	.01
☐ 67	Jason Timewell	.15	.06	.01
☐ 68	Pat Meehan	.15	.06	.01
☐ 69	Mike Leduc	.15	.06	.01
☐ 70	Brad Koopmans	.15	.06	.01
☐ 71	Guy Prince	.15	.06	.01
☐ 72	Dorel Gecse	.15	.06	.01
☐ 73	Scott Salmond	.15	.06	.01
☐ 74	Brian Zakall	.15	.06	.01
☐ 75	Mike Josephson	.15	.06	.01
☐ 76	Derek Harper	.15	.06	.01
☐ 77	John Graham	.15	.06	.01
☐ 78	Dan Morrissey	.35	.14	.03
☐ 79	Glenn Calder	.15	.06	.01
☐ 80	Jason Northard	.15	.06	.01
☐ 81	Chris Kerr	.15	.06	.01
☐ 82	Bill Muckalt	.25	.10	.02
☐ 83	Greg Hunt	.15	.06	.01
☐ 84	Paul Kariya	3.00	1.20	.30
	1990-91 All-Star Team			
☐ 85	Dean Rowland	.15	.06	.01
☐ 86	Paul Kariya (Skating)	5.00	2.00	.50
☐ 87	David Kilduff	.15	.06	.01
☐ 88	Jeff Tory	.15	.06	.01
☐ 89	Mike Newman	.15	.06	.01
☐ 90	Tyler Boucher	.15	.06	.01
☐ 91	Paul Kariya (Skating with stick)	3.00	1.20	.30
☐ 92	Phil Valk	.15	.06	.01
☐ 93	Paul Kariya (Passing)	3.00	1.20	.30
☐ 94	Bob Lewis	.15	.06	.01
☐ 95	Steve Williams	.15	.06	.01
☐ 96	James Pelzer	.15	.06	.01
☐ 97	Shawn Carter	.15	.06	.01
☐ 98	Ryan Erasmas	.35	.14	.03
☐ 99	John Dehart	.15	.06	.01
☐ 100	David Green	.15	.06	.01
☐ 101	Derek Gecse	.15	.06	.01
☐ 102	Brian Barnes	.15	.06	.01
☐ 103	Jason Given	.15	.06	.01
☐ 104	Jason Podollan	.75	.30	.07
☐ 105	Brian Veale	.15	.06	.01
☐ 106	Rob Tallas	.35	.14	.03
☐ 107	Bob McBurnie	.15	.06	.01
☐ 108	Paul McMillan	.15	.06	.01
☐ 109	Ryan Donovan	.15	.06	.01
☐ 110	Kevin Robertson	.15	.06	.01
☐ 111	Milt Mastad	.35	.14	.03
☐ 112	Kees Roodbol	.15	.06	.01
☐ 113	Carey Causey	.15	.06	.01
☐ 114	Patrick O'Flaherty	.15	.06	.01
☐ 115	Chad Vestergaard	.15	.06	.01
☐ 116	Tyler Quiring	.35	.14	.03
☐ 117	Loui Mellios	.15	.06	.01
☐ 118	Bob Bell	.15	.06	.01
☐ 119	Rob Tallas	.35	.14	.03
☐ 120	Clint MacDonald	.15	.06	.01
☐ 121	Bart Taylor	.15	.06	.01
☐ 122	Mark Basanta	.15	.06	.01
☐ 123	Don McCusker	.15	.06	.01
☐ 124	Jason Howse	.15	.06	.01
☐ 125	Mike McKinlay	.15	.06	.01
☐ 126	Trevor Pennock	.15	.06	.01
☐ 127	Dean Shmyr	.25	.10	.02
☐ 128	Chris Kerr	.15	.06	.01
☐ 129	Erin Thornton	.15	.06	.01
☐ 130	Dennis Archibald	.15	.06	.01
☐ 131	Brian McDonald	.15	.06	.01
☐ 132	Bob Quinnell	.15	.06	.01
☐ 133	Clint Black	.25	.10	.02
☐ 134	Jason Peters	.15	.06	.01
☐ 135	Doug Ast	.15	.06	.01
☐ 136	Jason Bilous	.35	.14	.03
☐ 137	Lee Schill	.15	.06	.01
☐ 138	Jason Sanford	.15	.06	.01
☐ 139	Jeff Hokanson	.15	.06	.01
☐ 140	Marc Gagnon	.15	.06	.01
☐ 141	Gunnar Henrikson	.15	.06	.01
☐ 142	Jamie Lund	.15	.06	.01
☐ 143	Jason White	.15	.06	.01
☐ 144	Jag Bal	.15	.06	.01
☐ 145	Brad Loring	.15	.06	.01
☐ 146	Mark Gagnon	.15	.06	.01
☐ 147	Brian Veale	.15	.06	.01
☐ 148	Checklist 1	.25	.10	.02
☐ 149	Checklist 2	.25	.10	.02
☐ 150	The Centennial Cup	.25	.10	.02
☐ 151	Brian Law	.15	.06	.01
☐ 152	Al Radke	.15	.06	.01
☐ 153	Andy Faulkner Jason Disiewich Darren Holmes Casey Hungle Chris Jones	.25	.10	.02
☐ 154	1982 Coastal Division	.25	.10	.02

Team Photo

☐ 155	Dusty McLellan	.25	.10	.02
	Roland Ramoser			
	Rick Eremenko			
	Sheldon Wolitski			
	Shawn Potyok			
	Scott Longstaff			
☐ 156	Hendrikson	.25	.10	.02
	Anchikoski			
	Marc Gagnon			
	Jason White			
☐ 157	John Graham	.25	.10	.02
	Dave Dunnigan			
☐ 158	Scott Chartier	.35	.14	.03
	Mike Zambon			
	Paul Taylor			
	Jason Lowe			
☐ 159	Jeff Tory	.25	.10	.02
	Tyler Boucher			
	David Kilduff			
	Lee Davidson			
	John Dehart			
	Burns			
☐ 160	Didmon	.25	.10	.02
	Bentham			
	Marsh			
	Walsh			
☐ 161	Lipsett	.25	.10	.02
	McNeill			
	Klyn			
	Eddington			
☐ 162	1991 Interior	.35	.14	.03
	All-Stars Team			
	Photo			
☐ 163	Johnson	.25	.10	.02
	Meek			
	Welker			
	Fitzpatrick			
	Collins			
	Sofikitas			
	Hutson			
	Herman			
☐ 164	John Dehart	.15	.06	.01
☐ 165	John Craighead	.15	.06	.01
☐ 166	Mike Josephson	.15	.06	.01
☐ 167	Wayne Anchikoski	.15	.06	.01
☐ 168	Paul Kariya	3.00	1.20	.30
	(Stars of the Future on the front)			
☐ 169	Jim Lessard	.15	.06	.01
☐ 170	Tommi Virkgunen	.15	.06	.01
☐ NNO	Wayne Anchikoski	.35	.14	.03
☐ NNO	John Craighead	.35	.14	.03
☐ NNO	Tommi Virkgunen	.35	.14	.03

1992-93 British Columbia JHL

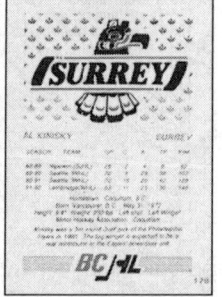

This 246-card set showcases players in the British Columbia Junior Hockey League. The cards measure the standard size (2 1/2" by 3 1/2") and feature color, action player photos with white borders. The player's name and position appear at the top. The team name is at the bottom. The backs carry the team logo in orange and black, statistics, and biographical information. The cards are numbered on the back and are in team order as follows: Bellingham Ice Hawks (1-23), Chilliwack Chiefs (24-45), Kelowna Spartans

(46-70), Merritt Centennials (71-92), Nanaimo Clippers (93-116, 240), Penticton Panthers (117-140), Powell River Paper Kings (141-163, 245), Surrey Eagles (164-188), Vernon Lakers (189-211), and Victoria Warriors (212-233). The set closes with an Alumni of the BCJHL subset (234-239, 241) and other miscellaneous cards (242-246).

		MINT	EXC	G-VG
COMPLETE SET (246)		25.00	10.00	2.50
COMMON PLAYER (1-246)		.15	.06	.01
☐ 1	Tom Wittenberg	.25	.10	.02
☐ 2	Kendel Kelly	.15	.06	.01
☐ 3	Gus Rettschlag	.15	.06	.01
☐ 4	Don Barr	.15	.06	.01
☐ 5	Dave Kirkpatrick	.25	.10	.02
☐ 6	Josh Flett	.15	.06	.01
☐ 7	Paul McKenna	.15	.06	.01
☐ 8	Brad Wingfield	.25	.10	.02
☐ 9	Derek Gesce	.15	.06	.01
☐ 10	Garry Gulash	.15	.06	.01
☐ 11	Tim Bell	.15	.06	.01
☐ 12	Dean Stork	.15	.06	.01
☐ 13	Wes Reusse	.25	.10	.02
☐ 14	Jason Peipmann	.15	.06	.01
☐ 15	Tyler Johnston	.15	.06	.01
☐ 16	Jason Delesoy	.15	.06	.01
☐ 17	The Ice Man	.25	.10	.02
☐ 18	Don Barr	.15	.06	.01
☐ 19	Brad Swain	.15	.06	.01
☐ 20	Wes Rudy	.15	.06	.01
☐ 21	Michael Sigouin	.15	.06	.01
☐ 22	Kevan Rilcof	.15	.06	.01
☐ 23	Brian Preston	.15	.06	.01
☐ 24	Doug Ast	.15	.06	.01
☐ 25	Knut Engqvist	.15	.06	.01
☐ 26	Zac George	.15	.06	.01
☐ 27	Clint Black	.15	.06	.01
☐ 28	Cameron Campbell	.15	.06	.01
☐ 29	Dan Davies	.15	.06	.01
☐ 30	Bryce Munro	.15	.06	.01
☐ 31	Ryan Dayman	.15	.06	.01
☐ 32	Kevin Kimura	.15	.06	.01
☐ 33	Paul Nicolls	.15	.06	.01
☐ 34	Thomas Kraft	.15	.06	.01
☐ 35	Erin Thornton	.15	.06	.01
☐ 36	Brad Loring	.15	.06	.01
☐ 37	Jag Bal	.15	.06	.01
☐ 38	Jeff Grabinsky	.15	.06	.01
☐ 39	Johan Ahrgren	.15	.06	.01
☐ 40	The Lethal Weapon	.25	.10	.02
☐ 41	Two Unidentified Players	.25	.10	.02
☐ 42	Judd Lambert	.15	.06	.01
☐ 43	Brian Schiebel	.15	.06	.01
☐ 44	Dennis Archibald	.25	.10	.02
☐ 45	David Longbroek	.15	.06	.01
☐ 46	Silverio Mirao	.15	.06	.01
☐ 47	Jason Haakstad	.15	.06	.01
☐ 48	Lee Grant	.15	.06	.01
☐ 49	Ryan Esselmont	.15	.06	.01
☐ 50	Steve Roberts	.15	.06	.01
☐ 51	Curtis Fry	.15	.06	.01
☐ 52	David Dollard	.15	.06	.01
☐ 53	Diano Zol	.15	.06	.01
☐ 54	Bob Needham	.15	.06	.01
☐ 55	Dustin Green	.15	.06	.01
☐ 56	Darren Tymchyshyn	.15	.06	.01
☐ 57	Peter Arvanitis	.15	.06	.01
☐ 58	Don Hearn	.15	.06	.01
☐ 59	Title Card (Unnumbered)	.25	.10	.02
☐ 60	Martin Masa	.15	.06	.01
☐ 61	Steffon Walby	.25	.10	.02
☐ 62	Joel Irwin	.15	.06	.01
☐ 63	Brent Bradford	.15	.06	.01
☐ 64	Dieter Kochan	.15	.06	.01
☐ 65	Brendan Kenny	.15	.06	.01
☐ 66	Marty Craigdallie	.15	.06	.01
☐ 67	Graeme Harder	.15	.06	.01
☐ 68	Pavel Suchanek	.15	.06	.01
☐ 69	Shane Johnson	.15	.06	.01
☐ 70	Burt Henderson	.15	.06	.01
☐ 71	Tyler Willis	.15	.06	.01
☐ 72	Mike Olaski	.15	.06	.01
☐ 73	David Green	.15	.06	.01
☐ 74	Tom Mix	.25	.10	.02
☐ 75	Walter(Guy) Prince	.15	.06	.01
☐ 76	Joseph Rybar	.15	.06	.01
☐ 77	Bill Muckalt	.25	.10	.02
☐ 78	Jason Mansoff	.15	.06	.01
☐ 79	Duane Puga	.15	.06	.01

□	80	Aaron Hoffman	.15	.06	.01
□	81	Dan Blasko	.15	.06	.01
□	82	Rob Szatmary	.15	.06	.01
□	83	Mike Minnis	.15	.06	.01
□	84	Pat Meehan	.15	.06	.01
□	85	Andre Robichaud	.15	.06	.01
□	86	The Terminator	.25	.10	.02
□	87	Derrek Harper	.15	.06	.01
□	88	Dan Morrissey	.15	.06	.01
□	89	Joey Kennedy	.15	.06	.01
□	90	Derrek Harper	.15	.06	.01
□	91	Lawrence Klyne	.15	.06	.01
□	92	Ryan Beamin	.15	.06	.01
□	93	Sjon Wynia	.15	.06	.01
□	94	Jason Disiewich	.15	.06	.01
□	95	Jason Sanford	.15	.06	.01
□	96	Casey Hungle	.15	.06	.01
□	97	Brent Murcheson	.15	.06	.01
□	98	Glenn Calder	.25	.10	.02
□	99	Jade Kersey	.15	.06	.01
□	100	Shawn York	.15	.06	.01
□	101	Bob Quinnell	.15	.06	.01
□	102	Geordie Dunstan	.15	.06	.01
□	103	Cory Crowther	.15	.06	.01
□	104	Jason Hodson	.15	.06	.01
□	105	Chris Jones	.15	.06	.01
□	106	Cory Green	.15	.06	.01
□	107	Chris Buie	.15	.06	.01
□	108	Shaun Peet	.15	.06	.01
□	109	Jason Wood	.15	.06	.01
□	110	Dan Murphy	.15	.06	.01
□	111	Jason Disiewich	.15	.06	.01
□	112	Cory Dayley	.15	.06	.01
□	113	Brian Veale	.15	.06	.01
□	114	Jason Northard	.15	.06	.01
□	115	Phil Valk	.25	.10	.02
□	116	Wade Dayley	.15	.06	.01
□	117	Brendan Morrison	.15	.06	.01
□	118	Marcel Sakac	.15	.06	.01
□	119	Tyler Boucher	.15	.06	.01
□	120	Ray Guze	.15	.06	.01
□	121	Brian Barnes	.25	.10	.02
□	122	Jason Given	.15	.06	.01
□	123	Michael Dairon	.15	.06	.01
□	124	Mike Newman	.15	.06	.01
□	125	Craig Fletcher	.15	.06	.01
□	126	Ty Davidson	.15	.06	.01
□	127	Miki Antonik	.15	.06	.01
□	128	Rob Pennoyer	.15	.06	.01
□	129	Dave Whitworth	.15	.06	.01
□	130	Steve Williams	.15	.06	.01
□	131	Robbie Trampuh	.15	.06	.01
□	132	Mark Filipenko	.15	.06	.01
□	133	Clint MacDonald	.15	.06	.01
□	134	Colin Ryder	.15	.06	.01
□	135	David Kilduff	.25	.10	.02
□	136	Mickey McGuire	.15	.06	.01
□	137	Randy Polacik	.15	.06	.01
□	138	Jeff Tory	.25	.10	.02
□	139	Chris Buckman	.15	.06	.01
□	140	Bill Moody	.15	.06	.01
□	141	Rick McLarren	.15	.06	.01
□	142	The Phantom	.25	.10	.02
□	143	Jason Zaichkowski	.15	.06	.01
□	144	Tony Hrycuik	.15	.06	.01
□	145	Cameron Knox	.15	.06	.01
□	146	Mike Warriner	.15	.06	.01
□	147	Robb Gordon	.35	.14	.03
□	148	Mike Pawluk	.35	.14	.03
□	149	Tim Harris	.15	.06	.01
□	150	Mike Bzdel	.15	.06	.01
□	151	Chad Wilson	.15	.06	.01
□	152	Andrew Plumb	.15	.06	.01
□	153	Andy MacIntosh	.15	.06	.01
□	154	Stefan Brannare	.15	.06	.01
□	155	Matt Sharrers	.15	.06	.01
□	156	Brent Berry	.15	.06	.01
□	157	Ryan Douglas	.15	.06	.01
□	158	Heath Dennison	.15	.06	.01
□	159	Chad Vizzutti	.15	.06	.01
□	160	Adam Lord	.15	.06	.01
□	161	Brad Klyn	.15	.06	.01
□	162	Andrew Young	.15	.06	.01
□	163	Casey Lemanski	.15	.06	.01
□	164	Mike McKinlay	.15	.06	.01
□	165	Derek Robinson	.15	.06	.01
□	166	Kees Roodbol	.15	.06	.01
□	167	Scott Boucher	.15	.06	.01
□	168	Shawn Gervais	.15	.06	.01
□	169	Ryan Schaffer	.15	.06	.01
□	170	Kevin Robertson	.15	.06	.01
□	171	Ryan Donovan	.15	.06	.01
□	172	Bart Taylor	.15	.06	.01
□	173	Greg Hunt	.15	.06	.01
□	174	Darcy George	.15	.06	.01
□	175	Shane Tidsbury	.15	.06	.01
□	176	Rob Smillie	.15	.06	.01
□	177	Chad Vestergaard	.15	.06	.01
□	178	Al Kinisky	.15	.06	.01
□	179	Patrick O'Flaherty	.15	.06	.01
□	180	Loui Mellios	.15	.06	.01
□	181	Lorin Murdock	.25	.10	.02
		(Unnumbered)			
□	182	Jason Genik	.15	.06	.01
□	183	Rob Herrington	.15	.06	.01
□	184	Loui Mellios	.15	.06	.01
□	185	Cal Benazic	.25	.10	.02
□	186	Richard Kraus	.15	.06	.01
□	187	Geoff White	.15	.06	.01
□	188	Kirk Buchanan	.15	.06	.01
□	189	Peter Zurba	.15	.06	.01
□	190	John Morabito	.15	.06	.01
□	191	Corey Kruchkowski	.15	.06	.01
□	192	Spencer Ward	.15	.06	.01
□	193	Danny Shermerhorn	.15	.06	.01
□	194	Mark Davies	.15	.06	.01
□	195	Jason Rushton	.15	.06	.01
□	196	Chad Buckle	.15	.06	.01
□	197	Serge Beauchesne	.15	.06	.01
□	198	Todd Kelman	.15	.06	.01
□	199	Jason Switzer	.15	.06	.01
□	200	Eon MacFarlane	.15	.06	.01
□	201	Terry Ryan	.15	.06	.01
□	202	Shawn Bourgeois	.15	.06	.01
□	203	Chad Schraeder	.15	.06	.01
□	204	Dusty McLellan	.15	.06	.01
□	205	The Predator	.25	.10	.02
□	206	Danny Shermerhorn	.15	.06	.01
□	207	Chris Godard	.15	.06	.01
□	208	Jason Chipman	.15	.06	.01
□	209	Christian Twomey	.25	.10	.02
□	210	Ryan Loxam	.15	.06	.01
□	211	Greg Buchanan	.15	.06	.01
□	212	Kees Roodbol	.15	.06	.01
□	213	Ryan Keller	.15	.06	.01
□	214	Kevin Paschal	.15	.06	.01
□	215	David Hebky	.15	.06	.01
□	216	Vince Devlin	.15	.06	.01
□	217	Mike Cole	.15	.06	.01
□	218	Daljit Takhar	.15	.06	.01
□	219	Scott Hall	.15	.06	.01
□	220	Derek Lawrence	.15	.06	.01
□	221	Mark Basanta	.15	.06	.01
□	222	Jan Kloboucek	.15	.06	.01
□	223	Randy Barker	.15	.06	.01
□	224	Kris Gailloux	.15	.06	.01
□	225	Tyson Scheuer	.15	.06	.01
□	226	Brent Wormald	.15	.06	.01
□	227	Vince Devlin	.15	.06	.01
□	228	Gus Miller	.15	.06	.01
□	229	Todd McKave	.15	.06	.01
□	230	Lawrence Oliver	.15	.06	.01
□	231	Scott Garvin	.15	.06	.01
□	232	Rob Milliken	.15	.06	.01
□	233	Roman Kobrc	.15	.06	.01
□	234	Dan Skene	.15	.06	.01
□	235	Blair Marsh	.15	.06	.01
□	236	Maco Balkovec	.15	.06	.01
□	237	Scott Kirton	.15	.06	.01
□	238	Blaine Moore	.15	.06	.01
□	239	Nigel Creightney	.15	.06	.01
□	240	Bill Zapt	.15	.06	.01
□	241	Jason Elders	.15	.06	.01
□	242	BCJHL Officials	.15	.06	.01
		(Unidentified Referee)			
□	243	Masks of the BCJHL	.25	.10	.02
		The Black Panther			
□	244	Masks of the BCJHL	.25	.10	.02
		The Puck Pirate			
		(Unnumbered)			
□	245	Mike Pawluk	.35	.14	.03
		BCJHL MVP			
□	246	Steffon Walby	.35	.14	.03
		Captains of the BCJHL			

1952-53 Juniors Blue Tint

The 1952-53 Junior set contains 182 cards measuring approximately 2" by 3". The cards have a blue tint and are numbered on the back. It is not known at this time who

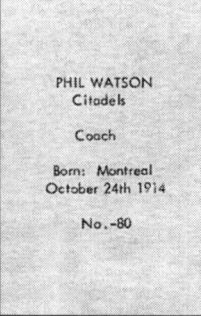

PHIL WATSON
Citadels

Coach

Born: Montreal
October 24th 1914

No. -80

sponsored this set. Key cards in this set are "Pre-Rookie Cards" of Al Arbour, Don Cherry, Charlie Hodge, John Muckler, Henri Richard, and Harry Sinden.

		NRMT	VG-E	GOOD
COMPLETE SET (182)		1500.00	600.00	150.00
COMMON PLAYER (1-182)		7.00	2.80	.70

	#	Name	NRMT	VG-E	GOOD
☐	1	Dennis Riggin	12.00	5.00	1.20
☐	2	Joe Zorica	7.00	2.80	.70
☐	3	Larry Hillman	12.00	5.00	1.20
☐	4	Edward(Ted) Reid	7.00	2.80	.70
☐	5	Al Arbour	50.00	20.00	5.00
☐	6	Marlin McAlendin	7.00	2.80	.70
☐	7	Ross Graham	7.00	2.80	.70
☐	8	Cumming Burton	7.00	2.80	.70
☐	9	Ed Palamar	7.00	2.80	.70
☐	10	Elmer Skov	9.00	3.75	.90
☐	11	Eddie Louttit	7.00	2.80	.70
☐	12	Gerry Price	7.00	2.80	.70
☐	13	Lou Dietrich	7.00	2.80	.70
☐	14	Gaston Marcotte	7.00	2.80	.70
☐	15	Bob Brown	7.00	2.80	.70
☐	16	Archie Burton	7.00	2.80	.70
☐	17	Marv Edwards	12.00	5.00	1.20
☐	18	Norman Defelice	7.00	2.80	.70
☐	19	Pete Kamula	7.00	2.80	.70
☐	20	Charles Marshall	7.00	2.80	.70
☐	21	Alex Leslie	7.00	2.80	.70
☐	22	Minpy Roberts	7.00	2.80	.70
☐	23	Danny Poliziani	7.00	2.80	.70
☐	24	Allen Kellogg	7.00	2.80	.70
☐	25	Brian Cullen	20.00	8.00	2.00
☐	26	Ken Schinkel	9.00	3.75	.90
☐	27	W. Hass	7.00	2.80	.70
☐	28	Don Nash	7.00	2.80	.70
☐	29	Robert Maxwell	7.00	2.80	.70
☐	30	Eddie Mateka	7.00	2.80	.70
☐	31	Joe Kastelic	7.00	2.80	.70
☐	32	Hank Ciesla	9.00	3.75	.90
☐	33	Hugh Barlow	7.00	2.80	.70
☐	34	Claude Roy	7.00	2.80	.70
☐	35	Jean-Guy Gamache	7.00	2.80	.70
☐	36	Leon Michelin	7.00	2.80	.70
☐	37	Gerard Bergeron	7.00	2.80	.70
☐	38	Herve Lalonde	7.00	2.80	.70
☐	39	J.M. Cossette	7.00	2.80	.70
☐	40	Jean-Guy Gendron	12.00	5.00	1.20
☐	41	Gamill Bedard	7.00	2.80	.70
☐	42	Alfred Soucy	7.00	2.80	.70
☐	43	Jean Leclerc	7.00	2.80	.70
☐	44	Raymond St.Cyr	7.00	2.80	.70
☐	45	Lester Lahaye	7.00	2.80	.70
☐	46	Yvan Houle	7.00	2.80	.70
☐	47	Louis Desrosiers	7.00	2.80	.70
☐	48	Douglas Lessor	7.00	2.80	.70
☐	49	Irvin Scott	7.00	2.80	.70
☐	50	Danny Blair	7.00	2.80	.70
☐	51	Jim Connelly	9.00	3.75	.90
☐	52	William Chalmers	7.00	2.80	.70
☐	53	Frank Bettiol	7.00	2.80	.70
☐	54	James Holmes	7.00	2.80	.70
☐	55	Birley Dimme	7.00	2.80	.70
☐	56	Donald Beattie	7.00	2.80	.70
☐	57	Terrance Chattington	7.00	2.80	.70
☐	58	Bruce Wallace	7.00	2.80	.70
☐	59	William McCreary	9.00	3.75	.90
☐	60	Fred Brady	7.00	2.80	.70
☐	61	Ronald Murphy	9.00	3.75	.90
☐	62	Lavi Purola	7.00	2.80	.70
☐	63	George Whyte	7.00	2.80	.70
☐	64	Marcel Paille	20.00	8.00	2.00
☐	65	Maurice Collins	7.00	2.80	.70
☐	66	Gerard(Butch) Houle	7.00	2.80	.70
☐	67	Gilles Laperriere	7.00	2.80	.70
☐	68	Robert Chevalier	7.00	2.80	.70
☐	69	Bertrand Lepage	7.00	2.80	.70
☐	70	Michel Labadie	7.00	2.80	.70
☐	71	Gabriel Alain	7.00	2.80	.70
☐	72	Jean-Jacques Pichette	9.00	3.75	.90
☐	73A	Camille Henry (Citadelles)	25.00	10.00	2.50
☐	73B	Camille Henry (New York)	150.00	60.00	15.00
☐	74	Jean-Guy Gignac	7.00	2.80	.70
☐	75	Leo Amadio	7.00	2.80	.70
☐	76	Gilles Thibault	9.00	3.75	.90
☐	77	Gaston Pelletier	7.00	2.80	.70
☐	78	Adolph Kukulowicz	9.00	3.75	.90
☐	79	Roland Leclerc	7.00	2.80	.70
☐	80	Phil Watson CO	35.00	14.00	3.50
☐	81	Raymond Cyr	9.00	3.75	.90
☐	82	Jacques Marcotte	7.00	2.80	.70
☐	83	Floyd(Bud) Hillman	9.00	3.75	.90
☐	84	Bob Attersley	7.00	2.80	.70
☐	85	Harry Sinden	50.00	20.00	5.00
☐	86	Stan Parker	7.00	2.80	.70
☐	87	Bob Mader	7.00	2.80	.70
☐	88	Roger Maisonneuve	7.00	2.80	.70
☐	89	Phil Chapman	7.00	2.80	.70
☐	90	Don McIntosh	7.00	2.80	.70
☐	91	Jack Armstrong	7.00	2.80	.70
☐	92	Carlo Montemurro	7.00	2.80	.70
☐	93	Ken Courtney	7.00	2.80	.70
☐	94	Bill Stewart	9.00	3.75	.90
☐	95	Gerald Casey	7.00	2.80	.70
☐	96	Fred Etcher	7.00	2.80	.70
☐	97	Orrin Carver	7.00	2.80	.70
☐	98	Ralph Willis	7.00	2.80	.70
☐	99	Kenneth Robertson	7.00	2.80	.70
☐	100	Don Cherry	250.00	100.00	25.00
☐	101	Fred Pletsch	7.00	2.80	.70
☐	102	Larry Thibault	7.00	2.80	.70
☐	103	James Robertson	7.00	2.80	.70
☐	104	Orval Tessier	15.00	6.00	1.50
☐	105	Jack Higgins	7.00	2.80	.70
☐	106	Robert White	7.00	2.80	.70
☐	107	Doug Mohns	25.00	10.00	2.50
☐	108	William Sexton	7.00	2.80	.70
☐	109	John Martan	7.00	2.80	.70
☐	110	Tony Poeta	9.00	3.75	.90
☐	111	Don McKenney	10.00	4.00	1.00
☐	112	Bill Harrington	7.00	2.80	.70
☐	113	Allen(Skip) Peal	7.00	2.80	.70
☐	114	John Ford	7.00	2.80	.70
☐	115	Ken Collins	9.00	3.75	.90
☐	116	Marc Boileau	9.00	3.75	.90
☐	117	Doug Vaughan	7.00	2.80	.70
☐	118	Gilles Boisvert	7.00	2.80	.70
☐	119	Buddy Horne	7.00	2.80	.70
☐	120	Graham Joyce	7.00	2.80	.70
☐	121	Gary Collins	7.00	2.80	.70
☐	122	Roy Greenan	7.00	2.80	.70
☐	123	Beryl Klynck	7.00	2.80	.70
☐	124	Grieg Hicks	7.00	2.80	.70
☐	125	Jack(Red) Novak	7.00	2.80	.70
☐	126	Ken Tennant	7.00	2.80	.70
☐	127	Glen Cressman	7.00	2.80	.70
☐	128	Curly Davies	7.00	2.80	.70
☐	129	Charlie Hodge	35.00	14.00	3.50
☐	130	Bob McCord	9.00	3.75	.90
☐	131	Gordie Hollinworth	7.00	2.80	.70
☐	132	Ronald Pilon	7.00	2.80	.70
☐	133	Brian Mackay	7.00	2.80	.70
☐	134	Yvon Chasle	7.00	2.80	.70
☐	135	Denis Boucher	9.00	3.75	.90
☐	136	Claude Buileau	7.00	2.80	.70
☐	137	Claude Vinet	7.00	2.80	.70
☐	138	Claude Provost	25.00	10.00	2.50
☐	139	Henri Richard	175.00	70.00	18.00
☐	140	Les Lilley	7.00	2.80	.70
☐	141	Phil Goyette	20.00	8.00	2.00
☐	142	Guy Rousseau	7.00	2.80	.70
☐	143	Paul Knox	7.00	2.80	.70
☐	144	Bill Lee	7.00	2.80	.70
☐	145	Ted Topazzini	9.00	3.75	.90
☐	146	Marc Reaume	9.00	3.75	.90
☐	147	Bill Dineen	30.00	12.00	3.00
☐	148	Ed Plata	7.00	2.80	.70
☐	149	Noel Price	9.00	3.75	.90
☐	150	Mike Ratchford	7.00	2.80	.70
☐	151	Jim Logan	7.00	2.80	.70
☐	152	Art Clune	7.00	2.80	.70

☐	153	Jerry MacNamara	7.00	2.80	.70
☐	154	Jack Caffery	9.00	3.75	.90
☐	155	Less Duff	7.00	2.80	.70
☐	156	Murray Costello	10.00	4.00	1.00
☐	157	Ed Chadwick	20.00	8.00	2.00
☐	158	Mike Desilets	7.00	2.80	.70
☐	159	Ross Watson	7.00	2.80	.70
☐	160	Roger Landry	7.00	2.80	.70
☐	161	Terry O'Connor	7.00	2.80	.70
☐	162	Ovila Gagnon	7.00	2.80	.70
☐	163	Dave Broadbelt	7.00	2.80	.70
☐	164	Sandy Monrisson	7.00	2.80	.70
☐	165	John MacGillvray	7.00	2.80	.70
☐	166	Claude Beaupre	7.00	2.80	.70
☐	167	Eddie Eustache	7.00	2.80	.70
☐	168	Stan Rodek	7.00	2.80	.70
☐	169	Maurice Mantha	9.00	3.75	.90
☐	170	Hector Lalonde	9.00	3.75	.90
☐	171	Bob Wilson	7.00	2.80	.70
☐	172	Frank Bonello	7.00	2.80	.70
☐	173	Peter Kowalchuch	7.00	2.80	.70
☐	174	Les Binkley	20.00	8.00	2.00
☐	175	John Muckler	35.00	14.00	3.50
☐	176	Ken Wharram	20.00	8.00	2.00
☐	177	John Sleaver	7.00	2.80	.70
☐	178	Ralph Markarian	7.00	2.80	.70
☐	179	Ken McMeekin	7.00	2.80	.70
☐	180	Ron Boomer	7.00	2.80	.70
☐	181	Kenneth(Red) Crawford	7.00	2.80	.70
☐	182	Jim McBurney	12.00	5.00	1.20

1951-52 Laval Dairy QSHL

The 1951-52 Laval Dairy QSHL set includes 109 black and white blank-back cards measuring approximately 1 3/4" by 2 1/2". These cards were issued in the province of Quebec and the Ottawa region. The cards are numbered and dated on the front. Key cards in this set are "Pre-Rookie Cards" of Jean Beliveau and Jacques Plante. The card numbering is organized by team as follows: Aces de Quebec (1-18 and 37), Chicoutimi (19-36), Sherbrooke (38-51), Shawinigan Falls (52-67), Valleyfield (68-84), Royals de Montreal (85-100), and Ottawa (101-109).

		NRMT	VG-E	GOOD
COMPLETE SET (109)		1000.00	400.00	100.00
COMMON PLAYER (1-109)		6.00	2.40	.60

☐	1	Jean Beliveau	250.00	100.00	25.00
☐	2	Jean Marois	6.00	2.40	.60
☐	3	Joe Crozier	9.00	3.75	.90
☐	4	Jack Gelineau	6.00	2.40	.60
☐	5	Murdo McKay	6.00	2.40	.60
☐	6	Arthur Leyte	6.00	2.40	.60
☐	7	W.(Bill) Leblanc	6.00	2.40	.60
☐	8	Robert Hayes	6.00	2.40	.60
☐	9	Yogi Kraiger	6.00	2.40	.60
☐	10	Frank King	6.00	2.40	.60
☐	11	Ludger Tremblay	6.00	2.40	.60
☐	12	Jackie Leclair	12.00	5.00	1.20
☐	13	Martial Pruneau	6.00	2.40	.60
☐	14	Armand Gaudreault	6.00	2.40	.60
☐	15	Marcel Bonin	9.00	3.75	.90
☐	16	Herbie Carnegie	15.00	6.00	1.50

☐	17	Claude Robert	6.00	2.40	.60
☐	18	Phil Renaud	6.00	2.40	.60
☐	19	Roland Hebert	6.00	2.40	.60
☐	20	Donat Duschene	6.00	2.40	.60
☐	21	Jacques Gagnon	6.00	2.40	.60
☐	22	Normand Dussault	6.00	2.40	.60
☐	23	Stan Smrke	9.00	3.75	.90
☐	24	Louis Smrke	6.00	2.40	.60
☐	25	Floyd Crawford	6.00	2.40	.60
☐	26	Germain Leger	6.00	2.40	.60
☐	27	Delphis Franche	6.00	2.40	.60
☐	28	Dick Wray	6.00	2.40	.60
☐	29	Guildor Levesque	6.00	2.40	.60
☐	30	Georges Roy	6.00	2.40	.60
☐	31	J.P. Lamirande	6.00	2.40	.60
☐	32	Gerard Glaude	6.00	2.40	.60
☐	33	Marcel Pelletier	9.00	3.75	.90
☐	34	Pete Tkachuck	6.00	2.40	.60
☐	35	Sherman White	6.00	2.40	.60
☐	36	Jimmy Moore	6.00	2.40	.60
☐	37	Punch Imlach	35.00	14.00	3.50
☐	38	Alex Sandalax	6.00	2.40	.60
☐	39	William Kyle	6.00	2.40	.60
☐	40	Kenneth Biggs	6.00	2.40	.60
☐	41	Peter Wright	6.00	2.40	.60
☐	42	Rene Pepin	6.00	2.40	.60
☐	43	Tod Campeau	9.00	3.75	.90
☐	44	John Smith	6.00	2.40	.60
☐	45	Thomas McDougall	6.00	2.40	.60
☐	46	Jos. Lepine	6.00	2.40	.60
☐	47	Guy Labrie	6.00	2.40	.60
☐	48	Roger Bessette	6.00	2.40	.60
☐	49	Yvan Dugre	9.00	3.75	.90
☐	50	James Planche	6.00	2.40	.60
☐	51	Nils Tremblay	6.00	2.40	.60
☐	52	Bill MacDonagh	6.00	2.40	.60
☐	53	Georges Ouellet	6.00	2.40	.60
☐	54	Billy Arcand	6.00	2.40	.60
☐	55	Johnny Mahaffy	9.00	3.75	.90
☐	56	Bucky Buchanan	6.00	2.40	.60
☐	57	Al Miller	6.00	2.40	.60
☐	58	Don Penniston	6.00	2.40	.60
☐	59	Spike Laliberte	6.00	2.40	.60
☐	60	Ernie Oakley	6.00	2.40	.60
☐	61	Jack Bownass	6.00	2.40	.60
☐	62	Ted Hodgson	6.00	2.40	.60
☐	63	Lyall Wiseman	6.00	2.40	.60
☐	64	Erwin Grosse	6.00	2.40	.60
☐	65	Mel Read	6.00	2.40	.60
☐	66	Lloyd Henchberger	6.00	2.40	.60
☐	67	Jack Taylor	6.00	2.40	.60
☐	68	Marcel Bessette	6.00	2.40	.60
☐	69	Jack Schmidt	6.00	2.40	.60
☐	70	Paul Saindon	6.00	2.40	.60
☐	71	J.P. Bisaillon	6.00	2.40	.60
☐	72	Eddie Redmond	6.00	2.40	.60
☐	73	Larry Kwong	9.00	3.75	.90
☐	74	Andre Corriveau	6.00	2.40	.60
☐	75	Kitoute Joanette	6.00	2.40	.60
☐	76	Toe Blake	75.00	30.00	7.50
☐	77	Georges Bougie	6.00	2.40	.60
☐	78	Jack Irvine	6.00	2.40	.60
☐	79	Paul Larivee	6.00	2.40	.60
☐	80	Paul Leclerc	6.00	2.40	.60
☐	81	Bertrand Bourassa	6.00	2.40	.60
☐	82	Jacques Deslauriers	6.00	2.40	.60
☐	83	Bingo Ernst	6.00	2.40	.60
☐	84	Gaston Gervais	6.00	2.40	.60
☐	85	Gerry Plamondon	6.00	2.40	.60
☐	86	Glen Harmon	6.00	2.40	.60
☐	87	Bob Friday	6.00	2.40	.60
☐	88	Rolland Rousseau	6.00	2.40	.60
☐	89	Billy Goold	6.00	2.40	.60
☐	90	Lloyd Finkbeiner	6.00	2.40	.60
☐	91	Cliff Malone	6.00	2.40	.60
☐	92	Jacques Plante	250.00	100.00	25.00
☐	93	Gerard Desaulniers	9.00	3.75	.90
☐	94	Arthur Rose	6.00	2.40	.60
☐	95	Jacques Locas	6.00	2.40	.60
☐	96	Walter Clune	6.00	2.40	.60
☐	97	Louis Denis	6.00	2.40	.60
☐	98	Fernand Perreault	6.00	2.40	.60
☐	99	Douglas McNeil	9.00	3.75	.90
☐	100	Les Douglas	6.00	2.40	.60
☐	101	Howard Riopelle	6.00	2.40	.60
☐	102	Vic Grigg	6.00	2.40	.60
☐	103	Bobby Roberts	6.00	2.40	.60
☐	104	Legs Fraser	6.00	2.40	.60
☐	105	Butch Stahan	6.00	2.40	.60
☐	106	Fritz Frazer	6.00	2.40	.60
☐	107	Bill Robinson	6.00	2.40	.60
☐	108	Eddie Emberg	6.00	2.40	.60
☐	109	Leo Gravelle	12.00	5.00	1.20

1951-52 Laval Dairy Subset

BILL RICHARDSON - Ottawa
No - 13 mars 1926 - Perth, Ont.
Aile Droite

The 1951-52 Laval Dairy Subset includes 66 skip-numbered black and white blank-back cards measuring approximately 1 3/4" by 2 1/2". Apparently, this set was intended to update the QSHL set and was issued after the QSHL set perhaps even as late as the 1952-53 season. The card numbering is organized by team as follows: Aces de Quebec (7-15 and 117), Chicoutimi (25-38), Sherbrooke (39-57), Shawinigan Falls (59-67, 89-90, 94-95, 115, 118, and 120), Valleyfield (68-84 and 116), Royals de Montreal (85-86, 92-93, and 96-97), and Ottawa (98-114, 119, and 121).

	NRMT	VG-E	GOOD
COMPLETE SET (66)	1000.00	400.00	100.00
COMMON PLAYER	12.00	5.00	1.20

		NRMT	VG-E	GOOD
☐ 4	Jack Gelineau SP	20.00	8.00	2.00
☐ 7	Al Miller	12.00	5.00	1.20
☐ 8	Walter Pawlyshyn	12.00	5.00	1.20
☐ 9	Yogi Kraiger SP	20.00	8.00	2.00
☐ 10	Al Baccari	12.00	5.00	1.20
☐ 12	Denis Smith	12.00	5.00	1.20
☐ 13	Pierre Brillant	12.00	5.00	1.20
☐ 14	Frank Mario	12.00	5.00	1.20
☐ 15	Danny Nixon	12.00	5.00	1.20
☐ 25	Leon Bouchard	12.00	5.00	1.20
☐ 26	Pete Taillefer	12.00	5.00	1.20
☐ 29	Bucky Buchanan	12.00	5.00	1.20
☐ 36	Marius Groleau	12.00	5.00	1.20
☐ 38	Fernand Perreault	12.00	5.00	1.20
☐ 39	Robert Drainville	12.00	5.00	1.20
☐ 40	Ronnie Matthews	12.00	5.00	1.20
☐ 44	Roger Roberge	12.00	5.00	1.20
☐ 46	Pete Wywrot	12.00	5.00	1.20
☐ 50	Gilles Dube	12.00	5.00	1.20
☐ 51	Nils Tremblay SP	20.00	8.00	2.00
☐ 52	Bob Pepin	12.00	5.00	1.20
☐ 53	Dewar Thompson	12.00	5.00	1.20
☐ 55	Irene St.Hilaire	12.00	5.00	1.20
☐ 56	Martial Pruneau	12.00	5.00	1.20
☐ 57	Jacques Locas	12.00	5.00	1.20
☐ 59	Nelson Podolsky	12.00	5.00	1.20
☐ 60	Bert Giesebrecht	12.00	5.00	1.20
☐ 61	Steve Brklaicich	12.00	5.00	1.20
☐ 65	Jack Hamilton	12.00	5.00	1.20
☐ 66	Dave Gatherum	12.00	5.00	1.20
☐ 67	Jean-Marie Plante	12.00	5.00	1.20
☐ 68	Gordie Haworth	12.00	5.00	1.20
☐ 69	Jack Schmidt SP	20.00	8.00	2.00
☐ 70	Bruce Cline	12.00	5.00	1.20
☐ 72	Phil Vitale	12.00	5.00	1.20
☐ 81	Carl Smelle	12.00	5.00	1.20
☐ 84	Tom Smelle	12.00	5.00	1.20
☐ 85	Gerry Plamondon	12.00	5.00	1.20
☐ 86	Glen Harmon	12.00	5.00	1.20
☐ 89	Frank Bathgate	12.00	5.00	1.20
☐ 90	Bernie Lemonde	12.00	5.00	1.20
☐ 92	Jacques Plante	250.00	100.00	25.00
☐ 93	Gerard Desaulniers	12.00	5.00	1.20
☐ 94	J.C. Lebrun	12.00	5.00	1.20
☐ 95	Bob Leger	12.00	5.00	1.20
☐ 96	Walter Clune	12.00	5.00	1.20
☐ 97	Louis Denis	12.00	5.00	1.20
☐ 98	Jackie Leclair	20.00	8.00	2.00
☐ 99	John Arundel	12.00	5.00	1.20
☐ 100	Leslie(Les) Douglas	12.00	5.00	1.20
☐ 103	Bobby Robertson	12.00	5.00	1.20
☐ 104	Ray Fredericks	12.00	5.00	1.20
☐ 106	Emile Dagenais	12.00	5.00	1.20
☐ 108	Al Kuntz	12.00	5.00	1.20
☐ 110	Red Johnson	12.00	5.00	1.20
☐ 111	John O'Flaherty	12.00	5.00	1.20
☐ 112	Jack Giesebrecht	12.00	5.00	1.20
☐ 113	Bill Richardson	12.00	5.00	1.20
☐ 114	Bep Guidolin	25.00	10.00	2.50
☐ 115	Roger Bedard	12.00	5.00	1.20
☐ 116	Renald Lacroix	12.00	5.00	1.20
☐ 117	Gordie Hudson	12.00	5.00	1.20
☐ 118	Dick Wray	12.00	5.00	1.20
☐ 119	Ronnie Hurst	12.00	5.00	1.20
☐ 120	Eddie Joss	12.00	5.00	1.20
☐ 121	Lyall Wiseman	12.00	5.00	1.20

1951-52 Laval Dairy Lac St. Jean

The 1951-52 Laval Dairy Lac St. Jean set includes 59 green-and-white tinted cards measuring approximately 1 3/4" by 2 1/2". The backs are blank. The cards are numbered on the front.

	NRMT	VG-E	GOOD
COMPLETE SET (59)	1000.00	400.00	100.00
COMMON PLAYER (1-59)	18.00	7.25	1.80

		NRMT	VG-E	GOOD
☐ 1	Eddy Daoust	25.00	10.00	2.50
☐ 2	Guy Gareau	18.00	7.25	1.80
☐ 3	Gilles Desrosiers	18.00	7.25	1.80
☐ 4	Robert Desbiens	18.00	7.25	1.80
☐ 5	James Hayes	18.00	7.25	1.80
☐ 6	Paul Gagnon	18.00	7.25	1.80
☐ 7	Gerry Perreault	18.00	7.25	1.80
☐ 8	Marcel Dufour	18.00	7.25	1.80
☐ 9	Armand Bourdon	18.00	7.25	1.80
☐ 10	Jean-Marc Pichette	25.00	10.00	2.50
☐ 11	Gerry Gagnon	18.00	7.25	1.80
☐ 12	Jules Racette	18.00	7.25	1.80
☐ 13	Real Marcotte	18.00	7.25	1.80
☐ 14	Gerry Theberge	18.00	7.25	1.80
☐ 15	Rene Harvey	18.00	7.25	1.80
☐ 16	Joseph Lacoursiere	18.00	7.25	1.80
☐ 17	Fernand Benaquez	18.00	7.25	1.80
☐ 18	Andre Boisvert	18.00	7.25	1.80
☐ 19	Claude Chretien	18.00	7.25	1.80
☐ 20	Norbert Clark	18.00	7.25	1.80
☐ 21	Sylvio Lambert	18.00	7.25	1.80
☐ 22	Lucien Roy	18.00	7.25	1.80
☐ 23	Gerard Audet	18.00	7.25	1.80
☐ 24	Jacques Lalancette	18.00	7.25	1.80
☐ 25	Maurice St.Jean	18.00	7.25	1.80
☐ 26	Camille Lupien	18.00	7.25	1.80
☐ 27	Rodrigue Pelchat	18.00	7.25	1.80
☐ 28	Conrad L'Heureux	18.00	7.25	1.80
☐ 29	Paul Tremblay	18.00	7.25	1.80
☐ 30	Robert Vincent	18.00	7.25	1.80
☐ 31	Charles Lamirande	18.00	7.25	1.80
☐ 32	Leon Gaudreault	18.00	7.25	1.80
☐ 33	Maurice Thiffault	18.00	7.25	1.80
☐ 34	Marc-Aurele Tremblay	18.00	7.25	1.80
☐ 35	Rene Pronovost	18.00	7.25	1.80
☐ 36	Victor Corbin	18.00	7.25	1.80
☐ 37	Tiny Tamminen	18.00	7.25	1.80
☐ 38	Guildor Levesque	18.00	7.25	1.80
☐ 39	Gaston Lamirande	18.00	7.25	1.80
☐ 40	Guy Gervais	18.00	7.25	1.80
☐ 41	Rayner Makila	18.00	7.25	1.80
☐ 42	Jules Tremblay	18.00	7.25	1.80
☐ 43	Roland Girard	18.00	7.25	1.80
☐ 44	Germain Bergeron	18.00	7.25	1.80
☐ 45	Paul Duchesne	18.00	7.25	1.80
☐ 46	Roger Beaudoin	18.00	7.25	1.80
☐ 47	Georges Archibal	18.00	7.25	1.80
☐ 48	Claude Basque	18.00	7.25	1.80
☐ 49	Roger Sarda	18.00	7.25	1.80
☐ 50	Edgard Gendron	18.00	7.25	1.80
☐ 51	Gaston Labossiere	18.00	7.25	1.80
☐ 52	Roland Clantara	18.00	7.25	1.80
☐ 53	Florian Gravel	18.00	7.25	1.80
☐ 54	Jean-Guy Thompson	18.00	7.25	1.80
☐ 55	Yvan Forton	18.00	7.25	1.80
☐ 56	Yves Laporte	18.00	7.25	1.80
☐ 57	Claude Germain	18.00	7.25	1.80
☐ 58	Gerry Brunet	18.00	7.25	1.80
☐ 59	Maurice Courteau	25.00	10.00	2.50

1992-93 MPS Photographics SJHL

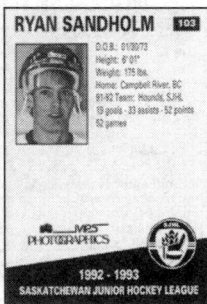

This 168-card set features players in the Saskatchewan Junior Hockey League. The cards are slightly larger than standard size, measuring 2 9/16" by 3 9/16." The fronts feature color action player photos with team color-coded borders at the top and bottom. The player's name and position appear in the top border. The team name and logo appear in the wider bottom border. The backs are white and carry a black-and-white close-up picture, biographical information, and a brief player profile. The sponsor logos are printed at the bottom of the card. The cards are numbered on the back and checklisted below according to teams: Estevan Bruins (1-14), Flin Flon Bombers (15-28, 58), Humboldt Broncos (29-42), Melfort Mustangs (43, 45-57, 59-70, 126), Melville Millionaires (44, 71-84, 95), North Battleford North Stars (85-91, 94, 96-98), Wilkie Youngbloods (92), Weyburn Red Wings (93), Notre Dame Hounds (99-112), Nipawin Hawks (113-125), Saskatoon Titans (127-140), Weyburn Red Wings (141-154), and Yorkton Terriers (155-168).

	MINT	EXC	G-VG
COMPLETE SET (168)	20.00	8.00	2.00
COMMON PLAYER (1-168)	.20	.08	.02

☐	1 Troy Edwards	.30	.12	.03
☐	2 Simon Oliver	.20	.08	.02
☐	3 Gerald Tallaire	.30	.12	.03
☐	4 Blair Allison	.20	.08	.02
☐	5 Mads True	.20	.08	.02
☐	6 Steve Brent	.20	.08	.02
☐	7 Jay Dobrescu	.20	.08	.02
☐	8 Dave Debusschere	.30	.12	.03
☐	9 Bryan Cossette	.20	.08	.02
☐	10 Brooke Battersby	.20	.08	.02
☐	11 Kyle Niemegeers	.20	.08	.02
☐	12 Darren McLean	.20	.08	.02
☐	13 Carson Cardinal	.20	.08	.02
☐	14 Bill McKay	.20	.08	.02
☐	15 Chris Hatch	.20	.08	.02
☐	16 Nolan Weir	.20	.08	.02
☐	17 Karl Johnson	.20	.08	.02
☐	18 Jason Brown	.20	.08	.02
☐	19 Tyler Kuhn	.20	.08	.02
☐	20 Daniel Dennis	.20	.08	.02
☐	21 Wally Spence	.20	.08	.02
☐	22 Rob Beck	.20	.08	.02
☐	23 Aaron Cain	.50	.20	.05
☐	24 Darryl Dickson	.20	.08	.02
☐	25 Travis Cheyne	.20	.08	.02
☐	26 Mark Leoppky	.20	.08	.02
☐	27 Jason Ahenakew	.20	.08	.02
☐	28 Kyle Paul	.20	.08	.02
☐	29 Dean Normand	.20	.08	.02
☐	30 Brett Kinaschuk	.20	.08	.02
☐	31 Darren Schmidt	.20	.08	.02
☐	32 Chris Schinkel	.20	.08	.02
☐	33 David Foster	.20	.08	.02
☐	34 Jason Zimmerman	.20	.08	.02
☐	35 Tom Perry	.20	.08	.02
☐	36 Kent Kinaschuk	.20	.08	.02
☐	37 Colin Froese	.20	.08	.02
☐	38 Shawn Zimmerman	.20	.08	.02
☐	39 Larry Empey	.20	.08	.02
☐	40 Curtis Knight	.20	.08	.02
☐	41 Blake Shipley	.20	.08	.02
☐	42 Cory Heon	.20	.08	.02
☐	43 Steve Pashulka	.20	.08	.02
☐	44 Rob Kinch	.20	.08	.02
☐	45 Dean Gerard	.20	.08	.02
☐	46 Matt Desmarais	.20	.08	.02
☐	47 Chad Rusnak	.20	.08	.02
☐	48 Brad Bagu	.20	.08	.02
☐	49 Cam Bristow	.20	.08	.02
☐	50 Derek Simonson	.20	.08	.02
☐	51 Ken Ruddock	.20	.08	.02
☐	52 Tyler Deis	.20	.08	.02
☐	53 Steve Tansowny	.20	.08	.02
☐	54 Bill Stait	.20	.08	.02
☐	55 Garfield Henderson	.20	.08	.02
☐	56 Lonny Deobald	.20	.08	.02
☐	57 Lyle Ehrmantraut	.20	.08	.02
☐	58 Layne Humenny	.20	.08	.02
☐	59 Darren Balcombe	.20	.08	.02
☐	60 Jeff McCutheon	.20	.08	.02
☐	61 Trevor Wathen	.20	.08	.02
☐	62 Derek Wynne	.20	.08	.02
☐	63 Matt Russo	.20	.08	.02
☐	64 Bruce Matatall	.20	.08	.02
☐	65 Derek Crimin	.20	.08	.02
☐	66 Chad Crumley	.20	.08	.02
☐	67 Mike Hillock	.20	.08	.02
☐	68 Art Houghton	.20	.08	.02
☐	69 Lee Materi	.20	.08	.02
☐	70 Nick Dyhr	.20	.08	.02
☐	71 Darren Maloney	.20	.08	.02
☐	72 Kurtise Souchotte	.20	.08	.02
☐	73 Noel Kamel	.20	.08	.02
☐	74 Trent Harper	.20	.08	.02
☐	75 Ted Grayling	.20	.08	.02
☐	76 Keith Harris	.20	.08	.02
☐	77 Corri Moffat	.20	.08	.02
☐	78 Travis Vantighem	.20	.08	.02
☐	79 Darren Houghton	.20	.08	.02
☐	80 Wade Welte	.20	.08	.02
☐	81 Dave Doucet	.20	.08	.02
☐	82 Jason Prokopetz	.20	.08	.02
☐	83 Gordon McCann	.20	.08	.02
☐	84 Clint Hooge	.20	.08	.02
☐	85 Glen McGillvary	.20	.08	.02
☐	86 Regan Simpson	.20	.08	.02
☐	87 Mike Masse	.20	.08	.02
☐	88 Jeremy Procyshyn	.20	.08	.02
☐	89 Jim Nellis	.20	.08	.02
☐	90 Todd Kozak	.20	.08	.02
☐	91 Brent Hoiness	.20	.08	.02
☐	92 Josh Welter	.20	.08	.02
	Jason Welter			
☐	93 Eldon Barker	.20	.08	.02
☐	94 Duane Vandale	.20	.08	.02
☐	95 Brad McEwen	.20	.08	.02
☐	96 Trent Tibbatts	.30	.12	.03
☐	97 Jody Reiter	.20	.08	.02
☐	98 Greg Moore	.20	.08	.02
☐	99 Jon Rowe	.20	.08	.02
☐	100 Mike Evans	.20	.08	.02
☐	101 Jason Krug	.20	.08	.02
☐	102 Jon Bracco	.20	.08	.02
☐	103 Ryan Sandholm	.20	.08	.02
☐	104 Darryl Sangster	.20	.08	.02
☐	105 Brett Colborne	.20	.08	.02
☐	106 Dean Moore	.20	.08	.02
☐	107 Chris Dechaine	.20	.08	.02
☐	108 Steve McKenna	.20	.08	.02
☐	109 Tony Bergin	.20	.08	.02
☐	110 Tim Murray	.20	.08	.02
☐	111 Casey Kesselring	.20	.08	.02
☐	112 Todd Barth	.20	.08	.02
☐	113 Ryan McConnell	.20	.08	.02
☐	114 Ian Adamson	.20	.08	.02
☐	115 Warren Pickford	.20	.08	.02
☐	116 Todd Murphy	.20	.08	.02
☐	117 Rob Phillips	.20	.08	.02
☐	118 Trevor Demmans	.20	.08	.02
☐	119 Jeff Greenwood	.20	.08	.02
☐	120 Kevin Messer	.20	.08	.02
☐	121 Dion Johnson	.20	.08	.02
☐	122 Rejean Stringer	.20	.08	.02
☐	123 Scott Mead	.20	.08	.02
☐	124 Jeff Lawson	.20	.08	.02
☐	125 Scot Newberry	.20	.08	.02
☐	126 Bill Reid	.20	.08	.02
☐	127 Chris Winkler	.20	.08	.02
☐	128 Kyle Girgan	.20	.08	.02
☐	129 Trevor Warrener	.50	.20	.05
☐	130 Richard Boscher	.20	.08	.02

☐	131	Tom Thomson	.20	.08	.02
☐	132	Mike Wevers	.20	.08	.02
☐	133	Barton Holt	.20	.08	.02
☐	134	Kent Rogers	.20	.08	.02
☐	135	Richard Gibbs	.20	.08	.02
☐	136	Jared Witt	.20	.08	.02
☐	137	Jamie Stelmak	.20	.08	.02
☐	138	Greg Wahl	.20	.08	.02
☐	139	J. Sotropa	.20	.08	.02
☐	140	Mark Pivetz	.20	.08	.02
☐	141	Travis Kirby	.20	.08	.02
☐	142	Jason Scanzano	.20	.08	.02
☐	143	Tyson Balog	.20	.08	.02
☐	144	Daryl Krauss	.20	.08	.02
☐	145	Mike Harder	.20	.08	.02
☐	146	Tyler McMillan	.20	.08	.02
☐	147	Darcy Herlick	.20	.08	.02
☐	148	Dave Zwyer	.20	.08	.02
☐	149	Craig McKechnie	.20	.08	.02
☐	150	Cam Cook	.20	.08	.02
☐	151	Derek Bruselinck	.20	.08	.02
☐	152	Travis Smith	.20	.08	.02
☐	153	Daryl Jones	.20	.08	.02
☐	154	Mike Savard	.20	.08	.02
☐	155	Jeremy Matthies	.20	.08	.02
☐	156	Michel Cook	.20	.08	.02
☐	157	Leigh Brookbank	.20	.08	.02
☐	158	Christian Dutil	.20	.08	.02
☐	159	Scott Heshka	.20	.08	.02
☐	160	Danny Galarneau	.20	.08	.02
☐	161	Jamie Dunn	.20	.08	.02
☐	162	Nigel Werenka	.30	.12	.03
☐	163	Steve Sabo	.20	.08	.02
☐	164	Tony Toth	.20	.08	.02
☐	165	Sebastien Moreau	.20	.08	.02
☐	166	Tim Slukynsky	.20	.08	.02
☐	167	Sheldon Bylsma	.20	.08	.02
☐	168	Stacy Prevost	.30	.12	.03

1988-89 ProCards AHL

This set of 348 cards features the 14 teams of the American Hockey League. The cards measure the standard size, 2 1/2" by 3 1/2". The fronts feature color player photos accented by a beige-colored hockey stick superimposed on the right and lower sides of the picture. The AHL logo appears in the lower left corner, and the photo is bordered on all sides by red. The back has player information in a black box, with the upper left corner cut out for the team logo. The cards are unnumbered and checklisted below alphabetically according to teams as follows (teams in alphabetical order and players listed alphabetically within each team): Adirondack Red Wings (1-25), Baltimore Skipjacks (26-48), Binghamton Whalers (49-72), Cape Breton Oilers (73-96), Halifax Citadels (97-119), Hershey Bears (120-147), Maine Mariners (148-169), Moncton Hawks (170-190), New Haven Nighthawks (191-222), Newmarket Saints (223-244), Rochester Americans (245-268), Sherbrooke Canadiens (269-299), Springfield Indians (300-324), and Utica Devils (325-348). Of all the teams, on the Hershey cards alone they failed to put the team name. Although the team sets were

originally sold with a suggested retail price of 3.00 per team set and packaged individually, they are listed below as one giant set. In many cases that was the way they were advertised and sold, i.e., as a complete set of all the teams in the AHL.

		MINT	EXC	G-VG
COMPLETE SET (348)		125.00	50.00	12.50
COMMON PLAYER (1-348)		.25	.10	.02

☐	1	Rob Nichols	.35	.14	.03
☐	2	Bill Dineen CO	.75	.30	.07
☐	3	Tim Paris Asst.TR	.25	.10	.02
☐	4	Glenn Merkosky	.35	.14	.03
☐	5	Mike Gober	.25	.10	.02
☐	6	Dave Casey TR	.25	.10	.02
☐	7	Sam St.Laurent	.50	.20	.05
☐	8	Mark Reimer	.25	.10	.02
☐	9	Dennis Smith	.25	.10	.02
☐	10	Lou Crawford	.35	.14	.03
☐	11	John Mokosak	.25	.10	.02
☐	12	Murray Eaves	.35	.14	.03
☐	13	Dave Korol	.25	.10	.02
☐	14	Miroslav Ihnacak	.50	.20	.05
☐	15	Dale Krentz	.25	.10	.02
☐	16	Brent Fedyk	1.50	.60	.15
☐	17	Dean Morton	.25	.10	.02
☐	18	Jeff Brubaker	.35	.14	.03
☐	19	Tim Cheveldae	7.50	3.00	.75
☐	20	Randy McKay	.50	.20	.05
☐	21	Peter Dineen	.25	.10	.02
☐	22	Rob Doyle	.25	.10	.02
☐	23	Daniel Shank	.50	.20	.05
☐	24	Joe Ferras	.25	.10	.02
☐	25	John Blum	.35	.14	.03
☐	26	Tim Bergland	.35	.14	.03
☐	27	Robin Bawa	.25	.10	.02
☐	28	Shawn Simpson	.25	.10	.02
☐	29	Chris Felix	.35	.14	.03
☐	30	Jeff Greenlaw	.35	.14	.03
☐	31	Frank Dimuzio	.25	.10	.02
☐	32	Tyler Larter	.25	.10	.02
☐	33	Rob Whistle	.25	.10	.02
☐	34	Dallas Eakins	.25	.10	.02
☐	35	Mark Hatcher	.25	.10	.02
☐	36	Dave Farrish	.35	.14	.03
☐	37	Bill Houlder	.75	.30	.07
☐	38	Doug Keans	.50	.20	.05
☐	39	Lou Franceschetti	.75	.30	.07
☐	40	Rob Murray	.50	.20	.05
☐	41	Terry Murray GM/CO	.75	.30	.07
☐	42	Steve Seftel	.25	.10	.02
☐	43	J.P. Mattingly TR	.25	.10	.02
☐	44	Mike Richard	.25	.10	.02
☐	45	Shawn Cronin	.75	.30	.07
☐	46	Scott McCrory	.25	.10	.02
☐	47	Mike Millar	.35	.14	.03
☐	48	Dave Sherrid TR	.25	.10	.02
☐	49	Marc Laforge	.25	.10	.02
☐	50	David O'Brien	.25	.10	.02
☐	51	Dave Rowbotham	.25	.10	.02
☐	52	Kay Whitmore	3.00	1.20	.30
☐	53	Richard Brodeur	1.25	.50	.12
☐	54	Mike Vellucci	.25	.10	.02
☐	55	Terry Yake	1.50	.60	.15
☐	56	Roger Kortko	.25	.10	.02
☐	57	Jon Smith TR	.25	.10	.02
☐	58	Lindsay Carson UER	.75	.30	.07
		(Misspelled Lindsy on card front)			
☐	59	Chris Brant	.25	.10	.02
☐	60	Claude Larose CO	.50	.20	.05
☐	61	Dallas Gaume	.25	.10	.02
☐	62	Charlie Bourgeois	.35	.14	.03
☐	63	Todd Krygier	1.00	.40	.10
☐	64	Gary Callahan	.26	.10	.02
☐	65	Mark Reeds	.25	.10	.02
☐	66	Al Tuer	.35	.14	.03
☐	67	Brian Chapman	.25	.10	.02
☐	68	Mark Lavarre	.25	.10	.02
☐	69	Mark Dumas	.25	.10	.02
☐	70	Jim Culhane	.25	.10	.02
☐	71	Larry Trader	.25	.10	.02
☐	72	Tom Mitchell GM	.25	.10	.02
☐	73	Rob MacInnis	.35	.14	.03
☐	74	John B. Hanna	.25	.10	.02
☐	75	Dan Currie	.75	.30	.07
☐	76	Dave Roach	.25	.10	.02
☐	77	Jamie Nicolls	.25	.10	.02
☐	78	Alan May	.75	.30	.07
☐	79	David Haas	.25	.10	.02
☐	80	Daryl Reaugh	.50	.20	.05

☐	81	Mike Ware	.25	.10	.02
☐	82	Mike Glover	.25	.10	.02
☐	83	Nick Beaulieu	.25	.10	.02
☐	84	Mario Barbe	.25	.10	.02
☐	85	Darren Beals	.25	.10	.02
☐	86	Kim Issel	.35	.14	.03
☐	87	Shaun Van Allen	.75	.30	.07
☐	88	Jim Ennis	.25	.10	.02
☐	89	Mark Lamb	.75	.30	.07
☐	90	Larry Floyd	.25	.10	.02
☐	91	Ron Shudra	.25	.10	.02
☐	92	Fabian Joseph	.50	.20	.05
☐	93	Selmar Odelein	.50	.20	.05
☐	94	Don Martin	.25	.10	.02
☐	95	Jim Wiemer	.50	.20	.05
☐	96	Brad MacGregor	.25	.10	.02
☐	97	Gerald Bzdel	.25	.10	.02
☐	98	Mike Hough	.75	.30	.07
☐	99	Ken McRae	.50	.20	.05
☐	100	Bobby Dollas	.75	.30	.07
☐	101	Joel Baillargeon	.25	.10	.02
☐	102	Ladislav Tresl	.25	.10	.02
☐	103	Jacques Mailhot	.25	.10	.02
☐	104	Dean Hopkins	.25	.10	.02
☐	105	Claude Julien	.25	.10	.02
☐	106	Brent Severyn	.75	.30	.07
☐	107	Keith Miller	.35	.14	.03
☐	108	Scott Shaunessy	.25	.10	.02
☐	109	Jaroslav Sevcik	.25	.10	.02
☐	110	Darin Kimble	.75	.30	.07
☐	111	Jean-Marc Routhier	.25	.10	.02
☐	112	Ken Quinney	.35	.14	.03
☐	113	Max Middendorf	.35	.14	.03
☐	114	Marc Fortier	.75	.30	.07
☐	115	Jean-Marc Richard	.25	.10	.02
☐	116	Mike Natyshak	.25	.10	.02
☐	117	Ron Tugnutt	2.50	1.00	.25
☐	118	Scott Gordon	1.00	.40	.10
☐	119	Doug Carpenter CO/GM	.50	.20	.05
☐	120	Jeff Harding	.25	.10	.02
☐	121	Jocelyn Perrault	.25	.10	.02
☐	122	Darryl Gilmour	.35	.14	.03
☐	123	John Stevens	.25	.10	.02
☐	124	Warren Harper	.25	.10	.02
☐	125	Chris Jensen	.35	.14	.03
☐	126	Mark Freer	.35	.14	.03
☐	127	Gordon Paddock	.25	.10	.02
☐	128	Bruce Randall	.25	.10	.02
☐	129	Glen Seabrooke	.35	.14	.03
☐	130	Mike Stothers	.35	.14	.03
☐	131	Dave Fenyves	.35	.14	.03
☐	132	Mark Lofthouse	.25	.10	.02
☐	133	Marc D'Amour	.50	.20	.05
☐	134	Shaun Sabol	.25	.10	.02
☐	135	Craig Kitteringham	.25	.10	.02
☐	136	J.J. Daigneault	1.00	.40	.10
☐	137	Don Biggs	.35	.14	.03
☐	138	Kent Hawley	.25	.10	.02
☐	139	Tony Horacek	.25	.10	.02
☐	140	Al Hill	.35	.14	.03
☐	141	Don Nachbaur	.35	.14	.03
☐	142	John Paddock CO	1.00	.40	.10
☐	143	Kevin McCarthy CO	.50	.20	.05
☐	144	Dan Stuck TR	.25	.10	.02
☐	145	Doug Yingst	.25	.10	.02
☐	146	Frank Mathers PR/GM	.25	.10	.02
☐	147	Brian Bucciarelli TR	.25	.10	.02
☐	148	Terry Taillefer	.25	.10	.02
☐	149	Paul Beraldo	.25	.10	.02
☐	150	Jeff Lamb	.25	.10	.02
☐	151	Mitch Molloy	.25	.10	.02
☐	152	Darren Lowe	.25	.10	.02
☐	153	Stephane Quintal	1.00	.40	.10
☐	154	Norm Foster	.50	.20	.05
☐	155	Jean-Marc Lanthier	.25	.10	.02
☐	156	Carl Mokosak	.25	.10	.02
☐	157	Mike Neill	.35	.14	.03
☐	158	Mike Jeffrey	.25	.10	.02
☐	159	Steve Tsujiura	.25	.10	.02
☐	160	Scott Drevitch	.25	.10	.02
☐	161	Paul Guay	.50	.20	.05
☐	162	Scott Wykoff ANN	.25	.10	.02
☐	163	John Carter	.75	.30	.07
☐	164	Phil Degaetano	.25	.10	.02
☐	165	Doug Foerster PB/TKTS	.25	.10	.02
☐	166	Bruce Shoebottom	.50	.20	.05
☐	167	Ray Podloski	.25	.10	.02
☐	168	Greg Hawgood	.75	.30	.07
☐	169	Joe Flaherty	.25	.10	.02
☐	170	Todd Flichel	.25	.10	.02
☐	171	Steven Fletcher	.25	.10	.02
☐	172	Len Nielson	.25	.10	.02
☐	173	Neil Meadmore	.25	.10	.02
☐	174	Gilles Hamel	.35	.14	.03
☐	175	Ron Wilson	.50	.20	.05
☐	176	Stu Kulak	.35	.14	.03
☐	177	Scott Schneider	.25	.10	.02
☐	178	Mike Warus	.25	.10	.02
☐	179	Jamie Husgen	.25	.10	.02
☐	180	Tom Draper	1.25	.50	.12
☐	181	Guy Gosselin	.25	.10	.02
☐	182	Guy Larose	.50	.20	.05
☐	183	Stephane Beauregard	1.00	.40	.10
☐	184	Brent Hughes	.75	.30	.07
☐	185	Sean Clement	.25	.10	.02
☐	186	Matt Hervey	.50	.20	.05
☐	187	Chris Norton	.25	.10	.02
☐	188	Rob Snitzer THER	.25	.10	.02
☐	189	Rick Bowness CO	.75	.30	.07
☐	190	Wayne Flemming MG	.25	.10	.02
☐	191	Tim Tookey	.35	.14	.03
☐	192	Ken Baumgartner	1.00	.40	.10
☐	193	John English	.25	.10	.02
☐	194	Darryl Williams	.25	.10	.02
☐	195	Hubie McDonough	.75	.30	.07
☐	196	Brad Hyatt	.25	.10	.02
☐	197	Phil Sykes	.50	.20	.05
☐	198	Mario Chitaroni	.35	.14	.03
☐	199	Tom Pratt	.25	.10	.02
☐	200	Sal Lombardi TR	.25	.10	.02
☐	201	Rick Dudley CO	.50	.20	.05
☐	202	John Tortorella CO	.35	.14	.03
☐	203	Chris Panek	.25	.10	.02
☐	204	Scott Green TR	.25	.10	.02
☐	205	Eric Germain	.25	.10	.02
☐	206	Bob Kudelski	2.50	1.00	.25
☐	207	Joe Paterson	.35	.14	.03
☐	208	Al Loring	.25	.10	.02
☐	209	Mark Fitzpatrick	2.50	1.00	.25
☐	210	Dan Gratton	.25	.10	.02
☐	211	Sylvain Couturier	.50	.20	.05
☐	212	Pat Hickey DIR	.50	.20	.05
☐	213	Petr Prajsler	.35	.14	.03
☐	214	Lyle Phair	.25	.10	.02
☐	215	Bob Logan	.25	.10	.02
☐	216	Francois Breault	.35	.14	.03
☐	217	Paul Kelly	.25	.10	.02
☐	218	Steve Richmond	.35	.14	.03
☐	219	Denis Larocque	.25	.10	.02
☐	220	Brian Wilks	.25	.10	.02
☐	221	Dave Pasin	.35	.14	.03
☐	222	Gordie Walker	.25	.10	.02
☐	223	Marty Dallman	.25	.10	.02
☐	224	Jim Ralph	.50	.20	.05
☐	225	Mike Blaisdell	.50	.20	.05
☐	226	Sean McKenna	.35	.14	.03
☐	227	Mark Kirton	.50	.20	.05
☐	228	Greg Gotham	.25	.10	.02
☐	229	Bill Root	.50	.20	.05
☐	230	Wes Jarvis	.35	.14	.03
☐	231	Daryl Evans	.25	.10	.02
☐	232	Jack Capuano	.35	.14	.03
☐	233	Tim Armstrong	.25	.10	.02
☐	234	Alan Hepple	.25	.10	.02
☐	235	Brian Blad	.25	.10	.02
☐	236	Ken Yaremchuk	.35	.14	.03
☐	237	Paul Gagne	.35	.14	.03
☐	238	Doug Shedden	.50	.20	.05
☐	239	Brian Hoard	.25	.10	.02
☐	240	Greg Terrion	.50	.20	.05
☐	241	Trevor Jobe	.50	.20	.05
☐	242	Jeff Reese	1.25	.50	.12
☐	243	Darryl Shannon	.75	.30	.07
☐	244	Tim Bernhardt	.75	.30	.07
☐	245	The Moose Mascot	.35	.14	.03
☐	246	Paul Brydges	.25	.10	.02
☐	247	Ken Priestlay	.75	.30	.07
☐	248	Jacques Cloutier	1.00	.40	.10
☐	249	Steve Smith	.25	.10	.02
☐	250	Jim Jackson	.35	.14	.03
☐	251	Grant Tkachuk	.25	.10	.02
☐	252	Kevin Kerr	.25	.10	.02
☐	253	Mark Ferner	.35	.14	.03
☐	254	Jeff Parker	.35	.14	.03
☐	255	Don McSween	.35	.14	.03
☐	256	Jim Hofford	.25	.10	.02
☐	257	Darcy Wakaluk	2.50	1.00	.25
☐	258	Scott Metcalfe	.25	.10	.02
☐	259	Richie Dunn	.35	.14	.03
☐	260	Wayne Van Dorp	.50	.20	.05
☐	261	Shawn Anderson	.50	.20	.05
☐	262	Jeff Capello	.25	.10	.02
☐	263	Mike Donnelly	1.00	.40	.10
☐	264	Mikael Anderson	.75	.30	.07
☐	265	Robert Ray	1.00	.40	.10
☐	266	Jody Gage	.75	.30	.07

☐ 267	Francois Guay	.35	.14	.03
☐ 268	John Van Boxmeer CO	.50	.20	.05
☐ 269	Jim Nesich	.25	.10	.02
☐ 271	J.J. Daigneault	1.00	.40	.10
☐ 272	Randy Exelby	.35	.14	.03
☐ 273	Jyrki Lumme	2.00	.80	.20
☐ 275	Francois Gravel	.35	.14	.03
☐ 276	Jacques Parent THER	.25	.10	.02
☐ 277	Bobby Boulanger MG	.25	.10	.02
☐ 278	Benoit Brunet	1.50	.60	.15
☐ 279	Martin Nicoletti	.25	.10	.02
☐ 280	Mark Pederson	.75	.30	.07
☐ 281	Stephan Lebeau	3.00	1.20	.30
☐ 282	Claude Larose CO	.50	.20	.05
☐ 283	Steve Bisson	.25	.10	.02
☐ 284	Scott Sandelin	.25	.10	.02
☐ 285	Rocky Dundas	.25	.10	.02
☐ 286	Serge Roberge	.25	.10	.02
☐ 287	Rob Bryden	.25	.10	.02
☐ 288	Marc Saumier	.25	.10	.02
☐ 289	Jean Hamel CO	.35	.14	.03
☐ 290	Mario Roberge	.50	.20	.05
☐ 291	Jocelyn Lemieux	1.00	.40	.10
☐ 292	Ron Chyzowski	.25	.10	.02
☐ 293	Martin Desjardins	.35	.14	.03
☐ 294	Steven Martinson	.35	.14	.03
☐ 295	Jose Charbonneau	.75	.30	.07
☐ 296	Stephane J.G. Richer Defenseman	.50	.20	.05
☐ 297	Sylvain Lefebvre	1.50	.60	.15
☐ 298	Donald Dufresne	.75	.30	.07
☐ 299	Luc Gauthier	.35	.14	.03
☐ 300	Shawn Evans	.35	.14	.03
☐ 301	Mike Stevens	.35	.14	.03
☐ 302	Bruce Boudreau	.50	.20	.05
☐ 303	Todd McLellan	.35	.14	.03
☐ 304	Jeff Hackett	2.00	.80	.20
☐ 305	Bill Berg	.75	.30	.07
☐ 306	Stu Burnie	.25	.10	.02
☐ 307	Duncan McPherson	.35	.14	.03
☐ 308	Jeff Finley	.50	.20	.05
☐ 309	Ralph Calvanese MG	.25	.10	.02
☐ 310	Rob DiMaio	.75	.30	.07
☐ 311	Chris Pryor	.25	.10	.02
☐ 312	Jim Roberts CO	.35	.14	.03
☐ 313	Vern Smith	.25	.10	.02
☐ 314	Mike Walsh	.25	.10	.02
☐ 315	Ed Tyburski TR	.25	.10	.02
☐ 316	Rod Dallman	.25	.10	.02
☐ 317	George Maneluk	.35	.14	.03
☐ 318	Richard Kromm	.50	.20	.05
☐ 319	Kerry Clark	.35	.14	.03
☐ 320	Hank Lammens	.50	.20	.05
☐ 321	Tom Fitzgerald	.50	.20	.05
☐ 322	Dale Henry	.35	.14	.03
☐ 323	Shawn Byram	.25	.10	.02
☐ 324	Doug Weiss	.25	.10	.02
☐ 325	John Walker	.25	.10	.02
☐ 326	Paul Ysebaert	2.00	.80	.20
☐ 327	Chris Cichocki	.35	.14	.03
☐ 328	Marc Laniel	.25	.10	.02
☐ 329	Kevin Todd	2.00	.80	.20
☐ 330	Dan Delianedis	.25	.10	.02
☐ 331	Robert Bill TR	.25	.10	.02
☐ 332	Jeff Croop TR	.25	.10	.02
☐ 333	Craig Billington	2.00	.80	.20
☐ 334	Alan Stewart	.35	.14	.03
☐ 335	Jeff Madill	.75	.30	.07
☐ 336	Scott Moon TR	.25	.10	.02
☐ 337	Neil Brady	.50	.20	.05
☐ 338	Murray Brumwell	.35	.14	.03
☐ 339	Anders Carlsson	.35	.14	.03
☐ 340	Dan Dorion	.35	.14	.03
☐ 341	Tom McVie CO	.75	.30	.07
☐ 342	David Marcinyshyn	.35	.14	.03
☐ 343	John Blessman	.26	.10	.02
☐ 344	Chris Terreri	3.00	1.20	.30
☐ 345	Eric Weinrich	1.00	.40	.10
☐ 346	Janne Ojanen	1.00	.40	.10
☐ 347	Tim Lenardon	.25	.10	.02
☐ 348	Jamie Huscroft	.50	.20	.05

1988-89 ProCards IHL

This set of 119 cards features players from the teams of the
International Hockey League. The cards measure the
standard size 2 1/2" by 3 1/2". The fronts feature color player

photos accented by a beige-colored hockey stick
superimposed on the right and lower sides of the picture.
The IHL logo appears in a circle in the lower left corner, and
the photo is bordered on all sides by red. The back has
player information in a black box, with the upper left corner
cut out for the team logo. The cards are unnumbered and
checklisted below alphabetically according to teams as
follows: Indianapolis Ice (1-22), Kalamazoo Wings (23-42),
Muskegon Lumberjacks (43-65), Peoria Rivermen (66-94),
and Saginaw Hawks (95-119). Although the team sets were
originally sold with a suggested retail price of 3.00 per team
set and packaged individually, they are listed below as one
giant set. In many cases that was the way they were
advertised and sold, i.e., as a complete set of all the teams
in the IHL.

		MINT	EXC	G-VG
COMPLETE SET (119)		80.00	32.00	8.00
COMMON PLAYER (1-119)		.25	.10	.02
☐ 1	Bob Lakso	.35	.14	.03
☐ 2	Rick Boyd	.25	.10	.02
☐ 3	Alan Perry	.35	.14	.03
☐ 4	Mark Teevens	.25	.10	.02
☐ 5	Gary Stewart	.25	.10	.02
☐ 6	Randy Taylor	.25	.10	.02
☐ 7	Scott Clements	.25	.10	.02
☐ 8	Chris McSorley	.75	.30	.07
☐ 9	Dave Allison	.25	.10	.02
☐ 10	Shane Doyle	.25	.10	.02
☐ 11	Darwin McCutcheon	.25	.10	.02
☐ 12	Geoff Benic	.25	.10	.02
☐ 13	Rich Oberlin TR	.25	.10	.02
☐ 14	Glen Johannesen	.25	.10	.02
☐ 15	Graeme Bonar	.25	.10	.02
☐ 16	Ron Handy	.35	.14	.03
☐ 17	Archie Henderson	.35	.14	.03
☐ 18	Brent Sapergia	.35	.14	.03
☐ 19	Brad Beck	.25	.10	.02
☐ 20	Paul Houck	.25	.10	.02
☐ 21	Jimmy Mann	.50	.20	.05
☐ 22	Rick Barkovich	.25	.10	.02
☐ 23	Scott McCrady	.25	.10	.02
☐ 24	Andy Akervik	.25	.10	.02
☐ 25	Rob Zettler	1.00	.40	.10
☐ 26	Jarmo Myllys	1.00	.40	.10
☐ 27	D'Arcy Norton	.25	.10	.02
☐ 28	Ken Hodge Jr.	.75	.30	.07
☐ 29	Emanuel Viveiros	.35	.14	.03
☐ 30	Scott Bjugstad	.35	.14	.03
☐ 31	Mike Berger	.35	.14	.03
☐ 32	Joe Lockwood	.25	.10	.02
☐ 33	Stephane Roy	.35	.14	.03
☐ 34	Randy Smith	.35	.14	.03
☐ 35	Mike McHugh	.35	.14	.03
☐ 36	Warren Babe	.35	.14	.03
☐ 37	Gary McColgan	.25	.10	.02
☐ 38	Darin Baker	.25	.10	.02
☐ 39	Neil Wilkinson	1.50	.60	.15
☐ 40	Kirk Tomlinson	.25	.10	.02
☐ 41	Larry Dyck	.35	.14	.03
☐ 42	Dave Schofield	.25	.10	.02
☐ 43	Brad Aitken	.35	.14	.03
☐ 44	Jock Callander	.75	.30	.07
☐ 45	Todd Charlesworth	.25	.10	.02
☐ 46	Jeff Cooper	.25	.10	.02
☐ 47	Jeff Daniels	.75	.30	.07

☐ 48	Greg Davies	.25	.10	.02
☐ 49	Lee Giffin	.25	.10	.02
☐ 50	Dave Goertz	.25	.10	.02
☐ 51	Steve Gotaas	.35	.14	.03
☐ 52	Scott Gruhl	.50	.20	.05
☐ 53	Doug Hobson	.25	.10	.02
☐ 54	Kevin MacDonald	.25	.10	.02
☐ 55	Pat Mayer	.25	.10	.02
☐ 56	Dave McLlwain	1.00	.40	.10
☐ 57	Dave Michayluk	.25	.10	.02
☐ 58	Glenn Mulvenna	.35	.14	.03
☐ 59	Jim Paek	1.00	.40	.10
☐ 60	Frank Pietrangelo	1.50	.60	.15
☐ 61	Bruce Racine	.35	.14	.03
☐ 62	Mark Recchi	20.00	8.00	2.00
☐ 63	Troy Vollhoffer	.25	.10	.02
☐ 64	Jeff Waver	.25	.10	.02
☐ 65	Mitch Wilson	.25	.10	.02
☐ 66	Mitch Messier	.50	.20	.05
☐ 67	Dave Lowry	.50	.20	.05
☐ 68	Tim Bothwell	.50	.20	.05
☐ 69	Sheryl Reeves	.25	.10	.02
	(Administrator)			
☐ 70	Shane MacEachern	.50	.20	.05
☐ 71	Glen Featherstone	1.00	.40	.10
☐ 72	Charlie Thompson MGR	.25	.10	.02
☐ 73	Wayne Thomas CO	.35	.14	.03
☐ 74	Dominic Lavoie	.75	.30	.07
☐ 75	Team Photo	.50	.20	.05
	Peoria Rivermen			
☐ 76	Scott Paluch	.25	.10	.02
☐ 77	Wayne Gagne	.25	.10	.02
☐ 78	Dave Thomlinson	.75	.30	.07
☐ 79	Tony Twist	.75	.30	.07
☐ 80	Brad McCaughey	.25	.10	.02
☐ 81	Kelly Chase	.75	.30	.07
☐ 82	Scott Harlow	.25	.10	.02
☐ 83	Peter Douris	.75	.30	.07
☐ 84	Cliff Ronning	5.00	2.00	.50
☐ 85	Lyle Odelein	2.00	.80	.20
☐ 86	Terry MacLean	.25	.10	.02
☐ 87	Darin Smith	.25	.10	.02
☐ 88	Skip Probst	.25	.10	.02
☐ 89	Ed McMurray MGR	.25	.10	.02
☐ 90	Greg Eberle TR	.25	.10	.02
☐ 91	Jim Vesey	.35	.14	.03
☐ 92	Toby Ducolon	.25	.10	.02
☐ 93	Pat Jablonski	2.00	.80	.20
☐ 94	Darrell May	.25	.10	.02
☐ 95	Ed Belfour	25.00	10.00	2.50
☐ 96	Bruce Cassidy	.35	.14	.03
☐ 97	Chris Clifford	.25	.10	.02
☐ 98	Mario Doyon	.35	.14	.03
☐ 99	Bill Gardner	.25	.10	.02
☐ 100	Mark Kurzawski	.25	.10	.02
☐ 101	Lonnie Loach	.50	.20	.05
☐ 102	Steve Ludzik	.50	.20	.05
☐ 103	David Mackey	.25	.10	.02
☐ 104	Dale Marquette	.25	.10	.02
☐ 105	Gary Moscaluk	.25	.10	.02
☐ 106	Marty Nanne	.25	.10	.02
☐ 107	Brian Noonan	1.50	.60	.15
☐ 108	Mark Paterson	.25	.10	.02
☐ 109	Kent Paynter	.25	.10	.02
☐ 110	Guy Phillips	.25	.10	.02
☐ 111	John Reid	.25	.10	.02
☐ 112	Mike Rucinski	.35	.14	.03
☐ 113	Warren Rychel	1.00	.40	.10
☐ 114	Everett Sanipass	1.00	.40	.10
☐ 115	Mike Stapleton	.50	.20	.05
☐ 116	Darryl Sutter	1.25	.50	.12
☐ 117	Jari Torkki	.25	.10	.02
☐ 118	Bill Watson	.50	.20	.05
☐ 119	Sean Williams	.50	.20	.05

1989-90 ProCards AHL

This set of 360 cards features the 14 teams of the American Hockey League. The cards measure the standard size, 2 1/2" by 3 1/2". Although the team sets were originally sold with a suggested retail price of 3.00 per team set and packaged individually, they are listed below as one giant set. In many cases that was the way they were advertised and sold, i.e., as a complete set of all the teams in the AHL. The numbering is by teams as follows: New Haven Nighthawks

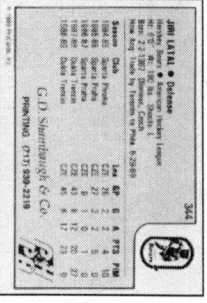

(1-27), Moncton Hawks (28-52), Maine Mariners (53-76), Baltimore Skipjacks (77-103), Newmarket Saints (104-128), Cape Breton Oilers (129-151), Halifax Citadels (152-178), Sherbrooke Canadiens (179-201), Utica Devils (202-228), Springfield Indians (229-254), Rochester Americans (255-282), Birmingham Whalers (283-305), Adirondack Red Wings (306-329), and Hershey Bears (330-360).

		MINT	EXC	G-VG
COMPLETE SET (360)		100.00	40.00	10.00
COMMON PLAYER (1-360)		.25	.10	.02
☐ 1	New Haven Checklist	.35	.14	.03
☐ 2	Francois Breault	.35	.14	.03
☐ 3	Paul Kelly	.25	.10	.02
☐ 4	Phil Sykes	.50	.20	.05
☐ 5	Ron Scott	.35	.14	.03
☐ 6	Micah Aivazoff	1.00	.40	.10
☐ 7	Sylvain Couturier	.50	.20	.05
☐ 8	Carl Repp	.25	.10	.02
☐ 9	Murray Brumwell	.35	.14	.03
☐ 10	Todd Elik	1.25	.50	.12
☐ 11	Darwin Bozek	.25	.10	.02
☐ 12	Eric Germain	.25	.10	.02
☐ 13	Scott Young	1.50	.60	.15
☐ 14	Chris Kontos	1.50	.60	.15
☐ 15	Scott Bjugstad	.50	.20	.05
☐ 16	Eric Ricard	.25	.10	.02
☐ 17	Ross Wilson	.25	.10	.02
☐ 18	Graham Stanley	.25	.10	.02
☐ 19	Chris Panek	.25	.10	.02
☐ 20	Nick Fotiu	.75	.30	.07
☐ 21	Rene Chapdelaine	.35	.14	.03
☐ 22	Gordie Walker	.35	.14	.03
☐ 23	Tim Bothwell	.50	.20	.05
☐ 24	Kevin MacDonald	.25	.10	.02
☐ 25	Darryl Williams	.25	.10	.02
☐ 26	John Van Kessel	.25	.10	.02
☐ 27	Paul Brydges	.25	.10	.02
☐ 28	Moncton Checklist	.35	.14	.03
☐ 29	Guy Larose	.50	.20	.05
☐ 30	Danton Cole	.75	.30	.07
☐ 31	Brent Hughes	.75	.30	.07
☐ 32	Larry Bernard	.25	.10	.02
☐ 33	Stu Kulak	.35	.14	.03
☐ 34	Bob Essensa	3.00	1.20	.30
☐ 35	Luciano Borsato	1.00	.40	.10
☐ 36	Guy Gosselin	.25	.10	.02
☐ 37	Todd Flichel	.25	.10	.02
☐ 38	Brian Hunt	.25	.10	.02
☐ 39	Neil Meadmore	.25	.10	.02
☐ 40	Matt Hervey	.35	.14	.03
☐ 41	Dallas Eakins	.25	.10	.02
☐ 42	Brad Jones	.50	.20	.05
☐ 43	Chris Norton	.25	.10	.02
☐ 44	Bryan Marchment	.75	.30	.07
☐ 45	Rick Tabaracci	2.00	.80	.20
☐ 46	Grant Richison	.25	.10	.02
☐ 47	Brian McReynolds	.50	.20	.05
☐ 48	Tony Joseph	.25	.10	.02
☐ 49	Dave Farrish	.35	.14	.03
☐ 50	Rob Snitzer	.25	.10	.02
☐ 51	Ron Wilson	.50	.20	.05
☐ 52	Scott Schneider	.25	.10	.02
☐ 53	Maine Checklist	.35	.14	.03
☐ 54	Dave Buda	.25	.10	.02
☐ 55	Paul Beraldo	.25	.10	.02
☐ 56	Lou Crawford	.35	.14	.03
☐ 57	Mark Montanari	.25	.10	.02
☐ 58	Don Sweeney	1.00	.40	.10

☐ 59	Jeff Sirkka	.25	.10	.02
☐ 60	Norm Foster	.50	.20	.05
☐ 61	Greg Poss	.25	.10	.02
☐ 62	Gord Cruickshank	.25	.10	.02
☐ 63	Bruce Shoebottom	.50	.20	.05
☐ 64	Mark Ziliotto	.25	.10	.02
☐ 65	Ron Hoover	.35	.14	.03
☐ 66	Scott Harlow	.25	.10	.02
☐ 67	Mike Millar	.35	.14	.03
☐ 68	Bob Beers	.75	.30	.07
☐ 69	Ray Neufeld	.50	.20	.05
☐ 70	Graeme Townshend	.50	.20	.05
☐ 71	Billy O'Dwyer	.35	.14	.03
☐ 72	Frank Caprice	.50	.20	.05
☐ 73	John Blum	.35	.14	.03
☐ 74	Jerry Foster	.25	.10	.02
☐ 75	Sutherland and Rick Bowness	.35	.14	.03
☐ 76	Scott Drevitch	.25	.10	.02
☐ 77	Baltimore Checklist	.35	.14	.03
☐ 78	John Purves	.50	.20	.05
☐ 79	Jeff Greenlaw	.35	.14	.03
☐ 80	Jim Taylor	.25	.10	.02
☐ 81	Alfie Turcotte	.35	.14	.03
☐ 82	Dan Redmond	.25	.10	.02
☐ 83	Chris Felix	.35	.14	.03
☐ 84	Bobby Babcock	.35	.14	.03
☐ 85	Steve Maltais	.50	.20	.05
☐ 86	Mike Richard	.25	.10	.02
☐ 87	Team Picture	.35	.14	.03
☐ 88	Bob Mason	.75	.30	.07
☐ 89	Mark Ferner	.35	.14	.03
☐ 90	Steve Seftel	.25	.10	.02
☐ 91	Brian Tutt	.25	.10	.02
☐ 92	Terry Murray	.50	.20	.05
☐ 93	Jim Hrivnak	1.50	.60	.15
☐ 94	Tyler Larter	.25	.10	.02
☐ 95	Tim Bergland	.50	.20	.05
☐ 96	Dennis Smith	.25	.10	.02
☐ 97	Steve Hollett	.25	.10	.02
☐ 98	Shawn Simpson	.25	.10	.02
☐ 99	Robin Bawa	.25	.10	.02
☐ 100	John Druce	.75	.30	.07
☐ 101	Kent Paynter	.25	.10	.02
☐ 102	Alain Cote	.50	.20	.05
☐ 103	J.P. Mattingly	.25	.10	.02
☐ 104	Newmarket Checklist	.35	.14	.03
☐ 105	Dean Anderson	.25	.10	.02
☐ 106	Wes Jarvis	.35	.14	.03
☐ 107	Brian Blad	.25	.10	.02
☐ 108	Derek Laxdal	.35	.14	.03
☐ 109	Kent Hulst	.25	.10	.02
☐ 110	Tim Bernhardt	.50	.20	.05
☐ 111	Brian Hoard	.25	.10	.02
☐ 112	Bill Root	.50	.20	.05
☐ 113	Paul Gardner	.35	.14	.03
☐ 114	Tim Armstrong	.25	.10	.02
☐ 115	Sean McKenna	.35	.14	.03
☐ 116	Tim Bean	.25	.10	.02
☐ 117	Alan Hepple	.25	.10	.02
☐ 118	Greg Hotham	.25	.10	.02
☐ 119	Scott Pearson	.75	.30	.07
☐ 120	Peter Ihnacak	.50	.20	.05
☐ 121	John McIntyre	1.00	.40	.10
☐ 122	Paul Gagne	.35	.14	.03
☐ 123	Darren Veitch	.50	.20	.05
☐ 124	Mark LaForest	.75	.30	.07
☐ 125	Doug Shedden	.50	.20	.05
☐ 126	Bobby Reynolds	.35	.14	.03
☐ 127	Tie Domi	2.00	.80	.20
☐ 128	Ken Hammond	.75	.30	.07
☐ 129	Cape Breton Checklist	.35	.14	.03
☐ 130	Wade Campbell	.35	.14	.03
☐ 131	Chris Joseph	.50	.20	.05
☐ 132	Marin Barbe	.25	.10	.02
☐ 133	Mike Greenlay	.25	.10	.02
☐ 134	Peter Soberlak	.25	.10	.02
☐ 135	Bruce Bell	.35	.14	.03
☐ 136	Dan Currie	.50	.20	.05
☐ 137	Fabian Joseph	.35	.14	.03
☐ 138	Stan Drulia	.35	.14	.03
☐ 139	Todd Charlesworth	.25	.10	.02
☐ 140	Norm Maciver	1.25	.50	.12
☐ 141	David Haas	.25	.10	.02
☐ 142	Tim Tisdale	.25	.10	.02
☐ 143	Eldon Reddick	2.00	.80	.20
☐ 144	Alexander Ryjnych	.25	.10	.02
☐ 145	Kim Issel	.35	.14	.03
☐ 146	Corey Foster	.50	.20	.05
☐ 147	Tomas Kapusta	.35	.14	.03
☐ 148	Brian Wilks	.25	.10	.02
☐ 149	John LeBlanc	.35	.14	.03
☐ 150	Ivan Matulik	.25	.10	.02
☐ 151	Shaun Van Allen	.75	.30	.07
☐ 152	Halifax Checklist	.35	.14	.03
☐ 153	Scott Gordon	.75	.30	.07
☐ 154	Trevor Steinburg	.35	.14	.03
☐ 155	Miroslav Ihnacak	.50	.20	.05
☐ 156	Jamie Baker	.50	.20	.05
☐ 157	Robbie Ftorek	.50	.20	.05
☐ 158	C. McQuaid and B.Smith	.25	.10	.02
☐ 159	Mario Brunetta	.35	.14	.03
☐ 160	Jean-Marc Routhier	.25	.10	.02
☐ 161	David Espe	.25	.10	.02
☐ 162	Ken Quinney	.35	.14	.03
☐ 163	Mark Vermette	.35	.14	.03
☐ 164	Dean Hopkins	.25	.10	.02
☐ 165	Claude Julien	.25	.10	.02
☐ 166	Claude Lapointe	1.00	.40	.10
☐ 167	Stephane Morin	1.00	.40	.10
☐ 168	Bryan Fogarty	1.00	.40	.10
☐ 169	Dave Pichette	.35	.14	.03
☐ 170	Kevin Kaminski	.50	.20	.05
☐ 171	Brent Severyn	.75	.30	.07
☐ 172	Max Middendorf	.35	.14	.03
☐ 173	Jean-Marc Richard	.25	.10	.02
☐ 174	Gerald Bzdel	.25	.10	.02
☐ 175	Ladislav Tresl	.35	.14	.03
☐ 176	Jaroslav Sevcik	.25	.10	.02
☐ 177	Greg Smyth	.35	.14	.03
☐ 178	Joel Baillargeon	.35	.14	.03
☐ 179	Sherbrooke Checklist	.35	.14	.03
☐ 180	Andre Racicot	1.50	.60	.15
☐ 181	Jean-Claude Bergeron	1.00	.40	.10
☐ 182	Jim Nesich	.25	.10	.02
☐ 183	Todd Richards	.25	.10	.02
☐ 184	Francois Gravel	.35	.14	.03
☐ 185	Lyle Odelein	1.50	.60	.15
☐ 186	Benoit Brunet	1.00	.40	.10
☐ 187	Mario Roberge	.50	.20	.05
☐ 188	Marc Saumier	.25	.10	.02
☐ 189	Norman Desjardins	.25	.10	.02
☐ 190	Dan Woodley	.25	.10	.02
☐ 191	Andrew Cassels	2.00	.80	.20
☐ 192	Roy Mitchell	.25	.10	.02
☐ 193	Guy Darveau	.25	.10	.02
☐ 194	Ed Cristofoli	.35	.14	.03
☐ 195	Stephane J.G. Richer Defenseman	.50	.20	.05
☐ 196	Jacques Parent	.25	.10	.02
☐ 197	Luc Gauthier	.35	.14	.03
☐ 198	John Ferguson	.50	.20	.05
☐ 199	Mathieu Schneider	2.00	.80	.20
☐ 200	Serge Roberge	.25	.10	.02
☐ 201	Jean Hamel	.35	.14	.03
☐ 202	Utica Checklist	.35	.14	.03
☐ 203	Jason Simon	.50	.20	.05
☐ 204	Jeff Madill	.35	.14	.03
☐ 205	Kevin Todd	1.50	.60	.15
☐ 206	Myles O'Connor	.75	.30	.07
☐ 207	Jon Morris	.50	.20	.05
☐ 208	Bob Hoffmeyer	.35	.14	.03
☐ 209	Paul Ysebaert	1.50	.60	.15
☐ 210	Steve Rooney	.50	.20	.05
☐ 211	Claude Vilgrain	1.00	.40	.10
☐ 212	Paul Guay	.35	.14	.03
☐ 213	Roland Melanson	.75	.30	.07
☐ 214	Tom McVie	.50	.20	.05
☐ 215	David Marcinyshyn	.35	.14	.03
☐ 216	Perry Anderson	.35	.14	.03
☐ 217	Jamie Huscroft	.50	.20	.05
☐ 218	Bob Woods	.25	.10	.02
☐ 219	Pat Conacher	.50	.20	.05
☐ 220	Jean-Marc Lanthier	.25	.10	.02
☐ 221	Chris Kiene	.25	.10	.02
☐ 222	Eric Weinrich	1.00	.40	.10
☐ 223	Brian Fitzgerald	.25	.10	.02
☐ 224	Craig Billington	1.00	.40	.10
☐ 225	Jim Thomson	.50	.20	.05
☐ 226	Tim Budy	.25	.10	.02
☐ 227	Marc Laniel	.25	.10	.02
☐ 228	Robert Bill	.25	.10	.02
☐ 229	Springfield Checklist	.35	.14	.03
☐ 230	Mike Walsh	.35	.14	.03
☐ 231	Dale Henry	.35	.14	.03
☐ 232	Bill Berg	.75	.30	.07
☐ 233	Hank Lammens	.50	.20	.05
☐ 234	Rob DiMaio	.50	.20	.05
☐ 235	Shawn Byram	.25	.10	.02
☐ 236	Jeff Hackett	1.25	.50	.12
☐ 237	Wayne McBean	.75	.30	.07
☐ 238	Tim Hanley	.25	.10	.02
☐ 239	Tom Fitzgerald	.50	.20	.05
☐ 240	Mike Stevens	.35	.14	.03
☐ 241	George Maneluk	.35	.14	.03

☐	242	Dean Ewen	.25	.10	.02
☐	243	Dale Kushner	.35	.14	.03
☐	244	Shawn Evans	.35	.14	.03
☐	245	Rod Dallman	.25	.10	.02
☐	246	Mike Kelfer	.25	.10	.02
☐	247	Sean LeBrun	.25	.10	.02
☐	248	Kerry Clark	.35	.14	.03
☐	249	Ed Tyburski	.25	.10	.02
☐	250	Derek King	2.00	.80	.20
☐	251	Marc Bergevin	.50	.20	.05
☐	252	Jeff Finley	.50	.20	.05
☐	253	Jim Roberts	.35	.14	.03
☐	254	Chris Pryor	.35	.14	.03
☐	255	Rochester Checklist	.35	.14	.03
☐	256	Robert Ray	1.00	.40	.10
☐	257	Ken Priestlay	.50	.20	.05
☐	258	Darcy Wakaluk	1.50	.60	.15
☐	259	Richie Dunn	.35	.14	.03
☐	260	Ken Sutton	.75	.30	.07
☐	261	Terry Martin	.25	.10	.02
☐	262	Scott Metcalfe	.25	.10	.02
☐	263	Joel Savage	.35	.14	.03
☐	264	Brad Miller	.35	.14	.03
☐	265	Donald Audette	2.00	.80	.20
☐	266	John Van Boxmeer	.50	.20	.05
☐	267	The Moose	.35	.14	.03
☐	268	Brian Ford	.25	.10	.02
☐	269	Darcy Loewen	.75	.30	.07
☐	270	Bob Halkidis	.50	.20	.05
☐	271	Steve Ludzik	.50	.20	.05
☐	272	Steve Smith	.25	.10	.02
☐	273	Francois Guay	.25	.10	.02
☐	274	Mike Donnelly	1.00	.40	.10
☐	275	Darrin Shannon	1.50	.60	.15
☐	276	Jody Gage	1.00	.40	.10
☐	277	Dave Baseggio	.25	.10	.02
☐	278	Bob Corkum	1.00	.40	.10
☐	279	Jim Jackson	.25	.10	.02
☐	280	Don McSween	.35	.14	.03
☐	281	Jim Hofford	.25	.10	.02
☐	282	Scott McCrory	.25	.10	.02
☐	283	Binghamton Checklist	.35	.14	.03
☐	284	Raymond Saumier	.25	.10	.02
☐	285	Mike Berger	.35	.14	.03
☐	286	Corey Beaulieu	.25	.10	.02
☐	287	Doug McKay	.25	.10	.02
☐	288	Blair Atcheynum	.35	.14	.03
☐	289	Al Tuer	.35	.14	.03
☐	290	Chris Lindberg	.50	.20	.05
☐	291	Daryl Reaugh	.50	.20	.05
☐	292	James Black	.75	.30	.07
☐	293	Vern Smith	.25	.10	.02
☐	294	Todd Krygier	.75	.30	.07
☐	295	Bob Joyce	.25	.10	.02
☐	296	Jon Smith	.25	.10	.02
☐	297	Michel Picard	.35	.14	.03
☐	298	Jim Culhane	.25	.10	.02
☐	299	Brian Chapman	.25	.10	.02
☐	300	Jim Ennis	.25	.10	.02
☐	301	Jacques Caron	.25	.10	.02
☐	302	Jim McKenzie	.50	.20	.05
☐	303	Kay Whitmore	1.50	.60	.15
☐	304	Terry Yake	1.00	.40	.10
☐	305	Mike Moller	.35	.14	.03
☐	306	Adirondack Checklist	.35	.14	.03
☐	307	Bob Wilkie	.35	.14	.03
☐	308	Chris McRae	.25	.10	.02
☐	309	Chris Kotsopoulos	.50	.20	.05
☐	310	Steve Sumner	.25	.10	.02
☐	311	Timothy Abbott	.25	.10	.02
☐	312	Gord Kruppke	.25	.10	.02
☐	313	Mike Gober	.25	.10	.02
☐	314	Al Conroy	.25	.10	.02
☐	315	Sam St.Laurent	.50	.20	.05
☐	316	Dave Casey	.25	.10	.02
☐	317	Yves Racine	1.50	.60	.15
☐	318	Randy McKay	.50	.20	.05
☐	319	Dale Krentz	.35	.14	.03
☐	320	Sheldon Kennedy	1.50	.60	.15
☐	321	Barry Melrose	2.00	.80	.20
☐	322	Dennis Holland	.25	.10	.02
☐	323	Glenn Merkosky	.35	.14	.03
☐	324	Murray Eaves	.35	.14	.03
☐	325	Mark Reimer	.25	.10	.02
☐	326	Tim Cheveldae	3.00	1.20	.30
☐	327	Peter Dineen	.25	.10	.02
☐	328	Dean Morton	.25	.10	.02
☐	329	Derek Mayer	.25	.10	.02
☐	330	Hershey Checklist	.35	.14	.03
☐	331	Don Biggs	.35	.14	.03
☐	332	Scott Sandelin	.35	.14	.03
☐	333	Shaun Sabol	.25	.10	.02
☐	334	Murray Baron	.50	.20	.05

☐	335	Dave Fenyves	.35	.14	.03
☐	336	Glen Seabrooke	.35	.14	.03
☐	337	Mark Freer	.50	.20	.05
☐	338	Ray Allison	.35	.14	.03
☐	339	Chris Jensen	.50	.20	.05
☐	340	Ross Fitzpatrick	.25	.10	.02
☐	341	Brian Dobbin	.35	.14	.03
☐	342	Darren Rumble	.35	.14	.03
☐	343	Mike Stothers	.35	.14	.03
☐	344	Jiri Latal	.50	.20	.05
☐	345	Don Nachbaur	.35	.14	.03
☐	346	John Stevens	.25	.10	.02
☐	347	Steven Fletcher	.25	.10	.02
☐	348	Kent Hawley	.25	.10	.02
☐	349	Bill Armstrong	.35	.14	.03
☐	350	Bruce Hoffort	.75	.30	.07
☐	351	Gordon Paddock	.35	.14	.03
☐	352	Marc D'Amour	.50	.20	.05
☐	353	Tim Tookey	.50	.20	.05
☐	354	Reid Simpson	.25	.10	.02
☐	355	Mark Bassen	.25	.10	.02
☐	356	Rocky Trottier	.35	.14	.03
☐	357	Harry Bricker	.25	.10	.02
☐	358	Dan Stuck	.25	.10	.02
☐	359	Al Hill	.35	.14	.03
☐	360	Kevin McCarthy	.35	.14	.03

1989-90 ProCards IHL

 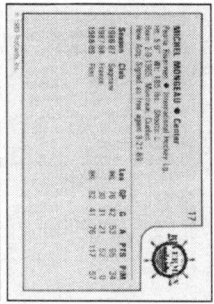

This set of 208 cards features the nine teams of the International Hockey League. The cards measure the standard size, 2 1/2" by 3 1/2". Although the team sets were originally sold with a suggested retail price of 3.00 per team set and packaged individually, they are listed below as one giant set. In many cases that was the way they were advertised and sold, i.e., as a complete set of all the teams in the IHL. The numbering is by teams as follows, Peoria Rivermen (1-23), Flint Spirits (24-48), Indianapolis Ice (49-73), Kalamazoo Wings (74-98), Phoenix Roadrunners (99-121), Fort Wayne Komets (122-141), Muskegon Lumberjacks (142-164), Milwaukee Admirals (165-189), and Salt Lake City Golden Eagles (190-208).

	MINT	EXC	G-VG
COMPLETE SET (208)	75.00	30.00	7.50
COMMON PLAYER (1-208)	.25	.10	.02

☐	1	Peoria Checklist	.35	.14	.03
☐	2	Darwin McPherson	.25	.10	.02
☐	3	Pat Jablonski	1.50	.60	.15
☐	4	Scott Paluch	.25	.10	.02
☐	5	Guy Hebert	3.00	1.20	.30
☐	6	Richard Pilon	.35	.14	.03
☐	7	Curtis Joseph	7.50	3.00	.75
☐	8	Robert Dirk	.75	.30	.07
☐	9	Darin Smith	.25	.10	.02
☐	10	Terry McLean	.25	.10	.02
☐	11	Kevin Miehm	.50	.20	.05
☐	12	Toby Ducolon	.25	.10	.02
☐	13	Mike Wolak	.25	.10	.02
☐	14	Adrien Plavsic	1.00	.40	.10
☐	15	Dave Thomlinson	.50	.20	.05
☐	16	Jim Vesey	.35	.14	.03

☐	17	Michel Mongeau	1.00	.40	.10
☐	18	Tom Nash	.25	.10	.02
☐	19	David O'Brien	.25	.10	.02
☐	20	Dominic Lavoie	.75	.30	.07
☐	21	Keith Osborne	.35	.14	.03
☐	22	Rob Robinson	.35	.14	.03
☐	23	Wayne Thomas	.35	.14	.03
☐	24	Flint Checklist	.35	.14	.03
☐	25	Jason Lafreniere	.50	.20	.05
☐	26	Rick Knickle	1.00	.40	.10
☐	27	Jerry Tarrant	.25	.10	.02
☐	28	Paul Broten	.75	.30	.07
☐	29	Kevin Miller	2.50	1.00	.25
☐	30	Jim Latos	.25	.10	.02
☐	31	Daniel Lacroix	.50	.20	.05
☐	32	Dennis Vial	.50	.20	.05
☐	33	Denis Larocque	.25	.10	.02
☐	34	Mike Golden	.25	.10	.02
☐	35	Mike Hurlbut	.50	.20	.05
☐	36	Scott Browter	.25	.10	.02
☐	37	Lee Giffin	.35	.14	.03
☐	38	Jeff Bloemberg	.50	.20	.05
☐	39	Simon Wheeldon	.35	.14	.03
☐	40	Rob Zamuner	1.00	.40	.10
☐	41	Joe Paterson	.35	.14	.03
☐	42	Barry Chyzowski	.25	.10	.02
☐	43	Peter Laviolette	.25	.10	.02
☐	44	Corey Millen	2.50	1.00	.25
☐	45	Darren Lowe	.25	.10	.02
☐	46	Peter Fiorentino	.25	.10	.02
☐	47	Soren True	.25	.10	.02
☐	48	Mike Richter	7.50	3.00	.75
☐	49	Ice Checklist	.35	.14	.03
☐	50	Sean Williams	.25	.10	.02
☐	51	Bruce Cassidy	.25	.10	.02
☐	52	Mark Kurawski	.25	.10	.02
☐	53	Bob Bassen	.75	.30	.07
☐	54	Marty Nanne	.25	.10	.02
☐	55	Jari Torkki	.25	.10	.02
☐	56	Ryan McGill	.75	.30	.07
☐	57	Mike Peluso	1.00	.40	.10
☐	58	Darryl Sutter	.50	.20	.05
☐	59	Dan Vincelette	.35	.14	.03
☐	60	Lonnie Loach	.50	.20	.05
☐	61	Mike Rucinski	.25	.10	.02
☐	62	Jim Playfair	.25	.10	.02
☐	63	Everett Sanipass	.35	.14	.03
☐	64	Dale Marquette	.25	.10	.02
☐	65	Gary Moscaluk	.25	.10	.02
☐	66	Mario Doyon	.35	.14	.03
☐	67	Ray LeBlanc	1.50	.60	.15
☐	68	Mike Eagles	.35	.14	.03
☐	69	Warren Rychel	.75	.30	.07
☐	70	Jim Johannson	.35	.14	.03
☐	71	Cam Russell	.75	.30	.07
☐	72	Mike McNeil	.35	.14	.03
☐	73	Jimmy Waite	2.00	.80	.20
☐	74	Kalamazoo Checklist	.35	.14	.03
☐	75	Kevin Schamehorn	.25	.10	.02
☐	76	Kevin Evans	.35	.14	.03
☐	77	D'Arcy Norton	.25	.10	.02
☐	78	Scott Robinson	.25	.10	.02
☐	79	Larry DePalma	.35	.14	.03
☐	80	Ed Courtenay	.50	.20	.05
☐	81	Rob Zettler	.75	.30	.07
☐	82	Dusan Pasek	.35	.14	.03
☐	83	Gary Emmons	.25	.10	.02
☐	84	Peter Lappin	.35	.14	.03
☐	85	Mario Thyer	.35	.14	.03
☐	86	Mike McHugh	.35	.14	.03
☐	87	Randy Smith	.35	.14	.03
☐	88	Link Gaetz	1.00	.40	.10
☐	89	Ken Hodge Jr.	.50	.20	.05
☐	90	Pat MacLeod	.75	.30	.07
☐	91	Neil Wilkinson	1.00	.40	.10
☐	92	Brett Barnett	.25	.10	.02
☐	93	Larry Dyck	.35	.14	.03
☐	94	Dean Kolstad	.50	.20	.05
☐	95	Jarmo Myllys	.50	.20	.05
☐	96	Paul Jerrard	.25	.10	.02
☐	97	Jean-Francois Quintin	.50	.20	.05
☐	98	Mitch Messier	.50	.20	.05
☐	99	Phoenix Checklist (110 Jeff Lamb not listed)	.35	.14	.03
☐	100	Bryant Perrier	.25	.10	.02
☐	101	Keith Gretzky	2.00	.80	.20
☐	102	Don Martin	.25	.10	.02
☐	103	David Littman	.50	.20	.05
☐	104	Mike DeCarle	.25	.10	.02
☐	105	Grant Tkachuk	.25	.10	.02
☐	106	Richard Novak	.25	.10	.02
☐	107	Chris Luongo	.50	.20	.05
☐	108	Bruce Boudreau	.35	.14	.03
☐	109	Nick Beaulieu	.25	.10	.02
☐	110	Jeff Lamb	.25	.10	.02
☐	111	Rob Nichols	.25	.10	.02
☐	112	Garry Unger	.50	.20	.05
☐	113	Larry Floyd	.25	.10	.02
☐	114	Brent Sapergia	.35	.14	.03
☐	115	Randy Exelby	.35	.14	.03
☐	116	Jim McGeough	.25	.10	.02
☐	117	Tom Karalis	.25	.10	.02
☐	118	Ken Spangler	.35	.14	.03
☐	119	Jacques Mailhot	.25	.10	.02
☐	120	Shawn Dineen	.25	.10	.02
☐	121	Dave Korol	.25	.10	.02
☐	122	Fort Wayne Checklist	.35	.14	.03
☐	123	Colin Chin	.25	.10	.02
☐	124	Scott Shaunessy	.25	.10	.02
☐	125	Bob Lakso	.25	.10	.02
☐	126	Duane Joyce	.25	.10	.02
☐	127	Joe Stephan	.25	.10	.02
☐	128	Ron Shudra	.25	.10	.02
☐	129	Bob Fowler	.25	.10	.02
☐	130	Steve Bisson	.25	.10	.02
☐	131	Craig Endean	.25	.10	.02
☐	132	Carl Mokosak	.25	.10	.02
☐	133	Carey Lucyk	.25	.10	.02
☐	134	Craig Channell	.25	.10	.02
☐	135	Frederic Chabot	.75	.30	.07
☐	136	Brian Hannon	.25	.10	.02
☐	137	Keith Miller	.25	.10	.02
☐	138	Al Sims	.35	.14	.03
☐	139	Stephane Beauregard	1.00	.40	.10
☐	140	Ron Handy	.25	.10	.02
☐	141	Byron Lomow	.25	.10	.02
☐	142	Muskegon Checklist	.35	.14	.03
☐	143	Jamie Leach	.35	.14	.03
☐	144	Chris Clifford	.25	.10	.02
☐	145	Dave Capuano	.50	.20	.05
☐	146	Jeff Daniels	.50	.20	.05
☐	147	Dave Goertz	.25	.10	.02
☐	148	Perry Ganchar	.25	.10	.02
☐	149	Mitch Wilson	.25	.10	.02
☐	150	Scott Gruhl	.35	.14	.03
☐	151	Randy Taylor	.25	.10	.02
☐	152	Bruce Racine	.35	.14	.03
☐	153	Dave Michayluk	.35	.14	.03
☐	154	Richard Zemlak	.50	.20	.05
☐	155	Brad Aitken	.35	.14	.03
☐	156	Paul Stanton	.50	.20	.05
☐	157	Darren Stolk	.25	.10	.02
☐	158	Jim Paek	.75	.30	.07
☐	159	Mark Kachowski	.25	.10	.02
☐	160	Dan Frawley	.35	.14	.03
☐	161	Mike Mersch	.25	.10	.02
☐	162	Glenn Mulvenna	.25	.10	.02
☐	163	Phil Russell	.25	.10	.02
☐	164	Blair McDonald	.35	.14	.03
☐	165	Milwaukee Checklist	.35	.14	.03
☐	166	Shaun Clouston	.25	.10	.02
☐	167	Steve Veilleux	.25	.10	.02
☐	168	Peter Bakovic	.25	.10	.02
☐	169	Peter DeBoer	.25	.10	.02
☐	170	Ernie Vargas	.25	.10	.02
☐	171	Keith Street	.25	.10	.02
☐	172	Rob Murphy	.50	.20	.05
☐	173	David Bruce	.75	.30	.07
☐	174	Shannon Travis	.25	.10	.02
☐	175	Jeff Rohlicek	.25	.10	.02
☐	176	Jay Mazur	.35	.14	.03
☐	177	Kevan Guy	.50	.20	.05
☐	178	Troy Gamble	2.00	.80	.20
☐	179	Ronnie Stern	.75	.30	.07
☐	180	Jim Revenberg	.25	.10	.02
☐	181	Jose Charbonneau	.75	.30	.07
☐	182	Ian Kidd	.25	.10	.02
☐	183	Todd Hawkins	.25	.10	.02
☐	184	Carl Valimont	.25	.10	.02
☐	185	Jim Agnew	.35	.14	.03
☐	186	Curtis Hunt	.25	.10	.02
☐	187	Dean Cook	.25	.10	.02
☐	188	Ron Wilson	.50	.20	.05
☐	189	Ron Lapointe	.25	.10	.02
☐	190	Salt Lake City Checklist	.35	.14	.03
☐	191	Brian Glynn	.50	.20	.05
☐	192	Stephane Matteau	1.00	.40	.10
☐	193	Rick Barkovich	.25	.10	.02
☐	194	Jeff Wenaas	.25	.10	.02
☐	195	Darryl Olsen	.25	.10	.02
☐	196	Rick Lessard	.25	.10	.02
☐	197	Kevin Grant	.25	.10	.02
☐	198	Rich Chernomaz	.35	.14	.03
☐	199	Stu Grimson	1.25	.50	.12

			MINT	EXC	G-VG
☐	200	Jamie Hislop and .... Bob Francis	.25	.10	.02
☐	201	Doug Pickell	.25	.10	.02
☐	202	Chris Biotti	.25	.10	.02
☐	203	Tim Sweeney	.75	.30	.07
☐	204	Ken Sabourin	.50	.20	.05
☐	205	Randy Bucyk	.25	.10	.02
☐	206	Wayne Cowley	.50	.20	.05
☐	207	Rick Hayward	.25	.10	.02
☐	208	Marc Bureau	1.00	.40	.10

1990-91 ProCards AHL/IHL

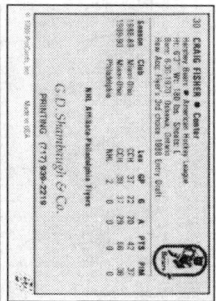

This 628-card set measures the standard size, 2 1/2" by 3 1/2", and features players who started or were expected to start the 1990-91 season in the minors. Players from the American Hockey League and the Internatonal Hockey League are included in this set. This set features red borders with a yellow hockey stick on the left side of the card diagonally framing a full-color picture of the player while the backs of the cards feature the basic factual information about the player as well as a complete statistical history. There are two number 99's: and the set is arranged by teams: Binghamton Rangers (1-25), Hershey Bears (26-53), Fredericton Canadiens (54-75), Peoria Riverman (76-99) Kalamazoo Wings (99-122), Maine Mariners (123-145), Newmarket Saints (146-170), Springfield Indians (171-194), Baltimore Skipjacks (195-219), Cape Breton Oilers (220-242), Moncton Hawks (243-264, 343-344), Rochester Americans (265-295), San Diego Gulls (296-321), Milwaukee Admirals (322-342), Phoenix Roadrunner (345-369), Muskegon Lumberjacks (370-392), Indianapolis Ice (393-414), New Haven Nighthawks (415-441), Halifax Citadels (442-468), Adirondack Red Wings (469-493), Capital District Islanders (494-514), Albany Choppers (515-535), Fort Wayne Komets (536-556), Utica Devils (557-581), Kansas City Blades (582-602), and Salt Lake City Golden Eagles (603-628). Each team has its own team checklist (TC) card as the last card in the team's numbering sequence. Although the team sets were originally sold with a suggested retail price of 4.00 per team set and packaged individually, they are listed below as one giant set.

		MINT	EXC	G-VG
COMPLETE SET (629)		125.00	50.00	12.50
COMMON PLAYER (1-629)		.25	.10	.02

☐	1	Rob Zamuner	.75	.30	.07
☐	2	Todd Charlesworth	.25	.10	.02
☐	3	Bob Bodak	.25	.10	.02
☐	4	Len Hachborn	.35	.14	.03
☐	5	Peter Fiorentino	.25	.10	.02
☐	6	Kord Cernich	.25	.10	.02
☐	7	Daniel Lacroix	.50	.20	.05
☐	8	Joe Paterson	.35	.14	.03
☐	9	Sam St.Laurent	.50	.20	.05
☐	10	Jeff Bloemberg	.35	.14	.03

☐	11	Mike Golden	.25	.10	.02
☐	12	Mike Hurlbut	.50	.20	.05
☐	13	Mark LaForest	.50	.20	.05
☐	14	Chris Cichocki	.35	.14	.03
☐	15	John Paddock	.50	.20	.05
☐	16	Peter Laviolette	.25	.10	.02
☐	17	Martin Bergeron	.25	.10	.02
☐	18	Rudy Poeschek	.50	.20	.05
☐	19	Eric Germain	.25	.10	.02
☐	20	Al Hill Asst.CO	.25	.10	.02
☐	21	Rick Bennett	.50	.20	.05
☐	22	Tie Domi	1.50	.60	.15
☐	23	Ross Fitzpatrick	.25	.10	.02
☐	24	Brian McReynolds	.50	.20	.05
☐	25	Binghampton Rangers CL	.35	.14	.03
☐	26	Mike Eaves CO	.35	.14	.03
☐	27	Lance Pitlick	.25	.10	.02
☐	28	Dale Kushner	.35	.14	.03
☐	29	Reid Simpson	.25	.10	.02
☐	30	Craig Fisher	.50	.20	.05
☐	31	Dominic Roussel	4.00	1.60	.40
☐	32	Dave Fenyves	.35	.14	.03
☐	33	Brian Dobbin	.25	.10	.02
☐	34	Darren Rumble	.50	.20	.05
☐	35	Murray Baron	.50	.20	.05
☐	36	Bruce Hoffort	.50	.20	.05
☐	37	Steve Beadle	.25	.10	.02
☐	38	Chris Jensen	.35	.14	.03
☐	39	Mike Stothers	.35	.14	.03
☐	40	Kent Hawley	.25	.10	.02
☐	41	Scott Sandelin	.25	.10	.02
☐	42	Guy Phillips	.25	.10	.02
☐	43	Mark Bassen	.25	.10	.02
☐	44	Steve Scheifele	.25	.10	.02
☐	45	Bill Armstrong	.35	.14	.03
☐	46	Shaun Sabol	.25	.10	.02
☐	47	Mark Freer	.35	.14	.03
☐	48	Claude Boivin	.50	.20	.05
☐	49	Len Barrie	.50	.20	.05
☐	50	Bill Armstrong	.35	.14	.03
☐	51	Tim Tookey	.35	.14	.03
☐	52	Harry Bricker Asst.CO	.25	.10	.02
☐	53	Hershey Bears TC	.35	.14	.03
☐	54	Alain Cote	.50	.20	.05
☐	55	Luc Gauthier	.35	.14	.03
☐	56	Eric Charron	.35	.14	.03
☐	57	Mario Roberge	.35	.14	.03
☐	58	Tom Sagissor	.25	.10	.02
☐	59	Brent Bobyck	.25	.10	.02
☐	60	John Ferguson	.35	.14	.03
☐	61	Jim Nesich	.25	.10	.02
☐	62	Gilbert Dionne	3.00	1.20	.30
☐	63	Herbert Hohenberger	.35	.14	.03
☐	64	Dan Woodley	.25	.10	.02
☐	65	Roy Mitchell	.25	.10	.02
☐	66	Frederic Chabot	.75	.30	.07
☐	67	Andre Racicot	1.00	.40	.10
☐	68	Paul DiPietro	1.25	.50	.12
☐	69	Norman Desjardins	.25	.10	.02
☐	70	Martin St.Amour	.25	.10	.02
☐	71	Jessie Belanger	1.50	.60	.15
☐	72	Ed Cristofoli	.35	.14	.03
☐	73	Patrick Lebeau	.75	.30	.07
☐	74	Paulin Bordeleau CO	.35	.14	.03
☐	75	Fredericton Canadiens TC	.35	.14	.03
☐	76	Keith Osborne	.25	.10	.02
☐	77	Richard Pilon	.35	.14	.03
☐	78	Alain Raymond	.25	.10	.02
☐	79	Rob Robinson	.35	.14	.03
☐	80	Andy Rymsha	.25	.10	.02
☐	81	Randy Skarda	.25	.10	.02
☐	82	Dave Thomlinson	.50	.20	.05
☐	83	Tom Tilley	.50	.20	.05
☐	84	Steve Tuttle	.35	.14	.03
☐	85	Tony Twist	.50	.20	.05
☐	86	David Bruce	.50	.20	.05
☐	87	Kelly Chase	.35	.14	.03
☐	88	Nelson Emerson	3.00	1.20	.30
☐	89	Guy Hebert	2.00	.80	.20
☐	90	Tony Hejna	.25	.10	.02
☐	91	Michel Mongeau	.75	.30	.07
☐	92	David O'Brien	.25	.10	.02
☐	93	Kevin Miehm	.50	.20	.05
☐	94	Darwin McPherson	.25	.10	.02
☐	95	Dominic Lavoie	.35	.14	.03
☐	96	Yves Heroux	.35	.14	.03
☐	97	Pat Jablonski	1.25	.50	.12
☐	98	Bob Plager CO	.75	.30	.07
☐	99A	Peoria Rivermen TC	.35	.14	.03
☐	99B	Jayson More	.50	.20	.05
☐	100	Kevin Evans	.35	.14	.03
☐	101	Warren Babe	.35	.14	.03

☐ 102	Mitch Messier	.50	.20	.05
☐ 103	John Blue	1.00	.40	.10
☐ 104	Larry Dyck	.35	.14	.03
☐ 105	Duane Joyce	.25	.10	.02
☐ 106	Kari Takko	.50	.20	.05
☐ 107	Brett Barnett	.25	.10	.02
☐ 108	Pat MacLeod	.50	.20	.05
☐ 109	Peter Lappin	.35	.14	.03
☐ 110	Link Gaetz	.75	.30	.07
☐ 111	Larry DePalma	.35	.14	.03
☐ 112	Steve Gotaas	.25	.10	.02
☐ 113	Mike McHugh	.35	.14	.03
☐ 114	Dan Keczmer	.50	.20	.05
☐ 115	Jackson Penney	.25	.10	.02
☐ 116	Ed Courtenay	.50	.20	.05
☐ 117	Jean-Francois Quintan	.25	.10	.02
☐ 118	Scott Robinson	.25	.10	.02
☐ 119	Mario Thyer	.35	.14	.03
☐ 120	Enrico Ciccone	.75	.30	.07
☐ 121	Kevin Constantine and John Marks	.35	.14	.03
☐ 122	Kalamazoo Wings TC	.35	.14	.03
☐ 123	Shayne Stevenson	.50	.20	.05
☐ 124	Jeff Lazaro	.75	.30	.07
☐ 125	Matt DelGuidice	.75	.30	.07
☐ 126	Ron Hoover	.35	.14	.03
☐ 127	John Mokosak	.25	.10	.02
☐ 128	John Blum	.35	.14	.03
☐ 129	Mike Parson	.50	.20	.05
☐ 130	Bruce Shoebottom	.50	.20	.05
☐ 131	Dave Donnelly	.35	.14	.03
☐ 132	Ralph Barahona	.35	.14	.03
☐ 133	Graeme Townshend	.50	.20	.05
☐ 134	Ken Hodge Jr.	.50	.20	.05
☐ 135	Norm Foster	.35	.14	.03
☐ 136	Greg Poss	.25	.10	.02
☐ 137	Brad James	.25	.10	.02
☐ 138	Lou Crawford	.25	.10	.02
☐ 139	Rick Allain	.25	.10	.02
☐ 140	Bob Beers	.50	.20	.05
☐ 141	Ken Hammond	.35	.14	.03
☐ 142	Mark Montanari	.25	.10	.02
☐ 143	Rick Bowness CO	.50	.20	.05
☐ 144	Bob Gould P/CO	.35	.14	.03
☐ 145	Maine Mariners TC	.35	.14	.03
☐ 146	Mike Stevens	.25	.10	.02
☐ 147	Greg Walters	.25	.10	.02
☐ 148	Mike Moes	.25	.10	.02
☐ 149	Kent Hulst	.25	.10	.02
☐ 150	Len Esau	.25	.10	.02
☐ 151	Darryl Shannon	.50	.20	.05
☐ 152	Bobby Reynolds	.25	.10	.02
☐ 153	Derek Langille	.25	.10	.02
☐ 154	Jeff Serowik	.35	.14	.03
☐ 155	Darren Veitch	.35	.14	.03
☐ 156	Joe Sacco	1.00	.40	.10
☐ 157	Alan Hepple	.25	.10	.02
☐ 158	Doug Shedden	.35	.14	.03
☐ 159	Steve Bancroft	.25	.10	.02
☐ 160	Greg Johnston	.50	.20	.05
☐ 161	Trevor Jobe	.25	.10	.02
☐ 162	Bill Root	.35	.14	.03
☐ 163	Tim Bean	.25	.10	.02
☐ 164	Brian Blad	.25	.10	.02
☐ 165	Robert Hornya	.25	.10	.02
☐ 166	Dean Anderson	.25	.10	.02
☐ 167	Damian Rhodes	1.50	.60	.15
☐ 168	Mike Millar	.35	.14	.03
☐ 169	Mike Jackson	.25	.10	.02
☐ 170	Newmarket Saints	.35	.14	.03
☐ 171	Cal Brown	.25	.10	.02
☐ 172	Michel Picard	.35	.14	.03
☐ 173	Cam Braumer	.25	.10	.02
☐ 174	Jim Burke	.25	.10	.02
☐ 175	Jim McKenzie	.50	.20	.05
☐ 176	Mike Tomlak	.35	.14	.03
☐ 177	Ross McKay	.25	.10	.02
☐ 178	Blair Atcheynum	.35	.14	.03
☐ 179	Chris Tancill	.75	.30	.07
☐ 180	Mark Greig	.75	.30	.07
☐ 181	Joe Day	.35	.14	.03
☐ 182	Jim Roberts CO	.35	.14	.03
☐ 183	Emanuel Viveiros	.25	.10	.02
☐ 184	Darryl Reaugh	.50	.20	.05
☐ 185	Tommie Eriksen	.25	.10	.02
☐ 186	Terry Yake	.75	.30	.07
☐ 187	Chris Govedaris	.50	.20	.05
☐ 188	Chris Bright	.25	.10	.02
☐ 189	John Stevens	.25	.10	.02
☐ 190	Brian Chapman	.25	.10	.02
☐ 191	James Black	.50	.20	.05
☐ 192	Scott Daniels	.25	.10	.02
☐ 193	Kelly Ens	.25	.10	.02
☐ 194	Springfield Indians TC	.35	.14	.03
☐ 195	Ken Lovsin	.35	.14	.03
☐ 196	Kent Paynter	.35	.14	.03
☐ 197	Jim Mathieson	.25	.10	.02
☐ 198	Bob Mendel	.25	.10	.02
☐ 199	Reggie Savage	1.00	.40	.10
☐ 200	Alfie Turcotte	.35	.14	.03
☐ 201	Victor Gervais	.25	.10	.02
☐ 202	Todd Hlushko	.75	.30	.07
☐ 203	Steve Seftel	.35	.14	.03
☐ 204	Thomas Sjogren	.25	.10	.02
☐ 205	Steve Maltais	.35	.14	.03
☐ 206	Bob Joyce	.50	.20	.05
☐ 207	Tyler Larter	.25	.10	.02
☐ 208	Mark Ferner	.35	.14	.03
☐ 209	Bobby Babcock	.35	.14	.03
☐ 210	Jeff Greenlaw	.25	.10	.02
☐ 211	Tim Taylor	.35	.14	.03
☐ 212	John Purves	.50	.20	.05
☐ 213	Chris Felix	.35	.14	.03
☐ 214	Jiri Vykoukal	.25	.10	.02
☐ 215	Shawn Simpson	.25	.10	.02
☐ 216	Jim Hrivnak	1.50	.60	.15
☐ 217	Rob Laird CO/GM	.25	.10	.02
☐ 218	Barry Trotz Asst.CO	.25	.10	.02
☐ 219	Baltimore Skipjacks TC	.35	.14	.03
☐ 220	David Haas	.25	.10	.02
☐ 221	Wade Campbell	.25	.10	.02
☐ 222	Dan Currie	.35	.14	.03
☐ 223	Shaun Van Allen	.75	.30	.07
☐ 224	Norm MacIver	.75	.30	.07
☐ 225	Mike Greenlay	.35	.14	.03
☐ 226	Peter Soberlak	.25	.10	.02
☐ 227	Tim Tisdale	.35	.14	.03
☐ 228	Mario Barbe	.25	.10	.02
☐ 229	Shjon Podein	.50	.20	.05
☐ 230	Trevor Sim	.25	.10	.02
☐ 231	Corey Foster	.50	.20	.05
☐ 232	Mike Ware	.25	.10	.02
☐ 233	Marc Laforge	.35	.14	.03
☐ 234	Bruce Bell	.35	.14	.03
☐ 235	Tomas Kapusta	.35	.14	.03
☐ 236	Alexander Tyjynch	.35	.14	.03
☐ 237	Tomas Srsen	.25	.10	.02
☐ 238	Collin Bauer	.25	.10	.02
☐ 239	Francois Leroux	.35	.14	.03
☐ 240	Don MacAdam CO	.25	.10	.02
☐ 241	Norm Ferguson Asst.CO	.25	.10	.02
☐ 242	Cape Breton Oilers TC	.35	.14	.03
☐ 243	Tony Joseph	.25	.10	.02
☐ 244	Brent Hughes	.75	.30	.07
☐ 245	Larry Bernard	.25	.10	.02
☐ 246	Simon Wheeldon	.35	.14	.03
☐ 247	Todd Flichel	.25	.10	.02
☐ 248	Craig Duncanson	.35	.14	.03
☐ 249	Iain Duncan	.50	.20	.05
☐ 250	Bryan Marchment	.50	.20	.05
☐ 251	Matt Hervey	.35	.14	.03
☐ 252	Chris Norton	.25	.10	.02
☐ 253	Dallas Eakins	.25	.10	.02
☐ 254	Peter Hankinson	.25	.10	.02
☐ 255	Grant Richison	.25	.10	.02
☐ 256	Lee Davidson	.25	.10	.02
☐ 257	Denis Larocque	.25	.10	.02
☐ 258	Scott Levins	.75	.30	.07
☐ 259	Guy Larose	.50	.20	.05
☐ 260	Scott Schneider	.25	.10	.02
☐ 261	Sergei Kharin	.50	.20	.05
☐ 262	Hawk	.35	.14	.03
☐ 263	Dave Farrish CO	.35	.14	.03
☐ 264	Moncton Hawks TC	.35	.14	.03
☐ 265	Kevin Haller	1.25	.50	.12
☐ 266	Joel Savage	.25	.10	.02
☐ 267	Scott Metcalfe	.35	.14	.03
☐ 268	Ian Boyce	.25	.10	.02
☐ 269	David Littman	.35	.14	.03
☐ 270	Dave Baseggio	.25	.10	.02
☐ 271	Ken Sutton	.50	.20	.05
☐ 272	Brad Miller	.35	.14	.03
☐ 273	Bill Houlder	.50	.20	.05
☐ 274	Dan Frawley	.50	.20	.05
☐ 275	Scott McCrory	.25	.10	.02
☐ 276	Steve Ludzik	.35	.14	.03
☐ 277	Robert Ray	.75	.30	.07
☐ 278	Darrin Shannon	1.00	.40	.10
☐ 279	Dale Degray	.35	.14	.03
☐ 280	Bob Corkum	.75	.30	.07
☐ 281	Grant Tkachuk	.25	.10	.02
☐ 282	Kevin Kerr	.25	.10	.02
☐ 283	Mitch Molloy	.25	.10	.02
☐ 284	Darcy Loewen	.50	.20	.05
☐ 285	Jody Gage	.75	.30	.07
☐ 286	Jiri Sejba	.35	.14	.03

☐ 287	Steve Smith	.25	.10	.02
☐ 288	Darcy Wakaluk	1.00	.40	.10
☐ 289	Donald Audette	1.00	.40	.10
☐ 290	Don McSween	.35	.14	.03
☐ 291	Francois Guay	.35	.14	.03
☐ 292	Terry Martin Asst.CO	.25	.10	.02
☐ 293	Don Lever CO	.35	.14	.03
☐ 294	The Moose	.35	.14	.03
☐ 295	Rochester Americans TC	.35	.14	.03
☐ 296	Mike O'Connell CO	.35	.14	.03
☐ 297	Paul Marshall	.25	.10	.02
☐ 298	Darin Bannister	.25	.10	.02
☐ 299	Rob Nichols	.25	.10	.02
☐ 300	Charlie Simmer P/CO	.50	.20	.05
☐ 301	Bob Jones	.25	.10	.02
☐ 302	Scott Brower	.25	.10	.02
☐ 303	Taylor Hall	.25	.10	.02
☐ 304	Carl Mokosak	.25	.10	.02
☐ 305	Glen Hanlon	.50	.20	.05
☐ 306	Peter Dineen	.25	.10	.02
☐ 307	Mike Sullivan	.50	.20	.05
☐ 308	Steven Martinson	.35	.14	.03
☐ 309	Dave Korol	.25	.10	.02
☐ 310	Darren Lowe	.25	.10	.02
☐ 311	Mark Reimer	.25	.10	.02
☐ 312	Mike Gober	.25	.10	.02
☐ 313	Al Tuer	.35	.14	.03
☐ 314	Dean Morton	.35	.14	.03
☐ 315	Jim McGeough	.25	.10	.02
☐ 316	Clark Donatelli	.35	.14	.03
☐ 317	Steven Dykstra	.35	.14	.03
☐ 318	Brent Sapergia	.35	.14	.03
☐ 319	Lloyd Floyd	.25	.10	.02
☐ 320	D'Arcy Norton	.25	.10	.02
☐ 321	San Diego Gulls TC	.35	.14	.03
☐ 322	Garry Valk	.75	.30	.07
☐ 323	Ian Kidd	.25	.10	.02
☐ 324	Todd Hawkins	.25	.10	.02
☐ 325	Carl Valimont	.25	.10	.02
☐ 326	Peter Bakovic	.25	.10	.02
☐ 327	Curt Fraser ACO	.35	.14	.03
☐ 328	David Mackey	.25	.10	.02
☐ 329	Jim Benning	.50	.20	.05
☐ 330	Peter DeBoer	.25	.10	.02
☐ 331	Steve Weeks	.50	.20	.05
☐ 332	Steve Veilleux	.25	.10	.02
☐ 333	Shaun Clouston	.25	.10	.02
☐ 334	Gino Odjick	1.00	.40	.10
☐ 335	Mike Murphy CO	.25	.10	.02
☐ 336	Cam Brown	.25	.10	.02
☐ 337	Patrice LeFebvre	.25	.10	.02
☐ 338	Eric Murano	.50	.20	.05
☐ 339	Jim Revenberg	.25	.10	.02
☐ 340	Don Gibson	.35	.14	.03
☐ 341	Steve McKichan	.25	.10	.02
☐ 342	Milwaukee Admirals TC	.35	.14	.03
☐ 343	Rick Tabaracci	1.25	.50	.12
☐ 344	Mike O'Neill	.75	.30	.07
☐ 345	Rick Hayward	.25	.10	.02
☐ 346	Sean Whyte	.25	.10	.02
☐ 347	Petr Prajsler	.35	.14	.03
☐ 348	John Van Kessel	.35	.14	.03
☐ 349	Mario Gosselin	.50	.20	.05
☐ 350	Kyosti Karjalainen	.35	.14	.03
☐ 351	Mikael Lindholm	.35	.14	.03
☐ 352	David Goverde	.35	.14	.03
☐ 353	Graham Stanley	.25	.10	.02
☐ 354	Stephane J.G. Richer Defenseman	.35	.14	.03
☐ 355	Brian Lawton	.50	.20	.05
☐ 356	Jerome Bechard	.25	.10	.02
☐ 357	Jeff Rohlicek	.25	.10	.02
☐ 358	Steve Jacques	.25	.10	.02
☐ 359	Chris Kontos	1.25	.50	.12
☐ 360	Sylvain Couturier	.50	.20	.05
☐ 361	Peter Sentner	.25	.10	.02
☐ 362	Steve Graves	.35	.14	.03
☐ 363	Daryn McBride	.25	.10	.02
☐ 364	Steve Rooney	.35	.14	.03
☐ 365	Mickey Volcan	.25	.10	.02
☐ 366	Kevin MacDonald	.25	.10	.02
☐ 367	Ralph Backstrom CO	.50	.20	.05
☐ 368	Garry Unger ACO	.50	.20	.05
☐ 369	Phoenix Roadrunners TC	.35	.14	.03
☐ 370	Rob Dopson	.50	.20	.05
☐ 371	Jock Callander	.50	.20	.05
☐ 372	Chris Clifford	.25	.10	.02
☐ 373	Sandy Smith	.25	.10	.02
☐ 374	Jim Kyte	.50	.20	.05
☐ 375	Mike Needham	.75	.30	.07
☐ 376	Mitch Wilson	.25	.10	.02
☐ 377	Dave Goertz	.25	.10	.02
☐ 378	Mark Kachowski	.25	.10	.02
☐ 379	Perry Ganchar	.25	.10	.02
☐ 380	Mark Major	.25	.10	.02
☐ 381	Joel Gardner	.25	.10	.02
☐ 382	Scott Gruhl	.35	.14	.03
☐ 383	Todd Nelson	.35	.14	.03
☐ 384	Darren Stolk	.25	.10	.02
☐ 385	Scott Shaunessy	.25	.10	.02
☐ 386	Mike Mersch	.25	.10	.02
☐ 387	Glenn Mulvenna	.35	.14	.03
☐ 388	Brad Aitken	.25	.10	.02
☐ 389	Dave Michayluk	.35	.14	.03
☐ 390	Blair MacDonald CO	.35	.14	.03
☐ 391	Phil Russell ACO	.35	.14	.03
☐ 392	Muskegon Lumber-jacks TC	.35	.14	.03
☐ 393	Sean Williams	.25	.10	.02
☐ 394	Ryan McGill	.50	.20	.05
☐ 395	Mike Eagles	.35	.14	.03
☐ 396	Jim Johannson	.35	.14	.03
☐ 397	Marty Nanne	.25	.10	.02
☐ 398	Jim Playfair	.25	.10	.02
☐ 399	Warren Rychel	.75	.30	.07
☐ 400	Cam Russell	.50	.20	.05
☐ 401	Jimmy Waite	1.00	.40	.10
☐ 402	Mike Stapleton	.35	.14	.03
☐ 403	Trevor Dam	.25	.10	.02
☐ 404	Tracey Egeland	.25	.10	.02
☐ 405	Owen Lessard	.25	.10	.02
☐ 406	Jeff Sirkka	.25	.10	.02
☐ 407	Mike Dagenais	.25	.10	.02
☐ 408	Alex Roberts	.25	.10	.02
☐ 409	Dominik Hasek	5.00	2.00	.50
☐ 410	Martin Desjardins	.25	.10	.02
☐ 411	Frantisek Kucera	.75	.30	.07
☐ 412	Carl Mokosak	.25	.10	.02
☐ 413	Dave McDowell	.25	.10	.02
☐ 414	Indianapolis Ice TC	.35	.14	.03
☐ 415	Paul Saundercock	.25	.10	.02
☐ 416	Darryl Williams	.25	.10	.02
☐ 417	Micah Aivazoff	.50	.20	.05
☐ 418	Robb Stauber	2.00	.80	.20
☐ 419	Tom Martin	.25	.10	.02
☐ 420	Billy O'Dwyer	.35	.14	.03
☐ 421	Scott Harlow	.25	.10	.02
☐ 422	Jim Thomson	.35	.14	.03
☐ 423	Jim Pavese	.35	.14	.03
☐ 424	Ron Scott	.35	.14	.03
☐ 425	Dave Pasin	.25	.10	.02
☐ 426	Serge Roy	.25	.10	.02
☐ 427	Darryl Gilmour	.35	.14	.03
☐ 428	Mike Donnelly	.75	.30	.07
☐ 429	Rene Chapdelaine	.35	.14	.03
☐ 430	Brandy Semchuk	.35	.14	.03
☐ 431	Paul Holden	.25	.10	.02
☐ 432	Bob Berg	.50	.20	.05
☐ 433	Ladislav Tresl	.25	.10	.02
☐ 434	Eric Ricard	.25	.10	.02
☐ 435	Murray Brumwell	.25	.10	.02
☐ 436	Shawn McCosh	.25	.10	.02
☐ 437	Ross Wilson	.25	.10	.02
☐ 438	Scott Young	.75	.30	.07
☐ 439	David Moylan	.25	.10	.02
☐ 440	Marcel Comeau CO	.25	.10	.02
☐ 441	New Haven Night-hawks TC	.35	.14	.03
☐ 442	David Espe	.25	.10	.02
☐ 443	Mario Doyon	.35	.14	.03
☐ 444	Gerald Bzdel	.25	.10	.02
☐ 445	Claude Lapointe	.75	.30	.07
☐ 446	Dean Hopkins	.25	.10	.02
☐ 447	Clement Jodoin	.25	.10	.02
☐ 448	Kevin Kaminski	.35	.14	.03
☐ 449	Jamie Baker	.50	.20	.05
☐ 450	Mark Vermette	.35	.14	.03
☐ 451	Iiro Jarvi	.50	.20	.05
☐ 452	Kip Miller	.75	.30	.07
☐ 453	Greg Smyth	.35	.14	.03
☐ 454	Serge Roberge	.25	.10	.02
☐ 455	Stephane Morin	.75	.30	.07
☐ 456	Brent Severyn	.75	.30	.07
☐ 457	Jean-Marc Richard	.25	.10	.02
☐ 458	Ken Quinney	.35	.14	.03
☐ 459	Jeff Jackson	.35	.14	.03
☐ 460	Jaroslav Sevcik	.25	.10	.02
☐ 461	David Latta	.35	.14	.03
☐ 462	Trevor Steinburg	.35	.14	.03
☐ 463	Miroslav Ihnacak	.35	.14	.03
☐ 464	Jim Sprott	.25	.10	.02
☐ 465	Mike Bishop	.25	.10	.02
☐ 466	Stephane Fiset	2.00	.80	.20
☐ 467	Scott Gordon	.50	.20	.05
☐ 468	Halifax Citadels TC	.35	.14	.03
☐ 469	Gord Kruppke	.25	.10	.02

☐	470	Glenn Merkosky	.35	.14	.03
☐	471	Dennis Holland	.25	.10	.02
☐	472	Chris McRae	.25	.10	.02
☐	473	Al Conroy	.50	.20	.05
☐	474	Yves Racine	.75	.30	.07
☐	475	Jim Nill P/CO	.35	.14	.03
☐	476	Barry Melrose CO	1.00	.40	.10
☐	477	Bob Wilkie	.50	.20	.05
☐	478	Guy Dupuis	.25	.10	.02
☐	479	Doug Houda	.35	.14	.03
☐	480	Tom Bissett	.25	.10	.02
☐	481	Bill McDougall	.75	.30	.07
☐	482	Glen Goodall	.25	.10	.02
☐	483	Kory Kocur	.50	.20	.05
☐	484	Chris Luongo	.35	.14	.03
☐	485	Serge Anglehart	.25	.10	.02
☐	486	Marc Potvin	.50	.20	.05
☐	487	Stewart Malgunas	.25	.10	.02
☐	488	John Chabot	.50	.20	.05
☐	489	Daniel Shank	.50	.20	.05
☐	490	Randy Hansch	.25	.10	.02
☐	491	Dave Gagnon	.35	.14	.03
☐	492	Scott King	.25	.10	.02
☐	493	Adirondack Red Wings TC	.35	.14	.03
☐	494	Derek Laxdal	.35	.14	.03
☐	495	Swan LeBrun	.25	.10	.02
☐	496	Shawn Bryan	.25	.10	.02
☐	497	Wayne Doucet	.35	.14	.03
☐	498	Rich Kromm	.35	.14	.03
☐	499	Chris Pryor P/CO	.25	.10	.02
☐	500	George Maneluk	.25	.10	.02
☐	501	Brad Lauer	.35	.14	.03
☐	502	Wayne McBean	.50	.20	.05
☐	503	Jeff Finley	.50	.20	.05
☐	504	Jim Culhane	.25	.10	.02
☐	505	Paul Cohen	.25	.10	.02
☐	506	Brent Grieve	.75	.30	.07
☐	507	Kevin Cheveldayoff	.35	.14	.03
☐	508	Dennis Vaske	.50	.20	.05
☐	509	Dave Chyzowski	.35	.14	.03
☐	510	Travis Green	.75	.30	.07
☐	511	Dean Chynoweth	.35	.14	.03
☐	512	Rob DiMaio	.50	.20	.05
☐	513	Paul Guay	.35	.14	.03
☐	514	Capital District Islanders TC	.35	.14	.03
☐	515	Rick Knickle	1.00	.40	.10
☐	516	Curtis Hunt	.25	.10	.02
☐	517	Bruce Racine	.35	.14	.03
☐	518	Yves Heroux	.35	.14	.03
☐	519	Joe Stefan	.25	.10	.02
☐	520	Torrie Robertson	.50	.20	.05
☐	521	Nick Beaulieu	.35	.14	.03
☐	522	Dave Richter	.50	.20	.05
☐	523	Jeff Waver	.25	.10	.02
☐	524	Gordon Paddock	.25	.10	.02
☐	525	Darryl Noren	.25	.10	.02
☐	526	Byron Lomow	.25	.10	.02
☐	527	Ivan Matulik	.25	.10	.02
☐	528	Dan Woodley	.25	.10	.02
☐	529	Dale Henry	.35	.14	.03
☐	530	Soren True	.25	.10	.02
☐	531	Stuart True	.25	.10	.02
☐	532	Rob MacInnis	.25	.10	.02
☐	533	Vern Smith	.25	.10	.02
☐	534	Paul Laus	.35	.14	.03
☐	535	Albany Choppers TC	.35	.14	.03
☐	536	Robin Bawa	.25	.10	.02
☐	537	Steven Fletcher	.25	.10	.02
☐	538	Lonnie Loach	.50	.20	.05
☐	539	Al Sims CO	.35	.14	.03
☐	540	Colin Chin	.35	.14	.03
☐	541	Bruce Boudreau P/CO	.35	.14	.03
☐	542	Bob Lakso	.25	.10	.02
☐	543	John Anderson	.35	.14	.03
☐	544	Kevin Kaminski	.35	.14	.03
☐	545	Bruce Major	.25	.10	.02
☐	546	Stephane Brochu	.25	.10	.02
☐	547	Peter Hankinson	.25	.10	.02
☐	548	Carey Lucyk	.25	.10	.02
☐	549	Tom Karalis	.25	.10	.02
☐	550	Bob Jay	.35	.14	.03
☐	551	Mike Butters	.25	.10	.02
☐	552	Brian McKee	.25	.10	.02
☐	553	Ray LeBlanc	.75	.30	.07
☐	554	Tom Draper	.75	.30	.07
☐	555	Steve Laurin	.25	.10	.02
☐	556	Fort Wayne Komets TC	.35	.14	.03
☐	557	Sergei Starikov	.50	.20	.05
☐	558	Claude Vilgrain	.50	.20	.05
☐	559	Jeff Sharples	.50	.20	.05
☐	560	Bob Woods	.25	.10	.02
☐	561	Perry Anderson	.35	.14	.03
☐	562	Brennan Maley	.25	.10	.02
☐	563	Mike Posma	.25	.10	.02
☐	564	Tom McVie GM/CO	.35	.14	.03
☐	565	Chris Palmer	.25	.10	.02
☐	566	Bill Huard	.50	.20	.05
☐	567	Marc Laniel	.25	.10	.02
☐	568	Neil Brady	.35	.14	.03
☐	569	Jason Simon	.50	.20	.05
☐	570	Kevin Todd	.75	.30	.07
☐	571	Jeff Madill	.50	.20	.05
☐	572	Jeff Christian	.35	.14	.03
☐	573	Todd Copeland	.25	.10	.02
☐	574	Mike Bodnarchuk	.25	.10	.02
☐	575	Chris Kiene	.25	.10	.02
☐	576	Myles O'Connor	.75	.30	.07
☐	577	Jamie Huscroft	.50	.20	.05
☐	578	Mark Romaine	.25	.10	.02
☐	579	Rollie Melanson	.50	.20	.05
☐	580	Utica Devils Team	.35	.14	.03
☐	581	Utica Devils TC	.35	.14	.03
☐	582	Ron Handy	.25	.10	.02
☐	583	Cam Plante	.25	.10	.02
☐	584	Lee Giffin	.50	.20	.05
☐	585	Jim Latos	.25	.10	.02
☐	586	Stu Kulak	.50	.20	.05
☐	587	Claude Julien	.25	.10	.02
☐	588	Rick Barkovich	.25	.10	.02
☐	589	Randy Exelby	.35	.14	.03
☐	590	Mark Vichorek	.25	.10	.02
☐	591	Darin Smith	.25	.10	.02
☐	592	Mike Kelfer	.25	.10	.02
☐	593	Andy Akervik	.25	.10	.02
☐	594	Mike Hiltner	.25	.10	.02
☐	595	Kevin Sullivan	.25	.10	.02
☐	596	Troy Frederick	.25	.10	.02
☐	597	Claudio Scremin	.35	.14	.03
☐	598	Kurt Semandel	.25	.10	.02
☐	599	Mike Colman	.25	.10	.02
☐	600	Jeff Odgers	.50	.20	.05
☐	601	Wade Flaherty	.35	.14	.03
☐	602	Kansas City Blades TC	.35	.14	.03
☐	603	Marc Bureau	.50	.20	.05
☐	604	Darryl Olsen	.25	.10	.02
☐	605	Rick Lessard	.35	.14	.03
☐	606	Kevin Grant	.25	.10	.02
☐	607	Rich Chernomaz	.25	.10	.02
☐	608	Randy Bucyk	.25	.10	.02
☐	609	Wayne Crowley	.25	.10	.02
☐	610	Ken Sabourin	.35	.14	.03
☐	611	Bob Francis CO	.25	.10	.02
☐	612	Jamie Hislop CO	.35	.14	.03
☐	613	Kevan Melrose	.25	.10	.02
☐	614	Scott McCrady	.25	.10	.02
☐	615	Corey Lyons	.25	.10	.02
☐	616	Martin Simard	.50	.20	.05
☐	617	C.J. Young	.50	.20	.05
☐	618	Mark Osiecki	.50	.20	.05
☐	619	Bryan Deasley	.25	.10	.02
☐	620	Kerry Clark	.35	.14	.03
☐	621	Paul Kruse	.35	.14	.03
☐	622	Darren Banks	.35	.14	.03
☐	623	Richard Zemlak	.50	.20	.05
☐	624	Todd Harkins	.25	.10	.02
☐	625	Warren Sharples	.35	.14	.03
☐	626	Andrew McKim	.50	.20	.05
☐	627	Steve Guenette	.50	.20	.05
☐	628	Salt Lake City Golden Eagles TC	.35	.14	.03

1991-92 ProCards AHL/CHL/IHL

This 620-card set was produced by ProCards and measures 2 1/2" by 3 1/2". Fronts feature a posed color photo enclosed by a white border. The player's name is in black within a gold bar at the top and the team name appears beneath in a yellow bar. The photo appears in a red and black speckled "frame" enclosed by a small blue border. The respective league logo (American Hockey League, Colonial Hockey League, or International Hockey League) appears in the lower right corner. The horizontal backs carry biographical and statistical information on a pale yellow background enclosed with blue and white borders. The cards are numbered on the back and checklisted below according to

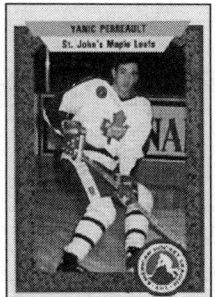
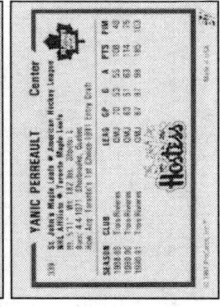

teams as follows: Rochester Americans (1-24), Peoria Rivermen (25-47), Maine Mariners (48-69), Fredericton Canadiens (70-92), Springfield Indians (93-117), Adirondack Red Wings (118-142), Kalamazoo Wings (143-163), Moncton Hawks (164-189), Binghamton Rangers (190-214), Cape Breton Oilers (215-238), Fort Wayne Komets (239-262), Hershey Bears (263-287), Muskegon Lumberjacks (288-310), San Diego Gulls (311-334), St. John's Maple Leafs (335-359), New Haven Nighthawks (360-383), Phoenix Roadrunners (384-407), Utica Devils (408-428), Flint Bulldogs of the Colonial Hockey League (429-451), Capital District Islanders (452-476), Indianapolis Ice (477-504), Kansas City Blades (505-527), Halifax Citadels (528-546), Baltimore Skipjacks (547-573), Salt Lake City Golden Eagles (574-594), and Milwaukee Admirals (595-620). Although the team sets were originally sold with a suggested retail price of 4.00 per team set and packaged individually, they are listed below as one giant set.

	MINT	EXC	G-VG
COMPLETE SET (620)	110.00	45.00	11.00
COMMON PLAYER (1-620)	.25	.10	.02

#	Player	MINT	EXC	G-VG
1	Bill Houlder	.50	.20	.05
2	Brian Curran	.35	.14	.03
3	Dan Frawley	.35	.14	.03
4	Darcy Loewen	.50	.20	.05
5	Jiri Sejba	.35	.14	.03
6	Lindy Ruff	.35	.14	.03
7	Chris Snell	.35	.14	.03
8	Bob Corkum	.75	.30	.07
9	Dave Baseggio	.25	.10	.02
10	Sean O'Donnell	.25	.10	.02
11	Brad Rubachuk	.25	.10	.02
12	Peter Ciavaglia	.35	.14	.03
13	Joel Savage	.25	.10	.02
14	Jason Winch	.25	.10	.02
15	Steve Ludzik	.35	.14	.03
16	Don McSween	.35	.14	.03
17	David DaVita	.25	.10	.02
18	Greg Brown	.35	.14	.03
19	David Littman	.35	.14	.03
20	Tom Draper	.75	.30	.07
21	Jody Gage	.75	.30	.07
22	Terry Martin	.25	.10	.02
23	Don Lever	.35	.14	.03
24	Rochester Checklist	.35	.14	.03
25	Jason Marshall	.75	.30	.07
26	Michel Mongeau	.75	.30	.07
27	Derek Frenette	.25	.10	.02
28	Kevin Miehm	.50	.20	.05
29	Guy Hebert	1.50	.60	.15
30	Greg Poss	.25	.10	.02
31	Dave Mackey	.35	.14	.03
32	Dan Fowler	.25	.10	.02
33	Mark Bassen	.35	.14	.03
34	Yves Heroux	.35	.14	.03
35	Harold Snepsts	1.00	.40	.10
36	Bruce Shoebottom	.50	.20	.05
37	Jaan Luik	.25	.10	.02
38	Alain Raymond	.25	.10	.02
39	Kyle Reeves	.25	.10	.02
40	Brian McKee	.25	.10	.02
41	Steve Tuttle	.35	.14	.03
42	Rob Tustian	.25	.10	.02
43	Richard Pion	.35	.14	.03
44	Joe Hawley	.25	.10	.02
45	Brian Pellerin	.25	.10	.02
46	Jason Ruff	.35	.14	.03
47	Rivermen Checklist	.35	.14	.03
48	Wes Walz	.50	.20	.05
49	Steve Bancroft	.25	.10	.02
50	John Blue	.75	.30	.07
51	Rick Allain	.25	.10	.02
52	Mike Walsh	.35	.14	.03
53	Dave Thomlinson	.35	.14	.03
54	Dennis Smith	.25	.10	.02
55	Jack Capuano	.35	.14	.03
56	Mike Rossetti	.25	.10	.02
57	Petr Prajsler	.35	.14	.03
58	Matt Glennon	.25	.10	.02
59	John Byce	.35	.14	.03
60	Howie Rosenblatt	.35	.14	.03
61	Brad Tiley	.25	.10	.02
62	Lou Crawford	.25	.10	.02
63	Matt Hervey	.35	.14	.03
64	Peter Douris	.35	.14	.03
65	Jeff Lazaro	.35	.14	.03
66	David Reid	.50	.20	.05
67	E.J. McGuire	.25	.10	.02
68	Frank Bathe	.25	.10	.02
69	Maine Checklist	.25	.10	.02
70	Paul DiPietro	1.00	.40	.10
71	Darcy Simon	.25	.10	.02
72	Patrick Lebeau	.50	.20	.05
73	Gilbert Dionne	1.25	.50	.12
74	John Ferguson	.35	.14	.03
75	Norman Desjardins	.25	.10	.02
76	Luc Gauthier	.35	.14	.03
77	Jean-Claude Bergeron	.50	.20	.05
78	Andre Racicot	.75	.30	.07
79	Steve Veilleux	.25	.10	.02
80	Patrice Brisebois	1.00	.40	.10
81	Tom Sagissor	.25	.10	.02
82	Lindsay Vallis	.25	.10	.02
83	Steve Larouche	.25	.10	.02
84	Sean Hill	1.00	.40	.10
85	Jesse Belanger	1.00	.40	.10
86	Stephane J.G. Richer	.35	.14	.03
	Defenseman			
87	Marc Labelle	.25	.10	.02
88	Pierre Sevigny	.50	.20	.05
89	Eric Charron	.35	.14	.03
90	Ed Ronan	.75	.30	.07
91	Paulin Bordeleau	.35	.14	.03
92	Fredrickson Checklist	.35	.14	.03
93	Daryl Reaugh	.50	.20	.05
94	Jergus Baca	.35	.14	.03
95	Karl Johnston	.25	.10	.02
96	Shawn Evans	.25	.10	.02
97	Scott Humeniuk	.25	.10	.02
98	Cam Brauer	.25	.10	.02
99	Scott Eichstadt	.25	.10	.02
100	Paul Cyr	.50	.20	.05
101	James Black	.50	.20	.05
102	Chris Govedaris	.35	.14	.03
103	Joe Day	.35	.14	.03
104	Chris Tancill	.50	.20	.05
105	Kerry Russell	.35	.14	.03
106	Denis Chalifoux	.25	.10	.02
107	Blair Atcheynum	.35	.14	.03
108	John Stevens	.25	.10	.02
109	Brian Chapman	.25	.10	.02
110	Chris Bright	.25	.10	.02
111	Jim Burke	.25	.10	.02
112	Scott Daniels	.25	.10	.02
113	Kelly Ens	.25	.10	.02
114	Mike Tomlak	.35	.14	.03
115	Mario Gosselin	.50	.20	.05
116	Jay Leach	.25	.10	.02
117	Springfield Checklist	.35	.14	.03
118	Allan Bester	.50	.20	.05
119	Daniel Shank	.50	.20	.05
120	Lonnie Loach	.50	.20	.05
121	Mark Reimer	.35	.14	.03
122	Kirk Tomlinson	.25	.10	.02
123	Stewart Malgunas	.25	.10	.02
124	Serge Anglehart	.25	.10	.02
125	Chris Luongo	.35	.14	.03
126	Keith Primeau	1.50	.60	.15
127	Ken Quinney	.35	.14	.03
128	Dave Flanagan	.25	.10	.02
129	Pete Stauber	.25	.10	.02
130	Mike Sillinger	.75	.30	.07
131	Micah Aivazoff	.50	.20	.05
132	Gary Schuchuk	.35	.14	.03
133	Bill McDougall	.50	.20	.05
134	Sheldon Kennedy	.75	.30	.07
135	Derek Mayer	.25	.10	.02

☐	136	Darin Bannister	.25	.10	.02	☐	229	Peter Soberlak	.25	.10	.02
☐	137	Guy Dupuis	.25	.10	.02	☐	230	Martin Rucinsky	.75	.30	.07
☐	138	Gord Kruppke	.25	.10	.02	☐	231	Tomas Kapusta	.35	.14	.03
☐	139	Jason York	.35	.14	.03	☐	232	Dean Antos	.25	.10	.02
☐	140	Barry Melrose	1.00	.40	.10	☐	233	Craig Fisher	.35	.14	.03
☐	141	Glenn Merkosky	.35	.14	.03	☐	234	Tomas Srsen	.25	.10	.02
☐	142	Adirondack Checklist	.35	.14	.03	☐	235	Don McAdam	.25	.10	.02
☐	143	Larry Dyck	.35	.14	.03	☐	236	Norm Ferguson	.25	.10	.02
☐	144	Roy Mitchell	.25	.10	.02	☐	237	Coaching Staff	.25	.10	.02
☐	145	Greg Spenrath	.25	.10	.02	☐	238	Cape Breton Checklist	.35	.14	.03
☐	146	Steve Herniman	.25	.10	.02	☐	239	Peter Hankinson	.25	.10	.02
☐	147	Brad Berry	.35	.14	.03	☐	240	Chris McRae	.25	.10	.02
☐	148	Jim Nesich	.25	.10	.02	☐	241	Craig Martin	.25	.10	.02
☐	149	Tim Lenardon	.25	.10	.02	☐	242	Carey Lucyk	.25	.10	.02
☐	150	Steve Guenette	.50	.20	.05	☐	243	Jean-Marc Richard	.25	.10	.02
☐	151	Paul Jerrard	.25	.10	.02	☐	244	Grant Richison	.25	.10	.02
☐	152	Cal McGowan	.35	.14	.03	☐	245	Mark Turner	.25	.10	.02
☐	153	Scott Robinson	.25	.10	.02	☐	246	Todd Flichel	.25	.10	.02
☐	154	Mitch Messier	.35	.14	.03	☐	247	Scott Shaunessy	.25	.10	.02
☐	155	Tony Joseph	.25	.10	.02	☐	248	Darin Smith	.25	.10	.02
☐	156	Steve Maltais	.35	.14	.03	☐	249	Ian Boyce	.25	.10	.02
☐	157	Steve Gotaas	.25	.10	.02	☐	250	Colin Chin	.35	.14	.03
☐	158	Doug Barrault	.35	.14	.03	☐	251	Bob Jones	.25	.10	.02
☐	159	Dave Moylan	.25	.10	.02	☐	252	Bob Jay	.35	.14	.03
☐	160	Mario Thyer	.35	.14	.03	☐	253	Kelly Hurd	.25	.10	.02
☐	161	Bob Hoffmeyer	.25	.10	.02	☐	254	Scott Gruhl	.35	.14	.03
☐	162	Wade Dawson	.25	.10	.02	☐	255	Kory Kocur	.35	.14	.03
☐	163	Wings Checklist	.35	.14	.03	☐	256	Steven Fletcher	.25	.10	.02
☐	164	Rob Murray	.35	.14	.03	☐	257	Bob Lakso	.35	.14	.03
☐	165	Chris Kiene	.25	.10	.02	☐	258	Dusty Imoo	.35	.14	.03
☐	166	Lee Davidson	.25	.10	.02	☐	259	Mike O'Neill	.75	.30	.07
☐	167	Rudy Poeschek	.50	.20	.05	☐	260	Bruce Boudreau	.35	.14	.03
☐	168	Kent Paynter	.25	.10	.02	☐	261	Al Sims	.35	.14	.03
☐	169	John LeBlanc	.35	.14	.03	☐	262	Komets Checklist	.35	.14	.03
☐	170	Dallas Eakins	.25	.10	.02	☐	263	Ray Letourneau	.25	.10	.02
☐	171	Claude Julien	.25	.10	.02	☐	264	Marc D'Amour	.50	.20	.05
☐	172	Bob Joyce	.35	.14	.03	☐	265	Dominic Roussel	3.00	1.20	.30
☐	173	Derek Langille	.25	.10	.02	☐	266	Bill Armstrong (LW)	.35	.14	.03
☐	174	Rob Cowie	.35	.14	.03	☐	267	Al Conroy	.50	.20	.05
☐	175	Warren Rychel	.75	.30	.07	☐	268	Dale Kushner	.35	.14	.03
☐	176	Tom Karalis	.25	.10	.02	☐	269	Toni Porkka	.25	.10	.02
☐	177	Kris Draper	.75	.30	.07	☐	270	Mike Stothers	.25	.10	.02
☐	178	Ken Gernander	.25	.10	.02	☐	271	Darren Rumble	.50	.20	.05
☐	179	Tod Hartje	.35	.14	.03	☐	272	Reid Simpson	.25	.10	.02
☐	180	Sean Gauthier	.25	.10	.02	☐	273	Claude Boivin	.50	.20	.05
☐	181	Tyler Larter	.25	.10	.02	☐	274	Len Barrie	.50	.20	.05
☐	182	Scott Levins	.75	.30	.07	☐	275	Chris Jensen	.35	.14	.03
☐	183	Jason Cirone	.25	.10	.02	☐	276	Pat Murray	.35	.14	.03
☐	184	Mark Kumpel	.35	.14	.03	☐	277	Eric Dandenault	.25	.10	.02
☐	185	Rick Tabaracci	1.00	.40	.10	☐	278	Rod Dallman	.25	.10	.02
☐	186	Luciano Borsato	.75	.30	.07	☐	279	Mark Freer	.35	.14	.03
☐	187	Dave Farrish	.35	.14	.03	☐	280	Bill Armstrong (D)	.35	.14	.03
☐	188	Dave Prior	.25	.10	.02	☐	281	Tim Tookey	.35	.14	.03
☐	189	Moncton Checklist	.35	.14	.03	☐	282	Jamie Cooke	.25	.10	.02
☐	190	Peter Fiorentino	.25	.10	.02	☐	283	Dave Fenyves	.35	.14	.03
☐	191	Glen Goodall	.25	.10	.02	☐	284	Steve Morrow	.25	.10	.02
☐	192	John Mokosak	.25	.10	.02	☐	285	Martin Hostak	.35	.14	.03
☐	193	Sam St.Laurent	.50	.20	.05	☐	286	Mike Eaves	.25	.10	.02
☐	194	Daniel Lacroix	.50	.20	.05	☐	287	Hershey Checklist	.35	.14	.03
☐	195	Guy Larose	.50	.20	.05	☐	288	Dave Michayluk	.35	.14	.03
☐	196	Mike Hurlbut	.50	.20	.05	☐	289	Glenn Mulvenna	.35	.14	.03
☐	197	Peter Laviolette	.25	.10	.02	☐	290	Jean Blouin	.25	.10	.02
☐	198	Eric Bennett	.25	.10	.02	☐	291	Jock Callander	.50	.20	.05
☐	199	Steven King	.75	.30	.07	☐	292	Perry Ganchar	.25	.10	.02
☐	200	Boris Rousson	.25	.10	.02	☐	293	Paul Laus	.35	.14	.03
☐	201	Jody Hull	.50	.20	.05	☐	294	Mark Major	.25	.10	.02
☐	202	Shaun Sabol	.25	.10	.02	☐	295	Bruce Racine	.35	.14	.03
☐	203	Joe Paterson	.25	.10	.02	☐	296	Daniel Gauthier	.25	.10	.02
☐	204	Rob Zamuner	.75	.30	.07	☐	297	Mike Needham	.75	.30	.07
☐	205	Don Biggs	.35	.14	.03	☐	298	Jeff Daniels	.50	.20	.05
☐	206	Chris Cichocki	.35	.14	.03	☐	299	Sandy Smith	.25	.10	.02
☐	207	Ross Fitzpatrick	.25	.10	.02	☐	300	Gilbert Delorme	.50	.20	.05
☐	208	Mark LaForest	.35	.14	.03	☐	301	Rob Dopson	.50	.20	.05
☐	209	Brian McReynolds	.35	.14	.03	☐	302	Eric Brule	.25	.10	.02
☐	210	Jeff Bloemberg	.35	.14	.03	☐	303	Alain Morissette	.25	.10	.02
☐	211	Kord Cernich	.25	.10	.02	☐	304	Paul Dyck	.25	.10	.02
☐	212	Ron Smith	.25	.10	.02	☐	305	Jason Smart	.25	.10	.02
☐	213	Al Hill	.35	.14	.03	☐	306	Gord Dineen	.35	.14	.03
☐	214	Binghamton Checklist	.35	.14	.03	☐	307	Todd Nelson	.35	.14	.03
☐	215	Francois Leroux	.35	.14	.03	☐	308	Jamie Heward	.25	.10	.02
☐	216	Marc Laforge	.25	.10	.02	☐	309	Paul Russell	.25	.10	.02
☐	217	Max Middendorf	.35	.14	.03	☐	310	Lumberjack Checklist	.35	.14	.03
☐	218	Shjon Podein	.50	.20	.05	☐	311	Soren True	.25	.10	.02
☐	219	Jason Soules	.35	.14	.03	☐	312	Murray Duval	.25	.10	.02
☐	220	Collin Bauer	.25	.10	.02	☐	313	Dmitri Kvartalnov	1.00	.40	.10
☐	221	Shaun Van Allen	.75	.30	.07	☐	314	Larry Floyd	.25	.10	.02
☐	222	Eldon Reddick	1.00	.40	.10	☐	315	Alan Legett	.25	.10	.02
☐	223	Eugeny Belosheiken	.75	.30	.07	☐	316	Alan Hepple	.25	.10	.02
☐	224	David Haas	.25	.10	.02	☐	317	Ron Duguay	.50	.20	.05
☐	225	Norm Foster	.35	.14	.03	☐	318	Len Hachborn	.35	.14	.03
☐	226	Greg Hawgood	.50	.20	.05	☐	319	Steve Martinson	.35	.14	.03
☐	227	Steven Rice	1.00	.40	.10	☐	320	Rick Knickle	.75	.30	.07
☐	228	Dan Currie	.50	.20	.05	☐	321	Darcy Norton	.25	.10	.02

#	Player				#	Player			
322	Keith Gretzky	1.50	.60	.15	415	Jeff Christian	.25	.10	.02
323	Brian Straub	.25	.10	.02	416	Corey Schwab	.35	.14	.03
324	Denny Lambert	.35	.14	.03	417	Kevin Dean	.25	.10	.02
325	Jason Prosofsky	.35	.14	.03	418	Todd Copeland	.25	.10	.02
326	Bruce Hoffort	.35	.14	.03	419	Mike Bodnarchuk	.25	.10	.02
327	Sergei Starikov	.35	.14	.03	420	Jason Miller	.25	.10	.02
328	Dave Korol	.25	.10	.02	421	Chad Erickson	.35	.14	.03
329	Robbie Nichols	.25	.10	.02	422	David Craievich	.25	.10	.02
330	Kord Cernich	.25	.10	.02	423	Jim Dowd	.75	.30	.07
331	Brent Sapergia	.35	.14	.03	424	Jamie Huscroft	.50	.20	.05
332	Don Waddell	.25	.10	.02	425	Myles O'Connor	.50	.20	.05
333	Charlie Simmer	.35	.14	.03	426	Jon Morris	.50	.20	.05
334	San Diego Checklist	.35	.14	.03	427	Valeri Zelepukin	2.00	.80	.20
335	Rob Mendel	.25	.10	.02	428	Utica Checklist	.25	.10	.02
336	Curtis Hunt	.25	.10	.02	429	Brad Beck	.25	.10	.02
337	Jeff Serowik	.35	.14	.03	430	Brett MacDonald	.25	.10	.02
338	Bruce Bell	.25	.10	.02	431	Jacques Mailhot	.25	.10	.02
339	Yanic Perreault	1.50	.60	.15	432	Francois Ouellette	.25	.10	.02
340	Brad Aitken	.25	.10	.02	433	Ron Kinghorn	.25	.10	.02
341	Keith Osborne	.25	.10	.02	434	Dennis Miller	.25	.10	.02
342	Todd Hawkins	.25	.10	.02	435	Darren Miciak	.25	.10	.02
343	Andrew McKim	.35	.14	.03	436	Tom Sasso	.25	.10	.02
344	Kevin McClelland	.35	.14	.03	437	Peter Corbett	.25	.10	.02
345	Mike Stevens	.35	.14	.03	438	Brian Horan	.25	.10	.02
346	Dave Tomlinson	.35	.14	.03	439	John Messuri	.25	.10	.02
347	Kevin Maguire	.35	.14	.03	440	E.J. Sauer	.25	.10	.02
348	Mike MacWilliams	.25	.10	.02	441	Tom Mutch	.25	.10	.02
349	Greg Walters	.25	.10	.02	442	Jason Simon	.50	.20	.05
350	Guy Lehoux	.25	.10	.02	443	Steve Sullivan	.25	.10	.02
351	Todd Gillingham	.25	.10	.02	444	Scott Allen	.25	.10	.02
352	Len Essau	.25	.10	.02	445	Stephane Brochu	.35	.14	.03
353	Greg Johnston	.35	.14	.03	446	Ken Spangler	.35	.14	.03
354	Felix Potvin	10.00	4.00	1.00	447	Lee Odelein	.25	.10	.02
355	Damian Rhodes	1.00	.40	.10	448	Antti Autere	.25	.10	.02
356	Joel Quenneville	.25	.10	.02	449	John Reid	.25	.10	.02
357	Marc Crawford	.35	.14	.03	450	Skip Probst CO	.25	.10	.02
358	Mike Eastwood	.50	.20	.05	451	Flint Checklist	.35	.14	.03
359	St.Johns Checklist	.35	.14	.03	452	Dean Ewen	.25	.10	.02
360	Lou Franceschetti	.35	.14	.03	453	Brent Grieve	.75	.30	.07
361	John Murray Anderson	.25	.10	.02	454	Jim Culhane	.25	.10	.02
362	Scott Schneider	.25	.10	.02	455	Joni Lehto	.25	.10	.02
363	Jerome Bechard	.25	.10	.02	456	Graeme Townshend	.50	.20	.05
364	Mario Doyon	.35	.14	.03	457	Danny Lorenz	.75	.30	.07
365	Jeff Jackson	.35	.14	.03	458	Phil Huber	.25	.10	.02
366	John Tanner	.75	.30	.07	459	Kevin Cheveldayoff	.35	.14	.03
367	Al Tuer	.25	.10	.02	460	Dennis Vaske	.35	.14	.03
368	Paul Willett	.25	.10	.02	461	Wayne Doucet	.25	.10	.02
369	Darryl Williams	.25	.10	.02	462	Greg Parks	.35	.14	.03
370	George Maneluk	.25	.10	.02	463	Dean Chynoweth	.25	.10	.02
371	Eric Ricard	.25	.10	.02	464	Lee Giffin	.50	.20	.05
372	Trevor Stienburg	.25	.10	.02	465	Richard Kromm	.35	.14	.03
373	Jerry Tarrant	.25	.10	.02	466	Derek Laxdal	.50	.20	.05
374	Michael McEwen	.50	.20	.05	467	Travis Green	.75	.30	.07
375	Brian Dobbin	.35	.14	.03	468	Iain Fraser	1.00	.40	.10
376	David Latta	.25	.10	.02	469	Rick Hayward	.35	.14	.03
377	Jim Sprott	.25	.10	.02	470	Jeff Finley	.35	.14	.03
378	Trevor Pochipinski	.25	.10	.02	471	Dave Chyzowski	.35	.14	.03
379	Stan Drulia	.35	.14	.03	472	Mark Fitzpatrick	1.00	.40	.10
380	Kent Hulst	.25	.10	.02	473	Hubie McDonough	.50	.20	.05
381	Brad Turner	.25	.10	.02	474	Sean LeBrun	.25	.10	.02
382	Doug Carpenter	.35	.14	.03	475	Chris Pryor	.25	.10	.02
383	New Haven Checklist	.35	.14	.03	476	Capital District CL	.35	.14	.03
384	Bob Berg	.25	.10	.02	477	Jeff Sirkka	.25	.10	.02
385	Steve Jaques	.25	.10	.02	478	Owen Lessard	.25	.10	.02
386	Chris Norton	.25	.10	.02	479	Jim Playfair	.25	.10	.02
387	Vern Smith	.25	.10	.02	480	Dan Vincelette	.35	.14	.03
388	Kevin MacDonald	.25	.10	.02	481	Tracey Egeland	.25	.10	.02
389	Ross Wilson	.25	.10	.02	482	Shawn Byram	.25	.10	.02
390	Shawn McCosh	.25	.10	.02	483	Trevor Dam	.25	.10	.02
391	Mike Vukonich	.25	.10	.02	484	Martin Desjardins	.25	.10	.02
392	Marc Saumier	.25	.10	.02	485	Milan Tichy	.50	.20	.05
393	Mike Ruark	.25	.10	.02	486	Cam Russell	.50	.20	.05
394	Kris Miller	.25	.10	.02	487	Mike Speer	.25	.10	.02
395	Tim Breslin	.25	.10	.02	488	Sean Williams	.25	.10	.02
396	Paul Holden	.25	.10	.02	489	Paul Gillis	.35	.14	.03
397	Jeff Rohlicek	.25	.10	.02	490	Brad Lauer	.35	.14	.03
398	Kyosti Karjalainen	.35	.14	.03	491	Trent Yawney	.50	.20	.05
399	David Goverde	.35	.14	.03	492	Craig Woodcroft	.35	.14	.03
400	John Van Kessel	.25	.10	.02	493	Justin LaFayette	.25	.10	.02
401	Sean Whyte	.25	.10	.02	494	Robb Conn	.25	.10	.02
402	Brent Thompson	.75	.30	.07	495	Frantisek Kucera	.50	.20	.05
403	Darryl Gilmour	.35	.14	.03	496	Mike Peluso	.75	.30	.07
404	Scott Bjugstad	.35	.14	.03	497	Roch Belley	.50	.20	.05
405	Ralph Backstrom	.35	.14	.03	498	Ryan McGill	.35	.14	.03
406	Rick Kozuback	.25	.10	.02	499	Kerry Toporowski	.35	.14	.03
407	Roadrunner Checklist	.35	.14	.03	500	Dominik Hasek	3.00	1.20	.30
408	Brent Severyn	.75	.30	.07	501	Adam Bennett	.35	.14	.03
409	Dean Malkoc	.25	.10	.02	502	Ray LeBlanc	.75	.30	.07
410	Matt Ruchty	.25	.10	.02	503	John Marks	.35	.14	.03
411	Jarrod Skalde	.75	.30	.07	504	Ice Checklist	.35	.14	.03
412	Brian Sullivan	.25	.10	.02	505	Mikhail Kravets	.35	.14	.03
413	Ben Hankinson	.50	.20	.05	506	Gary Emmons	.25	.10	.02
414	Bill Huard	.50	.20	.05	507	Ed Courtenay	.50	.20	.05

☐ 508	Claudio Scremin	.25	.10	.02
☐ 509	Jarmo Myllys	.50	.20	.05
☐ 510	Mike Coleman	.25	.10	.02
☐ 511	Kevin Evans	.35	.14	.03
☐ 512	Troy Frederick	.25	.10	.02
☐ 513	Ron Handy	.25	.10	.02
☐ 514	Murray Garbutt	.25	.10	.02
☐ 515	Gordon Frantti	.25	.10	.02
☐ 516	Dale Craigwell	.75	.30	.07
☐ 517	Wade Flaherty	.35	.14	.03
☐ 518	Dean Kolstad	.35	.14	.03
☐ 519	Rick Lessard	.50	.20	.05
☐ 520	Craig Coxe	.35	.14	.03
☐ 521	Jeff Madill	.35	.14	.03
☐ 522	Peter Lappin	.35	.14	.03
☐ 523	Duane Joyce	.25	.10	.02
☐ 524	Larry DePalma	.35	.14	.03
☐ 525	Pat MacLeod	.50	.20	.05
☐ 526	Andy Akervik	.25	.10	.02
☐ 527	Blades Checklist	.35	.14	.03
☐ 528	Mike Dagenais	.25	.10	.02
☐ 529	Gerald Bzdel	.25	.10	.02
☐ 530	Stephane Fiset	1.00	.40	.10
☐ 531	David Espe	.25	.10	.02
☐ 532	Patrick Lebrecque	.25	.10	.02
☐ 533	Niclas Andersson	.35	.14	.03
☐ 534	Jon Klemm	.25	.10	.02
☐ 535	Denis Chasse	.35	.14	.03
☐ 536	Stephane Charbonneau	.25	.10	.02
☐ 537	Ivan Matulik	.25	.10	.02
☐ 538	Serge Roberge	.25	.10	.02
☐ 539	Daniel Dore	.25	.10	.02
☐ 540	Sergei Kharin	.35	.14	.03
☐ 541	Jamie Baker	.50	.20	.05
☐ 542	Ken McRae	.35	.14	.03
☐ 543	David Marcinyshyn	.35	.14	.03
☐ 544	Clement Jodoin	.25	.10	.02
☐ 545	Dean Hopkins	.25	.10	.02
☐ 546	Checklist	.35	.14	.03
☐ 547	Jeff Greenlaw	.25	.10	.02
☐ 548	Byron Dafoe	.50	.20	.05
☐ 549	Jim Hrivnak	1.00	.40	.10
☐ 550	Olaf Kolzig	.75	.30	.07
☐ 551	John Purves	.50	.20	.05
☐ 552	Bobby Reynolds	.25	.10	.02
☐ 553	Simon Wheeldon	.35	.14	.03
☐ 554	Jim Mathieson	.25	.10	.02
☐ 555	Trevor Halverson	.50	.20	.05
☐ 556	Steve Seftel	.25	.10	.02
☐ 557	Ken Lovsin	.35	.14	.03
☐ 558	Victor Gervais	.25	.10	.02
☐ 559	Steve Martell	.35	.14	.03
☐ 560	Chris Clarke	.25	.10	.02
☐ 561	Brent Hughes	.50	.20	.05
☐ 562	Jiri Vykoukal	.25	.10	.02
☐ 563	Tim Taylor	.25	.10	.02
☐ 564	Richie Walcott	.25	.10	.02
☐ 565	Harry Mews	.25	.10	.02
☐ 566	Craig Duncanson	.35	.14	.03
☐ 567	Todd Hlushko	.50	.20	.05
☐ 568	Mark Ferner	.35	.14	.03
☐ 569	Bobby Babcock	.35	.14	.03
☐ 570	Reggie Savage	1.00	.40	.10
☐ 571	Rob Laird	.25	.10	.02
☐ 572	Barry Trotz	.25	.10	.02
☐ 573	Baltimore Checklist	.35	.14	.03
☐ 574	Kevan Melrose	.25	.10	.02
☐ 575	Kevin Grant	.25	.10	.02
☐ 576	Kevan Guy	.50	.20	.05
☐ 577	Darryl Olsen	.25	.10	.02
☐ 578	Kevin Worthman	.25	.10	.02
☐ 579	Darren Stolk	.25	.10	.02
☐ 580	Bryan Deasley	.25	.10	.02
☐ 581	Paul Kruse	.50	.20	.05
☐ 582	Darren Banks	.35	.14	.03
☐ 583	Corey Lyons	.25	.10	.02
☐ 584	Kenny Clark	.25	.10	.02
☐ 585	Todd Strueby	.35	.14	.03
☐ 586	Rich Chernomaz	.25	.10	.02
☐ 587	Tim Harris	.25	.10	.02
☐ 588	Shawn Heaphy	.25	.10	.02
☐ 589	Todd Harkins	.35	.14	.03
☐ 590	Richard Zemlak	.50	.20	.05
☐ 591	Warren Sharples	.35	.14	.03
☐ 592	Jason Muzzatti	.50	.20	.05
☐ 593	Dennis Holland	.25	.10	.02
☐ 594	Salt Lake City Checklist	.35	.14	.03
☐ 595	Shawn Antoski	.50	.20	.05
☐ 596	Peter Bakovic	.25	.10	.02
☐ 597	Robin Bawa	.35	.14	.03
☐ 598	Cam Brown	.25	.10	.02
☐ 599	Neil Eisenhut	.35	.14	.03

☐ 600	Jason Herter	.35	.14	.03
☐ 601	Ian Kidd	.25	.10	.02
☐ 602	Troy Neumeier	.25	.10	.02
☐ 603	Carl Valimont	.25	.10	.02
☐ 604	Phil Von Stefenelli	.25	.10	.02
☐ 605	Andrew McBain	.50	.20	.05
☐ 606	Eric Murano	.35	.14	.03
☐ 607	Rob Murphy	.35	.14	.03
☐ 608	Brian Blad	.25	.10	.02
☐ 609	Randy Boyd	.25	.10	.02
☐ 610	Don Gibson	.25	.10	.02
☐ 611	Paul Guay	.35	.14	.03
☐ 612	Jay Mazur	.35	.14	.03
☐ 613	Jeff Larmer	.35	.14	.03
☐ 614	Ladislav Tresl	.25	.10	.02
☐ 615	Dennis Snedden	.25	.10	.02
☐ 616	Corrie D'Alessio	.35	.14	.03
☐ 617	Bob Mason	.35	.14	.03
☐ 618	Jack McIlhargey	.35	.14	.03
☐ 619	Curt Fraser	.25	.10	.02
☐ 620	Admirals Checklist	.35	.14	.03

1992-93 Quebec Int. Pee-Wees

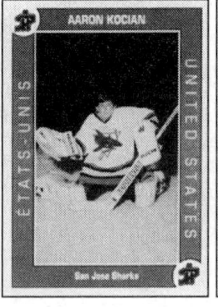 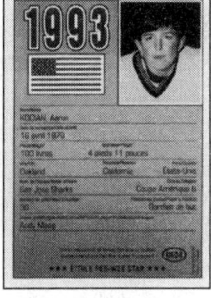

This 1808-card set measures the standard size (2 1/2" by 3 1/2") and features posed, color player photos of Pee-Wee players from international teams at the Quebec International Pee-Wee Tournament. The pictures are framed by a wide stripe that is purple at the top and blends to a pinkish-purple shade toward the bottom. The player's name is printed in white in the purple border above the photo, while the team name is printed below. The player's country is printed on both sides of the photo. The backs have the same purple color scheme and carry a small, close-up photo along with biographical information and the appropriate national flag. The cards are numbered on the back and checklisted below according to teams as follows: Ambassadeurs de la Vallee (1-16), Lakeshore Braves (17-32), Leafs de Verdun (33-48), Sphinx de St-Marc-des-Carrieres (49-63), Eperviers de Mascouche M.L.L. (64-80), National La Presqu'lle (81-97), Caravelles de l'Erable (98-114), Sherbrooke Metropolitain (115-131), Tigres Lac St-Louis Ouest (132-148), Banff Pee-Wee Bears (149-165), Calgary Flames (166-181), Mount Pearl Blades (182-199), L'Excel Centre Mauricie (200-216), Victoriaville (217-235), Les Canotiers de Montmagny (236-252), Harfangs de Beauport (253-270), Ladufo Cote de Beaupre (271-287), Les Seigneurs de Beaubourg (288-304), Charny-Bernieres (305-321), Lac-Megantic Bestar (322-340), Elite Beauce-Amiante (341-373), Beauce-Centre (374-407), Champlain du Richelieu (408-423), Faucons Pointe-Levy (424-440), Les Regents Rive-Sud (441-457), Elans de Charlesbourg (458-474), Toronto Young Nationals (475-489), North York Canadiens (490-505), Halifax Hawks (506-522), Charlevoix (523-541), Petersborough (542-559), Maple Leafs de Toronto (560-575), Smith Falls Bears (576-591), South Shore Kings (592-609), Sharks San Jose (610-

625), Lynnfield Pioneers (626-642), Boston Jr. Braves (643-663), Syracuse Stars (664-682), Boston Jr. Bruins (683-702), Chicago Blackhawks (703-720), New Jersey Devils (721-737), Tampa Bay Lightning (738-756), Pittsburgh Penguins (757-772), Hershey Cubs (773-792), Buffalo Sabres (793-809), Hartford Whalers (810-827), Beverly (828-846), Michigan Nationals (847-865), Minnesota North Star (866-883), St-Louis Blues (884-901), Selects du Nord (910-917), St-Georges (918-934), Lac-Etchemin (935-951), Cascades -- Amos (952-967), Selects de Sainte-Foy (968-984), Royaux de Sainte-Foy (985-1000), Les Epaulards (1001-1020), Pointe-Levy (1021-1037), Seigneurs Des Mille Iles (1038-1054), Bellechasse (1055-1071), Frontenac de Quebec (1072-1088), Cavaliers de Sainte-Foy (1089-1106), Nordiques de Quebec (1107-1123), Sagueneens de Chicoutimi (1124-1140), Edmonton Oilers (1141-1158), Richmond Hill (1159-1175), Oakville (1176-1192), Beresford (1193-1210), North River (1211-1226), Langley Eagles (1227-1242), California Kings (1243-1260), Washington Capitals (1261-1280), New York Rangers (1281-1298), Detroit GPD (1299-1315), Chicago Young Americans (1316-1332), Elites Rive-Nord (1333-1349), Alma (1350-1367), Citadelle de Quebec (1368-1384), Canadiens de Montreal (1385-1401), Toronto Red Wings (1402-1416), Don Mills Flyers (1417-1431), Vancouver Thunderbirds (1432-1462), Toronto Wexford (1463-1480), Pologne (1481-1520), Autriche (1521-1542), Bratislava (1543-1569), Philadelphia Little Flyers (1570-1588), Draveurs de la Mauricie (1589-1604), Vancouver Canucks (1605-1619), Team Zurich Suisse (1620-1640), Aquitains de Bordeaux (1641-1659), Philadelphia Jr. Flyers (1660-1680), Mississauga Senators (1681-1696), Slovaquie (1697-1723), Detroit Red Wings (1724-1764), and Slovenie (1765-1808). Card numbers 1446, 1499, 1570, 1736, 1738, 1741, 1744, 1746, 1747, 1757, 1780, are missing. Card 1758 Donald Pierce is listed as 1757 on the checklist card.

	MINT	EXC	G-VG
COMPLETE SET (1808)	90.00	36.00	9.00
COMMON PLAYER (1-1808)	.08	.03	.01

		MINT	EXC	G-VG
☐ 1	Vincent Dionne	.15	.06	.01
☐ 2	Bryan Ouellet	.08	.03	.01
☐ 3	Simon Gagnon	.08	.03	.01
☐ 4	Jerome Landry	.08	.03	.01
☐ 5	Sylvain Guenette	.08	.03	.01
☐ 6	Francois Paquet	.08	.03	.01
☐ 7	Martin-Benoit Leclerc	.08	.03	.01
☐ 8	Michel Theriault	.08	.03	.01
☐ 9	Frederick Pilote	.08	.03	.01
☐ 10	Dany Doucet	.08	.03	.01
☐ 11	Carl Dancause	.08	.03	.01
☐ 12	Simon Paquet	.08	.03	.01
☐ 13	Kaven McNicoll	.08	.03	.01
☐ 14	David Dupere	.08	.03	.01
☐ 15	Sebastien Caron	.08	.03	.01
☐ 16	Les Ambassadeurs de la Valle (Team photo and CL)	.15	.06	.01
☐ 17	Marc Scheuer	.08	.03	.01
☐ 18	Derek Legault	.08	.03	.01
☐ 19	Valerie Desjardins	.08	.03	.01
☐ 20	Eric Langill	.08	.03	.01
☐ 21	Sean Landry	.08	.03	.01
☐ 22	Jeremy Maher	.08	.03	.01
☐ 23	Stephane White	.08	.03	.01
☐ 24	Martin Dubeau	.08	.03	.01
☐ 25	Francois Duffy	.08	.03	.01
☐ 26	Steven Cote	.08	.03	.01
☐ 27	Mathieu Soulier	.08	.03	.01
☐ 28	Louis Archambault	.08	.03	.01
☐ 29	Robbie Boivin	.08	.03	.01
☐ 30	Wesley Scanzano	.08	.03	.01
☐ 31	Shawn Scanzano	.08	.03	.01
☐ 32	Lakeshore Braves (Team photo and CL)	.15	.06	.01
☐ 33	Eric Fragapane	.08	.03	.01
☐ 34	Francis Gagnier	.08	.03	.01
☐ 35	Jan Marcogliese	.08	.03	.01
☐ 36	Marc-Andre Guay	.08	.03	.01
☐ 37	Maxime Venne	.08	.03	.01
☐ 38	Arduino Patuli	.08	.03	.01
☐ 39	Shean Briffey	.08	.03	.01
☐ 40	Michael Scalzo	.08	.03	.01
☐ 41	Dino Fabrizio	.08	.03	.01
☐ 42	Sebastien Dorval	.08	.03	.01
☐ 43	Marco Painchaud	.08	.03	.01
☐ 44	Marc Simon	.08	.03	.01
☐ 45	Patrick Sagala	.08	.03	.01
☐ 46	Martin Prince	.08	.03	.01
☐ 47	Sean McLean	.08	.03	.01
☐ 48	Leafs de Verdun (Team photo and CL)	.15	.06	.01
☐ 49	Eric Petitclerc	.08	.03	.01
☐ 50	Tommy Tessier	.08	.03	.01
☐ 51	Mathieu Perreault	.08	.03	.01
☐ 52	Eric Trottier	.08	.03	.01
☐ 53	Jean-Francois Garnea	.08	.03	.01
☐ 54	Martin Naud	.08	.03	.01
☐ 55	Steve Durocher	.08	.03	.01
☐ 56	Frederic Boutin	.08	.03	.01
☐ 57	David Matte	.08	.03	.01
☐ 58	Jeremy Soler	.08	.03	.01
☐ 59	Pierre-Olivier Cantin	.08	.03	.01
☐ 60	Remy Marcotte	.08	.03	.01
☐ 61	Jasmin Naud	.08	.03	.01
☐ 62	Jonathan Perron	.08	.03	.01
☐ 63	Sphinx de St-Marc-des-Carrieres (Team photo and CL)	.15	.06	.01
☐ 64	Monelle Quevillon	.08	.03	.01
☐ 65	Hugo Lusignan	.08	.03	.01
☐ 66	Patrick Girard	.08	.03	.01
☐ 67	Mathieu St-Marc	.08	.03	.01
☐ 68	Sacha Paquette	.08	.03	.01
☐ 69	Dany Cloutier	.08	.03	.01
☐ 70	Mike Pistilli	.08	.03	.01
☐ 71	Martin Bourgeois	.08	.03	.01
☐ 72	Dominic Ranzi	.08	.03	.01
☐ 73	Jocelyn Dubord	.08	.03	.01
☐ 74	Ugo Larouche	.08	.03	.01
☐ 75	Marc-Andre Menard	.08	.03	.01
☐ 76	Jonathan Dionne	.08	.03	.01
☐ 77	Benoit Dumont	.08	.03	.01
☐ 78	Francois Boucher	.08	.03	.01
☐ 79	Benoit Poirier	.08	.03	.01
☐ 80	Eperviers de Mascouche M.L.L. (Team photo and CL)	.15	.06	.01
☐ 81	John Volk	.08	.03	.01
☐ 82	Jason Roy	.08	.03	.01
☐ 83	Manuel Frechette	.08	.03	.01
☐ 84	Vincent Parent	.08	.03	.01
☐ 85	Steve Madison	.08	.03	.01
☐ 86	Patrice Di Cola	.08	.03	.01
☐ 87	Jeremy Welik	.08	.03	.01
☐ 88	Benoit Chenier	.08	.03	.01
☐ 89	Marc Belhumeur	.08	.03	.01
☐ 90	Olivier Lebrun	.08	.03	.01
☐ 91	Martin Frechette	.08	.03	.01
☐ 92	Cedrick Noel	.08	.03	.01
☐ 93	Mathieu Lefrancois	.08	.03	.01
☐ 94	Richard Sweezey	.08	.03	.01
☐ 95	Eric Legault	.08	.03	.01
☐ 96	Jean-Francois Tousignant	.08	.03	.01
☐ 97	National La Presqu'Ile (Team photo and CL)	.15	.06	.01
☐ 98	Dominic Rouleau	.08	.03	.01
☐ 99	Steve Allaire	.08	.03	.01
☐ 100	Jean-Philippe Beaudoin	.08	.03	.01
☐ 101	Yannick Rousseau	.08	.03	.01
☐ 102	Eric Fortier	.08	.03	.01
☐ 103	Ghislain Robichaud	.08	.03	.01
☐ 104	Alexandre Beaudoin	.08	.03	.01
☐ 105	Francois Beauchesne	.08	.03	.01
☐ 106	Serge Crochetiere	.08	.03	.01
☐ 107	Dominic Gouin	.08	.03	.01
☐ 108	Jean-Philippe Parent	.08	.03	.01
☐ 109	Frederic Paris	.08	.03	.01
☐ 110	Eric Vigneault	.15	.06	.01
☐ 111	Sebastien Faucher	.08	.03	.01
☐ 112	Tommy Sevigny	.08	.03	.01
☐ 113	Hugues Fillion	.08	.03	.01
☐ 114	Caravelles de l'Erable (Team photo and CL)	.15	.06	.01
☐ 115	Jonathan Baillargeon	.08	.03	.01
☐ 116	Eric Chouinard	.08	.03	.01

☐ 117	David Boissinot	.08	.03	.01
☐ 118	Francis Cote	.08	.03	.01
☐ 119	Sylvain David	.08	.03	.01
☐ 120	Francois Desrosiers	.08	.03	.01
☐ 121	Simon Francoeur	.08	.03	.01
☐ 122	Jasmin Gaudet	.08	.03	.01
☐ 123	Jean-Francois Gagne	.08	.03	.01
☐ 124	Yannick Gilbert	.08	.03	.01
☐ 125	Alexandre Landry	.08	.03	.01
☐ 126	Dave Laurendeau	.08	.03	.01
☐ 127	Pierre-Yves Lemelin	.08	.03	.01
☐ 128	Alexandre Lessard	.08	.03	.01
☐ 129	Jean-Francois Pichette	.15	.06	.01
☐ 130	Francis Trudeau	.08	.03	.01
☐ 131	Sherbrooke Metropolitain (Team photo and CL)	.15	.06	.01
☐ 132	Alexandre Tomaras	.08	.03	.01
☐ 133	Martin Lavergne	.08	.03	.01
☐ 134	Allen Morris	.08	.03	.01
☐ 135	Nicholas Bilotto	.08	.03	.01
☐ 136	Patrick Soucy	.08	.03	.01
☐ 137	James Desmarais	.08	.03	.01
☐ 138	Christian Pichette	.08	.03	.01
☐ 139	Ryan Lubell-Smith	.08	.03	.01
☐ 140	Marc Lauzon	.08	.03	.01
☐ 141	Antoine Lejeune	.08	.03	.01
☐ 142	Simon Prieur	.08	.03	.01
☐ 143	John Lachance	.08	.03	.01
☐ 144	James Davidson	.08	.03	.01
☐ 145	Justin Humes	.08	.03	.01
☐ 146	Shaun McCarthy	.08	.03	.01
☐ 147	Jonathan Lamy	.08	.03	.01
☐ 148	Tigres Lac St-Louis Ouest (Team photo and CL)	.15	.06	.01
☐ 149	Charlie Powderface	.15	.06	.01
☐ 150	Paul Grygorasz	.08	.03	.01
☐ 151	Mineki Yamada	.08	.03	.01
☐ 152	Matt Stambaugh	.08	.03	.01
☐ 153	Cody Seguin	.08	.03	.01
☐ 154	Jared Smyth	.08	.03	.01
☐ 155	Bobby Myson	.08	.03	.01
☐ 156	Ken Okabe	.08	.03	.01
☐ 157	Takeshi Miyazoe	.08	.03	.01
☐ 158	Shane Mooney	.08	.03	.01
☐ 159	Marty Goulet	.08	.03	.01
☐ 160	Taisuke Hasumi	.08	.03	.01
☐ 161	Mike DeMichele	.08	.03	.01
☐ 162	Patrick Goon	.15	.06	.01
☐ 163	Michael Campbell	.08	.03	.01
☐ 164	Warren Beddow	.08	.03	.01
☐ 165	Banff Pee-Wee Bears (Team photo and CL)	.15	.06	.01
☐ 166	Oliver Addington	.08	.03	.01
☐ 167	Craig Dow	.08	.03	.01
☐ 168	Mark Darrah	.08	.03	.01
☐ 169	Ryan Epp	.08	.03	.01
☐ 170	David Duncan	.08	.03	.01
☐ 171	Matthew Johnson	.08	.03	.01
☐ 172	Bobby Kendall	.08	.03	.01
☐ 173	Derek Kogut	.08	.03	.01
☐ 174	Colin Mah	.08	.03	.01
☐ 175	Lawrence Nycholat	.08	.03	.01
☐ 176	Darren Malin	.08	.03	.01
☐ 177	Riley Papero	.08	.03	.01
☐ 178	John Stady	.08	.03	.01
☐ 179	Michael J. Zimmer	.08	.03	.01
☐ 180	Joshua Woitas	.08	.03	.01
☐ 181	Calgary Flames (Team photo and CL	.15	.06	.01
☐ 182	Cory Benson	.08	.03	.01
☐ 183	Stephen Murphy	.08	.03	.01
☐ 184	Ian Daley	.08	.03	.01
☐ 185	Keith Rickert	.08	.03	.01
☐ 186	Francis Mooney	.08	.03	.01
☐ 187	Brad Kerrivan	.08	.03	.01
☐ 188	Adam Nolan	.08	.03	.01
☐ 189	Wesley McGuire	.08	.03	.01
☐ 190	Matthew McGuire	.08	.03	.01
☐ 191	Blair Evans	.08	.03	.01
☐ 192	Chris Furlong	.08	.03	.01
☐ 193	Chad Jarvis	.08	.03	.01
☐ 194	Ryan Lauzon	.08	.03	.01
☐ 195	Clark Scott	.08	.03	.01
☐ 196	Douglas Spurrell	.08	.03	.01
☐ 197	Keith Evans	.08	.03	.01
☐ 198	Mark Steele	.08	.03	.01
☐ 199	Mount Pearl Blades (Team photo and CL)	.15	.06	.01
☐ 200	Pascal Langevin	.08	.03	.01
☐ 201	Steve Van Den Elzen	.08	.03	.01
☐ 202	Daniel St-Amant	.08	.03	.01
☐ 203	Maxime Samson	.08	.03	.01
☐ 204	Martin Quessy	.08	.03	.01
☐ 205	Benoit St-Hilaire	.08	.03	.01
☐ 206	Steve Mongrain	.08	.03	.01
☐ 207	Francois Pichette	.08	.03	.01
☐ 208	Francis Mongrain	.08	.03	.01
☐ 209	Sebastien Huard	.08	.03	.01
☐ 210	Jean-Francois Hamel	.08	.03	.01
☐ 211	Tommi Houde	.08	.03	.01
☐ 212	Marc-Andre Garceau	.08	.03	.01
☐ 213	Hugo Gelinas	.08	.03	.01
☐ 214	Simon Dessureault	.08	.03	.01
☐ 215	Yanick Dupuis	.08	.03	.01
☐ 216	L'Excel Centre Mauricie (Team photo and CL)	.15	.06	.01
☐ 217	Francis Rheault	.08	.03	.01
☐ 218	Yannick Allaire	.08	.03	.01
☐ 219	Jonathan Picard	.08	.03	.01
☐ 220	Samuel St-Pierre	.08	.03	.01
☐ 221	Eric Cote	.08	.03	.01
☐ 222	Michael Cote	.08	.03	.01
☐ 223	David Roberge	.08	.03	.01
☐ 224	Martin Tanguay	.50	.20	.05
☐ 225	David Bilodeau	.08	.03	.01
☐ 226	Yannick Bouchard	.08	.03	.01
☐ 227	Eric Lecompte	1.00	.40	.10
☐ 228	Simon Roy	.25	.10	.02
☐ 229	Francois Olivier Lafon	.08	.03	.01
☐ 230	Jean Regis	.08	.03	.01
☐ 231	Dominic Vincent	.08	.03	.01
☐ 232	Vincent Daigle	.15	.06	.01
☐ 233	Francois Cloutier	.08	.03	.01
☐ 234	Simon Mailhot	.08	.03	.01
☐ 235	Victoriaville (Team photo and CL)	.15	.06	.01
☐ 236	Jean-Philippe Morency	.08	.03	.01
☐ 237	Jerome Morin	.08	.03	.01
☐ 238	Dominic Jacques	.08	.03	.01
☐ 239	Martin Guinard	.08	.03	.01
☐ 240	Guillaume Boulet	.08	.03	.01
☐ 241	Francois Corriveau	.08	.03	.01
☐ 242	Daniel Gaudreau	.08	.03	.01
☐ 243	Reaume Caron	.08	.03	.01
☐ 244	Jean-Francois Dube	.08	.03	.01
☐ 245	Jean-Philippe Caron	.08	.03	.01
☐ 246	Mathieu Lapierre	.08	.03	.01
☐ 247	Steve Bernier	.08	.03	.01
☐ 248	Alexandre Thibault	.08	.03	.01
☐ 249	Yves Gagnon	.08	.03	.01
☐ 250	Vincent Boulet	.08	.03	.01
☐ 251	Mathieu Ringuet	.08	.03	.01
☐ 252	Les Canotiers de Montmagny	.15	.06	.01
☐ 253	Kavin Coulombe	.08	.03	.01
☐ 254	Jean-Francois Collin	.08	.03	.01
☐ 255	David Lachance	.08	.03	.01
☐ 256	Simon Villeneuve	.08	.03	.01
☐ 257	Christian Zounimbiat	.08	.03	.01
☐ 258	Dominic Paradis	.08	.03	.01
☐ 259	Joe Bussieres	.08	.03	.01
☐ 260	Nicolas Lemelin	.08	.03	.01
☐ 261	Carl Labbe	.08	.03	.01
☐ 262	Francis Dumont	.08	.03	.01
☐ 263	Cedric Pouliot	.08	.03	.01
☐ 264	Jean-Daniel Lavoie	.08	.03	.01
☐ 265	Dominic Latouche	.08	.03	.01
☐ 266	Frederic Parent	.08	.03	.01
☐ 267	Daniel Jobin	.08	.03	.01
☐ 268	Jean-Francois Gauthier	.08	.03	.01
☐ 269	Jonathan Fournier	.08	.03	.01
☐ 270	Harfangs de Beauport (Team photo and CL	.15	.06	.01
☐ 271	Sebastien Malenfant	.08	.03	.01
☐ 272	Simon Lajeunesse	.15	.06	.01
☐ 273	Jasmyn Laroche	.15	.06	.01
☐ 274	Danny Labbe	.08	.03	.01
☐ 275	Dany Racine	.08	.03	.01
☐ 276	Karl Giguere	.08	.03	.01
☐ 277	Carl Ferland	.08	.03	.01
☐ 278	Frederick Verret	.08	.03	.01
☐ 279	Claude Lachance Jr.	.08	.03	.01
☐ 280	Eric Paquet	.15	.06	.01
☐ 281	Alexandre Tremblay	.08	.03	.01
☐ 282	Jean Langevin	.08	.03	.01
☐ 283	Carl Bussiere	.08	.03	.01
☐ 284	Bruno Julien	.08	.03	.01
☐ 285	Claude Boucher	.08	.03	.01
☐ 286	Frederic Couture	.08	.03	.01
☐ 287	Ladufo Cote de	.15	.06	.01

Beaupre (Team photo and CL)

☐ 288	Sylvain Turgeon	.15	.06	.01
☐ 289	Jerome Tremblay	.08	.03	.01
☐ 290	Michael Thomassin	.08	.03	.01
☐ 291	Frederick Marcotte	.08	.03	.01
☐ 292	Jean-Francois Lavoie	.08	.03	.01
☐ 293	Philippe Lord	.08	.03	.01
☐ 294	Simon Gauthier	.08	.03	.01
☐ 295	Jimmy Lapointe	.08	.03	.01
☐ 296	Francois Fortier	.08	.03	.01
☐ 297	Patrick Fournel	.08	.03	.01
☐ 298	Mathieu Chicoine	.08	.03	.01
☐ 299	Daniel Chapados	.08	.03	.01
☐ 300	Philippe De Carvalho	.08	.03	.01
☐ 301	Frederic Brindamour	.08	.03	.01
☐ 302	Karl Bedard	.08	.03	.01
☐ 303	Eric Boucher	.08	.03	.01
☐ 304	Les Seigneurs de	.15	.06	.01

Beaubourg (Team photo and CL)

☐ 305	Jean-Francois Ruel	.08	.03	.01
☐ 306	Nicolas Pelletier	.08	.03	.01
☐ 307	Jean-Rene Ouellet	.08	.03	.01
☐ 308	David Paradis	.08	.03	.01
☐ 309	Eric Martineau	.08	.03	.01
☐ 310	Eric Lapierre	.08	.03	.01
☐ 311	Alexandre Langlois	.08	.03	.01
☐ 312	Eric Laflamme	.15	.06	.01
☐ 313	Eric Genest	.08	.03	.01
☐ 314	Jerome Hinse	.08	.03	.01
☐ 315	Marc Dubreuil	.08	.03	.01
☐ 316	Sebastien Dubois	.08	.03	.01
☐ 317	Jean-Francois	.08	.03	.01

Cantin

☐ 318	Laurent Bilodeau	.08	.03	.01
☐ 319	Jerome Allard	.08	.03	.01
☐ 320	Mathieu Bergeron	.08	.03	.01
☐ 321	Charny-Bernieres	.15	.06	.01

(Team photo and CL)

☐ 322	Mathieu Therrien	.08	.03	.01
☐ 323	Simon Bilodeau	.08	.03	.01
☐ 324	Jean-Francois Drouin	.08	.03	.01
☐ 325	Eric Turmel	.08	.03	.01
☐ 326	Jean-Francois Hallee	.08	.03	.01
☐ 327	Berthier Poulin	.08	.03	.01
☐ 328	Jerome Morin	.08	.03	.01
☐ 329	Vincent Morin	.08	.03	.01
☐ 330	Luc Tanguay	.08	.03	.01
☐ 331	Julien Dostie	.08	.03	.01
☐ 332	Remy Gosselin	.08	.03	.01
☐ 333	Michel Demers	.08	.03	.01
☐ 334	Frederic Michaud	.08	.03	.01
☐ 335	Marc-Andre Lacroix	.08	.03	.01
☐ 336	Jonathan Clusiault	.08	.03	.01
☐ 337	Steve Fortier	.08	.03	.01
☐ 338	Marc Charbonneau	.08	.03	.01
☐ 339	Francis Pare	.08	.03	.01
☐ 340	Lac-Megantic Bestar	.15	.06	.01

(Team photo and CL)

☐ 341	Patrick Alain	.08	.03	.01
☐ 342	Simon Gagne	.08	.03	.01
☐ 343	Dominick Samson	.08	.03	.01
☐ 344	Dominic Soulard	.08	.03	.01
☐ 345	Jonathan Beaulieu	.08	.03	.01
☐ 346	Carl Menard	.08	.03	.01
☐ 347	Steve Boutet	.08	.03	.01
☐ 348	Jean-Francois	.08	.03	

Damphousse

☐ 349	Benoit Dusablon	.08	.03	.01
☐ 350	Sebastien Bedard	.08	.03	.01
☐ 351	Marc-Andre Cantin	.08	.03	.01
☐ 352	Mathieu Julien	.08	.03	.01
☐ 353	Alexandre Rioux	.08	.03	.01
☐ 354	Frederic Thibault	.08	.03	.01
☐ 355	Pierre-Mathieu	.08	.03	.01

Vaillancourt

☐ 356	Les Gouverneurs de	.08	.03	.01

Sainte-Foy

☐ 357	Not Known	.08	.03	.01
☐ 358	Philippe Cloutier	.08	.03	.01
☐ 359	Mike Allen	.08	.03	.01
☐ 360	Eric Binet	.08	.03	.01
☐ 361	Karl Fortier	.08	.03	.01
☐ 362	Jean-Philippe Cliche	.08	.03	.01
☐ 363	Marco Lachance	.08	.03	.01
☐ 364	Philippe Cliche	.08	.03	.01
☐ 365	Jason Lehoux	.08	.03	.01
☐ 366	Jerome Nadeau	.08	.03	.01
☐ 367	Charles Pare	.08	.03	.01
☐ 368	Martin Roy	.08	.03	.01
☐ 369	Kevin Marcoux	.08	.03	.01
☐ 370	Jean-Francois	.08	.03	.01

Tanguay

☐ 371	Francis Binet	.08	.03	.01

☐ 372	Vincent Boulianne	.08	.03	.01
☐ 373	Elite Beauce-Amiante	.15	.06	.01

(Team photo and CL)

☐ 374	David Boudreault	.08	.03	.01
☐ 375	Patrice Morin	.08	.03	.01
☐ 376	Jean-Francois Minier	.08	.03	.01
☐ 377	Michael Harvey	.08	.03	.01
☐ 378	Cedric Boivin	.08	.03	.01
☐ 379	Daniel Maltais	.08	.03	.01
☐ 380	Jean-Philippe Gagne	.08	.03	.01
☐ 381	Dave McNicoll	.08	.03	.01
☐ 382	Steve Gagne	.08	.03	.01
☐ 383	Steve Laberge	.08	.03	.01
☐ 384	Marc-Andre Boivin	.08	.03	.01
☐ 385	Patrice Boudreault	.08	.03	.01
☐ 386	Pierre-Luc Gobeil	.08	.03	.01
☐ 387	Eric Belanger	.08	.03	.01
☐ 388	Sebastien Tremblay	.08	.03	.01
☐ 389	Donald Lavoie	.08	.03	.01
☐ 390	National de La Baie	.08	.03	.01
☐ 391	Frederic Pare	.08	.03	.01
☐ 392	Jonathan Poulin	.08	.03	.01
☐ 393	Julien Veilleux	.08	.03	.01
☐ 394	Jerome Roy	.08	.03	.01
☐ 395	Charles Fortin	.08	.03	.01
☐ 396	Junior Lessard	.08	.03	.01
☐ 397	Pierre-Jean Lajoie	.08	.03	.01
☐ 398	Keven Cloutier	.08	.03	.01
☐ 399	Jean-Pierre Lessard	.08	.03	.01
☐ 400	Mathieu Lachance	.08	.03	.01
☐ 401	Simon Veilleux	.08	.03	.01
☐ 402	Philippe Boily	.08	.03	.01
☐ 403	Dominic Bourret	.08	.03	.01
☐ 404	Maxime Paris	.08	.03	.01
☐ 405	Julien Boureault	.08	.03	.01
☐ 406	Vincent Maheux	.08	.03	.01
☐ 407	Beauce-Centre	.15	.06	.01

(Team photo and CL)

☐ 408	Steve Farnham	.08	.03	.01
☐ 409	David St-Germain	.08	.03	.01
☐ 410	Olivier Fontaine	.08	.03	.01
☐ 411	Yann Joseph	.08	.03	.01
☐ 412	Louis-Alexandre	.08	.03	.01

Lehoux

☐ 413	Patrice Boijoli	.08	.03	.01
☐ 414	Etienne Page	.08	.03	.01
☐ 415	Alexandre Lessnick	.08	.03	.01
☐ 416	Olivier Duguay	.08	.03	.01
☐ 417	Jean-Francois Boulay	.08	.03	.01
☐ 418	Jason Mihalik	.08	.03	.01
☐ 419	Steve Simoes	.08	.03	.01
☐ 420	Nicolas Rousseau	.08	.03	.01
☐ 421	Guy Lamontagne	.08	.03	.01
☐ 422	Jonathan Pilotte	.08	.03	.01
☐ 423	Champlain du	.15	.06	.01

Richelieu (Team photo and CL)

☐ 424	Dominic Vincent	.08	.03	.01
☐ 425	Jean-Sebastien	.08	.03	.01

Trudelle

☐ 426	Jerome Fournier	.08	.03	.01
☐ 427	Eric Carrier	.08	.03	.01
☐ 428	Pierre-Luc Hins	.08	.03	.01
☐ 429	Marc-Andre Fournier	.08	.03	.01
☐ 430	Martin Brisson	.08	.03	.01
☐ 431	Jerome Dumont	.08	.03	.01
☐ 432	Sebastien Caron	.08	.03	.01
☐ 433	Jean-Philippe Guay	.08	.03	.01
☐ 434	Jean-Philippe Dion	.08	.03	.01
☐ 435	Germain Chamberland	.08	.03	.01
☐ 436	Maxime Demers	.08	.03	.01
☐ 437	Pascal Aubut	.08	.03	.01
☐ 438	Gregoire Leblanc	.08	.03	.01
☐ 439	David Guerette	.08	.03	.01
☐ 440	Faucons Pointe-Levy	.15	.06	.01

(Team photo and CL)

☐ 441	Nicolas Bougie	.08	.03	.01
☐ 442	Martin Poirier	.08	.03	.01
☐ 443	Brian Laflamme	.08	.03	.01
☐ 444	Sebasten Allard	.08	.03	.01
☐ 445	Pierre Julien	.08	.03	.01
☐ 446	Jerome Marcotte	.08	.03	.01
☐ 447	Simon-Pierre Blouin	.08	.03	.01
☐ 448	Nicolas Demers	.08	.03	.01
☐ 449	Louis-Charles Warren	.08	.03	.01
☐ 450	Simon Fontaine	.08	.03	.01
☐ 451	Jonathan Roy	.08	.03	.01
☐ 452	Martin Gionet	.08	.03	.01
☐ 453	Tommy Larochelle	.08	.03	.01
☐ 454	Patrick Boivin	.08	.03	.01
☐ 455	Patrick Boulay	.08	.03	.01
☐ 456	Maxime Boucher	.08	.03	.01
☐ 457	Les Regents Rive-Sud	.15	.06	.01

(Team photo and CL

☐ 458	Hugo Welsh	.08	.03	.01
☐ 459	Jonathan Verreault	.08	.03	.01
☐ 460	Simon-Pierre Gingras	.08	.03	.01
☐ 461	Sebastien Letourneau	.08	.03	.01
☐ 462	Olivier Morin	.08	.03	.01
☐ 463	Dominick Giguere	.08	.03	.01
☐ 464	Yanick Berube	.08	.03	.01
☐ 465	Frederick Pepin	.08	.03	.01
☐ 466	Nicolas Dore	.08	.03	.01
☐ 467	Patrick Mathieu	.08	.03	.01
☐ 468	Jocelyn Dugre	.08	.03	.01
☐ 469	Marc Lafrance	.08	.03	.01
☐ 470	Eric Grenier	.08	.03	.01
☐ 471	Vincent Roy	.08	.03	.01
☐ 472	Bryan Cooper	.08	.03	.01
☐ 473	Olivier Simard	.08	.03	.01
☐ 474	Elans de Charlesbourg	.15	.06	.01

(Team photo and CL)

☐ 475	Andrew Robillard	.08	.03	.01
☐ 476	Stewart Gowans	.08	.03	.01
☐ 477	Mike De Petrillo	.08	.03	.01
☐ 478	Cody Leibel	.08	.03	.01
☐ 479	Jamie Drover	.08	.03	.01
☐ 480	Giancarlo Innoncentin	.08	.03	.01
☐ 481	Greg Willers	.08	.03	.01
☐ 482	Michael Laceby	.08	.03	.01
☐ 483	Brett Cerqua	.08	.03	.01
☐ 484	Craig Mumby	.08	.03	.01
☐ 485	Eddie Fines	.08	.03	.01
☐ 486	Andrew Kirwin	.08	.03	.01
☐ 487	Marc Ancheloni	.08	.03	.01
☐ 488	Bryan Pandovski	.08	.03	.01
☐ 489	Toronto Young	.15	.06	.01

Nationals
(Team photo and CL)

☐ 490	Michael Ignatz	.08	.03	.01
☐ 491	Jason Hurlbut	.15	.06	.01
☐ 492	Adriano Fiacconi	.08	.03	.01
☐ 493	Jeremy Wenzel	.08	.03	.01
☐ 494	Andrew Ritchie	.08	.03	.01
☐ 495	Robert Meanchoff	.08	.03	.01
☐ 496	Craig Telfer	.08	.03	.01
☐ 497	Willis Shawana	.08	.03	.01
☐ 498	Anton Strgacic	.08	.03	.01
☐ 499	David Delmonte	.08	.03	.01
☐ 500	Andrew Taylor	.08	.03	.01
☐ 501	Ken Fox	.08	.03	.01
☐ 502	Colin Nash	.08	.03	.01
☐ 503	Simon Bieber	.08	.03	.01
☐ 504	Morris Fabrizi	.08	.03	.01
☐ 505	North York Canadiens	.15	.06	.01

(Team photo and CL)

☐ 506	Tom Baxter	.08	.03	.01
☐ 507	Pat Berrigan	.08	.03	.01
☐ 508	Paul Dunphy	.08	.03	.01
☐ 509	Matt Fry	.08	.03	.01
☐ 510	Matt Jardine	.08	.03	.01
☐ 511	Alex Johnstone	.08	.03	.01
☐ 512	Peter Lawrence	.08	.03	.01
☐ 513	Andrew Lowery	.08	.03	.01
☐ 514	Scott McPhee	.08	.03	.01
☐ 515	Pat Miller	.08	.03	.01
☐ 516	Tim Moran	.08	.03	.01
☐ 517	Anthony Purchase	.08	.03	.01
☐ 518	Mike Quackenbush	.08	.03	.01
☐ 519	Matt Stephens	.08	.03	.01
☐ 520	Jeff Sutherland	.08	.03	.01
☐ 521	John Walker	.08	.03	.01
☐ 522	Halifax Hawks	.15	.06	.01

(Team photo and CL)

☐ 523	Alex Tanguay	.08	.03	.01
☐ 524	Frederic Bergeron	.08	.03	.01
☐ 525	Pascal McNicoll	.08	.03	.01
☐ 526	Pascal Lavoie	.08	.03	.01
☐ 527	Alexandre Vigneault	.08	.03	.01
☐ 528	Sebastien Harvey	.08	.03	.01
☐ 529	Mathieu Boulianne	.08	.03	.01
☐ 530	Ian Belisle	.08	.03	.01
☐ 531	Daniel Boulianne	.08	.03	.01
☐ 532	Pascal Turcotte	.08	.03	.01
☐ 533	Frederic Harvey	.08	.03	.01
☐ 534	Jerome Tremblay	.08	.03	.01
☐ 535	Patrick Sullivan	.08	.03	.01
☐ 536	Yan Chouinard	.08	.03	.01
☐ 537	Pascal Fillion	.08	.03	.01
☐ 538	Sylvain Plamondon	.08	.03	.01
☐ 539	Jean-Luc Neron	.08	.03	.01
☐ 540	Martin Dufour	.08	.03	.01
☐ 541	Charlevoix	.15	.06	.01

(Team photo and CL)

☐ 542	Robert Kitchen	.08	.03	.01
☐ 543	Shaun Hartwick	.08	.03	.01
☐ 544	Adam Collins	.08	.03	.01

☐ 545	Scott Johnson	.08	.03	.01
☐ 546	Chris Kerr	.08	.03	.01
☐ 547	Scott Self	.08	.03	.01
☐ 548	Aaron Shill	.08	.03	.01
☐ 549	Kelly Sullivan	.08	.03	.01
☐ 550	Josh Burdick	.08	.03	.01
☐ 551	Darren Mahoney	.08	.03	.01
☐ 552	Stephen Evans	.08	.03	.01
☐ 553	Nick Robinson	.08	.03	.01
☐ 554	Jay Legault	.08	.03	.01
☐ 555	Joel Johnston	.08	.03	.01
☐ 556	Brad McCamus	.08	.03	.01
☐ 557	Craig O'Brien	.08	.03	.01
☐ 558	Joey Lester	.08	.03	.01
☐ 559	Peterborough	.15	.06	.01

(Team photo and CL)

☐ 560	Joey Arko	.08	.03	.01
☐ 561	Luke MacBride	.08	.03	.01
☐ 562	Daniel Tkaczuk	.08	.03	.01
☐ 563	Steve Montador	.08	.03	.01
☐ 564	Matt Sirman	.08	.03	.01
☐ 565	Peter Sarno	.08	.03	.01
☐ 566	Sam Katsuras	.08	.03	.01
☐ 567	Darryl Slaney	.08	.03	.01
☐ 568	Damien Medina	.08	.03	.01
☐ 569	Brad Gladwish	.08	.03	.01
☐ 570	Justin Norwood	.08	.03	.01
☐ 571	Darryl Somerville	.08	.03	.01
☐ 572	Brant Somerville	.08	.03	.01
☐ 573	Danny Nicoletti	.08	.03	.01
☐ 574	Erik Epner	.08	.03	.01
☐ 575	Maple Leafs de	.15	.06	.01

Toronto (Team photo
and CL)

☐ 576	Matte Thake	.08	.03	.01
☐ 577	Mason Black	.08	.03	.01
☐ 578	Jed Thomson	.08	.03	.01
☐ 579	Larry Leadbeater	.08	.03	.01
☐ 580	Kris Loughren	.08	.03	.01
☐ 581	Robert Garvin	.08	.03	.01
☐ 582	Dan Stranberg	.08	.03	.01
☐ 583	Greg Pilon	.08	.03	.01
☐ 584	Keith Abbass	.08	.03	.01
☐ 585	Ryan Poll	.08	.03	.01
☐ 586	Derrick Rathwell	.08	.03	.01
☐ 587	Jon Hull	.08	.03	.01
☐ 588	David Ambler	.08	.03	.01
☐ 589	Shaun Johnston	.08	.03	.01
☐ 590	Jason Fielding	.08	.03	.01
☐ 591	Smith Falls Bears	.15	.06	.01

(Team photo and CL)

☐ 592	Paul Nahigian	.15	.06	.01
☐ 593	Ryan Murray	.08	.03	.01
☐ 594	Mike Murray	.08	.03	.01
☐ 595	Mike Morrison	.08	.03	.01
☐ 596	Nick Mosca	.08	.03	.01
☐ 597	Paul Mara	.08	.03	.01
☐ 598	Mike Maturo	.08	.03	.01
☐ 599	R.J. Longchamps	.08	.03	.01
☐ 600	Pat Lubitz	.08	.03	.01
☐ 601	Geoff Koch	.08	.03	.01
☐ 602	Chris Knight	.08	.03	.01
☐ 603	Bob Gordon	.08	.03	.01
☐ 604	Mike Higgins	.08	.03	.01
☐ 605	Lauren Goldstein	.15	.06	.01
☐ 606	Chris Dyment	.08	.03	.01
☐ 607	Adam Bouchard	.08	.03	.01
☐ 608	John Petricig	.08	.03	.01
☐ 609	South Shore Kings	.15	.06	.01

(Team photo and CL)

☐ 610	Nic Guida	.08	.03	.01
☐ 611	Ryan Jones	.08	.03	.01
☐ 612	Andy Quandt	.08	.03	.01
☐ 613	Jim Truitt	.08	.03	.01
☐ 614	Gary Levy	.08	.03	.01
☐ 615	Tye Nielsen	.08	.03	.01
☐ 616	Morgan McShan	.08	.03	.01
☐ 617	George Kiessling	.08	.03	.01
☐ 618	John McGuire	.08	.03	.01
☐ 619	Jason Luker	.08	.03	.01
☐ 620	C.J. MacDonald	.08	.03	.01
☐ 621	Scott Feeney	.08	.03	.01
☐ 622	Tommy Reed	.08	.03	.01
☐ 623	Billy Cox	.08	.03	.01
☐ 624	Aaron Kocian	.08	.03	.01
☐ 625	San Jose Sharks	.15	.06	.01

(Team photo and CL)

☐ 626	Todd Boling	.08	.03	.01
☐ 627	Tom Manning	.08	.03	.01
☐ 628	Sean McKeever	.08	.03	.01
☐ 629	Bernie Caniff	.08	.03	.01
☐ 630	Taylor Morrison	.08	.03	.01
☐ 631	Michael Brainerd	.08	.03	.01

☐ 632	Joe Burns	.08	.03	.01
☐ 633	James Aborn	.08	.03	.01
☐ 634	Ben Santonelli	.08	.03	.01
☐ 635	Scott Conley	.08	.03	.01
☐ 636	Danny Skinner	.08	.03	.01
☐ 637	Eric Silva	.08	.03	.01
☐ 638	Justin Stone	.08	.03	.01
☐ 639	Jamie Dalton	.08	.03	.01
☐ 640	Michael Wendt	.08	.03	.01
☐ 641	Brendon Hughes	.08	.03	.01
☐ 642	Lynnfield Pioneers	.15	.06	.01
	(Team photo and CL)			
☐ 643	John Vereker	.08	.03	.01
☐ 644	Mike Di Mella	.08	.03	.01
☐ 645	Nick De Monico	.08	.03	.01
☐ 646	Joey Roy	.08	.03	.01
☐ 647	Jeff Perry	.08	.03	.01
☐ 648	Carl Corazzini	.08	.03	.01
☐ 649	T.J. Scaparotti	.08	.03	.01
☐ 650	Tim Vafides	.08	.03	.01
☐ 651	Eddie Owens	.08	.03	.01
☐ 652	Jim Quigley	.08	.03	.01
☐ 653	Nick Kreus	.08	.03	.01
☐ 654	Jackie Wallace	.08	.03	.01
☐ 655	Ryan Bailey	.08	.03	.01
☐ 656	Chris Gannon	.08	.03	.01
☐ 657	Dan Genovese	.08	.03	.01
☐ 658	Tom Gottwald	.08	.03	.01
☐ 659	Eric Langley	.08	.03	.01
☐ 660	Bob Donovan	.08	.03	.01
☐ 661	Darrell Doucette	.08	.03	.01
☐ 662	Ben Oberto	.08	.03	.01
☐ 663	Boston Jr. Braves	.15	.06	.01
	(Team photo and CL)			
☐ 664	Tim Connolly	.08	.03	.01
☐ 665	Justin Brown	.08	.03	.01
☐ 666	Chris Ellis	.08	.03	.01
☐ 667	Jon Downs	.08	.03	.01
☐ 668	Brian Ford	.08	.03	.01
☐ 669	Nicole Kirnan	.15	.06	.01
☐ 670	Brad Wolcott	.08	.03	.01
☐ 671	Rob Krenrich	.08	.03	.01
☐ 672	Brett Merritt	.08	.03	.01
☐ 673	Chris Madden	.08	.03	.01
☐ 674	Bill Palmer	.08	.03	.01
☐ 675	Matt Murley	.08	.03	.01
☐ 676	Dominick Sereno	.08	.03	.01
☐ 677	Don Patrick	.08	.03	.01
☐ 678	Matt Weber	.08	.03	.01
☐ 679	Tim Stay	.08	.03	.01
☐ 680	Dana Hopps	.08	.03	.01
☐ 681	Tom Williams	.08	.03	.01
☐ 682	Syracuse Stars	.15	.06	.01
	(Team photo and CL)			
☐ 683	Ben Weiss	.08	.03	.01
☐ 684	J.P. Berkery	.08	.03	.01
☐ 685	Scott Cooper	.08	.03	.01
☐ 686	Jay Gleason	.08	.03	.01
☐ 687	Tim Wood	.08	.03	.01
☐ 688	Bobby Young	.08	.03	.01
☐ 689	Joseph Russo	.08	.03	.01
☐ 690	Ryan Maher	.08	.03	.01
☐ 691	Greg Mitchell	.08	.03	.01
☐ 692	John Lynch	.08	.03	.01
☐ 693	Eric Wood	.08	.03	.01
☐ 694	Chris Goulart	.08	.03	.01
☐ 695	Adam Aguilar	.08	.03	.01
☐ 696	Matt Langille	.08	.03	.01
☐ 697	Jonathan Morse	.08	.03	.01
☐ 698	Jason LeBlanc	.08	.03	.01
☐ 699	Greg Berks	.08	.03	.01
☐ 700	Brian Beaton	.08	.03	.01
☐ 701	Brendon Cashman	.15	.06	.01
☐ 702	Boston Jr. Bruins	.15	.06	.01
	(Team photo and CL)			
☐ 703	Chris Cichon	.08	.03	.01
☐ 704	Nik Tselios	.08	.03	.01
☐ 705	Mike Chesney	.08	.03	.01
☐ 706	Dan Cotuno	.08	.03	.01
☐ 707	Darren Malia	.08	.03	.01
☐ 708	Chris Henning	.08	.03	.01
☐ 709	Paul Caponigri	.08	.03	.01
☐ 710	Kevin Spiewak	.08	.03	.01
☐ 711	Marc Harris	.08	.03	.01
☐ 712	Eric T. Richardson	.08	.03	.01
☐ 713	William Phillip Rutherford	.08	.03	
☐ 714	Chris Knupp	.08	.03	.01
☐ 715	Matt Snyder	.08	.03	.01
☐ 716	Alex Katz	.08	.03	.01
☐ 717	Matt Doman	.08	.03	.01
☐ 718	Kris Koski	.08	.03	.01
☐ 719	Chris Campbell	.08	.03	.01
☐ 720	Chicago Blackhawks	.15	.06	.01
	(Team photo and CL)			
☐ 721	Craig Casella	.08	.03	.01
☐ 722	Derek Fisher	.08	.03	.01
☐ 723	Philip Lagola	.08	.03	.01
☐ 724	Kyle Frigon	.08	.03	.01
☐ 725	Jesse Elhai	.08	.03	.01
☐ 726	Bryan Eberenz	.08	.03	.01
☐ 727	Tommy Nastasi	.08	.03	.01
☐ 728	Joshua Mandel	.08	.03	.01
☐ 729	Gary Tashjian	.08	.03	.01
☐ 730	Scott Dutcher	.08	.03	.01
☐ 731	Nick Vlasidis	.08	.03	.01
☐ 732	Danny Perry	.08	.03	.01
☐ 733	Michael Sweeney	.08	.03	.01
☐ 734	Joshua Goldfarb	.08	.03	.01
☐ 735	Andor Kish	.08	.03	.01
☐ 736	Michael Sarro	.08	.03	.01
☐ 737	New Jersey Devils	.15	.06	.01
	(Team photo and CL)			
☐ 738	Jesse Goldstein	.08	.03	.01
☐ 739	Scott Driscoll	.08	.03	.01
☐ 740	Jason Fogelson	.08	.03	.01
☐ 741	Derek Nowak	.08	.03	.01
☐ 742	David Dymnicki	.08	.03	.01
☐ 743	David Saunders	.08	.03	.01
☐ 744	Sean O'Neill	.08	.03	.01
☐ 745	Curt Colarullo	.08	.03	.01
☐ 746	Kayser Dixon	.08	.03	.01
☐ 747	Scott Lensky	.08	.03	.01
☐ 748	David Cohen	.08	.03	.01
☐ 749	Tim Neary	.08	.03	.01
☐ 750	Jaime Moorhead	.08	.03	.01
☐ 751	Christian Sturz	.08	.03	.01
☐ 752	John Boynton	.08	.03	.01
☐ 753	Ryan Fitzgerald	.08	.03	.01
☐ 754	Jeff Giuliano	.08	.03	.01
☐ 755	Chris Lombardo	.08	.03	.01
☐ 756	Tampa Bay Lightning	.15	.06	.01
	(Team photo and CL)			
☐ 757	Jordon Spallone	.08	.03	.01
☐ 758	Gene Spadaro	.08	.03	.01
☐ 759	Michael Roth	.08	.03	.01
☐ 760	Derek Powell	.08	.03	.01
☐ 761	Sean Murphy	.08	.03	.01
☐ 762	Michael Conley	.08	.03	.01
☐ 763	Nathan Kush	.08	.03	.01
☐ 764	Marty Martorelli	.08	.03	.01
☐ 765	Justin Kenepp	.08	.03	.01
☐ 766	Ryan Boilard	.08	.03	.01
☐ 767	Jeff Bevacqua	.08	.03	.01
☐ 768	Kevin Barefoot	.08	.03	.01
☐ 769	Brandon Marlan	.08	.03	.01
☐ 770	Ryan Patrick	.08	.03	.01
☐ 771	Josh Allison	.08	.03	.01
☐ 772	Pittsburgh Penguins	.15	.06	.01
	(Team photo and CL)			
☐ 773	Seth Schell	.08	.03	.01
☐ 774	Eric Schork	.08	.03	.01
☐ 775	Ryan Nade	.08	.03	.01
☐ 776	Ryan Haley	.08	.03	.01
☐ 777	Bruce Bingaman	.08	.03	.01
☐ 778	Zach Stauffer	.08	.03	.01
☐ 779	Roald Llado	.08	.03	.01
☐ 780	Nate Tulli	.08	.03	.01
☐ 781	Sean Knaub	.08	.03	.01
☐ 782	Tony Morrell	.08	.03	.01
☐ 783	Ethan Holmes	.08	.03	.01
☐ 784	B.J. Heckendorn	.08	.03	.01
☐ 785	David Thomas	.08	.03	.01
☐ 786	Teague Willits-Kelley	.08	.03	.01
☐ 787	John Heitsenrether	.08	.03	.01
☐ 788	Dan Zorger	.08	.03	.01
☐ 789	Nick Castelli	.08	.03	.01
☐ 790	Jon Kuhn	.08	.03	.01
☐ 791	Kevin Hollenbush	.08	.03	.01
☐ 792	Hershey Cubs	.15	.06	.01
	(Team photo and CL)			
☐ 793	David Cavanaugh	.08	.03	.01
☐ 794	Keith Kashuba	.08	.03	.01
☐ 795	Rick Poveromo	.08	.03	.01
☐ 796	Blue Hill	.08	.03	.01
☐ 797	Ron Smith	.08	.03	.01
☐ 798	Justin Spicer	.08	.03	.01
☐ 799	Jeremy Osborne	.08	.03	.01
☐ 800	Scott Wojcinski	.08	.03	.01
☐ 801	Nik Fattey	.08	.03	.01
☐ 802	Nick Wierzba	.08	.03	.01
☐ 803	Mark D'Agostino	.08	.03	.01
☐ 804	Mike Kauzala	.08	.03	.01
☐ 805	Sean Lafferty	.08	.03	.01
☐ 806	Jonathan Obstarczyk	.08	.03	.01

☐ 807	Jason Snusz	.08	.03	.01
☐ 808	Jeff Arlotta	.08	.03	.01
☐ 809	Buffalo Sabres	.15	.06	.01
	(Team photo and CL)			
☐ 810	Eric Albano	.08	.03	.01
☐ 811	Aaron Solesky	.08	.03	.01
☐ 812	Joe Carpenter	.08	.03	.01
☐ 813	Ryan Beauvais	.08	.03	.01
☐ 814	Scott Cunningham	.15	.06	.01
☐ 815	Luke Earl	.08	.03	.01
☐ 816	R.J. Gates	.08	.03	.01
☐ 817	Eric Gustafson	.08	.03	.01
☐ 818	Craig Laramee	.08	.03	.01
☐ 819	Chuck Kaiton	.08	.03	.01
☐ 820	Greg Reynholds	.08	.03	.01
☐ 821	Kris Vrolyk	.08	.03	.01
☐ 822	B.L. Reid	.08	.03	.01
☐ 823	Justin Picone	.08	.03	.01
☐ 824	Mike Mello	.08	.03	.01
☐ 825	Jon Veisor	.15	.06	.01
☐ 826	Rob Martin	.08	.03	.01
☐ 827	Hartford Whalers	.15	.06	.01
	(Team photo and CL)			
☐ 828	Chris Maniatis	.08	.03	.01
☐ 829	Myles Dudley	.08	.03	.01
☐ 830	Chris Torri	.08	.03	.01
☐ 831	Nick Stead	.08	.03	.01
☐ 832	Mick Philbin	.08	.03	.01
☐ 833	Peter Catalano	.08	.03	.01
☐ 834	T.C. Harris	.08	.03	.01
☐ 835	Nicholas Dimitrakos	.08	.03	.01
☐ 836	Shawn Sutter	.08	.03	.01
☐ 837	Al Salvia	.08	.03	.01
☐ 838	Brian Marcaurelle	.08	.03	.01
☐ 839	Peter Metcalf	.08	.03	.01
☐ 840	Adam Kozlowski	.08	.03	.01
☐ 841	Mark Nunan	.08	.03	.01
☐ 842	Sean Donahue	.08	.03	.01
☐ 843	Gary Ford	.08	.03	.01
☐ 844	Chris Connolly	.08	.03	.01
☐ 845	D.J. Gravell	.08	.03	.01
☐ 846	Beverly	.15	.06	.01
	(Team photo and CL)			
☐ 847	Mike Vililante	.08	.03	.01
☐ 848	Jeff Reynaert	.08	.03	.01
☐ 849	Jeff Pustulka	.08	.03	.01
☐ 850	J.P. Pointek	.08	.03	.01
☐ 851	Jesse Paul	.08	.03	.01
☐ 852	Larry Mylek	.08	.03	.01
☐ 853	Ryan Melnechuk	.08	.03	.01
☐ 854	Jerod Lutz	.08	.03	.01
☐ 855	Josh Johnson	.08	.03	.01
☐ 856	Brandon Love	.08	.03	.01
☐ 857	Jake Heisler	.08	.03	.01
☐ 858	Patrick Jesue	.08	.03	.01
☐ 859	Brad Fraser	.08	.03	.01
☐ 860	David Hague	.08	.03	.01
☐ 861	Jesse Cortez	.08	.03	.01
☐ 862	Chris Desjardine	.08	.03	.01
☐ 863	Scott Abraham	.08	.03	.01
☐ 864	Jeremy Bachusz	.08	.03	.01
☐ 865	Michigan Nationals	.15	.06	.01
	(Team photo and CL)			
☐ 866	Lou Ferrari	.08	.03	.01
☐ 867	Chris Dietz	.08	.03	.01
☐ 868	Sean Corcoran	.08	.03	.01
☐ 869	Gerry Snyder	.08	.03	.01
☐ 870	Anthony Scorsone	.08	.03	.01
☐ 871	Don Phillips	.08	.03	.01
☐ 872	Shaun McSweeney	.08	.03	.01
☐ 873	B.J. Busch	.08	.03	.01
☐ 874	Kyle Langdon	.08	.03	.01
☐ 875	Chuckie Healey	.08	.03	.01
☐ 876	Cameron Boyd	.08	.03	.01
☐ 877	Brian Gionta	.08	.03	.01
☐ 878	Justin Booth	.08	.03	.01
☐ 879	Shawn Fowler	.08	.03	.01
☐ 880	Scott Behrens	.08	.03	.01
☐ 881	Mark Hodges	.08	.03	.01
☐ 882	Justin Knight	.08	.03	.01
☐ 883	Minnesota North Star	.15	.06	.01
	(Team photo and CL)			
☐ 884	Bobby Hern	.08	.03	.01
☐ 885	Brian Elder	.08	.03	.01
☐ 886	Andrew Geiger	.08	.03	.01
☐ 887	Christopher Kellogg	.08	.03	.01
☐ 888	Matt Knop	.08	.03	.01
☐ 889	Trevor Rice-Wood	.08	.03	.01
☐ 890	Brad Bokal	.08	.03	.01
☐ 891	Mark Turnipseed	.08	.03	.01
☐ 892	Tom Kaiman	.08	.03	.01
☐ 893	Gary Opitz	.08	.03	.01
☐ 894	Geoff Hartwig	.08	.03	.01
☐ 895	Justin Baisch	.08	.03	.01
☐ 896	Joseph Cabo	.08	.03	.01
☐ 897	Mike Summers	.08	.03	.01
☐ 898	Timothy Carbery	.08	.03	.01
☐ 899	Mike Jost	.08	.03	.01
☐ 900	Travis Rice-Wood	.08	.03	.01
☐ 901	St-Louis Blues	.15	.06	.01
	(Team photo and CL)			
☐ 902	Benoit Vezina	.15	.06	.01
☐ 903	Jonathan Girard	.08	.03	.01
☐ 904	Patrick Leveille	.08	.03	.01
☐ 905	Guillaume Barbe	.08	.03	.01
☐ 906	Francis Lalande	.08	.03	.01
☐ 907	Benoit Laroche	.08	.03	.01
☐ 908	David Ouellette	.08	.03	.01
☐ 909	Dominic St-Germain	.08	.03	.01
☐ 910	Daniel Brouillard	.08	.03	.01
☐ 911	Eric Bertrand	.08	.03	.01
☐ 912	Luc Vachon	.08	.03	.01
☐ 913	Eric Pinoul	.08	.03	.01
☐ 914	Guillaume Marcoux	.08	.03	.01
☐ 915	Julien Louis-Seize	.08	.03	.01
☐ 916	Eric Desjardins	.15	.06	.01
☐ 917	Selects du Nord	.15	.06	.01
	(Team photo and CL)			
☐ 918	Alexandre Mottard	.08	.03	.01
☐ 919	Jean-Francois Lavoie	.08	.03	.01
☐ 920	Eric Talbot	.08	.03	.01
☐ 921	Pascal Paradis	.15	.06	.01
☐ 922	Frederic Deblois	.08	.03	.01
☐ 923	Marco Grondin	.08	.03	.01
☐ 924	David Lessard	.08	.03	.01
☐ 925	Mathieu Pouliot	.08	.03	.01
☐ 926	Vincent Gonthier	.08	.03	.01
☐ 927	Sebastien Vachon	.08	.03	.01
☐ 928	Remy Doyon	.08	.03	.01
☐ 929	Jean-Pierre Talbot	.08	.03	.01
☐ 930	Steve Leclair	.08	.03	.01
☐ 931	Louis-Jean Labbe	.08	.03	.01
☐ 932	Marc Poulin	.08	.03	.01
☐ 933	Eric Grenier	.08	.03	.01
☐ 934	St-Georges	.15	.06	.01
	(Team photo and CL)			
☐ 935	Remi Gilbert	.08	.03	.01
☐ 936	Patrice Giguere	.08	.03	.01
☐ 937	Pierre Bouchard	.08	.03	.01
☐ 938	Alexandre Audet	.08	.03	.01
☐ 939	Dominic Drouin	.08	.03	.01
☐ 940	Philippe Deblois	.08	.03	.01
☐ 941	Jean-Francois Cote	.08	.03	.01
☐ 942	Marco Bouffard	.08	.03	.01
☐ 943	Johny Carrier	.08	.03	.01
☐ 944	Philippe Deblois	.08	.03	.01
☐ 945	Pierre-Luc Begin	.08	.03	.01
☐ 946	Jean-Philippe Chabot	.08	.03	.01
☐ 947	Sylvain Carbonneau	.08	.03	.01
☐ 948	Stephane Turcotte	.08	.03	.01
☐ 949	Jerome Drouin	.08	.03	.01
☐ 950	Bernard Lachance	.08	.03	.01
☐ 951	Lac-Etchemin	.15	.06	.01
	(Team photo and CL)			
☐ 952	Terry Rankin	.08	.03	.01
☐ 953	Christian Viens	.08	.03	.01
☐ 954	Luis Arseneau	.08	.03	.01
☐ 955	Herve Gagnon	.08	.03	.01
☐ 956	Jean-Francois Caron	.08	.03	.01
☐ 957	Daniel Masse	.08	.03	.01
☐ 958	Dave McCann	.08	.03	.01
☐ 959	Jerome Petit	.08	.03	.01
☐ 960	Jonathan Audet	.08	.03	.01
☐ 961	Simon Lavoie	.08	.03	.01
☐ 962	Martin Rondeau	.08	.03	.01
☐ 963	Jonathan Lemerise	.08	.03	.01
☐ 964	Benoit Constantineau	.08	.03	.01
☐ 965	Sebastien Audet	.08	.03	.01
☐ 966	Michel Bolduc	.08	.03	.01
☐ 967	Cascades -- Amos	.15	.06	.01
	(Team photo and CL)			
☐ 968	Alexis Beaudin	.08	.03	.01
☐ 969	Francois Houde	.08	.03	.01
☐ 970	Marc-Michel Lavoie	.08	.03	.01
☐ 971	Mathieu Louder	.08	.03	.01
☐ 972	Marc Fortier	.08	.03	.01
☐ 973	Francois Beland	.08	.03	.01
☐ 974	Dominci Jolin	.08	.03	.01
☐ 975	Jean-Rene Plante	.08	.03	.01
☐ 976	Jean-Patrick Emard	.08	.03	.01
☐ 977	Martin Bouffard	.08	.03	.01
☐ 978	Jean-Philippe Cote	.08	.03	.01
☐ 979	Mathieu Ouellet	.08	.03	.01
☐ 980	Luc Brisson	.25	.10	.02
☐ 981	Paul Blanchard	.08	.03	.01
☐ 982	Jean-Francois Plante	.08	.03	.01

☐ 983	Steve Jobidon	.08	.03	.01
☐ 984	Selects de Sainte-Foy	.15	.06	.01
	(Team photo and CL)			
☐ 985	Marc-Andre Poirier	.08	.03	.01
☐ 986	Jean-Sebastien Poulin	.08	.03	.01
☐ 987	Charles Gelinas	.08	.03	.01
☐ 988	Vincent Lecompte	.08	.03	.01
☐ 989	Guillaume Brochu	.08	.03	.01
☐ 990	Dennis Burns	.08	.03	.01
☐ 991	Kevin Belanger	.08	.03	.01
☐ 992	Alexandre Borne	.08	.03	.01
☐ 993	Dave Gagnon	.08	.03	.01
☐ 994	Jean-Francois Doyon	.08	.03	.01
☐ 995	Patrick Lachance	.08	.03	.01
☐ 996	Louis-Vincent Lemelin	.08	.03	.01
☐ 997	Santino De Toni	.08	.03	.01
☐ 998	Gilles-Charles Gosselin	.08	.03	.01
☐ 999	Yanick Fiset	.08	.03	.01
☐ 1000	Royaux de Sainte-Foy	.15	.06	.01
	(Team photo and CL)			
☐ 1001	Jean-Phillipe Cote	.08	.03	.01
☐ 1002	Simon Bussieres	.08	.03	.01
☐ 1003	Kim Cloutier	.08	.03	.01
☐ 1004	Jean-Luc Martin	.08	.03	.01
☐ 1005	Mathieu Lelievre	.08	.03	.01
☐ 1006	Jasmin Thibault	.08	.03	.01
☐ 1007	Steve Fortin	.08	.03	.01
☐ 1008	Eric Martin	.08	.03	.01
☐ 1009	Jonathan Harbour	.08	.03	.01
☐ 1010	Martin Fournier	.08	.03	.01
☐ 1011	Sami Jalbert	.08	.03	.01
☐ 1012	Francois Monier	.08	.03	.01
☐ 1013	Kevin Lapointe	.08	.03	.01
☐ 1014	Jean-Francois Dionne	.08	.03	.01
☐ 1015	Frederic Dreyer	.08	.03	.01
☐ 1016	Gyslain Thibault	.08	.03	.01
☐ 1017	David Whittom	.08	.03	.01
☐ 1018	David Cantin	.08	.03	.01
☐ 1019	Jean-Francois Sylvain	.08	.03	.01
☐ 1020	Les Epaulards	.15	.06	.01
	(Team photo and CL			
☐ 1021	Charles Latulippe	.08	.03	.01
☐ 1022	Frederic Nadeau	.08	.03	.01
☐ 1023	Jean-Francois Nolet	.08	.03	.01
☐ 1024	Maxime L'Hebreux	.08	.03	.01
☐ 1025	Louis-Charles Garant	.08	.03	.01
☐ 1026	Vincent Lemelin Ramsay	.08	.03	.01
☐ 1027	Jean-Philippe Morin	.08	.03	.01
☐ 1028	Mario Vallieres	.08	.03	.01
☐ 1029	Jerome Levasseur	.08	.03	.01
☐ 1030	Nicolas Carrier	.08	.03	.01
☐ 1031	Maxime Perreault	.08	.03	.01
☐ 1032	Jerome Guay	.08	.03	.01
☐ 1033	Dave Labrecque	.08	.03	.01
☐ 1034	Nicolas Vaillancourt	.08	.03	.01
☐ 1035	Eric Carrier	.08	.03	.01
☐ 1036	Louis-Olivier Gervais	.08	.03	.01
☐ 1037	Pointe-Levy	.15	.06	.01
	(Team photo and CL)			
☐ 1038	Jean-Francois Gamelin	.08	.03	.01
☐ 1039	Jean-Francois Fortin	.08	.03	.01
☐ 1040	Cedric Bourgeois	.08	.03	.01
☐ 1041	Pascal Brazeau	.08	.03	.01
☐ 1042	Alexandre Lachance	.08	.03	.01
☐ 1043	Benoit Lacasse	.08	.03	.01
☐ 1044	Michel Lachance	.08	.03	.01
☐ 1045	Pascal Dupuis	.08	.03	.01
☐ 1046	Frederic Girard	.08	.03	.01
☐ 1047	David Comeau	.08	.03	.01
☐ 1048	Sylvain Deschatelets	.08	.03	.01
☐ 1049	Jonathan Cecile	.08	.03	.01
☐ 1050	Jean-Philippe Cloutier	.08	.03	.01
☐ 1051	Mathieu Villeneuve	.08	.03	.01
☐ 1052	Sebastien Matte	.08	.03	.01
☐ 1053	Philippe Sauve	.08	.03	.01
☐ 1054	Seigneurs Des Mille Iles	.15	.06	.01
	(Team photo and CL)			
☐ 1055	Joel Couture	.08	.03	.01
☐ 1056	Vincent Caron	.08	.03	.01
☐ 1057	Stephane Blouin	.08	.03	.01
☐ 1058	Steve Bedard	.08	.03	.01
☐ 1059	Olivier Moreau	.08	.03	.01
☐ 1060	Sebastien Thivierge	.08	.03	.01
☐ 1061	Richard Lamontagne	.08	.03	.01
☐ 1062	Patrice Labrecque	.08	.03	.01
☐ 1063	Jean-Francois Roy	.08	.03	.01

☐ 1064	Jonathan Argouin	.08	.03	.01
☐ 1065	Rejean Gagne Jr.	.08	.03	.01
☐ 1066	Olivier Dumais	.08	.03	.01
☐ 1067	Patrice Lachance	.08	.03	.01
☐ 1068	Mathieu Patry	.08	.03	.01
☐ 1069	Vincent Gravel	.08	.03	.01
☐ 1070	Philippe Raby	.08	.03	.01
☐ 1071	Bellechasse	.15	.06	.01
	(Team photo and CL)			
☐ 1072	Yannick Turcotte	.08	.03	.01
☐ 1073	Denis Vaillancourt	.08	.03	.01
☐ 1074	Carl Rousseau	.08	.03	.01
☐ 1075	Mathieu Tanguay	.08	.03	.01
☐ 1076	Jonathan Petit	.08	.03	.01
☐ 1077	Olivier Marier	.08	.03	.01
☐ 1078	Martin Legare	.08	.03	.01
☐ 1079	Justin Lemay	.08	.03	.01
☐ 1080	Jean-Francois Fortin	.08	.03	.01
☐ 1081	Eric Dumont	.08	.03	.01
☐ 1082	Luc Dantinne	.08	.03	.01
☐ 1083	Stephane Demers	.08	.03	.01
☐ 1084	Sebastien Cimon	.08	.03	.01
☐ 1085	Francois Cantin	.08	.03	.01
☐ 1086	Marie-Claude Allard	.15	.06	.01
☐ 1087	Nicholas Brown	.08	.03	.01
☐ 1088	Frontenac de Quebec	.15	.06	.01
	(Team photo and CL			
☐ 1089	Dave Tessier	.08	.03	.01
☐ 1090	Vincent Ruel	.08	.03	.01
☐ 1091	Martin Roy	.08	.03	.01
☐ 1092	Jerome-Olivier Frechette	.08	.03	.01
☐ 1093	Jean-Sebastien Angers	.08	.03	.01
☐ 1094	Jasmin Fiset	.15	.06	.01
☐ 1095	David Barabe	.08	.03	.01
☐ 1096	Nelson Levesque	.08	.03	.01
☐ 1097	Nicolas Jolin	.08	.03	.01
☐ 1098	Korren Rivers	.08	.03	.01
☐ 1099	Francis Mainguy	.08	.03	.01
☐ 1100	Francois Mecteau	.08	.03	.01
☐ 1101	Daniel Auclair	.08	.03	.01
☐ 1102	Jerome Lessard	.08	.03	.01
☐ 1103	Dominic Carignan	.08	.03	.01
☐ 1104	Chantale Maheux	.15	.06	.01
☐ 1105	David Grenier	.08	.03	.01
☐ 1106	Cavaliers de Sainte-Foy	.15	.06	.01
	(Team photo and CL)			
☐ 1107	Simon Isabelle	.08	.03	.01
☐ 1108	Francois Latulippe	.08	.03	.01
☐ 1109	Carl Gosselin	.08	.03	.01
☐ 1110	Benoit Langlois	.08	.03	.01
☐ 1111	Patrice Auger	.08	.03	.01
☐ 1112	Philippe Grondin	.08	.03	.01
☐ 1113	Francois Fortin	.08	.03	.01
☐ 1114	Tommy Thibault	.08	.03	.01
☐ 1115	David Cote	.08	.03	.01
☐ 1116	Danny Bernier	.08	.03	.01
☐ 1117	Dominic Laflamme	.08	.03	.01
☐ 1118	Louis De Beaumont	.08	.03	.01
☐ 1119	Jean-Francois Fillion	.08	.03	.01
☐ 1120	Mathieu Deslauriers	.08	.03	.01
☐ 1121	Sylvain Desnoyers	.08	.03	.01
☐ 1122	Guy Roy	.08	.03	.01
☐ 1123	Nordiques de Quebec	.15	.06	.01
	(Team photo and CL)			
☐ 1124	Sebastian Melancon	.08	.03	.01
☐ 1125	Charles Turgeon	.08	.03	.01
☐ 1126	Philippe Matteau	.08	.03	.01
☐ 1127	Jean Etienne	.08	.03	.01
☐ 1128	Jean Hamel	.08	.03	.01
☐ 1129	Luc Langlois	.08	.03	.01
☐ 1130	Etienne Guay	.08	.03	.01
☐ 1131	Pascal Gauthier	.08	.03	.01
☐ 1132	Jean-Michel Drolet	.08	.03	.01
☐ 1133	Erik Gagnon	.08	.03	.01
☐ 1134	Patrice Cote	.08	.03	.01
☐ 1135	Eric De Champlain	.08	.03	.01
☐ 1136	Simon Boivin	.08	.03	.01
☐ 1137	Alexandre Boutin	.08	.03	.01
☐ 1138	Dominic Boily	.08	.03	.01
☐ 1139	Charles Boily	.08	.03	.01
☐ 1140	Sagueneens de Chicoutimi	.15	.06	.01
	(Team photo and CL)			
☐ 1141	Mark Woytiuk	.08	.03	.01
☐ 1142	Pat Stachniak	.08	.03	.01
☐ 1143	Mike Starrett	.08	.03	.01
☐ 1144	Tim Salter	.08	.03	.01
☐ 1145	Andy Penny	.08	.03	.01
☐ 1146	Oliver McGee	.08	.03	.01

☐ 1147 Charles Metcalfe	.08	.03	.01
☐ 1148 Shane McCooeye	.08	.03	.01
☐ 1149 Jeremy Glasgow	.08	.03	.01
☐ 1150 Joey Bastien	.08	.03	.01
☐ 1151 Mike Graves	.08	.03	.01
☐ 1152 Mike Comrie	.08	.03	.01
☐ 1153 Greg Dowell	.08	.03	.01
☐ 1154 Rick Dowell	.08	.03	.01
☐ 1155 Paul Esdale	.08	.03	.01
☐ 1156 Lloyd Fobes	.08	.03	.01
☐ 1157 Richard Forest	.08	.03	.01
☐ 1158 Edmonton Oilers	.15	.06	.01
(Team photo and CL)			
☐ 1159 Richard Charter	.08	.03	.01
☐ 1160 Sean Hodges	.08	.03	.01
☐ 1161 Phillip Barski	.08	.03	.01
☐ 1162 Robert Diblasio	.08	.03	.01
☐ 1163 John Gallo	.08	.03	.01
☐ 1164 Kevin Baker	.08	.03	.01
☐ 1165 Jeffrey Morrison	.08	.03	.01
☐ 1166 Adrian Firmani	.08	.03	.01
☐ 1167 Dominic Walters	.08	.03	.01
☐ 1168 Thomas Jason Hill	.08	.03	.01
☐ 1169 Steven Pocock	.08	.03	.01
☐ 1170 Anthony Doria	.08	.03	.01
☐ 1171 Gregory Dunlap	.08	.03	.01
☐ 1172 Kenneth Dunlap	.08	.03	.01
☐ 1173 Trevor Padgett	.08	.03	.01
☐ 1174 Peter Genua	.08	.03	.01
☐ 1175 Richmond Hill	.15	.06	.01
(Team photo and CL)			
☐ 1176 Adam Rosso	.08	.03	.01
☐ 1177 Todd McNaught	.08	.03	.01
☐ 1178 Adam Richards	.08	.03	.01
☐ 1179 Scott Nelson	.08	.03	.01
☐ 1180 Andre Kalata	.08	.03	.01
☐ 1181 Jeff Kubacki	.08	.03	.01
☐ 1182 Kirk Joudrey	.08	.03	.01
☐ 1183 Sasha Frankovic	.08	.03	.01
☐ 1184 Jeff Wilson	.08	.03	.01
☐ 1185 Chad Blundy	.08	.03	.01
☐ 1186 Jason Gauthier	.08	.03	.01
☐ 1187 Chris Kline	.08	.03	.01
☐ 1188 Michael Muldoon	.08	.03	.01
☐ 1189 Ross Fiore	.08	.03	.01
☐ 1190 Curtis Hamilton	.08	.03	.01
☐ 1191 Brad McDonald	.08	.03	.01
☐ 1192 Oakville	.15	.06	.01
(Team photo and CL)			
☐ 1193 Jeanot Savoie	.08	.03	.01
☐ 1194 Christian Roy	.08	.03	.01
☐ 1195 Eric Roy	.08	.03	.01
☐ 1196 Paul Ross	.08	.03	.01
☐ 1197 Martin Pare	.08	.03	.01
☐ 1198 Sebastien Paradis	.08	.03	.01
☐ 1199 Andrew Milton	.08	.03	.01
☐ 1200 Erik Gionet	.08	.03	.01
☐ 1201 Kule Jamieson	.08	.03	.01
☐ 1202 Jim Gallant	.08	.03	.01
☐ 1203 Stephane Fortin	.08	.03	.01
☐ 1204 Philippe Cormier	.08	.03	.01
☐ 1205 Ricky Doucet	.08	.03	.01
☐ 1206 Craig Branch	.08	.03	.01
☐ 1207 Ghislain Bryar	.08	.03	.01
☐ 1208 Andre Leblanc	.08	.03	.01
☐ 1209 Hughes Michaud	.08	.03	.01
☐ 1210 Beresford	.15	.06	.01
(Team photo and CL)			
☐ 1211 Ryan Gallant	.08	.03	.01
☐ 1212 Billy Frizzell	.08	.03	.01
☐ 1213 Mike McLaine	.08	.03	.01
☐ 1214 Kent Macissac	.08	.03	.01
☐ 1215 Nathan Carragher	.08	.03	.01
☐ 1216 Alex MacPherson	.08	.03	.01
☐ 1217 Kevin Crozier	.08	.03	.01
☐ 1218 Billy Murphy	.08	.03	.01
☐ 1219 Jonathan Stavert	.08	.03	.01
☐ 1220 Robbie Roberts	.08	.03	.01
☐ 1221 Joshua Proud	.08	.03	.01
☐ 1222 Donnie Mackinnon	.08	.03	.01
☐ 1223 Mark McKenzie	.08	.03	.01
☐ 1224 Jasmin Barrett	.15	.06	.01
☐ 1225 Kris Macphee	.08	.03	.01
☐ 1226 North River	.15	.06	.01
(Team photo and CL)			
☐ 1227 Jason Labarbera	.15	.06	.01
☐ 1228 Wes Jorundson	.08	.03	.01
☐ 1229 Steve Harrington	.08	.03	.01
☐ 1230 Tyler Jackson	.08	.03	.01
☐ 1231 Jeff Webster	.08	.03	.01
☐ 1232 Jordan Landry	.08	.03	.01
☐ 1233 Jesse Swett	.08	.03	.01
☐ 1234 Jeremy Johnson	.08	.03	.01

☐ 1235 Jeff Franklin	.08	.03	.01
☐ 1236 Brad Fehr	.08	.03	.01
☐ 1237 Peron Desnoyers	.08	.03	.01
☐ 1238 Curtis Cunningham	.08	.03	.01
☐ 1239 Mark Ewing	.08	.03	.01
☐ 1240 Brodie Norman	.08	.03	.01
☐ 1241 Peter Mihalech	.08	.03	.01
☐ 1242 Langley Eagles	.15	.06	.01
(Team photo and CL)			
☐ 1243 Alex Kim	.08	.03	.01
☐ 1244 Stephen Faulk	.08	.03	.01
☐ 1245 Shane Warschaw	.08	.03	.01
☐ 1246 Scott Holsinger	.08	.03	.01
☐ 1247 Noah Clarke	.08	.03	.01
☐ 1248 Patrick Johnson	.08	.03	.01
☐ 1249 Jon Wilkins	.08	.03	.01
☐ 1250 Jay Tyacke	.08	.03	.01
☐ 1251 Manu Mau'u	.08	.03	.01
☐ 1252 Justin Morrison	.08	.03	.01
☐ 1253 Micah Wouters	.08	.03	.01
☐ 1254 Garrett Stafford	.08	.03	.01
☐ 1255 Eric DeJong	.08	.03	.01
☐ 1256 Stephen Novodor	.08	.03	.01
☐ 1257 Garrett Yokoyama	.08	.03	.01
☐ 1258 Justin Dixon	.08	.03	.01
☐ 1259 Trevor Martin	.08	.03	.01
☐ 1260 California Kings	.15	.06	.01
(Team photo and CL)			
☐ 1261 Justin Roe	.08	.03	.01
☐ 1262 Matthew Kim	.08	.03	.01
☐ 1263 Paul R. Tilch	.08	.03	.01
☐ 1264 Corey Segal	.08	.03	.01
☐ 1265 Bobby M. Dameron	.08	.03	.01
☐ 1266 Jeff Sepanski	.08	.03	.01
☐ 1267 Zakary Thomas	.08	.03	.01
LeBlanc			
☐ 1268 Michael Abner	.08	.03	.01
☐ 1269 Cam Donahue	.08	.03	.01
☐ 1270 Michael Goldkind	.08	.03	.01
☐ 1271 Tom Daniel	.08	.03	.01
☐ 1272 Adam David McKenzie	.08	.03	.01
☐ 1273 Brian Rice	.08	.03	.01
☐ 1274 Tyler Scott	.08	.03	.01
☐ 1275 David Crenshaw	.08	.03	.01
☐ 1276 Zachary Christian	.08	.03	.01
Jackson			
☐ 1277 Michael Weyermann	.08	.03	.01
☐ 1278 Kevin B. Knupp	.08	.03	.01
☐ 1279 John Lee	.08	.03	.01
☐ 1280 Washington Capitals	.15	.06	.01
(Team photo and CL)			
☐ 1281 Lenny Raimondi	.08	.03	.01
☐ 1282 Brandan Tvohy	.08	.03	.01
☐ 1283 Chris Wolff	.08	.03	.01
☐ 1284 Craig Sliva	.08	.03	.01
☐ 1285 Andrew Townsend	.08	.03	.01
☐ 1286 David Gibson	.08	.03	.01
☐ 1287 Keith Anthony	.08	.03	.01
☐ 1288 Chris Migliore	.08	.03	.01
☐ 1289 Matt Celentano	.08	.03	.01
☐ 1290 Geoff Barlow	.08	.03	.01
☐ 1291 Chris Dunn	.08	.03	.01
☐ 1292 Jack Kennedy	.08	.03	.01
☐ 1293 John Longo	.08	.03	.01
☐ 1294 Erik Mikan	.08	.03	.01
☐ 1295 Scott Savenelli	.08	.03	.01
☐ 1296 Joe Snecinski	.08	.03	.01
☐ 1297 Derek Saunders	.08	.03	.01
☐ 1298 New York Rangers	.15	.06	.01
(Team photo and CL)			
☐ 1299 Mike Swistak	.08	.03	.01
☐ 1300 Erik Wright	.08	.03	.01
☐ 1301 Dustin Kuk	.08	.03	.01
☐ 1302 Terry Brennan	.08	.03	.01
☐ 1303 Tim Hearon	.08	.03	.01
☐ 1304 Matt Prater	.08	.03	.01
☐ 1305 Jason Bruneel	.08	.03	.01
☐ 1306 David Tigay	.08	.03	.01
☐ 1307 Scot Curtin	.08	.03	.01
☐ 1308 Phil Osaer	.08	.03	.01
☐ 1309 Dwayne McGowan	.08	.03	.01
☐ 1310 Nicholas Jardine	.08	.03	.01
☐ 1311 Jeff Bassett	.08	.03	.01
☐ 1312 Shaun Fisher	.08	.03	.01
☐ 1313 Mike Porter	.08	.03	.01
☐ 1314 Chris Tom	.08	.03	.01
☐ 1315 Detroit GPD	.15	.06	.01
(Team photo and CL)			
☐ 1316 Jejuan Collins	.08	.03	.01
☐ 1317 Michael Gingue	.08	.03	.01
☐ 1318 Toby Grahouec	.08	.03	.01
☐ 1319 John Johnson	.08	.03	.01
☐ 1320 Jeremiah Kimento	.08	.03	.01

☐ 1321	Nick Kalwinski	.08	.03	.01
☐ 1322	Adam Rogowin	.08	.03	.01
☐ 1323	Kraig Roberts	.08	.03	.01
☐ 1324	Anthony Battaglia	.08	.03	.01
☐ 1325	David Schneider	.08	.03	.01
☐ 1326	Peter Chelios	.15	.06	.01
☐ 1327	Nick Chin	.08	.03	.01
☐ 1328	Kenny Marsch	.08	.03	.01
☐ 1329	Gabe Polsky	.08	.03	.01
☐ 1330	Troy Linna	.08	.03	.01
☐ 1331	Brent Kozel	.08	.03	.01
☐ 1332	Chicago Young	.15	.06	.01
	Americans			
	(Team photo and CL)			
☐ 1333	Didier Tremblay	.08	.03	.01
☐ 1334	Alexandre Mathieu	.08	.03	.01
☐ 1335	Frederick Jean	.08	.03	.01
☐ 1336	Francis Morin	.08	.03	.01
☐ 1337	Jean-Martin Raymond	.08	.03	.01
☐ 1338	Francis Lessard	.08	.03	.01
☐ 1339	Marc Ouimet	.15	.06	.01
☐ 1340	Tom Dessureault	.08	.03	.01
☐ 1341	Christian Ringuet	.08	.03	.01
☐ 1342	Sebastien Cyr	.08	.03	.01
☐ 1343	Jean-Francois	.08	.03	.01
	Normand			
☐ 1344	Stephane Girard	.08	.03	.01
☐ 1345	Steve Vendette	.08	.03	.01
☐ 1346	Jonathan Dionne	.08	.03	.01
☐ 1347	Sebastien Fournier	.08	.03	.01
☐ 1348	Alexandre Guy	.08	.03	.01
☐ 1349	Elites Rive-Nord	.15	.06	.01
	(Team photo and CL)			
☐ 1350	Mathieu Bouchard	.08	.03	.01
☐ 1351	Sebastien Renaud	.08	.03	.01
☐ 1352	Sylvain Lacroix	.08	.03	.01
☐ 1353	Frederic Boily	.08	.03	.01
☐ 1354	Pierre-Marc Cote	.08	.03	.01
☐ 1355	Dany Prive	.08	.03	.01
☐ 1356	Frederick Cote	.08	.03	.01
☐ 1357	Marc Fortin	.08	.03	.01
☐ 1358	Steve Vandal	.08	.03	.01
☐ 1359	Alexandre Plourde	.08	.03	.01
☐ 1360	Sebastien Gaudreault	.08	.03	.01
☐ 1361	Eric Malaison	.08	.03	.01
☐ 1362	Parice Gagnon	.08	.03	.01
☐ 1363	Andre Tremblay Jr.	.08	.03	.01
☐ 1364	Pierre-Luc Gagne	.08	.03	.01
☐ 1365	Michael Villeneuve	.08	.03	.01
☐ 1366	Alexandre Cote	.08	.03	.01
☐ 1367	Alma	.15	.06	.01
	(Team photo and CL)			
☐ 1368	Erik St-Hilaire	.08	.03	.01
☐ 1369	Eric Simon	.08	.03	.01
☐ 1370	Simon Roy	.08	.03	.01
☐ 1371	Marc-Andre Proulx	.08	.03	.01
☐ 1372	Simon Ouellet	.08	.03	.01
☐ 1373	Eric Moreau	.08	.03	.01
☐ 1374	Tony McHugh	.08	.03	.01
☐ 1375	Pascal Mercier	.08	.03	.01
☐ 1376	Luc Live	.08	.03	.01
☐ 1377	Pascal Levesque	.08	.03	.01
☐ 1378	Dominic Lachance	.08	.03	.01
☐ 1379	Christian Lessard	.08	.03	.01
☐ 1380	Frederic Cloutier	.08	.03	.01
☐ 1381	Alexandre Garant	.08	.03	.01
☐ 1382	Nicolas Berryman	.08	.03	.01
☐ 1383	Donald Blouin	.08	.03	.01
☐ 1384	Citadelle de Quebec	.15	.06	.01
	(Team photo and CL)			
☐ 1385	Karl Guieseppe	.08	.03	.01
	Parenti			
☐ 1386	Benoit Heroux	.08	.03	.01
☐ 1387	Marc Parent Lavoie	.08	.03	.01
☐ 1388	Steve Sousa	.08	.03	.01
☐ 1389	Benjamin Denis-	.08	.03	.01
	Cartier			
☐ 1390	Patrick Heroux	.08	.03	.01
☐ 1391	Mike Ribeiro	.08	.03	.01
☐ 1392	Eric Cyr	.08	.03	.01
☐ 1393	Netema Ndunigidi	.08	.03	.01
☐ 1394	Yves Engler	.08	.03	.01
☐ 1395	Jean Themens	.08	.03	.01
☐ 1396	Jonatan Turcot	.08	.03	.01
☐ 1397	Francis Leclerc	.08	.03	.01
☐ 1398	Patrick Desrosiers	.08	.03	.01
☐ 1399	Jean-Francois	.08	.03	.01
	Fecteau			
☐ 1400	Stephane Villandre	.08	.03	.01
☐ 1401	Canadiens de Montreal	.15	.06	.01
	(Team photo and CL)			
☐ 1402	Jay Greer	.08	.03	.01
☐ 1403	Matt Laxton	.08	.03	.01
☐ 1404	Randy Fitzgerald	.08	.03	.01
☐ 1405	Chris Heron	.08	.03	.01
☐ 1406	Tommy Kotsopoulos	.15	.06	.01
☐ 1407	Shane Nash	.08	.03	.01
☐ 1408	Adam Colagiacomo	.08	.03	.01
☐ 1409	Greg Jossa	.08	.03	.01
☐ 1410	Mark Valcic	.08	.03	.01
☐ 1411	Scott Crawford	.08	.03	.01
☐ 1412	Clarke Walford	.08	.03	.01
☐ 1413	Greg Dunn	.08	.03	.01
☐ 1414	Robert Mulick	.08	.03	.01
☐ 1415	Terry Lenyk	.08	.03	.01
☐ 1416	Toronto Red Wings	.15	.06	.01
	(Team photo and CL)			
☐ 1417	Michael Ryder	.08	.03	.01
☐ 1418	Aaron Fox	.08	.03	.01
☐ 1419	Anthony Angelo Dynak	.08	.03	.01
☐ 1420	Adam Neave	.08	.03	.01
☐ 1421	Cerrone P. Natale	.08	.03	.01
☐ 1422	Michael Ioannou	.08	.03	.01
☐ 1423	George Lopes	.08	.03	.01
☐ 1424	Christopher Hunter	.08	.03	.01
☐ 1425	Adam Murray	.08	.03	.01
☐ 1426	Tommy Kotsopoulos	.15	.06	.01
☐ 1427	Trevor Tuckey	.08	.03	.01
☐ 1428	Robert Burns	.08	.03	.01
☐ 1429	Jerry Rusin	.08	.03	.01
☐ 1430	Mario Baleno	.08	.03	.01
☐ 1431	Don Mills Flyers	.15	.06	.01
	(Team photo and CL)			
☐ 1432	Mark Meredith	.08	.03	.01
☐ 1433	Trevor Mader	.08	.03	.01
☐ 1434	Ryan Duke	.08	.03	.01
☐ 1435	Vince Carinci	.08	.03	.01
☐ 1436	Jamie McKeracher	.08	.03	.01
☐ 1437	Joey Bizzarro	.08	.03	.01
☐ 1438	Matthew Stronach	.08	.03	.01
☐ 1439	Chris Gram	.08	.03	.01
☐ 1440	Alexander Boyle	.08	.03	.01
☐ 1441	Matt Zultek	.08	.03	.01
☐ 1442	Mike Lepp	.08	.03	.01
☐ 1443	Jason Spalding	.08	.03	.01
☐ 1444	Ron Greco	.08	.03	.01
☐ 1445	J.R. Mayers	.08	.03	.01
☐ 1446	Not Known	.00	.00	.00
☐ 1447	Gary Toor	.08	.03	.01
☐ 1448	Paul Dustin	.08	.03	.01
☐ 1449	Ben Ngui	.08	.03	.01
☐ 1450	Judd Medak	.08	.03	.01
☐ 1451	Chris McKane	.08	.03	.01
☐ 1452	Lee Kerasiotis	.08	.03	.01
☐ 1453	Abraham Jang	.08	.03	.01
☐ 1454	Chad Hahn	.08	.03	.01
☐ 1455	Chris Daum	.08	.03	.01
☐ 1456	Paul Condon	.08	.03	.01
☐ 1457	John Buchanan	.08	.03	.01
☐ 1458	Scott Arnold	.08	.03	.01
☐ 1459	Brian Alexander	.08	.03	.01
☐ 1460	Tyrone Lingley	.08	.03	.01
☐ 1461	Jason Lang	.08	.03	.01
☐ 1462	Vancouver Thunder-	.15	.06	.01
	birds (Team photo and CL)			
☐ 1463	Kyle Adams	.08	.03	.01
☐ 1464	Geoff Anderson	.08	.03	.01
☐ 1465	Brett Barrer	.08	.03	.01
☐ 1466	Scott Cuthbertson	.08	.03	.01
☐ 1467	Wes Harkin	.08	.03	.01
☐ 1468	Colin McKenna	.08	.03	.01
☐ 1469	Brian McDonough	.08	.03	.01
☐ 1470	Mike McLoughlin	.08	.03	.01
☐ 1471	David Oh	.08	.03	.01
☐ 1472	David Runge	.08	.03	.01
☐ 1473	Matt Selby	.08	.03	.01
☐ 1474	Chris Sinopoli	.08	.03	.01
☐ 1475	Cory Somerville	.08	.03	.01
☐ 1476	Michael Thompson	.08	.03	.01
☐ 1477	Alex Tzountzouris	.08	.03	.01
☐ 1478	Jamie Ward	.08	.03	.01
☐ 1479	Mike Weisz	.08	.03	.01
☐ 1480	Toronto Wexford	.15	.06	.01
	(Team photo and CL)			
☐ 1481	Mathieu Bellet	.08	.03	.01
☐ 1482	Mathieu Salamand	.08	.03	.01
☐ 1483	Yorick Treille	.08	.03	.01
☐ 1484	Arnaud Goetz	.08	.03	.01
☐ 1485	Cyril Trabichet	.08	.03	.01
☐ 1486	Laurent Meunier	.08	.03	.01
☐ 1487	Julien Staeger	.08	.03	.01
☐ 1488	Gautier Fontanel	.08	.03	.01
☐ 1489	Maxime Augris	.08	.03	.01
☐ 1490	Thibault Fontanel	.08	.03	.01
☐ 1491	Philippe Combe	.08	.03	.01
☐ 1492	Philippe Guers	.08	.03	.01

☐ 1493	Marc Billieras	.08	.03	.01
☐ 1494	Thomas Bergamelli	.08	.03	.01
☐ 1495	Roland Fougere	.08	.03	.01
☐ 1496	Benoit Sarzier	.08	.03	.01
☐ 1497	Clement Berruex	.08	.03	.01
☐ 1498	Nicolas Golleret	.08	.03	.01
☐ 1499	Not Known	.00	.00	.00
☐ 1500	Arkadiusz Bizub	.08	.03	.01
☐ 1501	Marek Raczka	.08	.03	.01
☐ 1502	Lukasz Bizubk	.08	.03	.01
☐ 1503	Jacek Sledzik	.08	.03	.01
☐ 1504	Robert Smreczynski	.08	.03	.01
☐ 1505	Piotr Fryzlewicz	.08	.03	.01
☐ 1506	Miroslaw Grzegorczyk	.08	.03	.01
☐ 1507	Jaroslaw Molenda	.08	.03	.01
☐ 1508	Tomasz Kajzer	.08	.03	.01
☐ 1509	Damian Slabon	.08	.03	.01
☐ 1510	Marcin Kolodziejczyk	.08	.03	.01
☐ 1511	Miroslaw Kolacz	.08	.03	.01
☐ 1512	Zdzislaw Zareba	.08	.03	.01
☐ 1513	Tomasz Golak	.08	.03	.01
☐ 1514	Pawel Slowakiewicz	.08	.03	.01
☐ 1515	Bartlomiej Iskrzycki	.08	.03	.01
☐ 1516	Grzegorz Brejta	.08	.03	.01
☐ 1517	Rafal Kowalski	.08	.03	.01
☐ 1518	Krzysztof Lipkowski	.08	.03	.01
☐ 1519	Marek Dabrowski	.08	.03	.01
☐ 1520	Pologne	.15	.06	.01
	(Team photo and CL)			
☐ 1521	Winfried Rac	.08	.03	.01
☐ 1522	Markus Peintner	.08	.03	.01
☐ 1523	Klaus Tschemernjak	.08	.03	.01
☐ 1524	Elger Oberwelz	.08	.03	.01
☐ 1525	Thomas Eichberger	.08	.03	.01
☐ 1526	Gerhard Gottfried	.08	.03	.01
☐ 1527	Jens Kraiger	.08	.03	.01
☐ 1528	Alexander Lichtblau	.08	.03	.01
☐ 1529	Gregor Baumgartner	.08	.03	.01
☐ 1530	Hans Peter Mitter	.08	.03	.01
☐ 1531	Christian Holler	.08	.03	.01
☐ 1532	Alexander Lechner	.08	.03	.01
☐ 1533	Reinhard Wolfgang	.08	.03	.01
☐ 1534	Gerhard Struger	.08	.03	.01
☐ 1535	Andre Drechsel	.08	.03	.01
☐ 1536	Andreas Kofler	.08	.03	.01
☐ 1537	Thomas Strauss	.08	.03	.01
☐ 1538	Patrik Schneider	.08	.03	.01
☐ 1539	Rene Vallant	.08	.03	.01
☐ 1540	Thomas Scheucher	.08	.03	.01
☐ 1541	Ludek Styblo	.08	.03	.01
☐ 1542	Autriche	.15	.06	.01
	(Team photo and CL)			
☐ 1543	Pavol Spila	.08	.03	.01
☐ 1544	Tomas Ziegler	.08	.03	.01
☐ 1545	Tomas Kurina	.08	.03	.01
☐ 1546	Martin Ochaba	.08	.03	.01
☐ 1547	Stanislav Pavlovic	.08	.03	.01
☐ 1548	Lubomir Pistek	.08	.03	.01
☐ 1549	Jaroslav Malik	.08	.03	.01
☐ 1550	Michal Krupa	.08	.03	.01
☐ 1551	Branislav Kosc	.08	.03	.01
☐ 1552	Marek Kristek	.08	.03	.01
☐ 1553	Alexander Jezo	.08	.03	.01
☐ 1554	Marian Hossa	.08	.03	.01
☐ 1555	Vladimir Hiadlovsky	.08	.03	.01
☐ 1556	Jan Holly	.08	.03	.01
☐ 1557	Miroslav Hala	.08	.03	.01
☐ 1558	Marek Havel	.08	.03	.01
☐ 1559	Adrian Daniel	.08	.03	.01
☐ 1560	Robert Dome	.08	.03	.01
☐ 1561	Martin Galik	.08	.03	.01
☐ 1562	Michal Cesnek	.08	.03	.01
☐ 1563	Jozef Capka	.08	.03	.01
☐ 1564	Robert Frajkor	.08	.03	.01
☐ 1565	Daniel Borik	.08	.03	.01
☐ 1566	Pavol Bolebruch	.08	.03	.01
☐ 1567	Jan Bezdek	.08	.03	.01
☐ 1568	Peter Bohunicky	.08	.03	.01
☐ 1569	Bratislava	.15	.06	.01
	(Team photo and CL)			
☐ 1570	Not Known	.00	.00	.00
☐ 1571	Kevin Meehan	.08	.03	.01
☐ 1572	Josh Spiegel	.08	.03	.01
☐ 1573	Anthony Switek	.08	.03	.01
☐ 1574	Paul Dorn	.08	.03	.01
☐ 1575	Rob Silvia	.08	.03	.01
☐ 1576	Tom McMonagle	.08	.03	.01
☐ 1577	Jimmy Henkel	.08	.03	.01
☐ 1578	James Laux	.08	.03	.01
☐ 1579	Russell Mocgut	.08	.03	.01
☐ 1580	Daniel Houck	.08	.03	.01
☐ 1581	John F. Larnerd	.08	.03	.01
☐ 1582	Jerramie Domish	.08	.03	.01

☐ 1583	Brian Wroble	.08	.03	.01
☐ 1584	Paul Dabrowski	.08	.03	.01
☐ 1585	Danny McDonald	.08	.03	.01
☐ 1586	Brendon Gallagher	.08	.03	.01
☐ 1587	Jeremy Bean	.08	.03	.01
☐ 1588	Philadelphia Little	.15	.06	.01
	Flyers			
	(Team photo and CL)			
☐ 1589	Hugues Gosselin	.08	.03	.01
☐ 1590	Jonathan Violy	.08	.03	.01
☐ 1591	Martin Beauchesne	.08	.03	.01
☐ 1592	Jonathan Blais	.08	.03	.01
☐ 1593	Jonathan Marchand	.08	.03	.01
☐ 1594	Jean-Francois Daneau	.08	.03	.01
☐ 1595	Francois Tanguay	.08	.03	.01
☐ 1596	Maxime Toupin	.08	.03	.01
☐ 1597	Benoit Cote	.08	.03	.01
☐ 1598	Mathieu Dubois	.08	.03	.01
☐ 1599	Pierre-Jean Gaudet	.08	.03	.01
☐ 1600	Jean-Francois Lemay	.08	.03	.01
☐ 1601	Francois Doucet	.08	.03	.01
☐ 1602	Maxime Hains	.08	.03	.01
☐ 1603	Martin Bilodeau	.08	.03	.01
☐ 1604	Draveurs de la	.15	.06	.01
	Mauricie			
	(Team photo and CL)			
☐ 1605	Jerry Merta	.08	.03	.01
☐ 1606	Ken Richmond	.08	.03	.01
☐ 1607	David Stewart	.08	.03	.01
☐ 1608	Justin Gough	.08	.03	.01
☐ 1609	Mike Greschner	.08	.03	.01
☐ 1610	Brent Giesbrecht	.08	.03	.01
☐ 1611	Ryan Killam	.08	.03	.01
☐ 1612	Jason Rich	.08	.03	.01
☐ 1613	Brian Lensen	.08	.03	.01
☐ 1614	Mike Morin	.08	.03	.01
☐ 1615	Chad Euverman	.08	.03	.01
☐ 1616	Cam Laker	.08	.03	.01
☐ 1617	Jon Cisecki	.08	.03	.01
☐ 1618	Ryan Allford	.08	.03	.01
☐ 1619	Vancouver Canucks	.15	.06	.01
	(Team photo and CL)			
☐ 1620	Olivier Stettler	.08	.03	.01
☐ 1621	Adrian Wichser	.08	.03	.01
☐ 1622	Daniel Seiler	.08	.03	.01
☐ 1623	Patrick Schraner	.08	.03	.01
☐ 1624	Ronald Schnuriger	.08	.03	.01
☐ 1625	Cornel Prinz	.08	.03	.01
☐ 1626	Beat Beier	.08	.03	.01
☐ 1627	Benjamin Pluss	.08	.03	.01
☐ 1628	Martin Hohener	.08	.03	.01
☐ 1629	Ronny Keller	.08	.03	.01
☐ 1630	Philipp Folghera	.08	.03	.01
☐ 1631	Marcel Franzi	.08	.03	.01
☐ 1632	Stefan Eberhard	.08	.03	.01
☐ 1633	Ronny Derrer	.08	.03	.01
☐ 1634	Marco Buhrer	.08	.03	.01
☐ 1635	Marco Bonderer	.08	.03	.01
☐ 1636	Moreno Bigliel	.08	.03	.01
☐ 1637	Peter Birrer	.08	.03	.01
☐ 1638	Oliver Aeschlimann	.08	.03	.01
☐ 1639	Fabio Beccareli	.08	.03	.01
☐ 1640	Team Zurich Suisse	.15	.06	.01
	(Team photo and CL)			
☐ 1641	Yannis Boudeau	.08	.03	.01
☐ 1642	Julien Valton	.08	.03	.01
☐ 1643	Yann Vonachen	.08	.03	.01
☐ 1644	Ludovic Hardouin	.08	.03	.01
☐ 1645	Mathieu Palav	.08	.03	.01
☐ 1646	Guillaume Arnoult	.08	.03	.01
☐ 1647	Dominic Carre	.08	.03	.01
☐ 1648	Jill Cauly	.08	.03	.01
☐ 1649	Stephane Labayle	.08	.03	.01
☐ 1650	Julien Hortholary	.08	.03	.01
☐ 1651	Clement Piedrafita	.08	.03	.01
☐ 1652	Alexandre Crampes	.08	.03	.01
☐ 1653	Paul-Edouard Bordas	.08	.03	.01
☐ 1654	Benoit Olivier	.08	.03	.01
☐ 1655	Etienne Lamande	.08	.03	.01
☐ 1656	Julien Barthelemy	.08	.03	.01
☐ 1657	Thomas Yulzari	.08	.03	.01
☐ 1658	Benoit Lubeigt	.08	.03	.01
☐ 1659	Aquitains de Bordeaux	.15	.06	.01
	(Team photo and CL)			
☐ 1660	Timothy Ralston	.08	.03	.01
☐ 1661	Jonathan Grabie	.08	.03	.01
☐ 1662	Jason James Taylor	.08	.03	.01
☐ 1663	Philip Cohen	.00	.00	.00
☐ 1664	James Whitacre	.08	.03	.01
☐ 1665	James R. Zitzer	.08	.03	.01
☐ 1666	Philip Amoroso	.08	.03	.01
☐ 1667	Kevin J. Audit	.08	.03	.01
☐ 1668	Blake Green	.08	.03	.01

☐ 1669	Kyle Neary	.08	.03	.01
☐ 1670	Zachary S. Bender	.08	.03	.01
☐ 1671	Rich Gorman	.08	.03	.01
☐ 1672	Bill Emerick	.15	.06	.01
☐ 1673	Matt Silverio	.08	.03	.01
☐ 1674	Philip A. Hagopian	.08	.03	.01
☐ 1675	Andrew R. Testa	.08	.03	.01
☐ 1676	Jimmy Gilbert	.08	.03	.01
☐ 1677	Matthew Herneisen	.08	.03	.01
☐ 1678	Gregory Marinari	.08	.03	.01
☐ 1679	Jonathan Drake	.08	.03	.01
☐ 1680	Philadelphia Jr. Flyers (Team photo and CL)	.15	.06	.01
☐ 1681	Eric Torresan	.08	.03	.01
☐ 1682	Steven Williams	.08	.03	.01
☐ 1683	Jared Gardner	.08	.03	.01
☐ 1684	Richard Williams	.08	.03	.01
☐ 1685	Colin Young	.08	.03	.01
☐ 1686	Chris Daigle	.15	.06	.01
☐ 1687	Mike Bournazakis	.08	.03	.01
☐ 1688	Lawrence Clarfield	.08	.03	.01
☐ 1689	Jeff Boyes	.08	.03	.01
☐ 1690	Mark Trafford	.08	.03	.01
☐ 1691	Peter John Spadafora	.08	.03	.01
☐ 1692	Matthew Thomas	.08	.03	.01
☐ 1693	Randy Stolec	.08	.03	.01
☐ 1694	Ryan Steele	.08	.03	.01
☐ 1695	Matthew Currah	.08	.03	.01
☐ 1696A	David Harrison	.15	.06	.01
☐ 1696B	Mississauga Senators (Team photo and CL)	.15	.06	.01
☐ 1698	Anthony MacLean	.08	.03	.01
☐ 1699	Kevin McKeown	.08	.03	.01
☐ 1700	Christopher McKeown	.08	.03	.01
☐ 1701	Tomas Baluch	.08	.03	.01
☐ 1702	Jozef Contofalsky	.08	.03	.01
☐ 1703	Tomas Schlosser UER (Name reversed on card)	.15	.06	.01
☐ 1704	Ladislav Nagy	.08	.03	.01
☐ 1705	Goczi Severin	.08	.03	.01
☐ 1706	Peter Smrek	.08	.03	.01
☐ 1707	Zoltan Batovsky	.08	.03	.01
☐ 1708	Martin Liba	.08	.03	.01
☐ 1709	Michal Jandel	.08	.03	.01
☐ 1710	Martin Kvietok	.08	.03	.01
☐ 1711	Simo Stanislav	.08	.03	.01
☐ 1712	Peter Grecko	.08	.03	.01
☐ 1713	Kristian Peter	.08	.03	.01
☐ 1714	Marian Bodnar	.08	.03	.01
☐ 1715	Peter Sejna	.08	.03	.01
☐ 1716	Marian Koleda	.08	.03	.01
☐ 1717	Jan Lasak	.08	.03	.01
☐ 1718	Peter Kassa	.08	.03	.01
☐ 1719	Jan Supuka	.08	.03	.01
☐ 1720	Stanislav Gejdos	.08	.03	.01
☐ 1721	Rastislav Jacico	.08	.03	.01
☐ 1722	Branislav Prasek	.08	.03	.01
☐ 1723	Slovaquie (Team photo and CL)	.15	.06	.01
☐ 1724	Brian Rocheford	.08	.03	.01
☐ 1725	J.P. Grianoli	.08	.03	.01
☐ 1726	Sean McQuade	.08	.03	.01
☐ 1727	Kevin Young	.08	.03	.01
☐ 1728	John Cappiello	.08	.03	.01
☐ 1729	Jon Olson	.08	.03	.01
☐ 1730	Ronnie D'Angelo	.08	.03	.01
☐ 1731	David Rush	.08	.03	.01
☐ 1732	Brett Hennings	.08	.03	.01
☐ 1733	Don Richardson	.08	.03	.01
☐ 1734	Ales Colinar	.08	.03	.01
☐ 1735	John Rombard	.08	.03	.01
☐ 1736	Not Known	.00	.00	.00
☐ 1737	Alan Steiger	.08	.03	.01
☐ 1738	Not Known	.00	.00	.00
☐ 1739	Matt Miracolo	.08	.03	.01
☐ 1740	Chris Wolff	.08	.03	.01
☐ 1741	Not Known	.00	.00	.00
☐ 1742	Ryan Bellina	.08	.03	.01
☐ 1743	Ted Schiff	.08	.03	.01
☐ 1744	Not Known	.00	.00	.00
☐ 1745	Blair Piggott	.08	.03	.01
☐ 1746	Not Known	.00	.00	.00
☐ 1747	Not Known	.00	.00	.00
☐ 1748	Brian Eovaldi	.08	.03	.01
☐ 1749	Ernie Hartlieb	.08	.03	.01
☐ 1750	Gregory Job	.08	.03	.01
☐ 1751	Jason B. Deskins	.08	.03	.01
☐ 1752	Joseph Gerbe	.08	.03	.01
☐ 1753	Mike Bozoian	.08	.03	.01
☐ 1754	Justin Brewer	.08	.03	.01
☐ 1755	Mark Brian Felker	.08	.03	.01
☐ 1756	Joseph R. Blackburn	.08	.03	.01

☐ 1757	Not Known	.00	.00	.00
☐ 1758	Donald Pierce (Listed as 1757 on checklist card)	.15	.06	.01
☐ 1759	Ronald Kolito	.08	.03	.01
☐ 1760	David A. Legwand	.08	.03	.01
☐ 1761	Rael Blair	.08	.03	.01
☐ 1762	Edward Close	.08	.03	.01
☐ 1763	Garrett M. Henkel	.08	.03	.01
☐ 1764	Detroit Red Wings (Team photo and CL)	.15	.06	.01
☐ 1765	Jiri Kratschmar	.08	.03	.01
☐ 1766	Christoph Jager	.08	.03	.01
☐ 1767	Sebastian Krause	.08	.03	.01
☐ 1768	Felix Jentzmik	.08	.03	.01
☐ 1769	Marc Wuhrer	.08	.03	.01
☐ 1770	Oliver Reimer	.08	.03	.01
☐ 1771	Matthias Vater	.08	.03	.01
☐ 1772	Steffen Karl	.08	.03	.01
☐ 1773	Marc Dell'Anna	.08	.03	.01
☐ 1774	Alexander Dexheimer	.08	.03	.01
☐ 1775	Sascha Goc	.08	.03	.01
☐ 1776	Tobias Zappe	.08	.03	.01
☐ 1777	Thomas Dolak	.08	.03	.01
☐ 1778	Norman Thimm	.08	.03	.01
☐ 1779	Thomas Jetter	.08	.03	.01
☐ 1780	Not Known	.00	.00	.00
☐ 1781	Anze Ulcar	.08	.03	.01
☐ 1782	Dusan Brulc	.08	.03	.01
☐ 1783	Jure Penkoc	.08	.03	.01
☐ 1784	Mitja Sivic	.08	.03	.01
☐ 1785	Aljosa Javor	.08	.03	.01
☐ 1786	Luka Rebolj	.08	.03	.01
☐ 1787	Gorazd Knezevic	.08	.03	.01
☐ 1788	Erik Blatnik	.08	.03	.01
☐ 1789	Martin Pirnat	.08	.03	.01
☐ 1790	Uros Peruzzi	.08	.03	.01
☐ 1791	Daniel Glumac	.08	.03	.01
☐ 1792	Ales Beton	.08	.03	.01
☐ 1793	Denis Samec	.08	.03	.01
☐ 1794	Edo Terglav	.08	.03	.01
☐ 1795	Matjaz Vodnjov	.08	.03	.01
☐ 1796	Tomaz Razinger	.08	.03	.01
☐ 1797	Tine Troha	.08	.03	.01
☐ 1798	Jure Rozman	.08	.03	.01
☐ 1799	Jurij Golicic	.08	.03	.01
☐ 1800	Marjan Bizjak	.08	.03	.01
☐ 1801	Miha Zbontar	.08	.03	.01
☐ 1802	Grega Matijasic	.08	.03	.01
☐ 1803	Luka Kamsek	.08	.03	.01
☐ 1804	Rudi Hiti	.08	.03	.01
☐ 1805	Gregor Pesjak	.08	.03	.01
☐ 1806	Bostjan Kolaric	.08	.03	.01
☐ 1807	Denis Kropec	.08	.03	.01
☐ 1808	Slovenie (Team photo and CL)	.15	.06	.01

1992-93 Quebec Int. Pee-Wees Gold

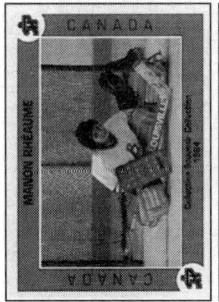 

This three-card insert set measures the standard size (2 1/2" by 3 1/2") and features color player photos with metallic-gold borders on white card stock. The player's name is printed in the border at the top, while the card title is printed below the picture. The backs carry a player profile against a metallic-gold background with white borders. Two of the cards are numbered, while one is not. The listing below reflects this numbering.

	MINT	EXC	G-VG
COMPLETE SET (3)	12.00	5.00	1.20
COMMON PLAYER (1-3)	1.00	.40	.10
☐ 1 Brad Park	4.00	1.60	.40
☐ 2 Manon Rheaume	9.00	3.75	.90
☐ NNO Guy Chouinard	1.00	.40	.10

1952-53 St. Lawrence Sales

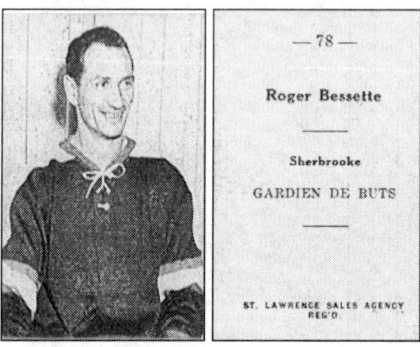

This 107-card black and white set (put out by St. Lawrence Sales Agency featured members of the QSHL. The card backs are written in French. The cards measure approximately 1 15/16" by 2 15/16" and are numbered on the back. The key cards in the set are cards of future (at that time) NHL greats Jean Beliveau and Jacques Plante. The complete set price includes both card # 17.

	NRMT	VG-E	GOOD
COMPLETE SET (108)	1000.00	400.00	100.00
COMMON PLAYER (1-108)	7.00	2.80	.70
☐ 1 Jacques Plante	250.00	100.00	25.00
☐ 2 Glen Harmon	7.00	2.80	.70
☐ 3 Jimmy Moore	7.00	2.80	.70
☐ 4 Gerard Desaulniers	7.00	2.80	.70
☐ 5 Les Douglas	7.00	2.80	.70
☐ 6 Fred Burchell	7.00	2.80	.70
☐ 7 Ed Litzenberger	12.00	5.00	1.20
☐ 8 Rollie Rousseau	7.00	2.80	.70
☐ 9 Roger Leger	7.00	2.80	.70
☐ 10 Phil Samis	7.00	2.80	.70
☐ 11 Paul Masnick	9.00	3.75	.90
☐ 12 Walter Clune	7.00	2.80	.70
☐ 13 Louis Denis	7.00	2.80	.70
☐ 14 Gerry Plamondon	7.00	2.80	.70
☐ 15 Cliff Malone	7.00	2.80	.70
☐ 16 Pete Morin	9.00	3.75	.90
☐ 17A Jack Schmidt	9.00	3.75	.90
☐ 17B Aldo Guidolin	15.00	6.00	1.50
☐ 18 Paul Leclerc	7.00	2.80	.70
☐ 19 Larry Kwong	9.00	3.75	.90
☐ 20 Rosario Joanette	7.00	2.80	.70
☐ 21 Tom Smelle	7.00	2.80	.70
☐ 22 Gordie Haworth	7.00	2.80	.70
☐ 23 Bruce Cline	7.00	2.80	.70
☐ 24 Andre Corriveau	7.00	2.80	.70
☐ 25 Jacques Deslauriers	7.00	2.80	.70
☐ 26 Bingo Ernst	7.00	2.80	.70
☐ 27 Jacques Chartrand	7.00	2.80	.70
☐ 28 Phil Vitale	7.00	2.80	.70
☐ 29 Renald Lacroix	7.00	2.80	.70
☐ 30 J.P. Bisaillon	7.00	2.80	.70
☐ 31 Jack Irvine	7.00	2.80	.70
☐ 32 Georges Bougie	7.00	2.80	.70
☐ 33 Paul Larivee	7.00	2.80	.70
☐ 34 Carl Smelle	7.00	2.80	.70
☐ 35 Walter Pawlyschyn	7.00	2.80	.70
☐ 36 Jean Marois	7.00	2.80	.70
☐ 37 Jack Gelineau	7.00	2.80	.70
☐ 38 Danny Nixon	7.00	2.80	.70
☐ 39 Jean Beliveau	250.00	100.00	25.00
☐ 40 Phil Renaud	7.00	2.80	.70
☐ 41 Leon Bouchard	7.00	2.80	.70
☐ 42 Dennis Smith	7.00	2.80	.70
☐ 43 Joe Crozier	12.00	5.00	1.20
☐ 44 Al Bacari	7.00	2.80	.70
☐ 45 Murdo MacKay	7.00	2.80	.70
☐ 46 Gordie Hudson	7.00	2.80	.70
☐ 47 Claude Robert	7.00	2.80	.70
☐ 48 Yogi Kraiger	7.00	2.80	.70
☐ 49 Ludger Tremblay	7.00	2.80	.70
☐ 50 Pierre Brillant	7.00	2.80	.70
☐ 51 Frank Mario	7.00	2.80	.70
☐ 52 Copper Leyth	7.00	2.80	.70
☐ 53 Herbie Carnegie	15.00	6.00	1.50
☐ 54 Punch Imlach	30.00	12.00	3.00
☐ 55 Howard Riopelle	7.00	2.80	.70
☐ 56 Ken Laufman	7.00	2.80	.70
☐ 57 Jackie Leclair	12.00	5.00	1.20
☐ 58 Bill Robinson	7.00	2.80	.70
☐ 59 George Ford	7.00	2.80	.70
☐ 60 Bill Johnson	7.00	2.80	.70
☐ 61 Leo Gravelle	7.00	2.80	.70
☐ 62 Jack Giesebrecht	7.00	2.80	.70
☐ 63 John Arundel	7.00	2.80	.70
☐ 64 Vic Gregg	7.00	2.80	.70
☐ 65 Bep Guidolin	12.00	5.00	1.20
☐ 66 Al Kuntz	7.00	2.80	.70
☐ 67 Emile Dagenais	7.00	2.80	.70
☐ 68 Bill Richardson	7.00	2.80	.70
☐ 69 Bob Robertson	7.00	2.80	.70
☐ 70 Ray Fredericks	7.00	2.80	.70
☐ 71 James O'Flaherty	7.00	2.80	.70
☐ 72 Butch Stahan	7.00	2.80	.70
☐ 73 Roger Roberge	7.00	2.80	.70
☐ 74 Guy Labre	7.00	2.80	.70
☐ 75 Gilles Dube	7.00	2.80	.70
☐ 76 Pete Wywrot	7.00	2.80	.70
☐ 77 Tod Campeau	7.00	2.80	.70
☐ 78 Roger Bessette	7.00	2.80	.70
☐ 79 Martial Pruneau	7.00	2.80	.70
☐ 80 Nils Tremblay	7.00	2.80	.70
☐ 81 Jacques Locas	7.00	2.80	.70
☐ 82 Rene Pepin	7.00	2.80	.70
☐ 83 Bob Pepin	7.00	2.80	.70
☐ 84 Tom McDougall	7.00	2.80	.70
☐ 85 Peter Wright	7.00	2.80	.70
☐ 86 Ronnie Matthews	7.00	2.80	.70
☐ 87 Irene St-Hilaire	7.00	2.80	.70
☐ 88 Dewar Thompson	7.00	2.80	.70
☐ 89 Bob Dainville	7.00	2.80	.70
☐ 90 Marvel Pelletier	7.00	2.80	.70
☐ 91 Delphis Franche	7.00	2.80	.70
☐ 92 Geo. Roy	7.00	2.80	.70
☐ 93 Andy McCallum	7.00	2.80	.70
☐ 94 Lou Smrke	7.00	2.80	.70
☐ 95 J.P. Lamirande	7.00	2.80	.70
☐ 96 Normand Dussault	7.00	2.80	.70
☐ 97 Stan Smrke	9.00	3.75	.90
☐ 98 Jack Bownass	7.00	2.80	.70
☐ 99 Billy Arcand	7.00	2.80	.70
☐ 100 Lyall Wiseman	7.00	2.80	.70
☐ 101 Jack Hamilton	7.00	2.80	.70
☐ 102 Bob Leger	7.00	2.80	.70
☐ 103 Larry Regan	9.00	3.75	.90
☐ 104 Erwin Grosse	7.00	2.80	.70
☐ 105 Roger Bedard	7.00	2.80	.70
☐ 106 Ted Hodgson	7.00	2.80	.70
☐ 107 Dave Gatherum	12.00	5.00	1.20

1989-90 7th Inn. Sketch OHL

This 200-card set which measures the standard, 2 1/2" by 3 1/2", was issued by 7th Inning Sketch featuring members of the Ontario Hockey League. The fronts of the cards have yellow borders which surround the player's photo and on the bottom of the front is the player's name. In the upper right hand corner, the team's name is featured. The backs of the cards feature statistical and biographical information. The set has been popular with collectors since it features early cards of Eric Lindros; most collectors consider card number 1 to be Lindros' regular card as opposed to the (Lindros) specials on cards 188, 195, and 196. The set was also issued on a limited basis (a numbered edition of 3000

sets) as a factory set; however, the factory set only included 167 cards as 33 cards were dropped and not included in the factory sets.

	MINT	EXC	G-VG
COMPLETE SET (200)	30.00	12.00	3.00
COMPLETE FACT.SET (167)	30.00	12.00	3.00
COMMON PLAYER (1-200)	.20	.08	.02

		MINT	EXC	G-VG
☐ 1	Eric Lindros	5.00	2.00	.50
	(Beware counterfeits)			
☐ 2	Jarrod Skalde	.50	.20	.05
☐ 3	Joe Busillo	.20	.08	.02
☐ 4	Dale Craigwell	.50	.20	.05
☐ 5	Clair Cornish	.20	.08	.02
☐ 6	Jean-Paul Davis	.20	.08	.02
☐ 7	Craig Donaldson	.20	.08	.02
☐ 8	Wade Simpson	.20	.08	.02
☐ 9	Mike Craig	.75	.30	.07
☐ 10	Mark Deazeley	.20	.08	.02
☐ 11	Scott Hollis	.20	.08	.02
☐ 12	Brian Grieve	.30	.12	.03
☐ 13	Dave Craievich	.20	.08	.02
☐ 14	Paul O'Hagan	.30	.12	.03
☐ 15	Matt Hoffman	.20	.08	.02
☐ 16	Trevor McIvor	.20	.08	.02
☐ 17	Cory Banika	.20	.08	.02
☐ 18	Kevin Butt	.30	.12	.03
☐ 19	Iain Fraser	.75	.30	.07
☐ 20	Bill Armstrong	.30	.12	.03
☐ 21	Scott Luik	.20	.08	.02
☐ 22	Brent Grieve	.75	.30	.07
☐ 23	Fred Brathwaite	.75	.30	.07
☐ 24	Paul Holden	.30	.12	.03
☐ 25	Trevor Dam	.20	.08	.02
☐ 26	Chris Taylor	.50	.20	.05
☐ 27	Mark Guy	.20	.08	.02
☐ 28	Louie DeBrusk	.75	.30	.07
☐ 29	John Battice	.20	.08	.02
☐ 30	Chris Crombie	.30	.12	.03
☐ 31	Sean Basilio	.20	.08	.02
☐ 32	Aaron Nagy	.20	.08	.02
☐ 33	Greg Ryan	.20	.08	.02
☐ 34	Steve Martell	.20	.08	.02
☐ 35	Scott MacKay	.20	.08	.02
☐ 36	Dennis Purdie	.30	.12	.03
☐ 37	Steve Boyd	.20	.08	.02
☐ 38	John Tanner	.75	.30	.07
☐ 39	David Anderson	.20	.08	.02
☐ 40	Rick Corriveau	.50	.20	.05
☐ 41	Todd Hushko	.50	.20	.05
☐ 42	Doug Synish	.20	.08	.02
☐ 43	Dan LeBlanc	.30	.12	.03
☐ 44	Dave Noseworthy	.20	.08	.02
☐ 45	Karl Taylor	.20	.08	.02
☐ 46	Jeff Hodgen	.20	.08	.02
☐ 47	Kelly/Agnew	.20	.08	.02
☐ 48	Wayne Maxner	.30	.12	.03
☐ 49	Brett Seguin	.50	.20	.05
☐ 50	Greg Walters	.20	.08	.02
☐ 51	Chris Snell	.50	.20	.05
☐ 52	Troy Binnie	.30	.12	.03
☐ 53	Joni Lehto	.20	.08	.02
☐ 54	Steve Kluczkowski	.20	.08	.02
☐ 55	Ryan Kuwabara	.50	.20	.05
☐ 56	Chris Simon	.75	.30	.07
☐ 57	Jerrett DeFazio	.30	.12	.03
☐ 58	Rob Sangster	.20	.08	.02
☐ 59	Greg Clancy	.20	.08	.02
☐ 60	Peter Ambroziak	.20	.08	.02
☐ 61	Jeff Ricciardi	.20	.08	.02
☐ 62	John East	.20	.08	.02
☐ 63	Joey McTamney	.20	.08	.02
☐ 64	Dan Poirier	.20	.08	.02
☐ 65	Gairin Smith	.20	.08	.02
☐ 66	Wade Gibson	.20	.08	.02
☐ 67	Checklist Card	.30	.12	.03
☐ 68	Andrew Brodie	.20	.08	.02
☐ 69	Craig Wilson	.20	.08	.02
☐ 70	Peter McGlynn	.20	.08	.02
☐ 71	George Dourian	.20	.08	.02
☐ 72	Bob Berg	.30	.12	.03
☐ 73	Richard Fatrola	.20	.08	.02
☐ 74	Craig Fraser	.20	.08	.02
☐ 75	Brent Gretzky	2.00	.80	.20
☐ 76	Jake Grimes	.30	.12	.03
☐ 77	Darren McCarty	.50	.20	.05
☐ 78	Ted Miskolczi	.20	.08	.02
☐ 79	Rob Pearson	1.00	.40	.10
☐ 80	Gordon Pell	.20	.08	.02
☐ 81	John Porco	.50	.20	.05
☐ 82	Ken Rowbotham	.20	.08	.02
☐ 83	Scott Thornton	.50	.20	.05
☐ 84	Shawn Way	.20	.08	.02
☐ 85	Steve Bancroft	.30	.12	.03
☐ 86	Greg Bignell	.20	.08	.02
☐ 87	Scott Boston	.20	.08	.02
☐ 88	Scott Feasby	.20	.08	.02
☐ 89	Derek Morin	.50	.20	.05
☐ 90	Sean O'Reilly	.50	.20	.05
☐ 91	Jason Skelet	.20	.08	.02
☐ 92	Greg Dreveny	.20	.08	.02
☐ 93	Jeff Fife	.20	.08	.02
☐ 94	Rob Stopar	.20	.08	.02
☐ 95	Joe Desrosiers	.20	.08	.02
☐ 96	Danny Flynn	.20	.08	.02
☐ 97	Dr. Vaughan	.20	.08	.02
☐ 98	Troy Stephens	.20	.08	.02
☐ 99	Dan Brown	.20	.08	.02
☐ 100	Mike Ricci	1.50	.60	.15
☐ 101	Brent Pope	.30	.12	.03
☐ 102	Mike Dagenais	.30	.12	.03
☐ 103	Scott Campbell	.20	.08	.02
☐ 104	Jamie Pegg	.20	.08	.02
☐ 105	Joe Hawley	.20	.08	.02
☐ 106	Jason Dawe	.75	.30	.07
☐ 107	Paul Mitton	.20	.08	.02
☐ 108	Mike Tomlinson	.20	.08	.02
☐ 109	Dave Lorentz	.20	.08	.02
☐ 110	Dale McTavish	.20	.08	.02
☐ 111	Willie McGarvey	.20	.08	.02
☐ 112	Don O'Neill	.20	.08	.02
☐ 113	Mark Myles	.20	.08	.02
☐ 114	Chris Longo	.30	.12	.03
☐ 115	Tom Hopkins	.20	.08	.02
☐ 116	Jassen Cullimore	.50	.20	.05
☐ 117	Geoff Ingram	.20	.08	.02
☐ 118	Twohey/Bovair	.20	.08	.02
☐ 119	Doug Searle	.20	.08	.02
☐ 120	Bryan Gendron	.20	.08	.02
☐ 121	Andrew Verner	.50	.20	.05
☐ 122	Todd Bocjun	.30	.12	.03
☐ 123	Dick Todd	.30	.12	.03
☐ 124	George Burnett	.30	.12	.03
☐ 125	Brad May	1.00	.40	.10
☐ 126	David Benn	.20	.08	.02
☐ 127	Brian Mueggler	.20	.08	.02
☐ 128	Todd Coopman	.20	.08	.02
☐ 129	Geoff Rawson	.20	.08	.02
☐ 130	Keith Primeau	2.00	.80	.20
☐ 131	Mark Lawrence	.30	.12	.03
☐ 132	Randy Hall	.20	.08	.02
☐ 133	Greg Suchan	.20	.08	.02
☐ 134	Ken Ruddick	.20	.08	.02
☐ 135	Jason Winch	.30	.12	.03
☐ 136	Paul Wolanski	.20	.08	.02
☐ 137	Dennis Scott	.20	.08	.02
☐ 138	Steve Udvari	.20	.08	.02
☐ 139	Rich Beley	.30	.12	.03
☐ 140	Don Pancoe	.20	.08	.02
☐ 141	Paul Bruneau	.20	.08	.02
☐ 142	Paul Laus	.30	.12	.03
☐ 143	Mike St. John	.20	.08	.02
☐ 144	John Johnson	.20	.08	.02
☐ 145	Greg Allen	.20	.08	.02
☐ 146	Don McConnell	.20	.08	.02
☐ 147	Andy Bezeau	.30	.12	.03
☐ 148	Jeff Walker	.20	.08	.02
☐ 149	John Spoltore	.50	.20	.05
☐ 150	Derek Switzer	.30	.12	.03
☐ 151	Tyler Ertel	.30	.12	.03
☐ 152	Shawn Antoski	.50	.20	.05
☐ 153	Jason Corrigan	.20	.08	.02
☐ 154	Derian Hatcher	1.00	.40	.10
☐ 155	John Vary	.20	.08	.02

☐	156	Jamie Caruso	.30	.12	.03
☐	157	Trevor Halverson	.75	.30	.07
☐	158	Robert Deschamps	.20	.08	.02
☐	159	Jeff Gardiner	.50	.20	.05
☐	160	Gary Miller	.20	.08	.02
☐	161	Shayne Antoski	.50	.20	.05
☐	162	John Van Kessel	.50	.20	.05
☐	163	Colin Austin	.20	.08	.02
☐	164	Tom Purcell	.20	.08	.02
☐	165	Joel Morin	.20	.08	.02
☐	166	Tim Favot	.20	.08	.02
☐	167	Checklist Card	.30	.12	.03
☐	168	Jason Beaton	.20	.08	.02
☐	169	Chris Ottmann	.20	.08	.02
☐	170	Mike Matuszek	.20	.08	.02
☐	171	Rob Fournier	.30	.12	.03
☐	172	Ron Bertrand	.30	.12	.03
☐	173	Bert Templeton	.30	.12	.03
☐	174	Casey Jones	.50	.20	.05
☐	175	Robert Frayn	.20	.08	.02
☐	176	Claude Noel	.20	.08	.02
☐	177	Sean Basilio Award	.30	.12	.03
☐	178	Chris Longo Rookie	.30	.12	.03
☐	179	Cory Keenan AS	.30	.12	.03
☐	180	Owen Nolan Award	1.50	.60	.15
☐	181	Steven Rice Award	.75	.30	.07
☐	182	Shayne Stevenson Scorer	.50	.20	.05
☐	183	Mike Ricci Award	.75	.30	.07
☐	184	Jason Firth Award	.50	.20	.05
☐	185	John Slaney Award	.50	.20	.05
☐	186	Iain Fraser Award	.30	.12	.03
☐	187	Steven Rice Star	.50	.20	.05
☐	188	Eric Lindros Scorer	2.50	1.00	.25
☐	189	Keith Primeau Scorer	.75	.30	.07
☐	190	Mike Ricci Award	.75	.30	.07
☐	191	Mike Torchia AS	.30	.12	.03
☐	192	Mike Torchia Star	.30	.12	.03
☐	193	Jarrod Skalde Champs	.30	.12	.03
☐	194	Paul O'Hagan Award	.30	.12	.03
☐	195	Eric Lindros (Where in 1991)	2.50	1.00	.25
☐	196	Eric Lindros AS	2.50	1.00	.25
☐	197	Jeff Fife Award	.30	.12	.03
☐	198	Iain Fraser MVP	.50	.20	.05
☐	199	Bill Armstrong Winner	.30	.12	.03
☐	200	Checklist Card	.30	.12	.03

1990 7th Inn. Sketch Memorial Cup

ERIC LINDROS

The 7th Inn. Sketch Memorial Cup Hockey set consists of 100 cards measuring the standard size (2 1/2" by 3 1/2"). The front features a borderless color posed photo of the player against an aqua blue background. The upper right corner of the picture is cut off and various hockey league logos are placed there. The back is printed in dark blue lettering on a yellow background and includes the card number, player information, the CHL logo, and the Coupe Memorial Cup logo. The set features players from the four semi-final teams in the 1990 Memorial Cup playoffs, Kamloops Blazers (1-25), Kitchener Rangers (26-49), Laval Titans (50-74), and Oshawa Generals (75-100). These cards were only issued as factory sets, with a numbered edition of

3000 sets. The set features cards of future NHL players Gilbert Dionne, Eric Lindros, Martin Lapointe, Scott Niedermayer, and Darryl Sydor.

			MINT	EXC	G-VG
		COMPLETE SET (100)	150.00	60.00	15.00
		COMMON PLAYER (1-100)	1.00	.40	.10
☐	1	Len Barrie	2.00	.80	.20
☐	2	Zac Boyer	1.50	.60	.15
☐	3	Dave Chyzowski	1.50	.60	.15
☐	4	Shea Esselmont	1.00	.40	.10
☐	5	Todd Esselmont	1.50	.60	.15
☐	6	Phil Huber	1.50	.60	.15
☐	7	Lance Johnson	1.00	.40	.10
☐	8	Paul Kruse	1.50	.60	.15
☐	9	Cal McGowan	2.00	.80	.20
☐	10	Mike Needham	2.50	1.00	.25
☐	11	Brian Shantz	1.00	.40	.10
☐	12	Daryl Sydor	4.00	1.60	.40
☐	13	Jeff Watchorn	1.00	.40	.10
☐	14	Jarrett Bousquet	1.00	.40	.10
☐	15	Todd Harris	1.00	.40	.10
☐	16	Deen Malkoc	1.00	.40	.10
☐	17	Joey Mittelstadt	1.00	.40	.10
☐	18	Scott Niedermayer	7.50	3.00	.75
☐	19	Clayton Young	1.00	.40	.10
☐	20	Trevor Sim	1.50	.60	.15
☐	21	Murray Duval	1.50	.60	.15
☐	22	Steve Yule	1.00	.40	.10
☐	23	Craig Bonner	1.50	.60	.15
☐	24	Dale Masson	1.50	.60	.15
☐	25	Corey Hirsch	4.00	1.60	.40
☐	26	Joe McDonnell	1.00	.40	.10
☐	27	Rick Chambers	1.00	.40	.10
☐	28	John Finnie	1.50	.60	.15
☐	29	Randy Pearce	1.00	.40	.10
☐	30	Mark Montanari	1.00	.40	.10
☐	31	Mike Torchia	1.50	.60	.15
☐	32	Jason York	2.00	.80	.20
☐	33	Jason Firth	1.50	.60	.15
☐	34	Jamie Israel	1.00	.40	.10
☐	35	Richard Borgo	1.50	.60	.15
☐	36	John Uniac	1.50	.60	.15
☐	37	Steve Smith	1.00	.40	.10
☐	38	Steven Rice	2.50	1.00	.25
☐	39	Gilbert Dionne	3.00	1.20	.30
☐	40	Cory Keenan	1.50	.60	.15
☐	41	Rick Allain	1.00	.40	.10
☐	42	John Copley	1.00	.40	.10
☐	43	Gib Tucker	1.00	.40	.10
☐	44	Chris LiPuma	2.00	.80	.20
☐	45	Brad Barton	1.00	.40	.10
☐	46	Rival Fullum	1.00	.40	.10
☐	47	Joey St.Aubin	1.50	.60	.15
☐	48	Jack Williams	1.00	.40	.10
☐	49	Shayne Stevenson	2.00	.80	.20
☐	50	Pierre Creamer	1.50	.60	.15
☐	51	Carl Mantha	1.00	.40	.10
☐	52	Julian Cameron	1.50	.60	.15
☐	53	Sandy McCarthy	2.00	.80	.20
☐	54	Gino Odjick	2.00	.80	.20
☐	55	Eric Raymond	1.50	.60	.15
☐	56	Carl Boudreau	1.00	.40	.10
☐	57	Greg MacEachern	1.00	.40	.10
☐	58	Allen Kerr	1.00	.40	.10
☐	59	Patrice Brisebois	2.00	.80	.20
☐	60	Eric Bissonnette	1.00	.40	.10
☐	61	Martin Lapointe	3.00	1.20	.30
☐	62	Michel Gingras	1.00	.40	.10
☐	63	Sylvain Naud	1.50	.60	.15
☐	64	Pat Caron	1.00	.40	.10
☐	65	Regis Tremblay	1.00	.40	.10
☐	66	Francois Pelletier	1.00	.40	.10
☐	67	Jason Brousseau	1.00	.40	.10
☐	68	Eric Dubois	1.00	.40	.10
☐	69	Claude Boivin	2.00	.80	.20
☐	70	Denis Chalifoux	1.50	.60	.15
☐	71	Jim Bermingham	1.00	.40	.10
☐	72	Daniel Arsenault	1.00	.40	.10
☐	73	Normand Demers	1.00	.40	.10
☐	74	Serge Anglehart	1.50	.60	.15
☐	75	Rick Cornacchia	1.50	.60	.15
☐	76	Kevin Butt	1.50	.60	.15
☐	77	Fred Brathwaite	2.00	.80	.20
☐	78	Paul O'Hagan	2.00	.80	.20
☐	79	Craig Donaldson	1.00	.40	.10
☐	80	Jean-Paul Davis	1.50	.60	.15
☐	81	Brian Grieve	2.00	.80	.20
☐	82	Bill Armstrong	1.50	.60	.15
☐	83	Wade Simpson	1.00	.40	.10
☐	84	Dave Craievich	1.00	.40	.10
☐	85	Dale Craigwell	2.00	.80	.20

☐ 86 Joe Busillo	1.50	.60	.15
☐ 87 Cory Banika	1.00	.40	.10
☐ 88 Eric Lindros	40.00	16.00	4.00
☐ 89 Iain Fraser	2.50	1.00	.25
☐ 90 Mike Craig	2.50	1.00	.25
☐ 91 Jarrod Skalde	2.00	.80	.20
☐ 92 Brent Grieve	2.50	1.00	.25
☐ 93 Scott Luik	1.00	.40	.10
☐ 94 Matt Hoffman	1.50	.60	.15
☐ 95 Trevor McIvor	1.00	.40	.10
☐ 96 Scott Hollis	1.50	.60	.15
☐ 97 Mark Deazeley	1.50	.60	.15
☐ 98 Clair Cornish	1.00	.40	.10
☐ 99 Oshawa Wins (Eric Lindros holding up Memorial Cup)	15.00	6.00	1.50
☐ 100 Checklist Card	2.50	1.00	.25

1990-91 7th Inn. Sketch OHL

The 7th Inning Sketch OHL Hockey set contains 400 cards measuring the standard size, 2 1/2" by 3 1/2". The front features a full color photo, enframed by different color borders. The player's position appears in a star at the lower left hand corner, with his name and "OHL" in the bar below the picture. The back has another color photo, with biographical information and career summary in a box running the length of the card. This set features a regular card (1) as well as a promo card of hockey star Eric Lindros. The promo version has the same front as Lindros' card number 1 but has an asterisk in the card number position on the card back. Players from the following teams are represented in this set: Oshawa Generals (1, 325-339, 341-345, 347-350), Belleville Bulls (2-10, 12-21, 23, 340, 346), Kingston Frontenacs (11, 51-75), Cornwall Royals (22, 24-50), Ottawa 67's (76-100, 230), Detroit Compuware Ambassadors (101-121, 123-125), North Bay Centennials (122, 301-324), London Knights (126-149), Sault Ste. Marie Greyhounds (150-173, 175-176), Windsor Spitfires (174, 177-200), Dukes of Hamilton (201-225), Kitchener Rangers (226-229, 231-250, 370), Niagara Falls Thunder (251-275), Owen Sound Platers (276-299), Peterborough Petes (351-369, 371-376), and Sudbury Wolves (377-400). First round picks (1991 NHL Draft) in this set include Eric Lindros (1), Alex Stojanov (7), Pat Peake (14), Glen Murray (18), and Trevor Halverson (21). First round picks (1992 NHL Draft rank indicated in parenthesis) in this set include Todd Warriner (4), Corey Stillman (6), Brandon Convery (8), Curtis Bowen (22), and Grant Marshall (23). A factory set, a numbered edition of 9000 sets, was produced and marketed separately.

	MINT	EXC	G-VG
COMPLETE SET (400)	18.00	7.25	1.80
COMPLETE FACT.SET (400)	20.00	8.00	2.00
COMMON PLAYER (1-400)	.10	.04	.01

☐ 1 Eric Lindros	3.50	1.40	.35
☐ 2 Greg Dreveny	.15	.06	.01
☐ 3 Belleville Checklist UER	.15	.06	.01
☐ 4 Richard Fatrola	.10	.04	.01
☐ 5 Craig Fraser	.15	.06	.01
☐ 6 Robert Frayn	.10	.04	.01
☐ 7 Brent Gretzky	1.00	.40	.10
☐ 8 Jake Grimes	.15	.06	.01
☐ 9 Darren Hurley	.10	.04	.01
☐ 10 Rick Marshall	.10	.04	.01
☐ 11 Checklist UER	.15	.06	.01
☐ 12 Darren McCarty	.25	.10	.02
☐ 13 Derek Morin	.15	.06	.01
☐ 14 Sean O'Reilly	.15	.06	.01
☐ 15 Rob Pearson UER (Listed on Oshawa CL but reverse says Belleville Bulls)	.50	.20	.05
☐ 16 John Porco	.15	.06	.01
☐ 17 Ken Rowbotham	.10	.04	.01
☐ 18 Ken Ruddick	.10	.04	.01
☐ 19 Jim Sonmez	.10	.04	.01
☐ 20 Brad Teichmann	.15	.06	.01
☐ 21 Chris Varga	.10	.04	.01
☐ 22 Checklist Card	.15	.06	.01
☐ 23 Larry Mavety CO	.10	.04	.01
☐ 24 Rival Fullum	.25	.10	.02
☐ 25 Nathan Lafayette	.50	.20	.05
☐ 26 Darren Bell	.10	.04	.01
☐ 27 Craig Brocklehurst	.10	.04	.01
☐ 28 Shawn Caplice	.10	.04	.01
☐ 29 Mike Cavanaugh	.10	.04	.01
☐ 30 Jason Cirone	.35	.14	.03
☐ 31 Chris Clancy	.10	.04	.01
☐ 32 Mark DeSantis	.10	.04	.01
☐ 33 Rob Dykeman	.15	.06	.01
☐ 34 Shayne Gaffar	.10	.04	.01
☐ 35 Ilpo Kauhanen	.15	.06	.01
☐ 36 Rob Kinghan	.10	.04	.01
☐ 37 Dave Lemay	.15	.06	.01
☐ 38 Guy Leveque	.35	.14	.03
☐ 39 Matt McGuffin	.10	.04	.01
☐ 40 Marcus Middleton	.10	.04	.01
☐ 41 Thomas Nemeth	.25	.10	.02
☐ 42 Rod Pasma	.15	.06	.01
☐ 43 Richard Raymond	.10	.04	.01
☐ 44 Jeff Reid	.10	.04	.01
☐ 45 Jerry Ribble	.10	.04	.01
☐ 46 Jean-Alain Schneider	.10	.04	.01
☐ 47 John Slaney	.50	.20	.05
☐ 48 Jeremy Stevenson	.35	.14	.03
☐ 49 Ryan VandenBussche	.25	.10	.02
☐ 50 Marc Crawford CO	.15	.06	.01
☐ 51 Tony Bella	.10	.04	.01
☐ 52 Drake Berehowsky	.50	.20	.05
☐ 53 Jason Chipman	.15	.06	.01
☐ 54 Tony Cimellaro	.10	.04	.01
☐ 55 Keli Corpse	.25	.10	.02
☐ 56 Mike Dawson	.10	.04	.01
☐ 57 Sean Gauthier UER	.10	.04	.01
☐ 58 Fred Goltz	.10	.04	.01
☐ 59 Gord Harris	.10	.04	.01
☐ 60 Tony Iob	.25	.10	.02
☐ 61 John Bernie	.10	.04	.01
☐ 62 Dale Junkin	.10	.04	.01
☐ 63 Nathan Lafayette	.50	.20	.05
☐ 64 Blake Martin	.10	.04	.01
☐ 65 Mark McCague	.10	.04	.01
☐ 66 Bob McKillop	.10	.04	.01
☐ 67 Justin Morrison	.15	.06	.01
☐ 68 Bill Robinson	.10	.04	.01
☐ 69 Joel Sandie	.10	.04	.01
☐ 70 Kevin King	.10	.04	.01
☐ 71 Dave Stewart	.10	.04	.01
☐ 72 Joel Washkurak	.10	.04	.01
☐ 73 Brock Woods	.10	.04	.01
☐ 74 Randy Hall CO	.10	.04	.01
☐ 75 John Vary	.10	.04	.01
☐ 76 Peter Ambroziak	.15	.06	.01
☐ 77 Troy Binnie	.15	.06	.01
☐ 78 Curt Bowen	.35	.14	.03
☐ 79 Andrew Brodie	.15	.06	.01
☐ 80 Ottawa Checklist	.15	.06	.01
☐ 81 Greg Clancy	.10	.04	.01
☐ 82 Jerrett DeFazio	.10	.04	.01
☐ 83 Kris Draper	.50	.20	.05
☐ 84 Wade Gibson	.10	.04	.01
☐ 85 Ryan Kuwabara	.20	.08	.02
☐ 86 Joni Lehto	.10	.04	.01
☐ 87 Donald MacPherson	.10	.04	.01
☐ 88 Grant Marshall	.50	.20	.05
☐ 89 Peter McGlynn	.15	.06	.01

☐ 90	Maurice O'Brien	.10	.04	.01
☐ 91	Jeff Ricciardi	.25	.10	.02
☐ 92	Brett Seguin	.25	.10	.02
☐ 93	Len DeVuono	.10	.04	.01
☐ 94	Gerry Skrypec	.10	.04	.01
☐ 95	Chris Snell	.35	.14	.03
☐ 96	Jason Snow	.10	.04	.01
☐ 97	Sean Spencer	.15	.06	.01
☐ 98	Brad Spry	.10	.04	.01
☐ 99	Matt Stone	.10	.04	.01
☐ 100	Brian Kilrea CO	.10	.04	.01
☐ 101	Kevin Butt	.25	.10	.02
☐ 102	Glen Craig	.10	.04	.01
☐ 103	Paul Doherty	.10	.04	.01
☐ 104	Mark Donahue	.10	.04	.01
☐ 105	Jeff Gardiner	.15	.06	.01
☐ 106	Trent Gleason	.10	.04	.01
☐ 107	Troy Gleason	.10	.04	.01
☐ 108	Mark Lawrence	.25	.10	.02
☐ 109	Trevor McIvor	.10	.04	.01
☐ 110	Paul Mitton	.10	.04	.01
☐ 111	David Myles	.10	.04	.01
☐ 112	Jeffery Nolan	.15	.06	.01
☐ 113	Rob Papineau	.10	.04	.01
☐ 114	Pat Peake	1.00	.40	.10
☐ 115	Chris Phelps	.10	.04	.01
☐ 116	John Pinches	.10	.04	.01
☐ 117	James Shea	.15	.06	.01
☐ 118	James Sheehan	.10	.04	.01
☐ 119	John Stos	.10	.04	.01
☐ 120	Tom Sullivan	.10	.04	.01
☐ 121	John Wynne	.10	.04	.01
☐ 122	Robert Thorpe	.10	.04	.01
☐ 123	David Benn	.10	.04	.01
☐ 124	Andy Weidenbach CO UER	.10	.04	.01
☐ 125	Detroit Checklist	.15	.06	.01
☐ 126	David Anderson	.10	.04	.01
☐ 127	Sean Basilio	.15	.06	.01
☐ 128	Brent Brownlee	.15	.06	.01
☐ 129	Rick Corriveau	.25	.10	.02
☐ 130	Derrick Crane	.10	.04	.01
☐ 131	Chris Crombie	.25	.10	.02
☐ 132	Louie DeBrusk	.25	.10	.02
☐ 133	Mark Guy	.10	.04	.01
☐ 134	Brett Marrietti	.15	.06	.01
☐ 135	Steve Martell	.10	.04	.01
☐ 136	Scott McKay	.10	.04	.01
☐ 137	Aaron Nagy	.25	.10	.02
☐ 138	Brett Nicol	.10	.04	.01
☐ 139	Barry Potomski	.25	.10	.02
☐ 140	Dennis Purdie	.25	.10	.02
☐ 141	Kelly Reed	.10	.04	.01
☐ 142	Gregory Ryan	.10	.04	.01
☐ 143	Brad Smyth	.10	.04	.01
☐ 144	Nick Stajduhar	.50	.20	.05
☐ 145	John Tanner	.50	.20	.05
☐ 146	Chris Taylor	.75	.30	.07
☐ 147	Mark Visheau	.15	.06	.01
☐ 148	Gary Agnew CO	.10	.04	.01
☐ 149	London Checklist	.15	.06	.01
☐ 150	Sault Ste. Marie Checklist	.15	.06	.01
☐ 151	David Babcock	.10	.04	.01
☐ 152	Drew Bannister	.35	.14	.03
☐ 153	Bob Boughner	.15	.06	.01
☐ 154	Joe Busillo	.15	.06	.01
☐ 155	Mike DeCoff	.10	.04	.01
☐ 156	Jason Denomme	.15	.06	.01
☐ 157	Adam Foote	.30	.12	.03
☐ 158	Kevin Hodson	.25	.10	.02
☐ 159	Shaun Imber	.10	.04	.01
☐ 160	Ralph Intranuovo	.50	.20	.05
☐ 161	Kevin King	.10	.04	.01
☐ 162	Rick Kowalsky	.15	.06	.01
☐ 163	Chris Kraemer	.10	.04	.01
☐ 164	Dan Lambert	.25	.10	.02
☐ 165	Mike Lenarduzzi	.25	.10	.02
☐ 166	Tom MacDonald	.10	.04	.01
☐ 167	Mark Matier	.10	.04	.01
☐ 168	David Matsos	.10	.04	.01
☐ 169	Colin Miller	.25	.10	.02
☐ 170	Perry Pappas	.10	.04	.01
☐ 171	Jarrett Reid	.25	.10	.02
☐ 172	Kevin Reid	.10	.04	.01
☐ 173	Brad Tiley UER	.20	.08	.02
☐ 174	Windsor Checklist	.15	.06	.01
☐ 175	Wade Whitten	.10	.04	.01
☐ 176	Ted Nolan	.10	.04	.01
☐ 177	Sean Burns	.10	.04	.01
☐ 178	Jason Cirone	.35	.14	.03
☐ 179	John Copley	.10	.04	.01
☐ 180	Tyler Ertel	.10	.04	.01
☐ 181	Brian Forestell	.10	.04	.01
☐ 182	Rival Fullum	.15	.06	.01
☐ 183	Steve Gibson	.20	.08	.02
☐ 184	Leonard MacDonald	.10	.04	.01
☐ 185	Mike Speer	.25	.10	.02
☐ 186	Kevin MacKay	.25	.10	.02
☐ 187	Ryan Merritt	.10	.04	.01
☐ 188	Doug Minor	.10	.04	.01
☐ 189	Rick Morton	.10	.04	.01
☐ 190	Sean O'Hagan	.15	.06	.01
☐ 191	Mike Polano	.15	.06	.01
☐ 192	Cory Stillman	.75	.30	.07
☐ 193	Jason Stos	.15	.06	.01
☐ 194	Trevor Walsh	.10	.04	.01
☐ 195	Todd Warriner	.75	.30	.07
☐ 196	Jeff Wilson	.15	.06	.01
☐ 197	Jason York	.30	.12	.03
☐ 198	Jason Zohil	.10	.04	.01
☐ 199	Steve Smith	.10	.04	.01
☐ 200	Brad Smith CO	.15	.06	.01
☐ 201	Jeff Bes	.75	.30	.07
☐ 202	Mike Blum	.10	.04	.01
☐ 203	Sean Brown	.10	.04	.01
☐ 204	Darcy Cahill	.10	.04	.01
☐ 205	Dale Chokan	.10	.04	.01
☐ 206	Chris Code	.10	.04	.01
☐ 207	George Dourian	.15	.06	.01
☐ 208	Todd Gleason	.15	.06	.01
☐ 209	Hamilton Checklist UER	.15	.06	.01
☐ 210	Michael Hartwick	.10	.04	.01
☐ 211	Scott Jenkins	.10	.04	.01
☐ 212	Rob Leask	.10	.04	.01
☐ 213	Gordon Pell	.10	.04	.01
☐ 214	Michael Reier	.10	.04	.01
☐ 215	Kayle Short	.10	.04	.01
☐ 216	Jason Skellett	.10	.04	.01
☐ 217	Gairin Smith	.10	.04	.01
☐ 218	Jeff Smith	.10	.04	.01
☐ 219	Jason Soules	.25	.10	.02
☐ 220	Alexandar Stojanov	.35	.14	.03
☐ 221	Dan Tanevski	.15	.06	.01
☐ 222	Gary Taylor	.10	.04	.01
☐ 223	Brent Watson	.10	.04	.01
☐ 224	Steve Woods	.10	.04	.01
☐ 225	Jay Johnston CO UER	.10	.04	.01
☐ 226	Mike Allen	.10	.04	.01
☐ 227	Brad Barton	.10	.04	.01
☐ 228	Richard Borgo	.10	.04	.01
☐ 229	Justin Cullen	.10	.04	.01
☐ 230	Lenny DeVuono	.10	.04	.01
☐ 231	Norman Dezainde	.15	.06	.01
☐ 232	Jason Firth	.25	.10	.02
☐ 233	Derek Gauthier	.10	.04	.01
☐ 234	Jamie Israel	.25	.10	.02
☐ 235	Chris LiPuma	.25	.10	.02
☐ 236	Tony McCabe	.10	.04	.01
☐ 237	Paul McCallion	.10	.04	.01
☐ 238	Shayne McCosh	.15	.06	.01
☐ 239	Rod Saarinen	.10	.04	.01
☐ 240	Steve Smith	.10	.04	.01
☐ 241	Joey St.Aubin	.15	.06	.01
☐ 242	Rob Stopar	.15	.06	.01
☐ 243	Jason Zohil UER	.10	.04	.01
☐ 244	Mike Torchia	.25	.10	.02
☐ 245	Gib Tucker	.10	.04	.01
☐ 246	John Uniac	.15	.06	.01
☐ 247	Jack Williams	.10	.04	.01
☐ 248	Joe McDonnell CO	.10	.04	.01
☐ 249	Steven Rice	.50	.20	.05
☐ 250	Mike Polano	.15	.06	.01
☐ 251	Greg Allen	.10	.04	.01
☐ 252	Roch Belley	.25	.10	.02
☐ 253	Andy Bezeau	.15	.06	.01
☐ 254	Derek Booth	.10	.04	.01
☐ 255	Kevin Brown	.20	.08	.02
☐ 256	Mark Cardiff	.10	.04	.01
☐ 257	Jason Coles	.10	.04	.01
☐ 258	Todd Coopman	.10	.04	.01
☐ 259	Richard Girhiny	.10	.04	.01
☐ 260	Brian Holk	.10	.04	.01
☐ 261	John Johnson	.10	.04	.01
☐ 262	Dan Krisko	.10	.04	.01
☐ 263	Manny Legace	.75	.30	.07
☐ 264	Brad May	.75	.30	.07
☐ 265	Don McConnell	.10	.04	.01
☐ 266	Niagara Falls Checklist UER (Nigara, sic)	.15	.06	.01
☐ 267	Aaron Morrison	.10	.04	.01
☐ 268	Cory Pageau	.10	.04	.01
☐ 269	Geoff Rawson	.10	.04	.01
☐ 270	Todd Simon	.35	.14	.03
☐ 271	Steve Staios	.35	.14	.03
☐ 272	Jeff Walker	.10	.04	.01

☐	273	Todd Wetzel	.10	.04	.01
☐	274	Jason Winch	.10	.04	.01
☐	275	Paul Wolanski	.10	.04	.01
☐	276	Owen Sound Checklist	.15	.06	.01
☐	277	Andrew Brunette	.35	.14	.03
☐	278	Wyatt Buckland	.10	.04	.01
☐	279	Jason Buetow	.15	.06	.01
☐	280	Jason Castellan	.10	.04	.01
☐	281	Trent Cull	.15	.06	.01
☐	282	Robert Deschamps	.10	.04	.01
☐	283	Chris Driscoll	.10	.04	.01
☐	284	Bryan Drury	.10	.04	.01
☐	285	Todd Hunter	.15	.06	.01
☐	286	Troy Hutchinson	.10	.04	.01
☐	287	Kirk Maltby	.35	.14	.03
☐	288	Geordie Maynard	.10	.04	.01
☐	289	Kevin McDougall	.15	.06	.01
☐	290	Ted Miskolczi	.15	.06	.01
☐	291	Steve Parson	.15	.06	.01
☐	292	Jeff Perry	.10	.04	.01
☐	293	Grayden Reid	.25	.10	.02
☐	294	Mike Speer	.15	.06	.01
☐	295	Mark Strohack	.10	.04	.01
☐	296	Mark Vilneff	.10	.04	.01
☐	297	Keith Whitmore	.10	.04	.01
☐	298	Jim Brown	.15	.06	.01
☐	299	Len McNamara CO	.10	.04	.01
☐	300	David Branch COMM	.25	.10	.02
☐	301	Shayne Antoski	.35	.14	.03
☐	302	Jason Beaton	.10	.04	.01
☐	303	Ron Bertrand	.15	.06	.01
☐	304	Michael Burman	.10	.04	.01
☐	305	Jamie Caruso	.25	.10	.02
☐	306	Allan Cox	.10	.04	.01
☐	307	Tim Favot	.10	.04	.01
☐	308	Trevor Halverson	.35	.14	.03
☐	309	Derian Hatcher	.50	.20	.05
☐	310	Bill Lang	.15	.06	.01
☐	311	Jason MacDonald	.10	.04	.01
☐	312	Gary Miller	.10	.04	.01
☐	313	Chris Ottmann	.15	.06	.01
☐	314	Chad Penney	.25	.10	.02
☐	315	Rick Pollard	.15	.06	.01
☐	316	Bradley Shepard	.10	.04	.01
☐	317	John Spoltore	.25	.10	.02
☐	318	Derek Switzer	.10	.04	.01
☐	319	Karl Taylor	.10	.04	.01
☐	320	John Vary	.10	.04	.01
☐	321	Kevin White	.10	.04	.01
☐	322	Billy Wright	.10	.04	.01
☐	323	Bert Templeton CO	.15	.06	.01
☐	324	North Bay Checklist	.15	.06	.01
☐	325	Oshawa Checklist UER	.15	.06	.01
☐	326	Jan Benda	.10	.04	.01
☐	327	Fred Brathwaite	.35	.14	.03
☐	328	Markus Brunner	.20	.08	.02
☐	329	Trevor Burgess	.15	.06	.01
☐	330	Clair Cornish	.10	.04	.01
☐	331	Mike Cote	.10	.04	.01
☐	332	Dave Craievich	.10	.04	.01
☐	333	Dale Craigwell	.35	.14	.03
☐	334	Jean-Paul Davis	.10	.04	.01
☐	335	Mark Deazeley	.10	.04	.01
☐	336	Mike Fountain	.25	.10	.02
☐	337	Brian Grieve	.20	.08	.02
☐	338	Matt Hoffman	.25	.10	.02
☐	339	Scott Hollis	.25	.10	.02
☐	340	Scott Boston	.15	.06	.01
☐	341	Scott Luik	.10	.04	.01
☐	342	Craig Lutes	.10	.04	.01
☐	343	William MacPherson	.20	.08	.02
☐	344	Paul O'Hagan	.25	.10	.02
☐	345	Wade Simpson	.10	.04	.01
☐	346	Jarrod Skalde UER	.35	.14	.03
		(Listed on Belleville CL but reverse says Oshawa Generals)			
☐	347	Troy Sweet	.10	.04	.01
☐	348	Jason Weaver	.25	.10	.02
☐	349	Rick Cornacchia CO	.10	.04	.01
☐	350	The Trophy	.25	.10	.02
☐	351	Greg Bailey	.15	.06	.01
☐	352	Ryan Black	.25	.10	.02
☐	353	Todd Bocjun UER	.25	.10	.02
		(Reversed negative on card front)			
☐	354	Toby Burkitt	.10	.04	.01
☐	355	Scott Campbell	.10	.04	.01
☐	356	Jassen Cullimore	.35	.14	.03
☐	357	Jason Dawe	.50	.20	.05
☐	358	Dan Ferguson	.10	.04	.01
☐	359	Bryan Gendron	.10	.04	.01
☐	360	Michael Harding	.10	.04	.01

☐	361	Joe Hawley	.10	.04	.01
☐	362	Peterborough Checklist UER	.15	.06	.01
☐	363	Geordie Kinnear	.15	.06	.01
☐	364	Chris Longo UER	.30	.12	.03
☐	365	Dale McTavish	.10	.04	.01
☐	366	Mark Myles	.10	.04	.01
☐	367	Don O'Neill	.10	.04	.01
☐	368	Jamie Pegg	.10	.04	.01
☐	369	Brent Pope	.15	.06	.01
☐	370	Kitchener Checklist UER	.15	.06	.01
☐	371	Doug Searle	.10	.04	.01
☐	372	Troy Stephens	.10	.04	.01
☐	373	Mike Tomlinson	.25	.10	.02
☐	374	Brent Tully	.25	.10	.02
☐	375	Andrew Verner	.30	.12	.03
☐	376	Dick Todd CO	.10	.04	.01
☐	377	John Tanner	.35	.14	.03
☐	378	Adam Bennett	.35	.14	.03
☐	379	Kyle Blacklock	.10	.04	.01
☐	380	Terry Chitaroni	.30	.12	.03
☐	381	Brandon Convery	.75	.30	.07
☐	382	J.D. Eaton	.10	.04	.01
☐	383	Derek Etches	.10	.04	.01
☐	384	Rod Hinks	.10	.04	.01
☐	385	Bill Kovacs	.10	.04	.01
☐	386	Alain Laforge	.10	.04	.01
☐	387	Jamie Matthews	.35	.14	.03
☐	388	Glen Murray	.75	.30	.07
☐	389	Dean Cull	.10	.04	.01
☐	390	Sean O'Donnell	.10	.04	.01
☐	391	Sudbury Checklist UER	.15	.06	.01
☐	392	Michael Peca	.35	.14	.03
☐	393	Shawn Rivers	.25	.10	.02
☐	394	Dan Ryder	.15	.06	.01
☐	395	Alastair Still	.25	.10	.02
☐	396	Michael Yeo	.10	.04	.01
☐	397	Barry Young	.10	.04	.01
☐	398	Jason Young	.25	.10	.02
☐	399	Ken MacKenzie CO	.10	.04	.01
☐	400	Bob Berg UER	.25	.10	.02
		(Missing draft eligibility information)			

1990-91 7th Inn. Sketch WHL

The 7th Inning Sketch WHL Hockey set contains 347 cards measuring the standard size, 2 1/2" by 3 1/2". The front features a full color photo, framed by different color borders. The player's position appears in a star at the lower left-hand corner, with his name and "WHL" in the bar below the picture. The back has another color photo, with biographical information and career summary in a box running the length of the card. Players from the following teams are represented in this set: Seattle Thunderbirds (1-22, 187), Medicine Hat Tigers (23-44), Swift Current Broncos (45-72), Saskatoon Blades (73-95), Tri-City Americans (96-120), Lethbridge Hurricanes (121-141), Moose Jaw Warriors (142-163), Regina Pats (164-186), Spokane Chiefs (188-213), Brandon Wheat Kings (214-236), Victoria Cougars (237-260), Prince Albert Raiders (261-283), Kamloops Blazers (284-309), and Portland

Winter Hawks (310-333). First round picks (1991 NHL Draft) in this set include Pat Falloon (2), Scott Niedermayer (3), Richard Matvichuk (8), Tyler Wright (12), Brent Bilodeau (17), and Dean McAmmond (22). First round picks (1992 NHL Draft) in this set include Mike Rathje (3), David Cooper (11), Jason Bowen (15), Jason Smith (18), and David Wilke (20). A factory set, a numbered edition of 6,000 sets, was produced and marketed separately.

	MINT	EXC	G-VG
COMPLETE SET (347)	18.00	7.25	1.80
COMPLETE FACT.SET (347)	20.00	8.00	2.00
COMMON PLAYER (1-347)	.10	.04	.01

□ 1	Brent Bilodeau	.50	.20	.05
□ 2	Craig Chapman	.10	.04	.01
□ 3	Jeff Jubenville	.15	.06	.01
□ 4	Al Kinisky	.10	.04	.01
□ 5	Kevin Malgunas	.10	.04	.01
□ 6	Andy MacIntyre	.15	.06	.01
□ 7	Darren McAusland	.15	.06	.01
□ 8	Mike Seaton	.10	.04	.01
□ 9	Turner Stevenson	.50	.20	.05
□ 10	Lindsay Valis	.25	.10	.02
□ 11	Dave Wilke	.15	.06	.01
□ 12	Jesse Wilson	.10	.04	.01
□ 13	Dody Wood	.25	.10	.02
□ 14	Bradley Zavisha	.25	.10	.02
□ 15	Vince Boe	.10	.04	.01
□ 16	Scott Davis	.10	.04	.01
□ 17	Troy Hyatt	.10	.04	.01
□ 18	Trevor Pennock	.10	.04	.01
□ 19	Corey Schwab	.20	.08	.02
□ 20	Scott Bellefontaine	.15	.06	.01
□ 21	Travis Kelln	.10	.04	.01
□ 22	Peter Anholt CO/GM	.10	.04	.01
□ 23	Sonny Mignacca UER	.15	.06	.01
□ 24	Chris Osgood	1.00	.40	.10
□ 25	Murray Garbutt	.10	.04	.01
□ 26	Kalvin Knibbs	.10	.04	.01
□ 27	Jason Krywulak	.20	.08	.02
□ 28	Jason Miller	.25	.10	.02
□ 29	Rob Niedermayer	1.50	.60	.15
□ 30	Clayton Norris	.25	.10	.02
□ 31	Jason Prosofsky	.25	.10	.02
□ 32	Dana Rieder	.10	.04	.01
□ 33	Kevin Riehl	.35	.14	.03
□ 34	Tyler Romanchuk	.10	.04	.01
□ 35	Dave Shute	.10	.04	.01
□ 36	Lorne Toews	.10	.04	.01
□ 37	Scott Townsend	.10	.04	.01
□ 38	David Cooper	.35	.14	.03
□ 39	Jon Duval	.10	.04	.01
□ 40	Dan Kordic	.30	.12	.03
□ 41	Mike Rathje	.75	.30	.07
□ 42	Tim Bothwell CO	.15	.06	.01
□ 43	Brent Thompson	.50	.20	.05
□ 44	Jeff Knight	.15	.06	.01
□ 45	Van Burgess	.10	.04	.01
□ 46	Kimbi Daniels	.35	.14	.03
□ 47	Curtis Friesen	.10	.04	.01
□ 48	Todd Holt	.25	.10	.02
□ 49	Blake Knox	.10	.04	.01
□ 50	Trent McCleary	.10	.04	.01
□ 51	Mark McFarlane	.10	.04	.01
□ 52	Eddie Patterson	.10	.04	.01
□ 53	Lloyd Pellitier	.10	.04	.01
□ 54	Geoff Sanderson	2.00	.80	.20
□ 55	Andrew Schneider	.25	.10	.02
□ 56	Tyler Wright	.75	.30	.07
□ 57	Joel Dyck	.10	.04	.01
□ 58	Len MacAusland	.10	.04	.01
□ 59	Evan Marble	.10	.04	.01
□ 60	David Podlubny	.10	.04	.01
□ 61	Kurt Seher	.50	.20	.05
□ 62	Jason Smith	.10	.04	.01
□ 63	Justin Burke	.15	.06	.01
□ 64	Kelly Thiessen	.25	.10	.02
□ 65	Todd Esselmont	.10	.04	.01
□ 66	Graham James CO/GM	.15	.06	.01
□ 67	Chris Herperger	.25	.10	.02
□ 68	Mark McCoy	.10	.04	.01
□ 69	Dean Malkoc	.10	.04	.01
□ 70	Dennis Sproxton	.15	.06	.01
□ 71	Centennial Civic Center	.15	.06	.01
□ 72	Kimbi Daniels	.25	.10	.02
□ 73	Shane Calder	.25	.10	.02
□ 74	Mark Franks	.25	.10	.02
□ 75	Greg Leahy	.10	.04	.01
□ 76	Dean Rambo	.10	.04	.01
□ 77	Scott Scissons	.25	.10	.02
□ 78	David Struch	.10	.04	.01
□ 79	Derek Tibbatts	.25	.10	.02
□ 80	Shawn Yakimishyn	.10	.04	.01
□ 81	Trent Coghill	.10	.04	.01
□ 82	Robert Lelacheur	.10	.04	.01
□ 83	Richard Matvichuk	.75	.30	.07
□ 84	Mark Raiter	.10	.04	.01
□ 85	Trevor Sherban	.10	.04	.01
□ 86	Mark Wotton	.10	.04	.01
□ 87	Cam Moon	.10	.04	.01
□ 88	Trevor Robins	.15	.06	.01
□ 89	Jeff Buchanan	.10	.04	.01
□ 90	Ryan Strain	.10	.04	.01
□ 91	Tim Cox	.10	.04	.01
□ 92	Terry Ruskowski CO	.15	.06	.01
□ 93	Saskatchewan Place	.15	.06	.01
□ 94	Darin Bader	.10	.04	.01
□ 95	Gaetan Blouin	.15	.06	.01
□ 96	Rick Kozuback CO/GM	.10	.04	.01
□ 97	Jason Bowen	.30	.12	.03
□ 98	Fran Deferenza	.15	.06	.01
□ 99	Terry Degner	.25	.10	.02
□ 100	Devin Derksen	.15	.06	.01
□ 101	Martin Svetlik	.10	.04	.01
□ 102	Jeremy Warring	.15	.06	.01
□ 103	Corey Jones	.15	.06	.01
□ 104	Dean Tiltgen UER	.25	.10	.02
□ 105	Ryan Fujita	.75	.30	.07
□ 106	Jeff Fancy	.10	.04	.01
□ 107	Terry Virtue	.10	.04	.01
□ 108	Dennis Pinfold	.10	.04	.01
□ 109	Kyle Reeves	.50	.20	.05
□ 110	Steve McNutt UER	.15	.06	.01
□ 111	Todd Klassen	.30	.12	.03
□ 112	Darren Hastman	.10	.04	.01
□ 113	Bill Lindsay	.75	.30	.07
□ 114A	Brian Sakic ERR (Misspelled Buan on card front)	.50	.20	.05
□ 114B	Brian Sakic COR	.50	.20	.05
□ 115	Dan Sherstenka	.10	.04	.01
□ 116	Don Blishen	.15	.06	.01
□ 117	Jason Marshall	.50	.20	.05
□ 118	Dean Zayonce	.10	.04	.01
□ 119	Brad Loring	.10	.04	.01
□ 120	No Card Issued	.00	.00	.00
□ 121	Darcy Austin UER	.15	.06	.01
□ 122	Darcy Werenka	.35	.14	.03
□ 123	Shane Peacock	.25	.10	.02
□ 124	Rob Hartnell UER	.25	.10	.02
□ 125	Brad Zimmer	.10	.04	.01
□ 126	Allan Egeland	.10	.04	.01
□ 127	Brad Rubachuk	.10	.04	.01
□ 128	Jamie Pushor	.25	.10	.02
□ 129	Jamie McLennan UER	.75	.30	.07
□ 130	Lance Burns	.15	.06	.01
□ 131	Ryan Smith	.25	.10	.02
□ 132	Jason McBain	.15	.06	.01
□ 133	Duane Maruschak UER	.15	.06	.01
□ 134	Kevin St.Jacques	.35	.14	.03
□ 135	Jason Sorochan	.10	.04	.01
□ 136	Jason Widmer	.15	.06	.01
□ 137	Bob Loucks CO	.15	.06	.01
□ 138	Jason Ruff	.35	.14	.03
□ 139	Pat Pylypuik	.10	.04	.01
□ 140	Scott Adair	.10	.04	.01
□ 141	Radek Sip	.35	.14	.03
□ 142	Russ West	.10	.04	.01
□ 143	Scott Thomas	.35	.14	.03
□ 144	Kent Staniforth	.10	.04	.01
□ 145	Travis Thiessen	.15	.06	.01
□ 146	Mark Hussey	.10	.04	.01
□ 147	Kevin Masters	.10	.04	.01
□ 148	Todd Johnson	.10	.04	.01
□ 149	Bob Loucks	.15	.06	.01
□ 150A	Rob Reimer ERR (Numbered 149 on back)	.25	.10	.02
□ 150B	Rob Reimer COR	.25	.10	.02
□ 151	Jeff Petruic	.10	.04	.01
□ 152	Chris Schmidt	.35	.14	.03
□ 153	Scott Barnstable	.10	.04	.01
□ 154	Ian Layton	.10	.04	.01
□ 155	Kevin Smyth	.25	.10	.02
□ 156	Kim Heck	.10	.04	.01
□ 157	Jason White	.10	.04	.01
□ 158	Peter Cox	.10	.04	.01
□ 159	Jeff Calvert UER	.15	.06	.01
□ 160	Paul Dyck UER	.10	.04	.01
□ 161	Derek Kletzel	.10	.04	.01
□ 162	Jason Fitzsimmons UER	.15	.06	.01
□ 163	Darcy Jerome	.10	.04	.01
□ 164	Hal Christiansen	.10	.04	.01

☐ 165	Terry Hollinger	.25	.10	.02
☐ 166	Mike Risdale	.25	.10	.02
☐ 167	Jamie Heward	.25	.10	.02
☐ 168	Louis Dumont	.10	.04	.01
☐ 169	Cory Dosdall	.10	.04	.01
☐ 170	Terry Bendera	.10	.04	.01
☐ 171	Jamie Hayden	.10	.04	.01
☐ 172	Kelly Chotowetz	.10	.04	.01
☐ 173	Brad Scott	.10	.04	.01
☐ 174	Jeff Shantz	.75	.30	.07
☐ 175	Kelly Markwart	.15	.06	.01
☐ 176	Gary Pearce	.10	.04	.01
☐ 177	Kerry Biette	.10	.04	.01
☐ 178	Jamie Splett	.10	.04	.01
☐ 179	Frank Kovacs	.10	.04	.01
☐ 180	Greg Pankewicz	.15	.06	.01
☐ 181	Colin Ruck	.10	.04	.01
☐ 182	Brad Tippett CO	.15	.06	.01
☐ 183	Dusty Imoo	.25	.10	.02
☐ 184	Derek Eberle	.10	.04	.01
☐ 185	Heath Weenk	.15	.06	.01
☐ 186	Mike Sillinger	.75	.30	.07
☐ 187	Erin Thornton	.10	.04	.01
☐ 188	Mike Chrun	.10	.04	.01
☐ 189	Pat Falloon	1.50	.60	.15
☐ 190	Bobby House UER	.25	.10	.02
☐ 191	Mike Jickling	.10	.04	.01
☐ 192	Trevor Tovall UER	.15	.06	.01
☐ 193	Steve Junker	.35	.14	.03
☐ 194	Shane Maitland	.10	.04	.01
☐ 195	Chris Lafreniere	.10	.04	.01
☐ 196	Frank Evans	.10	.04	.01
☐ 197	Jon Klemm	.10	.04	.01
☐ 198	Shawn Dietrich UER	.15	.06	.01
☐ 199	Dennis Saharchuk UER	.15	.06	.01
☐ 200	Mark Woolf	.15	.06	.01
☐ 201	Ray Whitney	.75	.30	.07
☐ 202	Scott Bailey	.15	.06	.01
☐ 203	Mark Ruark	.10	.04	.01
☐ 204	Brent Thurston	.10	.04	.01
☐ 205	Dan Faassen	.10	.04	.01
☐ 206	Kerry Toporowski	.35	.14	.03
☐ 207	Des Christopher	.15	.06	.01
☐ 208	Geoff Grandberg	.10	.04	.01
☐ 209	Bryan Maxwell CO	.15	.06	.01
☐ 210	Cam Danyluk	.10	.04	.01
☐ 211	Bram Vanderkracht	.10	.04	.01
☐ 212	Calvin Thudium	.10	.04	.01
☐ 213	Mark Szoke UER	.15	.06	.01
☐ 214	Kelly McCrimmon CO/GM	.10	.04	.01
☐ 215	Kevin Robertson UER	.15	.06	.01
☐ 216A	Brian Purdy ERR	.25	.10	.02
	(Misspelled Puroy on card front)			
☐ 216B	Brian Purdy COR	.25	.10	.02
☐ 217	Hardy Sauter	.10	.04	.01
☐ 218	Dwayne Gylywoychuk	.10	.04	.01
☐ 219	Bart Cote	.10	.04	.01
☐ 220	Merv Priest	.10	.04	.01
☐ 221	Jeff Hoad	.10	.04	.01
☐ 222	Glen Gulutzan	.10	.04	.01
☐ 223	Johan Skillgard	.10	.04	.01
☐ 224	Byron Penstock	.15	.06	.01
☐ 225A	Mike Vadenberghe ERR	.25	.10	.02
	(Misspelled Vandenberghe on card front)			
☐ 225B	Mike Vadenberghe COR	.25	.10	.02
☐ 226	Trevor Kidd	1.00	.40	.10
☐ 227	Dan Kopec	.10	.04	.01
☐ 228	Greg Hutchings	.10	.04	.01
☐ 229	Chris Constant	.10	.04	.01
☐ 230	Glen Webster	.10	.04	.01
☐ 231	Rob Puchniak	.10	.04	.01
☐ 232	Calvin Flint	.10	.04	.01
☐ 233	Stuart Scantlebury	.10	.04	.01
☐ 234	Jason White	.10	.04	.01
☐ 235	Gary Audette	.25	.10	.02
☐ 236	Kevin Schmalz	.10	.04	.01
☐ 237	Dwayne Newman	.10	.04	.01
☐ 238	Chris Catellier	.10	.04	.01
☐ 239	Todd Harris	.10	.04	.01
☐ 240	Mike Shemko	.10	.04	.01
☐ 241	John Badduke	.10	.04	.01
☐ 242	Mark Cipriano	.10	.04	.01
☐ 243	Brad Bagu	.10	.04	.01
☐ 244	Ross Harris	.10	.04	.01
☐ 245	Dino Caputo	.10	.04	.01
☐ 246	Cam Bristow	.10	.04	.01
☐ 247	Jarret Zukiwsky UER	.15	.06	.01
☐ 248	Jason Knox	.10	.04	.01
☐ 249	Gerry St.Cyr	.25	.10	.02
☐ 250	Larry Woo	.10	.04	.01
☐ 251	Jason Peters	.10	.04	.01
☐ 252	Shane Stangby	.10	.04	.01
☐ 253	Dave McMillen	.10	.04	.01
☐ 254	Colin Gregor UER	.15	.06	.01
☐ 255	Steve Passmore	.15	.06	.01
☐ 256	Shayne Green UER	.30	.12	.03
☐ 257	Kevin Koopman	.15	.06	.01
☐ 258	Larry Watkins UER	.15	.06	.01
☐ 259	Scott Fukami UER	.25	.10	.02
☐ 260	Rick Hopper CO	.10	.04	.01
☐ 261	Laurie Billeck	.10	.04	.01
☐ 262	Rob Daum CO/GM UER	.15	.06	.01
☐ 263	Mark Stowe	.10	.04	.01
☐ 264	Curtis Regnier	.25	.10	.02
☐ 265	David Neilson	.10	.04	.01
☐ 266	Brian Pellerin	.10	.04	.01
☐ 267	Dean McAmmond	.75	.30	.07
☐ 268	Darren Van Impe	.15	.06	.01
☐ 269	Troy Neumeier	.10	.04	.01
☐ 270	Mike Langen	.15	.06	.01
☐ 271	Dan Kesa	.30	.12	.03
☐ 272	Travis Laycock	.15	.06	.01
☐ 273	Scott Allison	.50	.20	.05
☐ 274	Jeff Gorman	.10	.04	.01
☐ 275	Lee J. Leslie	.50	.20	.05
☐ 276	Jason Kwiatkowski	.25	.10	.02
☐ 277	Donevan Hextall UER	.60	.24	.06
☐ 278	Shane Zulyniak	.10	.04	.01
☐ 279	Darren Perkins	.10	.04	.01
☐ 280	Chad Seibel	.10	.04	.01
☐ 281	Jeff Nelson	.75	.30	.07
☐ 282	Troy Hjertas	.10	.04	.01
☐ 283	Jamie Linden	.50	.20	.05
☐ 284	Zac Boyer	.50	.20	.05
☐ 285	Jarret Bousquet	.10	.04	.01
☐ 286	Steven Yule	.10	.04	.01
☐ 287	Tommy Renney CO UER	.15	.06	.01
	(Renny on back)			
☐ 288	Lance Johnson	.10	.04	.01
☐ 289	Scott Niedermayer	1.50	.60	.15
☐ 290	Ryan Harrison	.10	.04	.01
☐ 291	Ed Patterson	.35	.14	.03
☐ 292	Jeff Watchorn	.15	.06	.01
☐ 293	Cal McGowan	.35	.14	.03
☐ 294	Dale Masson	.15	.06	.01
☐ 295	Joey Mittelsteadt UER	.15	.06	.01
☐ 296	Scott Loucks	.25	.10	.02
☐ 297	Shea Esselmont	.10	.04	.01
☐ 298	Craig Bonner	.15	.06	.01
☐ 299	Mike Mathers	.25	.10	.02
☐ 300	Fred Hettle	.10	.04	.01
☐ 301	Craig Lyons	.10	.04	.01
☐ 302	Murray Duval	.10	.04	.01
☐ 303	Jamie Barnes	.10	.04	.01
☐ 304	Bryan Gourlie	.10	.04	.01
☐ 305	Chad Berezniuk	.10	.04	.01
☐ 306	Corey Hirsch	1.00	.40	.10
☐ 307	Darryl Sydor	.75	.30	.07
☐ 308	Jarrett Deuling	.25	.10	.02
☐ 309	Cory Stock	.10	.04	.01
☐ 310	Chris Rowland	.25	.10	.02
☐ 311	Mike Ruark	.10	.04	.01
☐ 312	Steve Konowalchuk	.50	.20	.05
☐ 313	Jeff Sebastian	.10	.04	.01
☐ 314	Brandon Smith	.10	.04	.01
☐ 315	Greg Gatto	.10	.04	.01
☐ 316	Brad Harrison	.10	.04	.01
☐ 317	Brantt Myhres	.35	.14	.03
☐ 318	Jamie Black	.35	.14	.03
☐ 319	Colin Foley	.10	.04	.01
☐ 320	Cam Danyluk	.15	.06	.01
☐ 321	Dean Dorchak	.10	.04	.01
☐ 322	Ryan Slemko	.10	.04	.01
☐ 323	Kim Deck	.10	.04	.01
☐ 324	Kelly Harris	.10	.04	.01
☐ 325	Murray Bokenfohr	.10	.04	.01
☐ 326	Dean Intwert	.15	.06	.01
☐ 327	Dennis Saharchuk UER	.15	.06	.01
☐ 328	Shane Seiker UER	.15	.06	.01
☐ 329	Terry Virtue	.10	.04	.01
☐ 330	Josh Erdman	.10	.04	.01
☐ 331	Layne Roland	.25	.10	.02
☐ 332	Michel Michon	.10	.04	.01
☐ 333	Scott Mydan UER	.15	.06	.01
☐ 334	Brandon Wheat Kings	.15	.06	.01
☐ 335	Moose Jaw Warriors	.15	.06	.01
☐ 336	Swift Current Broncos	.15	.06	.01
☐ 337	Regina Pats UER	.15	.06	.01
☐ 338	Saskatoon Blades	.15	.06	.01
☐ 339	Medicine Hat Tigers	.15	.06	.01
☐ 340	The Goalmouth	.15	.06	.01
☐ 341	Portland Winter Hawks	.15	.06	.01
☐ 342	Kamloops Blazers UER	.15	.06	.01
☐ 343	Victoria Cougars	.15	.06	.01

☐ 344	Tri City Americans	.15	.06	.01
☐ 345	Spokane Chiefs	.15	.06	.01
☐ 346	Seattle Thunderbirds	.15	.06	.01
☐ 347	Lethbridge Hurricanes	.15	.06	.01
☐ 348	Prince Albert Raiders	.15	.06	.01

1990-91 7th Inn. Sketch QMJHL

This 268-card set was produced by 7th Inning Sketch featuring players from the Quebec Major Junior Hockey League. The cards are standard size, 2 1/2" by 3 1/2". First round picks (1991 NHL Draft) in this set include Patrick Poulin (9), Martin Lapointe (10), and Philippe Boucher (13). There were no 1992 NHL Draft first round picks in this set. A factory set, a numbered edition of 4,800 sets, was produced and marketed separately.

	MINT	EXC	G-VG
COMPLETE SET (268)	15.00	6.00	1.50
COMPLETE FACT.SET (268)	15.00	6.00	1.50
COMMON PLAYER (1-268)	.10	.04	.01

☐ 1	Patrick Poulin	.75	.30	.07
☐ 2	Steve Lupien	.15	.06	.01
☐ 3	Pierre Gagnon	.10	.04	.01
☐ 4	Eric Plante	.10	.04	.01
☐ 5	Stephane Desjardins	.15	.06	.01
☐ 6	Peter Valenta	.10	.04	.01
☐ 7	Alexander Legault	.15	.06	.01
☐ 8	Patrice Brisebois	.75	.30	.07
☐ 9	Martin Charrois	.10	.04	.01
☐ 10	Eric Dandenault	.15	.06	.01
☐ 11	Claude Juiras Jr.	.10	.04	.01
☐ 12	David Pekarek	.10	.04	.01
☐ 13	Denis Chasse	.35	.14	.03
☐ 14	Ian Laperriere	.50	.20	.05
☐ 15	Roger Larche	.10	.04	.01
☐ 16	Dave Paquet	.25	.10	.02
☐ 17	Pascal Lebrasseur	.10	.04	.01
☐ 18	Eric Meloche	.10	.04	.01
☐ 19	The Face Off	.15	.06	.01
☐ 20	Sylvain Rodrique	.15	.06	.01
☐ 21	Dary Giarard	.10	.04	.01
☐ 22	Eric Rochette	.10	.04	.01
☐ 23	Steve Gosselin	.10	.04	.01
☐ 24	Martin Lavalle	.10	.04	.01
☐ 25	Martin Lapointe	.75	.30	.07
☐ 26	Eric Brule	.35	.14	.03
☐ 27	Richard Boivin	.10	.04	.01
☐ 28	Patrice Martineau	.10	.04	.01
☐ 29	Dave Trembley	.10	.04	.01
☐ 30	Steve Larouche	.10	.04	.01
☐ 31	Danny Beauregard	.10	.04	.01
☐ 32	Francois Belanger	.15	.06	.01
☐ 33	Michel St.Jacques	.35	.14	.03
☐ 34	Patric Sissillan	.10	.04	.01
☐ 35	Felix Potvin	5.00	2.00	.50
☐ 36	Sebastien Parent	.10	.04	.01
☐ 37	Eric Duchesne	.25	.10	.02
☐ 38	Gilles Bouchard	.10	.04	.01
☐ 39	Martin Gagne	.15	.06	.01
☐ 40	Stephane Charboneau	.15	.06	.01
☐ 41	Martin Beaupre	.10	.04	.01
☐ 42	Daniel Paradis	.25	.10	.02
☐ 43	Joe Canale	.25	.10	.02
☐ 44	Georges Vezina Arena	.15	.06	.01

☐ 45	Francois Leblanc	.15	.06	.01
☐ 46	Martin Chaput	.35	.14	.03
☐ 47	Marc Beaucage	.10	.04	.01
☐ 48	Carl Mantha	.15	.06	.01
☐ 49	Jim Bermingham	.25	.10	.02
☐ 50	Philippe Boucher	.75	.30	.07
☐ 51	Denis Chalifoux	.10	.04	.01
☐ 52	Sylvain Naud	.15	.06	.01
☐ 53	Jean Roberge	.10	.04	.01
☐ 54	Sandy McCarthy	.50	.20	.05
☐ 55	Eric Dubois	.10	.04	.01
☐ 56	Jean Blouin	.10	.04	.01
☐ 57	Jason Brousseau	.10	.04	.01
☐ 58	Pierre Sandke	.10	.04	.01
☐ 59	Benoit Larose	.10	.04	.01
☐ 60	Yanick Frechette	.10	.04	.01
☐ 61	Pierre Calder	.10	.04	.01
☐ 62	Patric Grise	.10	.04	.01
☐ 63	Martin Balfeux	.10	.04	.01
☐ 64	Boris Rousson	.25	.10	.02
☐ 65	Martin Trudeli	.10	.04	.01
☐ 66	Carl Leblanc	.10	.04	.01
☐ 67	Martin Broche	.15	.06	.01
☐ 68	Benoit Terrien	.10	.04	.01
☐ 69	QMJHL Action	.15	.06	.01
☐ 70	Pascal Vincent	.10	.04	.01
☐ 71	Christian Tardi	.10	.04	.01
☐ 72	Christian Campeau	.10	.04	.01
☐ 73	Eric Raymond	.15	.06	.01
☐ 74	John Kovacs	.10	.04	.01
☐ 75	Steve Areas	.10	.04	.01
☐ 76	Pascal Dufalt	.10	.04	.01
☐ 77	Greg MacEachern	.10	.04	.01
☐ 78	Remi Belliveau	.10	.04	.01
☐ 79	Jocelyn Langlois	.10	.04	.01
☐ 80	Carl Menard	.15	.06	.01
☐ 81	Sebastein Foneir	.10	.04	.01
☐ 82	Jean-Franco Gregoire	.10	.04	.01
☐ 83	Normand Demers	.10	.04	.01
☐ 84	Nicolas Lefebvre	.10	.04	.01
☐ 85	Dominic Maltais	.10	.04	.01
☐ 86	Mario Therrien	.10	.04	.01
☐ 87	Daniel Thibault	.10	.04	.01
☐ 88	Jean-Francois Labbe	.75	.30	.07
☐ 89	Alain Cote	.25	.10	.02
☐ 90	Eric Prillo	.10	.04	.01
☐ 91	Patrick Nadeau	.15	.06	.01
☐ 92	Claude Poner	.10	.04	.01
☐ 93	Stephane Julier	.10	.04	.01
☐ 94	Patrice Rene	.10	.04	.01
☐ 95	Francis Coutineir	.10	.04	.01
☐ 96	Guy Lefebvre	.10	.04	.01
☐ 97	Carl Boudreau	.25	.10	.02
☐ 98	Jacques Parent	.10	.04	.01
☐ 99	Stephane Bouquet	.10	.04	.01
☐ 100	Yanic Perreault	.75	.30	.07
☐ 101	Yvan Bergeron	.10	.04	.01
☐ 102	Jean-Francois Rivard	.15	.06	.01
☐ 103	Daniel Laflamme	.10	.04	.01
☐ 104	Francois Bourdeau	.10	.04	.01
☐ 105	Yvan Charrois	.10	.04	.01
☐ 106	Patric Genest	.10	.04	.01
☐ 107	Herve Lapointe	.10	.04	.01
☐ 108	Jean-Francois Jamphe	.25	.10	.02
☐ 109	Marc Tardiff	.15	.06	.01
☐ 110	Eric Cardinal	.10	.04	.01
☐ 111	Denis Cloutier	.10	.04	.01
☐ 112	QMJHL Action	.15	.06	.01
☐ 113	Alain Samscartier	.10	.04	.01
☐ 114	Marquis Mathieu	.10	.04	.01
☐ 115	Stephan Tartari	.10	.04	.01
☐ 116	QMJHL Action	.15	.06	.01
☐ 117	QMJHL Action	.15	.06	.01
☐ 118	Martin Ray	.10	.04	.01
☐ 119	David Boudreault	.10	.04	.01
☐ 120	Mario Durroulin	.10	.04	.01
☐ 121	Jean-Francis Dieard	.10	.04	.01
☐ 122	QMJHL Action	.15	.06	.01
☐ 123	QMJHL Action	.15	.06	.01
☐ 124	Mausime Gagne	.10	.04	.01
☐ 125	Stephane Guellet	.10	.04	.01
☐ 126	Steven Paiement	.10	.04	.01
☐ 127	Francois Olympique	.10	.04	.01
☐ 128	Eric Coci	.10	.04	.01
☐ 129	Simon Toupin	.10	.04	.01
☐ 130	Shane Doirrin	.10	.04	.01
☐ 131	Todd Sparks	.25	.10	.02
☐ 132	Bruno Lajeunesse	.15	.06	.01
☐ 133	Marcel Cousineau	.35	.14	.03
☐ 134	Claude-Charl Sauirol	.10	.04	.01
☐ 135	Eric Bellerose	.35	.14	.03
☐ 136	QMJHL Action	.15	.06	.01
☐ 137	QMJHL Action	.15	.06	.01

☐ 138	Martin Lepage	.25	.10	.02
☐ 139	Michael Langauer	.10	.04	.01
☐ 140	Fredric Boivin	.15	.06	.01
☐ 141	Steven Dion	.10	.04	.01
☐ 142	QMJHL Action	.15	.06	.01
☐ 143	QMJHL Action	.15	.06	.01
☐ 144	Dan Paolucci	.10	.04	.01
☐ 145	Bruno Villeneuve	.25	.10	.02
☐ 146	Checklist Card	.25	.10	.02
	(Yanic Perreault)			
☐ 147	Checklist Card	.15	.06	.01
☐ 148	Stefan Simoes	.10	.04	.01
☐ 149	Joel Blain	.10	.04	.01
☐ 150	Eric Lavigne	.50	.20	.05
☐ 151	Checklist Card	.15	.06	.01
☐ 152	Checklist Card	.25	.10	.02
	(Patrick Poulin)			
☐ 153	Robert Malanson	.10	.04	.01
☐ 154	Brian Rogger	.10	.04	.01
☐ 155	Checklist Card	.15	.06	.01
☐ 156	Checklist Card	.15	.06	.01
☐ 157	Francois Ouellette	.35	.14	.03
☐ 158	QMJHL Action	.15	.06	.01
☐ 159	Checklist Card	1.00	.40	.10
	(Felix Potvin)			
☐ 160	Checklist Card	.15	.06	.01
☐ 161	Checklist Card	.15	.06	.01
☐ 162	Checklist Card	.15	.06	.01
☐ 163	QMJHL Action	.15	.06	.01
☐ 164	QMJHL Action	.15	.06	.01
☐ 165	Checklist Card	.15	.06	.01
☐ 166	Checklist Card	.15	.06	.01
☐ 167	QMJHL Action	.15	.06	.01
☐ 168	QMJHL Action	.15	.06	.01
☐ 169	Pierre Fillon	.10	.04	.01
☐ 170	Yanick Degrace	.20	.08	.02
☐ 171	Paul Daigneault	.10	.04	.01
☐ 172	Stacy Dellaire	.10	.04	.01
☐ 173	Steve Searles	.10	.04	.01
☐ 174	Todd Gillingham	.35	.14	.03
☐ 175	Yves Sarault	.50	.20	.05
☐ 176	Jason Downey	.10	.04	.01
☐ 177	Paul Brousseau	.50	.20	.05
☐ 178	Raymond Delarosbi	.10	.04	.01
☐ 179	Yvan Corbin	.10	.04	.01
☐ 180	Gaston Drapeau	.15	.06	.01
☐ 181	Celebration	.25	.10	.02
☐ 182	Reginald Brezeault	.10	.04	.01
☐ 183	Eric Lafrance	.10	.04	.01
☐ 184	Martin Lavalle	.20	.08	.02
☐ 185	Sebastein Lavallere	.10	.04	.01
☐ 186	Martin Lefebvre	.10	.04	.01
☐ 187	Richard Hamelin	.10	.04	.01
☐ 188	Eric Beauvois	.10	.04	.01
☐ 189	Hughes Mongeon	.50	.20	.05
☐ 190	Alaine Cole	.10	.04	.01
☐ 191	Eric Desrochers	.10	.04	.01
☐ 192	Eric Joyal	.10	.04	.01
☐ 193	Steve Dortigny	.10	.04	.01
☐ 194	Fredrick Lefebvre	.10	.04	.01
☐ 195	Patrick Hebert	.10	.04	.01
☐ 196	Johnny Lorenzo	.15	.06	.01
☐ 197	Sylvain Cornier	.10	.04	.01
☐ 198	QMJHL Action	.15	.06	.01
☐ 199	Dave Morissette	.10	.04	.01
☐ 200	Yanick Dupre	.35	.14	.03
☐ 201	Eric Marcoux	.10	.04	.01
☐ 202	Bruno Ducharme	.10	.04	.01
☐ 203	Martin Caron	.10	.04	.01
☐ 204	Yves Meunier	.10	.04	.01
☐ 205	Eric Bissonette	.20	.08	.02
☐ 206	Jason Underhill	.10	.04	.01
☐ 207	Dave Belliveau	.10	.04	.01
☐ 208	Steve Lapointe	.10	.04	.01
☐ 209	Dean Melanson	.10	.04	.01
☐ 210	Trevor Dehaime	.10	.04	.01
☐ 211	Jacques Leblanc	.10	.04	.01
☐ 212	Normand Pacquet	.25	.10	.02
☐ 213	Huges Laliberte	.15	.06	.01
☐ 214	Craig Prior	.10	.04	.01
☐ 215	Patrick Labrecque	.15	.06	.01
☐ 216	Patrick Cloutier	.10	.04	.01
☐ 217	Michael Bazinet	.10	.04	.01
☐ 218	Christian Proulx	.25	.10	.02
☐ 219	QMJHL Action	.15	.06	.01
☐ 220	Charles Poulin	.50	.20	.05
☐ 221	Christian Larivierre	.10	.04	.01
☐ 222	Martin Brodeur	2.00	.80	.20
☐ 223	Yanick Lemay	.20	.08	.02
☐ 224	Dennis Leblanc	.10	.04	.01
☐ 225	Francois Groleau	.35	.14	.03
☐ 226	Pierre Sevigny	.75	.30	.07
☐ 227	Pierre Allard	.10	.04	.01

☐ 228	Craig Martin	.10	.04	.01
☐ 229	Karl Dykhuis	.35	.14	.03
☐ 230	Etienne Lavoie	.10	.04	.01
☐ 231	Stan Malanson	.10	.04	.01
☐ 232	Dominic Rheaume	.25	.10	.02
☐ 233	Mario Nobili	.30	.12	.03
☐ 234	Martin Gendron	.50	.20	.05
☐ 235	Stephane Menard	.15	.06	.01
☐ 236	David St.Pierre	.25	.10	.02
☐ 237	Yan Arsenault	.25	.10	.02
☐ 238	Norman Flynn	.10	.04	.01
☐ 239	QMJHL Action	.15	.06	.01
☐ 240	David Chouinard	.25	.10	.02
☐ 241	Robert Guilliet	.35	.14	.03
☐ 242	Martin Lajeunesse	.15	.06	.01
☐ 243	Nichol Cloutier	.10	.04	.01
☐ 244	Joel Brouchard	.10	.04	.01
☐ 245	Donald Brashear	.35	.14	.03
☐ 246	Sebastein Trembley	.10	.04	.01
☐ 247	Dominique Grandmaison	.10	.04	.01
☐ 248	Nicolas Lefebvre	.10	.04	.01
☐ 249	Joseph Napolitano	.20	.08	.02
☐ 250	Marc Savard	.25	.10	.02
☐ 251	Alain Gauthier	.15	.06	.01
☐ 252	Patrick Cole	.10	.04	.01
☐ 253	Richard Aimonette	.10	.04	.01
☐ 254	Martin Laitre	.10	.04	.01
☐ 255	Carl Lamonthe	.25	.10	.02
☐ 256	QMJHL Action	.15	.06	.01
☐ 257	Andre Durocher	.10	.04	.01
☐ 258	Jocelyn Martel	.10	.04	.01
☐ 259	Jeanot Ferlard	.10	.04	.01
☐ 260	Claude Savoire	.10	.04	.01
☐ 262	Denis Beauchamp	.10	.04	.01
☐ 263	Jean-Francois Gagnon	.15	.06	.01
☐ 264	Andre Boulaine	.15	.06	.01
☐ 265	Paul-Emile Exantus	.10	.04	.01
☐ 266	Danny Nolet	.10	.04	.01
☐ 267	Jean Lebreau	.10	.04	.01
☐ 268	Claude Barthe	.15	.06	.01

1991 7th Inn. Sketch
CHL Award Winners

This 30-card boxed set features Canadian Hockey League Award Winners. Each box has on its back a checklist and the set serial number. The cards measures the standard size (2 1/2" by 3 1/2") and feature action color player photos with gray borders against a black card face. The player's specific achievement is printed in gray in the black margin at the top. His name and team appear in white at the bottom. The horizontal backs show a close-up player picture on one half of the card. A white panel of the same size takes up the rest of the card face and features the player's name, achievement, and sponsor logos. The picture and panel are outlined by a thin black line. The cards are numbered on the back.

	MINT	EXC	G-VG
COMPLETE SET (30)	10.00	4.00	1.00
COMMON PLAYER (1-30)	.25	.10	.02

		MINT	EXC	G-VG
☐ 1	Eric Lindros	2.50	1.00	.25
	(In Oshawa Generals uniform)			
☐ 2	Dale Craigwell	.35	.14	.03
☐ 3	Nathan Lafayette	.50	.20	.05
☐ 4	Chris Snell	.25	.10	.02
☐ 5	Cory Stillman	.35	.14	.03
☐ 6	Mike Torchia	.25	.10	.02
☐ 7	George Burnett	.25	.10	.02
☐ 8	Eric Lindros	2.50	1.00	.25
	(Blue and white Generals uniform, facing front)			
☐ 9	Sherwood Bassin	.25	.10	.02
☐ 10	Eric Lindros	2.50	1.00	.25
	(Blue and white Generals uniform, slightly angled position)			
☐ 11	Scott Neidermayer	.75	.30	.07
	(Front shot)			
☐ 12	Pat Falloon	.60	.24	.06
☐ 13	Scott Neidermayer	.75	.30	.07
	(Left side forward)			
☐ 14	Darryl Sydor	.50	.20	.05
☐ 15	Donevan Hextall	.50	.20	.05
☐ 16	Jamie McLennan	.50	.20	.05
☐ 17	Tom Renney	.35	.14	.03
☐ 18	Frank Evans	.25	.10	.02
☐ 19	Bob Brown	.25	.10	.02
☐ 20	Ray Whitney	.35	.14	.03
☐ 21	Phillippe Boucher	.35	.14	.03
☐ 22	Yanic Perreault	.50	.20	.05
☐ 23	Benoit Larose	.25	.10	.02
☐ 24	Patrice Brisebois	.35	.14	.03
☐ 25	Phillippe Boucher	.35	.14	.03
☐ 26	Felix Potvin	2.00	.80	.20
☐ 27	Joe Canale	.25	.10	.02
☐ 28	Christian Lariviere	.25	.10	.02
☐ 29	Roland Janelle	.25	.10	.02
☐ 30	Yanic Perreault	.50	.20	.05

1991 7th Inn. Sketch Memorial Cup

Félix Potvin

The 1991 7th Inn. Sketch Memorial Cup Hockey set captures the four teams that participated in the Canadian junior hockey championship, with one team each from the OHL and WHL, and two from the QMJHL (the host league). The cards measure the standard size (2 1/2" by 3 1/2") and feature on the fronts color action player photos enclosed by silver borders. The upper right and lower left corners are cut off to permit space for the CHL and '91 Memorial Cup logos respectively. The player's name in the bottom silver border rounds out the card face. The backs carry a second color player photo, with the card number, player's name, and biographical information in a box alongside the picture. The set is skip-numbered due to the fact that several cards were withdrawn from the set after only a few sets had been released. These 17 card numbers are 21, 36 (Rob Dykeman), 96 (Eric Lindros), 106 (Pat Peake), 107 (Steve Staios), 110 (Alex Stojanov), 111 (Glen Murray), 113 (Jason Dawe), 114 (Nathan Lafayette), 116 (Guy Leveque), 118 (Shayne Antoski), 119 (Eric Lindros), 120 (Dennis Purdie), 121 (Terry Chitaroni), and 124 (Jamie Matthews).

		MINT	EXC	G-VG
	COMPLETE SET (130)	150.00	60.00	15.00
	COMPLETE SHORT SET (113)	15.00	6.00	1.50
	COMMON PLAYER (1-130)	.15	.06	.01
	COMMON PLAYER SP	2.50	1.00	.25
☐ 1	Mike Lenarduzzi	.50	.20	.05
☐ 2	Kevin Hodson	.35	.14	.03
☐ 3	OHL Action	.25	.10	.02
	Sault Ste. Marie vs. Oshawa			
☐ 4	Bob Boughner	.25	.10	.02
☐ 5	Adam Foote	.50	.20	.05
☐ 6	Brad Tilley	.15	.06	.01
☐ 7	Brian Goudie	.15	.06	.01
☐ 8	Wade Whitten	.15	.06	.01
☐ 9	Jason Denomme	.15	.06	.01
☐ 10	David Matsos	.15	.06	.01
☐ 11	Rick Kowalsky	.15	.06	.01
☐ 12	Jarret Reid	.35	.14	.03
☐ 13	Perry Pappas	.15	.06	.01
☐ 14	Tom MacDonald	.15	.06	.01
☐ 15	Mike DeCoff	.15	.06	.01
☐ 16	Joe Busillo	.25	.10	.02
☐ 17	Denny Lambert	.35	.14	.03
☐ 18	Mark Matier	.15	.06	.01
☐ 19	Shaun Imber	.25	.10	.02
☐ 20	Ralph Intranuovo	.50	.20	.05
☐ 21	Not Known SP	2.50	1.00	.25
☐ 22	Tony Iob	.35	.14	.03
☐ 23	Colin Miller	.75	.30	.07
☐ 24	Ted Nolan	.25	.10	.02
☐ 25	Sylvain Rodrigue	.35	.14	.03
☐ 26	Felix Potvin	4.00	1.60	.40
☐ 27	Martin Lavallee	.15	.06	.01
☐ 28	Eric Brule	.75	.30	.07
☐ 29	Steve Larouche	.50	.20	.05
☐ 30	Michel St-Jacques	.15	.06	.01
☐ 31	Patrick Clement	.15	.06	.01
☐ 32	Patrick Bisailon	.15	.06	.01
☐ 33A	Checklist 62-131 SP	2.50	1.00	.25
☐ 33B	Checklist 62-131	.25	.10	.02
	(Withdrawn numbers omitted)			
☐ 34	Gilles Bouton	.25	.10	.02
☐ 35	Eric Rochette	.15	.06	.01
☐ 36	Rob Dykeman SP	2.50	1.00	.25
☐ 37A	Checklist 1-61 SP	2.50	1.00	.25
☐ 37B	Checklist 1-61	.25	.10	.02
	(Withdrawn numbers omitted)			
☐ 38	Patrice Martineau	.15	.06	.01
☐ 39	Danny Beauregard	.35	.14	.03
☐ 40	Francois Belanger	.15	.06	.01
☐ 41	Sebastien Parent	.35	.14	.03
☐ 42	Martin Gagne	.15	.06	.01
☐ 43	Stephane Charbonneau	.25	.10	.02
☐ 44	Martin Beaupre	.15	.06	.01
☐ 45	Daniel Paradis	.25	.10	.02
☐ 46	Joe Canale	.15	.06	.01
☐ 47	OHL Action	.25	.10	.02
	Sault Ste. Marie vs. Oshawa			
☐ 48	Jubilation	.15	.06	.01
☐ 49	Steve Lupien	.50	.20	.05
☐ 50	Pierre Gagnon	.50	.20	.05
☐ 51	Alexandre Legault	.15	.06	.01
☐ 52	Martin Charrois	.15	.06	.01
☐ 53	Eric Dandenault	.25	.10	.02
☐ 54	Denis Chasse	.35	.14	.03
☐ 55	Guy Lehoux	.35	.14	.03
☐ 56	Ian Laperriere	.50	.20	.05
☐ 57	Hugo Proulx	.50	.20	.05
☐ 58	Dave Whittom	.15	.06	.01
☐ 59	Yanick Dupre UER	.50	.20	.05
☐ 60	Eric Plante	.15	.06	.01
☐ 61	Stephane Desjardins	.35	.14	.03
☐ 62	Patrice Brisebois	.50	.20	.05
☐ 63	Rene Corbet	.75	.30	.07
☐ 64	Marc Savard	.35	.14	.03
☐ 65	Claude Jutras Jr.	.15	.06	.01
☐ 66	David Pekarek	.15	.06	.01
☐ 67	Roger Larche UER	.50	.20	.05
	(Name misspelled Larohe on front)			
☐ 68	Dave Paquet	.75	.30	.07
☐ 69	Eric Meloche	.15	.06	.01
☐ 70	CHL Action	.25	.10	.02
	Spokane vs. Lethbridge			
☐ 71	Celebration	.35	.14	.03
	Ed Chynoweth PRES Jon Klemm			
☐ 72	Felix Potvin MVP	2.00	.80	.20
☐ 73	Scott Bailey	.75	.30	.07
☐ 74	Trevor Kidd	1.00	.40	.10
☐ 75	Chris Lafreniere	.15	.06	.01

		MINT	EXC	G-VG
☐ 76	Frank Evans	.15	.06	.01
☐ 77	Jon Klemm	.15	.06	.01
☐ 78	Brent Thurston	.15	.06	.01
☐ 79	Jamie McLennan	.75	.30	.07
☐ 80	Steve Junker	.50	.20	.05
☐ 81	Mark Szoke	.25	.10	.02
☐ 82	Ray Whitney	.75	.30	.07
☐ 83	Geoff Grandberg	.15	.06	.01
☐ 84	Cam Danyluk	.15	.06	.01
☐ 85	Kerry Toporowski	.25	.10	.02
☐ 86	Trevor Tovell	.15	.06	.01
☐ 87	Pat Falloon	1.00	.40	.10
☐ 88	Bram Vanderkracht	.15	.06	.01
☐ 89	Mike Jickling	.15	.06	.01
☐ 90	Murray Garbutt	.25	.10	.02
☐ 91	Calvin Thudium	.15	.06	.01
☐ 92	Mark Woolf	.25	.10	.02
☐ 93	Shane Maitland	.15	.06	.01
☐ 94	Bart Cote	.15	.06	.01
☐ 95	Bryan Maxwell	.15	.06	.01
☐ 96	Eric Lindros SP	50.00	20.00	5.00
☐ 97	Scott Niedermayer	1.50	.60	.15
☐ 98	Patrick Poulin	.75	.30	.07
☐ 99	Brent Bilodeau	.50	.20	.05
☐ 100	Pat Falloon	1.50	.60	.15
☐ 101	Darcy Werenka	.75	.30	.07
☐ 102	Martin Lapointe	.75	.30	.07
☐ 103	Philippe Boucher	.75	.30	.07
☐ 104	Jeff Nelson	.50	.20	.05
☐ 105	Rene Corbet	.75	.30	.07
☐ 106	Pat Peake SP	5.00	2.00	.50
☐ 107	Steve Staios SP	3.50	1.40	.35
☐ 108	Richard Matvichuk	.50	.20	.05
☐ 109	Dean McAmmond	.50	.20	.05
☐ 110	Alex Stojanov SP	2.50	1.00	.25
☐ 111	Glen Murray SP	5.00	2.00	.50
☐ 112	Tyler Wright	.50	.20	.05
☐ 113	Jason Dawe SP	3.50	1.40	.35
☐ 114	Nathan Lafayette SP	3.50	1.40	.35
☐ 115	Yanic Perreault	1.00	.40	.10
☐ 116	Guy Leveque SP	2.50	1.00	.25
☐ 117	Darren Van Impe	.50	.20	.05
☐ 118	Shawn Antoski SP	2.50	1.00	.25
☐ 119	Eric Lindros SP	50.00	20.00	5.00
☐ 120	Dennis Purdie SP	2.50	1.00	.25
☐ 121	Terry Chitaroni SP	2.50	1.00	.25
☐ 122	Jamie Pushor	.50	.20	.05
☐ 123	Chris Osgood	1.50	.60	.15
☐ 124	Jamie Matthews SP	2.50	1.00	.25
☐ 125	Yves Sarault	.50	.20	.05
☐ 126	Yanic Dupre UER	.50	.20	.05
☐ 127	Brad Zimmer	.25	.10	.02
☐ 128	Copps Coliseum	.25	.10	.02
☐ 129	Jason Widmer	.25	.10	.02
☐ 130	Marc Savard	.25	.10	.02

1991-92 7th Inn. Sketch OHL

Brent Gretzky
91-92 OHL   Bulls

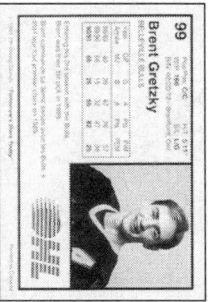

This 384-card set, which measures the standard size (2 1/2" by 3 1/2"), was issued by 7th Inning Sketch featuring players of the Ontario Hockey League. The production run was limited to 9,000 factory sets, with each set individually numbered "X of 9,000." On a white card face, the fronts feature color action player photos enclosed by different color frames. The corners of the picture are cut out to permit space for gold stars. The player's name, the year and league, and the team name appear below the picture. In a horizontal format, the backs have biography, statistics, and player profile in French and English. The cards are numbered on the back and checklisted below according to teams as follows: Cornwall Royals (1-26), Detroit Ambassadors (27-50), North Bay Centennials (51-73), Kitchener Rangers (74-98), Belleville Bulls (99-122), Peterborough Petes(123-147), Oshawa Generals (148-172), Windsor Spitfires (173-196), Niagara Falls Thunder (197-221), Kingston Frontenacs (222-243), Sudbury Wolves (244-268), Owen Sound Platers (269-290), Ottawa 67's (291-312), S.S. Marie Greyhounds (313-339), Guelph Storm (340-360), and London Knights (361-383). The team name has been given below for card 000, which is listed out of team order.

		MINT	EXC	G-VG
	COMPLETE SET (384)	15.00	6.00	1.50
	COMMON PLAYER (1-383)	.10	.04	.01
☐ 000	Chris Shushack	.15	.06	.01
	Kitchener Rangers			
☐ 1	John Slaney	.35	.14	.03
☐ 2	Jason Meloche	.10	.04	.01
☐ 3	Mark DeSantis	.10	.04	.01
☐ 4	Richard Raymond	.10	.04	.01
☐ 5	Dave Lemay	.10	.04	.01
☐ 6	Matt McGuffin	.10	.04	.01
☐ 7	Sam Oliveira	.10	.04	.01
☐ 8	Jeremy Stevenson	.20	.08	.02
☐ 9	Todd Walker	.10	.04	.01
☐ 10	Jean-Alain Schneider	.10	.04	.01
☐ 11	Guy Leveque	.35	.14	.03
☐ 12	Shayne Gaffar	.15	.06	.01
☐ 13	Mike Prokopec	.15	.06	.01
☐ 14	Nathan LaFayette	.35	.14	.03
☐ 15	Larry Courville	.10	.04	.01
☐ 16	Chris Clancy	.15	.06	.01
☐ 17	Tom Nemeth	.15	.06	.01
☐ 18	Jeff Reid	.25	.10	.02
☐ 19	Ilpo Kauhanen	.15	.06	.01
☐ 20	Rob Dykeman	.20	.08	.02
☐ 21	Rival Fullum	.15	.06	.01
☐ 22	Ryan VandenBussche	.15	.06	.01
☐ 23	Gordon Pell	.15	.06	.01
☐ 24	Paul Andrea UER	.10	.04	.01
	Team affiliation says Generals; should say Royals			
☐ 25	John Lovell CO UER	.10	.04	.01
	Team affiliation says Generals; should say Royals			
☐ 26	Alan Letang	.10	.04	.01
☐ 27	Chris Phelps	.10	.04	.01
☐ 28	John Wynne	.10	.04	.01
☐ 29	Rob Kinghan	.10	.04	.01
☐ 30	Glen Craig	.10	.04	.01
☐ 31	Eric Cairns	.25	.10	.02
☐ 32	John Pinches	.10	.04	.01
☐ 33	Todd Harvey	.75	.30	.07
☐ 34	Craig Fraser	.10	.04	.01
☐ 35	Pat Peake	.75	.30	.07
☐ 36	Chris Skoryna	.10	.04	.01
☐ 37	Bob Wren	.50	.20	.05
☐ 38	Chris Varga	.10	.04	.01
☐ 39	David Benn	.10	.04	.01
☐ 40	Mark Lawrence	.25	.10	.02
☐ 41	Jeff Kostuch	.10	.04	.01
☐ 42	J.D. Eaton	.25	.10	.02
☐ 43	Derek Etches	.15	.06	.01
☐ 44	Jeff Gardiner	.25	.10	.02
☐ 45	James Shea	.10	.04	.01
☐ 46	Brad Teichmann	.10	.04	.01
☐ 47	Jim Rutherford CO	.15	.06	.01
☐ 48	Derek Wilkinson	.15	.06	.01
☐ 49	OHL Action	.15	.06	.01
☐ 50	OHL Action	.15	.06	.01
☐ 51	Sandy Allan	.15	.06	.01
☐ 52	Ron Bertrand	.15	.06	.01
☐ 53	Brad Brown	.25	.10	.02
☐ 54	Dennis Bonvie	.10	.04	.01
☐ 55	Bradley Shepard	.10	.04	.01
☐ 56	Allan Cox	.10	.04	.01
☐ 57	Jack Williams	.20	.08	.02
☐ 58	Chad Penney	.25	.10	.02
☐ 59	Jason Firth	.25	.10	.02
☐ 60	Bill Lang	.20	.08	.02

☐ 61	Ryan Merritt	.15	.06	.01
☐ 62	Michael Burman	.10	.04	.01
☐ 63	Billy Wright	.15	.06	.01
☐ 64	Dave Szabo	.10	.04	.01
☐ 65	James Sheehan	.10	.04	.01
☐ 66	John Spoltore	.35	.14	.03
☐ 67	Paul Rushforth	.10	.04	.01
☐ 68	Jeff Shevalier	.10	.04	.01
☐ 69	Robert Thorpe	.10	.04	.01
☐ 70	Drake Berehowsky	.35	.14	.03
☐ 71	Patrick Barton	.10	.04	.01
☐ 72	Bert Templeton CO	.15	.06	.01
☐ 73	Wade Gibson	.10	.04	.01
☐ 74	C.J. Denomme UER	.10	.04	.01
	Name spelled C. Jay on back			
☐ 75	Mike Torchia	.15	.06	.01
☐ 76	Mike Polano	.15	.06	.01
☐ 77	Tony McCabe	.10	.04	.01
☐ 78	Chris Kraemer	.10	.04	.01
☐ 79	Tim Spitzig	.15	.06	.01
☐ 80	Trevor Gallant	.15	.06	.01
☐ 81	Yvan Corbin	.20	.08	.02
☐ 82	Norman Dezainde	.15	.06	.01
☐ 83	Marc Robillard	.10	.04	.01
☐ 84	Derek Gauthier	.10	.04	.01
☐ 85	Gib Tucker	.15	.06	.01
☐ 86	Paul McCallion	.10	.04	.01
☐ 87	Eric Manlow	.20	.08	.02
☐ 88	Jamie Caruso	.25	.10	.02
☐ 89	Gary Miller	.10	.04	.01
☐ 90	Jason Stevenson	.15	.06	.01
☐ 91	Shayne McCosh	.10	.04	.01
☐ 92	Jason Gladney	.10	.04	.01
☐ 93	Brad Barton	.10	.04	.01
☐ 94	Chris LiPuma	.25	.10	.02
☐ 95	Justin Cullen	.10	.04	.01
☐ 96	Bill Smith SCOUT	.10	.04	.01
☐ 97	Joe McDonnell CO	.15	.06	.01
☐ 98	Not printed	.00	.00	.00
☐ 99	Brent Gretzky	.75	.30	.07
☐ 100	Gairin Smith	.10	.04	.01
☐ 101	Blair Scott	.10	.04	.01
☐ 102	Daniel Godbout	.15	.06	.01
☐ 103	Dan Preston	.10	.04	.01
☐ 104	Ian Keiller	.10	.04	.01
☐ 105	Rick Marshall	.10	.04	.01
☐ 106	Aaron Morrison	.10	.04	.01
☐ 107	Dominic Belanger	.10	.04	.01
☐ 108	Kevin Brown	.25	.10	.02
☐ 109	Tony Cimellaro	.20	.08	.02
☐ 110	Larry Mavety CO	.10	.04	.01
☐ 111	Jake Grimes	.25	.10	.02
☐ 112	Greg Dreveny	.15	.06	.01
☐ 113	Darren McCarty	.35	.14	.03
☐ 114	Doug Doull	.10	.04	.01
☐ 115	Scott Boston	.15	.06	.01
☐ 116	Dale Chokan	.10	.04	.01
☐ 117	Darren Hurley	.10	.04	.01
☐ 118	Brian Mielko UER	.10	.04	.01
	Card misnumbered 61			
☐ 119	Richard Gallace UER	.10	.04	.01
	Card misnumbered 65			
☐ 120	Shayne Antoski	.25	.10	.02
☐ 121	Greg Bailey	.10	.04	.01
☐ 122	Keith Redmond	.10	.04	.01
☐ 123	Dick Todd CO	.15	.06	.01
☐ 124	Scott Turner	.10	.04	.01
☐ 125	Colin Wilson	.10	.04	.01
☐ 126	Mike Tomlinson	.15	.06	.01
☐ 127	Dale McTavish	.10	.04	.01
☐ 128	Chris Longo	.20	.08	.02
☐ 129	Chad Lang	.35	.14	.03
☐ 130	Brent Tully	.35	.14	.03
☐ 131	Shawn Heins	.10	.04	.01
☐ 132	Geordie Kinnear	.20	.08	.02
☐ 133	Jeff Walker	.10	.04	.01
☐ 134	Chris Pronger	2.00	.80	.20
☐ 135	Chad Grills	.10	.04	.01
☐ 136	Michael Harding	.25	.10	.02
☐ 137	Matt St.Germain	.10	.04	.01
☐ 138	Don O'Neill	.10	.04	.01
☐ 139	Dave Roche	.25	.10	.02
☐ 140	Doug Searle	.10	.04	.01
☐ 141	Bryan Gendron	.15	.06	.01
☐ 142	Kelly Vipond	.25	.10	.02
☐ 143	Andrew Verner	.35	.14	.03
☐ 144	Ryan Black	.25	.10	.02
☐ 145	Jason Dawe	.50	.20	.05
☐ 146	Jassen Cullimore	.25	.10	.02
☐ 147	Not printed	.00	.00	.00
☐ 148	Jason Arnott	2.50	1.00	.25
☐ 149	Jan Benda	.10	.04	.01
☐ 150	Todd Bradley	.10	.04	.01
☐ 151	Markus Brunner	.20	.08	.02
☐ 152	Jason Campeau	.10	.04	.01
☐ 153	Mark Deazeley	.15	.06	.01
☐ 154	Matt Hoffman	.15	.06	.01
☐ 155	Scott Hollis	.20	.08	.02
☐ 156	Neil Iserhoff	.10	.04	.01
☐ 157	Darryl Lafrance	.10	.04	.01
☐ 158	B.J. MacPherson	.25	.10	.02
☐ 159	Troy Sweet	.10	.04	.01
☐ 160	Jason Weaver	.20	.08	.02
☐ 161	Stephane Yelle	.10	.04	.01
☐ 162	Trevor Burgess	.15	.06	.01
☐ 163	Joe Cook	.10	.04	.01
☐ 164	Jean-Paul Davis	.10	.04	.01
☐ 165	Brian Grieve	.15	.06	.01
☐ 166	Rob Leask	.15	.06	.01
☐ 167	Wade Simpson	.10	.04	.01
☐ 168	Kevin Spero	.10	.04	.01
☐ 169	Fred Brathwaite	.25	.10	.02
☐ 170	Mike Fountain	.25	.10	.02
☐ 171	Rick Cornacchia	.15	.06	.01
☐ 172	Checklist 1-98	.15	.06	.01
☐ 173	Todd Warriner	.75	.30	.07
☐ 174	Reuben Castella	.10	.04	.01
☐ 175	Cory Stillman	.50	.20	.05
☐ 176	Steve Gibson	.20	.08	.02
☐ 177	Trent Cull	.15	.06	.01
☐ 178	John Copley	.10	.04	.01
☐ 179	Craig Binns	.10	.04	.01
☐ 180	Ryan O'Neill	.10	.04	.01
☐ 181	Matthew Mullin	.15	.06	.01
☐ 182	Todd Hunter	.10	.04	.01
☐ 183	Jason Stos	.15	.06	.01
☐ 184	Robert Frayn	.10	.04	.01
☐ 185	Leonard MacDonald	.10	.04	.01
☐ 186	Tom Sullivan	.10	.04	.01
☐ 187	Steve Smith	.10	.04	.01
☐ 188	Bill Bowler	.25	.10	.02
☐ 189	James Allison	.15	.06	.01
☐ 190	Kevin MacKay	.20	.08	.02
☐ 191	David Myles	.10	.04	.01
☐ 192	Wayne Maxner GM CO	.15	.06	.01
☐ 193	Dave Prpich CO UER	.10	.04	.01
	Windsor on front; should say Spitfires			
☐ 194	Brady Blain	.15	.06	.01
☐ 195	Eric Stamp UER	.10	.04	.01
	Windsor on front; should say Spitfires			
☐ 196	OHL Action	.15	.06	.01
☐ 197	David Babcock	.10	.04	.01
☐ 198	Brad Love	.10	.04	.01
☐ 199	Dale Junkin	.10	.04	.01
☐ 200	Rick Corriveau	.25	.10	.02
☐ 201	Scott Campbell	.10	.04	.01
☐ 202	Jason Clarke	.10	.04	.01
☐ 203	George Burnett	.10	.04	.01
☐ 204	Ryan Tocher	.10	.04	.01
☐ 205	Dennis Maxwell	.10	.04	.01
☐ 206	Greg Scott	.15	.06	.01
☐ 207	Mark Tardiff	.15	.06	.01
☐ 208	Neil Fewster	.10	.04	.01
☐ 209	Jason Coles	.10	.04	.01
☐ 210	Randy Hall CO	.10	.04	.01
☐ 211	Todd Simon	.50	.20	.05
☐ 212	Ethan Moreau	.75	.30	.07
☐ 213	Todd Wetzel	.10	.04	.01
☐ 214	Tom Moores	.10	.04	.01
☐ 215	Geoff Rawson	.10	.04	.01
☐ 216	Dan Krisko	.10	.04	.01
☐ 217	Manny Legace	.50	.20	.05
☐ 218	Kevin Brown	.25	.10	.02
☐ 219	Steve Staios	.35	.14	.03
☐ 220	Checklist 99-196	.15	.06	.01
☐ 221	Checklist 197-290	.15	.06	.01
☐ 222	Tony Bella	.10	.04	.01
☐ 223	Shawn Caplice	.10	.04	.01
☐ 224	Keli Corpse	.25	.10	.02
☐ 225	Chris Gratton	2.00	.80	.20
☐ 226	Gord Harris	.10	.04	.01
☐ 227	Cory Johnson	.10	.04	.01
☐ 228	Kevin King	.10	.04	.01
☐ 229	Justin Morrison	.25	.10	.02
☐ 230	Alastair Still	.15	.06	.01
☐ 231	Chris Scharf	.10	.04	.01
☐ 232	Brian Stagg	.10	.04	.01
☐ 233	Mike Dawson	.10	.04	.01
☐ 234	Rod Pasma	.15	.06	.01
☐ 235	Craig Rivet	.10	.04	.01
☐ 236	Dave Stewart	.15	.06	.01
☐ 237	John Vary	.10	.04	.01
☐ 238	Jason Wadel	.10	.04	.01

☐ 239	Joel Yates	.10	.04	.01
☐ 240	Marc Lamothe	.15	.06	.01
☐ 241	Pete McGlynn	.10	.04	.01
☐ 242	OHL Action	.15	.06	.01
☐ 243	Checklist 291-383	.15	.06	.01
☐ 244	Joel Sandie	.10	.04	.01
☐ 245	Glen Murray	.50	.20	.05
☐ 246	Derek Armstrong	.20	.08	.02
☐ 247	Michael Peca	.30	.12	.03
☐ 248	Barry Young	.10	.04	.01
☐ 249	Bernie John	.10	.04	.01
☐ 250	Terry Chitaroni	.25	.10	.02
☐ 251	Jason Young	.25	.10	.02
☐ 252	Rod Hinks	.15	.06	.01
☐ 253	Michael Yeo	.10	.04	.01
☐ 254	Kyle Blacklock	.10	.04	.01
☐ 255	Dan Ryder	.15	.06	.01
☐ 256	Doug Mason CO	.10	.04	.01
☐ 257	Jamie Rivers	.50	.20	.05
☐ 258	Brandon Convery	.50	.20	.05
☐ 259	Barrie Moore	.10	.04	.01
☐ 260	Shawn Rivers	.25	.10	.02
☐ 261	Jamie Matthews	.25	.10	.02
☐ 262	Tim Favot	.10	.04	.01
☐ 263	Bob MacIsaac	.10	.04	.01
☐ 264	Sean Gagnon	.10	.04	.01
☐ 265	Ken MacKenzie GM CO	.15	.06	.01
☐ 266	George Dourion	.15	.06	.01
☐ 267	Brian MacKenzie	.10	.04	.01
☐ 268	Jason Zohil	.20	.08	.02
☐ 269	Rick Tarasuk	.10	.04	.01
☐ 270	Jamie Storr	1.50	.60	.15
☐ 271	Sean Basilio	.20	.08	.02
☐ 272	Rick Morton	.10	.04	.01
☐ 273	Jason Hughes	.10	.04	.01
☐ 274	Scott Walker	.15	.06	.01
☐ 275	Willie Skilliter	.10	.04	.01
☐ 276	Shawn Krueger	.10	.04	.01
☐ 277	Jason MacDonald	.15	.06	.01
☐ 278	Kirk Maltby	.25	.10	.02
☐ 279	Brock Woods	.15	.06	.01
☐ 280	Troy Hutchinson	.10	.04	.01
☐ 281	Geordie Maynard	.10	.04	.01
☐ 282	Luigi Calce	.10	.04	.01
☐ 283	Steven Parson	.25	.10	.02
☐ 284	Andrew Brunette	.35	.14	.03
☐ 285	Robert MacKenzie	.10	.04	.01
☐ 286	Jason Buetow	.10	.04	.01
☐ 287	Wyatt Buckland	.10	.04	.01
☐ 288	Jim Brown	.15	.06	.01
☐ 289	Gord Dickie	.10	.04	.01
☐ 290	Jeff Smith	.10	.04	.01
☐ 291	Peter Ambroziak	.20	.08	.02
☐ 292	Mark O'Donnell UER	.10	.04	.01
	Name spelled			
	O'donnell on back			
☐ 293	Not printed	.00	.00	.00
☐ 294	Grayden Reid	.50	.20	.05
☐ 295	Sean Spencer	.15	.06	.01
☐ 296	Gerry Skrypec	.10	.04	.01
☐ 297	Billy Hall	.10	.04	.01
☐ 298	Sean Gawley	.10	.04	.01
☐ 299	Grant Marshall	.50	.20	.05
☐ 300	Michael Johnson	.10	.04	.01
☐ 301	Brett Seguin	.25	.10	.02
☐ 302	Chris Coveny	.10	.04	.01
☐ 303	Ryan Kuwabara	.35	.14	.03
☐ 304	Jeff Ricciardi	.25	.10	.02
☐ 305	Curt Bowen	.35	.14	.03
☐ 306	Zbynek Kukacka	.10	.04	.01
☐ 307	Chris Gignac	.15	.06	.01
☐ 308	Steve Washburn	.10	.04	.01
☐ 309	Brian Kilrea CO	.15	.06	.01
☐ 310	Mike Lenarduzzi	.15	.06	.01
☐ 311	Matt Stone	.10	.04	.01
☐ 312	Ken Belanger	.10	.04	.01
☐ 313	Chris Simon	.50	.20	.05
☐ 314	Kiley Hill	.10	.04	.01
☐ 315	Chris Grenville	.10	.04	.01
☐ 316	Aaron Gavey	.75	.30	.07
☐ 317	Briane Thompson	.10	.04	.01
☐ 318	Ted Nolan CO	.15	.06	.01
☐ 319	Perry Pappas	.10	.04	.01
☐ 320	Kevin Hodson	.25	.10	.02
☐ 321	Colin Miller	.25	.10	.02
☐ 322	Tom MacDonald	.10	.04	.01
☐ 323	Shaun Imber	.20	.08	.02
☐ 324	Jarret Reid	.25	.10	.02
☐ 325	Tony Iob	.20	.08	.02
☐ 326	Mark Matier	.10	.04	.01
☐ 327	Drew Bannister	.25	.10	.02
☐ 328	Jason Denomme	.15	.06	.01
☐ 329	David Matsos	.10	.04	.01

☐ 330	Rick Kowalsky	.15	.06	.01
☐ 331	Tim Bacik	.10	.04	.01
☐ 332	Ralph Intranuovo	.40	.16	.04
☐ 333	Jonas Rudberg	.15	.06	.01
☐ 334	Jeff Toms	.10	.04	.01
☐ 335	Jason Julian	.10	.04	.01
☐ 336	Brian Goudie	.10	.04	.01
☐ 337	Gary Roach	.10	.04	.01
☐ 338	Brad Baber	.10	.04	.01
☐ 339	Todd Gleason UER	.15	.06	.01
	Team affiliation says			
	Greyhounds; should			
	say Storm			
☐ 340	Chris McMurty	.10	.04	.01
☐ 341	Matt Turek	.10	.04	.01
☐ 342	Shane Johnson	.10	.04	.01
☐ 343	Grant Pritchett	.10	.04	.01
☐ 344	Mike Cote	.10	.04	.01
☐ 345	Duane Harmer	.10	.04	.01
☐ 346	Jeff Bes	.35	.14	.03
☐ 347A	Wade Whitten	.10	.04	.01
☐ 347B	Dan Tanevski UER	.10	.04	.01
	(Should be number 360)			
☐ 348	Bill Kovacs	.20	.08	.02
☐ 349	Kayle Short	.10	.04	.01
☐ 350	Sylvain Cloutier	.50	.20	.05
☐ 351	Brent Watson	.10	.04	.01
☐ 352	Brent Pope	.20	.08	.02
☐ 353	Craig Lutes	.10	.04	.01
☐ 354	Michael Hartwick	.10	.04	.01
☐ 355	Kevin Reid	.10	.04	.01
☐ 356	Toby Burkitt	.10	.04	.01
☐ 357	Todd Bertuzzi	.35	.14	.03
☐ 358	Angelo Amore	.10	.04	.01
☐ 359	Jeff Pawluk	.15	.06	.01
☐ 360	Not issued	.00	.00	.00
	(See card 347)			
☐ 361	Gordon Ross	.10	.04	.01
☐ 362	Dennis Purdie	.25	.10	.02
☐ 363	Dave Gilmore	.10	.04	.01
☐ 364	Brent Brownlee	.10	.04	.01
☐ 365	Aaron Nagy	.20	.08	.02
☐ 366	Barry Potomski	.20	.08	.02
☐ 367	Steve Smillie	.10	.04	.01
☐ 368	Kelly Reed	.10	.04	.01
☐ 369	Gary Agnew CO	.10	.04	.01
☐ 370	Chris Taylor	.25	.10	.02
☐ 371	Brett Marietti	.10	.04	.01
☐ 372	Cory Evans	.10	.04	.01
☐ 373	Brian Stacey	.10	.04	.01
☐ 374	Chris Crombie	.25	.10	.02
☐ 375	Derrick Crane	.10	.04	.01
☐ 376	Scott McKay	.20	.08	.02
☐ 377	Gregory Ryan	.10	.04	.01
☐ 378	Mark Visheau	.25	.10	.02
☐ 379	Gerry Arcella	.10	.04	.01
☐ 380	Nick Stajduhar	.35	.14	.03
☐ 381	Jason Allison	1.00	.40	.10
☐ 382	Sean O'Reilly	.10	.04	.01
☐ 383	Paul Wolanski	.15	.06	.01

1991-92 7th Inn. Sketch WHL

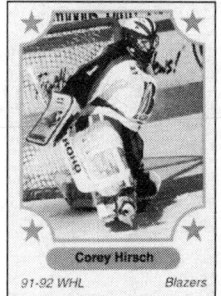

This 361-card set, which measures the standard size (2 1/2"
by 3 1/2"), was issued by 7th Inning Sketch featuring
players of the Western Hockey League. The production run
was limited to 7,000 factory sets, with each set individually

numbered "X of 7,000." On a white card face, the fronts feature color action player photos enclosed by different color frames. The corners of the picture are cut out to permit space for gold stars. The player's name, the year and league, and the team name appear below the picture. In a horizontal format, the backs have biography, statistics, and player profile in French and English. The cards are numbered on the back and checklisted below according to teams as follows: Spokane Chiefs (1-25), Portland Winter Hawks (26-49), Victoria Cougars (50-73), Kamloops Blazers (74-97), Saskatoon Blades (98-121), Seattle Thunderbirds (122-145), Tacoma Rockets (146-173), Swift Current Broncos (174-195), Brandon Wheat Kings (196-217), Regina Pats (218-242), Prince Albert Raiders (243-266), Moose Jaw Warriors (267-287), Tri-City Americans (288-311), Medicine Hat Tigers (312-335), and Lethbridge Hurricanes (336-360). The team name has been given below for card 000, which is listed out of team order.

	MINT	EXC	G-VG
COMPLETE SET (361)	15.00	6.00	1.50
COMMON PLAYER (1-360)	.10	.04	.01

		MINT	EXC	G-VG
☐ 000	Garfield Henderson	.15	.06	.01
	Moose Jaw Warriors			
☐ 1	Valeri Bure	1.50	.60	.15
☐ 2	Hardy Sauter	.10	.04	.01
☐ 3	Bryan Maxwell CO	.10	.04	.01
☐ 4	Scott Bailey	.25	.10	.02
☐ 5	Mike Gray	.10	.04	.01
☐ 6	Mark Szoke	.10	.04	.01
☐ 7	Mike Jickling	.10	.04	.01
☐ 8	Frank Evans	.10	.04	.01
☐ 9	Steve Junker	.35	.14	.03
☐ 10	Greg Gatto	.10	.04	.01
☐ 11	Jared Bednar	.10	.04	.01
☐ 12	Justin Hocking	.25	.10	.02
☐ 13	Paxton Schulte	.50	.20	.05
☐ 14	Brad Toporowski	.15	.06	.01
☐ 15	Shane Maitland	.10	.04	.01
☐ 16	Aaron Boh	.15	.06	.01
☐ 17	Ryan Duthie	.25	.10	.02
☐ 18	Craig Reichert	.25	.10	.02
☐ 19	Danny Faassen	.10	.04	.01
☐ 20	Randy Toye	.10	.04	.01
☐ 21	Geoff Grandberg	.10	.04	.01
☐ 22	Jeremy Warring	.10	.04	.01
☐ 23	Tyler Romanchuck	.10	.04	.01
☐ 24	Jamie Linden	.15	.06	.01
☐ 25	1990-91 Champs	.15	.06	.01
☐ 26	Corey Jones	.10	.04	.01
☐ 27	Brandon Smith	.10	.04	.01
☐ 28	Mike Williamson	.10	.04	.01
☐ 29	Adam Murray	.10	.04	.01
☐ 30	Steve Konowalchuk	.35	.14	.03
☐ 31	Shawn Stone	.10	.04	.01
☐ 32	Adam Deadmarsh	.50	.20	.05
☐ 33	Rick Mearns	.10	.04	.01
☐ 34	Chris Rowland	.15	.06	.01
☐ 35	Brandon Coates	.10	.04	.01
☐ 36	Dave Cammock	.10	.04	.01
☐ 37	Colin Foley	.15	.06	.01
☐ 38	Dennis Saharchuk	.10	.04	.01
☐ 39	Jiri Beranek	.15	.06	.01
☐ 40	Chad Seibel	.10	.04	.01
☐ 41	Kelly Harris	.10	.04	.01
☐ 42	Layne Roland	.15	.06	.01
☐ 43	Cale Hulse	.15	.06	.01
☐ 44	Ken Hodge CO	.15	.06	.01
☐ 45	Peter Cox	.10	.04	.01
☐ 46	Joaquin Gage	.25	.10	.02
☐ 47	Brent Peterson CO	.10	.04	.01
☐ 48	Jason McBain	.10	.04	.01
☐ 49	John Badduke	.10	.04	.01
☐ 50	Rick Hopper	.10	.04	.01
☐ 51	Dave Hamilton	.10	.04	.01
☐ 52	Dwayne Newman	.10	.04	.01
☐ 53	Chris Catellier	.10	.04	.01
☐ 54	Fran Defrenza	.15	.06	.01
☐ 55	Randy Chadney	.10	.04	.01
☐ 56	David Hebky	.15	.06	.01
☐ 57	Craig Fletcher	.10	.04	.01
☐ 58	Kane Chaloner	.10	.04	.01
☐ 59	Ross Harris	.15	.06	.01
☐ 60	Mike Barrie	.10	.04	.01
☐ 61	Steve Lingren	.10	.04	.01
☐ 62	Shea Esselmont	.10	.04	.01
☐ 63	Matt Smith	.10	.04	.01
☐ 64	Gerry St.Cyr	.25	.10	.02
☐ 65	Andrew Laming	.10	.04	.01
☐ 66	Jeff Fancy	.10	.04	.01
☐ 67	Ryan Pellaers	.10	.04	.01
☐ 68	Steve Passmore	.15	.06	.01
☐ 69	Scott Fukami	.20	.08	.02
☐ 70	Darcy Mattersdorfer	.10	.04	.01
☐ 71	Chris Hawes	.10	.04	.01
☐ 72	The Goalies I	.15	.06	.01
☐ 73	Checklist 1-97	.15	.06	.01
☐ 74	Riverside Coliseum	.15	.06	.01
☐ 75	Tom Renney	.10	.04	.01
☐ 76	Corey Hirsch	.60	.24	.06
☐ 77	Scott Ferguson	.10	.04	.01
☐ 78	Steve Yule	.10	.04	.01
☐ 79	Todd Johnson	.15	.06	.01
☐ 80	Jarrett Bousquet	.10	.04	.01
☐ 81	Mike Mathers	.15	.06	.01
☐ 82	Rod Stevens	.10	.04	.01
☐ 83	Lance Johnson	.10	.04	.01
☐ 84	Zac Boyer	.30	.12	.03
☐ 85	Craig Lyons	.20	.08	.02
☐ 86	Dale Masson	.15	.06	.01
☐ 87	Scott Loucks	.20	.08	.02
☐ 88	Darcy Tucker	.10	.04	.01
☐ 89	Shayne Green	.25	.10	.02
☐ 90	Michal Sup	.10	.04	.01
☐ 91	Craig Bonner	.10	.04	.01
☐ 92	Jeff Watchorn	.10	.04	.01
☐ 93	Jarrett Dueling	.25	.10	.02
☐ 94	Ed Patterson	.25	.10	.02
☐ 95	David Wilkie	.25	.10	.02
☐ 96	The Goalies III	.15	.06	.01
☐ 97	A Goal	.15	.06	.01
☐ 98	Andy MacIntyre	.15	.06	.01
☐ 99	Rhett Trombley	.10	.04	.01
☐ 100	Lorne Molleken CO	.10	.04	.01
☐ 101	Trevor Robins	.15	.06	.01
☐ 102	Jeff Buchanan	.20	.08	.02
☐ 103	Mark Raiter	.10	.04	.01
☐ 104	Bryce Goebel	.10	.04	.01
☐ 105	Paul Buczkowski	.10	.04	.01
☐ 106	James Startup	.10	.04	.01
☐ 107	Chad Rusnak	.10	.04	.01
☐ 108	Sean McFatridge	.10	.04	.01
☐ 109	Shane Calder	.20	.08	.02
☐ 110	Ryan Fujita	.35	.14	.03
☐ 111	Derek Tibbatts	.20	.08	.02
☐ 112	Glen Gulutzan	.15	.06	.01
☐ 113	Richard Matvichuk	.35	.14	.03
☐ 114	Chad Michalchuk	.10	.04	.01
☐ 115	Mark Wotton	.10	.04	.01
☐ 116	Mark Franks	.15	.06	.01
☐ 117	Norm Maracle	.35	.14	.03
☐ 118	Jason Becker	.10	.04	.01
☐ 119	Shawn Yakimishyn	.15	.06	.01
☐ 120	Ed Chynoweth PRES	.10	.04	.01
☐ 121	Checklist 98-195	.15	.06	.01
☐ 122	Craig Chapman	.15	.06	.01
☐ 123	Jeff Jubenville	.10	.04	.01
☐ 124	George Zajankala	.15	.06	.01
☐ 125	Turner Stevenson	.35	.14	.03
☐ 126	Rob Tallas	.25	.10	.02
☐ 127	Ryan Brown	.10	.04	.01
☐ 128	Andrew Kemper	.10	.04	.01
☐ 129	Brendan Witt	.60	.24	.06
☐ 130	Troy Hyatt	.10	.04	.01
☐ 131	Mike Kennedy	.25	.10	.02
☐ 132	Jesse Wilson	.10	.04	.01
☐ 133	Kurt Seher	.25	.10	.02
☐ 134	Dody Wood	.25	.10	.02
☐ 135	Darren McAusland	.20	.08	.02
☐ 136	Jeff Sebastian	.15	.06	.01
☐ 137	Eric Bouchard	.10	.04	.01
☐ 138	Joel Dyck	.15	.06	.01
☐ 139	Blake Knox	.25	.10	.02
☐ 140	Peter Anholt CO	.10	.04	.01
☐ 141	Chris Wells	.50	.20	.05
☐ 142	Andrew Reimer	.25	.10	.02
☐ 143	Along the Boards	.15	.06	.01
☐ 144	Which Way Is Up	.15	.06	.01
☐ 145	Checklist 196-287	.15	.06	.01
☐ 146	Tacoma Dome	.15	.06	.01
☐ 147	Opening Ceremonies	.15	.06	.01
☐ 148	Marcel Comeau CO	.10	.04	.01
☐ 149	Donn Clark CO	.10	.04	.01
☐ 150	John Varga	.25	.10	.02
☐ 151	Joey Young	.10	.04	.01
☐ 152	Laurie Billeck	.15	.06	.01
☐ 153	Jeff Calvert	.15	.06	.01
☐ 154	Tuomas Gronman	.35	.14	.03
☐ 155	Jason Knox	.10	.04	.01

☐	156	Kevin Malgunas	.15	.06	.01
☐	157	Dave McMillen	.10	.04	.01
☐	158	Darryl Onofrychuk	.10	.04	.01
☐	159	Miek Piersol	.10	.04	.01
☐	160	Lasse Pirjeta	.10	.04	.01
☐	161	Drew Schoneck	.10	.04	.01
☐	162	Corey Stock	.10	.04	.01
☐	163	Ryan Strain	.10	.04	.01
☐	164	Michal Sykora	.35	.14	.03
☐	165	Scott Thomas	.10	.04	.01
☐	166	Toby Weishaar	.10	.04	.01
☐	167	Jeff Whittle	.20	.08	.02
☐	168	The Rockettes	.15	.06	.01
☐	169	Allan Egeland	.35	.14	.03
☐	170	Van Burgess	.15	.06	.01
☐	171	Trever Fraser	.10	.04	.01
☐	172	Jamie Black	.25	.10	.02
☐	173	WHL Action	.15	.06	.01
☐	174	Andy Schneider	.35	.14	.03
☐	175	John McMulkin	.10	.04	.01
☐	176	Rick Girard	.35	.14	.03
☐	177	Shane Hnidy	.10	.04	.01
☐	178	Jason Krywulak	.25	.10	.02
☐	179	Jeremy Riehl	.20	.08	.02
☐	180	Brent Bilodeau	.30	.12	.03
☐	181	Mark McCoy	.10	.04	.01
☐	182	Matt Young	.10	.04	.01
☐	183	Dan Sherstenka	.10	.04	.01
☐	184	Jarrod Daniel	.15	.06	.01
☐	185	Lennie MacAusland	.10	.04	.01
☐	186	Keith McCambridge	.10	.04	.01
☐	187	Jason Horvath	.10	.04	.01
☐	188	Kevin Koopman	.15	.06	.01
☐	189	Chris Herperger	.25	.10	.02
☐	190	Trent McCleary	.20	.08	.02
☐	191	Tyler Wright	.35	.14	.03
☐	192	Todd Holt	.20	.08	.02
☐	193	Ashley Buckberger	.35	.14	.03
☐	194	Bram Vanderkracht	.10	.04	.01
☐	195	Ken Zilka	.10	.04	.01
☐	196	Chris Osgood	.75	.30	.07
☐	197	Rob Puchniak	.10	.04	.01
☐	198	Todd Dutiaume	.10	.04	.01
☐	199	Mike Maneluk	.25	.10	.02
☐	200	Shawn Dietrich	.10	.04	.01
☐	201	Chris Johnston	.15	.06	.01
☐	202	Brian Purdy	.25	.10	.02
☐	203	Mike Chrun	.10	.04	.01
☐	204	Dan Kopec	.10	.04	.01
☐	205	Ryan Smith	.75	.30	.07
☐	206	Marty Murray	.50	.20	.05
☐	207	Merv Priest	.10	.04	.01
☐	208	Bobby House	.25	.10	.02
☐	209	Chris Constant	.20	.08	.02
☐	210	Dwayne Gylywoychuk	.10	.04	.01
☐	211	Stu Scantlebury	.10	.04	.01
☐	212	Mark Kolesar	.10	.04	.01
☐	213	Craig Geekie	.10	.04	.01
☐	214	Terran Sandwith	.25	.10	.02
☐	215	Jeff Hoad	.10	.04	.01
☐	216	Kelly McCrimmon	.10	.04	.01
☐	217	Carlos Bye	.10	.04	.01
☐	218	Trevor Hanas	.10	.04	.01
☐	219	Jeff Shantz	.35	.14	.03
☐	220	Heath Weenk	.15	.06	.01
☐	221	Nathan Dempsey	.10	.04	.01
☐	222	Louis Dumont	.20	.08	.02
☐	223	Garry Pearce	.15	.06	.01
☐	224	Terry Bendera	.10	.04	.01
☐	225	Hal Christiansen	.10	.04	.01
☐	226	Jason Smith	.25	.10	.02
☐	227	Karry Biette	.10	.04	.01
☐	228	Barry Becker	.15	.06	.01
☐	229	Derek Eberle	.15	.06	.01
☐	230	Ken Richardson	.10	.04	.01
☐	231	Niklas Barklund	.15	.06	.01
☐	232	Frank Kovacs	.25	.10	.02
☐	233	Not Issued	.00	.00	.00
☐	234	Not Issued	.00	.00	.00
☐	235	Lloyd Pelletier	.20	.08	.02
☐	236	Dale Vossen	.10	.04	.01
☐	237	A.J. Kelham	.10	.04	.01
☐	238	Mike Risdale	.15	.06	.01
☐	239	Brad Bagu	.10	.04	.01
☐	240	Niko Ovaska	.10	.04	.01
☐	241	Brad Tippett CO	.10	.04	.01
☐	242	The Goalies II	.15	.06	.01
☐	243	Lee J. Leslie	.35	.14	.03
☐	244	Darren Perkins	.10	.04	.01
☐	245	Jason Kwiatkowski	.15	.06	.01
☐	246	Jason Renard	.10	.04	.01
☐	247	Dan Kesa	.25	.10	.02
☐	248	Jason Klassen	.10	.04	.01
☐	249	Nick Polychronopoulus	.10	.04	.01
☐	250	David Neilson	.15	.06	.01
☐	251	Merv Haney	.10	.04	.01
☐	252	Troy Hjertaas	.10	.04	.01
☐	253	Curt Regnier	.20	.08	.02
☐	254	Dean McAmmond	.35	.14	.03
☐	255	Travis Laycock	.15	.06	.01
☐	256	Jeff Lank	.10	.04	.01
☐	257	Barkley Swenson	.10	.04	.01
☐	258	Darren Van Impe	.25	.10	.02
☐	259	Ryan Pisiak	.10	.04	.01
☐	260	Jeff Gorman	.10	.04	.01
☐	261	Stan Matwijiw	.15	.06	.01
☐	262	Mike Fedorko	.10	.04	.01
☐	263	Mark Odnokon	.10	.04	.01
☐	264	Shane Zulyniak	.10	.04	.01
☐	265	Jeff Nelson	.35	.14	.03
☐	266	Donevan Hextall	.25	.10	.02
☐	267	Kevin Masters	.10	.04	.01
☐	268	Chris Schmidt	.20	.08	.02
☐	269	Jeff Budai	.10	.04	.01
☐	270	Bill Hooson	.10	.04	.01
☐	271	Fred Hettle	.10	.04	.01
☐	272	Kent Staniforth	.10	.04	.01
☐	273	Travis Stevenson	.15	.06	.01
☐	274	David Jesiolowksi	.10	.04	.01
☐	275	Mike Babcock CO	.10	.04	.01
☐	276	Scott Allison	.25	.10	.02
☐	277	Travis Thiessen	.20	.08	.02
☐	278	Marc Hussey	.10	.04	.01
☐	279	Kevin Smyth	.35	.14	.03
☐	280	Jason Fitzsimmons	.25	.10	.02
☐	281	Jeff Petruic	.10	.04	.01
☐	282	Russ West	.10	.04	.01
☐	283	Derek Kletzel	.25	.10	.02
☐	284	Jarret Zukiwsky	.10	.04	.01
☐	285	Jason Carey	.15	.06	.01
☐	286	Close Checking	.15	.06	.01
☐	287	Checklist 288-360	.15	.06	.01
☐	288	Jason Bowen	.50	.20	.05
☐	289	Dean Tiltgen	.25	.10	.02
☐	290	Terry Degner	.30	.12	.03
☐	291	Jodie Murphy	.10	.04	.01
☐	292	Brian Sakic	.35	.14	.03
☐	293	Jamie Barnes	.10	.04	.01
☐	294	Darren Hastman	.10	.04	.01
☐	295	Todd Klassen	.25	.10	.02
☐	296	Mirsad Mujcin	.10	.04	.01
☐	297	Trevor Sherban	.10	.04	.01
☐	298	Chadden Cabana	.10	.04	.01
☐	299	Adam Rettschlag	.10	.04	.01
☐	300	Mark Toljanich	.10	.04	.01
☐	301	Kory Mullin	.10	.04	.01
☐	302	Byron Penstock	.10	.04	.01
☐	303	Vladimir Vujtek	.50	.20	.05
☐	304	Bill Lindsay	.60	.24	.06
☐	305	Jeff Cej	.10	.04	.01
☐	306	Mike Busniak CO	.10	.04	.01
☐	307	Todd Harris	.10	.04	.01
☐	308	Cory Dosdall	.20	.08	.02
☐	309	Jason Smith	.15	.06	.01
☐	310	Mark Dawkins	.15	.06	.01
☐	311	Dan O'Rourke	.10	.04	.01
☐	312	Darby Walker	.10	.04	.01
☐	313	Olaf Kjenstadt	.25	.10	.02
☐	314	Sonny Mignacca	.50	.20	.05
☐	315	Jon Duval	.10	.04	.01
☐	316	Lorne Toews	.10	.04	.01
☐	317	Dana Rieder	.10	.04	.01
☐	318	Clayton Norris	.25	.10	.02
☐	319	David Cooper	.35	.14	.03
☐	320	Lanny Watkins	.15	.06	.01
☐	321	Evan Marble	.10	.04	.01
☐	322	Scott Lindsay	.25	.10	.02
☐	323	Ryan Petz	.10	.04	.01
☐	324	Jeramie Heistad	.10	.04	.01
☐	325	Scott Townsend	.10	.04	.01
☐	326	Stacy Roest	.15	.06	.01
☐	327	Rob Niedermayer	1.50	.60	.15
☐	328	Tim Bothwell CO	.15	.06	.01
☐	329	Kevin Riehl	.50	.20	.05
☐	330	Mike Rathje	.60	.24	.06
☐	331	Bryan McCabe	.25	.10	.02
☐	332	MHT Tiger MASCOT	.15	.06	.01
☐	333	Dean Intwert	.10	.04	.01
☐	334	Mike Vandenberghe	.15	.06	.01
☐	335	Cam Danyluk	.10	.04	.01
☐	336	Darcy Austin	.10	.04	.01
☐	337	Jason Knight	.10	.04	.01
☐	338	Lee Sorochan	.15	.06	.01
☐	339	Al Kinisky	.10	.04	.01
☐	340	Rob Hartnell	.15	.06	.01
☐	341	Radek Sip	.25	.10	.02

☐ 342	Jamie Pushor	.20	.08	.02
☐ 343	Shane Peacock	.20	.08	.02
☐ 344	Cadrin Smart	.15	.06	.01
☐ 345	Maurice Meagher	.10	.04	.01
☐ 346	Lance Burns	.10	.04	.01
☐ 347	Dominic Pittis	.25	.10	.02
☐ 348	Todd MacIsaac	.10	.04	.01
☐ 349	Brad Zimmer	.15	.06	.01
☐ 350	Jason Sorochan	.15	.06	.01
☐ 351	Darcy Werenka	.35	.14	.03
☐ 352	Kevin St.Jacques	.25	.10	.02
☐ 353	David Trofimenkoff	.15	.06	.01
☐ 354	Terry Hollinger	.25	.10	.02
☐ 355	Travis Munday	.10	.04	.01
☐ 356	Slade Stephenson	.10	.04	.01
☐ 357	Jason Widmer	.10	.04	.01
☐ 358	Brad Zavisha	.25	.10	.02
☐ 359	Bob Loucks CO	.10	.04	.01
☐ 360	Brantt Myhres	.25	.10	.02

1991-92 7th Inn. Sketch QMJHL

 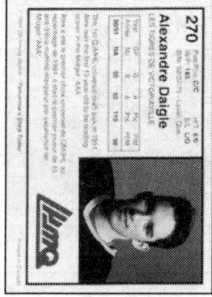

Alexandre Daigle
91-92 LHJMQ   Les Tigres

This 298-card set, which measures the standard size (2 1/2" by 3 1/2"), was issued by 7th Inning Sketch featuring players of the Quebec Major Junior Hockey League. The production run was limited to 4,000 factory sets, with each set individually numbered "X of 4,000." On a white card face, the fronts feature color action player photos enclosed by different color frames. The corners of the picture are cut out to permit space for gold stars. The player's name, the year and league, and the team name appear below the picture. In a horizontal format, the backs have biography, statistics, and player profile in French and English. The cards are numbered on the back and checklisted below according to teams as follows: St. Hyacinthe Laser (1-28), Granby Bisons (29-52), Shawinigan Cataractes (53-77), Chicoutimi Sagueneens (78-101), Trois Rivieres Draveurs (102-125), Verdun College Francais (126-150), St. Jean Lynx (151-172), Beauport Harfangs (173-198), Hull Olympiques (199-223), Laval Titan (224-248), Victoriaville Tigres (249-273), and Drummondville Voltigeurs (274-298).

	MINT	EXC	G-VG
COMPLETE SET (298)	15.00	6.00	1.50
COMMON PLAYER (1-298)	.10	.04	.01

☐ 1	Martin Brodeur	1.50	.60	.15
☐ 2	Normand Paquet	.20	.08	.02
☐ 3	David Desnoyers	.10	.04	.01
☐ 4	Carlo Colombi	.10	.04	.01
☐ 5	Stephane Menard	.15	.06	.01
☐ 6	Sebastien Berube	.10	.04	.01
☐ 7	Marc Desgagne	.10	.04	.01
☐ 8	Mil Sukovic	.25	.10	.02
☐ 9	Patrick Belisle	.10	.04	.01
☐ 10	Patrick Poulin	.75	.30	.07
☐ 11	Martin Trudel	.10	.04	.01
☐ 12	Charles Poulin	.50	.20	.05

☐ 13	Etienne Thibault	.15	.06	.01
☐ 14	Pierre Allard	.10	.04	.01
☐ 15	Francois Gagnon	.15	.06	.01
☐ 16	Stephane Huard	.10	.04	.01
☐ 17	Yannik Lemay	.10	.04	.01
☐ 18	Dany Fortin	.10	.04	.01
☐ 19	Carl Menard	.10	.04	.01
☐ 20	Serge Labelle	.10	.04	.01
☐ 21	Dean Melanson	.10	.04	.01
☐ 22	Yves Meunier	.15	.06	.01
☐ 23	Pierre Petroni CO	.10	.04	.01
☐ 24	Mario Pouliot CO UER	.10	.04	.01
	(Team affiliation says Bisons; should say Laser)			
☐ 25	Alain Cote UER	.25	.10	.02
	(Team affiliation on front says Bisons; should say Lasers; Back erroneously says Kingston Frontenancs)			
☐ 26	Hugues Laliberte	.15	.06	.01
☐ 27	Martin Gendron	.50	.20	.05
☐ 28	Stan Melanson	.10	.04	.01
☐ 29	Carl Leblanc	.15	.06	.01
☐ 30	Patrick Grise	.15	.06	.01
☐ 31	Yves Charron	.10	.04	.01
☐ 32	Hughes Mongeon	.40	.16	.04
☐ 33	Christian Tardif	.10	.04	.01
☐ 34	Patrick Tessier	.10	.04	.01
☐ 35	Christian Campeau	.10	.04	.01
☐ 36	Mario Hermann	.10	.04	.01
☐ 37	Martin Balleux	.15	.06	.01
☐ 38	Joel Brassard	.10	.04	.01
☐ 39	Sebastien Fortier	.15	.06	.01
☐ 40	Jocelyn Langlois	.10	.04	.01
☐ 41	Giuseppe Argentos	.10	.04	.01
☐ 42	Sylvain Brisson	.10	.04	.01
☐ 43	Philippe Boucher	.35	.14	.03
☐ 44	Martin Brochu	.25	.10	.02
☐ 45	Marc Rodgers	.20	.08	.02
☐ 46	Pascal Gagnon	.10	.04	.01
☐ 47	Benoit Therrien	.10	.04	.01
☐ 48	Robin Bouchard	.15	.06	.01
☐ 49	Michel Savoie	.10	.04	.01
☐ 50	Jean-Sebastien Boiteau	.10	.04	.01
☐ 51	Patrick Lamoureux	.10	.04	.01
☐ 52	Stephane Giard	.10	.04	.01
☐ 53	Maxime Jean	.10	.04	.01
☐ 54	Alain Cote	.25	.10	.02
☐ 55	Francois Groleau	.25	.10	.02
☐ 56	Richard Hamelin	.20	.08	.02
☐ 57	Eric Beauvis UER	.15	.06	.01
	(Name misspelled Beavis on back)			
☐ 58	Steve Laplante	.10	.04	.01
☐ 59	Yves Meunier	.10	.04	.01
☐ 60	Steve Dontigny	.15	.06	.01
☐ 61	Simon Roy	.25	.10	.02
☐ 62	Jean-Francois Laroche	.10	.04	.01
☐ 63	Patrick Traverse	.10	.04	.01
☐ 64	Eric Joyal	.10	.04	.01
☐ 65	Jean-Francois Gregoire UER	.15	.06	.01
	(Name misspelled Jean-Fracois on front)			
☐ 66	Jocelyn Charbonneau	.15	.06	.01
☐ 67	Jean Imbeau	.20	.08	.02
☐ 68	Francois Bourdeau	.10	.04	.01
☐ 69	Alain Savage Jr.	.15	.06	.01
☐ 70	Johnny Lorenzo	.20	.08	.02
☐ 71	Patrick Lalime	.10	.04	.01
☐ 72	Patrick Melfi	.10	.04	.01
☐ 73	Marc Tardif	.15	.06	.01
☐ 74	Marc Savard	.10	.04	.01
☐ 75	Alain Sanscartier CO	.10	.04	.01
☐ 76	Pascal Lebrasseur	.15	.06	.01
☐ 77	Checklist 1-101	.15	.06	.01
☐ 78	Dany Girard	.15	.06	.01
☐ 79	Eddy Gervais	.15	.06	.01
☐ 80	Dave Tremblay	.10	.04	.01
☐ 81	Dany Larochelle	.10	.04	.01
☐ 82	Michel St.Jacques	.20	.08	.02
☐ 83	Rodney Petawabano	.10	.04	.01
☐ 84	Eric Duchesne	.25	.10	.02
☐ 85	Patrick Clement	.10	.04	.01
☐ 86	Steve Gosselin	.15	.06	.01
☐ 87	Patrick Lacombe	.10	.04	.01
☐ 88	Patrice Martineau	.15	.06	.01
☐ 89	Danny Beauregard	.20	.08	.02
☐ 90	Martin Lamarche	.10	.04	.01
☐ 91	Sebastien Parent	.20	.08	.02
☐ 92	Christian Caron	.10	.04	.01
☐ 93	Sylvain Careau	.15	.06	.01

☐ 94	Martin Beaupre	.15	.06	.01
☐ 95	Daniel Paradis	.20	.08	.02
☐ 96	Sylvain Rodrigue	.20	.08	.02
☐ 97	Joe Canale CO	.10	.04	.01
☐ 98	Patrick Lampron	.10	.04	.01
☐ 99	Carl Blondin	.15	.06	.01
☐ 100	Carl Wiseman	.10	.04	.01
☐ 101	Hugo Hamelin	.15	.06	.01
☐ 102	Claude Poirier	.10	.04	.01
☐ 103	Charles Paquette	.35	.14	.03
☐ 104	Carl Fleury UER	.15	.06	.01
	(Name spelled FLeury on front)			
☐ 105	Paolo Racicot	.15	.06	.01
☐ 106	Sebastien Moreau	.10	.04	.01
☐ 107	Pascal Trepanier	.10	.04	.01
☐ 108	Dominic Maltais	.35	.14	.03
☐ 109	Steve Ares	.10	.04	.01
☐ 110	Daniel Thibault	.10	.04	.01
☐ 111	Eric Messier	.10	.04	.01
☐ 112	Stephane Julien	.15	.06	.01
☐ 113	Dave Paquet	.15	.06	.01
☐ 114	Nicolas Turmel	.10	.04	.01
☐ 115	Pascal Rheaume	.25	.10	.02
☐ 116	Carl Boudreau	.35	.14	.03
☐ 117	Dave Boudreault	.10	.04	.01
☐ 118	Eric Bellerose	.35	.14	.03
☐ 119	Steve Searles	.10	.04	.01
☐ 120	Patrick Nadeau	.25	.10	.02
☐ 121	Stephan Viens	.10	.04	.01
☐ 122	Jean-Francois Labbe	.35	.14	.03
☐ 123	Jocelyn Thibault	1.00	.40	.10
☐ 124	Gaston Drapeau CO	.10	.04	.01
☐ 125	Checklist 102-198	.15	.06	.01
☐ 126	Martin Lajeunesse	.20	.08	.02
☐ 127	Etienne Lavoie	.10	.04	.01
☐ 128	Dominic Rheaume	.15	.06	.01
☐ 129	Robert Guillet	.15	.06	.01
☐ 130	Francois Rivard	.10	.04	.01
☐ 131	Phillippe DeRouville	.35	.14	.03
☐ 132	Andrej Dobrota	.10	.04	.01
☐ 133	Pierre Gendron	.10	.04	.01
☐ 134	Dave Chouinard	.20	.08	.02
☐ 135	Martin Tanguay	.25	.10	.02
☐ 136	Jacques Blouin	.15	.06	.01
☐ 137	Martin Larochelle	.10	.04	.01
☐ 138	Jean-Martin Morin	.10	.04	.01
☐ 139	Donald Brashear	.25	.10	.02
☐ 140	Stephane Paradis	.10	.04	.01
☐ 141	Jan Simcik	.10	.04	.01
☐ 142	Yan Arsenault	.25	.10	.02
☐ 143	Joel Bouchard	.10	.04	.01
☐ 144	Jean-Sebastien Lefebvre	.10	.04	.01
☐ 145	David St. Pierre UER	.25	.10	.02
	(Name misspelled St-Pierre on front)			
☐ 146	Mario Nobili	.20	.08	.02
☐ 147	Stacy Dallaire	.10	.04	.01
☐ 148	Carl Lamothe	.20	.08	.02
☐ 149	Andre Bouliane	.10	.04	.01
☐ 150	Simon Arial	.10	.04	.01
☐ 151	Stephane Madore	.10	.04	.01
☐ 152	Hughes Bouchard	.10	.04	.01
☐ 153	Steve Decaen	.10	.04	.01
☐ 154	Jason Downey	.10	.04	.01
☐ 155	Raymond Delarosbil	.10	.04	.01
☐ 156	Lino Salvo	.15	.06	.01
☐ 157	Reginald Brezeault	.10	.04	.01
☐ 158	Nathan Morin	.10	.04	.01
☐ 159	Samuel Groleau	.25	.10	.02
☐ 160	Patrick Carignan	.20	.08	.02
☐ 161	Stephane St-Amour	.10	.04	.01
☐ 162	Marquis Mathieu	.15	.06	.01
☐ 163	Yves Sarault	.25	.10	.02
☐ 164	Dave Belliveau	.10	.04	.01
☐ 165	Trevor Duhaime	.10	.04	.01
☐ 166	Eric O'Connor	.10	.04	.01
☐ 167	Christian Proulx	.25	.10	.02
☐ 168	Martin Lavallee	.10	.04	.01
☐ 169	Jean-Francois Gagnon	.15	.06	.01
☐ 170	Eric Lafrance	.10	.04	.01
☐ 171	Enrico Scardocchio	.10	.04	.01
☐ 172	David Bergeron	.10	.04	.01
☐ 173	Guillaume Morin	.10	.04	.01
☐ 174	Charlie Boucher	.10	.04	.01
☐ 175	Martin Rozon	.10	.04	.01
☐ 176	Brandon Piccarreto	.10	.04	.01
☐ 177	Simon Toupin	.20	.08	.02
☐ 178	Jamie Bird	.10	.04	.01
☐ 179	Herve Lapointe	.10	.04	.01
☐ 180	Ian Mclntyre	.15	.06	.01
☐ 181	Jean-Francois Rivard	.10	.04	.01
☐ 182	Alain Chainey	.10	.04	.01
☐ 183	Daniel Laflamme	.10	.04	.01
☐ 184	Patrice Paquin	.10	.04	.01
☐ 185	Patrick Deraspe	.10	.04	.01
☐ 186	Martin Roy	.10	.04	.01
☐ 187	Jeannot Ferland	.10	.04	.01
☐ 188	Patrick Genest	.15	.06	.01
☐ 189	Matthew Barnaby	.75	.30	.07
☐ 190	Jean-Guy Trudel	.10	.04	.01
☐ 191	Eric Moreau	.10	.04	.01
☐ 192	Eric Cool	.25	.10	.02
☐ 193	Alexandre Legault	.10	.04	.01
☐ 194	Gregg Pineo	.10	.04	.01
☐ 195	LHJMQ Action	.15	.06	.01
☐ 196	Radoslav Balaz	.10	.04	.01
☐ 197	Stefan Simoes	.10	.04	.01
☐ 198	LHJMQ Action	.15	.06	.01
☐ 199	Francois Paquette	.10	.04	.01
☐ 200	Paul Macdonald	.10	.04	.01
☐ 201	Shane Doiron	.10	.04	.01
☐ 202	Michal Longauer	.10	.04	.01
☐ 203	Joe Crowley	.10	.04	.01
☐ 204	Joey Deliva	.15	.06	.01
☐ 205	Pierre-Francois Lalonde	.15	.06	.01
☐ 206	Paul Brousseau	.50	.20	.05
☐ 207	Martin Lepage	.10	.04	.01
☐ 208	Yanick DeGrace	.25	.10	.02
☐ 209	Jim Campbell	.50	.20	.05
☐ 210	Sebastien Bordeleau	.15	.06	.01
☐ 211	Marc Legault	.15	.06	.01
☐ 212	Joel Blain	.15	.06	.01
☐ 213	Claude Jutras	.20	.08	.02
☐ 214	Eric Lavigne	.35	.14	.03
☐ 215	Todd Sparks	.25	.10	.02
☐ 216	Sylvain Lapointe	.10	.04	.01
☐ 217	Eric Lecompte	.75	.30	.07
☐ 218	Thierry Mayer	.10	.04	.01
☐ 219A	Harold Hersh ERR	.35	.14	.03
	(Jim Campbell photo on back)			
☐ 219B	Harold Hersh COR	.15	.06	.01
☐ 220	Frederic Boivin	.10	.04	.01
☐ 221	Steven Dion	.10	.04	.01
☐ 222	Alain Vigneault	.10	.04	.01
☐ 223	Checklist 199-298	.15	.06	.01
☐ 224	Petr Valenta	.10	.04	.01
☐ 225	LHJMQ Action	.15	.06	.01
☐ 226	Jim Bermingham	.20	.08	.02
☐ 227	Yanick Dube	.75	.30	.07
☐ 228	Sandy McCarthy	.30	.12	.03
☐ 229	Dany Michaud	.10	.04	.01
☐ 230	Jason Brousseau	.10	.04	.01
☐ 231	Marc Beaucage	.15	.06	.01
☐ 232	Eric Cardinal	.10	.04	.01
☐ 233	Martin Chaput	.10	.04	.01
☐ 234	Jean Roberge	.10	.04	.01
☐ 235	Philip Gathercole	.10	.04	.01
☐ 236	Michael Gaul	.15	.06	.01
☐ 237	Yannick Frechette	.10	.04	.01
☐ 238	Sylvain Blouin	.10	.04	.01
☐ 239	David Pekarek	.10	.04	.01
☐ 240	John Kovacs	.10	.04	.01
☐ 241	Eric Raymond	.10	.04	.01
☐ 242	Emmanuel Fernandez	.75	.30	.07
☐ 243	Yan St. Pierre	.15	.06	.01
☐ 244	Brant Blackned	.10	.04	.01
☐ 245	Eric Veilleux	.25	.10	.02
☐ 246	Pascal Vincent	.10	.04	.01
☐ 247	Benoit Larose	.15	.06	.01
☐ 248	Olivier Guillaume	.10	.04	.01
☐ 249	Alain Gauthier	.10	.04	.01
☐ 250	Bruno Ducharme	.10	.04	.01
☐ 251	Patrick Charbonneau	.15	.06	.01
☐ 252	Daniel Germain	.10	.04	.01
☐ 253	Pascal Chiasson	.10	.04	.01
☐ 254	Marc Thibeault	.10	.04	.01
☐ 255	Martin Woods	.10	.04	.01
☐ 256	Not printed	.00	.00	.00
☐ 257	Dominic Grand'maison	.10	.04	.01
☐ 258	Carl Poirer	.10	.04	.01
☐ 259	Stephane Larocque	.10	.04	.01
☐ 260	Mario Dumoulin	.10	.04	.01
☐ 261	Yan Laterreur	.10	.04	.01
☐ 262	Claude Savoie	.25	.10	.02
☐ 263	Denis Beauchamp	.10	.04	.01
☐ 264	Patrick Bisaillon	.15	.06	.01
☐ 265	Pascal Bernier	.10	.04	.01
☐ 266	Nicolas Lefebvre	.15	.06	.01
☐ 267	LHJMQ Action	.15	.06	.01
☐ 268	Joseph Napolitano	.15	.06	.01
☐ 269	Sebastien Tremblay	.10	.04	.01
☐ 270	Alexandre Daigle	4.00	1.60	.40

☐ 271	Pierre Pillion	.10	.04	.01
☐ 272	Yves Lambert	.10	.04	.01
☐ 273	Pierre Aubry	.10	.04	.01
☐ 274	Yves Loubier	.10	.04	.01
☐ 275	Pierre Sandke UER	.10	.04	.01
	(First name Peter			
	on back)			
☐ 276	Louis Bernard	.10	.04	.01
☐ 277	Alain Nasreddine	.15	.06	.01
☐ 278	Sylvain Ducharme	.10	.04	.01
☐ 279	Jeremy Caissie	.10	.04	.01
☐ 280	Eric Meloche	.10	.04	.01
☐ 281	Ian Laperriere	.50	.20	.05
☐ 282	Hugo Proulx	.35	.14	.03
☐ 283	Dave Whittom	.15	.06	.01
☐ 284	Yanick Dupre	.25	.10	.02
☐ 285	Eric Plante	.15	.06	.01
☐ 286	Stephane Desjardins	.15	.06	.01
☐ 287	Rene Corbet	.50	.20	.05
☐ 288	David Lessard	.10	.04	.01
☐ 289	Eric Marcoux	.10	.04	.01
☐ 290	Alexandre Duchesne	.10	.04	.01
☐ 291	Maxime Petitclerc UER	.10	.04	.01
	(Name misspelled			
	Peticlerc on front)			
☐ 292	Pierre Gagnon	.15	.06	.01
☐ 293	Roger Larache UER	.10	.04	.01
	(Name misspelled			
	Larche on back)			
☐ 294	Jean Hamel	.15	.06	.01
☐ 295	Alexandre Gaumond	.10	.04	.01
☐ 296	Paul-Emile Exentus	.10	.04	.01
☐ 297	LHJMQ Action	.15	.06	.01
☐ 298	LHJMQ Action	.15	.06	.01

1961-62 Union Oil WHL

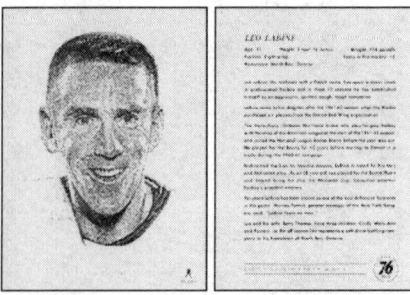

This 12-drawing set features players from the Los Angeles Blades (1-8) and the San Francisco Seals (9-12) of the Western Hockey League. The black-and-white drawings by artist Sam Patrick measure approximately 6" by 8" and are printed on textured white paper. The back of each drawing carries the player's career highlights and biographical information. The Union Oil name and logo at the bottom round out the backs. The cards are unnumbered and listed below alphabetically within teams. Reportedly only eight cards were issued to the public, making four of the cards extremely scarce.

		NRMT	VG-E	GOOD
COMPLETE SET (12)		75.00	30.00	7.50
COMMON PLAYER (1-8)		6.00	2.40	.60
COMMON PLAYER (9-12)		6.00	2.40	.60
☐ 1	Jack Bownass	6.00	2.40	.60
☐ 2	Ed Diachuk	6.00	2.40	.60
☐ 3	Leo LaBine	7.50	3.00	.75
☐ 4	Willie O'Ree	12.00	5.00	1.20
☐ 5	Bruce Carmichael	6.00	2.40	.60
☐ 6	Gordon Haworth	6.00	2.40	.60
☐ 7	Fleming Mackell	10.00	4.00	1.00
☐ 8	Robert Solinger	6.00	2.40	.60
☐ 9	Gary Edmundson	6.00	2.40	.60
☐ 10	Al Nicholson	6.00	2.40	.60
☐ 11	Orland Kurtenbach	12.00	5.00	1.20
☐ 12	Tom Thurlby	6.00	2.40	.60

1993-94 Amos Les Forestiers AAA Midget

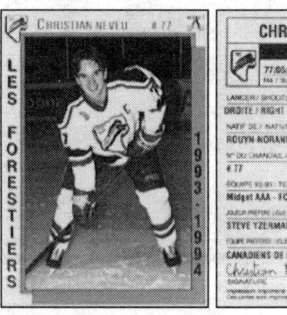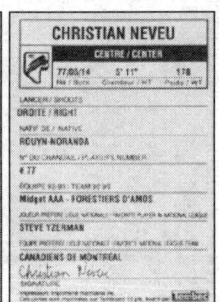

This 26-card standard-size (2 1/2" by 3 1/2") set features Les Forestiers, a Midget AAA team in the province of Quebec. Les Forestiers is one of ten teams in the province from which the junior teams pick their players. The production run was reportedly 505 sets, including 60 autographed sets randomly placed in the lot. On a white card face, the fronts display posed color player photos framed by blue on the left and top and by magenta on the right and bottom. Player identification is printed in the top border, and the team name is printed in the left border. The backs present biographical and trivia information. Also each player signed the back at the bottom. This set includes cards featuring Christian Neveu, who played on Team Quebec when it won the gold medal at the midget world hockey challenge. The cards are unnumbered and checklisted below in alphabetical order.

		MINT	EXC	G-VG
COMPLETE SET (26)		10.00	4.00	1.00
COMMON PLAYER (1-26)		.50	.20	.05
☐ 1	Jean-Francois Belley	.50	.20	.05
☐ 2	Carl Benoit	.50	.20	.05
☐ 3	Martin Biron	.50	.20	.05
☐ 4	David Bolduc	.50	.20	.05
☐ 5	Martin Bradette	.50	.20	.05
☐ 6	Dave Fontaine	.50	.20	.05
☐ 7	Paul-Sebastien Gagnon	.50	.20	.05
☐ 8	Eric Germain	.75	.30	.07
☐ 9	Eric Houle	.50	.20	.05
☐ 10	Jacques Larrivee ACO	.50	.20	.05
☐ 11	Yannick Lavoie	.50	.20	.05
☐ 12	Mathieu Letourneau	.50	.20	.05
☐ 13	Vincent Levasseur	.50	.20	.05
☐ 14	Jonathan Levesque	.50	.20	.05
☐ 15	Eric Naud	.50	.20	.05
☐ 16	Christian Neveu	2.50	1.00	.25
☐ 17	Patrick Pelchat	.50	.20	.05
☐ 18	John Pyliotis	.50	.20	.05
☐ 19	Luc St-Germain	.50	.20	.05
☐ 20	Frederick Servant	.50	.20	.05
☐ 21	Philippe Tremblay	.50	.20	.05
☐ 22	Serge Trepanier CO	.50	.20	.05
☐ 23	Dany Villeneuve	.50	.20	.05
☐ 24	Les Veterans	.75	.30	.07
	Christian Neveu			
	Mathieu Letourneau			
☐ 25	Checklist	.75	.30	.07
☐ 26	Title card	.50	.20	.05

1990-91 Arizona Icecats

Produced by the Ninth Inning, this 16-card set measures the standard size (2 1/2" by 3 1/2") and features members of the Arizona Icecats. Production was reportedly limited to 2,150

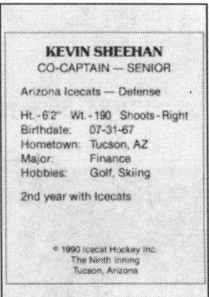

sets, obtainable either at the Tucson Convention Center Ice Arena on game days or at the Ninth Inning (a card shop). The front features a posed color photo of the player, with thin black border on white card stock. The upper left and lower right hand corners of the picture are cut out, with the year and the team logo inserted in these spaces respectively. The back presents biographical information in a black box. Although the individual cards are unnumbered, they are checklisted below according to the numbering assigned to them on the checklist card.

	MINT	EXC	G-VG
COMPLETE SET (16)	8.00	3.25	.80
COMMON PLAYER (1-16)	.50	.20	.05
☐ 1 Leo Golembiewski CO	.75	.30	.07
☐ 2 Icecat Leaders	1.00	.40	.10
Kevin Sheehan			
John Allen			
Leo Golembiewski CO			
Kelly Walker			
John Wegener			
☐ 3 John Allen	.75	.30	.07
☐ 4 Don Carlson	.50	.20	.05
☐ 5 Dan Divjak	.75	.30	.07
☐ 6 Frank DeMaio	.50	.20	.05
☐ 7 Jeremy Goltz	.75	.30	.07
☐ 8 Aaron Joffe	.50	.20	.05
☐ 9 Dan O'Day	.50	.20	.05
☐ 10 Dan Olberg	.50	.20	.05
☐ 11 Cory Oleson	.75	.30	.07
☐ 12 Kevin Sheehan	.75	.30	.07
☐ 13 Dean Sives	.50	.20	.05
☐ 14 Kelly Walker	.75	.30	.07
☐ 15 John Wegener	.75	.30	.07
☐ 16 Logo Card	.75	.30	.07
(Checklist)			

1991-92 Arizona Icecats

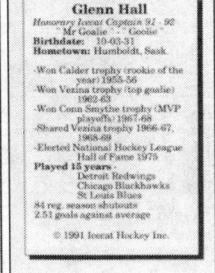

This 20-card set measures the standard size (2 1/2" by 3 1/2") and features members of the Arizona Icecats. The front features a posed color photo of the player, with thin blue border and a blue shadow-border on white card stock. The player's name appears in the bottom shadow- border. The back presents biographical information and statistics in a black shadow-bordered box. Though the individual cards are unnumbered, they are checklisted below according to the numbering assigned to them on the checklist card.

	MINT	EXC	G-VG
COMPLETE SET (20)	10.00	4.00	1.00
COMMON PLAYER (1-20)	.50	.20	.05
☐ 1 Leo Golembiewski CO	.75	.30	.07
☐ 2 Don Carlson	.50	.20	.05
☐ 3 Kelly Walker	.75	.30	.07
☐ 4 Cory Oleson	.75	.30	.07
☐ 5 Drew Sibr	.50	.20	.05
☐ 6 Dan Divjak	.75	.30	.07
☐ 7 Jeremy Goltz	.75	.30	.07
☐ 8 Aaron Joffe	.50	.20	.05
☐ 9 Tommy Smith	.75	.30	.07
☐ 10 Dan Anderson	.75	.30	.07
☐ 11 Dean Sives	.50	.20	.05
☐ 12 Steve Hutchings	.50	.20	.05
☐ 13 Shane Fausel	.50	.20	.05
☐ 14 Greg Mitchell	.50	.20	.05
☐ 15 Ricky Pope	.50	.20	.05
☐ 16 Nate Soules	.50	.20	.05
☐ 17 Flavio Gentile	.50	.20	.05
☐ 18 Icecats Leaders	1.00	.40	.10
Leo Golembiewski CO			
Kelly Walker			
Cory Oleson			
Jeremy Goltz			
Dan Divjak			
☐ 19 Glenn Hall	2.50	1.00	.25
Honorary Captain			
☐ 20 Logo Card	.75	.30	.07
(Checklist)			

1992-93 Arizona Icecats

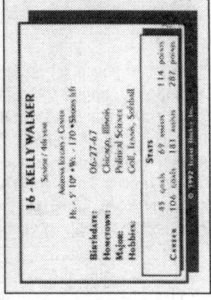

This 16-card set features the Arizona Icecats hockey team. Measuring the standard size (2 1/2" by 3 1/2"), each front displays a posed color player photo with multiple blue drop borders. The player's name appears in a royal blue stripe across the bottom of the picture. The backs carry biographical information and statistics in a black shadow-bordered box. Though the individual cards are unnumbered, they are checklisted below according to the numbering assigned to them on the checklist card.

	MINT	EXC	G-VG
COMPLETE SET (20)	8.00	3.25	.80
COMMON PLAYER (1-20)	.50	.20	.05
☐ 1 Leo Golembiewski CO	.75	.30	.07
☐ 2 Kelly Walker	.75	.30	.07
☐ 3 Cory Oleson	.75	.30	.07
☐ 4 Tommy Smith	.50	.20	.05
☐ 5 John Allen	.75	.30	.07
☐ 6 Dan Anderson	.75	.30	.07
☐ 7 Aaron Joffe	.50	.20	.05
☐ 8 Dan Divjak	.75	.30	.07

☐	9	Jeremy Goltz	.75	.30	.07
☐	10	Steve Hutchings	.50	.20	.05
☐	11	Greg Mitchell	.50	.20	.05
☐	12	Ricky Pope	.50	.20	.05
☐	13	Nate Soules	.50	.20	.05
☐	14	Matt Glines	.50	.20	.05
☐	15	Mark Thawley	.50	.20	.05
☐	16	Andre Zafrani	.50	.20	.05
☐	17	Chris Noga	.50	.20	.05
☐	18	Jim Kolbe	.50	.20	.05
		Honorary Captain			
☐	19	Coach and Top Gun Line	1.00	.40	.10
		Cory Oleson			
		Leo Golembiewski CO			
		Kelly Walker			
		Tommy Smith			
		John Allen			
		Dan Anderson			
☐	20	Logo Card	.75	.30	.07
		(Checklist)			

1983-84 Belleville Bulls

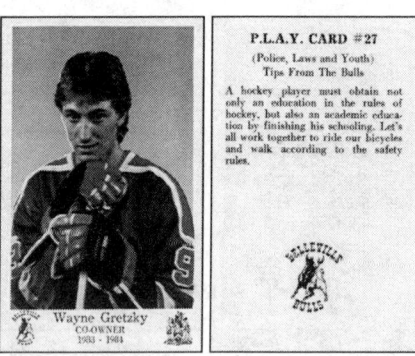

This 30-card police set measures approximately 2 5/8" by 4 1/8" and was sponsored by the Board of Commissioners of Police and other local organizations. The fronts feature posed color player photos with white borders. The player's name and position appear at the bottom. The backs carry P.L.A.Y. (Police, Laws and Youth) Card Tips from The Bulls which consist of a hockey term and relate it to everyday life. The cards are numbered on the back.

			MINT	EXC	G-VG
	COMPLETE SET (30)		50.00	20.00	5.00
	COMMON PLAYER (1-30)		.75	.30	.07
☐	1	Belleville Bulls Logo	1.50	.60	.15
☐	2	Quinte Sports Centre	.75	.30	.07
☐	3	Dan Quinn	3.00	1.20	.30
☐	4	Dave MacLean	.75	.30	.07
☐	5	Scott Gardiner	.75	.30	.07
☐	6	Mike Knuude	.75	.30	.07
☐	7	Brian Martin	.75	.30	.07
☐	8	R. Vaughan (Co-Owner)	.75	.30	.07
☐	9	John McDonald	.75	.30	.07
☐	10	Brian Small	.75	.30	.07
☐	11	Mike Savage	.75	.30	.07
☐	12	Dunc MacIntyre	.75	.30	.07
☐	13	Charlie Moore	.75	.30	.07
☐	14	Jim Andanoff	.75	.30	.07
☐	15	Mario Martini	.75	.30	.07
☐	16	Rick Adolfi	.75	.30	.07
☐	17	Mike Vellucci	.75	.30	.07
☐	18	Scott McMichel	.75	.30	.07
☐	19	Ali Butorac	.75	.30	.07
☐	20	Al Iafrate	15.00	6.00	1.50
☐	21	Rob Crocock	.75	.30	.07
☐	22	Craig Coxe	2.50	1.00	.25
☐	23	Grant Robertson	.75	.30	.07
☐	24	Craig Billington	3.00	1.20	.30
☐	25	Darren Gani	.75	.30	.07
☐	26	Tim Bean	.75	.30	.07
☐	27	Wayne Gretzky	30.00	12.00	3.00

☐	28	Russ Soule TR	.75	.30	.07
☐	29	Larry Mavety CO/GM	.75	.30	.07
☐	30	Team Photo	3.00	1.20	.30

1984-85 Belleville Bulls

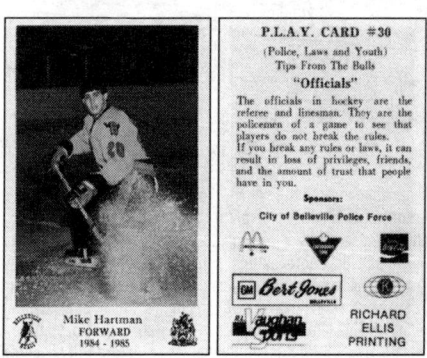

This 31-card police set measures approximately 2 5/8" by 4 1/8" and was sponsored by the City of Belleville Police Force and other local organizations. The fronts feature posed color player photos with white borders. The player's name, position, and the season (1984-85) appear at the bottom. The backs carry P.L.A.Y. (Police, Laws and Youth) Card Tips from The Bulls which explain a hockey term and relate it to everyday life. The cards are numbered on the back.

			MINT	EXC	G-VG
	COMPLETE SET (31)		20.00	8.00	2.00
	COMMON PLAYER (1-30)		.75	.30	.07
☐	1	Belleville Bulls	2.00	.80	.20
		(Team photo)			
☐	2	R. Vaughan	.75	.30	.07
		(Co-Owner)			
☐	3	Larry Mavety CO/MG	.75	.30	.07
☐	4	Dunc MacIntyre	.75	.30	.07
☐	5	Belleville Bulls Logo	1.50	.60	.15
		Card			
☐	6	Mike Knuude	.75	.30	.07
☐	7	John Purves	1.50	.60	.15
☐	8	Charlie Moore	.75	.30	.07
☐	9	Stan Drulia	1.50	.60	.15
☐	10	Craig Billington	4.00	1.60	.40
☐	11	Dave MacLean	.75	.30	.07
☐	12	Darren Moxam	.75	.30	.07
☐	13	Shane Doyle	.75	.30	.07
☐	14	Larry VanHerzele	.75	.30	.07
☐	15	Tim Bean	.75	.30	.07
☐	16	Kent Brimmer	.75	.30	.07
☐	17	Angelo Catenaro	.75	.30	.07
☐	18	Steve Linesman	.75	.30	.07
☐	19	Grant Robertson	.75	.30	.07
☐	20	John Reid	.75	.30	.07
☐	21	Dean Whyte	.75	.30	.07
☐	22	Darren Gani	.75	.30	.07
☐	23	Roger Robertson	.75	.30	.07
☐	24	Gary Callaghan	.75	.30	.07
☐	25	John Tamer	.75	.30	.07
☐	26	Todd Hawkins	.75	.30	.07
☐	27	Jim Andanoff	.75	.30	.07
☐	28	Chris Rutledge TR	.75	.30	.07
☐	29	Matt Taylor	.75	.30	.07
☐	30	Mike Hartman	2.00	.80	.20
☐	NNO	Title Card	1.50	.60	.15

1982-83 Brandon Wheat Kings

This 24-card set measures approximately 2 1/4" by 4" and features posed color player photos with thin yellow borders.

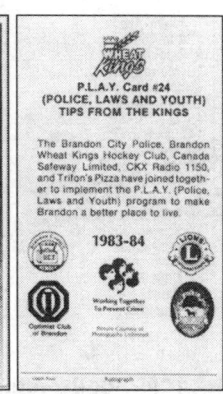

on a white card face. The player's name appears on the picture at the bottom. The backs carry P.L.A.Y. (Police, Laws and Youth) Tips From The Kings, which consist of a hockey term and relates it to a real life situation. Sponsor logos appear on the lower portion of the back. The cards are numbered on the back.

	MINT	EXC	G-VG
COMPLETE SET (24)	25.00	10.00	2.50
COMMON PLAYER (1-24)	.75	.30	.07
□ 1 Wheat Kings Logo	1.50	.60	.15
□ 2 Kevin Pylypow	.75	.30	.07
□ 3 Dean Kennedy	2.00	.80	.20
□ 4 Sonny Sodke	.75	.30	.07
□ 5 Darren Schmidt	.75	.30	.07
□ 6 Cam Plante	.75	.30	.07
□ 7 Sid Cranston	.75	.30	.07
□ 8 Bruce Thomson	.75	.30	.07
□ 9 Dave McDowall CO	.75	.30	.07
□ 10 Bill Vince	.75	.30	.07
□ 11 Kelly Glowa	.75	.30	.07
□ 12 Tom McMurchy	.75	.30	.07
□ 13 Ed Palichuk	.75	.30	.07
□ 14 Roy Caswell	.75	.30	.07
□ 15 Allan Tarasuk	.75	.30	.07
□ 16 Brent Jessiman	.75	.30	.07
□ 17 Randy Slawson	.75	.30	.07
□ 18 Gord Smith	.75	.30	.07
□ 19 Mike Sturgeon	.75	.30	.07
□ 20 Larry Bumstead	.75	.30	.07
□ 21 Kirk Blomquist	.75	.30	.07
□ 22 Ron Loustel	.75	.30	.07
□ 23 Ron Hextall	12.00	5.00	1.20
□ 24 Brandon Police Logo	1.50	.60	.15

1983-84 Brandon Wheat Kings

This 24-card set measures approximately 2 1/4" by 4" and features color posed action player photos with thin yellow borders on a white card face. The player's name is printed on the picture at the bottom. The backs carry P.L.A.Y. (Police, Laws and Youth) Tips From The Kings. Sponsor logos appear in the lower portion of the card. The cards are numbered on the back.

	MINT	EXC	G-VG
COMPLETE SET (24)	30.00	12.00	3.00
COMMON PLAYER (1-24)	.75	.30	.07
□ 1 Brian Wells	.75	.30	.07
□ 2 Jim Agnew	1.25	.50	.12
□ 3 Gord Paddock	.75	.30	.07
□ 4 John Dzikowski	.75	.30	.07
□ 5 Kelly Kozack	.75	.30	.07
□ 6 Byron Lomow	.75	.30	.07
□ 7 Pat Loyer	.75	.30	.07
□ 8 Rob Ordman	.75	.30	.07
□ 9 Brad Wells	.75	.30	.07

□ 10 Dave Thomlinson	1.50	.60	.15
□ 11 Cam Plante	.75	.30	.07
□ 12 Jay Palmer	.75	.30	.07
□ 13 Boyd Lomow	.75	.30	.07
□ 14 Brent Jessiman	.75	.30	.07
□ 15 Paul More	.75	.30	.07
□ 16 Stacy Prtt	.75	.30	.07
□ 17 Brandon Wheat Kings Brandon City Police	1.50	.60	.15
□ 18 Jack Sangster CO	.75	.30	.07
□ 19 Derek Laxdal	2.00	.80	.20
□ 20 Ray Ferraro	6.00	2.40	.60
□ 21 Allan Tarasuk	.75	.30	.07
□ 22 Randy Cameron	.75	.30	.07
□ 23 Dave Curry	.75	.30	.07
□ 24 Ron Hextall	10.00	4.00	1.00

1984-85 Brandon Wheat Kings

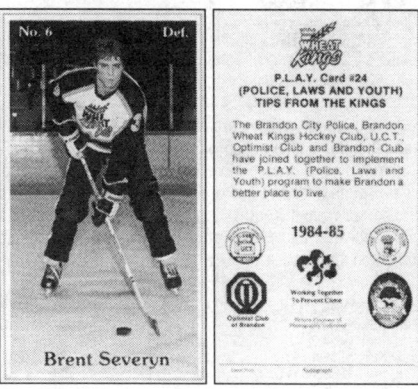

This 24-card set measures approximately 2 1/4" by 4" and features color posed action player photos with thin yellow borders on a white card face. The player's name is printed on the picture at the bottom. The backs carry P.L.A.Y. (Police, Laws and Youth) Tips From The Kings. Sponsor logos appear on the lower portion of the card. The cards are numbered on the back.

	MINT	EXC	G-VG
COMPLETE SET (24)	15.00	6.00	1.50
COMMON PLAYER (1-24)	.75	.30	.07
□ 1 Garnet Kazuik	.75	.30	.07
□ 2 Brent Mireau	.75	.30	.07
□ 3 Byron Lomow	.75	.30	.07
□ 4 Dean Shaw	.75	.30	.07
□ 5 Dean Sexsmith	.75	.30	.07
□ 6 Brad Mueller	.75	.30	.07

☐ 7	John Dzikowski	.75	.30	.07
☐ 8	Artie Feher	.75	.30	.07
☐ 9	Pat Loyer	.75	.30	.07
☐ 10	Murray Rice	.75	.30	.07
☐ 11	Derek Laxdal	1.50	.60	.15
☐ 12	Perry Fafard	.75	.30	.07
☐ 13	Lee Trim	.75	.30	.07
☐ 14	Dan Hart	.75	.30	.07
☐ 15	Trent Ciprick	.75	.30	.07
☐ 16	Jeff Waver	.75	.30	.07
☐ 17	Brandon Wheat Kings Brandon City Police	1.50	.60	.15
☐ 18	Jack Sangster CO	.75	.30	.07
☐ 19	Darwin McPherson	.75	.30	.07
☐ 20	Pokey Reddick	2.50	1.00	.25
☐ 21	Boyd Lomow	.75	.30	.07
☐ 22	Dave Thomlinson	1.50	.60	.15
☐ 23	Paul More	.75	.30	.07
☐ 24	Brent Severyn	2.00	.80	.20

1985-86 Brandon Wheat Kings

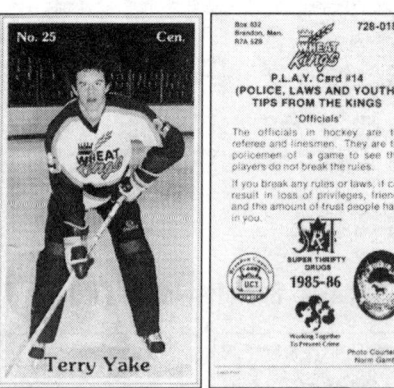

This 24-card set measures approximately 2 1/4" by 4" and features color posed action player photos with thin yellow borders on a white card face. The player's name is printed on the picture at the bottom. The backs carry P.L.A.Y. (Police, Laws and Youth) Tips From The Kings. Sponsor logos appear in the lower portion of the card. The cards are numbered on the back.

		MINT	EXC	G-VG
COMPLETE SET (24)		12.50	5.00	1.25
COMMON PLAYER (1-24)		.75	.30	.07
☐ 1	Kelly Hitchins	.75	.30	.07
☐ 2	Brent Mireau	.75	.30	.07
☐ 3	Byron Lomow	.75	.30	.07
☐ 4	Bob Heeney	.75	.30	.07
☐ 5	Dean Sexsmith	.75	.30	.07
☐ 6	Dave Curry	.75	.30	.07
☐ 7	John Dzikowski	.75	.30	.07
☐ 8	Artie Feher	.75	.30	.07
☐ 9	Kevin Mayo	.75	.30	.07
☐ 10	Murray Rice	.75	.30	.07
☐ 11	Derek Laxdal	1.25	.50	.12
☐ 12	Al Cherniwchan	.75	.30	.07
☐ 13	Lee Trim	.75	.30	.07
☐ 14	Terry Yake	2.50	1.00	.25
☐ 15	Trent Ciprick	.75	.30	.07
☐ 16	Jeff Waver	.75	.30	.07
☐ 17	Team Photo	1.50	.60	.15
☐ 18	Jack Sangster CO	.75	.30	.07
☐ 19	Mike Morin	.75	.30	.07
☐ 20	Jason Phillips	.75	.30	.07
☐ 21	Rod Williams	.75	.30	.07
☐ 22	Dave Thomlinson	1.25	.50	.12
☐ 23	Shane Eirickson	.75	.30	.07
☐ 24	Randy Hoffart	.75	.30	.07

1988-89 Brandon Wheat Kings

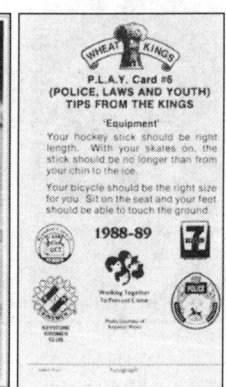

This 24-card set measures approximately 2 1/4" by 4" and features posed, color player photos with a thin yellow border stripe against a white card face. The backs carry P.L.A.Y. (Police, Laws and Youth) Tips from the Kings and sponsor logos. The cards are numbered on the back.

		MINT	EXC	G-VG
COMPLETE SET (24)		12.50	5.00	1.25
COMMON PLAYER (1-24)		.50	.20	.05
☐ 1	Kevin Cheveldayoff	1.00	.40	.10
☐ 2	Bob Woods	.50	.20	.05
☐ 3	Dwayne Newman	.50	.20	.05
☐ 4	Mike Vandenberghe	.50	.20	.05
☐ 5	Brad Woods	.50	.20	.05
☐ 6	Gary Audette	1.00	.40	.10
☐ 7	Mark Bassen	.50	.20	.05
☐ 8	Troy Frederick	.50	.20	.05
☐ 9	Troy Kennedy	.50	.20	.05
☐ 10	Barry Dreger	.50	.20	.05
☐ 11	Bill Whistle	.50	.20	.05
☐ 12	Jeff Odgers	1.25	.50	.12
☐ 13	Sheldon Kowalchuk	.75	.30	.07
☐ 14	Chris Robertson	.50	.20	.05
☐ 15	Don Laurin	.50	.20	.05
☐ 16	Curtis Folkett	.50	.20	.05
☐ 17	Team Photo (With Mascots and Police)	1.25	.50	.12
☐ 18	Kelly McCrimmon ACO	.50	.20	.05
☐ 19	Doug Sauter CO	.50	.20	.05
☐ 20	Kelly Hitchins	.50	.20	.05
☐ 21	Trevor Kidd	4.00	1.60	.40
☐ 22	Pryce Wood	.50	.20	.05
☐ 23	Cam Brown	.50	.20	.05
☐ 24	Greg Hutchings	1.00	.40	.10

1989-90 Brandon Wheat Kings

This 24-card P.L.A.Y. (Police, Laws and Youth) set measures approximately 2 1/4" by 4". The fronts display color posed action photos inside of yellowish-orange borders. The player's name is printed in black across the bottom of the picture. In addition to sponsor logos, the backs carry "P.L.A.Y. Tips from the Kings" in the form of safety messages. The cards are numbered on the back.

		MINT	EXC	G-VG
COMPLETE SET (24)		12.50	5.00	1.25
COMMON PLAYER (1-24)		.50	.20	.05
☐ 1	Trevor Kidd	3.00	1.20	.30
☐ 2	Troy Frederick	.50	.20	.05
☐ 3	Kelly Thiessen	.75	.30	.07
☐ 4	Pryce Wood	.50	.20	.05

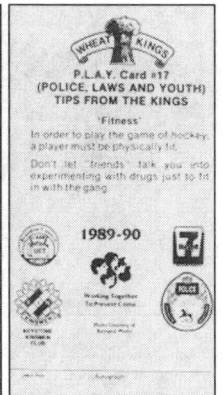

		MINT	EXC	G-VG
☐ 5	Mike Vandenberghe	.75	.30	.07
☐ 6	Chris Constant	.50	.20	.05
☐ 7	Hardy Sauter	.50	.20	.05
☐ 8	Cam Brown	.50	.20	.05
☐ 9	Bart Cote	.50	.20	.05
☐ 10	Jeff Hoad	.50	.20	.05
☐ 11	Kevin Robertson	.50	.20	.05
☐ 12	Dwayne Newman	.50	.20	.05
☐ 13	Calvin Flint	.50	.20	.05
☐ 14	Glen Webster	.50	.20	.05
☐ 15	Greg Hutchings	.75	.30	.07
☐ 16	Rob Puchniak	.50	.20	.05
☐ 17	Gary Audette	.75	.30	.07
☐ 18	Kevin Schmalz	.50	.20	.05
☐ 19	Dwayne Gylywoychuk	.50	.20	.05
☐ 20	Jeff Odgers	1.00	.40	.10
☐ 21	Brian Purdy	.50	.20	.05
☐ 22	Merv Priest	.50	.20	.05
☐ 23	Doug Sauter CO	.50	.20	.05
☐ 24	Team Photo with	1.00	.40	.10
	Safety Mascots			

1992-93 Brandon Wheat Kings

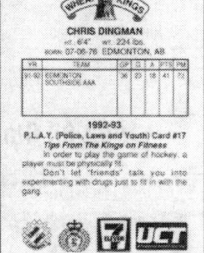

These 24 standard-size (2 1/2" by 3 1/2") cards feature color player action shots on their fronts. Each picture is trimmed in white and has its corners blacked out, giving the impression of a mounted photograph. The player's uniform number and position are printed at the bottom, within the light mustard-colored border surrounding the picture. The player's name in white lettering appears near the bottom within an elongated mottled-green capsule. The white back carries the Wheat Kings name and logo at the top, with the player's name and biography just beneath, followed by a stat table, year of issue (1992-93), and P.L.A.Y. safety tips. The logos for the Brandon City Police, 7-Eleven stores, and the

U.C.T. and Kinsmen organizations finish the card. The cards are unnumbered and checklisted below in alphabetical order.

		MINT	EXC	G-VG
	COMPLETE SET (24)	12.00	5.00	1.20
	COMMON PLAYER (1-24)	.50	.20	.05
☐ 1	Aris Brimanis	.75	.30	.07
☐ 2	Colin Cloutier	1.00	.40	.10
☐ 3	Chris Dingman	.75	.30	.07
☐ 4	Mike Dubinsky	.50	.20	.05
☐ 5	Todd Dutiaume	.50	.20	.05
☐ 6	Mark Franks	.50	.20	.05
☐ 7	Craig Geekie	.50	.20	.05
☐ 8	Dwayne Gylywoychuk	.50	.20	.05
☐ 9	Scott Hlady	.50	.20	.05
☐ 10	Jeff Hoad	.50	.20	.05
☐ 11	Bobby House	.75	.30	.07
☐ 12	Chris Johnston	.50	.20	.05
☐ 13	Mark Kolesar	.50	.20	.05
☐ 14	Scott Laluk	.50	.20	.05
☐ 15	Mike Maneluk	.75	.30	.07
☐ 16	Sean McFatridge	.50	.20	.05
☐ 17	Marty Murray	1.00	.40	.10
☐ 18	Byron Penstock	.50	.20	.05
☐ 19	Darren Ritchie	.50	.20	.05
☐ 20	Trevor Robins	.50	.20	.05
☐ 21	Ryan Smith	1.50	.60	.15
☐ 22	Jeff Staples	.50	.20	.05
☐ 23	Darcy Werenka	1.00	.40	.10
☐ 24	Willie (Mascot)	.50	.20	.05

1987-88 Brockville Braves

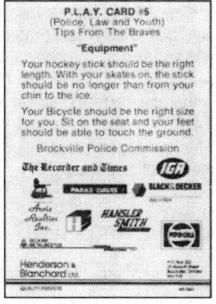

This 25-card set is printed on thin card stock, measures 2 5/8" by 3 5/8", and features posed color player photos with red studio backgrounds. The pictures are set on a white card face and show the player's name, position, and season in the white margin below the photo. The backs are white and carry public service messages in the form of P.L.A.Y. (Police, Law, and Youth) Tips From The Braves. Sponsor logos are shown on the back. The cards are numbered on the back.

		MINT	EXC	G-VG
	COMPLETE SET (25)	12.50	5.00	1.25
	COMMON PLAYER (1-25)	.75	.30	.07
☐ 1	Title Card	1.25	.50	.12
☐ 2	Steve Harper TR	.75	.30	.07
☐ 3	Peter Kelly TR	.75	.30	.07
☐ 4	Mac MacLean CO/MG	.75	.30	.07
☐ 5	Mike McCourt	.75	.30	.07
☐ 6	Paul MacLean	1.00	.40	.10
☐ 7	Mark Michaud	.75	.30	.07
☐ 8	Alain Marchessault	.75	.30	.07
☐ 9	Tom Roman	.75	.30	.07
☐ 10	Darren Burns	.75	.30	.07
☐ 11	Scott Halpenny	.75	.30	.07
☐ 12	Ray Gallagher	.75	.30	.07
☐ 13	Bob Lindsay	.75	.30	.07
☐ 14	Brett Harkins	1.50	.60	.15
☐ 15	Dave Hyrsky	.75	.30	.07
☐ 16	Richard Marchessault	.75	.30	.07

			MINT	EXC	G-VG
☐ 17	Scott Boston		.75	.30	.07
☐ 18	Steve Hogg		.75	.30	.07
☐ 19	Chris Webster		.75	.30	.07
☐ 20	Stuart Birnie		.75	.30	.07
☐ 21	Brett Dunk		.75	.30	.07
☐ 22	Charles Cusson		.75	.30	.07
☐ 23	Pat Gooley		.75	.30	.07
☐ 24	Andy Rodman		.75	.30	.07
☐ 25	Peter Radlein		.75	.30	.07

1988-89 Brockville Braves

This 25-card set is printed on thin card stock, measures 2 5/8" by 3 5/8", and features posed color player photos with pale blue studio backgrounds. The pictures are set on a white card face and show the player's name, position, and season in the white margin below the photo. The backs are white and carry public service messages in the form of P.L.A.Y. (Police, Law, and Youth) Tips From The Braves. Sponsor logos are shown on the back. The cards are numbered on the back.

		MINT	EXC	G-VG
COMPLETE SET (25)		12.50	5.00	1.25
COMMON PLAYER (1-25)		.75	.30	.07
☐ 1	Ray Gallagher	.75	.30	.07
☐ 2	Peter Kelly TR	.75	.30	.07
☐ 3	Steve Harper TR	.75	.30	.07
☐ 4	Winston Jones ACO	.75	.30	.07
☐ 5	Mac MacLean CO/GM	.75	.30	.07
☐ 6	Kevin Doherty	.75	.30	.07
☐ 7	Stuart Birnie	.75	.30	.07
☐ 8	Charles Cusson	.75	.30	.07
☐ 9	Paul MacLean	1.00	.40	.10
☐ 10	Bob Lindsay	.75	.30	.07
☐ 11	Darren Burns	.75	.30	.07
☐ 12	Rick Pracey	.75	.30	.07
☐ 13	Mike Malloy	.75	.30	.07
☐ 14	Dave Hyrsky	.75	.30	.07
☐ 15	Rob Percival	.75	.30	.07
☐ 16	Jarrett Eligh	.75	.30	.07
☐ 17	Pat Gooley	.75	.30	.07
☐ 18	Michael Bracco	.75	.30	.07
☐ 19	Ken Crook	.75	.30	.07
☐ 20	Brad Osborne	.75	.30	.07
☐ 21	Todd Reynolds	.75	.30	.07
☐ 22	Mike McCourt	.75	.30	.07
☐ 23	Chris Webster	.75	.30	.07
☐ 24	Kevin Lune	.75	.30	.07
☐ 25	Title Card	1.25	.50	.12

1991-92 Cincinnati Cyclones

The 1991-92 Cincinnati Cyclones of the East Coast Hockey League are represented in this 25-card set, which was sponsored by Cincinnati Bell Telephone and 19XIX Fox. The cards measure 2 3/8" by 3 1/2" and feature posed color

action shots enclosed by a white border. The team logo and year appear across the top of the card face, with the team name in silver outlined in red. The white front bottom portion of the card carries player information, the 19XIX Fox logo, and the Cincinnati Bell Telephone logo. Horizontally oriented backs carry biography and statistics in a white box surrounded by a gray border. The cards are unnumbered and checklisted below in alphabetical order.

		MINT	EXC	G-VG
COMPLETE SET (25)		10.00	4.00	1.00
COMMON PLAYER (1-25)		.50	.20	.05
☐ 1	Dan Beaudette	.75	.30	.07
☐ 2	Steve Benoit TR	.50	.20	.05
☐ 3	Steve Cadieux	.50	.20	.05
☐ 4	Craig Charron	.50	.20	.05
☐ 5	David Craievich	.75	.30	.07
☐ 6	Doug Dadswell	.75	.30	.07
☐ 7	Dennis Desrosiers CO	.50	.20	.05
☐ 8	Terry Ficorelli ANN	.50	.20	.05
☐ 9	Jeff Hogden	.50	.20	.05
☐ 10	Kevin Kerr	.50	.20	.05
☐ 11	Jaan Luik	.50	.20	.05
☐ 12	Scott Luik	.50	.20	.05
☐ 13	Chris Marshall	.50	.20	.05
☐ 14	Daryn McBride	.50	.20	.05
☐ 15	Doug Melnyk	.50	.20	.05
☐ 16	David Moore	.50	.20	.05
☐ 17	Tom Neziol	.50	.20	.05
☐ 18	Mark Romaine	.50	.20	.05
☐ 19	Jay Rose	.50	.20	.05
☐ 20	Martin St. Amour	.50	.20	.05
☐ 21	Kevin Scott	.50	.20	.05
☐ 22	Peter Schure	.50	.20	.05
☐ 23	Steve Shaunessy	.50	.20	.05
☐ 24	Blaine Stoughton CO	1.00	.40	.10
☐ 25	Bobby Wallwork	.75	.30	.07

1992-93 Clarkson Knights

 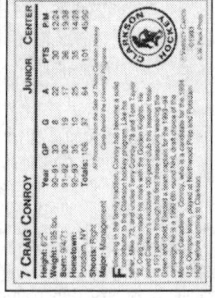

Issued in 1993 at the end of the hockey season, this 24-card set features the Clarkson Knights of the ECAC (Eastern Collegiate Athletic Conference). The cards measure the standard size (2 1/2" by 3 1/2") and feature on-ice player action and posed photos on the fronts. The pictures are on a white card face with the Clarkson hockey logo and name at the top and the player's name and position at the bottom. The horizontal backs carry biography, statistics for the '91-'92 and '92-'93 seasons, and career summary. The Clarkson hockey logo appears in the lower right. The cards are unnumbered and checklisted below in alphabetical order.

	MINT	EXC	G-VG
COMPLETE SET (24)	10.00	4.00	1.00
COMMON PLAYER (1-24)	.50	.20	.05
☐ 1 Josh Bartell	.50	.20	.05
☐ 2 Hugo Belanger	.75	.30	.07
☐ 3 Craig Conroy	.50	.20	.05
☐ 4 Jason Currie	.50	.20	.05
☐ 5 Steve Dubinsky	.75	.30	.07
☐ 6 Shawn Fotheringham	.50	.20	.05
☐ 7 Dave Green	.50	.20	.05
☐ 8 Ed Henrich	.50	.20	.05
☐ 9 Chris Lipsett	.50	.20	.05
☐ 10 Todd Marchant	2.00	.80	.20
☐ 11 Brian Mueller	1.00	.40	.10
☐ 12 Kevin Murphy	.50	.20	.05
☐ 13 Martin d'Orsonnens	.75	.30	.07
☐ 14 Steve Palmer	.50	.20	.05
☐ 15 Patrice Robitaille	.50	.20	.05
☐ 16 Chris Rogles	.75	.30	.07
☐ 17 Jerry Rosenheck	.50	.20	.05
☐ 18 Chris de Ruiter	.50	.20	.05
☐ 19 Guy Sanderson	.50	.20	.05
☐ 20 David Seitz	.50	.20	.05
☐ 21 Mikko Tavi	.50	.20	.05
☐ 22 Patrick Theriault	.50	.20	.05
☐ 23 Marko Tuomainen	1.00	.40	.10
☐ 24 Men's Hockey 1992-93	.75	.30	.07
Martin d'Orsonnens			
Steve Dubinsky			

1960-61 Cleveland Barons

This 19-card set of oversized cards measures approximately 6 3/4" by 5 3/8". The set commemorates the Cleveland Barons 1959-60 season which ended with the team in fourth place after elimination in the Calder Cup Playoffs. The white-bordered fronts display action, black-and-white player photos. A facsimile autograph is printed near the bottom of the photo on all the cards except the team photo card. The backs are blank. Since the cards are unnumbered, they are checklisted below alphabetically.

	NRMT	VG-E	GOOD
COMPLETE SET (19)	100.00	40.00	10.00
COMMON PLAYER (1-19)	5.00	2.00	.50
☐ 1 Ron Attwell	5.00	2.00	.50
☐ 2 Les Binkley	10.00	4.00	1.00
☐ 3 Bill Dineen	7.50	3.00	.75
☐ 4 John Ferguson	10.00	4.00	1.00
☐ 5 Cal Gardner	6.00	2.40	.60
☐ 6 Fred Glover	6.00	2.40	.60
☐ 7 Jack Gordon	6.00	2.40	.60

☐ 8 Aldo Guidolin	6.00	2.40	.60
☐ 9 Greg Hicks	5.00	2.00	.50
☐ 10 Wayne Larkin	5.00	2.00	.50
☐ 11 Moe Mantha	6.00	2.40	.60
☐ 12 Gil Mayer	5.00	2.00	.50
☐ 13 Eddie Mazur	5.00	2.00	.50
☐ 14 Jim Mikol	5.00	2.00	.50
☐ 15 Bill Needham	5.00	2.00	.50
☐ 16 Cal Stearns	5.00	2.00	.50
☐ 17 Bill Sutherland	5.00	2.00	.50
☐ 18 Tom Williams	7.50	3.00	.75
☐ 19 Team Photo	7.50	3.00	.75

1992-93 Cleveland Lumberjacks

Issued to commemorate the Lumberjacks' first season in Cleveland, these 25 cards feature on their fronts red-trimmed and white-bordered color player action shots and measure 2 3/8" by 3 1/2". The player's name, uniform number and position appear beneath the photo in the lower white margin. The team logo and season are displayed in the margin above the photo. The logos for the two sponsors, WKNR radio and Rusterminator, rest at the bottom. The horizontal backs display the player's name, uniform number, position, biography and stats within the central white rectangle. In the wide gray border, the logos for the team and the sponsors round out the card. The cards are numbered on the back.

	MINT	EXC	G-VG
COMPLETE SET (25)	10.00	4.00	1.00
COMMON PLAYER (1-25)	.50	.20	.05
☐ 1 Title Card	.75	.30	.07
☐ 2 Larry Gordon GM	.50	.20	.05
☐ 3 Paul Laus	.75	.30	.07
☐ 4 Travis Thiessen	.50	.20	.05
☐ 5 Phil Russell CO	.75	.30	.07
☐ 6 Gilbert Delorme CO	.50	.20	.05
☐ 7 Jamie Heward	.50	.20	.05
☐ 8 Greg Andrusak	.50	.20	.05
☐ 9 David Quinn	.60	.24	.06
☐ 10 Perry Ganchar	.50	.20	.05
☐ 11 George Zajankala UER	.50	.20	.05
(Birthplace misspelled			
Revelstroke on back)			
☐ 12 Todd Nelson	.60	.24	.06
☐ 13 Dave Michayluk	1.00	.40	.10
☐ 14 Bruce Racine	.75	.30	.07
☐ 15 Rob Dopson	.75	.30	.07
☐ 16 Bert Godin TR	.50	.20	.05
☐ 17 Ed Patterson	1.00	.40	.10
☐ 18 Justin Duberman	1.00	.40	.10
☐ 19 Sandy Smith	.50	.20	.05
☐ 20 Jason Smart	.75	.30	.07
☐ 21 Ken Priestlay	.75	.30	.07
☐ 22 Daniel Gauthier	.50	.20	.05
☐ 23 Robert Melanson	.50	.20	.05
☐ 24 Mark Major	.50	.20	.05
☐ 25 Paul Dyck	.60	.24	.06

1993-94 Cleveland Lumberjacks

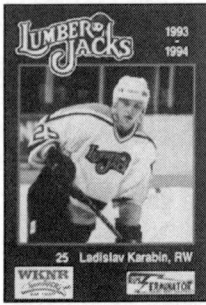 

 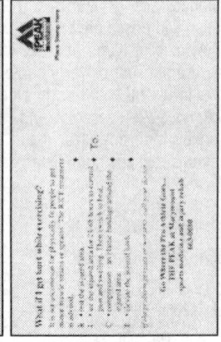

These 24 black-bordered cards feature the 1993-94 Cleveland Lumberjacks of the IHL (International Hockey League). The cards measure approximately 2 3/8" by 3 1/2" and display on their fronts color player action shots framed by red lines. The player's name, uniform number, and position are shown in white lettering in the black margin below the photo. The logos for sponsors WKNR SportsRadio and RusTerminator Electronic Rust Control rest at the bottom. The gray and white horizontal back carries the player's uniform number, name, position, biography, and statistics. The cards are numbered on the back.

		MINT	FXC	G-VG
	COMPLETE SET (24)	10.00	4.00	1.00
	COMMON PLAYER (1-24)	.50	.20	.05
☐ 1	Title Card	.75	.30	.07
☐ 2	Rick Paterson CO	.50	.20	.05
☐ 3	Gilbert Delorme ACO	.50	.20	.05
☐ 4	Paul Dyck	.50	.20	.05
☐ 5	Travis Thiessen	.50	.20	.05
☐ 6	Mike Dagenais	.50	.20	.05
☐ 7	Chris Tamer	.75	.30	.07
☐ 8	Greg Andrusak	.50	.20	.05
☐ 9	Todd Hawkins	.50	.20	.05
☐ 10	Jamie Black	1.00	.40	.10
☐ 11	Justin Duberman	1.00	.40	.10
☐ 13	Jock Callander UER (Misspelled Jack on front)	.75	.30	.07
☐ 14	Leonid Toropchenko	.75	.30	.07
☐ 15	Victor Gervais	.50	.20	.05
☐ 16	Perry Ganchar	.50	.20	.05
☐ 17	Ed Patterson	1.00	.40	.10
☐ 18	Ladislav Karabin	1.00	.40	.10
☐ 19	Dave Michayluk	.75	.30	.07
☐ 20	Jamie Heward	.50	.20	.05
☐ 21	Pat Neaton	1.00	.40	.10
☐ 22	Rob Dopson	.75	.30	.07
☐ 23	Steve Bancroft	.50	.20	.05
☐ 24	Olie Sundstrom	.50	.20	.05

1993-94 Cleveland Lumberjacks Postcards

These 21 black-bordered cards feature the 1993-94 Cleveland Lumberjacks of the IHL (International Hockey League). The cards measure approximately 3 1/2" by 5 1/2" and display on their fronts color player action shots. The player's name, uniform number, position, and biography are shown in yellow lettering within a black rectangle beneath the picture. Sponsor logos for WMMS Radio and The Peak (a sports

medicine and injury rehab facility) also appear on the front. The white horizontal back carries a tip on how to treat a minor muscle sprain. The cards are unnumbered and checklisted below in alphabetical order.

		MINT	EXC	G-VG
	COMPLETE SET (21)	10.00	4.00	1.00
	COMMON PLAYER (1-21)	.50	.20	.05
☐ 1	Greg Andrusak	.50	.20	.05
☐ 2	Steve Bancroft	.50	.20	.05
☐ 3	Jamie Black	1.00	.40	.10
☐ 4	Jock Callander	.75	.30	.07
☐ 5	Mike Dagenais	.50	.20	.05
☐ 6	Gilbert Delorme ACO	.75	.30	.07
☐ 7	Rob Dopson	.75	.30	.07
☐ 8	Justin Duberman	1.00	.40	.10
☐ 9	Paul Dyck	.50	.20	.05
☐ 10	Perry Ganchar	.50	.20	.05
☐ 11	Todd Hawkins	.50	.20	.05
☐ 12	Jamie Heward	.50	.20	.05
☐ 13	Ladislav Karabin	1.00	.40	.10
☐ 14	Dave Michayluk	.75	.30	.07
☐ 15	Pat Neaton	1.00	.40	.10
☐ 16	Rick Paterson CO	.50	.20	.05
☐ 17	Ed Patterson	1.00	.40	.10
☐ 18	Olie Sundstrom	.50	.20	.05
☐ 19	Chris Tamer	.75	.30	.07
☐ 20	Travis Thiessen	.50	.20	.05
☐ 21	Leonid Toropchenko	.75	.30	.07

1992-93 Dallas Freeze

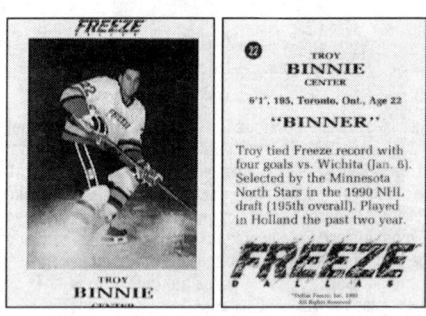

This 20-card set features the Dallas Freeze of the Central Hockey League. White-bordered color player photos adorn the fronts of these standard-size (2 1/2" by 3 1/2") cards. The Freeze logo appears on both sides of the card. In the border beneath the photo are the player's name and position. The jersey number on the card back appears in white in a black circle at the top left. Brief biographical information and career summary fill out the back. The cards are unnumbered and checklisted below in alphabetical order.

	MINT	EXC	G-VG
COMPLETE SET (20)	9.00	3.75	.90
COMMON PLAYER (1-20)	.50	.20	.05
☐ 1 Wayne Anchikoski	.75	.30	.07
☐ 2 Gary Audette	.75	.30	.07
☐ 3 Jeff Beaudin	.50	.20	.05
☐ 4 Troy Binnie	.50	.20	.05
☐ 5 Brian Bruininks	.50	.20	.05
☐ 6 Derek Crawford	.50	.20	.05
☐ 7 Dave Doucette	.75	.30	.07
☐ 8 Don Dwyer	.50	.20	.05
☐ 9 Joe Eagan	.50	.20	.05
☐ 10 Ron Flockhart CO	.75	.30	.07
☐ 11 Frank Lascala	.50	.20	.05
☐ 12 Robert Lewis	.50	.20	.05
☐ 13 Joey Mittelsteadt	.50	.20	.05
☐ 14 Rico Rossi	.50	.20	.05
☐ 15 Dean Shmyr	.50	.20	.05
☐ 16 Doug Sinclair	.50	.20	.05
☐ 17 Greg Smith	.50	.20	.05
☐ 18 Jason Taylor	.50	.20	.05
☐ 19 Mike Zanier	1.00	.40	.10
☐ 20 Team Photo	.75	.30	.07

1993-94 Detroit Jr. Red Wings

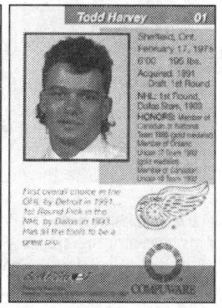

Sponsored by Compuware and printed by Slapshot Images Ltd., this standard size (2 1/2" by 3 1/2") 26-card set features the 1993-94 Detroit Jr. Red Wings. On a geometrical red and white background, the fronts feature color action player photos with thin black borders. The player's name, position and team name, as well as the producer's logo, appear on the front. The backs carry a close-up color player portrait, and biographical information, along with team and sponsor's logos. The cards are numbered on the back. Included in this set is a Slapshot ad card with a 1994 calendar on the back.

	MINT	EXC	G-VG
COMPLETE SET (26)	10.00	4.00	1.00
COMMON PLAYER (1-25)	.35	.14	.03
☐ 1 Todd Harvey	2.00	.80	.20
☐ 2 Jason Saal	.50	.20	.05
☐ 3 Aaron Ellis	.50	.20	.05
☐ 4 Chris Mailloux	.35	.14	.03
☐ 5 Robin Lacour	.35	.14	.03
☐ 6 Mike Rucinski	.35	.14	.03
☐ 7 Eric Cairns	.50	.20	.05
☐ 8 Matt Ball	.35	.14	.03
☐ 9 Dale Junkin	.35	.14	.03
☐ 10 Bill McCauley	.50	.20	.05
☐ 11 Jeremy Meehan	.35	.14	.03
☐ 12 Mike Harding	.35	.14	.03
☐ 13 Brad Cook	.35	.14	.03
☐ 14 Jeff Mitchell	.50	.20	.05
☐ 15 Jamie Allison	.75	.30	.07
☐ 16 Dan Pawlaczyk	.35	.14	.03
☐ 17 Kevin Brown	.75	.30	.07
☐ 18 Duane Harmer	.35	.14	.03

☐ 19 Gerry Skrypec	.35	.14	.03
☐ 20 Shayne McCosh	.50	.20	.05
☐ 21 Sean Haggerty	.75	.30	.07
☐ 22 Nic Beaudoin	.35	.14	.03
☐ 23 Paul Maurice CO	.35	.14	.03
☐ 24 Pete DeBoer ACO	.35	.14	.03
☐ 25 Bob Wren	.75	.30	.07
☐ NNO Ad Card	.35	.14	.03

1993-94 Drummondville Voltigeurs

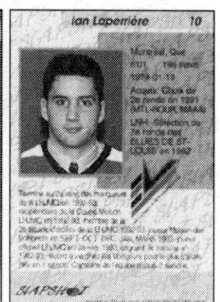

Printed by Slapshot Images Ltd., this standard size (2 1/2" by 3 1/2") 28-card set features the 1993-94 Les Voltigeurs de Drummondville. On a geometrical purple and green background, the fronts feature color action player photos with thin grey borders. The player's name, position and team name, as well as the producer's logo, appear on the front. The backs carry a close-up color player portrait, and biographical information in French only, along with team logo. The cards are numbered on the back. Included in this set is a Slapshot ad card with a 1994 calendar on the back.

	MINT	EXC	G-VG
COMPLETE SET (28)	8.00	3.25	.80
COMMON PLAYER (1-28)	.35	.14	.03
☐ 1 Title Card	.35	.14	.03
Checklist			
☐ 2 Stephane Routhier	.35	.14	.03
☐ 3 Yannick Gagnon	.35	.14	.03
☐ 4 Sebastien Bety	.35	.14	.03
☐ 5 Martin Latulippe	.35	.14	.03
☐ 6 Nicolas Savage	.35	.14	.03
☐ 7 Sylvain Ducharme	.35	.14	.03
☐ 8 Yan St. Pierre	.35	.14	.03
☐ 9 Emmanuel Labranche	.35	.14	.03
☐ 10 Ian Laperriere	1.00	.40	.10
☐ 11 Louis Bernard	.35	.14	.03
☐ 12 Stephane St. Amour	.50	.20	.05
☐ 13 Vincent Tremblay	.35	.14	.03
☐ 14 Denis Gauthier Jr.	.35	.14	.03
☐ 15 Eric Plante	.75	.30	.07
☐ 16 Christian Marcoux	.35	.14	.03
☐ 17 Patrice Charbonneau	.50	.20	.05
☐ 18 Raymond Delarosbil	.35	.14	.03
☐ 19 Patrick Livernoche	.35	.14	.03
☐ 20 Luc Decelles	.35	.14	.03
☐ 21 Francois Sasseville	.35	.14	.03
☐ 22 Steve Tardif	.50	.20	.05
☐ 23 Mathieu Sunderland	.35	.14	.03
☐ 24 Alexandre Duchesne	.50	.20	.05
☐ 25 Jean Hamel CO GM	.35	.14	.03
☐ 26 Mario Carrier ACO	.35	.14	.03
☐ 27 Me Andre Lepage TR	.35	.14	.03
☐ 0 <NNO Ad Card>	.35	.14	.03

1991-92 Ferris State Bulldogs

This 30-card standard-size (2 1/2" by 3 1/2") set features the 1991-92 Ferris State Bulldogs. The cards were available in the Ferris State University Pro Shop at the arena. The cards are unnumbered and checklisted below in alphabetical order.

	MINT	EXC	G-VG
COMPLETE SET (30)	8.00	3.25	.80
COMMON PLAYER (1-30)	.35	.14	.03

		MINT	EXC	G-VG
☐ 1	Aaron Asp	.35	.14	.03
☐ 2	Seth Appert	.35	.14	.03
☐ 3	J.J. Bamberger	.35	.14	.03
☐ 4	Kevin Beals ACO	.35	.14	.03
☐ 5	Scot Bell	.35	.14	.03
☐ 6	Brad Burnham	.35	.14	.03
☐ 7	Dan Chaput	.75	.30	.07
☐ 8	Tim Christian	.35	.14	.03
☐ 9	Bob Daniels	.35	.14	.03
☐ 10	Colin Dodunski	.35	.14	.03
☐ 11	Mick Dolan	.35	.14	.03
☐ 12	John Duff	.35	.14	.03
☐ 13	Daryl Filipek	.35	.14	.03
☐ 14	John Gruden	.75	.30	.07
☐ 15	Luke Harvey	.35	.14	.03
☐ 16	Jeff Jestadt	.35	.14	.03
☐ 17	Dave Karpa	.75	.30	.07
☐ 18	Gary Kitching	.35	.14	.03
☐ 19	Mike Kolenda	.35	.14	.03
☐ 20	Craig Lisko	.35	.14	.03
☐ 21	Mike May	.35	.14	.03
☐ 22	Pat Mazzoli	.35	.14	.03
☐ 23	Robb McIntyre	.35	.14	.03
☐ 24	Kevin Moore	.35	.14	.03
☐ 25	Greg Paine	.35	.14	.03
☐ 26	Dwight Parrish	.35	.14	.03
☐ 27	Val Passarelli	.35	.14	.03
☐ 28	Keith Sergott	.35	.14	.03
☐ 29	Doug Smith	.35	.14	.03
☐ 30	The Bulldog (Mascot)	.50	.20	.05

1988-89 Flint Spirits

This 22-card set measures the standard size (2 1/2" by 3 1/2") and features posed color player photos. The pictures are set at an angle on the card with green borders on the top and bottom. The player's name appears in the lower green border, while the team appears above. A thin blue line borders the front. The horizontal backs carry the player's name, biographical information, statistics, and career highlights. The cards are unnumbered and checklisted below in alphabetical order.

	MINT	EXC	G-VG
COMPLETE SET (22)	12.00	5.00	1.20
COMMON PLAYER (1-22)	.60	.24	.06

		MINT	EXC	G-VG
☐ 1	Dean Anderson	.60	.24	.06
☐ 2	Rob Bryden	.60	.24	.06
☐ 3	John Devereaux	.60	.24	.06
☐ 4	Stephane Giguere	.60	.24	.06
☐ 5	Steve Harrison	.60	.24	.06
☐ 6	Yves Heroux	1.00	.40	.10
☐ 7	Mike Hoffman	.60	.24	.06
☐ 8	Peter Horachek	.60	.24	.06
☐ 9	Guy Jacob	.60	.24	.06
☐ 10	Bob Kennedy	.60	.24	.06

		MINT	EXC	G-VG
☐ 11	Gary Kruzich	.60	.24	.06
☐ 12	Lonnie Loach	1.50	.60	.15
☐ 13	Brett MacDonald	.60	.24	.06
☐ 14	Mike MacWilliam	.60	.24	.06
☐ 15	Moe Mansi	.60	.24	.06
☐ 16	Mike Mersch	.60	.24	.06
☐ 17	Michel Mongeau	2.00	.80	.20
☐ 18	Ken Spangler	.60	.24	.06
☐ 19	Three Amigos	1.00	.40	.10
	Steve Harrison			
	Mike Mersch			
	Mike Hoffman			
☐ 20	Mark Vichorek	.60	.24	.06
☐ 21	Troy Vollhoffer	.60	.24	.06
☐ 22	Don Waddell GM	1.00	.40	.10

1992-93 Fort Worth Fire

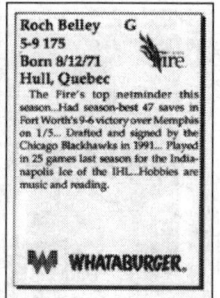

Sponsored by Whataburger, this 18-card set was issued as a cut set and also as a sheet. The sheet was rimmed on the left and right sides by a row coupons redeemable at Whataburger. Card strips featuring three player cards sandwiched between two coupons were also produced. The cards measure the standard size (2 1/2" by 3 1/2") and feature posed, color player photos with either a peach or a white studio background on white card stock. The picture is set off-center on a white area framed by a thin black line and shadow-bordered. The player's name and uniform number are printed above the photo, while "Whataburger" is printed in burnt orange below. The backs carry biographical information and career highlights. The cards are unnumbered and checklisted below in alphabetical order.

	MINT	EXC	G-VG
COMPLETE SET (18)	9.00	3.75	.90
COMMON PLAYER (1-18)	.50	.20	.05

		MINT	EXC	G-VG
☐ 1	Ron Aubrey	.50	.20	.05
☐ 2	Roch Belley	.75	.30	.07
☐ 3	Jason Brousseau	.50	.20	.05
☐ 4	Eric Brule	.50	.20	.05
☐ 5	Todd Drevitch	.50	.20	.05
☐ 6	Trevor Duhaime	.50	.20	.05
☐ 7	Steve Harrison ACO	.50	.20	.05
☐ 8	Ernest Hornak	.50	.20	.05
☐ 9	Alex Kholomeyev	.75	.30	.07
☐ 10	Curt Krolak	.50	.20	.05
☐ 11	Ryan Leschasin	.50	.20	.05
☐ 12	Peter Mahovlich CO	1.50	.60	.15
☐ 13	Mike McCormick	.50	.20	.05
☐ 14	Mike O'Hara	.50	.20	.05
☐ 15	Pat Penner	.50	.20	.05
☐ 16	Paolo Racicot	.50	.20	.05
☐ 17	Dan Rolfe	.50	.20	.05
☐ 18	Mike Sanderson	.50	.20	.05

1981-82 Fredericton Express

This 26-card set was issued by the team and endorsed by the Fredericton City Police, R.C.M.P., New Brunswick

 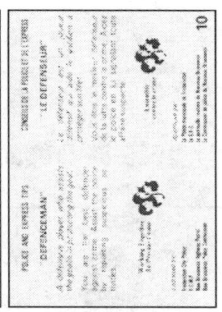

Basil McRae

Clint Malarchuk

Highway Patrol, and New Brunswick Police Commission. The cards measure approximately 2 1/2" by 3 3/4" with a white border on the front. The fronts also carry a posed color player photo with the player's name printed below. The CFNB and Pepsi logos are printed in the lower left and right corners respectively. The horizontal backs are bilingual and carry a brief message relating to the game of hockey and a safety tip or public service announcement. The cards are numbered on the back.

	MINT	EXC	G-VG
COMPLETE SET (26)	25.00	10.00	2.50
COMMON PLAYER (1-26)	.75	.30	.07
☐ 1 Team Photo	2.00	.80	.20
☐ 2 B.J. MacDonald	.75	.30	.07
☐ 3 Sylvain Cote	2.50	1.00	.25
☐ 4 Michel Bolduc	.75	.30	.07
☐ 5 Gary Lupul	.75	.30	.07
☐ 6 Clint Malarchuk	5.00	2.00	.50
☐ 7 Tony Currie	1.50	.60	.15
☐ 8 Tim Tookey	1.50	.60	.15
☐ 9 Anders Eldebrink	.75	.30	.07
☐ 10 Basil McRae	4.00	1.60	.40
☐ 11 Kelly Elcombe	.75	.30	.07
☐ 12 Jacques Demers	5.00	2.00	.50
☐ 13 Frank Caprice	3.00	1.20	.30
☐ 14 Terry Johnson	.75	.30	.07
☐ 15 Grant Martin	.75	.30	.07
☐ 16 Andre Chartrain	.75	.30	.07
☐ 17 Marc Crawford	1.50	.60	.15
☐ 18 Gaston Therrien	.75	.30	.07
☐ 19 Andy Schliebener	1.50	.60	.15
☐ 20 Christian Tanguay	.75	.30	.07
☐ 21 Art Rutland	.75	.30	.07
☐ 22 Jean Marc Gaulin	.75	.30	.07
☐ 23 Neil Belland	.75	.30	.07
☐ 24 Andre Cote	.75	.30	.07
☐ 25 Jim MacRae	.75	.30	.07
☐ 26 Scott Beckingham Marty Flynn	.75	.30	.07

1982-83 Fredericton Express

Sponsored by CFNB and Pepsi, this 26-card set measures approximately 2 1/2" by 3 3/4" and features posed, color player photos with white borders. The player's name and sponsor logos appear in the lower white margin. The horizontal backs carry Police and Express Tips relating to hockey skills and personal safety. The text is presented in both French and English. Sponsors are listed at the bottom. The cards are numbered on the back.

	MINT	EXC	G-VG
COMPLETE SET (26)	20.00	8.00	2.00
COMMON PLAYER (1-26)	.75	.30	.07
☐ 1 Team Photo	2.00	.80	.20
☐ 2 B.J. MacDonald	.75	.30	.07
☐ 3 Sylvain Cote	1.00	.40	.10
☐ 4 Michel Bolduc	.75	.30	.07
☐ 5 Gary Lupul	.75	.30	.07

☐ 6 Clint Malarchuck	4.00	1.60	.40
☐ 7 Tony Currie	.75	.30	.07
☐ 8 Tim Tookey	1.00	.40	.10
☐ 9 Anders Elderbrink	.75	.30	.07
☐ 10 Basil McRae	3.00	1.20	.30
☐ 11 Kelly Elcombe	.75	.30	.07
☐ 12 Jacques Demers	4.00	1.60	.40
☐ 13 Frank Caprice	2.00	.80	.20
☐ 14 Terry Johnson	.75	.30	.07
☐ 15 Grant Martin	.75	.30	.07
☐ 16 Andre Chartrain	.75	.30	.07
☐ 17 Marc Crawford	.75	.30	.07
☐ 18 Gaston Therrien	.75	.30	.07
☐ 19 Andy Schliebener	.75	.30	.07
☐ 20 Christian Tanguay	.75	.30	.07
☐ 21 Art Rutland	.75	.30	.07
☐ 22 Jean-Marc Gaulin	.75	.30	.07
☐ 23 Neil Belland	.75	.30	.07
☐ 24 Andre Cote	.75	.30	.07
☐ 25 Jim MacRae	.75	.30	.07
☐ 26 Scott Beckingham TR and Marty Flynn TR	.75	.30	.07

1983-84 Fredericton Express

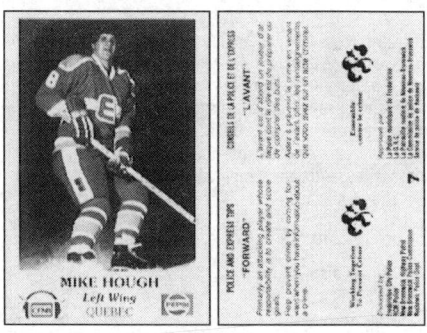

MIKE HOUGH
Left Wing
QUEBEC

This 27-card set measures 2 1/2" by 3 3/4" and features posed action color player photos with white borders. The player's name, position, and NHL affiliation appear below the picture in the white margin. The horizontal backs are white and carry Police and Express Tips in French and English. The cards are numbered on the back.

	MINT	EXC	G-VG
COMPLETE SET (27)	12.50	5.00	1.25
COMMON PLAYER (1-26)	.60	.24	.06
☐ 1 Team Photo	1.50	.60	.15
☐ 2 Frank Caprice	1.00	.40	.10

☐ 3	Michel Dufour	.60	.24	.06
☐ 4	Brian Ford	.60	.24	.06
☐ 5	Jean-Marc Lanthier	.60	.24	.06
☐ 6	Jim Dobson	.60	.24	.06
☐ 7	Mike Hough	1.50	.60	.15
☐ 8	Rick Lapointe	1.00	.40	.10
☐ 9	Michel Bolduc	.60	.24	.06
☐ 10	Christian Tanguay	.60	.24	.06
☐ 11	Tony Currie	.60	.24	.06
☐ 12	Moe Lemay	1.00	.40	.10
☐ 13	Bruce Holloway	.60	.24	.06
☐ 14	Neil Belland	.60	.24	.06
☐ 15	Richard Turmel	.60	.24	.06
☐ 16	Claude Julien	.60	.24	.06
☐ 17	Andre Chartrain	.60	.24	.06
☐ 18	Grant Martin	.60	.24	.06
☐ 19	Rejean Vignola	.60	.24	.06
☐ 20	Andre Cote	.60	.24	.06
☐ 21	Jean-Marc Gaulin	.60	.24	.06
☐ 22	Andy Schliebener	.60	.24	.06
☐ 23	Stu Kulak	1.00	.40	.10
☐ 24	Mike Eagles	1.50	.60	.15
☐ 25	Earl Jessiman CO/GM	.60	.24	.06
☐ 26	Marty Flynn TR	.60	.24	.06
	Scott Beckingham TR			
☐ NNO	Checklist	1.00	.40	.10

☐ 24	Andy Schliebener	.50	.20	.05
☐ 25	Earl Jessiman CO/GM	.50	.20	.05
☐ 26	Yvon Vautour	.50	.20	.05
☐ 27	Craig Coxe	.75	.30	.07
☐ 28	Blake Wesley	.75	.30	.07

1985-86 Fredericton Express

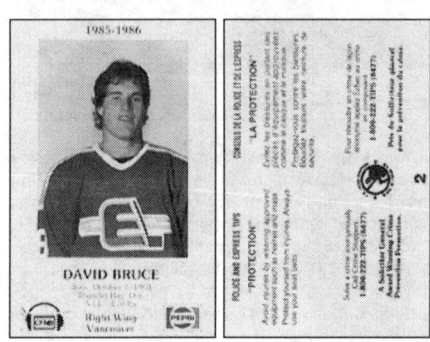

This 28-card set measures 2 1/2" by 3 3/4" and features posed color player photos against a white card face. The player's name, biography, position, and NHL affiliation appear in black print below the picture. Sponsor logos are in the lower corners. The horizontal backs are white and carry Police and Express Tips in French and English. The cards are numbered on the back.

	MINT	EXC	G-VG
COMPLETE SET (28)	10.00	4.00	1.00
COMMON PLAYER (1-28)	.50	.20	.05

☐ 1	Scott Tottle	.75	.30	.07
☐ 2	David Bruce	1.00	.40	.10
☐ 3	Team Photo	1.00	.40	.10
☐ 4	Marc Crawford	.50	.20	.05
☐ 5	Mike Stevens	.75	.30	.07
☐ 6	Gary Lupul	.50	.20	.05
☐ 7	Alain Lemieux	.75	.30	.07
☐ 8	Mike Hough	1.00	.40	.10
☐ 9	Tony Currie	.50	.20	.05
☐ 10	Dunc MacIntyre	.50	.20	.05
☐ 11	Jere Gillis	.50	.20	.05
☐ 12	Wendell Young	1.00	.40	.10
☐ 13	Jean-Marc Lanthier	.50	.20	.05
☐ 14	Ken Quinney	.75	.30	.07
☐ 15	Claude Julien	.50	.20	.05
☐ 16	Michel Petit	.75	.30	.07
☐ 17	Luc Guenette	.50	.20	.05
☐ 18	Andy Schliebener	.50	.20	.05
☐ 19	Mark Kirton	.50	.20	.05
☐ 20	Gord Donnelly	.75	.30	.07
☐ 21	Tom Karalis	.50	.20	.05
☐ 22	Daniel Poudrier	.50	.20	.05
☐ 23	Neil Belland	.50	.20	.05
☐ 24	Dale Dunbar	.50	.20	.05
☐ 25	Marty Flynn TR	.50	.20	.05
	Scott Beckingham TR			
☐ 26	Jean-Marc Gaulin	.50	.20	.05
☐ 27	Al MacAdam	.75	.30	.07
☐ 28	Andre Savard CO/GM	.75	.30	.07

1984-85 Fredericton Express

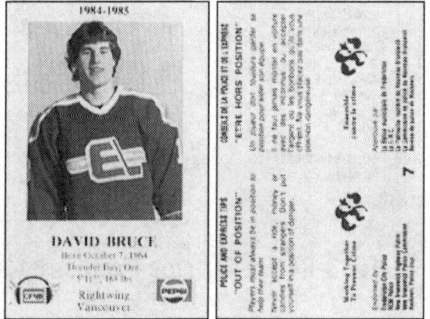

This 28-card set measures approximately 2 1/2" by 3 3/4" and features posed color player photos against a white card face. The player's name, biography, position, and NHL affiliation appear in black print below the picture. Sponsor logos are in the lower corners. The horizontal backs are white and carry Police and Express Tips in French and English. The cards are numbered on the back.

	MINT	EXC	G-VG
COMPLETE SET (28)	10.00	4.00	1.00
COMMON PLAYER (1-28)	.50	.20	.05

☐ 1	Dave Morrison	.75	.30	.07
☐ 2	Dave Shaw	1.00	.40	.10
☐ 3	Bruce Holloway	.50	.20	.05
☐ 4	Roger Haegglund	.50	.20	.05
☐ 5	Neil Belland	.50	.20	.05
☐ 6	Gord Donnelly	1.00	.40	.10
☐ 7	David Bruce	1.00	.40	.10
☐ 8	Claude Julien	.50	.20	.05
☐ 9	Dan Wood	.50	.20	.05
☐ 10	Clint Malarchuk	2.00	.80	.20
☐ 11	Jere Gillis	.75	.30	.07
☐ 12	Mike Hough	1.00	.40	.10
☐ 13	Michel Bolduc	.50	.20	.05
☐ 14	Peter Loob	.50	.20	.05
☐ 15	Steve Driscoll	.50	.20	.05
☐ 16	Newell Brown	.50	.20	.05
☐ 17	Jim Dobson	.50	.20	.05
☐ 18	Wendell Young	1.50	.60	.15
☐ 19	Mark Kumpel	.75	.30	.07
☐ 20	Mike Eagles	1.00	.40	.10
☐ 21	Tom Thornbury	.50	.20	.05
☐ 22	Grant Martin	.50	.20	.05
☐ 23	Marc Crawford	.50	.20	.05

1986-87 Fredericton Express

This 26-card set measures 2 1/2" by 3 3/4" and features posed color player photos against a white card face. The player's name, biography, position, statistics, and NHL

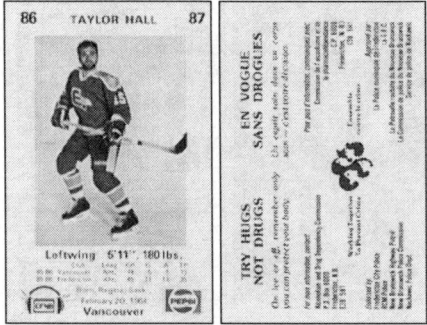

affiliation appear in black print below the picture. Sponsor logos are in the lower corners. The horizontal backs are white and carry public service messages in French and English. The cards are unnumbered and checklisted below in alphabetical order.

	MINT	EXC	G-VG
COMPLETE SET (26)	8.00	3.25	.80
COMMON PLAYER (1-26)	.40	.16	.04
□ 1 Jim Agnew	.75	.30	.07
□ 2 Brian Bertuzzi	.40	.16	.04
□ 3 David Bruce	.75	.30	.07
□ 4 Frank Caprice	.75	.30	.07
□ 5 Marc Crawford	.40	.16	.04
□ 6 Steven Finn	.75	.30	.07
□ 7 Marty Flynn TR	.40	.16	.04
Scott Beckingham TR			
□ 8 Jean-Marc Gaulin	.40	.16	.04
□ 9 Scott Gordon	.40	.16	.04
□ 10 Taylor Hall	.75	.30	.07
□ 11 Yves Heroux	.75	.30	.07
□ 12 Mike Hough	.75	.30	.07
□ 13 Tom Karalis	.40	.16	.04
□ 14 Mark Kirton	.75	.30	.07
□ 15 Jean-Marc Lanthier	.40	.16	.04
□ 16 Jean LeBlanc	.40	.16	.04
□ 17 Brett MacDonald	.40	.16	.04
□ 18 Duncan MacIntyre	.40	.16	.04
□ 19 Greg Malone	.75	.30	.07
□ 20 Terry Perkins	.40	.16	.04
□ 21 Daniel Poudrier	.40	.16	.04
□ 22 Jeff Rohlicek	.40	.16	.04
□ 23 Andre Savard CO	.75	.30	.07
□ 24 Mike Stevens	.40	.16	.04
□ 25 Trevor Stienburg	.40	.16	.04
□ 26 Team Photo	1.00	.40	.10

1992-93 Fredericton Canadiens

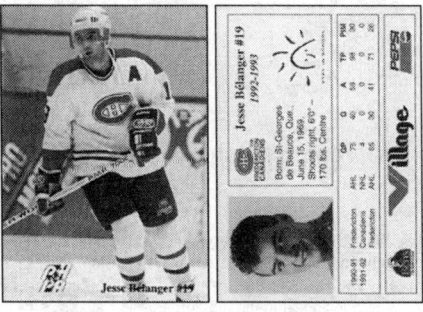

Printed on thin card stock, these 28 standard-size (2 1/2" by 3 1/2") cards feature borderless color player action photos on the fronts. Each has the player's name and uniform

number printed near the bottom and carries the Professional Hockey Player's Association logo. The white horizontal back displays a black-and-white posed player head shot in the upper left. The player's name, uniform number, and biography appear in a rectangle in the upper right, along with the Canadiens and Stay in School logos. A stat table is placed beneath, and the Pepsi, Village, and Ben's logos at the bottom round out the card. The cards are unnumbered and checklisted below in alphabetical order.

	MINT	EXC	G-VG
COMPLETE SET (28)	12.00	5.00	1.20
COMMON PLAYER (1-27)	.50	.20	.05
□ 1 Jesse Belanger	1.50	.60	.15
□ 2 Paulin Bordeleau CO	.50	.20	.05
□ 3 Donald Brashear	.75	.30	.07
□ 4 Patrik Carnback	1.00	.40	.10
□ 5 Eric Charron	.75	.30	.07
□ 6 Frederic Chabot	.75	.30	.07
□ 7 Alain Cote	.75	.30	.07
□ 8 Paul Dipietro	1.50	.60	.15
□ 9 Craig Ferguson	.50	.20	.05
□ 10 Gerry Fleming	.75	.30	.07
□ 11 Luc Gauthier	.50	.20	.05
□ 12 Robert Guillet	.50	.20	.05
□ 13 Patric Kjellberg	.50	.20	.05
□ 14 Les Kuntar	.75	.30	.07
□ 15 Ryan Kuwabara	.50	.20	.05
□ 16 Patrick Langlois TR	.50	.20	.05
□ 17 Steve Larouche	.50	.20	.05
□ 18 Jacques Parent TR	.50	.20	.05
□ 19 Charles Poulin	.50	.20	.05
□ 20 Oleg Petrov	1.50	.60	.15
□ 21 Yves Sarault	.75	.30	.07
□ 22 Pierre Sevigny	1.25	.50	.12
□ 23 Darcy Simon	.50	.20	.05
□ 24 Turner Stevenson	1.25	.50	.12
□ 25 Tricolo (Mascot)	.50	.20	.05
□ 26 Lindsay Vallis	.50	.20	.05
□ 27 Steve Veilleux	.50	.20	.05
□ 28 Title card	.50	.20	.05

1991-92 Greensboro Monarchs

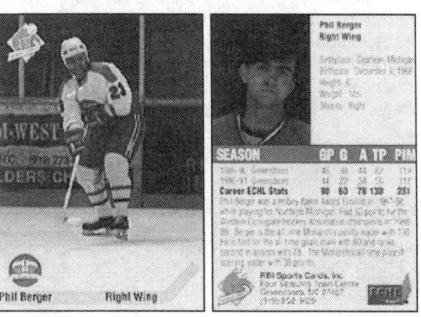

Sponsored by RBI Sports Cards Inc., this 19-card set features the Greensboro Monarchs of the East Coast Hockey League. The cards measure the standard size (2 1/2" by 3 1/2") and feature borderless, posed and action color player photos. The player's name and position appear on a mustard-colored hockey stick design at the bottom. The backs are subdivided by a red stripe and carry a close-up picture with biographical information above the stripe, and statistics and career highlights below it. The cards are unnumbered and checklisted below in alphabetical order.

	MINT	EXC	G-VG
COMPLETE SET (19)	8.00	3.25	.80
COMMON PLAYER (1-19)	.50	.20	.05
□ 1 Rob Bateman	.75	.30	.07
□ 2 Phil Berger	.50	.20	.05

☐ 3	Mike Butters	.50	.20	.05
☐ 4	John Devereaux	.50	.20	.05
☐ 5	Eric Dubois	.50	.20	.05
☐ 6	Todd Gordon	.50	.20	.05
☐ 7	Chris Laganas	.50	.20	.05
☐ 8	Eric LeMarque	.50	.20	.05
☐ 9	Timo Makela	.50	.20	.05
☐ 10	Greg Menges	.50	.20	.05
☐ 11	Daryl Noren	.50	.20	.05
☐ 12	Peter Sentner	.50	.20	.05
☐ 13	Boyd Sutton	.50	.20	.05
☐ 14	Nick Vitucci	.50	.20	.05
☐ 15	Shawn Wheeler	.50	.20	.05
☐ 16	Scott White	.50	.20	.05
☐ 17	Chris Wolanin	.50	.20	.05
☐ 18	Dean Zayonce	.50	.20	.05
☐ 19	Team Photo	1.00	.40	.10
	(Photo of Jeff Brubaker CO on back)			

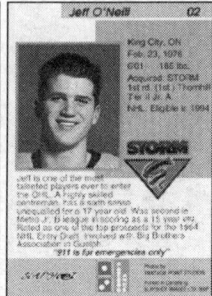

1992-93 Greensboro Monarchs

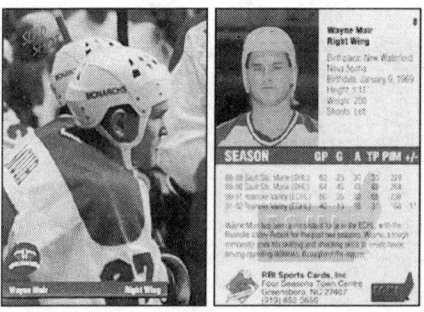

Sponsored by RBI Sports Cards Inc., this 19-card set measures the standard size (2 1/2" by 3 1/2") and features full-bleed, color, action player photos. The player's name and position appear in a blue and red stripe near the bottom. The backs display a close-up picture alongside biographical information. A red stripe below the photo divides the card in half and serves as a heading for statistics. A player profile appears below the statistics. The cards are numbered on the back.

		MINT	EXC	G-VG
COMPLETE SET (19)		8.00	3.25	.80
COMMON PLAYER (1-19)		.50	.20	.05
☐ 1	Team Photo	1.00	.40	.10
☐ 2	Chris Wolanin	.50	.20	.05
☐ 3	Bill Horn	.50	.20	.05
☐ 4	Brock Woods	.50	.20	.05
☐ 5	Phil Berger	.50	.20	.05
☐ 6	Dan Bylsma	.50	.20	.05
☐ 7	Davis Payne	.50	.20	.05
☐ 8	Wayne Muir	.50	.20	.05
☐ 9	Andrei Iakovenko	.50	.20	.05
☐ 10	Roger Larche	.50	.20	.05
☐ 11	Jamie Nicolls	.50	.20	.05
☐ 12	Darryl Noren	.50	.20	.05
☐ 13	Todd Gordon	.50	.20	.05
☐ 14	Claude Maillet	.50	.20	.05
☐ 15	Dave Burke	.50	.20	.05
☐ 16	Jamie Steer	.50	.20	.05
☐ 17	Greg Capson	.50	.20	.05
☐ 18	Chris Lappin	.50	.20	.05
☐ 19	Greg Menges	.75	.30	.07

1993-94 Guelph Storm

Sponsored by Domino's Pizza and printed by Slapshot Images Ltd., this standard size (2 1/2" by 3 1/2") 31-card set

features the 1993-94 Guelph Storm. On a geometrical blue and grey background, the fronts feature color action player photos with thin black borders. The player's name, position and team name, as well as the producer's logo, appear on the front. The backs carry a close-up color player portrait, and biographical information, along with team and sponsor's logos. The cards are numbered on the back. Included in this set is a Slapshot ad card with a 1994 calendar on the back.

		MINT	EXC	G-VG
COMPLETE SET (31)		10.00	4.00	1.00
COMMON PLAYER (1-31)		.35	.14	.03
☐ 1	Title Card	.35	.14	.03
☐ 2	Jeff O'Neill	2.50	1.00	.25
☐ 3	Mark McArthur	.50	.20	.05
☐ 4	Kayle Short	.35	.14	.03
☐ 5	Ryan Risidore	.50	.20	.05
☐ 6	Mike Rusk	.50	.20	.05
☐ 7	Regan Stocco	.35	.14	.03
☐ 8	Duane Harmer	.35	.14	.03
☐ 9	Sylvain Cloutier	1.00	.40	.10
☐ 10	Eric Landry	.50	.20	.05
☐ 11	Jamie Wright	.50	.20	.05
☐ 12	Todd Norman	.35	.14	.03
☐ 13	Mike Pittman	.35	.14	.03
☐ 14	Ken Belanger	.35	.14	.03
☐ 15	Viktor Reuta	.35	.14	.03
☐ 16	Mike Prokopec	.50	.20	.05
☐ 17	Jeff Williams	.50	.20	.05
☐ 18	Chris Skoryna	.35	.14	.03
☐ 19	Stephane Lefebvre	.35	.14	.03
☐ 20	Jeff Cowan	.35	.14	.03
☐ 21	Murray Hogg	.35	.14	.03
☐ 22	Andy Adams	.35	.14	.03
☐ 23	Todd Bertuzzi	1.25	.50	.12
☐ 24	Grant Pritchett	.35	.14	.03
☐ 25	Rumun Ndur	.75	.30	.07
☐ 26	Jeff O'Neill	1.50	.60	.15
☐ 27	Paul Brydges ACO	.35	.14	.03
☐ 28	John Lovell CO	.35	.14	.03
☐ 29	Team Photo	.50	.20	.05
	Checklist			
☐ 30	Sponsor Card	.35	.14	.03
	Gurinder Saini Domino's Pizza			
☐ NNO	Ad Card	.35	.14	.03

1990-91 Halifax Citadels

This 28-card set measures approximately 2 3/4" by 4 1/4" and features color, posed-action player photos with white borders. The Farmers Co-Operative Dairy Limited and the 92/CJCH logo appear in the top border. The player's name is printed on a red ribbon that intersects a red star design. The star contains the player's jersey number. The backs display the player's name, biographical information, and "Sports Tips That Make Our Communities Safe." The cards are unnumbered and checklisted below in alphabetical order.

	NRMT	VG-E	GOOD
COMPLETE SET (18).........................	20.00	8.00	2.00
COMMON PLAYER (1-18)................	1.00	.40	.10
☐ 1 Jack Anderson	1.00	.40	.10
☐ 2 Mike Clarke	1.00	.40	.10
☐ 3 Greg Clause............................	1.00	.40	.10
☐ 4 Joe Contini.............................	1.00	.40	.10
☐ 5 Mike Fedorko	1.00	.40	.10
☐ 6 Paul Foley	1.00	.40	.10
☐ 7 Greg Hickey............................	1.00	.40	.10
☐ 8 Tony Horvath	1.00	.40	.10
☐ 9 Mike Keating	1.00	.40	.10
☐ 10 Archie King	1.00	.40	.10
☐ 11 Ted Long..............................	1.00	.40	.10
☐ 12 Dale McCourt........................	5.00	2.00	.50
☐ 13 Dave Norris...........................	1.00	.40	.10
☐ 14 Greg Redquest	1.00	.40	.10
☐ 15 Glen Richardson	1.00	.40	.10
☐ 16 Ron Roscoe	1.00	.40	.10
☐ 17 Ric Seiling............................	2.00	.80	.20
☐ 18 Danny Shearer	1.00	.40	.10

	MINT	EXC	G-VG
COMPLETE SET (28)........................	12.00	5.00	1.20
COMMON PLAYER (1-28)................	.50	.20	.05
☐ 1 Jamie Baker	.75	.30	.07
☐ 2 Mike Bishop	.50	.20	.05
☐ 3 Gerald Bzdel	.50	.20	.05
☐ 4 Daniel Dore	.50	.20	.05
☐ 5 Mario Doyon	.50	.20	.05
☐ 6 Dave Espe	.50	.20	.05
☐ 7 Stephane Fiset........................	2.00	.80	.20
☐ 8 Scott Gordon..........................	.75	.30	.07
☐ 9 Stephane Guerard	.75	.30	.07
☐ 10 Dean Hopkins ACO...............	.50	.20	.05
☐ 11 Miroslav Ihnacak...................	.75	.30	.07
☐ 12 Jeff Jackson	.75	.30	.07
☐ 13 Clement Jodoin CO/MG........	.50	.20	.05
☐ 14 Claude Lapointe	1.00	.40	.10
☐ 15 Dave Latta	.50	.20	.05
☐ 16 Chris McQuaid EQ MG	.50	.20	.05
☐ 17 Kip Miller.............................	.75	.30	.07
☐ 18 Stephane Morin......................	1.00	.40	.10
☐ 19 Ken Quinney.........................	.50	.20	.05
☐ 20 Jean-Marc Richard.................	.50	.20	.05
☐ 21 Serge Roberge	.50	.20	.05
☐ 22 Jaroslav Sevcik	.50	.20	.05
☐ 23 Brent Severyn	.75	.30	.07
☐ 24 Mike Shuman TR	.50	.20	.05
☐ 25 Greg Smyth..........................	.50	.20	.05
☐ 26 Jim Sprott............................	.50	.20	.05
☐ 27 Trevor Stienburg	.50	.20	.05
☐ 28 Mark Vermette	.50	.20	.05

1975-76 Hamilton Fincups

This 18-card set measures the standard size (2 1/2" by 3 1/2") and features sepia-tone player portraits. The player's name and position are printed in the lower border, which is also sepia-tone. The team name is superimposed over the picture at the bottom center. The backs are blank and grayish in color. The cards are unnumbered and checklisted below in alphabetical order.

1992-93 Hamilton Canucks

Created by Diamond Memories Sportscards to commemorate the Canucks' inaugural season, these 30 standard-size (2 1/2" by 3 1/2") cards feature black-bordered color player action photos on the fronts. The photos are offset toward the lower right, with the player's name and position in white lettering placed vertically on the left side, and the team name at the top, with "Hamilton" in white lettering and "Canucks" in yellow and red. The player's uniform number appears in black within a white-trimmed band that grades from yellow to red from left to right. The gray-bordered white horizontal back carries the player's name, uniform number, biography, and stat table. The Y95 Radio, Diamond Memories Sportscards, and Hamilton Canucks logos on the bottom round out the card. The cards are unnumbered and checklisted below in alphabetical order.

	MINT	EXC	G-VG
COMPLETE SET (30)........................	15.00	6.00	1.50
COMMON PLAYER (1-30)................	.50	.20	.05
☐ 1 Shawn Antoski	1.00	.40	.10
☐ 2 Robin Bawa............................	.75	.30	.07
☐ 3 Jamie Carlson TR....................	.50	.20	.05
☐ 4 Jassen Cullimore....................	.75	.30	.07
☐ 5 Alain Deeks	.50	.20	.05
☐ 6 Neil Eisenhut	.75	.30	.07
☐ 7 Mike Fountain	1.00	.40	.10
☐ 8 Troy Gamble	1.00	.40	.10
☐ 9 Jason Herter	.50	.20	.05
☐ 10 Pat Hickey PR	.75	.30	.07
☐ 11 Dane Jackson........................	.50	.20	.05
☐ 12 Dan Kesa.............................	.75	.30	.07
☐ 13 Jeff Lumby ANN....................	.50	.20	.05
☐ 14 Mario Marois UER................	.75	.30	.07
(Last name misspelled Marios on front)			
☐ 15 Bob Mason...........................	.75	.30	.07

			MINT	EXC	G-VG
☐	16	Mike Maurice	.50	.20	.05
☐	17	Jay Mazur	.75	.30	.07
☐	18	Jack McIlhargey CO	.50	.20	.05
☐	19	Sandy Moger	.50	.20	.05
☐	20	Stephane Morin	1.00	.40	.10
☐	21	Eric Murano	.75	.30	.07
☐	22	Troy Neumeier	.50	.20	.05
☐	23	Matt Newsom GM	.50	.20	.05
☐	24	Libor Polasek	.50	.20	.05
☐	25	Phil von Stefenelli	.50	.20	.05
☐	26	Doug Torrel	.50	.20	.05
☐	27	Doug Tretiak TR	.50	.20	.05
☐	28	Rick Vaive CO	1.00	.40	.10
☐	29	Opening Night	.75	.30	.07
		Puck-Drop			
		Mario Marois			
		Pat Hickey PR			
		AHL President			
☐	30	Team Photo	1.25	.50	.12
		(Checklist)			

1981-82 Indianapolis Checkers

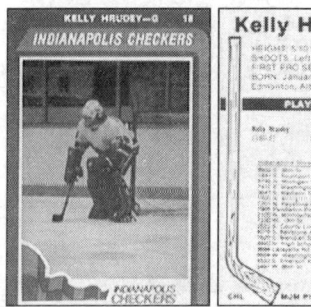
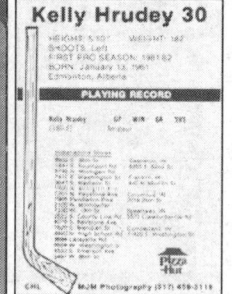

Sponsored by Pizza Hut, this 20-card standard-size (2 1/2"
by 3 1/2") set features the Indianapolis Checkers of the CHL.
The cards were available singly at Pizza Hut restaurants and
Checkers games on alternate weeks. On a blue background,
the fronts have color action player photos with thin white
borders. The team name appears above the photo in an
orange border that extends down the right side. The player's
name, position, and number are printed above the photo. On
a white background, the backs carry player biography,
statistics, and addresses of Indianapolis Pizza Huts. The
cards are unnumbered and checklisted below in alphabetical
order.

			MINT	EXC	G-VG
	COMPLETE SET (20)		30.00	12.00	3.00
	COMMON PLAYER (1-20)		1.50	.60	.15
☐	1	Bruce Andres	1.50	.60	.15
☐	2	Frank Beaton	1.50	.60	.15
☐	3	Kelly Davis	1.50	.60	.15
☐	4	Kevin Devine	1.50	.60	.15
☐	5	Glen Duncan	1.50	.60	.15
☐	6	Mats Hallin	2.50	1.00	.25
☐	7	Neil Hawryliw	1.50	.60	.15
☐	8	Bob Holland	1.50	.60	.15
☐	9	Mike Hordy	1.50	.60	.15
☐	10	Kelly Hrudey	10.00	4.00	1.00
☐	11	Randy Johnston	1.50	.60	.15
☐	12	Red Laurence	1.50	.60	.15
☐	13	Tim Lockridge	1.50	.60	.15
☐	14	Garth MacGuigan	1.50	.60	.15
☐	15	John Marks	2.50	1.00	.25
☐	16	Darcey Regier	1.50	.60	.15
☐	17	Charlie Skjodt	1.50	.60	.15
☐	18	Lorne Stamler	1.50	.60	.15
☐	19	Steve Stoyanovich	1.50	.60	.15
☐	20	Monty Trottier	2.00	.80	.20

1982-83 Indianapolis Checkers

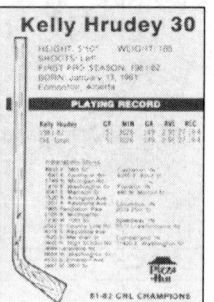

Sponsored by Pizza Hut, this 21-card standard-size (2 1/2"
by 3 1/2") set features the Indianapolis Checkers of the CHL.
The cards were available singly at Pizza Hut restaurants and
Checkers games on alternate weeks. On a red-orange
background, the fronts have color action player photos with
thin white borders. The team name appears above the photo
in an orange border that extends down the right side. The
player's name, position, and number are printed above the
photo. On a white background, the backs carry player
biography, statistics, and addresses of Indianapolis Pizza
Huts. The cards are unnumbered and checklisted below in
alphabetical order.

			MINT	EXC	G-VG
	COMPLETE SET (21)		30.00	12.00	3.00
	COMMON PLAYER (1-21)		1.50	.60	.15
☐	1	Kelly Davis	1.50	.60	.15
☐	2	Kevin Devine	1.50	.60	.15
☐	3	Gord Dineen	2.50	1.00	.25
☐	4	Glen Duncan	1.50	.60	.15
☐	5	Greg Gilbert	3.00	1.20	.30
☐	6	Mike Gredder	1.50	.60	.15
☐	7	Mats Hallin	2.50	1.00	.25
☐	8	Dave Hanson	1.50	.60	.15
☐	9	Rob Holland	1.50	.60	.15
☐	10	Scott Howson	1.50	.60	.15
☐	11	Kelly Hrudey	10.00	4.00	1.00
☐	12	Randy Johnston	1.50	.60	.15
☐	13	Red Laurence	1.50	.60	.15
☐	14	Tim Lockridge	1.50	.60	.15
☐	15	Garth MacGuigan	1.50	.60	.15
☐	16	Darcey Regier	1.50	.60	.15
☐	17	Dan Revell	1.50	.60	.15
☐	18	Dave Simpson	1.50	.60	.15
☐	19	Lorne Stamler	1.50	.60	.15
☐	20	Steve Stoyanovich	1.50	.60	.15
☐	21	Monty Trottier	2.00	.80	.20

1992-93 Indianapolis Ice

This 26-card set measures the standard size (2 1/2" by 3
1/2"). On a light blue background, the fronts feature posed,
color action photos with a thin red border. The team logo
appears on the bottom left side, while the player's number,
name and position appear in black letters on the right side.
The horizontal backs carry biographical and statistical
information. The cards are unnumbered and checklisted
below in alphabetical order.

			MINT	EXC	G-VG
	COMPLETE SET (26)		9.00	3.75	.90
	COMMON PLAYER (1-26)		.35	.14	.03
☐	1	Alexandr Andrievski	.35	.14	.03
☐	2	Steve Bancroft	.35	.14	.03

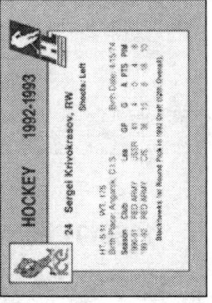

☐ 3 Zac Boyer	.75	.30	.07
☐ 4 Rod Buskas	.50	.20	.05
☐ 5 Shawn Byram	.35	.14	.03
☐ 6 Joe Cleary	.35	.14	.03
☐ 7 Rob Conn	.35	.14	.03
☐ 8 Joe Crowley	.35	.14	.03
☐ 9 Trevor Dam	.35	.14	.03
☐ 10 Ivan Droppa	.75	.30	.07
☐ 11 Tracy Egeland	.35	.14	.03
☐ 12 Dave Hakstol	.35	.14	.03
☐ 13 Kevin Hodson	.50	.20	.05
☐ 14 Tony Horacek	.35	.14	.03
☐ 15 Tony Hrkac	.50	.20	.05
☐ 16 Sergei Krivokrasov	1.25	.50	.12
☐ 17 Brad Lauer	.50	.20	.05
☐ 18 Ray LeBlanc	.75	.30	.07
☐ 19 Owen Lessard	.35	.14	.03
☐ 20 Jim Playfair ACO	.50	.20	.05
John Marks CO			
☐ 21 Kevin St. Jacques	.50	.20	.05
☐ 22 Michael Speer	.50	.20	.05
☐ 23 Milan Tichy	.50	.20	.05
☐ 24 Kerry Toporowski	.50	.20	.05
☐ 25 Sean Williams	.35	.14	.03
☐ 26 Craig Woodcroft	.50	.20	.05

1986-87 Kamloops Blazers

This 24-card sheet was issued in nine four-card sheets. Six of the panels feature two cards and an advertisement, while the other three panels feature four cards per panel. The sheets are perforated vertically but not horizontally, which produces two-card stripes. If cut, the cards would measure the standard size (2 1/2" by 3 1/2"). On a white card face, the fronts display posed action photos inside a bright blue border. The team logo and player information is presented in the wider bottom border. The backs carry "Tips from the Blazers," which consist of pointers about hockey and public service announcements. The cards are unnumbered and checklisted below in alphabetical order.

	MINT	EXC	G-VG
COMPLETE SET (24)	40.00	16.00	4.00
COMMON PLAYER (1-24)	.75	.30	.07
☐ 1 Warren Babe	1.00	.40	.10
☐ 2 Robin Bawa	1.00	.40	.10
☐ 3 Rob Brown	2.50	1.00	.25
☐ 4 Dean Cook	.75	.30	.07
☐ 5 Scott Daniels	.75	.30	.07
☐ 6 Mario Desjardines	.75	.30	.07
☐ 7 Bill Harrington	.75	.30	.07
☐ 8 Greg Hawgood	2.00	.80	.20
☐ 9 Serge Lajoie	.75	.30	.07
☐ 10 Dave Marcinyshyn	1.50	.60	.15
☐ 11 Len Mark	.75	.30	.07
☐ 12 Rob McKinley	.75	.30	.07
☐ 13 Casey McMillan	.75	.30	.07
☐ 14 Darcy Norton	.75	.30	.07
☐ 15 Kelly Para	.75	.30	.07
☐ 16 Doug Pickell	.75	.30	.07
☐ 17 Rudy Poeschek	1.50	.60	.15
☐ 18 Mark Recchi	25.00	10.00	2.50
☐ 19 Don Schmidt	.75	.30	.07
☐ 20 Ron Shudra	.75	.30	.07
☐ 21 Chris Tarnowski	.75	.30	.07
☐ 22 Steve Wienke	.75	.30	.07
☐ 23 Rich Wiest	.75	.30	.07
☐ 24 Team Photo	2.50	1.00	.25

1987-88 Kamloops Blazers

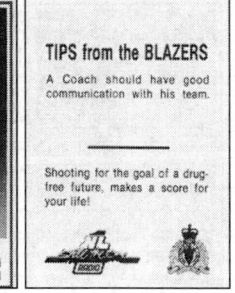

This 24-card set was issued in three-card perforated strips each consisting of two player cards and one advertisement or coupon card. (As listed below, two of these advertisement cards display team logos on the front). The strips measure 7 1/2" by 3 1/2", and if cut, the individual cards would measure 2 1/2" by 3 1/2". The features a color posed-action player photo with thin blue borders on a white card face. The player's name, jersey number, and position appear in the white bottom margin. The team logo overlaps the picture at the lower left. The backs carry Tips from the Blazers consisting of hockey tips and anti-drug messages. The cards are unnumbered and checklisted below in alphabetical order.

	MINT	EXC	G-VG
COMPLETE SET (24)	30.00	12.00	3.00
COMMON PLAYER (1-24)	.60	.24	.06
☐ 1 Warren Babe	.60	.24	.06
☐ 2 Paul Checknita	.60	.24	.06
☐ 3 Dave Chyzowski	1.50	.60	.15
☐ 4 Dean Cook	.60	.24	.06
☐ 5 Greg Davies	.60	.24	.06
☐ 6 Kim Deck	.60	.24	.06
☐ 7 Todd Decker	.60	.24	.06
☐ 8 Bill Harrington	.60	.24	.06
☐ 9 Phil Huber	.60	.24	.06
☐ 10 Steve Kloepzig	.60	.24	.06
☐ 11 Willie MacDonald	.60	.24	.06
☐ 12 Pat MacLeod	2.00	.80	.20
☐ 13 Glenn Mulvenna	1.00	.40	.10
☐ 14 Mike Needham	2.50	1.00	.25
☐ 15 Darcy Norton	.60	.24	.06
☐ 16 Devon Oleniuk	.60	.24	.06

		MINT	EXC	G-VG
☐ 17	Doug Pickell	.60	.24	.06
☐ 18	Garth Premak	.60	.24	.06
☐ 19	Mark Recchi	15.00	6.00	1.50
☐ 20	Don Schmidt	.60	.24	.06
☐ 21	Alec Sheflo	.60	.24	.06
☐ 22	Team Photo	2.50	1.00	.25
☐ 23	Logo Card	1.50	.60	.15
☐ 24	Logo Card	1.50	.60	.15

1988-89 Kamloops Blazers

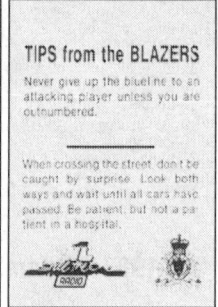

TIPS from the BLAZERS

Never give up the blueline to an attacking player unless you are outnumbered.

When crossing the street, don't be caught by surprise. Look both ways and wait until all cars have passed. Be patient, but not a patient in a hospital.

BLAZERS   Corey Hirsch
(35) Goal

This 36-card set was issued in three-card perforated strips that measure approximately 7 1/2" by 3 1/2". After perforation, the individual cards measure approximately 2 1/2" by 3 1/2". One of the cards on each three-card strip has the Kamloops logo in blue and orange on the front and the back contains a coupon. Several of the coupon cards have coupon information on both sides. The regular player cards have white borders with an inner royal blue line surrounding a posed player photo. The Kamloops logo is superimposed on the photo in the lower left corner with the player's name, team position, and number printed in the lower right corner. The white backs carry "Tips from the Blazers" in the form of public service announcements. The NL Radio station logo and the Royal Canadian Mounted Police emblem round out the back. The cards are unnumbered and are checklisted below in alphabetical order.

		MINT	EXC	G-VG
	COMPLETE SET (36)	20.00	8.00	2.00
	COMMON PLAYER (1-24)	.50	.20	.05
	COMMON AD CARD (25-36)	.25	.10	.02
☐ 1	Cory Anderson	.50	.20	.05
☐ 2	Pat Bingham	.50	.20	.05
☐ 3	Ed Bertuzzi	.50	.20	.05
☐ 4	Zac Boyer	1.00	.40	.10
☐ 5	Trevor Buchanan	.50	.20	.05
☐ 6	Dave Chyzowski	1.00	.40	.10
☐ 7	Dean Cook	.50	.20	.05
☐ 8	Cory Crichton	.50	.20	.05
☐ 9	Kim Deck	.50	.20	.05
☐ 10	Ryan Harrison	.50	.20	.05
☐ 11	Brad Heschuk	.50	.20	.05
☐ 12	Corey Hirsch	4.00	1.60	.40
☐ 13	Phil Huber	.50	.20	.05
☐ 14	Len Jorgenson	.50	.20	.05
☐ 15	Paul Kruse	.75	.30	.07
☐ 16	Dave Linford	.50	.20	.05
☐ 17	Pat MacLeod	1.50	.60	.15
☐ 18	Darwin McClelland	.50	.20	.05
☐ 19	Cal McGowan	1.00	.40	.10
☐ 20	Mike Needham	1.00	.40	.10
☐ 21	Don Schmidt	.50	.20	.05
☐ 22	Brian Shantz	.50	.20	.05
☐ 23	Darryl Sydor	4.00	1.60	.40
☐ 24	Steve Yule	.50	.20	.05
☐ 25	Hasty Market	.25	.10	.02
	Advertisement			
☐ 26	McDonalds	.25	.10	.02
	Advertisement			
☐ 27	Mr. Mike's Steakhouse	.25	.10	.02

		MINT	EXC	G-VG
	Advertisement			
☐ 28	The Yellow Submarine	.25	.10	.02
	Advertisement			
☐ 29	Blazers Logo	.25	.10	.02
☐ 30	Blazers Logo	.25	.10	.02
☐ 31	Blazers Logo	.25	.10	.02
☐ 32	Blazers Logo	.25	.10	.02
☐ 33	Blazers Logo	.25	.10	.02
☐ 34	Blazers Logo	.25	.10	.02
☐ 35	Blazers Logo	.25	.10	.02
☐ 36	Blazers Logo	.25	.10	.02

1990-91 Kansas City Blades

This 20-card set measures the standard size (2 1/2" by 3 1/2") and features posed, color player photos on a black card face. The pictures are bordered on three sides by a red design similar to a shadow border. Player information appears below the photo in the red border. The year and team name are printed at the upper left corner. The backs are white and carry the words "the jones store co.", the year, team logo, and the player's name and biography. One red star accents each corner. The cards are numbered on the back.

		MINT	EXC	G-VG
	COMPLETE SET (20)	9.00	3.75	.90
	COMMON PLAYER (1-20)	.50	.20	.05
☐ 1	Claudio Scremin	.75	.30	.07
☐ 2	Jeff Odgers	1.00	.40	.10
☐ 3	Wade Flaherty	.75	.30	.07
☐ 4	Rick Barkovich	.50	.20	.05
☐ 5	Ron Handy	.50	.20	.05
☐ 6	Kevin Sullivan	.50	.20	.05
☐ 7	Randy Exelby	.50	.20	.05
☐ 8	Darin Smith	.50	.20	.05
☐ 9	Stu Kulak	.75	.30	.07
☐ 10	Andrew Akervik	.50	.20	.05
☐ 11	Scott White	.50	.20	.05
☐ 12	Claude Julien	.50	.20	.05
☐ 13	Mike Hiltner	.50	.20	.05
☐ 14	Michael Colman	.50	.20	.05
☐ 15	Kurt Semandel	.50	.20	.05
☐ 16	Mike Kelfer	.50	.20	.05
☐ 17	Mark Karpen	.50	.20	.05
☐ 18	Lee Giffin	.75	.30	.07
☐ 19	Cam Plante	.50	.20	.05
☐ 20	Jim Latos	.75	.30	.07

1984-85 Kelowna Wings

This 56-card safety set was sponsored by A and W, Pizza Patio, CKIQ (a radio station), and the Kelowna Wings. The cards measure the standard size (2 1/2" by 3 1/2") and feature black-and-white posed and action player photos. The words "Kelowna Wings 1984-85" are at the top of card numbers 2-22, while the words "Junior Hockey Grads"

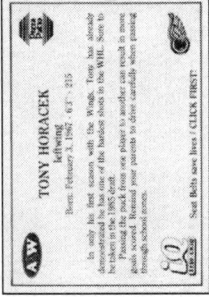

1981-82 Kingston Canadians

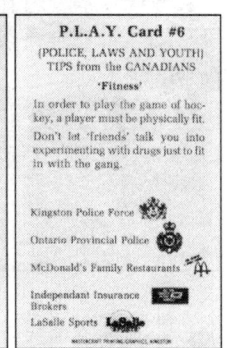

PHIL BOURQUE
Defence

appear at the top of card numbers 1 and 23-56. The player's name, position, and the card number are at the bottom. The backs feature biographical and statistical information in red print. After a checklist card, the set is ordered by Kelowna players (2-22) and WHL graduates to the NHL (23-56). The cards are numbered on the front in the lower right corner.

	MINT	EXC	G-VG
COMPLETE SET (56)	60.00	24.00	6.00
COMMON PLAYER (1-56)	.60	.24	.06
☐ 1 Checklist	1.50	.60	.15
☐ 2 Darcy Wakaluk	2.50	1.00	.25
☐ 3 Stacey Nickel	.60	.24	.06
☐ 4 Jeff Sharples	1.00	.40	.10
☐ 5 Greg Zuk	.60	.24	.06
☐ 6 Daryn Sivertson	.60	.24	.06
☐ 7 Randy Cameron	.60	.24	.06
☐ 8 Mark Fioretti	.60	.24	.06
☐ 9 Ron Viglasi	.60	.24	.06
☐ 10 Ian Herbers	.60	.24	.06
☐ 11 Mike Wegleitner	.60	.24	.06
☐ 12 Terry Zaporzan	.60	.24	.06
☐ 13 Dwaine Hutton	.60	.24	.06
☐ 14 Rod Williams	.60	.24	.06
☐ 15 Jeff Rohlicek	.60	.24	.06
☐ 16 Brent Gilchrist	2.00	.80	.20
☐ 17 Rocky Dundas	.60	.24	.06
☐ 18 Grant Delcourt	.60	.24	.06
☐ 19 Cam Laroruk	.60	.24	.06
☐ 20 Tony Horacek	1.25	.50	.12
☐ 21 Mark Wingerter	.60	.24	.06
☐ 22 Mick Vukota	1.50	.60	.15
☐ 23 Danny Gare	1.50	.60	.15
☐ 24 Rich Sutter	1.50	.60	.15
☐ 25 Alfie Turcotte	.60	.24	.06
☐ 26 Bryan Trottier	6.00	2.40	.60
☐ 27 Bill Derlago	1.00	.40	.10
☐ 28 Stan Smyl	1.25	.50	.12
☐ 29 Brent Sutter	2.00	.80	.20
☐ 30 Mel Bridgman	1.25	.50	.12
☐ 31 Paul Cyr	1.00	.40	.10
☐ 32 Gary Lupul	.60	.24	.06
☐ 33 Ray Neufeld	1.00	.40	.10
☐ 34 Brian Propp	2.50	1.00	.25
☐ 35 Bob Nystrom	1.50	.60	.15
☐ 36 Ryan Walter	1.00	.40	.10
☐ 37 Russ Courtnall	5.00	2.00	.50
☐ 38 Larry Playfair	.60	.24	.06
☐ 39 Ron Delorme	.60	.24	.06
☐ 40 Ron Sutter	1.25	.50	.12
☐ 41 Bobby Clarke	6.00	2.40	.60
☐ 42 Bob Bourne	1.00	.40	.10
☐ 43 Cam Neely	10.00	4.00	1.00
☐ 44 Murray Craven	1.50	.60	.15
☐ 45 Clark Gillies	2.50	1.00	.25
☐ 46 Ron Flockhart	1.00	.40	.10
☐ 47 Harold Snepsts	3.00	1.20	.30
☐ 48 Duane Sutter	1.25	.50	.12
☐ 49 Garth Butcher	2.00	.80	.20
☐ 50 Bill Hajt	.60	.24	.06
☐ 51 Jim Benning	.60	.24	.06
☐ 52 Ray Allison	.60	.24	.06
☐ 53 Ken Wregget	2.00	.80	.20
☐ 54 Phil Russell	.60	.24	.06
☐ 55 Brad McCrimmon	2.00	.80	.20
☐ 56 Dan Hodgson	1.00	.40	.10

This 25-card set measures approximately 2 5/8" by 4" and features posed, color player photos on thin white card stock. The player's name, position, and the team logo are printed in black below the picture. The backs carry P.L.A.Y. (Police, Laws and Youth) Tips from the Canadians, which consist of public service messages. Sponsor logos are printed at the bottom. The cards are numbered on the back.

	MINT	EXC	G-VG
COMPLETE SET (25)	30.00	12.00	3.00
COMMON PLAYER (1-25)	.75	.30	.07
☐ 1 Canadians Logo	1.50	.60	.15
☐ 2 Scott MacLellan	.75	.30	.07
☐ 3 Dave Courtemanche	.75	.30	.07
☐ 4 Mark Reade	.75	.30	.07
☐ 5 Shawn Babcock	.75	.30	.07
☐ 6 Phil Bourque	2.50	1.00	.25
☐ 7 Ian MacInnis	.75	.30	.07
☐ 8 Neil Trineer	.75	.30	.07
☐ 9 Syl Grandmaitre	.75	.30	.07
☐ 10 Carmine Vani	1.00	.40	.10
☐ 11 Chuck Brimmer	.75	.30	.07
☐ 12 Mike Linseman	.75	.30	.07
☐ 13 Steve Seguin	.75	.30	.07
☐ 14 Dan Wood	.75	.30	.07
☐ 15 Kirk Muller	15.00	6.00	1.50
☐ 16 Jim Aldred	.75	.30	.07
☐ 17 Rick Wilson	1.50	.60	.15
☐ 18 Mike Siltala	.75	.30	.07
☐ 19 Howie Scruton	.75	.30	.07
☐ 20 Mike Stothers	1.00	.40	.10
☐ 21 Dennis Smith	.75	.30	.07
☐ 22 Steve Richey	.75	.30	.07
☐ 23 Mike Moffat	1.50	.60	.15
☐ 24 Jim Morrison CO/MG	.75	.30	.07
☐ 25 Randy Plumb	.75	.30	.07

1982-83 Kingston Canadians

This 27-card set measures approximately 2 5/8" by 4 1/8" and features posed action, color player photos with white borders on thin white card stock. The player's name, position, and year of issue appear below the picture between the team logo and the Kingston Police Force insignia. The backs carry hockey tips and public service messages in the form of P.L.A.Y. (Police, Laws and Youth) Tips from the Canadians. Sponsor logos appear on the lower portion of the card. The cards are numbered on the back.

	MINT	EXC	G-VG
COMPLETE SET (27)	12.50	5.00	1.25
COMMON PLAYER (1-27)	.50	.20	.05

P.L.A.Y. Card #3

(POLICE, LAWS AND YOUTH)
TIPS from the CANADIANS
'Forward'

Primarily an attacking player whose responsibility is to create and score goals.

Help attack crime by coming forward when you have information about a crime.

SPONSORS

Beatrice Foods   Coca Cola   Empire Life

Independent Insurance Brokers

Legion No.9, No.560, No.631

Curtis Collin
FORWARD
1982 - 1983

		MINT	EXC	G-VG
COMPLETE SET (30)		12.50	5.00	1.25
COMMON PLAYER (1-30)		.50	.20	.05
☐ 1	Kingston Police Crest (Checklist)	1.00	.40	.10
☐ 2	Dennis Smith	.50	.20	.05
☐ 3	Ben Levesque	.50	.20	.05
☐ 4	Arie Moraal (Constable)	.50	.20	.05
☐ 5	Tom Allen	.50	.20	.05
☐ 6	Mike Plesh	.50	.20	.05
☐ 7	Roger Belanger	.50	.20	.05
☐ 8	Jeff Chychrun	1.00	.40	.10
☐ 9	Mike King	.50	.20	.05
☐ 10	Scott Metcalfe	.75	.30	.07
☐ 11	David Lundmark	.50	.20	.05
☐ 12	Tim Salmon	.50	.20	.05
☐ 13	Ted Linesman	.50	.20	.05
☐ 14	Chris Clifford	.50	.20	.05
☐ 15	Todd Elik	1.00	.40	.10
☐ 16	Kevin Conway	.50	.20	.05
☐ 17	Barry Burkholder	.50	.20	.05
☐ 18	Joel Brown	.50	.20	.05
☐ 19	Steve King	1.00	.40	.10
☐ 20	Craig Kales	.50	.20	.05
☐ 21	John Humphries TR	.50	.20	.05
☐ 22	David James	.50	.20	.05
☐ 23	Dav Simurda	.50	.20	.05
☐ 24	Allen Bishop	.50	.20	.05
☐ 25	Jeff Hogg	.50	.20	.05
☐ 26	Rick Cornacchia CO	.50	.20	.05
☐ 27	Ken Slater Director of Player Personnel	.50	.20	.05
☐ 28	Bill Dextater (Constable)	.50	.20	.05
☐ 29	Canadians Crest	.75	.30	.07
☐ 30	International Hockey Hall of Fame logo	.75	.30	.07

☐ 1	Jim Morrison MG	1.00	.40	.10
☐ 2	Dennis Smith	.50	.20	.05
☐ 3	Curtis Collin	.50	.20	.05
☐ 4	Joel Brown	.50	.20	.05
☐ 5	Ron Handy	.50	.20	.05
☐ 6	Carmine Vani	.50	.20	.05
☐ 7	Al Andrews	.50	.20	.05
☐ 8	Mike Siltala	.50	.20	.05
☐ 9	Syl Grandmaitre	.50	.20	.05
☐ 10	Steve Seguin	.50	.20	.05
☐ 11	Brian Dobbin	1.00	.40	.10
☐ 12	Mark Reade	.50	.20	.05
☐ 13	John Kemp	.50	.20	.05
☐ 14	Dan Mahon	.50	.20	.05
☐ 15	Keith Knight	.50	.20	.05
☐ 16	Ron Sanko	.50	.20	.05
☐ 17	John Landry	.50	.20	.05
☐ 18	Chris Brant	.50	.20	.05
☐ 19	Dave Simurda	.50	.20	.05
☐ 20	Mike Lafoy	.50	.20	.05
☐ 21	Scott MacLellan	.50	.20	.05
☐ 22	Brad Walcot	.50	.20	.05
☐ 23	Steve Richey	.50	.20	.05
☐ 24	Rod Graham CO	.50	.20	.05
☐ 25	Ben Levesque	.50	.20	.05
☐ 26	Canadians Logo	1.00	.40	.10
☐ 27	International Hockey Hall of Fame	1.00	.40	.10

1983-84 Kingston Canadians

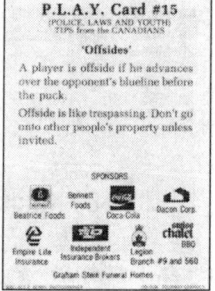

P.L.A.Y. Card #15

(POLICE, LAWS AND YOUTH)
TIPS from the CANADIANS

'Offsides'

A player is offside if he advances over the opponent's blueline before the puck.

Offside is like trespassing. Don't go onto other people's property unless invited.

SPONSORS

Bennett Foods   Coca Cola   Bacon Cans

Beatrice Foods

Empire Life   Independent Insurance Brokers   Legion Branch #9 and 560   chalet BBQ

Graham Stock Funeral Homes

Todd Elik
FORWARD
1983-1984

This 30-card set measures slightly larger than standard at 2 5/8" by 3 5/8" and features posed color player photos with white borders on thin card stock. The player's name, position, and year appears below the picture between the Canadians logo and the Kingston Police Force insignia. The backs carry public service messages in the form of P.L.A.Y. (Police, Laws and Youth) Tips from the Canadians. Sponsor logos fill out the lower portion. The cards are numbered on the back.

1984-85 Kingston Canadians

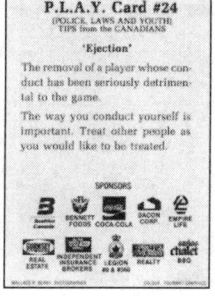

P.L.A.Y. Card #24

(POLICE, LAWS AND YOUTH)
TIPS from the CANADIANS

'Ejection'

The removal of a player whose conduct has been seriously detrimental to the game.

The way you conduct yourself is important. Treat other people as you would like to be treated.

SPONSORS

BENNETT FOODS   COCA-COLA   BACON CORP   EMPIRE LIFE

REAL ESTATE   INDEPENDENT INSURANCE BROKERS   LEGION #9 & #560   REALTY   chalet BBQ

Herb Raglan
FORWARD
1984-1985

This 30-card set measures 2 5/8" by 3 5/8" and features color, posed action player photos with white borders. The player's name, position, and year appear at the bottom. The backs carry public service messages in the form of P.L.A.Y. (Police, Laws and Youth) Tips from the Canadians. Sponsor logos round out the lower portion of the back. The cards are numbered on the back.

		MINT	EXC	G-VG
COMPLETE SET (30)		12.50	5.00	1.25
COMMON PLAYER (1-30)		.50	.20	.05
☐ 1	Kingston Police Force Crest	.75	.30	.07
☐ 2	Rick Cornacchia CO	.50	.20	.05
☐ 3	Arie Moraal (Constable)	.50	.20	.05
☐ 4	Ken Slater Director of Player Personnel	.50	.20	.05
☐ 5	Kingston Canadians Crest	.50	.20	.05

		MINT	EXC	G-VG
☐ 6	Scott Metcalfe	.75	.30	.07
☐ 7	Chris Clifford	.50	.20	.05
☐ 8	Todd Elik	1.25	.50	.12
☐ 9	Len Spratt	.50	.20	.05
☐ 10	Mike Plesh	.50	.20	.05
☐ 11	Marc Lyons	.50	.20	.05
☐ 12	Barry Burkholder	.50	.20	.05
☐ 13	Rick Fera	.50	.20	.05
☐ 14	David Hoover	.50	.20	.05
☐ 15	Andy Rivers	.50	.20	.05
☐ 16	Marc Laforge	.75	.30	.07
☐ 17	Peter Viscovich	.50	.20	.05
☐ 18	Jeff Chychrun	1.00	.40	.10
☐ 19	Wayne Erskine	.50	.20	.05
☐ 20	Todd Clarke	.50	.20	.05
☐ 21	Darren Wright	.50	.20	.05
☐ 22	Tony Rocca	.50	.20	.05
☐ 23	Brian Verbeek	.50	.20	.05
☐ 24	Herb Raglan	.75	.30	.07
☐ 25	Daril Holmes	.50	.20	.05
☐ 26	Len Coyle TR	.50	.20	.05
☐ 27	Ted Linesman	.50	.20	.05
☐ 28	International Hockey Hall of Fame logo	.75	.30	.07
☐ 29	Troy MacNevin	.50	.20	.05
☐ 30	Peter Campbell TR	.50	.20	.05

1985-86 Kingston Canadians

 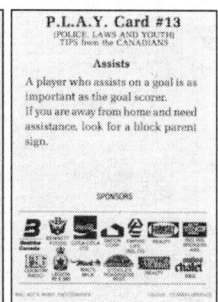

This 30-card measures approximately 2 5/8" by 3 5/8" and features color, posed action player photos with white borders. The player's name and position appear at the bottom. The backs carry public service messages in the form of P.L.A.Y. (Police, Laws and Youth) Tips from the Canadians. Sponsor logos fill the lower portion of the back. The cards are numbered on the back.

		MINT	EXC	G-VG
	COMPLETE SET (30)	10.00	4.00	1.00
	COMMON PLAYER (1-30)	.50	.20	.05
☐ 1	Kingston Police Force Crest	.75	.30	.07
☐ 2	Dale Sandles ACO	.50	.20	.05
☐ 3	Arie Moral (Constable)	.50	.20	.05
☐ 4	Fred O'Donnell GM/CO	.50	.20	.05
☐ 5	Kingston Canadian Crest	.50	.20	.05
☐ 6	Scott Metcalfe	.75	.30	.07
☐ 7	Chris Clifford	.50	.20	.05
☐ 8	Steve Seftel	.50	.20	.05
☐ 9	Andy Pearson	.50	.20	.05
☐ 10	Jeff Cornelius	.50	.20	.05
☐ 11	Marc Lyons	.50	.20	.05
☐ 12	Barry Burkholder	.50	.20	.05
☐ 13	Bryan Fogarty	1.00	.40	.10
☐ 14	Jeff Sirkka	.50	.20	.05
☐ 15	Scott Pearson	1.00	.40	.10
☐ 16	Marc Laforge	.50	.20	.05
☐ 17	Peter Viscovich	.50	.20	.05
☐ 18	Jeff Chycrun UER (Name misspelled Chycren)	.75	.30	.07

		MINT	EXC	G-VG
☐ 19	Wayne Erskine	.50	.20	.05
☐ 20	Todd Clarke	.50	.20	.05
☐ 21	Darren Wright	.50	.20	.05
☐ 22	Mike Maurice	.50	.20	.05
☐ 23	Brian Verbeek	.50	.20	.05
☐ 24	Mike Fiset	.50	.20	.05
☐ 25	Daril Holmes	.50	.20	.05
☐ 26	Len Coyle TR	.50	.20	.05
☐ 27	Ted Linesman	.50	.20	.05
☐ 28	International Hockey Hall of Fame	.75	.30	.07
☐ 29	Troy MacNevin	.50	.20	.05
☐ 30	Peter Campbell TR	.50	.20	.05

1986-87 Kingston Canadians

 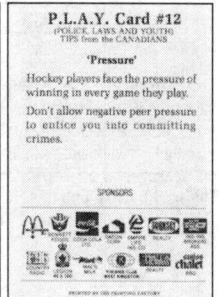

This 30-card set measures approximately 2 5/8" by 3 5/8" and features color, posed player portraits with blue studio backgrounds set on a white card face. The player's name, position, and year appear at the bottom. The backs carry public service messages in the form of P.L.A.Y. (Police, Laws and Youth) Tips from the Canadians. Sponsor logos fill the lower portion of the card. The cards are numbered on the back.

		MINT	EXC	G-VG
	COMPLETE SET (30)	10.00	4.00	1.00
	COMMON PLAYER (1-30)	.50	.20	.05
☐ 1	Kingston Canadians Crest	.75	.30	.07
☐ 2	Fred O'Donnell GM/CO	.50	.20	.05
☐ 3	Arie Moraal (Constable)	.50	.20	.05
☐ 4	Dale Sandles CO	.50	.20	.05
☐ 5	Kingston Police Force Crest	.50	.20	.05
☐ 6	Brian Tessier	.50	.20	.05
☐ 7	Franco Giammarco	.50	.20	.05
☐ 8	Peter Liptrott	.50	.20	.05
☐ 9	Chris Clifford	.50	.20	.05
☐ 10	Scott Metcalfe	.75	.30	.07
☐ 11	Scott Pearson	.75	.30	.07
☐ 12	Bryan Fogarty	1.00	.40	.10
☐ 13	Daril Holmes	.50	.20	.05
☐ 14	Andy Rivers	.50	.20	.05
☐ 15	Troy MacNevin	.50	.20	.05
☐ 16	Marc Laforge	.50	.20	.05
☐ 17	Wayne Erskine	.50	.20	.05
☐ 18	Peter Viscovich	.50	.20	.05
☐ 19	Mike Maurice	.50	.20	.05
☐ 20	Steve Seftel	.50	.20	.05
☐ 21	Chad Badaway	.50	.20	.05
☐ 22	Marc Lyons	.50	.20	.05
☐ 23	Jeff Sirkka	.50	.20	.05
☐ 24	Mike Fiset	.50	.20	.05
☐ 25	John Battice	.50	.20	.05
☐ 26	Len Coyle TR	.50	.20	.05
☐ 27	Sloan Torti	.50	.20	.05
☐ 28	Alain Laforge	.50	.20	.05
☐ 29	Ted Linesman	.50	.20	.05
☐ 30	Peter Campbell TR	.50	.20	.05

1987-88 Kingston Canadians

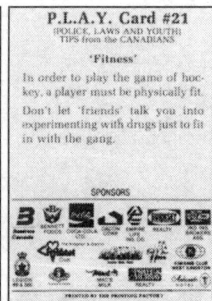

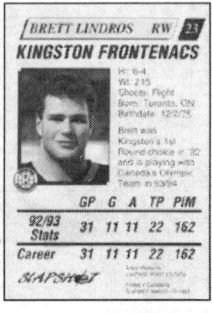

This 30-card P.L.A.Y. (Police, Laws and Youth) set measures approximately 2 3/4" by 3 5/8" and features color player portraits with blue studio backgrounds. The fronts are accented by white borders. The player's name, position, and the season year appear in the white border at the bottom. The backs carry public service messages in the form of "Tips From The Canadians." The cards are numbered on the back.

	MINT	EXC	G-VG
COMPLETE SET (30)	10.00	4.00	1.00
COMMON PLAYER (1-30)	.50	.20	.05
☐ 1 Arie Moraal	.75	.30	.0/
(Constable)			
☐ 2 Gord Wood GM	.50	.20	.05
☐ 3 Kingston Canadians	.50	.20	.05
Kingston Police			
Crests			
☐ 4 Jacques Tremblay CO	.50	.20	.05
☐ 5 Rhonda Sheridan	.50	.20	.05
Public Relations			
☐ 6 Jeff Wilson	.50	.20	.05
☐ 7 Franco Giammarco	.50	.20	.05
☐ 8 Peter Liptrott	.50	.20	.05
☐ 9 David Weiss	.50	.20	.05
☐ 10 Joel Morin	.50	.20	.05
☐ 11 Mark Turner	.50	.20	.05
☐ 12 Jeff Sirkka	.50	.20	.05
☐ 13 James Henckle	.50	.20	.05
☐ 14 Mike Bodnarchuk	.50	.20	.05
☐ 15 Mike Cavanaugh	.50	.20	.05
☐ 16 Darcy Cahill	.50	.20	.05
☐ 17 Kevin Falesy	.50	.20	.05
☐ 18 Dean Pella	.50	.20	.05
☐ 19 Brad Gratton	.50	.20	.05
☐ 20 Steve Seftel	.50	.20	.05
☐ 21 Bryan Fogarty	1.00	.40	.10
☐ 22 Scott Pearson	1.00	.40	.10
☐ 23 Tyler Pella	.50	.20	.05
☐ 24 Mike Fiset	.50	.20	.05
☐ 25 John Battice	.50	.20	.05
☐ 26 Len Coyle TR	.50	.20	.05
☐ 27 Geoff Schneider	.50	.20	.05
☐ 28 Chris Lukey	.50	.20	.05
☐ 29 Trevor Smith	.50	.20	.05
☐ 30 Peter Campbell TR	.50	.20	.05

1993-94 Kingston Frontenacs

Printed by Slapshot Images Ltd., this standard size (2 1/2" by 3 1/2") 25-card set features the 1993-94 Kingston Frontenacs. On a team color-coded background with black stripes, the fronts feature color action player photos with thin black borders. The team name is printed diagonally in the upper left corner of the photo, while the player's name

and number appear in a yellow bar in the bottom edge of the photo. The team and producer's logos on the bottom round out the front. The white backs carry a close-up color player portrait, biography and statistics, along with team and sponsor's logos. The cards are numbered on the back. Included in this set is a Slapshot ad card with a 1994 calendar on the back.

	MINT	EXC	G-VG
COMPLETE SET (25)	12.00	5.00	1.20
COMMON PLAYER (1-25)	.35	.14	.03
☐ 1 Greg Lovell	.35	.14	.03
☐ 2 Marc Lamothe	.35	.14	.03
☐ 3 T.J. Moss	.50	.20	.05
☐ 4 Marc Moro	.35	.14	.03
☐ 5 Trevor Doyle	.35	.14	.03
☐ 6 Jeff Dacosta	.35	.14	.03
☐ 7 Gord Walsh	.50	.20	.05
☐ 8 Brian Scott	.35	.14	.03
☐ 9 Jason Disher	.35	.14	.03
☐ 10 Alexander Zhurik	.50	.20	.05
☐ 11 Ken Boone	.35	.14	.03
☐ 12 Cail MacLean	.35	.14	.03
☐ 13 Bill Maranduik	.35	.14	.03
☐ 14 Martin Sychra	.75	.30	.07
☐ 15 Duncan Fader	.35	.14	.03
☐ 16 David Ling	.50	.20	.05
☐ 17 Chad Kilger	.50	.20	.05
☐ 18 Greg Kraemer	.35	.14	.03
☐ 19 Trent Cull	.50	.20	.05
☐ 20 Steve Parson	.35	.14	.03
☐ 21 Craig Rivet	.50	.20	.05
☐ 22 Keli Corpse	1.00	.40	.10
☐ 23 Brett Lindros	6.00	2.40	.60
☐ 24 David Allison CO	.35	.14	.03
Michael Allison ACO			
☐ NNO Ad Card	.35	.14	.03

1982-83 Kitchener Rangers

This 30-card set measures approximately 2 3/4" by 3 1/2" and features posed action color player photos with black inner borders and white outer borders. The backs are divided into three rectangular sections, each outlined by a thin black border. The upper section contains the player's name and biographical information. The middle section carries Tips from the Rangers and the Waterloo Regional Police. The bottom section contains sponsor logos. The cards are numbered on the back.

	MINT	EXC	G-VG
COMPLETE SET (30)	30.00	12.00	3.00
COMMON PLAYER (1-30)	.60	.24	.06
☐ 1 Waterloo Regional Police Crest	1.25	.50	.12
☐ 2 Harold Basse Chief of Police	.60	.24	.06
☐ 3 Sponsors' Card	.60	.24	.06
☐ 4 Joe Crozier GM/CO	1.50	.60	.15
☐ 5 Checklist	1.50	.60	.15
☐ 6 Kerry Kerch	.60	.24	.06
☐ 7 Tom St.James	.60	.24	.06
☐ 8 Wendell Young	2.50	1.00	.25
☐ 9 David Shaw	2.00	.80	.20
☐ 10 Darryl Boudreau	.60	.24	.06
☐ 11 David Bruce	2.00	.80	.20
☐ 12 Wayne Presley	2.00	.80	.20
☐ 13 Garnet McKechney	.60	.24	.06
☐ 14 Kevin Petendra	.60	.24	.06
☐ 15 Brian Wilks	.60	.24	.06
☐ 16 Jim Quinn	.60	.24	.06
☐ 17 Al MacInnis	15.00	6.00	1.50
☐ 18 Dave Nicholls	.60	.24	.06
☐ 19 Mike Eagles	1.50	.60	.15
☐ 20 Mike Hough	2.00	.80	.20
☐ 21 Greg Puhalski	.60	.24	.06
☐ 22 Darren Wright	.60	.24	.06
☐ 23 Todd Steffen	.60	.24	.06
☐ 24 John Tucker	2.00	.80	.20
☐ 25 Kent Paynter	.60	.24	.06
☐ 26 Andy O'Brien	.60	.24	.06
☐ 27 Les Bradley TR	.60	.24	.06
☐ 28 Scott Biggs	.60	.24	.06
☐ 29 Chris Martin TR	.60	.24	.06
☐ 30 Dave Webster	.60	.24	.06

1983-84 Kitchener Rangers

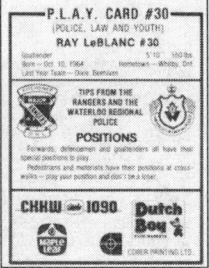

The Kitchener Rangers of the OHL are featured in this 30-card P.L.A.Y. (Police, Law and Youth) set, which was sponsored by the Waterloo Regional Police in conjunction with several company sponsors. The cards measure approximately 2 3/4" by 3 1/2" and are printed on thin card stock. The fronts feature color photos with the players posed in action stances. The photos are framed by black and white borders, and a facsimile autograph is inscribed across the bottom of the picture. The backs have biography, safety tips, and sponsors' logos, except for card number 18, which has a blank back. The cards are numbered on the back.

	MINT	EXC	G-VG
COMPLETE SET (30)	15.00	6.00	1.50
COMMON PLAYER (1-30)	.50	.20	.05
☐ 1 Joe Mantione	1.00	.40	.10
☐ 2 Jim Quinn	.50	.20	.05

☐ 3 Kitchener Rangers logo Checklist	1.00	.40	.10
☐ 4 Rob MacInnis	.50	.20	.05
☐ 5 Louie Berardicurti	.50	.20	.05
☐ 6 Neil Sandilands	.50	.20	.05
☐ 7 Darren Wright	.50	.20	.05
☐ 8 Tom Barrett CO/GM	.50	.20	.05
☐ 9 Brian Wilks	.50	.20	.05
☐ 10 Garnet McKechney	.50	.20	.05
☐ 11 David Bruce	1.00	.40	.10
☐ 12 Kent Paynter	.50	.20	.05
☐ 13 Sponsor's card P.L.A.Y. Rules	.50	.20	.05
☐ 14 Scott Kerr	.50	.20	.05
☐ 15 Greg Puhalski	.50	.20	.05
☐ 16 Wayne Presley	1.00	.40	.10
☐ 17 Carmine Vani	.50	.20	.05
☐ 18 Shawn Burr	1.50	.60	.15
☐ 19 Dave Latta	1.00	.40	.10
☐ 20 John Tucker	1.50	.60	.15
☐ 21 Mike Stevens	.50	.20	.05
☐ 22 Harold Basse Chief of Police	.50	.20	.05
☐ 23 Waterloo Regional Police	.50	.20	.05
☐ 24 Peter Bakovic	.50	.20	.05
☐ 25 Brian Ross	.50	.20	.05
☐ 26 Brad Balshin	.50	.20	.05
☐ 27 David Shaw	1.00	.40	.10
☐ 28 Chris Trainer TR	.50	.20	.05
☐ 29 Les Bradley TR	.50	.20	.05
☐ 30 Ray LeBlanc	2.00	.80	.20

1984-85 Kitchener Rangers

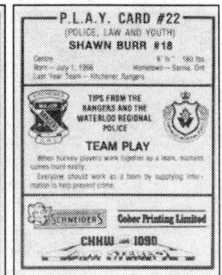

The Kitchener Rangers of the OHL are featured in this 30-card P.L.A.Y. (Police, Law and Youth) set, which was sponsored by the Waterloo Regional Police in conjunction with several company sponsors. The cards measure approximately 2 3/4" by 3 1/2" and are printed on thin card stock. The fronts feature color photos with the players posed in action stances. The photos are framed by black and white borders, and a facsimile autograph is inscribed across the bottom of the picture. The backs have biography, safety tips, and sponsors' logos. The cards are numbered on the back.

	MINT	EXC	G-VG
COMPLETE SET (30)	10.00	4.00	1.00
COMMON PLAYER (1-30)	.50	.20	.05
☐ 1 Waterloo Regional Police Crest	.75	.30	.07
☐ 2 Harold Basse Chief of Police	.50	.20	.05
☐ 3 Garnet McKechney	.50	.20	.05
☐ 4 Tom Barrett GM/CO	.50	.20	.05
☐ 5 Kitchener Rangers logo Checklist	.75	.30	.07
☐ 6 Mike Bishop	.50	.20	.05
☐ 7 Craig Wolanin	1.00	.40	.10
☐ 8 Steve Marcolini	.50	.20	.05
☐ 9 Peter Langlois	.50	.20	.05
☐ 10 Dave Weiss	.50	.20	.05
☐ 11 Ken Alexander	.50	.20	.05

		MINT	EXC	G-VG
☐ 12	Ian Pound	.50	.20	.05
☐ 13	Doug Stromback	.50	.20	.05
☐ 14	Joel Brown	.50	.20	.05
☐ 15	Brian Wilks	.50	.20	.05
☐ 16	Robin Rubic	.50	.20	.05
☐ 17	Kent Paynter	.50	.20	.05
☐ 18	Jon Helinski	.50	.20	.05
☐ 19	Greg Puhalski	.50	.20	.05
☐ 20	Wayne Presley	1.00	.40	.10
☐ 21	Dave McLlwain	1.00	.40	.10
☐ 22	Shawn Burr	1.00	.40	.10
☐ 23	Dave Latta	.75	.30	.07
☐ 24	John Keller	.50	.20	.05
☐ 25	Mike Stevens	.75	.30	.07
☐ 26	Sponsors' Card	.50	.20	.05
☐ 27	Richard Adolfi	.50	.20	.05
☐ 28	Grant Sanders	.50	.20	.05
☐ 29	Les Bradley TR	.50	.20	.05
☐ 30	Sponsors' Card	.75	.30	.07

1985-86 Kitchener Rangers

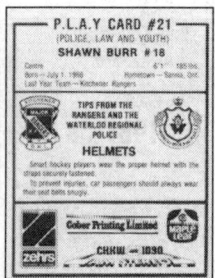

This 30-card set measures approximately 2 3/4" by 3 1/2" and is printed on thin card stock. The fronts feature posed, color player photos with thin black borders on a white card face. A facsimile autograph is inscribed across the picture. The backs carry the player's name, biographical information, and public service messages from the Rangers and the Waterloo Regional Police. The cards are numbered on the front and back.

		MINT	EXC	G-VG
	COMPLETE SET (30)	10.00	4.00	1.00
	COMMON PLAYER (1-30)	.50	.20	.05
☐ 1	Waterloo Regional Police Crest	.75	.30	.07
☐ 2	Harold Basse Chief of Police	.50	.20	.05
☐ 3	Sponsors' Card	.50	.20	.05
☐ 4	Tom Barrett GM/CO	.50	.20	.05
☐ 5	Kitchener Rangers logo Checklist	.75	.30	.07
☐ 6	Dave Weiss	.50	.20	.05
☐ 7	Steve Marcolini	.50	.20	.05
☐ 8	Kevin Gant	.50	.20	.05
☐ 9	Ken Alexander	.50	.20	.05
☐ 10	Mike Volpe	.50	.20	.05
☐ 11	Ian Pound	.50	.20	.05
☐ 12	Brett MacDonald	.50	.20	.05
☐ 13	Scott Taylor	.50	.20	.05
☐ 14	Greg Hankkio	.50	.20	.05
☐ 15	Mike Morrison	.50	.20	.05
☐ 16	Mike Wolak	.50	.20	.05
☐ 17	Craig Booker	.50	.20	.05
☐ 18	Jeff Noble	.50	.20	.05
☐ 19	Shawn Tyers	.50	.20	.05
☐ 20	Peter Lisy	.50	.20	.05
☐ 21	Shawn Burr	1.00	.40	.10
☐ 22	David Latta	.75	.30	.07
☐ 23	Ron Sanko	.50	.20	.05
☐ 24	Doug Jones	.50	.20	.05
☐ 25	Paul Penelton	.50	.20	.05
☐ 26	Blair MacPherson	.50	.20	.05
☐ 27	Richard Hawkins	.50	.20	.05

		MINT	EXC	G-VG
☐ 28	Brad Sparkes	.50	.20	.05
☐ 29	Ron Goodall	.50	.20	.05
☐ 30	Kevin Duguay TR	.50	.20	.05

1986-87 Kitchener Rangers

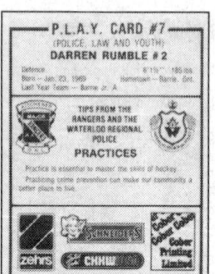

The Kitchener Rangers of the OHL are featured in this 30-card P.L.A.Y. (Police, Law and Youth) set, which was sponsored by the Waterloo Regional Police in conjunction with several company sponsors. The cards measure approximately 2 3/4" by 3 1/2" and are printed on thin card stock. The fronts feature color photos with the players posed in action stances. The photos are framed by black and white borders. The player's name appears in the lower right corner. The backs have biography, safety tips, and sponsors' logos. The cards are numbered on both sides.

		MINT	EXC	G-VG
	COMPLETE SET (30)	10.00	4.00	1.00
	COMMON PLAYER (1-30)	.50	.20	.05
☐ 1	Waterloo Regional Police Crest	.75	.30	.07
☐ 2	Harold Basse Chief of Police	.50	.20	.05
☐ 3	Sponsor's Card	.50	.20	.05
☐ 4	Tom Barrett GM/CO	.50	.20	.05
☐ 5	Checklist	.75	.30	.07
☐ 6	Dave Weiss	.50	.20	.05
☐ 7	Darren Rumble	1.00	.40	.10
☐ 8	Kevin Grant	.50	.20	.05
☐ 9	Len Fawcett	.50	.20	.05
☐ 10	Darren Beals	.50	.20	.05
☐ 11	Ed Kister	.50	.20	.05
☐ 12	Scott Taylor	.50	.20	.05
☐ 13	Darren Moxam	.50	.20	.05
☐ 14	Paul Epoch	.50	.20	.05
☐ 15	Richard Borgo	.50	.20	.05
☐ 16	Allan Lake	.50	.20	.05
☐ 17	Jeff Noble	.50	.20	.05
☐ 18	Mark Montanari	.50	.20	.05
☐ 19	Jim Hulton	.50	.20	.05
☐ 20	Kelly Cain	.75	.30	.07
☐ 21	Craig Booker	.50	.20	.05
☐ 22	David Latta	.75	.30	.07
☐ 23	Doug Jones	.50	.20	.05
☐ 24	Gary Callahan	.50	.20	.05
☐ 25	Bruno Lapensee	.50	.20	.05
☐ 26	Scott Montgomery TR	.50	.20	.05
☐ 27	Ron Goodall	.50	.20	.05
☐ 28	Discount Card	.50	.20	.05
☐ 29	Steve Ewing	.50	.20	.05
☐ 30	Joe McDonnell ACO	.50	.20	.05

1987-88 Kitchener Rangers

This 30-card set measures approximately 2 3/4" by 3 1/2" and was sponsored by Waterloo Region Optimist Clubs. The cards, which are printed on thin card stock, feature color posed action player photos with white borders. The card

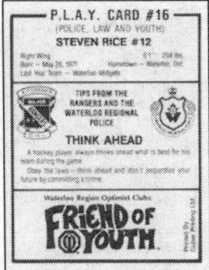

number, the player's name, and the season year appear in black print across the bottom of the photo. The backs are divided by thin black lines into three sections and carry player biography, tips from the Rangers and the Waterloo Regional Police, and the sponsor logo. The cards are numbered on both sides.

	MINT	EXC	G-VG
COMPLETE SET (30)	10.00	4.00	1.00
COMMON PLAYER (1-30)	.50	.20	.05
☐ 1 Waterloo Regional Police Crest	.75	.30	.07
☐ 2 Harold Basse Chief of Police	.50	.20	.05
☐ 3 Children's Bonus Card	.50	.20	.05
☐ 4 Joe McDonnell GM/CO	.50	.20	.05
☐ 5 Kitchener Ranger logo Checklist	.75	.30	.07
☐ 6 Gus Morschauser	.50	.20	.05
☐ 7 Rick Allain	.50	.20	.05
☐ 8 Kevin Grant	.50	.20	.05
☐ 9 Rob Thiel	.50	.20	.05
☐ 10 Darren Beals	.50	.20	.05
☐ 11 Cory Keenan	.75	.30	.07
☐ 12 Rival Fullum	.50	.20	.05
☐ 13 Tony Crisp	.50	.20	.05
☐ 14 Tyler Ertel	.50	.20	.05
☐ 15 Richard Borgo	.50	.20	.05
☐ 16 Steven Rice	1.50	.60	.15
☐ 17 Rob Sangster	.50	.20	.05
☐ 18 Jeff Noble	.50	.20	.05
☐ 19 Mark Montanari	.50	.20	.05
☐ 20 Jim Hulton	.50	.20	.05
☐ 21 Craig Booker	.50	.20	.05
☐ 22 Doug Jones	.50	.20	.05
☐ 23 Randy Pearce	.50	.20	.05
☐ 24 Darren Rumble	.75	.30	.07
☐ 25 Joe Ranger	.50	.20	.05
☐ 26 Optimist's Sponsor Card (A-K)	.50	.20	.05
☐ 27 Ron Goodall	.50	.20	.05
☐ 28 Allan Lake	.50	.20	.05
☐ 29 Scott Montgomery TR	.50	.20	.05
☐ 30 Optimist's Sponsor Card (L-W)	.50	.20	.05

1988-89 Kitchener Rangers

The Kitchener Rangers of the OHL are featured in this 30-card P.L.A.Y. (Police, Law and Youth) set, which was sponsored by the Waterloo Regional Police in conjunction with several area Optimist Clubs. The cards measure approximately 2 3/4" by 3 1/2" and are printed on thin card stock. The fronts feature color photos with the players posed in action stances. The photos are framed by black and white borders. The backs have biography, safety tips, and sponsors' logos. The cards are numbered on both sides.

	MINT	EXC	G-VG
COMPLETE SET (30)	10.00	4.00	1.00
COMMON PLAYER (1-30)	.50	.20	.05
☐ 1 Waterloo Regional Police Crest	.75	.30	.07

☐ 2 Harold Basse Chief of Police	.50	.20	.05
☐ 3 Children's Bonus Card	.50	.20	.05
☐ 4 Joe McDonnell GM/CO	.50	.20	.05
☐ 5 Kitchener Rangers logo Checklist	.75	.30	.07
☐ 6 Mike Torchia	.75	.30	.07
☐ 7 Rick Allain	.50	.20	.05
☐ 8 John Uniac	.75	.30	.07
☐ 9 Rob Thiel	.50	.20	.05
☐ 10 Gus Morschauser	.50	.20	.05
☐ 11 Cory Keenan	.75	.30	.07
☐ 12 Rival Fullum	.50	.20	.05
☐ 13 Jason Firth	.75	.30	.07
☐ 14 Joey St. Aubin	.50	.20	.05
☐ 15 Richard Borgo	.50	.20	.05
☐ 16 Steven Rice	1.50	.60	.15
☐ 17 Rob Sangster	.50	.20	.05
☐ 18 Gilbert Dionne	2.00	.80	.20
☐ 19 Mark Montanari	.50	.20	.05
☐ 20 Shayne Stevenson	1.00	.40	.10
☐ 21 Pierre Gagnon	.50	.20	.05
☐ 22 Kirk Tomlinson	.50	.20	.05
☐ 23 Randy Pearce	.50	.20	.05
☐ 24 Brad Barton	.50	.20	.05
☐ 25 Chris LiPuma	1.00	.40	.10
☐ 26 Optimist's Sponsor's Card (A-K)	.50	.20	.05
☐ 27 Steve Herniman	.50	.20	.05
☐ 28 Darren Rumble	.75	.30	.07
☐ 29 Rick Chambers TR	.50	.20	.05
☐ 30 Optimist's Sponsor's Card (L-W)	.50	.20	.05

1990-91 Kitchener Rangers

The Kitchener Rangers of the OHL are featured in this 30-card P.L.A.Y. (Police, Law and Youth) set, which was sponsored by the Waterloo Regional Police in conjunction with several area Optimist Clubs. The cards measure approximately 2 3/4" by 3 1/2" and are printed on thin card stock. The fronts feature color photos with the players posed in action stances. The photos are framed by black and red borders. The backs have biography, safety tips, and sponsors' logos. The cards are numbered on both sides.

		MINT	EXC	G-VG
COMPLETE SET (30)......................		8.00	3.25	.80
COMMON PLAYER (1-30)................		.40	.16	.04
☐ 1	Waterloo Regional..................	.75	.30	.07
	Police Crest			
☐ 2	Harold Basse......................	.40	.16	.04
	Chief of Police			
☐ 3	Joe McDonnell GM/CO..........	.40	.16	.04
☐ 4	Rick Chambers TR	.40	.16	.04
☐ 5	Kitchener Rangers logo..........	.75	.30	.07
	Checklist			
☐ 6	Mike Torchia	.75	.30	.07
☐ 7	Len DeVuono	.40	.16	.04
☐ 8	John Uniac........................	.60	.24	.06
☐ 9	Steve Smith........................	.40	.16	.04
☐ 10	Rob Stopar........................	.40	.16	.04
☐ 11	Tony McCabe	.40	.16	.04
☐ 12	Jason Firth.........................	.75	.30	.07
☐ 13	Joey St. Aubin......................	.40	.16	.04
☐ 14	Richard Borgo......................	.40	.16	.04
☐ 15	Norm Dezainde	.60	.24	.06
☐ 16	Jeff Szeryk.........................	.40	.16	.04
☐ 17	Derek Gauthier....................	.40	.16	.04
☐ 18	Jamie Israel........................	.40	.16	.04
☐ 19	Shayne McCosh	.75	.30	.07
☐ 20	Gib Tucker........................	.40	.16	.04
☐ 21	Paul McCallion	.40	.16	.04
☐ 22	Mike Allen	.40	.16	.04
☐ 23	Brad Barton........................	.40	.16	.04
☐ 24	Chris LiPuma	.75	.30	.07
☐ 25	Justin Cullen	.40	.16	.04
☐ 26	Optimist's Sponsor's	.40	.16	.04
	Card (A-K)			
☐ 27	Rod Saarinen......................	.40	.16	.04
☐ 28	Jack Williams......................	.40	.16	.04
☐ 29	Steven Rice........................	1.25	.50	.12
☐ 30	Optimist's Sponsor's	.40	.16	.04
	Card (K-W)			

☐ 3	Darryl Whyte........................	.35	.14	.03
☐ 4	Greg McLean.......................	.35	.14	.03
☐ 5	Jason Hughes	.35	.14	.03
☐ 6	Gord Dickie........................	.35	.14	.03
☐ 7	Travis Riggin.......................	.50	.20	.05
☐ 8	Norm Dezainde....................	.50	.20	.05
☐ 9	Tim Spitzig.........................	.50	.20	.05
☐ 10	Trevor Gallant	.50	.20	.05
☐ 11	Chris Pittman	.50	.20	.05
☐ 12	Ryan Pawluk.......................	.50	.20	.05
	UER Name spelled			
	Pawluck on back			
☐ 13	Jason Morgan......................	.35	.14	.03
☐ 14	James Boyd	.35	.14	.03
☐ 15	Todd Warriner	1.00	.40	.10
☐ 16	Mark Donahue.....................	.35	.14	.03
☐ 17	Peter Brearley	.35	.14	.03
☐ 18	Andrew Taylor	.50	.20	.05
☐ 19	Jason Gladney.....................	.50	.20	.05
☐ 20	Wes Swinson	.50	.20	.05
☐ 21	Matt O'Dette.......................	.50	.20	.05
☐ 22	Darren Schmidt....................	.35	.14	.03
☐ 23	Jason Johnson.....................	.35	.14	.03
☐ 24	Eric Manlow	.75	.30	.07
☐ 25	Jeff Lillie...........................	.35	.14	.03
☐ 26	Sergei Olympiev...................	.50	.20	.05
☐ 27	Joe McDonnell CO	.35	.14	.03
☐ 28	Rick Chambers TR	.35	.14	.03
☐ 29	Andrew Taylor	.50	.20	.05
	Travis Riggin			
	David Belitski			
	Top Prospects			
☐ 30	Sponsor Card	.35	.14	.03
	Domino's Pizza			
☐ NNO	Ad Card............................	.35	.14	.03

1993-94 Kitchener Rangers

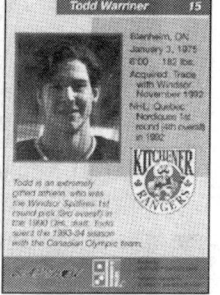

1993-94 Knoxville Cherokees

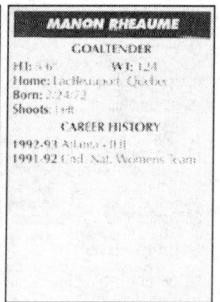

This 20-card set measures the standard size (2 1/2" by 3 1/2") and features the Knoxville Cherokees. On a black background with white borders, the fronts have color action and posed player photos with thin teal borders. The team name appears above the photo, while the player's name, position, and the team logo are under the photo. The white backs carry the player's name, position, biography, and career history. The cards are unnumbered and checklisted below in alphabetical order.

Sponsored by Domino's Pizza and printed by Slapshot Images Ltd., this standard size (2 1/2" by 3 1/2") 31-card set features the 1993-94 Kitchener Rangers. On a geometrical blue and red background, the fronts feature color action player photos with thin grey borders. The player's name, position and team name, as well as the producer's logo, appear on the front. The backs carry a close-up color player portrait, and biographical information, along with team and sponsor's logos. The cards are numbered on the back. Included in this set is a Slapshot ad card with a 1994 calendar on the back.

		MINT	EXC	G-VG
COMPLETE SET (31)......................		9.00	3.75	.90
COMMON PLAYER (1-31)................		.35	.14	.03
☐ 1	Eric Manlow	.50	.20	.05
	Jason Gladney			
	Tim Spitig			
	Checklist			
☐ 2	David Belitski	.50	.20	.05

		MINT	EXC	G-VG
COMPLETE SET (20)......................		9.00	3.75	.90
COMMON PLAYER (1-20)................		.35	.14	.03
☐ 1	Scott Boston	.35	.14	.03
☐ 2	Cory Cadden	.35	.14	.03
☐ 3	Tim Chase	.35	.14	.03
☐ 4	Steven Flomenhoft	.35	.14	.03
☐ 5	Scott Gordon......................	.50	.20	.05
☐ 6	Jon Larson........................	.35	.14	.03
☐ 7	Carl LeBlanc	.35	.14	.03
☐ 8	Kim Maier	.35	.14	.03
☐ 9	Wes McCauley	.35	.14	.03
☐ 10	Scott Metcalfe	.35	.14	.03

☐ 11	Mike Murray	.35	.14	.03
☐ 12	Hayden O'Rear	.35	.14	.03
☐ 13	Jeff Reid	.35	.14	.03
☐ 14	Manon Rheaume	5.00	2.00	.50
☐ 15	Marc Rodgers	.35	.14	.03
☐ 16	Doug Searle	.35	.14	.03
☐ 17	Barry Smith CO	.35	.14	.03
☐ 18	Martin Tanguay	.75	.30	.07
☐ 19	Nicholas Vachon	.35	.14	.03
☐ 20	Bruno Villeneuve	.35	.14	.03

1991-92 Lake Superior State Lakers

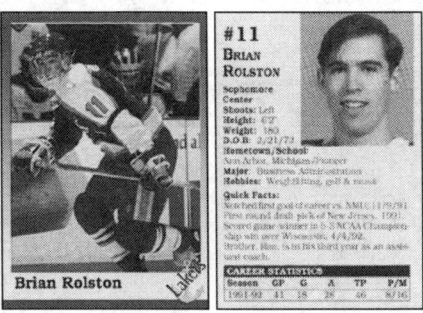

This 33-card set features the 1992 NCAA Champion Lake Superior State Lakers. The cards measure the standard size (2 1/2" by 3 1/2") and feature color, action player photos with gradated blue borders. The player's name and the Lakers logo appears below the picture. The backs carry black-and-white close-up photos along with biographical information, quick facts, and statistics. The cards are unnumbered and checklisted below in alphabetical order.

		MINT	EXC	G-VG
COMPLETE SET (33)		12.50	5.00	1.25
COMMON PLAYER (1-33)		.50	.20	.05
☐ 1	Team Photo	1.50	.60	.15
	1992 NCAA Champions			
☐ 2	Team Photo	1.00	.40	.10
	1992 CCHA Champions			
☐ 3	Keith Aldridge	.50	.20	.05
☐ 4	Dan Angelelli	.50	.20	.05
☐ 5	Mark Astley	.50	.20	.05
☐ 6	Mike Bachusz	.50	.20	.05
☐ 7	Steven Barnes	.50	.20	.05
☐ 8	Clayton Beddoes	1.00	.40	.10
☐ 9	David Gartshore	.50	.20	.05
☐ 10	Tim Hanley	.50	.20	.05
☐ 11	Matt Hansen	.50	.20	.05
☐ 12	John Hendry	.50	.20	.05
☐ 13	Dean Hulett	.75	.30	.07
☐ 14	Jeff Jackson	.75	.30	.07
☐ 15	Blaine Lacher	1.50	.60	.15
☐ 16	Darrin Madeley	1.50	.60	.15
☐ 17	Mike Matteucci	.50	.20	.05
☐ 18	Scott McCabe	.50	.20	.05
☐ 19	Kurt Miller	.50	.20	.05
☐ 20	Mike Morin	.50	.20	.05
☐ 21	Jay Ness	.50	.20	.05
☐ 22	Gino Pulente	.50	.20	.05
☐ 23	Brian Rolston	2.50	1.00	.25
☐ 24	Paul Sass	.50	.20	.05
☐ 25	Michael Smith	.50	.20	.05
☐ 26	Wayne Strachan	.50	.20	.05
☐ 27	Sean Tallaire	.75	.30	.07
☐ 28	Adam Thompson	.50	.20	.05
☐ 29	Jason Trzcinski	.50	.20	.05
☐ 30	Rob Valicevic	.50	.20	.05
☐ 31	Jason Welch	.50	.20	.05
☐ 32	Darren Wetherill	.50	.20	.05
☐ 33	Brad Willner	.50	.20	.05

1989-90 Lethbridge Hurricanes

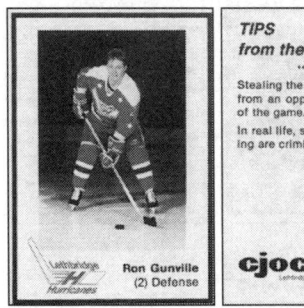

Showing signs of perforation, this 24-card set was issued in strips of several cards each. The cards measure the standard size (2 1/2" by 3 1/2") when separated and feature posed, color player photos. The photos are set on a white card face with a heavy black line framing the edge of the card, leaving white space between the line and the picture. The player's name, jersey number, and position appear in the white margin at the bottom. The backs carry "Tips from the Hurricanes," which are hockey tips and public service messages. The cards are unnumbered and checklisted below in alphabetical order.

		MINT	EXC	G-VG
COMPLETE SET (24)		18.00	7.25	1.80
COMMON PLAYER (1-24)		.60	.24	.06
☐ 1	Doug Barrault	1.00	.40	.10
☐ 2	Peter Berthelsen	.60	.24	.06
☐ 3	Bryan Bosch	.60	.24	.06
☐ 4	Kelly Ens	.60	.24	.06
☐ 5	Mark Greig	2.00	.80	.20
☐ 6	Ron Gunville	.60	.24	.06
☐ 7	Rob Hale	.60	.24	.06
☐ 8	Neil Hawryluk	.60	.24	.06
☐ 9	David Holzer	.60	.24	.06
☐ 10	Dusty Imoo	1.50	.60	.15
☐ 11	Darcy Kaminski ACO	.60	.24	.06
☐ 12	Bob Loucks CO	.60	.24	.06
☐ 13	Corey Lyons	.60	.24	.06
☐ 14	Duane Maruschak	.60	.24	.06
☐ 15	Jamie McLennan	3.00	1.20	.30
☐ 16	Shane Peacock	1.00	.40	.10
☐ 17	Pat Pylypuik	.60	.24	.06
☐ 18	Gary Reilly	.60	.24	.06
☐ 19	Brad Rubachuk	.60	.24	.06
☐ 20	Jason Ruff	1.50	.60	.15
☐ 21	Kevin St. Jacques	1.00	.40	.10
☐ 22	Wes Walz	2.00	.80	.20
☐ 23	Darcy Werenka	2.00	.80	.20
☐ 24	Brad Zimmer	.60	.24	.06

1985-86 London Knights

The London Knights of the OHL are featured in this 30-card P.L.A.Y. (Police, Law and Youth) set, which was sponsored by the London Crime Prevention Committee in conjunction with area businesses. The cards measure approximately 2 3/4" by 3 1/2" and are printed on thin card stock. The fronts feature color photos with the players posed in action stances. A facsimile autograph is inscribed at the bottom of the picture. The photos are framed by black and white borders. The backs have the player's name, safety tips, and sponsors' logos. The cards are numbered on the back.

		MINT	EXC	G-VG
COMPLETE SET (30)		25.00	10.00	2.50
COMMON PLAYER (1-30)		.50	.20	.05

		MINT	EXC	G-VG
COMPLETE SET (30)......................		18.00	7.25	1.80
COMMON PLAYER (1-30)................		.50	.20	.05
☐ 1	LaVerne Shipley......................	.50	.20	.05
	Chief of Police			
☐ 2	Tom Gosnell (Mayor).............	.50	.20	.05
☐ 3	Kellogg's Ad..........................	.50	.20	.05
	Checklist			
☐ 4	Wayne Maxner CO/GM...........	.50	.20	.05
☐ 5	Harry E. Sparling...................	.50	.20	.05
	Superintendent			
☐ 6	Brendan Shanahan..................	10.00	4.00	1.00
☐ 7	Pat Vachon............................	.50	.20	.05
☐ 8	Brad Schlegel.........................	.75	.30	.07
☐ 9	Barry Earhart..........................	.50	.20	.05
☐ 10	Jean Marc MacKenzie	.50	.20	.05
☐ 11	Jason Simon	.50	.20	.05
☐ 12	Jim Sprott.............................	.50	.20	.05
☐ 13	Bill Long VP...........................	.50	.20	.05
☐ 14	Murray Nystrom......................	.50	.20	.05
☐ 15	Shayne Stevenson..................	1.00	.40	.10
☐ 16	Don Martin............................	.50	.20	.05
☐ 17	Ian Pound	.50	.20	.05
☐ 18	Peter Lisy	.50	.20	.05
☐ 19	Steve Marcolini	.50	.20	.05
☐ 20	Craig Majaury........................	.50	.20	.05
☐ 21	Trevor Dam	.50	.20	.05
☐ 22	Dave Akey.............................	.50	.20	.05
☐ 23	Dennis McEwen	.50	.20	.05
☐ 24	Shane Whelan	.50	.20	.05
☐ 25	Greg Hankkio	.50	.20	.05
☐ 26	Pat Kelly TR	.50	.20	.05
☐ 27	Stephen Titus	.50	.20	.05
☐ 28	Fred Kean..............................	.50	.20	.05
	Director of PR			
	and Marketing			
☐ 29	Chris Somers	.50	.20	.05
☐ 30	Gord Clark MD	.50	.20	.05

☐ 1	LaVerne Shipley......................	.50	.20	.05
	Chief of Police			
☐ 2	Joe Ranger.............................	.50	.20	.05
☐ 3	Kellogg's Ad..........................	.50	.20	.05
	Checklist			
☐ 4	Don Boyd GM/CO..................	.50	.20	.05
☐ 5	Harry E. Sparling...................	.50	.20	.05
	Superintendent			
☐ 6	Murray Nystrom......................	.50	.20	.05
☐ 7	Bob Halkidis	1.00	.40	.10
☐ 8	Morgan Watts	.50	.20	.05
☐ 9	Brendan Shanahan.................	15.00	6.00	1.50
☐ 10	Brian Dobbin	.75	.30	.07
☐ 11	Ed Kister	.50	.20	.05
☐ 12	Darin Smith...........................	.50	.20	.05
☐ 13	Greg Puhalski........................	.50	.20	.05
☐ 14	Dave Haas	.50	.20	.05
☐ 15	Pete McLeod	.50	.20	.05
☐ 16	Frank Tremblay	.50	.20	.05
☐ 17	Matthew Smyth.......................	.50	.20	.05
☐ 18	Glen Leslie	.50	.20	.05
☐ 19	Mike Zombo...........................	.50	.20	.05
☐ 20	Jamie Groke..........................	.50	.20	.05
☐ 21	Brad Schlegel.........................	.75	.30	.07
☐ 22	Kelly Cain.............................	.50	.20	.05
☐ 23	Tom Allen..............................	.50	.20	.05
☐ 24	Rod Gerow............................	.50	.20	.05
☐ 25	Pat Vachon............................	.50	.20	.05
☐ 26	Paul Cook ACO......................	.50	.20	.05
☐ 27	Jeff Reese.............................	1.25	.50	.12
☐ 28	Fred Kean..............................	.50	.20	.05
	Dir. of PR/Marketing			
☐ 29	Scott Cumming.......................	.50	.20	.05
☐ 30	John Williams ACO	.50	.20	.05

1986-87 London Knights

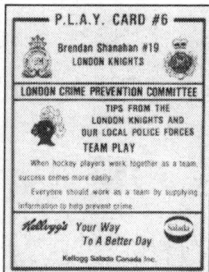

The London Knights of the OHL are featured in this 30-card P.L.A.Y. (Police, Law and Youth) set, which was sponsored by the London Crime Prevention Committee in conjunction with area businesses. The cards measure approximately 2 3/4" by 3 1/2" and are printed on thin card stock. The fronts feature color photos with the players posed in action stances. The photos are framed by black and white borders. The backs have biography, safety tips, and sponsors' logos. The cards are numbered on the back.

1992-93 Maine Black Bears

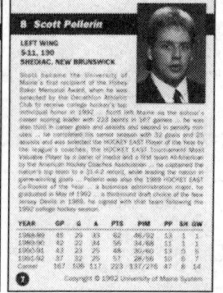

Featuring the Maine Black Bears, this 36-card set was issued as two series (1-16 and 17-36). The cards measure the standard size (2 1/2" by 3 1/2") and feature color, action player photos with light blue, dark blue, and white borders. A black stripe near the bottom carries the player's name and position in white print. The team logo is superimposed on the picture. The backs carry biographical information, career highlights, and statistics. The cards are numbered on the back.

		MINT	EXC	G-VG
COMPLETE SET (36)......................		30.00	12.00	3.00
COMMON PLAYER (1-16)...............		.50	.20	.05
COMMON PLAYER (17-36).............		.50	.20	.05
☐ 1	Title Card..............................	1.00	.40	.10
☐ 2	Mike Dunham.........................	3.00	1.20	.30
☐ 3	Andy Silverman......................	.50	.20	.05
☐ 4	Matt Martin	1.50	.60	.15
☐ 5	Chris Imes.............................	1.00	.40	.10
☐ 6	Jason Weinrich	.50	.20	.05
☐ 7	Scott Pellerin........................	1.50	.60	.15
☐ 8	Dan Murphy	.50	.20	.05

☐ 9	Dave LaCouture	.50	.20	.05
☐ 10	Patrice Tardif	.75	.30	.07
☐ 11	Eric Fenton	.50	.20	.05
☐ 12	Jim Montgomery	2.00	.80	.20
☐ 13	Kent Salfi	.50	.20	.05
☐ 14	Jean-Yves Roy	1.00	.40	.10
☐ 15	Garth Snow	1.50	.60	.15
☐ 16	Cal Ingraham	.75	.30	.07
☐ 17	Title Card	1.00	.40	.10
☐ 18	Mike Dunham	2.00	.80	.20
☐ 19	Chris Imes	1.00	.40	.10
☐ 20	Paul Kariya	10.00	4.00	1.00
☐ 21	Mike Latendresse	.75	.30	.07
☐ 22	Dan Murphy	.50	.20	.05
☐ 23	Dave MacIsaac	.50	.20	.05
☐ 24	Dave LaCouture	.50	.20	.05
☐ 25	Chris Ferraro	1.50	.60	.15
☐ 26	Peter Ferraro	3.00	1.20	.30
☐ 27	Jim Montgomery	2.00	.80	.20
☐ 28	Brad Purdie	1.00	.40	.10
☐ 29	Lee Saunders	.50	.20	.05
☐ 30	Justin Tomberlin	.75	.30	.07
☐ 31	Chuck Texeira	.50	.20	.05
☐ 32	Martin Mercier	.50	.20	.05
☐ 33	Garth Snow	1.50	.60	.15
☐ 34	Cal Ingraham	.75	.30	.07
☐ 35	Greg Hirsch	.50	.20	.05
☐ 36	Jamie Thompson	.50	.20	.05

1993-94 Maine Black Bears

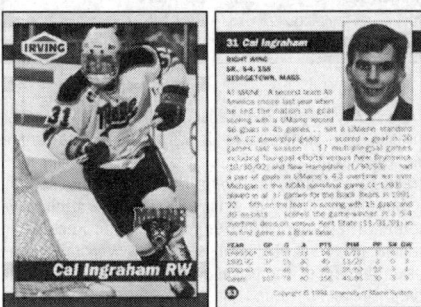

Measuring the standard size (2 1/2" by 3 1/2"), this 26-card set features the Maine Black Bears. The fronts feature color action player photos with light blue, dark blue, and white borders. A black stripe near the bottom carries the player's name and position in white print. The team logo is superimposed on the picture. The backs carry biographical information, career highlights, and statistics along with a small black-and-white player headshot. The cards are numbered on the back. The numbering continues where the previous year's numbering left off.

	MINT	EXC	G-VG
COMPLETE SET (25)	20.00	8.00	2.00
COMMON PLAYER (37-61)	.50	.20	.05
☐ 37 Paul Kariya	2.50	1.00	.25
Leo Wlasow			
Title Card			
☐ 38 Andy Silverman	.50	.20	.05
☐ 39 Jason Weinrich	.75	.30	.07
☐ 40 Jason Mansoff	.50	.20	.05
☐ 41 Paul Kariya	6.00	2.40	.60
☐ 42 Mike Latendresse	.75	.30	.07
☐ 43 Barry Clukey	.50	.20	.05
☐ 44 Wayne Conlan	.50	.20	.05
☐ 45 Dave MacIsaac	.50	.20	.05
☐ 46 Patrice Tardif	.75	.30	.07
☐ 47 Brad Purdie	.75	.30	.07
☐ 48 Dan Shermerhorn	.50	.20	.05
☐ 49 Lee Saunders	.50	.20	.05
☐ 50 Justin Tomberlin	.75	.30	.07
☐ 51 Chuck Texeira	.50	.20	.05
☐ 52 Tim Lovell	.50	.20	.05

☐ 53	Cal Ingraham	.75	.30	.07
☐ 54	Leo Wlasow	.50	.20	.05
☐ 55	Blair Allison	.50	.20	.05
☐ 56	Blair Marsh	.50	.20	.05
☐ 57	Marcel Pineau	.50	.20	.05
☐ 58	Trevor Roenick	2.00	.80	.20
☐ 59	Reg Cardinal	.50	.20	.05
☐ 60	Paul Kariya	6.00	2.40	.60
☐ 61	Jim Montgomery	2.50	1.00	.25
	Paul Kariya			
	Division I Champions			

1982-83 Medicine Hat Tigers

These 21 blank-backed cards measure approximately 3" by 4" and feature white-bordered, black-and-white posed studio head shots of the WHL Tigers on the left halves of the cards. The player's name, jersey number and biography, along with a space for an autograph, appear on the right half. The cards are unnumbered and checklisted below in alphabetical order.

	MINT	EXC	G-VG
COMPLETE SET (21)	25.00	10.00	2.50
COMMON PLAYER (1-21)	1.00	.40	.10
☐ 1 Al Conroy	1.50	.60	.15
☐ 2 Murray Craven	5.00	2.00	.50
☐ 3 Mark Frank	1.00	.40	.10
☐ 4 Kevan Guy	1.50	.60	.15
☐ 5 Jim Hougen	1.00	.40	.10
☐ 6 Ken Jorgenson	1.00	.40	.10
☐ 7 Matt Kabayama	1.00	.40	.10
☐ 8 Brent Kisilivich	1.00	.40	.10
☐ 9 Mark Lamb	2.00	.80	.20
☐ 10 Mike Lay	1.00	.40	.10
☐ 11 Dean McArthur	1.00	.40	.10
☐ 12 Brent Meckling	1.00	.40	.10
☐ 13 Shawn Nagurny	1.00	.40	.10
☐ 14 Kodie Nelson	1.00	.40	.10
☐ 15 Al Pederson	1.50	.60	.15
☐ 16 Todd Pederson	1.00	.40	.10
☐ 17 Jay Reid	1.00	.40	.10
☐ 18 Gord Shmyrko	1.00	.40	.10
☐ 19 Brent Steblyk	1.00	.40	.10
☐ 20 Rocky Trottier	1.00	.40	.10
☐ 21 Dan Turner	1.00	.40	.10

1983-84 Medicine Hat Tigers

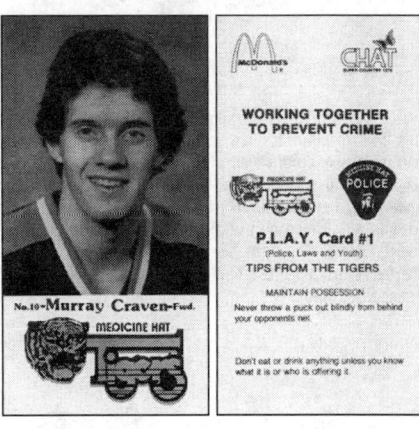

This 23-card P.L.A.Y. (Police, Laws and Youth) set measures approximately 2 3/4" by 5" and features color player portraits with a wide white bottom border. The border contains the player's jersey number and name. The team logo is also printed in this area. The backs carry sponsor logos and public service "Tips From The Tigers." The cards are numbered on the back.

	MINT	EXC	G-VG
COMPLETE SET (23)	35.00	14.00	3.50
COMMON PLAYER (1-23)	1.50	.60	.15
☐ 1 Murray Craven	5.00	2.00	.50
☐ 2 Shane Churla	6.00	2.40	.60
☐ 3 Don Herczeg	1.50	.60	.15
☐ 4 Gary Johnson	1.50	.60	.15
☐ 5 Brent Kisilivich	1.50	.60	.15
☐ 6 Blair MacGregor	1.50	.60	.15
☐ 7 Terry Knight	1.50	.60	.15
☐ 8 Mark Lamb	2.50	1.00	.25
☐ 9 Al Pederson	2.00	.80	.20
☐ 10 Trevor Semeniuk	1.50	.60	.15
☐ 11 Dan Turner	1.50	.60	.15
☐ 12 Brent Steblyk	1.50	.60	.15
☐ 13 Rocky Trottier	1.50	.60	.15
☐ 14 Kevan Guy	2.00	.80	.20
☐ 15 Bobby Bassen	2.50	1.00	.25
☐ 16 Brent Meckling	1.50	.60	.15
☐ 17 Matt Kabayama	1.50	.60	.15
☐ 18 Gord Hynes	2.00	.80	.20
☐ 19 Daryl Henry	1.50	.60	.15
☐ 20 Jim Kambeitz	1.50	.60	.15
☐ 21 Mike Lay	1.50	.60	.15
☐ 22 Gord Shmyrko	1.50	.60	.15
☐ 23 Al Conroy	2.00	.80	.20

1985-86 Medicine Hat Tigers

This 24-card set measures approximately 2 1/4" by 4" and features posed, color player photos on white card stock. The player's name and the team logo are printed in the larger white margin at the bottom. The player's jersey number and position are printed on the picture in the upper corners. A thin red line encloses the picture, player's name, and logo. The backs display P.L.A.Y. (Police, Laws, and Youth) tips and sponsor logos. The cards are numbered on the back.

	MINT	EXC	G-VG
COMPLETE SET (24)	20.00	8.00	2.00
COMMON PLAYER (1-24)	.75	.30	.07
☐ 1 Mike Claringbull	.75	.30	.07
☐ 2 Doug Houda	1.50	.60	.15
☐ 3 Mark Kuntz	.75	.30	.07
☐ 4 Guy Phillips	.75	.30	.07
☐ 5 Rob DiMaio	1.50	.60	.15
☐ 6 Al Conroy CAPT	1.50	.60	.15
☐ 7 Craig Berube	2.50	1.00	.25
☐ 8 Doug Sauter CO	.75	.30	.07
☐ 9 Dean Chynoweth	1.50	.60	.15
☐ 10 Scott McCrady	.75	.30	.07

	MINT	EXC	G-VG
☐ 11 Neil Brady	1.50	.60	.15
☐ 12 Dale Kushner	1.50	.60	.15
☐ 13 Jeff Wenaas	.75	.30	.07
☐ 14 Wayne Hynes	.75	.30	.07
☐ 15 Troy Gamble	3.00	1.20	.30
☐ 16 Bryan Maxwell ACO	.75	.30	.07
☐ 17 Gord Hynes	1.50	.60	.15
☐ 18 Wayne McBean	1.50	.60	.15
☐ 19 Mark Pederson	1.50	.60	.15
☐ 20 Darren Cota	.75	.30	.07
☐ 21 Randy Siska	.75	.30	.07
☐ 22 Dave Mackey	.75	.30	.07
☐ 23 Mark Fitzpatrick	3.00	1.20	.30
☐ 24 Doug Ball TR	.75	.30	.07

1993-94 Michigan State

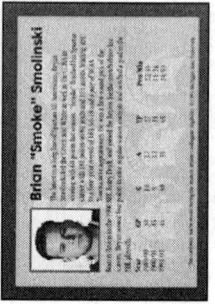

Produced by Phipps Sports Marketing, Inc., this 32-card set measures the standard size (2 1/2" by 3 1/2") and features the 1993-94 Michigan State Spartan hockey team. On a green background, the fronts have a mix of posed and action player photos in glossy color, within a thin silver border. The words "1993-94 MSU Spartan Hockey" are printed above the photo, while the player's name appears inside the photo. The player's position and number under the photo, along with a large block-style "S" round out the front. Printed on a light green background with ghosted Spartan helmet logos and a dark green border, the horizontal backs carry a black-and-white player portrait, along with biography and personal information. The cards are unnumbered and checklisted below in alphabetical order.

	MINT	EXC	G-VG
COMPLETE SET (32)	12.50	5.00	1.25
COMMON PLAYER (1-32)	.35	.14	.03
☐ 1 Matt Albers	.35	.14	.03
☐ 2 Michael Burkett	.75	.30	.07
☐ 3 Mike Buzak	.35	.14	.03
☐ 4 Anson Carter	2.00	.80	.20
☐ 5 Brian Clifford	.75	.30	.07
☐ 6 Brian Crane	.35	.14	.03
☐ 7 Steve Ferranti	.35	.14	.03
☐ 8 Ryan Fleming	.35	.14	.03
☐ 9 Steve Guolla	.35	.14	.03
☐ 10 Kelly Harper	.50	.20	.05
☐ 11 Eric Kruse	.35	.14	.03
☐ 12 Ron Mason CO	.50	.20	.05
☐ 13 Mike Mattis	.35	.14	.03
☐ 14 Rem Murray	.35	.14	.03
☐ 15 Steve Norton	.50	.20	.05
☐ 16 Nicolas Perreault	.75	.30	.07
☐ 17 Tom Ross	.50	.20	.05
Spartan Great			
☐ 18 Chris Slater	.35	.14	.03
☐ 19 Chris Smith	.35	.14	.03
☐ 20 Brian Smolinski	5.00	2.00	.50
☐ 21 Sparty (Mascot)	.35	.14	.03
☐ 22 Chris Sullivan	.35	.14	.03
☐ 23 Steve Suk	.35	.14	.03
☐ 24 Bart Turner	.50	.20	.05
☐ 25 Tony Tuzzolino	.50	.20	.05

		MINT	EXC	G-VG
☐ 26	Bart Vanstaalduinen	.35	.14	.03
☐ 27	Mike Ware	.35	.14	.03
☐ 28	John Weidenbach	.35	.14	.03
☐ 29	Josh Wiegand	.35	.14	.03
☐ 30	Scott Worden	.35	.14	.03
☐ 31	Munn Arena	.35	.14	.03
☐ 32	Title Card	.35	.14	.03

1990-91 Michigan Tech Huskies

This 31-card set was sponsored by The Daily Mining Gazette and showcases the Michigan Tech Huskies of the WCHA. Reportedly only 500 sets were produced. The cards measure the standard size (2 1/2" by 3 1/2") and are printed on thin cardboard stock. Borderless high gloss player photos grace the fronts, with the jersey number, team name, player name, and position given in a black stripe at the bottom of the card face. On a black and pale yellow background, each back has a black and white head shot, biography, statistics, and career summary. A "Huskies Hockey Quick Fact" completes the card back. The cards are unnumbered and checklisted below in alphabetical order.

		MINT	EXC	G-VG
COMPLETE SET (31)		15.00	6.00	1.50
COMMON PLAYER (1-31)		.50	.20	.05
☐ 1	Jim Bonner	.75	.30	.07
☐ 2	Newell Brown CO	.75	.30	.07
☐ 3	Dwight DeGiacomo	.50	.20	.05
☐ 4	Rod Ewacha	.50	.20	.05
☐ 5	Peter Grant	.50	.20	.05
☐ 6	Tim Hartnett	.50	.20	.05
☐ 7	Mike Hauswirth	.50	.20	.05
☐ 8	Kelly Hurd	.75	.30	.07
☐ 9	Kelly Hurd	.75	.30	.07
	Red Wings			
☐ 10	Layne Lebel	.75	.30	.07
	Jeff Hill			
☐ 11	Randy Lewis	.50	.20	.05
☐ 12	Jay Luknowsky	.50	.20	.05
☐ 13	Ken Martel CO	.50	.20	.05
	Mark Leach CO			
☐ 14	Darcy Martini	.75	.30	.07
☐ 15	Reid McDonald	.50	.20	.05
☐ 16	Hugh McEwen	.75	.30	.07
	Jim Storm			
	Kevin Manninen			
☐ 17	Don Osborne	.50	.20	.05
☐ 18	Greg Parnell	.50	.20	.05
☐ 19	Davis Payne	.75	.30	.07
☐ 20	Kirby Perrault	.75	.30	.07
	Darren Brkic			
☐ 21	Ken Plaquin	.75	.30	.07
☐ 22	Damian Rhodes	2.00	.80	.20
☐ 23	Geoff Sarjeant	1.00	.40	.10
☐ 24	Jamie Steer	.50	.20	.05
☐ 25	Rob Tustian	.50	.20	.05
☐ 26	Scott Vettraino	.75	.30	.07
	Jamie Ram			
☐ 27	Tim Watters	.75	.30	.07
	(black and white)			

		MINT	EXC	G-VG
☐ 28	John Young	.50	.20	.05
☐ 29	John Young	.75	.30	.07
	Kelly Hurd			
☐ 30	1991 MacInnes Cup	.75	.30	.07
☐ 31	1975 NCAA Champions	1.00	.40	.10

1991-92 Michigan Tech Huskies

This 36-card set features the 1992-93 Michigan Tech Huskies. Reportedly approximately 2,000 sets were produced. Measuring the standard size (2 1/2" by 3 1/2"), the fronts features full-bleed color action player photos. A gray and yellow stripe at the bottom contains the player's name. The Huskies logo overlaps the picture and the stripe. The backs are divided into three sections. The upper section is bright yellow and displays a black-and-white head shot, an action shot, and biographical information. A white middle section carries a player profile. The lower yellow section contains statistics. The player's name and uniform number are printed vertically in a black stripe on the left edge. Some players have two cards, the second of which is distinguished by a subtitle. The cards are unnumbered and checklisted below in alphabetical order.

		MINT	EXC	G-VG
COMPLETE SET (36)		15.00	6.00	1.50
COMMON PLAYER (1-36)		.50	.20	.05
☐ 1	Jim Bonner	.75	.30	.07
☐ 2	Darren Brkic	.50	.20	.05
☐ 3	Rod Ewacha	.50	.20	.05
☐ 4	Tim Hartnett	.50	.20	.05
☐ 5	Mike Hauswirth	.50	.20	.05
☐ 6	Jeff Hill	.50	.20	.05
☐ 7	Layne LeBel	.50	.20	.05
☐ 8	Randy Lewis	.50	.20	.05
☐ 9	Randy Lewis	.50	.20	.05
	Hit Squad			
☐ 10	John MacInnes CO	.50	.20	.05
☐ 11	Darcy Martini	.75	.30	.07
☐ 12	Darcy Martini	.75	.30	.07
	Rink Blaster			
☐ 13	Reid McDonald	.50	.20	.05
☐ 14	Hugh McEwen	.50	.20	.05
☐ 15	Bob Olson ANN	.50	.20	.05
☐ 16	Don Osborne	.50	.20	.05
☐ 17	Greg Parnell	.50	.20	.05
☐ 18	Davis Payne	.75	.30	.07
☐ 19	Kirby Perrault	.50	.20	.05
☐ 20	Ken Plaquin	.75	.30	.07
☐ 21	Jamie Ram	.75	.30	.07
☐ 22	Geoff Sarjeant	1.00	.40	.10
☐ 23	Geoff Sarjeant	1.00	.40	.10
	WCHA Student-Athlete			
☐ 24	Jamie Steer	.50	.20	.05
☐ 25	Jamie Steer	.50	.20	.05
	Blade Runner			
☐ 26	Jim Storm	1.50	.60	.15
☐ 27	Scott Vettraino	.50	.20	.05
☐ 28	John Young	.50	.20	.05
☐ 29	Credits (Team	.50	.20	.05
	huddling on ice)			
☐ 30	Freshman	.75	.30	.07

Justin Peca
Liam Garvey
Randy Stevens
Brent Peterson
Travis Seale

		MINT	EXC	G-VG
☐ 31	Great Lakes	.50	.20	.05
	Invitational			
☐ 32	Home Ice	.50	.20	.05
	MacInnes Student Ice Arena			
☐ 33	Team Photo	1.00	.40	.10
☐ 34	NHL Draft	1.50	.60	.15

Darcy Martini
Davis Payne
Geoff Sarjeant
Ken Plaquin
Jim Storm
Jamie Ram
Jamie Steer
Jim Bonner

		MINT	EXC	G-VG
☐ 35	Pep Band	.50	.20	.05
☐ 36	Michigan Tech Univ.	.75	.30	.07

1981-82 Milwaukee Admirals

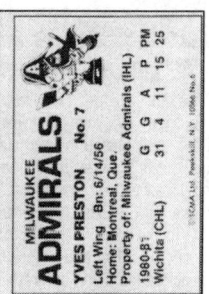

This 15-card set was produced by TCMA and features the members of the Milwaukee Admirals. The cards measure the standard size (2 1/2" by 3 1/2") and are made of thick card stock. On the front, a black-and-white player photo with thin black borders is framed in bright yellow. The team name appears in the yellow border above the photo, while the player's name, jersey number, and position appear below. The horizontal backs carry biography and statistics. The cards are numbered on the back.

		MINT	EXC	G-VG
COMPLETE SET (15)		12.00	5.00	1.20
COMMON PLAYER (1-15)		1.00	.40	.10
☐ 1	Pat Rabbitt	1.00	.40	.10
☐ 2	Real Paiement	1.00	.40	.10
☐ 3	Fred Berry	1.00	.40	.10
☐ 4	Blaine Peerless	1.00	.40	.10
☐ 5	John Flesch	1.00	.40	.10
☐ 6	Yves Preston	1.00	.40	.10
☐ 7	Bruce McKay	1.00	.40	.10
☐ 8	Dale Yakiwchuk	1.00	.40	.10
☐ 9	Lorne Bokshowan	1.00	.40	.10
☐ 10	Danny Lecours	1.00	.40	.10
☐ 11	Sheldon Currie	1.00	.40	.10
☐ 12	Doug Robb	1.00	.40	.10
☐ 13	Rob Polman Tuin	1.00	.40	.10
☐ 14	Bob Collyard	1.00	.40	.10
☐ 15	Tim Ringler TR	1.00	.40	.10

1991-92 Minnesota Golden Gophers

Sponsored by MCI, this 26-card set measures the standard size (2 1/2" by 3 1/2") and features the 1991-92 Minnesota Golden Gophers. On a maroon background, the horizontal

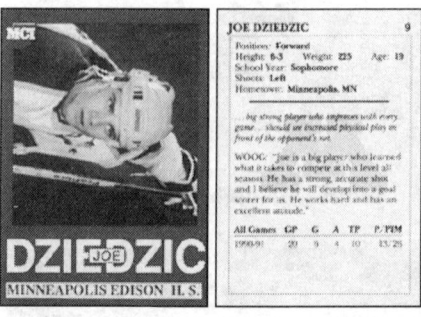

and vertical fronts have color action player photos along with the player's name and the name of the high school he attended. The white backs carry the player's name, number, biography, and profile. The cards are unnumbered and checklisted below in alphabetical order.

		MINT	EXC	G-VG
COMPLETE SET (26)		12.50	5.00	1.25
COMMON PLAYER (1-26)		.35	.14	.03
☐ 1	Scott Bell	.35	.14	.03
☐ 2	Tony Bianchi	.35	.14	.03
☐ 3	John Brill	.75	.30	.07
☐ 4	Jeff Callinan	.35	.14	.03
☐ 5	Joe Dziedzic	1.50	.60	.15
☐ 6	Sean Fabian	.35	.14	.03
☐ 7	Jed Fiebelkorn	.50	.20	.05
☐ 8	Nick Gerebi	.35	.14	.03
☐ 9	Darby Hendrickson	1.50	.60	.15
☐ 10	Craig Johnson	1.50	.60	.15
☐ 11	Trent Klatt	2.00	.80	.20
☐ 12	Cory Laylin	.35	.14	.03
☐ 13	Steve Magnusson	.50	.20	.05
☐ 14	Chris McAlpine	.50	.20	.05
☐ 15	Justin McHugh	.35	.14	.03
☐ 16	Eric Means	.35	.14	.03
☐ 17	Mike Muller	.50	.20	.05
☐ 18	Tom Newman	.35	.14	.03
☐ 19	Jeff Nielsen	.35	.14	.03
☐ 20	John O'Connell	.35	.14	.03
☐ 21	Larry Olimb	.50	.20	.05
☐ 22	Travis Richards	1.00	.40	.10
☐ 23	Brandon Steege	.35	.14	.03
☐ 24	Jeff Stolp	.35	.14	.03
☐ 25	Todd Westlund	.35	.14	.03
☐ 26	Doug Zmolek	1.00	.40	.10

1992-93 Minnesota Golden Gophers

Featuring the 1992-93 Minnesota Golden Gophers hockey team (WCHA), this 25-card set measures the standard size (2 1/2" by 3 1/2"). The fronts feature full-bleed, posed, color player photos. A gray bar at the top (or right edge) displays the school name, while the player's name is printed in maroon lettering in a yellow bar at the bottom. The horizontal backs carry biographical information, a player profile, and statistics, along with a photo of the player in action. The cards are unnumbered and checklisted below in alphabetical order.

	MINT	EXC	G-VG
COMPLETE SET (25)	10.00	4.00	1.00
COMMON PLAYER (1-25)	.35	.14	.03

☐ 1 Scott Bell	.35	.14	.03
☐ 2 Jesse Bertogliat	.50	.20	.05
Brian Bonin			
☐ 3 Tony Bianchi	.35	.14	.03
☐ 4 John Brill	.75	.30	.07
☐ 5 Jeff Callinan	.35	.14	.03
☐ 6 Bobby Dustin	.50	.20	.05
Dave Larson			
☐ 7 Joe Dziedzic	1.25	.50	.12
☐ 8 Jed Fiebelkorn	.50	.20	.05
☐ 9 Darby Hendrickson	1.25	.50	.12
☐ 10 Craig Johnson	1.25	.50	.12
☐ 11 Steve Magnusson	.50	.20	.05
☐ 12 Chris McAlpine	.50	.20	.05
☐ 13 Justin McHugh	.35	.14	.03
☐ 14 Eric Means	.35	.14	.03
☐ 15 Jeff Moen	.35	.14	.03
☐ 16 Tom Newman	.35	.14	.03
☐ 17 Jeff Nielsen	.35	.14	.03
☐ 18 Travis Richards	1.00	.40	.10
☐ 19 Brandon Steege	.35	.14	.03
☐ 20 Matt Stelljes	.50	.20	.05
Ryan Alstead			
☐ 21 Dan Trebil	.50	.20	.05
Greg Zwakman			
☐ 22 Charlie Wasley	.50	.20	.05
Mike McAlpine			
☐ 23 Todd Westlund	.35	.14	.03
☐ 24 Dan Woog	.50	.20	.05
Jim Hillman			
☐ 25 Doug Woog CO	.50	.20	.05

1993-94 Minnesota Golden Gophers

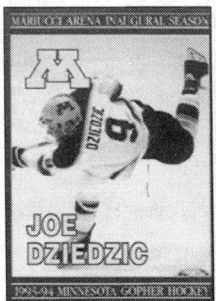 

This 30-card set measures the standard size (2 1/2" by 3 1/2"). On a maroon background, the fronts feature posed, color action player photos and portraits with a thin yellow border. The player's name is printed in yellow letters with a maroon outline on the bottom of the photo. The words "Mariucci Arena Inaugural Season" are printed above the photo, while "1993-94 Minnesota Gopher Hockey" is printed below it. On a maroon background, the horizontal backs carry biographical information, a player profile, statistics, and a drawing of the team mascot, along with a black-and-white player portrait. The cards are unnumbered and checklisted below in alphabetical order.

	MINT	EXC	G-VG
COMPLETE SET (30)	10.00	4.00	1.00
COMMON PLAYER (1-30)	.35	.14	.03

| ☐ 1 Brett Abrahamson | .35 | .14 | .03 |
| ☐ 2 Jesse Bertogliat | .35 | .14 | .03 |

☐ 3 Tony Bianchi	.35	.14	.03
☐ 4 Brian Bonin	.35	.14	.03
☐ 5 Andy Brink	.50	.20	.05
☐ 6 Jeff Callinan	.35	.14	.03
☐ 7 Nick Checco	.50	.20	.05
☐ 8 Bobby Dustin	.35	.14	.03
☐ 9 Joe Dziedzic	.75	.30	.07
☐ 10 Jed Fiebelkorn	.50	.20	.05
☐ 11 Brent Godbout	.35	.14	.03
☐ 12 Dan Hendrickson	.50	.20	.05
☐ 13 Jim Hillman	.35	.14	.03
☐ 14 John Hillman	.35	.14	.03
☐ 15 Brian LaFleur	.35	.14	.03
☐ 16 Dave Larson	.35	.14	.03
☐ 17 Steve Magnusson	.35	.14	.03
☐ 18 Chris McAlpine	.50	.20	.05
☐ 19 Mike McAlpine	.35	.14	.03
☐ 20 Justin McHugh	.35	.14	.03
☐ 21 Eric Means	.35	.14	.03
☐ 22 Jeff Moen	.35	.14	.03
☐ 23 Jeff Nielsen	.35	.14	.03
☐ 24 Brandon Steege	.35	.14	.03
☐ 25 Dan Trebil	.50	.20	.05
☐ 26 Charlie Wasley	.75	.30	.07
☐ 27 Dan Woog	.35	.14	.03
☐ 28 Doug Woog CO	.50	.20	.05
☐ 29 Greg Zwakman	.50	.20	.05
☐ 30 Title Card	.35	.14	.03

1985-86 Minnesota-Duluth

 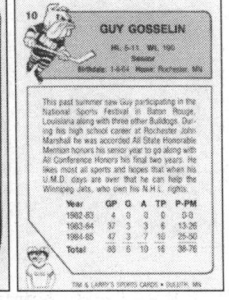

This 36-card set measures the standard size (2 1/2" by 3 1/2") and features color action player photos with rounded corners and black borders against a white card face. An oval inset at the lower right shows a head shot. The player's name is printed in black at the bottom. The backs carry biographical information, career highlights, and statistics. The cards are numbered on the back. It has been reported that this set may have been reprinted to take advantage of the popularity of Brett Hull.

	MINT	EXC	G-VG
COMPLETE SET (36)	30.00	12.00	3.00
COMMON PLAYER (1-36)	.50	.20	.05

☐ 1 Skeeter Moore	1.00	.40	.10
☐ 2 Terry Shold	.50	.20	.05
☐ 3 Mike DeAngelis	.50	.20	.05
☐ 4 Rob Pallin	.50	.20	.05
☐ 5 Norm Maciver	2.50	1.00	.25
☐ 6 Wayne Smith	.50	.20	.05
☐ 7 Dave Cowan	.50	.20	.05
☐ 8 Darin Illikainen	.50	.20	.05
☐ 9 Rick Hayko	.50	.20	.05
☐ 10 Guy Gosselin	1.00	.40	.10
☐ 11 Paul Roff	.50	.20	.05
☐ 12 Jim Toninato	.50	.20	.05
☐ 13 Tom Hanson	.50	.20	.05
☐ 14 Mike Cortes	.50	.20	.05
☐ 15 Matt Christensen	.50	.20	.05
☐ 16 Bruce Fishback	.50	.20	.05
☐ 17 Mark Odnokon	.50	.20	.05
☐ 18 Brian Johnson	.50	.20	.05
☐ 19 Bob Alexander	.50	.20	.05
☐ 20 Tom Lorentz	.50	.20	.05

☐ 21	Roman Sindelar	.50	.20	.05
☐ 22	Jim Sprenger	.50	.20	.05
☐ 23	Dan Tousignant	.50	.20	.05
☐ 24	Sean Toomey	.50	.20	.05
☐ 25	Brian Durand	.50	.20	.05
☐ 26	John Hyduke	.50	.20	.05
☐ 27	Brian Nelson	.50	.20	.05
☐ 28	Brett Hull	20.00	8.00	2.00
☐ 29	Joe DeLisle	.50	.20	.05
☐ 30	Pat Janostin	.50	.20	.05
☐ 31	Ben Duffy	.50	.20	.05
☐ 32	Sean Krakiwsky	.50	.20	.05
☐ 33	Mike Sertich	.50	.20	.05
☐ 34	Coaching Staff	.50	.20	.05
	Jim Knapp ACO			
	Glenn Kulyk ACO			
	Tim McDonald ACO			
	Mike Valesano ACO			
	Rick Menz EQUIP			
	Dale Hoganson EQUIP			
	Betty Fleissner TR			
☐ 35	Cheerleaders	.75	.30	.07
☐ 36	Jay Jackson (Mascot)	.75	.30	.07
	The Maroon Loon			

1993-94 Minnesota-Duluth

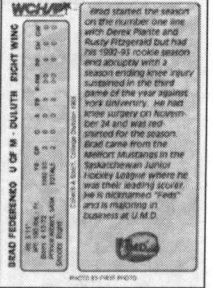

These 30 standard-size (2 1/2" by 3 1/2") cards feature on their fronts white-bordered color player action shots. The player's name and position, along with the Minnesota Bulldog logo, appear within the brown stripe across the bottom of the photo. The back carries the player's name, position, biography, and statistics on the left. His career highlights appear on the right. The set was produced by Collect-A-Sport and features a card of Chris Marinucci, 1993-94 Hobey Baker winner. The cards are unnumbered and checklisted below in alphabetical order.

		MINT	EXC	G-VG
COMPLETE SET (30)		10.00	4.00	1.00
COMMON PLAYER (1-30)		.35	.14	.03
☐ 1	Rod Aldoff	.35	.14	.03
☐ 2	Niklas Axelson	.35	.14	.03
☐ 3	David Buck	.35	.14	.03
☐ 4	Jerome Butler	.35	.14	.03
☐ 5	Brian Caruso	.50	.20	.05
☐ 6	Matt Christian	.50	.20	.05
	Chet Culic			
☐ 7	Marc Christian	.35	.14	.03
☐ 8	Joe Ciccarello	.35	.14	.03
☐ 9	Kyle Erickson	.50	.20	.05
	Adam Roy			
☐ 10	Brad Federenko	.35	.14	.03
☐ 11	Rusty Fitzgerald	.75	.30	.07
☐ 12	Jason Garatti	.35	.14	.03
☐ 13	Greg Hanson	.50	.20	.05
☐ 14	Don Jablonic	.35	.14	.03
☐ 15	Kraig Karakas	.35	.14	.03
☐ 16	Brett Larson	.50	.20	.05
☐ 17	Taras Lendzyk	.35	.14	.03
☐ 18	Derek Locker	.35	.14	.03
☐ 19	Chris Marinucci	2.50	1.00	.25

☐ 20	Todd Mickolajak	.50	.20	.05
	Chris Snell			
☐ 21	Rod Miller	.35	.14	.03
☐ 22	Rick Mrozik	.50	.20	.05
☐ 23	Aaron Novak	.35	.14	.03
☐ 24	Corey Osmak	.35	.14	.03
☐ 25	Sergei Petrov	.75	.30	.07
☐ 26	Jeff Romfo	.50	.20	.05
☐ 27	Mike Sertich CO	.35	.14	.03
☐ 28	Chris Sittlow	.35	.14	.03
☐ 29	Joe Tamminen	.50	.20	.05
☐ 30	Title Card	.50	.20	.05
	Roster			

1993-94 Minnesota-Duluth Commemorative

These four standard-size (2 1/2" by 3 1/2") cards feature black-and-white fronts with color photos on the backs. The set was produced by Collect-A-Sport to commemorate the 1992-93 WCHA champs.

		MINT	EXC	G-VG
COMPLETE SET (4)		6.00	2.40	.60
COMMON PLAYER (1-4)		1.00	.40	.10
☐ 1	Trophy Card	2.00	.80	.20
	(Chris Marinucci			
	with trophy)			
☐ 2	Derek Plante	4.00	1.60	.40
☐ 3	Brett Hauer	1.00	.40	.10
☐ 4	John Rohloff	2.00	.80	.20

1983-84 Moncton Alpines

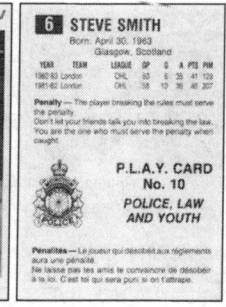

The Moncton Alpines are featured in this 28-card P.L.A.Y. (Police, Law and Youth) set, which was sponsored by the Moncton Police in conjunction with several company sponsors. The cards measure approximately 2 1/2" by 3 3/4" and are printed on thin card stock. The fronts feature color photos with the players posed in action stances. The photos are framed by white borders. The player's name and position are printed below the picture between Coke and Hostess logos. The backs have biography, statistics, and safety tips in English and French. The cards are numbered on the back.

		MINT	EXC	G-VG
COMPLETE SET (28)		15.00	6.00	1.50
COMMON PLAYER (1-27)		.50	.20	.05
☐ 1	Doug Messier CO	1.00	.40	.10
☐ 2	Chris Smith	.50	.20	.05

☐	3 Marco Baron	1.00	.40	.10
☐	4 Mike Zanier	1.00	.40	.10
☐	5 Dwayne Boettger	.50	.20	.05
☐	6 Lowell Loveday	.50	.20	.05
☐	7 Joe McDonnell	.50	.20	.05
☐	8 Peter Dineen	.50	.20	.05
☐	9 John Blum	1.00	.40	.10
☐	10 Steve Smith	5.00	2.00	.50
☐	11 Reg Kerr	1.00	.40	.10
☐	12 Tom Rowe	1.00	.40	.10
☐	13 Ross Lambert	.50	.20	.05
☐	14 Pat Conacher	1.25	.50	.12
☐	15 Paul Miller	.50	.20	.05
☐	16 Bert Yachimel	.50	.20	.05
☐	17 Tom Gorence	1.00	.40	.10
☐	18 Jeff Crawford	.50	.20	.05
☐	19 Serge Boisvert	1.00	.40	.10
☐	20 Todd Strueby	1.00	.40	.10
☐	21 Todd Bidner	.50	.20	.05
☐	22 Den Dachyshyn	.50	.20	.05
☐	23 Ray Cote	.50	.20	.05
☐	24 Shawn Babcock	.50	.20	.05
☐	25 Shawn Dineen	.50	.20	.05
☐	26 Marc Habscheid	1.25	.50	.12
☐	27 Charlie Lavalee TR Kevin Ferris TR	.50	.20	.05
☐	NNO Checklist Card	1.50	.60	.15

1984-85 Moncton Golden Flames

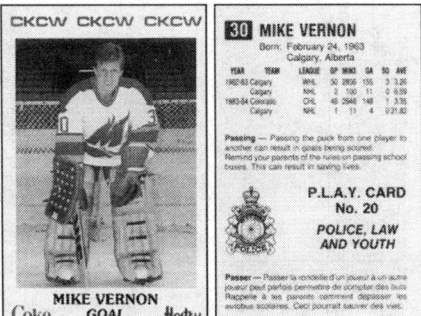

The Moncton Golden Flames are featured in this 26-card P.L.A.Y. (Police, Law and Youth) set, which was sponsored by the Moncton Police in conjunction with several company sponsors. The cards measure approximately 2 1/2" by 3 3/4" and are printed on thin card stock. The fronts feature color photos with the players posed in action stances. The photos are framed by white borders. The player's name and position are printed below the picture between Coke and Hostess logos. The backs have biography, statistics, and safety tips in English and French. The cards are numbered on the back.

		MINT	EXC	G-VG
	COMPLETE SET (26)	25.00	10.00	2.50
	COMMON PLAYER (1-26)	.60	.24	.06
☐	1 Brian Patafie TR	.60	.24	.06
☐	2 Mike Bianni TR	.60	.24	.06
☐	3 Pierre Page CO	1.25	.50	.12
☐	4 Neil Sheehy	1.00	.40	.10
☐	5 George White	.60	.24	.06
☐	6 Mark Lamb	1.25	.50	.12
☐	7 Dan Kane	.60	.24	.06
☐	8 Dan Bolduc	1.00	.40	.10
☐	9 Lou Kiriakou	.60	.24	.06
☐	10 Joel Otto	5.00	2.00	.50
☐	11 Dale Degray	1.00	.40	.10
☐	12 Mike Clayton	.60	.24	.06
☐	13 Mickey Volcan	.60	.24	.06
☐	14 Ted Pearson	.60	.24	.06

☐	15 Mario Simioni	.60	.24	.06
☐	16 Keith Hanson	.60	.24	.06
☐	17 Yves Courteau	.60	.24	.06
☐	18 Dan Cormier	.60	.24	.06
☐	19 Todd Hooey	.60	.24	.06
☐	20 Mike Vernon	10.00	4.00	1.00
☐	21 Dave Meszaros	.60	.24	.06
☐	22 Bruce Eakin	.60	.24	.06
☐	23 Tony Stiles	.60	.24	.06
☐	24 Ed Kastelic	1.25	.50	.12
☐	25 Pierre Rioux	.60	.24	.06
☐	26 Gino Cavallini	2.00	.80	.20

1985-86 Moncton Golden Flames

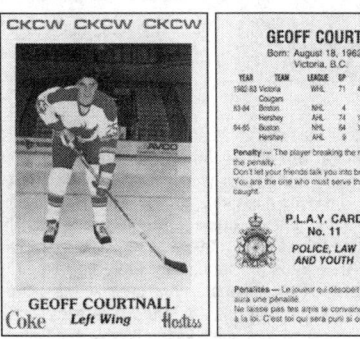

The Moncton Golden Flames are featured in this 28-card P.L.A.Y. (Police, Law and Youth) set, which was sponsored by the Moncton Police in conjunction with several company sponsors. The cards measure approximately 2 1/2" by 3 3/4" and are printed on thin card stock. The fronts feature color photos with the players posed in action stances. The photos are framed by white borders. The player's name and position are printed below the picture between Coke and Hostess logos. The backs have biography, statistics, and safety tips in English and French. The cards are numbered on the back.

		MINT	EXC	G-VG
	COMPLETE SET (28)	15.00	6.00	1.50
	COMMON PLAYER (1-28)	.60	.24	.06
☐	1 Terry Crisp GM/CO	1.50	.60	.15
☐	2 Dan Bolduc ACO	.60	.24	.06
☐	3 Terry Crisp GM/CO Dan Bolduc ACO	1.00	.40	.10
☐	4 Al Pedersen	1.00	.40	.10
☐	5 Dave Meszaros	.60	.24	.06
☐	6 George White	.60	.24	.06
☐	7 Mark Lamb	1.25	.50	.12
☐	8 Doug Kostynski	.60	.24	.06
☐	9 Brian Bradley	5.00	2.00	.50
☐	10 Rob Kivell	.60	.24	.06
☐	11 Geoff Courtnall	5.00	2.00	.50
☐	12 Tony Stiles	.60	.24	.06
☐	13 Jim Buettgen	.60	.24	.06
☐	14 Cleon Daskalakis	1.00	.40	.10
☐	15 Rick Kosti	.60	.24	.06
☐	16 Kevan Guy	1.00	.40	.10
☐	17 John Blum	1.00	.40	.10
☐	18 Brian Patafie Mike Baiani Jamie Druet	.60	.24	.06
☐	19 Greg Johnston	1.00	.40	.10
☐	20 Dale Degray	1.00	.40	.10
☐	21 John Meulenbroeks	.60	.24	.06
☐	22 Dave Reid	1.50	.60	.15
☐	23 Jay Miller	1.50	.60	.15
☐	24 Yves Courteau	.60	.24	.06
☐	25 Robin Bartel	.60	.24	.06
☐	26 Benoit Doucet	.60	.24	.06
☐	27 Pete Bakovic	.60	.24	.06
☐	28 Team Photo	2.00	.80	.20

1986-87 Moncton Golden Flames

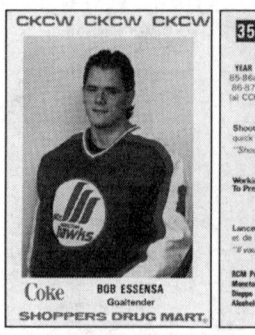

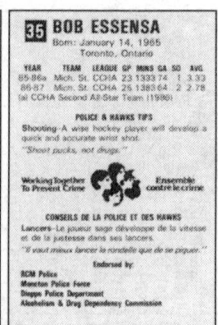

The Moncton Golden Flames are featured in this 28-card P.L.A.Y. (Police, Law and Youth) set, which was sponsored by the Moncton Police in conjunction with several company sponsors. The cards measure approximately approximately 2 1/2" by 3 3/4" and are printed on thin card stock. The fronts feature color photos with the players posed in action stances. The photos are framed by white borders. The player's name and position are printed below the picture between Coke and McDonald's logos. The backs have biography, statistics, and safety tips in English and French. The cards are numbered on the back. This set includes first pro cards of Brett Hull, Gary Roberts, Bill Ranford, and Lyndon Byers.

	MINT	EXC	G-VG
COMPLETE SET (28)	60.00	24.00	6.00
COMMON PLAYER (1-28)	.60	.24	.06
☐ 1 Terry Crisp CO/GM	1.50	.60	.15
☐ 2 Danny Bolduc ACO	.60	.24	.06
☐ 3 Doug Dadswell	.60	.24	.06
☐ 4 Doug Kostynski	.60	.24	.06
☐ 5 Bill Ranford	12.00	5.00	1.20
☐ 6 Brian Patafie TR	.60	.24	.06
☐ 7 Dave Pasin	.60	.24	.06
☐ 8 Darwin McCutcheon	.60	.24	.06
☐ 9 Team Photo	2.50	1.00	.25
☐ 10 Kevan Guy	1.00	.40	.10
☐ 11 Kraig Nienhuis	.60	.24	.06
☐ 12 Gary Roberts	8.00	3.25	.80
☐ 13 Ken Sabourin	1.25	.50	.12
☐ 14 Marc D'Amour	.75	.30	.07
☐ 15 Don Mercier	.60	.24	.06
☐ 16 Wade Campbell	.60	.24	.06
☐ 17 Mark Paterson	.60	.24	.06
☐ 18 Cleon Daskalakis	.75	.30	.07
☐ 19 Lyndon Byers	1.25	.50	.12
☐ 20 Brett Hull	40.00	16.00	4.00
☐ 21 Bob Sweeney	1.50	.60	.15
☐ 22 Gord Hynes	1.00	.40	.10
☐ 23 Peter Bakovic	.60	.24	.06
☐ 24 Dave Reid	1.25	.50	.12
☐ 25 Mike Rucinski	.60	.24	.06
☐ 26 Ray Podloski	.60	.24	.06
☐ 27 Bob Bodak	.60	.24	.06
☐ 28 John Carter	1.25	.50	.12

1987-88 Moncton Hawks

Sponsored by Coke, Shoppers Drug Mart, and CKCW, this 25-card set measures approximately 2 1/2" by 3 3/4" and features posed, color player photos with white studio backgrounds. The fronts have white borders with sponsor names printed in red above and below the picture. The player's name and position are printed in black just below the photo. The backs are white and carry biographical information, statistics, and "Police and Hawks Tips" in French and English. The cards are unnumbered and checklisted below in alphabetical order.

	MINT	EXC	G-VG
COMPLETE SET (25)	12.50	5.00	1.25
COMMON PLAYER (1-25)	.50	.20	.05
☐ 1 Joel Baillargeon	.50	.20	.05
☐ 2 Rick Bowness CO	1.00	.40	.10
☐ 3 Rick Carrano TR	.50	.20	.05
Wayne Flemming EQUIP			
☐ 4 Bobby Dollas	1.00	.40	.10
☐ 5 Peter Douris	1.00	.40	.10
☐ 6 Iain Duncan	.75	.30	.07
☐ 7 Bob Essensa	2.50	1.00	.25
☐ 8 Todd Flichel	.50	.20	.05
☐ 9 Rob Fowler	.50	.20	.05
☐ 10 Randy Gilhen	1.00	.40	.10
☐ 11 Matt Hervey	.75	.30	.07
☐ 12 Brent Hughes	1.00	.40	.10
☐ 13 Jamie Husgen	.50	.20	.05
☐ 14 Mike Jeffrey	.50	.20	.05
☐ 15 Guy Larose	1.00	.40	.10
☐ 16 Chris Levasseur	.50	.20	.05
☐ 17 Len Nielson	.50	.20	.05
☐ 18 Roger Ohman	.50	.20	.05
☐ 19 Dave Quigley	.50	.20	.05
☐ 20 Ron Pesetti	.50	.20	.05
☐ 21 Steve Penney	1.00	.40	.10
☐ 22 Scott Schneider	.50	.20	.05
☐ 23 Ryan Stewart	.50	.20	.05
☐ 24 Gord Whitaker	.50	.20	.05
☐ 25 Team Photo	1.50	.60	.15

1990-91 Moncton Hawks

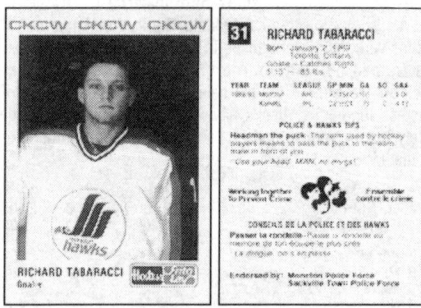

These 25 cards measure approximately 2 7/16" by 3 5/8" and feature on their fronts white-bordered posed-on-ice color shots of the '90-91 Moncton Hawks. The player's name and position appear at the lower left. The logos for the set's sponsors, Hostess, Frito Lay, and CKCW Radio, also appear on the front. The white back carries the player's name and uniform number at the top, followed below by biography, '89-90 statistics, and bilingual safety messages from the Hawks and Moncton Police. The cards are unnumbered and checklisted below in alphabetical order.

	MINT	EXC	G-VG
COMPLETE SET (25)	10.00	4.00	1.00
COMMON PLAYER (1-25)	.35	.14	.03

		MINT	EXC	G-VG
☐ 1	Larry Bernard	.35	.14	.03
☐ 2	Lee Davidson	.35	.14	.03
☐ 3	Iain Duncan	.75	.30	.07
☐ 4	Craig Duncanson	.50	.20	.05
☐ 5	Dallas Eakins	.50	.20	.05
☐ 6	Dave Farrish CO/GM	.35	.14	.03
☐ 7	Wayne Flemming EQUIP	.35	.14	.03
☐ 8	Todd Flichel	.35	.14	.03
☐ 9	Peter Hankinson	.35	.14	.03
☐ 10	Matt Hervey	.50	.20	.05
☐ 11	Brent Hughes	.75	.30	.07
☐ 12	Anthony Joseph	.35	.14	.03
☐ 13	Sergei Kharin	.50	.20	.05
☐ 14	Denis Larocque	.35	.14	.03
☐ 15	Guy Larose	.75	.30	.07
☐ 16	Scott Levins	.75	.30	.07
☐ 17	Bryan Marchment	1.00	.40	.10
☐ 18	Chris Norton	.35	.14	.03
☐ 19	Mike O'Neill	1.00	.40	.10
☐ 20	Grant Richison	.35	.14	.03
☐ 21	Scott Schneider	.35	.14	.03
☐ 22	Rob Snitzer TR	.35	.14	.03
☐ 23	Rick Tabaracci	2.00	.80	.20
☐ 24	Simon Wheeldon	.50	.20	.05
☐ 25	Team Card	1.00	.40	.10

1991-92 Moncton Hawks

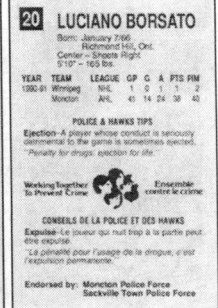

This 28-card set measures approximately 2 1/2" by 3 5/8" and was sponsored by the Moncton Police Force, the Sackville Police Force, and the Hostess/Frito Lay company. The fronts feature color photos with the players posed in action stances. The photos are framed by white borders. The player's name and position appear in the lower left corner, while the Hostess/Frito Lay logo is in the lower right corner. The backs carry biography, statistics, and safety tips in French and English. The cards are unnumbered and checklisted below in alphabetical order.

	MINT	EXC	G-VG
COMPLETE SET (28)	12.00	5.00	1.20
COMMON PLAYER (1-28)	.50	.20	.05

		MINT	EXC	G-VG
☐ 1	Luciano Borsato	1.00	.40	.10
☐ 2	Jason Cirone	.75	.30	.07
☐ 3	Rob Cowie	.50	.20	.05
☐ 4	Lee Davidson	.50	.20	.05
☐ 5	Kris Draper	1.00	.40	.10
☐ 6	Dallas Eakins	.50	.20	.05
☐ 7	Dave Farrish GM/CO	.50	.20	.05
☐ 8	Wayne Flemming EQUIP	.50	.20	.05
☐ 9	Sean Gauthier	.75	.30	.07
☐ 10	Ken Gernander	.50	.20	.05

		MINT	EXC	G-VG
☐ 11	Tod Hartje	.75	.30	.07
☐ 12	Bob Joyce	.75	.30	.07
☐ 13	Claude Julien	.50	.20	.05
☐ 14	Chris Kiene	.50	.20	.05
☐ 15	Mark Kumpel P/ACO	.50	.20	.05
☐ 16	Derek Langille	.50	.20	.05
☐ 17	Tyler Larter	.50	.20	.05
☐ 18	John LeBlanc	.50	.20	.05
☐ 19	Scott Levins	1.00	.40	.10
☐ 20	Rob Murray	.75	.30	.07
☐ 21	Kent Paynter	.50	.20	.05
☐ 22	Rudy Poeschek	.75	.30	.07
☐ 23	Dave Prior CO	.50	.20	.05
☐ 24	Warren Rychel	1.00	.40	.10
☐ 25	Rob Snitzer TR	.50	.20	.05
☐ 26	Rick Tabaracci	1.50	.60	.15
☐ 27	The Hawk (Mascot)	.50	.20	.05
☐ 28	Darren Veitch	.75	.30	.07

1989-90 Nashville Knights

This 23-card set measures the standard size (2 1/2" by 3 1/2") and was sponsored by Lee's Famous Recipe Country Chicken (a restaurant chain). The fronts feature color photos with the players in a variety of action and still poses. White borders enhance the front, and the player's name appears in the border below the picture. The corners of the picture are cut off to give the appearance of circular picture holders. The backs carry biography and advertisement information. The cards are unnumbered and checklisted below in alphabetical order.

	MINT	EXC	G-VG
COMPLETE SET (23)	8.00	3.25	.80
COMMON PLAYER (1-23)	.50	.20	.05

		MINT	EXC	G-VG
☐ 1	Pat Bingham	.50	.20	.05
☐ 2	Andre Brassard	.50	.20	.05
☐ 3	Mike Bukta	.50	.20	.05
☐ 4	Chris Cambio	.50	.20	.05
☐ 5	Chick-E-Lee (Mascot)	.75	.30	.07
☐ 6	Glen Engevik	.50	.20	.05
☐ 7	Matt Gallagher	.50	.20	.05
	Dir. Player Development			
	Scott Greer AGM			
☐ 8	Archie Henderson CO	.75	.30	.07
☐ 9	Billy Huard	.75	.30	.07
☐ 10	Craig Jenkins ANN	.50	.20	.05
	Dave Cavaliere TR			
☐ 11	Todd Jenkins	.50	.20	.05
☐ 12	Brock Kelly	.50	.20	.05
☐ 13	Paul Krayer	.50	.20	.05
☐ 14	Garth Lamb	.50	.20	.05
☐ 15	Rob Levasseur	.50	.20	.05
☐ 16	Dan O'Brien	.50	.20	.05
☐ 17	Bob Polk OWN	.50	.20	.05
	Ron Fuller OWN			
☐ 18	John Reid (In action)	.50	.20	.05
☐ 19	John Reid (Portrait)	.50	.20	.05
☐ 20	Jeff Salzbrunn	.50	.20	.05
☐ 21	Mike Schwalb	.50	.20	.05
☐ 22	Ron Servatius	.50	.20	.05
☐ 23	Jason Simon	.50	.20	.05

1990-91 Newmarket Saints

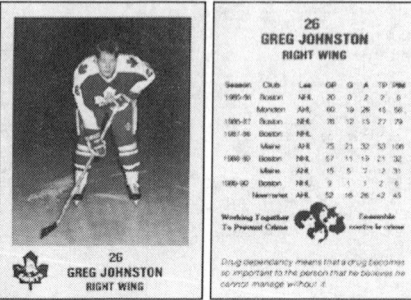

This 26-card set features the 1990-91 Newmarket Saints of the AHL (American Hockey League). Measuring approximately 2 1/2" by 3 3/4", the fronts feature on-ice color posed action shots. The pictures are framed by white borders; the team insignia and player information are printed in black in the bottom wider border. In addition to player information and season-by-season record, the backs carry a bilingual slogan ("Working Together To Prevent Crime" and "Ensemble contre le crime) and anti-drug or alcohol messages. The cards are unnumbered and checklisted below in alphabetical order.

	MINT	EXC	G-VG
COMPLETE SET (26)	10.00	4.00	1.00
COMMON PLAYER (1-26)	.35	.14	.03
☐ 1 Frank Anzalone CO	.35	.14	.03
☐ 2 Tim Bean	.35	.14	.03
☐ 3 Brian Blad	.35	.14	.03
☐ 4 Bryan Cousineau	.35	.14	.03
Deputy Chief			
☐ 5 Alan Hepple	.35	.14	.03
☐ 6 Donald Hillock	.35	.14	.03
Chief of Police			
☐ 7 Robert Horyna	.35	.14	.03
☐ 8 Kent Hulst	.35	.14	.03
☐ 9 Mike Jackson	.35	.14	.03
☐ 10 Greg Johnston	.75	.30	.07
☐ 11 Eldred King	.35	.14	.03
Chairman of Regional			
Municipality			
☐ 12 Frank Kovacs	.35	.14	.03
Police Sergeant			
☐ 13 Derek Langille	.35	.14	.03
☐ 14 Lanny	.35	.14	.03
Police Dog			
☐ 15 Mike Millar	.35	.14	.03
☐ 16 Mike Moes	.35	.14	.03
☐ 17 Bill Purcell ACO	.35	.14	.03
☐ 18 Bobby Reynolds	.35	.14	.03
☐ 19 Damian Rhodes	1.50	.60	.15
☐ 20 Bill Root	.50	.20	.05
☐ 21 Joe Sacco	.75	.30	.07
☐ 22 Darryl Shannon	.75	.30	.07
☐ 23 Doug Shedden	.75	.30	.07
☐ 24 Mike Stevens	.50	.20	.05
☐ 25 Darren Veitch	.75	.30	.07
☐ 26 Greg Walters	.35	.14	.03

1988-89 Niagara Falls Thunder

This 25-card set measures approximately 2 5/8" by 4 1/8" and was sponsored by the Niagara Falls Fire Department and area businesses. The cards are printed on thin card stock. The fronts have a white card face and feature color action player photos with two thin black lines forming a border. The player's name is printed in red on the picture at the

bottom. The team name appears below the picture. The backs carry biography and fire safety tips. The cards are numbered on the back.

	MINT	EXC	G-VG
COMPLETE SET (25)	30.00	12.00	3.00
COMMON PLAYER (1-25)	.60	.24	.06
☐ 1 Title Card	1.50	.60	.15
☐ 2 Brad May	6.00	2.40	.60
☐ 3 Paul Wolanski	.60	.24	.06
☐ 4 Keith Primeau	9.00	3.75	.90
☐ 5 Mark Lawrence	.75	.30	.07
☐ 6 Mike Rosati	.60	.24	.06
☐ 7 Dennis Vial	1.50	.60	.15
☐ 8 Shawn McCosh	.60	.24	.06
☐ 9 Jason Soules	1.00	.40	.10
☐ 10 Rob Fournier	.60	.24	.06
☐ 11 Scott Pearson	2.50	1.00	.25
☐ 12 Jamie Leach	1.00	.40	.10
☐ 13 Colin Miller	.60	.24	.06
☐ 14 Bryan Fogarty	2.00	.80	.20
☐ 15 Keith Osborne	1.00	.40	.10
☐ 16 Stan Drulia	1.00	.40	.10
☐ 17 Paul Laus	1.00	.40	.10
☐ 18 Adrian Van Der Sloot	.60	.24	.06
☐ 19 Greg Allen	.60	.24	.06
☐ 20 Don Pancoe	.60	.24	.06
☐ 21 Alain LaForge	.60	.24	.06
☐ 22 Bill LaForge GM/CO	.60	.24	.06
☐ 23 Steve Locke	.60	.24	.06
☐ 24 Benny Rogano ACO	.60	.24	.06
☐ 25 Heavy Evason ACO	.60	.24	.06

1989-90 Niagara Falls Thunder

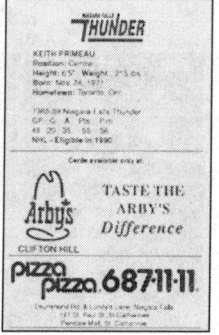

Sponsored by local Arby's and Pizza Pizza stores, these 25 cards measure approximately 2 5/8" by 4 1/8" and feature on their fronts white-bordered posed-on-ice color shots of the 1989-90 Niagara Falls Thunder. The player's name appears in red lettering within the white bottom margin. The white back carries the player's name and position at the top, followed by biography and 1989 statistics. The cards are unnumbered and checklisted below in alphabetical order.

	MINT	EXC	G-VG
COMPLETE SET (25)	15.00	6.00	1.50
COMMON PLAYER (1-25)	.50	.20	.05
☐ 1 Greg Allen	.50	.20	.05
☐ 2 Roch Belley	.75	.30	.07
☐ 3 David Benn	.50	.20	.05
☐ 4 Andy Bezeau	.50	.20	.05
☐ 5 George Burnett CO	.50	.20	.05
☐ 6 Todd Coopman	.50	.20	.05
☐ 7 Randy Hall ACO	.50	.20	.05
☐ 8 John Johnson	.50	.20	.05
☐ 9 Paul Laus	.75	.30	.07
☐ 10 Mark Lawrence	.75	.30	.07
☐ 11 Brad May	2.50	1.00	.25
☐ 12 Don McConnell	.50	.20	.05
☐ 13 Brian Mueggler	.50	.20	.05
☐ 14 Don Pancoe	.50	.20	.05

☐	15	Keith Primeau	3.50	1.40	.35
☐	16	Geoff Rawson	.50	.20	.05
☐	17	Ken Ruddick	.50	.20	.05
☐	18	Greg Suchan	.50	.20	.05
☐	19	Trainers	.50	.20	.05
		Paul Bruneau			
		Dennis Scott			
☐	20	Steve Udvari	.50	.20	.05
☐	21	Jeff Walker	.75	.30	.07
☐	22	Jason Winch	.75	.30	.07
☐	23	Paul Wolanski	.50	.20	.05
☐	24	Title Card	.50	.20	.05
☐	25	Checklist Card	.75	.30	.07

1993-94 Niagara Falls Thunder

 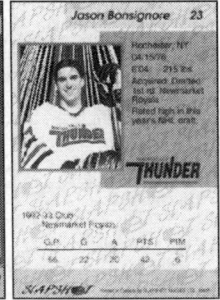

Printed by Slapshot Images Ltd., this 29-card set features the 1993-94 Niagara Falls Thunder. The cards measure standard size (2 1/2" by 3 1/2"). On a geometrical purple and green background, the fronts feature color action player photos with thin grey borders. The player's name, position and team name, as well as the producer's logo, appear on the front. The backs carry a close-up color player portrait, biography and statistics, along with team and sponsor's logos. The cards are numbered on the back. Included in this set is a Slapshot ad card with a 1994 calendar on the back.

			MINT	EXC	G-VG
	COMPLETE SET (29)		12.00	5.00	1.20
	COMMON PLAYER (1-29)		.35	.14	.03
☐	1	Title Card/Checklist	.35	.14	.03
☐	2	Jimmy Hibbert	.35	.14	.03
☐	3	Darryl Foster	.35	.14	.03
☐	4	Gerry Skrypec	.35	.14	.03
☐	5	Greg de Vries	.35	.14	.03
☐	6	Tim Thompson	.35	.14	.03
☐	7	Joel Yates	.35	.14	.03
☐	8	Yianni Ioannou	.50	.20	.05
☐	9	Steve Nimigon	.50	.20	.05
☐	10	Jeff Johnstone	.35	.14	.03
☐	11	Brandon Convery	1.50	.60	.15
☐	12	Dale Junkin	.35	.14	.03
☐	13	Ethan Moreau	2.00	.80	.20
☐	14	Derek Grant	.35	.14	.03
☐	15	Neil Fewster	.35	.14	.03
☐	16	Jason Reesor	.35	.14	.03
☐	17	Tom Moores	.35	.14	.03
☐	18	Matthew Mayo	.35	.14	.03
☐	19	Bogdan Savenko	.50	.20	.05
☐	20	Corey Bricknell	.35	.14	.03
☐	21	Derek Sylvester	.50	.20	.05
☐	22	Anatoli Filatov	.35	.14	.03
☐	23	Jason Bonsignore	3.00	1.20	.30
☐	24	Mike Perna	.35	.14	.03
☐	25	Manny Legace	1.25	.50	.12
☐	26	Randy Hall CO GM	.35	.14	.03
☐	27	Chris Johnstone CO	.35	.14	.03
☐	28	Jason Bonsignore	1.25	.50	.12
		Ethan Moreau			
		Brandon Convery			
		Towering Prospects			
☐		NNO Ad Card	.35	.14	.03

1982-83 North Bay Centennials

This 23-card set was printed on thick card stock. The fronts feature a mix of action poses and portraits bordered in white. The backs carry biographical information and sponsor logos, Aunt May's City Bakery (Northern) Limited and CFCH-600 Radio. The cards are unnumbered and checklisted below in alphabetical order.

			MINT	EXC	G-VG
	COMPLETE SET (24)		20.00	8.00	2.00
	COMMON PLAYER (1-24)		1.00	.40	.10
☐	1	Allen Bishop	1.00	.40	.10
☐	2	John Capel	1.00	.40	.10
☐	3	Rob Degagne	1.00	.40	.10
☐	4	Phil Drouillard	1.00	.40	.10
☐	5	Jeff Eatough	1.00	.40	.10
☐	6	Tony Gilliard	1.00	.40	.10
☐	7	Paul Gillis	1.50	.60	.15
☐	8	Pete Handley	1.00	.40	.10
☐	9	Mark Hatcher	1.00	.40	.10
☐	10	Tim Helmer	1.00	.40	.10
☐	11	Craig Kales	1.00	.40	.10
☐	12	Bob LaForest	1.00	.40	.10
☐	13	Mark LaForest	2.00	.80	.20
☐	14	Bill Maguire	1.00	.40	.10
☐	15	Andrew McBain	2.00	.80	.20
☐	16	Ron Meighan	1.00	.40	.10
☐	17	Rick Morocco	1.00	.40	.10
☐	18	Alain Raymond	1.00	.40	.10
☐	19	Joe Reekie	2.00	.80	.20
☐	20	Joel Smith	1.00	.40	.10
☐	21	Bert Templeton CO	1.00	.40	.10
☐	22	Kevin Vescio	1.00	.40	.10
☐	23	Peter Woodgate	1.00	.40	.10
☐	24	Don Young	1.00	.40	.10

1983-84 North Bay Centennials

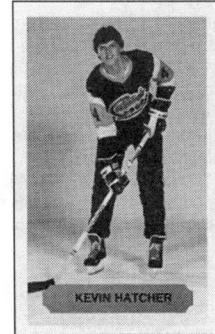 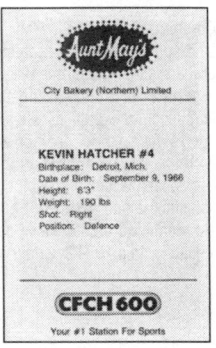

This 25-card set measures approximately 2 1/2" by 4" and is printed on thin card stock. The fronts carry color, posed action player photos with white borders. The player's name appears in a butterscotch-colored plaque that is superimposed over the picture. The backs carry biographical information and sponsor logos, Aunt May's City Bakery (Northern) Limited and CFCH-600 Radio. The cards are unnumbered and checklisted below in alphabetical order.

			MINT	EXC	G-VG
	COMPLETE SET (25)		25.00	10.00	2.50
	COMMON PLAYER (1-25)		.75	.30	.07
☐	1	Sponsor's Card	1.25	.50	.12
☐	2	Peter Abric	.75	.30	.07
☐	3	Richard Benoit	.75	.30	.07
☐	4	Scott Birnie	.75	.30	.07
☐	5	John Capel	.75	.30	.07

☐ 6	Curtis Collin	.75	.30	.07
☐ 7	Rob Degagne	.75	.30	.07
☐ 8	Kevin Hatcher	15.00	6.00	1.50
☐ 9	Mark Hatcher	.75	.30	.07
☐ 10	Tim Helmer	.75	.30	.07
☐ 11	Jim Hunter	.75	.30	.07
☐ 12	Kevin Kerr	.75	.30	.07
☐ 13	Nick Kypreos	1.50	.60	.15
☐ 14	Mike Larouche	.75	.30	.07
☐ 15	Greg Larsen	.75	.30	.07
☐ 16	Mark Lavarre	1.00	.40	.10
☐ 17	Brett MacDonald	.75	.30	.07
☐ 18	Wayne Macphee	.75	.30	.07
☐ 19	Peter McGrath	.75	.30	.07
☐ 20	Rob Nichols	.75	.30	.07
☐ 21	Ron Sanko	.75	.30	.07
☐ 22	Kevin Vescio	.75	.30	.07
☐ 23	Mike Webber	.75	.30	.07
☐ 24	Peter Woodgate	.75	.30	.07
☐ 25	Bert Templeton CO/GM	.75	.30	.07

1993-94 North Bay Centennials

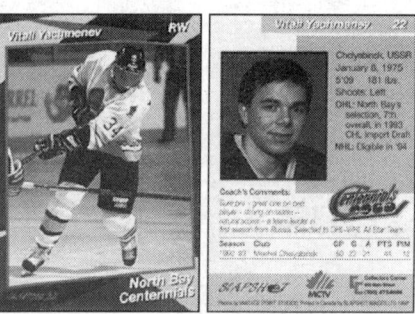

Co-sponsored by MCTV and Collectors Corner and printed by Slapshot Images Ltd., this standard size (2 1/2" by 3 1/2") 26-card set features the 1993-94 North Bay Centennials. On a geometrical yellow and black background, the fronts feature color action player photos with thin grey borders. The player's name, position and team name, as well as the producer's logo, appear on the front. The team color-coded backs carry a close-up color player portrait, biography and statistics, along with team and sponsors' logos. The cards are numbered on the back. Included in this set is a Slapshot ad card with a 1994 calendar on the back.

		MINT	EXC	G-VG
	COMPLETE SET (26)	10.00	4.00	1.00
	COMMON PLAYER (1-26)	.35	.14	.03
☐ 1	Brad Brown	1.00	.40	.10
☐ 2	Sandy Allan	.75	.30	.07
☐ 3	Rob Lave	.35	.14	.03
☐ 4	Steve McLaren	.35	.14	.03
☐ 5	Andy Delmore	.35	.14	.03
☐ 6	Corey Neilson	.35	.14	.03
☐ 7	Jason Campeau	.35	.14	.03
☐ 8	Jim Ensom	.35	.14	.03
☐ 9	Bill Lang	.50	.20	.05
☐ 10	Ryan Gillis	.35	.14	.03
☐ 11	Michael Burman	.35	.14	.03
☐ 12	Stefan Rivard	.35	.14	.03
☐ 13	B.J. MacPherson	.50	.20	.05
☐ 14	Lee Jinman	1.00	.40	.10
☐ 15	Scott Cherrey	.75	.30	.07
☐ 16	Damien Bloye	.35	.14	.03
☐ 17	Denis Gaudet	.35	.14	.03
☐ 18	Bob Thornton	.35	.14	.03
☐ 19	John Guirestante	.35	.14	.03
☐ 20	Jeff Shevalier	.75	.30	.07
☐ 21	Scott Roche	.50	.20	.05
☐ 22	Vitali Yachmenev	1.00	.40	.10
☐ 23	Bert Templeton CO	.35	.14	.03
☐ 24	Rob Kirsch ACO	.35	.14	.03

☐ 25	Brad Brown Vitali Yachmenev Top Prospects	.50	.20	.05
☐	NNO Ad Card	.35	.14	.03

1977-78 Nova Scotia Voyageurs

Sponsored by the Farmers Twin Cities Co-op Dairy Ltd., this 24-card set measures approximately 2 1/8" by 4 1/2" and features the Nova Scotia Voyageurs of the American Hockey Association. The fronts feature posed action player photos bordered in white. In the top border appears "Nova Scotia Voyageurs 1977-78," while the player's name, facsimile autograph, sponsor name and logo, and team logo are printed below the picture. The backs are blank. The cards are unnumbered and checklisted below in alphabetical order.

		NRMT	VG-E	GOOD
	COMPLETE SET (24)	20.00	8.00	2.00
	COMMON PLAYER (1-24)	1.00	.40	.10
☐ 1	Bruce Baker	1.00	.40	.10
☐ 2	Maurice Barrette	1.00	.40	.10
☐ 3	Barry Borrett	1.00	.40	.10
☐ 4	Tim Burke	1.00	.40	.10
☐ 5	Jim Cahoon	1.00	.40	.10
☐ 6	Norm Dupont	1.50	.60	.15
☐ 7	Greg Fox	1.50	.60	.15
☐ 8	Mike Hobin	1.00	.40	.10
☐ 9	Bob Holland	1.00	.40	.10
☐ 10	Don Howse	1.00	.40	.10
☐ 11	Pat Hughes	1.50	.60	.15
☐ 12	Chuck Luksa	1.00	.40	.10
☐ 13	Dave Lumley	1.50	.60	.15
☐ 14	Al MacNeil CO	1.50	.60	.15
☐ 15	Gord McTavish	1.00	.40	.10
☐ 16	Rick Meagher	2.50	1.00	.25
☐ 17	Mike Polich	1.00	.40	.10
☐ 18	Moe Robinson	1.00	.40	.10
☐ 19	Gaeton Rochette	1.00	.40	.10
☐ 20	Pierre Roy	1.00	.40	.10
☐ 21	Frank St.Marseille	1.00	.40	.10
☐ 22	Derrick St.Marseille TR	1.00	.40	.10
☐ 23	Rod Schutt	1.00	.40	.10
☐ 24	Ron Wilson	1.50	.60	.15

1983-84 Nova Scotia Voyageurs

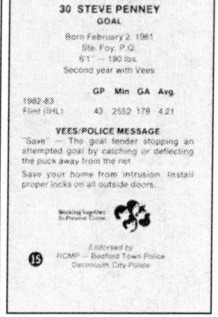

This 24-card police set features the Nova Scotia Oilers of the American Hockey League. The cards measure approximately 2 1/2" by 3 3/4" and were sponsored by Q104 (an FM radio station), Coca-Cola, and Hostess. The cards display posed color player photos on a white card face. The player's name and jersey number appear at the top. The three sponsors' logos are in the bottom white border. The backs are white and carry biography, statistics, and public service messages. The cards are numbered on the back in the lower left corner.

	MINT	EXC	G-VG
COMPLETE SET (24)	12.50	5.00	1.25
COMMON PLAYER (1-24)	.50	.20	.05
☐ 1 Mark Holden	.75	.30	.07
☐ 2 Bill Kitchen	.50	.20	.05
☐ 3 Dave Allison	.50	.20	.05
☐ 4 Stephane Lefebvre	.50	.20	.05
☐ 5 Stan Hennigar	.50	.20	.05
☐ 6 Steve Marengere	.50	.20	.05
☐ 7 John Goodwin	.50	.20	.05
☐ 8 John Newberry	.50	.20	.05
☐ 9 Bill Riley	.50	.20	.05
☐ 10 Norman Baron	.75	.30	.07
☐ 11 Brian Skrudland	2.00	.80	.20
☐ 12 Mike Lalor	1.00	.40	.10
☐ 13 Blair Barnes	.50	.20	.05
☐ 14 Remi Gagne	.50	.20	.05
☐ 15 Steve Penney	1.00	.40	.10
☐ 16 Michel Therrien	.50	.20	.05
☐ 17 Dave Stoyanovich	.50	.20	.05
☐ 18 Brian Patafie TR	.50	.20	.05
Lou Christian TR			
☐ 19 Mike McPhee	2.50	1.00	.25
☐ 20 Wayne Thompson	.50	.20	.05
☐ 21 Ted Fauss	.50	.20	.05
☐ 22 Jeff Teal	.50	.20	.05
☐ 23 Larry Landon	.50	.20	.05
☐ 24 Greg Moffett	.75	.30	.07

1984-85 Nova Scotia Oilers

This 26-card police set features the Nova Scotia Oilers of the American Hockey League. The cards measure approximately 2 1/2" by 3 3/4" and were sponsored by Q104 (an FM radio station), Coca-Cola, Hostess, and the Bedford Town Police, and the Halifax City Police. The cards display posed color player photos on a white card face. The player's name and position appear at the bottom. The three sponsors' logos are across the top and in the bottom two corners. The backs are white and carry biography, statistics, and public service messages. The cards are numbered on the back.

	MINT	EXC	G-VG
COMPLETE SET (26)	10.00	4.00	1.00
COMMON PLAYER (1-26)	.50	.20	.05
☐ 1 Mark Holden	.75	.30	.07
☐ 2 Dave Allison	.50	.20	.05
☐ 3 Dwayne Boettger	.50	.20	.05
☐ 4 Lowell Loveday	.50	.20	.05
☐ 5 Rejean Cloutier	.50	.20	.05
☐ 6 Ray Cote	.50	.20	.05
☐ 7 Pat Conacher	.75	.30	.07
☐ 8 Ken Berry	.75	.30	.07
☐ 9 Steve Graves	.50	.20	.05
☐ 10 Todd Strueby	.75	.30	.07
☐ 11 Steve Smith	2.00	.80	.20
☐ 12 Archie Henderson	.75	.30	.07
☐ 13 Dean Dachyshyn	.50	.20	.05
☐ 14 Marc Habscheid	1.00	.40	.10
☐ 15 Larry Melnyk	.50	.20	.05
☐ 16 Raimo Summanen	.75	.30	.07
☐ 17 Jim Playfair	.50	.20	.05
☐ 18 Mike Zanier	.75	.30	.07
☐ 19 Ian Wood	.50	.20	.05
☐ 20 Dean Hopkins	.50	.20	.05
☐ 21 Norm Aubin	.50	.20	.05
☐ 22 Tony Currie	.50	.20	.05
☐ 23 Ross Lambert	.50	.20	.05
☐ 24 Terry Martin	.50	.20	.05
☐ 25 Ed Chadwick CO	.50	.20	.05
Larry Kish CO			
Bob Boucher CO			
☐ 26 Lou Christian TR	.50	.20	.05
Kevin Farris TR			

1985-86 Nova Scotia Oilers

This 28-card police set features the Nova Scotia Oilers. The cards measure approximately 2 1/2" by 3 3/4" and were sponsored by Coca-Cola, Hostess, Q104 (an FM radio station), IGA foodstores, and the Halifax City Police. The fronts display color action photos on a white card face. The sponsor logos appear across the top and in the lower corners. The player's name and position is below the picture. The backs carry biographical information, statistics, and public service messages. The cards are numbered on the back.

	MINT	EXC	G-VG
COMPLETE SET (28)	12.00	5.00	1.20
COMMON PLAYER (1-28)	.50	.20	.05
☐ 1 Dean Hopkins	.75	.30	.07
☐ 2 Jeff Larmer	.50	.20	.05
☐ 3 Mike Moller	.50	.20	.05
☐ 4 Dean Dachyshyn	.50	.20	.05
☐ 5 Bruce Boudreau	.75	.30	.07
☐ 6 Ken Solheim	.50	.20	.05
☐ 7 Jeff Beukeboom	1.00	.40	.10
☐ 8 Mark Lavarre	.50	.20	.05
☐ 9 John Ollson	.50	.20	.05
☐ 10 Lou Crawford	.50	.20	.05
☐ 11 Warren Skorodenski	.75	.30	.07
☐ 12 Dwayne Boettger	.50	.20	.05
☐ 13 Daryl Reaugh	.75	.30	.07
☐ 14 John Miner	.50	.20	.05
☐ 15 Jim Ralph	1.00	.40	.10
☐ 16 Wayne Presley	.75	.30	.07
☐ 17 Steve Graves	.50	.20	.05
☐ 18 Tom McMurchy	.50	.20	.05
☐ 19 Darin Sceviour	.50	.20	.05
☐ 20 Kent Paynter	.50	.20	.05
☐ 21 Larry Kish GM/CO	.50	.20	.05
☐ 22 Jim Playfair	.50	.20	.05
☐ 23 Kevin Farris TR	.50	.20	.05
Ralph Mosher TR			
☐ 24 Mickey Volcan	.50	.20	.05
☐ 25 Ron Low ACO	.75	.30	.07
☐ 26 Don Biggs	.75	.30	.07
☐ 27 Bruce Eakin	.50	.20	.05
☐ 28 Team Photo	1.00	.40	.10

1992-93 Oklahoma City Blazers

This 18-card set measures the standard size (2 1/2" by 3 1/2") and was sponsored by TD's Sports Cards (a Tulsa baseball card store) and Planters Nuts and Snacks. Ten thousand were sets were produced. Randomly inserted throughout the sets were 350 autographed cards of each player. The cards feature color action player photos with white borders. The player's name is superimposed on the photo at the bottom. The backs carry biography, career highlights, and the Planters logo. The cards are unnumbered and checklisted below in alphabetical order.

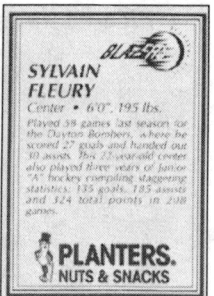

	MINT	EXC	G-VG
COMPLETE SET (18)	8.00	3.25	.80
COMMON PLAYER (1-18)	.50	.20	.05

		MINT	EXC	G-VG
☐ 1	Title Card	.75	.30	.07
☐ 2	Carl Boudreau	.50	.20	.05
☐ 3	Joe Burton	.50	.20	.05
☐ 4	Sylvain Fleury	.75	.30	.07
☐ 5	Brendan Garvey	.50	.20	.05
☐ 6	Guy Girouard	.50	.20	.05
☐ 7	Sean Gorman	.50	.20	.05
☐ 8	Jamie Hearn	.50	.20	.05
☐ 9	Craig Johnson	.75	.30	.07
☐ 10	Paul Krake	.75	.30	.07
☐ 11	Chris Laganas	.50	.20	.05
☐ 12	Daniel Larin	.50	.20	.05
☐ 13	Mark McGinn	.50	.20	.05
☐ 14	Alan Perry	.75	.30	.07
☐ 15	Steve Simoni	.50	.20	.05
☐ 16	Jim Solly	.50	.20	.05
☐ 17	Boyd Sutton	.50	.20	.05
☐ 18	Team Photo	1.00	.40	.10

1980-81 Oshawa Generals

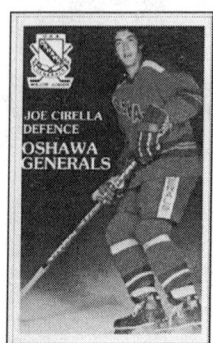
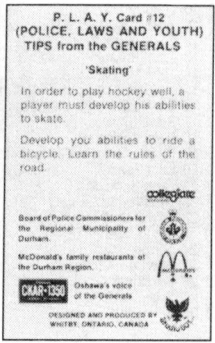

This 25-card P.L.A.Y. (Police, Laws and Youth) set measures approximately 2 5/8" by 4 1/8" and features color posed action player photos and is bordered by white borders accented by a thin red line. The player's name, position, and team are superimposed in white letters on the picture. The backs carry "Tips from the Generals" that include a hockey tip and its application to a life situation. The cards are numbered on the back and concludes with some former Generals' players (23-25).

	MINT	EXC	G-VG
COMPLETE SET (25)	150.00	60.00	15.00
COMMON PLAYER (1-25)	3.00	1.20	.30

		MINT	EXC	G-VG
☐ 1	Generals Logo	5.00	2.00	.50
☐ 2	Ray Flaherty	3.00	1.20	.30
☐ 3	Craig Kitchener	3.00	1.20	.30
☐ 4	Dan Revell	3.00	1.20	.30
☐ 5	Bob Kucheran	3.00	1.20	.30
☐ 6	Patrick Poulin	3.00	1.20	.30
☐ 7	Dave Andreychuk	40.00	16.00	4.00
☐ 8	Barry Tabobondung	3.00	1.20	.30
☐ 9	Steve Konroyd	5.00	2.00	.50
☐ 10	Paul Edwards	3.00	1.20	.30
☐ 11	Dale Degray	4.00	1.60	.40
☐ 12	Joe Cirella	5.00	2.00	.50
☐ 13	Norm Schmidt	3.00	1.20	.30
☐ 14	Markus Lehto	3.00	1.20	.30
☐ 15	Mitch Lamoureux	4.00	1.60	.40
☐ 16	Tony Tanti	7.50	3.00	.75
☐ 17	Bill Laforge	3.00	1.20	.30
☐ 18	Greg Gravel	3.00	1.20	.30
☐ 19	Mike Lekun	3.00	1.20	.30
☐ 20	Chris Smith	3.00	1.20	.30
☐ 21	Peter Sidorkiewicz	7.50	3.00	.75
☐ 22	Greg Stefan	5.00	2.00	.50
☐ 23	Tom McCarthy	5.00	2.00	.50
☐ 24	Rick Lanz	4.00	1.60	.40
☐ 25	Bobby Orr	60.00	24.00	6.00

1981-82 Oshawa Generals

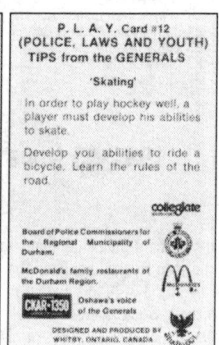

This 25-card P.L.A.Y. (Police, Laws and Youth) set measures approximately 2 5/8" by 4 1/8" and features color posed action player photos. The backs carry "Tips from the Generals" that include a hockey tip and its application to a life situation. The cards are numbered on the back.

	MINT	EXC	G-VG
COMPLETE SET (25)	75.00	30.00	7.50
COMMON PLAYER (1-25)	2.00	.80	.20

		MINT	EXC	G-VG
☐ 1	Generals Logo	4.00	1.60	.40
☐ 2	Chris Smith	2.00	.80	.20
☐ 3	Peter Sidorkiewicz	6.00	2.40	.60
☐ 4	Ali Butorac	2.00	.80	.20
☐ 5	Dan Revell	2.00	.80	.20
☐ 6	Mitch Lamoureux	2.50	1.00	.25
☐ 7	Norm Schmidt	2.00	.80	.20
☐ 8	Paul Edwards	2.00	.80	.20
☐ 9	Dan Nicholson	2.00	.80	.20
☐ 10	John Hutchings	2.00	.80	.20
☐ 11	Dave Gans	2.00	.80	.20
☐ 12	Dave Andreychuk	25.00	10.00	2.50
☐ 13	Mike Stern	2.00	.80	.20
☐ 14	Dale Degray	3.00	1.20	.30
☐ 15	Mike Lekun	2.00	.80	.20
☐ 16	Greg Gravel	2.00	.80	.20
☐ 17	Dave MacLean	2.00	.80	.20
☐ 18	Tony Tanti	7.50	3.00	.75
☐ 19	John MacLean	15.00	6.00	1.50
☐ 20	Jim Uens	2.00	.80	.20
☐ 21	Guy Jacob	2.00	.80	.20
☐ 22	Jeff Steffan	2.00	.80	.20
☐ 23	Paul Theriault	2.00	.80	.20
☐ 24	Sherry Bassin	2.00	.80	.20
☐ 25	Durham Regional Police Logo	2.00	.80	.20

1982-83 Oshawa Generals

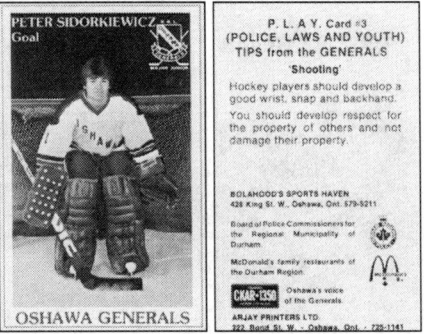

This 25-card set measures approximately 2 5/8" by 4 1/8" and features color, posed action player photos framed by thin red border lines that rest on a white card face. The player's name, position, and the team logo are superimposed across the top of the picture in white lettering. The team name appears below the photo in red. The backs carry P.L.A.Y. (Police, Laws and Youth) public service messages and hockey tips. Sponsor logos and name are printed on the lower portion of the card. The cards are numbered on the back.

	MINT	EXC	G-VG
COMPLETE SET (25)	35.00	14.00	3.50
COMMON PLAYER (1-25)	1.25	.50	.12

		MINT	EXC	G-VG
☐ 1	Generals Logo	2.00	.80	.20
☐ 2	Jeff Hogg	1.25	.50	.12
☐ 3	Peter Sidorkiewicz	5.00	2.00	.50
☐ 4	Dale Degray	1.50	.60	.15
☐ 5	Joe Cirella	2.50	1.00	.25
☐ 6	Todd Smith	1.25	.50	.12
☐ 7	Scott Brydges	1.25	.50	.12
☐ 8	Jeff Steffen	1.25	.50	.12
☐ 9	Don Biggs	2.00	.80	.20
☐ 10	Todd Hooey	1.25	.50	.12
☐ 11	Tony Tanti	5.00	2.00	.50
☐ 12	Danny Gratton	1.50	.60	.15
☐ 13	Steve King	1.25	.50	.12
☐ 14	Dan Defazio	1.25	.50	.12
☐ 15	John MacLean	10.00	4.00	1.00
☐ 16	Tim Burgess	1.25	.50	.12
☐ 17	Mike Stern	1.25	.50	.12
☐ 18	Dan Nicholson	1.25	.50	.12
☐ 19	David Gans	1.25	.50	.12
☐ 20	John Hutchings	1.25	.50	.12
☐ 21	Norm Schmidt	1.25	.50	.12
☐ 22	Todd Brydges GM	1.50	.60	.15
☐ 23	Paul Theriault CO	1.25	.50	.12
☐ 24	Sherry Bassin GM	1.25	.50	.12
☐ 25	Durham Regional Police Logo	1.25	.50	.12

1983-84 Oshawa Generals

This 30-card P.L.A.Y. (Police, Laws and Youth) set measures approximately 2 5/8" by 4 1/8" and features color posed action player photos. The backs carry "Tips from the Generals" that include a hockey tip and its application to a life situation. The cards are numbered on the back.

	MINT	EXC	G-VG
COMPLETE SET (30)	30.00	12.00	3.00
COMMON PLAYER (1-30)	1.00	.40	.10

		MINT	EXC	G-VG
☐ 1	Peter Sidorkiewicz	4.00	1.60	.40
☐ 2	Kirk McLean	12.00	5.00	1.20
☐ 3	Todd Charlesworth	1.00	.40	.10

		MINT	EXC	G-VG
☐ 4	Ian Ferguson	1.00	.40	.10
☐ 5	John Hutchings	1.00	.40	.10
☐ 6	Generals Logo	1.50	.60	.15
☐ 7	Mark Haarmann	1.00	.40	.10
☐ 8	Joel Curtis	1.00	.40	.10
☐ 9	Dan Gratton	1.00	.40	.10
☐ 10	Steve Hedington	1.00	.40	.10
☐ 11	Scott Brydges	1.00	.40	.10
☐ 12	CKAR Radio	1.00	.40	.10
☐ 13	Brad Walcot	1.00	.40	.10
☐ 14	Paul Theriault CO	1.00	.40	.10
☐ 15	Jon Jenkins Chief of Police	1.00	.40	.10
☐ 16	Sherry Bassin GM	1.00	.40	.10
☐ 17	Craig Morrison	1.00	.40	.10
☐ 18	Bolahood's	1.00	.40	.10
☐ 19	Bruce Melanson	1.00	.40	.10
☐ 20	Mike Stern	1.00	.40	.10
☐ 21	Gary McColgan	1.00	.40	.10
☐ 22	Lee Giffin	1.50	.60	.15
☐ 23	Brent Maki	1.00	.40	.10
☐ 24	Ronald McDonald	1.50	.60	.15
☐ 25	Jeff Steffen	1.00	.40	.10
☐ 26	John Stevens	1.00	.40	.10
☐ 27	David Gans	1.00	.40	.10
☐ 28	Don Biggs	1.50	.60	.15
☐ 29	Chip Crandall	1.00	.40	.10
☐ 30	Durham Police Logo	1.00	.40	.10

1991-92 Oshawa Generals

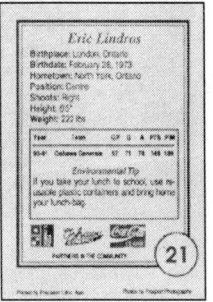

This 32-card set was sponsored by Coca-Cola and Domino's Pizza and measures the standard size (2 1/2" by 3 1/2"). The cards feature color action player photos framed by a royal blue double line. A white circle at the lower right corner carries the player's jersey number or the season year '91-'92. The upper left corner of the picture is cut off to permit space for the team name. The player's name is printed in red at the lower left corner. The backs display biographical information, statistics, environmental tips, and sponsor logos within a royal blue double line design like that on the front. The cards are numbered on the back.

	MINT	EXC	G-VG
COMPLETE SET (32)	20.00	8.00	2.00
COMMON PLAYER (1-32)	.50	.20	.05

		MINT	EXC	G-VG
☐ 1	Mike Fountain	1.00	.40	.10
☐ 2	Brian Grieve	.75	.30	.07
☐ 3	Trevor Burgess	.50	.20	.05
☐ 4	Wade Simpson	.50	.20	.05
☐ 5	Ken Shepard	.50	.20	.05
☐ 6	Stephane Yelle	.50	.20	.05
☐ 7	Matt Hoffman	.50	.20	.05
☐ 8	Neil Iserhoff	.50	.20	.05
☐ 9	Rob Leask	.50	.20	.05
☐ 10	Kevin Spero	.50	.20	.05
☐ 11	Scott Hollis	.50	.20	.05
☐ 12	Sean Brown	.50	.20	.05
☐ 13	Todd Bradley	.50	.20	.05
☐ 14	Darryl LaFrance	.50	.20	.05
☐ 15	Markus Brunner	.75	.30	.07
☐ 16	B.J. MacPherson	.50	.20	.05
☐ 17	Jason Campeau	.50	.20	.05

		MINT	EXC	G-VG
☐ 18	Jason Weaver	.50	.20	.05
☐ 19	Jan Benda	.50	.20	.05
☐ 20	Jason Arnott	6.00	2.40	.60
☐ 21	Eric Lindros	6.00	2.40	.60
☐ 22	Wayne Daniels	.50	.20	.05
	Dir. of Operations			
☐ 23	Joe Cook	.50	.20	.05
☐ 24	Can't Beat the Real	.50	.20	.05
	Thing (Coke Ad)			
☐ 25	Experience the	.50	.20	.05
	Domino's Effect			
	(Pizza Ad)			
☐ 26	Mark Deazeley	.50	.20	.05
☐ 27	Jean-Paul Davis	.50	.20	.05
☐ 28	Brian Grieve	.75	.30	.07
☐ 29	Oshawa Generals	2.50	1.00	.25
	Team Photo			
☐ 30	Ian Young CO	.50	.20	.05
	Larry Marson CO5			
	Rick Cornacchia CO			
☐ 31	Sponsor Ads	.50	.20	.05
	Checklist			
☐ 32	Prosport's Action	.50	.20	.05

1991-92 Oshawa Generals Sheet

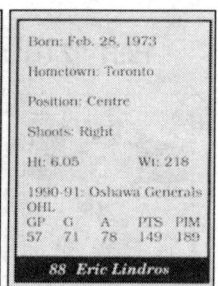

This 18" by 12" sheet was sponsored by the 8th Annual United Way Face-Off Breakfast. The front features posed, color player cards with the players' names printed in a black stripe that appears below each picture. The center of the sheet carries the words "8th Annual United Way Face-Off Breakfast" in sky blue print. The team name also appears in the center, along with the year, the individual sheet number, and the production run (5,000). The back displays the card backs which have biographical information and statistics. The card backs are white with black print. The players are checklisted below as they appear from left to right.

		MINT	EXC	G-VG
COMPLETE SET (26)		20.00	8.00	2.00
COMMON PLAYER (1-26)		.50	.20	.05
☐ 1	Scott Hollis	.50	.20	.05
☐ 2	Jan Benda	.50	.20	.05
☐ 3	Joe Cook	.50	.20	.05
☐ 4	Wade Simpson	.50	.20	.05
☐ 5	B.J. MacPherson	.50	.20	.05
☐ 6	David Anderson	.50	.20	.05
☐ 7	Stephane Yelle	.50	.20	.05
☐ 8	Troy Sweet	.50	.20	.05
☐ 9	Matt Hoffman	.50	.20	.05
☐ 10	Trevor Burgess	.50	.20	.05
☐ 11	Jason Weaver	.50	.20	.05
☐ 12	Craig Lutes	.50	.20	.05
☐ 13	Darryl LaFrance	.50	.20	.05
☐ 14	Jason Arnott	6.00	2.40	.60
☐ 15	Eric Lindros	6.00	2.40	.60
☐ 16	Brian Grieve	.75	.30	.07
☐ 17	Mark Deazeley	.50	.20	.05
☐ 18	Mike Cote	.50	.20	.05
☐ 19	Markus Brunner	.75	.30	.07
☐ 20	Kevin Spero	.50	.20	.05
☐ 21	Todd Bradley	.50	.20	.05
☐ 22	Mike Fountain	1.25	.50	.12
☐ 23	Fred Brathwaite	1.25	.50	.12
☐ 24	Jean-Paul Davis	.50	.20	.05

☐ 25	Jason Campeau	.50	.20	.05
☐ 26	Neil Iserhoff	.50	.20	.05

1992-93 Oshawa Generals Sheet

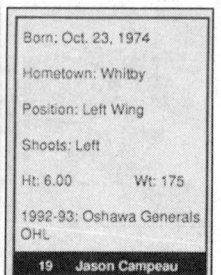

This 18" by 12" sheet was sponsored by the 9th Annual United Way Face-Off Breakfast. The front features posed, color player cards with the players' names printed in a black stripe that appears below each picture. The center of the sheet carries the words "9th Annual United Way Face-Off Breakfast" in black print. The team name also appears in the center, along with the year, the individual sheet number, and the production run (5,000). The back displays the card backs which have biographical information. The card backs are white with black print. The players are checklisted below as they appear from left to right.

		MINT	EXC	G-VG
COMPLETE SET (26)		12.00	5.00	1.20
COMMON PLAYER (1-26)		.50	.20	.05
☐ 1	Wade Simpson	.50	.20	.05
☐ 2	Jamie Kress	.50	.20	.05
☐ 3	Sean Brown	.50	.20	.05
☐ 4	Jason Arnott	5.00	2.00	.50
☐ 5	Mark Brooks	.50	.20	.05
☐ 6	Rob McQuat	.50	.20	.05
☐ 7	Joe Cook	.50	.20	.05
☐ 8	Chris Hall	.50	.20	.05
☐ 9	Jason McQuat	.50	.20	.05
☐ 10	Jason Julian	.50	.20	.05
☐ 11	Kevin Spero	.50	.20	.05
☐ 12	Steve Haight	.50	.20	.05
☐ 13	B.J. MacPherson	.50	.20	.05
☐ 14	Billy-Jay Johnston	.50	.20	.05
☐ 15	Stephane Soulliere	.50	.20	.05
☐ 16	Todd Bradley	.50	.20	.05
☐ 17	Darryl Lafrance	.75	.30	.07
☐ 18	Aaron Albright	.50	.20	.05
☐ 19	Trevor Burgess	.50	.20	.05
☐ 20	Scott Hollis	.50	.20	.05
☐ 21	Serge Dunphy	.50	.20	.05
☐ 22	Joel Gagnon	.75	.30	.07
☐ 23	Brian Kent	.50	.20	.05
☐ 24	Stephane Yelle	.50	.20	.05
☐ 25	Jason Campeau	.50	.20	.05
☐ 26	Neil Iserhoff	.50	.20	.05

1993-94 Oshawa Generals

Printed by Slapshot Images Ltd., this standard size (2 1/2" by 3 1/2") 27-card set features the 1993-94 Oshawa Generals. Reportedly only 3,000 of these sets were produced; the title card also serves as a Certificate of Authenticity and has the number 3,000 printed in the lower right corner. On a geometrical team color-coded

background, the fronts feature color action player photos with thin black borders. The player's name, position and team name, as well as the producer's logo, appear on the front. The backs carry a close-up color player portrait, biography and statistics, along with team and sponsor's logos. The cards are numbered on the back. Included in this set is a Slapshot ad card with a 1994 calendar on the back.

	MINT	EXC	G-VG
COMPLETE SET (27)	9.00	3.75	.90
COMMON PLAYER (1-27)	.35	.14	.03
☐ 1 Title Card	.35	.14	.03
Checklist			
☐ 2 Joel Gagnon	.75	.30	.07
☐ 3 Ken Shepard	.50	.20	.05
☐ 4 Jan Snopek	.50	.20	.05
☐ 5 David Froh	.35	.14	.03
☐ 6 Brandon Gray	.35	.14	.03
☐ 7 Damon Hardy	.35	.14	.03
☐ 8 Sean Brown	.50	.20	.05
☐ 9 Jeff Andrews	.35	.14	.03
☐ 10 Stephane Yelle	.50	.20	.05
☐ 11 Stephane Soulliere	.35	.14	.03
☐ 12 Andrew Power	.35	.14	.03
☐ 13 Todd Bradley	.35	.14	.03
☐ 14 Darryl Lafrance	.75	.30	.07
☐ 15 Darryl Moxam	.35	.14	.03
☐ 16 Robert Dubois	.35	.14	.03
☐ 17 Kevin Vaughan	.35	.14	.03
☐ 18 Rob McQuat	.50	.20	.05
☐ 19 B.J. Johnston	.35	.14	.03
☐ 20 Paul Doherty	.35	.14	.03
☐ 21 Eric Boulton	.50	.20	.05
☐ 22 Marc Savard	.50	.20	.05
☐ 23 Chris Hall	.35	.14	.03
☐ 24 Jason McQuat	.35	.14	.03
☐ 25 Ryan Lindsay	.35	.14	.03
☐ 26 Rick Cornacchia CO	.35	.14	.03
Wayne Daniels DIR			
Brian Drumm ACO			
☐ NNO Ad Card	.35	.14	.03

1982-83 Ottawa 67's

Sponsored by Coke and Channel 12, this 25-card set measures approximately 2 5/8" by 4 1/8" and features posed, color player photos with white borders. The player's name and jersey number are printed in black across the bottom of the picture. The backs carry biographical information, the team played for the previous year, and the player's school classification. Sponsor logos are printed at the bottom. The cards are unnumbered and checklisted below in alphabetical order.

	MINT	EXC	G-VG
COMPLETE SET (25)	20.00	8.00	2.00
COMMON PLAYER (1-25)	.75	.30	.07

		MINT	EXC	G-VG
☐ 1	Bruce Cassidy	.75	.30	.07
☐ 2	Greg Coram	.75	.30	.07
☐ 3	Adam Creighton	3.00	1.20	.30
☐ 4	Bill Dowd	.75	.30	.07
☐ 5	Gord Hamilton ACO	.75	.30	.07
☐ 6	Scott Hammond	.75	.30	.07
☐ 7	Alan Hepple	.75	.30	.07
☐ 8	Alan Hepple	.75	.30	.07
☐ 9	Jim Jackson TR	.75	.30	.07
☐ 10	Mike James	.75	.30	.07
☐ 11	Brian Kilrea CO	.75	.30	.07
☐ 12	Paul Louttit	.75	.30	.07
☐ 13	Brian McKinnon	.75	.30	.07
☐ 14	Don McLaren	.75	.30	.07
☐ 15	John Ollson	.75	.30	.07
☐ 16	Darren Pang	2.00	.80	.20
☐ 17	Mark Paterson	.75	.30	.07
☐ 18	Phil Patterson	.75	.30	.07
☐ 19	Larry Power	.75	.30	.07
☐ 20	Gary Roberts	7.50	3.00	.75
☐ 21	Brian Rome	.75	.30	.07
☐ 22	Darcy T. Roy	.75	.30	.07
☐ 23	Brad Shaw	2.00	.80	.20
☐ 24	Doug Stewart	.75	.30	.07
☐ 25	Jeff Vaive	.75	.30	.07

1984-85 Ottawa 67's

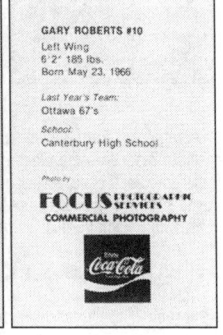

This 28-card set was sponsored by Coca-Cola and Focus Photographic Services Commercial Photography. The cards measure approximately 2 5/8" by 4 1/8" and feature color, full-length, posed player photos with white borders. The player's name and jersey number are superimposed on the bottom of the picture. The backs are white and carry biographical information, last year's team, and the player's high school. Sponsor logos are printed at the bottom. The cards are unnumbered and checklisted below in alphabetical order.

	MINT	EXC	G-VG
COMPLETE SET (28)	12.00	5.00	1.20
COMMON PLAYER (1-28)	.50	.20	.05

		MINT	EXC	G-VG
☐ 1	Tom Allen	.50	.20	.05
☐ 2	Graydon Almstedt	.50	.20	.05
☐ 3	Bill Bennett	.50	.20	.05
☐ 4	Bruce Cassidy	.75	.30	.07
☐ 5	Greg Coram	.50	.20	.05
☐ 6	Bob Ellett CO	.50	.20	.05
☐ 7	Tony Geesink	.50	.20	.05
☐ 8	Bob Giffin	.50	.20	.05
☐ 9	John Hanna	.50	.20	.05
☐ 10	Tim Helmer	.50	.20	.05
☐ 11	Andy Helmuth	.50	.20	.05
☐ 12	Steve Hrynewich	.50	.20	.05
☐ 13	Rob Hudson	.50	.20	.05
☐ 14	Jim Jackson TR	.50	.20	.05
☐ 15	Steve Kayser	.50	.20	.05
☐ 16	Bill Kuchma	.50	.20	.05
☐ 17	Mike Larouche	.50	.20	.05
☐ 18	Tom Lawson MG	.50	.20	.05
☐ 19	Richard Lessard	.50	.20	.05
☐ 20	Gary Roberts	4.00	1.60	.40
☐ 21	Jerry Scott	.50	.20	.05
☐ 22	John Shepherd Dir. of Public Relations and Marketing	.50	.20	.05
☐ 23	Steve Simoni	.50	.20	.05
☐ 24	Greg Sliz	.50	.20	.05
☐ 25	Gord Thomas TR	.50	.20	.05
☐ 26	Chris Vickers	.50	.20	.05
☐ 27	Bert Weir	.50	.20	.05
☐ 28	Dennis Wigle	.50	.20	.05

☐ 10	Mark Edmundson	.50	.20	.05
☐ 11	Billy Hall	.50	.20	.05
☐ 12	Mike Johnson	.50	.20	.05
☐ 13	Brian Kilrea GM/CO	.50	.20	.05
☐ 14	Grayson Lafoley	.50	.20	.05
☐ 15	Grant Marshall	1.50	.60	.15
☐ 16	Cory Murphy	.50	.20	.05
☐ 17	Mike Peca	1.50	.60	.15
☐ 18	Greg Ryan	.50	.20	.05
☐ 19	Jeff Salajko	.50	.20	.05
☐ 20	Gerry Skrypec	.75	.30	.07
☐ 21	Sean Spencer	.50	.20	.05
☐ 22	Steven Washburn	.50	.20	.05
☐ 23	Mark Yakabuski	.50	.20	.05
☐ 24	Title Card	.75	.30	.07

1992-93 Peoria Rivermen Coke/Kroger

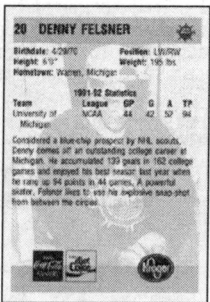

Sponsored by Coca-Cola and Kroger, this 30-card set measures the standard size (2 1/2" by 3 1/2"). The fronts feature color player photos with a white border. The team logo, the player's name, and position appear in a gray bar under the photo, while "1992" is printed in white letters on a blue triangle in the top right corner of the photo. The backs display biographical information, statistics, and sponsor logos against a light gray-in-gray player photo with a white border. Included in this set is a Coca-Cola coupon. The cards are unnumbered and checklisted below in alphabetical order.

	MINT	EXC	G-VG
COMPLETE SET (30)	9.00	3.75	.90
COMMON PLAYER (1-30)	.35	.14	.03

		MINT	EXC	G-VG
☐ 1	Jeff Batters	.35	.14	.03
☐ 2	Parris Duffus	.75	.30	.07
☐ 3	Greg Eberle TR	.35	.14	.03
☐ 4	John Faginkrantz MG	.35	.14	.03
☐ 5	Denny Felsner	.75	.30	.07
☐ 6	Derek Frenette	.35	.14	.03
☐ 7	Ron Handy	.35	.14	.03
☐ 8	Joe Hawley	.35	.14	.03
☐ 9	Terry Hollinger	.75	.30	.07
☐ 10	Ron Hoover	.35	.14	.03
☐ 11	Daniel LaPerriere	.75	.30	.07
☐ 12	Lee J. Leslie	.50	.20	.05
☐ 13	Dave Mackey	.35	.14	.03
☐ 14	Jason Marshall	.50	.20	.05
☐ 15	Brian McKee	.35	.14	.03
☐ 16	Rick Meagher CO	.50	.20	.05
☐ 17	Kevin Miehm	.50	.20	.05
☐ 18	Brian Pellerin ACO	.35	.14	.03
☐ 19	Mark Reeds	.35	.14	.03
☐ 20	Kyle Reeves	.50	.20	.05
☐ 21	Rob Robinson	.35	.14	.03
☐ 22	Jason Ruff	.50	.20	.05
☐ 23	Geoff Sarjeant	.75	.30	.07

1992 Ottawa 67's 25th Anniversary

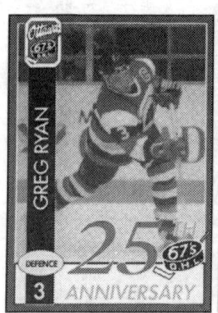
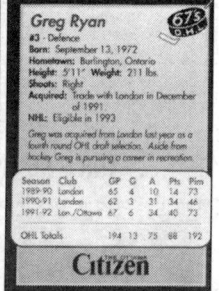

Celebrating the 25th anniversary of the Ottawa 67's, this 24-card set measures the standard size (2 1/2" by 3 1/2") and features color posed and action player photos with purple borders. The player's name, position, and jersey number appear in a black vertical stripe on the left side of the card. The phrase "25th Anniversary" is printed at the bottom in large red and blue letters. The letters overlap the photo and a white bar at the bottom of the photo. The backs carry biographical information, a player profile, and statistics against a gradated sky blue background with yellow and black borders. The cards are unnumbered and checklisted below in alphabetical order.

	MINT	EXC	G-VG
COMPLETE SET (24)	10.00	4.00	1.00
COMMON PLAYER (1-24)	.50	.20	.05

		MINT	EXC	G-VG
☐ 1	Ken Belanger	.50	.20	.05
☐ 2	Curt Bowen	1.00	.40	.10
☐ 3	Rich Bronilla	.50	.20	.05
☐ 4	Mathew Burnett	.50	.20	.05
☐ 5	Shawn Caplice	.50	.20	.05
☐ 6	Mike Carr	.50	.20	.05
☐ 7	Chris Coveny	.50	.20	.05
☐ 8	Howard Darwin (Founder)	.50	.20	.05
☐ 9	Shean Donovan	.50	.20	.05

		MINT	EXC	G-VG
☐	24 Richard Pion	.35	.14	.03
☐	25 Darren Veitch	.50	.20	.05
☐	26 Doug Wickenheiser	.50	.20	.05
☐	27 Shawn Wheeler	.35	.14	.03
☐	28 Checklist	.35	.14	.03
☐	29 Coca Cola Coupon	.35	.14	.03
☐	30 Title Card	.35	.14	.03

1993-94 Peoria Rivermen

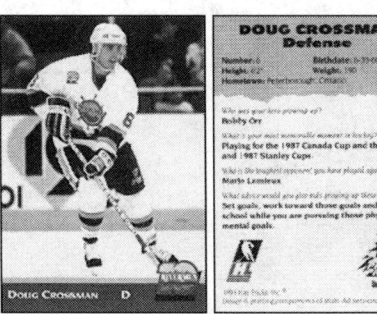

Produced by 1993 Hat Tricks, Inc., this 31-card D.A.R.E. (Drug Abuse Resistance Education) set measures approximately 2 3/8" by 3 1/4" and celebrates the tenth anniversary of the Peoria Rivermen (International Hockey League). The fronts feature full-bleed color action photos, except at the bottom where an orange stripe separates a thicker blue stripe carrying player information. The 10th anniversary logo in the lower right corner completes the front. In black print on a gray and white background, the backs present biography and additional information in a question-and-answer format. The cards are unnumbered and checklisted below in alphabetical order.

		MINT	EXC	G-VG
	COMPLETE SET (31)	9.00	3.75	.90
	COMMON PLAYER (1-31)	.35	.14	.03
☐	1 Mark Bassen	.35	.14	.03
☐	2 Jeff Batters	.35	.14	.03
☐	3 Rene Chapdelaine	.50	.20	.05
☐	4 Doug Crossman	.50	.20	.05
☐	5 Parris Duffus	.75	.30	.07
☐	6 Greg Eberle TR	.35	.14	.03
☐	7 Doug Evans	.50	.20	.05
☐	8 Kevin Evans	.35	.14	.03
☐	9 John Faginkrantz EQ MG	.35	.14	.03
☐	10 Denny Felsner	.75	.30	.07
☐	11 Derek Frenette	.35	.14	.03
☐	12 Terry Hollinger	.75	.30	.07
☐	13 Ron Hoover	.35	.14	.03
☐	14 Butch Kaebel	.35	.14	.03
☐	15 Nathan Lafayette	.75	.30	.07
☐	16 Dan Laperriere	.75	.30	.07
☐	17 Dave Mackey	.35	.14	.03
☐	18 Paul MacLean CO	.50	.20	.05
☐	19 Michel Mongeau	.75	.30	.07
☐	20 Brian Pellerin	.35	.14	.03
☐	21 Rick Pion	.35	.14	.03
☐	22 Vitali Prokhorov	.50	.20	.05
☐	23 Mark Reeds ACO	.35	.14	.03
☐	24 John Roderick	.35	.14	.03
☐	25 Geoff Sarjeant	.75	.30	.07
☐	26 Steve Staios	.50	.20	.05
☐	27 Darren Veitch	.50	.20	.05
☐	28 Nick Vitucci	.35	.14	.03
☐	29 Title card	.35	.14	.03
	(Team history on back)			
☐	30 Checklist	.35	.14	.03
☐	31 Alcohol is its own	.35	.14	.03
	punishment			
	(Eight Ways to Say No)			

1991-92 Peterborough Petes

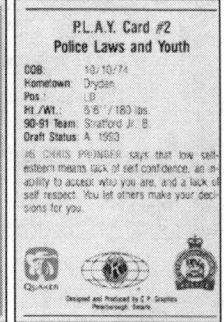

This 30-card P.L.A.Y. (Police, Laws and Youth) set measures approximately 2 1/2" by 3 3/4" and features posed, color player photos with bright blue and white borders. The player's name is printed on the picture in white letters in the upper left corner. The team logo appears in the upper right corner. The backs carry biographical information and public service messages.

		MINT	EXC	G-VG
	COMPLETE SET (30)	20.00	8.00	2.00
	COMMON PLAYER (1-27)	.50	.20	.05
☐	1 Jason Dawe	1.50	.60	.15
☐	2 Chris Pronger	7.50	3.00	.75
☐	3 Scott Turner	.50	.20	.05
☐	4 Chad Grills	.50	.20	.05
☐	5 Brent Tully	.75	.30	.07
☐	6 Mike Harding	.75	.30	.07
☐	7 Chris Longo	.75	.30	.07
☐	8 Slapshot (Mascot)	.50	.20	.05
☐	9 Doug Searle	.50	.20	.05
☐	10 Mike Tomlinson	.75	.30	.07
☐	11 Bryan Gendron	.50	.20	.05
☐	12 Andrew Verner	1.25	.50	.12
☐	13 Ryan Black	.75	.30	.07
☐	14 Don O'Neill	.50	.20	.05
☐	15 Jeff Twohey MG/CO	.50	.20	.05
☐	16 Dale McTavish	.50	.20	.05
☐	17 Jeff Walker	.50	.20	.05
☐	18 Matt St. Germain	.50	.20	.05
☐	19 Dave Roche	.75	.30	.07
☐	20 Colin Wilson	.50	.20	.05
☐	21 Jassen Cullimore	1.25	.50	.12
☐	22 Chad Lang	1.00	.40	.10
☐	23 Dick Todd MG/CO	.50	.20	.05
☐	24 Geordie Kinnear	.75	.30	.07
☐	25 Shawn Heins	.50	.20	.05
☐	26 John Johnson	.50	.20	.05
☐	27 Kelly Vipond	.75	.30	.07
☐	NNO Peterborough Police	.50	.20	.05
	Crest			
☐	NNO Kiwanis Sponsor Card	.50	.20	.05
☐	NNO Quaker Sponsor Card	.50	.20	.05

1993-94 Peterborough Petes

Sponsored by Cardboard Heroes and printed by Slapshot Images Ltd., this standard-size (2 1/2" by 3 1/2") 31-card set features the 1993-94 Peterborough Petes. Only 3,000 of these sets have been produced; the first card also serves as a Certificate of Authenticity and has the number 3,000 printed in the upper left corner. On a grey background, the fronts feature color action player photos with thin maroon borders. The player's name, position and team name, as well as the producer's logo, appear on the front. The team

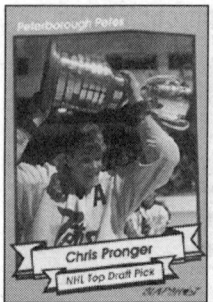
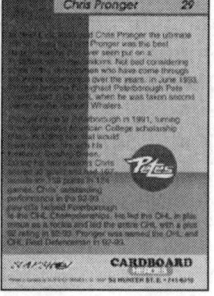

color-coded backs carry a close-up color player portrait, and biographical information, along with team and sponsors' logos. The cards are numbered on the back. Included in this set is a Slapshot ad card with a 1994 calendar on the back.

	MINT	EXC	G-VG
COMPLETE SET (31)	10.00	4.00	1.00
COMMON PLAYER (1-31)	.35	.14	.03
☐ 1 1992-93 OHL Champions	.75	.30	.07
☐ 2 Jonathan Murphy	.35	.14	.03
☐ 3 Dave Roche	.50	.20	.05
☐ 4 Rob Giffin	.35	.14	.03
☐ 5 Mike Harding	.50	.20	.05
☐ 6 Tim Hill	.35	.14	.03
☐ 7 Darryl Moxam	.35	.14	.03
☐ 8 Pat Paone	.35	.14	.03
☐ 9 Brent Tully	.75	.30	.07
☐ 10 Zac Bierk	.50	.20	.05
☐ 11 Chad Grills	.35	.14	.03
☐ 12 Matt St. Germain	.35	.14	.03
☐ 13 Henrik Eppers	.50	.20	.05
☐ 14 Rick Emmett	.35	.14	.03
☐ 15 Chad Lang	.75	.30	.07
☐ 16 Cameron Mann	.35	.14	.03
☐ 17 Steve Hogg	.35	.14	.03
☐ 18 Mike Williams	.35	.14	.03
☐ 19 Ryan Nauss	.50	.20	.05
☐ 20 Jamie Langenbrunner	2.00	.80	.20
☐ 21 Ryan Douglas	.50	.20	.05
☐ 22 Matt Johnson	.50	.20	.05
☐ 23 Kelvin Solari	.35	.14	.03
☐ 24 Dan Delmonte	.35	.14	.03
☐ 25 Quade Lightbody	.35	.14	.03
☐ 26 Adrian Murray	.35	.14	.03
☐ 27 Jason Dawe	.75	.30	.07
☐ 28 Mike Harding	.50	.20	.05
☐ 29 Chris Pronger	2.00	.80	.20
☐ 30 Sponsor Card	.35	.14	.03
Cardboard Heroes			
Greg Ball			
Kevin Ball			
☐ NNO Ad Card	.35	.14	.03

1992-93 Phoenix Roadrunners

Sponsored by Safeway, this 28-card standard-size (2 1/2" by 3 1/2") set features color action photos on the front edged by a blue border on the top and left margins, with full bleed on the bottom and right. The IHL logo is in the top right corner. The player's name and jersey number are printed in red at the bottom while the team name is printed in white immediately above. The team logo is in the lower right and the player's position is printed in red inside a hockey puck in the lower left. The horizontal backs have the team logo in the top left with biographical information beneath a red line. Statistics are presented in a red box and the red sponsor logo appears in the lower left. The cards are unnumbered and checklisted below in alphabetical order.

	MINT	EXC	G-VG
COMPLETE SET (28)	10.00	4.00	1.00
COMMON PLAYER (1-28)	.50	.20	.05
☐ 1 Tim Bothwell CO	.75	.30	.07
☐ 2 Frank Breault	.75	.30	.07
☐ 3 Tim Breslin	.50	.20	.05
☐ 4 Rene Chapdelaine	.50	.20	.05
☐ 5 Sylvain Couturier	.75	.30	.07
☐ 6 Phil Crowe	.75	.30	.07
☐ 7 Darryl Gilmour	.75	.30	.07
☐ 8 David Goverde	.50	.20	.05
☐ 9 Ed Kastelic	.75	.30	.07
☐ 10 Rick Kozuback ACO	.50	.20	.05
☐ 11 Ted Kramer	.50	.20	.05
☐ 12 Robert Lang	1.50	.60	.15
☐ 13 Guy Leveque	.75	.30	.07
☐ 14 Jim Maher	.50	.20	.05
☐ 15 Brad McCaughey	.50	.20	.05
☐ 16 Shawn McCosh	.50	.20	.05
☐ 17 John Mokosak	.50	.20	.05
☐ 18 Keith Redmond	.50	.20	.05
☐ 19 Mike Ruark	.50	.20	.05
☐ 20 Brandy Semchuk	.75	.30	.07
☐ 21 Dave Stewart	.50	.20	.05
☐ 22 Brad Tiley	.75	.30	.07
☐ 23 Dave Tretowicz	.50	.20	.05
☐ 24 Mike Vukonich	.50	.20	.05
☐ 25 Tim Watters	.75	.30	.07
☐ 26 Sean Whyte	.50	.20	.05
☐ 27 Darryl Williams	.50	.20	.05
☐ 28 Rocky Roadrunner	.50	.20	.05
(Mascot)			

1993-94 Phoenix Roadrunners

This 25-card set measures the standard size (2 1/2" by 3 1/2"). On a black and white marbleized background, the fronts feature color action player photos with rounded corners and a thin blue border. The player's name, position, and number appear under the photo, along with the team logo. On a white background, the horizontal backs carry the player's name, number, biography, and statistics. The cards are unnumbered and checklisted below in alphabetical order.

	MINT	EXC	G-VG
COMPLETE SET (25)	8.00	3.25	.80
COMMON PLAYER (1-25)	.35	.14	.03

		MINT	EXC	G-VG
☐ 1	Tim Breslin	.35	.14	.03
☐ 2	Brian Chapman	.35	.14	.03
☐ 3	Stephane Charbonneau	.35	.14	.03
☐ 4	Dan Currie	.50	.20	.05
☐ 5	Rick Dudley CO	.50	.20	.05
☐ 6	Marc Fortier	.50	.20	.05
☐ 7	David Goverde	.50	.20	.05
☐ 8	Kevin Grant	.35	.14	.03
☐ 9	Mark Hardy P/CO	.50	.20	.05
☐ 10	Dean Hulett	.35	.14	.03
☐ 11	Pauli Jaks	.75	.30	.07
☐ 12	Bob Jay	.75	.30	.07
☐ 13	Rick Knickle	.75	.30	.07
☐ 14	Guy Leveque	.75	.30	.07
☐ 15	Eric Lavigne	.50	.20	.05
☐ 16	Dominic Lavoie	.50	.20	.05
☐ 17	Jim Maher	.35	.14	.03
☐ 18	Brian McReynolds	.50	.20	.05
☐ 19	Rob Murphy	.35	.14	.03
☐ 20	Keith Redmond	.50	.20	.05
☐ 21	Dave Stewart	.35	.14	.03
☐ 22	Dave Thomlinson	.50	.20	.05
☐ 23	Brad Tiley	.35	.14	.03
☐ 24	Jim Vesey	.35	.14	.03
☐ 25	Darryl Williams	.35	.14	.03

1987-88 Portland Winter Hawks

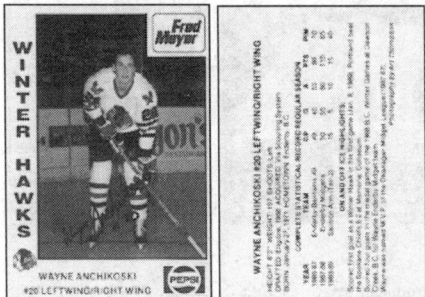

Sponsored by Fred Meyer and Pepsi, this 21-card standard-size (2 1/2" by 3 1/2") set features the 1987-88 Portland Winter Hawks of the Western Hockey League. Inside white borders, the fronts feature posed color player photos shot on the ice at the stadium. The wider left border carries the team name, while the upper right corner of the picture has been cut off to allow space for the sponsor logo. Player information and the Pepsi logo are presented beneath the picture. The horizontal backs have biography, statistics, and a section titled "On and Off Ice Highlights." The cards are unnumbered and checklisted below in alphabetical order.

		MINT	EXC	G-VG
COMPLETE SET (21)		10.00	4.00	1.00
COMMON PLAYER (1-21)		.50	.20	.05
☐ 1	Wayne Anchikoski	.75	.30	.07
☐ 2	Eric Badzgon	.50	.20	.05
☐ 3	Chad Biafore	.50	.20	.05
☐ 4	James(Hamish) Black	.75	.30	.07
☐ 5	Terry Black	.50	.20	.05
☐ 6	Shaun Clouston	.50	.20	.05
☐ 7	Byron Dafoe	1.00	.40	.10
☐ 8	Brent Fleetwood	.50	.20	.05
☐ 9	Rob Flintoft	.50	.20	.05
☐ 10	Bryan Gourlie	.50	.20	.05
☐ 11	Mark Greyeyes	.50	.20	.05
☐ 12	Dennis Holland	.75	.30	.07

☐ 13	Kevin Jorgenson	.50	.20	.05
☐ 14	Greg Leahy	.50	.20	.05
☐ 15	Troy Mick	.75	.30	.07
☐ 16	Roy Mitchell	.50	.20	.05
☐ 17	Joey Mittelsteadt	.75	.30	.07
☐ 18	Mike Moore	.50	.20	.05
☐ 19	Scott Mydan	.50	.20	.05
☐ 20	Calvin Thudiun	.50	.20	.05
☐ 21	Pepsi Ad Card	.50	.20	.05

1950 Quebec Citadelle

These 19 blank-backed photos of the Quebec Citadelle measure 4" by 6" and feature cream-bordered sepiatones of the suited-up players posed on the ice. The players' facsimile autographs appear near the bottom of the pictures. The photos are unnumbered and checklisted below in alphabetical order.

		NRMT	VG-E	GOOD
COMPLETE SET (19)		200.00	80.00	20.00
COMMON PLAYER (1-19)		7.50	3.00	.75
☐ 1	Neil Amodio	7.50	3.00	.75
☐ 2	Jean Beliveau	100.00	40.00	10.00
☐ 3	Bergeron CO	7.50	3.00	.75
☐ 4	Bruce Cline	12.00	5.00	1.20
☐ 5	Norm Divining	7.50	3.00	.75
☐ 6	Guy Gervais	7.50	3.00	.75
☐ 7	Bernard Guay	7.50	3.00	.75
☐ 8	Hanworth	7.50	3.00	.75
☐ 9	Camille Henry	20.00	8.00	2.00
☐ 10	Gordie Hudson	7.50	3.00	.75
☐ 11	Wildor Larochelle	12.00	5.00	1.20
☐ 12	Bernie Lemonde	7.50	3.00	.75
☐ 13	Paul Legault	7.50	3.00	.75
☐ 14	Copper Leyce	7.50	3.00	.75
☐ 15	R. Makila	7.50	3.00	.75
☐ 16	Marcel Paille	20.00	8.00	2.00
☐ 17	Jean-Marie Plante	7.50	3.00	.75
☐ 18	Sanecal	7.50	3.00	.75
☐ 19	J.C. Tremblay	20.00	8.00	2.00

1963-64 Quebec Aces QSHL

This 22-card set features the Quebec Aces of the Quebec Senior Hockey League. The cards measure approximately 3 1/2" by 5 1/2" and have black and white posed action photos with white borders. The player's name is printed in black at the bottom. The backs are blank. The cards are unnumbered and checklisted below in alphabetical order.

	NRMT	VG-E	GOOD
COMPLETE SET (22)	100.00	40.00	10.00
COMMON PLAYER (1-22)	3.00	1.20	.30

RINO ROBAZZA

		MINT	EXC	G-VG
COMPLETE SET (22)		15.00	6.00	1.50
COMMON PLAYER (1-22)		.90	.36	.09
☐ 1	Marc Bertrand	.90	.36	.09
☐ 2	Jacques Chouinard	.90	.36	.09
☐ 3	Roger Cote	.90	.36	.09
☐ 4	Gaston Drapeau CO	.90	.36	.09
☐ 5	Claude Drouin	.90	.36	.09
☐ 6	Gaetan Duchesne	2.00	.80	.20
☐ 7	Scott Fraser	.90	.36	.09
☐ 8	Jean-Marc Lanthier	.90	.36	.09
☐ 9	Jean Paul Lariviere	.90	.36	.09
☐ 10	Andre Larocque	.90	.36	.09
☐ 11	Roberto Lavoie	.90	.36	.09
☐ 12	Marc Lemay	.90	.36	.09
☐ 13	Stephane Lessard	.90	.36	.09
☐ 14	Paul Levesque	.90	.36	.09
☐ 15	Richard Linteau	.90	.36	.09
☐ 16	Patrice Masse	.90	.36	.09
☐ 17	David Pretty	.90	.36	.09
☐ 18	Guy Riel	.90	.36	.09
☐ 19	Daniel Rioux	.90	.36	.09
☐ 20	Roberto Romano	1.50	.60	.15
☐ 21	Michel Therrien	1.50	.60	.15
☐ 22	Gilles Tremblay	1.50	.60	.15

☐ 1	Don Blackburn	3.00	1.20	.30
☐ 2	Skippy Burchell	3.00	1.20	.30
☐ 3	Billy Carter	3.00	1.20	.30
☐ 4	Floyd Curry CO	10.00	4.00	1.00
☐ 5	Bill Dineen	10.00	4.00	1.00
☐ 6	Wayne Freitag	3.00	1.20	.30
☐ 7	Jean Gauthier	3.00	1.20	.30
☐ 8	Terry Gray	5.00	2.00	.50
☐ 9	John Hanna	3.00	1.20	.30
☐ 10	Doug Harvey	20.00	8.00	2.00
☐ 11	Wayne Hicks	3.00	1.20	.30
☐ 12	Charlie Hodge	15.00	6.00	1.50
	(Standing before net)			
☐ 13	Charlie Hodge	15.00	6.00	1.50
	(Spread out before net in defensive posture)			
☐ 14	Ed Hoekstra	5.00	2.00	.50
☐ 15	Frank Martin	3.00	1.20	.30
☐ 16	Jim Morrison	5.00	2.00	.50
☐ 17	Cleland Mortson	3.00	1.20	.30
☐ 18	Gerry O'Drowski	3.00	1.20	.30
☐ 19	Rino Robazza	5.00	2.00	.50
☐ 20	Leon Rochefort	3.00	1.20	.30
☐ 21	Bill Sutherland	5.00	2.00	.50
☐ 22	Lorne Worsley	25.00	10.00	2.50

1992-93 Raleigh Icecaps

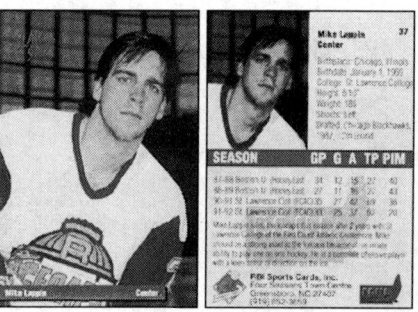

1980-81 Quebec Remparts

(11)
Gaétan Duchesne

This 22-card set measures approximately 2" by 3" and features posed color player photos. The cards were issued as part of a contest. The pictures are full-bleed except for a white bottom border that contains the team logo, player's name, and jersey number. The backs are blank. The collector who obtained the entire set and turned it in became eligible to enter a contest in which the grand prize was a trip to Disneyworld. The cards are unnumbered and checklisted below in alphabetical order.

Produced by RBI Sports Cards Inc. (Greensboro, North Carolina), this 19-card set features the Raleigh Icecaps of the East Coast Hockey League. The cards measure the standard size (2 1/2" by 3 1/2") and feature glossy, borderless, posed and action, color player photos. The player's name and position appear in a shadow-bordered bar that shades from blue to red near the bottom of the picture. The backs carry a small, close-up player photo, biographical information, statistics, and player profile. The cards are numbered on the back.

		MINT	EXC	G-VG
COMPLETE SET (19)		8.00	3.25	.80
COMMON PLAYER (20-38)		.50	.20	.05
☐ 20	Team Photo	1.00	.40	.10
☐ 21	Bruno Villeneuve	.50	.20	.05
☐ 22	Jeff Robison	.50	.20	.05
☐ 23	Jim Powers	.50	.20	.05
☐ 24	Derek Linnell	.50	.20	.05
☐ 25	Chris Marshall	.50	.20	.05
☐ 26	Kris Miller	.50	.20	.05
☐ 27	Joel Gardner	.50	.20	.05
☐ 28	Stan(Smokey) Reddick	1.00	.40	.10
☐ 29	Jim Mill	.50	.20	.05
☐ 30	Alan Leggett	.50	.20	.05
☐ 31	Brian Tulik	.50	.20	.05
☐ 32	Kirby Lindal	.50	.20	.05
☐ 33	Sean Cowan	.50	.20	.05
☐ 34	Lyle Wildgoose	.50	.20	.05

			MINT	EXC	G-VG
☐	35	Todd Person	.50	.20	.05
☐	36	Chic Pojar	.50	.20	.05
☐	37	Mike Lappin	.50	.20	.05
☐	38	Doug Bacon	.50	.20	.05

1989-90 Rayside-Balfour Jr. Canadiens

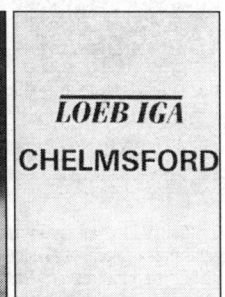

LOEB IGA

CHELMSFORD

This 20-card set is printed on thin card stock and measures approximately 2 3/8" by 3 3/8." The cards feature full-bleed, color, posed player photos. The player's name and jersey number are printed in black at the bottom. The team logo and name are printed at the top. The backs are white and carry sponsor information. The cards are unnumbered and checklisted below in alphabetical order.

		MINT	EXC	G-VG
COMPLETE SET (20)		8.00	3.25	.80
COMMON PLAYER (1-20)		.50	.20	.05

			MINT	EXC	G-VG
☐	1	Team Photo	1.00	.40	.10
☐	2	Dave Barrett	.50	.20	.05
☐	3	Dan Baston	.50	.20	.05
☐	4	Rick Chartrand	.50	.20	.05
☐	5	Simon Chartrand	.50	.20	.05
☐	6	Ron Clark	.50	.20	.05
☐	7	Brian Dickinson	.50	.20	.05
☐	8	Trevor Duncan	.50	.20	.05
☐	9	Don Gauthier	.50	.20	.05
☐	10	Shawn Hawkins	.50	.20	.05
☐	11	Roy Hildebrandt	.50	.20	.05
☐	12	Al Laginski	.50	.20	.05
☐	13	Eric Lanteigne	.50	.20	.05
☐	14	Mike Leblanc	.50	.20	.05
☐	15	Kevin MacDonald	.50	.20	.05
☐	16	Mike Mooney	.50	.20	.05
☐	17	Rick Potvin	.50	.20	.05
☐	18	Rick Poulin	.50	.20	.05
☐	19	Steve Prior	.50	.20	.05
☐	20	Scott Sutton	.50	.20	.05

1990-91 Rayside-Balfour Jr. Canadiens

This 23-card set is printed on thin card stock and measures approximately 2 3/8" by 3 1/4." The cards feature full-bleed, color, posed player photos. The player's name and jersey number are printed in black at the bottom. The team logo and name are printed at the top. The backs are white and carry sponsor information. The cards are unnumbered and checklisted below in alphabetical order.

		MINT	EXC	G-VG
COMPLETE SET (23)		8.00	3.25	.80
COMMON PLAYER (1-23)		.50	.20	.05

North West Lumber

286 ERRINGTON STREET
CHELMSFORD, ONT.
Tel. 855-4573 • 855-4574

			MINT	EXC	G-VG
☐	1	Dan Baston	.50	.20	.05
☐	2	Jon Boeve	.50	.20	.05
☐	3	Jordan Boyle	.50	.20	.05
☐	4	Serge Coulombe	.50	.20	.05
☐	5	Mike Dore	.50	.20	.05
☐	6	Denis Gosselin	.50	.20	.05
☐	7	Mike Gratton	.50	.20	.05
☐	8	Jason Hall	.50	.20	.05
☐	9	Grant Healey	.50	.20	.05
☐	10	Marc Lafreniere	.50	.20	.05
☐	11	Alain Leclair	.50	.20	.05
☐	12	Mike Longo	.50	.20	.05
☐	13	Troy Mallette	1.00	.40	.10
		1985-86 Rookie Card			
☐	14	Matthew Mooney	.50	.20	.05
☐	15	Virgil Nose	.50	.20	.05
☐	16	Trevor Oystrick	.50	.20	.05
☐	17	Steve Proceviat	.50	.20	.05
☐	18	Chris Puskas	.50	.20	.05
☐	19	Yvon Quenneville	.50	.20	.05
☐	20	Michael Sullivan	.75	.30	.07
☐	21	Trevor Tremblay	.50	.20	.05
☐	22	Sean Van Amburg	.50	.20	.05
☐	23	Title Card	.75	.30	.07

1991-92 Rayside-Balfour Jr. Canadiens

STEELCRAFT MANUFACTURING & HEAT TREATING

880 Lapointe
Sudbury, Ontario

phone 705-560-7794
FAX 705-566-5247

This 23-card set measures approximately 2 3/8" by 3 5/16" and is printed on thin card stock. The fronts feature color, full-bleed, posed action player photos. The player's name and jersey number are printed in black at the bottom. The team logo appears in either red or white at the upper left corner. The backs are white with black print and carry advertisements from local businesses. The cards are unnumbered and checklisted below in alphabetical order.

		MINT	EXC	G-VG
COMPLETE SET (23)		8.00	3.25	.80
COMMON PLAYER (1-23)		.50	.20	.05

			MINT	EXC	G-VG
☐	1	Dan Baston	.50	.20	.05
☐	2	Don Cucksey	.50	.20	.05

☐	3	Dean Cull	.50	.20	.05
☐	4	Mike Dore	.50	.20	.05
☐	5	Denis Gosselin	.50	.20	.05
☐	6	Jason Hall	.50	.20	.05
☐	7	Grant Healey	.50	.20	.05
☐	8	Marc Lafreniere	.50	.20	.05
☐	9	Mike Longo	.50	.20	.05
☐	10	Scott Maclellan	.50	.20	.05
☐	11	Matt Mooney	.50	.20	.05
☐	12	Rob Moxness	.50	.20	.05
☐	13	Virgil Nose	.50	.20	.05
☐	14	Trent Oystrick	.50	.20	.05
☐	15	Jon Stewart	.50	.20	.05
☐	16	Jon Stos	.50	.20	.05
☐	17	Dave Sutton	.50	.20	.05
☐	18	Scott Sutton	.50	.20	.05
☐	19	Trevor Tremblay	.50	.20	.05
☐	20	Jaak Valiots	.50	.20	.05
☐	21	Sean Van Amburg	.50	.20	.05
☐	22	Jason Young Stickboy	.50	.20	.05
☐	23	Title Card	.75	.30	.07

1981-82 Regina Pats

No. 5 - Garth Butcher - Def.

This 25-card set measures approximately 2 5/8" by 4 1/8" and is printed on thin card stock. The fronts feature color, posed action player photos with white borders accented by a thin red line. The player's jersey number, name, and position appear in black print across the bottom of the picture. The backs carry P.L.A.Y. (Police, Laws and Youth) public service messages and sponsor logos. The cards are unnumbered and checklisted below in alphabetical order.

	MINT	EXC	G-VG
COMPLETE SET (25)	25.00	10.00	2.50
COMMON PLAYER (1-25)	.90	.36	.09

☐	1	Pats Logo	2.00	.80	.20
☐	2	Garth Butcher	5.00	2.00	.50
☐	3	Lyndon Byers	3.00	1.20	.30
☐	4	Jock Callander	2.00	.80	.20
☐	5	Marc Centrone	.90	.36	.09
☐	6	Dave Goertz	.90	.36	.09
☐	7	Evans Dobni	.90	.36	.09
☐	8	Dale Derkatch	1.50	.60	.15
☐	9	Jeff Crawford	.90	.36	.09
☐	10	Jim Clarke	.90	.36	.09
☐	11	Jayson Meyer	.90	.36	.09
☐	12	Gary Leeman	3.00	1.20	.30
☐	13	Bruce Holloway	.90	.36	.09
☐	14	Ken Heppner	.90	.36	.09
☐	15	Taylor Hall	1.50	.60	.15
☐	16	Wally Schreiber	1.50	.60	.15
☐	17	Kevin Pylypow	.90	.36	.09
☐	18	Ray Plamondon	.90	.36	.09
☐	19	Brent Pascal	.90	.36	.09
☐	20	Dave Michayluk	2.00	.80	.20
☐	21	Barry Trotz	.90	.36	.09
☐	22	Al Tuer	1.50	.60	.15
☐	23	Tony Vogel	.90	.36	.09
☐	24	Martin Wood	.90	.36	.09
☐	25	Regina Police Logo	.90	.36	.09

1982-83 Regina Pats

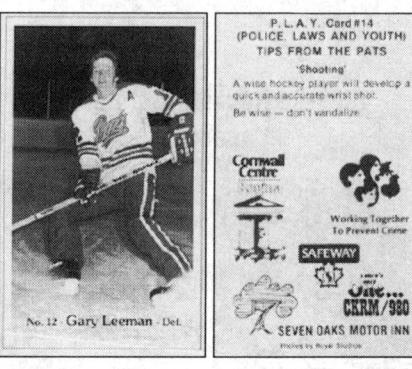

No. 12 - Gary Leeman - Def.

This 25-card set measures approximately 2 5/8" by 4 1/8" and features color, posed action player photos on white card stock. The pictures are framed by a thin red line. The player's name, jersey number, and position are printed in black on the photo. The backs carry P.L.A.Y. (Police, Laws, and Youth) public service and hockey tips. Sponsor logos are printed on the lower portion of the card back. The cards are numbered on the back.

	MINT	EXC	G-VG
COMPLETE SET (25)	18.00	7.25	1.80
COMMON PLAYER (1-25)	.75	.30	.07

☐	1	Regina Pats and Police Logo	1.00	.40	.10
☐	2	Todd Lumbard	.75	.30	.07
☐	3	Jamie Reeve	.75	.30	.07
☐	4	Dave Goertz	.75	.30	.07
☐	5	John Miner	.75	.30	.07
☐	6	Doug Trapp	.75	.30	.07
☐	7	R.J. Dundas	.75	.30	.07
☐	8	Stu Grimson	2.50	1.00	.25
☐	9	Al Tuer	1.25	.50	.12
☐	10	Rick Herbert	.75	.30	.07
☐	11	Tony Vogel	.75	.30	.07
☐	12	John Bekkers	.75	.30	.07
☐	13	Dale Derkatch	1.25	.50	.12
☐	14	Gary Leeman	2.00	.80	.20
☐	15	Nevin Markwart	1.25	.50	.12
☐	16	Kurt Wickenheiser	.75	.30	.07
☐	17	Jeff Frank	.75	.30	.07
☐	18	Marc Centrone	.75	.30	.07
☐	19	Taylor Hall	1.00	.40	.10
☐	20	Lyndon Byers	2.00	.80	.20
☐	21	Jayson Meyer	.75	.30	.07
☐	22	Jeff Crawford	.75	.30	.07
☐	23	Don Boyd CO	.75	.30	.07
☐	24	Barry Trapp ACO	.75	.30	.07
☐	25	K-9 Big Blue (Mascot)	.75	.30	.07

1983-84 Regina Pats

This 25-card set measures approximately 2 5/8" by 4 1/8" and features color, posed action player photos with white borders accented by a thin red line. The player's name is superimposed at the bottom of the picture. The backs carry P.L.A.Y. (Police, Laws and Youth) public service messages in the form of "Tips From The Pats." Sponsor logos appear on the lower portion of the card. The cards are numbered on the back.

	MINT	EXC	G-VG
COMPLETE SET (25)	12.00	5.00	1.20
COMMON PLAYER (1-25)	.60	.24	.06

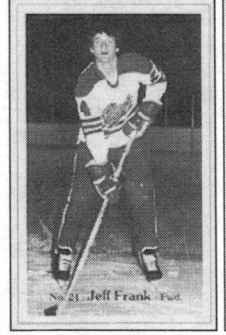

☐ 1	Title Card	.75	.30	.07
☐ 2	Todd Lumbard	.60	.24	.06
☐ 3	Jamie Reeve	.60	.24	.06
☐ 4	Dave Goertz	.60	.24	.06
☐ 5	John Miner	.60	.24	.06
☐ 6	Doug Trapp	.60	.24	.06
☐ 7	R.J. Dundas	.60	.24	.06
☐ 8	Stu Grimson	1.50	.60	.15
☐ 9	Al Tuer	1.00	.40	.10
☐ 10	Rick Herbert	.60	.24	.06
☐ 11	Tony Vogel	.60	.24	.06
☐ 12	John Bekkers	.60	.24	.06
☐ 13	Dale Derkatch	1.00	.40	.10
☐ 14	Gary Leeman	1.50	.60	.15
☐ 15	Nevin Markwart	1.00	.40	.10
☐ 16	Kurt Wickenheiser	.60	.24	.06
☐ 17	Jeff Frank	.60	.24	.06
☐ 18	Marc Centrone	.60	.24	.06
☐ 19	Taylor Hall	.75	.30	.07
☐ 20	Lyndon Byers	1.50	.60	.15
☐ 21	Jayson Meyer	.60	.24	.06
☐ 22	Jeff Crawford	.60	.24	.06
☐ 23	Don Boyd CO	.60	.24	.06
☐ 24	Barry Trapp ACO	.60	.24	.06
☐ 25	K-9 Big Blue (Mascot)	.60	.24	.06

1987-88 Regina Pats

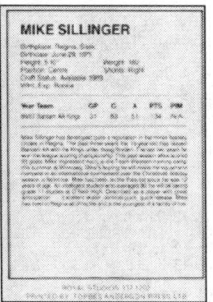

Produced by Royal Studios, this 28-card set measures the standard size (2 1/2" by 3 1/2") and features color, posed action player photos with red and white borders. The player's name is printed in red in the bottom white margin along with the team name and year, which are printed in black. The backs carry biographical information, statistics, and player profile within a box formed by a thin black line. The cards are unnumbered and checklisted below in alphabetical order.

	MINT	EXC	G-VG
COMPLETE SET (28)	15.00	6.00	1.50
COMMON PLAYER (1-28)	.60	.24	.06

☐ 1	Kevin Clemens	.60	.24	.06
☐ 2	Gary Dickie	.60	.24	.06
☐ 3	Milan Dragicevic	.60	.24	.06
☐ 4	Mike Dyck	.60	.24	.06
☐ 5	Craig Endean	.60	.24	.06
☐ 6	Kevin Gallant	.60	.24	.06
	Dir. of Marketing and Public Relations			
☐ 7	Jamie Heward	1.00	.40	.10
☐ 8	Rod Houk	.60	.24	.06
☐ 9	Mark Janssens	1.25	.50	.12
☐ 10	Trent Kachur	.60	.24	.06
☐ 11	Craig Kalawsky	.60	.24	.06
☐ 12	K-9 (Mascot)	.60	.24	.06
☐ 13	Frank Kovacs	.60	.24	.06
☐ 14	Darren Kwiatkowski	.60	.24	.06
☐ 15	Brian Leibel	.60	.24	.06
☐ 16	Tim Logan	.60	.24	.06
☐ 17	Jim Mathieson	.60	.24	.06
☐ 18	Darrin McKechnie	.60	.24	.06
☐ 19	Rob McKinley	.60	.24	.06
☐ 20	Brad Miller	.60	.24	.06
☐ 21	Cregg Nicol	.60	.24	.06
☐ 22	Doug Sauter CO	.60	.24	.06
☐ 23	Dan Sexton	.60	.24	.06
☐ 24	Mike Sillinger	2.50	1.00	.25
☐ 25	Dennis Sobchuk	.75	.30	.07
☐ 26	Stanley Szumlak TR	.60	.24	.06
☐ 27	Mike Van Slooten	.60	.24	.06
☐ 28	Team Photo	1.25	.50	.12

1988-89 Regina Pats

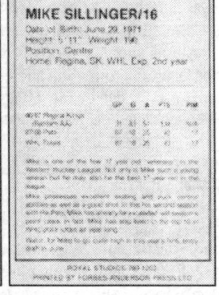

This 24-card set measures the standard size (2 1/2" by 3 1/2") and features color, posed action player photos with red and white borders. The player's name is printed in red in the bottom white margin along with the team name and year, which are printed in black. The backs carry biographical information, statistics, and a player profile within a box formed by a thin black line. The cards are unnumbered and checklisted below in alphabetical order.

	MINT	EXC	G-VG
COMPLETE SET (24)	15.00	6.00	1.50
COMMON PLAYER (1-24)	.60	.24	.06

☐ 1	Shane Bogden	.60	.24	.06
☐ 2	Cam Brauer	.60	.24	.06
☐ 3	Scott Daniels	.60	.24	.06
☐ 4	Gary Dickie	.60	.24	.06
☐ 5	Mike Dyck	.60	.24	.06
☐ 6	Dave Gerse	.60	.24	.06
☐ 7	Kevin Haller	2.00	.80	.20
☐ 8	Jamie Heward	1.00	.40	.10
☐ 9	Terry Hollinger	1.00	.40	.10
☐ 10	Rod Houk	.60	.24	.06
☐ 11	Frank Kovacs	.60	.24	.06
☐ 12	Brian Leibel	.60	.24	.06
☐ 13	Bernie Lynch CO	.60	.24	.06
☐ 14	Kelly Markwart	.60	.24	.06
☐ 15	Jim Mathieson	.60	.24	.06
☐ 16	Brad Miller	.60	.24	.06
☐ 17	Dwayne Monteith TR	.60	.24	.06
☐ 18	Curtis Nykyforuk	.60	.24	.06
☐ 19	Darren Parsons	.60	.24	.06

		MINT	EXC	G-VG
☐ 20	Cory Paterson	.60	.24	.06
☐ 21	Jeff Sebastian	.60	.24	.06
☐ 22	Mike Sillinger	2.00	.80	.20
☐ 23	Chad Silver	.60	.24	.06
☐ 24	Jamie Splett	.60	.24	.06

1989-90 Regina Pats

Sponsored by Mr. Lube, this 19-card set measures approximately 4" by 6" and is printed on thin card stock. The fronts feature black-and-white posed action photos with royal blue borders. The player's jersey number and name are printed in white in the bottom margin along with the team and sponsor logo. The backs are white and carry biographical information and a message from Bruce Olesen, general manager of Mr. Lube. The cards are unnumbered and checklisted below in alphabetical order.

		MINT	EXC	G-VG
	COMPLETE SET (19)	10.00	4.00	1.00
	COMMON PLAYER (1-19)	.75	.30	.07
☐ 1	Kelly Chotowetz	.75	.30	.07
☐ 2	Hal Christiansen	.75	.30	.07
☐ 3	Scott Daniels	.75	.30	.07
☐ 4	Wade Fennig	.75	.30	.07
☐ 5	Jason Glickman	.75	.30	.07
☐ 6	Jamie Heward	1.00	.40	.10
☐ 7	Terry Hollinger	1.00	.40	.10
☐ 8	Frank Kovacs	.75	.30	.07
☐ 9	Kelly Markwart	.75	.30	.07
☐ 10	Jim Mathieson	.75	.30	.07
☐ 11	Cam McLellan	.75	.30	.07
☐ 12	Troy Mick	.75	.30	.07
☐ 13	Greg Pankewicz	1.00	.40	.10
☐ 14	Cory Paterson	.75	.30	.07
☐ 15	Garry Pearce	.75	.30	.07
☐ 16	Mike Risdale	.75	.30	.07
☐ 17	Colin Ruck	.75	.30	.07
☐ 18	Mike Sillinger	2.00	.80	.20
☐ 19	Jamie Splett	.75	.30	.07

1935-36 Rhode Island Reds

Printed on thin card stock, this ten-card set measures approximately 2 1/4" by 3 1/2". The fronts feature black-and-white player photos bordered in white. The player's name and position are printed beneath the picture, along with the statement "A New 'Reds' Picture Every Amateur Hockey Night". Unlike the other nine cards, the name of the player on card 10 is not printed beneath his picture. From his facsimile autograph on the picture, his first name may be "Jacques," but his last name remains unidentified. The backs are blank. The cards are unnumbered and checklisted below in alphabetical order.

		EX-MT	VG-E	GOOD
	COMPLETE SET (10)	300.00	120.00	30.00
	COMMON PLAYER (1-10)	25.00	10.00	2.50
☐ 1	Bobby Bauer	35.00	14.00	3.50
☐ 2	Paddy Byrne	25.00	10.00	2.50
☐ 3	Woody(Porky) Dumart	50.00	20.00	5.00
☐ 4	Jackie Keating	25.00	10.00	2.50
☐ 5	Art Lesieur	25.00	10.00	2.50
☐ 6	Bert McInenly	25.00	10.00	2.50
☐ 7	Gus Rivers	25.00	10.00	2.50
☐ 8	Milt Schmidt	75.00	30.00	7.50
☐ 9	Jerry Shannon	25.00	10.00	2.50
☐ 10	Player Unidentified	25.00	10.00	2.50

1990-91 Richmond Renegades

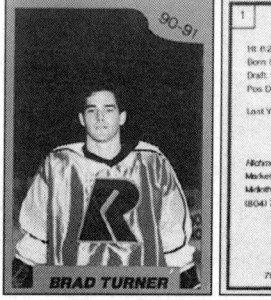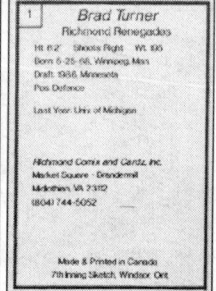

Produced by 7th Inning Sketch and sponsored by Richmond Comix and Cardz Inc., this 18-card set measures the standard size (2 1/2" by 3 1/2") and features posed color player photos with red borders. The player's name appears at the bottom. The year is printed diagonally in the upper right corner. The red border dips into the picture at this point to provide a background for the year. The backs carry biographical information within a black box. The cards are numbered on the back.

		MINT	EXC	G-VG
	COMPLETE SET (18)	8.00	3.25	.80
	COMMON PLAYER (1-18)	.50	.20	.05
☐ 1	Brad Turner	.75	.30	.07
☐ 2	Victor Posa	.50	.20	.05
☐ 3	Antti Autere	.50	.20	.05
☐ 4	Phil Huber	.50	.20	.05
☐ 5	Steve Spott	.50	.20	.05
☐ 6	Kelly Mills	.50	.20	.05
☐ 7	Paul Cain	.50	.20	.05
☐ 8	Shawn Lillie	.50	.20	.05
☐ 9	Kirby Lindal	.50	.20	.05
☐ 10	Dave Aiken	.50	.20	.05
☐ 11	Terry McCutcheon	.50	.20	.05
☐ 12	Jordan Fois	.50	.20	.05
☐ 13	Brad Beck	.50	.20	.05
☐ 14	Doug Pickell	.50	.20	.05
☐ 15	Frank Lascala	.50	.20	.05
☐ 16	John Haley	.50	.20	.05
☐ 17	Peter Harris	.50	.20	.05
☐ 18	Chris McSorley CO	1.00	.40	.10

1991-92 Richmond Renegades

Sponsored by "Bleacher Bums" Sports Cards Inc. and Domino's Pizza, this 20-card set was issued as a trifold sheet, one 12 1/2" by 7" team photo and two sheets with ten standard-size (2 1/2" by 3 1/2") player cards per sheet. The fronts feature color action player photos accented by a border design that shades from orange at the top to black at

the bottom. The player's name and position appear below the picture as do sponsor names. The team name appears above the picture. Inside a thin black border, the backs have the team name and logo on an orange panel with biography and sponsor logos below. The cards are numbered on the back.

	MINT	EXC	G-VG
COMPLETE SET (20)	9.00	3.75	.90
COMMON PLAYER (1-20)	.50	.20	.05
☐ 1 Rob Vanderydt	.75	.30	.07
☐ 2 Larry Rooney	.50	.20	.05
☐ 3 Brendan Flynn	.50	.20	.05
☐ 4 Scott Drevitch	.50	.20	.05
☐ 5 Joni Lehto	.50	.20	.05
☐ 6 Todd Drevitch	.50	.20	.05
☐ 7 Paul Rutherford	.50	.20	.05
☐ 8 Dave Aiken	.50	.20	.05
☐ 9 Pat Bingham	.50	.20	.05
☐ 10 Trevor Jobe	.50	.20	.05
☐ 11 Bob Berg	.50	.20	.05
☐ 12 Mark Kuntz	.50	.20	.05
☐ 13 Joe Capprini	.50	.20	.05
☐ 14 Trevor Converse	.50	.20	.05
☐ 15 Steve Scheifele	.50	.20	.05
☐ 16 Jon Gustafson	.50	.20	.05
☐ 17 Marco Fuster	.50	.20	.05
☐ 18 Guy Gadowsky	.50	.20	.05
☐ 19 Dave Allison CO	.50	.20	.05
☐ 20 Jamie McLennan	1.50	.60	.15
☐ xx Large Team Photo	3.00	1.20	.30

1992-93 Richmond Renegades

Sponsored by "Bleacher Bums" Sports Cards Inc. and Kellogg's, this 20-card set was issued as a trifold sheet, one 12 1/2" by 7" team photo and two sheets with ten standard-size (2 1/2" by 3 1/2") player cards per sheet. The fronts feature color action player photos accented by a black and orange border design. The picture itself is rimmed by an orange and white frame. Outside the frame is an orange design with varying sizes of stripes against a black

background. The player's name and position appear below the picture as do sponsor names. The team name appears above the picture. The backs carry a player biography and sponsor logos. The cards are unnumbered and checklisted below in alphabetical order.

	MINT	EXC	G-VG
COMPLETE SET (20)	8.00	3.25	.80
COMMON PLAYER (1-20)	.50	.20	.05
☐ 1 Will Averill	.50	.20	.05
☐ 2 Frank Bialowas	.75	.30	.07
☐ 3 Scott Drevitch	.50	.20	.05
☐ 4 Brendan Flynn	.50	.20	.05
☐ 5 Guy Gadowsky ACO	.50	.20	.05
☐ 6 Jon Gustafson	.50	.20	.05
☐ 7 Phil Huber	.50	.20	.05
☐ 8 Mike James	.50	.20	.05
☐ 9 Jeffery Kampersal	.50	.20	.05
☐ 10 Mark Kuntz	.50	.20	.05
☐ 11 Sean LeBrun	.50	.20	.05
☐ 12 Kevin Malgunas	.50	.20	.05
☐ 13 Jim McGeough	.50	.20	.05
☐ 14 Ed Sabo	.50	.20	.05
☐ 15 Jeff Saterdalen	.50	.20	.05
☐ 16 Alan Schuler	.50	.20	.05
☐ 17 Martin Smith	.50	.20	.05
☐ 18 Roy Sommer CO	.50	.20	.05
☐ 19 Jeff Torrey	.50	.20	.05
☐ 20 Ben Wyzansky	.50	.20	.05
☐ xx Large Team Photo	2.50	1.00	.25

1993-94 Richmond Renegades

Sponsored by "Bleacher Bum" Collectibles, Inc., radio station XL102, and Kellogg's, this 20-card set features the 1993-94 Richmond Renegades. The cards measure the standard size (2 1/2" by 3 1/2") and are printed on thin card stock. On a team color-coded background, the fronts feature color action player photos with purple borders, along with the player's name, position and team name. The white backs carry a short player biography and team and sponsors' logos. The cards are numbered on the back.

	MINT	EXC	G-VG
COMPLETE SET (20)	9.00	3.75	.90
COMMON PLAYER (1-20)	.50	.20	.05
☐ 1 Ken Weiss	.50	.20	.05
☐ 2 Guy Phillips	.50	.20	.05
☐ 3 Alexander Zhdan	.50	.20	.05
☐ 4 Alan Schuler	.50	.20	.05
☐ 5 John Craighead	.50	.20	.05
☐ 6 Colin Gregor	.50	.20	.05
☐ 7 Rob MacInnis	.50	.20	.05
☐ 8 Devin Derksen	.75	.30	.07
☐ 9 Jason Renard	.50	.20	.05
☐ 10 Peter Allen	.50	.20	.05
☐ 11 Roy Sommer CO	.50	.20	.05
☐ 12 Milan Hnilicka	1.00	.40	.10
☐ 13 Oleg Santurian	.50	.20	.05
☐ 14 Brendan Flynn	.50	.20	.05
☐ 15 Ken Blum	.50	.20	.05

☐ 16 Steve Bogoyevac..................	.50	.20	.05
☐ 17 Eric Germain	.50	.20	.05
☐ 18 Chris Foy.............................	.50	.20	.05
☐ 19 Darren Colbourne.................	.50	.20	.05
☐ 20 Jon Gustafson......................	.50	.20	.05

1963-64 Rochester Amerks

Printed on thin paper stock, this set of ten photos measure approximately 4" by 6" and features borderless black-and-white posed or action shots of the AHL (American Hockey League) Amerks. The white back carries the player's name, age, height, weight, and statistics from previous years in the minors. The cards are unnumbered and checklisted below in alphabetical order.

	NRMT	VG-E	GOOD
COMPLETE SET (10)......................	75.00	30.00	7.50
COMMON PLAYER (1-10)................	5.00	2.00	.50
☐ 1 Lou Angotti	7.50	3.00	.75
☐ 2 Al Arbour..............................	12.50	5.00	1.25
☐ 3 Gerry Cheevers UER..............	30.00	12.00	3.00
(Misspelled Jerry on card back)			
☐ 4 Mike Corbett	5.00	2.00	.50
☐ 5 Jack Curran TR	5.00	2.00	.50
☐ 6 Les Duff	5.00	2.00	.50
☐ 7 Eddie Lawson........................	5.00	2.00	.50
☐ 8 Jim Pappin	7.50	3.00	.75
☐ 9 Darryl Sly	5.00	2.00	.50
☐ 10 Stan Smrke	6.00	2.40	.60

1991-92 Rochester Americans Dunkin' Donuts

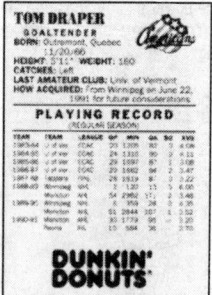

Sponsored by Dunkin' Donuts, this 20-card set measures the standard size (2 1/2" by 3 1/2"). It was issued in four

perforated strips, each consisting of four player cards and a Dunkin' Donuts coupon. On white card stock, the fronts feature color action player photos. Blue and red border stripes edge the picture on the bottom and half way on each side. The player's name is printed in a red-lined box above the picture, while logos and additional player information appear beneath it. In black print on a white background, the backs carry biography, statistics, and sponsor logo. The cards are unnumbered and checklisted below in alphabetical order.

	MINT	EXC	G-VG
COMPLETE SET (20)........................	10.00	4.00	1.00
COMMON CARD (1-20)	.50	.20	.05
☐ 1 Greg Brown..........................	.75	.30	.07
☐ 2 Peter Ciavaglia	.75	.30	.07
☐ 3 Bob Corkum.........................	1.00	.40	.10
☐ 4 Brian Curran	.50	.20	.05
☐ 5 David DiVita	.50	.20	.05
☐ 6 Tom Draper..........................	1.00	.40	.10
☐ 7 Jody Gage	.75	.30	.07
☐ 8 Dan Frawley	.75	.30	.07
☐ 9 Dave Littman.........................	.75	.30	.07
☐ 10 Darcy Loewen......................	.75	.30	.07
☐ 11 Don McSween......................	.75	.30	.07
☐ 12 Brad Rubachuk	.50	.20	.05
☐ 13 Lindy Ruff...........................	.75	.30	.07
☐ 14 Joel Savage	.50	.20	.05
☐ 15 Jiri Sejba.............................	.50	.20	.05
☐ 16 Chris Snell...........................	.75	.30	.07
☐ 17 Coupon Dunkin' Donuts........	.50	.20	.05
☐ 18 Coupon Dunkin' Donuts........	.50	.20	.05
☐ 19 Coupon Dunkin' Donuts........	.50	.20	.05
☐ 20 Coupon Dunkin' Donuts........	.50	.20	.05

1991-92 Rochester Americans Kodak

The 1991-92 Rochester American Team Photo and Trading Card Set was co-sponsored by Kodak and Wegmons Photo Center. It consists of three 11 1/4" by 9 1/2" sheets joined together and tri-folded. The first sheet displays a team photo of the players dressed in street clothes. The second and third sheets consist of 15 cards each arranged in three rows of five cards. The last four slots of the third sheet display sponsor coupons. After perforation, the cards would measure approximately 2 1/4" by 3 1/8". The player photos on the fronts have rounded corners and are poses shot from the waist up against a studio background. Team color-coded (red and blue) stripes edge the pictures on the bottom and each side. The player's name, position, and the team logo are above the picture, while sponsor logos and the uniform number are below it. In red and blue print, the backs carry biography and statistics. The cards are checklisted below as they are arranged in the album, with coaches presented first and then the players in alphabetical order.

	MINT	EXC	G-VG
COMPLETE SET (26)	10.00	4.00	1.00
COMMON PLAYER (1-26)	.35	.14	.03
☐ 1 Don Lever CO	.50	.20	.05
☐ 2 Terry Martin ACO	.35	.14	.03
☐ 3 Ian Boyce	.35	.14	.03
☐ 4 John Bradley	.35	.14	.03
☐ 5 Greg Brown	.75	.30	.07
☐ 6 Keith Carney	.50	.20	.05
☐ 7 Peter Ciavaglia	.75	.30	.07
☐ 8 Bob Corkum	1.00	.40	.10
☐ 9 Brian Curran	.35	.14	.03
☐ 10 David DiVita	.35	.14	.03
☐ 11 Lou Franceschetti	.50	.20	.05
☐ 12 Dan Frawley	.50	.20	.05
☐ 13 Jody Gage	.75	.30	.07
☐ 14 Kevin Haller	.75	.30	.07
☐ 15 Dave Littman	.50	.20	.05
☐ 16 Darcy Loewen	.50	.20	.05
☐ 17 Steve Ludzik	.50	.20	.05
☐ 18 Don McSween	.50	.20	.05
☐ 19 Brad Miller	.50	.20	.05
☐ 20 Sean O'Donnell	.35	.14	.03
☐ 21 Brad Rubachuk	.35	.14	.03
☐ 22 Lindy Ruff	.50	.20	.05
☐ 23 Joel Savage	.35	.14	.03
☐ 24 Jiri Sejba	.35	.14	.03
☐ 25 Chris Snell	.50	.20	.05
☐ 26 Jason Winch	.50	.20	.05

1992-93 Rochester Americans Dunkin' Donuts

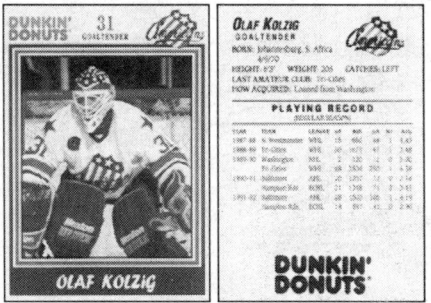

Sponsored by Dunkin' Donuts, this 20-card set measures the standard size (2 1/2" by 3 1/2"). It was issued in four perforated strips, each consisting of five player cards. On white card stock, the fronts feature color action player photos framed by team color-coded (red and blue) border stripes. Logos, jersey number, and position are printed above the picture, while the player's name is printed on the wider blue stripe beneath the picture. In black print on a white background, the backs carry biography, statistics, and sponsor logo. The cards are unnumbered and checklisted below in alphabetical order.

	MINT	EXC	G-VG
COMPLETE SET (20)	10.00	4.00	1.00
COMMON PLAYER (1-20)	.50	.20	.05
☐ 1 Peter Ambroziak	.50	.20	.05
☐ 2 Greg Brown	.75	.30	.07
☐ 3 Peter Ciavaglia	.75	.30	.07
☐ 4 Jozef Cierny	1.00	.40	.10
☐ 5 David DiVita	.50	.20	.05
☐ 6 Dan Frawley	.75	.30	.07
☐ 7 Jody Gage	.75	.30	.07
☐ 8 Andrei Jakovenko	.50	.20	.05
☐ 9 Olaf Kolzig	1.00	.40	.10
☐ 10 Doug Macdonald	.50	.20	.05
☐ 11 Mike McLaughlin	.50	.20	.05

	MINT	EXC	G-VG
☐ 12 Sean O'Donnell	.50	.20	.05
☐ 13 Bill Pye	.50	.20	.05
☐ 14 Brad Rubachuk	.50	.20	.05
☐ 15 Bruce Shoebottom	.75	.30	.07
☐ 16 Todd Simon	.75	.30	.07
☐ 17 Jeff Sirkka	.50	.20	.05
☐ 18 Chris Snell	.75	.30	.07
☐ 19 Scott Thomas	.75	.30	.07
☐ 20 Jason Young	.50	.20	.05

1992-93 Rochester Americans Kodak

The 1992-93 Rochester American Team Photo and Trading Card Set was co-sponsored by Kodak and Wegmons Photo Center. It consists of three 11 1/4" by 9 1/2" sheets joined together and tri-folded. The first sheet displays a team photo of the players in uniform. The second and third sheets consist of 15 cards each arranged in three rows of five cards. (The last four slots of the third sheet display sponsor coupons.) After perforation, the cards would measure approximately 2 1/4" by 3 1/8". The player photos on the fronts have rounded corners and are poses shot from the waist up against a studio background. Team color-coded (red and blue) stripes edge the pictures on the top and each side. The player's name, position, and the team logo are above the picture, while sponsor logos and the uniform number are below it. In red and blue print, the backs carry biography and statistics. The cards are checklisted below as they are arranged in the album, with coaches presented first and then the players in alphabetical order.

	MINT	EXC	G-VG
COMPLETE SET (26)	10.00	4.00	1.00
COMMON PLAYER (1-26)	.35	.14	.03
☐ 1 John Van Boxmeer CO	.50	.20	.05
☐ 2 Terry Martin ACO	.35	.14	.03
☐ 3 Peter Ambroziak	.35	.14	.03
☐ 4 Greg Brown	.75	.30	.07
☐ 5 Peter Ciavaglia	.75	.30	.07
☐ 6 Jozef Cierny	.50	.20	.05
☐ 7 David DiVita	.35	.14	.03
☐ 8 Dan Frawley	.75	.30	.07
☐ 9 Jody Gage	.75	.30	.07
☐ 10 The Moose (mascot)	.35	.14	.03
☐ 11 Tony Iob	.50	.20	.05
☐ 12 Olaf Kolzig	1.00	.40	.10
☐ 13 Doug MacDonald	.35	.14	.03
☐ 14 Mike McLaughlin	.35	.14	.03
☐ 15 Sean O'Donnell	.35	.14	.03
☐ 16 Brad Pascall	.35	.14	.03
☐ 17 Bill Pye	.35	.14	.03
☐ 18 Brad Rubachuk	.35	.14	.03
☐ 19 Joel Savage	.35	.14	.03
☐ 20 Bruce Shoebottom	.50	.20	.05
☐ 21 Todd Simon	.75	.30	.07
☐ 22 Jeff Sirkka	.35	.14	.03
☐ 23 Chris Snell	.50	.20	.05
☐ 24 Scott Thomas	.50	.20	.05
☐ 25 Jason Winch	.50	.20	.05
☐ 26 Jason Young	.35	.14	.03

1992-93 St. John's Maple Leafs

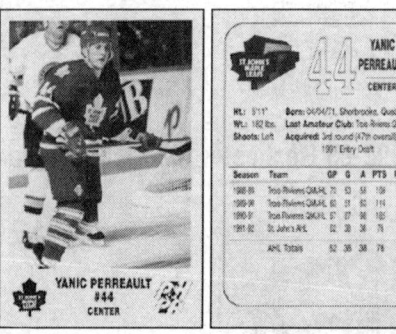

cartoon starring Smokey the Bear. Card number 10 was never issued. The cards are numbered on the back.

Measuring approximately 2 1/2" by 3 3/4", this 25-card set features the St. John's Maple Leafs of the American Hockey League. The fronts display color action player photos framed by white borders. In the wider bottom border, the player's name, uniform number, position, and logos are printed in black. On a white background inside a thin blue border, the backs present biographical and statistical information. The team logo in blue is printed at the upper left corner. The cards are unnumbered and checklisted below in alphabetical order.

	MINT	EXC	G-VG
COMPLETE SET (25)	10.00	4.00	1.00
COMMON PLAYER (1-25)	.35	.14	.03
☐ 1 Patrik Augusta	.35	.14	.03
☐ 2 Drake Berehowsky	1.00	.40	.10
☐ 3 Robert Cimetta	.50	.20	.05
☐ 4 Marc Crawford CO	.35	.14	.03
☐ 5 Ted Crowley	.50	.20	.05
☐ 6 Mike Eastwood	.50	.20	.05
☐ 7 Todd Hawkins	.35	.14	.03
☐ 8 Curtis Hunt	.35	.14	.03
☐ 9 Eric Lacroix	.50	.20	.05
☐ 10 Guy Lehoux	.35	.14	.03
☐ 11 Kent Manderville	1.00	.40	.10
☐ 12 Kevin McClelland	.75	.30	.07
☐ 13 Ken McRae	.50	.20	.05
☐ 14 Brad Miller	.35	.14	.03
☐ 15 Yanic Perreault	1.00	.40	.10
☐ 16 Rudy Poeschek	.50	.20	.05
☐ 17 Joel Quenneville ACO	.35	.14	.03
☐ 18 Damian Rhodes	1.00	.40	.10
☐ 19 Joe Sacco	.75	.30	.07
☐ 20 Jeff Serowik	.50	.20	.05
☐ 21 Scott Sharples	.35	.14	.03
☐ 22 Dave Tomlinson	.50	.20	.05
☐ 23 Nick Wohlers	.35	.14	.03
☐ 24 Team Photo	1.00	.40	.10
☐ 25 Buddy (Mascot)	.35	.14	.03

	MINT	EXC	G-VG
COMPLETE SET (24)	20.00	8.00	2.00
COMMON PLAYER (1-23)	.75	.30	.07
☐ 1 Rick Barkovich	1.00	.40	.10
☐ 2 Michael Dark	.75	.30	.07
☐ 3 Terry Perkins	.75	.30	.07
☐ 4 Peter Lappin	1.00	.40	.10
☐ 5 Wayne Cowley	.75	.30	.07
☐ 6 Rich Chernomaz	1.00	.40	.10
☐ 7 Steve Smith	.75	.30	.07
☐ 8 Theoren Fleury	12.00	5.00	1.20
☐ 9 Dave Reierson	.75	.30	.07
☐ 10 Not Issued	.00	.00	.00
☐ 11 Martin Simard	1.50	.60	.15
☐ 12 Stu Grimson	3.00	1.20	.30
☐ 13 Darwin McCutcheon	.75	.30	.07
☐ 14 Doug Clarke	.75	.30	.07
☐ 15 Doug Pickell	.75	.30	.07
☐ 16 Randy Bucyk	.75	.30	.07
☐ 17 Jim Johannson	.75	.30	.07
☐ 18 Rick Lessard	1.50	.60	.15
☐ 19 Ken Sabourin	1.50	.60	.15
☐ 20 Chris Biotti	.75	.30	.07
☐ 21 Jeff Wenaas	.75	.30	.07
☐ 22 Mark Holmes	.75	.30	.07
☐ 23 Bob Bodak	.75	.30	.07
☐ 24 Marc Bureau	1.50	.60	.15
☐ NNO Cover Card	1.50	.60	.15
(Smokey the Bear)			

1992-93 San Diego Gulls

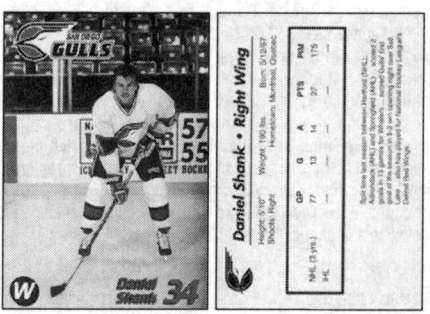

1988-89 Salt Lake City Golden Eagles

Commemorating the 20th anniversary of the Salt Lake City Golden Eagles, this 25-card set measures the standard size (2 1/2" by 3 1/2") and features color close-up shots against a light blue background. The player's name and position are printed diagonally in black across the front. The set was sponsored by the USDA Forest Service and Utah State Lands and Forestry agency. The backs are white with black print and include player statistics and a fire prevention

This 24-card set measures the standard size (2 1/2" by 3 1/2") and features full-bleed, color player photos. The player's name is superimposed on the picture in red lettering. The player's position appears in a black circle in the lower left corner. The horizontal backs carry biographical information, statistics, and a player profile. The cards are unnumbered and checklisted below in alphabetical order.

	MINT	EXC	G-VG
COMPLETE SET (24)......................	10.00	4.00	1.00
COMMON PLAYER (1-24)..............	.50	.20	.05
☐ 1 John Anderson........................	.75	.30	.07
☐ 2 Perry Anderson......................	.50	.20	.05
☐ 3 Scott Arniel...........................	.75	.30	.07
☐ 4 Michael Brewer......................	.50	.20	.05
☐ 5 Dale DeGray..........................	.75	.30	.07
☐ 6 Gord Dineen..........................	.75	.30	.07
☐ 7 Rick Dudley CO	.75	.30	.07
☐ 8 Larry Floyd............................	.50	.20	.05
☐ 9 Keith Gretzky.........................	2.00	.80	.20
☐ 10 Peter Hankinson....................	.50	.20	.05
☐ 11 Bill Houlder..........................	.75	.30	.07
☐ 12 Andrei Iakovenko	.50	.20	.05
☐ 13 Rick Knickle	1.00	.40	.10
☐ 14 Denny Lambert	.75	.30	.07
☐ 15 Mitch Lamoureux	.50	.20	.05
☐ 16 Clint Malarchuk	1.00	.40	.10
☐ 17 Steve Martinson....................	.50	.20	.05
☐ 18 Hubie McDonough	.75	.30	.07
☐ 19 Don McSween......................	.75	.30	.07
☐ 20 Mitch Molloy.........................	.50	.20	.05
☐ 21 Robbie Nichols......................	.50	.20	.05
☐ 22 Lindy Ruff	.75	.30	.07
☐ 23 Daniel Shank	.75	.30	.07
☐ 24 Sergei Starikov.....................	.75	.30	.07

1981-82 Saskatoon Blades

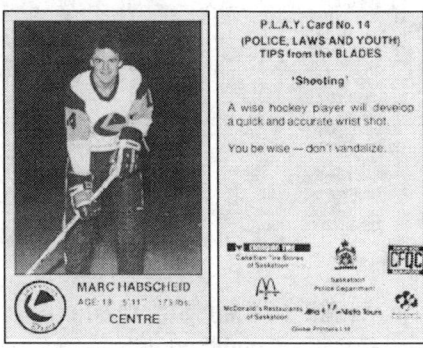

This 25-card P.L.A.Y. (Police, Laws and Youth) set was sponsored by the Saskatoon Police Department and area businesses. The cards measure approximately 2 1/2" by 3 3/4" and are printed on thin card stock. The fronts feature white-bordered color photos with the player's posed in action stances. The player's name, biographical information, and position appear in the bottom white margin. The team logo appears in the lower left corner. The backs carry public service messages in the form of "Tips from the Blades." Sponsor logos appear at the bottom. The cards are numbered on the back.

	MINT	EXC	G-VG
COMPLETE SET (25)..........................	15.00	6.00	1.50
COMMON PLAYER (1-25)...................	.75	.30	.07
☐ 1 Blades Team Photo	2.00	.80	.20
☐ 2 Daryl Stanley........................	1.00	.40	.10
☐ 3 Leroy Gorski	.75	.30	.07
☐ 4 Donn Clark	.75	.30	.07
☐ 5 Brad Duggan	.75	.30	.07
☐ 6 Dave Chartier	.75	.30	.07
☐ 7 Dave Brown..........................	2.00	.80	.20
☐ 8 Adams Thompson..................	.75	.30	.07
☐ 9 Bruce Eakin..........................	.75	.30	.07
☐ 10 Brian Skrudland	2.00	.80	.20
☐ 11 Roger Kortko........................	.75	.30	.07
☐ 12 Ron Dreger	.75	.30	.07
☐ 13 Daryl Lubiniecki	.75	.30	.07
☐ 14 Marc Habscheid	1.50	.60	.15
☐ 15 Saskatoon Police Logo.........	.75	.30	.07
☐ 16 Todd Strueby	.75	.30	.07

☐ 17 Craig Hurley	.75	.30	.07
☐ 18 Bill Hlynsky	.75	.30	.07
☐ 19 Lane Lambert........................	1.50	.60	.15
☐ 20 Mike Bloski	.75	.30	.07
☐ 21 Bruce Gordon.......................	.75	.30	.07
☐ 22 Perry Ganchar	.75	.30	.07
☐ 23 Ron Loustel..........................	.75	.30	.07
☐ 24 Blades Logo	1.00	.40	.10
☐ 25 Checklist Card......................	1.50	.60	.15

1983-84 Saskatoon Blades

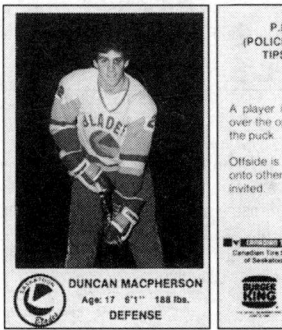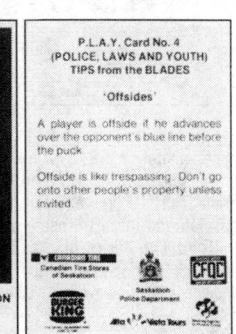

This set contains 24 P.L.A.Y. (Police, Law and Youth) cards and features the Saskatoon Blades of the Western Hockey League. The cards measure approximately 2 7/16" by 3 3/4". The fronts feature a color posed action shot with white borders. The team logo appears in the lower left corner, with player information to the right in black lettering. The backs have sponsors' logos at the bottom and "Tips from the Blades," which consist of definitions of hockey terms paralleled by public service or anti-crime messages. The cards are numbered on the back.

	MINT	EXC	G-VG
COMPLETE SET (24)......................	25.00	10.00	2.50
COMMON PLAYER (1-24)..............	.75	.30	.07
☐ 1 Team Photo........................	2.00	.80	.20
☐ 2 Trent Yawney	1.50	.60	.15
☐ 3 Grant Jennings.....................	1.50	.60	.15
☐ 4 Duncan MacPherson............	1.00	.40	.10
☐ 5 Greg Holtby.........................	.75	.30	.07
☐ 6 Dan Leier	.75	.30	.07
☐ 7 Dwaine Hutton	.75	.30	.07
☐ 8 Wendel Clark.......................	12.50	5.00	1.25
☐ 9 Kerry Laviolette	.75	.30	.07
☐ 10 Dave Chartier	.75	.30	.07
☐ 11 Dale Henry	.75	.30	.07
☐ 12 Randy Smith	.75	.30	.07
☐ 13 Kevin Kowalchuk	1.00	.40	.10
☐ 14 Todd McLellan	.75	.30	.07
☐ 15 Title Card............................	.75	.30	.07
Saskatoon Police			
☐ 16 Larry Korchinkski..................	.75	.30	.07
☐ 17 Curtis Chamberlin	.75	.30	.07
☐ 18 Greg Lebsack	.75	.30	.07
☐ 19 Ron Dreger	.75	.30	.07
☐ 20 Doug Kyle	.75	.30	.07
☐ 21 Rick Smith	.75	.30	.07
☐ 22 Joey Kocur..........................	3.00	1.20	.30
☐ 23 Allan Larochelle...................	.75	.30	.07
☐ 24 Mark Thietke	1.00	.40	.10

1981-82 Sault Ste. Marie Greyhounds

Sponsored by Blue Bird Bakery Limited, Coke, 920 CKCY radio, and Canadian Tire, this 28-card set measures

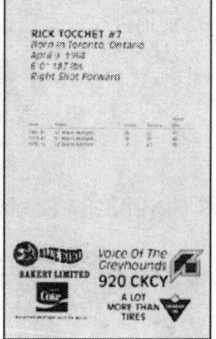

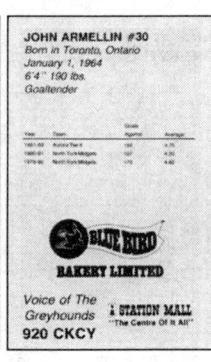

approximately 2 1/8" by 4 1/8" and features posed, color player photos with white borders. The player's name is printed in white on the picture, above the player's head. His position and the team name are printed in fuchsia at the bottom. The backs display biographical information, statistics, and sponsor logos. The cards are unnumbered and checklisted below in alphabetical order.

	MINT	EXC	G-VG
COMPLETE SET (28)	50.00	20.00	5.00
COMMON PLAYER (1-28)	.75	.30	.07

		MINT	EXC	G-VG
☐ 1	Jim Aldred	.75	.30	.07
☐ 2	Dave Andreoli	.75	.30	.07
☐ 3	Richard Beaulne	.75	.30	.07
☐ 4	Bruce Bell	.75	.30	.07
☐ 5	Chuck Brimmer	.75	.30	.07
☐ 6	Tony Cella	.75	.30	.07
☐ 7	Kevin Conway	.75	.30	.07
☐ 8	Terry Crisp CO	3.00	1.20	.30
☐ 9	Marc D'Amour	1.00	.40	.10
☐ 10	Gord Dineen	1.50	.60	.15
☐ 11	Chris Felix	1.00	.40	.10
☐ 12	Ron Francis	15.00	6.00	1.50
☐ 13	Steve Graves	.75	.30	.07
☐ 14	Wayne Groulx	.75	.30	.07
☐ 15	Huey Larkin	.75	.30	.07
☐ 16	Ken Latta	.75	.30	.07
☐ 17	Mike Lococo	.75	.30	.07
☐ 18	Jim Pavese	1.00	.40	.10
☐ 19	Dirk Rueter	.75	.30	.07
☐ 20	Steve Smith	3.00	1.20	.30
☐ 21	Terry Tait	.75	.30	.07
☐ 22	Rick Tocchet	15.00	6.00	1.50
☐ 23	John Vanbiesbrouck	15.00	6.00	1.50
☐ 24	Harry Wolfe	.75	.30	.07
	Voice of the Greyhounds			
☐ 25	J.D. Yari	.75	.30	.07
☐ 26	Bluebird Bakery	.75	.30	.07
	Limited Logo			
☐ 27	Canadian Tire Logo	.75	.30	.07
☐ 28	Coca-Cola Ad	.75	.30	.07

1982-83 Sault Ste. Marie Greyhounds

Sponsored by Blue Bird Bakery Limited and 920 CKCY radio station, this 25-card set measures approximately 2 1/2" by 4" and feature color, posed player photos with white borders. The player's name is superimposed on the photo in white lettering. His position is in black at the bottom. The backs carry biographical information, statistics, and sponsor logos. The cards are unnumbered and checklisted below in alphabetical order.

	MINT	EXC	G-VG
COMPLETE SET (25)	30.00	12.00	3.00
COMMON PLAYER (1-25)	.75	.30	.07

		MINT	EXC	G-VG
☐ 1	Jim Aldred	.75	.30	.07
☐ 2	John Armelin	.75	.30	.07
☐ 3	Richard Beaulne	.75	.30	.07
☐ 4	Jeff Beukeboom	2.00	.80	.20
☐ 5	Tony Cella	.75	.30	.07
☐ 6	Kevin Conway	.75	.30	.07
☐ 7	Terry Crisp	1.50	.60	.15
☐ 8	Chris Felix	1.00	.40	.10
☐ 9	Steve Graves	.75	.30	.07
☐ 10	Gus Greco	.75	.30	.07
☐ 11	Wayne Groulx	.75	.30	.07
☐ 12	Sam Haidy	.75	.30	.07
☐ 13	Tim Hoover	.75	.30	.07
☐ 14	Pat Lahey	.75	.30	.07
☐ 15	Huey Larkin	.75	.30	.07
☐ 16	Mike Lococo	.75	.30	.07
☐ 17	Mike Neill	.75	.30	.07
☐ 18	Ken Sabourin	1.50	.60	.15
☐ 19	Steve Smith	2.50	1.00	.25
☐ 20	Terry Tait	.75	.30	.07
☐ 21	Rick Tocchet	10.00	4.00	1.00
☐ 22	John Vanbiesbrouck	10.00	4.00	1.00
☐ 23	Harry Wolfe	.75	.30	.07
☐ 24	Station Mall Sponsor	.75	.30	.07
☐ 25	Bluebird Bakery Ltd.	.75	.30	.07

1983-84 Sault Ste. Marie Greyhounds

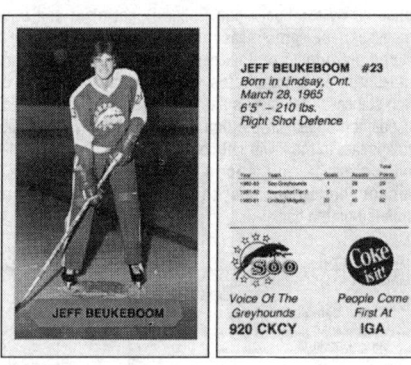

Sponsored by 920 CKCY radio, Coke, and IGA, the cards in this 25-card set measure approximately 2 1/2" by 4" and feature color, posed player photos with white borders. The player's name appears in an orange bar at the bottom of the picture. The backs carry biographical information, statistics, and sponsor logos. The cards are unnumbered and checklisted below in alphabetical order.

	MINT	EXC	G-VG
COMPLETE SET (25)......................	20.00	8.00	2.00
COMMON PLAYER (1-25)................	.75	.30	.07
☐ 1 Jeff Beukeboom	2.00	.80	.20
☐ 2 Graeme Bonar	.75	.30	.07
☐ 3 Chris Brant	.75	.30	.07
☐ 4 John English	.75	.30	.07
☐ 5 Chris Felix	1.00	.40	.10
☐ 6 Rick Fera	.75	.30	.07
☐ 7 Marc Fournier	.75	.30	.07
☐ 8 Steve Graves	.75	.30	.07
☐ 9 Gus Greco	.75	.30	.07
☐ 11 Wayne Groulx	.75	.30	.07
☐ 11 Sam Haidy	.75	.30	.07
☐ 12 Tim Hoover	.75	.30	.07
☐ 13 Jerry Iuliano	.75	.30	.07
☐ 14 Pat Lahey	.75	.30	.07
☐ 15 Mike Lococo	.75	.30	.07
☐ 16 Jean-Marc MacKensie...........	.75	.30	.07
☐ 17 Mike Oliverio	.75	.30	.07
☐ 18 Brit Peer	.75	.30	.07
☐ 19 Joey Rampton.......................	.75	.30	.07
☐ 20 Ken Sabourin	1.00	.40	.10
☐ 21 Jim Samec	.75	.30	.07
☐ 22 Rick Tocchet	8.00	3.25	.80
☐ 23 Harry Wolfe..........................	.75	.30	.07
☐ 24 IGA Sponsor Card	.75	.30	.07
☐ 25 Coke Sponsor Card	.75	.30	.07

1984-85 Sault Ste. Marie Greyhounds

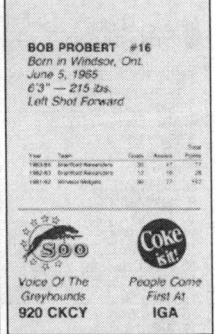

Sponsored by 920 CKCY radio, Coke, and IGA, this 25-card set measures approximately 2 1/2" by 4" and features white-bordered, posed, color photos of the players on ice with a blue studio background. The player's name appears on a bright red plaque near the bottom. The backs carry biographical information, statistics, and sponsor logos. The cards are unnumbered and checklisted below in alphabetical order.

	MINT	EXC	G-VG
COMPLETE SET (25)......................	18.00	7.25	1.80
COMMON PLAYER (1-25)................	.75	.30	.07
☐ 1 Marty Abrams	.75	.30	.07
☐ 2 Jeff Beukeboom	1.50	.60	.15
☐ 3 Graeme Bonar	.75	.30	.07
☐ 4 Chris Brant	.75	.30	.07
☐ 5 Terry Crisp CO	1.25	.50	.12
☐ 6 Chris Felix	1.00	.40	.10
☐ 7 Scott Green	.75	.30	.07
☐ 8 Wayne Groulx	.75	.30	.07
☐ 9 Steve Hollett	.75	.30	.07
☐ 10 Tim Hoover	.75	.30	.07
☐ 11 Derek King	2.50	1.00	.25
☐ 12 Tyler Larter	.75	.30	.07
☐ 13 Jean-Marc MacKenzie	.75	.30	.07

	MINT	EXC	G-VG
☐ 14 Scott Mosey......................	.75	.30	.07
☐ 15 Mike Oliverio	.75	.30	.07
☐ 16 Brit Peer............................	.75	.30	.07
☐ 17 Wayne Presley	1.00	.40	.10
☐ 18 Bob Probert........................	6.00	2.40	.60
☐ 19 Brian Rome	.75	.30	.07
☐ 20 Ken Sabourin	1.00	.40	.10
☐ 21 Rob Veccia	.75	.30	.07
☐ 22 Harry Wolfe........................	.75	.30	.07
Voice of the Greyhounds			
☐ 23 Rob Zettler	1.50	.60	.15
☐ 24 IGA Ad	.75	.30	.07
☐ 25 Coca-Cola Ad	.75	.30	.07

1987-88 Sault Ste. Marie Greyhounds

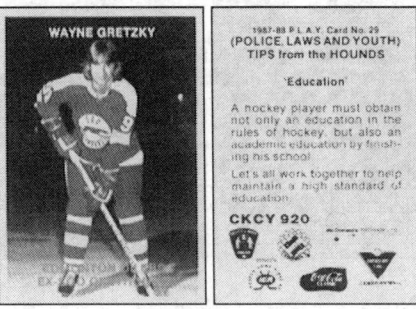

Printed on thin card stock, this 35-card set features players from the 1987-88 season of the Sault Ste. Marie Greyhounds and also past Greyhounds players who have gone on to NHL fame, such as Wayne Gretzky. The fronts feature white-bordered posed-on-ice color player photos. The player's name appears in white lettering near the top; his position and the team name appear in blue lettering near the bottom. The white back carries a hockey tip and a safety tip. Multiple sponsor logos at the bottom round out the back. The cards are numbered on the back.

	MINT	EXC	G-VG
COMPLETE SET (35)......................	75.00	30.00	7.50
COMMON PLAYER (1-35)................	.75	.30	.07
☐ 1 Barry King............................	.75	.30	.07
Chief of Police			
☐ 2 Dan Currie............................	1.25	.50	.12
☐ 3 Mike Glover	.75	.30	.07
☐ 4 Tyler Larter	1.25	.50	.12
☐ 5 Bob Jones	.75	.30	.07
☐ 6 Lyndon Slewidge...................	.75	.30	.07
National Anthem Singer			
☐ 7 Brad Jones	1.00	.40	.10
☐ 8 Ron Francis..........................	5.00	2.00	.50
☐ 9 Dale Turnbull........................	.75	.30	.07
☐ 10 Don McConnell	.75	.30	.07
☐ 11 Chris Felix	1.25	.50	.12
☐ 12 Steve Udvari........................	.75	.30	.07
☐ 13 Shawn Simpson	.75	.30	.07
☐ 14 Rob Zettler	1.25	.50	.12
☐ 15 Phil Esposito	5.00	2.00	.50
Co-owner			
☐ 16 John Vanbiesbrouck	5.00	2.00	.50
☐ 17 Mike Oliverio	.75	.30	.07
☐ 18 Colin Ford	.75	.30	.07
☐ 19 Steve Herniman....................	.75	.30	.07
☐ 20 Troy Mallette	1.25	.50	.12
☐ 21 Craig Hartsburg....................	1.25	.50	.12
☐ 22 Don Boyd CO/GM.................	.75	.30	.07
☐ 23 Peter Fiorentino	.75	.30	.07
☐ 24 Jeff Columbus	.75	.30	.07
☐ 25 Brad Stepan	.75	.30	.07
☐ 26 Rick Tocchet	5.00	2.00	.50
☐ 27 Shane Sargant.....................	.75	.30	.07
☐ 28 Wayne Muir.........................	.75	.30	.07

☐ 29	Wayne Gretzky	50.00	20.00	5.00
☐ 30	Gary Luther	.75	.30	.07
☐ 31	Harry Wolfe ANN	.75	.30	.07
☐ 32	Rod Thacker	.75	.30	.07
☐ 33	Coaches Card	.75	.30	.07
	Terry Tait			
	Ted Nolan			
	Mark Pavoni			
☐ 34	Brian Hoard	.75	.30	.07
☐ 35	Glen Johnston	.75	.30	.07

1993-94 Sault Ste. Marie Greyhounds

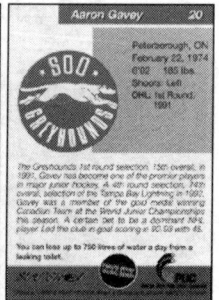

Sponsored by Pino's Food Trunk Road and Sault Ste. Marie Public Utilities Commission, and printed by Slapshot Images Ltd., this standard-size (2 1/2" by 3 1/2") 30-card set features the 1993-94 Sault Ste. Marie Greyhounds. On a geometrical team color-coded background, the fronts feature color action player photos with thin black borders. The player's name, position and team name, as well as the producer's logo, also appear on the front. The team color-coded backs carry biographical player information, along with team and sponsors' logos. A fire safety message also appears on the back. The cards are numbered on the back.

		MINT	EXC	G-VG
COMPLETE SET (30)		10.00	4.00	1.00
COMMON PLAYER (1-30)		.35	.14	.03
☐ 1	Andrea Carpano	.50	.20	.05
☐ 2	Ryan Douglas	.35	.14	.03
☐ 3	Dan Cloutier	1.50	.60	.15
☐ 4	Oliver Pastinsky	.35	.14	.03
☐ 5	Scott King	.35	.14	.03
☐ 6	Drew Bannister	.75	.30	.07
☐ 7	Sean Gagnon	.35	.14	.03
☐ 8	Andre Payette	.35	.14	.03
☐ 9	Peter MacKellar	.50	.20	.05
	UER Name spelled			
	Mackellar on front			
☐ 10	Richard Uniacke	.35	.14	.03
☐ 11	Steve Zoryk	.35	.14	.03
☐ 12	Brad Baber	.35	.14	.03
☐ 13	Gary Roach	.50	.20	.05
☐ 14	Jeff Gies	.35	.14	.03
☐ 15	Tom MacDonald	.75	.30	.07
☐ 16	Rhett Trombley	.35	.14	.03
☐ 17	Joe VanVolsen	.35	.14	.03
☐ 18	Andrew Clark	.35	.14	.03
☐ 19	Briane Thompson	.35	.14	.03
☐ 20	Aaron Gavey	1.50	.60	.15
☐ 21	Wade Gibson	.50	.20	.05
☐ 22	Chad Grills	.35	.14	.03
☐ 23	Jeff Toms	.75	.30	.07
☐ 24	Steve Sullivan	.75	.30	.07
☐ 25	Jeremy Stevenson	.75	.30	.07
☐ 26	Corey Moylan	.35	.14	.03
☐ 27	Steve Spina	.35	.14	.03
☐ 28	Dave Mayville GM	.35	.14	.03
☐ 29	Ted Nolan CO	.35	.14	.03
☐ 30	Dan Flynn ACO	.35	.14	.03
	Mike Zuke ACO			

1969-70 Seattle Totems WHL

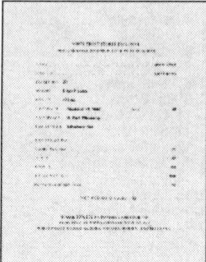

A White Front Stores exclusive at stores in Aurora, Tacoma, Burien, and Bellevue, this set of 20 team photos measures approximately 8" by 10". The set features members of the Seattle Totems of the Western Hockey League. Printed on thin paper, the front features a posed color player photo with a studio background. The pictures have white borders, and the player's signature is inscribed in the lower right corner. In black print on white, the backs present biography and statistics from the past season. The pictures are numbered on the back.

		NRMT	VG-E	GOOD
COMPLETE SET (20)		250.00	100.00	25.00
COMMON PLAYER (1-20)		10.00	4.00	1.00
☐ 1	Don Head	20.00	8.00	2.00
☐ 2	Chuck Holmes	10.00	4.00	1.00
☐ 3	Bob Courcy	10.00	4.00	1.00
☐ 4	Marc Boileau	20.00	8.00	2.00
☐ 5	Gerry Leonard	20.00	8.00	2.00
☐ 6	Art Stratton	10.00	4.00	1.00
☐ 7	Gary Kilpatrick	10.00	4.00	1.00
☐ 8	Don Ward	10.00	4.00	1.00
☐ 9	Jack Michie	10.00	4.00	1.00
☐ 10	Ronald Ingram	10.00	4.00	1.00
☐ 11	John Hanna	10.00	4.00	1.00
☐ 12	Ray Larose	10.00	4.00	1.00
☐ 13	Jack Dale	10.00	4.00	1.00
☐ 14	Tom McVie	25.00	10.00	2.50
☐ 15	Gerry Meehan	25.00	10.00	2.50
☐ 16	Chris Worthy	10.00	4.00	1.00
☐ 17	Bobby Schmautz	20.00	8.00	2.00
☐ 18	Dwight Carruthers	10.00	4.00	1.00
☐ 19	Pat Dunn TR	10.00	4.00	1.00
☐ 20	Bill MacFarland CO	10.00	4.00	1.00

1993-94 Seattle Thunderbirds

This 30-card standard-size (2 1/2" by 3 1/2") set features the 1993-94 Seattle Thunderbirds of the Western Hockey League (WHL). On a white card face, the fronts display posed color player photos. The pictures are edged by a row of blue stars on the left and by "Thunderbirds" in green print on the right. At the top left corner appears the team logo, while the player's name and position are printed in black beneath the photo. In black print on white, the horizontal backs present biography and a player profile. The cards are unnumbered and listed in alphabetical order.

		MINT	EXC	G-VG
COMPLETE SET (30)		10.00	4.00	1.00
COMMON PLAYER (1-30)		.35	.14	.03

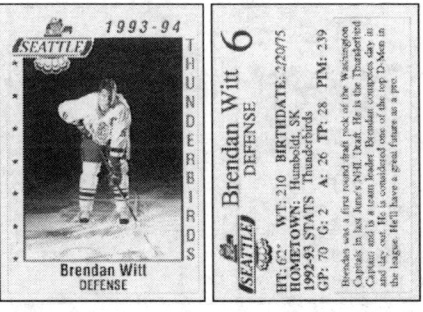

☐	1	Mike Barrie	.50	.20	.05
☐	2	Doug Bonner	.35	.14	.03
☐	3	Davie Carson	.35	.14	.03
☐	4	Jeff Dewar	.35	.14	.03
☐	5	Brett Duncan	.35	.14	.03
☐	6	Shawn Gervais	.50	.20	.05
☐	7	Chris Herperger	.75	.30	.07
☐	8	Troy Hyatt	.35	.14	.03
☐	9	Curt Kamp TR	.35	.14	.03
☐	10	Olaf Kjenstad	.50	.20	.05
☐	11	Walt Kyle CO	.35	.14	.03
☐	12	Milt Mastad	.50	.20	.05
☐	13	Larry McMorran	.35	.14	.03
☐	14	Jim McTaggart ACO	.35	.14	.03
☐	15	Regan Mueller	.35	.14	.03
☐	16	Kevin Mylander	.35	.14	.03
☐	17	Drew Palmer	.50	.20	.05
☐	18	Jeff Peddigrew	.35	.14	.03
☐	19	Darryl Plandowski ACO	.35	.14	.03
☐	20	Deron Quint	1.00	.40	.10
☐	21	Darrell Sandback	.35	.14	.03
☐	22	Chris Schmidt	.35	.14	.03
☐	23	Lloyd Shaw	.35	.14	.03
☐	24	Alexandre Matvichuk	.50	.20	.05
☐	25	Darcy Smith	.35	.14	.03
☐	26	Rob Tallas	.50	.20	.05
☐	27	Paul Vincent	.50	.20	.05
☐	28	Chris Wells	1.00	.40	.10
☐	29	Brendan Witt	1.50	.60	.15
☐	30	Team photo	.75	.30	.07

☐	11	Terry Mulroy	1.00	.40	.10
☐	12	Sam Nelligan	1.00	.40	.10
☐	13	Julian Nixon	1.00	.40	.10
☐	14	Mike Noel	1.00	.40	.10
☐	15	Jim Peck	1.00	.40	.10
☐	16	Bogdan Podwysocki	1.50	.60	.15
☐	17	John Saville P/CO	1.00	.40	.10
☐	18	Alex Shibicky Jr.	2.00	.80	.20
☐	19	Bob Thomerson	1.00	.40	.10
☐	20	Jim White	1.00	.40	.10

1989-90 Spokane Chiefs

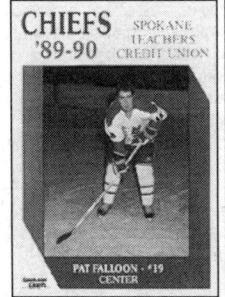

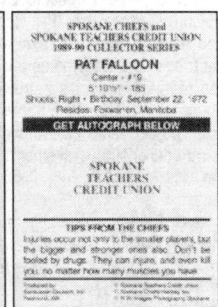

1974-75 Sioux City Musketeers

This 20-card set is printed on yellow stock. According to the producer, the cards were intended to be standard size (2 1/2" by 3 1/2"), but actually came out a little larger. The fronts feature bordered, posed player photos that have a dark green tint to them. In dark green lettering, the team name is printed above the picture while the player's name is printed below it. Green and gold were the Musketeers' team colors. The horizontal backs have the uniform number, brief biographical information, and player profile. The set year in the lower right corner rounds out the back. The cards are unnumbered and checklisted below in alphabetical order. Reportedly only 250 sets were made and they were originally sold at home games for 2.50.

		NRMT	VG-E	GOOD
COMPLETE SET (20)		15.00	6.00	1.50
COMMON PLAYER (1-20)		1.00	.40	.10
☐	1 Steve Boyle	1.00	.40	.10
☐	2 Dave Davies	1.00	.40	.10
☐	3 Steve Desloges	1.00	.40	.10
☐	4 Greg Gilbert	1.00	.40	.10
☐	5 Barry Head	1.00	.40	.10
☐	6 Steve Heathwood	1.00	.40	.10
☐	7 Dave Kartio	1.00	.40	.10
☐	8 Ralph Kloiber	1.00	.40	.10
☐	9 Pete Maxwell	1.00	.40	.10
☐	10 Randy McDonald	1.00	.40	.10

Sponsored by the Spokane Teachers Credit Union, this 20-card standard-size (2 1/2" by 3 1/2") set of the 1989-90 Spokane Chiefs features color posed-on-ice player photos on its fronts. The photos are bordered in team colors (red, white, and blue). The player's name, uniform number, and position appear within the blue border below the picture. The white back carries the player's name, position, and uniform number near the top, followed below by biography, a space for an autograph, and an antidrug message from the Chiefs. The cards are unnumbered and checklisted below in alphabetical order. Reportedly only 3,600 sets were made.

		MINT	EXC	G-VG
COMPLETE SET (20)		15.00	6.00	1.50
COMMON PLAYER (1-20)		.50	.20	.05
☐	1 Mike Chrun	.50	.20	.05
☐	2 John Colvin	.50	.20	.05
☐	3 Shawn Dietrich	.50	.20	.05
☐	4 Milan Dragicevic	.50	.20	.05
☐	5 Frank Evans	.50	.20	.05
☐	6 Pat Falloon	6.00	2.40	.60
☐	7 Scott Farrell	.50	.20	.05
☐	8 Jeff Ferguson	.50	.20	.05
☐	9 Travis Green	1.00	.40	.10
☐	10 Mike Hawes	.50	.20	.05
☐	11 Bobby House	.75	.30	.07
☐	12 Mike Jickling	.50	.20	.05
☐	13 Steve Junker	1.00	.40	.10
☐	14 Jon Klemm	.75	.30	.07

			MINT	EXC	G-VG
☐	15	Chris Rowland	.50	.20	.05
☐	16	Dennis Saharchuk	.50	.20	.05
☐	17	Kerry Toporowski	.75	.30	.07
☐	18	Trevor Tovell	.50	.20	.05
☐	19	Bram Vanderkracht	.50	.20	.05
☐	20	Ray Whitney	2.00	.80	.20

1983-84 Springfield Indians

Produced by Card Collectors Closet (Springfield, MA), this 25-card set measures the standard size (2 1/2" by 3 1/2") and features black-and-white player portraits on a white card face. The team name and year are printed in black at the top. The player's name and position appear at the bottom. The pictures are framed by a royal blue border while a red border encloses the photo and text. The backs carry the producer's advertisement. The cards are numbered on the back.

		MINT	EXC	G-VG
COMPLETE SET (25)		12.00	5.00	1.20
COMMON PLAYER (1-25)		.50	.20	.05

			MINT	EXC	G-VG
☐	1	Gil Hudon	.75	.30	.07
☐	2	Jim Ralph	1.00	.40	.10
☐	3	Todd Bergen	.75	.30	.07
☐	4	Len Hachborn	.75	.30	.07
☐	5	John Ollson	.50	.20	.05
☐	6	Steve Tsujiura	.50	.20	.05
☐	7	Gordie Williams	.50	.20	.05
☐	8	Dave Brown	1.00	.40	.10
☐	9	Dan Frawley	.75	.30	.07
☐	10	Tom McMurchy	.50	.20	.05
☐	11	Dave Michayluk	.75	.30	.07
☐	12	Bob Mormina	.50	.20	.05
☐	13	Perry Pelensky	.50	.20	.05
☐	14	Andy Brickley	1.50	.60	.15
☐	15	Ross Fitzpatrick	.75	.30	.07
☐	16	Florent Robidoux	.50	.20	.05
☐	17	Jeff Smith	.50	.20	.05
☐	18	Rod Willard	.50	.20	.05
☐	19	Darrell Anholt	.50	.20	.05
☐	20	Steve Blyth	.50	.20	.05
☐	21	Don Dietrich	.50	.20	.05
☐	22	Steve Smith	.50	.20	.05
☐	23	Daryl Stanley	.75	.30	.07
☐	24	Taras Zytynsky	.50	.20	.05
☐	25	Doug Sauter CO	.50	.20	.05

1984-85 Springfield Indians

Produced by Card Collectors Closet (Springfield, MA), this 25-card set measures the standard size (2 1/2" by 3 1/2") and features black-and-white player portraits on a white

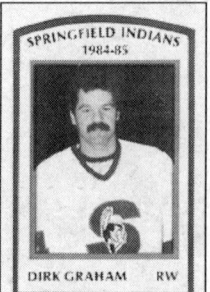
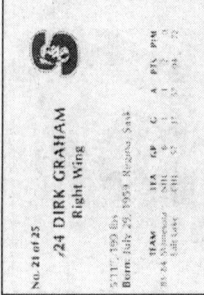

card face. The team name and year are printed in black at the top. The player's name and position appear at the bottom. The pictures are framed by a royal blue border while a red border encloses the photo and the text. On a white background, the horizontal backs carry the player's name, number, position, short biography, and statistics. The cards are numbered on the back as "x of 25."

		MINT	EXC	G-VG
COMPLETE SET (25)		12.00	5.00	1.20
COMMON PLAYER (1-25)		.50	.20	.05

			MINT	EXC	G-VG
☐	1	Mike Sands	.75	.30	.07
☐	2	Lorne Molleken	.50	.20	.05
☐	3	Todd Lumbard	.50	.20	.05
☐	4	Randy Velischek	.75	.30	.07
☐	5	David Jensen	.75	.30	.07
☐	6	Ken Leiter	.50	.20	.05
☐	7	Vern Smith	.50	.20	.05
☐	8	Alan Kerr	.75	.30	.07
☐	9	Scott Howson	.50	.20	.05
☐	10	Tim Coulis	.50	.20	.05
☐	11	Terry Tait	.50	.20	.05
☐	12	Tim Trimper	.75	.30	.07
☐	13	Rob Flockhart	.75	.30	.07
☐	14	Ron Handy	.50	.20	.05
☐	15	Jiri Poner	.50	.20	.05
☐	16	Chris Pryor	.50	.20	.05
☐	17	Dale Henry	.75	.30	.07
☐	18	Mark Hamway	.50	.20	.05
☐	19	Monty Trottier	.50	.20	.05
☐	20	Miroslav Maly	.50	.20	.05
☐	21	Dirk Graham	2.50	1.00	.25
☐	22	Roger Kortko	.50	.20	.05
☐	23	Bob Bodak	.50	.20	.05
☐	24	Lorne Henning CO	.75	.30	.07
☐	25	Checklist	.75	.30	.07

1984-85 Sudbury Wolves

This 16-card set measures approximately 3 1/2" by 6" and features color, action player photos accented by a hockey stick graphic design in white, green, gray, and red. The player's name and sponsor logos are printed on the design. A discount coupon for 2.50 off any children's admission to a game is attached at the bottom and can be torn along perforations. The card measures approximately 5 1/4" tall when the coupon is removed. The backs carry biographical information and sponsor logos. The cards are numbered on the front near the right edge.

		MINT	EXC	G-VG
COMPLETE SET (16)		15.00	6.00	1.50
COMMON PLAYER (1-16)		.75	.30	.07

			MINT	EXC	G-VG
☐	10	Dave Moylan	.60	.24	.06
☐	11	Brent Daugherty	.60	.24	.06
☐	12	Glenn Greenough	.60	.24	.06
☐	13	Mario Chitaroni	1.00	.40	.10
☐	14	Ken McRae	1.00	.40	.10
☐	15	Mike Hudson	1.50	.60	.15
☐	16	Andy Paquette	.60	.24	.06
☐	17	Ed Lemaire	.60	.24	.06
☐	18	Mark Turner	.60	.24	.06
☐	19	Craig Duncanson	.60	.24	.06
☐	20	Jeff Brown	4.00	1.60	.40
☐	21	Team Photo	1.50	.60	.15
☐	22	Max Middendorf	1.00	.40	.10
☐	23	Keith Van Rooyen	.60	.24	.06
☐	24	Brad Walcot	.60	.24	.06
☐	25	Rob Wilson	.60	.24	.06
☐	26	Bill White	.60	.24	.06

			MINT	EXC	G-VG
☐	1	Andy Spruce CO	.75	.30	.07
☐	2	Sean Evoy	.75	.30	.07
☐	3	Mario Martini	.75	.30	.07
☐	4	Brent Daugherty	.75	.30	.07
☐	5	Mario Chitaroni	1.50	.60	.15
☐	6	Dan Chiasson	.75	.30	.07
☐	7	Jeff Brown	7.50	3.00	.75
☐	8	Todd Sepkowski	.75	.30	.07
☐	9	Brad Belland	.75	.30	.07
☐	10	Glenn Greenough	.75	.30	.07
☐	11	John Landry	.75	.30	.07
☐	12	Max Middendorf	1.50	.60	.15
☐	13	David Moylan	.75	.30	.07
☐	14	Jamie Nadjiwan	.75	.30	.07
☐	15	Warren Rychel	2.00	.80	.20
☐	16	Ed Smith	.75	.30	.07

1985-86 Sudbury Wolves

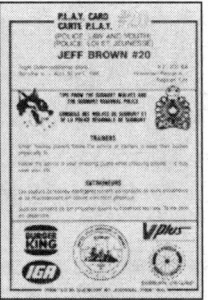

This 26-card set measures approximately 2 3/4" by 4" and features color, posed player photos with white borders. A facsimile autograph is inscribed across the bottom of the picture. The backs carry biographical information, P.L.A.Y. (Police, Laws and Youth) public service messages in English and French, and sponsor logos. The cards are numbered on the back.

			MINT	EXC	G-VG
	COMPLETE SET (26)		15.00	6.00	1.50
	COMMON PLAYER (1-26)		.60	.24	.06
☐	1	Sudbury Regional Police Crest	.75	.30	.07
☐	2	Sponsors' Card	.60	.24	.06
☐	3	Sudbury Wolves logo Checklist	1.00	.40	.10
☐	4	R. Zanibbi Chief of Police	.60	.24	.06
☐	5	Wayne Maxner CO	.60	.24	.06
☐	6	Sean Evoy	.60	.24	.06
☐	7	Todd Lalonde	.60	.24	.06
☐	8	Costa Papista	.60	.24	.06
☐	9	Robin Rubic	.60	.24	.06

1987-88 Sudbury Wolves

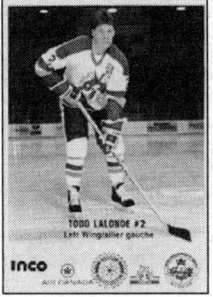
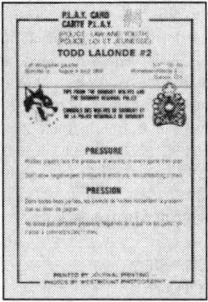

This 26-card set measures approximately 3" by 4 1/8" and features color, posed action player photos with white borders. The player's name, jersey number, and position are superimposed on the photo at the bottom. Sponsor logos in the white bottom border are INCO, Air Canada, Rotary International, Pure Spring Ginger Ale, and the Sudbury chapter of the United Steel Workers of America. The backs carry biographical information and P.L.A.Y. (Police, Laws and Youth) public service messages. The cards are numbered on the back.

			MINT	EXC	G-VG
	COMPLETE SET (26)		12.00	5.00	1.20
	COMMON PLAYER (1-26)		.60	.24	.06
☐	1	Checklist Card (Pictures two children with large toy police car)	1.00	.40	.10
☐	2	Ted Mielczarek	.60	.24	.06
☐	3	Dan Gatenby	.60	.24	.06
☐	4	Todd Lalonde	.60	.24	.06
☐	5	Justin Corbeil	.60	.24	.06
☐	6	Jordan Fois	.60	.24	.06
☐	7	Rodney Lapointe	.60	.24	.06
☐	8	Dave Akey	.60	.24	.06
☐	9	Jim Smith	.60	.24	.06
☐	10	Fred Pennell	.60	.24	.06
☐	11	Joey Simon	.60	.24	.06
☐	12	Luciano Fagioli	.60	.24	.06
☐	13	Robb Graham	.60	.24	.06
☐	14	John Uniac	.75	.30	.07
☐	15	Dave Carrie	.60	.24	.06
☐	16	Pierre Gagnon	.60	.24	.06
☐	17	Peter Hughes	.60	.24	.06
☐	18	Scott McCullough	.60	.24	.06
☐	19	Dean Guitard	.60	.24	.06
☐	20	Pat Holley	.60	.24	.06
☐	21	Chad Badawey	.60	.24	.06
☐	22	Paul DiPietro	3.00	1.20	.30
☐	23	Derek Thompson	.60	.24	.06
☐	24	Scott Luce	.60	.24	.06
☐	25	Rob Wilson	.60	.24	.06
☐	26	R. Zanibbi Chief of Police	.60	.24	.06

1988-89 Sudbury Wolves

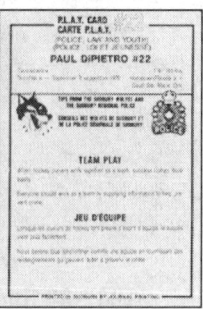

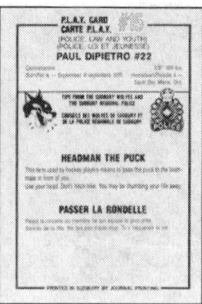

This 26-card set measures approximately 3" by 4 1/8" and features color, posed action player photos with white borders. The player's name, jersey number, and position are superimposed on the photo at the bottom. Sponsor logos in the white bottom border are INCO, Loeb, IGA, Air Canada, Air Ontario, Rotary International, Pizza Hut, and the Sudbury chapter of the United Steel Workers of America. The backs carry biographical information and P.L.A.Y. (Police, Laws and Youth) public service messages. The cards are numbered on the back.

	MINT	EXC	G-VG
COMPLETE SET (26)......................	12.00	5.00	1.20
COMMON PLAYER (1-26)................	.50	.20	.05
☐ 1 Checklist	1.00	.40	.10
(Pictures two children			
with large toy police car)			
☐ 2 David Goverde........................	1.00	.40	.10
☐ 3 Ted Mielczarek	.50	.20	.05
☐ 4 Adam Bennett	1.00	.40	.10
☐ 5 Kevin Grant	.50	.20	.05
☐ 6 Jordan Fois	.50	.20	.05
☐ 7 Sean O'Donnell	.50	.20	.05
☐ 8 Kevin Meisner	.50	.20	.05
☐ 9 Jim Smith	.50	.20	.05
☐ 10 Red Pennell..........................	.50	.20	.05
☐ 11 Tyler Pella	.50	.20	.05
☐ 12 Dean Pella	.50	.20	.05
☐ 13 Darren Bell...........................	.50	.20	.05
☐ 14 Derek Thompson...................	.50	.20	.05
☐ 15 Terry Chitaroni	1.00	.40	.10
☐ 16 Sean Stansfield	.50	.20	.05
☐ 17 Alastair Still	.50	.20	.05
☐ 18 Jim Sonmez	.50	.20	.05
☐ 19 Shannon Bolton	.50	.20	.05
☐ 20 Andy Paquette	.50	.20	.05
☐ 21 Mark Turner	.50	.20	.05
☐ 22 Paul DiPietro	2.00	.80	.20
☐ 23 Robert Knesaurek	.50	.20	.05
☐ 24 Todd Lalonde	.50	.20	.05
☐ 25 Scott Herniman	.50	.20	.05
☐ 26 R. Zanibbi.............................	.50	.20	.05
Chief of Police			

1989-90 Sudbury Wolves

This 25-card set measures approximately 3" by 4 1/8" and features color, posed action player photos with white borders. The player's name, jersey number, and position are superimposed on the photo at the bottom. Sponsor logos in the white bottom border are Coke, INCO, Air Canada, Air Ontario, Rotary International, Pizza Hut, and the Sudbury chapter of the United Steel Workers of America. The backs carry biographical information and P.L.A.Y. (Police, Laws and Youth) public service messages. The cards are numbered on the back.

	MINT	EXC	G-VG
COMPLETE SET (25)......................	12.00	5.00	1.20
COMMON PLAYER (1-25)................	.50	.20	.05
☐ 1 Checklist NNO	1.00	.40	.10
(Pictures two children			
with large toy police car)			
☐ 2 Alastair Still	.50	.20	.05
☐ 3 Bill Kovacs	.50	.20	.05
☐ 4 Darren Bell	.50	.20	.05
☐ 5 Scott Mahoney	.50	.20	.05
☐ 6 Glen Murray	3.00	1.20	.30
☐ 7 Alain Laforge	.50	.20	.05
☐ 8 Jamie Matthews.....................	1.00	.40	.10
☐ 9 Jon Boeve	.50	.20	.05
☐ 10 Adam Bennett	1.00	.40	.10
☐ 11 Derek Etches	.50	.20	.05
☐ 12 Marcus Middleton	.50	.20	.05
☐ 13 Jim Sonmez	.50	.20	.05
☐ 14 Leonard MacDonald..............	.50	.20	.05
☐ 15 Paul DiPietro	1.50	.60	.15
☐ 16 Neil Ethier	.50	.20	.05
☐ 17 Sean O'Donnell	.50	.20	.05
☐ 18 Andy MacVicar	.50	.20	.05
☐ 19 David Goverde.......................	1.00	.40	.10
☐ 20 Jason Young	.50	.20	.05
☐ 21 Wade Bartley.........................	.50	.20	.05
☐ 22 Barry Young	.50	.20	.05
☐ 23 R. Zanibbi.............................	.50	.20	.05
Chief of Police			
☐ 24 Terry Chitaroni	1.00	.40	.10
☐ 25 Rob Knesaurek	.50	.20	.05

1990-91 Sudbury Wolves

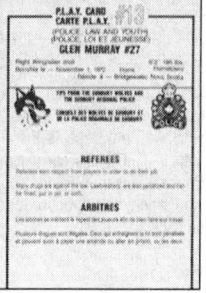

This 25-card P.L.A.Y. (Police, Laws and Youth) set measures approximately 3" by 4 1/8" and features color posed action player photos with white borders. The player's name and position is superimposed on the picture at the bottom. Sponsor logos in the white bottom border are Coke, INCO, Air Ontario, Rotary International, Pizza Hut, and the Sudbury chapter of the United Steel Workers of America. The backs carry biographical information and Tips From The

Sudbury Wolves and the Sudbury Regional Police. For the most part, the cards are numbered on both sides after the player's jersey number (except for card number 7 and 18).

	MINT	EXC	G-VG
COMPLETE SET (25)	10.00	4.00	1.00
COMMON PLAYER (1-25)	.50	.20	.05

		MINT	EXC	G-VG
☐ 1	Darryl Paquette	.75	.30	.07
☐ 2	Adam Bennett	.75	.30	.07
☐ 3	Barry Young	.50	.20	.05
☐ 4	Jon Boeve	.50	.20	.05
☐ 5	Kyle Blacklock	.50	.20	.05
☐ 6	Sean O'Donnell	.50	.20	.05
☐ 7	Dan Ryder	.50	.20	.05
☐ 8	Wade Bartley	.50	.20	.05
☐ 9	Jamie Matthews	.75	.30	.07
☐ 10	Rod Hinks	.50	.20	.05
☐ 11	Derek Etches	.50	.20	.05
☐ 12	Brandon Convery	1.50	.60	.15
☐ 13	Glen Murray	2.00	.80	.20
☐ 14	Bill Kovacs	.50	.20	.05
☐ 15	Terry Chitaroni	.75	.30	.07
☐ 16	Jason Young	.50	.20	.05
☐ 17	Alastair Still	.50	.20	.05
☐ 18	Shawn Rivers	.75	.30	.07
☐ 19	Alain Laforge	.50	.20	.05
☐ 20	J.D. Eaton	.50	.20	.05
☐ 21	Mike Peca	1.50	.60	.15
☐ 22	Howler (Mascot)	.50	.20	.05
☐ 23	Mike Yeo	.50	.20	.05
☐ 24	Not Known	.50	.20	.05
☐ 25	R. Zanibbi	.50	.20	.05
	Chief of Police			

		MINT	EXC	G-VG
☐ 13	Dan Ryder	.50	.20	.05
☐ 14	Derek Armstrong	.75	.30	.07
☐ 15	Terry Chitaroni	.75	.30	.07
☐ 16	Brandon Convery	1.50	.60	.15
☐ 17	Tim Favot	.50	.20	.05
☐ 18	Rod Hinks	.50	.20	.05
☐ 19	Jamie Matthews	.75	.30	.07
☐ 20	Barrie Moore	.50	.20	.05
☐ 21	Glen Murray	1.50	.60	.15
☐ 22	Michael Peca	1.50	.60	.15
☐ 23	Michael Yeo	.50	.20	.05
☐ 24	Jason Young	.50	.20	.05
☐ 25	Jason Zohil	.50	.20	.05

1992-93 Sudbury Wolves

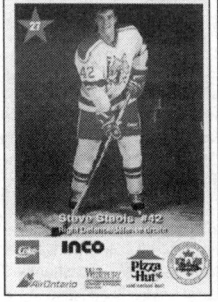
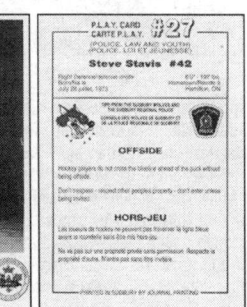

1991-92 Sudbury Wolves

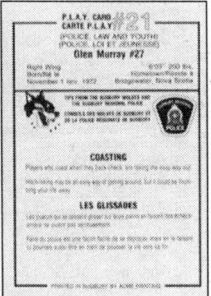

This 25-card set measures approximately 3" by 4 1/8" and features color, posed action player photos with white borders. The player's name, jersey number, and position are superimposed on the photo at the bottom. Sponsor logos in the white bottom border are Coke, INCO, Air Ontario, The Westbury (a Howard Johnson Plaza-Hotel), Pizza Hut, and the Sudbury chapter of the United Steel Workers of America. The backs carry biographical information and P.L.A.Y. (Police, Laws and Youth) public service messages. The cards are numbered on the front in a star and on the back.

	MINT	EXC	G-VG
COMPLETE SET (25)	10.00	4.00	1.00
COMMON PLAYER (1-25)	.50	.20	.05

		MINT	EXC	G-VG
☐ 1	R. Zanibbi	.75	.30	.07
	Chief of Police			
☐ 2	Howler (Mascot)	.50	.20	.05
☐ 3	Team Photo	1.00	.40	.10
☐ 4	Kyle Blacklock	.50	.20	.05
☐ 5	Sean Gagnon	.50	.20	.05
☐ 6	Bernie John	.50	.20	.05
☐ 7	Bob MacIsaac	.50	.20	.05
☐ 8	Mike Rivers	1.00	.40	.10
☐ 9	Shawn Sandie	.75	.30	.07
☐ 10	Joel Sandie	.50	.20	.05
☐ 11	Barry Young	.50	.20	.05
☐ 12	George Dourian	.50	.20	.05

These 27 oversized bilingual cards measure approximately 3" by 4 3/16" and feature on their fronts white-bordered color posed-on-ice player photos. The player's name, jersey number, and position are displayed on each card in white lettering at the bottom of the photo. Beneath the photo, on the broad white bottom margin, appear the logos for Coke, Air Ontario, The Westbury Hotel, INCO, Pizza Hut, and the Sudbury local of the United Steel Workers of America. The white back carries the player's name, jersey number, and biography near the top. The Wolves' and Sudbury Regional Police logos along with a P.L.A.Y. (Police, Law and Youth) safety tip appear beneath. The cards are numbered on both sides.

	MINT	EXC	G-VG
COMPLETE SET (27)	10.00	4.00	1.00
COMMON PLAYER (1-27)	.50	.20	.05

		MINT	EXC	G-VG
☐ 1	Howler and Lil Rookie	.75	.30	.07
	(Toy mascot and police car)			
☐ 2	Sudbury Regional Police	.50	.20	.05
	Chief R. Zanibbi			
☐ 3	Bob MacIsaac	.50	.20	.05
☐ 4	Joel Sandie	.50	.20	.05
☐ 5	Rory Fitzpatrick	.50	.20	.05
☐ 6	Mike Wilson	.50	.20	.05
☐ 7	Shawn Frappier	.50	.20	.05
☐ 8	Bernie John	.50	.20	.05
☐ 9	Jamie Rivers	1.00	.40	.10
☐ 10	Jamie Matthews	.75	.30	.07
☐ 11	Zdenek Nedved	1.00	.40	.10
☐ 12	Ryan Shanahan	.50	.20	.05
☐ 13	Corey Crane	.50	.20	.05
☐ 14	Matt Kiereck	.50	.20	.05
☐ 15	Rick Bodkin	.50	.20	.05
☐ 16	Derek Armstrong	.75	.30	.07
☐ 17	Barrie Moore	.50	.20	.05
☐ 18	Rod Hinks	.50	.20	.05
☐ 19	Kayle Short	.50	.20	.05
☐ 20	Michael Yeo	.50	.20	.05
☐ 21	Gary Coupal	.50	.20	.05
☐ 22	Dennis Maxwell	.50	.20	.05
☐ 23	Steve Potvin	.50	.20	.05
☐ 24	Joel Poirier	.50	.20	.05
☐ 25	Greg Dreveny	.50	.20	.05
☐ 26	Mark Gowan	.50	.20	.05
☐ 27	Steve Staios	1.00	.40	.10

1993-94 Sudbury Wolves

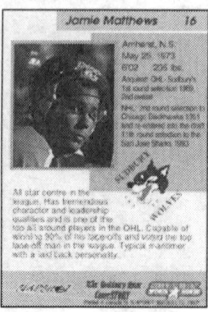

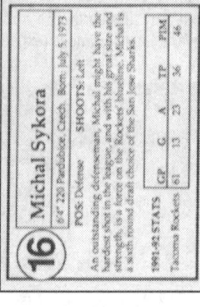

player profile with 1991-92 stats presented in a box. The cards are unnumbered and checklisted below in alphabetical order.

Sponsored by The Sudbury Star, CoverStory, and Sudbury Sports North, and printed by Slapshot Images Ltd., this standard-size (2 1/2" by 3 1/2") 25-card set features the 1993-94 Sudbury Wolves. On a geometrical team color-coded background, the fronts feature color action player photos with thin grey borders. The player's name, position and team name, as well as the producer's logo, also appear on the front. The backs carry a close-up player portrait and biographical information, along with team and sponsors' logos. The cards are numbered on the back. Included in this set is a Slapshot ad card with a 1994 calendar on the back.

	MINT	EXC	G-VG
COMPLETE SET (25)	10.00	4.00	1.00
COMMON PLAYER (1-25)	.35	.14	.03
☐ 1 Shawn Silver	.50	.20	.05
☐ 2 Jeff Melnechuk	.50	.20	.05
☐ 3 Jay McKee	.35	.14	.03
☐ 4 Chris McMurtry	.35	.14	.03
☐ 5 Rory Fitzpatrick	.75	.30	.07
☐ 6 Mike Wilson	.75	.30	.07
☐ 7 Shawn Frappier	.35	.14	.03
☐ 8 Jamie Rivers	1.00	.40	.10
☐ 9 Zdenek Nedved	.75	.30	.07
☐ 10 Ryan Shanahan	.50	.20	.05
☐ 11 Sean Venedam	.35	.14	.03
☐ 12 Andrew Dale	.35	.14	.03
☐ 13 Mark Giannetti	.35	.14	.03
☐ 14 Rick Bodkin	.50	.20	.05
☐ 15 Barrie Moore	.50	.20	.05
☐ 16 Jamie Matthews	.75	.30	.07
☐ 17 Gary Coupal	.35	.14	.03
☐ 18 Ilya Lysenko	.35	.14	.03
☐ 19 Simon Sherry	.35	.14	.03
☐ 20 Steve Potvin	.35	.14	.03
☐ 21 Joel Poirier	.50	.20	.05
☐ 22 Mike Yeo	.35	.14	.03
☐ 23 Bob MacIsaac	.35	.14	.03
☐ 24 Paul DiPietro	.50	.20	.05
☐ NNO Slapshot Ad Card	.35	.14	.03

1992-93 Tacoma Rockets

This 30-card standard-size (2 1/2" by 3 1/2") set features hatch-bordered, posed-on-ice color player photos. In a white field under the photo are the player's name, and in the right corner, the team logo of crossed red rockets. The uniform number appears in turquoise to the lower left in a circle that straddles the picture and the white field. The team name appears in a diagonal across the top left corner of the photo and the player's position is in blue letters across the top. The horizontal backs have the encircled player number in the top left with the player's name and biography boxed just to the right. The center portion of the card contains a

	MINT	EXC	G-VG
COMPLETE SET (30)	10.00	4.00	1.00
COMMON PLAYER (1-30)	.50	.20	.05
☐ 1 Alexander Alexeev	.75	.30	.07
☐ 2 Jamie Black	.75	.30	.07
☐ 3 Jamie Butt	.75	.30	.07
☐ 4 Jeff Calvert	.50	.20	.05
☐ 5 Don Clark ACO	.50	.20	.05
☐ 6 Marcel Comeau CO	.50	.20	.05
☐ 7 Duane Crouse TR	.50	.20	.05
☐ 8 Allan Egeland	1.00	.40	.10
☐ 9 Marty Flichel	.75	.30	.07
☐ 10 Trever Fraser	.50	.20	.05
☐ 11 Jason Kwiatkowski	.50	.20	.05
☐ 12 Todd MacDonald	.50	.20	.05
☐ 13 Dave McMillen	.50	.20	.05
☐ 14 Tony Pechthalt TR	.50	.20	.05
☐ 15 Ryan Phillips	.50	.20	.05
☐ 16 Mike Piersol	.50	.20	.05
☐ 17 Dennis Pinfold	.50	.20	.05
☐ 18 Kevin Powell	.50	.20	.05
☐ 19 Tyler Prosofsky	.75	.30	.07
☐ 20 Stu Scantlebury	.50	.20	.05
☐ 21 Drew Schoneck	.50	.20	.05
☐ 22 Adam Smith	.50	.20	.05
☐ 23 Corey Stock	.50	.20	.05
☐ 24 Barkley Swenson	.50	.20	.05
☐ 25 Michal Sykora	1.00	.40	.10
☐ 26 Dallas Thompson	.50	.20	.05
☐ 27 John Varga	1.00	.40	.10
☐ 28 Toby Weishaar	.50	.20	.05
☐ 29 Michal Sykora IA	.75	.30	.07
☐ 30 Cover Card (Team Logo)	.75	.30	.07

1993-94 Tacoma Rockets

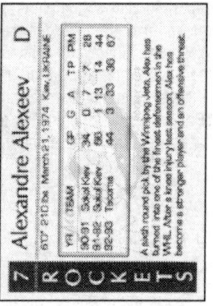

This 30-card standard-size (2 1/2" by 3 1/2") set features the 1993-94 Tacoma Rockets. The set is printed on thin card stock. The fronts have hatch-bordered color action player photos, with the player's name and position printed in white letters in a dark turquoise shadowed border above the

photo. The team name also appears in a dark turquoise shadowed bar to the left of the photo. Printed on a ghosted grey team logo background, the horizontal backs carry player biography and statistics. The cards are unnumbered and checklisted below in alphabetical order.

	MINT	EXC	G-VG
COMPLETE SET (30)	9.00	3.75	.90
COMMON PLAYER (1-30)	.35	.14	.03

		MINT	EXC	G-VG
☐ 1	Alexandre Alexeev	.75	.30	.07
☐ 2	Jamie Butt	.50	.20	.05
☐ 3	Trevor Cairns	.35	.14	.03
☐ 4	Jeff Calvert	.35	.14	.03
☐ 5	Marcel Comeau CO	.35	.14	.03
☐ 6	Jason Deleurme	.35	.14	.03
☐ 7	Allan Egeland	.75	.30	.07
☐ 8	Marty Flichel	.50	.20	.05
☐ 9	Trever Fraser	.35	.14	.03
☐ 10	Michal Grosek	.50	.20	.05
☐ 11	Lada Hampeis	.35	.14	.03
☐ 12	Tavis Hansen	.75	.30	.07
☐ 13	Burt Henderson	.35	.14	.03
☐ 14	Jeff Jubenville	.35	.14	.03
☐ 15	Todd MacDonald	.35	.14	.03
☐ 16	Kyle McLaren	.35	.14	.03
☐ 17	Kory Mullin	.35	.14	.03
☐ 18	Steve Oviatt TR	.35	.14	.03
☐ 19	Ryan Phillips	.35	.14	.03
☐ 20	Mike Piersol	.35	.14	.03
☐ 21	Dennis Pinfold	.35	.14	.03
☐ 22	Tyler Prosofsky	.50	.20	.05
☐ 23	Jamie Reeve ACO	.50	.20	.05
☐ 24	Adam Smith	.35	.14	.03
☐ 25	Corey Stock	.35	.14	.03
☐ 26	Dallas Thompson	.35	.14	.03
☐ 27	John Varga	.75	.30	.07
☐ 28	Team Photo	.75	.30	.07
☐ 29	The Tacoma Dome	.35	.14	.03
☐ 30	The Tacoma Rockets In Action Marty Flichel	.35	.14	.03

1993-94 Toledo Storm

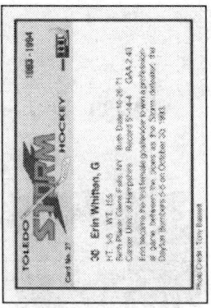

This 29-card set features the 1992-93 Riley Cup Champions Toledo Storm of the ECHL (East Coast Hockey League). The cards measure the standard size (2 1/2" by 3 1/2"). Inside a white and a thin red border, the fronts feature color action player photos with the player's name and position in a red border at the bottom of the card. The team logo also appears at the bottom. The horizontal backs carry the player's name, number and position, biographical information, statistics, career highlights, and team logo. The cards are numbered on the back.

	MINT	EXC	G-VG
COMPLETE SET (29)	10.00	4.00	1.00
COMMON PLAYER (1-29)	.35	.14	.03

		MINT	EXC	G-VG
☐ 1	Checklist Card	.35	.14	.03
☐ 2	Chris McSorley CO	.75	.30	.07
☐ 3	Barry Soskin PRES	.35	.14	.03

		MINT	EXC	G-VG
☐ 4	Tim Mouser MG	.35	.14	.03
☐ 5	Jeff Gibbons ANN	.35	.14	.03
☐ 6	Scott Luhrmann TR	.35	.14	.03
☐ 7	Nick Vitucci	.50	.20	.05
☐ 8	Andy Suhy	.50	.20	.05
☐ 9	Pat Pylypuik	.35	.14	.03
☐ 10	Chris Belanger	.35	.14	.03
☐ 11	Mike Markovich	.35	.14	.03
☐ 12	Darren Perkins	.35	.14	.03
☐ 13	Dennis Snedden	.35	.14	.03
☐ 14	Mark Deazeley	.50	.20	.05
☐ 15	Mark McCreary	.35	.14	.03
☐ 16	Jeff Rohlicek	.50	.20	.05
☐ 17	Chris Bergeron	.35	.14	.03
☐ 18	John Hendry	.35	.14	.03
☐ 19	Greg Puhalski	.50	.20	.05
☐ 20	Bruce MacDonald	.35	.14	.03
☐ 21	Marc Lyons	.35	.14	.03
☐ 22	Rick Judson	.50	.20	.05
☐ 23	Alex Hicks	.35	.14	.03
☐ 24	Barry Potomski	.50	.20	.05
☐ 25	Rick Corriveau	.75	.30	.07
☐ 26	Kyle Reeves	.75	.30	.07
☐ 27	Erin Whitten	3.50	1.40	.35
☐ 28	Brian Schoen	.35	.14	.03
☐ 29	Riley Cup Champions	.35	.14	.03

1992-93 Tulsa Oilers

This 18-card set measures the standard size (2 1/2" by 3 1/2") and was sponsored by Crown Auto World. Ten thousand were sets were reportedly produced. Randomly inserted thoughout the sets were 350 autographed cards of each player. The cards measure the standard size (2 1/2" by 3 1/2") and feature color photos of players in action and still poses. The pictures have white borders, and the player's name is printed in black on the photo at the bottom. The backs carry the team logo, the player's nickname, name, and biographical information. The sponsor logo is at the bottom. All the information on the back is framed by a border of three black lines of varying thicknesses. The cards are unnumbered and checklisted below in alphabetical order.

	MINT	EXC	G-VG
COMPLETE SET (18)	8.00	3.25	.80
COMMON PLAYER (1-18)	.50	.20	.05

		MINT	EXC	G-VG
☐ 1	Mike Berger	.75	.30	.07
☐ 2	Pat Cavanagh	.50	.20	.05
☐ 3	Shaun Clouston	.50	.20	.05
☐ 4	Brian Fiatt Tony Martino	.50	.20	.05
☐ 5	Tony Fiore	.50	.20	.05
☐ 6	Taylor Hall	.75	.30	.07
☐ 7	Tom Karalis	.50	.20	.05
☐ 8	Greg MacEachern	.50	.20	.05
☐ 9	Terry MacLean	.50	.20	.05
☐ 10	Al Murphy	.50	.20	.05
☐ 11	Sylvain Naud	.75	.30	.07
☐ 12	Mario Nobili	.75	.30	.07
☐ 13	Jody Praznik	.50	.20	.05
☐ 14	E.J. Sauer	.50	.20	.05
☐ 15	Craig Shepherd	.50	.20	.05
☐ 16	Garry Unger	1.00	.40	.10

☐ 17	Team Photo	1.00	.40	.10
☐ 18	Title Card	.75	.30	.07

1981-82 Victoria Cougars

This 16-card set was sponsored by the West Coast Savings Credit Union and Saanich Police Department Community Services. The cards measure approximately 3" by 5" and feature posed, color player photos with white borders. The player's name, position, and biographical information appear at the bottom. The backs carry public service messages that relate a hockey term to a life situation. The cards are unnumbered and checklisted below in alphabetical order.

	MINT	EXC	G-VG
COMPLETE SET (16)	20.00	8.00	2.00
COMMON PLAYER (1-16)	.75	.30	.07
☐ 1 Bob Bales	.75	.30	.07
☐ 2 Greg Barber	.75	.30	.07
☐ 3 Ray Benik	.75	.30	.07
☐ 4 Rich Chernomaz	2.00	.80	.20
☐ 5 Daryl Coldwell	.75	.30	.07
☐ 6 Geoff Courtnall	9.00	3.75	.90
☐ 7 Paul Cyr	2.00	.80	.20
☐ 8 Wade Jenson	.75	.30	.07
☐ 9 Stu Kulak	2.00	.80	.20
☐ 10 Peter Martin	.75	.30	.07
☐ 11 John Mokosak	.75	.30	.07
☐ 12 Mark Morrison	.75	.30	.07
☐ 13 Bryant Seaton	.75	.30	.07
☐ 14 Jack Shupe	.75	.30	.07
☐ 15 Eric Thurston	.75	.30	.07
☐ 16 Randy Wickware	.75	.30	.07

1982-83 Victoria Cougars

Featuring current and past players, this 23-card set was sponsored by the West Coast Savings Credit Union, GFAX 1070 Radio, and the Greater Victoria Police Departments. The cards measure approximately 3" by 5" and feature color player portraits with red and blue borders on a white card face. The player's name, position, and biographical information appear at the bottom. Past player cards have the words "Graduation Series" stamped in the lower right corner of the picture (card numbers 7, 8, 13, 20-21). The backs carry a brief player profile and public service messages. The cards are unnumbered and checklisted below in alphabetical order.

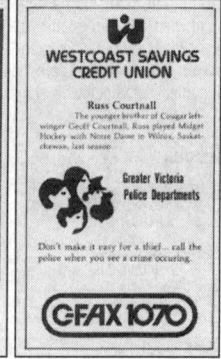

	MINT	EXC	G-VG
COMPLETE SET (23)	35.00	14.00	3.50
COMMON PLAYER (1-23)	.75	.30	.07
☐ 1 Steve Bayliss	.75	.30	.07
☐ 2 Ray Benik	.75	.30	.07
☐ 3 Rich Chernomaz	1.50	.60	.15
☐ 4 Geoff Courtnall	7.50	3.00	.75
☐ 5 Russ Courtnall	10.00	4.00	1.00
☐ 6 Paul Cyr	2.00	.80	.20
☐ 7 Curt Fraser	1.50	.60	.15
☐ 8 Grant Fuhr	12.00	5.00	1.20
☐ 9 Shawn Green	.75	.30	.07
☐ 10 Fabian Joseph	1.00	.40	.10
☐ 11 Stu Kulak	1.00	.40	.10
☐ 12 Brenn Leach	.75	.30	.07
☐ 13 Gary Lupul	1.00	.40	.10
☐ 14 Jack MacKeigan	.75	.30	.07
☐ 15 Dave Mackey	1.00	.40	.10
☐ 16 Mark McLeary	.75	.30	.07
☐ 17 Dan Moberg	.75	.30	.07
☐ 18 John Mokosak	.75	.30	.07
☐ 19 Mark Morrison	.75	.30	.07
☐ 20 Brad Palmer	1.00	.40	.10
☐ 21 Barry Pederson	4.00	1.60	.40
☐ 22 Eric Thurston	.75	.30	.07
☐ 23 Ron Viglasi	.75	.30	.07

1983-84 Victoria Cougars

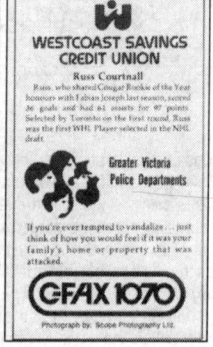

Featuring current and past players, this 24-card set was sponsored by the West Coast Savings Credit Union, GFAX 1070 Radio, and the Greater Victoria Police Departments. The cards measure approximately 3" by 5" and feature color player portraits with red and blue borders on a white card face. The player's name, position, and biographical information appear at the bottom. Past player cards have the words "Graduation Series" stamped in the lower right corner of the picture (card number 2 and 20). The cards are unnumbered and checklisted below in alphabetical order.

	MINT	EXC	G-VG
COMPLETE SET (24)	20.00	8.00	2.00
COMMON PLAYER (1-24)	.75	.30	.07

		MINT	EXC	G-VG
☐ 1	Misko Antisin	.75	.30	.07
☐ 2	Murray Bannerman	1.50	.60	.15
☐ 3	Steve Baylis	.75	.30	.07
☐ 4	Paul Bifano	.75	.30	.07
☐ 5	Russ Courtnall	6.00	2.40	.60
☐ 6	Greg Davies	.75	.30	.07
☐ 7	Dean Drozdiak	.75	.30	.07
☐ 8	Jim Gunn	.75	.30	.07
☐ 9	Richard Hajdu	1.00	.40	.10
☐ 10	Randy Hansch	.75	.30	.07
☐ 11	Matt Hervey	1.00	.40	.10
☐ 12	Fabian Joseph	1.00	.40	.10
☐ 13	Rob Kivell	.75	.30	.07
☐ 14	Brenn Leach	.75	.30	.07
☐ 15	Jack Mackeigan	.75	.30	.07
☐ 16	Dave Mackey	1.00	.40	.10
☐ 17	Tom Martin	.75	.30	.07
☐ 18	Darren Moren	.75	.30	.07
☐ 19	Adam Morrison	.75	.30	.07
☐ 20	Gord Roberts	1.00	.40	.10
☐ 21	Dan Sexton	.75	.30	.07
☐ 22	Randy Siska	.75	.30	.07
☐ 23	Eric Thurston	.75	.30	.07
☐ 24	Simon Wheeldon	1.00	.40	.10

1984-85 Victoria Cougars

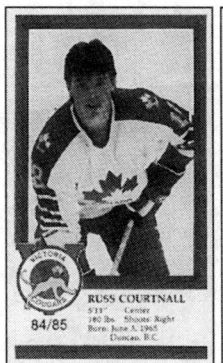

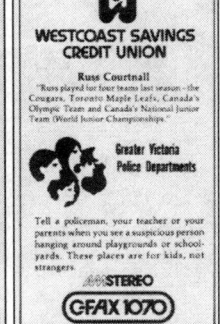

Featuring current and past players, this 24-card set was sponsored by the West Coast Savings Credit Union, GFAX 1070 Radio, and the Greater Victoria Police Departments. The cards measure approximately 3" by 5" and feature color player portraits with red and blue borders on a white card face. The player's name, position, and biographical information appear at the bottom. Past player cards have the words "Graduation Series" stamped in the lower right corner of the picture (card numbers 6 and 20). The backs carry a brief player profile and public service messages. The cards are unnumbered and checklisted below in alphabetical order.

	MINT	EXC	G-VG
COMPLETE SET (24)	15.00	6.00	1.50
COMMON PLAYER (1-24)	.60	.24	.06

		MINT	EXC	G-VG
☐ 1	Misko Antisin	.60	.24	.06
☐ 2	Greg Batters	.60	.24	.06

		MINT	EXC	G-VG
☐ 3	Mel Bridgman	1.25	.50	.12
☐ 4	Chris Calverly	.60	.24	.06
☐ 5	Darin Choquette	.60	.24	.06
☐ 6	Geoff Courtnall	4.00	1.60	.40
☐ 7	Russ Courtnall	5.00	2.00	.50
☐ 8	Rick Davidson	.60	.24	.06
☐ 9	Bill Gregoire	.60	.24	.06
☐ 10	Richard Hajdu	1.00	.40	.10
☐ 11	Randy Hansch	.60	.24	.06
☐ 12	Rob Kivell	.60	.24	.06
☐ 13	Brad Melin	.60	.24	.06
☐ 14	Jim Mentis	.60	.24	.06
☐ 15	Adam Morrison	.60	.24	.06
☐ 16	Mark Morrison	.60	.24	.06
☐ 17	Kodie Nelson	.60	.24	.06
☐ 18	Ken Priestlay	1.00	.40	.10
☐ 19	Bruce Pritchard	.60	.24	.06
☐ 20	Torrie Robertson	1.00	.40	.10
☐ 21	Trevor Semeniuk	.60	.24	.06
☐ 22	Dan Sexton	.60	.24	.06
☐ 23	Randy Siska	.60	.24	.06
☐ 24	Chris Tarnowski	.60	.24	.06

1989-90 Victoria Cougars

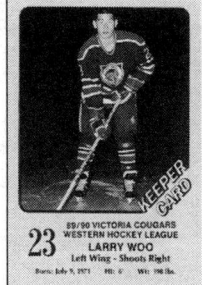

Sponsored by Safeway and Romeo's, this 21-card set measures approximately 2 3/4" by 4" and was sponsored by Flynn Printing and other area businesses. The cards feature color, posed action player photos with rounded corners on a yellow card face. The lower right corner of the picture is cut off and the words "Keeper Card" are written diagonally. The player's name, position, and biographical information appear below the picture. The backs carry sponsor logos in red and black print. A public service message appears in a wide red stripe near the middle of the card. The cards are unnumbered and checklisted below in alphabetical order.

	MINT	EXC	G-VG
COMPLETE SET (21)	9.00	3.75	.90
COMMON PLAYER (1-21)	.50	.20	.05

		MINT	EXC	G-VG
☐ 1	John Badduke	.50	.20	.05
☐ 2	Terry Bendera	.50	.20	.05
☐ 3	Trevor Buchanan	.50	.20	.05
☐ 4	Jaret Burgoyne	.50	.20	.05
☐ 5	Dino Caputo	.50	.20	.05
☐ 6	Chris Catellier	.50	.20	.05
☐ 7	Mark Cipriano	.50	.20	.05
☐ 8	Milan Drag	.50	.20	.05
☐ 9	Dean Dyer	.50	.20	.05
☐ 10	Shayne Green	.50	.20	.05
☐ 11	Ryan Harrison	.50	.20	.05
☐ 12	Corey Jones	.50	.20	.05
☐ 13	Terry Klapstein	.50	.20	.05
☐ 14	Jason Knox	.50	.20	.05
☐ 15	Curtis Nykyforuk	.50	.20	.05
☐ 16	Jason Peters	.50	.20	.05
☐ 17	Blair Scott	.50	.20	.05
☐ 18	Mike Seaton	.50	.20	.05
☐ 19	Rob Sumner	.50	.20	.05
☐ 20	Larry Woo	.50	.20	.05
☐ 21	Jarret Zukiwsky	.50	.20	.05

1993-94 Waterloo Black Hawks

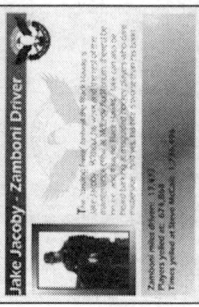

This 27-card set features the Waterloo Black Hawks of the USHL (United States Hockey League). The cards measure the standard size (2 1/2" by 3 1/2"). The fronts feature color action player photos, with the team name and logo in a red border above the photo, and the player's name, number, and position beneath it. The horizontal backs carry a black-and-white player portrait, the player's name and number, biographical information, statistics, a career summary, and the team logo. The cards are unnumbered and checklisted below in alphabetical order.

	MINT	EXC	G-VG
COMPLETE SET (27)	8.00	3.25	.80
COMMON PLAYER (1-27)	.35	.14	.03
☐ 1 Brent Bessey	.35	.14	.03
☐ 2 Jason Blake	.35	.14	.03
☐ 3 Scott Brand GM	.35	.14	.03
☐ 4 Eric Brown	.35	.14	.03
☐ 5 Rod Butler	.35	.14	.03
☐ 6 Chris Coakley	.35	.14	.03
☐ 7 Austin Crawford	.35	.14	.03
☐ 8 Doug Dietz ACO	.35	.14	.03
☐ 9 Jon Garver	.35	.14	.03
☐ 10 Brian Folden	.35	.14	.03
☐ 11 Bobby Hayes	.35	.14	.03
☐ 12 Jake Jacoby	.35	.14	.03
☐ 13 Terry Jarkowsky	.35	.14	.03
☐ 14 Jeff Kozakowski UER	.35	.14	.03
(Misspelled Kozakowskl on front)			
☐ 15 Josh Lampman	.35	.14	.03
☐ 16 Marty Laurila	.35	.14	.03
☐ 17 Steve McCall ANN	.35	.14	.03
☐ 18 Bill McNelis	.35	.14	.03
☐ 19 Rich Metro	.35	.14	.03
☐ 20 Scott Mikesch CO	.35	.14	.03
☐ 21 Barry Soskin PR	.35	.14	.03
☐ 22 Ben Stadey	.35	.14	.03
☐ 23 Ed Stanek	.35	.14	.03
☐ 24 Todd Steinmetz	.35	.14	.03
☐ 25 Scott Swanjord	.50	.20	.05
☐ 26 Miles Van Tassel	.35	.14	.03
☐ 27 Supporting Staff	.35	.14	.03
Dave Christians			
Mike Christians			
Bill Eggers			

1992-93 Western Michigan

These 30 standard-size (2 1/2" by 3 1/2") cards feature color player photos on their fronts, some are action shots, others are posed. These photos are borderless on the sides. The player's name and position appear in a brown bar upon a yellow stripe across the bottom. His uniform number appears within a brown stripe across the top. The back carries a color player head shot at the upper left. A brief

player biography appears alongside on the right. Below are his career highlights and, within a yellow panel, 1991-92 and career statistics. Aside from the players' uniform numbers appearing on the front and back, the cards are unnumbered and checklisted below in alphabetical order.

	MINT	EXC	G-VG
COMPLETE SET (30)	9.00	3.75	.90
COMMON PLAYER (1-30)	.35	.14	.03
☐ 1 Chris Belanger	.50	.20	.05
☐ 2 Joe Bonnett	.35	.14	.03
☐ 3 Brent Brekke	.50	.20	.05
☐ 4 Chris Brooks	.35	.14	.03
☐ 5 Craig Brown	.35	.14	.03
☐ 6 Jeremy Brown	.35	.14	.03
☐ 7 Tom Carriere	.35	.14	.03
☐ 8 Scott Chartier	.50	.20	.05
☐ 9 Ryan D'Arcy	.35	.14	.03
☐ 10 Pat Ferschweiler	.35	.14	.03
☐ 11 Brian Gallentine	.35	.14	.03
☐ 12 Jim Holman	.35	.14	.03
☐ 13 Derek Innanen	.35	.14	.03
☐ 14 Jason Jennings	.50	.20	.05
☐ 15 Mikhail Lapin	.50	.20	.05
☐ 16 Francois Leroux	.35	.14	.03
☐ 17 Jamal Mayers	.75	.30	.07
☐ 18 Kevin McCaffrey ACO	.35	.14	.03
☐ 19 Dave Mitchell	.35	.14	.03
☐ 20 Brian Renfrew	.35	.14	.03
☐ 21 Mike Schafer ACO	.35	.14	.03
☐ 22 Derek Schooley	.35	.14	.03
☐ 23 Neil Smith	.50	.20	.05
WMU Hall of Fame			
☐ 24 Colin Ward	.35	.14	.03
☐ 25 Dave Weaver	.35	.14	.03
☐ 26 Mike Whitton	.35	.14	.03
☐ 27 Bill Wilkinson CO	.35	.14	.03
☐ 28 Peter Wilkinson	.35	.14	.03
☐ 29 Byron Witkowski	.35	.14	.03
☐ 30 Lawson Arena	.35	.14	.03

1993-94 Western Michigan

These 30 standard-size (2 1/2" by 3 1/2") cards feature color player photos on their fronts, some are action shots, others are posed. These photos are borderless on three sides. The player's name and uniform number appear vertically in the brown left margin. The back carries a black-and-white player head shot at the upper left. A brief player biography appears alongside on the right. Below are his career highlights and 1992-93 statistics. Aside from the players' uniform numbers appearing on the front and back, the cards are unnumbered and checklisted below in alphabetical order.

	MINT	EXC	G-VG
COMPLETE SET (30)	9.00	3.75	.90
COMMON PLAYER (1-30)	.35	.14	.03
☐ 1 David Agnew	.35	.14	.03
☐ 2 Brent Brekke	.50	.20	.05
☐ 3 Chris Brooks	.35	.14	.03
☐ 4 Craig Brown	.35	.14	.03
☐ 5 Jeremy Brown	.35	.14	.03
☐ 6 Justin Cardwell	.35	.14	.03
☐ 7 Tom Carriere	.35	.14	.03
☐ 8 Tony Code	.35	.14	.03
☐ 9 Matt Cressman	.35	.14	.03
☐ 10 Jim Culhane ACO	.35	.14	.03
☐ 11 Ryan D'Arcy	.35	.14	.03
☐ 12 Brian Gallentine	.35	.14	.03
☐ 13 Matt Greene	.35	.14	.03
☐ 14 Rob Hodge	.50	.20	.05
WMU Hall of Fame			
☐ 15 Jim Holman	.35	.14	.03
☐ 16 Derek Innanen	.35	.14	.03
☐ 17 Mark Jodoin	.35	.14	.03
☐ 18 Brendan Kenny	.35	.14	.03
☐ 19 Misha Lapin	.50	.20	.05
☐ 20 Darren Maloney	.35	.14	.03
☐ 21 Jamal Mayers	.75	.30	.07
☐ 22 Dave Mitchell	.35	.14	.03
☐ 23 Brian Renfrew	.35	.14	.03
☐ 24 Mike Schafer ACO	.35	.14	.03
☐ 25 Derek Schooley	.35	.14	.03
☐ 26 Colin Ward	.35	.14	.03
☐ 27 Mike Whitton	.35	.14	.03
☐ 28 Bill Wilkinson CO	.35	.14	.03
☐ 29 Peter Wilkinson	.35	.14	.03
☐ 30 Shawn Zimmerman	.35	.14	.03

1992-93 Wheeling Thunderbirds

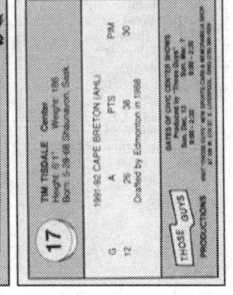

This 24-card set measures the standard size (2 1/2" by 3 1/2") and features color, posed action player photos. The pictures are set on a gray card face with a red banner above the photo that contains the year and the manufacturer name (Those Guys Productions). The player's name, position, and team name are printed below the picture. The horizontal backs have white borders and are divided into three sections by a gray, white, and gray stripe design. The upper gray area contains the player's name and biographical information. The middle white section holds statistics from the previous season. The lower gray section carries promotional information. The cards are numbered on the back.

	MINT	EXC	G-VG
COMPLETE SET (24)	9.00	3.75	.90
COMMON PLAYER (1-24)	.50	.20	.05
☐ 1 Title Card	.75	.30	.07
☐ 2 Claude Barthe	.50	.20	.05
☐ 3 Joel Blain	.50	.20	.05
☐ 4 Derek DeCosty	.50	.20	.05
☐ 5 Marc Deschamps	.50	.20	.05
☐ 6 Tom Dion	.50	.20	.05
☐ 7 Devin Edgerton	.50	.20	.05
☐ 8 Pete Heine	.50	.20	.05
☐ 9 Kim Maier	.50	.20	.05
☐ 10 Mike Millham	.50	.20	.05
☐ 11 Cory Paterson	.50	.20	.05
☐ 12 Trevor Pochipinski	.50	.20	.05
☐ 13 Tim Roberts	.50	.20	.05
☐ 14 Mark Rodgers	.50	.20	.05
☐ 15 Darren Schwartz	.50	.20	.05
☐ 16 Trevor Senn	.50	.20	.05
☐ 17 Tim Tisdale	.50	.20	.05
☐ 18 John Uniac	.75	.30	.07
☐ 19 Denny Magruder MG	.50	.20	.05
☐ 20 Chuck Greenwood	.50	.20	.05
Jim Smith (Producers)			
☐ 21 Larry Kish VP/MG	.50	.20	.05
☐ 22 Doug Sauter CO	.50	.20	.05
☐ 23 T-Bird (Mascot)	.50	.20	.05
☐ 24 Doug Bacon	.50	.20	.05

1989-90 Windsor Spitfires

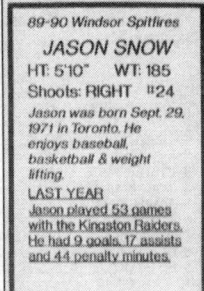

This 22-card set measures the standard size (2 1/2" by 3 1/2") and features members of the 1989-90 Windsor Spitfires of the Ontario Hockey league (OHL). The fronts feature posed shots of the players in front of their lockers. The backs carry biography, date of birth, personal interests, and a "last year" feature. The cards are unnumbered and checklisted below in alphabetical order.

	MINT	EXC	G-VG
COMPLETE SET (22)	10.00	4.00	1.00
COMMON PLAYER (1-22)	.60	.24	.06
☐ 1 Sean Burns	.60	.24	.06
☐ 2 Glen Craig	.60	.24	.06
☐ 3 Brian Forestell	.60	.24	.06
☐ 4 Chris Fraser	.60	.24	.06
☐ 5 Trent Gleason	.60	.24	.06
☐ 6 Jon Hartley	.60	.24	.06
☐ 7 Ron Jones	.60	.24	.06
☐ 8 Bob Leeming	.60	.24	.06
☐ 9 Kevin MacKay	.60	.24	.06
☐ 10 Kevin McDougall	.75	.30	.07
☐ 11 Ryan Merritt	.60	.24	.06
☐ 12 David Myles	.60	.24	.06
☐ 13 Sean O'Hagan	.60	.24	.06
☐ 14 Mike Polano	.70	.28	.07
☐ 15 Jason Snow	.60	.24	.06
☐ 16 Brad Smith CO	.75	.30	.07
☐ 17 Jason Stos	.60	.24	.06
☐ 18 Jon Stos	.60	.24	.06
☐ 19 Jamie Vargo	.60	.24	.06
☐ 20 Trevor Walsh	.60	.24	.06
☐ 21 K.J. White	.75	.30	.07
☐ 22 Jason Zohl	.60	.24	.06

1992-93 Windsor Spitfires

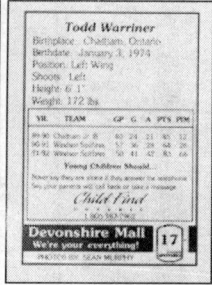

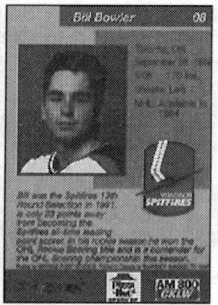

Sponsored by the Devonshire Mall, these 31 cards measure approximately 2 5/8" by 3 5/8" and feature on their fronts posed-on-ice color shots of the 1992-93 Windsor Spitfires bordered in red, white, and blue. The player's name and the Spitfires logo appear in the white area above the photo. The white back is framed by a black line and carries the player's name at the top, followed below by biography, statistics, and a safety message for children. The cards are numbered on the back.

	MINT	EXC	G-VG
COMPLETE SET (31)	10.00	4.00	1.00
COMMON PLAYER (1-31)	.35	.14	.03
☐ 1 Team Card/Checklist	.50	.20	.05
☐ 2 Mike Martin	.35	.14	.03
☐ 3 Luke Clowes	.35	.14	.03
☐ 4 Jason Haelzle	.35	.14	.03
☐ 5 Adam Graves	1.50	.60	.15
☐ 6 Craig Lutes	.50	.20	.05
☐ 7 David Pluck	.35	.14	.03
☐ 8 Colin Wilson	.35	.14	.03
☐ 9 Bill Bowler	.75	.30	.07
☐ 10 Ryan O'Neill	.35	.14	.03
☐ 11 Adam Young	.35	.14	.03
☐ 12 Gerrard Masse	.35	.14	.03
☐ 13 Daryl Lavoie	.35	.14	.03
☐ 14 Peter Allison	.35	.14	.03
☐ 15 Ernie Godden RET	.50	.20	.05
☐ 16 Brady Blain	.50	.20	.05
☐ 17 Todd Warriner	1.00	.40	.10
☐ 18 Rick Marshall	.35	.14	.03
☐ 19 Craig Johnson	.50	.20	.05
☐ 20 Kelly Vipond	.50	.20	.05
☐ 21 Devy Bear MASCOT	.35	.14	.03
☐ 22 Stephen Webb	.35	.14	.03
☐ 23 Scott Miller RET	.35	.14	.03
☐ 24 Dennis Purdie	.50	.20	.05
☐ 25 Steve Gibson	.50	.20	.05
☐ 26 Mike Hartwick	.35	.14	.03
☐ 27 Shawn Heins	.35	.14	.03
☐ 28 David Benn	.35	.14	.03
☐ 29 Matt Mullin	.50	.20	.05
☐ 30 David Mitchell	.35	.14	.03
☐ 31 The Dynamic Duo	.75	.30	.07
Todd Warriner			
Cory Stillman			

player photos with thin grey borders. The player's name, position and team name, as well as the producer's logo, also appear on the front. The backs carry a close-up color player portrait and biographical information, along with team and sponsors' logos. The cards are numbered on the back. Included in this set is a Slapshot ad card with a 1994 calendar on the back.

	MINT	EXC	G-VG
COMPLETE SET (27)	12.00	5.00	1.20
COMMON PLAYER (1-27)	.35	.14	.03
☐ 1 Ed Jovanovski	4.00	1.60	.40
☐ 2 Shawn Silver	.35	.14	.03
☐ 3 Travis Scott	.75	.30	.07
☐ 4 Mike Martin	.35	.14	.03
☐ 5 Daryl Lavoie	.35	.14	.03
☐ 6 Craig Lutes	.50	.20	.05
☐ 7 David Pluck	.35	.14	.03
☐ 8 Bill Bowler	.75	.30	.07
☐ 9 David Green	.35	.14	.03
☐ 10 Adam Young	.35	.14	.03
☐ 11 Mike Loach	.50	.20	.05
☐ 12 Brady Blain	.50	.20	.05
☐ 13 Shayne McCosh	.35	.14	.03
☐ 14 Rob Shearer	.50	.20	.05
☐ 15 Joel Poirier	.50	.20	.05
☐ 16 Cory Evans	.35	.14	.03
☐ 17 Vladimir Kretchine	.75	.30	.07
☐ 18 Dave Roche	.50	.20	.05
☐ 19 Ryan Stewart	.35	.14	.03
☐ 20 Dave Geris	.50	.20	.05
☐ 21 Dan West	.35	.14	.03
☐ 22 Luke Clowes	.35	.14	.03
☐ 23 John Cooper	.35	.14	.03
☐ 24 Akil Adams	.35	.14	.03
☐ 25 Sponsor Card	.35	.14	.03
Pizza Hut			
☐ 26 Sponsor Card	.35	.14	.03
Steve Bell			
Radio station AM 800			
☐ NNO Slapshot Ad Card	.35	.14	.03

1993-94 Windsor Spitfires

Co-sponsored by Pizza Hut and radio station CKLW AM 800, and printed by Slapshot Images Ltd., this 27-card set features the 1993-94 Windsor Spitfires. The cards measure standard size (2 1/2" by 3 1/2"). On a geometrical team color-coded background, the fronts feature color action

Acknowledgments

Each year we refine the process of developing the most accurate and up-to-date information for this book. I believe this year's Price Guide is our best yet. For that, you can thank all of the contributors nationwide (listed below) as well as our staff here in Dallas.

Those who have worked closely with us on this and many other books have again proven themselves invaluable in every aspect of producing this book: Ab D Cards (Dale Wesolewski), Action Packed (Laurie Goldberg), Mike Aronstein, Chris Benjamin, Erwin Borau, Bill Bossert (Mid-Atlantic Coin Exchange), John Bradley (JOGO), John Brenner (Lookin' For Heroes Comics and Sportscards), Milt Byron, Cartomania (Joseph E. Filion), Cartophilium (Andrew Pywowarczuk), Michael Chark, Classic (Ken Goldin), Collection de Sport AZ (Ronald Villanueve), Ken Collins, Mike Cramer (Pacific Trading Cards), Bill and Diane Dodge, Donruss/Leaf (Vince Nauss), Fleer (Jeff Massien and Ted Taylor), Gervise Ford, Steve Freedman, Larry and Jeff Fritsch, John Furniss, Gary Gagen (Let's Collect), Dick Gariepy, Dick Gilkeson, Mike and Howard Gordon, George Grauer, John Greenwald, Wayne Grove, Gene Guarnere, Bill Haber, Jerry and Etta Hersh, Mike Hersh, Sean Isaacs (Billings Coin and Currency), Dennis Kannokko, Paul and Anna Kannokko, Alex Klenman (CAN-AM Card Company), Lew Lipset, Paul Marchant, Branson H. McKay, Michael Moretto, Brian Morris, O-Pee-Chee (Malcolm Bull), Jean-Guy Pichette, Pinnacle (Roy Whitehead), Jack Pollard, Tom Reid, Gavin Riley, Alan Rosen (Mr. Mint), Rotman Productions, John Rumierz, San Diego Sport Collectibles (Bill Goepner and Nacho Arredondo), Kevin Savage (Sports Gallery), Angelo Savelli, Mike Schechter (MSA), Richard Scott, Richard Sherman, Gary Silkstone (Bleachers), Gerry Sobie (Foots), John Spalding, Phil and Joan Spector, Nigel Spill (Oldies and Goodies), Sports Collectors Store (Pat Quinn and Don Steinbach), Frank Steele, Murvin Sterling, Topps (Marty Appel, Sy Berger, and Bob Ibach), Upper Deck (Rich Bradley), Shirl Volk, Pete Wooten, Kit Young, and Robert Zanze.

Finally, we give a special acknowledgment to Dennis W. Eckes, "Mr. Sport Americana," whose untimely passing in 1991 was a real loss to the

Remerciements

Chaque année nous améliorons notre technique pour assembler les renseignements les plus corrects et courants pour ce livre. Je crois que le Guide des prix de cette année est meilleur que jamais. Pour cela, vous pouvez remercier tous nos collaborateurs du pays entier (listés ci-dessous), ainsi que notre personnel à Dallas.

Ceux qui nous ont aidé avec ce projet et plusieurs autres, ont, cette fois-ci encore, prouvé leur valeur durant chaque phase de production de ce livre: Ab D Cards (Dale Wesolewski), Action Packed (Laurie Goldberg), Mike Aronstein, Chris Benjamin, Erwin Borau, Bill Bossert (Mid-Atlantic Coin Exchange), John Bradley (JOGO), John Brenner (Lookin' For Heroes Comics and Sportscards), Milt Byron, Cartomania (Joseph E. Filion), Cartophilium (Andrew Pywowarczuk), Michael Chark, Classic (Ken Goldin), Collection de Sport AZ (Ronald Villanueve), Ken Collins, Mike Cramer (Pacific Trading Cards), Bill and Diane Dodge, Donruss/Leaf (Vince Nauss), Fleer (Jeff Massien and Ted Taylor), Gervise Ford, Steve Freedman, Larry and Jeff Fritsch, John Furniss, Gary Gagen (Let's Collect), Dick Gariepy, Dick Gilkeson, Mike and Howard Gordon, George Grauer, John Greenwald, Wayne Grove, Gene Guarnere, Bill Haber, Jerry and Etta Hersh, Mike Hersh, Sean Isaacs (Billings Coin and Currency), Dennis Kannokko, Paul and Anna Kannokko, Alex Klenman (CAN-AM Card Company), Lew Lipset, Paul Marchant, Branson H. McKay, Michael Moretto, Brian Morris, O-Pee-Chee (Malcolm Bull), Jean-Guy Pichette, Pinnacle (Roy Whitehead), Jack Pollard, Tom Reid, Gavin Riley, Alan Rosen (Mr. Mint), Rotman Productions, John Rumierz, San Diego Sport Collectibles (Bill Goepner and Nacho Arredondo), Kevin Savage (Sports Gallery), Angelo Savelli, Mike Schechter (MSA), Richard Scott, Richard Sherman, Gary Silkstone (Bleachers), Gerry Sobie (Foots), John Spalding, Phil and Joan Spector, Nigel Spill (Oldies and Goodies), Sports Collectors Store (Pat Quinn and Don Steinbach), Frank Steele, Murvin Sterling, Topps (Marty Appel, Sy Berger, and Bob Ibach), Upper Deck (Rich Bradley), Shirl Volk, Pete Wooten, Kit Young, and Robert Zanze.

Enfin, nous avons une dette de reconnaissance particulière envers Dennis W. Eckes, « Monsieur

hobby and to me personally. The success of the Beckett Price Guides has always been the result of a team effort.

Many other individuals have provided price input, illustrative material, checklist verifications, errata, and/or background information. At the risk of inadvertently overlooking or omitting these many contributors, we would like to personally thank Jerry Adamic, Bren Adams, James F. Amick, Neil Armstrong (World Series Cards), Walter Baran, Brent Barnes, Frank and Vivian Barning), Robert Beaudoin, Todd Bellerose, Beulah Sports (Jeff Blatt), Brian L. Bigelow, Ki Billy, Chad Blick, Michel Bolduc, Peter Borkowski, Luc Boucher, B. Jack Bourland III, Tony Bouwman, Jim Boyne, Bob Bruner, Dan Bruner, Eric Burgoyne, Scott Burke, Jim Cappello, Danny Cariseo, Greg Caskey, Dwight Chapin, Check-Swing Sportcards Inc., Steve Chiaramonte, Susan Christensen, Allan E. Cohen, Shane Cohen (Grand Slam), Barry Colla, Matt Collett, Joe Conte, Dan Conway, Ryan Cope, Michael J. Cox, Taylor Crane, Wil Curtis, Allen Custer, Kenneth Daniels, Steven Danver, Leo Davis, Dee's Baseball Cards, Normand Desroches, Larry DeTienne, Dave Deveney, Leon Dill, Mario DiPastena, Marc Dixon (International Sports Investibles), Charles Dugre, John Duplisea, D. Ellis, Don Ellis, Danny Ellwood, Michael Esposito, Evelyn Ettinger, Doak Ewing, Dave Feltham, Frank Fox, Craig Frank, Mark Franke, Kathryn Friedlander, James Funke Jr., Tony Galovich, Jim Galusha, Michael R. Gionet, Brian Goldstein, Jeff Goldstein, Renvel Gonsalves, Rynel Gonsalves, Seth Gordon, Erik Gravel, Pierre-Luc Gravel, Hall's Nostalgia, Tom Harrett, Ron Heller, Bill Henderson, Chick Hershberger, Gerald Higgs, Clay Hill, Gary Hlady, Shawn Hoagland, Keith Holtzmann, Joseph Horgan, D. Howery Jr., Richard Irving, John James, Robert Jansing, Cliff Janzen, Leslie Jezuit, Robert Kantor, Jay and Mary Kasper, Alan Kaye, John Kelly, Rick Keplinger, Larry Kerrigan, Dean Konieczka, Chuck Kucera, Rob Kuhlman, Thomas Kunnecke, Ted Larkins, Scott LeLievre, Irv Lerner, Howie Levy, Stephane Lizotte, Nicholas LoCasto, Tim Loop, Karoline K. Lowry, Steven J. Loy, Thierry Lubenec, Jim Macie, Joe Marasco, Chris Mayhew, Michael McDonald (The Sports Page), Blake Meyer, John Meyer, Dick Millerd, Ben Mitchell, Paul V. Mohrle, Joe Morano, Michel Morin, Kevin Mudrak, Todd Nelkin, Leandre Normand, David Nystrom, John O'Hara, Nelson Paine, Andrew Pak, David

Sport Americana », dont le décès prématuré en 1991 fut une grande perte pour le monde du hockey et pour moi personnellement. La réussite des « Guide des prix Beckett » a toujours été le résultat d'un effort d'équipe.

Plusieurs autres personnes ont contribué des données sur les prix, des illustrations, des contrôles, des listes de vérification, des errata, et/ou des renseignements généraux. Au risque d'omettre le nom de certains de ces collaborateurs, nous voulons remercier personnellement Jerry Adamic, Bren Adams, James F. Amick, Neil Armstrong (World Series Cards), Walter Baran, Brent Barnes, Frank and Vivian Barning), Robert Beaudoin, Todd Bellerose, Beulah Sports (Jeff Blatt), Brian L. Bigelow, Ki Billy, Chad Blick, Michel Bolduc, Peter Borkowski, Luc Boucher, B. Jack Bourland III, Tony Bouwman, Jim Boyne, Bob Bruner, Dan Bruner, Eric Burgoyne, Scott Burke, Jim Cappello, Danny Cariseo, Greg Caskey, Dwight Chapin, Check-Swing Sportcards Inc., Steve Chiaramonte, Susan Christensen, Allan E. Cohen, Shane Cohen (Grand Slam), Barry Colla, Matt Collett, Joe Conte, Dan Conway, Ryan Cope, Michael J. Cox, Taylor Crane, Wil Curtis, Allen Custer, Kenneth Daniels, Steven Danver, Leo Davis, Dee's Baseball Cards, Normand Desroches, Larry DeTienne, Dave Deveney, Leon Dill, Mario DiPastena, Marc Dixon (International Sports Investibles), Charles Dugre, John Duplisea, D. Ellis, Don Ellis, Danny Ellwood, Michael Esposito, Evelyn Ettinger, Doak Ewing, Dave Feltham, Frank Fox, Craig Frank, Mark Franke, Kathryn Friedlander, James Funke Jr., Tony Galovich, Jim Galusha, Michael R. Gionet, Brian Goldstein, Jeff Goldstein, Renvel Gonsalves, Rynel Gonsalves, Seth Gordon, Erik Gravel, Pierre-Luc Gravel, Hall's Nostalgia, Tom Harrett, Ron Heller, Bill Henderson, Chick Hershberger, Gerald Higgs, Clay Hill, Gary Hlady, Shawn Hoagland, Keith Holtzmann, Joseph Horgan, D. Howery Jr., Richard Irving, John James, Robert Jansing, Cliff Janzen, Leslie Jezuit, Robert Kantor, Jay and Mary Kasper, Alan Kaye, John Kelly, Rick Keplinger, Larry Kerrigan, Dean Konieczka, Chuck Kucera, Rob Kuhlman, Thomas Kunnecke, Ted Larkins, Scott LeLievre, Irv Lerner, Howie Levy, Stephane Lizotte, Nicholas LoCasto, Tim Loop, Karoline K. Lowry, Steven J. Loy, Thierry Lubenec, Jim Macie, Joe Marasco, Chris Mayhew, Michael McDonald (The Sports Page), Blake Meyer, John Meyer, Dick Millerd, Ben Mitchell, Paul V. Mohrle, Joe Morano,

Paolicelli, Tom Parker, Clay Pasternack, Alan Peace, Len Pottie, Red River Coins and Cards, Randall Reese, Ralph Reitsma, Dorothy Reznik (Discount Dorothy), Owen Ricker, John Wayne Roman, Charles Rooke, Francis Rose, Jim Routly, Joe Rubert II, Terry Sack, Joe Sak, Alan Karl Samuelson, Claire Samuelson, Cheryl Sauve, Chris Sklener, Lyle Skrapek, Slapshot Sports Collectibles, Carl Specht, Cary Stephenson, Dan Stickney, Dave Sularz, Fred Suzman (Suzman's Minors), George Tahinos, Danny Tarquini, Paul S. Taylor, Lee Temanson, Chuck Thomas, Joe Tomasik, Upper Deck Card Shop, Michel Vaillancourt, Variete Sports Verville Enr., Clayton Vigent, Jonathan Watts, David Weiner, Andrew B. Weisenfeld (Rocky Mtn. Trading Card Co.), Kermit B. Wells, Bill Wesslund, Bob Wilke (The Shoe Box), Kelly Wionzek (Coty Collectibles), Brian Wobbeking, Thomas L. Wujek, Yaz's Sports Memorabilia, Gerard Yodice, Christina Zawadzki, and Bill Zimpleman .

Every year we make active solicitations for expert input. We are particularly appreciative of the help (however extensive or cursory) provided for this volume. We receive many inquiries, comments and questions regarding material within this book. In fact, each and every one is read and digested. Time constraints, however, prevent us from personally replying. But keep sharing your knowledge. Your letters and input are part of the "big picture" of hobby information we can pass along to readers of our books and magazines. Even though we cannot respond to each letter, you are making significant contributions to the hobby through your interest and comments.

The effort to continually refine and improve this book also involves a growing number of people and types of expertise on hour home team. Our company boasts a substantial Technical Services team, which strengthens our ability to provide comprehensive analysis of the marketplace. Technical Services capably handled numerous technical details and provided able assistance in the preparation of this edition.

Our hockey analysts played a major part in compiling this year's book, travelling thousands of miles during the past year to attend sports card shows and visit card shops around the United States and Canada. The Beckett hockey specialists are Jeff Allison, Tom Layberger, Allan Muir and Dave Sliepka. Their baseline analysis and careful proofreading were key contributions to the accuracy of

Michel Morin, Kevin Mudrak, Todd Nelkin, Leandre Normand, David Nystrom, John O'Hara, Nelson Paine, Andrew Pak, David Paolicelli, Tom Parker, Clay Pasternack, Alan Peace, Len Pottie, Red River Coins and Cards, Randall Reese, Ralph Reitsma, Dorothy Reznik (Discount Dorothy), Owen Ricker, John Wayne Roman, Charles Rooke, Francis Rose, Jim Routly, Joe Rubert II, Terry Sack, Joe Sak, Alan Karl Samuelson, Claire Samuelson, Cheryl Sauve, Chris Sklener, Lyle Skrapek, Slapshot Sports Collectibles, Carl Specht, Cary Stephenson, Dan Stickney, Dave Sularz, Fred Suzman (Suzman's Minors), George Tahinos, Danny Tarquini, Paul S. Taylor, Lee Temanson, Chuck Thomas, Joe Tomasik, Upper Deck Card Shop, Michel Vaillancourt, Variete Sports Verville Enr., Clayton Vigent, Jonathan Watts, David Weiner, Andrew B. Weisenfeld (Rocky Mtn. Trading Card Co.), Kermit B. Wells, Bill Wesslund, Bob Wilke (The Shoe Box), Kelly Wionzek (Coty Collectibles), Brian Wobbeking, Thomas L. Wujek, Yaz's Sports Memorabilia, Gerard Yodice, Christina Zawadzki, and Bill Zimpleman .

Chaque année nous sollicitons activement la collaboration de spécialistes. Nous sommes particulièrement reconnaissants de l'aide (si étendue ou si modeste soit elle) apportée à la mise en place de ce volume. Nous recevons de nombreuses demandes de renseignements, des appréciations, et des questions concernant les éléments de ce livre. En fait, toutes sont lues et examinées. Toutefois, les contraintes de temps nous empêchent d'y répondre personnellement. Mais que cela ne vous empêche pas de nous communiquer vos connaissances. Vos lettres et votre collaboration font partie intégrale des renseignements sur ce passe-temps que nous pouvons passer aux lecteurs dans nos livres et magazines. Même si nous ne pouvons pas répondre à chaque lettre, votre contribution est importante grâce à vos commentaires et intérêt.

Le processus continu d'amélioration de ce livre est basé en partie sur la croissance de notre équipe et de nos compétences. Par exemple, nous avons aujourd'hui un important département Services techniques qui renforce nos capacités d'analyser le marché à fond. L'équipe des Services techniques a fourni de nombreux détails techniques et une assistance compétente durant l'établissement des prix pour cette édition du guide annuel.

Nos analystes du hockey ont joué un rôle majeur dans la compilation du livre de cette année,

this annual.

Tom Layberger's coordination of the pricing of sets listed in *Beckett Hockey Monthly* helped immeasurably, as did *BHM* title analyst Allan Muir's knowledge of junior and minor league sets. Dave Sliepka contributed many hours of pricing and proofing, and book title analyst Rich Klein employed his encyclopedic knowledge and meticulous attention to detail.

The effort was directed by Technical Services manager Rich Olivieri. He was ably assisted by the rest of the Price Guide analysts: Theo Chen, Ben Ecklar, Dan Hitt, Mike Jaspersen, Grant Sandground and Steve Smith. Also contributing to Technical Services functions were Keith Pentico, Travis Raczynski, Gabriel Rangel and Brett Setter.

The price gathering and analytical talents of this fine group of hobbyists have helped make our Beckett team stronger, while making this guide and its companion monthly Price Guide more widely recognized as the hobby's most reliable and relied upon sources of pricing information.

Granted, the production of any book is a total team effort. However, I owe special thanks to the members of our Book Team who demonstrated extraordinary contributions to this massive undertaking. Managing editor Steve Wilson supervised a dedicated staff that continues to grow in number and expertise. He set up initial schedules and ensured that all deadlines were met, while looking for all the fine points to improve our process and presentation throughout the cycle.

Scott Layton, assistant manager of Special Projects, served as point man in the demanding area of new set entry and was a key person in the organization of both technological and people resources for the book. He was ably assisted by Beverly Mills, Maria Neubauer and Peter Tepp, who entered new sets, ensured the proper administration of our contributor Price Guide surveys and performed various other tasks. Also contributing to the Book Team effort were assistant manager Mary Gregory, Julie Grove, Teri McGahey and Stacy Olivieri.

Our computer experts, Rich Olivieri and Jordan Gallagher, spent countless hours programming, testing and implementing new software to simplify the handling of thousands of prices that must be checked and updated for each edition of this book.

Computer Services manager Airey Baringer made sure that paginating and typesetting the text

voyageant des milliers de kilomètres durant toute l'année pour assister aux salons des cartes de sport et visiter des boutiques de cartes partout aux États-Unis. Les experts du hockey à Beckett sont Jeff Allison, Tom Layberger, Allan Muir et Dave Sliepka. L'année durante, ce groupe suit le marché des cartes de hockey, et par ses analyses de base et relectures soigneuses, a énormément contribué à l'exactitude de ce livre.

Tom Layberger nous a infiniment assisté en coordonnant les données de l'équipe et en établissant les prix des jeux listés dans "Beckett Hockey Monthly" ainsi qu'Allan Muir (analyste pour "Beckett Hockey Monthly") par sa connaissance des jeux des ligues cadettes et minimes. Dave Sliepka a contribué beaucoup d'heures de la détermination des prix et l'inspection de groupes spécifiques de joueurs et Rich Klein (analyste pour les livres) a contribué ses connaissances très étendues et sa relecture précise et méticuleuse.

Le directeur des Services techniques, Rich Olivieri, a été assisté par les autres analystes du Guide des prix : Theo Chen, Ben Ecklar, Dan Hitt, Mike Jaspersen, Grant Sandground et Steve Smith. Keith Pentico, Travis Raczynski, Gabriel Rangel et Brett Setter ont également contribué aux efforts de nos Services techniques.

Cette équipe accomplie de spécialistes en la matière, par ses talents d'analyse et d'établissement de prix, a contribué à l'établissement d'une équipe Beckett encore plus énergique, tout en faisant de ce guide et de ses compagnons, les guides mensuels, des sources d'information de prix davantage reconnues comme les plus fiables et dignes de confiance.

Il est évident que la production d'un livre requiert les efforts d'une équipe entière. Je veux cependant tout particulièrement remercier les membres de notre « Book Team », dont les contributions à ce livre ont été extraordinaires.

Notre éditeur exécutif, Steve Wilson, a mené une équipe dévouée qui croît encore en nombre et en expertise. Il a organisé l'emploi du temps et a assuré l'observation des dates limites, tout en recherchant chaque détail pouvant améliorer notre processus et présentation à travers le cycle.

Scott Layton, directeur adjoint des Projets spéciaux, a été responsable de l'enregistrement des nouveaux jeux et s'est montré indispensable durant l'organisation des ressources technologiques et humaines requises par ce livre. Beverly Mills, Maria Neubauer et Peter Tepp lui ont prêté leurs compé-

layout ran smoothly, checking the myriad details involved in that process. Paul Kerutis was responsible for much of the typesetting, as well as many of the card photos you see throughout the book. Matt Bowling contributed his design skills to enhance readability.

Carrie Ehrhardt spent tireless hours on the phone attending to the wishes of our dealer advertisers under the direction of Customer Service assistant manager Patti Harris. Once the ad specifications were delivered to our offices, John Marshall used his computer skills to turn raw copy into attractive display advertisements.

In the years since this guide debuted, Beckett Publications has grown beyond any rational expectation. A great many talented and hard working individuals have been instrumental in this growth and success. Our whole team is to be congratulated for what we together have accomplished. Our Beckett Publications team is led by Associate Publisher Claire Backus, Vice Presidents Jeff Amano, Joe Galindo and Fred Reed, Editorial Director Pepper Hastings, and Senior Managers Beth Harwell and Reed Poole. They are ably assisted by Dana Alecknavage, Theresa Anderson, Alan Andrews, Jeff Anthony, Kelly Atkins, Kaye Ball, Marvin Bang, Barbara Barry, Nancy Bassi, James R. Beane, Therese Bellar, Christa Bencomo, Louise Bird, Cathryn Black, Amy Brougher, Bob Brown, Janel Bush, Chris Calandro, Randy Calvert, Emily Camp, Mary Campana, Susan Catka, Tim Chamberlain, Jud Chappell, Albert Chavez, Evelyn Clark, Tommy Collins, Belinda Cross, Randy Cummings, Patrick Cunningham, Marlon DePaula, Gail Docekal, Alejandro Egusquiza, Paulo Egusquiza, Eric Evans, Craig Ferris, Jorge Field, Sara Field, Jean Paul Figari, Jeany Finch, Kim Ford, Blain Fowler, Gayle Gasperin, Loretta Gibbs, Anita Gonzalez, Rosanna Gonzalez-Olaechea, Jeff Greer, Jenifer Grellhesl, Jenny Harwell, Mark Harwell, Joanna Hayden, Chris Hellem, Barbara Hinkle, Tracy Hinton, Tim Jaksa, Deliese Jaspersen, Julia Jernigan, Heidi Johnson, Jay Johnson, Rudy Klancnik, Frances Knight, Jane Ann Layton, Sara Leeman, Benedito Leme, Lori Lindsey, Stanley Lira, Sara Maneval, Louis Marroquin, Kaki Matheson, Mike McAllister, Kirk McKinney, Omar Mediano, Lisa Monaghan, Sherry Monday, Robert Moore, Mila Morante, Daniel Moscoso Jr., Mike Moss, Randy Mosty, Hugh Murphy, Shawn Murphy, Steve Naughton, Michael O'Hara, Lisa O'Neill, Mike

tences en enregistrant des nouveaux jeux (en nombre record cette année), assurant l'administration correcte de nos sondages des collaborateurs au Guide des prix et accomplissant beaucoup d'autres tâches. Mary Gregory, directrice adjointe, Teri McGahey, Julie Grove et Stacy Olivieri ont aussi contribué aux efforts de ce livre.

Nos experts de Services informatiques Rich Olivieri et Jordan Gallagher ont passé des mois à programmer, tester et faire fonctionner du logiciel neuf pour simplifier la manipulation de milliers de prix devant être vérifiés et mis à jour à chaque parution de ce livre.

Airey Baringer, directeur des Services informatiques, a assuré que la pagination et la mise en page du texte se passe correctement, vérifiant les innombrables détails impliqués dans cette procédure. Paul Kerutis est responsable de beaucoup de photos de cartes que vous voyez dans ce livre, ainsi que de la direction du collage. Matt Bowling a contribué ses talents en arts graphiques.

Carrie Ehrhardt a vaillamment passé maintes heures au téléphone pour satisfaire les souhaits de nos distributeurs voulant placer une publicité, sous la supervision de notre directrice adjointe des Services clientèle, Patti Harris. John Marshall a utilisé ses talents d'informaticien pour transformer les épreuves en publicités attirantes.

Au fil des années, depuis les origines de ce guide, les Editions Beckett ont pris une extension au-delà de toute attente raisonnable. De nombreuses personnes de talent, travaillant inlassablement, ont contribué à cet accroissement et réussite. Notre équipe au complet mérite d'être félicitée pour ce que nous avons accompli ensemble. L'équipe Beckett Publications est dirigée par notre éditrice associée, Claire B. Backus, nos vice-présidents Jeff Amano, Joe Galindo et Fred Reed III, notre directeur de rédaction, Pepper Hastings et nos directeurs supérieurs, Reed Poole et Beth Harwell.

Ils ont profité de l'assistance capable de Dana Alecknavage, Theresa Anderson, Alan Andrews, Jeff Anthony, Kelly Atkins, Kaye Ball, Marvin Bang, Barbara Barry, Nancy Bassi, James R. Beane, Therese Bellar, Christa Bencomo, Louise Bird, Cathryn Black, Amy Brougher, Bob Brown, Janel Bush, Chris Calandro, Randy Calvert, Emily Camp, Mary Campana, Susan Catka, Tim Chamberlain, Jud Chappell, Albert Chavez, Evelyn Clark, Tommy Collins, Belinda Cross, Randy Cummings, Patrick Cunningham, Marlon DePaula, Gail Docekal,

Pagel, Wendy Pallugna, Laura Patterson, Mike Payne, Tim Polzer, Fran Poole, Bob Richardson, Tina Riojas, Gary Santaniello, Janice Seydel, Elaine Simmons, Lynn Smith, Sheri Smith, Jeff Stanton, Laura Steele, Margaret Steele, Marcia Stoesz, Cindy Struble, Doree Tate, Diane Taylor, Jim Tereschuk, Jana Threatt, Patrick Wascovich, Cindy Waisath, Carol Weaver and Mark Zeske. The whole Beckett Publications team has my thanks for jobs well done. Thank you, everyone.

I also thank my family, especially my wife, Patti, and our daughters, Christina, Rebecca, and Melissa, for putting up with me again.

Alejandro Egusquiza, Paulo Egusquiza, Eric Evans, Craig Ferris, Jorge Field, Sara Field, Jean Paul Figari, Jeany Finch, Kim Ford, Blain Fowler, Gayle Gasperin, Loretta Gibbs, Anita Gonzalez, Rosanna Gonzalez-Olaechea, Jeff Greer, Jenifer Grellhesl, Jenny Harwell, Mark Harwell, Joanna Hayden, Chris Hellem, Barbara Hinkle, Tracy Hinton, Tim Jaksa, Deliese Jaspersen, Julia Jernigan, Heidi Johnson, Jay Johnson, Rudy Klancnik, Frances Knight, Jane Ann Layton, Sara Leeman, Benedito Leme, Lori Lindsey, Stanley Lira, Sara Maneval, Louis Marroquin, Kaki Matheson, Mike McAllister, Kirk McKinney, Omar Mediano, Lisa Monaghan, Sherry Monday, Robert Moore, Mila Morante, Daniel Moscoso Jr., Mike Moss, Randy Mosty, Hugh Murphy, Shawn Murphy, Steve Naughton, Michael O'Hara, Lisa O'Neill, Mike Pagel, Wendy Pallugna, Laura Patterson, Mike Payne, Tim Polzer, Fran Poole, Bob Richardson, Tina Riojas, Gary Santaniello, Janice Seydel, Elaine Simmons, Lynn Smith, Sheri Smith, Jeff Stanton, Laura Steele, Margaret Steele, Marcia Stoesz, Cindy Struble, Doree Tate, Diane Taylor, Jim Tereschuk, Jana Threatt, Patrick Wascovich, Cindy Waisath, Carol Weaver and Mark Zeske.

J'adresse mes remerciements à l'ensemble de l'équipe des Editions Beckett pour un travail bien fait. Merci à chacun de vous.

Enfin, je veux remercier ma famille, et en particulier ma femme Patti, et nos filles Christina, Rebecca et Melissa de m'avoir cette fois-ci encore soutenu.

822

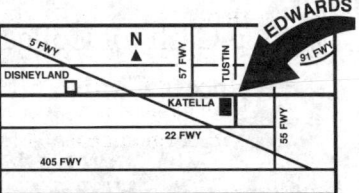

Don't forget to enclose a self-addressed,
stamped envelope when responding
to advertisers in this book.

And mention that you saw their ad in
The Sport Americana Hockey Card Price Guide!

"Sign Language"

Dedicated to the autograph collector, this column appears periodically in Beckett® monthly magazines giving helpful hints for obtaining autographs, choosing a pen, and storing and displaying collections. You'll always find a monthly Price Guide, awesome hobby coverage and more in *Beckett Basketball Monthly*!

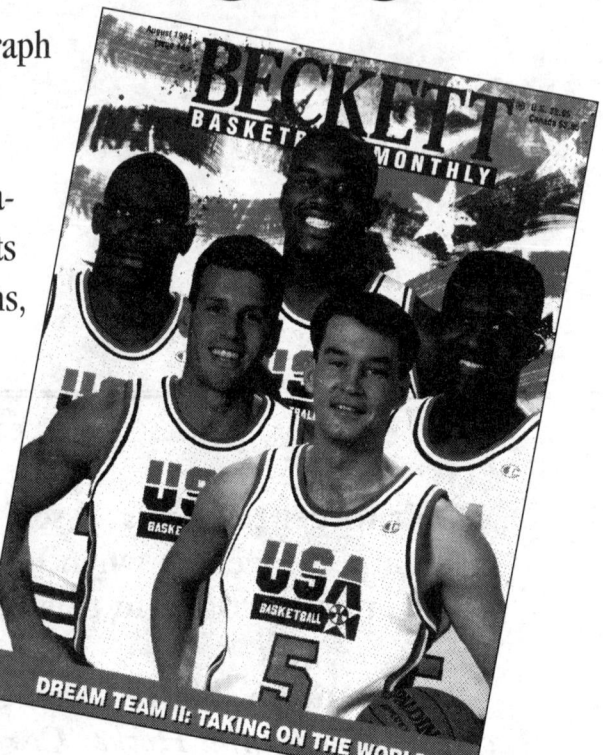

Subscribe today!

"Prime Time Talent"

Providing a unique perspective, the "Prime Time Talent" column compares a young star in one of the four major team sports to a successful superstar and to a player whose career just didn't measure up. Find a monthly Price Guide and more in *Beckett Focus on Future Stars®.*

Subscribe today!

"Collecting In The '90s"

Today's collectors keep on the leading edge of the hobby with "Collecting In The '90s." This informative column addresses issues of concern to all collectors. It is a recurring column in all five Beckett® monthly titles. Get a monthly Price Guide, great hobby coverage and more in *Beckett Baseball Card Monthly*!

Subscribe today!

Beckett – What You Want From Your Hobby Magazine

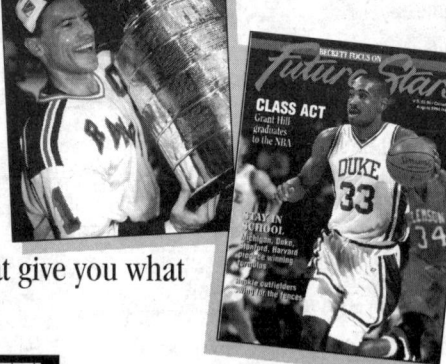

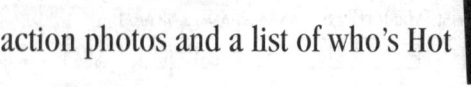
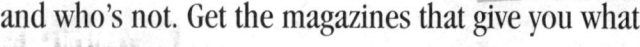